# THE DICTIONARY OF SCOTTISH ART AND ARCHITECTURE

# THE DICTIONARY OF SCOTTISH ART AND ARCHITECTURE

Peter J M McEwan

GLENGARDEN PRESS

ISBN 0-9547552-1-9



British Library Cataloguing-in-Publication Data
A catalogue record for this book is available from the British Library

Published by Rhod McEwan at
GLENGARDEN PRESS
Ballater, Aberdeenshire AB35 5UB
Scotland
www.dictionaryofscottishart.com
Tel: 013397 55429

---

Frontispiece: *Self portrait* by William Ewart Lockhart RSA, courtesy of Aberdeen AG
Title page: *Deerhound Head* by Sir Edwin Landseer RA, private collection
Front panel dustjacket: *The MacDonald Boys* attrib to William Mosman, courtesy of SNPG
Rear panel dustjacket: *The Pharos in the Sound of Mull* by F C B Cadell, private collection
Spine: *Bonnie Prince Charlie* Albion Collection, courtesy of Bonhams Auctioneers
Front endpaper: *Princes Street with the commencement of the building of the Royal Institution* by Alexander Nasmyth, courtesy of SNPG
Rear endpaper: *The Letter* by Stuart Luke Gatherer, private collection

---



Printed in China through Colorcraft Ltd., Hong Kong

# CONTENTS

# ACKNOWLEDGEMENTS

For a project that has been pursued intermittently over twenty years it is possible to thank only a limited few of those whose help has been so warmly appreciated and so necessary.

Correspondents about individual artists included surviving spouses, relatives, descendants, unrelated enthusiasts and archivists. They wrote from around the world offering an invaluable store of hitherto unrecorded information and corrections to errors replicated in the literature. Unhappily the list is too long to identify everyone but when identification has been requested this is shown in the text. Five respondents must be singled out, however, because of their extended help over a series of entries. Dr D Le Poidevin of Aberdeen gave me the benefit of his private archive dealing with some of the lesser known artists of that city; Colonel Charles Napier helped me unravel some of the tangled skeins of his remarkable family's history; the art critic and writer Mrs Ailsa Tanner who has spent a lifetime immersed in the artistic life of Scotland often pointed me in useful directions, especially in the project's formative period; Krystyna Malcharek of Poland provided guidance about several important Scottish emigrés to her country; and Mr William Wallace granted access to his archive dealing with the artists of Hamilton. Peter Hodgkiss of the Ernest Press provided valuable insight and unstinting expert assistance in production of the book. Without the help of all these and many other kind people, important biographical details would have remained hidden.

Contemporary artists were invited to contribute essential autobiographical information. To the large majority who replied I owe a sincere debt of gratitude. Gaps inevitably remain so that any further information about both the living and previous generations would always be appreciated.

Many private and public galleries and museums responded - often more than once - most helpfully, also some individuals. These included Aberdeen AG (especially the Librarian and her assistant), Airdrie Public Library, Alloa Public Library, Angus District Libraries, Arbroath Public Library, Argyll & Bute District Council, Banff Public Library, Bergen AG (Norway), Roger Billcliffe, William Birrell, Dr Louise Boreham, Brechin Public Library, Bridge of Allan Public Library, Brighton AG, Mr I Brown of Ettrick & Lauderdale Museums Services (Selkirk), Miss R Brown of Borders Regional Library Service, Mrs Rosie Capper (Roxburgh District Curator), Carnegie Dunfermline Trust, Carnoustie Public Library, Christchurch (Dorset) Public Library, Thora Clyne, Mr T R Collin (ex-Stewartry Museum, Kirkudbright), Bill & Marion Craigie, Cunninghame District Library (Ardrossan), Ann Dallas, Valerie Dean, Moi Deicke, Dr Devereaux of the Stewartry District Council (Kirkudbright). Dundee AG, Dunfermline District Museum, Edinburgh Public Library, Elgin Library, Ewart Library (Dumfries), Robin Fanshawe, Martin Farrelly, Forfar Public Library, Fraserburgh Public Library, Glasgow AG, Priscilla Gordon-Duff, Gracefield Studios (Dumfries & Galloway District Council), Grampian Region Archivist, Kathleen Hannay, Dr Janice Helland, Mr Graham Hopner of Dumbarton District Libraries, Brian Howison, Jean Hubbard, Inverness Public Library, Mr Bill Jackson (The Scottish Gallery), Roger Jackson, Alistair Keith, Mrs Jane Kidd (Paisley AG), Kilmarnock Public Library, Kirkcaldy Museum and AG, Kyle & Carrick District Library & Museum Services (Ayr), Lille AG (Milngavie), Col W G McHardy, Mr Hugh Mackay (Hawick Public Library), Dr Judith McLaren, McLean Museum and AG (Greenock), John MacWhirter, Manchester AG, Peter Manson, Mr Duane Mead (Rendezvous Gallery), Dr Jennifer Melville, Jack Meredith, Val Morrocco, Montrose Library, Nairn Public Library, the National and main provincial Galleries of Australia, Canada, Ireland, New Zealand and South Africa, National Gallery of Scotland, North East of Scotland Library Service, Oban Public Library, Anthony G G Oliver, Mr Andrew Patrick (The Fine Art Society), Perth & Kinross District Council, Peterhead Public Library, Mr Robin Rodger (Perth AG), Lorna Rose, Royal Academy (especially Miss Charlotte Stirling), Royal Canadian Academy of Arts, Royal Naval Museum (Greenwich & Portsmouth), Royal Scottish Academy (especially the late Esme Gordon & Mrs Joanna Soden), Royal Scottish Society of Watercolourists, Rozelle Galleries (Ayr), Sandeman Library (Perth), Scottish Arts Council, Scottish National Gallery of Modern Art, Scottish National Portrait Gallery, Scottish National Trust, Society of Scottish Artists, Mr David Scruton of The McManus Galleries (Dundee), St Andrews Public Library, Stavanger AG (Norway), Stirling Smith AG (Stirling), Thurso Heritage Society, Rev Professor Ian R Torrance, Mrs Jean Walsh (Glasgow Museums and AG), His Honour David Wild, and Yale University (Paul Mellon collection).

My greatest debt of all is to the small dedicated band who made the project possible. Vivien Macmillan prepared essential information for a substantial number of entries, her extensive and often difficult voyages of discovery far exceeded the call of duty. Without her sustained help over several years many entries would have been woefully limited or missing altogether.

My family, Feona, Malcolm and Rhod read through many pages of early proofs and checked especially the sporting literature; Kate Rigby, Margaret Charles and Jane Grey deciphered my interminable jottings and recorded my tapes with remarkable accuracy, stamina and good humour; my wife Dorothy constantly gleaned information from the most unexpected quarters, encouraged and criticised while keeping hope alive that one day the project really would be finished. Without her encouragement and support in the face of all disruptions and distractions the work could never have been completed.

Responsibility for any errors and omissions is of course mine alone.

# GUIDE TO USERS

Entries are in alphabetical order. When the surname is the same the order is in accordance with first and second christian names and where only initials are known these precede full names. Thus, for example, 'SMITH, J' appears before 'SMITH, J Arthur' while 'SMITH, James' would come later and 'SMITH, James Arthur' after that.

Married lady artists appear according to their most frequently preferred professional name, with the prefix 'Mrs' when the husband's name is used and he too is an artist. When the husband of a lady artist is not himself an artist but the family name has been sometimes used by his wife, this is shown in parenthesis. 'Miss' rather than 'Ms' indicates unmarried status since most entries lived when that was the customary mode and it happens also to be less ambiguous. Where more than one name has been used professionally during a lifetime, mention is made of the alternative. When a male entry has more than one professional name or has a publicly used soubriquet these are shown in parentheses.

No differentiation has been made between 'Mc' and 'Mac' both of which have been placed before all other 'M's.

Names appearing in bold within the text refer to individuals of minor importance about whom little is known but who nevertheless had a full or part-time occupation falling within the scope of the Dictionary.

Where dates of birth and death are not known the flugit (fl) dates refer to the period of recorded activity. When there is no date following the hyphen this indicates that the entry is still active. A question mark following the hyphen implies that although deceased the exact year of death is not known. The prefixing of circa (c) before a date indicates that the precise year is unclear.

References within the text to other entries are followed by a parenthesized qui vive (qv).

The sources of direct quotations are given in square brackets, further details being provided in the individual bibliographies. For reasons of space the bibliographies are not exhaustive but provide details of only the most important works. Where bibliographic references are shown this does not imply that any or all of the biographical details have been taken from any or all of them.

References have been given wherever possible to places open to the public in which examples of an entry's work may be seen.

The use of the term 'amateur' should not be regarded as in any sense derogatory but refers only to the fact that as far as can be ascertained an active pursuance of the arts was not the main source of income. Inevitably, there may be an overlap with the term 'part-time'. In many cases artistic achievement/recognition has been gained only after retirement from other work so that a single career might encompass several descriptions, applicable at different period of life.

# ABBREVIATIONS

| | |
|---|---|
| AAS | Aberdeen Artists' Society |
| ARE | Associate Royal Society of Painter Etchers |
| ARHA | Associate Royal Hibernian Academy |
| ARIAS | Associate of the Royal Incorporation of Architects in Scotland |
| ARIBA | Associate Royal Institute of British Architects |
| ARMS | Associate Royal Society of Miniature Painters |
| ARPE | Associate Royal Society of Painter-Etchers |
| ARSA | Associate Royal Scottish Academy |
| ARWS | Associate Royal Society of Painters in Watercolours |
| FAS | Fellow Antiquarian Society |
| FBA | Fellow British Academy |
| FRIAS | Fellow of the Royal Incorporation of Architects in Scotland |
| FRS | Fellow Royal Society |
| FRSA | Fellow Royal Society of Arts |
| FRSE | Fellow of the Royal Society of Edinburgh |
| FRSSA | Fellow of the Royal Scottish Society |
| FSA | Fellow of Royal Society of Artists (before 1791) |
| FRSA | Fellow of Royal Society of Antiquaries |
| GI/RGI | (Royal) Glasgow Institute of the Fine Arts |
| HRCA | Honorary Member Royal Cambrian Academy |
| HRHA | Honorary Member Royal Hibernian Academy |
| HRSA | Honorary Member Royal Scottish Academy |
| NG | National Gallery |
| NLS | National Library of Scotland |
| NPG | National Portrait Gallery |
| NWS | New Water Colour Society |
| OWS | 'Old Water Colour Society' or Society of Painters in Watercolours, later Royal Society of Painters in Watercolours |
| PRA | President Royal Academy |
| PRCA | President Royal Cambrian Academy |
| PRHA | President Royal Hibernian Academy |
| PRI | President Royal Institute of Painters in Water Colours |
| PRMS | President Royal Miniature Society |
| PRSA | President Royal Scottish Academy |
| RA | Royal Academy; Royal Academician |
| RBA | Royal Society of British Artists, Suffolk Street |
| RCA | Member Royal Cambrian Academy |
| RCanA | Royal Canadian Academy |
| RE | Fellow Royal Society of Painter Etchers |
| RHA | Royal Hibernian Academy; Royal Hibernian Academician |
| RI | Royal Institute of Painters in Water Colours |

| | |
|---|---|
| RIBA | Royal Institute of British Architects |
| RMS | Royal Society of Miniature Painters Sculptors and Engravers |
| ROI | Royal Institute of Oil Painters |
| RSA | Royal Scottish Academy; Royal Scottish Academician |
| | Royal Society of Arts |
| RSW | Royal Scottish Society of Painters in Water Colours |
| RWA | Royal West of England Academy |
| RWS | Royal Society of Watercolour Painters |
| SA | Society of Artists (incorporated in 1765) |
| SBA | Society of British Artists (Royal Society of British Artists) |
| SM | Society of Miniaturists |
| SNGMA | Scottish National Gallery of Modern Art |
| SNPG | Scottish National Portrait Gallery |
| SS (see RBA) | Suffolk Street |
| SSA | Scottish Society of Artists |
| SSWA | Scottish Society of Women Artists |
| V&A | Victoria and Albert Museum |
| VPRI | Vice President Royal Institute of Painters in Water Colours |
| VPRR | Vice President Royal Society of Miniature Painters, Sculptors & Engravers |
| WIAC | Women's International Art Club |

# INTRODUCTION

The intention has been to provide the most relevant details of all painters, engravers and etchers who met a comprehensive range of criteria, and all architects, carvers, designers, draughtsmen, embroiderers, illustrators, jewellery designers, masons, photographers and stained glass window designers who met slightly more rigorous criteria.

In the case of 'artists', the criteria are twofold: to be or have been [A] Scottish - by birth, direct near ancestry, or marriage and/or to have had an important association (e.g. Sam Bough) and/or influence (e.g. Sir Edwin Landseer) on Scottish artistic tradition; *and* to have been [B] an exhibitor in a major public institution (e.g. RSA, RA, RSW, RGI, RWS, AAS, Paisley Institute) or to have executed at least one known work of repute. Although inevitably introducing a judgmental element, the last criterion is necessary in order to encompass those who never exhibited either because (i) they lived too early, (ii) died prematurely, (iii) made no attempt to exhibit, or (iv) their work was of an inappropriate kind.

Even within these broad parameters there are anomalies. Early records do not distinguish between painters of coats of arms, house and palace interiors, gun battlements, manuscripts or portraits. The earliest portrait painters in Scotland came from overseas, while the first Scottish artist to be described as a painter of pictures was John Smith in 1609. Doubtful cases have been included with evidence of their activity. Admission to the title of 'burgess' has always been noted because during the fifteenth, sixteenth and seventeenth centuries this was a necessary qualification before being allowed to work for any civic authority.

Early masons have also presented a difficulty. They have been included whenever a work of contemporary importance has been recorded; often their contribution was inextricably bound up with a trained architect.

As group practices became increasingly common within the architectural profession so it has been progressively more difficult to attribute responsibility to any one partner. Accordingly, the number of architects practising this century who have been included is a smaller proportion than in earlier centuries.

In Victorian and Edwardian times it was fashionable for ladies to paint, especially in watercolours. Many travelled extensively and were greatly talented but few sought to have their work exhibited. Their modesty has made the posthumous recording of their achievement difficult but the effort has been made. Victims of male establishment bias, many deserve a recognition yet to be awarded.

The greatest difficulty has been with contemporaries. Although alive to tell the tale some have shown remarkable reluctance to do so whilst others have suggested entries of voluminous proportions. Furthermore, whilst personal prejudice must be excluded from a work of this nature, it has sometimes been undeniably difficult to identify any artistic component. The principal criterion has again been at least one acceptance in a major exhibition whilst not excluding artists of recognised merit who for one reason or another have not yet exhibited.

For so small a country, although perhaps because of it, Scotland has produced a surprising number of artistic dynasties. Foremost were the Faeds, Napiers, Nasmyths, Nories and Patersons while in architecture there were the incomparable Adam family, the Stevensons, and the Mylne dynasty of masons. In the case of the Nories a genealogy has been shown to help illustrate the uncertain contributions made by the different generations.

Many secondary sources have been used and the details extracted have been checked in order to minimise the perpetuation of reiterated error (of which the introduction of a second initial for James Giles is a prime example). In addition to the bibliographic notes, on account of their comprehensive span, special acknowledgements are due to Robert Brydall's *Art in Scotland; its Origins & Progress* (1889), Sir James Caw's *Scottish Painters 1620-1908* (1908), Grant M Waters's *Dictionary of British Artists 1900-1950,* David & Francina Irwin's *Scottish Painters 1700-1900* (1975), M R Apted & S Hannabuss's *Painters in Scotland 1301-1700* (1978), Julian Halsby's *Scottish Watercolourists 1740-1940* (1986) and - less compendious but most erudite - Duncan Macmillan's *Scottish Art 1640-1990* (1990). Apart from variations in the periods covered, the treatment and emphases of these writers has been so different that the contrasts are often as enlightening as the contents.

Whenever reliable evidence has permitted, reference has been made to character and personality as well as to outstanding or unusual autobiographical detail not necessarily in itself artistic.

In human affairs, passion attaches to opinion in a measure inversely proportionate to the potential for objectivity. Thus art criticism, whether voiced by 'experts' or exemplified as popular esteem, shares the kind of self-confident assertion often found in religious and political utterances. Judgement of quality in artistic endeavour is open to many influences. Art criticism in Scotland, for example, has neglected marine painting just as it has ignored sporting and wildlife art; the market place is controlled and sometimes manipulated by the buyers prepared to spend most; academic art as taught in our leading art schools is a slave to its own contemporary fashion while the leading public academies have too often been guilty of parochialism and self-advancement.

The length of an entry has been determined by what is known and should be regarded as reflecting in only the broadest way the verdict of history - certainly not any personal whim.

Artists of all kinds and talents need to be constantly appraised in a manner undeterred by the views of the art establishment and uninfluenced by the market place. The shifting verdict of history and individual taste fashioned by constant communion with artistic work are the best guides. In bringing to public attention many artists hitherto neglected, it is hoped that this work will enhance and extend the scope for informed judgement whilst at the same time expanding the field for further research.

PJM McEwan MA PhD
Glengarden
Ballater
Aberdeenshire

# PREFACE TO SECOND EDITION

The purpose of preparing a second edition, in addition to making the Dictionary again available, has been twofold: to correct an occasional error and to bring the work up to date.

Recognised errors of both omission and commission appearing in the first edition were happily few, the most serious being the inexplicable omission of an entire page of original text and recording the death of an artist who is still happily very much alive. Also, there were several renowned painters who had been originally excluded because their Scottishness or Scottish involvement, since confirmed, had been unclear or unknown.

Bringing entries up to date proved more difficult. This was not only because contemporary artists range from the silently reclusive to the compulsively self-promotional, though this is certainly true, but because of a growing tendency among highly competent artists to bypass Academy recognition. Academic fashion, both at Colleges of Art and at the Academies, seem largely out of step with popular taste. This means that many painters prefer to exhibit at commercial galleries, where the monitoring procedures are less strict and the financial rewards greater, regardless of peer group or academic recognition. Whereas until the middle of the last century it was highly probable that the best practitioners exhibited at one or other of the principal public galleries, this is no longer the case. And since the number of professional painters currently working is remarkably high, when determining entries personal judgement has had to be taken into account in addition to objective criteria.

There is now an extensive bibliography, missing from the first edition.

Some confusion and irritation was caused by the use of the term 'amateur'. The correct use of this term, to mean someone who is not primarily dependent on artistic endeavour for a living, has been retained; it is **not** used in the pejorative sense of someone whose art is thought to be somehow inferior.

The initials GI and RGI are synonymous. From its foundation in 1861 until 1896, when it was granted a royal charter, it was the Glasgow Institute of the Fine Arts (GI), thereafter it became the Royal Glasgow Institute of the Fine Arts (RGI).

A final heartfelt word of thanks to two people without whose extensive help the revision would not have been possible. Vivien Macmillan has again been responsible for harvesting the details of many contemporaries, fielding many enquiries in the process, and keeping me in touch with Academy developments. My son Rhod who, as well as typesetting and editing the revised text, has overcome the many complexities of transferring the text from one computer system to another, in addition to amending the pagination and headings, different from the original on every one of over 600 pages. Two very considerable necessary tasks. Their respective help has been essential and to both I am deeply indebted, and to Dorothy, my long-suffering wife, for her endless patience and wise counsel.

# PORTRAITS OF SOME SCOTTISH ARTISTS

This selection of portraits of some of the best known Scottish artists is not intended to be exhaustive but represents those for whom suitable illustrations were readily available. Some are self-portraits, some painted by fellow artists and one or two are taken from photographs. As indicated in the acknowledgements, the large majority are taken from the National Galleries of Scotland for whose permission to have them reproduced we are most grateful.

*Robert Adam by James Tassie*

*John Alexander, self portrait*

*William Aikman, self portrait*

*Sir William Allan by William Nicholson*

*William Bonnar, self portrait*

*John Brown by William Delacour*

*John Burnett by Stephen Denning*

*Sir David Young Cameron by Alfred Kingsley Lawrence*

*George Paul Chalmers by John Pettie*

*Robert Colquhoun by Robert MacBryde*

*James Cowie by John Lawrie*

*Joseph Crawhall by Edward Arthur Walton*

*Stanley Cursiter with wife by Stanley Cursiter, detail*

*William Delacour, self portrait*

*Sir William Reid Dick by Reginald Greenville Eves*

*John Milne Donald by Alexander Duff Robertson*

*Joan Eardley, photograph by Audrey Walker.*
*Courtesy Mrs P.M. Black*

*Joseph Farquharson, self portrait.*
*Courtesy Mr & Mrs Angus Farquharson*

*Thomas Faed by Sir William Fettes Douglas*

*David Foggie, self portrait*

*John Duncan Fergusson, self portrait*

*Andrew Geddes, self portrait*

*Sir William Gillies, self portrait*

*Sir James Guthrie, self portrait*

*Sir Francis Grant by John Prescott Knight*

*Gavin Hamilton by Archibald Skirving*

*Sir George Harvey by Robert Herdman*

*John Henning by Robert Scott Lauder*

*George Henry by Thomas C Dugdale*

*Robert Herdman by Robert Duddingston Herdman*

*David Octavius Hill by Amelia Robertson Hill*

*Violet Kennedy Erskine Jacob by an unknown artist*

*George Jamesone, self portrait*

*Robert Scott Lauder by John Hutchison*

*Sir John Lavery by James Kerr-Lawson*

*William McCance, self portrait*

*Dugald Sutherland MacColl by Donald MacLaren*

*Horatio McCulloch by Sir Daniel Macnee*

*Hannah Clarke Preston MacGoun, self portrait*

Robert Ranald McIan by John Stone

Charles Rennie Mackintosh by Francis Henry Newbery

William Darling McKay, self portrait

Duncan MacLaren by Edward John Gregory

Kenneth Macleay by John Gibson

*Sir David MacNee by James Macbeth*

*Sir William MacTaggart by William Gillies*

*David Martin, self portrait*

*John MacWhirter by Sir Hubert Herkomer*

*Sir John Baptiste de Medina, self portrait*

*John Mylne by an unknown artist*

*Charlotte Nasmyth by William Nicholson*

*James Nasmyth, self portrait*

*Erskine Nicol, self portrait*

*James Campbell Noble by John Pettie*

*James Norie, self portrait*

*Patric Park by Kenneth Macleay*

James Paterson, self portrait

Sir Joseph Noel Paton by Ranald Noel Paton

Samuel John Peploe, self portrait

Waller Hugh Paton by George Paul Chalmers

John Pettie by George Paul Chalmers

*John Phillip, self portrait*

*Sir Henry Raeburn by Thomas Campbell*

*Allan Ramsay, self portrait*

*Anne Redpath, self portrait*

*Sir George Reid by John Bowie*

*David Roberts by Robert Scott Lauder*

*Andrew Robertson, self portrait*

*Alexander Ignatius Roche, self portrait*

*Alexander Runciman by John Brown*

*William Bell Scott by David Scott*

*Charles Kirkpatrick Sharpe by Thomas Fraser*

*Robert Sivell by Hamish Paterson*

*William Strang, self portrait*

*Sir John Steell by Robert Scott Lauder*

*Archibald Skirving by Andrew Geddes*

*John Syme, self portrait*

*Sir Robert Strange by Jean Baptiste Greuze*

*Phoebe Anna Traquair by James Pittendrigh Macgillivray*

*Rev John Thomson by William Wallace*

*Edward Arthur Walton by Helen Walton*

*Scottie Wilson by Marie Levy*

*Richard Waitt, self portrait*

*Sir David Wilkie, self portrait*

*William Yellowlees, self portrait*

*Alexander Macdonald by Sir George Reid*

*Sir William Fettes Douglas by Sir George Reid*

*Thomas Faed by John Pettie*

*Peter Graham, self portrait*

*Robert Herdman, self portrait*

*John Hutchison by Sir George Reid*

*William McTaggart by Sir George Reid*

*William Calder Marshall by John Pettie*

Sir David Murray by James Couttes Michie

Alexander Nasmyth by James Nasmyth

Sir Joseph Noel Paton by Sir George Reid

Sir John Steel by Sir George Reid

*Thomas Alexander Ferguson Graham, self portrait*

*Colin Hunter, self portrait*

*Sir William Quiller Orchardson, self portrait*

**ABBEY, Heather** **fl 1964**
Aberdeen painter of landscape and still life. Exhibited AAS(3) from 73 Braemar Place.

**ABBO GROUP**
An Aberdeen group of artists who exhibited together. Formed shortly after the second World War. members included Eric Auld(qv), William P Baxter(qv), Donald Buyers(qv) and W T Ord.

**ABBOT, Richmond** **fl c1855-1865**
Painter in oil of figures, interiors and still life. First known at a Welsh address in Gresford, Denbighshire, exhibited on a number of occasions at the RSA, once in 1858 and twice (from a Liverpool address) 1861.

**ABBOTT, Stewart** **fl 1880-1882**
Glasgow artist; exhibited GI(2).

**ABBOTT, William B** **fl 1880-1890**
Edinburgh painter in watercolours; domestic genre. In c1888 moved to Dundee. Exhibited RSA 1883 and 1884; also RI(1).

**ABELL, William A** **fl 1917-1940**
Glasgow watercolour painter. Exhibited RSW(2) & GI(12).

**ABERCROMBIE, Douglas** **1934-**
Born Glasgow. Painter in oils and acrylic; abstract in the expressionist tradition, also figurative, portraits; scene designer. Studied at GSA 1952-1956. Awarded a travelling scholarship, he spent some time on the continent before touring with Bertram Mills Circus 1957. The following year was painter-designer at the Glasgow Citizens Theatre and in 1964 moved to London. Shortly after graduating exhibited RSA (1956 and 1957) portraits and still lifes. In 1964 he worked at the Royal Opera House in Covent Garden and from 1965-67 lived in Barcelona and Minorca where he painted in an increasingly abstract style. Greatly influenced by North American abstract painters (especially Louis Olitski and Noland) but developed his own expressive style. He has exhibited at the GI and was included in the 1977 Exhibition of '25 Years of British Painting' at the RA.
**Bibl:** Hardie 179.

**ABERCROMBIE, James** **fl 1723**
Early portrait painter. Appointed second King's Limner for Scotland after the death of George Ogilvie - much to the disappointment of William Aikman(qv). Apart from the fact that Abercrombie came from Glasgow and subsequently served in the army in the Colonies, nothing is known of his life or work.

**ABERCROMBIE, John Brown** **1843-1929**
Edinburgh painter of figures, genre and landscape, husband of Jessie Abercrombie. Living in Edinburgh for a time, from 1866. Exhibited RA in 1873 and 1896, and at the GI in 1904. Exhibited a total of 95 works at the RSA. In 1872 one of his Academy pictures was a curious portrayal of the verse:
Bonnie Jockie, blythe and gay kiss'd young Jenny makin hay;
the lassie blush'd, and frowning cried,
'Na, na, it winna dae';
I canna, canna, winna, mauna buckle tae".
Among his other works was a powerful portrayal of 'The Assassin's Bursting Open the Door to Murder James I of Scotland, 1437' (1883). In 1899 exhibited a portrait of the artist G W Johnston RSA. (His name is incorrectly spelt by Graves). Also exhibited AAS 1894-1923.

**ABERCROMBY, J R** **1908-1961**
Arbroath and Edinburgh painter in oil and watercolour, mostly topographical scenes in and around Edinburgh, also genre. Exhibited regularly at the RA between 1908 and 1961. May have studied at Hospitalfield, Arbroath since this is the address given in his earlier exhibited works. Appears to have visited Spain, three Spanish landscapes being exhibited RSA in 1914, 1916 and 1918.

**ABERCROMBY(IE), Jessie** **fl 1878-1893**
Edinburgh painter in oils who specialised in portraits, literary figures and landscapes. Wife of John Abercrombie(qv). Her style was similar to her husband's although the craftsmanship was weaker and the colour sense perhaps a little more sensitive. Exhibited RSA 1878-1883.

**ABERCROMBY, Robert C** **fl 1906-1961**
Painter in oil who exhibited regularly RSA 1908 & 1961, AAS 1906-1923. Represented in Paisley AG.

**ABERDEEN ARTISTS SOCIETY** **1885-**
Founded Jan 3, 1885 when Sherwood Hunter(qv) presided over an inaugural meeting attended by Archibald Reid, James Cadenhead, James Coutts Michie, John Philip Fraser, John Mitchell, George Russell Gowans, Garden Smith, Alex Mackenzie and John Duthie (who became secretary). 'Non-resident' artists invited to join were Sir John Steel, George Reid, G B MacDonald, Sam Reid, Joseph Farquharson, J Fraser Taylor, John Burr, Alex Burr, A D Longmuir, J Stirling Dyce, J G Laing, William Baird, Thomas Bunting, Joseph Milne, Colin Phillip and Peter Graham. The leading spirits were Cadenhead and Russell Gowans. The principal aim has always been to promote art and the artists of the north-east, mainly by means of an annual exhibition. The Society languished during and after WW2 until being resuscitated by Ian Fleming in 1958. In 1992 a non-practising artist was elected President for the first time.

**ABERDENE, John de** **fl 1364**
Little is known of this early Scottish painter beyond the fact that he is listed as a herald painter to the Courts of the Lord Lyon in 1364.

**ABINGER, Lord** **1878-1943**
Amateur landscape painter in oil. Would never sell a picture as he did not wish to compete with professional artists whose livelihood depended on selling their work. Close friend of Lamorna Birch with whom he often painted in the Highlands. Exhibited a landscape at the RSA in 1932, a work still in the possession of the artist's family. Lived at Inverlochy Castle, Fort William.

**ABOYNE, E** **fl c1865-1875**
Edinburgh painter in oils. Specialised in landscapes especially Swiss and continental scenes. Exhibited RSA 1868-1872.

**ACADEMY OF ST LUKE (ROME)** **17th Cent-**
Famous Roman teaching academy which provided inspiration and instruction to visiting Scottish artists of whom in the second part of the eighteenth century there were usually at least ten at any one time. The Academy was born of the University of Painters, Miniaturists & Embroiderers (1478). It now holds over one thousand paintings and sculptures. Members of the Academy staffed and supervised the Accademia del Nudo which opened in 1754 in a room in the Capitoline Gallery. Competitions were held, the most important being the Concorsi Clementini, held annually but after 1721 triennially, for architects, artists and sculptors under 25. In 1763 there was also the Concorsi Balestra. In 1758 Robert Mylne(qv) won the principal prize for architecture, an achievement repeated by James Byres(qv) four years later. David Allan(qv) won the gold medal at the Concorsa Balestra in 1773 for his 'Departure of Hector', a work which has remained in St Luke's. Other students included Gavin Hamilton(qv), Jacob More(qv) and Sir Robert Strange(qv). The Academy was the model for the short-lived Edinburgh Academy of the same name(qv).
**Bibl:** Basil Skinner, Scots in Italy, SNPG 1966.

**ACADEMY OF ST LUKE (EDINBURGH)** **1729-1731**
Short-lived Academy inspired by the Academy of the same name in Rome. Founded by Allan Ramsay(qv), William Adam(qv), both James Nories(qv), John Alexander(qv) and the English engraver Richard Cooper, then an Edinburgh resident, elected Treasurer. Cooper was the eldest statesman of the group and almost certainly used some of his own collection to instruct other members, notably Robert Strange(qv).

**ACHESON, Miss Annie Crawford** **1882-1962**
Sculptress. Exhibited a figurative work at the RSA in 1944.

**ACHESOUN, James** **fl 1675**
Engraver. In 1675 he was made a Burgess of Edinburgh.

**ACHESOUN, Johnne** **fl 1553**
Engraver, Master of the Mint. Known as the 'Maister Cunyeour' for his work in Paris cutting dies with portraits of Queen Mary used for the extremely rare testoons and half-testoons, the only known coins of that time.
**Bibl:** Brydall 62; Proc. of Scottish Antiquaries.

**ACTON, Meriel** **fl 1964-1965**
Amateur portrait painter based in Dingwall who exhibited twice at the RSA in 1964 and again the following year, latterly living in Perthshire.

**ADAIR, John** **fl 1683-d1722**
Engraver, map maker and surveyor. Commissioned by the Privy Council 1683 to survey the Scottish shires. In 1703 published *The Description of the Sea-coast and Islands of Scotland,* part i, Folio. But the work was never completed although many maps and charts of Scotland were undertaken.
**Bibl:** Bushnell; DNB.

**ADAIR, Agnes** **fl 1883-1886**
Stranraer painter in oil of fruit and still life. Exhibited at the RA in 1883 and again in 1886.

**ADAM the PAINTER** **fl 1628**
Portrait painter. Portraits of Lord Erroll, Lady Hay and James Maxwell were executed during 1628, also a commissioned work of the 3rd Earl of Winton.
**Bibl:** Apted II, 12.

**ADAM, Miss C C** **fl 1885-1886**
Glasgow watercolour painter of flowers. Exhibited RSA in 1886 & GI.

**ADAM, Charlotte E L** **fl 1893-1896**
Dunblane and Glasgow figurative painter. Exhibited once at the RSA in 1895 from 227 West George Street & GI(4).

**ADAM, David Livingstone** **1883-1924**
Born Glasgow, died Chicago. Known to have been in Glasgow 1908-1909. Exhibited three pictures at the GI.

**ADAM, George** **fl 1861-1865**
Edinburgh painter in oil, landscapes and coastal scenes. He was particularly fond of the east coast and in 1861 exhibited 'Dysart Harbour', in 1862 'Buckhaven', a London scene in 1863 and 'On the Clyde' in 1864 - all from 20 Clarence Street, Edinburgh.

**ADAM, James** **1732-1794**
Born Edinburgh 21 Jly; died London. Painter in watercolours, architect. Third son of William Adam and younger brother of Robert Adam. Early sketchbooks include one for the design of Gunsgreen House, Eyemouth (c.1755). In 1760 completed his architectural education by touring Italy in the company of George Ritson. In Venice he was joined by Clerisseau and together they went to Rome and to Naples and Paestum. His journal was printed in the *Library of Fine Arts* ii, 9-13, 1831. A visit to Italy demonstrated a critical attitude towards Palladio and evinced an interest in 'grotesque and Pompeian decoration'. Returned to London and joined the family partnership in 1763 where he acted as junior partner although sharing the credit for the buildings jointly designed and erected with Robert. These included Mellerstain (for George Baillie of Jarviswood, 1770-8), Wedderburn (for Patrick Home, 1770-8), Culzean (for the 10th Earl of Cassillis, 1777-90), Pitfour (1784), Seton (1789-91) and Stobs (1792) with its square rather than rounded towers and surrounding Scottish crowtops with Latin-Cross finials. Works executed independently included Cullen House, Banffshire for the 3rd Earl of Seafield (1763), Hertfordshire Town Hall (1767-9) and the facades of Portland Place, London (1776). He must have been mainly responsible for four Glasgow buildings erected after Robert's death including the Royal Infirmary (1792-94 - demolished 1910) the Tron Church (1794), the Barony Church (1798 - now demolished) the first Assembly Rooms (1796-98 - demolished c1890), and the surviving Trades Hall. In 1769 he succeeded his brother as architect to King George III, a position he retained until its abolition in 1782. He also wrote a number of books, the principal being *Practical Essays on Architecture.* His work was included in the RA Exhibition of Scottish Art in 1939. A portrait by Allan Ramsay is in the SNPG. Represented by a selection of drawings in Sir John Soane's Museum and by architectural sketchbooks at Penicuik House, Midlothian.
**Bibl:** Colvin; Dunbar 109,113,120-1,124; John Fleming, Robert Adam & his circle, 1962; Gifford 38,277,332; A Gomme & D Walker, Architecture in Glasgow, London 1987(rev), 13,18,46n,60-5,284; Halsby 245; Rykwert, The Brothers Adam, 1985.

**ADAM, James** **fl 1813**
Edinburgh joiner and amateur draughtsman. An ink and wash drawing of 'The West Front of the Royal Palace of Holyrood House', executed on 8 Dec 1813, is in the collection of the City of Edinburgh.

**ADAM, James** **fl 1858**
Aberdeen landscape painter in oil. Exhibited a North Wales scene at the RSA in 1858.

**ADAM, Mrs Jean Miller** **fl 1935-1940**
Amateur Glasgow artist, exhibited GI(13) & SWA(2).

**ADAM, John** **1721-1792**
Born Kirkcaldy. Architect. Eldest son of William(qv). With his brother Robert(qv), he formed the link between the early and mid-Georgian eras of Scottish architecture. As he inherited the family estate at Blair Adam, near Kinross, as well as the family's business concerns in Scotland, he remained north of the border until his brother Robert's miscalculations involved him in London. On the death of their father, John and Robert had the task of decorating Hopetoun House, an accomplishment that exceeded in excellence anything of its kind done before in Britain. The brothers were also engaged in extensions to Arniston, but most of the work at this time was with the Ordnance, John having become Master to the Board. The main examples of this work are at Fort Augustus and Fort George. John was appointed architect of the first improvement to the public works of Edinburgh, specifically the new Exchange, now the City Chambers (1753-1761). Another important activity at this time was extensive work at Inverary for the Duke of Argyll (1754). Later, working on his own, John designed Douglas Castle, Lanark, the interior being not at all Gothic (1757-1761) and although never completed, the unfinished building was demolished 1939. Other important works were the rebuilding of Banff Castle, (1750-1752), Dumfries House, Ayrshire, (1754-1759), Hawkhill, Edinburgh (1761-62), Moffat House (1762), The Tolbooth Steeple, Banff (1764-67), additions to Castle Grant (1765), the remodelling of Broomhall, Fife (1766-77) and Pitfour Castle, Perthshire c1785, enlarged by Wm Burn(qv) 1825. He was an extremely able and influential interior designer. An example of his fastidiousness was his concern over the looking-glasses in Tweeddale Castle, the Edinburgh home of the Hay's; he wished to refurbish the glasses 'to make them much more genteel', and to preserve a screen by covering it with glass to keep it 'from dust and from being handled by curious people'.
**Bibl:** Colvin; Cosh, 'The Adam Family and Arniston' Arch Hist 27, 1984, 214 ff; Dunbar 104,106,109-111,135; Gifford 47,56,102,161, 176,184,209,271,273,286 (illus); Irwin 61,63,101; Lees-Milne, The Age of Adam, 1947; Ian G Lindsay & Mary Cosh, Inverary and the Dukes of Argyll, 1973; Rowan, 'The Building of Hopetoun', Arch Hist, 27, 1984, 183 ff; Rykwert, The Brothers Adam, 1985; SAC 'Robert Adam and Scotland. The Picturesque Drawings', (Ex Cat by A A Tait, 1972); Swarbrick, Robert Adam and His Brothers, 1915; Tait, 'The Picturesque Drawings of Robert Adam', Master Drawings, IX, 2, 1977, 161-171; Bruce Walker & W S Gauldie, Architects and Architecture on Tayside, Dundee 1984, 63-5.

**ADAM, John** **fl 1874-1881**
Edinburgh painter, mostly in watercolour; portraits, wild flowers, still life, coastal scenes and landscape. He exhibited at the RSA(4) 1874-1881, but having moved to London in 1880 his professional association with Scotland seems then to have ceased.
**Bibl:** Irwin 61,128.

**ADAM, Joseph** **fl 1858-1916**
Born Glasgow. Landscape painter in oils and watercolours. Father of Joseph Denovan Adam(qv). Worked in London during the second half of the 19th century exhibiting frequently at the RA between 1858 and 1880, mostly landscapes in Cumbria, the Scottish Highlands, and the outer fringes of London. He signed his work 'J Adam'. Exhibited

RSA regularly 1872-1916, once at the RA, and ten pictures at the GI. Represented in Glasgow AG, Victoria (Australia) AG 'Balmoral'.

**ADAM, Joseph Denovan RSA RSW** **1842-1896**
Born Glasgow, Sep 19; died Glasgow, Apr 22. Painter in oil and occasionally watercolour of animals and landscape, occasional still lifes. Received early tuition from his father, the landscape painter, subsequently studied at South Kensington and in the RA life class. Quickly evinced an interest in animal painting. Having spent holidays in Scotland went to live in Crieff 1870. Following the death of his wife 1873 moved to Edinburgh, re-marrying 1876. In 1887 settled near Stirling, founding the School of Animal Painting at Craigmill. Here he specialised in painting Highland cattle, generally in moorland settings, but also depicted sheep and occasional landscapes. He was a precursor of the Glasgow School. Elected RSW 1880, ARSA 1884, RSA 1892. "His natural taste in colour was rather crude and garish, and his drawing more facile and vigorous than stylish and constructive; his compositions inclined to be crowded and tumultuous, and the vigour of his brushwork although not unpainter-like, was truculent and at times repellent. Yet in his later pictures, in part due to maturing powers, and in part, to the influence of the more decorative ideals pursued by some of the young Glasgow painters...these elements while remaining characteristic became confused into a style which, if lacking in refinement and distinction, was coherent and distinctive" (Caw). Regular exhibitor at both RA 1860-1892 & RSA from 1871 annually until 1896. Also GI, SS, Paris & Munich where he won a gold medal. Exhibited AAS 1893 & Paris Salon 1894. Represented in NG, NGS(4), Glasgow AG (Balmoral-Autumn), Paisley AG; McLean Museum (Greenock), Riga Museum (Latvia), Smith AG (Stirling), Ulster Museum (Belfast) (a ravishing still life).
**Bibl:** Bryan; Caw 338-339; Halsby 245; Maria Devaney, 'Joseph Denovan Adam - Mountain, Meadow, Moss and Moor', Ex Cat, Smith AG (Stirling), 1996

**ADAM, Joseph Denovan Jnr** **1879-1931**
Animal painter in oil. Son of Joseph Denovan Adam(qv); worked for his father on the Craigmill Farm and became an animal painter. Sometimes collaborated with his father although his watercolour technique is looser and more fluid than that of his more famous parent. Exhibited RSA(22) & GI(55), also at the inaugural exhibition of the AAS 1885. Represented Smith AG (Stirling).
**Bibl:** Halsby 245.

**ADAM, Margaret** **?-1820**
Amateur draughtswoman. Unmarried sister of Robert Adam(qv). Represented in the Blair Adam Collection (Kinross) with 'Rocky Landscape with Trees and a Classical Building in the Distance'.
**Bibl:** Halsby 245.

**ADAM, Matthew** **fl 1904-1922**
Paisley-based landscape painter in oil. Founder member, Paisley Art Club and captain of his local golf club, he was a quiet, unassuming and popular man. Exhibited French and English landscapes RSA in 1916, 1921 and 1922; GI(5), and in 1921 exhibited a portrait at the AAS. Represented in Paisley AG.

**ADAM, Patrick William RSA** **1854-1929**
Born Edinburgh; died North Berwick 27 Dec. Painter of portraits, landscapes, subject pictures, still life, interiors. Second son of Patrick Adam(qv). Studied at Edinburgh Academy then in London before returning to Scotland to complete his formal studies at the RSA School under George Paul Chalmers and William McTaggart. In 1872 at the age of 18 he first exhibited at the RSA, eventually showing there 164 pictures. Won the Maclaine-Watters medal for the best painting from life. Elected ARSA 1883, RSA 1894. Travelled abroad extensively and worked in Rome, Venice and Russia. Prominent member of the Society of Eight(qv) in Edinburgh, where his pictures were always a special feature. Keen supporter of the Scottish Artists Benevolent Association, he became its first honorary secretary and later a vice-president. His artistic interests were varied, now best remembered for his tenderly portrayed interiors painted from 1908 onwards when he was living in North Berwick. Exhibited 12 works at the RA between 1878 and 1896, also RSA(47) 1872-1883, GI(42) & AAS 1886-1926. Represented in NGS, Aberdeen AG, Dundee AG, Paisley AG, City of Edinburgh collection.
**Bibl:** Caw 423; Halsby 245; Hardie 142.

**ADAM, R S** **fl 1871**
Edinburgh painter in oils, exhibited a Highland landscape at the RSA in 1871.

**ADAM, Robert** **1728-1794**
Born Kirkcaldy; died London. Architect, interior designer, water-colourist and draughtsman in pen and wash. Son of William Adam(qv), brother of James(qv) and brother-in-law of John Clerk of Eldin(qv). Educated at Edinburgh University. In the company of Allan Ramsay(qv) enjoyed the patronage of the Hope family, visiting Rome to further his architectural studies 1754, sketching the classical ruins of that city. Later they were both employed by Lord Bute, Adam designing Luton Hoo and what is now Lansdowne House in Berkeley Square. Appointed architect to King George III in 1762 and with his brothers built the Adelphi in London 1769-71 as well as various other buildings and mansions in both town and country. He was an accomplished though amateur watercolourist fascinated by chiaroscuro. Influenced by Clerisseau and also by Paul Sandby, meeting the latter when Sandby was studying in Edinburgh 1747. In 1758 he returned to London and although immersed in many other activities continued to draw classical studies of landscapes with castles or ruins. One example, 'Landscape with Castle and Lake', is now in the SNG. Designed Charlotte Square, Edinburgh (1791). In addition to the Adam 'castles', designed with his brother James, was responsible for more modest but equally impressive private buildings. His mature style is best observed in his country houses, Newliston, West Lothian for Thomas Hogg, (1789-92) and Gosford, East Lothian (for the 7th Earl of Wemyss), although the latter was changed in the course of execution. Also responsible for Register House, Edinburgh began in 1774. Shortly before his death he was commissioned to rebuild the University of Edinburgh (illus Dunbar 113) but by 1793 lack of money aborted further work. Considering his varied activities he was a prolific artist and after his death 200 drawings were found in his London home, the majority of which are now in four collections, the NGS, Sir John Soane's Museum, the Blair Adam Collection (Kinross) and the Royal Museum of the Fine Arts, Copenhagen; other examples may be seen in the V&A. [See also James Adam]
**Bibl:** Arthur Thomas Bolton, The Architecture of Robert and James Adam 1758-1794, 2 Vols 1922; Dunbar 106,109,112-3,116-7,120-1,124; John Fleming, Robert Adam and his Circle in Edinburgh and Rome, 1962; Gifford passim; A Gomme & D Walker, Architecture of Glasgow, London 1987(rev), 13,18,46n,60-5,71n,82,109,284; Halsby 15-19,33; Hardie 13; Irwin 134 et passim; Paul Oppe, 'Robert Adam's Picturesque Compositions', Burlington Mag LXXX, 1942, 56-59; A A Tait, 'Robert Adam and Scotland. The Picturesque Drawings', SAC (Ex Cat 1972); 'The Picturesque Drawings of Robert Adam', Master Drawings,IX,2,1971.

**ADAM, Stephen** **1847-1910**
Architect and stained-glass window designer. The pioneer of modern stained glass window design in Scotland. Founded the firm of Adam & Small in 1870, producing windows of the highest standard to his own designs (eg Pollockshields parish church and the Clark memorial church, Largs). Exhibited at the RA between 1892 and 1899 from a Glasgow address including a design for a stained-glass window for Crathie Church at Balmoral, Aberdeenshire (1894). Other important work included the N transept window at Culross Abbey (1906), scenes from the Life of Christ at New Kilpatrick Church, Bearsden (c1909), the parish church of Pollockshields, and 'The Healing of the Sick' in the ante chapel of Glasgow Royal Infirmary. Exhibited RSA in 1896, 1897 and 1898(2), RSW(1) & GI(33).
**Bibl:** Painton Cowen, Stained Glass in Britain, 1985, 228,231,234-5,237-8; M. Donnelly, Glasgow Stained Glass, a preliminary study, 1981.

**ADAM, Stephen Jnr** **1873-1960**
Stained glass window designer. Son of Stephen Adam(qv). Two of his best known designs are a highly coloured window of an old man praying for The People's Palace, Glasgow (c1900) and a series of biblical subjects for the Episcopal church of St. James, Bishopsbriggs (c1900). Exhibited GI(3).
**Bibl:** Painton Cowen, Stained Glass in Britain, 1985, 238; Gifford 45,259,525.

**ADAM, Mrs Thomas** **fl 1896-1902**
Aberdeen painter in oil. Between the above years exhibited two

Venetian scenes and 'Tilquhillie Castle' at the AAS from 16 Albyn Place and after 1901 from Denmore.

**ADAM, William** **1689-1748**
Born Kirkcaldy, Oct 24. Architect; also property developer and speculative builder. Son of a local stonemason; father of four sons including John(qv), James(qv) and Robert(qv) and six daughters. The most successful and important architect working in Scotland between the two uprisings of 1715 and 1745. He combined great artistic ability with a shrewd business sense and a congenial temperament. Early in his career he gained the confidence of two influential patrons, the 2nd Earl of Stair and Sir John Clerk (11th baronet of Penicuik). Through them he obtained important commissions and in 1728, having become a burgess of Edinburgh, he was appointed Clerk and Storekeeper to the Works, being elevated two years later to Mason to the Board of Ordnance in North Britain. Whilst never neglecting his prosperous business interests, he nurtured the idea of publishing engravings of his architectural designs together with those of other architects but the plan remained unrealised until 64 years after his death - when *Vitruvius Scoticus* was published by his grandson in 1812. 'His work is remarkable as much for its eclecticism as for its unevenness of quality. His indebtedness to Gibbs and Vanbrugh is manifest, while Dutch and French sources seem also to have been laid under tribute from time to time. For the severities of English Palladianism...Adam had little taste, although he could when called upon - as for example at Newliston and Haddo (1732-5) - express himself convincingly enough in that idiom' [Dunbar]. His most important works include Mavisbank (c1727), a small but innovative country house for Sir John Clerk; Drum (built for Lord Somerville shortly afterwards); Airdrie House, Fife; the Anglo-Palladian villa of Dun (for David Erskine, Lord Dun 1730), the latter two having impressively rich stucco work executed by **Samuel CALDERWOOD**; and his two grandest conceptions: the enlargement of Bruce's original Hopetoun, and Duff House, Banff (for William Duff, later Earl of Fife 1730-2). Adam was also responsible for a number of important public buildings including the old Edinburgh Infirmary (1738, now demolished) and the College Library, Glasgow (1732, demolished). His most interesting church is Hamilton Parish church(1732), incorporating a 'wheel-cross' design that Dunbar suggests may have been borrowed from the fifth book of Serlio's *Architettura.* 'By utilising one limb of the building as a portico and vestry, and imposing the familiar T-plan arrangement upon the remainder, the architect showed considerable ingenuity in reconciling Renaissance theory with the realities of Presbyterian worship'. He had hoped to build a circular church at Inverary but, although pursued by his son John, it never materialised. Among his best known garden designs are Arniston in Midlothian (1726, for Robert Dundas) and Chatelherault in Lanarkshire (1732 for the 5th Duke of Hamilton). In 1740 he was responsible for redecorating the same Duke's apartments at Holyroodhouse, commissioning the landscape paintings and frames from the Nories(qv); also the design of General Wade's bridge at Aberfeldy(1733) and Gartmore House, Perthshire(c1740-5). Adam was one of the original signators of the Academy of St Luke(qv). After his death the prospering family business was successfully tended by his sons John(qv) and Robert(qv).
**Bibl:** Brydall 174; Cosh, 'The Adam Family and Arniston', Arch. History, 27, 1984; Dunbar 89,103-111,135; Gifford passim; Gomme & D Walker, Architecture of Glasgow, London 1987(rev) 58n,65-7,81n,284,291; Irwin 126; Lees-Milne, The Age of Adam, 1947; Bruce Walker & W S Gauldie, Architects and Architecture on Tayside, Dundee 1984, 61-3.

**ADAM, William** **1846-1917**
Born Tweedmouth. Painter in oils who specialised in street scenes and landscapes in Egypt, Holland and Scotland. Spent most of his working life in Glasgow. Exhibited 3 pictures at the RSA & GI(33).

**ADAMS, Charles** **fl 1953**
Exhibited one oil painting at the RSA in 1953, from an Aberdeen address.

**ADAMS, Charles Aston** **1932-**
Born in Aberdeen 25 Feb. Painter in oil and watercolour, designer; landscapes and portraits. Educated Robert Gordon's (1937-1949) and Gray's School of Art, Aberdeen (1949-1953). Combined teaching with painting. Illustrated a number of books, also designed a puppet series of children's programmes for Grampian TV. His work is conventionally representational with a good sense of atmosphere. Since retiring from teaching in 1988 has devoted himself full-time to his art. Exhibited RSA(1) 1953. Represented in the collection of the Queen Mother by 'The Bridge at Cambus O'May'.

**ADAMS, Eleanor (Mrs Stuart Macrae)** **fl 1951**
Exhibited one oil painting at the RSA in 1951, from a Dumbarton address.

**ADAMS, John** **fl 1849**
Painter in oils. This Edinburgh portraitist exhibited three paintings at the RSA in 1849.

**ADAMS, Joseph** **fl 1859**
Landscape painter. Exhibited a view of Grasmere at the RSA.

**ADAMS, Miss Mary L** **fl 1889**
Glasgow artist. Exhibited once at the RSA in 1889 & GI(3).

**ADAMS, W Douglas** **1853-1920**
Painter in oil; animals, landscape. Although based in London, most of his work was Scottish in character. Liked especially Highland cattle in broadly painted mountainous settings. The draughtsmanship was weak and the colours overly strong but he conveyed atmosphere well. Illustrated Gathorne Hardy's *The Salmon* (1898). His occasional golfing scenes achieved acclaim, 'The Drive' and 'The Putting Green' were engraved and published by Henry Graves (1984). Exhibited RA(32) from 1880 including 'Return of the Stalker' (1900) and 'Straight for the Guns', also GI(7).
**Bibl:** Wingfield.

**ADAMS, W R** **fl 1928**
Amateur Glasgow artist; exhibited GI(1).

**ADAMS, William** **fl 1921**
Amateur Glasgow artist; exhibited GI(1) and once at Liverpool.

**ADAMSON, David Comba** **1859-1926**
Born Ayrshire. Painter of domestic scenes and portraits, also occasional sculptor. He studied in Paris under Carolus Duran and Constant, returning there to live and work in the early 1890s. Exhibited twice at the RA, a domestic interior from a Glasgow address in 1889 and a portrait from a Paris address in 1893, also at the RSA(3) from a Paris address in 1896, and once more in 1898; and at the GI(5). Represented in Dundee AG.

**ADAMSON, John** **fl 1876-1902**
Edinburgh landscape painter in oil. Exhibited RSA 1876-1883. Possibly the same John Adamson who exhibited RA 1890-1902 from London addresses.

**ADAMSON, R Crawfurd** **1953-**
Born Edinburgh. Painter in oil of figurative and abstract subjects. Trained Dundee College of Art 1971-1976. After visiting Canada and France 1976-8 on a travelling scholarship he settled in Kent in 1979, although his first exhibition at the RSA that year gives a Dundee address. Held several successful shows in England and Scotland and in 1984 his work was shown at the XVIII PRIX International d'Art Contemporain de Monte-Carlo and at the John Player Portrait Exhibition at the National Portrait Gallery in 1987. Interested in 'the undefined inter-personal narratives, the non-verbal language of attraction and repulsion...in the single figure attempting to translate the figure into terms of paint and colour, without compromising the anatomy, but retaining its structure implicitly within the paint, rather than relying on anatomical delineation'. Solo exhibition in London 1989. Exhibits RSA since 1979 and ROI from 1984. Lives at St Leonard's-on-Sea, Sussex.

**ADAMSON, Robert** **1821-1848**
Photographer. Early exponent of the calotype process. Too delicate to continue his chosen career as an engineer, he was trained by his brother 1841-42 and by 1843 was beginning to exploit the new photographic technique commercially. Between May and August 1843, living in Edinburgh, he was introduced to David Octavius Hill(qv) by Sir David Brewster. A partnership began which produced work of the highest quality. Among their finest work are calotypes of Greyfriars churchyard and the fisherfolk of Newhaven, also a series

taken in Bonaly Tower (1846). In September 1843, Hill and Adamson attended the second assembly of the Free Church held in Glasgow and there took studies of groups and individual portraits which eventually were used for Hill's painting 'The Disruption of the Church of Scotland'. Adamson provided the technical expertise for the partnership. Groups of calotype studies were exhibited at the Royal Scottish Academy in 1884, '85 and '86 as the work of "Robert Adamson, under the artistic direction of D O Hill". They were presented not as photographs but as a kind of mezzotint. Adamson became ill in the autumn of 1847 and died in the autumn of 1848 when still only 27 years old.
**Bibl:** Halsby 85; Irwin 287,301; Duncan Macmillan [GA] 185-6;[SA] 194-197; Sara Stevenson,'DO Hill and Robert Adamson', Cat of Calotypes (SNPG 1981) 8-9.

**ADAMSON, Sarah Gough (Mrs Walker)** **1888-1963**
Born Manchester. Narrative and landscape painter, also flowers and occasional portraits; embroiderer. Studied at Edinburgh College of Art. It would seem that until 1915 she worked in Edinburgh and thereafter moved to London. She appears to have been related to Robert Adamson whose wife's portrait she painted in 1934. She was a frequent exhibitor at the RSA showing a total of 29 pictures from 1911-1915, then intermittently from 1917-1949; also RA(3), GI(5), RSW(3) & Paris Salon. Exhibited local landscapes at the AAS in 1912 and 1931.

**ADAMSON, Sydney** **fl 1892-1914**
Born Dundee. Painter of landscapes, portraits and public scenes; illustrator. Worked in London, illustrating for the leading magazines in the 1890s. Showed 44 works at the Baillie Gallery. Exhibited '*Military Service in St Giles Cathedral, Edinburgh*' at the RA 1908; Liverpool 1914, from 278 Blvd Raspail, Paris. Represented in V & A.
**Bibl:** Houfe 43-4.

**ADAMSON, Thomas** **fl 1886-1889**
Painter in oil; still-life and interiors. All that is known of this artist is that from 3 Braidburn Terrace, Edinburgh he exhibited 5 paintings at the RSA, a still-life and a French landscape in 1886, an interior of P W Adams' studio in 1888 and 2 evening landscapes in 1889; also once at the GI.

**ADAMSON, Miss Una Duncan** **fl 1929-1939**
Probably Scottish. All her exhibits were in Scotland, at the RSA in 1936 and 1937, RSW(6) & GI(3).

**ADAMSON, W M** **fl 1885-1886**
Landscape painter. Exhibited RSA, 1885 and 1886.

**ADAMSON, William** **fl 1853**
Landscape painter. Exhibited 'Sketch at Newbattle' at the RSA in 1853.

**ADCROFT, Frank** **fl 1932-1955**
Painter of landscape. Exhibited views of Fife at the RSA in 1932 and 1955, from a Glasgow address, also GI(5).

**ADDISON, Donald S** **fl 1967-1987**
Aberdeen painter in oil of landscape and semi-abstracts. Concentrates on form and chiaroscuro. Commissioned by British Petroleum to depict, in a series of panels, the land route taken by BP Forties export pipeline in NE Scotland. Vice-President of the AAS 1975 and President 1976-77. Exhibited RSA in 1983 and 1986 and regularly at the AAS 1967-87, from 11 Albert Street.

**ADLER, Jankel** **1845-1949**
Born Lodz, Poland; died Glasgow. Painter in watercolour and pen and ink of figurative studies and decorative work. Attended School of Applied Arts in Wuppertal, Germany. In 1922 he helped to organise the Union of Progressive International Artists Congress in Dusseldorf. From 1935-1937 he lived in Poland and at the outbreak of war joined the Polish army. After the evacuation of Dunkirk he settled in Glasgow in 1941 where he shared a studio with Benno Schotz(qv) and then with William Crosbie(qv) and J D Fergusson(qv). Instrumental in founding the New Scottish Group, November 1942, together with Josef J O Herman(qv) and J D Fergusson(qv) who became its first President. Moved to London 1943 but not before his influence had been felt by other artists such as Robert Colquhoun(qv). Hardie points out that 'Adler acted as a vivid channel of the Synthetic Cubism of Picasso, and his drawing of the figure is given a certain indefinably central-European Weltschmerz by emotive distortions which surface again in Colquhoun's work at its most stark'.
**Bibl:** Hardie 167-170, 173-174.

**ADLINGTON, Esther C** **fl 1885-1896**
Aberdeen landscape painter of 31 Albyn Place. In 1896 she moved to St Paul's Studios, Aberdeen. Exhibited AAS(5).

**AESTHETIC CLUB** **1851-?**
An Edinburgh club devoted to the arts, philosophy, science and theology. At a dinner party held at the home of Mr D R Hay(qv) of Jordan Bank, Morningside, it was resolved to institute an Aesthetic Club with the prime object of 'elucidating the principles of beauty and reducing them to a science'. The first President was Professor Kelland with Hay (who had one of the finest collection of Scottish paintings and who was described in the Edinburgh Directory of 1840 as Housepainter and Decorator to the Queen) as Secretary. The artist James Ballantyne(qv) was a founder member. The Minute book is in the library of the RSA.
**Bibl:** The Artist 1902; Chambers Journal 1906.

**AFFLECK, Andrew F** **1869-1935**
Ayr painter and etcher of architectural subjects, landscape and topographical scenes. Although Scottish he travelled and worked very widely including long stays in England, Belgium, France and Spain. He appears to have lived in Scotland in 1904, to have been in France in 1905, back in Scotland c1907 and sometime shortly afterwards he finally settled in London. His work shows fine attention to detail and considerable competence in the practice of etching, without ever achieving the front rank. His artistic imagination was not the equal of his technical skill. He exhibited on ten occasions at the RSA and on three occasions at the RA between 1904 and 1923; also GI(20). Represented in Paisley AG.
**Bibl:** Conn 462; DBA 1880-1940.

**AFFLECK, Norman James** **1917-**
Angus artist who exhibited a landscape at the RSA in 1943. Represented in Dundee AG.

**AGNEW, Miss Constance** **fl 1887-1909**
Painter in oil of figurative subjects. A quiet, unaffected painter who depicted subjects such as 'Meditation', 'Old Age' and 'Blacksmiths at work'. Exhibited RA in 1904 and again in 1908, RSA and in 1887 and 1888 GI(2).

**AGNEW, Eric Munro** **1888-1951**
Born Kirkcaldy. Painter of landscapes and portraits, also designer. Studied architecture and later art at the Glasgow School of Art and at the Slade School. Thereafter he remained most of his life in England. During the war he reached the rank of Captain while serving with the Argyll and Sutherland Highlanders, winning the Military Cross. In World War 2 he served as a staff officer with the rank of Major. Lived in London and exhibited at the Royal Society of Portrait Painters and at the International Society of Sculptors, Painters and Engravers. His style was forthright, strongly pictorial, with a good sense of design though sometimes lacking in finesse. Exhibited frequently at the RA 1924-1939.

**AGNEW, G C** **fl 1896**
Edinburgh still-life painter who exhibited once at the RSA in 1896.

**AGNEW, Miss Harriet** **fl 1880-1885**
Glasgow painter in oils; flowers and still life. After exhibiting at the RSA, exhibited four times at the GI.

**AGNEW, Michael** **1968-**
Printmaker, based in Aberdeen. Studied Gray's School of Art 1986-90. Won First prize, Gray's sketch club exhibition 1988 and was awarded a George Davidson travelling scholarship 1990/1. Exhibited RSA 1990, exhibits AAS.

**AGNEW, Lady Swanzie** **fl 1944**
Sculptress. Based in Edinburgh, she exhibited a portrait bust at the RSA.

**AHRENS, Lynn** **Cont**
Edinburgh-based painter. Exhibits AAS.

**AIKEN, Janet Macdonald** **1873-1941**
Painter in watercolour and pen and ink. Studied at the Glasgow School of Art then at Colarossi's in Paris, and Spain where she produced many lively and colourful sketches. Her watercolours were principally of Ayrshire and London where she latterly lived. Member of the Glasgow Society of Lady Artists, the SSWA and the Women's Instructional Art Club. Represented in Paisley AG.

**AIKEN, John Macdonald RSA RI ARE ARCA** **1880-1961**
Born Aberdeen. Painter in oils and watercolours; etcher and stained-glass artist. After serving a six years apprenticeship as a draughtsman with the lithographer Robert Gibb(qv) he studied at Gray's School of Art in Aberdeen and at the Royal College of Art under Gerald Moira as well as in Florence. He became Head of Gray's School of Art in 1911-1914 before devoting himself full-time to the practice of art. Awarded the silver medal at the Paris Salon in 1923 for his portrait of Harry Townend, previously exhibited at the RA in 1921 and shown yet again at the French Artists' Salon of 1929. Lived for a time in London before returning to Aberdeenshire. Although his earlier work showed the great influence of Moira's decorative technique he gradually developed his own distinctive style. He produced more than 100 etchings, 8 of which are identified in Guichard's *British Etchers.* After the death of his wife settled in Aboyne, Aberdeenshire. Elected ARSA 1923, ARE 1924, RSA 1935, RI 1944. Exhibited regularly RA(25), RSA(127), RI(8), RE(19), RSW(2), GI(49) & AAS 1898-1959. Represented in Aberdeen AG, Dundee AG, Perth AG, Leith Hall (NTS).
**Bibl:** Halsby 245.

**AIKEN, John P** **1920-1966**
Died 2 Jan. Dumbarton painter in oil and watercolour of landscape; also etcher and teacher. Trained Glasgow School of Art 1939-1943, graduating with distinction. Influenced by Joan Eardley and David Donaldson, he was a close friend of the conductor Dr Ian Whyte and was himself a highly competent freelance violinist. Travelled extensively in Europe but his favourite scenes remained in Lennox, and the Balloch and River Leven regions. He turned increasingly to oil as his favoured medium. Died in tragic circumstances. Exhibited RSA 1942-1958. Represented in Dundee AG, Glasgow AG Sydney AG (Australia).

**AIKMAN, A F** **c1790-c1840**
Edinburgh engraver. Prepared a number of plates for Dibdin's *Bibliographical...Tour,* 1838, including a view of the West Port and South Street, St Andrew's, after J McLea(qv).
**Bibl:** Bushnell.

**AIKMAN, George Matthew** **fl 1881-1889**
Edinburgh painter in watercolour; buildings, landscapes and genre. Exhibited regularly RSA 1881-1887.

**AIKMAN, George W ARSA RSW** **1831-1905**
Born Edinburgh, 20 May, died Edinburgh, 8 Jan. Painter in oil and watercolour of landscapes, town scenes and portraits; engraver. After leaving Edinburgh Royal HS, he studied at Trustees School of Design under Robert Scott Lauder(qv). Initially he worked with his father, training as an engraver. He contributed illustrations to the *Encyclopedia Brittanica.* Specialised in moorland and woodland scenes, often using sombre browns; his coastal and harbour views were rather brighter with the use of silvery grey tones showing the influence of the Hague School. He illustrated the now much sought after book by Smart, *A Round of the Links* (1893), also Chapman and Strathesk: *The Midlothian Esks* (1895). The V&A holds a series of architectural studies of Edinburgh for an unidentified book. Elected RSW 1878, ARSA 1880. Exhibited RA(5) 1874-1904, RSA(144) 1866-1905, RSW(19) & GI(28). Represented in City of Edinburgh collection by 32 watercolour Edinburgh street scenes.
**Bibl:** Butchart 78; Halsby 245; Wingfield.

**AIKMAN, John** **1713-1731**
Figure painter. Only son of William Aikman(qv) who died the same year, it is said from the shock of his son's death. The only known works are studies of heads.

**AIKMAN, L J** **fl 1880-1890**
Amateur Glasgow painter. Lived in Partick. Exhibited GI(6).

**AIKMAN, Mrs P H** **fl 1890-1895**
Amateur artist who lived at Hillhead and exhibited twice at the GI.

**AIKMAN, William** **1682-1731**
Born Cairnie, Aberdeenshire 24 Oct; died London, 14 Jan (4 Jne according to Walpole). Painter in oils and etcher; portraits. Nephew of Sir John Clerk of Penicuik(qv). Originally destined by his father for the law he was determined to follow a career in art. After studying portraiture in Edinburgh for three years with Sir John Medina(qv) he went for a short time to London before selling the paternal estate in 1706. Encouraged by his uncle he visited Rome, Constantinople and Syria. He returned to Scotland in March 1711 when he succeeded to Medina's practice, becoming Scotland's leading portrait painter largely under the patronage of John, 2nd Duke of Argyll (1680-1743). He returned to London in 1723, becoming a friend of Walpole, Swift, Gay, Pope and Thomson. He was painting the royal family for Lord Burlington in 1730 when ill-health intervened. Opinion about his work is varied, Armstrong speaks of "a certain weak amiability", McKay refers to "a capable draughtsman...he lacked the strength of character to substitute an outlook of his own for the conventions by which he was surrounded". Virtue found "his manner of designing very easy, graceful and genteel, his colouring natural and lively". More recently, Holloway has written "a comparison with the works painted by Aikman in Italy with his earlier portraits shows a refining of his style and the emergence of what became the hallmark of his mature portraiture - a certain melancholy and introspection...while Medina's men and women were robustly depicted in confidently handled paint and rich colour Aikman's delicate and tentative portraits penetrate the public mask to the personality behind". His own portrait is in the Uffizi Gallery. Represented in the SNPG, SNG, Brodie Castle (NTS), House of Dun (NTS), Chatsworth.
**Bibl:** William Aikman (The Bee, 6 Nov 1793); William Aikman (Scottish Masters 9) Edinburgh 1988; James Anderson, 'Biographical Sketches of Eminent Scottish Artists, Bee, Edinburgh, 6 Nov 1793; Armstrong 6-7; Brydall 104-6; Caw 23-26,474; Holloway, 'Patrons & Painters' (SNPG 1989); Irwin 41-4 et passim; McKay 9, 13-15 Irwin; Macmillan [GA]; Macmillan [SA]; Wilton-Ely, 'Lord Burlington and The Virtuoso Portrait', Architectural History, Vol 27, 1984; Wingfield.

**AIKMAN, William** **fl 1887-1924**
Edinburgh flower and landscape painter in oils; also designer of stained glass windows. Exhibited RSA from Edinburgh 1887 before moving to London from where he exhibited further works between 1896 and 1899. Thereafter exhibited RA(26) & GI(2). Represented in Dundee AG.

**AIMER, James** **fl 1905**
Amateur Melrose artist. Exhibited once at the RSA in 1905.

**AINGER, Miss E Caroline M** **fl 1931**
Exhibited once at the RSA in 1931 from an Edinburgh address.

**AINSLEY, Sam** **1950-**
Born North Shields, Tyne & Wear. Tapestry designer. Trained in Leeds and Newcastle-upon-Tyne Polytechnic. In 1975 spent six weeks in Japan studying Sukiya architecture and the use of natural materials in Japanese art became an important influence. Wall-hangings of the late 1970s incorporate canvas, cotton bindings and wood in ways which suggest Japanese costumes. In 1977 moved to Edinburgh to study tapestry at the College of Art and currently teaches at Glasgow School of Art. More recently has begun using brighter colours and abstract shapes, employing canvas materials overlaid and sewn together. In 1983 produced a 30-ft tapestry for General Accident's head office in Perth. The following year she made five 20-ft banners for the opening of the SNGMA new building in Edinburgh. Since 1985 Ainsley has carried on working on the theme of women in contemporary society, depicting stylised female forms constructed from pieces of canvas woven together and painted with acrylics. Represented in SNGMA.
**Bibl:** Hardie 215; Hartley 114; TEC, Glasgow, 'Why I Chose Red', Sam Ainsley (Ex Cat, 1987); TRAC, Edinburgh, Three artists, 1979.

**AINSLIE, John** **c1750-1834**
Engraver and surveyor probably of Edinburgh. In 1755 published a map of Fife and Kinross with the rivers Forth and Tay, engraved by himself. In c1780 he surveyed and published a plan of Edinburgh and in 1804 another plan of Edinburgh and Leith 'engraved by the surveyor and John Craig his assistant'.
**Bibl:** Bushnell.

**AINSLIE, John** **fl 1807-1835**
Edinburgh painter in oil; portraits and still life. Although probably the same John Ainslie who exhibited twice at the RSA in 1827 and 1829 his career is generally unrecorded. The Irwins noted his winning the second premium at the Trustees Academy in 1807 and his painting a number of portraits for the Duke of Buccleuch at Bowhill. One, of the Duke's chef, Joseph Florance, dated 1817 is a very skilful portrait of the man who had the honour to be in charge of the catering for George IV when he stayed at Dalkeith House in 1822. "The chef's crisply painted white coat is relieved against a green-grey background and the face with its broken teeth is meticulously observed. The overall pattern, with the copper saucepans, still life arrangement of dead game and fish on the table in front of him, points to a Dutch prototype, and evidently derives from the 17th century paintings of fish-stalls with the vendor behind the counter. Ainslie also exhibited genre pieces, and 'The Drunken Smith' (1809) likewise suggests a Dutch source". [Irwin].
**Bibl:** Irwin 216-7; Macmillan [SA], 180-181.

**AINSLIE, R** **fl 1896**
Turriff amateur artist. Exhibited 'Spanish Cigarette Maker' at the AAS from Dalgety Castle.

**AINSWORTH, Graciela** **1960-**
Sculptress and sculpture conservationist. Trained Univ. of Northumbria 1979-82 and City of Guilds of London Art School 1982-85. Works mainly in stone. Commissions include heraldic panel for National Museums of Scotland, a finial Cross for Iona Abbey and important conservation in Prague. Exhibits AAS. Lives in Edinburgh.

**AIRD, Charles** **fl 1904-d 1927**
Kilmarnock painter in oils of pastoral scenes. Exhibited RA(1), RSA(12) between 1915 and 1927, GI(24) & AAS 1923-26.

**AIRD, Michael S** **fl 1961**
Stornoway painter. Exhibited a portrait and 3 local topographical scenes at the AAS, all in the above year, from 1 Torquil Terrace.

**AITCHISON, A W** **fl 1902**
Hawick amateur artist who exhibited once at the RSA in 1902.

**AITCHISON, Craigie RA** **1926-**
Born Edinburgh. Portrait and figurative painter; semi-abstracts most usually based upon portraits, still lifes or crucifixions, with occasional dogs. The son of a Lord Justice Clerk of Scotland, his early life was spent in Scotland and in c1950 he moved to London to study law but quickly abandoned the idea in favour of art, proceeding to study at the Slade School of Art 1952-1954. In 1955 he won a scholarship to study in Italy. On returning to London, where he has remained, he began exhibiting there in 1954 and has held frequent exhibitions since. His paintings are almost minimalist, often featuring just one or two simple elements. He seldom signs on the front so as not to upset the balance of the composition. His preferred subjects are animals, plants and, from 1963, portraits. He has also produced a number of religious works. First solo exhibition in London, 1959. Latterly divides his time between London and Italy. Elected ARA 1978. Represented in Tate AG, SNGMA, Aberdeen AG, Perth AG, Newcastle AG (Australia), Walker Gallery (Liverpool).
**Bibl:** Hardie 183; Hartley 114; SAC,'Craigie Aitchison' Ex Cat 1975; Serpentine, London, 'Craigie Aitchison' Ex Cat 1981, text by Helen Lessore and John McEwen; Lucy Sweet, *Exactingly Ambiguous*, Sunday Times, 10.viii.03

**AITCHISON, Jessie G A** **fl 1901-1902**
An Edinburgh miniature painter who exhibited one portrait miniature at the RSA in 1902; possibly related to A W Aitchison(qv) who exhibited the same year from Hawick.

**AITCHISON, Thomas S** **fl 1863-1868**
Edinburgh painter in oil; landscapes. All that is known of this artist is that he exhibited five paintings in the RSA in 1863(1), 1867(2) & 1868(2).

**AITKEN, Mrs Elizabeth M** **fl 1934-1952**
Painter of landscapes and portraits. Exhibited RSA 1934-1952, also RA(2), ROI(4).

**AITKEN, George Shaw** **1836-1921**
Born Dundee. Architect. Worked for J Dick Peddie(qv) in Edinburgh. Founder member of the Edinburgh Architectural Association. Returned to Dundee where he continued to practise until 1880 when he went back to Edinburgh. Exhibited RSA(8) 1898-1900, including designs for Glasgow Municipal Buildings (1883), Lady Stair's House in the Lawnmarket, as restored for the Earl of Rosebery (1898), a proposed National Gallery on Calton Hill (1907), Glasgow Cathedral, and Holyrood Abbey Chapel (1910).
**Bibl:** Colvin; Gifford 196-7,488,491.

**AITKEN, Miss H** **fl 1868**
Amateur Edinburgh landscape painter. Sister of Miss M Aitken(qv). Exhibited RSA 1868.

**AITKEN, J D** **fl 1887-1888**
Amateur Glasgow artist who exhibited once at the GI and once in Liverpool.

**AITKEN, Mrs James** **fl 1864**
Edinburgh-based painter in oil of still life. Probably wife of James Alfred Aitken(qv). Exhibited once at the RSA.

**AITKEN, James** **fl c1880-1935**
Born Newburgh, Fife. Painter, mainly in oil of landscape and river scenes but occasional watercolours & pencil. Father of John Ernest Aitken(qv). As well as painting in England and Scotland he made several visits to the continent executing landscapes in France, Italy and Switzerland. Pencil works include 'In Home Waters' and 'Across the Western Ocean'. He lived at Port St Mary on the Isle of Man. Exhibited at the RA(7), RSA(2), GI and elsewhere in the provinces and was a member of the Liverpool Academy of Arts. Represented in the Manx Museum.

**AITKEN, James Alfred ARHA RSW** **1846-1897**
Born Edinburgh; died Glasgow, 21 Dec. Painter in oil and watercolour, principally of landscapes. Went to Dublin as a young man where he first studied art. In 1866 he returned to Glasgow, becoming a pupil of Horatio McCulloch(qv). Later travelled widely both in Europe and the United States. Towards the end of his life he became increasingly attracted to watercolours and was a founder member of the RSW. Painted views of the Highlands and Scottish coastal scenes using bright evocative colour; also painted a number of Venetian views which are regarded as some of his best work. Elected ARHA 1871 (resigned 1890), RSW 1878. Exhibited regularly RSA 1866 until the year of his death, RA in 1874 and more frequently at the RSW(67) & GI(46).
**Bibl:** Halsby 245.

**AITKEN, Miss Janet Macdonald WIAC** **1873-1941**
Born Glasgow. Painter in oils of landscapes and portraits; also metal work designer. She was the daughter of Robert Aitken the lithographer. After studying at the Glasgow School of Art 1887-1902 she went to Paris where she continued her studies at the Academie Colarossi. She lived in Glasgow and then in Troon. A member of Charles Rennie Mackintosh's circle and a leading member of the Glasgow Society of Lady Artists(qv). 'Her designs in *The Magazine* incorporate flowing lines of hair, dresses and feathers, and flowers growing from large bulbs, with frequent rhythmic repetition of the human figure. Her patterns are bold, with the generous use of black and hints of the oriental in a hair style and its bare sharply twisting branches, showing a marked affinity to Toorop' [Burkhauser]. Her monochromatic sketches of Glasgow scenes were confidently executed, several being reproduced as postcards. In 1930 an exhibition of her work was held at the Beaux Artes Galleries which included 40 landscapes. Exhibited regularly RSA(33), GI(55), SWA(3) L(6), and - mainly portraits - AAS 1900-1931.
**Bibl:** Burkhauser 49,60,76,77,79,88(fig 97); Halsby 246.

**AITKEN, John Ernest RSW RCAMA ARWA** **1880-1957**
Born Liverpool; died Isle of Man, 15 Jne. Son of the Scottish landscape painter James Aitken(qv) under whom he studied before continuing further studies in Manchester, Liverpool and Wallasey. He was a member of the Liverpool Academy of Arts and of the Manchester Academy of Fine Arts. Painted widely in Holland, Belgium, France, Switzerland, Italy, Wales and Scotland. Exhibited widely, RA(9), RSA(3), RI(33), RSW(42) & Royal Cam A(70). Latterly lived near Port St Mary in the Isle of Man. Represented in Manx Museum.
**Bibl:** Halsby 245.

**AITKEN, John Morgan** **?-1923**
Architect. His principal works were in Shetland. Responsible for the Baptist church, Lerwick 1894-95, the chancel of St Columba, Lerwick 1895, the Isleburgh Community Centre 1901-02, Lerwick's Clydesdale Bank 1892, and two interesting concrete piers for Symbister harbour 1895.

**AITKEN, Katherine D** **fl 1894**
Amateur Glasgow artist who exhibited once at the GI.

**AITKEN, Miss M** **fl 1868**
Edinburgh painter of oil and landscapes. Sister of Miss H Aitken(qv). Exhibited RSA 1868.

**AITKEN, William** **fl 1928-d1981**
Larbert painter in oil and watercolour of landscape. While art master at Riverside High School, Stirling, he did much to promote the use of film in schools. He designed the coat-of-arms for Falkirk Technical College and the railings that surround the War Memorial in Larbert. President of Falkirk Archaeological Society. Exhibited RSA annually between 1928 & 1932 and irregularly between 1941 and 1960, always landscapes, and at the Grafton Galleries, New York. A drawing 'Carron Estuary, Grangemouth', dated 1933, is in Falkirk AG.

**AITKEN, William Alexander** **1893-1975**
Born & died Aberdeen. Lithographic artist and watercolour painter of buildings, townscapes & landscapes, especially Aberdeenshire and the NW coast. Trained Robert Gordon Technical College. graduating with distinction. Married with two daughters. Close friend of Henry Jackson Simpson(qv). Partner, George & Augustus Robb, Aberdeen lithographic printers. His architectural drawings are particualrly fine and his landscapes always sensitively portrayed. Exhibited regularly at AAS from 1912 from the family home, 47 Hilton Drive.

**AITKENHEAD, Lindsay** **fl 1965**
Glasgow sculptor; exhibited RSA(1).

**AKERBERG, Mrs Verna** **fl 1920-1930**
Amateur Swiss artist who lived for a time in Corstorphine and exhibited four paintings RSA between 1923 and 1928.

**ALABASTER, Vera (née Petschatkinoz)** **1889-1964**
Born St. Petersburg. Painter of landscapes and figure studies. Studied in St. Petersburg, Florence and then Munich. Married a British customs official and went to live in Shanghai where she became friendly with Anna Hotchkis(qv). When her husband retired they moved to France but with the onset of WW2 migrated to Jamaica. Widowed, she settled in Kirkcudbright, beside Hotchkis. Painted in Jamaica. Exhibited intermittently RSA 1951-1963 and in Kirkcudbright. Lived in Fisher's Close.

**ALAN the PAINTER** **fl 1453-d1454**
Painted the king's guitar for which he received one shilling. An 'Allan Pantour' was chronicled as 'the most ingenious man in Scotland, and most subtle in divers things'; slain by an arrow at the siege of Abercorn Castle on St. George's Day.
**Bibl:** Apted; Brydall 31; Exchequer Rolls,v,603.

**ALDRIDGE, Thomas** **Cont**
Edinburgh-based artist. Exhibits AAS.

**ALEXANDER, Aileen** **fl 1983**
Landscape painter. Exhibited RSA in 1983 from a Falkirk address.

**ALEXANDER, Alan M** **1936-1996**
Edinburgh artist, ballet dancer, restauranteur; teacher. Studied Edinburgh College of Art whilst also training at the Scottish Ballet School. Taught Edinburgh College of Art. Exhibited RSA 1961 & 1977.

**ALEXANDER, Alexander** **fl 1901-1915**
Portobello artist who exhibited eight landscapes at the RSA 1901-1915. An interesting example of his work was sold in London at Sotheby's, 26 March 1974.

**ALEXANDER, Miss Ann(ie) Dunlop** **fl 1917-1966**
Glasgow based painter in watercolours; book illustrator and ceramic designer. Trained at Glasgow School of Art where she was strongly influenced by the decorative, delicate constructions of Jessie King(qv) and Ann MacBeth(qv). Regular exhibitor RSA(11) 1919-1966, mostly literary paintings, often from Tennyson, & GI(19).
**Bibl:** Halsby 246.

**ALEXANDER, Cosmo John** **1724-1772**
Died in Edinburgh. Portrait painter. Son and pupil of John Alexander, great grandson of George Jamesone(qv). His first known work is a copy of Jamesone's portrait of George Keith 5th Earl Marischal. Like his father, he fought on the Jace side during the '45 Rebellion and remained in Rome, whence he had fled in 1746, until 1751. There he became friendly with George Chalmers, and all the while he was studying and copying the Old Masters, especially Caracci. In 1751 he left Rome, travelling to Paris via Bologna and Venice, and there painted members of the Scottish community. In 1754 he inherited a furnished London house from his friend James Gibb(qv), the architect, but, returning to the UK and finding that the competition from rival portrait painters such as Ramsay and Reynolds limited the number of commissions, he concentrated on Scottish sitters. During the late 1750s and early 1760s Alexander commuted between London and Scotland painting in both places. He visited Holland in 1763, becoming a member of the Guild of Painters in The Hague, who fined him for not paying his dues. There followed a tour of the United States between 1768 and 1772, spending the winter of 1768/9 with William Franklyn, the Governor of New Jersey, and most of 1771 travelling in the southern States where he was joined as an assistant by his only known pupil, Gilbert Stuart(qv), with whom he returned to Scotland shortly before his death. Together with his father, he was pre-eminently the painter of the leading Catholic and Jacobite Scottish families of his time. A competent rather than highly talented artist who painted accurately if in a rather commonplace manner. Represented in NGS, SNG, SNPG, Aberdeen AG, The Binns (NTS), Drum Castle (NTS).
**Bibl:** Caw 28; 'Cosmo Alexander in America', Art Quarterly XXVI, Autumn 1963; 'Cosmo Alexander in Holland', Oud Holland LXXIX (1964) 1 (85); Geddy. MacL. 'Cosmo Alexander's Travels and Patrons in America', Antiques 112 Nov 1977; Gavin Maitland Goodfellow, The Art, Life and Times of Cosmo Alexander (MA Thesis Oberlin, 1961); Holloway; Irwin 46-7; Macmillan [SA], 93-94, 'Patrons and Painters'.

**ALEXANDER, Daniel** **c1800-1864**
Glasgow born portrait painter who settled in Edinburgh, also painted genre. Established a prosperous career. His versatility was illustrated by the variety of his 56 exhibits at the RSA between the above years including for example, a portrait of a Hindu (1835), 'William Rhind' (1837) and several paintings of antique Rome. A series of wash drawings of city views are in Glasgow AG, based mainly on a visit he made in 1824 to Italy and Switzerland.
**Bibl:** Halsby 49.

**ALEXANDER, David R** **fl 1933-1937**
Aberdeen painter in oil of local scenes. Exhibited AAS.

**ALEXANDER, Dennis Samuel Johnston** **fl 1964-1985**
Glasgow painter of coastal and local scenes. Exhib regularly AAS.

**ALEXANDER, E** **fl 1873**
Edinburgh painter who exhibited 'At the trysting place', at the RSA in 1873.

**ALEXANDER, Edwin John RSA RSW RWS** **1870-1926**
Born Edinburgh, 1 Feb; died Musselburgh, 23 Apr. Painter in oil and

watercolour; birds, flowers, animals, Arabian subjects. His watercolours are generally done on silk, linen or heavily grained paper. Son of Robert Alexander(qv). In 1887, when he was 17, he visited Tangier with his father and Joseph Crawhall(qv), the latter coming to have a profound influence on his artistic career. In 1891 he studied in Paris with Robert Burns(qv) under Fremiet. The following year, in the company of Erskine Nicol jnr(qv), he visited Egypt where he remained until 1896, living for much of the time on a houseboat on the Nile. He lived among the people becoming fluent in Arabic. His work at this time was characterised by soft tones and quiet understatements whilst at the same time evoking the shimmering heat and the intense light of the country. In 1904 he married, settling at Inveresk where he kept exotic birds in his garden and from which he frequently visited the west coast of Scotland, especially Kirkcudbright and the Hebrides. In 1913 he travelled to Amsterdam to sketch in the local zoo. During the war he taught at the Edinburgh College of Art but a stroke in 1917 severely curtailed any further work. Although never a member of the Glasgow School, their decorative ideas and especially the masterly restraint of Crawhall, is reflected in all his art, as is the influence of the Japanese style. A quiet, reserved man his place as one of Scotland's most masterly animal painters is secure. He exhibited once at the RA in 1896, frequently at the RSA between 1887 and 1916, also GI(15), RWS(49), RSW(42) & AAS 1906-1923. Represented in the NG, Tate Gallery, NGS(7), Dundee AG, Glasgow AG, City of Edinburgh collection, Perth AG.
**Bibl:** AJ 1898, 71, PL 69; Caw 438-440; Halsby 147-9 et al; Martin Hardie, Watercolour Painting in Britain, vol III, London 1968,207; OWS Annual IV (1926); J Patterson, Edwin Alexander; Who's Who 1906; Wood, T Martin 'Some Recent Watercolours by Edwin Alexander' Studio, 53, 1911, 90-100; Studio, 45,1909,116; Wingfield.

**ALEXANDER, E Martin** **1881-**
Born Edinburgh. Sculptor, especially in bronze. Spent most of his life in London. Exhibited RA(9), RSA(18) & GI(4).

**ALEXANDER, Elizabeth Haen** **1868-1942**
Glasgow sculptress and watercolourist. Exhibited RSA 1901-1904 and again in 1910, also RSW(1) & GI(15).

**ALEXANDER, Ella** **fl 1890-1895**
Amateur Glasgow artist who exhibited three times at the GI.

**ALEXANDER, Mrs Euphen PPSSWA** **1917-**
Born Rangoon 13 Jan. Painter in oil of botanical subjects. Studied under her husband James Alexander(qv), she also undertook private tuition in landscape with David Cox and in flower painting with Sir Cedric Morris. Much influenced in her youth by Kate Cameron(qv) and Margaret Laing(qv). She painted wild flowers in many parts of the world including Australia, Austria, the Algarve, Elba, Madeira, Iceland and Shetland. A series of 63 paintings 'Little Gems of the Royal Botanic Garden, Edinburgh' gained her the silver Grenfell Award of the Royal Horticultural Exhibition in London (1975) and again in 1981. President, SSWA 1972-1975. Held exhibitions in Adelaide, Melbourne, New Zealand and Edinburgh. Lives and works near Selkirk.

**ALEXANDER, George FRBS** **1881-1942**
Born Glasgow. Sculptor. Attended Allan Glen's School and studied at Glasgow School of Art and the RA School in London where he won several distinctions. Specialised in ornamental and figure work including many examples of famous public buildings among them the London County Council headquarters, the Civic Centre, Southampton and Hammersmith Town Hall. Among his better known works were four bas-reliefs in stone of an ibex, a moose, a parrot and a cobra, and a tiger killing a snake, in an art deco style, tho' clearly influenced by Barye. Worked at the Justice Studios, 4-6 Justice Walk, London SW3. Elected a member of the Royal Society of British Sculptors. Frequent exhibitor RA(7), once at the RSA & GI(5). Some London city companies have examples of his work.

**ALEXANDER, J W** **fl 1899**
Artist, probably Scottish. Lived in Paris from where he exhibited RSA(1).

**ALEXANDER, J Scott** **fl 1893**
Amateur Glasgow artist who exhibited once at the GI.

**ALEXANDER, James** **fl 1660-1697**
Early painter. Son of Patrick Alexander(qv). Apprenticed 1660 to John Tailyfier (painter). Paid £15 by Edinburgh town council 1667 for 'helping and painting of the great drawght of the good toun presently hanging in the laich councill house'. Two years later he entered upon the first of four marriages and in 1675 became a Burgess of Edinburgh and a member of the Incorporation of St Mary's. Between 1676 and 1685 Alexander was working at Holyroodhouse, including painting in the room occupied by the Princess, Lady Anne. In 1685 he is found working at Edinburgh Castle 'collouring the drawbridges, timber and iron railles, tirlise doores, centrie boxes, taxfalles and all the magasen windres'. James Hamilton(qv) was a pupil. At this time, specialisation in painting had not been established so that it was common for the same person to paint a portrait one month and a window grille the next.
**Bibl:** Apted 21-22.

**ALEXANDER, James** **fl 1902**
Amateur Aberdeen painter. Exhibited a local view at the AAS.

**ALEXANDER, James B** **fl 1894-1906**
Glasgow artist. Exhibited GI(5).

**ALEXANDER, James Stuart Carnegie** **1900-1952**
Born nr Selkirk, 13 Feb; died Jly. Watercolour painter; landscapes and flowers. Educated at Haileybury School, he was self-taught in painting though greatly encouraged by his friends Edwin(qv) and Robert Alexander(qv), and by Tom Scott(qv). Married Euphen Alexander(qv) 1943. Latterly lived in Hawick. Exhibited RA(5), RSA from 1921(13), also RSW(30), RI(8),GI(3) & AAS(1). Represented Kirkcaldy AG, Liverpool AG, Manchester AG.
**Bibl:** Halsby 246.

**ALEXANDER, Jean** **fl 1904-1905**
Edinburgh artist. Exhibited twice at the RSA in 1904 and 1905.

**ALEXANDER, John** **1658-1682**
Born Aberdeen; died Wurzburg, 25 May. Little is known about the art of this interesting person who had such a short life. In October 1677 he left Scotland with Bernard Maxwell, a Scottish monk, to enter the priesthood and in May 1679, he travelled to Amsterdam entering the Monastery at Wurzburg in October, having borrowed money from Sir James Kennedy, later Conservator of the Scottish Stable at Bera. At Wurzburg he assumed the name of Brother John. His paintings appear to have been done before travelling to the continent.
**Bibl:** Dilworth Mark, Scots in Franconia, Edinburgh 1974, 116-7, 281; Ratisbon Archives, 'Letters of Bernard Maxwell'; The Innes Review, ix, 199;

**ALEXANDER, John** **1686-c1766**
May have been born in Aberdeen. Portrait painter, engraver and etcher. Maternal grandson of George Jamesone(qv) and father of Cosmo Alexander(qv). The circumstances of his early life and training are unknown. He seems to have travelled at an early age for by 1710, when he was studying in London copying portraits, he had already visited Paris. In 1711 he travelled to Italy and at Leghorn he executed the fine miniature self-portrait now in the SNPG. Whilst in Rome he painted portraits of visiting British notables, for example Lord Chief Justice Coke was a sitter in 1714, and took the opportunity of copying many of the Italian Old Masters and of studying with Guiseppe Bartolomeo Chiari. He published a set of engravings after Raphael, some of which were dedicated to Cosimo de Medici. Alexander was patronised by the Marquis of Huntly (later 2nd Duke of Gordon) and by the Jacobite Earl of Mar. In 1720 he returned to Scotland and although based in Edinburgh, he embarked upon a commission for the Duke of Gordon decorating the ceiling staircase at Gordon Castle "the most ambitious baroque ceiling in Scotland", following a basic design of Chiari's 'The Rape of Proserpine'. During the 1730s he extended his practise in the north east of Scotland having in 1723 married Isobel Innes of Tillyfour, Aberdeenshire and travelling among his former aristocratic friends. In 1728 he engraved George Jamesone's self-portrait and the following year in association with his friends, James Norie(qv) and son, he helped establish the Academy of St Luke in Edinburgh. He was out in the 1745 Rebellion and declared a wanted man after Culloden in 1746 but by 1748 he was working again. His renowned portrait of George Drummond, Lord

Provost of Edinburgh and founder of the Royal Infirmary, painted in 1752, was exhibited at the RSA in 1880 and now hangs in the Royal Infirmary. At the time of his death he was painting 'The Escape of Queen Mary from Loch Leven' in which the landscape was executed from nature. The fact that this work was never completed is sad as it was perhaps the first Scottish landscape to have been painted out of doors. He was a very able, if somewhat rather stiff portraitist, his later work being looser and more relaxed in style. At his best he was undoubtedly one of the finest Scottish portrait painters of the 18th century. Caw found his drawing hard and unsympathetic but expressing a considerable grasp of character and form while his handling of paint was fluid enough but without style or expressiveness, his "colour harsh, the flesh being bricky in its reds, if transparent and fused as a whole". Represented in the BM, NGS, SNPG.
**Bibl:** Apted; Armstrong 7; Brockwell 29; Brydall 101-3; Caw 27; Holloway 85-92, et al; Irwin 45-6, 99-100; McKay 10.

**ALEXANDER, John** **fl 1875-1892**
Glasgow painter in oils and watercolour; landscape and townscapes. Exhibited twice at the RSA 1875-1881 and four times at the GI.

**ALEXANDER, L** **fl 1894-1909**
Glasgow painter in oil. Exhibited RSA(5), GI(23) & L(2).

**ALEXANDER, Lena M (Mrs Lees Duncan)** **1899-1983**
Born Glasgow, Dec 9. Painter in watercolour and pastel; mainly flowers, but also landscapes, often views of Venice and Paris as well as portraits. Trained Edinburgh School of Art and Paris. Moved with her parents first to Broughty Ferry, then Kirkcudbright 1939 near her friends Dorothy and Miles Johnston. Painted in a broad style with intense colour and confident, expansive washes. Exhibited RA(1) and regularly RSA 1919-1925, 1936, and 1943-1972, also GI(20) and Kirkcudbright. Represented in Castle Douglas AG.
**Bibl:** Halsby 246.

**ALEXANDER, Louise J** **fl 1979-1981**
Aberdeen avant garde jewellery designer. Exhibited AAS(3) sometimes in collaboration with Mark Blackadder.

**ALEXANDER, Miss Margaret** **fl 1910-1921**
Aberdeen painter of portraits and local landscape. Exhibited AAS in 1910 and again in 1921 from 1 Queen's Cross.

**ALEXANDER, Miss Margaret A** **fl 1964**
Aberdeen jewellery and metalwork designer. Lived at 181 Hardgate from where exhibited AAS(2).

**ALEXANDER, Patrick** **fl 1666-1670**
Aberdeen portrait and heraldic painter. Father of James Alexander(qv), possibly related to George Jamesone. Little is known of his work. In 1666, the year his child died in Aberdeen, he was paid £25 for painting armes of the funeral of Sir Robert Farquhar and in 1670 described as a 'portrait drawer'. He was arrested for the murder of one William Harvie.
**Bibl:** Analecta Scotica, 2, 165-6; Apted 22.

**ALEXANDER, R J** **fl 1839-1849**
Obscure Edinburgh painter of portraits and humorous figurative scenes. In 1839 exhibited at the RSA, 'The Poacher Detected' and in 1840, 'Miser Alarmed'.

**ALEXANDER, Robert L RSA RSW** **1840-1923**
Born Kilwinning, Ayrshire; died Edinburgh, 2 Jly. Animal painter in oil and occasionally watercolour. Father of Edwin(qv). The arrival of Robert Alexander heralded a new direction in Scottish animal painting. With him this branch of art became real and vital. Previously animal painting in Scotland had been essentially realistic, portraying domestic animals as breed specimens; any pictorial quality was introduced accidentally but with Alexander's work the pictorial element is primary. He was apprenticed to a Kilmarnock house painter who also painted landscape but from 1868 he devoted himself to painting dogs and horses. A short visit to the continent in 1875 was followed by many more and these helped to develop his faculty in watercolour. In 1878 he exhibited the first of four painting between then and 1888 at the RA in London. By that time he was living in Edinburgh and painting animals on commission for such patrons as the Duke of Portland. He exhibited at the RSA from 1868 until 1893. In 1887 he visited Tangier with Joseph Crawhall(qv), Pollok Nisbet(qv) and his own son Edwin(qv). Perhaps his greatest works are 'The Happy Mother' of 1887 and 'Two Mothers' of the following year; at the time they were regarded as 'the most masterly piece of animal painting yet produced in Scotland'. In 1900 a study of dogs and cats was exhibited in the Paris Salon. Writing in 1898 in the AJ, Caw said "his work is more refined than strong. His drawing is sensitive rather than distinguished...but the result is invariably harmonious, pleasant in colour, refined in tone, and expressive in draughtsmanship, while it reveals a subtle and sympathetic observation of animal life. He does not endow animals with qualities they do not possess, but uses their beauty of form and colour associated with some simple motive of action or repose for a pictorial purpose". Elected ARSA 1878, RSA 1888 and RSW 1900 but resigned in 1901. Father-in-law of Alexander Roche(qv) who married his daughter Jean in 1906. "Most of his work has been done in oils but the watercolours he has painted are exceedingly charming and possess to the full that delicate sense of form, colour and tone used to express a sympathetic observation of animal life which gives vital interest to his pictures. In its combination of artistic accomplishment and facility with refined and unforced sentiment, Alexander's achievement claims a high place in modern painting, and no native of these Isles has done quite so finely in the particular domain he has chosen for the exercise of his gifts" [Caw]. Exhibited RA(2), RSA(125), RSW(4), GI(10) & AAS 1893-1923. Represented in NGS(4), Dundee AG, City of Edinburgh collection(3), Victoria AG (Australia) 'The Two Mothers'.
**Bibl:** Caw 335-8; Halsby 146,148,150,246; Studio 49,1910,230; Wingfield.

**ALEXANDER, Mrs Rosemary E** **fl 1965-1983**
Aberdeen painter of still life and semi-abstracts. Exhibited frequently at the AAS from 8 Forest Avenue.

**ALEXANDER, Sally D (Mrs Eric Dott)** **fl 1927-1972**
Musselburgh portrait painter in oil and watercolour; and sculptress. Exhibited regularly at the RSA 1927-1972, RSW(11) & GI(1).

**ALEXANDER, Sheena Helen Johnston** **fl 1974-1980**
Painter in oil of local scenes. Exhibited AAS from 1 Falcon Buildings, Dunbar Street, Old Aberdeen.

**ALEXANDER, Simon** **fl 1978-1979**
Glasgow painter. Exhibited twice at the RSA in 1978 and 1979.

**ALEXANDER, Vivien** **fl 1963-**
Edinburgh painter. Portraits, interiors, still life, topographical. Studied Edinburgh College of Art where she was awarded an Andrew Grant Scholarship. Visited Greece on a travelling sholarship. A major exhibition of her work was held at the Edinburgh City Art Centre 1990. Recent solo exhibitions in Edinburgh, Kirkcaldy, Galashiels and at the Lyth Arts Centre, Wick, and in the group shows in London, Edinburgh and Mainhill Gallery, Ancrum, Roxburghshire. One reviewer (Richard Jacques) referred to her early work with its 'Bratby-like exuberance...the wall to wall brushstrokes encompass [a variety of subjects]'. Exhibits regularly at the RSA & SSA since 1963. Represented in City of Edinburgh collection. Lives and works at Kirk Lodge, Yarrow.

**ALEXANDER, William** **1841-1904**
Dundee architect. Worked in the Renaissance manner. Designed Victoria Chambers, Victoria Rd, Dundee(1874).
**Bibl:** Gifford 517; Bruce Walker & W S Gauldie, Architects and Architecture on Tayside, Dundee 1984, 138-141.

**ALEXANDER, William** **fl 1926**
Paisley artist. Exhibited Paisley Institute & AAS.

**ALEXANDER, William Lyon** **fl 1838-1843**
Edinburgh miniature painter. Exhibited RSA 1938-1843. No record remains of his work.

**ALGIE, Miss Jessie** **1859-1927**
Flower painter in oil and watercolour. Studied at Glasgow School of

Art and later went to live near Stirling where she became associated with the Cambuskenneth(qv) and Craigmill(qv) circles of artists. In 1899 she had two pictures in the RSA and in 1908 she shared an exhibition of flower pictures in London with Annie Muir(qv), Jessie King(qv) and Louise Perman(qv). Her work is finely detailed, nicely coloured but lacking in imaginative flair. The latter part of her life was spent at Kirn, Argyllshire. Exhibited RSA(19), RSW(3), ROI(6), GI(53), L(24) & AAS 1900-1912. Represented in Glasgow AG.
**Bibl:** Halsby 246.

**ALGIE, Miss Lucie** **fl 1905-1910**
Amateur Stirling artist. Sister of the better known Jessie Algie(qv). Exhibited two flower pictures at the SWA in 1908.

**ALISON, D** **1785-1807**
Portrait painter in oil. Son of a Perth Baillie. Pupil of Raeburn. There is a portrait of Sir James Dunsmore, 75th Regt, signed with monogram 'DA' and dated 1807 now in the Gordon Highlanders' Museum, and another of the surgeon Alexander Wood (1725-1807) in the SNPG.

**ALISON, David RSA RP** **1882-1955**
Born Dysart, Fife; died in Edinburgh, 14 Jan. Portrait painter. Brother of Henry Young A(qv). He studied first with a lithographer then at Glasgow School of Art before continuing his studies in Italy for one year and then attending the Painting School of the RSA. Enjoying travel, he embarked on further painting expeditions to Paris and Spain where Velasquez made a marked impression. In 1912 he was one of eight painters who formed the Society of Eight (the others being T W Adam, F C B Cadell, James Cadenhead, James Paterson, Harrington Mann, Sir John Lavery, and A G Sinclair). The following year he was appointed to the staff of the Edinburgh College of Art and at the outbreak of war joined the Royal Scots being wounded at Gallipoli. On his return he was appointed Head of Painting at the Edinburgh College of Art and elected a member of the Royal Society of Portrait Painters. In 1916 he was elected ARSA and in 1944 resigned from his teaching position, going to London for a short time before returning to Edinburgh prior to his death. An artist of great integrity who constantly reappraised his own work. Among the distinguished sitters were the Duke of Roxburghe, the Earl of Mar and Kellie, and the Earl of Strathmore. He also painted group portraits. His finest work was the portraits of his family and close friends. Elected RSA 1922. Exhibited widely including RA(31), RSA(95), RSW(7), GI(72), AAS 1906-37. Represented in Dundee AG, City of Edinburgh coll(3), Perth AG.
**Bibl:** Halsby 148,211,222; Hardie 142.

**ALISON, Henry Young** **1889-1972**
Born Dysart, Fife, 21 Sep; died 9 Mar. Painter of portraits and figure studies. Son of a master joiner and brother of David Alison. Trained at the Glasgow College of Art. His first exhibit at the RSA was in 1916 executed whilst on active service during which time he was wounded spending some time as a prisoner of war. In 1921 he exhibited a portrait of Joseph Lee at the RSA and in 1928 joined the staff of the Glasgow School of Art becoming Registrar (1930) and Interim Director (1945-6). In 1946 he retired to Pinherry, Ayrshire to devote himself full-time to family. Exhibited RA(1), RSA(37), GI(54) & AAS 1926-1929. Represented in Glasgow AG, Perth AG.

**ALISON, James Pearson FRIBA FSA (Scot)** **1862-1932**
Born Eskbank; died Hawick, Nov. Architect, responsible for much of the architecture of Hawick including several churches, mansions and factories. Exhibited RSA(1) & GI(3).
**Bibl:** Scott, Trans Hawick Archaeol Soc, 1986, 24-29.

**ALISON, J T** **fl 1885**
Amateur Dalkeith artist. Exhibited once at the RSA 1885. Son of the Chief Magistrate of Dalkeith and brother of Thomas Alison(qv).

**ALISON, Mrs M** **fl 1925-1930**
Amateur Edinburgh artist. Exhibited 3 landscapes in Liverpool during the 1920s.

**ALISON, Thomas Jnr** **fl 1881-1899**
Dalkeith painter in oils and watercolours; landscapes and portraits. Son of the chief magistrate of Dalkeith and brother of J T Alison(qv). Spent most of his life in that town. In 1882 exhibited a portrait of his father and in 1899 'The fishmarket at Bergen, Norway'. Exhibited RSA(54) between 1881 & 1899, RSW(2) & AAS.

**ALISON, Walter** **fl 1939**
Amateur Kirkcaldy artist. Exhibited RSA 1939.

**ALLAN, Alexander RSW** **1914-1972**
Born Dundee, 26 Oct; died Dundee, 22 Sep. Painter in oil, pen and ink and gouache; also portraits in pastel. Educated at Harris Academy, Dundee. Studied art at Dundee College of Art 1932-38 under J McIntosh Patrick(qv) and Edward Baird(qv); also at the Reimann School in London, Hospitalfield (1939) and the Westminster School of Art under Mark Gertler. Worked for the Forestry Commission 1940-46 before becoming a full-time artist. Held several one man shows in Glasgow and Edinburgh. Elected RSW 1965 and awarded an Arts Council travel grant in 1968. His work was mostly landscapes especially those of East Fife, Angus, North West Scotland, Lake Lugano and Ostend. At his best, expressing complexity from simple restrained means, showing the influence of oriental delicacy "the nuance, the indication rather than the description, a heavy mass of ink balanced by thin type pen strokes in an infinite emptiness of space" [S Goodsir Smith]. He died at the summit of his powers. Exhibited RA(2), RSA(4) and regularly at the RSW. Represented in Dundee AG, Glasgow AG, City of Edinburgh collection, Sheffield AG.

**ALLAN, Alexander S** **1830-?**
Little known Edinburgh-based landscape painter in oils. Trained Trustees Academy 1848-49. Exhibited RSA 1847-49.

**ALLAN, Andrew** **1863-1940**
Ayrshire painter in watercolour, and illustrator; also silver point, landscapes, still life, figures. He was influenced by the style of the French fin-de-siecle. Exhibited RSA once in 1895 from a Glasgow address and thereafter from 1897 whilst living at Ardrossan, contributing a total of 34 works there during his lifetime, as well as exhibiting GI(73), RSW(15), L(77) & AAS 1900-1935. Represented in Glasgow AG.
**Bibl:** Halsby 246.

**ALLAN (ALLEN), Andrew** **?-1740**
Scottish portrait painter. Known to have been working in Edinburgh c1730. Although his portraits of Sir Walter Pringle, Lord of Session and William Carteret were both engraved by Cooper and highly regarded, his reputation is that of a minor portrait painter of his period. His portrait of Lord Newhall is in the SNPG.

**ALLAN, Archibald Russell Watson RSA** **1878-1959**
Born Glasgow, 6 Mar; died Stirling, 24 May. Painter in oil, watercolour and pastel; mostly landscapes. Educated at Collegiate School (Glasgow) and Greenock Academy. Studied art under Joan Spiers(qv), the Glasgow portrait painter, at the Glasgow School of Art, and in Paris, at Julian's and Colarossi's. Elected ARSA 1931, RSA 1937. Lived for many years in Stirling. Particularly fond of domestic and garden scenes, often with animals. Exhibited RSA in 1909 and regularly 1920-1959. Represented in Glasgow City Collection, Dundee AG, Perth AG, South African National Gallery (Capetown).
**Bibl:** Halsby 246.

**ALLAN, Arthur** **fl 1931**
Amateur Helensburgh painter. Exhibited 'Thistledown' at the AAS.

**ALLAN, Catharine** **fl 1865-1870**
Painter in oil; landscapes. Sister of Christina Allan(qv) and related to David Allan(qv). Lived most of her life in Glasgow. Exhibited RSA 1865 and 1868(2).

**ALLAN, Christina G** **fl 1865-1870**
Glasgow painter in oils; landscapes and seascapes. Sister of Catharine Allan(qv) and related to David Allan(qv). Exhibited RSA 1865(2), 1869(2) and 1870(3).

**ALLAN, David** **1744-1796**
Born Alloa; died Edinburgh. Painter of portraits, portrait miniatures and figure subjects. Father of Scottish genre painting and pioneer of Scottish aquatinting. When only 11 years old he was expelled from school for caricaturing a master. The following year attended Foulis Academy, Glasgow. After leaving Glasgow he attracted the attention of some wealthy people in Alloa, including Lord Cathcart. They combined to send him to Italy where he stayed for eleven years. He

began by painting incidents drawn from ancient history and in 1773 was awarded a gold medal by the Academy of St Luke in Rome, the first Scottish painter since Gavin Hamilton(qv) to obtain the Award. This picture 'The Origin of Painting' was subsequently engraved by Cunego and is now in the SNG. In 1777 he returned to London but disillusioned with the prospects there he settled in Edinburgh in 1779. Four prints of early Edinburgh are of particular interest: 'The General Assembly of the Kirk of Scotland' (issued 1783), 'View of the High St' (1793), 'View of the High St before the removal of the luckenbooths' (1793) and 'Laying the Foundation Stone of the New College, Edinburgh, November 16, 1789'. Mention must also be made of his golfing print for the Honourable Company of Edinburgh Golfers done in 1787, reproduced in volume 18 of the *Book of the Old Edinburgh Club.* In 1785 he succeeded Alexander Runciman(qv) as master of the Trustees Academy, a position he combined with running his own drawing school where Hugh Grecian Williams(qv) was one of his pupils. The same year saw his famous portrait group of the Cathcart family playing cricket at Schawpark House, nr Alloa. His illustrations for *The Gentle Shepherd* (1788) attracted immediate acclaim and after Paul Sandby had published a series of prints taken from Allan's Sketches of the Roman Carnival the latter was dubbed 'the Scottish Hogarth'. He etched some plates for the *Songs of the Lowlands of Scotland* (1798). A fine watercolour 'Curlers at Canonmills Loch, Edinburgh' (c1795) is the first known picture of the sport. His influence on subsequent generations of Scottish genre painters, especially Alexander Carse(qv) and Walter Geikie(qv) was considerable. Although not generally regarded as a miniaturist the SNPG does have a pencil and watercolour portrait signed by Allan and dated 1774. Another miniature was exhibited as no 811 in the Exhibition of Scottish Art at Burlington House in 1939. Represented in NGS, Dundee AG, City of Edinburgh collection (4, 3 of them having been removed from the chapel of St Peter, Roxburgh Place, Edinburgh), Perth AG, Fyvie Castle (NTS).
**Bibl:** Butchart 28-31,36; Caw 50-3,59,94,96,477,482; T Crouther Gordon, David Allan of Alloa, Alva 1951; Bryan; Lindsay Errington, David Allan's Seven Sacraments (NGS 1982); Halsby 27-32 et passim; Irwin 68-72,114-123; Macmillan [GA]; Macmillan [SA]; W G Blaikie Murdoch, 'The Prints of David Allan', Print Collector's Quarterly,XIV,Oct 1927; Allan Ramsay, The Gentle Shepherd illus by David Allan (Glasgow 1788); Allan Ramsay, The Gentle Shepherd, Newhall edition, including a memoir of David Allan and other notes on Scottish paintings, 2 vols (Edinburgh 1808); Basil Skinner, 'The Indefatigable Mr Allan' SAC (Ex cat 1973); D R Fawcett Thompson, 'The Indefatigable Mr Allan', Conn. CLXXIII,1970; Wingfield.

**ALLAN, David** **fl 1868**
Glasgow landscape painter in oil. Possibly brother of Catharine(qv) and Christina(qv). Exhibited RSA(1) in 1868.

**ALLAN, Elise V** **1957-**
Born Scotland. Trained Glasgow School of Art 1974-8 and at Cyprus School of Art 1981-2. Worked as an art therapist 1978-81 and held her first solo exhibition in Glasgow 1981. Emphasises the inner life and mystical experience in large, powerful oils. Exhibited Inverclyde Biennial 1988.
**Bibl:** Alastair Paterson, 'Masculine & Feminine: Archetypes in Development in the painting of Elise V. Allan', J. Theosoph. Soc. in Scotland, no. 10, autumn 1989.

**ALLAN, Eliza Spence** **fl 1886-1898**
Glasgow painter of landscapes. Exhibited one watercolour of a scene near Dordrecht at the RSA in 1897 & GI(7).

**ALLAN, Mrs Graham** **fl 1893-1895**
Amateur Glasgow artist. Exhibited A Study in Scarlet at the RSA in 1895 & GI(4) 1893-95.

**ALLAN, H** **fl 1890-1905**
Competent amateur Glasgow landscape artist, he settled at Killin c1900. Exhibited 4 times at the RSA & GI(26).

**ALLAN, Hugh** **1862-1909**
Glasgow painter in oil and watercolour; landscapes, figures, rustic scenes. Exhibited regularly RSA(10) 1867-1897 - mostly west coast scenes and seascapes of the Clyde; also RSW(3) & AAS.

**ALLAN, J A O** **fl 1927**
Amateur Aberdeen artist. Exhibited once at the RSA in 1927.

**ALLAN, Mrs J Anderson** **fl 1875-1877**
Helensburgh painter in oils and watercolours; landscapes. Exhibited RSA 1875-1877.

**ALLAN, J K** **fl 1921**
Amateur Glasgow artist. Exhibited once at the RSA in 1921.

**ALLAN, J McGrigor** **fl 1853**
He exhibited 'A Scottish Lassie' at the RSA in 1853 from Edinburgh.

**ALLAN, J W A** **fl 1915-1919**
Portrait painter who exhibited a portrait drawing at the RSA in 1915 from Leith, and two other pictures in 1917 and 1919.

**ALLAN, Miss Jessie R** **fl 1889-1923**
Glasgow painter in oil and watercolour; flowers, figures and landscape. Exhibited RSA(9), GI(26), RSW(3), L(2) & AAS(3).

**ALLAN, John** **fl 1921-1938**
Coatbridge artist. Exhibited GI(3) & 'Fishing boats off Eyemouth' at the AAS 1921.

**ALLAN, K G** **fl 1888**
Amateur Glasgow painter. Exhibited GI in 1888.

**ALLAN, Laura M** **fl 1970**
Aberdeen landscape painter. Exhibited AAS from 56 Queen's Road.

**ALLAN, Mrs Margaret** **fl 1897**
Glasgow flower painter who exhibited twice at the RSA in 1913 and 1940, & GI(18).

**ALLAN, Miss Mary R P** **1917-**
Painter in oils of still life. Lived at Helensburgh. Exhibits regularly RSA & GI. Represented in Glasgow AG.

**ALLAN, Maxwell** **fl c1930-c1950**
Decorative sculptor. Responsible for the panels on the N and S faces of the wings of the National Library of Scotland and for the capitals at the west end of Robin chapel, Edinburgh.
**Bibl:** Gifford 184,538.

**ALLAN, Robert Weir RSA RWS RSW** **1852-1942**
Born Glasgow 11 Nov; died London. Painter in oil and watercolour; landscape, seascape and occasional portraits. Son of a lithographer. His subjects were mainly landscapes of the north-east coast of Scotland, fishing villages and cliffs. Working first near Glasgow, he exhibited at the Glasgow Institute in 1873 and at the RA from 1875 onwards. Although mainly self-taught, after moving to Paris in 1875 he studied for a short time at the Beaux Arts and at the Atelier Julian. From there he sent many plein-air landscapes to the RA and other English exhibitions. Settled in London in 1881 and continued to sketch frequently in Holland, Belgium, France and Italy, touring India in 1891-92 and Japan in 1907. His seascapes and harbour scenes have been likened to those of Colin Hunter but his foreign scenes reflect more his Paris training. His work in watercolour is sometimes likened to that of Melville(qv) and although without that artist's talent as a draughtsman the technique is similar. Most of Allan's compositions include the human figure though painted incidentally rather than as the focal point. He was particularly interested in depicting atmosphere and colour with the subject matter of secondary importance. A regular exhibitor in the French Salon, winning medals in 1899 and 1900 and an hors de concours. One of the first watercolourists to be influenced by the French Impressionists. His output was prolific, he exhibited over 1,100 works in his lifetime in Britain alone. In 1934 he executed a portrait of Lloyd George. Elected RSW 1880, ARWS 1887, RWS 1886, VPRWS 1908-10. Exhibited RA(83), RSA(89), RSW(166), RWS(403), GI(121) & regularly at the AAS. Represented in Glasgow AG, Paisley AG, Leeds AG, Liverpool AG, Manchester AG, Sydney(Australia) AG.
**Bibl:** AJ 1904, 197; Bell, 'Robert Weir Allan', Studio, Vol 23, 1901, 228-237; Caw 329-331; Halsby 133-136 et passim; Hardie III 193; Studio, vol 46, 1909, 89-100.

**ALLAN, Tom** **fl 1960**
Exhibited once at the RSA in 1960 from a Glasgow address.

**ALLAN, Ugolin** **fl 1893-1902**
Glasgow painter in oil and watercolour; figurative subjects. Exhibited once at the RSA in 1899, RSW(2), GI(11) & AAS(2).

**ALLAN, W H** **fl 1889**
Amateur Glasgow artist who exhibited once at the GI.

**ALLAN, Wilkie** **fl 1891-1892**
Painter of interiors. Exhibited once at the RSA in 1891 from an Edinburgh address.

**ALLAN, Sir William RA PRSA** **1782-1850**
Born and died Edinburgh. Painter in oils of historical scenes, Russian subjects, portraits. Apprenticed as a coach painter, studied under Graham(qv) at the Trustees Academy with Wilkie(qv), John Burnett(qv) and Alexander Fraser(qv) before entering the RA Schools in London. Disappointed with his progress there, where he had taken Opie as his model - 'Gipsy Boy and Ass' shown at the RA(1805) being the prime example - Allan decided to go to St Petersburg (1805) but his ship was driven into Poland by bad weather. There he painted portraits to earn his keep, staying at the residence of Count Felix Potocki at Tulczyn. For the Count he also painted landscapes and genre pictures in both oil and watercolour and executed six landscapes intended as illustrations to the poem "Opisanie Zofiiofki". These drawings were engraved by Schlotterbeck. Having arrived in St Petersburg he made the acquaintance of Sir Alexander Crichton, physician to the Imperial family. He then travelled to Turkey and Tartary studying the Cossacks and Circassians and collecting subjects for many future pictures. In 1814 he returned to Edinburgh and the following year exhibited 'Circassian Captives' which was subscribed to by Sir Walter Scott and his friends. Later Allan painted scenes of Scottish history suggested by the Waverley novels. These proved more popular than his Russian subjects. In 1826 he became Master of the Trustees Academy but in 1828 an eye infection caused a pause in his work so he set off for Italy and thence to Asia Minor. This was followed by a trip in 1834 to Spain and North Africa and a return in 1844 to Russia. In 1843 he had exhibited 'The Battle of Waterloo' from the English Side at the Royal Academy, subsequently purchased by the Duke of Wellington. When in St Petersburg in 1844 he painted 'Peter the Great Teaching his Subjects the Art of Ship Building' for the Czar's Winter Palace. In addition to his historical and portrait work Allan painted one or two miniatures, one of which is in the SNPG and another in the V&A. In 1841 he succeeded Wilkie as Limner for the Queen in Scotland and was knighted the following year. In spite of these honours none of his paintings was added to the Royal Collection. It was the fate of Sir William Allan to be eclipsed in reputation and popularity by some of those who came after him, several of whom had been his pupils. Allan's work is more interesting as inaugurating a new development in Scottish painting than on its own account; but it possesses some intrinsic merit, considerably more than is indicated by the pictures which represent him in public collections. 'His colour possessed no particular quality or charm, as a draughtsman he was rather mincing and neat, as a designer his merit, although considerable, was more anecdotal than decorative, and weakness of drawing and smallness of parts contradicted the vigour and spirit with which he occasionally arranged his subject; but, when compared with the standard of his day, his technique was respectable and his conception of incident intelligent and straightforward' [Caw]. He was the first in Scotland to study correctness of historical costume, and in this respect his work was always abreast of the best contemporary knowledge. Elected ARA 1825, RA 1835, RSA 1829, PRSA 1838. Altogether exhibited 48 pictures at the RA 1803-49 and almost as many at the RSA 1830-50. Represented in NG, NGS, Edinburgh City collection, Haddo House (NTS).
**Bibl:** AJ 1849, 109; 1850, 100; 1903, 53; Armstrong 33; Bryan; Caw 108-110; Foskett 136; Halsby 62-3 et passim; Hardie 39,41-2,45; Irwin 204-213 et passim; McKay 142-146, Rd; Macmillan [GA]; Macmillan [SA].

**ALLAN, William James Jnr** **fl 1902-1928**
Leith painter who exhibited at the RSA in 1918 and 1928, once at the GI & Evening at the AAS in 1902.

**ALLAN, William K** **fl 1963-1976**
Edinburgh-based painter. Exhibited RSA during the above years.

**ALLAN, W M** **fl 1888**
Amateur Glasgow painter. Exhibited 2 pictures at the GI in 1888.

**ALLAN-FRASER, Patrick HRSA** **1813-1890**
Born and died Arbroath. Although a painter of portraits and genre his main claim to fame was his patronage of artists during and after his lifetime. Apprenticed to a housepainter before proceeding to Edinburgh where he studied under Scott Lauder(qv). Then travelled to Rome where he was subsequently instrumental in reviving the British Academy of Art, becoming its President. In 1839 he returned to Arbroath and soon obtained important portrait commissions. He then travelled again to Paris and to London before returning to Arbroath when he was invited to do a series of sketches for Cadell's edition of the Waverley novels, especially *The Antiquary.* He built the mansion of Hospitalfield used as the prototype for Monks Barns. Married Elisabeth Fraser of Hospitalfield and assumed her name to become Allan-Fraser. Having taken up residence there he proceeded to purchase paintings and sculptures from contemporary artist friends and he bequeathed Hospitalfield with sufficient funds for "the assistance and encouragement of young men not having means of their own who shall be desirous of following up one or more of the professions of painting, sculpture, carving in wood, architecture and engraving". Exhibited four times at the RA in 1852, 1871, 1874 and 1878 and 32 works at the RSA 1852-80.

**ALLARDYCE, Archibald McN** **fl 1929**
Amateur Glasgow painter who exhibited once at the GI.

**ALLARDYCE, Samuel** **c1760-c1830**
Engraver. Apprenticed to Robert Scott(qv). He emigrated to Philadelphia where he became die-sinker to the USA Mint. In 1790 he engraved a bookplate for the Library Company of Baltimore. Engraved a large number of plates in Dobson's edition of A Rees's *Cyclopaedia,* 1794-1803.
**Bibl:** Bushnell; D M Stauffer, American Engravers, vol i, 8, vol ii, p11.

**ALLEN, Charles John** **1862-**
Sculptor. Exhibited a portrait bust at the RSA in 1917.

**ALLEN, Colin** **fl 1959-1965**
Painter. Exhibited figurative works at the RSA 1959-1965 from an address in Carlisle.

**ALLEN, Miss Constance** **fl 1893-1894**
Amateur Edinburgh painter. Exhibited a still life at the GI in 1893 and another at the AAS in 1894, from 5 Stowan Terrace, Trinity.

**ALLEN, Sylvia** **1951-**
Born Glasgow. Painter in oils and watercolour; mostly landscapes using strong colour and with expressive movement. Subjects often around the Ayrshire coastline. Trained Glasgow School of Art 1970-1974, where she was tutor in Life Drawing 1986-94. Held solo exhibitions in Scotland, Germany and the USA. Exhibits RSA & RGI.

**ALLISON, Miss Jeannie** **fl 1895**
Edinburgh artist. Exhibited one picture 'Largo Pier' at the RSA in 1895.

**ALLISON, Robert** **fl 1926-1940**
Glasgow painter. Exhibited 7 times at the GI between the above years.

**ALLINSON, Thomas Jnr** **fl 1885-1894**
Dalkeith based painter of pastoral scenes. Exhibited AAS in the above years.

**ALLSOP, Harry S** **fl 1931-1950**
Ayrshire artist who specialised in local landscapes and portraits, exhibiting RSA 1931-1948 and again in 1950, also GI(6) & AAS(7).

**ALLSOP, John** **fl 1856**
He exhibited a Highland landscape at the RSA in 1856.

**AL(L)SOP, Frederick** **1839-c1890**
Born Edinburgh. Animal painter in oil, also landscape. Son of an Edinburgh doctor he entered the Trustees Academy in Edinburgh in 1854, having been recommended by David Octavius Hill. At the end of a year he left to continue studies on his own and began exhibiting at the RSA 1853. This may have been the Frederick Alsop who exhibited a landscape at the RA in 1853 from Milngavie.

**ALMOND, Henry Nicholas FRSA** **1918-**
Born nr Bishop Auckland, Co Durham. Painter in oil of landscape; teacher. Trained Newcastle-upon-Tyne School of Art under Alex Mainds, Robert Lyon(qv) and Sir Robin Darwin. From 1940-46 he served in the Royal Navy. He was formerly Head of Art and Design at the Mason College of Education in Ambleside 1962-1978 and was elected to the Lake Artists Society in 1963, becoming its President in 1971-77, and again from 1983-1989. Specialises in winter landscapes most often of the Lake District and the Scottish Highlands. Strongly affected by a visit to Australia in 1988 as illustrated in his 'Aspect of Ayers Rock', exhibited in the RSA 1989. Frequently exhibits in Sydney, Australia and has exhibited RA & RSA since 1953.

**ALSTON, Gavin G C** **fl 1953-1963**
Painter. Exhibited RSA 1953, 1956 and annually 1960-1963 from addresses in Edinburgh and Glasgow.

**ALSTON, I W** **1785-1795**
Scottish painter mainly in watercolour of figurative studies and genre.

**ALSTON, Jane** **fl 1961-1970**
Sculptress. Exhibited RSA 1961-1962 and again in 1970.

**ALSTON, Thomas** **c1780-c1830**
Halsby lists an artist of this name who painted landscapes 'in a neat topographical style'.
**Bibl:** Halsby 246.

**ALSTON, I W** **18th Cent**
Watercolour painter listed by Halsby as producing genre works 'in rustic settings'.
**Bibl:** Halsby 246.

**ALSTON, William** **fl 1962-1970**
Painter of portraits and still lifes. Exhibited RSA in 1962, 1965-66 and 1970.

**ALVES, James** **1738-1808**
Born Inverness; died Inverness, 27 Nov. Miniaturist and portraitist in crayons. Came from a well known Inverness family. He won a gold medal from the Edinburgh 'Society of Arts' in 1756, after which he spent eight years studying in Rome. He is known to have practised in London. Besides miniatures he painted small portraits in crayons and mythological subjects, including two Roman history compositions, exhibited at the RA in 1775. There is a miniature of Lord Keith at Windsor Castle, signed 'I A' which may be by Alves. A portrait 'Hugh Rose, 20th Laird of Kilravock' (1780-1827) is in the collection of Rose of Kilravock House. Exhibited at the RA every year between 1775 and 1779.
**Bibl:** Brydall 141; Foskett; Graves, RA, Scottish Notes and Queries, March 1926, 64; Long 4; Philip Yorke, Baker's Diary, 1931.

**AMBROZEVICH, Carmen Moira** **fl 1975-1989**
Aberdeen designer. Exhibited regularly AAS from 48 Stanley Street.

**AMOUR, Elizabeth Isobel (Mrs G P H Watson)** **1885-1945**
Edinburgh painter and potter. Founded 'Bough Pottery' in Edinburgh. Exhibited 6 pictures at the RSA 1937-1939.

**ANCILL, Joseph** **1896-c1940**
Painter and engraver. Exhibited RSA in 1919, 1921, 1940 and in 1961, also GI(5).

**ANCRUM, Marion (Mrs G Turnbull)** **fl 1885-1919**
Edinburgh painter in watercolours; interiors, landscapes, townscapes. Specialised in watercolours of Old Edinburgh some of which can be seen in the City of Edinburgh Art Collection. Exhibited RA(1) 1891, RSA 1887-1910, RSW(15), GI(2) & AAS 1894-1898. Represented in City of Edinburgh collection (3 watercolours of Old Edinburgh streets).
**Bibl:** Halsby 246.

**ANCRUM, Miss Mary** **fl 1887-1898**
Edinburgh artist. Exhibited 'A Sunny Day on the Moor' at the RA in 1891, also RSA(10), RHA(2) & GI(7).

**ANDERSON -** **fl 1760-1770**
Sculptor. Between the above years executed a number of decorative carvings at Penicuik House, Midlothian. A 'Mr Anderson' exhibited 'a tripod from the original design of Mr Stuart's' at the Free Society of Artists in 1761.

**ANDERSON, A** **fl 1881**
Amateur Edinburgh artist who exhibited once at the RSA in 1881.

**ANDERSON, Miss A Jane** **fl 1866-1871**
Dalkeith flower painter. Appears to have moved to Edinburgh c1870. Exhibited RSA 1861-1872.

**ANDERSON, Alexander** **1775-1870**
Born New York; died Jersey City. Scottish parentage. First wood engraver to practice the art in North America where he became known as the Bewick of America. Began life as a physician, graduating in 1796, but soon abandoned medicine in order to devote himself full-time to art. Among his most important works are those in Webster's *Spelling Book,* Bell's *Anatomy,* Josephus's *History* and Shakespeare's *Plays,* all from original designs. An engraving of 'The Last Supper', made between 1820 & 1830, was his last work on copper. When he was 93 years old he engraved illustrations for Barbour's *Historical Collections of New Jersey.*
**Bibl:** AJ, 1858, 271; Bryan; Bushnell; D M Stauffer, American Engravers, vol i, 8, vol ii, 11.

**ANDERSON, Anne (Mrs Alan Wright)** **1874-c1930**
Born in Scotland. Painter in watercolours, etcher, book illustrator, specialising in children's books. After a childhood in Argentina her family moved to Berkshire. In 1911 she met the artist/illustrator Alan Wright whom she married 1912. Influenced by the work of Mabel Lucie Attwell and Jessie M King(qv), she was responsible for illustrating over one hundred children's books, many in collaboration with her husband. Writing in *Book Collector*, Maleen Matthews praised her work having "all the qualities which make her so incomparable a children's artist...from the point of view of creating for a child's mind she is perhaps more important than either [Rackham or Charles Robinson]". Her work has a gentle feel both in its colour and drawing. Books include Underdown: *Aucassin and Nicolette* (1911), *The Gateway to Chaucer* (1912), *Old Nursery Songs* (nd), *Old French Nursery Songs* (nd), *The Sleepy Song Book* (nd), Garrett: *Rip* (1919), Strang: *My Big Picture Book* (et al, 1920), Talbot: *The Cosy-Comfy Book* (1920), Eliot: *The House Above the Trees* (1921), Barnes: *Fireside Stories* (1922), Herbertson: *Sing Song Stories* (1922), Joan: *Cosy-Time Tales* (1922), *Grimm's Fairy Tales* (1922), Anderson: *Fairy Tales* (1924), Garrett: *Wanda and the Garden of the Red House* (124), Kingsley: *The Water Babies* (1924), Morrison: *Cosy Chair Stories* (1924), Spyri: *Heidi* (1924), Strang: *Little Rhymes for Little Folk* (1925), Heward: *Mr Pickles and the Party* (1926), *The Old Mother Goose Nursery Rhyme Book* (1926), Southwold: *Once Upon a Time Stories* (1927), Crossland & Parrish: *The Children's Wonder Book* (1933), *My Big New Book* (et al, 1938). She contributed regularly to *Blackie's Children's Annual, Cassell's Children Annual, Mrs Strang's Annuals, Playbox Annual* and *Wonder Annual.*
**Bibl:** M Matthews: *"An Illustrator of the Nineties",* Book Collector, 28,4,(1979); Horne; Peppin.

**ANDERSON, Anne M A** **fl 1948-1956**
Born Trinidad. Educated in Scotland, trained at Glasgow School of Art. Winner of the Lauder Award with the Glasgow Society of Women Artists and commended by the Council of the Institute of Painters and Watercolours for the most distinguished work by a non-member. Has exhibited regularly at the RSA, RI, GI, the SSWA, the Glasgow Society of Women Artists and the Glasgow Art Club. Lives at Killearn, Stirlingshire.

**ANDERSON, Archibald** **fl 1864-1891**
Sculptor and painter in oils; landscapes and portraits. Exhibited regularly RSA 1864-1891, sometimes landscapes and sometimes medallion portraits;also exhibited sculpture in 1869, 1872 and 1873.

**ANDERSON, Blair** **fl 1988**
Painter of figurative, landscape and semi-abstract paintings in oil. Trained Gray's School of Art. Won Elizabeth Greenshields award. First solo exhibition, Edinburgh 1990. Exhibits RSA & AAS.

**ANDERSON, Charles** **fl 1962**
Painter. Exhibited once at the RSA in 1962. Represented in Paisley AG(7).

**ANDERSON, Christina S** **fl 1890-1896**
Glasgow artist. Exhibited a life study at the RSA in 1893; also 3 pictures at the GI & RI(1).

**ANDERSON, Sir D C** **fl 1883**
Amateur Glasgow artist who exhibited 2 pictures at the GI in 1883.

**ANDERSON, D Leuchars** **fl 1889-1892**
This Glasgow artist exhibited twice at the RSA in 1891 and 1892, having moved to Temple-by-Gorebridge in 1890; also GI(1).

**ANDERSON, D M** **fl 1902-1925**
Painter. Exhibited mostly foreign scenes at the RSA in 1909 and again in 1918 from an address in Dunbar; also L(2).

**ANDERSON, Miss Daisy M G** **fl 1935-1951**
Amateur Glasgow painter. Exhibited GI(4). Represented in Dundee AG.

**ANDERSON, Daniel** **fl 1983-1984**
Aberdeen painter in the modern idiom. Exhibited AAS(3) from 190 Ferrier Crescent.

**ANDERSON, David** **c1799-1847**
Born Perthshire (christened in Perth, Aug 25); died Liverpool, Oct. Sculptor. A self-taught Perthshire carver who had a considerable local success with his statue of Tam O'Shanter. Father of William Anderson(qv). In 1847 went to Liverpool to exhibit his groups in stone of Tam O'Shanter and Kirkton Jean, and 'The Parting between Watty and Meg'. Died of typhus in October of the same year. The *Gentleman's Magazine* considered him 'a man of great ability as an artist' while the *Liverpool Mercury,* in its obituary, stated that 'like most men of genius he was modest, retiring, plain and unassuming'. Anderson was buried in Perth. The statues of Prince Charlie and Flora Macdonald at Fingask, sometimes attributed to him, were by **Charles SPENCE**. A number of his groups illustrating Scottish poems including Scott's *Last Minstrel* and *The Highland Drover,* Burns's *Three Jolly Boys* and Alexander Wilson's *Watty and Meg* which now stand in the grounds of Fingask Castle, near Perth.
**Bibl:** Gunnis; Gent Mag vol II, 1847, 668; Liverpool Mercury, Oct, 1847.

**ANDERSON, David** **fl 1882-1883**
Glasgow artist. Exhibited once at the RSA and twice at the GI. Not to be confused with an English artist of the same name who was painting angling scenes at about the same time.

**ANDERSON, David R RSW** **1883-1976**
Born Glasgow. Watercolourist. Trained Glasgow School of Art followed by a spell at Glasgow University and Ecole des Beaux Arts, Paris. A journalist and editor by profession, an amateur artist by inclination. Maintained a studio at Gareloch on the Clyde. In mid-life moved to Edinburgh. After retirement settled in Ilkley and devoted himself full-time to the practice of art. Executed powerful watercolours as well as chalk drawings, mostly landscapes. His earlier work was influenced by Muirhead Bone(qv) but his later work was characterised by the development of his own style. Exhibited regularly RA, RSW & GI.
**Bibl:** Halsby 246.

**ANDERSON, Douglas N** **1927-**
Born Glasgow. Paints in watercolour and monochrome. Primarily a commercial artist, specialises in military uniform. Studied Glasgow School of Art. Published many illustrations, mostly of Scottish costume. Represented in City of Edinburgh collection.

**ANDERSON, Elspeth M** **fl 1928-1935**
Exhibited twice at the RSA in 1929 and again in 1931 from Dunbartonshire; also GI (5) & L(2).

**ANDERSON, G G** **fl 1892-1925**
Glasgow painter in oil of portraits, landscapes and marines. Exhibited 4 pictures at the RSA 1900-1904, also GI(44) & RSW(3). A work of his was included in the Exhibition of Modern Scottish Artists at Brighton AG 1906.

**ANDERSON, G W** **fl 1826-1852**
Landscape painter in oils. Son of the Scottish marine painter William Anderson. Lived near London and for a time at 15 Orchard Street, Aberdeen. Exhibited 13 works in London, mostly landscapes near London, including 7 at the RA. Occasionally painted sea pieces such as A Boat Adrift (RA 1846) and A View on the Coast with Boats and a Breeze (RA 1852); also GI(44), RSW(3) & AAS(4).

**ANDERSON, Helen Carrick**
**[see CARRICK-ANDERSON, Helen]**

**ANDERSON, Hilda** **fl c1910-c1925**
Portrait painter, probably Scottish. Little is now known about her. Worked mainly in France, exhibiting Salon of French Artists 1913 and National Salon 1924.

**ANDERSON, Hugh** **c1790-c1830**
Born Scotland. Probably related to Alexander A(qv). Emigrated and settled in Philadelphia where he is said to have executed good line and stipple work 1815-1825.
**Bibl:** Bushnell; D M Stauffer, American Engravers, vol i, 9, vol ii, 15.

**ANDERSON, Ida Katherine** **fl 1904-1938**
Dunbartonshire painter of portrait miniatures. Trained Glasgow School of Art. Exhibited once at the RA, also RSA(3), GI(16) & L(4).

**ANDERSON, Mrs J P RMS** **fl 1897**
Miniature painter. Lived at Strathmiglo, Fife, exhibiting 4 miniatures at the RMS 1897.

**ANDERSON, J S** **fl 1874**
Painter. Exhibited once at the RSA in 1874 from an Edinburgh address.

**ANDERSON, James** **fl 1866-1884**
Painter in oils of landscapes and still life. Exhibited RSA 1866, 1868 and 1884 from Paisley.

**ANDERSON, James** **fl 1883-1907**
Glasgow artist. Exhibited RSA(2), GI(9) & L(4).

**ANDERSON, James** **fl 1883-1924**
Paisley artist and (certified) teacher of art. Exhibited Paisley Art Institute 1878-1924 and committee member 1879-1914. A prolific artist, more interested in supporting his local exhibitions than in exhibiting widely afield.

**ANDERSON, James Bell RSA** **1886-1938**
Born Edinburgh; died Glasgow, Nov. Portrait painter. Educated Bo'ness Academy and trained Edinburgh School of Art where he won a scholarship in his first year; also studied at Hospitalfield, Arbroath for four years under George Harcourt before continuing his studies at Julian's in Paris under Jean Paul Laurens. Upon returning to Britain set up a studio in Glasgow 1912, devoting himself entirely to portraiture. One of his first commissions was from Lord Strathclyde, then Lord Advocate. Commissioned by the Constitutional Club to complete a portrait of Bonar Law, which had been started by Sir James Guthrie. Elected ARSA 1932, RSA 1938. Exhibited regularly RA(3), RSA(45) occasionally still lifes as well as portraits, RSW(2), GI(74) & AAS(1).

**ANDERSON, James Lawrie** **fl 1881**
A little known Edinburgh painter. Specialised in watercolour townscapes, exhibiting RSA(1) 1881.

**ANDERSON, Miss Jane McGillivray** **fl 1883-1886**
Pilrig portrait painter in oils. Exhibited twice at the RSA in 1883 and 1886.

**ANDERSON, Janette** **fl 1965-1977**
Glasgow painter. Exhib RSA from 1965 to 1971 and again in 1977.

**ANDERSON, Miss Jessie J** **fl 1881-1885**
Helensburgh artist. Exhibited 11 pictures at the GI between the above dates.

**ANDERSON, John** **fl 1600-1665**
Early painter. Elected Burgess of Aberdeen 1601. In 1611 received £69.13 4d from the City of Edinburgh for painting and gilding the Netherbow Clock in Edinburgh and the same year was made a Burgess of Edinburgh. On May 27, 1612 George Jamesone was apprenticed to him in Edinburgh and in 1617 Anderson was working for the Marquis of Huntly at Strathbogie (Huntly Castle) and in March of that year was instructed by the Privy Council to go to Falkland Palace for the King's impending visit. Anderson seems to have attended to this summons rather peremptorily for he was ordered to appear 'under the pane of rebellioun'. Later that year he was working also at Edinburgh Castle, redecorating the room in which James VI was born. Apted points out that as he was summoned for this purpose from Huntly it seems reasonable to suppose that he was also responsible for the emblematic paintings traces of which survive at Huntly Castle. In 1633 he painted the Council house at Holyrood. The following year he carried out work in St Nicholas, Aberdeen, and also at Ballachastell for Sir John Grant of Freuchie, where he painted the gallery ceiling. In 1647 and 1649 there are records of him selling properties in Aberdeen. Little is known of his life, he had a son Adam and a daughter Euphemia who married an advocate. Nothing further is heard of him until 1663 when he was working again at Holyrood Palace.
**Bibl:** Apted 14-15; M R Apted, Painted Ceilings of Scotland, Edinburgh 1966, 89,93; Edinburgh Records for 1611; Macmillan [SA] 57-62; Register of Edinburgh Apprentices for 1612, Roll of Edinburgh Burgesses 1612; Duncan Thomson, Painting in Scotland 1570-1650; George Jamesone, Oxford 1974.

**ANDERSON, John** **c1780-c1830**
Born Scotland. Wood engraver. Little is known about him except that he was a pupil of Bewick's and illustrated the poem 'Grove Hill'. According to Redgrave he showed great talent but gave up art prematurely.
**Bibl:** Bushnell; DNB; Redgrave.

**ANDERSON, John** **c1780-c1830**
Edinburgh engraver. Apprenticed to James Johnston(qv). Opened his own business at 9 Picardy Place but in about 1816 entered into partnership with George Walker. They engraved Marshall's *Scottish Airs* 1822 and their names appear on many of the sheet music publications of the time.
**Bibl:** Bushnell; D Cook, Scottish Notes and Queries, Nov 1928.

**ANDERSON, John** **fl 1844-1849**
Obscure painter of sporting scenes. A study of a horse-drawn carriage and groom(1844) and the portrait of a Highland sportsman with his Pony and Dog recently appeared on the market (CSK 1985 & Sotheby 1984 respectively).
**Bibl:** Wingfield.

**ANDERSON, John** **fl 1880-1891**
Landscape painter and etcher. Having exhibited 5 times at the RA he moved from London to Glasgow 1887 concentrating on Scottish landscapes. Exhibited RSA in 1887, GI(5), RE(3) and at the inaugural exhibition of the AAS in 1885.

**ANDERSON, John Farquharson** **fl 1877-1882**
Painter in oils and watercolours; topographical, landscapes. Exhibited RSA in 1877, 1879 and 1881-2, latterly from Dundee.

**ANDERSON, Mrs K B** **fl 1880-1881**
Amateur Glasgow painter; exhibited twice at the GI.

**ANDERSON, Mrs L T** **fl 1902**
Glasgow-based painter. Exhibited RSA(1) in 1902.

**ANDERSON, Margaret D** **fl 1893**
Amateur Largs artist. Exhibited once at the GI 1893.

**ANDERSON, Martin ('Cynicus')** **1854-1932**
Born Leuchars, Fife; died Balmullo, Fife, Apr. Painter in oil and watercolour of landscape; also cartoonist, using the pseudonym 'Cynicus'. Educated Madras College; apprenticed for seven years to a designer in Glasgow and whilst there attended evening classes at Glasgow School of Art. Devoted much of his time to landscape painting becoming a contributor to local art exhibitions. Between 1878 and 1880 exhibited at the RSA from Cambuslang. Worked for a time with Leng Publications in Dundee, contributing numerous sketches and newspaper illustrations. In the late 1880s moved to London and in 1890 published his first book *The Satires of Cynicus,* followed by *The Humours of Cynicus* (1891), *Symbols and Metaphors, The Fatal Smile: A Fairy Tale* (1892) and *Cartoons Social and Political* (1893). Returned to Scotland c1890 setting up a studio at Tayport, Fife where he was sufficiently successful to engage copyists to reproduce his work. Posthumous exhibition, St Andrews Museum 1994. Built 'Castle Cynicus' at Balmullo where he died. Exhibited 'The Music Lesson' at the RSA 1878. Six works are in Dundee AG.
**Bibl:** Caw 468; Halsby 246; Houfe; E Reid & F Davidson *The Fortunes of Cynicus.*

**ANDERSON, Miss Minnie** **fl 1898-1909**
At the time of her first exhibit this artist was living in Dunbar but by 1898 had moved to Greenock. Exhibited twice at the RSA & GI(13).

**ANDERSON, Muriel** **fl 1971-1974**
Sculptress. Exhibited RSA 1971-72 and again in 1974 from an address in Perth.

**ANDERSON, Nettie** **fl 1902**
Amateur painter of local landscapes. Exhibited AAS from 55 Westburn Road.

**ANDERSON, Miss Nina** **fl 1889-1898**
Edinburgh painter of flower pieces and portraits, pastels. Exhibited once at the RSA in 1889 & GI(1).

**ANDERSON, Miss Nora D** **fl 1915**
Exhibited once at the Walker AG, Liverpool from her home at Knockderry Cove, Dunbartonshire.

**ANDERSON, Patricia E** **fl 1965-1966**
Minor Aberdeen portrait painter. Exhibited several works at the AAS from 24 Ellon Road, Bridge of Don.

**ANDERSON, Rev R P R** **fl 1940**
Amateur watercolourist. Exhibited twice at the RSW.

**ANDERSON, Richard** **c1930-2002**
Landscape painter. Worked from Glasgow. Enjoyed rugged and dramatic, especially mountainous, scenes. Exhibited *'Cape Horn'* at RGI (1954). The Cairngorm Club have a scene in the Grampians on semi-public display.

**ANDERSON, Robert** **fl 1897-1903**
Edinburgh painter principally in watercolour of landscape and figures. Exhibited RSA(10) 1897-1903.

**ANDERSON, Robert L ARSA RSW** **1842-1885**
Born Edinburgh; died 24 Apr. Line engraver and watercolour artist. Acquired a reputation as an engraver but towards the end of his life devoted his time to watercolour painting. Specialised in the depiction of churches and large, often powerful watercolours of fishing vessels and fishermen. Also attracted to scenes of rural life in Brittany and Holland. In recent years his reputation seems to have inexplicably declined. Elected RSW 1878, ARSA 1879. Exhibited once at the RA 'Curling on Duddingston Loch' and every year at the RSA between 1869 and his death in 1885; also at the NWS, RSW(18) & GI(8). Represented in Manchester AG, Sydney AG (Australia).
**Bibl:** Caw 324; Halsby 246-7.

**ANDERSON, Sir Robert Rowand ARSA** **1835-1921**
Born Forres; died Colinton, 1 Apr. Edinburgh architect. Son of a

lawyer, after an early education at George Watson's Hospital he left a solicitor's office to study in the Ornamental Department of the Trustees School under William Christie, also under R S Lauder(qv). Apprenticed in Edinburgh with John Lessels he then went to France, Italy and Holland before working in London with Sir Gilbert Scott. Published *Examples of the Municipal, Commercial and Street Architecture of France and Italy* (nd). First exhibited RA 1860, by which time he had established his own business in Edinburgh. Received an Honorary LLD from Edinburgh University 1884 and the same year exhibited at the RA plans for an Edinburgh University extension and for the Central Station Hotel, Glasgow (1884), one of the city landmarks. Elected ARSA 1876 but resigned 1883 in protest against the neglect of architecture in the election of academicians. Subsequently a more proportional representation at each level was maintained. Elected HRSA 1896. Taught at the School of Applied Art. His re-modelling of Broughty Castle, Angus(1860-1) and St Vigeans church, Angus(1893) influenced a generation of Scottish architects. It was through his initiative that the Institute of Scottish Architects was founded, and he became its first President. In 1916 received the Institute's gold medal (on the recommendation of J.J.Burnet), the highest available award to a British architect. In early professional life his works were almost entirely ecclesiastical but from the middle 1870s his practise became more varied. His lay work was executed in one or other of the forms of the Renaissance and his churches in the Gothic style. Inaugurated the National Art Survey. Exhibited RA(4), RSA(37) 1860-1916, GI(4) & AAS(1).
**Bibl:** Caw 217,224; Dunbar 149, 163-5; Gifford passim; A Gomme & D Walker, Architecture of Glasgow, London 1987(rev), 13,67,177n,193f,201,284,286; Peter Savage, Lorimer and the Edinburgh Craft Designers, Edinburgh 1980; Bruce Walker & W S Gauldie, Architects and Architecture on Tayside, Dundee 1984, 157.

**ANDERSON, Steven** **1975-**
Born Feb 28, Paisley. Painter, primarily in oils. Trained Glasgow School of Art 1993-97. Exhibits RSA & RGI since 1996.

**ANDERSON, Thomas Alexander** **fl 1927-1940**
Paisley painter, poster designer and wood engraver. Trained Glasgow School of Art 1924-1927 where he obtained a special award for portrait painting. Unable to make a sufficient living from his unpretentious but competent work, he combined it with teaching, becoming second master at Doncaster School of Arts and Crafts. Exhibited only once, at the GI in 1930.

**ANDERSON, Trevor N** **fl 1892-1902**
Edinburgh painter in oil and watercolour of landscapes. Exhibited RA in 1896 and 1899, RSA(4), RSW(2), GI(7) & L(1) in 1898.

**ANDERSON, T R** **fl 1891**
Edinburgh painter. Exhibited 3 works at the RSA in 1891.

**ANDERSON, Valerie** **1965-**
Born Edinburgh. Painter in watercolour, charcoal, pastel. Trained 1982-87 at the Edinburgh College of Art graduating with distinction. Awarded a Hospitalfield Scholarship 1985 and in 1986 the John Kinross Scholarship, earning her three months in Florence. Has participated in various travelling exhibitions in Britain and Italy. Favours still lifes and interiors. Her first exhibited works were in 1987 at the RSA, SSA & SSWA.

**ANDERSON, William James** **1863-1900**
Glasgow architect. Apprenticed to Gillespie of St Andrews(qv). Arrived Glasgow from Dundee c1882. Assistant to T L Watson(qv) and William Leiper(qv). Won Thomson travelling scholarship 1887. Became Director, Dept of Architecture, Glasgow School of Art 1894. Increasingly depressed by the death of six workmen during the construction of the 5th floor of Napier building which eventually caused him to abandon any further work. Author of *Architectural Studies in Italy* (1890), *The Architecture of the Renaissance in Italy* (1896) and *The Architecture of Greece and Rome* (completed posthumously by Phene Spiers). Exhibited GI(10) 1891-1897.
**Bibl:** A Gomme & D Walker, Architecture of Glasgow, London 1987(rev), 222-4,228,266n,284f,303.

**ANDERSON, William** **1757-1837**
Born Sutherland, 27 May. Painter of marine subjects and coastal views. Originally trained as a shipwright and had a lifelong experience of ships and shipping. His watercolour seascapes are highly valued for their clean execution and accurate drawing. His oils are comparable to his contemporaries Brooking and Cleveley. A friend of J C Ibbotson whose influence can be seen in Anderson's rare landscapes. Produced many types of composition from 'The Lifeboat Off Tynemouth' (1824) to 'The British Squadron Going Into the Tagus with Spanish Captured Ships'. Painted an interior of Westminster Abbey and his 'Five Views of the Battle of the Nile' was engraved in aquatint by W Aliss. His son G W Anderson(qv) was a landscape artist. Marine paintings, like sporting paintings, have been comparatively neglected by art historians, largely accounting for the scant attention given to Anderson who was undoubtedly one of the finest marine artists Scotland has produced. Sir Geoffrey Callender said that "in his most characteristic work Anderson displays an airy quality and a soft sense of colour reminiscent of Van de Capelle. His work is unequal. He is at his best when portraying ships in light airs, but in some of his drawings he develops a hardness comparable with that found in the later work of Pocock". He made skilful use of the sharp point of a knife to indicate wave forms. Exhibited at the RA almost annually from 1789 to 1834. Represented in the BM, V&A.
**Bibl:** Binyon; Brydall 311; Cundall; DNB; Graves, RA; Halsby 49-50; Redgrave; TB 21,63; VAM; Williams; Windsor.

**ANDERSON, William** **fl 1845-1865**
Perthshire portrait sculptor. Exhibited RSA 1858, a bust of Neil Gow in 1861, and another work in 1865. Exhibited a portrait bust of the Duke of Atholl 1866 which, together with Neil Gow, suggests that he at least knew the Duke and was probably commissioned by him.

**ANDERSON, William** **fl 1845-1854**
Inverness sculptor. Son of David Anderson(qv). Exhibited at the Great Exhibition of 1851 a figure of a Highlander throwing the 'putting-stone', while on the pedestal are reliefs of figures 'further illustrative of Highland Games'. In 1853 he carved the bust of Peel for the memorial erected at Forfar and in the following year he executed a heroic statue of Burns which he presented to his native town, described by *The Builder* as of 'manly make'. It now stands above a public house in County Place. Anderson's statues of Prince Charles Edward Stuart and Flora Macdonald, carved in about 1845, are in the grounds of Fingask Castle, nr Perth.
**Bibl:** Gunnis.

**ANDERSON, William S** **fl 1917-1930**
Painter. Although living in Hexham, moved to Glasgow before 1930. All his exhibits were in Scotland, at the RSA(9), RSW(1) & GI(9).

**ANDREWS, Miss Anna** **fl 1830-1838**
Edinburgh portrait miniaturist who exhibited annually at the RSA from an Edinburgh address between 1830 and 1838. Recorded by neither Long nor Foskett.

**ANDREWS, Charlotte J** **fl 1898**
Amateur Melrose oil painter of landscapes, exhibited a picture of Knaresborough at the RSA in 1898.

**ANDREWS, D A (R?)** **fl 1831-1849**
Dundee painter in oil and watercolour; historical subjects, portraits and still life. Exhibited RSA(16) between the above years. Became the first drawing master at the Dundee Seminaries (later Dundee HS).

**ANEILL, Joseph** **fl 1929**
Amateur Glasgow artist. Exhibited GI(2).

**ANGELL, Helen Cordelia RWS** **1847-1884**
English watercolourist. Received her first lessons from her brother William S Coleman. Specialised in the delicate depiction of fruit, flowers and birds. Queen Victoria patronised her work and appointed her Flower Painter in Ordinary 1879, the same year Angell was elected RWS. Her claim for inclusion here is that during her short life much of her best work was done in Scotland. Exhib 21 times at RSW.

**ANGUS, Catherine** **fl 1978**
Amateur painter. Exhibited a Sutherland landscape from an Edinburgh address RSA 1978.

**ANGUS, Miss Dorothy** **1890-1979**
Aberdeen-based embroiderer & occasional painter of genre; teacher.

Trained under Louisa Chart(qv) at Edinburgh College of Art. Following four years teaching at the Carnegie Craft School, Dunfermline, joined the staff of Gray's School of Art, Aberdeen, where she remained for thirty-five years. Imbued with Chart's love of stitchery conjoined with a strong design sense she inspired her students to 'create a fusion between drawing, fabric and stitchery...a sense of vitality and line were the qualities she sought' [Kathleen Whyte]. Among her best works are an heraldic bedspread for Lord Glentanar and two panels *Fiery Furnace* and *War Impressions* completed in 1939. Member, Modern Embroidery Society 1921-39 and closely associated with the Needlwork Development Scheme that continued to encourage Scottish embroidery until 1961 when it closed. Exhibited at the Walker Gallery, Liverpool 1925 while still a student, and annually between 1929 and 1935 at the AAS.
**Bibl:** R Oddy, *Embroideries from the Needlework Development Scheme*, Royal Scottish Museum, 1965; Margaret Swain 147,171-3; K Whyte, *'Dorothy Angus in Aberdeen'*, Embroidery, vol XXIV, no 3, Autumn 1973, p73.

**ANGUS, George** **1796-1840**
Edinburgh architect. Responsible for designing Dundee High School (1832-4), one of the most imposing school buildings erected during the resurgence of activity in the building of educational establishments that took place between 1818 and 1845; also designed Reform Street, Dundee. Won a competition for a new gaol and courthouse in Dundee (1833, completed 1863); also responsible for the British Linen Bank, Kirriemuir, Angus (1841-43). In Edinburgh he remodelled 17-19 Hill St (1825-8) to become the Subscription Baths and Drawing Academy, now Edinburgh Lodge Number One. Represented in Dundee AG.
**Bibl:** Dunbar 150; Gifford 330; Bruce Walker & W S Gauldie, Architects and Architecture on Tayside, Dundee 1984, 75,89.

**ANGUS, William Magnus** **fl 1983**
Aberdeen painter, associated with Gray's School of Art. Exhibited AAS(1) from 136 Victoria Street, Dyce.

**ANNADALE, E A** **fl 1896**
Amateur watercolour artist who exhibited once at the RSW.

**ANNAN, James** **fl 1867**
Edinburgh sculptor of portrait busts. Exhibited RSA(1) 1867.

**ANNAN, Thomas** **1829-1887**
Born Dairsie, Fife. Photographer and engraver. One of the great pioneers of early photography. Fifth child of a farming family. Apprenticed as a lithographic writer and engraver in Cupar (1845-1849), he then joined the firm of Joseph Swan in Glasgow. Becoming interested in photography in 1855 he and a friend set up in business as a 'collodian calotypist'. Two years later he started his own business at 116 Sauchiehall Street and in 1859 opened a printing works in Hamilton. Became expert in photographing works of art. In 1862 the Glasgow Art Union commissioned him to reproduce three paintings by respectively J E Millais, Joseph Noel Paton(qv), and James Sant(qv). These photographs were exhibited in Edinburgh by Alexander Hill, brother of David Octavius Hill(qv). This led in 1865 to Hill commissioning Annan to produce large numbers of photographs in three sizes of Hill's painting of 'The Signing of the Deed of Demission'. By adopting a carbon process developed by Joseph Wilson Swan, (not the same Joseph Swan as had employed Annan), Annan had succeeded in endowing photographs with a permanency that opened the way to book illustration. But it is for his own poetic skills as a photographer of townscapes and portraits that he is best remembered, of which the portrait of David Livingstone 1864 is the best known. His remarkable series of photographs of Glasgow city were taken in 1868-1871. These chronicled the depths of Victorian urban decay. It took three years to take 35 photographs, having to carry all the chemicals around with him and to coat the plates immediately the photographs were taken. "The photographs are undeniably beautiful. Annan used his knowledge and control of collodian process to achieve the same kind of subtle light and detail that appears in his landscape photographs" [Stevenson]. The obituary in the *British Journal of Photography* spoke of Annan's honesty and exquisite work 'honourable in feeling and fastidious in taste, he was utterly intolerant of shams...he was the personification of truth, and the soul of honour'.
**Bibl:** William Buchanan, Thomas and James Craig Annan, 1990; Fisher, 'Thomas Annan's "Old Closes and Streets of Glasgow"' Scottish Photography Bulletin, Spring and April 1987 and Spring 1988; Harker 'Annan's of Glasgow', British Journal of Photography, 12 Oct 1973, 932-5 and 19 Oct 1973 960-69; Harker, 'From Mansion to Close: Thomas Annan, Master Photographer', Photographic Collector, Vol 5, No 1, 81-95; Mozley, Photographs of the Old Closes and Streets of Glasgow, 1977; Sara Stevenson, 'Thomas Annan', Scottish Masters series) no. 12, 1990.

**ANNAN, William R** **fl 1870**
Amateur Murrayfield landscape painter in oil. Exhibited once at the RSA in 1870.

**ANNAND, Barbara N** **fl 1912-1921**
Aberdeen etcher of landscape and figurative subjects. Exhibited AAS regularly from 11 Osborne Place.

**ANNAND, David Andrew** **1948-**
Born Insch, Aberdeenshire 30 Jan. Sculptor; best known for his life-size animal sculptures and portraits. Trained at Duncan of Jordanstone College of Art. His work is rooted in the tradition of figurative representation, generally in bronze. Won several awards including the Latimer Award, RSA (1976), Benno Schotz Award RSA (1978), the Ireland Alloys Award RSA (1982) and the Sir Otto Beit Medal of the RSBS for his 'Deer Leap', now in Dundee Technology Park. Exhibits frequently at RSA & once at AAS. His work can be seen in the Edinburgh Botanic Gardens, Dundee Technology Park and Edinburgh City AG. More recently has sculpted the characters for the Beatrix Potter(qv) memorial garden at Birnam, Perthshire.

**ANNAND, Louise Gibson (also known as Richard or Dick Annand)** **1915-**
Born Uddingston, Lanarkshire 27 May. Painter in oil, watercolour and chalk; landscape and figurative subjects; also abstracts in the 1940s. Obtained an honours degree in English, University of Glasgow 1937 and Museum Diploma in Fine Art 1956. As a young artist was influenced by J D Fergusson(qv), being associated with the New Scottish Group(qv). Founder member of the New Art Club. Early in her artistic life was most interested in portraits and drawings of people, but around 1950 this changed to more abstract work exemplified in the abstract personalised symbolism of her 'New Art Club Meeting' (1944), and the use of wild places for inspiration. In about 1969 she became pre-occupied with the Glasgow townscape and latterly, combining her work as a painter with an appointment as Education Officer with Glasgow Museums, has worked increasingly in watercolour and chalk returning to the media she favoured at the outset of her career. President, SSWA (1963-1965) and Glasgow SWA 1977-79. President of the J D Fergusson Foundation. Regular exhibitor RSA & AAS(1). Represented in Glasgow AG, Newport AG, Perth AG.
**Bibl:** Hardie 171-2(illus).

**ANSON, Peter Frederick** **1889-1975**
Born Portsmouth; died Nunraw, East Lothian. Painter in oil, watercolour, pencil portraits and illustrator; churchman and author of many books on the fishing industry and on religious subjects. Son of an admiral. Trained Architectural Association 1908-1910. Became an Anglican monk on Caldey Island 1910, later received into the RC church. Awarded Papal knighthood of the Order of St Gregory the Great. Moved to Glasgow 1925 and after returning to England finally settled in Macduff 1938-51, 1952-58. He regarded the work he completed during a visit to Italy in the summer of 1924 as the best. 'His art has a technical accuracy...but the human figures have a uniformly faceless qualty: fishermen anonymously controlled by the rhythms of the boat and the sea, as monks are ruled by their own order. He chose to belong to his own notion of a secular order of fishermen, dressing and living like one, and forming brotherhoods of his own' [George Murdoch]. His autobiography *Life on the Low Shore* was published in 1969. Lived at Harbour Head, 2 Low Shore, Macduff. During his final years moved between an ancestral home in Montrose and an island monastery off the coast of South Wales. Exhibited harbours and coastal scenes RA(2), RSA 1926-1948 (15), RSW(2), RHA(7), GI(2) & L(4). Represented in Buckie Museum with 400+ watercolours.
**Bibl:** The Leopard, Aberdeen, June 1994 26-7.

**ANSON, Richard F** **fl 1919-1925**
Lived for a time in Glasgow from where he exhibited 3 pictures at the RSA in 1924 and 1925.

**APPLEBEY, Wilfred Crawford** **1889-?**
Born Dudley, Worcestershire 28 Jan. Painter and etcher; architectural subjects, portraits and landscapes. Trained Glasgow School of Art where he won a bursary and 4 scholarships. Worked chiefly in Scotland but also in London, France and Italy. Lived in Glasgow and exhibited regularly at the RSA(14), GI(48), at the AAS 1919-1936, & in the provinces and overseas.

**APPLEBY, Malcolm Arthur** **1946-**
Born Beckenham, Kent. Silversmith, jewellery and metal designer. Works in gold, silver, iron, steel and stone. Trained Beckenham School of Art, Ravensbourne College of Design, Central School of Art & Design, Sir John Cass College & RCA. Littledale Scholar 1969. Developed new silver engraving techniques. Commissioned to complete a cruet set for the Silver Trust 1989, 500th Anniversary Silver Cup for London Assay Office, and a standing cup and cover for the Nat. Mus. of Scotland. Exhibited AAS 1974-1980 from his workshop at Crathes, Aberdeenshire. Represented in V&A, RSM(Edin), Aberdeen AG, Perth AG, Goldsmiths Hall, Royal Armouries, Tower of London, Iceland Museum.
**Bibl:** Eliz Benn, Daily Telegraph, 11 Nov 1979; Rick Carr, The Guardian, 18 May 1976; Prudence Glynn, The Times, 27 May 1975; Graham Hughes, Arts Rev, 9 Mar 1990; Edwin Luie-Smith, 'The Critics Eye', Crafts, May/June 1991.

**APPLEYARD, Annie Burr** **?-1947**
Scottish heraldic artist and embroiderer. Trained Edinburgh College of Art. On two occasions responsible for the embroidered cushion of the reddendo of three arrows presented by the Royal Company of Archers to Their Majesties King George V 1927 and George VI 1937. Created many Rolls of Honour, genealogical trees etc, and executed shields for bishops in St John's Church, Edinburgh. Shortly before her death carried out interesting historical work as part of the restoration at Eilean Donan Castle, Wester Ross.

**ARCHER, Alexander** **fl 1848-1870**
Edinburgh genre and animal painter. Exhibited a horse portrait at the RSA in 1848. Represented City of Edinburgh collection ('Dog mourning its little Master' 1866.

**ARCHER, Miss** **fl 1852**
This artist showed six medallion portraits at the RSA in 1852 from an Edinburgh address. Recorded by neither Foskett nor Long.

**ARCHER, Miss Ann** **fl 1882**
Painter. Exhibited once at RSA in 1882.

**ARCHER, J Wallace** **fl 1904**
Amateur Edinburgh artist. Exhibited RSA 1904.

**ARCHER, James** **fl 1786**
Bushnell records an engraver of this name working in Edinburgh in 1786. Married a Janet Lathem on 25 August 1786.
**Bibl:** Edin Marr Reg 1751-1800

**ARCHER, James RSA** **1823-1904**
Born Edinburgh; died Haslemere 3 Sep. Painter in oils and water-colours; genre, landscapes, historical scenes and portraits. Studied at the Trustees Academy, Edinburgh under Sir William Allan(qv) before moving to London 1864. At first he painted chalk portraits but in 1849 exhibited his first historical picture at the RSA 'The Last Supper'. Circa 1859 he began to paint a series of Arthurian subjects, for example 'Sir Lancelot', 'Queen Guinevere,' 'La Morte d'Arthur', which show marked pre-Raphaelite influence. Settled in London 1862 and turned mainly to sentimental scenes and portraits, becoming the first Victorian painter to execute children's portraits in period costume. In 1884 visited the United States and 1886 went to India. By 1889 he was back in London. An original member, with the Faeds(qv), John Ballantyne(qv) and Fettes Douglas(qv) of the Edinburgh group 'The Smashers'(qv), founded 1848 and later reconstituted with the addition of Andrew Maclure(qv), Erskine Nicol(qv) and John Stirling as the Auld Lang Syne Group(qv) 1863. Archer exhibited his first picture at the RSA 1842 'The Child St John in the Wilderness'. At this time scriptural subjects were alternating with fantastic and romantic themes as well as a large number of portraits, many of them in chalk. His most important work was done between 1854 and 1877. Although influenced by the same literary works as Noel Paton(qv) he was less affected by the pre-Raphaelites. Some of his oil paintings achieved an opalescent quality in keeping with the character of his subjects although at times this could be overdone. Elected ARSA 1850, RSA 1858. Exhibited 108 works at the RA between 1840 and 1904 as well as many at the British Institute and Suffolk Street, AAS 1896-1902 and annually at the RSA from 1842 until his death. Two portraits, a death mask of Sir Walter Scott, and 2 figure paintings can be seen in the NGS; 10 portraits of contemporary fellow artists, including a self-portrait, are in the SNPG, and 5 works in Dundee AG.
**Bibl:** AJ 1871, 97-99; Caw 170-171; Halsby 66,247; Hardie 45,55,57; Irwin 306; Maas 231; Macmillan [SA] 212-214; McKay 340-343; Ruskin, Acad Notes 1875.

**ARCHER, James I** **fl 1899**
Edinburgh landscape painter in oils. Exhibited RSA in 1899.

**ARCHIBALD, Gordon R RSW** **1905-1980**
Born Falkirk. Painter in oil and watercolour, mainly the latter; landscapes. Studied at Glasgow School of Art in the early 1920s and later joined the staff. Settled in Aberdeen shortly before WW2 where he was art adviser to Aberdeen Education Committee. A compulsive sketcher, filling many notebooks. Developed a distinctive style, the drawings heightened with a watercolour wash. Held a firm conviction of the probity and value of naturalistic drawing, his work often carrying a rich vein of humour. Elected RSW 1953. Exhibited RSA 1929-1970(10), mostly landscapes of Aberdeenshire and north east Scotland, also GI(12), a portrait as well as many local landscapes at the AAS 1959-1979, from 31 Whitehall Road and latterly 156 Midstocket Road, Aberdeen. Represented in Dundee AG.

**ARCHIBALD, J L** **1890**
Amateur Edinburgh painter. Exhibited a pastoral scene at the AAS.

**ARCHIBALD, James** **fl 1846-1873**
Painter in oil; landscapes, especially scenes around Edinburgh. Exhibited frequently RSA during the years 1846-1873 from Edinburgh.

**ARCHIBALD, John** **fl 1846**
Edinburgh landscape painter in oil. Exhibited RSA(1) 1846.

**ARCHIBALD, John S** **fl 1929**
Amateur painter who migrated to Montreal as a very young man, from where he exhibited twice at the GI.

**ARCHIBALD, Phyllis M C (Mrs Clay)** **1880-1947**
Born Tunbridge Wells. Sculptress. Trained Glasgow School of Art. Formerly in Glasgow later lived at Bletchingly, Surrey. In Edinburgh designed a bronze memorial tablet with low relief bust in the Kirk O'Field memorial to A H Charteris. Exhibited RA(6), RSA between 1908-1933 (11), GI(37), SWA(3) & L(5).
**Bibl:** Gifford 240.

**ARCHIBALD, William** **fl 1801-1811**
Edinburgh engraver. The fine engraver William Miller(qv) was one of his pupils. Executed a portrait of Burns in 1801 edition of the *Poems,* vol i.
**Bibl:** Bushnell; Butchart 62.

**ARCHIBALD, William** **fl 1858**
Edinburgh landscape painter in oil; exhibited once at the RSA 1858.

**ARMOUR, A J R** **fl 1907**
Exhibited once at the GI in the above date.

**ARMOUR, Brownlee** **fl 1964-1989**
Aberdeen artist. Exhibited AAS in 1964, 1986 and 1989 from 46A Union Street.

**ARMOUR, George Denholm OBE** **1864-1949**
Born Waterside, Lanark 30 Jan; died Wiltshire 17 Feb. Painter in oil and watercolour; horses and hunting scenes. Son of a cotton broker.

Keen hunting man, hunted regularly with the Lanark amd Renfrewshire hunts, and a fine horseman, for two years ran a stud in Hertfordshire with Joseph Crawhall(qv). Spent his early life in Liverpool before returning to Scotland for schooling in Fife. After studying at St Andrew's University he proceeded to Edinburgh, training at the School of Art and RSA Schools. There he met Robert Alexander(qv) who exerted a strong influence. Together they went to Tangier where Armour was later to meet Joseph Crawhall. On his return to London, where he shared a studio with Phil May, he contributed drawings of sporting and rustic humour to *Punch,* conveyed most simply in muddy and wet settings. Also illustrated in colour two books, *Jorrocks* and Beckford's *Thoughts on Hunting*. His first work was published in *The Graphic* 1890. Met Phil May who introduced him to *Punch* for whom he remained a contributor for 35 years. During WW1 he commanded the Remount Depot in Salonika 1917-1919. Awarded OBE 1919. In his equestrian portraits, of which 'The Dowager Duchess of Beaufort' is perhaps the best example, he captures the quintessential character of both horse and rider in the Leech tradition. In 1910 visited Austro-Hungary to study military horse procedures at the Spanish Riding School in Vienna. His first wife died 1924 and two years later he married Violet Burton(qv). While hunting he always carried a sketch book. At home, one side of his studio was converted into a stable. His draughtsmanship was very direct, with freedom in paint portraying a true, natural and very strong representation of the animal. Main illustrated works were John Masefield's *Reynard the Fox,* John Fortescue's *The Story of a Red Deer, Handley Cross* (1908), *Foxiana* (1929), *Humour in the Hunting Field* (1928), and *Sport and There's the Humour of It* (1935). His principal contributions were for *The Graphic* (1892), *The Pall Mall Budget* (1893), *Pick-Me-Up* (1896), *The New Budget* (1895), *The Unicorn* (1895), *The Pall Mall Magazine* (1897), *The Longbow* (1895), *The Butterfly* (1899), *Sporting and Dramatic News, The Windsor Magazine* and *Judge* (NY). Retired to Wiltshire. Exhibited regularly RA 1884-1896 (16), RSA 1882-1887 (63), RSW(2), GI(34), L(21) & AAS. Represented in V&A, Glasgow AG.
**Bibl:** Caw 464-5; Halsby 146,149-150; Mitchell, R G Price, A History of Punch, 1955, 176,205-6; Wingfield.

**ARMOUR, Hazel Ruthven (Mrs John Kennedy) 1894-1985**
Born Edinburgh. Painter of flower pieces but principally a sculptress. Trained Edinburgh College of Art, then in Paris. After her marriage in 1921 she retained studios in both Edinburgh and London, visiting South Africa twice to make studies of native heads. Commissioned to design 'The Tunnellers' Friends' panel in the Scottish National War Memorial. Working from an Edinburgh address exhibited at the RSA 1914-1961.

**ARMOUR, Mrs Mary Nicol Neill (née Steel) RSA RSW 1902-2000**
Born Blantyre, Lanarkshire 27 Mar, died 5 July. Painter in oil and watercolour; landscape and still life. Educated at Blantyre and Hamilton Academy, trained Glasgow School of Art under Forrester Wilson(qv) and Maurice Greiffenhagen(qv) 1920-1925. Received Guthrie Award 1927 and the GI's Cargill Award 1972. Taught still life at Glasgow School of Art 1951-1962. Early in her career was greatly influenced by the French Impressionists, particularly Pissarro, Bonnard and Vuillard. Best known as a still life painter, her diploma work typifies her individual contribution to this field showing her prediliction for rich colour, coruscating light and assured paint texture. Her best work has a parallel in the finest examples of William McTaggart(qv). Her landscapes do not achieve quite the same effect but are nevertheless always interesting compositions in which the configuration is nicely blended with an accentuation of natural colour. Married William Armour(qv). Elected ARSA 1941, RSW 1956, RSA 1958. Elected hon. Vice-President, Paisley Art Institute and in 1983 hon. President RGI. Exhibited regularly RA, RSA, RSW, SSA and GI. Represented in Aberdeen AG, Glasgow AG, City of Edinburgh collection, Dundee AG, Greenock AG, Paisley AG, Perth AG, Victoria(Australia) AG.
**Bibl:** Halsby 247; Anon, Obituary, RSA Annual Report 2000.

**ARMOUR, William RSA RSW 1903-1979**
Born Paisley, 20 Aug. Painter in oil, watercolour and pastel, also a wood engraver; portraits, landscapes and figurative subjects. Son of Hugh Armour, a designer. Educated first in Paisley and then Glasgow School of Art (1918-1923) under Maurice Greiffenhagen(qv). Joined the staff of the Glasgow School of Art 1947 becoming Head of Drawing and Painting in 1955. Retired 1957. The influences which remained with him until the end of his life were, in the field of watercolour, Cotman, de Wint, and Turner; in oil it was Velasquez, and in drawing Holbein and Degas. His many pastel portraits were informed by a fine command of draughtsmanship. Married Mary Armour(qv) 1927. Elected RSW 1941, ARSA 1958, RSA 1966. Represented in SNGMA, Aberdeen AG, Dundee AG, Glasgow AG, Greenock AG, Lille AG (Milngavie), Paisley AG, Perth AG, SAC & Belfast AG.
**Bibl:** Halsby 247.

**ARMSTRONG, Anthony E 1935-**
Born Dundalk, Ireland. Painter in oil, pastel and watercolour of landscapes, townscapes, figure subjects and semi-abstracts. Trained Glasgow School of Art. Has published a series of prints entitled 'The Glasgow Collection'. Commissioned by the RAC for Glasgow Museum of Transport. Formerly combined his work as an artist with that of a dealer but has latterly returned to full-time painting in Blairgowrie, Perthshire. Author & illustrator, *Paintings & Drawings of Anthony Armstrong. The Glasgow Collection*, 1990. Exhibits RGI.

**ARMSTRONG, James C fl 1934-1940**
Amateur Bearsden painter; exhibited RSA(1) & GI(6).

**ARMSTRONG, John fl 1880-1883**
Edinburgh architect. Exhibited a competitive design for the new municipal buildings for the City of Glasgow at the RSA 1881. Designed the massive Carrubbers Close Mission (1883) on the Royal Mile described in *The Builder* as 'a miserable production' as well as the rather more interesting Old Waverley Hotel (1883) with its Peterhead granite shafted windows.
**Bibl:** Gifford 205,311.

**ARMSTRONG, Roy fl 1962-1967**
Edinburgh landscape painter. Exhibited RSA 1962-1967.

**ARMSTRONG, Snowden fl 1918**
Glasgow painter. Exhibited RSA(1) 1918.

**ARMSTRONG, Tim 1945-**
Born Cambridge, 27 Jly. Landscape painter in oil; illustrator and teacher. Educated at St Mark's Vicarage, Newnham, Cambridge, then studied art at Cambridgeshire College of Arts and Technology 1962-64 under Bill Darrell and Nottingham College of Art 1964-1967 under John Powell and the guidance of visiting tutor Bridget Riley. From 1967 to 1969 studied at the Slade School under Robyn Denny. Illustrated *Physiology of Mammals and other Vertebrates* (1965) and obtained a post-graduate diploma in art from London University in 1969. During the early 70s he was appointed to the staff of the Glasgow College of Art, where he has exerted a strong influence on succeeding generations of students. Influenced by optic-kinetic art, the construction methods of Islamic patterns on oriental carpets, medieval manuscripts and architecture and the use of symbols. In 1966-67 concentrated on monochromatic kinetic drawings and constructions and for two years introduced colour made from print-collages and reeded plastic. Since 1969 has turned mainly to print-making. Exhibited extensively in England, Scotland, Germany, France and the USA. Represented in Doncaster AG, the collection of Glasgow Corporation & Canberra AG (Australia).

**ARMSTRONG, Walter fl 1871**
Amateur Dumfries landscape painter in oil; exhibited RSA(1) 1871.

**ARMSTRONG, Walter fl 1895-1900**
Amateur Ayr artist. Exhibited GI(4).

**ARMSTRONG, William fl 1887-1896**
Glasgow artist whose work still occasionally appears. Exhibited GI(7).

**ARNEILL, Brian 1953-**
Born Ireland. Bird painter. Studied animal behaviour and physiology in Belfast and London. Spent a year teaching in Manchester before moving to SW Scotland, first as a shepherd manager, then as a Nature Reserve Warden before turning to full-time painting 1990. Selected for 'Birds in Art' at the Leigh Yawkey Woodson Museum, USA 1991

& 1993; also at the Int. Festival of Animal Art, St Laurent Loire, France and Wild In De Natuur, Enschede, Holland 1990, 1991,1992 & 1993. Lives and works in Galloway.

**ARNOLD, Mrs Annie Merrylees** **fl 1894-1937**
English painter of portrait miniatures. She had a strong following in Scotland, based largely on her patronage by the Erskine family. Her work was highly regarded, especially in the Glasgow area, where she was best known. Exhibited under her maiden name Merrylees until marriage in 1898 to the English portrait miniaturist Reginald E Arnold. Exhibited two portrait miniatures at the RSA in 1903, one of the Earl of Mar and Kellie and the other portrait of a girl, also RA(46), RI(21), RMS(16) & GI(6).

**ARNOLD, Miss Edith May** **fl 1869-1870**
Edinburgh landscape painter in oil. Lived also in London and probably in Dublin. Exhibited RA(1) & RSA(2) 1869-1870.

**ARNOT, A** **fl 1858**
Edinburgh oil painter, exhibited once at the RSA 1858.

**ARNOT, E L** **fl 1879-1880**
Amateur Edinburgh landscape painter. Exhibited RSA 1879 & 1880.

**ARNOT, Miss Jessie Adeline** **fl 1881-1882**
Glasgow portrait painter in oil. Exhibited RSA(2) 1882 & GI(1).

**ARNOTT, Adam C** **fl 1937**
Amateur Kirkcaldy painter; exhibited once at the RSA in 1937.

**ARNOTT, Alexander Reid** **fl 1831-1832**
Edinburgh portrait and animal painter. Exhibited RSA in 1831 & 1832.

**ARNOTT, Miss Annie A** **fl 1917-1919**
Edinburgh artist. Exhibited RSA annually between 1917 & 1919.

**ARNOTT, Miss Elizabeth S** **fl 1849-1879**
Edinburgh painter in watercolour; landscape and still life. Exhibited RSA in 1849 and in 1864 by which time she had moved to Edinburgh.

**ARNOTT, Ian ARSA RIBA ARIAS** **1929-**
Edinburgh architect. Designed the Scottish Financial Centre in Castle Terrace, Edinburgh. Exhibited RSA in 1978, 1988 & 1989.

**ARNOTT, James** **fl 1880-1891**
Kirkcaldy painter in oil of figurative subjects. Exhibited RSA on a number of occasions between 1880 and 1891.

**ARNOTT, J A** **fl 1939**
Amateur Edinburgh painter; exhibited RSA(1) 1939.

**ARNOTT, James Alexander** **1871-1950**
Edinburgh architect and watercolourist. Architectural subjects and buildings. With Auldjo Jamieson(qv) was responsible for the E extension to the Church of Scotland offices in George St (1932-3). Exhibited RSA(5) 1897-1899 & GI(1).
**Bibl:** Gifford 306.

**ARNOTT, James George McLellan** **1855-1923**
Born Dumfries; died Dumfries, 26 Oct. Painter in oil and watercolour; figurative, landscape and portraits. From his earliest years was devoted to art and while still very young commenced studies with the Dumfries painter J R Fergusson(qv). In 1873 proceeded to London to study at Heatherley's before going on to Antwerp. By this time he had become friendly with Hornel(qv), Alexander Roche(qv) and James Paterson(qv). Returning from Antwerp, Arnott established a studio in London, exhibiting at the RA 1892. This was 'Semiramis' which depicted the legend of a young Queen of Assyria. The picture was reproduced in the *Graphic* the same year and prints were published. A number of other fine works formed the series 'Views in the Burns Country'. Eventually settled in Dumfries in the early 1880s. Although suffering from chronic ill-health played an active role in the artistic and religious life of the area, being especially devoted to the Dumfries and Maxwelltown Industrial School for boys and to the Benedictine Convent in Maxwelltown in which he was art master 1890-1920. Began exhibiting RSA 1884 when still in London, and continued to do so regularly until 1920 (9), also at the GI(9). Examples of his work can be seen in altar-pieces in St Andrew's pro-cathedral at Dumfries and in St Mary's Church, New Abbey. A portrait 'Bishop Turner', present whereabouts unknown, aroused much favourable attention when first seen.

**ARNST, Adam** **fl 1858-1876**
Edinburgh painter in oil and chalk, also watercolour; landscapes and portraits. Exhibited coastal scenes and portraits RSA between 1858 & 1876. Fond of the Cramond area of Edinburgh.

**ARROLL, James** **fl 1883-1909**
Helensburgh landscape painter in oil and watercolour. Exhibited RSA(10) between 1883 and 1899, RSW(1), GI(23) & L(2).

**ARROLL, Richard Hubbard** **1853-**
Born Helensburgh, 24 May. Painter in oil, watercolour, and pen and ink; genre and landscapes. Lived in Bridge of Weir before moving to Ayr in the early 1920s. Exhibited 2 pictures at the RSA in 1886 from a Helensburgh address, also GI(16) & Paris Salon.

**ARTHUR, Anne Knox** **fl c1925-1940**
Glasgow embroiderer and teacher. One of an active group of designers working in Glasgow during the 1920s and 30s. In 1928 succeeded Ann Macbeth(qv) as head of the embroidery department, Glasgow School of Art, a post she relinquished in 1981 in order to establish the 'Arthur Studios' at 15 Rose Street. Friend of Mary Sturrock(qv) and closely associated with Helen Paxton Brown(qv) and Margaret Swanson(qv). Author of *An Embroidery Book.*
**Bibl:** Burkhauser 73,154-5,182,184.

**ARTHUR, Miss Emily** **fl 1903**
Amateur Glasgow painter; exhibited a landscape at the Walker Gallery, Liverpool 1903.

**ARTHUR, J** **fl 1919**
Amateur Glasgow painter; exhibited once at the RSA 1919.

**ARTHUR, Miss Jean** **fl 1913-1914**
Amateur artist from Lamshaw, Stewarton. Exhibited once at the RSA and twice at the Walker Gallery, Liverpool between the above dates.

**ARTHUR, John M** **fl 1924-1926**
Amateur Airdrie artist; exhibited once at the RSA and once at the GI.

**ARTUS, Charles** **fl 1926-1930**
Exhibited 5 pictures at the RSA and 4 at the GI between the above dates.

**ARUS, R** **fl 1883**
Amateur painter. Exhibited once at the GI in 1883.

**ASHBURN, Marian** **1954-**
Painter. Studied Edinburgh College of Art 1971-2. Exhibits RSA and SSA, of which she is a member. Lives and works on Orkney.

**ASHBY, Derek Joseph** **1926-**
Painter and sculptor. Father of Nina A(qv). Trained Edinburgh College of Art and at the RA Schools 1948-56. Lecturer in painting at Gray's School of Art, Aberdeen and at Robert Gordon's Institute of Technology. Makes three-dimensional constructions exploring the tonal surfaces of various metals. Exhibited regularly at the RSA 1955-1979 specialising in Aberdeenshire landscapes also many works at the AAS 1959-1983 at first from 3 Foreman Drive, Peterhead, latterly from Old Invery, Banchory.

**ASHBY, Mrs Nina Catriona Morrison** **1956-**
Born Aberdeen, Nov 21. Amateur painter & textile designer, also a student of nursing. Daughter of Derek Joseph A(qv). Graduated in Philosophy & Eng Lit, Edinburgh, followed by a postgraduate course in Industrial Admin. Worked for a time with Peacock Printmakers in Aberdeen. Exhibited RSA(2), AAS since 1981, awarded First Prize 1992. Lives in Aberdeen.

**ASHTON, Gertrude Annie (Mrs C J Lauder)** **?-1918**
Died Lanarkshire, 8 Aug. Painter in oil and watercolour; flowers and

wildlife. Married Charles James Lauder(qv). Born in the Glasgow area, spent most of her life in England before returning to Scotland at the turn of the century. Moved to Thorntonhall, Lanarkshire c1910. Exhibited RSA(3), RSW(2), GI(23) & L(3).

**ASHWORTH, Miss Susan A** **fl 1864-1873**
Edinburgh painter in oil and watercolour; flowers, still life and landscapes. Best known for having succeeded R S Lauder(qv) as Head of the Trustees Academy. Exhibited annually RI(27) 1864-1873, also SWA(2). Lived in London before returning to Edinburgh.

**ASSOCIATED SOCIETY OF ARTISTS** **1808-1816**
A second attempt by Alexander Nasmyth and Raeburn to establish an exhibiting organisation in the capital, the first having failed in 1791. The first exhibition was held 1808. Between 1809-1813 the annual show was held in Raeburn's studio. The Association ended with the establishment of the Edinburgh Exhibition Society(qv).
**Bibl:** Alexander Campbell, A Journey from Edinburgh through Parts of North Britain, London 1810, 276; Macmillan [SA] 161-2.

**ASSOCIATION FOR THE PROMOTION OF THE FINE ARTS IN SCOTLAND** **1833-1897**
The first society of its kind in Britain, it was introduced by D. O. Hill(qv) Sir John Steell(qv) and Sheriff Glassford Bell (who devised the constitution) with the aim of fostering a Scottish school of painting mainly by keeping Scottish artists at home through the purchase of their works and the distribution of engravings and prints. This gave the committee considerable power since it was they who made the selections. In 1837 a short-lived rival appeared: the **NEW ASSOCIATION FOR THE PROMOTION OF THE FINE ARTS IN SCOTLAND**, changing its name in 1842 to the **ART UNION OF SCOTLAND**. Its charter of incorporation was granted in 1848 and a royal charter followed in 1850. In 1860 thin volumes of engravings were published, mostly of subjects taken from Scottish history and literature, especially Burns and Scott. At one time the Association's annual revenue had exceeded £7,000 but when this fell to only several hundred pounds the society was dissolved. It had played a significant part in the establishment of a recognisable Scottish School of painting. A parallel **Association** related to the West of Scotland Academy(qv) was briefly formed in Glasgow (c1841) from which stemmed the **GLASGOW ART UNION**.
**Bibl:** Brydall 371-2; Caw 66-7; Irwin 285-6,323-4 et passim.

**ASSAFREY, Miss Alma G M** **fl 1913**
Amateur Glasgow painter exhibited once at the Walker Gallery, Liverpool.

**ATHERTON, Barry** **fl 1973-**
Painter and sculptor. Trained Manchester College of Art and Design 1961-65 having been awarded a Leverhulme Research Scholarship, followed by a spell at the RA Schools 1966-69. Since 1973 lecturer, Glasgow School of Art. Several one man shows in London and Glasgow. Specialises in the human figure including portraiture in painting, sculpture, pastel and print-making. Married to Linda A(qv). Exhibits regularly GI and with the Glasgow League of Artists. Began exhibiting RSA 1980. Represented in Aberdeen AG.

**ATHERTON, David John** **fl 1988-**
Born Northwich, Cheshire 10 Apr. Aberdeen-based printmaker. Studied at Manchester Polytechnic 1974-1978 and Slade School 1978-1980. Exhibited an etching of the Thames Barrier at the RSA 1988. Represented in V&A, Aberdeen AG, Australian Nat. Gall.

**ATHERTON, Mrs Linda** **fl 1986-**
Glasgow painter. Married Barry Atherton(qv). Exhibited Self-portrait at the RSA 1986.

**ATHOLL, Charlotte, Duchess of** **?-1805**
Embroiderer. Daughter of the 2nd Duke of Atholl, she married her cousin (John Murray of Strowan) 1753 who became 3rd Duke 1764. Believed responsible for a set of twelve chairs, still at Blair Castle, and certainly responsible for a broomwood pole screen in tent stitch, dated 1759, also still in the castle.
**Bibl:** Margaret Swain 71.

**ATKINS, C** **fl 1917**
Amateur Glasgow painter; exhibited GI(1).

**ATKINS, James** **1799-1883**
Born Belfast; died Valetta, Malta, Dec. Miniature and portrait painter. Son of a Scottish coach-painter from Stranraer. As a boy assisted his father with heraldic painting. Studied at Belfast Academical Institution 1814-1818 where he was a pupil of Goetano Fabbrini, being awarded a gold medal in his final year for an oil portrait. His first exhibits at the Institution received favourable attention and a number of patrons, among them the Marquis of Londonderry, sent him to Italy 1819 where he remained until 1832, copying old masters in Florence, Rome and Venice. Visited Constantinople to paint a portrait of the Sultan, but whilst in quarantine in Malta on the way home he contracted consumption and died. Exhibited twice at the RA, 1831 and 1833.
**Bibl:** Long 10; Strickland.

**ATKINSON, Emily** **fl 1885-1889**
Brigg, Midlothian painter in watercolour. Exhibited 'Stampede' at the RSA in 1885 and 2 other pictures subsequently.

**ATKINSON, George** **c1830-?**
Glasgow painter in oil; literary subjects and genre. Trained at the Trustees Academy in Edinburgh 1848-53. Little more is known except for two works at the RSA in 1853 and 1855 exhibited from an Edinburgh address.

**ATKINSON, Marilyn Gore** **1946-**
Born Yorkshire. Trained 1964-1968 Manchester College of Art and Design and from 1968-1971 at the Royal College in London. After leaving art school concentrated on pencil and charcoal drawings, changing to small intense pencil landscape studies tinted with watercolour. Moved to Scotland 1974 when her work became more varied in mood with particular regard to the changing seasons and with a quiet tranquillity and poetic feel for the natural scene.

**ATKINSON, William** **c1773-1839**
English architect. Pupil of James Wyatt, he designed three notable asymmetrical neo-Gothic houses, Scone Palace, Perthshire (1803-6), Rossie Priory (1810, demolished) and Tuliallan, Fife (1817-20), now the Scottish Police Training College. With Edward Blore he was also responsible for Abbotsford, Roxburghshire, its conical roofed angle turrets and crow-stepped gables foreshadowing the early Victorian revival of the Scottish Baronial style.
**Bibl:** Dunbar 122,124; Dunlop 127-129; Bruce Walker & W S Gauldie, Architects and Architecture on Tayside, Dundee 1984, 69-72.

**'AUBREY, John' (Isabella Margaret Chalmers)** **1909-1985**
Born 1 May; died 12 Jne. Oil painter; portraits. Lossiemouth artist. Daughter of a Fochabers doctor. John Aubrey was the pseudonym used by Isabella Margaret Chalmers. Trained Nottingham School of Art for 3 years before spending 5 years at the RA Schools in London. Held many highly successful solo shows, mainly in Edinburgh. Active member of the Moray Arts Club of which she was co-founder in 1962. During the war worked as a bank clerk in Fochabers and Keith before returning to full-time painting. Elected Fellow, RSA 1960. Whilst staying in London exhibited her first painting at the RA in 1938 entitled 'Grey Lady'. Regularly exhibited RA & RSA, the latter from 1962, also AAS 1959 and 1966. Also showed at RSPP, RSW, RSBA & GI. Represented in the collection of the Royal Academy of Music, London, Loughborough Col of Tech, Royal Collection (Holyrood House). A studio sale was held at Christie's, Glasgow, May 1986.

**AUCHINVOLE, Miss Gladys M** **fl 1929**
Amateur Kilmacolm portrait painter. Exhibited once at the RSA in 1929.

**AUDUBON, John James HRSA** **1785-1851**
Born Haiti, 26 Apr; died Minnie's Land, New York 27 Jan. Probably the best known of all the world's bird illustrators, both for the superb quality of *Birds of America* and for the very romantic life he led. Audobon had two significant incursions into the art life of Scotland for the first of which he was elected an Honorary Member of the RSA. The illegitimate son of a French sailor and a Creole lady from San Domingo, the children were legalised by act of adoption at Nantes 1800. At the age of 15 he had already started to draw French birds and

at 16 he was sent to Military School for a year followed by a spell in Paris where it is said he worked for a few months in the studio of Jacques-Louis David. In 1803 he sailed for America and the following year he arrived at a plantation near Philadelphia owned by his father. He became engaged to an English girl and after a quarrel with his father's agent he walked to New York, borrowed some money from his fiancee's uncle and returned to France. Back in Europe he joined forces with the son of one of his father's business associates and together they returned to America in 1806. After an unsuccessful venture at reviving a lead mine Audubon returned to New York and entered his fiancee's uncle's business. However, town life did not appeal to him and he and his friend Rozier bought a general store in Louisville, Kentucky. There followed an extraordinary meeting with Alexander Wilson(qv), the Scottish born 'Father of American Ornithology', who by chance came into the shop. At that time neither knew of the other's existence but the feud that developed between the two ornithologists acted as a great spur to Audubon. After being jailed for debt, although allowed to keep his bird drawings, he began drawing portraits for $5 a time and then the idea of publishing his bird drawings became serious. In 1824 he returned to Philadelphia to find a publisher and received tuition in the use of oil paint from Thomas Sully. Advised to seek a publisher in Europe and set sail for Liverpool from where he travelled to Edinburgh. Here he was very well received, being elected a member of the Royal Society of Edinburgh, and meeting W H Lizars(qv) and Sir Walter Scott. Earned his keep in Edinburgh by painting and selling oil copies of his own drawings (the originals not being for sale as they were needed by the engraver). In 1827 he moved from Edinburgh to London but found the latter less congenial. Having lost the services of Lizars because of a strike after the first 10 plates had been produced, he was fortunate in meeting the English engraver Robert Havell. Returned to Edinburgh 1834 and continued work on his other magnum opus *Ornithological Biography* being helped with the text by MacGillivray. Returning shortly afterwards to North America c1840 his eyesight began to fail. During his last years became increasingly apathetic and introverted.
**Bibl:** J J Audubon, Birds of America, 1827-1838; Maria Audubon, Audubon and his Journals, London 1898; Howard Corning (Ed), Journal of J A Audubon, made while obtaining subscriptions to his 'Birds of America' 1840-1943. Boston 1929; Irwin 219,220,222; Constance Rourke, Audubon, London 1936 esp 210-222; Peyton Skipwith, The Great Bird Illustrators, London 1979,34-47.

**AULD, Eric** **1931-**
Born Aberdeen. Painter in oil and pastels. Studied Gray's School of Art 1948-1953. In his final year awarded a travelling scholarship enabling him to visit France, Spain, Holland and Italy. Following a period teaching art at Aberdeen Academy became principal teacher at Kincorth Academy, Aberdeen. Specialises in local landscapes with a nice sense of colour and accurate depiction of pictorial elements, if somewhat unimaginative and occasionally flat. Received Arts Council award 1967. Prints of his Deeside landscapes have proved popular. Exhibits regularly at the AAS since 1959. Represented in Lillie AG, Milngavie.

**AULD, John Leslie M** **1914-**
Born Belfast, 21 Jan. Goldsmith and art teacher. Educated at Methodist College, Belfast; studied art at Belfast College of Art 1931-35 and Royal College of Art, London 1935-39. Exhibited in London, Brussels, Paris, New York, and Stockholm. Head of the art department, Municipal Technical College, Londonderry 1940-1946. Moved to Glasgow to become senior lecturer, Glasgow School of Art, remaining there until his retirement 1974. In Glasgow exercised great influence in the development of the goldsmith art in Scotland. Published *Your Jewellery.* Represented in Goldsmiths' Company Hall, London, New York City Corporation collection.

**AULD LANG SYNE CLUB** **1863-?**
A London sketching club limited to Scottish artists. Formed by members of The Smashers' Club(qv) who had moved to London and were no longer able to attend meetings in Scotland. Erskine Nicol(qv), John Stirling(qv) and Andrew MacLure(qv) became members while regular guests included Peter Graham(qv), William Orchardson(qv) and John Pettie(qv). Other members included William Fettes Douglas(qv) and Thomas Faed(qv). A group portrait of members, painted by themselves, is in private hands. The Minutes are in the library of the RSA.
**Bibl:** Martin Hardie, John Pettie, London 1908, 44-5; and in The Artist, January 1902; and Chambers's Journal, January 1906; Mary McKerrow, The Faeds, Edinburgh 1982,

**AULD, Mrs Margaret** **fl 1959-1971**
Aberdeen flower painter, also occasional portraits and landscape. Exhibited RSA 1960, 1965 & AAS 1959-1971.

**AULD, Patrick Campbell** **1813-1866**
Ayr painter in oil; landscape, often castles most especially in the north-east of Scotland including upper Deeside. Moved to Aberdeen c1844. Influenced by John Phillip(qv), James Giles(qv) and Sir John Steell(qv). Prints were published of his work showing accurate and sensitive portrayal of the local scenes. Exhibited RSA including the 'Mill at Auchendryne, Braemar' (1849). Visited Arran 1862 and three of the works painted whilst there were shown in the RSA the following year. Represented in Aberdeen AG.
**Bibl:** Halsby 247.

**AULDJO, John W** **fl 1970**
Aberdeen artist. Exhibited AAS from 2 Cottage Brae.

**AUSTEN, Frank** **fl 1901-1911**
Amateur Glasgow painter. Exhibited GI(5).

**AWLSON, Walter** **1949-**
Born Galashiels, 1 Sep. Painter in oil, also potter and ceramic sculptor. Graduated from Edinburgh College of Art in furniture design and sculpture 1970 and from 1972 until 1978 taught art and design. Since 1978 has been lecturer in art, Falkirk College of Technology. Influenced by the Flemish School and by photography, his main interests are in the human figure and ceramic sculpture, in the style of photo-realism. Exhibits regularly at the RSA.

**AYERS, Rev J F** **fl 1935**
Amateur painter. Minister of Turriff, Aberdeenshire, from where he exhibited a Fife landscape at the AAS.

**AYLES, C Nunn** **fl 1837-1913**
Amateur Glasgow artist who moved to Ayr around the turn of the century. Exhibited GI(9).

**AYLING, Joan (Mrs Rees) RMS** **1907-**
Born Edinburgh, 16 Sep. Miniature painter of portraits; etchings. Educated in St Mary's Hill, Mill Hill and Kilburn Polytechnic. Studied art at Birmingham School of Arts and Crafts and etching at Slade School under F L Griggs. Awarded silver medal at the Paris Salon 1952 and gold medal 1957. Painted Bertrand Russell and many other notables including several bishops. Her main influence was the work of Nicholas Hilliard. Lived latterly in Wembley, Middlesex. Not recorded by Foskett or Long. Exhibited regularly RA, Paris Salon & Walker AG, Liverpool.

**AYR SKETCH CLUB** **1901-**
Founded by a group of artists led by Thomas Bell(qv), Thomas Bonar Lyon(qv) and James MacMaster RSW(qv), for the primary purpose of mutual analysis and criticism. Membership limitied to sixty. Annual exhibitions held at McLaurin Gallery, Ayr.

**AYRES, C Harold** **fl 1933**
Amateur watercolourist who exhibited twice at the RSW.

**AYRTON, Antony M** **fl 1933-1935**
Edinburgh painter who moved to London. Exhibited RSA 1933-1935.

**AYTON, William** **fl c1630-d1645**
Born Inchdairnie. Edinburgh master mason. Descendant of the poet W.E. Aytoun. Superintended the construction of much of Heriot's Hospital (together with William Wallace(qv) and John Mylne jnr(qv) who worked respectively before and after Ayton). Employed by the Innes family to 'draw the form of a House on paper', for which he was paid £26.13.4d Scots. Thus was born Innes House, Morayshire (1640-1653), where it is thought Ayton carved much of the ornamental detail himself. Described as 'one of the most substantial

houses of its class. The treatment of the elevations resembles that of Hill House but the detail is better carved and of more pronounced Scottish renaissance character'[Dunbar]. Erected the monument to George Foulis of Ravelston with its headless figures of Justice and Religion(1636). Gifford remarks on the similarity of Winton House (Lothian) and Castle Gogar (Midlothian) to Innes House suggesting that Ayton may have designed all three.
**Bibl:** Dunbar 60,100; Gifford 159,180,590; Robert S. Mylne, The Master-Masons of the Crown of Scotland, 1883, 116.

**AYTO(U)N, George** **fl 1861-1864**
Amateur Edinburgh landscape painter in oil. Exhibited RSA between 1861 and 1864.

**AYTOUN, Janetta M** **fl 1887**
Amateur Edinburgh watercolour painter. Possibly related to George Aytoun(qv). Exhibited RSA 1887.

# B

**BABIANSKA, Isabel Brodie** **[see BRODIE, Isobel]**

**BACHELOR, Mary** **fl 1990-**
Helensburgh painter in oils and acrylic. Studied at Glasgow School of Art under Peter Howson(qv), David Linley(qv) and Norrie Kirkham(qv). Paints extravagantly coloured compositions based upon known landscapes in an ebullient, imaginative manner. Member of Paisley Art Institute, associate of the RGI. Exhibits RSA, RGI and at galleries throughout Scotland.

**BACHOP, (or BAUCHOP) Tobias** **?-1710**
Alloa master mason. Undertook considerable work for the government, mainly at Stirling Castle. Succeeded Mylne as Bruce's master mason and was associated with the building of Logie church (Stirlingshire), Cortachy Castle and Panmure House; with Bruce he helped build Craigiehall (1698-9) and Mertoun (1703-9). Instrumental in the spread of Bruce's ideas on classical form. In addition to his contractual works seems to have designed buildings, among them Dumfries Town House (the Midsteeple, completed c1708) and his own premises in Alloa. His son **Charles BACHOP** continued the family business after his death.
**Bibl:** Dunbar 79-80,89,102.

**BACK, Robert** **1922-**
Edinburgh painter; exhibited once at the RSA in 1941.

**BADENOCH, Margaret J S** **fl 1890-1902**
Aberdeen painter in oil, flowers, local landscapes and pastoral scenes. Exhibited AAS during the above years. In 1890 was living at 189 Holburn Street and 1894 went to London, returning to 19 Justice Mill Lane, Aberdeen 1898.

**BAIKIE, Constance N** **fl 1921**
Edinburgh based landscape painter in oil. Exhibited AAS(2).

**BAILEY, Catherine C** **fl 1953**
Sculptress. Exhibited once at the RSA in 1953 from an Edinburgh address.

**BAILEY, Chris** **1960-**
Born Oxford, 9 Apr. Sculptor. Trained Cambridge College of Art 1978-79 and at Sheffield City Polytechnic 1979-82, obtaining first-class honours in fine art (sculpture). Opened a studio in Sheffield and two years later joined other artists to form Pitt Street Studios in the city. In 1985 moved to the Peak District when his art changed from large scale applications to wood carving. Two years later opened another studio in Sheffield with two friends and in 1985 became Curator of the Yorkshire Sculpture Club. Most recently he moved to Scotland, working in close collaboration with the Scottish Sculpture Workshop in Aberdeenshire. Influenced by the Vorticist movement and the sculptures of Gaudier-Brzeska & Jacob Epstein. Exhibits annually RSA since 1989.

**BAILEY, Miss D E** **fl 1900-1910**
Invergloy, Inverness-shire landscape artist. Exhibited in various galleries, mostly in England, between the above dates.

**BAILEY, Renee** **fl 1955**
Sculptress. Exhibited RSA 1955.

**BAILEY, Wellesley** **fl 1901-1936**
Edinburgh architect and watercolour draughtsman; exhibited RSA(8) & RSW(1), including design for Gogar House, Midlothian (1901) and some watercolour sketches made in Italy.

**BAILEY, William Charles** **fl 1953-1988**
Edinburgh sculptor, though currently living in Marple, Lincs. Mainly female figures and torsos in bronze and terracotta. Exhibited RSA in 1953 and 1976, 1977 and 1979-88.

**BAILLIE, Alexander** **c1710-1777**
Edinburgh based engraver about whom little is known. His earliest recorded work is dated 1735. Engraved Barsanti's *Collection of Old Scots Tunes,* 1742. Also plates representing the Holy Family and St Cecilia, both after Francesco Fernandi, 1764, and a portrait of Field Marshal Keith after Pesne, 1751. Known to have engraved a map of Kincardineshire 1776, as well as other maps. Appears to have visited Rome in 1764 and to have exhibited an engraving at the Society of Artists from an Edinburgh address 1765. Later settled in Edinburgh where, in addition to the plates mentioned above, he engraved several portraits, including 'Doctor Robert Simon' (1766). In 1768 Lord Gardenstone arrived in Naples and was delighted to find there several of his compatriots - 'Sir Hugh Munro, Mr Dunbar, Mr Oliphant and Mr Baillie'. Represented in Glasgow AG.
**Bibl:** Bryan; Bushnell.

**BAILLIE, Charles Cameron** **fl 1925-1931**
Glasgow Art Deco artist and designer. An incisive portraitist and interior designer, sometimes painting on glass. Worked for several shipping companies designing the decor for luxury liners. Best remembered for Rogano's Restaurant in Glasgow's Royal Exchange Place. Exhibited RSA(1) & GI(4).
**Bibl:** Hardie 157-8.

**BAILLIE, Douglas G** **fl 1909-1921**
Paisley landscape artist in oil; moorland and upland scenes. Exhibited RSA(1), GI(4), also Paisley Art Institute 1910-1920 of which he was a member 1913-1917.

**BAILLIE, Lady Isabel** **fl 1897-1921**
Miniature painter. Lived at Whitburn, West Lothian and for a time at Dinard in France. Exhibited 3 portrait miniatures at the RSA and 2 at the RMS.

**BAILLIE, James** **fl 1900**
Amateur Edinburgh landscape painter; exhibited a local scene at the RSA in 1900.

**BAILLIE, J T** **fl 1905**
Amateur Edinburgh sculptor. Exhibited a mural monument, erected at Inveresk, at the RSA in 1905.

**BAILLIE, Martin** **1920-?**
Born Edinburgh. Painter in oil; genre and urban life art critic and teacher. Educated Royal High School and Edinburgh College of Art. During WW2 served with the RAF in Burma and India. Immediately after the war he studied in France, Italy and Spain, having been awarded the Andrew Grant and Andrew Carnegie travelling scholarships. Teacher of drawing, Edinburgh College of Art 1947 and in 1950 became senior lecturer in painting at Leeds CA before returning to Scotland to take up a senior lectureship in art history at Glasgow University, remaining there 1954-1985. Between 1970 & 1980 art critic of the *Glasgow Herald.* Exhibited in the Scottish Genre Paintings Exhibition 1700-1952 organised by the Arts Council (1952), and regularly at the RSA & GI. Represented SAC, Nuffield Foundation.

**BAILLIE, Richard** **fl 1931-1932**
East Lothian landscape painter from Pencaitland who exhibited 3 works at the RSA 1932.

**BAILLIE, William** **fl 1900-1913**
Glasgow artist. Exhibited once at the RSA & GI(5).

**BAILLIE, William** **1905-1999**
Born Larkhall, Lanarkshire 22 Nov; died Jne 10. Painter in oil and watercolour; figurative subjects. Studied Glasgow College of Art under Haswell Miller(qv). An early appreciation of the human figure as a source of inspiration developed into consideration of the figure as a medium in itself. Some of his earliest works were watercolour, mostly landscapes, but he quickly turned to figure painting. By 1922 a desire for structure returned, as reflected in his first exhibit at the RSA (1925). Began teaching in 1928 and in 1930 became interested in photography; elected member of the Scottish Photographic Society. His work was almost entirely figurative, not being consciously based on any external data. In the 1930s some pastels were purchased to decorate SS Monarch of Bermuda. Exhibited RSA(12) & GI(3). Represented in Hamilton Museum, Perth AG.
**Bibl:** Hardie 180-1.

**BAILLIE, William Carlisle** **fl 1887-1920**
Edinburgh landscape painter in watercolour. Exhibited 6 works at the RSA between 1887-1899, GI(3) & AAS in 1902.

**BAILLIE, William James Laidlaw PRSA PPRSW RGI HRA** **1923-**
Born Edinburgh. Painter in oil, watercolour, pencil; flowers, landscape, still life. Studied Edinburgh College of Art 1941-50 where he was an Andrew Grant Scholar. His studies were interrupted by war service spent in the Royal Corps of Signals, mainly in the Far East 1942-47. Elected SSA 1953. Resident tutor, National Gallery of Canada's summer school 1955, and in 1960 appointed to the staff of the Edinburgh College of Art where he became senior lecturer 1968-88. Travelled extensively overseas. Elected RSW 1963, ARSA 1968, President RSW 1974, RSA 1979, Treasurer RSA 1980-1990, President RSA 1990-. Exhibits regularly at RSA and RSW, mainly flowers and still life but also landscapes. Represented in SNGMA, Aberdeen AG, Glasgow AG, Kirkcaldy AG, City of Edinburgh collection, RSA, SAC.

**BAIN, Alex M** **fl 1928-1932**
Mauchline artist who exhibited 3 works at the GI between the above dates.

**BAIN, Bob** **fl 1989-**
Aberdeen-based printmaker. Exhibited a print 'Lovers by the river' at the RSA 1989, from 13 Deemount Gardens.

**BAIN, Donald** **1904-1979**
Born Kilmacolm, Renfrewshire 12 Mar. Painter in oil and watercolour; landscapes, semi-abstract figurative subjects, still life; also theatre designer. In 1918 his family moved to Harrogate and subsequently to Liverpool before settling in Matlock, Derbyshire. In 1920 he met W Y MacGregor(qv) who introduced him to the work of J D Fergusson(qv). In 1928 Bain visited Paris where he was particularly impressed by the work of Matisse. Returned to Glasgow 1940 where he worked in the shipyards. He immediately contacted Fergusson and became involved in the formation of the New Scottish Group(qv) 1942. His work at this time, highly coloured still lifes and landscapes, was much influenced by Fergusson and Hunter(qv). In 1946 returned to France where he remained until 1948, meeting Picasso, with whom he appears to have got on very well, and Matisse. Exhibited at the major salons in Paris and on the Côte d'Azur. Bain's paintings of this period show the concerns of contemporary French landscape artists for tightly co-ordinated structure, bright colour and rich paint texture, in the manner of Cézanne. In 1948 Fergusson's wife commissioned Bain to design a decor for the ballet A Midsummer Night's Dream. Although he had a retrospective exhibition which toured Scotland in 1973 and received the medal and diploma of honour at the Annual International Italian Art Exhibition 1968, an honourable mention at Ancona in 1968-69 and at the Grande Prix de New York 1969, ill health curtailed his work so that he faded gradually from public notice. Award of The Queen's Jubilee Medal for services to the arts (1977) revived interest and his work has become increasingly well regarded since that time. "Bain's pictures can be uncomfortable and positively fierce, but his best work is adventurous, animated and unambiguous - like his conversation" [W R Hardie]. A regular exhibitor at the RSA as well as at various salons overseas. Represented in Glasgow AG, Perth AG, Museum of Contemporary Art, Skopje (Yugoslavia), Dundee AG, City of Edinburgh collection, Gulbenkian Museum (Lisbon).
**Bibl:** Dundee AG 'Donald Bain' (Ex Cat 1972); Glasgow Print Studio 'Donald Bain Memorial Exhibition' (Ex Cat 1972); Hardie 169-171; Hartley 114-115; MacLellan, Donald Bain, 1950; Macmillan [SA], 370, 401; Williamson, 'Donald Bain Scottish Painter' Studio, Vol CXLIII, No 708, Mar 1952.

**BAIN, Donald** **1959-**
Born Glasgow 1959. Works in oil, watercolour, pen & ink; printmaker. Studied Glasgow School of Art 1977-81 and Royal College of Art 1981-3. Established 'The Cloth' studio 1983. Influenced by Pablo Picasso. Spent some time in Australia. First solo exhibition in London 1983 and first exhibit at the RA the following year.

**BAIN, George** **1881-1968**
Born Caithness. Painter in oil and watercolour; teacher. At an early age went to Edinburgh where he studied at the Edinburgh College of Art, later going to London for further studies at the Royal College of Art. During WW1 was with the 26th Division in Greece and sketched incidents of the war in Salonica. In 1918 he was appointed head teacher of art, Kirkcaldy HS, a position he held until retiring in 1946. Had a lifelong interest in Celtic art and wrote an important monograph on the subject in 1951, published in Glasgow by McLellan. As well as his Greek landscapes, enjoyed painting the Scottish countryside. A retrospective exhibition of his work was held in Kirkcaldy 1978. Exhibited Paris Salon, RSA(13), RSW(1), GI(1), L(1) & AAS(1) between 1901 and 1958. Represented in Kirkcaldy AG (4).
**Bibl:** Halsby 247; Kirkcaldy AG (Ex Cat 1978).

**BAIN, Miss Jean** **fl 1910-1917**
Born Wick. Painter in oil and watercolour of figurative studies and portraits. Exhibited AAS 1910 from 37 Dempster Street, Wick before moving to Edinburgh. From there she exhibited RSA(5) & RSW(1) between 1912 and 1917.

**BAIN, John D** **fl 1938-1939**
Bathgate artist who exhibited RSA(2) & RSW(2).

**BAIN, John Maxie** **fl 1965-1980**
Painter in oil; mainly portraits, also some exotic figurative subjects. Originally from Aberdeen, where he resided at 34 Rosemount Place. Exhibited RSA & AAS 1966-75, and from Salisbury, whence he had moved 1978-80.

**BAIN, Robert Bruce** **1949-1989**
Aberdeen portrait painter and engraver. Lived at 133 Garthdee Drive, Aberdeen from where he exhibited RSA 1975-1989 & AAS 1973-1988.

**BAIN, S (or J) H** **fl 1849**
Edinburgh watercolour painter of still life. Exhibited RSA 1849.

**BAIN, Walter** **fl 1902**
Amateur Stirling artist who exhibited once at the RSA.

**BAIN, William** **fl 1849**
Edinburgh landscape painter in oil. Exhibited RSA 1849. Represented by 10 works in SNPG.

**BAIN, William** **fl 1817-1862**
Scottish medallist working first half 19th century - most prolific of his time, producing over a dozen pieces. Mosly Scottish themes including memorials to Francis Horner 1817 and to the death of 2nd Duke of Sutherland 1840. Also designed medals of Scott and Mary Somerville and 3 medals of Charles Rennie the engineer (following his death in 1821), later to commemorate his work on Sheerness Docks and London Bridge. For the Royal visit of 1822, Bain produced 3 medals, one of them for the National Monument.
**Bibl:** Virtue & Vision, Sculpture & Scotland 1540-1990, NGS 1991.

**BAIRD, Edward MacEwan** **1904-1949**
Born Montrose. Painter in oil and draughtsman in pencil, war subjects especially aircraft; also portraits and still life. Trained Glasgow School of Art 1923-1927, graduating with the Newbery Medal (for the best student of the year), awarded for a study of Roman rooftops. Won a travelling scholarship which enabled him to visit Western Europe, most significantly to Italy where the meticulous detail of early Renaissance painting affected his subsequent style. An acute asthma sufferer and a recluse, he returned to Montrose and apart from war service with the Ministry of Information spent the rest of his life in his home town. In the 1930's he incorporated surrealist elements in his pictures which are close to Nash and Wadsworth. From 1938 to 1940 taught at Dundee College of Art but otherwise spent long periods working on his own. His 'Local Defence Volunteer', shown at the RA 1941, is a moving depiction of the role of the civilian in war time. The painting, begun in 1937, depicts a young man with a rifle, the sitter being "Pumphy" Davidson, a well known local poacher. But with the onset of war Baird added an LDV armband, Davidson having been an early recruit to the service. Examples of his work were included in the Contemporary Scottish Painting Exhibition 1951. Other principal works are 'Mrs Ogilvie' (1932), 'The Birth of Venus' (1934) and what some regard as his masterpiece, 'Unidentified Aircraft' (1942).

His paintings demonstrate a fine grasp of detail, and the draughtsmanship is crisp and competent but at times his tonalities may be a little weak. His work - only 33 paintings have been recorded - remained virtually unknown until the SAC mounted a retrospective exhibition in 1968. In 1992 a selection of his paintings was shown at the SNGMA and 'Portrait of a Young Scotsman' at the Fleming Collection exhibition 2004. Exhibited RA(1), RSA(9) & AAS 1933. Represented in Aberdeen AG, Dundee AG, Glasgow AG, Paisley AG. There is a panoramic view of Montrose by him in Montrose Public Library.
**Bibl:** Patrick Elliott, Edward Baird, Scottish Masters series, Edinburgh 1992; Hardie 155-6; Hartley 115; Macmillan [SA], 341-2,372; Montrose Public Library, 'Edward Baird' (Ex Cat 1981); SAC, 'Edward Baird and William Lamb' (Ex Cat 1968); Andrew Williams, The Times, 15 May, 1992; Derwent May, 'Tribute to Scotland's forgotten realist', The Times, May 4 2004.

**BAIRD, Edwin** **fl 1940**
Montrose artist; exhibited once at the RA.

**BAIRD, Hamish** **1959-**
Born Aberdeen. Figurative painter. Trained Gray's School of Art 1977-81. Compositions largely autobiographical, haunting and sometimes troubled, reflecting what the artist has described as "a certain isolation and loneliness...being brought up in a children's home". Influenced by Stanley Spencer and Lucien Freud, also by James Cowie(qv) and Ken Currie(qv). Exhibits regularly at AAS from Alford, Aberdeenshire.

**BAIRD, George** **1876-c1938**
Perth painter in watercolour and illustrator; portraits and topographical subjects. Apprenticed to a lithographer, worked in this medium before developing his skills in watercolour. Illustrated Peter Baxter's *The Drama in Perth* (c1929). Exhibited at the Perth Arts and Crafts exhibition of 1904 and Perth Artists exhibition 1937/8. Represented by a portrait in Perth AG.

**BAIRD, George** **fl 1957**
Aberdeen landscape painter in oil. Exhibited AAS from 63 Braemar Place.

**BAIRD, George A** **fl 1967**
Amateur landscape painter in oil. Lived at Elderslie, Renfrewshire and exhibited AAS in the above year.

**BAIRD, Hugh** **1770-1827**
Edinburgh architect and engineer. Responsible for the eight arches with battered piers of the Union Canal Aquaduct (1818) which runs beside Lanark Road.
**Bibl:** Gifford 512.

**BAIRD, Hugh John** **fl 1851-1865**
Musselburgh based landscape painter in oil. Exhibited Preston Harbour at the RSA in 1859, latterly from a Leith address.

**BAIRD, James** **fl 1882-1888**
Glasgow painter. Exhibited GI(3) & RHA(1).

**BAIRD, John** **1798-1859**
Born Dalmuir, Dumbartonshire. Glasgow architect and teacher. Apprenticed to SHEPHERD (d 1818). Used an exposed iron frame of hammerbeam construction to roof the Argyle Arcade in Glasgow, also designed Gardner's, an edifice warehouse (36 Jamaica Street). Alexander Thomson(qv), who designed the Buck's Head, Argyle St and the Egyptian Halls in Union Street, worked in his office. His portrait, by Macnee(qv), is in Glasgow AG.
**Bibl:** Dunbar 141; A Gomme & D Walker, Architecture in Glasgow, London 1987(rev), 88,92,114n,242,249,274,285.

**BAIRD, John** **1816-1893**
Glasgow architect. Un-related to previous entry. Married the daughter of M A Nicholson(qv); brother-in-law of Alexander Thomson(qv). Entered partnership with Thomson under name of Baird & Thomson 1849-1857. Short association with James Smith(qv). Designed churches and private houses.
Bibl: A Gomme & D Walker, Architecture of Glasgow, London 1987(rev), 102,134,285,299,301.

**BAIRD, Johnstone** **fl c1900-d1935**
Born Sorn, Ayrshire. Painter in oils and etcher; architectural subjects. Studied at Glasgow School of Art in 1900. Naval architect with the Admiralty 1917-1919. Lived in London. His principal works include paintings of Waterloo Bridge, Loch Lomond and Edinburgh Castle. Exhibited twice at the RSA, also L(1) & Paris Salon. Represented in Paisley AG.

**BAIRD, Miss Maureen** **1931-**
Born Glasgow. Studied as a postgraduate at Edinburgh College of Art in 1954. An oil painting 'Grouse Beating' was exhibited at the Exhibition of Contemporary Scottish Painting 1954.

**BAIRD, Nathaniel Hughes John ROI** **1865-1936**
Born Yetholm, Roxburghshire, 20 Aug. Painter in oil, watercolour and pastel, also an engraver; portraits, landscape and rural scenes with animals, especially horses. As a young man he left Roxburghshire to study in Paris under Bouguereau and Duran before going to the the Herkomer School at Bushey, Herts. First exhibited at the Royal Scottish Academy in 1878 and continued to do so until the end of the century. In the 1880s published *Antiquities of Exeter,* reproduced by J G Commin, the originals of which were acquired by the V & A. After a spell in Devon he went to live at Rodmell, nr Lewes, finally settling in Reading. An outstanding painter of farm horses, his landscapes were characterised by tranquillity and a subtle transfusion of atmosphere. Principal works include 'The Chestnut Team', 'The Favourite' and 'The Forest Team'. "His work displays a tremendous feel for sunlight and the elements, and his pictures are free and strong. His horses are powerful and realistic, shown at their natural best and most sensitively painted...an outstanding artist" [Mitchell]. Elected ROI 1897. Exhibited 32 works at the RA between 1882 and 1892, also RSA(20), ROI(60), RI(29), RBA(3), GI(11) & L(18). Represented in V&A, Exeter AG.
**Bibl:** Mitchell.

**BAIRD, Miss Nina** **fl 1904-1912**
Stonehaven painter in oil; portraits, interiors and figurative subjects. Her sitters included Sir Alexander Baird of Urie (possibly her father). Exhibited RSA(6) & AAS.

**BAIRD, R G** **fl 1827-1829**
Painter in oil; figurative subjects, genre, portraits and animals. Exhibited RSA 1827-1829 from Edinburgh.

**BAIRD, Robert** **fl 1872-1881**
Edinburgh painter in oil and watercolour; landscapes, figures. Exhibited RSA 1875-1881 & GI(1).

**BAIRD, Ruth** **fl 1978-1979**
Painter. Exhibited RSA(3) 1978 and 1979 from 2 Glenisla Gardens, Edinburgh.

**BAIRD, William** **fl 1879-1887**
Portobello painter in watercolours; interiors and landscapes. Exhibited RSA from 1879 to 1887 including a study of Windsor Castle and 'The Lairig Ghru, below Ben Macdhui'.

**BAIRD, William** **fl 1978**
Aberdeen ceramic designer and potter. Exhibited AAS from 116 Craigiebuckler Avenue.

**BAIRTRUM, (or Bairhum) Andrew** **fl 1538-1541**
Painter of altar pieces and chambers. From 1538 until 1541 was working at Kinloss Abbey for Bishop Reid. Said to have been 'outstanding in his craft but a man who was difficult to handle and cantankerous, struggling with a violent temper no less than with a weak body and lame in both feet'. Whilst at Kinloss he decorated 'with three separate panels painted in a simple but beautiful manner three chapels in its church, those of Mary Magdalene, John the Evangelist and St Thomas of Canterbury. He also painted, but in the lighter style of painting now customary throughout Scotland, the Abbot's Cell and Oratory, and at the same time a large chamber in front of the stair which leads to the Abbot's Cell'. Brydall suggests that he may also have been responsible for the frescoes formerly in St.

Congan's, Turriff (Aberdeenshire), the similar paintings at Pluscardine Priory (at the top of the gate leading to the chancel), and those in the parish church at Guthrie.
**Bibl:** Apted; Billings; Brydall 57; 'Ferrerii Historia Abbatum de Kynlos', Bannantyne Club, 1839, 50-51; Macmillan [SA], 35-6; Proceedings of the Scot. Antiquaries, vols ii & vi.

**BAKER, Arthur P** **fl 1882-1886**
Edinburgh painter in watercolour; landscape and flowers. Exhibited RSA between the above years.

**BAKER, Caroline M** **fl 1921-1951**
Scottish painter living in London. Artist of considerable competence; although exhibiting throughout the United Kingdom the majority of her work was in Scotland. Exhibited RSA(11) & GI 1921-1938.

**BAKER, Edmund** **fl 1880-1910**
Stirling painter in oil and watercolour; landscape and coastal scenes, especially the Clyde coast. His watercolours are painted in broad washes as favoured by the Dutch school. Exhibited two works at the RSA in 1898 and again in 1899; also GI(1) and 'Macduff's Cave, Elie' at the AAS (1894).
**Bibl:** Halsby 247.

**BAKER, Evangeline (Eve)** **fl 1890-1915**
Kirriemuir painter in oil and watercolour; landscape, seascape (especially harbours), portraits, occasional domestic scenes and miniatures. Studied in London and Paris. Her first exhibit at the RSA was in 1896 where she continued to show for a number of years. In 1898 opened an atelier in Albany Chambers, Glasgow. In 1909 exhibited a miniature from a Glasgow address at the RA. A militant suffragist she left Glasgow 1915 after which time there is no further recorded work. Altogether she showed 33 works at the RSA; also GI(29), RI(1), RBA(9), AAS(14) & L(10).
**Bibl:** Halsby 277.

**BAKER, Leonard** **1831-1911**
Born Holloway, London; died 20 Sep, Stirling. Painter in oil; landscape, portraits and coastal scenes. Studied under Alfred Stevens at the London School of Design. Sent to Dunfermline 1854 to instruct designers in connection with the linen trade. From 1857 to 1904 art master, Stirling HS. Baker inaugurated the Stirling Fine Arts Association in 1882. In *Eight Centuries of Scottish Education* it is recorded that owing to Baker's "boundless energy and enthusiasm, the art classes in the High School of Stirling have long been recognised by competent authorities as unsurpassed by any similar classes in the country". Reputedly the first person in Scotland to introduce clay modelling. Twice married. Exhibited mostly Scottish landscapes at the Stirling Fine Art Exhibitions in oil and watercolour 1900-10, also RSA 1861-1884.
**Bibl:** Stirling Observer, Obituary, 26 Sep 1911.

**BAKER, S Howard** **fl 1932-1936**
Amateur Glasgow painter; exhibited 2 works at the GI in 1932 and 1936.

**BAKER, T E** **fl 1893**
Amateur Coldingham painter of country scenes; exhibited at both the GI and AAS in the above year.

**BAKER, W** **fl 1823-1832**
Little is known of this architect and architectural draughtsman beyond the fact that he left Scotland at an early age. Exhibited three times at the RSA during the years 1823 to 1832, always architectural subjects, on one occasion the design for an undisclosed church in Inverness.

**BALDERSTANE** **fl 1707**
A Lanarkshire account records that on the 10 January 1707, a Mr Balderstane was paid twenty-five pounds sixteen pence "for going out to Carno, taking the mould of (Sir John Hamilton of Halcraig's) face and drawing his picture in wax".

**BALDRY, John** **fl 1870**
Edinburgh landscape painter in oil; exhibited RSA 1870.

**BALDWIN, Rosalind** **fl 1973-**
Trained Glasgow School of Art 1969-73. Works in gouache, oil and pastel. Specialises in equestrian and wildlife subjects. Work ranges from delicate miniatures to large portraits. Published many prints. Elected an Associate of the Society of Equestrian Artists.

**BALFOUR, Alexander** **fl 1859-1870**
Dunfermline painter in oil; landscape and figurative. Exhibited RSA, usually Highland scenes in Inverness-shire, during the above years.

**BALFOUR, Andrew** **fl 1901-1905**
Amateur Glasgow artist; exhibited GI(4).

**BALFOUR, Miss Margaret** **fl 1859-1866**
Dunfermline painter in oil, chalk; landscape and portraits. Exhibited two pictures at the RSA in 1859 and 1866.

**BALFOUR-BROWNE, Vincent Robert Stewart Ramsey** **1880-1963**
Born London, 30 May. Painter in watercolour and pencil; stalking scenes and wildlife. Lived in Dumfriesshire. Pupil and friend of the artist and naturalist George Lodge(qv). Working mostly in watercolour, his favourite subjects were Highland stalking scenes but was equally proficient at portraying the birds and mammals of Scotland, generally painted on a small scale with finely delineated detail. He leased a deer forest for stalking and sketching purposes in various parts of the west coast for many years although most of his best work was done in the Blackmount area of Argyll. Illustrated several books including Patrick Chalmers' *Mine Eyes Unto the Hills. The Stalking Letters and Sketches of V.R. Balfour-Browne,* first published in 1978, was an immediate success, providing a fine illustrative account of his oeuvre. Prints of his work, often produced during his lifetime in circular form to simulate the view from a telescope, have always been in demand. One of the finest Scottish sporting and wildlife artists of any period and arguably the finest painter of red deer. Exhibitions of his work were held annually during his lifetime in London, often shared with the English wildlife artist Barrington-Browne.
**Bibl:** Halsby 247.

**BALFOUR-MELVILLE B** **fl 1908**
Miniature painter from Leith who exhibited once at the RSA in 1908 & RSW(1). Recorded in neither Foskett nor Long.

**BALL, Harrison** **fl 1921-1923**
Aberdeen painter of townscapes. Lived at 13 Beechgrove Avenue from where he exhibited AAS(4).

**BALL, Susan Jennifer** **1951-**
Born England, 24 Aug. Sculptress and scenic artist. After studying at Stafford and Wolverhampton CAs attended Gray's School of Art, Aberdeen specialising in ceramics and sculpture. Her early work was mainly figurative, using clay, plaster and fibreglass. In the 1980s her work became increasingly abstract, using cut wood and sheet metal with surface drawing in wood die, ink and pencil. Designed the Fountain in Rubislaw Terrace, Aberdeen. Exhibited RSA 1990 & AAS from Rose Cottage, Methlick.

**BALLANTYNE, Alexander** **fl 1907-1909**
Member of the family firm of stained glass window designers of 42 George Street, Edinburgh. Exhibited RSA 1907 and 1909.

**BALLANTYNE, Miss Edith J** **fl 1866-1884**
Painter in oil and watercolour of figurative and literary works. Daughter of John Ballantyne(qv). Her first exhibit there was of the interior of a Kensington house, subsequently purchased by John Phillip(qv). Exhibited RA(3) between 1866 and 1884 during the whole of which time she appears to have been living with her father under whom she studied: also exhibited at the RSA from 1867 until 1885, RBA(2) & L(2).

**BALLANTYNE, James** **1808-1877**
Stained glass window designer, specialising in church work. In 1837 founded the firm Ballantyne (James) & Son responsible for several comprehensive schemes in Edinburgh among them the decoration in the choir of St Giles' Cathedral (1874-77), suggested by Joseph Noel Paton(qv) and Robert Herdman(qv) and executed under Herdman's supervison. The design depicts scenes from the life of Christ. His quartet of heraldic windows in the Scott Memorial (c1845) are

regarded by Cowen as being 'on the stodgy side'; other works include eight windows in Old Greyfriars, Edinburgh and in Glasgow cathedral. Exhibited RSA 1848.
**Bibl:** Gifford 44,179,208,316,368,387,418; Painton Cowen, Stained Glass in Britain, 1975, 228,232,237.

**BALLANTY(I)NE, James FSA (Scot)** **1878-1940**
Born Edinburgh. Stained glass window designer, son of Alexander Ballantyne(qv). The third generation to become a stained glass designer. Pupil at Edinburgh Academy before continuing his studies in London, Paris and Dresden. His particular interest was ancient continental glass about which he lectured and broadcast. Designed for many churches and cathedrals in Scotland and other parts of the world including the Reid Memorial Church in Edinburgh and the stained glass for the central staircase of the Caledonian Insurance Company in St Andrew's Square. Lived in North Berwick and wrote a *Short History of Church Stained Glass.* William Watson(qv), later to become the leading stained glass artist in Scotland, was one of his apprentices. Died as the result of an accident. Prize winner at the RSA Life School and exhibited RSA over many years.
**Bibl:** Gifford 44,241,278,454,485,617-8,629; Macmillan [SA], 361; Scotsman Obit, 25.11.1940.

**BALLANTYNE, John RSA** **1815-1897**
Born Kelso, Apr 25; died Melksham, Wiltshire, 12 May. A painter in oil of portraits and historical genre. Educated Edinburgh Academy, trained Trustees School, Edinburgh under Sir William Allan(qv) and Thomas Duncan(qv). After his first exhibit at the RSA in 1831 he studied in London, where William Etty introduced him to the RA schools, Paris and Rome. Returned to Edinburgh 1839 and painted numerous pictures. Went back to London 1864 and exhibited no more in Scotland after 1887. An original member of the group known as 'The Smashers'(qv), formed in Edinburgh in 1848, and later reconstituted in London as the 'Old Lang Syne Club(qv), ARSA 1841, RSA 1860. Ballantyne liked to paint portraits of artists in their studios. R S Lauder(qv) appointed him his assistant in the antique and life classes at the Academy 1848, thus beginning a memorable partnership between the two. After Duncan's death in 1845 the prestige of the Trustees Academy had been deteriorating and it was therefore especially timely when under Lauder's commanding influence he and Ballantyne began the task of restoring its fine tradition. While Lauder was the inspiration and the devotee of colour, Ballantyne provided the academic draughtsmanship and drive toward fulfilment. In London, he rented a flat in The Mall, Kensington where he completed a series of 17 paintings of artists' studios, these receiving detailed coverage in the *Art Journal* followed by a London exhibition 1865. In collaboration with Heywood Hardy, painted the portrait of George Glennie, captain of Royal Blackheath GC and the R & A. Exhibited RA(5), RBA(1) & RSA(5) between 1831 and 1889, RSW(1) & AAS. A prolific artist, his work can be seen at the NPG, depicting Landseer at work on the Lions at Trafalgar Square, also represented in SNPG(5), Glasgow AG, City of Edinburgh collection.
**Bibl:** Bryan; Caw 230-1; Halsby 104; Hardie 45; Irwin 306; McKay 355; NPG Cat 1903; Studio 1907; Lizzie Darbyshire, The studios of celebrated Painters'; a series of portraits by John Ballantyne RSA, Apollo, May, 1998.

**BALLANTYNE, John** **fl 1889-1906**
Edinburgh landscape painter in oil and watercolour; exhibited RSA in 1889(165), 1905 and 1906(6), RSW(2) & GI(1).

**BALLANTYNE, Mary (Mrs R Wilkie)** **fl 1920-1939**
Painter. Exhibited RSA(11) between 1920 and 1939 & GI(1) from an address in Glasgow.

**BALLANTYNE, Robert Michael** **1825-1894**
Born Edinburgh. Author and painter in oil and watercolour; landscapes, figures, coastal; also some sporting subjects. Nephew of James Ballantyne(qv). Began as a clerk with the Hudson Bay Company before joining the Edinburgh offices of the publisher Thomas Constable. Prolific author of over 100 titles. Also worked in Europe moving to Harrow, Middlesex c1880. One painting 'The Mosstrooper' (1868), was sold to the Association for the Encouragement of the Fine Arts. Exhibited RSA(46) 1866-1887. Represented in Edinburgh City collection (including 'Self-portrait').
**Bibl:** Halsby 247.

**BALLARD, Miss** **fl 1893**
Amateur Selkirk artist who exhibited once in England.

**BALLARDIE, J de Caynoth** **fl 1887-1888**
Amateur Glasgow artist of French extraction. Exhibited a landscape at the RSA, also GI(1).

**BALLEMENT, Miss D** **fl 1902**
Amateur Greenock artist. Sister of L Alexandra Ballement(qv). Exhibited RSA 1902.

**BALLEMENT, L Alexandra** **fl 1900-1902**
Greenock miniature painter. Sister of Miss D Ballement(qv). Exhibited RSA(1), GI(2) & L(1). Recorded by neither Foskett nor Long.

**BALLINGALL, Alexander** **1870-1910**
Edinburgh painter in oil and watercolour; townscapes and coastal scenes. Specialised in watercolours of coastal scenes in a style similar to G D Taylor(qv), Andrew Black(qv) and J D Bell(qv). His drawings were precise but hard and his colour indelicate and strong. Also worked for a time in Venice and in 1883 exhibited a domestic scene at the NW. Exhibited RSA(73), RI(1) & GI(1) between 1871 and 1899.
**Bibl:** Caw 331; Halsby 247.

**BALLINGALL, John** **fl 1896-1899**
Largo painter in watercolour of seascapes; exhibited RSA(3) between 1896 and 1899.

**BALMAIN, Elizabeth B** **fl 1947-1976**
Painter in oil; local scenes. Exhibited RSA from an address in Edinburgh & AAS in 1967, 1969 & 1976.

**BALMAIN, Kenneth Field** **1890-1957**
Born Edinburgh, Jan. Landscape painter in oil, mostly of the East Lothians; also photographer. Served in the RAF during WW1 1914-1919, thereafter settling in North Berwick. Studied Edinburgh College of Art and at the RSA Life School. Exhibited RSA(10), also AAS & SSA.

**BALMER, Barbara (Mrs Mackie) ARSA RSW RGI** **1929-**
Born Birmingham 23 Sep. Painter in oil and watercolour; landscape and decorative items, also occasional murals. Educated Solihull HS for Girls, studied at Coventry School of Art 1947-8 and Edinburgh College of Art 1949-52 under William Gillies(qv), Robin Philipson(qv), Robert Henderson Blyth(qv) and John Hunter(qv) winning a travelling scholarship enabling her to visit France and Spain. First visited Italy 1973, where the fresco paintings made a profound influence, reinforcing a natural inclination toward "on the wall" flatness through the use of close tone and line. Became visiting lecturer at Gray's School of Art, Aberdeen while maintaining a studio in Edinburgh. Married George Mackie(qv). Has a preference for using pale colours. A large mural was commissioned for the new Cumbernauld Town Hall. Over seventy commissioned portraits, many of children. Lives in Stamford, Lincs with frequent visits to Tuscany. Elected RSW 1966, ARSA 1973. Exhibited regularly at both RSA & RSW, also AAS 1959-1980. Represented in Aberdeen AG, Glasgow AG, Perth AG and Lillie AG (Milngavie), SAC, Royal College of Physicians, Edinburgh.

**BALMER, William** **fl 1861-1871**
Jedburgh landscape painter in oil especially local scenes. Exhibited regularly RSA 1861-1871.

**BAMBOROUGH, James** **fl 1866-1885**
Edinburgh painter in oil; figures, portraits. Exhibited 'Self-portrait' at the RSA 1866, and another work 1885.

**BANBURY, William RBS** **1871-c1932**
Born Leicester; moved to Aberdeen c1908. Sculptor in metal, wood and stone, also landscape painter in oil. Settled in Aberdeen, first at 26 Irvine Place and then at Gowanlee, Hammerfield Avenue, and in 1931 at The Knoll, Oakhill Road. Exhibited RA(6), RSA(13) and annually 1908-31 at the AAS.

**BANFORD, James** **fl 1927**
Amateur Glasgow artist who exhibited once at the GI.

**BANKHEAD, Austin** **fl 1976**
Exhibited three paintings at the RSA in 1976.

**BANKS, A L** **fl 1904-1905**
Amateur Edinburgh artist who exhibited twice at the RSA.

**BANKS, Miss Annie P** **fl 1937**
Edinburgh painter, exhibited once at the RSA.

**BANKS, E G** **fl 1881**
Glasgow landscape painter in watercolour. Exhibited RSA(1).

**BANKS, George** **fl 1909**
Amateur Edinburgh watercolourist; exhibited RSW(1).

**BANKS, Henry** **fl 1859**
Minor portrait painter. Exhibited two portraits at the RSA from an Edinburgh address 1859.

**BANKS, John** **fl 1938**
Amateur painter. Exhibited GI(1).

**BANKS, Leslie** **1962-**
Born Scotland, based in Aberdeen. Painter in oil of portraits and figure compositions. Studied Glasgow School of Art 1980-84. A Greenshields scholarship took her to Amsterdam for six months. Recipient of many awards including the RGI's David Cargill Award 1990 and their Scottish Amicable Award 1991, Levehulme Trust Award, facilitating a visit to Italy, 1996. First solo exhibition in Glasgow, 1991. Treats her work as a social commentary, profiling the same women in different settings, mostly in urban environments. Exhibits regularly at the RSA, RGI & AAS. Represented in Aberdeen AG, Lillie AG, Museum of Modern Art, Glasgow.

**BANKS, Lizzie Jane** **fl 1882-1883**
Edinburgh flower painter; exhibited twice at the RSA 1882-1883 from 48 Grange Loan.

**BANKS, Martin** **1962-**
Born Bellshill, Lanarks. Painter mainly in acrylic of abstract designs often based upon the cell with images taken from electron microscopes; also teacher. Trained Glasgow School of Art 1980-84. First solo exhibition in Glasgow 1998. Exhibits RSA, RGI, AAS.

**BANKS, Violet** **1869-?**
Born Kinghorn, Fife, 3 Mar. Painter in oil and watercolour of figure subjects and interiors; also skilled pottery decorator. Studied Edinburgh College of Art. Friend of Ernest Lumsden(qv). Lived for a spell in Kirkcaldy before going to Edinburgh 1928 to become Art mistress at the now defunct St Ornan's School. Exhibited RSA(6), RSW(9), GI(1) & L(1); also SSA, SSWA, AAS and in the provinces.
**Bibl:** Halsby 248.

**BANKS, William** **fl 1874-1884**
Edinburgh painter in oil and watercolour; literary and figurative subjects, also townscapes. Exhibited RSA(13) 1874-1884.

**BANNATYNE, Annie M** **fl 1888**
Amateur Edinburgh painter in oil; exhibited once at the RSA from 15 Lansdowne Crescent.

**BANNATYNE, J G** **fl 1888**
Painter. Possibly related to Annie Ballantyne(qv). Exhibited RI(1) & GI(3) from an English address.

**BANNATYNE, John James RSW** **1836-1911**
Scottish born landscape painter in oil and watercolour. His favourite subjects were views of Scottish lochs. His work is not often seen. Although all his RA exhibits were Highland scenes, generally in Perthshire and on Loch Lomondside, he resided in London. Exhibited RA(5), RSA(28) 1861-1897, RSW(70), RSA, ROI(10), RI(13), RBA(9), GI(84) & L(8).
**Bibl:** Halsby 108,248.

**BANNER, Alexander** **fl 1868-1890**
Glasgow painter in oil and art teacher; still life. Exhibited RSA(1) 1868; also GI(2).

**BANNER, Hugh Harwood** **1865-**
Born Glasgow, 14 Oct. Painter in oil and watercolour of portraits and landscape; also etcher and mezzotinter. Trained Glasgow School of Art and City of London Art School. Living in Edinburgh 1887 but had moved to Maxwelltown, Dumfries by 1906 and to Carlisle in the 1920s. Exhibited GI(2), L(4) & in the provinces.

**BANNERMAN, Cameron L** **fl 1953-1961**
Glasgow painter. Exhibited RSA 1953-1961.

**BANNERMAN, Charles** **fl 1933**
Amateur Aberdeen artist; exhibited RSA(1).

**BANNERMAN, Helen Brodie Cowan** **1863-1946**
Born Edinburgh; died Edinburgh, 13 Oct. Author and illustrator of children's books. Daughter of an army chaplain. As a young girl travelled extensively with her family including a stay of ten years in Madeira. Educated St Andrews University and in Germany and Italy. Married an army doctor and lived for thirty years in India. In 1899, while returning to India after leaving her two young daughters at school in Scotland, she wrote and illustrated *The Story of Little Black Sambo.* Subsequently wrote and illustrated more children's stories based on Indian life, the best known being *The Story of the Teasing Monkey* (1906). Others were *Story of Little Black Mingo* (1901), *Story of Little Black Quibba* (1903), *Story of Little Kettle-head* (1904). *Pat and the Spider* (1905), *Story of Little Black Quasha* (1908) and *Story of Little Black Bobtail* (1910). After the death of her husband she returned to live in Edinburgh and in 1936 her American publisher persuaded her to write a sequel to her first book. *Sambo and the Twins* was the result. A MS entitled *Little White Squibba* was discovered after her death and published in 1966.
**Bibl:** B.E. Mahony et al, Illustrators of Children's Books 1744-1945, Boston (USA) 1947, 273-4; Elizabeth Hay, *Sambo Sahib: The Story of Helen Bannerman* 1981; Alderson; Carpenter; Horne 89; Peppin.

**BANNISTER, W E** **fl 1919**
Glasgow painter; exhibited once at the GI.

**BANZIE, Marie de** **1918-?**
Painter in oil; murals. Studied Glasgow School of Art 1937-41 and Hospitalfield 1941-2. Also trained as a ballet dancer with the Celtic Ballet Company (established by Margaret Morrison, wife of JD Fergusson). Founder member of the New Art Club and Secretary to the New Scottish Group 1943-5. Sometimes collaborated with Isabel Brodie(qv).
**Bibl:** Macmillan [SA], 369,370.

**BARBOUR, Margaret Stewart (Mrs D Cowan)** **1887-c1960**
Born 12 Aug. Amateur Pitlochry watercolourist. Member of the Barbour family of Bonskeid, daughter of Rev R W Barbour, Minister of Cults. Studied social work before enrolling on a short course at Edinburgh College of Art. Married Rev D Cowan, minister of Anderston Church, Glasgow 1931, later of Huntly and Dervaig, Mull. Died without issue. Travelled widely, always sketching on her journeys. One fine drawing done in Kashmir remains in the family; exhibited RSW 1925.

**BARBOUR, Marie** **1963-**
Born Scotland. Lithographer, specialises in linocuts and woodcuts; concentrates on the the female figure within an urban context. Studied Glasgow School of Art 1981-5. First solo exhibition Greenock 1986. Her work was included in the Inverclyde Biennial 1988. Represented Greenock AG.

**BARCLAY, Miss Ada Mary** **fl 1879-1914**
Edinburgh painter in oil and watercolour, portraits and landscapes. Moved to London 1910. Exhibited RA(1) & RSA(14) 1879-1885.

**BARCLAY, Albert Paterson** **1912-1998**
Born Edinburgh, Sep 30; died Perth, Aug 15. Painter of figurative studies and landscape; schoolmaster. Trained Edinburgh College of Art 1930-35 under S J Peploe(qv), David Sutherland(qv), David Foggie(qv) and Gillies(qv). Contemporary of Charles McCall(qv) whose portrait of Barclay is in Perth AG. Art master, Perth Academy 1938-50 becoming senior art master 1950-75 in which capacity he was responsible for the introduction of the Scottish Cert. for Sixth Year studies in art. Exhibited RSA 1934 & 35. His work seldom

appears although several paintings came up at auction in April 2004, entered by the family. Represented in Perth AG.

**BARCLAY, David** **1846-1917**
Glasgow architect. Less talented brother of Hugh B(qv). The brothers collaborated on a number of schools and churches including Glasgow Academy(1878). After Hugh's death he designed Royal College of Science and Technology(1901).
**Bibl:** A Gomme & D Walker, Architecture of Glasgow, London 1987(rev), 122n,163,195,258n,294,298,300.

**BARCLAY, Eliza M** **fl 1887**
Edinburgh painter in watercolour of fruit and still life. Exhibited RSA 1887.

**BARCLAY, Graham H** **fl 1880-1885**
Edinburgh painter in oil; exhibited 3 works at the RSA in 1885.

**BARCLAY, H** **fl 1905**
Glasgow artist; exhibited 3 works at the GI 1905.

**BARCLAY, Miss Helen Lee** **fl 1940-1944**
Edinburgh sculptress. Exhibited RSA(3) 1940, 1942 and 1944, also GI(1).

**BARCLAY, Herbert A** **fl 1933**
Amateur Aberdeenshire painter of rustic scenes, sometimes with farm animals. Exhibited AAS from Woodend, Newmachar.

**BARCLAY, Hugh** **1828-1892**
Glasgow architect. Brother and partner of David B(qv). Pupil of William Spence(qv). Became James Sellars's master and lifelong friend. Specialised in school design, including Glasgow Academy(1878).
**Bibl:** A Gomme & D Walker, Architecture of Glasgow, London 1987(rev), 116,118,163-7,195,262,285f,294,298,300.

**BARCLAY, Isabella F** **fl 1900-1910**
Aberdeen painter in oil of local scenes. Exhibited AAS during the above years.

**BARCLAY, James** **fl 1888-1899**
Glasgow artist. Occasional hunting and sporting subjects in watercolour. Exhibited GI(1).

**BARCLAY, James Mclean** **1929-**
Stirlingshire sculptor. Exhibited mostly portrait busts at the RSA 1952-1966, from East Kilbride.

**BARCLAY, James R** **fl 1989-**
Angus painter. Exhibited two works at the RSA in 1989, and one in 1990 from Kettlehill, nr Cupar.

**BARCLAY, John MacLaren RSA** **1811-1886**
Born Perth, Feb 27; died Edinburgh, Dec 1. Educated Perth Academy, his father entered him in the office of a civil engineer but he soon left in order to study art at the Board of Trustees School under Sir William Allan(qv). Returned to Perth having become reasonably proficient before moving to Edinburgh where he produced several subjects taken from Scottish history. For twelve years a Visitor of The Life School and for the last two years of his life Treasurer and Trustee of the Academy. Lifelong friend of D O Hill(qv) and Thomas Duncan(qv). Elected ARSA 1863, RSA 1871, Treasurer RSA 1884-1886. Caw was rather disparaging 'he displayed considerable accomplishment, if no distinction'. Exhibited 13 times at the RA from 1850 until 1875 from a Perth address, RSA(130) 1846-1886, GI(1) & AAS(1). Represented by 6 works in SNPG, Leith Hall (NTS), Brodie Castle (NTS), Perth AG.
**Bibl:** Caw 178.

**BARCLAY, John Rankine** **1884-1963**
Born Edinburgh 22 Oct. Worked in oil and watercolour, also etcher; landscape and architectural subjects. Studied Edinburgh and on the continent, visiting Paris in 1911. Awarded Carnegie Travelling Scholarship and Guthrie Award 1922. Moved to St Ives in Cornwall in the late 1930s. The most painterly of the Edinburgh Group, his work included golfing and ice skating subjects. Exhibited regularly at the RSA between 1910 & 1939 (52 works), also RA(1), RSW(2) & GI(8). Represented in SNGMA.
**Bibl:** Mungo Campbell, 'The Line of Tradition', Nat Gall Scot, Ex cat, 1993; Halsby 193,222; Macmillan [SA], 332,351.

**BARCLAY, Miss Mabel** **fl 1922-1927**
Edinburgh painter in oil and watercolour; exhibited RSA(3) & RSW(1).

**BARCLAY, Margaret S** **fl 1921**
Aberdeenshire enamellist. Exhibited two designs at the AAS from the Schoolhouse, Kepplehills, Bucksburn.

**BARCLAY, Stephen** **1961-**
Born Ayrshire. Painter. Studied Glasgow School of Art 1980-85. First one-man exhibition in London c1983. Featured in 'The New Image Glasgow' exhibition organised by Alexander Moffat 1985. Fascinated by 'haunted landscapes or interiors where the human presence may only be suggested' [Hardie]. Represented in Australian National Gallery.
**Bibl:** Hardie 206.

**BARCLAY, Thomas** **fl 1801-1807**
Building designer and mason. Worked at Balbirnie, Fife. Designed the Classical Town House, Falkland, Fife (1801-2) and was probably responsible for the Manse, Falkland, Fife (1806-7).
**Bibl:** Bruce Walker & W S Gauldie, Architects and Architecture on Tayside, Dundee 1984, 83.

**BARCLAY, William** **fl 1865**
Stirling sculptor. Exhibited a marble portrait bust at the RSA in 1865.

**BARCLAY, William** **fl 1867-1906**
Dundee painter in oil and watercolour; landscapes, local scenes. One of his finest works was 'Dunnottar', shown at the RA in 1873. Exhibited regularly at the RSA between 1867 and 1898. Represented in V&A.

**BARCLAY, William James** **fl 1880**
Amateur Fife painter from Cupar; exhibited RSA(1) 1880.

**BARCLAY, William Jnr** **fl 1863-1870**
Aberlady artist who exhibited landscapes at the RSA from 1863 (from a London address) until 1870.

**BARGER, Miss Margaret** **fl 1937**
Edinburgh artist. Exhibited once at the RSA from 48 St. Alban's Road.

**BARKER, E Conyers** **fl 1923**
Scottish painter in watercolour; exhibited RSW(2).

**BARKER, Henry Aston** **1774-1856**
Born Glasgow; died Bilton, near Bristol 19 Jly (according to the *AJ*, in London 26 Feb). Painter and engraver of panoramas. Son of the Irish portrait and miniature painter Robert Barker(qv), he studied at the Royal Academy schools, London, where he became a friend of Robert Kerr Porter and J M W Turner. When only twelve he assisted his father in producing a panorama of the Calton Hill in Edinburgh, which eventually became a whole circle view of the city. [See Robert Barker]. His own first work was a painting 'Panoramic View of London' 1792. Made several extensive overseas visits to make drawings for panoramas including trips to Constantinople, to Palermo 1799, Copenhagen 1801 (in both of these places he met Lord Nelson), and in 1810 visited Malta. Married the eldest of the six daughters of Admiral Bligh 1802. Assisted Messrs Burford in their panoramas of the Peninsular Actions of the Battle of Waterloo. In 1802 visited Paris and quickly made his mark with some fine Parisian panoramas. During the Peace of Amiens he was introduced to Napoleon. His last work in this genre before his retirement 1826 was the 'Procession of the Coronation of George IV' (1822). In 1829 he was in Venice, and never returned to Scotland.
**Bibl:** Brydall 311-313; Bryan; Butchart.

**BARKER, Robert** **1739-1806**
Born Kells, Co Meath, Ireland; died in Lambeth, London 8 Apr. After

failure of a business enterprise in Dublin he took up miniature painting but being unsuccessful he went to Edinburgh, setting up practice as a miniaturist and portrait painter. Became interested in landscape and invented a system of painting panoramas of curvilinear perspective, a technique which he subsequently taught. This perspective was applied to a concave subject so as to appear level from a certain point. Working to this plan he drew his panoramic view in six large sections which were then engraved in aquatint by J Wells. Each of the sections measures 21'7" x 16'7" and, when mounted together, occupy a wall space of approximately 11 feet. These illustrate quite precisely the lower part of the city in 1793 as seen in different directions from the Calton Hill. The key issued with them enables one to identify the outstanding buildings. This key is an unusual production, being issued later from Leicester Square whither Barker had moved. Beyond the central circle Barker had listed 49 items of interest supplemented by concise little drawings on the outer fringes. His great panoramic sweep begins at the foot of the Canongate where it takes in the Canongate Church and the Tolbooth, Surgeon's Hall, the Infirmary and other famous landmarks. Thereafter it continues its circular progression around the city until the sixth and last part of the tour shows the new Observatory, Portobello, Musselburgh, and the background of Arthur's Seat and the Salisbury Crags. The view of Calton Hill, Edinburgh had suggested the idea and in 1787, assisted by his son Henry(qv), then only 12 years old, he made drawings of a half-circle view of the hill, eventually completing a full-circle view of Edinburgh. This was exhibited in Edinburgh and later in 1788. In London it was such a success that he painted several other views in the same way.
**Bibl:** AJ, 1857 46; Bryan; Brydall 311-312; Butchart 80-82; DNB; Foskett i, 149; Irwin 143; Long, 15; Macmillan [SA], 145; Rb; Strickland.

**BARKER, Thomas Jones** **1815-1882**
Painter in oil of historical scenes, landscape, and portraits. It is not certain if he was Scottish by birth but many of his exhibits at the Royal Academy 1845-1876 were of Scottish subjects including 'Edinburgh after Culloden' (1850), 'Colonel Locket MP of Lanark' (1860), 'The Moss-trooper' (1869), while all his exhibits at the RSA between 1844 and 1852 were Scottish portraits and scenes, some of them from an Edinburgh address. A prolific and competent artist although his work is not often seen. Represented by a portrait of the 1st Lord Clyde in the SNPG, also Glasgow AG.

**BARKIS, Miss Annie** **fl 1880-1888**
Coldstream painter in oil and watercolour; portraits and landscape. Exhibited RSA(6) & SWA(1).

**BARLOW, Richard M** **fl 1958-1970**
Dalkeith sculptor; exhibited RSA 1958-1970.

**BARMAN, L** **fl 1898-1909**
Amateur Glasgow artist; exhibited GI(3) & L(2). Married to an artist who also exhibited, although rather later.

**BARMAN, Mrs L** **fl 1917-1919**
Amateur Glasgow painter. Married L Barman(qv). Exhibited GI(4).

**BARNARD, Katherine** **fl c1910**
Edinburgh watercolourist specialising in landscape. signed her work 'KB' or 'K', sometimes 'K Barnard'; exhibited RSA.

**BARNARD, Margaret** **fl 1922-1939**
Painter in oil of figures, and portraits. Trained in Glasgow, moved to Kelso in 1923 and then to London in the early 1930s. During this period exhibited RA(2), RBA(1) & GI(2).

**BARNARD, Marjorie (Mary) Baylis (Mrs MacGregor Whyte)** **1870-1946**
Born Wiltshire. Flower painter in oil and watercolour. Trained in Paris. Married the artist Duncan McGregor Whyte(qv) 1901, with whom from 1910 she shared a studio in Oban and later Tiree where they spent a large part of each year. Moved from London to Glasgow 1900. Highly competent still-life flower painter with a fine colour sense, delicately portraying flowers, generally in vases on tables. Also painted occasional landscapes and interiors. Exhibited RA(2), RSA(6) 1903-1913), GI(13), RBA(3), ROI(1) & L(4).

**BARNES, A W H** **fl 1920-1938**
Glasgow artist in oil and watercolour; landscapes and topographical subjects. Moved from Glasgow to London 1930, then to Cambridge 1932. Exhibited 1920-1938 at the RSA(2), RSW(2), GI(13), L(3) & AAS(2).

**BARNES, Miss Ellen** **fl 1875-1885**
Edinburgh painter in watercolour; still life and figurative subjects. Exhibited RSA 1875(2), 1876 and 1879, and at the SWA 1884-5 from 8 St Anne's Villas, Notting Hill, London.

**BARNES, Sir Harry Jefferson** **fl c1945-d1982**
Painter in oil of landscapes and townscapes; administrator. After a spell teaching at the Royal Masonic Senior School, Bushey moved to Glasgow, becoming Principal, Glasgow School of Art and founder of the Charles Rennie Mackintosh Society. Exhibited RSA(1) 1945 & RBA(3).

**BARNES, Samuel John** **1847-1901**
Birmingham artist who paid several prolonged visits to Scotland. Exhibited RA(2) and Scottish landscapes at the RSA in 1883, 1884(3) & 1886, RHA(3) & L(2).

**BARNET, Isabel M ('Belle')** **1895-1983**
Scottish embroiderer & teacher. Assistant to and influenced by Dorothy Angus(qv), in 1922 she joined the staff of Dundee College of Art. Member, Modern Embroidery Society in which capacity she exhibited RSA 1934.

**BARNETT, Catriona** **fl 1965-1966**
Aberdeenshire painter. Exhibited 'Dorit' and 'Jamaica Way' at the AAS from The School House, Tornaveen, Torphins.

**BARNETT, Francis** **fl c1850-c1870**
Leith stained glass window designer. Responsible for the Anderson Memorial window in the N aisle, Old Greyfriars, Edinburgh; abstract designs in St Patrick's Chapel, Cowgate; two tall windows beside the pulpit in St Mary's, Bellevue Crescent, and three windows depicting respectively Abraham and Isaac, St John the Baptist and the Resurrection on the N side of the nave in St James', Constitution St (1868). In late career was joined in partnership with her son **William Collingridge BARNETT,** continuing to specialise in ecclesiastical work.
**Bibl:** Gifford 155,169,338,452,454,455.

**BARNS-GRAHAM, Wilhelmina HRSW** **1912-2004**
Born St Andrews, Fife, 3 Jly; died Jan 22. Painter in oil, gouache, collage and line drawings but best known for painted reliefs. Studied at Edinburgh College of Art 1931-1936 under Gillies(qv), Maxwell(qv) and Moodie(qv), where her fellow students included Gear(qv), Mellis(qv), Denis Peploe(qv) and Charles Pulsford. From 1936 to 1940 had a studio in Edinburgh and in 1940 went to St Ives in Cornwall on a scholarship. In Cornwall she became a friend of Borlase Smart and met Nicholson and Hepworth. Joined the Newlyn Society of Artists and the St Ives Society of Artists in 1942 and became a founder-member of the Penwith Society 1949, the year she married the writer David Lewis. A visit to Switzerland 1948 resulted in a series of drawings and paintings of glaciers which made a great and lasting impression. She wrote 'this likeness to glass and transparency combined with solid rough ridges made me wish to combine in a work all angles at once, from above, through and all round, as a bird flies, a total experience'. For the next two years worked on large gouaches and also began to work on small abstract white reliefs. During an Italian government scholarship in 1955 she met Poliakoff and, returning through Paris, visited Brancusi and Arp. Taught at Leeds School of Art from 1956-57 and from 1961-63 maintained a studio in London. In 1960 she inherited a house in St Andrews and subsequently divided her time between there and Cornwall. Her stylistic development, always on the margins of abstraction and realism, continued throughout her life. In the words of her obituary, 'it is difficult to think of any other artist whose work has remained, after sixty years, not only vital but actually surprising'. Held many solo exhibitions and exhibited regularly RSA. Elected HRSW 1998. Represented in Tate AG, V&A, SNGMA, Sydney AG, University of Michigan, Whitworth AG (Sheffield), Plymouth AG, Aberdeen AG, Dundee AG, Kirkcaldy AG, Glasgow AG.

**Bibl:** Mungo Campbell, 'The Line of Tradition, Nat Galls of Scot, Ex cat, 1993; City Art Centre, Edinburgh, 'W Barns-Graham Retrospective, 1940-1989' (Ex Cat 1989); Hardie 180; Hartley 115-6; Macmillan [SA], 358; Scottish Gallery, Edinburgh, 'W Barns-Graham' (Ex Cat 1956, W McLellan Text); Intro by Alan Bowness; Tate Gall, 'St Ives, 25 years of painting, sculpture and pottery' (Ex Cat 1985); The Times, Obit, 28 Jan 2004.

**BARR, Agnes Crawford** **fl 1884-1905**
Glasgow painter. Exhibited RSW(2) & GI between the above dates, a total of 10 works.

**BARR, Alexander** **fl 1850-1851**
Little known Edinburgh painter; exhibited twice at the RSA 1850-1851.

**BARR, George** **fl 1927-1940**
Glasgow artist; exhibited 16 works at the GI between the above years & AAS(1).

**BARR, Miss Helen** **fl 1887**
Amateur Uddingston artist who exhibited once at the GI.

**BARR, James** **fl 1861-1889**
Glasgow oil painter of Scottish landscapes. Exhibited RSA 1861(2) and 1889, also GI(4).

**BARR, James** **fl 1931-1938**
Glasgow painter in oil; exhibited RSA(6) & GI(8).

**BARR, James ARSA ARBS** **1911-1969**
Born Rinning Park, Glasgow; died 6 Jan. Educated Bellahouston Academy, then entered the offices of Govan shipyard. Thoroughly disliking this work but enjoying evening art classes he decided to enrol full-time at Glasgow School of Art where he was taught by Archibald Dawson. Awarded Haldane Scholarship 1931, John H Burnett prize 1932, and in 1933 a maintenance scholarship to study for a fifth year. Also won an RSA Carnegie travelling scholarship. In 1938 joined the staff of the Glasgow School of Art but when this was closed in 1939 he took employment as a rivetter. Readmitted to the Art School 1945. After the retirement of Benno Schotz(qv) he presented the diploma students for five years. Associate Member, Society of British Sculptors, elected ARSA 1963. Designed figure panels on the wings of the National Library of Scotland. A portrait in marble was included in the touring exhibition of Scottish Sculpture, 1965. Exhibited regularly RSA.
**Bibl:** Gifford 184.

**BARR, Miss L** **fl 1898**
Perthshire landscape painter in oil. Lived at Tigh-na-Beithe, Birnam. Exhibited AAS.

**BARR, Miss Robina** **fl 1919-1938**
Glasgow sculptress. Studied Glasgow School of Art. Remained in Glasgow, exhibiting 19 works at the GI and 7 at the Walker Gallery, Liverpool between the above years from 26 Holyrood Crescent.

**BARR, Shona S M** **1965-**
Born Glasgow. Studied at Glasgow School of Art 1984-88, winning the landscape prize in 1987 and the Armour prize for still life in 1988. After graduating spent a year in Oslo on a scholarship from the Norwegian Research Council. Upon her return immediately exhibited at the RSA and RSW with a one-man exhibition in Edinburgh 1989 followed by London 1990 and 1993. Further studies Winchester School of Art 1991-2, although based in Barcelona. Her work is mainly based on landscape, often with flowers. Works with a water-based mixed media executed in the open air from which are developed abstracted oils in the studio, preferring strong colours. Also undertakes occasional portraiture and still life.

**BARR, Thomas** **1834-1903**
Perth architect. Best remembered for his design of the West Station, Union St, Dundee(1888-1889, dem 1960s).
Bibl: Bruce Walker & W S Gauldie, Architects and Architecture on Tayside, Dundee 1984, 138.

**BARR, Tom** **fl 1903-1926**
Rutherglen artist who moved to Glasgow in the 1920s and exhibited 3 times at the GI.

**BARR, William Beaton** **1867-1933**
Born Glasgow, Apr 26; died San Francisco, Feb 25. Painter in oil and occasional watercolours and illustrator. Trained Paisley Government School of Design 1881-85 at which time he was elected an artist member of Paisley Art Institute where he continued to exhibit annually throughout his life. Continued his training under Fra Newbery at Glasgow School of Art 1893-96. Committee member, Paisley Art Institute 1899-1914, serving alongside JE Christie(qv), Robert Cochran(qv), Archibald Kay(qv) and William Pratt(qv). Lived first in Paisley then in Glasgow, joining the Glasgow Art Club 1904, proceeding shortly afterwards to a further spell of training in Paris at the Academy Julian under Jean-Paul Lauren. His group portrait of 136 leading Paisley worthies (1910) is perhaps his most memorable Scottish work. Visited San Francisco 1912 where he eventually settled 1915. A rather neglected artist, better known and respected in USA than in his native land. A rare appearance of his work in UK was a painting sold at Sotheby's Feb 25, 1975. Exhibited RSA(3), RSW(3), GI(17), L(6) & AAS 1900-1906. Represented by 6 works in Paisley AG.
**Bibl:** Sandra Barr, 'William Barr - a Paisley School Artist', Univ of Glasgow dissertation, 1996.

**BARRIE, Mardi RSW** **1931-**
Born Kirkcaldy. Painter in oil and watercolour; landscape, semi-abstract. Studied Edinburgh University and Edinburgh College of Art 1948-1953 and taught at Broughton High School, Edinburgh. Paints oils in a loose, free style, using strong impasto and colour, reminiscent of Joan Eardley(qv). Accorded great success in Australia, Europe and South Africa as well as in the UK. First solo exhibition Edinburgh 1963. Elected RSW 1968. Regular exhibitor RSA & RSW since 1960, also AAS 1964-1966. Represented in SNGMA, RSA, Glasgow AG, Laing(Newcastle) AG, City of Edinburgh collection, Municipality of Ridderkerk (Holland), SAC, Duke of Edinburgh private collection.

**BARRIE, Muirhead** **fl 1900**
Glasgow painter; exhibited RSA(2) 1900.

**BARRIE, Stuart** **fl 1960-1965**
Engraver. Exhibited RSA 1960-1965.

**BARRON, Mrs** **fl 1893-1894**
Aberdeen painter of flower studies. Mother of Jeannie B(qv). Exhibited AAS from 46 Carden Place.

**BARRON, Alexander** **fl 1830-1855**
A minor Edinburgh portrait painter who exhibited regularly at the RSA 1830-1855.

**BARRON, Miss E J** **fl 1888-1889**
Amateur artist, possibly related to the Barron family of Inverness. Exhibited RA(4), all of them Scottish subjects, RSA(2) & GI(2), all from The Homestead, East Dulwich Road, London.

**BARRON, Gladys Caroline ARSA (née Logan)** **1885-1967**
Born India. Painter and sculptress; portrait busts mostly in bronze. Studied under Gertrude Bayes and St John's Wood School of Art. Moved to Inverness in the 1920s, marrying Dr Barron, editor and proprietor of the *Inverness Courier.* Portrait busts in bronzes of Dr Kurt Hahn, Sir Murdoch Donald, Sir Alexander McEwan, and a memorial plaque to Neil Gunn are in Inverness Town House. Frequent exhibitor at both RA & RSA. Her work may also be seen in the University libraries of Edinburgh and Aberdeen.
**Bibl:** Scotsman, Obituary, 19.1.67.

**BARRON, Isobel** **1893-1894**
Aberdeen painter in oil of flower pieces. Exhibited AAS, first from 67 Rose Street, and latterly 202 Union Grove.

**BARRON, James** **fl 1858-1862**
Edinburgh landscape painter predominantly of local views; exhibited RSA 1858 and 1862.

**BARRON, Miss Jeannie C** **fl 1894**
Amateur Aberdeen artist. Daughter of Mrs Barron(qv). Exhibited 2 still lifes from 46 Carden Place.

**BARRON, Miss W** **fl 1880-1882**
Amateur St Andrew artist; exhibited once at the RSA, once at the GI.

**BARRON, Westill A** **fl 1880-1885**
Portobello flower painter; exhibited twice at the RSA in 1880 and 1885.

**BARRON, William** **fl 1873**
Edinburgh landscape painter in oil; exhibited once at the RSA in 1873.

**BARRY, Andrew** **fl 1537-1538**
Painter and gilder who during 1537-1538 was working at Holyrood being paid 42s 'for painting and gilding pogybeer with reformyng and clenging of the hale gret armis' - presumably referring to the Royal Coat of Arms.
**Bibl:** Apted 26.

**BARRY, William** **fl 1883-1901**
Midlothian landscape painter in oil and watercolour. Working until 1883 from Leith before moving to Picardy Place, Edinburgh, where he shared a studio with J Michael Brown(qv). For some years successfully practised his art in Inverness, painting a large variety of striking if rather heavy Highland landscapes. His studies of mountain scenery, particularly Ben Nevis, are especially powerful. Exhibited 18 works at the RSA between the above dates.

**BARSON, Anthony** **fl 1957**
Edinburgh painter; exhibited RSA(3) 1957.

**BARTHOLOMEW, Miss Betty** **fl 1927-1931**
Amateur Edinburgh painter who exhibited 6 works at the RSA between the above years.

**BARTLETT, Miss Josephine Hoxie** **fl 1888-1899**
Painter in oil of landscape, still life and portraits. Exhibited a landscape of Glen Sannox in Arran at the RA in 1894, a portrait at the RSA in 1896, 4 other works at the RSA in 1897 and 1899, and a further 7 paintings thereafter, also AAS(2).

**BARTON, Ernest** **fl 1897**
Amateur painter. Exhibited GI(1).

**BATCHELOR, Graham Dallachie** **1943-**
Born Arbroath, studied Dundee College of Art 1961-67. Awarded Keith Prize. Travelled extensively in Western Europe and Russia studying the techniques of the Old Masters. Lives in Glasgow. Exhibited 2 still lifes at the RSA 1966.

**BATCHELOR, Robert (Bob) William** **1928-**
Born Georgetown, Guyana. After schooling in Guyana he enrolled at Gray's School of Art 1946-50 and Moray House, Edinburgh. Remained in Scotland embarking on a teaching career which took him to Alloa, Clackmannanshire, Macduff, Banffshire and Harlaw Academy 1966-86, Aberdeen. Became a full-time painter and printmaker 1985; landscape, flowers, interiors, portraits. The flower paintings are bold, colourful and powerful evocations of sunshine and exotica. "In Bob's work", wrote the botanist Gordon Smith, "the effects of a tropical childhood burst through the cold muted colours of a temperate northern climate". Exhibited RA, RSA between 1955 and 1988 and regularly at the AAS since 1965, elected President 1990. Represented in Aberdeen AG, Manchester AG.

**BATE, Miss Emily Spence** **fl 1893-1908**
Glasgow painter in oil. Moved to London c1900. Exhibited RA(1), RSA(1), RBA(1), SWA(5), GI(3) & L(1).

**BATHGATE, George** **fl 1880-1889**
Edinburgh painter in oil; portraits, interiors, street scenes. Brother of Hattie Ellen B(qv). Exhibited four figures at the RA and eleven at the RSA between 1881 and 1886, including two continental scenes, one in Munich and the other in Venice; also RBA(1) & L(6).

**BATHGATE, Miss Hattie Ellen** **fl 1886-1914**
Edinburgh painter in oil of flowers, fruit and occasional equestrian portraits. Sister of George B(qv). Exhibited 'A Summer Day in June' at the RA in 1888 and two works at the RSA in 1886, with four more thereafter; also Liverpool 1911-1914.

**BATHGATE, John** **1949-**
Born Lauder. Semi-abstract landscape artist, based mainly on Scottish subjects, executed in the manner of Japanese prints. Exhibited RSW 1989 from East Lothian.

**BATMAN, L** **fl 1904**
Amateur Glasgow painter; exhibited one work at the Walker Gallery, Liverpool.

**BATTEN, Mark Wilfred PRBS RBA** **1905-c1965**
Born Kirkcaldy 21 Jly. Painter in oil and sculptor in stone, marble and granite. Trained Slade School of Art and Chelsea School of Art under Jowett. Until 1934 he painted in oils but thereafter worked almost exlusively as a sculptor. Published *Stone Sculptor by Direct Carving* (1957), *Direct Carving in Stone* (1966). Elected ARBS 1950, FRBS 1960, PRBS 1959-1961, RBA 1962. The last years of his life were spent at Dallington, Sussex. Exhibited widely after 1936, at the RA, RSA(2) in 1953 and 1954, GI & Paris Salon.

**BATTY, Derek** **fl 1978**
Sculptor from West Lothian; exhibited RSA(1).

**BATTY, Miss J** **fl 1875**
Glasgow landscape painter in oil; exhibited RSA(1).

**BAUER, Edmund** **fl 1872**
Aberdeen landscape painter in oil; exhibited RSA(1).

**BAXTER, Douglas Gordon RSW SSA** **1920-**
Born Kirkcaldy 6 Oct. Landscape and wild-life painter in oil, watercolour, pastel and gouache. Studied at Edinburgh College of Art 1946-1950; received a travelling scholarship enabling him to go to Paris in 1948, Scandinavia in 1949, Spain 1950. From a base in Musselburgh taught part-time at Loretto School and is an occasional exhibitor at the RSA, although not since 1962. Elected SSA 1961 and RSW but resigned shortly afterwards. Represented in City of Edinburgh collection.

**BAXTER, Mrs E** **fl 1888**
Amateur Forfar painter; exhibited RSA(1).

**BAXTER, Mrs Ena** **fl c1970-**
Flower painter of Fochabers, Morayshire; business executive. Studied at Gray's School of Art under D M Sutherland(qv) and Robert Sivell(qv) in the 1940s. Art Teacher at Fochabers Academy. Married Gordon Baxter 1952 and joined the flourishing family business. After an early interest in portraiture turned exclusively to flower painting. Most often her pictures are of cut flowers in vases executed with a fine eye for colour and delicate form, similar in style to that of her friend Cecil Kennedy(qv) whom she had first met in the 1970s. Business and family commitments severely curtailed her output until the late 1970s after which her output began to increase. Frst solo exhibition at Duff House 1998.

**BAXTER Mrs Frances W** **fl 1872-1888**
Broughty Ferry painter in oil; figurative subjects. Exhibited RSA 1872-1873, and again in 1888.

**BAXTER, Graeme William** **1958-**
Painter of golfing subjects. Trained Glasgow School of Art. Exhibition Perth 1988. Managed by his father, his accurate if rather photographic depictions of golf courses and golfing scenes have achieved international recognition. Prints of his work are extremely popular. Official artist for the Open, Ryder Cup, Professional Golfers' Association, Solheim Cup, President's Cup, World Championship. Represented in Muirfield GC and Augusta (USA).

**BAXTER, John Jnr** **c1732-1798**
Celebrated Scottish architect and draughtsman. Associated with Sir James Clerk of Penicuik in the design of Penicuik House, Midlothian

(c1761, gutted by fire 1899). His other main claims to attention are the fine Parish Church at Fochabers (1798) and its contemporary flanking blocks which fit in so well with the new town, laid out on a grid-pattern by command of the Duke of Gordon, although the remaining streets were not completed until some years later, also the Old Merchant Hall in Edinburgh and Galloway House (1730-50). Involved in the building of Haddo House for the 2nd Earl of Aberdeen (1732). Visited Rome 1761 where he became a member of the Academia di San Luca. Designed the Cowgate Chapel, Edinburgh (now St Patrick's (RC) (1771-4) and was responsible for major reconstruction to the Tron church (1785-7) while in the Assembly Rooms he executed the large roses over the chandeliers and the fluted Corinthian pilasters (1796). May also have been responsible for Mortonhall House (1769). Friend of Alexander Runciman(qv) whose profile portrait he painted, now in NGS.
**Bibl:** Mungo Campbell, 'The Line of Tradition', Nat Galls of Scotland, Ex cat, 1993; Dunbar 110; Gifford 38,168,174,234,282, 448,474,490.

**BAXTER, John Jnr** **fl 1769-1787**
Architect, son of John Baxter(qv). Visited Italy, where he acted as sculpture dealer on behalf of Sir James Clerk. Designed the Old Merchants' Hall, Hunter Square, Edinburgh, and additions to Ellon Castle, Aberdeenshire 1781-1787 for the 3rd Earl of Aberdeen. Also designed Gordon Castle, Morayshire, built for Alexander, 4th Duke of Gordon 1769-1782; dem. 1961. A watercolour of Ellon castle is in NLS.
**Bibl:** Dunbar 124.

**BAXTER, John** **fl 1886-1887**
Edinburgh landscape painter in watercolour; exhibited twice at the RSA 1886-1887.

**BAXTER, Lawrence** **fl 1975**
Midlothian painter in oil; semi-abstract in the current idiom. Exhibits RSA intermittently since 1975.

**BAXTER, Miss Muriel F** **fl 1927**
Amateur painter from 134 Meadowpark Street, Dennistoun, Glasgow; exhibited once in Liverpool.

**BAXTER Nellie (Mrs John Kippen)** **fl c1895-**
Dundee textile designer and book illustrator. During her early working life lived in Tayport with her sister Rosa when she formulated a plan to open a school of embroidery in association with Elizabeth Burt. Studied under John Duncan(qv) and became a member of The Evergreen circle 1895-97. Contributed head pieces and tail pieces to several issues and one full page decoration (Vol IV: *The Book of Winter,* p5: Almanac). Executed Celtic motifs for John Duncan's murals in Ramsay Lodge, Edinburgh. Exhibited occasionally at the Dundee Graphic Arts Association 1898 until her marriage in the early 1900s. A finely produced large appliqué embroidery, signed HK, is in the possession of the Dundee Art Society.
**Bibl:** Irwin 406.

**BAXTER, William C** **fl 1892-1897**
Amateur Hamilton artist; exhibited GI(1) from Comrie Cottage; also at the opening of Hamilton Liberal Club 1892.

**BAXTER, William Melville** **1902-1974**
Born Greenock. Son of a journeyman painter. Part-time painter in oils and watercolour; talented violinist and professional precision engineer. Employed at the RN Torpedo factory, Greenock and Admiralty Argyll works, Alexandria. Painted mainly landscapes, often in the Clyde area. Represented in Greenock AG.

**BAXTER, William P** **1931-**
Born Aberdeen. Painter in oil and watercolour, and printmaker. Portraits, figurative works and landscape. Studied Grays School of Art 1948-50 and, with the aid of an Andrew Grant scholarship, continued his studies at Edinburgh College of Art. Exhibits AAS.

**BAYES, Miss Jessie RMS** **fl c1920-1950**
Miniature painter and mural decorator. Lived in London and in Edinburgh. Exhibited RA, RMS, SSA & widely abroad including the Paris Salon.

**BAYNE, J** **fl 1892-1908**
Miniature painter from Bridge of Allan. Moved to Edinburgh 1895, thence to Burntisland 1908. Exhibited portrait miniatures on ivory at the RSA in 1900, 1902, 1903 and 1908, also GI(2). Recorded by neither Foskett nor Long.

**BAYNE, James** **fl 1867-1910**
Edinburgh landscape painter in oil and watercolour. Exhibited carefully produced pictorial scenes and tightly composed watercolours at the RSA 1867-1879.
**Bibl:** Halsby 248.

**BEALE, Miss Evelyn** **1870-1944**
Sculptress and potter. Trained Slade School. Moved from Edinburgh to North Shields 1907 and the following year returned to Scotland to live in Portobello before moving to Rothesay 1910, finally settling at 15 Woodside Terrace, Glasgow, c1918. Exhibited intermittently RSA(18) from a Glasgow address 1904-1931, specialising in memorial panels and medallions; also GI(36), RSW(1), AAS(2) & L(31).

**BEAR, George Telfer** **1876-1973**
Born Greenock, 30 Oct. Painter in oil, pastel and watercolour; flowers, landscape and architectural subjects. Trained Glasgow College of Art under Fra Newbery(qv) before spending several years in Saskatchewan. Produced many powerful charcoal and wash drawings more highly thought of during his lifetime than they have been since. Married 1906 and in the early 1920s returned to Scotland settling first in Whistlefield, nr. Garelochhead, before moving to Kirkcudbright. At this time he resumed a friendship with James Kay(qv) as well as acquiring new friends among his neighbours including E A Hornel(qv), Charles Oppenheimer(qv), E A Taylor(qv) and Taylor's wife, Jessie M King(qv). In 1931 was one of six artists to exhibit as 'Les Peintres Écossais' at the Galeries Georges Petit in Paris. Member of the Society of Eight(qv) and influenced by his contact there with Cadell(qv). In 1901 moved from Glasgow, where he had been an active council member of the Arts Club, to Kilmacolm remaining there until the death of his wife. His principal works include 'Langsyde Street', 'The Green Scarf', 'Day Dreams', 'Nocturne' and 'Mill on Green Water'. Exhibited regularly RSA(32), GI(54), AAS(2), Royal Cambrian Academy & overseas. Represented in Paris (Louvre), Glasgow AG, Greenock AG, Edinburgh City Collections.
**Bibl:** Hardie 130,139.

**BEARDSWORTH, Ruth** **fl 1981-1988**
Aberdeen figurative painter, her subjects often contain a macabre element. Trained at Gray's School of Art, Aberdeen. Exhibited AAS regularly between the above years from 5 Chattan Place.

**BEATON, Catriona** **fl 1977**
Aberdeen sculptress. Exhibited 'Wood Map' at the AAS from 70 Ashvale Place.

**BEATON, Miss Penelope ARSA RSW** **1886-1963**
Born and died Edinburgh. Painter in oil and watercolour of landscape, flowers and genre, occasional embroiderer. Trained Edinburgh College of Art, gaining diploma 1917 and joining the staff 1919. During the interval taught at Hamilton Academy where among her colleagues were two whose work had a considerable influence on her own: Donald Moody(qv) and A B Thompson(qv). Mary Armour(qv) was one of her pupils. Especially fond of painting east coast harbours and Iona. Her work was included in the Exhibition of Scottish Genre Painting 1700-1952, and when teaching commitments allowed, occasionally at the RSA. Sometimes likened to her contemporary Anne Redpath(qv). During mid-career her watercolour painting was influenced by the expressionist style of Gillies(qv) although her colours were gentler. By the 1940s she acquired a more regulated style. Working member of the Modern Embroidery Society, exhibited with the Society, RSA 1934. Elected RSW 1952, ARSA 1957. Exhibited RSA(102), RSW(1), GI(4), AAS(1) & L(1).
**Bibl:** Halsby 219; Macmillan [SA], 332.

**BEATON, Robert J** **fl 1898**
Amateur Glasgow painter; exhibited GI(1).

**BEATON, Rosemary** **1950-**
Glasgow painter of portraits and figurative studies. Trained Glasgow School of Art 1981-86, including a scholarship to Hospitalfield 1984, the year that she won the National Portrait Award. Painter of rare distinction. Commissioned to paint the portraits of Sir Robin Day for the NPG and Lord Provost Gray for the City of Glasgow 1985. Exhibited at the Edinburgh Festival 1987. Member of the Glasgow Group(qv). Represented in NPG.

**BEATON (BETOUN, BEATOUN), William** **?-1620**
Scottish embroiderer. The King's Embroiderer in Scotland, possibly responsible for the panel bearing the royal coat of arms, now in the Royal Museum of Scotland. Among his commissions were items of clothing for Lady Ogilvie 1582. Believed also to have undertaken heraldic work. Other embroiderers working in Edinburgh at the time include **James (Sr)**, **James (Jr)** and **William WHITE**, all of whom became burgesses; also **Alexander BARNES, Hew TOD, Adam GORDON, Thomas FORRESTER** and **Robert PORTEOUS** (who undertook the Royal Arms for the High Court House 1661).
**Bibl:** Margaret Swain 43-44.

**BEATON, Wilson** **fl 1894-1902**
Glasgow painter; exhibited 10 works at the GI between the above dates. Represented in Glasgow AG.

**BEATSON, Helena (Lady Oakeley)** **1763-1839**
Scottish amateur painter usually in crayon. Niece and pupil of Katherine Read(qv), whose manner she copied. She had a precocious talent, exhibiting at the RA 1774 when aged 11 and again in London the following year. In 1777 she went with her aunt to India where she married and subsequently appears to have abandoned painting. Her husband became Sir Charles Oakeley Bt 1790.
**Bibl:** Sir William Foster, British Artists in India 1760-1820, Walpole Society, XIX (1931), 64; Waterhouse, 44.

**BEATTIE, Alexander B** **fl 1923-1937**
Painter in oil of north-east landscapes. Lived in various towns of the north-east including Elgin, Huntly 1931 and latterly 262 Union Street, Aberdeen. During the above years exhibited regularly at the AAS and in 1927 at the GI.

**BEATTIE, Charles** **fl 1863-1869**
Aberdeen landscape painter in oil; exhibited RSA in 1863, 1867-69. Possibly the same **Charles F BEATTIE** who between 1890-1931 exhibited landscapes, historical compositions and occasional portraits at the AAS from 19 Richmond Street and, in 1931, from 14 St Mary Street, Peterhead.

**BEATTIE, Charles J Jnr** **fl 1890-1902**
Aberdeen painter in oil of local landscapes. Probably son of Charles F Beattie(qv). In 1890 was living at 19 Richmond Street moving in 1900 to 8 Wallfield Place. Exhibited Aberdeenshire scenes at the AAS regularly between the above years.

**BEATTIE, E** **fl 1878**
Glasgow painter in oil; figurative subjects. Exhibited RSA(1).

**BEATTIE, George** **1810-1872**
Edinburgh architect. Partner in George Beattie & Son. Brother of Thomas Hamilton B(qv) and **George Lennox BEATTIE**(1862-?). Exhibited a number of important designs for buildings at the RSA 1867-72, also posthumously 1873.
**Bibl:** Gifford.

**BEATTIE, Miss Jane** **fl 1844-1855**
Edinburgh painter in watercolour of flowers and still life. Exhibited four paintings at the RSA between the above dates.

**BEATTIE, Reuben** **fl 1902**
Aberdeen painter in oil of local landscapes. Exhibited AAS from 22 Thistle Street.

**BEATTIE, Thomas** **c1861-1933**
Edinburgh architectural modeller who worked at the Dean Studio; exhibited once at the RSA. Specialised in richly modelled ceilings. Worked with Robert Lorimer(qv) since the beginning of the latter's career, often in conjunction with **Sam WILSON**. Responsible for the carved friezes and octagonal piers in the Scottish National War Memorial; also the plaster centrepiece in the Auditorium of the Usher Hall.
**Bibl:** Gifford 100,262; Peter Savage, Lorimer and the Edinburgh Craft Designers, Edinburgh 1980, passim.

**BEATTIE, William** **fl 1829-1867**
Sculptor; portrait busts and figures. Exhibited RA 1829-1864 including an embossed silver plaque 'Knox admonishing Mary Queen of Scots', a model of Lord Bacon (1844), and a bronze medallion of Lord Elcho (1863). Most of the time he lived in London but working in Edinburgh 1839 and again 1858. Exhibited RSA(3), in 1856, 1858 and 1867.

**BEATTIE, William** **fl 1877-1883**
Glasgow landscape painter in oil; exhibited RSA in 1877, 1878 and 1883, also GI(3).

**BEATTIE, William Francis FRSA** **fl 1912-1914**
Edinburgh sculptor; exhibited RSA(2). Exhibited a sketch for Hawick War Memorial 1914.

**BEATTIE, William Hamilton** **1840-1898**
Edinburgh based architect, specialising in hotels; partner in firm George Beattie & Son. Brother of George B(qv) and George Lennox B. Responsible for the North British Hotel (1895), the Calton Hotel (1898), the internal remodelling of 13 George St in Renaissance style, 18 George St (1879), Jenners (1893-5), the Albert Buildings - built as the Albert Gallery - 22-30 Shandwick Place (1876-7) and the Braids Hills Hotel (1886). Exhibited RSA 1880-1896 including designs for a new North Berwick Railway Hotel and head offices, 1896.
**Bibl:** Gifford 71,72,231,285,299,301,310,311,312,380,419,447, 500,624,644 (pl 106).

**BEATTIE-SCOTT, John** **c1865-1925**
Obscure Aberdeen painter in watercolour and etcher; local views and coastal scenes. Second son of John Scott, barber, he worked from 57 Osborne Place before retiring to Thornton, Fyvie. Painted in a tight, rather garish style. His work is now seldom seen. A catalogue of his etchings appeared in 1917 and published a play 1924. President of the Aberdeen Art Guild. Most of his works were of local scenes and his etchings were weak. Exhibited RA(2) & RSA(2).
**Bibl:** Halsby 248.

**BEATY, Mrs Moira** **1922-**
Born Prestwick, Ayrshire. Painter in oil and watercolour; still-life, landscape and floral studies - but latterly preoccupied with genre painting, often with children, executed in the 'direct' Glasgow manner. Educated Hutchesons Girls' GS, Glasgow and one year under Hugh Adam Crawford(qv), alongside Joan Eardley(qv), before the onset of WW2 intervened. From 1942 to 1945 was an enigma code breaker at Bletchley. Resumed her studies at Glasgow School of Art 1947. Married R Stuart Beaty(qv) 1951 and moved to Hawick remaining there until retiring to Dalbeattie 1989. Her work shows the lasting influence of the Glasgow School, Joan Eardley and the Impressionist movement. Elected SSWA 1974. Exhibited RSA 1955 and 1965.

**BEATY, R Stuart ARBS FSA** **fl 1954-1958**
Born Saltcoats, Ayrshire. Sculptor, mainly in bronze and wood; textile designer. Educated Ardrossan Academy. During WW2 served with the RAF. With the advent of peace entered Glasgow School of Art, studying sculpture under Benno Schotz(qv). Awarded Carnegie scholarship and as a result visited Mexico, studying pre-Columbian sculpture. Joined the knitwear company Pringle of Scotland 1951 becoming design director and remaining with them until 1974. Commissioned work includes a suite of 19 decorative panels in wood for the Scottish Development Agency, a relief carving in wood Lion Rampant for Hawick rugby club, and two three-figure groups Baptism and Resurrection, for St Joseph's Church, Selkirk. Influenced by Henry Moore and Brancusi, his forms have smooth, polished surfaces imbuing them with tactile as well as visual qualities. Cordelia Oliver refers to his 'consummate skills...the matching of a witty idea to the perfect form in the right material'. Elected ARBS 1980, FSA (Scot) 1984. Moved from Hawick to Dalbeattie 1989.

Exhibited figurative works at the RSA 1954-1958. Represented in Birmingham City AG.

**BEAUMONT, Bina J L** **fl 1893**
Amateur Aberdeen painter. Exhibited a portrait and a flower piece at the AAS from Blackhall Cottage.

**BECKHAM, James Sinclair** **fl 1873**
Portobello oil painter, figurative subjects; exhibited once at the RSA.

**BEDGOOD, Miss Jane McG** **fl 1928**
Amateur Renfrew painter; exhibited GI(1).

**BEECH, Alexander** **fl c1735-d1749**
Edinburgh painter. Son of Joseph Beech(qv). All that is known of him is that he was elected Burgess of Edinburgh in 1738 and enrolled as a member of the Incorporation of St Mary's 1739. In 1742 he took as an apprentice George Wilson. No recorded work of his remains.

**BEECH, Joseph** **c1670-1724**
Painter. Son of a perfumer, he was made a Burgess of Edinburgh as an apprentice in 1695 and also a member of the Incorporation of St Mary's from 1695-1724, having become a Guild brother of Edinburgh 1699. The same year he painted a landscape for St Mary's Chapel, Edinburgh. In 1700 took as his first apprentice John Reoch (Beech), possibly his brother, and in 1702 he married. Other work was of a more pedestrian nature such as painting the aisle and door of Colinton Church (1705). In 1707 took as another pupil J Robertson.
**Bibl:** Apted 26.

**BEENS, Mrs F S** **fl 1830-1834**
Edinburgh portrait painter. Exhibited RSA in 1830(2) and 1834.

**BEGBIE, Patrick** **fl 1770-1780**
Edinburgh engraver. Lived at Blyth's Close, Castle Hill 1773-1774. In 1770 he engraved a bookplate for a Dr John Boswell. Appears to have left Edinburgh and settled in London c1776, residing at least until 1780 at Dukes Court, St Martin's Lane. While in London he engraved a number of bookplates, some recorded by Fincham.
**Bibl:** Bushnell; H W Fincham, Artists and Engravers of British and American Bookplates, 1897.

**BEGG, Charles** **fl 1950s**
Painter. Exhibited two pictures at the RSA 1956.

**BEGG, David** **fl 1860-1869**
Glasgow landscape painter in oil; exhibited RSA two pictures in 1860 and 1869.

**BEGG, F S** **fl 1970**
Thurso painter. Exhibited two pictures at the RSA 1970.

**BEGG, Ian McKerron** **1925-**
Edinburgh architect. Unusually imaginative in his designs although generally directed towards comparatively modern developments. Has exhibited regularly at the RSA since 1964. Restored the ruin of Muckrach Castle, nr Dulnain Bridge, originally built 1598 (1978-85); built the tower house Ravens' Craig, Plockton (1987-89) and further down the same hill, the earlier and more commonplace Craig (1963). His most recent work is the Nordic Scanda hotel, built in the Scottish baronial style, completed 1989.
**Bibl:** Gifford, H & I, 54,95,549

**BEGG, James L** **fl 1896-1909**
Glasgow painter in oil and watercolour; exhibited twice at the RSA in 1907 and 1909; also RSW(1), GI(7) & L(1).

**BEGG, Miss Jane P** **fl 1892-1906**
Paisley artist moved to Glasgow c1897. Exhibited 11 works at the GI & AAS(1).

**BEGG, John FRIBA** **1864-1937**
Architect. Trained with H.J. Blanc(qv) in Edinburgh. Honorable mention for the Pugin Prize 1889, winning it the following year and winning the Ashpital Prize 1891. Worked with Alfred Waterhouse of London. Runner-up for the Soane Medallion 1892, winning the silver medal 1894. Outstanding draughtsman who collaborated closely with Robert Lorimer(qv), drawing several of his RSA exhibits including the first garden layout scheme for Earlshall 1896. Worked in South Africa but returned to Edinburgh during the Boer War. Appointed consulting agent for Bombay 1901 and to the Government of India 1908-21. Entered into a partnership with Lorne Campbell in Edinburgh 1921 and the next year was appointed Head of the School of Architecture, Edinburgh College of Art. Responsible, with Campbell, for the Edinburgh Dental Hospital(1925-7).
**Bibl:** Gifford 179,501; Peter Savage, Lorimer and the Edinburgh Craft Designers, Edinburgh 1980, 7,11,13,27,40,49.

**BEGG, Mrs Marjory** **fl 1949-1952**
Landscape painter; exhibited RSA between the above years.

**BEGG, Mary Strachan** **fl 1900s**
Painter in oil, also carver and embroiderer. Member of a family of seven, all five sisters being accomplished artists. Mary was the only one to receive formal training, attending morning classes at Glasgow School of Art from the age of sixteen. She specialised in embroidery, a silk tea-cosy being in the collection of Glasgow AG.
**Bibl:** Burkhauser 166.

**BEGG, Nita (Mrs William Gallacher)** **c1920-?**
Born Mount Vernon, Lanarkshire. Painter in oil and acrylic; portraiture and still life. Fascinated by perspective in the anatomy of the human figure. Attended Laurel Bank School for Girls before studying drawing and painting at Glasgow School of Art 1938-42 under Hugh Adam Crawford(qv), and Hospitalfield House, Arbroath, under James Cowie(qv) 1946-47. Launched herself upon a full-time painting career and in 1949 married the Glasgow portrait painter William Gallacher(qv). Member of the Glasgow Society of Women Artists 1960, winning the Gertrude Annie Lauder Award 1962. Member SSWA. Exhibited regularly RSA from 1954, also GI, SWA and various provincial galleries. Represented in Glasgow AG, Royal collection.

**BEGG, Robert William CBE** **1922-**
Born 19 Feb. Glasgow painter in oil and pastel; administrator. Portraits, landscape and still-life. Educated Glasgow University and at evening classes, Glasgow School of Art, subsequently becoming a governor and eventually chairman. Married Sheena Begg(qv). President of RGI 1990. Exhibited RSA 1980-87, occasionally RSW.

**BEGG, Sheena Margaret** **1921-**
Born 27 Nov. Glasgow painter in oil, gouache; flowers, still life, landscape and wildlife. Married Robert William B(qv). Exhibited RSA 1981 and more regularly at the RSW.

**BEHENNA, Mrs Kathleen (?Katherine)** **fl 1897**
Born Scotland. Miniaturist and illustrator. Probably left Scotland at an early age as we first learn of her as a pupil in New York where she studied under George Forest Brush. Proceeded to Paris to study under Febvre. Returning to England, she was elected to the RSM in London as well as to the Art Students League in New York, and eventually to membership of the RWS in London. Exhibited 2 portraits at the RA in 1897, one of them of HRH Princess Louise, Marchioness of Lorne. The present whereabouts of her major works are unknown.

**BEHRENS, Reinhard** **1951-**
Born Hanover, Germany. Painter in oil, watercolour and acrylic; etcher. Sometimes uses lead pencil with colour highlights on board and acrylic, with layers of thin oil paint glazes on top. Trained Hamburg College of Art 1971- 1978 and in 1979 came to Edinburgh as a postgraduate student at the Edinburgh College of Art. He remained there 1982-84 as part-time teacher and in 1987 moved to Pittenweem, Fife to become a full-time artist. Has exhibited widely in Scotland since 1982. In 1980 he received the Andrew Grant Major Award of the ECA, Benno Schotz Award 1983; and the Educational Institute of Scotland Award of the RSA 1986. Exhibits regularly RSA. Represented in Glasgow AG, Royal Edinburgh Hospital, Eden Court Theatre, Inverness, Department of Ancient Monuments, Countryside Commission for Scotland.

**BELFRAGE, Miss Elaine** **fl 1937-39**
Amateur Edinburgh artist of 14, Eglington Crescent; exhibited RSA between the above years.

**BELKNAP, A W** **fl 1978**
Painter in oil. Exhibited a figurative work at the AAS from Craigentath, Blairs, by Aberdeen.

**BELL, Mrs A M** **fl 1845-1848**
Edinburgh watercolour painter of portraits and figure studies. Exhibited 15 drawings at the RSA during the above period.

**BELL, A P** **fl 1893**
Aberdeen amateur artist in oil. Exhibited Tilquhilly Castle, nr Banchory and a coastal scene at the AAS, from 46 Holburn Road.

**BELL, Alexander PRMS PRCP** **fl c1750-c1780**
Engraver. Lived in Edinburgh. The most notable examples of his work are 'Sir Hew Dalrymple of Drumnor (1652-1737) Lord President', after a painting attributed to Sir John Medina; 'Sir George Drummond (1687-1766), Lord Provost of Edinburgh' after a painting by Sir George Chalmers; 'Andrew Duncan (1744-1828), President of the Royal Medical Society and of the Royal College of Physicians', after David Martin; and 'Alexander Duncan', after Allan Ramsay.
**Bibl:** Bushnell.

**BELL, Alexander Carlyle** **fl 1847-1893**
Painter in watercolour and occasionally oils; landscape and topographical. Appears to have been quite prolific and to have spent most of his time in London although all recorded exhibits were in Scotland, the majority being of Scottish subjects. Exhibited three Swiss scenes in 1866 and again in 1867 (from a Tranent address), and a fine study 'Ben Slioch at evening' 1868. One of his last exhibits was a study of Traquair House, Perthshire 1884. Also exhibited RA 1884-1889 (drawings of Ben Cruachan and Santa Maria Salute, and 'Loch Rannoch, with Schiehallion in the distance'); RSA 1847-84, ROI(8), RBA(4), GI(2) & L(4).

**BELL, Alison F FRSA** **1961-**
Born Scotland, 17 Jne. Painter in watercolour and gouache; printmaker, often on silk. Trained Dundee College of Education and Duncan of Jordanstone 1970-74. Art teacher 1978-92; thereafter lectures part-time including workshops on silk painting. Her work is generally small scale often employing ancient, mythological symbolism, but also inspired by natural forms and the Scottish countryside. Solo exhibitions in England, Scotland since 1993. Exhibits RSA. Lives and works in north Ayrshire.

**BELL, Andrew** **1726-1810**
Born Edinburgh; died Lauriston, Jne 10. Engraver. Based in Edinburgh, he studied under Richard Cooper. Married the daughter of the painter John Scougal(qv). His work was mostly book illustrations. Supposedly began by engraving names and crests on plates and dog collars. Early in his career he became friendly with Smellie, founder of the *Encyclopaedia Britannica.* Subsequently became its proprietor (with Colin MacFarquhar), amassing a small fortune in the process. He did important engravings for Smellie's translation of Buffon in 1782. Although suffering serious physical disability he continued to teach apprentices, the best known being Francis Legat(qv). The stories told of him in Kay's *Portraits* indicate that Bell was a popular and much loved figure in Edinburgh society. His portrait, by George Watson(qv), is in the SNPG.
**Bibl:** Brydall 202-3; Bushnell; Butchart 15-6,18,37.

**BELL, Ann C Beatson** **fl 1896-1901**
Edinburgh watercolour painter of portraits and figures. Exhibited twice at the RSA in 1896 and 1899 and three more thereafter.

**BELL, Arthur George** **1849-1916**
Edinburgh oil painter; landscape, often in winter. Exhibited RSA 1879-1883.

**BELL, Benjamin** **fl 1926**
Engraver and etcher; exhibited an etching at the RSA 1926.

**BELL, Sir Charles** **1774-1842**
Born Edinburgh; died Hallow Park, nr Worcester, 8 Apr. Amateur painter in oil and watercolour; neurologist and teacher. Endowed with a brilliant and enquiring mind. As a boy studied drawing with David Allan(qv) and as a medical student at Edinburgh University was a pupil of his brother John Bell and of the philosopher Dugald Stuart. Arriving in London as a young scientist, he embarked upon a series of lectures on the subject of anatomy and the portrayal of expression for artists. Wilkie persuaded a number of his academy friends to attend. The lectures were subsequently published as *Essays in the Anatomy of Expression* (1806); in the third edition (1845) the relationship between Wilkie and Bell is recorded, Wilkie contributing one of the illustrations. Bell warned his students against reliance on the posed academy figure on the one hand and blind imitation of the antique on the other. He argued that a knowledge of the muscles of expression and the nerves controlling them was essential for painting emotion and that this must be combined with observation of emotional states. The antique should only be used as "a corrective of his taste, after having laid a sure ground work in the study of anatomy and a close observation of nature...in natural action there always is a consent and symmetry in every part. When a man clenches his fist in passion the other arm does not lie in elegant relaxation. When the face is stern and vindictive, there is energy in the whole frame. When a man rises from his seat in impassioned gesture, there pervades every limb and feature a certain tension and straining". Wilkie's whole development as a painter was much affected by these lectures. It is possible that Bell would also have been known to Geikie(qv) and Nasmyth(qv). When reviewing the art of the twentieth century it is salutary to consider Bell's comment 'it is only when the enthusiasm of an artist is strong enough to counteract his repugnance to scenes in themselves harsh and unpleasant, when he is careful to seek all occasions of storing his mind with images of human passion and suffering, when he philosophically studies the mind and affections as well as the body and features of man, that he can truly deserve the name of a painter'. Several of Bell's watercolour landscapes are in the British Museum. A sketch of three reclining figures executed in pen, pencil and wash is in the NGS.
**Bibl:** Sir Charles Bell, Essays in the Anatomy of Expression 1806; Letters to Sir Charles Bell selected from his correspondence with his brother George Joseph Bell 1870; Irwin 167, 170-171; Macmillan [GA], 157-9 et passim.

**BELL, David** **fl 1840s**
Architect, specialising in railways, often in collaboration with the engineer John Miller. Considering that the designs for both the Waverley and Haymarket(1840) stations are attributed to him remarkably little is known of his life and career.
**Bibl:** Gifford 290,369.

**BELL, David S** **fl 1971-1986**
Sculptor. Worked in Monifieth, Angus. Exhibited RSA 1971- 1973, and again in 1986.

**BELL, Mrs E M** **fl 1893**
Amateur Stirling artist; exhibited GI(1) 1893.

**BELL, Eileen** **fl 1955**
Amateur artist. A painting of wild flowers was exhibited at the RSA 1955.

**BELL, Miss Elizabeth H** **fl 1881**
Broughty Ferry watercolour painter; landscape. Exhibited RSA(1).

**BELL, Eric Sinclair** **1884-?**
Born Warrington 1 Sep. Architect and etcher of architectural subjects. Trained Glasgow School of Art, also in Stirling, Aberdeen and London. Apprenticed as an architect under Sir J J Burnet(qv). Based in Stirling, he exhibited twice at the RSA (1920), also in the USA & GI(1).

**BELL, Miss F** **fl 1868**
Edinburgh painter in oil of animal subjects especially dogs; sister of Miss J C Bell(qv), related to A C Bell(qv). Exhibited RSA 1868.

**BELL, Harold Fraser** **fl 1880-1892**
Edinburgh landscape painter in oil. Exhibited RSA(21) 1881-1890 & GI(7).

**BELL, Miss Helen P** **fl 1934**
Exhibited two paintings at the RSA in 1934 from a Glasgow address.

**BELL, Henry Johnson** **1863-1925**
Edinburgh landscape painter in oil and watercolour. Exhibited 6 paintings at the RA in 1894, 1895 and 1899, including a fine broadly painted study of Eilan Donan Castle; also RSA(20) 1887-1916, generally Scottish landscapes and rural scenes; also GI(11), regularly at the AAS 1893-1921 & L(2). His last years were spent in Dundee.

**BELL, J C** **fl 1860**
Painter in oil; exhibited five pieces at the RSA in 1860 from an Edinburgh address.

**BELL, J C** **fl 1927**
Dumfriess-shire artist. Exhibited a landscape at the RSA 1927.

**BELL, James Torrington** **1898-1970**
Painter in oil; landscape, principally in Angus and surrounding countryside. Native of Leven, Fife. Son of a bank manager, he served as a lieutenant in the Royal Navy during WWI. Combined being a bank manager with the practice of art. Attended Edinburgh College of Art as a part-time student. A keen golfer and JP. Favourite subjects were Highland scenes, often with cattle and horses and sometimes rustic buildings. Demonstrated a high degree of professional balance and harmony in composition in a strongly naturalistic vein, if a trifle bland. Commissioned by the County of Angus to paint 'The Valley of Strathmore' as a wedding gift to the Queen. Some of his best work remains in his branch of the National Bank of Scotland, Carnoustie. Exhibited RA(10), RSA(15) 1934-1969, also GI, Royal Cambrian Academy & AAS(1). Angus Library and Museum have 3 of Bell's paintings in their collection: 'Carnoustie Links' (1955), 'Carnoustie House' (1962) and 'The Braes of Downie' (1938).

**BELL, J Brownridge** **fl 1885-1887**
Edinburgh watercolour painter of townscapes; exhibited RSA(2).

**BELL, J Currie** **fl 1904-1929**
Edinburgh portrait and figure painter; oil and pastel. Exhibited RSA 1904-5, but continued painting until at least 1929, generally portraits and studies of attractive young ladies.

**BELL, Miss Jane Campbell (Clara)** **fl 1857-1869**
Edinburgh artist who latterly lived in London. Painted literary scenes in oil. Exhibited RSA 1857, 1861 and 1869.

**BELL, John** **fl c1840-1860**
Landscape painter in both oil and watercolour; probably Scottish. Lived for a time in Manchester. Two Edinburgh views are in the City of Edinburgh collection.

**BELL, John D RSW** **fl 1874-1910**
Edinburgh painter in oil and watercolour; landscapes, especially of the north-west of Scotland, figures and shipping scenes. Prolific artist, most of his marine and coastal views are in watercolour, often fishing villages and boats gusting along under sail along the Scottish coast. Also worked on the Isle of Man and occasionally in the north-west. Elected RSW 1878 but resigned in 1902. Exhibited annually RSA(42) 1874-1899, also RSW(70) & GI(25).
**Bibl:** Halsby 248.

**BELL, John M** **fl 1894-1940**
Liverpool painter in oil and watercolour. Moved to Glasgow in the 1900s. Exhibited RSA 1924 and 6 works between 1925 and 1927; also RSW(2), GI(34) & L(3), always from a Glasgow address.

**BELL, John T Scott** **fl 1925-1932**
Painter in oil of landscape. Exhibited thirteen paintings at the RSA between 1925 and 1932, mostly Edinburgh scenes and French landscapes.

**BELL, John Zephaniah RSA** **1794-1885**
Born Dundee. Painter in oil of Scottish domestic and historical scenes, also portraits. Unfortunately the details of his life and the whereabouts of most of his paintings are unclear. Studied at the RA Schools in London and then under Martin Archer Shee(qv) with whom he travelled on the continent. He never belonged to the artistic establishment in Edinburgh and in 1837 travelled to England to become head of the government school of design in Manchester. Spent some time in Paris working in the studio of Gros and in 1825-6 spent a year in Rome. A fine double portrait of David Ogilvie, 9th Earl of Airlie with his daughter Clementina, in which the French influence is clearly seen, dates from 1829. An interest in fresco work had been aroused when in Rome where he would have seen the frescos being painted by the Nazarenes. In 1833 decorated the ceiling of two rooms in the new Muirhouse mansion near Edinburgh of which only the central oval now remains. Nine years after these had been completed the plaster used by Bell was analysed and the outcome published in the *Art Union*. In 1834 Wilkie visited Muirhouse to see the frescos which "pleased me greatly". He referred to Bell as the reviver of fresco painting in Scotland. Bell competed in the Westminster Hall competition in 1843 winning £200; and, although never carried out in fresco, the oil version can be seen in the Tate Gallery. When in London he was friendly with Pettie(qv) to whom his work has sometimes been compared. When visiting Portugal he painted Queen Maria II, now in the Town Hall, Oporto. His work is more highly deserving of praise and study than it has hitherto been accorded. Exhibited 28 pictures in the RA, also BI, SS, regularly RSA 1834-1876 & Royal Manchester Institution sporadically between 1836 and 1870. Represented in SNGMA, Tate AG, Dundee AG, Perth AG, Fettes College (a portrait of David Bryce the architect).
**Bibl:** Mungo Campbell, 'The Line of Tradition', Nat Galls of Scotland, Ex cat, 1993; Gifford 626; Irwin 203-204; Macmillan [SA], 202; Helen Smailes, Scottish Masters series, no. 13, 1990.

**BELL, Jonathan Anderson** **1809-1865**
Born Glasgow. Architect and watercolourist. Studied at Edinburgh University and in Rome 1929-30. Painted highly coloured watercolours of Italian scenes and buildings and architectural engravings of Scottish buildings and Cambridge colleges where he was sometime resident. Practised in Birmingham and Edinburgh. Exhibited a design for New College, Edinburgh at the RA and regularly at the RSA 1834-61, two of them, in collaboration with John Burbridge, for a new Corn Exchange at Leith and Victoria Buildings in Glasgow. Represented in NGS(4).

**BELL, Joseph John** **fl 1883-1908**
Painter in watercolour, local landscapes. Probably of Roslyn. Exhibited RSA(10) 1883-1908, AAS 1890-1898 & GI(6).

**BELL, Kate F** **fl 1898-1900**
Amateur Glasgow artist; exhibited GI(2).

**BELL, Lawrence** **fl 1921-1922**
Glasgow artist who lived in London and exhibited at the GI twice.

**BELL, Lizzie** **fl 1895-1896**
Amateur Glasgow painter; exhibited 2 works at the GI.

**BELL, L S** **fl 1899**
Amateur Glasgow artist; exhibited GI(1).

**BELL, Miss M L** **fl 1878**
Painter in watercolours of flowers. Exhibited RSA(1) 1878 from a Hawick address.

**BELL, Mary (May) Montgomerie** **c1900-1905**
Miniature portrait painter. Her early life was spent at 72 Great King Street, Edinburgh from where she exhibited two portrait miniatures at the RSA in 1901 and another in 1902. In 1903 she exhibited an unidentified young lady at the RA.

**BELL, Robert Anning RA RWS** **1863-1933**
Born London. Painter, modeller for coloured relief, black and white illustrator and designer of stained glass and mosaics. Studied Westminster & RA Schools. Gained sculptural experience by sharing a studio with Sir George Frampton. Head of Design Section, Glasgow School of Arts. Professor of Design, Royal College of Art and instructor in painting and design, University College, Liverpool. Married to the French artist Laura Anning Richard-Troncy (1867-1950), a pastellist. Member, Society of Twenty-Five. Several paintings of his were purchased by the Chantrey Bequest including 'The Listener' 1906, 'Mary and the House of Elizabeth' 1918, and 'Her Son' 1934. Among his most distinguished windows are

Radstock (Avon), the four lancets of the west window in St Mary, Slough over which he probably collaborated with Alfred Wolmark and which constituted a landmark in the evolution of stained glass design, the St Dorothy window on the north side of St Peter & St Paul, Cattistock (Dorset), the four British saints in Bradford City AG 1925, a five light window in the Arts and Crafts tradition in Crathie church, Aberdeenshire (figures of Christ, St Margaret, St Andrew, St Columba and Bridget), a window in St Margaret church, Dalry (Strathclyde) and in the parish church of Pollockshields, Glasgow. Elected ARA 1914, RA 1922, ARWS 1901, RWS 1904. Settled in Glasgow c1912. Exhibited regularly throughout Britain, including RA(59), RSA(11), RSW(6), RWS(97), ROI(4), RHA(3), RBA(5), GI(14), AAS(10) & L(59).
**Bibl:** Painton Cowen, Stained Glass in Britain, 1975; Halsby 227; Chivers.

**BELL, Robert Charles** **1806-1872**
Born Edinburgh 15 Sep; died 7 Sep. Draughtsman and engraver. Father of Robert Purves Bell(qv). Pupil of John Beugo(qv). Attended Trustees Academy. Best known for his engravings of 'The Widow' (after Sir William Allan), 'Le Sou Attendu' (after Alexander Fraser), and many illustrations after Mulready, Wilkie, Leslie and the Faeds, all for the *Art Journal.* His last work was a large reproduction of Sir William Allan's 'Battle of Prestonpans'. Exhibited RSA 1837-38. Represented in SNPG(2), City of Edinburgh collection.
**Bibl:** Brydall 214.

**BELL, Robert Grant** **fl 1909**
Edinburgh artist; exhibited once at the RSA.

**BELL, Robert Purves ARSA** **1841-1931**
Born Edinburgh, 6 Feb; died Hamilton, 22 Mar. Painter in oil of genre, portraits and figures. Son of Robert Charles Bell(qv). Educated at Newington Academy and studied at the RSA Schools. He lived at Tayport and then Hamilton from 1891 before returning again to Tayport. In 1875 he submitted his works to the Scottish Academy from Algiers. He was a friend of George Paul Chalmers(qv) and painted very much in the manner of that school. His most important works were probably 'Highland Mother' (1880) and 'The Chess Players'. Elected ARSA in 1880. Exhibited about 80 works at the RSA almost annually between 1863 and 1907, and at the GI(3). Represented in SNPG.

**BELL, Samuel** **c1739-1813**
Dundee architect. Greatly influenced by William Adam(qv). In association with James Craig of Edinburgh was responsible for the town church of St Andrew's, Dundee(1772), Trades Hall, Dundee(1776), Theatre Royal, Castle St, Dundee(1807-1810) and Trinity House, Dundee(1790).
**Bibl:** Dunbar 124; Bruce Walker & W S Gauldie, Architects and Architecture on Tayside, Dundee 1984, 65,80,85.

**BELL, Stanley Fraser** **fl 1970s**
Lecturer, Glasgow School of Art. Produced many murals in the Hamilton district.

**BELL, Susan** **fl 1985-**
Aberdeen abstract sculptress.

**BELL, Thomas Currie** **fl 1892-1925**
Edinburgh oil painter of genre and landscape. Spent several years in London before returning to Scotland c1904. Exhibited RA(1), RSA(21) including a Perthshire view in 1897, GI(4), AAS 1910, when his address was Synod Hall, Castle Terrace, Edinburgh, & L(1).

**BELL, Thomas S** **fl 1908-1910**
Ayr part-time artist. Professional musician in Hamilton Hippodrome orchestra. Exhibited GI & Hamilton Art Society 1908.

**BELL, William G** **fl 1963-1970**
Painter. Although an Englishman living in Lancashire he came from a Scottish family and spent a considerable amount of time in Scotland during the 1960s. Exhibited RSA between 1963 and 1970, none of Scottish subjects.

**BELL, William H** **fl 1885-d c1902**
Edinburgh painter principally of watercolour landscapes. Lived for a time in London before returning to Edinburgh and later Dumfries. Exhibited RA(1), Dumfriesshire views at the RSA in 1885, 1886 and 1887 and a sketch of the Seine in 1890 (altogether 5 works), also ROI(1), & GI(1).

**BELL, William S** **fl 1891-1892**
Painter in oil. Exhibited twice at the RSA in 1891 and 1892 from an Edinburgh address.

**BELL-IRVING, E O** **fl 1885**
Edinburgh portrait painter; exhibited three works at the RSA in 1885.

**BELLANY, John CBE RA HRSA LLD(Lon)** **1942-**
Born Port Seton, 18 Jne. Son and grandson of fishermen. Trained Edinburgh College of Art in 1960-1965 under Robin Philipson(qv), gaining the Andrew Grant Scholarship 1962 which enabled him to travel to Paris where he greatly admired the work of Gustav Courbet. 1965-68 found him at the Royal College of Art studying under Carol Weight and Peter de Francia. At first his work drew inspiration from the fishing industry as carried on around his home village, but by the late 1960s, becoming increasingly concerned with the social aspects of art, he began developing a complex symbolism. A visit to the Max Beckmann retrospective show in London 1965 and to East Germany 1967 when he visited Buchenwald concentration camp, deeply affected him. In 1968 he joined the staff of Brighton College of Art and the following year went to Winchester College of Art until 1973 when he was appointed head of the faculty of painting at Croydon College of Art, London 1973-1978 and lecturer at Goldsmith's College 1978. In 1983 he spent a year as Artist in Residence at the Victoria College of Art, Melbourne, Australia. What have been described as his claustrophobic paintings of the early 1970s eventually gave way to the use of acid tones and broader brush strokes, the works becoming less descriptive and more idiosyncratic. By 1982 he was applying paint so aggressively and freely that his work approached abstraction. Since then his symbolism remained but became more moderately rendered. During the 1980s he produced a large number of watercolour portraits many in the wake of serious illnesses suffered in 1984 and 1988. A series executed after major surgery was shown at the SNGMA 1989 followed by a solo exhibition there 1994 which included a portrait of Peter Maxwell Davis commissioned by the Gallery. Retrospective shows in 1983 (touring Australia and the United States), in New York 1988, in Germany 1988-89, and Italy 2002. Awards include the Wollaston Award (NG) 1987 and the Korn/Ferry Picture of the Year (RA) 1993. CBE 1994, hon. doctorates of universities of Edinburgh 1996 and Heriot Watt 1998. Elected ARA 1986, RA 1991 and HRSA 1986. There is a coarseness in the work which is neither appealing nor beautiful nor even particularly painterly; that in these respects it corresponds to the spirit of their time accounts for their reputation although many critics differ. Peter Fuller, for example, regarded him 'emerging as the most outstanding British painter of his generation'. Currently lives and works in London. 'Self-portrait' is in the City of Edinburgh Art Collection. Represented in NPG ('Ian Botham'), SNPG, SNGMA, Tate AG, Glasgow AG, Kirkcaldy AG, City of Edinburgh collection, Aberdeen AG, British Museum, Dundee AG, Ferens AG (Hull), Fitzwilliam (Cambridge), Kassa Kasser Museum (NY), Leeds AG, Leicester AG, Ayr AG, Metropolitan Museum of Art (NY), Middlesborough AG, Museum of Boca Raton (Florida), Museum of London, Museum of Modern Art (NY), National Gallery, Gdansk, NGMA (Dublin), Nat Gall of Art (Poland), Perth AG, Sheffield AG, Southampton AG, Swindon AG, V & A, Manchester AG, Wolverhampton AG, Zuider Zee Museum (Holland).
**Bibl:** Fischer FA, London, 'John Bellany', (Ex Cat 1986); Peter Fuller, Modern Painters (ed by John McDonald), London, 1993, 157-162; Hardie 198,202-5,206-7; Hartley, 116-7; Ikon Gall, Birmingham, 'John Bellany: Paintings 1972-1982' (Ex Cat); Macmillan [SA], 401-4, 406-8 et passim; NPG,'John Bellany', (Ex Cat 1986); SNGMA 'John Bellany', (Ex Cat 1986).

**BELSKIE, Abraham** **fl 1925**
Amateur Glasgow painter; exhibited once at the GI.

**BENEDUCE, Giuseppe** **fl 1931-1932**
Edinburgh sculptor of Italian extraction. Exhibited RSA(2) & GI(1).

**BENJAMIN, Benjamin B** **fl 1901-1903**
Edinburgh artist who exhibited three works at the RSA 1901-1903, all

of them pen and ink sketches.

**BENNETT, Alexander P** **fl 1953-1977**
Edinburgh artist. Moved to West Linton 1973 and exhibited Scottish scenes and landscapes at the RSA 1953-1977.

**BENNETT, Charles Bell** **fl 1892-1912**
Glasgow artist who moved to Bridge of Allan c1909. Exhibited RSA(1), GI(1) & L(2).

**BENNETT, Eileen V** **fl 1948-1953**
Edinburgh artist who exhibited at the RSA during the above period.

**BENNETT, Emily J** **fl 1892**
Amateur Glasgow artist; exhibited GI(1) 1892.

**BENNETT, Eve Reid** **fl c1970-**
Born Edinburgh. Painter in oil and watercolour. Studied design at the Edinburgh College of Art and remained in the city until 1968 when she emigrated to Canada, studying ceramics, painting and printmaking at the Vancouver School of Art. Whilst there she held several successful exhibitions. Returned to Edinburgh 1985 although living and painting in Greece during the summer months of the early 1970s. Exhibited a 'decorative' abstract at the RSA 1989.

**BENNETT, J Gilchrist** **fl 1937-1938**
Amateur Glasgow painter who exhibited 2 works at the GI.

**BENNETT, John B** **fl 1828-1843**
Edinburgh landscape painter in oil; exhibited RSA 1828-1843.

**BENNETT, John W** **fl 1925**
Amateur landscape painter from Markinch, Fife; exhibited RSA 1925.

**BENNETT, Margaretann** **1968-**
Painter in mixed media and collage techniques, using hand-painted and often handmade papers. Trained Glasgow School of Art 1987-1991. Works in a highly individualistic style, colourful with idiosyncratic features in composition. Achieved Scottish Arts Council Award for Individual Development 1997. First solo exhibition Glasgow 1997. Member SSA. Exhibits RSA, RSW, RGI from Cartvale Rd, Langside, Glasgow.

**BENNIE, Elspeth** **1962-**
Stirling sculptress. Graduated in fine art with first class hons from Glasgow School of Art 1983, then proceeded to study for two more years at St Martin's School of Art, London before taking up a residency at the Scottish Sculpture workshop in Lumsden, Aberdeenshire. As well as being a sculptress works as an artist blacksmith. All her sculptures are made from forged steel. When she began in the medium her main source was the human figure but has recently been moving away from this on to a series based on symbols and images associated with the legends of the god of blacksmithing, Haphaestus. Received Benno Schotz Award (RSA) 1987. Exhibited RSA 1986 and 1987, also in the USA.

**BENNIE, Maggie M** **fl 1897**
Bridge of Weir part-time artist. Taught Hamilton Academy 1903. Exhibited GI(2).

**BENSON, Mrs Dorothy Martin** **fl 1935-1969**
Amateur Crieff watercolour artist. Exhibited RSA in 1947, 1951, 1958, 1961 and 1969, also RSW(3).

**BENSON, James** **fl 1910**
Amateur Glasgow artist; exhibited twice at the GI.

**BENTLEY, Alfred** **fl 1913-d1923**
Engraver. Exhibited two drypoints of Edinburgh scenes at the RSA in 1913 and a French landscape in 1922, both from a London address.

**BENTZ, Frederick G** **fl 1877-1885**
Edinburgh painter in oil; landscape including continental scenes. Exhibited RA 1880-1885, RSA 1881-1885, also in the provinces. Settled in Manchester.

**BENZIE, Anne R** **fl 1960-**
Born Fraserburgh. Studied at Gray's School of Art, travelled extensively abroad sketching in Spain and Brittany. Held her own exhibitions in oil and watercolour in Aberdeen, also in Edinburgh and London. Her attention has recently turned to collages. Two of her works, a portrait and a figure study, were included at the AAS in 1964 when living at 33 Strichen Road, Fraserburgh.

**BENZIE, Michael G** **fl 1959-1965**
Aberdeen painter in oil of topographical subjects. Exhibited AAS from 64 Sclattie Park, Bucksburn.

**BERGIN, Michael Joseph** **fl 1967-1977**
Edinburgh painter in oil; exhibited 1967-1977.

**BERNET, C F** **fl 1850-1851**
Edinburgh painter; exhibited RSA 1850 and 1851.

**BERRY, Jonah** **fl 1965-1966**
Edinburgh painter; exhibited RSA 1965 and 1966.

**BERRY, Miss Mary Elizabeth** **fl 1885-1933**
Painter in oil and watercolour; landscape, Scottish interiors and portraits. Lived for a while in London before returning north of the border first to Leith c1888 and then c1899 to Edinburgh. Exhibited RA(1), RSA(11), RSW(6), SSA, AAS 1898-1912 & GI(5).

**BERRY (BERRIE), William** **1730-1783**
Died Jne 3. Edinburgh seal cutter. Pupil of a Mr Proctor in Edinburgh. Set up business on his own account. According to Bushnell, executed a number of heads remarkable for their delicacy and precision, among them 'Oliver Cromwell', 'Julius Caesar' and 'Queen Mary'. Brydall records that 'although possessed of talents unequalled in their kind in Britain, an industrious worker and economical liver, he died in far from affluent circumstances'. A portrait of him was executed in 1765 by William Delacour(qv) and engraved 1793, from a copy by Archibald Skirving. The drawing is now in SNPG.
**Bibl:** Brydall 215-6; Bushnell.

**BERSTECHER, Harry RSW** **1893-1983**
Born Glasgow 15 Jne. Landscape painter in oil, etcher; watercolour and tempora. Son of a furrier. Educated Hillhead HS. After spending a year learning the family business, entered Glasgow School of Art. One of the many Scottish watercolourists who were painting fishing villages on the east coast of Scotland in the early part of the 20th century. He has a refreshing style combining watercolour with the use of charcoal reminiscent of the work of W H Clark and William Crozier. Served in the Pioneer Corps during WW1. Exhibited alongside J D Fergusson(qv) and David Foggie(qv). Visited India for two years during which time he received many commissions. On returning to Pittenweem he found financial success difficult and became a professional photographer. Elected RSW 1926. Married 1941 and moved to Anstruther, Fife. A stroke in 1970 forced him to abandon painting. Exhibited regularly RSA(6), RSW(40), GI(34), also AAS 1923-1926 & SSA. Represented in Glasgow AG.
**Bibl:** Halsby 248; RSW Obituary by John Fleming, 1984.

**BERTRAM, H T** **fl 1882-1906**
Glasgow painter. Exhibited 7 works at the GI between the above dates.

**BETHUNE, Susan M** **fl 1980s**
Aberdeen-based jeweller, designing in the modern idiom. Exhibited AAS in 1980 from 212 Holburn Street.

**BEUGO, John** **1759-1841**
Born Edinburgh. Engraver. Best known for his two engravings Portrait of 'Dr Nathaniel Spens', and his friend 'Robert Burns' (after Alexander Nasmyth). Also did some engravings after Sir Joshua Reynolds and exhibited an historical scene at the British Institute 1830. Robert Charles Bell(qv) was one of his students. Published anonymously *Poetry, Miscellaneous and Dramatic* 1797, 'by an Artist'. Work was exhibited posthumously RSA in 1887 and 1926. Three portraits of him are in the SNPG. Represented in Glasgow AG.
**Bibl:** Brydall 206; Macmillan [GA], 143.

**BEVIN, Peter A** **fl 1983**
Landscape painter in oil. Exhibited AAS from 5 Steeple Square, Kilbarchan, Renfrewshire.

**BEVERIDGE, A T Gordon** **fl 1894-1900**
Aberdeen painter in oil of local landscapes. Exhibited AAS(6) latterly from 82 Crown Street.

**BEVERIDGE, Allan** **fl 1982-1984**
Artist living in Broughty Ferry. Exhibited AAS.

**BEVERIDGE, Andrew C** **fl 1944-1947**
Cowdenbeath amateur painter. Exhibited RSA(5) in 1944, 1945 and 1947.

**BEVERIDGE, D Drysdale** **fl 1901**
Amateur Edinburgh painter; exhibited GI(1).

**BEVERIDGE, Erskine** **c1885-1972**
Painter in oil and watercolour; seascapes, coastal scenes and landscape. Lived in Glasgow, moved in 1912 to Helensburgh and later to North Berwick. A colourful watercolourist whose work has been likened to that of Robert Clouston Young(qv). Exhibited RSA (31) between 1908 and 1939, RSW(4), ROI(4) GI(11) & L(5).
**Bibl:** Halsby 248.

**BEVERIDGE, James Symone** **1864-?**
Born Catrine, Ayrshire 27 Jly. Landscape painter in oil and watercolour. In the 1920s moved to Dorchester then for a time to Oxford before returning to Scotland, settling in Hurford, Kilmarnock. His work has been undeservedly neglected. Exhibited RSA(11), RSW(3), RA(2), GI(78) & L(1).

**BEVERIDGE, Laurence** **fl 1879**
Edinburgh architect. Exhibited the design for the Tain Memorial at the RSA 1879.

**BEVERIDGE, Miss Millicent** **fl 1908-1914**
Kirkcaldy painter. Moved to Paris in the early 1910s. Exhibited a variety of works in both oil and watercolour, sometimes at the Paris Salon (1910), also at the Exhibition of French artists (1911), London Salon(5) & RSA(1) 1914.

**BEVERIDGE, Thomas Johnston ARSA FRIBA** **1888-1964**
Born Edinburgh; carver. Son of a law clerk, he joined the firm of Scott Morton serving for one year in the carving shop and four years in the drawing office whilst at the same time attending classes at the Edinburgh College of Art. Awarded national art survey scholarship 1908 and a travelling bursary 1910. During WWI served in the Argyll and Sutherland Highlanders, thereafter setting up practice at 22 Ainslie Place. In 1924 moved to Glasgow where he remained for the rest of his life. His main interest was in domestic buildings of traditional character. He had an exceptional knowledge of Scottish architectural detail in timber and stone as well as traditional architectural practice. All his works show a painstaking regard for subtle detail and fine craftsmanship, illustrating the influence of Lutyens and Lorimer(qv). He had a flair for ecclesiastical woodwork, a fine example of which can be seen in Glasgow Cathedral. Responsible for Jacobean carvings in the N aisle of St Giles'. Elected ARSA 1957. Exhibited RSA occasionally between 1940 and 1948 and then annually 1956-1965.
**Bibl:** Gifford 115,616.

**BEVERIDGE, William** **fl 1915-1919**
Barrhead, Glasgow painter; exhibited 6 works at the GI.

**BEWARS, W Herbert** **fl 1907-1921**
English watercolour painter, probably from Manchester. Settled Newton Mearns, Renfrewshire 1910. Exhibited RSW(1), GI(1) & L(4), also 3 works at the London Salon.

**BEWS, James F R** **fl 1959-1970**
Aberdeen painter in oil, specialising in local scenes. Studied Gray's School of Art 1956-1959. Exhibited AAS from 29 St John's Road.

**BEYFUS, Edie** **fl 1889**
Amateur Glasgow painter; exhibited GI(2).

**BIGGAR, Helen Manson** **1909-1953**
Born 25 May; died 28 Mar. Sculptress. Eldest daughter of Hugh Biggar, she studied at the Glasgow School of Art 1926-1931. Initially was most interested in textile design. Continued her studies in Glasgow in order to concentrate on sculpture, being taught by James Gray(qv) and Alexander Proudfoot(qv). Became interested in stage design and was involved with Herbert Marshall, James Barke and others in the formation of the Glasgow Unity Theatre. Also designed costumes, including those for the pageant commemorating the centenary of the Co-operative Society of Glasgow 1944. In 1946 married the Glasgow artist and musician Eli Montlake. A sculpture 'The Leaning Girl' was included in the third exhibition of the New Scottish Group. Influenced by the Cubist sculptor Henri Laurens. Her 'Self-portrait' is now at Portmeiron, Wales. Suffered a stroke when only 44 years old and died the following day. Exhibited one work at the GI.

**BIGGINS, Miss Joan Forest (Mrs R S Renton)** **1935-**
Born Sunderland. Studied at Edinburgh College of Art 1953-1957 taking a postgraduate diploma 1957. Awarded travelling scholarship 1958 which enabled her to visit France, Italy and Spain. Lives and works in Edinburgh, member SSA. Exhibited Scottish landscapes at RSA 1960-1962, including a view of Gruinard Bay.

**BILLINGS, Robert William** **1813-1874**
Born London; died Putney, 4 Nov. Architect, landscape painter and illustrator in oil and watercolour. Although an Englishman based in London and exhibiting at the RA, his most important work was of Scottish subjects. Between 1834 and 1837 he was working in Bath. Among his exhibits at the RA from 1845 to 1872 14 were of Scottish subjects including castles, cathedrals and churches. Best known for *The Baronial and Ecclesiastical Antiquities of Scotland* (1845-52). This was originally planned in collaboration with William Burn(qv) but subsequently completed alone. It contains 240 of his own illustrations which influenced a generation of taste. Also illustrated other works. His crisply delineated watercolours and pencil drawings of Scottish buildings may be found in several art galleries in Scotland. One of the finest architectural draughtsman who has ever worked in Scotland, aided in historical aspects by his friend the antiquary Patrick Chalmers of Auldbar. Other works include *Britton's Cathedrals* (1832-36), *Architectural Illustrations of Carlisle Cathedral* (1840), *Architectural Illustrations of Durham Cathedral* (1843), *Architectural Illustrations of Kettering Church* (1843). Responsible for two buldings in Glasgow, the facades for 118-128 Brunswick St (1854) and 102-104 Brunswick St (1860). Towards the end of his life he was invited to supervise the restoration of the chapel at Edinburgh Castle. Six of his original illustrations are in the NGS, also represented in City of Edinburgh collection, Bath AG.
**Bibl:** Butchart 75; Dunbar 149,161; A Gomme & D Walker, Architecture of Glasgow, London 1987(rev), 20,27n,29,286; Halsby 248.

**BINNIE, Andrew H** **1935-**
Born Port Glasgow, 7 Jne. Educated Largs HS, Ardrossan Academy and Glasgow School of Art (1952-56). Moved to Kelso 1960. Has always stressed the importance of pictorial structure in his landscapes. Exhibited mainly Border landscapes, generally in oil, 1964-87, GI 1959-82 & SSA 1960-65. Represented in Dept of the Environment.

**BINNIE, Frederick** **fl 1771**
Scottish portrait painter. Waterhouse records a 'quite competent head at Prestonfield of Sir William Dick' signed on the back: 'Fredk (the k is just a little offset on the line above) Binnie PXT 1771 after a drawing of Mr Ramsay's.' The original drawing must have been made in the late 1730s.
**Bibl:** Waterhouse 53.

**BINNIE, (BINNING) John** **fl 1610-1633**
Early painter. Apprenticed to John Sawels the elder(qv). Enrolled as a Burgess of Edinburgh in 1628. He worked at Falkland Palace and at Stirling Castle. In 1630 he took one John Marshall as an apprentice and among the work he did in 1633 was painting in Linlithgow Palace in collaboration with James Workman the elder(qv). This included 'gilting with gold the haill foir face of the new walk with the timber windows and window brodis, staine windowis and crownellis with ane brod for the kingis armes and houssing...and for gilting and laying over with oyle the cullour the four oderis abone the other yet...and

laying over the two unicornes and gilting of thane.'
**Bibl:** Apted 27; Accounts of the Master of Works, vol i, 76,77,269,369-370, vol ii, 76,77,269,369-370, ed H.M.Paton, Edinburgh 1957.

**BINNIE, Maureen** **1958-**
Born Glasgow. Painter in oil and pastels, and etcher. Landscapes in bright colours, showing the influence of John Reid Murray(qv) and George Henry(qv). Graduate of Glasgow University (BA, 1st class hons in fine art), and Glasgow School of Art 1975-80. In 1980-83, aided by a Greenshields scholarship, studied in Paris at Atelier 17 with Stanley Hayter and attended classes at La Grande Chaumière. Much of her printmaking done on Orkney. Lectured in Glasgow but is now a full-time artist. The paintings are mostly landscape and derive from journeys in her native Scotland and around the USA. Awarded an Arts Council Residency Award 1983, and in 1984 won the Latimer Award at the RSA; also the Lady Artist's Club Trust Award, Cargill and Torrance Awards of the RGI, both in 1985. In 1986 won the RSA Guthrie Gold Medal and awarded a fellowship at the Frans Masereel atelier, Belgium 1987. This was followed by the Betty Davies award (SSWA) 1988 and Ireland Alloys award (RSA) 1988. Visiting Artist, Syracuse University Program Abroad (Florence) 1990-2. Regular exhibitor RSA since 1984, also GI.

**BINNIE, Richard Lionel** **fl 1951-1952**
Stirlingshire painter; exhibited RSA 1951(3) and 1952.

**BINNIE, William** **1941-**
Dundee painter, mostly in watercolour; landscape and flower studies. Trained Duncan of Jordanstone College of Art 1959-63, winning the Stuart Prize at the RSA 1963. After graduating taught until 1970 when he became a full-time working artist. Reclusive by nature and naturalistic rather than academically contemporary in style, he has never sought entry into any of the professionally organised exhibitions, preferring to satisfy private clients. The landscapes are generally of the Angus, Fife and Upper Deeside areas, depicted in sensitively drawn and delicate detail. His tightly painted flower and still life studies, meticulously drawn with a strong design element, are sometimes reminiscent of Andrew Nicholl. A set of six flower studies were published by Valentine 1970; other published works include 'The Tay Road Bridge', 'Bridge at Kenmore, Loch Tay', and 'The 17th Hole, Old Course, St. Andrews' (featured in *Golfing Art,* 1989).

**BINNING, Alexander** **fl 1916**
Amateur painter from Anniesland, Glasgow; exhibited GI(1).

**BINNING, Alfred Bathurst** **fl 1921-1938**
Amateur Glasgow artist; exhibited 3 works at the GI during the above years.

**BINNING, Robert** **fl 1538-1547**
Early painter. In partnership with Sir Thomas Cragy(qv) carried out work at Holyrood House 1538. Still working in Edinburgh 1547, 'paynting of the speiris' for Corpus Christi day.
**Bibl:** Apted 27; Accounts of the Masters of Works, vol 1,224, ed H.M. Paton, Edinburgh 1957.

**BINNING, Thomas** **fl 1563-d c1586**
Painter and glasswright. Specialised in painting stained glass including a design in 1563 for the new Tolbooth and Council House in Edinburgh. Described in the *Wardrobe Inventories,* (190-1) as a servant of Lord St John in 1573. Had as apprentice **William PINKERTON** who joined him in 1586 when he was still working in Edinburgh.
**Bibl:** Apted 27-8; Edinburgh Burgh Accounts,i,432,437,492,513.

**BINNING, Walter** **fl 1540-1594**
Like most artists of his time he seemed to combine painting portraits with painting guns and being generally employed in both interior and exterior decorating. Thus in 1540 he was painting artillery in Edinburgh Castle, in 1545 he painted a portrait and in 1548 was painting a ceiling. Between 1548 and 1553 he was working for the Regent Arran in Edinburgh, Hamilton and Linlithgow. He painted a suit of arms on glass in Hamilton 1550 and worked at Chatelherault, Edinburgh 1551. In 1558 he was engaged on a triumph for the marriage of Mary Queen of Scots and in 1560 a list of what is believed to be the Queen Dowager's household at the time of her death includes a note of various payments to Binning. In 1566 he was paid £4 'for painting of the King of Francis Armys, and of oure Soverane lord lawin armys, quhen His Majestie ressapit the ordour of kokle' that is in February that year when the French Ambassador invested Darnley with the Order of St Michael, known as the Cockle. His last known work was in 1577 when he was involved in painting the Arms of the Abbots of Arbroath and Paisley and other forfeited persons.
**Bibl:** Apted; M R Apted, Painted Ceilings of Scotland, Edinburgh 1966, 3; Macmillan [SA], 48; Thomson, George Jameson 1974, 48.

**BINNY, Graham RSW** **c1870-1929**
Born Edinburgh; died 15 Dec. Edinburgh watercolourist of portraits and figures. His work is not often seen. Elected RSW 1909. Studied in Antwerp, Munich and Paris, specialising in portraits and figures. Exhibited chiefly in Scotland including work at the RSA 1896-1919, also RSW(5), RHA(3), GI(4) & L(2).
**Bibl:** Halsby 248.

**BIRCH, Downward** **1827-1897**
Landscape painter. Exhibited RSA from 1856-1859, first from an Edinburgh address and latterly from London.

**BIRCH, Geraldine R (Mrs W Galloway Duncan)** **fl 1883**
Dundee etcher. Exhibited 3 works at the London Salon in 1883.

**BIRD, Cyril Kenneth (Fougasse)** **1887-1965**
Born 17 Dec. English black and white artist. Best known for his cartoons using the pseudonym 'Fougasse'. Also produced serious work in watercolour and in pen and ink. Educated at Cheltenham College and King's College, London, became art editor of *Punch* 1937 and was largely responsible for modernising the paper's image; editor 1949-52. During WW2 achieved considerable fame as a poster artist with his series 'Careless Talk Costs Lives'. Married the artist Mary Holden B(qv). Together they established a home-cum-studio at Morar, Inverness-shire and it was here that most of his serious watercolours, including his academy work, was done. Exhibited RSA(6), all in 1926. A retrospective exhibition was held at the Fine Art Society 1966.
**Bibl:** Houfe, 308; R G Price, A History of Punch, 1957, 285-6,300-301,illus.

**BIRD, David D** **1964-**
Born 20 Mar. Edinburgh painter and sculptor. Moved to Edinburgh at the age of 7 and in 1980 studied at Dundee School of Art, graduating with honours in drawing and painting 1982. Whilst there he was influenced by Will MacLean(qv) and experimented by using the 'box construction' format. His works are in the modern idiom using wooden boxes with printed paper and materials of all kinds and paint, wall hanging rather than free standing. Exhibits RSA and London.

**BIRD, Miss Hamilton** **fl 1845**
Amateur Edinburgh flower painter. Exhibited RSA 1845.

**BIRD, J B** **fl 1833**
Edinburgh engraver; exhibited an engraving of a portrait of the Rev David Marr, after William Bonnar, at the RSA 1833. Represented in Glasgow AG.

**BIRD, Mrs Mary Holden** **?-1978**
Although English, and married to the cartoonist 'Fougasse', much of her best work was done at her home in Morar, Inverness-shire, painting the white sands of Arisaig and other views and waterways along the north-west shores. Her style showed great skill in watercolour although at times the result was a little inconsequential. She knew the west coast so well that her colours generally portrayed the ever-changing climate faithfully. Signed with a monogram. Her work has often been reproduced. Exhibited RSA(7) each year between 1927-31; also RSW(10), RA(4) & L(3).
**Bibl:** Halsby 248.

**BIRLEY, Mary** **fl 1964-1966**
Amateur painter of Mansefield House, Craigellachie, Banffshire. Exhibited pastoral scenes at the RSA in 1964 and at both the RSA and AAS in 1966.

**BIRLEY, Sir Oswald Hornby Joseph RP ROI** **1880-1952**
Born Auckland, New Zealand 31 Mar; died 6 May. Educated at Harrow and Trinity College Cambridge, studied art in Dresden, Florence and in Paris under Marshall Baschet and at the Academie Julien. Worked most of his life in London in a manner similar to that of John Singer Sargent. Painted a large number of Scottish sitters and paid regular visits to Scotland where he was well-known among the Scottish portrait painters of the period. During his working life he visited US, Mexico, Thailand and India. Exhibited regularly at the RSA between 1903 and 1943. Represented SNPG by '1st Lord Reith'.

**BIRNIE, Archibald (D)** **fl 1820s**
Miniature portrait painter on ivory. Known to have been working in Aberdeen 1820, Inverness 1822 and again in 1823, conducting drawing classes at 79 Church Street. Also worked in Elgin, Forres and Tain. Long suggests that this might be the same artist known to have painted portrait miniatures in London in 1834.
**Bibl:** Inverness Courier 9.1.25; Long, 32.

**BIRNIE, Jeananne** **fl 1976**
Aberdeen painter of pastoral landscape, especially trees. Exhibited AAS from 490 King Street.

**BIRNIE, William RSW** **1929-**
Born Bathgate, Midlothian. Painter of landscape in oil and watercolour. Studied at Glasgow School of Art 1946-51 and at Hospitalfield. Awarded various travelling scholarships. Became head of the art department, Douglas Academy, Milngavie 1974. Member of the Glasgow Group(qv). Elected SSA 1952, RSW 1965. Exhibited regularly RSA 1951-1985. Represented in Glasgow AG, Paisley AG, SAC, Royal collection.

**BIRRELL, A** **c1770-c1820**
Scottish engraver. Engraved a portrait of John Home Douglas, after Raeburn; also various plates for Pinkerton's *Iconographia Scotica and Scottish Gallery,* also for *Biographical Magazine,* 1794 and for Smith's *Iconographia Scotica,* 1798. Known to have been living in London in 1816.
**Bibl:** Bushnell.

**BIRRELL, E Martin** **fl 1896**
Amateur Edinburgh painter; exhibited GI(1).

**BIRRELL, Ebenezer** **1801-1888**
Painter of landscape and portraits. Emigrated to Canada 1834 settling in Pickering, Ontario. Exhibited Scottish and Canadian landscapes at Upper Canada provincial exhibitions. Also a prominent agriculturalist and lieutenant-colonel, commanding the 4th Battalion Ontario Militia. A religious fantasy painted in Canada was discovered 1964. This makes him one of the earliest figures in Ontario's pre-Confederation art. An interesting pastoral scene 'Good Friends', with ponies and dairy cattle in the manner of Gourlay Steell, is in Hamilton AG.

**BIRRELL, George** **1949-**
Born Glasgow, Nov 22. Abstract and landscape painter; teacher. Trained Glasgow School of Art 1967-71. Paints in oil, mixed media (acrylic based). Influenced by William Birnie(qv), William Crosbie(qv) and John Piper(qv). Enjoys bright colours upon recognisable shapes, especially buildings and boats, although in later years has become increasingly abstract with bolder colours and forms. Exhibits RSA, RGI, from 16 Ladybank Rd, Kingskettle, Fife.

**BIRRELL, Mrs James** **[see DALYELL, Amy]**

**BIRRELL, Ronald** **fl 1964-1976**
Painter. Exhibited RSA in 1964, 1965, 1968 and 1976.

**BIRRELL, William** **1945-**
Born Glasgow, 26 Oct. Painter in oil, also pen and ink; studied Glasgow School of Art 1964-66 & 1968-70. Son of Agnes Davidson B, brother of Ronald B(qv), both of whom influenced him. Preoccupied with symbolism and surrealism, often with ethereal female forms and clouds like smoke, usually with a light palette. Worked as a graphic artist in Canada for 3 years before returning to Glasgow. Exhibited RSA 1987 & GI.

**BIRSE, Miss Isobel** **fl 1940**
Hamilton painter, probably sister of Mabel B(qv). Exhibited RSA(1) & GI(1).

**BIRSE, Miss Mabel** **fl 1940-1943**
Amateur Hamilton artist. Probably sister of Isobel B(qv). Exhibited RSA from 1940-1943.

**BIRSS, Charles** **fl 1894-1914**
Edinburgh painter in pastel, oil and watercolour; landscape and portraits. Exhibited 2 pictures at the RSA in 1898 and a further 9 thereafter, also RSW(4) & AAS(1) 1910.

**BISHOP, Miss Molly (Lady George Scott)** **fl 1943-1945**
Painter of portraits and figure studies. Exhibited RSA 1943-1945.

**BISSET, Douglas Robertson** **1908-?**
Born Strichen, Aberdeenshire 25 May. Sculptor. Trained Glasgow School of Art 1930-1933, Royal Danish Academy 1933 and British School, Rome 1933-1934. On his return from Italy settled in London. Regular exhibitor RA, mainly of portrait busts. Taught at Brighton School of Art 1939 and subsequently at Leeds College of Art. Exhibited RA(1) & GI(8).

**BISSET, Miss Helen Kerr** **fl 1916-1919**
Edinburgh painter of still life and flower studies. Exhibited RSA(2) 1916, 1917 and 1919(2).

**BISSET, Miss Isabella** **fl 1848-1850**
Pittenweem artist; exhibited landscapes and rural scenes at the RSA in 1848 (2) and 1850.

**BISSET, James** **1760 (or 1762?)-1832**
Born Perth; died Leamington, 17 Aug. Miniature painter and engraver. He moved to England early in life training in Birmingham as an artist's apprentice. In 1785 was practising as a portrait painter in Newmarket and in Birmingham 1793. According to Redgrave he was back in Birmingham soon after 1800 where he produced medallions and opened a museum. Illustrated his own *Poetic Survey round Birmingham,* with emblematical and topographical designs 1800. In later life he opened a museum and painting gallery in Leamington.
**Bibl:** DNB; Long 32; Rd.

**BISSET(T), Robert** **fl 1887**
Fraserburgh painter. Exhibited once at the AAS.

**BISSETT, Peter Thomson** **1923-1961**
Born Jly 13; died Jly 7. Perth watercolour painter of landscapes, especially of the north-east; also Perthshire and some continental scenes. Educated Sharp's Institution and Perth Academy. Left school early in order to join the RAF during WW2. After the war he resumed studies at Dundee Art College and after teacher training joined the staff of Perth Academy 1950, remaining there until his early death. An active member of the **PERTH ART ASSOCIATION**, he was on the committee 1957-8 and President 1959, dying in office. A retrospective memorial exhibition was held at Perth AG 1963. His wife, **Mrs E S BISSET** was also a painter. Represented in Perth AG(4).

**BLACK, Alexander** **1798-1858**
Architect and teacher. Most active in Edinburgh where he designed the outdoor Heriot Schools in Society Square, the Old Fishmarket Close at the foot of Cowgate, Young St and Broughton St. Introduced important improvements in ventilation. In his early years he was involved with the Art School, becoming its honorary librarian. George Hay(qv) and Hugh Cameron(qv) were among his pupils.
**Bibl:** The Builder, 10 June 1882; Gifford 181,182,187,204,225,340, 341,342, 362,382,422.

**BLACK, Andrew RSW** **1850-1916**
Born Glasgow, 11 May; died Glasgow, 16 Jly. Painter in oil and watercolour; landscape and marines. Trained Glasgow School of Art and Paris, worked for 11 years as a designer before turning to full-time painting 1877. Exhibited at the main London Galleries from 1883. His work now seems a little lugubrious but he undoubtedly

understood the sea and those who gain their livelihood from fishing. Elected RSW 1884. Exhibited RSA(16) 1871-1899, RA(8), RSW(56), GI(100), AAS(1) & L(8). Represented in Paisley AG.
**Bibl:** Halsby 161,248.

**BLACK, Miss Ann Spence RSW SSA** **1861-1947**
Born Dysart, Fifeshire. Watercolour painter of landscape, flowers and fruit. Prolific artist, she lived in Edinburgh most of her life. Her favourite places were around Falkland, Culross and the east coast. Enjoyed bright colours laid on in pure washes without white or bodycolour. Elected RSW 1917, SSA 1940. Exhibited a large number of works at the RSA 1896-1946, also GI(38), RSW(95), AAS(2) & L(2). Represented in Kirkcaldy AG, City of Edinburgh collection.

**BLACK, Dorothy** **1963-**
Born Forfar. Painter and printmaker. Studied at the Edinburgh College of Art 1981-1985, awarded a Diploma in 1986 and the Young Artists prize at the Inverclyde Biennial 1987. 'A surrealist instinct seems to lie beneath even her most objective and straightforward surfaces. Lobster claws cling to a portrait then find their way on to a plate. Fresh flowers are painted black. Dorothy Black paints right between the eyes, unafraid of contradiction and discovery' [Alice Bain]. Exhibited 'Dancing Girl' at the RSA in 1986 and another work in 1987. Represented in Jean F Watson Bequest, City of Edinburgh.

**BLACK, Emma L (Mrs J D K Mahomed)** **fl 1881-1936**
Painter in oil; portrait, figures and local landscapes. Lived for many years at Leuchars House, Elgin. Exhibited RA(8), RBA(4), RI(4), AAS(3) & L(8).

**BLACK, E Rose** **fl 1920-1939**
Landscape watercolourist who worked in a free style. Probably husband of Mrs W Rose B(qv) who worked from Elgin.
**Bibl:** Halsby 249.

**BLACK, Francis Mollison** **1836-c1900**
Born Angus (christened at Monikie, Nov 28). Came to Perth from Kilmarnock to become art master, Perth Academy 1878-99. Exhibited RSA(2) 1864.

**BLACK, Franciszek Ksawery** **1881-1959**
Born Warsaw, 3 Dec; died Paris, Aug. Sculptor and occasional painter. Grandson of a Scottish engineer who settled in Poland. In 1900 he left Poland, travelling via Vienna and Zurich to England. From 1901 studied woodcarving in London at the Art School of Decorative Woodcarving. In 1903 moved to Paris for further studies at the Ecole Nationale des Beaux-Arts under Antoine Mercier. Invited by Ignacy Paderesski to Rion Basson, near Lausanne, he remained there until 1911. After WWI he returned to France, settling in Paris. Among his earliest known works are two small bas-reliefs: 'An Embroiderer' (1904) and 'A Man Playing a Mandolin' (1905). Between 1907 and 1910, together with B Balzukiewicz, he helped with work on the Grunwald Monument in Cracow. This was executed partly in Paris but the monument was destroyed during the war and reconstructed in 1976. In 1908 he began to exhibit in Paris at the Societe Nationale des Beaux-Arts and, from 1920, at the Societe des Artistes Français, and at the Salon d'Autumne, where he had regular exhibitions until 1949, having been elected a member 1925. His period of most intense work was during his stay in Switzerland 1917-1919 when he concentrated on genre studies and female nudes in marble, bronze and plaster. Also sculptured portraits, including a number of historical Polish personalities, among them Chopin 1934, Adam Mickiewicz 1933, Samlicki 1924, and Paderewski 1936. Engaged in monumental sculpture, winning 3rd prize in Paris 1929 for the design of a monument to Simon Bolivar. The same year he undertook some bas-reliefs for the Bolivar Pantheon in Caracas, Venezuela. A monument to Col. Edward House was executed in 1932 in bronze and granite for the Paderewski Park in Warsaw. He also executed a monument to Leopold Sudre in 1933 for the Mont Parnasse Cemetery, Paris, the monument of J Hoene-Wronski 1937 in bronze and stone for the Cemetery at Neuilly and several other similar works for cemeteries in France and Switzerland. His work is of a classical character revealing great precision in modelling, especially in the heads where he took great pains to render accurately the character and expression of the sitter. His first one-man exhibition of painting was in Paris 1922.
**Bibl:** Slowlik Artystow Polskich i Obcych w Polsce dzialajacych, Wroclaw-Warszawa-Krakow-Gdansk 1971, vol 1A.

**BLACK, Hugh** **fl 1885**
Amateur Glasgow painter; exhibited GI(1).

**BLACK, James** **?-1841**
Architect. Arrived Dundee 1833 and designed the Barrack St Gateway to the Howff, Dundee 1833-4. Laid out West Bell St in the same city 1839. Responsible for the fine Greek Revival School Wynd church, Dundee (1824) later known as Kidd's Rooms and now sadly demolished.
**Bibl:** Bruce Walker & W S Gaudie, Architects and Architecture on Tayside, Dundee 1984, 82,89(illus).

**BLACK, John** **1959-**
Born Dumbarton. Self-taught wildlife painter in oil. Began full-time painting career in 1981, working from a studio in Inverness-shire. Specialises in painting Highland landscapes with red deer and game birds usually prominent. His paintings have a strong dramatic impact without deferring to the brightly picturesque. Mist is more common than sunlight while occasional shafts of sunshine add to the realism - the reason for the artist's established reputation both in Britain and North America. Several works have illustrated front covers of sporting publications.

**BLACK, Philip S** **fl 1981-**
Edinburgh artist; exhibited portrait heads at the RSA 1981 and 1982.

**BLACK, Robert Milligan** **fl 1981-1984**
Aberdeen artist of semi-abstracts. Trained Gray's School of Art, Aberdeen. Exhibited RSA 1984 & AAS 1981-1984, latterly from 51E Nelson Street.

**BLACK, Robert R ARSA** **fl 1970-**
Dundee architect, associated with Baxter, Clark and Paul. His main work has been in the re-development of streets and housing estates. Among the most notable have been the Ferguson Park housing estate, Blairgowrie (1972), and the Castle Street redevelopment in Fraserburgh. Elected ARSA 1989; exhibited regularly RSA from 1970.

**BLACK, Professor Sam RSW** **1913-1998**
Born Ardrossan, 5 Jne; died Apr 23. Painter in oil and watercolour of landscapes and architectural subjects; art teacher. Studied Glasgow School of Art, subsequently in Belgium and France. Lived at West Kilbride before going to Canada to take up an appointment at the University of British Columbia. Held many one-man shows from 1961 and received the Canadian Centennial Medal 1967. In 1975 elected vice-president, International Society for Education through Art. In addition to other media, worked also in acrylic and graphics and in welded metals. The work is characterised by vigorous bold design, strong colour and overall vitality. Lived on Bowen Island, Vancouver. Elected RSW 1953, CSDW 1963, CSG 1964. Exhibited regularly RSA 1940-58. Represented in Dundee AG, Glasgow AG, Vancouver AG, Seattle AG, London AG (Ontario), Edmonton AG, Sarnia AG.

**BLACK, Thomas** **fl 1830-1838**
Little known Edinburgh animal painter in oil. Specialised in portraits of dogs. In 1830 he exhibited a copy of Landseer's Athole family group and a number of dog studies in 1837 and 1838.

**BLACK, Tom** **fl 1880-1907**
Painter from Partick, Glasgow; exhibited 15 works at the GI during the above period.

**BLACK, W Milne** **fl 1908-1912**
Amateur Glasgow painter; exhibited 4 works during the above dates.

**BLACK, Mrs W Rose** **fl 1906-1921**
Elgin painter in oil and watercolour. Probably wife of E Rose B(qv). Specialised in paintings of the north-west coast and the north-east. Exhibited regularly AAS between the above years, first from Hythehill, Elgin and after 1915 from Correilwood, Elgin.

**BLACK, William S** **fl 1875-1905**
Edinburgh painter in oil. Possibly the W S Black responsible for designing and preparing the Queen's Own Cameron Highlanders South African War Memorial(1905) in St Giles. Exhibited RSA(13) 1875-1895.

**BLACK, William Williams** **fl 1921-1935**
Turriff painter in oil. Exhibited mainly moorland scenes at the AAS in 1921, 1931, 1933 and 1935 from 4 Sunnybrae.

**BLACKADDER, Dame Elizabeth Violet (Mrs Houston) OBE RA RSA RSW RGI D Litt** **1931-**
Born Falkirk, Stirlingshire, 24 Sep. Painter in oil and watercolour; interiors and still life in stylised semi-abstract manner, often with vegetation and animals, especially cats. From 1949 to 1954 studied art at Edinburgh University (obtaining a first-class hons degree) and Edinburgh College of Art where her teachers included Penelope Beaton(qv), Robert Henderson Blyth(qv), Robin Philipson(qv) and William MacTaggart(qv). But the teacher who had the greatest influence on her work was William Gillies(qv). In 1954 won a Carnegie Travelling Scholarship enabling her to visit Greece, Italy and Yugoslavia. She was impressed by Byzantine architecture and mosaics which came to affect much of her later work. During a postgraduate scholarship year she spent nine months in Italy studying the work of the early Italian Masters as well as contemporary artists such as Morandi and Sironi. In 1956 she married John Houston(qv) and took up a teaching appointment at Edinburgh College of Art. Travelled widely with her husband in most European countries, USA and Japan, sometimes painting but always immensely aware of the rich welter of images that travel generated. Subjects include landscapes, portraits and still life but the quintessential foci of her art are such everyday domestic scenes as cut flowers (especially irises), cats and other household objects. She also produces tapestries, stained glass and lithographs. Although working occasionally in oil her most important innovative work has been in watercolour. In 1978 she began a series of delicately observed watercolours of flowers. One of her great strengths is the idiosyncratic nature of her work, untrammelled by direct association with any established school, and the way in which she arranges objects in space. A quiet, intense, highly intelligent person of great integrity and originality, although it seems that in later life she finds it hard to break the mould of the ouevre that has made her best known. "Whether she is painting the human figure, landscape, still life objects or flowers, Blackadder's special achievement lies in her capacity to organise and realise deeply felt experiences...its twentieth-century melody is sometimes melancholy and disturbing, but more frequently it celebrates an experience of post-war Britain that exudes a sense of increasing luxury and well-being" [Bumpus]. Since 1986 her public work has been in great demand including the design of a new window for the National Library of Scotland, a poster design for Henley Festival, a lithograph for the RSA, ceramic designs for the RA in London. She has remained resident in Edinburgh throughout her working life. The first woman to be an Academician of both the RA and RSA. Elected ARSA 1963, RSW 1961, ARA 1971, RSA 1972, RA 1976. Received the Guthrie Award RSA 1962, OBE 1982, DBE 2003. Joint winner of the RA's Watercolour Foundation Award 1988. Hon. member of the RWA, RWS, Royal Soc. of Printers; Hon. Fellow RIAS, Royal Soc. of Edinburgh; granted hon. doctorates from the Univs of Edinburgh, Aberdeen, Strathclyde & Heriot Watt. Although she has exhibited in many parts of the world, the most regular exhibits have been at the RA, RSA(113), RSW & AAS 1964-1983. Represented in SNPG, Tate AG, Glasgow AG, Aberdeen AG, Carlisle AG, Kirkcaldy AG, Paisley AG, Reading AG, Sheffield AG, Teeside AG, Doncaster AG, Huddersfield AG, Bolton Museum and AG, Atkinson AG (Southport), Scottish Arts Council, Hove Museum and AG, UK Government Art Collection, Heriot-Watt University (Edinburgh), City of Edinburgh collection(4), Perth AG, Towner AG (Eastbourne), Chatsworth House, Museum of Modern Art (New York), National Museum of Women in the Arts (Washington).
**Bibl:** Bumpus, Elizabeth Blackadder 1988; Coia 'Elizabeth Blackadder ARA' Scottish Field Nov 1966, 60-61; Elder Dickson 'Scottish Painting: the Modern Spirit', Studio International, Dec 1963, 236-243; Hall, 'Elizabeth Blackadder', The Scottish Art Review, Vol IX, 4, 1964, 9-12 and 31; Hardie 183,202; Hartley 117; Macmillan [SA], 214-5; Vann 'R A Travel: Eastern Eden. Elizabeth Blackadder RA tells Philip Vann of her Japanese inspirations', RA Magazine, 15, 1987, 46-48.

**BLACKBURN, Mrs Hugh (Jemima Wedderburn)** **1823-1909**
Born Edinburgh, 1 May; died 9 Aug. Painter in watercolour, illustrator and author; animals, birds, landscapes and portraits; occasional stained-glass window designer. A most interesting, mainly self-taught and highly prolific artist who received little public recognition in her life-time but whose edited, attractively produced biography 'Jemima', published in 1988, has begun to stimulate some of the recognition she richly deserves. Her mother was related to Clerk of Penicuik(qv); her father, who belonged to one of Scotland's most distinguished families and became Solicitor-General, died before she was born. Her importance is based less on the quality or originality of her work than on the fact that she sketched almost daily during a life that coincided with the full span of the Victorian age. Moreover, her friends included many of the notables of the day among them the Duke of Wellington, Sir Edwin Landseer(qv), whom she first met in London 1843, John Ruskin(qv), Peter Graham(qv) and John Everett Millais. Landseer wrote that he had nothing to teach her in the painting of animals while Ruskin went so far as to refer to her as 'the best artist he knew'. Other family friends included Disraeli, the Prince of Wales, Trollope, and James Clerk Maxwell (her cousin). Although she travelled extensively in western Europe, North Africa and Iceland, her home and greatest love was the Western Highlands. The watercolours are those of a highly competent amateur, richly coloured, a little naive, brimful of personal and sometimes social significance and always with animals or birds or people prominent and sensitively delineated. Her bird paintings were less successful although well observed. Published a number of works of which the best known is the *Birds of Moidart* 1896; others were *Scenes from Animal Life and Character* (1858), *Birds Drawn from Nature* (1862), *A Few Words About Drawing For Beginners* (1893), *The Crows of Shakespeare, Illustrations of Scripture, Instructions on Drawing by one who has experienced its difficulties* (1892), and *Bible Beasts and Birds.* In 1878, in collaboration with Anthony Trollope, she published privately *How the Mastiffs went to Iceland.* In addition she illustrated A White's *The Instructive Picture Book* and W J M Rankin, *Songs and Fables* (1874). Frequent contributor to the popular magazine *Good Words.* Her stained-glass windows for St Finan (Episcopal) church, Kinlochmoidart c1859 were among the first stained glass designs to appear in highland Scotland; she also designed the elaborate cornice in the drawing room of her home Roshven, nr Arisaig. Happily married to Hugh Blackburn, Professor of Mathematics at Glasgow University. Recently many volumes of her drawings came to light. Exhibited 3 works at the RA between 1863 and 1875 & RSA 1861. Represented in BM, NPG, British Library, Natural History Museum, Royal Collection, James Clerk-Maxwell Foundation.
**Bibl:** Fairley, Jemima, Edinburgh 1988; Houfe, 236; Lutyens, Millais and the Ruskins, 1967, 113 n.; Macmillan [SA], 214-5; G Du Maurier, Social Pictorial Satire, 1898, 84.

**BLACKBURN, Miss Grace** **[see Countess of Wemyss]**

**BLACKBURN, Miss Isabella** **fl 1863-1864**
Edinburgh portrait painter in oil; exhibited 3 works at the RSA between the above dates.

**BLACKBURN, Samuel** **fl 1837-1857**
Edinburgh painter in oil; historical, portraits and figurative. His work was competent but not exciting; in some ways in the tradition of John Pettie(qv). Exhibited 3 works at the RA: 'The Earl of Stafford in the Tower, receiving intelligence from Carlton, secretary to Charles I, that the King had assented to his death' (1842); 'The Disinterestedness of Calvin - Geneva in the Distance' (1845) and 'Cromwell, Milton, and Mary Powell his wife' (1854). Also exhibited a number of historical scenes at the RSA 1837-56, and in various other provincial galleries.

**BLACKER, William Charles** **1949-**
Born Glasgow. Painter in watercolour and engraver. Trained Glasgow School of Art and in northern Italy. Gained the Latimer Award (RSA) 1972 and Scottish Young Contemporaries Print Prize the same year. Most of his work has been shown with the Glasgow Print Studio. Moved to Barra 1979. Exhibited five works at the RSA in 1972 and 1973.

**BLACKIE, Agnes H** **fl 1887-1890**
St Boswells painter; exhibited RSA(2).

**BLACKLEY, Alexander** **fl 1834-1838**
Edinburgh painter in oil, watercolour and pastel; portraits. Exhibited 8 works at the RSA between the above dates, most of them portraits, some in chalk.

**BLACKLOCK, Thomas Bromley** **1863-1903**
Born Kirkcudbright; died 28 Sep. Painter in oil, watercolour, pen and ink: landscapes, interiors, flowers, portraits, figures; also illustrator and author. Trained Edinburgh. His early work was landscape, 'marked by feeling for the sentiment of tranquillity in nature and refined in colour and handling, if conceived with little passion or distinction'. In 1896, however, into one of those autumn evening landscapes he introduced a fairy-like figure of 'kilmeny' and over the next few years, working in Kirkcudbright, he developed a personal variant on the themes of children and landscape which Hornel(qv), MacGeorge(qv) and others were painting. 'Borrowing, but more through stimulus than invitation, some of Hornel's brilliance of colour and inventiveness of pattern he added a touch of fantasy of his own. He developed into a painter of fairy-tales. He painted pleasant tender fancies expressed with a daintiness of colour and design and an ingenuity and quaintness in costume and accessory which, if occasionally verging upon mere prettiness, gave his pictures a definite if modest place among the more realistic or more artistically powerful and decorative work of the time' [Caw]. Author & illustrator of *East Lothian Illustrated*, 1892. He was a close friend of the Blairgowrie painter Ewan Geddes(qv) who helped Blacklock over the last few years when the latter was afflicted with a spinal disease that eventually drove him to suicide. Exhibited RA(2), RSA(81) 1882-1899, AAS 1890-1898, GI(28) & L(5). Some late works exhibited posthumously RSA in 1926.
**Bibl:** Caw 406; Halsby 249; Hardie 101(illus).

**BLACKLOCK, William Kay** **1872-c1922**
Painter in oil, romantic landscapes and figurative subjects. Although an English painter his period as a staff member at the Edinburgh School of Art in the early 1900s had great impact. Since his primary interest was in the romantic depiction of evening scenes and attractive young people, the location of his works was of little significance so that most of them, including those in Scotland, were of non-Scottish subjects. All delicately portrayed in a strictly conventional mould. Married the flower painter Nellie Blacklock. Exhibited RA(16), RSA(19), GI(12), ROI(6), L(15) & AAS 1906.

**BLACKWELL, Mrs Elizabeth** **fl 1735-1739**
Botanical illustrator and printmaker. Daughter of an Aberdeen merchant, she married and eloped secretly to London with Thomas Blackwell, brother of the first Professor of Greek at Aberdeen. When her husband was imprisoned for debt she began to produce flower paintings for publication and, there being no proper herbal at that time, she received encouragement from Sir Hans Sloan, Dr Mead and other eminent medical men. In 1737 she published a large folio volume containing 250 plates. This was followed by a second volume in 1739. Also engraved and hand-coloured the prints. The income from these works was sufficient to secure her husband's release.
**Bibl:** Brydall 171-2; Caw 50.

**BLAIKIE, Mrs** **fl 1863-1864**
Burntisland landscape painter in oil. Exhibited twice at the RSA during the above period.

**BLAIKIE, Agnes Helen** **1863-1932**
Born St Boswells, 16 Jne; died Selkirk, 1 Sep. Painter in oil and watercolour; birds and still life. Sister of Frances Blaikie(qv) and cousin of the author and poet Andrew Laing; another sister was the writer Jean Laing. Exhibited 'The Linnet's Nest' at the RSA in 1890. Represented by 3 works in SNPG.

**BLAIKIE, Andrew** **fl c1800**
Paisley engraver. His name appears on the title page of Murphy's *Collection of Irish Airs and Jiggs,* c1809. Frequent references to him also occur in Dauney's *Ancient Scottish Melodies.*
**Bibl:** Bushnell; D Cook, Scottish Notes and Queries, Nov 1928.

**BLAIKIE, Miss Frances Margaret Brunton** **1869-1915**
Born Bowden, Roxburghshire, 17 Oct; died London, 1 May. Painter in oil; animals, especially horses, rural scenes, illustrator. Younger sister of Agnes Blaikie(qv) and cousin of the writer Andrew Laing. Trained Glasgow School of Art and in 1892 went with her friend Amy Steedman to study at Denovan Adam's School of animal painting at Craigmill(qv). During the winter of 1895 and some subsequent winters she studied figure painting under Robert McGregor(qv) in Edinburgh. Went to Paris 1895 where she studied under Colarossi and Whistler. Illustrations began to appear in places as far apart as *Punch* and an almanack in New York, also for a children's book *Wicked Willie*. In 1905 she began an association with Mrs Jack in Edinburgh which led to commissions for illustrating many children's books including *Gulliver's Travels, Don Quixote* and *The Arabian Nights* as well as the *Complete Children's Dickens.* Moved to London 1908 where the illustrations continued. At her best illustrating nursery rhymes, benefitting from her gift of benevolent caricature. Immensely popular and widely loved, sadly she died just after an important contract had been signed. "Wherever she went - the various Art Schools, in Paris, at the Club in London, at the Flats - her wonderful gift of kindly caricature made her widely known, and those who were admitted to her inner circle give thanks for having known the most helpful, loyal, and true friend that ever lived. The testimony of all who knew her is the same 'strong, faithful, tender - a rock to lean on'" [Will Ogilvie].
**Bibl:** W Ogilvie, Border Magazine, XXI, 245, 1916, 97-100.

**BLAIKIE, Jeanie** **fl 1899**
Hawick artist; exhibited GI(1).

**BLAIKLEY, Alexander** **1816-1903**
Born Glasgow. Painter in oil, crayon and watercolour; portraits and figurative subjects. During mid-career lived in London but returned to Edinburgh 1841 where he taught drawing. This long-lived, prolific artist exhibited about 100 works at the RSA 1837-1889, among them Edinburgh scenes, portraits of men and women and, in 1884, a view of Niagara; also RA 1842-67 & GI. Represented in SNPG.
**Bibl:** Mungo Campbell, 'The Line of Tradition', Nat Galls of Scotland, Ex cat, 1993.

**BLAIN, James** **fl 1906-1945**
Kilmarnock artist who moved to Glasgow c1935; exhibited RSA(2), RSW(1) & GI(5).

**BLAIR, Andrew** **1817-1892**
Painter in oil and watercolour; landscapes, especially the Trossachs. This Dunfermline artist was the son of a weaver. Started life as a house-painter and opened his own business very early in his career retaining it throughout his life. Studied art at the Board of Manufacturers Schools. Devoted to the study and depiction of nature, toured the Highlands in 1847 being especially attracted to the area around Oban. His work, especially in watercolour, is noted for its mastery over light and shade. He produced a series of extremely popular Highland loch scenes subsequently published by Raphael Tuck; also a rare depiction of the game of quoits (BI 1847). A close and life-long friend of Sir Joseph Noel Paton(qv) who wrote of Blair's "kindly nature...I can recall nothing that does not reflect honour on his character". He exhibited 90 works at the RSA between 1849 and 1891, also RI and Walker Gallery, Liverpool.
**Bibl:** Wingfield.

**BLAIR, E Scott** **fl 1884**
Amateur Edinburgh flower painter in oil and watercolour; exhibited 2 works at the RSA.

**BLAIR, Miss Frances M** **fl 1925-1952**
Edinburgh painter and engraver in oil and watercolour; landscapes. Travelled to France shortly after the war and while there painted a number of French landscape studies. Exhibited spasmodically 9 works at the RSA between 1925 and 1952, also RSW(9), GI(5) & L(7). Between 1926 and 1933 she exhibited a number of delicate coloured woodcuts at the AAS including 'Old Mill of Gairn' (1929).

**BLAIR, Gorrie McLeich** **fl 1885**
Amateur Edinburgh painter; exhibited RSA(1).

**BLAIR, Miss Isa R** **fl 1870**
Amateur Edinburgh landscape painter in oil; exhibited RSA(1).

**BLAIR, Janet T R** **fl 1899-1913**
Glasgow painter who exhibited once at the GI and 5 works at the Walker Gallery, Liverpool.

**BLAIR, John** **1850-1934**
Born Hatton, Berwickshire; died Edinburgh. Painter in oil but mostly watercolour; landscape, figures, topography, especially of the east coast of Scotland, still life. A prolific artist, now best known for his pleasantly painted, colourful watercolours of the south-east coastline of Scotland. A variable artist, at his best he painted with atmosphere and integrity the pleasing scenes of his own land, generally in the summertime or autumn. But often there is evidence of undue haste perhaps due to an increasing demand for his work in the mid-1870s. His later work had stronger colour being somewhat reminiscent of Hamilton Glass(qv). Exhibited regularly RSA(83) 1870-1920, also RSA(4), RI(3), RHA(2), GI(10) & AAS 1893-1912.

**BLAIR, Miss Margaret I** **fl 1941-1943**
Amateur Dundee portrait painter. Sister of Rosemary Blair(qv). Exhibited RSA(4) between the above dates.

**BLAIR, Miss Rosemary** **fl 1944**
Amateur Dundee sculptress; exhibited once at the RSA.

**BLAIR, William Charles** **1883-1887**
Edinburgh painter from Kincardine-on-Forth of landscape and portraits in oil. Seems to have travelled extensively; in 1883 he exhibited from Paris and in 1884 from an address in Madeira. He showed 8 works at the RSA, GI(3) & L(1).

**BLAKE, Miss Dorothea Frances** **1895-?**
Born Greenock, 18 Jan. Painter in oil; landscape, portrait and figures. Although born in Scotland she was trained at the Byam Shaw and Vicat Cole Schools of Art and at the RA School in England. As a student won silver and bronze medals. Remained in London throughout her working life. Exhibited RA(3), ROI(2) & L(1).

**BLAKE, Frederick Donald RI** **1908-**
Born Greenock. Painter in oil, watercolour and acrylic of coastal scenes and local landscape; also etcher. Trained at Camberwell Goldsmith's College, spent his working life in England. Probably brother of Dorothea Blake(qv). Elected RI 1952. Exhibited RSA, ROI & RI.

**BLAKELOCK, Katherine Percy** **fl 1894-1914**
Arbroath landscape painter in oil and watercolour who moved to Carnoustie c1904 before settling in Buxton, Derbyshire, finally moving to London in 1913. Exhibited RHA(9), RI(2) & London Salon(15).

**BLAKEMAN, Charles** **fl 1936-1941**
Edinburgh sculptor; exhibited 2 works at the RSA in 1936 and 1941.

**BLANC, Hippolyte Jean RSA FRIBA** **1844-1917**
Born Belgium, 18 Aug; died Edinburgh, 12 Mar. Architect of French parentage, educated George Heriot School and in Edinburgh where he lived most of his life. Father of the architect **Frank Edward BLANC**. By 1877 was chief assistant in His Majesty's Office of Works in Edinburgh. Designed churches all over Scotland being the most successful Gothic church architect of his time, also domestic buildings and such works as the Baths and Gymnasium at Dunfermline, and Bangour Lunatic Asylum. Restored the Argyll Tower and Parliament Hall in Edinburgh Castle. President, Edinburgh Architectural Association 1871-72, 1899-1900 and 1906-07. In 1866 awarded a medal at the Edinburgh Exhibition and a gold medal in Paris. Elected Fellow of the Royal Institute of British Architects 1889, ARSA 1892, RSA 1896 and Treasurer 1907-17. Exhibited 6 works at the RA including the Coates Memorial Church, Paisley (1892), St Matthew's Church, Edinburgh (1893) and St Cuthbert's Church, Edinburgh (1894). Exhibited RSA(82) 1873-1915; RHA(12) & GI(1).
**Bibl:** Gifford 42,88,91,95,98,208,223,264,274,275,301,311,312, 321,333,366, 386,435,499,500,521,556,611,613,616,617,619,635 (pl 38).

**BLATCH, Miss Lucy Helen** **fl 1868-1873**
Perth painter in oil; portraits and landscape. Related to the Rev. William Blatch. Exhibited 3 works at the RSA between the above years.

**BLATHERWICK, Dr Charles RSW** **fl 1867-d1895**
Amateur Helensburgh painter in oil and watercolour; landscapes. Involved in founding the RSW 1878 before moving to Highgate, London, where he practised medicine. In 1865 returned to Scotland to take up a position at Rhu as Chief Inspector of Alkali and Chemical works for Scotland and Northern Ireland. His landscapes were tightly painted and his watercolours generally bright and colourful. Arran was a favourite place. Twice married; his daughter from his first marriage, Lily Blatherwick(qv), married his stepson A S Hartrick(qv). Elected RSW 1878 and President of the Glasgow Art Club 1981-1983. Exhibited 4 times at the RA between 1875 and 1882 and RSA(7) but mainly RSW(51), GI(14) & RI(1).

**BLATHERWICK Lily RSW (Mrs A S Hartrick)** **1854-1934**
Born Richmond, London; died Fulham, London 26 Nov. Painter in oil and watercolour; flowers, also lithographer. Daughter of Charles Blatherwick(qv). Moved to Scotland with the family in 1865. Founder member of the RSW. Painted landscapes and flowers in both oil and watercolour in a natural, unmannered and effective style. Spent some time on the continent, exhibiting a winter scene at the Paris Salon in 1912. After her marriage to A S Hartrick(qv), son of her father's widow by her first marriage, they moved south to Acton Turville and Tresham in Gloucestershire. In 1906 they returned to London in order for her husband to take up a teaching appointment at Camberwell School of Art. It was when in London that she took up lithography, exhibiting a number of exquisite flower prints with the Senefelder Club(qv) 1923. In his autobiography her husband wrote that his wife 'painted the feeling and spirit of flowers in a way that was unique'. Elected RSW 1878, ASWA 1886, SW 1898. Exhibited in many places including no fewer than 161 works at the RSW, RA(25),RSA(13), SWA(33), ROI(12), RBA(1), GI(61) & L(7).
**Bibl:** Halsby 249; A S Hartrick, A Painter's Pilgrimage Through Fifty Years, 1939, 179.

**BLAYLOCK, Thomas Todd ARCA (Lond)** **1876-1929**
Born Langholm. Painter, etcher and woodcut engraver. Studied at the RCA and received his Diploma in 1903. Won a bronze medal at the Milan International Exhibition 1906. Lived most of his life in England moving from London to Leek, Staffs in 1907 thence to Poole, Dorset, before settling finally in Salisbury. Exhibited RA(6), RBA(1) & L(56).

**BLAXTER, Sir Kenneth** **fl 1966-d1989**
Amateur landscape artist who lived for many years at Wardenhill, Bucksburn, Aberdeen. Knighted for his scientific work as Director of the Rowett Institute, Aberdeen. Retired to Suffolk but retained a home in Strathdon, Aberdeenshire. Exhibited 3 landscapes at the AAS.

**BLEASE, Elizabeth** **fl 1977-1978**
Amateur painter of 'St Leonards', Johnshaven. Exhibited 2 local views at the AAS.

**BLEIER, Heinrich (Henry)** **fl 1876-1878**
Almost certainly of German origin. Worked in oil, specialising in portraits and figure studies. Lived for some years in Edinburgh. Exhibited RSA(9) 1876-1878.

**BLISS, Douglas Percy ARCA (Lond)** **1900-1984**
Born Karachi, 28 Jan; died Mar 11. Although an Englishman, Bliss spent most of his professional life in Scotland where he became strongly influential as Director of the Glasgow College of Art. Landscape artist and engraver, administrator and teacher, as well as a wise judge of character and professional ability. Many students had a great deal for which to thank him. Educated Watson's College, Edinburgh 1912-18 and Edinburgh University 1918-22, he studied painting at the Royal College of Art under Sir William Rothenstein and Eric Ravilious 1922-25, also wood engraving under Sir Frank Short. Published and illustrated *Border Ballads* while still a student (1925). Wrote *A History of Wood Engraving* (1928) and became the London art critic for *The Scotsman.* Taught part-time at Hornsey School of Art 1932-1940 and Blackheath 1934-40. In 1934 he was

elected a member of the Society of Wood Engravers. From 1946 until his retirement in 1964 Director, Glasgow School of Art. During this time he illustrated 12 books and published many essays in such publications as *The Studio, The Print Collector's Quarterly* and *Art World.* Other published work included illustrations for *The History of Rasselas, Prince of Abyssinia* (1926), *Salamander in Spring* (1933), *The Devil in Scotland* (1934), Poe's *Tales of Mystery and Imagination* (1938) and the *Memoirs of Prince Alexy Haimetoff* (1952). His work is meticulously detailed in the pre-Raphaelite manner. During World War I served with the RAF. Partial to bright colours and the scenery of the West Highlands which he portrayed romantically. The texture of dyke stones and old crofts particularly fascinated him. Horne notes that "the difficulty of getting satisfactory results by 'dropping' engravings into a page of text persuaded [Bliss] to try his hand at line drawings, sometimes with stencilled colour. The pen and ink illustrations for Painter's *Palace of Pleasure* 1929, with their visual wit, demonstrate his skill". John Russell Taylor thought that Bliss's finest hour was with his watercolours in the 1980s. Married Phyllis Dodd. His principal works include 'Summer in the Hebrides' and 'Windy Day'. Elected RBA 1939. Exhibited RA(24), RSA(12), RBA(6), GI(2) & L(3). Represented in SNGMA, Glasgow AG, Perth AG.
**Bibl:** Alpine Gallery, London, 'Douglas P Bliss. Paintings, Watercolours and Wood Engravings' (Ex Cat 1980); Blond Fine Art, London, 'Douglas P Bliss: Watercolours and Wood Engravings' (Ex Cat 1980); Albert Garrett, A History of British Wood Engraving, 1978; Hartley, 117-118; John Russell Taylor: "How the Modern Classics Confront Their Own Eighties", The Times 8 Jly 1980; Balston; Deane; Garrett 1 & 2; Horne 108-9; Times Obit Mar 20 1984.

**BLISS, Rosalind** **1937-**
Born London. Glasgow-based painter and printmaker. Daughter of Douglas Percy B(qv). Trained as a mural painter, worked also as a potter. Taught engraving by her father. Exhibited Greek scenes RSA 1963-4.

**BLORE, Edward FRS FSA** **1787-1879**
Born Rutland. Architect and architectural draughtsman. Eldest son of Thomas Blore, historian of Rutland. Based for a time in Edinburgh, he was responsible with William Atkinson for re-building Abbotsford in the Gothic style for Sir Walter Scott (1816-23). His friendship with the author resulted in his employment as 'manager' of *The Provincial Antiquities & Picturesque Scenery of Scotland* for which he contributed all the architectural drawings. He was made a 'special architect' to William IV and Queen Victoria in which capacity he completed Buckingham Palace 1831-37. Surveyor of Westminster Abbey 1827-49, and designed Corehouse, Lanarkshire. He left 48 volumes of architectural drawings, now in the British Museum, including his designs for Buckingham Palace; also represented in V&A, Society of Antiquaries.
**Bibl:** Colvin 78-82; Dunbar 124; Houfe 237.

**BLUNT, Miss Sybil Allan** **1880-**
Painter, etcher and black and white artist. Studied at the Byam Shaw School of Art and Edinburgh College of Art. First exhibit was from an address in Edinburgh 1911 but in the 1920s moved to the south of England. Exhibited RSA(3), RA(4) & L(3).

**BLYTH, John W** **fl 1948-1981**
Edinburgh watercolourist and stained glass window designer. Studied under and became assistant to William Wilson(qv). Designed and executed two windows in Beauly parish church, Ross-shire, in collaboration with William Wilson(qv), also in St Andrew's, Alyth, (c1952); also the War Memorial lights in Dalry church (now St Bride's Community Centre)(1949) and Holyrood Abbey church (1949). Two lights 'Suffer the little children' are in St James church, Rosefield Place, Edinburgh. Regularly exhibited RSA 1948-1957, and again 1971.
**Bibl:** Gifford 44,504,555,651; Painton Cowen, Stained Glass in Britain, 1985, 232,238.

**BLYTH, Robert Henderson RSA RSW** **1919-1970**
Born Newlands, Glasgow 21 May; died Aberdeen, 18 May. Landscape painter in oil, watercolour and gouache. Trained Glasgow School of Art under Forrester Wilson(qv) 1934-1939 and at Hospitalfield Art College, Arbroath under James Cowie 1938. During World War 2 served in the Royal Army Medical Corps and continued to paint while in France, Belgium, Holland and Germany. First exhibited RSA 1937. Won the RSA's Guthrie Award 1945. Joined Edinburgh School of Art as an assistant to Gillies(qv) in 1946, then Gray's School of Art, Aberdeen 1954, becoming head of drawing and painting 1960. Fond of broad sweeps of tightly controlled, sometimes garish colour. Elected SSA 1949, ARSA 1949, RSW 1949, RSA 1958. Exhibited RSA(171) & AAS 1959-1969 from 106 Desswood Place, Aberdeen. Represented in Aberdeen AG, Dundee AG, Glasgow AG, Perth AG, Paisley AG, Nottingham AG, City of Edinburgh collection. There was a retrospective exhibition 1987.
**Bibl:** Halsby 231,249; Macmillan [SA], 364.

**BLYTH(E), Charles A** **fl 1846-1849**
Edinburgh landscape painter in oil. Exhibited RSA in 1846 and having moved to Peebles, again in 1849.

**BLYTH(E), James** **fl 1934-1941**
Leith artist. Exhibited RSA(4).

**BOAG, Andrew** **1870-1915**
Greenock landscape artist and engraver. Conducted an engraving and stationery business at 3 Barton St, Greenock in the 1880s. Exhibited GI(1) & locally 1899-1915.

**BOAG, Francis** **1948-**
Born Dundee. Painter, primarily in acrylic and oils; teacher. Trained Duncan of Jordanstone College of Art 1965-69, studying under Alberto Morrocco(qv) and David McClure(qv). Art teacher, Dundee 1970-76 before being appointed Head of Art, Aberdeen GS 1989-2001. Following a series of successful exhibitions in London, Dublin and Scotland, he abandoned teaching in order to paint full-time in 2001. A prolific artist, he paints in the Scottish colourist tradition, revelling in vibrant colours depicting landscapes in stylistic patchworks of brilliant colour and texture. His work is extremely popular with items exhibited in New York and Seattle, as well as in Germany, France and Spain, and throughout Britain. Began exhibiting RSA 1999, RSW 1999, RGI 1999, AAS and Paisley (invited) 2002. Scottish representative in *Work Small, Learn Big!* (2003) in which 17 international artists offer advice on painting skills.
**Bibl:** 'Technicolour Dreamcoat', *International Artist*, 23, Feb/Mar 2002, 86-93, illus.

**BOARDMAN, J A C** **fl 1896**
Dumfries artist; exhibited GI(1).

**BODEN, Leonard FRSA** **1911-1993**
Born Greenock. Portrait painter. Educated at Sedbergh and trained Glasgow School of Art and Heatherley's in London. Painted three official portraits of Queen Elizabeth II, four of Prince Philip, and a large 9 ft x 6 ft portrait of Pope Pius XII now in the Vatican. Also many other eminent figures of the day from his London studio. Married Margaret Boden(qv). Member of the Council of the Royal Society of Portrait Painters. Made a Freeman of the City of London. Exhibited a number of portraits RSA 1950-53. Represented in NPG.

**BODEN, Margaret FRSA** **c1912-2002**
Born Ecclesmachen. Painter of portraits in oil and pastel. Educated at Dowanhill; studied art at Glasgow School of Art and Heatherley's in London. Spent some time in France where she was influenced by the work of Rembrandt, Rubens, Velasquez and the French Impressionists. Many distinguished sitters, among them Sir Charles Forte, Beryl Grey and Eileen Joyce. Also painted animals and children. Married to Leonard Boden(qv). Exhibited Paris Salon where she received an honourable mention, frequently at the RA, ROI, RI, & RP. Represented in Bradford AG, Royal Collection.

**BODLEY, George Frederick** **1827-1907**
Dundee architect responsible for St. Salvador's Episcopal church "which combines simplicity of form with rich interior decoration in gesso, stencilwork and painted glass' [Dunbar]. Robert Lorimer(qv) worked for a spell in his office.
**Bibl:** Dunbar, 151,165.

**BOGLE, John H(?)** **c1746-1803**
Born West of Scotland, probably Glasgow; died Edinburgh.

Miniature painter. Bogle has been described as 'one of the most important Scottish artists of the 18th Century'. Son of an excise officer whose wife was sister to the 'beggar Earl of Menteith'. The Earldom became dormant on the death of the 8th Earl in 1694 and the succession was obscure. John Bogle was the heir presumptive but made no claim, though his sister Mary styled herself Lady Mary Bogle. Bogle studied at the drawing school in Glasgow founded in 1753 by Robert and Andrew Foulis(qv). In 1769 he married the beautiful daughter of a Nithsdale merchant. The same year he was working in Edinburgh and exhibited at the Society of Artists from an Edinburgh address in 1769 and again in 1770. That year he went to London and began exhibiting at the Royal Academy in 1772 continuing to exhibit there until 1794. Returned to Edinburgh 1800. Most of his miniatures are small but the larger ones are especially good. His technique is not easy to describe; 'he painted with a soft colouring shaded with a minute stippling which, particularly in the treatment of the hair, often produces a curiously woollen effect when viewed under a lens. His draughtsmanship was good, and the sitters costumes well painted. He often painted a small area of dark shading over the sitters head' [Foskett]. Long found his work "very deliberate and painstaking, lacking in fluency and dash; often charming and showing a certain naiveté. His colouring, usually restrained, is harmonious and good...his touch soft". Painted an attractive portrait of Fanny Burney in whose company he attended the trial of Warren Hastings in the Great Hall of Westminster 1783, in which the author's humour is beautifully portrayed. It is inscribed on the reverse "Miss Bunny" (the diarist's nickname) indicating that Bogle knew her well. A portrait of Mary Queen of Scots, formerly in Alloa Tower, was copied by Bogle and mentioned by J Stoddart in his book *Remarks on...Scotland,* II, 232. An ivory of a man in a plum coloured suit, bearing the inscription on the background 'Sam L Foote/Born Truro/AUG 24-17-21/J(?I)-H-BOGLE/PINXT' is in the Holburne Museum, Bath; Long described it as a good miniature "the stippling of the features being somewhat like that of Galloway". Allan Cunningham noted that Bogle lived in difficulty and died in poverty, 'he loved to paint the heads of ladies which no-one did more gracefully. His portrait of Lady Eglinton, to whom the 'Gentle Shepherd' is inscribed, may be compared with any miniature of modern times. He excelled in small likenesses, was a little lame man, very proud, very poor and very singular'. Exhibited London Academy 1775,1776,1777 & 1787. Examples of Bogle's work are in SNG, V & A, SNPG, City of Edinburgh collection, Holburne (Bath) AG, National Gallery of Eire (Dublin).
**Bibl:** Brydall 220; Caw 45; Foskett 1,169; Long 33-35; Macmillan [SA], 150; McKay 323.

**BOGLE, Mrs Margaret** **fl 1873-1880**
Edinburgh oil painter of figurative subjects. Exhibited 5 times at the RSA, always from Edinburgh except in 1878 from an address in Dusseldorf. Married to William Lockhart Bogle(qv).

**BOGLE, William Lockhart** **fl 1881-d1900**
Born in the Highlands; died 20 May. Portrait and figure painter, also illustrator. Also an accomplished archaeologist and a champion wrestler. Member of the Gilmorehill family, he studied at Glasgow University and after seven years apprenticeship to a lawyer moved to London to study painting at Bushey School of Art under Herkomer. Heavy in technique and monochromatic in colour although as a pen draughtsman his illustrations for *Good Words* carry a certain conviction, especially those which represent the romantic side of Highland life in Jacobite times. A portrait of William Thackeray (1900) is in Trinity College, Cambridge. Signed his work 'Lockhart Bogle' or 'LB'. Contributed illustrations to *Illustrated London News* (1886-1889); *The Graphic* (1882-1889) and to *Good Words* (1891-1894). In addition to his exhibits at the RSA(6), including an arresting study 'The Skye Crofter' (1885), he showed 20 works at the RA, also RBA(6), GI(6) & L (6). Represented in V & A.
**Bibl:** Caw 272; Houfe 238.

**BOGUE, Thomas H** **fl 1882-1884**
Edinburgh landscape painter in oil; also scene painter. Worked for the Theatre Royal in Edinburgh and exhibited at the RSA during the above years.

**BOHM, H R** **fl 1887**
A Broughty Ferry artist; exhibited RSA(2).

**BONAR, Thomas** **fl 1858**
Amateur Edinburgh oil painter of figurative subjects; exhibited RSA(2).

**BOND, Marj RSW** **1939-**
Fife artist, mainly in watercolour; also printmaker. Studied Glasgow School of Art under Alex Dick(qv), David Donaldson(qv), Mary Armour(qv) and Benno Schotz(qv). Received Anne Redpath Award 1984. Elected SSWA 1975, SSA 1989, RSW 1989. In 1988 a visit to India stimulated her to work more with hand-made paper. Her work is fresh in colour, bold in design and sometimes coarse in texture. Council member of the SSWA 1980-83. Exhibits regularly RSA & GI.

**BOND, R S** **fl 1861-1866**
Hamilton landscape painter in oil who exhibited 2 works at the RSA.

**BONE, Miss Freda C** **fl 1928-1935**
Helensburgh-based artist and wood engraver. Daughter of the master-mariner and author Captain David Bone (Commodore of the Anchor Line in 1915) and niece of Muirhead Bone(qv). Trained Glasgow School of Art 1928-32. Illustrated a number of books including D W Bone: *Capstan Bards: Nautical Songs* (1931), O'Brien: *Without My Cloak* (1931), Tunstall: *The Shining Night* (1931), A Bone: *Bowsprit Ashore* (1932), and Holden: *Grace O'Light* (1935). Horne found her work sometimes reminiscent of Gwendolen Raverat and Joan Hassall. Moved with her father to 5 Grosvenor Terrace, Glasgow 1932. Exhibited RSA during the above period.
**Bibl:** Horne 110.

**BONE, John Craigie** **fl 1911-1914**
Lived at 45 Marchmont Road, Edinburgh; exhibited 5 works at the RSA during the above years, all ecclesiastical illustrations.

**BONE, Sir Muirhead HRSA HRWS HARIBA HRE LLB D Litt** **1876-1953**
Born Partick, Glasgow, 23 Mar; died Oxford, 21 Oct. Painter of portraits and topographical subjects, also etcher and draughtsman. Son of a journalist. Attended evening classes at Glasgow School of Art under Fra Newbery(qv), having been persuaded to go there by his schoolmaster, Archibald Kay(qv). Brother of the master-mariner and author Captain David Bone, father of Stephen Bone(qv) and uncle of Freda Bone(qv). In 1901 he moved to London, becoming a member of the Society of Twelve. Married 1903 Gertrude Dodd, sister of Francis Dodd. From 1902 he was a member of the NEAC having exhibited with them from 1898. His first set of Glasgow etchings 1898 drew upon the prints of Meryon and Whistler. In 1901, following his series of etchings for the International Exhibition in Glasgow, he moved to London. Embarked on frequent continental tours with his wife, resulting in a number of books written by her and illustrated by him. Much of his best work was done in his capacity as official artist on the western front and with the Fleet during the second half of WW1 and during WW2 as official war artist to the Admiralty 1940-43. A distinguished print maker, he was an excellent draughtsman especially of architectural subjects. Trustee of the Tate Gallery from 1927, also of the National Gallery and the Imperial War Museum, supporting young artists such as Epstein. 'As a painter he was distinguished, as an etcher he was outstanding in a generation that knew great etchers, but it is by his drawings in a wide range of mediums that he will be best remembered. He had an uncanny gift in rendering the complexities of crowded scenes. The immensities of industrial or constructional schemes, the confused order of shipyards, the bustle and excitement of great occasions...he had, above all, the gift of rendering the feeling and emotional content of his subject matter and...the mystery of night in Spain, the grim realities of war in Flanders, the uncertainties of mist and discomforts of drizzle on shipping in the sea approaches'[Houfe]. Moved to Oxford in the 1930s; knighted 1937. Illustrated *Glasgow* in 1901 (1901), *Children's Children* (1908), *Glasgow, Fifty Drawings* (1911), *The Front Line* (1916), *Merchant Men-at-Arms* (1919), *The London Perambulator, Days in Old Spain* (1938), *London Echoing* (1948), *Merchant Men Rearmed* (1949), *The English and Their Country* (1951), and *Come to Oxford* (1952). Also contributed to *The Yellow Book* (1897). Exhibited in many places including RA(17), RSA(100+), RSW(3), GI(50), AAS 1923-1933 and over 500 works in various other London Galleries. Represented in V & A, NGS(18

landscapes), SNGMA, Tate AG, Paisley AG, City of Edinburgh collection, Brodie Castle (NTS), Perth AG.
**Bibl:** M Bone 'Talks with great Scots', Scotland, Spring 1937; M Bone 'From Glasgow to London', Artwork, 1929, 143-164; C Dodgson, Etchings and Drypoints of Muirhead Bone (1897-1907) London 1909; C Dodgson, 'The Later Drypoints of Muirhead Bone (1908-1916)', Print Collector's Quarterly, Feb 1922, 173-200; Crawford Centre for the Arts, St Andrews, 'Muirhead Bone, Portrait of the Artist' (Ex Cat 1986) - Essay by Peter Trowles; Halsby 238-9,249; Hartley 118; Houfe 238; Macmillan [SA], 303-7 et passim.

**BONE, Miss Phyllis Mary RSA** **1894-1972**
Born Hornsby, Lancashire, 15 Feb; died Kirkcudbright, 12 Jly. Sculptress, specialising in animals. Trained Edinburgh College of Art, Paris and Rome. After education at St George's School 1907 she entered her name at the Royal Institute of Art and in 1910 at the New College of Art where she became a student in 1912 gaining a Diploma in Sculpture in 1918. In Paris she studied under the animal sculptor Nevallier. On her return to Scotland assisted Pilkington Jackson(qv) in Edinburgh for some time, before directing commissions by Sir Robert Lorimer(qv) for the animal sculpture on the Scottish National War Memorial enabled her to launch an independent career. Responsible for sculpting the animals on the elaborate Ecology building at Edinburgh University, as well as many other commissions including embellishments for the chapel at Stowe school and the lion and unicorn reliefs at the entrance to St Andrew's House. She executed a succession of animal statuettes in bronze widely exhibited in Britain and Paris. Her last 23 years were spent in Kirkcudbright. Throughout her life she suffered the burden of lameness made no easier by the knowledge that it could have been corrected if properly treated when a child. The first woman to be elected ARSA 1940, RSA 1944. Exhibited RSA(140) & AAS 1959-1967.
**Bibl:** Gifford 100,441; Peter Savage, Lorimer and the Edinburgh Craft Designers, Edinburgh 1980, 150, 162.

**BONE, Stephen** **1904-1958**
Born Chiswick Nov 13; died London 15 Sep. Painter of landscape and portraits, illustrator, wood engraver and writer. Son of Sir Muirhead Bone(qv), he lived all his life in England being educated at Bedales School (during which he had a drawing accepted by the NEAC), and studying at the Slade under Henry Tonks and exhibited only rarely in Scotland (twice at the GI) and on a few occasions with the Fine Art Society. During the War he worked for the Civil Defence Camouflage Establishment, later becoming an official Naval Artist. Awarded Gold Medal, Paris 1926. Author of several books including *Guide-Book to the West Coast of Scotland* (1938, rev.1952), *An Artist's Britain* (1939, rev. 1949) and *Oil Painting* (1956). In 1948 became art critic of the *Manchester Guardian.* Married the designer Mary Adshead 1929 with whom he collaborated on several children's books. Illustrated G Bone (his mother): *The Furrowed Earth* (1921), *Mr Paul* (1921), Bourne: *A Farmer's Life* (1922), Davies: *Selected Poems*, G Bone: *Oasis* (1924), *Of the Western Isles* (1925), *The Hidden Orchis* (1928), *The Cope* (1930), Brooke: *The Military Orchid* (1948). Exhibited mostly in London including RA(12), also RSA(3) in 1945 and 1947, AAS(1) in 1929, also at the Galerie Moderne (Stockholm). Represented in Tate AG, Glasgow AG, Dundee AG, Paisley AG, Manchester AG, National Gallery of Eire (Dublin).
**Bibl:** Horne 110; Ian Jaffray; *The British Landscape 1920-1950* (1984); The Times Obituary 16 Sep 1958; Harries; Peppin, Waters.

**BONE, William Drummond RSW ARSA** **1907-1979**
Born Ayr; died Ayr, Nov. Painter in oil and watercolour, also pencil; genre and landscape. An early interest in art was encouraged by his uncle Sir Muirhead Bone(qv). From 1928-1931 trained Glasgow School of Art, a travelling scholarship enabled him to visit Italy and later Germany and Holland. Best known for his wartime watercolours, his portraits and landscapes in oil and his figurative drawings. Usually signed his work in capitals. Exhibited many works at the RSA, also GI(5). Elected ARSA 1969, RSW 1950. Represented in Aberdeen AG, RSA, Royal collection.

**BONIMAN, James** **fl 1895**
Painter. Lived at 38 Cambridge Gardens, Edinburgh and exhibited 2 works at the RSA in 1895.

**BONNAR, Mrs** **fl 1896**
Amateur artist. Exhibited RSA(1) from 7 Fingal Place, Edinburgh.

**BONNAR, Archibald** **fl 1852-1854**
Edinburgh portrait painter who exhibited at the RSA during the above period.

**BONNAR, John** **fl 1743-1782**
Edinburgh decorative painter. Apprenticed to Robert Norie on 8 Mar, 1743 for 8 years, being discharged on 28 Feb 1751. He became a Master Painter in 1756. Completed the work at Penicuik House begun by Alexander Runciman with paintings of mythological subjects on the ceiling of one of the staircases signed and dated 1782. This is recorded in a watercolour drawing at the Royal Commission for Ancient and Historical Monuments in Scotland. Jacob More(qv) may have been apprenticed to him.
**Bibl:** John Gray, Description of Art Treasures at Penicuik House; Macmillan [SA], 54.

**BONNAR, John A T** **fl 1885-1889**
Edinburgh painter in oil and watercolour of historical and figurative subjects. Among his exhibits at the RSA in 1885 was 'The Trial of Queen Caroline' and 'The Downfall of Wolsey'. An interesting painter of considerable skill but his output was limited and his work is now seldom seen. Exhibited RSA(13) & AAS(1) 1886.

**BONNAR, Mrs Jessie (née Rhind)** **fl 1896**
Edinburgh illustrator. Married Thomas Bonnar(qv). Exhibited designs for a book illustration at the RSA in 1896.

**BONNAR, Miss Mary C** **fl 1892-1905**
Amateur painter of figurative subjects and landscape. Lived in the Abbot's House, Dunfermline and exhibited once at the GI, but more frequently with Dunfermline Fine Art Association where the prices she commanded compared favourably with such better known artists as William Mouncey(qv) and Marshall Brown(qv).

**BONNAR, Thomas** **?-1847**
Edinburgh architect and architectural administrator. Succeeded William Sibbald(qv) as City Superintendent of Works 1809 but was removed from office 1818. Three years later appointed Surveyor to the Heriot Trust in which capacity he was responsible for general development on the W side of the new town including most specifically 2-40 Albany St, much of Barony St, the design of Bellevue Crescent and Atholl Crescent(1825).
**Bibl:** Gifford 205,336,340-9,351,361,370,422,437,478,641.

**BONNAR, Thomas** **1810-1873**
Edinburgh decorative artist. Father of Thomas(qv). Worked for D R Hay & Co before becoming establishing the firm Bonnar & Co. Specialised in painted ceilings, including work with Robert Lorimer(qv) at Earlshall. Responsible for miniature oval pastoral scenes in gilt arabesques at Mortonhall c1840 and may have executed the neo-Jacobean ceilings in St Leonard's, Pollock Halls, Edinburgh 1869-70. Exhibited RSA(2) 1872.
**Bibl:** Gifford 490,638.

**BONNAR, Thomas Jnr** **?-1899**
Edinburgh designer and painter in oil and watercolour; stained glass windows, ceilings, figurative subjects. Son of Thomas(qv). Responsible for elaborate painted ceiling in McMorran house on the Royal Mile(1898), the ceiling and corner roundels for the chapel of George Watson's Hospital, the sumptuously decorated ceiling in the old Council Chamber, Leith Town Hall(1891-2) and the heraldic decorations(1892) within Liberton House. Exhibited RSA(17) including a decoration for the roof at Falkland Palace, a library ceiling for Inchdrewer House, Colinton (1896) and additional ceilings for Falkland Palace (1897), also several designs at the AAS in 1893, from 127 George Street, Aberdeen.
**Bibl:** Gifford 200,260,404,443,465,489.

**BONNAR, Thomas A** **fl 1843-1858**
Scottish painter of portraits, nature studies and subject paintings. The Darnley Conspirators shown at the RSA in 1858, received considerable attention.

**BONNAR, Thomas Kershaw** **fl 1897**
Edinburgh architect and architectural draughtsman. related to Thomas Bonnar(qv). Exhibited RSA(1).

**BONNAR, William RSA** **1800-1853**
Born and died Edinburgh. Father of William Bonnar Jnr(qv). This artist, who spelt his name 'Bonar' until 1829, had a career of three distinct parts. He was a house-decorator, then a painter of domestic subjects, genre and historical works and finally - and most successfully - a portrait painter. Caw thought that his pastoral pieces and children were better suited to his talent than his more ambitious historical pieces. His genre subjects showed a marked Wilkie influence. Although primarily a painter of genre in terms of the number of works executed, in later years his portraits showed the full flowering of his genius. In 1822 he assisted David Roberts in decorating the Assembly Rooms for the visit of George IV. His first important picture was 'The Tinkers', exhibited in 1824, followed a short time later by a major work 'John Knox Administering the Sacraments'. Brydall considered that although not possessing much power or originality of conception and expression, Bonnar's pictures often suffered from a crudenesss of colour. Elected RSA 1929. Exhibited RSA(105). The NGS possesses his 'Self-portrait' and also one of G M Kemp, the ill-fated architect of the Scott Monument. Represented by 8 works in the SNPG, Perth AG and an attributed work in the City of Edinburgh collection.
**Bibl:** AJ 1853, 76; Armstrong 46; Brydall 377-378; Caw; DNB; Halsby 62; Hardie 40(illus); Mackay 259; Macmillan [SA], 183-4.

**BONNAR, William Jnr** **fl 1849**
Edinburgh landscape painter in oil. Son and pupil of William B(qv). Exhibited RSA(2).

**BONTINE, James** **fl 1674-1686**
Son of the Town Clerk of Dumbarton. Probably a herald painter having been apprenticed in 1674 to George Porteous(qv). In 1686 he raised an unsuccessful criminal procedure against the Deacon of Wright's and George Porteous for robbing his house and taking away his colours, imprisoning him and threatening him with torture. Subsequently Porteous pursued Bontine for attacking him in the High Street and beating him.
**Bibl:** Apted 30; Historical notices of Scottish affairs, selected from the mss of Sir John Lauder of Fountainhall Bt, Bannatyne Club 1848.

**BOOTH, Mrs H (Isabella) Gore** **fl 1856-1884**
Sculptress. Worked for many years in London before moving to Scotland in c1857. Specialised in portrait busts and also figurative subjects. Among her 10 works exhibited at the RA (1856-1878) was a marble bust of James Smith FRS. In about 1889 moved to Manchester. Exhibited RSA 1878-1883 and occasionally in Glasgow at the GI.

**BOOTH, William** **1807-1845**
Born Aberdeen. Miniaturist. Encouraged by his friend and probably teacher Andrew Robertson(qv), he went to London 1825. Entered the RA Schools the same year and two years later was exhibiting at the RA and the Society of British Artists, continuing to do so until 1845. Won silver medal 1827. His portrait of John Constable was exhibited at the RA in 1836. Specialised in children and serving officers. His work has been likened to that of Thorburn Ross(qv) and to Edward Robertson(qv). Sometimes painted full-scale miniatures as large as ten inches often with a lot of gum. In 1865 Mrs William Angus loaned three ivory miniatures by Booth to an exhibition at the South Kensington Museum, one of them a portrait of the artist's son and another of his sister, both dated 1843. Exhibited RSA between 1829 and 1844 and also posthumously in 1880.
**Bibl:** Foskett 1. 173-4; Long 42; Rb.

**BORLACH(K), John** **fl c1710**
Scottish draughtsman and watercolourist. A perspective drawing of Kinross House which differs significantly from Edward's sketch of 1645 is in the possession of Mrs C Purvis Russell Montgomery. An engraving of the work appeared in William Adam's *Vitruvius Scoticus* (1810).

**BORLAND, Christine** **1965-**
Born Darvel, Ayrshire. Studied Glasgow School of Art before graduating at the Univ. of Ulster 1988. First solo exhibition, Glasgow 1992. Has exhibited in Berlin, at the Venice Biennale 1995, Münster 1997, Luxembourg 1998 and in 1998-9 had a retrospective exhibition at De Appel, Amsterdam, also Zurich and Porto. She strives to straddle the borders of art and science, emotion and logic. In her most recent work, she painted bone china skulls in a manner and patterning to evoke issues of cloning and genetic engineering. The problem inherent in such modern attempts of fusion is that contrivance replaces beauty.
**Bibl:** Macmillan 2001, 171,178, illus 195.

**BORLAND, Miss M E** **fl 1883-1888**
Amateur Castle Douglas painter. Probably daughter of W D Borland(qv). Exhibited 3 works at the GI during the above period.

**BORLAND, W D** **fl 1866-d-1877**
Born Castle Douglas; died Newton Stewart, 13 Oct. Amateur artist, member of a family business of house painters. Married late, in 1875. Probably father of Miss M E Borland(qv). Exhibited a Kircudbright landscape at the RSA 1866.

**BORRIE, Miss Eleanora Anderson (Mrs Henderson) SSA** **1917-**
Born Edinburgh, 22 Jne. Painter in oil; landscape, flowers. Trained Edinburgh College of Art 1935-1940. Exhibited RA 1933-34, 'Chrysanthemums' at RSA 1943 and 'A view over Dean Mews' 1944, also RBA, all from her London studio.

**BORROWMAN, Lt Col Charles Gordon RSW** **1892-1956**
Born Edinburgh, 30 May; died Dunkeld, 14 Oct. Painter in watercolour; animals, figures and landscape. Educated at Edinburgh University and at the Edinburgh College of Art 1912-1917 and 1920, under William Walls(qv), David Alison(qv) and Robert Burns(qv). Embarked upon a full-time army career becoming a company commander with the 4th Gurkha Rifles, providing the opportunity to paint many Indian subjects. First commissioned 1912 and after retirement settled in Dunkeld. First president, reconstituted Pershshire Art Association 1952-56. A memorial exhibition of his work was held in Perth 1959. Elected RSW 1945. Exhibited RSA(35), RSW(21), GI(5), L(1) & SSA. Represented in Glasgow AG, Perth AG.
**Bibl:** Halsby 249.

**BORTHWICK, Alfred Edward RSA PRSW ARBA ARE** **1871-1955**
Born Scarborough. Painter in oil and watercolour; portraits, landscapes and religious studies; also occasional stained glass window designer. Trained at Edinburgh College of Art, in London and at the Academie Julian in Paris. Settled in Edinburgh. Served in both the Boer War and WW1. Employed a free, wet and typically Scottish technique, in the manner of the Hague School. Both his daughters, Marjorie(qv) and Miss G R B(qv), painted. Designed the W rose window 'Christ as teacher' for Christ Church, Bruntsfield Place (1926). Elected ARE 1909, RSW 1911, ARBA 1927, RSA 1938, President of the RSW 1932-1951. Exhibited RA(7), RSA(88), GI(33), RSW(93), RI(1), AAS(12) 1893-1923 & L(8). Represented in SNPG, NGS(two landscapes), Glasgow AG, Kirkcaldy AG, Paisley AG, Edinburgh City collection(5), Perth AG.
**Bibl:** Gifford 616; Halsby 249.

**BORTHWICK, Miss Hannah C** **fl 1894-1896**
Amateur oil painter of landscape. Exhibited AAS from Cornhill-on-Tweed.

**BORTHWICK, Miss G R** **fl 1927**
Edinburgh watercolourist. Daughter of Alfred Edward Borthwick(qv). Exhibited RSW(1).

**BORTHWICK, Ian T** **fl 1981**
Painter in oil of 55A Nelson Street, Aberdeen. Exhibited AAS.

**BORTHWICK, John** **fl 1828-1843**
Edinburgh portrait and landscape painter; exhibited intermittently at the RSA between the above years.

**BORTHWICK, Miss Marjorie E** **fl 1933-1940**
Edinburgh watercolour painter. Daughter of Alfred Edward Borthwick(qv). Exhibited RSW(14), RSA(1) & GI(7).

**BOSE, Fanindra Nath ARSA** **?-1926**
Born Calcutta; died Edinburgh, 1 Aug. Sculptor of figurative subjects. The first sculptor of Indian nationality to receive official

recognition in Great Britain. Came to study art at Edinburgh College of Art at the age of 15 under Percy Portsmouth(qv). Obtained all possible honours including a travelling scholarship which enabled him to visit France. When in Paris he was introduced to Rodin who took a great interest in the young Indian. Worked from the Dean Studios. Among his exhibits was 'The Snake Charmer' 1922, [lent by the Gaekwar of Baroda], and 'St John the Baptist', designed for a memorial shrine at St John's Church, Perth 1926. Settled in Edinburgh, having married a Scot. Occasionally visited India where he had a number of patrons including, most importantly, the Gaekwar of Baroda. A keen angler, he died whilst on a fishing trip to Peebles. Portsmouth said of his work 'Bose excelled in small sculpture; he had a phenomenal control of minutiae. It was most interesting to watch his beautiful hands manipulate his sculpture...he was an excellent craftsman, a true artist, showing delicacy and taste in everything he did.' Elected ARSA 1925. Exhibited regularly a total of 22 works at the RSA between 1909 and 1927, also RA(4) & GI(2).

**BOSSE, Edward** **fl 1848-1851**
Edinburgh portrait painter who exhibited 5 works at the RSA between the above dates from 16 Albany Street.

**BOSTON, Thomas** **fl 1884-1886**
Glasgow portrait painter; exhibited GI(2) between the above dates. Represented in SNPG.

**BOSWALL, Alexander** **?-1752**
Obscure early heraldic painter. Painted the back of the lower tier in the chancel of Magdalen Chapel, Cowgate(c1725) with the arms of the trades forming the Incorporation of Hammermen, and a ceiling in the same Chapel, now lost.
**Bibl:** Gifford 164,165n.

**BOSWELL, Elizabeth of Balmuto** **fl c1820-1830**
Painter in oil of flowers. Trained under Patrick Syme(qv) with whom she eloped and married. A tinted pencil drawing of her in 1817 by Andrew Geddes survives in a private collection.
**Bibl:** Halsby 51.

**BOSWELL, George A** **fl 1829-1833**
Amateur Glasgow painter. Exhibited GI(3) between the above dates.

**BOSWELL, Georgina L D** **fl 1898**
Painter in oil of pastural scenes. Exhibited AAS from Carralan, Cumnock, Ayrshire.

**BOSWELL, James E** **1906-1971**
Exhibited topographical works and landscape at the RSA in 1955, 1959 and 1961. His last address was Longformacus.

**BOTHWELL, Margaret K** **fl 1959**
Aberdeen portrait painter in oil. Exhibited AAS from 139 Forest Avenue.

**BOTTOMLEY, John William** **1816-1900**
Probably English, although in the 1860s was living at 31 Nelson Street, Edinburgh. Trained in Munich and Dusseldorf. Exhibited 4 animal studies and several Scottish landscapes at the RSA & GI(1).

**BOUCHER, James** **c1832-1906/7**
Glasgow architect. Apprenticed alongside James Cousland(qv) to Charles Wilson(qv). After Cousland's early death Boucher became associated with the Saracen Ironworks. From c1876 entered partnership with **Henry HIGGINS**. Among other major Glasgow buildings he designed Wm Teacher's, 14-18 St Enoch Sq and the Carron building, 123-129 Buchanan St.
**Bibl:** A Gomme & David Walker, Architecture of Glasgow, London 1987, 217(illus),247(illus),286.

**BOUGH, Samuel RSA** **1822-1878**
Born Carlisle, 8 Jan; died Edinburgh, 19 Nov. Painter in oil and watercolour, also illustrator; landscape and coastal/harbour scenes. Although strictly speaking he was not a Scot, he came from Border ancestry and all his later associations were Scottish; it was as a member of the RSA that he won success and fame while the influence he exerted over the artistic community was most strongly found in Scotland. Son of a Carlisle shoemaker who encouraged him to become an artist and arranged training at a minor academy run by a local cobbler and amateur painter, John Dobson. When aged 15 Bough went to learn the art of landscape-engraving from Thomas Allom's mother in London. Bough was a restless young man and at the age of 18 returned to Carlisle where he contributed nine drawings to an illustrated edition of the *History of Leath Wood in the County of Cumberland* (1840). He appears to have been rather feckless, entering into all kinds of scrapes. In 1845 he took a position as scene-painter at the Theatre Royal, Manchester. The first scene which he painted, a backcloth, about 40 feet in width, showing a large oak in a woodland, so pleased the manager that the young man's salary was at once raised by 5 shillings. Whilst there he worked towards the exhibition of the Royal Manchester Institution 1847 to which he contributed 5 works, winning a silver medal for the best watercolour. Towards the end of 1848 he moved to Glasgow becoming scene-painter at the new Princess Theatre. At this time he married but fell out with the theatre manager and the following year was working at the Adelphi Theatre in Edinburgh. There he had another quarrel and was again thrown upon his own resources. His first well-known work, 'Barncluith', now in Glasgow AG, dates from this time. Leaving the world of theatre, Bough moved to Hamilton in order to be close to Cadzow forest. In 1851 he painted the forest in oil, winning the West of Scotland Fine Art Association's gold medal for the best Scottish landscape. In 1855 he was at 2 Upper Dean Terrace, Edinburgh later moving to 5 Malta Terrace, Stockbridge. This was the year he exhibited 6 works at the RSA. Elected ARSA 1856. Because of his difficult personality election to full membership of the Academy was delayed until 1875. Between 1848 and 1855 he often painted in and around Cadzow with his friend Alexander Fraser(qv). It has been said that vitality lies at the back of what is best in his art. His watercolours, with their affinity to Muller and Cox, was perhaps his finest medium. A prolific worker, composing with great speed, he often completed a picture in a single day. Became increasingly enamoured with the bustle of crowded ports, but seldom went abroad apart from an occasional visit to a few French harbours. Because his best period was regarded as 1855-1870 he was known to have signed '1857' on many very much later works. The free use of turpentine imparts something of the watercolour treatment to his finest oils. R L Stevenson said that a painting by Bough was an act of dashing conduct like the capture of a fort in war. McKay spoke of 'facile hand and unrivalled power of drawing which gave him a rare command over the ever-shifting panorama of sky and cloudland, whilst his dramatic instinct enabled him swiftly to seize the arrangement and composition most appropriate for the subject under treatment'. He seldom attained Cox's purity of colour but in other ways he outstripped his great predecessor. His work was of unequal merit, the colour sometimes cold and murky with the intrusion of harsh and jarring notes. His chief teachers, apart from nature, were Muller, Cox, Constable and Turner. He was given to promiscuous hospitality, welcoming visitors even when working. In the words of his biographer, 'of chaff and nonsense and all sorts of whims, Bough had abundance and to spare; and these were often indulged in to an extent altogether beyond the bounds of reason and decorum. Keeping little or no restraint upon his sayings or doings, he was apt to drift into too much pawky forwardness to be at all times an agreeable companion. He broke down and set at nought all sorts of class barriers; paid no respect to the manners and customs of the day; could be very open and plain with his saxon speech; and was an adept at rapping out a good mouth-filling oath'. The *AJ* was severe, 'his intentions and his choice of subject defied contamination, though his technique suffered. By nature he saw broadly but his mental growth was cramped so that he rarely expresses essential facts with the unhampered directness of great art'. He provided the illustrations for the 1875 edition of Robert Burns' *Poems and Songs* and R L Stevenson's *Edinburgh-Picturesque Notes* (1879). Exhibited RA between 1886 and 1876 but kept his best and by far the largest number of exhibits for the annual shows of the RSA, exhibiting over 200 items 1844-1887. Represented in BM, V & A, NGS, Aberdeen AG, Dundee City AG, Fitzwilliam, Glasgow AG; Greenock AG, Kirkcaldy AG, Paisley AG, Manchester City AG, City of Edinburgh collection, Ulster Museum, The Binns (NTS), Brodie Castle (NTS).
**Bibl:** AJ 1871, and 1894, 59; S Armstrong 66-68; Brydall 378-381; Cundall; DNB; Gilpin, Sam Bough, 1905; Halsby 112-16 et passim; Hardie, III, 183-186; Irwin 360-1; Macmillan [SA], 229-30 et passim.

**BOUMPHREY, Mrs Pauline (née Firth)** **1886-?**
Sculptress. It seems that after her marriage she lived in Cheshire until

moving in the 1940s to Killiecrankie. From there she exhibited 3 equestrian statues at the RSA, also RA(4), RSA(3), GI(4) & L(7).

**BOURDON, Eugene** **c1890-1916**
Painter. As a young man was an enthusiastic member of Glasgow Art Club(qv). Sadly he was killed in action on August 1st 1916. The whereabouts of none of his work is recorded.

**BOURHILL, James E** **fl 1866-1887**
Edinburgh painter in oil and watercolour; fruit, animals, buildings and figurative subjects. Exhibited 12 works at the RSA between the above years, including 'Goats on the Hillside' (1884).

**BOURNE, Peter RSW** **1931-**
Born Madras. Perthshire-based artist in oil, watercolour and gouache; printmaker. Trained at Glasgow School of Art where he subsequently taught for many years. Elected RSW 1982, awarded the Highland Society of London's Prize at the RSA 1984. His main interests are colour and bold design with an emphasis on formal and abstract elements in a figurative context. His interest in printmaking is primarily combining aspects of screen printing and painting. Regular exhibitor RSA since 1975, also RSW & RGI. Represented in City of Edinburgh collection.

**BOW, Robert H** **fl 1871**
Edinburgh topographical painter in oil; exhibited 2 works at the RSA.

**BOWEN, Emanuel** **fl 1773-1774**
Bushnell records a Scottish engraver of this name who engraved maps and plans of Scottish Counties and towns.

**BOWER, Alexander** **fl 1831-1832**
Edinburgh portrait painter; exhibited RSA during the above years.

**BOWER, J St Clair Lt RN** **fl 1878**
Edinburgh amateur coastal painter in oil; exhibited RSA(1).

**BOWES, Alistair** **fl 1966**
Aberdeen landscape painter in oil. Exhibited AAS from 3 Mosman Place.

**BOWICK, Miss Winifred** **fl 1937**
Aberdeen portraitist. Exhibited AAS from 69 Gray Street.

**BOWIE, Jessie** **fl 1884**
Amateur Glasgow painter; exhibited GI(2).

**BOWIE, John (Dick) ARSA** **1864-1941**
Born Edinburgh; died Edinburgh, 8 Oct. Portrait and landscape painter, also occasionally flowers and a limited number of still lifes. After attending George Watson's College he studied at Edinburgh College of Art going on to the RSA Life School and then the Academie Julian in Paris, under Bouguereau and Fleury. Subsequently visited Haarlem and Madrid. A fine portrait painter whose work has never received the recognition that it seemed to be achieving during his lifetime. Thus his portrait of Principal Rainy was regarded as one of the great Scottish portraits 'its simple dignity, its characterisation of the distinguished churchman, the subtlety of the hands and the accomplishment of the painting generally are notable elements in this remarkable achievement'. He also produced a fine portrait of the artist William Beattie-Brown at the RSA in 1899. Moved to London 1905. Elected ARSA 1903, RP 1905. Exhibited 10 works at the RA and no fewer than 133 at the RSA; also GI(59), L(6) & AAS 1919-1926. Represented by 2 works in SNPG.
**Bibl:** Caw 430-1.

**BOWIE, Thomas Taylor** **fl 1931-1948**
Edinburgh sculptor who latterly moved to Falkland, Fife. Exhibited occasional works at the RSA between the above dates. An example of his work was included in the 1983 RSA Exhibition posthumously.

**BOWIE, William** **c1860-pre1940**
Aberdeen watercolour painter. May have received some training at the Mechanics Institute where he exhibited in 1881 and 1882. Worked as a plumber, acquiring his own business in 1908 from which he retired in 1922. Thereafter he spent much of his time painting landscapes and topographical subjects of the Aberdeen region. Lived at 67 Bon Accord Street. Worked in strong bold colours. Exhibited AAS 1919-1933. Represented by 4 works in Aberdeen AG and another at the Aberdeen Maritime Museum.
**Bibl:** Halsby 249.

**BOWMAN, Bella** **fl 1885-1896**
Aberdeen painter in oil of figurative subjects and landscape. Exhibited AAS between the above years from 31 Belvidere Crescent and latterly 6 Henry Place.

**BOWMAN, James** **fl 1884**
Glasgow painter. Held a number of one man shows in London and Sydney, Australia, as well as in his native Scotland, and always his talent as a draughtsman shines through. Represented in Paisley AG, Museum of Primitive Art, Ecuador.

**BOWMAN, Margaret H** **c1860-1931**
Portrait painter in oil, and woodcut artist; landscapes and portraits. Trained RA Schools, Paris and Glasgow School of Art 1890-94. Exhibited most of her work from Skelmorlie, Renfrewshire but appears to have spent prolonged spells in London during her later years. Exhibited RA(2), RSA(5), ROI(5), GI(16) & L(2).

**BOWMAN, Sheena May** **fl 1976-1980**
Aberdeen painter of allegorical and figurative works. Exhibited AAS from 19 Hartington Road.

**BOWMAN, Thomas S** **fl 1921-1926**
Possibly an English artist, living in Edinburgh 1926. From there he exhibited 2 studies of Beverley Minster at the RSA, having exhibited at the RA five years earlier.

**BOYCE, W S** **fl 1888**
Paisley artist; exhibited GI(2).

**BOYD, Miss Agnes S** **fl 1866-1898**
Edinburgh painter in watercolour; birds, flowers and figurative works. Sister of Miss M Boyd(qv). Exhibited regularly RSA 1866-1887, also SWA(6).

**BOYD, Alexander Stuart RSW** **1854-1930**
Born Glasgow, 7 Feb; died New Zealand, 21 Aug. Painter of landscape, genre, marine and coastal subjects; also flower painter and illustrator. Practised in his home city until c1890, contributing humorous drawings to *Quiz* and *The Bailie of Glasgow* under the pseudonym 'Twym'. After moving to London drew for most of the leading magazines of the time specialising in accurately portrayed parliamentary subjects. Regularly contributed to *Punch* and was for a time on the staff of *The Graphic* and *The Daily Graphic*. He and his wife, a writer, collaborated on a number of books. He provided the illustrations for his friend Charles Blatherwick's novel *Peter Stonnor* (1884), *The Birthday Book of Solomon Grundie* (1884), J K Jerome's *Novel Notes* (1893), *At the Rising of the Moon* (1893), *Ghetto Tragedies* (1894), *A Protegée of Jack Hamlin's* (1894), *The Bell Ringer of Angels* (1894), *John Engelfield* (1894), *The Sketchbook of the North* (1896), *Rabii Saunderson* (1898), R L Stevenson's *Lowden Sabbath Morn* (1898), *Days of Auld Lang Syne* (1898), *Gillian the Dreamer* and *Horace in Homespun* (1900), *Our Stolen Summer* (1900), *A Versailles Christmas-Tide* (1901), with his wife *The Fortunate Isles; Wee Macgregor, Jess and Co, Cottars Saturday Night* and *Hamewith.* In 1905 published a series of sketches under the title *Glasgow Men and Women.* Member of Glasgow Art Club. Elected RSW 1885. Shortly after 1914 emigrated to Takapuna, near Auckland, New Zealand. President, Auckland Society of Artists. Exhibited RA(7), RSA(11), RSW(66), GI(62) & L(4). Represented in V & A, Glasgow AG (170 flower paintings dating from 1915), City of Edinburgh collection (4 drawings for R L Stevenson).
**Bibl:** Halsby 249-50; Houfe 239,illus 240; M H Spielmann, The History of Punch, 1895, 567.

**BOYD, Donald** **fl 1935-1936**
Glasgow artist. Exhibited RSA(1) & GI(1).

**BOYD, Elizabeth Frances** **fl 1896-1935**
Born Skelmorlie, Ayrshire. Painter and woodcut artist. Moved to

Dublin at an early age. All her works were exhibited from addresses in Dublin, London and, latterly, Rye, Sussex. Specialised in Italian landscapes and flower paintings. Exhibited RA(1), RSA(1), GI(1) & London Salon(20).

**BOYD, George** **fl 1889-1893**
Kilmarnock artist who exhibited 4 works at the GI during the above years.

**BOYD, James** **fl 1893-1905**
Hamilton artist; exhibited RSA(2) & GI(7).

**BOYD, James ARE** **1943-**
Born Dundee. Engraver and etcher. Trained Duncan of Jordanstone College of Art (1959-63) and Hospitalfield (1963). Founder member, Dundee Printmakers Workshop. Recently worked solely on etchings, using copper-plates, irregularly shaped by hand. Especially interested in the interaction between light and the urban architecture of northern Europe. Elected ARE 1982. Exhibited RSA 1972, 1976 (2), 1981-83 and 1987, also RPE, SSA & International Print Exhibitions in Korea, China (1983 & 89), France (1983) & Finland (1987). Represented in Hunterian Museum (Glasgow), Inverness AG, SAC.

**BOYD, James Davidson FSA (Scot) FRSA** **1917-?**
Born Glasgow, 10 Aug. Painter in watercolour, oil, collage, enamels; also administrator. Educated Falkirk High School and Technical Schools, trained Glasgow School of Art 1936-1940. Author of a number of works on art history. Staff member of Glasgow Art Galleries and Museums under Dr T J Honeyman during 1946-49, afterwards becoming Director of Dundee Art Galleries and Museums. Influenced by Alexander Rhind(qv), Henry Allison(qv), Campbell Mackie(qv) and T J Honeyman(qv). Represented in Australian, English and Scottish collections.

**BOYD, John G RP RGI** **1940-2001**
Born Stonehaven. Glasgow painter in oil of still life, landscape, biblical scenes and portraits. Attended Gray's School of Art 1958-62 and Hospitalfield. In 1962 awarded a travelling scholarship and in 1972 received the Latimer Award, the Eastwood Publications Award, 1990, and Armour Award, 1993, both from the RGI. Some of his best work was done in the last few years of his life. His portrayal of fishermen, often with model size boats was inspired by early Italian paintings of prelates holding models of their churches. Influenced by David Donaldson(qv) and William Crosbie(qv). Bourne Fine Art held a retrospective 2001. First solo exhibition Edinburgh 1967 followed regularly by London, Glasgow, Edinburgh, Eton & Johannesburg. Elected RGI 1982, RP 1989. Exhibited regularly RSA 1961-2000, AAS 1959. Represented in Paisley AG, Lillie AG (Milngavie).

**BOYD, John S** **fl 1938**
Amateur Glasgow artist; exhibited once at the GI.

**BOYD, Miss Marianne** **fl 1868-1880**
Edinburgh painter in oil and watercolour; fairies, literary, portrait and figurative subjects. Sister of Agnes Boyd(qv). Lived for many years at Gairneyfield, Corstorphine, Edinburgh. Exhibited annually RSA 1868-1876 and again in 1878.

**BOYD, Mrs Mary Syme** **1910-1997**
Born Edinburgh. Sculptress. Pupil of Navellier, she was particularly skilful in animal sculptures, exhibiting at the Salon des Artistes Françaises 1934. Exhibited design for a carved oak angel in memory of Sir Hugh Walpole for St Margaret's Episcopal Church, Corstorphine 1953. Exhibited RSA(9), RGI(4), from 14 Belford Mews, Edinburgh. Represented in SNGMA.

**BOYD, Ronald** **1946-**
Dundee portrait painter. Trained Duncan of Jordanstone School of Art 1964-9 and Royal College of Art 1969-72. First one-man exhibition in London 1978. Exhibited 3 works at the RSA 1969.

**BOYD, Miss Sophia** **fl 1883-1887**
Amateur Edinburgh watercolour painter of domestic interiors. Exhibited RSA in 1883(2) and again in 1887(2), from 41 Moray Place.

**BOYD, Stephen C** **fl 1981-**
Glasgow painter who in the mid 1980s moved to Stoke-on-Trent. Exhibited RSA 1981, 1983(4) & 1984(2).

**BOYD, Stuart** **1887-1916**
Painter in oil of landscape and figures. Son of the artist Alexander Stuart B(qv). Most of his brief life was spent in England. Victim of WW1 which tragically cut short the life of this most promising young artist. Exhibited RA(2), GI(7), L(3) & 8 works at the London Salon.

**BOYD, Thomas** **fl c1785-1800**
Dumfries architect whose main work was the beautifully proportioned private house of Glenae, Dumfriesshire, designed in 1789, one of the few documented houses of its class. Boyd was also responsible for alterations to Cally House, Kirkcudbrightshire in 1794.

**BOYD, Walter Scott** **fl 1883-1899**
Glasgow painter. Went to England in the 1880s before moving to Dolgelly in Wales c1899. Specialised in interiors and figurative subjects. Exhibited 4 works at the RA whilst resident in Glasgow including the Great Gallery, Aston Hall (1883), also ROI(1).

**BOYD, William Wilson** **fl 1883-1900**
Glasgow watercolour painter; exhibited GI(6) & RSW(1) during the above period.

**BOYES, Sidney T** **fl 1907-1931**
Aberdeen sculptor who lived at 51 St Swithin Street before moving to the south of England 1910. Exhibited a bust of the Rev Alexander Webster at the RSA in 1907, 11 works at the RA, also AAS 1906-1908 & L(1).

**BOYLE, Lady A** **fl 1901**
Amateur Argyllshire artist who exhibited 2 works from an address in Fairlie.

**BOYLE, Charles** **fl 1974**
Glasgow painter who exhibited once at the RSA in the above year.

**BOYLE, James** **1872-1935**
Born Stockport but moved to Perth at an early age where he studied art. Gifted amateur. Manager of Pullars of Perth and during his time with the firm painted many local landscapes in watercolour. Member of Perth Art Club. Taught evening classes in Perth Academy. Committee member, Perth Art Association 1923-1929. Exhibited Perth and Dundee between c1904 and his death in 1935.
**Bibl:** Halsby 250.

**BOYLE, James A** **fl 1908**
Amateur Partick painter; exhibited GI(1).

**BOYLE (or BOYLL) John** **fl 1632-1633**
Little is known of this artist beyond the fact that he married in 1632 and was elected a Burgess Painter of Edinburgh 1633.
**Bibl:** Apted 30.

**BOYLE, John** **fl 1982**
Dundee painter. Exhibited AAS.

**BOYLE, Mark** **1934-**
Born Glasgow. Sculptor. After three years in the army 1950-53 and a year studying law at Glasgow University 1955-56 he began getting involved in performance art in the early 1960s. His first exhibitions were in Edinburgh, Glasgow and London 1963-65. With his companion and collaborator Joan Hills(qv) the first replica of a section of ground surface was made in 1964. 'This was the start of a project 'Journey to the Surface of the Earth' begun in 1969 to duplicate one thousand randomly selected parts of the earth's surface. Darts were thrown at a map to pinpoint proposed sites, a T-square was then thrown to mark the precise section to be duplicated...a plastic substance is spread over the ground, allowed to dry and then peeled away, carrying with it the imprint of the ground together with the surface debris. A fibreglass cast is made which is then painted to provide an exact duplicate of the original. Smells and sounds are sometimes added'[Hartley]. From 1967-68 he collaborated with the rock musicians Jimi Hendricks and Soft Machine, lighting their stage

shows. Since 1970 the earth-surface studies have been widely exhibited throughout the world including a central position in the British Pavilion at the 1978 Venice Biennale. Other exhibitions have been held at the Institute of Contemporary Art, Boston and at the San Francisco Museum of Modern Art. A painted fibreglass exhibit is in SNGMA.
**Bibl:** Hardie 194(illus); Hartley 118-119; Hayward Gallery, London, 'Beyond Image: Boyle Family' (Ex Cat 1986); Hovikodden, Henie-Onstad Foundation, Boyle Family Archives, Oslo 1985; ICA, London, 'Journey to the Surface of the Earth' (Ex Cat 1969); Macmillan [SA], 401; D Thompson, Journey to the Surface of the Earth: Mark Boyle's Atlas and Manual, London 1970.

**BOYLE, Miss Mina** **fl 1883-86**
Watercolour painter from Methven, Perthshire who exhibited once at the RSA. In 1886 she exhibited a figurative painting and the portrait of a local lady landowner, from Methven Castle, where the artist may have been employed.

**BOYLE, The Hon Mrs Richard ('EVB') (Eleanor Vere Gordon)** **1825-1916**
Born Aberdeenshire; died Maidenhead, Bucks, 30 Jly. Illustrator and draughtswoman; children's books and poetry. Youngest daughter of Alexander Gordon of Ellon Castle, Aberdeenshire. In 1845 she married the Hon Rev Richard Boyle, Chaplain in Ordinary to Queen Victoria, thereafter living at the vicarage in Marston Bigott, Somerset. Apparently self-taught, she was advised by Boxall and Eastlake; her work as an illustrator gained the appreciation of the pre-Raphaelites. Often inspired by the work of Holman Hunt and Millais her books appeared between 1853 and 1908. Described as 'full of wide-eyed love of nature and a quirky charm of their own...her decorations and mystical pictures come directly from Arthur Hughes or are softened fantasies from Doyle'. Writing in 1908 *The Bookman* said 'EVB is an aesthete of Ruskin's school, a lover of beautiful things, of what is decent and quiet and old, of gardens, of nature in selections, and of art'. Houfe regards her as the only woman illustrator of competence to have emerged before the 1860s. In middle life she lived at Maidenhead. Signed her work with a monogram. Illustrated *A Children's Summer* (1853), *Child's Play* (1858), *The May Queen* (1861), *Woodland Gossip* (1864), coloured plates for *The Story Without An End* (1868), Andersen's *Fairy Tales* (1872), *Beauty and The Beast* (1875), *The Magic Valley* (1877), *The New Child's Play* (1880), *A Book of Heavenly Birthdays* (1894), *Seven Gardens and a Palace* (1900), and *The Peacock's Pleasaunce* (1908). Also contributed several beautiful illustrations for the Christmas number of the *Illustrated London News* (1863).
**Bibl:** Houfe 239, illus 241; B Peppin, Fantasy Book Illustrators, 1975, 8, 11,57, illus 60.

**BOYS, John Philip RSA FRIBA FRIAS** **1928-2000**
Born Kirriemuir, Aug 23; died Dec 30. Architect. Completed his studies at Glasgow School of Architecture. After graduating joined Keppie, Henderson 1953, resigning five years later to set up Lothian Barclay, Jarvis & Boys. After the practice was dissolved he continued in practice until 1993. Founder, New Glasgow Society (an urban amenity group), member of Council, RIAS and Glasgow Inst of Architects. Elected ARSA 1983. His work is scattered across Scotland, including an interesting conversion at Armadale Castle 1979-84. Exhibited regularly RSA from 1964 from 19 Woodside Pl, Glasgow.
**Bibl:** Anon, Obituary, RSA Annual Report 2000.

**BOYSE, Peter Paul** **17th Century**
Born in Holland. Skilled carver, brought to London by the Duke of Queensberry to make a marble statue of James VII for Holyrood. The project was abandoned and he was next heard of working for Sir William Bruce, Kinross House, then for the Duke of Queensberry at Drumlanrig.
**Bibl:** John Dunbar 'Lowlanders in the Highlands: Dutch Craftsmen in Restoration Scotland', Country Life, 8 Aug 1974, 372-376.

**BOZZI, Giovanni** **fl 1895-1901**
Lived in Edinburgh. This sculptor exhibited 13 portrait busts at the RSA and one in Liverpool. In 1896 another artist, **Lorenzo BOZZI**, exhibited a work at the RSA from a Paris address. As Giovanni also exhibited once from Paris in 1901 the two may have been brothers.

**BRACKETT, Nancy A** **1907-?**
Edinburgh based painter in oil; animals especially horses. Studied under William Walls(qv) at Edinburgh College of Art. Exhibited 4 horse paintings at the RSA 1950, 1964, 1965 & 1967. Represented in City of Edinburgh collection.

**BRADFORD, Clare** **fl 1978-1979**
Aberdeen painter of figures. Exhibited AAS from 27 College Bounds, Old Aberdeen.

**BRADSHAW, E** **fl 1890**
Glasgow painter; exhibited GI(1).

**BRADY, Emmet** **fl 1896-1928**
Born Glasgow; painter and etcher. Studied at South Kensington and in Paris, winning the Owen Jones Medal and two National silver and two bronze Medals. Assistant master, Glasgow School of Art before becoming art master at Kelvinside Academy, Glasgow. Principal works include 'Shipbuilding on the Clyde', 'Evening on the Clyde', 'The Pool, London' and 'The Harbour, Scarborough'. Exhibited widely including RSA(10), RSW(3), RHA(6), GI(31), AAS 1906-1912, L(1), & London Salon(2).

**BRADY, Ian Gerrard** **fl 1982-1986**
Aberdeen painter of symbolic and semi-abstract subjects. Exhibited AAS from 85 Menzies Road, Torry and latterly 258 Holburn Street.

**BRADY, Miss Katharine M** **fl 1929**
Kelvinside artist; exhibited GI(2) 1929.

**BRAHAM, Philip** **1959-**
Born Glasgow. Painter. Trained Dundee College of Art 1976-80 and Royal Academy of Fine Art, Holland 1980-1. Appointed visiting artist, University of California at Los Angeles 1981-2. 'His work has more in common with abstract expressionism than with that of Scottish painterliness'. Participated in International Exchange Workshop, Valencia 1989. Appointed part-time lecturer, Gray's School of Art 1994. Received Guthrie Award (RSA) 1995. His work has recently moved closer to the western romantic landscape tradition. First one-man exhibition Glasgow 1984. Exhibited RSA 1985-87. Represented in SNGMA, Lillie AG (Milngavie).
**Bibl:** Macmillan 2001, 147,184-4, illus 195; Hardie 215; Clare Henry, 'Phil Braham & Ian Hughes' Main Fine Art, Glasgow Herald, 1 April, 1986; The Vigorous Imagination, 1987, 54-57,118.

**BRAMAH, Bruce** **fl 1937-1938**
Amateur Glasgow painter from Giffnock. Exhibited GI during the above years.

**BRAND, Jane C** **fl 1890-1903**
Amateur artist from Baillieston. Exhibited 8 works at the GI during the above years.

**BRASH, John** **?-1838/9**
Glasgow architect. Associated with the building of Blythswood Square (1823-9) and several conventionally classic churches including Tolcross Central (1806) and Macmillan Calton (1819) although his precise role in the former is unclear.
**Bibl:** A Gomme & David Walker, Architecture of Glasgow, London 1978, 74,75-8(illus),286.

**BREBNER, Elizabeth Margaret** **fl 1884-1925**
Edinburgh watercolour painter; flowers and still life. Probably related to Hugh Brebner(qv). Exhibited RA(5), RSA(21), GI(13), SWA(3), L(2), & 8 times at the London Salon.

**BREBNER, George** **fl 1885**
Aberdeen artist who exhibited a landscape at the inaugural exhibition of the AAS.

**BREBNER, Hugh** **fl 1875-1879**
Edinburgh painter in oil and watercolour; landscape, continental as well as Scottish, and portraits. Probably father of Elizabeth B(qv). Exhibited 'Torry Lighthouse, Aberdeen' at the RSA in 1875 and other works during the succeeding four years.

**BREBNER, James** **fl 1886-1887**
Amateur painter of Drumlithie, Fordoun, Kincardineshire. Exhibited AAS(3).

**BREDA, Miss E M K** **fl 1932**
Amateur painter working at Colinton. Exhibited RSA(2) 1932.

**BREMNER, Aidan** **1946-**
Born Edinburgh. Painter in watercolour, engraver, sculptor & teacher. Trained Edinburgh College of Art (1963-68). Taught in Uganda as a Voluntary Service Overseas assignment. Since 1977 teacher at Royal School for the Blind. Member of Edinburgh Sculpture Workshop. Enjoys seascapes and urban scenes from everyday life, often spiced with a touch of humour. His etchings are good on atmosphere, perceptive in detail, occasionally derivative, often moody, always interesting. Exhibited RSA 1988.

**BREMNER, Mrs G S** **fl 1840-1843**
Edinburgh portrait and miniature painter. Exhibited 6 portraits RSA during the above years. Recorded by neither Foskett nor Long.

**BREMNER, Lizzie** **fl 1885-1891**
Edinburgh painter in watercolour; landscape and shore scenes. Exhibited 2 studies of Loch Leven at the RSA in 1885, twice again in 1886, in 1890 'A View on the Forth', also AAS(1), all from 11 Scotland Street.

**BRENNAN, Archie** **1931-**
Born nr Edinburgh. Weaver. Trained as a tapestry weaver at the Edinburgh Tapestry Company 1947-53 (Dovecot Studios) and at the Golden Targo Studio in Edinburgh. 1954-6 spent travelling in France. After national service studied drawing and printed textiles at the Edinburgh College of Art and in 1962 established a tapestry department at the College. Active in the SSA of which he became a Council member 1968. His work is conceived in terms of drawing, painting and construction which is the way all his work is started before being committed to weaving. Currently weaving director at Dovecot Studios.

**BREWSTER, Andrew Smith** **fl 1860-1877**
Edinburgh sculptor and portrait painter. Brother of David Brewster(qv). Exhibited 22 works mostly portrait medallions, at the RSA between the above dates.

**BREWSTER, David** **fl 1870**
Edinburgh portrait painter in oil. brother of Andrew Brewster(qv). Exhibited portrait busts at the RSA during the above years.

**BRICHTA, Frank F** **fl 1897-1898**
Edinburgh watercolour painter; figures, Scottish and Italian landscape. Exhibited 14 works at the RSA including one of the Bay of Naples (1890), another of Sorrento (1898); also GI(8) & L(1).

**BRIDGE, Aline Sybil** **fl 1887-1913**
Born Ryde, Isle of Man. Painter in oil; figurative subjects. Went to Edinburgh in the 1890s to study under Robert McGregor(qv) before proceeding to Paris to work under Lucien Simon. As well as exhibiting at the RSA(2), GI(2), London Salon(6) and Walker Gallery, Liverpool(4), she showed at the Salon des Artistes Français, (1911) and on a number of occasions with the Salon d'Automne, notably 'La Femme seule' and 'La Tour'.

**BRIDGE, Eoghan Thomas** **1963-**
Born Edinburgh. Sculptor in bronze & ceramics. Studied Harrogate School of Art (1981-82) and Leeds Polytechnic (1982-85). His work is centred upon the human figure and on equine shapes, showing the influence of ancient Greek, Chinese and Egyptian work. Received the Ireland Alloys Award 1989. Exhibited RSA from 1987.

**BRIDGE, Thomas James Joseph** **fl 1961-1969**
Edinburgh sculptor. Exhibited annually at the RSA between the above dates, figures, heads and portrait busts.

**BRIDGEHOUSE, Robert** **fl 1874**
West Gorton oil painter, figurative subjects; exhibited once at the RSA.

**BRIDGEWATER, Phyllida Scott** **fl 1929**
Aberdeen painter of figurative and literary subjects. Exhibited 2 works after Christina Rossetti at the AAS from 15 Ashley Park South.

**BRIDGLAND, Judith I** **1962-**
Born Horsham, Victoria (Australia), Oct 6. Landscape painter in oils. Trained Univ of Glasgow 1980-84, graduating in Eng Lit and History of Fine Art. Won McRoberts Open Prize 1999. Elected member, Paisley Art Institute 1997. Paints in a very bold, colourful manner in which form remains recognizable although secondary to the strong overall effect. Exhibits RGI, Lillie AG (Milngavie), Greenock AG, Paisley Art Institute. Known internationally with work in collections in England, Ireland, France, Germany, Switzerland, Scotland, Sweden, Italy, Russia, the Netherlands, Turkey, Mexico, Canada, USA, Australia and the UAE.

**BRIERLEY, Argent** **fl 1914**
Edinburgh painter. Exhibited RSA 1914. Three Scottish landscapes were exhibited at the RSA (posthumously) 1944-1945.

**BRIGGS, Charles Henry** **fl 1879**
Edinburgh watercolourist of figurative subjects; exhibited RSA(1).

**BRIGGS, Ernest Edmund RI RSW** **1866-1913**
Born Broughty Ferry, 12 Jan; died Dunkeld, 4 Sep. Landscape watercolourist specialising in angling and river scenes. Studied at the Slade School under Legros between 1883 and 1887, having given up a career in mining engineering for health reasons. Author and illustrator of *Angling and Art in Scotland* (1912), one of the illustrators for *Fishing at Home and Abroad* (1913). His output was comparatively small and he worked mainly in Scotland, favouring especially the area around Glendochart. Often worked alongside his close friend Norman Wilkinson. Excelled in portraying moving water and it is this aspect of his art which has earned the greatest praise. Towards the end of his life he lived at Dalbeattie House, Dunkeld. Elected RI 1906, RSW 1913. Exhibited RA every year from 1889 until 1913, also RI & RSW.

**BRIGGS, John** **fl 1883-1889**
Edinburgh painter in oil and watercolour; flowers and landscape. Appears to have moved to London c1888. Exhibited RSA(8), RA(1), L(1) & AAS.

**BRIGGS, John** **fl 1925**
Exhibited 'The Harbour, St Monan's' at the RSA.

**BRIGGS, Nan C** **fl 1894-1899**
Edinburgh watercolour painter of portraits and figures. Exhibited RSA(3) & GI(6).

**BRIGHT, Miss Beatrice** **fl 1896-1902**
Scottish born figurative painter. Lived in Aberdeen in the 1890s before moving to London c1900 from where she worked at 26 Yeoman's Row Studio. Exhibited AAS(8).

**BRINKLEY, R** **fl 1880-1886**
Glasgow painter; exhibited 4 works during the above period, at the GI.

**BRISTOWE, Ethel Susan Graham (née Paterson)** **1866-1952**
Born London, 13 Oct; died Balmaclellan, Kirkcudbright, 2 Mar. Painter of still life and flowers in watercolour and occasional oils, also some portraits and landscapes. Studied watercolour painting under Claude Hayes. Author of books on Assyriology and Egyptology. Exhibited in Berlin, Paris, Rome and Stockholm and held her first one-man show in London 1907. Moved to Scotland 1903 settling in Balmaclellan. Temporarily abandoned painting in 1914 only resuming 1929 when she preferred using oils as her medium. In 1938 she bequeathed an art gallery to the people of Castle Douglas in which several of her works now reside.

**BROCKETT, Macfarlane** **fl 1910-1929**
Painter of landscape in oil, especially woodland scenes. Lived at Hillhead, Glasgow from where he exhibited AAS 1921-2929, GI(5) & L(9) 1910-1926.

**BROCKIE, Keith** **1955-**
Born Fife, 5 Dec. Wildlife artist, especially of birds, in watercolour, pen and ink, pencil. Educated at Bell Baxter High School, Fife 1968-74, trained Duncan of Jordanston College of Art 1974-78, gaining a diploma in illustration and printmaking and in 1977 being awarded the George Duncan of Drumford travelling scholarship. After graduating he worked as an illustrator for Dundee Museum and Art Gallery 1978-79 since when he has worked freelance primarily as an illustrator and author of natural history books. Published and illustrated *Wildlife Sketchbook* (1981), *One Man's Island* (1984) and *The Silvery Tay* (1988). Prepared the illustrations for Harris' *The Puffin* (1984); Stone's *Studies on the Tihamah* (1985); Newton's *The Sparrowhawk* (1986), Busby's *Drawing Birds* (1986); Rayfield's *Painting Birds* (1988) and Village's *The Kestrel* (1990). Has taken part in many important natural history expeditions including the Cambridge/Norwegian (1978), the Tihamah North Yemen (1982), British Schools Expedition to Greenland in which he was the art leader (1982), Tanzania (1984), Scandinavia (1986), and art leader again with the British Schools Expedition to Greenland (1988). Illustrated many fine Scottish native farm animals for Polly Pullar, *Rural Portraits*, The Langford Press, 2003. Currently working on a series of lithographs for publication in America and on a textbook on ptarmigan and mountain hare. His work is characterised by the fine meticulous attention to detail necessary for small-scale work intended for illustrations. Exhibitions of his work have been held at the RSM, Dundee Museum and Ville Vauban, Luxembourg. Studio at Fearnan, Loch Tay, Perthshire.

**BRODERICK, Laurence ARBS FRSA** **1935-**
Born Bristol. English sculptor of Scottish ancestry. Specialises in wildlife and occasional portraiture. Trained Regent Street Polytechnic under Geoffrey Deeley, and Hammersmith School of Art under Sidney Harpley and Keith Godwin. Works predominantly in bronze and stone. Among many commissions are those from the International Tennis Federation (World Champion trophies and a portrait of past President Philip Chatrier), Royal Caribbean Cruise Line, Otter Trust, and a massive bull for the Birmingham Bullring. Has held an annual exhibition on Skye, where he maintains a studio, since 1985. Joint President, International Otter Survival Fund. Elected ARBS 1991. Exhibits RA, RSA, RSBA, SWA & RWEA.

**BRODERICK, William** **fl 1839-1851**
Painter of field sports and country subjects. Living Edinburgh 1839, moving to Belford, Northumberland 1842. Between 1849 and 1851 he exhibited 13 works at the RSA including such titles as 'The Trap', 'The Keeper's Victim' and 'The Reclaimed Falcon'.

**BRODIE, Alex** **fl 1953-1968**
Edinburgh landscape painter; exhibited at the RSA between the above years.

**BRODIE, Alexander** **1830-1867**
Born Aberdeen; died 30 May, Aberdeen. Sculptor, mainly worked in marble. Brother of William Brodie(qv) under whom he studied. In 1863 he carved the statue of the Duke of Richmond to be erected at Huntly and, in 1865, began the statue of Queen Victoria for Aberdeen although it was later finished by his brother William for exhibition at Dublin Museum. The original is in Aberdeen AG. His 'Oenone' was exhibited at the International Exhibition 1862. Exhibited 2 figure sculptures at the RA in 1864, also RSA 1858 and 1861. His portrait of Queen Victoria is in the SNPG. Died by his own hand when only 37.
**Bibl:** Daily Free Press 31.10.1981; Gunnis 62.

**BRODIE, Alexander Kenneth** **fl 1898**
Born Edinburgh; painter of interiors, exhibited a Breton interior at the RA from his home at 15 Rutland Square, Edinburgh. In 1897 he received an honourable mention at the French Salon.

**BRODIE, Bill** **1943-**
Born Armadale, West Lothian. Painter in oil, acrylic and watercolour. Trained Edinburgh College of Art 1961-66, awarded travelling scholarship 1965-6 enabling him to visit Italy. Won the Keith prize 1968. Since concentrating on acrylic as his preferred medium his compositions have become more hard-edged and his style semi-expressionist. In 1990 there was a return to watercolour. Exhibited at RSA from 1987, also RSW & GI.

**BRODIE, C E** **fl 1884**
Exhibited once at the RSA from 37 Raeburn Place, Edinburgh.

**BRODIE, George E** **fl 1884**
Edinburgh watercolourist of rustic scenes; exhibited one work at the RSA.

**BRODIE, Miss Isabel (Babianska)** **fl 1940**
Amateur Glasgow painter. Studied at Hospitalfield 1941. Member of the New Scottish Group formed in 1943 with J D Fergusson as president. Work of the group reflects the expressionism of Van Gogh and Sontine - as seen in Babianska's 'Fiesta' of 1943 - a group of grotesque faces crowded together, reminiscent of Sontine. Exhibited GI(1).
**Bibl:** Macmillan [SA], 370.

**BRODIE, James** **fl c1736-37**
Portrait painter in oil. Member of the Brodie family of Brodie castle, possibly the son of Ludovic Brodie of Whythfield WS and his wife Helen Grant. Among the family sitters were 'James Brodie of Syne, father of James Brodie of Brodie 1744-1824' (1736), 'Ian Brodie' (1737) and 'Francis Brodie' (1737). All known surviving works are portraits of the family. 'Arresting and distinctive, they are quite unlike any other portraits painted in Britain at that time - in fact their closest parallels are in northern Italy' [Holloway]. Represented only in Brodie Castle (NTS) where he is catalogued as 'Joseph Brodie'.
**Bibl:** Irwin 66; Thomson.

**BRODIE, James** **fl 1833-1870**
Edinburgh painter in oil; landscape. Brother of John Brodie(qv). A house painter in his early career, he was elected a Burgess of Edinburgh in 1841. Exhibited twice at the RSA, in 1868 and 1870.

**BRODIE, Miss Jessie A** **fl 1867-1892**
Edinburgh painter in oil and watercolour; portraits, figures, coastal scenes and landscapes. Exhibited regularly between the above years at the RSA a total of 15 works including two studies of Banff in 1877 and three Normandy landscapes in 1881.

**BRODIE, John** **fl 1853-1873**
Edinburgh landscape painter in oil. Brother of James B(qv). Specialised in scenes near Edinburgh, exhibiting 9 works at the RSA between the above years.

**BRODIE, J Lamont** **fl 1846-1864**
Painter in oil; portraits and figures. Exhibited RSA between the above years.

**BRODIE, Mrs Kate S** **fl 1891-1900**
Glasgow painter in oil and watercolour; landscape and interiors. Exhibited altogether 11 works at the RSA and 9 at the GI. In c1892 appears to have moved to Edinburgh before returning c1895 to Glasgow.

**BRODIE, Kathleen R M** **fl 1981**
Aberdeen painter of still life, also printmaker. Exhibited AAS from 10 Bonnymuir Place.

**BRODIE, Miss Mary** **fl 1858-1864**
Edinburgh portrait painter. Exhibited 5 works at the RSA during the above period.

**BRODIE, William RSA** **1815-1881**
Born Banff, 22 Jan; died Edinburgh, 30 Oct. Sculptor. Son of John Brodie, a ship-master of Banff. Was only about 6 years old when his family moved to Aberdeen. Apprenticed to a plumber, in his spare time studied at the Mechanics' Institute, where he enjoyed casting lead figures of well-known people. Soon began modelling small medallion portraits which attracted the attention of a Mr John Hill Burton who encouraged him to go to Edinburgh in 1847. 'Here Brodie studied for 4 years at the Trustees' School of Design, learning to model on a larger scale and also executing a bust of one of his earliest patrons Lord Jeffrey. In about 1853 he went to Rome, where he studied under Lawrence Macdonald, and with his assistance Brodie modelled 'Corinna the Lyric Muse', a work which Copland reproduced in miniature in Parian 4 years later' [Gunnis]. Elected

ARSA 1852, RSA 1859, and in 1876 appointed Secretary of the RSA, a position he held until his death. In 1875 he executed a group 'A Peer And His Lady Doing Homage', for the Prince Consort Memorial in Edinburgh. At the Great Exhibition of 1851 he showed a group of 'Little Nell and Her Grandfather'. In Edinburgh he executed the statue of Sir James Simpson (1877), the Memorial to the 93rd Sutherland Highlanders Indian Mutiny on the W wall of the South aisle in St Giles(c1860), Lord Cockburn(1863) in the NE corner of the Law Courts, several monumental busts in the Canongate churchyard, the Greyfriars Bobby fountain(1872), a portrait bust Rev. John Paul in St Cuthbert's church, several of the statues in the Scott Memorial, the statuary group in West Princes St Gardens 'The Genius of Architecture crowning the Theory and Practice of Art' and the monument on Calton Hill to Dugald Stewart (1860). From time to time he transferred his models in clay to marble. He undertook all kinds of portraiture including children, reproducing the soft features and evanescent expressions of the young in their most captivating aspects. 'In portraiture Brodie had a peculiarly happy knack of catching the likeness. Furthermore, it was almost always a pleasing and characteristic likeness elevated without being over idealised, 'hard', 'wooden', 'vulgar', were epithets never applied to his work' [RSA obit]. Exhibited 3 works at the RA 1850-1881, and over 250 works at the RSA 1847-1881, also GI(6). Represented in NGS, SNPG(13 portraits), Glasgow AG,Kirkcaldy AG, Paisley AG, City of Edinburgh collection(7 including a marble portrait of Queen Victoria), Westminster Abbey, Collection of Glasgow Corporation, NGS, and Scottish Museum of Antiquities. Other statues include the Prince Consort (1864) in Perth, John Graham Gilbert (1870) in the Kelvingrove AG, Glasgow, and a statue of George Brown (1880) in Toronto, Canada. A portrait bust of Queen Victoria is in the grounds of Balmoral Castle.
**Bibl:** Brydall 191; Gifford 48,116,123,150,168,226,276,294,316-7, 331,389,390; Gunnis; RSA Obit.

**BROGAN, Elizabeth R** **fl 1972-1973**
Glasgow sculptress. Lived at 19 Balfluig Street, Provanhill. Exhibited RSA during the above dates.

**BROMHEAD, Horatio K** **fl 1897-1915**
Amateur Glasgow artist who exhibited at the GI in 1897 and again in 1915.

**BROMMER, Wies** **fl 1982-1984**
Dutch-born sculptor who lived for a number of years in Aberdeen. Exhibited portrait maquettes from 4 Milltimber Brae East.

**BRONDUM-NIELSON, Birgitte RI SSWA (née Bocher)** **1917-?**
Born Copenhagen. Painter in watercolour, pen and ink; Scottish landscape, interiors and still life. Educated in Copenhagen, she studied art at the College of Arts and Crafts in that City before moving to London and then to Scotland, settling in Alloa 1955. Illustrated several song books for Danish children, also *Fairy tales from many lands, Switzerland,* and others. In addition to exhibiting at the RA, RSA (1959-81) and RSW, showed regularly at Charlottenborg (Copenhagen), and the Salon International de Vichy. Signs her works 'BITTE B-N'. Represented in Glasgow AG.

**BRONKHORST, Arnold or Arthur van** **fl 1565-1598**
Born Flanders. Portrait painter and miniaturist in oil. An interesting artist whose name is variously spelt Bronchorst, Brounckhurst, Brackhorst, Brownchurst or, most commonly in Scotland, Bronkhorst. First name is sometimes incorrectly recorded as Arthur. His cousin, Cornelius de Vos, "a most cuninge pictur maker, and excellent in arte for triall of meneralls and menerall stones, sometimes dwelling in London" and the great English miniaturist Nicholas Hilliard joined in 1572 to despatch Bronkhorst to Scotland to prospect for gold under special licence. Bronkhorst "searched sundry moores and found gold in sundry places" but the Regent Murray, on behalf of the minor James VI, refused to allow him to bring the gold into England. After futile legal action, Bronkhorst "was forced to become ane of His Majestie's sworne servants at ordinary in Scotland, to draw all the small and great pictures for his Majestie". In 1580 he was paid £64 for painting three portraits, two of them of James VI of Scotland and one of George Buchanan, and the same year was given 100 marks "as ane gratitude for his repairing to this country" (Scotland), and was appointed King's Limner for Scotland. An oil painting of the 1st Baron St John of Bletso, signed 'AR BRONCKORST FECIT. 1578', wrongly attributed for some years, has recently been rediscovered. Other works by Bronkhorst can be seen in the SNPG and in The Hague.
**Bibl:** Apted 26-7; Stephen Atkinson, The Discoverie...of the Gold Mynes in Scotland, 1619, Bannatyne Club, 1825, 33; Erna Auerbach, Tudor Artists, a study of painters in the royal service, London 1954; Brydall 69-70, 100; R W Cochran-Patrick, Early Records relating to Mining in Scotland, 1878 XVI etc; Long 49; Macmillan [SA], 44-5; Duncan Thomson 22-24.

**BROOKE, Major Edward Alston Pierrepoint** **1858-1942**
Born Pabo Hall, Carnarvonshire, Aug 6; died Llandudno, May 22. Son of a Sheriff of London, competent amateur landscape painter in oils; army career. Educated Eton & Cambridge. Joined 93rd Highlanders 1879, exchanged to Cameron Highlanders 1889 when he commanded The Royal Guard at Ballater 1890. Remained on Deeside from where he exhibited at AAS 1894; also a series of river scenes at Woodend and Glassel which were probably commissioned. Continued exhibiting in Aberdeen from Edinburgh Castle 1900 and Conway 1902. Retired from the army 1896 but in 1914 rejoined as Major with the 11th Battalion Argyll & Sutherland Highlanders. Keen golfer, captain and later secretary, Carnarvon Golf Club.

**BROOKS, Miss F C** **fl 1882-1884**
Although showing from a London address she exhibited exclusively in Scotland, once at the RSA and once in Glasgow.

**BROTCHIE, James Rainy** **1909-1956**
Glasgow painter of Scottish landscapes. Studied at Glasgow School of Art, being a prizeman in 1930 and 1931. Appointed Assistant Curator of the Art Department, Kelvingrove AG 1932-1936. Exhibited RSA 1938-40, also GI(1).

**BROTCHIE, Theodore Charles Ferdinand** **1868-1937**
Born Ceylon. Painter in oil and watercolour; landscapes. Also a writer on art. Studied at Edinburgh School of Art becoming Director of Glasgow AGs 1920. Father of James Rainy B(qv). Exhibited GI(21) 1915-1927.
**Bibl:** Halsby 250.

**BROTHERSTON, William ARSA** **1943-**
Born Edinburgh. Sculptor. Studied History and Fine Art at Cambridge University 1962-65 and sculpture at Edinburgh College of Art until 1971. Prefers working on a small scale, based on animal and plant forms, a preference shared with Jake Kempsall(qv) and Bill Scott(qv). 'In early works Brotherston dedicated much time to exploring traditional ways of making sculpture out of metal. He took a particular delight in the 'lost-wax' process of bronze casting and in surfaces this process creates. His imagery, which at one glance appears simple and highly refined, is referring to very complex structures. That which at one glance appears simple, geometric, symmetrical and inanimate can be after a while complicated, organic, asymmetrical and human' (Demarco). Elected SSA 1973, ARSA 1979. Exhibits RSA regularly since 1975. Represented in SAC.
**Bibl:** Demarco, 'Brotherston, Kempsall and Scott'.

**BROUGH, Miss Cecilia** **fl 1883-1884**
Dundee landscape painter in oil. Exhibited twice at the RSA, in 1884 a view of St Paul's from Hampstead Heath.

**BROUGH, J Carruthers-Smith** **fl 1887**
Amateur Perthshire painter in watercolour, and designer; landscape. Exhibited 2 works at the RSA from Comrie.

**BROUGH, Robert RA ARSA** **1872-1905**
Born Invergordon, Ross-shire, 20 Mar; died Sheffield, 22 Jan. Painter in oil, watercolour and crayon of portraits, landscape and figure subjects. Studied at Aberdeen Art School under J P Fraser, working there as an engraver with Andrew Gibb and Co, with whom Sir George Reid had also once been an apprentice. Proceeded to study at the RSA Schools, completing his studies in Paris under Laurens and Benjamin Constant. Won silver medal at the Universal Exhibition 1900. In his first year at the RSA Life School he took 3 prizes, the Chalmers Bursary, Stuart prize for figure composition, and the Maclaine Watters medal. Returned to Aberdeen from Paris 1894.

Spent part of 1897 in London; visited Paris regularly and sketched in Brittany. First attracted general attention with 'Lu-lu' and a male portrait in the Grafton Galleries 1896; a male portrait of W D Ross Esq was exhibited both in Glasgow and in Munich where it won Brough a gold medal, and is now in the collection of the SNPG. Writing in the *AJ*, 1898 Pinnington said '[Brough] shot above the London horizon somewhat suddenly from the North. The possession of a distinctive and brilliant style attracted attention, won him critical recognition and welcome, and created a hope that he might remain. Should he fulfil the expectation which he has excited, his success is likely to be as phenomenal as his appearance.' Referring to his self-portrait of 1889, a contemporary critic noted 'the chiaroscuro is managed with a subtlety and deftness most remarkable in an untrained youngster'. Later his 'Fantaisie' was regarded as one of the cleverest and most genuinely inspired works that had appeared in either Academy for years, 'marked by dash and artistic abandon and in its unity absolutely perfect'. He contributed an interesting illustration for *The Evergreen* in 1896. In 1904 he travelled to north Africa through Spain, producing paintings reminiscent of Melville (eg 'Spanish Shawl', 1904). Elected RA 1900, ARSA 1904. When only 33 he was killed in a railway accident, prematurely ending one of the most meteoric rises in the history of Scottish art. Exhibited RA(7), RSA(24), GI(12), AAS (20+) & L(10). Represented in SNPG, Aberdeen AG, Dundee AG.
**Bibl:** AJ 1898, 71, 146-149; Halsby 250; Hardie 104-5,123,129; Houfe, 246; Macmillan [SA], 310,312.

**BROUN-MORISON, Guye ROI** **fl 1910-1925**
Oil painter. Lived in London, later moving to Paris and finally settling in Errol, Perthshire c1910. Died by his own hand when only 37. Exhibited ROI(21) & L(1).

**BROWN, A** **fl 1880**
Amateur Edinburgh painter of local landscapes he exhibited 2 works at the RSA.

**BROWN, Mrs A T** **fl 1902**
Scottish artist who exhibited at the SWA(2) from Whamp Hill.

**BROWN, Mrs Alex(ander)** **fl 1898**
Amateur Aberdeen painter. Exhibited a local town scene and a study of wild flowers from 460 Great Western Road.

**BROWN, Alexander Kellock RSA RSW RI** **1849-1922**
Born Edinburgh, 11 Feb; died Lamlash, Arran 9 May. Painter in oil and watercolour; landscape and flowers. Studied at Haldane Academy, Glasgow, then at Glasgow School of Art. Brother of Kellock B(qv). Subsequently worked as a textile designer and studied at Heatherley's in London. Almost all his works were Scottish scenes, the only important exception being the 'Temple of Com-oriba, Egypt', exhibited in 1879. In common with a number of his contemporaries such as Waller Hugh Paton(qv), he loved the landscape of Arran, where he died. Co-founder of the Scottish Artist's Benevolent Association(qv), becoming its President until 1922. Associated with Glasgow for most of his life, for many years President of the Glasgow Art Club(qv). Writing in *The Studio* Pinnington said 'he works largely in semitones in russets, grey, green and soft shades of blue. A leaning towards low tones is accompanied by a frequent choice of evening, moonlight and winter effects. He loves to look dreamily across moorland when the sun is low, when the clouds absorb the dying light and the world reposes in shadow'. Caw found his landscapes 'delightful in their truth, delicacy and simplicity'. Active in the development of the watercolour technique using broad washes, sometimes called 'wet', that was common especially among Glasgow painters of the time, in which the influences of James Docharty(qv) and the Hague School were apparent. Elected RI 1878, RSW 1878, ARSA 1892, RSA 1908. Exhibited RA(31), RSA(121), RSW(125), RI(20), GI(115), RBA(6) & L(54). Represented in Glasgow AG, Paisley AG.
**Bibl:** AJ 1898, 71; 1901, 101; 1904, 172,174; 1909, 153; Caw 300-301; Halsby 25,139,250; Studio 1917-18, 16.

**BROWN, Andrew** **fl 1875-1878**
Edinburgh painter in oil and watercolour; buildings, still life. Exhibited 6 works at the RSA, 1 in 1875 and 5 in 1878.

**BROWN, Miss B May** **fl 1918-1947**
St Andrews watercolour painter of considerable talent though she was largely untrained. Moved to London in the early 1930s but continued to exhibit at the RSA showing there irregularly between the above years. In addition to Scottish landscapes she painted in France and Canada before finally settling in London. Exhibited RSA(19), RSW(20) & GI(5).

**BROWN, Major Cecil RA RBS** **1868-1926**
Born Ayr. Painter, sculptor and illustrator. Educated at Harrow and Oxford, studied art in London and Paris. Elected RBS 1909; secretary of the St John's Wood Art Club for two years. From 1907-1910 Art Master at Charterhouse School. An authority on horses and horsemanship, writing several articles and illustrating *The Horse in Art and Nature* (1896) as well as many sketches for *Illustrated London News*. At the outbreak of war, although well over military age, he enlisted as a trooper in the Middlesex Yeomanry and because of his knowledge of horses soon won a commission in the RASC, serving with the Egyptian Expeditionary Force in Egypt and Palestine. After the war he became Art Master at Bedford School where he remained for the rest of his life. Designed a medal for the International Medical Congress in London 1913. Amongst his major works was the Camel Corps Memorial in the Victoria Embankment Gardens. Died after a heart attack whilst hunting. 'Brown's work is superb but comparatively unknown. He included polo among his subjects and sometimes painted on silk laid on board. His bronzes are amongst the finest to be seen by any British sculptor' [Mitchell]. In 1895 he had an oil painting accepted by the RA but thereafter concentrated increasingly on sculpture, almost always of horses. Also exhibited Paris Salon.
**Bibl:** Houfe 246; Mitchell.

**BROWN, Charles Sidney** **fl 1889-1895**
Amateur Edinburgh painter in oil and watercolour of 17 Gilmore Place. Exhibited 9 works at the RSA including 'Fagot Gatherer' and 'A Harvester' in 1890, RSW(2), GI(3) & AAS(3).

**BROWN, Colin** **1962-**
Born Dundee. Painter in various media; teacher. After schooling in Kingussie, moved to Dundee where he was trained at Duncan of Jordanstone College of Art 1982-87, winning a John Kinross scholarship 1987, enabling him to study in Florence. Won Pollock-Krasner Award (Pollock-Krasner Foundation, New York) 1996. Following a spell in Dusseldorf 1991-95, he returned to Scotland, settling in Stonehaven from where he combines a lectureship at Gray's School of Art with painting. Solo exhibitions in Germany & Scotland since 1989. Fascinated by materials and surfaces, feels himself more in the broad European rather than Scottish tradition. Generally prefers subdued colour with subtle contrasts and shading and frequent use of collage. Exhibits RSA & AAS 1995-.
**Bibl:** 'Colin Brown', Ex Cat, Nord/LB, Hanover & Galerie Bongartz (Hanover) 1997.

**BROWN, Colin C** **fl 1939-1961**
Edinburgh painter and stained glass window designer. Lived at Corstorphine. Exhibited RSA 1939, 1940 and again in 1961.

**BROWN, Cormack** **fl 1853-1887**
Edinburgh watercolourist; townscapes, buildings and figurative subjects. Exhibited 12 works at the RSA including one of the Wee'est Kirk on the Lyne (1886).

**BROWN, Davina S** **fl 1904-1938**
Glasgow painter; exhibited regularly GI(65) and L(2).

**BROWN, Diana E** **1929-**
English wildlife painter and illustrator. Works mainly in watercolour, pen and ink, pencil but occasionally in oils. Has lived and worked in Scotland since c1970. Trained Tunbridge Wells School of Art 1947 and studied under the Danish animal painter Leis Jensen. Illustrated *Hunter and Hunted*, Cambridge Univ Press 2004, as well as books on deer, foxes, ponies and wild otters. Particularly skilful at capturing movement. Also illustrates in magazines, often humorously, including *The Observer* and for 27 years had a weekly illustration in a Sussex newspaper. Exhibits regularly at Society of Wild Life Artists.

**BROWN, Dorothy** **1887-1965**
Amateur Glenrothes watercolourist; exhibited two landscapes at the SWA in 1917.

**BROWN, E M** **fl 1899**
Exhibited 'Solitude' at the RSA in 1899 from 19 Douglas Crescent, Edinburgh.

**BROWN, Eleanor** **fl 1860**
Exhibited a Perthshire landscape at the RSA in the above year.

**BROWN, G Taylor** **fl 1883-d1930**
Edinburgh and Glasgow painter in oil and watercolour of landscapes. Painted mostly in south-west Scotland and lived for many years at Stewarton, Ayrshire. Exhibited RA(1), RSA 1883 & GI.

**BROWN, George** **c1600-?**
Early painter. His parents came from West Gordon and he was apprenticed to William Ramsay, an Edinburgh painter 1622. Probably brother of **James BROWN**. Nothing of his work is now known.
**Bibl:** Apted 31.

**BROWN, George** **fl 1866-1911**
Landscape painter in oil and watercolour. Birthplace unknown, though he worked for a time at Lasswade, also in Aberdeen (1892), Paisley (1893) and Glasgow (1895). Particularly fond of scenes around the Esk, and in Bute and Arran. Exhibited RSA(25), RSW(2), GI(8) & L(2).

**BROWN, Professor Gerald Baldwin ARIBA FSA(Scot)** **1849-1932**
Amateur artist, educated Uppingham School and Oriel Coll, Oxford, subsequently becoming a Fellow of Brasenose. Best known as Professor of Ancient History, RSA 1911 and first incumbent of Watson Gordon Chair of Fine Art at Edinburgh University 1880-1930, author of *The Glasgow School of Painters* (1908). Close associate of Patrick Geddes on the Social Union formed in Edinburgh 1885, a key event in the introduction of arts and crafts ideas into Scotland. Elected ARIBA 1887; appointed Commissioner, Board of Ancient Monuments 1909. Hon. RSA 1911. Exhibited once at the RSA 1882 and once in Liverpool 1883.
**Bibl:** Macmillan [SA], 273-6; Peter Savage, Lorimer and the Edinburgh Craft Designers, Edinburgh 1980, 4.

**BROWN, Helen Paxton ('Nell')** **1876-1956**
Born Glasgow. Portrait painter in oil and watercolour, also embroiderer. Trained Glasgow School of Art. Became close friend of Jessie M King(qv) and other members of that circle. Shared a studio flat at 101 St Vincent Street with Jessie King c1898-1907. In 1904 went to London where she successfully sold an illustration for the cover of *Girl's Realm.* Later the same year she travelled to Paris, the first of many visits. Elected to the Glasgow Society of Artists, a group started by Alexander Frew(qv). Began teaching needlework in 1904 at the School of Art as part of a team which including Jessie Newbery(qv) and Ann Macbeth(qv) which had given the school an international reputation in the craft of embroidery. From 1911 to 1913 she taught book-binding. From the 1920s she was known for preparing 'snapshot' watercolour sketches of children done very quickly. At about the same time became increasingly fascinated by the use of strong colour and form in both her embroideries and paintings. Won Lauder Award 1923. In 1925 commissioned to prepare 12 murals of nursery rhymes for Mount Blow, Dalmuir. Some of her embroidery designs, similar in style to Annie French(qv), were reproduced in *The Studio.* Her most important works were her portraits for which she had great flair. Enjoyed painting groups of figures in cafes, demonstrating something of her humour and warm personality. Retired to Kirkcudbright. Exhibited regularly RSA(18), RSW, GI(34) & L(12). Represented in Glasgow AG.
**Bibl:** Burkhauser 173-4; Halsby 250.

**BROWN, Henrietta** **fl 1902**
Amateur Glasgow artist who exhibited twice at the GI.

**BROWN, Henry** **1847-1871**
Edinburgh painter mainly of coastal scenes. Lived at 23 Union Place and exhibited at the RSA 5 works during the above years.

**BROWN, Henry James Stuart** **1871-1941**
Born Bathgate 1 Mar; died Torpichen, Linlithgow 1 Apr. Painter in watercolour and etcher. Educated Inverness and Glasgow. Attracted to the wide open flatlands of East Anglia and the Netherlands. Lived for many years at Torpichen. Exhibited RA(1), RSA(2), RSW(1), GI(3) but mainly with the London dealer Colnaghi (113 works). Represented by 24 etchings in the Print Room at the British Museum, also Glasgow AG.
**Bibl:** Halsby 250.

**BROWN, Henry K** **fl 1879-1883**
Scottish landscape painter who lived in both Edinburgh and Glasgow. Exhibited Scottish scenes at the RSA between the above years.

**BROWN, H W Jennings** **fl 1869-dc1887**
Landscape and portrait painter. Birthplace unknown although he lived for some years in Eastbourne before moving to Scotland in the mid-1880s. In addition to landscape painting he executed figurative work and portraits. Almost all his exhibited works were in Scotland, 23 works at the RSA between 1869 and 1887, and one at the RHA. A painting of Clovelly and another of Normandy were among 5 works shown RSA 1885.

**BROWN, Iain Nigel Stuart Robertson** **fl 1941-1947**
Born Edinburgh 29 Jly. Painter, sculptor, engraver & teacher. Trained Edinburgh College of Art 1938-42 followed by studies in music & singing in Britain and France. Obtained a licentiate at the Royal Academy of Music and subsequently a BA(Hon) in art history, added to subsequent studies in theology and country dancing. Friend of Anne Redpath(qv) and godson of Joan Hassall, both of whom have had a strong influence on his painting. Art master at Merchiston School, Edinburgh for 20 years and at Sherborne School for Girls for 27 years. Changed his name to Robertson 1950. Exhibited at RSA regularly 1942-47 and for several years engraved the fortnightly programmes at the Gateway Theatre, Edinburgh.

**BROWN, Isabella (Isabel)** **fl 1876-1894**
Edinburgh watercolour painter of wildlife and figurative subjects. Exhibited a number of drawings at the RSA between the above years.

**BROWN, J H O** **fl 1883**
Amateur Ayr painter who exhibited at the GI. Possibly the same **J O BROWN** whose sketch of a collapsed tenement in the High St, Edinburgh (24 Nov 1861) is in City of Edinburgh collection.

**BROWN, Miss J M** **fl 1886**
Amateur Edinburgh watercolourist; exhibited a study of flowers at the RSA from 2 Erldon Street.

**BROWN, J S C McEwan** **fl 1922-1936**
Painter in oil and watercolour of landscape, and occasional sculptor. Although of Scottish extraction (his mother was Scottish), spent most of his life near Christchurch, Hampshire. Studied for a time in the studio of the sculptor J A Warrington Hogg. Held annual exhibitions at his own beautiful studio at Lark's Gate, Thorney Hill. Revelled in views of the open sea, especially off the Cornish coastline, these together with scenes in the New Forest and cloud effects across large expanses of sky were his main exhibits. A contemporary critic wrote of his 1936 exhibition 'it is refreshing to dwell upon the works of a painter who scorns affectation or any cult...seldom has the charm and spiritual meaning of the Forest been so mastered by the brush'. His 'Storm Clouded the Restless Sea' was exhibited at the Paris Salon 1935. His wife was also a landscape painter. Most of his exhibits were at the Walker Gallery in London with whom he showed 548 works during the above years.

**BROWN, Mrs J W** **fl 1861**
Landscape painter in oil. Exhibited at the RSA in the above year. Possibly the same Mrs J W Brown who exhibited 3 works at the Walker Gallery, Liverpool 1882-83.

**BROWN, J Hoffman** **fl 1849**
Edinburgh landscape painter of 4 St James's Square who exhibited 'Gannochy Bridge, Forfarshire' at the RSA in the above year.

**BROWN, J Taylor** **fl 1893-1940**
Stewarton, Ayrshire painter in oil of landscape and rustic genre. Exhibited 8 works at the RSA, but mainly GI(57); also L(12).

**BROWN, James** **c1729-1807**
Edinburgh architect, involved in the design of the new town. His most important work was the laying out of Buccleuch Place and the design of 1-6 c1790, and the laying out of George Square in 1766.
**Bibl:** Gifford 250-1.

**BROWN, James** **fl 1870**
Edinburgh landscape painter in oil. Brother of John Brown of Dollar(qv). Exhibited at the RSA in the above year.

**BROWN, James** **fl 1928**
Glasgow painter of 48 Benview, Firhill. Exhibited once at the GI.

**BROWN, James ('Jim')** **1951-**
Born Edinburgh. After training as an architect studied art at Dundee 1971-5 specialising in design. Worked for a spell among architects in Argyll. Launched his own business 1980 designing interiors, brochures, pub signs and Celtic carpets. Turned to painting seriously 1985, living nomadically in the Highlands before settling in Glasgow 1987. Paints powerful figurative and conversation paintings in strong colour and bold realism, also occasional portraits in both oils and watercolour. "I feel totally compelled and able to use all the experience of my life as a resource. Not in a conceited way but I have reference to times on an open road, times in privileged marble mansions, times in the gutter and times just struggling to be normal. I attempt to relate all this through a form of poetic story telling using symbols that are sometimes carefully calculated and others unconsciously formulated". First solo exhibition Glasgow 1990, first major show Lillie AG (Milngavie) 1993.
**Bibl:** Cat (ed. by Helen Anne Gillespie), Art 2000, Bearsden, 1993.

**BROWN, James Michael** **1853-1947**
Edinburgh artist in oil and watercolour; portraits, landscapes, coastal and golfing scenes. Son of the Fife engraver Tom Brown. Schooled at George Watson's and trained at the RSA Schools, being awarded a travelling scholarship 1885/6 enabling him to travel to Florence & Venice. While there he completed a number of attractive watercolour sketches. Keen golfer and founder member of the Mortonhall Golf Club in Edinburgh, it is for his golfing scenes that he is now best remembered. These were delineated with an eye for detail and sensitive feel for atmosphere that bore the hallmark of a practised golfer. Between 1890 and 1920 he painted 28 golfing scenes for the Life Association Company (whose managing director was also a member of Mortonhall). Of these, 24 remain in the company's collection. Most were later printed and in 1914 one of his golfing etchings was used by Mortonhall Golf Club for its Christmas card. His studio was in Picardy Place, Edinburgh. Owing to the growing demand for golfing pictures the financial value of this branch of his art has spiralled, bearing little reference to artistic merit. The artist himself looked upon the landscapes and portraits as his best work. His portrait 'Miss Jane Grahame of Claverhouse', exhibited in London, remains in the artist's family. Brown painted many landscapes and seascapes when on holiday at St Cyrus, often incorporating his dog 'Hector'. Exhibited five works at the RA 1890-1900, but mainly at the RSA (80 works between 1879 & 1897), GI(31), RBA(3), RHA(2), L(17) and regularly at the AAS 1890-1902. Represented in Dundee AG (an oil 'Three children at the seaside', on long loan to City of Edinburgh collection).
**Bibl:** Halsby 250; Wingfield.

**BROWN, Jane R** **fl 1964**
Aberdeen textile designer. Exhibited AAS from 11 North Anderson Drive.

**BROWN, Miss Jean D** **fl 1935**
Aberdeenshire amateur portrait painter. Exhibited AAS from Kintore.

**BROWN, Miss Jessie C** **fl 1937**
Amateur Glasgow artist who exhibited once at the GI.

**BROWN, John** **1752-1787**
Born Edinburgh, 18 Jne; died Leith, 5 Sep. Miniaturist and portrait painter, also etcher and writer of music. Son of a jeweller and watchmaker, after a good early education he studied painting under Alexander Runciman(qv) becoming a close friend of the family. Studied at the Trustees Academy, probably with Delacour(qv) and Charles Pavillon(qv). In 1769 went to London. In 1771, travelling as draughtsman for Townley and William Young, he proceeded to Italy, encompassing a tour of Sicily in the company of David Erskine, whose cousin Charles Erskine was an important Vatican luminary able to effect introductions into the cultural circles of Rome. In Rome he made many sketches of statues in the Roman Galleries and studies of street scenes now in the V & A. Henry Fuseli seems also to have accompanied him on this trip. In 1776-79 he was in Florence, copying works in the Uffizi. After he returned to Edinburgh he devoted himself to portraiture, specialising in the use of pencil. The SNPG have in their possession a series of 31 drawings executed during the winter of 1780/1 at the request of the Earl of Buchan(qv), founder and first President of the Society of Antiquaries in Scotland. These consist of pencil portraits of members of the Society, each drawing made at a sitting lasting an hour for a fee of one guinea. In 1786 he married and moved to London where he exhibited at the RA as a miniaturist in 1786, also drawing members of the Royal family and being briefly employed again by Townley to draw his notable collection of marbles. Known to have made a number of etchings and also to have written on music. After his death Lord Monboddo published his *Letters on the Poetry and Music of the Italian Opera* for the benefit of the artist's widow. Previously there has been no reason to connect Brown and Scoular but recently Foskett has unravelled Brown's somewhat complicated family history so that we now know that these two artists were second cousins, their grandmother's being half-sisters, as well as first cousins, their parents being brother and sister. Foskett records that three miniatures by John Brown still remain in the family. In addition to the miniatures in the SNPG, the Scottish Society of Antiquaries have retained about twenty portraits, including a pencil miniature of David Deuchar the seal engraver, and one of Alexander Runciman, drawn in pencil from life (1785). Brown deserves to be much better known, having suffered from bearing an undistinguished name and the fact that most of his work was done in Scotland rather than in London or continental Europe. In addition to his artistic work, Brown must have been generally well cultivated. Monboddo recorded that he was 'not only known as an exquisite draughtsman, he was also a good philosopher, a sound scholar and endowed with a just and refined taste in all the liberal and polite arts and a man of consummate worth and integrity'. Died from seasickness following a return voyage to Leith from London. The NGS holds ten works including 'An Italian Farm House and Maxentius', 'Rome with a murder being perpetrated in the foreground'; also in Fyvie Castle (NTS).
**Bibl:** Armstrong 8; John Brown, Letters on the Italian opera, with intro by James Burnett, Lord Monboddo, Edinburgh 1792; Brydall, 169; Caw 44; European Magazine Vol 17 page 91, (with engraved fp 163); Foskett, i, 183, and Foskett 206; John M Gray, 'John Brown The Draughtsman', Mag of Art, July 1889, 310-315; Halsby 247; Irwin 79-80,112-3; Long 50; Macmillan [SA], 125-6, 150-2 et passim; McKay 326; N Powell, 'Brown and Women of Rome', Signature XIV, 1952, 40-50; Rb; Basil Skinner, 'John Brown and the Antiquarians', Country Life 150, Aug 1971.

**BROWN, John** **fl 1846-1871**
Landscape painter who lived most of his life in Dollar. Brother of James Brown(qv). Fond of the scenes around Glen Devon and Loch Lomondside. Exhibited RSA(34).

**BROWN, John Jnr** **fl 1936-1937**
Hamilton painter in oil and watercolour. Exhibited RSA(1) & RSW (2) from Woodhay, Dalmeny Road.

**BROWN, John Caldwell RSW** **1945-**
Painter, primarily in watercolours; schoolmaster. Trained Glasgow School of Art under William Armour(qv), David Donaldson(qv) and Duncan Shanks(qv). After a short spell of full-time painting, he joined the staff of Fettes as Art Master 1966-68, moved to Malvern College 1968-88, returning to Edinburgh Academy 1988. Specialises in landscapes, portraits and occasional still lifes, in the Colourist manner. Elected RSW 1996. Exhibits RSA, RSW, RGI.

**BROWN, John Crawford ARSA** **1805-1867**
Born Glasgow; died Edinburgh. Educated in Glasgow and, returning from a period on the continent, spent some years in London before finally settling in Edinburgh 1842. Younger brother of William B(qv), art master of Perth Academy. Most of his works were landscapes, often with figures prominently depicted. Whilst in

Holland, Belgium and Spain he completed a number of continental scenes. Exhibited a Kentish landscape at the RA in 1833 but most of his exhibits were at the RSA where he showed a total of 128 works, being elected ARSA 1843.
**Bibl:** McKay 318.

**BROWN, John George** **1831-1913**
Painter of genre. Although born in Scotland he lived and worked all his life in London with occasional visits to the continent. Associated with Goupil & Co. Exhibited 'The Passing Show' at the RA (1880) and 'Free from Care' (1885). In 1889 he exhibited and gained an honourable mention at the Universal Exposition.

**BROWN, John Lewis** **1829-1890**
Born Bordeaux of Scottish descent. Best known for his horse paintings. Studied under Belloc and Roqueplan. Exhibited RGI(3).

**BROWN, John Osborne** **fl 1856-1871**
Edinburgh painter who exhibited Scottish landscapes, often of Glen Affric, and narrative scenes at the RSA(30) during the above years.

**BROWN, Joseph** **fl 1885-d1923**
Painter in oil and watercolour of landscape, shipping and coastal scenes. It is not known where he was born or indeed whether he was Scottish but he was living in Edinburgh 1885 and exhibited almost exclusively in Scotland. He showed 23 works at the RSA between 1885 and 1899, and GI(4).

**BROWN, Kate C** **fl 1893-1894**
From St Andrews Manse, Kirkintilloch, she exhibited GI for two consecutive years.

**BROWN, Miss Kathleen R H** **fl 1921-1929**
Edinburgh portrait painter. Lived at 24 York Place. Exhibited 3 works at the RSA, twice in 1921 and once in 1929.

**BROWN, Kellock** **1856-1934**
Born Glasgow 15 Dec; died Glasgow 20 Feb. More of a decorator than a sculptor, he did some charming repoussé work. Also a sculptor of bronze figures. Brother of Alexander Kellock Brown(qv). Trained Glasgow School of Art, Royal College of Art under Lanteri and RA Schools. Undertook many commissions for memorials and monuments and in later life taught at the Glasgow School of Art. Exhibited 8 works at the RA in 1887 and 1893 his 'Ju-Jitsu' was purchased by the Chantrey Bequest 1924. Exhibited 35 works at the RSA of which perhaps the best known is 'Flora Macdonald' (1893), also showed regularly in Glasgow at the GI(89), RSW(1) & L(6). Represented in the City of Edinburgh collection by a bronze, 'Dr Neil Munro' (1864-1930).

**BROWN, Miss L J** **fl 1879-1882**
Amateur Edinburgh oil painter of still life and buildings. Lived at Bell's Mill House, Dean. Exhibited 3 works at the RSA during the above dates.

**BROWN, Lindsay M** **1969-**
Born Edinburgh, Jan 5. Sculptress, using photography. Trained Gray's School of Art 1998-2001 and Duncan of Jordanstone (Dundee). Involved in experimental work using a variety of media within a sculptural context. Her work has been shown at the NGS (Duff House), Aberdeen AG and RSA (Student Exhibition). Began exhibiting AAS 2002.

**BROWN, M** **fl 1849-1895**
Edinburgh landscape painter in oil and watercolour; exhibited RSA intermittently between 1849 and 1889, also RSW(1) & GI(9).

**BROWN, Miss Mabel J** **fl 1918-1930**
Trained Edinburgh College of Art, moved to Liverpool in the 1920s from where she exhibited at the Walker Gallery. Exhibited twice at the RSA, in 1918 and 1919.

**BROWN, Margaret Campbell (née Maclachlan)** **1877-1951**
Born 25 Mar; died Tobermory 9 Dec. Painter in oil and etcher. Signed her work either Rita Maclachlan, M C Maclachlan or M C Sandy Brown. Shortly after her husband's death she preferred to be known as 'Mrs Sandy Brown'. One of her landscape etchings was included in the Anglo-German Exhibition of 1913. She had a sad life, her husband was killed playing polo in 1931 and their only child suffered from Down's Syndrome dying at the age of 26. When she returned to Scotland she settled in Connel, Argyllshire. Her first work was exhibited at the RHA 1912.

**BROWN, Margaret 'Maggie' H** **fl 1902-1940**
Musselburgh flower painter; exhibited two works at the RSA and 7 watercolours at the RSW, also 4 at the Walker Gallery, Liverpool where she lived before returning to Edinburgh.

**BROWN, Margaret K** **fl 1906**
Amateur Glasgow painter; exhibited GI(1).

**BROWN, Miss Margaret T** **fl 1910**
Lived at Denney, Selkirk; exhibited RSA(1).

**BROWN, Marion Miller** **fl 1893-1945**
Musselburgh painter. Possibly related to Margaret H Brown(qv). Exhibited 16 works at the RSA between 1895 and 1945, some Scottish landscape and shore scenes but mostly flower paintings; also RSW(1), GI(10) & L(1).

**BROWN, Marshall** **fl 1890-1899**
Edinburgh painter in oil and watercolour of figures, landscapes, seascapes and townscapes. Brother of Charles Sidney Brown(qv). Exhibited 'Highland Washing and Bait Diggers' at the RSA in 1890, and 16 works between 1896 and 1899. Not to be confused with William Marshall Brown.

**BROWN, Mary A** **fl 1970-1971**
Glasgow painter who exhibited west coast Scottish landscapes at the RSA in 1970 and in 1971.

**BROWN, Maude Baldwin** **fl 1884-1913**
Edinburgh flower painter in oil and watercolour. Moved to Nottingham c1913. Exhibited RSA in 1884, and thereafter in English provincial galleries until 1913.

**BROWN, Mrs May Marshall (née Robertson) RSW** **1887-1968**
Born Edinburgh 5 Mar. Painter in oil but mainly watercolour and etcher; landscapes and architectural subjects. Studied at Edinburgh College of Art and The Royal Institute of Edinburgh; subsequently worked in France, Holland and Ireland before settling in Edinburgh where she married William Marshall Brown(qv). Her work shows the great influence of her husband. Enjoyed drawing fishing villages and boats in a fresh style with a lively handling of the paint. Elected RSW 1936. Exhibited RSA(62) 1915-1966, all of them coastal, market or harbour scenes on the east coast of Scotland, in Holland and in France; also RSW(44), GI(22) & L(2).
**Bibl:** Halsby 251.

**BROWN, Meta G Napier** **fl 1903-1906**
Enamellist. Lived at 13 Cambridge Street, Edinburgh and exhibited cases of enamels at the RSA in 1903 and 1904. During the above period also exhibited 14 works at the Walker Gallery, Liverpool.

**BROWN, Michael** **1923-1996**
Born Edinburgh, May 8; died Cotswolds, Feb 20. Architect, specialising in environmental and landscape designs; teacher and writer. Trained Edinburgh College of Art 1946-51. After war service in India his first post was with the schools division, London County Council, before joining a private practice. A scholarship in 1955 enabled him to undertake further studies at the Univ of Pennsylvania where he was influenced by Ian McHarg. Whilst working in a Vermont practice he was involved in the Saarinen House, Ohio and the Rockefeller Institute, New York. He then spent a short time teaching back in Pennsylvania before returning to London. After a period with Sir Eric Lyons he set up his own practice 1962. This expanded rapidly until by 1974 it was one of the largest landscape offices in the country, responsible for *inter alia* the Brunel Estate (Paddington), Beavers Farm (Hounslow) and the large Graham Park Estate (Hendon). Consultant to the group designing the New Town of Redditch. In the early 1980s he moved to Devon, while continuing to embark on overseas lecture tours, where he set up a study centre in ecology and landscape design. Contributed to *Urban Landscape*

*Handbook* 1972 and *City Landscape* 1983. Also wrote *Ideas for a Sustainable Village - and its relevance for a* rapidly *changing world.*
**Bibl:** The Times, Obituary, Feb 1996.

**BROWN, Miss N F** **fl 1920**
Stirling artist; showed once at the GI.

**BROWN, Miss Nana** **fl 1938-1944**
Kilmarnock landscapist in oil, she exhibited 5 Scottish landscapes at the RSA during the above dates and once at the GI in 1938.

**BROWN, Neil Dallas ARSA** **1938-2003**
Born Elgin; died St Andrews, Jan 14. Educated at Bell-Baxter's High School, Cupar. Moved to Fife at the age of seven and after school trained at Dundee College of Art 1954-58, Hospitalfield for a year and a further two years of study at the RA Schools in London. From there he won travelling scholarships to France, Italy and Spain, winning the David Murray Scholarship 1959 and 1961, Leverhulme Award 1960, and Chalmers Bursary 1962. Visited New York 1967. Won first prize in the Arts Council of North Ireland painting competition, Belfast 1970. Lived and worked at Newport-on-Tay, and was a visiting tutor at Duncan of Jordanstone College of Art, Dundee. Found frequent inspiration for his work in dreams; paintings often have an erotic quality 'a quite unashamed ode to the love act'. 'He is predominantly concerned with the human figure which he regards with a wide eye and scale of a landscape painter, making people his landscapes and imbuing them with a lyrical ambience and warm, sympathetic comment' [Gage]. Elected ARSA 1975, resigned 1990. Like Philipson(qv), he occasionally introduced animals, especially dogs, as a symbolic bestiary drawing attention to the brutal nature running through many of his fantasies. Represented in Dundee AG, Kirkcaldy AG, Perth AG, Liverpool AG, Nottingham AG, Skopje AG (Yugoslavia).
**Bibl:** Gage 61,62,75; Hardie 198.

**BROWN, Neil Macalister** **fl 1869-1871**
Amateur Edinburgh painter in oil of coastal scenes and landscape. Exhibited 3 works at the RSA during the above period.

**BROWN, Patrick** **fl 1544**
Herald painter. Received 54s for decorating standards for the Regent Arran 1544.
**Bibl:** Apted 32; Accounts of the Lord High Treasurer of Scotland, ed T Dickson et al, Edinburgh 1877-1916.

**BROWN, Peter** **fl 1935-1960**
Dalkeith portrait painter and stained glass window designer. Exhibited a portrait of Anne Redpath at the RSA in 1960 having exhibited there previously in 1935.

**BROWN, R W** **fl 1827**
Edinburgh portrait painter who exhibited 2 works at the RSA in the above year.

**BROWN, Robert** **c1790-1860**
Architect. Responsible for the design of Melville St, Edinburgh(1814), Haddington Place, Queen's Hall(1823), the original scheme for Coates Crescent(1813), the E side of Manor Place, possibly Stafford St and William St(1824-5), most of St. Stephen St and the aborted Hopetoun Crescent(1825). Also involved in the development of Portobello and Joppa.
**Bibl:** Gifford 61,243,249,322,347,359,371,375,377,381,383,411, 412,415,420,429-30,555,559,658,pl.104.

**BROWN, Robert H** **fl 1964-1965**
Glasgow painter; exhibited 3 street scenes at the RSA during the above years from 29 Prosen Street, Tollcross.

**BROWN, Robert William** **1890-1944**
Born Hamilton, the son of a master builder. Painted in oils, sculpted stone figures. Carried on the family business as a building contractor and stonemason. He lived at Wark, near Dunning from where, in 1911/12, he exhibited two landscapes and a figurative composition at the Perth Fine Art Exhibition. In 1918 he married Evelyn Thompson(qv) and in the same year joined the 4th Batt., King's Own Scottish Borderers as a 2nd Lt. In 1919 he moved to Hamilton before settling in Ayrshire, where he died. Exhibited GI(3), RI(1) & London Salon (3).

**BROWN, T Michael** **fl 1898**
Edinburgh painter; exhibited AAS from 51 Nile Grove.

**BROWN, Taylor** **fl 1900-1912**
Ayrshire landscape painter in oil. Exhibited RSA in 1900 and a number of local scenes at the AAS 1906-1912 from Stewarton.
**Bibl:** Caw 389.

**BROWN, Thomas Jnr** **fl 1844-1880**
Edinburgh painter in oil of interiors and landscapes, especially Perthshire, Northern Highlands and East Lothian. Son of Thomas Brown snr(qv). Exhibited 112 works at the RSA between above dates.

**BROWN, Thomas** **c1781-1850**
Architect. Sometime Prison Board architect. Designed Edinburgh's Royal Crescent after succeeding Thomas Bonnar(qv) as City Superintendent of Works; also Nicholas Square Methodist church (1815-6), St Mary's church, Bellevue Crescent, the N side of both Cumberland and Northumberland Streets (1822) and in Leith the Assembly Rooms (1809-10) and Trinity House (1816-8), Inverness District Court (formerly the Jail) (1846-48), the Sheriff Courts of Dingwall (1842-45), Stornoway (1843) & Tain (1848-49), Dornoch Jail (1842-44). Toward the end of his career, entered into partnership with James Maitland Wardrop(qv).
**Bibl:** Gifford 61,189,229,240,250,336-7,341-2,345,350,353,411-2,438,464,466, 577,579.613,pls.30,31; Gifford, H & I, 66,197,399,406,460,567,630,pl.103.

**BROWN, Thomas Jnr** **fl 1879-80**
Edinburgh painter. Son of Thomas B snr(qv). Exhibited two angling pictures at the RSA from 3 Castle Terrace.

**BROWN, Thomas Snr** **fl 1848-1855**
Painter of portraits and architectural subjects and engineer. Studied under Robert Scott(qv). Brown abandoned a career in engraving on obtaining a captain's commission. Author of several works on natural history. Father of Thomas Brown jnr(qv). Exhibited RSA during above years.

**BROWN, Thomas Austen ARSA RSW RI** **1857-1924**
Born Edinburgh, 18 Sep; died Boulogne, 9 Jun. Painter of genre and landscape, illustrator, also an etcher and woodcut artist. Son of a drawing-master. Outstanding student at the RSA School attracting early attention by the pleasing and deft quality of his work. 'Bright in colour, joyous in sentiment and marked by considerable grace in design, drawing, and handling, they were scenes of country life much in the mood and manner of R W Macbeth's work of that period, with a soupçon of Orchardson's elegance and colour added' [Caw] He possessed a very individual style, the figures are sketchy and ill-defined, the buildings wavy in soft tints. Illustrated with lithographs *Bits of Old Chelsea* (1922) and contributed to *Illustrated London News* 1899. Keenly interested in the work of the French artists, the influence of Bastien Lepage being very evident in much of his work. Always interested in experiment. Painted a lot at Largo, Blairgowrie, and near Stirling where for a time he was associated with the artistic community active in and around Cambuskenneth. It was from here that he painted his well known 'A Gypsy Encampment'. But from 1897 most of his work was done in France. Travelled extensively in Spain, Morocco, Italy, Holland, Belgium and Germany and spent a year in America. Influenced also by his association with the Glasgow School he began to imitate Millet, Jacques and Israels, the mood and subjects changing from young daintily clad rustic girls set in summer fields to aged labourers and ragged herds tending cattle, to sad shepherdesses and bedraggled tinkers. The main criticism that can be levelled is that he never developed a style of his own. Signed 'TAB' in monogram. Elected RI in 1888, RSW 1889, ARSA 1889. Associate of the Beaux Art Société of Paris, Honorary Member of the Brussels Academy, won gold medals in Barcelona, Budapest, Dresden, and Munich. Exhibited RA(31), RSA(100+), RI(13), GI(34), ROI(9), AAS regularly 1886-1921 & L(46). Represented in BM, V & A, Glasgow AG, Brussels AG, Leeds AG, Munich AG.
**Bibl:** Armstrong 79; Caw 300-301 et passim; Halsby 250; Houfe, 247; Who Was Who, 1916-28.

**BROWN, Thomas P** **fl 1897-1898**
Amateur Glasgow watercolourist; exhibited RSW(1) & GI(1).

**BROWN, Thomas S** **fl 1853-1879**
Edinburgh painter in oil and watercolour of landscapes, interiors, genre, architectural subjects. Exhibited 22 works at the RSA between the above years. Probably the same Thomas Brown who exhibited a drawing at the RSA in 1849. Not to be confused with Thomas Brown Snr or Thomas Stirling Brown.

**BROWN, Thomas Stirling** **fl 1902-1915**
Oil painter of Scottish extraction who moved from East Anglia to Glasgow in c1909. Enjoyed painting romantic moonlit landscapes. Lived latterly at Drumchapel, Nr Glasgow. Exhibited RA(2), RSA(2), ROI(6), GI(2) & L(7).

**BROWN, Thomas Wyman** **1868-1930**
Perth artist; painted landscapes and flowers in oil and watercolour, being locally well known for his fish paintings. Employed by Mallochs of Perth as a cast-painter. Member of the Perth Art Association committee 1927-1929. Exhibited locally in Dundee and Perth between c1904 and 1929. Represented in Perth AG.
**Bibl:** Halsby 250.

**BROWN, Tom** **fl 1907-1910**
Amateur Glasgow painter exhibited a landscape at the AAS from 146 Broomhill Road, Aberdeen, & GI(1).

**BROWN, William** **1798-1874**
Born Glasgow; died Perth, Oct 30. Painter in oil and watercolour and teacher; landscapes. Taught at the Drawing Academy (4 Maxwell Street and subsequently 49 & 52 Virginia Street, Glasgow), 1822-30. Brother of John Crawford B(qv). In 1830 appointed Art Master at Perth Academy. Exhibited Scottish landscapes at the RSA between 1830 and 1841. Illustrated Jamieson's *Select Views of the Royal Palaces of Scotland* (1830) and in 1843 provided eight views for Hooker's *Perthshire Illustrated,* later engraved by Swan. An elder of the kirk, he was secretary of the Literary and Antiquarian Society of Perth (1845-69) and author of *The Stormontfield Experiment on the Salmon* (1862). Represented in Perth AG.

**BROWN, William** **fl 1958-1968**
Parkhead, Midlothian painter who exhibited mainly still lifes at the RSA between the above years.

**BROWN, William** **fl 1893**
Amateur Glasgow painter; exhibited once at the GI.

**BROWN, William** **fl 1940**
Amateur Glasgow painter of 63 Clouston Street, exhibited twice at the GI in the above year.

**BROWN, William Beattie RSA** **1831-1909**
Born Haddington; died Edinburgh 31 Mar. Father of William Beattie Brown Jnr(qv). Starting as a restorer of paintings, he was educated at Leith High School and Trustees Academy studying under James Ballantine(qv) of Edinburgh, the glass cutter. Visited France, Belgium and Holland but painted mostly in Scotland, living in Edinburgh. Most of his work was in oil; Scottish views using a dark palette and sombre Highland scenes in a style similar to Peter Graham(qv). 'The painter depicts Scottish scenery with a great amount of quiet, reposeful charm and excels in the rendering of the varied gradations of clear and obscure atmosphere which were abundantly found in lowland glen and on Highland mountain peak. His perspective is invariably excellent; in the painting of scrubby hillside, of pastureland and of running water he is equally at home, and blends the various elements of scenery with taste and harmony. His colouring is rich, fresh, and natural, rather than brilliant, and is generally applied with scrupulous attention to detail' [James Webster]. Elected ARSA 1871, RSA 1884. Exhibited 23 works at the RA from 1863 to 1899. In 1862 'Sunrise - the Carrier's Cart' enhanced his reputation. Also exhibited RSA(170), GI(60), ROI(3), RI(2), RHA(4), AAS in 1896 & L(9). Represented in NGS.
**Bibl:** Caw 298; Halsby 251.

**BROWN, William Beattie Jnr** **fl 1895-1915**
Edinburgh architect and occasional painter in oil and watercolour; landscapes and architectural scenes. Son of William Beattie Brown(qv). Painted in a similar style to his father's but with less success. Served in the Armed Forces during WWI. Shortly before he died he entered a competition for the design of Perth City Hall. Exhibited 20 works at the RSA between 1899 and 1910. Represented in Brodie Castle (NTS).
**Bibl:** Halsby 251.

**BROWN, William Chalmers** **fl 1939-1965**
Aberdeen painter of landscape and harbour scenes. Lived at 11 North Anderson Drive. Worked mostly in oil and invariably painted Scottish scenes. Exhibited intermittently at the RSA between 1940 and 1965, & RSW(1).

**BROWN, William Fulton RSW** **1873-1905**
Born Glasgow; died Glasgow 27 Jan. Painter in watercolour, illustrator. Studied with his uncle David Fulton(qv) and Glasgow Art School. After a distinguished career as a student he first came to prominence with 'A Gentleman of France', exhibited RSA 1898. The following year his study 'The Magician' again achieved prominence. Won silver medal at Saltzburg, 1904. Elected RSW 1894. During his short life he exhibited RSA(20), RSW(29), GI(31), RI(3) & L(4). Glasgow AG has his 'Orpheus' and Paisley AG (20).
**Bibl:** Caw 429; Halsby 251.

**BROWN, William Marshall RSA RSW** **1863-1936**
Born and died Edinburgh. Painter in oil and watercolour; fruit, figurative and landscapes. Attended evening classes Edinburgh School of Art and at the RSA Life School while working as a wood engraver and book illustrator. Won the Chalmers Bursary and Stewart Prize. Subsequently awarded the bronze medal for anatomical studies in South Kensington. Elected ARSA 1909, RSA 1928, RSW 1929. Most of his exhibited work was in oil, his coastal scenes in watercolour are pedestrian, dominated by a slightly over-brown if rather pleasant mellow grey. They are carefully studied and the figure incidents which he incorporates help to convey a good sense of atmosphere. Founder member, SSA and chairman 1905. Kept a studio at Cocksburnpath where he painted many large figure subjects. Exhibited RA(2), RSA(171), RSW(45), GI(78), RCA(3) & L(19). Represented in City of Edinburgh collection, Paisley AG, Kirkcaldy AG, Harrogate AG. The RSA owns his Diploma work 'A Breton Washing Pool' and 'Washing, Volendam'.
**Bibl:** Caw 333; Halsby 251; Macmillan [SA] 309.

**BROWN, Yvonne Lindsay** **fl 1959-1960**
Portobello artist. Exhibited twice at the RSA during the above years.

**BROWNE, Alexander** **fl 1660-1677**
Obscure Scottish heraldic painter, probably of Edinburgh.

**BROWNE, Charles Francis** **fl 1890-1904**
Artist who lived at the turn of the century in Paris before settling in Kirkcudbright; exhibited GI(2).

**BROWNE, George Elmer** **fl 1909**
Watercolour painter of Scottish extraction; exhibited RSW(1).

**BROWNE, Sir George Washington PRSA FRIBA, PRA, HRA, HRMS LLD** **1853-1939**
Born Glasgow 21 Sep; died Sambrook, Shropshire 18 Jun. Architect. Acquired his early training and education in Glasgow, continuing an apprenticeship in London, winning the Pugin Travelling Scholarship, the first time this award had gone to a Scot. Settled in Edinburgh 1879 as principal assistant to Rowand Anderson(qv). Much of his work lay in library design, his initial assignment being the Edinburgh public library, the first of the Carnegie libraries to be built in Scotland. He was the architect for the Edinburgh Sick Children's Hospital and designed the operating theatres for the Royal Infirmary. In 1899 designed the Royal Bank of Scotland on the corner of High St and Castle St, Dundee - the first commercial building in the new style influenced by new metal technologies. Appointed architect for a new Thames bridge but the war intervened. When he was elected President of the RSA in 1930 he was the first architect to have been so honoured. Fellow of the Royal Institute of British Architects, President, Association of Architects, and a member of the Royal Fine Art Commission for Scotland. As part of the celebrations of the centenary of the RSA Browne was honoured with an LLD Edinburgh

University. Robert Lorimer(qv) respected his work deeply 'because he could do the whole thing'. Elected HRA 1924, HRMS 1931, ARSA 1892, RSA 1902, Treasurer RSA 1917-24, RSW 1933, PRSA 1930, knighted 1927. Exhibited RSA(60), RA(1) & GI(9).
**Bibl:** Dunbar 149; Gifford passim; Peter Savage, Lorimer and the Edinburgh Craft Designers, Edinburgh 1980, 4,5,6,30,93,114; Bruce Walker & W S Gauldie, Architects and Architecture on Tayside, Dundee 1984, 163.

**BROWNE, K M** **fl 1936-1939**
Scottish amateur artist who spent much of his life in London. Exhibited once at both the RSA and GI.

**BROWNE, Mrs Marmaduke** **19th Century**
Miniature painter. Little is known of her beyond the fact that the SNPG has a competently executed miniature portrait of Dr James Atkinson, painted in watercolour on ivory, oval, 4" x 3 1/8" signed on the front 'M B Browne' and on the reverse 'Mrs Browne/Pinxit James Atkinson EDINB'. A paper placed behind the miniature bears the inscription: 'Painted by Mrs Marmaduke Browne, Calcutta'. Schidlof records seeing a miniature in the collection of the Marchioness of Hastings signed 'M B Browne'.
**Bibl:** Foskett i 184; Long 51; Schidlof.

**BROWNE, Peter C** **fl 1900**
Amateur Edinburgh artist who exhibited once at the RSA.

**BROWNE, Ronald G** **1937-**
An amateur Edinburgh artist, better known as a member of the folk-singing group 'The Corries'. Exhibited RSA 1960 and again in 1961 from at 5 West Cross Causeway.

**BROWNHILL, John** **fl 1530-1532**
Master-Mason. Appointed Master Mason to the King for life in January, 1531. He appears to have been ousted from James V's favour shortly afterwards by Thomas Franche(qv).

**BROWNLIE, Geanieh** **fl 1893**
Amateur Lenzie artist; exhibited GI(1).

**BROWNLIE, James Miller** **fl 1895-1921**
Glasgow painter in oil and watercolour. Spent part of his early life in Strathbungo. Exhibited RSA 1901, RSW(2), GI(12) & L(4).

**BROWNLIE, Miss L** **fl 1883**
Amateur Glasgow painter exhibited one work at the GI.

**BROWNLIE, Robert Alexander ('RAB') RSW** **fl 1880-d1897**
Born in England but worked most of his life in Scotland, mainly in Glasgow. Painter in oil and watercolour, also illustrator; landscape, flowers, coastal views and fishing villages. Talented caricaturist, contributing spirited cartoons to *The Sketch* (1893-5), *St Paul's, Judy* (1893), *The Pall Mall Magazine* (1893), and *The English Illustrated Magazine* (1894-6). Painter of limited output whose attractive watercolours were recognised by his being elected a member of the RSW 1890. Exhibited 5 works at the RSA, 3 of them in 1890. Also GI(7) & L(3). Represented in V & A.
**Bibl:** Halsby 251; Houfe 249.

**BROWNLOW, George Washington** **1835-1876**
Painter in oil of landscape and narrative paintings. Although not a Scotsman he lived for a time in Edinburgh and a number of his most important works, especially in the early part of his career, were undertaken north of the border. He was not prolific and examples of his work are seldom seen but at his best he was a fine draughtsman with a good colour sense and with the ability to handle large crowd scenes capturing the spirit of the occasion. His smaller studies, although attractive, were less successful. Exhibited 8 works at the RA including 'The Mother's Lesson', 'Cottage Interior at Wishaw, Lanarkshire' (1860) and 'A Findon Fisherman's Fireside' (1866) but his most important work was undoubtedly his large-scale painting of 'A Revivalist Preaching at Ethword Church, Lincolnshire' (1860). At the RSA he exhibited 11 works, mostly Scottish scenes, 1859, 1860 and 1868.

**BRUCE, Andrew** **fl 1887**
Amateur Edinburgh watercolourist; exhibited a study of buildings at the RSA.

**BRUCE, Eldred H Home** **fl 1919-1939**
Amateur oil painter. Shortly after WW1 he moved to Penzance, Cornwall. Exhibited once at the RSA in 1919 and on a number of occasions in English provincial galleries.

**BRUCE, Frederick William** **fl c1890-1910**
Born Edinburgh. Spent most of his life in France and England. A pupil of Ernest Laurent. Exhibited several works at the Paris Salon, notably a portrait and a still life, both in 1905. Never exhibited in his native country.

**BRUCE, George** **fl 1834**
Leith miniature and profile painter. One of only three Scotsmen to excel at painting silhouettes (the others being J Smith(qv) and Bruce's partner, S Houghton(qv)). His principal business was that of a jeweller and frameworker in South Bridge St, Edinburgh. Learned the art of profilism from Houghton who had newly returned from an apprenticeship with Miers(qv) in Leeds. The two set up in partnership 1792. Exhibited a frame containing 9 miniatures at the RSA 1834. Two of his works, which more closely resembled Miers than did Houghton's, have recently been discovered. 'Robert Burns' is in SNPG.
**Bibl:** Arthur Mayne, British Profile Miniaturists, London 1970, 67,Pl 40.

**BRUCE, Hamish** **fl 1955-1959**
Falkirk painter who exhibited 2 works during the above period.

**BRUCE, Miss Harriet C** **fl 1876-1899**
Highly competent Edinburgh watercolour painter who in later life went to live at Lochgilphead, Argyllshire. Specialised in landscapes, coastal scenes, still life and figurative subjects. In 1887 exhibited a study of the Post Office at Ford, Loch Awe, at the RA. She showed 27 works at the RSA between 1876 and 1899 as well as exhibiting SWA(3), GI(10) & L(6).
**Bibl:** Halsby 108,251.

**BRUCE, Miss Jenny** **1943-**
Born Berriedale, Caithness. Painter in oil and mixed media with a tendency toward seascapes - ecological and historical. Studied Grays School of Art 1961-66. Awarded Bryne scholarship and between 1965 and 1969 worked as a freelance textile designer. In 1972-74 lecturer in art, University of Johannesburg and 1974-1976 at the University of Witwatersrand, South Africa. Returned to live in Glasgow and teaches in Dunbartonshire. Exhibited RSA 1989.

**BRUCE, John** **fl 1876-1880**
Edinburgh landscape painter in watercolour. Exhibited 3 works at the RSA between the above years before moving c1880 to London. No further exhibits are recorded.

**BRUCE, John S** **fl 1936**
Amateur Glasgow painter; exhibited GI(1).

**BRUCE, Martin Brydon** **fl 1885-1899**
Edinburgh landscape painter in watercolour and oil. Moved from Edinburgh to Reidhaven Street, Elgin c1890 and then to London c1894. Exhibited RA(2), RSA(7), RBA(22), ROI(2), GI(5) & AAS(2).

**BRUCE, Mary Maggie** **fl 1900-1923**
Aberdeen painter of local landscape in oil. Exhibited frequently at the AAS during the above years, at first from Viewpark, Deemount Terrace and latterly from View Mount, West Cults.

**BRUCE, Matt RI** **1915-?**
Born Shanghai, 17 Nov. Landscape painter in oil and watercolour; art teacher. Educated at Dollar Academy, trained Edinburgh College of Art 1932-39 under Gillies(qv) and Maxwell(qv). Taught at Victoria College, Jersey and Brighton College of Art until ill-health led to early

retirement. His style is impressionistic, the compositions figurative including portraiture, flowers, but especially landscapes, marines and occasional flat-racing scenes. Forced to retire in 1977 by ill-health but recovered and resumed full-time work. Council member of both RI and PS. Some work has been published by the Hamlyn Group and by Harlands of Hull.
**Bibl:** Wingfield.

**BRUCE, Mirabel** **fl 1964**
Aberdeen gem and metalwork designer. Exhibited AAS from 70 Ashvale Place.

**BRUCE, Peter Ross** **fl 1899-1915**
Greenock landscape artist and bank agent who exhibited 5 works of Scottish genre and landscapes at the RSA during the above years and GI(3), also locally 1899-1915. 'An Arran hillside', completed in 1913, is in Greenock AG.

**BRUCE, Mrs T E (or F G)** **fl 1935**
Aberdeen amateur painter. Exhibited 'The Thicket' at the AAS from Fairford, Cults.

**BRUCE, Sir William** **c1630-1710**
Scottish architect of eminence and influence. Founded the school of classical architecture in Scotland. Sir John Clerk of Penicuik wrote that Bruce was "the introducer of Architecture in this country" (1717). Younger son of a minor Perthshire landowner, Robert Bruce of Blairhall, whose wife was the daughter of a neighbouring laird, Sir Robert Preston of Valleyfield. His early training is unclear but it is known that he visited the continent in 1663 and was often in London. The works of Palladio were in his library. In about 1660 he married Mary, daughter of Sir James Halket of Pitfirrane. In later life one of his children married into the family of the influential Earl of Rothes. He may have studied intermittently at St Andrews University. In 1671-1678 Surveyor-General of the Royal Works in Scotland. In 1663 after the Restoration he was honoured with a baronetcy. Following the death of Charles II he lost favour and spent the remainder of his life in political exile. From 1686 he concentrated on developing his estates in Fife and Kinross, completing the magnificant Kinross House. In 1699 his wife died and he quickly remarried, leaving Kinross House to his son. Ambitious but principled, supporting the house of Stuart until his death, he became increasingly autocratic as financial problems intensified and his son (who died within a year of his own death) produced no heir. He was fond of all the arts and also of horticulture in which he retained an innovative interest. Bruce's influence in the development of Scottish architecture in the 17th century was gained partly through his own work and partly through his personal influence obtained as much by his position in society as by his repute. He designed at least ten major buildings including Holyrood House (with Mylne) and Lauder Church, but mostly country houses. Dunkeld (1676-84) and Moncreiffe (1675-9, demolished by fire 1957) saw Bruce experiment with the compact 'oblong square' type plan, more fully developed at Hopetoun and Kinross. In Edinburgh, Craigiehall(c1695) 'marks the emergence of the rectangular piend-roofed house type which was to dominate 18th century Edinburgh country house and villa design' [Gifford]. Among his patrons were the Dukes of Queensberry and Hamilton. Through them he influenced the many other architects they employed. Several important Scottish architects gained early experience by assisting Bruce, among them James Smith(qv) (later to become a rival), Alexander Edward(qv) and Robert Mylne(qv). "Bruce was more than a competent imitator and his best work shows considerable originality. No English house of the period achieved the same serene dignity as Kinross, and few could show as much sophistication of design as Hopetoun, with its cross-in-square plan, convex quadrant-colonnades and francophile elevations. Three qualities in Bruce's work command attention...a grandeur of conception, an ability to envisage house, gardens and landscape as related components of an integral design...a sensitivity in the selection and handling of materials, and in particular an aptitude for harnessing the distinctive properties of Scottish sandstone to achieve effects of great subtlety and refinement and lastly a respect for medieval tradition" [John Dunbar].
**Bibl:** John G Dunbar,'Sir William Bruce', SAC (Ex Cat); Dunbar 75-81,83-6,88-92 et passim; Gifford 55,126-8,142,143,145-6,180,191,209, 557, 591-2,pl.62; Macmillan [SA], 74,77,79 et passim; Colin McWilliam, The Buildings of Scotland et passim; Bruce Walker & W S Gauldie, Architects and Architecture on Tayside, Dundee 1984, 45-51.

**BRUCE, Winifred Bella Ironside** **c1920**
Exhibited a landscape at the AAS from North Bank House, Wick.

**BRUCE-LOCKHART, John Harold** **1889-1956**
Born Beith, Ayrshire, 4 Mar; died Jun. Painter in watercolour; landscapes. Educated at Sedbergh, Jesus College, Cambridge and in France and Germany. His life was divided between his teaching responsibilities - in 1936 he was appointed headmaster of Sedbergh - and his painting. Active member of the Lake Artists' Society. Exhibited several times at both the RA and the RSA. Multi-talented, in addition to art and teaching he was a keen sportsman representing Scotland at both rugby 1913-1920 and cricket 1909-1910.

**BRUFORD, Joan** **fl 1951**
Edinburgh artist who exhibited 2 works at the RSA in the above year.

**BRUMBY, William** **fl 1834-1843**
Edinburgh engraver. Working at 72 Rose Street, specialised in landscape and historical scenes. Thus in 1834 he exhibited an engraving of George Harvey's painting 'The Covenanters', and a landscape; exhibited again RSA in 1843.

**BRUNTON, Miss Elizabeth York** **1880-c1960**
Sculptress, painter and engraver. Studied Edinburgh College of Art and in Paris where she was a pupil of Nevellier. Painted continental market scenes, sometime using linen as a ground. In 1925 exhibited a statuette at the Paris Salon as well as engravings at the Autumn Salon in Paris of 1929 and 1930. Member of the Colour Woodcut Society, her coloured wood engravings earning international recognition. In addition to many exhibits in France she showed 15 works at the RSA, RSW(2), GI(19), AAS(1) & L(5).
**Bibl:** Halsby 251.

**BRUNTON, John** **fl 1875-1884**
Edinburgh landscape painter in oil. Exhibited 7 times at the RSA during the above years, moving to a Liverpool address in 1881.

**BRUNTON, Miss Mabel M** **fl 1916-1926**
Scottish painter who went to live in Leeds before returning to Scotland, settling in Kirkcudbright 1926. Exhibited RCA(2).

**BRUNTON, Mary Campbell** **fl 1885-1934**
Born Glasgow. Painter in oil of landscape and portraits. After a brief spell at Glasgow School of Art she continued her studies in Paris under Benjamin Constant, J P Laurens, J Lefevre and T R Fleury. A number of her portraits were shown at the French Salon during 1929 to 1934. Exhibited RSA(11) 1890-1911 & GI(35).

**BRYAN, Edward C** **fl 1970-1982**
Edinburgh sculptor; exhibited at the RSA between the above years.

**BRYCE, Alexander Joshua Caleb RBA** **1868-c1938**
Painter in oil; landscape and portraits. Trained Glasgow School of Art, Manchester and Paris. Spent most of his working life in England, finally settling in Witham, Essex. Elected RBA 1914. Exhibited RA(9), RSA(3), ROI(13), RI(1), GI(3) & L(4), but mainly at the RBA(180).

**BRYCE, David RSA FRIBA** **1803-1876**
Born Edinburgh; died Edinburgh, 7 May. Architect and painter in watercolours. Elder brother of David(qv). Educated at the High School and professionally in the office of Burn(qv) whose partner he became 1841, running the Scottish branch of the practice. A great Scottish romantic and one of the finest architects of modern times. In 1844 their association was dissolved allowing him to follow more thoroughly his own ideas which led to a modification of the Gothic generally called 'the Scotch Baronial'. In this style, for the revival of which his fame is mainly due, he erected Cortachy, Blair Castle, The Glen House, and Castlemilk(1864), while leaving his impress on additions and modifications to many others. Worked in many other styles including Scottish Jacobean, T-shaped vernacular, Picturesque, Early English Gothic and classical French chateau (Meikleour,

Perthshire, 1869). Designed the Edinburgh and Glasgow bank in George Street and Fettes College. His main Glasgow buildings are Tolcross House (1848) and the Scottish Widows' Fund Building (112-4 W George St), since altered. In Tayside he was responsible for the 'spectacular adaptation' of Mylne's(qv) Panmure House, Angus(1852-7), reconstructed Playfair's Kinnaird Castle, Angus(1854-6) in a French Gothic chateau style, designed the Royal Exchange Building, Dundee; Fotheringham, Angus(1859); Balbirnie House, Fife(1874) and many others. Founder of the short-lived Architectural Institute of Scotland. He was Grand Architect for Scotland. Among his pupils were James Maclaren(qv), Andrew Heiton(qv), David Smart(qv) and John Milne(qv). Elected ARSA 1855, RSA 1856. Exhibited RSA 1851-1880, not only architectural designs but also precisely drawn topographical subjects.
**Bibl:** Dunbar 147,149,151,158-63; Gifford see index; Gomme & Walker 1987(rev), 286; Halsby 251; Irwin 204; Peter Savage, Lorimer and the Edinburgh Craft Designers, Edinburgh 1980, 6,29,93,154,163; Bruce Walker & W S Gauldie, Architects and Architecture on Tayside, Dundee 1984, 125-131.

**BRYCE, David Jnr** **1815-1874**
Architect. Younger brother of David B(qv). Designed the memorial to George Lorimer in St Giles(1867); Merchants' Hall, Hanover St and an interesting large farm group Meadowhead on Liberton Drive (1854-5).
**Bibl:** Gifford 71,115,263,307,311,491.

**BRYCE, Gordon RSA RSW** **1943-**
Born Edinburgh, Jne. Painter in oil and watercolour, printmaker and teacher. Specialises in strongly coloured, vibrant landscape and still life, generally of flowers. His palette is predominantly red, yellow and green most effectively used in a bold, highly structured compositional style, in the Mary Armour tradition. Educated Watson's College and Edinburgh Academy, he studied drawing and painting at Edinburgh College of Art under Gillies(qv) and Philipson(qv) 1960-65, being awarded the Andrew Grant Scholarship enabling him to visit Spain 1965, the same year as his first solo exhibition in Edinburgh. Won Keith prize 1964, Chalmers Bursary 1965 and first prize for painting in France (Pernod) 1967. Taught for a year before taking up an appointment as lecturer in printmaking at Gray's School of Art in 1968 and head of fine art 1986. Began painting full-time 1995, since when his work has become increasingly abstract, his technique looser but without losing pictorial authenticity. Won the Latimer Award 1968 and first prize in the Arbroath Painting Competition 1970. Founder member and secretary of the Peacock Printmaker's Workshop, Aberdeen. Regular exhibitor RA, RSA, RSW, SSA, AAS. Elected RSW, ARSA, RSA 1993. Represented in SNGMA, Aberdeen AG, Perth AG, City of Edinburgh Collection, Darlington AG, Leeds City AG, Arbroath Town Council.

**BRYCE, Helen Bryne** **fl 1918-1931**
Born Glasgow. Painter in oil; still life, flowers and architectural subjects. Studied at St John's Wood School of Art and lived almost all her life in England, first at Burford, Oxfordshire then in London. Exhibited RA(5), ROI(3) & SWA(1) - mainly in the 1920s, but never in Scotland.

**BRYCE, Miss Jessie** **fl 1850-1851**
Amateur Edinburgh painter of Scottish landscapes; exhibited twice at the RSA during the above years.

**BRYCE, John** **c1805-1851**
Edinburgh architect. Settled in Glasgow in the 1820s. Among his pupils were John Carrick(qv) and William Spence(qv). Designed some important Scottish houses of which the best known is Major Scott's Mansion at Gala, the designs for which were exhibited at the RSA 1877. Responsible for the Necropolis(1833) in Cathedral Square, Glasgow.
**Bibl:** A Gomme & D Walker, Architecture in Glasgow, London 1987(rev), 286.

**BRYCE, John** **?-1922**
Edinburgh architect. Nephew of David Bryce(qv). Completed Edinburgh Royal Infirmary (1876-9) begun by his uncle, similarly the Bank of Scotland in George St; also designed the Concert hall for Fettes College(1878).
**Bibl:** Gifford 259,282,288,302,303,574.

**BRYCE, Mrs T H** **fl 1890**
Amateur Kelvinside artist; exhibited GI(1).

**BRYCE, W T P** **fl 1933**
Amateur Edinburgh artist; exhibited RSA(1) from 40 Melville Street.

**BRYCE, William Snodgrass** **fl 1887-d1944**
Paisley painter in oil and watercolour of coastal and fishing scenes, especially those around St Monance where he had a studio. Studied at Glasgow School of Art. Lived for a time at 11 Hunter Street, Paisley where he was a member of the Art Institute Committee before moving to West Kilbride in the 1920s. Exhibited RSA(9) 1901-1911, RSW(1) & GI(31). Represented in Paisley AG, AAS.

**BRYDALL, Robert** **1839-1907**
Born in Glasgow. Painter in oil and watercolour and art historian; continental scenes and landscapes, also figurative. Studied Glasgow School of Art under Charles Heath Wilson(qv) becoming in due course a member of the staff. Probably best known for his book *Art in Scotland - Its Origins and Progress* (1889). Exhibited frequently at the RSA between 1866 and 1884, mostly landscapes, many of them executed on his visits to Italy and Switzerland. Exhibited RA(1), RSA(53), RSW(15), AAS(2) & GI(66). Represented by 25 works in Glasgow AG.

**BRYDALL, Mrs Robert** **fl 1868-1901**
Glasgow painter in oil and watercolour; fruit and still life. Wife of Robert Brydall(qv). Exhibited RSA once in 1868 followed by a considerable pause before in later life she began exhibiting at the GI.

**BRYDEN, Agnes C B H** **fl 1954**
Ayrshire painter. Sister of Nan Bryden(qv). Exhibited RSA(1) 1954.

**BRYDEN, Nan** **fl 1956**
Ayrshire born artist. Sister of Agnes Bryden(qv). Exhibited RSA(1) 1956.

**BRYDEN, Robert RE** **1865-1939**
Born Coylton, Ayrshire; died Ayr, 22 Aug. Engraver and sculptor; painter; etcher of architectural subjects and portraits. Educated Coylton and Ayr Academy. Worked for some years in an architect's office before moving to London. Trained Royal College of Art and RA Schools. Visited Belgium, France and Italy 1894, Spain 1896 and Egypt 1897. In 1899 produced a series of woodcuts 'Men of Letters of the 19th Century' and in 1916 'Twenty Etched Portraits from Life'. His *Etchings of Ayrshire Castles* were published in three volumes between 1899 and 1910. Also published *Etchings in Italy* (1894), *A Series of Burns Etchings* (1896), *Etchings in Spain* (1896), *Auld Ayr and some Ayr Characters* (1897), *Woodcuts of Men of Letters of the 19th century* (1899), *Workers, or Waning Crafts* (1912), *Edinburgh Etchings* (1913), *Glasgow Etchings* (1914), *Ayrshire Monuments* (1915), *Ayr Etchings* (1922) and *Parables of Our Lord* (1924). Two busts by Bryden, of Wallace and Bruce, stand at each side of the main entrance to Ayr Town Hall. A quiet man, he never married and seldom travelled far from home after 1900. Elected ARE 1891, RE 1899. His early etchings were small and delicate; his later work is on a larger scale with what Caw described as "somewhat rude but expressive rigour of conception, light and shade of handling". His later woodcuts used a novel method of printing from two blocks, producing an unusual portrayal of light and shade. Exhibited RA(1), RSA(36), RE(155) & GI(30). Represented by 2 works in SNPG including a portrait of Sir James Caw, Perth AG, and by 72 works in Glasgow AG.
**Bibl:** Caw 463; Houfe 250.

**BRYDEN, Robert Alexander** **1841-1906**
Glasgow architect. Entered partnership with George Bell jnr(qv) c1883. Best remembered for his Ocean Chambers, 190 W George St.
**Bibl:** A Gomme & D Walker, Architecture of Glasgow, London 1987(rev), 258n,290.

**BRYDEN, William** **fl 1964**
Amateur Inveresk painter; exhibited 'The Shoot' at the RSA in the above year.

**BRYDON, Arthur McKenzie** **fl 1906**
Glasgow painter exhibited once at the GI.

**BRYDON, Charles** **fl 1880-1901**
Edinburgh based painter in oil and watercolour; coastal scenes, local townscapes and topographical. His best known work was 'HMS Edinburgh lying off Queensferry' shown RSA in 1896. Exhibited RSA(34), RSW(1) & GI(3), also exhibited landscapes including several views of Rothiemay at the AAS 1890-1894 when living at Denholm, Roxburghshire.

**BRYDON, John McKean** **1840-1901**
Scottish architect. Most of his career and best work was in England. Trained in Liverpool, Edinburgh (with David Bryce) and Glasgow (with Campbell Douglas). Became assistant to Shaw and Nesfield in London c1880. It was Brydon who recommended Robert Lorimer for the ARIBA. Elected Vice-President, RIBA 1899-1901.
**Bibl:** Peter Savage, Lorimer and the Edinburgh Craft Designers, Edinburgh 1980, 156,163.

**BRYDON, M L** **fl 1890**
Glasgow painter of 15 Dalhousie Street who exhibited once at the GI.

**BRYMNER, William CMG PRCA RMS** **1855-1925**
Born Greenock; died Wallasey, Cheshire. Miniature portrait painter, also figurative subjects and occasional landscapes. Migrated to Canada 1857 and although exhibiting occasionally at the ROI and at Manchester City AG his professional life was spent in Canada. Studied architecture in Ottawa and sometime after 1878 paid a visit to Paris where he studied at the Academie Julien and with Carolus-Duran. Honorary member, RMS 1916. His visit to France was part of a general wave of Canadian artists who were party to a new fashion to study in France and largely responsible for many unwieldy, sentimental, narrative figure pictures that dominated the RCA until the end of the 19th century. Whilst in France he filled several sketch books with architectural studies and before going to Julien spent three months working on parts of the human anatomy under Pinet. He remained in Paris for six years achieving a remarkable facility in the precise and recognised manner of drawing and painting the nude, often praised by Carolus-Duran. His works were sent for sale to Ottawa. On his return to Canada in 1886 he replaced Harris as Head of the Art Association of Montreal Classes. There he taught many of that city's best known early 20th century artists emphasising the importance of draughtsmanship. Awarded the Gold medal at the Buffalo Pan American Exhibition of 1901. In later life contact with Maurice Cullen, the first Canadian to exploit Impressionism, gradually modified his style. A newer freedom of technique is most apparent in 'The Vaughan Sisters' (Hamilton AG). His later landscapes are almost impressionistic. Director of the Art Association of Montreal 1886-1921, elected ARCA 1883, RCA 1886, PRCA 1909-1918, RMS 1916 and awarded the CMG in 1916. His 'With Dolly at the Sabot-Maker's' is now in the National Gallery of Canada.

**BRYNING, Hugh** **fl 1973-1985**
Broughty Ferry painter and sculptor. Exhibited RSA between the above dates.

**BRYSON, Ian** **fl 1973-1984**
Dundee painter. Exhibited a number of works at the RSA between the above dates.

**BRYSON, John M** **fl 1932-1934**
Glasgow painter; exhibited RSA 1934 & GI 1932.

**BRYSON, Nathaniel** **fl 1905-1910**
Edinburgh watercolourist and stained glass window designer. His studio was in 8 Leith Street Terrace. The 'pensive' Annunciation in St Mary, Bellevue has been described as 'a revolutionary work for its date' [Gifford]. Another remarkable example is the pair of lights 'Consider the Lilies' in the SE nave of Old Parish church, Kirk Loan. Exhibited RSA 1905 and 1910, also GI(1).
**Bibl:** Gifford 44,338,515,524.

**BRYSON, Robert M** **fl 1852-1854**
Glasgow landscape painter in oil. Exhibited at the RSA annually during the above years.

**BUCHAN, 10th Earl of** **[see Erskine, David]**

**BUCHAN, 11th Earl of** **[see Erskine, Charles]**

**BUCHAN, Alex** **fl 1868**
Edinburgh figurative painter in oil; exhibited RSA(1).

**BUCHAN, Andrew G P** **fl 1954-1956**
Amateur Kirkcaldy sculptor; exhibited RSA 1954 and 1956. Represented in Kirkcaldy AG.

**BUCHAN, Archibald** **fl 1898**
Edinburgh topographical painter. Exhibited AAS(1).

**BUCHAN, Dennis RSA** **1937-**
Born Arbroath. Studied at Dundee College of Art 1954-58 and Hospitalfield (1959), obtaining a post-graduate diploma in 1958-59 and an RSA Award in the same year. Part-time lecturer in Dundee College of Art 1962-65 before becoming a full-time lecturer, retiring 1994. Awarded Keith prize at the RSA 1962 and Latimer Award 1963. Holds many one man shows in Edinburgh, Glasgow and Dundee. Elected SSA 1961, ARSA 1975, RSA 1990. Teaches at Dundee College of Art. "He has returned to paraphrase and re-arrange separate elements from his everyday experience in a bold, rumbustious, calligraphic language that is very much his own and involves orchestrations of hue where chords of red or grey, for instance, are laid on a black ground base. Varied in scale and still broadly handled, these vigorous pictures are so physical and full of energetic activity that the noise they make is splendid" [Gage]. Exhibits regularly RSA since 1959 interiors and coastal scenes before becoming increasingly abstract. Represented in SAC, Dundee College of Education, Leicester University.
**Bibl:** Gage 57-9; Hardie 198; *'The Society of Scottish Artists - the First 100 Years'*, 1991; Macmillan [SA].

**BUCHAN, Elizabeth** **fl 1933-1937**
Aberdeen landscape painter of 3 Devanha Terrace. Exhibited AAS during the above years.

**BUCHAN, Peter** **1790-1854**
Peterhead engraver. Remarkably versatile figure, in addition to engraving he was author, bookseller, historian and printer. Kinsman of the 10th Earl of Buchan(qv). Drew and engraved the plates illustrating his *Annals of Peterhead* 1819, which he also printed on his own press. Published poems and wrote historical tracts.
**Bibl:** Bushnell; DNB.

**BUCHAN, William Hamilton** **fl 1896-1899**
Aberdeen painter of portraits and figure subjects. Exhibited AAS 1896 from King Street & RSA 1899 from 43 Summer Street.

**BUCHANAN, A** **fl 1915-1921**
Amateur Glasgow painter; exhibited GI(3).

**BUCHANAN, A M** **fl 1919-1928**
Amateur Edinburgh watercolourist. Lived at 23 Willowbrae Avenue. Exhibited RSA(1) & RSW(1), both during the above period.

**BUCHANAN, Alexander Mitchell** **fl 1919**
Amateur Edinburgh painter; exhibited RSA(1).

**BUCHANAN, Allan** **fl 1878-1900**
Glasgow painter in oil and watercolour; landscape and seascape. One of many artists to enjoy working on Arran. Exhibited an Arran landscape 1878 and another in 1885, also GI(12) & AAS(1)
**Bibl:** Halsby 251.

**BUCHANAN, Archibald** **fl 1886-1898**
Edinburgh watercolour painter of landscape; exhibited RSA(3).

**BUCHANAN, David McC** **fl 1873-1874**
Amateur Glasgow painter of figures and landscapes; exhibited RSA(2).

**BUCHANAN, Elspeth** **1915-?**
Born Bridge of Weir, 29 Nov. Painter in oils and watercolours; landscape and buildings, also occasional portraiture. Educated at St George's, Edinburgh. Daughter of Evelyne Oughtred Buchanan(qv). Trained Edinburgh College of Art 1933-38. Awarded a travelling scholarship. Lived in Edinburgh for some years and taught from 1956 Cranley School. Her first show was held at the

Fine Art Society 1972. Illustrated *Land Air Ocean*. Influenced by R H Westwater and Sir Norman Reid who was her contemporary at the College of Art. Worked as a cartographer for naval intelligence during the war, coming under the influence of the Russian artist Bernard Meninsky. Most of her later work was watercolour drawings of Scottish landscape and buildings, modest but agreeable. Member SSA & SSWA. Exhibited RA, RSA, GI & AAS.

**BUCHANAN, Miss Etta** **fl 1932**
Amateur painter. Lived at Firgrove, Bridge of Allan. Exhibited RSA(1).

**BUCHANAN, Evelyne Oughtred** **1883-c1975**
Born Stockton-on-Tees, 21 Jan. Painter in oil and watercolour; landscape, flowers and portraits. An adopted Scot, she was trained in Edinburgh and remained there for the rest of her life. Studied for one term at Glasgow College of Art, also privately at Newlyn under Stanhope Forbes 1910 and portraiture under R H Westwater. Influenced greatly by Laura Knight, Lamorna Birch and Peploe(qv). Mother of Elspeth Buchanan(qv). Shared an exhibition in Edinburgh with her daughter and son-in-law Nicholas Horsfield 1971. After abandoning painting for many years, she began again in 1933, continuing until 1972 when failing eyesight made it no longer possible. Her watercolours are in the style of Gillies(qv). Exhibited RA(2), RSA(7), SWA(4), ROI(2), RBA(1) & GI(2). Represented in Glasgow AG.
**Bibl:** Halsby 251.

**BUCHANAN, George F** **fl 1848-1864**
Scottish born landscape painter in oil. Lived all his life in London though frequently visited the Highlands. Enjoyed grand scenes painted in dramatic context either in early morning or twilight and often during the autumn when the colours are at their most dramatic. Almost all his exhibits were Scottish scenes, mainly in Argyllshire and Perth. His wife was also a landscape painter. Apart from exhibiting at the British Institute and in Suffolk Street, all his principal work was shown at the RA where he exhibited 27 items between 1848 and 1864. 'Loch Leven Castle' is in Capetown AG while 'Helen's Isle, Loch Katrine', and 'Lake Scene with Castle Ruins' are in Nottingham AG.

**BUCHANAN, Mrs George F** **fl 1865**
Landscape painter in oil. Married George Buchanan(qv). Spent most of her life in London, exhibiting 'Loch Long, Argyllshire' at the RA 1865.

**BUCHANAN, Hugh** **1958-**
Painter, principally in watercolour, favouring architectural themes conveyed in rich coloured washes. Trained Edinburgh College of Art 1976-1980, gaining an Andrew Grant scholarship 1981. Started in the baroque manner but became more classical. Guy Peploe found similarities in Buchanan's earlier work with John Piper and the Scottish 'blottists' Arthur Melville and JW Herald, but Buchanan gradually developed a quite distinctive style of his own. One-man exhibition in Edinburgh 1991. Lives and paints near Crail, Fife. Represented in City of Edinburgh collection, House of Commons, NTS.

**BUCHANAN, James** **fl 1849-1867**
Bonhill painter of genre in oil. Exhibited RSA(9).

**BUCHANAN, James** **1889-1951**
Born Largs, Ayrshire, 26 Jne. Landscape painter in oil and watercolour, also collector. Eldest of five children. Educated at Glasgow Academy, trained Glasgow School of Art. Travelled extensively in North Africa. Lived in Largs for many years and was a founder member of Largs Art Club. In about 1960 moved to Cowdenbeath. Entered business with his father, managing the Govan Croft Pottery. His early street scenes of Morocco were evocative, faithfully capturing the heat and brilliant light. He was attracted by Scottish scenery often painted at sunset. He never married and although not a professional artist his pictures became extremely popular after WW2. In addition to art and collecting, his other great interest was sailing, owning his own racing yachts. Exhibited RSW(3), GI(2) & AAS in 1926 and 1935.
**Bibl:** Halsby 251.

**BUCHANAN, John** **1819-1898**
Born Levenside, Dunbartonshire. Painter in oil; landscape and genre. Originally a pattern designer at a dye factory, he became increasingly interested in painting. Before 1849 his particular interest had focused upon botanical subjects. In the 1850s he migrated to New Zealand where he continued to paint, mostly in watercolour. His 'Milford Sound, looking north-west from Freshwater Basin' (1863) is in the Hocken Library, University of Otago, Dunedin.

**BUCHANAN, Dr John** **fl 1893-1908**
Amateur Aberdeen painter of wild flowers and local scenes. Exhibited AAS from 56 St Swithin Street.

**BUCHANAN, John C** **fl 1932**
Amateur artist from Kilmacolm, Renfrewshire; exhibited GI(1).

**BUCHANAN, Mary** **1876-1958**
Born Glasgow. Sculptress. Her first exhibits were from Paisley 1910. Went to Paris to study 1911, exhibiting that year at the French Salon. In 1912 exhibited at the Salon of French Artists where she was awarded an honourable mention for a portrait study 'Head of a Child'. In 1931 exhibited designs at the Autumn Salon. Returned to live in Chipstead, Surrey c1925 and thereafter exhibited mainly in England. Exhibited RA(3), RSA(4), GI(7) & SWA(3). Represented in Glasgow AG, Paisley AG, City of Edinburgh collection(2).

**BUCHANAN, Patricia** **fl 1977**
Aberdeen landscape painter, trained at Gray's School of Art. Exhibited AAS from 42 Whitehorse Terrace, Balmedie.

**BUCHANAN, Peter S** **fl 1860-1911**
Glasgow painter in oil and watercolour; landscape, especially coastal and harbour scenes. Exhibited 20 works at the RSA between 1871 and 1883, thereafter moving to London before a further sojourn at Windermere 1891, finally settling in Trefriw, North Wales 1905. Exhibited RA 1887 and 1888, GI(34) & RCA(4).
**Bibl:** Halsby 251.

**BUCHANAN, Robert T** **fl 1890**
Amateur Aberdeen artist who exhibited a pastoral scene at the AAS from David Cottage, Auchmill.

**BUCHANAN, Roderick** **1965-**
Born Glasgow. Video artist. Trained Glasgow School of Art. Winner of Beck's Futures prize 2000. According to Jean-Marc Huiford, Buchanan's work, which often uses sporty themes, "deals with today's crucial questions in a way that refuses cynicism or ironic distancing and enthusiastically embraces and commits itself to the world" (*Arts Press*). Exhibits internationally.
**Bibl:** Macmillan 2001, 177-8.

**BUCHANAN, William** **fl c1760**
Engraver. Pupil of Foulis Academy in Glasgow, together with his brother **Ralston BUCHANAN**. Remembered for his engravings for the Raphael *Bible.*
**Bibl:** Brydall 129.

**BUCHANAN, William Cross** **fl 1881**
Helensburgh watercolour painter of landscapes. In 1881, from 6 Sutherland Crescent, Helensburgh, he exhibited a South American scene at the RSA.

**BUCHANAN-DUNLOP, Lt-Col A H OBE** **1874-1947**
Professional soldier and amateur artist. Father of Ian B-D(qv). Served with the Royal Berkshires in South Africa and during both world wars. Keen golfer, captain of Royal Musselburgh, his best known watercolour portraits are of famous golfers including Cyril Tolley, Gene Sarazen, Walter Hagen, Reginald Whitcombe, Bernard Darwin and Sandy Herd.
**Bibl:** Wingfield.

**BUCHANAN-DUNLOP, Brigadier Ian CBE** **1908-**
Born Whitefield, Lancashire. Painter in watercolour and Indian ink; landscapes. Son of A H B-D(qv). Educated Loretto School; self-taught in art. Influenced by J C T Willis and the events of his early life spent in India, Malaysia and Hong Kong. His style is consistently

representational, increasingly aimed at the depiction of light. In its honest unpretentiousness, its clarity and its deftness in dealing with light, his work is a beacon in contemporary Scottish art.

**BUCK, Anne Lillias** **fl 1900-1925**
Painter of portraits and portrait miniatures, specialising in women and children. Although born in Somerset, settled in Scotland where her best work was done. Exhibited RA(1), RSA(5) & L(1).

**BUCKLEY, Jim** **fl 1984-**
Glasgow sculptor in steel of emblematic shapes. In their angularity and ugliness they reflect their position in both time and space. Invited for inclusion in New Directions in Scottish Sculpture at the Barbican Art Gallery, London 1990. Exhibits regularly RSA since 1984.

**BUCKNER, Alfred** **fl 1864-1875**
Edinburgh painter in oil; landscapes, especially the Scottish Highlands. One of many artists to enjoy painting on Arran. Exhibited annually at the RSA a total of 31 works between the above dates.

**BUCKNER, Frank S** **fl 1881-1886**
Amateur Edinburgh painter in oil and watercolour of Old Edinburgh scenes and landscape. Exhibited RSA(3) & GI(1).

**BUDD, Helen Margaret (née Mackenzie) ROI** **fl 1905-1939**
Born Elgin. Painter, etcher and engraver. Studied Royal College of Art, London where she remained most of her life, having married the English artist Herbert Ashwin Budd. Signed her work 'Helen Mackenzie'. Elected ROI 1922, ASWA 1918, SWA 1923. Achieved some eminence mainly through her etchings, exhibiting 22 works at the RA, also ROI(46), SWA (38), GI(7) & L(1).

**BUICK, Alan** **fl 1958**
Amateur painter from Alyth, Perthshire. Exhibited once at the RSA.

**BUIST, Charles E** **fl 1943**
Amateur Roxburgh painter; exhibited RSA(2).

**BULL, Clive S** **fl 1910**
Aberdeen painter of local topographical subjects. Exhibited AAS(1) from 80 Great Western Road.

**BULL, Mrs Clive S** **fl 1910**
Aberdeen amateur painter of landscapes and figure subjects. Married Clive B(qv). Exhibited AAS(3).

**BULL, Frederick** **1936-**
Born Aberdeen. Landscape painter; draughtsman and teacher. Trained Gray's School of Art 1954-59. For many years Head of Art, Craigie College of Education, Ayr before becoming national development officer in Art and Design, Scottish Dept. of Education. Influenced by Henderson Blyth(qv) and Joan Eardley(qv). Interested particularly in tone and distance with a penchant for the landscape of north-east Scotland. Retired to Aberdeenshire. Has held several solo exhibitions and exhibits RSA & RGI.

**BULLICK, Molly** **1941-**
Born Belfast. Painter and engraver of religious and Scottish landscape subjects. Studied architecture at Belfast College of Art before entering Edinburgh College of Art 1962-65. Became increasingly interested in print-making, winning various awards culminating in the Mini Print International Cadaques, Spain 1983. Finely concentrated detail if at times her colour is a little muddy. Exhibited RSA 1977 & 1979-83 from the Stables, Stow, nr Galashiels, also SSA & SSWA.

**BULLO, James** **c1680-c1730**
Little known Edinburgh early painter. Married 1703 and subsequently became a painter burgess of Edinburgh.
**Bibl:** Edinburgh Marriage Registry for 1703; Roll of Edinburgh Burgesses.

**BULMER, Frederick C (K)** **fl 1964**
Aberdeen painter of local scenes. Exhibited AAS from 73 Braemar Place.

**BUNTEN, Mrs P B** **fl 1868**
Amateur Glasgow flower painter in oil; exhibited twice at the RSA in the above year.

**BUNTING, Miss Annie** **fl 1919**
Aberdeen painter of landscape and local coastal scenes. Sister of Julia B(qv) and probably related to Thomas B(qv). Exhibited AAS(2) from 40 Thomson Street.

**BUNTING, Mrs Jessie** **fl 1912**
Aberdeen landscape painter. Wife of Thomas B(qv). Exhibited a local scene at the AAS from 25 Beaconsfield Place.

**BUNTING, Miss Julia** **fl 1921**
Aberdeen painter of interiors and genre. Sister of Annie B(qv) and probably related to Jessie and Thomas B(qv). Exhibited an interior at the AAS from 40 Thomson Street.

**BUNTING, Thomas** **1851-1928**
Aberdeen painter in oil and watercolour; landscape, mainly local. Specialised in Aberdeenshire and Perthshire scenes, often with rivers or the sea in ivory tones. In his early years he exhibited from the home of James Winkley(qv) whose protégé he was. Founder member of the Aberdeen Society of Artists(qv) 1885. His work was competent but a little nondescript. Earned the reputation of being difficult. His later work is looser, lighter and less interesting. Among the 18 works exhibited at the RSA 1874-95 was 'Evening at Braemar' (1879); also GI(6) & regularly AAS 1885-1929.
**Bibl:** Halsby 251.

**BUNTING, Thomas J** **fl 1908**
Amateur Dingwall painter. Exhibited a local scene at the AAs from 1 Mansfield.

**BUNTING, William** **1951-**
Modern abstract painter, pupil of William Baillie(qv). Shares the fashionable modern view that 'art begins where imitation representation ends, and that all art is abstract'. Hardie describes his work as employing 'a closely related vocabulary with a personal accent of interlocking forms defined by taut lines and modelled by subtle gradations of light, rather than texture'.
**Bibl:** Hardie 180-1(illus).

**BURBRIDGE, John** **fl 1858-1894**
Glasgow painter in oil and watercolour; landscape, and architectural subjects. Exhibited RSA 1858 and 1861 from Glasgow and again 1881 having moved to London. Occasionally collaborated with J A Bell(qv) the architect. Exhibited Walker Gallery, Liverpool 1894.

**BURCHELL, Carolyn A** **1961-**
Born Edinburgh; painter in oil, crayon, wax, gouache; subject studies, murals. Studied at Edinburgh College of Art 1979-83; gained post-graduate scholarship enabling her to visit Florence 1984. Commissioned to provide murals for Bruntsfield Hotel, Edinburgh 1983-87. Fascinated by the texture of old buildings. Exhibited RSA from 1984.

**BURDEN, Archibald** **fl 1710-1722**
Scottish engraver. Engraved plates for Nisbet's *System of Heraldry* 1720. A number of his bookplates are recorded in Fincham.
**Bibl:** Bushnell; John Orr, Ex Libris Journal, vol 6, 13.

**BURGESS, Dawn** **fl 1981**
Edinburgh painter of 123 Saunders Street. Exhibited a figurative composition at the AAS.

**BURGESS, James** **fl 1865-1875**
Edinburgh painter in oil; sporting, landscape and coastal scenes. Exhibited 14 works at the RSA between the above dates.

**BURGESS, James G** **1865-1950**
Amateur artist. Studied at Dumbarton Art School. Possibly related to James Burgess(qv). Started a firm of interior decorators and became friendly with some of the Glasgow Boys. Lived in Helensburgh and painted local scenes generally in watercolour. Exhibited RSA(4), RSW(2) & GI(3).

**BURGESS, Jenny** **1949-**
Born Scotland, Aug 29. Weaver and jewellery designer. Trained Gray's School of Art. Awarded RSA First Prize bursary. Became

personal assistant to Sir Nicholas Sekers at Lister & Co (Bradford). Since 1992 has lived, taught (City & Islington College, Islington), and worked in London. Solo exhibitions of handwoven textiles in Aberdeenshire 2003. Lives at 37 Cleveleys Rd, London E5 9JW, with summers in rural Aberdeenshire.

**BURGESS, William** **1805-1861**
Edinburgh artist who exhibited once at the RSA in 1850.

**BURGOYNE, Joan** **fl 1963-**
Aberdeen painter of still life, flowers and genre. Trained at Gray's School of Art. Married to John B(qv). Vice-President, Aberdeen Artists' Society 1979-81. Exhibited RSA(6) between 1963 and 1966 but much more regularly, since 1964, at the AAS from 3 Polmuir Road and latterly 41 Mount Street.

**BURKE, Andrew** **1947-**
Born Glasgow, 7 Apr. Trained Carlisle College of Art 1967-8 and Edinburgh School of Art 1968-71. Travelling scholarships enabled him to visit Amsterdam. Influenced by American Realist and Dutch genre painting, his favoured medium is acrylic in which he produces highly detailed landscapes in restricted colour but with a full range of tone. Has exhibited RSA since 1984, also RSW & GI. Represented in Duke of Edinburgh's collection.

**BURLISON, John** **1843-1891**
Stained glass window designer. Partner in firm of Burlison & Grylls. Responsible for windows in both St Giles and St Mary's Cathedrals.
**Bibl:** Gifford 44,117,366.

**BURN, Miss Hilda Marion** **fl 1920-1948**
Edinburgh painter, designer and pottery worker. Lived at 6 Murrayfield Road. Exhibited mainly Scottish landscapes at the RSA 1943-1948, also GI(1) & L(7).

**BURN, William (RSA)** **1789-1870**
Born Edinburgh; died London. Architect. Educated Edinburgh HS, he was a pupil of Sir Robert Smirke 1808-11. Responsible for a number of important buildings in Scotland. Between 1811 and 1826 'he did more to establish the Hellenism of Sir Robert Smirke and William Wilkins as the 'modern' style of architecture for public and urban building in Scotland than anyone else' [Dunbar]. In 1816 he was narrowly defeated by Playfair in competition for the completion of Edinburgh University, thus beginning a lifelong rivalry but by 1830 had the largest practice in Scotland. Foundation member, Institute of British Architects 1835. In 1840 he agreed to become vice-president of the proposed Institute of Architects in Scotland, but resigned after a quarrel regarding the eligibility of Bryce(qv). Before his departure for London 1841 (when David Bryce took over the Edinburgh practice) Burn was the leading country house architect in Scotland. Worked in a Tudor and later a Jacobean style, with occasional forays into the Gothic middle ages as, for example, his design of Saltoun Hall, East Lothian and the Scottish vernacular. In Tayside alone he designed over fifty buildings built 1822-1847 including Murray Royal Hospital, Perth(1822-7), Camperdown House, Angus(1824-6); also Faskally, Perthshire(1829) and Madras College, St Andrews(1832-4). Several of his drawings are in the National Library of Scotland. Examples of his work are Tyninghame House, built for the 9th Earl of Haddington (1829) & alterations to Raehills, Dumfries-shire, the home of the Earl of Hopetoun. Responsible for popularising 'Tudor Gothic', among the best examples being the mansion houses at Carstairs, Lanarkshire (1820) and Blairquhan, Ayrshire (1824). Also responsible for church architecture including the Abbey Kirk, Dunfermline (1821) - a fully developed cruciform structure with a crossing tower. In Edinburgh the Doric style was evidenced in Burns' design of John Watson's School (1825) and Edinburgh Academy (1823-1836). Unique in the annals of British architecture 'epitomising in a single career the whole course of 19th century architecture from Greek revival to Scottish Baronial'. Elected RSA 1829 but resigned before taking up membership. Exhibited RSA only in 1926.
**Bibl:** Dunbar 123,126,129,160,166,207; Gifford see index; Peter Savage, Lorimer and the Edinburgh Group of Designers, Edinburgh 1980, 3,29,85,108,154,163; Bruce Walker & W S Gauldie, Architects and Architecture on Tayside, Dundee 1984, 125.

**BURN-MURDOCH, Miss D** **fl 1905**
Amateur painter. Related to William Gordon(qv) and Morag Burn-Murdoch(qv). Exhibited RSA(1).

**BURN-MURDOCH, Sarah Jessie Cecilia ('Morag')** **1862-1916**
Edinburgh painter in oil and watercolour; landscape and figures. lived for a short time in Paris c1901. Sister of William Gordon B-M(qv), related also to Miss D B-M(qv). Exhibited RSA(10), GI(8) & RSW(1).

**BURN-MURDOCH, William Gordon RCA FRSE** **1862-1939**
Born Edinburgh; died Edinburgh, 19 Jly. Painter in oil and watercolour, lithographer, etcher and writer. Specialised in Polar scenery and historical subjects; also sculptor, writer, sportsman, antiquarian and Scottish nationalist. Brother of Morag B-M(qv). Educated in Edinburgh, trained in art at Antwerp Academy under Verlat, in Paris under Carolus Duran and in Florence, Naples and Madrid. In 1892 he went to the Antarctic on a Dundee whaler with his friend the explorer Dr W S Bruce. Author of *From Edinburgh to the Antarctic, Modern Whaling and Polar Bear Hunting,* and *From Edinburgh to India and Burmah.* Contributed to *The Evergreen - The Book of Spring* (1895) and *The Book of Summer* (1896), published by Patrick Geddes. Illustrated Lang: *Angling Sketches.* Among his 55 exhibits at the RSA were portraits of 'My Wife' (1882), 'Hamilton Bryce LLD' (1890), a dramatic scene 'Antarctic expedition steering south through chain of Icebergs' (1896) and in 1897 exhibited the originals of his illustrations for H J Bull's *Cruise of the Antarctic.* At the suggestion of his friend Patrick Geddes, wrote, illustrated & published *A Procession of the Kings of Scotland...*1902. Exhibited a portrait of his wife at the RA in 1891, also GI(6) & L(6). Represented in SNPG, City of Edinburgh collection (a watercolour 'Hansoms at Night - Mount St, London') and Perth AG (a watercolour portrait of the clarsach player Pattuffa Kennedy-Fraser and a large oil of the Chelsea Art Ball).
**Bibl:** Halsby 251.

**BURNET, Miss Edith** **fl 1919**
Aberdeen etcher and draughtswoman. Exhibited AAS(4) from 59 Queen's Road.

**BURNET, Frank** **1848-1923**
Glasgow architect. Apprenticed to John Carrick(qv). In 1901 joined with his former assistant **James CARRUTHERS**(1872-?) designing in a style similar to the unrelated J J Burnet(qv).
**Bibl:** A Gomme & D Walker, Architecture of Glasgow, London 1987(rev),190,258n,263,286-7.

**BURNET, James M** **1788-1816**
Born Musselburgh; died Lee, Kent, 27 Jly. He was apprenticed to Liddel, a woodcarver, and later worked under John Graham at the Trustees Academy. Established a reputation as a cattle painter before leaving Edinburgh 1810 to join his brother John(qv) in London. Thereafter abandoned carving in favour of full-time painting. Regarded Cuyp and Paul Potter as his masters. His work shows talent but his tragically premature death precluded its fulfilment. His subjects were pastoral scenes in which cattle predominated. Some work was engraved by his brother to illustrate a book on landscape and painting in 1849. His brother also referred to him as 'Knox' in his thinly veiled book *Progress of a Painter in the Nineteenth Century.* Allan Cunningham, who devoted a chapter to Burnet in his *Lives of the Most Eminent British Painters,* compared him to Bonington. His best works were 'Taking cattle to shelter during a storm', now in the NGS, 'Crossing the Brook' and 'Cattle by a pool in summer'. Died of tuberculosis. Exhibited RA until the year of his death. Represented in NGS, Aberdeen AG.
**Bibl:** Armstrong 32-33; Brydall 268-270; Caw 159; Allan Cunningham, Lives of the Most Eminent British Painters 6 vols, 1823-6; Halsby 251; Irwin 237-8; McKay 157.

**BURNET, John HRSA** **1784-1868**
Born Fisherrow, Musselburgh, Mar 20; died Stoke Newington, 29 Apr. Painter in oil of genre and narrative works, engraver. Brother of Sir John James Burnet(qv) & James M(qv). His fame rests upon his engravings of many of Wilkie's pictures, especially 'Pensioners celebrating the Battle of Waterloo', printed for the Duke of Wellington in 1837. Burnet also wrote on art subjects. Pupil of Robert

Scott(qv) and studied at the Trustees Academy with Wilkie(qv) and David Allan(qv). In 1806 paid his first visit to London and immediately met Wilkie. He engraved 'The Jew's Harp' in the style of Philippe Le Bas, and 'The Blind Fiddler' in the style of Cornelius Vischer. These were followed by many more of Wilkie's paintings. In 1814 he visited Paris and in 1817 his painting 'Cow's Drinking' together with 'The Fish Market at Hastings' of the following year form part of the Sheepshank collection now in the NG. Published several books, classics of their kind, with his own illustrations, including *Practical Treatise on Painting* (1827), *Practical Hints on Light and Shade* (1838), *On Colour in Painting* (1843), *Rembrandt and his works* (1849), and *Turner and his works* (1852). His most important original work was probably 'Greenwich Hospital and Naval Heroes', painted for the Duke of Wellington as a companion to 'Chelsea Pensioners'. Elected HRSA 1832. Published a series of popular handbooks on art including *Practical Hints on Painting, Light and Shade* and the *Principles of Composition, Education of the Eye, Letters on Landscape Painting* and the *Principles of Portrait Painting* and *Turner and his Works*. Illustrated a volume on Rembrandt and published *Progress of a Painter through the Nineteenth Century* (1854) in which his younger brother James appears as the hero 'Knox'. He died poor. Exhibited 5 works at the RA between 1808 and 1823. Represented in NG, NGS(9), Dublin AG, Glasgow AG, City of Edinburgh collection, Fyvie Castle (NTS, 'Trial of Charles I'), Culzean Castle (NTS).
**Bibl:** Armstrong 30-32; Bryan; Brydall 207-9; John Burnet, Practical essays on various Branches of the Fine Arts etc, London 1848; also 'Autobiography of John Burnet' AJ, 1850; 'Recollections of my contemporaries' AJ, 1860; Bushnell; DNB; Halsby 61-2,79,97; Irwin 195-6 et passim; Macmillan [SA], 181-3; McKay 156-157.

**BURNET, John snr** **1814-1901**
Born Craighead House, Kirk of Shotts. Father of Sir John James B(qv). Educated Dunipace parish school. Was successively a carpenter, clerk of works and architect 1844. After a classical beginning his designs became closer to the Italian Renaissance, always with a fastidious eye for detail. Elected FRIBA 1876; President, Glasgow Institute of Architects 1876-8. Joined by his son 1877. Responsible for Clydesdale Bank (30 St. Vincent Place)(1870), Glasgow Eye Infirmary (1871) and east section of the Glasgow Stock Exchange (1875).
**Bibl:** Gifford 168; A Gomme & D Walker, Architecture of Glasgow, London 1987(rev),78,88,157-161,178,255,287.

**BURNET, Sir John James RA RSA FRIBA** **1857-1938**
Born Glasgow. Architect. Son of John B(qv); nephew of the London architect William B. Graduated Ecole des Beaux Arts, Paris 1874-77. Became a partner with his father 1878 and in 1886 J A Campbell(qv) joined the firm which became Burnet Son and Campbell. Travelled widely on the continent studying museum design 1895 and the following year visited USA to examine hospital and laboratory design, journeys that had a lasting influence. In 1903 he was chosen to design the Edward VII Gallery at the British Museum, forming the resolve to transfer to London. Moving there 1905 he established a large practice with Thomas Tait (who had joined Burnet two years earlier) and Francis Lorne, while retaining his offices in Glasgow. 'Following his visit to the United States in 1896 he began to experiment with a more functional style in which the underlying steel framework of a building was increasingly allowed to govern the composition of the facade, a development which was to lead to his extremely influential design for the Kodak building in London. [He] also succeeded in finding a satisfactory formula for the tall narrow-fronted buildings that commercial pressures were imposing...one of the earliest (being) the former Athenaeum Theatre, Buchanan Street (1891)' [Dunbar], designed in collaboration with J A Campbell(qv). In 1882 he exhibited at the RA his design for the Glasgow Institute for Fine Art and 1885 his plans for the new Drumsheugh Baths in Edinburgh. Collaborated with H P Nenot over the League of Nations building, Geneva. Knighted 1914. Principal architect with the Imperial War Graves Commission 1918-26. 'A Frenchified Scotsman, extraordinarily nice, with a tremendous love of order and system. He never lost hold of the essentials and thought no-one in England knew anything about them...no interest in style as such...really was a great man' [Goodhart-Rendel]. Exhibited RA(29), RSA(55), GI(36) & L(2).
**Bibl:** Dunbar 143-5; Gifford 72,285,304,310,396,520,571,645; A Gomme & D Walker, Architecture of Glasgow, London 1987(rev), 175-7,200-5,209-210,266, 287-9; Goodhart-Rendel in Architectural Review, Oct 1965, 261; Hardie 39,80-1; Peter Savage, Lorimer and the Edinburgh Craft Designers, Edinburgh 1980, 92,135,156,163.

**BURNETT, Al (Alan Burnett-Leys)** **1921-**
Born South Africa. Marine painter of primarily naval craft. Scottish parents. Trained Royal College of Art 1938-41. Began serious painting 1947. Returned to Scotland 1985. Works mainly on commission, often for naval associations and their members; has never sought to exhibit. Represented in Royal Navy Museum, Portsmouth.

**BURNETT, Andrew** **fl 1874-1879**
Edinburgh painter in oil and watercolour; figurative, flowers and landscape. Lived for a time in Aberdeen before returning to Edinburgh. Exhibited 11 works at the RSA between the above dates.

**BURNETT, David Duguid** **fl 1919-1940**
Edinburgh landscape watercolourist. Exhibited RSA(9) & RSW(13).
**Bibl:** Halsby 252.

**BURNETT, Dorothy** **fl 1977-**
Aberdeen landscape and semi-abstract artist. Married to Sydney B(qv). Sometime lecturer in Design, Aberdeen College. Gray's School of Art & latterly the Northern Coll. of Education. Specialises in woven wall panels. Exhibited AAS(2) from 237 Westburn Road.

**BURNETT, Gordon** **fl 1976**
Aberdeenshire metalwork designer. Exhibited AAS from 23 Seaview Park, Murcar.

**BURNETT, Miss J S** **?-1962**
Painter in watercolour of flowers and landscape. Part of her early life spent in London.
**Bibl:** Halsby 252.

**BURNETT, John G C** **fl 1937-1977**
Aberdeen painter of landscape in oil. Exhibited RSA(2) in the 1950s when living in Banff but has shown more regularly, generally landscapes of the north-east at the AAS, in 1937, 1957, 1966, 1977, latterly from 21 Park Road, Cults.

**BURNETT, L E** **fl 1899**
Amateur St Andrews watercolourist. Lived at Moncrieff House. Exhibited RSA(1).

**BURNETT, Mary** **fl 1966**
Edinburgh artist of 58 Polwarth Terrace.

**BURNETT, Sydney** **1941-**
Born Aug 13. Aberdeen painter and sculptor. Son of Sydney A B(qv). Trained Gray's School of Art 1959-1964 winning the Hector Memorial prize 1960, a Byrne travelling scholarship (which took him to Paris) 1962, the Former Pupils' Prize 1963 and a Robert Brough travelling scholarship (taking him to Greece, Egypt, Jordan & Israel) 1965. Won the Saltire Award for sculpture related to architecture 1972, and in 1993 received a research grant to examine the computer-aided design of wind powered gyratory structures. Married to Dorothy B(qv). Exhibits regularly at RSA, AAS. Represented in Aberdeen AG and many private collections at home and overseas.

**BURNETT, Sydney A** **1896-1975**
Aberdeen landscape painter in oil. Father of Sydney B(qv). Trained Gray's School of Art. Principal art teacher, Fraserburgh Academy. Best known for his paintings of north-east fishing villages. Exhibited frequently at the AAS during the above years mainly from 2 Loanhead Terrace.

**BURNETT, Thomas Stuart ARSA** **1853-1888**
Born Edinburgh; died Edinburgh, 3 Mar. Sculptor. Son of a lithographic printer. Studied under William Brodie(qv) and at the School of Board of Trustees. In 1876 he entered the RSA Life School and subsequently studied abroad. Worked mostly in bronze and marble. In 1875 awarded gold medal at the School of Trustees. Among other prizes for modelling was a share of the Stuart prize in

1880. Responsible for panels depicting incidents in the life of the Duke of Buccleuch in Parliament Square, small statues in the Scott Memorial and a neo-Greek memorial to Robert Bryson in Warriston Cemetery. Elected ARSA 1883. Exhibited RA(6) 1885-1887, RSA(49) 1875-1887 & GI(16). Statues by him of General Gordon and Rob Roy are in SNG.
**Bibl:** Gifford 203,316,577.

**BURNETT, Miss Winnie Stuart** **fl 1908-1912**
Edinburgh landscape painter who lived at 17 Luton Place. Exhibited 5 works of genre and Scottish scenery at the RSA between the above dates.

**BURNIE, David B** **fl 1890-1893**
Edinburgh architect and draughtsman. Specialised mainly in church design. Exhibited RSA(3) 1890-1892 & GI(2).

**BURNS, Agnes** **fl 1880-1890**
Amateur painter from Ibrox, Glasgow; exhibited GI(6).

**BURNS, Alexander ('Alastair') S RSW** **1911-1987**
Born Newmills, Ayrshire, 17 Sep; died Aberdeen 6 Dec. Painter in oil, charcoal and pastel but mostly watercolour; landscape, often in winter, and portraits. Painted a lot on Skye, Arran, the western seaboard and in Provence. Son of a GP who was also Provost of Stonehaven, he came to that town when he was two. Educated Mackie Academy, Stonehaven. Trained at Gray's School of Art 1929-33 under D M Sutherland(qv). Helped by a travelling scholarship he went for further training to Paris. In addition to the influence of Sutherland he was deeply affected by de Vlaminck. Always fascinated by the north-east of Scotland 'the rugged intensity of marginal land', including its coastline to which he returned in mid-career. Spent most of 1937 restoring the heraldic wall panels at Monymusk House. In 1938 joined the staff of the Central School in Belmont Street, Aberdeen remaining there until his retirement. In 1940 married an art teacher, Kathleen McLean. During WW2 he served in the RAF, producing a memorable series of drawings of comrades. Elected RSW 1957. Exhibited frequently AAS 1933-85, RSA(6) & GI(2), latterly from Norwood, Stonehaven. Represented in Glasgow AG, Aberdeen AG, Paisley AG, Caird Institute (Greenock), Newport AG (Monmouthshire).

**BURNS, Miss Jean Douglas** **1903-**
Born Cumbernauld, 15 Jne. Painter and engraver. Trained at Glasgow School of Art. Exhibited RSA(5), SWA(1), GI(2) & L(2).

**BURNS, John** **fl 1865-1873**
Edinburgh landscape painter in oil; exhibited RSA 1865, 1869 and 1871-1873.

**BURNS, Joseph** **fl 1927**
Amateur Glasgow painter; exhibited GI(1).

**BURNS, Matthew Robert** **fl c1820-1830**
Edinburgh lithographic artist. Possibly related to Robert Burns(qv). His reputation rests on his *Six Original Lithographic Prints* published in 1829. These are 'Covenanters Tomb in Greyfriars', 'Old Building, foot of Libberton's Wynd, Cowgate', 'West Bow', 'An old Building, foot of the High School Wynd, Cowgate', 'Castlehill, Edinburgh' and 'Regent Murray's Place, Canongate'. Though not of great artistic merit they illustrate some original vantage points in the City of Edinburgh with informative notes. The collection showed an originality of choice and treatment with such an interest in the minutiae of history that it is surprising not more is known about him.
**Bibl:** Butchart 52-3.

**BURNS, Robert ARSA (res)** **1869-1941**
Born Edinburgh, 9 Mar; died 30 Jan. Painter in oil and watercolour; portraits and figurative, also designer of stained glass. Studied at South Kensington and Paris 1890-1892, at the Academy Delacluse, and drawing from life in the Jardin des Plantes. On his return settled for a time in Edinburgh working as a commercial artist producing designs for stained glass windows and interiors. Inherited a great interest in Scots ballads from his family and intended producing an illustrated book. In 1936 his *Scots Ballads by Robert Burns, Limner* (1939) appeared. Illustrated the *Song of Solomon*. His work always showed a marked sense of design being influenced latterly by Vorticism as well as by the Russian ballet. His mural decorations executed under the influence of Charles Mackie adorned Darlings shop in Edinburgh (now demolished). In addition to his work as an illustrator, in which he was one of the leading modern Scottish exponents, his landscapes were of less significance being generally painted in rather sombre hues although a journey to Morocco 1920 led to the use of brighter colours whilst retaining a strong sense of design. Particularly good in portraying crowded scenes built up densely as in a medieval tapestry. Elected ARSA 1902 but resigned shortly afterwards. His appointment as head of drawing and painting at Edinburgh College of Art also came to an abrupt end due to disagreement over his methods of teaching. President, Society of Scottish Artists(qv). Worked for Patrick Geddes's *Evergreen* (1895), contributing a most impressive illustration 'Naturans' to accompany Geddes's article 'Life and its Science', interesting as one of the earliest examples of art nouveau. His 'Young Girl' was illustrated in *Ver Sacrum*, II, 7 in 1899. A fine late example of his stained glass work is 'Presentation in the Temple' (1924) in St Mary, Bellevue Crescent. Exhibited frequently RSA(68), RSW(6), RSA(1), GI(36), AAS 1893-1926, L(8) & RHA(2). Represented in NGS by a most attractive ink drawing of sailing ships and mermaids, Dundee AG, Glasgow AG, Kirkcaldy AG, City of Edinburgh collection(2).
**Bibl:** Bourne Fine Art, 'Robert Burns', (Ex Cat 1982 intro by Martin Forrest); Caw 411-12; Fine Art Soc, 'Robert Burns Limner' (Ex Cat 1978 intro by Paul Stirton); Gifford 336; Halsby 190-2; Hardie 39,109,122-3; Irwin 406,408-10; Macmillan [SA], 288,297,298,317, 331,347,366; Studio, Vol 81, 1921, 86-90.

**BURNS, Robert** **fl 1965-**
Glasgow photographer, mainly of portraits but also landscape. Trained Glasgow School of Art. Solo exhibition at Glasgow School of Art 1987. Founder member of the Glasgow Photography Group. In 1989 became the first photographer to be elected to the Glasgow Group(qv).

**BURNS, Thomas James** **1888-c1940**
Born Edinburgh, 14 Oct. Sculptor. Studied at Edinburgh School of Art and Royal College of Art, London. Exhibited 14 works at the RSA including 'The Sirens', 'St Columba', and 'Corporal Tom Hunter VC'.

**BURNS, William** **fl 1934-1935**
Amateur Glasgow painter; exhibited RSA(1) and a landscape at the AAS from Cailnagreine, Kilmacolm.

**BURNS, William Alexander RSA RSW RI** **1921-1972**
Born Newton Mearns, 31 May; died Aberdeenshire, 14 Oct. Landscape painter in oil and watercolour. Educated in Glasgow under David Donaldson(qv) and Ian Fleming(qv) 1944-1948, and Hospitalfield 1947-1949. Received the Torrance Award from the GI 1952 and the Guthrie Award RSA 1953. Lived at Balmedie. Principal lecturer in art, Aberdeen College of Education 1955-1970. Served in the RAF during WW2. Possessed a very fine colour sense with a predilection for schemes based on red. Resigned from his teaching appointment 1970 in order to concentrate full-time on his painting. He died off the Kincardineshire coast when returning on a solo flight from Dundee to Aberdeen. Aberdeen harbour was his principal theme and his love of flying affected his compositional outlook. The lyricism of his earlier landscapes and mountain scenes of the north gave way later to the more pronounced and abstracted works of the north east, particularly harbour scenes. Elected SSA 1952, RI 1953, ARSA 1957, RSW 1957, RSA 1970. Exhibited extensively RSA, RSW & AAS. Represented in Kirkcaldy AG, Paisley AG, City of Edinburgh collection(2).
**Bibl:** Gage 40-1; Hardie 196.

**BURNSIDE, Cameron** **fl 1923**
Scottish landscape painter. Lived for many years at 86 rue Notre Dame des Champs from where he exhibited 2 landscapes at the AAS.

**BURR, Alexander Hohenlohe** **1835-1899**
Born Edinburgh. Scottish genre and historical painter, in oil and occasionally watercolour. Studied Trustees' Academy where he was a pupil of Robert Lauder(qv) and John Ballantyne(qv). In 1861 went to London with his brother John Burr(qv). Fond of painting children,

often at play, and was in many ways his brother's understudy, painting in a very similar manner. Generally, Alexander Hohenlohe's works were more expansive, pitched in a higher key with often a combination of pinkish-red, citrous, or orange-yellow colour. Also less anecdotal and rather less inventive than his elder brother and his handling softer and less assured. Worked on illustrations for an edition of Burns' *Poems* and many of his works were subsequently engraved. Exhibited RA(16), ROI(10), RBA(5), GI(3) & L(3). His scene illustrating Tennyson's *Dora,* exhibited RA 1863 is in Perth AG, his 'Kite Flying' in Glasgow AG, and 'Prayers before the meal' in Sheffield AG; also represented in Paisley AG.
**Bibl:** AJ 1870, 309-311; Caw 262; Clement and Hutton; Lindsay Errington, Masterclass: Robert Scott Lauder and his pupils, NGS exhib 1983; Halsby 69,252; Hardie 38,54-5(illus); Irwin 350; McKay 359; Macmillan [SA], 231.

**BURR, George Gordon** **1862-?**
Born Aberdeen. Painter mainly in watercolour of landscapes and very occasional portraits. Educated at Robert Gordon's. Became a clerk at the Town House 1876 where he remained until 1892. Best remembered for his large watercolours of Aberdeen buildings and streets as illustrated in *Landmarks of Old Aberdeen,* published with his colleague and contemporary A M Munro, later City Chamberlain, 1885. Appears still to have been active in 1894 although mental illness seriously limited his later output. Exhibited watercolours at the AAS 1886 and 1893. The last recorded work is dated 1922. Variously signed himself 'B', 'GB', 'G Burr' and 'G G Burr'. Represented in Aberdeen AG.

**BURR, John RBA ROI ARWS** **1831-1893**
Born Edinburgh; died London. Scottish genre painter in oil and occasionally watercolour. Elder brother of Alexander Hohenlohe B(qv). In 1853 studied at the Trustees Academy in Edinburgh under Robert Lauder(qv) before moving to London 1861. Began painting commercially at the age of 14, travelling from town to town painting landscapes as well as the occasional portrait. His first two exhibits completed during his second year as a student were favourably received. 'The Housewife', painted in 1857, was purchased by the APFA in Scotland as was 'The Strolling Musician' painted the following year. In 1866, accompanied by his brother, he went to Paris working in the Studio Hébert. Some of his best work was never exhibited. One of his most enthusiastic collectors purchasing pictures before they could be shown publically was Edward Hargitt(qv). Visited Holland 1869. The *AJ* described his work as 'painstaking, genuine and able.' He was master of the doleful and rarely produced a picture without a story. 'He paints and polishes an idyll and while mixing his colours with pathos does not forget the more purely artistic beauty of the painted phrase'. Like Thomas Faed(qv), John Burr painted some excellent watercolours especially of young girls in Highland scenery or by the seaside. His 'Domestic Troubles', exhibited RA 1875, was engraved by W Greatbach and featured in the *AJ* 1869, 272. In Caw's opinion Burr 'lacked the tenderness of Thomas Faed, the rich humour of Erskine Nicol, or the intellectual quality of Robert Herdman'. Elected RBA 1875, ROI 1883. Exhibited RA(18), RSA(2), RWS(9), GI(4), ROI(14), RBA(15) & L(6). 'Peepshow', exhibited RA 1864, is now in the Forbes Magazine Collection (New York), two pictures are in Glasgow AG, 'The Fifth of November', (1871) and 'The Dominie's Visit' (1879), and a 'Self-portrait' is in SNPG. Also represented in Paisley AG, City of Edinburgh collection.
**Bibl:** AJ 1869,272,337-339; 1898, 370; Caw 262; Celtic Annual, 1916 (illus 79); Clement and Hutton; Lindsay Errington, Masterclass: Robert Scott Lauder and his pupils, NGS 1983; Halsby 69,252; Hardie 38,54-6; Irwin 350; McKay 359; Macmillan [SA], 231.

**BURROWS, J Paterson** **fl 1885-1886**
Edinburgh painter who exhibited AAS.

**BURTON, Edward** **fl 1846-1865**
Engraver from Colinton, Edinburgh. Exhibited an engraving of the self-portrait of Sir Watson Gordon at the RA 1865.

**BURTON, (Elias Haliburton) James** **1761-1837**
Scottish architect. As a young man went to England working at first with a builder in Southwark where in 1786 he designed and built the Leverian Museum, afterwards known as the Surrey Institution, in Blackfriars Road. Became the most enterprising and successful London builder of his time, largely responsible for the development of Foundling and Bedford Estates in Bloomsbury, where he built Russell Square (1800-1814), the east side of Tavistock Square (dem 1938), Burton Street and Burton (now Cartwright) Crescent. Also built Waterloo Place and many of Nash's terraces in Regent's Park, besides a large number of houses in Regent's Street itself. His readiness to tackle sites in this way did much to make the Regent Street scheme a financial success. In return Nash assisted his son Decimus Burton in an architectural career. During 1805-1807 Burton was concerned with an important housing estate at Tunbridge Wells, and in 1828 he turned his attention to St Leonard's-on-Sea, for whose development he was largely responsible. Among the buildings he erected were the Assembly Rooms, now the Masonic Hall, and the Royal Victoria Hospital (remodelled in 1903). According to a local source he designed the Gothic Church built at St Leonard's 1831-1834. In Bloomsbury, he was responsible for the design of the Russell Institution in Great Coram Street. His own houses, 'The Holme' in Regent's Park (1818) and at Quarry Hill, nr Tonbridge, were both designed by his son Decimus. An elder son, James, became a pupil of Sir John Soane, but gave up architecture in favour of Egyptology. Burton was Master of the Tylers' and Bricklayers' Company 1801-1802. He died in St Leonard's and is commemorated there by a monument with a profile portrait [After Colvin].
**Bibl:** Colvin; Dobie, The History of the United Parishes of St Giles in the Fields and St George Bloomsbury 1829, 144-149; Gents Mag, 1837 (i), 669; Summerson, John Nash, 1935, passim.

**BURTON, Miss J H** **fl 1845-1847**
Edinburgh amateur painter who lived at 20 Scotland Street. Exhibited RSA(2) during the above years.

**BURTON, Miss M R Hill** **fl 1885-1898**
Edinburgh painter in oil and watercolour of continental and local landscapes, figures, flowers and garden scenes. Possibly related to Nancy Jane Burton(qv). Lived at various times in Inverness-shire, Edinburgh and London. Exhibited RA 1892 an 'Iris garden at Tokyo', but more frequently at the RSA 1885-1898 including Japanese scenes, crocuses, and 'Edinburgh Castle'. In 1899 was living in Foyers. Exhibited AAS, RSA(22), RSW(2), GI(8), ROI(3) & L(2).

**BURTON, Mungo ARSA** **1799-1882**
Born Colinton; died 1 Nov. Painter in oil and watercolour of portraits and figurative subjects. Possibly related to Edward Burton(qv). Displayed an early taste for art. His first professional attempts being likenesses in watercolour. His principal works in portraiture were in oil whilst occasionally he produced figure pictures of Scottish homely life. Elected ARSA 1845. His amiability and kindliness secured the general esteem of his professional colleagues. Exhibited RSA many times between 1838 and 1880 including 'John McIver, Provost of Dingwall' (1856) which excited contemporary critical accclaim. Represented in Paul Mellon collection (Yale Univ.,USA) by a portrait of John Logan Campbell(1817-1912) in the club dress of the Edinburgh Allcion Archers (1838).
**Bibl:** Wingfield.

**BURTON, Nancy Jane RSW** **1891-1972**
Born Ardgour, Argyll; died, Aberfoyle, Perthshire 15 Aug. Animal painter mainly in watercolour, occasionally in oil. Studied Glasgow School of Art under Murray Thomson(qv). Received Lauder Award 1924. Lived first at Aberfoyle before moving to a farm near Tyndrum. In the early 1930s visited her sister in Kashmir, and went to Afghanistan, painting many watercolours along the way. Close friend of Kate Cameron(qv) and Helen Lamb(qv). A person of great integrity, a life-long friend recorded that 'Nancy Burton would never allow any painting to be exhibited unless she had made it as perfect as she knew how, nor would she ever be influenced by the passing faction in art'. One of Scotland's leading animal painters of the first half of the twentieth century, her work is still greatly admired. Elected RSW 1932. Exhibited AAS 1926-1937, RSW(38), RSA(27), GI(45) & L(3).
**Bibl:** Halsby 252.

**BURTON, Rose Hill** **fl 1881-1887**
Lothian painter in oil and watercolour; wild flowers and landscape. Possibly related to Miss M R Hill Burton(qv). Exhibited 8 works at the RSA between the above years, also GI(5).

**BURTON, William Paton RSW** **1828-1883**
Born Madras; died Aberdeen. Edinburgh architectural draughtsman and landscape painter in oil and watercolour, especially continental and Egyptian scenes. Son of an Indian Army Officer. Educated in Edinburgh before joining the architectural office of David Bryce(qv). Devoted most of his time to painting in watercolour and travelled widely, visiting India and Egypt. Moved from Edinburgh to southern England in the 1860s and painted many Surrey scenes. Eventually retired to Cults, Aberdeenshire. His work was confident although generally uninspired. Elected RSW 1882. Exhibited RA(23), RSA(19) RBA(9), RI(1), GI(8) & L(1).
**Bibl:** Halsby 252.

**BUSBY, John P ARSA RSW** **1928-**
Born Bradford, Yorkshire. Painter in oil and watercolour; also illustrator; wildlife, especially birds. Studied at Leeds 1948-52 and Edinburgh College of Art 1952-54. Having received a travelling scholarship shortly after graduating he toured France and Italy before settling in Scotland. Member of the Council of the SSA, becoming President 1973-76. Founder member of the Society of Wildlife Artists. One of few artists to have spanned the credibility gap between academic and wildlife art. Most of his work has a strong abstract structure, hence his links with the two disparate worlds. Lecturer in painting and drawing, Edinburgh College of Art since 1956. Illustrated over 20 books on natural history including *The Living Birds of Eric Ennion* (1982), *Drawing Birds* (1986) and *Birds of Mallorca* (1988). Married to the singer Joan Busby. He has also undertaken occasional church work including a mural 'Christ in Majesty' in St Columba's by the Castle, Edinburgh 1959 and carvings for St Martin's Church, Bradford 1962. Elected RSW 1982, ARSA 1987. Represented in Glasgow AG, City of Edinburgh collection, Abbots Hall AG (Kendal), Belfast Museum, Wakefield AG.
**Bibl:** Gage 46-7; Gifford 168.

**BUSHE, Christopher RSW** **1958-**
Born Aberfeldy. Landscape painter in oils & watercolour. Trained Gray's School of Art 1980-84. SAC Award 1997, Glasgow Arts Club Fellowship 1998, Russell Flint Trust 1998. Elected RSW 1999. While still training his landscapes were often of the Torridon region, subsequently he has enjoyed the intense light and vibrant colours of the Greek Islands, Spain and the Balearics. Exhibited RSA since 1992, regularly at RSW and in his early career at AAS.

**BUSHE, Frederick RSA** **1931-**
Born Coatbridge, 1 Mar. Sculptor in welded and cast metals, and concrete. Educated at Motherwell High School; studied at Glasgow School of Art 1949-53 under Benno Schotz(qv), at the University of Birmingham and School of Art Education 1966-7. First one-man show was held in Edinburgh in 1962, thereafter at Liverpool four years later and the Demarco Gallery in Edinburgh 1971. Exhibits in London and all over Scotland. Received the SAC Major award 1977/8. Draws and paints in ink and watercolour at the same time as he works on sculptures. Also makes small macquettes. Concentrates on a broad sense of mood usually suggested by the title and often associated with death. Lecturer in sculpture, Aberdeen College of Education. Received Scottish Arts Council Awards 1971 and 1973. In 1980 established the Scottish Sculpture Workshop, and in 1981 'Scottish Sculpture Open'. His work is characterised by a combination of bold and flowing lines very much in the modern idiom. Although he lives in Lumsden, Aberdeenshire, his work is clearly grounded in the industrial age with all the coarse directness that this implies. Elected ARSA 1977, RSA 1986. Exhibited RSA(43), 1952-1989 & AAS 1973-1989. Represented in Aberdeen AG, SAC.

**BUSHE, Stephen** **fl 1978**
Aberdeen painter. Exhibited a fishing scene at the AAS, from 121 Rosemount Pl.

**BUSHELL, Francis** **fl 1879**
Amateur Edinburgh oil painter of figurative subjects; exhibited RSA(3).

**BUSKENS, J** **fl 1917**
Glasgow painter; exhibited once at the GI from 46 Windsor Terrace.

**BUTLER, E T** **fl 1880-1888**
Glasgow painter. Exhibited GI(6).

**BUTLER, Vincent RSA RGI** **1933-**
Born Manchester; has lived in Scotland since 1963. Sculptor of figures and portraits in bronze, stone, terracotta and wood, also of animals. Trained Manchester School of Art under Tocher and Edinburgh College of Art before finishing his formal studies in Milan under Marini. Teacher at Edinburgh College of Art until his retirement in 1990, he held his first one man show in Edinburgh 1963 and thereafter in London 1969 and Manchester 1973. His work possesses a rugged almost chunky quality in the modern idiom, his main interest being in the naturalistic figurative mould, concentrating largely on the human figure. Does most of the bronze casting himself. 'Stations of the Cross' in high-relief bronzes on flat panels are in St Mark's (RC), Oxgangs Ave, Edinburgh. Published *'Casting for Sculptors'* 1997. Elected ARSA 1972, RSA 1977. Regular exhibitor RSA since 1964; also AAS(1), RA & GI. Represented in SNPG (bust of Benno Schotz), City of Edinburgh collection (2 bronzes).
**Bibl:** Gifford 567,625.

**BUTTBERG, Miss Victorine** **fl 1933-1966**
Edinburgh painter in oil, Scottish landscape and figure subjects. Lived for many years at 23 Findhorn Place. Exhibited RSA between the above years.

**BUTTERWORTH, E** **fl 1824-1829**
Bushnell records a Scottish engraver of this name who engraved maps of Scottish counties.

**BUTTERWORTH, Howard** **1945-**
Born Rochdale. English painter of landscape in oils. Self-taught. Concentrates on the scenery of upper Deeside, where he lives, and topographical scenes in Spain which he often visits in the winter. Has a strong local reputation. Publishes prints of his own work. An exhibition of his work was held at Duff House, 2003.

**BUYERS, Donald Morison RSW** **1930-2003**
Born Aberdeen, 29 Dec; died Aberdeen, 29 Dec. Painter in oil and watercolour, the latter since 1970; also teacher and art therapist. Studied at Gray's School of Art, Aberdeen, becoming lecturer at the College of Domestic Science in that city. From 1954 to 1961 painted largely abstracts showing the influence of Paul Klee; between 1961 and 1968 he was mainly personalistic and confined to landscape, with particular interest in American abstract expressionism. Having received an Arts Council award 1968 for the next six years developed a preoccupation with representational landscape, gradually becoming closer to the Scottish School. Began working in watercolour in 1970, elected RSW 1973. Vice-President, AAS 1978. Exhibited regularly RSA, SSA, AAS & elsewhere with one-man shows in Aberdeen and Edinburgh. Represented in Aberdeen AG, SAC, Royal Collection.

**BUYERS, Donna** **1956-**
Born Aberdeen 1 Jne. Painter, embroiderer, stained-glass window designer, costume designer and teacher. Daughter of Donald B(qv). Trained Gray's School of Art, Aberdeen and at the Central School of Art and Design in London. Her painting is abstract showing the influences of Klee and Miro. Combines her artistic work with being a wardrobe supervisor the the BBC in Scotland and costume designer for theatre and television, also part-time lecturer in art and design, Aberdeen College of Commerce. Exhibited SSWA & Acrobats at the AAS from 96 Gray Street.

**BYRES, Miss Isabel** **fl 1865-1876**
Grange painter in watercolour; landscape, fruit and flowers. Exhibited regularly at the RSA a total of 19 works during the above years.

**BYRES, James** **1734-1817**
Born and died Tonley, Aberdeenshire. Although not a professional artist, Byres played an unusual role in the history and development of Scottish painting. He was the eldest son of Jacobite parents from Aberdeenshire. As a young man he joined Ogilvie's Regiment in the French service but quickly abandoned thoughts of a military career in order to study architecture and painting in Rome, whence he travelled in 1758 remaining until 1761 during which time he studied under Mengs, assisting him on the nave ceiling of S Eusebio. In 1762 he won the prime architectural prize at the Concorso Clementino and continued to practice architecture spasmodically throughout his long life. His clients included the Duke of Gordon, Sir Laurence Dundas

and the College of Physicians in Edinburgh. In 1763 he became an antiquary, among his 'pupils' being Edward Gibbon, Charles Townley and the Dukes of Hamilton and Northumberland. As a practising archaeologist Byres' greatest interest was Etruscan antiquity. His plates for *Hypogaei or Sepulchral Caverns of Tarquinia* were published after his death. Between 1766 and 1790 his operations were wide and varied, including the purchase of the Portland vase for Sir William Hamilton and Poussin's first series of the 'Seven Sacraments' for the Duke of Rutland. When the French arrived in Italy Byres returned to Britain. Raeburn was one artist to benefit in more ways than one from Byres. He always treasured the advice 'never to copy any object from memory, but from the principal figure to the minutist accessory and to have it placed before him', and it was Byres who arranged Raeburn's commission to paint a miniature portrait for Lord Spencer. Another artist he helped was David Allan(qv) whose work 'The Origin of Painting' (now in the NGS) Byres had purchased, retaining it in Italy after Allan's return to Scotland. Byres followed the early career of Alexander Nasmyth, sharing an enthusiastic fascination for volcanoes with Jacob More(qv), and had been a student at Anton Meng's studio alongside Charles Cunningham(qv), James Nevey(qv) and George Willison(qv). Byres' influence as a cultural catalyst was strong and lasting although because it was largely informal and personal it is difficult to assess its extent.
**Bibl:** Caw 30,74n; Irwin 151-2 et passim; Macmillan [SA], 117,128; Basil Skinner, Scots in Italy, 1966, 16-17,28-9.

**BYRES, Keith** **fl 1978-1988**
Aberdeen portrait painter. Exhibited regularly in the above years at the AAS from 56 Caisdykes Road, Kincorth.

**BYRNE, Herbert J** **fl 1928**
Newton Mearns painter; exhibited GI(1).

**BYRNE, John (Patrick)** **1940-**
Born Glasgow. Painter in oil and illustrator. Educated Glasgow School of Art 1958-61 and Edinburgh College of Art 1961-62 before returning for further study to Glasgow 1962-63. Won the Newbery Medal 1963, the W O Hutcheson prize for drawing and the Bellahouston Scholarship. Visited Perugia 1963-64, being much influenced by the work of Giotto in Assisi, as well as Cucico and the Italian Primitives. On his return to Scotland he went back to the carpet factory where he had worked before art college, as a designer. At this time he sent some naive paintings to a London gallery pretending them to be the work of his father. Then worked as a graphic artist for Scottish Television. Professional painter since 1968 holding a number of one-man shows in London and Sydney, Australia, as well as in his native Scotland. Always his considerable talent as a draughtsman shines through. Hardie refers to his 'quixotic brilliance'. Painted, in his pop style, a study of 'The Beatles' for the *Illustrated Beatle Lyrics* (c1969). Represented in Paisley AG, Museum of Primitive Art, Ecuador.
**Bibl:** Hardie 193-4,206(illus); Macmillan [SA] 117, 128.

**BYTAUTAS, Alfons ARSA** **1955-**
Born 30 Oct. Watercolour painter and engraver. Studied at Edinburgh College of Art 1972-76. In 1978 appointed lecturer in printmaking, Edinburgh College of Art and in 1983 studied at Atelier 17 with S W Hayter. In 1986 appointed printmaker-in-residence at Soulisquay Printmakers, Kirkwall, Orkney. Published 'Inchcolm' in limited edition folio (1988) and provided etchings for a published poem by the contemporary Scots poet Alexander Hutchison. Associated with the Scottish Printmakers Workshop. Artist-in-residence, Les Roncontres Internationales de L'Aquarelle Hirson, Thiérache, France. Elected ARSA 1994. Exhibits RSA from 1988, also RSW & SSA. Represented in Royal Collection, Leeds AG, SAC, National Library, Edinburgh.

**CABLE, William Lindsay** **fl 1944-1949**
Dundee painter. Exhibited RSA(2) 1944 and 1949.

**CADELL, Agnes Morison** **1873-1958**
Born Dounton, Wiltshire 9 Apr. Painter in oil and watercolour; portraits, landscapes, animals. Sister of Florence Cadell(qv). Painted almost entirely in oil and in addition to work in Edinburgh frequently visited Paris where she had trained as a portrait painter, also went to Malta. In 1921 'Study of a Cat' at the Salon de la National achieved considerable attention. Most of her later work was done at Crail, Fife where she lived with her sister. By this time her output was almost entirely land and seascapes. Exhibited French Salon 1914-1922, and again 1924-1929, also RA(1) & RSA(3). Represented by 'The Orange Hat' in City of Edinburgh collection.

**CADELL, Florence St John** **1877-1966**
Born Australia, 14 Aug. Sister of Agnes Cadell(qv) and distant cousin of F C B Cadell(qv). Early in life returned with her father to Edinburgh and as a young girl she and her sister began painting seriously, specialising in animals, especially goats. In the 1920s she began exhibiting in Edinburgh and Perth. Rebuilt Whinmill Brae House on the Water of Leith, designed around a large studio. Painted some portraits although in later years her output was mainly of finer landscapes especially in Kintail. The best works are very bright sun-filled watercolours and continental market places of Paris as well as sensitive if sometimes rather contrived studies of young children. Her still lifes are less effective. Exhibited RSA 1900-1965, one of the few artists whose output increased with age. Exhibited RSA(25), RSW(1), GI(25), L(1) & AAS 1933-1937.
**Bibl:** Halsby 252.

**CADELL, Frances Campbell Boileau RSA RSW** **1883-1937**
Born Edinburgh, 12 Apr; died Edinburgh, 6 Dec. Son of an Edinburgh doctor. Educated Edinburgh Academy and studied art at the RSA Life School. Disillusioned with the teaching there, he was encouraged by Arthur Melville(qv), a close family friend, to go to Paris where he enrolled at Julian's. After three years in Paris, learning the importance of tonal values, then the principal tenet of French teaching, and having had a watercolour exhibited at the Paris Salon in 1899, he returned to Scotland. His first exhibit at the RSA was in 1902. He was becoming much influenced by Whistler, modified by Melville, John Lavery(qv) and the colours of William McTaggart(qv). Spent two years in Munich 1906-8, and in 1909 bought his first studio at 130 George Street. In 1910, financed by a school friend and patron, he visited Venice. There his work became more vibrant, responding to the intensity of light and the inspiration of being able to paint in an atmosphere of novelty. Although his Italian paintings were not at first well received in Edinburgh, for the next five years he concentrated on portrait commissions and upper-middle class interiors becoming, as Billcliffe has it, "the perfect recorder of that glorious period in well-to-do British society that preceded the First World War". The colour he found in Italy, the fluid brush work, were retained in the depiction of drawing room silver and ornament. In 1912, disliking the artistic establishment, he founded the Society of Eight(qv) with Patrick Adam(qv), David Alison(qv), James Cadenhead(qv), John Lavery(qv), Harrington Mann(qv), James Paterson(qv) and A G Sinclair(qv)). In 1915 he joined the Royal Scots, serving in France, and declined a commission until 1918 when he was transferred to the Argyll and Sutherland Highlanders. Two years earlier his sketches of army life, originally sold for the Red Cross, were collated in the form of a book and published as *Jack and Tommy*. After the War every summer was spent on Iona, which he had first discovered 1912. The tranquil landscape, where he was often joined by his friend Peploe, were much more to post-war taste than interiors, thus providing an added commercial incentive to enjoy the west. In the spring of 1923, and again in 1924, he returned to the luminosity of the Mediterranean, this time to Southern France. Although by now accepted by the artistic establishment, having been elected ARSA 1931, RSW 1935 (the only Colourist to be elected) and RSA 1936, his work was not selling well and he died poor, having applied in 1936 for financial assistance from the Nasmyth Fund for the Relief of Decayed Scottish Artists. His personality has been lovingly described by his friend Stanley Cursiter(qv) "..in many ways the complete antithesis of Peploe. He was only of medium height and stout, his face was large and round and ran to chins - someone described him as like a vegetable marrow. He was voluble and even boisterous. He loved bright clothes, shepherd-tartan trousers, lemon-yellow waistcoats, cobalt blue scarves. He was very witty and wrote Rabelaisian verse with great facility. He had many ups and downs and reversals of fortune which he accepted with boyish good humour." His place in Scottish art is now firmly established. The only one of the Colourists who looked favourably upon the Glasgow Boys, especially Lavery(qv). Hardie identifies four distinct styles "the early interiors and still-lifes are painted with great verve and brilliant use of whites, and dashes of orange and mint green. The white sand and bright green stretches of water characteristic of the east shore of Iona in certain conditions of weather provided a pretext for the bold colour schemes of his earlier Iona pictures. Cadell's later Iona paintings of the 20's, when he was working with Peploe, are more quietly coloured and more precisely drawn. The elegance and sophistication of the earlier studio interiors...give way to a more contrived style...Here, the paint is thinly applied in large panels of self-colour. The Croft House interiors of the early 30s employ a style reminiscent of L C Taylor's work in their evocation of the airy atmosphere of a beautiful room; but Cadell is a more satisfying designer than Taylor". Exhibited RSA(77), RSW(12), GI(66) AAS in 1908 and 1919-1935, also L(15). Represented in SNGMA, Aberdeen AG, Gracefield AG(Dumfries), Dundee AG, Glasgow AG, Greenock AG, Kirkcaldy AG, Paisley AG, Brodie Castle (NTS), Manchester AG, Rochdale AG, City of Edinburgh collection (3 including a portrait of Lady Lavery), Perth AG, National Gallery of South Australia (Adelaide).
**Bibl:** Roger Billcliffe, The Scottish Colourists 1989, 25-26,37-38,54-58 et al; Roger Billcliffe, 'F C B Cadell, a Centenary exhib;, Fine Art Society, Glasgow 1983; Halsby, 205-206 et al; Hardie 133-4 et passim; Hartley 119-120; Tom Hewlett, Cadell, A Scottish Colourist, 1988; T J Honeyman, Three Scottish Colourists 1950; Macmillan [SA], 310-11 et passim.

**CADELL, Gilbert Laurie** **fl 1930-1937**
Edinburgh artist in oil and watercolour. Latterly moved to London. Exhibited RSA, mostly Scottish landscapes 1930-1937; also RSW(9).

**CADELL, Col Henry Mowbray RE** **1892-1967**
Amateur watercolour painter. No formal training. Father of William A Cadell(qv). Exhibited once at the RSA in 1925 from The Grange, Linlithgow.

**CADELL, Miss Isabel Mowbray** **fl 1900-1943**
Edinburgh landscape artist in oil and watercolour. Exhibited RSA between 1900 and 1905 and then again in 1930 and 1943; also RSW(4) and 2 monochrome drawings at the AAS from 27 Rutland Square.

**CADELL, Miss Mary E** **fl 1887**
Amateur flower painter. Exhibited GI(1) from Busby, Lanarkshire.

**CADENHEAD, James RSA RSW** **1858-1927**
Born Aberdeen 12 Jan; died Edinburgh 22 Jan. Painter in oil and watercolour; etcher and lithographer; landscapes. Son of a Procurator Fiscal. Educated at Aberdeen Grammar School, Dollar Academy and Aberdeen University and subsequently at the RSA Life Schools. After completing his studies in Edinburgh went to Paris to work under Carolus Duran 1882-1884. Influenced by Whistler and the Aesthetic movement in London and by Japanese art. Founder member, New English Art Club 1886. Working from Edinburgh, where he settled in 1891, his paintings in oil and watercolours were mainly landscapes using strong colours and with a marked decorative element somewhat reminiscent of Japanese painting. Sometimes he produced very large canvases, one of which is in the City of Edinburgh Art Collection. In later life, with the waning influence of the Glasgow School, he returned to a more realistic manner, his landscapes becoming more romantic although his various scenes of Deeside do not compare favourably with other artists of the period. Founder member, NEAC 1889. An accomplished printmaker, his few book illustrations show the influence of the Japanese print. Illustrated Ford: *Pixie* (1891); *Master Rex* (1891) and Stephens: *Hell's Piper* (nd). Elected RSW 1893, ARSA 1902, RSA 1921. Exhibited regularly at the RSA(148)

from 1880 onwards, also RSW(4), GI(27), & AAS 1885-1931. Represented in SNPG (a portrait of Robert Brough), NGS, City of Edinburgh Collection (9), Glasgow AG, Kirkcaldy AG, Perth AG, Manchester AG.
**Bibl:** Caw 387; Halsby 169-70,252; Hardie 105,142; *The Studio*, 10, 1897, p67 illus; vol 55, 1912, pp10-20 illus; Houfe 85.

**CADENHEAD, William Collie Milne** **1934-**
Born Aberdeen; painter in oils, pastel and watercolour; landscapes. Trained Dundee College of Art 1952, Hospitalfield 1955, Royal Academy Schools 1957-61. Obtained a postgraduate scholarship enabling him to travel in Europe. On his return he studied for a further four years at the RA schools in London. Elected SSA 1969. Currently lecturer in drawing and painting at Duncan of Jordanstone College of Art. Many solo exhibitions, the first in Forfar 1958. His work is based upon landscape, favouring atmospheric snow-clad mountain groups. Regular exhibitor RSA since 1954, and elsewhere in the provinces. Represented in Dundee AG, Paisley AG, SAC, collection of HM Queen Mother.

**CADOGAN, Sidney Russell** **?-1911**
Painter of landscapes in oil. Born in England, but especially fond of Scotland. Many of his subjects were of the Scottish countryside and coast. He had a great love of trees and forest life. As a young man visited Corsica and Algeria. A fine raconteur. Most of his paintings were landscapes of Perthshire and the south of England. Lived for a time at St Andrews, then Sevenoaks, Kent. Exhibited RSA 1877-1895.

**CADZOW, James** **1881-1941**
Born Carluke, Lanarkshire, 30 Oct. Painter and etcher; oils, watercolours, charcoal and pencil; landscape, mainly Scottish. Studied at Edinburgh College of Art before becoming head of the art department, Dundee HS. Worked occasionally in watercolours but also produced fine pencil drawings and etchings. Lived at Leebank, Broughty Ferry. President, Dundee Arts Society. Exhibited RSA(32), GI(32), L(23), also harbour scenes and a view of the herring fleet at the AAS 1933-1935. Represented by 13 works in the NGS, Glasgow AG.
**Bibl:** Halsby 252.

**CAIN, Antony** **fl 1976-1977**
Painter. Maintained a studio in Plockton, Wester Ross. Exhibited RSA 1976 and 1977 (2), all Scottish landscapes.

**CAINE, Anisa** **c1963-**
Born Uganda. Landscape painter in watercolours; also flowers. Trained in Berne, Stuttgart, Basle & Paris, now settled in Newtonmore. Greatly influenced by colour and the vagaries of light. First solo exhibition Berne 1994. Her work is in private collections in Australia, Austria, Belgium, Canada, France, East & Southern Africa, Switzerland, Thailand and the USA. Orchidee Lodge in Basle has a large collection of her paintings of orchids. Exhibits RSW from Neadaich, Newtonmore.

**CAIRD, Miss Marjorie Rorie** **fl 1918-1933**
Edinburgh painter of 13 Charlotte Square and later 58 Queen Street. Little known beyond the fact that she exhibited 2 narrative paintings at the RSA in 1918 and again 2 in 1919. Exhibited 'Orion' at the AAS in 1933.

**CAIRD, Mrs** **fl c1823**
Miniature painter. Thought to have come from Edinburgh. Foskett records having in her own collection a miniature portrait inscribed on the reverse 'Mrs Caird/about 1823'. The miniature is of 'Henry VIII, Mary I (his daughter) and Will Somers the Court jester holding a dog'. The original of this painting is in Lord Spencer's collection at Althorp. The picture is a composite one executed by an unknown 16th century artist of the English School; the portrait of Henry VIII is after Holbein, Mary I is after Mor and the portrait of Somers is possibly from life. Foskett reports a suggestion that it was made for Somers on his retirement from royal service. This is the only recorded work by this artist.
**Bibl:** Foskett.

**CAIRN, Thomas Francis** **fl 1867**
Landscape painter in oil, exhibited RSA(1) 1867.

**CAIRNCROSS, Alastair D** **fl 1962**
Exhibited 2 watercolours, both of the river Kirkaig at the GI from 1 Brompton Terrace, Perth.

**CAIRNCROSS, Charles** **fl 1900-1909**
Edinburgh landscape painter, especially fond of moorland and coastal scenes. Lived at 4 Bruntsfield Avenue, moving in 1906 to 41 Morningside Park. Exhibited RSA 1901(2), 1903 and 1909; GI(1), L(1) & AAS.

**CAIRNCROSS, George** **?-1819**
Died Edinburgh, Jan. Edinburgh architect. Son and pupil of Hugh Cairncross(qv). In 1815 he provided the Lord Provost of Edinburgh with a copy of Robert Adam's(qv) elevation for the west side of Edinburgh University, and in the same year 'Mr. Cairncross, an Ordained Surveyor, measured work at the new Signet Library'. Involved with his father in the early development of Gayfield Place. Buried in Greyfriars Cemetery.
**Bibl:** Gifford 427.

**CAIRNCROSS, Hugh** **?-1808**
Born Edinburgh; died Melrose, 21 Jly. Edinburgh architect practising during the reign of George III. Father of George Cairncross(qv). Pupil or assistant to Robert Adam(qv), under whom he acted as clerk of works at Culzean and Dalquharran castles. At the former there is a design for a timber bridge signed 'H Cairncross, 1796'. In December, 1791, Adam appointed him to be clerk of works for the new University Building, Edinburgh, replacing John Paterson, and Cairncross continued this work for at least ten years. In 1797 he designed Ardgowan House, Renfrewshire for Sir John Shaw-Stewart, the original drawings for which are now in the collection of Paul Mellon. Involved with his son in the early development of Gayfield Place, Edinburgh, designing 12-32 Gayfield Square, Edinburgh. In 1801 he was paid 'for measuring and valuing the work in the finishing of the English and Gaelic Churches at Inveraray' and in the same year he submitted a design for rebuilding Falkirk Church which was not adopted owing to a dispute among the parishioners.
**Bibl:** Gifford 427-9,517.

**CAIRNCROSS, Michael** **1958-**
Born Edinburgh, May 12. Sculptor, painter in oil and watercolour; teacher. Trained Dundee College of Art 1977-81, qualifying as a teacher 1986. Won Highland Society award (RSA) 1997. Since 1995, when, after a spell in Italy, he settled in Ross-shire, most of his work is sculpture. Works in a variety of materials including Ledmore marble, Portsoy stone, metal and wood. Exhibits RSA & RGI from Glenweir, Barbaraville, Invergordon.

**CAIRNEY, Alan Neil** **fl 1977**
Aberdeen landscape painter in oil. Trained Gray's School of Art. Exhibited AAS from 7 Alan Street.

**CAIRNEY, John, Jnr** **fl 1872-1906**
Glasgow painter in oil and watercolour; landscapes, churches, rustic scenes. Exhibited annually RSA between 1872 and 1887, also GI(45), RHA(5) & AAS 1893-1902.

**CAIRNS, Professor David** **fl 1973**
Amateur Aberdeen painter of local scenes. Exhibited AAS from 1 St Swithin Street.

**CAIRNS, Miss Hildegarde M** **fl 1939-1942**
Glasgow based painter in oil of landscapes and still life. Lived at Bearsden exhibited GI(4), mostly scenes on Skye.

**CAIRNS, Hugh** **fl 1890-1891**
Glasgow artist; exhibited twice at the GI.

**CAIRNS, James** **fl 1935-1939**
Amateur Edinburgh watercolour painter of 75a Hanover Street; exhibited RSW(4).

**CAIRNS, John** **fl 1845-1867**
Edinburgh painter in oil and watercolour; coastal scenes, especially Arran, north-east Scotland and Holland. Had a dynamic, slightly rough style capturing the light and harshness of the North Sea. Exhibited regularly RSA between 1845 and 1867. There is a

watercolour 'Silly-sur-Somme', painted in 1845/7 in NGS; also in Paisley AG.
**Bibl:** Halsby 108,252.

**CAIRNS, Joyce Winifred RSA RSW** **1947-**
Born Haddington. Painter in oil; Scottish scenes, portraits and genre, also teacher. Studied at Gray's School of Art, Aberdeen 1966-71 followed by three years at the Royal College of Art and a fellowship course, Gloucester College of Art and Design. Among her awards were the Hospitalfield Prize 1969, RSA Student Prize 1970, RSA Latimer Award 1978, 1st Prize in the Morrison Portrait Competition, RSA 1989. A Carnegie Travelling Scholarship 1971 enabled her to travel to the USA. In 1985 became the first women President of Aberdeen Artists, being twice re-elected. Since 1977 has taught at Gray's School of Art and been occasional visiting lecturer in Dundee and Glasgow Schools of Art. First solo exhibition Glasgow 1980. 'Her paintings combine graphic and painterly qualities within a densely packed picture surface to depict part biographical and part fictional experiences'. Another critic referred to the 'distressed disorder' of her work. Elected RSW 1979, ARSA 1985, RSA 1998. Regular exhibitor RA, RSA, RGI, RSW, AAS since 1979 & SSA. Represented in Aberdeen AG, Glasgow AG, SAC, Sheffield AG, Perth AG (The Deadly Wars), Glasgow Museum of Modern Art, McMaster Museum (Hamilton, Ontario).
**Bibl:** The Compass Gall, Edinburgh, 'The Compass Contribution; 21 Years of Contemporary Art 1969-1990', (Ex Cat 1990); Bill Hare, Contemporary Painting in Scotland, Edinburgh 1993.

**CAIRNS, Robert Dickie** **1866-1944**
Dumfries artist and teacher. Mainly landscapes in oil and watercolour, often of the western Highlands. Pleasing use of colour. Founder member, Dumfries & Galloway Art Society. Art master, Dumfries Academy 1889-1927. Friend of Chris Fergusson(qv), EA Hornel(qv) and E A Taylor(qv). Quiet man who shunned publicity. Minor studio sale Edinburgh 1993 extremely successful. Moved to Bearsden in 1929. Exhibited RSA(1), AAS(1) & GI(8).

**CAKE, Miss Dorothy F** **fl 1935-1939**
Amateur watercolour and pen and ink painter of landscape. Attracted to Arran. Lived at Cragdarroch, Cove-on-Clyde, Dunbartonshire. Exhibited RSW(1) & GI(4).

**CAKLY H** **fl c1840**
Little known artist, possibly of Perth. Represented in Perth AG by an oil painting 'Crieff from the South'.

**CALDER, Miss Bell(e) W** **fl 1896**
Amateur flower painter of Midtown, Barras, Stonehaven. Exhibited AAS(1).

**CALDER, Helen** **fl 1964-1965**
Aberdeen watercolour painter of figure subjects. Exhibited AAS from 6 Jasmine Place.

**CALDER, Rev J J** **fl 1896**
Amateur Aberdeenshire-based painter in oil of landscape and rustic scenes. Exhibited 'An old cottage' at the AAS from The Manse, Rhynie.

**CALDER, Lady Renate** **fl 1966**
Amateur Morayshire painter of landscape and still life. Exhibited AAS(3) from Braemoriston House, Elgin.

**CALDER, Thomas** **fl 1700-1720**
Edinburgh engraver. Engraved a bookplate for John Scott in 1710 and the armorial bearing of the Rt Hon James, Lord Somervell (1720).
**Bibl:** Bushnell.

**CALDER, Thomas** **1927-**
Glasgow painter of landscape, figurative subjects and pastoral scenes, primarily of a Scottish nature, in oil, watercolour, ink and scraperboard. Also semi-professional jazz musician. Studied Glasgow School of Art and Hornsey. Principal awards include First Prize: Glasgow Civic 1965, First prize, Scottish Drawing competition 1995. Titles include 'Backyards in Motherwell', 'Tarpaulins in scaffolding', 'Church at Honfleur'. Exhibited RSA 1954, 1964 (2), 1965-1966, 1983-1984, & GI(15). Represented in Glasgow AG. Lives and works in Glasgow.

**CALDER, W Y** **fl 1893-1894**
Glasgow painter of 209 St Vincent Street. Worked in oil and watercolour, mainly portraits. Exhibited GI(2), including a portrait of Sheriff-Substitute Aitken. Represented in Glasgow AG.

**CALDERWOOD, Mrs A L R** **fl 1933-1940**
Amateur watercolour and occasional oil painter of flower studies and still life. Lived at 35 Harriet Street, Glasgow. Exhibited RSW(4) & GI(14).

**CALDERWOOD, Samuel** **c1687-1735**
Plasterer of considerable artistry and skill. His finest extant work can be seen in the entrance hall of The Drum, Edinburgh.
Bibl: Gifford 56,558n,583,pl. 67.

**CALDERWOOD, William Leadbetter** **1865-1950**
Born Glasgow 19 Feb. Painter in oils; portraits, landscape. Author and renowned fisherman. Studied at Edinburgh College of Art, worked in Italy, Spain and USA. Author of *The Life of the Salmon* (1907) and *The Salmon Rivers of Scotland* (1909). Lived in Edinburgh and signed his work WLC. Exhibited landscapes at the RSA in 1897 and 1898 and again 1913-23, mostly portraits, including 'Margaret, the daughter of Fiddes Watt' (1916) and 'The Hon Lord Sands' (1919); also a portrait of the Inspector of Salmon Fisheries in Scotland at the GI.

**CALDOW, James (Hugh)** **fl 1919**
Amateur watercolour painter of 61 Exeter Drive, Partick, Glasgow. Exhibited a landscape at GI.

**CALDWALL or (CALDWELL), James** **fl 1790-1830**
Edinburgh designer, engraver and possibly miniaturist. Brother of John Caldwall(qv). His most celebrated work is the fine aquatint 'View of the City of Edinburgh' after a drawing by Adam Callender (1799), of which the proof copy, dedicated to the Earl of Hardwicke, is in Edinburgh Central Library. A James Caldwall was noted by Long as having practised as a miniature painter from 1809 to 1830 at New Street, Canongate, Edinburgh. Represented in City of Edinburgh Art Collection (an aquatint, engraving and lithograph), Glasgow AG.
**Bibl:** Butchart 38-9.

**CALDWALL or (CALDWELL), John** **c1738-1819**
Said to have been born in London although sometimes stated as Scotland. Brother of James Caldwell the engraver(qv). Practised as a miniaturist in Scotland, working sometimes in crayon. Lived for a spell in Blackfriars Wynd (Edinburgh Directory, 1793/4), and in the Canongate until 1816. Died in February 1819 when, according to a note in the SNPG, he was in his eighty-first year. A miniature of an unknown man signed on reverse on a piece of paper 'Caldwall', is in V & A.
**Bibl:** Foskett 1,192.

**CALDWELL, Miss Lizzie** **fl 1900**
Amateur landscape artist of 36 Carluke Street, Glasgow. Exhibited GI.

**CALDWELL, Thomas M R** **fl 1951-1963**
Amateur Renfrewshire watercolourist. Exhibited 4 local landscapes at the GI latterly from 10 Duff Avenue, Inverkip.

**CALDWELL, William Taylor** **fl 1854-1900**
Edinburgh painter in oils and watercolour; landscapes, especially loch scenes. Stimulated by the area around Loch Lomond. Regular exhibitor RSA(23) 1856-1888 & GI(38). Possibly the same William Caldwell who exhibited AAS 1906 from a Glasgow address.

**CALLAGHAN, Gerald** **fl 1976**
Amateur Dundee artist. Exhibited 'Low Peak' at the RGI from 13 Dura Street.

**CALLENDER, Adam** **fl 1780-1811**
Scottish born landscape painter in oil and watercolour. It is not known when he travelled to London but all his exhibited work was done from London addresses at the RA and BI. Between the above years he

exhibited 51 works at the RA from 6 Baker Street, Queen Anne Street and after 1799 from 1 New Cavendish Street. Subjects included a number of Scottish scenes including 'Inverary, the seat of the Duke of Argyll' (1782), 'Kilchurn Castle on Loch Awe '(1786), 'The town and castle of Stirling' (1790), 'Loch Lomond' (1793), 'Ravenshow Castle' (1800) as well as views of St Helena, Capetown, Tenerife, a number of Welsh castles and romantic scenery in various parts of England. His 'View of the City of Edinburgh' was engraved by J Caldwall(qv) in 1799.
**Bibl:** Butchart 38; Waterhouse 68.

**CALLENDER, Robert ARSA** **1932-**
Born Mottingham, Kent. Painter in oil and sculptures in board. Studied South Shields Art School. Arrived Edinburgh 1951, attended Edinburgh University 1951-1954 and Edinburgh College of Art 1954-1959. In 1959 awarded an Andrew Grant Scholarship enabling him to study at the British School in Rome. Also visited France, teaching for a time at the Institute for American Universities in Aix-en-Provence, and in Spain. In the 1960's he began constructing works from cardboard. These were not sculptures in any traditional sense but likened to theatrical stage designs being composed of painted layers of board arranged in 3-dimensional space. In the 1970s and 1980s, besides continuing his work as a painter Callender began reconstructing objects, often sailing boats, in cardboard and painting them to produce realistic replicas. Since 1980 he has used balsa-wood, paper and card in making miniature models. Received the Latimer Award 1964, Guthrie Award 1965. Elected ARSA 1966 but resigned three years later. Lives in Edinburgh and teaches at Edinburgh College of Art. President, SSA 1969-1973. Exhibited GI(4). Represented in City of Edinburgh Art collection (oil and 2 lithographs), Teeside Museum.
**Bibl**: Callender, Robert & Ogilvie, Elizabeth, "Watermarks" SAC Fruit Market Gall., Edin. 1980; Gage 133,489; Hardie 194,196; Hartley 120; Macmillan [SA], 396, 398-9; Mayor Gall, London, 'Robert Callender Constructions' (Ex Cat 1986); TRAC, Edinburgh, 'Sea Salvage' (Ex Cat 1989);

**CALLUM, Ian** **fl 1957**
Amateur artist of 47 Stirling Avenue, Bearsden. Exhibited a townscape at GI.

**CALVERLEY, Mrs Charles C** **fl 1868**
Amateur landscape Edinburgh painter in oil. Exhibited RSA(1) 1868.

**CALVERT, Edward** **?-1914**
Edinburgh architect. Responsible for many rather undistinguished and often fussy tenement blocks and villas especially in the Bruntsfield area. Perhaps the most interesting are 20 Colinton Rd (1888) designed for the builder Peter Craig Renton and 32 Colinton Rd, a spired Jacobean house for Sir James Steel.
**Bibl:** Gifford 64,224,339,396,499-504,564,654.

**CALVERT, Edwin Sherwood RSW** **1844-1898**
Scottish painter in oil and watercolour; pastoral scenes, portraits and figurative works. Disciple and follower of Corot. Began by painting coastal and fishing scenes, but his later work, much of it in watercolour, was pastoral in nature and idyllic in character. Frequently painted in the north of France, using grey and slightly drab colour schemes, closely following Corot in the general balance of foliage, shepherdesses and sheep. These works were often given general titles rather than identifying specific places. Elected RSW 1878. Exhibited Salon des Artists Français 1896, Berlin Art Exhibition 1896, and (posthumously) in Munich 1899. Also exhibited regularly RSA 1872-1896 (in 1886, one of his exhibits was 'Millet's studio, Barbizon'), RA(14), RSW(36), GI(46), RHA(3), RBA(1), AAS & L(17), mainly from Glasgow latterly 113 Douglas Street.
**Bibl:** Caw 301; Halsby 252.

**CALVERT, S S** **fl 1882**
Glasgow painter residing at 1 Doune Terrace, Kelvinside; exhibited GI(1).

**CALVERT, Wilfred** **fl 1946**
Amateur watercolour painter of flowers. Exhibited GI(1) from Seaview, Dougall Street, Tayport, Fife.

**CAMBUSKENNETH** **c1880-1920**
Stirlingshire village much frequented by artists especially during the above period. Best known for the gatherings of several of the Glasgow Boys(qv) notably E A Walton(qv), who kept a studio in the village, William Kennedy(qv), who resided for several summers at Abbey Road, Sir James Guthrie(qv), who stayed as the guest of a Mr Robertson (owner of the local ropeworks), Arthur Melville(qv), also with a studio in the village, Joseph Crawhall(qv) and John Lavery(qv), friends of Kennedy, T Millie Dow(qv), T C Morton(qv) and J Downie(qv). Others not directly connected with the Glasgow group who came included Archibald Kay(qv), A K Brown(qv), Henry Morley(qv), William Wells(qv), Crawford Shaw(qv) and the Milne brothers(qv). The Craigmill school of animal painting(qv) was only a few miles away and several artists, notably Kennedy, mingled between the two places.
**Bibl:** Stirling Smith AG, 'Craigmill and Cambuskenneth' (Ex Cat, text by Fiona Wilson), 1978.

**CAMERON, Agnes M** **fl 1933-1937**
Aberdeen landscape painter in oil, rejoiced in rugged Highland scenes often with fast flowing rivers. Probably sister of Annie J C(qv). Exhibited AAS from 45 Victoria Street.

**CAMERON, Alexander** **fl 1921-1951**
Borders landscape painter in oil, watercolour and pen; generally Scottish scenes especially of the west coast. Lived at Seton House, Jedburgh, until moving in 1926 to Port Ellen, Islay and finally to 12 Bute Terrace, Coatbridge, Lanark. Exhibited RSA in 1921, 1922, 1929 and 1951, also GI(3) & AAS(2).

**CAMERON, Alexander G Beauchamp** **fl 1944-1952**
Edinburgh painter in oil and pastel; flowers and portraits, of 16 Torpichen Street. Exhibited RSA between 1944 and 1952 & GI(1).

**CAMERON. Alexander K** **fl 1889**
Exhibited two still lifes at the GI from 42 Dundas Street, Glasgow.

**CAMERON, Allan** **fl 1798-1799**
Edinburgh engraver known to have been working in 1798, the year of his marriage. Engraved Alexander Runciman's 'East View of the Porch of Holyrood House' used in Arnot's *History of Edinburgh.*
**Bibl:** Bushnell; Butchart 17; Canongate Reg Marr 1654-1800.

**CAMERON, Allan Rose** **fl 1951-1967**
Balloch sculptor in sandstone, terracotta and wood; mainly figure studies and portait busts. Exhibited two works at the RSA in 1952 and 1958 & GI(15).

**CAMERON, Annie Esther** **fl 1880**
Amateur landscape painter from Milton House, Sutherland. Exhibited RSA 1880.

**CAMERON, Miss Annie J** **fl 1908-1945**
Amateur Aberdeen painter in oil and watercolour of landscape, especially Deeside. Probably sister of Agnes M C(qv). Exhibited RSA between 1938 and 1945 from 45 Victoria Street, GI(2), and regularly AAS 1908-1937.

**CAMERON, B** **fl c1670**
Scottish portrait painter. Waterhouse records 'a rustic painter who executed a portrait of a peasant with a mug of ale, lettered 'Will' Howyson by B Cameron, more or less life size and with a certain rude power', which is at Gosford and listed in the 1771 catalogue.
**Bibl:** Waterhouse 68.

**CAMERON, Miss C Josephine** **fl 1912**
Amateur Glasgow artist of 30 Lansdowne Crescent. Exhibited 'The Houses on the Rock' at the AAS.

**CAMERON, Charles** **1743-1811/12**
Architect to Catherine the Great. Probably son of Walter Cameron, a carpenter and Scottish builder established in London. Apprenticed to his father in 1760, but subsequently became a pupil of the architect, Isaac Ware. When Ware died in 1766, Cameron completed a project which Ware had formed for a new edition of Lord Burlington's *Fabbriche Antiche.* Cameron proposed to go to Rome in order to

correct and complete the imperfect drawings of the Roman baths by Palladio which Burlington had used in an earlier publication. He exhibited six proof prints of ancient Thermae at the Free Society of Artists in London 1767. Visited Rome 1768 to carry out excavations on the Baths of Titus. Returned to London for periods in 1771 and 1772. In 1772 he published *The Baths of the Romans;* the same year he exhibited three views of the Antonine Baths in the Society of Artists giving the address 'Corner of White House Street, Piccadilly.' Nothing further is heard until 1779 when he was working for Empress Catherine the Great at Tsarskoe Seloe. There he worked with the head gardener, John Bush of Hackney, whose daughter he married sometime between 1781 and 1784. He spent 15 years building the complex, including the Cold Baths, the Agate Rooms or Pavilion, the Gallery or Colonnade (the Cameron Gallery) and ten rooms of private apartments. Between 1782 and 1786 was also engaged in building the Palace of Pavlovsk for the Grand Duke Paul. Cameron was a superb decorator and set up workshops to train Russian workmen. He worked for three Russian sovereigns, much in the Chinese style; he was also responsible for the Church of Santa Sophia, alterations to the Palace of Bakhtchi-Serai in the Crimea and a triumphal arch, a drawing of which by J S Bond was exhibited at the RA 1793. Like Adam(qv), he insisted on designing all the furniture in the buildings for which he was responsible. At Tsarkoe Seloe he produced some of the most exquisitely elegant interiors in 18th century Europe. His use of colour was particularly effective. In the Agate Pavilion he set red agate columns with gilt bronze capitals against green jasper walls to achieve a rich polychromatic effect. Although in some respects still a Palladian, Cameron was a pioneer of the Greek Revival in Russia, notably in the Greek Doric Temple of Friendship at Pavlovsk, designed c1780. He was a difficult man, and on 9th December, 1796 he was dismissed by the Grand Duke Paul over disagreements about rising costs. In 1800 he was allowed to return to Tsarskoe Seloe where he lived in Bush's former house. He then built the Pavilion of the Three Graces and the Elizabeth Gallery and in 1802 was appointed Architect-in-Chief to the Admiralty, with accommodation in Mikhailovski Castle. He died sometime between 1811 and 1812. In November, 1812, his widow sold his books, pictures and scientific instruments. She died five years later when most of Cameron's architectural drawings were returned to England, but in 1820 they were purchased by the Tsar to help with restoration work at Tsarkoe Seloe, which had been damaged by fire. They were to prove their worth again in the loving restoration of Cameron's buildings after severe damage suffered in WW2. The main collection of Cameron's surviving drawings is in the Hermitage State Museum, St Petersburg. Other drawings in Russian collections are listed in the Arts Council Catalogue. There is a design for a ceiling by Cameron in Sir John Soane's Museum and a small sketch in Glasgow University Library. A portrait by A O Orlovsky, dated 1809, is reproduced in the Supplement to the AC Catalogue and in Rae's biography.

**Bibl:** Arts Council (Ex Cat 1967-8); Loukmski, Charles Cameron, 1943; Rae, Charles Cameron, Architect to the Court of Russia, 1971; Shividovsky, 'The Empress and the Architect' Country Life, Nov 16, 1989, 90-95; Taleporovski, Charles Cameron, Moscow 1939 (in Russian).

**CAMERON, D** **fl 1866**

Amateur Dundee landscape painter in oil. Exhibited RSA(1).

**CAMERON, Sir David Young RA RSA RWS RSW RE1865-1945**

Born Glasgow, 28 Jne; died Perth, 16 Sep. Painter, watercolourist and etcher. Son of a Glasgow minister. After a short, rather unhappy time spent in business, he studied at the Glasgow School of Art during the evening and in 1885 joined the Life School of the RSA in Edinburgh as a full time student. Lived in Edinburgh until 1898 when he moved to Kippen. His early paintings and watercolours are eclectic, showing a variety of influences including those of Velasquez, Whistler, the Barbizon school, and Dutch artists of the 19th century Revival, particularly Mathew Maris. In the 1890s he became known for his etchings and it was not until 1893 that there was evidence of the development of a very personal style. The landscapes of this period have a great feeling of weight and grandeur conveying the immensity of the structure. The breadth of handling is monumental and an air of mysticism is conveyed. At the end of the first decade of this century, Cameron tended to eliminate the brighter colours from his paintings preferring cool browns, strong blacks and pale greys. This sombre mood was not always in evidence as, for example, his painting 'Ben Ledi' in 1914 with its feeling for the crisp, cool springtime air. In about 1916 he began a series of architectural subjects of outstanding quality, the predominant feature of which was the definite geometrical pattern made on the canvas by the 'close-up' technique giving an exciting immediacy to the unpopulated scene. This style continued into the early 1920s, when he was concentrating on the landscape and buildings of Provence and Italy. His colours began to intensify. It is generally thought that while his French landscapes are artistically his most successful, it is the paintings of his native Scotland that showed his poetic majesty at its best. He was a master etcher, able to conjure up subtle colour, atmosphere and the vastness of the scene before him with a wonderful economy of line. Many of his etchings were used to illustrate Seton Gordon's *Highways & Byways of Central Scotland* (1937) and *Highways & Byways of the Western Highlands* (1935); also Herbert Maxwell's *The Story of the Tweed* (1905) and the 1902 edition of *The Compleat Angler*. Other illustrations he provided were for *Old Glasgow Exhibition* (1894); *Charterhouse Old and New* (1895); Buchan: *The Scholar Gypsies* (1896); Stevenson: *An Elegy & Other Poems* (1896), as well as producing a number of portfolios: *The Clyde Set* (1890); *North Holland* (1892); *North Italy* (1896); *The London Set* (1900); *Paris Etchings* (1904); *Etchings in Belgium* (1907). It is as a print maker that Cameron reached the greatest height of his artistic achievements. Regular exhibitor at both the RA and the RSA and was the recipient of many medals abroad. Elected RWS and RSW 1906, RSA 1918, RA 1920, knighted 1924. He was honoured with doctorates of the Universities of Glasgow (1911), Manchester (1923), Cambridge (1928), and St Andrews (1936). Appointed King's Painter and Limner in Scotland 1933. Trustee of the National Gallery of Scotland and the Tate Gallery, Vice-President of the Scottish Modern Arts Association, and closely associated with the British School of Rome. Not only a fine artist, he was also a fine human being. Many people remember his generosity, kindness and compassion, given without stint or consideration for himself. Although some books list him as one of the Glasgow Boys, he was not associated with the group in its formative years and the emphatic colour contrasts in his later landscapes, quite undetermined by decorative considerations, make him atypical of the movement. His sister **Elizabeth CAMERON** was a watercolour artist. She donated twelve drawings depicting each month of the year to Kippen Church where they continue to be displayed on each appropriate month. Exhibited RA(71), RSA(80), GI(59). RSW(10), ROI(8), RHA(4), RE(139), AAS(36) & L(92). Represented in NGS(4), Tate AG, V & A, SNGMA, City of Edinburgh Art collection, RA, Aberdeen AG, Dundee AG, Paisley AG, Perth AG, Glasgow AG, Kilmarnock AG, Kirkcaldy AG, Ashmolean Museum, Oxford, Birmingham AG, Bradford AG, Fitzwilliam Museum, Cambridge, Liverpool AG, Manchester AG, Rochdale AG, Nat. Gall. of Canada (Ottawa), Nat. Gall. of New Zealand (Wellington), Victoria AG (Australia).

**Bibl:** Apollo, 1929; Arts Council of GB, Scottish Committee, Sir DYC 1865-1945, Centenary exhib 1965; Caw 457-60; Halsby 151-2 et al; Hardie III, 65,211 (pl 245); Arthur M Hind, The etchings of DYC, London 1924; Frank Rinder, DYC, an illustrated catalogue of his etchings and drypoints 1887-1932, Glasgow 1932; Scottish Arts Council Centenary Exhibition 1919; The Studio, 1925, 'Modern Masters of Etching, no. 7, DYC' - intro by Malcolm Salaman; The Studio, 'The Paintings of David Young Cameron' 1919; Houfe 87; *Modern Book Illustrators and Their Work*, The Studio 1914; *Print Collectors' Quarterly*, 11, no.1, 1924, pp44-68; Bill Smith, D Y Cameron - The Vision of the Hills, Atelier, 1992.

**CAMERON, Duncan** **?-1899**

Architect. An idiosyncratic design was the single storey villa, Heatherlie, Strathpeffer (1895-97). Became partner with J Russell **BURNETT** (d.1921), responsible for the Phipps Institute, Beauly (1901-03), and together they designed, inter alia, the large Highland Hotel, Strathpeffer (1909-11).

**Bibl:** Gifford, H&I, 69,166,180,200,203,214,242-3 et passim,pl 117.

**CAMERON, Duncan** **1837-1916**

Painter in oil; landscapes. Spent most of his life in Stirling although also lived for a time in Dundee and between 1883 and 1908 at 149 Warrender Park Road, Edinburgh. Specialised in landscapes of the Scottish Highlands, including the western isles. Prolific. Especially attracted to and competent at depicting harvest fields with mountains looming overhead, and the subtle luminosity of autumnal light in the

Highlands. His work was varied, at its best it was very good in the traditional Scottish style of landscape painting after Horatio McCulloch(qv) but his minor works give evidence of having been done rather quickly with little attention to draughtsmanship. Exhibited RA(22) 1872-1900, including scenes in Arran, Perthshire and Glencoe, also RSA(85) between 1863 (when he was living in Dundee) and 1907; also RHA(3), GI(33), RBA(5), AAS 1893-1910 & L(5).
**Bibl:** Caw 303.

**CAMERON, E Josephine (Mrs Miller)** **1890-1975**
Artist, generally in black and white, of 30 Lansdowne Crescent, Glasgow. . Married A E Haswell M(qv). Exhibited townscapes at the GI(2) & L(1). Represented in Glasgow AG.

**CAMERON, Elizabeth** **1915-**
Born Nov 28, London. Painter, primarily in watercolours of botanical subjects, and latterly landscape. Enrolled at the Slade 1938 but, with the imminence of war and not being allowed into the "life" room, she walked out. Attended life classes for one year at St John's School of Art. Her first painting was accepted by the RA 1938 and shortly after began exhibiting RSA. An extremely modest but determined person, in 1970 she turned to botanical work, specialising in accurate, delicate studies of flowers and vegetables for which she won 3 RHS gold medals. Her work was included in the 5th Int. Exhibition at the Hunt Institute, Pittsburgh. Has held several solo shows in London. Lives at Allangrange, Munlochy, Ross & Cromarty.

**CAMERON, Emily** **fl 1864**
Burntisland painter; exhibited Dunkeld Cathedral at the RSA in 1864.

**CAMERON, Eunice Gavin** **fl 1970-1972**
Sculptress based in Kirkcaldy, Fife. Exhibited two portrait busts at the RSA in 1970 and again in 1972. Represented in Kirkcaldy AG.

**CAMERON, Ewan D A** **fl 1967-1982**
Ross-shire artist who exhibited at the RSA in 1967 (2), 1976 (3) and 1982.

**CAMERON, George** **fl 1770-1773**
Edinburgh engraver. Engraved maps of Breadalbane and Lanarkshire in 1773 from Borthwick's Close, Edinburgh.
**Bibl:** Bushnell.

**CAMERON, George C** **fl 1932-1944**
Amateur landscape painter in oil and watercolour from Glasgow. Exhibited three works at the RSA from 15 The Oval, Clarkston, & GI(2).

**CAMERON, Gordon Stewart RSA** **1916-1994**
Born Aberdeen, 27 Apr; died Apr. Painter in oil and illustrator. Educated Robert Gordon's College, Aberdeen, studied art at Gray's School (1925-1940) under D M Sutherland(qv) and Robert Sivell(qv). Awarded a travelling scholarship in 1939, Guthrie Award 1944 and a Carnegie Travelling scholarship 1946. After travelling in France & Holland, he became a part-time lecturer at Gray's and, as assistant to Sivell, worked on a series of murals for the new Aberdeen Student Union 1939-54, Sivell being responsible for the designs and Cameron for most of the painting. The owner of the only custom-built studio in Aberdeen, this became a meeting place for artists. Joined the staff of Duncan of Jordanstone School of Art 1952. Influenced by Vuillard. Husband of Ellen Malcolm(qv). From his home at 56 Forest Avenue he retired to 7 Auburn Terrace, Invergowrie, Perthshire c1965. His best known illustrations were for Lockhart's *Anatomy of the Human Body.* In later years became increasingly entranced by Cezanne and like him, Cameron was self-critical, never seeking public approbation. Elected ARSA 1958, RSA 1971. Exhibited RSA regularly since 1942, also RGI(26) & AAS 1937, 1957 and 1965. Represented in Aberdeen AG, Dundee AG, Glasgow AG, Paisley AG, Perth AG.
**Bibl:** Alberto Morrocco, Obituary, RSA Annual Report, 1994.

**CAMERON, Hugh RSA RSW ROI** **1835-1918**
Born Edinburgh, 4 Aug; died Edinburgh, 15 Jly. Painter in oil; landscape, genre and portraits. At the age of 14 apprenticed to an architect but preferring to pursue art he entered the Trustees Academy 1815, studying under Scott Lauder(qv). Continued his training in London 1876-1888 having visited the Riviera in c1880. His work developed in parallel with that of George Paul Chalmers(qv) and McTaggart(qv), but with its own more gentle individuality. Apart from portraits, his favourite subjects were homely genre, especially scenes of childhood and old age; some of his earlier works have a pre-Raphaelite finish. Settled in London 1876 but from 1888 spent his summers at Largs and winters in Edinburgh. Also painted a few Italian scenes. Armstrong called him 'a master of tone and atmosphere', while Caw spoke of his drawing which 'lacks decision and emphasis, his technique, fullness and grip, his ideas are not sufficiently materialised, tendencies which are more marked in his later work. On the other hand, his sentiment is often charming, and always refined and with it his delicate sense of colour is in full sympathy...In the works of Israels, for example, the spectator feels that the atmosphere is bitterly cold, and that the little ones were shivering; but Cameron's world is an abode of happiness'. The influence of McTaggart in both colour and composition is very clear, especially during his later period. 'He lingers between passion and pathos, and rarely leaves the refinement of soothing semi-tones...The modesty of reserve, the tuneful suggestiveness of native airs. In portaiture he seeks the normal mood, the habitual expression, and reads character by divination...He possesses exceptional intellectual breadth and strong, reflective tendencies...He wanders thoughtfully by the shore of Largo Bay, and there dreaming his picture, like Corot, he paints his dream'. During his final years the colours became brighter and more transparent. He contributed illustrations to Nimmo: *Pen and Pencil Pictures from the Poets* (1867), and *Good Words*. Elected ROI 1883, ARSA 1859, RSA 1869, RSW 1878, HRSW 1916. Exhibited RA(25) 1871-1892, RSA from 1871 until his death in 1918 and thereafter posthumously in 1919, 1926 and 1976 amounting to a total of almost 200 works, also RSW(9), RWS(1), GI(52), AAS regularly between 1890 and 1912, ROI(8) & L(1). Represented NGS(10), Kirkcaldy AG, Paisley AG, Perth AG, City of Edinburgh collection(4), Brodie Castle (NTS).
**Bibl:** AJ 1898, 46,86,342,370; Caw 259-261, et al; Lindsay Errington, Masterclass: Robert Scott Lauder and his pupils, NGS exhib 1983, biog of Hugh Cameron; Halsby 167,241; Hardie 54,57,64-7,77-8(illus); Irwin 348-9,365-6(illus); Macmillan [SA], 231,232,244,253; Who was Who, 1916-1928; Houfe 87.

**CAMERON, Hugh Armstrong** **fl 1901-1923**
Painter in oil and watercolour. Lived at Largo, Fife, before moving to Edinburgh c1907. Served overseas during WWI. Exhibited RSA(12), RSW(2) & L(1).

**CAMERON, Hugh Mackay** **fl 1855**
Amateur Edinburgh artist who exhibited one landscape at the RSA.

**CAMERON, Isabel Armstrong** **fl 1908**
Sculptress based in Edinburgh. Exhibited once at the RSA in 1908 from 45 George Square.

**CAMERON, J** **fl 1888-1889**
Amateur artist of 15 Hill Street, Garnet Hill, Glasgow; exhibited GI(2).

**CAMERON, J Bruce Jnr** **fl 1936**
Amateur watercolour artist. Son of J Bruce C(qv). Exhibited a landscape at the GI.

**CAMERON, J Bruce** **fl 1902-1939**
Painter, draughtsman, etcher and engraver of Crannoch, Addesleigh Avenue, Milngavie. Exhibited regularly at the RSA(16) between 1922 and 1937, generally landscapes, often with Scottish castles, also GI(31).

**CAMERON, James C** **fl 1958-1959**
Amateur Dumbarton landscape painter in watercolour. Exhibited GI(3) from 19 White Avenue.

**CAMERON, Mrs Jean M** **fl 1980**
Printmaker of 15 Castle Avenue, Balloch, Dunbartonshire, exhibited once at the GI.

**CAMERON, Mrs Jessie T** **fl 1896**
Amateur Edinburgh watercolour landscape painter of 9 Merchison Place. Exhibited RSA(1).

**CAMERON, John** **fl 1888-1931**
Painter in watercolour, also engraver and etcher, especially drypoint. Lived in Inverness before moving to Costorphine 1918. Exhibited RSA regularly in the first decade of this century (16), also at the International Society of Sculptors, Painters and Engravers, GI(8), RHA(2) & L(5). Represented in Paisley AG. A coloured drawing for *Treasure Island* is in the Witt Photo Library.
**Bibl:** Houfe 87.

**CAMERON, John D** **fl 1899**
Painter in oil. Spent the early part of his career in Paris from where he exhibited 'Stranger at Versailles' in 1899.

**CAMERON, Katherine (Kate) (Mrs Arthur Kay) RSW RE** **1874-1965**
Born Glasgow, 26 Feb. Painter in oil, watercolour and gouache; also book illustrator and etcher; flowers and landscape. Sister of Sir David Young Cameron(qv), and fourth daughter among seven surviving children of a country minister and his artistic wife who painted watercolours. Direct descendant of Dr Archibald Cameron, 'The Gentle Lochiel' of the '45 rebellion. Studied Glasgow School of Art 1890-1893 under Francis Newbery(qv) and Paris at Colarossi's under Gustave Courtois. Returning home she was invited to illustrate two books of fairy tales. Her first solo exhibition in Glasgow 1900. Writing in the *AJ* H C Marillier praised the romantic way Cameron painted romantic subjects 'because she loves them, and because they are a vital part of her existence. She has the true race feeling of the Celt for love and legend'. This exhibition included detailed studies of bees and illustrations for several Scottish ballads. A short time later she moved to Stirling there illustrating her first book, *In Fairyland* (1904), also Kingsley's *Water Babies* (1905), MacGregor: *Stories of King Arthur's Knights* (1905), followed a year later by her illustrations for Louey Chisholm's *The Enchanted Land*. In 1908 she travelled to Italy to prepare illustrations for Steedman's *Legends and Stories of Italy* (1909). Other illustrations included those for *Madonna* (1908), *Stella Maris* (1908), *Aucassin Nicolette* (1908), *Celtic Tales* (1910), Thomas: *The Flowers of Love* (1916); Aitken: *In a City Garden* (1913); Williams: *Where the Bee Sucks* (1929); Flora Grierson's *Haunting Edinburgh* (1929); and her own book *Iain The Happy Puppy* (1934). In 1928 married the writer and collector Arthur Kay and returned to live in Edinburgh. Her early watercolours were influenced by the Glasgow Symbolists although her work was always less stylized. Her best known paintings are her flower studies, the earlier of which used stronger colour and more frequently flowers in bowls whereas the later work was freer, more delicate and portray the flowers in their natural environment. The influence on the later work of Edwin Alexander(qv) is evident. Lifelong member of the Glasgow Lady Artists Club(qv). Elected RSW 1897, RE 1964. In addition to exhibiting in Munich and Berlin, she exhibited at the RA from 1921 (18), RSA from 1894 (107), RSW(130), SWA(1), RE(39), GI(188), regularly at the AAS 1908-1937 & L(58). Represented in V & A, BM, Glasgow AG, Kirkcaldy AG, City of Edinburgh collection(3), Perth AG and by 30 etchings in the Library of Congress, Washington.
**Bibl:** Burkhauser 218-221 et passim; Caw 415-6; Halsby 183-6,252; Hardie 103,117; Irwin 403; Bertha E Mahony, Illustrators of Children's Books, 1744-1945, Boston (USA), 1947, 189; H C Marillier, 'The Romantic Watercolours of Katherine Cameron', AJ, 1900, 149; H Wright: *The Etchings of Kate Cameron*, International Studio, 1975.

**CAMERON, Kenneth** **fl 1978-1979**
Aberdeen artist who exhibited 4 works at the AAS from 9b Ferrier Gardens.

**CAMERON, Miss Lou V** **fl 1932-1937**
Artist in oil and chalk, also engraver, of Meiklehill, Kirkintilloch. Exhibited 5 flower paintings at GI.

**CAMERON, Margaret Kerr** **fl 1899**
Amateur Edinburgh painter of portraits in watercolours. Related to Jessie Cameron(qv). Exhibited RSA(1) from 9 Merchiston Place.

**CAMERON, Margaret P** **fl 1897-1902**
Amateur flower painter in watercolour of 140 Govan Street, Glasgow. Exhibited RSA & GI(1).

**CAMERON, Miss Marion L** **fl 1932-1934**
Sculptress in bronze and plaster of animals and figures of Strathaven, Lanarkshire. Moved to 15 Lynedoch Street 1933. Exhibited RSA(1) & GI(3).

**CAMERON, Mary (Mrs Alexis Miller)** **c1865-1921**
Born Edinburgh. She painted in oil and watercolour; animals, landscape, figure compositions, portraits. Studied at the Edinburgh School of Art and in Paris under L Sargent, Gustave Courtois and J A Rixens. Fond of Spanish scenes and equestrian portraits, often large. Also known for her early painting of military subjects and bull fighting scenes painted during the time she was living in Madrid and Seville 1900. In Spain she met and for a time studied under Ignacis Zuloaga. Solo exhibition at the Galleries des Artistes Modernes, Paris 1911. Her portrait 'Mme Blair et ses borzois' received an honourable mention at the French Salon 1904. Exhibited Paris Salon 1904, 1905 and 1914, also RA(2) 1900, RSA(53) 1886-1919, GI(17), L(12) & AAS, latterly from 12 Clarendon Crescent. Represented in City of Edinburgh collection(5).
**Bibl:** Caw 429; Halsby 252-3; Wingfield.

**CAMERON, Mary Emily** **fl 1864-1865**
Amateur Burntisland painter in oil and watercolour of landscapes and buildings. Exhibited RSA(2) 1864 and 1865 when living at St Ninian's Vicarage, Glenurquhart, Inverness-shire, & GI(2).

**CAMERON, Mary F** **fl 1867**
Amateur watercolour painter of 5 Ardgowan Street, Greenock. Exhibited a landscape at the GI.

**CAMERON, R Christie** **1944-**
Born Greenock. Figurative artist with landscape backdrops in a stylised manner. Trained Glasgow School of Art 1978-82. Many solo exhibitions beginning in 1983 and group shows in Germany & Yugoslavia. Exhibits RSA & RSW since 1993. [Not to be confused with Robert Christie Cameron]

**CAMERON, Reginald Henry** **fl 1896-1908**
Amateur Edinburgh painter. Exhibited landscapes, generally of the Lothians, at the RSA between 1896 and 1908.

**CAMERON, Richard** **fl 1833-1839**
Edinburgh marine painter. Exhibited RSA in 1833, 1835 and 1839.

**CAMERON, Robert Christie** **fl 1938-1940**
Greenock watercolour painter of 130 Drumfrochar Road; exhibited RSW(1) & GI(1).

**CAMERON, Robert Macfarlane** **fl 1883-d1921**
Edinburgh architect and draughtsman. Designed The Jolly Arms, West Register St (1896), a modernised interior for Bruntsfield Golf Tavern, The old Outpatients building for Western General Hospital (1912) and the Royal Burgess Golf Club (1896-7). Also responsible for Holyrood Abbey church (1899) and St Columba's RC church, Upper Gray St (1888). Exhibited a pencil sketch of an interior at the RSA in 1883 and two works subsequently.
**Bibl:** Gifford 330,498,503,512,532,548,555,580-1,636.

**CAMERON, Roger** **fl 1966-1970**
Edinburgh painter. Exhibited RSA between 1966 and 1970.

**CAMERON, Roy** **fl 1969-1970**
Painter. Exhibited twice at the RSA from an Edinburgh address in 1969 and 1970.

**CAMERON, Samuel Rose** **fl 1923-1938**
Sculptor. Exhibited portrait busts and religious subjects in marble and bronze at the RSA from 1923-28, 1930 and 1938.

**CAMM, C H D** **fl 1893**
Stained glass window designer; exhibited RSA(1).

**CAMM, Miss Florence** **1874-1960**
Stained glass window designer, related to C H D Camm(qv) and also to James(qv), Robert(qv) and Walter Herbert Camm(qv) who were members of the same business carried on from Birmingham, and who also lived for a time in Largs. Exhibited GI(1).

**CAMM, James F P** **fl 1892-1902**
Edinburgh stained glass window designer; exhibited RSA in 1902 and RHA.

**CAMM, Robert** **1878-1954**
Studied Birmingham School of Art. Possibly the head of the family firm based in Birmingham. Subsequently moved to Largs. Brother of Florence C(qv) and Walter Herbert C(qv). Exhibited RA(13) & RSA 1922.

**CAMM, Walter Herbert** **1876-?**
Brother of Robert(qv) and Florence C(qv). Member of family firm of stained glass window designers, founded by his father Thomas William C. Exhibited RA(47), RSA 1919 and 1920, GI(2) & L(4).

**CAMPBELL, Miss** **fl 1832**
Amateur Edinburgh painter, exhibited once at the RSA.

**CAMPBELL, Alexander** **1764-1824**
Topographical painter in watercolour, pencil and sepia; also musician and writer. Best known as the author of *Journey from Edinburgh through Parts of North Britain* (1802). NGS has a collection of 15 views, mostly Highland.

**CAMPBELL, Alexander RSA RSW** **1932-**
Born Edinburgh. Landscape painter. Studied Edinburgh School of Art 1951-7 winning an Andrew Grant travelling scholarship enabling him to visit Italy, Spain and Morocco. Won Guthrie Award 1963. First one-man show in Bradford, 1966. Elected ARSA 1970, RSW 1976, RSA 1981. Exhibited irregularly at the GI(4) and often at the RSA, from 8 Barnton Park Grove. Represented in SAC, Keighley AG,
**Bibl:** Halsby 253.

**CAMPBELL, Alexander Buchanan FRIAS ARSA FRIBA** **1914-**
Born Findochty, 14 Jne. Studied architecture at Glasgow School of Architecture 1930-1937 under Professor Harold Hughes and J A Coia. Interested in modern design. Elected FRIAS and FRIBA 1955, ARSA 1972. Exhibited regularly RSA from 1956 onwards.

**CAMPBELL, Alexander Lorne** **c1871-1944**
Edinburgh architect and designer. Partner in firm of Begg & Lorne Campbell and later Scott (JN) & Lorne Campbell. Designed Lochend Parish church (1929); also the woodwork in the old Free High Church on the Mound when converted into a library(1934-6).
**Bibl:** Gifford 185,617,660.

**CAMPBELL, Alexander Stewart RSA RSW** **1932-**
Born Edinburgh. Painter in oil, watercolour, gouache and especially acrylic. Educated at Edinburgh University where he obtained MA honours degree in fine art. Teaches drawing and painting at Edinburgh College of Art. Received Guthrie award 1963, John Maxwell Award 1981. Librarian, RSA 1983-1988. 'Has a liking for restrained, harmonious colour schemes where greys predominate, and a preference for regarding subjects idiosyncratically from unexpected angles which emphasise the artistic and compositional virtues' [Gage]. His typical compositions are harbours and fishing boats, often without figures, or parts of boats; also fishermen penned in by deck furniture and rigging. Interested in off-beat arrangements of abstract design, often using the frame to slice and cut as Degas did. 'He paraphrases rather than describes structures so that the appearance of the work is casual and unfussy.' Elected ARSA 1970, RSA 1988. Represented in Edinburgh City collection(2).

**CAMPBELL, Archibald** **fl 1861-1868**
Glasgow painter in oil of figurative subjects. Moved to London c1864. Exhibited twice at the RSA in 1861 and 1864, & GI(13).

**CAMPBELL, Archibald** **1914-**
Painter in oil, probably born in Perth. Local landscapes and figure subjects.

**CAMPBELL, C Wylie** **fl 1946-1947**
Amateur watercolour painter of landscape. Exhibited GI(5).

**CAMPBELL, Miss Carrie** **fl 1921**
Amateur Glasgow artist. Exhibited a black and white study of Kirkwall Cathedral at the GI from 220 West Regent Street.

**CAMPBELL, Catriona J** **1940-**
Born Dollar. Painter in oil; portraits, occasional still life and latterly figure compositions. Daughter of Ian C(qv). Trained Glasgow School of Art 1957-61 being taught by Mary Armour(qv) and David Donaldson(qv). Council member of SWA, she has also exhibited with the RSPP. A recent 'Self-portrait' won the Anne Redpath Award, SSWA exhibition 1988. Exhibits RSA regularly since 1964, also RGI since 1958 and at the Royal Society of Portrait Painters(3). Represented in private collections worldwide.

**CAMPBELL, Charles Moss** **fl 1865-1868**
Amateur landscape artist of coastal scenes and seascapes. Exhibited RSA from 1865 to 1868.

**CAMPBELL, Colen** **1676-1729**
Died 13 Sep. Architect. Eldest son of Donald Campbell, Laird of Boghole and Urchany (and younger brother of Sir Hugh Campbell of Cawdor Castle, Nairnshire). Campbell inherited the estates in 1680 on the death of his father. Had a liberal education and was possibly the Colen Campbell who graduated from Edinburgh University 1695. In 1715/ 16 was in Italy - in a petition to George I he referred to having 'studied architecture here and abroad for several years'. Then became a lawyer, practising in Edinburgh but made the transition to architecture, perhaps through an association with James Smith(qv) (c1645-1731) whom he described in *Vitruvius Britannicus* as 'the most experienced architect in Scotland'. Campbell may have been Smith's pupil, and probably Smith directed Campbell's attention to the architecture of Palladio. In any event, Campbell proceeded to make his name as the leading propagandist of the Palladian movement in British architecture. Published *Vitruvius Britannicus* in three folio volumes, each containing 100 plates (1715, 1717 and 1725). The main purpose of the book seems to have been to assert the superiority of 'antique simplicity' over the "affected and licentious" forms of the Baroque. It also served as an advertisement for Campbell's own ability - all his own works were included among the illustrations. Volume I was dedicated to the King. However, it was the patronage of William Benson, Surveyor General of the Works, which Campbell sought for architectural position. He wanted to be Master of Works for Scotland, an office previously held by William Bruce(qv) and then James Smith(qv), but he failed although ten years later he was appointed Chief Clerk and Deputy Surveyor 1718. Unfortunately, Benson was corrupt and Campbell shared in his disgrace, losing his appointment. In 1719 he was appointed Architect to the Prince of Wales but this failed to lead to any new commissions. He was then patronised by Lord Burlington who employed Campbell to remodel his London home in the Palladian style 1719. Campell acquired some influential patrons, including Sir Robert Walpole, Henry Hoare, and the Earl of Pembroke. In 1728 he succeeded Vanburgh as Surveyor of Greenwich Hospital and published a revised version of Palladio's *First Book of Architecture* reissued the following year as *The Five Orders of Architecture*. Campbell was an outstanding figure in late 18th century English architecture, responsible for some of the most important buildings of the Palladian movement, including Wanstead House, Essex (c1714-20, demolished 1824), Stourhead, Wiltshire (1720-24), and Houghton Hall, Norfolk (1722-1735).
**Bibl:** Brydall 173-4; Colvin; Dunbar, 86-7,102,104; Macmillan [SA], 96-7.

**CAMPBELL, Colin** **fl 1820-1830**
Edinburgh miniature painter. Although Foskett reports having no information other than that the artist was working in 1820 at 187 High Street, Edinburgh, he exhibited portrait miniatures at the RSA in 1827 (3), 1828 (3), and 1830 (2) from an address at 5 College Street, Edinburgh.

**CAMPBELL, Colin Cairness Clinton** **1894-**
Portrait and flower painter in oil. Studied in New York and at Byam Shaw School and Slade in London. Between 1932 and 1938 he lived in Argyll before moving to Oakhall, Hythe, Kent. Exhibited RSA in 1936, 1938 (3) and 1939 (3), GI(65) & AAS 1935.

**CAMPBELL, Colin W** **fl 1963-1964**
Amateur Glasgow watercolourist. Exhibited 4 landscapes at the GI from 7 Mossview Quadrant.

**CAMPBELL, Lady Constance (Duchess of Argyll)** **fl 1891**
Exhibited one painting at the Dudley Gallery, Birmingham from Inverary Castle.

**CAMPBELL, Crawford** **fl 1984-1987**
Painter of harbour scenes. Exhibited RSA in 1984 and 1986(2), also GI(2).

**CAMPBELL, D** **fl 1879-1893**
Glasgow painter in oil and watercolour of town and landscapes. Exhibited GI(4).

**CAMPBELL, Daniel C S** **fl 1954**
Amateur Glasgow watercolour painter. Exhibited a beach scene at the GI from 1071 Sauchiehall Street.

**CAMPBELL, Donald W MacK** **fl 1965**
Amateur Dumbarton watercolourist. Exhibited a winter landscape at the GI from 11 Ramsay Crescent.

**CAMPBELL, Dugal** **?-1757**
Architect. Responsible for the Governor's House in the New Barracks of Edinburgh Castle (1742). This was used as three homes, one for the Governor, one for the storekeeper and one for the master gunner.
Bibl: Gifford 192.

**CAMPBELL, Duncan** **fl 1872**
Glasgow portrait miniaturist. Exhibited 2 portrait medallions, one of Charles Dickens, at the GI from 16 Herbertson Street.

**CAMPBELL, Mrs Eleanora Corbett** **fl 1882-1886**
Edinburgh amateur painter in oils of fruit and landscape. Exhibited RSA 1882, 1884 and 1886, also GI(1), & AAS in 1885, from 6 West Maitland Street.

**CAMPBELL, Miss Fiona A S** **fl 1987**
Amateur Stirling painter. Exhibited 'The Plough' at the GI from 36 James Street.

**CAMPBELL, George (The Duke of Argyll)** **fl 1882-1888**
Amateur artist living at his ancestral home, Inverary Castle, Argyll. Married Constance(qv). Exhibited two pictures at the RSA in 1882 & GI(1).

**CAMPBELL, Gershom** **fl 1901**
Amateur Edinburgh artist; exhibited RSA.

**CAMPBELL, Gillies** **fl 1974-**
Artist from Whitburn in West Lothian; exhibited three pictures at the RSA in 1974.

**CAMPBELL, Gordon** **fl 1974-**
Fife painter from Leven; exhibited RSA in 1974 and 1979.

**CAMPBELL, Miss Helen McD** **fl 1935-1946**
Portrait painter in oil. Lived in London and exhibited RSA in 1945 'Sir Alexander Fleming' and 'Lord McMillan' 1946. Also exhibited RA(3) & SWA(1). Represented in Manchester AG by a portrait of the Slade Professor 'Henry Tonks' (1943).

**CAMPBELL, Hugh** **fl 1928-1932**
Greenock landscape painter in watercolour. Exhibited RSW(1) & GI(1), from 20 Union Street.

**CAMPBELL, Ian** **1902-1984**
Born Oban. Portrait painter in oil also engraver. Trained Glasgow School of Art 1921-1926, received the Guthrie Award for a self-portrait at the RSA in 1931 and the following year exhibited the first of two portraits at the RA. Father of Catriona C(qv). In 1930 moved to Dollar to become head of the art department at the local Academy 1937-1968. At his best he was a fine, sensitive portrait painter with a wonderful eye for a likeness without being overly flattering. His drawing of the late 'Cosmo Lang, Archbishop of Canterbury', is in the NPG in London; Dumfries AG also has a portrait and the Smith Institute in Stirling holds a figure composition entitled 'Westward' exhibited in the Canadian National Exhibition, Toronto 1931. Exhibited RSA(23), GI(33), RI, SSA & ROI.

**CAMPBELL, Ian** **fl 1978**
Amateur painter of 31 Adams Avenue, Saltcoats, Ayrshire. Exhibited GI(1).

**CAMPBELL, Ina D D (Mrs E J Unthoff)** **fl 1916-1922**
Amateur Glasgow painter of portraits and landscape in oil and monochrome. Exhibited RSA(2) & GI(5) from 1 James Street.

**CAMPBELL, J G** **fl 1829-1831**
Amateur Edinburgh painter who exhibited genre paintings at the RSA from 1829 to 1831.

**CAMPBELL, J Valentine** **fl 1951-1968**
Edinburgh painter of town scenes; exhibited RSA from 1951 to 1968, & GI(3).

**CAMPBELL, James** **fl 1853-1896**
Glasgow based painter in oil and watercolour; landscapes, portraits and narratives. The portraits were generally of Glasgow characters while his drawings were often sepia studies of Glasgow and Ayrshire scenes. Exhibited RSA(9) 1861, 1865 and 1873, & GI(23).
Bibl: Halsby 253.

**CAMPBELL, James/John** **fl 1854-1856**
Painter who exhibited subject paintings at the RSA in 1854-5, six of them from a Liverpool address.

**CAMPBELL, James D** **fl 1977**
Glasgow painter of landscape and shipping scenes. Exhibited GI(2) from 58 Ormonde Avenue.

**CAMPBELL, Miss Jane C** **fl 1881-1883**
Perthshire watercolour painter; interiors and landscape. Appears to have moved from Crieff where she was in 1881, to Ayr where she was in 1883. Visited South Africa and whilst there painted landscapes. Exhibited twice at the RSA from Sauchie House, Crieff.

**CAMPBELL, Jean B** **fl 1965-1967**
Artist in watercolour and pen and ink, mainly portraits. Exhibited GI(4) from 42 Kingshill Drive, Glasgow.

**CAMPBELL, Jenny (Mrs Roland Hipkins)** **1888-1966**
Ayrshire landscape painter; studied at the Edinburgh College of Art. Moved to London in the early 1920s. Exhibited GI(2). Represented in National Art Gallery of New Zealand ('Spring').

**CAMPBELL, John** **fl 1698**
Engraver. Son of a Glasgow merchant. Apprenticed to Henry Fraser in 1698. None of his work is known to have survived.
**Bibl:** Apted 32.

**CAMPBELL, John (Joshua?)** **fl 1746-1754**
Watercolourist and engraver. Known primarily as one of the few important Scottish engravers of the early 18th century, specialising in producing plates after Rembrandt, there is a miniature watercolour portrait of Duncan Forbes of Culloden, dated 1746, in the SNPG.
**Bibl:** Bryan; Brydall 202; Bushnell 9.

**CAMPBELL, John** **fl 1879-**
Edinburgh painter in oil; figurative. Exhibited RSA(1).

**CAMPBELL, John** **fl 1888-1907**
Cathcart painter in oil and watercolour of figure subjects and landscape. Exhibited GI(6), latterly from 5 Gordon Terrace, Glasgow.

**CAMPBELL, John** **fl 1930-1937**
Glasgow engraver. Exhibited an aquatint and lithograph at GI.

**CAMPBELL, John Archibald FRIBA** **1859-1909**
Glasgow architect. Apprenticed to John Burnet & Sons 1877-1880, then at Ecole des Beaux Arts, Paris 1880-3. Tite Prizeman 1885, elected FRIBA 1895. Entered into partnership with J.J. Burnet(qv) in Glasgow 1886-97, thereafter practised alone except for taking on **A D HISLOP** shortly before his death. Interested in the design of unusual buildings. Responsible for an extensive enlargement to Dawick, Peebles-shire, a house originally built by Burn(qv) and later further

altered by Robert Lorimer(qv). Dunbar mentions the Barony Church, Castle St, Glasgow, designed by Burnet and Campbell in 1886 "a fine Early Pointed composition with a most impressive interior on the Gerona model". One should also mention the treatment of windows of the Athenaeum Theatre, Glasgow, unorthodox, impressive and a forerunner of later work executed in similar vein. Remained unmarried, living in an imposing large house at Bridge of Weir. Exhibited RSA(15), including a design for Dalekairth House, Dumfries-shire, & GI(25).
**Bibl:** Dunbar 143-5; A Gomme & D Walker, Architecture of Glasgow, London 1987(rev), 175-7,204-5,210,211,214,289; Peter Savage, Lorimer and the Edinburgh Craft Designers, Edinburgh 1980, 108,163.

**CAMPBELL, John Francis** **fl 1841-1862**
Painter of landscape and figure drawings in oil and watercolour, also designer. In the NGS there is a large album containing many Scottish views and costume studies as well as sketches from the artist's travels: 'Trieste' 1841, 'Naples and Sicily' 1842, 'Spain' (including copies from pictures in the Prado) 1842, 'Germany' and 'Czechoslovakia' 1846 and 'Avranches', France 1848.

**CAMPBELL, John Hay** **fl 1937-1938**
Amateur Lanarkshire artist of flower studies and portraits in oil. Of 30 Cadzow Street, Hamilton and later 22 Auchingramont Road. Exhibited RSA(1) & GI(10).

**CAMPBELL, John Hodgson** **fl 1855-1927**
Edinburgh painter in oil and watercolour; buildings, portraits, landscape, genre. In c1883 he moved to Newcastle-on-Tyne. Exhibited RA(5), RSA(11) between 1879 and 1900, also RI(7) & L(1).

**CAMPBELL, John Thomson** **fl 1873-1874**
Amateur landscape painter in oil. Lived most of his adult life in Newcastle. Exhibited twice at the RSA, in 1873 and 1874.

**CAMPBELL, Joseph** **fl 1953**
Amateur Glasgow artist who exhibited 'Study of a Head' at the GI from 38 Katewell Avenue.

**CAMPBELL, Joshua** **[see CAMPBELL, John]**

**CAMPBELL, Miss Margaret M** **fl 1936-1955**
Glasgow watercolour painter of flowers and still life. Exhibited RSA 1938, 1948-9 and 1955, RSW(4) & GI(14) from 31 Glasgow Road, Clydebank, Dunbartonshire.

**CAMPBELL, Miss Mary Frances** **fl 1881-1888**
Edinburgh painter in watercolour of portraits, usually women. Exhibited RSA(13) between the above dates.

**CAMPBELL, Patrick Maitland** **fl 1919-1928**
Amateur Edinburgh painter in watercolour. Exhibited RSA 1919 & RSW 1928.

**CAMPBELL, Reginald Henry** **1877-?**
Born Edinburgh, 2 Dec. Painter in oil; portraits and landscape. Studied at the RA Schools in Edinburgh winning the Maclaine-Watters medal 1899, a Keith bursary and the Chalmers Jervise prize. Appears to have moved to London about the turn of the century. Exhibited RA(1), RSA(19), GI(7) & AAS in 1900.

**CAMPBELL, Robert** **1883-1967**
Born Dumbarton; died Edmonton, Canada. Landscape painter in watercolour. Received no formal art training. Worked in Scotland as an apprentice plasterer before migrating with his family to Canada 1906. In 1914 returned to Britain and while stationed at Bramshott, met and studied under the English watercolourist Victor Burnand. After the war Campbell returned to Edmonton where he obtained work as a dental technician while continuing to paint and sketch. At about this time he met and went on painting expeditions with the Canadian painter A C Leighton, depicting mainly the local landscape and views of a metropolis that was already changing. The latter work has become a valuable historical record of old Edmonton. Founder member, Edmonton Art Club. Represented in Edmonton Provincial Museum and AG (Canada).
**Bibl:** Edmonton AG, 'Robert Campbell' (Ex Cat) nd.

**CAMPBELL, Robert G** **fl 1942-1974**
Paisley painter in oil, watercolour and pencil of portraits, still life and landscape. Exhibited RSA & GI(17). Represented by 2 works in Paisley AG including 'Self-portrait'.

**CAMPBELL, Robert J** **fl 1962-1986**
East Kilbride sculptor. Exhibited 9 portrait heads in terracotta, plaster and ciment fondu at the GI from 189 Quebec Drive.

**CAMPBELL, Ronald** **fl 1839-1845**
Edinburgh portrait painter in oil. Exhibited regularly at the RSA between the above years.

**CAMPBELL, Miss Rosemary B** **fl 1974-1977**
Glasgow artist who exhibited 2 figure studies at the GI.

**CAMPBELL, Samuel** **fl 1848-1860**
Amateur Edinburgh landscape painter; exhibited RSA in 1848, 1852(4) and 1860(3).

**CAMPBELL, Scott** **1924-**
Born 10 Jly. Works primarily in oil, also occasional wood assemblage and etching. Figurative and non-figurative subjects. Educated Bradford Grammar School and King's College, University of Durham. Served in WW2 1942-47 and thereafter trained as a painter, graduating as a mature student with a master's degree 1982. Assistant Regional Director of the Arts Council 1953-55, Administrative Assistant, Department of Fine Art, King's College, Durham 1952-61 and lecturer there until his retirement 1989. His first one-man exhibition in London 1960 followed by another 1963. Exhibits RSA. Lives in Newcastle.

**CAMPBELL, Steven** **1953-**
Born Glasgow. After leaving school he spent several years working as an engineer but at the age of 25 enrolled at Glasgow School of Art. In 1982 won a Fulbright Scholarship which enabled him to visit New York. Whilst there he held two successful exhibitions, the first of many further shows in that country and in Europe. Remained in New York until 1986, when he returned to Glasgow. Spent 1990 as resident Artist, New South Wales AG. Creative Scotland Award winner 2000. His paintings are characterised by surreal and highly esoteric symbolism. 'Birds, beasts and men compete in a hostile garden environment, performing strange rituals which defy nature's logic. The precise arcane titles which Campbell gives his works are often at odds with the painted image, recalling Max Ernst's exploitation of the gulf between word and image'. He works quickly, painting directly on to canvas. In the late 1980s achieved national renown when Leeds City AG purchased his 'Three Men of Exactly the Same Size in an Unequal Room' (1989). Campbell is, in his rough Glaswegian way, a social commentator. Inspired by images taken from P G Wodehouse and others, he views the world with amusing, pithy cynicism. For example, England seen as a dying culture, in 'Elegant Gestures of the Drowned' after Max Ernst - even while drowning the figures continue to pose and gesture as if nothing is happening. Campbell emphasises the point by introducing a line of sheep following each other and ending up beside the Union Jack. As one critic has said 'His mind tends to work by association rather than by strict logic, one idea triggering another at breakneck speed. He is fascinated by powerful mythologies on the one hand and by scientific and pseudo-scientific discoveries on the other'. Represented in SNGMA, Glasgow AG.
**Bibl:** Hardie 209-13(illus); Hartley 120; Macmillan [SA], 404-5; Malborough FA, London, 'Steven Campbell: Recent Paintings' (Ex Cat 1987); Marlborough Gall, New York 'Steven Campbell: Recent Paintings' (Ex Cat 1988); Riverside Studios, London and FMG, Edinburgh 'Steven Campbell: New Paintings' (Ex Cat 1984); Duncan Macmillan, Steven Campbell, the story so far, 1993; Murdo Macdonald, Scottish Art, 2000; Macmillan 2001, 9,143,145,147-50,157-8,163,173,176,183, illus 161,192,201.

**CAMPBELL, Miss T C** **fl 1880**
Amateur Edinburgh painter who exhibited two pictures at the RSA in 1880.

**CAMPBELL, Thomas** **1790-1858**
Born Edinburgh, 1 May; died London, 4 Feb. Sculptor. Apprenticed alongside William Mossman(qv) to John Marshall, a marble cutter, in

Edinburgh. Whilst helping to carve a chimney-piece in the St. Andrew Square home of a Mr Gilbert Innes the owner was sufficiently impressed by the young apprentice to provide the means for his visit to London. There Campbell studied at the RA Schools and, helped once more by Mr Innes, from 1818-1830 he was in Rome. Among the patrons acquired there was the Duke of Devonshire for whom he executed a statue of Napoleon's beautiful sister, Princess Pauline Borghese. This became the sensation of the Paris Salon of 1855. Returning to London 1830 he continued exhibiting annually in the Academy until the year before his death, while retaining a studio in the Piazza Mignanelli, Rome whence he frequently visited to superintend numerous commissions. Described as a man of middle stature, robust and lively, but sometimes brisk and with a boisterous manner that concealed a natural shyness and occasional depression. Exhibited RSA 1835 and 1856; also posthumously 1863 and 1880. Two public statues are in Edinburgh, Frederick, Duke of York(1839) on Castlehill and the 4th Earl of Hopetoun(1824) in front of the Royal Bank in St Andrew Square; a statue of Queen Victoria is at Windsor. Carved dripstone heads decorate a door in St Mary's Cathedral, Edinburgh. SNG has a bust of Sir James Gibson, while the NPG has busts of Sarah Siddons and William Cavendish Bentinck, and the SNPG holds 2 works including Sir Henry Raeburn; also represented in BM, V & A.
**Bibl:** AJ, 1858 107-8 (obit); Brydall 188-190; Thomas Campbell, Letterbook, NLS MS146; Gifford 48,90,279,326; Theophile Gautier, Les Beaux Arts en Europe, Paris, 1855; Gunnis; Helen E Smailes, Virtue and Vision. Sculpture in Scotland 1540-1990, ch vi, Edinburgh 1991.

**CAMPBELL, Thomas** **fl 1830**
Amateur Greenock portrait painter. Exhibited five portraits at the RSA in 1830.

**CAMPBELL, Thomas** **fl 1901-1943**
Paisley and Glasgow artist in oil and watercolour; landscapes often Arran. Exhibited RSA(3), GI(40) & L(5) from 314 Renfrew Street.

**CAMPBELL, Col Thomas Hay** **fl 1872**
Amateur Edinburgh portrait painter in oil. A Colonel in the Royal Artillery, he exhibited at the RSA in 1872.

**CAMPBELL, Tom** **1865-1943**
Craigton and Glasgow landscape and topographical watercolourist. Specialised in views of the west coast and islands in a straightforward, strongly coloured style, often with children playing on the beach. Portrayed the sands of the west in a convincing and straightforward manner and was quite prolific. Exhibited RSA 1930 'The Three Pilchards Inn, Polperro', also at the AAS 1931. Represented in Paisley AG.
**Bibl:** Halsby 253.

**CAMPBELL, William** **fl 1862-1863**
Edinburgh sculptor. Exhibited small medallions at the RSA in 1862 and 1863.

**CAMPBELL, William jnr** **fl 1873**
Exhibited a landscape with classical ruins at GI from Tulliechewan, Alexandria, Dunbartonshire.

**CAMPBELL, William Wright** **fl 1940-1969**
Cambuslang painter in oil; landscape and portraits. Exhibited regularly at the RSA between 1940 and 1951; landscapes, often of Highland scenes, especially Loch Earn and Loch Awe; also GI(42), from Ashfield, Beach Avenue.

**CAMRASS, David** **1939-**
Born Israel. Glasgow-based sculptor. Lived in Israel and served in the Israeli army 1957-9, then moved to Glasgow to work with Benno Schotz(qv). Exhibited abstract works in metal at the RSA in 1964 and 1965, & GI(4).

**CANDOW, William** **fl 1924-1933**
Edinburgh painter of landscapes, especially of scenes in the Stirling area whence he moved c1928. Exhibited RSA in 1924, 1930 and 1933, & GI(1).

**CANNON, Cedric J** **fl 1950-1951**
Amateur Broughty Ferry painter who exhibited at the RSA in 1950 and 1951.

**CANTLAY, Miss Constance A** **fl 1919**
Amateur Aberdeen artist of buildings. Exhibited at the AAS(2) including 'Glascoure Castle' from 37 Devonshire Road.

**CANY, Miss Christine M** **fl 1977**
Amateur Dunbartonshire painter. Exhibited 'Flasher' at RGI from 28 Balloch Road, Balloch.

**CAPPER, Stewart Henbest RCanA** **1859-1924**
Edinburgh-trained architect. Among his designs were the University Hall extension, the first stage of Castlehill, Edinburgh (1892-3), an L-plan very Scottish in style, 'a cluster of gabled towers, the largest laden with a doubly jettied oriel and clasped by a battlemented stair-turret'; Robbie Burns Land, Lawnmarket, Edinburgh (1894), and a commemorative marble pulpit for the Church of the Sacred Heart, Lauriston (1895); also Nos 453-461 Lawnmarket, for Patrick Geddes (1892) and for the same patron the restructuring of Riddle's Close (1893). In 1895 he designed Edzell Lodge, 34 Inverleith Terrace. Sometime thereafter he migrated to Canada, becoming a Royal Canadian Academician. Exhibited designs for projects in and around Edinburgh RSA 1891- 1895, also GI(4).
**Bibl:** Gifford 191,195,197-9,256,531,579-80.

**CAPPON, Thomas Martin** **fl 1895-1915**
Dundee architect, he exhibited five times at the RA, including designs for the Panmure Arms Hotel, Edzell, the Meffan Institute, Forfar, and the Ramsay Arms, Fettercairn, also once at the RSA.

**CARBERRY, Nicola** **1970-**
Glasgow-based painter and illustrator. Trained Glagow School of Art 1987-91. Won Elizabeth Greenshields Award 1993 and the visual arts category of the Young Scot award 1995. Member, Hanging Together group(qv). Travels extensively in Europe, also visited Australia & Indonesia. Worked for a spell as resident artist, Coldstream. Illustrated for the *Glasgow Herald.*

**CARDONNEL, Adam M de** **c1760-1820**
Important amateur etcher and archaeologist. Joined Grose on his Scottish journeys making sketches along the way. The result was the picturesque *Antiquities of Scotland* (1788) comprising a series of plates of famous ecclesiastical and baronial edifices. Under each etching are notes outlining historical and other features, all prepared most meticulously. Cardonnel executed other forms of engraving and made an important contribution to numismatics with his sheets of plates for *Numismata Scotiae* (1786). He became the first Curator for the Society of Antiquaries of Scotland, 1782-1784. When he succeeded to the Chirton estate, he changed his name to Lawson. There are 3 engravings in the City of Edinburgh Collection and a pen and pencil sketch of the north-west view of St Monan's Church, Fife at the NGS.
**Bibl:** Bushnell; Butchart 26; DNB.

**CARDOSI, George** **fl 1985**
Bearsden painter. 'Exhibited On His Return from the Biennial' at the GI from 42 Switchback Road.

**CARDROSS, Lord** **fl 1760s**
Etcher. Studied at the University under Adam Smith and at the Foulis Academy(qv) while serving with his regiment in Glasgow 1762. Etched drawings of Iona made by William Lilliman of the Royal Engineers which later appeared in *Transactions of the Society of Antiquaries of Scotland.* Redgrave describes him as an amateur and says that 'among his later works were some portraits, and these etchings were respectable'.
**Bibl:** David Murray, Robert and Andrew Foulis, Glasgow 1913; Redgrave.

**CAREY, Alice S T** **fl 1884**
Amateur painter. Exhibited a townscape at the GI from 6 Belhaven Terrace, Glasgow.

**CAREY, Miss Anne** **fl 1978**
Amateur Paisley artist. Exhibited a moonlight scene at GI from 12 Greenlaw Avenue.

**CAREY, June** **fl 1985-**
Edinburgh painter in oil and mixed media. Exhibits RSA from 1985 and RGI. Abandoned Glasgow School of Art 1962 but returned to training 1978 at Edinburgh College of Art. She works in themes. Travels in Indonesia, Bali and Singapore led to the use of exotic symbolism.

**CARFRAE, J(?G)** **fl 1787-1799**
Two watercolour landscapes, one signed and dated 1799, are in the NGS. Most probably the same **G CARFRAE** who exhibited 'Scene in the rebellion of 1715' at the RA (1787) from 2 Ely Place, Holborn and is represented in the BM.

**CARFRAE, John Alexander** **1868-1947**
Edinburgh architect. Specialised in schools developing what Gifford has called a 'Board School Baroque style', his most distinguished design being Leith Academy Annexe(1903), also Boroughmuir and Tollcross schools (1911) and St Thomas Aquinas school (1913) overlooking Holyrood. Exhibited RSA 1894-1921 including a design for the War Memorial at George Watson's College (1921).
**Bibl:** Gifford 75,187,193,244,261,323,392,426,437,495-7,506-8,520,557,580,642,645,650,653,pl 95.

**CARFRAE, Miss Mary** **fl 1891-1892**
Edinburgh artist in watercolour of landscape. Exhibited RSA(1) and twice at the GI in 1892 from Montrose Villa, Murrayfield.

**CARGILL, Robert** **1940-**
Born Arbroath. Painter in oil. Studied at Duncan of Jordanstone College of Art, Dundee. In 1969 received an SAC Award and in 1970 a Greenshields Award which enabled him to visit Canada. Has exhibited widely including RSA, RSW, GI(1) & SSA, from 52 High Street.

**CARLAW, Miss Effie** **fl 1883-1887**
Glasgow painter of flower studies in watercolour and oil. Exhibited RSA(1) & GI(4).

**CARLAW, John RSW** **1850-1934**
Born Glasgow; died Helensburgh, 20 Apr. Painter in oil but mostly watercolour, also etcher; animals and landscape. Studied Glasgow School of Art. His early career was as a designer at the Saracen Foundry, Glasgow. Brother of William C(qv) and friend of the Glasgow Boys although never actually joined the group. Influenced by their wet technique of watercolour painting. His best works show a controlled, fluent handling of multicoloured washes, but sometimes can be inadequately drawn and weak in technique. Elected RSW 1885. Exhibited RA(14), RSA from 1882 (13), RSW(63), GI(46), AAS(2) & RHA(4). Glasgow AG has two watercolours.
**Bibl:** Caw 341; Halsby 253; Wingfield.

**CARLAW, Miss Lizzie** **fl 1883-1884**
Amateur Glasgow artist, related to Effie(qv) and John C(qv). Exhibited two flower studies at the GI in the above years from 385 Sauchiehall Street.

**CARLAW, Sally** **1964-**
Painter in oil and watercolour; teacher. Won several prizes while still at school and enrolled at Glasgow School of Art 1980 winning the J D Kelly Prize for the most promising student. A scholarship enabled her to travel extensively in Europe. Recently took up a teaching appointment on Mull. Exhibits GI.

**CARLAW, William RSW** **1847-1889**
Glasgow painter in oil and watercolour; landscapes, figures. Brother of John Carlaw(qv). Associated with the Glasgow School. Specialised in marine subjects in and around the coast of Scotland and the west of England 'with freshness and power' [Caw]. Elected RSW 1878. Exhibited eight landscapes at the RA between 1883 and 1891 and was a regular exhibitor at the RSA between 1872 and 1887. Also exhibited at the RSW(33), RI(1) & GI(42). Represented in Glasgow AG.
**Bibl:** Caw 324; Halsby 253.

**CARLE, Margaret B** **fl 1933**
Amateur painter of 83 Ashley Road, Aberdeen. Exhibited AAS(1).

**CARLISLE, Fiona** **1954-**
Born Wick, Caithness. Paints in watercolour, oil and acrylic, often figure compositions and marine-associated works. Studied Edinburgh College of Art 1972-1976. One of Scotland's most talented young artists. Awarded post-graduate scholarship 1976. Held her first exhibition in Edinburgh 1978. Achieved considerable international reputation having taken part in several successful exhibitions in the USA and her work having been shown in Paris and Geneva. Has lived in Crete since 1983, her love of Greece and its people is reflected in large vibrant landscapes and figure compositions. Widely travelled, has executed paintings in China and America as well as in Europe. Uses flat areas of colour and black contour lines to portray groups of women vigorously rendered. Exhibited RSA 1978, '79 and '82. Represented in SNGMA, Dundee AG, City of Edinburgh collection, SAC.
**Bibl:** 369 Gallery, Edinburgh (Ex Cat 1980, 1982, 1983, 1986); Hardie 214; Hartley 121.

**CARLISLE, G** **fl 1828**
Amateur Edinburgh painter. Exhibited a portrait at the RSA in 1828.

**CARLISLE, G M** **fl 1948**
Amateur Girvan oil painter. Exhibited GI(1).

**CARLISLE, Jeremy** **fl 1989-**
Exhibited 'Still Life with Mirror' at the RSA in 1989 from Twynholm, Kirkcudbrightshire.

**CARLOS, Patricia** **fl 1969-1978**
Aberdeen painter of landscape and representational studies. Exhibited regularly at the AAS during the above years from 20 Ferryhill Place.

**CARLYLE, Miss** **fl 1887**
Amateur Greenock painter of domestic interiors. Exhibited GI(2) from 44 Esplanade.

**CARLYLE, Frederick W** **fl 1933-1987**
Glasgow painter. Exhibited RSA 1933, local scenery and Fife coastal scenes, then in 1983 (2) and 1987; also GI(11), from 7 Huntershill Road, Bishopbriggs.

**CARLYLE, James T** **fl 1968-**
Edinburgh painter; exhibited RSA 1968.

**CARLYLE, R** **fl 1829**
Amateur Edinburgh painter; exhibited RSA(1).

**CARLYLE, Thomas snr** **c1771-c1843**
Miniature painter. Brother of Robert Carlyle (1773-1825). Father was a sculptor who encouraged his son to become interested in art. Possibly had lessons with the only miniaturist in Carlisle, Matthew Wilkinson, for he soon showed an ability for this branch of painting. After working as a pattern drawer for a Carlisle firm, moved to Edinburgh where he quickly established a reputation. Exhibited 32 portrait miniatures at the Carlisle Academy between 1823 and 1828, also at the RSA, Dumfries and Liverpool, where he eventually settled.

**CARMICHAEL, C** **18th century**
Painter of figurative subjects. Said to have been a pupil of Alexander Runciman(qv). A pen drawing of a hermit, after Salvator Rosa, is in the NGS.

**CARMICHAEL, Charles** **fl 1865**
Edinburgh painter in oil; seascapes. Exhibited once at the RSA.

**CARMICHAEL, David** **fl 1912**
Amateur Paisley artist. Exhibited an autumn landscape at the GI from 34 Causewayside.

**CARMICHAEL, Lady Gibson (Miss Mary Helen Elizabeth Nugent)** **fl 1901-1904**
Silversmith and enamellist. Whilst in Balerno, Italy 1901 had an enamel casket accepted for the RSA followed three years later by two further enamelled caskets each mounted on copper-gilt.

**CARMICHAEL, Miss Helen B** **fl 1846-1866**
Edinburgh painter in oil and watercolour; landscapes. Exhibited RSA 1846-1865 including a sketch of the Bass Rock and a study of Blackness Castle.

**CARMICHAEL, James F** **fl 1833-1853**
Edinburgh based painter in oil and watercolour of coastal and local scenes, also figurative and mystical subjects. Some of his work had similar subjects eg 'A light breeze off the Bass Rock' (1841) to those of the English marine artist John Wilson Carmichael who was exhibiting at the RSA at the same time. Taught drawing in Edinburgh. Exhibited RSA(55) between the above years from a variety of Edinburgh addresses.

**CARMICHAEL, Rodick** **1931-**
Born Edinburgh. Author and painter in oil. Studied at Edinburgh College of Art 1948-53 and at British School, Rome 1956-57. Awarded Chalmers Bursary 1958. Visited Salzburg and Vienna 1960. Has held various one man exhibitions, mostly in Edinburgh. Themes are concerned with 'identity, the detachment of individuals and time-warped events'. Included in Four Young Scottish Painters' Exhibition, 1960. Author of *Common Factors/Vulgar Fractions,* with J Nuttal, (1980), *The Iconic Language of Painting* (1981), *Orienteering, Painting in the Landscape* with Makin & Wellesley, (1982), *Arts and Actuality* (1984), *Artisan & High Technology* (1985). Exhibited RSA from 1963. Represented in Glasgow AG.
**Bibl:** SAC, 'Rodick Carmichael; an antipodean decade 1978-1988' (Ex Cat).

**CARMICHAEL, Stewart** **1867-1950**
Born Dundee; died Nov. Painter in oil and watercolour, architect, decorator and engraver, portraits and architectural subjects. Began to train as an architect before becoming a black and white artist with a London publishing firm. In 1888 studied in Antwerp under Verlat before proceeding to Brussels where he studied with Lieven Herremans, thence in Italy. In Belgium he was elected a member of L'Areopage, a Brussels art society. While retaining a studio in Edinburgh, he visited the Continent frequently. In 1926 went to Lithuania where he executed many fine studies of local folk and architecture. Returned to Dundee 1890 and began to concentrate upon mystical and romantic Scottish historical subjects. These were more successful than his Belgian landscapes. An associate of Nellie Baxter(qv), John Duncan(qv), Alec Grieve(qv) and George Dutch Davidson(qv), like them he exhibited regularly at the Dundee Graphic Arts Association. Member, SSA and founder member of Dundee Art Society and part of the artistic circle working in Dundee in the 1890s which included John Duncan(qv), George Dutch Davidson(qv) and David Foggie(qv). Served on the Fine Arts Committee of Dundee Galleries and was for fourteen years Governor of the Institute of Art and Technology, Dundee. Exhibited widely in Paris, Brussels, London, RSA(71), GI(9), AAS 1893-1935 & L(4). A large oil, entitled 'The Model', is represented in Forfar Public Library and lithographs are in Dundee AG, also Glasgow AG, Paisley AG.
**Bibl:** Caw 415; Halsby 197.

**CARMICHAEL-ANSTRUTHER, Lady** **fl 1962**
Exhibited a still life at the RGI.

**CARNDUFF, D McQueen** **fl 1918**
Amateur Paisley artist of 1 Johnston Street; exhibited a winter landscape at the GI.

**CARNEGIE, Lady Agnes** **1790-1875**
Born Kinnaird Castle (Angus), 18 Sep; died 8 Mar. Portrait painter and landscapist. A fine pastel study of her four daughters is in the collection of her kinsman the Earl of Southesk at Kinnaird Castle, Brechin, where there is also a small watercolour of the castle.

**CARNEGIE, Miss M S** **fl 1943**
Amateur Perth artist; exhibited RSA.

**CAROLAN, Eugene** **fl 1937-d1990**
Edinburgh artist. Taught for a period at Edinburgh College of Art. Exhibited regularly at the RSA between the above dates, such subjects as 'Reverie' (1942), 'Psyche' (1958) and 'Resurrexit' (1963), and a Border landscape at the AAS in 1937.

**CARPENTER, Miss Jane Henrietta** **fl 1847-1857**
Miniature painter. Daughter of Margaret-Sarah Carpenter(qv), by whom she was taught. Exhibited RA(10) during the above dates, specialising in portraits of women and children.

**CARPENTER, Mrs Margaret-Sarah (née Geddes)** **1793-1872**
Born Salisbury; died London, 13 Nov. Painter of portraits, fancy subjects and miniatures in oil, watercolour and crayon. Daughter of Captain Geddes of Edinburgh; another daughter married the artist William Collins RA. Studied portraiture at Lord Radnor's collection in Longford Castle. Went to London 1814 and exhibited at the RA and BI under her maiden name 1814-1817 and as Mrs Carpenter 1819-1866. Married the Keeper of Prints and Drawings at the BM, upon whose death in 1866 Queen Victoria conferred upon her a pension of £100 per annum. Her daughter Jane Henrietta Carpenter(qv) and her son William Carpenter Jnr(qv), were among her pupils. The fact that she worked almost exclusively in London and exhibited only in England has prevented her from receiving the recognition from her native country that her artistic skill and fervour justify. Among her RA exhibits were the 'Archbishop of Canterbury', 'Dr Waagen, Director of the Royal Gallery Pictures in Berlin', the 'Countess of Kintore' and many other notables, both men and women. Awarded the Gold Medal of the Society of Arts. Exhibited altogether 145 pictures at the RA before retiring from full-time art in 1866. Exhibited only twice in Scotland, both at the RSA in 1832, one a portrait of the Duke of Roxburgh.
**Bibl:** Foskett 195; Long.

**CARPENTER, William jnr** **1818-1899**
Born in London of Scottish descent. Portrait and miniature painter. The son of Margaret-Sarah Carpenter(qv). In addition to portraits, among them one of Lady Campbell and another of the Earl of Antrim, he was interested in historical subjects. Pepys wrote of his fine painting in 1848 of Charles II in Holland before the Restoration 'this afternoon Mr Edward Pickering told me in what a sad, poor condition for clothes and money the King was'. The whereabouts of this work is not now known. It is interesting to note, although the reason is not clear, that he ceased to exhibit the same year that his mother retired. In 1855 he travelled with the Punjab Irregular Force to Afghanistan, and sketched extensively in India. Lived in London until 1862, when he went to Boston. Exhibited 25 paintings at the RA 1840-1866. An exhibition of his Indian work was held at South Kensington, 1881. Represented in BM, V & A, Ashmolean Museum, Oxford.

**CARR, Allan Eric John** **1914-fl 1954**
Edinburgh painter in oil; fruit, flowers, domestic genre, rustic scenes and figurative. Exhibited RSA during the above periods, & GI(5).

**CARR, David** **fl 1958-1971**
Edinburgh architect. Exhibited RSA 1958-71, including designs for Seton and Hope houses at Loretto School; also Cramond Primary school (1967-71).
**Bibl:** Gifford 517,548,615,635.

**CARR, Tom** **1912-1977**
Painter of hunting and racing scenes. Although born in Durham, where in early life he worked as a blacksmith at Priestman Collieries. His claim for inclusion here is that his best work was done in the Scottish borders where he lived for a number of years. Due to an injury sustained by an underground fall he was hospitalized and there became aware he could draw and paint. He abandoned colliery work and with the aid of compensation money studied art at King's College, Newcastle-upon-Tyne, being awarded a certificate of Fine Art 1950. Studied drypoint etching under G B Stokes. Specialising in all kinds of hunting scenes, he was patronised by the Dukes of Beaufort and Northumberland. His best work was done in the Braes of Derwent and the Jedforest. Produced limited edition prints of his hunting scenes published by Dickens of London, also illustrated several books including *A Hunting Man's Rambles*, by Stanislaus Lynch. Said to have been a most charming man, full of warmth, humour and common sense, 'a real countryman'. Married with two daughters, he was not prolific and his work is only rarely seen. One of his paintings hangs in Durham Cathedral.
**Bibl:** Mitchell; Wingfield.

**CARRICK, Alexander RSA LBS** **1882-1966**
Born Musselburgh; died Galashiels, 26 Jan. Sculptor; bronze, stone

and marble. Trained as a stone carver under Birnie Rhind(qv) in Edinburgh before proceeding to Edinburgh College of Art and RCA, London. Before WW1 he carved and modelled in stone, and between 1918 and 1942, when he left for the Borders, he taught at Edinburgh College of Art, succeeding Portsmouth as head of the sculpture department. Received frequent commissions for work on buildings bringing him into close contact with architecture, steadily increasing his awareness of the relationship between sculptor and building. Monumental commissions during the inter-war years included the Animal Wall extensions of 1923 at Cardiff Castle for the 4th Marquis of Bute, War Memorials at Ayr, Berwick upon Tweed, Dornoch, Forres, Fraserburgh and Killin, the carved exterior figures of 'Justice' and 'Courage' and interior bronze reliefs to the Royal Artillery and the Royal Engineers, 1924-1927, for the Scottish National War Memorial, the Wallace Statue 1928 for Edinburgh Castle, the 1932 figurative relief of 'Geology' for the University of Edinburgh, an exterior carved stone relief of 'Christ and the Woman of Samaria at the Well' in 1934 for the Cloister of the Reid Memorial Church, Edinburgh, the carved pediment of 1936 for the Sheriff courthouse, Edinburgh, the carving of Reid Dick's designs for St Andrew's House, Edinburgh 1936, and two bronze figures - 'Safety' and 'Security' for an insurance company in St Andrew's Square, Edinburgh. Carrick was an inspiring teacher of a generation of Scots sculptors including Mary Boyd, Elisabeth Dempster, Murray McCheyne, George Mancini and Hew Lorimer. Elected ARSA 1918, RSA 1929. Exhibited regularly RA(6), RSA(46), GI(18) & AAS. Represented in City of Edinburgh collection, permanent collection of RSA.
**Bibl:** Gifford 90,100-1,188,441,485,487,524,536; Glasgow Herald, Obit, 28 Jan 1966; Hartley 121; Macmillan [SA], 331,352; Peter Savage, Lorimer and the Edinburgh Craft Designers, Edinburgh 1980, 149,150,163; Studio, lxxxviii, 379, Oct 1924, 224.

**CARRICK, Anne M (Mrs R M Scott)** **1919-**
Born Edinburgh. Daughter of the sculptor Alexander C(qv). Studied Edinburgh College of Art and London Central School of Art under Janetta Cochrane. Painter of genre, flower pieces and still life, also occasional landscape; theatrical designer. Worked at theatres in Rugby, Northampton, Perth and Edinburgh. Settled in Melrose 1947. Exhibited RSA irregularly between 1955 and 1967; also GI(11), from The Pendstead, Melrose. Represented in City of Edinburgh collection by a dressed wire sculpture of 'A Highland Chieftain'.

**CARRICK, John** **1819-1890**
Born Denny, Stirlingshire. Architect. Articled to John Bryce(qv) 1831. Draughtsman with **John HERBERTSON**, spent some time in England before returning to Glasgow 1839, entering into partnership with **James BROWN** (d 1878) 1839-54. Worked mainly in the west end of Glasgow. Appointed Superintendent of Streets 1844 (precursor of the Master of Works and City Architect).
**Bibl:** A Gomme & D Walker, Architecture of Glasgow, London 1987(rev), 88,173n,289-290.

**CARRICK, John Mulcaster** **fl 1854-1878**
Landscape painter, sometimes with fishing scenes; illustrator. Brother of Robert C(qv). Illustrated Charles MacKay's *The Home Affections* (1858).
**Bibl:** Wingfield.

**CARRICK, Robert RI ROI** **1829-1904**
Born West of Scotland. Painter in oil and watercolour; genre and landscape. Brother of John Mulcaster C(qv). Details of his training are unclear, but in the 1840s he moved to London and began to exhibit RA almost immediately. 'Thoughts of the Future' (1857) and 'Weary Life' (1858), were much admired by John Ruskin(qv). He painted rather in the manner of the pre-Raphaelites. His landscape 'In The Highlands' was engraved by E Brandard and featured in the *AJ* of 1869 (p302). 'A boldness of treatment lending force and vigour of touch and handling in harmony with itself. The foreground and middle ground are equally clear, a hard light emphasises the contrast between the shaft of sunlight overhead and the distant storm, while the human touch is added by the cowherd, his dog and the Highland cattle'. Elected ANWS 1848, NWS 1850, ARI 1848, RI 1850, ROI 1883. Exhibited RA 1853-1880; also ROI(19), RI(37) & L(2). Represented in Manchester City AG. Not to be confused with the Glasgow painter of the same name.
**Bibl:** AJ 1859, 162, 1869, 302; Halsby 82,253; McKay 359; Ruskin, Acad Notes 1857-8.

**CARRICK, Robert** **fl 1845-1885**
Glasgow artist who worked in the same lithographic studio as William 'Crimean' Simpson(qv) and painted in a similar style. Lithographed two drawings of Edinburgh by David Roberts(qv) which later appeared in Lawson's *Scotland Delineated.* Specialised in minor watercolours of Glasgow and its environs. Not to be confused with the landscape painter, Robert Carrick(qv). Exhibited an engraving at the GI. Represented in Glasgow AG, City of Edinburgh collection.
**Bibl:** Butchart 58.

**CARRICK, William** **1827-1878**
Born Edinburgh, Dec 31; died St Petersburg, Nov. Photographer and watercolourist. Migrated to Russia as a baby with his parents 1828, his father having a timber business there. Studied architecture and drawing at St Petersburg Academy of Arts 1844-53. Preferred drawing portraits to architecture. Visited Rome 1853-6 associating with the artistic community and painting architectural and landscape subjects. On returning to Russia he found the family business faltering and turned to photography, studying with James Good Tunny in Edinburgh 1857-8. Back in St Petersburg, opened a studio at 19 Malaya Morskaya in partnership with John MacGregor(qv). Through the appreciation of Tsar Alexander IIs son Nicholas, they collaborated with the Court watercolourist Mihaly Zichy(qv). His renown is based on depicting Russian rural peasantry at work, an approach most probably influenced by his militant, feminist, Nihilist wife Markelova whom he adored. 'Carrick brought to his subjects a view of the world characterised by humour and affection. Direct polemic is absent, and instead of general issues, the particular and the individual claim his interest' [Lawson]. A successful exhibition of his work was held in London 1878 and at the SNPG 1987.
**Bibl:** Felicity Ashbee & Julie Lawson, William Carrick, (Scottish Masters series), Edinburgh, 1987.

**CARRICK, William Arthur Laurie** **1879-1964**
Born Glasgow, 6 Jne. Painter in oil and watercolour; landscape and coastal scenes. Served apprenticeship under Sir J J Burnett(qv) and practised architecture in Glasgow for several years before giving it up for health reasons. He then turned to painting in watercolour. Particularly enjoyed coastal and beach scenes which he executed in an unrestrained and sometimes convincing manner. Lived for a time in Lanarkshire then Lancashire before settling in Findhorn, nr Forres, 1937 and finally retiring to Ardgowan, Kingussie, Inverness-shire. Exhibited RSA(10), RSW(13), GI(89), AAS(1) & L(9). Represented in Glasgow AG.
**Bibl:** Halsby 253.

**CARRICK-ANDERSON, Helen M** **1909-**
Born 16 May. Painter in oil and watercolour; landscape and 'humanity'. Graduated at Glasgow University in 1930. Trained as a mature student Glasgow School of Art 1947-49 where she was much influenced by James Robertson(qv) and greatly encouraged by William(qv) and Mary Armour(qv). Most enjoyed portraying Scottish landscapes with figures. President, Glasgow Society of Women Artists in its centenary year. Exhibited regularly RSA (since 1966), GI (since 1963), RSW & Paisley Art Institute.

**CARRUTHERS, A** **fl 1718**
Edinburgh engraver. His name appears on the list of subscribers to Nisbet's *Essay on...Armories,* 1718 where he is listed as 'A. Carruders'.
**Bibl:** Bushnell.

**CARRUTHERS, Frank J C** **fl 1890-1896**
Dumfries architect. In 1896 exhibited a design for Milkbank House, Dumfries-shire at the RA and in 1890 a design for the new Town Hall, Lockerbie at the RSA from 25 Buccleuch St.

**CARRUTHERS, Mrs J R** **fl 1896**
Amateur artist of View Park, Partick, Glasgow; exhibited a woodland scene at GI.

**CARRUTHERS, James** **fl 1909-1911**
Glasgow artist in oil of figure compositions and still life. Exhibited GI(2) & L(1) from 42 Sinclair Drive.

**CARRUTHERS, The Hon Mrs Mary** **1878-**
Landscape and flower painter. Moved to Berner Hall, King's Lynn, Norfolk upon her marriage but continued to exhibit in Scotland at the RSA in 1940 (3) and 1950-52, & RBA(1).

**CARRUTHERS, Stephen James** **fl 1986**
Exhibited 'Dancing Figure' at the GI from 16 Gibson Street, Glasgow.

**CARRUTHERS, Victoria M** **fl 1892-1894**
Lanarkshire painter in oil and watercolour of 82 Langside Road, Crosshill; exhibited GI(2).

**CARRUTHERS, William Laidlaw** **?-1914**
Architect. Designed St Stephens, Inverness (1895). According to Gifford, Carruthers 'gave Inverness the best array of Arts and Crafts suburban villas in Scotland'. He added a Queen Anne porch to Cluny Castle (1891) and a 'pompous' balustraded porch to Balavil House (1899). Perhaps his best legacy is the Inverness house he designed for himself in Annfield Rd, Lethington (1892). Formed a partnership in late career with Ballantyne, Cox & Taylor.

**CARSE, Alexander** **c1770-1843**
Born and died Edinburgh. Painter in oil of genre and country life. Called 'Old Carse', he was a pupil of David Allan(qv), and had been employed by him to copy drawings which Allan later touched up. Allan's influence remained strong in his work which falls some way between that artist and Sir David Wilkie(qv). Entered the Trustees Academy 1806 and two years later contributed five genre scenes to the first exhibition of the same year. Several were selected for favourable comment by the *Scots Magazine* with whom Carse later collaborated in preparing illustrations. His 'Arrival of the Country Relations' was exhibited in Edinburgh in 1812, and later that year the artist moved to London showing the 'Itinerant Preacher' at the RA. He continued to exhibit there and at the BI until 1820, when he returned to Scotland, thereafter exhibiting in Edinburgh until 1837. Much of his work suffered from a darkness of tone and heaviness of touch. Executed many sketches of domestic life in Scotland with a frequent introduction of humour, reminiscent of Geikie(qv). In *Memorials,* Cockburn wrote 'some pretended to call him the Tenniers of Scotland...But though he certainly had humour, I doubt if he would ever have got the better of the coarseness and bad training, both in colour and drawing'. A large sketch of Edinburgh from the South-east was engraved by Robert Scott(qv). Allan Cunningham believes that the tone of Wilkie's earlier pictures was taken from those of Carse and, as Caw points out 'if this is so, it can be traced in the 'Blind Fiddler' rather than in 'Pitlessie Fair''. Where Wilkie would have chosen the more subtle humour of the situation, Carse 'seized at its broadest grin, and forced expression until it became caricature. His pictures raise immediate laughter, but leave no ripple of merriment behind: you never recur to them in memory. Yet honestly observed and full of character they are racy and realistic and completely free from the pseudo-pastoral flavour which detract from David Allan's more original work. And while he was not much of a craftsman, he handled paint with some vigour and gusto. Artistically the best quality in his pictures is their tone, which is wonderfully free from the prevalent brown, and now and then he attained considerable unity in virtue of the rather atmospheric, if too cold, greenish-grey of his choice'. Elected Artist Associate of the Royal Institution 1831. Represented in NGS, SNPG, Glasgow AG, City of Edinburgh collection.
**Bibl:** Armstrong 20; Brydall 267-8; Butchart 35-6,43; Caw 106; Lindsay Errington, Alexander Carse NGS, 1987; Halsby 59-60,61; Irwin 190-1 et passim; McKay 141; Macmillan [SA], 141,165,179-80,183,189.

**CARSE, James Howe** **c1819-1900**
Painter. Almost certainly the son of Alexander Carse(qv), he painted similar subjects in an inferior manner. There is evidence that he did some work in Scotland prior to moving to London 1860. Exhibited twice in London between 1860 and 1862 before emigrating to Australia in the mid-1860s.

**CARSE, W Crichton** **fl 1871-1873**
Amateur Edinburgh landscape painter in oil; exhibited at the RSA 'Coast scene, Prestonpans' (1871) and 'Old bridge at Duntocher' (1873), from 1 Sciennes Hill Pl.

**CARSE, William** **c1800-1845**
Painter in oil; domestic subjects, genre, cattle pieces, narrative subjects; also copies of Wilkie 'The letter of introduction' (1832) and 'The cottar's Saturday night' (1831 & 1845). Probably son of Alexander Carse(qv). There is reason to believe that he spent a part of his life in Edinburgh - during the 1830s and 1840s he exhibited from the same address as Alexander C(qv), but his biographical details remain vague. Exhibited four times at the RA from a London address between 1820 and 1829 and at the RSA 1820-1831, three of his works were shown posthumously at the RSA in 1880 and 1882. His 'Tam O'Shanter' is in Edinburgh City collection.
**Bibl:** Caw 106.

**CARSEWELL, James** **fl 1863**
Painter in oil and watercolour of continental and Highland landscape. Exhibited 9 works at the GI, all in the same year, from Cove, Lochlong, by Greenock.

**CARSLAW, Evelyn J L (née Workman)** **1881-1968**
Born Glasgow. Landscape painter in oil, watercolour and pencil. Studied at Glasgow School of Art and in Paris, travelling extensively on the Continent painting many views in Holland, Italy and Spain. Her husband, a Glasgow surgeon, was a keen yachtsman and she illustrated his book *Leaves from Rowan's Logs* 1944, being an account of a cruise around the north-west coast of Scotland. Close friend of Norah Gray(qv). Exhibited GI(8) from 4 Loch Drive, Helensburgh.
**Bibl:** Halsby 253.

**CARSON, Thomas Ogilvie** **1888-1948**
Born Stirling May 31; died Glasgow. Landscape painter in oils and watercolour, especially fond of the southern Highlands. Exhibited a landscape at the GI from 34 Albert Place, Stirling.

**CARSON, William M** **fl 1884-1895**
Glasgow artist in oil and watercolour of domestic genre, figurative works and landscape. Exhibited GI(18) & L(1), from 128 Hope Street.

**CARSTAIRS, A L** **fl 1866-1870**
Amateur Edinburgh landscapist in oil. Father of Elizabeth Carstairs(qv). Exhibited RSA in 1866 and 1869.

**CARSTAIRS, Miss Elizabeth L** **fl 1870s**
Amateur Edinburgh oil painter of still life. Daughter of A L C(qv). Exhibited RSA 1873.

**CARSTAIRS, J L** **fl 1926**
Amateur Glasgow artist; exhibited a landscape drawing at the GI from 20 Lansdowne Crescent.

**CARSWELL, Mary F** **fl 1882-1885**
Amateur Glasgow painter in oil; flowers and figures. Exhibited RSA(3) 1883-1885, & GI(1), from 61 Sardinia Place.

**CARTER, Charles** **fl 1833-1834**
Portrait painter who exhibited at the RSA in 1833 (2) and 1834 (2).

**CARTER, Christopher ARIBA ARIAS** **1926-**
Born Wimbledon, 10 Mar. Architect and watercolourist. Educated at George Watson's College, Edinburgh and Edinburgh College of Art where he became much influenced by the work of William Gillies(qv). Prefers landscape in which natural topographical lines predominate over individual natural features. Husband of Susan Carter(qv). Began serious painting as a hobby 1972. Founder member of the Scottish Society of Architect Artists (SSAA). Retired 1992. Exhibits RSA, RSW, RIAS, RIBA. Lives in Tyninghams, East Lothian.

**CARTER, Christopher** **1944-**
Edinburgh painter of landscape, foreign as well as Scottish. Exhibited 15 works at the RSA between 1973 and 1986 including views in Orkney, Spain and the Middle East.

**CARTER, D Broadfoot** **fl 1904-1910**
Glasgow painter, designer and illustrator in oil and pencil. Studied

Glasgow School of Art and Paris. Settled in London as a professional lithographer. Exhibited GI(5) from 136 Wellington Street.

**CARTER, Capt F M** **fl 1850s**
Amateur Edinburgh painter. Exhibited a picture of 'Elcho' and 'Kinfauns Castles' at the RSA in 1851.

**CARTER, Lieutenant J** **fl 1839**
Amateur painter in oil; served in the Royal Regiment. Exhibited four landscapes at the RSA in 1839.

**CARTER, Pam** **c1960-**
Born in Tanzania. Painter of landscapes in oils. Scottish father, Austrian mother. Arrived in Scotland aged 13. Strong broad sweeps of subtle colour give her landscapes an unusual serenity. Prints of her work are popular. Exhibits RGI.

**CARTER, Susan** **1925-1993**
Painter in watercolour and pastel, mainly animals and birds. Trained as an architect at Edinburgh College of Art. Wife of Christopher(qv). Exhibited RSA(2) 1986.

**CARTER, William Allan** **fl 1868-1892**
Edinburgh architect and painter in oil and watercolour; landscapes. Exhibited 10 works at the RSA including 'Neidpath Castle' and 'Loch Lubnaig', both in 1887. Represented in Paisley AG.

**CARTWRIGHT, John** **fl 1940s**
Amateur Edinburgh painter. Exhibited a landscape at the RSA in 1944.

**CARUS-WILSON, C D** **fl 1925-1927**
Edinburgh architect. In 1925 exhibited at the RSA a design for the Bank of Chile in Valparaiso; also a competitive design for a new Dundee War Memorial and Anglo-South American Bank in Santiago, Chile. In 1927 exhibited his design for a new cenotaph for the City of Sheffield.

**CASSELS, Jonathan** **1965-**
Born Glasgow, 22 May. Printmaker. Studied Glasgow School of Art 1987-91, specialising in printmaking. As a student exhibited regularly with the Glasgow Print Studio & RSA. Lives in Glasgow.

**CASSEL(L)S, William** **fl 1893**
Amateur Glasgow watercolour artist. Exhibited a landscape of Arran at the RA in 1893, also RSW(1) and 'Loch Ranza' at the GI from Belleview Villa, Bishopbriggs.

**CASSIDY, Victoria** **1965-**
Born Glasgow. Watercolour artist and silkscreen printmaker. Studied Glasgow School of Art 1983-87. In 1987 received the Friends of the RSA Purchase Prize, and awards at the GSA and SSA. Her drawings and prints mimic the mottled surface and delicate deckle edge of handmade paper, 'her new works masquerade as time worn fragments of ornate gilded images'. First solo exhibition 1989. Recently engaged in producing a livre d'artiste of nine lithographic images on paper made by herself. Her work included in 1990 exhibition 'Five Girls from Glasgow' as part of the Glasgow Festival year. Exhibited RSA 1990 & GI(4) 1986-1987, from 96 Farmington Avenue.

**CASSIE, James RSA RSW** **1819-1879**
Born Keith Hall, Inverurie; died Edinburgh, 11 May. Painter in oil and watercolour; landscape and coastal scenes; also occasional portraits. Eldest son of a tea and spirit merchant. In the late 1820s, when still very young, moved with his family into Aberdeen. Shortly afterwards he was seriously injured in a street accident, the injuries disabling him for the rest of his life. Although largely self-taught, he did receive some instruction from James Giles(qv). Began earning his living as an artist by painting animals and portraits. In the 1860s he turned increasingly to seascapes and coastal scenes, especially at dawn and sunset. He was always outside the mainstream of academic painting. As a man he was enormously popular, renowned for his wit. His first exhibit at the RA in 1854 'On the Road to the Linn of Dee - Braemar, Aberdeenshire' was succeeded by 21 further works shown almost annually until 1879. At the RSA he exhibited with similar regularity from 1840 until the year of his death. Fond of bright creamy colours, he painted in both oil and watercolour with clearly delineated detail. His oil paintings tended to be large and his watercolours small, the latter often being signed with a monogram and in sombre tones which sometimes render them hard to identify. McKay spoke of his 'dainty but somewhat soft and mellowed brushwork'. The aims of Roeloff and Mollinger in Holland are discernible, though he always remained comparatively subdued and sympathetic in his treatment. His reputation suffered comparative neglect until a retrospective exhibition at Aberdeen AG in 1979 helped to reinstate his deserved position as an important artist. He was not himself a sailor, and the coastal scenery is generally viewed from the land with as much attention to the coastline as to the sea itself. 'Dumbarton Castle at Sunset' (1874) was very favourably received at the RSA. Ranks beside Joseph Farquharson(qv) and James Giles(qv) as arguably the three finest portrayers of the Deeside landscape. Elected ARSA 1869, the year he moved to Edinburgh, RSW 1878, RSA 1879. Exhibited RA(21) 1854-1879, RSA (195) 1840-1880, RSW & GI(54). Represented in NGS(5), Aberdeen AG.
**Bibl:** Aberdeen AG (Ex Cat 1979); Armstrong 62; Brydall 381-2; Caw 324; Halsby 87-8; Hardie 26; McKay 316-7.

**CASSIE, Ma(r)y (Mrs Charles Blakeman)** **fl 1940-1942**
Portrait sculptress; exhibited RSA 1940-42 from 29 George Street, Edinburgh.

**CASTELLANETA, Miss Erica** **fl 1896-1902**
Edinburgh artist; exhibited RSA(1), GI(1) & L(5).

**CATCHPOLE, Neil M** **1904-1994**
Born Glasgow, Aug 15; died Dundee, July. Painter in oils, watercolour and acrylic; also stained glass and mural decoration; teacher. Friend and contemporary of James McIntosh Patrick(qv) and James Reville(qv). Before entering Glasgow School of Art 1923, he had won bronze, silver and gold medals at Kelvingrove Art Gallery's annual competitions 1918-21. He then completed teacher training at Jordanhill College, becoming Principal Art Teacher, Greenock HS. Moved to Dundee 1944 as Principal Lecturer in Arts & Crafts, Dundee College of Education. After retirement in 1970 he devoted himself full-time to painting, remaining an influential and highly respected figure in the artistic life of Dundee. Exhibited RGI(17). Represented in Dundee AG.
**Bibl:** Neil Catchpole and Friends, ex cat McManus Galleries, Dundee, 1994.

**CATHRO, George S** **fl 1929**
Amateur Montrose painter in oil of figure studies and landscape. Exhibited AAS(2) from 12 Panmure Place.

**CATTANACH, Alexander** **c1857-1928**
Architect, based at Kingussie. Responsible for many of the larger buildings in Strathspey. These include the Duke of Gordon Hotel, Kingussie (1906), Kincraig United Free Church, now Badenoch Christian Centre (1909), the 'ambitious but unloveable' UF Church Kingussie (1908-09) and the village Post Office (1909), various buildings in Newtonmore including Craigmhor Hotel (1909), the Hall (1912-13) and the Primary School (1910).
**Bibl:** Gifford, H & I, 69,80,89-92,96.

**CATTERNS, Edward R** **fl 1871-1907**
Glasgow painter in oil and watercolour; portraits, figurative and landscape. Exhibited a portrait of the 'Very Rev Marshall Lang, Principal of Aberdeen University', at the RA in 1904 and regular exhibitor RSA 1871-1896, including two studies of Loch Maree and one of a croft on Arran. Also exhibited RSW(1), GI(43) & L(1).

**CATTRELL, Annie** **c1960-**
Glasgow painter. One of a wave of promising young women painters absorbed with the human figure. Exhibited at the Edinburgh Festival 1987.
**Bibl:** Hardie 215.

**CAUNTER, Robert** **fl 1846-1868**
Edinburgh painter in oil and chalk; landscape, genre still life and literary subjects. Visited Amalfi and Naples in 1847. Exhibited once at the RA and at least 14 works at the RSA.

**CAVE, Joseph** **fl 1718-d1756**
Edinburgh engraver. Engraver to the Scottish Mint. Designed the monument to William Carstaires (d1727) on the W wall of Greyfriars churchyard. In Nisbet's *Essay on...Armories,* 1718, he is described as 'His Majesty's Engraver'. Possibly the **Joseph CAVIE** who had a child buried 26 May 1660 in Greyfriars, Edinburgh.
**Bibl:** Apted 32; Gifford 160; Register of Interments in the Greyfriards Burying Ground, Edinburgh, 1656-1700, ed H. Paton, Scot. Rec. Soc. 1902.

**CAW, James** **fl 1839-1884**
Edinburgh based painter in oil; portraits and landscape. Exhibited regularly RSA 1839-1884, often portraits but also some Scottish scenes. Represented in Paisley AG.

**CAW, Sir James Lewis HRSA** **1864-1950**
Born Ayr; died Lasswade, Midlothian. Painter in oil and watercolour; children, portraits, landscapes and figurative. Also painted landscapes in pastel and watercolour, often coastal subjects. Trained Glasgow School of Art, in Edinburgh and also abroad. Published *Scottish Painting Past and Present* 1908, the most comprehensive work on Scottish art published up to that time, also other studies of Scottish artists including the biography of his father-in-law, William MacTaggart, and *Scottish Portraits,* 1903. Curator, SNPG 1895-1907, Director, National Galleries of Scotland 1907-1930. Responsible for arranging important exhibition of Scottish art at the Royal Academy 1939. Exhibited RSA(29) from 1887; also RSW(3) & GI(24). Represented NGS(7).
**Bibl:** Halsby 253.

**CAWOOD, Charles J** **fl 1902**
Amateur Edinburgh landscape painter in oil. Exhibited AAS(1) from 4 Oxford Street.

**CAY, Isabella** **fl 1883-1913**
Painter in oil and watercolour; figures and portraits. Travelled a great deal, exhibiting RA(1), RSA(9), GI(3) & L(4), in 1883 from an Edinburgh address, in 1905 from Paris and in 1913 from Venice.

**CAY, William Dyce** **fl 1885-1887**
Amateur Edinburgh painter in watercolour; landscape. Exhibited a drawing 'South Breakwater Works, Aberdeen' at the RSA in 1887, three other works previously, and once at the AAS in 1886.

**CAYZER, Dora (Mrs S Brownrigg)** **1923-**
Amateur Angus artist. Daughter of Sir James Cayzer of Kinpurnie. Exhibited RSA(1) 1941.

**CELTIC REVIVAL**
Refers to an apparently spontaneous re-emergence of Celtic inspired art forms and images that appeared in Glasgow in the work of Frances Macdonald(qv), Margaret Macdonald(qv), Charles Rennie Mackintosh(qv) and Herbert MacNair(qv). In the east, Dundee was the centre, for a number of artists illustrated Sir Patrick Geddes's *The Evergreen*(qv) using Celtic mannerisms, a development pursued by Stewart Carmichael and David Foggie(qv) in their drawings for Thomas Foulis's occasional journal *The Blue Blanket.*
**Bibl:** Timothy Neat, Part Seen, Part Imagined: Meaning and Symbolism in the Work of Charles Rennie Mackintosh and Margaret Macdonald, 1994; The Wind in the Pines: A Celtic Miscellany, TN Foulis, 1925.

**CEMENTARIUS, Richard** **13th century; d c1294**
Aberdonian master mason and burgess. Something of a mystery figure, reputedly the first provost of Aberdeen and builder of the Castle of Drum. Evidence for Aberdeen's early aldermen is often dubious, being dependent upon secondary sources. However, a charter of 1294 recorded in the *Registrum Epicopatus Aberdonensis* refers to the foundation in 1277 of the altar of S John the Evangelist and Apostle within the church of St Nicholas by "magister Ricardus cementarius quondam burgensis de Aberden". Another contemporary reference in the *Exchequer Rolls* return for Aberdeen 1264 again refers, in the context of work being carried out on Aberdeen's castle, to "Magistro Ri. cementario".
**Bibl:** Siobhan Convey (Aberdeen City archivist), *personal correspondence*

**CENTER, Edward Kenneth** **1903-**
Born Aberdeen, 24 Jly. Painter in oil; landscape, portrait and figure painter. Studied at Gray's School of Art, Aberdeen and Allan Fraser Art College, Arbroath. Lived in Aberdeen, retired to Sussex. Assistant to Sir Frank Brangwyn. Exhibited ROI(2) and regularly at the AAS 1919-1935.

**THE CENTRE** **1941-1942**
Founded by the bibliophile David Archer in Glasgow, it combined a gallery, bookshop and coffee room. Many members of the New Art Club joined The Centre in an endeavour to replicate an Institute of Contemporary Arts. Artist members included Adler(qv), Benjamin Creme(qv) - who assumed its management - William Crosbie(qv), Taylor Elder(qv) and Herman(qv). Its premises were taken over by the Unity Theatre and shortly afterwards the New Scottish Group(qv) came into existence.
**Bibl:** Dennis Farr, 'New Painting in Scotland' SAC (Ex Cat 1968); Hardie 168-9.

**CERFOLA, -** **fl 1891-1892**
A painter of this name exhibited at the RSA(2) through an Edinburgh agent (Nelson of 19 Hanover Street).

**CHALK, Timothy** **fl 1974**
Edinburgh painter of figurative and flower studies. Specialises in public art displays with Paul Grime under the title 'Chalk and Grime'. Exhibited GI(2) from 7 Belmont Crescent.

**CHALMER, Alexander** **fl 1506-1532**
Herald and ship painter. Decorator to King James IV in which capacity he worked on the Royal Castles of Stirling and Falkland. In 1506 he was commissioned to paint part of the King's Ship and in 1507 was paid by the Lord Treasurer for work in connection with the Tournament of the Black Lady. This included painting 'pieces of canvas with wooden wings...and for the battering of the best hedis for the feild...for making the said bestis and for making his part of cote armouris and banaris'. In 1511-1513 he was painting ships, notably the *Great Michael* and also for the *James and Margret.* In 1515 a service was held in St Giles to commemorate the death of James IV for which Chalmer was commissioned to paint the Arms. In 1532 he was employed at Holyrood with Sir John Kilgour(qv).
**Bibl:** Apted 32-34; Armstrong 3; Brydall 53; Glamis Book of Records (SHS); Macmillan [SA], 30-31,48.

**CHALMERS, Mrs Charles** **fl 1914**
Amateur Bathgate painter; exhibited 'The Oboe' at the RSA 1914.

**CHALMERS, Lady Elizabeth (née Graham)** **fl 1894-1945**
Edinburgh painter of flowers and portraits. Exhibited RSA 1904, 1907(2), 1924 and 1945, also SWA(3), RBA(1) & L(2).

**CHALMERS, Miss Evelyn Caroline** **fl 1909-1936**
Brechin artist of Aldbar Castle. Flowers, still life and portraits. Moved to Montrose c1929. Exhibited RA(3), RSA(7) 1917-1936; also AAS & London Salon, (6), latterly from Munross House, Montrose.

**CHALMERS, George** **fl 1880-1881**
Glasgow painter. Exhibited twice at the RSA from 25 Hayburn Crescent.

**CHALMERS, Sir George (of Cults)** **c1720-1791**
Born Edinburgh; died London. Son of Roderick Chalmers(qv). 4th Baronet, son of a herald painter to the Lyon Court. Descendant of Jamesone(qv) through the Alexanders. Studied with Allan Ramsay(qv). His earliest known works, all portraits, date from 1738. In 1751 he was in Florence and Minorca, having gone there probably because of his Jacobite sympathies since a Jacobite exile was one of his main patrons. In about 1760 he settled in Edinburgh, assuming the baronetcy about 1764. Married Cosmo Alexander's sister Isabella 1768. Became a successful portrait painter, producing his best works around 1770. For reasons that are unclear in 1778 he went to live in Hull, remaining there until 1781. From 1784 until his death he was in London. His work was praised by Hudson and Batoni. His best although uncharacteristic work was perhaps his portrait 'The Captain of the Honourable Company of Edinburgh Golfers William St Clair of Roslin' (1771). This painting is now in the Hall of the Royal Company

of Archers, Edinburgh. The influence of Ramsay is sometimes discernible as, for example, in 'Anne Kennedy' (1764) now at Blairquhan, Ayrshire. Another portrait can be seen in the Huntly House Museum, Edinburgh. The portraits are competent showing considerable power of characterisation but, in the words of Caw 'err in excessive projection of the features, and while fair in tone, [are] rather hard in handling and negative in colour'. An interesting sideline is afforded by an important article which appeared in the *Weekly Magazine or Edinburgh Amusement,* 16 January 1772, forty years after the elder Scougal's death, reporting the fact that he had a son and discussing aspects of the family. Although not altogether reliable, the document is of considerable historical interest. At Minorca he met General Blakeney whose portrait he painted. Exhibited 24 works at the RA between 1775 and 1790, mostly portraits of gentlemen, especially army officers, but also one or two ladies. In addition to the works mentioned above he is represented in NGS, SNPG(2), City of Edinburgh collection, Drum Castle (NTS), Fyvie Castle (NTS), Victoria (Australia) AG.
**Bibl:** Brydall 171; Bulloch, Life of Jamesone; Caw 17,48; Irwin 73-4(illus); Macmillan [SA], 94.

**CHALMERS, George Paul RSA RSW** **1833-1878**
Born Montrose; died Edinburgh, 28 Feb. Painter in oil and watercolour; domestic genre, portrait and landscape. Son of a captain of a coasting vessel, he was apprenticed to a ship's chandler and in 1853 went to Edinburgh where, aged 20, he enrolled at the Trustees Academy studying under R Scott Lauder(qv) and becoming friendly with his fellow student McTaggart(qv). In his second year won fifth prize and in his third year first prize. In 1857 he returned to Montrose but two years later went back to Edinburgh and a year later, in 1860, exhibited his first picture. In Edinburgh he led a quiet and uneventful life working at his art, interspersed by occasional sketching trips to Ireland, the Continent, Skye and his favourite Glenesk. A visit to Brittany in 1862 with Pettie(qv) and Tom Graham(qv), and a short trip to Paris and the Low Countries in 1874, when he became re-acquainted with Josef Israels whom he had met once before in Aberdeen in 1870, were important events. These were the only visits to mainland Europe that he ever made. His genre paintings and portraits are usually of single figures seated in dimly lit interiors, often placed in strong light and shade reminiscent of Scott Lauder(qv). Friend of the Aberdeen connoisseur and collector, John Forbes Whyte. Whyte was a patron of Bosboom, Mauve, Monninger and especially Israel. Chalmers' acquaintance with these painters almost certainly affected his technique and choice of palette. His portrait of Israels in Aberdeen AG is inscribed 'A notre ami Whyte'. Although always sensitive to colour, it was a long time before he threw off an early looseness. Disinterested in politics and literature and knowing very little history, he was nevertheless a fine and influential artist who has received more attention commensurate with the quality of his work than perhaps any other Scottish painter. Pinnington wrote that for Chalmers 'art was a mysterious problem awaiting solution. He aimed at a perfection beyond human attainment, and spent his life in a dream of beautiful colour and the transformations of light...To him the better part of art resided in colour. His every study is an experiment in analysis. He probes the mystery concealed in light: how it touches a young cheek with the bloom of the peach; turns yellow hair to living gold, and ashen rocks to silver. He seeks the secret in the shady pool, in the mists of the mountain side and Highland valley and in the veiled glories of the Scottish gloaming. He is an alchemist seeking the elixir of light. His aim was always purely artistic, whether his theme were a face, a flower, a landscape, or took him into the undefined field of genre. He stands by himself in a single-hearted devotion of pure art'. The *AJ* of 1894 spoke of him as 'a greater man than Reid'. Being so preoccupied with light and colour, his figures were sometimes weakly drawn but with a soft and mysterious charm. As a man he was warmly, even intensely, loved by his fellows. 'It is difficult for anyone who did not know him personally to understand fully the fascination he seems to have possessed for those who did' and goes on to relate how one of his friends once said 'we could have better spared a better man supposing we had had one' [Caw]. This emphasizes the sadness caused by Chalmers' premature death at the age of 55 in an accident, the probability being that he was murdered. Although his watercolour output was limited, Halsby suggests that he may have used watercolour for preliminary sketches as did his friend McTaggart. Married a miniature painter(qv). Founder member of the RSW in the year of his death. Elected ARSA 1867, RSA 1871, RSW 1878. Exhibited six works at the RA between 1863 and 1876 but principally at the RSA, almost continuously between 1855 and 1879, GI(31) & AAS 1886-1926. A rare watercolour sketch 'The Legend' is in Aberdeen AG. Represented in NGS(10), SNPG(6), including 'Self-portrait', Aberdeen AG, Glasgow AG, Kirkcaldy AG, Paisley AG, Perth AG.
**Bibl:** AJ 1897, 83-8; 1878, 124 (obit); 1880, 39F; 1898, 342; Armstrong 69-72; Brydall 382-4; Caw 244-247; Lindsay Errington, Masterclass: Robert Scott Lauder and his pupils, NGS, 1983; Halsby 118,124,253; Hardie 64-7,74-6; Irwin 344-348; Halsby 124; Macmillan [SA], 231,240-44,263; McKay 358-9; 1872, 192; Edward Pinnington, George Paul Chalmers and the Art of his Times, 1896; Portfolio 1887, 189; The Studio 1907.

**CHALMERS, Mrs George Paul** **fl 1858-1863**
Edinburgh portrait miniaturist. Wife of George Paul Chalmers(qv). Exhibited a portrait miniature at the RSA in 1858 and two further miniatures in 1863 although at this time she was using a different address from her husband. Recorded by neither Foskett nor Long.

**CHALMERS, Hector** **1849-1943**
Died Edinburgh, 1 Apr. Painter in oil and watercolour; landscape, topographical, genre and figurative, also an occasional portrait. Studied at Trustees Academy with McTaggart(qv) and G P Chalmers(qv) also at the RSA School. Mainly a landscape painter. Lived in Edinburgh. Member of the Scottish Arts Club and the Pen and Pencil Club. His work was straightforward and unimaginative but at his best he painted attractive landscapes with figures incorporated harmoniously with their surroundings. Fond of harvest scenes in the Tayside area which have always remained popular. A minor figure but not without interest. Extremely prolific exhibiting 176 works at the RSA in addition to RSW(5), GI(68), RHA(2) & AAS 1893-1931. Represented in Glasgow AG(2), Paisley AG.
**Bibl:** Caw 303; Halsby 253; Scotsman, Obit, 2 April 1943.

**CHALMERS, Hector Louis** **fl 1887-1901**
Amateur Edinburgh watercolour painter of interiors and Eastern scenes. Exhibited Cairo Bazaar at the RSA in 1887 and one other picture the same year. Represented in City of Edinburgh collection.

**CHALMERS, Isabella Margaret** **[see AUBREY, John]**

**CHALMERS, Isabel Maclagan (née Scott)** **1900-?**
Born Glasgow, 9 Sep. Engraver, designer and figure painter. Latterly went to live in Nottingham and was elected an Associate of the Nottingham Society of Artists 1930. Exhibited RSA & GI in the 1920s.

**CHALMERS, Ivan M** **fl 1931**
Minor Aberdeen etcher. Exhibited an etching of King's College at the AAS from 115 Hamilton Place.

**CHALMERS, James** **fl 1885-1913**
Glasgow artist of topographical and architectural drawings. Exhibited GI(9) from 93 Hope Street.

**CHALMERS, Miss Jean(ie) Jamieson** **fl 1876-1890**
Edinburgh oil painter specialising in landscapes, flowers and figures. Exhibited regularly at the RSA(15) between 1876 and 1890 from 19 Union Street, & AAS(1).

**CHALMERS, John** **fl 1856-1933**
Glasgow painter in oil and watercolour; figures, landscape and coastal scenes. Exhibited RSA annually between 1856 and 1859 and then less frequently until 1883; also GI(13), latterly from 22 Eaglesham Street. Possibly the same **John CHALMERS** who was a professional photographer in John St, Hamilton 1881-1933, exhibited Glasgow Art Club 1924 and represented by three works in Hamilton Museum.

**CHALMERS, Miss Mary H** **fl 1881-1882**
Amateur painter in oil; portraits and figures. Exhibited RSA 1881 and again 1882; also RBA(2).

**CHALMERS, Peter MacGregor** **1859-1922**
Scottish architect designer and scholar. Studied under Honeyman(qv). Specialised in Romanesque churches and

restorations, the best known being the choir walls and the base of the tower at Paisley Abbey, a task in which he succeeded Rowand Anderson(qv) in 1911 and was himself succeeded by his cousin Robert Lorimer(qv). Rebuilt the nave of Iona Cathedral. His most original design was the Neptune Building, 470 Argyle St, (1905, demolished 1966). In Edinburgh he designed the Romanesque St Anne's church, Corstorphine; the late Scots Gothic church part of Lady Glenorchy's, Roxburgh Place; the War Memorial chapel within St Cuthbert's Parish church (1921); St Luke's, East Fettes Ave (1907-8); and St Columba's, Queensferry Rd (1903). His studies of architectural history were well received, especially *A Scots Medieval Architect*. Influenced and restricted by an architecturally trained but dominant wife.
**Bibl:** Gifford 43,240-1,276,525,529,572,pl.46; A Gomme & D Walker, Architecture of Glasgow, London 1987(rev), 180,224,290; Peter Savage, Lorimer and the Edinburgh Craft Designers, Edinburgh 1980, 140-1.

**CHALMERS, Robert** **1873-1877**
Argyll painter in oil; coastal and sporting scenes and portraits. Exhibited RSA 1873-1877 & GI(5), from Auchinellan House, Kirn.

**CHALMERS, Roderick** **c1685-1746**
Portrait painter in oil. Son of Charles Chalmers, W.S. In 1701 apprenticed to Henry Fraser and in 1708 became Burgess of the City of Edinburgh. In 1721 he painted 'The Edinburgh Trades', placed over the chimney piece of the hall in St Mary's Chapel, Niddry's Wynd, belonging to the Incorporate Trades (incorporation of St Mary's). In 1724 he was working as a heraldic painter in Edinburgh. A full-length portrait of the freeman of each of the above arts was painted, working in the operative dress of his profession, and was exhibited in the Great Square West Front of Holyrood Palace. It was removed when the Great Hall was pulled down and was purchased in c1780 by the Earl of Buchan. The picture is now in the College of the Incorporate Trades of Edinburgh; a pen and wash drawing of the original is in NGS.
**Bibl:** Brydall 112; Edinburgh Evening Courant, May 26, 1814; Macmillan [SA], 84,85,88,91,92,94.

**CHALMERS, Mrs W H** **fl 1958-1963**
Edinburgh portrait miniaturist. Exhibited RSA.

**CHAMBERLAIN, Dawson J** **fl 1887-1912**
Glasgow watercolour artist, also painted occasionally in oil. Won competition for chapter heading in *The Studio* vol 12, 1898, illus. Exhibited land and seascapes at the RSW(3) & GI(8).

**CHAMBERS, Sir William RA** **1723-1796**
Born Gothenburg; died London, 8 Mar. Scottish architect. Son of John Chambers, a merchant established at Gothenburg, and grandson of Dr Patrick Chambers, Laird of Hazelhead, Aberdeen. His mother was a Scotswoman, Sarah Elphinstone. Sent him to school at Ripon 1728 and at the age of 16 returned to Sweden where he entered the service of the Swedish East India Company, making a voyage in one of the Company ships as a cadet c1740. A second voyage followed in 1743-5 and in 1748-9 he visited Bengal and China. His duties on these trips were not burdensome. He wrote that during the voyages he was able to study 'modern languages, mathematics and the free arts, but chiefly civil architecture, for which I have from my earliest years felt the strongest inclination'. Furthermore, he had been able to visit Scotland, Holland, Flanders and a part of France. While in Canton he made some sketches of Chinese costume and architecture and in 1749 left the company and went to Paris to study architecture under F F Blondel. Toward the end of 1750, having decided to make architecture his profession, he journeyed to Italy and remained there five years. As well as meeting French architects, he befriended Joshua Reynolds and Joseph Wilton the sculptor, and was elected a member of the Florentine Academy. In 1755 his ambitions centered upon England rather than Scotland and he returned there to commence practice. By this time he was married and had two children. Almost at once he had the good fortune to be recommended to Lord Bute as someone who might fill the post of architectural tutor to the Prince of Wales (later George III). Also employed by the Princess Dowager of Wales to landscape the grounds at Kew and to embellish them with a variety of pavilions and temples. These designs were published in 1763 as *Plans, Elevations, Sections and Perspective Views of the Gardens and Buildings at Kew in Surrey.* In 1757 he published his first book *Designs of Chinese Buildings, Furniture, Dresses etc* and in 1759 produced the first part of *A Treatise on Civil Architecture.* By 1760 he was well established in practice and rivalry was forming between him and the other leading architect of the day, fellow Scot Robert Adam(qv). With Adam, he became the second 'Architect of the Works' appointed by the Crown at a salary of £300. In 1769 made Comptroller of the Works and in 1782 the first Surveyor-General and Comptroller. It was in this official capacity that he designed Somerset House and the Royal State Coach, still used for coronations. In 1770 the King allowed him to assume the rank and title of knight on receiving the Order of the Polar Star from the King of Sweden. Subsequently he made designs for the royal castle at Swartso, near Stockholm (1775), one of 19 exhibits at the RA between 1769 and 1777. In 1776 he was elected a member of the Swedish Academy of Sciences; he was also a member of the French Academy of Architecture and an FRS 1776. Exhibited Society of Artists 1761-1768 and in the latter year played a leading role in founding the RA, becoming its first Treasurer. For nearly 30 years he was a dominant figure in the management of the RA, indeed Sir Joshua Reynolds, the President, said that 'Sir William was Viceroy over me'. He published a dissertation on *Oriental Gardening* (1772), a book of which it was said 'its immediate influence was small, it had an important place in the history of picturesque theory, and in some way anticipates the ideas of Payne Knight and Uvedale Price' [Colvin]. Toward the end of his life, he retired from public works and lived in a small house in Norton Street, where he died, being buried in Westminster Abbey. Among his pupils were Thomas Hardwick, Thomas Whetton and John Read. His portrait by Reynolds is in the RA. There is also a marble bust by Westmacott in Sir John Soane's Museum, where a collection of his drawings is housed, including the working drawings for Somerset House. A number of his best drawings are in the V & A while others are in the Fitzwilliam Museum, Cambridge and the Royal Library, Windsor. Four of his letter-books are in the BM. Among the most famous public buildings he designed were Somerset House, London (1776-1786), the Observatory at Old Deer Park, Richmond (c1768), the Town Hall at Woodstock, Oxford for the Duke of Marlborough (1766), altered and enlarged premises in The Strand, London, the stables at Goodwood House, Sussex, the Temple of Diana at Blenheim Palace, and the Queen's Lodge at Windsor for Queen Charlotte (1778-1782; dem 1823). In Scotland he was responsible for only one Scottish mansion, Duddingston, Midlothian (1763-1768), built for the Earl of Abercorn "a most advanced design which exerted a considerable influence throughout Britain and beyond. Essentially a re-interpretation of the Palladian villa in neo-classical terms the house comprised a square two-storeyed block with a temple portico, the omission of the customary basement allowing direct access to the principal floor" [Dunbar]. Also designed two town houses in St Andrew's Square, one of them the home for Laurence Dundas which is now the Royal Bank of Scotland (1771-1772).
**Bibl:** Colvin; Dunbar 113; Gents Mag, lxvi 1796 (i 259) obit; Gifford 18,56-7, 323-5,559,pls.69,116; Mrs H M Martienseen, An Inquiry concerning the Architectural Theory and Practice of Sir William Chambers RA (1951); Pevsner, 'The Other Chambers' Arch Rev, Jne 1947.

**CHAMBERS, William** **fl 1870-1880**
Glasgow sculptor and painter of figure studies and landscape. Exhibited RSA(1) 1872 & GI(4), from 36 Houston Street.

**CHANDLER, J W** **fl 1785-c1805**
Miniature painter. Although not Scottish, being the natural son of Lord Warwick, he spent a considerable amount of his working life in Scotland. Worked in Aberdeenshire in the early 1800s before moving to Edinburgh. He subsequently attempted to commit suicide but died in confinement in 1804 or 1805. Exhibited RA 1787-1791 while residing in London and (in 1791) from Warwick Castle. Several engravings and portraits by this artist can be seen in the BM.
**Bibl:** Graves, RA; Long, 66; Rd.

**CHANLER, Albert** **1880-**
Born Glasgow, 13 May. Painter in watercolour and etcher of architectural subjects. Studied at Glasgow School of Art and Royal Institute, Edinburgh. Worked in Venice, Coventry, Edinburgh and on the Thames. Exhibited RSA(1), RBA(2) & GI(2).

**CHANNING, William** **fl c1848-1860**
Born England; died Leith. He started life as a scene painter at the Theatre Royal, Manchester before moving to Scotland. In Edinburgh it seems he was employed in the same capacity at the Theatre Royal. Sam Bough(qv) was among his pupils and at the end of his life Channing was cared for by his former pupil. There are three volumes of his work, containing 147 watercolour sketches of Edinburgh and district comprising the Cowan Bequest, in the Edinburgh City Library. Dr Savage concluded that 'topographically, they were excellent because the artist was careful in drawing the details which enabled the topographers to identify the buildings'. At Sam Bough's studio sale in 1879 a book of drawings of military and other costumes by Channing sold for 5 guineas.
**Bibl:** Butchart 72-3; Gilpin, Sam Bough RSA, 1905.

**CHAPEL, Miss Helen Kay** **1861-1949**
Died Arbroath, 9 Nov. Painter in oil and watercolour; portraits and landscapes. Sister of Sir Wm Chapel, Provost of Arbroath, sister of Jeannie Chapel(qv). Educated Arbroath HS. Lived at Caenlochan later moving with her two spinster sisters to Westlands, Salisbury Place, Arbroath. Illustrated Adams' *Lunan Water*. A quiet, refined, reserved disposition reflected in her unassuming art. Exhibited RSA 1901-1905 and again in 1921 and 1929.

**CHAPEL, Miss Jeannie K** **fl 1900-1901**
Sister of Helen Chapel(qv). Exhibited twice at the RSA during the above dates.

**CHAPMAN, Agnes T** **fl 1891-1897**
Edinburgh artist, specialising in pencil studies of heads, also flower studies and landscape. Exhibited RSA 1891-1897, & GI(5), from 30 Inverleith Row.

**CHAPMAN, Miss Elizabeth L** **fl 1941**
Painter. Exhibited a portrait at the RSA in 1941.

**CHAPMAN, Laura M** **fl 1878-1890**
Glasgow painter in oil; landscape and flowers. In 1880 moved to Burgh Hill, Hereford. Exhibited RSA 1878-1881 & GI(11).

**CHAPMAN, Vivien K (Mrs Mrszynska)** **fl 1946-1966**
Castle Douglas painter specialising in genre scenes. Exhibited RSA during the above years, & GI(4), latterly from Allanbank, Balmaclellan. An oil painting 'Patchwork' is in Abbot Hall AG (Kendal).

**CHAPMAN, William** **1749-1832**
Architect, specialising in docks and harbours. Designed extensions to Leith piers (1826-30). These developments, including plans for a breakwater to form an outer harbour (1829) resulted in the bankruptcy of Edinburgh City 1833.
**Bibl:** Gifford 460.

**CHAPMAN, William** **fl 1890**
Amateur artist. Exhibited 'Roses' at the GI from Agnew Villa, Helensburgh.

**CHARLES, Miss Catherine L** **fl 1928-1946**
Edinburgh painter of landscape, figure subjects and portraits. Exhibited RSA intermittently between the above dates, also GI(4), L(2) & AAS from the Studio, 45 Frederick Street.

**CHARLES, George Hay** **fl 1906**
Amateur Aberdeen painter of domestic genre. Exhibited AAS(2) from Glenesk House, Grampian Road, Torry.

**CHARLES, Henry W W** **fl 1887-1892**
Amateur Edinburgh painter of townscapes, figure subjects and landscape. Exhibited RSA 1889-1891, scenes in Edinburgh closes, also GI(2) & AAS(3), from 2 Blacket Place.

**CHARLES, William** **?-1820**
Scottish engraver. Worked most of his life in America. Went to New York in 1800, died in Philadelphia.
**Bibl:** Bushnell; Stauffer, American Engr vol i, 45, vol ii, 54.

**CHARLTON, Louise** **1981-**
Born Aberdeen May 4. Printmaker. Trained Gray's School of Art 1999-2003. Fascinated by Scottish and Danish landscapes, and discarded objects. Received Cross Trust travelling scholarship 2003. Exhibits AAS from 16 Lilac Place, Aberdeen.

**CHART, Helga (Mrs Robinson) RSW** **1926-fl 1979**
Edinburgh woodcut artist of landscape and figure subjects. Studied Edinburgh College of Art 1962-1966. Undertook further training in painting & printmaking. Received RSA Stuart Award 1967, RSA City of Edinburgh Award 1985, RSW Council Award 1998. Elected RSW 1994, Vice-President SAAC, 1998. Exhibited RSA intermittently 1968-1986, & RGI(3), latterly from 30 Summerside Place.

**CHART, Mrs Katherine** **1913-1997**
Born North Queensferry. Heraldic painter. Trained Edinburgh College of Art. Worked in embroidery studio of Louisa M Chart(qv) 1935-1940. Became Herald Painter Ordinary, Court of the Lord Lyon 1947; appointed Principal Herald Painter 1959-1971.

**CHART, Miss Louisa M** **1880-1963**
Born Hampton Court. Edinburgh-based embroiderer. Trained at the Royal School of Needlework, London. Founder member, the Embroiderer's Guild 1906; taught at Edinburgh College of Art until 1947 whilst maintaining a studio in George Square, where, assisted by her designer nephew, **John R CHART**, she undertook many private commissions. 'She was an inspiring teacher with a rich sense of colour, and brought not only the professional methods used at the Royal School, but a passionate interest in stitchery' [Swain]. Responsible for the Speaker's Faldstool in the House of Commons, she undertook several important heraldic commissions as well as supervising much restoration of the furnishings at Holyrood and restoring some of Mary Queen of Scots' panels bought for Holyrood 1961. Closely involved with the Needlework Development Scheme in Scotland.
**Bibl:** L M Chart, *Mary Queen of Scots Panels*, Embroidery, vol XII, no 2, Summer 1961, p50; Margaret Swain 147,171-3.

**CHEALE, Mrs M J** **fl 1942**
Amateur painter of flowers in watercolour. Exhibited GI(1) from 38 S Mains Road, Milngavie, Dunbartonshire.

**CHEAPE, Evelyn J** **fl 1958-1964**
Dundee Sculptress. Exhibited portrait heads at the RSA during the above years.

**CHEAPE, Malcolm** **c1963-**
Painter of maritime-related and industrial subject matter. Works in oil and mixed media. Studied Duncan of Jordanstone School of Art 1982-6, followed by postgraduate years studying 1987-9. Recently begun to exhibit at both the RSA & AAS.

**CHESSER, John** **1820-1892**
Edinburgh architect of 1 Chalmers Street. In his capacity as Heriot Trust architect, responsible for designing a number of the later streets in Edinburgh New Town including Glencairn and Eglington Crescents(1872), Douglas and Magdala Crescents (1875-9) together with Coates Gardens (1871-6) and arguably the finest terrace of all and the first with bay windows, Buckingham Terrace (1860); also the memorial to Rev. Robert Nisbet (d1874) on the W wall of the N porch in St Giles, Heriot's School, Davie St (1875). Schools were included in his repertoire among them Regent Road school (now Moray House) (1874), and what Gifford has described as a 'showy baronial country house' Southfield Hospital in Lasswade Rd (1875). Exhibited a design for Heriot Watt College at the RSA.
**Bibl:** Gifford 58,115,182,243,362,371,373-4,377,382,397-9,404, 419,422,439,444,447,475,486,515,599,Pls.72,126; Dunbar 147.

**CHEVERTON, Mrs Lottie (née Ramsden)** **1960-1991**
Born England 16 Jan; died Edinburgh 17 Sep. Painter and teacher. Educated Marlborough College where she was one of the most outstanding pupils of her generation. Won a scholarship to study art at the Slade School in London and whilst there organised a student protest against what she saw as a lack of teaching. 'A naturally expressive draughtswoman and a painter whose richly coloured works, often composed in different mediums, had a grave spiritual

dignity that compelled respect' [Obituary]. Married Mark C(qv) 1982. Settled in Scotland where she taught part-time at Fettes as well as exhibiting nationally. In 1988 she and her husband founded the Leith School of Art(qv). Died tragically in a car accident.
**Bibl:** The Times, Obit, 24 Oct 1991.

**CHEVERTON, Mark** **1952-1991**
Born England 23 Apr; died Edinburgh 17 Sep. Painter and teacher. Educated Exeter University where he was the first person to be awarded a double first in English and Art. Taught for six years at Marlborough College (where he met his wife(qv)) before moving to Scotland to be head of the art department at Edinburgh Academy. With his wife, founded the Leith School of Art(qv) 1988. Died tragically in a car accident.
**Bibl:** The Times, Obit, 24 Oct 1991.

**CHEYNE, Alexander (Sandy)** **fl 1967-1980**
Aberdeen painter in oil of local landscapes and portraits; also printmaker. Exhibited AAS(9) from 54 Whitehall Place and latterly 17 Park Road, Cults.

**CHEYNE, E J** **19th Cent**
Obscure portrait painter, possibly Scottish. A monogrammed portrait of an unknown sitter is in the City of Edinburgh collection.

**CHEYNE, Edith** **fl 1908**
Amateur Aberdeen painter of 1 Bon Accord Square. Exhibited a rural scene at the AAS.

**CHEYNE, George** **fl 1983-1989**
Aberdeen painter in oil. Trained at Gray's School of Art. Exhibited AAS from Nelson Street.

**CHEYNE, Ian Alec Johnson** **1895-1955**
Born Broughty Ferry, 10 May. Painter in oil and watercolour also wood engraver. Educated at Glasgow Academy, studied at Glasgow School of Art under Maurice Greiffenhagen(qv). Although originally a painter he became increasingly interested in colour woodcuts of Scottish, Spanish and French landscapes. Resided in Bearsden, Glasgow. Exhibited in the Scottish Section of the 1949 Exposition Internationale de la Gravure Contemporaire in Paris. One of the founders of the Society of Artist-Printmakers, subsequently elected treasurer; also Associate of the Society of Graver-Printers in Colour. In addition to most of the important home exhibitions he exhibited in Chicago and Toronto and was awarded one of the principal prizes in the former. 'His colour woodcuts have an Art Deco quality in their use of flat planes and curved forms combined with the perspective found in Japanese woodcuts' [Garton & Cooke]. Exhibited RSA regularly between 1920 and 1955, Highland landscapes, still life, flowers, and colour woodcuts; also at the RSW, GI(21) & AAS, latterly from High Thorn, Bearsden. Represented in SNGMA, Glasgow AG, City of Edinburgh collection, Perth AG.
**Bibl:** Mungo Campbell, 'The Line of Tradition', Nat Galls of Scotland, Ex cat, 1993; Garton and Cooke, London, 'British Colour Woodcuts and Related Prints' Ex Cat 35, 1986; Hartley 121; Macmillan [SA], 359.

**CHEYNE, Miss Lizzie** **fl 1908**
Amateur painter of Mill of Kelly, Tarves, Aberdeenshire. Exhibited 'Coming rain' at the AAS.

**CHILTON, Miss Margaret Isobel** **1875-1962**
Designer of stained glass windows, also painter. Lived at Fettes Row, Edinburgh, having moved north from Bristol; then moved to Glasgow before returning to the capital establishing a practice with Marjorie Kemp(qv). A sparkling set of lights may be seen in the now disused N Morningside church depicting bibular trees; also in the City Chambers; in the hall of the SNPG; St Cuthbert's church (1935) and Melville & Stewart's College (1921). Exhibited regularly RSA(35) 1923-1957, also RA(2), RI(1), GI(2) & L(2). Represented by a window in St John's church, Perth.
**Bibl:** Gifford 44-5,177-8,284,388,452,515,572,618,628,634.

**CHINN, David** **fl 1973-1976**
Exhibited at the AAS from 65 Mile-end Avenue, Aberdeen.

**CHIPAROUS, Demeter** **fl 1930**
Sculptor. Exhibited RSA(1).

**CHISHOLM, Alexander FSA** **1792-1847**
Born Elgin, died Rothesay, 3 Oct. Painter in oil and occasional watercolour; historical romances, portraits, miniatures. His father intended him to be a weaver and he worked in that trade for some time at Peterhead. But, not liking this occupation, he walked to Aberdeen where his portrait sketches were quickly noticed. Received encouragement, his drawing of the Synod, which happened to be meeting in the city, attracted favourable attention and the young man was commissioned to paint it. However, he had to decline, owing to his total ignorance of the use of colour. In about 1809 went to Edinburgh where he obtained the patronage of Lord Elgin and the Earl of Buchan. For some time an assistant in the Trustees' Academy where he met and married Susanna Fraser. Appointed to the staff and in 1818 moved to London. From 1820 until 1846 he exhibited regularly at the RA; his earlier exhibits were mostly portraits including the 'Earl of Buchan' (1822) and 'Major-General Theophilus Pritzler' (1824). After a gap between 1827 and 1837 he concentrated more on historical work with the occasional portrait. One exhibit in 1844 depicted Charles II offering to purchase some miniatures from Mrs Oliver, wife of Isaac Oliver, the miniature painter. His last Academy exhibit depicted the Minister of Kinneff and his wife concealing the Scottish regalia in their church. Executed an oil sketch of George Buchanan's skull and a copy of Lord Buchan's portrait of Buchanan by Titian, now at St Andrew's University. Both oil sketches are dated 1816 and in the possession of the Faculty of Advocates, Edinburgh. Long reports having seen one of his miniatures. Suffered ill health for most of his life and died at a comparatively young age. In 1829 became an associate of the Water-Colour Society. Exhibited regularly BI & OWCS 1820-1847. Represented in V & A.
**Bibl:** Bryan; Brydall 277-8; Foskett; Halsby 62; Long.

**CHISHOLM, Miss Anne** **fl 1880-1890**
Portrait painter in oil. Exhibited RSA in 1881, 1889, 1890 and again the following year. An A Chisholm exhibited 'The Lords of the Congregation' at the GI in 1862.

**CHISHOLM, Archibald** **fl 1745**
Glasgow sculptor. Exhibited a plaster relief at the GI from 10 Newlands Road.

**CHISHOLM, David John** **1885-1949**
Edinburgh Architect. Lived at 1 Mayfield Road and was for most of his professional life with Dick Peddie(qv), Todd & Jamieson. Carried out a substantial amount of work on the Continent and in 1919 exhibited a design for the tomb of Count Hugo of Tuscany at the RSA.
**Bibl:** Gifford 455.

**CHISHOLM, Miss E Grace** **fl 1934-1935**
Artist of Redhurst, Coatbridge; still life and flowers in watercolour and oil. Exhibited RSA in 1934 and 1935, & GI(4).

**CHISHOLM, Rev James** **fl 1942-d1988**
Edinburgh painter in watercolour who exhibited figurative studies and fantasies at the RSA. Taught in extra-mural department of Edinburgh University. Exhibited RSA in 1942(2), 1947, 1948 and 1950, & GI.

**CHISHOLM, John M A** **fl 1917-1925**
Edinburgh painter of genre, landscape and portraits. Exhibited RSA 1917-1925 (4), also RSW(2) & GI(1), from 85 Hanover Street.

**CHISHOLM, Miss Nancy S** **fl 1937-1951**
Lanarkshire watercolour painter of still life, interior and flowers. Exhibited GI(4) from 17 Douglas Drive, Garrowhill, By Baillieston.

**CHISHOLM, Sheila M** **fl 1964-1966**
Amateur Lasswade painter of still life. Exhibited twice at the RSA during the above years, & GI(2), from Dundas Cottage.

**CHISHOLME, J** **fl 1827**
Edinburgh portrait painter who exhibited once at the RSA in 1827.

**CHISNELL, Edward H** **fl 1962-1973**
Glasgow sculptor. Exhibited 2 figure studies at the GI, latterly from 192 Wilton Street.

**CHOLMONDELEY, Miss Lettice** **fl 1937-1939**
Amateur Hamilton artist in watercolour of Fairholm, Larkhall. Exhibited four paintings at the RSA in 1937 and 1938, and 'Shere Khan' at the GI.

**CHORLEY, Leslie Frank** **fl 1965-1966**
Sculptor who exhibited at the RSA in 1965 from Stonieshiel Hall, Reston, Eyemouth, Berwickshire, & GI(1).

**CHRISTEN, Rodolphe** **c1859-1906**
Born St Imier, Switzerland 26 Apr; died Ballater, Aberdeenshire, 7 Sep. At the age of 14 he ran away from home and apprenticed himself to an engraver of watch-backs in Neuchatel. After completing a four year apprenticeship he went to Paris, first painting buttons, then working with the engraver Wolf. He met the Swiss artist Louis Guillaume at Julian's Academy and together they visited Aberdeen, teaching painting at Desclayes' Collegiate School and befriending Garden G Smith(qv). Christen fostered his career as a popular teacher by accepting an appointment at Delacluse's Academy in Paris. He painted extensively in Italy, Switzerland, Spain and France; generally landscape but also portraits and animal studies and pencil sketches, and crayon. In 1902 he settled in the Highlands, having married an amateur Irish artist comparatively late in life. His work was warm, strong and highly competent. Greatly loved by all who knew him, a laughing cavalier, fond of human company, in harmony with nature and accompanied everywhere by his devoted dog 'Hans'. His biography, *Rodolphe Christen; An Artist's Life* (1910), written by his widow(qv), contains many illustrations of his work. Not a prolific artist, being heavily committed to teaching and interrupted too readily by the demands of his many friends. Exhibited RHA(1), a portrait of the Aberdeenshire naturalist George Sim, also GI & AAS(1) 1890.
**Bibl:** S.M. Christen, Rodolphe Christen, London 1910.

**CHRISTEN, Madame Sydney Mary** **fl 1887-dc1935**
Born Ireland; died Aberdeen. Watercolour painter of landscape and still life. Wife and biographer of Rodolphe C(qv). Exhibited AAS 1887. Several of her watercolours are in Belfast AG.

**CHRISTIE, Adam** **1869-1950**
Born Cunningsburgh, Shetland; died Montrose. Painter in oil and watercolour, sculptor. Although he never exhibited in the recognised places this amateur artist is an interesting figure on account of his unconventional life and methods. At the age of seven he entered Sunnyside Asylum in Montrose and there spent the rest of his life painting often portraits and religious subjects, also carving in stone. He made his own paint brushes and used any kind of paint that he could lay his hands on. According to Keddie 'sacking from empty flour bags was the only source of canvas that he had'.
**Bibl:** Kenneth Keddie, The Gentle Shetlander, 1984.

**CHRISTIE, Alexander ARSA** **1807-1860**
Born Edinburgh; died Edinburgh, 5 May. Decorative subjects, portraits, miniatures. Began life as a lawyer but when he was 26 years old decided to become an artist; studied under Sir William Allan(qv) at the Trustees Academy. After a short spell in London he returned to Edinburgh and in 1843 was appointed an assistant at the Trustees' Academy. In 1845, on the death of Thomas Duncan(qv), was appointed first Master of the ornamental Department in the Trustees' School, a position from which he was able to greatly influence the study of decorative art in Scotland. One of his most notable works was a portrait of Oliver Cromwell exhibited at the RSA 1843. At his best his work was reminiscent of the early Erskine Nicol(qv). He drew well and painted with great vigour although the result was often a little hard, 'strong in his manner'. One miniature of an unknown lady was painted in 1832. Tom Faed(qv) and J Macdonald(qv) were among his pupils. Elected ARSA 1848. In 1847 he submitted a painting 'Sir John Moore being carried from the Field of Corunna' at the Westminster Hall competition. Exhibited once at the RA 1853, regularly at the RSA 1839-1860 & BI 1838-40. Represented in NGS(2), SNPG.
**Bibl:** Armitage 63; Bryan; Brydall 384-5; McKay 259.

**CHRISTIE, Alexander** **1901-1946**
Born Aberdeen, 28 Feb. Painter in oil; landscapes, interiors and portraits. Studied at Grays School of Art, Aberdeen and at the RA Schools gaining the Byrne Scholarship, the Robert Brough Studentship and a Scottish Education Department Travelling Studentship in 1926, the latter enabling him to undertake further studies in France and Spain. Best known for his sympathetic and accurately presented portraits. Among his sitters were Lord Fisher, Archbishop of Canterbury; the Duchess of Sutherland; a fine family group now at Kinnaird Castle; and Lord Olivier. His talent was tragically cut short by an early death. Exhibited RA(7), RSA(4), GI(1), & AAS 1921-1937.
**Bibl:** Revue Moderne, 30 Jly 1937.

**CHRISTIE, Arthur S** **1854-1944**
Born Rothesay; died Lasswade, 27 Mar. Trained as an architect, he turned to music and was organist of Rothesay New Parish Church for 53 years. In later life he devoted increasing time to watercolour and occasional oil painting. Exhibited RSA(3), GI(8) & RSW(5) 1938-1940 when living at 1a Battery Place, Rothesay; also exhibited in Paisley and Gourock.

**CHRISTIE, Miss Clyde** **fl 1904-1929**
Portrait painter, miniaturist, illuminator and illustrator. Lived in Glasgow before moving to London in 1915. Exhibited RA(1), GI(12) & L(5).

**CHRISTIE, Miss Diana** **fl 1957-1962**
Clydebank painter in oil and watercolour of landscape. Exhibited GI(6) from 9 and later 3 Drumry Road.

**CHRISTIE, Mrs Eleanor G** **fl 1953**
Amateur sculptress. Exhibited a self-portrait in terracotta at the GI.

**CHRISTIE, Ella** **fl 1888-1890**
Landscape painter. Exhibited RSA(1) from 31 College Bounds, Old Aberdeen and a coastal scene at the AAS in 1890 from 19 Hamilton Place.

**CHRISTIE, Fyffe W G** **1918-1979**
Glasgow painter in oil and watercolour also chalk; figure studies and landscape. Exhibited RSA(6) 1944-1955, & GI(9).

**CHRISTIE, Mrs S F (Georgina)** **fl 1965**
Amateur sculptress. Exhibited 'African Buffalo' in terracotta at the GI from Blackhills, Moray.

**CHRISTIE, Herbert** **fl 1931**
Turriff painter. Trained Gray's School of Art, Aberdeen. Exhibited 'Delgaty Castle' at the AAS from 'The Auld Hoose'.

**CHRISTIE, Ian Gordon** **fl 1967**
Aberdeen sculptor. Exhibited AAS from 48A Fonthill Road.

**CHRISTIE, J** **fl 1847**
Exhibited the portrait of a piper at the RSA in 1847. Possibly the same as John Christie(qv).

**CHRISTIE, James Elder** **1847-1914**
Born Guardbridge, Fife; died London. Painter in oil of poetical and literary subjects and portraits. Studied in Paisley under William Stewart(qv) and after 1874 at South Kensington and the RA School, obtaining gold medal for historical painting 1877. Went to Paris 1882-85, working under Bouguereau. On returning to London he joined the NEAC and disappointed the prophets by producing work 'in the best opposition style'. In 1893 he went to Glasgow but by that time his best work had already been done. In Glasgow he became an 'occasionally uproarious' member of the Glasgow Art Club, known for his recitations of Tam O'Shanter. His bust usually stands in the Club's entrance hall. Although only a peripheral member of the Glasgow School, he exhibited with them at Munich ('Hallowe'en'), then in the USA ('The Red Fisherman'). These works show much of the freshness and influence of the Glasgow Boys. Finally returned to London 1906 having obtained an honourable mention at the Paris Salon the previous year. Founder member of the Chelsea Arts Club and President of the Glasgow Art Club 1899-1901. Illustrated Bret

Harte: *Susy* (1897). Exhibited extensively including RA(21), RSA (13), RBA(5), ROI(1), GI(91), L(30) & AAS. Represented in NGS, Glasgow AG, Paisley AG(22).
**Bibl:** Caw 274; DNB; Halsby 150; Hardie 105; Irwin 373,375,391; Martin 3-6; SAC, 'The Glasgow Boys' (Ex Cat 1968); The Studio ii (1897) 121.

**CHRISTIE, James M** **fl 1956-1957**
Lanarkshire painter. Exhibited a portrait and a fishing scene at the GI from 29 Barrowfield Street, Coatbridge.

**CHRISTIE, Jean Lyal, (Mrs James Gray)** **fl 1922-1934**
Edinburgh watercolour painter; exhibited RSA(4) 1922-1933, RSW(9), GI(1) & L(2) from 63 Morningside Park.

**CHRISTIE, John** **fl 1854**
Edinburgh painter. Exhibited 'The Milkmaid' at the RSA in 1854.

**CHRISTIE, John** **fl 1890**
Aberdeen amateur painter of 21A Richmond Street. Exhibited a coastal scene at the AAS.

**CHRISTIE, Mrs Mabel** **fl 1937**
Glasgow watercolour artist; exhibited 'Sunshine' at the GI from 111 Randolph Road.

**CHRISTIE, Mrs Major** **fl 1939**
Edinburgh painter. Exhibited once at the RSA in 1939.

**CHRISTIE, Miss Mamie M** **fl 1932**
Sculptress. Exhibited two portrait busts at the RSA in 1932.

**CHRISTIE, Mary M M (Mrs A B Robertson)** **1933-**
Born Wishaw, Lanarkshire, 14 Apr. Painter in oil and watercolour; landscape, still life and ornate detail from buildings. Studied Glasgow School of Art 1950-1955, receiving a highly commended post-diploma endorsement in her final year, enabling her to travel. Member, Glasgow Art Club. Began exhibiting RSA 1963, GI(19). Member, SSA and Scottish Society for Art History. Returned to painting following a long absence in the late 70's after bringing up her family. In later years her interest has been in the self and nature and the interaction between the two. Lived for many years at 2 College Park, Barassie, Troon, Ayrshire.

**CHRISTIE, Norman** **fl 1969-1971**
Angus watercolour painter of The Cottage, Fettercairn House, Laurencekirk. Exhibited local landscape and figure studies at the AAS.

**CHRISTIE, Robert** **fl 1887-1903**
Edinburgh painter; exhibited 4 works at the RSA from 170 Leith Walk. Also from St John's Wood in 1887 (2), 1888 and 1889 & GI(2).

**CHRISTIE, Robert John** **fl 1863-1870**
Edinburgh painter in oil and watercolour; landscape, portraits, still life and fruit. Exhibited RSA during the above dates including a painting of the 'Monks' Cave, Aberdeen' (1864) and 'Water Melon-Garden in Chile' (1869) & GI(5).

**CHRISTIE, Shonagh** **fl 1985-1986**
Edinburgh painter. Exhibited RSA 1985-1986.

**CHRISTIE, William S** **fl 1890-1929**
Exhibited intermittently at the AAS from a variety of Aberdeen addresses, mainly still life and interiors, latterly from 74 Great Western Road.

**CHRISTIE, Winifred** **fl 1901-1908**
Edinburgh portrait miniaturist in watercolour and pen and ink. Lived at 181 Morningside Road. Exhibited ten miniatures at the RSA between 1901 and 1908, also two at the GI.

**CHRISTINE, James** **fl 1972**
Amateur Glasgow painter. Exhibited a figurative study at the GI from 58 Montford Avenue.

**CHRISTISON, David** **fl 1874**
Edinburgh landscape painter in oil; exhibited RSA in 1874.

**CHRISTISON, James** **fl 1905**
Edinburgh painter; exhibited RSA(1) 1905, from 22 Fettes Row.

**CHRISTMAS, E W** **fl 1902**
Amateur Glasgow landscape painter. Exhibited GI(1) from Willowbank Crescent.

**CHRISTY, Robert** **fl 1901-1903**
Exhibited three landscapes at the RSA in 1901 and 1903.

**CHRYSTAL, Arthur B** **1904-1978**
Montrose painter in watercolour and pencil, and engraver. Also lived in Perth and moved to Edinburgh c1930, then to Stanley, Perthshire in the 1940s before returning to Montrose where he established a studio at 180 High Street. Exhibited 10 works at the RSA between 1926 and 1971, mostly landscapes and some figure studies, also five works at the GI and regularly at the AAS 1931-1978.

**CHRYSTAL, Jessie** **fl 1908-1912**
Amateur Aberdeen painter. Lived for a time at the United Free Manse, Bucksburn before moving to 115 Hamilton Place. Exhibited AAS(6).

**CHRYSTAL, Mrs Katherine D** **fl 1971**
Amateur Montrose watercolour painter of landscape. Exhibited AAS from 2 Dorward Place.

**CHRYSTAL, Margaret** **fl 1910-1920**
Sculptress. Worked most of the time in France. Her most common works were portrait busts, statuettes and 'masques'. Exhibited at the National Salon 1910-1920, then at the French Salon 1913.

**CHURCH, Miss E M** **fl 1879-1885**
Glasgow painter of still life and flowers; exhibited GI(4) from 2 Southpark Terrace.

**CHURCHILL, Martin** **1954-**
Born Glasgow, 18 Nov. Painter of mostly architectural subjects and abstract, personal symbolism. Educated Edinburgh College of Art 1972-77, winning the Adam Bruce Thomson Prize. Moved from Edinburgh to London c1985. Taught at Gloucester CA 1981-82, 1980 Latimer Award, 1981 Guthrie Award, 1982 Greenshields Award, Canada, 1983 Cargill Award RGI. Influenced by Bastien-Lepage. Exhibited regularly at the RSA since 1980, RSW, & GI(7). Represented in Hunterian Museum, Glasgow. Edinburgh City collection.

**CIAPPA, Giovanni** **fl 1894**
Lived at 95 Bath Street, Glasgow and exhibited once at the GI.

**CINA, Colin** **1943-**
Born Glasgow. Painter in oil; abstracts. Studied Glasgow School of Art 1961-1963 before settling in London. In 1966 awarded a Stuyvesant Bursary enabling him to travel in the USA. There the paintings of contemporary American colour-field artists such as Barnett Newman and Joseph Albers influenced him. In the mid 1960s he was combining geometric abstraction with Surrealist imagery in works akin to Pop art. From 1967-68 he eliminated external influences to concentrate on totally abstract work, often using unusually shaped angular canvases. In the 1970s he returned to painting on rectangular surfaces, giving them a unified surface colouring. In the 1980s he reintroduced fragments of quasi-surrealist imagery into his paintings, after the style of Kandinsky. Formerly head of fine art at Chelsea School of Art. Represented in V & A, SNGMA, Israel Museum (Jerusalem), Bristol AG, Laing AG (Newcastle), SAC.
**Bibl:** Gage 69-70,134; Hardie 130; Hartley 122; TEC, Glasgow 'Colin Cina Paintings and Drawings 1966-75' (Ex Cat 1975).

**CLAPPERTON, Annie A** **fl 1890**
Amateur artist of Drumslea, Greenock; exhibited a still life at the GI.

**CLAPPERTON, Bruce** **fl 1962-1968**
Dumfries-shire painter of interiors and nudes. Exhibited regularly at

the RSA 1962-1969, and then again 1979 and 1980, also GI(1), from 17 Ladysmith Road, Eastriggs.

**CLAPPERTON, Thomas John FRBS** **1879-1962**
Born Galashiels, 14 Sep; died Sussex. Sculptor, widely known as 'The Border Sculptor'. Son of a photographer/naturalist. In 1896 began his artistic studies at the Galashiels Mechanics Institute where he developed an aptitude for drawing under the influence of James Huck(qv), winning a bronze medal in 1898 and a silver medal and scholarship in 1899. The latter enabled him to study at Glasgow School of Art 1899 and 1901-1903 at the City of Guilds in London Institute, before proceeding to the RA Schools 1904-5 where he won a gold medal and travelling studentship for sculpture. In London he worked under Sir William Goscombe John, the most eminent sculptor of the day. Travelled and studied in Italy and Paris. Completed 2 bronze panels for the Mungo Park Memorial in Selkirk. In 1906 he returned to London establishing a studio in Chelsea. Commissions came flooding in, among them a large 'literature' statue for the Mitchell Library, Glasgow, and 5 statues for the British Pavilion of Applied Arts in London, a war memorial for Selkirk, a statue for Cardiff City Hall and a large work on the theme 'Mining and Shipping' for the National Museum of Wales. Other memorials included those in Hexham, Minto, Canonbie, Earlston and Galashiels as well as several commissions in New Zealand. Also prepared a gigantic frieze for Liberty's in London and a statue of Robert the Bruce for Edinburgh Castle. During WW1 served in India. His last major bust was of 'Lord Tweedsmuir, Governor General of Canada', now in the SNPG. In 1913 elected a member of the Royal Society of British Sculptors, Associate 1928, Fellow 1938. Exhibited many works at the RSA 1910-46, RA(24), GI(24) & L(6).
**Bibl:** Graeme D R Cruickshank, Thomas Clapperton, the Border Sculptor.

**CLARK, Agnes Wilson (Mrs Finlay)** **fl 1899-1912**
Scottish painter in oils and watercolours; landscape, generally Highlands sometimes Arran. Appears to have travelled a lot within Scotland, living at Rutherglen in 1899, Newton 1904, Pollokshields 1908, and Bridge of Weir 1909. After her marriage in 1911, moved again, to Wemyss Bay 1912. Exhibited RSA(2) & GI(22), from Craig na Luittie, Skelmorlie, Ayrshire.

**CLARK, Allan** **fl 1951-1960**
Sculptor who lived at 36 Borgie Crescent, Cambuslang. Specialised in portrait heads, mostly in plaster. Exhibited four times at the RSA between the above years.

**CLARK, Arthur Melville** **fl 1942-1949**
Edinburgh topographical artist; exhibited RSA between the above years.

**CLARK, David** **fl 1842-1856**
Musselburgh painter in oil; landscapes and topographical scenes, especially in East Lothian. Exhibited RSA 1842-1856.

**CLARK, Donald** **1965-**
Born Irvine, Scotland. Educated Edinburgh College of Art 1983-7. Received Andrew Grant travelling scholarship in 1986 enabling him to visit France, Germany and Italy. His interest is in landscape, sea, mortality and the passage of time. Uses natural and man-made objects found on beaches giving his paintings a representational approach, often with trompe de l'oeil devices and elements of surrealism. Began exhibiting RSA 1989 & SSA 1988.

**CLARK, Miss Elliot O** **fl 1893-1910**
Aberdeen painter of coastal scenes and mountains, fond of painting Deeside. Exhibited AAS during the above years from 27 Albyn Place.

**CLARK, Forbes ARCA** **fl 1898-1908**
Aberdeen landscape painter. Exhibited AAS 1898 from Ashbank, Broadford Place and in 1908 from Maberley Street.

**CLARK, George** **fl 1847**
Glasgow painter; exhibited a view of Little France, nr Edinburgh at the RSA in 1847.

**CLARK, Mrs Gilchrist** **fl 1878**
Thornhill watercolour painter of flowers; exhibited once at the RSA.

**CLARK, Harry** **fl 1943-1949**
Carnoustie landscape painter. Exhibited scenes in Perthshire and Fife at the RSA between the above years.

**CLARK, I** **fl 1772-1824**
Aquatintist and engraver. In 1773-1774 was living opposite the Tolbooth. Several views of Edinburgh, including 3 aquatints after A Kay(qv), are in City of Edinburgh collection.

**CLARK, J** **fl 1703-1727**
Engraver of maps including one of Scotland, also the Firth of Tay, Montrose Basin and Roman Camps in Scotland, all between the above dates.

**CLARK, J** **fl 1829**
A painter of this name exhibited a view near Dunedin at the RSA in 1829.

**CLARK, James** **fl 1681-1690**
Scottish engraver. Executed the title page in the portrait of Charles II in Murray of Glendook's *Acts of Parliament of Scotland,* 1681. The same signature appears on an engraving of 'The Burning Bush' in *The Principal Acts of the General Assembly of the Church of Scotland...1690* (1691).
**Bibl:** Bushnell; J C Guy, Edinburgh Engravers in the book of the old Edinburgh Club, Vol 9, 1916.

**CLARK, James** **fl 1868-1886**
Glasgow painter in oil and watercolour of landscapes, coastal scenes and figures. Particularly fond of moorland scenes in the central Highlands. Exhibited RSA 1873-1886, & GI(6), from 11 Miller Street.

**CLARK, James** **fl 1889-1909**
Glasgow landscape painter in oil, especially Highland scenes often Perthshire. Exhibited GI(36) from 79 West Regent Street.

**CLARK, James** **fl 1898**
Amateur Edinburgh painter in oil; exhibited once at the RSA from 123 George Street.

**CLARK, James** **fl 1913-1929**
Edinburgh painter in oil; exhibited RSA(9) between the above dates.

**CLARK, James** **fl 1939-1944**
Engraver and etcher of Ayr. Portraits and landscape. Exhibited GI(3) from 24 Carrick Park.

**CLARK, James Dickson** **fl 1843-1879**
Amateur Edinburgh painter in oil and watercolour of landscape. Moved in late life to North Shields. Exhibited RSA 1843, & GI(1).

**CLARK, James Harvey ARSA** **1885-1980**
Sculptor. Lived in Edinburgh. Last of the 'Old Guard' of Scottish sculptors. After leaving school he served a six year apprenticeship with the Edinburgh printing firm of McLagan and Cumming as their lithographic artist. Studied drawing and modelling at the RSA School, one of the first to be transferred to the New Edinburgh College of Art where he gained an Academy award (Stewart Prize) for the best figurative composition of the year. Worked for two years in an ornamental sculptor's studio to gain knowledge of 'the styles'. From 1914-18, served in France, becoming a 2nd Lieut in the King's Own Scottish Borderers. After demobilisation, worked as an assistant to several monumental sculptors including J Beattie, J Hayes and Mrs Alice Meredith Williams (who worked on the Scottish National War Memorial). In 1929 he set up on his own, designing and carving a variety of mainly heraldic and monumental works for leading Edinburgh architects, also figurative works and portrait busts. Some of his most important work was the modelling of maquettes from which the woodcarvers W & A Clow(qv) worked. Elected ARSA 1934. Exhibited many times at the RSA between 1913 and 1981. A fine portrait bust of 'John Massey Rhind' (1962) was included in the touring exhibition of Scottish Sculpture 1965; also RA(1) & GI(43), latterly from 1 Belford Road.

**CLARK, James N C** **fl 1931-1959**
Amateur Peterhead artist, schoolmaster and baillie; worked in oil and

watercolour, also etcher. Rector of Peterhead Academy, later moved to Troon. Exhibited RSA(1), GI(20) all since 1952, & AAS(1) 1957.

**CLARK, Jane** **fl 1884-1890**
Glasgow watercolour painter of flowers. Exhibited once at the RSA (1884) & GI(9) between the above dates, from 9 Wilton Crescent.

**CLARK, John** **?-1857**
Edinburgh architect. Although a native of the capital, he spent his entire working life in England. In 1826 he was successful in a competition for a design for the Commercial Buildings at Leeds. This led to other commissions in the area and Clark remained in practice in Leeds until shortly before his death. All his domestic work was classical in style, but he built at least one Gothic church. Among the main works in Leeds were the Commercial Buildings (1826) & St George's Church (1837-8); also responsible for Airedale College, near Bradford, the Cheltenham Pump Room at Harrogate (1835), the Victoria Baths, Harrogate and Gledhow Grove, near Leeds. In 1848 a design for a new Roman villa for a Scottish patron was exhibited at the RA.
**Bibl:** Colvin 141; The Building Chronicle, Edinburgh, May 1857, 197(obit).

**CLARK, John Heaviside ('Waterloo Clark')** **c1771-1863**
Thought to have been born in Scotland; died Edinburgh, Oct 1863. Engraver, landscape and seascape painter, miniaturist. He was in London in 1802-1832, where he counted Rowlandson and Pether among his friends. Exhibits at the RA between 1812 and 1832 were principally of maritime subjects and landscapes. Best known for his engravings of Scottish towns and cities, historically important for their accurate attention to detail and aesthetically pleasing for their uncluttered clear depiction of space, and for his sketches of the battlefield of Waterloo, later published as coloured engravings. These gave rise to his nickname 'Waterloo Clark'. Published several books on painting including instructions on the art of miniature painting incorporated in his *Elements of Drawing and Painting,* 1851, pp139 et seq. Illustrated *Foreign Field Sports* (1814). Three of the finest aquatints in Sir John Carr's *Caledonian Sketches* were 'Clark's View of the Old Town, Taken From Clarke's Circulating Library, South Street Andrew Street', 1812, 'View of the Old Town, Taken From Princes Street', 1814, and 'City of Edinburgh', 1824. In the last, taken from the north-east, delicately traced trees in the park adorn the foreground, while a group of elegant ladies and gentlemen add a lively touch to the soft-toned scene, completed by the Castle, Calton Hill, Nelson Monument and Arthur's Seat. Represented in Glasgow AG, Fyvie Castle (NTS).
**Bibl:** Athenaeum 10.10.1863; Thieme Becker; Bryan; Butchart 41-2; Halsby 50; Long 72.

**CLARK, John K** **1957-**
Born Dumbarton. Stained glass window designer. Trained Glasgow School of Art, 1975-81 and apart from working for two years as a part-time lecturer at Glasgow School of Art, began working as a full-time designer almost immediately thereafter. By 1990 he had become one of Scotland's leading and busiest designers. In 1988 he received two Saltire Society awards for art in architecture. Represented Britain at the European Commission Crafts Exhibition in Palais des Papes, Avignon, 1990 and in the same year won another Saltire award for his window in Paisley Abbey. Designed the Lockerbie Memorial window (1990) and two windows to celebrate the release of the hostage John McCarthy. Enjoys vibrant colours, capturing mood most evocatively. The three dimensional effect of his 'Flock of Fishes' in the Cafe Gondolfi, Glasgow (1987), which won him the first of three Saltire awards, is deeply impressive. To date his other major works have been the James Shaw memorial window (five lancets) in Paisley Abbey (1988), a large tryptich window and half dome in Queen's Park Synagogue, Glasgow (1990-1) and the Lockerbie memorial window in the Lesser Town Hall, Lockerbie (1991). Works from lla Maxwell Drive, Pollokshields, Glasgow and from Germany.

**CLARK, John M** **fl 1894**
Amateur Buckie painter of secluded landscapes. Exhibited AAS(2) from Bridge End.

**CLARK, John McKenzie** **1928-**
Born Dundee, 29 Nov. Painter in oil, watercolour and ink; portraits, landscape and pastoral scenes. Son of a commercial artist, he was educated at Harris Academy, Dundee and Dundee College of Art 1945-1950, Norwich Art College 1950-51, Hospitalfield 1953 and St Martin's Art School 1955-56. Held regular one man shows in Dundee and Edinburgh and has exhibited RA, RSA, RSW, SSA & GI(6) from 2 Birchwood Place.

**CLARK, Joseph** **fl 1977**
Amateur East Kilbride painter. Exhibited a figurative work at the GI from 32 Glenfalloch, St Leonard's.

**CLARK, Mrs Linda** **fl 1981**
Amateur still life painter of 6 Wallace Road, Renfrew. Exhibited GI(2).

**CLARK, Lindsay Scott** **fl 1957-**
Born Forfar, Angus. Raised in Glasgow, began painting when in Edmonton, Alberta in the 1930s, exhibiting at Edmonton Art Club. Returned to Kirriemuir 1938, studied music. P-o-w in Burma during WW2. Taught music after the war and resumed painting 1959, becoming full-time artist 1969. Studied under Frank Spenlove-Spenlove and Jack Merriott. Exhibited RSA, RSW, GI(3), RWS & RI, mainly watercolours.

**CLARK, M** **fl 1873-1874**
Edinburgh landscape painter in oil, exhibited twice at the RSA between the above dates.

**CLARK, Neil R S Dockrill** **fl 1966-1988**
Glasgow painter and sculptor. Exhibited still life and figure subjects at the RSA regularly between 1966 and 1988, & GI(11), latterly from 9 Fintry Gardens, Bearsden.

**CLARK, R** **fl 1851**
Edinburgh sculptor. His design for a monument to the late George Bentinck to be erected in Manfield Market Place and intended for a small market house, was exhibited at the RSA in 1851.

**CLARK, Robert Peacock** **fl 1883-1884**
Edinburgh painter of interior and furniture designer. Exhibited RSA between the above dates from 6 Thistle Place.

**CLARK, Sarah R** **fl 1894**
Amateur Aberdeen landscape painter. Exhibited 2 local scenes at the AAS from 40 Whitehall Road.

**CLARK, Thomas** **fl 1740s**
Dunkeld mason and designer. In the mid-eighteenth century a number of Renaissance type churches appeared in Scotland. The church at Killin, Perthshire (1744) was a vernacular variant built by Clark. Although altered in 1831 and again 1900 something of its original attractive appearance remains.
**Bibl:** Bruce Walker & W S Gauldie, Architects and Architecture on Tayside, Dundee 1984, 88.

**CLARK, Thomas ARSA** **1820-1876**
Born Edinburgh, 14 Nov; died Aberfoyle, Perthshire, 7 Oct. Painter in oil; landscape, coastal scenes and interior designs. Skilful landscape painter who delighted in nature and was always most conscientious in his depiction of detail. Moved to London c1838 before returning to Scotland 1860 from which time his compositions were almost always Scottish. Although wintering in the south, he continued to paint English landscapes. Among his best known works are 'Waiting for the Ferry', 'A Quiet Morning on Loch Awe' and 'Hambledon Common'. Elected ARSA 1865. First exhibited RSA at the age of 20 when living in Edinburgh. A short time later he moved to London and between 1830-1870 exhibited 12 works at the RA, all of them English landscapes, except for a theatre design (1830), 'Highland salmon river' (1862) and an interior of an old private chapel at the Moat (1870); also GI(32), latterly from 12 Castle Terrace, Edinburgh. Represented in Melbourne AG.
**Bibl:** AJ 1877, 20,38(obit); Clement and Hutton; DNB.

**CLARK, William** **fl c1790-1800**
Obscure painter, probably Scottish. A painting of the 'Hall of the Old Tolbooth c1795' is in the collection of the City of Edinburgh.

**CLARK, William** **fl 1846-1858**
Edinburgh landscape painter in oil; exhibited three works at the RSA between the above dates.

**CLARK, William** (of Greenock) **1803-1883**
Born Greenock, 26 Jne; died Greenock, 11 Nov. Painter of ships in oil and watercolour. Son of a seaman. Became a house painter but an interest in ships and a desire to paint pictures resulted in his becoming a ship portraitist of high quality. Worked all his life in Greenock. One of the best examples of how Scottish marine artists have been so neglected by art historians and, to a lesser degree, by the art market. Sometimes thought that there were two William Clarks, a junior and a senior, but there was probably only one, the better works having been described in the past as by 'senior' while the lesser works have been attributed to 'junior'. Some of his resplendent yacht racing scenes were engraved by Edward Duncan(qv) including 'Regatta of the Royal Northern Yacht Club'. Exhibited regularly RSA 1829-1864, and in 1871 at the GI(2) from Seafield, Greenock. The National Maritime Museum, Greenwich has seven ship portraits by him and the Liverpool Gallery has one, the National Library of Art in Canberra has a ship portrait as does the Peabody Museum of Salem, Massachusetts.
**Bibl:** Halsby 88,244; Hardie 26(illus); Wingfield.

**CLARK, William D** **fl 1848-1849**
Bonhill landscape painter in oil; exhibited RSA in 1848 and 1849 landscapes of Highland views.

**CLARK, William N** **fl 1931-1937**
Amateur Edinburgh watercolour painter; exhibited 'The Wood in Spring' at the RSA 1934 & RSW(3).

**CLARKE, Derek ARSA RSW RP** **1912-**
Painter in oil and watercolour; landscape, figurative studies, portraits. Lives in Edinburgh. Studied 1947-1950 at Slade School, London, subsequently joining the Edinburgh College of Art as a lecturer. Lived for a short time in Ireland. Latterly a full-time painter of landscape, portraits and a designer of stained glass windows for churches. Has held many one-man exhibitions. Elected RP 1950, ARSA 1989. Exhibited regularly RSA since 1950, & GI(4), from 8 Magdala Crescent. Represented in Dunfermline AG, University of Edinburgh, SAC.

**CLARKE, Edward Francis C** **fl 1866-1887**
Edinburgh painter and architect; landscape and topographical scenes. Moved to London c1870. Among his designs were the Priory House Hotel, Walsall, a new chancel at Christchurch, Wolverhampton, and the new church of St Mary, Woolwich. In Edinburgh he painted the nine saints that adorn St James' church, Constitution St and also designed the Reredos. Exhibited regularly at the RA 1872-1881, RSA intermittently 1866-1885, also RBA(7) & L(1).
**Bibl:** Gifford 455.

**CLARKE, James** **c1745/50-1799**
Born Inverness. Scottish portrait painter and copyist. Came from a poor family. After acquiring some skill as a painter, in 1767 he executed a number of works similar to those of William Millar(qv). Went to Italy 1768 to study painting through the support of two patrons, Sir Ludovic Grant of Grant and Sir Hew Dalrymple (later the 5th Earl of Stair). At Naples he received travellers, recommended by Byres and Moir, and arranged for them to buy prints and pictures. In 1783, having returned to Italy through the support of Lord Findlater, he introduced Allan Ramsay(qv) and his son to various important collections. From 1798-99 he was engaged in listing and packing the entire collections of Sir William Hamilton. After his death he bequeathed a 'Holy Family', attributed to Sassoferrati, to the town of Inverness. His entrepreneurial work took precedence over his art.
**Bibl:** Basil Skinner, Scots in Italy, Edinburgh 1966, 15,20-1,25; Waterhouse 82.

**CLARKE, John** **c1650-c1697**
Born in Scotland, this engraver was active in Edinburgh where in 1690 he made a portrait medallion in profile of William III and Mary II, said to be as pleasing as were the seven portrait heads (1670) on one page of Charles II, his wife Katherine of Braganza and the Princes William of Orange and Rupert, the Dukes of York and Monmouth and General George Monk. Walpole and Strutt have attributed to him engraved portraits of the jurist Sir Matthew Hale (d1676), the writer Andrew Marvell (1678), the historian Humphrey Prideaux (1648-1724), and the Swedish Minister Baron Georg Heinrich von Goertz-Schultz (beheaded in 1719). Thieme Becker believes the last should more probably be attributed to John Clerk of Eldin(qv) with whom the artist John Pine collaborated. Also engraved 'The Humours of Harlequin' and 'Les Amours de Columbine and Harlequin' from his own drawings.
**Bibl:** Bryan; Brydall 193; Bushnell.

**CLARKE, Marian Eagle (Mrs Richard N Coulson)** **fl 1908-1927**
Edinburgh land and seascape painter in oil and watercolour. Travelled widely, settling at Airthrey, Ayrshire, c1921. Married the ornithologist and Keeper of Natural History at the Royal Scottish Museum, William Eagle Clarke, in whose volumes *Studies of Bird Migration* (1912) she has two illustrations: one, the frontispiece for vol 1, taken from a painting of the 'Eddystone Lantern, 12th October 1901', and as frontispiece for volume 2 her drawing of the 'Kentish Knock Lightship'. Exhibited at the RSA in 1921 'Bees on Catkins' and again in 1920 'Bees on Bell Heather'; also RSW(1), but mainly at Walker's Gallery, London(65).

**CLARKE, W R** **fl 1947**
Amateur Glasgow artist, he exhibited 'Irish Idyll' in carbon at the GI from 1101 Aitkenhead Road.

**CLARKE, William** **1809-1899**
Glasgow architect. Apprenticed to David Bryce(qv). Entered partnership with George Bell snr(qv). They won a competition to build the City & County Buildings (40-50 Wilson St), (1842) and the practice took off. 'Their earliest works are refined neo-Greek or neo-Tudor, moving into refined Italianate and a rather crude early pointed later. By the 1880s their work had become free Renaissance' [Gomme & Walker].
**Bibl:** A Gomme & D Walker, Architecture of Glasgow, London 1987(rev), 54,62,72,101,122n,290.

**CLARKE, William Hanna** **1882-1924**
Born Glasgow; died Kirkcudbright, 1 May. Painter in oil of landscape, rustic scenes and figurative subjects. Began his career as a dentist. Worked from a London address in 1911, then appears to have moved to Milngavie 1913 before settling in Kirkcudbright 1916. Almost all his works were country scenes, especially of Kirkcudbright and Stirlingshire at the brighter times of year. Writing in *The Studio* E A Taylor observed 'Never have I known an artist who works more assiduously early and late...each new canvas shows a marked technical and assured advance. Having an idyllic sense of colour, sunlight and the pastoral life surrounding farm steadings and the intimate woodlands captivate him most...in his smaller spontaneous figure pastorals especially there is a charm that endures'. Victim of a fatal accident in his home. Exhibited regularly RSA(17), also RSW(2), GI(35) & L(2). Represented in Glasgow AG.
**Bibl:** Halsby 218,226-7; Studio 1922.

**CLARKSON, Kathleen** **1950-**
Painter in oil. Her 'Jetty One' was purchased through the Pernod Art Competition 1972 for the collection of the City of Edinburgh.

**CLAUSTON, Mrs T S** **fl 1902**
Amateur Edinburgh painter. Exhibited RSA(1) from 11 Braid Road, Morningside.

**CLAY, Miss Patricia Thomson** **fl 1925-1946**
Edinburgh painter in oil and watercolour; landscape, flowers, still life. Lived in Florence during the mid-1920s before returning to Edinburgh. Exhibited 18 works at the RSA 1925-1946, mostly still life and flowers during the earlier years, but increasingly Scottish landscapes and rustic scenes during her later period; also RSW(24), GI(1), & L(1), from 18 S Learmounth Gardens.

**CLAYTON, John** **c1860-1894**
Born Keith; died Algeria, 3 Sept. Painter in oil of continental landscapes; photographer. Educated Keith Parish School. Spent most of his life in Paris where his sister was married to a Professor and

government minister, and from where he exhibited once at the RSA in 1876; often at the Paris Salon. Killed in an accident.

**CLAYTON, John Richard** **1827-1913**
Stained glass window designer. Partner with **Alfred BELL** (1832-1895), **John Clement BELL** (1860-1944), **Reginald Otto BELL** (1864-1950 and **Michael Charles Farrar BELL** (1911-1993) in the firm Clayton & Bell. Responsible for windows in many Edinburgh churches including St Peter's, Lutton Place; St Mary's Cathedral; St John's, Princes St; St Andrew Place Church and North Morningside church. Michael B, trained Edinburgh College of Art, exhibited RA and installed nearly all the windows in Her Majesty's Chapel of the Mohawks in London.
**Bibl:** Gifford 44,242,278,366,455,618; The Times, Obit, 14 Jne 1913.

**CLAYTON, Thomas** **fl 1710-1760**
Plasterer, specialising in finely executed stucco work. Son of Thomas Varsallis C(qv). Believed to have worked in Brunstane House, Edinburgh and extensively in William Adam's Drum House.
Bibl: Gifford 56,558-9,584.

**CLAYTON, Thomas Varsallis** **1743-1793**
Plasterer. Son of Thomas C(qv). Responsible for extensive work around the dome of Register House, Edinburgh, re-decorated 1973-4.
**Bibl:** Gifford 287.

**CLEGG, Leo** **fl 1947-1967**
Glasgow sculptor. Moved to Aberdeen in the 1950s. Exhibited 2 plaster heads at the GI, & AAS(2), latterly from 1 Ruthrieston Road.

**CLEGG, Thora** **fl 1964**
Sculptress. Probably related to Leo C(qv). Exhibited a portrait bust at the AAS from 47 Rubislaw Park Terrace.

**CLEGHORN, Alex** **fl 1926-1931**
Aberdeenshire-based etcher of continental and local townscapes. Exhibited AAS(3) from Drumrossie, Insch.

**CLELAND, A** **fl 1818-1819**
Edinburgh painter of still life and interiors. Lived at 15 Hanover Street. Seems never to have exhibited in Scotland but did so twice at the RA during the above dates, and once at the BI.

**CLELAND, Archibald B** **fl 1880**
Amateur Edinburgh painter; exhibited RSA(1) from 16 India Street.

**CLELAND, Peter** **fl 1834-1901**
Edinburgh painter in oil and watercolour; flowers, still life and most especially Scottish landscapes. Prolific artist who was for a time lecturer at Gray's School of Art, Aberdeen. Moved to Edinburgh c1868. A picture showing the arrival of Queen Victoria and her family at Aberdeen harbour on the occasion of their first visit to Balmoral, is in Aberdeen Town House. Small oil studies were made of the notables portrayed in the painting, two sets of which adorned Douglas Simpson's room in Aberdeen University library. Exhibited 61 works at the RSA between the above dates, including 'The Pass of Ballater' (1866), 'Traquair House', in which the figures were painted by Erskine Nicol (1876), and 'Doune Castle' (1898). Also exhibited GI(1) & several times at the AAS, from 2 Albany Street, Edinburgh.

**CLELLAND, David** **fl c1730-c1750**
Early painter. Son of a Merchant Burgess of Edinburgh. In 1737 he married the daughter of the Minister of the North Kirk, Edinburgh. Admitted to the Academy of St Luke 1729. Member of the Incorporation of St Mary's 1735-42. In 1735 he was made a Burgess of Edinburgh and in 1741 took his first pupil, a J Weir, followed in 1745 by a second, George MacFarquhar. Nothing is now known of his work.

**CLELLAND, David** **fl 1932-1979**
Born Larkhall. Landscape painter in oil and watercolour, often worked in Kincardineshire and Orkney. His early training was at the Academy in Larkhall before proceeding to Glasgow School of Art. In 1929 he took first place for drawing and painting in the diploma examination and won a maintenance scholarship enabling him to travel to Italy, France, Belgium and Holland. Enjoyed using rich colour. Exhibited 'Jessie' at the RSA (1933), also 'Still Life' (1934) and 'Myrtle Walk, Cambuslang' (1947), & GI(20), from a 13 Old Glasgow Road, Uddingston, Lanarkshire.

**CLELLAND, Peter** **fl 1884**
Amateur Edinburgh landscape painter. Exhibited a Perthshire view at the GI from 16 India Street.

**CLEPHANE, Hunter** **c1825-?**
Scottish ornamental painter. Entered Trustees' Academy 1850 but left after only five days.

**CLERK, Alexander** **c1650-c1737**
Portrait painter. Younger brother of Sir John Clerk of Penicuik(qv). Studied portrait painting under John Alexander(qv) and Imperiali, and during 1733 in London under Pond and Hysing. Together with the two Alan Ramsays, the two Norries, the English-born engraver Richard Cupar, the art dealer Andrew Hay, William Adam the architect and two portrait painters (William Robertson and William Denune), he signed an agreement to form the Edinburgh School of St Luke(qv) 'for encouragement of the arts of painting, sculpture, architecture, etc and improvement of the Students'.
**Bibl:** Douglas, Baronage of Scotland; John Fleming, Robert Adam and his Circle in Edinburgh and Rome, 1962, 328n; Macmillan [SA], 99; SRO Clerk of Penicuik Papers, 4661-4,4667,4671-5,4677; Waterhouse 82.

**CLERK, Sir George** **late 18th C**
Amateur watercolour painter. According to Halsby he painted in dark washes with dramatic chiaruscuro, and was related to Clerk of Eldin.
**Bibl:** Halsby 253-4.

**CLERK, Sir James of Penicuik** **1710-1782**
Painter and architect. 3rd Baronet of Penicuik. Sent to London in 1727 to study under Aikman(qv). His principal fame is based upon his patronage of the arts. Designed Hailes House, Hailes Ave, Edinburgh (c1765).
**Bibl:** John Fleming, Robert Adam and his Circle in Edinburgh and Rome, 1962, 28; Gifford 509; Waterhouse 82.

**CLERK, John** **c1670-**
Little is known of this painter. In 1698 he was made Burgess of Edinburgh and in 1710 had taken on as an apprentice John Mark. Not to be confused with **Sir John CLERK** (1676-1755) who designed the park for Cammo mansion, Edinburgh 1710-1726.
**Bibl:** Roll of Edinburgh Burgesses; Reg of Edin Apprentices, app 58.

**CLERK, John ('of Eldin')** **1728-1812**
Born Penicuik; died Edinburgh. Known as Clerk of Eldin. Etcher and engraver. Seventh son of Sir John Clerk of Penicuik. Educated at Dalkeith Grammar School. He set up as a draper, later becoming Secretary to the Commissioners on the Annexed Estates in Scotland. He and his family were close friends of the Adam family and he married Susannah Adam in 1753. With Robert Adam(qv), he befriended Paul Sandby who had arrived in Scotland with the Board of Ordnance in 1747. By the 1770s, when he made his first plates, he had developed a style more characteristic of etching, with busy, loping strokes to build up textures and tones. Fond of wide-angle views, framed with dark foliage. Writing in the *Print Collector's Quarterly* (Vol 12), Lumsden spoke of Clerk's 'extraordinary technical proficiency in etching proper, particularly in the long series of plates hardly larger than a visiting card. Of these, 'Sherriff Hall' and 'Lauriston Castle' are two of the finest'. His larger works are notable for their superb treatment of trees and country landscapes, and for their softness of tone. Greatly interested in the sea, his *Essay on Naval Tactics* (1782), includes the first successful aquatints as well as being a remarkable work in its own right. In ten years he produced over 100 plates of etchings in many of which the influence of Hollar is readily seen. Twenty-eight of these plates were published in large folio in 1825 by the Bannatyne Club, reprinted in 1855 with additional etchings discovered by his son in an old cupboard. Although more than an able amateur, his prints are bound by the constraints of strictly topographical draughtsmanship while his depiction of Scottish scenery is highly stylised. If at times he may seem over anxious and his plates over worked, the delicacy and detailed precision of his work

still makes a strong impression. Represented in NGS(17), SNPG (Lord Newton), BM, Glasgow AG.
**Bibl:** Geoffrey Bertram, John Clerk of Eldin, Edinburgh 1978; Bryan; Bushnell; Butchard 31-3; John Clerk of Eldin, Etchings, chiefly of views of Scotland, Bannatyne Club, 1825; DNB; Halsby 18-20 et al; Irwin 135; Macmillan [SA], 139,149-51,300; PCQ vol xii, 15, Feb 1925 and vol xiii, 97, Feb 1926.

**CLERK, Mrs Pauline** **fl 1984**
Exhibited 3 portraits in oil at the AAS from Mossgiel House, Mary Street, Stonehaven.

**CLERK, T** **fl 1810-c1830**
Scottish engraver. Engraved a map of the soils and roads of Perthshire in January 1810 issued with Morison Morison's *Guide to the City and County of Perth*, 4th ed, 1828. Also executed numerous maps and plans of Scottish towns 1814-1830.
**Bibl:** Bushnell.

**CLERK, William** **fl 1828**
Amateur Edinburgh painter; exhibited St Bernard's Well at the RSA in 1828.

**CLIFFORD, Henry Edward** **1852-1932**
Architect and watercolour painter. Apprenticed to John Burnet snr(qv). Although won a competition for the design of the Royal Glasgow Infirmary(1901), the work went to James Miller(qv). Specialised in late Gothic churches and domestic buildings. Partner in the firm of Clifford and Lunan. Exhibited designs and sketches of interiors RSA(1), GI(25) & RHA(1).
**Bibl:** A Gomme & D Walker, Architecture of Glasgow, London 1987(rev), 180,190,290-1; H Muthesius, Das Englische Haus, 1911 (transl 1979).

**CLIFFORD, John Grant ARSA** **1944-**
Born Perth, 14 Apr. Fife painter in oil; figurative subjects, portraits and abstracts. Studied at Duncan of Jordanstone College of Art, Dundee and Royal College of Art, London. Won Guthrie Award 1975, Robert Colquhoun Prize 1978 and the Gillies Award 1987. His earlier exhibited works have been almost all subject paintings, eg 'The Shepherdess', 'Seafarer', 'Couple Crying in the Web of Love and Hate', but recently he has become rather more abstract, using symbolic embryonic shapes with a propensity for the use of bright greens. Lectures Duncan of Jordanstone College of Art. In addition to his own creative work has played a significant role in promoting Scottish east coast artists. Chairman of the Dundee Group of Artists and since 1976 a professional member of the SSA as well as an active supporter of the Dundee WASPS Printmakers. In 1986 became involved in an exhibition of designs and models for Dundee Development and Public Art Project. Elected ARSA 1979. Exhibits regularly RSA since 1971. Represented Perth AG.

**CLIFTON, Robert Walter** **fl 1889-1890**
Amateur Edinburgh painter in oil. Exhibited twice at the RSA between the above dates.

**CLIMIE, Mrs Barbara Fortune** **fl 1938**
Amateur Glasgow watercolour painter. Exhibited GI(1), from Southpark, Lowndes Street, Barrhead.

**CLINSKILL, Miss L S** **fl 1884-1889**
Amateur Glasgow flower and figure painter in oil and watercolour. Exhibited RSA(1) & GI(10), latterly from Bienvenue, Bridge of Weir, Renfrewshire.

**CLINTON, Marjorie (or Margery) I** **fl 1954-1985**
Born Glasgow. Painter in oil and watercolour, also lithographer and potter; landscape, seascape, genre and semi-abstracts. Studied Glasgow School of Art and after a spell of teaching moved to London in the 1970s to study at the Royal College of Art. Became fascinated by reduction lustre glazes. Her pottery is decorated with gold and irridescent red lustres, a technique that goes back to the 9th century. Lives and works in Haddington, East Lothian. Exhibited RSA in 1954, 1958-59 and 1964-5, & GI(18). Represented Aberdeen AG.

**CLOUSTON, Brenda Mairi ARBS (Mrs Brittain)** **fl 1952-1988**
Edinburgh sculptress. Professional member, SSWA. Exhibited regularly RSA 1952-1971, again in the 1980s mainly portraits or figure compositions in stone and plaster. Exhibited a plaster statuette of a girl at the GI in 1956, from Bieldside House, Aberdeen.

**CLOUSTON, Robert Stewart** **1857-1911**
Born Orkney; died Sydney, Australia 25 Apr. Painter in oil, engraver; portraits, mezzotints, still life, figures, landscape and genre. Son of a minister, educated at the Universities of St Andrews and Edinburgh. In 1876 entered RSA Art School before proceeding to Bushey to study under Herkomer. There he learned competence in mezzotinting. Also painted portraits at which he had a remarkable skill in obtaining likenesses. Highly regarded as a mezzotint artist. *The Daily Graphic* said that this 'apostle of mezzotinting is one of the greatest living followers of that branch of art...his plates after Raeburn, Reynolds, Gainsborough and Watts being very fine'. Shortly after his death his mezzotints were viewed at the RSA as fine examples of recent Scottish art. An enthusiastic antiquary, spending much time digging a chambered dwelling or tomb at Unston, Stenness, the results of which are now in the Scottish Museum of Antiquities. Regular contributor to *The Connoisseur,* wrote *A Standard Book of Eighteenth Century Furniture, A Life of Arthur Melville,* and *Robert Mannering, The Designer* (this last containing 100 pencil illustrations). His landscapes were competent, traditional and unoriginal but it is as a mezzotinter that he is best remembered. Exhibited regularly RSA a total of 18 works, often using local models, also GI(2) & AAS(1) in 1886.

**CLOW, Alexander** **1861-1946**
Wood carver. Resided in Edinburgh and, in association with his brother **William CLOW**, was employed in much church and domestic wood carving in both Scotland and England. Established a business 1891, met Robert Lorimer(qv) the next year and went on to work exclusively for the celebrated architect. The two of them were responsible for all the carving in the Knights of the Thistle Chapel (except only the crests surmounting the stalls) and all the oak carving in the Scottish War Memorial Chapel. After WWI, carved the War Memorial for Westminster School sadly destroyed in 1941. He did much work for the late J Pierpont Morgan in St John's Church, Lattingtown. In 1931 Christopher Hussey, quoted by Savage, described them as 'two identical middle-aged men, looking, in their long grey overalls, like Tweedledum and Tweedledee grown spare and kindly'. They were linguists with a scholarly approach to their work, travelling Europe together to draw and measure and generally inspect. According to Hussey they achieved a virtuosity unsurpassed since the Middle Ages, often working from maquettes supplied by Deuchars(qv), Hayes and latterly Meredith-Williams and Pilkington Jackson(qv).
**Bibl:** Colvin; Christopher Hussey, The Work of Sir Robert Lorimer, 1831; Peter Savage, Lorimer and the Edinburgh Craft Designers, Edinburgh 1980, passim.

**CLOY, James** **fl 1883**
Amateur Glasgow painter; exhibited GI(1).

**CLUNESS, George E A** **fl 1941-1946**
Edinburgh sculptor. Specialised in figurative works. Exhibited RSA 1941-1946.

**CLYDE, Miss Helen F** **fl 1932-1939**
Glasgow painter of flowers and rustic scenes. Exhibited RSA(4) & GI(5), latterly from 6 Larchfield Avenue, Newton Mearns, Renfrewshire.

**CLYDE, Dr William M** **fl 1939-1941**
Amateur Dundee watercolourist. Member, Dundee Art Society; Head of English Department, University College, Dundee. Exhibited RSW(2) 1939 from 7 Beechwood Terrace.

**CLYNE, Arthur** **fl 1874**
Perth amateur painter and draughtsman. Exhibited RSA(1).

**CLYNE, Henry Horne** **1930-**
Born Wick, Caithness, 5 Mar. Sculptor and teacher. Trained at Edinburgh College of Art 1948-54 and Moray House 1954-55; awarded Harkness Fellowship to visit USA 1959-61. He has taught in Scotland and England and was recently Head of the sculpture

department at Winchester. Now retired and living in England. Brother of Thora C(qv). Exhibited RSA 1954, 1955, 1972(3) and 1974(2).

**CLYNE, Thora** **1937-**
Born Wick, Caithness, 10 Nov. Painter in oil, watercolour, pastel, pen and ink; landscape, figures, interiors, animals. Sister of Henry C(qv). In 1960 graduated with an hons. degree in fine art, Edinburgh University and Edinburgh College of Art and the following year gained Andrew Grant postgraduate scholarship enabling her to travel overseas. In 1961-62 was principal assistant, Aberdeen AG, before going to Boulder, Colorado to study printmaking. On her return in 1963, appointed part-time lecturer at Edinburgh College of Art until her retirement in 1993, and in 1979 received the Anne Redpath Award from the SSWA. Won Morrison Portrait Award (RSA) 1991 and again in 1995. Continues to travel, visits to Montenegro and Serbia influenced her landscape painting. Some of her interiors have shown a particular fondness for cats, impressionistically but characteristically portrayed. Formerly married to Robin Philipson(qv), now married to the composer Gareth Clemson. Member, Edinburgh Printmakers Workshop since 1995. Exhibits regularly RSA, RSW, SSWA & RGI from Perthshire.

**CLYNE, William D** **1922-1981**
Born Stirkoke Farm, Caithness, Jly 22; died Jan 23. Painter of landscapes & portraits; teacher; farmer. Brother of Henry(qv), with whom he shared a studio in the 1950s, and of Thora(qv). Trained Edinburgh College of Art 1940-42 before serving in the Fleet Air Arm in South Africa. Resumed training 1946-48, followed by a year at Hospitalfield House, Arbroath. Teacher, Banff Academy 1949-50. First solo exhibition 1950. Returned to Caithness in 1972. Known to his family and friends as 'Dan', he signed sometimes 'William D Clyne' and sometimes 'D Clyne'. "A stylist of great charm who excels in the fashionable devices of candle-grease and pen and ink upon damp paper...influenced by the delicate tints and nervous calligraphy of Anthony Gross and the shrill, excited scribblings of Topolski" [Douglas Percy Bliss]. Began exhibiting RSA & RSW 1951.
**Bibl:** Who's Who in Art 1952; John O'Groat Journal, Jly 1952 & Aug 1995; Caithness Courier, Aug 8, 1995 [From notes kindly supplied by Thora Clyne].

**COATES, Margaret** **fl 1969**
Amateur Edinburgh painter. Exhibited RSA(1).

**COATS, Janie H** **fl 1889**
Amateur Paisley artist; exhibited two flower studies at the GI from Ellangowan.

**COATS, Jessie** **fl 1889-1890**
Amateur Paisley artist, possibly related to Janie H Coats(qv). Exhibited four works at the GI between the above dates from Ferndean, Castlehead.

**COATS, Mary** **fl 1899-1910**
Born Paisley. Painter and ceramic artist. Studied Paisley School of Art, Glasgow School of Art and in the United States. On her return, became headmistress, West Public School, Paisley. Lived at Glenview, Barterholm. Most of her work was directed towards teaching and ceramic painting. Exhibited a flower study at the GI in 1899.

**COCHRAINE, M** **fl 1827**
Edinburgh artist; exhibited 'Roslin Castle' and 'Loch Lomond' at the RSA in 1827.

**COCHRAN, Miss Constance M** **fl 1960**
Amateur Glasgow artist; exhibited a continental landscape at the GI from 518 Castlemilk Road.

**COCHRAN, Miss Euphen F** **fl 1942-1943**
Selkirk watercolour painter of flowers; exhibited once at the RSA and twice at the GI from Ashkirk House, Ashkirk.

**COCHRAN, John** **fl c1750**
Probably Scottish. This engraver undertook a line and wash portrait of 'Jeremiah Dyson MP'. A large number of plates are attributed to him in O'Donoghue's *British Engraved Portraits.*
**Bibl:** Bushnell.

**COCHRAN, John** **fl 1929**
Amateur Glasgow watercolour artist; exhibited GI(1) from 37 Whitby Street, Parkhead.

**COCHRAN, Robert RSW** **c1850-1914**
Amateur Paisley watercolourist. Travelled extensively in Egypt and painted watercolours of that country. Also worked in Holland and France but was particularly fond of scenes in the Western Isles and along the Fife coast. Sometime Provost of Paisley. Elected RSW 1910. Exhibited five works at the RSA in 1895, 1901-2, 1909-10, 1913, RSW(13), GI(19), AAS from 1902-1908 & L(1). Represented in Paisley AG.
**Bibl:** Halsby 254.

**COCHRAN, William** **1738-1785**
Born Strathaven, Clydesdale 12 Dec; died Glasgow 23 Oct. Portrait painter, also occasional historical subjects and landscape. Studied Glasgow Academy of painting under Robert and Andrew Foulis(qv) 1754. In 1761, went to Rome continuing his studies under Gavin Hamilton(qv) before returning to Glasgow 1766. There he devoted himself to miniatures as well as portrait paintings on a large scale. Also occasionally executed historical subjects, eg 'Daedalus and Icarus' and 'Diana and Endymion', completed in Italy. Brydall records a landscape 'after Van Niest', which was at Newhall House. Eventually returned to Glasgow to join his elderly mother, establishing a thriving portraiture practice. Described by Bryan as a modest man who never exhibited his works nor put his name to them. Buried Glasgow Cathedral. An inscription on his gravestone reads 'The work of his pencil and this marble bear record to an eminent artist and a virtuous man'. Exhibited RSA 1846. Two of his works are in Glasgow AG, a large portrait of 'James Watt' and 'Sir James Dunbar of Mauchrum'.
**Bibl:** Bryan; Brydall 129-130; Caw 50; David Murray, Robert and Andrew Foulis, Glasgow 1913; Redgrave; Waterhouse, 83.

**COCHRAN, William** **fl 1883**
Amateur Glasgow painter; exhibited an orchard scene at the GI from 12 St James's Street, Paisley Road.

**COCHRANE, John** **fl 1837-1841**
Edinburgh sculptor; exhibited the model of a 'Gentleman in Highland Regimental Dress' at the RSA in 1837 and a three quarter bust of Sir Walter Scott in 1841.

**COCHRANE, John** **fl 1699-d1726**
Son of a gardener burgess, he was apprenticed to Walter Melville, painter, in 1699. He was working on St Mary's Chapel between 1713 and 1726 the year of his death.
**Bibl:** Apted 34.

**COCHRANE, John S** **fl 1913-1915**
Greenock artist in black and white. Exhibited figure studies at the RSA(3) & GI(1) during the above period from 9 Finnart Street.

**COCHRANE, Miss Mary L M** **fl 1966-1968**
Painter in oil and watercolour of still life and townscapes. Exhibited GI(2) from 43 Lambie Crescent, Newton Mearns, Renfrewshire.

**COCHRANE, William** **fl 1846**
Edinburgh landscape artist; exhibited RSA(1).

**COCKBURN, Alexander** **fl 1906**
Glasgow sculptor; exhibited a portrait of 'James Shaw Maxwell' at the GI from 120 West Campbell Street.

**COCKBURN ASSOCIATION** **1875-**
Founded as 'A popular Association for preserving and increasing the attraction of the city and its neighbourhood'. In 1849 Lord Cockburn published a pamphlet entitled *A letter to the Lord Provost on the best ways of spoiling Edinburgh* being a moderate diatribe against such architectural monstrosities as Waverley Station. In his biography published in 1874, ten years after his death, the letter was reprinted. Public opinion was aroused and the Association was born. It has continued ever since to exert an active and beneficial influence on architecture not only within the city but throughout Scotland.

**COCKBURN, Gordon** **1944-**
Born Maybole, Ayrshire. Draughtsman and painter, his best work to

date being executed in ink. Educated Carrick Academy. First solo exhibition 1977. Exhibits mainly landscape at the GI from 4 Masonhill Place.

**COCKBURN, Major-General James Pattison** **1778-1847**
Born New York; died Woolwich. Scottish parentage. Artillery officer, author, amateur draughtsman and illustrator. Entered Woolwich in 1793 and left two years later during which time he studied under Paul Sandby(qv). Served at the capture of the Cape of Good Hope and was in India 1798 and Copenhagen 1807. Director of Royal Laboratory, Woolwich 1838-1846, promoted major-general 1846. Following the peace of 1815 he was stationed in Malta and from there visited Italy and Switzerland. His watercolours are of high quality and have considerable charm, with a preponderance of greys, blues and greens. Cockburn wrote several travel books for which he also executed the illustrations including: *A Voyage to Cadiz & Gibraltar* (1815) with 30 coloured plates, *Swiss Scenery* (1820) with 62 plates, *The Route of the Simplon* (1822), *The Valley of Aosta* (1823) and a folio volume *Pompeii Illustrated* (1827). Represented in BM.
**Bibl:** Bryan.

**COCKBURN, Jane** **fl 1980-**
Flower painter, also occasional landscape and topography, mainly in watercolour. Studied glass engraving under Majella Taylor; mainly self-taught as a painter although trained for a time in botanical drawing by Anne-Marie Evans. First solo exhibition Edinburgh 1986. Won RHS silver medal for botanical painting, 1987. Lives and works in Edinburgh, dividing her time between painting, teaching and framing, from 30 Moray Place.

**COCKBURN, John** **fl 1889**
Exhibited study 'Moorland Scene at Evening' at the RSA in 1889.

**COCKBURN, Miss Laelia Armine RSW** **fl 1913-1963**
Animal painter in oil and watercolour. Studied at Kemp-Welch School at Bushey. Painted richly coloured oils, watercolour and pastels of animals, especially horses, and also landscapes. Moved home quite regularly, living first in North Berwick 1913, then Crianlarich 1919, Edinburgh 1924-1932, Ottery St Mary, Devon 1928, back to Midlothian in 1930, Balerno in 1936, and after 1943 from 3 East Fettes Avenue, Edinburgh. Her colours and technique were light and competent. Received Guthrie Award of the RSA 1925, having been elected RSW the previous year. Exhibited RA(2), RSA(77), RSW(51), GI(81), ROI(3), SWA(1), RI(1) & L(8).
**Bibl:** Halsby 254.

**COCKBURN, Marion** **1937-fl 1977**
Sculptress. She studied at Edinburgh College of Art, specialising in figures and torsos. Exhibited RSA 1962-1968 and again in 1977 by which time she had moved to Sunderland, & GI(1) 1964.

**COCKBURN, Timothy** **fl 1977-1983**
Portrait and narrative painter in Edinburgh; exhibited RSA 1977-8 and 1983.

**COCKBURN, W Laughland** **fl 1909-1938**
Paisley artist in oil and watercolour of landscape. Exhibited RSA(5), GI(15), AAS(3) & L(2) from Maryton, Oldhall and later from 4 Oldhall Road. Represented in Paisley AG.

**COCKER, Douglas ARSA** **1945-**
Born Perthshire. Sculptor. Studied at Duncan of Jordanstone College of Art, Dundee 1963-68. In 1966, awarded an SED enabling him to travel to Greece and Italy, and in 1968 a further Fellowship facilitated a visit to New York and a return to Greece. From 1972-1981 lived in Northampton, returning to Scotland to take up an appointment at Gray's School of Art, Aberdeen. Winner of a number of awards including Benno Schotz prize (RSA) 1967, Latimer Award (RSA) 1970, Gillies Award (RSA) 2001. Until 1972 he made sculptures in metal but after that date he preferred making box constructions incorporating wood and collage elements. 'By 1980 their coded meanings were becoming increasingly complex as texts and sound subjects were added. From the early 1980s he started on larger quasi-architectural works designed for outdoor exhibitions. Like his boxes, these were precisely machined structures made from wood; a series was also designed for interior wall-mounting. In 1985 he began making still larger works of rough wooden logs, inspired by classical architecture'. Elected ARSA 1984, Chairman of the Federation of Scottish Sculptors 1985. Exhibited annually RSA from 1966, also GI(10) & AAS 1969 onwards from Aboyne, Aberdeenshire, moved to Angus c2002. Represented in Glasgow AG, SAC, RSA, Hunterian AG (Glasgow), Peterborough AG, Northampton AG, Kirkcaldy AG, Perth AG, Ballinglen Archive (Ballycastle, Co Mayo).
**Bibl:** Hartley 122; TEC Glasgow, 'Doug Cocker; Sculpture and Related Works 1976-1986' (Ex Cat 1986).

**COCKERELL, Charles Robert** **1788-1863**
Joint architect with W H Playfair(qv) of the National Monument in Edinburgh, designed an exact imitation of the Parthenon in Athens, 1822. Cockerell's task was to ensure precision being appointed 1823, a year before Playfair's appointment as resident architect. Basil Hall likened the two to Phidias and Callicrates and refers to Cockerell's 'extensive and accurate knowledge of all the details of this wonderful building'.
**Bibl:** Dunbar 117; Gifford 48,67,437,pl.52.

**COGAN, R O** **fl 1866**
Glasgow landscape painter in watercolour who lived at 21 Woodside Terrace. One of the large number of artists who painted during the summer in Arran. Exhibited RSA(1) & GI(1).

**COHEN, David** **fl 1965-**
Sculptor, mainly abstract forms. Member of Glasgow Group. Exhibitions held in London, USA and Scotland. Exhibits RSA since 1965. Represented in Aberdeen AG, Dundee AG, Glasgow AG, Paisley AG, Perth AG, Leeds AG, HM The Queeen Mother.

**COIA, Emilio Hon LLD** **1911-1997**
Born Gasgow, Apr 13; died Jne 17. Portrait painter in oil and watercolour, also pastel and occasionally black and white; caricaturist and art critic. Educated at St Mungo's Academy, trained Glasgow School of Art 1926-31. Eloping with Mary, his future wife, to London with £12 between them, he became the regular cartoonist with the *Sunday Chronicle* until the editor fired him for his treatment of a particular friend, the novelist Ethel Mannin. After working in Kent during the war he moved back to Scotland where, following a brief spell in the shoe trade in Kilmarnock, he joined *The Scotsman* as regular cartoonist which included covering the Festival personalities. Among his many sitters were D H Lawrence, George Bernard Shaw, Henry Moore, Augustus John, Max Beerbohm, Shostakovich, Daniel Barenboim, Herbert von Karajan and Yehudi Menuhin. Menuhin thought Coia "every musician's favourite caricaturist [with a wonderful sense] of compassion, tragedy and concern". Artistic Adviser to Scottish Television. An intensely popular Glaswegian, he was three times elected President, Glasgow Art Club. Fellow, Royal Society of Edinburgh. Exhibited RGI(11) from 1 Kelvinside Terrace West including a portrait of 'Sir Robin Philipson' (1978). Represented by several works in the SNPG.
**Bibl:** The Times, Obituary, April 1977.

**COIA, Jack CBE RSA FRIBA PPRIAS** **1898-1981**
Born Wolverhampton. Sculptor. Son of Giovanni Coia, who became a sculptor when he left the family farm near Naples; his mother was a circus artist and dancer. Jack Coia was christened Giacomo Antonio. His father bought a barrel organ when he was a year old and placing Coia in a basket on the organ worked his way to Glasgow performing musical acts, incidentally opening one of the first Italian cafes in Glasgow. With no formal education, he obtained a position as an architect's apprentice in 1915 with J Gaff Gillespie(qv). Subsequently entered the Glasgow School of Architecture in which early baroque influenced him. After leaving Gaff Gillespie, he worked with A N Paterson, being responsible for a large number of war memorials in the vicinity of Glasgow. Later worked with the semi-traditionalist, A D Hislop, and in 1923 visited Italy making a number of detailed drawings. He then worked for a time in London for Herbert Welch but in 1927 returned to Glasgow to rejoin Gillespie's firm which had become known as Gillespie, Kidd and Coia and with them he remained for the rest of his working life. His first commission was in 1928, a design in the latent Art Nouveau style for a Glasgow hairdresser. In addition to his practice, he was an inspirational teacher at Glasgow School of Art where he lectured in design, his intimate knowledge of architectural tradition being especially appreciated. He

sketched everywhere, it is said he used to draw even on the tablecloth at Glasgow Art Club. According to P J Nuttgens, Coia made at least three major contributions to architecture: '1) work and design belonged to the fascinating transition through the re-interpretation of historical styles to a radical modern of the most uncompromising kind; 2) he expressed in himself a passionate concern for architecture as such, not for subordinate activities like management and organisation - design for its own sake as expression of people's needs and aspirations; and 3) he was one of the greatest experts in the assembling of a team of designers with whom he created unmistakeable new concepts distinguished by their individuality and uncompromising clarity'. Received many awards including the Saltire Award 1952, the RIBA Bronze Regional Award 1963 and again in 1966, the Royal Gold Medal in 1969 and honorary doctorates of Glasgow University 1970 and Strathclyde University 1976. Elected ARSA 1954, RSA 1962. His principal works were the Festival of Britain Exhibition at the Kelvin Hall, especially the ship building and railways pavilion (1951), the BEA offices in Buchanan Street, Glasgow (1970). Bellshill Hospital and Nurses Home (1962), the Caldoro in Union Street, Glasgow (1927), and a library extension and residential accommodation at Wadham College, Oxford. Exhibited GI(11).
**Bibl:** Patrick J Nuttgens, The Story of Architecture, Phaidon Press, Oxford 1995.

**COIA, Mrs Marie** **fl 1960-1968**
Flower painter. Married to Emilio Coia(qv). Exhibited at the RSA between the above years, also GI(1).

**COKIE, William (or Cockie)** **fl 1610-1617**
Early painter. Worked at Greyfriars churchyard, Edinburgh. Received £213. 6s 8d 'for his warkmanschip at the Netherbow'.
**Bibl:** Apted 34; Gifford 157; Mylne 106.

**COLAM, Mrs Cecilia** **fl 1926-d 1964**
Born & died Helensburgh. Artist in watercolour and pen and ink of still life and flowers. Mother of Kirstie C(qv). Lived for a spell in Craigmillar in the 1920s. Exhibited RGI(3) from Peffermill House, Edinburgh.

**COLAM, Kirstie P SSWA** **1929-**
Born Edinburgh. Works in embroidery and fabric collage. Daughter of Cecilia C(qv). Studied design, Edinburgh College of Art 1949-52. Attracted to the theatre, designing costumes for the Wilson Barrett Company, Perth Repertory, Glasgow Citizens Theatre, and Howard Wyndham before becoming a costume designer for television 1957. Moved from Glasgow to Edinburgh c1973 after which she free-lanced for television and theatre. Visiting lecturer in Costume, Queen Margaret College, Edinburgh 1889-1993. Lives at 8 Lynedoch Place, Edinburgh.

**COLCLOUGH, Frank** **fl 1981**
Born Wick, Caithness. Draughtsman & landscape painter primarily in oils. Lived in London, studying art at Camberwell, before settling in Alloway, Ayrshire. Originally a design draughtsman he began painting professionally 1981. Strongly influenced by the Scottish Colourists, his depiction of the north-western seaboard captures the light with great accuracy and strong colour. Exhibits regularly at RSA, RSW & RGI.

**COLDSTREAM, Sir William Menzies KBE DE Litt** **1908-1987**
Born Belford, Northumberland, 28 Feb; died London. Painter in oil, art administrator and teacher; figurative subjects, landscapes, and portraits. Youngest son of an austere Scottish doctor. After suffering rheumatic fever in 1919 he was educated at home. At the age of 18 he enrolled at the Slade and there he was remembered by Rodrigo Moynihan as 'a luminary...those that mattered, Tonks and Steer, knew he was good, and his reputation was riding high in the life rooms'. In the early 1930s abstractionism began to appear in the work of his contemporaries but Coldstream, dissatisfied with this development, abandoned participation in a 1934 exhibition 'Objective Abstraction'. He gave up painting and joined John Grierson's GPO Film Unit. There W H Auden was among his confederates. Coldstream's first film was 'The King's Stamp' for which he persuaded Benjamin Britten to write the score. The aim of the group was to provide an alternative to abstractionism based on dispassionate realism and the objective study of what lay in front of them. At the outbreak of WW2 he joined the Royal Artillery and became an official war artist in 1943. Posted to Cairo, he executed a series of portraits of Indian soldiers. Later transferred to Rome and thence to Capua and Rimini, where his landscapes painted from high vantage points over the war-torn cities attained a degree of delicacy and balance that mark, with their use of unaffected colour, the style by which he became known. After the war Parsmore invited Coldstream to teach at Camberwell and in 1949 he was appointed Slade Professor. Auden had encouraged the artist toward portrait painting and from the early 50s until his retirement he painted no more significant landscapes. Portrait commissions came steadily and at the same time demands for his services as an administrator increased. In addition to being Slade Professor of Fine Art he was Vice Chairman of the Arts Council of Great Britain, Trustee of both the National and Tate Galleries, Director of the Royal Opera House, Chairman of the British Film Institute, Joint Founder of the British Film School and author of the *Coldstream Report* which has formed the basis for art education in Britain since 1960. A retrospective exhibition of his work was held at the Tate, 1990-91. 'Man with a Beard' was purchased by the Chantrey Bequest 1940. Created CBE 1952, knighted 1956. Exhibited regularly at the London Galleries. Represented in Tate AG, V & A.

**COLERIDGE, Captain F G** **fl 1868-1914**
Glasgow landscape painter. Joined the army becoming an officer in 25th Kings Own Borderers and eventually moving to Twyford, Berkshire where he remained for the rest of his days. Exhibited a painting of Niagara at the RSA in 1868. Subsequently turned his attention increasingly to England where he exhibited a total of over 350 works, mostly at the Dudley Gallery and Walker's Gallery, London.

**COLES, Frederic Rhenius** **fl 1873-1889**
Edinburgh landscape painter in oil, he moved to Kirkcudbright in c1882. Exhibited RSA(5).

**COLEY, Nathan** **1967-**
Born Glasgow. Studied Glasgow School of Art, specialising in Environmental Art. His work, difficult to classify, endeavours to reveal, by means of slide projections and videos, the implicit codes of perception that emanate from physical structures. For example, *Fourteen Churches of Munster, 2000,* is a video portrayal of the churches of a German city prepared from an aerial tour that seeks to illustrate, through interpretative imagination, the significance of religious buildings for our cultural identity regardless of their explicit spiritual significance. Coley uses visual imagery, selected from the 'real' world, to capture our attention of intrinsic values and to sensitise the viewer to hidden significances that might otherwise be masked by unthinking familiarity. First solo exhibition in St Andrews 1992. His work has been exhibited in Glasgow, Aberdeen, Stockholm, Berlin, Oslo and at the SNGMA. In 2001 won the Scottish Art Council's Creative Scotland Award and the Henry Moore Sculpture Fellowship at Duncan of Jordanstone College of Art, Dundee, in which city he lives and works.

**COLEY, Richard** **fl 1973-1975**
Glasgow sculptor in metal and glass-fibre; exhibited twice at the RSA in 1973 and 1975, & GI(7), from 28 Queen's Drive.

**COLLIE, James Robertson** **fl 1855-1877**
Edinburgh painter in oil of buildings, genre, often Continental. Exhibited RSA(15) during the above period, also GI(5), from Peffermill, Liberton, Edinburgh.

**COLLIE, John** **fl 1756**
A miniature watercolour 'Mrs Katherine Hay', signed and dated 1756, is in the SNPG.

**COLLIE, John** **fl 1829-1847**
Scottish narrative and landscape painter. Exhibited regularly RSA between the above years.

**COLLIE, Miss Leys** **fl 1898-1910**
Portrait painter in oil of Harlaw, Inverurie. Exhibited frequently at the AAS during the above years.

**COLLIE, W Stewart G** **fl 1906-1919**
Glasgow painter in oil and pencil. Exhibited GI(3) between the above dates from 16 Burnbank Gardens.

**COLLIE, William** **fl 1830**
Edinburgh painter. Exhibited RSA(1) from Thistle Street.

**COLLIER, W F Jnr** **fl 1877-1878**
Amateur Glasgow painter; exhibited two country scenes at the GI from 12 Belmont Crescent.

**COLLINGBOURNE, Stephen** **1943-**
Born Dartington, Devon. Abstract sculptor and painter, usually in steel and on a small scale. Trained Bath Academy of Art 1961-4, becoming a lecturer at Dartington College of Art 1965-70. In 1970 he decided to pursue his studies, attending a foundry course at the Royal College of Art and in 1972 became assistant to Robert Adams. At the end of that year until the end of 1973 he lived in Malaysia, returning as a Fellow in sculpture, University College of Wales. He left there to take up a position at the Edinburgh College of Art. His constructions have been mainly in steel and linear in concept. 'My lasting preoccupation with contrasting curved and straight forms stems from Chinese and Japanese architecture and calligraphy...I am less interested in instant visual impact than in making sculpture which is capable of giving changing visual experience'. Received Ireland Alloys Award 1977. Founder member, Federation of Scottish Sculptors 1982-88. Exhibited RSA 1977-1981. Represented Leicester City AG, SAC.

**COLLINS, Hugh** **fl 1860-d1896**
Born Dundee. Painter in oil and watercolour; portraits, genre and military history, figurative. Lived most of his life in Edinburgh apart from a short spell in the 1880s in Dundee. Exhibited three works at the RA: 'In Close Pursuit of a Deserter', 'The 42nd Highlanders' (1868), and portraits of his daughter (1890) and his wife (1891). Both his daughters, Janet(qv) and Maria(qv), were also artists. Altogether, he exhibited 102 works at the RSA 1860-1891 & GI(17). Two of his works are in the Victoria AG, Australia, one in SNPG.

**COLLINS, Miss Jennett (Janet)** **fl 1881-1900**
Broughty Ferry oil painter of domestic scenes. Daughter of Hugh Collins(qv). Exhibited RA(3) 1892-1897, RSA(16), GI(2) & AAS(2), from 28 Forth Street, Edinburgh.

**COLLINS, Miss Maria** **fl 1885-1890**
Edinburgh painter in oil of English and Continental landscapes. Daughter of Hugh Collins(qv). Exhibited The Old Mill, Vichy at the RA in 1889 & RSA(8) 1885-1900, from 38 Moray Place.

**COLLINS, Peter G RSA** **1935-**
Born Inverness. Studied art at Edinburgh College of Art 1952-1956. Awarded post-diploma scholarship 1957, also an Andrew Grant travelling scholarship the same year. This enabled him to visit Italy and Switzerland 1957-8. Won Latimer Award, RSA 1962. The year before he had been appointed lecturer at Dundee College of Art, a position he retained for many years. Particularly impressed in Italy by the Pompeiian frescoes. An unashamed eclectic in his early artistic development, the paintings later evolved into a style of metaphysical realism. Elected SSA 1959, ARSA 1966, RSA 1974. Librarian RSA. Regular exhibitor RSA, also GI(2), from 44 Leamington Terrace East, Edinburgh. Represented in Aberdeen AG, Glasgow AG, Dundee AG, Perth AG, SAC.
**Bibl:** Gage 61-2;134; Hardie 198.

**COLLISON, Jan** **fl 1664-1665**
Believed to have been born in Aberdeen, although Apted notes that he may have been a member of the Scottish community living in Poland and may never have visited Scotland. All that is now certainly known is that on 30 October 1664, in Warsaw, King John Casimir bestowed on him the title of Court Painter and Royal Servitor, giving him permission to paint anywhere in Poland.
**Bibl:** Apted 34-5; Krystyna Malcharck, personal communications to James Holloway and Peter McEwan.

**COLOMBO, Russell** **1947-**
Born London. Abstract painter and art therapist. Trained Edinburgh College of Art 1969-73 and St Albans College of Art 1980-1. Lives and works nr Edinburgh. Regards his work as 'an attempt to find a visual metaphor for the unnamable'. Solo exhibition Edinburgh 1990.
**Bibl:** Bill Hare, Contemporary Painting in Scotland, Edinburgh 1993.

**COLONE, Adam de** **fl 1622-1628**
Portrait painter in oil. Almost certainly the son of the court painter Adrian Vanson(qv) and his wife Susanna de Colone. The family was of Dutch origin. Adrian Vanson had four children between 1595 and 1601. Adam must therefore have been born before 1595. 'On approaching manhood he went to the low countries 'for his better inhabling' in his father's craft. He spent several years there before returning to seek employment at the court in London. This was probably in 1622 when he painted a copy of Gheeraerts's portrait of the 1st Earl of Dunfermline. In 1623 he was paid £60 for two portraits of the King, presumably the full length portraits dated 1623 now at Hatfield and Newbattle. According to his Royal protector, de Colone had been in Scotland several months before seeking permission to travel to Flanders for business purposes. He did not leave immediately for the dated portraits appear down to the year 1628. These are generally of the more central figures among the Scottish aristocracy when compared to the patrons of his rival during this time, George Jamesone(qv); it remains unclear whether they were painted in Scotland or in London. The most significant of these patrons so far as establishing the artist's identity is concerned was George Seaton, 3rd Earl of Winton, who in 1628 paid to 'Adam the painter' a total of £40 for a number of portraits including his own which may have been the one now at Traquair dated 1628' [Thomson]. There is a certain aloof character to his work and a sensitive rendering of the nuances of flesh and expression which justify numbering him among the most important portrait painters working in Europe of his time. All Colone's principal pictures have a weight of pigment unusual for the time and there are signs that his influence was strong especially 'when he acted as a channel conveying the Jacobean manner to Jamesone, but it waned after about 1630 when the latter moved to a manner rather less circumscribed...while de Colone's portraits have a quiet depth and authority...they rather lack physical atmosphere' [Thomson]. Represented by five works in SNPG including James VI & I.
**Bibl:** Apted 35; Macmillan [SA], 58-60 et al; Thomson 50-55, also Thomson, The Life and Art of George Jamesone, 1974, 55-59 et passim.

**COLQUHOUN, Miss Lucy B** **fl 1866-1868**
Rothesay painter who lived in Kames Castle. Primarily a landscape painter; exhibited RSA(3) during above period.

**COLQUHOUN, Robert** **1914-1962**
Born Kilmarnock, 14 Dec; died London, 20 Sep. Painter, lithographer and theatrical designer. Educated Kilmarnock Academy, studied Glasgow School of Art 1932-7 under Hugh Crawford(qv) and Ian Fleming(qv), winning a travelling scholarship that enabled him to visit France and Italy. There he became a lifelong friend of Robert MacBryde(qv). After serving in WW2, and being invalided out in 1941, settled in London, driving ambulances for the Civil Defence and painting in the evenings. First one man exhibition was in London 1943. Designed for the theatre and was represented in the British Pavilion at the Venice Biennale 1954. A retrospective exhibition (1942-1958) was held at Whitechapel AG 1958. A follower of Cézanne and influenced by Picasso, painting mostly figures. Stimulated by French painting exhibitions in Glasgow, spent his post-diploma year at Hospitalfield. Shared a studio in London with John Minton and Robert MacBryde(qv), meeting other artists there including Michael Ayrton, Lucien Freud and Dylan Thomas. In 1943 he and MacBryde were joined in their London home by Jankel Adler(qv), the Polish artist and friend of Klee. Adler encouraged Colquhoun to forget landscape and concentrate on the figure alone set within a shallow picture space. Colquhoun was probably at the peak of his powers in the mid 1940s, his best known works being 'Woman with Leaping Cat' (1945-6) and 'Woman with Birdcage' (1946). 'The figures in these paintings have an underlying feeling of desolation and detachment which runs throughout Colquhoun's work.' In 1946 he began to experiment with monotypes and visited Ireland. In 1947 they were evicted from their studio and lived in Lewes being commissioned by Caroline Lucas and Frances Byng

Stamper, owners of Miller's Press. Thereafter his fortunes began to decline, partly as a result of alcoholism and ill-health. After moving to Essex 1949, where they lived in the home of the poet George Barker, he concentrated on animal painting but with less success than hitherto. Occasionally one sees the suggestion of an influence from Wyndham Lewis. After a period in Italy in 1949 he returned to Essex, finalising with MacBryde designs for the Scottish ballet 'Donald of Burthens', produced by Massine; he also designed George Levine's Stratford production of King Lear in 1951 before returning to London 1954. The sixteen lithographs for Turner & Shannon: *Poems of Sleep and Dream* (1947) are bizarre and appear unrelated to the text. A Colquhoun Memorial Gallery was opened in Kilmarnock 1972, with an annual Art Prize being also offered in his name. Exhibited RSA 1940. Represented in Tate AG ('Woman with leaping Cat',1945-6), SNPG, City of Edinburgh collection, Aberdeen AG, Glasgow AG, Dundee AG, Perth AG, Bradford City AG ('Woman with Birdcage', 1946), Bristol AG, Manchester AG, Sydney AG (Australia), Nat. Gall of Canada (Ottawa), Vancouver AG, Albright AG (Buffalo), Michigan AG, Metropolitan Museum of Modern Art (New York).
**Bibl:** Barbican Art Gall, London 'A Paradise Lost. The neo-Romantic Imagination in Britain 1935-55' (Ex Cat 1987, edited by David Mellor); Andrew Brown, Robert Colquhoun CEAC, 1981; CAC, Edinburgh 'Robert Colquhoun' (Ex Cat 1981, text by Andrew Brown); Gage 31-2,134-5; Hartley, 122-123 et passim; Macmillan [SA], 372-3,403; Mayor Gall, London 'Robert Colquhoun and Robert MacBryde, (Ex Cat 1977, text by Richard Shone); Harold Osborne(ed), Twentieth Century Art, 1988, 119; Rothenstein, 170 (pl 148); Whitechapel Art Gall, London 'Robert Colquhoun' (Ex Cat 1958); Malcolm Yorke, The Spirit of Place. Nine Neo-Romantic Artists and their Times, London 1988; Horne 118.

**COLSTON, Alexander** **fl 1863-1870**
Grange (Edinburgh) oil painter of landscape. Exhibited six works at the RSA between the above dates.

**COLSTON, John** **fl 1893-1906**
Glasgow painter of country scenes. Exhibited GI(2), latterly from 61 Westerland Street.

**COLTART, G A** **fl 1878-1882**
Dunoon watercolour painter; landscapes of local scenes. Moved to 24 Windsor Street, Edinburgh c1881. Exhibited twice at the RSA and three works at the GI between the above dates.

**COLVILLE, Miss Marilyn** **fl 1959-1962**
Stirlingshire sculptress who exhibited 2 works at the RSA: Bird Feeder and Mary Brown, and at the GI(2), from Gribloch, Kippen.

**COLVIN, Callum OBE** **1961-**
Born Glasgow. Painter and sculptor; photographer. Studied at Duncan of Jordanstone College of Art, Dundee 1979-1983. Initially in the painting department, he changed to sculpture and subsequently developed a great interest in photography. All three elements became apparent in his work. From 1983-85 he studied photography at the RCA in London. Research fellow in Digital Imaging, Univ. of Northumbria 1995-96 and in 2002 appointed Professor of Fine Art Photography. Awarded OBE 2001. Awards include 13th Higashikawa Overseas Photographer 1997, Creative Scotland Award 2000 and a Leverhulme Fellowship 2000. Has held solo exhibitions in Japan, Spain, USA and Portugal. Thereafter began to make constructions out of junk objects photographed in situ using large-format cameras. He painted on to the objects, first representing figures by a single black outline and then incorporating colour and layering objects in a highly sophisticated and complex way. His 'Constructed Narratives' are composed over a period of several days, painted over to give a bizarre and highly ambiguous reading of three-dimensional space, and then photographed. The elements in the composition are selected to construct an open-ended narrative dealing with male desire, fantasy and hero-worship. Represented in SNGMA, Aberdeen AG, Chicago Art Institute, Arnolfini Collection Trust (Bristol), Edinburgh City AC, Metropolitan Museum of Art (NY), Houston Museum of Fine Arts, SNPG, V&A.
**Bibl:** Alba, 1987 40-41; Hartley 124; The Photographer's Gall, London, 'Constructed Narratives: Photographs by Callum Colvin and Ron O'Donnell' (Ex Cat 1986); SNGMA, 'The Vigorous Imagination' (Ex Cat 1987); David A Mellor, Callum Colvin, Fruitmarket AG, ex cat; 'Light from the Dark Room', NGS cat 1995; James Lawson, 'Sacred and Profane', NGS ex cat 1998; Macmillan 2001, 161,163-4,167,180-1, illus 185,194.

**COLVIN, Meta** **fl 1881-1888**
Glasgow oil painter. Exhibited On the Alert at the RSA in 1881 and, having moved to Kilcreggan c1885, exhibited GI(5).

**COMFORT, Charles Fraser** **1900-1994**
Born Edinburgh. Migrated to Winnipeg, Canada 1912. Trained at Winnipeg School of Art and Art Student's League, New York, moving to Toronto 1925, inspired to become a painter by a visit to a Group of Seven exhibition in Toronto. Studied under Frank Johnstone. During WW2 appointed head Canadian war artist serving with the army in both the UK and Italy, subsequently publishing a book of his experiences *Artists at War* 1956. Regarded as a brilliant technician in both oil and watercolour. When he moved to Toronto his talents were widely recognised, being regarded as the virtuoso of the day. A fine achievement was his portrait of 'Carl Schaefer' (painted during the depression and now in Hart House, University of Toronto). During the depression he established a successful art studio in Toronto producing watercolours of enormous size as well as a series of oil paintings of the lower St Lawrence and Saguenay River landscapes in the 1930s. Elected member, Canadian Group of Painters 1933. In 1960 appointed Director of the National Gallery of Canada, a post he retained until 1965. Represented in NGS, Hamilton AG.
**Bibl:** Chivers.

**COMPER, Sir (John) Ninian** **1864-1960**
Born Aberdeen 10 Jne; died 22 Dec. Architect and stained glass window designer. Son of the founder and incumbent of St. Margaret's, Aberdeen. Educated Glenalmond and Ruskin School, Cambridge. Studied architecture at the Royal School of Art, South Kensington and with the window designer C E Kempe. Articled with G F Bodley and T Garner. The leading and most influential stained glass window designer of his time, although mostly worked in England. Possibly his best work in Scotland are the three windows at the E end of the chapel in Edinburgh's Theological College, Rosebery Crescent (originally Coates Hall). Knighted 1950. Principal works include windows for St Mary's, Wellingborough, St Crispin's Yerendawna, Poona, India (1903), the Warrior's Chapel, window, Canterbury Cathedral (1954) and the Welsh National War memorial, Cardiff (1928). Published *Of the Atmosphere of a Church* (1947) and *Of the Christian Altar and the Buildings which contain it* (1950). Wrote many articles in the transactions of ecclesiological societies.
**Bibl:** Gifford 368; Painton Cowen, Stained Glass in Britain,London 1985, passim.

**COMPTON, Miss Emma** **fl 1840-1854**
Edinburgh artist who painted landscape, still life and flowers. Exhibited RSA between the above dates.

**COMPTON, Mary Jane** **fl 1851-1861**
Edinburgh flower painter in oil. Possibly related to Emma(qv) and also to Thomas Compton(qv). Exhibited RSA in 1851, 1857 and 1861.

**COMPTON, Thomas** **fl 1837-1848**
Edinburgh landscape painter; exhibited 9 works at the RSA between the above years.

**COMRIE, Colin** **fl 1932**
Amateur Glasgow painter. Exhibited an interior at the GI from 4 Finnieston Quay.

**COMRIE, Minnie M** **fl 1898**
Glasgow painter. Exhibited GI(1) from 220 Longside Road, Crosshill.

**CONDAMINE, Mrs De la** **fl 1873**
Edinburgh landscape painter in oil. Possibly related to Henry Condamine, a painter of interiors, who exhibited RA 1894. Exhibited RSA(2) 1873.

**CONDIE, George** **fl 1960**
Amateur Stirling painter and schoolmaster. Exhibited a watercolour of a market place at the GI from The Schoolhouse, East Plean.

**CONDIE, Robert Hardie** **1898-1981**
Born Kirkcaldy but moved to Brechin at an early age. Painter of landscapes and harbour scenes in oil, watercolour and carbon. Taught in Brechin for many years. Best known for his large, broadly painted and colourful harbour scenes along the Aberdeenshire, Fife and Angus coasts. Exhibited regularly at the RSA between 1937-1971 from 10 Cookston Road and other Brechin addresses, and at the GI(59), latterly from 40 Bank Street, & AAS 1937-1973. Represented in Glasgow AG.

**CONELY, Miss Mary** **fl 1957**
Amateur Glasgow painter of still life. Exhibited GI(1) from 137 Templeland Road.

**CONGREVE, Miss D** **fl 1908-1923**
Nairn landscape painter in oil. Almost certainly related to Frances Dora C(qv). Exhibited regularly at the AAS during the above period, from Janefield.

**CONGREVE, Miss Frances Dora** **1869-c1935**
Nairn painter in oil and watercolour of landscapes and marines. Studied art in Rome, Naples and Edinburgh. Her principal works include 'Racing Yachts', 'The Rivals', 'Start of Race', 'Loch Ness'. Elected SSA 1909. Exhibited RSA, GI & AAS(1) from Millford.

**CONLAN, James** **fl 1963-1968**
Stirling landscape and genre painter. He exhibited 5 works between the above dates at the GI from 3 Forth Crescent.

**CONN, Adam** **fl 1960-1967**
Glasgow landscape painter; exhibited GI(8) from 11 Kildary Avenue.

**CONN, James** **1879-1946**
Dalry painter in oil. Brother of Thomas C(qv). Exhibited GI(3) from Wellington Villa.

**CONN, Thomas** **1872-1955**
Dalry artist. Influenced by James Houston(qv). Favoured landscapes executed in both oil and watercolour. Brother of James C(qv). Exhibited six works at the RSA 1913-1935 and GI(27) 1905-1946.

**CONNAL, John** **fl 1860-1876**
Edinburgh painter in oil and watercolour; topographical and town scenes. Exhibited nine works at the RSA between the above dates.

**CONNELL, Anne** **fl 1963-1967**
Edinburgh landscape and topographical painter in watercolour. Exhibited four works at the RSA 1963-1966, and a continental scene at the GI in 1967 from 5 Murrayfield Avenue.

**CONNELL, Christopher Thomas** **fl 1973-1976**
Aberdeen painter of local buildings and interiors. Exhibited AAS from 64 Bon Accord Street.

**CONNELL, James** **fl 1967-**
Dundee sculptor in wood, ceramics, steel and terracotta. Fascinated by the action of the sea on the surface of found materials. Member of the Glasgow Group(qv). Latterly his work has become more informed by a study of the construction of the violin family. In c1970 he moved to Helensburgh, exhibiting regularly at the RSA between 1979-1983 and again in 1989, and at the GI(3) from 26 Bain Crescent, also at the AAS(1). Represented in Glasgow AG, SAC.

**CONNELL, Leonard Shafto** **fl 1885**
Edinburgh painter in oil. Exhibited a portrait of 'Miss Ada Connell' at the RSA in 1885 from 22 Inverleith Row.

**CONNELL, Miss Marion S** **fl 1953**
Glasgow sculptress; exhibited a plaster head at the GI from 1048 Cathcart Road.

**CONNELL, R S** **fl 1870**
Amateur painter from Bridge of Weir, Renfrewshire; exhibited a study of a dog's head at the GI.

**CONNER, William Tait** **fl 1895-1901**
Painter living at 121 West Regent Street, Glasgow. Exhibited 4 works at the GI between the above dates.

**CONNOLLY, John** **fl 1960-1965**
Glasgow sculptor. Exhibited the statuette of an owl and a head of a man in metal at GI from 199 Thornton Street.

**CONNOLLY, Peter J** **fl 1973-1976**
Amateur Bearsden painter. Exhibited 4 figurative works at the GI from 4 Milverton Avenue.

**CONNON, William John** **1929-**
Born Turriff, Aberdeenshire, 11 Dec. Studied Gray's School of Art, Aberdeen 1956-59 and spent his post-diploma year at Hospitalfield. Travelling scholarship 1961 enabled him to visit France and Italy. After a short spell of teaching at Dunfermline, appointed to the staff of Gray's School of Art from where he retired 1993. Influenced by James Cowie(qv). Paints mostly in oil, figurative paintings in which the formal elements are given increasing emphasis. Elected SSA. Vice-President of Aberdeen Artists' Society 1971-74, President 1975 and 1993-4. Exhibits regularly AAS 1957-1985, many West Highland landscapes and coastal scenes, from 35 Albert Street, Aberdeen. Represented in Aberdeen AG and as part of the David Muirhead Bequest at the RSA.

**CONROY, Stephen** **1964-**
Born Helensburgh. Studied painting at GSA 1982-87. In 1986 won first prize at the RA's British Institute Fund Awards and the same year held a one-man exhibition of commissioned work under the auspices of Dumbarton District Council. 'Unlike the majority of his contemporaries who prefer loose brush work and violent colour, Conroy works in the classical tradition, meticulously planning each painting with detailed preparatory drawings and compositional studies. Employing chiaroscuro and compressing his subjects into a shallow pictorial space, he succeeds in evoking a claustrophobic Edwardian world in which communication between the figures is minimal and highly enigmatic.' There are recurring suggestions of the influence of such artists as Degas, Seurat, Sickert and Cowie(qv). Exhibits GI(2) from 14 Station St, Renton, Dunbartonshire. Represented in SNGMA.
**Bibl:** Hartley 124; Marlborough Fine Art, London, 'Stephen Conroy, Living the Life', (Ex cat 1989); SNGMA 'The Vigorous Imagination' (Ex Cat 1987).

**CONSOLIDATED SKETCHING CLUB** **c1848-c1860**
Edinburgh-based club formed by pupils of R.S. Lauder(qv). Lauder was perhaps the single most influential teacher in the history of Scottish art, not only through his own exertions but also by the friendly emulation and comradeship among many of his most outstanding students. The **DOUAY COLLEGE** and the **DILETTANTI SOCIETY** of the eighteenth century, as well as the Aesthetic Club(qv), had already created a tradition of communal artistic endeavour and social intercourse. The Consolidated club was formed by Hugh Cameron(qv), Joseph Ebsworth(qv), Peter Graham(qv), John Hutchison the sculptor(qv), John MacWhirter(qv), William McTaggart(qv) and W.Q. Orchardson(qv), the prime mover. Meetings were held weekly with subjects being drawn and painted according to a theme announced at the beginning of each session. After about a year there was a threatened split on the grounds of exclusiveness but this was avoided by adding further members including, among others, George Paul Chalmers(qv), George Hay(qv) and John Pettie(qv). It continued in this form for about ten more years before being replaced by the contemporaneous group The Smashers(qv), subsequently the Auld Lang Syne(qv) group.
**Bibl:** Caw 234.

**CONSTABLE, Agnes Maria** **1857-?**
Born Kirkmichael, Perthshire. Watercolour painter of flowers. One of two sisters, living at Balmyle, Blairgowrie who in c1888 moved to Carlisle. Exhibited RSA & AAS both in 1887.

**CONSTABLE, James Lawson** **1890-?**
Born Hamilton, 28 Jan. Painter of portraits and landscapes in oil. Studied Glasgow School of Art before becoming a member of the Glasgow Society of Painters and Sculptors. Married Margaret Constable(qv). From Chantinghall Road, Hamilton exhibited RSA(9), GI(5) & L(1).

**CONSTABLE, Jane Bennett** **1867-c1935**
Born Kirkmichael, Perthshire, 16 Sep. Painter of genre and landscape. Sister of Agnes Maria C(qv). Pupil of Frank Calderon and Walter Donne. She spent some time in France, exhibiting at the Salon des Artistes Français 1926-1931. Favourite compositions were genre, such works as 'Field Labour', 'Going Home' and 'Hard Times'. Exhibited a landscape of Loch Long at the RSA 1887 and showed quite regularly in the provinces, Paris Salon & SWA(7). Exhibited RSA in 1887 and 1888 and again in 1925 and 1929. Also AAS 1887-1935, formerly from Balmyle, Blairgowrie.

**CONSTABLE, Margaret (née Taylor)** **fl 1932**
Landscape artist. Wife of James Lawson Constable(qv). Lived at Hamilton. Exhibited a continental landscape in watercolour at the GI from 9 Chantinghall Road.

**CONSTABLE, Norman** **fl 1973**
Amateur Aberdeen painter. Exhibited AAS from 10 Rosemount Square.

**CONSTANTINIDES, D L** **fl 1901**
Amateur Edinburgh portrait painter. Exhibited a portrait of J R M Muir at the GI from 20 South Frederick Street.

**CONVERY, Francis** **1956-**
Born Paisley. First class hons in painting, Edinburgh College of Art 1979-83, with postgraduate diploma and distinction 1983-86, taught ECA, and from 1988 at Gray's School of Art, Aberdeen becoming Head of Painting 1997. Began life as an apprentice mechanical engineer. After art school he won a series of awards including the Keith Prize 1983 and Latimer Award 1984. His work pays scant regard to perspective, draughtsmanship or texture but depends rather upon the interpretation of juxtapositions and composition with which it happens to be endorsed by the observer. Following the figurative nature of his earlier work he has become a master of tonality. First solo exhibition 1984. Exhibited RSA 1984, 1986, 1988 and 1990.
**Bibl:** John Griffiths, Scottish Gallery, Edinburgh (Ex Cat 1991).

**CONWAY, Melton** **fl 1860**
Edinburgh painter. 'The Castle of Chillon' was shown at the RSA in 1860.

**COOK, Mrs Alice May** **1876-1960**
Edinburgh painter in oil; portraits and topographical subjects. Exhibited twice at the RSA before WW2 and twice thereafter.

**COOK, Ashley** **1964-**
Born Edinburgh. In 1986 studied at Glasgow School of Art, from which he graduated with a first class honours degree. Mainly interested in printmaking using silk screens and collage. Portrays the female form showing an Indian influence in colour, pose and composition. Teaching staff, Glasgow School of Art (silkscreen printing). Exhibits RSA.

**COOK, Cyril J** **fl 1952**
Amateur Glasgow landscape painter. Exhibited a watercolour study of Gardenstown, Banff from 4 Elm Road, High Burnside.

**COOK, David** **1957-**
Born Dunfermline. Painter and sculptor. Still life, semi-abstracts, cats and flowers, collages. Worked as a bricklayer 1973-7 before enrolling at Duncan of Jordanstone School of Art 1979-84. A travelling scholarship enabled him to visit Paris, Amsterdam, Belgium and Cyprus. Received Guthrie Award 1983. First one-man exhibition in 1982 followed by his first exhibit at the RSA the following year. Stylistically close to the Art Brut primitivism of Buffet, especially in the use of vibrant colour.
**Bibl:** Enid Gauldie, 369 Gallery (Ex Cat 1989).

**COOK, David Mackie** **fl 1983-**
Dundee painter. Exhibiting RSA since 1983, & GI(1).

**COOK, Miss Eveline M** **fl 1949**
Amateur Paisley painter of watercolours. Exhibited a Swiss landscape at the GI from 16 Woodland Avenue, Potterhill.

**COOK, Helen A** **fl 1909-1912**
Watercolour artist of Carrick House, Earlsferry; exhibited RSW(1) & GI(1).

**COOK, Herbert Moxon** **1844-c1926**
Landscape and coastal painter. Although originally from Manchester, this prolific artist spent an increasing amount of time in Scotland, particularly on Arran and the west coast. Among his 7 RA exhibits, although 5 were submitted from London addresses, all except one were Highland subjects. His portrayal of the mountains in sombre, glowering mood was more successful than the animals and figures that were sometimes included. Exhibited widely including RA(7), RSA(6), ROI(1), RI(10), GI(15), RBA(6) & RHA(1).

**COOK, Ian RI RSW** **c1952-**
Born Paisley. Painter in oil and watercolour. Studied GSA 1969-1972, being awarded the Hutchison Drawing Prize 1972. Aided by a post-diploma award, travelled to Spain and North Africa 1974. His landscapes are semi-impressionistic with a sure but light touch and a fine sense of tonal harmony. Exhibited GI(64) since 1976; from 1983 living at 3 Falside Road, Paisley; also exhibits RA & RSW since 1978, as well as in Eire, France & Spain.

**COOK, James** **fl 1904-1905**
Paisley landscape artist from Englethwaite, Castlehead. Exhibited coloured sketches at the Paisley Art Institute 1904-1905 & GI(1).

**COOK, James B** **fl 1917-1962**
Kilbirnie, Ayrshire, landscape and coastal artist in oil and watercolour. Exhibited 'Cullen Harbour' at the RSA in 1921 for which he received an honourable mention in the Studio. Moved to Motherwell 1958. In addition to Scottish subjects, also painted French views. Exhibited RSA 1919-1946, GI(38) & L(3).
**Bibl:** Halsby 254.

**COOK, John Kingsley** **1911-**
Edinburgh landscape and genre painter. Head of School of Design, Edinburgh College of Art. Exhibited RSA 1946-1956.

**COOK, Joseph** **fl 1931-1932**
Amateur Inverness watercolour painter and engraver of 7 Muirfield Road, he specialised in harbour scenes, showing 4 during the above years, including one at the RA.

**COOK, Margaret B** **fl 1897-1913**
Painter and illustrator. Oil and pencil; portraits. Lived in Ardrossan before moving to London c1905. Exhibited once at the RA, also RSA(6), GI(6) & RBA.

**COOK, Marion** **1910-**
Clarkston painter of 2 Woodbank Crescent; exhibited landscapes at the RSA in 1970-76 and again from 1982 until her husband died 1990.

**COOK, Rev Thomas** **fl 1917-1921**
Minister of Levern Manse, Nitshill. Exhibited four black and white topographical studies, including one of 'Durham Cathedral' at the GI during the above years.

**COOK, Walter J R** **fl 1934-1941**
Polmont, Stirlingshire artist who moved to Edinburgh shortly before WW2. Exhibited RSA(6) between 1934-41, mostly designs for stained glass memorial windows.

**COOKE, F H** **fl 1907**
Painter. Exhibited RSA(1) from the Parsonage, Dalkeith.

**COOKE, George Ernest** **fl 1880-1881**
Edinburgh painter in oil; exhibited RSA(4) between the above years.

**COOKE, Thomas Etherington** **fl 1863-1895**
Edinburgh landscape, coastal and interior painter in oil and watercolour. Lived in Portobello before latterly moving to Glasgow. Exhibited 13 works at the RSA 1863-1871, & GI(1), from West Arthurlie, Renfrewshire, & AAS 1890.

**COOKESLEY, Mrs Margaret Murray** **c1850-1927**
Edinburgh painter in oil; landscape and figure painter. Visited the Middle East in the 1880s exhibiting 'Seller of Pottery, Cairo' at the RSA 1885, 14 years after her first exhibit there. In the mid 1880s moved to London where she remained until 1891 before going to Salisbury, eventually settling in Bath 1915. Her painting of 'Ellen Terry as Imogen', exhibited in 1898, made quite a stir at the time, similarly her last exhibit, 'A Thing of Beauty' (1902). In addition to RA(24), exhibited RI(18), ROI(39), SWA(9) & L(31).

**COOMBER, Miss June** **fl 1976**
Amateur Edinburgh artist. Exhibited a landscape at the GI from Millburn Lodge, Gogarburn.

**COOPER, Mrs** **fl 1837-1838**
Amateur painter from Drummond Place in Edinburgh who exhibited at the RSA twice in 1837 and once the following year.

**COOPER, Miss Eleanor** **fl 1868**
Edinburgh landscape painter in oil; exhibited once at the RSA in the above year.

**COOPER, Francis ARCA** **fl 1926-1933**
Painter. Member of the staff of Dundee School of Art; exhibited AAS 1926 and again 7 years later.

**COOPER, Frederick L** **fl 1928-1960**
Glasgow painter in oil and watercolour. Moved to Rutherglen c1935 and in 1960 was living at 37 Carolside Avenue. Exhib GI(7) & L(1).

**COOPER, G Sidney** **fl 1846**
Edinburgh landscape painter in oil; exhibited RSA 1846.

**COOPER, Hugh** **fl 1896**
Amateur Glasgow watercolourist. Exhibited RSW(1) from 9 Elder Park Street, Govan.

**COOPER, J C** **fl 1912**
Painter. Exhibited a local townscape in oil at the GI from Euclid, Bothwell Road, Hamilton, Lanark.

**COOPER, Joan Ophelia Gordon** **1915-**
Born Scotland, 1 July. Sculptress and watercolourist. Daughter of Lawrence Bell the engraver, and pupil of H Brownsword, Violet E Gibson and Geoffrey Duley. Generally signs her work 'Ophelia Gordon Bell'. Exhibited regularly at the RA, GI, RSA and Lake Artists Society.

**COOPER, John C** **fl 1941**
Amateur Lanarkshire watercolourist; exhibited 'In the Woodlands' at the GI from Greenside, Bothwell.

**COOPER, Leslie F** **fl 1957**
Amateur Lanarkshire sculptor. A wood statuette of 'Janus' was exhibited at the GI from 28 Kylepark Crescent, Uddingston.

**COOPER, Lindsay Ewan** **fl 1983**
Aberdeen abstract painter in the modern manner; exhibited AAS from 22 Springfield Gardens.

**COOPER, Marion M** **fl 1949-1957**
Edinburgh painter. Mostly landscape and portraits. Exhibited RSA 1949-1957.

**COOPER, Richard Snr** **1705-1764**
Born probably in Yorkshire. Artist and engraver who came to Edinburgh during the early years of the century, initially to visit Alexander Guthrie. He liked the city and remained there, having married the daughter of an Edinburgh merchant. Involved in the Edinburgh Guild of St Luke(qv) from its establishment 1729, becoming its first Treasurer. Studied under John Pine. Sir Robert Strange(qv) and Andrew Bell(qv) were among his pupils. A few years later, in 1735, he established his own academy, known as the Winter Academy as it only met at that time of year. 'Artists paid an annual subscription of half a guinea, how long this Academy lasted is not known, but he would have made available to students his fine collection of engravings after Old Masters, as indeed he may have already done at the Academy of St Luke, where he had been the only senior artist in the position to really instruct the younger ones' [Irwin]. Best known for his engravings of contemporary portraits, also many bookplates including a design for Lord Elphinstone. In Vol II of *The Book of the Old Edinburgh Club,* there is a coloured reproduction of Cooper's engraving of Prince Charles Edward, drawn in 1745. An earlier and scarcer print, dated 1742, shows the surrender of Mary Queen of Scots to the Confederate Lords at Carberry Hill, a small version of which was published in Grant R Francis' *Mary of Scotland.* The original was in Kensington Palace, having been presented to the Royal Family by the Earl of Pomfret in 1738. Represented in Glasgow AG and the City of Edinburgh collection.
**Bibl:** Brydall 112,171,194; Bushnell; DNB; Halsby 24; Irwin 83-4; Macmillan [SA], 92-3,118,149.

**COOPER, Richard, Jnr** **1730-1820**
Born Edinburgh, son of Richard Cooper Snr, the engraver. Mainly a portrait painter but little is now known of either his life or his work. He was a pupil of Le Bas in Paris. Neither he nor his father should be confused with the English miniature painter of the same name working at about the same time. Settled in Charles Street, St James's Square, London, c1787, where he remained for the rest of his life.
**Bibl:** Halsby 24.

**COOPER, Robert** **fl 1875-1884**
Glasgow painter in oil of genre and landscape. Exhibited three works at the RSA & GI(8), latterly from Ashburn Lodge, Partickhill.

**COOPER, Robert Maxwell** **c1813-c1853**
Born Edinburgh, died London. Landscape and figurative painter in oil. After working for a time in Glasgow where he gave lessons, went to London, perhaps because of domestic unhappiness. There he was employed as a scene painter with Grieve and the Wilsons, and by Telkin. A fine portrait of the poet, Montgomery, was engraved. His last work was on some of the scenery at Windsor Castle theatre, for performances by Charles Kean, executed for Prince Albert. A notable landscape is the large 'Inveruglas', shown at the Glasgow Dilettanti Exhibition. 'Gifted with extraordinary talent, whose pictures, possessed of rare merit, are seldom to be met with...His landscapes are full of rich, deep, warm colour, great breadth, and free masterly execution - in such respects very closely resembling the work of Muller' (Brydall). Died from food poisoning. Exhibited at the RSA throughout the 1840s.
**Bibl:** Brydall 385-6.

**COOPER, Waistel** **1921-2003**
Born Ayr, April 19; died Penzance, Jan 15. Painter, potter & teacher. Educated Ayr Academy, Hospitalfied Coll. of Art & Edinburgh Coll. of Art. Influenced by Robert Colquhoun(qv), Robert McBryde(qv), Barbara Hepworth and Henry Moore. Injured during the war, he returned to academic life in Edinburgh. In the early 1950s he received a commission from Iceland to undertake a series of portraits; whilst there he met the Icelandic sculptor Gestur Thorgrimsson who invited Cooper to set up a pottery. Intent on further development, he returned to Britain 1950 creating a studio in Somerset. After two years of private experimentation he became increasingly fascinated by the contrast between glazed and unglazed surfaces. His first solo exhibition of pottery was at Henry Rothschild's Primavera Gallery 1955. Best known for his white stoneware based upon a mix of South Devon ball clay and Cornish calcined kaolin, signed 'Waistel'. A retrospective exhibition of his work was held at Manchester City AG 1994. Represented in Royal Museum of Scotland and the V&A.
**Bibl:** The Times, Obit, 1.ii.03

**COOPER, William** **fl 1866**
Amateur Edinburgh painter; exhibited an interior at the RSA on the above date.

**COPE, Samuel** **fl 1859-1865**
Glasgow oil painter of still life, flowers and fruit, exhibited three works at the RSA in 1859, 1860 and 1863, also GI(10), from 10 Minerva Street.

**COPELAND, Enoch** **fl 1869-1870**
Glasgow sculptor of portrait busts. Exhibited GI(3), latterly from 13 Holmhead Street.

**COPLAND, Alick D** **fl 1910**
Amateur Aberdeen painter of wildlife; exhibited AAS(1) from 38 Grosvenor Place.

**COPLAND, John** **1854-1929**
Born Kirkcudbright, 9 Jne; died 30 Oct. Painter in oil, watercolour and pencil, also book illustrator; landscapes, figurative. Descended on his father's side from Sir John Copland of Nevills Cross, Durham, and on his mother's side from the Greys of Eskdale, one of whom was Surgeon Grey who attended Napoleon on St Helena, and more recently from a number of sculptors in the USA. In 1883, Copland went to Liverpool intending to study marine engineering but decided on art instead, whereupon he proceeded to London. Attracted to the traditional English masters of landscape, he studied under William Gill. Then travelled extensively throughout Britain, settling in Dundrennan, Kirkcudbright when the Kirkcudbright School was coming to life. He was also a book illustrator, executing 40 illustrations for his school friend S R Crockett. Illustrated Wood's *Smuggling in Galloway* and *Witchcraft in Galloway.* His work has sometimes been likened to that of Mouncey(qv). He travelled in a car designed and built by himself. Exhibited regularly RSA(13) 1903-1921, & GI(5).

**CORBET, William** **fl 1873-1880**
Edinburgh painter in oil and watercolour; landscape. Exhibited RSA between the above dates latterly from 6 Royal Park Terrace.

**CORBETT, Hubert** **fl 1970-1971**
Sutherland sculptor who has lived and worked for most of his life at Shinness. Exhibited three abstract paintings at the RSA in 1970 and 1971. Best known for his 'Sutherland' pottery.

**CORBOULD, Alfred** **fl 1835-1875**
Painter of sporting subjects, including stalking scenes, often in the Highlands. Member of a well-known family, probably the brother of Aster C(qv). Exhibited RA(22) including 'Duncan and the Deer' (1838) from the Waverley novels, and perhaps his best known work 'At Home in the Highlands' (1868).

**CORBOULD, Aster R C** **fl 1850-1874**
London painter in oil and watercolour. Member of a well-known artistic family several of whose members were actively exhibiting throughout the nineteenth century. Exhibited RA(35) 1850-1874 including a number of Highland subjects, mostly sporting scenes and occasional portraits. Between 1861 and 1870 he exhibited 12 works at the GI, all of them Highland scenes.

**CORD, George H** **fl 1973**
Amateur Dundee artist; exhibited AAS(1).

**CORDINER, Rev Charles** **1746-1794**
Painter, illustrator and author; clergyman. Father of Rev James C(qv). One of the few pupils known to have studied at the Foulis Academy(qv), Glasgow between 1763 and 1766. During his spell there, he and a student friend, Robert Paul, embarked upon various tours giving particular attention to castles and old bridges which were drawn in pencil and gouache in a delicate, refined and highly competent manner. During his time as a Minister in Banff, he published the *Antiquities and Scenery of the North of Scotland* (1780) and *Remarkable Ruins and Romantic Prospects of North Britain* (1795). His 'Bothwell Castle' is in the Hunterian Museum, Glasgow.
**Bibl:** Caw 50; Halsby 32; Irwin 86,90(illus).

**CORDINER, Rev James** **1775-1836**
Topographic artist, cleric and illustrator. Son of the Rev Charles C(qv). Graduated Aberdeen Univ 1793. Army chaplain in Madras 1797 and then at Colombo 1798-1804. In 1807 settled in Aberdeen becoming minister of St Paul's Episcopal Church 1807-1834. Illustrated *A Description of Ceylon* (1807) and *A Voyage to India* (1820).
**Bibl:** Houfe 100.

**CORMAC, Richard J S** **fl 1946**
Amateur Glasgow watercolour painter of animals. Exhibited GI(1) from 244 Langside Road.

**CORMACK, Neil** **1793-?**
Miniature painter. Considerably more is known about his life than his work. It is not known for certain even that he was Scottish although given his name and the fact that his brother was minister of Stow in Midlothian it seems highly probable. Entered RA Schools 1816 before taking up an appointment in Bombay with the East India Company where he also practised as a miniature painter. While there he wrote an account of female infanticide in Gujarat and other similar works. He gave the Earl of Fife and Mr Charles Forbes as securities. In 1823 went to Madras but does not appear to have stayed there long as he is next heard of in Bombay 1819-1827. He must have returned to Madras c1831 for he advertised from 10 Stringer Street on 27 January that he was willing to paint miniatures and sell drawing materials. On March 31 he again advertised, this time that he had moved to a garden opposite the Pantheon formerly owned by a Dr Filson. Cormack stated that he had reduced his charges to "30 pagodas and upwards according to style". He was living in Madras until 1837 after which time nothing more was heard. Exhibited five miniature portraits at the RA between 1814 and 1816.
**Bibl:** Annals of the Fine Arts, II, 569; Foskett 1,218,219; Graves RA.

**CORNER, James M** **fl 1849**
Edinburgh landscape portrait painter; illustrator. Illustrated frontispiece for Crombie's *Braemar.* Exhibited RSA(1).

**CORNET, James** **fl 1889**
Dalmuir amateur painter; exhibited a local scene at the GI in the above year.

**CORNWALL, J Steel(e)** **fl 1902-1937**
Aberdeen painter in oil and watercolour of local and continental landscapes. Exhibited AAS from The Birches, Milltimber and later from Clydeburn, Gordondale Road.

**CORRIGAN, Kathleen** **fl 1965-1966**
Amateur sculptress of 10 Stirling Drive, Garve, Ross-shire. Exhibited several works at the AAS during the above years.

**CORRUDES, James (or John)** **fl 1670-1680**
Variously spelled Corrudez, Corrodus, Caruduse and Carrudus. Painter living in the Canongate, Edinburgh. In 1671 he was paid £84 Scots by Lord Chancellor Rothes for a picture and the same amount by the 3rd Duke of Hamilton. The following year he received £36 Scots from Sir William Bruce and in 1673 he painted a portrait of the Duchess of Lauderdale.
**Bibl:** Apted 36; Brydall 94; Fraser, The Lords Elphinstone of Elphinstone, i, 215; Kinross House Muniments, GD.29/262/3-4; Lauderdale Muniments, Thirlestane, 6/11.

**CORSON, Miss Margaret A** **fl 1921-1923**
Painter in oil and watercolour. Exhibited three figure compositions at the RSA in 1922 and two works at the RSW from 45 Frederick Street, Edinburgh; also AAS(2).

**COSGROVE, James** **1939-**
Born Glasgow. Joined the army in 1955 as a cartographic draughtsman. Then worked for ten years in the telecommunications industry before deciding to study art, concentrated on prints and textiles at the GSA 1967-71. Appointed to the staff, becoming head of department in the mid 1970s. In 1980 held his first one man exhibition. Has also exhibited ceramics and sculptures, although concentrating mainly on painting. Shows regularly RSA & GI(7), latterly from 16 Gordon Street, Paisley. Represented in SNGMA, Glasgow AG, Perth AG, SAC.
**Bibl:** Hartley 124.

**COSGROVE, Paul** **1961-**
Glasgow sculptor. Preferred medium is wood. Graduated 1983 with an honours degree in fine art from Glasgow University and School of Art. Winner of various awards including Ireland Alloys Award, RSA (1985) and Benno Schotz Award of the GI (1986). In 1988 was Artist-in-Residence at Aberdeen AG and the following year held a two months' residency at the Centrum Rzezby Polskiej in Poland. Elected SSWA 1988. Exhibits RSA & GI(5), since 1986 from Cuttieburn House, Craig, Rhynie, Aberdeenshire. Represented in Aberdeen AG.

**COSSMAN, M** **fl 1875**
Edinburgh oil painter of interiors, exhibited RSA(1).

**COTTER, Miss Katherine** **fl 1881-1891**
Edinburgh painter in oil and watercolour; flowers, still life and buildings. Exhibited five works at the RSA between the above years.

**COTTERELL, Miss Lorraine** **fl 1986**
Amateur Glasgow painter; exhibited a flower study at the GI from 48 Glencairn Drive.

**COTTIER, Daniel** **1838-1891**
Painter in oil of interior scenes, stained glass window designer. Lived for some years in Edinburgh. Exhibited RSA(1) 1865. Represented by two windows (the west window and one at the east end of the nave) in St Giles Cathedral, Edinburgh; a very Victorian window on the choir south side at St. Michael's, Linlithgow; some portrait pieces transferred from Dowanhill convent to St. Andrew's college, Bearsden; a panel in the People's Palace, Glasgow; 'Hope' in the Old West Kirk, Greenock and, most importantly, in the Cairndhu hotel, Helensburgh; the east window in Paisley Abbey; and three portrait panels in Colearne House (Ruthven Hotel), Auchterarder, Perthshire.
**Bibl:** Gifford 117,400; Painton Cowen, Stained Glass in Britain, 1985, 233-5,237-8.

**COTTON, Niall** **fl 1983**
Aberdeen watercolour painter of semi-abstracts; exhibited AAS(2) from 91 Holburn Street.

**COTTON, R Jane** **fl 1975**
Amateur Helensburgh painter; exhibited a coastal scene at the GI from 141 West Princes Street

**COTTRELL, Mrs Lily** **fl 1940-1967**
Dalkeith artist of 26 Lasswade Road, Liberton. Exhibited landscapes and pastoral scenes at the RSA 1940 and 1959-1967.

**COULBORN, May** **fl 1894-1897**
Glasgow artist; flowers studies and landscape. Moved to Kent 1896. Exhibited GI(3) & L(2), after 1895 from Beckenham.

**COULING, Arthur Vivian** **1890-c1952**
Born Shantung, China, 13 Nov. Painter in oil and watercolour, etcher of landscapes and marines. Son of a missionary. Studied Edinburgh College of Art remaining there for many years. Exhibited RSA(28), GI(21) & L(1), from 14 Northumberland Street, Edinburgh. Represented in Glasgow AG.

**COULLIE, J E** **fl 1859-1861**
Edinburgh amateur painter in oil of figurative subjects, exhibited RSA(2) in 1859, 1860 (2), and again in 1861 (2).

**COULOURIS, Mary Louise** **1939-**
Born New York. Linlithgow-based engraver and muralist. Studied Slade School under Anthony Gross. A French government scholarship took her to Paris where she developed her own colour etching technique. Influenced by the French Impressionists and by Riego Riviero. Lived at 5 Strawberry Bank, Linlithgow. Exhibited RSA 1978 and again twice in 1983; also RA. Represented in Sheffield AG, Trinity College Oxford, New York Public Library.

**COULTON, Kevin John** **fl 1969-1975**
Pencaitland sculptor. Exhibited twice at the RSA, in 1969 and 1975.

**COUPAR, Finlay** **fl 1974-**
Edinburgh sculptor; exhibited RSA(1).

**COUPER, May Coventry** **fl 1896-1905**
Edinburgh portrait and figurative painter in oil and watercolour. Exhibited 'Study of a Roman Catholic Priest' at the RSA in 1905 and a watercolour at the RSW in 1896 from 3 Charlotte Square.

**COUPER, M N** **fl 1890**
Glasgow painter in oil of still life; exhibited GI(1) from 37 Landsdowne Crescent.

**COURT, Sydney A** **fl 1906**
Amateur Aberdeen painter of coastal scenes. Exhibited AAS(1) from 14 Grosvenor Place.

**COURTNEY, Miss D A** **fl 1910-1921**
Artist who lived at 9 Chenies Street, Glasgow. Exhibited three works at the GI during the above years.

**COUSIN, David** **1808-1878**
Edinburgh architect. Partner in the firm Cousin and Lessels. Among his main works in Edinburgh are the Moray Chapel (1864) in St Giles, the Dunedin Room in the City Chambers (c1870), Free Church College (1858-63), Reid School of Music (1858), elevations for the entire N side of Chambers St (much altered in construction), the E side of St Mary's St (1869), the 'large and purposeful' India Buildings in Victoria St, St Catherine's Convent in Lauriston Gdns, St Thomas, Rutland Place (now a heritage centre) (1842-3), Royal Caledonian Horticultural Society Hall (1842-3), the re-organisation of E Princes Gdns after the building of the railway (1849-50), the grand nos. 1-19 Mayfield Gdns and his own home no.7 Greenhill Gdns. Exhibited RSA 1830-1876, including a design for the New British Linen Bank, Paisley (1867), and a musical classroom in Edinburgh University, 1868.
**Bibl:** Gifford 116,154,177,179,182,186,196,208,220-1,223,227, 233,237,241,256,307,314,341,367,369,396,403,506,547,576,593, 621,634,636,643-4.

**COUSIN, Jeff** **1947-**
Born Kincardine-on-Forth. Studied Duncan of Jordanstone College of Art (1968-73). From 1974 taught art in Falkirk. Early influences on his work include McTaggart(qv), Emile Nolde and Cézanne. More recently affected by Braque, Max Ernst and Ranchenberg. During the 1980s he worked in isolation, experimenting with themes, styles and technique. Only since 1988 has he begun again to produce work exploring architectural themes in an expressionist style. Has painted figures and figurative compositions in the manner of William Crosbie(qv). Exhibited RSA 1989.

**COUSLAND, Mrs J A** **fl 1873-1874**
Amateur flower painter in oil, exhibited RSA(2) during the above years.

**COUSTON, A S** **fl 1884**
Amateur portrait painter in oils from 265 High Street, Kirkcaldy. Exhibited RSA(1).

**COUTTS, George Reid** **fl 1910-1912**
Amateur Aberdeen painter of landscape and portraits. Exhibited AAS(2) from The Square, Ellon.

**COUTTS, Gordon** **1875-1943**
Born Glasgow; died San Francisco. Painter of landscapes, portraits and figure subjects. Studied at Glasgow School of Art, RA Schools and Academie Julian in Paris. At an early age settled in Australia and taught art in Sydney. Represented in the Australian Artists Exhibition held at Brighton AG 1925. Exhibited RA, RP, Paris Salon & GI(4).

**COUTTS, Hubert** **c1850-1921**
Although an English painter from Ambleside in the Lake District, this oil and watercolour landscapist concentrated so much on his Scottish scenes, particularly those in the Western Isles and Highlands, that he is indelibly identified with Scotland. Changed his name from Hubert Coutts Tucker in order to distinguish himself more emphatically from his brother and fellow artist, Arthur Tucker. Exhibited RSA 'Loch Maree from Poolewe' (1884), 'The Smithy, Kinlochewe' (1885) and other works, also regularly at the RA from 1876-1903, very often scenes of Arran, RI(55), GI(4) & L(77).

**COUTTS, Ian** **fl 1974-**
Edinburgh artist of 4a St Bernard's Crescent; has so far exhibited once at the RSA.

**COUTTS, Ian T G** **fl 1967-1969**
Aberdeen sculptor. Exhibited several works at the AAS from 121 Stewart Crescent.

**COUTTS, J** **fl 1880-1889**
Edinburgh artist; exhibited 6 works at the GI during the above years.

**COUTTS, J H** **fl 1821**
Buckie painter of landscapes and teacher. Taught art at the local school. The work was finely done and such was the popularity of his scenes in his native Banffshire that he never sought to exhibit elsewhere. One interesting painting of Buckie recently appeared on the market. Lived in Church Road. Father of James C(qv). Exhibited RHA(1).

**COUTTS, James** **fl 1870-1889**
Born Kincardine O'Neil, Aberdeenshire. Painter in oil; figurative subjects and landscape. Settled in Edinburgh. Son of J H Coutts(qv). Exhibited RSA 1871-1874, also GI(12), latterly from 17 Standon Crescent.

**COUTTS, Miss Mary Anne** **fl 1876**
Edinburgh sculptress; exhibited a marble bust at the RSA.

**COUTTS, R Glen** **1957-**
Born Glasgow. Painter in oil, acrylic, pastel and mixed media. Semi-abstract compositions. Studied Glasgow School of Art 1975-79. Since 1982 has taught art and design becoming Head of Department in Port Glasgow HS. Exhibits RSA, RSW, GI(6) & SSA, from 52 Dunvegan Ave, Eldersley, Renfrewshire.

**COUTTS, William G** **fl 1867-1885**
Edinburgh portrait painter and sculptor. Latterly he lived in London. In 1867 he exhibited a portrait bust at the RA of 'Henry Pelham-Clinton, Duke of Newcastle', and regularly at the RSA between 1867 and 1876.

**COUZENS, James C** **fl 1952**
Amateur Edinburgh painter. Exhibited 'The Mill' at the RSA.

**COVENTRY, Gertrude Mary (Mrs E Robertson)** **1886-1964**
Born Glasgow 2 Nov. A fine painter of portraits, landscapes, marine and harbour scenes in oil and watercolour. Studied at Glasgow School of Art and subsequently travelled to Holland and Belgium with her father, Robert McGown Coventry(qv). Married 1915, moved to Bangor and then, in 1934, to Manchester. Eventually migrated to Canada, where she died. Exhibited RA(1), RSA(20), RCA(5) & GI(47), 1916-21 from Inveresk and 1922-24 from Bangor.
**Bibl:** Halsby 254.

**COVENTRY, Robert McGown ARSA RSW** **1855-1941**
Born Glasgow, 25 Jly; died Glasgow, 29 Mar. Studied Glasgow School of Art under Robert Greenlees(qv) and in Paris under Bouguereau and Fleury. Father of Gertrude Coventry(qv). Lived in Glasgow and travelled much abroad but painted principally fishing and harbour scenes of the east of Scotland. Many of his pictures depict busy quayside subjects with a wonderful sense of colour and compositional harmony. The use of subtle greens and blues show Continental influences. His figures have been described as 'dumpy' and were generally incidental to the scene, indicating bustle and adding human interest. Worked in Belgium and Holland, views in the vicinity of Dordrecht and Amsterdam were among his regular exhibits at the RSW, and in the 1890s he visited the Middle East. Elected ARSA 1906, RSW 1889. Exhibited RA(5), RSA(27), RSW(65), GI(82) and regularly at the AAS 1900-1912. Represented in Glasgow AG, Kirkcaldy AG, Paisley AG.
**Bibl:** Caw 332; Halsby 153,243,254.

**COVENTRY, Robin W** **1944-**
Kirkintilloch engraver and watercolourist. Exhibited RSA 1964 and 1965, & GI(8) from 1 Burnside Avenue, Westermains. Represented in Glasgow AG.

**COVRIG, Doru** **fl 1983**
Foreign born sculptor. Based for a time at Scottish Sculpture Workshop in Lumsden, Aberdeenshire from where he exhibited at the AAS.

**COWAN, Adam** **1862-1896**
Born Ayr; died Ayr, 2 Nov. Was only 34 when he died. Exhibited a study GI 1889 from Edenarroch.

**COWAN, Rev Arthur A** **fl 1924-1958**
Amateur painter in watercolour and pen and ink of English, Scottish and Continental landscape. Minister of Inverleith, Edinburgh for many years. Exhibited RSA, RSW(12) & GI(20).

**COWAN, Georgina** **fl 1904-1927**
Edinburgh watercolour painter, sculptress and miniaturist. Lived at 30 Dick Place, then from 1923 at 130 George Street. Exhibited RSA 1904, 1923-25, also RSW(5).

**COWAN, James** **fl 1875-1899**
Glasgow painter in oil of landscape and figures. Exhibited 5 works at the RSA between 1876 and 1899, & GI(11), latterly from 6 Hampden Terrace.

**COWAN, Jean Mildred Hunter SSA (née Hore)** **1882-1967**
Born Edinburgh. Portrait sculptress and painter in oil and watercolour. Educated St Leonards School, St Andrews and the Karlsruhe Conservatorium; studied art under R H Westwater. Had a more variously accomplished life than perhaps any other Scottish artist. In addition to her work as sculptor and painter, including many sketches completed when serving with the French Ambulance Organisation in France during WW1, she regularly exhibited at the SSWA, and was President 1951-1958. Elected member, SSA 1945. Exhibited RSA(5) & RSW(4). She was the first Scottish woman to fly solo 1911, an amateur violinist of repute, winner of the ladies golf championship of India 1924, ladies doubles tennis champion of Malaysia 1924, and founder president of the Women's Section of the Edinburgh Society of Musicians 1927. Also exhibited bronzes and watercolours at the GI(7), all from 31 Drumsheugh Gardens.

**COWAN, Jennifer R** **fl 1957**
Edinburgh sculptress, exhibited a seated figure at the RSA in 1957.

**COWAN, Jessie B** **fl 1900-1927**
Edinburgh landscape painter in oil who lived at 7 East Fettes Avenue. Exhibited RSA(1) & AAS(1). Probably the Jessie Cowan who exhibited at the RI(3) and Walker Gallery, Liverpool(8) between 1911 and 1927 from addresses in Birkenhead, London and Bombay.

**COWAN, John** **fl 1773-1777**
Edinburgh engraver. Executed a plan of Leith in 1777. Lived 'Opposite the Guard'.
**Bibl:** Bushnell; Edin Directory, suppl. 1773-1774.

**COWAN, John** **fl 1847-1856**
Leith portrait painter. Most of his sitters are unidentified except for a chalk study of 'A Clergyman' 1849 and in 1850 'Dr Shaw of the Bengal Army' and 'Master John Farquharson'. Exhibited RSA(24) between the above years.

**COWAN, Ralph** **1917-1977**
Painter, architect and designer. Worked in oil and watercolour and was also a stained glass designer; figure subjects and landscapes, sometimes with a religious theme. Designed the Architecture Building (1961) for Edinburgh College of Art and collaborated with Alan Reiach(qv) in the Agriculture building as part of the King's Buildings, Edinburgh University. Exhibited GI(20), after 1967 from Dunira, Uplawmoor, Renfrewshire.
**Bibl:** Gifford 259,487.

**COWAN, T Donald** **fl 1955**
Sculptor. Exhibited 2 statuettes in wood at the GI, one representing motherhood, the other a panther, from 14 McNeil Street, Larkhall, Lanarkshire.

**COWAN, William** **fl 1907-1925**
Glasgow landscape painter. Moved to 34 Allan Street Douglas, Isle of Man c1920. Exhibited 4 works at the GI and two in Liverpool.

**COWAN, Wilson** **?-c1918**
Corstorphine painter. Served in the Royal Flying Corps during WWI. It is not clear whether he died in the War but his last exhibit was in 1918. Painted pastoral scenes and portraits. Exhibited RSA(6) & GI(1) 1912.

**COWAN-DOUGLAS, Miss Lilian Horsburgh** **1894-c1960**
Born Calgary, Mull. Painted flower pieces, often depicted in their habitat and landscape, sometimes in oil but more frequently in watercolour. Trained Edinburgh College of Art. Lived at Corbet Tower, Kelso. Exhibited RSA(17) 1930-1944, RSW(21), GI(24) & AAS(6).
**Bibl:** Halsby 254.

**COWARD, Charles R** **fl 1773-1781**
Aberdeen artist in watercolour and pen and ink. Trained Gray's School of Art. Exhibited AAS from 71 Fonthill Avenue.

**COWERN, Anna M** **fl 1972-1973**
Landscape Painter. Possibly related to Raymond Teague Cowern RA. Exhibited Greek views at the RSA during the above period.

**COWIE, Alan** **fl 1970-**
Painter from Munlochy, Ross-shire; exhibited twice at the RSA in 1978 again in 1981 and at the AAS since 1970 from various Aberdeen addresses.

**COWIE, Bel** **1943-1983**
Born Dundee, 15 Aug. Painter in oil and screen-printer. Trained at Gray's School of Art and Ceramische Fachschule, Berne. Her work illustrates a fascination with Japanese prints and weaving designs. There is a gentle delicacy in all she does, a warmer feel for line than for colour. Lived for long spells in Allardyce Castle, nr Montrose and Kirkside, Westhills, Skene. Exhibited regularly RSA 1974-1982, GI(4) & AAS 1971-1981. Represented in Aberdeen AG.

**COWIE, George M** **fl 1883-1885**
Amateur Edinburgh painter of townscenes in watercolour. Exhibited RSA 1883 & AAS 1885 from 34 St Andrew's Square.

**COWIE, H** **fl 1871**
Amateur Edinburgh portrait painter in oil; exhibited RSA(1).

**COWIE, James** **fl 1880-1884**
Edinburgh painter in oil; landscape and figurative. Curiously, this painter exhibited nine works during the above five year period including two continental scenes in 1882 and 'The Harem's languid hours of listless ease' (1884), but at no other time.

**COWIE, James RSA LLD** **1886-1956**
Born Cuminestown, Aberdeenshire, 16 May; died Netherton of Delgaty, nr Cuminestown, Aberdeenshire, 18 Apr. Painter in oil, occasional watercolour; portraits, landscape and figurative studies. One of the most idiosyncratic Scottish artists of the twentieth century. Started an English course at Aberdeen University, but failed to graduate and became art master at Fraserburgh Academy. In 1912, resigned his post in order to enrol at Glasgow School of Art where he studied painting under Morris Greiffenhagen(qv) and became friendly with Robert Sivell(qv) and Archibald McGlashan(qv), his fellow students. Thereafter, resumed a teaching career in conjunction with his painting, becoming art master at Bellshill Academy, Lanark for more than twenty years. His work was marked by intense individuality. He belonged to no particular group. He was a traditionalist in his pursuit of searching and intimate drawing but modern in the free way he dealt with the subject and the introduction of transparent planes and other details which he incorporated into his compositions with the greatest ingenuity. In some ways he was akin to that other idiosyncratic Scottish painter, John Quinton Pringle(qv). He had a highly original and very thoughtful mind. Percy Bliss wrote of him 'Scottish painters take pride in bold handling, gay colour, frank design and a feeling for the medium whether it be oil or watercolour. They are so concerned with painterly qualities that they tend to neglect tone, drawing and the architectonic qualities in picture-making. Cowie's work, on the other hand, was based squarely on drawing. He was less interested in colour than tone, and cared not a rush for painterly qualities. He even tended to mix his media...little in common with other leading Scottish painters of his time...He cherished his own strongly felt convictions and went his own way.' He had the ability to find significance in everyday appearance. During WWI he was a conscientious objector, working with the Pioneer Corps. After the War he resumed his teaching at Bellshill. In 1935 was appointed Head of Painting at Grays School of Art, Aberdeen, before becoming Warden of the Patrick Allan Fraser School of Art at Hospitalfield, Arbroath 1937, a post from which he retired in 1948. The 'still formality of Cowie's paintings of the 1920's and 1930's, products of elaborate preparatory studies in the manner of the Old Masters, gave way in the 1940's to an interest in Surrealism. Paul Nash, in particular, inspired Cowie to take liberties with perspective and to incorporate picture-within-a-picture devices into his work to highly idiosyncratic effect. His passion for centralising compositions around plaster-cast figures, often enigmatically placed in landscape, contains echoes not only of Nash, but also of de Chirico'. Succeeded David Foggie(qv) as Secretary of the RSA 1948. In 1952 he suffered a severe stroke from which he never fully recovered. Elected ARSA 1936, RSA 1943, LLD (University of Edinburgh) 1948. Exhibited RA(4), GI(57) & often at the AAS. Represented in Aberdeen AG, Glasgow AG, Liverpool (Walker AG), Paisley AG, Perth AG (incl 2 of the 3 prints he ever executed), RSA.
**Bibl:** Arts Council GB, 'James Cowie; Memorial Exhibition' (Ex Cat 1957); Richard Calvocoressi, James Cowie, SNGMA, Edinburgh 1979; Cyril Gerber Fine Art, James Cowie; Paintings & Drawings, Glasgow 1988; Halsby 229-231,244,254; Hartley 125; Macmillan [SA], 338-46,360-1,372,395,400 et passim in final chs; Cordelia Oliver, James Cowie, Edinburgh 1980; Cordelia Oliver, James Cowie; the artist at work, SAC, Glasgow & elsewhere, 1981.

**COWIE, Mrs Nancy** **fl 1921**
Glasgow portrait and still life painter. In the same year she exhibited RSA(3), GI(1) & AAS(1), all from 41 St Andrew's Drive, Pollockshields.

**COWIE, R** **fl 1871**
Edinburgh painter; exhibited a study of 'A Gypsy' at the RSA.

**COWIE, Robert Jnr** **fl 1864-1871**
Dundee landscape painter in oil; exhibited RSA(4) between the above dates.

**COWIE, Robert A** **fl 1848-1869**
Edinburgh painter in oil and watercolour; figures, castles, and portraits. Exhibited RSA(6) 1848-1857 & GI(3) when living in Glasgow.

**COWIE, William** **fl 1878-1879**
Edinburgh landscape watercolourist; exhibited RSA(2) during the above period.

**COWIESON, Agnes Margaret** **1855-1940**
Born Nov 11, 215 Clerk St, Edinburgh; died Edinburgh, May 10. Painter in oil and watercolour; animals, figures, interiors and landscapes. Daughter of an Edinburgh printseller. Lived most of her life in Edinburgh, although in the mid 1890s she travelled to Java, Malaysia and South Africa. Many of her watercolours were figures on beaches and in interiors, a favourite place being Portobello sands. Sympathetic painter, especially of animals. It is surprising that examples of her quite prolific output are not more frequently seen. Exhibited eight works at the RA including 'Kaffir Women Washing, Kimberley' (1900). At the RSA, where she exhibited 73 works, in 1897 she exhibited 'Bullock Wagon on the Veldt (South Africa)'. Also exhibited RSW(3), GI(46), AAS(16) & L(7), latterly from 14 Esplanade Terrace, Joppa, where she lived for many years with her sister Alice.
**Bibl:** Caw 443; Halsby 254.

**COWPER, James R** **fl 1911-1912**
Amateur Helensburgh artist in oil and watercolour of figure studies. Exhibited GI(2) from Dounebank.

**COWPER, Max** **1860-1911**
Born Dundee. Worked as an illustrator for the *Dundee Courier* before moving to Edinburgh 1894 and thence to London from 1901, joining the staff of the *Illustrated London News*. According to Houfe, Cowper made illustrations for a large number of magazines, "his ink drawing is very good and his grey wash drawings are delicate, but he sometimes swamps his fine line with wash". He provided illustrations for *Fun* (1892-93); *St Pauls* (1894); *The Rambler* (1897); *The Longbow* (1898); *Pick-Me-Up* (1899); *Illustrated Bits* (1899); *The Quiver* (1899). Painted market scenes and figures in both oil and

watercolour. Exhibited RA(8), RSA(3), GI(4) & L(1), latterly from Iona, Finchley Road, London.
**Bibl:** Halsby 254; Houfe 101.

**COWPER, William Hay** **fl 1885-1892**
Edinburgh painter. Painted in oil and charcoal; portraits and figures. Exhibited RSA(16) & GI(5), from 7 Scotland Street.

**COX, Mrs Bertram** **fl 1894-1896**
English portrait painter. Exhibited RA(1) 1894 before moving to Glasgow in 1896. From there exhibited GI(2) & L(1).

**COX, James Cox** **1849-1901**
Born Dundee. Amateur painter in oil and photographer; local landscapes, figurative. Eldest son of a prosperous Dundee jute merchant with extensive property interests in the Lochee district of that city and in Perthshire. Although Cox successfully exhibited his oil paintings, he is best known for his remarkable work in photography. Four albums of his photographs are in the SNPG showing an obvious affinity with Bastien-Lepage, recollecting the hard stresses of life among the poorer fishing communities of the east coast. His main photographic work was in the fishing villages of Auchmithie and West Haven. Probably well acquainted with William McTaggart(qv) who had a copy of one of Cox's early seascape photographs; the fact that they both worked in the same area, being similarly interested in light and movement lends further circumstantial evidence of an association. One is also reminded of the paintings of Robert McGregor(qv) and David Murray(qv). "James Cox was one of the interesting figures in the history of art who was eccentric because he was in advance of his time. His photographs would sit easily in a context ten or even 40 years after he took them. He was acquainted with the Glasgow painters but made the successful connection with Bastien-Lepage before then producing Scottish 'realist photographs' in advance of the 'realist' paintings...the story-telling element is missing from his photographs. The emotional feeling behind them is there without him spelling the words out for us. The photograph of the landscape with a small photograph of a crying child in the margin, which was reviewed and condemned in 1886 as incomprehensible, was presumably one of Cox's more explicit statements - the expression of an idea that the landscape or the seascape were not objects of simple prettiness, but in human terms the makers of a hard life, the dealers of sorrow and of death...Cox's photographs have so many blurred movements, particularly turning heads, that he must have positively enjoyed the effect. Taking photographs in dull light conditions would have increased this kind of distortion, so he was not just accepting it as an accident but deliberately incorporating it into his idea of photographic truth. Cox's taste for this kind of oddity and his respect for its reality, marks him out from his immediate contemporaries...He stands as a man who could make competent, skilled, professional pictures with conventional modes of portraiture or landscape that was capable of a more significant sympathy with the uncomfortable realities of his time". [Sara Stevenson]. Exhibited RSA(11) 1881-1886, RHA(3), GI(4) in 1884 & 1885 & L(5).
**Bibl:** Sara Stevenson, James Cox, Scottish Masters, 1988.

**COYLE, Maurice** **fl 1971**
Amateur painter. Exhibited a still life at the GI whilst at Glasgow School of Art.

**COYLE, Peter** **fl 1971**
Amateur Pittenweem artist; exhibited 'Self portrait' at the GI from School Wynd.

**COYLE, Thomas** **fl 1978**
Bearsden painter in oil of landscape and coastal scenes, especially Caithness, Deeside, Orkney and Wester Ross. Exhibited GI(27), latterly from 25 Mosshead Road.

**CRABB, James** **fl 1866**
Amateur Glasgow portrait painter; exhibited GI(1) from 42 Cadogan Street.

**CRABB, William** **1811-1876**
Born Laurencekirk; died Laurencekirk 20 Jly. Painter of portraits and historical scenes. Known as 'Crabb of Laurencekirk'. One of the most under-rated Scottish painters. Studied at the Trustees Academy when very soon his work attracted the attention of Sir Francis Grant(qv) who employed him as an assistant to paint draperies and the like. Singularly retiring, in later life became totally blind, dying in his sister's house. In 1851 his 'Ahab Naboth's Vineyard', which portrayed Ahab and Queen Jezebel being surprised by Elijah, received special mention in the *AJ* which referred to the'striking originality in the costumes of the figures which have been adopted from the Ninevah remains, and remarkable for its decided style, unexceptional drawing and powerful colour.' Referring to his very first exhibit, a portrait of 'Richard Milnes, MP,' (RA 1848), Brydall thought it 'very notable, not only for its striking likeness to the original, but for its artistic qualities of natural pose and movement, forceable execution, and happy constrast between the stiffness of the dress and the ease of the head'. The same critic regarded his work as 'sometimes of almost equal quality to that of Raeburn'. 'Fitz-James and Roderick Dhu after the Combat' was exhibited at the Edinburgh International Exhibition of 1886. Numerous portraits still exist in many large Scottish houses, although the SNPG appears to be without an example. Among his known works are 'James Ogilvy Mack, an Edinburgh magistrate' (1846), 'Alexander Hill', publisher and print seller to the Queen (1847), 'Lord Fullarton' (1847), 'Lord Ardmillan' (1857), 'John Philip' (1874), and 'Alexander Hill' (1880). Exhibited RA(9) 1848-1857, among the portraits and historical subjects Jacob Refusing to be Comforted (1873) receiving particular praise. Exhibited a love scene in watercolour at the GI 1861 and 4 others over the ensuing twelve years. Represented in Kellie Castle (attrib, NTS).
**Bibl:** AJ 1851; Brydall 386-7; Mackay 319-320.

**CRAGG, Keith** **fl 1969**
Edinburgh painter; exhibited RSA(1).

**CRAGY, Sir Thomas** **fl 1538**
Early painter. Associate of Robert Binning(qv) with whom he was involved in 'gilting of the gret stane armis on the est quarter of the palice that wes put up of befor gold and cuiloris finding of all costs' for which they were paid $12 during the summer of 1538.
**Bibl:** Accounts of the Lord High Treasurer of Scotland, ed. T. Dickson et al, Edinburgh, 1877-1916; Accounts of the Masters of Works, vol i, ed. H.M. Paton, Edinburgh 1957; Apted 36.

**CRAIG, Ailsa** **1895-1967**
Painter and illustrator, specialising in lettering and illumination. Studied at Glasgow School of Art. Friend of Helen(qv) and Mildred Lamb(qv). Lived in Glasgow at 3 Foremount Terrace, Downshill. Lecturer in lettering, Glasgow School of Art. Published the authoritative work on the history of the subject. Exhibited widely and lived latterly in Bridge of Allan.

**CRAIG, Alex A** **fl 1889**
Amateur Glasgow painter; exhibited 'A Backwater of the Tay' at the GI from 7 Holland Place.

**CRAIG, Alexander** **fl 1834-d1878**
Glasgow artist, mostly of portraits, who spent the last few years of his life in London. Exhibited portraits at the RSA 1834-1854, & GI(2) in 1861.

**CRAIG, Mrs Clara L** **fl 1912-1938**
Glasgow painter in watercolour of flower studies; exhibited GI(2) & L(2) from 3 Athole Gardens.

**CRAIG, Miss Esther** **fl 1950-1982**
Glasgow painter in oil, chalk and pastel of figure subjects and landscape. Moved to Knaresborough, Yorkshire 1955. Exhibited RSA 1951 and again in 1982, & GI(6).

**CRAIG, Mrs Ethel** **fl 1917-1944**
Glasgow painter of still life, flowers, topographical subjects and landscapes. Mother of Ethel C(qv). Exhibited regularly at the RSA between 1932 and 1944, also GI(5) 1917-1938 & AAS(1) in 1935, from 26 Belmont Drive, Giffnock.

**CRAIG, Miss Ethel** **fl 1935-1966**
Giffnock painter. Worked in oil, watercolour, chalk and charcoal. Daughter of Ethel C(qv). Exhibited 21 landscapes and flower pieces

at the GI and 2 still lifes at the AAS, all from the same addresses as her mother.

**CRAIG, George** **c1852-1928**
Architect. Specialised in rather dull, portentous school buildings of which the most imaginative is Trinity Academy (1891). Architect to the Leith School Board.
**Bibl:** Gifford 75,462-4,466-7,473,603.

**CRAIG, George** **fl 1833**
Portrait miniaturist. Exhibited two portrait miniatures at the RSA 1833.

**CRAIG, H F** **fl 1860**
Landscape painter. Probably English. Exhibited two Scottish views at the RSA 1860.

**CRAIG, Ian** **fl 1964-1965**
Painter in oil and watercolour of 467 Shields Road, Glasgow. Exhibited GI(2).

**CRAIG, James** **1740-1795**
Born Edinburgh; died Edinburgh, 23 Jne. Architect, watercolourist and engraver. Son of an Edinburgh merchant and nephew on his mother's side to the poet of the 'Seasons'. In 1772 prepared designs for the Town Church at St Andrews, Dundee, in association with the local architect, Samuel Bell. This was one of the most attractive town churches of its time, incorporating a steeple, a pattern first introduced in the London city churches a generation or more earlier. In Edinburgh, the City Fathers had organised a competition for the layout of a proposed new town in 1766. In this James Craig was successful and what proved to be the first of a series of urban layouts that carried the city boundaries northwards almost to the Water of Leith and eastwards beyond the Calton Hill was begun. Craig's work can be seen in St Andrew's Square and Queen Street. The NLS has a set of his drawings for the proposed renovation of St Giles. In 1786 Craig published an ambitious but subsequently rejected scheme for improvements to the Old Town which would have linked the High Street with the road from the North Bridge, thus forming a large octagon around the Tron Kirk. Represented in NGS by a watercolour signed and dated 1777, and in City of Edinburgh Art Collection by a sepia engraving and two ink plans for the New Town.
**Bibl:** Brydall 180; Colvin; Dunbar 116, 124; Gifford 60,231,271, 273,289,300-1, 309,326,328,332,436,480; Irwin 69; Wilson, Memorials of Edinburgh; Youngson, The Making of Classical Edinburgh, 1966 et passim.

**CRAIG, James** **fl 1851-1853**
Glasgow painter who exhibited works on classical themes at the RSA during the above years.

**CRAIG, James Richardson** **1857-1914**
Born Gourock. A wool and cloth manufacturer in Glasgow and amateur painter. Illustrated a book on the history of Gourock, *Notes About Gourock* (1880), written by his brother-in-law, the Rev David Macrae. The Corporation of Gourock own a large oil Old Gourock Pier. This shows the town in about 1873 when the horse-tram service started from Greenock, and before 1889 when the railway to the Pier was opened by the Caledonia Railway Company. The painting is historically important, probably portraying the well-known Glasgow character 'Old Malabar' as a juggler.

**CRAIG, Jean** **fl 1897**
Glasgow painter of 7 Ardgowan Terrace; exhibited a study of chrysanthemums at the GI.

**CRAIG, Miss Jean R** **1927-**
Born London. Painter in oil and watercolour and etcher. Studied at Kingston School of Art before settling in Edinburgh 1950. Attended Edinburgh College of Art as a mature student. Works in various mediums including acrylic and pen and ink. Exhibited RSA 1981 and again in 1988, GI(2) 1958 and regularly at SSWA.

**CRAIG, John** **fl 1804-1818**
Edinburgh engraver. A surveyor who assisted John Ainslie(qv).
**Bibl:** Bushnell.

**CRAIG, John** **fl 1827-1838**
Prolific Edinburgh landscape painter in both oil and watercolour. Specialised in East coast scenes and exhibited almost annually at the RSA between the above dates from 6 James Court.
**Bibl:** Halsby 254.

**CRAIG, Robert** **fl 1887-1890**
Painter. Exhibited five landscapes at the RSA, also GI(1) & AAS(1), during the above dates from Dalkeith.

**CRAIG, Robert** **fl 1968**
Amateur Edinburgh landscape painter in watercolour. Exhibited a winter scene at the GI from 44 Vandeleur Avenue.

**CRAIG, Ronald A H** **1927-**
Born Renfrewshire. Painter in oil of landscape. Graduated in art with distinction at Gray's School of Art, Aberdeen. Particularly interested in recording the effects of light and weather on the Scottish landscape especially in autumn and winter. Art master at Glenalmond College 1956-1987. Since his retirement as a teacher has been engaged in part-time lecturing as well as continuing to paint. Fellow, RSA. Exhibited RSA 1953-1984 & GI(2) 1960.

**CRAIG, Thomas John** **fl 1959-1962**
Amateur Glasgow painter in oil and watercolour. Exhibited GI(3).

**CRAIG, William Marshall** **fl 1787-c1834**
Painter in oil and watercolour of miniatures, portraits, landscapes, figurative subjects. Probably brother of the Edinburgh architect James Craig(qv) and father of W Craig(qv) and J K Craig(qv). Appointed Painter in Watercolour to the Queen and Miniature Painter to the Duke and Duchess of York. The Earl of Morton clearly thought highly of Craig for this was the miniaturist commissioned to tutor Sarah Biffin, an artist born without arms, hands or feet who went on to win a silver medal from the Society of Artists and to exhibit regularly at the RA. A miniature of an officer signed on the reverse and dated '1815', is in the V & A and is reproduced in Foskett (pl 66). Elected a member of Associated Artists in Water-Colours 1810. Exhibited in Liverpool 1787, working in Manchester 1788 before moving to London c1791. Exhibited RA 1788-1827, and at the Associated Artists in Water-Colours from 1808-1812. Represented in V & A, BM (who have numerous engraved portraits by him).
**Bibl:** Foskett 225.

**CRAIG, W Wood** **fl 1907-1913**
Edinburgh painter; exhibited GI(2) between the above years from 5 Maurice Place.

**CRAIG, William W** **fl 1871-1873**
Minor Hamilton watercolour painter of landscape. Exhibited at GI(3) from 8 Miller Street.

**CRAIG-BARR, Miss Nancy** **fl 1942-1944**
Amateur Paisley artist in oil and pen and ink of landscape and figure subjects. Exhibited GI(3) from Garail, Thornley Park.

**CRAIG-WALLACE, Robert** **1886-1969**
Glasgow painter in oil and watercolour also etcher. Mainly interested in views of shipping and yachting on the Clyde and the Argyll coast. His work invokes the mood of the period remarkably well; a keen yachtsman, many works being completed on the family yacht 'Calmara'. Exhibited RA(1), RSA(15) 1930-1954 & GI(92), from 5 Westercraigs, Dennistoun. Represented in Glasgow AG.
**Bibl:** Halsby 254; Wingfield.

**CRAIGIE, James Hoey** **1870-1930**
Born May 7. Glasgow architect. Associated with George Bell jnr(qv), becoming partner in Clark, Bell &-Craigie. Specialised in neo-Greek, German Baroque and art nouveau, the last exemplified in The Exchequer, formerly the Roost Bar, 59 Dumbarton Rd, Partick 1899 and the Corona Bar, Shawlands Cross, Glasgow 1912-13. Involved in the reconstruction of Glasgow Law Courts and designed Lewis's in Argyle St, Glasgow.
**Bibl:** W Craigie (personal communication); A Gomme & D Walker, Architecture in Glasgow, London 1987(rev), 70,145,290; R Kenna &-A-Mooney, People's Palaces 1983, 109-110.

**CRAIGIE, John** **fl 1833**
Portobello painter who exhibited a still life at the RSA in 1833.

**CRAIGIE, Patrick** **fl 1679-1713**
In 1679 a painter of this name was apprenticed to James Anderson. From 1691 until 1713 he was an active member of the Incorporation of St Mary's and in 1694 took on a John Yates as apprentice. No work of his is known to have survived.
**Bibl:** Apted 36.

**CRAIGMILE, William** **fl 1905-1913**
Landscape artist. Lived for a time in Banchory, Kincardineshire c1907. Exhibited two works at the RCA; also eight works at the London Salon.

**CRAIGMILL SCHOOL OF ANIMAL PAINTING** **1887-c1896**
Established near Stirling by Joseph Denovan Adam(qv). Based on a farm where the livestock provided the models, especially the Highland cattle and mountain sheep so loved by its founder. The 60 x 30 ft studio had glass sides enabling the students to paint regardless of weather. There were up to 25 students at any one time. In addition to the Adam family, there were visits from the thriving artistic communities of Cambuskenneth(qv) and Stirling. John Lochhead(qv) and John Roberts(qv) both stayed for several years and Tom Austen Brown(qv) painted 'A Gypsy Encampment at the School'. Other guests included William Kennedy(qv) (who met his wife Lena Scott there), John MacWhirter(qv) and John Smart(qv). Pupils included a number of Scottish animal painters of note including David Gourlay Steell jnr(qv) and Robert Monro(qv).
**Bibl:** Stirling Smith AG, 'Craigmill and Cambuskenneth', (Ex Cat text by Fiona Wilson), 1978.

**CRAMER, Mrs Belle** **fl 1917-1939**
Born Scotland. Painter of landscape, figures, flowers and still life. Pupil of Ruth Dugget's at Edinburgh School of Art. Exhibited extensively including ROI(3), SWA(6) and nine at the London Salon. But most of her work was sold in commercial galleries.

**CRANSTON, Andrew** **fl 1933-1944**
Glasgow watercolour artist of landscape. Exhibited RSW(7) before WW2 from 63 Kintore Road, and GI(1) 1944 from 8 Suffolk Street, Helensburgh.

**CRANSTON, Miss M B** **fl 1910**
Amateur Aberdeen painter of coastal views. Exhibited AAS(1) from 340 Holburn Street.

**CRANSTOUN, James Hall** **1821-1907**
Born Edinburgh; died Perth, Jne 8. Painter of landscapes in oil and watercolour. Studied at the Slade before returning to Scotland to live in Perth. Painted Scottish landscapes, often in Perthshire, in both oil and watercolour in a careful but not over-worked manner. His watercolours have been likened in style to those of Thomas Fairbairn(qv) and his oils to McNeil McLeay(qv). Friend of Sir W Q Orchardson(qv). Visiting art master, Glenalmond College. Exhibited 63 works at the RSA between 1844 and 1893, & GI(1) from 3 Athole Street in 1861. Represented Perth AG.
**Bibl:** Halsby 254.

**CRAPELLI, G L** **fl 1885**
Edinburgh artist. Exhibited RA(1) when living at 23 Moray Place.

**CRASTER, J Wellington** **fl 1892-1893**
Penicuik artist, in oil and watercolour of landscape and flower studies. Exhibited GI(3).

**CRAWFORD, Alexander Hunter** **fl 1892-1911**
Edinburgh architect and watercolourist; churches, schools. Friend and associate of Robert Burns(qv). His most important work was the new Freemasons' Hall, George St (1910-12); also responsible for Murrayfield Parish church (1905) and Lady Haig's poppy factory (1912). Later joined the family bakery firm. Exhibited 12 designs at the RSA including a school nr Pitlochry 1897.
**Bibl:** Gifford 282,609,628,648; Halsby 191.

**CRAWFORD, Alistair** **fl 1964**
Amateur Fraserburgh artist. Exhibited Lemon Grove at the GI from 28 Glenbuchty Place.

**CRAWFORD, Andrew** **d.c1605**
Master of Works. Worked for Patrick Stewart, Earl of Orkney and involved in the building and most probably the design of Muness Castle (Unst), begun in 1598, and Scalloway Castle 1600.

**CRAWFORD, Ann (née Bruce)** **1932-**
Born of Scottish parents in Penang. Painter & sculptress. Educated Malaysia, Australia & England. Trained at Chelsea School of Commercial Art 1951-54, winning the Burrough-Johnson prize for Life Drawing. In 1985 left Malaysia to live in Edinburgh where she remained until moving to Sussex 1994. Awarded the Ottile Helen Wallace scholarship (RSA) for the best work by a woman sculptor 1994. Elected SSWA & SAAC 1988. Exhibits regularly at the RSA, RGI, RSW, SSA, SSWA. Her work is in many private collections in Australia, Britain, Hong Kong, Ireland, Malaysia, Singapore, Taiwan & the USA. Represented in Univ. of Paisley (sculpture), Vanderbilt Foundation NY (painting).

**CRAWFORD, Col Archibald** **fl 1866**
Professional soldier and amateur landscape artist of Roseburn, Ayr. Exhibited a watercolour of a Highland landscape at the GI.

**CRAWFORD, Brodie** **fl 1906-1908**
Amateur Aberdeen painter of figurative compositions. Exhibited a number of works at AAS from Polmuir Avenue.

**CRAWFORD, Cara McKinnon** **c1963-**
Born Campbelltown, Argyll. Painter of landscape, still life and figure studies. Daughter of John McKinnon C(qv). Trained Glasgow School of Art 1980-84. First solo exhibition Glasgow 1985. A strong handling of intense colour characterises rich landscapes of her native north-west Scotland as well as the quieter fields of Tuscany and breezy Cornish pastures. In 2002 invited by the Colonsay Art Trust to illustrate this inner Hebridean island in May, the only Scottish member on the team of seven European artists. Currently involved in a large scale project *21st Century Clyde* for completion in 2006. Exhibits RSA 1987- & RGI 1983- from 4 Wester Leddriegreen Rd, Blanefield.

**CRAWFORD, Charles Paul** **fl 1891-1893**
Glasgow artist in oil and watercolour of landscape and flowers. Exhibited three works at the GI from 3 Westminster Terrace. Ibrox.

**CRAWFORD, David** **fl 1887**
Amateur Kilmacolm artist; exhibited a landscape at the GI from George Villa.

**CRAWFORD, David William** **fl 1899-1912**
Edinburgh designer and painter in oil. Lived at 12 Calton Street and exhibited four works at the RSA between the above dates.

**CRAWFORD, Mrs Dorothy** **1923-**
Glasgow painter in oil, watercolour and charcoal - especially the latter. Portraits and figure studies; occasional landscape. Wife of John T C(qv). After the early death of her husband returned to painting full-time. Member, Glasgow Society of Women Artists. Exhibited RSA 1965 & GI(5) from 66 Oakfield Avenue. Lives nr Moniaive.

**CRAWFORD, Edmund Thornton RSA** **1806-1885**
Born Cowden, nr Dalkeith; died Lasswade, 29 Sep. Painter in oil and watercolour; Scottish landscape, coastal and shipping scenes, harbours. Son of a surveyor. As a boy was apprenticed to a house painter in Edinburgh before proceeding to study at Trustees Academy where among his fellow students were R Scott Lauder(qv), D O Hill(qv), John Wilson(qv) and William Simson(qv), the latter becoming a close friend. In 1831 visited Holland where he studied Dutch 17th century paintings, becoming preoccupied with tone. Influenced by John Wilson and John Thompson(qv) but most by Van de Velde in seascapes and Hobbema in landscapes. His work has been likened in its spirit and period to that of Patrick Nasmyth(qv). It is 'eminently sane and healthy. Crawford was a capable craftsman always, though both in method and subject his work was somewhat restricted; his work has little variety of surface, the material being of a rather monotonous consistency throughout' [McKay]. His work conveyed a fine sense of movement and the composition was

generally pleasing. Scottish marine painting has not received the same recognition as other branches of art, a fact which has undoubtedly restricted the rightful recognition of Crawford's work. Foundation Associate, RSA 1826 but one of nine artists who withdrew after the first meeting; re-elected ARSA 1839, RSA 1848. Exhibited regularly at the RSA between 1829 and 1886; in 1836 exhibited a view of the port and fortifications of Callao, with the capture of the Spanish frigate *Esmeralda,* at the RA. Also at the GI(9) & AAS posthumously. Represented in NGS and Brodie Castle (NTS).
**Bibl:** Brydall 387-8; Caw 161-2; Halsby 88,254; McKay; Macmillan [SA], 209,229,254.

**CRAWFORD, Hugh Adam RSA** **1898-1982**
Born Busby, Lanarkshire, 28 Oct. Painter in oil of portraits and figure subjects and occasional landscapes. Studied under Greiffenhagen(qv) at Glasgow School of Art from which he graduated 1923 before undertaking further studies in London until 1925. Runner-up in the Prix de Rome 1926. A man of great charisma who dominated the art scene in Glasgow during the 1930s. He changed the hard line monochromatic training of Greiffenhagen, producing his best paintings when a young man, brilliantly drawn and suffused in colourful light. An inspiring teacher, among his students being David Donaldson(qv) and Joan Eardley(qv). He once wrote 'art for me is an adventure not the supplying of a demand'. Elected ARSA 1938, RSA 1956. Exhibited regularly RSA 1931-1984, from his home Carronmhor, Blanefield, Stirlingshire, GI(29) & AAS(1). Represented in Glasgow AG, Paisley AG.
**Bibl:** Ian Fleming, RSA (obit); Glasgow Art Club, Hugh Adam Crawford RSA', (Ex Cat 1971); Hartley 125; SAC,' Painters in Parallel', (Ex Cat by Cordelia Oliver, 1978); Third Eye Centre, Glasgow 'Crawford and Company, selected works 1928-1978', (Ex Cat by Cordelia Oliver, 1978).

**CRAWFORD, J D** **20th Cent**
Amateur Glasgow watercolour painter of landscape. Exhibited GI(2) from 18 Newton Street.

**CRAWFORD, J M** **fl 1904-1915**
Glasgow watercolour painter, exhibited RSW(3) & GI(5) between the above years.

**CRAWFORD, J R** **fl 1961-1965**
Cumbernauld painter of landscape and portraits. Exhibited GI(6) from 3 Little Lairdshill.

**CRAWFORD, Jeanie W** **fl 1888-1890**
Hayfield, Rutherglen painter in oil and watercolour of still life and flowers; showed four times at the GI between the above years.

**CRAWFORD, Jethro B** **fl 1863-1867**
Glasgow sculptor, exhibited RSA(1) & GI(7) from 117 Eglington Street.

**CRAWFORD, Johanne M** **1968-**
Born Falkirk. Printmaker and etcher. Studied Glasgow School of Art and was still a student when he embarked upon a printmaking career with the emphasis on etching. His work has included portraiture, figures and architectural materials, often demonstrating a fascination for mirrors and the effects of reflected light. Received Latimer Award of the RSA 1989 and Saltire Society Purchase Award the same year. Began exhibiting at the GI 1988.

**CRAWFORD, John** **fl 1846**
Glasgow landscape painter; exhibited RSA(1).

**CRAWFORD, John** **fl 1860**
Edinburgh painter in oil, exhibited a landscape in Co Antrim at the RSA in 1860.

**CRAWFORD, John** **fl 1886**
Glasgow sculptor. Father of Thomas Hamilton C(qv). Exhibited 2 works in wood at the GI from 39 Cranston Street.

**CRAWFORD, John FSA(Scot)** **1932-**
Born Edinburgh, 22 Oct. Painter of landscapes, mainly in watercolour; also printmaker. Father of Kenna Crawford(qv). Trained Edinburgh College of Art 1951-55. His favourite place is the Hebrides. In 1969 published *Introducing Jewellery Making, Creer de Bijoux* (1970), *Elaboracion de Joyas* (1971) and *Precious Stones* (1972). Author of *The Sandhill Site on the Isle of Coll,* published in the Proceedings of the Soc. of Antiquaries of Scotland, 1997. Latterly favours painting in acrylics. In addition to painting and printmaking is an active antiquarian, elected FSA (Scot) 1981. Lives in Edinburgh. Retired from teaching 1989. Exhibits RSA since 1957 and RSW since 1960, also exhibited 2 interiors and 2 prints at the GI 1967-1986. Represented in SAC.

**CRAWFORD, John D** **fl 1845-1855**
Glasgow painter of pastoral scenes and landscapes, often in Perthshire and Fife. Exhibited regularly at the RSA between the above years.

**CRAWFORD, John Gardiner RBA RSW RI** **1941-**
Born Fraserburgh. Painter in oil, watercolour and acrylic; landscapes and occasional still life. Trained at Gray's School of Art, Aberdeen 1959-63, and at Hospitalfield, Arbroath. In 1961 awarded the Governor's Award for painting and three years later a bursary award from the RSA. Has taught in Aberdeenshire schools and at Dundee College of Education and in 1980-81 was artist tutor at Newcastle Abbey College, Midlothian. Elected RSW 1974. Since 1980 has devoted himself full-time to painting. Regular exhibitor RSA, also GI(4) & AAS(2). Represented in Aberdeen AG, Arbroath AG, Dundee AG, Newcastle AG, SAC.

**CRAWFORD, John M** **fl 1915**
Stirlingshire engraver; exhibited 3 works at the GI from The Tower, Torrance.

**CRAWFORD, John McKinnon** **fl 1952-**
Born Campbelltown, Argyllshire. Painter in oil, watercolour, gouache and crayon; landscape. Father of Cara McKinnon C(qv). Studied Glasgow School of Art, under Mary Armour, and St Mary's College of Art 1948-54. Also trained in art education and has been principal adviser in Art and Design to the Highland Regional Education Committee since it was founded. Now paints almost exclusively in the north-east of Scotland apart from occasional visits to Northern France. His work is imbued with quiet but rich tonal qualities. Exhibited local scenes and figures RSA 1958-1961, & RGI(28), often fishing and harbour scenes, latterly from Beechcroft, Strathpeffer, Ross-shire.

**CRAWFORD, John T** **1913-1965**
Landscape painter in oil and gouache; potter and teacher. Trained Glasgow School of Art. Married Dorothy C(qv). Six war years serving the Navy. Joined staff, Glasgow School of Art 1946 remaining there until his premature death. From 1949 he was in charge of the reconstituted pottery department. Active member, Glasgow Art Club. Exhibited RSA(1) & RGI from 31 Jacks Road, Saltcoats.

**CRAWFORD, Joseph** **fl 1973-1979**
Glasgow painter in oil of landscape, especially the west coast of Scotland. Exhibited GI(16).

**CRAWFORD, Julia** **fl 1937-1938**
Scottish artist living in London; exhibited RSA(1) & RBA(1) during the above years.

**CRAWFORD, Kenna** **1959-**
Born Edinburgh, 3 Oct. Watercolourist. Daughter of John Crawford(qv). Began exhibiting at the RSW when only 16 years old. Exhibits regularly there and at the RSA.

**CRAWFORD, Lesley J** **fl 1964**
Amateur Aberdeen landscape painter. Exhibited AAS(1) from 15 Fonthill Road.

**CRAWFORD, Margaret W M** **fl 1948-1951**
Troon sculptress, exhibited portrait heads at the RSA in 1948 and again in 1951.

**CRAWFORD, Peter** **fl 1905-1911**
Glasgow painter in oil of landscape, generally in the Highlands, often

evocative seasonal scenes especially in winter. Exhibited GI(10), latterly from 60 Seymour Street.

**CRAWFORD, Robert** **fl 1950**
Edinburgh painter, exhibited RSA(1).

**CRAWFORD, Robert Cree RSW** **1842-1924**
Born Govanbank. Painter in oil, but mainly watercolour; landscapes, seascapes, portraits and flower subjects. Studied at Glasgow University before moving to Canada. Later returned to Scotland and earned a local reputation for his oil portraits. Also painted watercolours of landscape and marine scenes, especially in and around the Clyde. Elected RSW 1878. Exhibited 15 works at the RA between 1880 and 1898, subjects as varied as a portrait of 'Professor W L Reid' (1891) and 'Wild Fowl Shooting' (1881), also regularly at the RSA(27) 1871-1896, but mostly at the GI(114) & occasionally AAS. Represented in Glasgow AG, Paisley AG, Perth AG.
**Bibl:** Halsby 254.

**CRAWFORD, Miss Robina S** **fl 1877-1878**
Amateur Edinburgh sculptress; exhibited a marble bust of 'General Sir John Campbell' at the RSA in 1877 which appeared again at the GI the following year, from 2 West Maitland Street.

**CRAWFORD, Stella (née Meredith)** **1921-1991**
Stirlingshire painter in oil and watercolour. Trained Grays School of Art & Glasgow School of Art. Exhibited Smith Biennial, Stirling 1981-88, RSW 1987-90, RGI 1986-87.

**CRAWFORD, Susan Fletcher ARE** **1863-1919**
Born Glasgow, 13 Jne; died 23 Apr. Painter and etcher. Studied at Glasgow School of Art under Newbery(qv) and subsequently in France, Germany, Holland and Spain. Contemporary of Sir D Y Cameron(qv). 'Her work translates into line the romantic and picturesque relics of old Scotland, chiefly in brooding sunshine or at night. One of her most original works was the 'Golf Links, St Andrews' in which the scattered buildings, in heavy sunlight, are placed with great daring, and the heavy shadow of the foreground bridge unites the picture.' Executed a series of etchings of Edinburgh buildings and a Rothenberg series of continental landscapes. Her work has a romantic beauty and charm showing great tenderness and sympathy. Taught etching for several years at Glasgow School of Art. Elected ARE 1893. Exhibited RA(3), RSA(51), RSW(1), GI(61), RE(104), L(3) & AAS 1900-1910. Represented in BM (Goff Bequest), Glasgow AG.
**Bibl:** Caw 463.

**CRAWFORD, Susan Louise (Mrs Jeremy Phipps)** **1941-**
Painter in oil of animals, especially horses. Daughter of a Haddington racehorse trainer. Studied in Florence under Signorina Simi (who also taught Annigoni). In addition to her studies of dogs, horses and cattle, has executed a number of portraits. Married with two children one of whom is the portrait painter **Jemma L R PHIPPS**, trained in Florence. Undertaken a number of commissions for the Royal family. Several limited editions of her work have been published including portraits of the racehorses Ribot and Arkle. Began her artistic career almost accidentally when asked to do a mural for the milk bar at a party in Edinburgh Assembly Rooms. Three more serious murals followed for the Ben shipping line, for Salvesen's, and in 1960s for the dining room of the new Forth Road Bridge Motel. After studying in Florence, went to Ireland for two years to paint horses. The Tryon Gallery, London became interested and her career blossomed. Painted every Derby winner between 1965 and 1975, using a mobile caravan as a studio. Her great artistic idols are Stubbs and Munnings. Among her most famous works are portraits of *'Nijinsky'* and *'Sir Ivor'*. Exhibits at the RSA, NPG, RA, RSPP, V&A, and at the Nat. Gall. of Malaysia.

**CRAWFORD, Thomas** **fl 1834**
Edinburgh painter; exhibited 'Study of Cattle' at the RSA in the above year.

**CRAWFORD, Thomas** **fl 1888**
Glasgow landscape painter in oil. Exhibited GI(1) from 3 Dundas Terrace, Crosshill.

**CRAWFORD, Thomas Hamilton RSW** **1860-1933**
Born Glasgow. Painter in oil and watercolour and engraver; portraits and architectural subjects. Son of the sculptor, John C(qv). Pupil of Hubert and V Herkomer, he studied at both Glasgow and Edinburgh Schools of Art. Painted church interiors and façades in Britain and on the Continent, prepared illustrations of Edinburgh for R L Stevenson's *A Picturesque Note.* Moved to London 1893, later going to Hertfordshire. Signed his work 'T Hamilton Crawford'. Elected RSW 1887. Exhibited six works at the RA between 1881 and 1899 including 'In St Pauls' (1891) and 'Interior of York Minster' (1898). Also exhibited RSA(3), RSW(27), RI(3), RE(2), GI(21), L(4) & on the Continent at the Salon des Artistes Française 1920-1928. Represented in Glasgow AG.
**Bibl:** Caw 393; Halsby 234.

**CRAWFORD, Miss Violet M** **fl 1958**
Amateur Dumbarton watercolour painter of flowers. Exhibited GI(1) from Dunalbyn, Round Riding Road.

**CRAWFORD, W** **fl 1909**
Edinburgh artist; exhibited RSA(2).

**CRAWFORD, Mrs W** **fl 1869**
Amateur Edinburgh painter. Exhibited three studies of 'Haddon Hall, Derbyshire' at the RSA in 1869.

**CRAWFORD, William ARSA** **1825-1869**
Born Ayr; died Edinburgh, 2 Aug. Painter in oil and watercolour; portraits and figures. Son of a minor poet, studied at Trustees Academy under Sir William Allan(qv). Gained a travelling bursary, chiefly for his copy of an Etty painting. This enabled him to study in Rome for two years. Mainly interested in small genre compositions and portraits. Taught drawing at Trustees Academy until 1858. Brydall likened his work to that of Geddes(qv). His best known works include 'A Highland Keeper's Daughter' and its companion piece 'Waiting for the Ferry'. During his lifetime, his crayon paintings were particularly popular. Original member of 'The Smashers Club'(qv) formed in Edinburgh 1848 and reconstituted in London 1863 as 'The Auld Lang Syne Club'(qv). Elected ARSA 1860. Exhibited 23 works at the RA between 1852 and 1868 including a portrait of 'Sir George Macpherson Grant' (1864), and 'Johnnie, the Son of Thomas Faed' (1867), also exhibited 198 works at the RSA, & GI(7), from 2 Lynedoch Place, Edinburgh. Represented in Glasgow AG.
**Bibl:** AJ 1869, 272; Brydall 388; Caw 178; Halsby 254; McKay 355.

**CRAWFORD, William Caldwell PSSA** **1879-1960**
Born Dalkeith, 3 Aug. Painter in oil and watercolour; landscapes. His family had moved to a farm near Dalkeith shortly before his birth, having come from Glasgow where his father ran a family foundry business. Father of the potter Joan Faithfull(qv). Educated Edinburgh Academy and Heriot Watt College where he was awarded a medal for technical engineering. Then attended the RA schools under Charles Hodder where he met Robert Burns(qv), Robert Alexander(qv) and F C B Cadell(qv). Went to France, studied in Paris before returning to Scotland when he was commissioned to paint a set of cruising ships. As a result of this, he discovered Mull and Iona (it is said that it was he who introduced Cadell and Peploe to that island). Certainly many colourist friends including Edwin Alexander(qv), Robert Burns(qv) and George Houston(qv) cruised around the western highlands with him. After WW2 settled in East Linton. Exhibited RSA & SSA, elected President of the latter 1928. In 1922 shared a studio in Ainslie Place with Cadell. His best paintings were of the west coast, always his first love. They are based on a sensitive appreciation of colour, atmosphere and a subtle feeling for composition. After 1900 his style changed, assimilating the influences of the colourists but retaining a delicate, personal, tranquil element in his landscapes. Undertook a series of lengthy voyages to Scandinavia and along the French canals. Declined RSA Associateship. Exhibited RSA(29) & GI(9).
**Bibl:** Halsby 255.

**CRAWFORD & BALCARRES, Constance, Countess of** **?-1947**
Scottish needlewoman and embroiderer. Wife of the 27th Earl, she was a prolific worker. Ten large bedcovers, worked c1914, are still at Balcarres. Her daughter **MARY** (b1903) carried on the tradition.
**Bibl:** Margaret Swain 155-6.

**CRAWHALL, Joseph E RSW** **1861-1913**
Born Morpeth, 20 Aug; died London, 24 May. Scottish by association rather than birth. Taught to draw from memory by his father, a Lord Mayor of Newcastle and close friend of Charles Keene of *Punch*. After schooling in London, he studied art for a short time in Paris under Aimé Morot, the apostle of painting from memory, before returning to Scotland. Worked at Brig O'Turk with James Guthrie(qv), E A Walton(qv) and George Henry(qv). Most of his paintings are in watercolour on silk or linen, his favourite subjects being horses, dogs, animals and birds. His technique of rapid wash drawings has often been compared to Oriental calligraphic art. Lived for many years in Tangier visiting there with Edward Alexander(qv). Later he settled at Brandsby, Yorkshire. Throughout his comparatively short life his output was small. He was a perfectionist, ruthlessly destroying work that failed to reach his self-imposed standard. A lifelong horseman and a keen huntsman, he also had an intimate knowledge of animals and birds. These were depicted with great simplicity and firmness of line, frequently in gouache on linen. One of the most important horse painters of the twentieth century. Described as quiet, reticent and uncommunicative but 'his pencil was to him what the tongue is to other men'. Happiest painting on brown holland, sketched with the point of his brush, owing nothing to teachers and imitating no-one, although he admired Whistler. 'He employed an economy of line coupled with a great spontaneity.' One picture, 'The Aviary', was thrown away, retrieved by a friend and ultimately awarded a gold medal in Munich. During the last ten years little work was done beyond humorous sketches for members of his family. Blessed with a photographic memory. Died from emphysema. One of the most individual and highly talented artists Scotland has produced. Occasionally illustrated books, the best known being some of the works of the naturalist and hunter Abel Chapman. Exhibited RA(2), RSA(22), RSW(22), GI(18) & L(12). Represented in NGS(2), V & A, Glasgow AG, Kirkcaldy AG, Newport AG.
**Bibl:** Apollo, LXVI, 1957; Bury, Joseph Crawhall, the Man and the Artist (1958); Caw 208,346,367,438,465; Halsby 143-147 et passim; Irwin 370-385 (illus); Macmillan [SA], 256,264,269-70,287; OWS Club, XXIII 1945; Walker, 'The Art of Joseph Crawhall', Studio, Vol 69, 1917, 16.; Vivien Hamilton: *Joseph Crawhall 1861-1913 One of the Glasgow Boys*, Glasgow Museums 1990.

**CRAWSHAW, Frances (née Fisher)** **1876-c1940**
Painter in oil and watercolour; flowers and pastoral scenes. Second wife of Lionel Townsend C(qv). Studied at Westminster School of Art and Scarborough School of Art and in Milan before moving to Edinburgh 1935. Lived at 10 Napier Road. Returned to England c1937, settling in Droitwich. Although not Scottish by birth, she met her husband in Edinburgh and much of her best work was done whilst in Scotland and in the company of many of the leading Scottish artists of her day. Exhibited RSA(37) 1933-1937, also RA(13), RSW(75), ROI(16), RI(9), GI(2) & L(9); also 'Edinburgh Ice Rink' and 'Skating at Craiglockart' at the AAS.
**Bibl:** Halsby 255.

**CRAWSHAW, Lionel Townsend RSW** **1864-1949**
Born Doncaster. Painter in oil and watercolour of figures and flowers. Studied law before taking up painting, thereafter studying art in Dusseldorf, Karlsruhe and Paris. Settled in Edinburgh where he met his second wife, Frances Crawshaw(qv). Painted a large number of different subjects including town scenes with figures and flowers. Elected RSW 1923. Exhibited RA(13), RSA(37) 1908-1938, RSW (75), RI(9), ROI(16), GI(19), AAS(1), London Salon(12) & L(9).
**Bibl:** Halsby 255.

**CRAYK, Fred** **1952-**
Born Portsmouth. Painter and schoolmaster. Early life spent in Inverness. Trained Duncan of Jordanstone School of Art 1972-6. Awarded SAC bursary. Uses thick impasto; powerful figurative painter opting to depict harsh industrial and urban conditions rather than the more peaceful rural scenes of Scottish life: the alienation of the human psyche. Exhibition Edinburgh 1991.
**Bibl:** Bill Hare, Contemporary Painting in Scotland, Edinburgh 1993.

**CREE, Alexander** **1929-**
Born Dunfermline, 24 Feb. Painter in oil, watercolour, pastel and pen; landscapes, interiors, portraits and rustic scenes. Studied Edinburgh College of Art 1946-1950 under Gillies(qv); awarded Andrew Grant Scholarship followed by a travelling scholarship 1951-52. Attracted to France and modern French art. From his studio in East Linton, exhibited regularly at the RSA 1950-1980, mainly East Lothian landscapes, also one or two genre and still life, & GI(10), after 1965 from Braeheads, East Linton, E Lothian.

**CREE, Miss Florence** **fl 1888-1902**
Amateur flower painter from Ingleside, Lenzie, nr Glasgow. Moved to Edinburgh c1902. Exhibited RSA(1) & GI(3).

**CREE, John Jnr** **fl 1842**
Glasgow painter; exhibited RSA(1).

**CREED, John** **1938-**
Born Heswall, Cheshire. Scottish-based sculptor in metal; silversmith. Trained Liverpool College of Art 1955-59 and after a year's apprenticeship and a further year in Austria, gained teaching diploma 1962. Lectured in various English art schools prior to joining teaching staff, Glasgow School of Art 1971-95 followed by part-time teaching Edinburgh College of Art 1996-2000. Opened studio in USA 2000. Many solo exhibitions in England, Scotland (first in Glasgow 1989) and Germany. "He allies the physical presence and linear qualities characteristic of works in base metals with the precision and attention to detail intrinsic to works in silver and gold"[Watt]. Exhibits RGI. Represented in National Museum of Scotland, Goldsmith's Hall, Aberdeen AG, Vatican, Princess Royal's collection.
**Bibl:** Rosemary Watt, 'John Creed', Ex Cat, Roger Billcliffe Gallery, Sept-Oct 1999.

**CREME, Benjamin** **fl1940-1965**
Glasgow painter. Member of the Centre(qv), taking over the management with Robert Frame 1941. Moved to London 1946, retaining a close association with Jankel Adler(qv). Hardie refers to his 'sinewy uninhabited landscapes'.
**Bibl:** Hardie 168,170,174.

**CRESSWELL, A E B** **fl 1861-1868**
Nairn landscape and portrait painter who exhibited four works at the RSA between the above dates, and 3 local landscapes at the GI.

**CRESSWELL, Constance W Baker** **fl 1881**
Amateur painter who lived at Walton Lodge, Crieff. Exhibited a figurative work at the RSA.

**CRESWICK, Charles** **?-1965**
Sculptor and silversmith. Originally a sculptor before becoming a full-time silversmith. Taught for 30 years at Edinburgh College of Art, during which time he accepted occasional commissions including the chalice and gospel lights for the Episcopal cathedral, Oban; the chalice and paten for All Saints, Edinburgh and the monstrance for St Margaret's RC church, Edinburgh.
**Bibl:** Scotsman, Obit, 28.v.1965

**CRESWICK, John** **fl 1922**
Edinburgh sculptor. In 1922, when living at 46 Torphichen Street, Edinburgh, exhibited a bronze group of dogs at the RSA.

**CREW, Dr Helen C** **fl 1938-1942**
Edinburgh painter in oil and watercolour of rural scenes. Lived at 41 Mansionhouse Road. Exhibited RSA 1940 and 1942, also RA(3), during the above period.

**CRIBBES, George Oswald** **1903-1967**
Painter in oil, also etcher; interiors, townscapes and landscape. Studied at Edinburgh College of Art under A B Thomson(qv), and worked in the low countries and France. His etchings, executed between 1922 and 1935 are of fine quality. In later life he turned to more abstract work. In the 1930s lived at 21 Viewforth Terrace. Exhibited landscapes, especially farm buildings and portraits, RSA(17) 1929-1937 & GI(2), from 74 Leamington Terrace, Edinburgh.

**CRICHTON, Alexander** **fl 1867**
Edinburgh sculptor of portrait medallions. Exhibited once at the RSA.

**CRICHTON, Edward J** **fl 1932-1937**
Edinburgh painter of interiors, still life and portraits, exhibited three works at the RSA between the above years. Lived at 32 Brinkbonny Gardens.

**CRICHTON, J Stewart** **fl 1945**
Amateur Glasgow artist; exhibited a topographical watercolour at the GI from 29 Gibson Street.

**CRICHTON, James** **fl 1873**
Edinburgh painter, exhibited two works at the RSA in the above year.

**CRICHTON, James Angus** **fl 1901**
Edinburgh painter living at 34 York Place. Exhibited RSA(1).

**CRICHTON, Miss Jane Mary** **fl 1869-1875**
Edinburgh painter in oil and watercolour; landscape and wildlife. Sister of Matilda C(qv). Exhibited annually at the RSA(8) 1869-1875, & GI(1), from 4 Henderson Row.

**CRICHTON, John P** **fl 1973**
Amateur Airdrie painter. Exhibited once at the GI from 4 Spey Court.

**CRICHTON, Miss Matilda** **fl 1872-1874**
Edinburgh painter in oil and watercolour; figures and still life. Sister of Jane Mary C(qv). Exhibited four works at the RSA between 1872 and 1874, & GI(1) from 3 Sumner Place.

**CRICHTON, Michael Hewan** **fl 1910-1924**
Sculptor, including portrait medallions. Lived for many years in the West Midlands, before moving to Edinburgh from where most of his exhibited works were completed. Lived at 26 Swanston Terrace. Exhibited RA(2) & RSA(6).

**CRICHTON, Robert (? Richard)** **1771-1817**
Edinburgh architect. Uncle of Richard and Robert Dickson(qv). Trained under the Adam brothers, becoming an able, versatile designer. Responsible for Rossie Castle, Angus (c1800;dem 1957) and, also on Tayside, the extensive Gothic Abercairny Abbey (c1805; dem 1960). Designed Gask House for Laurence Oliphant (1801), a restrained composition somewhat in the manner of Robert Adam; also Balbirnie, Fife for General Robert Balfour (1820), characterised by the entrance portico being positioned on one of the short sides of the house. A fine drawing of the 'Elevation of the Approach to the Calton Hill by Wellington Bridge' was reproduced as an aquatint by Robert Scott(qv) 1814.
**Bibl:** Dunbar 124; Gifford 164,188n,219,285,442,516,517n; Bruce Walker & W S Gauldie, Architects and Architecture on Tayside, Dundee 1984, 69.

**CRICHTON-STUART, Frances** **fl 1977-**
Portrait and mural painter, also interiors, still life, flowers and animals. Daughter of Major and Mrs Michael Crichton-Stuart of Falkland Palace. Trained St Martin's School of Art, London. In 1977 she executed a mural for the New Charing Cross Hospital, London, sponsored by an Arts Council Award grant. Travels widely in Europe, South America and Australia. Lives in London.

**CRIGHTON, Hugh Ford** **fl 1853-1882**
Glasgow portrait painter. Moved to Edinburgh. Exhibited RSA(28) between the above years, & GI(11).

**CROALL, Annie A** **fl 1886**
Lanark watercolour painter of interior scenes, exhibited RSA91).

**CROALL, Senga** **fl 1984**
Amateur Clydebank painter; exhibited GI(1) from Marden House.

**CROCKETT, Josephina** **fl 1976-1982**
Aberdeen painter of figurative subjects. Trained at Gray's School of Art. Exhibited AAS during the above years from 68 Hardgate.

**CROCKETT, William** **fl 1981**
Aberdeen painter. Exhibited a representational work at the AAS from 1 Pinewood Avenue.

**CROEBAR, Paul O (or Q)** **fl 1913**
Amateur Edinburgh portrait painter, exhibited RSA(1) from 9 Palmerston Place.

**CROFT, Paul John** **fl 1986-**
Edinburgh painter, exhibited RSA 1986.

**CROFT-SMITH, David** **fl 1968-1973**
Amateur Tarbolton artist. Exhibited GI(4) from 32 Fail Avenue & AAS(2) 1973 from Troon, Ayrshire.

**CROIL, Gladys M** **fl 1910-1912**
Aberdeenshire painter of Scottish and continental landscape, townscape and coastal scenes. The first of 4 exhibits at the AAS was in 1910 when living at Balquhidder, Murtle; shortly afterwards moved to 381 Union Street from where she also exhibited at the NEAC.

**CROLL, Francis (Frank)** **1827-1854**
Born and died Edinburgh. Engraver. Apprenticed to the Edinburgh naturalist and engraver T Dobbie. Subsequently studied for two more years with J A and William Bell; also attended drawing classes given at the Scottish Academy by Sir William Allan. Besides engraving many portraits in the city, Croll engraved 'The Tired Soldier', after Goodall, for the Vernon gallery. The Scottish Society for the Encouragemnent of Art commissioned him to engrave one of the series of plates from the designs of John Faed for *The Cottar's Saturday Night,* a task left unfinished at his tragically premature death. Exhibited RSA 1850, 1851(2) and 1852, mostly sketches from nature in Argyll and Perthshire. Two of his engravings are in the City of Edinburgh collection.
**Bibl:** Brydall 214; Bryan.

**CROMBIE, Benjamin William** **1803-1847**
Born Fountainbridge, Edinburgh, 19 Jly. Miniature portrait painter, etcher and lithographer. Son of a solicitor. Interested in art from an early age, in 1825, when only 22 years old, published a series of drawings *Portraits of the Members of the Scottish Bench and Bar* for Constable. At the same time he was commissioned to undertake a set of portraits with the title *Contemporary Portraits,* but these were never published. Then turned to illustrating members of the dock rather than the bench. Burke, the murderer, was drawn from life with the prisoner's own 'consent' in the lock-up house the day before his execution. In 1830 he exhibited at the RSA for the first time, three unnamed miniatures. His main work was done between 1837 and 1847 when he produced a remarkable series of etched caricatures. These were issued in parts until 1839, the first edition appearing in 1844. After his death the etched copper plates were purchased from his widow by H Paton and used to produce further editions, the last of which was edited by William Scott Douglas in 1882. Douglas regarded the etchings as superior in treatment and less given to caricature than any others. These subsequently appeared as *Modern Athenians* 1839-1851. Between 1835 and 1837 he had been engaged in a series of *Fine Heads of Legal Luminaries* published by Alexander Hill, printseller to the RSA, and in 1843 a composite portrait 'Leaders of the Secession' (Drs Candlish, Guthrie, Gordon and Cunningham). Represented in SNPG (including a sketch book, caricature sketches and 18 other works), City of Edinburgh Art collection, Edinburgh Public Library.
**Bibl:** Brydall 213; Butchart 90,94-5; McKay 326; Houfe 105; Veth; *Comic Art in England*, 1930, p41, illus.

**CROMBIE, David A** **fl 1802-1889**
Edinburgh architect. Exhibited a number of designs at the RSA including one for Hawick Baptist church.

**CROMBIE, Ethel** **fl 1900-1923**
Miniature portrait painter. Although spending most of her life in York, she was of Scottish extraction and the majority of her works were shown at the Society of Miniaturists 1900-1910 and RSA 1906-1921. Also exhibited GI(8), RHA(12), RI(1), RCA(15) & L(17).

**CROMBIE, Mrs Frances A** **fl 1936-1937**
Amateur Glasgow watercolourist. Exhibited two works at the RSW during the above years from 11 Cranworth Street.

**CROMBIE, James A** **fl 1947-1955**
Edinburgh stained glass window designer, exhibited RSA during the above years.

**CROMBIE, Robert** **fl 1854-1860**
Amateur Edinburgh landscape painter in oil, exhibited 3 works at the RSA including a study of the 'Old Kirk, Innerleithen' (1860) from 13 West Nicholson Street.

**CROMBIE, Thomas** **fl 1788**
Scottish portrait painter. Two portraits are recorded, one of 'a man' and one of 'a child' in a private collection in Dorset.

**CROMBIE, Thomas** **fl 1862**
Edinburgh landscape painter. Lived at 13 West Nicholson Street. Exhibited RSA(2) in the above year.

**CROMBIE, William** **fl 1858-1866**
Dalkeith painter in oil; landscapes. Exhibited RSA in the above years, including two American scenes in 1858, suggesting a visit there around that time.

**CROME, William Henry** **1806-1873**
Edinburgh landscapist; exhibited RSA(9) 1842-1847.

**CROMPTON, Edward** **fl 1893-1921**
Sculptor who came from England in c1900. Trained under Sir Alfred Gilbert. In 1909 joined the staff of the College of Art as assistant to Percy Portsmouth(qv). From there he did most of his best work. Specialised in portrait sculptures and bronze and plaster medallions. Lived at 47 Colinton Dell and later 3 Whitehouse Loan, Edinburgh. Exhibited a portrait bust of 'General Booth' at the RA in 1893 and 10 works at the RSA 1909-1921.
**Bibl:** Scotsman, Obit, 7 May 1936.

**CROOKS, Samuel** **fl 1882-1883**
Edinburgh painter in oil of landscapes and buildings; exhibited for two years at the RSA.

**CROSBEE, Miss Sarah A** **fl 1941-1942**
Edinburgh-based portrait painter. Daughter of Eric Crosbee, an architect, and her mother(qv) who also exhibited paintings. Specialised in portraits, showing at the RSA during the above years.

**CROSBEE, Mrs W G** **fl 1927**
Painter. Mother of Sarah Crosbee(qv). Married Eric Crosbee, the architect. Exhibited RSA in 1927 from 21 Claremont Crescent.

**CROSBIE, William RSA RGI** **1915-1999**
Born Hankow, China, Jan 31; died Perth, Jan 15. Painter and art historian. Educated Glasgow Academy and Glasgow School of Art 1932-35, winning a Haldane Travelling Scholarship that enabled him to visit Athens, Rome, Brussels and to study at the Academy des Beaux Arts, Paris under Fernand Léger. Also studied under Aristide Maillol and at the Sorbonne. His main interest was the history and theory of techniques in which he obtained postgraduate qualifications. Remained in the studios of Léger and Maillol in Paris until WW1 during which he served in the Ambulance Service and at sea. For many years he worked in D Y Cameron's old studio at 12 Ruskin Lane. Mainly influenced by the Flemish school, works mostly in oil with design & texture usually dominating the composition. One unusual commission was to execute a model wind tunnel for the Royal Technical College, Glasgow. After the war his first exhibition in London was shared with the English surrealist John Armstrong 1946. He received many commissions for murals and altarpieces, largely through his association with Basil Spence(qv) and Jack Coia(qv). He was also involved in book illustrations and once designed a ballet set for George Chisholm. Lived in Glasgow from the end of WW2 until 1980 when he moved to Hampshire. Retrospective exhibitions were held in Edinburgh 1980, Glasgow 1990 and at Perth AG 1990. Exhibited regularly RSA 1937-1990 and GI(148). Elected ARSA 1953, RSA 1974. Represented in SNGMA, SNPG (*'Duncan Macrae'*), Edinburgh City Collection, SAC, Glasgow AG, Paisley AG, Perth AG (self-portrait and a large surrealist work, La Vie Distraite), Sydney (Australia) AG, Newport AG (Monmouth), Hunterian Museum (Glasgow University), Royal Collection.
**Bibl:** William Crosbie 'Oriental and Occidental Art', Scottish Art & Letters 3, 1947; Hartley 126; Macmillan [SA], 369-70; Scottish Gall, Edinburgh, (Ex Cat 1980); Anon, Obituary notice, RSA Annual Report 1999.

**CROSHER, Miss S A G** **fl 1937**
Amateur Glasgow painter, exhibited RSA(1) from 30 Blairgowrie Road, Cardonald.

**CROSS, Frederick A** **fl 1933**
Amateur watercolourist, exhibited RSW(2).

**CROSS, Miss M Dehane** **fl 1908**
Amateur Forfar painter. Exhibited a pastoral scene at the AAS from Auchenreich House, and Tuchbare, Forfarshire.

**CROSSLAND, J Brian** **fl 1957-1968**
Born Lancaster. Painter in oil, watercolour and pen of figurative compositions and landscape; author. Studied Lancaster Art College and Edinburgh School of Art. Worked in Scotland as a town planner and in advertising for Scotsman Publications. Published *Victorian Edinburgh* (1966) and *Looking at Whitehaven* (1971). Lived in Ayr and Edinburgh from both of which he exhibited at the GI(6). Represented in City of Edinburgh collection by two drawings of the Canongate.

**CROW, Mrs Louise** **fl 1952**
Watercolour painter of landscape. Exhibited GI(1) from 12 Parkgrove Terrace, Glasgow.

**CROWE, Miss Sheena** **fl 1971**
Exhibited an abstract painting at the AAS from 11 Laxford Lane, Broughty Ferry.

**CROWE, Victoria ARSA RSW** **1945-**
Born Kingston-upon-Thames. Painter of still life, interiors, landscape and portraits, works in both oil and watercolour, also drawings in charcoal and pencil and etcher. Studied Kingston School of Art and the Royal College of Art (1961-65). Since 1968, when invited by Robin Philipson to become a part-time lecturer at the Edinburgh College of Art, she has lived in Scotland. Highly versatile artist. Lives in the moorland countryside south of Edinburgh which she finds a powerful, evocative environment. Although not a specialist portrait painter, she undertakes several commissions each year. Received the Anne Redpath Award 1973. Following the tragic early death of her son in 1995, her work has become increasingly reflective. Among her sitters have been 'Tam Dalyell, MP', 'Tom Morgan, Lord Provost of Edinburgh' (1988), and 'Principal Johnston of Heriot Watt University' (1988/9). In 1989 commissioned by the National Trust of Scotland to paint their retiring President, 'The Earl of Wemyss and March'. Elected RSW 1982, ARSA 1987, winning the Daler-Rowney Prize for Watercolour at the RA in London the same year. Included in *500 Years of Scottish Portraiture* at the National History Museum, Frederiksborg, Denmark 1998. Exhibits annually at the RSA since 1969 also RA, RSW & GI(4), from Monksview, Carlops, Penicuik. Represented in NPG, SNPG, SNGMA, Edinburgh City Art Coll., Danish Nat. Hist. Museum (Frederiksborg), RA, Smith AG (Stirling).

**CROZIER, Pamela J** **fl 1978-1979**
Amateur Aberdeen painter. Exhibited AAS(3) from 43 Wallfield Crescent.

**CROZIER, Robert** **1940-**
Born Buckie. Painter and sculptor. Trained Edinburgh College of Art 1958-62. Awarded Andrew Grant scholarship 1960. Taught for several years in Bathgate. First solo exhibition Dundee 1968. Exhibited a portrait head in ciment fondu at the GI from 78 Deanburn Park, Linlithgow.
**Bibl:** SAC, Edinburgh 'Scottish Realism' (Ex Cat 1971).

**CROZIER, William ARSA** **1897-1930**
Born Edinburgh, 20 Jne; died 19 Dec. Painter and etcher. Studied Edinburgh College of Art and RSA School. As the result of gaining the Chalmers Bursary and Carnegie Travelling Scholarship, spent much time in France and Italy, painting chiefly landscapes. In 1923 went to Paris and with Gillies(qv) and Geissler studied under André

Lhôte. In 1928 shared the Guthrie Award for 'The Cello Player', one of his few figure pictures. In the 1920s shared a studio with William MacTaggart(qv) with whom he visited France, Italy and Holland. A haemophiliac, his tragically early death cut short a highly promising career which in its short time exerted a strong influence on the development of art in Edinburgh. Exhibited RSA(41), RSW(3) & GI(10). Represented in SNGMA, Glasgow AG, City of Edinburgh collection, Perth AG.
**Bibl:** Halsby 218-9; Hardie 159; Hartley 126; Macmillan [SA], 348,351-2; Scotsman, Obit, 20 Dec 1930; Harvey Wood, Sir William MacTaggart, Edinburgh, 1974.

**CROZIER, William** **1933-**
Born Yoker, nr Glasgow. Painter in oil of representational and abstract work. Studied Glasgow School of Art 1949-53, since then he has lived in London, Paris, Malaga and London. Head of the Department of Fine Art at Winchester School of Art. Divides his time between London and Winchester. Exhibited in the National Gallery of Canada, San Francisco Museum of Art and in Cologne, Copenhagen, New York and Madrid. Better known overseas than in his native country. Represented in V & A, Aberdeen AG, Copenhagen Museum of Modern Art, SNGMA, Glasgow AG, National Gallery of Australia, National Gallery of Canada, Warsaw Museum of Modern Art, Carnegie Institute (Pittsburgh).
**Bibl:** Gage 54,135; Gage, The Eye in the Wind (1978); Hardie 200; Hartley 127; Kirkwood, Interview with W C in Artlog No. 6, 1979; Macmillan [SA], 394; Parry-Crooke 'Contemporary British Artists', 1979; Herbert Read, 'Contemporary British Art', 1964; Scottish Gall, Edinburgh 'William Crozier: Paintings' (Ex Cat 1985).

**CRUDEN, John** **fl c1665-1700**
Born Aberdeen. At an early age he settled in Poland. From 1667 to 1687 he was assistant to Claude Callot and worked at Breslau after the death of his master. Callot had bequeathed all his books, engravings and paintings to Cruden and on 28th May, 1691, he was granted the patent as the Bishops' Court Painter. Believed to have painted the epitaph to Callot once in the Church of St Vincent in Warsaw which since 1890 has been in the Polish National Museum, Cracow. In the Weigel Kunstlagerkat of 1838, there is an engraving (no.6312) executed in the manner of J v Somer after a painting by Cruden. This is a portrait of a premonstratensian abbot seated in an armchair surrounded by books. (After notes provided by Krystyna Chalcharek).
**Bibl:** Apted 37; Bushnell; Krystyna Malcharck, personal communications to James Holloway, 1975 and Peter McEwan 1990; Macmillan [SA], 78; PCQ, vol xvi, 63.

**CRUICKSHANK, Bella B** **fl 1893**
Amateur Macduff artist; exhibited an oil study of a fish at the AAS from 5 Union Street, Macduff.

**CRUICKSHANK, Miss Catherine Gertrude** **fl 1868-1889**
Scottish miniaturist and landscape painter; daughter and pupil of Frederick Cruickshank(qv) and sister of Grace C(qv). Lived most of her life in London and exhibited 15 works at the RA between 1868 and 1889 including a portrait of 'Lady Eva Greville' (1888); also GI(2) 1870.

**CRUICKSHANK, Doris M L** **fl 1926-1927**
Banff painter in watercolour. Moved to Glasgow c1927. Exhibited RSA(2) & GI(3) from St Leonard's.

**CRUICKSHANK, Mrs Elizabeth H M** **b1898-fl 1953**
Glasgow painter who exhibited at the RSA between 1944 and 1946, also at the GI(6), between 1938 and 1953 from 2 Park Circus and after 1944 from 54 Turnberry Road.

**CRUICKSHANK, Francis** **fl 1825-1881**
Edinburgh based portrait painter, also genre. Studied at Trustees Academy 1845-52. Exhibited two works at the RA, one in 1852 and a portrait 'John Finlay of the 78th Highlanders' in 1855. Most exhibits, however, were at the RSA including 38 works between 1849 and 1881 among them a portrait of 'Lord Palmerston' (1858), now in the NPG.

**CRUICKSHANK, Frederick** **1800-1868**
Born Aberdeen. Painter of portrait miniatures and portraits in watercolour. Studied under Andrew Robertson(qv) whose work his own resembled. Although Cruickshank lived for a long time in Manchester, most of his working life was spent in Scotland where he enjoyed many commissions, often staying with the sitter's family. Among his pupils were the miniaturists Mrs F Dickson (née Cowell) and Margaret Gillies, also two of his daughters, Catherine Gertrude and Grace C. Foskett regards Cruickshank as 'a good artist whose miniatures show character. The features are painted in detail, but the costume is often washed in, with a full brush of paint, only lightly indicating the folds of the material'. Exhibited 149 portraits at the RA between 1822 and 1860, including many famous sitters, among them 'John Audubon' (1835) and 'Admiral of the Fleet Sir James Hawkins Whitshed Bt' (1844). Represented in V&A, Greenwich, Manchester City AG.

**CRUICKSHANK, George** **1792-1878**
Born Bloomsbury, Sept 27; died London, Feb 1. Painter and engraver. Younger son of Isaac Cruickshank(qv). His first wish was for a career at sea but this was discouraged by his mother who persuaded her husband to offer the young man instruction in art. But sadly his father died shortly afterwards and the young man thereupon began to finish some woodcuts which his father had started. Became a radical commentator of the social scene & political life in the Regency period and one of the truly great, inventive caricaturists and illustrators. After failing to secure an acting job, he was invited to try painting scenery but chose the art of caricature instead whilst occasionally appearing on stage as an amateur. Provided a monthly publication *The Scourge* with caricatures and also one of which he was the co-founder called *The Meteor.* But his earliest work of outstanding importance was related to Egan's famous *Life in London,* the original suggestion for which is said to have been made by Cruickshank. The completion of the plates was left to his brother Robert(qv). He next illustrated *The Humourist* and between 1823 & 1826 completed several fine illustrative etchings for Grimm's *German Popular Stories* and *Fairy Tales.* Also responsible for a curious set of comic prints called *Points of Humour.* In 1847 published a series of eight woodcuts called *The Bottle* which were immediately successful. The following year he added 'The Drunkard's Children', 'Sunday in London', 'The Gin Trap', and 'The Gin Juggernaut'. Other books he illustrated were *Hans of Iceland* (1825), *Mornings at Bow Street* (1825), *Punch & Judy* (1828), *John Gilpin,* by Cowper, (1828), *The Epping Hunt* (1830), *The Novelist's Library* (1831-2), *My Sketch Book* (1833-4), 35 illustrations for *Don Quixote,* designed and etched by his brother Robert (1834), *The Comic Almanac* (1835-52), *Sketches by 'Boz'* (Charles Dickens) (1836-7), *Memoirs of Joseph Grimaldi* (1838), *Jack Sheppard* (1839), *Oliver Twist* (1839), *The Ingoldsby Legends* (18407), *Windsor Castle* (1847), *The Miser's Daughter* (1848), *Three Courses and a Dessert* (1849), *The Loving Ballad of Lord Bateman* (1851), *The Tower of London* (1854) and *Guy Fawkes* (1857). Claimed to have given his friend Dickens the idea, including all the characters, for *Oliver Twist.* After a second marriage c1840 he abandoned drink & became a reforming teetotaller. No children by either marriage but nine children by a mistress. Exhibitions of his work were held at the V & A 1978 and at the Museum of the Order of St John, London 1992. Buried in St Paul's Cathedral. Represented in NG, V & A.
**Bibl:** Kenneth Baker, The Times, Oct 24, 1992; Bryan; Cruickshank (ed by Patten), 1973; DNB; Robert L Patten, George Cruickshank's Life, Times & Art, vol I 1792-1835, Lutterworth Press 1992; G W Reid, Descriptive catalogue of the works of George Cruickshank, 1871.

**CRUICKSHANK, George** **fl 1895-1909**
Edinburgh painter in oil of domestic genre, portraits and landscape, but best known for his still life paintings on ivory. In 1909 moved to Polmont Station, Stirlingshire. Exhibited RSA(18) between the above dates, & GI(4). Not to be confused with the Linlithgow artist of the same name(qv).

**CRUICKSHANK, George** **fl 1916-1922**
Linlithgow painter and teacher of drawing, exhibited 'September

Afternoon' at the RSA 1921. Lived at Norwood, Edinburgh Road. Not be confused with the Edinburgh-based painter of the same name(qv).

**CRUICKSHANK, Grace** **fl 1860-1894**
Scottish miniaturist. Daughter and pupil of Frederick C(qv) and sister of Catherine Gertrude C(qv). Spent most of her life in London except for a spell in Manchester. Exhibited 10 portraits at the RA between 1860 and 1894, mostly children and young ladies.

**CRUICKSHANK, Isaac** **1756-1811**
Born Leith; died London. Son of a customs officer and artist. Father of George C(qv) and Robert Isaac C(qv). Entirely self-taught apart from the hints he must have received from his father. Occasionally painted sporting scenes but was better known as an etcher and watercolourist. Went to London toward the end of the 18th century and began to earn his living drawing caricatures and designing stamps of a political nature. The first was a defence of Pitt in 1796, after the politician had suffered an assault from Gillray. Illustrated works of Jonathan Swift, Joseph Miller and John Browne. Early death induced by alcohol. In 1789 exhibited 'Return to Lochaber' at the RA, followed by another work 1790 and the 'Distresses and Triumphs of Virtue' 1792. Represented in the V & A, BM. (Not to be confused with Isaac Robert Cruickshank (1789-1856)
**Bibl:** Bryan; Brydall 254; DNB; F Marchmont, *The Three Cruickshanks*, 1897; E B Krumbhar, *Isaac Cruickshank Catalogue Raisonné*, 1996; Burlington Magazine, April 1928.

**CRUICKSHANK, J N** **fl 1941**
Amateur Glasgow watercolourist. Exhibited the study of a farmstead at the GI from 2 Park Circus.

**CRUICKSHANK, Keith** **fl 1929**
Amateur Aberdeen painter. Exhibited 2 figure studies at the AAS from Cults.

**CRUICKSHANK, R A** **fl 1887-1904**
Painter who lived at Kilmun, Argyll. Painted Highland landscape, mostly in oil. Exhibited RSA(4), RBA(2), GI(10) & L(10).

**CRUICKSHANK, Robert Isaac** **1789-1856**
Portrait and figurative painter in oil and watercolour; also engraver. Son of the Leith painter Isaac C(qv), and brother of George(qv). Spent all his life in England but always retained an interest in Scottish work. His first job was that of a midshipman on the East India company's vessel *Perseverance.* Illustrated Cumberland's *British Theatre* and the same author's *Minor Theatre.* His first exhibit at the RA 1811 was a portrait of one of the Loyal North Britons Riflemen, and in the same year a watercolour portrait of the same rifle company skirmishing. Associated with his brother George in illustrating *The Universal Songster* (1828) and *Cruickshank at Home,* followed by a supplementary volume *The Odd Volume* in association with Robert Seymour. Achieved great popularity with his illustrations for *Life in London*, adapted from the play he himself designed at the Adelphi Theatre. Also illustrated *The English Spy*; Moore: *Age of Intellect* (1819), *Lessons of Thrift* (1820), *Nightingale's Memoirs of Queen Caroline* (1820), *Radical Chiefs* (1821), *The Commercial Tourist* (1822), *Annals of Sporting and Fancy Gazette* (1822-25), Ramsey: *New Dictionary of Anecdote* (1822), *My Cousin in the Army* (1822), Westmacott: *Points of Misery* (1823), *Spirit of the Public Journals* (1823-24), *Life and Exploits of Don Quixote* (1824), *Punster's Pocket Book* (1826), *London Characters* (1827), *Grimm's Fairy Tales* (1827), Thompson: *Life of Allen* (1828), Smeeton: *Doings in London* (1828), *British Dance of Death* (1828, fp), *Spirit of the Age* (1828), *London Oddities* (1828), *The Finish to the Adventures of Tom, Jerry and Logick* (1828). He died in poverty of bronchitis. According to Bryan 'his designs on wood were often excellent but generally spoilt by the engraver'. Exhibited RA(8). Represented in British Museum.
**Bibl:** Bryan; Bushnell; DNB; F Marchmont: *The Three Cruickshanks*, 1897; W Bates: *George Cruickshank, the Artist, the Humorist and the Man, with some account of his brother Robert*, 1878; Everitt: *English Caricaturists,* 1893, 89-124.

**CRUICKSHANK, Robert J** **fl 1910**
Amateur Aberdeen artist. Exhibited 2 summer Highland landscapes at the AAS from 27 South Mount Street.

**CRUICKSHANK, Ronald** **fl 1933**
Edinburgh painter, exhibited a seascape at the RSA in the above year from 7 Ardmillan Terrace.

**CRUICKSHANK, William RCanA** **1849-1922**
Born Broughty Ferry; died Kansas City. Painter in oil and watercolour. Described as 'an eccentric old batchelor...undoubtedly one of the greatest yet least appreciated 19th-century painters in Canada'. Nephew of George C(qv). Settled in Toronto 1857 after studying at the RSA Schools in Edinburgh and the RA Schools in London under Leighton and Millais and the French historical painter Yvon in Paris. Returned to Toronto 1873 where he taught at the Central Ontario School of Art before moving to Kansas City in 1919. For many years an illustrator for the publishers Cassels and Scribner's, *London Graphic,* and *Saint Nicholas Magazine.* As a teacher he was a rigid disciplinarian, frightening his students, but beneath this gruffness there was great kindness. A fine draughtsman and a remarkable technician. In his portraits, such as 'Anne Cruickshank' (now in Ontario AG) he painted more than a simple character study using imaginative grouping with a fine tonal sense and alluring colour. Late in life he turned to purely Canadian subjects, a fine example of which is 'Breaking a Road', now in the National Gallery of Canada. Member of Toronto Art Club, enlivening the proceedings with his 'caustic, dry Scot's wit'. Elected ARCA 1884, RCA 1894.
**Bibl:** Colin S MacDonald, A Dictionary of Canadian Artists, 4 vols, Ottawa 1967-1974.

**CRUICKSHANK, Mrs Winifred** **fl 1943**
Amateur Rothesay flower painter. Exhibited 2 gouaches at the GI from 57 Barone Road.

**CRUTTWELL, Miss Grace** **fl 1903-1940**
Lived for a spell in St Andrews at the end of WW1. Exhibited mostly narrative paintings at the RA(1), RSA(4) & RCA(7).

**CUADRAS, Joaquin** **fl 1870-1874**
Edinburgh painter who had his studio for some years at 8 Albert Place. He exhibited a 'Cuban interior' at the RA in 1872 and 11 works at the RSA between 1870 and 1874, including landscapes and portraits in oil, & GI(2).

**CULLEN, Alexander** **fl 1891-1929**
Scottish architect and draughtsman. County Architect of Inverness-shire. Although the buildings for which he is responsible are not especially noteworthy, he was a frequent exhibitor of drawings, showing RA(2), RSA(8) & GI(46).

**CULLEN, Inez** **fl 1967**
Amateur Huntly artist; exhibited AAS(1) from 19 Park Street North.

**CULLEN, John** **fl 1872-1876**
Edinburgh oil painter of landscapes; exhibited RSA(14) during the above years.

**CULLEN, John** **fl 1906**
Glasgow figure painter who exhibited at the RI three times in the above year from 461 Albert Road, Langside, & GI(1) from 461 Albert Road.

**CUMMING, Mrs Ann B** **fl 1938-1959**
Glasgow flower painter who lived at 46 Clarence Drive. Exhibited GI(13).

**CUMMING, Archibald** **fl 1957-1964**
Amateur Glasgow watercolourist of landscape. Exhibited GI(2) from 259 Churchill Drive.

**CUMMING, B J** **fl 1929**
Amateur Aberdeen painter. Exhibited a figurative work at the AAS from 43 Bon Accord Street.

**CUMMING, Mrs Belle Skeoch** **1888-1964**
Edinburgh painter and watercolourist who lived for many years at 31 Buckingham Terrace. Wife of William Skeoch C(qv). Exhibited figurative works and landscapes at the RSA between 1939 and 1943, also RSW(2) & GI(8).
**Bibl:** Halsby 255.

**CUMMING, Bertie J** **fl 1948**
Nairn painter. Exhibited RSA(1) 1948.

**CUMMING, Betty** **fl 1959**
Amateur Edinburgh flower painter; exhibited RSA(1).

**CUMMING, Miss Constance Fredericka ('Eka') Gordon** **1837-1920**
Painter of landscape and watercolour. Daughter of Sir A P Gordon Cumming of Altyre and Gordonstoun. Lived for many years at Glencairn House, Crieff and also Edinburgh. Toured the Far East 1870. Fond of portraying sunsets and the use of vermilion. Author of *At Home in Fiji, A Lady's Cruise in a French Man-of-War,* and *Fire Fountains, the Kingdom of Hawaii,* 2 vols (1883). Governess to the family of Governor Gordon and accompanied them on tours of Fiji 1875-1880. Exhibited 27 works at the RSA 1870-1910 including two Indian and one Egyptian scenes in 1871, views around her ancestral home in Forres in 1867, & GI(12). Represented in Perth AG by 20 works of Hawaii, several of which were illustrations for *Fire Fountains,* and in the Gauguin Museum, Tahiti.

**CUMMING, J** **fl 1862**
Amateur Glasgow watercolour painter of landscape. Exhibited GI(1) from 5 Franklyn Terrace.

**CUMMING, James** **1732-1793**
Painter in oil and antiquarian. Apprenticed to Robert Norie and Co in 1747. Admitted to the Incorporation of St Mary's 1765. Close friend of Alexander Runciman(qv) and member of the Cashe Club (founded in 1764 for socio-artistic intercourse). Alexander Nasmyth was among his pupils, joining in 1782. Cumming was much attracted to *Ossian.* His portrait of 'William Macgregor', an Edinburgh porter, now in the City's Art collection, reflects the imagery that captured the artist's imagination.
**Bibl:** Macmillan [SA], 88,110,122,133,137,180.

**CUMMING, James** **fl 1833**
Edinburgh portrait painter. Entered in the Edinburgh Directory 1840-4 as living at Mound Place. Among the Airlie papers are recorded 4 portraits for which the Countess paid £27.6.0 in 1855.
**Bibl:** SRO Airlie Papers.

**CUMMING, James M** **fl 1919-1920**
Figure and miniature portrait painter who lived at Kilncroft, Helensburgh, exhibited three portraits at the RSA in 1919, also RA(1) & GI(1).

**CUMMING, James W H RSA RSW** **1922-1991**
Born Dunfermline, 24 Dec; died Edinburgh, 22 Jan. Painter in oil, gouache and watercolour; genre, portraits, landscape and abstracts. Educated Dunfermline HS. Studied at Edinburgh College of Art 1939-41 and 1946-50 winning a scholarship enabling him to spend most of 1950 on the Isle of Lewis. Also visited France, Spain, Italy and Belgium. Subsequently joined the staff of the ECA 1950, teaching mural painting. After graduating he spent his travelling scholarship on the Isle of Lewis. During WW2 served in the RAFVR training as a pilot in Texas and subsequently flying in India and Burma. Influenced by Mondrian. Held more than 25 solo exhibitions in England and Scotland. Memorial exhibition, Roger Billcliffe Gallery (Glasgow), 1995. Elected RSW 1962, ARSA 1962, RSA 1970, appointed 20th Treasurer, RSA 1973 and Secretary 1978-80. President, SSA 1958-61. Represented in SNGMA, Aberdeen AG, Glasgow AG, Kirkcaldy AG, Perth AG, City of Edinburgh collection, Eastbourne AG, Toronto AG.
**Bibl:** Mungo Campbell, 'The Line of Tradition', Nat Galls of Scotland, Ex cat, 1993 (but confused with James M Cumming); Gage 40-42,135-6; Scotsman, Obit, Jan 24 1991.

**CUMMING, Jane Ferguson** **fl 1889**
Portobello artist; exhibited RSA(1) from 1 Bath Place.

**CUMMING, John** **fl 1969-1975**
Painter. Exhibited AAS 1969 and again six years later.

**CUMMING, John Begg** **1884-1968**
Portrait painter. Studied Edinburgh College of Art. 'Self-portrait' in oil in collection of the City of Edinburgh.

**CUMMING, Marion Gordon** **fl 1907-1920**
London based miniature painter of Scottish extraction. Exhibited three works at the RA between 1907 and 1920, one of her sitters being 'Lieut-Gen Sir Bryan Milnan'.

**CUMMING, Miss Nanzie** **fl 1952-1959**
Glasgow painter of still life and landscape, generally in oil. Exhibited GI(3) from 46 Clarence Drive.

**CUMMING, R J** **fl 1892-1909**
Landscape painter in oil and watercolour of landscape and coastal scenes. He seems to have frequently moved, with various addresses: Dalmuir 1892, Glasgow 1902, Lenzie 1904 and Bridge of Allan 1907. Exhibited RSA 1898, GI(15) & AAS(2).

**CUMMING, William** **fl 1885**
Exhibited a shipping scene at the AAS from 2 East Broughton Place, Edinburgh.

**CUMMING, William Skeoch** **1864-1929**
Born Edinburgh. Painter in watercolour; portraits and military subjects, also designer of tapestries, woven in Lord Bute's studios at Corstorphine. Studied Edinburgh School of Art and RSA School. Served in the Boer War, sketching incidents of the campaign in watercolours, also painted portraits. Lived at 28 Queen Street before moving to 31 Buckingham Terrace. Works include scenes from Scottish military history including the Afghanistan campaign and portraits. Contributed designs in the early days of the Dovecot Tapestry Company. Member, Society of Scottish Artists from 1906. His work was strong, colourful and bold, in keeping with the subjects he portrayed. His wife Belle Skeoch C(qv) was also an artist. Exhibited at the RA 'The Black Watch on the trek' (1903) and 'Defence of a Kraal: First Lifeguards at Diamond Hill, 11 June, 1900' (1904), also RSA(48) 1885-1928. Represented in SNPG by 2 portraits, both of the surgeon Thomas Keith (1827-1895), and by two military group portraits in watercolour in City of Edinburgh collection.
**Bibl:** Caw 272; Halsby 255.

**CUMMINGS, Albert Runciman** **1936-**
Painter of classical scenes, landscape and figure subjects, often in watercolour, also in mixed media and egg tempera. Indirectly descended from the Runciman family of artists. His work is exquisitely detailed, classical in form and feel.

**CUMMINGS, R** **fl c1780-c1800**
English sculptor, but settled in Edinburgh. The SNPG has a portrait bust of the antiquarian and naturalist William Smellie in plaster of Paris signed 'R Cummings, Sculptor, Edinburgh'. This is probably the 'very pleasing creation' mentioned by Campbell in his *Journey from Edinburgh through parts of North Britain* (1811, rev ed).

**CUNDALL, C E** **fl 1832-1842**
Leith portrait painter; exhibited RSA(5) during the above years.

**CUNNINGHAM, Miss A B** **fl 1845-1846**
Amateur Coldstream landscape painter. Exhibited four works at the RSA during the above time.

**CUNNINGHAM, Miss Aileen** **fl 1972**
Amateur Falkirk portrait painter. Exhibited a 'self-portrait' at the GI from 119 Thornbridge Road.

**CUNNINGHAM, Annie** **fl 1863-1867**
Amateur Glasgow landscape painter in oil and watercolour, exhibited two works at the RSA in 1867 & GI(4), from 22 Grove Street.

**CUNNINGHAM, Arthur Wellesley** **fl 1883-1887**
Edinburgh landscape painter in watercolour. Exhibited three works at the RSA 1886-1887 & GI(2) from 25 Royal Crescent.

**CUNNINGHAM, Edward Francis (called 'Il Bolognese')** **c1741-1793**
Born Kelso; died Berlin. Painter in oil; portraits and historical scenes especially the battles of Frederick the Great, the finest being 'The Battle of Hochkirk, Oct 14, 1758'. Studied in Palma, Rome, Venice and Paris, becoming a very good portraitist. Father was a nobleman

who fled to Bologna with his son after the '45 Rebellion. Followed the Duchess of Kingston to Russia and later worked in the Russian Court and subsequently in Berlin where he enjoyed great success being made 'premier painter' by Katherine II. Also known as Francesco Calza or Calze under which name he studied at Palma. In Rome he studied with the antiquary James Byres(qv), the portraitist George Willison(qv) and the history painter James Nevay(qv) under Anton Mengs and Battoni, then in Naples under Franceschiello. In 1763 won an Academy prize for Drawing at Guiseppe Baldrighi's School in Parma. When in Paris painted the portrait of the King of Denmark (fortuitously in the city at the time), a chance encounter which led to many commissions. Visited London twice between 1764 and 1781, exhibiting RA(14) 1770-81. Returning to the continent, this time to Berlin, he was much in demand; became an honorary member of the Kgl Akademie der Kunst, winning the Gold Medal known as 'Merentibus' 1792. In the catalogue of the Kgl Akademie there is mentioned a decoration in the Queen's new apartments depicting mythological and symbolic scenes 1790. In 1791 he executed an historical scene for the King's private box at the Charlottenburg theatre. The portrait of 'General Amslaini' was engraved by Giovanni Fabbri 1756. According to Thieme-Becker he died in Berlin 28 April 1793 but Redgrave says that he died in poverty in London 1795. Among the few of his works remaining in public collections are an oil portrait 'The Queen of Prussia' in Hampton Court Palace, pastel portraits of 'Field Marshall von Millerdorf' and 'General von Zeithen' (c1786) in Kgl Schloss, Berlin and three works - including 'The Death of Field Marshal Keith' in the Stadtschloss, Potsdam.
**Bibl:** Bryan; Brydall 161-2; Caw 39; McKay 24; Redgrave; Waterhouse 96.

**CUNNINGHAM, Miss Ellen** **fl 1974**
Dumbarton based textile designer and embroiderer. Exhibited GI(1) from 115 Dumbuck Crescent.

**CUNNINGHAM, James (Jim)** **fl 1968-1982**
Sculptor. Exhibited GI(7) from 26 Arran Crescent, Beith, Ayrshire.

**CUNNINGHAM, Jane** **fl 1886-1897**
Glasgow painter in oil and watercolour of flowers. Exhibited RSA 1886 & GI(8) from 50 Kelvingrove Street.

**CUNNINGHAM, Miss Jessie C** **fl 1879-1880**
Edinburgh painter in oil of domestic animals of Ettrick Road. Exhibited RSA during the above years.

**CUNNINGHAM, John** **fl c1800-c1840**
Scottish architect. Best known for the impressively domed Court House in Greenlaw commemorating the burgh's former status as a county town.

**CUNNINGHAM, John RGI D.Litt** **1926-1998**
Born Lanarkshire. Painter in oil; landscapes, portraits, still life and figurative works. Studied at Glasgow School of Art 1946-50. Taught at Glasgow School of Art 1967-85 and painted extensively in France and Spain. But his greatest love, and the inspiration for his best work, was the west coast of Scotland. Taught Glasgow School of Art 1967-85. Elected RGI 1980. Former President, Glasgow Art Club, where he was granted a retrospective exhibition 1996. Exhibited regularly at the RSA 1954 until 1995 & RGI(101). Represented in Glasgow AG.

**CUNNINGHAM, Miss Lin** **fl 1987**
Glasgow painter; exhibited GI(2) from 7 Devonshire Terrace.

**CUNNINGHAM, Miss Mary L Dorothy** **fl 1891-1892**
Painter. Exhibited two interiors from Liberton House, Midlothian.

**CUNNINGHAM, Mern E C** **1893-?**
Born Dundee. Educated at Edinburgh College of Art 1911-12, and for three years at Swanley Horticultural College, where she was particularly interested in garden design 1921-1924. Later became a landscape architect. In her painting work concentrated on watercolours, especially of houses, old buildings and gardens in Europe, Australia and USA. Frequent exhibitor RSW & SSW from her studio in Edinburgh.

**CUNNINGHAM, Miss Sarah Sparrow** **fl 1886-1900**
Glasgow flower and landscape painter. Lived in Pollockshields 1886 before moving to Glasgow 1892. Exhibited RSA(5), GI(5) & AAS(1), from 181 Pitt Street.

**CUNNINGHAM, Thomas M Ewan** **fl 1882-1892**
Edinburgh painter in watercolour of rural landscapes; exhibited 12 works at the RSA during the above years from 16 Spittal Street, & AAS(2).

**CUNNINGHAM, Walter** **fl 1949-1965**
Edinburgh painter of figurative subjects in oil. Exhibited GI(3) & AAS(1) from 45 East Trinity Road.

**CUNNYNGHAME, D** **fl 1782**
Watercolour artist. A watercolour sketch of Edinburgh Castle is in NGS, signed and dated 1782.

**CUNYNGHAM, Helen Dick** **fl 1888**
Amateur Aberdeen painter. Exhibited RSA(1) from Caskieben.

**CUNYNGHAM, Mrs V Dick** **fl 1939**
Painter. Daughter-in-law of Helen Dick C(qv). Exhibited RI(1).

**CUNYNGHAME, Eleanor A Blair** **fl 1903**
Amateur Edinburgh miniaturist. Exhibited RSA(1) from 18 Rothesay Place.

**CURDIE, John** **fl 1851-1878**
Kilmarnock painter in oil; landscapes, especially Ayrshire and Arran. One of many painters of his time who enjoyed painting Arran, showing two landscapes of the island at the RSA in 1864. Exhibited 31 works at the RSA 1851-1878, & GI(6) from 74 King Street.

**CURR, Amy J** **fl 1885-1894**
Flower and portrait painter of Seafield, Aberdeen; exhibited GI(2) & AAS(6).

**CURR, James B S** **fl 1934-1953**
Amateur Paisley artist and engraver. Exhibited a nude at the Paisley Art Institute in 1953 from 3 Dunchurch Road, Oldhall, also landscapes in 1934-36 and 1939; & GI(1) from 7 Wellmeadow Street.

**CURR, Miss Muriel C S** **fl 1943-1966**
Edinburgh painter of flowers, landscape (especially Arran), still life and portraits. Exhibited nine works at the RSA between the above years from 14 East Claremont Street, & GI(7).

**CURR, Thomas** **1952-1962**
Edinburgh portrait and landscape painter in oil. Among his sitters was the 'Rt Hon J Westward, Secretary of State for Scotland' (1946). Designed the plaque commemorating the pupillage of R L Stevenson(qv) at what is now the Youth Centre of Dublin St Baptist Church, Canonmills. Exhibited regularly RSA 1944-1958, & GI(10).

**CURRAN, Francis** **fl 1952-1981**
Bonnyrigg painter of landscapes, mostly of the West Coast, who exhibited at the RSA regularly throughout the above period.

**CURRER, John D** **fl 1947-1950**
Amateur Ayr painter in watercolour and pencil; landscape and portraits. Exhibited GI(4) from 24 Elba Street.

**CURRIE, Andrew** **1813-1891**
Born Ettrick Forest; died Edinburgh, 28 Feb. Self-taught Melrose sculptor and antiquarian. Son of a farmer. Responsible for the Ettrick Monument at St Mary's Loch (1860) and the Bruce statue at Stirling Castle. Wood carvings by him can be seen at Abbotsford. A fine craftsman. After abandoning an apprenticeship and serving at Chatham dockyard for several years, he turned to sculpture. Executed in wood the famous fancy flower-stand descriptive of Thomas the Rhymer, exhibited at the RSA, now in Methven House. Other work in wood includes a very fine carved oak mantelpiece, exhibited in Melbourne, now in a private house in Larro, Victoria and the pulpit for the RC church, Galashiels. Carved a statue of 'Mungo Park', Selkirk 1839. Executed a sandstone figure of 'Old Mortality' which he decided to raffle. The winner, a Dr Sinclair, was killed on the day of the draw and his executors presented the work to the Observatory at Dumfries where an octagonal temple was built to receive it. Currie's

group 'Old Mortality renewing the Inscription on the grave stones of the Covenanters' was exhibited at Liverpool, and in 1840 the sculptor also showed 'Edie Ochiltree and Douster Swivel' in London. His figures 'Dominie Sampson' and 'Meg Merrilees' are, or were, in the grounds of Carlton House, near Kirkcudbright. Exhibited a portrait bust at the RA in 1877 and twice at the RSA in 1877 and 1878, also GI(1). Represented in City of Edinburgh collection by a marble statue of an unknown girl holding flowers.
**Bibl:** Border Mag Vol XI, 1906, 4-5; Gifford 316; Gunnis 119 (where his Christian name is incorrectly given as John).

**CURRIE, Hilary** **fl 1969-1980**
Aberdeen artist of flowers and landscape. Wife of Joseph C(qv). Exhibited AAS from 19 St Swithin Street.

**CURRIE, Isabella** **fl 1885**
Edinburgh-based artist; exhibited RSA(1) from 16 Roxburgh Street.

**CURRIE, J C** **fl 1934-1937**
Glasgow painter who exhibited 5 works at the GI from 35 West Graham Street. Represented in Paisley AG.

**CURRIE, James** **fl 1846**
Obscure portrait painter. Portraits of several members of the Brodie family, all signed and dated 1846, can be seen in Brodie Castle (NTS).

**CURRIE, Jessie C** **fl 1937**
Amateur Aberdeen artist. Exhibited 3 local scenes at the AAS from The Manse of Newhills, Bucksburn.

**CURRIE, John** **fl 1912-1915**
Amateur Kilmarnock painter of 5 John Dickie Street. Exhibited GI(3).

**CURRIE, Joseph G** **fl 1967**
Aberdeen landscape painter, works also in enamels. Staff member, Gray's School of Art. Husband of Hilary C(qv). Exhibited AAS(2) from 19 St Swithin Street.

**CURRIE, Ken** **1960-**
Born in North Shields. Painter in oil of figurative and narrative subjects. Studied social science at Paisley College 1977-78 before going to Glasgow School of Art 1978-1983 winning the Newbery medal and Greenshields Foundation Scholarship 1982. Awarded the SAC Young Artist Bursary in 1985 and from that time worked as a full-time artist. A politically committed commentator, seeking involvement in the struggle for a more just society. After graduating he became increasingly dissatisfied with traditional landscape and turned to figure painting. Encouraged by Alexander Moffat, he turned the values of the Scottish colourist tradition on their head 'instead of colour being the prime quality and content being placed last in the order of priorities, Currie put content first and colour last. Ideas were to supersede sensuality' [Hartley]. After working on two community based films about Glasgow and industry on the Clyde 1983-5, he began to base his subject matter on the current social and industrial conditions of the city with particular reference to the shipyards. In his preoccupation with art as a social statement rather than as a vehicle for the expression of beauty he is very much a child of his age. His work is coarse like so many Scottish painters of the time but there is considerable originality in conception and dour solidity that reflects the environment in which he works. Visiting tutor, Glasgow School of Art 1991; visiting Artist, Art Institute of Chicago 1992. Commission for Glasgow Royal Concert Hall completed 1995. Represented in SNGMA, Gulbenkian Foundation, Lisbon, City of Edinburgh collection, Perth AG, SAC, British Council, London, People's Palace Museum (Glasgow).
**Bibl:** Hartley 70-73,121; Macmillan [SA], 406; TEC, Glasgow, 'Ken Currie' (Ex Cat 1988); Ken Currie, 'Notes by the Artist', ex cat, Boukamel Contemporary Art, 1999.

**CURRIE, Miss Maud** **fl 1912-1916**
Edinburgh painter of small animals and flowers. Exhibited RSA(1) & GI(2) during the above period from Millbank, Grange Loan.

**CURRIE, Robert** **fl 1872-1885**
Fifeshire painter and etcher in oil of landscape and wildlife. Exhibited 'A Group of Herons on the Earn' at the RA (1885) and several landscapes at the RSA as well as etchings at the RE. Also executed two landscapes of the Australian Bush 1868.

**CURRIE, William** **fl 1846-1868**
Edinburgh landscape painter, sometimes of southern England. Exhibited 14 works at the RSA between the above years.

**CURRIE, William** **fl 1938**
Greenock watercolourist and etcher of still life and landscapes. Exhibited GI(2) from 52 Murdieston Street

**CURSITER, James Grant** **fl 1982**
Minor Edinburgh painter. Exhibited 'The Fading' at the AAS from 5 Bellevue Road.

**CURSITER, Stanley CBE RSA RSW** **1887-1976**
Born Kirkwall, 29 Apr; died Stromness, Orkney. Painter in oil and watercolour; portraits, figures and landscapes. Also art administrator and writer. His apprenticeship was served as a chromolithographic designer before becoming a full-time student at Edinburgh College of Art. Much taken with the post-impressionist and futurist works seen in London 1912 and 1913, encouraging him to paint his own series of futurist pictures in the latter year. During this period he was fascinated with the design of futurist type compositions. An intellectual appreciation of design, style and technique was stimulated during his spell as Keeper of the SNPG and subsequent innovative work in art education and picture restoration as Director of NGS 1930-1948. Executed landscapes in the South of France and in Orkney. Also embarked upon society and group portraits as well as a wide range of subjects through lithography. Helped organise the major shows of Scottish art at the RA in 1939 and during WW2 mounted an important series of exhibitions of child art and contemporary art from abroad at the NGS. In 1948 appointed King's Painter and Limner in Scotland, retiring to Orkney where he devoted himself to landscape painting and recording Orcadian life. Author of *Peploe: An Intimate Memoir of an Artist and His Work* (1947); *Scottish Art at the Close of the Nineteenth Century* (1949); and *Looking Back: Book of Reminiscences* (1974). Curiously, it is only recently, with the great increase in interest in Scottish art and with the oil industry endowing a number of Orcadians with the resources to purchase original works, that Cursiter has achieved full and proper recognition. Elected ARSA 1927, RSA 1938, RSW 1914. Awarded CBE 1948. Exhibited RA(9), RSA(69), RSW(45), GI(30), RHA(6), L(28) & AAS(6). Represented in NGS, SNGMA, Glasgow AG, Kirkcaldy AG, Paisley AG, Perth AG, The Binns (NTS).
**Bibl:** Eddington, 'The Paintings and Lithographs of Stanley Cursiter', The Studio, Vol LXXXII, 340, July 1921, 21-25; Halsby 20,255; Hartley 127-8; Macmillan [SA], 305,311; Pier Arts Centre, Stromness, Orkney 'Stanley Curstier Centenary Exhib', (Ex Cat 1987); The Scotsman, Obit, 23.4.1976.

**CURTIS, Miss Ada N** **fl 1886-1887**
Painter of Ebberly, Greenock. Sister of Ellen C(qv). Exhibited GI(2) during the above period.

**CURTIS, Miss Ellen** **fl 1879-1887**
Greenock landscape painter in oil. Sister of Ada N C(qv). Exhibited 7 works at the GI from Greenbank.

**CURTIS, E M** **fl 1887**
Greenock painter of 27 Bentinck Street; exhibited a flower study at the GI.

**CURWEN, Edward** **fl 1922-1930**
Painter in watercolour. Moved around the south-west of Scotland, in Glasgow 1922, Rutherglen 1923 and Greenock 1927. Exhibited RSA(1) & GI(4).

**CUTHBERT, Mrs Elspeth M** **fl 1962-1972**
Painter of portraits and flowers. Exhibited GI(5) from Kerrix Cottage, Killearn, Stirlingshire.

**CUTHBERT, Gwen** **fl 1922-1923**
Illustrator of 38 Bingham Terrace, Dundee; exhibited RSA(1) & GI(1).

**CUTHBERT, James G** **fl 1862-1876**
Arbroath painter in oil; landscape and figures. During the above years exhibited 12 works at the RSA, in 1876 from a Braco address, & GI(1) from 1 Howard Street, Arbroath.

**CUTHBERT, Margaret A M** **fl 1973**
Clackmannan landscape painter. Exhibited RSA(2) 1973.

**CUTHBERTSON, Miss Alice** **fl 1863-1887**
Edinburgh painter in oil and watercolour; landscape, especially Perthshire. Also painted flowers. Living in Rome 1880. Exhibited 8 works at the RSA between the above dates, & SWA(4).

**CUTHBERTSON, Dr David P** **fl 1939-1954**
Glasgow landscape painter of 3 Wilmot Street. Exhibited RSA, RSW(2) & GI(12). Became increasingly active as a painter after moving to Aberdeen, exhibiting a number of landscapes, many of the Cairngorms, at the AAS.

**CUTHBERTSON, J** **fl 1887-1893**
Amateur Kilmarnock painter in oil and watercolour of landscapes. Exhibited GI(4) during the above years.

**CUTHBERTSON, Kenneth J** **fl 1920-1952**
Painter who came to live in Barnton, Edinburgh, mainly in watercolour and most often landscapes. Lived in Midlothian, changing his address from Inveresk to Corstorphine. Sometimes worked abroad, particularly in Italy. Exhibited 17 works at the RSA 1920-1952, also RSW(6), GI(9) & L(3), from West Winds, Drum Brae North, Barnton. **Bibl:** Halsby 255.

**CUTHBERTSON, Mrs W** **fl 1891-1914**
Edinburgh painter. Exhibited RSA(6) & GI(2).

**CUTHBERTSON, William Alexander** **fl 1902-1920**
Edinburgh painter of portraits and genre who in c1909 moved to Glasgow and in c1920 south to Croydon. In addition to one exhibit at the RA, he showed a number of works at the RSA between 1902 and 1914, after 1909 from 65 West Regent Street in Glasgow, also GI(2) including 'The Golfer' (1906).

**CUTHIL, Miss Joan W** **1921-**
Born Arbroath, 18 Dec. Painter in oil, watercolour, pastel, gouache and pencil; flowers, landscape, portraits and still life, also embroiderer. First solo exhibition while still a schoolgirl in 1939, with frequent sequels, mostly in Scotland, the last one in 2000. Taught art at Falkirk Technical School, Morrison's Academy, Crieff, Dundee HS and Arbroath HS. Responsible for the lettering and illumination of the Roll of Honour on Dundee War Memorial and in 1961 provided the illuminated lettering for a Book of Names commemmorating pupils killed in WW2. One time secretary of Arbroath Art Society and President of Arbroath Business and Professional Women's Club. Exhibited local Angus scenes at the RSA in 1945 and 1947(2).

**CUTHILL, Walter M** **fl 1929-1946**
Edinburgh painter of landscape. Exhibited 6 works at the RSA between the above years, usually landscapes, living latterly at 4 Magdala Mews and then Cragbrook Avenue.

**'CYNICUS'** **[see ANDERSON, Martin]**

**D, J R** **fl 1866-1868**
Anonymous Edinburgh-based artist who exhibited seven landscape paintings in oil, mostly of Perthshire scenes, at the RSA between 1866 and 1868 from Dreghorn College, Colinton.

**DACKER, Herbert** **fl 1960-1968**
Edinburgh sculptor. In 1968 he showed a portrait head of 'Professor George Scott, FRCSE FRCPE FRSE' at the RSA. Exhibited several cold cast copper and bronze portrait heads at the RSA during the above years, also GI(4), from 21 Lauder Road.

**DAINTY, Charles T J** **fl 1950**
Amateur Edinburgh watercolourist of flowers. Exhibited GI(1) from 168 Colinton Mains Drive.

**DAKERS, Robert Alexander** **fl 1913-1924**
Landscape painter. Living at Haddington 1913, moved to Castle Douglas then to Edinburgh c1920 and then Alnwick where he was living 1924. Between the above years he exhibited 28 landscape and rustic paintings at the RSA, many of them scenes in Galloway.

**DALBY, Joy Claire Allison (née Longbotham) RWS RE** **1944-**
Born St Andrews, 20 Nov. Painter in watercolour and pen and ink; also wood engraver, calligrapher and illustrator, mostly botanical. A meticulous draughtswoman, specialising in churches, trees, interiors and flower studies. Daughter of Charles Longbotham, RWS. Educated at Haberdashers' Aske's School, London, studied art at the City and Guilds, London 1964-67. Awarded Greenshields Memorial scholarship 1961 and David Murray Studentship 1966. Held her first one-man show at the Clarges Gallery, London 1968 and again in 1972. Her wood engravings are generally of buildings and farm machinery, all with a fine attention to detail and sense of atmosphere. Influenced by Joan Hassall and Thomas Bewick. Illustrated Alvin: *The Observer's Book of Lichens* (1977), Angel & Wolseley: *The Family Water Naturalist* (1982), and Downie: *Even the Flowers* (1989). Elected ARWS 1973, RWS 1977, ARE 1978, RE 1982. Exhibits regularly RA, RWS, RE & NEAC.
**Bibl:** *Claire Dalby's Picture Book* 1989; Brett; Horne 163; Jaffé.

**DALE, Robert** **fl 1861**
Amateur Glasgow painter. Exhibited a local landscape at the GI from 71 North Street.

**DALE, William** **fl 1862-1870**
Helensburgh artist; exhibited one landscape in oil at the RSA in the above years, & GI(3), from 40 Queen Street.

**DALGLEISH, Andrew Adie** **fl 1867-1904**
Glasgow painter in oil and later increasingly watercolour, mainly landscape. Exhibited RSA(11), including a study on Arran, (1875) and 2 of Cadzow forest (1879); also RSW(5) & GI(29), mostly from 21 Princes Street.

**DALGLEISH, Edmore** **fl 1967**
Aberdeen jewellery and metalwork designer; exhibited AAS(2) from 25 Albyn Place.

**DALGLEISH, Lizzie** **fl1901**
Amateur painter of 108 Woodlands Road, Glasgow; exhibited 'Cloister doorway of Iona Cathedral' at the GI.

**DALGLISH, William** **1857-1909**
Born Glasgow; died Glasgow, Mar. Landscape painter in oil and watercolour. Began art studies under A D Robertson, a local teacher who had a studio in Dundas Street; continued his studies at Glasgow School of Art. Preferred marine subjects, generally in watercolour, drawn in a manner similar to his Glaswegian contemporary, J D Taylor(qv). Exhibited RSA(17) 1875-1901. These included a watercolour sketch of an Arran scene (1875) and two Spanish scenes (1885). In 1898 exhibited 'Across Renfrewshire' at the RA. Also exhibited elsewhere in London from 1891 until his death, also RSW(6), GI(60), AAS 1885 & RI(3) from 26 Renfield Street. Represented in Paisley AG.
**Bibl:** Halsby 255.

**DALKEITH, Thomas Alison** **fl 1880s**
Painter of coastal scenes. Exhibited RSA.

**DALL, John** **fl 1897-1924**
Glasgow painter in oil of figure subjects. Exhibited RSA 1898 & GI(5) between the above years. Possibly the same as the architect responsible for several houses on Ravelston Dykes, Edinburgh including no. 72 and nos. 78-84 (all 1924).

**DALLAS, Alastair A K** **1898-1983**
Born Berlin, 24 Sep; died Aberfeldy, Perthshire, 20 Dec. Painter in oil and watercolour of landscapes; also teacher. Son of a minister of the Church of Scotland. The family returned to Edinburgh when the artist was seven. There he attended the Royal High School and George Heriot's before joining the army in 1916, becoming a junior officer in the 17th Lancers and serving under General Allenby in Palestine. Then posted to France where he was wounded and seconded to the Royal Air Force in which he helped ferry new aircraft to Belgium and France. After WW1 studied civil engineering at Edinburgh University but left without completing his degree and joined the Control Commission in Germany. On his return to Scotland he enrolled at Edinburgh School of Art. In the late 1920s he became official artist to the King of the Belgians' Expedition led by Colonel Gregory across Africa in search of the tsetse fly, journeying from the Gold Coast via Lake Chad to Mombasa. Thereafter he resumed duties as an official artist, this time for the King of Sweden's Meteorological Expedition in the Gobi Desert, crossing into China where he remained six months. Returning to Edinburgh he worked for a time in a commercial art studio in George Street, and for two years, 1932-34, was art and games master at a school in Nottingham. From 1934 until the outbreak of WW2 he devoted his time exclusively to watercolour landscape painting in Scotland. Exhibited RSA most years, also at the RSW. In 1940 he helped in the evacuation from Dunkirk and thereafter joined the Merchant Navy serving first on fishing trawlers then becoming a cook on the Panamanian oil tanker *Quernica.* This was chased by a German U-Boat and ran aground on the African coast west of the Kalahari Desert. With the rest of the crew Dallas escaped overland. In 1945 he married Ann(qv) and settled in Kirkcudbright. There he spent many years painting and working as a printer and binder. His last exhibits at the RSA were studies of Loch Tayside and Inverary 1944, also a local landscape at the GI. [From notes provided by the family].
**Bibl:** Halsby 255.

**DALLAS, Mrs Ann** **1908-**
Born Newbiggin, Northumberland Jan 10. Kirkcudbright-based oil and watercolour painter of local landscape, seascapes, portraits and flower pieces; also teacher. Trained King Edward VII School of Art, Newcastle. Taught at Gosforth GS 1929-45. Married Alastair(qv) 1945. Last survivor of Kircudbright school. Exhibited GI(1) from Glenhead, Auchencairn, by Castle Douglas and every year between 1945 and 1990 exhibited in Kircudbright, Laing AG (Newcastle).

**DALLAS, Annie C** **fl 1908-1912**
Amateur Aberdeen painter of figure studies and flowers; exhibited AAS(5), initially from 15 Albert Street and later from 3 Albyn Terrace.

**DALLAS, Emslie William** **1809-1879**
Edinburgh painter in oil of buildings, figurative subjects and portraits. Exhibited RSA 1842-59 (35) - almost all Italian scenes, mostly around Rome including some subject paintings, also posthumously in 1880.

**DALRYMPLE, Charles Elphinstone** **1817-1891**
There is an ink drawing of 'Prince Charles Edward Stuart', dated 1887, in the SNPG.

**DALRYMPLE, John** **fl 1861-1866**
Glasgow painter of local landscapes; exhibited GI(3) from 214 New City Road.

**DALTON, Miss Carrie** **fl 1885**
Painter of Dennistoun, Greenock. Exhibited two oil paintings of figurative subjects at the RSA in the above year.

**DALTON, Charles William** **fl 1920**
Edinburgh engraver of 4 Royston Terrace; exhibited a monotype at the RSA.

**DALYELL, Amy (Mrs James Birrell) RSW** **fl c1875-d1962**
Artist based in Edinburgh, later moved to Wimbledon. Painted in oil and watercolour, mainly the latter. Exhibited frequently RSW. Elected RSW 1883. Sister of Gladys D(qv). Favourite subjects were landscape, often with figures, but also painted coastal scenes and portraits. Exhibited RSA(27) 1901-1925, RSW(53), GI(5) & AAS(1) 1910.
**Bibl:** Halsby 255.

**DALYELL, Miss Gladys** **fl 1910-1920**
Edinburgh watercolour painter. Sister of Amy D(qv). Exhibited eight works at the RSA between 1912 and 1919, always Scottish landscapes; also RSW(1) & GI(1), from 10 Merchiston Crescent.

**DALZELL, A** **fl 1907**
Amateur Edinburgh artist; exhibited an Edinburgh townscape at the GI from 10 Murchiston Crescent.

**DALZELL (DALZIEL), Robert** **1810-1842**
Glasgow portrait miniaturist. As a young man he studied in Edinburgh with John Thomson(qv), dividing his time between Glasgow and London. Exhibited RSA in 1838 and 1839 - no fewer than seven portrait miniatures on the latter occasion. Recorded by neither Long nor Foskett.

**DALZIEL, Miss Caroline A** **fl 1906-1910**
Edinburgh miniaturist and watercolour painter of topographical subjects. Exhibited GI(3) & L(1) from 76 Thirlestane Road, also RSA 1907 & 1908. Represented in City of Edinburgh collection by a watercolour of Edinburgh Castle (1910).

**DALZIEL, Catherine J (Renée) (née Muirhead)** **1899-1994**
Born Scotstoun, Glasgow, 29 Dec. Painter in oil and watercolour of landscapes and portraits; sculptress. Jane Burns Muirhead(qv) was her great aunt. Before leaving school aged 15 she was left an orphan. Trained at Glasgow School of Art 1915-18. After graduating taught at Queen's Park Secondary School until her marriage in 1929. Sculpted a number of heads of members of the family and friends although these were never exhibited. In 1949 she began painting again, more seriously than hitherto. Working almost invariably in oil until the 1980s she exhibited regularly at the RSA and Lillie AG, Milngavie. Signed her work 'Renée J Dalziel'. As a student she had been influenced by Henderson Blyth(qv) and had a marked respect for Anne Redpath(qv). Affected by her surroundings and experiences gained in travel. Intrigued by light and shade and the contrast to be found within the qualities of light - sunlit hill slopes seen through the dim closes of Peebles or the darkness that epitomises the heart of a wood. Held regular one-man exhibitions in the John D Kelly Gallery, Glasgow. Her last exhibit at the RSA was in 1979. Also exhibited 6 oils and watercolours at the GI 1957-1980, from Kittochside House, By Busby.

**DALZIEL, Henry** **[see DANIEL, Henry]**

**DALZIEL, John** **fl 1940**
Barrhead, Renfrewshire artist of 35 Commercial Road; exhibited GI(1).

**DALZIEL, John Borland** **fl 1939-1953**
Painter in watercolour; exhibited once at the RSA (1952), & GI(11) from Hayhill Cottage, Gartcosh, Lanarkshire.

**DALZIEL, Miss Nan** **fl 1923-1931**
Painter in oil and engraver who lived in Glasgow before spending some time in Paris in the early 1930s. Exhibited RSA(1), GI(5) & L(1), also at the Paris Salon.

**DAMER, Anne Seymour (née Conway)** **1749-1828**
Died 28 May. Sculptress. Half Scottish, being the only child of Field Marshal Conway and his wife, Lady Caroline Campbell, daughter of the 4th Duke of Argyll. It is said that when still a child, David Hume rebuked her for laughing at the work of an itinerant Italian modeller and told her that she could not do anything similar, a remark which prompted the young modeller to go home and model a head in wax, a performance she later repeated in stone. Studied under Ceracchi and John Bacon, and in 1767 married John Damer, the eldest son of Lord Milton, later Earl of Dorchester. Her husband, heir to a considerable fortune, was a hopeless spendthrift who, in 1765, committed suicide in a Covent Garden tavern. After her husband's death, she devoted herself to sculpture, being encouraged by her lifelong friend, Horace Walpole, who held an exaggerated opinion of her talent. Her busts of Charles James Fox and Nelson, both of which she presented to Napoleon, were not considered very well done by Farington, the painter, when he visited the Tuileries in 1802. He thought them 'not very good likenesses, but they might be known'. Walpole bequeathed his home to Mrs Damer for life and a sum of £2,000 to keep it in repair. She stayed there until 1811 when it was sold to Lord Waldegrave. Her best known works are the Portland-stone heads of the rivers Thames and Isis for Henley Bridge (1785), her statue of Apollo for Drury Lane Theatre (1792, destroyed by fire 1809) and a statue of George III (1795) now in the Office of the Registrar General, Edinburgh. Busts of herself and her husband are at Drayton, Northants, while 'Self-portrait' is in the British Museum. She also executed the busts of Nelson, the Duchess of Argyll (in Sundridge Church, Kent), the Duke of Richmond (a plaster cast at Goodwood), the Duchess of Devonshire, and Mrs Siddons. 'Two Sleeping Dogs' is at Goodwood, Sussex, and 'Two Kittens' at Came House, Dorset. Exhibited RA(32) 1784-1818.
**Bibl:** Allan Cunningham, Lives of the Painters, vol III; Gifford 287; Gunnis, 120-121; Percy Noble, Anne Seymour Damer, A Woman of Art & Fashion, Kegan Paul 1908.

**DANCZYSZAK, John** **fl 1976**
Aberdeen-based amateur sculptor. Exhibited a portrait head at the AAS from 22A Stafford Street.

**DANDIE, Alex** **fl 1925**
Portobello artist of 5 Joppa Road; exhibited 'Mist on the Brae' at the RSA in the above year.

**DANFORD, C G** **fl 1885-1886**
Painter. Exhibited at the inaugural AAS exhibition and again the following year from an (unspecified) address in Banchory, Kincardineshire.

**DANIEL, Henry Wilkinson** **fl 1906-1957**
Painter in oil and watercolour, mostly of landscapes; also etcher. Studied at the Slade School before becoming art master at Trinity College, Glenalmond and a governor of the Allan-Fraser Art College at Hospitalfield, Arbroath. Retired to Glenholm, Glenmore Road, Oban. Exhibited RA(6), RSA(30) 1916-1946, RSW(5), ROI(2), AAS(1) & GI(18).

**DANIEL, Miss Nicola** **fl 1983-1985**
Painter of interiors and architectural topography; exhibited GI(2) from 115 Mugdock Road, Milngavie, Dunbartonshire.

**DANIELS, William** **fl 1923**
Edinburgh artist of 16A Broughton Street; exhibited RSA(1).

**DANSEY, Herbert** **fl 1903**
Edinburgh painter. Exhibited RSA(1).

**DANSKIN, Fiona Couttie** **1964-**
Born Dundee, 1 Oct. Paints in oil, charcoal and chalk, also etcher. Trained Duncan of Jordanstone College of Art, Dundee. Influenced by the theatre, interested in the nature of dreams and the element of mystery even in ordinary subjects. Exhibits regularly RSA & SSA.

**DANSON, F Sybil** **fl 1908-1910**
Amateur Aberdeen painter of country scenes; exhibited AAS(3) from 19 Bon Accord Crescent.

**DAPRÉ, Dom Vincent** **fl 1966-1967**
Member of the Dominican Order and an amateur artist of Pluscarden Priory, Elgin; exhibited 2 religious works at the AAS.

**DARNELL, E A** **fl 1889**
Amateur Edinburgh artist of Cargilfield, Trinity; exhibited RSA(1).

**DARNEY, Miss Lilian Dalzell** **fl 1891-1909**
Miniature portrait painter from Kinghorn, Fife, later moving to Colinton c1894 and subsequently to Witney, Oxfordshire c1909. Exhibited RA(3) 1891-1894, also six miniatures at the RSA & GI(2). Recorded by neither Foskett nor Long.

**DAVENPORT, Mrs Enid** **fl 1921**
Amateur painter of miniatures, exhibited 'The coming of Spring' at the GI from 37 Montgomery Terrace, Mount Florida, Glasgow.

**DAVID, Miss Agnes** **fl 1910-1914**
Aberdeen artist in oil; figurative subjects, portraits and portrait miniatures. Daughter of Henry F D(qv). Among works shown at the RSA were 'The Black Hat' (1913) and a portrait 'Letamai, the daughter of E O Arbuthnott'. Exhibited RA(6), RSA(5) & GI(4), all between the above years, also GI(4), latterly from 74 Osborne Place, & AAS(3).

**DAVID, Henry F** **fl 1908-1910**
Amateur Aberdeen painter of portraits and continental landscape. Father of Agnes D(qv). Exhibited AAS(5) from 35 Desswood Place.

**DAVID, Michelle** **1968-**
Painter of abstract landscapes in the modern idiom. Inspired by the raw forces of the natural environment. Trained Glasgow School of Art 1986-90 winning the John & Mabel Craig Bequest 1990. Artist-in-Residence, Shetland Isles 1992; visited Australia 1996-7. Exhibits RSA, winning the Andrew Salveson prize 1998.

**DAVIDSON, Agnes** **fl 1896**
Amateur Aberdeen painter; exhibited AAS(1) from 89 Fountainhall Road.

**DAVIDSON, Alexander** **fl 1834-1842**
Painter of rural scenes and narrative works, including incidents from the *Waverley Novels.* Exhibited RSA including a landscape in 1834 and scenes from the *Fortunes of Nigel* 1842.

**DAVIDSON, Alexander RSW** **1838-1887**
Stirling and Glasgow painter in oil and watercolour, also illustrator; landscape, mostly Scottish, interiors, portraits, figures and still life. Specialised in historical subjects and genre, similar to those of his friend Duncan McKellar(qv). Fascinated by scenes in the life of Bonnie Prince Charlie and in the texture and history of old buildings. The watercolours are often large and sometimes overworked. Elected RSW 1883. Illustrated an edition of the *Waverley Novels.* Exhibited four works at the RA 1873-1876 including 'Harvest time-Glenlochay, Perthshire' (1876) and 'Scarinish Harbour, Isle of Tiree' (1886). Also exhibited 139 works at the RSA between 1863 and 1885, RSW(26), RBA(2), L(3), AAS(2) & GI(56). Represented in Glasgow AG.
**Bibl:** Caw 272; Halsby 253.

**DAVIDSON, Alexander** **fl 1864**
Edinburgh sculptor. Exhibited designs for a monument in memory of the wife of William Hunter of Liverpool at the RSA.

**DAVIDSON, Alister James** **fl 1921-1926**
Aberdeen landscape painter in oil, especially fond of the west Highlands. Exhibited AAS(4) from Balnagask.

**DAVIDSON, Andrew** **fl 1877-d 1925**
Inverness sculptor; Davidson's many-sided productions in the domain of sculptor have been recognised for their artistic beauty and classic refinement. Responsible for the Flora Macdonald statue on Castle Hill, Inverness, for the bust of Rev Dr Macdonald of the High Church in Inverness Town Hall and the fine marble font in St Andrew's Cathedral, modelled after Thorwaldsen's famous font in Copenhagen Cathedral. Became senior partner in D & A Davidson. Exhibited three works at the RA, a marble medallion of Master James Augustus Grant (1878), a marble bust of a lady (1879) and a marble medallion portrait of a lady (1881). Also exhibited RSA from 1877, & AAS 1887.
**Bibl:** Gifford, H & I, 42,180,88-9,192,194,197,240-1,278,404,427, 460

**DAVIDSON, Andrew Williamson** **fl 1890-1908**
Edinburgh landscape painter in watercolour. Was in Berwick-on-Tweed c1903 and Devon 1908. Exhibited RSA(9), RSW(2), GI(4) & AAS(3).

**DAVIDSON, Arthur** **fl 1914**
Amateur Dunbartonshire sculptor. Exhibited GI(1) from Lilybank, Garelochhead.

**DAVIDSON, Bessie** **1880-1965**
Born Adelaide, Australia. Painter in oil and watercolour of interiors, landscape and flower pieces. Related to David Scott(qv), studied art in Munich and Paris where she maintained a studio. Spent extended periods in Scotland, working in Edinburgh and Perth. Represented in City of Edinburgh collection.

**DAVIDSON, Charles** **fl 1875-1897**
Landscape painter of uncertain origin who settled in Paisley in the early 1890s. Exhibited GI(8).

**DAVIDSON, Charles James** **fl 1876-1880**
Edinburgh artist of 24 Caledonian Crescent. Painter in oil and watercolour of buildings and topographical subjects. Exhibited RSA(8) 1876-1880.

**DAVIDSON, Charles Lamb** **1897-1948**
Born Brechin, Forfarshire. Painter in oil and watercolour, also stained glass designer, interior decorator and cartoonist. Studied at Glasgow School of Art where he was awarded the Haldane Travelling Scholarship in 1920. Married J Nina Miller(qv). Designed at least one light depicting the Beautitudes (1922) in Mayfield Church, Edinburgh. Exhibited 'Stretcher Bearers' at the RSA in 1920 while still a student, & GI(4) from 25 Northland Drive, Glasgow. Represented in Glasgow AG.
**Bibl:** Gifford 635.

**DAVIDSON, Daisy** **fl 1894-1896**
Amateur Aberdeenshire painter of flowers and fruit; exhibited AAS(2) from Woodbank, Cults.

**DAVIDSON, Daniel Pender** **1855-1933**
Born Camelon, Falkirk, 2 Oct. Painter in oil; portraits, figures, landscape, flowers and still life. Studied at Glasgow School of Art, also in Brussels, Munich, France and Italy. Moved to Milngavie 1916 before settling in London at the end of WWI. Principal works include 'Death of the Year', 'The Lotus-Land', 'The Sons of the Typhoon' and 'The Four Horsemen'. Exhibited RA(1), GI(1) & L(6), from Lochen, Bardowie, Nr Milngavie.

**DAVIDSON, Duncan** **fl 1893-d1907**
Born Aberdeenshire; died Gairnshiel, Aberdeenshire 13 Mar. Amateur painter in oil and watercolour of local landscape and occasional portraits. His principal occupation is unknown but was probably a gamekeeper on the Invercauld estate. Exhibited 15 works at the AAS between 1893 and the year of his death, including a portrait of the 'Hon Stuart R Erskine' (1900), from 'Rinloan', Glengairn, Ballater. An example of his work remains in Invercauld Castle.

**DAVIDSON, Edward M** **fl 1901-1904**
Amateur Dundee painter in oil and watercolour of figurative subjects; exhibited GI(3) from 30 Lilybank Road.

**DAVIDSON, Miss Effie** **fl 1886**
Amateur painter of Rose Cottage, Broughty Ferry, near Dundee. Exhibited a local landscape at the RSA in the above year.

**DAVIDSON, Elspeth M** **fl 1931-1937**
Aberdeen painter in oil of landscape and topographical subjects. Exhibited AAS during the above period from 22 Forest Avenue.

**DAVIDSON, George** **1872-1910**
Aberdeen painter in oil of landscape, especially the West Highlands,

and genre. Between 1905 and 1910 he travelled extensively throughout France, Holland, Belgium, Spain and North Africa, especially Morocco. Noted locally for his treatment of light and shade, frequently demonstrated in his portrayal of trees in a heavily wooded landscape. Trained for a time in Paris. Some of his early life has been likened to Gaugin's Brittany period, although his vibrant palette was adopted before he visited France. One of his most important works is Whitehills, Banff. At the time of his death he was regarded as the leading figure in the Northern Arts Club. Unfortunately his recognition has been limited by his tragically short life. His pencil studies in the classical tradition occasionally appear on the market. Exhibited 3 works at the RA including 'To Invergordon' (1904), RSA(4) 1904-1908, London Salon(5), GI(8) & AAS(44), latterly from 10 Thistle Street. Represented in Aberdeen AG.

**DAVIDSON, George** **fl 1921**
Dundee based landscape painter in oil. Exhibited AAS(1) from 2 Airlie Terrace.

**DAVIDSON, George Dutch** **1879-1901**
Born Goole, Yorkshire, 12 Aug; died Dundee. Painter in oil, watercolour, grisaille, pencil, crayon, and ink; figurative subjects, portraits, complex decorative and imaginative. Only child of Scottish parents, he returned with his family to Dundee when only a few months old. As a very young man a severe bout of influenza severely affected his heart causing him to abandon engineering studies and, contrary to the advice of his doctor, he enrolled in art classes at Dundee HS. There he met local artists including Frank Laing(qv), David Foggie(qv), John Duncan(qv), Alex Grieve(qv) and Stuart Carmichael(qv). By 1898 he had become a pupil of Duncan's and in 1899 went to London, Antwerp and France in four hectic, productive months accompanied by his mother and David Foggie. Returned to Scotland 1900 but tragically died five months later. According to Hardie, all his designs were produced in a period of less than three years between the spring of 1898 and January 1901, and so painstaking were his methods that the total of completed works during this period was only approximately 30. Of these, 18 works can still be accounted for. Close friend of David Foggie and John Duncan and greatly influenced by both. Davidson had no artistic progeny. The little group of which he was briefly the centre in Dundee had already lost Duncan to Chicago by 1901. "The art nouveau in Edwardian Dundee was restricted to architecture...but in Davidson's work Dundee may be said to have made an original contribution to the iconology of that quixotic movement with its combination of intensity and refinement and its syncretic use of several decorative influences, it is one of the rarest blooms in the hothouse" [Hardie]. A retrospective exhibition of his work was held in Glasgow 1973. Represented in Dundee AG.
**Bibl:** Caw 418; Dundee Graphic Art Association (David Foggie, John Duncan and others), George Dutch Davidson, A Memorial Volume, Dundee 1902; Halsby 197-9; Hardie 123-6; W R Hardie; Scottish Art Revue Vol XIII No 4 1972; Irwin 409-10; Macmillan [SA], 296.

**DAVIDSON, Gordon** **fl 1976**
Amateur Aberdeen painter. Exhibited AAS(1) from 104 Auchmill Road, Bucksburn.

**DAVIDSON, Hugh** **fl 1867**
Scottish landscape painter in oil. Lived for a time in Edinburgh. Exhibited RSA(1).

**DAVIDSON, Ian Winsted** **fl c1937-c1986**
Born Aberdeen. Portrait and occasional landscape painter. When he was five years old moved to 33 Gladstone Place, Aberdeen remaining there until his death 76 years later. Studied chemistry at Aberdeen University but two years later exposure to laboratory fumes caused a chronic lung condition which led him to follow an artistic career. Began by drawing shipping on the Thames. Returning to Aberdeen, studied part-time at Gray's School of Art and later at Bournemouth Art School. Visited New Zealand 1983 and the next year Brazil. Some of his townscapes illustrate parts of his native city which no longer exist. His wife **Flora** (d 1979) was also an artist. A number of his works are in Aberdeen University. A retrospective exhibition was held in Aberdeen 1986. Exhibited RSA 1937-43 & at the AAS.

**DAVIDSON, J** **fl 1976**
Exhibited 'The Warf' at the GI from 50 Drumry Lane Court, Calderwood, East Kilbride.

**DAVIDSON, Miss J T** **fl 1884-1887**
Amateur painter who lived in Paris for some years but moved to Glasgow c1886; exhibited GI(2) & L(1).

**DAVIDSON, Jack A** **fl 1981**
Aberdeen artist. Exhibited AAS(2) from 53D Nelson Street.

**DAVIDSON, James** **fl 1852-1886**
Edinburgh painter in oil and watercolour; mostly Scottish landscapes also genre, still life and portraits. Exhibited 33 works at the RSA between the above dates & GI(1), from 16 Valleyfield Street.

**DAVIDSON, James S** **fl 1884-1889**
Amateur landscape artist of Partick, Glasgow; exhibited GI(4).

**DAVIDSON, Jennie G** **fl 1897-1904**
Edinburgh painter in oil of figure subjects, genre and landscape including continental views. Exhibited RSA(7), GI(1) & AAS(3) from 128A George Street.

**DAVIDSON, John** **fl 1858-1895**
Edinburgh painter of portraits, landscape and figure compositions, often around the Pentlands, generally in oil but sometimes in watercolour. A prolific artist, he exhibited more than 50 works at the RSA between the above years, in the English Provinces, at the GI(7) & AAS(1), from 2 West Laurieston Place.

**DAVIDSON, Margaret (Majel) Elizabeth** **1885-1969**
Born Cults, Aberdeen. Painter of wild flowers & interiors and potter. Studied at Gray's School of Art 1904-1907 and on the proceeds of a scholarship visited Paris studying under Guerin 1908-09. In 1923 a visit to Toronto brought her into contact with members of the Group of Seven as a result of which her work became bolder and more impressionistic. After WW2 she became involved in pottery but in the 1950s joined a group of women friends near Stirling and resumed painting. Exhibited AAS(6) from Birchwood, Cults.
**Bibl:** Hardie 144-5.

**DAVIDSON, Martin McLean** **fl 1965-1989**
Aberdeen painter of still life and figure studies. Exhibited AAS from various addresses in the city and latterly from 33 Grange Road, Edinburgh.

**DAVIDSON, Mrs Marianne** **fl 1940-1943**
Edinburgh portrait sculptress of 34 Cambridge Gardens; exhibited RSA during the above years.

**DAVIDSON, Mary** **fl 1994-**
Born Dundee. Painter of varied interests and techniques; particularly attracted to still life, flowers, interiors and Scottish landscape. Studied Glasgow School of Art. Stimulated by chiaroscuro. Began full-time painting 1994. Exhibits RSA & RGI.

**DAVIDSON, Miss Mary C RSW** **1865-1951/2**
Born Aberdeenshire; died Edinburgh. Painter in watercolour and occasional oil, she specialised in landscapes in Scotland and France and in flower studies. One of ten children of a well known Deeside family. Spent her early years in Aboyne, and was a friend of Joseph Farquharson(qv). In 1908 she went to Edinburgh to look after her ageing parents and it was only after their death that she was able to devote herself to art. A competent artist, using light colours but sometimes rather weak in drawing. Also painted a group of Indian landscapes following a visit to that country in 1936, the year she was elected RSW. Exhibited 24 works at the RSA, 1906-1936, mostly pastoral and topographical subjects including a number of mosque scenes. Thus in 1913 there was 'The Spring Mosque at Kohat', in 1928, 'A Neglected Afridi Mosque, Kohat' and in 1928 'The Call to Prayer, Kohat Mosque'. Toward the end of her life failing eyesight led to her having to abandon painting. Exhibited RSW(44), RA(1), GI(12) & AAS 1906-1923. One of her works decorates the Victory Hall, Aboyne.
**Bibl:** Halsby 255.

**DAVIDSON, Miss Nellie** **fl 1896-1898**
Amateur Aberdeen painter of portraits and flowers. Exhibited AAS(3) from 21 Queen's Road.

**DAVIDSON, Mrs Nina Miller** **1895-1957**
Glasgow painter in watercolour, also stained glass window designer. Worked as a stained glass designer with Guthrie & Wells Ltd. Responsible for a window 'The Life of St Giles' in the S transept of St Peter's (RC) Church, Edinburgh, 'flashy and mannered' [Gifford]. Exhibited GI(11).
**Bibl:** Gifford 619.

**DAVIDSON, Noel** **fl 1981**
Aberdeen printmaker. Trained at Gray's School of Art. Exhibited AAS from 60 Aulton Court, Seaton.

**DAVIDSON, Peter Wylie** **fl 1906-1940**
Born Bridge of Allan, Stirlingshire. Sculptor in bronze and wood, goldsmith, leather worker and decorative artist. Studied at Glasgow School of Art, London and Paris. Settled in Glasgow where he taught at the School of Art c1910. Exhibited RSA 1915-1917, mostly ornamental jewellery, also GI(30), AAS(2) & L(5), from 3 Ruskin Square, Bishopbriggs.

**DAVIDSON, Robert G** **fl 1902-1923**
Edinburgh artist of 164 Montgomerie Street. Exhibited topographical scenes in and around the city of Edinburgh at the RSA in 1903 and 1908 and many landscapes at the AAS, latterly from Belskavie, Drumoak.

**DAVIDSON, Miss Sara M** **fl 1880**
Balerno artist of Dean Park; exhibited a sketch of the staircase at Skene House, Aberdeen at the RSA in the above year.

**DAVIDSON, Susan** **fl 1893-1937**
Aberdeen painter of local landscape. Exhibited regularly at the AAS during the above time from 58 Hamilton Place and Denville, Forest Road.

**DAVIDSON, T Furlong** **fl 1893**
Amateur painter of 76 Montgomerie Street, Kelvinside, Glasgow; exhibited 2 continental pastoral scenes at the GI.

**DAVIDSON, T W** **fl 1935**
Aberdeen artist. Exhibited 2 local landscapes at the AAS from 33 Gladstone Place.

**DAVIDSON, Taffy** **fl 1919-1937**
Aberdeen painter who lived at 8 Thistle Street; portraits, landscape and figurative subjects. Exhibited RSA(5) 1923-1935 and regularly at the AAS 1919-1937.

**DAVIDSON, Thomas** **fl 1880-1890**
Glasgow painter in oil and watercolour, of 5 Spring Gardens, Kelvinside; exhibited GI(4).

**DAVIDSON, Thomas L** **fl 1923**
Brechin artist who lived at Ellenlea; exhibited GI(1).

**DAVIDSON, Ursula** **fl 1961-1967**
Edinburgh portrait sculptress of 28 Moray Place, Edinburgh; exhibited during the above years including a portrait bust of Sir Compton McKenzie (1961), which attracted considerable attention.

**DAVIDSON, W Armstrong** **fl 1907-1912**
Glasgow artist. Collaborated with Kate W Thomson(qv) to produce 10 works, all exhibited at the Walker Gallery, Liverpool between the above years.

**DAVIDSON, W Meldrum** **fl.1951-54**
Painter of 47 Glenprosen Terrace, Dundee; exhibited 3 still lifes at the RSA, & GI(4).

**DAVIDSON, Walter D** **fl 1913-1919**
Amateur sculptor of portrait heads from Brechin; exhibited GI(4) from his studio in Southesk Street.

**DAVIDSON, William** **fl 1868-1932**
Edinburgh architect and decorative painter; writer on architecture, sculpture and decorative art, taught architecture at Edinburgh College of Art. Early exhibits were mostly landscapes and topographical scenes, later more designs for churches and war memorials including the War Memorial in Old Parish Church, Kirk Loan, Edinburgh (1919-23). Exhibited RSA(37), RA(3), RSW(7) & GI(6).
**Bibl:** Gifford 524.

**DAVIE, Alan CBE HRSW** **1920-**
Born Grangemouth, 28 Sep. Family were artistically inclined, his father being a painter and etcher. Studied at Edinburgh College of Art 1938-40 under John Maxwell(qv). In addition to an interest in painting, experimented in textile design, pottery and jewellery-making. Received Guthrie Award of the RSA 1942. While serving in the Royal Artillery 1940-1946, his chief interests were writing poetry and playing jazz. Although holding his first one-man exhibition in Edinburgh 1946 and taking up a travelling scholarship to visit Italy 1948 (where he held one-man exhibitions in Florence and Venice), France, Switzerland and Spain, in 1951 he abandoned painting in order to become a professional jazz musician. In 1947 married the artist/potter Janet Gaul. In Venice he met Peggy Guggenheim who introduced him to the early work of American Abstract Expressionism, including Pollock and Rogko. Resumed an active interest in painting and held the Gregory Fellowship in Painting at the University of Leeds 1956-1959. His early abstract painting shows the influence of Pollock, Gorky and Appel, also Picasso and Klee. 'What distinguished Davie was a highly developed personal philosophy which viewed art as a ritualistic process geared to the attainment of spiritual enlightenment. He expressed these ideas through an elaborate range of symbols appropriated from non-Western cultures; he had become interested in Zen Buddhism and Oriental mysticism from the middle of the 1950s. Since the 1960s he consolidated his international reputation'[Hartley]. 'His work is extremely personal in character, incorporating in an abstract framework images of a magical or ambiguous nature. Latterly he made more and more use of pictographs taken either from the Carib Indians or from modern European life...often set against an unmodulated monochromatic or two-colour background' [Osborne]. Won prize for the best foreign painter at the VII Bienal at Sao Paulo, Brazil 1963, and first prize at the International Print Exhibition at Cracow 1966. His latest works are less expressionistic in character and more formally coherent. He once wrote 'Art and religion could be conceived to be very much the same thing. What I have called the Evocation of the Inexpressible by images, symbols, sounds, movements, or rituals'. Held a major exhibition at the RSA in 1972 and a major retrospective exhibition in Glasgow 1992. Elected Senior Fellow, RCA 1991; awarded doctorates by Heriot Watt Univ. 1994 & Hertfordshire Univ. 1996, elected HRSW 1998. A retrospective exhibition was held in New York 1997 & SNGMA the same year. Now lives in England. Exhibited GI(6). Represented in Tate, V & A, SNGMA, Dundee AG, Glasgow AG, Lillie AG (Milngavie), Manchester AG, Abbot Hall AG (Kendal), Nat Gall of Canada (Ottawa), Nat Gall of South Australia (Adelaide), Stedlijk Museum (Amsterdam), Staatliche Kunsthalle (Baden-Baden), Bedford AG, Berne Kunsthalle, Bristol Museum, Albright Museum (Buffalo, USA), Institute of Art (Detroit), Tanner AG (Eastbourne), Eindhoven Museum, Hull AG, Leeds AG, Museum of Modern Art (New York), Israel Nat Gall (Tel Aviv), Gemeonte Museum (The Hague), Museum of the 20th Century (Vienna), Wakefield AG.
**Bibl:** Alan Bowness, Alan Davie, 1967; Alan Davie 'Interview with Keith Patrick' The Green Book, iii, 3, Bristol 1989; Gimpel Fils, London, 'Alan Davie, Major Works of the Fifties', (Ex Cat 1987, Harold Osborne(ed)); Peter Fuller, Modern Painters (ed by John McDonald), London, 1993, 192-8; Gage 39; Hardie 185-9; Hartley 128; Michael Horovitz, Alan Davie, 1963; Macmillan [SA], 369, 375-82 et passim in ch xx & xxi; Twentieth Century Art, 1988, 146-7.

**DAVIE, Helen Craig** **fl 1951-1970**
Glasgow painter of portraits, still life and Continental landscapes. Exhibited RSA(11) from 10 Kew Terrace.

**DAVIE, James William** **1889-fl 1942**
Grangemouth painter and etcher; portraits, mostly children, also still life and landscape. Studied at Glasgow School of Art and also in London and Paris. Working from Laraben, Grangemouth, he exhibited regularly at the RSA between 1925 and 1942, also GI(3), AAS & L(4).

**DAVIE, Joseph (Joe)** **1965-**
Born Glasgow. Painter of rural scenes; teacher. Trained Glasgow School of Art 1983-87. Founded the Lighthouse Studio, Glasgow 1987 which continued until 1995 when he joined the staff of Jordanhill 1994-2001 before becoming assistant principal art teacher, Fife 2001. Principal awards include a Carnegie Travel Scholarship 1987, Guthrie Prize (RSA) 1990, David Cargill Award (RGI) 1992, the Arthur Anderson Award (RGI) 1997 and the May Marshall Brown Prize (RSW) 1997. Solo exhibitions in London, Toronto & Scotland since 1991. Represented in Kelvingrove AG, Hunterian Museum (Glasgow), Dick Institute (Kilmarnock), Glasgow Museum of Modern Art, Smith Institute (Stirling).

**DAVIES, David** **fl 1988-**
An engraver from Wormit, Fife; exhibited RSA(2) 1988.

**DAVIES, Douglas RSW** **1946-**
Ceramic artist. Lives and works in Glasgow. Educated Edinburgh College of Art 1966-70; studied ceramics under Katie Horsman and glass design under Helen Monroe Turner. Visited Italy on a postgraduate scholarship 1970-1, returning to join the staff of Moray House College of Education. The following year appointed lecturer in ceramics at Glasgow School of Art. Designed fireplace mural for Hugh Duncan, Gyles House, Pittenweem (NTS), also worked for the President of Austria. Member of Academia Italia. In all his work the classical renaissance influence is strong. Elected RSW 2000. Represented in Royal Scottish Museum, Paisley AG.

**DAVIES, Hugh Llewelyn** **fl 1977-1978**
Aberdeen jewellery designer; exhibited AAS(3) from 21 Summerfield Terrace.

**DAVIS, Anna** **1989-**
Exhibited 'Twilight' at the RSA in 1989 from 103 Otago Street, Glasgow.

**DAVIS, Miss Doreen E** **fl 1974**
Paisley artist of mainly small wildlife studies. Exhibited GI(2) from 14 Oakshaw Street.

**DAVIS, James (Jim) S RSW** **1954-**
Glasgow figurative painter in oils. Trained Glasgow School of Art 1962-67. His studies often evoke his early memories as a child in Glasgow. Elected RSW 2003. Exhibits RSA, RSW & RGI. Represented in the collection of HRH The Duke of Edinburgh.

**DAVIS, Louis** **1861-1941**
English stained glass window designer; did most of his best work in Scotland in association with Sir Robert Lorimer(qv) whom he met at Oxford and stayed with at Kellie 1902. Executed a window in the parish church at Colmonell, Ayrshire (1899), and most of the windows (except the E. window) in the Thistle Chapel, Edinburgh; also at Paisley Abbey.
**Bibl:** Gifford 118; Peter Savage, Lorimer and the Edinburgh Craft Designers, Edinburgh 1980, 20,23,67,87,110,141,164.

**DAVISON, Jeremiah** **1695-1745**
Born London; died London, Dec. Portrait painter in oil. Of Scottish parentage, he was one of a number of artists in London (Allan Ramsay was another) who employed the services of the drapery painter, Joseph van Haecken(qv). He studied in Lely's studio and had access to the royal collection where he made copies. In 1730 he painted Frederick, Prince of Wales, and Anna Maria Poyntz in 1735. The following year, having met the Duke of Atholl at a masonic gathering, he was persuaded to go north and settled in Edinburgh. The Atholl family continued to patronise him and through them he received commissions from other aristocratic families in the north of Scotland. Generally regarded with Allan Ramsay as the first Scottish painter to invigorate the portrait tradition with a new human quality of robustness, refreshing and honest. An uneven artist, it has been said 'Davison at times almost attains the quality of early Ramsay in both feeling and colouring, but he was never so fine in modelling. Davidson is always harder and never approaches Ramsay's soft pastel transition of flesh tones...Ramsay's most immediate and important Scottish precursor' [Irwin]. The Morton Group is an interesting record of an artist working in two conflicting styles, one backward and the other forward looking - an indication of the changes that were taking place in portraiture in both Scotland and England during the 1740s. The year before his death, he returned to London. His work may be seen at Abercairny where he painted the very fine full length marriage portraits in 1737 of 'James Moray and his wife Christian'; also at Blair Castle where there are portraits of 'John Murray "3rd Lord Nairne"' (1738) and an undated portrait of 'Duncan Forbes of Culloden.' At Dalmahoy House, there is a portrait of 'James, 13th Earl of Morton and family' commissioned by the Earl of Morton in 1740, now in the SNPG, while the Tate Gallery has his study of 'The Graham children' (1742). Six works are in SNPG.
**Bibl:** Brockwell, 6; Caw 50; Holloway 106-7, 141-2; Irwin 47-49 et al (illus); Macmillan [SA], 99-100; McKay 10; Vertue; Waterhouse 103.

**DAVISON, T Raffles Hon ARIBA** **1853-1937**
Topographical draughtsman. A black and white view of Edinburgh is in the collection of the City of Edinburgh(1912).

**DAWSON, Archibald C ARSA** **1894-1938**
Born Hamilton, Lanark. Studied Glasgow School of Art. Glasgow sculptor and carver. Most of his exhibits were portrait busts but he also devoted much time to architectural work executing wood carvings and stone mouldings for the Memorial Chapel, Glasgow University, figures on the Scottish Legal Life Assurance building, Glasgow, and those on a new block of the Western Infirmary. During the war he served with the Glasgow Battalion of the Highland Light Infantry. After being demobilised received many commissions for plaques and other types of memorial. Head of Sculpture, Glasgow School of Art. Responsible for the giant figure of 'St Andrew' for the Scottish Pavilion at the Empire Exhibition of 1938. Elected ARSA 1936. Exhibited regularly RSA 1924-1938 & GI(23).

**DAWSON, Miss Ethel** **fl 1929**
Amateur portrait painter of 104 West George Street, Glasgow; exhibited GI(1).

**DAWSON, George A** **fl 1931-1935**
Glasgow watercolourist and artist in pen and ink; exhibited RSW(2) & GI(3) from 2 Leebank Drive.

**DAWSON, J Allan** **fl 1893-1936**
Edinburgh painter in oil; figurative, literary and angling subjects. Exhibited RA(1), RSA(26), GI(15), AAS(3), RHA(1) & L(1), from 6 St Vincent Street.

**DAWSON, Miss Mabel RSW SSA** **1887-1965**
Born Edinburgh, 13 Oct. Painter in watercolour and tempera; birds and animals, also landscape, children, flowers and interiors; also occasional embroiderer. Studied Edinburgh College of Art under Robert McGregor(qv), also in London under Frank Calderon and William Walls(qv). Lived in Edinburgh for many years. In addition to animal paintings, depicted east coast fishing villages, in a fluent, wet style not unlike Emily Paterson(qv). Also noted for her embroidery, exhibiting RSA 1934 with the Modern Embroidery Society of which she was a member. Kept a studio at 8 Palmerston Place after moving from 130 George Street in 1943. Elected SSA 1907, RSW 1917. Exhibited RA(1), RSA(78), RSW(95), GI(91), AAS(3) & L(10).
**Bibl:** Halsby 253.

**DAWSON, Marion** **fl 1908**
Aberdeen painter of portraits, especially children, and figure studies. Exhibited AAS(2) from 28 Gladstone Place.

**DAWSON, Rev Roy** **fl 1908**
Edinburgh artist of Ramsay Gardens; exhibited RSA(1).

**DAWSON, William** **fl 1929-1937**
Forgandenny painter. Exhibited AAS(6) from Airds Cottage.

**DAWSON, William** **fl 1931**
Amateur Aberdeen painter in oil of coastal and river scenes. Exhibited AAS(2) from 45 Hilton Street.

**DAY, Barclay** **fl 1877-1881**
Flower painter. Exhibited RSA(1) 1877 from a London address, and GI 1881.

**DAY, William Inglis** **fl 1937-1938**
Sculptor who lived in Bute Cottage, Bruce Street, Dumbarton. Exhibited two works in wood at the GI, also AAS(2).

**DEAN, Alexander Davidson** **fl 1861**
Glasgow engraver. Probably the same A D Dean who co-founded Gilmour and Dean. Exhibited 2 architectural studies at the GI from 105 Breadalbane Terrace.

**DEAN, Ann (Mrs A S Young)** **fl c1970-**
Aberdeen painter and school teacher. Trained Gray's School of Art, Aberdeen but it was only after the birth of her son and breakdown of her marriage that she turned seriously to painting. Specialises in landscape painted in bold, strong colours. Exhibits AAS since 1970, latterly from West Lediken, Insch.

**DEAN, Christopher** **fl 1895-1925**
Born Glasgow. Painter in oil and watercolour, also illustrator and book decorator. Worked in Glasgow until 1895, then moved to Marlow, Bucks and in 1925 transferred to Chelsea. Designed illustrations and book covers in a bold Celtic style, showing the clear influence of the Glasgow school with distinctive, interlaced borders to the page plates. Prepared designs for *Hans Sachs, His Life and Work,* c1910 and *The Odes of Anacreon* (c1910). Exhibited RSA(2) & GI(3).
**Bibl:** Houfe; Studio, vol 12, 1898, 183-187; illus Winter number 1900-1901, 64.

**DEAN, Fiona ARSA** **1962-**
Born Glasgow. Sculptress. Studied Glasgow School of Art 1979-83, obtaining also BA Hons in Fine Art (Sculpture). In 1983/4 awarded a diploma in postgraduate studies. Received Benno Schotz Award for drawing 1983 and again in 1984, and the John Keppie Travel Scholarship 1984 enabling her to visit Greece. Other awards have included the Ottile Wallace scholarship for sculpture, RSA 1985, the Ireland Alloys prize 1984, Guthrie Award 1987 and James Torrance Memorial Award of the RGI 1987. Recent commissions include maquette for a sculpture at Newcraighall, Edinburgh and for the Rubislaw Terrace fountain in Aberdeen. Invited to exhibit at the first International Exhibition of Sculpture at Odense, Denmark 1988. Elected ARSA 1988. Exhibits regularly at the RSA & GI(4), from Cuttieburn House, Craig, By Huntly, Aberdeenshire. Represented in Oronsko Museum (Poland), Odense Magistrat offices (Fyn, Denmark), RSA.

**DEAN, Stansmore Richmond Leslie (Mrs Macaulay Stevenson)** **1866-1944**
Born Glasgow, 3 Jne. Painter of portraits and figure studies. Daughter of Alexander Davidson D(qv), a master engraver of Aberdeen and co-founder of the firm Gilmour and Dean. Youngest of six children. Studied Glasgow School of Art 1883-1889 where she was a contemporary of Charles Rennie Mackintosh(qv), David Gauld(qv), Bessie MacNicol(qv) and Margaret Rowat(qv), the latter becoming a close friend. In 1890 beame the first woman to win a Haldane Travelling Scholarship. This enabled her to spend some time in Paris studying under August Courtois at Colarossi's. Shortly after her return to Glasgow she opened a studio at 180 West Regent Street. Most summers were spent in the South of France, Brittany and Holland. In 1902 she became the second wife of Robert Macaulay Stevenson(qv). Her early work may have been influenced by James McNeill Whistler who was President of the International Society at the time Dean's work was exhibited there. In 1905/6, as well as continuing to exhibit at the Paris Salon, she executed a portrait of Neil Munro (now in the SNPG), the first painting the gallery purchased from a living artist. Ailsa Tanner records that as a member of the Society of Lady Artists she was elected convener of their decoration Committee in 1908 formed to supervise alterations to their property at 5 Blythswood Square. She was convinced that the work should be given to Charles Rennie Mackintosh but the President and Council disagreed so Dean resigned. Although subsequently asked to return she and her husband had by this time gone to live in France where they remained until 1926. In 1927 they returned to their home in Robinsfield and she resumed painting. Beset again by financial difficulties they moved in 1932 to Kirkcudbright staying in a succession of hotels. A neglected artist, the delicacy and quality of whose work will undoubtedly find her reinstated. First exhibited at the GI in 1894, she continued to exhibit there until 1900 and again 1928-1932. Also exhibited RSA(1), Walker Gallery, Liverpool & twice at the International Society in London. Represented in SNPG.
**Bibl:** Burkhauser 191,207-9.

**DEANE, -** **fl 1799**
Scottish engraver probably of Glasgow. Bushnell records that a 'Deane Sculpt' is appended to the vignette of the engraved title-page to *The Polyhymnia,* printed and sold by John Murdoch of Glasgow. In one of the issues of this scarce collection Burns's 'Bonny Lass of Ballochmyle' first appeared in 1799.
**Bibl:** Bushnell.

**DEANS, Colin N** **fl 1965-1966**
Aberdeen sculptor; exhibited AAS(4) from 1 Golf Road, Bieldside.

**DEANS, Hugh A** **fl 1967**
Amateur Inverness painter; exhibited a local townscape at the AAS from Helen's Lodge, Inshes.

**DEAS, William M** **1876-c1945**
Born Perth, 10 Aug. Painter in watercolour and tempera; landscapes and interiors. Lived in Forgandenny. Pupil of William Proudfoot(qv) in Perth, he was an amateur painter until 1923 when he devoted himself full-time to art, holding one-man exhibitions in London and Perth. Painted mainly Perthshire landscapes in a fresh style. Principal works include 'Cottage Interior', 'Glen Ure' and 'The Smithy'. Exhibited RSA(5), RSW(20), RI(2), GI(5), AAS(4), RBA(2) & L(1) from Airds, Forgandenny. Represented in Perth AG.
**Bibl:** Halsby 255.

**DE BELLE, Charles** **fl 1900-1911**
Although possibly an Irish artist, he lived for many years in Scotland and exhibited at the RSA. In 1900 he was living in Dublin and was known to have been in Glasgow 1907 and Kilbride 1909, before moving to London c1911. Exhibited RSA(3), RA(1) & RHA(1).

**DE BREANSKI, Alfred Snr** **fl 1869-c1925**
Painter in oil and occasionally watercolour; landscape and river scenes. Son of a Polish landowner who migrated to Britain c1848, becoming tutor to the son of the Duke of Cambridge. Trained at St Martin's School under Cecil Rea and later in Paris under Whistler. He most enjoyed painting mountainous scenes with rivers running through rocky gorges and is best known for his Highland and Welsh landscapes often at sunset in which distant cattle, sheep and anglers are sometimes seen. Although never exhibiting at the RSA, his Scottish landscapes are among the most popular of his works even though the topographical detail is often repetitious. Also worked in the Lake District and Thames valley. Brother of the coastal and marine artist Gustave (1860-1899), father of Alfred Jnr(qv) and Arthur (b1879), the last emigrating to Canada at an early age. Exhibited RA(24), RBA(80), ROI(12), RHA(2), RI(3), L(11), GI(6) & RCA(8), latterly from Glendale, Church Road, London SE. Represented in Paisley AG.

**DE BREANSKI, Alfred (Fontville) Jnr** **1877-1957**
Born London, Aug 28; died Tonbridge Wells, Apr 17. Landscape painter, primarily in oils. Son of Alfred Snr(qv). Painted in a similar though slightly sweeter style than his father, mainly Highland scenes, often from a base in the Trossachs. Depicted scenery more accurately than his father, as evidenced by the many cards he illustrated. Following a lawsuit, in order to distinguish his work from that of his father he took on the name 'Fontville'. Exhibited RA, Suffolk Street. [From notes provided by John Motley].

**DE COLONE, Adam** **[see COLONE]**

**DEES, Stephanie RSW** **1974-**
Born Hoxham. Edinburgh-based painter mainly in mixed media and watercolours. Particularly drawn to the coastal regions and harbours of south-east Scotland and Cornwall. Visits to Prague, Italy and France have extended her architectural and atmospheric treatment of her preferred subjects. Elected RSW 2003.

**DEEVAR, Isa M** **fl 1888**
Dingwall artist; exhibited RSA(1).

**DEFOSSE, Patrick** **fl 1981-1982**
Aberdeenshire painter. Exhibited 3 rural interiors at the AAS latterly from Little Haddo Farmhouse, Newburgh.

**DEKKERT, Eugene** **fl 1899-1940**
Painter in oil and watercolour of landscape and coastal scenes. Probably of Dutch origin, he lived in Glasgow 1899-1903, before moving to St Monance. Specialised in coastal scenes, generally of the north-east, using thin, often dull coloured washes in a slightly coarse manner. Clearly influenced by the Hague school. Exhibited RSA(12), RSW(3), GI(26), L(8) & AAS(4).
**Bibl:** Halsby 255.

**DELACOUR, William** **fl 1740-d1768**
Born France; died Edinburgh. Portrait and landscape painter in oil and pastel; also scene painter. Worked in London as a portrait painter and theatre designer. In the 1740s he published eight *Books of Ornament* and by 1753 had moved to Dublin where he advertised that he had changed his address from Ormonde Quay to College Green. His stay in Ireland was not a great success and by 1757 he had settled in Edinburgh where he remained for the rest of his life. In addition to continuing to work as a scene painter, he also painted portraits and landscapes in both oil and watercolour. He decorated Lord Milton's House in the Canongate (4 landscapes survive in the stairwell of Milton House School) and, having reached Edinburgh at the time of James Norie's death, Delacour obtained commissions in his place to embellish several of the more important houses built by John and Robert Adam. An enthusiastic teacher and capable administrator, in 1760 he was appointed the first Master of the Trustees' Academy, a post he retained until 1767 but which interfered with his drama work, for in 1763 he had been abandoned by managements in both Edinburgh and Glasgow. In 1764 some of his foliage drawings were used in Aberdeen by the Academy being established there by Lord Deckford with William Mosman(qv) as director. His work is sometimes confused with that of the Nories, but there were generally more foliage in Delacour's compositions. His landscapes painted on plaster often had painted frames to imitate a spirally carved wooden picture frame, and bring to mind the work of Claude. Accused of charging high prices he defended himself publicly in the *Edinburgh Evening Courant* (March, 1763) in which he said he was paid benefits, 'any surplus being retained by the Managers'. Executed some fine landscapes, the compositions being of classical ruins and statues, with figures walking and sitting among them as can still be seen in the Saloon of Yester House. They are stylistically close relatives to Pannini but the lightness of touch and prettiness is quintessentially French. The Irwins regard the room as 'charmingly elegant, Rococo interior, one of the best of its kind in Scotland'. A panel with an imaginary landscape in Drylaw House, Edinburgh has been attributed to Delacour. A good 'Self-portrait' is among 3 works in the SNPG and a portrait of 'John Brown' is in the NGS; other works are in Edinburgh City collection, University of Edinburgh and Yester House, East Lothian.
**Bibl:** Brydall 109,144; Caw 35; J Fleming, 'Enigma of a rococo artist',Country Life, 24 May 1962, 1224-6; Halsby 24-5; Fraser Harris, 'William De la Cour, Painter, Engraver and Teacher of Drawing', Scottish Bookman Vol I, No 5, 1936; James Holloway 118-121; Gifford 626; Irwin 91-3,121,128 (illus); Macmillan [SA], 118,125,226; J Simpson 'Lord Alemoor's Villa at Hawk Hill', Bulletin of the Scottish Georgian Society, 1972, Vol I, 2-9; Strickland.

**DE LAUTOUR, Amelia Cate** **fl 1925-1931**
Born in Scotland. Sculptress. Studied Bournemouth School of Art and Central School Arts and Crafts in London. All her work was centred on the London region, mostly bronzes and paintings of animals. Exhibited RA(3), RMS(1) & L(6).

**DELAVAULT, Pierre** **fl 1887-1903**
French artist who spent some time in Aberdeen. Earlier he had been an art master at Inverness Academy. There he produced 20 original watercolours of old Inverness subsequently published as *Pictures of old Inverness* (1903). Most of the subjects have long since disappeared and the portfolio, dedicated to the Provost and Magistrates of the town, has long been out of print. The illustrations are those of an accomplished if unexciting watercolourist. Exhibited a Normandy scene at the GI giving his address as 259 Union Street; also exhibited several landscapes of the Inverness area at the AAS 1887-1890.

**DELVILLE, Jean** **1867-1953**
Belgian symbolist painter in oil and teacher. Founder of the Salon pour l'Art, furthered the ideas of Peladan through the Salon de la Rose Croix in Paris. Continued to apply Peladan's precepts in Belgium even after the latter's withdrawal from public life. Interested in the occult and mysticism; important member of the Symbolist movement. Appointed by Fra Newbery(qv) in 1900s to Glasgow School of Art to teach drawing and painting as part of the latter's programme which brought fame to the School. Although he spoke no English his influence was considerable and can be seen most markedly in the work of Nora Gray(qv), Frances MacDonald(qv) and Herbert MacNair(qv). Author of *New Mission for Art* (c1913). Returned to Brussels 1905 to teach at the Academie des Beaux-Arts before retiring 1937. Two important works from 1929: *'Les Fruits nos Entrailles'* and *'L'Ecole du Silence'* were sold in London 1995. During his stay in Glasgow exhibited RSA & GI(1).

**DEMARCO, Richard OBE RSW HRSA** **1930-**
Born Edinburgh. Painter and entrepreneur from an Italian immigrant family. Trained Edinburgh College of Art 1949-53 and after National Service, during which he served as art master at Duns Scotus Academy, Edinburgh, in 1963 became founder member of the Traverse Theatre, Vice-Chairman of the Traverse Committee of Management and Director of the Traverse AG. His own early work was mainly as a murallist in which he studied under Leonard Rosoman. In 1966 founded the Richard Demarco Gallery which flourished for twenty years at various venues in Edinburgh. Director of 'Edinburgh Arts' 1972-74, an international summer school that functioned during the Edinburgh Festival. Received Gold Award of the Polish People's Republic 1976 in recognition of services for developing cultural relations between Britain and Poland. Elected RSW 1969, SSA 1969. Awarded OBE 1984, Cavaliere della Republica d'Italia 1987, elected HRSA 2003. During the late 1960s exhibited his own work at the RSA. Represented in V & A, SNGMA, Cracow University, Philadelphia Museum of Art, SAC.

**DEMPSTER, Elizabeth Strachan ARSA** **1909-1987**
Born Greenock. Sculptress. Orphaned at an early age, came to Edinburgh in 1930 to be near her cousin the Very Rev Dr Charles Warr. Studied at Edinburgh College of Art under Alexander Carrick(qv) and Norman Forrest(qv). One of a distinguished group of students including Hew Lorimer(qv), Scott Sutherland(qv) and Tom Whalen(qv). Continued her studies in London and Munich. Throughout life remained a carver especially in wood and stone. Commissioned by the Clyde Navigation Trust 1938 to execute a large silver seahorse for the Empire Exhibition in Glasgow; later undertook three large oak figures for the High Kirk of St Giles. After WW2 carved four symbols representing the four elements for the quarters of an austere cross in St Giles War memorial chapel. Worked with Pilkington Jackson(qv) for the Royal Scots memorial in Princes Street Gardens and assisted Hew Lorimer in carving seven of the exterior carvings for the National Library of Scotland, including the Archangels Gabriel and Michael, behind the altar in St Giles. Elected ARSA 1960.

**DEMPSTER, Ivor J R** **fl 1961-1964**
Amateur Hamilton painter in oil and watercolour of landscape and domestic genre; exhibited GI(3) from 7 Lilybank Street.

**DEMPSTER, M J** **fl 1884-1910**
Stirling painter of landscape, figure subjects and flowers; exhibited RSA(2), GI(6), AAS(1) & L(2) from 6 Albert Place.

**DEMPSTER, Margaret (Mrs Robert Buchan Nisbet)** **fl 1885-1932**
Painter in oil of portraits, portrait miniatures and flowers. Studied at the Royal Institution, Edinburgh and in Paris. Married R B Nisbet(qv). Came from Edinburgh and 1898 moved to Comrie, Perthshire and c1904 to Crieff. Exhibited a portrait of a lady at the RA in 1891, also RSA(37), GI(15), RI(7), L(5), RVA(1), London Salon(4) & AAS, from 4 Glenfinlas Street, Edinburgh

**DEMPSTER, Robert** **fl 1942-1966**
Amateur watercolourist; also singer. President, Hamilton Art Club 1965. Exhibited a landscape at the GI from 7 Portland Park, Hamilton.

**DENERLEY, Helen Susan** **1956-**
Born Roslin, Midlothian. Sculptress. Trained Gray's School of Art 1969-73. Specialises in large metal sculptures, often of wildlife. Since receiving her first commission in 1977 from Aberdeen District Council, she has had important commissions almost every year including one for a lifesize whale to be made from local scrap metal on South Georgia 2004. Her work is renowned for its striking animation and strong feeling of movement. Many solo exhibitions in Scotland, England, Ireland & Belgium. Exhibits regularly at the SSA of which she was elected a professional member 1995, and at the RGI.

**DENHOLM, James** **1772-1818**
Born Scotland; died Glasgow, 20 Apr. Miniature painter in oil, he taught at the Glasgow Drawing and Painting Academy, Argyle Street and was a member of the Glasgow Philosophical Society from 1803 and President 1811-1814. Author of topographical works on Glasgow. Prepared a set of drawings of Edinburgh for the *Edinburgh Magazine* 1785-1800. Practised as a miniaturist and landscape painter at M'Ausland's Land, Trongate, Glasgow 1801.
**Bibl:** Butchart 40; DNB; Long 121.

**DENHOLM, James** **fl 1885-1894**
Dunbar painter in oil and watercolour of landscapes; exhibited RSA(3) & L(1).

**DENHOLM, Robert** **fl 1897-1927**
Edinburgh painter in oil, also etcher. Exhibited a painting of Arran at the RA 1897 and two Hebridean scenes at the RSA in 1899, also 1900-1904 - silver-point drawings of landscapes and birds.

**DENNIS (or DENYS), Robert** **fl 1542**
Early painter. In December, 1542 preparations for the funeral of James V included £4 to 'Robert Denys, painter, for colloring of the Dolorus Chapell witht the clubbis, speris, chandelaris and uther wark in the kirk'.
**Bibl:** Apted 38.

**DENNISS, Ann** **fl 1976-1984**
Edinburgh painter who studied at Edinburgh University. Exhibited RSA during the above dates from 27 Castle Terrace.

**DENNISTOUN, F E** **fl 1876-1880**
Helensburgh painter in oil and watercolour of rustic scenes. Although a member of the Dennistoun family of artists the exact relationship is unclear. Exhibited six works at the RSA 1876-1877 & GI(5) from Rowmore Cottage, Rhu, Dunbartonshire.

**DENNISTOUN, Mrs R** **fl 1880**
Helensburgh painter, wife of William Dennistoun(qv). Exhibited GI(1).

**DENNISTOUN, William I** **1838-1884**
Old Kilpatrick painter in oil and watercolour of landscapes, buildings and interiors. Trained as an architect, painted topographical subjects in watercolour. First President, Glasgow Art Club 1867-8. Later moved to the Isle of Capri in Italy. Died in Venice. Early works were in and around Glasgow and Helensburgh whilst his later watercolours are of Italian buildings and landscape. The style is not immediately attractive, although competent and accurate. Exhibited RSA(8), RI(1) & GI(9). Represented in Glasgow AG.
**Bibl:** Halsby 255.

**DENNY, Stephen** **fl 1814**
Little known Scottish miniaturist, Foskett records and illustrates a miniature, now in an American collection, of an unknown Scotsman in uniform, wearing a scarlet coat, sash, green bonnet and white epaulettes and signed on the reverse 'Stephen Denny - Pinxit-1814-No 11 Alfred Street - Newington'. The colouring is good and the work is competent, if a touch coarse.
**Bibl:** Foskett.

**DENT, Rupert Arthur** **fl 1891-1892**
Painter in oil and watercolour of animals and rustic scenes. Exhibited RSA(5) during the above years, also GI(3), from 1 Balcarres Street, Edinburgh.

**DENUNE, William L** **c1712-1750**
Born Edinburgh, died Dumfries, Jne. Son of a Canongate surgeon. Youngest of those who signed the Charter of the Academy of St Luke in 1729. His first recorded work was a portrait of the Rev Archibald Gibson dated 1735. During his short life Denune established a thriving practice in Edinburgh and especially Dumfries-shire, with studio sales held in both areas after his premature death. The Duke of Hamilton was a patron. Although an artist of limited resource, his influence in provincial Scotland was considerable. His reputation has suffered by the brevity of his life. Represented in SNPG(2), NGS(2), and by an attributed portrait in the collection of Edinburgh City.
**Bibl:** Holloway 112-114,142; Macmillan [SA], 92,99.

**DE RUSETT, Mrs Wendy** **fl 1986**
Amateur Glasgow artist. Exhibited GI(2) from 11 Jedburgh Gardens.

**DES CLAYES, Miss Alice AR(Can)A** **1891-?**
Born Aberdeen 22 Dec. Painter of animals, pastoral and sporting subjects. Studied at Bushey under Rowland Wheelwright, and in France under Dudley Hardy. Lived near London at Chorleywood, Hertfordshire and later at Newton Abbot before migrating to Canada where she was subsequently elected an associate of the Royal Canadian Academy. Highly competent artist among whose principal works are 'Toilers of the Shore after a Hard Day' and 'Bonsecours Market'. Her work is attractive with a lovely sense of colour and vitality. Sister of Berthe(qv) and Gertrude(qv). Exhibited RA(5), GI(2) & L(1).

**DES CLAYES, Miss Berthe** **fl 1905-1927**
Born Aberdeen. Landscape and figure painter. Worked in the style of her sisters Alice(qv) and Gertrude(qv). Exhibited RA(3), RI(2), ROI(1) & L(5).

**DES CLAYES, Miss Gertrude** **fl 1905-1960**
Born Aberdeen. Portrait and landscape painter who at an early age went to live in London. Member of a most talented family of sisters(qv). Studied at RA School, Paris Salon and subsequently in Canada. Painted The Duke and Duchess of Connaught and other leading figures of her time. Exhibited RA(7), ROI(2), L(8) & GI(1).

**DES GRANGES, David** **1611-1671/2**
Born Guernsey; died England. Miniature painter, portraitist and engraver. Baptised in London, his first known work is an engraving of Raphael's 'St George and the Dragon'. Painted many portrait miniatures of the English aristocracy and in 1640 completed one of his best works, a miniature copy of Titian's 'Marquis del Guasto with his Mistress', the original of which is in the Louvre. His position in Scottish art was due to his employment by Charles I and Charles II, the latter bringing him to Scotland in 1650 and 1651 and appointing him His Majesty's Limner in Scotland. As a result, Des Granges undertook other commissions in Scotland including the portraits of the 'Duke of Buccleuch' and the 'Earl of Haddington'. His miniature portrait of Charles II, watercolour on vellum, based on Hannerman's portrait painted two years earlier, is a work of high quality, used by the King to present to ambassadors and others. In 1671, Des Granges having become impoverished, petitioned the King for £76 due for several pieces of work done in Scotland "delivered to sundry persons of quality by order of the King, for which the artist had received nothing except 40s sent to him when he lay ill at St Johnston's (Perth) and £4 thereafter'. He therefore prayed for payment of the residue 'to relieve the pressing necessities of himself and miserable children; his sight and labour failing him in his old age; whereby he is enforced to rely on the charity of well-disposed persons". The petition was accompanied by a schedule of 13 pictures delivered in 1651 during the King's residence in Perth. On November 11, 1671 the King referred the petition to the English Treasury in respect of the "poor and necessitous condition" for which the painter and his family were reduced, but there is no record of any payment having been received. He was an uneven artist, at his best extremely good, and very prolific. Represented in the Rijksmuseum, NPG, V & A, Windsor Castle.
**Bibl:** Apted 43; Calendar of Treasury Papers 1557-1696, London 1868, 7 (transcript in EUL, La.IV.26); Foskett,i,242-3; Holloway 143; Long, British Miniaturists (1520-1860), London 1929; J Murdoch et al The English Miniature, New Haven, Conn 1982; Waterhouse, 40.

**DESSURNE, Mark B A** **fl 1851-1865**
Glasgow painter in oil and watercolour of landscape and figurative subjects. Moved to London early in his career. Exhibited two works at the RA, 'The Maid of Judah' in 1851 from 102 North Frederick Street, Glasgow and a scene from Paradise Lost in 1863 from a London address. Also exhibited RSA 1847, 1850, 1858 and 1859; & GI(10).

**DESTON, Adam** **fl 1871**
Fife painter. Exhibited a topographical oil at the RSA from Leven.

**DEUCHAR, Miss Christina R** **fl 1872-1887**
Edinburgh artist who lived at 22 Morningside Place and exhibited flowers, still life and dead birds in both oil and watercolour at the RSA between the above dates.

**DEUCHAR, David** **1745-1808**
Born nr Montrose, Angus. Seal-engraver and etcher of Edinburgh. Friend of James Gilliland, silversmith, tutor of Raeburn. Finding Raeburn one day gazing intently into a small mirror, Deuchar said 'Hello, Henry, are you admiring your good looks?' 'No' said the boy, 'but I am trying to draw a likeness of myself.' As a result of this incident Deuchar introduced Raeburn to David Martin(qv). Deuchar is now best known for his publication *A Collection of Etchings after the Most Eminent Masters of the Dutch and Flemish Schools - Particularly Rembrandt, Ostade, Cornelius Bega and Van Vliet...*(1803). This collection includes both open air scenes of village festivals in the style of the Dutch masters and tavern interiors as well as a few compositions by Deuchar himself, including one of a Scottish Penny Wedding. Although somewhat derivative and comparatively crude, it is nevertheless a most interesting collection, a landmark in the development of etching in Scotland. Deuchar also produced a series of etchings after Holbein's *Dance of Death* (1788), published in Edinburgh 1803. There is strong evidence to suppose that Deuchar had an influence on Raeburn's early work; for example, the pose of the portrait of James Hutton has been likened to that of the female figure in an etching that Deuchar made after Ostade which was also the basis of Wilkie's portrait of his parents 30 years later. Raeburn's admiration for Deuchar was shared by Wilkie. A portrait of Deuchar by Raeburn is in the NGS and two pencil portraits of him are in the SNPG. Represented by 55 prints in Glasgow AG.
**Bibl:** Caw 70; Irwin 169,175; Macmillan [GA], 74-6 et passim; Macmillan [SA], 150-2,165-66,185,300; Walter Shaw Sparrow, A Book of British Etching, London 1926, 122-3.

**DEUCHAR, Miss Elizabeth R** **fl 1849-1867**
Edinburgh portrait painter and miniaturist; exhibited RSA(28) during the above period.

**DEUCHAR, Lossie E** **fl 1887**
Amateur Aberdeen artist; exhibited AAS(1) from 34 Bank Street.

**DEUCHARS, Louis Reid** **1870-1927**
Born Comrie, Apr 4; died Edinburgh, Sep 9. Sculptor and painter in oils. Landscape painter, generally in oil, and sculptor. Divided his time between the south of England and the north of Scotland. Studied Glasgow School of Art 1887-?, and in London under G F Watts. Modelled the cherubs' heads and all the figures and animals which were subsequently carved in oak and stone for the Thistle Chapel in Edinburgh. Later undertook similar work with Lorimer(qv) at Dunblane Cathedral, for whom he designed model cartouches for several chimneypieces. Designed six fauns for Robert McEwan's music room at Marchmont, Berwickshire. Living in Surrey 1898 and 1899, Inverness 1901, back in London 1903-1908 and then Edinburgh/Leith 1908 remaining there for the rest of his life. His paintings are fine but sometimes a little overworked. A stone 'Madonna and Child' is in the E nave wall of Old St Paul Church, Jeffrey St, Edinburgh. Exhibited six works at the RA including one of 'Loch Ness in Winter' (1901) from an address in Dores, Inverness, also RSA(20), RSW(1), L(5) & GI(5). Represented in NPG, Walker AG, Harris AG, Preston AG. [From notes provided by Dr Louise Boreham].
**Bibl:** Gifford 167,295; Peter Savage, Lorimer and the Edinburgh Craft Designers, Edinburgh 1980, 54,118,164; Louise M Boreham, Louis Reid Deuchars (1870-1827) and the Relationship between Sculptors and Architects, PhD thesis, Edinburgh College of Art, 1998.

**DEVERIA, Eugene** **fl 1850-1856**
Portrait painter who although he seemed to divide his time between Edinburgh (he had a studio at 22 Home Street) and Pau, France, exhibited 35 works at the RSA 1850-56, almost all of them portraits from Edinburgh. In 1851 the portrait of 'James Buchanan' was exhibited at the RA and in 1856 'The Birth of Edward VI and the Death of his Mother, Jane Seymour'.

**DEVINE, Miss Eliza** **fl 1870-1874**
Edinburgh painter in oil, member of a gifted family. Painted landscapes and figurative subjects. Exhibited RSA(7).

**DEVINE, Miss Katherine (Katie)** **fl 1873-1894**
Edinburgh painter in oil of landscape and portrait miniatures. One of three artistically talented sisters. Exhibited RA(3) & RSA.

**DEVINE, Miss Mary** **fl 1870-1874**
Edinburgh painter of subject paintings and topographical scenes. Probably sister of Katherine D(qv). Exhibited RSA during the above years.

**DEVINE, Peter** **fl 1851-1862**
Edinburgh portrait miniaturist; exhibited 43 portraits at the RSA during the above period. Recorded by neither Foskett nor Long.

**DEVLIN, George RSW** **1937-**
Born Glasgow, 8 Sep. Painter in oil and watercolour; art teacher. Brother of **Duncan DEVLIN**, also an artist. Educated Albert Secondary School, Glasgow, studied art at Glasgow School of Art 1955-60 under David Donaldson(qv). Scholarship studies in Greece and Italy (1960) and North and West Africa (1961). Arts Council extra-mural lecturer, Glasgow University. Received RSA Chalmers Bursary 1959 and a Haldane Scholarship 1960, also Carnegie travelling scholarship and Maclaine-Watters medal 1961. Travelled in the Sahara and in West Africa. Founded his own summer school 1969. Holds one-man shows regularly in Edinburgh and at Glasgow Art Club since 1970. Lecturer in design department, Glasgow College of Building and Printing. Elected RSW 1964. In 1972 presented series on art for STV and in 1977 elected chairman of Glasgow League of Artists. In 1981 commissioned to paint Sir Alexander Cairncross and 1982 winner of 'Images of Today' competition. Artist-in-residence, Dinan, France 1991. President, Glasgow Art Club 1997. Holds regular solo exhibitions in London & Edinburgh since 1991. Exhibits RSA, RSW & GI(68) from 6 Falcon Terrace Lane. Represented in SNGMA, Lillie AG (Milngavie), Aberdeen AG, Edinburgh City collection, Royal collection.

**DEVLIN, May (Mrs Alex F Dale)** **fl 1922-1936**
Born Dumbarton. Painter in watercolour of landscapes and coastal subjects. Studied at Glasgow School of Art. Art Mistress, Bearsden Academy for many years. Moved to London for a time in the 1930s before returning again to Glasgow. Principal works include 'Evening Solitude', 'The Old Coal Cart', 'Moorland' and 'A Painted Ship on a Painted Ocean.' Exhibited RSA(5), RSW(7) & GI(7), from 125 Cheyne Walk, Glasgow and after her marriage from Cuileann, Houston Road, Bridge of Weir.

**DEWAR, Alexander C** **fl 1884**
Edinburgh artist. Exhibited a drawing of an interior at the RSA from 34 Marchmont Crescent, Edinburgh.

**DEWAR, Andrew S** **fl 1973-**
Aberdeen sculptor. Vice-President, Aberdeen Artists' Society 1985-7, President 1982-4, 1988-9. Exhibited RSA 1978 and 1979 and regularly at the AAS, latterly from Gladhaven, Elrick, Skene.

**DEWAR, Deborah** **fl 1969-1976**
Edinburgh painter. Exhibited RSA during the above years from 2 NE Circus Place, Edinburgh.

**DEWAR, Isabel M** **fl 1887-1891**
Dingwall portrait and landscape painter. Exhibited RSA(4) between the above years from West Lodge, Dingwall.

**DEWAR, J Stewart** **fl 1849-1885**
Edinburgh painter in oil of landscape, portraits and figurative

subjects. Exhibited RSA(8) irregularly during the above years. Not to be confused with John S Dewar(qv).

**DEWAR, John S** **fl 1873-1889**
Glasgow painter of 227 West George Street. Exhibited Scottish landscapes and portraits at the RSA during the above years, also GI(16). Not to be confused with John Stewart Dewar(qv).

**DEWAR, Miss Margaret de Courcy Lewthwaite ('Kooroovi')** **1878-1959**
Born Kandy, Sri Lanka. Designer, enamellist, watercolourist, draughtswoman, teacher and author. Studied Glasgow School of Art 1891-1908 and Central School of Arts and Crafts, London. First came to notice in *The Studio* for a candle sconce and white metal casket shown at the School of Art Exhibitions of 1899 and 1900. Shortly after graduating acquired her own studio on the 6th floor of 93 Hope Street, Glasgow, remaining there until 1926 when she moved to 15 Woodside Terrace. Appointed lecturer in enamelling by Fra Newbery. Became associated in the School with Anne Macbeth(qv), Jessie King(qv), Dorothy Carleton Smyth(qv), John Delville(qv) and the sculptor Kellick Brown(qv). She herself had been influenced by the designer Peter Wylie Davidson(qv) with whom she had studied metalwork in the late 1890s. Later, having a studio in the same building, they designed together. Dewar was responsible for having Davidson's expertise made available to the students over a protracted period 1910-1935. A presentation casket, currently on loan to Glasgow AG, was illustrated in Davidson's book *Applied Design in Precious Metals* and received the Society of Lady Artists' Lauder Award, 1935. Throughout her working life she was a shrewd observer of the pulsating artistic scene of the time and in 1950 published *The History of the Glasgow Society of Lady Artists* of which she had been President. Active in the suffragette movement and in the forefront of the inspirational involvement of women in the development of Scottish Art 1880-1920, chronicled by Burkhauser. All her work was characterised by bold use of colour and vigorous outline. During WW2 she was influential in establishing a Scottish-Czechoslovak Club in Glasgow. This involvement is evidenced in her change of style and informed her work. In 1924 she painted one of twenty-three panels for the Forestry Hall at the Wembley Exhibition. 'Until the end of her life Dewar stretched the boundaries of the possible, often challenging the status quo' [Burkhauser]. Exhibited RSA 1903-09, 1917-18 & 1929. Also RSW(6), GI(9), L(14) & regularly at the AAS 1912-1935 from 15 Woodside Terrace. Represented in Glasgow AG.
**Bibl:** Burkhauser 159-163 et passim; Halsby 256.

**DEWAR, Mrs William A** **fl 1850-1852**
Edinburgh portrait painter and miniaturist. Exhibited at the RSA no fewer than 16 portrait miniatures in 1850 with further works in 1852 from 3 Leopold Place.

**DEY, Derek** **fl 1973-1975**
Amateur Aberdeen artist; exhibited AAS(4) from 61 Auchinyell Road.

**DEY, James** **fl 1894-1921**
Painter of Scottish landscape and topographical scenes. Lived at Rosemount, Corstorphine, Edinburgh; exhibited RSA 1901-05 and again in 1921, & AAS(1).

**D'HARDIVILLER, Chevalier** **fl c1835-1840**
Little known French artist who lived for a time in Edinburgh. Drew and engraved a view of the Assembly Rooms with the title 'Bal Celtique'. This portrayed an important social event in the life of the city which took place in late January 1836 in aid of the Highland Society. Laure D'Hardiviller, who exhibited at the London Salon in 1909, may have been his grandaughter. In 1835 he wrote and illustrated *Souvenirs des Highlands; Voyage a la suite de Henri V en 1832*, dedicated to the Duchesse de Berri. Exhibited RSA(3) 1837 including a portrait of the daughter of the Duc de Berri.
**Bibl:** Butchart 66-7.

**DIAZ(S), Robert** **fl 1880-1896**
Painter in oil and watercolour of buildings and interiors. Spent part of his life in Edinburgh and later in Glasgow, his final exhibits coming from 138 West Graham Street. Work similar in scope to George Aikman(qv). Exhibited RSA 1885 and 1886 including a study of John Knox's house in the High Street, also other works in 1889-90 and 1891-2, RSW(1) & GI(2). Approximately 20 works of his are in the Edinburgh Room at the Edinburgh Central Library and at Huntly House. Probably the **G DIAZ** who has two watercolour drawings of Edinburgh townscapes in the collection of the City of Edinburgh.

**DIBDIN, Henry E** **fl 1843-1854**
Edinburgh landscape painter. Mostly Scottish scenes but also painted some in Cumbria. Exhibited several paintings at the RSA during the above period.

**DIBDIN, Sara Beatrice (née Guthrie)** **1874-?**
Painter and metal worker from Glasgow. Studied at Glasgow School of Art and then in Munich. Second wife of Edward Rimbault D. Exhibited RSA(1), RSW(2), RA(1), RCA(26), L(101), ROI(5) & GI(1).

**DICHMONT, James** **fl 1933**
Watercolour painter. Exhibited RSW(1).

**DICK, A** **fl 1908**
Selkirk painter of 20 Tower Street; exhibited RSA(1).

**DICK, A M** **fl 1861**
Amateur Glasgow portrait painter. Exhibited GI(1) from 1 South Portland Street.

**DICK, Alan Graham** **fl 1975**
Aberdeen printmaker. Exhibited AAS(3) from 117D Gerrard Street.

**DICK, Alexander L** **c1805-**
Scottish engraver. Pupil of Robert Scott(qv) in Edinburgh. Migrated to the United States c1833. There he developed a highly successful business employing many engravers.
**Bibl:** Stauffer, American Engravers, vol 1, 65.

**DICK, Beverley** **fl 1975**
Amateur Aberdeen flower painter. Married Alan Graham D(qv). Exhibited AAS(1).

**DICK, Dorothy J (née Swan)** **fl 1911-1920**
Sculptress. Married the English artist Stewart D. Probably mother of Dorothy Dick(qv). Exhibited RSA(1), RA(3), GI(1), L(2), SWA(1) & LS(11).

**DICK, Dorothy** **1932-**
Born Glasgow. Sculptress in concrete, bronze, marble and wood. Probably daughter of Mrs Dorothy J D(qv). Exhibited figure studies regularly at the RSA since 1963 & GI(19), from 38 Earlspark Avenue, Glasgow.

**DICK, Eliza Izzett** **fl 1869-1882**
Edinburgh painter in oil, but mainly watercolour; landscape and flowers of 17 Elm Row. Exhibited RSA(10) & GI(3) during the above period.

**DICK, Fiona Buchan** **fl 1982-1984**
Edinburgh printmaker. Exhibited AAS(4) from 5 Leamington Road.

**DICK, Gary** **fl 1986-**
Edinburgh painter. Began exhibiting at the RSA in 1986 from 6 Beaverbank Place, Edinburgh.

**DICK, Hans V** **fl 1859-1860**
Painter. Exhibited still life works at the RSA in the above years.

**DICK, J Stevenson** **fl 1876-1880**
Glasgow landscape painter in oil; exhibited RSA 1876 & GI(1) in 1880, from 18 Berkeley Street.

**DICK, Jessie Alexandra ARSA** **1896-1976**
Born Largs. Glasgow painter of oil and watercolour; portraits and still life. Studied Glasgow School of Art 1915-1919 and was a member of

staff 1921-1959. Active member of the Ladies Art Club. Painted in Glasgow and Arran. Signed her work 'J Alix Dick'. Elected ARSA 1960. Exhibited RSA 1924-76, also RSW, RE, GI(86) & L1.
**Bibl:** Halsby 256.

**DICK, John** **fl 1873**
Edinburgh painter in black and white; exhibited RSA(1).

**DICK, John** **fl 1905**
Sculptor of 36 James Street, Perth. Exhibited bust of a child at the GI.

**DICK, John T** **fl 1892-1896**
Glasgow landscape painter; exhibited GI(3) from 24 Battlefield Avenue.

**DICK, Thomas** **fl 1837-1874**
Scottish engraver. Exhibited engravings after William Dyce(qv) and J Watson Gordon(qv) at the RSA during the above years. Represented in Glasgow AG.

**DICK, Sir William Reid KCVO RA HRSA** **1879-1961**
Born Glasgow. Studied Glasgow School of Art. Moved south c1908, being employed as a carver. During the 1914-18 war was in the services and resumed work as a sculptor immediately thereafter. Sculptor to King George VI, and Queen's Sculptor-in-Ordinary for Scotland 1938-1952. Trustee of the RA, member, Royal Fine Art Commission, also member of the Mint Advisory Committee and trustee of the Tate Gallery 1934-1941. His 'Androdus' was purchased by the Chantrey Bequest 1919. Most notable works include the tomb of George V at Windsor Chapel and a memorial bust of George V at Crathie Church, Aberdeenshire; also the Kitchener memorial in St Paul's Cathedral and war memorials in various parts of the country including the London Embankment, a large bronze eagle for the Royal Air Force memorial, and the lion at the Lenin Gate. Responsible for the equestrian group at Unilever House, Blackfriars, the Lord Leverhulme memorial in Port Sunlight, a nine foot statue of Lord Halifax now in Delhi and one of Lord Willingdon, also in Delhi, the statue of Livingstone at Victoria Falls (for which he journeyed up the Zambesi to study the site). Collaborated with Sir Charles Gilbert Scott over the George V memorial in Old Palace Yard, Westminster. Elected ARA 1921, RA 1928, HRSA 1939. Knighted 1935. As well as over 100 exhibits at the RA and 31 at the RSA 1912-1960, exhibited GI(51), RSW(2), RI(3) & L(32). Represented in the City of Edinburgh collection.
**Bibl:** Gunnis; RSA(obit).

**DICKIE, Miss Janet A** **fl 1925-1926**
Glasgow sculptor of figures. Exhibited GI(2) from Burnbank, Yoker.

**DICKIE, Miss K M** **fl 1923-1929**
Jewellery designer of Scottish-Irish extraction. Moved to Edinburgh 1929. Exhibited L(15).

**DICKIE, Rev William** **fl 1896-1928**
Amateur Glasgow artist in oil and watercolour; mainly landscapes, especially Perthshire. Exhibited RSW(2), GI(5) & L(1), from Lynwood, Partickhill.

**DICKINSON, Thomas** **fl 1890-1919**
Born near Lancaster. Trained Royal College of Art, London where he was a distinguished student. After a short stay in Bury, Lancashire came to Dunfermline where for 12 years he was the art master at Dunfermline HS before dying from war wounds. His special skill was as a designer, his work showing qualities of imagination and poetic intensity which placed him far above the rank of the ordinary drawing master. Also a very fine draughtsman and a successful decorative artist of acknowledged ability, much admired by Sir Edwin Abbey with whom he was associated in the preparation of several designs and schemes of decoration. Walter Crane had employed some of his designs to illustrate his textbook *Ideals in Art.* At the time of his death he was under consideration for senior appointments at both Edinburgh and Glasgow Schools of Art. A sympathetic and generous person always ready to encourage his students. Also taught evening classes at the Lauder Technical School. Exhibited once at the RSA from his home at 129 Brucefield Avenue 1919 and a local landscape at the AAS in 1890 when living at David Cottage, Auchmill.

**DICKINSON, W C** **fl 1868**
Edinburgh painter of sporting subjects in oil; exhibited RSA(1).

**DICKSON, Adelaide C** **fl 1889-1908**
Edinburgh landscape and flower painter, moved to London c1902. Exhibited two Dutch scenes at the RA, also RSA(2) & L(3).

**DICKSON, Alexander** **fl 1871-1876**
Edinburgh portrait painter, exhibited four works at the RSA during the above period.

**DICKSON, Miss Edith G K** **fl 1900-1902**
Edinburgh miniaturist who lived for a time at 3 Royal Circus before moving to Glasgow and then back again to Edinburgh. Painted mainly portrait miniatures on ivory, exhibiting RSA 1900-1902.

**DICKSON, Mrs Elizabeth Gillespie** **fl 1881-1902**
Edinburgh painter in watercolour and chalk of figurative subjects and portraits. Moved to Glasgow 1883 before returning to Edinburgh. 'The Arisaig Weaver', exhibited in 1885, attracted considerable notice. Exhibited RSA(8) & GI(3).

**DICKSON, Heather** **fl 1982**
Aberdeen artist. Exhibited AAS(2) from Flat B3, Viewfield Road.

**DICKSON, Major J** **c1893-?**
Huntly-based professional soldier and amateur etcher. Served in World War I with the 6th Batt. The Gordon Highlanders, fighting with distinction at Givenchy 1915. Transferred to the RAMC 1916/17. His etching of Robecq provides the fp in D Mackenzie's *The Sixth Gordons in France and Flanders* (1921).

**DICKSON, J A C** **fl 1858-1865**
Edinburgh oil painter of local landscape and still life; exhibited RSA(10) between the above years.

**DICKSON, James Marshall** **fl 1978-1989**
Fife painter. Exhibited GI(4) from 44 Main Street, Lochgelly.

**DICKSON, Miss Jeanie** **fl 1880-1886**
Edinburgh painter in oil and watercolour of landscape, figurative subjects. Exhibited RSA(17) 1881-1886, also GI(8) & AAS(2).

**DICKSON, John** **fl 1896-1919**
Aberdeenshire lawyer and amateur etcher, mainly of local scenes around Huntly. Exhibited AAS(6) during the above period.

**DICKSON, Malcolm** **fl 1984**
Glasgow painter. Exhibited GI(1) from 45 Cecil Street.

**DICKSON, Miss Lalia C P** **fl 1936-1957**
Edinburgh painter, of 1 Inverleith Row. Religious subjects and stained glass window designer; exhibited RSA 1936-7, 1940 and 1957, & RSW(1).

**DICKSON, Margaret** **fl 1932-1935**
Amateur painter of portraits and local landscape. Exhibited GI(2) latterly from 15 Woodside Terrace, Rutherglen.

**DICKSON, Richard** **1792-1857**
Edinburgh architect. Nephew of the architect Richard Crichton(qv). In partnership with his brother **Robert DICKSON** (c1794-1865), he specialised in designing Georgian Gothic country houses. Their best known house was Millearne, Perthshire, executed in the Tudor style "exquisitely" [Dunbar] 1820-4, since demolished. Together the brothers designed Leith Sheriff Court (1827, since rebuilt); rebuilt the Tron Church, Edinburgh (1828); designed Gardner's Crescent, Edinburgh (1822) and designed the imposing asymmetrical Tudor gothic mansion Muirhouse, Marine Drive (1830-2).
**Bibl:** Dunbar 124; Gifford 67,174,265,460,463,465,626,633, pls.70,94.

**DICKSON, Thomas Elder PPSSA FRSE** **1899-?**
Born Barrhead, Renfrew, 26 Aug. Painter in oil and watercolour. Studied Glasgow School of Art under Greiffenhagen 1920-24. Lectured on the History of Art at Edinburgh College of Art from 1943

to 1949. Published *Elements of Design, An Introduction to Colour, Sir William Gillies* and *Contemporary French Painting*. Head of the art department, George Watson's Ladies College 1927-1949 and vice-principal, Edinburgh College of Art 1949-1970. Founder member of the Scottish Crafts Centre. Lived at 12 Bank Terrace, Corstorphine until 1954, then at 25 Belgrave Road, Corstorphine. President SSA 1946-49. Exhibited RSA(58) & RSW(3).
**Bibl:** Halsby 256.

**DICKSON, William** **fl 1883-1898**
Blairgowrie landscape and still life painter in oil. Friend and associate of William Geddes(qv). Exhibited two works at the RSA in 1898 from Maybank & at Perth Fine Art exhibition(3) 1883.

**DICKSON, William B** **1871-1950**
Professional photographer and amateur portrait painter. Known to have painted at least two portraits of Sir Harry Lauder.

**DICKSON, William J (T?) Gillespie** **fl 1883**
Amateur painter of Westfield House, Partickhill, Glasgow. Exhibited GI(1).

**DILETTANTI CLUB** **1850s**
Edinburgh group of artists and art lovers. Members included William Allan, the brothers Ballantyne, Andrew Geddes, Alexander Nasmyth, William Nicholson, Henry Raeburn, Walter Scott, John Schletky, John Thomson, David Wilkie, Hugh 'Gregian' Williams. Allan painted a full meeting. Important as a precursor to other artistic societies in Edinburgh, notably the Society of Artists(qv). Separate from Glasgow Dilettanti Society(qv).
**Bibl:** Esmé Gordon, The Royal Scottish Academy 1826-1976, Edinburgh 1976; Irwin 188; James Nasmyth, An Autobiography, London 1883.

**DIMAMBRO, Francesco** **fl 1943-1947**
Hamilton based sculptor in plaster and sandstone. Exhibited GI(7) from 252 Quarry Street.

**DINGLEY, Humphrey J** **fl 1883-1891**
Glasgow landscape painter in oil who moved c1888 to Dunoon. Exhibited RSA(2), RHA(3) & GI(11) latterly from Glengyle, Dunoon.

**DINGWALL, Miss Helen Cooper** **1859-c1948**
Born Helensburgh, 1 Sep. Flower painter. Daughter of an Auchtermuchty architect. Sister of Isabella(qv) and John D(qv). Appears to have taken over 'The Glennan' from her mother in 1918 and to have remained there until 1939. Exhibited GI(3) and elsewhere 1883-1890 from 'The Glennan'.

**DINGWALL, Isabella (Mrs Hassall)** **1865-c1945**
Painter. Born Helensburgh, 2 Mar. One of six children, sister of Helen(qv) and John D(qv). Exhibited GI(3).

**DINGWALL, John** **1869-c1949**
Born Helensburgh, 27 Dec. Amateur artist. Brother of Isabella(qv) and Helen D(qv). In 1906 acquired 47 William Street, Helensburgh as a home and studio but later moved frequently in the Glasgow area and was for a time in Eastleigh, Hampshire 1925-1934. Exhibited Fancy Fair at the RSA 1896.

**DINGWALL, Kenneth** **1938-**
Born Devonside, Clackmannan. Painter in oil, acrylic, watercolour, also constructions. Trained Edinburgh College of Art 1955-60 under W G Gillies(qv), John Maxwell(qv) and Robin Philipson(qv). After being awarded an Andrew Grant postgraduate scholarship 1959-60 was in Greece 1961-2, studying at the Athens School of Fine Art. Returning to Scotland, assumed a teaching post at Edinburgh College of Art 1963 and from 1973-4 was visiting Professor at Minneapolis College of Art and Design. Whilst in the States he executed his first abstract colour-field paintings. Influenced by American artists such as Robert Ryman, his paintings of the 1970s contain rich surface texture and subtle modulations of colour. In the mid 1970s he produced a series of small minimalist wooden constructions painted in a uniform colour. Held his first one-man exhibition in Greece 1962 followed by his first UK exhibition in Edinburgh 1969. In 1988 became Professor of Painting in Cleveland Institute of Art. Represented in SNGMA, Aberdeen AG, Glasgow AG, Lillie AG (Milngavie), Middlesborough AG, Perth AG, Portsmouth City AG, Southampton AG, Minneapolis Art Institute, USA,
**Bibl:** Gage 69-71; Hartley 129; SAC Gallery, Edinburgh, 'Kenneth Dingwall' (Ex Cat 1977).

**DINGWALL, Sandra Elizabeth** **fl 1975-1977**
Aberdeen artist. Trained at Gray's School of Art. Specialised in collages. Exhibited AAS(4), latterly from 26 Rosemount Place.

**DINKEL, Emmy G M (née Keet)** **fl 1948-1950**
Painter of illustrative works. Lived at 15 Greenhill Place. Wife of Ernest Michael D(qv). Exhibited RSA during the above years.

**DINKEL, Ernest Michael RWS ARCA** **1894-?**
Born Huddersfield. Painter in oil, watercolour and tempera of flower pieces and Scottish landscape; teacher. Head of Design, Edinburgh College of Art. Became widely known for his knowledge of the wall paintings of Canterbury Cathedral. Married Emmy D(qv). Exhibited annually RSA 1948-1961.

**DINNIE, Mrs Catherine** **fl 1966-1967**
Aberdeen painter of flowers and town views especially in evening time. Exhibited at AAS(3) from 72 Beaconsfield Place.

**DINSDALE-YOUNG, Jean** **c1938-**
Watercolour artist, cartoonist and printmaker. She has lived and worked in Inverness-shire since 1976. Trained Liverpool College of Art and Wimbledon School of Art, gaining national diplomas in illustration and art teaching. First Prize, Scottish Field's Cartoon competition 1991 and in 1993 a silver medal for silver design presented to 10 Downing St for state banquets. Member, Highland Printmakers with whom she exhibits. Paintings in collections in Australia, Canada, Cayman Islands and throughout the UK. In the artistic tradition of Cynicus, she is probably best known for her humorous portrayal of the eccentricities of country life and its pursuits, with cartoons using the pseudonym 'Creswell'. Worked as cartoonist for *Glasgow Herald*. Lives and works from Kiltarlity, Inverness-shire.

**DISTON, Adam** **fl 1858-1878**
Leven landscape painter in oil; exhibited three works at the RSA during the above years.

**DISTON, J** **fl 1885**
Exhibited once at the RSA from 21 Raeberry Street, Glasgow.

**DITCHBURN, Mrs Ursula** **fl 1966**
Amateur artist. Exhibited watercolour study of a squirrel at the GI from 21 Pitbauchlie Road, Dunfermline.

**DIXON, Miss Anna RSW** **1873-1959**
Born Scotland; died Edinburgh, 6 Feb. Painter in oil and watercolour. Studied art at the RSA Life School under E A Walton(qv), Charles Mackie(qv) and William Walls(qv). Specialised in watercolour studies of flowers and landscape. Worked in France, especially Brittany. Painted in a fluent manner, often of the crofting townships of Western Scotland. Frequently painted donkeys and horses, often with children. Taught for a brief spell at Moray House Training College. Elected RSW 1917. President SSWA 1930-42. Exhibited RSA(94), RSW(98), GI(107), RA(2), L(4) & AAS regularly 1898-1935, latterly from 6 Spring Gardens, Abbeyhill. Represented in Paisley AG.
**Bibl:** Caw 426; Halsby 256; Scotsman 7 Feb 1959(obit).

**DIXON, Arthur Percy** **fl 1884-1917**
Edinburgh painter in oil and watercolour, portraits and figurative subjects. In 1887 his 'Edinburgh Castle' received favourable mention as did his study of 'An Edinburgh flower market' in 1899. Exhibited RSA(57), GI(26), RSW(1), AAS(2) & L(2) from 47 York Place. Represented in City of Edinburgh collection.

**DIXON, Craig** **fl 1871-1873**
Glasgow landscape painter in oil; exhibited twice at the RSA, both in the same year & GI(4) from 19 Elmbank Crescent.

**DIXON, Miss Edna M** **fl 1919-1951**
Portrait miniaturist and landscape painter in oil and watercolour, also occasionally animals and flowers of The Studio, Clarkston. Exhibited RSA(5) from 1931-37, also RA(1), GI(33) & L(1).

**DIXON, Miss Elspeth Mary** **1920-1977**
Born Glasgow, 20 Mar; died Dumbarton, 22 Sep. Amateur landscape artist; exhibited locally in Helensburgh and in Inverness; & GI(1) from Dhunan, Portincaple.

**DIXON, James** **fl 1854-1855**
Edinburgh landscape painter from 81 Leith Street; exhibited a Dutch scene in 1854 at the RSA and 'Ravensheugh Castle' in 1855.

**DIXON, Mrs Marion Isabel** **fl 1968**
Amateur watercolour artist; exhibited a landscape at the GI from Ard Mor, Dunrobin Glen, Golspie, Sutherland.

**DOAR, M Wilson** **1898-?**
Little known Scottish sculptress of animals, often dogs, carved in wood; also animal painter.

**DOBBIE, Miss Christina J** **fl 1887-1898**
Glasgow flower painter. Exhibited GI(5) from Ayrshire and 24 West Cumberland Street.

**DOBBIE, Isa** **fl 1896**
Flower painter of Laurel Bank, Ayr. Probably sister of Christina J D(qv). Exhibited GI(1).

**DOBBIE, John** **fl 1920-1935**
Glasgow portrait painter of 65 West Regent Street. In 1932 exhibited a portrait of an ex-Moderator of the Church of Scotland at the RSA. Exhibited RSA 1920-33 & GI(9), latterly from Greenbank, Helensburgh.

**DOBBIE, T** **fl 1820**
Edinburgh engraver. Engraved a view of Edinburgh Castle after D O Hill, 1820.

**DOBBIE, Thomas** **fl 1930-1942**
Edinburgh portrait painter and engraver. Etched 'Wilkie's Parliament Close and Public Characters, of Edinburgh fifty years since'. Exhibited at the RSA during the above years from Sciennes Court.
**Bibl:** Butchart 24.

**DOBBIE, Thomas** **fl 1972**
Amateur Dunbartonshire painter; exhibited GI(1) from 72 Salisbury Place, Clydebank.

**DOB(B)IE, William J** **fl 1954-1959**
Falkirk based landscape painter in oil and watercolour. Exhibited a view near Brodick, Arran at the RSA & GI(1), from Glasgow Road, Uddingston.

**DOBIE, Miss Matilda Isabel** **fl 1883**
Amateur painter of 1 Buchanan Terrace, Paisley. Exhibited a flower study at the GI, & L(1), both during the above year.

**DOBSON, Mrs B** **fl 1966**
Amateur watercolourist. Married to E Carey D(qv). Exhibited a landscape at the AAS from 81 Murray Terrace, Aberdeen.

**DOBSON, Cowan RBA** **1893-1980**
Born Bradford, 28 Jne. Portrait painter in both oil and watercolour. Son of Henry John D(qv). Although born in England of Scottish parents, he spent most of his life in Scotland. Educated in Edinburgh. Many society sitters were among his clients. He painted in a conventional manner emphasising the ordinariness of sitters rather than concentrating on any specific quality or aspect of symbolism. Elected ARBA 1919, RBA 1922. Exhibited RA from the age of 19 also RSA(23), RSW(6), GI(63), RBA(18), RCA(6) & L(5), latterly from 62 Edwardes Square, London W8. Represented in SNPG(2), Paisley AG.
**Bibl:** Halsby 256.

**DOBSON, E Carey** **fl 1964**
Aberdeen painter of local landscapes and metalwork designer. Exhibited AAS(2) from 81 Murray Terrace.

**DOBSON, Henry John RSW RCanA** **1858-1928**
Born Innerleithen, Peebleshire. Painter in oil and watercolour of interiors and genre. Both his sons, Cowan(qv) and Henry Raeburn(qv) were artists. Studied School of Design, Royal Institution and RSA Life Schools. Although he exhibited six works at the RA, most of his exhibits were at the RSA, concentrating on homely scenes of Scottish life. In 1911 visited Canada and the USA. Lived in Edinburgh and Kirkcudbright. Occasionally worked in watercolours with considerable success. In 1900 shared an exhibition at the Scottish Gallery with A K Brown(qv). Illustrated Sandison's *Scottish Life and Character,* although, in Caw's opinion, the illustrations rather overdid the homely and pathetic and "as W E Henley said of Tom Faed's pictures, 'are tremulous with bleat'". Elected RSW 1890. Exhibited RA(6), RSA(62), RSW(55), RCA(54), GI(48), L(3) & regularly AAS 1906-1912.
**Bibl:** Caw 468; Halsby 256; Reynolds.

**DOBSON, Henry Raeburn RCanA** **1901-**
Born Edinburgh, 29 May. Portrait and figure painter. Studied at Edinburgh College of Art. Son of Henry John D(qv). Lived in Edinburgh. Painted both portrait and figurative subjects in oil and watercolour. Some of his drawings of old Scottish characters are reminiscent of those by Henry Wright Kerr(qv). Moved to London c1928. Elected ARCanA 1920. Exhibited RA(6), RSA(24), RSW(5), RCA(23) & L(4). Represented in City of Edinburgh collection by Lord Provost Sir Herbert Brechin.
**Bibl:** Halsby 256.

**DOBSON, Mrs J L Herbert** **fl 1885-1940**
Glasgow painter in oil and watercolour, mainly the latter. Appears to have worked at two widely separated periods of her life. In 1885 and 1893 she exhibited landscapes at the AAS but not again until 1939-40 when she showed 4 landscapes at the GI from 5 Newton Terrace.

**DOBSON, Miss Margaret Stirling ARE** **fl 1905-1936**
Born Galashiels. Painter, etcher and authoress. Studied at Edinburgh College of Art. Moved to London c1912. Elected ARE 1917. Exhibited RA(5), RSA(4), RI(1), RE(12) & L(3).

**DOBSON, William Loudon** **fl 1884-1932**
Glasgow painter of figure studies and landscape. Exhibited over a wide span of time at the GI(4), latterly from 26 Agnes Street.

**DOCHARTY, Alexander Brownlie** **1862-1940**
Glasgow landscape painter mainly in oils, occasionally also in watercolour. Nephew of James D(qv). Studied part-time at GSA under Robert Greenlees(qv), and after a period spent designing calico, took up painting professionally in 1892, having studied in Paris 1884. Lived and worked in Kilkerran, Ayrshire. 'For long his home was in the lovely district where Thomson of Duddingston had his first charge and painted his early pictures, and amid the park-like pastures and the tree-fringed meadows, and on the sylvan watersides of the Girvan he found material for very good pictures. Latterly, however, the landscape of Carrick figured less frequently than that of the nearer Highlands. He was an all-the-year-round landscape man, although perhaps he liked the green summer best. Painted with gusto, but not without refinement, in frank, fresh and harmonious colour, and good in drawing and design, Docharty's landscapes preserved the aroma of a sincere, if unimpassioned, love of the simple and everyday aspects of Nature and awakened pleasant memories of the country'[Caw]. Exhibited RA(12), RSA(19), GI(155) & AAS 1893-1912. Represented in Glasgow AG, Paisley AG.
**Bibl:** Caw 390; Halsby 256.

**DOCHARTY, James ARSA** **1829-1878**
Born Bonhill, Dunbartonshire; died Egypt, Apr. Glasgow landscape painter. Son of a calico block-cutter. Served his apprenticeship as a pattern designer for calico printing. In 1861 gave up designing in order to concentrate on painting landscape from a studio in Glasgow. In the spring of 1876, his health fading, he went to Egypt, via Italy and France, and died shortly after his return. All his paintings are of

Scottish views, his style is realistic, natural and true to nature. The *AJ* of 1874 noted 'The Fishing Village and The Cuchullan Hills leave nothing to desire; James Docharty lays his hand, not metaphorically like Byron, but materially, upon Nature's elements, and shows many secrets of her witchery'. His best works have a quiet harmony of colour and a sympathy but often fail as compositions. Influenced by J M Donald(qv). Caw found his work 'less poetic than Wintour's, less vivacious and effective than Bough's and less charming and accomplished than Fraser's, [but with] a modest merit of their own'. 'Salmon Stream' painted 1878 and now in Glasgow AG is generally regarded as his masterpiece. This shows the roaring River Lochy with Ben Nevis towering over all. Brydall said that 'while his works rose far above mediocrity, they never aspired to or touched the sublimer aspects of Nature...He was an earnest student of Nature and an industrious worker, his efforts being spurred on by the fact that his children were mostly mutes'. Elected ARSA 1877. Exhibited RSA, GI(102) and had 13 works accepted at the RA 1865-1877. Represented in Paisley AG.
**Bibl:** AJ 1878, 155; Armstrong 73-4; Brydall 389-90; Caw 193-4; DNB; Halsby 70,125; Irwin 356; McKay 359; Wingfield.

**DOCHARTY, James L C** **fl 1875-c1915**
Glasgow landscape painter in oil and occasional watercolour. Specialised in West Highland scenes. Exhibiting RSA(9) 1879-1900; also GI(79) & RSW(3) from 134 Bath Street & AAS 1893-1910.
**Bibl:** Halsby 256.

**DOCHERTY, Frank** **fl 1985**
Amateur Renfrewshire artist of figure studies. Exhibited GI(1) from Calderbank Cottage, Lochwinnoch.

**DOCHERTY, George** **fl 1965-1973**
Glasgow painter. Exhibited figure studies at the GI(5) from 23 Glasgow Street.

**DOCHERTY, Michael ARSA** **1947-**
Born Alloa. Trained Edinburgh College of Art 1964-68. Received an Andrew Grant scholarship 1968 enabling him to travel to France and Spain. Although primarily a painter, he works in mixed media and in modern jargon has been described as a 'minimalist'. Often works with found objects such as metal cans and buckets and pieces of wood, on to which he paints objects for their special relevance to a particular location which then form a kind of diary of his travels. Often the work seems artificially contrived. Elected ARSA. Teaches at Edinburgh College of Art. Exhibited RSA since 1979 & GI(2). Represented in SNGMA.
**Bibl:** Hartley 129; SAC,'Scottish Art Now' (Ex Cat 1982).

**DOCHERTY, R McKendrick** **fl 1959**
Ayr based sculptor. Exhibited a plaster group at the GI from 31 Orchard Avenue.

**DODD, Frances E** **fl 1892-1951**
Glasgow painter in watercolour, charcoal and pen and ink; portraits, figurative subjects and landscape. Exhibited GI(9), after 1904 from London.

**DODD, Phyllis, (Mrs D P Bliss)** **fl 1948-1955**
Glasgow painter of figurative compositions and portraits. Wife of Douglas Percy Bliss(qv). Studied at the RCA in London. Exhibited RSA 1948-1955 & GI(24).

**DODDS, Albert Charles RSW** **1888-1964**
Born Edinburgh, 28 May. Landscape and portrait painter in oil and watercolour, mostly Scottish views but also occasionally on the continent, and occasional flower studies. Studied Edinburgh College of Art and RSA Life School, where he received the Carnegie travelling scholarship 1914. Had only one arm. Drawing Master at Edinburgh Academy for many years. Painted on the Continent, especially in France, also in southern England and in Scotland. His work shows a firm grasp of both media. Elected RSW 1937. Exhibited RSA(44), RSW(24), GI(38), AAS(1) & L(2) from 4 Albert Terrace, Edinburgh. Represented in Glasgow AG, Paisley AG, City of Edinburgh collection.
**Bibl:** Halsby 256.

**DODDS, Andrew** **1927-**
Born May 5, Gullane. Painter, illustrator and teacher. Educated in England, studied art at North-East Essex Technical College 1941-43 and at Colchester School of Art 1943-45. After service in the Royal Navy 1945-47, he returned to art school studying under Bernard Meninsky, Keith Vaughan and John Minton at the Central School of Arts and Crafts 1947-50. Began his working life with the Hulton Press 1950, illustrating the *Eagle*. After teaching at Ipswich School of Art in 1980, became Principal Lecturer and Deputy Head at Suffolk College School of Art & Design. Contributed over 300 illustrations for the *Radio Times* between 1951 & 1970, his first being for the Archers series, his mother being the model for Doris Archer. Provided illustrations for Benham: *Essex Ballads* (1960), Armstrong: *Island Odyssey* (1963), 'Miss Read': *Country Bunch* (1963), Armstrong: *The Big Sea* (1964), Allen: *Smitty and the Plural of Cactus* (1965), Morgan: *The Casebook of Capability Morgan* (1965), 'Miss Read': *Hob and the Horse Bat* (1965), Allen: *Smitty and the Egyptian Cat* (1966), Naughton: *A Roof Over Your Head* (1967), Vaughan-Thomas: *Madly in All Directions* (1967), Hibbert: *London* (et al, 1969), Reder: *Epitaphs* (1969), Nendick: *Silver Bells and Cockle Shells* (1971), Ward: *The Blessed Trade* (1971), *The Hospice Book of Poems* (1989). Also illustrated and wrote *East Anglia Drawn* (1987). First solo exhibition Studio Club 1961 followed later at the Aldeburgh Festival 1989.
**Bibl:** Driver; Horne 168-9; Peppin; Ryder; Usherwood.

**DODDS, John Innes** **fl 1958**
Edinburgh sculptor. Exhibited a group in wood at the GI from 6 West Savile Terrace.

**DODDS, William** **fl 1881-1910**
Galashiels watercolour painter of landscape. Exhibited RSA(13), RSW(2), GI(3), ROI(3) & RBA(1).

**DODMAN, Frank E** **fl 1932-1939**
Although English, this etcher spent his most active professional years working in Scotland from his home at Blackhall, near Edinburgh. Exhibited RA(2), RSA(7) & L(3).

**DODS, Andrew ARSA FRVS** **1898-1976**
Born Edinburgh 10 May; died Edinburgh 9 Feb. Sculptor. Educated at Boroughmuir School. Apprenticed to Beattie's, an Edinburgh firm of masons. At the outbreak of WW1 he enlisted in the Gordon Highlanders but was withdrawn on his mother's insistence as being under age; he eventually returned as a sniper and was twice wounded. After the war he studied at Edinburgh College of Art, showing great ability in clay modelling and stone carving. Appointed assistant to Pittendreigh MacGillivray(qv), learning the techniques of working in plaster and bronze whilst executing complex works in the neo-classical style. After MacGillivray's death he joined the staff of the Edinburgh College of Art remaining there for the rest of his life. Specialised in modelling portrait heads, often of his own family. Member of a team gathered together by Sir Frank Mears to work on the Royal Scots Memorial in Princes Street Gardens, he was responsible for the design and carving of two of the seven monoliths. Among other works was a model for Joseph Greave's design of the Christopher Columbus memorial in San Domingo which won an international competition. Elected ARSA 1957. Exhibited frequently RSA & GI(15) from 10 Merchiston Gardens.
**Bibl:** RSA 1976 (Obit).

**DODS, Isabella** **fl 1899-1900**
Dunbar painter of landscape and flower studies in oil and watercolour; exhibited RSA & AAS from Hedderwick.

**DODS, John Wilson** **fl 1893-c1912**
Dumfries sculptor, specialising in portrait heads. Made several working visits to Palestine, Egypt, Greece and Rome. Published an important guide for monumental sculptors *A Series of Alphabets, Symbols and Abbreviations, with hints on punctuation,* 1911. From St Mary's Place, exhibited RSA(4) including a portrait head of the African explorer Joseph Thomson (1896), also RA 1894 & GI(12).

**DODS, Robin Smith** **1868-1920**
Born Dunedin, New Zealand. Architect. Both parents were Scottish. Arrived in Edinburgh 1886 to train with Hay and Henderson. Become

one of Sir Robert Lorimer's closest friends. Four years later he moved to London to work with Aston Webb and Ingress Bell, and later for William Dunn. Awarded a special prize 1893, honourable mention for the Sloane Prize 1894. An excellent draughtsman, he executed some of Lorimer's early exhibition drawings. Returned to Australasia 1896, taking up an appointment with Francis Hall in Brisbane, moving to Sydney 1911. At the time of his death he was considering the offer of a partnership from Lorimer(qv).
**Bibl:** Peter Savage, Lorimer and the Edinburgh Craft Designers, Edinburgh 1980, 7,19,49,68,72,131,133-5,164.

**DOEG, Robert E** **fl 1903**
Amateur painter. Exhibited RSA(1) from 4 Craighall Terrace, Musselburgh.

**DOHERTY, Miss Katherine** **fl 1944**
Exhibited a plaster statuette at the GI from 39 Earnock Street, Glasgow.

**DOIG, Margaret Henderson** **[see MACLEOD, Margaret]**

**D'OLIER, Mrs** **fl 1858**
Edinburgh-based painter in pencil and watercolour of portraits. Possibly related to Florence D. who exhibited at the RHA 1912-22 from Knocklina, Bray, Ireland. Exhibited RSA(1).

**DONACHIE, John J** **fl 1975-1987**
Sculptor in bronze and wood. Exhibited GI(6) from Norwood, Tigh-na-bruich, Argyll.

**DONALD, Adam T** **fl 1934**
Painter. Exhibited RSA from Dundonald Arms, Culross, nr Dunfermline.

**DONALD, Alex** **fl 1843**
Glasgow painter; exhibited 3 views of Argyllshire at the RSA in the same year.

**DONALD, Miss Anne** **1941-**
Glasgow painter in oil and watercolour, also printmaker. English, Scottish and continental landscape, flowers and still life. Trained Glasgow School of Art under David Donaldson(qv) and W Drummond Bone(qv) 1959-1963. Worked at Glasgow AG 1965-1991, latterly as keeper of Fine Art. Works mainly in a traditional style, seeking inspiration in her still lifes, particularly from her collection of 19th century ceramics. Fond of Tuscany landscapes. Exhibits regularly at the RSA & RGI. Exhibited GI(48) from 38 Victoria Crescent Road. Represented in Glasgow AG, Lillie AG(Milngavie).

**DONALD, Gabriel** **fl 1950-1958**
Glasgow flower painter. Exhibited GI(2) from 70 Douglas Park Crescent, Bearsden.

**DONALD, George RSA RSW** **1943-**
Born Ootacamund, South India. Painter in oil and printmaker. Came to Aberdeen and studied at Edinburgh College of Art 1963-7. A postgraduate scholarship enabled him to visit Afghanistan, India, Iran, Nepal, Pakistan & Turkey 1968. Spent the following year at Benares Hindu University before returning for a further year's study at Hornsea College of Art 1968-9 and subsequently Edinburgh College of Art 1977-80. Awarded Scottish Arts Council grant which led him to the USA 1981. Married Alexander Fraser's(qv) sister. Lecturer at the Edinburgh College of Art since 1971 and visiting Professor of Art at the University of Central Florida 1981. Lives at Bankhead, by Duns, Berwickshire. His works are mostly of a semi-abstract and colourful nature in the modern idiom, generating a glowing rhythm likened by Gage to a balleric line of dance. Keen amateur fiddle player. RSA 1992. Exhibited regularly RSA since 1967 & AAS 1971-73. Represented in Glasgow AG, Aberdeen AG, collection of Edinburgh City, SAC.
**Bibl:** Gage 72-3.

**DONALD, Ian G** **fl 1947-1960**
Giffnock painter in oil and watercolour of landscape and flower studies. Exhibited GI(5) from 5 Huntly Avenue.

**DONALD, J M** **fl 1888-1894**
Amateur Edinburgh painter. Exhibited RSA(1) & GI(1) from 8 Leslie Place.

**DONALD, John** **fl 1968**
Glasgow watercolour artist. Exhibited GI(2) from 93 Petershill Drive.

**DONALD, John Hutcheon** **1916-1997**
Born Banff. Architect and painter in oils and watercolour. Trained Gray's School of Art. Apprenticed to Allan, Ross & Allan. Architect to the Scottish Dept of Agriculture & Fisheries. Studied painting under Ian MacInnes(qv) and T Archie Sutter Watt(qv). Exhibited until 1992 at AAS & Gracefield AG, Dumfries.

**DONALD, John Milne** **1819-1866**
Born Nairn; died Glasgow. Painter in oil and watercolour; landscape. His parents moved to Glasgow shortly after his birth. Apprenticed to a house painter in Glasgow, in about 1840 he visited Paris, after which he settled for a short time in London, meeting Samuel Rogers who commissioned two pictures. Whilst in London he worked in the shop of a picture restorer learning the techniques of oil painting. By 1844 had established himself in Glasgow, painting mostly Highland landscapes with a northern boldness combined with lowland softness. Many of his pictures show tracts of broken ground, with patches of colour and scattered flocks of sheep, and in the distance rugged mountainsides. 'His colour, though seldom brilliant, was nearly always delicate and luminous...His landscapes are mostly well composed, though often showing signs of haste' [Armstrong]. He was a reserved, even diffident man. Also painted panels for ships built on the Clyde, many on glass, some being later transferred on to canvas. From the middle 1850s, possibly through an association with Sam Bough(qv), there is an awakening to the charmed variety of natural lighting rather than to the elaboration of detail. At the same time his output grew in vitality. Shortly before he died he suffered a mental illness which curtailed his work. Bough thought that Milne might have excelled him. 'His pictures are characterised by great truth to nature, fine colour, and beauty of execution. A keen observer, he reverences nature too deeply to use any liberties, and hence his works yield that amount of pleasure which accords with the appreciation of nature possessed by the spectator. His best works are those of a smaller size; he saw too keenly to paint to be seen at a distance, and he saw too wisely to paint anything but what conveyed the impression without the slavish hollowing of nature. Ideality and impressionism form no part of his creed, and for him did not exist...To take Donald at his best, as an executant, he is unapproached by any of his predecessors and by few of his successors' [Brydall]. Although little appreciated in his lifetime, his influence on landscape painting in Scotland was substantial and his work an important link in the history of the Scottish tradition of landscape art. Except for Graham Gilbert the portrait painter, Milne was the first artist of real ability to spend his whole life in Glasgow. Exhibited regularly RSA and twice at the RA (1844 and 1846), also GI(23). Represented in NGS, Paisley AG.
**Bibl:** Armstrong 73; Brydall 390-1; Caw 146-7 et al; Halsby 113,125,256; Irwin 356; McKay 313-6.

**DONALD, Miss Mary** **fl 1874-1886**
Edinburgh painter in oil; landscape, often with buildings. Exhibited at least twice at the RSA from 9 Whitehouse Terrace.

**DONALD, Robert E** **fl 1971-1986**
Aberdeen painter; exhibited AAS regularly during the above years from 7 Albert Terrace.

**DONALD, Thomas William RSW** **1853-1883**
Glasgow painter in oil and watercolour of landscapes. Worked in the west highlands and along the western coast. Founder member of the RSW but died tragically young only five years later, before the full flourish of his talent had been realised. Elected RSW 1878. Exhibited RSA(19), mostly Argyll and Perthshire landscapes, RSW(18) & GI(37).
**Bibl:** Halsby 256.

**DONALD-SMITH, Miss Helen** **fl 1883-1929**
Born in Scotland. Portrait and landscape painter. Studied at Kensington, in Paris and at Herkomer's School in Bushey, Herts. From a Kensington, London address exhibited widely including RA(10), RSA(3), RBA(4), RI(20), ROI(20), SWA(20) & L(13).

**DONALDSON, A F** **fl 1933**
Scottish painter, born in Scotland but spent most of his life in England. Exhibited from The Shieling, Heatherdene Road, West Kirby, Lancs.

**DONALDSON, Andrew** **1790-1846**
Born Comber, nr Belfast; died Glasgow. Landscape painter in oil, but mainly watercolour and pencil; also teacher. As a young man he came to Glasgow, apprenticed to his father's spinning business. As a result of a serious injury he turned to art c1810. At first he worked in pencil and watercolour painting mainly Glasgow views but as his travelling increased so did his repertoire. Augmented his income by occasional teaching, Thomas Fairbairn(qv) being a pupil. The heaviness of his earlier work gave way to a lighter touch in the 1820's. In 1828 exhibited twelve works at the first exhibition of the Dilettanti Society, Glasgow(qv). Exhibited RSA(57) 1831-1846 mostly castles, ruins and cottages executed in a controlled but accurate and picturesque manner. Represented in NGS(2), People's Palace (Glasgow).
**Bibl:** Brydall 310; Halsby 34,48-9,82,88.

**DONALDSON, Miss Annie** **fl 1867-1878**
Edinburgh painter in oil and watercolour of landscape, flowers and still life. Exhibited RSA(9) during the above years.

**DONALDSON, David Abercrombie RSA RP LLD** **1916-1996**
Born Chryston, Glasgow, 29 Jne; died 22 Aug. Painter in oil and occasional watercolour; portraits, landscape and still life. Studied Glasgow School of Art 1931-8. Received the Guthrie Award 1941. Joined the staff at Glasgow School of Art in 1940, becoming head of painting 1967-81. Although he painted still life and compositions of allegorical fantasy, it is as a portrait painter that he gained a national reputation. In 1977 he was appointed Limner to the Queen in Scotland; a portrait of the Queen is at Holyrood. "In all his work David's approach to the subject was one of direct confrontation - he never worked from preparatory drawings or kept sketches, he favoured the poetic or instinctive approach combining a strong imaginative vision and the senusal quality of the paint itself" (James Robertson). Lived latterly at 5 Clifton Drive, Glasgow. Elected ARSA 1951, RSA 1962, RP 1964 and in 1971 received honorary doctorates from Strathclyde and Glasgow Universities. Exhibited regularly RSA, RGI(104) & AAS 1964. A major retrospective exhibition, Glasgow 1996. Represented in Aberdeen AG, Glasgow AG, Lillie AG(Milngavie), Paisley AG, Perth AG, SAC, Edinburgh City collection, Royal Collection.
**Bibl:** Roger Billcliffe 'David Donaldson RSA', GAGM, 1983; Hardie 181-3; Macmillan [SA], 360,392,401; James D Robertson, Obituary, RSA Annual Report 1996; W Gordon Smith, *David Donaldson*, 1996; The Times, *Obituary*, Aug 30, 1996.

**DONALDSON, Haswell** **fl 1883-1891**
Edinburgh painter of landscape and figure studies and portraits; exhibited RSA(15) & GI(4) from 32 Stafford Street.

**DONALDSON, James** **fl 1954-1956**
Wick painter of local scenes. Exhibited GI from 19 Thurso Street.

**DONALDSON, John FSA** **1737-1801**
Born Edinburgh; died Islington, London, 11 Oct. Painter in water-colour on ivory, enamel and Worcester porcelain, also drew in black lead and was an occasional etcher, especially studies of beggars after Rembrandt. Son of a glovemaker, he was self-taught. Copied engravings and sold miniature portraits in Indian ink. In 1757-8 awarded drawing prizes by the Edinburgh Society of Arts. Came to London 1764 before moving north to Newcastle 1768. In 1764 and 1768 he received two awards from the Society of Arts for enamel paintings and exhibited four works at the RA in 1775 and 1791. According to McKay, he had 'socialistic notions' which led him to look on art, including his own, with contempt. One of the earliest Scottish artists to paint portraits in watercolour, also caricatures, and one of only a few miniaturists working in Scotland during the mid 18th century, being a contemporary of James Ferguson(qv). Early skill at drawing was encouraged by his father, and he is reputed to have earned money when he was only 12. In the early stages of his life, he was supported by the Earl of Buchan. Among his pupils were John Gow(qv), Richard Learmonth(qv) and Adam Robertson(qv). Married Margaret Donald, daughter of a weaver, 1768. A man of unsettled habits and interests, he took up chemistry and patented a method of preserving vegetables and meat. Published a volume of *Poems* (1786) and an essay on the *Elements of Beauty* (1780). In 1786 he was a candidate for Mastership of the Trustees Academy. He became partially blind and suffered some sad last years, dying in Islington, London, abandoned by many of his relatives and friends on account of his difficult temperament. Few of his works are signed. According to Foskett, although attribution of his miniatures is sometimes difficult 'characteristics appear to be the use of a rather pink and white flesh colour, the face shaded with a bluish-grey, especially round the eyes, and a deeper bluish-grey is apparent on the hair which is drawn in lines, made partly by the use of a scraper and partly with opaque white. The red on the lips is usually still bright and the general effect pleasing.' In 1761 he went to London, exhibiting at the Free Society of Artists 1761-4. Elected member of the Society 1764. Died impoverished. Represented in the NGS where there is a portrait miniature of a lady, loaned to the Edinburgh Exhibition 1965.
**Bibl:** Brydall 165-7; Bushnell; Caw 44; Foskett 249; Halsby 256; McKay 27.

**DONALDSON, John** **fl 1884-1912**
Glasgow painter of portraits and local landscapes. Exhibited GI(2) & RI(1) from 196 St Vincent Street.

**DONALDSON, John R** **fl 1863-1875**
Edinburgh landscape painter in oil; exhibited 18 works at the RSA between the above years, mostly views in Fife and around Glen Devon.

**DONALDSON, Mabel** **fl 1937**
Aberdeenshire porcelain painter. Exhibited AAS(1) from East Brae, Abbotshall Road, Cults.

**DONALDSON, Mrs M Lynn** **fl 1980-**
Glasgow painter of flowers, landscape and semi-abstract. Exhibited GI(22) from 1 Kilmardinny Crescent, Bearsden.

**DONALDSON, Miss Margaret E** **fl 1905-1942**
Painter in watercolour of landscape, flowers and portraits; also portrait miniaturist. Lived in Glasgow 1905 before moving north to Killearn 1911, finally settling at Auchenenden, Blanefield, Stirlingshire 1929. Exhibited RSW(1) & GI(8).

**DONALDSON, Mrs Marysia (Maria)** **fl 1961-1989**
Glasgow painter of portraits, still life and flowers. A painter in the modern semi-abstract style, often with strong colour, she has a popular following. Exhibits regularly RSA since 1963, & GI(39), from 5 Cleveden Drive.

**DONALDSON, N** **fl 1898**
Amateur painter; exhibited a study of an old woman at the GI from 5 Crown Terrace, Downhill.

**DONALDSON, Peter** **fl 1758**
Scottish painter about whom very little is known. In 1758 he won an Edinburgh Society of Arts drawing prize for the best landscape by a boy under 18.

**DONALDSON, Thomas** **c1742-?**
Edinburgh engraver, contemporary of the Runcimans, who in about 1775 produced 'View of the New Bridge of Edinburgh', with the adjacent buildings of the old and new town from the west. The print was engraved again, though less successfully, by Daniel Lizars, a pupil of Andrew Bell, and was used as an illustration in Arnot's *History of Edinburgh.* In 1756-9 he won drawing prizes at the Edinburgh Society of Art but unable to manage his finances, he took sanctuary as a debtor in Holyrood on a number of occasions, in 1763, 1765, 1773 and again in 1780. Living in the house of a Thomas Millar 1780. Represented in City of Edinburgh Art Collection.
**Bibl:** Butchart 18.

**DONALDSON, Prof Thomas Leverton** **fl 1816-1864**
Architect of Scottish extraction. Professor of Architecture at King's College, London. According to DNB, Donaldson was the nephew of the architect Thomas Leverton. Exhibited RA(27) including the Monument to the Duke of York (1831), a design for the Nelson

Monument (1840), Hallyburton House, Angus, the seat of Lord Douglas Hallyburton (1842) and three designs for the Prince Consort Memorial at the RSA 1864.
**Bibl:** DNB.

**DONALDSON, Virginia** **fl 1899**
Exhibited a landscape painting in oil at the RSA from 5 Crown Terrace, Glasgow.

**DONALDSON, William** **1882-c1945**
Edinburgh architectural sculptor. Worked from the Dean Studio after retiring as a teacher of modelling at Glasgow School of Art. Studied at Inverness, Glasgow and Edinburgh. Exhibited portrait busts and heads at the RSA in 1914-44, also GI(1) & L(1).

**DONALDSON, William H** **fl 1860-1878**
Edinburgh painter in oil and watercolour; landscape, fruit, flowers and dead birds. Exhibited RSA(17) & GI(4).

**DONATI, Colin** **1962-**
Born Dalbeattie, 27 Jan. Artist, writer and musician. Self-taught artist, he was brought up in rural surroundings in the south of Scotland and for a time in Morayshire. Graduated from Aberdeen University 1984. Now most active as an etcher, seeking a synthesis of poetry and artwork in the style of Chinese, medieval and Rennaisance 'notebooks'. Lives in Edinburgh. A poem he wrote in honour of the Forth Rail Bridge centenary received considerable acclaim. Exhibited RSA 1990.

**DONN, Robert** **fl 1902-1906**
Dundee artist who exhibited illustrative and biblical scenes at the RSA during the above years from 1 Westfield Lane, Dundee.

**DONNACHIE, J J** **20th Cent**
Sculptor. A bronze 'Natalie' is in the Lillie AG(Milngavie).

**DONNAN, Frank A** **20th Century**
Painter and sculptor. Exhibited landscapes and a wooden statuette at the GI from 66 Wallace Street, Grangemouth.

**DONNAN, Robert** **fl 1888-1951**
Painter, etcher, applied art designer and potter; landscapes and topographical subjects in Scotland, especially Iona, but mostly Cornwall. Studied South Kensington and l'Acadamie Delacluse, Paris, becoming Art Master at Allan Glen's School, Glasgow. Exhibited RSA 1909-51, GI(39) & L(1), living latterly at 14 Montrose Gardens, Milngavie. Represented in Lillie AG(Milngavie).

**DONNELLY, William A** **fl c1860-1870**
Watercolour painter of birds, land, seascapes and figurative works. Based for many years at Milton, Bowling, Dunbartonshire. Exhibited GI(9) including a painting of the 'Braemar Gathering' in 1870.

**DOON, J A** **fl 1890**
Glasgow artist; exhibited GI(2) from 27 Carnarvon Street.

**DORAN, Mrs** **fl 1881-1890**
Glasgow painter of still life. Exhibited GI(2) from 12 Windsor Terrace.

**DORAN, James** **fl 1971**
Glasgow sculptor. Exhibited 2 bronzes at the GI from 413 North Woodside Road.

**DORMAN, Miss Dorothy** **fl 1926-1927**
Ceramic designer and occasional watercolour painter of figure studies. A stoneware, crackle glazed jar won her the Lauder Award in 1934. This was thought to be a greater accomplishment technically than the painted china shown in the 1890s. Sister of Frances D(qv). Exhibited GI(3) from 13 Westcraigs, Dennistoun, Glasgow.

**DORMAN, Frances C** **fl 1926-1930**
Sculptress. Sister of Dorothy D(qv). Exhibited portrait busts at the RSA, also GI(3).

**DORNBERGER, C T Adam** **fl 1889**
Leith based painter. Exhibited RSA(1) from 30 North Fort Street.

**DORRAN, Godfrey S** **fl 1961-1980**
Glasgow watercolour painter and draughtsman in pen and ink of figurative compositions. Exhibited GI(9) from 137 Hyndland Road.

**DORRIAN, Patrick** **fl 1977-**
Glasgow painter of figure studies. Perhaps his best known work is 'Magician's Assistant'. Exhibited GI(23) 1977-1990 from 13 Huntly Gardens.

**DOTT, Mrs David** **fl 1894**
Musselburgh painter. Exhibited RSA(1) from Windsor Cottage.

**DOTT, Jean** **fl 1914-1918**
Edinburgh portrait and flower painter; exhibited RSA(3) from Hailes Brae, Colinton.

**DOTT, Miss Jessie W** **fl 1882-1918**
Edinburgh based painter in watercolour of still life, flowers and landscapes. Exhibited RSA(3) & SSA.

**DOTT, John L** **fl 1875-1887**
Edinburgh painter in watercolour; landscape and coastal scenes. Exhibited RSA(3).

**DOUGALL, Margaret S** **fl 1927-1931**
Glasgow sculptress. Exhibited mainly human figures at the GI(5) latterly from Queenswood, Hatfield, Herts.

**DOUGALL, Peter F** **fl 1869**
Edinburgh sculptor. Exhibited a portrait medallion at the RSA.

**DOUGLAS, Alexander Wallace Jnr** **1840-1914**
Born Perth, Mar 8; died Jan 14. Painter in oil and watercolour. Possibly related to the Douglas firm of painters and decorators of Charlotte Street, Perth. Exhibited 'Balvaird Castle' at the RSA from 40 Main Street, Bridgend. Represented in Perth AG by two oils and a watercolour.

**DOUGLAS, Andrew RSA** **1870-1935**
Born Midlothian, 7 Apr; died Edinburgh, 21 Feb. Painter in oil and watercolour of landscape and cattle. Attended a private school and later the old School of Art on the Mound. For further development he visited Belgium, Holland and France, before making an extensive tour of America. Began painting comparatively late, it was not until 1897 that he won his first award, a bronze medal at the Academy Life Class, and the Keith prize. His favourite painting grounds were in Perthshire and around East Linton although he also did important work in Berlin, Vienna & Munich. Principal works include 'Autumn Sunshine', 'Maternal Instinct', 'Ben Venue' and 'Loch Tay'. Elected ARSA 1920, RSA 1933. Exhibited RA(2), RSA(119), RSW(1), GI(78), AAS 1893-1933 & L(13), from 5 Picardy Place. Represented in Paisley AG, Brodie Castle (NTS).
**Bibl:** Caw 443.

**DOUGLAS, Miss Anna** **fl 1844-1850**
Edinburgh portrait and landscape painter in oil and watercolour. Exhibited three works at the RSA during the above years.

**DOUGLAS, Anna Dawson** **fl 1894-1910**
Fife landscape & miniature painter. Lived in Tayport. Married James D(qv). Exhibited RSA between the above years, latterly from 130 George Street, Edinburgh.

**DOUGLAS, Miss Archibald Ramsay** **1807-1886**
Born Edinburgh, 23 Apr; died Edinburgh, 25 Dec. Painter of portrait miniatures. Daughter of William D(qv). Lived at 13 Hart Street, Edinburgh where she died. Exhibited four works at the RA 1834-41, and RSA(9) 1835-1847.

**DOUGLAS, Arthur** **fl 1933**
Amateur Edinburgh painter. Exhibited AAS(1).

**DOUGLAS, Bessie** **fl 1901**
Glasgow flower painter. Exhibited GI(1) from Ashlea, Bellahouston.

**DOUGLAS, Campbell** **1828-1910**
Glasgow architect. Apprenticed to J T Rochead(qv) 1842-7. After a

spell in Newcastle returned to Glasgow 1856. Partnership with J J Stevenson(qv) 1860-9, specialising in churches. In the early 1870s Sellars joined them whereafter a large number of buildings were designed, including fifty-three churches. Assistants included William Leiper(qv), George Wahington Browne(qv), William Flockhart(qv), John Keppie(qv) and J M Brydon(qv). Because of the large number of partners and the length of his career it is difficult to assess his professional career. His last partner, A N Paterson(qv) considered that he had a share in most of the designs attributed to James Sellars(qv). Among the works most certainly attributed to him are Townhead parish church(1865), Cowcaddens church(1872), Citizens' Theatre (121-129 Gorbals St)(1878) and the Discharged Prisoners' Aid Society building at 28-32 Cathedral Square while in Edinburgh he designed North Leith Free Church (1858-9). A generous man with a most convivial nature. Exhibited GI(1) from 266 St Vincent Street.
**Bibl:** Gifford 453,633; A Gomme & D Walker, Architecture of Glasgow, London 1987(rev), 174,266,291.

**DOUGLAS, Caroline Lucy** **1784-1857**
Portrait painter in oil and watercolour. Second daughter of the 1st Baron Douglas of Douglas. In 1807 married Admiral Sir George Scott and the same year executed a self-portrait in watercolour, signed 'CLD'. Also painted a watercolour portrait of her brother 'George Douglas, RN' (1788-1838).

**DOUGLAS, Daniel** **fl 1884**
Glasgow landscape painter. Exhibited GI(1) from 135 Caledonian Road.

**DOUGLAS, Edwin James** **1848-1914**
Born Edinburgh, died London. After studying at the RSA school, and lived in Edinburgh until 1872, then went to London remaining there for the rest of his days. Painted sporting animal and genre subjects, somewhat in the style of Landseer whom he imitated. Although little inferior to Landseer in technique, he was far behind in inventive power, design and in what Caw described as 'humanising sympathy'. Works at the RSA included 'The Deer Path' (1866) described at the time as being nearly as good as James Giles(qv) and in some respects better. In 1875 illustrated *Poems and Songs of Robert Burns.* One of his best known works was a portrait of the Triple Crown winner of 1896, 'Persimmon', drawn in a stable interior. Exhibited RA(41) 1869-1900, RSA(40), GI(9) & ROI(14).
**Bibl:** AJ 1885, 193, 213; Caw 340; Clement & Hutton; Wingfield.

**DOUGLAS, Elizabeth** **fl 1980-**
Selkirk painter who exhibited at the RSA 1980-1986, figurative subjects in a semi-abstract manner.

**DOUGLAS, George** **fl 1887**
Edinburgh artist. Exhibited RSA(1) from 272 Causewayside.

**DOUGLAS, George Cameron** **fl 1908-1909**
Dundee artist. Exhibited LS(8) from 41 Reform Street.

**DOUGLAS, Georgina** **fl 1885**
Helensburgh painter; exhibited 'Autumn leaves' at the GI from Bellevue Bank.

**DOUGLAS, Gordon** **fl 1892-1893**
Aberdeen artist; exhibited RHA(3) & L(1) from 64 Dee Street. Curiously, he never exhibited with the AAS.

**DOUGLAS, Miss Helen** **fl 1982-1985**
Milngavie painter of flowers and still life. Exhibited GI(2) from 6 Breadie Drive.

**DOUGLAS, Isabel** **fl 1899-1902**
Lanarkshire portrait painter; exhibited GI(2) from Blair Villa, Lenzie.

**DOUGLAS, Isabella H L** **fl 1938-1939**
Stained glass window designer. Exhibited two designs at the RSA(2) from 53 Frederick Street, Edinburgh.

**DOUGLAS, J** **fl 1890**
Partick portrait painter; exhibited GI(1) from 105 Byres Road.

**DOUGLAS, James** **fl 1837-1843**
Edinburgh painter. Lived at Hill Square and exhibited a number of portraits and subject paintings at the RSA during the above years.

**DOUGLAS, James RSW** **1858-1911**
Born Dundee; died Liff, nr Dundee. Artist in oil, but more especially watercolour; landscape and interiors; occasional golfing subjects. Close friend of Thomas Marjoribanks Hay(qv), his watercolour style is fresh, although his palette brighter and more vibrant than Hay's. Between 1895 and 1897 lived and worked in Rothenburg, Germany, and from 1904 until 1908 exhibited at the Tayport Art Circle with his wife Anna(qv) and artistic associates Stewart Carmichael(qv), David Foggie(qv), Alex Grieve(qv), Frank Laing(qv), W B Lamond(qv) and C L Mitchell(qv). During the postcard boom many of his drawings were reproduced by 'Cynicus'(qv). Lived in various parts of Britain including Edinburgh, Applethwaite, Chilworth and London before settling at Spring Cottage, Tayport 1906. Elected RSW 1900 but struck off in 1907 as a result of mental illness which led to his confinement. Exhibited RA(5), RSA(76) 1881-1907, RSW(15), 3 English landscapes at the AAS 1906-1908, GI(5) & L(3). Represented in collection of the City of Edinburgh(5). [From notes provided by James Barnes.]
**Bibl:** Caw 303; Halsby 168,257; James Douglas RSW A Scottish Watercolourist, James S.W. Barnes, Perth Museum & Art Gallery 2002.

**DOUGLAS, James** **fl 1967**
Glasgow landscape painter in oil and watercolour. Exhibited GI(2) from 66 St Vincent Crescent.

**DOUGLAS, Miss Jean** **fl 1941-1943**
Edinburgh painter of topographical scenes and flower studies. Exhibited RSA(3) between the above years.

**DOUGLAS, John** **1867-1936**
Born Kilmarnock, 12 Dec; died Ayr, 27 Aug. Painter in oil and watercolour of landscape and genre. Son of a Kilmarnock tweed manufacturer and local magistrate. Educated Kilmarnock Academy. Entered the drapery trade and after a few years went to Edinburgh to join Jenners. Subsequently migrated to the United States where he remained for several years. On returning to Scotland he enrolled at the Glasgow School of Art becoming a close associate of several members of the Glasgow School, especially Sir John Lavery(qv), subsequently one of his closest friends. Member of the Kilmarnock Sketch Club and the Ayr Sketch Club of which he became President. One of his best known works 'The Irish Boat' is in Ayr Carnegie Library. Other principal works are 'The Mill', 'A View of Old Kilmarnock' and 'The Carriers'. Exhibited RSA, RSW(3), GI(12) & L(1).

**DOUGLAS, John Scott** **fl 1877**
Edinburgh watercolour painter of rustic scenes; exhibited RSA(1).

**DOUGLAS, Miss Margaret W** **fl 1875-1902**
Aberdeen painter in oil of landscape and local scenes and figures. Exhibited RSA(3), a contemporary townscape at the GI in 1880 from Aberdeen & AAS(2) 1902 from Tigh-na-bruich, Aberfeldy, Perthshire.

**DOUGLAS, Marguerite France (née Dommen)** **1918-?**
Born Switzerland, 12 Jly. Painter in oil and watercolour; also farmer. Daughter of a Swiss engineer. Educated at Cheltenham Ladies College before studying art at Derby under Ernest Townsend. Spent a year at the Ecole des Beaux Arts, Lausanne 1935 and 1936-39 studied at the RA schools under Walter Russell, Tom Monnington and Ernest Jackson. In 1959 became a corresponding member of the International Institute of Arts and Letters and in 1968 exhibited in Ancona, being awarded a diploma of merit. Illustrated a number of books. Signs her work 'MFD'. Came to live and work at Glenderg, Galashiels; active in the artistic life of the area. Frequently exhibited landscape and portraits with RSW & SSA under the name Douglas.

**DOUGLAS, Murray** **fl 1978**
Aberdeen printmaker of 27 Spa Street. Exhibited AAS(1).

**DOUGLAS, N** **fl 1820-1822**
Scottish engraver of topographical subjects. Engraved a plan of St Andrews in 1820 and one of Brechin in 1822.

**DOUGLAS, R** **fl 1937**
Glasgow stained-glass window designer. Exhibited a design for a memorial window at GI from 167 West Graham Street, Glasgow.

**DOUGLAS, Robert** **fl 1890**
Leith designer; exhibited a portrait medallion at the RSA in the above year.

**DOUGLAS, Robert Smeaton FSA** **fl 1900-d1912**
Died Ayr, 27 Nov. Painter of portraits, flower studies and landscapes, also sculptor and art teacher. Primarily remembered as an outstanding art master at Ayr Academy 1902-1912. Came to Ayr from St Andrews and lived at 37 Bellevue Crescent. His life was dedicated to teaching for which he had an outstanding aptitude. One of his pupils spoke of how his tone and method was 'free, human, unconventional'. Less a teacher than an educator, less interested in impressing himself upon his pupils than anxious to educate 'what by individual power and perception might be in the pupils themselves...spirits like his, informed with the sense of beauty, raised by a certain native dignity above the pursuit of position and self, are hard to find in a mercantile and material age' [Obit]. Exhibited RSA(8) & GI(5). Represented in Ayr AG.

**DOUGLAS, Miss S B** **fl 1900-1902**
Edinburgh artist. Exhibited 3 genre and pastoral scenes at the RSA from 22 Drummond Place,

**DOUGLAS, Sholto Johnstone** **1871-1958**
London based artist, son of a Lockerbie landowner, primarily a portrait painter. Studied at the Slade under Tonks and Steer and in Paris at the Academie Julian as well as in Antwerp. During WW1 he served as a war artist and 1926 settled in Southern France. Later works, often in watercolour, charcoal and pastel were mainly landscapes executed in a loose manner. Returned to Scotland 1939. Exhibited RA(13) from 1902 including a portrait of 'Sir Herbert Maxwell' and another of 'Mrs Russell, a New York snake charmer'. Exhibited RSA 1904-20, GI(3), AAS 1906, LS(2) & L(8).
**Bibl:** Caw 432.

**DOUGLAS, Thomas H** **fl 1875-1878**
Edinburgh landscape painter in oil and watercolour, also coastal scenes. Exhibited RSA(4), and Rosyth Castle at the GI.

**DOUGLAS, William** **fl 1935**
Exhibited a lithograph 'Pentland Landscape' at the RSA from 10 Polwarth Crescent, Edinburgh.

**DOUGLAS, William** **1780-1832**
Born Glenbervie, Kincardineshire, 14 Apr, died Edinburgh, 30 Jan. Landscape painter and portrait miniaturist; in later life excelled in animal miniatures. Descended from the Douglases of Glenbervie. Brought up in Edinburgh. Pupil of Robert Scott the engraver(qv). His first known work was a print of 'John Hully' who rescued the crew of the wreck *Janet of Macduff* off St Andrews - although awkwardly drawn, it was subsequently engraved by Robert Scott. Executed paintings and drawings on commission for the 9th Earl of Dalhousie, mostly full-length drawings with heads finished in watercolour or crayon. In 1808-9 exhibited in Edinburgh where he worked and contributed to all but the last of the exhibitions of the Society of Associated Artists, mostly with miniatures and full-length drawings of sitters and their favourite dogs or horses; also exhibited several purely animal studies. Showed a few landscapes and often has detailed landscape used as background to portraits, sometimes incorporating a view associated with the sitter. Thus 'Admiral Robert Wauchope of Niddrie as a boy holding a golf club', dated 1808, has Arthur's Seat in the background. This watercolour sold for £65,520 in Jan 2004. Appointed Miniature Painter in Scotland to HRH Prince Leopold of Saxe-Coburg 1817. The Prince had a miniature of 'Princess Charlotte Augusta', only child of George IV. Douglas then visited London undertaking several commissions for William Balliol Best of Chilston Park, Kent. He returned to Edinburgh, but continued to exhibit at the RA 1818-1826. His main clientele consisted of the Edinburgh middle classes and some Lowland and south Highland aristocratic families, including the McLeans and McLeods. In 1822 he painted a miniature of Sir Walter Scott's son Walter. Commissioned to paint copies of 'Napoleon' (1823, after Isabey) and a miniature of 'Mary Queen of Scots' (probably a copy of a 19th century engraving). Father and teacher of Miss Archibald Ramsay D(qv). [After notes by Miss Mary Middleton]. Exhibited RSA 1808-9. A miniature of Mary, Dowager Lady Molesworth, painted on ivory (1809) was in the South Kensington Exhibition 1865. Schidlof quotes two miniatures sold in Amsterdam in 1924. Represented by 2 miniatures in NGS, SNPG, Glasgow AG, BM (engraved portrait of the Rev H Gray).
**Bibl:** Brydall 204,245; Caw 22; DNB; Foskett 250; Graves RA; Halsby 257; Irwin 80,216(illus); Long 130; RD.

**DOUGLAS, Sir William Fettes PRSA** **1822-1891**
Born Edinburgh; died Newburgh, Fife. His mother was the grand-niece of Sir William Fettes, founder of Fettes College. From Royal HS, Edinburgh he entered the Commercial Bank, working for ten years as a bank clerk. Mainly self-taught, his earliest works were mostly portraits which he soon abandoned in favour of genre subjects. After visiting Italy in 1857, became a keen antiquarian and collector of books, coins, medals, antiquities, ivories and enamels, used as accessories in his pictures. His first watercolours date from late 1870s after ill health prevented him from working on larger oils. When visiting Belgium and the Low Countries in 1878 he was influenced by the Dutch school. This can be seen in in his delicate watercolour landscapes with subtle greens and blues under dark, pearly skies. Most enjoyed painting interiors of studies with antiquarians pouring over books, manuscripts and similar objects. The detail and quality of his still life painting has often been compared to the pre-Raphaelites, but being more interested in accessories, his figures are often rather weak and lifeless. Original member of the Edinburgh group The Smashers(qv). Although remaining a member of the re-constituted Auld Lang Syne Group(qv) in London he was never much attracted to the city being a typical product of the Scottish capital. Visits to Italy broadened his perspective so that in the paintings of the 1870s there is a more visual approach with less stress on content. 'His technique differs from that of his Scottish contemporaries as his temperament and conceptions differ. There is a minimum of that play of the brush and of the varying consistencies of paint in which they mostly delight...yet it has all the native deftness and dress; no Fleming or Dutchman had a hand more agile...and few had a keener conception of certain aspects, or could render them with such unerring precision in the physiognomy of conspirator, astrologer, or fanatic'[McKay]. Influenced by Duncan(qv) and Maudeis, although when he painted domestic life Douglas deals mostly with its lighter side, his deeply moving 'When the Sea Gives Up its Dead' (1873) being an exception. Landscape became a later interest although briefly attempted during his stay at Prestonpans in 1860 but it was not until the exhibitions of 1875-6 that scenic subjects became important to him. 'Stonehaven from the Bervie Braes' and 'Early Morning - Herring Boats Entering Stonehaven' are typical of his work at this time. It was in his watercolours that his landscape showed to best advantage. Monteith, Lochmaben and East Neuk were favourite places. Said never to have copied a painting in his life, he was a thinking and painstaking artist. Elected ARSA 1851, RSA 1854, knighted 1882. Curator of the NGS 1877-82, but resigned in order to succeed Sir Daniel MacNee(qv) as President of the RSA 1882-91. Exhibited nine works at the RA 1862-75 and 260 works at the RSA, also occasionally at the RSW, GI(10) & AAS intermittently 1885-1894. Represented in NGS(19), SNPG(4), V & A, Aberdeen AG, Dundee AG, Glasgow AG, Perth AG.
**Bibl:** AJ 1892, 288; 1868, 137-9; Armstrong 82; Caw 172-4; DNB; John Gray, Sir William Fettes Douglas, 1885; Halsby 127 et al; Hardie III 189-90; Irwin 305-7(illus); Macmillan [SA], 187,215-6,234; McKay, 334-340.

**DOUGLAS-IRVINE, Miss Lucy Christina** **1874-?**
Born Viginia Water, Surrey, 20 Apr. Painter mostly in watercolour of cattle and barn interiors, also pencil studies. Studied art at Clifton, Glasgow School of Art and the Kemp-Welch School of Painting. Lived at Pittenweem. Exhibited widely including RSA(1), RSW(3), RHA(2), RCA(2) & L(1).

**DOUTHWAITE, Patricia** **1939-2002**
Born Glasgow July 28; died Dundee, July 26. Painter in oil and watercolour of figurative and allegorical subjects, and dramatic art. No formal training. Educated at Kilmacolm, Renfrew. Between 1952 and 1955 studied mime and dance with Margaret Morris(qv) whose husband, J D Fergusson(qv), encouraged Douthwaite to paint. In 1954 she embarked on a dancing tour through America and two years later joined the Gate Theatre, Dublin. Painted throughout these years, her first solo show being held in Edinburgh 1958. In 1959 went to

live in Sussex devoting herself to full-time painting. She experimented with a variety of mediums, but it was the idiomatic primitivism of Jean Dubuffet that appealed most. She became pre-occupied with the human predicament as personally manifested by her insecurity and the professional rivalries which haunted her. In 1960 she married Paul Hogarth but after ten years the marriage broke up. From that time, until her health deteriorated, Douthwaite led a restless nomadic life. In Edinburgh she was seriously assaulted, leaving a permanent mental scar which increased further her social and psychological alienation. Notwithstanding her depression and financial impoverishment, she embarked on journeys alone to North Africa, India and Peru until ill-health made further travel impossible. Her final move was to Dundee where she found work with a printmaker. Worked in isolation from 1960 and in 1963 visited Majorca. She was married to the illustrator, Robert Graves. Has been called the 'High Priestess of the Grotesque in British Art'. Executed a collection of drawings entitled 'Alphabet Book of Greek Goddesses'. Interested in dance and drama. Worked extensively on series of paintings, such as those based on the aviator 'Amy Johnson' and the painter 'Gwen John'. 'The tortured, twisted figures recall the works of Egon Schiele and evoke a similar sense of anguish and neurosis'. Represented in SNGMA, Edinburgh City collection, SAC.
**Bibl:** Gage 59-60; Hartley 129; TEC, Glasgow, 'Pat Douthwaite' (Ex Cat 1988); Obit, *The Times* 1 Aug 02.

**DOW, Alexander Warren RBA** **1873-1948**
Of Scottish descent. Painter of landscape and still life, etcher and art critic. Studied under Norman Garstin, Frank Brangwyn, also at Heatherley's and in France. Resident in London. Elected RBA 1919. Exhibited RA(2), RSA in 1922 and again 1946, RBA(181), RHA(4), RI(4), ROI(8), LS(9) & L(20).

**DOW, Catherine M** **fl 1965**
Amateur Carnoustie painter. Exhibited a still life at the AAS from 38 High Street.

**DOW, David Simpson** **fl 1880-1905**
Painter in oil and watercolour of local landscapes. Lived in Perth 1880, moving to Edinburgh c1898. Exhibited RSA(16).

**DOW, George** **fl 1976-1981**
Aberdeenshire painter of figurative compositions. Exhibited a number of times at the AAS from 13 Cairnvale Crescent, Kincorth.

**DOW, James William** **fl 1877-1885**
Edinburgh painter in oil and watercolour of landscapes. Exhibited RSA(9) from 10 Claremont Place, Edinburgh.

**DOW, Mary A** **fl 1885-1892**
Amateur watercolour painter of Glasgow and Moffat; mostly landscape, also flowers. Exhibited RSA(1) from Beech Grove, Moffat, & GI(9), mostly from Glasgow.

**DOW, Thomas Millie RSW** **1848-1919**
Born Dysart, Fife; died St Ives, Cornwall. Painter in oil and watercolour; historical and classical subjects, also landscape. Son of a Town Clerk. Began to study law in Edinburgh but abandoned this in order to study in Paris at the Ecole des Beaux-Arts under Jerome and at the Atelier of Carolus Duran. Returned to Fife where he continued working for some years before settling in Glasgow 1890. In 1880, after returning from France, began to exhibit regularly at the GI. Landscapes such as 'Hudson River', 'Spring in Morocco' and 'Valley of the Appenines' as well as flower pieces in oil and watercolour with their tonal richness and decorative qualities staked his claim as a member of the new movement becoming known as the Glasgow Boys. In about 1890 he undertook a considerable body of work in pastel creating the same effects as with oil rather than as a medium in its own right. Moved to St Ives, Cornwall in 1896. An enthusiastic traveller, he spent winters in Canada, Italy and Tangiers, always painting landscapes and an occasional portrait. In 1893 he turned to romantic allegorical subjects similar in conception to those of his friend William Scott of Oldham, whose work was seen in Glasgow 1883 and in Edinburgh 1886 and whose portrait of Millie Dow is now in the NGS. 'Dow's execution in figurative subjects as in landscape, remains refined and delicate with great sensitivity to decorative possibilities, appropriateness of colour and to the total variations within one or a very small range of colours' [Sara Henderson]. Writing in *The Studio,* Gastin (quoted by Halsby) said of Dow's watercolours 'He is not occupied by the topographical facts of landscape, except for his own purposes of design, but each picture portrays some exquisitely seen scheme of colour and effect, some opalescent morning, some evening of amber and gold, some twilight of shimmering blues and violets.' Elected RSW 1885. Exhibited RSA(28), RSW(24), ROI(4), RBA(4), GI(45), AAS 1885-1900, & L(17). Represented in Glasgow AG, Kirkcaldy AG, Edinburgh City collection, Liverpool AG, Leeds AG, Manchester AG.
**Bibl:** Caw 408-410; Garstin: The Work of T Millie Dow; Halsby 152-3; Hardie 91-3; Macmillan [SA], 259; SAC, The Glasgow Boys, 17 et passim; 'Studio' Vol 10, 1897, 145-52.

**DOWDEN, Miss Anna** **fl 1908-1911**
Edinburgh painter. Exhibited RSA(1) & RHA(1) from 13 Learmonth Terrace.

**DOWELL, Charles R RSW** **-d1935**
Born Glasgow. Painter of portraits and interiors in oil and watercolour, especially the latter. Studied at Glasgow School of Art under Fra Newbery(qv). Won a travelling scholarship to Rome. After his return he devoted himself to painting seascapes in oil and watercolour, also portraiture, landscapes, interiors, still life and silhouettes. Often portrayed the east coast of Scotland around Pittenweem, St Monance and the Firth of Forth, generally done in bright, sparkling colours. Vice-President, Glasgow Art Club. Elected RSW 1933. Exhibited RSW(21), RSA(14), GI(76), a harbour scene at the AAS in 1921 & L(2). Represented in Glasgow AG.
**Bibl:** Halsby 229-257.

**DOWER, Miss Siobhan** **fl 1984**
Amateur East Kilbride artist. Exhibited a figure study at the GI from 4 Livingstone Drive.

**DOWIE, A L** **fl 1858-1869**
Glasgow landscape painter specialising in Clyde views. Exhibited RSA(5) and 'Moonlight' at the GI from 19 Abbotsford Place.

**DOWNIE, Helen (née Cochran)** **fl 1895-1897**
Flower painter who lived in Paisley. Married Patrick D(qv). Exhibited RSA(1), GI(5), AAS(2) & L(1) from Ladyburn Villa.

**DOWNIE, Mrs Isobel** **fl 1976-1986**
Dumbarton sculptress in bronze and plaster. Exhibited GI(10) from 4 Hillside Road, Cardross.

**DOWNIE, John Patrick RSW** **1871-1945**
Born Glasgow; died Edinburgh, 4 Apr. Portrait, genre and landscape painter in oil and watercolour, especially the latter. Studied at the Slade School under Legros 1889 and in Paris. Spent some time painting in Holland, principally at Laren, where Mauve was working, with the result that Downie paid more attention to tone than to colour. Influenced by the Hague School. Exhibited mainly in Scotland but also at the principal London Galleries and on the Continent. Elected RSW 1903. Exhibited RSA(24), RSW(51), RWS(2), GI(118), L(14) & AAS 1906-1931. Represented in Paisley AG, Hamilton Museum. Not to be confused with Patrick Downie(qv).
**Bibl:** Caw 428; Halsby 257.

**DOWNIE, Kate** **1958-**
Born N. Carolina. Trained extensively abroad and at Gray's School of Art, Aberdeen. Awarded SAC Residency in Amsterdam 1983-4. Settled in Edinburgh, with a spell in Paris 1988-9. Specialises in highly expressive depictions of human life in the big cities 'echoing the dynamism of film and photography'. Exhibited RSA 1980-83 & AAS.

**DOWNIE, Miss Margaret** **fl 1872**
Amateur Glasgow oil painter of landscape; exhibited RSA(1) & GI(1) from 13 Clarendon Place, New City Road.

**DOWNIE, Patrick RSW** **1854-1945**
Born Greenock; died 16 May. Landscape painter in oil and watercolour. In early life he had been a postman but turned to art. Although mainly self-taught, studied for a short time in Paris. Married

Helen D(qv). Began exhibiting 1885. Painted widely around Glasgow, particularly views of the Clyde and in the vicinity of Gourock. His strength was in capturing the corruscations of light on water, often with the peaks of Arran beyond. Like his contemporary James Kay(qv), he was knowledgeable about the many types of craft then to be seen on the Clyde so that his watercolours are accurate in detail, redolent of the white horses of the western Atlantic. Lived in Greenock, Paisley, Skelmorlie and Glasgow. Won gold medal at the Paris Salon in 1901. Exhibited RA(16), RSA(54), RSW(126), RI(4), GI(133) & AAS. Represented in Glasgow AG, Paisley AG(10).
**Bibl:** Caw 334; Halsby 160,257.

**DOWSE, Frederick W H** **fl 1872-1880**
Edinburgh painter in oil and watercolour of landscape, especially local scenes; exhibited RSA(6).

**DOYLE, Charles Altamont** **1832-1893**
Born London; died Dumfries, 10 Oct. Painter in watercolour of fantasies, literary subjects, sporting subjects and humorous sketches; illustrator. Fourth son of the caricaturist, John Doyle (1797-1868), brother of Richard Doyle, and father of Sir Arthur Conan Doyle. An adopted Scot, he is the only member of the family to justify inclusion. From early childhood he showed a talent for drawing which was encouraged by his father. In 1849 became assistant to the surveyor in the Scottish Ofice of Works in Edinburgh. Between 1849 and 1876, in collaboration with Robert Matheson(qv), he designed many public monuments in the capital. In his leisure hours he painted many strange fantasies with elves, horses and figures. Encouraged by his brother and the need to provide for an expanding family, following his marriage in 1855 to his landlady's daughter Mary Foley, and the subsequent arrival of ten children, he illustrated Bunyan's *Pilgrim's Progress* and produced many illustrations for *London Society* (1862-64) and *The Graphic* as well as other humorous books, including 60 illustrations for Jean Jambon: *Our Trip to Blunderland* 1877. From 1883 he lived nr Montrose but turned increasingly to alcohol and was eventually committed to the Montrose Royal Lunatic Asylum where epilepsy was diagnosed. Whilst in the Asylum he continued to work but most of this was inward-looking and brooding. In his autobiography Conan Doyle laments 'my father's life was full of tragedy, of unfulfilled powers and undeveloped gifts'. Exhibited light hearted, competently drawn, humourous sketches at the RSA 1875-1887 from 23 George Square. One of his humorous watercolours 'Curling Match on Duddingston Loch' is in Edinburgh City collection and 'Bank Holiday' is in the National Gallery of Ireland.
**Bibl:** Halsby 257; Houfe; Maas, 155; Univ Cat of Books on Art (Vam 1870), 1, 189 (under Bunyan); Wingfield.

**DOYLE, Christine** **1951-fl 1977**
Renfrewshire painter of still life often with small animals. Exhibited RSA(2) & GI(9) from 25 Hawthorn Avenue, Johnstone. Represented in Glasgow AG.

**DRANSART, Penelope** **fl 1978**
Amateur Aberdeen artist. Exhibited an exotic landscape at the AAS from 16 Fountainhall Road.

**DRAPER, Ralph** **fl 1940**
Amateur painter. Exhibited RSA(1) and a seascape at the GI from 17 Maxwell Avenue, Garrowhill, Ballieston, Edinburgh.

**DRAPER, Simon** **fl 1983**
Sculptor. Exhibited a semi-abstract work at the AAS from the Sculpture Workshops, Lumsden, Aberdeenshire.

**DREGHORN, Allan** **1706-1764**
Glasgow architect and merchant. Worked with **James CRAIG** on the Town Hall, Trongate, Glasgow(1737). Much influenced by James Gibbs(qv), as can be seen in his St Andrew Church, Glasgow (c1760). Its portico and elegant steeple, and the rusticated window-architraves, have been likened to St Martin-in-the-Fields in London. Baillie of Glasgow 1741. The first Glaswegian to maintain a four-wheeled carriage.
**Bibl:** Dunbar 111; A Gomme & D Walker, Architecture of Glasgow, London 1987(rev), 52-3,57,60,291.

**DRENNAN, Jean C (Mrs Jean Harkness)** **1938-1998**
Watercolour painter. Mother of the watercolourist **Lorna Claire HARKNESS**. Secretary, Perthshire Art Association. Exhibited two works at the RSA, 'Autumn Trees at Barskimming' (1964) and 'Broken Dyke' (1965), both from 21 Gray Street, Prestwick, Ayrshire. Died Dundee.

**DRENNAN, Miss Rosalind** **fl 1973-1980**
Glasgow painter of semi-abstracts. Exhibited GI(4) from 12 Colchester Drive.

**DREW, Miss J** **fl 1889-1891**
Glasgow painter of still life generally with flowers. Exhibited GI(3) from 4 Crown Circus.

**DREW, Mrs Nell** **fl 1912**
Exhibited a banner for the General Assembly Hall - 'The Royal Arms'. This seems to have been commissioned by HM Office of Works to whom it was loaned for the exhibition. Lives at 32 Comely Bank, Edinburgh.

**DRON, James A** **fl 1892-1929**
Glasgow painter of portraits and local landscapes also engraver. Exhibited mainly GI(16), also RSA(1) & RSW(1).

**DRUMMOND, Mrs A** **fl 1886-1900**
Painter. Exhibited RSA(1) and elsewhere in the Provinces, latterly living in Edinburgh.

**DRUMMOND, Christine J** **fl 1982-1983**
Painter of large, colourful abstracts. Trained at Gray's School of Art. Exhibited AAS(3) from 12 Manor Place, Cults.

**DRUMMOND, David** **fl 1911**
Amateur artist. Exhibited LS(2) from Drymen, Stirlingshire.

**DRUMMOND, Miss Eliza Anne** **fl 1820-1843**
Born London of Scottish descent. Daughter of Samuel D(qv). Four sisters were also portrait miniaturists(qv). Won a premium at the Society of Arts 1822 and again in 1823. A pastel of 'Charles John Kean' is in the NPG. Exhibited 11 works at the RA between 1820 and 1837.

**DRUMMOND, Miss Ellen (? F)** **fl 1836-1860**
Miniature portrait painter. Daughter of Samuel D(qv). Exhibited 16 works at the RA (1838-1860) latterly from 5 Clarendon Place. In 1847 there was a portrait exhibited at the RSA by a Miss Drummond.

**DRUMMOND, Helen** **fl 1887-1894**
Aberdeen landscape painter. Exhibited local scenes at the AAS(2) from 359 Great Western Road.

**DRUMMOND, Ian** **fl 1959**
Amateur Dundee flower painter. Exhibited GI(1) from 8 Haldane Avenue.

**DRUMMOND, James RSA** **1816-1877**
Born Edinburgh (in John Knox's House); died Edinburgh, 13 Aug. History painter, especially of Edinburgh. Son of an Edinburgh merchant, he was born and lived in John Knox's house in the Canongate. Studied at the Trustees Academy under Sir William Allan(qv) and from an early age became steeped in Scottish archaeology and history. Began as a book illustrator for Captain Brown whilst still a student. After qualifying, he taught drawing. His great knowledge of Scottish arms, costume and customs enabled him to make his pictures extremely accurate, although he lacked the ability to breathe dramatic life into figures and groups. Nevertheless, his work often showed bustling vitality and draughtsmanship of high quality, of which 'Porteous Mob 'in the NGS is a prime example. His first RSA exhibit was 'Waiting for an Answer' (1835). Only once did he exhibit a portrait at the RSA. A series of 95 drawings in the SNPG of localities and buildings that have now gone are of great interest. Represented in the International Exhibition in London 1862 and in 1850 his two companion works 'Peace' and 'War' were purchased by Prince Albert. Appointed Librarian of the RSA 1857 and Curator of the NGS 1868-77. Member of the Society of Antiquaries in Edinburgh. His privately printed *Medieval Triumphs and Processions* was illustrated by himself. He was also the author of two classic works, *Ancient Scottish Weapons* (1881) and *Sculptured Monuments in Iona*

*and the West Highlands* (1881), either of which would have alone accorded him a place in Scottish history. A folio volume of his illustrations was published as *Old Edinburgh.* Also contributed a sketch of the interior of St. Giles Cathedral for Sir Daniel Wilson's *Memorials of Edinburgh in the olden time.* His diploma painting for the RSA (1852) shows 'James I of Scotland while a prisoner'. Elected ARSA 1845, RSA 1852. Exhibited five works at the RA (1847-1865), the last of them an important portrait 'Graham of Claverhouse and the Duke of Gordon'. Exhibited 126 works at the RSA (1835-1877) with six works exhibited posthumously in 1880 and 1887 and at the GI(8) from 30 Hamilton Place. Represented in NGS(4), SNPG, V & A, Glasgow AG, City of Edinburgh collection(5), Blackburn AG, Huntly House, Edinburgh, Royal Collection.
**Bibl:** AJ 1877, 336 (obit); Armstrong 63; Brydall 391-3; Butchart 74; Caw 118-9; Elizabeth Cumming, James Drummond RSA: Victorian Antiquary and Artist of old Edinburgh, Cannongate, Tolbooth Museum, Edinburgh 1977; DNB; Gifford 183,316,577; Halsby 72,89-90,257; Hardie 41-5,55,57; Irwin 304; Macmillan [SA], 187,191-2,212-13, 231-2; McKay 396-6; 'Sculptured Monuments in Iona and the West Highlands', Archaeologica Scotia, supplementary vol, Edinburgh 1881.

**DRUMMOND, Miss Jane** **fl 1819-1833**
Born London of Scottish descent. Portrait miniature painter. Daughter of Samuel D(qv). Her first exhibit at the RSA was 'Portrait of a Highlander' (1819). The Society of Arts awarded her a silver medal for a fixed crayon portrait in 1821 and a silver Isis medal 1826. Foskett regards her as an artist 'of only average ability.' Like her sisters Eliza Anne(qv), Rose Emma(qv), Rose Myra(qv) and Eliza Ellen(qv), she favoured painting portraits of members of the theatrical profession. Altogether exhibited 14 works at the RA (1819-33), the last of which was a portrait of 'Kasiprasadh Ghosh', the celebrated Hindu poet, painted at 6 Wellesley Place, Calcutta.
**Bibl:** Foskett; Long.

**DRUMMOND, Jean** **fl 1943**
Glasgow textile designer. Exhibited GI from 164 Arisaig Drive.

**DRUMMOND, John of Auchterarder** **fl 1529**
Wood carver. Sometime Master of the King's Works. Responsible for the fine carved roof of the presence chamber at Stirling Castle, executed with the assistance of Andrew Wood. Brydall recorded in 1889 that 38 of these panels of heads and figures were at that time still preserved.
**Bibl:** Armstrong 3; Brydall 50.

**DRUMMOND, John Henry** **1802-1889**
Born Edinburgh. Eldest son of Admiral Sir Adam D of Megginch and Lady Charlotte Murray. Professional soldier, amateur painter; watercolours more skilled than his oils. Landscape and occasional country sporting subjects. Studied for a time under Alexander Nasmyth. Entered Sandhurst 1818. Commissioned by Queen Victoria but did not exhibit in any major public gallery.
**Bibl:** Wingfield (where referred to as John Murray Drummond).

**DRUMMOND, Joyce** **fl 1958**
Glasgow painter. Exhibited a work entitled 'Hobby Horses' at the GI from 254 Corsaig Drive.

**DRUMMOND, Miss Linda** **fl 1971**
Textile designer. Exhibited 2 designs from Glasgow School of Art at the GI.

**DRUMMOND, Miss Rose Emma** **fl 1815-1835**
Born in London of Scottish extraction. Daughter of Samuel D(qv). Her three sisters were also portrait painters. In 1823 she was awarded a silver medal by the Society of Arts for an historical composition. Exhibited 18 works at the RA during the above years.

**DRUMMOND, Miss Rose Myra** **fl 1833-1849**
Born in London of Scottish descent. Daughter of Samuel D(qv) and sister of the Misses Jane(qv), Eliza Anne(qv), E Ellen(qv) and Rose Emma D(qv). Her principal work was a portrait of 'Charles Kean in the character of Hamlet' (1838). Also painted portraits of normal size and exhibited under the Christian name 'Myra'. Exhibited nine works at the RA between 1833 and 1849, most of them, like her sisters, members of the theatrical profession.

**DRUMMOND, Samuel ARA** **1765-1844**
Born London, 25 Dec; died London, 6 Aug. Scottish descent. Portrait and miniature painter in oil and crayon, also historical subjects and a lithographer. Son of a partisan of Bonnie Prince Charlie. Ran away to sea but later devoted himself to art. Elected ARA 1808. Exhibited almost annually a total of no fewer than 306 works at the RA, 1791-1844. A miniature portrait of 'Elizabeth Fry' is in the NPG, who also have oil portraits by him. There is a portrait of 'Gen Sir David Dundas' (1735-1820) in the SNPG. Engravings after some of his works are in the BM.

**DRUMMOND, Sarah-Jane** **1989-**
Glasgow painter of coastal and shore scenes in an impressionistic style. Exhibited RSA 1989 from 3 Alfred Terrace, Hillhead.

**DRYBURGH, Dorothy** **fl 1910**
Amateur Edinburgh artist; exhibited AAS(1).

**DRYSDALE, Miss Mary** **1912-**
Architect and watercolour painter. Trained Edinburgh College of Art and exhibited two Italian scenes at the RSA in 1932 from Heathersett, Crieff, Perthshire.

**DRYSTER, Will** **fl 1919-1921**
Aberdeen painter and jewellery designer. Trained at Gray's School of Art. Exhibited AAS(4) from 101 Holburn Street.

**DUCE, George Raymond** **fl 1937-1948**
Hamilton sculptor and draughtsman. Trained Edinburgh College of Art. Exhibited portrait busts at the RSA during the above years from 226 Ferry Road, Edinburgh.

**DUCKWORTH, Christopher** **fl 1883**
Edinburgh artist. Exhibited an oil painting of a hunting scene at the RSA from 3 Summer Place, Inverleith Row.

**DUDGEON, Thomas** **fl 1831-1878**
Edinburgh artist of genre and topographical subjects. Exhibited RSA 1831 and 1833. 'The Clyde from Denottar Hill' is in Glasgow AG.
**Bibl:** Halsby 257.

**DUESBURY, Lillie** **fl 1895-1896**
Paianter. Exhibited RSA(1) & RBA(2) from Inverkeithing, having moved there from Hull in 1895.

**DUFF, Allan** **fl 1970**
Glasgow sculptor. Exhibited a ciment fondu portrait of a head at the GI from 65 Gardiner Street.

**DUFF, Allan G** **fl 1952**
Wigtownshire portrait painter. Exhibited 2 works at the GI, one a self-portrait, from East Challoch, Dunragit.

**DUFF, Dorothy A** **fl 1908-1912**
London based artist with Aberdeenshire connections. Exhibited AAS during the above years.

**DUFF, George** **1888-**
Born Glasgow. Portrait and subject painter in oil and watercolour. Exhibited RSA(6), RSW(1), GI(2), & L(1) from 1381 Argyle Street, Glasgow.

**DUFF, George Henry Grant** **fl 1921-1923**
Turriff artist of figurative subjects and landscape. Exhibited twice at the AAS, one in collaboration with his wife Rachel(qv), the other entitled 'The Black Rabbit', from Dalgety Castle, Turriff, Aberdeenshire.

**DUFF, Miss Heather** **fl 1900-1937**
Landscape painter who divided her time between 11 Eaton Place, London SW and Fetteresso Castle, Kincardineshire. Exhibited regularly during the above years at the AAS.

**DUFF, Miss Helen A Gordon** **fl 1935-1937**
Keith painter who exhibited local scenes at the AAS from Davietown.

**DUFF, Major Hugh Robert** **1771-1832**
Architect. Designed and owned Muirtown House, Charleston Pl, Inverness. "Unique in combining quite so many styles, Palladian, neo-Greek, castellated and Gothick in one not very large house." (Gifford). Gifford quotes Joseph Mitchell "[Duff] was an able man but somewhat eccentric. He had been one of Bonaparte's *detenus*, and was confined in a church in France for six months, which he gave as an excuse for not afterwards attending divine service at home. He occupied his time in building his houses and laying out the plantations around it."
**Bibl:** Gifford, H & I, 52,204,pl 86.

**DUFF, Mrs J Helen** **fl 1965**
Aberdeen textile designer. Exhibited AAS(1) from 42 Westholme Avenue.

**DUFF, John Robert Keitley RI RE** **1862-1938**
Died London, 26 Sep. Scottish painter and etcher; also lawyer. Landscape and game in oil, watercolour and pastel. Lived all his life in England. Educated Bishop's Stortford and Sidney Sussex College, Cambridge, where he took a law degree. Studied art at Westminster School under Fred Bram and at the Slack School under Legros. Elected RI 1913, ARE 1914, RE 1919. Author of *Pastel. A Manual for Beginners*. His work shows an affinity with the Dutch School in tone, colour and treatment. Exhibited RA(24), RE(61), RI(113), GI(2) & L(2), mostly from Sunningfield, Hendon, Middlesex.
**Bibl:** Caw 443; DBA; Waters.

**DUFF, Miss Maria Garden** **fl 1900s**
Exhibited 3 continental townscapes at the AAS c1900 from Clifton Cottage and later Fair Lawn, Banchory.

**DUFF, Mrs Rachel Ainslie Grant** **fl 1919-1933**
Aberdeenshire portrait painter, also occasional landscapes. Exhibited AAS(4), one a portrait of Mrs Ainslie of Dalgety and another in collaboration with her husband(qv), all from Dalgety Castle, Turriff.

**DUFFES, Honor (Mrs Arthur P)** **fl 1915-1920**
Edinburgh painter in oil and watercolour. Exhibited RSA(3), GI(2) & L(2) from 24 Queen Street.

**DUFFIN, Stuart R ARSA RE** **1959-**
Glasgow printmaker and engraver. Lived, educated and worked in Glasgow 1963-78, before studying at Gray's School of Art, Aberdeen 1978-82. Currently a member of staff at Glasgow Print Studios, working primarily in etching and mixed media. The main influences on his work have been Byzantine, medieval and renaissance art and architecture. Gained 1st prize, irish Miniature Print Exhibition 1986, SAC travel award 1987. Elected ARE 1991, ARSA 1996. Exhibits regularly at the RSA since 1982 as well as abroad, also GI 1985, from 103 Woodford Street, Glasgow and latterly from 40 Cromarty Ave.

**DUFFUS, Kenneth Thomson** **fl 1976**
Amateur Aberdeen still life painter. Exhibited AAS(1) from 7 Northfield Place.

**DUFFY, Daniel J** **1878-c1945**
Landscape, portrait and still life painter in oil. Studied Glasgow School of Art and in Italy. Lived in Glasgow and Coatbridge and exhibited RA(5), RSA(5), RHA(2), GI(40), ROI(8) & L(4), latterly from Dunbeth Lodge, Coatbridge.

**DUFFY, Ken** **1946-**
Printmaker and teacher. Trained Edinburgh College of Art 1964-8. An SAC scholarship enabled him to study lithography at the Tamarind Institute, New Mexico. Director, Printmakers Workshop, Edinburgh 1969-87.

**DUFTY, Miss L M** **fl 1943-1946**
Paisley artist in watercolour and crayon. Literary and figure subjects. Exhibited GI(2) from Meersbrook, Meikleriggs.

**DUGAN, Henry C** **fl 1910-1929**
Aberdeen painter of mountain scenery, especially the Cairngorms. Exhibited regularly at the AAS during the above years from 38 Whitehall Road and 5 Argyll Crescent.

**DUGMORE, John R** **fl 1946-1972**
Painter of landscapes (mostly local scenes), rustic scenes and portraits. First exhibited a watercolour at the RSA in 1936 whilst still serving in the army. After WW2 retired to live at Dalbeattie and painted in oil and watercolour. Influenced by John Maxwell(qv). Held his first-one man exhibition at the Gracefield Gallery, Dumfries. Also painted rustic scenes and several miniatures. Held a one-man exhibition in Mombasa, Kenya and illustrated a number of works including *The Game Birds of East Africa* and *Shotgun and Sunlight*. Also an etcher, an exhibition of his dry points of African birds and animals was held at the Greatorex Gallery. Exhibited a number of portraits at the RSA and one at the RA.

**DUGUID, Andrew** **fl 1858**
Amateur painter. Exhibited an oil painting of buildings at the RSA in the above year.

**DUGUID, Miss E F M** **fl 1906-1931**
Aberdeenshire artist of local landscape. Sister of Dora D(qv). Exhibited regularly at the AAS during the above years from the same addresses as her sister.

**DUGUID, Gladys D (Mrs Innes Thomson)** **fl 1944**
Painter in oil, exhibited a landscape of Arran at the RSA from a West Linton address.

**DUGUID, Henry G** **fl 1828-1860**
Edinburgh painter in oil and watercolour; buildings and landscape. In 1851 he prepared two sepia aquatints of Edinburgh city which, seen together, present a panoramic view from the Calton Hill. In the same year he sketched 'Edinburgh from the Braid Hills'. This was engraved by Christian Rosenberg. This scarce print shows Donaldson's Hospital and the three noted churches of St John's, St Cuthbert's and St George's, also the Castle, while in the distance can be seen the coast of Fife. Exhibited RSA(81) 1828-1860. Represented in NGS by a large collection of 78 watercolour sketches of Old Edinburgh; SNPG by a wash drawing of 'Sir Walter Scott'; Edinburgh City collection.
**Bibl:** Butchart 85-6; Halsby 90.

**DUGUID, Jessie Ann** **fl 1894-1926**
Aberdeen landscape painter. Exhibited many local scenes at the AAS during the above period from 84 Skene Square and later from 123 Union Street.

**DUGUID, John** **20th Cent**
Painter in oil and watercolour and charcoal of figurative subjects. Represented by two oil paintings and two charcoal drawings in Abbot Hall AG(Kendal).

**DUGUID, Miss M Dora** **fl 1906-1931**
Aberdeenshire painter of local landscapes. Sister also an artist(qv). Exhibited regularly AAS at first from Balnacraig, Kincardine O'Neil and then from Manor, Inverurie.

**DUGUID, Norman George** **fl 1977**
Aberdeen abstract painter; exhibited AAS(1) from 3 Deemount Avenue.

**DUKE, George** **fl 1900**
Hamilton watercolour artist. Exhibited a continental scene at the GI from Peacock Cross.

**DUKE, Harvey** **fl 1989-**
Dundee painter in oil; exhibited RSA.

**DUMBRECK, Miss Kate** **fl 1896-1893**
Hawick artist, mainly in watercolour. Lived in Teviotside House, Hawick, where for a time in the 1870s she ran a boarding school for young ladies. Exhibited RSA(1) and 'Watching the sunset' at the GI from Craigholm, Colinton, Midlothian.

**DUN, John** **fl 1863-1908**
Edinburgh painter in oil and watercolour of landscapes, figures, portraits, domestic animals and literary subjects. Studied at the RSA schools in Edinburgh. His work was particularly strong in colour. In 1867 an exhibited drawing 'The Gate of the City of Refuge' was

awarded a prize of £18 from Lady Stuart of Allanbank's Endowment for students currently at the RSA school. In 1871 a portrait of his mother and a landscape were both hung on the line at the RSA. Exhibited RA(3) 1872-1884, RSA(100+), GI(32), AAS(2) & L(1) latterly from 6 Nile Grove.

**DUNACHIE, Mrs Lyn B** **fl 1987-**
Glasgow painter. Exhibited a study of domestic fowl at the GI from 12 Rowallan Gardens.

**DUNBAR, David** **1782-1866**
Born Dumfries. Sculptor, mostly in marble. Worked in Cumberland 1811 before entering the studio of Sir Francis Chantrey in London. After nine years he returned to Carlisle to work for Paul Nixon. Nixon was interested in furthering the arts in Carlisle and it was Dunbar's suggestion that an Academy of Arts should be built. Studied for a time in Italy. As well as preparing the exhibitions, Dunbar acted as secretary for the Dumfries exhibitions of 1828 and 1830 and, after leaving Carlisle, held his own exhibitions in Newcastle and Durham. Contributed to Carlisle Academy and between 1823 and 1833 exhibited 40 pieces of sculpture. Among his best known works are busts of 'Earl Grey', 'Lord Durham' and 'Grace Darling'. Represented in SNPG (Robert Burns), Carlisle AG.
**Bibl:** Brydall 191.

**DUNBAR, Francis B** **fl 1958-1971**
Ayr architect, landscape painter and sculptor. Exhibited GI(10) from 35 Lochlea Drive.

**DUNBAR, George P** **fl 1908**
Amateur Aberdeen painter. Exhibited a country scene at the AAS from Sclattie, Bucksburn.

**DUNBAR, James Ernest Lindsay** **1949-**
Born Mambasa, Congo, 18 Feb. Painter. Came home to Scotland to study at the Duncan of Jordanstone College of Art, Dundee 1970-1974. In 1972 received the Chalmers Jervise Award of the RSA as well as a travelling scholarship and in 1973 won the Keith award as well as additional travelling scholarships. These were followed by the Latimer Award 1979. Recently commissioned by Tayside Regional Council to execute a portrait of 'Dr Fitzgerald', past convener of Tayside. Has held frequent exhibitions of his oil paintings and mixed media drawings of portraits, still life and landscapes. Exhibits regularly RSA, RGI & AAS from 21 Lochly Street, Carnoustie, Angus. Represented in Hunterian AG (Glasgow Univ).

**DUNBAR, Miss Jean** **fl 1943**
Textile designer. Exhibited GI(3) from 1 Woodburn Cottages, Stevenston, Ayr.

**DUNBAR, John S** **fl 1863**
Amateur Glasgow watercolourist. Exhibited a study of boats at the GI from 34 Paterson Street.

**DUNBAR, Lennox Robert ARSA** **1952-**
Born Aberdeen. Studied at Gray's School of Art, Aberdeen 1969-74 winning a postgraduate scholarship and working also at Hospitalfield 1973. Travelled to Belgium, France and Holland 1973, and to Italy 1974. Won the Mary Oppenheimer Prize at the RSA 1976, the Latimer Award 1978 and the Gillies Award (RSA) 1999 enabling him to visit Santa Fe. In 2003 awarded first equal prize at the International Print Biennale in Varna, Bulgaria. Shortly afterwards set up an Amsterdam studio in association with the SAC. Won Guthrie Award 1984 and a prize at the Paisley Art Institute for drawing in 1985 and first prize Paisley drawing competition 1987. Works in drawing, etching and painting, his prime interests being in construction, responses or inspiration from his immediate environment taking into account historical and agricultural references. Head of Printmaking, Gray's School of Art. Founder member of SAC Awards panel 1984-87 and a board member of Peacock Printmakers. Exhibits regularly RSA since 1976 from Old Bourtree Farm, Newtonhill, Kincardineshire & AAS from 1973. Represented in Aberdeen AG, Paisley AG, RSA.

**DUNBAR, N M** **fl 1870-1881**
Landscape painter in oil and watercolour; exhibited RSA(5) & GI(10) from various addresses in Glasgow.

**DUNBAR, Peter** **fl 1861-1875**
Glasgow painter of landscape, mostly Argyll and Perthshire. Moved c1864 to Paisley and 1873 to London. Exhibited RSA(23) & GI(28).

**DUNBAR, Robert Brassey** **fl 1886-1912**
Landscape painter. Exhibited GI(12), mostly country scenes, whilst living in Glasgow.

**DUNBAR, Lady Sophia (of Duffus) (née Orred)** **c1820-1909**
Born Tranmere, Lancs. Painter of landscapes and flowers in both oil and watercolour. Studied under the marine painter John Le Capelain. Exhibited in London and Edinburgh from 1863. Married Sir Archibald Dunbar, Bt of Northfield, Elgin 1840. Her landscapes were international in scope including Algeria, Corsica, Gibraltar, France, Switzerland and Scotland. Visited Algeria with Barbara Bodichon who had a house there and sketched many subjects in watercolour. Whilst there undertook trips to Corsica and the French Riviera. Painted in a solid, traditional style with good colour and accurate detail. Exhibited RSA(40) 1867-1886, GI(18), SWA(5) & AAS(3). A retrospective exhibition was held in Aberdeen AG 1989.

**DUNBAR, W Nugent** **fl c1825-1842**
Scottish artist, known to have been living in Rome in the early 1820s. Exhibited watercolour landscapes of Italy at the RSA 1840-42.
**Bibl:** Halsby 257.

**DUNBAR-NASMITH, Sir James (Duncan) KBE RIBA PPRIAS FRSA FRSE** **1927-**
Born Mar 15. Architect, administrator & teacher. Educated Winchester and Cambridge Univ, trained Edinburgh College of Art and RIBA. Served in the Scots Guards 1945-48. President, Royal Incorporation of Architects in Scotland 1971-73, Council member, RIBA 1967-73, Professor Heriot Watt Univ and head of dept, Edinburgh College of Art 1978 until his retirement 1988. Partner, Law & Dunbar Nasmith.
**Bibl:** Burke's Peerage & Gentry 2004.

**DUNCAN, Alexander** **fl 1958-1979**
Montrose painter of topographical and local scenes, mainly in watercolour. Exhibited annually at the RSA from 107 High Street; also regularly at the AAS until 1965, mainly fishing villages of the north east, & GI(5) latterly from Three Wells, Hillside, Montrose.

**DUNCAN, Alexander C W** **fl 1884-1932**
Landscape and flower painter in oil and watercolour. Moved to Colinsburgh, Fife c1908. Exhibited two works at the RA in 1896 and 'Summer - Across to Arran' in 1902, also RSA(9), RSW(3), GI(68) & L(3). Not to be confused with Alexander D(qv).

**DUNCAN, Miss Carol** **fl 1984**
Amateur Glasgow painter. Exhibited 'Still life with fruit' at the GI from 123 Buccleuch Street.

**DUNCAN, Charles** **fl 1874-1885**
Edinburgh painter in oil and watercolour of landscapes, interiors and buildings. Exhibited RSA(37) including two Continental landscapes 1884 and a fine scene of Arran 1881, also GI(6), from Pentland Villa, Ferry Road.

**DUNCAN, D M** **fl 1880-1882**
Glasgow painter of figure studies and genre; exhibited GI(8) from 6 Springfield Road.

**DUNCAN, David** **1868-1943**
Born Edinburgh. Painter in oil landscapes and marines, also etcher. Studied in Dunfermline, where he was for a time chief damask designer for the Victoria Linen Works. In his early days was the head damask designer with Inglis and Co. Later concentrated on producing aquatints, first in black and white and as his technique developed, in colour. Subjects were generally the landscapes of south-west Scotland. Known affectionately as Davie he was for many years President of Dunfermline Art Club. Lived at Grieve Street, Dunfermline. His best known works are 'Bridge at Strathyre', 'Highland Farm, near Strathyre' (both exhibited in 1942), 'In Glen Croe', 'Evening over Highland Moor' and 'Sky Clearing over Ben Venue'. Exhibited RSA(22), RSW(1), GI(30) & L(12). Represented in Walker AG, Liverpool.

**DUNCAN, Mrs Dorothy** **fl 1909-1938**
Dundee based painter of landscape in oil. Wife of John D. RSA(qv). Exhibited RSA(3) & ROI(3).

**DUNCAN, E Pittendreich** **fl 1912**
Amateur Turriff painter. Exhibited AAS(1) from the Crown Hotel.

**DUNCAN, Miss Elizabeth Ann** **fl 1940-1941**
Alloa etcher. Exhibited RSA(2) & GI(2) from 2 Coningsby Place.

**DUNCAN, Ella P** **fl 1933**
Minor Banff painter. Exhibited a view of the 'Cluny, nr Braemar' at the AAS from Cairnfield, Clochan.

**DUNCAN, Frank M** **fl 1975**
Amateur Aberdeen watercolourist. Exhibited AAS(2) from 85 Bon-Accord Street.

**DUNCAN, George** **fl 1845-1861**
Edinburgh animal painter; exhibited RSA(3).

**DUNCAN, George W** **fl 1897-1904**
Glasgow painter of country scenes and townscapes. Exhibited GI(4) from 180 West George Street.

**DUNCAN, Gideon** **fl 1885-1889**
Glasgow painter of landscape and figurative studies. Exhibited GI(5) & AAS(1) from 45 Dumbarton Road.

**DUNCAN, Isa** **fl 1893**
Amateur Edinburgh artist; exhibited AAS(2).

**DUNCAN, J C** **fl 1889**
Exhibited 'On the Clyde, near Kenmure' at the RSA from 8 Clydeview Terrace, Glasgow.

**DUNCAN, James** **1946-**
Born 18 Sep. Works mainly in oil, paints landscapes, figurative works, genre and semi abstracts. Trained at Gravesend School of Art, Kent and at Edinburgh College of Art 1964-67. Held exhibitions in London, Majorca, Carolina and Granada, Spain. Received bronze medal at the International Exhibition of Contemporary Art, Paris, 1984. Since 1988 has been combining art work with the restoration of a 13th century Banffshire castle. Exhibited at the RSA from 1983.

**DUNCAN, James Allan** **fl 1888-1910**
Milngavie landscape painter in oil and watercolour, also illustrator, decorator and designer. Worked in Glasgow 1895-97, at Milngavie 1902. Regular contributor to magazines, an illustrator of children's books and designer of alphabets for the Chiswick Press c1899. Illustrated *Children's Rhymes* (1890). Exhibited RSA(2) & RGI(4), latterly from Montrose Gardens.
**Bibl:** Houfe 1126; *The Studio* 15, 1899, 1884-89.

**DUNCAN, James S R** **fl 1914**
Dunbartonshire portrait painter. Exhibited GI(1) from Bonnington, Milngavie.

**DUNCAN, John** **fl 1890-1896**
Glasgow watercolour painter of landscape and figure subjects, eg 'A Highland Croft near Dunkeld'. Exhibited RSA(2).

**DUNCAN, John RSA RSW** **1866-1945**
Born Dundee; died Edinburgh, 24 Nov. Painter in oil, tempera, charcoal and watercolour of landscapes, genre and historical subjects; mural decorator, illustrator and stained-glass designer; teacher. At the age of 11 enrolled at Dundee School of Art remaining there seven years. After a spell in Dusseldorf returned to Dundee where he painted several portraits. Spent a winter in Italy before settling finally in Chicago where he was Professor of Art 1902-1904. Returned to Dundee to undertake an important commission for a group of panels in a French chateau. A considerable part of his decorative work was ecclesiastical - altar pieces, stations of the Cross, and wall decorations. His diploma work, 'Ivory, Apes and Peacocks' is an excellent example of work in tempera and shows clearly his characteristic fantasy. Throughout his life Celtic subjects remained his chief inspiration, although much of his earlier work shows the strong influence of Japanese art, especially Japanese prints. Close friend of Patrick Geddes(qv), he produced illustrations for *The Evergreen* (1895). From 1898 worked on a decorative scheme for mural decorations in Geddes's Edinburgh home. Settled in Edinburgh 1902. Married Dorothy D(qv). Designed the 'awesome' war memorial in Edinburgh's North Morningside Church (1935); an Art Nouveau fountain at Castlehill reservoir (1894); scenes from Scottish history in the Common Room of Ramsay Lodge; a vast mural in St Cuthbert's (1931) and eleven stations of the Cross in St Peter (RC), Falcon Avenue, now lost. Elected ARSA 1910, RSA 1923, RSW 1930. Librarian, RSA 1925-45. Exhibited once at the RA in 1903, regularly RSA from 1896 onwards, & AAS 1919-33. Represented in Edinburgh University where he executed the decorations in the former University Hall (now Ramsay Lodge); also in Dundee AG, Glasgow AG, Kirkcaldy AG, Paisley AG, Edinburgh City collection (10), Perth AG. Not to be confused with John McKirdy Duncan(qv).
**Bibl:** Margaret Armour 'Mural decoration in Scotland, Part I', Studio x, 1987; The Artist, 1898, 146-152; Barbican AG, London, 'The Last Romantics; The Romantic Tradition in British Art' (Ex Cat 1989) - essay 'Celtic Elements in Scottish Art at the Turn of the Century', Lindsay Errington; Gifford 45,176, 192,275-6,618,619n; Patrick Geddes, John Duncan, Interpretation of the Pictures at University Hall, Edinburgh 1928; Halsby 257; Hardie 123-6 et passim ch VII; Hartley 129-130; Houfe; Irwin 406-410(illus); John Kemplay, John Duncan, CEAC 1987; Macmillan [SA], 296-8,315,326,331,337-8; NGS, 'John Duncan' (Ex Cat 1941, Essay by Stanley Cursiter); Peter Savage, Lorimer and the Edinburgh Craft Designers, Edinburgh 1980, 100,164; Scotsman, 24 Nov 1945 (obit).

**DUNCAN, John** **fl 1915-1938**
Watercolour painter of birds. Often composed in circles and ovals. An artist of moderate ability, usually dark and a little coarse and suffering in technique although some works are quite appealing. Exhibited GI(3) from Glasgow.

**DUNCAN, Joseph** **fl 1868-1870**
Edinburgh oil painter of landscape, especially Banffshire. Exhibited RSA(3).

**DUNCAN, Leslie S** **1932-**
Glasgow flower and wild-life painter. Exhibited GI(1) from 35 Havelock Street. Represented in the Lillie AG(Milngavie).

**DUNCAN, Mrs Margaret S** **fl 1948**
Amateur Milngavie watercolourist. Exhibited a local landscape at the GI from Mugdock Road.

**DUNCAN, Miss Mary** **fl 1904-1925**
Pollokshields painter of oil and watercolour of interiors and figure subjects. Exhibited RSA(8), GI(7) & L(5).

**DUNCAN, Mrs Mary S** **fl 1964-1970**
Glasgow painter of 14 Kelvin Drive. Worked in oil and pastel, painting landscapes with considerable verve, though sometimes repetitive. Her pastel studies are generally smaller than her oils and more successful. Lives in Fife. Married Robert D(qv). Exhibited RSA(3) & AAS(1) 1964 and 1970.

**DUNCAN, Richard** **fl 1963**
Fife painter, exhibited 'Red Boats' at the RSA from 2 Glebe Street, Leven.

**DUNCAN, Robert** **20th century**
Fife watercolour artist. Usually paints landscapes, generally incorporating figures. A critic referred to his 'fragmentation - explosions, radiations and flutterings - that remind us of the Rayonism invented by the Russian painter Larionov'. Married Mary D(qv).

**DUNCAN, T G McGill** **fl 1946-1961**
Midlothian based painter in oil and watercolour of beach and harbour scenes. Particularly attracted to Portobello beach, most of his 15 exhibits at the RSA being in the area - there is even a 'Portobello Beach - 22'. Also exhibited at the GI(13), latterly from High Tide, Gatehouse-of-Fleet, whence he moved in 1961.

**DUNCAN, Thomas ARA RSA** **1807-1845**
Born Kinclaven, Perthshire, May 4; died Edinburgh, Apr 25. Painter of historical subjects and portraits in oil. First studied law before entering the Trustees Academy, Edinburgh where he worked under William Allan(qv). Although his style and subjects are typical of the period, Duncan painted with remarkable freedom of technique and strong sense of colour. Most of his subjects were taken from Scottish history, especially the 1745 rebellion. Has strong claims to be regarded in the forefront of Scottish artists even though his life came to a tragically early end at the age of thirty-eight. His first painting at the RA was 'Prince Charles entering Edinburgh', a work that was to become famous and was engraved by Bacon 1845. His second famous picture was shown three years later - 'Prince Charles Edward asleep in one of his hiding places, after the Battle of Culloden, protected by Flora Macdonald and Highland outlaws, who are alarmed on their watch'. In 1844 succeeded Sir William Allan as Headmaster of the Trustees Academy. One of his finest works is a three-quarter length 'Self-portrait', the last of his paintings to be exhibited at the RA 1845, now in the SNPG. This was subsequently purchased by a consortium of fifty Scottish artists and given to the RSA. An unfinished sketch left at his desk 'George Wishart dispensing the Sacrament in the Castle of St Andrews' was believed by many to have been an advance on anything he had hitherto accomplished, now in Perth AG. 'He seldom used blue, delighted in varieties of maroon, cherry and puce, and in harmonising or contrasting such with olives, ruddy browns or a full note of yellow'. Although his compositions may lack a little in largeness of design, it is this which contributes to their dignity and impressiveness. 'The Waefu' Heart' (exhibited RA 1841) is now in the V & A and a sketchy little picture 'Jeannie Deans and the Robbers' is in the NGS. His study of 'Bran', a celebrated deerhound, was lent by the Lord Advocate and exhibited (1844) while his studies of young ladies demonstrate his appreciation of feminine beauty. Lord Cockburn spoke of his portrait of 'Dr Chalmers' as being the best likeness ever made of that clergyman. His portrait of 'Lady Stuart of Allanbank' is in the NGS. A recent decline in appreciation of history and tradition together with Duncan's short life has led to his comparative neglect in recent years. This is bound to be corrected over time. In an earlier period, Caw commented 'the defects of Duncan's art in conception and execution are those of his day, but they are less obvious than in most of his fellows, and they are redeemed by a refinement of feeling, fine colour, and a sense of beauty. If without the fertility of invention and the breadth of intellect which makes the historical pieces of Daniel Maclise(qv) interesting in spite of obvious and great faults, Duncan's idea of the less rhetorical in themselves were controlled by finer taste and a more pictorial conception of treatment. Compared with Wilkie or Allan or Harvie, again, he had acute perception of the beautiful and developed colour sense. His women are charming of face and elegant in person; the poses of his figures are often graceful; his drawing, if lacking the vivacity of Wilkie's, is dainty and refined; his design satisfying within its range and intention; his colour nearly always delightful in quality, and in the subtle ways in which its dominant chords are repeated so as to form with the brownish fond of the period, from which he did not wholly escape, a clearly conceived colour scheme' [Caw]. His work 'Anne Page and Slender' led to his election ARSA. Elected ARA and RSA 1843. Became an original member of RSA by the Hope-Cockburn Settlement 1829, becoming 'Royal' 1838. Exhibited 102 works at the RSA and its predecessors 1828-1846, including a number of portraits of ladies, gentlemen and occasionally animals. Represented in V & A, NGS(20, including the original study for 'Prince Charles Edward entering Edinburgh, 22 Sept 1745'), SNPG(6), Glasgow AG(11).
**Bibl:** Armstrong 62-3; AU 1847, 380; Brydall 394-7; Caw 110-2; Halsby 257; Hardie 41-4; Irwin 213-215 et passim; Macmillan [SA], 187,192,209; McKay 205-211; Portfolio 1887, 179; R H Rodger, The Remarkable Mr Hill, David Octavius Hill, Perth AG, 2002.

**DUNCAN, William S** **fl 1869**
Inverness painter in oil of figurative subjects; exhibited RSA(1).

**DUNCAN OF JORDANSTONE COLLEGE OF ART, DUNDEE** **1975-1994**
Named after James Duncan of Jordanstone and Drumfork who, in 1909, bequeathed a large legacy to found a school of industrial art and a women's institute. The College emerged as a separate body from the Dundee Institute of Art & Technology(qv) 1975, to become the largest college of art and design in Scotland, with courses in architecture, environmental management, ceramics, catering, graphic and textile design, metalwork and painting. In 1994 it merged with the University of Dundee.

**DUNDAS, Miss Agnes** **fl 1865-1884**
Painter in oil of birds, animals, especially dogs, and still life. Lived in London, of Scottish descent. Most of her work was exhibited at the RSA where she showed 20 works between the above years; also GI(17), many from Dawlish, Devon, & SWA.

**DUNDEE ART GALLERY** **c1888-**
The first exhibition in the town was in 1857 followed by a second ten years later. In 1873 a special wing was opened within the Albert Institute for the display of paintings with permanent annual exhibitions starting in 1877. A new gallery was built in 1888 at a cost of £15,000 raised by public subscription. Received generous gifts from J G Orchar(qv) and other local residents including the Keiller family.

**DUNDEE INSTITUTE OF ART AND TECHNOLOGY** **1911-1975**
Evolved from the Dundee Technical Institute (est 1888) whose first full-time art teacher was **Thomas Delgaty DUNN**. Although classes had been held while the building in Bell St was completed, formal establishment took place in 1911 under the Institute's previous name, Dundee Technical Institute and School of Art. The name Dundee Institute of Art and Technology came into being 1933. The Art division was often known as the Dundee College of Art and, following a bequest from James Duncan of Jordanstone 1909, as the Duncan of Jordanstone College of Art(qv). In 1975 the Institute divided into separate Colleges of Art and Technology.

**DUNDEE PRINTMAKERS WORKSHOP** **1976-**
Youngest of the Scottish print workshops that have recently been flourishing. Located in the Dudhope Arts Centre. Facilities for etching, lithography, relief painting and photography are available for beginners and established artists alike.

**DUNDEE SEVEN** **1970**
Seven artists who became members of staff at the Duncan of Jordanstone College of Art at about the same time and who in 1970 shared an exhibition. In the catalogue Hardie pointed to additional links between them which imbued the seven with an aesthetic identity 'setting them apart from their contemporaries in Scotland and especially from the new realists in Edinburgh...all tended...towards great restraint in the use of colour and a high degree of refinement of handling and finish...[with] a general unwillingness to abandon a figurative mode of expression'. The artists were Neil Dallas Brown, Dennis Buchan, Peter Collins, Ian Fearn, James Howie, Jack Knox and James Morrison. Although the course of their subsequent development diverged, the label has remained, valid over a short but significant span of time.
**Bibl:** Hardie 198-9; W Hardie 'Seven Painters in Dundee', SAC (Ex Cat 1970).

**DUNKLEY, Keith** **1942-**
Kelso painter. Exhibited four works at the RSA since 1985 from 70 The Linn.

**DUNLOP, A** **fl 1862-1863**
Amateur Helensburgh watercolour painter of landscape. Exhibited GI(3) from Jordanhill Cottage.

**DUNLOP, David** **fl 1861-1866**
Glasgow landscape painter in oil and watercolour; exhibited RSA(1) & GI(7) from 82 Hospital Street.

**DUNLOP, Gilbert P** **fl 1939**
Dundee artist; exhibited RSA(1) from 1 Blackness Avenue.

**DUNLOP, Iain** **fl 1978-1979**
Aberdeen printmaker. Exhibited AAS(2) from 9C Station Road, Woodside.

**DUNLOP, J K** **fl 1880**
Exhibited 'Tarner Island, Isle of Skye' at the RSA from 16 Hope Street, Edinburgh.

**DUNLOP, J Y** **fl 1873-1874**
A Partick painter in oil of fruit; exhibited RSA(3).

**DUNLOP, James M** **fl 1900-1915**
Glasgow painter; exhibited RSA(2) & GI(2).

**DUNLOP, James Norton** **fl 1900-1905**
Glasgow portrait painter; exhibited RSA(2) & GI(2), from 5 Kelvingrove Terrace.

**DUNLOP, Jessie I (Mrs Wilson)** **fl 1925-1939**
Paisley painter in oil of figurative and religious subjects, also portraits. Studied Glasgow School of Art. After 1936 she lived at Woodstock, Largs, Ayrshire. Exhibited RSA(2), AAS(1), Paisley Art Institute(12) & L(1) from Oldhall.

**DUNLOP, John Rankin** **fl 1870-1908**
Edinburgh portrait painter; exhibited RSA(4) before moving to 34 Tait Street, Carlisle.

**DUNLOP, Mrs Rachael R B** **fl 1912-1921**
Glasgow painter of landscape and portrait miniatures. Exhibited RA(3) & GI(4), latterly from The Crossways, Helensburgh where she was living in 1920.

**DUNN, Ian G D** **fl 1939**
Little known painter. Exhibited RSA(1). Represented in Kirkcaldy AG.

**DUNN, James** **1929-1986**
Perthshire portrait sculptor; painter, draughtsman; teacher. Educated Perth Academy, trained Dundee College of Art under D S Sutherland(qv). Member, Perthshire Art Association for many years. Principal art teacher, Denny HS. Exhibited RSA(3) from 56 Townhead, Auchterarder.

**DUNN, James Bow RSA** **1861-1930**
Edinburgh architect. Partner with James Findlay(qv). Among his major projects were extensions or modifications to Edinburgh Public Library; Haggerston Castle, Northumberland; Middleton Hall, Northumberland; Blair Drummond, Perthshire; Solicitors' Library, Edinburgh with its large oriel windows, gargoyles and clustered chimneys; the War Memorial in the Gatehouse (1922), Lauriston Place; Charteris Memorial Church (now Kirk o'Field) in the Pleasance (1910-2) and George Watson's College (1930). Also various designs for a number of Scottish war memorials and additions to the Scotsman building, Edinburgh. Elected ARSA 1918, RSA 1931. Exhibited regularly at the RSA from 1888 until the year of his death, also occasional designs at the GI(3).
**Bibl:** Gifford 121,124,182,233,240,495,519,552,624.

**DUNN, Joyce V** **fl 1929**
Glasgow sculptress. Exhibited a study of a head at the GI from 19 Huntly Gardens.

**DUNN, Normand R** **fl 1937**
Amateur watercolour artist; exhibited RSW(1).

**DUNN, Patrick S** **fl 1873-1918**
Glasgow painter in oil and watercolour of landscapes often with figures. Exhibited RSA(1), RSW(1) & GI(39), including a fine study of 'Glenbuchat Castle', 1909.

**DUNN, S F** **fl 1885-1887**
Edinburgh painter in watercolour of landscape and portraits. Exhibited RSA(2) from 13 Glengyle Terrace.

**DUNN, Thomas F** **fl 1896-1912**
Exhibited 2 figure studies and a view of 'Harbottle Castle, Northumberland' at the GI from Garngilloch House, Cumbernauld in 1896 and after 1906 from the Theatre Royal, Glasgow where he may have been employed as a scene painter.

**DUNN, William** **1859-1934**
Architect. Worked with William Flockhart(qv) before joining James Maclaren(qv). In 1890 he entered into partnership with Robert Watson(qv). They continued Maclaren's work less imaginatively but consistently. An early exponent of reinforced concrete, he influenced Lorimer's use of it in most of his country mansions. Examples of his designs are Fortingall Inn (1891) and Glenlyon House (1891), both in collaboration with Robert Watson(qv).
**Bibl:** Dunbar 165; Peter Savage, Lorimer and the Edinburgh Craft Designers, Edinburgh 1980, 7,92,154,164.

**DUNN, William** **1862-c1932**
Helensburgh painter of rustic scenes and landscapes. Exhibited RSA(8) 1899- 1925 & GI(19) from Davies O'the Mill, Beith, Ayr, and frequently at the AAS 1902-1912. Between 1920 and 1927 lived in New Rumney, Kent. Represented in Glasgow AG.

**DUNN, William E** **fl 1893-1897**
Watercolour painter from Ayrshire; exhibited RSW(1), GI(4) & L(1) from the village of Galston and latterly 352 N Woodside Drive, Glasgow.

**DUNNETT, Dorothy** **[see HALLIDAY, Dorothy]**

**DUNNETT, Miss J Florrie** **fl 1936-1937**
Sculptress; exhibited three figure subjects at the RSA during the above years from 52 Argyle Square, Wick, Caithness.

**DUNSMOIR, Miss Dorothy E** **fl 1968**
Amateur Lanarkshire landscape artist. Exhibited 'Ben Slioch reflected in Loch Maree', at the GI from 8 Glenbank Road, Lenzie.

**DUNSMORE, William** **fl 1934-1940**
Glasgow watercolourist and engraver of landscapes and figure compositions. Exhibited RSA(1) & GI(4) from 71 Cartvale Road, Langside.

**DUNSMUIR, James** **fl 1885-1896**
Edinburgh watercolour painter; exhibited RSA(1) & RSW(1) from 10 Coates Crescent.

**DUPERNE, M B A** **fl 1849**
Glasgow figurative painter in oil; exhibited RSA(1).

**DURHAM, J** **fl 1827-1829**
Edinburgh painter of genre and portraits; exhibited RSA(7) from Broughton Street, Edinburgh.

**DURHAM, Nellie E** **fl 1893-1896**
Stonehaven painter of landscape and flowers. Exhibited AAS(6) from 64 Allardyce Street.

**DURNFORD, F Andrew** **fl 1840-1848**
Edinburgh painter of harbour and coastal scenes, often in Fife, sometimes in Holland and occasionally on the Thames. Exhibited RSA(18) from 40 North Bridge.

**DURWARD, Dorothy Weir** **fl 1963-1964**
Edinburgh painter of landscape and Italian scenes; exhibited four works at the RSA from 21 Hillview Drive.

**DURWARD, Graham** **c1955-**
Painter of expressive, semi-figurative works. Trained Edinburgh College of Art 1973-8. His work demonstrates a reaction against the mainstream Edinburgh tradition of the 1970s and 1980s of 'restraint and delicate nuance rather than the uncompromising statement' [Hartley], illustrating what has been called a strong muscular post-Cubist art in the line of Picasso, Léger and Pollock. First solo exhibition 1979. Represented in Aberdeen AG.
**Bibl:** Hartley; SAC 'Scottish Art Now' (Ex Cat 1982).

**DURWARD, J Edmonston** **fl 1872-1876**
Edinburgh (Joppa) painter in oil and watercolour of landscape, especially local coastal scenes. Exhibited RSA(4).

**DURWARD, Miss Janette** **fl 1876-1883**
Edinburgh painter in oil and watercolour of still life, flowers and landscape; exhibited RSA(4) from 1 Clerk Street.

**DURY, Colonel Theodore** **1661-1742**
Military architect, possibly Scottish. Worked extensively in Edinburgh: designed an officers' barracks (1708) now the Scottish United Services Museum; gun platforms along Telfer's Wall (1715); below the summit to the N of the Castle gun emplacements known as Dury's Battery (1708-13); and just beyond the outer perimeter of the castle an ambitious scheme of hornwork known as Le Grand Secret abandoned 1710 after the threat from a French fleet off the coast had receded.
**Bibl:** Gifford 84,86,90,98.

**DUTHIE, A Spottiswood(e)** **fl 1885-1930**
Aberdeen painter of portrait and genre in oil and watercolour, also landscapes and figurative subjects. Lived in Glasgow, London, Cults and at Pitmedden House, Udny, Aberdeenshire. Exhibited RSA(3), RA(9) 1896-1901, RBA from 1892 (7), L(4) & AAS.

**DUTHIE, Alexia M McCombie** **fl 1908**
Amateur Aberdeenshire painter. 'Exhibited Low Tide' at the AAS from The Manse, Ellon.

**DUTHIE, Arthur Louis** **fl 1892-1898**
Granton, Edinburgh, painter and stained glass artist who lived at 36 Rawlings Street, London SW c1892-98. Exhibited RSA(2), RA(1) & GI(2).

**DUTHIE, Charlotte C** **fl 1907-1909**
Exhibited 2 Italian scenes at the RSA from The Presbytery, North Berwick.

**DUTHIE, Hilary** **fl 1975**
Aberdeen painter. Trained Gray's School of Art. Exhibited AAS(1) from 35 Victoria Street.

**DUTHIE, John Alexander** **fl 1935**
Amateur Aberdeen painter of townscapes. Exhibited an Aberdeen scene at the AAS from 16 Newlands Crescent.

**DUTHIE, Miss Mary E** **fl 1872-1887**
Edinburgh and Perthshire painter in oil of landscape and flowers; exhibited RSA(2) & SWA(3).

**DUTHIE, Phillip G** **fl 1980-1986**
Aberdeen painter. Trained Gray's School of Art. Exhibited several works at the AAS from 15 E Mains Avenue.

**DUTHIE, R G B** **fl 1959**
Aberdeen medical consultant and amateur painter in watercolour. Exhibited AAS(2) from his holiday home Geallaig Lodge, Crathie.

**DUTHIE, R J** **fl 1959**
Amateur watercolour landscape painter. Wife of R G B D(qv). Exhibited a continental scene and a Deeside view at the AAS.

**DUTHIE, William** **fl 1886-1919**
Stonehaven painter in oil of landscape, coastal and shipping scenes, also portraits. Member of the well-to-do Aberdeenshire shipping family after whom the Duthie Park, Aberdeen is named. Exhibited RSA(5) & GI(2) first from Ashley Lodge, Aberdeen before moving to London (1892), also at the AAS throughout his working life. A shipping scene is in the Director's room of the Aberdeen Maritime Museum.

**DUTHIE, Wilma Alexander** **fl 1975-1979**
Amateur Aberdeen abstract painter. Probably sister of Hilary D(qv). Exhibited AAS from 35 Victoria Street.

**DYAS, James W** **fl 1959-1971**
Aberdeen painter of local landscape. Exhibited a number of works at the AAS between the above years, often of Upper Deeside, from 56 Beaconsfield Place.

**DYCE, Iain M** **fl 1960-1965**
Stirling watercolour artist of Highland landscape. Exhibited GI(5) from 16 Cleuch Road.

**DYCE, James Irvine** **fl 1918-1919**
Sculptor. Exhibited 2 portraits at the RSA from 27 Albany Street, Edinburgh.

**DYCE, J Neil** **fl 1839-1867**
Lanark-based landscape painter and draughtsman. A collection of drawings of the vicinity of Balmoral and Braemar, dated 1839, recently appeared in Aberdeen. Exhibited RSA(1) 1867.

**DYCE, J Stirling** **?-1900**
Landscape and portrait painter in both oil and watercolour. Painted landscapes in England, France and Scotland. Son of William D(qv). Lived most of his life in England but retained his links with Aberdeen. His style shows the influence of meticulous Pre-Raphaelite landscape. In 1894 he showed 'The Roe's Pot, Banchory'. All other exhibits were oil and watercolour landscapes of France, especially in Giverny and Normandy, and two portraits. Exhibited AAS(14) 1894-1906, RA(5) & GI(1) from 154 Cheyne Court, London SW.
**Bibl:** Halsby 257.

**DYCE, William RA ARSA** **1806-1864**
Born Aberdeen, 19 Sep; died Streatham, London 14 Feb. Painter, etcher, scientist, philosopher, sculptor and designer. Educated at Aberdeen Grammar School 1814-1819 and from 1819-1823 at Marischal College. Studied medicine and theology while secretly practising art. In 1824 went to London where he received encouragement from Sir Thomas Lawrence RA. The following year, together with Alexander Day, he visited Rome and remained there nine months studying particularly the works of Poussin and Titian. On his return in 1826, he decorated a room in his father's Aberdeen house with arabesque designs, and also had his first RA exhibit 'Bacchus Mused by the Nymphs of Nyssa'. In 1827 he was back in Italy, making contact with the Nazarenes. At this time his interest in science remained strong and in 1829 received the Blackwell prize at Marischal College for his famous essay *The Relations between Electricity and Magnetism and the Consequences deducable from these Relations*. Also an etcher, illustrating Sir Thomas Dick Lauder's *The Morayshire Floods* (1830). During the period 1830-1837 he based himself in Edinburgh and concentrated on portrait painting. This was interrupted by a further trip to Italy in 1832 and another series of etchings, completed in 1837, for Lauder's *The Highland Rambler*. The same year he was appointed Master of the Trustees Academy, Edinburgh and found time to visit Prussia, Bavaria, Saxony and France on behalf of the London School of Design. In 1838 he was appointed Superintendent of the Schools of Design, Somerset House, London and two years later was elected Professor of the Theory of Fine Art at King's College, London. As if these varied interests and activities were not sufficient, he became deeply involved in church music and ritual, founding the Motet Society for the study, practise and re-printing of church music of the 16th and 17th centuries. The same year he composed a long essay *Ecclesiastical Architecture; a Defence of Anglican Usage*. In 1842, in the company of William Etty, he attended Taylor's Art School. It is hardly surprising that having found the time to publish an edition of the *Book of Common Prayer* (to which he added an additional essay), he then resigned from his Directorship of the Schools of Design and was in 1844 elected ARA and given the subject 'The Baptism of Ethelbert' by the Commission on the Fine Arts for the decoration of the central space behind the throne in the House of Lords. Prince Albert commissioned him to execute one of the eight frescoes for the Pavilion at Buckingham Palace. In 1845-6 he was back in Italy studying frescoes of the Old Masters. Shortly thereafter he was invited to decorate the Queen's Robing Room at the Palace of Westminster and in 1848 was elected RA. On 17th Jan 1850 Dyce married Jane, daughter of James Brand of Milnathorpe, by whom he had two sons and two daughters. During the rest of his life became increasingly engaged in writing and travel. In 1856 he designed a beautiful stained glass window, 'St Paul and St Barnabus, Preaching at Antioch' which adorns St Paul's Church, Alnwick. By the time of his death, five of the seven panels for the Queen's Robing Room had been completed. Dyce was undoubtedly the most comprehensively accomplished painter Scotland has ever produced. There were two slight flaws that render any claim that he was the greatest Scottish painter questionable. The first was an inner doubt about his powers coupled with chronic uncertainty about which was his greatest talent. He seems to have been aware of these problems himself for after he had been painting

portraits in Edinburgh for seven years with great distinction he wrote to a friend that he had considered "at more than one period the intention of abandoning the practice of art except as a matter of private gratification chiefly because I doubted whether my talent for painting was original enough to obtain the reputation which I had the vanity to suppose my general ability or various studies warranted me to aspire to". The second flaw was a certain coldness of which some of his friends were aware. Charles Carter summarised it well "the correct High Churchman could have done with the enthusiasm of an evangelical. Admire as we will the tenderness and delicacy of his touch, the soundness of his modelling, the movement, grace and purity of his line, the quiet simplicity of his arrangement, the poetic feeling of which he was sometimes capable, his work is always cool and calculated. He was capable of warmth but shied away from it as though he was afraid of life". Dyce was a classicist, tinged with pre-Raphaelite attention to detail, (it was Dyce who converted Ruskin to the movement) but his main source of inspiration was 15th century Italian. In Italy it was Gozzoli, Raphael, Peregino and Pintoricchio who most attracted him. Among his studio paintings, although he executed over 100 portraits being particularly sympathetic in his treatment of women and children and many landscapes, his religious subjects illustrated the greatest flowering of his genius. 'His finest works can be numbered among the masterpieces of British paintings'. His work may be seen in many public places including the NGS(11), SNPG, Tate Gallery, V&A, City of Edinburgh Art Collection, Aberdeen AG, Glasgow AG, Perth AG (The Daughters of Jethro defended by Moses, 1829), Houses of Parliament, RA, Royal Collection.

**Bibl:** Aberdeen AG 'Centenary exhib of the work of William Dyce', 1964; AJ, 1860, 293-6; Keith K Andrews, discusses Dyce's relations with the German Nazarenes in The Nazerenes: A Brotherhood of German Painters in Rome; Armstrong, 53-56; Q Bell, The School of Design, London, 1963, mainly 79-83; T S R Boase, The Decoration of the New Palace of Westminster, 1841-63; J Warburg and Courtauld Inst, vol XVII Nos 3-4, 1954, 315 et seq; Brydall, 397 et seq; Caw, 128-135 et al; Austin Chester, 'The Art of William Dyce RA', Windsor Mag, 1909, 576-590; J Stirling Dyce, Papers, Aberdeen AG, typescripts with his emendations by the artist's son, intended to be 'The Life Correspondence and Writings of William Dyce RA (1806-1864)'; Halsby 94-97 et al; Hardie, passim, intro & ch I; Irwin 244-262,317-8 et passim; Macmillan [SA], 202,205,208-13,218,229,252; McKay, 233-4 and 244-256; R Muther, The History of Modern Painting, London, 1896, vol 2, 565-6; Redgrave, 529 and 551 et seq, cq; Marcia Pointon 'Dyce's Pegwell Bay' Art History, i, 1989; Marcia Pointon 'William Dyce', Oxford, 1979; A Staley, 'William Dyce and Outdoor Naturalism', Burlington Mag CV, 470 et seq; J Steegman, Consort of Taste, 1950, several references; R J B Walker, Catalogue of Paintings and Drawings of Palace of Westminster, vol 1b, 1962, 27-36,157-159,164-6.

**DYCE-SHARP, Daphne** **1924-**

Edinburgh sculptress of portraits and horses. Trained Edinburgh College of Art. Exhibited RSA(6) from 53 George Street before emigrating to Canada. Returned to live in Rumbling Bridge, Perthshire 1963.

# E

**EADIE, Miss A S** **fl 1903**
Exhibited a continental watercolour at the GI from 70 Barnaby Rd, London.

**EADIE, Mrs Anne** **fl 1951**
Glasgow amateur portrait painter; exhibited G(1), from 5 Kingsley Ave.

**EADIE, Charles** **fl 1877-1891**
Glasgow painter and sculptor; portraits and landscape, especially Arran, in oils and watercolour. Exhibited GI(11), from Westbank Quadrant, Hillhead.

**EADIE, Ian Gilbert Marr** **1913-1973**
Born Dundee. Painter in oil and watercolour, etcher, teacher; portraits, landscapes, genre. Studied Dundee College of Art 1931-5, in Paris at the Ecole des Beaux Art 1937 and Westminster School of Art 1939. Studied under J McIntosh Patrick(qv). Taught at Duncan of Jordanstone College of Art, Dundee. His talent as a designer brought wide recognition, commissions including murals for the Glasgow Empire Exhibition of 1938, the Overgate shopping precinct in Dundee, and the Aviemore recreation centre. Painted a number of notable portraits, as well as landscapes, continental scenes, some abstract works, and a number of large decorative murals. During WW2 he served as an officer in the 51st Highland Division in North Africa, Sicily and north-west Europe. In later years lived at 432 Blackness Rd, Dundee. Exhibited RA(3), RSA(46), RSW(1) & GI(9) 1936-1973, first of all mainly portraits and after the war mostly continental scenery. Represented in Glasgow AG, Imperial War Museum.

**EADIE, James** **fl 1856-1863**
Glasgow painter in oil and watercolour; exhibited genre and local landscapes at the RSA(3) & GI(3), from 21 Argyle St.

**EADIE, John** **fl 1877-1894**
Glasgow painter in oil and watercolour, mostly the latter. Coastal and harbour scenes. Exhibited GI(12), after 1889 from 5 Wendover Crescent.

**EADIE, Miss K Veronica** **fl 1930-1937**
Glasgow painter of Highland landscape, portraits and genre. Exhibited GI(1) & AAS(3) latterly from 71 Queen Margaret Drive.

**EADIE, Nadia T** **fl 1948-1950**
Amateur painter who lived at 6 Cluny Gardens, Edinburgh; exhibited 2 topographical works at the RSA in 1948 and 1950.

**EADIE, Robert RSW** **1877-1954**
Born Glasgow 16 Mar. Painter in oil and watercolour; architectural subjects, townscapes, portraits and landscape, also poster artist and lithographer. Educated in Glasgow, continued his studies in Munich and Paris. Lived in Glasgow and Cambuslang. Best known for his landscapes painted in a broad, wet, straightforward style, with more attention to general effect than to detail, sometimes elegant, always decorative. Elected RSW 1916. Exhibited RA(1), RSA(43), RSW(95), GI(127), AAS(1), Paris Salon & L(9), latterly from 1 Royal Terrace, Glasgow. Represented in Glasgow AG, Paisley AG, City of Edinburgh collection.
**Bibl:** Halsby 226,228,257.

**EADIE, Roland H** **fl 1935**
Amateur Aberdeen watercolourist. Exhibited once at the AAS from 134 Hardgate.

**EADIE, William** **fl 1868-1893**
Paisley painter in oil; landscape, fruit and domestic subjects. Taught at Paisley School of Art for many years. In the mid-1870s he spent some time in London and Cornwall before returning to Paisley. Exhibited 4 works at the RSA during the above period, and GI(10) 1872-1893, after 1887 from St. Ives, Cornwall. Represented in Paisley AG.

**EAGLE, Robert Haldane** **fl 1878-1886**
Edinburgh painter in watercolour of landscape and coastal scenes. Resided for many years at 19 Brunswick Street, Hillside. Exhibited RSA(6).

**EARDLEY, Joan Kathleen Harding RSA** **1921-1963**
Born Warnham, Sussex, 18 May; died Killearn hospital, nr Glasgow, 16 Aug. Painter in oil, watercolour, pencil; landscape and figurative subjects. Father was an army officer turned farmer, who took his life when she was only eight years old; her mother was Scottish. Left Blackheath School 1938, enrolling in Goldsmith's School of Art but staying there only one or two terms before the family moved to Glasgow 1940. There she began studying at Glasgow School of Art under Hugh Adam Crawford(qv) and in 1943 was awarded the Guthrie prize for portraiture. At the end of that year she enrolled at Jordanhill College of Education in Glasgow but left after the first term to become a carpenter's mate. At about this time began visiting Corrie on Arran. After spending two years as an artisan she returned in 1947 to study art at Hospitalfield, Arbroath under James Cowie(qv) and there met Angus Neil who became a life-long friend. In 1948 she went back to Glasgow to resume a postponed post-diploma scholarship. Two further awards enabled her to visit Paris and Italy. In 1950 she discovered Catterline, whence she moved 1956. The previous year she had been elected ARSA and in 1963 became a full Academician, the youngest lady artist to have achieved the honour. Although in 1956 she suffered from neck problems which made it impossible for her to work, she fully recovered, but developed a terminal illness in 1962, dying the following year. It is hard to realise that the whole of her achievement was encompassed within the span of only fourteen fully creative years. Whilst her output cannot be separated into periods, it can be divided into two compositional types. These were the Townhead children of Glasgow, especially the archetypal Samson family whom she painted so sympathetically and so beautifully, and the broader more elemental work done at Catterline. Those who prefer the latter speak of 'the fullest flowering of (her) talent stimulated by the coast of Kincardineshire. There, something not only in the physical form of the place within its ambience set her imagination alight'. To those who prefer her Glasgow paintings the Catterline landscapes have found a smaller public, generally amongst those who were informed upon developments in painting...popular taste in acclaiming the Townhead works may prove to have the greater insight. When at Catterline she used a derelict cottage as her studio and much of her work was completed in the open. It has been said that 'her work is remarkable in that while it is 'contemporary' in feeling it is completely unmannered. It proclaims allegiance to no school, it is technically as foreign to the self-conscious disciplines of hard-edge abstraction as it is to the spontaneous abandon of abstract expressionism...it is restrained in both colour and tone, yet strangely rich in both. It defies the jargon so adroitly applied to much contemporary art'[Oliver]. In the words of her biographer 'Eardley's life was a paradox. She was shy and gentle yet powerful; she understood the lives of children, yet had none of her own; she painted not only the city, but also the sea and the seasons of the year; and while her creative power was flowing fiercely her life was extinguished'. Exhibited regularly at the RSA, GI(20) & AAS(4) 1959-1961, from 170 Drymen Rd, Bearsden and after 1960 from 18 Catterline. Represented in SNGMA, Aberdeen AG, Bedford AG, Birmingham AG, Cambridge AG, Coventry AG, Dundee AG, Glasgow AG, Gracefield (Dumfries) AG, Lillie AG (Milngavie - where there is an important collection of 60 works), Huddersfield AG, Kendal AG, Kettering AG, Kirkcaldy AG, Middlesborough AG, Paisley AG, Perth AG, Reading AG, Rugby AG, National Art Gallery of New Zealand, Wellington (NZ) AG, RSA, City of Edinburgh collection, British Library, South London AG.
**Bibl:** Percy Bliss in Studio, 1953; William Buchanan, Joan Eardley, 1976; Gage 38-9; Halsby 231; Hardie 174-8,181,202,206 et passim Ch x & xi; Hartley 130; Macmillan [SA], 367,373-5,377,391-4 et passim in ch xxi; McIsaac in Studio, August 1967; Cordelia Oliver, 'Joan Eardley' (Ex Cat May 1975); Fiona Pearson, Joan Eardley 1921-1963, NGS, Edinburgh 1988; Scot Art Rev, VI, 2, 1957, 2-6.

**EAST, Sir Alfred RA RI PRBA RE** **1849-1913**
Born and died Kettering, Northamptonshire. Landscape painter in oil and watercolour. Also became an etcher and aquatinter. English by birth, he travelled to Glasgow as a very young man and studied in the evenings at Glasgow School of Art. Later he went to Paris studying

at the Ecole des Beaux Arts, subsequently joining Julian's Studio and working under Bouguereau and Tony Fleury. Before then the first of 24 RSA exhibits was in 1878 and he continued to show there until 1912, mostly rural Scottish scenes especially in the kingdom of Fife. Spent some time at Barbizon and Grez and on returning had his first exhibit at the RA 1883. Travelled extensively abroad visiting France, Spain, Italy, Morocco, Ceylon, Japan and the USA. In 1889 he remained in Japan for six months during a round the world voyage. Works resulting from this journey were shown in 1895 and received considerable acclaim. Thereafter Far Eastern influences were always present in his work. A gallery in Kettering attached to his home is now open to the public. Elected RE 1885, RI 1887, ARA 1899, PRBA 1906, knighted 1910 and elected RA on his death bed 1913. Exhibited RA(108), RSA(24), GI(49), RI(30), ROI(27), RE(67), RBA(66), L(65) & AAS, latterly from 2 Spencer St, London. Represented in BM, V & A, Accrington AG, Ashmolean Museum, Oxford, Dudley AG, Eastbourne AG, Kettering AG, Leeds AG, Newport AG, Paisley AG, Wakefield AG, Nat Gall of Canada (Ottawa).
**Bibl:** Halsby 143; Laing AG, Newcastle (Ex Cat 1914).

**EASTON, H G** **fl 1947**
Glasgow watercolourist; exhibited GI(1), from 11 Kirklee Rd.

**EASTON, James** **fl 1961-1962**
Glasgow painter of Highland landscape; exhibited GI(2), from 45 Union St.

**EASTON, Margaret (Meg) H (Mrs Viols)** **fl 1920-1939**
Edinburgh watercolourist; painted landscapes between the wars in a free, wet style, characteristic of the period. During the late 1930s she settled in Kent. Exhibited 2 topographical works at the RSA in 1927 and again in 1945, RSW(5) & AAS 1933-1937.

**EBBUTT, Thomas Kerr** **fl 1906**
Edinburgh-based sculptor. Exhibited RSA(1) from 98, Hanover St.

**EBSWORTH, Joseph Woodfall** **1824-1908**
Edinburgh painter in watercolour and oil and lithographer; historical, landscape and literary. Studied Trustees Academy under Sir William Allan(qv) and David Scott(qv). Four watercolours by Ebsworth, now in Huntly House, Edinburgh, drawn in 1847, depict Edinburgh from the top of the Scott Monument. These are animated works with active street scenes and the wide countryside beyond. Three sketches of soldiers marching down The Mound, Calton Hill, the railway station, and the skyline of the Old Town, were used by J N A Macdonald to illustrate his *Life Jottings of an old Edinburgh Citizen.* Artistic Director of the Manchester Inst of Lithography, later taught at Glasgow School of Art. In later life he abandoned art for the church and is now almost forgotten. Exhibited 22 works at the RSA between 1848 and 1859, mostly narrative paintings, one of which was entitled 'Shakespeare's Last Visit to London', 1615. Represented in SNPG ('Self-portrait'), City of Edinburgh Collection.
**Bibl:** Butchart 84; Halsby 90,92,258.

**ECCLESTON, Philip E** **fl 1937-1948**
Glasgow watercolour painter who resided at 25 Reston Drive. Exhibited two works at the RSA in 1944 & GI(3), including two views of Succoth golf course; latterly from 451 Edinburgh Rd.

**EDGAR, Alexander** **fl 1906**
Exhibited a design for a memorial window at the GI.

**EDGAR, Archibald** **fl 1959-1970**
Aberdeen landscape painter in oil, mostly scenes of north-east Scotland. Exhibited AAS regularly during the above years from 3 King's Gate.

**EDGAR, David** **fl 1893-1907**
Kilmarnock landscape artist; exhibited GI(2), 1893 and 1907, the latter from Kilmarnock Academy where he was probably a member of staff.

**EDGAR, J B** **fl 1863-1870**
Glasgow-based landscape painter in oil and watercolour; exhibited GI(8) in 1870, from Uplawmoor, Renfrewshire.

**EDGAR, James** **1819-1876**
Born Liverpool. Painter in oil and watercolour; genre, landscape, (especially castles) and portraits. Two of his sepia drawings are in the NGS, one entitled 'Robert Burns at an evening party of Lord Monboddo's' (1854) and a portrait of 'Robert Burns at Professor Adam Ferguson's House 1787'. The former is a drawing of a more elaborate work in the SNPG, both studies for an oil painting which until 1957 was in the possession of Lady Invernairne of Flickarty House, Inverness. Exhibited RSA(81), GI(5) & BI 1870, from 22 India St. A portrait of 'Thomas Weston Milne' is in the Victoria AG, Australia and 'Lord Provost Sir John Melville' is in the City of Edinburgh collection.
**Bibl:** Butchart 75.

**EDGAR, Norman B** **1948-**
Born Paisley. Gourock painter of genre, still-life, coastal scenes and portraits. Trained Glasgow School of Art 1966-70. After a short spell teaching took up painting full-time. President, Glasgow Art Club 1993. Paints in the modern colourist tradition. One-man exhibitions in Scotland and London regularly from 1977. Exhibits RSA, RGI, RPS. Represented in Gourock AG, several Royal collections.

**EDIE, R** **fl 1923**
Amateur Glasgow artist; exhibited once at the Walker Gallery, Liverpool.

**EDINBURGH COLLEGE OF ART** **1906-**
The present College evolved directly from the old Trustees Academy and the Edinburgh School of Arts for the teaching of mechanics, craft and trades which had changed its name in 1852 to the **WATT INSTITUTION AND SCHOOL OF ARTS**. In 1902 the condition of the Board of Manufacturers' School was examined by a departmental committee and four years later, in a manner previously suggested by the Scottish Education Department, arrangements were made with the city fathers to establish a new school of art. £30,000 was contributed by the Education Department and £10,000 by the Board of Manufacturers - on the understanding that a matching figure would be forthcoming from local sources. This was achieved, thanks partly to the city providing a site valued at £15,000 and Andrew Grant of Pitcorthie donating £10,000. The building was designed mainly by Pittendrigh Macgillivray(qv) and John More Dick Peddie(qv). From the beginning diplomas were awarded in drawing and painting, design and crafts, sculpture and architecture; town and country planning was added in 1945. Links with the new Heriot Watt University were forged in 1968.

**EDINBURGH DRAWING INSTITUTION** **1825-?**
Little known and short-lived drawing academy 'established for the instruction, upon moderate terms, of Young Ladies and Gentlemen in the various branches of Drawing, upon the general system of the Academies on the Continent. Also in Landscape Painting in Oil and Watercolours and Military pen drawing'. Apparently established in Hill St and equipped with busts, casts and drawings "selected with the most scrupulous care so as to avoid anything the least objectionable". Subscribers included Sir Walter Scott, Sir Henry Raeburn, Lord Cockburn, Francis Jeffrey, James Skene and Andrew Wilson (at that time teaching at the Trustees Academy). Several University professors were also associated.

**EDINBURGH ETCHING CLUB** **1866-?**
Short-lived grouping of Edinburgh-based etchers. Founder members were William Bonnar, Alexander Christie, David Octavius Hill and William B Johnstone.

**EDINBURGH GROUP** **1912-1933**
Formed at a time when it was fashionable for groups of artists to join together. Original members were David Alison (also a member of the Group of Eight), J R Barclay, Hugh Cameron, William Glass, W O Hutchison, Eric Robertson, J G Spence Smith, J W Somerville, A R Sturrock and D M Sutherland. Their first exhibition took place in Doig, Wilson and Wheatley's gallery in George St. The following year they moved to a new Gallery in Shandwick Place. Alison departed and was replaced by Cecile Walton. After a quiescent period during WW1 the group was resuscitated in 1919 when Dorothy Johnstone and Mary Newbery joined. The group attracted some notoriety, largely on account of Eric Robertson's work and lifestyle

and his association with Cecile Walton. Writing in *National Outlook* 1920, Frederick Quinton observed 'half Edinburgh goes to Shandwick Place, secretly desiring to be righteously shocked and the other half goes feeling deliciously uncertain. It may be disappointed by not finding anything sufficiently shocking'. The first three Guthrie awards went to members of the Group. In 1933 D M Sutherland and his wife Dorothy Johnstone moved to Aberdeen and W O Hutchinson went to Glasgow; thus dispersed, the Group came to an end. (See also under individual artists)
**Bibl:** Hardie 142-3.

**EDINBURGH PRINTMAKERS WORKSHOP** **1967-**
Limited non-profit making company financed by sales, fees and subscriptions, and by grants from the SAC (since 1967) and the City of Edinburgh (since 1971). Also specialises in edition printing for artists and publishers. Premises include a gallery. Open seven days a week to paid-up members and hirers at 29 Market St (TN 031-225 1098).

**EDINBURGH SOCIAL UNION** **1885-?**
Formed by Patrick Geddes and dedicated to the improvement of the city. Largely responsible for introducing the Arts and Crafts movement to Edinburgh.

**EDINBURGH SOCIETY FOR THE ENCOURAGEMENT OF ARTS, SCIENCES & MANUFACTURES** **1755-1759**
Also known as the Edinburgh Society. After first visiting Rome and before moving to London Allan Ramsay and David Hume had formed in 1754 an élite Edinburgh coterie called the **SELECT SOCIETY**, the natural precursor of the Academy of the Board of Trustees(qv). Upon going to London Ramsay wrote to Hume "What chiefly renders us considerable is a project of engrafting on the Society a scheme for the encouragement of Art and Science and Manufactures in Scotland by premiums, partly honorary and partly lucrative...Nine managers have been chosen and to keep the business distinct from our reasoning, the first Monday of every month is set apart for these transactions". The idea of offering premiums for improved products and methods had first been introduced by the Board of Manufacturers for Scotland in 1727 in order to administer a grant made to Scotland under the Act of Union as an equivalent for the additional taxation due to the English national debt. The managers were headed by the Duke of Hamilton and the first awards were made in 1756 including a gold medal to James Alves(qv) of Inverness, 3 guineas for 2nd prize to William Jamieson of Kilmarnock and 2 guineas for equal 3rd prize to George Willison(qv) and Thomas Donaldson(qv) of Edinburgh. In 1757 prizes for design were introduced. Donaldson won again, this time for landscapes executed by boys under 18, while Richard Cooper jnr(qv) won best statue by anyone under twenty. No designs were offered in either 1758 and in 1759 only one prize was awarded. The first literary award had gone to the Aberdeen philosopher, Alexander Gerard, for his *Essay on Taste*, published in 1759. No further notices of the Society appeared although in 1761 the Select Society were still meeting, finally disappearing c1765.
**Bibl:** Brydall 140-142; Caw 29,33; Irwin 61,75.

**EDMONSTON, Miss Agnes** **1885-1921**
Edinburgh painter in oil and watercolour. Lived at 2 Kilgraston Road, Exhibited mainly Highland landscapes but also interior and figurative subjects at the RSA(52), RSW(4), GI(18), L(1) & AAS(1).

**EDMONSTON, Miss Anne B D** **fl 1879-1898**
Edinburgh painter in oil and watercolour; birds, buildings, wildlife and landscape. Daughter of Samuel E(qv) and sister of Janet E(qv). Lived in Joppa, Annan and Edinburgh. Exhibited RSA(13) between the above years.

**EDMONSTON, F** **fl 1830**
Minor Edinburgh engraver. Executed bookplates for Dalrymple Hamilton and also for Scott of Melby both in 1830; also for a Mr Sibbald.

**EDMONSTON, Janet** **fl 1859-1863**
Edinburgh painter in oil of interiors and landscape. Daughter of Samuel E(qv) and sister of Anne(qv). Worked in a dark, rich slightly dramatic style with much bitumen. Exhibited RSA(8) 1859-1863.

**EDMONSTON, Samuel** **1825-?**
Edinburgh painter in oil, watercolour and chalk; literary, landscape (especially in the Highlands) and animals. Studied Trustees Academy 1845-1853 under William Allan(qv) and Thomas Duncan(qv). Father of Anne(qv), Janet(qv) and W Douglas E(qv). Specialised in pictures of Scottish rural life and although achieving considerable success in his own life-time, has become sadly neglected, partly due to the fact that late in life he emigrated to the USA. Contributed illustrations for *Pen and Pencil Pictures from the Poets* (1866); *Burns Poems* (nd). Exhibited twice at the RA from his studio at 17 London Street, Edinburgh: 'Music hath charms' (1862) and 'The fisherman's return' (1864). But kept almost all of his best work for the RSA, exhibiting 106 works there between 1845 and 1887, also GI(11) & AAS(1), after 1871 from North Bridge. Represented in NGS(3).
**Bibl:** Chatto & Jackson: *Treatise on Wood Engraving*, 1861, 599.

**EDMONSTON, W Douglas** **fl 1887**
Edinburgh painter in watercolour of landscapes and interiors. Son of Samuel E(qv). Exhibited 2 works at the RSA in the above year, one a study of the druidical stones nr Pitlochry, Perthshire.

**EDMONSTONE, Robert HRSA** **1794-1834**
Born Kelso; died Kelso, 21 Sep. Painter in oil of portraits and figurative and historical studies. After a short apprenticeship with a watchmaker he persuaded his father to send him to Edinburgh to study art, enrolling at the Trustees Academy. His work was praised by Hume who became one of his closest friends. C1820 he painted a clever picture of 'Jamie the Showman', an Edinburgh character well-known from an engraving. In 1818 he became a student at the Royal Academy in London, exhibiting his first picture there the same year. Contributed in 1824, 1825 and 1827 to the annual exhibition of the GI. Also spent several years in Rome and other Italian cities. 'Ceremony of Kissing the Chains of St Peter', painted in Rome, was exhibited and sold in the British Gallery 1833. Whilst in Italy he contracted a fever which required his return to London 1832. Unable to work again he finally settled in his native Kelso. His early death was deeply regretted by his contemporaries, who recognised his considerable talent. Elected HRSA 1829. Exhibited RA(23) 1818-1834, most of them portraits, especially children; also RSA(8) 1829-1834, and 3 of his works were included posthumously in 1863.
**Bibl:** Brydall 279.

**EDNIE, Andrew** **fl 1904**
Architect and interior designer. Brother of John E(qv). Exhibited an interior for a banqueting hall at the GI.

**EDNIE, John** **fl 1903-1910**
Architect, interior designer and watercolourist. Lived at Bishopton in 1904 and later Edinburgh. Trained Edinburgh School of Art before joining Wylie & Lochhead in Glasgow as an interior designer. One of his first commissioned works was an interior for the firm's pavilion at the Glasgow exhibition of 1901. As a watercolourist was influenced by Charles Rennie Mackintosh(qv). Husband of Lily E(qv). Exhibited RSA(2) & GI(5), in 1910 from the Technical College, Glasgow where he was most probably a member of staff.
**Bibl:** Halsby 188.

**EDNIE, Mrs Lily R** **fl 1904-1908**
Landscape painter. Wife of John E(qv). Exhibited RSA(1) & GI(1).

**EDOUART, Augustin Amant Constant Fidele** **1789-1861**
Born Dunkirk; died Guisnes, nr Calais. Portrait miniaturist and silhouettist. Although French he established himself in London 1813 painting animals and then concentrating on silhouettes. Regarded by many as the finest of all silhouettists. Whilst in London he exhibited at the RA 1815-16. Then visited Scotland where he remained several years, teaching his art in Edinburgh, before proceeding to Ireland and then America. Appointed silhouettist to the Royal family of France. Represented by no fewer than 74 works in the SNPG; also in V & A, National Gallery of Ireland.

**EDWARD, Albert** **fl 1876**
Dundee painter who exhibited a still-life in watercolour at the RSA in 1876. Possibly the Albert Edward who exhibited at the RI from 27 Park Lane, London 1885.

**EDWARD, (Rev) Alexander** **1651-1708**
Architect, cleric and garden designer. Son of the minister of Murroes, Angus. Graduated from St. Andrews University 1670. Parish Minister of Kemback, Fife until ousted as a non-juror in 1689. The plans, elevation and garden layout for Kinross House were drawn by Edward for Sir William Bruce c1684, possibly scale drawings made after the architect, now in the possession of Edinburgh College of Art. Edward undertook similar work at Melville House. With funds provided by two of his leading patrons, the Earls of Mar and Panmure, he visited London in 1701/2, before proceeding to France and the Netherlands. On his return he was to give each of his sponsors three drawings of their choice and spend three days a year with each of them. The only known surviving drawing is a plan of Marly now in the Gibbs collection. His notes reveal a cultivated and enquiring mind with a serious interest in botany, engravings and scientific instruments. Worked at Kellie Castle, Angus 1699-1705 and was involved in the building of Rossie House, Angus 1700. Involved in the remodelling of Brechin Castle for the Earl of Panmure and prepared a series of interesting garden designs for the 4th Earl of Southesk at Kinnaird Castle. Also concerned with designing the layout of the gardens at Hopetoun as well as designing an exuberant memorial to the 1st Marquis of Atholl at Dunkeld Cathedral.
**Bibl:** Dunbar 81-3,87-9,93; Bruce Walker & W S Gauldie, Architects and Architecture on Tayside, Dundee 1984, 48-50.

**EDWARD, Alfred S RBA** **1852-1915**
Born Dundee; died 15 May. Landscape and marine painter. Apprenticed to an architect he then studied art in Edinburgh, moving to London early in his career. Exhibited at the principal London galleries from 1876. Member of the London Sketch Club and the Hogarth Club. Lived London and Puckeridge, Hertfordshire. Painted in France, Holland, Spain, the Canaries and Africa. Among his 8 exhibits at the RA between 1879 and 1900 all, save one, were Scottish coastal scenes eg 'On the West Coast, Sutherlandshire', 1879, 'On the Kincardine Coast', 1889. Elected RBA 1894. Exhibited RSA(14), RBA(216) & GI(28), after 1900 from 10 Kyverdale Rd, London.

**EDWARD, Maggie W** **fl 1889**
Amateur Glasgow artist; exhibited 'An Autumn Spray' at the GI.

**EDWARD, William** **fl c1760**
Edinburgh engraver. Referred to on the only known copy of the first edition of *A Collection of Scots Reels...Composed by John Riddle at Ayr,* published in about 1760.
**Bibl:** Davidson Cook in Scottish Notes & Queries, Nov, 1928.

**EDWARDS, Brian William MSC ARIBA ARIAS FSA (Scot)1944-**
Born Orpington, Kent, 26 Jly. Architect and draughtsman. Educated Canterbury College of Art and Edinburgh College of Art. Influenced most strongly by Paul Hogarth and Gordon Cullend. Settled in Scotland and lives in the Lothians where he is active in the field of conservation. His principle interest in painting is capturing the mood and character of historic buildings and towns with an emphasis on the picturesque. Represented in Leeds AG.

**EDWARDS, Catherine D** **fl 1935**
Amateur painter of 13 Dalhousie Street, Brechin. Exhibited RSA(1).

**EDWARDS, Evan** **fl 1928-1932**
Landscape painter. Lived at 16 Ainslie Place, Edinburgh. Exhibited 4 works at the RSA between the above dates, all local coastal scenes painted in oil.

**EDWARDS, Joseph B** **1933-**
Born Aberdeen, Feb 4. Painter in oil and tempera of portraits, genre and farming scenes; also lithographer. Trained Gray's School of Art, Aberdeen 1950-4 under Robert Sivell(qv). Commissioned by Aberdeen Council to paint the portrait of 'ex Lord Provost Collie'. Turned increasingly to more abstract work concerned with the perspective of colour. Exhibited RSA 1959-1970, GI(19) & AAS 1959-1972, after 1965 from Speedwell Cottage, Fairley, Kingswells.

**EDWIN, John** **fl 1885-1890**
Glasgow landscape painter in oil and watercolour. Exhibited RSA(1) & GI(5), latterly from 1 Valeview, Battlefield, Langside.

**EDWIN, Richard** **fl 1870-1876**
Glasgow watercolourist; exhibited Highland landscapes at the GI(3).

**EGGINTON, Robert** **c1960-**
Scottish-based landscape painter in watercolours and occasionally oils. Paints mainly Scottish scenes in an accurate pictorial manner and a slightly sweet palette. Nephew of the artist **Frank EGGINTON** and grandson of **Wycliffe EGGINTON RI**. Exhibits regularly in London & Edinburgh, from Grantown-on-Spey.

**EGLIN, Jane M** **fl 1888**
An amateur Glasgow flower painter who resided at 370 Great Western Road, and exhibited two works at the GI in 1888.

**ELDER, Andrew Taylor** **1908-1966**
Painter in oil and watercolour; landscapes and figure subjects. Studied at Edinburgh College of Art 1927-31. After winning a travelling scholarship undertook further studies under André Lhôte in Paris. Following working trips around France and Spain he settled in Glasgow 1940, exhibiting at The Centre(qv).
**Bibl:** Hardie 168.

**ELDER, Clarence** **fl 1919-1921**
Painter. Lived at 136 Wellington Street, Glasgow. Exhibited 4 genre paintings in oil at the RSA 1920(2) and 1921(2); also GI(1) & L(1).

**ELDER, Miss Grace** **fl 1882**
Edinburgh painter of 5 St Bernard's Row, in watercolour. Exhibited an interior at the RSA.

**ELDER, J F** **fl 1896-1898**
Glasgow painter of flowers and landscape; exhibited GI(3) from 33 Monteith Road.

**ELDER, James** **fl 1879-1901**
Glasgow painter of landscape and figurative works in watercolour and oil; exhibited RSW(1) & GI(11), latterly from 37 Bentinck St.

**ELDER, John** **fl 1883-1901**
Scottish painter in oil of pastoral scenes. He lived at various times in Glasgow Cathcart and 21 George Street, Stirling. Exhibited GI(6) & AAS(3).

**ELDER, Ralph H** **fl 1880-1885**
Glasgow painter of local landscapes; exhibited RSA(3) & GI(5) from 274 Renfrew Street, Garnet Hill.

**ELDER, William** **fl 1681**
Scottish engraver. Mentioned by Walpole, for whose *Anecdotes* he provided some of the illustrations, as 'contemporary with Robert White, and a Scotchman Vertue had seen some writing graved by him in a book in 1681. He made two engravings of himself. His best plate is of 'Ben Jonson'; also did heads of 'Pythagoras'; 'Dr de Mayerne'; 'John Ray'; 'Dr Morton'; 'Archbishop Sancroft'; 'George Parker'; 'Charles Snell'; 'Admiral Russell'; and 'Judge Pollexfen'.
**Bibl:** Bryan; Brydall 193-4; The Book of the Old Edinburgh Club, vol 9, Edinburgh 1916.

**ELLEN, Anne M** **fl 1969**
Amateur Nairn watercolour artist. Exhibited a mother and child at the AAS from Ardlinnhe, Albert Street.

**ELLERMAN, Cecil** **fl 1885-1890**
Aberdeen painter in oil. Exhibited at the AAS harbour scenes and titles such as 'The Wreck' from 6 Crown Terrace.

**ELLIOT, Miss Ann** **fl 1984**
Exhibited an untitled work at the GI while still a student at the Glasgow School of Art.

**ELLIOT, Archibald** **1761-1823**
Architect. One of the most notable exponents of castellated Gothic architecture of his time. This important contribution, with his brother James(qv), did not prevent the establishment of an extensive country house practice. The finest of their surviving works is the main block

of Taymouth Castle, completed for the 4th Earl of Breadalbane 1806-1810, following the dismissal of the Edinburgh architect John Paterson(qv). An impressive feature of Taymouth is that it is Gothic inside as well as outside, most noteworthy being the elegant fan-vaulted staircase hall, decorated by the Italian plasterer, Bernasconi c1810. The Elliot brothers also directed the construction of Stobo Castle, Peeblesshire (1805-1811) and Lindertis, Angus (1815-6). Archibald was responsible for Newbyth, East Lothian, built for General Sir David Baird (1817-1819). This was the original design with high octagonal angle-towers and a rib-vaulted and arcaded portico, but having a Gothic interior. Other buildings of interest are the Governor's House for the Old Calton Jail in Edinburgh, Waterloo Place (1815), St. Paul's Episcopal church, Edinburgh (1816), Broughton Place church (1821) and the complicated radial plan Jedburgh Jail (1823). His son **Archibald ELLIOT II** (d1843) was also an architect.
**Bibl:** Brydall 181; Dunbar 121,127,194,207; Gifford 39,67,106,120, 123,280,286,324-5,361,379,425,433,437-8,442-3,448,Pls.9,33; Bruce Walker & W S Gauldie, Architects and Architecture on Tayside, Dundee 1984, 69.

**ELLIOT, Miss Euphemia Moffat** **1883-1954**
Born Blackhaugh of Meigle, 13 Mar; died Durness, 21 Dec. Landscape painter in oil. Lived near Galashiels before settling Durness, Sutherland c1945. Exhibited Sutherland landscapes at the RSA annually between 1940 and 1953. Represented by 9 works in Glasgow AG.

**ELLIOT, James** **1770-1810**
Architect. Younger brother of Archibald E(qv).
**Bibl:** Dunbar 121,125; Bruce Walker & W S Gauldie, Architects and Architecture on Tayside, Dundee 1984,69.

**ELLIOT, M Scott** **fl 1881**
Edinburgh painter who exhibited a flower painting in oil at the RSA in the above year from 34 Regent's Terrace.

**ELLIOT, Mabel** **fl 1909-1915**
Ayrshire watercolour painter, latterly living at Barrhill; exhibited RSW(1) & RSA(3) between the above years.

**ELLIS, David** **fl 1974-1975**
Glasgow painter of portraits and figure works; exhibited GI(2), from 4 Kennoway Drive.

**ELLIS, Mrs Dewi** **fl 1918**
Amateur Glasgow painter of portrait miniatures; exhibited GI(1) from 79 W. Regent St.

**ELLIS, Miss Dora** **1902-**
Glasgow based portrait and glass painter, also teacher. Worked mainly in watercolour. Studied Glasgow School of Art and lived at 62 Great George Street, 1925-26. Exhibited GI(2).

**ELLIS, Jean(ie) Wright (née Paulin)** **fl 1911-1932**
Portrait and animal painter, also black and white artist. Studied at Glasgow School of Art. Sister of the sculptor, George Henry Paulin(qv). Lived at Milngavie 1917, moving to Bearsden c1930. Exhibited two portraits at the RSA in 1911 and 1919 & GI(8) 1917-1932, after 1930 from Thorn Rd, Bearsden.

**ELLIS, Lindsay James Paxton** **1953-**
Painter in gouache and oil with a strong emphasis on design and colour. Trained Duncan of Jordanstone College of Art, Dundee 1973-77. Thereafter taught in various London schools 1978-89. At the beginning of 1990 returned to Scotland and began painting full-time. Influenced by Alberta Morrocco(qv) and David McClure(qv). Exhibited a 'Self-Portrait with Colour Bowl' at the RSA in 1990.

**ELMSLIE, Alex** **fl 1887**
Amateur Aberdeen artist; exhibited AAS(1) from Headcroft Place.

**ELMSLIE, Sandra** **Cont**
Born Elgin. Landscape painter in oil on canvas and paper; occasional watercolour. Trained Aberdeen College and Gray's School of Art. The early death of her husband caused the abandonment of doctoral studies in the history of art, leading instead to work as a full-time artist. Inspired by the colours and patterns of nature and the north-east countryside. Her work is characterised by a strong colour sense allied to a sensitivity for the history and significance of place.
**Bibl:** John Ward "Confronting the Challenges...", Scottish Connections, Jly 2003, pp22-23.

**ELPHINSTONE, Hon John** **1706-1753**
Important engraver. Son of Lord Elphinstone, he predeceased his father and so never inherited the title. Sometime before 1740 he completed 15 sketches issued in book form under the title *Fifteen Views of the Most Remarkable Buildings of the City of Edinburgh.* These views were used again to illustrate Arnot's *History of Edinburgh,* 1779. Published a map of Britain in 1744, and in 1745 a map of Scotland that was far in advance of any that had previously appeared and which was widely used by both sides during the 1745 rebellion. Represented in City of Edinburgh Art Collection.
**Bibl:** Butchart 15-16.

**ELRICK, A W** **fl 1898-1926**
Aberdeen painter of country scenes. Exhibited frequently at the AAS between the above years from Ruthrieston.

**ELRICK, Mary A** **fl 1959**
Aberdeen painter of domestic genre and still life. Exhibited AAS(2) from 39 Charles Street.

**ELTON, Lady** **[see Mary STEWART]**

**ELWES, Windsor Cary** **fl 1885**
Portobello watercolour miniature painter. Exhibited RSA(3) 1885, from 4 Durham Road, Portobello.

**ELYAN, Jessica** **fl 1934**
Glasgow figurative painter; exhibited 'Musing' at the GI from 596 Clarkston Road.

**EMMOTT, Lady Constance H** **fl 1896-1921**
Probably English. Exhibited her first works in London and was living at Thorpe Hall, Barnard Castle in 1908, before moving to Inverary c1912 and Edinburgh c1918. Exhibited 3 landscapes at the RSA in 1917, 1919 and 1920; also RA(2), GI(2), 3 Scottish landscapes (one of Aboyne), at the AAS, when living at 24 Belgrave Crescent, 1919-1921. Represented by an oil painting in City of Edinburgh collection.

**EMSLEY, Alexander** **fl 1927-1934**
Glasgow portrait painter in oil; exhibited twice at the RSA, one a self-portrait 1934, & GI(2) from 71 Chancellor Street, Partick.

**EMSLIE, Grace** **fl 1926**
Amateur Aberdeen painter; exhibited AAS(1) from 82 Mile-end Avenue.

**ERSKINE, Colin** **c1704-post 1743**
Scottish born portrait painter, resident in Rome. His son, later Cardinal Charles Erskine, was born in Rome while his father was still there in 1743.
**Bibl:** Waterhouse, 120.

**ERSKINE, David Steuart (11th Earl of Buchan)** **1742-1829**
Born Scotland, 1 Jne. Antiquarian, art patron, engraver and etcher. Eldest son of Henry David E(qv). Privately tutored, partly by his mother, before entering Glasgow University. During his time in Glasgow also studied design, engraving and etching at Foulis Academy(qv). Then joined the army, serving for several years with the 32nd Cornwall Regiment of Foot. Became an ardent Methodist but following the death of his father in 1767 moved to Scotland, there becoming increasingly interested in Scottish antiquities and history. Visited Rome with his friend John Brown(qv) 1771. In 1780 founded the Society of Antiquities of Scotland(qv) and in 1786 purchased the estate of Dryburgh. There he erected an Ionic temple with a statue of Apollo and the bust of the poet James Thomson of Ednam and later a Parian urn in memory of Burns. Friend of Sir Walter Scott and frequent contributor to various publications. Patronised several artists, notably John Brown and James Howe(qv). An etching by Erskine of the Abbey of Icolmkill appeared beside his account of the

abbey in *Transactions of the Society of Antiquities of Scotland* (vol 1). SNPG has a pencil drawing of the mathematician 'James Short' (1710-1768) and no fewer than 30 copies of other sitters.
**Bibl:** Halsby 25,27; Irwin 78-9,191-3 et al.

**ERSKINE, Henry (Harry)** **fl 1884-1929**
Glasgow painter in oil and watercolour. Exhibited landscapes, still life and flower paintings at the RSA(3), RSW(11) & GI(11) from 37 Barclay Terrace.

**ERSKINE, Henry David (10th Earl of Buchan)** **1710-1767**
Born Scotland. Draughtsman and engraver. Father of David Steuart E(qv). Thought to have had connections with Glasgow Academy. A pen portrait of 'Henry Scougal, Professor of Divinity at Aberdeen', signed and dated, is in the NGS.
**Bibl:** Bryan; Brydall 129; DNB.

**ERSKINE OF TORRY INSTITUTE** **1872-**
Founded by Mrs Sharpe-Erskine, the youngest daughter of General Sir William Erskine of Torrie, and sister of Sir James Erskine who donated the Torrie bequest to the University of Edinburgh 1835. She bequeathed a small but select collection of mainly Flemish paintings, and a library of over 4,000 volumes, together with a sum to cover maintenance, for a permanent display at Dunimarle castle, near Culross, Fife.
**Bibl:** Brydall 369; Caw 222.

**ERSKINE, William Charles Chitty** **fl 1873-1881**
Painter in oil and watercolour; landscapes, often in winter, portraits and figures. Exhibited 'A glen in winter', at the RA in 1879 from 21 India Street, Edinburgh and RSA(6) 1873-1881.

**ESPLENS, Charles and John** **fl c1750**
Edinburgh engravers. The two brothers were in partnership. Together they engraved portraits of 'Lord President Forbes' and 'George Heriot'.
**Bibl:** J Chaloner Smith, British Mezzotint Portraits, 1878-1883, 264.

**ESPLIN, Tom** **1915-**
Born Motherwell, Nov 26. Painter in oil and watercolour until 1955, principally the latter; also teacher. Educated Buckhaven HS, Edinburgh University and Edinburgh College of Art where he was an Andrew Grant scholar. As the result of a travelling scholarship in 1952 he visited New Zealand and settled there permanently in 1954 being appointed Senior Lecturer in Design at the Univ of Otago. Promoted to Associate Professor 1978, remaining until his retirement in 1985. Member of the New Zealand Society of Industrial Designers and the NZ Academy of Fine Arts. Professor of Design at the Univ. of Otago 1978 until his retirement in 1980. Exhibited a watercolour at the RSW from Links Road, Leven in 1935 and subsequently in New Zealand, mostly with the Otago Art Society. Lived at 3 Prospect Row, Sawyers Bay, Otago. Represented in Otago AG and other institutions throughout New Zealand.

**EVANGELISTA, Raymond** **fl 1971**
Ceramic sculptor. Exhibited GI(4), from 10 Clyde Place, Corseford, Johnstone.

**EVANS, David Pugh RSA RSW ARCA** **1942-**
Born Llanfrechfa, Gwent. Painter in oil and occasionally watercolour; figurative and narrative subjects, landscapes. Trained at Newport College of Art 1959-1962 and Royal College of Art 1965 where he was awarded a silver medal for painting. Much affected by his immediate environment, he is a lover of delicate hue, sharp angles and subtle tonal contrasts, with a hint of Magritte and a distant influence of Edward Hopper. Photographic realism with silent mood, sombre palette and a strong story line. Elected ARSA 1974, RSA 1989, RSW 1975. Lives in Edinburgh and teaches at Edinburgh College of Art. Exhibits regularly at the RSA since 1967, & GI(8) from 17 Inverleith Gdns. Represented in Carlisle AG, Edinburgh City collection, Municipality of Ridderkerk (Holland), SAC.
**Bibl:** Gage 63-5.

**EVANS, J M** **fl 1895**
Glasgow artist; exhibited 'December' at GI, from 136 Wellington St.

**EVANS, Marjorie RSW (Res) (Mrs A Scott Elliot)** **c1850-1907**
Aberdeen based painter in oil and watercolour of flowers, still life, landscape and occasional portraits. Travelled frequently between Aberdeen, London, Greenock and Surrey. Elected RSW 1891, but resigned 1902. Exhibited two paintings of roses at the RA, in 1892 from a London address and again in 1895; also RA(2), RSA(4), RSW & AAS, after 1893 from 16 Albyn Place, Aberdeen.
**Bibl:** Halsby 258.

**EVANS, Merlyn O** **fl 1929**
Glasgow painter of informal portraits; exhibited GI(1) from 15 Abbotsford Ave, Rutherglen.

**EVANS, Rufus Easson** **fl 1902-1940**
Painter in oil and watercolour of rustic scenes and landscapes. Lived at Newcastleton, Roxburghshire. Exhibited regularly at the RSA between 1904 and 1916, also RSW(15) & GI(1).

**EVERGREEN: A NORTHERN SEASONAL** **1895-1897**
Influential quarterly magazine founded and edited in Edinburgh by the biologist, social philosopher and town planner Patrick Geddes(qv). The title echoes Allan Ramsay's collection of ancient Scots poetry of 1724. Its importance lay not only in its literary content - although Geddes and others contributed significant essays including 'The Scots Renascence' published in the opening issue - but also in its dissemination through illustration and design of the Celtic Revival and Edinburgh art nouveau, notably by Robert Burns(qv) and John Duncan(qv). The theme for each quarter was the relevant season of the year appearing within covers designed by Charles Hodge Mackie(qv) while the general motif was a return to the old Celtic traditions of Scotland in art and literature.
**Bibl:** Patrick Geddes(ed), Evergreen; A Northern Seasonal, Dundee 1895-6; Irwin 404-410; Macmillan [SA], 301,304-5,309-310,324.

**EWAN, Alfred W** **fl 1934-1936**
Angus painter. Exhibited a still life in 1934 and a portrait in 1936 at the RSA from Dundee and Lundin Links.

**EWAN, Alison ARIAS** **1933-**
Bron Aberdeen. Architect, watercolour painter and teacher. Fascinated by old rural buildings and structures which have become blended with the landscape. Member, Scottish Society for Architecture Artists. Paints flowers, country buildings and landscape in a colourful, decorative, loose and modest manner. Keen on stagecraft and music, she is a member of the Deeside Orchestra and for many years designed and painted stage sets for the Deeside Musical Society. Founder member of the Society of Artists of Upper Deeside, 1992. Exhibits RSA, RIAS and at galleries throughout Scotland from her home in Aboyne.

**EWAN, Donald** **fl 1969**
Dundee ceramic designer. Exhibited AAS(1) from 19 Black Street.

**EWAN, M M** **fl 1906**
Amateur Edinburgh painter. Exhibited 2 landscapes at the AAS from 66 Hanover Street.

**EWAN, Marion C** **fl 1935**
Edinburgh painter. Exhibited RSA(1) from 13 Warrender Park Crescent.

**EWAN, R** **1885-1891**
Amateur Glasgow painter; exhibited GI(2).

**EWANS, David J RSW** **1942-**
Edinburgh painter of landscape. His work often had a brooding quality with titles such as 'Before the storm'. Living in Dumfries 1965 but returned to Edinburgh c1970. His landscapes, often of Fife and Kirkcudbrightshire, were exhibited at the RSA 1955-1970, GI(10) & AAS(2), latterly from 22 Dublin St, Edinburgh.

**EWART, Charles** **fl 1913**
Engraver and etcher. Exhibited an etching of 'Cockenzie harbour' at the RSA from an Edinburgh address.

**EWART, David Shanks ARSA** **1901-1965**
Born Shettleston, Glasgow, 21 Dec; died Glasgow, 12 Oct. Landscape and portrait painter in oil. Spent a year in business before entering Glasgow School of Art under Maurice Greiffenhagen(qv) and Fra Newbery(qv) in 1919. Awarded a travelling scholarship enabling him to study in France and Italy. Shortly after his return he received the Guthrie Award (1926) and the Lauder Award (1927). In his early years painted mainly the scenery of the Cuillins, Loch Coruisk in Skye and the three sisters of Glencoe, but he soon concentrated on portraiture. Member Glasgow Art Club 1925. Visited the US between 1946 and 1964, for six months each year he painted portraits of wealthy industrialists and their wives. Elected ARSA 1934. Lived all his life in Glasgow. Exhibited 80 portraits at the RSA including 'Lord Provost Sir Ian Johnson-Gilbert' and the 'Moderator of the Church of Scotland', RA(2), GI(74 including 'Members of the Glasgow Art Club' (1933), AAS(1) & L(4), latterly from 2 Royal Terrace. Represented in SNGMA, City of Edinburgh collection.
**Bibl:** Glasgow Herald 13 Oct 1965(obit); Hartley 130-1.

**EWART, Miss Freida M** **fl 1947**
Renfrewshire painter; exhibited GI(1), from Am Fasgadh, Kilmarnock Rd, Newton Mearns.

**EWBANK, John Wilson RSA** **1779-1847**
Born Gateshead; died Edinburgh, 28 Nov. Landscape and seascape painter in oil. He started work as an apprentice to a housepainter but after a short while, having lost his parents at a very young age and being adopted by a wealthy uncle who pointed the young man in the direction of training for the priesthood, absconded in favour of a house-painter called Coulcon. When the latter moved to Edinburgh his young apprentice went too. There he studied under Alexander Nasmyth. Also for a time under W H Lizars(qv) who did much of his engraving including Ewbank's illustration for Dr James Browne's *Picturesque Views of Edinburgh.* Influenced by Dutch painting of the 17th century, particularly Van der Velde. His best work was from his early years, after about 1810 his work badly deteriorated. Described as 'a painter of considerable talent with...a fine sense of composition, an evenness of surface well suited to the moderate scale on which the best of them are painted...something emasculated in its chiaroscuro while the opposition of brown with whitish tones imparts an anaemic aspect to the scenes depicted. When more positive colour is used it breaks out in spots like the hectic blush of the consumptive'[McKay]. Held a prominent position in landscape and marine art in the ten years that followed the establishment of the RSA. His inland scenes and large historical works are not the equal of his marines. Late in life he developed bad habits and a career of great promise ended prematurely from typhus in 1847. Elected RSA 1826. Exhibited 27 works in Carlisle Academy 1825-1833, mostly shipping and coastal views. Exhibited twice at the RA and many times at the RSA. Represented in BM, NGS (6 drawings, a watercolour and 2 oils), City of Edinburgh collection, Brodie Castle (NTS), Accrington AG, Laing AG (Newcastle).
**Bibl:** AJ 1848, 51; Brydall 308-9; Butchart 51-2; Caw 160 ff, 322; Halsby 88; Macmillan [SA], 140-1,143; McKay 116-7.

**EWING, George Edwin** **1828-1884**
Glasgow sculptor in marble; portraits and portrait busts. Important sculptor of his time with a most distinguished clientele but never quite received due recognition. Lived all his life in Glasgow. Among his sitters were the artists 'Daniel Macnee' (1862 and again in 1866), 'Thomas Faed' (1863), the 'Duke of Sutherland', the 'Prince and Princess of Wales' (all in 1869), the 'Lord Provost of Glasgow' (1870), 'Princess Victoria of Teck' (1871), the 'Duke of Teck' (1872), and the 'son of the painter Dr Blatherwick' (1876). Exhibited 45 works at the RA 1862-1877, RSA(40+) 1861-1878, including a marble bust of the 'daughter of Denovan Adam' (1879), another of 'Thomas Faed' (1878); also GI(73), latterly from 287 Bath St. Represented in Paisley AG.

**EWING, J G Leckie** **fl 1890-1904**
Amateur painter of seascapes, landscapes and harbour scenes. Lived in Glasgow (1890), London (1893), settled St Andrews 1897 at 11 Murray Park. Painted a number golf scenes in St Andrews, usually rather grey and woolly. Exhibited RSA(2) 1901, studies of Nairn and Newhaven harbours; also GI(5), latterly from Ballancleroch, Campsie Glen, Stirlingshire.

**EWING, James A** **fl 1879-1898**
Glasgow sculptor; figures and busts, often in marble. Possibly related to his Glasgow contemporary **Hugh EWING**. Exhibited RSA(8) 1879-1888 but mostly at the GI(38), latterly from 24 Woodlands Rd. Represented in Paisley AG.

**EWING, Michael** **fl 1899-1907**
Landscape painter in oil of 265 Kenmure Street, Pollockshields; exhibited RSA(5) & GI(4).

**EWING, Sandra Mary** **1943-**
Born Johannesburg, South Africa. Came to Scotland in 1961, studied at Glasgow School of Art, specialising in textile design in which she obtained a diploma. 1965-1975 working on embroidery, pastels and monochrome drawings, all widely exhibited. In 1975 began painting in gouache. Her main interest is in Scottish landscape and still life. Among the many influences in her work have been the Impressionist Klimt, Joan Eardley(qv), Duncan Shanks(qv), and Stanley Spencer. Her paintings are concerned with colour, shape and pattern, clearly showing her training and interest in textile design. The landscapes also show a great awareness of texture. Her paintings became simpler and broader with a heightened interest in still life. Exhibited 'a study of gladioli' at the RSA in 1989 from East Kilbride, also RSW & GI(22), after 1970 from 58 Scalpay, St. Leonards, East Kilbride.

**EWING, William** **fl 1818-1826**
Miniaturist. An ivory medallion portrait miniature of the artist 'William Yellowlees' signed and dated 1818 is in the SNPG.

# F

**FAED, Frank** **1905-1949**
Painter in watercolour and etcher in drypoint. Son of William Cotton F(qv). Was becoming known as an artist when he succumbed to a polio epidemic. Nothing is now known of his work.

**FAED, George** **1830-1852**
Born Barley Mill, 4 Nov; died Edinburgh, 12 Mar. Engraver and portrait painter in oil and pencil. The earliest record is when, as a youth of about 17, he was asked by his brother James(qv) to go to Edinburgh to help with background work on his plates. George quickly showed that he too had a talent for engraving. James noted 'he worked at it for a year or two and did some work on his own account that I could not take in hand. With a little help from me he did them very well but his fingers were more suited for the brush and the pencil than the engraving tools. His taste was also more suited. So he spent a great deal of time in his room at night doing ideal heads and I will say that no other member of the family showed more refined taste and fine sentiment in his female heads than he did'. He died at 21, and had he lived would have been a high class artist in a style of his own. 'All his heads had a delicate look, a consumptive look as he had himself, but he was a most handsome fellow in every feature, and tall'. An unsigned oil 'My Memory Come to Me', was sold at auction after the death of Susan F(qv) 1909. Engravings by George of three portraits are in the print room of the SNPG. These are 'Rev Prof S Macgill' (after Sir Henry Raeburn), 'Dr David Moir' (after Sir John Watson Gordon), and 'Rev John Cumming' (after William M Tweedie). Represented in the SNPG by a portrait of Thomas Faed.
**Bibl:** McKerrow, The Faeds, 1982 132-133.

**FAED, James** **1821-1911**
Born Barley Mill, Kirkcudbrightshire, 4 Apr; died Edinburgh, 23 Sep. Painter in oil and watercolour, engraver; landscape, portrait miniatures, genre and portraits. Younger brother of John(qv) and Thomas F(qv). As a young man demonstrated remarkable talent with his hands. He made toy pistols, musical instruments, dressed salmon flies and in the winters turned to gun-making and boat-building. After the death of his father in 1843, he joined his brothers John and Thomas in Edinburgh, helping John paint miniatures. Through John he met the mezzotint engraver John Bonnar(qv). This encouraged him in the art and his first plate was his own portrait, painted by Thomas. His second plate was after Caracci's 'The Entombment', the ground for which was done by a machine of his own invention. Shortly afterwards he was commissioned by John Watson Gordon(qv), the start of a regular stream of commissions that continued to flow in throughout his life. Never elected an academician, perhaps because he had never served an apprenticeship, but generally regarded as the finest mezzotinter of his time after Samuel Cousins. Engraved at least 133 plates including 'John Watson Gordon'(qv) and 'Sir Francis Grant'(qv). Exhibited RA(37) 1855-1904, among them engravings of 'Sam Bough'(qv) and his wife 'Isabella', copies of which are in the SNPG. His last exhibited plate at the Academy was 'The Earl of Home', grandfather of the present Earl, after Sir George Reid(qv). In 1850 he was invited by Queen Victoria to engrave Winterhalter's picture of 'The Queen and Prince Arthur'. This led to further work and visits to Balmoral. Soon after his marriage in 1852 to Mary, a member of the Cotton tobacco family, he moved from Comely Bank, Edinburgh to 7 Chalcott Terrace, St John's Wood, London but returned north in 1855 to Overshiel House, Mid Calder, West Lothian, then to 14 Comely Bank in 1861, buying the estate of Craigenveoch, Glenluce for farming and holiday purposes in the early 1870s, an adventure he was to repeat in 1898, this time with an estate in Peebleshire. 'One forms the impression from his notes written at the age of 80 that he was egotistical, irascible, quick to take offence, given to self-praise and meticulously careful about his personal appearance. A man of high principle, he had absolute confidence in himself, was dogmatic, intolerant, but scrupulously correct in all his dealings' [McKerrow]. Exhibited RSA(144), GI(33) & AAS(2) from 7 Barnton Terrace. Represented in SNPG, City of Edinburgh Art collection, Royal library, Windsor, Stranraer PL, Wigtown County Library, Aberdeen AG, Glasgow AG, Carberry Tower, Musselburgh, Sheriff Court Room, Kircudbright, Town Hall, New Galloway, Leicestershire AG, Yale Centre for British Art, New Haven (USA), University of Poona (India).
**Bibl:** Halsby 66,167,241,243,258; Macmillan [SA] 216; McKerrow, The Faeds, 1982 47-81 et passim.

**FAED, James Jnr** **1856-1920**
Born Mid Calder, West Lothian, 6 Oct; died New Galloway, 17 Feb. Painter in oil, but mainly watercolour, portraits and moorland landscapes. Elder surviving son of James Faed(qv). Became interested in art at an early age but never attended art school. By the age of twenty he was exhibiting in the RSA, 'A corner in the keeper's kitchen' being exhibited 1876. He quickly discovered that the subjects of greatest attraction for him were the hills of Galloway. These he took particular delight in depicting with special regard to the varying shades of heather through the seasons. Exhibited eight pictures at the RA 1880-1902 one of which, 'The Town Park' (1893), now hangs in the Town Hall, New Galloway. Married Eleanor Herdman and lived for many years in London. On one occasion at a tea-party in the garden of his London studio Harry Lauder was a guest and wishing to purchase a watercolour by Faed of a winding road with a bend at the top, was denied it because Mrs Faed was too fond of it. A short time later, at another studio afternoon, Harry Lauder sang the well-known song, 'Keep right on to the end of the road', which he had composed in the meantime, inspired by the picture. In 1912 Faed built a house in New Galloway where he settled shortly after WWI, dying there 1920. Twenty watercolours were published as *Galloway Watercolours* (1919); also illustrated Sloan's *Galloway* (1908). Exhibited RSA(50), GI(37) & AAS, from 7 Barnton Terrace and after 1899 from 1 Clifton Hill Studios, Abbey Rd, London. Represented in the Town Hall, New Galloway.
**Bibl:** Halsby 258; McKerrow, The Faeds, 1982 134-136.

**FAED, John RSA** **1819-1902**
Born Barley Mill, Kirkcudbright, 31 Aug; died Kirkcudbright, 22 Oct. Painter in oil and indian ink; portrait miniatures, genre and historical subjects. Attended Girthon Parish School but his school days ended when, aged only 11, he was refused permission to place his name beneath a map of Italy. Entirely self-taught, his first serious miniatures were painted when he was ten. A portrait of the local minister, 'painted from likeness' rather than life is now in the NGS. Viscount Kenmure had chanced to see some of the boy's ink drawings and was so impressed he visited the family. He found John finishing an engraving of Lord Byron that was better than the original. The artist's report of what followed is quoted in McKerrow (p6). 'I found him in the Bay Horse surrounded with some good watercolour drawings of ships, seaviews and seascapes, all of his own producing. He told me he was going to give up painting and wished to give me his paint box. No amount of language could convey the satisfaction and delight I had in carrying the box home. I had never seen a cake of watercolour in my life before, but to be the possessor of such a number of colours was wealth indeed. I took them to bed with me, so that when daylight came I might examine them one by one. It is needless to say that after that, I deserted my old friend indian ink'. Between the ages of 11 and 12 he was touring Galloway as a miniature painter, painting the aristocracy and notables including William Nicholson the poet. The five miniatures painted in about 1836 of James McKeachie, his wife and three daughters, are now in the Stewartry Museum, Kirkcudbright. They are astonishingly mature work for a sixteen year old. Being prevented by his father from travelling with a friend to London, he took his pictures to Kircudbright where they were sold by raffle. He remained there for about 18 months painting more miniatures. Studied Trustees Academy in Edinburgh and his first picture to be accepted by the RSA 'Portrait of a Gentleman', was shown a year after his arrival in the city together with four miniatures. Nine miniatures were exhibited in 1842 and 10 more in 1843. Exhibited a further 36 portraits and 6 miniatures at the RSA 1844-46. Thereafter he became more interested in painting larger portraits and fewer miniatures. One portrait (1847) of the children of Dr Bennie now called 'The Evening Hour', described 'as an extraordinary if improbable rendering of an early Victorian ideal view of juvenile behaviour, and brimful of unheard music', is in the NGS. Elected ARSA 1847, winning a bronze medal the same year, and RSA 1851, winning a silver medal. In 1848 was a founder member of The Smasher's Club(qv). Some of the sketches done there by John and Thomas Faed are now in the print room of the Glasgow AG. Fifteen years later, when several of the artists had won

fame in England, the Faeds moved south and the club was reconstituted under the title 'Auld Lang Syne'(qv), when they were joined by Erskine Nicol(qv), John Stirling(qv) and Andrew Maclure(qv). Faed illustrated *The Cottar's Saturday Night, Tam O'Shanter* and *The Soldier's Return* for the Fine Arts Association. The six Tam O'Shanter illustrations were used in the centenary edition of the *Poetry of Robert Burns* (1896). Wood carvings of the pictures were made by Thomas Tweedie two of which are in the Portsonachan Hotel, Loch Awe, Argyll. After a visit to the continent in 1857 he became occupied with eastern and biblical subjects and the following year painted one of his most famous works 'The Wappenschaw'. His first exhibits at the RA were in 1861 - 'Pastimes in times past' and 'Queen Margaret's Defiance of the Scottish Parliament'. In 1864 he illustrated *Legend of St Swithin - A Rhyme for Rainy Weather,* a book of amusing verse by the Aberdeen poet George Davidson. In 1864 he moved to London but after five years decided to return to Scotland, building a house in Gatehouse-of-Fleet. In 1869 and 1870 he departed from Scottish tradition by painting two full-length portraits of a young lady in a long brocade dress, the second of which is now in the Art Institute of Chicago entitled 'The Young Duchess'. Although nominated several times for an associateship of the RA he was never elected but in 1899 became President of the Kirkcudbright Fine Art Association. He loved his work and although never driven by ambition was always happiest when painting, 'never allowing anything to leave his hands without the last finishing touch, often one of the greatest delicacy'. Four of his children became artists. Altogether he exhibited 40 works at the RA 1855-1893 and 235 works at the RSA 1841-1895; also GI(8). Represented in SNPG(7), NGS(11+ scrapbook), V & A, Highland Tolbooth Church, Lady Stair Museum, NTS, RSA, Royal Society of Edinburgh, Gatehouse School, Gatehouse-of-Fleet, Glasgow AG, Torosay Castle, Isle of Mull, Broughton House, Kirkcudbright, Stewartry Museum, Kirkcudbright, Town Hall, Castle Douglas, Perth AG, Wigtown County Library, Stranraer, Bradford AG, Bury AG, Sheffield AG, Royal Shakespeare Theatre, Stratford-upon-Avon, Wolverhampton AG, York AG, Chicago Art Institute, Cleveland Museum, Ohio, St Mary's Art Guild, Detroit, Michigan.
**Bibl:** AJ 1865, 1867-9, 1871, 1872, 1874, Armstrong, 81; Art Review 27.2.1864; Bryan; Caw 166; DNB 2, Supp II 1912; Foskett; Sproate, 'John Faed RSA', Gallovidian Mag Spring 1902; Halsby 66,167,241,243,258; Hardie 38,45,48-9; Irwin 300-304 et passim; Macmillan [SA] 215-7; McKerrow The Faeds, 1982.

**FAED, John Francis** **1859-1904**
Painter in oil and watercolour of seascapes. Only son of Thomas(qv) & Frances F. Lived with his parents in St John's Wood, London until his marriage to Mary Bernaby. In 1881 she gave birth to a still-born son and a year later to a still-born daughter. Their first child to survive died when he was only six. The loss of three children in such quick succession precipitated him to abandon painting, and to drink himself to a tragically premature death. Exhibited RA(8) 1883-1892, all of them tempestuous sea scenes, also at least once at the RSA (1885) & GI(3), all between 1833 and 1836 and all from 24A Cavendish Rd, London. A watercolour 'Ardrach Castle' is in Broughton House, Kirkcudbright.
**Bibl:** McKerrow, 1982, 139-141.

**FAED, Miss Susan Bell** **1827-1909**
Born Barley Mill, Kirkcudbright, 8 Jne; died Gatehouse 19 May. Painter in oil and watercolour of portrait miniatures and animal studies. Only daughter of James and Mary Faed. Said to have been a strikingly beautiful girl and a natural model for her brothers. A portrait by her brother James provides a good idea of this description. The only daughter, she remained with her mother until at least 1852 whom she continued to look after until her mother's death 1866. According to brother James 'Susan painted some beautiful heads and would have risen to eminence if she had worked, but she would not work. It was always a marvel to me that she could do such good things with studying so little'. However, in 1866 she exhibited 'The Country Lass' at the RA followed by 'Rose Bradwardine' in 1867 (sold in Edinburgh 1959) and 'Remember the Sweeper' (1868). That year she had also exhibited three works at the RSA following two she had shown there in 1867. Enjoyed a late marriage and at the end of her life looked after her brother John, continuing to live in the house until her own death. 'She was remembered as an old lady of grace, intelligence and of particular charm'. At an auction of paintings at Faed House after her death 10 of her works were included. Exhibited at least 3 works at the RA, RSA(9) & GI(4), latterly from 24 Cavendish Rd, London.
**Bibl:** McKerrow, 129-131.

**FAED, Thomas RA HRSA** **1826-1900**
Born Barley Mill, Kirkcudbright, 8 Jne; died St John's Wood, London, 17 Aug. Painter in oil and watercolour, portraits, genre, interiors and domestic scenes. Older brother of John(qv) and James F(qv). His interest in art became apparent at a very early age, indeed his first oil picture, 'Interior with figures' was painted at the age of 12 and is now in Glasgow AG. When 16 he was sent to work as an apprentice draper in Castle Douglas but very soon his artistic talent proved too strong and he moved to Edinburgh to help his brother John with the miniatures. However, this did not fully express his burgeoning talent and he entered the Trustees Academy, studying under Sir William Allan(qv) and, most influentially, Thomas Duncan(qv) who took the colour class. Presented his dramatic portrait of 'John Mungo', the prize painting in the live class in 1847, to Sir Thomas Dick Lauder(qv). Among fellow students were W Q Orchardson(qv), Erskine Nicol(qv) and Robert Herdman(qv). The earliest exhibited work was a watercolour, 'A Scene from the *Old English Baron*' shown at the RSA when he was only 18. It soon became clear that his greatest strength lay in painting pictures of rural life and the more pathetic and sentimental aspects of Scottish domestic life. In the late 1840s he illustrated Walter Scott's *Heart of Midlothian,* gaining the Heywood gold medal at Manchester. In 1847 exhibited 'The Draught Players', an outstanding example of domestic genre. Each of the figures is an individual study whilst the sharpening of the lighting is of great interest. This encouraged him to enter 3 pictures for the RA, thus beginning a long stream of exhibits totalling 98 between 1851 and 1893. Also exhibited RSA(71) 1844-1885 & AAS from 1887. His greatest success was in 1855 when his painting 'The Mitherless Bairn' was hailed by most critics as the picture of the season and universally acknowledged, partly as a result of the engravings that made it famous world-wide. The original is now in the National Gallery of Victoria, Australia. After his McGeoch relations had emigrated to Canada he decided to paint a trilogy of pictures having a Canadian background. The first of these, 'First Letter from the Emigrants', was exhibited at the RSA in 1849, the second 'The Scottish Emigrant's Sunday in the Back Wood', appeared ten years later with its now more familiar title 'Sunday in the Back Woods', while the third, 'O why have I left my hame?', did not appear until 27 years later. The most productive years were 1860-1870. In 1867 he exhibited 'The Last of the Clan' (now in a private collection in Hamburg) painted when he was at the height of his powers, and 'Evangeline', the heroine of Longfellow's poem of that name, which was engraved by James F in 1856 and became immensely popular across the Atlantic. Longfellow wrote to Faed thanking him. His diploma work 'Ere Care Begins', was painted in Argyll when on holiday. With his brother, was an original member of the Edinburgh Smasher's Club (1848) reconstituted in London (1863) as the Auld Lang Syne Club (see John F). Marion Hepworth Dickson said of him, 'there are painters who observe and paint what they see and others who paint what they are instructed to see or what they conceive the masters painted before them. The first speak with the personal, the intimate note; the second with often the mere parrot voice of artistic convention. That the output of Thomas Faed belongs to the former category is a matter which hardly needs demonstration'. In 1892 failing sight compelled him to give up painting. His last exhibit at the RSA was 'Of What Is The Wee Lassie Thinking ?' Continued exhibiting at the RSA for the next 10 years until his last picture 'A Rustic Bather', originally in the 1885 exhibition, reappeared in 1893; also GI(24). Marion Dickson's notes in the *Magazine of Art* (1893) summed up 'Mr Faed is a poet who uses a brush instead of a pen...he is a realist. Life is not with him a mere desperate struggle for existence. Into the lot of the meanest and poorest there enter compensations begotten of love, and unselfishness and faith. Mr Faed is one of the most popular of the brigade of London/Scottish artists that include so many distinguished men. Success had not spoiled him or weakened his personality. There is a fine sturdy commonsense in all his ways and words as refreshing as the breeze that blows over the moors and mosses of his native Galloway'. Caw pointed out that 'he was more concerned with the fact of a thing than with its pictorial significance...yet his work marked an advancing realism, an entire absence of affectation, in both sentiment and method, saves his simple and naive art from

reproaches...from first to last his idea of picture making, if less artfully carried out, was the same as Wilkie's before the latter went to Spain...adopting a more delicate and suave, though still precise manner, early in the 50s, he thereafter attained finer colour and richer and more fused tonal effects based upon a skilful use of chiaroscuro...these were the qualities which dominated his practice during his prime, and it follows that his most successful pictures are those dealing with indoor incidents'. Elected ARA 1861, RA 1864. Represented in NGS, SNPG, Tate AG, Aberdeen AG, Broughty Ferry AG, Dundee, Dumfries AG, Dundee AG, Glasgow AG, Kirkcaldy AG, Manchester AG, Paisley AG, Salford AG, Sheffield AG, St Andrews AG, Stranraer AG, Sunderland AG, Wolverhampton AG, York AG, City of Edinburgh collection, Old Bridge House Museum, Lady Stair Museum, Edinburgh, Broughton House, Kirkcudbright, Town Hall, Castle Douglas, Brodie Castle (NTS), Queen's University, Belfast, Royal Albert Memorial Museum, Exeter, Royal Holloway College, Egham, Surrey, The Ashmolean Museum, Oxford, Guildhall Library, City of London, National Gallery of Victoria, Melbourne (Australia), Museum of Fine Arts, Montreal (Canada), Vancouver AG (Canada), Kamatibagh Museum, Baroda (India), Durban (South Africa).
**Bibl:** Academy Notes 1876, 1877, 1878; AJ 1851-61, 1863-8, 1870-2, 1876, 1880, 1906; Armstrong 81; Bryan; Caw 164-6; DNB, Suppl I Vol II; Halsby 66-9,167,241,243,258; Hardie 46-8,57; Irwin 300-303 et passim; Macmillan [SA], 186,212-18,231,243,276,374; McKay 343-6; McKerrow 1982 83-127,152-153; NGS, Notes and Sketchbooks of Thomas Faed; NLS, Letters of Thomas Faed.

**FAED, William Cotton** **1858-1937**
Born Mid Calder, 20 Jly; died Jersey, 22 Nov. Painter in oil and watercolour of portraits, landscape and figurative subjects. Second surviving son of James Faed(qv). Became interested in art when still young. Produced a very competent oil of a Spanish girl when only 10. Little is known of his early career. As a young man he went to Australia with the object of making a living by painting prosperous wool-producing settlers. While there he met and married Janet Armstrong. They returned to England settling in Dulwich, before going to live in the Channel Islands. A number of eastern subjects reflects the time he spent in the Middle East and North Africa. Also painted portraits of his family, one of his father being engraved by him. Did little work after migrating to the Channel Islands, much to the disappointment of his father who was convinced that he was sufficiently gifted to attain renown. Father of Frank F(qv), who died when only 44. Exhibited regularly at the RSA 1883-1889, three works at the RA, one in 1884 and two in 1891, also AAS 1886 & GI(23), latterly from 51 Carson Rd, W. Dulwich.
**Bibl:** McKerrow 138-9.

**FAGEN, Graham** **fl 1988-**
Glasgow sculptor. Exhibited a wire and stone figure at the GI, from Flat 7D, Gorget Quadrant.

**FAHRENHOLT, Mateus** **1964-**
St Andrews painter, sculptor and printmaker. Trained at Gray's School of Art, Aberdeen 1984-88 and in 1991 was appointed Resident Artist, Aberdeen AG. His most recent work is box-type constructions, a combination of 'thought-provoking objects and images on the theme of exile'. His prints and constructions have been exhibited in Poland as well as in Scotland.

**FAILL, Miss Ina** **fl 1883-1885**
Amateur Glasgow painter of portrait heads. Sister of Margaret S F(qv). Exhibited GI(3) from 5 Derby Crescent.

**FAILL, Miss Margaret ('Maggie') S** **fl 1883-1889**
Amateur Glasgow landscape and still life painter. Sister of Ina F(qv). Exhibited GI(7) from 5 Derby Crescent.

**FAIRBAIRN, C** **fl c1909**
Obscure Scottish painter of angling subjects and sporting fish.
**Bibl:** Wingfield.

**FAIRBAIRN, Henry** **fl 1877-1880**
Edinburgh painter of 16 Drumdryan Street who exhibited three works at the RSA (1877-9) & RHA(1).

**FAIRBAIRN, Nicholas QC** **1933-2000**
MP, lawyer, self-proclaimed wit, amateur painter in oil, crayon, gouache and chinese ink in the modern idiom. Educated Loretto School and University of Edinburgh. Lived at Fordell Castle, by Dunfermline. Former Solicitor General for Scotland. Published *A Life is Too Short* (1987). Vice-President SSWA 1987. Exhibited RSA 1967 & RGI 1961.

**FAIRBAIRN, Thomas RSW** **1820-1885**
Born Campsie, nr Glasgow; died Glasgow, Oct. Landscape painter in oil, watercolour and chalk. Lost his father at an early age. Began working life as a shop assistant with a firm of dyers during which time he attended art classes in Glasgow, studying under Gilfillan(qv) and Andrew Donaldson(qv). Shortly afterwards he married and in 1850 moved to Hamilton, occasionally visiting England. Far more proficient in watercolour than in oil. Especially fond of portraying forest scenery, often Cadzow forest, in the company of his friends Alexander Fraser(qv) and Sam Bough(qv). Among his best work is a series of watercolours of Glasgow 1844-9, first published in 1849 and reprinted 1884. From about 1871 he suffered from creeping paralysis, although a partial recovery c1878 led to some of his best work 'more tender in colour and softer in manipulation than some of his earlier pictures' [Brydall]. John Mossman(qv) and Robert Greenlees(qv) organised an exhibition of his works in which were included many sketches of old houses and areas around Glasgow as well as a number of Highland burns. Elected RSW 1882. Exhibited RSA(40), RSW(32) & GI(64), after 1879 from Parkview, Clydesdale St, Hamilton. Represented in SNPG by portraits of 'Sam Bough' and 'Alexander Fraser', Glasgow AG, People's Palace, Glasgow.
**Bibl:** Brydall 404-6; Halsby 88-9.

**FAIRFAX-LUCY, Norah, Lady Ramsay** **?-1980**
Amateur embroiderer. Designed and worked one of the largest and most interesting Scottish panels of the twentieth century. Inspired by the Jedforest Hunt, it measures approximately 25 by 3 ft. It is said that every figure of man and horse is a portrait including the embroiderer and her sister and dog standing beside a Landrover.
**Bibl:** Margaret Swain 167-8.

**FAIRFOWL, Miss Kathleen M** **fl 1923-1927**
Edinburgh miniature portrait painter on ivory; exhibited RSA 1923 and 1927 from 12 St Peter's Place.

**FAIRGRIEVE, James H ARSA RSW** **1944-**
Born Prestonpans, East Lothian. Painter in oil and watercolour; landscape and figurative works. Trained at Edinburgh College of Art 1962-68 obtaining Andrew Grant open scholarship 1963. Moved to London where he was awarded the David Murray landscape scholarship (RA) 1968 and another Andrew Grant travelling scholarship 1969 enabling him to visit Italy. Recipient of the Gillies prize (RSW) and again in 1997, the Gillies Travel award (RSA) 1991, and the Maud Gemmell Hutchison prize (RSA) 1993. The same year he was elected a member of the Society of Scottish Artists and in 1975 ARSA and RWS. In 1978 elected President of the Society of Scottish Artists. Currently teaches at Edinburgh College of Art. Exhibits regularly RSA since 1975, RSW & GI(9) from Burnbrae, Gordon, Berwickshire. Represented in Lillie AG, Milngavie, Perth AG, Edinburgh Royal College of Physicians, Edinburgh City collection, SAC and with the First National Bank, Chicago.
**Bibl:** Gage 75-6; *Scottish Watercolour Painting*, J Firth.

**FAIRHOLME, Mrs** **fl 1866**
Animal and historical painter. Exhibited RSA(2) 1866. Possibly the artist who exhibited two works at the SWA in 1855 from Elm Tree House, Shrivenham, Berkshire and perhaps related to Adele Fairholme, the animal painter, who exhibited at the RA, RSA and elsewhere 1899-1936.

**FAIRLEY, Miss Dorothy M** **1894-?**
Wood engraver, etcher and landscape painter in oil. Of Scottish ancestry, she studied at Richmond Art School and Regent Street Polytechnic before settling at Holmhurst, Knell Road, Robertsbridge, Sussex. Exhibited Scottish landscapes, especially scenes around St. Mary's Loch, and in Perthshire and Inverness-shire; RA(4), RSA 1927-63; ROI(5), GI(11 including 'Loch Muick'), SWA(5) & L(6).

**FAIRLEY, George** **1920-?**
Born Dunfermline 16 Dec. Painter and sculptor. Educated

Dunfermline High School and Edinburgh College of Art where he studied under David Alison(qv), Gillies(qv) and A B Thomson(qv). Lived in Horsham, Sussex. After teaching at Swansea School of Art for 15 years, he moved to Croydon College of Art showing in London and the home counties with the 56 Group of which he was a member. Exhibited with the London group and elsewhere in London.

**FAIRLEY, James Graham** **1846-1934**
Edinburgh architect, especially of churches. Among his designs have been the pavilion for Edinburgh University AC, Buccleuch memorial (Hawick) and a large residence in Massachusetts. Also Alardale School in West Lothian (1894) and the Senior School, West Calder, Midlothian (1896). Exhibited RA(6), RSA(38) & GI(7).

**FAIRLEY, Madge B** **fl 1905-1912**
Edinburgh portrait miniature painter; specialised in finely executed heads of children. Exhibited from her studio in 12 Shandwick Place, at the RSA 1905, RHA(4), SWA(1) & London Salon (4).

**FAIRLEY, Robert** **fl 1891**
Engraver, from 7 Minto Street, Edinburgh; exhibited an etching 'Faggot gathering' at the RSA in 1891.

**FAIRLIE, Joseph** **fl 1929**
Amateur Glasgow painter. Exhibited 'The grey February day' at the AAS.

**FAIRLIE, R N** **fl 1883-1894**
Painter from Ayr who moved to Dollar c1885 before returning to Ayr. Painted country scenes and figurative subjects in oil, exhibited 2 works at the RSA & 3 at the GI, all between the above dates.

**FAIRLIE, Reginald RSA LLD FRIBA** **1883-1952**
Born Myres Castle, Auchtermuchty, Fife. Architect. Educated Oratory School, Birmingham. Received early training in the office of Robert Lorimer(qv). After extensive foreign travel he commenced his own architectural practice in Edinburgh 1909, designing St James' RC Church, St Andrews (1910). During WW1 he serviced with the Royal Engineers. Afterwards began to receive numerous commissions for church and domestic designs including war memorials and the restoration of St Andrew's University Chapel. Served as academic representative on the ECA Board of Management. Took over work at Kilmany, Fife (1914-9) after the owner's disagreement with Lorimer; also Hutton Castle nr Berwick, after Burrell had fallen out with Lorimer, although the result attracted unfavourable critical comment. An interesting design was for the small church, Our Lady Star of the Sea, Tayport, Fife (1939). One of his most important commissions was for a new National Library of Scotland (1934-6), but not built until 1955 after simplification by A R Conlon. Chairman, Ancient Monuments Advisory Board, Scotland, member of the Society of Antiquities of Scotland and Council for Art in Industry 1934-39. Received an honorary doctorate from St Andrew's University. Elected ARSA 1923, RSA 1934. Exhibited RSA regularly 1911-1953 & GI(7) including a design for the new Abbey church, Fort Augustus (1925) and work on Iona (1936).
**Bibl:** Gifford 169,184,279,387,568,574,582,601,615,636; Peter Savage, Lorimer and the Edinburgh Craft Designers, Edinburgh 1980 26,87,121,164; Bruce Walker & W S Gauldie, Architects and Architecture on Tayside, Dundee 1984, 161.

**FAIRMAN, James** **1826-c1890**
Born Glasgow; died Chicago. Painter in oil of landscape and historical scenes. Son of a Swedish officer named Fehrman and a Scottish mother. After his father died the family moved to New York where he enrolled in Fred Agate's Academy of Design studying law at the same time. After participating in the Civil War resumed painting in 1863. In 1867 his 'Androscoggin Valley' won a competition and in 1871 Fairman returned to Europe. Recognising how much he had still to learn, especially from the Old Masters, he studied in Dusseldorf and Paris for three years followed by two more years in London. When in Germany he became interested in meteorology, finding the subject invaluable for the treatment of light and space. Completed a number of works in Europe, including 'The Entry of Prince Charles Edward Stuart into Edinburgh', 'Adieu to the land', and 'The White Mountains nr Bethel, N. America' all at the GI (1973), from 212 Fifth Avenue, New York. Finally departed Europe 1881, settling in Chicago.

**FAIRWEATHER, Adam Burnett** **fl 1883-1896**
Perthshire oil painter of local scenes. Lived at Bridgend, Blairgowrie and in Dundee. Exhibited RSA(12), GI(1), GI(1) & 3 landscapes at Perth Art Exhibition 1883.

**FAIRWEATHER, Ian** **1891-1974**
Born Bridge of Allan, 29 Sep; died Australia. Painter of figures and landscapes. Extremely important figure in the development of modern art in Australia. His interest in painting was aroused by a Dutch artist with whom he shared a billet during WW1. In 1920 he enrolled at the Slade School becoming interested in oriental art. Returned to Germany 1924 and in 1927 visited Canada. After a spell of three years in Shanghai he toured Asia and Bali. In 1934 his wanderings took him to Melbourne where he met the art bookdealer Gino Nibbi and through him received a commission to paint a mural for the Menzies Hotel, Melbourne. When a critic compared it to the style of Brangwyn he destroyed the work and set sail for the Philippines. In 1934 the Tate acquired 'Bathing Scene, Bali' and the next year Fairweather entered a contractual arrangement with the Redfern Gallery of London. Worked in Peking 1935, then spent several more years in Northern Australia and the Philippines. Served as captain in the Indian Army 1940-2 but was invalided out. After a stay in Melbourne he settled near Darwin. An attempt to sail the Timor Sea on a raft made of softwood and petrol drums in 1952 led to an obituary appearing in the Melbourne Herald (13 May). Landing on a Timor beach, he was transported to Singapore and housed in a home for destitutes but following the intervention of the British authorities he was able to sail to England. But once there the climate was not to his liking and he returned to Sydney 1953, constructed a hut for himself on Bribie Island, off the Queensland coast, near Brisbane, where he studied animal life and forestry. A student of Chinese, he translated *The Drunken Buddha* based on the 1894-5 edition. Achieved wide influence and recognition in Australia as one of that country's leading artists. 'Fairweather painted mainly in earth colours used by the artists of South-East Asia and the Pacific and was one of the first artists to assimilate aboriginal art into his own personal style...a master of a fluent, semi-abstract, calligraphic style in which the values of East and West are united in a manner that has rarely been achieved' [Osborne]. Exhibited over 30 works at the Redfern Gallery between 1935 and 1937. Represented in all the main Australian public collections.
**Bibl:** Harold Osborne(ed), Twentieth Century Art, 1988, 183.

**FAIRWEATHER, John** **fl 1920s**
Glasgow architect. Best remembered for the Playhouse Theatre, Edinburgh (1927-9), refurbished 1978-80.
**Bibl:** Gifford 439.

**FAITHFULL, Joan Margaret Caldwell (née Crawford)** **1953-**
Born East Linton, East Lothian, 17 May. Potter. Daughter of William Caldwell Crawford(qv). Educated privately in Edinburgh, studied Edinburgh College of Art under Katie Horsman(qv). Lives at Eskbank, Midlothian. Has been a member of the Scottish Craft Centre since 1953. Frequently exhibits SSA & SSWA.

**FALCONER, Miss Agnes Trotter** **1883-c1967**
Born Edinburgh, 4 Mar. Landscape, townscape, coastal and flower painter in oil and watercolour, also lithographer. Studied at Edinburgh College of Art, becoming lecturer with the NGS for touring parties. Exhibited RSA(42) 1917-1967, GI(10), AAS(4) & L(2), after 1956 from 2 Ainsley Place.

**FALCONER, Hugh David** **fl 1976**
Scottish potter. Exhibited AAS(1).

**FALCONER, Miss Isabella** **fl 1866**
Amateur watercolour painter of Belvidere, Aberdeen; exhibited 'The Old Church, Aberdeen' at the GI.

**FALCONER, John M** **1820-1903**
Painter and etcher. Emigrated to New York c1880. Exhibited RE(10) & L(4).

**FALCONER, Pearl** **fl 1945-**
Born Dundee. Painter of murals, fashion designer and book illustrator. Trained St Martin's School of Art and Central School of Arts and Crafts under Bernard Meninsky. Prepared murals for three

pavilions at the Festival of Britain 1951. Latterly has concentrated on illustrating children's books in a style reminiscent of Osbert Lancaster. Books illustrated include Phillips: *Ask Me Another* (1945), *Meet William Shakespeare* (1949), *The Hubert Phillips Annual* (1951), Aldiss: *The Brightfount Diaries* (1955), Carson: *The Happy Orpheline* (1960), Farmer: *The China People* (1960), Treadgold: *The Winter Princess* (1962), Carson: *The Orphelines in the Enchanted Castle* (1963), *A Pet for the Orphelines* (1963).
**Bibl:** Horne 184; Jacques; Peppin; Ryder; Usherwood.

**FALLON, Miss Sarah W M** **fl 1877-1895**
Edinburgh painter in oil of domestic scenes, portraits, animals and flowers. Exhibited 'Mending Nets' at the RA (1895), also RSA(10), RBA(5), SWA(7) & GI(1).

**FAN, Joe ARSA** **c1965-**
Painter of landscape, figurative and surreal works, often favouring a dark palette. Trained Gray's School of Art in the 1980s, subsequently lecturing there 1990-98; also visiting teacher at the Cyprus College of Art 1994. First solo exhibitions in Paris and Aberdeen 1989. Elected Young Scottish Artist of the Year 1988, enabling him to spend a year in Paris; winner Guthrie Award (RSA) 1994, Morrison Portrait Award 1995, Portland Gallery Award (RSA) 1997. Elected ARSA 2003. Exhibits regularly RSA, AAS. Represented in Aberdeen AG, SAC collection, Unilever Art Collection.

**FANNER, Miss** **fl 1856**
Portrait painter. Exhibited RSA(3) from 28 India Street.

**FANNER, Henry George** **fl 1854-1888**
Portrait painter of Scottish descent; worked mainly in watercolour. Lived in London in the 1880s moving to Glasgow 1888. Exhibited RSA(7) & GI(4), latterly from 90 St. Vincent St. Represented in Glasgow AG.

**FANSHAW, H Valentine** **fl 1933**
Amateur watercolour painter; exhibited RSW(1).

**FARLEY, Mrs Turner** **fl 1894-1898**
Kincardineshire painter of local landscape and sporting subjects. Exhibited AAS(4) from Cairnton, Banchory.

**FARLOW, Harry M** **fl 1929**
Exhibited 2 still life paintings at the RSA in 1929 from 33 London Street, Edinburgh.

**FARM, A** **fl 1879**
Glasgow watercolour painter of landscape and genre; exhibited GI(2) from 15 Ruthven St.

**FARQUHAR, Archibald** **fl 1877-1882**
Painted landscapes in oil and watercolour from Birmingham. Of Scottish descent, birthplace unclear. Exhibited RSA 1877-78 & Royal Society of Artists Birmingham(1) 1882.

**FARQUHAR, Emily ('Dee') (Mrs Godfrey Bird)** **1885-1975**
Born Southsea, Hants; died Sussex. Middle of three daughters of Admiral and Mrs Richard Farquhar of Aboyne, Aberdeenshire. Landscape painter in watercolour, also occasional portraits and sometimes in charcoal and oils. Always known as 'Dee' after her beloved river Dee. Privately educated, trained at the Slade c1911-1914. Joined the Hydrographic Department of the Admiralty 1914. Married 1918 and thereafter her artistic career remained subordinated to her family. Sketched extensively when on holiday, usually on Deeside but also in North Africa, Malta, Greece and southern England. Generally worked on a modest scale, competent, colourful and totally without pretension. Exhibited a portrait at the Royal Society of Portrait Painters. [From notes provided by the family.]

**FARQUHARSON, Mrs Mary Anne (née Girdwood)** **1838-1914**
Amateur Kincardineshire artist. Wife of Dr Francis Farquharson, laird of Finzean, and step-mother of Robert and Joseph(qv). Travelled to Egypt on at least one occasion with Joseph and exhibited 'Our home on the Nile' at the AAS. This is her only recorded work, it seems probable that her step-son collaborated in its execution.

**FARQUHARSON, David ARA ARSA RSW ROI** **1840-1907**
Born Blairgowrie, Perthshire; died Birnam, Perthshire, 12 Jly. Painter in oil and watercolour of landscapes. Began life as an apprentice decorator and moved to Edinburgh 1872. To a large extent he was self-taught although for a time studied in London under William Geddes. Began exhibiting at the RSA in 1868. Elected ARSA 1882. In London 1886-1894. Whilst often revisiting Scotland he established a studio at Sennen's Cove, nr Land's End. His early pictures deal mostly with the border land between Perth and Forfar, and in the Braemar and Glen Shee areas. Painted shipping on the rivers and estuaries of the Maas and Scheldt in addition to his Scottish and English scenes. His work shows a continuous development, the best pictures belonging to the later years. Equally at home with oil and watercolour although his output was far greater in the former. Studied Dutch art. His last works became facile and sometimes superficial. Elected ARSA 1882, ARA 1905, RSW 1885, ROI 1904, ARA 1905. Exhibited RA(32) 1877-1904, RSA(63); also ROI(1), RSW(2), RHA(1), GI(37), L(6) & AAS 1883-1926. Represented in NG, NGS, Tate Gallery, Paisley AG, Manchester AG.
**Bibl:** AJ 1907, 197, 283, 360; 1908, 231; Caw 306-7; DNB; Halsby; RA Pictures 1891-6; 1906-8; Studio, vol 38, no 10, 1839.

**FARQUHARSON, Douglas McLean** **fl 1976**
Aberdeenshire painter in oil of local landscapes. Trained at Gray's School of Art, Aberdeen. Exhibited 2 works at the AAS from 12 Northfield Place, Ellon.

**FARQUHARSON, Evelyn Gordon** **fl 1961-1988**
Amateur painter in oil of landscapes and figure subjects. Exhibited RSA 1962-1963 & AAS(2) in 1961 and 1988, latterly from 13 Silverbank Crescent, Banchory.

**FARQUHARSON, James** **fl 1949-1966**
Paisley watercolour painter of Scottish, English and some Italian landscapes. Exhibited GI(12), from 57 Clydesdale Ave.

**FARQUHARSON, John** **fl 1880-1905**
Edinburgh painter in watercolour and oil of landscape and animal subjects. Son of David F(qv). Specialised in coastal views of Scotland and the west country but also painted other subjects with dexterity and sensitivity. Lived at 3 Wycombe (or Wychcombe) Villas, Haverstock Hill, London 1890. Exhibited RSA(16), GI(1), AAS(1) & L(1). Represented in City of Edinburgh collection by two watercolour drawings of The Pleasance.
**Bibl:** Halsby 258.

**FARQUHARSON, Joseph RA** **1846-1935**
Born Edinburgh, 4 May; died Finzean, Aberdeenshire, 15 Apr. Painter in oil and sometimes watercolour of landscape, garden scenes and occasional portraits. Renowned for his snow scenes. Son of Francis F, laird of Finzean and medical practitioner in Kincardineshire. His brother Robert, a much respected physician and local Member of Parliament, bore a claim to the chieftainship of the clan but this was never pressed. His mother, a celebrated beauty, was an Ainslie. Early days were spent in his father's house in Northumberland Street below Queen Street Gardens and later at Eaton Terrace beyond the Dean Bridge, Edinburgh and at Finzean. Until he was 12 Joseph was allowed to paint only on Saturdays when he was permitted to use his father's paints. On his twelfth birthday he was presented with his first box of paints, a gift he was quick to celebrate the following summer by submitting a picture to the RSA which was accepted. The popular Scottish landscape painter and teacher Peter Graham(qv) was a family friend, under whose tutelage the young man studied for twelve years. Most of his early subjects were inspired by the countryside around his home. Aged 16 he entered the Board of Manufacturers School in Edinburgh under the guidance of Hodder and in 1880 studied in Paris under Carolus Duran. Between 1885 and 1893 he paid several visits to Egypt. Among the works exhibited at this time were 'The Egyptian', 'On the Banks of the Nile Outside Cairo', and perhaps the best of his Egyptian work, 'He Drove them Wandering o'er the Sandy Way'. His first major portrait was of 'Miss Alice Farquhar', exhibited 1884. His first exhibit at the RA, 'Day's Dying Glow', was in 1873. In common with other leading Aberdeen artists eg John Philip(qv) and William Dyce(qv), Edinburgh and Glasgow were leap-frogged in favour of London. Walter Sickert wrote an essay comparing Farquharson's treatment of snow scenes to

those of Courbet and praised the former's lightness of touch, 'the mark of the real painter'. Farquharson had a deep understanding of people as well as of landscape. The finest works often included a human figure, generally men and women of the land going about their daily labour. As he grew older his work became more impressionistic, less pictorially precise. The mood began to transcend the particulars. His place in British art is secure, no-one has painted the north-east of Scotland with greater integrity and understanding, nor with less pretence. He was a totally honest man, free from sycophancy, whose joy it was to portray the natural beauties around him and to let his paintings speak for themselves. Although pre-eminently a painter of snow and winter landscapes his ability to catch the warmth and light, the sun-filled sandy atmosphere and the dazzling bazaars of north Africa as well as sunny autumn days in the Highlands are equally evocative. Elected ARA 1890, RA 1915. In addition to exhibiting over 200 works at the RA he showed RSA(73), RCA(1), GI(32), L(47) & 181 works at the Fine Art Society, after 1916 from Finzean, Kincardineshire. Represented in Tate AG, NGS, SNPG (portrait of 'George Paul Chalmers'), Aberdeen AG, Bristol AG, Nottingham AG, Dundee AG, Hartlepool AG, Manchester AG, Paisley AG, Perth AG, Bournemouth AG, Burnley AG, Liverpool AG, Birkenhead AG.
**Bibl:** Aberdeen AG (Ex Cat, text by Francina Irwin, 1985); AJ 1890, 158; 1893, 153; 1905, 175; Caw 306; Conn XXXVI 59 ff; Holloway 43-45,143; Irwin 363-4 et al; Macmillan [SA], 77-78; W R Sickert, A Free House, (ed Osbert Sitwell) 1947, 204-6; W M Sinclair, Art Annual Christmas 1912; Studio 'Art in 1898', index, 1905-8,1910-12; The Globe 5.8.1908.

**FARQUHARSON, Linda A** **1963-**
Born Aberdeen, April 22. Printmaker and illustrator. Trained Duncan of Jordanstone College of Art, Dundee, winning the Sekalski prize for printmaking. Childhood spent on a farm at Fettercairn. In 1990 she purchased an 1850 Columbian press which she restored and works from an Edinburgh studio. Her work decorates several hospitals. Began exhibiting RSA 1995 & RGI 1996.

**FARQUHARSON, Myrtle J ('Mo')** **1931-**
Born Aberdeen, Nov 9. Painter in oil and watercolour; printmaker & teacher. Educated Broomhill School, trained Gray's School of Art 1950-54. Awarded Steel Cornwall scholarship and the George Davidson gold medal. Travelled in Italy, Spain and France 1955, in September of that year took up a teaching post at Northfield Academy. Her early work was mainly landscape, and wildlfower and fruit studies. Took early retirement 1978 and discovered Peacock Printmakers, working with Beth Fisher(qv), and later screen printing with Jonathan Jones. Exhibits RSA, AAS.

**FARQUHARSON, Robert C** **fl 1867-1878**
Dundee artist in oil of animals and country subjects. Some of his work was strongly painted and deserves wider recognition than has hitherto been granted. A striking portrait of a ram's head appeared on the market 1974. Exhibited Dundee Fine Art Exhibition quite often, also RSA 1867-78.

**FARRAN, Miss Lulu** **fl 1887-1892**
Portrait and figure painter; lived in London and Gibraltar before moving to Glasgow in 1889. Exhibited RSA(1), RA(1), GI(4) & L(2), latterly from 40 Penywerm Rd, Earls Court, London.

**FARRELL, Frederick Arthur** **1882-1935**
Self-taught etcher and watercolourist of portraits and topographical subjects. Produced powerful watercolours of the Battle of Ypres in 1917. Helped to illustrate *The 51st Highland Division War Sketches* (1920). Before beginning to etch he studied civil engineering. Later he etched views of London, Glasgow, Paris and other European cities. Influenced greatly by Muirhead Bone(qv). Principal works include 'Danzig Fishmarket', 'Nice terraces' and 'The Bank of England'. Exhibited RA(3), RSA(1), GI(43) & L(10), mostly from Glasgow but after 1927 from 22 Buckingham Chambers, Greencoat Place, London. Represented by 54 works in Glasgow AG, Paisley AG.
**Bibl:** Halsby 258.

**FARRELL, Joseph J** **fl 1948-1962**
Paisley watercolourist, also worked occasionally in pencil. Landscape and farming scenes. Exhibited GI(18), after 1952 from 50 Linnwell Crescent.

**FARREN, Hugh** **fl 1975**
Aberdeen metal work designer especially of jewels. Exhibited AAS(1).

**FARREN, Robert H** **fl 1867-1889**
Lived in Cambridge. Painter and etcher. Although not a Scot he painted in Scotland and in the 1870s was a member of the artistic community that congregated on the Isle of Arran during the summer. Exhibited RA(16) 1872-89, including two views on Arran 1872 and again 1873; Highland subjects appeared also in 1875; & RSA 1867, 1868 and 1870, including views of 'The Cobbler', 'Head of Loch Long' and 'A Spate at Inversnaid, Loch Lomond'.

**FAULDS, Alan C FRIAS** **1951-**
Born Glasgow, Oct 30. Architect and sculptor. Educated Strathclyde Univ. 1970-76. Sculpting polychromed imaginative figurative woodcarving, often incorporating circus or medieval themes. Elected Royal Incorporation of Architects in Scotland 1977. Exhibits RSA from 1988.

**FAULDS, James G** **fl 1896-1938**
Glasgow painter in oil and occasional watercolour of figurative subjects, also illustrator. Contributed the *The Graphic* 1903. Exhibited at the RSA(1), RSW(1) but mainly at the GI(37), after 1928 from 21 Stirling Dr, Rutherglen. Represented in Glasgow AG.

**FAULDS, Jane L** **fl 1877-1878**
Glasgow flower painter in watercolour. Exhibited GI(3) from 8 Elgin Villas, Shawlands.

**FAULDS, John F C** **fl 1971**
Kilmarnock painter and etcher; exhibited RSA(1) & GI(1) from 7 Mayfield Avenue, Hurlford.

**FAULKNER, Iain** **1972-**
Portrait and figurative painter in oils. Trained Glasgow School of Art. Lived for a time on Cyprus. Fascinated by the ancient cultures of the icon and mosaic with the frequent inclusion of ballet dancers, chess and card players. Exhibitions in London, Edinburgh, Glasgow & Stirling. Exhibited RSA. Commissions received include the Glasgow Chamber of Commerce, St Andrews Society and the Royal College of Pharmaceutical Medicine.
**Bibl:** Albemarle Gallery catalogue 1998.

**FEARN, Ian** **1934-**
Born Newport-on-Tay. Painter of figurative studies in a semi-abstract manner, influenced by Tapies. Uses photography directly 'transferring a carefully composed image with an air gun through an organdie screen on to the canvas, making delicate alterations to the image in the process'[Hardie]. Lecturer, Dundee College of Art. Exhibited RSA, SSA and in 'Three Centuries of Scottish Painting', Canada 1968. Represented in Glasgow AG.
**Bibl:** Hardie 198.

**FEARNSIDE, Norma** **fl 1969**
Amateur Glasgow painter; 2 works at the RSA from 10 Belmont Street, Hillhead.

**FELL, Miss Clara** **fl 1866-1871**
Edinburgh painter in oil of figurative subjects. Exhibited RSA(5) during the above years.

**FENDER, Maggie T** **fl 1889-1892**
Berwickshire painter of landscape and coastal scenes. Latterly lived in Northfield, Ayton, Berwickshire. Exhibited RA(2), RSA(2), AAS(2) & GI(2).

**FENTON, James** **fl 1911-1919**
Landscape painter in oil and watercolour. In the mid-1910s moved to Ythan Bank, West Newport. Exhibited GI(3), from Clifton Park, Newport-on-Tay.

**FENTON, Roxburgh** **fl 1901**
Amateur landscape painter; exhibited GI(2) from 14 Thomson Street, Dundee.

**FENWICK, Horace G** **fl 1847-1851**
Dundee artist; exhibited landscapes in oil at the RSA during the above years first from Dudhope Terrace, Dundee and latterly from 4 Douglas Terrace, Broughty Ferry.

**FENWICK, Thomas** **fl 1835-d1849**
Born Gateshead. An Englishman who practised in Edinburgh and was a pupil of John Ewbank(qv). Showed all the merits and demerits of his teacher 'the luminous skies and fine aerial distances, marred by forcing of effect and colour in the former, and by the ruddy brown tones of the dark foreground in the latter' [McKay]. Exhibited regularly RSA 1833-1850, mostly Scottish landscapes, especially of the Highlands.
**Bibl:** Caw 161; McKay 199.

**FERGUS, John** **fl 1750s**
Edinburgh architect and builder. Member of a trades consortium 'Gentlemen of Mary's Chappel' contracted to build Edinburgh City Chambers (the only 18th Century public building on the Royal Mile). In this capacity Fergus produced a modified elevation of the John Adam original, responsible for 'a shallower entablature above the windows, and unfluted pilasters' [Gifford].
**Bibl:** Gifford 176.

**FERGUS, Winifred (Mrs Richardson)** **1961-**
Born Pitcaple, Aberdeenshire. Painter of still life and interiors. Trained Gray's School of Art 1979-84, awarded Founder's Prize in her final year, used to travel in Egypt. Awarded John Murray Thomson prize (RSA) 1998. Exhibits RSA. Represented in Aberdeen AG.

**FERGUSON, Miss A B Ochiltree** **fl 1895-1898**
Dunbartonshire amateur oil and watercolour painter of village life and scenes; exhibited RSW(2) & GI(2) from Benburb House, Lenzie.

**FERGUSON, Alexander Snr** **fl 1809**
Edinburgh painter, apprenticed to James Bryce(qv). Father of Alexander F Jnr(qv). Burgess of Edinburgh 1809.

**FERGUSON, Alexander Jnr** **fl 1816-1823**
Son of Alexander F Snr(qv). Burgess of Edinburgh soon after his father's election. In 1816 took on his first apprentice John Cameron, followed by Daniel Taylor 1817 and Duncan Irvine 1823.

**FERGUSON, Annie M** **fl 1902**
Portrait painter. Exhibited RSA from 31 George Square, Edinburgh, and the same year a miniature portrait of an officer in a red coat at the AAS.

**FERGUSON, Miss C M** **fl 1897-1900**
Amateur painter. Exhibited SWA(4) from 16 Lennox Street, Edinburgh during the above years.

**FERGUSON, Charles S R** **fl 1895-1897**
Glasgow flower and landscape painter, generally in oil. Exhibited GI(3), after 1896 from 79 W. Regent St.

**FERGUSON, Daniel** **fl 1873-1896**
Glasgow sculptor and medallionist. Carvings in bronze and wood of portrait busts and decorative items. Exhibited GI(31), including a portrait of Gladstone (1886)), latterly from 13 Carnarvon St.

**FERGUSON, Daniel ROI** **1910-**
Born Motherwell. Painter in oil and watercolour and colour printer; still life and birds, genre and portraits. Brother of Roy F(qv). Educated Dalziel HS, Motherwell and Glasgow School of Art under Revel(qv), Hutchison(qv), Crawford(qv) and Wilson(qv). Lived in Glasgow for many years before moving to Motherwell. Awarded silver medal, Paris Salon 1961. A strong feeling for texture. 'The Tam O'Shanter Jug', an important example of his work, is in a private collection. Elected ROI 1958. Exhibited regularly RSA 1946-1980, RSW, ROI, RI, GI(44) & Paris Salon, from Redyett, Manse Rd, Motherwell. Represented in Glasgow AG, Paisley AG.

**FERGUSON, Danny RSW** **1925-1993**
Born Lanarkshire; died Jne 18. Painter in oil and watercolour of domestic scenes, landscapes, portraits; also teacher. Educated Airdrie Academy 1936-41 and Glasgow School of Art 1941-43. Awarded the Torrance and Cargill prizes of the RGI. During WW2 served in the RAF before joining the staff of Glasgow School of Art 1947, remaining there for two years. Moved to Jordanhill Training College for a year. After a further spell of 18 years teaching in Glasgow schools combined with being a visiting staff member of the Glasgow School of Art, he returned full-time to the School of Art 1968-86. Elected RSW 1969. Exhibited regularly RSA(12) from 1961 including a self-portrait in 1989, RSW & GI(88), from 87 Balshagray Ave. Represented in Lillie AG (Milngavie), Royal Collection.

**FERGUSON, Mrs Emma (of Raith)** **fl 1860**
Watercolourist. Portrait attributed to her of 'Caroline Norton, later Lady Stirling-Maxwell', is in SNPG.

**FERGUSON, Mrs G Munro** **fl 1889-1891**
Amateur landscape painter of Assynt, Novar, Ross-shire. Moved to London 1890. Exhibited RSA(1) & Dudley Gallery, Birmingham(3).

**FERGUSON, Hugh** **fl 1932-1944**
Glasgow painter in oil, watercolour and sometimes charcoal; exhibited RSA(1) & GI(2), latterly from 160 Byres Rd.

**FERGUSON, Hugh C S** **fl 1971**
Painter. Exhibited St. James St, SW1 at the GI when at the University of Strathclyde.

**FERGUSON, Ian** **fl 1930-1933**
Edinburgh painter; exhibited RSA(4) during the above years.

**FERGUSON, James** **1710-1776**
Born nr Keith, Banffshire, 25 Apr. Portrait miniaturist, mostly in Indian ink. His parents were poor and, apart from learning to read, he seems to have had no formal education. Began life as a farm labourer before discovering he had an aptitude for mathematics. Studying the sky at night he became known locally as 'Ferguson the astronomer'. Friends and patrons, notably Sir James Dunbar of Drum, enabled him to study in Edinburgh. In the early 1740s he moved to London and in 1746 advertised that he had moved from Compton Street to 'The White Perriwig in Great Pultney Street, London, drawing "pictures as usual for 9 shillings, or goes abroad to do them for one half guinea"'. His work was usually small, and finely drawn. Foskett records that 'the sitters' upper eyelids and eyebrows are usually strongly delineated'. His work was seldom if ever signed. A fine pen and ink portrait of "Prince Charles Edward Stuart', 2" in diameter, was sold in London, 1972. Represented in V & A, NGS.
**Bibl:** Bryan; Foskett 269.

**FERGUSON, James** **fl 1817-1868**
Probably born Edinburgh. Landscape painter in oil. Moved to England at an early age, first to Keswick and then to 21 King Street, Covent Garden, London, before eventually retiring to Barnard Castle. Exhibited regularly RSA 1827-68, mostly Scottish and north-east English landscapes; also RA(10) 1817-23, several of these being Scottish scenes, including 'View near Doune Lodge, Perthshire, the seat of the Earl of Moray', 1820.

**FERGUSON, James Matheson** **fl 1938-1949**
Glasgow painter of portraits and Scottish landscapes. Exhibited RSA 1938 and 1947-49 from 173 West Graham Street.

**FERGUSON, James T** **fl 1952-1965**
Painter in oil and engraver of still life, flowers, genre and portraits. Exhibited RSA 1952-56 and 1963-65 from 23 Swanston Avenue, Edinburgh.

**FERGUSON, James W** **fl 1915-1963**
Glasgow painter in oil and watercolour of portraits and narrative pictures. Exhibited regularly RSA, RSW(3), GI(93) & L(6) during the above years, mostly from 24 Daleview Avenue, Kelvindale.

**FERGUSON, Miss Jean** **fl 1950-1951**
Lanarkshire flower painter; exhibited GI(3), from 56 Manse Rd, Motherwell.

**FERGUSON, John Gow** **fl c1880-c1895**
Edinburgh-based painter in oil of figure and historical studies.

**FERGUSON, John Knox** **fl 1878-1891**
Edinburgh painter in mostly watercolour; figurative, portraits and landscapes. Exhibited 2 historical works at the RA in 1886 and 1887, RSA(20) 1878-91, AAS(1) & L(2).

**FERGUSON, Mrs Margaret** **fl 1965-1966**
Glasgow sculptress of figure subjects. Exhibited GI(2), from 65 Buchanan Dr, Bearsden.

**FERGUSON, Mrs Margaret R** **fl 1974**
Glasgow embroiderer. Married to Danny F(qv). Exhibited GI(1) from 87 Balshagray Ave.

**FERGUSON, Robert John Jnr** **fl 1878-1890**
Edinburgh oil painter of landscapes, especially in the Highlands. Exhibited 6 works at the RSA between the above years, his 'Cubaig Loch, Sutherland' shown in 1890 attracted much attention.

**FERGUSON, Roy Young RSW** **1907-1984**
Born Motherwell. Landscape painter in watercolour and black and white, also caricaturist and illustrator. Brother of Daniel F(qv) with whom he lived. Educated Dalziel HS, Motherwell, studied Glasgow School of Art under Revel(qv) and Crawford(qv). Also a naturalist. Author of several works on natural history and some poetry. Exhibited widely including Paris Salon where he obtained a silver medal in 1952, RA, RSA(56) 1941-1981, RBA, RSW & GI(76). Represented in Glasgow AG, Newport AG, Monmouthshire.

**FERGUSON, T Barclay** **fl 1950**
Ayrshire landscape painter; exhibited GI(1), from Avonlea, Low Fenwick.

**FERGUSON, W** **fl 1912**
Amateur painter of Knowes Mill, East Linton, Prestonkirk, East Lothian; exhibited L(1).

**FERGUSON, W Harding** **fl 1884-1889**
Edinburgh painter in watercolour of landscapes, marines and flowers. Exhibited 7 works at the RSA during the above years including 'Edinburgh Castle from the Pentlands' 1886.

**FERGUSON, Walter** **fl 1843**
Edinburgh painter of 42 George Street who exhibited 'Above Aberdour - Incholm' and 'Edinburgh in the Distance and Newhaven fishwives' at the RSA.

**FERGUSON, William Snr** **fl 1848-1881**
Painter of east coast landscapes and occasional flower studies from both Glasgow and Edinburgh addresses. Probably father of William F Jnr(qv). Exhibited RSA(4) between the above years, also GI(2) from Cambuslang.

**FERGUSON, William Jnr** **fl 1884-1917**
Edinburgh based painter in oil and watercolour of landscapes, especially views in Perthshire and the Lothians. Exhibited 46 works at the RSA during the above years including the occasional flower painting and still life, also RA(1) 1892, RSW(1), GI(4) & AAS 1883-1885, from 13 Dean Park Mews.

**FERGUSON, William** **fl 1984-**
East Lothian topographical artist; exhibited GI(3), from Tayview, Veitch Pk, Haddington.

**FERGUS(S)ON, William Forbes** **fl 1929-1940**
Glasgow landscape painter in oil and watercolour; exhibited landscapes of Perthshire and the south-west Highlands at the RA(1), RSA(1), RSW(15), GI(43) & L(2). Moved to Killearn, Stirlingshire 1941.

**FERGUSON, William Gouw** **c1632-c1690**
Born and probably trained in Scotland; died London. Left for Europe while still young, first staying in Italy before taking up residence at The Hague 1660-68 and then Amsterdam 1681. Married in the Netherlands. Painted dead game and still life in the manner of the Dutch school. Sometimes mistaken for Jan Weenix. Three of his pictures 'A Curious Piece Still Life with Small Birds', 'Birds with a Kingfisher' and 'A Curious Piece of Ruins', were included in a sale in Edinburgh on 3rd March 1693. Represented in NGS(4), Glasgow AG(2), Brodie Castle (NTS), Manchester AG, Berlin AG, Kunsthalle (Hamburg), The Hermitage (Leningrad), Rijksmuseum (Amsterdam).
**Bibl:** Apted 39; Brydall 98; Caw 16-17,196; McKay 10.

**FERGUSSON, A C** **fl 1888**
Glasgow amateur flower painter; exhibited GI(2).

**FERGUSSON, Charles** **fl 1894**
Amateur Aberdeen painter of local landscapes and portraits. Exhibited one year only at the AAS(6) from 77 Skene Street.

**FERGUSSON, Christine Jane (née Stark)** **1876-1957**
Born Lucknow Place, Dumfries, 14 Sep; died Dumfries, 5 Jan. Painter in oil and watercolour principally of landscapes, occasionally flowers and portraits. Third daughter of a family of five, father was a Dumfries solicitor, mother came from Wigtownshire. Educated Dumfries Academy where she distinguished herself especially in painting and watercolour drawing. Attended Crystal Palace School of Art, London and Glasgow School of Art where she studied under Fra Newbery and subsequently taught before becoming Principal Art Mistress at Glasgow High School for Girls. Won the Windsor and Newton prize for painting 1902. In 1908 returned to Dumfries, married a local solicitor and set up home in the town. This was furnished in the current art nouveau style then popular in Glasgow, some of the pieces being made by Fergusson herself. In the early 1920s, with Hornel(qv), Jessie King(qv), E A Taylor(qv), Charles Oppenheimer(qv) and others she formed the Dumfries and Galloway Fine Art Society whose first exhibition was held 1922. In 1924 *The Studio* commented upon the 'vividly spontaneous watercolour by Chris Fergusson showing The Nith, Dumfries, in its artistic attractiveness and lyrical spontaneity'. Many of her best works were done in the 1920s and the early 1930s following the birth of her three children. Travelled widely in Scotland painting as she went and was one of many artists with a particular affection for the Isle of Arran, which she visited regularly in the 1930s. Also associated with the East Neuk of Fife (1923) and St Abb's, Berwickshire (1937). Signed her works variously 'Chris J Stark, Chris J Stark Fergusson, Chris J Fergusson and C J Fergusson'. Regular supporter of the Glasgow School of Lady Artists, winning the Lauder Award for the best painting in their exhibition 1933, 1938 and 1954. Writing in *The Studio* E A Taylor said 'there is no feeling in any of her drawings of the artist having fumbled for effect, but always one of directness and open air liveliness...her vision and taste being entirely her own'. Principal works include 'Moonlight in the Village', 'Rocks of Whithorn', 'Corner of Pittenweem' and 'Winter in Dumfries'. In 1952 116 of her works were exhibited in Dumfries and in 1957 there was a retrospective exhibition at Gracefield Centre, Dumfries, and again in 2002. In 1986 about 70 of her works were exhibited at the Robert Burns Centre, Dumfries, as part of the town's Octocentenary and thereafter were shown at Broughton House (Hornel's home in Kircudbright). Exhibited RA(2), RSA(28), RSW(10), GI(63) & L(4) from Southdean, Rotchell Rd, Dumfries. 'The Brig-end of Dumfries' and 'Salutation Inn, Dumfries', both dated from about 1925, are in the Dumfries Council Chamber Room. Represented in Gracefield Art Centre, Dumfries [From notes provided by W James C Henderson, grandson].
**Bibl:** W J C Henderson: *Chris J Fergusson, a Dumfries and Galloway Artist,* Gracefield Arts Centre Cat, 2002.

**FERGUSSON, David D** **fl 1832**
Painter. Exhibited a study of Hawthornden at the RSA.

**FERGUSSON, Miss Isa R Gillon** **fl 1876-1902**
Edinburgh painter of oil and watercolour; small scale landscapes, domestic scenes and flowers. Exhibited 6 works at the RSA from 31 Chester Street, Edinburgh.

**FERGUSSON, Mrs James** **fl 1968**
Dumfriesshire portrait painter. Exhibited GI(1), from 44 Drumlanrig St, Thornhill.

**FERGUSSON, John Duncan RBA** **1874-1961**
Born Leith, 9 Mar; died Glasgow, 30 Jan. Landscape and figure painter. After initially studying medicine in Edinburgh 1894 he turned to art, being influenced by members of the Glasgow School especially Arthur Melville(qv). Like Melville, he visited Spain and Morocco where he executed many sketches. Spent much time in Paris, studying briefly at the Academie Colarossi in the late 1890s, eventually settling there 1907-1914. Interested in music and movement, in particular the Ballets Russes seen in Paris, this affected his art and in 1913 he married the dancer and painter Margaret Morris(qv). After a spell in London resumed life in Paris between the wars and settled there again before returning to Scotland in 1939. In 1905 held his first one man show at the Baillie Gallery. The nude became the dominant feature of his work in about 1910. He persevered with the Fauvist method of echoing the figure in the background but his colours grew less strident and his outlines more emphatic. In 1911 he was made a member of the Salon des Independants. The outbreak of war brought him back to London and in 1918 he joined the navy, undertaking a series of war paintings of Portsmouth dockyards. In the 1920s his exhibitions with Cadell, Hunter and Peploe led to the term 'Scottish Colourists' being coined. In the 1930s he was elected President, Groupe des Artistes Anglo-Americains in Paris and in 1940 became President of the New Scottish Group. In 1940 founded the New Art Club in Glasgow and 1942 founded the New Scottish Group. His book, *Modern Scottish Painters,* appeared in 1943. For many years art editor of *Scottish Art and Letters.* Received LLD from Glasgow University 1950. Elected RBA 1903. Exhibited at the Salon d'Automne 1907-12, RBA 1899-1912, but never at the RA; also RSA(8), RBA(74), GI(14), RI(4), AAS (in 1935), London Salon(19) & L(5). The largest collection of his work and copyright of all his work is held by Perth & Kinross Council, and housed in The Fergusson Gallery, Perth. Represented in Luxembourg, Tate AG, Ayr AG, Belfast AG, Dundee AG, Glasgow AG, Greenock AG, Kirkcaldy AG, Leeds AG, Paisley AG, City of Edinburgh collection, Manchester AG, Sydney AG (Australia).
**Bibl:** Arts Council of GB (Scottish Committee) J D Fergusson 1874-1961, Memorial exhib of Painting and Sculpture, Edinburgh 1961; R Billcliffe, The Scottish Colourists 1989, passim; R Billcliffe, J D Fergusson, A centenary exhib, Fine Art Society, Glasgow 1974; J D Fergusson 'Chapter from an Autobiography' Saltire Review VI No. 21, 1960; Halsby, 208-210; Hardie 127-137; Hartley 131-2; Macfall, 'The Paintings of John D Fergusson RBA' Studio, Vol 40, 1907, 202-10; Macmillan [SA], ch xvii-xx, et passim; Nigel McIsaac 'J D Fergusson' Scottish Art Review n.s.7, 1959; Margaret Morris, The Art of J D Fergusson. A Biased Biography 1974; John Middleton Murray Between two Worlds, London 1935; Harold Osborne(ed), Twentieth Century Art, 1988, 188; SAC, 'J D Fergusson, Memorial Exhibition' (Ex Cat 1961, Text by A Maclaren Young); SAC, 'Colour, Rhythm and Dance. Paintings and drawings by J D Fergusson and his circle in Paris' (Ex Cat, Essays by Eliz. Cumming, Sheila McGregor & John Drummond); Diana Sykes 'J D Fergusson 1905-15' Crawford Art Centre, St Andrews (Ex Cat 1982); K Simister, Living Paint. J D Fergusson 1874-1961, Mainstream 2001; Louis Annand, J D Fergusson in Glasgow 1939-1961, Alex Parker 2003.

**FERGUSSON, John R** **fl 1871-1872**
Dumfries painter in oil and crayon, portraits. Taught J G M Arnott(qv). Exhibited RSA(2).

**FERGUSSON, Nan (Agnes) Stark (Mrs James Henderson)** **1910-1984**
Born Dumfries 9 May; died Edinburgh, 8 Jan. Painter in oil and watercolour; landscape, mainly Scottish especially of Galloway and Arran, also still life. Elder daughter of Christine Jane F(qv). Educated at the Convent School, Maxwelltown, Dumfries and Edinburgh College of Art where she obtained three travelling scholarships as well as a post-diploma award. Continued her studies at the Academie Scandinave in Paris, visiting Florence, Venice, Rome and Sienna 1935. In 1937 married the artist James Henderson(qv) with whom she exhibited in Edinburgh and elsewhere. When resident in the Borders she helped to found Galashiels Studio Club 1949. In the mid 1970s was President of the SSWA. From 1963-71 teacher of art at George Watson's Ladies College, Edinburgh. Her landscapes were marked by great individuality with special regard for design and well considered composition. Signed her work 'Nan S Fergusson'. Exhibited regularly RSA & GI(2). [From notes provided by W James C Henderson].

**FERGUSSON, W F** **fl 1933-1935**
Amateur painter of mainly Highland lochs. Exhibited at the AAS latterly from St Margaret's, Killearn, Stirlingshire, whence he moved c1934.

**FERGUSSON, William** **fl 1882**
Edinburgh painter of local landscape; exhibited GI(2), from The Tower, Murrayfield.

**FERNANDEZ, Roberto Gonzalez** **fl 1980**
Glasgow-based painter and engraver. Exhibited GI(1), from 24 Regent Terrace.

**FERNBANK, R** **fl 1938**
Glasgow painter of flowers and church interiors; exhibited GI(4), from 152 Renfrew St.

**FERNIE, Maureen (Mrs John Mooney)** **1947-**
Born 7 Jne. Painter of still life and figurative works. Trained Edinburgh College of Art 1965-70. Lives Earlston, Berwickshire. Represented in City of Edinburgh collection by three oils.

**FERNIE, William** **fl 1981**
Edinburgh painter; exhibited 'Three Yachts at Rye' at the GI, from 3 St. Clair Rd.

**FERNS, Philip** **fl 1973**
Glasgow painter; exhibited GI(1), from 89 N. Park St.

**FERRARI, Giuseppe** **fl 1875-1883**
Italian painter who settled for a time in Edinburgh before moving to Bude, Cornwall. Oil painter of figurative subjects. Exhibited RSA(9), RA(2), GI(1) & L(2).

**FERRIER, Arthur** **1891-1973**
Born Scotland; died London, May. Portrait painter, illustrator and theatrical cartoonist. After a short spell in the pharmaceutical trade in Glasgow he moved to London. Most illustrations were of a humorous, theatrical nature, often featuring slender long-legged ladies. Driver suggested that he created the dolly bird and the mini skirt before their time. Regular contributor to the *Radio Times* and *News of the World.*
**Bibl:** Driver; Horne 188; The Times Obit 29 May 1973.

**FERRIER, C Moira RSW** **fl 1959-**
Born Angus. Educated Brechin HS, studied at Gray's School of Art. Influenced by Ian Fleming(qv), Henderson Blyth(qv) and Joan Eardley(qv) and later by Chagall. In 1975 held her first solo exhibition. Sometimes paints local landscapes often with superimposed symbolism and an enchanting dream-like quality. Employs a subtle use of colour and independent form, finding inspiration from the scenery of the north-east of Scotland. Her work has been purchased by various public authorities. Exhibits regularly RSW & AAS.

**FERRIER, George Strat(t)on RI RSW RE** **1852-1912**
Painter and etcher. Son of James F(qv). The first member of the family to use the name Strat(t)on which eventually became hyphenated. Worked most of the time from Edinburgh, painting primarily in watercolour, Highland and continental landscape with a particular fondness for depicting trees, broad landscapes and seascapes with a preponderance of sky at which he was especially good, also interiors. Also a fine etcher. Influenced by the Hague School. Most exhibits at the RSA were Highland subjects particularly around Perthshire and the Western Highlands, including Iona. Also executed a number of angling, golfing and shooting scenes. Contributed four marines to *The Portfolio,* 1879. An interesting informal portrait of a red-coated golfer made £15,500 in 1992. **John Deloitte STRATON-FERRIER** of Thornhill, painter of castles and large country houses, is a direct descendant. Elected RE 1881, RI 1898, RSW 1881. Exhibited 4 works at the RA 1878-93, all of them Scottish subjects including a fine etching, 'The Herring Fleet leaving Wick Harbour' (1880), RSA(92), RSW(68), RE(4), RI(92), AAS (1893) & GI(34), after 1903 from 34 Queen St, Edinburgh.
**Bibl:** Caw 303, Halsby 258; Wingfield.

**FERRIER, James Stratton** **fl 1849-d1883/4**
Edinburgh painter of landscape, oils but mainly watercolour painted

in the grand manner. Especially fond of Highland scenes often in Argyll, Perthshire, and Wester Ross. Worked in a broad, detailed manner somewhat in the style of McNeil MacLeay(qv), although finer. 'The Bridge of Feugh, Kincardineshire', 1858, was a well received academy painting. Father of George Stratton F(qv). Exhibited 58 works at the RSA, among them an especially fine landscape of 'Flowerdale, Gairloch' (1873) purchased by James Brown of Selkirk, and many others of the Gairloch and Loch Maree areas which he frequently visited. Exhibited GI(18), latterly from 30 Danube St. Represented City of Edinburgh collection.
**Bibl:** Halsby 106,258.

**FERRIS, Richard** **fl 1885-1906**
Glasgow sculptor of portrait busts. Exhibited GI(5), from 129 W. Regent St.

**FIDDES, Alexander M** **fl 1964**
Amateur Aberdeen landscape painter. Exhibited AAS(1) from 2 Ellon Road, Bridge of Don.

**FILLANS, James B** **1808-1852**
Born Wilsontown, Lanark; died Glasgow, 18 Aug. Sculptor. Brother of John(qv) and probably related to Wilhelmina F(qv). Apprenticed to a Paisley mason before turning his attention to sculpture. In 1836 moved to London before returning to Glasgow 1852. His best work was done in the south from where he exhibited 25 works, mostly marble busts at the RA 1837-50, among them 'Sir Walter Scott', the engineer 'Robert Napier', and a commissioned work for the town of Paisley, 'Professor Wilson' (1845). Persuaded to return to Scotland to execute a large statue of 'Sir James Shaw' (1846) at Kilmarnock, the 'Blind Girls' (in plaster), and a beautiful life-sized 'Rachel weeping for her Children' adopted as a monument over his grave in Paisley cemetery. Shortly after reaching Scotland he died prematurely and his work is now almost lost to the Scottish public. Represented in SNPG, Paisley AG.
**Bibl:** Brydall 191.

**FILLANS, James D** **fl 1878**
Glasgow sculptor; probably related to James F(qv). Exhibited a plaster bust of 'James Couper, Bailie of Provan,' at the GI from 36 Watt St.

**FILLANS, John** **c1817-1867**
Sculptor, usually on a small scale. Brother of James(qv) and probably related to Wilhelmina(qv). A wax medallion of the poet William Motherwell (1797-1835) is in SNPG.

**FILLANS, Miss Wilhelmina** **fl 1869-1879**
Glasgow sculptress specialising in portrait medallions and busts. Probably related to James and John F(qv). Exhibited RSA(2) & GI(10), latterly from 30 Berkeley St.

**FILSON, J** **fl 1974**
Ayr painter; exhibited a study of rocks at GI, from 14 Prestwick Rd.

**FIMISTER, Miss Ellen F** **fl 1926-1935**
Aberdeen painter of local landscape. Exhibited AAS(4) from 42 Whitehall Road.

**FINDLATER, Lydia** **fl 1908-1927**
Edinburgh topographical painter in oil and watercolour; exhibited RSA(8) & RSW(2) from 74 and 130 George Street.

**FINDLAY, Miss Anna R** **1885-1968**
A linocut and lithographic artist who also painted in watercolours; mostly topographical works. Exhibited RSA(8) 1926-42, GI(10) & L(7), after 1938 from Eastrigg, Killearn, Stirlingshire. In 1931 exhibited 'Chepstow Castle' at the AAS.

**FINDLAY, Mrs C Mary** **fl 1898-1900**
Amateur Aberdeen portrait painter. Exhibited AAS(3) from 2 Queen's Terrace.

**FINDLAY, C T L** **fl 1950-1962**
Banffshire wood sculptor. Exhibited GI(4) from Aikenway, Craigellachie.

**FINDLAY, Mrs Edna M W** **fl 1965-1966**
Glasgow flower painter. Exhibited GI(2) from 22 Dalziel Drive.

**FINDLAY, James** **fl 1830**
Edinburgh painter. Exhibited 'Highland Outlaws Retreating', at the RSA from 9 Queensferry Street.

**FINDLAY, Jane Leslie** **fl 1889-1891**
Edinburgh watercolour painter of interior scenes; exhibited RSA(3) from 3 Rothesay Terrace.

**FINDLAY, Miss M M** **fl 1912-1929**
Aberdeen flower painter. Exhibited AAS(6) from 85 Gray Street.

**FINDLAY, Margaret Ann** **fl 1968-**
Banffshire sculptress of figurative subjects; exhibited RSA 1968-76 from 35 Park Crescent, Portsoy.

**FINDLAY, Miss Margaret C P** **1902-1968**
Sculptress in bronze, lead, cement and plaster of portraits, figurative subjects and genre. Exhibited regularly RSA 1928-1934 from 30 Falkland Mansions, Glasgow W2, also RA(1), GI(13) & L(3).

**FINDLAY, Miss Mary A** **fl 1930s**
Watercolour artist of rustic scenes and landscape especially of the Moray Firth area. Exhibited at the AAS from a variety of addresses, latterly from Mansefield, Hatton, Aberdeenshire.

**FINDLAY, Sheila Anne Macfarlane (Mrs Hackney) RWS** **1928-**
Born Auchlishie, Kirriemuir 22 Apr. Painter in oil and watercolour, illustrator. Educated Webster's Seminary, Kirriemuir and at Edinburgh College of Art 1945-51 under Maxwell(qv), Sir William MacTaggart(qv) and Rosoman(qv). Awarded postgraduate travelling scholarship 1950-51 enabling her to visit France, Italy and Sweden. Illustrated many children's books which became her speciality. Elected ARWS 1971; RWS 1968. Married Alfred Hackney and lived in Kent. Exhibited widely, especially RA and RWS.

**FINDLAY, William** **1875-1960**
Born Glasgow; died Los Angeles. Painter of portraits, figurative works and murals in oil, also etcher. Son of a general practitioner and author, educated Glasgow HS and Glasgow School of Art, later studying in Paris. Returned to Glasgow and set himself up as a portrait painter although at the same time interested in murals, examples of which are in the banqueting hall of Glasgow City Chambers where the frieze is decorated with four murals depicting the four principal Scottish rivers. In 1928 he visited USA and settled in Los Angeles, acquiring American citizenship and marrying an American. Illustrated several of his father's books and executed a number of competent etchings. Exhibited RA(1), RSA(13), RSW(2) & GI(69). Represented in Glasgow AG.

**FINE ART SOCIETY OF KIRKCALDY** **c1872-?**
A pioneer among the smaller Scottish towns in the organisation of annual exhibitions, the first of which was held in 1872.

**FINLAY, Alex** **fl 1887**
West Lothian painter; exhibited 'The Last Basket' at the GI, from Linlithgow.

**FINLAY, Alexander** **fl 1868-1896**
Glasgow painter in oil and watercolour of figurative subjects and sea pieces, including fishing scenes. Exhibited 'The Harbour Kemaquhair', at the RA (1879) and another work in 1881, also RSA(5), GI(30) & AAS, after 1892 from 25 Belmont St, Glasgow.

**FINLAY, Miss Anne Bannatyne** **1898-1963**
Painter in oil and watercolour; landscape, genre and figure especially children and young women. Studied at Edinburgh College of Art before moving to London. Friend of Dorothy Johnstone(qv), Eric Robertson(qv) and Cecile Walton(qv). Elected ASWA 1939. Exhibited RA(17), RSA(56), SWA(15), RBA(1) & GI(2) from 3 Primrose Hill Road, London, and during the war from Temple Farm, Leyburn, Yorks.

**FINLAY, Miss Helen** **fl 1885-1887**
Glasgow figure and portrait painter; exhibited GI(6) from 5 Colebrook Terrace, Hillhead.

**FINLAY, Miss Helen** **fl 1972-1975**
Glasgow landscape painter; exhib GI(4), from 261 Churchill Drive.

**FINLAY, Ian Hamilton** **1925-**
Born Bahamas. Scottish parentage. Sculptor, lithographer, dramatist and poet. Came to Helensburgh 1927. Left school at 14, employed by the Forestry Commission. In 1944 he joined the army and from 1947-59 lived at Comrie, Perthshire. In 1954 began writing short stories and plays and then poetry in 1959. In 1969 launched the Wild Hawthorn Press. Since 1965 he has lived at Dunsyre, Lanarkshire writing concrete poetry since 1962, usually on glass or silk screen. His 'garden of concrete poetry' (if such is possible) at his home in Dunsyre is still being developed. Many exhibitions in Europe and United States. Awarded an honorary doctorate, University of Aberdeen, and presented with a bust of Saint-Just by the French Communist Party. Permanent landscape installations can be seen in the Schweizergarten, Vienna; Kroller Muller Sculpture Garden, Holland; Museum of Modern Art, Strasbourg; Furka Pass, Switzerland; Forest of Kerguehannec, Brittany; Forest of Dean, England; Celle (near Florence); University of California, San Diego; Eindhoven, Holland. His short stories have been published in the *Oxford Book of Scottish Short Stories* and Penguin's *Scottish Short Stories.* Represented in SNGMA, City of Edinburgh Collection, Manchester AG.
**Bibl:** Yves Abrioux, Ian Hamilton Finlay - A Visual Primer, London; Stephen Bann Ian Hamilton Finlay, an illustrated essay, SNGMA 1972, Arts Council GB (Serpentine Gall, London 1977); Biobibliography Ian Hamilton Finlay, Frankfurter, Kunstverein 1991; Francis Edeline, Ian Hamilton Finlay, Belgium; Ian Hamilton Finlay, 'The Garden on the Hill', Pont La Vue Press, New York; Hardie 197-8; Hartley 132; Macmillan [SA], 350,377-8,386-90 et passim in ch xx & xxi; Christopher McIntosh, Coincidence in the work of Ian Hamilton Finlay, Edinburgh 1980.

**FINLAY, Janetta** **fl 1888**
Glasgow landscape painter; exhibited GI(1) from 4 Spring Gardens, Kelvinside.

**FINLAY, Miss Jill (Mrs G Fullerton)** **fl 1980-**
Glasgow painter of portraits, still life and interiors. Trained Glasgow School of Art 1952-56. Awarded the Lauder prize (RGI) 1996. Works mainly in oil and pastel. Exhibited RSA, RGI from 5 Colquhoun Drive, Bearsden and latterly Denbrae Lodge Stables, St Andrews.

**FINLAY, Kirkman John** **fl 1852-1889**
Edinburgh based painter. Moved to London and then to Stirling. Worked in oil and watercolour, especially landscapes and some figure subjects. In the 1880s he moved again, this time to Dolgelly, North Wales. Illustrated *By the Loch and Riverside* 1866. Exhibited RSA(50) & GI(11), after 1867 from Springfield, Ryde, Isle of Wight.

**FINLAY, M L** **fl 1893**
Amateur artist. Exhibited AAS(1) from Edinburgh.

**FINLAY, Peter** **fl 1867-1868**
Edinburgh topographical painter in oil; exhibited RSA(2) & GI(1), from 16 Colville Place.

**FINLAY, R Hunter** **fl 1883**
Glasgow animal painter. Exhibited 'Head of a Pug' at the GI(1) from 13 Hill Street, Garnethill, Glasgow.

**FINLAY, S S** **fl 1933**
Scottish watercolour painter; exhibited RSW(1).

**FINLAY, Mrs William** **fl 1871-1872**
Edinburgh painter in oil of landscapes, especially east coast scenes; exhibited RSA(3).

**FINLAY, William R** **fl 1932-1947**
Painter of still life, interiors; exhibited RSA(4) & GI(3) from 18 Thorburn Road, Colinton, Edinburgh.

**FINLAYSON, Clifford** **fl 1933**
Edinburgh etcher. Exhibited GI(1) from 4 Haymarket Terrace.

**FINLAYSON, J D** **fl c1850**
Possibly the same as **John Findlayson**, an Edinburgh painter apprenticed to James Gibson in 1829. A pencil drawing signed 'J D Finlayson' is in the SNPG.

**FINLAYSON, James A** **c1901-1978**
Painter in oil and watercolours of portraits and landscapes, also teacher. Brought up in Perth, studied Edinburgh College of Art before taking up a teaching appointment at Harris Academy, Dundee. From there moved to Hawick as Principal Art Master 1928 remaining there until his retirement almost 40 years later. Fine draughtsman and accomplished artist. In the 1930s he and Anne Redpath(qv), a college contemporary, were active members of the Hawick Art Club. Although unsuccessful in their aim of acquiring a permanent gallery in the town, many years later the Scott Gallery was opened. As well as his artistic work Finlayson was an ardent member of the Hawick Archaeological Society (from 1929) serving on the committee and becoming Secretary and President; also President of the local branch of the Scottish Nationalist Party and Secretary, Hawick Archaeological Society 1942-51 and President 1957-69. In retirement he became a member of what was then Hawick Town Council, serving as Dean of Guild. Toward the end of his life he was injured in a car accident which prevented any further painting. Exhibited a number of portraits at the RSA 1940-47, & GI(1) in 1946 from 29a Bridge St, Hawick. A portrait of 'William Soutar' is in Perth AG.

**FINLAYSON, James M** **fl 1859-1866**
Glasgow painter of Highland landscape in oil and watercolour, mainly the latter. Exhibited 'A Rustic Cottage, Arran', at the RSA(1859); also GI(6), from 1 Newhall Terrace.

**FINLAYSON, John** **1730-1736**
Scottish engraver. Most of his working life was spent in London. Engraved several portraits in mezzotint including one of 'Maria, Countess of Coventry', half-length after C Read, 1771, the 'Duke of Northumberland' (after Hamilton) and his own work 'Candaulus, King of Libya, showing his Queen coming out of the Bath to his favourite gygas', and some historical subjects. In 1773 he received a premium from the Society of Arts.
**Bibl:** Bryan; Bushnell.

**FINLAYSON, John D** **fl 1904-1907**
Landscape painter in oil, generally winter and storm scenes; exhibited RSA(2) & AAS, from Longniddry, East Lothian.

**FINLAYSON, Kenneth** **fl 1920**
Glasgow painter. Exhibited a still life at the RSA from 28 West End Park Street.

**FINLAYSON, Peter** **fl 1889-1893**
Glasgow landscape painter, fond of atmospheric effects. Exhibited GI(5), latterly from 150 Byres Rd.

**FINLAYSON, Thomas B** **fl 1870-1874**
Edinburgh landscape painter in oil, etcher. Exhibited RSA(7). An etching, 'The Lawnmarket, Edinburgh' is in the collection of City of Edinburgh.

**FINLAYSON, W J** **fl 1882**
Renfrewshire painter of genre and sporting subjects. Exhibited GI(2) from The Oaks, Johnstone.

**FINN, Miss Maureen** **fl 1985**
Argyll painter; exhibited GI(1), from Gleaner Lea, Stronvar Rd, Campbeltown.

**FINNIE, John RE** **1829-1907**
Born Aberdeen; died Aberdeen 27 Feb. Landscape and portrait painter, etcher and engraver. In London 1853-6. Headmaster of the Mechanics Institute and the School of Art, Liverpool, until 1896. Elected ARE 1887, RE 1895. Exhibited 48 works at the RA 1861-

1902, mostly landscapes, until 1897 from a Liverpool address before moving to Fairview, Tywyn, Llandudno. Also exhibited RSA(15), RI(12), RE(61), RBA(18), GI(33) & L(84).
**Bibl:** Halsby 107-8.

**FIRTH, Helen** **fl 1972-1984**
Fife painter. Exhibited annually during the above period (except for 1982 and 1983) at the RSA from 87 Hepburn Gardens, St Andrew's.

**FIRTH, John (Jack) B RSW** **1917-**
Edinburgh landscape painter, mainly of the Scottish Highlands and in France; author. After a spell painting in both oil and watercolour, from 1958 he has worked only in the latter. Studied at Edinburgh College of Art 1935-9 under Gillies(qv), Lintott, Maxwell(qv) and Bruce Thomson(qv). Taught art from 1946-1963 before becoming art adviser to Lothian Region 1963. Published *Scottish Watercolour Painting* 1979. Elected RSW 1961; since 1979 President of the Scottish Artists Benevolent Association. Exhibited RSA(40) 1952-1984, RSW, GI(6), SSA & in 1964 at the AAS from 37 Traquair Park West. Represented in City of Edinburgh collection.

**FIRTH, John Humphrey** **fl 1960**
Edinburgh painter; exhibited RSA(1) from 62 Hanover Street.

**FISHER, Mrs Beth L ARSA** **1944-**
Born Portland, Maine, USA. Printmaker; children a favourite subject. Although born in the United States has lived in Britain since 1970 becoming an integral part of the artistic scene in her adopted country. Graduated from the University of Wisconsin 1967, spending a year at Oxford with the Ruskin School of Drawing and Fine Art 1964-5. After a brief return to Wisconsin where she studied etching 1967-70, trained in printmaking at Oxford Polytechnic 1970-73, etching at Glasgow School of Art 1975-6 and printmaking at Gray's School of Art, Aberdeen 1983. In 1985 she returned to the States as Associate Professor, University of Wisconsin but continued to take seminars in Scotland. In 1986 was guest lecturer at the Chelsea College of Art and at the Ruskin School of Art in Oxford, and 1971-1975 administrator at Glasgow Print Studio. Since 1976 has been a member of the Peacock Printmakers, Aberdeen and served on a variety of committees in Scotland. As a printmaker she has achieved considerable success, being represented in public collections at home and abroad. She has described her work over twenty-five years as "the pull between domestic and a professional life...I have made work from the conflict and combination of elements in everyday family life. Each work is documentation but not a documentary, the work chronicles an epsode, or a time of feelings, rather than an event. I am interested in small, unremarkable personal experiences translated, made iconic". Elected member of the Printmaker's Council 1971, AAS 1979, ARSA 1989. Represented in SNGMA.
**Bibl:** Mungo Campbell, 'The Line of Tradition', Nat Galls of Scotland, Ex cat, Edinburgh, 1993; Rendezvous Gallery Ex Cat, 'Academicians', Dec 2002.

**FISHER, David** **fl 1871-1884**
Glasgow painter in oil and watercolour of local landscapes and figure subjects. Exhibited RSA(5) & GI(2), originally from Glasgow but moved in 1882 to Callander, Perthshire.

**FISHER, David Harley** **fl 1957-1965**
Fife painter of still life. Exhibited RSA 1957-1962 and 1965 from 1 Dalmahoy Crescent.

**FISHER, Edgar** **fl 1919-1920**
Edinburgh animal painter in watercolour. Exhibited RSA(1) & GI(1) from 31 Great King Street.

**FISHER, Gareth ARSA** **1951-**
Born Keswick, Cumbria. Sculptor. Initially trained at the Carlisle College of Art 1968-69, travelled to Scotland 1969 enrolling as a student at Edinburgh College of Art 1969-76. Prize-winner 1972. Subsequent travelling scholarships enabled him to travel overseas and 1979-1981 chairman of the 'New Fifty-Seven' gallery. His work is a young sculptor's perception of the changing physical world around him, 'he brings together disparate objects which communicate the coming together of different cultures and visual stimuli in our modern urban world'. A strong decorative feel to his work 'with particular overtones of a certain decadent gratuitous enjoyment of colour and shape in their own right'. Incorporates his constructional past in the assemblages as literally and metaphorically a base for the final image. Has taught at Duncan of Jordanstone College of Art since 1982. First solo exhibition in Edinburgh 1977, subsequently in Toronto 1984 and at the Abbot Hall AG (Kendal) 1986. Elected ARSA 2003.
**Bibl:** Third Eye Centre, Glasgow, 'Scatter' (Ex Cat 1989).

**FISHER, Hilary Ann** **1963-**
Born Kirkcaldy, 2 Jly. Painter of landscapes and interiors, also printmaker. Studied Edinburgh College of Art 1981-86 obtaining a postgraduate diploma in printmaking, and a scholarship enabling her to travel to Austria, Germany and Switzerland. In 1986 received a John Kinross scholarship from the RCA enabling her to visit and study in Florence. Lives at The Laurels, Newtonmore Road, Kingussie, Inverness-shire. Embarked on teacher training 1986-87. Exhibits RSA since 1988 & SSA since 1986.

**FISHER, Miss Jessie C** **fl 1886**
Glasgow painter. Exhibited GI(2) from 24 Bank Street, Hillhead.

**FISHER, James A S** **fl 1935-1940**
Edinburgh painter of genre and narrative subjects; exhibited RSA(3) from 55 Hillview Crescent, Corstorphine.

**FISHER, John T** **fl 1858-1859**
Edinburgh oil painter of figurative subjects; exhibited RSA(2).

**FISHER, Morgan** **fl 1978**
Exhibited 'Study of an old boat - Arran' at the GI, from Ceol-na-Mara, Lochranza.

**FISHER, Robert B** **fl 1936-1950**
Glasgow painter in chalk and watercolour of landscape, informal portraits and figurative works. Trained Glasgow School of Art 1932-6, winning a Haldane travelling scholarship. Exhibited RSA(1) & GI(3), from 4 Kemp St, Hamilton. Represented in Hamilton Museum.

**FISHER, Mrs Robert Macaulay (née McLaurin)** **fl 1880-1888**
Landscape painter in watercolour. Daughter of Duncan McLaurin(qv). Ran a drawing-class with her husband at 5 Campbell Street, Helensburgh. Sometimes collaborated with her father-in-law. Taught the piano. Married Robert Macaulay Fisher(qv). In addition to exhibiting GI(1) , showed many times at local exhibitions from Blair Athole Villa, Helensburgh.

**FISHER, Robert Macaulay** **fl 1881-1890**
Helensburgh painter in oil of landscape and shore scenes, particularly fond of Arran. Sometimes collaborated with his father-in-law Duncan McLaurin(qv). Ran a local drawing class with his wife from 5 Campbell Street. Exhibited RSA(4) & GI(12), after 1887 from Belle Vue, Helensburgh.

**FISK, John R** **fl 1949**
Rutherglen painter; exhibited 'Bombed House in Herts' at the GI, from 172 Brownside Rd, Burnside.

**FISKEN, Jessie M** **fl 1886-1888**
Amateur Glasgow landscape and flower painter in oil and watercolours. Exhibited AAS(1) & GI(3), from 24 Bank Street.

**FITCH, Mrs Elizabeth C** **fl 1926**
Aberdeenshire artist. Exhibited AAS(2) from Heathview, West Cults.

**FITZPATRICK, Miss J A** **fl 1949-1954**
Paisley watercolourist of landscape and figurative works. Exhibited GI(8), after 1952 from 60 Endrick Dr, Paisley.

**FITZPATRICK, Paula** **fl 1973-1974**
Glasgow painter. Exhib RSA(2) from 100 Herries Road, Shawlands.

**FLANNAGAN, Craig McEwan** **fl 1983-1984**
Aberdeen painter in the modern style, figure subjects. Exhibited AAS from 41 George Street.

**FLATTELY, Professor Alastair F** **1922-**
Born Inverness, 20 Nov. Landscape painter in oil and watercolour,

and monochrome. Educated at Reading and Glasgow Universities where he read engineering before studying at Edinburgh College of Art 1945-50. As a student he was influenced by Sir William Gillies(qv) and Leonard Rosoman. Developed an interest in panoramic landscapes during war service as an artillery surveyor. Awarded Andrew Grant Fellowship in painting 1953-1955. Vice-principal and head of fine art at Gloucestershire College of Art (Cheltenham) 1960-72. Head of Gray's School of Art, Aberdeen 1972-1987. During WW2 was a surveyor with the Royal Artillery, obtaining many long distance views from hill tops later used in his work. From 1949-1952 he painted direct from landscapes but from 1953-1955 became semi-abstract, depicting fantasy landscapes. Since 1955 he has returned again to work directly from the view before him. His prime concern is lighting and colour. Member of the Royal West of England Academy. Settled in Beaminster, Dorset. Exhibits RSA, RSW, GI(13) & AAS, from Briar Lodge, Westerton Place, Cults. Represented in Aberdeen AG, Dundee AG, Glasgow AG.

**FLEMING, A G** **fl 1933-1935**
Edinburgh watercolour artist; exhibited RSW(7) from 50 Ann Street.

**FLEMING, Agnes Bell** **fl 1886-1902**
Aberdeen artist; exhibited regularly AAS from 17 Bon-Accord Terrace.

**FLEMING, Ian RSA RSW RWA RGI LLD Hon DArt 1906-1994**
Born Glasgow, Nov 19; died Aberdeen, Jly 24. Landscape painter in oil and watercolour, also etcher. Landscape, portraiture, genre and semi-abstracts. Studied Glasgow School of Art 1924-1929, specialising in engraving, colour woodcuts and lithography. After further studies in Paris toured southern France and Spain before returning to teach at Glasgow School of Art 1931-47 with a wartime break that saw him first as a Glasgow reserve policeman (recorded in a series of etchings) and from 1941 in the Pioneer Corps, demobbed 1946 with the rank of major. In Aberdeen he rescucitated the AAS 1958. After retirement in 1971, founded Peacock Printmakers and Artspace. Warden of Patrick Allan Fraser Art College, Arbroath, 1948-54. Head of Gray's School of Art, Aberdeen 1954. Lived in Aberdeen for many years. One of Scotland's most important twentieth century etchers. Prepared some memorable scenes of wartime Glasgow. Elected RSW 1946, ARSA 1947, RSA 1956. Exhibited RSA almost annually from 1929, RA(4), GI(93) & frequently at the AAS 1959-1978. Represented in SNGMA, Belfast AG, Bradford AG, Dundee AG, Glasgow AG, City of Edinburgh collection(2), Lillie AG (Milngavie), Liverpool AG, Newcastle AG, Paisley AG, Perth AG, RSA, Biblioteque-Nationale, Paris.
**Bibl:** Aberdeen AG,'Great Scottish Etchers' (Ex Cat 1981, Text by Ian Fleming, Cat by Anny Whyte); Aberdeen AG, 'Ian Fleming: Graphic Work' (Cat 1983, incl an autobiographical essay); 'Ian Fleming', Peacock Printmakers, Aberdeen 1982; Hartley 132-3; Macmillan [SA] 308,358,360-3,371-2,359.

**FLEMING, Ian** **fl 1961**
Glasgow painter; exhibited 'Objects in a Classical Landscape' at the GI from 309 Chirnside Rd, Hillington.

**FLEMING, Mrs J Arnold** **fl 1932-1941**
Helensburgh flower painter in watercolours. Exhibited GI(5) from Locksley, Helensburgh.

**FLEMING, J Edith F** **fl 1897-1902**
Edinburgh painter in oil, informal portraits, landscape and flowers; lived first in Edinburgh with a short spell at the turn of the century in Campbelltown, Argyll. Exhibited RSA(7) & GI(4),

**FLEMING, Jean RSW** **1937-1988**
Born Burnside, Glasgow. Painter, now based in Fife although has lived most of her life in the west of Scotland. Trained Glasgow School of Art 1954-8. Won Newbery medal for painting and Guthrie Award of the RSA 1959. Her work shows a strong sense of design. Killed in a road accident. Exhibited genre, interiors, portraits, still life and local scenes at the RSA 1958-1987, GI(44) & AAS(1), after 1986 from 9 Pinkerton Road, Crail. Represented in Glasgow AG, Paisley AG.

**FLEMING, John** **1792-1845**
Born Greenock. Landscape painter, also occasional portraits. Known as 'Fleming of Greenock'. Began exhibiting locally in 1813, and in Glasgow from 1820, his first subject having a strong religious motif 'Peter Denying Christ', alongside several landscapes. Best remembered for works painted to illustrate Swan's *Select Views of Glasgow and its environs,* 1828, *Views on the Clyde,* 1830, and *The Lakes of Scotland,* 1834. His work possesses great charm. The treatment of scenery is highly vertical but often the beauty of the distance and middle-distance is marred by a rather conventionally treated foreground. His favourite views were in Ayrshire and the Highlands. Exhibited in Glasgow, becoming a member of the West of Scotland Academy. Represented in Edinburgh City collection by a portrait, 'Robert Andrew MacFie' (1811-1893).
**Bibl:** Caw 146; Halsby 258; McKay 276-7.

**FLEMING, John** **fl 1880-1881**
Glasgow landscape and animal painter in oil and watercolours, mainly the latter. Exhibited GI(5) from 1 Scotland Street.

**FLEMING, John Baxter RSW** **1912-1986**
Born Dumbarton. Painter in oil and watercolour and book illustrator; marine, landscapes, especially churches, also some continental scenes and in Connecticut. Educated Dumbarton Academy, trained Glasgow School of Art and Art Student's League in New York. Became a follower of Eric Ravilious, John Nash, Gillies(qv) and Wilson. During WW2 he served at sea, providing the experience and knowledge on which his later marine paintings were based. Senior tutor Glasgow School of Art for many years. Reputedly 'witty, inventive, moodily dramatic'. Illustrated Glasier: *As the Falcon Her Bells* (1963), Niall: *A Galloway Shepherd* (1970), Lernihan: *Science in Focus* (1975), *Science in Action* (1979)*, Pioneers of Science, Human Engineering.* Elected RSW 1960. Outstanding contributor to the affairs of the RGI, serving as secretary for many years. Exhibited regularly RSA 1948-85 & GI(101) 1947-86, after 1981 from Rockhouse, 23 Shoregate, Crail, Fife. Represented in Dundee AG, Glasgow AG, Paisley AG.
**Bibl:** Horne 194; Who 1986 edtn.

**FLEMING, William C** **1804-fl 1848**
Glasgow painter of landscapes and coastal scenes; exhibited RSA(10) 1844-1848, including 'The Mill, Castleton of Braemar'.

**FLETCHER, Alan** **1930-1958**
Born Glasgow; died Milan. Painter and sculptor; still life, objects and portrait busts. After completing national service in 1951 studied at Glasgow School of Art including sculpture under Benno Schotz 1952-55. Won John Keppie travelling scholarship. Most of his paintings, showing the influence of N de Stael, date from the last two years of his life. His work has a haunting quality capturing the mood of his time. 'One of the most exciting young artists of his generation...uses unusual and sombre colours made from a recipe including printer's ink, and invariably restricts his palette to three, four or five colours which are never mixed or modulated. His treatment of the edge is one of the fascinations of his work, as he achieves a sense of spatial ambiguity by reserving foreground objects in the underpainting of the picture'[Hardie]. Granted a memorial exhibition at the MacLellan Galleries, Glasgow, arranged by the SAC. While in Milan he suffered a fatal accident. During his short life exhibited RSA, his terracotta bust 'John McGlashan' 1956 attracting critical acclaim; also GI(3), from 144 W. Graham St, Glasgow, and New York and Moscow. Represented in Dundee AG.
**Bibl:** Hardie 179.

**FLETCHER, Angus** **1799-1862**
Edinburgh sculptor. Specialised in marble busts, exhibiting 6 at the RA 1831-39 including a bust of the 'Duke of Argyll' (1831) and another of 'Charles Dickens' (1839). Also RSA(20) 1829-40 from 20 Fettes Row.

**FLETCHER, Frank Morley** **1866-1949**
Born Whiston, Lancashire; died California, 2 Nov. Portrait painter, engraver and teacher. Brother of the architect Sir Bannister Fletcher. Studied art in Paris at the Atelier Cormon. Exhibited at the principal London Galleries from 1888. Member, Council of the International Society of Sculptors 1903-1909. Head, art department at University College, Reading 1898-1906 before moving to Edinburgh where he was Principal of the Edinburgh College of Art 1908-1923. After retiring emigrated to California and became a naturalised citizen three

years later. Whilst in Edinburgh published *Wood-block printing* 1916. Often chose rather morbid subjects which detracted from the public appeal of his work. Exhibited RA(2) 1892-1893, also RSA(1), ROI(1), L(2), Paris Salon & the USA. Represented in SNGMA.
**Bibl:** Garton & Cooke, London 'British Colour Woodcuts and Related Prints', (Ex Cat 1986); Hartley 133; Grant M Waters, Dictionary of British Artists working 1900-1950, Eastbourne 1975.

**FLETCHER, Hanslip 1874-1949**
Born London; died London, 21 Feb. Etcher, watercolour painter and illustrator. Educated Merchant Taylors' School. Member of the Art Workers' Guild. His drawings appeared in the *Daily Telegraph, Sunday Times* and elsewhere. Worked in Scotland. Exhibited RA, and 'The Senate Room, St Andrews' at the RSA 1916. Represented in City of Edinburgh collection by two drawings, 'Edinburgh from the Calton Hill' (1910) and 'Morning Drawing Room, Holyrood Palace' (1910).

**FLETCHER, John fl 1862-1867**
Edinburgh landscape painter; exhibited RSA(2) & GI(2).

**FLETT, Alex Edward Campbell 1914-?**
Born Findochty, Morayshire, 11 Aug. Painter in oil and watercolour; mainly coastal and fishing scenes and still life. Studied at Gray's School of Art under D M Sutherland(qv). Exhibited RA, RSA, ROI, NEAC & SSA from a London base.

**FLETT, Una fl 1970**
Edinburgh sculptress. Exhibited a portrait group at the RSA from 8 Lee Crescent.

**FLIGEL, Leonard fl 1968-1982**
Glasgow painter in oils and occasionally pen and ink. Painted genre and still life. Exhibited GI(2) from 12 Blairhill Ave.

**FLINT, Miss Amelia fl 1848**
Edinburgh artist; who exhibited 2 flower paintings at the RSA from Greenhill Bank.

**FLINT, Francis Murray Russell RWS RSW 1915-?**
Born 3 Jne. Landscape and coastal painter in oil and watercolour. Son of Sir William Russell F(qv). Educated at Stubbington, Cheltenham and HMS Conway. Studied at RA Schools under Sir Thomas Monnington and at Beaux Artes, Paris. Official War Artist in the Far East when serving with the RNVR during WW2. Sketches, made when aide-de-camp to Sir Winston Churchill, were the basis for his painting of the cruiser *HMS Belfast* during bombardment off the Normandy coast in 1944. This was commissioned by the *HMS Belfast* Trust and displayed aboard the ship 1972. Flint, a Lieutenant Commander in 1939, was on *HMS Thanet* when she was sunk; his painting '*HMS Thanet's Last Fight*' was exhibited at the RA after the War. Devoted to his father, he painted in a style somewhat similar although the subject matter was generally different. In 1972, when Francis held an exhibition of his work in Brighton at the same time as a posthumous exhibition of his father's work in London, the public and press acknowledged that both had the same mastery of technique as well as the ability to record a personal statement of facts as observed. One critic wrote 'he has succeeded in following in father's footsteps'. Francis's first love was undoubtedly watercolour painting, and spoke of his 'feeling for the tenderness and delight of watercolour'. In the words of his father's biographer 'the work of both painters encourages contemplation and expresses the union between life and peace'. Lived in Burgess Hill, Sussex and exhibited RA, RSA, RWS & RGI(8). Represented in Lillie AG (Milngavie).

**FLINT, Francis Wighton fl 1874-1888**
Edinburgh painter and commercial designer in oil. Father of Sir William Russell F(qv) and Robert Purves F(qv). Lived for many years at 5 Rosefield Place, Portobello and exhibited at the RSA a study of bird's nests in 1874 and the 'Smithy nr Grantshouse' 1888.
**Bibl:** Halsby 235.

**FLINT, Robert Purves RSW ARWS 1883-1947**
Born Edinburgh, 22 Nov. Landscapes and coastal scenes in oil and watercolour, also etchings. Son of Francis Wighton F(qv), brother of Sir William Russell F(qv). Educated Daniel Stewart's College, Edinburgh. First one man show was at the Leicester Galleries 1926. Worked extensively abroad, particularly in France. Served in the army during WW1, wounded in Flanders 1917. Latterly lived in Whitstable, Kent. Elected RSW 1918, ARWS 1932, RWS 1937. Exhibited extensively RA(4), RSA(3), RSW(72), RWS(82), RHA(13), GI(76), L(18) since 1928 from Littlemead, Joy Lane, Whitstable, Kent & AAS 1912-1937. Represented in Glasgow AG, City of Edinburgh collection, Brodie Castle (NTS).
**Bibl:** Halsby 235,238,253.

**FLINT, Stanley R fl 1957**
Edinburgh amateur landscape painter in watercolour. Exhibited a townscape at the GI from 104 Baird Dr.

**FLINT, Sir William Russell PRA PRWS RSW ROI RE 1880-1969**
Born Edinburgh 4 Apr; died London, 27 Dec. Landscape and figure painter in watercolour and oil, etcher and illustrator. Described by his biographer Ralph Lewis as one of the finest watercolour artists who ever lived, he was certainly one of the finest watercolourists that Scotland has ever produced. Son of Francis Wighton F(qv) and elder brother of Robert Purves F(qv). Greatly influenced by *The Studio* and by the Dutch School. Studied at Daniel Stewart's College, Edinburgh. Aged 14 became apprenticed to a firm of lithographers where, in spite of the tedium, he remained six years. From 1895 he began studying under Hodder at RI School of Art evening classes, where he also came under the influence of Arthur Melville(qv). A visit to the continent with his brother 1900 resulted in painting watercolours in Dordrecht, Amsterdam and Volendam. In 1900 went to London where he was at first employed to undertake medical drawings, later joining the staff of the *Illustrated London News* 1903-1907. During this period he studied at Heatherley's Art School in the evenings. Became interested in book illustration, his first work being for Haggard's *King Solomon's Mines.* Elected ROI 1901 although resigned shortly afterwards. Visited Italy 1912-13 and about this time took up etching which he studied at Hammersmith School of Art 1914, having already won a silver medal at the Paris Salon 1913. During WW1 served as a Lieutenant in the RNVR and later as a Captain in the RAF. After the war he painted extensively all over Europe especially in France, Italy, Scotland, Spain and Switzerland producing many fine etchings 1928-32. Best known for his semi-nudes in French or Spanish settings, many of which have been widely reproduced. Also painted many pure landscapes and was an excellent animal draughtsman, especially during the early part of his career. Happily married, he found it almost impossible to work after his wife died in 1960. One of the most popular artists who embellished the London scene. Adrian Bury wrote 'I have always regarded Sir William Russell F as a great artist and a great man (the two are not always synonymous), in the sense that he planned life so as to make the most of his many talents, to add more beauty to the world, and give happiness to his dependents, friends and humanity at large. I have known quite a few art geniuses so-called, some of them true to the popular idea that a genius is a gifted but irresponsible, not to say reprehensible, person unable to adapt himself to normal standards of civilisation...not so Sir William Russell Flint, there was nothing Bohemian about him. He was always dressed in a tidy conventional way, wearing none of the sartorial insignia often associated with artists. He had a gentle conversational style, with a slight Scottish accent, a spontaneous, whimsical sense of humour, discussed things with a careful choice of words, and was a good listener. One was always at ease in his company for he never made one conscious of his celebrity. Rather the reverse...his way of life was well-ordered and systematic. A constant practice throughout a lifetime resulted in a faultless style. The refined vision was the artist's birthright'. Published an autobiography, *In Pursuit* (1970). Other works he wrote and illustrated included *Models of Propriety* (1951), *Minxes Admonished* (1955), *Pictures from the Artist's Studio* (1962), *Shadows in Arcady* (1965), *The Lisping Goddess* (1968), *Breakfast in Perigord* (1968). Also illustrated *King Solomon's Mines* (1905), *Of the Imitation of Christ* (1908), *Song of Songs* (1909), *The Savoy Operas,* 2 Vols (1909-10), *Marcus Aurelius Antoninus* (1909), *Le Morte D'Arthur,* 4 Vols (1910-11), *The Scholar Gypsy* (1910), *The Heroes* (1912), *The Canterbury Tales,* 3 Vols, (13), *Rabbi Ben Ezra* (1913), *Theocritus Bion and Moschus* 2 Vols (1922), *The Odyssey* (1924), *Judith* (1928), *Airmen or Noahs* (1928), *Tobit and Susanna* (1929), and Herrick's *Poems* (1955). Exhibited GI(86). Represented in V & A, BM, City of Edinburgh Art collection, Lillie AG(Milngavie), Aberdeen AG, Blackburn AG, Darlington AG,

Glasgow AG, Greenock AG, Harrogate AG, Leeds AG, Leicester AG, Maidstone AG, Newport AG, Paisley AG, Perth AG, Nat Gall of Canada (Ottawa), Nat Gall of New Zealand (Wellington).
**Bibl:** Baldry, 'A Romanticist Painter: W Russell Flint', The Studio vol 60, 1914, 252-63; Halsby 234-238; Lewis, Sir William Russell Flint (1880-1969), 1980; Palmer, 'More Than Shadows: A Biography of W Russell Flint', The Studio, 1943; RA 'London Works by Sir William Russell Flint' (Ex Cat 1962); Sandilands, 'Famous Watercolour Painters: W Russell Flint', The Studio 1928.

**FLOCKHART, Helen** **1963-**
Born East Kilbride. Painter of figurative work in oils. Trained Glagow School of Art 1979-84 and at Poznan. Winner of prestigious Pollock-Krasner Award from the New York Foundation of that name. One of a group of promising young lady artists whose work was included in the 'Vigorous Imagination' exhibition at the Edinburgh Festival 1987. Exhibited RGI(1) from 76 Buccleuch St.
**Bibl:** Hardie 215.

**FLYNN, Peter** **fl 1893**
Amateur Carnoustie painter. Exhibited AAS(1) from 1 Westfield Place.

**FLYNN, Theresa RSW** **fl 1961-1986**
Glasgow based watercolour painter, also worked sometimes in oil. Reticent about her work, little is known of her life beyond the regular exhibits at the RSA(10) during the above years, also RSW & GI(28), since 1986 from 6 Rosebery Crescent. Represented Lillie AG (Milngavie).

**FOGARTY, R** **fl 1919-1937**
Aberdeen painter of landscape, including Indian scenes, and figure subjects. Many exhibits at the AAS during the above years from 18 Elm Place.

**FOGGIE, David RSA RWS** **1878-1948**
Born Dundee; died Edinburgh, 2 Jne. Painter in oil, watercolour, pastel and charcoal; portraits and figures. Educated Dundee High School under William Grubb, he was a close friend of George 'Dutch' Davidson(qv). A smooth effortless style emerged from his studies abroad in Antwerp, Florence, Paris and Holland. Began his career as an artist in Leuchars and Dundee where he developed a close association with Stewart Carmichael(qv), John Duncan(qv) and Alexander Grieve(qv). In 1920 he went to Edinburgh to take up a part-time teaching appointment in the College of Art. Secretary, RSA 1932. Enjoyed painting members of the lower class, those described as 'robust types of Scottish people, very typical'. Some of his work was extremely tasteful, beautifully harmonious in colour and conception, with fine draughtsmanship. Elected RSW 1918, ARSA 1925, RSA 1930. Exhibited RA(5), RSA(114), RSW(91), GI(100), AAS 1908-1937 & L(6). Represented in SNPG(44) (including a 'self-portrait'), Dundee AG, City of Edinburgh collection, Brodie Castle (NTS).
**Bibl:** Halsby 197-9; Hardie 123,142; Wingfield.

**FOGGIE, Neil** **fl 1935-1979**
Edinburgh painter of Scottish landscapes and topographical subjects. Lived in Dollar until about 1937 then in Galashiels, Edinburgh and Toronto 1954. Married Margaret McLeod Hendry(qv). Exhibited RSA(35), GI(33) & frequently at the AAS 1959-1973, from 1955 at Craigielea, Lawyer's Brae, Galashiels.

**FOGO, J L** **fl 1971-1983**
Glasgow painter of churches in oil; exhibited RSA(1) & GI(4), from 133 W. George St.

**FOJCIK, Brian Joseph** **1960-**
Born Kirkcaldy. Studied at Duncan of Jordanstone College of Art, Dundee 1979-83 where he received the John Milne Purvis prize for painting and a travelling scholarship. First one man show at Kirkcaldy Museum 1987. In 1986 received a Young Artist bursary. Other awards include the Drumfork travelling scholarship (Duncan of Jordanstone College of Art), Elizabeth Greenshields travel award 1988, Maud Gemmell Hutchison prize (RSA). Elected SSA 1992. Exhibits RSA.

**FOLAN, Colm Edward** **fl 1985-**
Painter of abstracts. Exhibited AAS(1) from 3 Pinkie Gardens, Newmachar.

**FOLEY, George Cameron** **fl 1938-1970**
Painter in oil of fishing scenes and figures. Lived shortly before the war in Falkirk latterly moving to 48 Castle Street, Duns, Berwickshire. Exhibited RSA at least 7 works over a broad span between 1938 and 1970.

**FOLLETT, Sidney G** **fl 1903-1907**
Edinburgh painter of architectural subjects; exhibited RSA from 12 Sylvan Place.

**FONSECA, Joseph Henry** **fl 1873**
Edinburgh landscape painter in oil, exhibited RSA(1).

**FOOT, Miss Victorine Anne (Mrs Schilsky)** **1920-?**
Born Penbury, Kent, 1 May. Oil painter and mural decorator. Educated at Oakdene School, studied at the Central School of Arts and Crafts 1938-1941, Chelsea School of Art and Edinburgh College of Art. Married to the sculptor Eric Schilsky(qv). Employed by Directorate of Camouflage during the War. Influenced by the early Florentines and Piero della Francesca, by her husband, by William Gillies(qv) and through her friendships with Anne Redpath(qv) and John Maxwell(qv). Best known for her depiction of Scottish landscape, often with cattle and as a setting for people, and for her portraits; fond of portraying biblical scenes. Lived in Edinburgh. Exhibited extensively RA, RSA and elsewhere.

**FOOTE, Edward Kilbourne** **fl 1886-1906**
Aberdeen painter in oil of landscape and townscape. Husband of Margaret F(qv). Many of his works were done in Egypt. Exhibited AAS during the above years.

**FOOTE, Mrs E K (Margaret Ingram)** **fl 1898-1902**
Painter in oil of landscape. Travelled with her husband in North Africa and Italy. Exhibited AAS(5) including 2 Venetian scenes.

**FOOTE, Robert** **fl 1919-1938**
Glasgow painter of still life. Exhibited GI(15), first from Cathcart, Glasgow and after 1929 from Mansewood, Overlea Rd, Clarkston, by Busby.

**FORBES, A** **fl 1953**
Glasgow portrait painter; exhibited GI(1), from 4 Corunna St.

**FORBES, Albert J** **fl 1950-1951**
Amateur painter who exhibited a still life and a local landscape at the RSA during the above years from 52 Harefield Road, Dundee.

**FORBES, Alexander** **fl 1690-1691**
Painter in oil. Probably father of **Alexander FORBES** known to have been painting in 1744. Responsible for topographical views of towns. The only one which can now be identified is a view of the old Coventry Cathedral. Represented in British Museum.

**FORBES, Alexander ARSA** **1802-1839**
Born Aberdeen; died Edinburgh. First made his mark in 1828 by exhibiting three pictures at the RSA while teaching art in Edinburgh. Animal painter to the forerunner of the Royal Highland Agricultural Society from whom he received many commissions for portraits of horses and dogs. These he painted with such sympathy that he became known as the 'Landseer of the north'. Gilbey considered him an artist of considerable ability who would have reached the front rank of animal painters. A small version of an engraved picture 'Much between the cup and the lip', demonstrates spirited action combined with free handling. Elected ARSA 1830. Exhibited RSA(64).
**Bibl:** Caw 198; McKay 355.

**FORBES, Anne** **1745-1834**
Born and died Edinburgh. Painter of portraits in oil and watercolour but mostly in crayon. Grand-daughter of William Aikman(qv). One of only a few women artists in the 18th century to have undergone full professional training, she studied in Rome c1767 and 1768 under Gavin Hamilton(qv), having received financial backing from a group

of friends. For a year she was required to gain 'mastery of the pencil' before being allowed by her teachers to use oils. Recorded as painting 'several good portraits from nature, copying Old Masters such as Guido Reni and Correggio' she found herself in the company of the Runciman brothers(qv), James Clark(qv) and the sculptor William Jeans(qv). Back in London her work was warmly commended by the Duke of Queensberry whose portrait she painted. By the autumn of 1772 she was beginning to struggle, partly on account of a weakness in painting drapery and failure to find anyone to help overcome the problem. Returning to Scotland she attracted a large following. Work by her is now scarce. The only RA exhibits were four portraits in 1772, one of a lady of quality, one an Italian girl, another 'a young girl' and the fourth an unidentified officer. Represented in SNPG by a portrait of 'David Allan' 1781, also in NGS.
**Bibl:** Caw 49; Forbes correspondence, MSS, NLS, Acc. 3081; Irwin 76-7; Macmillan [SA], 114,116214; McKay 27; Basil Skinner, Scots in Italy, Edinburgh 1966, 19,22,25,29,33; Waterhouse.

**FORBES, Miss Annie** **fl 1869-1876**
Edinburgh painter in oil and watercolour of landscape and figurative subjects, exhibited RSA(4).

**FORBES, Archibald** **fl 1932**
Perthshire portrait painter; exhibited GI(2), from Edengrove, Braco.

**FORBES, Donald** **1952-**
Painter of still life and semi-abstract landscape; exhibited RSA 1982-84 & GI(12) since 1977, from 19 Wardlaw Street, Edinburgh.

**FORBES, Miss Georgina E** **fl 1850-1865**
Edinburgh landscape painter in oil; exhibited RSA(9) between the above years, mostly of Aberdeenshire especially Braemar.

**FORBES, J C** **fl 1874**
Glasgow landscape painter in oil, exhibited RSA(2), both painted whilst the artist was in Canada.

**FORBES, James** **1797-1881**
Born Lonmay, Aberdeenshire; died Plainwell, USA. Painter in oil of landscape, figure studies and portraits. Largely self-taught, at different times lived in Brora, London and Peterhead before settling in Aberdeen. In the mid 1850s emigrated to Chicago. Probably married to Mary F(qv). Exhibited landscape and figurative studies at the RSA 1852-1854, whilst living at Invernettie, nr Peterhead.

**FORBES, Professor James David** **1809-1868**
Draughtsman and glaciologist. Elected FRSE 1828, was a joint founder of the British Association 1831 and elected FRS 1832. Professor of Natural Philosophy, Edinburgh Univ., 1833, Principal of St Andrews Univ, 1859. Alpinist. Illustrated *Travels to The Alps of Savoy* (1843), *Norway and its Glaciers* (1853).
**Bibl:** Fergus Fleming, Killing Dragons; The Conquest of the Alps, Granta Books, London pp126-7 et passim; Houfe 139.

**FORBES, James Grellier** **c1800-1857**
Portrait painter and cartographic artist of Scottish descent. Trained at the RA Schools, London. Member of a Manx banking family and brother of Professor Edward Forbes of Edinburgh University. Exhibited RA(1) 1853, RSA(3) 1852-4 & British Institution 1857. Artist to the Ordnance Survey. Represented in Manx Museum, Chicago Art Institute (portrait of 'A N Fullerton'). Died Douglas, IOM. His brother was a naturalist and minor artist, several of whose cartoons and scientific drawings are in the Manx Museum.

**FORBES, Karen** **fl 1988-**
Glasgow-based sculptress. Exhibited GI(1) in glass fibre and terracotta, from 6 Doune Terrace.

**FORBES, Marie** **fl 1886**
Edinburgh painter in oil; exhibited a townscape at the RSA from 15 Stafford Street, Edinburgh.

**FORBES, Mary** **fl 1851-1854**
Painter of narrative subjects; exhibited RSA 1851 and 1854 from Peterhead.

**FORBES, P** **fl 1834**
Exhibited 3 narrative works at the RSA from Crown Court, Aberdeen.

**FORBES, Ronald ARSA** **1947-**
Born Braco, Perthshire, 22 Mar. Painter in oil and acrylic, and film-maker. Figurative subjects, genre and still life. Studied Edinburgh College of Art 1964-69, awarded postgraduate scholarship 1968-69. In 1971 founded the Glasgow League of Artists and elected its first chairman. After living in Cork, where he was head of painting at the Crawford School of Art 1974-78, he returned to Scotland as artist-in-residence at Livingston, joining the staff of Glasgow School of Art 1979-83; since 1966 has been Head of Painting at Duncan of Jordanstone College of Art, Dundee. Preoccupied with the portrayal of rural life and landscape through the imagery of the townsman, the way we perceive relative to tradition and the manner in which we think we see things. Has held one man exhibitions in London, Glasgow, Dublin and Dundee. Elected ARSA 1996. Exhibits regularly RSA, AAS & GI(7). Represented in Perth AG, Hunterian AG (Glasgow Univ), Cork Municipal AG, Dundee AG, Smith AG (Stirling), RSA (SAC bequest), Museum Narodowecz (Poland), Gdansk AG (Poland).

**FORBES, Sheena** **fl 1975**
Aberdeen watercolour artist and printmaker. Exhibited AAS(2) from 1 Ruthrie Terrace.

**FORBES, Thomas** **fl 1720-1730**
Aberdeen engraver. Engraved bookplates for a Thomas Forbes 1720 and for a Mr Joseph Stewart in 1730.
**Bibl:** Bushnell.

**FORBES, William** **?-1826**
Aberdeenshire engraver. Son of Sir William Forbes, 7th Bt of Pitsligo. Army Captain. Engraved his own bookplate; died unmarried.

**FORBES, William** **fl 1934**
Watercolour painter. Exhibited RSW(2) from 9 Rutland Street, Edinburgh.

**FORBES-DALRYMPLE, Arthur Ewan** **1912-?**
Born Edinburgh, 22 Oct. Painter in oil, watercolour, gouache and pastel. Studied at Heatherley's under Henry Massey 1930-32 and at Goldsmith's College School under Clive Gardiner 1932-34. Signs his work 'Forbes'. Elected NS 1937. His exhibition 'Sketchbook in Provence' was opened by Anne Redpath(qv) in Edinburgh 1951. Exhibited RA, RSA, RHA, ROI, RBA & Paris Salon from a London address.

**FORBES-ROBERTSON, Eric** **fl 1885-1891**
Landscape painter of Scottish extraction; dramatic scenery effects. Son of an Aberdonian who came to London as an art critic and journalist, and brother of the actor and amateur artist Sir Johnston F-R(qv). Exhibited RA 1885 and 1891 & GI(3), from 25 Charlotte St, Bedford Sq, London.

**FORBES-ROBERTSON, Sir Johnston** **1853-1937**
Born London, 16 Jan. Professional actor and amateur portrair painter. Son of John F-R, an Aberdonian journalist who went to London as an art critic; brother of Eric(qv). Educated Charterhouse, attended the RA Schools 1870 but, like both his brothers and sister, soon turned to drama although continued to regard himself as primarily an artist. A handsome man, he sat for D G Rossetti, Ford Madox Brown and other artists. Among his sitters was the actor 'Samuel Phelps in the character of Wolsey', now in the Garrick Club. Married an American actress. His own portrait was painted by Alfred Collins and by Meredith Frampton, the latter for the Shakespeare Memorial Theatre, Stratford. John Perceval Gulich's drawing of Forbes-Robertson in his most famous role - Hamlet - appeared in 1897 and was the basis for Spy's cartoon in *Vanity Fair* (1895). Exhibited GI(2) from 25 Charlotte St, Bedford Sq, London.
**Bibl:** DNB.

**FORBES-ROBERTSON, Margaret** **fl 1892-1894**
Portrait miniaturist. Sister of Eric(qv) and Johnston(qv). Exhibited RA(5) from 22, Bedford Square, London.

**FORD, George M** **fl 1885-1888**
Topographical painter. Exhibited RSA(2) from 1 Vanburgh Place, Leith Links, Edinburgh.

**FORD, Mrs Jean M** **fl 1958-1962**
Glasgow sculptress and watercolour painter. Exhibited GI(3), from 15 Randolph Crescent.

**FORD, John A** **fl 1881-1923**
Leith painter in oil and watercolour of portraits, figures, interiors and landscapes. One striking portrait was of the 'Edinburgh prison chaplain' (ex 1898). President, SAC 1919-1922. Exhibited RA(1) from Picardy Place, Edinburgh, also RSA(79), RSW(2), GI(38, including a portrait of 'James Caw' (1903) & AAS (including 'Self-portrait'). Represented in City of Edinburgh collection, Paisley AG.
**Bibl:** Caw 290.

**FORD, Miss M N M** **fl 1964-1965**
Glasgow watercolour painter and sculptress. Daughter of Jean F(qv). Exhibited GI(3).

**FORDE, Edward** **fl 1909**
Amateur painter. Exhibited GI(1) from 65 West Regent Street, Glasgow.

**FORDYCE, Mrs Betsy B** **fl 1948**
Glasgow landscape painter. Exhibited 'Snow in Darjeeling' at the GI from 10 Hotspur St.

**FORDYCE, George** **fl 1900-1902**
Aberdeen painter of landscape, townscape and architectural subjects. Exhibited AAS latterly from Arthur Cottage, Prince Arthur Street.

**FOREMAN, Miss H Dorothy** **fl 1929-1935**
Perthshire flower painter. Exhibited several works at the AAS during the above years from Cloquhat, Bridge of Cally.

**FOREMAN, William** **1939-**
Born London, 18 Mar. Painter in oil of landscape and genre. Although born in London, claims a Scottish grandmother and settled in Scotland 1970. Entirely self-taught and devoted to the art and landscape of France. His work shows the clear influence of the post-impressionists and pointillism. First exhibition Gibraltar 1961 and almost regularly in London and New York ever since. Lives and works in Aberdeenshire but continues to visit France two or three times a year, especially the areas of Provence, Cote d'Azur, Rouen and Normandy.

**FORGAN, Winifred M** **fl 1921-1929**
Aberdeen painter in watercolour of still life and figure subjects. Exhibited AAS(3) from 2 Hamilton Place.

**FORMAN, Miss Dorothy** **fl 1951-1953**
Ayrshire painter in oils and watercolour of genre, figurative works and townscapes. Exhibited GI(3), from The Hut, Fairlie.

**FORRES, Lady Freda** **fl 1926-1938**
Sculptress of Glenogil, Kirriemuir, Forfarshire, usually in bronze. Also lived at 41 Trafalgar Sq, Chelsea, London (1937). Exhibited 'Study of a Faun' at the RSA in 1926, also RA, ROI & GI(1).

**FORREST, Archibald** **1869-1963**
Born Greenwich. Scottish parentage. Painter in oil & watercolour; illustrator, landscape & figurative works. Studied Edinburgh College of Art and at Westminster School of Art under Fred Brown. Keen observer of character. Worked in Blackheath 1908 and at Lymington, Hants, 1926, concentrating on monochromatic work in the 1890s before turning to colour in the 1900s and pure landscapes from about 1910. Illustrated Koebel: *South America*, Bensusan: *Morocco*, Henderson: *The West Indies* (1905). Worked for *Today* and prepared the illustrations for Marshall's *Island Story,* also illustrated *Uncle Tom's Cabin* and *Robin Hood* as well as narrative works about Portugal & Mexico. Lived in Sussex. Exhibited RBA(2) & LS(5).
**Bibl:** Caw 487-8; Waters.

**FORREST, Archie RGI** **1950-**
Born Glasgow. Painter of landscapes, still life and figurative subjects; also sculptor in bronze, plaster & terracotta. Trained Glasgow School of Art 1969-73, subsequently a staff member 1978-85, terminating the appointment in order to paint full-time. Elected RGI 1998. Influenced by Robin Philipson(qv) and David Donaldson(qv). Uses strong brilliant colours, partly the effect of travelling in India and France. His work expresses a natural balance with a sensual harmony in colour and tone. Solo exhibitions in France (1981), Italy (1983), USA (1985), as well as in London & Edinburgh. Began exhibiting RSA 1984 and RGI 1973. Represented in National Museum of Scotland, SNPG, Glasgow AG, Glasgow Art Club, NTS.

**FORREST, Arthur** **fl 1973**
Exhibited 2 Angus landscapes at the RSA from 59 Abbeyhill, Edinburgh.

**FORREST, Ian B** **c1814-1870**
Born Aberdeenshire; died Hudson County, NJ (USA). Scottish miniature painter and engraver. Apprenticed to Thomas Pry, a London engraver, remaining in his employ until 1837, when he went to Philadelphia to engrave for the National Portrait Gallery. Later began miniature painting at which he achieved some success. Long suggests that he may be the same as the F B Forrest who was awarded a silver Isis medal by the Society of Arts 1826/27 for an engraved portrait.
**Bibl:** Fielding, Transactions of the Society of Artists; Long 157,158.

**FORREST, John S** **fl 1961**
Perthshire artist; exhibited 'Rock Pool' at the GI from Woodlea, Ancaster Rd, Callander.

**FORREST, Miss Kathleen** **fl 1956**
Paisley painter of figure susbjects and landscape in oil. Exhibited GI(3), from 3 Drummond Drive, Ralston.

**FORREST, Marianne** **1957-**
Born London. Scottish father. Jeweller, silversmith & teacher. Trained Middlesex Polytechnic and Royal College of Art 1979-83. Her work is characterised by its clarity, crispness and unfussy individualistic design. Has exhibited in New York, Japan, London and Germany; an exhibition of her timepieces in Glasgow 1998. Lecturer, RCA and various English Universities. Made a Freeman of the City of London 1994. Represented in V & A, Royal Museum of Scotland, Goldsmith's Hall, London Museum, Hampshire Museum.

**FORREST, Martin Andrew FSA (Scot)** **1951-**
Born Musselburgh, East Lothian, 7 Jan. Painter of poetical, figurative subjects and portraits, mainly in oil. Also art historian and art dealer. Studied Birmingham Polytechnic before returning to Scotland. Paints mainly subjects in which he is influenced by European subjective traditions. Regular exhibitor RSA & GI(4). Lives at 75 High Street, East Linton, East Lothian.

**FORREST, Norma Tait** **fl 1948-1948**
Edinburgh portrait painter; exhibited 4 works at the RSA from 37 Chambers Street.

**FORREST, Norman John ARSA ARBS** **1898-1972**
Born Edinburgh, 30 Sep; died Edinburgh, 10 Nov. Sculptor in wood, bronze, plaster and stone. Studied at Edinburgh College of Art under the sculptor Thomas Good at the same time as apprenticed to an architectural sculptor. Produced a series of statuettes in walnut and limewood for the liners *Queen Mary, Queen Elizabeth* and *Queen of Bermuda.* Created some large wood carvings for various churches. Member, Board of Governors for Edinburgh College of Art 1963-68. Lived for many years in Edinburgh. Elected ARSA 1943. Exhibited RSA(60), GI(21), AAS & SSA, from 16 Regent Terrace.

**FORREST, Robert** **c1789-1852**
Born Carluke, Lanarkshire; died 29 Dec. Sculptor, working mainly from a greyish sandstone known as liver-rock, excavated from a quarry in Lesmahagow. Originally a mason, he first began carving secretly in a secluded glade in woodland near the Clyde. In about

1817 a Colonel Gordon, whilst out shooting, came upon the sylvan studio. This led a friend, Mr Robertson of Hallcraig, to commission Forrest to undertake a life-size Highland chieftain. He executed portrait busts of many celebrities including Napoleon, Duke of Wellington, Sir William Wallace for the town of Lanark, as well as other equestrian statues. Undertook Chantrey's design for the statue which surmounts the column in St Andrew's Square, Edinburgh, the first public monument to be erected in the New Town. Responsible for a large sculptured group 'James V at Cramond Bridge' (c1836) at Braehead Mains, formerly at the demolished Clermiston House. In about 1832 there was an exhibition of his work beside the National Monument on Calton Hill, Edinburgh. Exhibited regularly RSA.
**Bibl:** Brydall 187-8; Gifford 48,322,593; Scotsman 20th Jly, 1938.

**FORREST, Robert Smith** **1871-1943**
Born Edinburgh, 29 Mar; died 9 Feb. Painter and engraver. Exhibited etchings and Edinburgh topographical scenes as well as narrative subjects and portraits at the RSA 1908-1959. Began life as a photographer, in 1906 rented the top flat at 32 York Place, Edinburgh known as Raeburn's Studio. Robert Hope(qv) and Ernest Lumsden(qv) had their studios at the same address. In 1911 was commissioned by the Royal Burghs to paint a watercolour portrait of the King and Queen for their convention at Holyrood, now in Edinburgh City Chambers. Also exhibited RSW(4). After 1927 Forrest turned increasingly to etching. One example, now in the NGS, is of King George V; also represented in City of Edinburgh collection(4).

**FORREST, William HRSA** **1805-1889**
Engraver. Elected Honorary Member, RSA 1877. His touched proof mezzotint after William Simson's 'Salmon Spearing' was exhibited posthumously at the RSA in 1826. Particularly associated with the work of Horatio McCulloch(qv). Brydall said that Forrest did for McCulloch(qv) what Miller did for Turner. Represented in Glasgow AG, City of Edinburgh Art collection.
**Bibl:** Brydall 214; Butchart 69; Irwin 354.

**FORREST, Mrs Winifred** **fl 1969-1970**
Aberdeen painter of local and French landscapes. Exhibited AAS(3) from 48 Craigiebuckler Terrace.

**FORRESTER, Alexander** **fl 1874-1883**
Edinburgh painter in oil and watercolour of interiors and townscapes. Exhibited RSA(8).

**FORRESTER, J** **fl 1865**
Glasgow landscape painter; exhibited GI(1), from 32 Eglinton St.

**FORRESTER, W** **fl 1890**
Edinburgh watercolour painter; exhibited 'Street Scene, Cairo' at the RSA.

**FORSTER, Elizabeth G** **fl 1885**
Exhibited Brambles at the RSA when employed by Fettes College, Edinburgh.

**FORSTER, J** **late 18th Century**
Edinburgh -based topographical draughtsman. Represented in NGS by 36 views.

**FORSTER, Percy HRSA** **fl 1828-1858**
Coldstream painter of figurative subjects, often with sporting associations. Said variously to have been the son of a former gamekeeper at Hulne Abbey, Alnwick, and the son of the Duke of Northumberland himself. As an itinerant portrait painter he frequented, in about 1833-1840, Yester House and the village of Gifford. 'Study of a hound' was exhibited at the RA 1845, and another work at the RSA 1846. On 8th April 1828 he was proposed by W Lizars(qv) and Samuel Joseph and duly elected honorary Member, RSA. Exhibited RA(1) & RSA 1828-31, all of them still life or fruit and dead game, apart from one animal portrait 1831; also 'Minnow Fishing on the Tweed' at the BI.
**Bibl:** Wingfield.

**FORSYTH, Alexander** **fl 1889**
Landscape painter; exhibited at the RSA sketches in York from 6 Roseneath Terrace, Edinburgh.

**FORSYTH, Amelia B (Mrs William Johnston)** **fl 1935-1945**
Glasgow based amateur figurative painter. Studied Glasgow School of Art 1931-1934, winning the Lauder Award of the Glasgow Society of Lady Artists in 1937. After her marriage in 1945 no further paintings recorded. Exhibited RSA(1) from 90 Springkell Avenue, Glasgow.

**FORSYTH, Miss C** **fl 1934**
Exhibited a nursery decoration for the Princess Margaret Rose Hospital, Edinburgh, at the RSA, in collaboration with Miss C Sutherland, from 27 Grange Loan, Edinburgh.

**FORSYTH, Gordon Mitchell RI ARCA (Lond)** **1879-1952**
Born Fraserburgh, 30 Oct; died nr Crewe, 19 Dec. Painter in watercolour and oil of landscape and architectural subjects, also pottery designer. Studied at Gray's School of Art and Royal College of Art where he received his diploma 1903. Best known for his work for the Pilkington Tile and Pottery Co. Painted watercolours of landscapes in ceramics which he usually signed with a monogram. Principal works include 'Polperro', 'The Great Pier, York' and 'St Pierre, Caen'. Adviser to the British Pottery Manufacturers Federation and art director, Stoke-on-Trent School of Art 1913-1940. Elected RI 1927. Exhibited RA(16), RI(63), GI(8) & L(4).
**Bibl:** Halsby 258-9.

**FORSYTH, Miss J S** **fl 1871-1874**
Edinburgh painter in oil of wild flowers and churches; exhibited RSA(6).

**FORSYTH, James** **fl 1880**
Glasgow painter of Highland scenery. Exhibited GI(2), from 189 Pitt St.

**FORSYTH, James Law** **fl 1921-1935**
Oil and watercolour painter, also etcher and stone carver. Exhibited RSA(1) 1935, RSW(1) & GI(5), from 7 Mulberry Road, Glasgow.

**FORSYTH, Moira** **1905-1991**
Born Stoke-on-Trent, May 5; died Mar 18. Stained-glass designer and (in early life) potter. Trained in ceramics Burslem School of Art. Daughter of the renowned Scottish ceramic designer and Head of Burslem School of Art, Gordon Forsyth. An example of her pottery was purchased by the Queen 1926. After the kilns she was working were closed down by the General Strike, she won a national scholarship and enrolled in the Royal College of Art, working in the glass department under Martin Travers. An ardent Roman Catholic, after graduation she pursued a life-long career in stained-glass window design. Her most important works are the transept window on the theme of Abraham and Melchizedek in Fort Augustus Abbey, the east rose window at St Columba's Church of Scotland, Pond St (London), the Benedictine window in Norwich Cathedral (possibly her favourite), several windows for Guildford Cathedral, eight armorial windows in Eton College Chapel, and windows for the Heath End Catholic Church, Farnham. During the war worked in the Research Department, Ministry of Town & Country Planning. Council Member, British Society of Master Glass Painters 1968-75, President, Society of Catholic Artists. Awarded Queen's Award for Service to the Arts 1974.

**FORSYTH, Peter** **fl 1866-1867**
Edinburgh painter in oil of landscapes and figure subjects; exhibited RSA(2).

**FORSYTH, R** **fl 1956**
Glasgow landscape and topographical painter. Exhibited 'A Paisley Street' at the GI, from 61 Croftcraig Rd.

**FORSYTH, Richard** **fl 1977**
Milngavie painter; exhibited 'Glasgow Fish Market' at the GI, from 52 Falloch Rd.

**FORTESCUE, Hon Henrietta Anne (née Hoare)** **c1745-1841**
Amateur painter in watercolour and pen and pencil of topographical scenes. Lived in Edinburgh for a time. Became Lady Acland.

**FORTIE, John Snr** **fl 1846-1868**
Edinburgh painter in oil and watercolour of figurative subjects and landscape, often coastal scenes. Father of John F Jnr(qv). Exhibited 'The old shepherd - scene near Pentland Hills' at the RA (1847), RSA(15) & GI(3) from 2 S. Charlotte St.

**FORTIE, John Jnr** **fl 1875-1876**
Landscape painter. Exhibited RSA(2) from the same address as his father John F Snr(qv).

**FORTUNE, Euphemia Charlton** **1885-?**
Born California. Painter in oil of landscapes, portraits and still life. Studied at St John's Wood School of Art, and Art Students' League, New York. Settled in Edinburgh c1911. Exhibited portraits, still life and landscape at the RSA 1911-23 and 'Monterey Bay, California' at the GI, from 47 Mardale Crescent, Edinburgh.

**FORTUNE, John** **fl 1983**
Gourock painter; exhibited GI(1), from 11 Clock Rd.

**FORTUNE, Susan** **fl 1972**
Aberdeen metalwork designer, especially jewellery. Exhibited AAS(1) from 47 Angusfield Avenue.

**FORTY-SEVEN GROUP** **1947-?**
Group of Aberdeen-based artists formed 1947. Founder members included Gordon Cameron(qv), Alberto Morocco(qv) and Daniel Stephen(qv).

**FOSTER, John** **fl 1871**
Coldstream painter of figurative subjects in oil; exhibited RSA(1).

**FOSTER, John J** **fl 1923-1930**
Glasgow printmaker; townscapes and buildings. Exhibited GI(4) from 35 Braemar Street, Langside.

**FOSTER, Marie** **fl 1887**
Edinburgh watercolour painter of landscapes; exhibited RSA(2).

**FOTHERGILL, George Algernon** **1868-1945**
Born Leamington, 13 May. Painter in watercolour, illustrator, physician and writer. Spent most of his life in Scotland after being educated at Uppingham School (where he obtained three drawing prizes), and Edinburgh University, graduating in medicine 1895. Silver medallist in physiology at the Royal College of Surgeons (Edin). Also gained 1st class hons degree in logic. Later became lecturer at Edinburgh University and resident clinical assistant in a mental hospital. In 1906 abandoned medicine in favour of art, archaeology and literature. Already he had published over 1,000 drawings, most of them in sporting magazines. From 1918-1919 he was medical officer to the 1st Cavalry Brigade. Among his patrons were the King, the German Emperor, the Duke of Leeds and the Earls of Lonsdale and Rosebery. As well as painting and illustrating, he painted on pottery and was an autolithographer, experimenting in collotype and tri-colour process printing. Among the books he wrote and illustrated were *A Riding Retrospect* (1895), *An Old Raibie Hunt Album* (1899), *Notes from the Diary of a Doctor, Sketch Artist and Sportsman* (1901), *A North Country Album* (1902). Lived at Cramond Bridge, West Lothian. Exhibited regularly RSA 1909-1920, mostly portraits, also L(11). Represented in City of Edinburgh collection (7 black and white drawings of local townscapes).

**FOTHERINGHAM, Leigh** **Cont**
Stirling-based jeweller and silversmith. Trained Glasgow School of Art. Won Carole Harper Memorial Award 1989 & 1990; also the Incorporation of Hammermen's Award. Exhibits widely across Britain and overseas, specialising in precious jewellery.

**FOTHERINGHAM, Miss Mary R** **fl 1959-1960**
Glasgow watercolour painter of still life, landscape and figure subjects; also occasionally worked in oil. Exhibited RSA(3), GI(1) & AAS(2), from 55 Dinart Street, Riddrie.

**FOTHERINGHAM, William S** **fl 1886-1887**
Aberdeen painter of landscape and historical subjects. Exhibited AAS from 48 Loanhead Terrace.

**FOULIS ACADEMY** **1753-1775**
Glasgow academy for the teaching of the fine arts founded by the brothers Andrew and Robert Foulis(qv), publishers of the **FOULIS PRESS**, which as well as pioneering the field of artistic instruction in Scotland (it predated the establishment of the RA in London by fifteen years) was the single most influential factor in the development of 18th century Scottish art. One of the principal reasons for its short-lived success was the fact that it was modelled on the Italian appproach to art instruction (based upon the brothers' direct experience) in contrast to the apprenticeship system and emphasis on industrial design of the Trustees Academy. 'Whatever nation has the lead in fashion, must previously have invention in drawing diffused, otherwise they can never rise above copying their neighbours' [Robert Foulis]. Having acquired an extensive collection of books, prints and original paintings (some of them Old Masters, as listed in the catalogues) from their several continental visits, and encouraged by several Glasgow merchants each of whom contributed £40 annually, the brothers took into partnership three businessmen (Campbell of Clathic, Glaseford of Dougalston and Archibald Ingram) for the purpose of establishing an academy. Four teachers were initially appointed: a Frenchman, Payien, for painting, another Frenchman, Françoise P Aveline, for engraving, an Italian, M Torrie, for sculpture and the Frenchman, M Dubois, for copper-plate printing. Students, who paid no fees but received a small wage, drew from a living model three evenings a week and from the antique also thrice weekly. In 1759 there was an exhibition of students' work held in the shop of Robert Fleming in Edinburgh and in a University room in Glasgow. Then, to mark the coronation of George III in 1761, the students' exhibition was that year open to the public. In 1775 Ingram died followed soon after by the death of Andrew. Although Andrew had been by far the less energetic and involved of the two brothers, the loss of these two central figures placed an impossible burden on Robert. In 1775 he closed the academy and in April 1776 took the remaining works to London for auction. Two months later he died. Students of the academy included David Allan(qv), Ralston(qv) and William Buchanan(qv), William Cochran(qv), Charles Cordiner(qv), David Erskine (Earl of Buchan, qv), Andrew MacLauchlan (who had married a Foulis daughter, qv), James Mitchell(qv), Andrew Paul(qv), John Paxton(qv), Alexander Runciman(qv), Hamilton and John Stevenson (who later started their own academy in South Carolina, qv), James Tassie(qv) and George Walker (who was to become landscape painter to the king, qv). The academy was before its time; travelling scholarships were awarded - antedating the RA equivalent by almost a generation, recipients spending two years in Rome c1760-1770. They included William Cochran(qv), Archibald McLauchlan(qv), James Maxwell(qv) and John Paxton(qv). A contemporary painting, subsequently engraved, of the academy at work, possibly by William Allan, is in Glasgow University.
**Bibl:** Brydall 121-130; Caw 34,50; R & A Foulis, A Catalogue of Pictures, Drawings, Prints, Statues and Busts, in plaster of Paris, done at the Academy in the University of Glasgow, Glasgow 1758; Robert Foulis, A Catalogue of Pictures, composed and painted chiefly by the most admired of the Roman, Florentine, Bolognese, Venetian, Flemish and French Schools, 3 vols, London 1776; Irwin 85-90; D Murray, Robert and Andrew Foulis, Glasgow, 1913.

**FOULIS, Andrew** **1712-1775**
Born Glasgow, 23 Nov. Classical scholar, printer, draughtsman and teacher. Son of a maltsman named Faulls. In 1738 he went with his brother Robert(qv) to Paris and by 1742 the two had set up a printing business in Glasgow. The less energetic of the two brothers. Established the short-lived but innovative Foulis's Academy(qv) in Glasgow 1753, the demise of which was hastened by Andrew's death. No record of his own artistic work remains. Not to be confused with Robert's son also called Andrew who continued the printing business. (See also **Foulis Academy)**
**Bibl:** Brydall 121-127 et passim; Irwin 85-90 et passim; Maitland Club Papers, 1831; D Murray, Robert and Andrew Foulis, Glasgow 1913; Scots Magazine, 1822.

**FOULIS, E** **fl 1885-1888**
Glasgow landscape painter in oil; often Iona and St.Andrews. Exhibited RSA(2) & GI(4) from 191 Hill Street, Glasgow.

**FOULIS, Miss Euphemia A** **fl 1927-1948**
Glasgow based painter and printmaker (wood engraver) of country

scenes both Scottish and continental. Until 1927 lived at Elie, Fife, thereafter in Glasgow. Exhibited regularly at the RSA also at the GI(12) & L(1), after 1935 from 35 Saltoun St. Not to be confused with Euphemia Foulis (d.1828), daughter of Robert Foulis(qv), although the two may have been related.

**FOULIS, Mrs H V** **fl 1879-1890**
Edinburgh oil painter of portraits and figure subjects; exhibited RSA(7) & AAS from 34 Heriot Row.

**FOULIS, Sir James (of Woodhall)** **1770-1842**
Born 9 Sep. Painter in oil of landscape and portraits. Nephew of Alexander Nasmyth(qv). Studied in Rome with Nasmyth, Skirving(qv) and others. After marriage in 1812 he joined the Edinburgh Regiment of Militia and later that year succeeded his cousin Sir James Harlis of Colinton and Ravelston. In 1808-1811 exhibited with Associated Artists. Represented in Edinburgh City collection by a portrait of 'James Gillespie', founder of Gillespie's Hospital.

**FOULIS, Robert** **1707-1776**
Born Glasgow 20 Apr; died Edinburgh, 2 Jne. Printer, painter, teacher, bookseller and collector. Son of a Glasgow maltsman named Faulls. None of his own work remains. Best remembered for the pioneering Foulis Academy(qv) which he and his brother Andrew(qv) opened in Glasgow 1753 and which numbered David Allan and James Tassie among its students. Not to be confused with the miniaturist of the same name. (See also **Foulis Academy**).
**Bibl:** Brydall 121-127 et passim; Irwin 85-90 et passim; D Murray, Robert and Andrew Foulis, Glasgow 1913; Scots Magazine 1822.

**FOULIS, Robert** **fl 1819-1853**
Miniature and portrait painter. Worked in Edinburgh and London and in about 1819 went to Halifax, Nova Scotia, where he started a drawing school. Nothing more seems to be known of this artist who was possibly the son of Robert F(qv).
**Bibl:** Bolton; Long 160.

**FOWKES, David Reeve** **1919-c1986**
Painter of landscape and topographical scenes in Britain and abroad. Lived at Home Farm Cottage, Muchalls, near Aberdeen but c1981 moved to York. Married Lorna A F(qv). Exhibited regularly RSA 1951-1986.

**FOWKES, Lorna A** **fl 1958-1980**
Painter of still life, landscape and domestic genre. Wife of David Reeve F(qv). Exhibited RSA & AAS throughout the above years.

**FOWLER, George** **fl 1890-1902**
Edinburgh landscape painter in oil and watercolour, mainly the latter. Exhibited RSA(8) & AAS.

**FOWLER, Iain D** **fl 1971**
Glasgow designer of stained glass. Exhibited GI(1) whilst at Glasgow School of Art.

**FOWLER, Marshall Robinson** **fl 1873-1876**
Pitlochry oil painter of landscape. Exhibited RSA(5) having moved to Stockton-on-Tees 1876.

**FOWLER, Robert RWS RI ARCA** **1853-1926**
Born Anstruther, Fife; died London, 28 Oct. Decorative painter in oil and watercolour of mythological and allegorical subjects. Studied in London. His figures were treated decoratively in pale colours, somewhat in the style of Albert Moore Leighton and Ferdinand Khnopff. Also influenced by the Japanese School. His studio in Liverpool was a focal point for artistic life. His work was at first principally watercolour, the subjects being taken from classical mythology and romantic poetry. Later he turned more to oils in which he enjoyed greater success. Began landscape painting 1902. Also designed posters. Many of his Welsh landscapes were reproduced in A & C Black's books. According to Caw he was 'different from most painters of myth and allegory, in this country at least, in virtue of the more abstract and less illustrative and didactic quality of his conception, his treatment of themes is generalised suggestive, and decorative rather than detailed, definite and academic'. Elected RI 1891, Associate, Royal Cambrian Academy. Exhibited RA(20) 1876-1903, RSA & GI(2). Represented in Bootle AG, Exeter AG, Liverpool AG, Magdebourg AG.
**Bibl:** Art in 1898, Summer number, 1900, 35; Caw 409-11; Halsby 259; RA Pictures 1897-1913; Studio Vol 9, 1897, 85-98; 32, 1904, 161; Who's Who 1914.

**FOWLER, William** **1796-1880**
Architect, etcher and architectural draughtsman. Exhibited RSA(5) including the interior of the dining-hall at Lochinver House for the Duke of Sutherland and shooting lodge at Loch Hope, both 1878. Lived at Dunrobin, Golspie, Sutherland.

**FOX, Miss H J Florence** **fl 1881-1884**
Portrait miniaturist from Halton, Montrose. Exhibited RSA(3) including a fine portrait on ivory of 'Lieut Col Rait, late RHA' (1881).

**FOX, Latricia L** **fl 1966**
Dundee sculptress. Exhibited AAS(1) from 149 Strathearn Road.

**FOY, Dympna** **fl 1959**
Amateur painter. Exhibited a still life at the RSA from 123 North Frederick Street, Glasgow.

**FRAIN, Robert** **fl 1830-1870**
Edinburgh portrait painter. In 1833 he was living at Francis Place. His best known portraits are of 'William Francis Forbes' (1860-1880) and 'John Francis Forbes' (1862-1863), the sons of William Forbes the 3rd of Callender. Two negatives from D O Hill calotype photographs of him are in the SNPG.

**FRAME, Miss Margaret** **fl 1852-1866**
Edinburgh painter in oil of conversational pieces; exhibited RSA(4).

**FRAME, Mark C** **fl 1946**
Paisley etcher. Exhibited GI(1), from 21 Queen St.

**FRANCHE, Thomas** **fl 1489-dc1545**
Master-mason. From a Linlithgow family, he was the most notable of three generations of architects and masons. Probably moved from Linlithgow to Aberdeen shortly after his father's death in 1489. There he became Master Mason to the Bishop of Aberdeen, who founded and endowed the University, and began to build the University as well as the Bridge over the Dee (widened 1841-4). A short time later, following the premature death of his son in 1530, he succeeded his father **John FRANCHE** (d. 1489) in the employ of King James V, undertaking work at the Palaces of Falkland and Linlithgow. For this he was appointed Master Mason to the Crown for life 1535. The long gallery on the south side of the inner quadrangle at Linlithgow was certainly his work as was most probably the gateway.
**Bibl:** Mylne 36-44.

**FRANCIS, David Alexander ARSA ARBS** **1886-1931**
Born Edinburgh. Sculptor. Began as a wood carver, studied art school on the Mound and after WW1 attended Edinburgh College of Art, subsequently joining the staff. Specialised in bronze and marble portrait busts working usually on a small scale. Elected ARSA 1927. Exhibited RSA(32), RA(2), GI(10) & L(4), from Young's Street Lane, North Edinburgh.

**FRANK, Hannah (Mrs Lionel Levy)** **1908-**
Born Glasgow. Painter and sculptress. Works in plaster, terracotta, bronze and paints sometimes in watercolour, sometimes in pen and ink. Portrait heads and figurative works. Educated Strathbungo School, Albert Road Academy and University of Glasgow from where she graduated in 1930. Poems and later drawings published under the pseudonym 'Al Aaraaf'. Attended Jordanhill Training College then taught mainly at Campbellfield School in Glasgow whilst attending evening classes at Glasgow School of Art 1930-45. Her work has often been favourably compared to that of Margaret(qv) and Frances Macdonald(qv) and Aubrey Beardsley. A Frank design chosen to front the UK Jewish Film Festival 2004. Her drawings appeared regularly at the GI(68) and from the 1950s at the RSA. Studied wood engraving and clay modelling under Paul Zunterstein, protégé of Benno Schotz(qv). Exhibition of her life's work held at Lancaster City Museum 2004. Since 1950 has turned exclusively to sculpture and continues to exhibit mainly figurative subjects at the RA, RSA and RGI from 40 First Avenue, Glasgow.

**Bibl:** 'Hannah Frank, A Glasgow Artist: Drawings and Sculpture', rev 2004.

**FRANKS, William** **fl 1973**
Rewnfrewshire painter; exhibited GI(1), from 9 Buchanan Drive.

**FRASER, Alexander Jnr RSA RSW** **1828-1899**
Born Woodcockdale, nr Linlithgow; died Musselburgh, 24 May. Son of Alexander George F(qv). Studied at Trustees Academy although largely self-taught being helped by Sir William Fettes Douglas(qv) and others. Until 1857, the year before he was elected ARSA, his subjects were mainly Scottish, but that year he visited Wales and for some time became preoccupied with Welsh landscape. Returned to Scotland to paint some of his finest pictures in Cadzow Forest alongside his friend Sam Bough, and on Loch Lomondside. In 1868-1869 he painted in Surrey and for the last 15 years of his life in Scotland. Particularly fond of summer and high noon in the forest, resembled the pre-Raphaelites in the attention he gave to detail. In 1846 exhibited his first picture at the RSA 'Gypsy Girl in Prison'. He was more of a colourist than a composer, being one of the first Scottish landscape painters to work directly from nature, a characteristic he shared with Waller Hugh Paton(qv). His technique is best shown in his Cadzow paintings. He positioned his figures well in the compositions. He said that he learnt nothing at Trustees Academy and that his real teachers were Muller and Cox. Author of the first biography of Horatio McCulloch(qv), whose work his own resembled, especially in later years. Toward the end of his life his work became less detailed. Elected ARSA 1858, RSA 1862, RSW 1878. Exhibited 11 works at the RA (1869-1885), RSA(200+), GI(96), RBA(5), L(2) & AAS from 1886-1893, after 1886 from 16 Eskside, Musselburgh. Represented in V & A, NGS, Glasgow AG, City of Edinburgh collection, Newport AG.
**Bibl:** AJ 1904, 375-9; 1906, 154ff; 1873, 101; Armstrong; Bryan; Caw 190ff; DNB; Irwin 305,355,356,361; Macmillan [SA], 227-230,253; McKay 304-8; Portfolio 1887, 208.

**FRASER, Alexander RSA RSW** **1940-**
Born Aberdeen. Portrait and figurative painter. Educated at Aberdeen Grammar School, studied at Gray's School of Art, Aberdeen, and Hospitalfield, Arbroath, 1958-1962. Awarded postgraduate diploma and travelling scholarship enabling him to visit France and Italy. Received Latimer Award 1964 and Guthrie Award 1969; also 1st prize in the Arbroath Open Competition the same year. Lecturer of long standing at Gray's School of Art retiring 1997 in order to paint full-time, travelling to Egypt, Russia, Mexico and the United States. An early fascination with abstraction has been succeeded by a distinctive imaginary world with incidents drawn from personal experience, expressed in a manner which challenges the viewer to explain or interpret. Visited Egypt 1979. Once said that he was a figurative painter 'primarily searching for the visual quality which will correspond to my judgement of the world. The images can look after themselves'. Married to Helen F(qv). His many portrait commissions include Provost Rae of Aberdeen (1989); Sir Kenneth Alexander, Chancellor of Aberdeen Univ. (1993); Sir Anthony Toft, Pres. Royal College of Physicians (1995); Principal MacFarlane of Heriot Watt Univ. (1996). Head of Drawing & Painting, Gray's School of Art 1987-97. First prizes include Morrison Scottish portrait competition 1991, Noble Grossart painting competition 1996. His return to figurative painting in later works was said to be not a reaction but "complementary development to the artist's involvement with abstraction...Fraser paints bizarre, theatrical scenes inhabited by curious creatures...whose contemporary dress belies universal personae." (Ian Gale). Lives at 9 Marine Terrace, Muchalls, Kincardineshire. Elected ARSA 1971, RSA 1989. Exhibited regularly at the RSA since 1964, also RA & AAS. Represented in Aberdeen AG, Dundee AG, Glasgow AG, Paisley AG, Sheffield AG, Edinburgh City collection, SAC.
**Bibl:** Gage 72; Ian Gale, 'Alexander Fraser, New Paintings', ex cat., Scottish Gallery 1998; Macmillan 2001, 112, illus 120.

**FRASER, Alexander (Alec) Coutts** **fl 1886-d1939**
Aberdeen painter in oil of portraits, figure studies landscapes and genre; also engraver. Son of an Aberdeen stonemason. Trained Glasgow School of Art, becoming its Head 1914-34, although not formally recognised until 1923. Also trained in London and Paris. Most of his landscapes were of coastal and pastoral subjects; in spite of his background he does not seem to have been interested in hills, but more in wide open spaces. Visited Belgium 1894. A prolific etcher, many of his subjects being taken from the Newtonhill region. In his earlier work the paint was handled smoothly but he later roughened the texture of the canvases and his treatment of impasto gives his latest works a luminosity which made them quite distinctive. Maintained a studio at 214 Union Street. Occasionally executed posters, several of which were used by the Great Western Railway, three of them appearing in the *AJ* 1906. Active member of the Northern Arts Club. Retired from teaching 1933. Exhibited regularly RSA(30) 1892-1912, GI(37), L(6) & AAS during most of the above years from 4b Crown Terrace, Aberdeen. Represented in Aberdeen AG, Glasgow AG.
**Bibl:** Caw 192; The Scotsman, 25 Apr 1939 (obit).

**FRASER, Alexander D** **fl 1876**
Edinburgh watercolour painter of local scenes; exhibited RSA(1).

**FRASER, Alexander George Snr ARSA** **1785-1865**
Born Edinburgh; died Wood Green, London, Feb 1865. Painter of domestic and historic genre. Studied at Trustees Academy under John Graham(qv). In 1810 he began exhibiting at the RA and settled in London 1813. Helped greatly by Wilkie in the painting of still life and other details in his pictures. In the early 1850s ill-health forced him to give up painting. Illustrated an edition of the *Waverley Novels.* His paintings are sometimes deficient in taste, his figures frequently verge on the vulgar and have been described as portraying 'coarseness with gusto'. Nevertheless he could produce striking colour effects as for example in the 'Moment of Victory', where the dishevelled plumage of the vanquished bird is particularly striking. In 1842 'Namaan cured of the Leprosy' was voted best picture of the year at the British Institute. 'Most of his pictures deal with social or convivial situations conceived in the spirit of Comedy' [Caw]. One of the first Associates of the RSA to be elected 1840. Exhibited RSA and its predecessors a total of 71 works 1809-1855. Represented in Tate AG, BM, NGS(11), Paisley AG, Brodie Castle (NTS).
**Bibl:** AJ 1865, 125; Armstrong 34; Brydall 266-7; Butchart 24; Caw 104; Allan Cunningham, Life of Sir David Wilkie; DNB; Gent Mag 1865, XVI, 653; Irwin 97,177,190,206; Macmillan [SA], 181-84; McKay 158; Portfolio 1887, 109.

**FRASER, Alice M** **fl 1876-1877**
Edinburgh watercolour painter of wild plants, exhibited RSA(5) & GI(2), from 8 Moray Place.

**FRASER, Alisdair** **fl 1974**
Amateur Aberdeen sculptor. Exhibited AAS(1) c/o 18 Sanday Road.

**FRASER, Ann (Lady Charles Fraser)** **c1962-**
Inveresk-based botanical artist. Trained at Edinburgh College of Art under Sir Robin Philipson, 1981-84, followed by a spell at the Royal Botanic Gardens, Edinburgh, with John Mooney(qv). First solo exhibition London 1991 was sold out. Represented in Botanical Artists of the World exhibition 1999.

**FRASER, Miss Annie** **fl 1879-1895**
Edinburgh landscape and figure painter in oil and watercolour. Exhibited RSA(21), RSW(2), GI(9) & L(1), from 7 London St.

**FRASER, Arthur Anderson** **1861-1904**
Landscape painter in watercolour. Son of Dr Robert F; five brothers also artists(qv). Signed his work 'Arthur Anderson' to prevent confusion. Painted in a soft style, often angling scenes. Exhibited SS, NWCS from Holywell.
**Bibl:** Wingfield.

**FRASER, Calum** **fl 1982**
Edinburgh painter; exhibited GI(2), from 230 Corstorphine Rd.

**FRASER, Miss Cynthia** **fl 1956-1974**
Edinburgh painter in oil and watercolour of flowers, animals, village scenes and still life. Exhibited RSA regularly during the above period & GI(2) from 20 Moray Place, Edinburgh.

**FRASER, Donald Hamilton ARA** **1929-**
Born London. Scottish parentage. Painter in oil, acrylic and water-

colour; author. Trained St. Martin's School of Art, London 1949-52 and, with the aid of a French government scholarship, in Paris 1953-4. First solo exhibition London 1953; since then in New York, Zurich, and Edinburgh; works selected for exhibitions in London, San Francisco, Dallas, Stuttgart, Florence, Paris and Jerusalem. Writer on painting and ballet, author of a book about Gauguin, *Vision after the Sermon,* 1968. Appointed tutor, RCA 1958. Elected FRCA 1969; ARA c1980. Regular exhibitor RA. Represented in Hull AG; Nottingham AG; Reading AG; Southampton AG; Boston Museum of Fine Art; Albright Knox AG (Buffalo); Carnegie Institute (Pittsburgh); City Art Museum (St Louis); Smithsonian Institute, Washington; Nat Gall of Canada (Ottawa); Nat Gall of Australia (Melbourne); Yale Univ AG (USA).

**FRASER, Donald** **fl 1955**
West Lothian watercolour artist; exhibited a local landscape at the GI, from 5 Dean Rd, Bo'ness.

**FRASER, Dorothy (or Dorothea)** **fl 1906-1912**
Renfrewshire portrait miniaturist. Exhibited RA(1), GI(4) & L(1) from Woodlands, Elderslie.

**FRASER, E** **fl 1884**
Glasgow landscape painter; exhibited GI(1).

**FRASER, Edith** **1933-**
Painter of landscape and still life. Daughter of N Stuart F(qv) and twin sister of Valerie(qv). Studied at the Edinburgh College of Art and worked extensively in France. Exhibited RSA(5) 1956-1959, and often at the SSWA.

**FRASER, Miss Ena** **fl 1945-1948**
Midlothian flower painter in watercolour. Exhibited GI(2) from Duncraig, Dalkeith.

**FRASER, Farquhar** **fl 1965**
Glasgow painter of townscapes. Exhibited GI(1), from 192 W. Princes St.

**FRASER, Miss Fiona** **fl 1984**
Lanarkshire landscape painter; exhibited GI(1), from 22 Kronborg Way, Whitehills, East Kilbride.

**FRASER, Francis Arthur Anderson** **1846-1924**
Edinburgh painter who settled in London at an early age. Eldest son of Dr Robert Winchester F; brother of George Gordon(qv), Garden Williams(qv), Arthur Anderson(qv), **Robert Winchester FRASER** and **Gilbert Baird FRASER**. Painted figurative subjects, animals especially hunting scenes, dogs and still life in oil and watercolour, also landscapes; illustrator. Delicate and sensitive draughtsman whose work is surprisingly little known. Used monogram FAF. Exhibited RSA(14) 1866-75, RBA(6) & L(2).
**Bibl:** Wingfield.

**FRASER, George** **fl 1890**
Amateur Aberdeen painter who exhibited two local town views at the AAS c/o 46 Marischal Street.

**FRASER, George Gordon** **1859-1895**
Landscape and figurative painter; illustrator. Son of Dr Robert F; brother of five artists(qv). Educated Bedford whence the family moved 1861. Probably trained under Bradford Rudge. Illustrated for *Strand, Judy, Fun* and *The Saturday Journal.*
**Bibl:** Wingfield.

**FRASER, Mrs Helen** **fl 1967-1986**
Muchalls based painter in oil and watercolour of animals and birds. Wife of Alexander F(qv). Exhibited AAS from 9 Marine Terrace.

**FRASER, Henry** **fl 1670-d1724**
Herald painter of Edinburgh. Son of Patrick Fraser, a Leith mason. In 1670 was apprenticed to George Porteous. In 1671 married Elizabeth Chalmers with whom he had five children, one of whom married James Syme(qv). Elected Burgess of Edinburgh 1675 and a member of the Incorporation of St Mary's 1675-1723. Appointed Ross Herald 1687. In 1693 he undertook work for the funeral of Lord Bargany. Working at Holyrood in 1776 when he was paid £25 for the furnishing of 'Inglish lead gold and guilding of two great and two lesser copper globs with their stocks fixed upon the tops of two turnepyekes above the lead platform of the east quarter'. In 1690 he was painting the Coat of Arms of Viscount Dundee, the Earl of Dunfermline and others forfeited for treason. Also worked for the funerals of the Countess of Moredun and was commissioned to gild and paint colours for the town of Leith. In 1705 he and Walter Melville were involved in a dispute with the town of Edinburgh over the provision and hiring of mort cloth for funerals; the mort cloth was purchased from them and they agreed not to use any other in future [Edinburgh Burgh Records, 1701-18].
**Bibl:** Apted 36-8; Hew Dalrymple, The Hamiltons of Bargany; Lyon Court 4,9,18; Reg of Edin Appr, 35; Roll of Edin Burgesses 111,193.

**FRASER, Herbert Ross** **fl 1909-1914**
Born Hamilton; died France. Painter of topographical scenes and interiors, mainly in Paris and Scotland; also engraver. Secretary, Hamilton Art Club 1911. Exhibited RSA(7) & GI(2) from 110 Cadzow St, Hamilton.

**FRASER, Miss Hilary** **fl 1973**
Milngavie landscape painter. Exhibited a farm scene at the GI from Duneaves, Drumclog Ave.

**FRASER, James** **fl 1873**
Edinburgh based landscape painter in oil. Possibly the James Fraser who is recorded as painting local scenes in the Perth area in the 1880s. Exhibited RSA(1). (See **James FRAZER**)

**FRASER, James Baillie** **1783-1856**
Born Reelick, Inverness, 11 Jne; died Reelick, 23 Jan. Traveller, man of letters and artist. Eldest son of Edward Satchell Fraser of Reelick. In early life he went to the West Indies and thence to India. In 1815, at the end of the war with Nepal he and his brother made a tour of exploration in the Himalayas, being the first Europeans to traverse that part of the country. The tour occupied two months in the course of which they penetrated as far as the sources of the rivers Jumna and Ganges. Later published his account *Journal of a Tour through part of the Himalaya Mountains, and to the Sources of the Rivers Jumna and Ganges* (1820). A folio volume of colour plates illustrating the scenery accompanied the work. In 1821 he accompanied Dr Jukes on a mission to Persia but finding the road blocked by disturbances they ended their travels at Tabriz. This expedition furnished him with material for two further books, *Narrative of a Journey into Khorasan in the years 1821 and 1822, including some Account of the Countries to the North-East of Persia* (1825) and *Travels and Adventures in the Persian Provinces on the Southern Banks of the Caspian Sea* (1826). This was followed by *The Kuzzilbash. A Tale of Khorasan* (1828), and a sequel *The Persian Adventurer* (1830). Then published *The Highland Smugglers* in 3 volumes (in 1832) followed by *Tales of the Caravanserai* (1833). The winter of 1833-4 he went on a diplomatic mission to Persia, riding a distance of 2,600 miles between Christmas 1833 and 8 March 1834. The story of this journey was published in 1836 as *A Winter's Journey from Constantinople to Teheran.* His *Travels in Kurdistan, Mesopotamia* (1840) 2 vols, describes the return journey. Other books include *Narrative at the Residence of the Persian Princes in London* (1835 and 1836) 2 vols, (1838). A 3 volume romance appeared in 1842 and the same year, *Mesopotamia and Assyria from the Earliest Ages to the Present Time.* Two more *Eastern Romances* followed. His last work was *Military Memoir of Lieutenant Colonel James Skinner* 2 vols (1851). Also illustrated *Views of Calcutta* (1824-1826) and *Views of the Hamala Mountains.* Most of his painting was in watercolour. Returning to Calcutta in 1816, whilst working up his sketches he met the professional artist William Havell to whom he credited his subsequent clear improvement. After departing from Calcutta in February 1819, James had further lessons from George Chinnery with whom, after returning to Scotland in 1823, he remained in close touch. When on a visit to Edinburgh in 1819, JMW Turner expressed his admiration for James's work. Sir Walter Scott, writing in the *Quarterly Review,* spoke of his genius 'scenes of active life are painted by the author with the same truth, accuracy, and picturesque effect which he displays in landscapes or single figures. In war especially he is at home; and gives the attack, the retreat, the rally, the bloody and desperate close combat, the flight, pursuit, and massacre, with all the current of a heavy fight, as one who must have witnessed such terrors'. Several of his drawings of eastern scenes have been engraved. In 1823 he

married his cousin, the youngest daughter of Lord Woodhouselee of Aldourie. Reelick was full of his own work and there were few days in which he did not handle the pencil. An ardent gardener, Reelick was planted with many rare Eastern trees and shrubs. Exhibited at the RSA 7 landscapes, most of them in Scotland but one each in India, Italy and Switzerland from Reelick, Inverness. The Fraser family papers have survived and are listed by the National Register of Archives. Represented in Glasgow AG.
**Bibl:** DNB vol vii, 651-652; Inverness Courier, Jan 24, 1856 (Obit); A Mackenzie, History of the Frasers, 1896, 713-715; Archer, M & Falk, T, *India Revealed: The Art and Adventures of James & William Fraser 1801-1835* (Cassell, 1989); Falk, T, "From Watercolour to Print. James Baillie and Views of Calcutta", in *Under the Indian Sun. British Landscape Artists*, eds. P Rohatgi & P Godrej (Bombay, JJ Bhabha for Marg Publications, 1995); Christie's catalogue, Longleat sale, June 13, 2002, pp175-178.

**FRASER, Mrs Jane Hyde** **fl 1902-1946**
Painter in oil and watercolour of Highland pastoral scenes, especially around Nairn and the Findhorn areas; moved from Forres to Nairn c1905. Exhibited RSA(6), RSW(8), GI(2) & SWA(7) from Grianach, Nairn.

**FRASER, Janet** **fl 1898-1902**
Painter of flowers, figure subjects and portrait heads. Exhibited GI(4) from Glasgow and Lenzie.

**FRASER, John** **fl 1868-1887**
Edinburgh painter in oil and watercolour of figurative subjects; exhibited RSA(6).

**FRASER, John P ARCA** **fl 1864-1912**
Flower, figure and landscape painter in oil and watercolour. Taught Gray's School of Art in 1881. Exhibited RSA(5) and frequently at the AAS 1885-1912, mainly local country scenes and views of the fishing fleet, from 46 Carden Place, Aberdeen.

**FRASER, John Simpson RSW** **fl 1870-1893**
Edinburgh painter in oil and watercolour of landscapes, figure subjects, still life and seascapes. In his early life he lived in Edinburgh but moved to Auchmithie, Forfarshire in about 1887. Elected RSW 1878. Exhibited RSA(32), GI(1) & RI(1).
**Bibl:** Halsby 259.

**FRASER, Keith Alexander** **fl 1980-1984**
Dundee based painter of figurative subjects and printmaker. Trained at Gray's School of Art, Aberdeen. Exhibited AAS latterly from 23 Findale Street, Dundee.

**FRASER, Malcolm** **fl 1947**
Exhibited The Muse, at the RSA from 24 Rennie Street, Kilmarnock and 'The Old Bakehouse' in watercolour at the GI the same year.

**FRASER, Mary M** **fl 1906-1908**
Aberdeen painter of interiors and country scenes. Exhibited AAS from Kenfield, Mannofield.

**FRASER, Miss Maureen** **fl 1969**
Glasgow sculptress. Animals and human figures. Exhibited GI(2), from 31 Kingsborough Gdns.

**FRASER, N** **fl 1893-1897**
Lanark painter in oils of topographical works and still life. Exhibited a French street scene at the RSA and two works at the GI, from Saffronhall Manse, Hamilton.

**FRASER, N Stuart** **fl 1963-1971**
Animal sculptor, mainly in bronze. Father of Edith(qv) and Valerie(qv). Exhibited RSA(2), an 'Otter' at the GI & AAS(2), from 87 St John's Road, Edinburgh.

**FRASER, Patrick Allen** **[see ALLAN-FRASER, Patrick]**

**FRASER, Peter** **1888-?**
Born Shetland, Nov 6. Watercolour painter, illustrator and author. Trained Central School of Arts and Crafts. Contributed many humorous animal drawings for *Punch*, wrote and illustrated *Funny Animals* (1921), *Tufty Tales* (1932), *Moving Day* (1945). Illustrated Harrison: *Humour in the East End* (1933), Fraser: *Chuffy* (1942), *Duckling to Dance* (1944), *Floppity-Hop* (1944), *Helping Mrs Wigglenose* (1944), *Jock and Jack's Great Discovery* (1944), *Billy Bobtail Goes to School* (1945), *Bunky the Bear Cub* (1945), *Camping Out* (1945), *The New Recruit* (1945), Rye: *The Blackberry Picnic* (1946), *Bevis and the Giant* (1948) and Fraser: *John and Ann* (1949).
**Bibl:** Horne 199; Peppin; Waters.

**FRASER, Mrs Phelia L** **fl 1847**
Edinburgh portrait painter; exhibited RSA(1).

**FRASER, R E** **fl 1881**
Edinburgh painter in oil of coastal scenes; exhibited RSA(1) from Barnton Lodge, Davidson's Mains, Edinburgh.

**FRASER, Rev Robert George** **fl 1868-1888**
Amateur Leith painter in watercolours and occasional oils of landscapes and rustic buildings. Exhibited RSA(9), RHA(3) & GI(3), from St Thomas's Manse. His last exhibit was 'In Glen Sannox, Arran' (1888).

**FRASER, Rose M** **fl 1908-1916**
Edinburgh painter and engraver of narrative subjects, still life and topographical scenes; exhibited regularly at the RSA(13) & GI(1) from 34 St Andrew's Square, Edinburgh, and later (1915) from 3 Queen Street.

**FRASER, Miss Sarah Frances** **fl 1879-1883**
Edinburgh painter in oil and watercolour of interior scenes; exhibited RSA(6) & GI(1), from 27 Elder St.

**FRASER, Simon John** **fl 1981-1984**
Nairn artist. Trained at Gray's School of Art, Aberdeen. Exhibited interiors and garden scenes at the AAS from Drum House, Lochloy Road, Nairn.

**FRASER, Tessa Campbell ARBA (Mrs Rory Bremner)** **1967-**
Born Edinburgh. Painter and sculptress. Trained Chelsea School of Art. Won Diana Brooks Award 1992, Chelsea Arts Society Award 1993, Winsor & Newton Turner Watercolour Award 1995. Married Rory Bremner, well known impressionist, 1999. Commissioned by HM The Queen 1992. Elected Associate Member, Royal Society of British Sculptors 2001. At the turn of the century, transferred her main creative allegiance from watercolours to sculpting large-scale animal works. Exhibited RA, RSW, Natural History Museum from her studio in Oxfordshire, 2004. Represented in Royal Collection, Knuthenborg Safari Park (Copenhagen), Household Cavalry (with 'Sefton').

**FRASER, Thomas** **fl 1825-d1851**
Edinburgh portrait painter. Most of his work was of unnamed sitters although in 1835 he showed 'The Helmsman' - the portrait of a seaman who fought under Nelson at Trafalgar. Exhibited 18 works at the RSA 1825-1843. Represented in SNPG(2).
**Bibl:** Brydall 242; Caw 90.

**FRASER, Valerie RSW** **1933-**
Painter in oil and watercolour, landscape and coastal scenes especially Fife and East Lothian. Daughter of N Stuart F(qv) and twin sister of Edith(qv). Studied at Edinburgh College of Art, travelled and sketched extensively in France. Regular exhibitor at the RSA 1956-84, AAS 1964-1973, RSW, RGI(11) since 1983.

**FRASER, William** **fl 1887**
Aberdeen artist; exhibited AAS(1) from 15 North Silver Street.

**FRASER, William** **fl 1929**
Aberdeen artist; exhibited AAS(1) from 7 Fraser Street.

**FRASER, William** **fl 1965**
Amateur Aberdeen portrait painter; exhibited 'Self-portrait' at the AAS from 262 Broomhill Road.

**FRASER, Mrs William N** **fl 1849-1864**
Edinburgh portrait painter in oil; exhibited RSA(3).

**FRASER-TYTLER, Miss K A** **fl 1882-1895**
Roslin (Midlothian) sculptress, most often in terracotta, sometimes marble and plaster. Related to James Baillie F(qv) whose wife was a Fraser-Tytler. Exhibited life studies at the RSA(12), GI(9) & L(10). Her last known address was Milton Bridge.

**FRATER, Henry** **fl 1899-1926**
Glasgow based topographical painter in oil and watercolours; exhibited GI(3), L(2) and, some years later, at the AAS, latterly from 29 Gibson Street.

**FRATER, Margaret** **fl 1893**
Glasgow based flower painter. Possibly related to Henry F(qv). Exhibited GI(1) from 44 Dumbarton Road, Glasgow.

**FRATER, William** **1890-1974**
Born Ochiltree, Linlithgow. Painter in oil and stained glass window designer. Educated Bridge End, Linlithgow and Glasgow School of Art under Greiffenhagen(qv) and in London under Anning Bell(qv). Visited Melbourne 1910 and attended life classes with the Victorian Artists' Society. Returned to Europe the following year, visiting London and Paris before resuming his studies for two more years at Glasgow School of Art 1912-3. In 1914 he migrated permanently back to Australia where he was employed by Brooks Robinson & Co as a stained glass window designer in Melbourne while continuing to paint. Interested in the theories of Max Meldrum he became increasingly influenced by Cézanne. Together with Arnold Shore he founded the Society of Twenty Painters (1917) but attracted little public favour. Mainly responsible, with Shore and George Bell, for the development of post-impressionism in Australia. Retrospective exhibition September 1966 at the National Art Gallery of Victoria. Represented in most Australian public collections.
**Bibl:** Harold Osborne (ed), Twentieth Century Art, 1988, 205.

**FRAZER, Andrew** **?-1792**
Architect. Professional soldier, Royal Engineers. Appointed Scottish Engineer-in-Chief 1779. Designed the oval at St. Andrew's church, George St, Edinburgh (1782-4).
**Bibl:** Dunbar 125; Gifford 38,273,Pl.28.

**FRAZER, James** **fl 1883**
Obscure landscape and topographical painter. Thought to have used photographs as source material. Exhibited 'Perth Railway Station' at the Perth Fine Art Exhibition 1883, now in Perth AG. (See **James FRASER**)

**FRAZER, William Miller RSA** **1864-1961**
Born Scone, Perth, 30 Sep; died Edinburgh, 7 May. Landscape painter. Educated at Perth Academy, Edinburgh Board of Manufacturer's School, and RSA Life School (1883-1887). Son of Baillie John Frazer. In 1890 travelled extensively on the continent visiting and working in Algeria, Holland, Italy and Norway. He had a Corot-like feeling for the atmospheric effects on landscape. Fond of the Norfolk broads, the Fens and the lowlands of Fife. Founder member of the SSA of which he was President 1908. President, Scottish Arts Club 1926-1927, one of the longest lived members both there and in the Academy, as well as being one of the most loved artistic figures of his day. Spent most of his life at Bridge of Earn, Perthshire. Elected ARSA 1909, PSSA 1908, RSA 1924 and Treasurer, RSA 1932-1937. Began exhibiting at the RSA 1884 and continued to do so throughout his life, a total of 182 works, also RA(3), RSW, GI(189), RHA(6), RBA(1), AAS 1887-1937 & L(13), after 1954 from 5 Lady Rd, Edinburgh. Represented in Paisley AG, City of Edinburgh collection, Brodie Castle (NTS).
**Bibl:** AJ 1903, 284; Macmillan [SA], 253,309; The Studio XLIV, 230, 232, LVIII, 66, LXV, 102; Who's Who 1914.

**FREEBAIRN, Alfred Robert** **1794-1846**
Scottish engraver. Best known for his engraving of Flaxman's 'Shield of Achilles'; also executed plates to illustrate Jenning's *Landscape Annual,* 1835.
**Bibl:** Bryan; Bushnell.

**FREELAND, David** **fl 1932-1933**
Edinburgh painter of figure studies and street scenes; exhibited RSA(2) & GI(2), from 65 Drygate St, Larkhall.

**FRENCH, Annie (Mrs G Wooliscroft-Rhead)** **1872-1965**
Lived in Clarkston, Glasgow. Illustrator and watercolourist, also an etcher. Fellow student and later staff colleague of Jessie King's at Glasgow School of Art. Primarily an illustrator of fairy tales and poems, also designed postcards and posters. Her style was remarkably similar in its accomplished decorative work to that of Jessie King, both illustrating the ethereal and elements of art nouveau 'sweetly intensified to a point where the world is reduced to a world of gossamer, a diadem of forget-me-nots, or a charm of finches, in which love-in-a-mist is personified as a pair of lovers, or where mermaids teach their babies to swim' [Hardie]. Seldom can two painters have developed a style so similar to each other and yet so different from everyone else. Her first exhibit had been at the Brussels Salon of 1903, when she was still a student under Jean Delville(qv). Illustrated a number of works including *The Picture Book, The Daisy Chain,* and *The Garland.* In 1914 she became the second wife of the English artist George Wooliscroft Rhead. Unfortunately the marriage only lasted 6 years for in 1920 Rhead died. Exhibited RSA(34), regularly 1904-14, RSW(2), RA(28), L(31), GI(52), RHA(3), RI(3), after 1914 from Eaglesmere, 25 Trinity Rise, London. Represented in NGS(5), SNGMA, V & A, Glasgow AG.
**Bibl:** Barbican AG, London, 'The Last Romantics; The Romantic Tradition in British Art' Ex Cat 1989, Text by John Christian); Hartley 133; Louise Annand in Burkhauser, 141-145.

**FRENCH, D M** **fl 1959**
Amateur Kincardineshire painter. Exhibited three country scenes at the AAS from Belmont, Stonehaven.

**FRENCH, Miss Imelda** **fl 1980**
Dumbartonshire painter; exhibited GI(1) from 16 George St, Helensburgh.

**FRENCH, Mrs Isabel M** **fl 1954**
Glasgow watercolourist; exhibited a landscape asnd a town view at the GI.

**FRENCH, R P** **fl 1838**
Painter of figurative and rustic scenes; exhibited RSA(2) from 153 Rose Street, Edinburgh.

**FRENCH, Stephen** **fl 1977-1978**
Dundee wildlife artist. Exhibited GI(2), from 2 Wilkies Lane.

**FREW, Alexander** **fl 1883-d1908**
Landscape and marine painter who lived in Glasgow and later in Helensburgh. Married Bessie MacNicol(qv). Keen sailor. Painted with rich tones, strong impasto and a closely-knit handling of paint, creating intense atmosphere. Exhibited RA(8) 1890-1898, RSA(3), GI(28) & L(7), from 12 St. James's Terrace, Glasgow. Represented in Glasgow AG.
**Bibl:** Caw 333.

**FREW, Hannah (Mrs T C Paterson)** **fl 1974**
Glasgow embroiderer; exhibited GI(1) from 50 Otago St.

**FREWIN, Kenneth G** **1936-**
Born Inverness, 10 Jne. Painter in oil and washes. Studied architecture for two years at Edinburgh College of Art and painting at Gray's School of Art, Aberdeen. Influenced by forces as diverse as the English landscape school, Modigliani, Joan Eardley(qv), and Magritte. Preoccupied with the development of landscape, moods and forms and the conflict of sea with coastline. Since 1970 involved with box forms encapsulating optical effects of mirrors and the superimposition of monoscopic images. Formerly married to Moira Ferrier(qv), lives at 45 Brighton Place, Aberdeen. Exhibits GI(6).

**FRIEND, George** **fl 1867**
Edinburgh landscape painter in oil; exhibited RSA(1).

**FRIER, Harry** **c1849-1919**
Born Scotland. Painter in oil and watercolour of landscapes and figurative subjects. French descent, a cousin of John Pettie(qv). Son of a Principal of Edinburgh University. Lost the sight of one eye in an accident. Served apprenticeship in Paris, returned to England, married in London and moved to Taunton. Although based periodically in

Edinburgh he finally settled in Taunton, Somerset. Exhibited RSA(24) & GI once in 1880, from 62 Queen St, Edinburgh.

**FRIER, Miss Jean Jamieson** **fl 1869-1883**
Edinburgh painter in oil of landscape especially around Perthshire. Sister of Jessie F(qv) and Robert F(qv). Exhibited RSA(9).

**FRIER, Miss Jessie** **1863-1912**
Edinburgh painter in oil but mainly watercolour. Landscapes, townscapes, interiors and coastal scenes, especially of Bute and Perthshire. Sister of Robert(qv) and Jean F(qv). A confident painter with the greatest talent in a talented family. Exhibited regularly RSA(63) 1863-1890, also GI(1) & SWA(7), from 62 Queen St.
**Bibl:** Halsby 108,259.

**FRIER, Miss Maggie E** **fl 1879-1880**
Another member of the talented Frier family. Painted landscapes in watercolours; exhibited RSA(2) from 62 Queen Street, Edinburgh.

**FRIER, Miss Mary** **fl 1877-1887**
Edinburgh watercolour painter of landscapes, townscapes especially churches and river scenes. Member of the Frier family of artists. Exhibited RSA(20), SWA(2) & GI(1).

**FRIER, Robert** **fl 1853**
Edinburgh painter in oil and watercolour of landscapes, especially Perthshire and the south west borders. Brother of Jean Jamieson(qv) and Jessie(qv), related to Harry Frier(qv). Turned increasingly to oil as his career developed. Largely preoccupied with Highland scenery. In 1879, for example, when his sisters were painting in Normandy, he went north completing four Highland scenes, all exhibited the same year RSA. His work was characterised by a fresh use of colour and keen observation, encompassing nearly all the Loch Tay area but also in the Lothians and Fife and 1882-1885 on Arran. Exhibited RSA(c155) & GI(7).
**Bibl:** Halsby 108,259.

**FRIER, Robert Hepburn** **fl 1888-1892**
Midlothian painter in watercolour of landscape. Exhibited 5 works at the RSA including 'Crail Harbour' (1890).

**FRIER, Walter** **fl 1705-1731**
Scottish portrait painter about whose life little is known. On 27 February 1705 married the daughter of an Edinburgh goldsmith and Burgess. Several of his portraits are at Prestonfield House, including 'Sir William Cunningham of Caprington Bt', (1664-1740). For this and for the following four pictures Frier received £180 Scots: 'Sir James Dick of Prestonfield, 1st Bt, Lord Provost of Edinburgh (1680-1682)'; 'Anne Cunninghame (1704-1776) second wife of Sir Robert Dalrymple of Castleton'; 'Janet Dick (1704-1776) wife of Sir William Cunningham of Caprington'; and 'Anne Paterson wife of Sir James Dick of Prestonfield the 1st baronet'. Signed his work 'WF' in monogram. Represented in SNPG by an 'Arab Princess, "Wife" of Sir John Henderson of Fordell, with a negro maid in attendance' 1731.

**FROMUTH, Charles Henry** **1861-c1925**
American artist in oils and watercolour, mainly of harbour and coastal scenes. Spent much of his life in the artist's colony of Concarneau, France and patronised the Scottish galleries. Using Aitken Dott and Son as his agent, exhibited RSA(4), GI(3) & RHA(4) in the 1920s.

**FROOD, Miss Hester** **fl 1919-1938**
Landscape painter in watercolour and monochrome. Sister of Millie F(qv). Exhibited GI(3), in 1919 from The Barton, Bideford, N. Devon and in 1938 from Dunleys, Odiham, Hants - 'Kilchurn Castle' and 'Ben Lomond'.
**Bibl:** Macmillan [SA], 370,383.

**FROOD, Miss Millie** **1900-1988**
Born Motherwell. Painter of genre and landscape. Social realist and painter of the forties. Sister of Hester F(qv). Trained at Glasgow School of Art. Founder member of the New Art Club and the New Scottish Group in Glasgow, in the circle of J D Fergusson(qv). Exhibited RSA(3) & RSW(1) from Hayfield, Hamilton Road, Motherwell.

**FRY, Christopher Edward** **fl 1977-1978**
Aberdeen printmaker. Exhibited AAS latterly from Whitehouse, Newburgh.

**FULFORD, Miss Julia** **fl 1867**
Edinburgh oil painter of wild life subjects; exhibited RSA(2).

**FULLARTON, Mrs Fay** **fl 1966**
Amateur portrait painter. Exhibited AAS(1) from Shannaburn Cottage, Blairs, Aberdeen.

**FULLARTON, James** **1946-**
Born Glasgow. Painter in oil and acrylic of portraits, still life, landscapes, semi-abstract and topographical subjects. Studied Glasgow School of Art under David Donaldson(qv) 1965-1969 since when he has been a full-time professional artist living and working in Ayrshire. In 1976 received the David Cargill Award and 1986 the Britoil Award, both from the RGI. Uses a broad sensual palette with colour as the dominant feature, his landscapes being in the Cadell-Peploe tradition. First solo exhibition in Glasgow 1975. Exhibited RSA(9) since 1978 & GI(48) from 1976 from 20 Dalmellington Road, Straiton, Ayrshire. Represented in Lillie AG (Milngavie), Greenock AG, Royal College of Physicians and Surgeons, Glasgow.

**FULLARTON, Julie Ann** **fl 1974-1975**
Glasgow based painter. Exhibited RSA(3) from 17 Belmont Crescent.

**FULLER, G G** **fl 1887**
Amateur Aberdeenshire painter. Exhibited AAS(1) from Dunvegan Cottage, Cults.

**FULLERTON, Mrs Elizabeth S** **fl 1881-1896**
Member of a well-known Paisley family of artists and art administrators. Mainly a flower painter in watercolour but also painted in oil, on porcelain; also sculptress. From 1881-1885 lived at Merksworth, Paisley. Exhibited two studies of rhododendrons at the RA (1890 and 1892), also RSA(4), ROI(3), RI(27), SWA(1), GI(13) & L(2), latterly from 1 Garthland Place.

**FULLERTON, J G** **fl 1929-1932**
Glasgow based painter of still life and interiors; exhibited RSW(1) & GI(3), from 6 Walmer Terrace.

**FULLERTON, Mrs John** **fl 1885-1896**
Paisley based painter, sculptress & engraver. Animals, flowers and fruit. Exhibited a terracotta relief of Christmas roses, at the RA in 1886 from Merksworth House & GI(16), since 1887 from 1 Garthland Place, Paisley.

**FULLERTON, Leonard** **fl 1929-d1968**
Fife painter of birds and genre, usually in watercolour. Father of Clare Smith(qv). Exhibited at RSA(10) & GI(2), sometimes from Aberdeen then from Dundee and latterly from The Castle, West Newport.

**FULLERTON, Miss Nina F** **fl 1882-1893**
Painter of flowers and landscape in oil and watercolour. Almost certainly a daughter of Elizabeth F(qv). Exhibited Paisley Art Institute(20), latterly from Fordbank, Milliken Park.

**FULTON, David RSW** **1848-1930**
Born Parkhead, Glasgow. Painter of landscapes, angling scenes, interiors and figure subjects mainly in watercolour. Studied Glasgow School of Art. Exhibited at the principal London Galleries from 1884, also overseas but mainly in Scotland. Favourite watercolour subjects were sun-drenched landscapes with figures, generally children, beneath trees or beside rivers. Elected RSW 1890. Exhibited RA(1), RSA(72), RSW(85), GI(156), L(17) & AAS 1906-1923. Represented in Paisley AG.
**Bibl:** Caw, 284; Halsby 155,259; Muther, Gesch der Engl Maler, 1903, 380; Fv Ostini, Die Gall Th Knorr in Munchen, 1901, 132,137; V Pica, L'Arte Mond a Venezia nel 1899, 30.

**FULTON, Miss E Duncan** **fl 1912-1918**
Glasgow based painter. Exhibited GI(4) & L(3), latterly from 136 Wellington Street.

**FULTON, James Black FRIBA** **1875-1922**
Scottish architect and watercolourist. Painted topographical views of Constantinople and Venice and flower studies. Trained in Glasgow where he was influenced by Mackintosh(qv) and Keppie(qv). Lived most of his life in London. Exhibited RA(1) & GI(1), from 28 Hazlitt Rd, London. Represented in Glasgow AG.
**Bibl:** Halsby 259.

**FULTON, Samuel** **1855-1941**
Born Glasgow, 26 Apr. Painter in oil and watercolour, of animals, especially dogs. Educated Glasgow HS. Active member of Glasgow Art Club when living in Renfrewshire. In 1881 he gained greatly from joining Crawhall(qv), Guthrie(qv) and Walton(qv) at Brig o' Turk. Exhibited RSA(10), RSW(3), GI(125), AAS(1) and in Venice, Prague and St Louis. Moved to Kilmacolm and then to his final home, Wateryetts, 1932. 'Fox-hounds' is in Glasgow AG, also represented Paisley AG.
**Bibl:** Halsby 145,259.

**FURNEAUX, James** **1935-**
Born 7 Jne. Painter in watercolour of landscape. Studied at Aberdeen School of Architecture, but in 1954 enrolled at Gray's School of Art, studying under Ian Fleming(qv) before transferring to sculpture where he studied under Leo Clegg. At this time he was inspired by Epstein and Bourdelle but drawn ultimately to expressionist anti-fascist artists like Emil Nolde. Declined a postgraduate scholarship in order to embark upon a teaching career. In 1958 won the Keith prize. In addition to painting, he is a printmaker working in association with Peacock Printmakers in Aberdeen. Confesses to liking places and situations that have marks and traces of man. Retains a romantic attachment to Van Gogh, Gauguin and Cézanne but drawn strongly to the work of Gore and Stanley Spencer. Exhibits regularly RSA & AAS since 1959, latterly from 11 Ashley Road, Aberdeen.

**FURNEAUX, Paul** **1962-**
Born Ellon, Aberdeenshire. Son of James F(qv). Studied Edinburgh College of Art 1982-86 obtaining a postgraduate diploma with distinction in 1987. Young Scottish Artist of the Year 1977-78, awarded Keith prize 1986. Works mostly in oil but also in acrylic and pastel on canvas. Owing much to the northern romantic tradition and the work of Blake and Samuel Palmer. A strong elemental force pervades his work. Exhibits RSA, GI(2), from 15a Cumberland St, Edinburgh. Represented in Aberdeen AG, City of Edinburgh collection.

**FYFE, Eric** **fl 1974**
Renfrew amateur artist who exhibited GI(1), from 3 Andrew Ave.

**FYFE, Jane (Mrs Cyril Wilson)** **1914-?**
Painter in oils, watercolours and gouache of flowers, still life, pastoral scenes, figurative studies and genre. Studied at Bournemouth College of Art. Married the painter Cyril Wilson(qv). Member, SSWA and Dumfries and Galloway Arts Society. From 1952-55 was a member of the Moray Arts Club and Inverness Arts Club. Held her first solo exhibition in Edinburgh 1969. Exhibited RSA 1957-65 and again in 1970 and 1975, also GI(30), from Sunny-Brae, Duncow, Dumfries. Represented in SAC, Bournemouth AG, Gracefield AG (Dumfries).

**FYFE, P** **fl 1736**
Glasgow engraver. Engraved the arms of Glasgow printed in McUre's *View of the City of Glasgow,* 1736.
**Bibl:** Bushnell.

**FYFE, Samuel H** **fl 1846-1872**
Greenock painter of coastal scenes and yacht portraits; exhibited RSA(2) & GI(2), latterly from 353 Paisley Rd, Glasgow.

**FYFE, William Baxter Collier** **1836-1882**
Born Dundee. Figure and portrait painter, and illustrator. Studied at the RSA Schools and in Paris 1857-8. In 1861 his first important picture 'Queen Mary resigning her crown at Loch Leven Castle' was shown at the RSA. The following year he was in Europe, studying in France, Belgium and Italy. Returned to London at about the same time as his friend and admirer John Faed(qv). A covenanting painting 'The Death of John Brown of Priesthill' attracted considerable notice. Member of the Council of the City of London Society of Artists, Savage Club and Scottish Artists' Club, also the Hogarth Club. Won international gold medals 1873 and 1875. Exhibited 26 works at the RA 1866-1882 including a portrait of 'John Faed' (1882) and an interesting historical scene, 'The raid of Ruthven, an incident in the life of James VI of Scotland' (1878). Contributed illustrations to *Good Words* in 1861. Exhibited also RSA(63) 1855-1882 mostly portraits including those of 'John Faed and his wife' (1868) & GI(8), from 25a Abbey Rd, London.
**Bibl:** Bryan; Scotsman 18 Sep 1882(obit).

# G

**GABBAIN, Ethel Leontine (Mrs John Copley) RBA ROI** **1883-1950**
Born Le Havre; died London, 30 Jan. Painter of portraits, figure subjects, and landscape; etcher and lithographer. Worked in oils, watercolour and monochrome. Studied Paris and at the Slade. Married the English artist John Copley 1913. Won the De Lazlo silver medal for portrait of 'Dame Flora Robson' (1933) now in Manchester AG. Official war artist 1940. Influenced by Manet. Elected RBA 1932, ROI 1933. In addition to regular exhibitions at the RA and elsewhere in England, showed annually at the GI(100) 1915-1950, missing only 1918. Her work, which included an evocative, powerful depiction of 'The Cairngorms' (1942) was a feature of the Glasgow show, regularly receiving favourable attention from both critics and artists. Lived at 10 Hampstead Square. Represented Glasgow AG, Manchester AG.
**Bibl:** Waters.

**GABBETT, Margaret C** **fl 1885-1887**
Edinburgh flower watercolourist. Exhibited RSA(5), RHA(2), GI(1), AAS(2) & L(1), from 24 Stafford Street.

**GADDUM, Mrs Jessie Graham** **fl 1880-1883**
Landscape painter of Highland and continental scenes. Possibly mother of **Edith Gaddum** who exhibited 46 landscapes at the Baillie Gallery, London 1910-1920. Exhibited GI(2).

**GAFFRON, F C** **fl 1882**
Minor artist. Possibly brother of William John G(qv). Exhibited a local scene AAS, 1882.

**GAFFRON, Horace C** **fl 1919-1921**
Aberdeen landscape painter. Related to, probably brother of, W J G(qv). Exhibited rather dull local landscapes at the AAS during the above years from 311 Holburn Street.

**GAFFRON, William John** **fl 1891-1912**
Aberdeen painter in oil and watercolour of figurative and landscape subjects. Son of a Prussian emigré William Frederick (1830-1890), head steward with a local shipping company. An active, founder member of the AAS, associated with Thomas Bunting(qv), John Mitchell(qv) and James Greig(qv). Painted in subdued tones, his best work is not without attraction, often featuring sheep in landscape settings at different seasons, occasionally done with delicacy and a good feeling for colour. His work is more decorative than naturalistic. Related to F C(qv) and Horace G(qv). Although he did not exhibit in any of the main institutions, he did so at the AAS, latterly from 311 Holburn Street.

**GAGE, Edward Arthur RSW** **1925-2000**
Born Gullane, East Lothian, 28 Apr; died March. Painter in oil and watercolour; also illustrator, journalist, broadcaster, art critic and teacher. Educated Royal High School, Edinburgh. Studied Edinburgh College of Art 1942 resuming after the war 1947-50, being awarded a travelling scholarship. During WW2 served with the Scots Guards and the Royal Scots, latterly as a staff officer in the Far East. Art master, Fettes College 1952-68; senior assistant Edinburgh College of Commerce, and a part-time lecturer at the Edinburgh College of Art. Art critic of *The Scotsman* 1966-? President of the SSA 1960-64. Author of *The Eye in the Wind (Scottish Painting since 1945)* 1977. His work is characterised by weak structure and strong colour without achieving the success that perhaps he might have wished. Best known for his sometimes strident but always illuminating criticism of the current art scene in which his main sympathies and understanding clearly lie with contemporary art, especially the *avant garde*. Writing of his own work while visiting Mallorca, "I was assisted by the kindly example and friendship of Robert Graves, who first taught me how to look for the significance behind events and occurrences, re-awakened my interest in the Greek and other Myths...as a student I was much more influenced by the work of artists like Diego Rivera, Stanley Spencer or Graham Sutherland than that of any of my instructors. There were exceptions, however, in the case of Rosoman and Maxwell. I share William Blake's belief about art being a spiritual activity; I think a painting primarily is a means of communicating my thoughts, ideas and observations by making an image a vehicle of metaphor in the same way as a poem is for the poet...neither have I any qualms about moving freely between real and imagined events, between things seen with what Blake called the 'outward' and the 'inward' eyes; nor in adopting whatever degree of representation or abstraction seems right for the matter in hand...my work is predominantly figurative, and even if the human figure is not actually there, its presence is generally felt, inferred or even symbolised...from the visible world, observed incidents of a bizarre or humourous disposition generally attract me; I find still-life of little interest, but the fanatic moods and forms of landscape, though I have been long in appreciating the immense furtive power of that subject, now absorb me deeply'. Elected RSW 1963. President, SSA 1960-4. Exhibited GI(21), from 6 Hillview. Represented in SNGMA, Glasgow AG, Edinburgh City collection, RSA, SAC.
**Bibl:** Mungo Campbell, 'The Line of Tradition', Nat Galls of Scotland, Ex cat, Edinburgh 1993; Gage 42; Driver; Horne 207; Usherwood; Waters; Who.

**GAHAN, George Wilkie** **1871-1956**
Born Newcastle-on-Tyne. Painter and etcher. Studied Dundee School of Art. Lived in the Dundee area with only short intervals elsewhere. Exhibited mainly topographical subjects at the RSA(4) & L(2) from Duncraig, Barnhill, Broughty Ferry.

**GAIR, Alice** **fl 1884-1902**
Falkirk painter in oil and watercolour; landscape, figurative subjects and animals. Fond of quiet pensive romantic subjects and peaceful genre scenes. Exhibited RSA(20), GI(16) & AAS(3), in 1901 from Edinburgh, from The Kilns, Falkirk and latterly Easterhope, Falkirk.

**GAIR, James A** **fl 1931-1934**
Aberdeen landscape painter in oil. Exhibited RSA(1), GI(1) & Barbados harbour view at the AAS, from 112 King Street.

**GALBRAITH, Alex B** **fl 1926-1930**
Glasgow landscape painter. Exhibited GI(4) & AAS(1), latterly from 106 Ardmay Crescent, Glasgow.

**GAILBRAITH, Alexander K** **fl 1890-1893**
Painter of genre and interiors. Exhibited GI(2) from Blairhoyle, Eltham Rd, Lee, Kent.

**GALBRAITH, Isobel** **fl 1888**
Glasgow flower painter. Exhibited GI(1) from 15 Lansdowne Crescent.

**GALBRAITH, Kate** **fl 1884-1892**
Glasgow flower and figure painter. Exhibited GI(8), from 23 Glasgow St.

**GALBRAITH, M S** **fl 1897**
Helensburgh artist. Exhibited GI(1) from St Bernard's.

**GALBRAITH, Robert** **fl 1539**
Early painter. In August 1539 he received £27.10/- from Sir John Kilgour for painting the Royal Boat.
**Bibl:** Accounts of the Lord High Treasurer of Scotland, vii, 189; Apted 40.

**GALBRAITH, Sir Thomas** **fl 1491-1512**
Decorator and illustrator to King James IV. A priest of the Lennox family. Worked on the Royal Palaces of Holyrood, Stirling and Falkland. Described as 'one of the clerks of the Chapel Royal, Stirling'. Illuminated books and documents for the king, notably the treaties of peace and marriage, executed 17th December 1502 before the marriage of James IV to Margaret Tudor; and a great 'porteus' (breviary) for the King's Chapel.
**Bibl:** Accounts of the Lord High Treasurer of Scotland, i, 349,351; ii, 58,340,350,358,379,383,416; Armstrong 3; Apted 39-41; Brydall 32,46; Macmillan [SA], 30,31,35,36,48.

**GALL, Rev James** **fl 1850-1864**
Edinburgh amateur sculptor; portrait busts, usually in marble, also parian. Exhibited RSA(35) 1850-1864.

**GALL, Robert** **fl 1870-1874**
Glasgow landscape painter; exhibited GI(2), from 24 West End Pk St.

**GALL, Robert R** **fl 1896-1919**
Aberdeen landscape painter in oil. Frequent exhibitor at the AAS during the above years. Formerly from 90 Rosemount Place and latterly 15 Union Terrace.

**GALLACHER, Frank B** **fl 1987**
Glasgow painter. Exhibited a domestic interior at the RSA from 32 Gilbert Street, Yorkhill.

**GALLACHER, James** **fl 1984**
Ayrshire etcher. Exhibited GI(1), from 30 Main St, Straiton.

**GALLACHER, William** **1920-1978**
Born New York, 11 Nov; died Glasgow, 29 Oct. Painter in oil, gouache, chalk, charcoal and pencil; portraits, figurative studies and murals; also lithographer. Born of Scottish parents, he came to Scotland while still a baby and remained there for the rest of his life. The family settled in Paisley, Gallacher attending Camphill School. Outside school hours both Paisley and Kelvingrove AG held drawing competitions which the young man entered, carrying off certificates and medals as evidence of early talent. Then attended Glasgow Art School but his studies were interrupted by WW2. Renouncing his right to remain uninvolved as an American citizen, he volunteered for the Royal Navy, serving on a minesweeper and ending the war with 7 medals. In 1945 returned to Glasgow School of Art graduating in 1947 after obtaining the Guthrie prize for best portrait. Changed to mural decoration; a large mural 'Salome' in the students' refectory, rich in design and combining strength with elegance, was much admired at the time. In 1948 he shared the Brough prize for interior design. Shortly afterwards appointed visiting lecturer in architecture at the GSA, becoming full-time member 1978. Received Torrance Memorial Award. A gentle, modest man, full of humour. His work is characterised by the sensitive portrayal of the character of his sitters, especially the young and beautiful. Left behind a large volume of work. Regular and active member of the Glasgow Art Club, a President of which wrote, 'his loss can never be replaced. He was one who was easy to like and as a long-standing and greatly respected member of the club for nearly 30 years his company was continually sought by artists and lay-member alike. His was a gentle and modest personality, full of humour. He was a friend to all and many were enriched beyond their immediate realisation and rewarded often beyond their expectation' [Stuart Paterson]. Retrospective exhibition was held at the Glasgow Art Club 1979. Exhibited RSA in 1952 & GI(37), from 28 Glasgow St.

**GALLAGHER, Miss Mary** **1953-**
Glasgow painter of informal portraits, flowers and still life. Trained Glasgow School of Art 1974-9. Several solo exhibitions in Glasgow and London. Her work has a delicate touch and sensitive intensity of feeling. Exhibits regularly GI, latterly from 2/2, 124 Maryhill Rd.

**GALLAWAY, Alexander** **fl c1794-1812**
Little known Glasgow based painter of portrait miniatures. Ran a drawing academy in Glasgow in collaboration with a Mr Williams, who painted landscape miniatures. The *Glasgow Courier* carried two announcements in the summer of 1794 of a change of address for the 'Drawing Academy'. In 1811 he moved to Edinburgh, having exhibited at the Society of Artists 1808 and painted 9 miniatures of the Muirhead family. His work was competent without being spectacular. Employed a minute, soft stippling sometimes signing in block capitals 'AG', or a cursive 'AG'. One characteristic feature is an occasional pillar or curtain in the background. Completed miniature portraits of Richard Brinsley Sheridan (1796) one of which is in a private collection in Zurich. Represented in V & A, Lincoln Museum.
**Bibl:** Foskett 283; Long 165-6.

**GALLAWAY, Mrs I McRae** **fl 1941**
Edinburgh based painter. Exhibited a domestic interior at the RSA from a Craigmillar address.

**GALLIE, Miss H N** **fl 1916**
Portobello based portrait miniaturist. Exhibited RSA(1) from 25 Regent Street.

**GALLOWAY, Miss Ann** **fl 1974**
Stirlingshire topographical artist. Exhibited 'Buckie' at the GI from 42 Branziert Rd, North Killearn.

**GALLOWAY, Elspeth Sybil** **1890-1980**
Painter of landscape and flower watercolourist. Traiend Edinbirgh College of Art before travelling to Italy 1956. First lady President, Perthshire Art Association 1962-77, remaining an hon. president until her death. Taught art Perth Academy. Died in Perth. Exhibited 'Iceland Poppies' at the RSA in 1963 & GI(2) 1965/6, from King's Well, 30 Burghmuir Rd, Perth. Represented Perth AG.

**GALLOWAY, Everett** **fl 1957-1962**
Perthshire landscape painter in oil and watercolour, mainly the latter. Exhibited GI(4), from, Inverleith, Callander.
**Bibl:** Halsby 259.

**GALLOWAY, G** **fl 1838-1839**
Scottish landscape painter. Exhibited RSA(3) including the 'Falls of Stonebyres on the Clyde', 'Loch Long', and 'Craikston Castle'.

**GALLOWAY, H G** **fl 1885**
Dunfermline based artist. Exhibited 2 Scottish landscapes at the RSA from Holyrood Place.

**GALLOWAY, Hugh G** **fl 1967-1969**
Brechin landscape and still life painter. Exhibited AAS(1) & GI(1) from 1 East Bank.

**GALLOWAY, Isobel** **fl 1925**
Hawick painter in watercolour. Exhibited RSW(1) from Minto Manse.

**GALLOWAY, John** **fl 1861-1871**
Glasgow painter in oil and watercolours; landscape, especially the Scottish Highlands. Exhibited RSA(13) including a scene in the Pyrenees (1871), & GI(8), after 1862 from 40 Claremont St.

**GALLOWAY, John Everett** **1890-c1968**
Born Dunfermline, 21 Jne. Painter and designer. Christened John Everett as a token of his father's admiration for the family friend John Everett Millais. Son of William G(qv). Apart from a brief spell at Belfast College of Art in 1908 received no formal training. The meticulous quality of his work was considerable, especially in his later years. Secretary, Belfast Art Society and regular exhibitor RSW & Perth Art Society. Represented in Perth AG.

**GALLOWAY, Lizzie E** **fl 1890-1893**
Aberdeen painter of portraits and landscape. Exhibited AAS from 207 Union Street.

**GALLOWAY, Mrs Sally** **fl 1965**
Glasgow sculptress. Exhibited 'A Covenant-group' in plaster at the GI, from 26 Russell Dr, Bearsden.

**GALLOWAY, William de B M** **fl 1865-1877**
Edinburgh landscape painter in oil and watercolour. Father of John Everett G(qv) and a close personal friend of John Everett Millais, also of George Vicat Cole and John Lavery(qv). Although quite a prolific artist his work is not often seen. Exhibited RSA(4) & a watercolour drawing of 'Maclean's Cross, Iona' at the GI.

**GALT, Alexander** **1827-1863**
Sculptor. Exhibited a marble bust at the RSA in 1860 when living in Florence.

**GALT, Alexander M** **1913-**
Painter of portraits, still life, genre, landscape - fond of depicting rivers and coastal scenery. Worked in oils and occasional watercolour. Lived formerly in Greenock, moving to Edinburgh where his last address was 1 Liberton Brae. Exhibited GI(116). Represented in Glasgow AG, Greenock AG, City of Edinburgh collection ('Vera').

**GALT, John** **fl 1878**
Edinburgh landscape painter in oil; exhibited RSA(1).

**GALT, John** **fl 1917**
Glasgow based painter. Exhibited a church interior at the GI from 225 St Vincent Street.

**GALZENATI, Charles** **fl 1912**
Edinburgh based painter. Exhibited RSA(1) from 42 Brunswick Street.

**GAMLEY, Andrew Archer RSW** **1869-1949**
Born Johnshaven, Kincardineshire. Watercolour painter, also worked occasaionally in oils. Portraits, shipping, harbour scenes, landscape and figurative subjects. Studied at RSA Schools gaining a Carnegie Travelling Scholarship and Keith Prize. Lived in Edinburgh before moving to Pittenweem, Fife, where he was working 1920, then Gullane, East Lothian c1934. Enjoyed painting harbour scenes, capturing the effects of light on water, generally favouring a rather delicate almost indeterminate approach, also golf scenes. Occasionally worked in Spain. Elected RSW 1924. Exhibited RA(1), RSA(83), RSW(80), GI(77), regularly AAS 1932-1935, & L(4), after 1933 from Gullane, East Lothian.
**Bibl:** Halsby 259; Wingfield.

**GAMLEY, Henry Snell RSA FRBS** **1865-1928**
Born Logie Pert, Montrose. Sculptor and medallionist. Studied Royal Institute in Edinburgh. Responsible for the memorial statue to Edward VII at Holyrood. Elected ARSA 1908, RSA 1920. Among the 86 works exhibited at the RSA were a bust of Major McCaig (of the Folly, Oban) 1904, a portrait bust of Fiddes Watt 1911, and a model for the bronze medallion of William Murdoch, the inventor of gas lighting, executed for his birthplace Lugar, Ayrshire 1916. A large statue of Robert Burns is in Wyoming. Executed war memorials at Cupar and Montrose. Work in Edinburgh includes the WW1 Memorial in the Albany Aisle, W wall, St Giles (1924); the bronze portrait bust of E M Salvesen in the N Choir Aisle of St Giles (1915); also the Heart of Midlothian War Memorial (1921-2) at the junction of Haymarket and Clifton Terraces, a bronze statue of Edward VII at Holyrood, a bronze relief in the Canongate Churchyard (1909), a bronze tablet to Sir Alexander Russell Simpson in Chalmers Close on the Royal Mile and two heroic figures - 'Musical Inspiration' and 'Achievement' on the Grindlay St wing of the Usher Hall. His St Andrew surmounts the central doorway of the Freemasons' Hall, George St. Exhibited RA(3), GI(17), AAS 1909-1926 & L(4), all from his Edinburgh studio, 7 Hope St Lane. A replica of the statue of Edward VII, executed in 1916, is in SNPG.
**Bibl:** Gifford 115,141,152,203,205,262,282,374.

**GAMLEY, Miss L Vince** **fl 1919-1922**
Edinburgh based painter and sculptress. Exhibited RSA(7) from 7 Montpelier Park.

**GAMLEY, Miss Lola** **fl 1934-1936**
Edinburgh based painter in oil and watercolour; mainly scenes of farming life. Exhibited GI(2) from 10 Wemyss Place.

**GANTER, Jo** **c1965-**
Etcher. Trained Edinburgh College of Art 1983-88. Although she has remained with this medium throughout her working life, her work has changed from being figurative to being increasingly abstract, with the addition of colour to the designs. Her technique is to place large semi-transparent layers of colour over abstract expressionist compositions. Awards include a John Kinross Scholarship 1988, Andrew Grant Scholarship 1989, British Council travel grant 1997. Has held solo exhibitions in Aberdeen, Edinburgh & Glasgow. Currently teaches Edinburgh & Glasgow Schools of Art. Exhibits RSA since 1991. Represented in Edinburgh City AG, New York PL, Jane Voorhees Zimmerli Museum (Rutgers, NJ), Antwerp Museum of Fine Arts.
**Bibl:** Elizabeth Cowling, 'Jo Ganter - Meeting Places', Glasgow Print Studio ex cat.

**GARAU, Dolores** **fl 1916**
Glasgow based painter. Exhibited GI(1) from 65 West Regent Street.

**GARCEAU, Gilbert Alec** **1908-c1985**
Born London, 6 Nov. Painter in oil, watercolour and charcoal; landscape especially north-west Scotland. Educated at St Paul's School, London where he twice won the John Watson prize for painting. Son of Edouard Garceau the noted tenor, amateur artist and professor at the Guildhall School of Music and Jeanne Douste, notable pianist and friend of Liszt. Influenced by von Hugel and in atmospheric appreciation by the Hebridean singing of Elfreda Bruce. Began painting exclusively in oil 1960 concentrating on Highland landscapes. As well as being an artist was a self-taught mineral analyst, earning the William Bolitho Gold Medal for Geology 1953. His painting, while emphasising the picturesque more than is currently fashionable, faithfully captures the evasive light of north-west Scotland. The depiction of expansive rock, sea and mountain torrent is masterly. There is no intrusion between the vision and the viewer except for clarity and sharp focus. Lived with his Scottish wife in Cornwall.

**GARDEN, Francis** **fl 1718-?**
Edinburgh engraver. Probably related to Francis Garden, Lord Gardenstone. Mentioned in Nisbet's *Essay on...Armories,* 1718. Probably the Francis Garden, engraver of coats-of-arms, crests, etc, who advertised in the *Boston Evening Post* 1745 that he had recently arrived in America.
**Bibl:** Bushnell.

**GARDEN, George D** **fl 1926**
Aberdeen painter of local landscapes and figure studies. Exhibited AAS(3) from 17 King's Crescent.

**GARDEN, Ivan M** **20th Cent**
Aberdeen painter of fishing boats, birds and coastal scenes. Exhibited AAS(3) from 7 Rose Place.

**GARDEN, James A** **fl 1927-1932**
Aberdeen painter of portraits and wildlife. Moved to Kirkcaldy 1932. Exhibited RSA(3) & AAS(3), latterly from 142 St Clair Street, Kirkcaldy, Fife.

**GARDEN, William** **fl 1893-1894**
Aberdeen painter in oil. Concentrated on Highland scenery. Exhibited AAS(3) from 4 Rubislaw Terrace.

**GARDEN, William Fraser** **1856-1921**
Born Edinburgh. Painter of landscape, mainly in watercolours. Son of Dr Robert Fraser, four of his six brothers(qv) were also artists. Changed his name to Garden to distinguish his work from that of his brothers. Educated Bedford, probably trained there under Bradford Rudge. Specialised in angling and country scenes on the river Ouse. Exhibited RA signing his work W F Garden. Exhibited RA(10).
**Bibl:** Wingfield.

**GARDINER, A L** **fl 1876**
Glasgow painter of genre; exhibited 'Little Mischief Maker' at GI, from 2 Craigton Ave.

**GARDINER, Annie** **fl 1881**
Glasgow based landscape painter. Exhibited GI(1) from 1 Lendel Terrace.

**GARDINER, Nicol** **fl 1687**
Linlithgow painter. Worked at Kinneil Castle for the 3rd Duke of Hamilton.
**Bibl:** Apted 41; Hamilton Archives, Lennoxlove, Fl/557/7.

**GARDINER, Stanley Horace** **1887-c1939**
Landscape painter and teacher. Studied at Allan Fraser Art College, Arbroath and exhibited RA(11) 1927-1939, RSA(1) & L(1) from Lamorna, nr Penzance, Cornwall.

**GARDINER, Thomas** **[see GARDNER, Thomas]**

**GARDINER, Viola M** **fl 1936**
Edinburgh based flower painter. Exhibited RSA(1) from 7 Leven Terrace.

**GARDNER, Mrs** **fl 1888**
Glasgow flower painter; exhibited GI(1), from 2 Kirklee Rd.

**GARDNER, Miss Agnes M** **fl 1886-1893**
Glasgow based painter of landscapes. Exhibited GI(6) & AAS(1)

latterly from 6 Huntly Terrace, Kelvinside.

**GARDNER, Miss Alexandra (Sandie)** **1945-**
Born Bellshill, Glasgow. Painter in oils, charcoal and pastel; portraits, still life, figurative subjects, flowers. Trained Glasgow School of Art 1963-68 returning as a lecturer 1969-89. Inspired by David Donaldson(qv). Received Lauder Award (GSA) 1974, SAC Travelling scholarship 1980 and in 1991 was a prize winner at the 5th Int. Drawing Biennale, Cleveland. "Her paintings have wit, an understanding (of her subject) that allows her to give sympathy to the grotesque, to confront them, edify and amuse, all in the same moment". Exhibited RSA, RSW & RGI since 1990, latterly from 7 Devonshire Terrace.

**GARDNER, Alex McInnes** **fl 1904-1932**
Glasgow based painter. Exhibited GI(13).

**GARDNER, Allan Constant** **1906-?**
Born Valparaiso. Painter of coastal and shipping scenes, also etcher and stained glass window designer. Studied at Edinburgh College of Art. Exhibited RA(8) & RSA(6), having moved to London from Kilmacolm 1932.

**GARDNER, Ivy H** **[see PROUDFOOT, Mrs Jane]**

**GARDNER, Miss Jean** **fl 1973-1984**
Glasgow based painter. Exhibited pastoral subjects at the RSA(4) & GI(22), since 1980 from 11 Glasgow Rd, Eaglesham.

**GARDNER, John** **fl 1950**
Glasgow watercolour painter of flowers; exhibited GI(1), from 96 Novar Dr, Glasgow.

**GARDNER, John C** **fl 1948-1949**
Glasgow painter in oils and sometimes pencil; portraits, figure studies and townscapes. Exhibited GI(4), from 271 Broadholm St.

**GARDNER, Mary** **fl 1887-1895**
Ayrshire based flower painter. Exhibited GI(12) & L(1) from Dunholme, Skelmorlie.

**GARDNER, Robert** **fl 1849-1863**
Edinburgh painter of landscape and seascapes in oil; exhibited RSA(1) 1849 and 'On the Gareloch' at GI 1863, from 2 W Regent St.

**GARDNER, Thomas** **fl 1861-1869**
Edinburgh painter in oil of townscapes especially topographical scenes in Fifeshire and the Lothians. Exhibited RSA(5).

**GARDNER, W & J** **fl 1830-1840**
Perthshire engravers who invariably worked together. Engraved bookplates for Hay, 1840, Richardson of Pitfour 1840, and documents for the Lord Provost, Magistrates and Town Council of the city of Perth 1830.
**Bibl:** Bushnell.

**GARDNER, William** **fl 1930-1976**
East Lothian painter in watercolour, linocut and stencil; mostly animal linocuts. Exhibited regularly RSA, 1957-1967 from 3 Leyden Gdns, Glasgow & GI(13) after 1965 from 77 Abbot's View, Haddington.

**GARDNER-McLEAN, G** **fl 1932-1937**
Glasgow based painter. Exhibited GI(4).

**GARDNER-McLEAN, Mrs Madge** **fl 1930-1951**
Glasgow based painter in oil and watercolour; landscapes, portraits and flowers. Married to G G-M(qv). Exhibited RA(1), RSA(1), RSW(3), RWS(1), GI(20) & L(2) and, 1931, from Drumahoe, Londonderry.

**GARDYNE, Major A D G** **fl 1906**
Amateur artist and army officer. Probably Scottish. Exhibited RA(1) while at Castlehill Barracks, Aberdeen.

**GARDYNE, Helen M Greenhill** **fl 1889-1896**
Tobermory painter in pastels of landscape; exhibited 'Loch Baa, Mull', at the RSA 1896 & GI(2) from Glenforsa, Aros.

**GARDYNE, J Bruce** **fl 1880**
Arbroath landscape painter. Exhibited a view 'Sonning, Berkshire' at the RSA from Middleton.

**GARDYNE, Maryel A G** **fl 1965-1967**
Angus painter in oil of landscape and figure subjects. Exhibited a river scene RSA & AAS(4) from The Milton, Finavon, Forfar.

**GARLAND, Henry** **1834-1913**
Born Oct 23; died Jan 22. English landscape and wildlife artist whose love of Scotland and Scottish landscapes merits his inclusion. Trained RA Schools 1853-57. Exhibited RA(30), BI(12), SS(67), RWS(1). His favourite subjects were Highland Cattle in Highland landscapes, often with a herdsman and dog in attendance. Represented in Sunderland AG, York City AG, Leicester AG, Lords AG.

**GARRAD, Daphne Joyce Bertha 'Buttercup' (Miss May Butterfield)** **1917-**
Born Great Chelford 20 Jan. Landscape painter mainly in watercolour. Educated Cambridge County School and Newnham College, Cambridge. Began painting seriously in 1945 when resident at Rock House, Calton Hill, Edinburgh. Her first exhibition was shared with her husband at the Scottish Gallery, Edinburgh 1953. Subsequently held a number of solo exhibitions in Edinburgh as well as exhibiting widely in France, especially in the Montpellier area where she had a home. Paints in a very broad and somewhat primitive style, strongly influenced by her experience of mediterranean colours. Lived in Howgate, Midlothian where, with her husband(qv), she ran a popular restaurant before retiring to her home in France.

**GARRAD, William R ('Bill')** **1918-**
Born Leeds 7 May. Painter in watercolour of interiors. Son of Canon Garrad of Bradford. Educated Marlborough school and Trinity Hall, Cambridge. Studied at the RA Schools 1943-47, becoming a stage designer for the Wilson Barratt Company. From 1947-51 Deputy Director, Edinburgh International House. Husband of Buttercup G(qv). First exhibition in Edinburgh with John Minton and Felix Kelly 1947 and, with his wife, in London 1952. In 1955 he took over the Howgate Restaurant outside Edinburgh, developing it into an internationally recognised centre of haute cuisine. Close friend of William Wilson(qv) and Anne Redpath(qv), whom he accompanied on a painting visit to Spain 1951. Retired to France. A watercolour exhibited at the RSA is now in the permanent collection of the SAC.
**Bibl:** W R Garrad, Howgate (c1970); Scotsman, 1.5.75.

**GARROW, Miss Jean (Jessie) Isobel** **fl 1919-1925**
Glasgow painter in watercolours and monochrome; engraver. Landscape and figurative subjects. Exhibited RSA(4), GI(10), RSW(1), AAS(5) & L(2) from 11 Montgomery Road, Newlands.

**GARROW, R T** **fl 1906**
Aberdeen architectural draughtsman. Exhibited AAS from 56 Albury Road.

**GARTSIDE, Frederick** **fl 1887**
Glasgow based artist. Exhibited GI(1) from The Studio, 71 Waterloo Street.

**GARVIE, Jeannie A** **fl 1894-1896**
Aberdeen flower painter. Exhibited AAS(5) from 1 Osborne Place.

**GASKELL, Ernest** **fl 1929-1931**
Kilmarnock painter of flowers and landscape. Exhibited AAS from 11 Dick Road.

**GATES, Cyril Hedgley** **fl 1933-1972**
Prolific and versatile amateur Aberdeen artist. Exhibited portraits, still life and landscape regularly at the AAS during the above years from 176 Broomhill Road and latterly 102 Devonshire Road.

**GATHERER, Stuart Luke** **1972-**
Figurative painter. Son of a Scottish father and Dutch mother, he spent most of his early life in Scotland. Educated Aboyne Academy, where his first artistic endeavours were encouraged by art teacher Miss Petrie; trained Edinburgh College of Art and Edinburgh University 1989-95. First London show 1997. Moved to London and after marriage in 2003 settled in Herefordshire. Using his friends and

relations as models, his compositions often carry allegorical and symbolic undertones although, in the artist's words, "my paintings are primarily aesthetic experiences rather than illustrations of pre-conceived narratives". His style is direct in its appreciation of texture, mood, and the subtleties of interior illumination. "Images which combine the Old Masters with the cinema" [Richard North]. Successful shows in London, New York and Scotland with an ever-widening following of collectors, and with an escalating commercial value he is established as one of Scotland's most exciting young painters, building on the classical tradition of figurative painting to develop his own unique style.
**Bibl:** Edward Lucie Smith: *Stuart Luke Gatherer*, Ex Cat, Albemarle Gallery 2002; Jackie McGlone, *Picture of Wealth*, Sunday Herald 13 Aug 2000; Phil Miller: *I'm alright Jack*, The Herald 16 Nov 2002.

**GAULD, David RSA** **1865-1936**
Born Glasgow 7 Nov; died Glasgow 18 Jne. Painter in oil and occasional watercolour of landscapes, portraits and cattle; also illustrator and stained glass window designer. In 1882 began work as an apprentice lithographer to Gilmour and Dean but soon turned his attention to black and white drawings for newspaper illustrations. These attracted early recognition, together with his work in stained glass design for the firm of Guthrie and Wells. Studied probably as an evening student at the Glasgow School of Art and Holbein Academy, attending classes until 1885, and again in 1889 as an apprentice artist when living at Risk, Lochwinnoch. In 1887 joined the staff of the *Glasgow Weekly Citizen* producing pen drawings to illustrate serial instalments of novels. Became friendly with Rennie Mackintosh(qv) who had given him a set of bedroom furniture as a wedding present in 1893. His early works in oil were of portraits, often ladies reclining beside streams, but his greatest success came as a painter of cattle and for his beautiful soft, pastel coloured landscapes often with the introduction of a mill or an old steading set amid trees and a stretch of quiet water. More concerned with the moods of nature than with mere transcription of facts. Primarily a decorative artist, his early paintings owing much to Rossetti and Burne Jones, while his cattle paintings were influenced by the tenderness and veracity that were the hallmark of James Maris. Rarely worked in watercolours except for preliminary studies for stained glass window designs. The secular works are considered his best, also the Praise Window at the east end of Upper Largo parish church, Bellahouston church and Skelmorlie church, but his most important stained glass work was the windows of St Andrew's Scottish Church in Buenos Aires, a commission which lasted ten years before its completion in 1910. Member of the Glasgow School(qv), sharing a studio for a time with Harrington Mann(qv). One of the most enigmatic members of the Group, bridging a gap, as Ailsa Tanner pointed out, between the Glasgow Boys and Art Nouveau, the clearest evidence of which is his art nouveau portrait en plein air of 'St Agnes' [illus Hardie,103]. In 1896 he painted an important series of landscapes at Grez, some with cattle, but more atmospheric in character than his later work. In the last year of his life he was made Director of Design, Glasgow School of Art. 'He was a quiet man, greatly respected and liked by his colleagues and friends, possessing a fine sense of humour'. Elected ARSA 1918, RSA 1924. Exhibited RSA continuously 1905-1939, a total of 44 works, as well as GI(96) & AAS 1921-1931. Represented in Aberdeen AG, Dumfries AG, Dundee AG, Edinburgh (RSA Diploma Coll), Glasgow AG, Greenock AG, Kilmarnock AG, Kirkcaldy AG, Liverpool AG, Paisley AG, Perth AG, City of Edinburgh collection.
**Bibl:** W Buchanan,'The Glasgow Boys' 2 vols, SAC (Ex Cat 1968 & 1971); Caw 450-1; Halsby 150,160,172-3; Hardie[SP] 102-3,104,109; Irwin 373,386,392(illus); Macmillan [SA] 282; 'David Gauld', Scottish Life & Letters, Sep-Nov 1903, 372-383.

**GAULD, Mrs David** **fl 1905**
Glasgow based flower painter. Wife of David G(qv). Exhibited GI(2) when living at 23 Belmont Street.

**GAVIN, Charles** **1944-**
Born Edinburgh. Painter. In 1970 entered the L'école des Beaux Arts, returning to Edinburgh two years later. After a short spell in London he moved to Spain, returning to Britain 1979. Held one-man exhibition in Edinburgh 1986.

**GAVIN, Hector Snr** **1748-1814**
Born Langton, Berwickshire, 7 May; died Edinburgh, 7 Jly. Edinburgh engraver. In 1775 he met Thomas Bewick in Edinburgh who described the encounter 'I next day called upon Hector Gavin, an engraver, in Parliament Close. This kind man - a stranger to me - after a bit of chat about the arts, threw down his tools, and was quite at my service. The warmth of his kindness I can never forget. He took me all over Edinburgh, and gave me a history and explanation of everything he thought worthy of notice'. Elected Burgess of the city of Edinburgh 1782. Among the many bookplates he engraved were those for Keith Urquhart 1760 and James Urquhart 1760. Some of the plates are signed 'Gavin', others 'H Gavin' or 'Hr Gavin'; it is not always easy to distinguish his work from that of his son. Acquired the property of Croft-an-Righ, near Holyrood. His son Hector(qv), whom he took into partnership, succeeded him.
**Bibl:** Bushnell; Cannongate Reg of Marr, 1564-1800.

**GAVIN, Hector Jnr** **1784-1874**
Born Croft-an-Righ, Edinburgh, 5 Oct; died Edinburgh 1 Mar. Engraver. Son, partner and successor of Hector G snr(qv). Married Marion Walker, sister of William Walker(qv) a contemporary engraver, 11 Nov 1814. Elected Burgess of the city of Edinburgh 1811, Guild Brother 1818, Member of the Merchant Company 1825 and Governor 1837. County maps of Scotland, engraved by him and his father were published in Edinburgh by Thomas Brown. In 1823 Bewick revisited Edinburgh when he paid his 'respects to the son and successor of my kind friend of former years...these, in my estimation, were doing credit to their instruction as engravers'. He had a large family but all his sons predeceased him and in 1856, having sold Croft-an-Righ 4 years earlier to the Crown, went to live with a married daughter in whose care he died. Buried on Calton Hill, Edinburgh.
**Bibl:** Bushnell.

**GAVIN, Hugh** **fl 1930-1940**
Glasgow based watercolourist. Landscapes, principally Highland and Irish scenery. Exhibited GI(30) latterly from 51 Kingston Rd, Bishopton, Renfrewshire. Represented in Paisley AG.

**GAVIN, James** **1928-**
Born Duns, Berwickshire. Painter of landscape and semi-abstracts in oil. Studied Edinburgh College of Art 1955-1959 and the following year visited Paris for further private studies. Subsequently appointed lecturer in foundation studies, Cumbria College of Art and Design. First solo exhibition Edinburgh 1961. Exhibits RSA from 1 Eyre Place, Edinburgh.

**GAVIN, Malcolm ARSA** **1874-1956**
Born Scotland; died London, 4 Apr. Painter of portraits, flowers and still life. Scottish parentage. His early education was in Edinburgh, then studied art South Kensington and RA Schools. Most successful in his portraits of women. Among his posthumous RSA exhibits in 1957 was a fine portrait of Hector Chalmers, lent by the SAC. Exhibited frequently in London but returned to Edinburgh and was a regular exhibitor at the RSA. Went back to London a few years before his death. Elected RP 1919, ARSA 1920. Exhibited RSA(42), GI(9) & L(6), from 31 Stafford St, Edinburgh.

**GAVIN, Robert RSA** **1827-1883**
Born Leith; died Newhaven, nr Edinburgh 6 Oct. Studied under Duncan(qv) at the Trustees Academy. Figure painter; at first he painted a variety of subjects until about 1865 when he visited New Orleans. Thereafter 'mulatto, quadroon and negro were his models'. When his American sketches were not too successful he moved to Tangiers, returning only shortly before his death. His work before 1865 is rarely seen so that he is now best known for his American and Moorish subjects. This is to be regretted because some of his early works show a fine talent, simple and direct. His diploma picture in the SNG entitled 'Moorish Maiden's First Love' was said to be lacking in southern light or colour. 'Technically he had considerable facility and power, drawing easily and painting with a full and fluent brush; at its best the colour was rich and harmonious, and he possessed an eye for pictorial setting and brilliant and bizarre costume. In susceptibility to the impressions of unfamiliar life and surroundings he was more kindred to Philip than to many of his contemporaries'[Brydall]. Elected ARSA 1855, RSA 1879. Exhibited RA(5) 1855-71, all of them from Edinburgh, RSA(137) 1868-1882 & GI(11), latterly from Cherry Bank, Newhaven St.
**Bibl:** Bryan; Brydall 406-7; Caw 166-7; McKay 351-2.

**GEAR, William** **1915-1997**
Born Methil, Fife, 2 Aug; died Feb 27. Abstract painter in oil, gouache and watercolour. Educated at Buckhaven HS, studied Edinburgh College of Art 1932-37 and fine art at University of Edinburgh 1936-37. As the result of a travelling scholarship he studied in Paris at the Academie Colarossi and under Fernand Leger 1937. The following year visited Italy, Greece and the Balkans. Exhibited internationally. Served with the Royal Corps of Signals 1939-46. While in the Middle East he had exhibitions in Jerusalem, Tel Aviv and Cairo, and when in Italy, at Siena and Florence. Immediately after the war he worked in the Control Commission for Germany's Monuments and Fine Arts Section and met the German artist Karl Otto Gotz; subsequently they both became members of the COBRA movement linking European artists sharing an interest in abstract and folk art. His first one man show began in 1944. After a period in London he moved to Paris becoming closely associated with such figures as Atlan, Soulages and Poliakoff at the École de Paris. First solo show there 1948, the same year as his first show in London. He evolved a personal style akin to stained glass design, using black lines surrounding bright colours. In 1957-59 visited New York and was Curator of the Art Gallery, Eastbourne 1959-1964 and Head of the Department of Fine Art, Birmingham Polytechnic from 1964. 'He constructs bold abstractions which are based mainly on the elements, like tree forms, taken from landscape and executed in a style that is immediately recognisable in its powerful visual impact. He wields a dark broad calligraphy, shows a marked interest in staccato rhythms and jagged edges and uses strong tonal constrast to produce a heightened sense of drama that is basically romantic' [Gage]. Exhibited RSA from East Wemyss, Fife in 1934 and 1937, then from Sussex 1962-1963 and from Birmingham 1967-1986, also RGI(4), after 1961 from 46 George St, Birmingham. Represented in Aberdeen AG, Dundee AG, Glasgow AG, Kirkcaldy AG, Birmingham AG, Brighton AG, Tate, V & A, Cambridge AG, Manchester AG, Newcastle AG, Oxford AG, Southampton AG, Eastbourne AG, SNGMA, National Gallery of Canada, Gallery of New South Wales, Buffalo AG, New York, Toronto AG, Toledo AG (Spain), Liege AG, Lima AG, Nelson AG (New Zealand), Tel Aviv AG.
**Bibl:** Arts Council of N. Ireland, 'William Gear: Paintings 1948-68', (Ex Cat 1968); Gage 34; Galerie 1900-2000, Paris, 'William Gear: Cobra Abstractions 1946-1949' (Ex Cat 1988); Gimpel Fils Gall, London, 'William Gear' (Ex Cat 1961); Hardie 185-7; Hartley 134; Macmillan [SA] 369,375-6 et passim in ch xx & xxi; Munich, Karl & Faber, 'William Gear' (Ex Cat, 1988); The Times, Obituary, Mar 1 1997.

**GEDDES, Andrew ARA** **1783-1844**
Born Edinburgh; died London 5 May. Portrait painter and etcher. Son of a deputy auditor in the Edinburgh Excise Office who was also a knowledgeable collector. After the death of his father in 1807, he entered the RA Schools joining a group which included Wilkie, Jackson and Haydon. Returned to Edinburgh, setting up as a portrait painter, but in 1814 was back in London where he remained for the rest of his life although continuing to wander between there, Edinburgh, Paris and Rome. Visited Holland 1839. In 1821 he exhibited a fine, large painting at the RA 'The discovery of the Regalia of Scotland'. No purchaser for this work was found so Geddes cut it up, selling the heads as individual portraits. Toward the end of his life religious subjects became more frequent but best remembered as an etcher. 'Even when his subject is ill-advised and his interest was half-excited, we find enough to delight us in the mere freedom of his line, in the instinct with which he seizes upon right ideas for translation with the paint, and a right way to set about the work'. His professional life was almost entirely devoted to portraiture his only genre painting being 'The Draught Players' (1809). An individualistic artist, follower of no-one, but always associated in the public mind with Wilkie. Honorary member of the Royal Institution but never associated with the Scottish Academy. His famous portrait of Wilkie dates from the time he was in Edinburgh. But perhaps his best known work is 'Summer', now in the NGS, in which one of Nasmyth's daughters appears. In 1826 he issued a series of 10 etchings. His etched portrait of Henry Broadwood induced Hamerton to include Geddes amongst his list of distinguished etchers. Geddes is one of those not infrequent in the annals of art and literature whose reputation seems never to have equalled ability. 'Perhaps there was a lack of that concentration which is one of the main elements of success'. Wilkie had said of him 'if Mr Geddes could once get the public applause on his side he would never lose it, his works are so far above what is called the fashion, and in this style of art, it is my decided opinion he has more taste than any artist in Britain'. Brydall considered that, with the exception of Wilkie, Geddes was the most successful etcher in Britain of his time 'and even for long after'. Exhibited RA(100) 1806-1845. No less than 22 of his works were exhibited posthumously at the RSA 1880-1949. Represented in NG, BM, V & A, NGS(22), SNPG(12, including two self-portraits), Glasgow AG, Kirkcaldy AG, Paisley AG, City of Edinburgh collection, Perth AG (set of 1826 etchings in original wrappers), Paul Mellon coll (Upperville, VA, USA - chalk drawing of a golfer and another of a figure skating).
**Bibl:** Bryan; Brydall 232-6; Caw 83-5 et al; Halsby 79; Irwin 197-202 et al; Macmillan [SA], 143,181-3,299; Walpole Society, vol 5, 1828, 19; Wingfield.

**GEDDES, Ewan RSW** **1865-1935**
Born and died Blairgowrie, Perthshire. Primarily a watercolourist, specialising in landscapes, homely scenes and country people. Trained in Edinburgh. Son of William G(qv). Very popular where he lived, being described as a 'thoroughly sweet person'. Friends and frequent guests at his home included Tom Blacklock(qv), William Frazer(qv), Andrew Gamley(qv) and Hannah Preston Macgoun(qv). Especially fond of the countryside around Muirton and Cramond. His landscapes are simple, poetic and personal, using subdued tones. Particularly adept at painting snow scenes. His paintings are popular in the USA. Lived all his working life at Gowanbrae, Blairgowrie, although his studio was always 108 George St, Edinburgh. An exhibition of his work was held in Blairgowrie 1974. Elected RSW 1902. Regular exhibitor RSA(151) from 1891, also RA(2), RSW(113), GI(72), RHA(5) & AAS 1885-1935. His watercolour 'The Fair Maid's House, Perth,' is in Perth AG; also represented in Glasgow AG, Kirkcaldy AG, City of Edinburgh collection.
**Bibl:** Caw 392; Halsby 259; personal family communication.

**GEDDES, Frances B** **fl 1919-1937**
Amateur Aberdeen painter of local landscape and wildlife subjects. Her two exhibits at the AAS were separated by a span of 18 years. Lived at Postcliffe, Peterculter.

**GEDDES, George W** **fl 1931**
Glasgow based painter. Exhibited GI(1) from 31 Rampart Avenue.

**GEDDES, Robert Smith** **1883-1951**
Occasional Blairgowrie landscape artist. Brother of Ewan G(qv) with whom he lived for many years, and son of William G(qv). During his incomplete studies at Edinburgh College of Art he completed many caricatures of his fellows including Stanley Cursiter(qv), Dorothy Johnston(qv), Walter Hislop(qv) and Albert Dods(qv). Brother Ewan considered 'Bob' the more talented of the two. Disappeared for years, finally settling with his sister in Portland, Oregon, where he died. His work is now seldom seen. A watercolour portrait of his brother was exhibited in the retrospective exhibition 1974. Several examples of his work remain in the collection of the family. Exhibited a watercolour at the GI & AAS(1), from the family home Gowanbrae, Blairgowrie.
**Bibl:** Family communication.

**GEDDES, William (of Blairgowrie)** **1840/1-1884**
Born and died Blairgowrie, Oct. Painter in oil and watercolour of landscapes and country life. In 1853 he started as a house painter earning two shillings a week. Married in Edinburgh but returned to Blairgowrie becoming indelibly associated with the town. Maintained a large fish tank at home, his early reputation rests largely on his meticulous studies of fish. In 1882 won a Gold Medal and £50 for the best genre painting in the RSA. Andrew Carnegie paid £500 for a crowd scene commemmorating Carnegie's visit to Dunfermline with his mother, a painting in which Andrew Blair(qv) provided the background street scene, which can now be seen in the Dunfermline Andrew Carnegie Birthplace Museum. In 1871, and again in 1875, he visited Paris, studying for two months in the Louvre. During his stay he was arrested as a spy. Friendly with many artists including David Farquharson(qv), George Whitton Johnstone(qv), Hugh Allan(qv), William Dickson(qv), Tom Scott(qv), Michael Brown(qv), James Spindler(qv), T Austen Brown(qv) and Thomas Burnett(qv). He had ten children, two of whom became artists. Exhibited RSA(40) 1865-

79, & GI(7). Represented in Perth AG(2), where there is also his portrait bust by T S Burnett.
**Bibl:** Dryerre, Blairgowrie, Stormont and Strathmore Worthies, 1933, 184,218-229; Macdonald, History of Blairgowrie 1899, 224 (port 216); family communication.

**GEDDIE, Miss Hope** **fl 1929-1935**
Aberdeen painter of continental and local landscapes. Daughter of Dr Watson G(qv). Living in London 1933 when she exhibited a Yugoslavian townscape. Regular exhibitor AAS during the above years.

**GEDDIE, Dr Watson** **fl 1900-1929**
Amateur Aberdeen etcher of portraits and local scenery. Father of Hope G(qv). Exhibited regularly AAS from 13 Golden Square.

**GEIKIE, George R** **fl 1941-1949**
Edinburgh landscape painter in oil. Exhibited 3 Ross-shire scenes at the RSA & GI(3 - all sea lochs), from 83 Colinton Road.

**GEIKIE, Miss Isabella L** **fl 1872-1874**
Newington sculptress. Daughter of Professor Geikie, the famous geologist and author. Exhibited 4 portrait busts at the RSA including a medallion of her father & GI(2) including a bust of her father.

**GEIKIE, Miss Lucy** **fl 1901-1904**
Landscape painter exhibited RA(2), including 'After a Wet Night: St Andrews' (1904).

**GEIKIE, Walter RSA** **1795-1837**
Born Edinburgh, 9 Nov; died Edinburgh. Trained Trustees Academy under John Graham(qv) and Patrick Gibson(qv). He recorded the ever-changing life of Edinburgh streets. Deaf and dumb since the age of two which seems to have heightened his awareness and sensitivity toward the social scene of his day. His character studies included such subjects as the cobbler at his stall, drunken men, a seasick dandy, and bargaining for fish. Colour was not his forte and his oil paintings failed to show the full flourish of his genius. His true metier was undoubtedly etching. Did much work at St Luke's Art Club. His lightning sketches of the idiosyncracies of many people known to the audience created great hilarity and must have helped him to forget his own physical defects. His greatest work was done with his friend, Sir Thomas Dick Lauder(qv), producing *Etchings Illustrative of Scottish Character and Scenery.* This appeared after his death, in 1841, with another edition in 1885. In 1830 he published *A Collection of Original Drawings of Edinburgh and Environs.* Geikie has been variously called the Scottish Rembrandt or at least the Van Ostade. 'Geikie was remarkable for the excellence and amiability of his disposition...his temper was extremely patient, and he bore every little annoyance with the best possible humour and with the most unruffled countenance...warm-hearted and affectionate' [Lauder]. Elected ARSA 1831, RSA 1834. Exhibited RA(2), 'Craigmillar Castle' (1818) and 'Dunstaffnage Castle' (1835). Also exhibited RSA and its predecessor (107) 1815-39. Represented in NGS (by 'Scottish Roadside Scene', 1825, a sketchbook and over 90 other works), Glasgow AG, City of Edinburgh collection (many examples).
**Bibl:** Armstrong 20; BM Cat of Drawings by Brit Artists, vol 2, 184; Bryan; Brydall 211-12; Bushnell; Butchart 42,43,54-5; DNB; Halsby 309; Irwin 1935 et al; Macmillan [GA], 173-4; Macmillan [SA], 142,148,183-5,196,201,216; Macmillan, Walter Geikie, TRG 1984; McKay 159; Roy Morris 'The etchings of Walter Geikie' Print Collectors Quarterly XXII, 1935.

**GEISSLER, William Hastie RSW** **1896-1963**
Edinburgh based painter in oil and watercolour of portraits and Scottish landscape. Trained Edinburgh College of Art alongside Crozier(qv) and his close friend Gillies(qv). With them he visited Italy and France in 1923 studying for a time in the studio of André Lhôte in Paris. His watercolour landscapes showed a strong sense of design and vivacious use of colour, indicating the influence of Lhôte. Became head of the Art Department, Moray House, Edinburgh and President SSA 1957. Founder member of the 1922 Group(qv). Exhibited RSA & RSW from 52 Audley Avenue. A copy after an unknown artist of a portrait of John Graham of Claverhouse is in SNPG, also a copy of Willem van Honthorst's portrait of the 1st Marquess of Montrose.
**Bibl:** Halsby 211,218,221-2; Hardie 160.

**GELLATLY, John** **fl 1830**
Edinburgh engraver. Exhibited 4 topographical scenes in Stirling area at the RSA from 8 Register Street. Two steel engravings of Edinburgh are in the City of Edinburgh collection, the better known being 'Leith from the Pier', after A S Masson(qv).
**Bibl:** Butchart 47.

**GELLATLY, William** **fl 1859-1860**
Edinburgh painter of pastoral scenes; exhibited RSA(2) from 3 Leopold Park.

**GELTON, T(?oussaint)** **fl 1672**
In 1672 he was paid 500 rix dollars (c£125) for pictures, by Sir William Bruce. Probably a Dutch painter working briefly in Edinburgh, most probably the Toussaint Gelton, painter to the King of Denmark 1673, who died 1680 and is represented in Copenhagen AG, Stockholm AG.
**Bibl:** Apted 42; SRO Kinross House Muniments, GD.29/263/4.

**GEMMELL, Agnes** **fl 1891**
Paisley sculptress. Exhibited a carved oak plaque at the GI, from Oaklea, Crookston.

**GEMMELL, David** **fl 1936-1944**
Edinburgh painter of genre. Exhibited RSA(4) from 48 Clermiston Road, Barnton.

**GEMMELL or (JEMELY), James** **fl 1720-1725**
Scottish portrait painter. Painted various sitters for Hopetoun House in the manner of Medina, among them a portrait of 'Lord Riccarton' (1722), the surgeon 'John Baillie '(1723) and several others including the 'Earl of Crawford'. A miniature copy by an unknown artist of a portrait by Gemmell of 'James Balfour' (1681-1737), first Laird of Pilrig, is in the SNPG.
**Bibl:** B Balfour-Melville, The Balfours of Pilrig, 1907, 71.

**GEMMELL, John Lewthwaite** **fl 1883-1885**
Glasgow watercolour landscape painter from 5 Woodville Place, Govan. One of the band of painters who spent summers sketching on Arran, one sketch exhibited RSA 1885. Exhibited RSA(2) & GI(4).

**GEMMELL, Marion** **fl 1887-1909**
Watercolour painter of domestic scenes, figure subjects and informal portraits. Exhibited RI(1), ROI(2), SWA(6), GI(1), L(5) & the London Salon (2) from various addresses in London and Glasgow.

**GEMMELL, Matthew** **fl 1888**
Glasgow watercolourist. Exhibited a pastoral scene at the GI, from 5 Sardinia Terrace.

**GEMMILL, William** **fl 1888**
Glasgow figure painter; exhibited GI(2), both entitled 'The Duellist'.

**GENOTIN, Frederick** **fl 1866**
Edinburgh painter of conversation pieces in oil. Exhibited RA(1) & RSA(2), all in the same year, from 11 Nelson Street.

**GENTLEMAN, Tom** **fl 1921-1929**
Landscape painter, engraver, poster and book engraver. Studied at the Glasgow School of Art. Married Winifred Murgatroyd. Lived in Glasgow until c1922 moving then to Coatbridge, finally settling in London c1929. Exhibited RSA(2) & GI(7).

**GENTLES, Maruk** **fl 1975-1978**
Aberdeen based painter who exhibited at the AAS during the above period from 1 Baillieswells Crescent, Bieldside.

**GEORGE, Frederick B** **fl 1846**
Glasgow landscape painter in oil; exhibited 7 works at the RSA, mostly Highland views.

**GEORGE, Frederick W** **fl 1919-1948**
Aberdeen sculptor of portraits and figures and painter of landscapes and Arab scenes. His wife, Mrs F G(qv) and Maude N(qv, his mother?) were also sculptors. Exhibited RSA(17) and often at the AAS 1919-1937 from 37 Salisbury Terrace, Aberdeen.

**GEORGE, Mrs Frederick** **fl 1923**
Amateur Aberdeen sculptress. Wife of Frederick G(qv). Exhibited a portrait bust at the AAS.

**GEORGE, Matthew S S** **fl 1974**
Dundee artist. Trained at Duncan of Jordanstone School of Art, Dundee. Exhibited AAS(4) from 244 Blackness Road.

**GEORGE, Mrs Maude N** **fl 1926-1935**
Aberdeen sculptress. Lived at the same address and probably mother of Frederick G(qv). Exhibited intermittently AAS during the above years.

**GERRARD, Miss W M** **fl 1882-1946**
Edinburgh miniature flower painter in oil; exhibited RSA(3) during the above years.

**GERRIE, A B** **fl 1923-1926**
Aberdeen painter of landscape and local coastal scenes. Exhibited AAS from 5 Marine Place.

**GEYER, Rev A H** **1857-1931**
Born Therring, Austria, 26 Jly; died Dunblane, Aug. Painter and etcher of landscape; also engineer and pastor. Came to Glasgow c1880 as a qualified engineer to work with John Brown Shipbuilders. Married a Glasgow girl 1886 and established the first German Protestant church in Kelvinside. Harrassed during WW1 on account of his name and origin he moved to Dunblane. To supplement his income painted mainly landscapes and etched. Attracted to the Trossachs and the scenery around Loch Lomond. Exhibited GI 1912 before leaving Glasgow, and subsequently from Dunblane. Represented in Paisley AG.

**GIBB, Andrew FSA(Scot)** **1821-1881**
Born Stonehaven. Draughtsman, lithographer and antiquarian. Partner in the Aberdeen firms of Keith & Gibb and its successor **Gibb & HAY**, 'Draughtsmen and lithographers' to Her Majesty'. With his partner J. Marley Hay(qv) he illustrated and described the first history of the valley of the Dee *The Scenery of the Dee* 1884. His best known work is *The Sculptured Stones of Scotland* 1884. Arguably the most talented draughtsman the north-east has produced.
**Bibl:** Fenton Wyness, Royal Valley, 1968, 287.

**GIBB, Mrs Audrey** **fl 1966-1969**
Glasgow sculptress; worked in cement and in plaster. Exhibited GI(6), from 140 Brownside Rd, Cambuslang.

**GIBB, Charles** **fl 1900**
Glasgow landscape painter. Exhibited GI(1) from 8 Whitevale Street.

**GIBB, Miss Constance** **fl 1953**
Glasgow watercolourist, especially of harbour scenes. Exhibited GI(1), from 42 Bellwood St.

**GIBB, Ethel A (Mrs Alex Cousins)** **fl 1912-1948**
Glasgow portrait miniaturist, usually on ivory. Married Alex Cousins in the 30s. Lived at Redhurst, 75 Drymen Rd, Bearsden. Exhibited GI(10) including a portrait of her husband (1939).

**GIBB, George** **fl 1895**
Edinburgh painter. Exhibited RSA(1) from 31 Joppa Road, Portobello.

**GIBB, Glen Hill** **1936-**
Born Kingston-upon-Hull, Aug 30. Architect and painter. Moved to Scotland c1971. Registered architect 1962 but ceased practising 1990 in order to devote himself to painting full-time. Exhibits RSA since 1991 and RSW since 1992. Lives in North Berwick.

**GIBB, Henry M** **fl 1931**
Glasgow watercolour painter; exhibited RSA(1) from 23 Kennoway Drive.

**GIBB, J** **fl 1827**
Edinburgh architect. Exhibited a design for the interior of the Gallery at Scone Palace, Perthshire at the RA in 1827.

**GIBB, James** **fl 1930s**
Hamilton amateur painter; joiner by trade. Collected paintings and gems, bequeathed to Hamilton Museum. Represented by a pastel 1930 in Hamilton Museum

**GIBB, John** **1831-1909**
Born Castlecary, Dunbartonshire. Painter in oil, seascape and landscape. Studied under John Mackenzie of Greenock(qv). Specialised most in seascapes. Probably the 'J Gibb' responsible for 'Curling', signed & dated 1860. In 1876 sailed to New Zealand in the *Merope,* and settled in Christchurch, where he was the guiding figure in Canterbury Art Society. Exhibited extensively in New Zealand and Australia and was noted for his treatment of the play of light on water. In his NZ Nat Gall picture 'The Wool Season', bales of wool are seen being conveyed by lighter from some sheep station near a wharf to the waiting coastal vessel. The reflections of the ships and the lazy smoke from the funnel of the gently rolling vessel establish the calm unhurried mood of the scene. Exhibited RSA(4) when living at Innellan, Argyll, and (2) when at Alnwick, Northumberland (1865); also GI(4) 1868-1872 from Innellan. Represented in Perth AG and National Gallery of New Zealand (Wellington).
**Bibl:** Brown and Keith, An Introduction to New Zealand Painting, 1837-1967; Collins 1969, 58.

**GIBB, Lewis Taylor** **fl 1922-1945**
English artist with Scottish connections. Landscape painter in oils. Based in London before moving 1931 to Holm, West Mersea, nr Colchester, Sussex. Painted many Highland scenes, especially around Loch Maree and in Perthshire. Exhibited RA, RSA & GI(23); also Paris Salon.

**GIBB, Peter James** **1951-**
Born Edinburgh. Painter of large semi-abstracts. Studied Duncan of Jordanstone College of Art. Represented in City of Edinburgh collection.

**GIBB, Robert RSA** **1801-1837**
Born Dundee. Landscape painter in oil and watercolour. Foundation Associate of the RSA but one of nine artists who withdrew after the first meeting. Re-elected Academician 1829, receiving the Hope and Cockburn Award. One of the first landscape painters in Scotland to work on location. Alexander Nasmyth jeeringly called him the Chief of the Docken School. The crudeness of his colours, especially green, combined with the brevity of his life to deny him the recognition expected of an academician. Exhibited 98 works at the RSA and its precursor, among them a magnificent 'View of Perth' (1829) now in Perth AG. Represented in NGS(8).
**Bibl:** Blackwood's Mag, 1827; Brydall 309-310; Caw 59; Halsby 50-1; McKay 199.

**GIBB, Robert RSA** **1845-1932**
Born Laurieston 28 Oct; died Edinburgh 11 Feb. Painter of romantic, historical, military subjects, also portraits. Brother of William G(qv). Limner to His Majesty for Scotland 1908-1932. Studied art at Edinburgh classes in the Life School of the RSA. His earlier paintings indicated an earnest approach to historical scenes often of a tragic nature while his later work shows him in a more romantic light. In 1878 he began a series of military pictures on which his reputation is now largely based. 'Comrades' was followed by the 'Retreat from Moscow', finished in Paris. In 1881 'The Thin Red Line' created a storm at the RSA and going on tour carried the artist's fame overseas. Other famous paintings include the 'Charge of the 42nd, Up the Heights of Alma', 'Saving the Colours' (an incident in the 3rd Crimean battle) and 'Hougomont' (1903). One of the finest British battle painters. Caw thought him 'the only one who can be compared with the military painters of France...the outstanding qualities of his art as a whole are the clarity and coherence of its conception on the intellectual side, and the high level of its accomplishment in certain technical respects, while the scale on which he works and the complexity of the material with which he deals are exceptional'. Keeper of the NGS 1895-1907 in which capacity he re-arranged and re-catalogued the collection, marking a landmark in its development. Exhibited RA(5) 1882-1886 from 15 Shandwick Place, Edinburgh and in 1893 from 2 Bruntsfield Crescent. The portrait of 'Stanley' (1886) and 'The Thin Red Line' (1882) were two of his most successful works. Elected ARSA 1878, RSA 1882. Exhibited

RSA(119) from 1867, also AAS 1890-1931 & GI(10). Represented in the NGS(15), City of Edinburgh collection, Perth AG.
**Bibl:** AJ, 1897 25ff; Caw 266-7; Halsby 50-1; Hardie III, 195; Studio Vol 65, 204; Who's Who, 1914.

**GIBB, Miss Sadie** **fl 1913-1916**
Glasgow painter. Exhibited L(19) from 93 Hope Street.

**GIBB, W Menzies** **1859-1931**
Born Innellan, Firth of Clyde. Watercolour landscape painter. Son of John G(qv). Represented in Nat Gall of New Zealand (Wellington).

**GIBB, William** **1839-1929**
Born Laurieston; died London. Landscape painter in watercolour and gouache, also lithographer. Brother of Robert G(qv). Originally trained in lithography he turned increasingly to painting relics, goldsmith's work etc with great clarity. His work has been described as the counterpart of Jacquemart's etchings in France. Best known for his accurate watercolours of objects of applied art in particular oriental porcelain in which the work is finely delineated if sometimes dull. Illustrated *Dundee: its Quaint and Historic Buildings* (1895). Exhibited RSA(21), GI(2) including 'Braemar' (1880) & AAS 1885-1921, from 6 Hillsborough Sq, Glasgow. Represented in NGS(4), Glasgow AG. His study of a Derby vase was reproduced as Pl 26 in B Rackham's *A Book of Porcelain,* 1921.
**Bibl:** Halsby 259.

**GIBBON, Anthony** **fl 1975**
Glasgow artist; exhibited GI(2), from 8 Birrell Rd, Milngavie.

**GIBBON, Myra Faith** **fl 1965-1970**
Kincardineshire landscape painter mainly of Highland scenes. Exhibited GI & AAS(1) from 13 Main Street, Johnshaven.

**GIBBONS, Miss Carole** **1935-**
Born Glasgow. Painter in oil, watercolour and gouache; figures, still life and portraits. Studied Glasgow School of Art 1953-57, lived in Spain 1965-1966. Travelled extensively in France and Belgium. In contrast to the abstract tendencies of most of her contemporaries she has always retained an interest in traditional subject matter. The scale of her work and the exhilarating boldness of execution gives a special significance and weight to everyday subjects. 'Superficially drab and even in tone, her paintings reveal startlingly intense colours rubbed and worked into each other all over the surface of the picture that create almost irridescent patterns' [McMillan]. Her first exhibition was in Glasgow 1986 and in Edinburgh the following year. Exhibited RGI(2) from 3 Bogany Terrace, Castlemilk. Represented in Aberdeen AG, SAC, J F Hendry Collection, Ontario.
**Bibl:** Duncan Macmillan, Five Scottish Artists Retrospective; McLellan Galleries (Ex Cat 1986).

**GIBBS, James** **1682-1754**
Born near Aberdeen, died in London. Distinguished architect. Only son of an Aberdeen merchant from Footdeesmire. When very young he left home for Holland, travelling through Flanders, France, Switzerland, and Germany to Italy. Was in Rome 1707-1709 and, determined to become an architect, entered the studio of Carlo Fontana. He was a Tory, a catholic, and probably a Jacobite. After returning to London his ideas from Italian mannerist and baroque sources combined with elements from Wren's work as exemplified in the Church of St Mary le Strand (1714-1717). This was badly received and thereafter Gibbs abandoned his Italian style. His only recorded work in Scotland is his design for a reconstructed church of St. Nicholas in Aberdeen which he presented to his native city. Without becoming a real Palladian he remained close to the style of Wren. His compositions generally consist of broad masses relieved by centre and end projections and uniformly fenestrated - a type of composition familiar in England since Pratt and in Scotland since Bruce(qv). The favourite architect of the Tory party, he worked for such patrons as the Earls of Oxford and Mar, Lord Bolingbroke, the Duke of Bolton and the Duke of Argyll. For Argyll he built Sudbroke House in 1718. From 1721 to 1726 he was engaged in the design of the Church of St Martin's-in-the-Fields. Although his domestic work is uniformly sober the church work was less restrained. Designed the Senate House and the Fellows Building at King's College, Cambridge, as well as the Radcliffe Library, Oxford (1739-49). These, together with St Martin's-in-the-Fields, are regarded as his finest achievements. Although strongly individualistic his influence was enormous, most especially through his books - *A Book of Architecture,* published in 1728, was the most widely used architectural book of the century; also wrote *Rules of Drawing for several Parts of Architecture* (1732). He belonged to no School and was once described as the delayed fulfilment of Wren. Friend of the Alexander family of painters, especially Cosmo(qv) to whom he bequeathed his furnished London home in Henrietta Street.
**Bibl:** Brydall 175-6; Allan Cunningham, Lives of the Most Eminent Painters, 1829-1833; Dunbar 82,89,93,103-4,111; John Summerson, Architecture in Britain 1530-1830, Penguin, 1953.

**GIBBS, Leonie** **1962-**
Born London 27 Oct. Sculptor and ceramic designer. Attended the Edinburgh College of Art Foundation Course 1980-82 and the Wimbledon School of Art 1982-84, since then has been working in ceramics. Commissioned to execute a life-size figure carved out of portland stone for *The Spectator* 1988. Major solo exhibition in London 1997. Elected FRSBS 1989. Many portrait commissions and generally large-scale work for gardens. Exhibits regularly, mainly in London, but also at the RSA in 1985, 1987 and 1989 from her home near Beauly, Inverness-shire.

**GIBROY, C** **fl 1881**
Painter, possibly Scottish. Represented in City of Edinburgh collection by 'Ye Auld Smithy, Roseburn', 1881.

**GIBSON, A S** **fl 1953-1957**
Ayrshire landscape painter; exhibited GI(2), from 36 Garnock St, Dalry.

**GIBSON, Alexander Roy** **fl 1912-1957**
Stirlingshire painter in oils but mainly watercolour of topographical and rural scenes, especially in Ayrshire and Fife; exhibited regularly RSA 1913-1944, RSW(1), GI(36), L(5) & AAS 1921-1935, latterly from 19 St Mirren's Road, Kilsyth.

**GIBSON, Bessie** **fl 1905-1926**
Miniature painter. Exhibited RA(14), RSA(1), RMS(2) & L(6), initially from Edinburgh but then from Paris whence she moved in 1906.

**GIBSON, Brenda** **fl 1959-1974**
Aberdeen watercolour painter of local landscapes and church interiors. Exhibited regularly AAS latterly from 50 Salisbury Terrace.

**GIBSON, Colin** **fl 1935-1948**
Angus painter in oil of portraits, landscapes and nudes. Lived for a time in Aberdeen and Arbroath before settling in Monifieth. Exhibited RA(1), RSA in 1935 and 1941-48 & AAS(5) from Adabank, 67 Princes Street, Monifieth.

**GIBSON, David** **fl 1828-1839**
Edinburgh miniaturist and engraver of mainly portraits. Exhibited RSA(21) from 8 St Andrew's Square during the above years.

**GIBSON, David Cooke** **1827-1856**
Born Edinburgh, 4 Mar. Painter in oil of portraits, literary and narrative subjects, occasional landscapes. Son of David G(qv) from whom he had his first art lessons. Studied at the RA Schools in London, then in Belgium and Paris. In 1840-41 living in Edinburgh having toured the continent in 1840. In 1852 he settled in London, visiting Spain 1856. Exhibited 19 works at the RSA between 1845 and 1854. The SNPG have his portrait of Sir Adam Ferguson and his wife.
**Bibl:** Bryan; W MacDuff, The Struggles of a Young Artist: Being a Memoir of David C Gibson, by a Brother Artist, 1858.

**GIBSON, David Livingstone** **fl 1869-1876**
Edinburgh painter in oil and watercolour of portraits, landscape, genre and buildings; exhibited RSA(17) & GI(1).

**GIBSON, George** **fl 1827-1854**
Edinburgh based portrait miniaturist. Lived for a time in Grangemouth. Exhibited 11 works, all of unnamed sitters, at the RSA in 1827, 1828 and then regularly between 1848 and 1854.

**GIBSON, George Selkirk** **fl 1899-1902**
Edinburgh figurative painter in oil; exhibited RSA(3) from 46 Polwarth Gardens.

**GIBSON, Helen** **fl 1988-**
Glasgow painter; exhibited RSA 1988 and 1989.

**GIBSON, James** **1948-**
Born Glasgow. Graduate of Edinburgh University. Taught English for several years while continuing to paint. First one-man show in Edinburgh 1978. His early work was largely graphic, later work shows an expressive use of paint and richness of texture. Mainly figurative subjects characterised by a 'feeling of loneliness, a sense of unease and vulnerability in a hostile world'. Exhibits RSA. Represented in Paisley AG.

**GIBSON, James Brown** **1880-c1961**
Born Glasgow, 26 Nov. Versatile artist; a painter in oils and watercolour; landscapes (mostly Highland), portraits and figure subjects; also etcher, lithographer and sculptor. Studied Glasgow School of Art. Lived at Milngavie and later at Killin, Perthshire. Executed many topographical works in London, France and Holland as well as in Scotland. Exhibited RSA(20), RSW(3), GI(53), AAS & L(3), after WW2 from his studio at Millmore, Killin.
**Bibl:** Halsby 260.

**GIBSON, John** **c1790-1854**
Edinburgh painter of genre who later moved to Newcastle-upon-Tyne; exhibited RSA(2).

**GIBSON, John D** **fl 1829-d1852**
Glasgow portrait painter. Exhibited mainly unidentified ladies and gentlemen at the RSA(11) but most often at the West of Scotland Academy, latterly from 54 West Nile Street. Died as the result of an accident. Represented in SNPG by a portrait of Kenneth McLeay.
**Bibl:** Bryan.

**GIBSON, Katharine Ballantyne Scott** **fl 1902**
Edinburgh based painter; exhibited a portrait at the RSA from 10 Belgrave Crescent.

**GIBSON, M** **fl 1879-1880**
Glasgow based still life and figurative painter. Exhibited GI(3) from 38 Burnbank Gardens.

**GIBSON, Miss Mary** **fl 1881-1888**
Flower painter in oil of still life, fruit and local landscape. Exhibited RSA(3), GI(4) & AAS from Rosebank, Doune, Perthshire.

**GIBSON, Mary Stewart** **fl 1930-1953**
Painter of rustic scenes and townscapes. Studied at Glasgow School of Art and in Paris. Exhibited GI(2), from 25 rue Jean Rolent, Paris.

**GIBSON, Miss Noel** **fl 1964**
Exhibited a Govan dockyard scene at the GI.

**GIBSON, Norman** **fl 1977-1986**
Abstract sculptor of 12 Jonquil Way, Carluke, exhibited RSA 1977-83 and 1986.

**GIBSON, Norman A M** **fl 1965-1974**
Aberdeen sculptor. Fascinated by rocks and stones. Exhibited AAS & GI(1) latterly from 58 Brackenhill Dr, Hamilton.

**GIBSON, Patrick RSA** **1782-1829**
Born and died Edinburgh. Landscape painter in oil and watercolour, etcher and author. Studied Trustees Academy and under Alexander Nasmyth. One of the members of the Society of Artists who exhibited in 1808; published in various periodicals some valuable notices on the history of art. Generally painted landscapes following the style of Poussin and Claude. In London 1805-9. Published a series of views of the Faroe Islands which he visited in the company of Sir George Mackenzie 1812. In 1817 he produced six etchings 'Select Views in Edinburgh'. Three of these - 'Regent Bridge and the New Jail from the West', 'Princes Street from Regent Bridge' and 'Edinburgh Castle from the Grassmarket' are of particular interest on account of the construction work in progress. Another attractive sketch was a 'View of Edinburgh' (from the Calton Hill) engraved and published in 1809. Helped to teach Geikie(qv). In 1816 wrote an interesting article in the *Edinburgh Annual Register* 'View of the Progress and Present State of the Arts of Design'. Art master, Dollar Academy 1824-1829. Together with Robert Gibb(qv) he was one of only two foundation members of the RSA who painted landscapes. Foundation Academician 1826. Exhibited RSA(56). Represented in NGS(16+ sketchbook), SNPG ('Self-portrait'), BM (volume of 26 Faroese views), Glasgow AG, City of Edinburgh collection (oil & 2 engravings).
**Bibl:** BM Cat of Drawings by Brit Artists, vol 2, 216; Bryan; Brydall 309; Bushnell; Butchart 42,54; DNB; Halsby 47-8; RSA (Obituary).

**GIBSON, R Mair** **fl 1908**
Aberdeen etcher. Exhibited AAS from 156 Hamilton Place.

**GIBSON, T Bowhill** **c1895-1949**
Edinburgh architect, partner in Gibson & Laing. Responsible for the County Cinema, Portobello (1938); St Anne's Hall (1928); Fairmile Inn (1938); Dominion Cinema (1937-8); Crewe Rd W in West Pilton and the County Cinema, Portobello (1938).
**Bibl:** Gifford 72,400,525,545,570,620,627,652.

**GIBSON, Thomas** **fl 1750-1754**
Architect. Known only as the architect in the Palladian style of Marchmont House, Berwickshire for the 3rd Earl of Marchmont (re-modelled by Robert Lorimer 1913-6 after its purchase in 1913 by Robert McEwan).
**Bibl:** Colvin; Dunbar 111; Peter Savage, Lorimer and the Edinburgh Craft Designers, Edinburgh 1980, 117,118,119,164.

**GIBSON, Thomas** **fl 1871-1886**
Portobello landscape painter in oil. Specialised in Latin American subjects. In 1886 showed 'Sheep and Cattle Station on the Plains of Buenos Aires'. Exhibited RSA(2).

**GIBSON, William** **fl 1830**
Edinburgh landscape painter of 56 Abbey Mount. Exhibited RSA(1).

**GIBSON, William** **fl 1862**
Edinburgh painter of landscapes of Whitefield Place, Leith Walk; exhibited RSA(2).

**GIBSON, William** **fl 1925**
Glasgow painter, exhibited GI(1).

**GIBSON, William Alfred** **1866-1931**
Born Glasgow, 19 Sep; died Glasgow, 6 Jan. Landscape painter in oil and watercolour. Educated at the Normal School and Glasgow University. Apart from a short spell of tutelage under a student of Corot's, he was self-taught. As a youth he made a careful study of many great paintings especially those in Glasgow AG. Entered his father's business but abandoned this shortly afterwards in order to paint full-time. In his unaided study Gibson revealed an affinity for the work of the great Dutch painters and for the Barbizon School, particularly Corot. Served in the Boer War with the 6th Battalion Scottish Imperial Yeomanry. His first exhibits were an oil and a watercolour at the GI in 1888. Throughout his life he was a keen member of the Glasgow Art Club. His paintings were characterised by great technical skill and subtle use of colour harmonies. His continental scenes were presented with sensitive and intimate charm incorporating delightful woodland landscapes and quiet waterways rich in poetic appeal. Also painted in France and England being particularly fond of Herefordshire and Gloucestershire, especially the Forest of Dean; in later life the landscape of Suffolk also inspired him. In 1902 was associated with the Glasgow artist and physician Alexander Frew(qv) in establishing the short-lived breakaway group Glasgow Society of Artists(qv). At their first exhibition most of the works were by him, Frew and Bessie MacNicol(qv). In the last two or three years of his life he painted increasingly on the west coast of Scotland, usually in Morar. He found expression mainly in low-toned harmonies ranging through grays, greens, silver whites and cool browns and although preserving these characteristics, in his later years he painted in a higher key. Warm-hearted and frank, he had great charm, being popular among a wide circle of friends. Exhibited

RA(3), RSA, GI(106), AAS 1906-1929 & L(27). Represented in Aberdeen AG, Glasgow AG, Greenock AG, Paisley AG, Hull AG, Bradford AG, Oldham AG.
**Bibl:** Caw 407; Halsby 260.

**GIERASIK, Susan** **1960-**
Born 4 Feb. Works in oil, gouache, collage, silk screen printing and etching. Trained Edinburgh College of Art 1984-88, receiving a postgraduate diploma 1988-89. In 1989 received an Indian National Trust Award for art and cultural heritage enabling her to spend a year at the University of Baroda. Greatly influenced by Indian miniature painting, Indian religion and mythology and holistic healing. Exhibits regularly at the RSA, SSA, SSWA & at the 1st International Art College Bienniale, Antwerp 1989, from 12 St Mary's Street, Edinburgh.

**GIFFORD, James G** **fl 1893-1894**
Amateur Aberdeen artist, fond of atmospheric effect. Exhibited AAS(2) from 265 Union Street.

**GIFFORD, M** **fl 1926**
Exhibited 'Moorish Castle' at the GI, from 9 Main St, Wishaw.

**GILBERT, David** **1928-**
Born Uxbridge. Sculptor. Resident on Arran since 1959. Studied English Literature, Cambridge Univ 1949-52 before art training at Penzance School of Art 1952-53. Travelled widely across France, Italy and Sweden before settling briefly in London 1954. Preferred material is wood with frequent use of Celtic imagery.

**GILBERT, George M** **fl 1936-1964**
Glasgow painter in oil, watercolour and chalk; topographical scenes and figure studies. Attracted to the areas around Stonehaven, Paisley and Glasgow. Exhibited RSA regularly, RSW(5), GI(13) & AAS, from 21 Cromwell Street before moving to England, finally settling at 74 Wyatt Rd, Sutton Coldfield, Warwicks.

**GILBERT, George Ronald RSW** **1939-**
Fife painter in watercolour, acrylic, pen and wash of local scenes especially East Neuk harbours, figure studies, interiors and still life. Graduated Glasgow School of Art 1961, postgraduate course 1961-62. Many one-man shows. Elected RSW 1973 and Council member, RSW 1994. Awards include Artstore prize (Paisley Art Institute) 1992, Sir W G Gillies award (RSW) 1993. Lived for a time in Glasgow and St Andrews and from 1988 at St Monans, Fife. Exhibited regularly at the RSA since 1966 & GI(15), in 1964 from Coull Schoolhouse, Aboyne but latterly from 44 Marketgate South, Crail, Fife. Represented in collection of Nuffield Foundation.

**GILBERT, Jeannie G** **fl 1894-1896**
Edinburgh painter in watercolour of flowers and local topography. Exhibited 'Bass Rock from Point Garry' at the RSA in 1896 & AAS 1894-1896, from 16 Glengyle Terrace, Edinburgh. Represented in Edinburgh City collection by 5 watercolour drawings of Old Edinburgh.

**GILBERT, John** **fl 1963-1965**
Dunfermline painter of still life and Scottish scenes. Exhibited RSA(7) & GI(2) from 52 Appin Crescent.

**GILBERT, Norman** **fl 1952-1960**
Glasgow-based topographical and landscape painter. Exhibited twice at the GI including 'Troon Golf Course' (1952), latterly from 16 Kenmore St.

**GILBERT, Stephen** **1910-**
Born Wormit, Fife, 15 Jan. Painter of abstract subjects, also sculptor and architectural designer. Educated University College School, London. Grandson of the sculptor Sir Alfred Gilbert. Studied Slade School 1929-32, concentrating first on architecture but turning to painting on the advice of Tonks. Exhibited from 1933 and at the RA from 1936, holding his first one man show in London 1938. At the end of that year he went to Paris, settling there permanently. Represented in Tate AG, Leicester AG, Sheffield AG, Alborg AG, Stedelijk AG (Holland).
**Bibl:** Chevalier, The Dictionnaire de la Sculpture Moderne; Read, A Concise History of Modern Sculpture; Seuphor, La Sculpture de cet Siècle.

**GILCHRIST, J D** **fl 1937**
Glasgow painter of genre. Exhibited GI(2) from 82 Ardshiel Road.

**GILCHRIST, Miss Martha M** **fl 1931-1934**
Glasgow painter and etcher of narrative subjects and genre. Exhibited RSA(3), GI(2) & AAS(1) from 8 Herries Road, Maxwell Park.

**GILCHRIST, Mary Smith** **fl 1883-1885**
Amateur Lanarkshire painter in oil and watercolour; flowers and landscape. Wife of the minister at Shotts. Exhibited RSA(3).

**GILCHRIST, Miss R R** **fl 1919**
Edinburgh artist who exhibited a work 'Withered and grim' at the RSA from 86 Inverleith Place, Edinburgh.

**GILDARD, Robert J** **fl 1899-1900**
Glasgow painter of townscapes and buildings; exhibited GI(2), from 23 Marchmont Crescent.

**GILDARD, Thomas** **1822-1895**
Glasgow architect. Probably father of Robert G(qv). Trained under the Hamiltons(qv) 1838-1843. Most of his working life was spent as assistant to John Carrick(qv). A literary bent led to his handling the Dean of Guild Court affairs and acting as correspondent for leading building journals. Later he wrote memoirs and biographies of Carrick(qv) and Alexander Thomson(qv), now in the Mitchell Library. Responsible for Britannia Music Hall, 115 Trongate, Glasgow.
**Bibl:** A Gomme & D Walker, Architecture in Glasgow, London 1987(rev), 291-2.

**GILDAWIE, James** **fl 1846-1856**
Minor portrait painter of 10 St Andrews Square, Edinburgh; exhibited 7 works at the RSA during the above years, also 'A Troubadour' at the RA 1836 when living in London. Probably father of James G(qv).

**GILDAVIE, James** **fl 1877-1880**
Edinburgh landscape portrait and figure painter in oil; exhibited RSA(4) from 31 Broughton Street. Probably son of James G(qv).

**GILES, James RSA** **1801-1870**
Born Woodside, Aberdeen, 4 Jan; died Aberdeen, 6 Oct. Painter of Scottish and continental landscape, sporting subjects and portraits. Son of a textile designer. At the age of 13 was painting miniature human and animal figures on snuff boxes. In 1820 he was teaching public drawing classes in Aberdeen. His first known sketch from nature, 'St Machar's Cathedral', dates from this time and was later lithographed and published. He combined teaching with a study of anatomy spending the summers sketching in the central and western highlands. In 1823, having married Clementina Farquharson, he received his first regular training in art, initially in London and then, in 1824, in Paris, where he studied under Regnault. Then travelled to Marseilles and on to Italy, visiting Genoa, Florence, Sienna and Rome. In 1825 was in Naples and Salerno before returning home via the Italian lakes, Switzerland and the Rhine. During the tour he completed over 1,000 watercolour sketches as well as 40 copies of famous works. A selection of these was shown at the Ashmolean Museum 1970. These early works express an original talent never quite recaptured. "A sensitivity to atmosphere and to effects of sun and cloud and storm, and the power of rendering his impressions freely and directly, that remind one inevitably of Turner at his best and boldest...his sky studies are strikingly original and his range of colours, in which blues and browns predominate, shows to special effect in his views of Aricceia and of the slope of Clitumnis reflected in the river" [Sparrow]. In 1826 Giles returned to Aberdeen, becoming increasingly known to a wide range of local lairds, many of them introduced by his friend Hugh Irvine of Drum. At about this time he became interested in landscape gardening. In 1830 he advised the 4th Earl of Aberdeen regarding the policies at Haddo House, also helped the Earl of Kintore. In 1827 he and Archibald Simpson(qv) founded the Aberdeen Artists Society(qv). In 1829 he became one of the 24 original full members of the RSA, exhibiting 304 paintings

there during his lifetime. In 1852 he was invited to submit perspective drawings for the new Balmoral Castle. Many Royal commissions followed, including landscaping at Balmoral. It is said that Giles twice declined a knighthood. All five children of his first marriage predeceased him and Clementine died 1866. His second wife was the daughter of the owner of Bridgeford Inn where he often fished, and they had two children. His reputation rests mainly on his paintings of deer and the landscape of upper Deeside, especially stalking scenes around Braemar, being himself an excellent stalker. The Earl of Aberdeen commissioned 85 drawings subsequently published in 1936 as *Drawings of Aberdeenshire Castles.* Among his many designs were the sculpture group 'Demeter' that now adorns the roof of the Clydesdale Bank in Castle Street, Aberdeen, damask table linen for Queen Victoria, and the deer park at Haddo House. He had an intense interest in history and was a founder member of the Spalding Club, Chairman of the Gas Light Company, and a keen churchman. At one period in his life became a close friend of Landseer whom he accompanied on a number of sketching trips. Sometimes given a second Christian name 'William' but this is incorrect; it is unclear whether or not the lithographer John West Giles was related. Painted many portraits including at least five self-portraits. Exhibited RA(2), RSA(329), GI(10) & AAS(2), from 62 Bon Accord St. Represented in NGS(2), BM, Aberdeen AG, Castle Fraser (NTS), Haddo House (NTS), Melbourne AG (Australia). [From notes provided by Mary B Herdman]
**Bibl:** AJ 1870, 343; Brydall 407-8; Caw 146,198; DNB XXI 1890; Halsby 73-5 et al; Irwin 312-314 et al; McKay 318.

**GILES, Peter** **?-1815**
Aberdeen painter in oil. In addition to his painting he worked as a pattern-designer with Gordon Barron and Co of Woodside, Aberdeen. Father of James G(qv). Married Jean Hector, who was related to the Bruces of Kennethmont. A contemporary described his work as having 'originality, taste and dispatch'. Taught drawing and painting at various Aberdeen schools and at one time opened his own studio at 1 John Street, Aberdeen. Started the practice of hiring out his pictures. He was a painstaking draughtsman, executing meticulous, colourful work, now seldom seen.

**GILES, Ursula** **fl 1952-1953**
Renfrewshire landscape painter in watercolour. Exhibited GI(2), from Cascaes, Bridge of Weir.

**GILES, William Gordon** **fl 1843-1844**
Aberdeen painter of portraits and Scottish landscapes. Son of James G(qv). An artist of great promise who tragically died when only 19. Exhibited RSA(5) from his parents' home 60, Bon Accord St.

**GILFEDDER, Michael Felix** **fl 1973**
Exhibited "The Tower' at the GI, from 88 Leslie St, Glasgow.

**GILFILLAN, Alexander** **fl 1951-1976**
Perth based painter in oil and sometimes watercolour of genre, still life; also stained glass designer and works in linocuts. Moved from Musselburgh 1951. Committee member of the Perth Art Association 1953-56. Exhibited RSA(2), GI(5) & PAA 1952-1958, from 1 Wilmot Rd, Glasgow.

**GILFILLAN, Arthur** **fl 1893-1938**
Glasgow landscape painter in oil and watercolour. Exhibited RSA(1), RSW(4), GI(5) & AAS, from Westerton.

**GILFILLAN, James R** **fl 1928**
Ayrshire watercolour painter of still life; exhibited GI(1) from Drumhart, Eglinton Street, Saltcoats.

**GILFILLAN, John Alexander** **1793-1863**
Born Jersey; died Australia. Painter in oil and watercolour of landscape, marines and townscapes. Studied at Edinburgh becoming an art master at the Andersonian University, Glasgow, for 15 years. Migrated to New Zealand in 1841, settling with his family in the Wanganui district. An able draughtsman, he was sympathetic towards Maori people and interested in achieving improvements in their life. His painting 'Interior of a Native Village or Pa in New Zealand', of which only a lithographic reproduction is now known, exemplifies this interest. Ironically, his wife and four children were all killed by the Maoris, causing him to seek a sad refuge in Australia. Before turning to art as a career he had served in the Navy and shortly after qualifying in Edinburgh concentrated mainly on marine subjects, sometimes on the grand scale and with fine detail and vitality. Also painted Glasgow scenes in watercolour in a cool style with silvery colours in ivory tones, handled with precision. His work is now scarce but greatly sought after both for its intrinsic quality and its historic interest. Exhibited RSA(5) 1829-1837 & once at the GI - 'New Zealanders Bartering with Settlers' (1862). Represented in V & A, SNPG (a portrait of 'Jean, wife of Robert Burns'), Glasgow AG.
**Bibl:** Brown & Keith, Painters of New Zealand, 1969, 17; Brydall 310; Halsby 260.

**GILFILLAN, Tom** **fl 1932-1953**
Glasgow based painter in oil, watercolour and tempera of landscape, portraits and figures. His golfing and racing scenes, including The Derby winner 'Pinza, with Sir Gordon Richards up' (1953), received some popularity. Exhibited rather pedestrian landscapes, in the style of Tom Campbell(qv), at the RSA(1) & GI(16), from 1 Carrick Ave, Ayr.
**Bibl:** Wingfield.

**GILKIE, Alexander** **fl 1791-1795**
Master builder and architect of Coldstream, Berwickshire. Carried out considerable works at Ford Castle, Northumberland for Lord Delaval during the above years. The great gateway, lodges and towers, among other buildings, were remodelled by him. One Nesbit, an architect of Kelso, afterwards of Edinburgh, made many of the drawings for Gilkie, and William Smeaton(qv) did the carving. Gilkie was recommended by Lord Delaval to Lord Strathmore for the re-building of Gibside. Among the drawings for Blackadder House, Berwickshire in the RIBA library are some marked 'by Messrs Gilkie and Waddle, including a Design of a Bridge for Mr Boswell over Blackadder Water' ascribed to 'A Gilkey'. [After Colvin.]
**Bibl:** Colvin; Proc Soc Antiquaries of Newcastle-on-Tyne, v 1891-2, 63.

**GILL, Alexander** **fl 1896-1900**
Aberdeen landscape artist. Probably father of Alexander G jnr(qv). Exhibited AAS from 74 Desswood Place.

**GILL, Alexander jnr** **fl 1919-1937**
Aberdeen painter of local scenes, especially Deeside. Probably son of Alexander G(qv). Exhibited AAS from 37 Argyll Place.

**GILL, Florence H** **fl 1912**
Milngavie watercourist of genre. Exhibited GI(1), from 3 Moor Rd.

**GILL, J D** **fl 1961-1967**
Aberdeenshire artist of figurative works. Exhibited AAS(5) from Elmbank, Primrosehill Road, Cults.

**GILL, Miss Janet M** **fl 1926-1927**
Aberdeen based artist. Exhibited L(6) from 141 Duthie Terrace.

**GILL, Margery Jean** **1925-**
Born Coatbridge, Apr 5. Etcher, engraver & illustrator. Trained Harrow School of Art and Royal College of Art 1945-48. Married 1946 while still a student. After a short period teaching at Maidstone College of Art 1955, wishing to remain at home with her children, she began illustrating children's books, becoming increasingly in demand. Illustrated Stevenson: *A Child's Garden of Verses* (1946), Pertwee: *Islanders* (1950), Tarn: *Treasure of the Isle of Mist* (1950), Pertwee: *Rough Water* (1951), Green: *Mystery at Mycenae* (1957), Guillot: *The Blue Day* (1958), Hamilton: *The Heavenly Carthorse* (1958), Streatfield: *Bertram* (1959), Kornitzer: *Mr Fairweather and His Friends* (1960), Burnett: *A Little Princess* (1961), Streatfield: *Apple Bough* (1962), Arthur: *Dragon Summer* (1962), Bingley: *The Story of a Tit-Be and his Friend* (1962), Lang: *Fifty Favourite Fairy Tales* (1963), Craig: *What Did You Dream?* (1964), Mayne: *Sand* (1964), *A Day Without Wind* (1964), Beresford: *The Hidden Mill* (1965), Boston: *The Castle of Yew* (1965), Barrett: *Midway* (1967), Cockette: *Twelve Gold Chairs* (1967), *The Wild Place* (1968), Rossetti: *Doves and Pomegranates* (1969), Arthur: *The Autumn Ghosts* (1973), *Candlemas Mystery* (1974), Mahy: *The Bus under the Leaves* (1974), Streatfield: *When the Siren Wailed* (1974), Cresswell:

*The Butterfly Chase* (1975), Cookson: *Mrs Flanagan's Trumpet* (1976), Crompton: *The House Where Jack Lives* (1978), Denton: *Catch* (1980), *Short Cut* (1980), Chapman: *Suzy* (1982), Thwaite: *Pennies for the Dog* (1985).
**Bibl:** Horne 218; Mahoney; Ryder; Peppin.

**GILL, Michael P** **fl 1961-1967**
Painter of figurative subjects. Moved from Aberdeen to Byways, Boorhill, Fife c1967. Exhibited Dutch landscapes at the AAS.

**GILL, W S** **fl 1902-1908**
Aberdeenshire painter in oil, watercolour and pastel, also mezzotinter. Exhibited AAS(3), latterly from Dalhebity, Bieldside.

**GILLAN, Alexander** **fl 1976**
East Kilbride painter of still life. Exhibited GI(2), from 80 Geddes Hill.

**GILLAN, Mrs Christine** **fl 1965**
East Kilbride etcher. Exhibited GI(2), from 29 Manitoba Crescent, Westwood.

**GILLAN, J R** **fl 1926**
Amateur Aberdeen artist. Exhibited 'Lac Leman' at the AAS from 335 Holburn Street.

**GILLAN, Mrs Margaret Dalrymple** **fl 1946-1948**
Glasgow based sculptress of portrait busts; exhibited RSA(3) & GI(2) from 357 Netherton Road.

**GILLANDERS, Mrs J B** **fl 1886-1893**
Aberdeen painter of flowers and church interiors. Exhibited 'Christmas roses' at the RSA in 1891 and a number of works at the AAS between the above years, latterly from 17 King's Crescent.

**GILLESPIE, Allan C** **fl 1954-1971**
Edinburgh painter in oil and watercolour of still life, genre and topographical subjects, mainly of Edinburgh and the Lothians. Exhibited regularly during the above years at the RSA & GI(8), since 1965 from 87 Balgreen Rd.

**GILLESPIE, Alexander Bryson** **fl 1898-1942**
Edinburgh painter in oil, watercolour and pastel, also engraver and etcher; landscape, especially mountain scenes and zoo animals including exotic birds. Fascinated by the wynds and old streets of Edinburgh and by many of the animals in the zoological gardens. Brother of Janetta(qv) and Floris G(qv). An exhibition of his work, jointly with his two sisters, was held in Edinburgh 1892. The later part of his life was spent in Strathyre. Two of his best known works are 'Morning Mist on Goat Fell, Arran' (1898) and 'Stuc-a-Cron - After Rain' (1899). Exhibited RSA(45) 1906-1942, RSW(17), GI(13), AAS & L(2), from Kilkerran, Strathyre, Stirlingshire.
**Bibl:** Halsby 260.

**GILLESPIE, Alexander L** **fl 1888-1899**
Edinburgh based painter in oil and watercolour. Exhibited RSA(3) & RSW(2) from 10 Walker Street.

**GILLESPIE, Dugald Hyndman** **fl 1936-1945**
Airdrie sculptor mainly portrait busts in plaster. Lived at 4 McAlister Avenue, Airdrie and latterly at 54 Shandwick Place, Edinburgh. Exhibited 6 portrait busts at the RSA during the above years & GI(9).

**GILLESPIE, Miss Floris Mary** **1882-1967**
Born Bonnybridge, Stirlingshire; died Edinburgh. Competent painter in oil and watercolour mainly of flowers, also still life and occasional landscape. Sister of Janetta(qv) and Alexander G(qv). Studied Glasgow School of Art. Lived for many years at Bonnybridge after a spell teaching at Stranraer High School. Exhibited RSA(13), RSW(14), GI(30) & L(3), from 1939 at Rosarnach, Bonnybridge, Stirlingshire.
**Bibl:** Halsby 260.

**GILLESPIE, H L** **fl 1895**
Edinburgh based flower painter; exhibited 'Daffodils' at the RSA from 4 Oxford Street.

**GILLESPIE, J** **fl 1829-1830**
Edinburgh landscape painter; exhibited RSA(3) from 10 Abbeyhill.

**GILLESPIE, J H** **fl 1790-1820**
Minor itinerant profilist. Worked in London, Liverpool and Edinburgh before migrating to Nova Scotia 1820. Painted on paper or card, often bust portraits with colour. His profiles were generally painted direct although sometimes the portraits were cut first and over-painted later. Bronzing when used he applied lightly.
**Bibl:** Arthur Mayne, British Profile Miniaturists, London 1970, 112.

**GILLESPIE, James** **fl 1903-1904**
Designer of exteriors and garden landscapes. Exhibited a sketch design for a formal garden and one other at the RSA from 6 Bruntsfield Gardens, Edinburgh.

**GILLESPIE, Miss Janetta Susan RSW** **1876-1956**
Born Bonnybridge, Stirlingshire. Painter in oil and watercolour, mainly of flowers, still life and sometimes landscape. A member of a highly talented family, both her sister Floris(qv) and her brother Alexander G(qv) were artists. The most talented member of the family. Trained at Glasgow School of Art. After graduating she taught for a time at Bonnybridge School, before concentrating on painting full-time. An attractive still life of flowers and fruit, 'Moon Pennies', received very favourable attention at the RSW 1952. Won the Lauder prize. An outstanding lady painter of her time, as a person she was unassuming and appealing, but in her work bold, vigorous and dashing with a highly developed sense of handling chiaroscuro. Elected RSW 1943. Exhibited RSA(27), RSW(20), GI(41), AAS(2) & L(2) mostly from Rosarnach, Bonnybridge, Stirlingshire.
**Bibl:** Halsby 260.

**GILLESPIE. Joan** **1954-**
Born Dundee, Apr 4. Painter. Trained Duncan of Jordanstone College of Art, Dundee 1972-75 followed by a year at Edinburgh College of Art. Exhibits widely in Scotland and France, RSA since 1993 from Roseneath Terrace, Edinburgh. Represented in City of Edinburgh AG.

**GILLESPIE, Kathleen** **fl 1935**
Amateur Aberdeen watercolour painter of country scenes. Exhibited AAS(1) from 44 Carden Place.

**GILLESPIE Mrs L** **fl 1881-1882**
Dumfries landscape painter. Exhibited GI(2) from Netherlea.

**GILLESPIE, Lex Bryson** **fl 1902-1935**
Edinburgh painter of country scenes. Exhibited many times at the AAS during the above years from 58 Mayfield Road.

**GILLESPIE, Rhona** **fl 1981**
Dumbarton painter and printmaker. Exhibited GI(1), from 45 Campbell Ave.

**GILLESPIE, Stirling** **fl 1947-1988**
Bute-based painter in oil and watercolour. Landscapes, especially the mountains and coasts of NW Scotland. Exhibited GI(66), since 1957 from Torwood, 21 Crichton Rd, Rothesay, Bute.

**GILLESPIE, Tony** **fl 1974-1977**
Edinburgh sculptor of figure studies. Exhibited AAS 1974 when living in Dundee and 2 works in bronze and aluminium resin RSA, the latter from 27 Guthrie Street.

**GILLIES, Herbert** **fl 1945-1954**
Edinburgh painter of genre, flowers, portraits and landscapes; exhibited RSA during the above years & GI(4), from 4 Ainslie Place.

**GILLIES, Margaret ARSW** **1803-1887**
Born London, 7 Aug; died Hampstead, London, Jly. Genre and miniature painter, usually in watercolour. Daughter of a Scottish merchant who settled in London. When still young she was orphaned and brought up in Edinburgh by her uncle Lord Gillies, a Scottish judge. Mixing in Edinburgh with many notables of the day, she resolved to make her own way in the world and went to Paris where she met the Scheffers, an influential Parisian family, under whose

auspices she pursued her studies. Returned to London 1823, studying under Frederick Cruickshank. Painted miniatures and watercolours of single figures often Scottish, in landscape settings. Her figures are often sentimental, like those of Robert Herdman(qv), showing the influence of the pre-Raphaelites. Went to London and later Hampshire but continued to visit Scotland frequently. She knew Sir Walter Scott and her sitters included 'Dickens', 'Leigh Hunt' (now in the NPG), and 'Wordsworth' (1839). She stayed with the Wordsworths for several weeks and painted a number of miniature portraits of their family. Employed a lot of gum arabic in her miniatures with a tendency to idealise her sitters. Her last years were spent at 25 Church Row, Hampstead, London. Elected ARSW 1852, the first woman to achieve the honour. Exhibited RSA(14) 1834-1852, RSW(7), GI(8) & L(1), from 25 Church Row, London. Represented in BM, V & A.
**Bibl:** Bryan; Brydall 247-8; Halsby 260.

**GILLIES, Miss Marie** **fl 1945**
Renfrewshire wood engraver; exhibited GI(2), from Woodside, Busby.

**GILLIES, Robert** **fl 1983-1984**
Edinburgh amateur still life painter. Exhibited GI(2), from 73 E. Claremont St.

**GILLIES, William George** **fl 1890-1924**
Glasgow painter in oil of portraits (usually young ladies), genre and occasional landscape. Exhibited 'Her love was one a-sailing' at the RSA and 28 works at the GI, all between the above years from 58 W. Regent St.

**GILLIES, Sir William George CBE LLD RSA PPRSW RA** **1898-1973**
Born Haddington, East Lothian, 21 Sep; died Temple, 15 Apr. Studied Edinburgh College of Art for two terms in 1916 before being called up for war service. Resumed studies in 1919, winning a scholarship enabling him to visit Italy and France. Founder member of the 1922 Group, young artists who exhibited together in Edinburgh for the following six years. In 1924 went to Paris with William Geissler(qv) and studied under André Lhôte. Taught art for a year at Inverness Academy, then joined the staff of Edinburgh College of Art where he remained for the next 40 years, becoming Head of Painting 1946 and Principal 1960. In 1925 he adopted a cubist idiom but gradually turned more to naturalistic treatment in his paintings of still life and Scottish landscapes. The Munich Exhibition of 1931 provoked him to the use of Expressionist brush work and colour, and toward the end of the 1930s the more controlled styles of Bonnard and Braque became apparent. In 1939 he moved to the village of Temple where the surrounding landscape furnished the principal motifs of his post-war work. A tireless man, estimated to have completed well over 2,000 works, he was one of the dominant influences in Scottish twentieth century art. Recognised as a leading Scottish watercolourists of his time. His work is characterised by solid draughtsmanship combined with fluent technique and he was not averse to sometimes appear almost primitive in his treatment of objects in landscapes. Elected ARSA 1940, RSA 1947, President, RSW 1963, CBE 1957, knighted 1970. Exhibited frequently RSA & GI(31), from Temple Cottage, Temple, by Gorebridge, Midlothian. Represented in SNPG ('Self-portrait'), SNGMA, Aberdeen AG, Dundee AG, Glasgow AG, Greenock AG, Kirkcaldy AG, Paisley AG, City of Edinburgh collection, Brodie Castle (NTS), Kellie Castle (NTS), SAC.
**Bibl:** T. Elder Dickson, W G Gillies 1974; Gage 27 et al; Halsby 211-3 et passim; Hardie 142 et passim ch ix,x & xi; Hartley 134-5; Macmillan [SA], 316,348,352,358,362-5 et passim in ch xx & xxi; Rothenstein 172; SAC, 'William Gillies and the Scottish Landscape', (Ex Cat 1980); SAC, 'W.G.Gillies; a Retrospective Exhibition', (Ex Cat, 1970); Alastair Smart, 'The Art of W G Gillies', Scottish Art Review, 1955, vol 5; W Gordon Smith, Sir William Gillies, Atelier, 1991.

**GILLILAND, Donald** **fl 1963-1964**
Angus sculptor, specialising in equestrian studies and groups; exhibited RSA(3) from 291 Hawkhill, Dundee.

**GILLIVERY, J P M** **fl 1883**
Painter of figure studies in oil; exhibited RSA(1) from 112 Bath Street, Glasgow.

**GILLON, William** **1942-**
Born Edinburgh. Painter of figurative subjects, interiors and semi-abstracts; usually oil on wood but sometime uses other media. Began to enjoy drawing at an early age and was encouraged by Ricky Demarco(qv) who persuaded him to enrol at the Edinburgh College of Art 1960-5, followed by a spell in France and Spain on the proceeds of a travelling scholarship. First one-man exhibition in Edinburgh 1970. 'In devastated landscapes, arbitrarily ritualised traps, and rigid dream-like mazes, people seem trapped and unable to express their humanity because of the unbearable social and emotional pressure on them...with his psychologically intense control and restrictive use of colour Gillon forces us to recognise the most unpleasant facts of what man does to man'.[Bold.]
**Bibl:** SAC, Edinburgh 'Scottish Realism' (Ex Cat 1971, Text by Alan Bold).

**GILLON-FERGUSSON, James** **1967-**
Born 1 Feb. Abstract works in oil. Trained Duncan of Jordanstone College of Art, 1985-9 where he obtained an upper 2nd class honours and continued with a postgraduate diploma course for which he was highly commended. In 1990 he visited Florence on a scholarship and the same year received the Betty Davis Award from the Society of Artists. Lives and works at 11 Cleghorn Street, Dundee. Exhibited RSA 1990 & SSA 1989.

**GILLRAY, James** **1757-1815**
Born Chelsea, London; died London, 1 Jne. Political caricaturist and occasional watercolourist. Son of a native of Culter, nr Biggar who joined the army and eventually became a Chelsea pensioner. Apprenticed to a letter engraver but ran away to join a company of strolling players before entering the RA Schools where he studied engraving under W W Ryland and Bartolozzi. The father of the political cartoon, too preoccupied with the English establishment to give more than scant attention to his Scottish roots. His political works date from 1780, the majority being published by Miss Humphrey with whom he lived at 29 St James's Street, Picadilly. His work was done mainly with pencil, pen and etching needle. 'The Very Slippy Weather' (1808) caricatures, now in the BM, filled each square of a bow window. Hardie points out that this was at a time when rival print shops advertised permanent exhibitions of 'the largest collection of caricatures in the world, entrance 1s' and when portfolios of political and personal satires, hot from the printing press, were hired out for the evening. Although much of his work was done before 1800 a group of splendid caricatures appeared later including 'Tiddy-Doll, the great French-Gingerbread Baker', 1806; 'Uncorking Old Sherry' 1805, 'The Plum-pudding in danger' in 1805 and most famous of all 'The King of Brobdingnag and Gulliver', drawn in 1803. His last work was engraved in 1811 shortly before he became insane. His watercolours are rare, most of his work being drawn directly on to plates. Some of his more serious figure drawings, especially those made for a series of military subjects painted in conjunction with P J de Loutherbourg, have often been attributed to the latter. Represented in BM, V & A, Ashmolean Museum, Glasgow AG, New York Public Library. Buried at St James's Church, Piccadilly.
**Bibl:** Country Life, Dec 5, 1952; Jan 12, 1967; D Hill, Fashionable Contrasts: Caricatures by JG (1966); D Hill, Mr G The Caricaturist (1965); Houfe; Ralph Nevill, 'James Gillray', Conn; Rhoda Spence, 'The Scot who made Europe laugh', Scotland's Mag, Dec 1957; T Wright, The Caricatures of JG (1851); T Wright, The Works of JG (1873).

**GILMER, John R** **fl 1875-1879**
Glasgow sculptor. Portrait busts and reliefs. Exhibited GI(4), latterly from 89 Bothwell St.

**GILMORE, Avril J D** **fl 1957-1983**
East Lothian painter in oil and pastel; portraits, still life, and landscapes generally in the Lothians; exhibited RSA regularly 1959-1966 and 1977-79, also GI(10), from Rose Cottage, Garvald, Haddington.

**GILMOUR, James** **c1867-1937**
Glasgow watercolour artist who painted landscape in a fresh rather loose style with strong redolent colour. Exhibited 'The Boats are In! - Eyemouth' at the RSA in 1935, also RSW(3), GI(7) & L(5), latterly from Crossmyloof, nr Glasgow. Represented in Glasgow AG.
**Bibl:** Halsby 260.

**GILMOUR, John** **fl 1908-1909**
Glasgow landscape painter; exhibited GI(2), from 81 Minard Rd.

**GILMOUR, Margaret** **1860-1942**
Born Glasgow. Painter in oil and watercolour; also metalwork designer. Studied at Glasgow School of Art. Established her own studio at 179 West George Street with her sister Mary(qv) c1893, a business that continued for about 50 years. The Gilmour Studio, as it was known, 'attracted a wide variety of craft students, beginners and experienced alike, from the surrounding neighbourhood, who wished to make useful and beautiful objects for their homes. The studio taught a range of crafts including metalwork in brass and pewter, embroidery, leatherwork, ceramic decoration, wood carving, wood staining and painting. Although successful and well known in the city, the Gilmours never promoted themselves beyond Glasgow' [Burkhauser]. Their characteristic design style included gem-like white and coloured enamel. Their exhibition of beaten brass and copy work was included in the 1901 Glasgow International Exhibition. Exhibited RSA(1) 1889 & GI(11) from her home at 4 Queensferry Terrace, Langside, and after 1900 from 179 W. George St. Represented in Glasgow AG.
**Bibl:** Burkhauser 165-6.

**GILMOUR, Mary Ann Belle** **1872-1938**
Glasgow based watercolour and monochrome artist; flowers and figurative works. Sister of Margaret Gilmour(qv). The younger sister, she concentrated more on production work than on design while the third sister Agnes kept the accounts. Exhibited RSW(1) & GI(3) from 8 Ailsa Drive, Langside. Represented in Glasgow AG.

**GILMOUR, Lady Montrave** **fl 1899**
Amateur Fife artist. Exhibited 3 works at the SWA from Leven.

**GILMOUR, Stuart** **fl 1988-**
Dundee based artist. Exhibited 'The magical snapdragon' at the RSA from 138 Seagate, Magnum House.

**GIRLING, Fred J** **fl 1954**
Glasgow watercolour painter of topographical subjects. Exhibited GI(2), from 24 Mansionhouse Rd, Langside.

**GIRVAN, Geraldine (Gerry)** **1947-**
Born Derby, Mar. Studied at Edinburgh University 1965-70, graduating with a fine arts degree before embarking on postgraduate studies at Edinburgh College of Art 1970-1 where she was influenced most strongly by Elizabeth Blackadder(qv), William Geddes(qv) and Robin Philipson(qv), and Moray House College of Education 1971-72. Since 1984 has painted full-time, mainly in watercolour although since 2000 has painted increasingly in oils. Her first solo exhibition was in 1988 followed by others in London and elsewhere in subsequent years. Her work has been published by Athena, the Cannsdown Press, the Robertson collection and Devon Editions, USA and is illustrated in *The Encyclopaedia of Watercolour Techniques.* Having lived in Scotland since her student days she has been much influenced by the Scottish School, enjoying direct observation with spirited paint handling and a traditional love of vibrant colour linking her work to the major French painters of the 20th century. Works in gouache and oil and delights in the use of strong colour and subjects with a strong patterned element such as still life and interiors. Has written and contributed illustrations for various publications including 'The Encyclopaedia of Watercolour Techniques', Quarto 1991; 'The Art of Drawing and Painting', Eaglemoss 1999. Her "paintings come out of enjoyment, and are clearly meant to give immediate enjoyment to other people...she would clearly subscribe to the views of Matisse on the life-enhancing qualities of colour and the legitimacy of sheer sensuous delight in painting, but Matisse was more complex than he appeared and so is she" [JR Taylor]. Lives and works from 103 Morningside Drive, Edinburgh since 1992. Exhibits often RSA.
**Bibl:** John Russell Taylor, *Geraldine Girvan*, Ex Cat, Chris Beetles Ltd, Oct-Nov 1989; Giles Auty, 'Geraldine Girvan', Ex Cat, Chris Beetles Ltd, 1993; Julian Halsby, 'Geraldine Girvan', Ex Cat, Chris Beetles Ltd, 1995.

**GIRVAN, Thomas Gerald** **1944-**
Aberdeen painter. Exhibited RSA(2) from 49 Regent's Quay in 1977 and 1978 & AAS(4) 1977-1980, from 26 Forbes Street.

**GITTLESON, Albert Abram** **fl 1911-1944**
Born Kovno, Russia. Painter of portrait, landscape, miniatures, genre and pastoral scenes, also teacher and restorer. Studied at Leeds School of Art and the Royal College of Art under Owen Bowen, and overseas. Settled in Glasgow in the early 1920s with his wife and son(qv) both of whom were artists. Exhibited RA, RSA(9), RHA & GI(4), from 47 Camphill Avenue, Langside, Glasgow.

**GITTLESON, Barnet** **fl 1931**
Glasgow painter, member of the Gittleson family (?son) all of whom exhibited from the same Glasgow address. Exhibited two landscapes at the GI.

**GITTLESON, Leonard** **fl 1943**
Glasgow artist. Almost certainly the son of Albert Abram(qv) and Sadie(qv) since he exhibited RSA(1) from the same address.

**GITTLESON, Mrs Sadie (née Nicholson)** **fl 1928-1945**
Glasgow based flower and landscape painter. Wife of Albert Abram G(qv); exhibited RSA(2) & GI(6).

**GIULIANI, Amadeo** **fl 1913-1915**
Italian sculptor in marble and bronze; settled in Glasgow and exhibited RSA(1) & GI(4) from 104 Bothwell St.

**GIVEN, David** **fl 1891**
Edinburgh based painter. Exhibited RSA(1) from 23 Ann Street.

**GLADSTONE, Miss Florence M** **fl 1947**
Glasgow portrait artist who worked mainly in pencil; exhibited GI(2), from 268 Albert Dr.

**GLADSTONE, Miss Mary Selina** **1842-1932**
Portrait painter. Member of the Gladstone family, niece of William Ewart G. Lived at Fasque, Laurencekirk throughout her life. Exhibited a portrait of the Countess of March at the RA 1879.

**GLADSTONE, Thomas** **1803-1832**
Scottish portrait painter, nephew of Robert Gladstone of Capenoch. Little is known about him but several portraits are documented at the SNPG. He painted 'Adam Steuart (1750-1820)', and his daughter 'Catherine Steuart (1779-1818)', who became the wife of Robert Gladstone (who died in 1835). Also painted the family portrait of 'Thomas Gladstone (1732-1809)', a Leith grain merchant and father of Sir Thomas Gladstone.

**GLANCY, Eileen** **fl 1956-1957**
Edinburgh painter of genre. Exhibited RSA(3) from 15 Strathfillan Road.

**GLASGOW ART CLUB** **1867-**
Initiated by nine artists including William Dennistoun(qv), David Murray(qv) and William Young(qv) who held monthly meetings at which members' work was circulated for review and discussion. Then in 1873, having added to its numbers, the first of many public exhibitions was held. With the advent of its own rooms in Bothwell Circus the group became the centre of art life in the city. In 1893 the club moved to more extensive premises in Bath St.
**Bibl:** Caw 211; Glasgow Art Club publications (various); Hardie 81; Irwin 393.

**GLASGOW DILETTANTI SOCIETY** **1825-1838**
Established following the demise of the Institution for Promoting and Encouraging the Fine Arts in the West of Scotland(qv) and stemming from the occasional meetings of James Davie(qv), Andrew Henderson(qv) and William Young(qv). The Society's first exhibition was held 1828 and included John Graham's head of Rebecca, four works by Horatio McCulloch(qv), one each from John Knox(qv) and Daniel McNee(qv) together with twenty local artists among them William Brown(qv), Andrew Donaldson(qv), John D Gibson(qv), John Gilfillan(qv) and Andrew Henderson(qv), while from Edinburgh came George Harvey(qv), William Simson(qv), John Ewbank(qv) and the sculptor John Steell(qv). The President was Dr William Young with the architect David Hamilton vice-president. A second exhibition was held in 1830. In the fourth show there were 400 works on display. A final exhibition followed 1832 and although

the average number of exhibits throughout its brief history had been 327 with exhibitors including William Allan(qv), David Cox, David Roberts(qv), Turner and David Wilkie(qv), the Society was dissolved in 1838 'through want of patronage'. The last Presidents had been John Houldsworth(1837) and James O Anderson(1838). In 1840 the organisation was reconstituted as the West of Scotland Academy(qv).
**Bibl:** Anon pamphlet, A Glance at the Glasgow Dilettanti Society's Exhibition (1835) quoted in anonymous A Criticism on the Pictures in the Glasgow Exhibition with a Letter to the President and Members of the Dilettanti Society, Glasgow, 1835,10; Brydall 362-4; Caw 67; Irwin 222,243,310,355,447n3.

**GLASGOW FOUR ('The Spook School') c1890-c1910**
This comprised Charles Rennie Mackintosh(qv), Herbert MacNair(qv) and the sisters Frances(qv) and Margaret Macdonald(qv). Their influence was cumulative because they worked and often exhibited together at, for example, the Glasgow School of Art Club exhibition of 1894. Although in common with the Arts and Crafts movement they gained inspiration from nature, practised simplicity of design and enjoyed craft work, they were rejected by their London counterpart who branded all art that failed to recognise or accept a socialist component as subscribing to the rival 'Aesthetic Movement'. Additional characteristics shared by the four were a permeating and enigmatic mysticism, a kind of resigned pessimism allied to a strain of whimsicality. They 'were captivated by the disquieting dream world of Maeterlinck, Rossetti, Gautier and other men of letters, and by publications such as The Yellow Book and The Evergreen[qv]. They were immersed in...the Celtic twilight and found visual stimulation in the work of the symbolists - Jan Toorop, Carloz Schwabe, Aubrey Beardsley and others...there was also a powerful undertow, a turbulent emotional conflict (representing) the age-old struggle of youth seeking to free itself from the shackles of tradition, of moral and religious repression in a world of rapid change' [Thomas Howarth]. During their most active period they won more recognition abroad than at home. In 1900, for example, they were invited to participate at the Secession Exhibition in Vienna and the following year the Austrian Secessionist journal *Ver Sacrum* devoted an entire issue to the Four. A further exhibition followed in Turin 1902. (See also individual entries)
**Bibl:** Burkhauser 22,60,85-89,111,131; Irwin 396-404; Alexander Koch in Dekorative Kunst (Darmstadt), 1897,1,1; Scottish Art Rev, new series XI,4,1968,13; XIV,4,1975,13; Studio 11,1897; special issue Modern British Domestic Architecture and Decoration,1901; Vienna, Ver Sacrum, 1901,No.23.

**GLASGOW GIRLS 1880-1920**
A recent notation, first coined by William Buchanan in 1968, to indicate the important, intrinsic role played by women artists and designers in the creation and development of the Glasgow School, the Glasgow Style and the fin de siecle strain of art nouveau, paralleling the existence of what now are generally referred to as the Glasgow Boys. Burkhauser's edited volume of illustrated essays expanded on this overdue omission. (See also **Spook School** and individual entries)
**Bibl:** Burkhauser.

**GLASGOW GROUP 1957-**
Formed in 1957 by a group of young Glasgow artists including Douglas Abercrombie(qv), Alan Fletcher(qv), Carole Gibbons(qv), Alasdair Gray(qv), Jack Knox(qv), Ian McCulloch(qv), Ewan McLauchlan(qv), James Morrison(qv), Anda Paterson(qv), James Spence(qv, the prime mover) and James Watt(qv). Born out of frustration with insufficient artistic activity and lack of encouragement in the Glasgow area at a time when the RSA was at its most Edinburgh-centric and the RGI was passing through its most conservative phase. It began life as 'The Young Glasgow Group' but dropped the 'Young' in 1966. From the beginning the annual exhibition has always been held in the McLellan Galleries, Glasgow with occasional supplementary shows in London, Aberdeen and Edinburgh. Limited to professional members and in its early days to those resident in the west of Scotland, recently its catchment area has been widened. Bill Birnie(qv) founded an offshoot body within the group in 1965. This continues to flourish and is known as the **GLASGOW GROUP SOCIETY.** Although the Group has received recognition and support from the SAC 1969-88 and, from 1967 Glasgow City Council, its influence has been strangely neglected by modern writers, probably because membership, limited to twenty professionals, has been based on friendship and propinquity rather than on shared artistic goals or a common style. (See also under individual artists)
**Bibl:** Glasgow Group 1958-1990, Sep 1990; Glasgow Group Ex Cats, especially 1978.

**GLASGOW INSTITUTION FOR PROMOTING AND ENCOURAGING THE FINE ARTS IN THE WEST OF SCOTLAND 1821-1823**
The first attempt by Glasgow to emulate the several exhibition societies that had arisen in Edinburgh. Formed 21st March 1821 with 43 founder members including the Lord Provost (JT Alston), the inaugural exhibition took place within the premises of a carver and gilder (Robert Finlay) at 2 South Maxwell St. 253 works were shown including examples by Andrew Donaldson(qv), John Fleming of Gourock, John Graham(-Gilbert, qv), Andrew Henderson(qv), D O Hill(qv) and R A Howard. Daniel MacNee(qv) exhibited for the first time and John Henning(qv) showed some small bas reliefs. This was followed by a second exhibition the following year before it was replaced, probably due to lack of patronage, by the Glasgow Dilettanti Society(qv).
**Bibl:** Brydall 359-360; Irwin 222.

**GLASGOW LEAGUE OF ARTISTS 1971-**
An artists' co-operative representing no particular didactic style. Its aim is to establish a large communal studio and workshop in central Glasgow with touring exhibitions taken not only to galleries but also to places not normally associated with the visual arts. A programme has been developed for exchanging exhibitions with similar groups in England, Ireland, Canada and the Netherlands.

**GLASGOW PRINT STUDIO 1972-**
A non profit-making organisation offering the use of equipment and technical assistance in the field of printmaking. Largely funded by SAC and the Gulbenkian Foundation. Facilities open to all, with a preference for artists of 'good standard'. Located at 128 Ingram St, Glasgow (Tel: 0141 552 0704).

**GLASGOW SCHOOL c1878-c1895**
A label first applied in 1890 and loosely referring to a Glasgow-based group comprising an indeterminate number of professional artists (and one sculptor), which (on the basis of a letter from the last survivor R Macaulay Stevenson(qv) to Dr Honeyman) is generally regarded as twenty-three, known collectively - and more accurately - as **THE GLASGOW BOYS**. They were Sir D Y Cameron (1865-1945), James Elder Christie (1847-1914), Joseph Crawhall (1861-1913), T Millie Dow (1848-1919), David Gauld (1865-1936), Sir James Guthrie (1859-1930), J Whitelaw Hamilton (1860-1932), George Henry (1858?-1943), E A Hornel (1864-1933), William Kennedy (1859-1918), Sir John Lavery (1856-1941), J Pittendrigh Macgillivray (1856-1938), W Y Macgregor (1855-1923), Harrington Mann (1864-1937), Arthur Melville (1855-1904), T Corsan Morton (1859-1928), Stuart Park (1862-1933), James Paterson (1854-1932), Sir George Pirie (1864-1946), Alexander Roche (1861-1921), R Macaulay Stevenson (1854-1952), Grosvenor Thomas (1855-1923) and E A Walton (1860-1922). They were in fact a loose-knit 'brotherhood' predating the Glasgow School of Art(qv) with which they are sometimes erroneously associated and/or confused, with their own distinctive styles, favouring differing compositions and using different mediums. They were approximate contemporaries who shared a profession and two grievances: a dissatisfaction with the picturesque romanticism common among their immediate elders (whom they christened **The Gluepots** on account of their predilection for heavy brown megilp varnish) and hostility toward Edinburgh's endemic parochialism as reflected in the exhibitions of the Royal Scottish Academy. Macaulay Stevenson summarised their aim as 'aspect is subject'. At the beginning there seem to have been three main characters with their own coterie of friends: Guthrie at Cockburnspath, Lavery in France and Macgregor in Glasgow and, a little later, Hornel in Kircudbright. In 1878 Macgregor and Paterson spent the summer painting together in Nairn, Stonehaven and St Andrews and the same year Crawhall, Guthrie and Walton met at the **St. MUNGO ART CLUB** in Glasgow. Over the next two years they were joined by Henry on painting trips to Brig O'Turk in the Trossachs and to Crowland, Lincs. In 1883 Guthrie and Walton discovered Cockburnspath, nr Dunbar where the group was joined by

Whitelaw Hamilton, Morton and Melville. During the winters they retreated to their Glasgow studios. The same year three paintings appeared at the Glasgow Institute(qv) which exerted an abiding influence on the group: Bastien-Lepage's 'Le Mendiant', William Stott's 'La Baignade' and Arthur Melville's 'Evie'. A parallel movement was occurring in England, the New English Art Club; with Lavery already having joined in 1887; Dow, Hamilton, Henry, Paterson and Walton also joined. When Guthrie emulated Melville in being elected an associate of the RSA in 1888 to be followed by Henry, Lavery and Macgillivray in 1892 'the Academy ate the not unwilling Glasgow Boys and was much better for the meal'. Also in 1888, Crawhall and Guthrie joined Walton at the latter's studio in Cambuskenneth with Kennedy closeted nearby. By 1895 most of the Boys had left Glasgow and the group was passing into history. They had rejuvenated Scottish art, influenced European artistic development (especially the Secession movements in Munich and Vienna) and left behind a lasting legacy now once again in favour, breaking ground which the Scottish Colourists(qv) were soon to follow. (See also individual entries)

**Bibl:** Martin Battersby, 'The Glasgow School', Art and Artists, vol 4,11; Roger Billcliffe, The Glasgow Boys, London 1985; Roger Billcliffe, The Glasgow Boys; the Glasgow School of Painting, London 1985; Elizabeth Bird, 'International Glasgow', Conn, Aug 1973; G Baldwin Brown, The Glasgow School of Painters, 1908; Gerard Baldwin Brown, The Glasgow School of Painters, Edinburgh 1889; William Buchanan et al, The Glasgow Boys, 2 vols, SAC 1968 & 1971; Caw 207-8,343-364,480-482,493-4; Caw 207-8,343-355,356-64,480-4; Hardie 82 et passim ch vi; W R Hardie (text) in Fine Art Society (Ex Cat), 'The Glasgow School of Painting',1970; Irwin 372-394; Horst-Herbert Kossatz, 'The Vienna Secession and its early relations with Great Britain', Studio International, Vol 181, no.929; David Martin, The Glasgow School of Painting, Glasgow 1897; Ronald Pickvance,'A Man of Influence: Alexander Reid, (Ex Cat, SAC, 1967); William Power, 'Glasgow and the Glasgow School', Scottish Art Review, 1946; Studio, vol XI,1897,86-100,225-236; X,47-51.

**GLASGOW SCHOOL OF ART** **1840-**

Founded in 1840 as a School of Design with premises in Ingram St. Charles Heath Wilson(qv) was Headmaster 1849-1864. Although well qualified - he had been Dyce's successor as Director and Secretary of the School of Art at Somerset House, London - his tenure produced little of note and in 1864 the Board of Trade Masterships were terminated. He was succeeded by Robert Greenlees(qv) who remained in office until 1881 during which time the School moved 1869 to the upper part of the Corporation Galleries in Sauchiehall St. The influence and general quality of the School dramatically and quickly reached its zenith with the arrival of Fra Newbery as Director 1885 and Sir James Fleming two years later as chairman. An appeal for funds resulted in a fine new building, opened in 1899, finished in 1909 and housing four departments: drawing & painting, architecture, modelling and design, and applied art. The building, designed by Charles Rennie Mackintosh, is an architectural landmark 'mostly austere and often dramatic'. In addition to the teaching programme there began at this time a flourishing **GLASGOW SCHOOL OF ARTS STUDENTS' CLUB** and an equally vibrant but short-lived publication *The Magazine*(qv), both contributing greatly to the development of Scottish art, especially the art nouveau movement and the rise of the Glasgow School(qv). After WW2, training in design was intensified and by 1963 additional buildings were completed.

**Bibl:** Burkhauser 59-60,71-5,67-9,238-9 et passim; Caw 224-5; Glasgow School of Art Press Cuttings Books; Irwin 399-400.

**GLASGOW SOCIETY OF LADY ARTISTS** **1882-1971**

Founded in 1882 by a group of eight women associated with the Glasgow School of Art(qv): Harriet Agnew(qv), Catherine Henderson(qv), Georgina Greenlees(qv), Jane Nisbet(qv), Elizabeth Patrick(qv), Elsie Prova(qv), Henrietta Roberton(qv) & Frieda Rohl(qv). It paralleled the **GLASGOW ART CLUB** open only to men. The first exhibition was in 1883. In 1893, having acquired new premises at 5 Blythswood Square and attracted 30 more members, enabling it to combine artistic and social activities, the name was changed to the Glasgow Society of Lady Artists' Club. Members now included Kate Cameron(qv), De Courcy Dewar(qv), Jessie M King(qv) and Agnes Raeburn(qv). Artist members were elected only by ballot. Special exhibitions were held of which the most notable was 'The Art of the Book' 1934, featuring especially the work of Jessie M King(qv). One important function of the Club was to enable artists no longer resident in the city (eg those who had migrated to Kircudbright) to maintain contact with artistic developments in Glasgow. The Club foundered after WW2 being replaced c1975 by the nomadic **GLASGOW SOCIETY OF WOMEN ARTISTS** which was in turn dissolved in 1987 when the Glasgow Art Club(qv) at last accepted women members.

**Bibl:** Burkhauser 19,31,47-8,184-5,207-8; Caw 212; De Courcy Lewthwaite Dewar, A History of the Glasgow Society of Lady Artists' Club, Glasgow 1950; Jean Kelvin, 'Clubs and Clubwomen' Glasgow Herald, 28 Mar 1936.

**GLASGOW SOCIETY OF PAINTERS AND SCULPTORS** **1919-c1921**

The idea of Robert Sivell(qv), other foundation members included James Cowie(qv), William McCance(qv), Archibald McGlashan(qv), Agnes Miller Parker (qv, McCance's wife) and Benno Schotz(qv). According to Schotz the aim was 'to strike back at the Art Union which ran a lottery in connection with the RGI exhibitions and which for some reason considered a certain group of painters as rebels and therefore rejected their work...perhaps because some of them thought many artists supporting the Union repeated themselves ad nauseam'. But the Society mounted only two exhibitions before internal discord so reduced the membership that its income dried up (see also under individual artists).

**Bibl:** Hardie 147-8; Benno Schotz, Bronze in my Blood - The Memoirs of Benno Schotz, Edinburgh 1981.

**GLASHAN, John** **1927-1999**

Born Glasgow, Dec 24; died Jne 15. Watercolour painter & cartoonist; also writer. Son of Archibald McGlashan(qv) and an Italian mother. When deciding to become primarily a cartoonist he dropped the 'Mc'. After National Service he trained at Glasgow School of Art in the late 1940s before moving to London. His first major breakthrough was when the American editor of *Lilliput* gave him three pages per issue. Work for *Punch* and *Queen* soon followed. Subsequently worked for most of the major newspapers as well as *Esquire* and *The New Yorker*. His 'Genius' cartoon strip in *The Observer* had a wide following. Held an exhibition of his landscapes in London 1979 and again in 1983, 1991 and 1994. With Jonathan Routh produced *The Good Loo Guides*, wrote and illustrated *The Mental Health Workout Book*, 1986 and *John Glashan's World* 1991.

**Bibl:** Horne 220; The Times, Obituary, June 1999.

**GLASS, John** **fl 1846**

Stirling landscape painter. Exhibited RSA(3) from Allan Park.

**GLASS, John James ARSA** **1820-1885**

Born Edinburgh; died Edinburgh, 12 Sep. Animal painter in oil, also topographical subjects; occasional watercolours. Began life as a house-painter, apprenticed to John Jackson who was described as an 'ornamental painter' working beside Thomas Fenwick. After studying at the Board of Trustees Academy, a Mr Joseph Young of Burntisland became one of his patrons and together they travelled to Europe sketching in many Royal stables. Showed an early aptitude and a predilection for animal painting, generally those involved in country sports such as foxhounds, ponies, keeper's dogs and Arabian thoroughbreds, also occasionally painted landscapes. Incorrectly catalogued in the RA lists though he did exhibit 2 works there, 'The Keeper's Pony' (1847) and 'Resting on the Moor; Portraits' (1859). Until 1865 his work was characterised by artistic qualities in composition and colour. Later developed a mental disorder which affected his work. Although he recovered, his painting ability unfortunately did not, a fact noticeable in his later works. A very gentle, unassuming man, full of stories about old Edinburgh. Elected ARSA 1849. Exhibited RSA annually 1840-1880 a total of 199 works, latterly from 3 Princes Street. His 'High School Yards', painted in the 1850s, hung in Huntly House. Represented in Edinburgh City collection(3).

**Bibl:** Butchart 77; Wingfield.

**GLASS, John Hamilton** **fl 1890-1925**

Painter in oil and watercolour, mainly the latter; landscapes, coastal and river scenes. Little is known about his personal life although his artistic output was large. Painted mostly in Scotland and Holland.

Lived in Musselburgh and often worked along the east coast, also sometimes on Iona. His work, although constant in style, was variable in quality. The colours tend to be brown and grey and the figures dumpy. His wife, **Mary Williams**, painted in a similar style. One of the reasons why so many of his works appear is that he often appended his signature to the work done at least partly by his wife. Exhibited RSA(19), RHA(4), GI (3) & L(1), after 1905 from Cadzow Studio, Pencaitland, East Lothian.
**Bibl:** Halsby 260.

**GLASS, William Mervyn RSA PSSA** **1885-1965**
Born Ellon, Aberdeenshire; died Edinburgh, 14 Aug. Painter of landscape and coastal views in oil and occasionally watercolour. Studied at Gray's School of Art, Aberdeen and the RSA Life School in Edinburgh, also in Paris and Italy. Lived almost all his life in Edinburgh where he settled 1906. Won Maclaine-Watters bronze medal and Chalmers Jervise prize. Painted chiefly in Iona and the Scottish Highlands and was particularly fond of portraying precipitous slopes and snow-clad mountain peaks. Elected ARSA 1934, RSA 1959. Exhibited RA(1), RSA(100+), GI(53), AAS & L(4), from 38 Drummond Place.
**Bibl:** Macmillan [SA], 326,332.

**GLEAVE, Joseph Lee RSA ARIBA** **1907-1965**
Architect. Studied at Manchester School of Architecture. In 1930 won the International Architectural Competition for a memorial to Christopher Columbus to be erected in the Dominican Republic. Two years later became senior assistant, Edinburgh School of Architecture and head of the School of Architecture and Town Planning 1935-1948, apart from a period during WW2 spent on active service. After the war he joined the practice of Graham Henderson in Glasgow, subsequently known as John Keppie and Henderson and Gleave, mainly engaged in housing and schools and the re-decoration of Bute Hall, Glasgow University. Other works include the Prestwick Air Terminal Buildings and Queen Mother's Hospital, Yorkhill, Glasgow. Consultant architect to Glasgow University and member of the panel advising Edinburgh Corporation on Princes Street development. Member, Royal Fine Art Commission for Scotland, also Historic Buildings Council. Past President SSA and council member, RIBA and RIAC. Elected ARSA 1953, RSA 1959. Frequent exhibitor RSA & GI(5).

**GLEN, Graham** **fl 1895-1925**
Edinburgh painter in oil and watercolour, figurative subjects and portraits. Exhibited chiefly in Scotland. Chairman SSA. In the early 1920s moved to London. Exhibited RSA(27) including a portrait of the 'Marchmont Herald' (1899), RA(2), GI(5), AAS(4) & L(1), latterly from 32 Dublin St. Represented in SNPG, City of Edinburgh collection.

**GLEN J Scott** **fl 1894**
Glasgow based flower painter. Exhibited GI(1) from 30 Lilybank Gardens, Hillhead.

**GLEN, James** **fl 1840-d1865**
Glasgow painter in oil and watercolour and teacher. Although not a distinguished artist, he contributed more to the artistic life of Inverness than probably any other single person. Arrived in the town from Glasgow 1845 bringing with him a number of landscape and figure subjects and in addition to holding private classes took up a post with the newly established Inverness Royal Academy. In 1851 he returned to Glasgow but the following year he went back to Inverness to take up the Drawing Mastership in the Academy. He was a most popular teacher and after his death his pupils erected a monument to his memory in Tomnahurich Cemetery.

**GLEN, James Kelso** **fl 1943**
Motherwell painter in pastel; exhibited 'Caravan' at the GI, from 27 Montalto Ave.

**GLEN, John Anderson** **fl 1921-1922**
Glasgow based sculptor. Exhibited portraits and figure subjects at the GI(5) from 72 Croft Street, Cambuslang.

**GLENDAY, James Barry** **fl 1875**
Dundee based landscape painter in oil; exhibited 'A peat moss, Kilchurn Castle' at the RSA.

**GLENDINNING, Miss Elizabeth** **fl 1954-1959**
Glasgow sculptress. Exhibited 4 plaster and terracotta heads at the GI, latterly from 5 Belhaven Terrace.

**GLIORI, Lionel** **fl 1949-1967**
Lanarkshire sculptor and painter, etcher and lithographer. Figure subjects, still life, portrait heads; in oil and watercolour. Exhibited GI(10), after 1964 from 4 Kirklee Terrace.

**GLISSMANN, Hans** **fl 1940**
Edinburgh based portrait painter. Exhibited RSA from 7 Kingsburgh Road.

**GLOAG, Miss Isobel Lilian ROI** **1865-1917**
Born Kensington, London; died Jan 5. Painter in oil and watercolour of classical subjects, still life, portraits and interiors. Of Scottish parentage. Studied at Slade School under Legros, St John's Wood Art School, South Kensington and in Paris. Undertook poster design and stained-glass work. Contributed to *The Graphic* (1910). At the time of her death had completed illustrations for projected editions of *William Tell* and *Love's Labour Lost.* Elected ROI 1910. Exhibited RA(18), ROI(21), RBA(2), GI(6), SWA(1) & L(8). Represented in City of Edinburgh collection.
**Bibl:** Houfe.

**GLOUCESTER, HRH The Duchess of (née Lady Alice Montagu-Douglas-Scott) RSW** **1901-**
Painter in watercolour of landscape and animal studies. Third daughter of 7th Duke of Buccleuch. Her first solo exhibition was at the Walker Gallery, London 1933 when 64 of her paintings were on view. Those attracting particular attention were 'Flat-topped Thorn Trees between Siola and Archer's Post' and 'Thomson's Gazelles'. *The Times* noted that 'in this clear light, with the sun vertically overhead, there is not much opportunity for indicating recession by atmospheric means, and by some instinct Lady Scott has relied upon the perspective of her planes of colour...she is particularly good in the treatment of the retiring surfaces, and the colour effects throughout the exhibition are intense without being garish'. A second exhibition two years later was still more successful. Elected RSW 1938. Some of her watercolours and drawings were included in her autobiography *Memories of Ninety Years* (1991). Exhibited RSW & GI(22) including 'Loch Muick' and 'Kamerin Escarpment, Kenya' (both in 1938), from St James's Palace, London.
**Bibl:** Alice, Duchess of Gloucester, Memories of Ninety Years, London 1991.

**GLOVER, Edmund** **1816-1860**
Painter in oil of landscape, seascapes and river scenes who lived at various times in both Edinburgh and Glasgow. Probably related to William Glover(qv). Also scene painter for among his recorded addresses were the Theatre Royal, Edinburgh and the Theatre Royal, Glasgow. Exhibited RSA(36) 1842-1865 mostly landscapes, sometimes in oils, generally in Scotland.

**GLOVER, John Hardy OBE RSA RIBA FRIAS** **1913-1994**
Born North Berwick, Feb 21; died Edinburgh 6 April. Architect. Educated at the local High School and Edinburgh College of Art. Joined the firm of Leslie Graham Thomson 1936. After serving in India during the war he joined Basil Spence(qv) 1947. Elected ARSA 1969; RSA 1981. Supported the team approach to design, he conducted the Scottish end of the practice. Among his major buildings are the Royal Highland Showground, the original Glasgow Airport, and buildings at the Universities of Dublin, Heriot Watt, Edinburgh, Newcastle, Liverpool and Aston. A quiet unassuming gentleman, he retired 1980, enjoying his family, fishing, and a cottage at Drumbeg, while retaining an active interest in his younger partners and proteges.
**Bibl:** Andrew Merrylees, Obituary, RSA Annual Report, 1994.

**GLOVER, John McC N** **fl 1904**
Dumfries artist. Occasionally painted on the continent. Exhibited a landscape at the RSA from Hazelwood.

**GLOVER, William RSW** **1848-1916**
Painter in oil and watercolour, mainly the latter, landscapes, especially in the Highlands. Possibly son of Edmund G(qv). For many years was Manager of the Theatre Royal, Glasgow. Also worked as a scene

painter. His coastal scenes and west coast landscapes were attractively composed but often showing a lack of skilled draughtsmanship. Patronised by John Watson of Earnock, Hamilton. Lived in Glasgow and latterly Cumbernauld. Elected RSW 1878. Exhibited RSA(21), RSW(34) & GI(63). Represented in Paisley AG, Hamilton Museum(2).
**Bibl:** Halsby 260.

**GLUE, Jane** **fl 1980-**
Orkney landscape and genre painter in both oil and watercolour, also local coastal scenes and wildlife. Studied art in London for three years before returning to Orkney where she runs her own gallery. Employs a bright, broad palette full of light and sunshine.

**GOALEN, Miss Delny** **fl 1955-1956**
Glasgow painter of landscape, figure subjects and still life; exhibited GI(3), from 12a Second Ave, Bearsden.

**GOBLE, Richard** **19th Cent**
Obscure Scottish watercolour painter of landscape and seascape who spent some years in Australia c1890. Sometimes signed 'Goble' and sometimes with a monogram. His family came from the Isle of Whithorn; a landscape of their farm 'Shaddock by Goble' is still with the family, also two NSW coastal scenes.

**GODBY, Frederick** **fl 1841-1854**
Edinburgh landscape, figurative and occasional portrait painter. Worked often on the coast around Newhaven, also Argyll, Fife and Perthshire. Exhibited RSA(42).

**GOGGS, Evelyn Dorothy** **1900-**
Born Edinburgh. Book-binder, textile designer and wood engraver. Studied at the Central School of Arts and Crafts. Exhibited L(4) from 11 Durrington Park Road, London.

**GOLD, Mrs Sheila G** **fl 1973**
Lanarkshire animal painter; exhibited 'A study of zebra' at the GI, from Hill of Birches, Thorntonhall.

**GOLDIE, Mrs** **fl 1871**
Edinburgh landscape painter in oil; exhibited RSA(3).

**GOLDIE, George** **fl 1963-1976**
Glasgow painter in oil, watercolour and conte. Mainly landscape, especially studies of trees. Exhibited GI(10), from 7 Holmhead Crescent.

**GOLDIE, Marjorie H** **fl 1936**
Artist. Exhibited a life drawing at the RSA from 7 Eyre Terrace, Edinburgh.

**GOLDIE, Mary E** **fl 1950**
Glasgow painter of still life; exhibited RSA(1) from Roslyn House, Kelvinside.

**GOLDIE, Patrick Carron** **fl 1875-1888**
Edinburgh flower and landscape painter in oil of figurative subjects buildings and landscape, sometimes with anglers. Exhibited RSA(10) & GI(6), latterly from 1 Glenbank Terrace, Lenzie, Dunbartonshire.

**GOLDIE, William** **fl 1867-1888**
Edinburgh painter in oil of landscape and fruit and coastal scenes. Exhibited RSA(21).

**GOLDRICKE, James** **fl 1897-1903**
Glasgow landscape painter in oil and watercolour; exhibited RSA 1898 and 1902 & GI(3), latterly from 118a Mains St.

**GOLDWAG, Hilda** **fl 1951-1985**
Glasgow based painter of still life, pastoral scenes and genre. Regular exhibitor RSA & GI(88), from 5 Archerhill Gardens.

**GOMME, Mrs Phyllis** **fl 1949-1956**
Glasgow painter of landscape and still life; exhibited GI(5), from 1 Melrose St.

**GOOD, James** **fl 1953**
Lanarkshire flower painter; exhibited GI(1), from 44 Belstane Rd, Carluke.

**GOOD, Thomas** **fl 1910-1944**
Edinburgh portrait sculptor. In 1918 exhibited a portrait medallion of Charles Maitland Pelham-Burn of the Seaforth Highlanders and in 1935 collaborated with Henry Lintott(qv) over a memorial to Dr Haig Ferguson. Designed the oak choir stalls, decorated with animal ends, in the Robin Chapel of the Thistle Foundation, Niddrie Mains Rd. Exhibited regularly RSA during the above years, GI(1) & Walker Gallery, Liverpool, latterly from 1 Ramsay Lane.
**Bibl:** Gifford 538.

**GOOD, Thomas Sword HRSA** **1789-1872**
Born and died Berwick-upon-Tweed. Painter of domestic genre. Studied under a house-painter, moved to London 1822 but returned north in 1824. Pupil of Wilkie(qv). Fond of painting fisherfolk and the coastal scenes around Berwick but in 1830 an inheritance persuaded him to abandon painting altogether. Exhibited RA 1820-1823 a total of 19 works, 5 works at Carlisle Academy 1825-1833 and one in Carlisle Athenaeum 1846; also RSA(11) 1828-1833 and again in 1850. Represented in SNPG by a self-portrait and a portrait of James Howe, BM, Tate AG, Berwick Guild Hall Museum, Berwick-upon-Tweed AG, Laing AG (Newcastle-upon-Tyne), Manchester AG, Castle Museum (Nottingham), National Maritime Museum (Greenwich), Nat Gall of Ireland (Dublin).
**Bibl:** AJ 1852, 94; 1901 293; P Edwin Bowes, In a Strong Light, the Art of Thomas Sword Good, Berwick 1989; 1985; Cust, The National Portrait Gallery, 1901-2, II, 12; DNB XXII; J Fleming,'Thomas Sword Good: A Disregarded Victorian Painter', Country Life, vol ciii, 23 Jan 1948; Liz Maxwell,'Doing a Good Deed at Berwick', Scotsman, 2 Aug 1989; B Poynter, National Gallery 1899-1900, III.

**GOODALL, Oscar Raymond** **1924-**
Painter in oil and teacher; mainly abstracts and semi-abstracts with a figurative element. Studied Dundee College of Art and Patrick Allan-Fraser Art College, Arbroath. Member, SSA. Art master Bell-Baxter School, Cupar, Fife. Exhibited RSA(21) 1951-62 and again in 1980 and 1981, also GI(2). Represented Perth AG.

**GOODENOUGH, Marie** **fl 1952-**
Sculptress and occasional watercolourist. Educated Edinburgh College of Art 1952-58, receiving a postgraduate major travelling award which enabled her to visit West Germany. Awarded the Harrie prize and Helen Wallace prize. Sculpts botanical and abstract subjects in wood. Her early work evolved by way of enlarged representations of plant forms into robust stylised animal forms. Employs strong use of colour inherent in the grain of the wood, enhanced by stained glass, resin, dye and coloured wax as well as paint. Also works in papier-mâché, plaster and resin. Member, SSWA. Exhibits RSA from various addresses in the north of England, most recently Warkworth, Northumberland.

**GOODFELLOW, David** **1871-1941**
Amateur watercolour flower painter. An artist of some competence specialising in flowers and landscape. He was in trade as a baker in Broughty Ferry living at 81 Gray Street. Exhibited RSA(2), RI(1) & GI(1).
**Bibl:** Halsby 260.

**GOODLET, Ms Sharon** **fl 1988-**
Glasgow-based portrait painter; exhibited a self-portrait at the GI, from 435 Sauchiehall St.

**GOODMAN, Walter** **1838-1889**
Edinburgh oil painter of church interiors, portraits and figurative subjects. Lived for a time in London and also in France. Exhibited RSA(4).

**GOODRICH, James B** **fl 1866**
Edinburgh landscape painter in oil; exhibited RSA(2).

**GOODRICH (or Guidrich or Gooderick), Matthew** **fl 1617-1654**
Early English painter. Worked extensively at Holyrood 1617. Remnants remain of a tempera frieze in Mary Queen of Scots' Outer

Chamber while the Inner Chamber has a similar frieze 'in blacks and greys with the Honours of Scotland, arabesques and cornucopias between guilloiche borders' [Gifford]. Also received 'tua hundreth pundis laughful money of England for paynting and gylting of his Majesteis chappell...and his Majesteis chamberis'.
**Bibl:** Apted 42; Croft-Murray, Decorative Painting, i, 202-4; Gifford 146,147; Reg. Privy Council, 1st ser, x, 593-4,xi, 6,65,67,84; Walpole Soc, vii, 43.

**GORAN, Maitland** **fl 1885**
Edinburgh based artist; exhibited RSA(1).

**GORDINE, Mrs Dora (The Hon Mrs Richard Hare)** **1906-1992**
Born St Petersburg, Russia, Apr 13; died London Jan 2. Sculptress. Father was Scottish (Mark Gordine) and her mother Russian. Until the age of 16 studied music but became interested in dance and increasingly in wood carving. In 1925 visited Paris intending to study art at an atelier but a chance meeting with the sculptor Aristide Maillol dissuaded her. Accepting his advice to work alone, within a year she was exhibiting at the Salon des Tuileries. Her first sale was to the influential, perceptive Swiss collector Dr Widner. First solo exhibition in London 1928. There Samuel Courtauld purchased her 'Mongolian Head' which he subsequently donated (anonymously) to the Tate; at the same exhibition the Colonial Office bought 'Torso' for University College, Gold Coast. A solo exhibition on the continent followed in Berlin 1929. During a spell in Singapore 1930-1935 her preference for the full rounded organic form developed; she was commissioned to decorate the interior of Singapore's new Town Hall. Returning to Britain, she married in 1936 and built a studio and sculpture gallery - Dorich House, Kingston Vale, London - to her own design. Spent most of 1947 in America. Her finest works are her oriental heads - compelling in their 'spiritual serenity'. Her obituary referred to her 'natural, untrained talent (which) created some of the most spiritual and engaging heads of modern times...a truly international artist'. Sitters included Freya Stark, Carol Reed, Emlyn Williams, Beryl Grey, Sir Kenneth Clark and Sir John Pope-Hennessy. Exhibited RA and RSBS every year 1937-1960 & GI(7) 1938-1961. Represented in Tate AG, Herron Museum of Art (Indianapolis), Senate House (London Univ), Singapore Town Hall, RIBA.
**Bibl:** The Times (obit), Jan 5, 1992.

**GORDON, Adam W** **fl 1889-1892**
Edinburgh portrait painter; exhibited RSA(2) from 11 Picardy Place.

**GORDON, Alexander** **fl 1890-1923**
Ayrshire watercolour painter of figure subjects, interiors and rustic scenes. Lived at Underbank Lodge, Largs, before moving to England to take up a position at the School of Art, Taunton 1891. Settled London 1897. Exhibited RA(4) 1891-1898, also RBA(2) & GI(8), in 1923 from 4 Waldemar Rd, London.

**GORDON, Alexander** **fl 1905-1914**
Glasgow based painter in oil and watercolour of rustic interiors and genre. Exhibited RA(1), RSA(3), RSW(2), RCA(2) & GI(1) from Gourock and Glasgow.

**GORDON, Alexander Esmé RSA FRIBA FRIAS** **1910-1994**
Born Edinburgh, 12 Sep. Architect and watercolourist of landscapes and town views. Educated Edinburgh Academy, Edinburgh College of Art 1928-34, studied under John Begg, John Summerson, E A A Rowse and A Bruce Thomson. Owen Jones Scholar 1934. Author of *A Short History of St Giles Cathedral, Edinburgh, The Principles of Church Building, The Royal Scottish Academy 1826-1976* (1976). Before retirement was in private practise as senior partner of Gordon and Bey having joined the firm 1936. Among his designs are the head offices of the Scottish Life Association and the South of Scotland Electricity Board; designs for the High Kirk of St Giles, the War Memorial Chapel, and the Memorial to King George VI in the Chapel of the Order of Thistle (1962). Before and after WW2 was a member of staff, School of Architecture at Edinburgh College of Art. During WW2 served with the Royal Engineers. Past president, Edinburgh Architectural Association. Friendly, jovial, kindly and popular. His watercolours show a great delicacy of feeling and an accurate portrayal of continental and Scottish scenes, brightly lit and generally painted in a happy mood. Elected FRIAS 1953, FRIBA 1956, ARSA 1956, RSA 1967. Secretary RSA 1973-78. Regularly exhibited RSA, occasional exhibitor RSW & GI(1).
**Bibl:** Gifford 111,114,118,149,182,274,485,577,582,621-2.

**GORDON, Anna** **c1971-**
Jeweller. Trained Edinburgh College of Art 1989-93. Specialises in geometric designs. Won Habitat UK Design Award 1994, 2nd prize, Ayrton Metals Platinum Award 1994. Received commission from Scottish Arts Council for their exhibition '4 in Motion' 1996. Exhibits widely in the UK and overseas.

**GORDON, Mrs Anne** **1941-**
Born Glasgow. Studied Glasgow School of Art. Stirlingshire painter of country scenes, landscape, flowers and still life in the tradition of the Scottish Colourists. Exhibited GI(20), from Balnakyle, Boquhan, by Balfron.

**GORDON, Boswell William** **fl 1863-1870**
Leith based painter of coastal scenes and landscapes in oil; exhibited RSA(4).

**GORDON, Mrs Carola** **1940-**
Born Lucknow, India. Painter, mainly townscapes in watercolour, designer of fabric collages. Studied University of Pietermaritzburg, South Africa 1958-1961 obtaining an honours degree in English, repeated at New Hall, Cambridge 1961-1963. Studied Edinburgh College of Art 1963-1965 and returned to lecture in South Africa 1966-1976 before settling in Scotland. Since then has worked in oils, watercolour and fabric collage, mainly landscape and buildings. Fine draughtswoman with a subtle sense of colour and an idiosyncratic style that captures atmosphere and mood. Exhibits RSA & GI(1), and RSW from 5 East Fettes Ave, Edinburgh. Her work is in private collections in Australia, Canada, Germany, South Africa, and the USA.

**GORDON, Daisy Violet Jessiman** **1906-1979**
Born Rhynie, Aberdeenshire. Painter in watercolour, pen and ink, also engraver and woodcuts. Painted mainly flower studies, also woodcuts of delicate art nouveau type. Lived at various times in Macduff and Aberdeen.

**GORDON, Douglas** **1966-**
Born Glasgow. Trained Glasgow School of Art 1984-88 and at the Slade School 1988-90. Avant-garde artist who uses film, video, sound, and the written word to depict aspects of memory, perception and interpretation. Winner of the Turner Prize and the Kunstpreis Niedersachen, Kunstverein, Hanover 1996, the Premio 2000 at the Venice Biennale 1997, and the Hugo Boss Prize (Guggenheim, NY) 1998.
**Bibl:** "Kidnapping Douglas Gordon", with Jan Debbaut, Stedelik van Abbemuseum, Einhoven, nd; Macmillan 2001, 171,177-8.

**GORDON, Edward** **fl 1880-1883**
Edinburgh painter in oil and watercolour of flowers and fruit. Exhibited RSA(2) from Coatbridge.

**GORDON, G Huntly** **fl 1836-1872**
Painter of landscapes in oil and watercolour. Working in Edinburgh 1836 when he exhibited 'Tower at Craigmillar Castle' at the RA. Latterly at Nairn from where he exhibited RSA(8). In 1868 exhibited 'Street of the Golden Mosque, Lahore' and GI(2) including 'Iashoch Castle, Nairn' and 'Nairn Harbour'.

**GORDON, H W** **fl 1890**
Amateur Edinburgh portrait painter. Exhibited a portrait of David West(qv) at the AAS.

**GORDON, Herbert Lewis** **fl 1930-1940**
Edinburgh based illustrator and illuminator, mainly of religious subjects. Exhibited regularly RSA during above dates & GI(3), from Murrayfield.

**GORDON, Rev I V James (of Rothiemay)** **fl 1647**
Engraver. Invited by Edinburgh City Council to survey the city, his 1647 drawing, published and engraved by Frederick de Wit in Amsterdam entitled 'Bird's Eye View of Edinburgh from the South' was subsequently reprinted many times. Later drew his well known

'prospects' of the city from the north and the south. Further drawings of Edinburgh followed, the best known being of 'The Castle', 'Holyrood House', 'Parliament House', and 'Heriot's Hospital'. Important figure in the history of Edinburgh. Represented in the City of Edinburgh Art collection.
**Bibl:** Brydall 85-6; Butchart 6-9,44.

**GORDON, J E** **fl 1918-1922**
Edinburgh watercolour painter; exhibited RSA(2) & RSW(2) from 3 Abercromby Place.

**GORDON, Mrs J W** **fl 1889**
Amateur artist. Exhibited Walker Gallery, Liverpool from Ellon, Aberdeen.

**GORDON, James Snr.** **fl 1820-1850**
Aberdeen artist who painted views of that city and its environs, often for reproduction. Father of James jnr(qv). Sound draughtsman, used a mixture of charcoal, pencil and wash in a fluent style. His work was illustrated in Nichol's *Cities and Towns of Scotland.* Produced 'Panoramic View from Nelson's Monument' c1850, subsequently engraved by his son.
**Bibl:** Butchart 85; Halsby 250.

**GORDON, James Jnr** **fl 1843-1889**
Painter in oil and watercolour of mainly topographical scenes especially in and around Edinburgh, and occasional portraits. Two Edinburgh views, 'Edinburgh from the North' and 'Princes Street, looking West, with proposed Scott Monument 1840', were engraved by Nichol(qv). Exhibited RSA 1843-1889, from a variety of Edinburgh addresses, & GI(2), from 2 Rockville St; also exhibited a number of portraits including 'Robert Jamieson of King's College, Aberdeen' (1852). Represented in the City of Edinburgh Collection.
**Bibl:** Butchart 66,85.

**GORDON, Jean A** **fl 1926**
Amateur Aberdeen painter of flowers and trees. Exhibited AAS(2) from 9 Queen's Road.

**GORDON, John** **fl 1902**
Amateur Aberdeen watercolour painter and portrait sculptor. Exhibited AAS(2) from Sunny Bank, Bieldside.

**GORDON, John Ross** **1890-?**
Born Ardland, Aberdeenshire. Etcher of landscapes and watchmaker. Studied Gray's School of Art. Lived in Aberdeen before moving to Edinburgh 1931. Principal works include 'Sunset: Bridge of Don', 'Stirlingshire Village' and 'Old Buchan Farmhouse'. Exhibited RA(1), RSA(19), AAS 1923-1926 & L(1), latterly from 21 Comelybank Street.

**GORDON, Mrs Nora Mary** **fl 1937-1940**
Minor Edinburgh sculptress. Exhibited 2 works at the AAS including a portrait bust 'Admiral of the Fleet Sir Edward Seymour OM' and GI(5), from 24 Murrayfield Avenue.

**GORDON, Patricia** **fl 1959**
Angus landscape painter. Exhibited GI(2), from 23 Keptie Rd, Arbroath.

**GORDON, Robert of Straloch** **1580-?**
Born Kinmundy, Aberdeenshire. Map-maker and surveyor. Second son of Sir John Gordon of Pitlurg and father of Gordon of Rothiemey(qv). The first person to use actual measurements in the preparation of topographical surveys. His *Atlas of Scotland,* commissioned by Charles I, appeared in 1648.
**Bibl:** Brydall 86.

**GORDON, Ronald J** **fl 1959**
Aberdeen portrait painter. Exhibited AAS(1) from 8 Holburn Road.

**GORDON, Miss Vivian** **fl 1943**
Glasgow textile designer. Exhibited GI(1), from 4 Ailsa Drive.

**GORDON, Walter** **fl 1744-1753**
Scottish painter working in Edinburgh. Elected Burgess of Edinburgh 1744 and a member of the Incorporation of St Mary's 1747. In 1753 apprenticed to Alexander Barwall, painter.

**GORDON, William** **fl 1834-1861**
Painter in oil of landscape and topographical. Lived for a time in Edinburgh before moving to Leith. Exhibited RSA(11) all 1834-1841 except for one in 1861.

**GORDON, William A** **fl 1970-1971**
Glasgow sculptor. Exhibited figure studies at the RSA(3) from 107 Queen Margaret Drive.

**GORDON, William G** **fl 1882-1931**
Aberdeen painter in oil of landscapes and portraits. Trained at Gray's School of Art 1888-1891 probably part-time. Taught art privately and at Aberdeen HS. Simple and direct in style combining a tradition somewhat sombre and reticent in colouring with a free style of drawing. Most of his landscapes were of local scenery. Known to have been living in Stonehaven 1921.

**GORDON, William Sinclair** **fl 1920**
Amateur Glasgow portrait painter. Exhibited RSA(2) from 83 Hill Street, Garnet Hill.

**GORDON-DUFF, Miss Helen A** **1897-1991**
Born 11 Downing St, London, 22 Sep; died Ebrington, Glos, Jan. Amateur landscape painter, etcher. Her uncle, Sir Michael Hicks-Beach, was Chancellor of the Exchequer. Trained at the Slade. Painted in many parts of the world especially north-east Scotland and Yugoslavia. Drove an ambulance in London during WW2. Practised as a faith healer and was a pioneer in organic foods. Retired to Ebrington where she spent her childhood. A very popular, kind, generous woman who had no enemies and very many friends. Exhibited two local scenes at the AAS 1935 from Davieburn, Keith.

**GORE-BOOTH, Mrs** **fl 1884**
Dumbarton portrait painter; exhibited GI(3), from Sea-Side House, Helensburgh.

**GORELL, Norman** **fl 1922-1923**
Glasgow based amateur painter. Exhibited GI(3) from 114 West Campbell Street.

**GORMAN, Des** **1961-**
Trained Glasgow School of Art. Glasgow painter of interiors, figurative subjects and semi-abstract still life; exhibited GI(4), from 159 Penilee Terrace.

**GORMAN, Miss Fiona** **fl 1984**
Ayrshire abstract painter. Daughter of James D A G(qv). Exhibited GI(2), from Belmar, Castle Rd, Skelmorlie.

**GORMAN, James** **1931-**
Born Gourock. Painter in oil, watercolour and acrylic; figurative subjects, landscape and decorative works. Studied Glasgow School of Art specialising in mural design under Walter Pritchard 1949-53. In 1979 appointed art master, Port Glasgow HS but in 1987 abandoned teaching to devote himself full-time to painting, moving to Arran. His training in murals was the basis of the major influences on his work - celtic art, symbolism, cubism, Stanley Spencer and English romantics of the 1930s and 40s. His style has become basically linear stressing tonalities and textures. Enjoys the human figure although this is usually secondary to ensuring overall balance. Most recently has concentrated on landscapes. Exhibited frequently RSA, RSW, GI(41) & Paisley Art Institute since 1987 from Alltbeag, Corriegills, Arran. Represented in Paisley AG, Newport AG, Monmouth AG.

**GORRIE, Helen** **fl 1925-1927**
Dunfermline based painter and teacher, taught at the Croft School, Dunfermline and embroidery at Dunfermline craft school c1912-c1940. Exhibited L(3) & Dunfermline Art Club in the early 1920s.

**GOSSMAN, Miss Mary** **fl 1939-1940**
Glasgow watercolourist; exhibited GI(2), from 49 Killermont Rd, Bearsden.

**GOUDIE, Alexander** **1933-2004**
Born Paisley, Nov 11; died Mar 9. Painter in oil, watercolour, chalk and wash of portraits, still life, landscapes (usually in Brittany); also sculptor in plaster and terracotta. Studied at Glasgow School of Art under David Donaldson(qv) and Benno Schotz(qv), the latter having encouraged him to become a portrait painter. Postgraduate scholarship enabled him to pay regular visits to Brittany to where he returned every year for three decades. His portraiture is in the Lavery(qv) tradition. His work has the same easy appearance as that of Cadell(qv) and in its bravura of handling is reminiscent of the Glasgow School. Regarded as a very professional painter. The first major exhibition of his Brittany paintings was held in Edinburgh 1966, leading to a commission to decorate the flagship of the Brittany Ferries fleet, *Bretagne*, 1987. Goudie completed a series of works illustrating *Tam O'Shanter* 1966. These paintings, together with 54 subsequently exhibited in Edinburgh, were purchased for Rozelle House, Alloway, where they remain on permanent display. Elected member, Royal Society of Portrait Painters, 1970. Awarded the Newbery Medal 1955. Collaborated with David Donaldson(qv) on a mural depicting the departure for France of Mary Queen of Scots. Began exhibiting RSA 1951 & GI(78) 1954-1987, from Arnewood House, 4 Clevedon Rd. A retrospective exhibition was held at the Fine Art Society 1983. Represented in Glasgow City Collection, Royal Collection, Paisley AG, Greenock AG, Lillie AG (Milngavie), Perth AG.
**Bibl:** Alexander Goudie, The Times, Obituary, 16 Mar 2004.

**GOUDIE, Miss Isobel Turner Maxwell** **1903-?**
Stained glass designer, potter and painter. Studied at the Glasgow School of Art and moved from Stirling to Edinburgh 1930. Exhibited regularly at the RSA between 1928 and 1946 & GI(4) including a portrait 'Sir Norman Macfarlane, President of the RGI' (1986), latterly from 50 Queen Street, Edinburgh. Represented by a window in St. John's Church, Perth and by 'The Servants of the Lord' (Duncan memorial window) in E bay of the N aisle of St Peter, Lutton Place, Edinburgh.
**Bibl:** Gifford 242.

**GOUDIE, John** **fl 1911-1917**
Renfrewshire landscape painter. Exhibited GI(4) from 1 Bank Street, Barrhead.

**GOUICK, William** **fl 1868-1869**
Edinburgh sculptor of medallion portraits. Exhibited RSA(3).

**GOUK, Alan** **1939-**
Born Belfast, Northern Ireland. Architect and painter in oil and acrylic. Moved to Glasgow 1944, studied architecture part-time at Glasgow School of Art 1957-59, completing his studies at Regent Street Polytechnic, London 1959-60. Thereafter he returned to study psychology and philosophy at Edinburgh University 1961-1964. From 1964-1967 was fine arts exhibition officer at the British Council and it was only in 1967 when appointed lecturer at St Martin's School of Art that he devoted himself to painting. Became head of advanced paintings and sculpture at St Martin's 1986. Lives in London. At first he was a pure abstractionist, much influenced by the American abstract expressionist school. During the 1970s he was one of a number of painters whose main concern was the physical quality of paint itself. From the mid-70s he abandoned acrylic for oil using increasingly thick, creamy paint and by 1981 the brush strokes had become broad and linear, the paint impasto. Represented in Tate AG, Gulbenkian Foundation, SAC.
**Bibl:** Hartley 136; Smith's Galleries, London, 'Alan Gouk' (Ex Cat 1986).

**GOULD, George T S** **fl 1937-1953**
West Lothian painter in oil but more often watercolour; genre, Scottish topographical, also French landscapes. Exhibited RSA 1937-44 and again in 1946, 1949, 1952 and 1953, & GI(10), from Broompark, Kelty Avenue, Bo'ness.

**GOURDIE, Thomas MBE** **1913-**
Born Cowdenbeath, 18 May. Painter in oil and watercolour, designer and calligrapher. Studied at Edinburgh College of Art 1932-37. Shortly before the outbreak of war became interested in industrial subjects, especially around East Lothian and West Fyfe. Served in the RAF during WW2 continuing occasionally to paint. In the light of post-war industrial development his pre-war paintings are now of considerable historical interest. Elected SSA 1945. Taught at Banff Academy before moving to Kirkcaldy HS 1947-1973. In the 1950s commissioned to design marquetry murals for several ocean liners including work in formica for the Greek liner *Olympia* 1952. Has become increasingly interested in calligraphy, especially the improvement of children's handwriting, work for which he was awarded an MBE 1959. Exhibited regularly RSA from 1953, & RSW & SSA since 1945. Represented in Kirkcaldy AG, Imperial War Museum.

**GOURLAY, Miss Midge** **fl 1974**
Stirling embroiderer; exhibited GI(1), from Morven, Gartmore.

**GOURLEY, Alan Stenhouse ROI** **1909-1991**
Born Ayr, 13 Apr; died Kent, Sep 9. Painter in oil; landscapes, mainly English but scenes in Spain, Morocco, Malta, Italy and Singapore, also occasional portraits and stained glass window designs. In 1932 his mother's poor health forced him to remove the family to South Africa and 1932-1937 he taught art at Johannesburg Technical College. There he received commissions to make large windows for the Anglican cathedral in Johannesburg and the Roman Catholic cathedral in Pretoria. Returning to Europe in 1938 he attended the Studio Sabatti in Paris 1938-1940. During most of the war was employed as an instructor in the Camouflage Corps. In 1945 entered the Slade School working under Randolphe Schwabe and Alan Gwynne-Jones. Settling in Bromley, Kent he depended on theatrical design for his principal income. Member of the European Group 1974. Held his first one-man show in London 1974. Member, ROI from 1963, president 1978-82; also president of Chelsea Art Society until 1989. Best known for his handling of light, controlled spontaneity and tonal accuracy. Exhibited regularly RA since 1946 & RSA(1) 1967. Represented in Johannesburg Anglican Cathedral, Pretoria RC Cathedral, Barclays Bank HO (Lombard St, London), South Africa House (by a carpet).
**Bibl:** Times, (obit),Sept 14, 1991.

**GOURLEY, W H** **fl 1956-1959**
Stirlingshire landscape painter; exhibited GI(4), from Balfron station, by Glasgow.

**GOVAN, Miss Mary Maitland** **fl 1884-1925**
Born Gibraltar. Painter in watercolour and oil of flowers, genre, portraits and landscape. Studied at Birkenhead, Antwerp and Edinburgh College of Art. First exhibit was at the RSA from Musselburgh in 1884. Moved to Edinburgh from where exhibited RA(2), RSA(51), RSW(2), GI(21), AAS(4) & London Salon.

**GOVAN, William** **fl 1951-1952**
Ayrshire animal sculptor, usually in wood. Exhibited GI(2), from 7 Polo Gdns, Troon.

**GOVANE, R Stewart** **fl 1876-1886**
Edinburgh painter in oil of continental and Scottish landscape and flowers. Exhibited RSA(11), GI(1) & L(1), from 7 Union St.

**GOW, Charles** **fl 1834-1863**
Portrait painter in watercolour; exhibited RSA(3) & GI(1), from 62 Portland St.

**GOW, David** **fl 1886-1908**
Glasgow landscape painter, mainly local subjects. Exhibited RSA(3), RI(5) & GI(11) from a London address until 1891, thereafter from 471 Sauchiehall Street, Glasgow.

**GOW, Hamish** **fl 1967-1968**
Dumbartonshire sculptor; usually worked in plaster and wood. Exhibited GI(3), from 33 Douglas St, Milngavie.

**GOW, James Forbes Mackintosh** **fl 1861-1898**
Edinburgh painter in oil and watercolour of portraits, landscapes, animal heads, coastal scenes and figure subjects. Coastal subjects were generally of the north-east Scottish coastline. Prolific artist, lived in Edinburgh before spending several years at Knocke sur Mer, Belgium in the 1890s. Exhibited RA(6) 1890-1898 including 'In the Beauly Firth' (1892), also RSA(47), GI(5) & AAS(2).

**GOW, John Cox** **fl 1965**
Dundee painter of girls in country settings; exhibited GI(2), from 5 Glenisla Rd, West Ferry.

**GOW, Mabel S** **fl 1929**
Glasgow based amateur watercolour painter. Exhibited RSW(1) from 29 Hamilton Park Terrace.

**GOWAN, Alexander** **early 18th century**
Edinburgh sculptor and pupil of Roubillac. Father of William G(qv). It was from Alexander Gowan that Robert Burns ordered the stone to be erected in Canongate Churchyard over the tomb of Robert Fergusson. Duddingston Parish Church has a finely carved urn with a low relief of a shipwreck dedicated to Patrick Haldane of Gleneagles. Unfortunately the marble facing became detached in 1981.
**Bibl:** Gifford 555.

**GOWAN, William** **1765-1828**
Edinburgh sculptor who carried on business from Abbey Hill. Son of Alexander G(qv). Several examples of Gowan's work are on tombstones in Inverness churchyard.

**GOWANS, Alexander A** **fl 1948-1972**
Glasgow watercolour landscape painter, also worked occasionally in oils. Often painted in Perthshire and on Arran. Exhibited GI(21), from 2 Gowanlea Ave.

**GOWANS, Charles** **fl 1884-1885**
Glasgow flower painter in oil and watercolour. Exhibited RSA(1) & GI(3) from Woodend, Langside.

**GOWANS, George Russell RSW** **1843/5-1924**
Born Aberdeen. Landscape painter in oil but mainly watercolour, also pastel and black and white. Often painted upper Deeside and in Picardy. Studied Aberdeen Art School, in London and Paris, at the Academie Julian under Bouguereau. Lived and worked most of his life in Aberdeen and was a foundation member of the AAS 1885. Painted powerful watercolours with broad skies and expansive views across fields and moorland, with more interest in mood than detail. One of his favourite sketching areas was Glen Gairn, upper Deeside in the company of his friend and local resident Rudolfe Christen(qv). Elected RSW 1893. Exhibited RA(4) 1877-1891, RSA(24) including 'On the Gairn near Ballater' (1875), RSW(28), RI(1), RBA(1), GI(22) & AAS 1886-1924, after 1905 from 119 Broomhill Ave.
**Bibl:** Caw 392; Halsby 260-1.

**GOWANS, Isabella de Grotte** **fl 1877-1883**
Edinburgh painter in oil and watercolour of landscapes including continental scenes. Sister of Sir James(qv). Exhibited RSA(5).

**GOWANS, Sir James de Grotte** **1822-1890**
Born Blackness, West Lothian. Architect and painter in oil of architectural subjects. Brother of Isabella de Grotte G(qv). Apprenticed to David Bryce(qv) in Edinburgh. Involved in railway construction in West and East Lothian c1847 and in designing houses for artisans; also quarry manager and town councillor. Spent much of his life in Crieff. One of the first to advocate University education for architects. 'It is hard to decide whether Gowans, with his obsession with rational planning and modular construction (the masonry of his house in Edinburgh was constructed in accordance with a standard two-foot grid), should be regarded as a pioneer or an eccentric' [Dunbar]. Designed Lochee station, Dundee (1861) where 'the polygonal stonework formed a mosaic of coral, red, rust and black highlighted with the occasional insertion of sparkling white quartz. Over this was superimposed a modular grid of raised bands in the form of identical moulded-timber brackets supporting the wooden platform roof. The whole composition enlivened by the use of decorative metalwork and ornate iron lamps' [Walker & Gauldie]. In Edinburgh he was responsible for the 'astonishing' tenement (1868) in Castle Terrace, and the characteristic Lammerburn, Spylaw Rd, Merchiston (1860). Appointed Lord Dean of Guild 1885. 'Obsessed by stone and by the elaboration of construction, especially at corners; this formula was based on a stone grid...with angles based on the diagonal or bisected diagonal of the square. His own house, Rockville (1858) had a five-stage tower with his initials on the wrought-iron railings' [Gifford]. Exhibited RSA(13), all architectural designs and paintings. Represented in City of Edinburgh collection.
**Bibl:** Duncan McAra, Sir James Gowans, Romantic Realist, 1975; Dunbar 149; Gifford 64,248,263,269,287,317,356,502,512,537, 643, Pl.128; Bruce Walker & W S Gauldie, Architects & Architecture on Tayside, Dundee 1984, 133-5.

**GOWANS, Mrs Jessie** **fl 1900-1921**
Aberdeen painter of flowers and landscape. Wife of George Russell G(qv). Exhibited GI(1) & AAS latterly from 36 Holburn Street.

**GRACIE, Miss K Jean** **fl 1938-1940**
Glasgow based figure painter, especially older folk. Exhibited GI(3) from 9 Clevedon Crescent.

**GRACIE, Miss Marion** **fl 1974**
Dundee artist. Exhibited GI(1), from 5 Hyndforth St.

**GRAEME (ROE), Colin** **1858-1910**
Painter in oil, animals, sporting subjects. Son of R H Roe, he changed his surname in order to distinguish himself from other members of the family. Painted rather ordinary portraits of horses, shooting dogs on the moors, and terriers with rabbits. Although not Scottish his work is indelibly associated with the country, almost all his better known works being done in the Highlands.

**GRAEVENITZ, Miss Pamela** **fl 1977**
Argyll-based artist. Exhibited 'Autumn in Argyll' at the GI, from Ardlamont, Tighnabruich.

**GRAHAM, A B** **fl 1881**
Edinburgh landscape painter in oil. Exhibited RSA(1) from Hazelbank, Murrayfield.

**GRAHAM, Miss Agnes** **fl 1943**
Glasgow embroiderer. Exhibited GI(1), from 9 Hillend Rd, Clarkston.

**GRAHAM, Alasdair J** **fl 1963-1964**
Berwickshire painter of local farm scenes and views. Exhibited GI(2), from Murrayfield, Gordon, Berwickshire.

**GRAHAM, Alex(ander) Steel** **1917-1991**
Born Glasgow, Mar 2; died Dec 3. Portraitist, watercolour artist, illustrator & cartoonist. Educated Dumfries Academy, trained Glasgow School of Art. Began professional life as a portrait painter, he served in the Argyll & Sutherland Highlanders during WW2, exhibiting a study of a fellow Highlander at the RGI 1942. Best known for his cartoon characters "Wee Hughie", "Briggs the Butler" and "Fred the Basset Hound". Wrote and illustrated: *Please Sir, I've Broken My Arm: A Sporting Commentary in Cartoons*, 1959; *The Eavesdropper*, 1961; *The Doctor and the Eavesdropper*, 1964; *Fred Bassett: The Hound That's Almost Human*, 1964-80; *Graham's Golf Club*, 1965; *Oh Sidney - Not the Walnut Tree: People in Cartoons*, 1966; *Normally I Never Touch It: People at Parties*, 1968; *I Do Like To Be...People at Leisure*, 1970; *It's Spring, Arthur*; *Spring*, 1973; *At Least, I'm Practically Alone*, 1973; *All The Other Men Have Mellowed*, 1975; *A Lively Retirement*, 1975; *Wurzel's neueste Abenteuer*, 1976; *Augustus and His Faithful Hound*, 1978. Illustrated Parkinson, *Football Daft*, 1968; Alexander: *Practice and Progress: An Integrated Course for Pre-Intermediate Students*, 1971; Eckersley, *English Commercial Practice and Correspondence: a first course for foreign students*, 1973; Schur, *British Self-Taught: With Comments in American*, 1974; Bendell: *Home and Dry: Confessions of an Unliberated Housewife*, 1974; Graham, *Fred Bassett and the Spaghetti*, 1977; Burghes, *Introduction to Control Theory, and Applications*, 1980. Sometime Captain, Rye Golf Club in whose clubhouse are many of Graham's golf cartoons.
**Bibl:** Bateman; Horne 223; Cartoonist Profiles, June 1976; [From notes provided by Alistair Keith].

**GRAHAM, Andrew Adam** **fl 1961-1965**
Edinburgh based painter. Exhibited 2 figurative studies at the RSA from 5 Dunsmore Court.

**GRAHAM, Miss Ann** **fl 1871**
Amateur Perthshire portrait painter in oil. Exhibited RSA(1) from a Blair Drummond address.

**GRAHAM, Anne Clare** **c 1955-**
Jeweller & silversmith. Trained Duncan of Jordanstone College of Art 1973-77. Important commissions include presentation pieces for The Prince and Princess of Wales and for Lady Thatcher. Exhibits RGI, Glasgow AG, Goldsmiths Hall and in the USA, France, Germany & Japan.

**GRAHAM, Archibald** **fl 1952-1954**
Ayrshire painter of portraits and genre. Exhibited RSA(2) & 'Self-portrait' at the GI, from 21 Briarhill, Prestwick.

**GRAHAM, C** **fl 1866**
Edinburgh portrait painter in oil, also studies of dogs. Exhibited RSA(4).

**GRAHAM, Edward Alexander** **fl 1980**
Glasgow sculptor. Exhibited a slate sculpture at the GI, from 160 Lincoln Ave.

**GRAHAM, Ellen E** **fl 1885**
Exhibited 'Homewards' at the AAS from Jessifield House, Newham Road, Edinburgh.

**GRAHAM, Fergus** **fl 1861**
Edinburgh painter of genre and conversation pieces. Exhibited GI(1), from 9 Malta Terrace. Represented Manchester AG.

**GRAHAM, George** **fl 1780-1799**
Scottish engraver. Mainly engraved portraits. Executed illustrations for Campbell's *Pleasures of Hope,* 1799. Mainly worked in stipple, including 'The Soldier's Farewell' and 'The Soldier's Return', after Morland. Also executed mezzotint plates of 'John, Earl of Bute' after Ramsay, 'Mrs Collier', after Sir Joshua Reynolds, 'Cornellius Van Tromp', after Rembrandt (c1780); engraved plates after Rowlandson, Westall and Hodges.
**Bibl:** Bushnell; Bryan; J Chaloner-Smith, British Mezzotint Portraits 1878-1883.

**GRAHAM, George H** **fl 1889-1914**
Glasgow based painter of landscape, still life and portraits. Exhibited GI(10), from 319 Sauchiehall St.

**GRAHAM, George William** **fl 1875-1889**
Glasgow painter in oil and sometimes watercolour; landscapes and coastal scenes with boats, especially of Loch Fyne and the Clyde. Painted on Arran. Exhibited RSA(11) & GI(8), from 94 Alison St. Represented in Paisley AG, Brodie Castle (NTS).

**GRAHAM, Miss Isabella J** **fl 1946**
Midlothian flower painter in watercolour. Exhibited GI(1), from 17 Mountcastle Drive S, Portobello.

**GRAHAM, Mrs J** **fl 1923**
Amateur watercolourist from Selkirk; exhibited RSW(1).

**GRAHAM, J L** **fl 1891-1898**
Edinburgh based artist. Exhibited RSA(1) & ROI(1) from Warrender Park Crescent.

**GRAHAM, James B** **fl 1870-1883**
Edinburgh painter of landscapes and seascapes; exhibited 'Kilchurn Castle' at the RSA from 31 Greenside Street; & Carrick Castle, Lochgoil at the GI in 1870.

**GRAHAM, James Gillespie** **1777-1855**
Scottish architect. Born Dunblane in humble circumstances, he rose from a joiner's bench to become one of the most accomplished exponents of the irregular Gothic house in Scotland. Early in life married Miss Graham of Orchill, an heiress from an old Perthshire family, coupling her name with his own. Had a great talent for imaginative composition and an ability to devise rich, Gothic interiors in carved stone, timber, paint and plaster. Even his ornamental detail generally had an authentic medieval character. Among the most distinguished works are the final series of alterations to Taymouth Castle which he superintended (1840), Duns, Berwickshire (c1812) and Dunninald, Angus (1819-1832). Also responsible for Dr Gray's Hospital, Elgin (1815-1819), Achnacarry Castle (1802-1837), the Tolbooth, St John's, Edinburgh (1844), Moray Place (1822) - showing that he was equally at home with classical compositions - and Haddington Town Hall (1830). In Glasgow he designed St Andrew's Catholic church(1814) - now the Cathedral - and George St church(1819). Occasionally worked with Pugin, whom he had befriended after Pugin had been shipwrecked off Leith, (eg Tolbooth, St John's, Edinburgh). He gave advice, (as well as his own set of compasses) to Pugin which the latter used for the rest of his life, as shown in Hubert's portrait. His ecclesiastical Gothic is best represented by Cambusnethan, Lanarkshire (1819). The rather grim figure of Graham was portrayed by Benjamin Crombie in his book *Modern Athenians.* The name of the subject was tactfully omitted from the original plate but after his death the plates were collected together and published in 1851 with the name added on the back cover. One of his more ambitious designs was Armadale Castle, Skye of which only a portion was completed for Lord Macdonald 1814-1822. The interest here was partly its irregular composition, demonstrated by clusters of high and variously shaped towers which are nevertheless in pleasing harmony with the dramatic landscape around them. Another example was St Andrew's Cathedral in Glasgow, thought at the time to be outrageous. Graham had already designed a Gothic chapel for the catholics of Edinburgh, but here was the largest Roman Catholic church in Scotland and the first neo-Gothic building to have a nave and aisles in imitation of the medieval. Unfortunately only the chapel was finished. His ornate Gothic chapel built for Sir William Drummond-Steuart beside Murthly Castle, Perthshire, completed 1846, was fully illustrated in lithographs published in Edinburgh 1850, Graham's design of the altar and all the carved work being illustrated as pl.xv. Also responsible for the Assembly Hall on the Mound.
**Bibl:** Brydall 181; The Builder, 10 Jne 1882; Dunbar 121,123-4,143,160; A Gomme & D Walker, Architecture in Glasgow, London 1987(rev), 170-2,292; Gifford, see index; Peter Savage, Lorimer and the Edinburgh Craft Designers, Edinburgh 1980, 29,164; Bruce Walker & W S Gauldie, Architects and Architecture on Tayside, Dundee, 1984, 72-3,85-7.

**GRAHAM, John** **1754-1817**
Born North of Scotland; died Edinburgh. Painter in oil of portraits and historical scenes; teacher. After serving an apprenticeship in Edinburgh as a coach-painter, went to London becoming a student at the RA Schools, eventually abandoning trade for art. Whilst in London befriended many of the most prominent artists and made a number of studies of the lions at the Tower. His ability as an animal painter was exemplified in an early work, 'The Disobedient Prophet'. When in later years as a teacher he wished to extol the virtues of painting direct from nature, he would unroll this canvas explaining how Gainsborough had praised the donkey which had been painted from life. In 1798 he was persuaded to return to Scotland to help found a Drawing Academy under the patronage of the Trustees Academy. From this time his main achievement was to be as a teacher. His pupils included Alexander Fraser(qv), Sir David Wilkie(qv), Walter Geikie(qv), William Horne Lizars(qv), Sir William Allan(qv), the Burnets(qv) and Sir John Watson Gordon(qv). The opening of this new Academy had a profound and unexpected effect. In 1800 the Trustees Academy and Graham's Academy were amalgamated with the intention of having the latter supersede 'the decorative or mechanical aims' of the former. To help reveal the true character and profound influence on the future development of Scottish Art of Graham's Academy, Irwin quotes a passage written by the secretary 'it is well known that drawing from nature, or from the antique statues, or from both, is universally considered by those conversant with the art to be the only proper mode of obtaining correctness and truth in drawing, and the only approved method of forming the artist; at least that nature, and statue, ought to be much more copied in pictures and drawings'. In 1799 the Academy purchased a collection of plaster casts of antique sculpture for better teaching, and in 1816 Graham persuaded the Trustees to buy a set of plasters of the Elgin Marbles as recommended by 'Grecian' Williams. One of Graham's major innovations was to introduce historical compositions. He was held in immense regard by most of his pupils. Wilkie wrote that he was 'the only person I have ever met in Scotland who could talk reasonably about art' while John Burnet recalled 'we were always lectured on the necessity of paying the greatest attention to the drawing of hands. Graham used to remind us that Michaelangelo was

great in defining the extremities'. William Allan(qv) said that Graham 'was the first to give an impulse to art and to move the enthusiasm of a rising class of artists of that period'. Exhibited RA(35) 1780-1797, most of them historical scenes but also several portraits. His 'Alderman John Boydell', exhibited RA 1792 still hangs in the Stationers' Hall, London. Represented NGS, Stationer's Hall (London).
**Bibl:** Armstrong 20-21; Bryan; Brydall 252-3; Caw 95; Irwin 94-7; McKay 99; Macmillan [SA] 165-6,201.

**GRAHAM, John** **fl 1880-1885**
Landscape painter; exhibited RSA(5) from Murrayfield, Edinburgh and from Hawick (1883).

**GRAHAM, John C** **fl 1848**
Exhibited two figure studies at the RSA in the above year from St Vincent Street, Glasgow.

**GRAHAM, Josephine** **fl 1869-1886**
Glasgow based painter of portraits, still life, genre and figure subjects mainly in oil but occasionally, especially early in his career, in watercolour. Exhibited RSA(3) & RI(3) from 338 Albert Drive, Pollockshields.

**GRAHAM, Kim Bonette** **fl 1983-1984**
Aberdeen painter of genre and still life. Exhibited AAS from 1A Milburn Street.

**GRAHAM, Mrs Lorna** **fl 1976**
Dumfriesshire flower painter; exhibited GI(1), from Kirkland, Courance, Lockerbie.

**GRAHAM, Miss Nancy** **fl 1922-1978**
Prolific landscape painter in oil and pencil; also painted genre and topographical subjects in Scotland, Belgium and Holland. Lived in Stirlingshire before moving c1935 to Polegate, Sussex. Later returned to Corshill, Thornhill, by Stirling. Exhibited regularly RSA, also RA(1), SWA(3), RBA(2), NEA(1), GI(11), L(1) & AAS 1965-1974.

**GRAHAM, Peter RA HRSA** **1836-1921**
Born Edinburgh; died St Andrews, 18 Oct. Painter in oil of landscape and rocky coastal scenes. Studied at Trustees Academy under Scott Lauder(qv). Went to London 1866 and leapt to fame with his first picture exhibited that year at the RA 'A Spate'. This had been described as 'a revelation of close observation, fresh colour, and pure atmosphere: to look at it was to be transported from the hot and crowded city to the heart of the Highlands in a day of wind and rain'[Caw]. His early pictures gave little indication of the genre with which he was later to become associated. In 1863 his 'In the Highlands' was hailed as a new departure in Scottish landscape painting. Friend and teacher of Joseph Farquharson(qv), he enjoyed painting the stormy coastal scenes of the north-east with titles such as 'Sea-girt Crags' and 'Lonely sea cliffs where the gannets find a Home'. His best work showed a coherent richness of line, rich and deep colour, the painting solid and masterly. 'His exhibit "Evening" was regarded as a personification of Scotland as it appeals not to the tourist, but to the native...the subtle spirit of the country to which he belongs, and by which his artistic nature has been shaped'. In 1891 he returned to Scotland settling in St Andrews. Elected ARSA 1860 but resigned in 1877 when he was made an HRSA, ARA 1877, RA 1881. Exhibited RA(83) 1866-1904, RSA(41) 1855-1922, GI(14) & AAS. Represented in NGS, Aberdeen AG, Glasgow AG, Kirkcaldy AG, Manchester AG, Perth AG, Worcester AG, Victoria AG (Australia).
**Bibl:** AJ Christmas Annual 1899; Armstrong 78-9; Caw 255-6; Lindsay Errington (text), 'Robert Scott Lauder and his pupils' NGS (Ex Cat 1983); Hardie 62-6; Irwin 362-3 et al; Macmillan [SA] 165-6,201; Mag of Art II, 144; Portfolio Nov 1887.

**GRAHAM, R Gore** **fl 1955-1961**
Landscape painter in oil exhibited 6 continental scenes at the RSA from Rathburne, Longformaclus, Berwickshire.

**GRAHAM, Robert** **fl 1896-1897**
Glasgow based figure painter in oil and watercolour; exhibited RSW(2) & GI(2), from 122 W. Campbell St.

**GRAHAM, Robert Brown** **fl 1858-1878**
Edinburgh painter in oil and watercolour of landscapes and subject paintings, also topographical subjects including castles and churches, also shipping scenes. One of his exhibits (1870) was a view of the deck of the steamer *Iona* which was both historically and artistically interesting, the latter on account of its unusual perspective. Exhibited RSA(35) & GI(5), from 50 George St.

**GRAHAM, Thomas** **fl 1896-1897**
Edinburgh based painter. Exhibited RSA(3) from 63 Comely Bank Avenue.

**GRAHAM, Thomas Alexander Ferguson HRSA** **1840-1906**
Born Kirkwall; died Edinburgh 24 Dec. Painter in oil of fishing, country life and portraits. Entered Trustees Academy in 1855 studying under Scott Lauder(qv) alongside Orchardson(qv) and Pettie(qv). Soon took a prominent place in this group which also included Chalmers(qv) and McTaggart(qv). Began to exhibit at the RSA 1859 but in 1863 joined Orchardson and Pettie in London. Spending more time abroad than his friends, in 1860 he went to Paris with McTaggart, Chalmers and Pettie, and in 1862 visited Brittany on his own. Was in Venice two years later and painted 'Kismet, Morocco' 1885. But it was the wild west coast of Scotland and the little fishing villages of Fife which were his favourite sketching grounds. Some of his work at this time shows the influence of the pre-Raphaelites, especially Millais. Exceptionally handsome, he was the model for the angry husband in 'The First Cloud', also appeared in Pettie's 'The Jacobites'. Best known work is the 'Landing Stage', now in the V & A, an oil sketch for which is in Bradford City AG. Contributed illustrations for *Good Words* 1861-1863. Elected ROI and HRSA 1883. In addition to many exhibits at the RSA, exhibited RA(43) 1863-1904, ROI(22), RBA(1), GI(29), L(23) & AAS, after 1904 from 96 Fellows Rd, London. Represented in V & A, NGS, Glasgow AG, Kirkcaldy AG, Perth AG, City of Edinburgh collection.
**Bibl:** AJ 1873, 208; 1874, 356; 1901, 92; 1902, 216; 1907, 36 (obit); Armstrong 589; Caw 244, 258-9, 479; Lindsay Errington (text), 'Robert Scott Lauder and his pupils', NGS (Ex Cat 1983); Halsby 118; Irwin 348 et al; Macmillan [SA] 231,233,239; Portfolio 87, 233; 1896, 146; Studio 40, 87; V & A, Cat of Oil Ptgs, 1907.

**GRAHAM, Thomas D** **fl 1953-1961**
Glasgow based sculptor; exhibited heads and torsos at the RSA(2) & GI(1), from 251 Wilton Street.

**GRAHAM-GILBERT, John RSA** **1794-1866**
Born and died Glasgow. Painter in oil of biblical and genre scenes but mainly portraits. Born John Graham, the son of a prosperous West Indies merchant, he was educated at the local grammar school before occupying a desk in his father's office. At the age of 24 he obtained consent to pursue art as his chosen profession. Enrolling as a student at the RA Schools in London where, in 1819, at the end of his first year, won a silver medal for drawing from the antique. Two years further study secured him the gold medal for a painting of the prodigal son. The next two years were spent in Italy. After his return he remained a short time in London exhibiting three portraits at the Academy 1823. In 1827 he settled as a portrait painter in Edinburgh at a time when the Scottish Academy was in its formative years. Became a member of the RI but left in order to join the Academy, and was elected Academician 1830. His portraits follow the Raeburn tradition although his backgrounds were more detailed than either his contemporaries or predecessors. Painted biblical and genre subjects showing the influence of the Italian Old Masters of which he was a celebrated collector. Married a niece of Mr Gilbert of Yorkhill 1834 and assumed the name of Gilbert, settling in Glasgow. Earned the reputation of being able to paint a pretty woman better than any Scottish artist before him. Watson Gordon(qv) and Colvin Smith(qv) were among his contemporaries and rivals. His 'Rebecca' was shown at the first exhibition of the Dilettanti Society of Glasgow(qv) where it received great plaudits. One of his earliest works was a portrait of 'William Murdoch', the inventor of gas illumination. 'He was fascinated by the effect of broad shadow, the construction of his faces little indicated by the brush work - an unusual technique for the period. His softer brush suits better the more refined modelling and delicate gradations of complexion...he was preoccupied with colour and fusion of surface, he failed sufficiently to note the underlying structure which gives individuality to form and feature...his treatment

of black has neither the grateful warmth of tone of Raeburn or Watson Gordon, nor does he observe so carefully or express so simply that incidence of light on it which gives form to mass' [McKay]. Contemporary critics found his art pleasing rather than satisfying. 'The admirably ordered and balanced ensemble, touched with beauty as it occasionally is, of his finer things even, is insufficiently supported by the more virile qualities of craftsmanship. His drawing, while facile and good enough to be pleasing, was neither stylish nor learned; his modelling, if suave and tender, was lacking in a sense of construction; and his actual handling of paint was deficient in gusto and expressiveness. But he had good taste, an instinct for beauty, whether subjective or pictorial, and the grace and refinement of his best pictures ensure him a definite place among the Scottish painters of his time' [Caw]. Bequeathed his collection of Old Masters and other pictures to the Corporation Gallery of Glasgow, now in Glasgow AG. President, West of Scotland Academy, one of the founders of the Glasgow Art Institute. Exhibited RA(10) 1844-1864, all from Yorkhill, Glasgow, RSA and its predecessors(187) 1812-1876 & GI(43). His portraits of 'Sir John Watson Gordon' and 'Joseph Home' are in the SNPG; also represented in NGS, V & A, Glasgow AG, City of Edinburgh collection, Drum Castle (NTS).
**Bibl:** AJ 1886, 217; Armstrong 45-6; Bryan; Brydall 238; Caw 85-7; DNB; McKay 118-124; Macmillan [SA] 163-4,256; Portfolio 1887, p139.

**GRAHAM-YOOLL, Miss Helen Annie** **fl 1880-1898**
Painter in oil and watercolour of domestic and rustic scenes and flowers. Exhibited RSA(10) & GI(1) from Pittenweem in her earlier years and latterly from Edinburgh.

**GRAHAM-YOOLL, Miss Katrine (Mrs H H Young)fl 1956-1983**
Aberdeen painter of genre, often with children, and figure subjects also designer. Worked in oil, pen and ink, charcoal. Exhibited RSA(9), GI(7) & regularly at the AAS, latterly from 1 Marchbank Road, Bieldside.

**GRAHAME, Alexander B** **fl 1871-1877**
Painter in oil of interiors, coastal scenes and landscape. Possibly brother of James(qv) and John G(qv). Exhibited RSA(10) & GI(2), from 40 Holland St, London.

**GRAHAME, James Barclay** **fl 1866-1882**
Edinburgh-based painter in oil of landscapes, sea scenes and figurative subjects. Brother of Alexander B(qv) and John B G(qv). Lived latterly at 7 West Castle Street. Exhibited RA(7) 1866-1875, all of them whilst living in London although most of them were Scottish scenes including an unidentified fishing harbour on the east coast of Scotland (1875); also RSA(18) & GI(3), latterly from 4 India St.

**GRAHAME, John Barclay** **fl 1875-1879**
Edinburgh based painter in oil and watercolour of portraits and figurative subjects. Brother of Alexander B(qv) and James Barclay G(qv). In addition to exhibiting RSA(5) & GI(4), exhibited RA(2) in London 1878-79 from 7 W. Castle Street.

**GRAHAME, S** **fl 1878**
Edinburgh watercolourist; exhibited 'A December bouquet' at the RSA in the above year.

**GRANGER, John** **fl 1882-1884**
Glasgow based artist. Painted mainly rustic scenes in oil. Exhibited GI(4) from 18 Shaftesbury Terrace.

**GRANGES, David des** **1611-1675**
Artist and miniature painter. Son of Sampson des Granges and Marie Bouvier of Guernsey. The Laing papers include a transcript of a petition from the artist who claims 'that he served yor majestie faithfully and diligently before yor restoration as yor limner in Scotland'. Also described as David de Grange, 'entertained Limner to His Majesty during the Royal Ye Abode at St Johnstones in Scotland' and submits an account for 13 portraits painted in 1651. The petition was accompanied by a schedule of the 13 pictures delivered there that year during the King's residence in Perth. On the 11 November 1671 the King referred the petition to the English treasury in respect of the 'poor and necessitous condition' to which the painter and his family were reduced, but there is no record of any further action. He was given employment by Charles I and Charles II and accompanied the latter to Scotland in 1651. He is said to have been a friend of Inigo Jones whose miniature he painted. Two portraits are known to exist, one in the collection of the Duke of Portland and the other with the Duke of Devonshire. The earliest known dated miniature is that said to represent Catherine Manners, Duchess of Buckingham, at Windsor Castle; this is signed 'DDG' in a triangle with a space between the D, the D and the G and dated '1639'. In 1671 ill-health, failing eyesight and increasing years persuaded him to petition Charles II. A signed miniature of an unknown lady is in the V&A, also represented in NPG, Ham House, Royal Collection.
**Bibl:** Apted 45; Brydall 100; Foskett 242-3; Goulding: 'Welbeck Abbey Miniature', Walpole Society, Vol IV.

**GRANT, 'Miss'** **19th century**
A watercolour drawing of a female figure with flowing drapery, in a doorway, is in the NGS. The back bears the inscription: ''Miss' Grant was a drawing mistress in Edinburgh, who later turned out to be a man'.

**GRANT, Alexander** **fl 1880-1881**
Fifeshire oil painter of castles and landscape. Exhibited RSA(2) from Buckhaven. Possibly the same Alexander Grant of 2 Esslemont Avenue, Aberdeen who exhibited Irish landscape at the AAS in 1902.

**GRANT, Alice E** **fl 1882-1900**
Crieff painter of still life and portraits in oil; exhibited RSA(2).

**GRANT, Alistair RBA ARCA (Lond)** **1925-1997**
Born London, 3 Jne. Portrait painter in oil; lithographer and etcher. Son of Duncan Grant(qv). Studied at Birmingham College of Art and at the Royal College of Art, London 1947-51. From 1955 taught printmaking at RCA becoming head of department 1970 and Professor of Printmaking 1984 until his retirement 1984. Exhibited regularly at the RA from 1952 & GI(1), from 13 Redcliffe Gdns, London. Represented in City of Edinburgh Art Collection (a lithograph and coloured etching), Glasgow AG, V & A.

**GRANT, Duncan James Corrour** **1885-1978**
Born Rothiemurchus, Inverness-shire, 21 Jan; died May 8. Painter in oil and watercolour; portraits, landscapes and still life; also decorator, illustrator, potter and designer of theatrical scenery. Lived in India until 1893 being educated at St Paul's School. Studied Westminster School of Art, in Italy, in Paris under J E Blanche 1906, then at the Slade School. Through his cousin, Lytton Strachey, he entered the Bloomsbury circle of Roger Fry, Vanessa Bell and Virginia Woolf. Lived in Paris 1907-9, visited Greece in 1910, Sicily and Tunisia 1911. Influenced toward abstract paintings by a visit to the 1910 London exhibition 'Manet and the Impressionists', prepared by Roger Fry. Member of the Camden Town Group 1911 and the London Group 1919. Worked for a time with Roger Fry in the Omega Workshop which, together with Woolf's sister Vanessa Bell and Fry, he founded. Often visited the south of France on sketching holidays, spending most of the summers between 1927 and 1938 at Cassis. Lived at Furl, Sussex for many years. 'Although Grant's intellectual predelictions make him intermittently responsive to the aesthetic doctrines of his friends his most personal gifts were not only for the poetic invention noted by Fry but for the representation of the real world, in particular for the richness of colour and the weight and texture of things' [Rothenstein]. His work evolved from an appreciation for the Fauves and Post-Impressionists. With Vanessa (with whom Grant lived for fifty years) and Quentin Bell he decorated the church at Berwick, Sussex 1943, both of whom were later involved in decorating Lincoln Cathedral. Provided illustrations for B Grant: *The Receipt Book of Elizabeth Raper* (1924), Garnett: *A Terrible Day* (1932), Coleridge: *The Rime of the Ancient Mariner* (1945), Wu Ch'eng-en: *Monkey* (1968), Rhodes: *In an Eighteenth Century Kitchen* (1968). His work was included in the British Pavilion at the Venice Biennale 1926 and again in 1932. 'The Kitchen' (1902) was purchased by the Chantrey Bequest 1959, 'The Tub' (1912) in 1965 and 'Girl at the Piano' in 1940. Exhibited widely throughout Britain including RA, RSA, GI(10) & RHA. A retrospective exhibition of his work was held at the Tate in 1959. Represented in Tate AG, SNGMA, Liverpool AG, Bucharest AG, Kirkcaldy AG, Glasgow AG, Manchester AG; Southampton AG, Nat Gall of Canada(Ottawa), Nat Gall of New Zealand (Wellington).

**Bibl:** Mortimer, Duncan Grant (Penguin Modern Painters 1944); Harold Osborne(ed), Twentieth Century Art 1988, 232-3; Rothenstein 18-19, 172 (pls 44 and 63); I Andscombe: *Omega and After: Bloomsbury and the Decorative Arts* 1981; *Landscape in Britain 1850-1950* (Arts Council 1983); Horne 224-6; Ian Jeffrey.

**GRANT, Edmund** **fl 1878**
Glasgow watercolourist. Exhibited GI(1), from 140 Mains St.

**GRANT, Edward** **fl 1938**
Glasgow based watercolour natural history artist. Exhibited RSW(1) & GI(1) from Pollok House.

**GRANT, Sir Francis PRA RSA** **1803-1878**
Born Edinburgh, 18 Jan; died Melton Mowbray, 5 Oct. Painter in oil of portraits, equestrian studies and sporting subjects. Fourth son of Francis Grant, Laird of Kilgraston, Perthshire and next younger brother of Lieutenant General Sir James Hope Grant. Originally educated for the Bar but a passionate love of art induced him to follow it as a profession and he began seriously to study when about 24. After having exhausted a patrimony of about £10,000, in 1834 he was forced to become a professional painter. Received some instruction from his friend Ferneley whose influence is more easily detected than that of Alexander Nasmyth who had instructed the artist as a very young man in Edinburgh. Grant was good at obtaining likenesses while able to portray horses with character. He himself was a handsome, well-connected and charming man which helped to rapidly attract notice for his equestrian groups, many being engraved. By 1837 he had become a leading London portrait painter. Three years earlier his 'Breakfast at Melton' at the RA, containing 12 portrait figures and an equestrian portrait of 'Capt Van de Leur of the Inniskilling Dragoons', attracted popular acclaim. Married the Duke of Rutland's niece which further developed his connections. In 1841 an equestrian portrait 'Queen Victoria attended by Lord Melbourne and others' was exhibited as in 1843 was a portrait of 'The Queen' herself. Exhibited portraits of his wife, 'Lady Beauclerk', 'Lady Rodney' and 'Lord John Russell' in the Paris Exhibition of 1855. His portrait of Queen Victoria made him the most sought after portraitist of his time and from then on he exhibited only at the RA. After Landseer had declined and Daniel Maclise had also refused the honour, following the death of Sir Charles Eastlake in 1866, Grant was elected PRA and duly knighted. As President he skilfully concluded negotiations with the Government that enabled the Academy to occupy Burlington House. Whilst at the top of his profession, he continued to divide his time between painting and fox-hunting. He shared with Landseer, whose portrait he painted, the distinction of being the only painter in London who had a studio expressly designed for painting animals. When he was knighted Queen Victoria commented 'she cannot say she thinks his selection a good one for art. He boasts of never having been in Italy or studied the Old Masters. He has decidedly much talent but it is much the talent of an amateur.' He had great talent though it was often superficial, and it was in his less important work that it was best revealed. It was said that the broad and restful management of light eluded him and that 'his horses are never painted, save they look as though they are stuffed!' Wishing to be buried at Melton Mowbray, the honour of a burial at St Paul's Cathedral was declined. Elected RSA 1830, ARA 1842, RA 1851. Exhibited RA(253), RSA(53) & GI(6), from Sussex Villa, Sussex Place, London. A memorial exhibition was held at SNPG 2003. Represented in NGS, SNPG(6), NPG, Glasgow AG, City of Edinburgh collection (an oil of 'Sir Walter Scott' and mezzotint of 'John Gibson Lockhart'), Perth AG, Brodick Castle (NTS, 'Susan, Countess of Lincoln, daughter of the 10th Duke of Hamilton'), Leicester AG.
**Bibl:** Armstrong 47; Bryan; Brydall 408-410; Caw 176-7; Grant 224-5, pl 117; Irwin 320-2; Maas 72-3; McKay 128-134; Macmillan [SA] 164; Steegman, 'Sir Francis Grant, PRA The Artist in High Society', Apollo LXXIX, 1964, 479-485.

**GRANT, George** **fl 1921**
Paisley based artist. Exhibited a study of 'The Thistle Chapel, St Giles, Edinburgh' at the RSA from 30 Williamsburg.

**GRANT, Gertrude M** **fl 1919-1929**
Aberdeen painter of landscape, engraver and etcher. Exhibited AAS, latterly from 69 Devonshire Place.

**GRANT, Ian Macdonald ARCA (Lond) FRSA** **1904-**
Born Coatbridge, Lanark, 6 Sep. Painter in oil of portraits and landscapes. Studied at Glasgow School of Art 1922-26, in Paris at Colarossi 1927 and Royal College of Art 1927-30. Influenced by Haswell Miller(qv) in Glasgow, by Severini and Leger in Paris as well as by the Diaghilev ballet. Went through a futurist/cubist phase 1926-35. Taught at School of Art, Southport 1936 and thereafter developed a more traditional style. His principal works include 'Self-portrait' and 'Cheshire Mill'. Painting master at Manchester School of Art for many years from 1937. Lived latterly at High Lane in Cheshire. Exhibited RA(3), RSA(9) & GI(6). Represented in Derby AG, Manchester AG, Salford AG, Southport AG.

**GRANT, J** **fl 1800-1809**
Edinburgh engraver. Engraved a map of the Zetland Islands which appears as a frontispiece in Edmondson's *View of the...Zetland Islands* 2 vols, 1809. Thought by Bushnell to be the same as the engraver who executed a stipple engraving in colours after Bigg.
**Bibl:** Bushnell.

**GRANT, James** **fl 1840-1855**
Artist, novelist, historian, draughtsman. Whilst a resident of Stockbridge, Edinburgh he brought together a volume of original drawings entitled *A Collection of Sketches, Plans, Details, etc from old buildings, particularly in and around Edinburgh, drawn by me, chiefly between 1840 and 1850.* Included among the sketches is a watercolour of 'Edinburgh Castle' drawn by Grant's mother Mary Anne Watson. His work made an important contribution to the topographical history of Edinburgh. Lived at 26 Danube St, Stockbridge.
**Bibl:** Butchart 21,32,67-8.

**GRANT, James** **fl 1886**
Glasgow based painter. Exhibited 'Homeward Bound' at the GI(1) from 21 West Nile Street.

**GRANT, James J** **fl 1890-1893**
Minor Aberdeen painter. Exhibited 'Harvest scene' at the AAS from 10 Esslemont Avenue.

**GRANT, Jane E** **fl 1884-1889**
Glasgow based flower painter in oil and watercolour. Exhibited GI(4), latterly from 79 West End Pk St.

**GRANT, John** **fl 1890-1893**
Aberdeenshire landscape painter. Exhibited mainly local scenes, also 'Tarbert Castle' at the AAS(4) from Haddo House.

**GRANT, John** **fl 1974**
Inverness-shire amateur artist. Exhibited 'Oak trees in winter' at the AAS from Canopus, Balmacaan Road, Drumnadrochit.

**GRANT, John (of Kilgraston)** **1798-1873**
Painter in oil and pen and ink of portraits and figure subjects. Elder brother of Sir Francis G(qv). An ink study of a knight with a lance on a galloping horse, drawn on blue notepaper, is in the NGS. Mitchell refers to a painting of 'John Walker, huntsman to the Fife Foxhounds with whips and hounds', signed and dated 1836. There is also a print published in 1845, drawn and engraved by John Grant 'Rocket Practice in the Marshes'.
**Bibl:** Mitchell.

**GRANT, John** **fl 1970-1981**
Ayrshire painter of still life and semi-abstracts in mixed media and oil. Exhibited GI(8), from 15 Stronsay Place, Wardneuk, Kilmarnock.

**GRANT, John M** **fl 1920**
Exhibited 'The Medical hut - waiting his turn' at the RSA from Archibald Place, Edinburgh.

**GRANT, Keith** **1960-**
Born Edinburgh. Painter and printmaker. Trained Gray's School of Art, Aberdeen 1978-82 followed by a post-graduate year. Exhibits since 1982 and in 1988 was a visiting lecturer at Gray's School of Art.

**GRANT, Lyn** **fl 1974**
Amateur Dundee artist who exhibited at the AAS.

**GRANT, Miss Margaret** **[see HISLOP, Margaret Ross]**

**GRANT, Miss Mary** **1830-1908**
Sculptress. Painter and embroiderer. Eldest daughter of John(qv) and Lucy Grant of Kilgraston and niece of Sir Francis G(qv). Studied Paris and afterwards under Foley in London. One of 13 children. Her nephew, Colonel Patrick Grant, wrote of her 'Mary Grant was a pioneer - if not the pioneer - amongst women to take up sculpture professionally, and to set up a studio of her own. In 1879 she was asked by the Prince of Wales to represent British Art at the Paris Exhibition. She was a lady of singular versatility, skilled at painting, embroidery, and with a touch of great charm on the piano. Many persons of note frequented her salon in Tithe Street, Chelsea. She was possessed with the gift of drawing the best out of people and making them feel vastly important - without herself being highly intellectual'. Some of her work remains at Kilgraston, including several busts, two plaster bas reliefs, an altarpiece and a small pastoral scene. Sculpted the memorial to Arthur Penrhyn Stanley in St. George's Chapel, Windsor, a replica of which is in the Preston aisle of St. Giles. Also in Edinburgh is her white marble relief of the Crucifixion on the reredos of St Mary's Cathedral. Exhibited RA for no fewer than 41 years, executing over 100 works; also RSA(8). Represented in SNPG.
**Bibl:** Gifford 115,365.

**GRANT, Robert** **fl 1871**
Edinburgh based painter. Exhibited 'Loch Leven Castle' at the RSA from 4 Leggats Land, Stockbridge.

**GRANT, Miss Robina B I** **fl 1940-1948**
Dumfriesshire landscape painter in oil. Exhibited mainly Solway landscapes at the RSA annually 1940-1944 and again in 1946 and 1948 from 3 Park Terrace, Annan.

**GRANT, Thomas** **fl 1887-1901**
Glasgow painter of landscape, townscapes and still life in oil and watercolour. Exhibited GI(5), after 1900 from Springfield Rd.

**GRANT, Thomas F** **fl 1868-1879**
Edinburgh oil painter of landscapes including Highland scenes, often with castles. Exhibited RSA(21) & at the GI 'Tantallon Castle' and 'Cockermouth Castle, Cumberland', from 90 George St. Represented in City of Edinburgh collecton.

**GRANT ROBERTSON, Fiona** **1953-**
Born West Lothian. Works in watercolour and mixed media using papermaking techniques to create paintings and boxes containing low relief images, frequently theatre related. Trained Edinburgh College of Art 1971-75, winning an Andrew Grant scholarship spent with the Royal Shakespeare Company. Became qualified teacher 1976 and since 1980 teaches at Trinity Academy, Edinburgh. First solo exhibition 1979 followed by one in Hong Kong and many in Edinburgh.

**GRANT-SUTTIE, Mrs G D** **[see HOSACK, Isobel]**

**GRASSBY, Charles B** **fl 1865-1884**
Glasgow based figurative sculptor. Exhibited GI(7) from 227 West Campbell Street.

**GRASSIE, Adam H** **fl 1948-1965**
Renfrewshire painter of still life and landscape in oil and watercolour. Exhibited GI(10), from 90 Sandy Rd, Renfrew.

**GRASSIE, George** **1922-1972**
Angus painter in oil and watercolour of portraits, landscape and topographical subjects, also teacher. A native of Arbroath he spent his childhood in Dundee being educated at Harris Academy. At the age of 16 he had an accident while playing football which required him to spend 5 years in hospital. There his artistic abilities were encouraged notably by James Cowie(qv). After leaving hospital he studied at Dundee College of Art gaining a postgraduate travelling scholarship allowing him to study for six months in France and Italy. Upon his return he took up a teaching appointment with Angus Education Committee and became principal art teacher at Mackie Academy, Stonehaven before joining the staff of his old school. Chairman of Arbroath Art Society, in 1969 a paper entitled 'The Individual as Subject and Source in the Teaching of Art' was presented at the World Congress of the International Society for Education Through Art in New York. One of the original eight members appointed in 1970 to serve on the Children's Panel in Arbroath. As well as being an outstanding teacher his artistic output was extensive and varied. In 1973 a retrospective exhibition was held in Dundee and among the works on show were realistic pastoral scenes as well as surrealistic studies. He experimented with still life after Mondrian and one work 'Wagonwheel' was executed with the painting continued on to the frame on all four sides. His greatest strengths, apart from his educational work, were an understanding of perspective and great skill in delineation and draughtsmanship. Machines also fascinated him and he often discovered most unlikely subjects for drawings in such places as railway sidings, factories and farm buildings. Exhibited RSA(7) & AAS(2).

**GRASSIE, Miss Marissa** **1963-**
Born 23 Dec. Printmaker, painter and lithographer in oil, charcoal, crayons, pen and ink. Favourite compositions are figures and portraits showing the influence of Bonnard, Matisse and Schiele. Daughter of Morris G(qv). Studied Edinburgh College of Art 1982-1986, obtaining a postgraduate diploma in 1986-1987. Attended Moray House 1987-88. In 1986, having won the Andrew Grant travelling award, visited Italy, followed in 1989 by winning the Greenshields award for drawing and painting. Exhibited RSA since 1988, & in 1989 'Self-portrait' at the GI, from 12A Brandon St.

**GRASSIE, Morris** **1931-**
Born Arbroath. Painter of still life and figurative works; also lithographer. Father of Marissa G(qv). Studied at Duncan of Jordanstone College of Art 1952, under Alberto Morrocco(qv), James Cowie(qv), and Ian Fleming at Hospitalfield(qv). Obtained a postgraduate travel award 1953, enabling him to visit Paris. Won Keith prize 1952. Has lectured extensively on art appreciation and in 1970-1975 was Convener of the Annual Conference of Lecturers in Art of the Scottish Colleges of Education. From 1981-1984 member of the Scottish Central Committee on Art and in 1987 member of the Design Council Curricula and Development in Resources Monitoring Group. In between these administrative duties he continued to paint. Lives in Edinburgh. Exhibited regularly RSA 1950-1969 then again from 1988, & GI(5) 1952-3. Represented in Arbroath AG, Dundee AG, Glasgow AG.

**GRASSOM, J** **fl 1817-1819**
Engraved maps of Stirling and Stirlingshire during the above years.
**Bibl:** Bushnell.

**GRAVES, Henry Richard** **fl 1867-1875**
Portrait painter. Exhibited RSA(4) including 'Col Douglas of Glenfinart' 1867.

**GRAY, Alasdair** **1934-**
Born Glasgow. Specialised in mural, narrative paintings, still life, figurative subjects and portraits; worked in oil and occasional watercolour. Studied Glasgow School of Art. Also an author, his best known work being *Lanark* (1981) for which he also provided the illustrations. Exhibited RSA(3) & GI(29), since 1979 from 39 Kersland St.

**GRAY, Miss Alice** **fl 1882-1904**
Portrait, flower and figure painter and miniaturist in oil and watercolour also interiors, birds and flowers, mostly miniatures on ivory. Exhibited RA 1891 and 1892, RSA(29), RBA(1), RI(1), L(1) & GI(13), after 1890 from 59 George St, Edinburgh.

**GRAY, Archibald** **fl 1955-1959**
Glasgow painter of portraits, flowers and landscape; exhibited GI(6), from 102 Cardowan Rd.

**GRAY, Archibald Gary** **fl 1953-1967**
Glasgow painter of genre and landscapes (especially in Cornwall); exhibited RSA(5) & GI(9), from Four Winds, Gargunnock.

**GRAY, Beaumont** **fl 1951-1953**
Edinburgh based painter of genre, interiors and topographical scenes. Exhibited RSA(3) from 10 Ann Street.

**GRAY, C** **fl 1867**
Glasgow painter; exhibited GI(1), from 14 Shamrock St.

**GRAY, Carol** **fl 1982-1987**
Aberdeen artist. Trained at Gray's School of Art, Aberdeen. Exhibited AAS during the above years from 44 Kintore Place.

**GRAY, Charles William** **fl 1925-1966**
Edinburgh architect. Responsible for some important work including the reconstruction of the interior of Aberdeen Cathedral (1966). In Edinburgh he designed St John the Baptist (RC) church, St Ninian's Rd (1926) and the 'pebbledashed, expressionist octagon' church of St Teresa, Niddrie Mains Rd (1963).
**Bibl:** Gifford 525,538.

**GRAY, Charlotte** **fl 1893-1896**
North Berwick painter of landscape and country scenes. Exhibited AAS from Brownrigg, N Berwick.

**GRAY, Chrissie (Lady Keith)** **fl 1921**
Amateur Aberdeen landscape painter. Married Sir Arthur Keith. Exhibited AAS from 8 South Crown Street.
**Bibl:** Arthur Keith, An Autobiography, Watts, London 1950.

**GRAY, D H** **fl 1873**
Glasgow-based sculptor; exhibited GI(1), from 4 W. Campbell St.

**GRAY, David** **1939-2003**
Born Shawlands, Glasgow; died Inverness. Painter & illustrator of flowers, landscape and fish. Married, with two sons and a daughter. After leaving school he joined a Glasgow advertising agency, working in the graphic department and enrolling in evening classes at the Glasgow School of Art. Won a prestigeous award at the Cannes Film Festival 1965. This led to a number of lucrative commissions for commercial designs, including labels for the Moniack Castle Winery and Bowmore Whisky. Other awards included a gold medal at the Cork International Film Festival and the Layton Press Award for poster design. Moved to Inverness 1981 to work with Michael Fraser associates, while continuing to visit and paint on Islay. One time champion and captain of Eastwood Golf Club.

**GRAY, David G M** **fl 1968**
Glasgow painter of townscapes and garden scenes. Exhibited GI(2), from 3 Gilmour St.

**GRAY, George** **fl 1866-1910**
Painter in oil and watercolour; landscapes, especially of the Highlands. Husband of Jessie G(qv). His earlier life was spent in Kirkcaldy before moving to Edinburgh and finally in c1898 to Musselburgh. A highly prolific and competent painter. His watercolours were more distinguished than his oils with a fine luminous use of colour although the compositions tend to be somewhat confining. Fond of working in the Trossachs. Exhibited RSA(100+), RSW(5), RHA(1), GI(15) & AAS 1893. Represented in City of Edinburgh collection(2).
**Bibl:** Caw 303; Halsby 261.

**GRAY, George H** **fl 1961**
Aberdeen landscape artist. Exhibited AAS(1) from 7 Ross Crescent.

**GRAY, Gerard** **fl 1974-1979**
Glasgow topographical artist; exhibited GI(2), from 11 Lockerbie Ave.

**GRAY, Hamish J** **fl 1964**
Stirlingshire etcher. Exhibited 'Glasgow Tram in Smog' at the GI (1964), from 4 Lendrick Ave, Falkirk.

**GRAY, Hugh** **fl 1866-1870**
Glasgow watercolourist of genre and landscape; exhibited GI(2), from 39 Clyde St.

**GRAY, Iain Donald Fraser** **fl 1970**
Aberdeenshire designer, mainly of jewellery. Exhibited AAS from Murcar.

**GRAY, Isabella** **fl 1892-1894**
Edinburgh based painter in oil and watercolour of portraits and genre. Married to J Leadbetter G(qv). Exhibited RSA(3) & RSW(1) from 1 Warrender Park Crescent.

**GRAY, J Leadbetter** **fl 1891**
Edinburgh based amateur portrait painter of 1 Warrender Park Crescent. Married to Isabella G(qv). Exhibited RSA(1).

**GRAY, Jack** **fl 1920-1922**
Edinburgh based landscape painter in watercolour. Exhibited RSA(4) & GI(2) from 43 Briarbank Terrace.

**GRAY, James** **fl 1893-1925**
Glasgow-based sculptor; worked mainly in bronze, occasionally plaster and metal especially pewter. Lived in Milngavie, trained Glasgow School of Art. Specialised in portrait busts and figure subjects. Exhibited a bronze statuette 'Les Reves' at the RA (1903) from 79 West Regent Street, Glasgow. Exhibited RSA(16) & GI(30), after 1916 from Auldhaven, Milngavie.

**GRAY, James RSW** **fl 1917-d1947**
Edinburgh flower painter in watercolour. His work was generally free and effective. His wife Jean Lyal Christie also painted in watercolours. Elected RSW 1936. Taught Edinburgh College of Art. Exhibited RSA(35) 1917-1945, RSW(38), RA(6), L(8), AAS(4) & GI(37), after 1933 from Green Steps, 22 Braid Farm Rd. Represented in Edinburgh City collection.
**Bibl:** Halsby 261.

**GRAY, Janice RSW** **1966-**
Born 15 Jne. Painter of old buildings, animal portraits and still life. Prefers to work in watercolour with extensive use of washes. Refers to herself as an illustrator rather than a painter. Trained Glasgow School of Art 1984-1988. Received the W O Hutchison Prize for Drawing and an Elizabeth Greenshields scholarship 1988. Major influence has been Joseph Beuys. Elected RSW 1995. Began exhibiting RSW 1986 & RSA 1989. Represented in Aberdeen AG, Perth AG.

**GRAY, Jeannie Cumming** **fl 1896-1911**
Painter in oil of portraits and flowers. Lived in Edinburgh, Dollar and Dundee. Exhibited RSA(5), including Lilies, & L(1).

**GRAY, Jessie Dixon (Mrs George Gray)** **fl 1881-1892**
Painter in oil and watercolour of portraits, rustic scenes, small animals and figurative subjects. Daughter of George G(qv). Exhibited regularly RSA(42) 1881-1890 including a portrait of Robert McGregor's daughter 1883. In 1892 exhibited 'A little maid' at the RA from 1 Warrender Park Crescent, Edinburgh; also GI(4).

**GRAY, John** **fl 1873-1882**
Glasgow based landscape painter in oil. Exhibited two views of Loch Awe at the RSA from 179 West George Street.

**GRAY, John RSW** **1877-1957**
Scottish watercolour painter of flowers, portraits and natural history subjects. During his career he lived in many places thus we find him in London 1885, Surrey 1890, Dorset 1899, Hawick 1910 and again 1925, Suffolk 1917 and Broughty Ferry 1937 before finally being heard of in Edinburgh. Probably best known for his early strongly painted coastal scenes, often worked on a large scale. Elected RSW 1941. Exhibited widely including works at the RA(23), RSA(4), RSW(26), RBA(10), ROI(4) & GI(5). Represented in Glasgow AG, Dundee AG.
**Bibl:** Halsby 234,261.

**GRAY, John C** **fl 1911-1912**
Minor Dundee artist. Exhibited a harvest scene AAS & GI(1) from Alexander Place, Downfield.

**GRAY, Joseph** **1890-1962**
Painter and etcher. Studied at South Shields School of Art before settling in Scotland. Undertook many sketching trips overseas including visits to Russia, Germany, Spain, France and Holland. During WW1 served with the Black Watch in Belgium and was war artist to *The Graphic*. During this time he undertook many sketches of

wartime Paris. After the arrival of peace he began exhibiting at the RSA (1919) 'Bivouac of the 4th Black Watch' and 'General Southey's Brigade after the Battle of Neve Chapelle 13.3.1915' (from a sketch on the spot). Exhibited again at the RSA 1924. His last address was Seacote, Kerrington Crescent, Barnhill, Broughty Ferry. Represented in Glasgow AG.

**GRAY, Joseph Crosbie** **1873-1958**
Glasgow based painter of genre and landscape in watercolour, sometimes in oil. Exhibited RSA(2), RSW(1), GI(8) & AAS (1935-1937), from 43 Lamb Street, Parkhouse.

**GRAY, Miss Kate** **fl 1867**
Glasgow painter of figurative subjects. Daughter of C G(qv). Exhibited GI(2), from 14 Shamrock St.

**GRAY, Leonard RSW** **1925-**
Born Dundee. Painter of landscapes and town scenes in oil and gouache. Trained 1949-53 at the Edinburgh College of Art from where he obtained a postgraduate scholarship. His particular interest is in bridges and domestic buildings including such places as hothouses and aquaria with emphasis on textural relationships. Many of his subjects are based on the coastal villages of Aberdeenshire, Fife and the North East, executed latterly with a mixed media technique with gouache predominant. Recently began investigating the possibilities of pure watercolour. In 1969 appointed lecturer in drawing and painting at the Northern Art College, retired 1989. Elected RSW 1968, also member of the SSA. Received the EIS Award (RSW) 1980, the May Marshall Brown Award (RSW) 1994 and the RSW Council's Major Award 1995. Exhibited regularly at the RSA since 1954, also RSW, GI(9) & AAS since 1973 from 27 Marchbank Road, Bieldside. Represented in Greenock AG, Edinburgh City collection.
**Bibl:** Frith 48 (83).

**GRAY, Leonard J** **1951-**
Born Glasgow. Painter in oils, primarily of fruit and vegetable still lifes on a comparatively small scale; also printmaker. Attended Glasgow School of Art 1968-72, gaining a post-graduate award 1973. Studied printmaking in London 1973 under Alastair Grant(qv) and Eduardo Paolozzi(qv). Exhibited British International Print Biennale 1982, 1986, 1990 and RSA since 1994.

**GRAY, Mabel** **fl 1906-1914**
Glasgow based portrait miniaturist. Exhibited GI(5) including portrait miniatures of Jessie M King (1907), after 1912 from 4 Claremont Terrace.

**GRAY, Mary Anderson** **fl 1879**
Edinburgh portrait painter and ceramic designer. Exhibited a portrait on porcelain at the RSA.

**GRAY, Mike** **fl 1978**
Aberdeen landscape painter. Exhibited 5 local views at the AAS from 56 Garthdee Road.

**GRAY, Miss Norah Neilson RSW** **1882-1931**
Born Helensburgh. Painter in oil and watercolour, also fashion-plate designer; portraits, figure subjects and fantasies. Daughter of a Glasgow shipowner, second youngest of seven children. After preliminary art studies at 'The Studio', Craigendoran, run by Madge Ross, she enrolled at Glasgow School of Art 1901-1906 studying under the Belgian Symbolist Jean Delville(qv). While still a student had her first exhibit at the RA, a portrait of her sister Gertie. Joined the staff of the GSA shortly after graduating as well as teaching at St Columba's School, Kilmacolm. In 1910 she acquired her own studio at 141 Bath Street. Four years later elected RSW, the same year that her watercolour illustrations for Wordsworth's *Ode on Intimations of Immortality* first appeared. In about 1915 she executed 'One of our Trawlers are Missing', now in Glasgow AG. Her most impressive works were completed over the next few years including 'The Country's Charge' c1915, exhibited at the RA and purchased by Joseph Bibby. 'The Belgian In Exile' also dates from this time, being exhibited at the GI 1916, RA 1917 and Paris Salon 1921 where it was awarded a bronze medal. In 1918 she went to France to work as a nurse at the Scottish Women's Hospital and in 1920 was commissioned by the Imperial War Museum to record the hospital. During the last year of the war she painted more wartime studies successfully capturing the stark atmosphere of those times. In 1923 won gold medal in Paris for 'La Jeune Fille'. After the war returned to Glasgow spending more time on portrait painting some of which found disfavour among contemporary critics because of the prominence given to decorative elements. In 1921 was the first woman elected to the RGI's hanging committee. In 1922 exhibited 'Little brother' at the RA, now in Glasgow AG, and that year contributed a miniature painting for the Queen's Dolls House. Later works became more modernist in feel with a tendency toward abstract expressionism. A hauntingly beautiful 'Self-portrait', now in the collection of a descendent, is illustrated in colour (fig 271) in Burkhauser. In spite of her early death she is established as a significant figure in European art, to a greater extent than was ever the case in her native country. 'Her distinctive colour schemes, unconventional placement of images upon the canvas and 'purple patch' shadow patterns were all trade marks'. Exhibited extensively including RA(7), RSA(27), RSW(55), GI(43) & L910). Represented in Glasgow AG, Perth AG, Brussels AG, Nice AG, Toronto AG.
**Bibl:** Burkhauser and Catriona Reynolds in Burkhauser, 201-206; Halsby 183-4,261.

**GRAY, Patrick** **fl 1964**
Minor Aberdeen landscape painter. Exhibited a local study at the AAS from 27 Marywell Street.

**GRAY, R** **fl 1830-1840**
Scottish engraver, probably of Edinburgh. Engraved bookplates for James Couper, 1840; John Couper, 1830; James Dobie, 1830; John Ross, 1840; and W Wood, 1830. Possibly one of the Glasgow firm of engravers who executed a number of plates to illustrate the 1830 edition of McUre's *View of the City of Glasgow*.

**GRAY, Robert** **fl 1865**
Glasgow waterolourist. Exhibited 'Dunbar Pier & Lighthouse' at the GI, from 2 Laurence Place.

**GRAY, Robert Campbell** **fl 1885-1887**
Painter in oil and watercolour of buildings and occasional subject studies. Exhibited RSA(9) from 72 Northumberland Street, Edinburgh, and latterly from 27 Ann Street.

**GRAY, Rosalie (née Campbell) RSW** **1883-1955**
Born Glasgow. Watercolourist and embroiderer. Studied Glasgow School of Art. Exhibited many decorative watercolours at the RSW.
**Bibl:** Halsby 261.

**GRAY, Miss Sheila** **fl 1950-1952**
Glasgow painter of flora and fauna. Related to William G(qv). Exhibited GI(3), from 30 Berryhill Drive, Giffnock.

**GRAY, Tom** **1841-1876**
Born Aberdeen. Painter in oil and watercolour of figures and portrait subjects. Nephew of James Cassie(qv) and father of Chrissie G(qv). He resolved to follow his uncle's footsteps and to that end went to London but met with only moderate success. Although an excellent musician and a very social person, his paintings were not greatly valued. However, became Secretary of the Hogarth Club of Fitzroy Square, frequented by most leading young artists of the day. In 1868 he married. By 1876 he had developed consumption and died shortly after. Exhibited RSA(17) including 'A Japanese Picture Book', purchased by James Cassie.
**Bibl:** Arthur Keith, An Autobiography, Watts, London 1950.

**GRAY, William** **fl 1887**
Exhibited 'Winter waves' at the AAS from 26 South Mount Street.

**GRAY, William** **fl 1933-1951**
Glasgow based landscape painter, principally views on Skye, Arran and in the region of St. Ives (Cornwall). Related to Sheila G(qv). Exhibited GI(20), from 30 Berryhill Drive, Giffnock.

**GRAY'S SCHOOL OF ART** **1885-**
Facilities for education in art and design existed in Aberdeen since 1852 when the first classes were developed under the auspices of the

Aberdeen Mechanics Institute. In 1885, through the munificence of John Gray, a local ironmaster, the School of Art opened on the site of the old Grammar School, adjoining the Art gallery, taking over and expanding the work being done by the Mechanics Institute. By 1901 it had become one of the four main centres of art education in Scotland. Now a component of Robert Gordon's Institute of Technology, in September 1988 the School joined the Scott Sutherland School of Architecture to become the new Faculty of Design.
**Bibl:** Caw 225.

**GREEN, Alexander** **fl 1849-1865**
Painter in oil of portraits, figure subjects and genre. Lived for a time in Edinburgh and after 1858 in Leith. Exhibited RSA(27), including a rare study of the game of shinty entitled 'Playing at Shinty' 1865; also GI(2). Represented City of Edinburgh collection(2).

**GREEN, Archibald** **fl 1872**
Minor Aberdeen portrait painter in oil. Exhibited 'John Dove Wilson, Sheriff-Substitute of Aberdeenshire' at the RSA.

**GREEN, Benjamin R** **fl c1838-1874**
Portrait, topographical and figure painter in watercolour and sometimes pencil; worked in Inverness in the late 1830s and again in 1840. His work was well received and the local newspaper spoke of its 'beauty and fidelity which were equally apparent'. Exhibited GI(9) 1863-1874, from 41 Fitzroy Sq, London.

**GREEN, Betty** **fl 1934**
Milngavie engraver. Exhibited a wood engraving at the RSA from Lochend, Bardowie.

**GREEN, Derek** **fl 1983-1988**
Glasgow painter and sculptor. Figures and flowers. Exhibited GI(5) including 'Sudanese girl' in terracotta at the GI, from 53 Fergus Drive.

**GREEN, Edward** **fl 1906**
Minor Aberdeen landscape painter. Exhibited AAS(1) from 6 Victoria Buildings.

**GREEN, George Kay** **fl 1899**
Edinburgh painter of interiors in oil, exhibited a study of the Upper Hall Signet Library, Edinburgh (1899) at the RSA from 42 Blacket Place.

**GREEN, Hugh** **fl 1944-1946**
Stirlingshire landscape painter. Exhibited GI(2), from Allan Bank, Bridge of Allan.

**GREEN, Madeline** **fl 1923**
Born London. Portrait and topographical painter. Studied at RA Schools. Exhibited Paris Salon winning a gold medal 1923. (Benezit erroneously records exhibited RA). There is a painting entitled 'Glasgow' in the Victoria AG (Australia) catalogued as Scottish, almost certainly by this artist.

**GREENE, T Garland** **fl 1933**
Watercolourist, exhibited RSW(1).

**GREENHILL, Alexander McDonald** **1907-**
Born Glasgow, 30 Dec. Painter in watercolour and etcher; landscapes and designer. Studied Glasgow School of Art as an evening student and whilst employed as a carpet designer for a Glasgow company began exhibiting at the RSW from his home at Hillhead, Glasgow.

**GREENLEES, Georgina Mossman (Mrs Graham Wylie) RSW** **1849-1932**
Born Glasgow. Painter in oil and watercolour of landscapes, still life, portraits, figure subjects and rustic scenes. Daughter of Robert Greenlees(qv). Studied Glasgow School of Art joining the teaching staff 1875-1880. Resigned with her father in protest at the absence of life-classes for women students. Second President, Glasgow Society of Lady Artists. A competent watercolourist. Painted continental views in Italy, Belgium and Switzerland. Elected RSW 1878. Exhibited twice at the RA, 'A corner of the forest, Inverary' (1878) from 150 Randolph Terrace, Glasgow and 'A Byepath - Corrie, Arran' (1880) from 136 Wellington Street; also RSA(29), RSW, GI(65) & AAS, after 1896 from Regent Park, Prestwick, Ayrshire.
**Bibl:** Halsby 261.

**GREENLEES, James** **fl 1860-1903**
Lived in Glasgow, Greenock and latterly in Dunblane. Painter of landscapes in oil and occasional watercolour in a meticulous manner with a fine eye to topographical shape and line. Brother of Marion L G(qv). Exhibited RSA(50), always Scottish landscape, mostly of the West Coast, Argyll, and some Perthshire scenes; also GI(46).

**GREENLEES, Miss Maggie L S** **fl 1884-1885**
Edinburgh watercolourist of landscapes; exhibited RSA(3) from 12 Cumin Place, Grange.

**GREENLEES, Marion L** **fl 1866-1867**
Glasgow oil painter of still life, flowers and fruit. Daughter of Robert G(qv), sister of Georgina(qv) and James(qv). Exhibited RSA(3) & GI(4), from 193 Sauchiehall St.

**GREENLEES, Robert David** **fl 1867-1889**
Glasgow painter of Highland scenery. Exhibited GI(4), from 4 Cumberland St.

**GREENLEES, Robert M RSW** **1820-1904**
Painter in oil of landscapes and narrative subjects. Painted landscapes in a distinctive, detailed, slightly fussy but often telling style in both oil and watercolour. Father of Georgina(qv) and James G(qv). Preceded Fra Newbery as Head of Glasgow School of Art. Resigned 1881 and the two lady members of staff left with him, one of them his daughter Georgina(qv). A meeting was called in his studio and a Book of Rules prepared, recommending the provision of life classes for female students. Elected RSW 1878. Exhibited RA(4) 1873-77, RSA(52), RSW(24), RHA(5), GI(112), AAS & L(7), after 1888 from 150 Hill St.
**Bibl:** Caw 224; Halsby 70,153,165,261.

**GREENLEES, William** **fl 1847-1850**
Edinburgh portrait painter and painter of conversation pieces in oil. Perhaps his best known portrait was the 'Hon Lady Charlotte MacGregor' (1848). Exhibited RSA(9), & 'Tantallon Castle' at the GI, from 23 Jamaica St. Represented in SNPG(2).

**GREENSHIELDS, John** **1795-1835**
Born Lesmahagow, Lanarkshire; died Ramapo, United States, 20 Apr. Sculptor. Mason by trade. Employed by Robert Forrest(qv) 1822 who at the time was working on a statue of Melville. This gave Greenshields an interest in sculpture and he began to study and model in clay. His first work was a figure of a dog carved in stone; also modelled likenesses in clay of his father and brother. Executed a small stone statue of Lord Byron, and in 1827 made a figure of Canning and followed this with a large statue of the Duke of York 1828. Leighton in his *Views on the River Clyde* (1830) remarked that 'it is truly surprising what a degree of dignity and grace has been given the figure and how admirably the most minute parts of the dress and decorations are executed'. Carved the stonework for the front of Hamilton Palace, designing and creating gateways and other ornaments. By 1828 he had become established, especially in Edinburgh. A friend of the publisher William Blackwood through whom he met many of his distinguished contemporaries. When visiting the Earl of Elgin he met the art patron, Sir James Steuart of Allanbank, who in turn informed Sir Walter Scott 1829. Scott was impressed by Greenshields' statue of George IV, but less so by the sculptor's 'caricatures' eg the 'Jolly Beggars'. At first Scott thought that Greenshields was wasting his talent but when he saw the finished group he expressed great admiration. Also undertook a large statue of 'Robert Burns' (from a portrait by Peter Taylor in the SNPG), now in Australia. In 1831 he had a last meeting with Scott and then made a posthumous statue working from Chantrey's bust and the memory of his last interviews in the library of Lockhart's Clydeside house. This took two years to complete. Executed a group from *Rob Roy* which now adorns the garden at Abbotsford. In 1834 he carved the statue of 'Prince Charles Edward' for Glenaladale, Inverness-shire. A small-scale model for a seated statue of 'Sir Walter Scott' (1832) is at Powderham Castle, Devon and another in the Advocate's Library, Edinburgh. His final work was Glasgow's monument to Sir Walter

Scott. Finally settled in the United States 1821 where fourteen years later he died on a farm, still only forty. A plaster bust of 'Sir Walter Scott' is in City of Edinburgh collection.
**Bibl:** Brydall 185-7; Gifford 123; Gunnis 180; Scots Mag April 1952.

**GREER, James** **fl 1958-1985**
Glasgow painter and engraver of genre and semi-abstracts; woodcuts, wood engravings and etchings. Father of Mark G(qv) and Simon G(qv); also a daughter **Ruth** who was trained at the Glasgow School of Art and worked with Glasgow Printmakers Studio. Exhibited regularly RSA since 1985 & GI(13) from 60 Cloan Crescent, Bishopbriggs.

**GREER, Mark** **fl 1986-**
Glasgow engraver. Son of James G(qv) & brother of Simon G(qv). Exhibited GI(5), from 60 Cloan Crescent, Bishopbriggs.

**GREER, Simon** **fl 1980-**
Glasgow painter of social themes in a semi-abstract manner. Son of James G(qv) & brother of Mark G(qv). Exhibited RSA since 1980 & GI(4) from 60 Cloan Crescent, Bishopbriggs.

**GREGORY, George** **fl 1838-1879**
Painter in oil of portraits and landscapes including some Deeside scenes. Exhibited RSA(6) from 4 Young Street, Edinburgh and latterly from the Isle of Wight.

**GREIFFENHAGEN, Maurice William RA** **1862-1931**
Born London; died St John's Wood, London, 26 Dec. Painter of portraits and occasional romantic allegories; also murallist, illustrator, administrator and teacher. Trained at the RA Schools where he won the Armitage prize. Appointed Director, Glasgow School of Art 1906 remaining there until 1929. Remembered for his cartoons, posters, book illustrations but most of all for his influence as an inspiring teacher. Founder member, NEAC. His 'Women by a Lake' was purchased by the Chantrey Bequest 1914 and 'Dawn' in 1926. What many regard as his best work, 'Idyll', was shown at the Walker Gallery, Liverpool 1891. During the early part of his career he worked almost entirely at book illustrations in which the influence of Phil May is apparent. Particularly associated with the illustrations for the novels of Rider Haggard and, curiously, appears to have been DH Lawrence's favourite artist. The former include *She* (1887), *Allan's Wife* (1889), *Cleopatra* (1889) and *Montezuma's Daughter* (1894). Between 1901 and 1912 exhibited at many of the important international exhibitions including Munich, Pittsburg and Venice. Executed some large murals for the Langside Library in Glasgow, the British Pavilion at the Paris Exhibition of 1925, in Dunedin and Antwerp 1930 and for the SS *Empress of Britain.* Commissioned by the LMS railway to prepare several posters. Illustrated *Vain Fortune* (1894) and contributed to *Judy* (1889-1890), *Black and White* (1891-1896), *Fun* (1892), *ILN* (1892-1898), *The Butterfly* (1893), *The Pall Mall Budget* (1894), *Daily Chronicle* (1895), *Pick-Me-Up* (1895), *The Unicorn* (1895), *Ally Sloper's Half Holiday; The Sketch; The Ladies Pictorial* and *The Windsor Magazine.* Elected RP 1909, ARA 1916, RA 1922. Exhibited regularly RA(104), RSA(12), AAS 1898 and 1919, & GI(47), after 1925 from 12 Loudoun Rd, London. Represented in the V & A, SNPG(3).
**Bibl:** AJ 1890, 150; 1894, 225ff; Halsby 227; Houfe 325; Fiona MacAulay 'Maurice Greiffenhagen'for Bourne Fine Art (Ex Cat 1992); Macmillan [SA] 337-8; J Pennel, Modern Illustration 1895; R Sketchley: English Book Illustration of Today; Studio, 9, 1897, 235-245, vol 63, 131,260; vol 68, 40,122; vol 69, 71; Who's Who 1921.

**GREIG, George M** **c1820-1867**
Born Edinburgh; died Edinburgh. Painter in occasional oil but primarily in watercolour; interiors and figure subjects. Painted picturesque buildings, interiors landscapes and Edinburgh views, also children and seaside scenes. The reputation he enjoyed during his lifetime has waned since his death. He exhibited over 50 works at the RSA including one purchased by John Faed and, in 1864, 4 landscapes of scenes at Balmoral and Glenmuick. Exhibited RA(3) 1865, 'Queen Mary's Bedchamber, Holyrood Palace'; 'The Drawing Room at 51 Albemarle Street'; and 'The State Secretary's room, Holyrood Palace, as used by HRH Prince Consort'; also GI(7), from 10 S. Charlotte Street.
**Bibl:** Bryan; Halsby 261.

**GREIG, Miss J Gordon** **fl 1884-1887**
Watercolour painter of flowers. Lived at the Free Church Manse of Kinfauns, Glencarse in 1884 before moving to Murrayfield, Edinburgh. Exhibited RSA(5).

**GREIG, J M** **fl 1884**
Dundee portrait painter, exhibited RSA(1).

**GREIG, James Wright RBA** **1861-1941**
Born Arbroath; died Brighton, 13 Oct. Painter, black and white artist and writer, also librarian, critic. Began his working life in a local tackle shop where his father was foreman. While still in Arbroath he had sketches published in *Piper o'Dundee* and in 1891 went to London as an assistant in Marylebone library, taking evening classes at Heatherley's School of Art. In 1895 studied at Colarossi's and Julien in Paris. Favoured town scenes and figures, including a number of Arab subjects. For many years art critic of *The Morning Post;* also worked as an illustrator. Published the *Life of Gainsborough, Life of Raeburn,* and edited *The Farrington Diaries,* 1922-1928. Contributed illustrations for *Black and White* (1892); *The English Illustrated Magazine* (1893-1896); *St Pauls* (1894); *The Sketch* (1895-1896); *The Temple* (1896); *Good Words* (1898-1899); *Punch* (1902-1903); *Castle's Family Magazine; The Ludgate Monthly; The Idler; The Pall Mall Magazine; The Windsor Magazine;* and *The Quiver.* Elected RBA 1898. His exhibiting seems to have been confined to the RBA 1897-1907. Represented in V&A.
**Bibl:** Caw 467; Houfe; J B Salmond,'Jimmy Greig - The journey of a hackle shop loon', Scots Mag, Nov 1941.

**GREIG, John Russell** **1870-1962**
Born Aberdeen, 24 Aug. Portrait, figure and landscape painter. Studied Gray's School of Art in Aberdeen, RSA School in Edinburgh and in Paris at the Academie Julien and Colarossi. The similarity of his early work to that of Robert Brough(qv) may be attributed to their having followed a similar path of study. For many years taught drawing and painting at Gray's School of Art in Aberdeen. Equally facile in oil and watercolour, he was an active early member of the Aberdeen Artists Society. Painted delicately and with great charm although was never a prolific artist. One characteristic was to leave the unprepared board as part of the painting. Exhibited RSA(35) 1898-1939, RA(2), GI(8), AAS(107) & 5 works at the London Salon, latterly from 21 Bridge Street.
**Bibl:** Caw 432.

**GREVILLE, Robert Kaye HRSA LLD** **1794-1866**
Botanist and painter in oil of landscapes. A man of many parts, he made his name primarily as a botanist for which he was awarded an honorary LLD. An accomplished oil painter, particularly of wild mountain scenes, most often in the Scottish Highlands but also in Wales and occasionally on the continent. Lived at 31 George Square, latterly moving to 33. Elected honorary Academician 1829. Exhibited 3 works at the RA, 'Conway Castle' (1844) and 2 Scottish scenes (1845 and 1852); also RSA(60) 1831 & 1859.

**GREY, Alfred RHA** **fl 1864-d1913**
Painter in oil of landscape and animal subjects. Son of Charles G(qv). Lived most of his life in Dublin although, unlike his father, exhibited RA(3) 1873-1886, & regularly at the RHA.

**GREY, Charles RHA** **c1808-1892**
Born Greenock. Painter in oil of landscapes and portraits. Father of Alfred(qv), Gregor and James(qv), all of whom were artists. When still a young man he went to Ireland, finding employment as a portrait painter in Dublin, especially among the Scottish community. From 1837 he exhibited at the RHA and was elected an associate 1838 and academician 1845. Early in his career he was taken up by Lord Londonderry and Lord Powerscourt, spending much time with them in the Scottish Highlands, mainly in Glenisla, Angus. A number of sketches of Irish noblemen were etched by John Kirkwood for *Dublin University Mag.* During the later part of his life he painted Scottish scenery almost exclusively. Among his principal works are 'Donald McLea, head forrester' (painted at Rhidorroch, Ross-shire for Lord Powerscourt 1859); 'Lord MacDuff' (1874); 'James McGlashan' (1849); 'Waiting for the return of the Deer-stalkers, Rhidorroch' (for the Marquess of Londonderry, 1862) and 'The Pass of Cairngorm'. Elected RHA 1846. Exhibited regularly RSA. Represented in Nat.

Gall. of Ireland, Ulster Museum, Trinity Coll (Dublin).
**Bibl:** Thieme Becker; Strickland; Wingfield.

**GREY, James RHA** **fl 1873-dc1890**
Painter of landscape and genre. Son of Charles G(qv). Lived and worked in Dublin sharing a studio with his brother Alfred(qv). Another brother Gregor was a minor artist while a third brother, Charles Malcolm, achieved some success as a wood engraver. Exhibited regularly RHA & RA(2) 1873 and 1875, from 4 Lower Gardiner Street, later moving to 1 Little Sherrard Street.

**GREY, John** **fl 1870-1887**
Glasgow based landscape painter. Exhibited 11 works at the RSA, generally of scenes in Argyll, Kirkcudbright and Ayrshire; also GI(50), after 1885 from Girvan, Ayrshire.

**GRIEG, Alan** **fl 1982**
Aberdeenshire painter. Trained at Gray's School of Art, Aberdeen. Exhibited AAS(1) from Balmedie Park, Belhelvie.

**GRIER, John Joseph** **fl 1877-1879**
Amateur Greenock landscape painter. Major and adjutant, 1st Batt. Renfrew Rifle Volunteers. Exhibited during the above years in London. His last entry in the Greenock Directory is 1884-5.

**GRIERSON, Colin** **fl 1950**
Dundee watercolour painter. Exhibited 'In the boat shed' at the GI, from Claremont, Wormit-on-Tay.

**GRIERSON, Miss Elizabeth** **fl 1852-1853**
Edinburgh amateur portrait painter. Exhibited RSA(4) from 50 Great King Street, one of them a landscape.

**GRIERSON, George** **fl 1863-1869**
Oil painter of Burntisland. Exhibited 4 local landscapes and 2 conversation pieces at the RSA during the above years.

**GRIERSON, Miss L Hamilton** **fl 1933-1939**
Edinburgh based painter of Scottish landscapes and still life. Exhibited RSA annually during the above years from 58 Queen Street; also AAS(1), GI(2) & SWA(2), from 4 Raeburn Cliff.

**GRIERSON, Mary Anderson** **1912-?**
Born Bangor, North Wales. Painter in watercolour of flowers and fruit. Both her parents were Scottish and she spent her school years exploring the mountains of North Wales searching for plants. During WW2 served in the WAAF as an interpreter for the Photographic Reconnaissance Unit where she first became familiar with chalkland flora. Later joined an aerial survey firm, becoming a skilled cartographer. A love of plants led her to study under John Nash RA and through his encouragement she became botanical illustrator at the Royal Botanic Gardens, Kew, remaining there until her retirement. Her work has appeared in many scientific journals including *Curtis's Botanical Magazine,* now the *Kew Magazine.* After retiring continued to work freelance and was invited by the Nature Reserve Authority to visit Israel to paint some of the endangered plants there. Visited Holland several times especially to paint tulips and from 1974 regular visits to Hawaii at the invitation of the National Tropical Botanic Garden in order to build up a collection of paintings of native and introduced plants. Awarded five gold medals by the Royal Horticultural Society including the Gold Veitch Memorial Medal and in 1986 was granted an honorary degree at the University of Reading. Among the works for which she provided illustration are A Huxley's *Mountain Flowers* (1967), Bean's *Trees and Shrubs of the British Isles* (1970), P F Hunt's *Orchidaceae* (1973), Brian Mathew's *The Genus Crocus* (1982), C Grey-Wilson's *The Genus Cyclamen* (1988), Brian Mathew's *The Genus Hellebore* (1989) and W T Stearn and C Bricknell, *An English Florilegium featuring 17th Century Plants* (1989).
**Bibl:** Spink (Ex Cat May 1990).

**GRIEVE, Alexander** **1864-1933**
Born and died Dundee. Painter in oil, watercolour and pastel, portraits and landscapes. Studied at Dundee Art College and in Paris under Colarossi. A founder with Frank Laing(qv), of the Tayport Art Circle. Principal works include 'Laboureur et les Corneilles', 'Dundee seen from Tayport', 'Solitude', 'Un Coin de Tayport'. Active member of the community of artists living in the area around the 1890s which included John Duncan(qv), George Dutch Davidson(qv) and David Foggie(qv). Exhibited RSA(15), RA(1), GI(5), L(2), AAS 1893-1908, after 1897 from West Lights, Tayport, Fife. Represented in Dundee AG, including a portrait of the mother of George Dutch Davidson (1902), Paisley AG, Edinburgh City collection.
**Bibl:** Halsby 261.

**GRIEVE, John** **fl 1866-1884**
Edinburgh painter in oil and watercolour of houses, townscapes and landscapes. Exhibited RSA(23), mostly of scenes around Edinburgh also in Perthshire, Peeblesshire and Fife.

**GRIEVE, Marion** **fl 1877-1912**
Glasgow painter in oil and watercolour of fruit, landscape and flowers. Exhibited RSA(19), RSW(1) & GI(43).

**GRIEVE, Walter Graham RSA RSW** **1872-1937**
Born Kirkliston, West Linton; died Edinburgh, 15 Mar. Painter in oil and watercolour, portraits, still life and landscape. Studied at Royal Institution and at the RSA Life School in Edinburgh 1896-1899. Began his career as a lithographer being appointed art adviser to Thomas Nelson and Son. As a painter Grieve was robust and dramatic in manner and rich in pigment and colour. A great many of his pictures were of groups of richly costumed figures in some arresting situations as in 'The Combat' and his diploma work 'The Cribbage Players'. His watercolours were competent and marked with fine mastery of the light technique of washes and dappling. Lived most of his life in Edinburgh. Elected ARSA 1920, RSA 1929, RSW 1934. Exhibited RSA(100+), RSW(11), GI(46), L(8) & AAS 1926-1935, from 31 Nelson St, Edinburgh.

**GRIFFITH, Arthur R** **fl 1948-1950**
Glasgow painter of figure subjects in watercolour and pen and ink. Exhibited GI(5), from 108 Renfield St.

**GRIFFITH, William Gladwell** **fl 1907**
Edinburgh landscape painter; exhibited a 'Highland landscape near Newtonmore' at the GI, from 45 Frederick St.

**GRIFT, Fanny Osbourne van de** **[see Mrs R L STEVENSON]**

**GRIGOR, Archibald M** **1889/90-1929**
Glasgow painter of shipping and occasional landscapes; also engraver often of topographical subjects. Exhibited RSA(2), AAS(1), L(3) & GI(3) from 701 Yoker Road, Scotstoun West. Represented in Glasgow AG.

**GRIME, Alison Moira** **fl 1980**
Aberdeen printmaker. Exhibited a study of flowers at the AAS from 330 Hardgate.

**GRIMMOND, Amelia G J** **fl 1889**
Glasgow based landscape painter. Wife of William G(qv). Exhibited a view on Arran at the GI from 271 Sauchiehall Street.

**GRIMMOND, William** **fl 1876-1914**
Glasgow oil painter; landscapes, rustic scenes, narrative subjects and portraits. Husband of Amelia G(qv). Active member, Glasgow Art Club. Exhibited RA(3) 1887-1891, RSA(6) 1876-1882 & GI(44), after 1906 from 94 Leith Mansions, Elgin Ave, London.

**GRIMSON, James** **1830-1857**
Hamilton painter of literary subjects, interiors and landscapes. Son of a needle manufacturer. Moved to Glasgow 1852. Exhibited RSA(20).

**GRIMSTONE, James** **fl 1898-1914**
Glasgow based painter of portraits and figurative works. Exhibited GI(10), after 1905 from 24 Blenheim Dr.

**GRISCHOTTI, Nina M** **fl 1891**
Glasgow based painter. Exhibited GI(1) from 12 Belmont Gardens, Hillhead.

**GROOM, Mary** **fl 1930**
Painter. Exhibited 'The Crucifixion' at the RSA.

**GROOM, Richard** **fl 1986-1987**
Edinburgh sculptor; exhibited RSA(2) from 21 Broughton Street.

**GROUNDS, James Nigel** **1962-**
Born Leigh, Lancs. Trained Gray's School of Art, Aberdeen 1982-86. Landscape painter in oil, watercolour and mixed media; mainly Scottish scenery. Influenced by the Scottish Colourists. First one-man exhibition Aberdeen 1986. Elizabeth Greenshields Foundation Award 1990, Howard Doris Trust Award 1991. Exhibits RSA since 1993, AAS since 1986. Represented in Paul Mellon Foundation, HRH Prince of Wales collection and in various major Scottish institutions. Lives and works at 2 Hamilton Place, Kyle, Wester Ross.

**GRUBB, William Mortimer** **fl 1875-1900**
Dundee oil and watercolour painter of landscapes and figurative subjects. Painted attractive domestic scenes and local views. Art master at Dundee High School in the 1880s. Exhibited RSA(6) from 5 Osborn Place.
**Bibl:** Halsby 261.

**GUAN HIN TAN** **fl 1976**
Glasgow-based artist. Exhibited two landscapes at GI, from 94 Hill St.

**GUDGEON, Ralston R B RSW** **1910-1984**
Born Ayr. Scottish painter in watercolour; birds and animals. Studied Glasgow School of Art 1928-33, winning the Torrance Memorial Award of the GI 1933. Showed early artistic talent and a passion for animals, especially birds. During WW2 he served in the Lovat Scouts and, following a climbing accident, in the King's Own African Rifles. Lived latterly at Milliken Park, Renfrewshire. His style was somewhat fanciful, highly coloured, decorative rather than accurate with a strong sense of design reminiscent of oriental art. Elected RSW 1936, at the time the youngest ever. Exhibited RSA(5), RSW(9) & GI(19), latterly from Kirkconnell Lea, Glencaple, Dumfries. Represented in Glasgow AG, Paisley AG, City of Edinburgh collection.
**Bibl:** Halsby 223,261.

**GUEST, George** **fl 1874-1876**
Helensburgh painter of landscapes and figurative subjects. Exhibited RSA(2).

**GUFFIE, David** **fl 1907-1908**
Ayrshire based landscape painter. Exhibited GI(2) from 38 Sharon Street, Dalry.

**GUIDRICH (GOODRICK), Matthew** **fl 1617-1654**
English painter, probably of London. Employed at Holyrood in 1617 for painting and gilding the chapel and 'His Majesties chamberis'. Other work done in England is recorded by Croft-Murray.
**Bibl:** Apted 42-3; E Croft-Murray, Decorative Painting in England, 1537-1837, 1962; Reg Privy Council, 1st series, x, 593-4, xi, 6,65,67,84; Walpole Soc, vii, 43.

**GUILD, Derrick** **1963-**
Born Perth. Trained Duncan of Jordanstone College of Art. Lecturer, Edinburgh College of Art and Duncan of Jordanstone College of Art. Represented Perth AG.

**GUILD, James Horsburgh** **fl 1885-1932**
Edinburgh painter mainly watercolour; landscape and figure subjects. Exhibited RSA(3) & L(1) from 1 Livingston Place.

**GUISE, Tom G M** **1916-?**
Born Cromarty, Aug. Painter in oil and watercolour also process engraving printer, lithographer; landscapes, abstracts. Educated Inverness and Edinburgh. Self-taught except for a period of attendance at evening classes and life drawing at Edinburgh College of Art immediately after the war. During WW2 served in the Royal Artillery and in 1948 received an RSA Award for life drawing. Held one-man shows in Edinburgh in 1966, California 1967 and 1968, and many subsequently. In 1947-58 his approach was conventional but he became increasingly subjective and quietist following an intensive two week period at Pittenweem 1957. Influenced by Seurat and Morandi. He is intrigued by the observation that animals, bottles and buildings are formally similar, and has sought to discover the synthesis between animal, vegetable and mineral in the content. 'The quietest painter with a miasmic technique compounded of Seurat's science and precision, he conjures from within his delicately tinted fogs, a luminous imagery, which is sometimes gentle, more often disturbing, always ambiguous' [Felix McCullough]. Exhibited from 1951-1966 at RSA, SSA, since 1948 at GI(3), AAS(1), and since 1968 at RSW, from 30 Comely Bank.

**GULLAND, David** **1934-**
Born Edinburgh. Glass engraver. Trained Edinburgh College of Art. Established a studio in Kircudbright 1979. Work is mainly copper-wheel engraving on lead crystal glass using sand-blasting to decorate larger items (eg windows). Responsible for several of the larger windows in St Mary's Cathedral, Aberdeen, and others in Morayshire and Galloway.

**GULLAND, Miss Elizabeth** **c1860-1934**
Born Edinburgh; died Bushey, Herts, 6 Nov. Painter in oil and engraver; portraits, still life and figurative subjects. Studied art in Edinburgh under Herkomer and at Bushey where she settled 1892 remaining there for the rest of her life. An accomplished and successful artist, exhibiting at the principal London galleries from 1886, RSA from 1878 and RA from 1887. Exhibited RA(15), including an engraving of a portrait of 'William Brooke' after Herkomer (1894), one of 'Mrs Whatman' after G Romney (1901), and 'Lady Hamilton Bacchante', also after Romney (1903); also RSA(20), GI(2), ROI(3) & L(6), from Kingsley Cottage, Bushey, Herts.

**GUNN, Barbara** **fl 1862**
Glasgow watercolourist; landscape and still life. Exhibited GI(3), from 113 Kensington Place, Sauchiehall St.

**GUNN, David W** **fl 1924-1929**
Dunfermline painter of subject studies. Member of 1922 Group(qv). Exhibited RSA(2) & L(1) from 20 Grieve Street.
**Bibl:** Hardie 160.

**GUNN, Dorothy B** **fl 1928-1939**
Kirkcudbright painter of flowers, still life in oil and watercolour. Exhibited RSW(2) & GI(3) from 'Margrie', Borgue.

**GUNN, Frederick J T** **fl 1889-1905**
Painter in oil and watercolour of landscapes often of Highland scenery painted in a bold manner. Exhibited widely including RA(4) 1891-1895 at first from various addresses in Edinburgh, RSA(9), RSW(5), GI(5), RHA(4), AAS(2) & L(4).

**GUNN, Gordon N RSBA** **1916-c1980**
Glasgow architect and watercolour landscape painter. Eldest son of Richard Gunn, the architect, and cousin of Sir James Gunn RA(qv). Educated Hillhead HS and Glasgow School of Art, where he was a pupil of Hugh Cameron Wilson(qv). Later influenced by Sir William O Hutchison(qv) and Ian Fleming(qv). His father died when he was 17 but Gunn remained close to his father's circle of friends, many of them architects. Received his first commission from Arthur Melville who died the day Gunn completed the work. Received a bursary to study architecture at the Royal Technical College in Glasgow and became a qualified surveyor in 1949. Designed camouflage for water pipes at Ben Nevis and later helped with the Spey Valley Development Scheme. Gunn has always preferred watercolour as a working medium. In 1952 completed 'Before the Cataclysm', his first 'Cosmic' painting, for which he has become best known. His first London exhibition was at the Walker Gallery 1957. The same year a watercolour was sold privately for what was then believed a record sum for a work by a living British artist. In 1969 Gunn had a one man show at the Federation of British Artists Galleries. In 1972 he moved from Inverness to Arisaig and the same year his work was exhibited at the 26th Edinburgh International Festival. Elected RSBA 1961. Exhibited for the first time at the RA in 1962 and the same year at the Royal Society of Marine Artists; also GI(4).
**Bibl:** N Rhind, Gordon Gunn; A Scottish Painter and his World, 1972.

**GUNN, Sir Herbert James RA PRP RSW** **1893-1964**
Born Glasgow, 30 Jne; died London 30 Dec. Painter in oil and watercolour of portraits and landscapes. Studied Glasgow School of Art, Edinburgh School of Art and Academie Julian in Paris under J P

Laurens. Began exhibiting at the age of 16. Shortly after graduating remained in Paris winning a gold medal at the Paris Salon 1939. Became increasingly popular with aristocratic and royal patrons who appreciated the elegant formality of his portraits. Painted the state portrait of 'Her Majesty the Queen' 1953-1954. Lived in London for most of his life. Elected RSW 1930. Exhibited occasionally RSA(24), although most of his work was seen in London including the RA(38), also GI(71), after 1956 from 7 Kidderpore Ave, Hampstead. Represented in SNPG(4), Glasgow AG, City of Edinburgh collection (3 including 'Lord Provost Sir W Y Darling').
**Bibl:** Halsby 211; Macmillan [SA] 332.

**GUNN, James Thomson** **1932-**
Born Gorebridge, 9 Apr. Landscape artist in oil, watercolour, gouache; designer. Educated Dalkeith HS. Studied Edinburgh College of Art 1953-1956, awarded Andrew Grant Travelling Scholarship 1950 with the help of which he visited Austria, France, Germany, Holland, Italy and Switzerland. Influenced by Turner, Gillies(qv), Henderson Blyth(qv) and Joan Eardley(qv). There have been two phases in his work, the use of impasto surfaces to create a concrete reality and the use of gouache and watercolour to capture the evanescent quality of atmosphere in landscape. Lives in Dalkeith, Midlothian. Exhibits frequently at the RSA since 1969, also RSW, GI(1) & SSA, from 3 Park Crescent, Dalkeith.

**GUNN, Miss Jessie** **fl 1887-1891**
Edinburgh flower painter in watercolour. Exhibited RSA(2) from 15 Glengyle Terrace.

**GUNN, Richard R** **fl 1901**
Amateur Glasgow landscape painter primarily in watercolour. Exhibited 'Glencairn Monument, Kilmaurs' in watercolour at the GI from 15 Windsor Street.

**GUNN, Miss Sandra** **fl 1976**
Lanarkshire artist. Exhibited 'Botanic Gardens' from 126 Carnwath Rd, Carluke.

**GUNN, William Archibald** **1877-?**
Born 26 February. Landscape painter in watercolour and pastel. Studied Glasgow School of Art 1897-1901. Lived in various parts of Britain including Newport, York and St Ives. Exhibited chiefly in the Midlands, Lancashire and Yorkshire, & L(2).

**GUNNING, Robert Bell** **c1830-1907**
Born and died Dumfries (interred Whitehaven). Painter in oil of portraits and landscapes, still life, fruit and flowers, and genre. Painted subjects in Cumberland and taught art at Whitehaven for over 40 years. Moved from Edinburgh to Whitehaven c1860. Exhibited regularly RSA 1852-1856 and again 1870-1871.

**GURNEY, David Russell** **fl 1975-1977**
Aberdeenshire painter of landscape and harbours, also printmaker. Exhibited AAS from Braecroft, Muiresk, Turriff.

**GUTHRIE, Alexander** **?-1753**
Edinburgh painter. Son of Alexander G, WS. All that is now known is that he married the daughter of a surgeon and in 1724 was elected a member of the Academy of St Luke(qv). Richard Cooper(qv) came originally to Edinburgh to see Guthrie who must have been a friend.
**Bibl:** Butchart 14.

**GUTHRIE, Mrs Annie M B** **fl 1908-1921**
Edinburgh portrait and subject painter in oil and watercolour, also did a number of street scenes in and around Edinburgh. Exhibited RA(1), RSA(15), RSW(1), L(6) & AAS 1910-1919 from Tresta, Colinton.

**GUTHRIE, George Collingworth ('Old George')** **1869-1944**
Painter, etcher, publisher and photographer. Worked mainly in pastel and watercolour. Educated Saltcoats Academy, Ardrossan Academy and George Watson's College, Edinburgh. A man of wide interests, grandson of the founder of the *Ardrossan and Saltcoats Herald.* He himself became editor of the newspaper in 1924 on the death of his father. Member of Ardrossan Town Council 1900-1903. Member of the **SOCIETY OF SIX** (the others being Albert Beard(qv), Tom Gilfillan(qv), C H Lilley(qv), Chris Meadowes(qv), and R Clouston Young(qv)). They held many exhibitions together, the principal one being at Saltcoats 1923. Especially fascinated by the sea, the glorious blue of the summer water and the blue opulent, irridescent skies. Also painted Highland scenery; his impressionist 'Wintry Sky' captured the quintessence of a winter day. In addition to his art he was a fine photographer, some of his studies of Old Ardrossan and Saltcoats are in North Ayrshire Museum.

**GUTHRIE, George Davidson ('Young George')** **1893-1962**
Drypoint artist and publisher. Member of a well-known local family of newspaper publishers he became editor on the death of his uncle 'old George C Guthrie(qv)' in 1944. Educated at Ardrossan Academy he became a draughtsman by profession but his main occupation was his 18 years as editor. Painted local scenes but was best known for his talented etchings principally of the area in which he lived. In addition to his artistic abilities he was a keen sportsman being a founder of the Ardrossan Cricket Club, member of the Eglinton Harriers and the local bridge club. Also belonged to and became President of the Rotary Club of Ardrossan and Saltcoats. Exhibited GI(2) & L(2), after 1925 from Tighnamara, Saltcoats, Ayrshire.

**GUTHRIE, Helen** **fl 1898-1915**
Painter in oil and watercolour of figures, still life and continental market scenes. Exhibited RSA(3), RSW(1), AAS(4), L(8) & GI(1), latterly from 6 Rochester Terrace.

**GUTHRIE, Ian** **fl 1968-1980**
Abstract painter and engraver. Exhibited RSA(7) & AAS from 17 Ann Street, Stonehaven, Kincardineshire.

**GUTHRIE, Sir James PRSA HRA RSW LLD** **1859-1930**
Born Greenock, 10 Jne; died 6 Sep. Painter in oil and watercolour of portraits, genre, figurative subjects. Instrumental in establishing the stained glass window firm of J & W Guthrie, responsible for executing many fine windows in Scottish churches including the churches of Upper Largo (Fife) and St. John's, Perth; also the People's Palace, Glasgow. Youngest son of an Evangelical Union clergyman, he attended Glasgow University but abandoned law studies in 1877 in favour of art after receiving encouragement from James Drummond(qv) and after John Faed(qv) had persuaded his father. When his father died in 1878 he settled with his mother in London and there he met John Pettie(qv). Through this contact Guthrie also met Orchardson(qv) and Tom Graham(qv) and although he soon abandoned the subject picture with literary sources associated with these men, he greatly valued their encouragement and advice. His first exhibited work at the RA was 'Funeral Service in the Highlands', 1882, followed by 'Goose Girl', (now in Aberdeen AG) at the GI in 1883. It was after painting the portrait of the 'Rev Andrew Gardiner' in 1885 that he turned mainly to portraiture. In 1882 he visited Paris the effect of which on his style was quite clear. His 'To Pastures New' painted during the winter of 1882-1883 after his return from France is 'full of plein air and colour showing unmistakable signs of inspiration resulting from the work of Bastien-Lepage'. By 1884 Guthrie was working at Cockburnspath with a number of others who felt the need to express themselves in a more positive way than their fellow countrymen. George Henry(qv), Joseph Crawhall(qv), Whitelaw Hamilton(qv), Corson Morton(qv) and Arthur Melville(qv) came to the Berwickshire village, painting and frankly criticising each other's work. The spirit engendered by this community of artists was something quite new in Scottish art and was an important influence in developing the strength of handling, richness of tone and colour, characteristic of the painting of the group. Although most of Guthrie's paintings of the early 1880s were landscapes or subject-pictures with strong regard for content, he had tackled the occasional portrait and it was to be in this field that he made his name. By the autumn of 1885 all his friends had returned to their town studios, Guthrie was lonely for social contact and starved of artistic impetus. Because of his despair with his painting of a large canvas (which he subsequently destroyed) of field-workers sheltering from rain, the problems of chiarascuro were seemingly insoluble. He decided to give up painting altogether and return to the study of law or medicine. His cousin James Gardiner fortunately dissuaded him and suggested that he return to Glasgow and paint his father's portrait. This Guthrie did and it was this work which proved the turning point of his career. From then until his death Guthrie painted a succession of dazzling and fluent portraits of men and women from the ranks of society,

commerce and politics' [W Buchanan et al]. With regard to his status as one of the Glasgow Boys, his 'position in the group was one of importance, both for his rare gift as a painter and for his own inestimable character and personality, which helped to win toleration if not complete acceptance for the movement. It is difficult to be sure who is the leader of this guild but it seems certain that in its early days, when in its formative state, Guthrie was the acknowledged leader'. [After A. Auld]. In 1902, on the resignation of Sir George Reid, he became the youngest ever President of the RSA, a position he retained until 1919. As a West of Scotland artist his election marked the end of the antagonism between the RSA and the Glasgow Boys. Personally responsible for collecting £10,000 toward a fund for securing the best examples of Scottish art for the NGS. Knighted 1903. Elected ARSA 1888, RSW 1890, RSA 1892, HROI 1903, HRSW 1903, RBA 1907, HRA 1912. Exhibited regularly RSA, RSW, GI(80) 1882-1929 & AAS. Represented in NGS(7), including three sketch books, SNPG(21, including 'Winston Churchill', 'Bonar Law', 'Campbell-Bannerman' and 'Lloyd-George'), NPG, Aberdeen AG, Arbroath AG, Dundee AG, Glasgow AG, Greenock AG, Kilmarnock AG, Kirkcaldy AG, Paisley AG, City of Edinburgh collection, RSA, Melbourne AG, Australia, Ghent AG.
**Bibl:** AJ 1894, 1903, 1909, 1911; Roger Billcliffe, The Glasgow Boys, London 1985; William Buchanan et al, 'The Glasgow Boys', 2 vols, SAC (Ex Cat 1968 & 1971); Caw 365-370 et al; Sir James L Caw, Sir James Guthrie, London 1932; Conn LXXXVI, 1930; Painton Cowen, Stained Glass in Britain, London 1985, 228,231, 237-9; FAS, Glasgow 'Guthrie and the Scottish Realists' (Ex Cat 1981); Grosvenor Notes, 1890; Halsby 138-9 et al; Hardie 82-84; Irwin 370-99,410 (illus); Macmillan [SA] 255-6,257-9,267-9,277, 285,291; Scotsman, Jly, 1974; Studio, Vol LIV, 1912; J Wayers 'Scottish painter of souls'.

**GUTHRIE, James Joshua** **1874-1952**
Born Glasgow, 11 Apr; died England, 25 Oct. Painter, illustrator, printer, author and poet. Father of Robin Craig G(qv). Best known in connection with his work at Pear Tree Press, Flansham, nr Bognor Regis, established 1899. Many of his paintings were illustrated by the Press, 'engaging in design and feeling and inventive in movement, the pattern being thought out and the sentiment expressed by a clever use of white lines and dots on a solid black ground'[Caw]. The poet Gordon Bottomley, quoted by House, reported on Guthrie's idiosyncratic work method: "He takes a piece of granulated cardboard and washes it over with a few brushfuls of a thin mixture of plaster of Paris. Then he digs into that with a pen and Indian ink. Then he puts on a film of Chinese White (Paris, India, China) what riches all at once". Guthrie founded and illustrated *The Elf* in 1895 as well as decorating rhyme sheets for Harold Monro's Poetry Bookshop. Franklin referred to Guthrie's poems *Frescoes from Buried Temples* (1928) as 'an extraordinary production from poet and artist alike...it strikes me as among the three or four monumental achievements of private presses in the twentieth century, and by its originality of concept and content, the highest'. Author of *The Proportional System of Typographical Composition, The Wild Garden, A Child's Good Day, Divine Discontent, An Album of Drawings* (1900) and *My House in the World* (1919). Illustrated Blatherwick: *Peter Stonor* (with Boyd, 1884), *The Elf* (1895-1904), de Passemere: *Wedding Bells* (1895), Low: *Little Men in Scarlet* (1896), Beardsell: *Pillow Fancies* (1901), Poe: *Some Poems* (1901-08), Williams: *The Floweret* (1902), Rossetti: *The Blessed Damozel and Hand and Soul* (1903), Beardsell: *Garden Fancies* (1904), Milton: *Hymn on the Morning of Christ's Nativity* (1904), Virgil: *Alexis* (1905), Bottomley: *Midsummer Eve* (1905), *The Beatitudes from the Sermon on the Mount* (1905), Radford: *In Summer Time* (1906), *A Second Book of Drawings* (1908), *The Poems of E A Poe* (1908), JDB: *Echoes of Poetry* (1908), Bottomley: *The Riding to Lithend* (1909), *The Paradise of Tintoretto* (1910), *The Blessed Damozel* (1911), Osmaston: *Art and Nature Sonnets* (1911), Eastaway: *Six Poems* (nd), Ellis: *Epode* (1915), Munro: *Trees* (1915), *Root and Branch* (1916), *Space and Man, The Castle of Indolence*, Bottomley: *Frescoes from Buried Temples* (1928), *The Viking's Barrow at Littleholme* (1930), Collins: *Ode to Evening* (1937), Blake: *Songs of Innocence* (1939). Exhibited RA(3), Arts and Crafts Society, the Barcelona International Exhibition winning a Gold Medal for his monochromatic work. Lived in Sussex. Represented in V & A.
**Bibl:** James Guthrie,'The Different Art of Hand-Printing', Modern Scotland, 1, 1930; Macmillan [SA] 301; Colin Franklin, "James Guthrie", *Private Library* 2nd s.,9,no.1 (Spring 1976); Bellamy; Horne 233; Peppin; Waters; Houfe; *The Artist*, May-Aug 1898, 238-241; illus Sept 1900, 197-202; *The Private Library*, Second Series, vol 9, 21, Spring 1976, with check list.

**GUTHRIE, John S B** **fl 1873-1905**
Glasgow painter in oil of landscape, genre and interiors; also stained glass window designer. Fond of Arran. Exhibited a formidable study of 'Dunnottar Castle'. Executed a memorial window for the United Free church, Forfar. Exhibited RA(1), RSA(6) & GI(15) from 395 Sauchiehall Street, Glasgow.

**GUTHRIE, Leonard Howe** **fl 1899-1930**
Lanarkshire architect, stained glass designer and landscape painter. Associated with the family firm of stained glass window designers W & G Guthrie. Exhibited 2 designs at the AAS in 1893 from 237 West George Street and a sketch design for a stained glass window at the RSA; also RA(10) & GI(10) from Lanarkshire until 1900, thereafter from London.

**GUTHRIE, Robin Craig** **1902-1971**
Born Harting, Sussex, 15 Jne; died Sussex, 27 Jan. Painter, mainly in oil of portraits, genre and landscapes. Son of James Joshua G(qv). Studied at Slade School 1918-22 under Tonks, Steer and Russell. Exhibited NEAC from 1923, becoming a member in 1928. Began exhibiting at the RA from 1931, the same year that he was appointed Director, Boston Museum School of Fine Arts, where he remained for 3 years. Instructor at St Martin's School of Art and the RCA 1951-54, and at the City and Guilds Art School. Published book illustrations from his London studio. Exhibited RA(11), RSA(5), GI(1) & L(1). Represented Manchester AG.

**GUTHRIE, Rome** **fl 1900-1902**
Draughtsman and illustrator. Awarded Alex Thomson Prize 1900. Illustrated H.I. Triggs' *Formal Gardens in England and Scotland* (1902).

**GUTHRIE, Miss Sara Beatrice (Mrs Dibdin)** **[see Mrs Dibdin]**

**GUTHRIE, Miss Susan M** **fl 1943**
Lanarkshire designer. Exhibited a screen-printed textile design at the GI from Carwood, 57 Adele St, Motherwell.

**GUTHRIE, William** **fl 1879-1897**
Glasgow landscape painter in oil; also stained glass designer. Specialised in Highland scenery, exhibiting 'Evening, Glenfinlas' and 'Quiet Day - Loch Ranza' at the RSA, both 1879, & GI(7).

**GUTHRIE, William** **fl 1920-1931**
Helensburgh-based landscape painter; often depicted Arran, Skye and Perthshire. Exhibited RSA(6) 1924-1931, & GI(13), from Royston, Herts.

**GWATKIN, Arthur L** **fl 1890-1899**
Landscape painter and frieze designer. Exhibited 10 works at the RA 1890-1899 latterly from 5 Clyde View, Partick, also RBA, GI(1) & at the Walker Gallery, Liverpool, though never at the RSA. Lived at 2 Thornwood Terrace, Glasgow.

**HACKSTOUN, William** **1855-1921**
Born Balbreakie, Kennoway, Fife; died London, 8 Jne. Painter of landscapes, architectural subjects and draughtsman; studied architecture in Glasgow under Horatio K Bromhead. Made his sketches in the manner of Cotman. Studied music in London at the Royal Academy of Music then in Italy with Campobello. He considered an operatic career but Ruskin encouraged him to return to drawing and he spent several years in London before moving to St Andrews. There he painted mainly local landscapes, also views in Perthshire. Some of his sketches were produced in *Potiva Tabella*, published on the occasion of the Quincentenary of St Andrews University. His work is distinctive in its treatment of clouds and hills, delineated in bold tones. Never exhibited at the RSA and only once at the GI (a watercolour of the Tay, nr Perth) in 1916, from 148 Hill St, Glasgow. Represented by three watercolours in the NGS, a watercolour of St Monan's in Kelvingrove AG, Glasgow and a St Andrews street scene in the collection of Edinburgh City.
**Bibl:** Halsby 261.

**HADDEN, James** **fl 1869-1871**
Exhibited 3 coastal scenes, all of the Firth of Forth at the RSA during the above period.

**HADDEN, Mary** **fl 1896-1900**
Amateur Aberdeen painter of landscape. Exhibited AAS(3) latterly from 200 Mid Stocket Road.

**HADDEN, Robert** **fl 1876-1880**
Landscape painter in oil; exhibited RSA(2) 1876 while living in Edinburgh and in 1880 after settling in London.

**HADDOW Miss Theo** **fl 1916-1941**
Glasgow-based flower painter. Exhibited GI(16) until 1916 from Fairhill, Uddingston, after 1933 from 175 Menock Rd, Glasgow.

**HAGART, William D** **fl 1835-1842**
Portobello painter of figure compositions; exhibited RSA(6), including a 'View of Arran from the sea' and 'Boys Bathing', the latter somewhat in the manner of Tuke.

**HAGGART, Donald Campbell** **fl 1869-1912**
Sculptor. Worked in marble, bronze and plaster, specialising in portrait busts. In 1882 exhibited 3 marble busts at the RA all of the family of Robert Hunter of Hunter. Lived and worked in Edinburgh until 1880, then moved to Glasgow with an interlude in Oban 1890. Exhibited RSA(31), among them 2 busts of daughters of the Earl of Glasgow (1876 and 1878), also GI(34), after 1906 from 28 Lansdowne Crescent, Glasgow.

**HAGGERTY, Ken** **1963-**
Born Maine, USA. Printmaker. 1982-86 studied at the Humberside College of Further Education, then became interested in print media, largely mono silkscreen. His images are concerned with Christian art and symbols showing the influence of the American abstract expressionists. Exhibited RSA 1989, and with the Printmakers Workshop, Edinburgh since 1987 and the Glasgow Printmakers since 1989.

**HAGGO, Matthew** **fl 1920**
Glasgow based painter; exhibited a watercolour at the GI from 12 Westfield Street.

**HAHNISCH, Anton** **1817-1897**
Born Vienna, 28 Oct; died Karlsruhe. Painted miniatures in ivory, porcelain, glass, pastel portraits, portraits in watercolour and also executed lithographs. Pupil at the Academy at Vienna where he lived until 1847, then went to Berlin and afterwards travelled extensively including Frankfurt, Paris, London 1850-62, Edinburgh 1955-57 and back to Berlin 1869. In Rome 1872-73 and from there went to Karlsruhe. Although not Scottish he lived for some years in Edinburgh and showed a number of important portraits at the RSA(10) 1855-1857 among them a portrait of 'Her Imperial Highness the Grand Duchess Marie-Nicola Jewna, Duchess of Leuchtenberg' (1856), from Castle Street and latterly York Place. He had a distinguished clientele including Prince Frederic of Prussia, the Princess Royal of Prussia and Lady Victoria Hamilton. Exhibited Vienna 1836-47 & RA 1851-69. Represented in BM, Vienna (Musée Historique), Karlsruhe AG.

**HAIG, Miss Evelyn Cotton RMS** **fl c1885-1920**
Edinburgh painter in oil and watercolour of portrait miniatures, rural and domestic scenes and occasional flowers, after 1897 from 87 Comely Bank Avenue. Related (? sister) to Florence H(qv). Exhibited RA from 1891, RSA(23), RMS(18), GI(16) & L(2).

**HAIG, Miss Florence E RBA** **fl 1886-1929**
Edinburgh oil painter of landscape, portraits and figures, who after 1911 was living in London. Related to Evelyn H(?sister, qv) with whom she shared a studio in Shandwick Place, Edinburgh in the early 1890s. Elected ARBA 1925, RBA 1926, SWA 1923. Exhibited RSA(12), SWA(16), GI(4), LS(3), RA(2), RBA(12) & AAS(1).

**HAIG, Rt Hon George Alexander Eugene Douglas (Earl Haig) OBE ARSA FRSA** **1918-**
Born Kingston Hill, London, 15 Mar. Painter in oil and watercolour, abstracts. Son of Field Marshal Earl Haig. Succeeded his father to the title 1928. Educated Stowe School 1931-5 and Christ Church, Oxford 1936-9. Studied at Camberwell School of Art 1945-47 under Pasmore, Gowring, Coldstream(qv), Rogers and William Johnstone(qv), and privately with Paul Maze. Lived in Melrose for many years. Began painting as a prisoner-of-war. Influenced by Morandi. 'The border landscapes are in an important sense the foundation of Haig's painting. Border atmosphere and light taught him, of necessity, a care for interval, the 'space between' which is as vital to painting as it is to handwriting...it is also in the Border landscapes that we can see best the working of the duel aspects just described...'only the land remains' and its rythms, intervals, distances, and silences have so far possessed him as to lead instinctively to a visual equivalent' [Douglas Hall]. Past member of the Royal Fine Art Commission for Scotland and Trustee, NGS. Awarded OBE 1966. Exhibited RSA regularly from 1950, also GI(4) & AAS(1), from Bemersyde, Melrose, Roxburghshire. Represented SNGMA, Abbot Hall (Kendal), City of Edinburgh collection, Imperial War Museum, SAC, Royal Collection, SNPG (self-portrait), Hunterian AG (Glasgow), Hawick AG, Aberdeen AG.
**Bibl:** Gage 39,143-4.

**HAIG, Henry** **fl 1840s**
It is unclear whether this aquatinter and engraver was English or Scottish. An aquatint of the 'Rev Alexander Keith of St Cyrus, Montrose' (1844), after Watson Gordon, and an engraving of 'Archibald Alison, Sheriff of Lanarkshire' and author of *The History of Europe,* are in the City of Edinburgh Collection. Specialised in engravings after Rubens as seen in *Engravings after the Best Pictures* 1841.

**HAIG, J E** **fl 1893**
Edinburgh artist; exhibited AAS during the above year.

**HAIG, James** **fl 1878-1885**
Cambuslang watercolour painter of bird subjects and landscape; exhibited RSA(1) & GI(3), latterly from 164 Bath St.

**HAIG, James Hermiston** **fl 1885-1919**
Landscape painter in oil and very occasional watercolour. Lived in Chirnside in Berwickshire, and in Glasgow. Most of his exhibits were landscapes and rustic scenes. Exhibited RSA(15), RSW(3), GI(56) & AAS in 1885. After 1900 was living at Allanton, Chirnside, Berwickshire. Represented in Paisley AG.

**HAIG, Miss Jessie Caroline** **fl 1874**
Edinburgh watercolour painter of buildings and landscape; exhibited RSA(1).

**HALDANE, Al(l)an J H** **fl 1953-1958**
Paisley painter and sculptor; specialised in portrait heads and animal studies, generally in plaster, stone or terracotta. Exhibited RSA(2) & GI(6), from 1 Main Rd, Castlehead, Paisley.

**HALDANE, James** **?-1832**
Edinburgh architect. Responsible for no major buildings but his Morrison development in the West Maitland St district of the city (1825) was commendable. 'Elegant but unlucky, its severe Neo-Greek palace-fronts unbalanced or incomplete, and many of the rusticated ground floors obscured by later shops' [Gifford].
**Bibl:** Gifford 269,361,383.

**HALDANE, Kathleen Margaret** **fl 1982**
Aberdeen artist. Exhibited AAS(2) from Edendee, Inchgarth Rd, Cults.

**HALDANE, Miss Mary Elizabeth** **fl 1881**
Edinburgh portrait painter in pastel; exhibited RSA(1) from 17 Charlotte Square, Edinburgh.

**HALDANE, Petronella** **fl 1970-**
Sculptress. Her portraits included a study of the 'Rev Richard Holloway' (1981). Exhibited RSA from an Edinburgh address in 1970 and 1981.

**HALE, Kathleen (Mrs McCleen) OBE** **1898-?**
Born Broughton, Peebleshire 24 May. Painter in oil and watercolour, lithographer, book illustrator & jacket designer specialising in children's books. Educated at Manchester High School for Girls, studied Manchester School of Art, Reading University under Seaby 1915-17, Central School of Arts and Crafts 1928-30 and East Anglian School of Painting and Drawing under Cedric Morris 1938. Began writing and illustrating 'Orlando the Marmalade Cat' books for her two sons. So popular did these become that 17 were eventually published, the last in 1972. Awarded OBE in 1976. Illustrated Harrower: *I Don't Mix Much With Fairies* (1928), E Waugh: *Basil Seal Rides Again* (1963). Wrote and illustrated *Orlando the Marmalade Cat: A Camping Holiday* (1938), *Orlando: A Trip Abroad* (1939), *Orlando's Evening Out* (1941), *Orlando Buys a Farm* (1942), *Orlando's Home Life* (1942), *Henrietta the Faithful Hen* (1943), *Orlando Becomes a Doctor* (1944), *Orlando's Invisible Pyjamas* (1947 & 64), *Orlando Keeps a Dog* (1949), *Puss-in-Boots: A Peep Show Book* (1951), *Manda* (1952), *Orlando's Zoo* (1954), *Orlando's Magic Carpet* (1958), *Orlando the Marmalade Cat Buys a Cottage* (1963), *Orlando and the Three Graces* (1965), *Orlando the Marmalade Cat and the Water Cats* (1972), *Henrietta's Magic Egg* (1973). Exhibited at NEAC, LG and several London galleries. Lived at Rabley Willow, South Minns, Herts.
**Bibl:** CA; Horne 235; Peppin; Waters.

**HALKERSTON, Charles** **?-1899**
Edinburgh painter in oil and watercolour of landscapes, figures especially cupids, interiors and genre. The landscapes are generally of a topographical nature, most of them in the Lothians. Exhibited RSA(97), RSW(2), L(1) & GI(21), latterly from 3 Fettes Row.

**HALKETT, Miss E A** **fl 1885**
Aberdeen painter. Daughter of George(qv) & Ellen H(qv). Exhibited a landscape at the AAS.

**HALKETT, Mrs Ellen J Frances** **fl 1880-1892**
Edinburgh painter in oil of coastal and domestic scenes, also landscape and figurative subjects. Wife of George Roland H(qv). Exhibited RSA(7) & AAS in 1885, from 12 Douglas Crescent.

**HALKETT, George Ro(w)land** **1855-1918**
Born Edinburgh, 11 Mar; died London, 4 Dec. Cartoonist, watercolourist and writer on art. Studied art in Paris. Returning to Edinburgh he concentrated on preparing caricatures for the national press, also book illustrations. In 1876 became art critic of the *Edinburgh Evening News,* joined the *Pall Mall Gazette* 1892 and was art editor *The Pall Mall Magazine,* 1897, and editor 1900-05. Best known for his caricatures of Gladstone issued in *New Gleanings From Gladstone* and a *Gladstone Almanack*; also for his illustrations in *The Irish Green Book* satirising the Home Rule debates of 1887. Houfe comments that his early style was of the portrait chargee type adopted by 'Ape', but in the 1900s there is a definite Beggarstaff influence with chalky black lines on toned paper. Husband of Ellen H(qv). Illustrated *The Elves and the Shoemaker,* contributed to *Punch* (1897-1903), *The Butterfly, Edin Univ Lib Ass* frontispiece (1883); *St Stephen's Review* (1885); *Budget* (1893); *Pall Mall Mag* (1897). Exhibited landscape and genre paintings at the RSA(14), GI(1) & AAS(3), from 5 Douglas Crescent. Represented in V & A, SNPG(3).
**Bibl:** Caw 467; Houfe.

**HALL, Alistair John** **fl 1967-1968**
Aberdeen painter; exhibited AAS during above years from 49 Esslemont Ave.

**HALL, Capt Basil RN** **1788-1844**
Traveller, author and amateur artist (mainly illustrator). Son of Sir James Hall of Dunglass. Responsible for *Illustrated Travels in the US,* published in Edinburgh 1829, for camera lucida sketches of Sir Walter Scott 1830, for *Account of a Voyage of Discovery to the West Coast of Corea and the Great Loo-Choo Island*; *Extracts From a Journal Written on the Coasts of Chili, Peru and Mexico in the Years 1820, 1821, 1822*; *Forty Etchings, From Sketches Made with the Camera Lucida in North America in 1827 and 1828*; *Fragments of Voyages and Travels* (3 vols); *Travels in India, Ceylon & Borneo*; *Skimmings, or a Winter at Schloss Hainfeld, in Lower Styria*; *Narrative of a Voyage to Java, China, and the Great Loo-Choo Island.*
**Bibl:** H G Rawlinson, Capt Basil Hall, 1931; *Travels in India, Ceylon & Borneo*, Routledge, London.

**HALL, Fergus** **1947-**
Born Paisley. Painter. Son of a scene painter. Trained Glasgow School of Art. Influenced by the colourful atmosphere of the theatre and fascinated by the bizarre and the curious, often portrayed in a fantasy world. First solo exhibition in London.

**HALL, George Wright** **1895-1974**
Born 10 Oct. Painter in oil and watercolour; portraits, flower pieces, domestic and rural scenes. Studied RSA School and Edinburgh College of Art. Awarded Keith Prize 1921. His landscapes were often scenes in Iona, Galloway and France. Member, 1922 Group(qv). Painting master in Manchester for many years. Director, Edinburgh Arts Centre from 1971 until his death. Lived in Edinburgh. Exhibited RA(1), RSA(41), RSW(2), GI(2) & L(3), after 1946 from 59 Melville St. Represented in Glasgow AG, City of Edinburgh collection.
**Bibl:** Halsby 211,222,261; Hardie 160.

**HALL, James W** **1797-1845**
Born Edinburgh; died Ashiestel, Selkirk. Son of Sir James Hall Bt. Advocate, amateur painter in oil, watercolour and chalk; landscape and portraits. Most of his landscapes were of Scottish and English scenes. Occasionally painted interiors. Befriended Wilkie, whose palette Hall presented to the National Gallery in London. Exhibited RA(8) including a portrait of the Duke of Wellington (1838) 1835-1853, from 40 Brewer St, also RSA 1830-34, 1844-45. Represented by three works in the SNPG, including 2 chalk studies of The Duke of Wellington, and an oil portrait in the Edinburgh City collection.
**Bibl:** Bryan.

**HALL, John C** **fl 1896-1937**
Stained glass window designer and watercolourist. Senior partner in the family firm John Hall & Co of 278 (later 305) St Vincent Street, Glasgow, specialising in stained glass window design. Exhibited RA(1), RSA(3) & GI(21).

**HALL, Miss Kate** **fl 1874-1894**
Aberdeen painter in oil of local landscapes, interiors & flowers. Probably the same Kate A Hall who was living in Birmingham 1882-1885 and exhibited flower paintings in England. Exhibited RSA(2) & AAS 1885-94 from 32 Desswood Place.

**HALL, Louie E** **fl 1901-1902**
Aberdeen painter of portraits and figure subjects. Exhibited GI(1) & AAS(3) from 461 Union St.

**HALL, Mabel G Blythe** **fl 1896-1898**
Glasgow painter in oil of portraits and portrait miniatures. Exhibited RSA(10), including portraits of 'Lady Maud Dundas', 'Lord George Dundas', and 'Viscount Melville'. Mentioned by neither Foskett nor Long.

**HALL, Miss Maureen** **fl 1974**
Paisley artist; exhibited GI(1), from 12 Stanley Court.

**HALL, Michael J** **fl 1981**
While living at Lumsden, Aberdeenshire, worked with the Scottish Sculpture Workshop. Exhibited AAS(1).

**HALL, Miss R** **fl 1872-1873**
Aberdeen landscape painter in oil. Exhibited RSA(3). One exhibit was a woodland scene purchased by Capt Lodder RN(qv), another bought by an anonymous Aberdeen collector.

**HALL, Rosalind F F** **fl 1965**
Fife sculptress. Exhibited AAS(1) from Manse of Criech, Cupar.

**HALL, Sidney** **fl 1820-1831**
Scottish engraver. Engraved Scottish maps and plans during the above dates. Mentioned in neither Bryan nor DNB.

**HALL, Stephen Alexander** **fl 1977**
Aberdeen artist. Exhibited AAS(1) from 54 Bedford Rd.

**HALL, Thomas** **fl 1848-d1888**
Edinburgh painter in oil and watercolour of landscape and topographical subjects especially castles and churches in the Lothians, and scenes on Arran. Among his exhibits were 'Borthwick Castle' (1859), 'Windsor Castle' (1861), 'Tantallon Castle' and 'Linlithgow Palace' (both in 1862) while his later works were of natural scenes such as 'Salmon pool on the Ken' (1884). Some confusion is caused by the fact that the painter Thomas Hall is referred to in the RSA records as 'Thomas Hall Jnr' whilst the RA records that from the same address - 8 George Street, Edinburgh - a Thomas Hall exhibited 4 architectural designs (1880-1896) including a decoration for the dining-room of Craig House nr Edinburgh (1880), United Presbyterian Hall (1881), staircase for 4 Ainslie Place (1887) and St Baldred's Church, North Berwick (1896). Exhibited RSA(63) 1848-1884 & GI(1), from 13 Gayfield Square.

**HALL, Tom** **fl 1970**
Milngavie-based painter of figurative compositions. Exhibited GI(1), from 25 James Watt Rd.

**HALLAM, J S** **fl 1933**
Watercolour painter; exhibited RSW(4).

**HALLEY, John** **fl 1850**
Edinburgh painter; exhibited still life and portraits at the RSA from 6 Charlotte Place.

**HALLEY, Mrs N** **fl 1893**
Amateur Aberdeen painter of rustic scenes and landcape. Exhibited AAS(2) from 27 Gladstone Place.

**HALLIDAY, Dorothy (Lady Dorothy Dunnett)** **1923-2001**
Born Dunfermline; died Edinburgh. Painter and novelist. Educated James Gillespie's HS, Edinburgh; trained at both the Edinburgh & Glasgow Schools of Art. Her early career was in the Civil Service as a Press Officer in Edinburgh 1940-1955. Married Alastair Dunnett, sometime editor of The Scotsman, 1946. Primarily a portrait painter in oils, she also painted figure studies and occasional still lifes. Exhibited regularly at the RSA.
**Bibl:** David Robinson, The Scotsman, Obituary, Dec, 2001.

**HALLIDAY, George** **fl 1888-1912**
Edinburgh sculptor. Moved to Sheffield in c1899 and then to Birmingham. Exhibited RA(3) & RSA(1).

**HALLIDAY, Irene May RSW** **1931-**
Born Kingsmuir, by Forfar, Angus, 26 Sep. Painter in oil but principally watercolour; landscape and flower studies. Educated Arbroath HS, Dundee College of Art, and Moray House College of Education. Received post-diploma scholarship 1953 and travelling scholarship 1954. Head of Art and Design, Didsbury College of Education and from 1972-73 Visiting Professor, State University of NY (at Buffalo). Abandoned full-time teaching 1979 in order to devote more time to painting. Elected RSW 1955. Lives and works in Manchester and Arbroath with frequent working visits to Scotland, Italy and the Greek Islands. Exhibiting regularly at the RSA since 1961, GI(65) & AAS 1964-76. Represented in Dundee AG, Glasgow AG, Greenock AG, Salford AG, Royal Collection.

**HALLIDAY, John Alexander** **1933-**
Born Kirkcudbright. Painter of portraits, landscape and murals. Studied Glasgow School of Art 1949-53. Won two RSA travelling scholarships enabling him to visit France and Italy. Executed the murals at Prestwick airport as well as for a number of properties belonging to the National Trust for Scotland, including several at Culzean Castle. Exhibited RSA(2) 1960 and 1964; & GI(8), most recently from The Old School, Dunsyre, by Carnwath, Lanarkshire.

**HALLIDAY, Thomas Symington MBE FRSA** **1902-1998**
Born Thornhill, Dumfriesshire, 11 Apr; Dundee, 22 May. Sculptor and etcher, stained glass designer, mural decorator. Painter of marines, aircraft, landscape (mostly in southern France) animals, especially birds, and figures. Also sculpted in wood, bronze and terracotta. Influenced by the work of Douglas Strachan(qv) and early French stained glass. Educated Ayr Academy, worked as a marine engineer on the Clyde before studying Glasgow School of Art under Anning Bell. Began sculpting after 1932, helped by Norman Forrest(qv). Art Master, Prestwick HS for a number of years and founder member, Guild of Aviation Artists. Commissioned by the RSA to paint a large mural of the 'Battle of Narvik' for the Royal Naval Canteen, Rosyth. Lived at Ayr before moving to Wormit, nr Dundee. One of Scotland's most versatile artists. He turned to sculpture, later specialising in animal carving, generally in wood. Exhibited RSA(88), RSW(6), GI(102) & L(2), from 6 Glebe Terrace, Alloa, Clackmannanshire. Represented in Imperial War Museum, Arbroath AG, Ayr AG, Derby AG, Glasgow AG, Edinburgh City AG, Dundee AG, Perth AG, Royal collection.

**HALSTEAD, Wendy** **1959-**
Sculptor and painter. Works in wood, jute, paper and bark. Enjoys recycling old material especially that collected on beaches and in woodlands. Studied on the foundation course at Lincoln 1977-78, textile design at Kidderminster College of Art 1978, theatre design at Birmingham Polytechnic 1979 and sculpture at Birmingham Polytechnic 1979-82. Also a graphic artist preferring to work in large bold energic botanical forms. Exhibits regularly at the RSA since 1983. First solo exhibition 1985. Represented in Aberdeen AG, Edinburgh City collection.

**HALSWELLE, Keeley RI ARSA** **1832-1891**
Born Richmond-on-Thames, 23 Apr; died Paris, 12 Apr. Born of Scottish parentage. Painter in oil of genre and landscape also illustrator. After studying at the BM and in Edinburgh, worked as an illustrator for the *Illustrated London News* and, returning to Edinburgh in 1856, became principal illustrator for the Edinburgh publishing company Nelson. Many of his pictures from this early period were scenes of fishing life around Newhaven. In 1868 he first visited Rome, providing him with Italian subjects for many years. As well as painting in oil he was a draughtsman on wood and a magazine and book illustrator. From 1869 he lived in Italy for several years, painting mainly peasant subjects, and also worked for a time in Paris. His pen and ink drawing 'A Child's Dream of Christmas' (1858) places him in the tradition of Richard Doyle. In the 1880s he abandoned figure painting and turned almost entirely to Highland landscapes and views on the Thames. 'His landscapes were often cold and false in colour, with a tendency sometimes to blackness, sometimes to the kind of lurid tone which nature puts on just before a thunderstorm. But they had personality. They embodied, almost always, a really pictorial idea, and they shared power both to select and to suppress' *[AJ]*. Elected ARSA 1865, RI 1882. Illustrated *The Princess Florella and the Knight of the Silver Shield* (1860), and *Six Years in a House-boat.* Also contributed to *Good Words* (1860); *Pen and Pencil Pictures from the Poets* (1866) and Scott's *Poems* (c1866). Exhibited 36 works at the RA between 1862 and 1891 including 'Lo Sposalizio; Bringing Home the Bride' (1875), a lively scene of a marriage procession of contadini, enlivened by the music of the Piferrari, who marched in front with their pipes. As evidence of the influence of Horatio MacCulloch(qv) there was in contrast to the above works, 'Inverlochy Castle and Ben Nevis' (1882). Continued exhibiting Highland scenes as late as 1890. Also RSA(122) 1852-1926, GI(21) & AAS in 1887. Represented in NGS, Tate AG, Nat Gall of Ireland, Glasgow AG, Leeds AG, Victoria AG (Australia).
**Bibl:** AJ, 1879, 49-52; 1894, 195; 1884, 59f; 1891, 192; 1893, 132;

1894, 195; Caw 274; Clement and Hutton; Cundall; DNB, 1890; Halsby 109,261; Houfe; Mag of Art IV, 406; Portfolio 1884, 24; Gleeson White 45,127,140.

**HAMBLETON, Andrew Denis** **fl 1982**
Dundee printmaker. Exhibited AAS from 58 Provost Rd.

**HAMBROUCK, H** **fl 1918**
Sculptor. Exhibited GI(1) from Southfield House, Newton Mearns, nr Glasgow.

**HAMILTON, Alexander** **fl 1862-1870**
Paisley painter in oil and occasional watercolour of figure subjects and genre/rural scenes. Exhibited RSA(10) & GI(6), from 57 Canal St.

**HAMILTON, Andrew** **fl 1846-1859**
Edinburgh based painter of landscape and topographical subjects. Exhibited RSA(15) during the above years.

**HAMILTON, Andrew H** **fl 1901**
Glasgow landscape painter, usually in watercolour. Exhibited GI(1), from 25 Armadale St.

**HAMILTON, C Winifred** **fl 1907-1912**
Sculptor. Exhibited GI(5) from Ardedynn, Kelvinside, Glasgow until 1908, thereafter from 19 Beaufort Gardens, London.

**HAMILTON, Catherine (Kate) (née Highet)** **1854-1948**
Born Ayrshire; died Newbattle, 31 Jan. Landscape painter. Studied painting at the RSA Classes. Her second marriage was to James Hamilton(qv). Exhibited RSA 1889, 1890 and 1900.

**HAMILTON, Charles William** **1670-1754**
Born Brussels, died Augsburg. Oil painter of hunting scenes, birds and reptiles. Son of James H(qv), the Edinburgh portrait painter who fled to Brussels. Brother of Ferdinand Philip(qv) and John George H(qv). Lived and worked in Germany. Signed his work 'CWDH'. Represented in Cologne AG, Helsinki AG, Lyon AG, Stuttgart AG.

**HAMILTON, Claud** **fl 1686-1690**
House painter. Lived at Westerhills. Between 1686 and 1690 was painting in Hamilton Palace and the Countess of Arran's burial place in Hamilton Parish Church.
**Bibl:** Apted 44; Hamilton Archives, Lennoxlove, 505/26/102.

**HAMILTON, Miss Constance M** **fl 1960**
Glasgow painter; exhibited 'Suddenly a house appeared' at the GI, from 162 Crofton Avenue.

**HAMILTON, Miss D** **fl 1931-1937**
Aberdeenshire watercolourist. Specialised in local scenes, especially around Dinnet and Aboyne. Exhibited AAS(6).

**HAMILTON, David** **1768-1843**
Architect. Son of a Glasgow mason. Turned to architecture c1800. Father of **William HAMILTON**(d c1827), watercolourist and draughtsman, who assisted his father until his early death. Versatile designer able to work in quite different styles. Influenced in part by the work of Sir John Soane at the Bank of England. Hutcheson's Hospital of 1802-5 was designed in the Adam-Wyatt manner but the Royal Exchange of 1827-30 was in the Greek tradition. Played an important part in the development of Aberdeen, being largely responsible for the construction of King St and Union St 1800-1805. The tall clustered chimneys and strapworked pediments of Dunlop, Ayrshire (1833) was one of the first buildings to show the reawakening of interest of the early Scottish renaissance. In 1822 he designed Castle House, Dunoon and the Town House designed for Falkirk in 1813. Another interesting design was his 'Norman Castle' at Lennox (1837-41) while in Edinburgh he was responsible for the interesting Tudor Gate-Piers to Barnton House (c1810; now dem.).
**Bibl:** Dunbar 118,124,138; A Gomme & D Walker, Architecture in Glasgow, London 1987(rev) 292 et al.

**HAMILTON, David** **fl 1876-1887**
Painter in oil of rustic genre; exhibited RSA(1) & GI(10), from Horsburgh Castle, nr Peebles whence he moved from London c1880.

**HAMILTON, Dorothy** **fl 1904**
Amateur painter of 6 James Place, Leith, exhibited 'A Japanese Doll', at the RSA.

**HAMILTON, Douglas** **fl 1944-1957**
Glasgow painter and stained glass window designer. Responsible, with Mary Wood(qv), for the set of richly coloured lights in Priestfield Church depicting the trees of the Bible (1912); also the war memorial in St Bernard's Free Church, Henderson Row (1949). Exhibited RSA & GI(21), after 1954 from 65 Hamilton Drive.
**Bibl:** Gifford 45,417,636.

**HAMILTON, Miss E** **fl 1896-1916**
Painter in oil and watercolour, principally the latter. Still life and landscape. Exhibited at various English galleries from Barncleuth, Hamilton.

**HAMILTON, Elizabeth P** **fl 1948-1982**
Painter and sculptress. Worked in oil and watercolour, plaster and wood, miniatures on ivory. Exhibited flower studies, figurative and symbolic works RSA(3) & GI(22). Moved from Edinburgh to Glasgow c1955 living latterly at 47 Westbourne Gdns, Glasgow.

**HAMILTON, Esther** **fl 1950-1959**
Edinburgh based painter of interiors and still life. Exhibited RSA(3) 1950 and 1959.

**HAMILTON, Miss F** **fl 1908**
Aberdeen flower painter. Exhibited Walker Gallery, Liverpool(1) & AAS from Skene House.

**HAMILTON, Ferdinand Philip** **1664-1750**
Born Brussels; died Vienna. Son of James H(qv), brother of Johan George(qv) and Karl Wilhelm(qv). Greatly influenced by the Dutch Masters, he specialised in animal painting and still life. Together with his brother Johan was commissioned by the Emperor Charles VI. Many critics considered him the most artistically talented member of a very talented family. His work has always been highly valued on the continent and can be seen in Berne AG, Besancon AG, Breslau AG, Budapest AG, Frankfurt AG, Gratz AG, Hermitage Museum, Leningrad AG, Munich AG, Stuttgart AG, Vienna AG.
**Bibl:** Caw 16.

**HAMILTON, Gavin** **1723-1798**
Born Murdieston House, Lanark; died Rome, 4 Jan. Oil painter, author, archaeologist and antiquarian; portraits, historical subjects. One of the great figures of Scottish art, member of a well-known local family distantly related to the Dukes of Hamilton through the Hamiltons of Murdieston in Lanarkshire. A polymath, immersed in the classical European cultural tradition and one of the founders of the neo-classical movement as painter, theorist and enlightened archaeologist. In 1738 graduated from Glasgow University, where he studied the humanities, and in 1744 visited Rome for the first time to study under Agostino Mesucci. Formed a friendship with Nicholas Revett and James Steuart, authors of *Antiquities of Athens.* With them he went to Naples 1748. Returning to London concentrated on portrait painting, at which he was a traditionalist, before turning to history painting at which he was an innovator. In his portraits he sought delicacy and elegance and was fascinated by surface texture. 'Elizabeth Gunning, Duchess of Hamilton' (Holyrood House), although an early example (1752-55), marks the apotheosis of his portrait painting. Other important works include 'Wood and Dawkins discovering Palmyra' (1758), now on loan to Glasgow University, the exiled Jacobite poet 'William Hamilton of Bangour', in the SNPG, two later portraits of 'Emma Hamilton' and a late group, now at Lennoxlove, of the '8th Duke of Hamilton with Dr John Moore and Ensign Moore'. This last was interesting in placing the sitters against a backcloth of classical ruins, reflecting the contemporary vogue for undertaking the Grand Tour. In about 1758 he returned to Rome, remaining there for the rest of his life. Now concentrated more on historical subjects, always with a moral theme. For him art served a moral purpose, enobling the spirit and releasing the understanding from time-warped prejudice. The first Homeric work 'Andromache bewailing the Death of Hector' 1760, marks a significant point in the

development of neo-classicism, being approved by Winckelmann for its good composition and truly Grecian heads but criticised for its hard colouring. As with the Homeric sequence that followed over the next ten years, the work was engraved by Domenico Cunego. In understanding Hamilton's approach to these Homeric subjects notice should be taken of four important books that had recently appeared and were probably known to the artist. Thomas Blackwell's *Inquiry into the life, times and writings of Homer,* had been published in 1755, George Turnbull's *Treatise on Ancient painting* appeared in 1740 (Turnbull was a pupil of Blackwell's in Aberdeen), Comte de Caylus' *Tableaux Tir de l' Iliade...de Homere,* published in 1757 and Robert Wood's *Essay on the Original Genius of Homer,* which appeared in 1769. Whilst these works were being completed Hamilton produced two other important paintings, 'The Oath of Brutus', commission for Lord Hope in 1763 and engraved in 1766 and 'Agrippina with the Ashes of Germanicus', commissioned by Earl Spencer in 1765 (RA 1772). Hamilton had charged highly for his paintings and was able to choose his patrons carefully. Among them were the Dukes of Dorset and Hamilton, the Earl of Hopetoun, Earl Spencer, Viscount Palmerston, James Boswell, Sir James Grant of Grant and Prince Borghese. The decoration of the Villa Borghese for the Prince was one of the most extensive projects of its time. As well as Hamilton, Jacob More(qv) was involved, although Hamilton was given the principal room for his Paris and Helen cycle. The three principal canvases are now in the Museo di Roma, the ceiling paintings can still be seen in the Villa. The monumental works painted for these patrons were to influence the course of 18th century culture and had a potent effect even upon David, the greatest neo-classical painter of his time. In Rome Hamilton was the leading Scottish artist. 'He is', said Lord Cathcart, 'the unsolicited friend of every artist'. Among the Scots were David Allan, William Cochran, Alexander Nasmyth and Henry Raeburn. He assisted others too, Canova and the American Benjamin West among them. As doyen of the British colony in Rome he found ready buyers for the finds unearthed by his excavations. Among these and other works exported by Hamilton were Leonardo's 'Virgin of the Rocks' and Raphael's 'Ansidei Madonna', the 'Warwick Vase', and the figure of Hermes, now in Copenhagen. The culmination of his archaeological work came after 1769, when he began excavations at Hadrian's Villa, until his last discoveries at Gabii in 1792. Published a volume of engravings, *Schola Italica Picturae.* Elected to the Academy of St Luke and to an élite literary group, the Arcadians. Exhibited RA(5) 1770-1788, 'Mary Queen of Scots Resigning Her Crown' (1776) being a commission for James Boswell. Represented in Villa Borghese, in which the ceiling paintings survive in situ, Museo di Roma, which has the large wall canvases of the 'Story of Paris', SNPG(3), and NGS(5). There is a sketch of a group of classical figures dating from 1759 at Manchester AG, 'The Earl of Strafford and his Family' (1732) at the Nat. Gall of Canada (Ottawa), and a large portrait of an unknown lady with a lyre at Drum Castle (NTS).
**Bibl:** James Anderson, 'Biographical Sketches of eminent Scottish Artists: Gavin Hamilton' The Bee, 10 July 1793; Art Bulletin XLIV, 1962, 87-102, by David Irwin; Brockwell 7-8; Bryan; Brydall 154-8,203; Caw 36-8; Edward, Early Conversation Pictures, 1954, 65,170(illus); Ferrara, 'LA "Stanza di Elena e Paride" nella Galleria Borghese', Rivista dell'Istitupo Nazionale d' Archaeologia e Storia dell' Arte, new series, AIII, 1954; Irwin 49-50, 101-4; Macmillan [GA] 31-42; Macmillan [SA] 114-17 et passim; McKay 25-6; Sir Ellis Waterhouse, 'The British Contribution to the neo-classical style of painting', Proceedings of the British Academy, XL,1954, Julia Lloyd Williams, Scottish Masters, no. 18, 1994.

**HAMILTON, Gavin** **1923-**
Born Rutherglen 19 Nov. Carpet designer. Educated Gallowflat School, studied art at Darlington School of Art 1945-6 and Glasgow School of Art 1946-9. Designs carpets internationally. Lives and works in London.

**HAMILTON, Gawen** **1698-1737**
Born in the West of Scotland nr Hamilton; died London, 28 Oct. Painter of conversation pieces and small full-length portraits. Studied under an obscure bird painter named Wilson. Worked in London from about 1830 and was one of Hogarth's chief rivals in conversation pieces. Thought by some contemporaries superior to Hogarth. Unfortunately so little of his work now remains that his reputation has suffered accordingly. Represented in NPG by his best known work 'A conversation of Virtuosi', Glasgow AG.
**Bibl:** Hilda Finberg, HF, 'Gawen Hamilton', Walpole Society, VI, 1917-18, 51ff; Irwin 69; Kerslake 340-342; Hamish Miles, 'Conversations and Histories', Scottish Art Review, new series, V, I, 1954, 26-8; Virtue.

**HAMILTON, George** **1882-1894**
Edinburgh watercolour painter of landscapes and townscapes. Exhibited RSA(3), all topographical paintings of Edinburgh Old Town.

**HAMILTON, Miss J** **fl 1799**
Landscape painter. An honorary exhibitor at the RA in 1799 showing 'View of Craigmillar Castle' and 'View of Roslin Castle'. Appears never to have exhibited elsewhere.

**HAMILTON, James** **c1640-1720**
Born Murdieston, Fife; died Brussels. Worked as a portrait painter in Edinburgh but fled to Brussels with the advent of the Commonwealth and settled there before moving on to Germany where he specialised in still life and fruit. He had three sons - Ferdinand Philip(qv), John George(qv) and Charles William(qv), all of whom were artists. His work is well known and appreciated on the continent. Represented in the NGS by a still life, signed and dated 1695.
**Bibl:** Apted 44; Caw 16; J Tonge, The Arts of Scotland, London 1938.

**HAMILTON, James** **fl c1678-d1691**
Early Edinburgh painter. Died Edinburgh, Mar. Apprenticed to the painter James Alexander(qv). Became painter burgess of Edinburgh 1684 and member, Incorporation of St Mary's. Worked at the Palace of Holyrood 1684; a perspective study of Holyrood was vetoed because Hamilton had not served a long enough apprenticeship but a second essay 'ane frontispiece of ane tomb, done in black and white upon a sheet of lumber paper' was more successful. Employed between 11 Sep and 11 Dec 1687 at Holyrood painting closets, bedchambers and rooms in the gatehouse. Took as an apprentice David Nicol 15 Aug, 1688.
**Bibl:** Apted 45; Laing MSS, Edinburgh PL, IV.26; Register of the Privy Council of Scotland, ed J.H. Burton et al, Edinburgh 1877-? 3rd series, xvi, 476.

**HAMILTON, James** **c1807-1862**
Glasgow architect. Son of David H(qv). After the death of his father entered partnership with James Smith(qv). The business failed 1844 but Hamilton continued to help behind the scenes. Responsible with his father and/or Smith for many important Glasgow buildings including Royal Exchange(1827) and Royal Exchange Square(1830), Hutcheson's GS, Western Club (147 Buchanan St)(1841); also Castle Toward, Argyll(1821). Won 3rd prize in 1835 competition for Houses of Parliament.
**Bibl:** A Gomme & D Walker, Architecture in Glasgow, London 1987(rev), 292 et al.

**HAMILTON, James ARSA** **1853-1894**
Born Kilsyth; died Edinburgh, 29 Dec. Student at the RSA Life School from 1874. Painted in oil and sometimes watercolour, chiefly incidents connected with Highland life, mainly Jacobite history and occasionally landscapes and genre subjects. His early promise was not fulfilled. Among his most successful works were 'Refugees of Glencoe', 'Leaving the mountains to follow Prince Charlie', and 'Annet Lyle'. Elected ARSA 1886. Exhibited RA(1) 1892, RSA(94) & GI(18), after 1893 from 3 Fettes Row, Edinburgh. Represented in Glasgow AG.
**Bibl:** Caw 272.

**HAMILTON, James Anderson** **1816-1875**
Architect. Little-known, what is preserved is commonplace. His best work was probably Old Newhaven Free Church (1852), Pier Pl, Newhaven, now in secular use.
**Bibl:** Gifford 471,476,479,601.

**HAMILTON, James Steedman** **fl 1922-1937**
Painter and stained glass window designer. Taught at Dundee School of Art 1922, lived in Aberdeen from 1931, teaching at Gray's School of Art. Exhibited RSA(2), including a window for the Arbilot Parish Church, Forfarshire (1922) & regularly AAS 1923-37.

**HAMILTON, James Whitelaw RSA RSW** **1860-1932**
Born Glasgow, 26 Nov; died Helensburgh, 16 Sept. Painter in chalk, pastel, oil and watercolour. Son of a wealthy Glasgow merchant, brother of Maggie(qv) and uncle of Viola Paterson(qv). Spent his early days in business before escaping to Paris with Joseph Crawhall(qv) and Alex Roche(qv) to study in the studios of Dagnan-Bouveret and Aimé Morot. His subjects were usually landscapes, generally in watercolour. Enjoyed painting the fishing villages and fields of Berwickshire, later in the North of England at Richmond, in Westmoreland and nearer home in Helensburgh and Glen Fruin. Exhibited on the continent as frequently as in the UK. Although generally regarded as a member of the Glasgow School, his association is not clearcut. He did indeed work alongside Crawhall, Guthrie and Walton at Cockburnspath as early as 1883, and again the following year with his sister Maggie(qv), but his style developed in its own way. Apart from the vigour of his handling of paint and his strength of colour, he owed little to the Glasgow movement. Capable administrator and organiser, his work helping to organise exhibitions of Scottish art in Italy led to him being honoured with the Order of the Crown of Italy 1901. Later became President, Scottish Artists Benevolent Fund. Also served on the Council of the RSA, and was Honorary Secretary, Glasgow Institute 1920. Member of the Society of 25 Artists. Elected ARSA 1911, RSA 1922, RSW 1895, RP 1901, SSA 1898. Awarded gold medal at the Munich Exhibition 1897. Exhibited RA(10), RSA(113), RSW(75), GI(129) & AAS 1906-1931, after 1893 from The Grange, Helensburgh. Represented in Glasgow AG, Paisley AG, Perth AG, Kirkcaldy AG, Lillie AG (Milngavie), Edinburgh City collection, RSA (Diploma coll.), Weimar AG (Germany).
**Bibl:** Caw 386; Halsby 139,145,150,261; Irwin 374-5; Scottish Country Life, Jan 1921; Studio Vol 6 1914 9-19.

**HAMILTON, Johann George** **1662-c1736**
Oil painter of hunting scenes, mainly stags and horses. Son of James Hamilton(qv), the Edinburgh portrait painter who fled to Brussels; brother of Ferdinand Philip(qv) and Charles William H(qv). Lived and worked in Germany; died in Vienna. Employed by Frederick I of Prussia and by the Emperor Charles VI. Represented in Vienna AG(5), Munich AG, Dresden AG.

**HAMILTON, Mrs John (Sybil)** **fl 1921**
Amateur painter. Exhibited two paintings of rustic genre at the AAS.

**HAMILTON, John Alexander** **fl 1885-1886**
Edinburgh draughtsman and watercolour painter of local landscapes and topographical subjects. Exhibited RSA(3) including 'Sunset from South Queensferry' 1885.
**Bibl:** Bryan; Caw 16.

**HAMILTON, John Guy** **?-1838**
Inverness portrait and landscape painter in oil. Celebrated drawing master at Inverness Academy. Laboured under the disadvantage of having neither fingers nor toes, his brush or pencil having to be strapped to the stump which served in place of a thumb. In her book *Inverness before Railways,* Isobel Anderson remarks upon Hamilton's great talent as a painter, 'his paintings of scenes in the neighbourhood of Inverness being exquisite, he especially excelled in delineating cloudy skies and lake and ocean scenery...as a teacher he could not be excelled, and the drawings of his pupils bear evidence of having been directed by a master hand'. His portrait of 'Dr Bethune' achieved local fame partly on account of the tragically early death of this much loved doctor and partly on account of the quality of the portrait itself. An engraving was subsequently published in 1824. In January 1823 Hamilton issued an elaborate prospectus of the series of lithographic sketches of Inverness scenery. It was intended that the work would extend to three or four numbers each containing six views: but only part 1 was published and that not until 1825 when it appeared under the imprint of Ackermann. The views included 'Loch Ness', 'the Pass of Inverfarigaig', 'the lower Fall of Foyers', 'Urquhart Castle' and 'Culloden House'. After his death, Hamilton left behind a large collection of original works that were eventually sold after his widow died in 1843. Exhibited RSA(3) 1833-35 including 'Culloden Moor, the spot where the battle was fought in 1745' (1835).

**HAMILTON, John McClure** **1853-1936**
Born Philadelphia. Portrait and figure painter of Scottish extraction. Studied at Pensylvannia Academy of Fine Arts before coming to Britain to continue his studies at the RA Schools with further study in Antwerp and Paris. Settled in London 1878. Elected NEA 1890, RP 1891. Exhibited RA(8), RSA(1) in 1929, GI(14) ROI(1), RI(1), RBA(1) & L(20). Represented in Glasgow AG.

**HAMILTON, Karl Wilhelm** **1668-1754**
Born Brussels; died Augsburg. Son of James Hamilton(qv) and brother of Ferdinand(qv) and Johan H(qv). Perhaps the least talented of the four although still well regarded in Austria where he died. Painter of hunting and sporting scenes, also birds and reptiles. Represented in Cologne AG, Dijon AG, Helsinki AG, Lyon AG, Stuttgart AG.

**HAMILTON, Margaret (Maggie) (Mrs Alexander Nisbet Paterson)** **1867-1952**
Born Glasgow, Sept 1; died Helensburgh, 21 Jan. Painter in oil and watercolour of still life, flowers and figures, also embroiderer. Sister of James Whitelaw H(qv) and mother of Viola P(qv). When a young girl her parents moved to Helensburgh. Although receiving no formal training in art she was associated through her brother with the Glasgow Boys and at their studio at Cockburnspath in 1883 was invited by James Guthrie's mother to help with domestic duties. There she was painted by Guthrie several times and his diploma work 'Midsummer' (1892) incorporates her portrait. In 1897 she married the architect Alexander Paterson. In the late 1890s her embroideries in Chinese silks achieved widespread acclaim. Her decoration of their home in Helensburgh, 'The Long Croft', included embroideries with floral designs in the Arts and Crafts tradition introduced into the wood panelling of the public rooms. Exhibited Glasgow International Festival 1901. Although preferring to paint flowers in oil rather than watercolour, in later years she moved towards still life in the Dutch manner with dark backgrounds and detailed realism. In 1937 was made an artist member of the Lady Artists Club and was twice elected Vice-President 1928-31 and 1937-40. Exhibited RSA(47), RA(4), GI(92) & L(4) from The Long Croft, Helensburgh. Represented in Glasgow AG and in the Royal Museum of Scotland.
**Bibl:** Burkhauser 222-3; Margaret Swain 159-162.

**HAMILTON, Miss Mary Elizabeth** **1875-1956**
Born Skene, Aberdeenshire. Landscape and flower painter, book plate and linocut artist and designer. Studied Byam Shaw School of Art. Lived in London for a time c1908 before finally coming to live in Murtle, Aberdeenshire. Exhibited RA(5), RSA(2), RI(2), SWA(1), L(20), GI(2) & AAS 1896-1937. Represented n Aberdeen AG.

**HAMILTON, Miss Maud E** **fl 1942-1948**
Glasgow painter of portraits, figure studies and flowers; exhibited RSA(9) & GI(5), from 3 Victoria Park Gardens, between the above years.

**HAMILTON, Noel** **fl 1972-1973**
Perth painter of landscape and town views. Exhibited two Perth townscapes at the GI, from 40 George St.

**HAMILTON, Mrs Rachel** **fl 1929-1932**
Edinburgh amateur watercolourist; exhibited RSW(1) from 25 Buckingham Terrace, and 'West Highland cottage' at the AAS 1929.

**HAMILTON, Thomas RSA** **1784-1858**
Born Edinburgh; died Edinburgh. Architect and watercolourist. Apprenticed to his father. Important figure in the architectural life of the capital, being responsible for the Royal HS (1825-9), the George IV Bridge (1829-34), the King's Bridge (over King's Stables Rd) (1829-32) and many other public buildings; also the Burns Memorial, Ayr (1820). As well as his architectural work he was an unusually good architectural draughtsman. Responsible for designing Ayr Town Hall (1828), with its particularly fine steeple. The Royal HS is 'by general consent, the finest monument of the Scottish Greek Revival, its massive stepped profile culminating most effectively in the Doric temple portico of the main hall, while for good measure rival variants of the Choragic Monument of Lysicrates, Athens, appeared on each flank'[Dunbar]. His attempt to combine neo-classical and baroque elements in direct apposition exemplified by the Dean Orphanage (1831-1833) was not entirely successful but the facade of the Physicians' Hall, Edinburgh (1844-46) achieved real

distinction. Foundation member of the RSA, being with William Nicholson (secretary, qv), James Stevenson(qv) and Patrick Syme(qv) one of the original four members of Council, Treasurer 1826-1829 and again 1846-1850. Represented by six watercolours in the NGS and by 4 ink drawings of old Edinburgh in the City collection.
**Bibl:** Brydall 334,338,342; Mungo Campbell, 'The Line of Tradition', Nat Galls of Scotland, Ex cat, Edinburgh 1993; Dunbar 117; Gifford see index; Halsby 261.

**HAMILTON, Thomas Crawford** **fl 1880-1900**
Glasgow painter in oil, watercolour and pencil of historical buildings, landscape, continental scenes, religious subjects and occasional portraits. Exhibited RSA(8), RSW(10) & GI(12). Represented in the SNPG (by a drawing of the exterior of the SNPG and a portrait study of the advocate 'George Seton' 1822-1908).
**Bibl:** Halsby 261.

**HAMILTON, Vereker Monteith** **1856-1931**
Born Hafton, Argyll. Painter of landscape, genre, military subjects and figure studies. Studied at the Slade School where he was awarded the landscape prize 1886. Married the sculptress Lilian V Hamilton. Frequently collaborated with Joseph Benwell Clark. Elected RE 1887. Exhibited RA(32) from 1888, GI(5), RHA(2), RE(6), LS(12) & NS(12). Represented in Cape Town AG, Sydney (Australia) AG.

**HAMILTON, William RA** **1751-1801**
Born Chelsea; died London, 2 Dec. Decorative, history and portrait painter. Father was the Scottish assistant to Robert Adam(qv), who sent the young man at an early age, to Rome. At first he was a pupil of Antonio Zucchi, possibly in Rome 1766 and certainly in London from 1768. Trained as an architectural draughtsman before attending the RA schools in 1769 after which he turned to figure painting. Produced a steady stream of narrative scenes, often small, in a romantic manner, and painted many pictures for Boydell's *Shakespeare Gallery,* Macklin's *Bible and British Poets,* and Bowyer's *English History.* Also designed cabinets and stained glass for William Beckford and others. His best portraits are of theatrical personages, including many of Mrs Siddons. Decorated the panels of Lord Fitzgibbon's state carriage, now in the V&A. His charming and mannered narrative scenes sometimes show the influence of Fuseli with whom he collaborated in illustrating Thomson's *Seasons.* His 'Mrs Siddons as Zara', formerly in Los Angeles County Museum, was sold in London 1947. First exhibited at the RA 1774, elected ARA 1784, RA 1789. His portrait of 'Henry Siddons' is in the SNPG; also represented in NPG, Derby AG, Dublin AG, V & A, Manchester AG, Nottingham AG.
**Bibl:** Bryan; Bushnell; Caw 40; DNB; Hanns Hammelmann Book Illustration in 18th Century England, 1975; Waterhouse, 158.

**HAMILTON, William** **fl 1901-1925**
Hamilton part-time painter and professional photographer. President, Hamilton Art Club 1925. Exhibited 'The old Mill' at the GI from Butterburn Park.

**HAMILTON, William** **fl 1932-1933**
Glasgow based painter and etcher. Exhibited two townscapes at the GI from 221 Renfrew Street.

**HAMILTON, William E** **fl 1870-1873**
Edinburgh oil painter of dead game and landscapes. Moved to London in 1873. Exhibited RSA(1).

**HAMMOND, Dorothy** **20th Cent**
Amateur Aberdeen painter. Exhibited 'The white chair' at the AAS from 29A Spa Street.

**HAMPTON, Mrs Irene** **fl 1969-1974**
Aberdeen painter of local landscapes and country scenes. Exhibited AAS from 188 Mid Stocket Rd.

**HAMSHERE, A S** **1946-**
Born Edinburgh. Painter and clockmaker. Trained Duncan of Jordanstone College of Art, Dundee 1963-68. Began making mechanical clocks 1970. His astronomical clocks commissioned and exhibited at Edinburgh City Arts Centre, Goldsmiths Hall (London), Carlisle and St Andrews. Awarded Saltire Award 1987 and Certificate of Excellence by the Clockmakers Company of London. Exhibits paintings at RSA & elsewhere with many in public collections worldwide. Lives at Balcanquhal Farmhouse, Gateside, Fife.

**HANBRIDGE, James E** **fl 1870-1908**
Glasgow landscape painter in oil and occasional watercolour, particularly fond of Highland scenes. Member of the community of artists who enjoyed sketching on Arran. Exhibited RSA(9), GI(68) & L(1), from 8 Balmoral Crescent.

**HAND, Ms Madeleine** **fl 1988-**
Perthshire painter of genre; exhibited GI(2), from 2 Water Wynd, Dunkeld.

**HANGING TOGETHER** **1993-**
A loose association of Stirling-based artists 'aiming to raise the profile of creative activity in central Scotland through creative engagement with the historical context and the present-day communities...the artists create and place their individual and collective art works in situations outside the normal gallery situations...the exercise is non-commercial; the works themselves are without value'. Those most involved are Val Shatwell(qv), Peter Russell(qv), Paul Eames (trained Camberwell School of Art 1983-87, combines working as an artist with an appointment with Falkirk Council), Nicola Carberry(qv), Karen Strong(qv), David Campbell (b 1967, trained Univ of Central Lancashire), Paula Ellis ('Charuta')(b 1972, trained Edinburgh School of Art), Carolyn Mason (b 1964 in Ayrshire, trained in tapestry and weaving, Camberwell School of Art), and Emma Scott-Smith (b 1977, Alloa).

**HANGINGSHAW, Mungo** **[see HINDSHAW, Mungo]**

**HANLEY, Cliff** **fl 1987**
Glasgow-based portrait painter; exhibited a portrait of his father at the GI, from 36 Munro Rd.

**HANLEY, Miss Geraldine** **fl 1975**
Glasgow painter; exhibited 'Turtle' GI, from 32 Helensburgh Drive.

**HANNAH, Andrew** **1907-?**
Born Glasgow, 13 Sep. Oil painter and art administrator; flowers, portraits and still life. Son of Andrew G H(qv). Educated Bearsden Academy and Glasgow University. Studied Glasgow School of Art 1932-5 under Revel(qv), W O Hutchison(qv) and Hugh Crawford(qv). Deputy Director of Glasgow Museum and Art Galleries, retired 1972 to take up curatorship of the Burrell Collection. Edited *Architectural Prospect.* Member, Glasgow Art Club(qv). Exhibited GI(4), from 84 Killermont Rd, Bearsden.

**HANNAH, Andrew G** **1872/3-1955**
Oil and watercolour painter, also some pastels. Flower pieces, landscape, figurative studies, farmyard and garden scenes. Father of Andrew H(qv). Exhibited RSA(2), from Milngavie, 'A Study of the Garden' in 1933 and 'The Mill' in 1948, also GI(57) & RSW(1), after 1929 from Coire-lie, Campbell Ave, Milngavie. Four of his works, including 'Self-portrait', are in Glasgow AG.

**HANNAH, E M** **fl 1891-1923**
Glasgow based painter in oil and watercolour. Exhibited RSA(3), RSW(1) & GI(15) from addresses in Glasgow and Helensburgh.

**HANNAH, Mrs Edith B** **fl 1931-1932**
Exhibited a portrait and study of 'A Catalpa Tree'at the RSA during the above years from The Whim, La Mancha, Midlothian.

**HANNAH, George** **1896-1947**
Born Renfrewshire. Painter in oil of landscapes and town scenes. Largely self-taught, he painted in the early years of WW2 and for a short time afterwards. Founder member, New Art Club and The New Scottish Group in Glasgow.
**Bibl:** George Hannah 'The Painting of George Hannah' Million, 1st col, Glasgow 1943; Macmillan [SA], 370-1,373,383.

**HANNAH, Miss Jean** **fl 1949**
Renfrewshire sculptress. Exhibited two plaster groups at the GI from 3 Cochrane St, Barrhead.

**HANNAH, Robert** **1812-1909**
Born Creetown, Kirkcudbright. Painter in oil of historical subjects and genre, also portraits. Influenced by John Faed(qv). Little is known of this artist who appears to have gone to London at an early age since his first exhibit was at the RA when aged 30, from Shrubbery House, Compton Road. Charles Dickens is known to have bought two of his works. His best known paintings were the 'Countess of Nithsdale petitioning George I' (1854), 'Master Isaac Newton in his garden' (1856), and a portrait of the artist 'J C Hook ARA' (1859). Exhibited RA(22) 1842-1872, also in Liverpool and Rome, but his only exhibits in Scotland were at the GI(2) in 1863, from 2 Alfred Place West. Represented in V & A, Glasgow AG, Castle Douglas AG (where his 'Astronomy' was originally thought to be a portrait of a single woman but cleaning recently revealed a narrative theme).

**HANNAH, T B** **fl 1975-1976**
Lanarkshire landscape artist. Exhibited GI(2), from 33 Gloucester Ave, Clarkston.

**HANNAN, William** **fl 1751-1772**
Probably born in Scotland; died West Wycombe in about 1775. Painter of topographical landscapes, decorative and historical works, in oil and watercolour. His most important patron was 'Sir Francis Dashwood' (Lord Le des Pencer) at West Wycombe Park, where he painted views of the house and grounds 1751 which were engraved 1754-57. Also executed several neo-classical ceiling decorations and a frescoe 'Chariot of Night' (1770) for the west portico. He may have had a former partnership with Guiseppe Borgnis (d1761) who also worked at West Wycombe. Waterhouse describes his views as in the manner of Lambert, but clumsier. Exhibited Society of Artists 1769-72, mainly views in the Lake District.
**Bibl:** Edward Croft-Murray, Decorative Painting in England 1537-1837, vol i, 1962; Waterhouse 158; West Wycombe Park, National Trust Guide Book.

**HANNAY, Alice (Alys) M** **fl 1908-1933**
Landscape figure and flower painter also etcher. Exhibited widely, sometimes from London, sometimes from Glasgow. Exhibited RSA(3), SWA(4), ROI(6), RBA(2), RA(2), L(5) & London Salon(5).

**HANNAY, Mrs E M** **fl 1891-1923**
Helensburgh painter in oil and watercolour, also monochrome. Topographical subjects, flowers and figure studies. Exhibited GI(17), from Muirtown.

**HANNAY, Mrs Kathleen** **1912-?**
Born Edinburgh. Painter in gouache and watercolour of flowers and landscape. Trained at Edinburgh College of Art. During WW2 served in the RAF. Ill health ended her painting career 1989. Exhibited RSW. Lived in Dunkeld, Perthshire.

**HANSEN, Miss Christine** **fl 1911-1926**
Painter of landscapes, especially of storm-ridden scenes. Exhibited RSA(2), RCA(1), LS(8), L(7), GI(2) & AAS, at first from Glasgow and after 1919 from Ben Rhydding, Yorkshire.

**HANSEN, Hans Jacob RSW** **1853-1947**
Born Copenhagen; died Essex, 4 Dec. Landscape and figure painter in watercolour. Educated Royal HS, Edinburgh having moved at an early age with his family to Leith. Took up painting at the age of 13. Studied in Edinburgh under R B Nisbet(qv) and J Ross(qv). Won silver medal at Salzburg International Exhibition. Worked a lot in Spain and Morocco and visited Russia in the 1890s. Lived for a time in Essex. His work was of varied quality, at his best he produced attractive, decorative views of eastern markets somewhat in the style of Arthur Melville(qv) whom he sought to copy, but at times his work was extremely dark and lacking in draughtsmanship. Elected ARSW 1893, RSW 1906 but struck off in 1913. Exhibited RA(13), RSA(37), RSW(49), ROI(2), RI(14), RHA(2), RBA(13), L(10), AAS 1893-1908 & GI(23), in 1911 from 2 Hurlingham Mansions, Hurlingham Rd, London. Represented in Glasgow AG.
**Bibl:** Halsby 155,262; Wingfield.

**HANSEN, Miss Helen K** **fl 1932-1935**
Painter of flowers and rustic landscapes. Exhibited RSA(4) & GI(2) from 12 Baliol St, Glasgow.

**HANSEN, Lys** **1935-**
Born Grangemouth. Painter specialising in female nudes and landscapes, living and working at Blairlogie, Stirlingshire. Works in oil, watercolour and gouache. Studied at Edinburgh College of Art under Robin Philipson(qv) and Sir William Gillies(qv). Won the Prix de Rome then studied at the British School in Rome before returning to study fine art at Edinburgh University and Moray House. Favours boldly coloured paintings of female nudes often set in landscapes. Her work has been described as 'brash, figurative expressionism'. Spends long sojourns in Berlin. Enjoys strident tones, arresting images, is at her best when profligacy of colour and texture is demanded. Exhibited RSA since 1961, GI(2) & AAS(2), from 13 Mayfield Crescent, Clackmannan. Represented in Kirkcaldy AG.

**HANSON, Edith Mary** **fl 1913-1940**
Born, studied and lived in Edinburgh. Painter in oil but primarily watercolour; portraits and figure subjects. Exhibited RA(1), RSA(7), RSW(4) & GI(3), from 5 Alva St.

**HARCOURT, Aletha** **fl 1932-1940**
Portrait painter. Daughter of George H(qv). Exhibited RA(5) from a London address.

**HARCOURT, Miss Anne SWA** **fl 1930-1938**
Born Arbroath. Portrait and landscape painter in oil. Daughter and pupil of George H(qv). Studied at Slade School under Bernard Adams. Exhibited RA(3), ROI, RBA & overseas. Lives at 34 Dorset Street, London and Bourne End, Bucks.

**HARCOURT, George RA RP** **1868-1947**
Born Dunbarton, 11 Oct; died 30 Oct. Portrait and figure painter in oil. Father of Aletha(qv), Anne(qv) and Mary H(qv). Married the artist Mary Lascelles Leesmith 1914. Studied for three years with Herkomer in England, then visited France where in 1923 he won a gold medal at Paris Salon. After spending a number of years as Herkomer's assistant was appointed Governor of Hospitalfield Art School, Arbroath 1901-1909. Thereafter returned to Bushey and in 1910 'The Birthday', a portrait group, won another gold medal, this time at the Amsterdam International Exhibition 1912. The work marked a new departure in the treatment of light and shade. The first pictures of note had been a landscape 'Evening Time' painted near Merryhill, Bushey, exemplifying the painter's love of subtle effects of light and colour and 'The Heir', demonstrating his inherent love of the dramatic. 'A good and strong, though not a stylish draughtsman, and a capable painter with a method at once powerful and complete, he shows distinct ability in the design and conduct of pictures complex in subject and of great size; while his colour, if not quite captivating, is usually sound and expressive' [Caw]. Principal works include 'The Leper's Wife' (1896), 'Goodbye! The 3rd Battalion Grenadier Guards leaving Waterloo Station 1899', (1900) and 'The Wanderer'. Elected ARA 1919, RA 1926. Exhibited RSA(6), RA(118), RBA(1), L(25) & GI(8, including 'Clement Attlee' (1946), from High Sparrows, Herne, Bushey. Represented in Arbroath Town Hall, Arbroath P.L., Sydney AG (Australia).
**Bibl:** Caw 424-5.

**HARCOURT, Miss Mary Edeva** **fl 1922-1927**
Portrait painter. Daughter of George(qv) and Mary H(qv). Studied RA Schools. Exhibited RA(2) from High Sparrows, Herne, Bushy, Herts.

**HARCOURT, Mary Lascelles (née Leesmith)** **fl 1892-1922**
Landscape figure and portrait painter. Wife of George H(qv), mother of Anne(qv), Aletha(qv) and Mary Edeva H(qv). Exhibited RSA(6), RA(11), RHA(1).

**HARDIE, Professor Alexander Merrie RWA** **1910-1989**
Born Aberdeen, 10 Feb. Painter in oil, watercolour, gouache and pastel; professional physicist. Painted mainly landscapes and still life, occasionally portraits. Educated Aberdeen Grammar School and Aberdeen University of which he was a Classical Golf Medallist. Received no formal art training but influenced by Anne Redpath(qv), Ian Fleming(qv), André Derain and Marc Chagall. Elected member of the Royal West of England Academy where he continued to exhibit after his retirement to Cromarty in 1975, winning the Award for the most distinguished exhibit 1981. A retrospective exhibition of his

work was held at the Univ. of Bath 1991 and a posthumous exhibition at the McEwan Gallery, Ballater 1995. Elected ARWA 1967, RWA 1970. For many years Professor of Physics at the University of Bath before retiring to Ross-shire. Exhibited RSA(28) 1957-1984, RSW, GI(2 watercolours in 1957) & AAS 1921-64. Represented in Aberdeen AG.

**HARDIE, Ann** **fl 1975-1978**
Aberdeenshire artist, married to James H(qv). Exhibited colourful semi-abstracts at the AAS during the above years from Fetternear Schoolhouse, by Kemnay.

**HARDIE, Annie** **fl 1910**
Amateur Glasgow figure painter; exhibited GI(1) from 2 Queen's Crescent.

**HARDIE, Charles Martin RSA** **1858-1916**
Born East Linton, 3 Sep; died Edinburgh. Painter of portraits, landscapes, interior, genre, country sports and historical scenes in oil and watercolour. Uncle of Martin H(qv). Worked as a carpenter in the family business. A family connection with John Pettie(qv) led him towards art and eventually to study at the Trustees Academy. Won the Stewart prize 1879 and the Keith prize the following year. Early in his career some pleasant watercolours were often used as preliminary studies for major historical pictures. His work closely followed Orchardson(qv) and often seems to be more concerned with the story than with artistic form. 'Intelligently conceived, carefully designed, and correctly drawn as the best of his pictures have been, their merits are to a considerable extent discounted by commonness of feeling, mechanical if competent painting, and want of refined tone and colour'. 'The Curling Match between North and South at Carsebreck' (1900) adorns the Royal Caledonian Curling Club, Edinburgh. Elected ARSA 1886, RSA 1895. Exhibited RA(13), RSA(161), RHA(2), RI(1), L(5), GI(25) & AAS, latterly from 1 Belford Rd. Represented in SNPG(6), Glasgow AG, Greenock AG, City of Edinburgh collection.
**Bibl:** Caw 270-1,273; Halsby 262; Wingfield.

**HARDIE, George** **fl 1970**
Aberdeenshire painter of portraits. Trained at Gray's School of Art, Aberdeen. In 1970 exhibited a portrait of his aunt 'Miss Katherine Forbes of Newe' at AAS, from 29 Marchbank Rd, Bieldside.

**HARDIE, Gwen** **1962-**
Born Newport, Fife. Trained Edinburgh College of Art 1979-83, obtaining a Hospitalfield Scholarship in 1982 and going on to receive postgraduate diploma at the ECA 1983-4. Received the Richard Ford Award, 1983. Lives and works in West Berlin. A decision in 1984 to go to Berlin to study was in order to work outside the Scottish tradition and to explore new ways of approaching painting. Studied at first under George Baselitz. She said that 'in 1983 came the realisation that painting is the construction of an idea, rather than the study of the object in space'. Her emphasis so far has been on the schematisation of the female figure, 'opening it up like a diagram to show the internal organs. It is the idea of a woman's body and of course the knowledge that the artist has of her own bodily functions, that she now depicts'. Explores aspects of femininity without resort to slogans or overt propaganda. Represented in Metropolitan Museum of Art(New York), SNGMA.
**Bibl:** Fruitmarket Gall, Edinburgh, 'Gwen Hardie Paintings and Drawings' (Ex Cat 1987); Hartley 136.

**HARDIE, James** **fl 1952-1954**
Grangemouth painter in gouache, pencil and wash; landscape and figure compositions. Exhibited GI(4), from Mayfield, Dalratho Rd.

**HARDIE, James Watterson** **1938-**
Born Motherwell. Studied Glasgow School of Art (1955-59) where he won the Keith Award and the Chalmers Bursary enabling him to travel to Holland and France. Also won Torrance Award. Appointed lecturer in Drawing and Painting, Aberdeen College of Education and since 1980 has been a lecturer at Glasgow School of Art, visiting Chicago 1989. His work has been of a rather abstract nature although his keeness on open spaces - he has held a pilot's licence since 1969 - shines through some of his work. Exhibited RSA regularly since 1958 & GI(44) 1962-1988, from Skelmorlie House, 7 The Crescent, Skelmorlie, Ayrshire. Represented in Tate AG, Aberdeen AG, SAC.

**HARDIE, Martin CBE RE RI VPRI RSW** **1875-1952**
Born London; died 20 Jan. Painter in oil and watercolour, etcher and author. Educated at St Paul's School and Trinity, Cambridge, he studied later under Sir Frank Short. Nephew of Charles Martin H(qv) and also of John Pettie(qv) in whose studio he spent much time and whose biographer he became. In 1898 joined the staff of the V & A becoming its Keeper of Painting and Engraving 1921-35. Began exhibiting RA 1908, producing many etchings and drypoints. There is a tranquil quality to his watercolours some of which are reminiscent of his friend McBey(qv). Although living most of the time and working in England, he retained strong links with Scotland and the Scottish tradition. A fine watercolourist, painting views in France and Italy and East Anglia, using a firm outline and a fluid technique. Wrote a number of books on the history of watercolours including the definitive *Water-colour Painting in Britain,* 1968. Elected ARE 1907, RE 1920, RI 1924, VPRI 1934, RSW 1934, CBE 1935. Exhibited RA(45), RSA(4), RSW(22), GI(9), L(52) & in many provincial galleries. Represented in Glasgow AG, Brodie Castle (NTS).
**Bibl:** Halsby 242.

**HARDING, James Duffield OWS** **1797-1863**
Born Deptford, England. Taught by his father, himself a pupil of Paul Sandby, and by Samuel Prout. Came to Edinburgh as a young man, apprenticed to a heraldic painter. Became friendly with David Roberts(qv) then working at the Theatre Royal. Twenty lithographs of quality are in Edinburgh PL. In 1854 he executed two lithographs after W L Leitch, 'Head of the West Bow' and 'St Bernard's Well'. Among his friends was George Cattermole(qv) whose sketches of Edinburgh scenes he engraved. The length of his stay in Scotland is not precisely known although since he was in Italy 1831 and 1834 he was probably only resident for a short time before returning again during the 1850s. Ruskin called him 'after Turner, unquestionably the greatest master of foliage in Europe'. Published a number of books on drawing the details of which appear in Roget. Represented in BM, V & A, Ashmolean, Cartwright Hall (Bradford), Fitzwilliam Museum, Glasgow AG, Leeds City AG, Manchester City AG, Laing AG (Newcastle), Newport AG, Portsmouth City Museum, Ulster Museum, City of Edinburgh collection (nine lithographs including an original of 'The Palace of Holyrood').
**Bibl:** AJ 1850, Sep 1856, Feb 1864; Butchart 58,59,70-1; Martin Hardie III 24-7; OWS Club XXXVIII, 1963; J L Roget, History of the old Water-Colour Society, 1891, II, 178-187.

**HARDING, Miss Monica** **fl 1974**
Glasgow embroiderer. Exhibited GI(1) from 35 Kingborough Gdns, London.

**HARDWICKE, Elizabeth Yorke, Countess of** **?-1858**
Died 26 May. Amateur artist and illustrator. Daughter of the 5th Earl of Balcarres; married Philip, 3rd Earl of Hardwicke 1782. Published and illustrated *The Court of Oberon or The Three Witches* (1831).

**HARDY, Miss Cecily A** **fl 1927**
Edinburgh artist. Exhibited a topographical Edinburgh landscape at the RSA from 18 Howard Place.

**HARDY, Henry** **1831-1908**
Edinburgh based architect and landscape painter in oil of architectural drawings and designs. Exhibited RSA(9).

**HARDY, John** **fl 1861**
Edinburgh painter in oil; exhibited 'A Sketch near Inverary - Argyllshire' at the RSA.

**HARGAN, Joseph R** **1952-**
Born Glasgow. Painter in oil, acrylic, gouache of landscapes, portraits figurative studies and minimal paintings; also teacher. Trained Glasgow School of Art. Member for many years of Glasgow Art Club and Council member, Paisley Art Institute since 1985; currently chairman/president. Founder member of Group '81 Artists. Awarded the painting prize, Glasgow AG 1972 and first prize, Stirling (Smith AG) 1978, Cargill Award GI 1982, Torrance Award GI 1984, Oppenheim Award RSA 1986. Exhibits RSA from 1984 & GI(38), from 40 Oakshaw St, Paisley. His wide ranging types of work are in several public collections including the BBC.

**HARGITT, Edward RI ROI** **1835-1895**
Born Edinburgh. Landscape, figurative and cattle painter in oil and watercolour. Also a renowned ornithologist. Pupil of Horatio MacCulloch(qv). Moved south as a young man and although most of his compositions were of Scotland and the Highlands, he is more akin to the English than the Scottish 'School'. His pre-Raphaelite concern with detail made him at his best an extremely competent landscape painter. Hardie thinks his 'Leixlip on the Liffey nr Dublin' (V&A) extremely good - like a Harpignies, it has breadth and subtle refinement in its low-toned scheme of gray and green'. Painted the Highlands, often below brooding skies, with distant Highland cattle adding to the atmosphere. Elected ARI 1865, RI 1867, ROI 1883. Exhibited RA(19) 1853-1881 but mainly RSA(84) 1851-1862, RI(68), ROI(22), L(6) & G(17). Represented in V & A, Glasgow AG, Manchester City AG, Paisley AG, Perth AG, Sydney AG.
**Bibl:** Binyon; Bryan; Cundall; Halsby 109,262; Hardie III, 163 (pl 190); Ottley; VAM.

**HARGITT, George F** **fl 1858-1871**
Landscape painter in oil and occasional watercolour. Brother of Edward H(qv). During early life lived in Liverpool and like his brother concentrated on Highland landscapes, moving to Scotland c1860 before settling back in Liverpool 1865. Exhibited RSA(50+) & GI(18), latterly from 18 Priory St, Liverpool.

**HARGREAVES, William J** **fl 1935**
Edinburgh painter; exhibited 'Cooling Stream' at the RSA from Foulis Crescent, Juniper Green, Edinburgh.

**HARGREAVES, William Y (or J?)** **fl 1895**
Exhibited 'Moorland' RSA from 24 Brougham Place, Edinburgh.

**HARKNESS, David** **fl 1886-1929**
Edinburgh painter in oil, also engraver; town views. Later moved to live in Clydebank 1928. Probably the David Harkness who exhibited a figurative painting at the RSA in 1929 from an address in Clydebank. Exhibited RSA(3) & GI(5), in 1951 from 50 Overtown Rd, Dalmuir, Dunbartonshire.

**HARKOM, A** **fl 1875**
Edinburgh oil painter of coastal scenes; exhibited RSA(1).

**HARLEY, A Ernest** **fl 1893-1928**
Edinburgh painter of still life, flowers and portrait studies; exhibited RSA(7), L(7), AAS(12) & GI(3), in 1921 from 27 Thistle Street.

**HARLEY, Miss Netty** **fl 1884-1905**
Landscape and flower painter. Exhibited GI(6) & L(1) from Coney Park, Uddingston, Lanarkshire, also at some time from Liverpool.

**HARLEY, Peter C** **fl 1880-1883**
Edinburgh landscape painter in oil; exhibited RSA(2) from 4 Richmond Lane.

**HARLEY, R** **fl 1830**
Dunfermline based painter; exhibited a study of Dunfermline Palace at the RSA in the above year.

**HARPER, Alexander (Alec)** **fl 1919**
Aberdeen flower painter; exhibited AAS(1) from 40 Woolmanhill.

**HARPER, Alison** **1964-**
Born Glasgow. Painter of semi-abstracts, often on a large scale (murals) in oil. Trained Glasgow School of Art, at the Oslo Academy of Fine Art 1985-86 and at the Univ of Baroda, India 1993-95. Awarded a scholarship by the Norwegian Government 1993. Part-time lecturer Glasgow School of Art 1986-93.
**Bibl:** Alexander Moffat, 'Angels wear Silver', Compass Gallery ex cat 1995.

**HARPER, John** **fl 1863-1868**
Edinburgh landscape painter in oil. Fond of sunset effects. Exhibited RSA(8).

**HARPER, Lillie J** **fl 1902**
Edinburgh painter; exhibited an interior and 2 townscapes at the AAS.

**HARPER, Lucy** **fl 1976**
Aberdeen painter. Exhibited a still-life at AAS from 46 Craigie Park.

**HARPER, Malcolm Maclachlan** **1839-1917**
Dumfries bank manager and amateur landscape painter in oil. Came from Castle Douglas. Friend of E A Hornel(qv) and W S McGeorge(qv). Author of *Rambles in Galloway* (1876). Exhibited local Kirkcudbrightshire scenes at the RSA(8) & GI(13), from Castle Douglas.

**HARPER, Robert** **fl 1971-1973**
Aberdeen painter. Exhibited AAS(4), latterly from 24 Balmoral Place.

**HARRIGAN, Claire RSW** **fl 1985-**
Watercolour painter of stylised, angular colourful garden scenes and landscape. Daughter of James H(qv) and Elspeth H(qv). Trained Glasgow School of Art 1981-86. Regular working expeditions to America, Europe, Asia, and the West Indies have influenced her flamboyant colourful style. Exhibits London, Hong Kong & Japan. Elected RSW 1992. Exhibits RSW & RGI.

**HARRIGAN, Elspeth** **1938-**
Born Kilmarnock. Botanical artist. Mother of Claire(qv), wife of James(qv). Trained Glasgow School of Art 1956-60. Works primarily as an illustrator, being noted for her accuracy and fine sense of colour and form. Commissioned to paint a page in the *Marie Curie Book of Hope*, displayed in the NLS. Solo exhibitions at Glasgow AG and elsewhere. Won Glasgow Lady Artists Trust award 1985, group award for watercolour (SSWA), the Lily McDougall prize (SSWA), RHS's bronze medal 1989, bronze medal at Glasgow Orchid Festival 1993 and the RHS's silver medal 1995 & 1996, David Cargill award (RGI) 1996 and Scottish Amicable award (Glasgow Soc. of Women Artists) 1996. Illustrated cover for *Guide to Crarae Garden* 1985 and Dr James Dickson's *Wild Plants of Glasgow* 1991.

**HARRIGAN, James** **fl 1960-**
Born Ayr. Painter of subject studies and landscape; teacher. Trained Glasgow School of Art where he met his wife Elspeth H(qv). Father of Claire(qv). Won Laing Prize. Has held many solo exhibitions based upon painting in France, Italy and Scotland. Exhibits RSA, RGI.

**HARRINGTON, Mrs Sybil** **fl 1961**
Glasgow flower painter in watercolour; exhibited GI(1), from 5 Great Western Terrace.

**HARRIS, -** **fl 1790-1810**
Scottish engraver who lived for much of his life at Kirkwoods, Stirling. Recorded as having engraved bookplates for James Elliot 1790, Capt Thomas Gilfillan 1800, and for Thomas Rhind 1810.
**Bibl:** Bushnell.

**HARRIS, Arthur** **fl 1891-1902**
Landscape and seascape painter based in Newport, Fife, executed mostly local scenes in oil and watercolour. Exhibited RSA(6), RSW(1), RA(1), GI(1) & AAS(2) from Elmbank House.

**HARRIS, Lawrie** **fl 1978**
Painter of semi-abstracts; exhibited RSA since 1978.

**HARRIS, Mary Packer** **1891-?**
Perthshire watercolour painter; exhibited RSW(1) 1919 from Ellangowan, Crieff.

**HARRIS, Miss Rachel** **fl 1988**
Glasgow sculptress. Exhibited two plaster figures of dogs at the GI, from 2/R, 54 Garnethill St.

**HARRISON, B** **fl 1831-1833**
Edinburgh landscape painter; exhibited RSA(3) including Crichton Castle (1833).

**HARRISON, Edward Stroud OBE** **1879-1979**
Born Edinburgh; died Elgin, 8 May. Painter in oil and watercolour, also engraver and photographer; landscapes and portraits. Painting was his principal hobby. Professionally a woollen manufacturer; Lord

Provost of Elgin 1942-1949. Awarded OBE 1963, subsequently granted the Freedom of Elgin. Founder and president of the Elgin Society; closely involved with both the Moray Music Festival and Elgin Museum. Founder-president of Elgin Rotary Club and a founder member of Elgin Golf Club. Frequent exhibitor at the Morayshire Arts and Crafts exhibitions winning 2nd prize for a portrait 1910. Most of his exhibited works were local scenes, and at the RSA they were mostly monotypes. Exhibited RSA(47), L(23) & GI(17), also in Paris, latterly from Newfield, Elgin.

**HARRISON, Miss Elizabeth W** **fl 1943**
Falkirk weaver. Exhibited two designs at the GI, from Camelon St.

**HARRISON, H P Cooper** **fl 1980**
Stirlingshire painter; exhibited a canal scene at the GI, from Corrieknowe, Blanefield, Stirling.

**HARRISON, H Scott** **fl 1929-1932**
Edinburgh painter. Exhibited a landscape and a colour linocut at the RSA during the above years from 87 Shandwick Place; also GI(2) & AAS(2).

**HARRISON, Mrs Helen G** **fl 1899-1902**
Edinburgh painter of landscape and still life; exhibited RSA(4) including two views of St Andrews, 'The Falls of Tummel', and 'Chrysanthemums' from 3 Napier Road.

**HARRISON, J** **fl 1861**
Glasgow watercolour painter of coastal scenery. Exhibited GI(2), from 71 St George's Rd.

**HARRISON, J E** **fl 1895-1907**
Glasgow landscape painter in oil and watercolour; exhibited GI(3), latterly from 32 Hamilton Park Terrace.

**HARRISON, Mary Kent (née May Marryat)** **1915-**
Studied Kingston School of Art 1933-5 and RA Schools 1937-8. Began exhibiting in 1940 when living in Aberdeen, then moved to Edinburgh until 1978 and thereafter south to 27 Meckleburgh Square, London. Sometimes signed her work 'Mary Kent'. Exhibited wild flowers and landscape RSA(9) & RA(1).

**HARRISON, Ronald** **fl 1937**
Glasgow artist; worked in monochrome, often in ink. Exhibited 'Autumn' at the RSA and 'The Market' at the GI from 26 Aytoun Rd.

**HARROWER, Jean H** **fl 1883-1886**
Painter. Of Scottish descent, lived at Wickham Hall, Gateshead. Painted domestic and rustic scenes in oil, exhibiting RSA(3).

**HART, Miss Anna** **fl 1953-1956**
Falkirk painter of flowers and still life; exhibited GI(2), from Kinneil House, Camelon.

**HART, Brian** **fl 1971-1981**
Trained Grays School of Art; exhibited AAS between above years.

**HART, E B** **fl 1898-1903**
Edinburgh based painter. Exhibited landscapes and portrait miniatures RSA(8) & RSW(2) from 10 Buckingham Terrace.

**HART, Elizabeth ASWA** **fl 1898-1921**
Landscape and portrait painter in oil and watercolour. Elected ASWA 1902. Exhibited RA(3), SWA(27), L(3) & GI(4) from Stirling and subsequently Bushey, Herts.

**HART, Margaret Ann** **fl 1982**
Amateur Aberdeen artist. Exhibited a Highland landscape at AAS from 7 Richmond Court

**HART, William Matthew** **1823-1894**
Born Paisley, 31 Mar. Painter in oil of landscape. Began working as a coach painter but soon emigrated to the United States where he began painting portraits, establishing a studio in New York 1853. Member of the National Academy in 1858 and later elected President, Brooklyn Academy of Design. He made a number of illustrations for the works of John Gould. A very important group of watercolours for Gould's *The Birds of Great Britain 1862-1873* were sold in 1994. Houfe gives his dates as 1830-1908. In 1851 he exhibited two landscapes at the RSA, 'A Scene in the Highlands near Killin', and 'Scene near Albany, New York State, US'.
**Bibl:** Houfe 169; *The Goodman Collection of Watercolours for John Gould's 'The Birds of Great Britain'*, Christie's cat., intro by Maureen Lambourne, 1994.

**HARTLEY, Albert A** **20th Cent**
Aberdeen painter. Exhibited AAS from Elm Place.

**HARTMANN, Sylvia von RSW** **1942-**
Born Hamburg, Germany, 8 Dec. Paints mainly in watercolour but also in gouache and wax pen. Educated at the Walddoerfer Schule, and at the Werkkunst Schule, Hamburg 1961-63. She studied at the Edinburgh College of Art 1963-5 gaining a highly commended diploma and doing further work at the Royal College of Art 1966 before completing her studies at Moray House, Edinburgh. Although critics suggest the influence of Chagall and Klee, she herself says that her work stems more from curiosity than from anything else. At the end of 1963 she came to Edinburgh and has remained there ever since. Received a number of prizes including the Anne Redpath Award 1980. Published *Living Light Books,* I, II and III. Lives at 35 Craiglockhart Grove, Edinburgh. Elected RSW 1983, also a member of SSA, SSWA. Exhibited RA, RSA, RSW & GI. Represented in SNGMA, City of Edinburgh collection.

**HARTRICK, Mrs A S** **[see BLATHERWICK, Miss Lily]**

**HARTRICK, Archibald Standish OBE RWS** **1864-1950**
Born Bangalore, Madras 7 Aug; died London 1 Feb. Painter and lithographer of figure subjects, urban scenes and landscapes; also illustrator. Son of an army captain. Educated Fettes College, Edinburgh and Edinburgh University. Studied Slade School 1884-5 under Legros and in Paris under Boulanger and Cormon 1886-7. Spent the summer of 1886 in Pont Aven, Brittany where he met Gauguin. After returning to Scotland he visited London joining the staff of the *Daily Graphic* 1890 and the *Pall Mall Magazine* 1893. Founder member and Vice-President of the Senefelder Club(qv). In 1896 he married his step-sister, the artist Lily Blatherwick(qv), moved to Gloucestershire, then to London where he taught at Camberwell School of Art and later at the Central School of Arts and Crafts. Although prolific, the quality of his work remained consistently high, especially his chalk drawings. Nevertheless, he did not consider himself primarily an illustrator, becoming an excellent watercolourist and significant lithographer. At his best depicting rural characters. A set of such drawings called Cotswold types was acquired by the BM. Author of *Lithography as a Fine Art* (1932) and *A Painter's Pilgrimage through 50 Years* (1939). Illustrated Kipling's *Soldiers Tales* (1896) and R L Stevenson's *The Body Snatcher.* Contributed to *The Graphic* (1889-95), *Daily Graphic* (1890), *The Pall Mall Budget* (1893), *Daily Chronicle, The Quiver, The New Budget* (1895), *Black and White* (1899-1900), *The Butterfly* (1899), *Castle's Family Magazine* (1899), *Fun* (1901), *The Yellow Book, The Ludgate Monthly, The Strand Magazine, Pearson's Magazine* and *The Pall Mall Magazine. The Penitents' Bench* (1904), was purchased by the Chantrey Bequest 1934. Elected NEAC 1893, IS 1906, ARWS 1910, RWS 1920. Exhibited RA(29), RSA(21), RWS(229), RHA(16), ROI(5), GI(100), AAS & L(33), after 1935 from 75 Clancarty Rd, London SW6. Represented in SNPG(2) including 'Self-portrait', BM, V & A, Aberdeen AG, Glasgow AG, Liverpool AG, Manchester AG, Melbourne AG, Sydney AG.
**Bibl:** Apollo, XXIV, 1936; Halsby 262; A S Hartrick, Painter's Pilgrimage through 50 Years; Houfe; Studio, Winter, 1900-01, 72, illus.

**HARVEY, Agnes Bankier** **1874-1947**
Painter, goldsmith and enameller; also teacher. Studied Glasgow School of Art 1894-1899 and London School of Silversmithing. From 1904-1908 taught silversmithing at Glasgow School of Art. Active member of the Glasgow Lady Artist's Club contributing regularly to their annual exhibition. Also studied the art of cloisonné in London under a Japanese master, after which time most of her work was done in the Japanese manner using wire outlining. 'In addition to fine enamel work, technically sound and constructionally solid, she

made objects in brass and beaten repousse and completed commissions for various badges as well as gun tompions for *HMS Ajax'* [Burkhauser]. Won a silver medal while still a student and again at the Women's Exhibition in London 1910. Exhibited internationally in Berlin, Budapest, Cork and Turin. In later life was a near neighbour of Jessie M King(qv) and E A Taylor(qv). Lived in Kirkcudbright and was a member of the 'Close coterie'. Possibly related to Marion Harvey(qv). Exhibited RSA(1) & GI(7), in 1916 from Braleckan, Gourock.
**Bibl:** Burkhauser 180.

**HARVEY, Douglas** **fl 1861-1876**
Portrait, landscape and subject painter in oil; exhibited RSA(14), including a portrait of 'William Bone' (1872).

**HARVEY, Ethel M** **fl 1961**
Aberdeen designer of gems and jewellery. Exhibited AAS(1) from 8 Hamilton Place.

**HARVEY, Miss Euphemia** **fl 1889-1894**
Stirling based artist, sister of Nellie(qv). Painted wild flowers; exhibited RSA(3), AAS(1) & GI(2) from Gowanbrae, Stirling.

**HARVEY, Miss Gail** **1954-**
Kilmacolm-based painter of domestic genre. Exhibited RSA(1) in 1990 & at the GI(4), latterly from Coubal, Dunrossness, Shetland.

**HARVEY, Sir George PRSA** **1806-1876**
Born St Ninians, nr Stirling, Feb; died Edinburgh 22 Jan. Painter of genre, historical scenes and landscape. Apprenticed to a bookseller in Stirling with whom he remained until 1824. Then went to Edinburgh and studied at the Trustees Academy under Sir William Allan(qv). Opinion is divided over his qualities but undoubtedly his work as a landscape and genre painter is rather different from his heavier religious subjects. He was much affected by Sir Walter Scott; although not a member of the national church he was a keen sympathiser with a reaction against the moderation of the 18th century to the more evangelical tenets of the preceding period. Illustrated Scottish life in a greater variety of its aspects than any other member of the School. The Covenanting and Disruption pictures appeared at intervals, beginning with 'The Preaching', 1829-30 to 'Sabbath in the Glen' about 30 years later. He had little training 'the ardour of a contemplative and imaginative spirit struggling with limited technical knowledge' [McKay]. By 1840 he found his métier. His famous 'Quitting the Manse', made popular by engravings, is now lost but 'Sabbath in the Glen' shows him at his best, especially in its unity of landscape and figures. 'The Curlers', long used by the Royal Caledonian Curling Club as its frontispiece, remains his best known work. As regards colour and handling Harvey was at his best during his middle period, in later work the fineness of surface was pushed to excess. He turned to landscapes when almost 60 and put much thought into their composition although it has been said that they lack a certain largeness which adds dignity. He was undoubtedly a master at portraying the 'pensive charm and pastoral melancholy of the Highland straths and the Lowland hills with insight and sympathy which make recollections of his landscapes a treasured possession'. From 1839-1849 he painted under severe disadvantage; he had been thrown from a gig on to his head causing depression, severe headache and failing eyesight. In 1848, after a holiday in Italy, he declared his work was done. Noel Paton(qv) persuaded him to seek medical advice and he was cured. From 1853 onward most of his work was landscape. In 1870 he wrote an interesting account of the early struggles of the RSA. 'As a draughtsman, Harvey's defects are a want of grace in his forms, and a distribution in his arabesques. His figures were squat, thick-set, and muffled in their clothes, while in too many cases they seemed crowded together like frightened sheep. As a colourist he is without one-ness. He has no idea of preserving the purity of a tint, and of keeping it in its place by consummate harmonisation. His colour, though often transparent, is monotonously low in tone. His defects are those which come in no slight degree from a narrow horizon in the absence of a great tradition' [Caw]. His place in Scottish art is as an important link in the tradition of genre painting between Wilkie's generation and exponents of more accurate pictorial representation of whom Thomas Faed(qv) was the major figure. His 'The Curlers' can be seen in the NGS. His last work was 'Muckrach Castle, Strathspey', (1875) then owned by Dick Peddie RSA. The castle has been restored and it would be interesting to know where the painting now resides. Elected ARSA at the unusually early age of 20 in 1826, RSA 1829. On the death of Sir John Watson Gordon(qv) he was elected PRSA 1867 and knighted the same year. Exhibited RSA(15) 1843-1873, RSA(125) 1826-1875, GI(8) & AAS posthumously in 1896. Represented in NGS(24), SNPG(5), Glasgow AG, City of Edinburgh collection, Sydney AG(Australia).
**Bibl:** AJ 1850, 341; 1858, 73-5 (obit) 1904; Armstrong 48-9; Brydall 410-414; Caw 112-114, 149-50 et passim; Halsby 85-6 et al; Hardie 44-47 et passim; Sir George Harvey, Note on the Early History of the Royal Scottish Academy, Edinburgh 1873; Irwin 299-300 et al; Macmillan [SA], 186,192,217,234-258; McKay 271-4; Portfolio, 1887, 152; A L Simpson, Harvey's Celebrated Paintings, 1870.

**HARVEY, Gordon L** **fl 1964-1983**
Inverness-based artist, probably teacher at the Inverness Royal Academy. Exhibited country views and northern landscapes at the AAS, latterly from 4 Aultnaskiach Ave.

**HARVEY, H E** **fl 1893**
Amateur painter; exhibited RSA(1) from 11 Howe Street, Edinburgh.

**HARVEY, J** **fl 1878**
Painter from Wardie, Edinburgh, exhibited 'Aberdeen harbour' at the RSA.

**HARVEY, Jake RSA** **1948-**
Born Kelso, 3 Jne. Sculptor. Studied at Edinburgh College of Art 1966-72 and having received an Andrew Grant Travelling Scholarship visited Greece. Received the RSA Latimer Award 1975 and the same year was elected a member of the SSA. In 1976 gained the Benno Schotz Award. Member Federation of Scottish Sculptors, erected a sculpture at Landmark 1983. Executed memorial sculpture to Hugh MacDiarmid 1985 and to Charles Rennie Mackintosh. Commissioned in 1988 to execute a symbol stone for the City of Glasgow. Elected ARSA 1977, RSA 1989. Regular exhibitor at RSA. Represented in Glasgow AG, Edinburgh City collection, SAC.

**HARVEY, James MacGregor** **fl 1950-1959**
Painter of still life and figurative subjects; exhibited RSA(4) from 28a Polwarth Terrace, Edinburgh. Represented in City of Edinburgh collection.

**HARVEY, Miss Marion Rodger Hamilton** **1886-1971**
Born Ayr. Animal painter, especially dogs, in oil, pastel, monochrome, but most often watercolour. Painted some very fine portraits showing excellent handling of paint and fine knowledge of breed conformation. Closely associated with her friends Jessie King(qv), E A Taylor(qv) and E A Hornel(qv) who together became known as the 'Close coterie'. Moved from Glasgow to Leadaig, Argyll 1959 and 1964 to 2 Branksome Park, Oban. Exhibited RSA(6), RSW(1), SWA(2), L(19), AAS(2) & GI(96). Represented in Glasgow AG.

**HARVEY, Nellie Ellen** **c1865-1949**
Stirling painter in watercolours, domestic interiors and bird painter. Sister of Euphemia(qv) and niece of Sir George H(qv). Studied under Denovan Adam(qv) at Craigmill and in Paris under Delacluse. Enjoyed particularly painting birds and domestic fowl. Exhibited RSA(18), RSW(5), SWA(3), RHA(3), AAS & GI(16), from Gowanbrae.
**Bibl:** Halsby 262.

**HARVEY, Miss R B** **fl 1883**
Edinburgh amateur painter; exhibited GI(1) from 32 George Square.

**HARVEY, R Jnr** **fl 1876**
Glasgow watercolourist. Exhibited a continental landscape at the GI, from Whithorn Villa.

**HARVEY, R L** **fl 1906-1907**
Glasgow amateur painter of flowers and landscape; exhibited GI(2) from Lyngarth, Bearsden.

**HARVEY, Winnie** **fl 1910-1913**
Edinburgh portrait painter and portrait miniaturist; exhibited RSA(4) from 31 Coniston Drive.

**HARVIE, J S** **fl 1804-1815**
Edinburgh miniaturist and portrait painter. Patronised by the nobility. Exhibited a portrait of the 'Earl of Buchan'(qv) at the RA in 1811. A miniature portrait of the 'first Marquis of Hastings', executed in 1804, is in the SNPG.
**Bibl:** Brydall 242-3; Long 193; Rose RA.

**HARVIE, James** **fl 1950**
Ayrshire painter; exhibited GI(1), from Speybank, 52 Dalry Rd, Kilwhinning.

**HARVIE, Rebecca B** **fl 1883**
Edinburgh flower painter. Exhibited GI(1), from 32 George Square.

**HARVIE, Robert** **fl 1761-d1781**
Portrait painter. In the mid-18th century he painted members of the Breadalbane family, and in 1759 the 'Hon George Baillie (Mellerstain)', also Sir Walter Scott's grandfather, 'Robert Scott of Sandyknowe' (1699-1775) and the novelist's father and his wife, 'Walter Scott' (1729-99) and 'Anne Rutherford', (1739-1819), still at Abbotsford. Represented in Glasgow AG.

**HARWOOD, Henry** **1803-1868**
Born in Ireland, reared in Dundee from an early age. Painter in oils of landscape, portraits, animals and genre. His sitters were all from Dundee including 'Major de Renzy, Barrackmaster' (1852), several Dundee Provosts and the well-known surgeon 'Matthew Nimmo' (1863). Not to be confused with the English artist Henry Harwood who was exhibiting 1892-1915. Exhibited RSA(19). Represented in Paisley AG.

**HASTIE, Grace H** **fl 1879-1889**
London-based flower painter, also pastoral subjects. Scottish descent. Exhibited GI(5), from 216 Camberwell Rd, London.

**HASTIE, Miss Margaret** **fl 1876-1889**
Renfrewshire watercolourist, mainly flowers. Exhibited GI(4), from Millhouse, Camphill, Paisley.

**HASTIE, William** **fl 1798**
Architect. Worked with Charles Cameron(qv) in Russia. His only documented work, according to Tait, is at the Palace of Bakhtchisari in the Crimea, of which drawings, dated 1798, were, or are, in the Marble Palace, Leningrad.
**Bibl:** Charles Cameron 1948; A Tait, British Architects in the service of Catherine II.

**HASTON, Elspeth (née McMurtrie)** **fl 1959-**
Aberdeen watercolour painter; daughter of Mary McMurtrie(qv). Specialises in country scenes in France and the north-east corner of Scotland in a broad, muted style with extensive washes. Exhibits AAS from Sunhoney, Milltimber.

**HASWELL, Miss Annie** **fl 1874**
Edinburgh oil painter; exhibited RSA(1).

**HASWELL, Miss Grace B** **fl 1915-1943**
Edinburgh painter in oil and watercolour of narrative pictures, landscape sketches and animals. Exhibited RSA(12), RSW(9) & GI(4) from 5 Midmar Gardens.

**HASWELL-SMITH, Hamish** **1928-**
Born Glasgow, Sept 20. Painter, principally in watercolour, and architect. Trained Edinburgh College of Art & Heriot Watt 1946-51. In 1955, after serving with the emergency forces in Kenya, he remained there, establishing his own architectural practice. Returned to Scotland 1960, again opening his own practice. Eventually retired from architecture to paint full time, holding his first solo exhibition in Edinburgh 1985. President of the Scottish Arts Club 1982-84; President of the Society of Architectural Artists 1987-94. Author & illustrator of *The Scottish Islands* 1996. Exhibits RSA, RSW.

**HATTON, Edward F** **fl 1861**
Edinburgh marine painter in oil, exhibited the 'Channel Fleet at Queensferry' at the RSA.

**HATWELL, Anthony** **1931-**
Sculptor and teacher. Studied at Bromley College of Art 1947-49, 1951-53, followed by a year at the Borough Polytechnic under David Bomberg. Then spent four years at the Slade School where he was awarded a Boyce Travelling scholarship 1956-58. After studying abroad he was appointed assistant to Henry Moore before being appointed to the part-time staff of the Bromley School of Art. Taught Chelsea School of Art 1960-63 and in 1969 was appointed head of the School of Sculpture at Edinburgh School of Art remaining there until his retirement 1990. Although occasionally executed some conventional portrait busts, usually female, his main work was 'constructivist'. Elected member of the London Group 1959, Vice-President 1961-1963. Exhibited RSA(3).

**HAUGH, W** **fl 1885**
Amateur artist, probably Scottish; exhibited RSA(2) from 22 Newman Street, Oxford Street, London.

**HAUGHTON, W T H** **fl 1926-1935**
Aberdeenshire portrait painter. Exhibited several works at AAS between the above years from Williamston, Insch.

**HAVERFIELD, John T** **fl 1869-1881**
Perthshire landscape painter in oil and watercolour. Exhibited 'A November Day in the Pass of Leany' at the RA 1871 from Flower Grove, Callender, and at the RSA the following year. Later RHA(3) & GI(13), after 1875 from Titley House, Titley, Herefordshire.

**HAWEIS, Stephen** **fl 1911-1914**
Landscape and figure painter. When in Edinburgh he lived at 26 South Castle Street. Exhibited RSA(2) & LS(6) but mainly at the Baillie Gallery, London (113).

**HAWKER, Yvonne** **1956-2001**
Born July 14; died July 28. Landscape painter in the modern idiom, often with a strong social element. Lived for many years in a stone shepherd's cottage behind Colmonell, Ayrshire. When Scottish Power planned a large electricity project involving 45 miles of pylons she ran the Stop the Overhead Powerlines campaign. During a public session she unveiled a painting of her threatened glen which she subsequently presented to Lord Mackay (senior counsel for Scottish Power) "to remind him forever of the valley his clients wished to desecrate". Invited by Chris Patten to visit Hong Kong as artist-in-residence 1994. There, her paintings became macabre and threatening with vibrant reds and blacks. On her return she settled in Stoer, north of Lochinver, where she transformed a remote cottage into an artist's retreat and solace.

**HAWKES, Mirabel Melville Gray (née Walker)** **1912-?**
Born Ceylon to a Fraserburgh family. Painter in oils, pastel and watercolour; also illustrator and author. Educated St Leonard's School, St Andrews where she received her only formal instruction in art. Examples of her work were exhibited in Holland while she was still at school. Published the first volume of her memoirs *Pearls, Palms and Riots* in 1986 which she also illustrated. Her first husband was killed in WW2 and in 1945 she married Tim Hawkes. Returned from Ceylon and settled in Buckie 1959. Severe arthritis restricted her work to pastel. Exhibited RA, Royal Institute London & in Ceylon. Her younger daughter **Mirabel SIMPSON** is also an artist, having been trained at Gray's School of Art, Aberdeen, and now lives in the Falklands where she teaches art.

**HAWKINS, James** **1954-**
English landscape painter in oils. Trained Wimbledon School of Art and Ruskin College. Settled in north-west Scotland 1978. Has an expansive colourful style with broad sweeps of colour.

**HAWORTH, Peter** **fl 1933**
Amateur watercolour painter, exhibited RSW(2).

**HAWORTH, Zenna** **fl 1933**
Amateur watercolour painter, possibly the wife of Peter H(qv); exhibited RSW(2).

**HAWTHORN, Charles G** **fl 1850**
Possibly a scene painter at the Theatre Royal, Edinburgh, he exhibited

2 architectural subjects at the RSA, 'The West Front of Sompting Church, near Worthing' and 'A Ruined Gothic Bridge'.

**HAXTON, William** **fl 1874-1881**
Painter of landscapes and buildings in oil and watercolour; exhibited RSA(2) & GI(1) first from Bowling and latterly from 31 Willowbank Crescent, Glasgow.

**HAY, A M** **fl 1884**
Edinburgh oil painter of portraits and landscape; exhibited RSA(2) from 37 Queensferry Street.

**HAY, Alec John** **1878-?**
Born Aberdeen, 5 May. Painter in oil and watercolour, stained glass window artist. Continental landscape and genre. Studied Edinburgh College of Art, obtaining a travelling scholarship. Became Supervisor of Art at Dunfermline elementary schools. Exhibited RSA(2), RSW(1) & GI(1) in 1932 from 24 John St, Dunfermline, also SSA & AAS 1923-31.

**HAY, Alexander** **fl 1855-1878**
Portrait and landscape painter. Lived in Edinburgh before moving c1878 to Birkenhead. His paintings were chiefly Edinburgh locations. Exhibited RSA 1855-1862, 1869, 1874 and 1878. Represented in City of Edinburgh collection.

**HAY, Alexander** **fl 1887**
Edinburgh painter. Exhibited two subject paintings at the RSA from 4 Charlotte Place.

**HAY, Andrew** **fl 1710-d1754**
Born Fife. Scottish portrait painter and dealer who in 1710 painted 'George Baillie of Jerviswood (1663-1738)' at Mellerstain. Baillie paid Hay for a number of portraits of himself intended for distribution among his friends. No other works by the artist, who worked in the manner of Medina(qv), are now known. By the 1720s he had abandoned painting in favour of dealing with the Italian market. Founder member of the Academy of St Luke(qv), made at least six visits to Italy, twice on foot, several times selling paintings he had collected. Instrumental in forming the collections of Sir Robert Walpole and the Duke of Devonshire.
**Bibl:** James Dennistoun, Memoirs of Sir Robert Strange and Andrew Lumsden, 2 vols, 1855; Basil Skinner, Scots in Italy, Edinburgh 1966, 30.

**HAY, Cecil George Jackson** **1899-?**
Born Sandgate, Kent. Painter in oil of portraits, still life, flowers and landscape, including French views. Fascinated by ceramics, especially oriental, which often appear in his compositions. Trained Glasgow School of Art and remained in Glasgow for several years after graduating. Returned to London c1922, finally settling in Canterbury, Kent 1960. Exhibited RA(12), RSA(9), GI(89).

**HAY, Constance Drummond** **c1862-fl c1899**
Amateur Perthshire watercolourist. Daughter of Captain Henry Maurice Drummond and Constance Hay of Seggieden, Perthshire. Over 100 of her drawings of flowers, fruit and fungi are in Perth AG.

**HAY, David** **fl 1868-1876**
Edinburgh oil painter of wildlife, fruit and landscape. Exhibited RSA(24).

**HAY, David** **1946-**
Exhibited a still life at the RSA in 1990 from Laret Cottage, Yetholm, Roxburghshire.

**HAY, David Ramsay** **1798-1866**
Born and died Edinburgh. Painter, house decorator and art collector. House painter protégé of Sir Walter Scott who advised him to turn to decorative painting. In 1822 he undertook the decoration of Abbotsford. Hay pioneered and popularised many new decorative painting techniques, the best known being his method of rendering 'imitation damask'. Noted for his theoretical writings on design and colour, including *The Laws of Harmonious Colouring* (1827). This was a creditable attempt to apply recent investigations in colour theory and perception to practical house decoration. Obtained a Scottish patent for his imitation damask. Tried to develop this invention in England through his agent David Roberts(qv) the artist, but the plan to sell the patent profitably went awry when Hay's angry partners presented Thomas Grace of Regent Street with written instruction for Hay's patent. According to the *Edinburgh Directory* 1840 he was Housepainter and Decorator to the Queen. Hay then set up business alone at 90 George Street, and remained the sole partner of D R Hay & Co, which continued until his death in 1866. He perfected the art of stippling. His patterns derived from an interest in mathematics and geometry. Fascinated with colour, it was this that made him reintroduce Adam's painted compartment ceilings. Rigorous scientific method governed his choice of juxtaposed colours. Exerted an influence throughout the UK. His decorative Watteauesuqe paintings in the dining room of 34, Gt King St were restored in 1956 while similar work in Lauriston Castle has been attributed. An accomplished painter, he exhibited a landscape at the RSA 1850.
**Bibl:** Bryan; Gifford 347,551; Ian Gow, 'The First Intellectual House Painter', Interiors, May 1984; Irwin 296,303,333,334.

**HAY, Miss Ella Edgar** **fl 1932**
Renfrewshire painter; exhibited a portrait at the GI, from 40 Oakshaw, Paisley.

**HAY, F R** **fl c1800-1820**
Edinburgh engraver. Pupil of Robert Scott(qv).
**Bibl:** J C Guy, The Book of the Old Edinburgh Club, vol 9, Edinburgh 1916.

**HAY, George RSA RSW** **1831-1912**
Born Leith Walk, Edinburgh, 21 Jne; died Edinburgh, 31 Aug. Painter in oil and watercolour of figure subjects, genre and historical works; also illustrator. After education at Edinburgh HS was apprenticed to Alexander Black, architect. Also studied modelling at the Watt School of Art under Gourlay Steell(qv). Subsequently enrolled at the Trustees Academy becoming a pupil of R S Lauder(qv). Painted mostly 18th century society, often taken from characters in the Waverley Novels. 'Never a sound draughtsman or a vigorous or expressive craftsman in paint, and seldom grasping the real significance of a situation, whether dramatic or humorous, the pictures and drawings of his best time seldom failed in delicacy of colour or in a certain touch of beauty...finding subjects chiefly in the past or in the Waverley Novels...he ensured picturesque costumes and setting for his incidents of gallantry, superstition, or adventure, and so added to their charm' [Caw]. Most of his life was spent living and working in Edinburgh. Illustrated *Pen and Pencil Pictures from the Poets* (1866); *Poems and Songs by Robert Burns* (1875) and Scott's *Redgauntlet* (1894). Elected RSA 1869, RSA 1876. Secretary RSA from 1881-1907. Honorary Academician 1910. Exhibited RSA (132), GI(15) & AAS 1885-1893, latterly from 7 Ravelston Terrace. Represented in Dundee AG, Glasgow AG, RSA Diploma Gallery.
**Bibl:** Caw 261; Halsby 262; Houfe; McKay 359.

**HAY, George Heron** **fl 1860-1871**
Edinburgh landscape painter in oil; exhibited RSA(8). Not to be confused with George Hay RSA.

**HAY, Miss Helen** **fl 1895-1953**
Flower painter in oil and watercolour, also charcoal. Associated with the Glasgow School. Contributed to *The Evergreen* 1895-1896. Exhibited RSA(3) & GI(7) from Paisley 1933, Eaglesham 1937 and after 1951 from Drumhead, Cardross, Dunbartonshire.

**HAY, J W** **fl 1859**
Edinburgh amateur portrait and genre painter; exhibited RSA(3) from 7 Richmond Place.

**HAY, James** **fl 1880-1914**
Minor Edinburgh painter of genre and figurative subjects in oil and watercolour, also landscapes and still life. Enjoyed introducing into his composition objects of applied art. Exhibited RA(2), RSA(12), RSW(1), RI(4), AAS(1), L(2) & GI(5), latterly from 57 Merchiston Crescent. Represented in City of Edinburgh collection.
**Bibl:** Halsby 262.

**HAY, John** **fl 1787**
Edinburgh engraver. The *Edinburgh Marriage Register* of 1751-

1800 records his marriage on 31 May 1787 to Margaret Scott in the High Kirk.

**HAY, John** **fl 1834**
Sculptor who exhibited a bust of the 'Rev Charles Fraser of St Peter's Chapel, Aberdeen' at the RSA.

**HAY, John** **fl 1889-1910**
Aberdeen amateur artist; exhibited RSA(2) moving to Edinburgh c1892. Also exhibited a local landscape at the AAS.

**HAY, John Arthur Machray RP** **1887-1960**
Born Aberdeen; died London, 24 Nov. Oil painter of portraits and genre. Studied Allan Fraser Art College. Concentrated mainly on members of the minor aristocracy. Elected RP 1929; member of the London Portrait Society. Exhibited RA(23) from 1919, GI(1) & L(5); also AAS 1906-1935, from 29 Salisbury Terrace, Aberdeen.

**HAY, John G** **fl 1873-1881**
Glasgow landscape painter in oil; exhibited RSA(4) & GI(10), latterly from Blantyre.

**HAY, Margaret D** **fl 1921**
Amateur Aberdeen landscape painter; exhibited once at the AAS from 61 Sunnyside Rd.

**HAY, Mrs Mary** **fl 1972-1975**
Brechin painter of continental market scenes; exhibited AAS(3), including 'Nigerian marketplace', from 15 Argyll St.

**HAY, Peter Alexander RI RSW** **1866-1952**
Born Edinburgh. Prolific painter in oil and watercolour, of portraits, landscape, still life and figure subjects. Studied RSA Schools, Academie Julian in Paris, and Antwerp. His landscapes were generally of Perthshire scenes although also painted in France in the early 1920s. His portraits show a fine touch of colour and a faithful depiction of the sitter. Elected RSW 1891, RI 1917. Exhibited RA(18) 1892-1904 using a London address from 1895 onwards, when the influence of Sargent on his work was most marked. The majority of his exhibits were at the RSW(136) & RI(126), but also RA(64), RSA(27), ROI(13), GI(33), RBA(10) & RHA(4).
**Bibl:** Caw 432; Halsby 262.

**HAY, R D** **fl 1850**
Edinburgh based oil painter. From 3 King's Place, Leith Walk, he exhibited 'Glen Finnan' at the RSA.

**HAY, R G B** **fl 1869-1870**
Edinburgh painter in oil and watercolour of landscapes and architectural sketches; exhibited RSA(2).

**HAY, Ralph William** **c1878-1943**
Edinburgh based painter in watercolour and teacher. Attended Gray's School of Art, Aberdeen in 1895 and the School of Design, Aberdeen 1895-1900 before continuing his studies at the London School of Arts and Crafts 1900-1902 and RSA Schools 1909-1913. In 1908 joined the staff of George Watson's Boys College, Edinburgh, becoming head of the art department. Painted mainly Lothian coastal scenes in a rather gloomy manner; also occasional flower pieces. Exhibited 'Anemones' at the RSA; also RSW(1) & AAS 1896-1919.

**HAY, Rhoda M M** **fl 1938**
Dundee-based painter; exhibited a still life at the RSA(1), from 3 Windsor Street.

**HAY, Robert HRSA** **1799-1863**
Architect, watercolourist and Egyptologist. He painted detailed watercolours of Egyptian scenes. Elected Honorary RSA 1841. Exhibited a design for a villa in 1852. In 1856 was living at Abbey Park Place, Dunfermline from where he exhibited a design for the north front of Fordell House, Fifeshire.
**Bibl:** Halsby 262.

**HAY, Thomas Marjoribanks RSW** **1862-1921**
Born and died Edinburgh. Almost exclusively a watercolourist, although in early career also designed stained glass windows. Travelled throughout Scotland painting mainly moorland and coastal scenery in finely delineated detail. Exhibited in Edinburgh and London. Hardie spoke of his 'feeling for atmospheric effect'. Used a wet style with a great deal of wash and as he developed so his style broadened. Close friend of James Douglas(qv). Exhibited RA(3) 1891-1893, all of them Highland scenes painted from 41 Charlotte Street, Edinburgh; also RSA(88), RSW(59), RI(12), RHA(3), L(6), GI(24) & AAS 1885-1919. Represented in NGS, Manchester AG.
**Bibl:** Caw 303; Halsby 168,262; Hardie.

**HAY, Thomas N** **fl 1949**
Ayrshire pastoral painter; exhibited GI(1), from 18 Morven Drive, Troon.

**HAY, William** **1811-1888**
Edinburgh architect and watercolour painter of local views and architectural designs, including interiors. In 1846 he worked for his father's partner John Henderson and subsequently as Clerk of Works for George Gilbert Scott at St. John's, Newfoundland. After practising in Chicago, Montreal and Toronto he returned to Edinburgh 1879, entering into partnership with George Henderson jnr. At one time he drew up plans for a side chapel at St. Giles', Edinburgh but these were superseded by Lorimer's design for what became the Thistle Chapel; however, the Moray Chapel (remodelled from a heating chamber by Burn), the arcade in the nave and the W doorway are by Hay (1884) as is a low vestry (1883), the organ chamber (1883), the Royal Pew (1885, later recast by Esmé Gordon), and a stone screen separating the church from the vestibule nr the North Transept (1891-3). Also in Edinburgh he was responsible, with George Henderson(qv), for the distinctive Old St Paul Church in Jeffrey St (1880-1905). Exhibited RSA(7) 1865-1874 including designs for the General Hospital, Toronto (1867), the interior of the High Church, Edinburgh (1871) and a residence at Abbotshill, Galashiels (1874).
**Bibl:** Gifford 106-8,111-4,116,166,654,657; Peter Savage, Lorimer and the Edinburgh Craft Designers, Edinburgh 1980, 84.

**HAY, William** **fl 1941**
Dundee artist; exhibited 'Willow Trees' at the RSA.

**HAY, William** **1859-1934**
Born Birkenhead. Nephew of William Hay (b 1811)(qv). Painter in oil and occasional watercolour; mostly landscape, generally in the Highlands, often west coast scenes. Studied Glasgow School of Art and in Paris, also worked in Belgium. Active member of Glasgow Art Club. Exhibited RSA(13) 1887-1933, also GI(97), RSW(5) & L(7).
**Bibl:** Halsby 262.

**HAY, William Hardie** **c1813-1900**
Liverpool architect. Son of **John HAY**(d 1861) and brother of **James Murdoch HAY** (c1823-1915). Undertook significant ecclesiastical work in Edinburgh. Together responsible for Augustine Bristo Congregational Church (1857-61) on George IV bridge in the 'best Liverpudlian free style, boldly mixing Romanesque, Renaissance and late Classical motifs' [Gifford]; also the old Free Church of Buccleuch and Greyfriars (1856-7). Exhibited RSA 1848-1864 including a design for Short's New Observatory on Calton Hill and for completing the National Monument on Calton Hill.
**Bibl:** Gifford 148,239,338,600.

**HAY, William Robert** **1886-?**
Born Glasgow 31 Oct. Painter, etcher and calligrapher. Studied at Westminster School of Art, where he was awarded the King's Prize for perspective, and at Chelsea. Exhibited 1911-1923 from London whence he had moved as a very young man. Exhibited RA(1), L(1) & 12 works at the London Salon.

**HAYCRAFT, Lillie Stacpoole (Mrs John Berny)** **fl 1888-1900**
Figure and landscape painter. Lived in Edinburgh in the late 1880s and in Cardiff from c1895. Exhibited RSA(5), RA(1) & L(1).

**HAYES, Charles** **fl 1862-1872**
Paisley oil painter of fruit and still life. Taught at Paisley School of Art in 1860s and early 1870s. Exhibited RSA(4) & GI(4).

**HAYES, James** **fl 1898**
Amateur Edinburgh watercolourist; exhibited RSW(2) from 41 Charlotte Square.

**HAYES, Joseph** **fl c1900-1920**
Sculptor, mainly in stone as architectural ornament. Responsible for some good church carvings in Edinburgh including examples in the Thistle Chapel, St Giles, Mercury and the figures of 'Night and Day' on the *Scotsman* buildings, detail on the Department of Employment, Lauriston Pl and 'intricate Byzantine carving' at Boroughmuir School and on the pedimented ends of the Public Library, Morningside Rd.
**Bibl:** Gifford 108,117,232,258,495,619-20.

**HAYES, Winifred (née Yule)** **fl 1913-1938**
Born London. Sculptress. Studied at Aberdeen School of Art and Edinburgh College of Art. Remained in Scotland for many years before returning to London c1927. Exhibited RSA(1), RA(14), GI(2) & SWA(2).

**HAYWARD, Alfred** **fl 1870**
Glasgow painter of local; landscape; exhibited GI(1), from Struin Terrace, Crosshill.

**HAZEL, John T** **fl 1937**
Edinburgh amateur watercolour painter; exhibited RSW(1) from 10 Forth Street.

**HEALY, Denis** **fl 1984**
Argyll painter; exhibited 'Parisian townscape' at the GI from Toberdhu, Tighnabruaich.

**HEARDEN, Mrs S A** **fl 1881-1884**
Broughty Ferry oil painter of landscapes; exhibited a view on the Tay at the RSA & SWA(1) from Douglas Terrace.

**HEATHERILL, Jessie** **fl 1887**
Glasgow painter; exhibited two landscapes at the GI, one Hebridean, one Swiss, from Marylea, Bearsden.

**HEATLEY, Tom** **fl 1969-1970**
Aberdeen ceramic designer. Exhibited AAS(2) from 77 Leadside Rd.

**HEATLIE, L C** **fl 1849-1851**
Leith landscape painter in oil, mostly coastal scenes, exhibited RSA(7) including the impressive 'Admiral Duncan's Victory over the Dutch Fleet in the North Sea, Oct 11, 1797' (1851).

**HEATLIE, William Jnr** **fl 1875-d1910**
Born Ettrick Brigend, nr Selkirk; died Newstead, Northumberland. Watercolour painter; still life, landscape and ecclesiastical subjects. At an early age he moved to Eildon Hall, Melrose where his father was gardener. After his father's death he moved with his mother and sister to The Cloisters, Melrose. Friend of Tom Scott(qv) with whom he enjoyed many sketching excursions around the Borders. Exhibited RSA(18) & AAS(2).

**HEBELER, Miss Phyllis M** **fl 1928-1929**
Portrait painter. Exhibited RSA(3) from 60 Castle Street, Edinburgh.

**HECTOR, Miss Gertrude Mary** **1888-**
Born Calcutta, India. Designer and craft worker. Studied Gray's School of Art, Aberdeen and Battersea Art School. Lived in Aberdeen 1916-1922. Daughter of the artists Maggie & James H(qv). Exhibited cloisonné enamels RSA(2), AAS & L(2).

**HECTOR, James A H** **1868-1940**
Aberdeen painter in oil & watercolour, also stained glass designer. Landscape, portraits and subject paintings. Trained Gray's School of Art, became an art teacher but in the mid-1890s went to study at the Atelier Julian in Paris and in Brittany. The experience left an indelible impression and he retained an affection for France for the best of his life. Opened a teaching studio in Union Row in collaboration with Rudolfe Christen(qv). Appointed principal lecturer in art, Aberdeen Training College 1904, a post he held for 30 years. Among his students was George Melvin Rennie(qv). Exhibited 'Hazy Morning, St Monans, Fife', at the RA 1916 and 'The Banners of Autumn' (1935). His stained glass window designs may be seen in Nigg Parish Church, St Ninian's Church, Aberdeen and Gordon Schools, Huntly. Married Maggie J S H(qv) but the marriage broke down in 1932. His daughter Gertrude(qv) was a jewellery designer. Exhibited RSA(24), RA(2), GI(9) & L(8) and AAS(17) of which he was elected a member 1908. Lived latterly at 44 Marischal St, Aberdeen.

**HECTOR, Mrs Maggie J S** **fl 1910-1937**
Aberdeen painter of coastal scenes, landscape & flowers. Wife of James H(qv) until their marriage ended in 1932; mother of Gertrude(qv). Exhibited quite often AAS from 41 Salisbury Terrace.

**HECTOR, W Cunningham** **fl 1900-1915**
Glasgow painter in oil and occasional watercolour; landscape, cathedrals, genre and an occasional portrait. Visited Katwijk 1905. Exhibited RSA(1), L(2), GI(11) including several Dutch scenes, Glasgow Society of Artists & 'Dutch canal scene' AAS 1910.

**HEDDERWICK, Mairi** **1939-**
Born Renfrewshire May 2. Author, draughtswoman and illustrator. Trained Edinburgh College of Art. After an early marriage settled on an Hebridean island with her husband but returned to the mainland nine years later to run her own art printing gallery. Authorship and book illustration gradually took over and her work is evocative and popular. She provided the illustrations for Godden: *The Old Woman Who Lived in a Vinegar Bottle* (1972), Duncan: *Brave Janet Reachfar* (1975), *Herself and Janet Reachfar* (1975), *Janet Reachfar and the Kelpie* (1976), *Janet Reachfar and the Chickabird* (1978), Body: *A Cat Called Rover; a Dog Called Smith* (1981), Miller: *Hamish and the Wee Witch* (1986), Wood & Pilling: *Our Best Stories* (1986). Her own illustrated books include *Mairi Hedderwick's Views of Scotland* (1981), *Katie Morag Delivers the Mail* (1984) and *Katie Morag and Big Boy* (1987).
**Bibl:** Horne 242; Mahoney.

**HEDDERWICK, Percy D** **fl 1878-1880**
Glasgow painter. Exhibited farming and pastoral scenes RSA(1) & GI(5) from 26 Newton Place.

**HEGGIE, Malcolm** **fl 1958**
Glasgow watercolour artist. Exhibited a landscape of Iona at the GI, from 104 Turret Rd.

**HEITON, Andrew G** **1823-1894**
Perth architect. Father of **Andrew HEITON** who designed the stations on the Perth-Coupar Angus line, the Station Master's house, Cargill, Perthshire (1849-50) and Birnam station, Dunkeld (1856). Probably related to John Heiton the builder responsible for nos. 1-10 Circus Place, Edinburgh. Trained in the office of David Bryce(qv). Entered partnership with his father **Andrew HEITON snr**(?-1858) who had designed Garth House, Perthshire (c1838), extensively restored by his son 1890. An enthusiasm for Early French gothic had been imparted by an erstwhile assistant William Leiper(qv). Responsible for designing the banqueting hall of Halliburton House, the tower of Lethendy, a design for a new Perth Public Library, the memorial library at Glenalmond School and for what Dunbar called the 'vast and showy' Castleroy (1867, now demolished), the largest of the 'Jute palaces', which 'set the tone' for Broughty Ferry, and for what is now the Atholl Palace Hotel, Pitlochry, Perthshire (1875); also Victoria Buildings (36-44 Tay St, Dundee)(1872) and the Savings Bank (26 Tay St)(c1873). His best known and most talented assistant was John Murray Robertson(qv). Exhibited RA 1895, RSA 1884, 1886, 1905, 1909 & GI(4).
**Bibl:** Dunbar 151,158; A Gomme & D Walker, Architecture of Glasgow, London 1987(rev), 294; B Walker & W Sinclair Gauldie, Architects and Architecture on Tayside, Dundee 1984, 136,149.

**HELLER, Caroline Frances** **fl 1982**
Aberdeenshire artist; exhibited AAS from a Maryculter address.

**HELLEWELL, Claire** **fl 1986-**
Edinburgh engraver. Exhibits RSA since 1986 from 50 Silverknowes Drive.

**HEM(M)INGWAY, Charles W** **fl 1929-1952**
Aberdeen painter of portraits, landscape and subject studies in oil, exhibited RSA(6), RA(2) & GI(3), latterly from 3 Strawberry Bank; also at the AAS 1929-37 from 24 Esslemont Ave.

**HEMMING, Edith** **fl 1904-1911**
Miniature portrait painter. Lived in London before moving in c1907

to Burmah Cottage, Dollar, Clackmannanshire. Exhibited RA(3), RSA(4), L(6) & GI(7).

**HENDERSON, Mrs A C** **fl 1888-1889**
Dunbartonshire painter of landscape and seascape in watercolour. Exhibited GI(2), latterly from Shandon.

**HENDERSON, A R** **fl 1879-1895**
Glasgow landscape painter in oil and watercolour, mostly the latter; worked in Paris 1879, Brazil 1889, Italy and Switzerland 1890/1, and South Africa 1895. Exhibited RSA(6) & GI(16), latterly from 60 North St.

**HENDERSON, Adam** **fl 1878**
Edinburgh landscape painter in oil; exhibited 'Gogar burn' 1878.

**HENDERSON, Alexander** **fl 1921**
Aberdeen artist. Exhibited 'Cattle grazing' at AAS from 22 College Bounds.

**HENDERSON, Alexander John** **fl 1889**
Edinburgh painter in oil of landscape; exhibited a sketch near Banff at the RSA from 20 Haddington Place.

**HENDERSON, Andrew** **1783-1835**
Born Blair Adam. Portrait painter. In 1796 he was an apprentice gardener and later employed by Lord Kinnoul at Dupplin in Hopetoun. Abandoned this craft for reasons of health and became a clothier but in 1789 went to London to study at the RA Schools. Returned to Scotland 1813, setting up a studio in Glasgow, mainly painting portraits for which he earned a local reputation. In 1832 published an excellent collection of Scottish periodicals. Co-author of the *Laird of Logan*. Inaugural president, Glasgow Dilettante Society(qv). Among his portraits was a 'Self-portrait', now in Glasgow Technical College. Exhibited RSA 1828-1830. A portrait of the poet 'William Motherwell (1797-1835)' is in SNPG.

**HENDERSON, Andrew Graham RSA** **1882-1963**
Born Auckland, NZ; died Pollockshields, Glasgow, 21 Nov. Architect. Came to Scotland at a very early age remaining for the rest of his life. Educated Irvine Royal Academy and Allan Glen's School, Glasgow, then studied at Glasgow School of Art with MacWhannell and Rogerson. In 1911 awarded the Arthur Coates prize. Worked as assistant with Charles Rennie Mackintosh(qv) in John Keppie's office. 'His many well-proportioned, cleverly planned buildings, show evidence of his inventive skill and versatility, and his building for the Bank of Scotland in Sauchiehall Street, Glasgow, is generally considered the best example of its kind in the country'. Elected PRIBA 1950; toured Canada and the USA. In WW1 he lost the use of his right arm and hand. Elected ARSA 1943, RSA 1953. Regular exhibitor RSA.

**HENDERSON, Ann RSA** **1921-1976**
Born Thurso, 11 Oct; died 13 Mar. Sculptress. Educated Miller Academy, Thurso and Edinburgh College of Art 1940-45. Proceeded to postgraduate study under Eric Schilsky(qv), a travelling scholarship enabled her to study in Paris 1947-48 at the Ecole des Beaux Arts under Gimond. In 1948 returned to Edinburgh College of Art to teach. An inspirational instructor, responsible for introducing courses which were at the time experimental. Had an abiding love for Caithness, especially the landscape in which rock and stone were so everywhere apparent and which provided the basic inspiration for her sculpture. In 1954 received Guthrie Award RSA for Composition (two figures looking at a cow). Her realism gave way to expressionism in cubist terms, using still figures and animals, eg 'Hen Woman' - simple elements alone in nature became apparent in her later work eg bird flight, plant growth or sea forms. Her abstract works, some in stone, were executed at the same period as works of a free kind cast in polyester resins and fibreglass. Shared several exhibitions with Henderson Blyth(qv), David Donaldson(qv) and Alberto Morrocco(qv). Involved in organising international open air exhibition of sculpture in Dunfermline and in 1972 organised 'Eight Edinburgh Sculptures'. Member, SAC panel. Among her publically visible works are the relief representing 'Agriculture' at the Department of Agriculture, University of Edinburgh, a fibreglass relief for the music pavilion at George Watson's College and a figurative group with Christ 'They knew him in the breaking of bread' (1969) for Nunraw monastery refectory. Elected ARSA 1968, RSA 1973. Exhibited RSA(68) 1947-1977 & GI(5 bronzes) from 5 Learmonth Gardens Mews, Edinburgh. Represented City of Edinburgh collection (bronze).
**Bibl:** RSA, Obituary, March 1976.

**HENDERSON, Mrs Ann H** **fl 1941**
Ayrshire watercolourist; flower studies. Exhibited GI(2), from Heywood Hotel, Skelmorlie.

**HENDERSON, Annie** **fl 1887**
Edinburgh watercolour painter of flowers; exhibited RSA(2) & AAS(1) from 4 Chalmers St.

**HENDERSON, Archibald** **fl 1926**
Aberdeenshire painter who exhibited 'Canal barges, Ceylon' at the AAS from 'Sirhowy', Cults.

**HENDERSON, Arthur Edward RBA FRIBA** **1870-1956**
Born Aberdeen 18 Apr; died Crawley Down, 8 Nov. Architect and painter of architectural subjects in oil and watercolour. Studied at the Architectural Association, also at the City and Guilds School. Won an Owen Jones travelling scholarship 1896 and settled for a time in Instanbul, working on the British excavations at the Temple of Diana of Ephesus, before returning to London 1896. Although born in Scotland spent all his student and working life in England and Turkey. Retired to Crawley Down, Sussex. Elected RBA 1901, FRIBA 1912. Exhibited regularly RA, RBA & United Artists.

**HENDERSON, Brian** **fl 1980-1981**
Painter from Lerwick, Shetland. Exhibited figurative works RSA(2).

**HENDERSON, Catherine** **fl 1881-1889**
Glasgow painter in oil and watercolour, mainly the latter; landscape, figurative compositions and flowers. Exhibited GI(7) from 17 Belhaven Terrace.

**HENDERSON, Miss D Y** **fl 1963**
Ayrshire painter; exhibited 'The green pool' at the GI, from Savoy House, Ayr.

**HENDERSON, David** **?-c1787**
Edinburgh mason. Father of John H(qv). Designed Inverleith House (1774).
**Bibl:** Gifford 56,282,286,575,610.

**HENDERSON, David RSW** **fl 1977-**
Aberdeen painter of landscape and conversation pieces; also etcher. Trained Gray's School of Art, Aberdeen. Exhibited RSA(3) & AAS since 1977, latterly from 13 Norfolk Rd.

**HENDERSON, Elizabeth ('Lizzie')** **fl 1896-1898**
Aberdeen painter of flowers and church interiors. Exhibited AAS(3) from 422 King St.

**HENDERSON, Miss Ella** **fl 1882**
Larbert painter in oil, continental landscapes; exhibited RSA(2).

**HENDERSON, George** **1846-1905**
Architect. Associated with William Hay(qv) of Edinburgh and the rediscovery of Scots Late Gothic exemplified by Craiglockhart Parish Church (1899); also designed the Masonic Hall, Queen's St (1894), the Lady Chapel in St Mary's Cathedral (1897-8), Duart Lodge (73, Colinton Rd) and the interior of the nave and most of the N aisle in Old Parish Church, Kirk Loan.
**Bibl:** Gifford 43,166-7,321,365-6,501,523-4,534-5,552.

**HENDERSON, Gordon** **fl 1977-**
Glasgow painter of flowers and still life. Exhibits GI(29), since 1988 from 42 Crosbie St.

**HENDERSON, Hamish** **fl 1961**
Aberdeen painter; exhibited at AAS(2) from Newton Rd, Newtonhill.

**HENDERSON, Irene** **fl 1910-1912**
Exhibited at the Walker Gallery, Liverpool(4) from Chisholme, Hawick, Roxburghshire.

**HENDERSON, Miss Ivy Craik** **fl 1951-1952**
Glasgow painter; exhibited 2 figurative subjects at the RSA.

**HENDERSON, J D** **fl 1964-**
Glasgow painter of landscape, portraits and flower studies in oil. Trained Sir John Cass School of Art in London and Glasgow School of Art. Has held many solo exhibitions in England & Scotland. Regular exhibitor at RSA, RGI and Paisley Institute. Exhibited GI(32), since 1979 from 8 Southern Ave, Rutherglen.

**HENDERSON, James** **1809-1896**
Born Aberdeen; died Aberdeen. Architect and builder. Attended the Mechanics' Institute. After the splitting of the Church of Scotland 1843, he worked unpaid for the Free Church, designing churches, manses and schools. Qualified as an architect 1850. Laid out Westfield Terrace, Aberdeen, designed alterations at Birkhall, Abergeldie Castle and Invercauld.
**Bibl:** Alison McCall, 'Railway station that might have been', Leopard, April 2003, 35-6.

**HENDERSON, James** **fl 1875-1889**
Edinburgh artist and designer. Painted mainly landscapes especially of the west coast and Iona. Exhibited RSA(8) 1875-1889 from 8 Graham Street and latterly 47 Great King Street.

**HENDERSON, James** **1908-?**
Born North Berwick, 4 Jan. Painter of landscape and portraits, mostly schoolgirls. Educated North Berwick High School and Edinburgh College of Art, obtained a travelling scholarship enabling him to visit France and Italy 1936. Head of the art department at Galashiels Academy 1948-49 moving to take up a similar position in George Watson's Ladies College, Edinburgh, remaining there until 1967. For the next 14 years was travelling lecturer with the SAC during which time he and his wife helped to found the Galashiels Art Club. Signed his work 'James Henderson'. Exhibited with his future wife Nan Fergusson(qv) RSA(6) 1934-1951, mostly portraits of girls at Galashiels Academy, also RGI from 1935 and at the SSA. [From notes by W James C Henderson]

**HENDERSON, James A** **1871-1951**
Born Glasgow; died Regina, Canada. Painter in oil, portraits and landscapes also lithographer. Studied Glasgow School of Art. Visited the Canadian Prairies 1910 and after a spell in Montreal settled in Saskatchewan 1916. Exhibited AAS(2) 1908-1910.

**HENDERSON, James C** **1858-1881**
Edinburgh painter of rustic scenes and figures in oil. Eldest son of Joseph H(qv). Studied Haldane Academy, Glasgow, and RSA Schools. Was about to travel to Paris to pursue further studies when he died. Exhibited 'The Village Well' at the RSA in 1881 & GI(2) from 21 St Andrew's Square.

**HENDERSON, James Lawrie** **fl 1878-1890**
Edinburgh landscape painter in oil and watercolour. Exhibited RSA(1) & L(1).

**HENDERSON, Jemima A** **fl 1902**
Aberdeen landscape painter in watercolour; exhibited AAS(1) from 15 Craigie St.

**HENDERSON, John** **?-1786**
Architect. Son of David H(qv). Spent some time in Rome. Designed the Assembly Rooms, one of the first 18th century public buildings in the New Town.
**Bibl:** Gifford 67,281-2,575,pl.81.

**HENDERSON, John** **1804-1862**
Edinburgh architect and designer. One of Scotland's foremost church architects, responsible for Trinity College, Glenalmond (1841-51), St. Mary's, Arbroath (1854), Montrose museum (1837), the large classical memorial column called the Panmure Testimonial, Monikie, Angus(1839), the Tudor Gothic Mechanics Institute, Brechin (1838-9) and many Episcopalian edifices. Exhibited RSA 1834-62 including a design for the Scott Monument (1837) and designs for the Chapel at Trinity College, Perthshire (1849). In Edinburgh he was responsible for a number of late Gothic churches including Newhaven (1836), Morningside (1838), Holyrood Free Church on Horse Wynd (1850), St Columba by the Castle (1846-7) and Holy Trinity (1837).
**Bibl:** Dunbar 149; Gifford 39,163,168,226,320,387,435,453,456, 601,615,617, 621-2,pl.34; Bruce Walker & W S Gauldie, Architects and Architecture on Tayside, Dundee 1984, 75,131.

**HENDERSON, John** **1860-1924**
Born Glasgow; died Busby, nr Glasgow. Painter in oil and watercolour of landscape, figure subjects and animals. Son of Joseph H(qv), brother of Joseph Morris(qv) and uncle of Betty McTaggart(qv). Studied at GSA under Robert Greenlees(qv). Director of Glasgow School of Art. Caw described his work as having 'a refined feeling for woodland and burnside landscape and a cultural ideal of design, in which balance of mass and rhythm of line are combined with respect for those tender and characteristic beauties of natural form and growth which charm one so in Nature'. Exhibited RSA(47), RSW(3), GI(102), AAS (1893-1912) & L(5), from 1903 at 207 W. Campbell St. Represented in Glasgow AG, Greenock AG.
**Bibl:** Caw 391; Halsby 263.

**HENDERSON, Joseph RSW** **1832-1908**
Born Stanley, Perthshire; died Ballintrae, Ayrshire 17 Jly. Painter in oil and watercolour of landscapes, genre, portraits and seascapes. Father of John(qv) and Joseph Morris(qv). Studied at Trustees Academy 1849-52, settling immediately thereafter in Glasgow, becoming a well-known and much loved figure in the artistic life of the city and an active member of the Glasgow Art Club. His early work was mostly in oils and in 1852 he exhibited 'Self-portrait' at the RSA. A private commission for a portrait launched his career as a professional painter. Portrait and genre were his early particular interests. But in 1870, while on holiday at Saltcoats, he met William McTaggart(qv) who encouraged him to turn his attention to seascapes. Diminishing the significance of his figures, his pictures gained freshness of colour and delicacy. His work is characterised by cool, silvery colour and by careful technique. Pinnington wrote 'he paints the sea of Scottish bays and firths, a living, jubilant, musical sea, which flings a veil of foam over jutting rocks, and throws itself in playful ripples on the sandy, pebbly shore...there is a beauty few painters catch in its changing hues of blue and gray-green within the bay and in the warmer tints borrowed from seaweed in the shallows, and from the grays and umbers of the beach'. In his watercolours he often allowed the white paper to come through, creating luminous effect. He remains one of Scotland's half-forgotton painters who deserves greater recognition than he has hitherto received. His daughter was William McTaggart's second wife. Founder member, RSW 1878. Exhibited RA(20) 1871-1886, mostly seascapes on the south western shores of Scotland, also RSW(47), RSA(25), GI(147), AAS 1900-1906, RBA(4) & L(3). Represented in Glasgow AG, Greenock AG, Kirkcaldy AG, Edinburgh City collection.
**Bibl:** AJ 1898, 371; Armstrong 78; Bate, The Art of Joseph Henderson, Glasgow, 1908; Caw 328-9; Halsby 123-4,131,263; Macmillan [SA], 253.

**HENDERSON, Joseph Morris RSA** **1864-1936**
Born and died Glasgow. Painter in oil and watercolour, mostly seascapes and coastal scenes. Son of Joseph(qv) and brother of John(qv). Educated Glasgow University and Glasgow School of Art, also learning much from his father. Influenced by his father's later style and favourite compositions. 'Summer Clouds' was his diploma work 1935. His chief pleasure was in flowery foregrounds 'and weeded watersides, pale blue streams rippling over white pebbles, and distances of hay fields or softly swelling country under bright skies' [Caw]. Closely associated with the Glasgow Art Club and a member of Committee of Management, Paisley Art Institute. Elected ARSA 1928, RSA 1935. President, Scottish Artists Benevolent Association. Exhibited RA(5), (erroneously listed as John Morris Henderson), RSA(80), RSW(3), AAS 1900-1912 & GI(129). Represented in Glasgow AG.
**Bibl:** Caw 391; Halsby 213.

**HENDERSON, Miss Katharine G** **fl 1943-1945**
Aberdeen landscape miniaturist; exhibited GI(4) including three

miniatures of scenes on Iona and one of Loch Katrine, from 29 Carlton Place.

**HENDERSON, Keith OBE RSW RWS ROI** **1883-1982**
Born Scotland, 17 Apr; died South Africa, Feb 24. Painter in oil but mostly watercolour; landscapes, figurative subjects, birds and other animals; flowers; also illustrator. After early days in Aberdeenshire, educated at Orme Square School, London, and Malborough College, Slade School and 1904 in Paris at L'Academie de la Grande Chaumiere. While there he shared accommodation with Norman Wilkinson and met Edmund Dulac. Associated with the Scottish school mainly through his later work, painted and exhibited in Scotland. Served with the forces in WW1, in WW2 was a war artist with the RAF. Lived for many years at Achneabhach, Glen Nevis, nr Fort William, and from 1942 in nearby Spean Bridge where he painted powerful, uncomplicated watercolours. First commissioned works were portraits, but also painted landscapes and murals in a variety of media. London Transport and the Empire Marketing Board commissioned posters, the latter sending him to Cyprus for a year. A lovely gentleman, full of charm and wit, a fine artist "perhaps the last of the great Victorian painters of his generation" (Times obituary). Illustrated and wrote *A Book of Whimsies* (with Whitworth, 1909), *Letters to Helen* (1917), *Palmgroves and Humming Birds* (1924), *Prehistoric Man* (1927), *Pastels* (1952), *Till 21* (1970). A book of Eastern European mythology *Creatures and Personages* occupied him for twenty years but remained unpublished. He illustrated Chaucer: *The Romaunt of the Rose* (with Norman Wilkinson, 1908), Hardy: *Under the Greenwood Tree* (1913), Eddison: *The Worm Ouroboros* (1922), Prescott: *The Conquest of Mexico* (2 vols, 1922), Eddison: *Styrbiorn the Strong* (1926), Hudson: *Green Mansions* (1926), *The Purple Land* (1929), Beith: *No Second Spring* (1936), Cunningham: *Buckaroo* (1936), Eddison: *Mistress of Mistresses* (1935), Beith: *Sand Castle* (1936), Fleming: *Christina Strang* (1936), Burns: *Burns - By Himself* [the author's favourite](1938), Gunn: *Highland Pack* (1949), *Recording Scotland* (with others, 1952), Eddison: *The Mezentian Gate* (1958), Piggott: *Scotland Before History* (1958). Received many honours, including RP 1912, ARSW 1930, ARWS 1930, ROI 1934, RSW 1936, RWS 1937, OBE. Exhibited RSA(35), RSW(18), RWS(83), ROI(20), RA(27), GI(25), AAS(2) & L(13). Represented in V & A, Kirkcaldy AG, Glasgow AG, Manchester AG(17), Preston AG, Birmingham AG, Worthing AG, Newport AG, Leamington AG, Dublin AG, City of Edinburgh collection.
**Bibl:** Halsby 263; Macmillan [SA] 332; Bertha E Mahony, Illustrators of Children's Books, 1744-1945, Boston (USA), 1947, 317; Geoffrey Whitworth 'Keith Henderson' Studio, 90, 1925; Who's Who; Stephen Constantine: *Buy and Build: The Advertising Posters of the Empire Marketing Board,* HMSO 1986; Harries; K Henderson: *Till 21*, Regency Press 1970; Horne 242-3; Keith Nicholson: "Conversations with Keith Henderson", *Antiquarian Book Monthly Review 2*, no.11, 1975; Peppin; The Times, Obituary, Feb 27 1982; Waters.

**HENDERSON, Kevin** **1963-**
Born Singapore. Sculptor. Abstract, often fragmented and sometimes painted, carefully modulated forms. Studied Gray's School of Art, Aberdeen 1981-6 followed by a year at Oregon State University. First one-man exhibition Inverness 1987. Exhibited AAS from Harbour Cottage, Cruden Bay; now lives in Edinburgh.
**Bibl:** Third Eye Centre, Glasgow 'Scatter' (Ex Cat 1989).

**HENDERSON, M A** **fl 1894**
Amateur painter; exhibited 'St. Martin's Cross, Iona' at the GI from Towerville, Helensburgh.

**HENDERSON, M Beatrice** **fl 1900-1905**
Painter of portraits and genre. Exhibited RSA(6), SWA(1), RA(1) & GI(1).

**HENDERSON, M Eadie** **fl 1893-1894**
Glasgow landscape painter; exhibited two views in the Dunblane area at the GI, from 19 Elmbank Place, Glasgow.

**HENDERSON, Margaret T** **fl 1900**
Glasgow amateur flower and fruit painter; exhibited GI(1) from 19 Princes Square, Strathbungo.

**HENDERSON, Miss Mary Reid** **1882-1964**
Born Glasgow. Painter, etcher, illuminator, enameller, embroiderer and metalworker. Studied Glasgow School of Art. Taught embroidery continuation classes at Motherwell Technical School after retiring as head teacher of art at Helensburgh and teacher of drawing and metalwork at Stirling. Concentrated on ecclesiastical subjects, exhibiting RSA(4), including an etching of Dunblane Cathedral, the Henry VII Chapel at Westminster, and the chancel of Roseneath Parish Church; also GI(14), AAS 1921-35 & L(5), latterly from Inchmahome, Auchenmaid Drive, Largs.

**HENDERSON, Matthew** **fl 1919-1949**
Born Glasgow. Etcher and drypoint artist, painter in oil and watercolour. Worked extensively in France and in Holland. Influenced by the Hague School. Executed such works as 'Dutch Fishing Smacks', 'Palace of the Popes, Avignon'. Exhibited RSA(10), GI(29), AAS(4) & L(7) after 1946 from 780 Crow Road.

**HENDERSON, Peter Lyle Barclay** **1848-1912**
Edinburgh architect. Practised at 122 George Street. Designed Minto House (1878). Exhibited a design for the new chapter house at 75 George Street for the Supreme Grand Royal Architectural Chapter of Scotland at the RSA 1901.
**Bibl:** Gifford 197,205,223,242,248,321-22,412,443,457,464,500, 545,563.

**HENDERSON, Richard** **fl 1911**
Glasgow painter of country scenes; exhibited GI(1), from 121 St. Vincent St.

**HENDERSON, Richard G** **fl 1897**
Glasgow amateur landscape painter; exhibited GI(1) from 345 New City Road.

**HENDERSON, Ronald G** **fl 1935-1937**
Forfar artist, mainly local views and country scenes. Exhibited AAS(2) latterly from 63, Hammersmith Rd, Aberdeen.

**HENDERSON, William** **fl 1860-d1926**
Landscape painter in watercolour and sometimes oil, often of Perthshire castles and Clydeside coastal scenes. 'A Member of the Honourable Company of Edinburgh Golfers' was published as a popular coloured mezzotint. Exhibited RSA(3) & GI(4), latterly from 86 North Frederick Street, Glasgow. Represented in Glasgow AG.

**HENDIL, Brigitte** **1944-**
Born Copenhagen, 4 Sep. Trained Edinburgh College of Art. Lives in Scotland. Painter and illustrator in oil, watercolour, gouache and pen; figures, portraits, birds, still life. First one-man exhibition in 1974. Has a remarkably delicate eye for detail with almost medieval concentration, but without fussiness. Influenced by Cranach, Holbein, Eworth and Bonnard. Began by depicting historical and imaginary people but in the early 1970s began to make small paintings of birds, sometimes with human figures added. One of the finest but academically neglected Scottish artists of her time. Lives in Stirling but visits Denmark regularly. Some of her best work is signed 'Livingston Morgan'.

**HENDRIE, Herbert** **1887-1947**
Born Manchester. Landscape painter in watercolour and stained glass designer. Studied Royal College of Art 1911 and Slade School. Head of design school, Edinburgh College of Art for many years from 1923. Exhibited RA(17), RSA(2) 1924, RSW(4), GI(3) & L(1), latterly from 5 Newton St, Greenock. Represented in Liverpool's Anglican Cathedral (including the NW transept featuring the Church of England), the South chapel east window of St. Peter Mancroft, Norwich, a fine window at the W end of St. Michael's, Linlithgow, Christ and the World's Work in a medieval mannered style in Glasgow cathedral, and windows in Paisley Abbey.
**Bibl:** Painton Cowen, Stained Glass in Britain, 1985, 150,158,234, 237-9.

**HENDRIE, John** **fl 1677**
Obscure painter. A large portrait of 'Charles I', measuring 94" x 61", painted for Glasgow City Council in 1677, is in Glasgow AG.

**HENDRY, Archibald Hunter** **1890-?**
Born North Leith, 6 Feb. Painter in oil and watercolour. Educated Canonmills, studied Edinburgh College of Art 1916-23 under Campbell Mitchell(qv), D M Sutherland(qv), E M Thompson(qv) and David Foggie(qv). Lived at Borthwick, Midlothian and later at nearby Middleton. Elected SSA. Exhibited RSA, RSW & SSA, latterly from 11 Leslie Road, Rosyth.

**HENDRY, Margaret McLeod (Mrs Neil Foggie)** **fl 1935-1940**
Edinburgh painter of landscapes and rural scenes around Edinburgh. Married to Neil Foggie(qv). Exhibited RSA(5) & GI(1) in 1939, from Cazimir, Cairnpark St, Dollar.

**HENDRY, William** **fl 1884**
Perthshire portrait painter; exhibited GI(1) from Burrell Square, Crieff. Possibly the artist whose portrait of James Grindlay is in Edinburgh City collection.

**HENDRY, William** **fl c1930-c1946**
Painter and teacher. Worked as a scenery painter in London; married the actress Maud Risdon. Member of Frank Benson's Shakesperean Company. Art master, Hamilton Academy in the mid-1930s. President, Hamilton Art Club 1946.

**HENLEY, Nicola** **Cont**
Textile designer of richly worked, stitched, collaged surfaces based upon her observation of British birds, imaginatively depicted. Although she has not sought to exhibit in the academic galleries holds regular one-man shows in Scotland.

**HENNESSY, Patrick** **fl 1939**
Landscape painter of 9 Bridge Street, Arbroath. Exhibited 'Self-portrait' and "Still life' at the RSA in 1939.

**HENNIKER, Mrs R (Katie)** **fl 1940-1943**
Edinburgh watercolour painter of 172 Craigleith Road; exhibited 'A study of fruit' at the RSA (1943) & RSW(2).

**HENNING the Elder, John HRSA** **1771-1851**
Born Paisley 2 May; died London 8 Apr. Sculptor and draughtsman. Son of a builder and carpenter, he learnt to draw plans and elevations from his father. In 1799 went to an exhibition of wax works in his native town and became fired with the idea of making wax busts himself. His first sitter was one of his father's workmen, but the result was not particularly successful. He would have given up his efforts had not the decline of his father's business forced him to seek an alternative livelihood. In 1800 he went to Glasgow and set up business as a modeller of wax portraits. Fortunate to attract the attention of the Duke of Hamilton, who was not only good natured enough to sit for his own portrait but also commissioned others of his wife and daughters. These helped greatly to establish Henning's reputation as an artist. On the strength of this he moved to Edinburgh where he made likenesses of many notables of the day including the 'Earl of Buchan', 'Sir William Forbes', 'Hector MacNeill' and 'Mr Allison'. Settled in Edinburgh 1803 and embarked upon studies at the Trustees Academy. There he made a number of portraits in enamel and wax of various distinguished contemporaries including Sir Walter Scott, The Earl of Lauderdale and The Duke of Gordon. In 1811 went to London but was disappointed with the city. However, when visiting Burlington House the Elgin Marbles made a great impression. Two years later, in a letter to Josiah Wedgwood, he said 'I felt my mind transfixed with admiration of them. In the hope of improving myself in art I began to draw from them. It struck me forcibly that from their superior excellence they might sometime or other become such an object of public curiosity that models of them, while they might be very improving to myself, might become objects of pecuniary advantage'. It took him twelve years to complete his models and a number of small plaster copies were later produced. Also executed large friezes based upon them for the Athenaeum Club (1830). Between 1820 and 1822 he produced a series of small plaster copies of the Raphael cartoons, completed with amazing delicacy and sharpness. The originals can be seen at Leeds, while replicas are in the Palace, Bishop Auckland. In his later years was assisted by his elder son. Founder, Society of British Artists. Elected HRSA 1827. Exhibited RA(17) 1821-28, Edinburgh Society of Artists 1808-13 & RSA 1827-29. Several attractive chalk drawings including a portrait of James Watt the engineer, painted in 1809, can be seen in the SNPG which has 53 works by the artist. There is a study in black chalk of a man's head and a pencil portrait 'John Francis Erskine of Mar' in NGS; also SNPG, Paisley AG and by an attributed plaster medallion in Edinburgh City collection.
**Bibl:** AJ 1849, 112; 1851, 212; Brydall 182-4; Builder 297; Gunnis 196-198; New Monthly Mag, Part I 1820, 455-459.

**HENNING, John Jnr** **1801-1857**
Eldest son of John H(qv) the Elder. In 1816 he received the Silver Isis Medal from the Society of Arts for a relief of 'The Good Samaritan'. In c1825 repaired the statue of Queen Anne outside St Paul's Cathedral after it had been damaged by vandals. Three years later, helped by his father and brother Samuel H(qv), he produced his most famous and lovely work, the classical reliefs on Decimus Burton's Triple Screen at Hyde Park Corner. In 1836 he carved the reliefs of 'Architecture, Painting and Sculpture', and 'Wisdom, Astronomy and Mathematics', for the front of Manchester Art Gallery. In 1845 executed the reliefs on the column erected at Holkham in memory of the Earl of Leicester and, the same year, the reliefs on the Colosseum, Regent's Park. In 1850 he completed reliefs based on Hogarth's pictures of the industrious and the idle apprentices for a school in Brixton. Henning showed a bust of 'Achilles' at SBA in 1925 and exhibited RA 1828-1852 including a bust of his father (1848). His bust of 'Anne, Duchess of Bedford', is at Woburn Abbey, and that of the '1st Duke of Marlborough' at Windsor Castle. There is also a monument by him to Charles Heaton Ellis at Wyddial, Hertfordshire (1857). A plaster bust of his father is in Paisley AG.
**Bibl:** Gunnis 198.

**HENNING, Samuel** **c1795-1832**
Sculptor. Younger son of John H(qv) the elder. Assisted his father in the restoration of the Elgin Marbles, at Hyde Park and the Atheneum. In 1818 he received a Silver Palette from the Society of Arts. Made impressions from the best Italian models in Flaxman's Collection which he then sold. Also responsible for the sarcophagus of Duncan Sinclair (c1832) in Kensal Green Cemetery. Died of cholera on November 2, apparently in poor circumstances. His widow was granted a pension which she continued to draw until 1851. Exhibited RA 1828-1831 & BI 1825-6.
**Bibl:** Gunnis 198.

**HENRY, Alice M** **fl 1884-1898**
Edinburgh draughtswoman in pencil, sketches and drawings, mainly wild flowers and trees, also occasional portrait studies. Sister of Kate H(qv). Exhibited RSA(16) & AAS(2).

**HENRY, Barclay** **fl 1891-d1946**
Died Arrochar, Argyll. Painter in oil and watercolour; landscape, coastal scenery and figurative works. Educated at Bonnington Park, Peeblesshire, then at Madras College, St Andrews. Associated for a time with the Craigmill School, Stirling. Moved to Arrochar 1892. Exhibited 'The flowing tide' at the RA 1899, 'The Shores of Skye' at the RSA 1899 from Fascadail, Arrochar, also GI(98) & RSW(2), after 1930 from Glenloin, Arrochar.
**Bibl:** Halsby 263.

**HENRY, Elizabeth** **fl 1969-1970**
Aberdeen painter of birds and flower studies. Exhibited AAS(1) from 34 Gray St.

**HENRY, George RA RSA RSW** **1858-1943**
Born Irvine, Ayrshire, probably 14 Mar; died London 23 Dec. Mystery surrounds his childhood about which he never spoke. His parents died when he was very young and he was brought up by an uncle. Studied for an unspecified time at Glasgow School of Art where he met, among others, Crawhall(qv), Guthrie(qv) and Walton(qv), with whom he began to paint at Brig o'Turk and Rosneath, as well as attending life class sessions at W Y MacGregor's(qv) studio in Bath Street. Began to exhibit GI 1882. In 1881 he was with Crawhall, Guthrie and Walton at Brig o'Turk in the Trossachs and in 1883 worked at Cockburnspath with Arthur Melville(qv). It was probably at this time that his interest in watercolour emerged. In 1885 he became acquainted with E A Hornel(qv) and together they painted in Galloway and Kirkcudbright. His 'A Galloway Landscape' (1889) was the

apotheosis of his work up to this time. By 1895 he had dropped his middle initial. With Hornel he subsequently shared a studio and together they produced two large works - 'The Druids' and 'Star in the East'. The former was particularly well received at the Grosvenor Gallery show 1890. The same year 'A Galloway Landscape', exhibited at the RSA 1891/2, was described as 'the nearest to a masterpiece ever painted by any of the Glasgow Boys'. Ian Finlay compared the painting with an ancient pictish carving, speaking of 'the strange rhythmic swirls, the same fundamental decorative sense which governed two far separated compositions...but the emphasis on colour and design to the exclusion of representation in the obvious sense was characteristic of northern peoples as a whole, particularly the Celtic people, from early times'. At the beginning of 1893, because of ill-health and helped financially by the Glasgow dealer Alexander Reid, Henry went to the Far East with Hornel to convalesce. The artistic effect of this visit has been variously regarded. Some critics have regarded the Japanese experience as a kind of release resulting in a more determined attempt towards pleasant decorative effects and a lighter, more pictorial touch. On the other hand, others, Cordelia Oliver for example, regard the result as 'unfortunate'. Gone was the youth with a 'twinkle in his eye, his mouth rather whimsically puckered, and wearing a bowler hat stuck on the back of his head, in the very long, brownish yellow ulster which somehow made him look like a jockey' [Caw] - and in its place came a typical southerner, a founder member of the Chelsea Arts Club, 'remembered for the glamorous figure he cut in a dress kilt'. Whatever one's conclusions, undoubtedly in his early period 'he sowed his artistic wild oats and despite the brilliance and beauty of the passion - flowers which here and there spangle his past, his most recent pictures stand on a higher and more distinguished plane, in these the colour problem has been handled in a way at once far subtler and more convincing than before, while the sentiment they embody in its sanity and grace is of a higher and more poetic order'. What is beyond dispute is that he was one of the principal guiding lights in the early days of the Glasgow Boys, and his work, especially his earlier landscapes, have had a lasting influence on subsequent generations. Elected ARSA 1892, RSA 1902, ARA 1907, RA 1920. Exhibited RA(121), RSA, RSW, AAS, RBA, ROI, GI(115), after 1904 from 26 Glebe Place, London SW. Represented in Aberdeen AG, Dundee AG, Perth AG, Stirling AG, Edinburgh AG, Glasgow AG, Paisley AG, Kirkcaldy AG, Manchester AG, Newcastle AG, Southport AG, Worthing AG, Nat Gall of Canada(Ottawa), Auckland AG, Nat Gall of South Africa (Cape Town).
**Bibl:** George Buchanan, 'A Galloway Landscape', Scottish Art Review no.7, 1960; William Buchanan, Mr Henry and Mr Hornel visit Japan, SAC, Edinburgh 1979; Caw 399-404 et al; Halsby 141-3 et al; Irwin 386-8, 389-90 et al (illus); Macmillan [SA], 256, 264, 266, 278-9, 283-5 et passim in ch xv & xvi; Studio 1897, 117; 1904 3-12; 68, 73ff.

**HENRY, George** **fl 1941-1954**
Arbroath painter of still life and local landscapes; exhibited RSA(8).

**HENRY, Gordon Edward** **1937-**
Born Elgin, 23 Sep. Educated Elgin Academy, trained Gray's School of Art and Aberdeen College of Education. Initially influenced by George Mackie(qv) and William Gillies(qv). Awarded Gold Medal 1959 and a postgraduate scholarship 1962-3. In 1960-62 taught art at Elgin Academy before joining the staff at Gray's School of Art. Involved as a designer with Aberdeen University Press 1964-8, becoming Director of the Press 1970-75. Director, Aberdeen Tourist Board 1982. His earlier work was mainly watercolour scenes of the north-east, particularly around Aberdeen. Latterly has turned increasingly to work in pen and wash, watercolour and gouache. His speciality is design and he has illustrated a number of books and dust jackets. Works in the tradition of R W Allan(qv) and William Eadie(qv). Exhibited AAS 1961-78 from 21 Pluscarden Rd, Elgin.

**HENRY, Mrs Grace** **[see Grace Mitchell]**

**HENRY, James** **fl 1866-1870**
Edinburgh oil painter of landscape and coastal scenes; exhibited RSA(4).

**HENRY, James Macintyre** **fl 1885-d1929**
Edinburgh architect. Specialised in hotel design. Designed Inveresk Parish Hall, New Palace Hotel, Edinburgh (1896), the new RB Hotel, Edinburgh (1896), the dining-room for the Balmoral Hotel in Edinburgh, the Club House at Tantallon Golf Club, the 'flabby Palladian' Lothian Regional Chambers (1900-5), and many other buildings for public purposes. Exhibited RSA(19) & GI(1).
**Bibl:** Gifford 71,183,270,310,313,331,502,526,650,653,pl.105.

**HENRY, Mrs John E W** **fl 1863-1866**
Edinburgh oil painter of town views and landscapes; exhibited RSA(3).

**HENRY, Kate M** **fl 1887**
Edinburgh painter of townscapes. Sister of Alice H(qv). Exhibited AAS(1).

**HEPBURN, Frances** **fl 1896-1900**
Edinburgh sculptor. Exhibited two portrait busts at AAS from 1 Wardie Rd.

**HEPBURN, Michael** **fl 1981-1984**
Glasgow-based wildlife and pastoral painter, especially wild flowers. Exhibited GI(4), from 1 Selkirk Rd, Port Glasgow.

**HEPBURN, Sir Ninian Buchan Bt** **1922-?**
Born Smeaton Hepburn, East Lothian. Painter in oil. Educated at Canford School, where he started painting under Sir William Coldstream and at the Byam Shaw School of Art, 1956-58. During WW2 served in India and Burma with the Queen's Own Cameron Highlanders. Specialised in Scottish and Italian landscape painted in a straightforward decorative style, with a good sense of colour and sensitive handling of water. Exhibited RA from 1964 & RSA in 1970.

**HEPBURN, T N** **fl 1908**
Amateur landscape painter; exhibited RSA(1) from 122 Marchmont Road, Edinburgh.

**HEPBURN, William** **fl 1835-1837**
Edinburgh based painter in oil of animals; exhibited RSA(2) from 1 Lothian Street.

**HEPPER, George** **fl 1866**
Portobello oil painter; exhibited 'The Gamekeeper's Kitchen' at the RSA.

**HERALD, James Watterston** **1859-1914**
Born Forfar. Watercolour painter of landscape and figurative subjects. Son of a shoemaker, he was schooled in Dundee and then apprenticed to a house painter in Forfar before becoming a clerk in a local textile mill. His artistic interest shone through and his parents eventually relented, enabling him to embark upon an artistic career. In 1884 moved with his family to Edinburgh. His only formal training was at Herkomer's School in Bushey, Hertfordshire, where he met William Nicholson(qv) and James Pryde(qv). It was about this time that he was influenced by the style and technique of Arthur Melville(qv), whom he may have met. In the 1890s he lived in London holding several exhibitions. In 1901, in spite of having made the acquaintance of a well-to-do patron, he returned to Arbroath and remained there for the rest of his days, becoming increasingly addicted to alcohol. Painted in a very personal style using a 'blottesque' technique. Loved the streets and harbour of Arbroath, capturing the colours and patterns created by the sails of fishing boats, the busy market scenes and figures painted darkly at dusk. The quality of his work declined markedly in his later years when the composition became loose and unstructured and the colours ever darker. But at his best he was a wonderfully sensitive, evocative artist. Capable of transcending commonplace scenes into the realm of religious mysticism as in 'The Saint', now in the V&A. Exhibited RSA(5) 1888-1911, posthumously in 1926, GI(3) & AAS 1902-06. Represented in BM, V & A, NGS, Arbroath AG, Dundee AG, Glasgow AG, Greenock AG, Kirkcaldy AG, Paisley AG.
**Bibl:** Caw 393; Halsby 155-8, 172, 177, 211, 213; Hardie 104; Macmillan [SA] 288; The Fine Art Society, James Watterston Herald, Edinburgh 1981.

**HERBERT, Alexander S** **fl 1894**
Glasgow amateur artist; exhibited GI(1) from 12 Derby Street.

**HERBERT, James** **fl 1892**
Edinburgh amateur artist; exhibited 'Pittenweem Harbour' at the RSA in 1892 from 71 Comiston Road.

**HERBERT, Joanna L (Mrs Dobson)** **fl 1902-1940**
Painter in oil and watercolour of landscape; exhibited RSA(2) from Glasgow in 1909 and 1915, RSW(6), RA(2), AAS, GI(12) & L(5) mostly from March Hill, Niddrie, Edinburgh.

**HERD, John Grosvenor** **fl 1916-1919**
Kirkcaldy portrait painter. Exhibited RSA(4) & AAS(1) from Whitebank.

**HERD, T** **fl 1883**
Minor Edinburgh landscape painter in oil; exhibited 'A scene near Banff' at the RSA from 6 Murdoch Terrace.

**HERDMAN, Robert RSA RSW** **1829-1888**
Born Rattray, Perthshire, 17 Sep; died Edinburgh, 10 Jan. Fourth and youngest son of a parish minister. After the early death of his father in 1838 the family moved to St Andrews where Herdman entered Madras College and subsequently St Andrew's University. A promising Greek scholar, he retained a love for the classics throughout his life. Left university prematurely. First exhibited RSA 1850 and two years later enrolled at the Trustees Academy under Scott Lauder(qv). In 1854 won the Keith prize for the best historical work by a student. Some of his early paintings illustrated biblical subjects, but after his return from another visit to the continent in 1855, - which provided him with several more Italian subjects including his diploma work 'La Culla' 1864 - his main source of inspiration became Scottish history and song, often patriotic subjects such as 'After the Battle' (1870), showing a severely wounded soldier among his family. Also executed a number of portraits and single figures, often Scottish peasant girls. Italian light and colour considerably influenced him and he clearly enjoyed the details of quattrocento painting as well as the richer colours of the Seicento. In Perth AG there is an early watercolour, 'Mandolin Player', which reveals the influence of his Italian experience. He did some delightful work in watercolour, many of the holiday sketches of wildflowers, boulders and seashores made in Arran retain great beauty. Certainly the best educated and cultured man in his group. He stood apart among Lauder's pupils in remaining uninfluenced by the naturalistic movement. His style is broad, simple, direct; unaffected by plein air or pre-Raphaelitism, generally with vivid colour and discrimination although the faces tend to be typified. Two days after his death a critic in *Scottish Leader,* quoted by Brydall, wrote 'the technical side of his painting evidenced the same powers and shortcomings as were characteristic of his mental side. Full of knowledge...his brush-work was always suave and apparently effortless, which gave the spectator a sense of his never being worried or flurried, but always at his ease. On the other hand...his technique (might) be seen as wanting in depth, in solidity, and in true rendering of textures and surfaces...ultimately (its) great charm was the realisation of his natural and inborn sense of the beautiful'. Member, Hellenic Club, president, Edinburgh Art Club and vice-president, Society of Antiquaries of Scotland. One of his interesting ventures was a collection of portraits of contemporary Scottish artists, now in Aberdeen AG. Illustrated Roscoe's *Legends of Venice,* 1841 and contributed illustrations for *Poems and Songs by Robert Burns* (1875). Father of Robert Duddingstone H(qv). Elected ARSA 1858, RSA 1863, RSW 1878. Exhibited RSA(150+), RA(8), AAS 1887 & GI(47), living latterly at St Bernard's, Bruntsfield Crescent, Edinburgh. Represented in NGS(3), SNPG(4), National Gallery of Victoria (Melbourne), Glasgow AG(10), Paisley AG, Perth AG, Aberdeen AG, and a portrait 'Lord Provost Sir James Falshaw Bt' is in Edinburgh City collection.
**Bibl:** AJ 1873, 376; Bryan; Brydall 414-8; Caw 349-50; DNB; Lindsay Errington, Robert Herdman, NGS 1988; Halsby 104-6 et al; Irwin 349-50 (illus); Macmillan [SA], 231, 240; McKay 352-5; Studio Special Number RSA 1907.

**HERDMAN, Robert Duddingstone ARSA** **1863-1922**
Born Edinburgh; died Edinburgh 9 Jne. Portrait, figure and genre painter in oil and watercolour. Second son of Robert H(qv). Studied art at the RSA Schools sharing the Keith prize in 1886 and 1887, and in Paris 1891 under Paul Delance and George Callot as well as at the Studio Colarossi. Visited Spain and Holland. First exhibited RSA 1886, a half-length portrait of his father. In 1898 was co-founder and first chairman of the SSA. Elected ARSA 1908. Exhibited RA(10), RSA(101), RSW(27), GI(37), AAS 1885-1900 & L(24). The SNPG has a portrait of Robert Herdman.
**Bibl:** Caw 290; Halsby 263.

**HEREFORD, Edward W** **fl 1884-1915**
Watercolour painter of Gourock, nr Greenock. Moved shortly after the turn of the century to England remaining there for the rest of his life. Exhibited RSA(1), RI(2) & L(2).

**HERIOT, George** **1766-1844**
Born Haddington. Amateur artist, son of the Sheriff-Clerk of East Lothian. A civil servant, later becoming Deputy Postmaster General of Canada 1799-1816. On his retirement returned to Scotland. Influenced by the work of Paul Sandby, he painted views of Spain, France, Wales, Scotland and the Thames Valley. Published *Travels through Canada* which he illustrated himself. Represented in Glasgow AG.
**Bibl:** Halsby 263.

**HERMAN, Josef** **1911-?**
Born Warsaw, 3 Jan. Painter in oil, watercolour, pen & ink. Figure subjects used as a vehicle for social realism. Studied Warsaw School of Art 1930-32, left Poland 1938 going first to Brussels, where he came under the influence of Parmeke, then to Glasgow 1940 and London. Became a naturalized British citizen 1948. Involved in the establishment of the New Art Club and the New Scottish Group 1942. Although resident in Scotland for only a short time his influence was considerable as seen, for example, in the work of Donald Bain(qv) and Millie Frood(qv). Exhibited GI(2). Lived in London and Suffolk.

**HERMAN, Miss L** **fl 1895-1896**
Glasgow flower painter. Exhibited GI(1) & Walker Gallery, Liverpool(2), first from Paris and later from Glasgow.

**HERON, James** **fl 1873-1919**
Edinburgh painter in oil and watercolour; landscapes, often Highland, buildings, architectural drawings, pastoral scenes. Father of William H(qv). Partial to autumnal scenes in the highlands of Perthshire, the north-west coast, and Aberdeenshire. His colour is restrained and sometimes of a surreal turn but his compositions are pleasing, if occasionally the draughtsmanship is rather slight. Exhibited RSA(105), including 'On the Dee near Ballater' (1896) & 'The River Dee' (1897); AAS & GI(11). Shared a studio at 16 Picardy Place, Edinburgh. Represented in City of Edinburgh collection.
**Bibl:** Halsby 263.

**HERON, William** **fl 1883-1896**
Edinburgh watercolour and oil painter of landscapes. Son of James H(qv). Later moved to Liverpool. Exhibited RSA(4), sometimes in watercolour, including a number of Australian scenes.

**HERRAGHTY, George** **fl 1975-1977**
Dundee-based painter exhibited two works at the RSA, one of them a study of a 'Rainbow Trout' 1977, from 50 Seafield Road.

**HERRIES James W** **fl 1932-1940**
Edinburgh painter. Exhibited RSA(4), mostly coastal scenes around Kippford, from 22 Findhorn Place.

**HERRIOT, James** **fl 1959-1968**
Glasgow landscape artist; exhibited GI(11), from 15 Quentin St.

**HERVEY, Jean** **fl 1964**
Aberdeenshire watercolour artist of local landscape and fishing scenes. Exhibited AAS(3) from Foucausie, Granholm.

**HESLOP, T A B** **fl 1966-1969**
Angus sculptor. Mainly figures & subjects associated with the sea. Exhibited AAS(4) from Ness House, Johnshaven, nr Montrose.

**HEUDE (HOOD), Nicholas** **fl 1672-d1703**
Born Le Mans, France; died Edinburgh, 30 Jan. French Huguenot painter. Member French Academy 1672 but in 1682 was expelled

from France on religious grounds and settled in England, becoming assistant to Verrio. Brought to Scotland by William, Duke of Queensberry c1688, to work at the latter's new home of Drumlanrig. Two circular ceiling paintings, 'Aurora and Diana' and 'Endymion at Caroline Park', Granton are attributed to him. The house, then known as Royston House, was rebuilt after 1685 by Viscount Tarbet, making it contemporary with Prestonfield. It has been suggested that 'Sacrifice of Iphigenia' at Dunnotar Castle may be his work. When in Edinburgh appears to have lived in World's End Close. At his death his property included 'the wholl pictours finished and unfinished within his house, together with his books (being most pairt Frence) and the abuilyiements of his bedie', realised £333 6s 8d at auction. A portrait painter who signed himself **L Heude**, and who painted a poor portrait of 'John Tran', now in Glasgow University, was probably related, although no son of that name is recorded.
**Bibl:** Apted 46-7; Brydall 94; Caw 20; E Croft-Murray, Decorative Painting in England, 1537-1837, 1962, i, 284b; Cursiter, Scottish Art, 23; Gifford 606-7; MacMillan [SA] 81, 87; SNPG, Hew Dalrymple Papers; Walpole, Anecdotes, ii, 192; Walpole Soc Vertue Notebooks, iv, 48, 103, 139, 145.

**HEUHAN, J** **fl 1810-1815**
Glasgow miniature painter. Exhibited four portraits at the RA 1810-1813, three of young ladies, and one of a gentleman.
**Bibl:** Graves, RA

**HEWETSON, Miss Annie** **fl 1886**
Edinburgh painter of domestic animals; exhibited RSA(1) from 9 Carlton Street.

**HEWIE, D William** **fl 1989-**
Dundee sculptor. Exhibited a waxen animal group at GI, from 318 Perth Rd.

**HEWSON, Miss Frances Ann** **fl 1865**
Wildlife painter. Exhibited 'Bullfinch and Flowers' at the RSA in the above year.

**HEX, Miss Jennifer E** **fl 1962-1974**
Ayrshire painter and engraver, also embroiderer. Etchings, linocuts and woodcuts. Trained Glasgow School of Art. Her first career was as a teacher in Argyll and Ayrshire. Became interested in embroidery 1970 and in 1980 left teaching to become a full-time embroiderer and weaver. Moved from Ayrshire to Argyll 1970. Exhibited RGI(10), latterly from Rhonadale, Carradale, Argyll.

**HEYS, Mary** **fl 1901**
Glasgow flower painter of Rockmount, Barrhead; exhibited GI(2).

**HIGHET, Kate** **fl 1883**
Ayrshire painter of local scenery. Exhibited GI(1), from Langlands, Troon.

**HILL, Alexander** **fl 1888-1889**
Lanarkshire painter of flowers and still life; oil and watercolour. Exhibited GI(3) from 13 Harriet Street, Pollockshields.

**HILL, Alexander Stuart** **1888-1948**
Born Perth; died Chelsea, Feb. Portrait painter in oil. Son of a Perth fish merchant. Lived in Chelsea, dressed like 'the complete dandy' and established himself as a recognised society portrait painter, exhibiting RA but only occasionally in Scotland at RSA & RGI(3). Represented in Perth AG.

**HILL, David** **fl 1814-1815**
Arbroath architect. Designed the Trades Hall, later the Sheriff Court House, Arbroath (1814-5).
**Bibl:** Bruce Walker & W S Gauldie, Architects and Architecture on Tayside, Dundee 1984, 80.

**HILL, David Octavius RSA** **1802-1870**
Born Perth, May 20; died Edinburgh, 17 May. Painter in oil and watercolour, landcapes and figurative subjects; pioneer photographer and illustrator. Son of a bookseller in Perth. Married Amelia Paton(qv). Studied at Trustees Academy, Edinburgh under Andrew Wilson(qv). Whilst still a student he exhibited 3 landscapes, all of scenes in or near his native city, at the Institution for the Encouragement of Fine Arts in Scotland 1821 and three more in 1822, including 'Brechin Castle'. In 1826 became a foundation associate of the newly formed Scottish Academy but was one of 9 artists who withdrew after the first meeting, although re-elected in 1829. In the late 1820s he began painting figurative groups leading very soon to portraits. In 1833 he initiated the Association for the Promotion of the Fine Arts in Scotland(qv), the first scheme of its kind in Britain, which received the Royal Charter 1850. The Irwins point out how interesting to speculate on the cross-currents of influence between Hill's calotypes and the generation of painters active in Edinburgh in the 1840s. Lady Eastlake, admiring Thomas Duncan's 'Self-portrait' in the RSA exhibition of 1845, declared it 'a most wonderful picture, evidently showing that he has learnt much from the calotypes - so broad, brown and true'. Occasionally he used photographs as preparation for his landscapes, as for example, his view of the new railway viaduct at Ballochmyle in Ayrshire (1851), now in Glasgow Museum of Transport. Secretary of the Scottish Academy, later becoming the RSA, 1830-69. Enjoyed illustrating the works of Burns and in 1841 published *The Land of Burns,* 60 illustrations engraved from his own landscapes. For several years he worked on a major group portrait 'Signing the Deed of Demission', a picture containing 470 portraits of the leaders of the Free Church of Scotland. This was completed in 1866 and is now in the hall of the Free Church in Edinburgh. He had more works engraved than any other Scottish artist. His 'View of Edinburgh from the Castle' and his very large 'Windsor Castle' continued to achieve enormous popularity long after his death. His principal claim to fame, however, is as one of the most outstanding portrait photographers of the 19th century. He first adopted photography in the painting of his largest canvases and over his work for the Free Church 1843-65. In 1843, with the chemist and photographer Robert Adamson, he began to take calotype photographs of people to appear in his painting. At the same time the two of them took the opportunity of opening a photographic business concentrating on portraits of the most eminent Scots of the day. In 1846 he published a series of calotype views of St Andrews. After Adamson's retirement in 1847, Hill returned to painting. Helped to found the NGS 1850. His photographic works were often compared to those of earlier masters and were largely instrumental in reducing both the quality and quantity of miniature portrait painting in Scotland. In personal appearance he was 'remarkable for his striking, classical, and manly features'. His work in support of the RSA during its early days was of inestimable value. In the words of a contemporary obituary 'as a friend and companion he will ever be remembered by those who knew him as one possessed of admirable talents for promoting the happiness of the society in which he moved, combining kindness, wit, and humour, with an innate modesty which never allowed him to say anything hard or uncharitable of anyone'. His family home on Calton Hill was for many years a focal point in the cultural life of the city. Contributed a series of 30 lithographic plates with the title *Sketches of Scenery in Perthshire* 1821-23 and illustrations for a number of books including *The Abbot, Redgauntlet* and *The Fair Maid of Perth; Poems and Songs by Robert Burns* (1875) and *The Land of Burns*. From its foundation in 1828 until his death in 1870 Hill exhibited annually at the RSA. Also showed 4 large landscapes at the RA (1852-1868), & GI(9) 1866-1873 from Newington Lodge, Mayfield Terrace, Edinburgh. Some of his pencil sketches of views in and around Edinburgh and the Firth of Forth, as well as the 'Tomb of Burns, Dumfries', are now in the NGS; represented also in SNPG(1), by 4 engravings - one of the artist James Giles - in City of Edinburgh collection, Glasgow AG, Perth AG, Birkenhead AG.
**Bibl:** AJ 1869, 317-9; 1870, 203 (obit); Armitage 42; Art Quarterly, Winter, 1958; D Bruce, Sun Pictures 1973; Brydall 418-21; Caw 145-6; DNB; Halsby 84-5, 263 et al; Irwin 285-288; Maas 191; McKay 198-9; Portfolio 1887, 135; Aaron Scharf, Art and Photography 1968, 27,29-31,59, 260; Heinrich Schwarz, D O Hill, 1932.

**HILL, Mrs David Octavius (Amelia Robertson Paton) 1820-1904**
Born Dunfermline, Jan 15. Sculptress. Described by a contemporary in the *AJ* as among the first rank of Scottish artists. Sister of Joseph Noel(qv) and Waller Hugh Paton(qv). One of her most notable sculptures was the seven and a half feet high bust of Dr Livingstone, exhibited RA 1869 of which a contemporary critic wrote 'personal likeness all his friends could wish for...vigorous...lifelike...lacking in all stiffness and formality'. This was later exhibited at the GI 1869

when a Scottish critic spoke of 'this noble, colossal statue'. It is now in East Princes St Gdns. In 1861 she executed a bust of John Fergus, for 12 years MP for Fife, now in Kirkcaldy Town Hall. Among other works at the RA 1863-1874 were portraits of the 'Countess of Elgin and Kincardine' (1864), 'James Wemyss of Wemyss MP' (presented to the Fife County Hall, Cupar 1866), 'Sir George Harvey, President of the RSA' (1867), and 'Thomas Carlyle', exhibited the same year. A marble portrait bust of her husband (1869) and of her brother 'Sir Joseph Noel Paton', executed after her husband had died in 1874, were exhibited from Newington Lodge, Edinburgh whence she had moved. In 1886 a bronze bust of her husband was erected in the Dean Cemetery. Exhibited RSA & GI(21). Represented in SNPG(7), including 3 of her husband and 3 of her brother Joseph. A plaster plaque of Ethel Margaret Paton, wife of her nephew Frederick(qv), remains in the artist's family. Represented in Perth AG.
**Bibl:** AJ 1869, 19,82; Caw 194; Gifford 314,316,380,390; David Octavius Hill; Bicentenary Festival, Scottish Society for the History of Photography 2002; R H Rodger, The Remarkable Mr Hill, David Octavius Hill, Perth AG 2002.

**HILL, Miss Elizabeth** **fl 1959**
Angus amateur painter; exhibited GI(1), from The School House, Glen Ogilvy, Forfar.

**HILL, Miss Gladys** **fl 1981**
Amateur Stirlingshire landscape artist. Exhibited 'Gathering storm' at the GI, from 26 Keir Hardie Ave, Laurieston, Falkirk.

**HILL, Miss Isa E** **fl 1925**
Amateur Glasgow painter; exhibited 'The Entombment' at the GI from St Vigeans, Giffnock.

**HILL, J A** **fl 1943-1951**
Dumbartonshire flower painter; exhibited 8 works at the GI, 6 of them 'Sweet Peas', from Dalnottar Ave, Old Kilpatrick.

**HILL, James** **fl 1934-1936**
Amateur Stirling watercolour painter of townscapes; exhibited RSW(2) & GI(1), from 3 The Esplanade, Stirling.

**HILL, John** **fl 1878**
Largs oil painter of seascapes; exhibited RSA(2).

**HILL, Kate T** **fl 1902-1921**
Forfar painter of landscape and figurative works. Exhibited GI(2) & AAS 1902-21, latterly from Broomfield, Forfar.

**HILL, Miss Lesley** **fl 1983**
Renfrewshire artist; exhibited a local townscape at the GI, from 3 Albion St, Paisley.

**HILL, Miss Pamela** **fl 1942-1944**
Glasgow engraver; linocuts and pen and ink sketches; exhibited GI(2), from 8 Sandyford Place.

**HILL, Patrick** **fl 1867**
Sculptor; exhibited 2 portrait medallions at the RSA 1867.

**HILL, Peter** **fl 1983-1986**
Scottish painter. Exhibited RSA(4) from a Glasgow address and since 1986 in Edinburgh; titles include 'The garden of the forking paths', 'The gargoyle and the plough'; also GI(1), from 13 Parkgrove Terrace.

**HILL, William** **fl 1879**
Unknown painter, possibly Scottish; exhibited a watercolour of cottages at Kintyre at the GI.

**HILL-SMITH, Doris** **fl c1970-**
Watercolour painter, mainly flowers. Studied Glasgow School of Art followed by a sculpture course at Loughborough College. First commissioned officer of drawing duties, Women's Royal Naval Service. Taught for several years in England before settling in Appin House, Dull, Perthshire. Exhibits RA, Society of Flower Painters & in France.

**HILLARY, William** **fl 1968-1973**
Edinburgh based sculptor. Exhibited semi-abstract works at the RSA(8) between the above years from 48 Merchiston Avenue. Titles include 'Minor movement', 'Uranus', 'Atlantis' and 'Magic Circle I'.

**HILLEARY, Alasdair ("Loon")** **1955-**
Scottish humorous cartoonist, usually depicts country pursuits in their madder moments and fantasies. Self-taught, educated Gordonstoun. Served briefly in the Scots Guards. Fine sense of humour balanced by a fine colour sense. Exhibits London, Australia, Hong Kong & Spain, from Easter Ross.

**HILLOCKS, James** **fl 1947**
Buckie painter. Exhibited a portrait of his mother and a schoolroom interior at the RSA from 5 Cluny Terrace.

**HINDSHAW (HENSHAW)/(HYNDSHAW), Mungo fl 1637-1681**
Early painter. In 1637 he was known to have been painting in Hamilton Palace. Married Margaret Weir 1642. In 1663-4 payment of £300 was made by the 3rd Duke of Hamilton to 'Mungo Henshaw picture drawer', for painting in and about Hamilton Palace. The following year he was known to be working at the Earl of Tweeddale's Edinburgh home and at Yester House. In 1681 he received 15s sterling from Mary's Chapel.
**Bibl:** Apted 47; Hamilton Archives, Lennoxlove, 435/1/7, F1/319/7, F1/319/16.

**HISLOP, Andrew** **fl 1880-1903**
Glasgow landscape painter; worked mostly in oil and mainly in the west and south-west of Scotland. Exhibited RA(1), RSA(12) & GI(32). In 1889 exhibited 'Cathcart Castle' at the RA.

**HISLOP, Andrew Healey** **1887-1954**
Born 7 Jly; died Edinburgh 6 Jly. Painter in oil and watercolour also etcher; subjects mainly farming scenes, flowers, landscape and fishing activities around the coast. Married Margaret Ross H(qv). Teacher of drawing Edinburgh College of Art where he studied 1908-13, winning a travelling scholarship which enabled him to spend a further year at the British School in Rome. During WW1 was interned in Germany. Prolific artist in both main mediums and fine draughtsman who for ten years did a great deal of etching before turning chiefly to oil. Lived in Edinburgh. Elected SSA 1922. Exhibited RSA(54), RSW(6), GI(35) & L(1), 1936-1952 from 18 Cluny Ave and after 1952 from 28 London St, Edinburgh.
**Bibl:** Halsby 263.

**HISLOP, Margaret Ross (née Grant) RSA RBA** **1894-1972**
Born West Calder, 27 Jne; died Edinburgh, 8 May. Painter in oil, watercolour and pastel; still life and portraits, also interiors and landscape, including scenes in Paris & Venice. Studied Westminster School of Art and Edinburgh College of Art, awarded diploma 1916. In 1921 married Andrew Hislop(qv). Travelled extensively in Canada, Ceylon, India and Egypt. Lived for many years in Edinburgh. Elected ARSA 1950, RSA 1964. Exhibited RA, RSA, GI(58) & a North African scene at the AAS 1926 when living at Lethendy Lodge, Grantown-on-Spey. Represented in Dundee AG, Glasgow AG, Greenock AG, Edinburgh City collection, a number of Australian and American Galleries.

**HISLOP, Miss Susan** **fl 1881-1890**
Edinburgh portrait painter; moved to Auchterarder c1886. Exhibited RSA(7) & GI(2).

**HISLOP, Walter B** **fl 1900-d1915**
Edinburgh landscape painter in oil but mainly watercolour. Studied Edinburgh College of Art. During WW1 served as a 2nd Lieutenant in the 5th Battalion of the Royal Scots and was killed at Gallipoli. Exhibited RSA(2), AAS(1), L(1) & SSA.

**HOBDEN, Miss Mildred** **fl 1942-1947**
Renfrewshire painter of still life and flower piueces, in oil and watercolour. Exhibited RSA(5) between the above years, mostly flower paintings and one nude, & GI(5), from 10 Collingwood Terrace, Gourock.

**HODDER, Charles D** **1835-1926**
Landscape, portrait and figure painter. Lived in Edinburgh, also for a time in Arran during the mid-1860s. Exhibited RSA(12) & RHA(1). Represented by 'Self-portrait' in SNPG.

**HODGE, Albert Hemstock** **1876-1918**
Glasgow painter and sculptor; figurative works and garden pieces. Father of Jessie H(qv). Exhibited RA(22), RSA(6), GI(17) & RI(1). One of his exhibits was a Soane medallion design for the Institute of Architects 1897.

**HODGE, Andrew** **fl 1863**
Glasgow landscape painter in oil and watercolour. Exhibited GI(2), from 9 Newton St.

**HODGE, David J F** **fl 1971-1976**
Kincardineshire designer of jewellery. Father of Linda H(qv). Exhibited AAS from 6 Portlethen. Moved to Orkney on retirement.

**HODGE, Miss Jessie Mary Margaret** **1901-?**
Painter and mural decorator. Works in oil and watercolour, narrative and symbolic works became increasingly interested in depicting birds. Studied RA Schools where she obtained a bronze medal for life painting and a Landseer scholarship. Daughter of Albert Hemstock H(qv). Exhibited regularly 1922-1940 RA(12), RSA(8), RSW(2), RMS(2), GI(21) & L(5), all from 53 Meadway, London NW11.

**HODGE, Linda M** **fl 1970-1979**
Kincardineshire metalwork designer. Trained Gray's School of Art, Aberdeen. Daughter of David H(qv). After marriage in the early 1970s, moved to the Middle East. Exhibited AAS during the above years from her home in Portlethen.

**HODGE, Maureen** **1941-**
Born Perth. Edinburgh-based designer and weaver. Trained Edinburgh College of Art, specialising in tapestry and stained glass window design 1959-1964. Between 1965 and 1973 assisted Archie Brennan in the tapestry department, Edinburgh College of Art, succeeding as head of department 1973. Member, SSA Council 1973-6. Worked with Dovecote Tapestries. Exhibited AAS(1) & in various galleries at home and overseas.

**HODGE, Simon Prince RI** **1903-?**
Born Glasgow, 19 Apr. Painter in watercolour and illustrator. Studied Glasgow School of Art 1919-24 and a short time thereafter settled in Johannesburg. President of Johannesburg Art Club 1931-2. Spending winters in South Africa he returned to spend the summers in London. Elected RI. Exhibited RA(4) & RI(2).

**HODGE, Thomas** **1827-1907**
Born Truro, Cornwall. Watercolour painter of golfing subjects and figurative scenes; caricaturist and illustrator. Keen golfer and member of the Royal & Ancient Golf Club, he went to Prestwick 1851, settling in St Andrews 1864. Won the autumn medal there three times and the spring medal once. Author of a book on military fortifications. Illustrated *Golf* for the Badminton Library series, also Andrew Lang's *Golfing Papers* (1891) and Robert Clark's *Golf - a Royal and Ancient Game.* Especially adept at capturing the idiosyncracies of his fellow players, he was the first specialist golfing artist. Exhibited two golfing paintings at the RSA 1878 and 1879 from West View, St Andrews. Represented in R & A, St Andrews by many examples, including a watercolour portrait of 'George Glennie' (1880).
**Bibl:** Wingfield; Harry Langton, 'Thomas Hodge, The Golf Artist of St Andrews', Sports Design International, London, 2000

**HODGES, Roberta (Mrs Sekalska)** **1903-1951**
St Andrews portrait, figure and landscape painter. Art teacher at St. Leonards School. Married the engraver Josef Sekalska(qv). Exhibited RSA(22), RHA(2), RBA(2) & AAS(2) from, 4 St Mary Street.

**HODGESON, E S** **fl 1887**
Dundee landscape painter, especially fond of sunsets and sunrises. Exhibited AAS(2) from Ward St.

**HODGETTS, Robert M** **fl 1801-1840**
Edinburgh engraver; landscape and portraits. Son of Thomas H(qv). Exhibited RSA(9), once 1827 and then 1833-1838. These include engravings after Poussin, Sir J W Newton, and John Syme(qv). In 1838 exhibited 'The Rt Hon David Boyle, Lord Justice Clerk', after a miniature by Sir John Newton. Lived at Comely Bank and latterly at Canonmills Cottage. Represented in Glasgow AG, City of Edinburgh collection (original engraving of Sir Walter Scott).

**HODGETTS, Thomas** **c1780-1846**
Edinburgh painter and engraver. Father of Robert M H(qv). Exhibited mainly portraits after Colvin Smith(qv), Raeburn(qv), John Syme(qv) and others 1827-1833. Many of his early prints bear the address Westbourne Green, Paddington. Probably pupil of, and certainly worked with, the engraver George Dawe. In 1827 his first work was shown at the RSA and in the *Edinburgh Directory 1837-38* he appears as an historical and portrait engraver living at Canonmills. In 1830 engraved the well-known portrait of 'King George IV' after the original by Sir Thomas Lawrence, from Comely Bank and later worked from Trinity Mains. Four portrait engravings were exhibited posthumously at the RSA 1926. Represented in City of Edinburgh collection by 3 aquatints and 4 mezzotints.
**Bibl:** Bushnell 23-24.

**HODGKINSON, Frank** **fl 1944**
Edinburgh painter; exhibited 3 landscapes at the RSA in the above year.

**HODSON, William** **fl 1870**
Glasgow watercolour portrait painter; exhibited a portrait of 'Richard Plantaganet' at the GI, from 176a Hope St.

**HOECK, Ebenezer T** **fl 1886-d1931**
Landscape painter and engraver; some lithography. Worked in Scotland, Belgium, France and Italy. Also painted church interiors in a rather heavy style. Lived in Glasgow 1885-1928, moved to 53 Hillview Terrace, Corstorphine, Edinburgh 1929. Exhibited RSA(2), GI(39), AAS(1) & L(1).

**HOFFIE, William** **fl 1883-1900**
Edinburgh painter in oil and watercolour of landscapes. Exhibited RSA(14) sometimes coastal scenes, such as 'The Beach, Newhaven' 1884,'Evening on the Esk near Musselburgh' 1890.

**HOG, Lady Mary** **?-1795**
Scottish embroiderer. Daughter of the 7th Earl of Lauderdale. In 1785 received drawing lessons form David Allan(qv). It is thought that he may have assisted Mary in the design of some of the important needlework panels used as wall hangings in the drawing room of Newliston, designed by Robert Adam(qv). Her technique of appliqué involved shapes cut out of a woven woollen fabric and applied to a ground of moreen, held down by tailor's silk and touched up with watercolour. Represented at Newliston and the Georgian House, Edinburgh.
**Bibl:** Margaret Swain 80; M Swain, *A Georgian Mystery, Lady Mary Hog and the Newliston Needlework,* Country Life, 12 Aug 1982, pp470-472.

**HOGARTH, Edward** **fl 1888**
Amateur painter, exhibited 'Cast ashore on a lonely bay' at the RSA from Glebe Street, Campbeltown.

**HOGARTH, Miss Lizzie RBA** **1879-c1942**
Born Old Aberdeen, 6 Jly. Painter in oil, watercolour and pastel of landscape, portraits and still life. Studied in Aberdeen under James Hector(qv) and St Martin's School of Art, London under Swan and Brangwyn. Lived in London, later Sherborne, Dorset. Exhibited 1900-1940 RSA(16), SWA(39), RBA(92), AAS (regularly 1896-1937), GI(2) including a pastel 'Self-portrait' 1900, ROI(1) & L(7).

**HOGARTH, Thomas Campbell** **fl 1863-1864**
Edinburgh oil painter of figurative subjects; exhibited RSA(3).

**HOGG, Archibald Williamson** **fl 1885-1903**
Edinburgh painter in oil and watercolour; landscape especially coastal scenes and lochs often in Perthshire, also in the Scottish lowlands and Northumberland. Exhibited 'A lowland stream' at the RA 1895, RSA(45) & RHA(3).

**HOGG, Douglas G** **fl 1973-**
Kelso stained glass window designer. There is a fine small panel by him in Culross Abbey that uses glass in a three-dimensional manner, placing it on edge to simulate a cross. Lived at 34 The Square, and exhibited regularly RSA including a design for the west window of St Giles Cathedral 1982; also in Good Shepherd Church, Murrayfield Ave (1977).
**Bibl:** Gifford 628.

**HOGG, James** **fl 1785**
Scottish engraver. Bryan gives his christian name as Jacob. Engraved 'The Hand-Maid' after H Walton (stipple) 1785, and a number of plates after Angelica Kauffmann, J R Smith, Morland, Wheatley and others.
**Bibl:** Bryan; Bushnell.

**HOGG, Mary** **fl 1911**
Dunbartonshire painter. Exhibited a 'Triptych of St. Patrick' at the GI from Ferncraig, Old Kilpatrick.

**HOGG, Thomas** **fl 1829-1830**
Minor Edinburgh portrait painter in oil. Exhibited 2 unidentified sitters at the RSA in the above years from Cumberland Street.

**HOG(G), William** **fl 1695-1717**
Son of William Hogg, indweller of Edinburgh, apprenticed to the painter burgess Thomas Warrender in 1695. In 1705 elected Burgess of Edinburgh and in 1717 a member of the Incorporation of St Mary's. In the role of members of 1717 he was said to have executed 'Ane piece of landscape to be done in propper colours'.
**Bibl:** Apted 47; Edin Univ Library, Laing MSS, IV, 26.

**HOGG, William A** **fl 1923-1953**
Hamilton engraver and sculptor; etching, plaster figure subjects, birds. Served in the RN. Secretary, Hamilton Art Club for many years. Exhibited 'At Sea' at the RSA in 1932, a portrait of 'A D J Wotherspoon RSA' 1953; also GI(7) & Hamilton AC 1923-1940, from Abbotsford, 40 Scott Street.

**HOGUET, Charles** **1821-1870**
Oil painter of landscapes who worked for a time in Edinburgh; exhibited RSA(2). Living in Berlin 1869 from where he sent to the RSA 'A View of Capri' but the following year was living in Edinburgh and exhibited 'After the Storm', also a coastal painting, at the GI 1863.

**HOLDER, Rayner** **fl 1938-1987**
Painter and engraver; portraits and military subjects. During WW2 was associated with the Royal Artillery, exhibiting several paintings depicting their action in wartime. Exhibited RSA(5) from 110 Lauriston Place, Edinburgh, later moving to Rowans, Methlick, Aberdeenshire from where he exhibited a number of times at the AAS.

**HOLE, Mrs** **fl 1867**
Edinburgh wildlife painter in oil; exhibited RSA(1).

**HOLE, Dora** **fl 1913-1935**
Amateur Edinburgh painter who exhibited at the RSA(4). Possibly daughter of William H(qv). Her portrait of 'William Brassey Hole' is in the SNPG.

**HOLE, William Brassey RSA RSW RE** **1846-1917**
Born Salisbury, 7 Nov; died Inverleith Terrace, Edinburgh 22 Oct. Painter and etcher of landscapes and genre; occasional sculptor and stained glass window designer. Educated Edinburgh Academy and Edinburgh University. First became a civil engineer but changed to professional art, studying at the Trustees School and RSA life class. As his career progressed he turned more to mural decorations and became known for his reproduced etchings. Awarded the RSA's Stuart prize 1870 for 'Night to be remembered - it is the sacrifice of the Lord's passover...' Professor Stevenson wrote of his etchings 'he succeeds best with the romanticists; for, like them, he never misses the aspect and the style of the subject, whether in any particular case he may or may not bestow attention upon the drawing of detail and the fineness of treatment. His large plate 'The jumping horse', after Constable, is perhaps the finest rendering ever given of any picture. No copiers could be freer with his brush than Mr Hole with his needle, or could render, at the same time, with a closer fidelity the character of Constable's tangled variety of execution'. Hole himself was especially delighted to meet Whistler in Paris and to be invited by the great artist to etch Whistler's self-portrait. As a man he had a remarkable sense of fun - his wife once said her husband was the youngest person she knew. A simple, religious man without delight in intellectual or moral subtleties, evasions or duplicities. He was greatly loved and very sadly missed. Responsible for many of the etchings appearing in W E Henley's memorial catalogue of the French and Dutch loan collection in the Edinburgh exhibition (Meadowes) of 1886 and for designing the mural decorations in the central hall of the SNPG. The Dutch loan collection contains some of the finest work of Millet, Corot, Diaz, Rousseau, Troyon, Monticelli as well as members of the Dutch school. His method was not normal etching, his much larger plates included works after Millet, Matthew Maris and Velasquez, described by a contemporary critic as 'perhaps the most wonderful translations of colour and handling, of design and conception in spirit into another artist medium ever made, and entitle their author to rank with creative artists of the highest class'. In the execution of original paintings, to which he returned towards the end of his career, he was particularly fond of episodes from Scottish history including Covenanting times and the 1745 rebellion. Among his murals are a series of historical scenes in Edinburgh City Chambers (1903-9), a painting of 'The Historical Cycle' now in the Central Hall, SNPG (1897-1901), a lettered frieze of the Te Deum on St James' Church, Inverleith Row (c1892-1902), a memorial fountain in Inverleith Park (1900) and a stained glass window, 'Christ the Light of the World', in the chapel of St Colm's College. Elected ARSA 1878, RSA 1889, RE 1885, RSW 1885. His watercolours were classical scenes occasionally of the north-west Highlands and around Edinburgh. Illustrated *A Widow in Thrums* (Barrie, 1892), *The Heart of Midlothian* (1893); Barrie's *The Little Minister* (1893), Barrie's *Auld Licht Idylls* (1895), *Kidnapped* (1895), *Catriona* (1895), *Beside the Bonnie Brier Bush* (1896), *The Poetry of Robert Burns* (1896) and *The Master of Ballintrae* (1897). Contributed to *The Quiver* (1882). Exhibited RA(16), RSA(111), RSW(11), RE(52), GI(23), RHA(1) & AAS. Represented in NGS, Glasgow AG.
**Bibl:** Armstrong 89; Caw 268-9; Gifford 178,284,571,575,579; Halsby 263; Hole, Memories of William Hole, 1920; Houfe; Irwin 410; R E D Sketchley, English Book Illustrations, 1903, 92, 151; Who Was Who 1916-1928.

**HOLIDAY, Henry** **1839-1927**
Stained glass window designer. Deserves greater recognition than he has hitherto received. Edinburgh has several fine examples including three lights depicting the Ascension in Holy Trinity, Dean Bridge (1899-1901), St Cuthbert (Episcopal) Church (1900), two in Fettes Chapel (1893) and two in 42, Colinton Rd ('Oberon and Titania' and 'Science, Art and Charity', 1902). There is a fine group of three panels in St David's (Episcopal), Granton (c1910).
**Bibl:** Gifford 45,387,501,574,601.

**HOLLOWAY, John M** **fl 1970**
Aberdeen painter; exhibited AAS(1) from 66 Kildrummy Rd.

**HOLME, Douglas L** **fl 1944**
Painter based in Joppa, Edinburgh; exhibited 'Delphiniums and Sunflowers' at the RSA.

**HOLMES, Miss E** **fl 1926**
Glasgow amateur painter; exhibited GI(1) from 40 Westbourne Gardens.

**HOLMES, John** **fl 1890-1928**
Glasgow figurative and portrait sculptor; exhibited GI(12), latterly from 81 Shamrock Street.

**HOLMES, John** **fl 1973**
An Edinburgh based painter who exhibited 2 landscapes at the RSA from Blantyre Terrace.

**HOLMES, John H** **fl 1888**
Glasgow sculptor; exhibited a portrait bust at the GI from 63 Sandyfauld Street.

**HOLMES, Marcus Henry** **fl 1896-1910**
Aberdeen painter of landscape, generally local scenes but also

sometimes of the Channel Islands. Exhibited during the above years at the AAS from 11 Bon-Accord Crescent.

**HOLMES, William Kersley** **fl 1943-1949**
Glasgow landscape watercolourist. Exhibited GI(5), from 17 Stanhope St.

**HOLMS, Alexander Campbell RSW** **1862-1898**
Paisley based painter in oil and watercolour and illustrator. Flowers, figurative works and religious subjects. Studied Glasgow School of Art and in Paris. Illustrated the poems of Rossetti, Spencer and Tennyson. Elected RSW 1893. Lived at Sandyford. Exhibited RSW, GI(10) & AAS. Represented in Paisley AG.
**Bibl:** Halsby 263.

**HOLMS, Miss Elfrida** **fl 1916-1926**
Glasgow-based landscape watercolour artist. Exhibited GI(2) from 38 Sardinia Terrace, Hillhead.

**HOLMS, Janette** **fl 1979-1980**
Exhibited AAS. Address unrecorded.

**HOLMS, Miss Lisette H D** **fl 1884-1888**
Glasgow artist; figure studies and literary subjects. Exhibited GI(6) from Hope Park, Partick.

**HOLT, Edmund (Ned)** **fl 1860-d1892**
Caricaturist and figure painter in the Crombie and Kay tradition. Painted characters of Edinburgh in watercolour. Little of his work survives although an album of 49 sketches is in Edinburgh Central Library.
**Bibl:** Halsby 263.

**HOLT, Gwynneth Cobden (Mrs Huxley Jones)** **1909-**
Sculptress & woodcutter; worked in wood and teracotta, also carved in ivory. Based in Cults, Aberdeenshire. In later years moved to England, first to Chelmsford and then to Oxford. Exhibited portraits and figures RSA(12) in terracotta, bronze and oak, GI(7) & AAS(3).

**HOLT, W** **fl 1961-1965**
Aberdeen textile designer. Exhibited AAS from 13 Forest Rd.

**HOMAN W Maclean** **fl 1918-1932**
Painter in oil of domestic, ecclesiastical and pastoral scenes. Exhibited RSA(8), L(3) & GI(3) formerly from Glasgow and in 1932 from Winchelsea, Sussex.

**HOME, Bruce James** **1830-1912**
Topographical Edinburgh artist. Studied Trustees Academy under R S Lauder(qv). Curator of the Outlook Tower and first Curator of Edinburgh City Municipal Museums. Painted pen and wash views of Edinburgh streets and courts. His *Old Houses in Edinburgh,* 2 vols, 1905-1907, has been described as 'an outstanding contribution to the artistic interpretation of local topography' [Butchart]. Exhibited RSA(5) from 5 Upper Gray Street, Edinburgh.
**Bibl:** Butchart 78; Halsby 263.

**HOME, David** **fl 1870-1879**
Edinburgh painter in oil but more frequently watercolour; topographical scenes, landscape and occasional buildings and still life. Exhibited RSA(8) & GI(11), latterly from 22 Oxford St.

**HOME, Mrs Evelyne Milne** **fl 1939**
Dumfries-shire amateur watercolour painter; exhibited RSW(2) from Canonbie.

**HOME, Gordon** **fl 1952**
Roxburghshire watercolour painter. Exhibited a Maltese scene at the GI, from Lessudden House, St. Boswells.

**HOME, Jean Mary Milne** **fl 1917-1929**
Watercolourist. Related to Evelyne Milne H(qv). Exhibited RSW(2) from Paxton, Berwick-on-Tweed.

**HOME, Robert PSSA** **1865-?**
Born Edinburgh 29 Jan. Landscape and portrait painter, illuminator, stained glass artist and book decorator. Painted mainly local scenery. President, SSA 1915-17. Lived at Ceres, Fife. Enjoyed painting interiors, for example, 'The old cupboard and staircase - Duchess of Gordon's house, Castlehill, under demolition' RSA 1887. Exhibited RA(2), RSA(46), GI(10) & AAS.

**HONEYMAN, John RSA** **1831-1914**
Born Glasgow, 11 Aug; died Bridge of Allan, 8 Jan. Architect and landscape painter in oil and watercolour. After abandoning a career in the church became articled to Alexander Munro. Established his own practice in Glasgow 1854. Specialised in church architecture, being an authority on medieval architecture with an intimate knowledge of Gothic. Responsible, inter alia, for the Free High Church, Partick (1868), Barony North Church (14-20 Cathedral Sq, Glasgow - 1878), Free West Church, Perth (1869). In Edinburgh his design for St Michael's Parish Church, Slateford Rd (1881-3) has been much admired, also to a lesser extent his St Philip's, Portobello. Restored the cathedrals of Brechin and Iona. Entered into partnership with John Keppie(qv) 1889, being joined the same year as a draughtsman by C R Mackintosh(qv). When Honeyman retired Mackintosh replaced him as a partner. Elected ARSA 1892, RSA 1896. Exhibited RA(2) 'A view at Skipness, Argyllshire' 1879 and Architectural study of the church at North Merchiston, Edinburgh 1880, RSA(14) & GI(14 + many from his firm) - in addition to works exhibited in collaboration with Keppie and Macintosh.
**Bibl:** Colvin; Dunbar 143; Gifford 42,505,652,pl.39; A Gomme & D Walker, Architecture of Glasgow, London 1987(rev), 293 et al; Halsby 175.

**HONY, William** **fl 1857**
Edinburgh painter in oil of landscape. Exhibited 'Loch Ard' at the RSA in the above year.

**HOOD, Duncan Craig** **fl 1982-1985**
Aberdeen sculptor and ceramic designer. Exhibited AAS from 3 Duthie Terrace, Mannofield.

**HOOD, Ernest Burnett** **1932-1988**
Born Edinburgh; died Glasgow. Painter in both mediums of industrial landscapes and topographical scenes, occasional portraits, still life and scenes from opera; also aquatintist and lithographer. Educated in Glasgow. After being apprenticed to a lithographer studied Glasgow School of Art where he was befriended by William and Mary Armour(qv). Following a period on the staff of the Glasgow School of Art worked as full-time painter concentrating on Glasgow scenes, sometimes in the form of etchings. Keen member of Glasgow Art Club and life-long friend of Alexander Goudie(qv). Exhibited RSA(10) 1956-1972 & GI(122). Lived for many years at 75 Clouston St.

**HOOD, W Geddes** **fl 1915-1985**
Painter in watercolour and oil. Related to the Geddes family(qv) of artists. Exhibited RSA(3) & RSW(1), latterly from Damacre Road, Brechin.

**HOODLESS, William Henry** **1841-1902**
Edinburgh painter in oil of landscape, mostly scenes in Cumbria. Exhibited RSA(8).

**HOOGERWERF, A** **fl 1942-1944**
Dutch painter of seascapes and pastoral scenes. During WW2 he settled in Dowanhill, Glasgow 1943. From there he exhibited GI(3).

**HOOLE, Gerald S** **fl 1918**
Amateur sculptor; exhibited GI(1) from Mamby, Garelochhead.

**HOOPS, Mrs Mostyn** **fl 1931**
Aberdeen painter. Exhibited a picture 'Arab fisherman in the Gulf of Suez' at the AAS from 19 Wellbrae Terrace.

**HOPE, Alexander** **fl 1827**
Scottish portrait painter; exhibited an unknown sitter at the RSA in the above year.

**HOPE, Diana** **fl 1984**
Edinburgh painter. Wife of the architect John H(qv). Exhibited

'Green Plant for a Daughter' at the RSA in the above year from St Bernard's Crescent.

**HOPE, Mrs Harry** **fl 1919**
Dunbar amateur painter; exhibited RSA(1) from Barneyhill.

**HOPE, Jane** **1776-1829**
Little known amateur painter in watercolour. Taught privately by David Allan(qv). According to Halsby may have been the daughter of the 2nd Earl of Hopetoun. Married Henry Dundas, later Viscount Melville 1793. A second marriage was to Thomas, 1st Lord Wallace. Described by a contemporary as an elegant woman.
**Bibl:** Halsby 264.

**HOPE, M** **fl 1892**
Helensburgh based little known painter who exhibited 'Pasture lands, Picardy' at the RSA from Westlea.

**HOPE, Miss Mary** **fl 1878-1888**
Edinburgh painter in oil of portraits, figure subjects and flowers. Lived latterly at Bourmount, Dunbar. Exhibited RSA(17) & GI(5).

**HOPE, Robert RSA** **1869-1936**
Born Edinburgh; died Edinburgh 10 May. Painter in oil of figure subjects, portraits and landscapes and decorative work including murals. Began as a lithographic draughtsman. Later worked at designs for printers and book illustration. Studied Edinburgh School of Design where he was awarded the national gold medal, and RSA Life School 1893-95, obtaining prizes for drawing and painting, and a Chalmers bursary. Then studied at Julian's Academie in Paris. His diploma work was a figure subject 'Glints of gold'. His output was very varied. The first notable commissions were to paint the ballroom of Manderston House, and 'The Blue Blanket' in Edinburgh City Chambers - illustrating James III gift of a banner, the famous blue blanket, to the craftsmen of the city. Enjoyed painting historical scenes demonstrating his ardent love of border ballads, songs and romance. Member, Scottish Art Club. Painted 'Christ in Glory' for the apse of St Cuthbert's Church, Edinburgh and in 1921 executed an important work for the General Assembly of the Church of Scotland when addressed by Earl Haig - a picture requiring a great many portrait studies of current notables. 'Bonnie Kilmeny' was purchased by the King of Romania. A tender painter, of great vitality and feeling for beauty and form. Elected ARSA 1911, RSA 1925. Exhibited RA(1), RSA(153), RSW(7), GI(96), AAS & L(20). Represented in Glasgow AG, Kirkcaldy AG, Paisley AG, Perth AG.
**Bibl:** Caw, 432; Gifford 275; Studio XLII, 63; L, 233; LVII, 54, 57; LXXIII, 74; 1909, 82, 84; Who's Who.

**HOPE-STEWART, James** **1830-1881**
Born Edinburgh and died Edinburgh. Studied in Italy. Reputedly worked from York but painted mainly Scottish landscape and portraits.

**HOPKINSON, Mary Barbara** **fl 1908**
Aberdeen painter of still life and fruit. Exhibited AAS(1) from Firbank.

**HORDON, J W** **fl 1854-1855**
Minor Edinburgh portrait painter. Exhibited RSA(2) in the above period.

**HORN, C Norrie** **fl 1926**
Aberdeen portrait painter. Exhibited AAS(2) from 41 Bedford Place.

**HORNE, Barbara** **fl 1938-1940**
Edinburgh-based watercolour painter. Exhibited RSA(2) & RSW(2) from 1 Westhall Gardens.

**HORNE, Miss Susan G** **fl 1912**
Aberdeen artist who exhibited a scene on the Deveron at the AAS from 41 Carden Place.

**HORNE, W D** **fl 1866-1870**
Glasgow painter in oil of still life, flowers and landscape especially in the Callander area; exhibited RSA(1) & GI(4), from 435 St. Vincent St.

**HORNEL, Edward Atkinson** **1864-1933**
Born Bacchus Marsh, Victoria, Australia, 11 Jly; died Kirkcudbright, 30 Jne. Both his parents were Scottish and he came to Britain at the age of two, settling with his parents in Kirkcudbright. Studied at the Trustees Academy, Edinburgh 1880-1883 and at the Academy in Antwerp in the company of W S MacGeorge(qv) under Verlat 1883-85. At the Academy, Edinburgh, with James Pryde(qv) and D Y Cameron(qv) among his contemporaries, his classmates included Denholm Armour(qv) and the Greenock artist Peter Kerr(qv). Whilst still a student he painted a little woodland scene, handled with some freedom and already showing an emphasis on two-dimensional pattern, which still exists. Member of the Glasgow School(qv). In 1883 'A View of Kirkcudbright', painted the previous year, appeared in the RSA. His work in Belgium confirmed his development in a broad landscape style, showing the influence of Jacob Maris and Anton Mauve. In 1885 met George Henry(qv) and formed a friendship which was to influence both of them for the rest of their lives. The two shared a studio in Glasgow and painted alongside one another at Kirkcudbright for several years before travelling to Japan together 1893-4. They developed a highly original style which concentrated on flat colour pattern detracting from any emphasis upon the subject. A rich impasto, low-key palette was the result and with minor variations remained his distinctive style making the paintings instantly recognisable. An early example of the mature style, before the arrival of the Japanese paintings with their expressionistic rhythms and powerful colouring, is 'The Dance of Spring'. Hardie finds a marked similarity between Hornel's curious, grotesque, 'The Brownie of Blednoch' 1899 and the Belgium expressionist James Ensor's early work. The Japanese paintings of 1893-4 are generally regarded as the artist's apotheosis. After his return we find an uncertain self-consciousness and the early signs of mannerism which detracted so much from his later work. 'The little girls become increasingly coy and well-behaved, the palette sweeter, the composition mechanical, and the figures static...yet (his) remarkable sense of colour rescued many of his later paintings from banality' [Hardie]. He enjoyed travel, visiting Ceylon 1907, Burmah and Japan again 1922. He continues to be an intensely popular Scottish artist and for many collectors it is a social cachet to possess a Hornel. Elected ROI 1904, having declined ARSA 1901; member, Society of 25 Artists(qv). Exhibited RSA, RA, RSW, ROI, GI(103), AAS & L(43). Represented in his own memorial gallery (Kirkcudbright), Aberdeen AG, Dundee AG, Glasgow AG, Paisley AG, Perth AG, Edinburgh AG, Kilmarnock AG, Kirkcaldy AG, Kirkcudbright AG, Bradford AG, Brighouse AG, Bury AG, Ghent AG, Huddersfield AG, Leeds AG, Liverpool AG, Manchester AG, Rochdale AG, Adelaide AG, St Louis AG, Buffalo AG, Toronto AG.
**Bibl:** AJ 1894, 76,78; 1898, 69; 1905, 352; 1906, 383; 1909, 95; Caw 400-403; Conn, 1911, 216; 1913, 111; Halsby 131, 143, 150, 159, 173; Hardie, Scottish Art Review, Vol XI, Nos 3 & 4 1968; Hardie, Cat of Glasgow Boys Exhibition 1968; Irwin 386-8 et al (illus); Martin 30ff; RA Pictures 1910-15; Studio, see Index 1901-14; Bill Smith, E A Hornel, Atelier, 1997.

**HORNER, Margaret F** **fl 1954-1970**
Painter in oil of portraits and rural scenes. Lived at Hamilton before moving to East Kilbride. Exhibited RSA(14) 1955-68 & GI(29), after 1964 from 30 New Plymouth, East Kilbride.

**HOROBIN, Peter** **fl 1967-1968**
Dundee artist. Exhibited GI(1) & AAS(2) from 37 Union St.

**HORSBURGH, A Moncrieff** **fl 1926-1929**
Glasgow sculptor; bronze and plaster. Animals, especially dogs, and figurative works. Exhibited GI(7) in 1929 from 8 Grove Pk St.

**HORSBURGH, Edith M** **fl 1900**
Fife painter of flower studies. Exhibited RSA(1) from Aberdour House, Aberdour.

**HORSBURGH, John** **1791-1869**
Born Prestonpans, 16 Nov; died Edinburgh, 23 Sep. Edinburgh engraver and etcher; minister of the original Baptist church in Edinburgh for thirty-seven years. Studied Trustees Academy having studied since the age of 14 under Robert Scott(qv), living with him for several years before establishing himself as a landscape engraver in Edinburgh, at first from 5 Archibald Place and later 18 Buccleuch

Place. Founder member of the Academy 1826. Among his best known works are a portrait 'Mackay, the actor, as Baillie Nicol Jarvie', after Sir William Allan, two portraits of 'Sir Walter Scott', one after Sir Henry Raeburn and the other after Sir Thomas Lawrence - the latter being published in the *AJ* 1858. Other important works include 'Prince Charles reading a Despatch' after Simson and a portrait of 'Burns', after Taylor, engraved for the Royal Scottish Association. Also engraved several plates including vignettes for the Waverley Novels and etched several plates in outline illustrating the life of Robert Bruce. Represented by 8 engravings in the City of Edinburgh collection.
**Bibl:** Bryan; Brydall 213; Bushnell; J C Guy, 'Edinburgh Engravers' The Book of the Old Edinburgh Club, vol 9, Edinburgh 1916; Thieme Becker.

**HORSBURGH, John** **fl 1878-1890**
Studio photographer and engraver. From his premises at 131 Princes Street he produced life-sized portraits finished in oil. Important figure in the development of Scottish studio photography. Foundation Associate Engraver of the Scottish Academy in 1826 but was one of the nine who withdrew after the first meeting. Represented in the SNPG by a portrait of the botanist 'John Hutton Balfour' (1808-1884), signed and dated 1878.

**HORSBURGH, Victor D** **c1860-c1935**
Architect. Savage records that he witnessed Lorimer's indenture at Wardrop, Anderson and Browne's in 1884. Won silver medal 1907. Member, advisory committee on the Town Planning and Housing supplement of the *Architectural Review* with Lorimer, Ashbee Crane and Macartney, 1910. Drew perspectives for Robert Lorimer(qv), a former colleague at Rowand Anderson's(qv), and may have shared premises in Edinburgh with Frank Deas(qv). Collaborated with Lorimer in providing the working drawings for a wooden house at Mandal, Norway, built for the Edinburgh shipping family Salvesen, and another at Brackenburgh, Cumberland. Migrated from Edinburgh to Toronto c1910 and remained there for the rest of his life. In the 1900s exhibited RSA(5); thereafter his work was confined to his Canadian designs the most important of which was a branch building for the Canadian Bank of Commerce, St Catherine Street, Montreal.
**Bibl:** Colvin; Gifford 297; Peter Savage, Lorimer and the Edinburgh Craft Designers, Edinburgh 1980, 26,45,51,165.

**HORSFALL, W B** **fl 1949**
Glasgow artist; exhibited 'The Slipway, Rutherglen' at the GI, from 39 County Ave, Cambuslang.

**HORSMAN, Miss Kathleen F ARCA** **fl 1948-1959**
Born London. A watercolour painter of landscape and topographical subjects. Settled in Scotland joining the staff of the Edinburgh College of Art. Studied Hornsey School of Art and the Royal College of Art. Exhibited RSA(12) 1948-1957, AAS, GI(4), SSA & SSWA, from 29 George Square.

**HOSACK, Isobel (Mrs G D Grant-Suttie)** **fl 1922-1935**
Sculptress. Member of a well known Scottish family. Worked in Crieff until the early 1930s when following her marriage she moved to Goring-on-Thames, Berkshire. Exhibited RA(1), RSA(1) and GI(1).

**HOSIE, David** **1962-**
Born Glasgow. Figurative painter. Trained Edinburgh College of Art 1980-85. Won Richard Ford Award (RA) 1985, Hutchison Award and Andrew Grant Award (RSA) 1986. In the tradition of Max Beckmann and Otto Dix, his paintings are symbolic, representing a congruence of associations and significance. Exhibits RSA & RGI.
**Bibl:** John Russell Taylor *in* Jill George Gallery Catalogue, London 1992.

**HOSIE, George J G** **fl 1964-1976**
Glasgow painter and engraver. Worked in aquatint, oil, chalk and linocut. Landscape, still life and flower studies. Exhibited GI(12), from 36 Kirkburn Ave, Cambuslang.

**HOSKYNS, Miss G** **fl 1918**
Minor Morayshire painter who exhibited at the SWA(2) from Nairn.

**HOSPITALFIELD SCHOOL OF ART**
[see ALLAN-FRASER, Patrick]

**HOSSACK, Alexander J** **fl 1954-1974**
Edinburgh painter in oil and occasional watercolour; landscape, flower pieces and coastal scenes. Married Anna H(qv). Exhibited RSA(22) & GI(7) from 4 Barony Terrace, Corstorphine.

**HOSSACK, Mrs Anna** **fl 1955-1964**
Edinburgh painter in both mediums of still life, landscape and figurative compositions. Married Alexander H(qv). Exhibited RSA(4) & GI(5) between the above years.

**HOSSACK, Ethel C** **fl 1893**
Banff flower painter. Exhibited AAS from St Catherine's.

**HOSSACK, James Wright** **1895-?**
Born Edinburgh, 20 Nov. Landscape, coastal and figure painter in oil. Studied Camberwell School of Arts and Crafts. Exhibited 1920-1931 RA(5) & L(2) from 18 Hall Road, Newlands, London.

**HOTCHKIS, Miss Anna Mary** **1885-1984**
Painter in oil, watercolour and pastel; also woodcut artist, figures and landscape. Sister of Isobel H(qv). Encouraged by her mother, herself an amateur watercolour painter, in spite of delicate health she enrolled at Glasgow School of Art 1906-1907, then studied in Munich with Hans Lasker and Edinburgh College of Art under Robert Burns(qv) 1907-1910. Opened a studio in Edinburgh and travelled widely to China and North America as well as around Europe. Went back to China with her friend the painter Mary Mulliken on a sketching tour 1922, remaining there to take up a teaching post at Yen Ching University, Peking 1922-24, and stayed in the country until 1937. As a result of her experience there she and Mulliken published *Buddhist Sculptures at the Yin Kang Caves* Henry Vetch, Peiping 1935 and *The Nine Sacred Mountains of China: An Illustrated Record of Pilgrimages Made in the Years 1935-1936,* Vetch & Lee, Hong Kong 1973. Active member, Glasgow Society of Lady Artists. Associated with the Green Gate Close coterie in Kirkcudbright where she rented a studio from Jessie King(qv). Through her early studying of landscape painting with E A Taylor(qv) in the 1920s, and visits in the 1940s, she settled in Kirkcudbright permanently. Published a number of works on Chinese art. In addition to works at the RSA(28), RSW(10), GI(38) & L(1), she also exhibited Los Angeles & Hong Kong. Represented in Castle Douglas AG.
**Bibl:** Halsby 220,264.

**HOTCHKIS, Miss Isobel** **1897-1947**
Born Crookston, nr Glasgow. Painter in oil and watercolour of portraits and landscape. Sister of Anna Mary H(qv). Studied Glasgow School of Art under Jean Delville(qv) and in Munich with her sister under Hans Lasker. Early in her career she visited South Africa and on her return lived for a time in Liverpool before settling in Edinburgh. Painted mainly portraits in oil until c1920 when, due to ill-health, she increasingly turned to watercolours. Exhibited RSA(10), RSW(15), GI(11) & L(7), after 1935 from Shamba, Twynholm, Kirkcudbrightshire.
**Bibl:** Halsby 264.

**HOUGHTON, George OBE** **1905-1993**
Born Perth. Illustrator, watercolourist, cartoonist & writer; also journalist having been a foreign correspondent with the *Daily Mail* based in Paris and later in Spain during the Civil War. Studied at Ecole des Beaux Arts, Paris and worked for some years in France and Spain. Best known for his humorous golf books of which he has written and illustrated over forty with sales over two million. Author of *Parade of Violence* (being the story of a Legionnaire and escaped criminal whom he had befriended) and *They flew through Sand* (his experiences as a group captain on the staff of Lord Tedder in North Africa during WW2). Introduced to golf as a young man by the famous old Scottish pro Joe Anderson. His *Golf Addicts Cartoon Calendar* has appeared annually without a break since 1952. Awarded OBE. Since 1975 concentrated mostly on painting the golf courses and scenery of Scotland in watercolour. Lived at Coneygar House, Bridport, Dorset.

**HOUGHTON, Laurence** **fl 1942**
Perthshire portrait painter. Exhibited the portraits of two servicemen,

both members of the RAOC, one in pencil, at the GI, from Altamont, Aberfoyle.

**HOUSMAN, James** **fl 1682**
All that is known of this painter is that in 1682 he painted a work for Lord Moray the account being dated Jan 24, 1683. Apted points out that this may refer to Jacob Hysman.
**Bibl:** Apted 48; SNPG Artist's File, quoting Darnaway MSS, 1955.

**HOUSTON, Charles** **fl 1881-1936**
Glasgow oil and watercolour painter of landscape and occasional flower studies who lived latterly at Rutherglen. Brother of John Rennie McKenzie H(qv). 'A Crofter's Pet Lamb' (1886) received very favourable reviews. Exhibited RSA(10), RSW(5) & GI(58).
**Bibl:** Halsby 264.

**HOUSTON, George RSA RSW RI** **1869-1947**
Born Dalry, Ayrshire, 20 Feb; died Dalry, 5 Oct. Painter in oil and watercolour, landscapes, especially Argyll, Loch Awe and Loch Fyne; also etcher. Served his time as a lithographic artist in Glasgow, subsequently illustrator with the *Glasgow Citizen.* Widely travelled, visiting Japan 1911. Prolific painter in both oil and watercolour with a simple direct vision. His finest work has a unity - visual, technical and emotional - which, in the words of his obituary, 'places it among the finest landscapes produced in Scotland'. Enjoyed wide expanses of loch or moorland painted against a backcloth of distant hills. Employed a bright palette in which strong blues, greens and yellows were dominant, and was notably successful in his depiction of snow. Member, London Society of 25. Elected ARSA 1900, RSW 1908, RI 1920, RSA 1925. Exhibited in Australia, Canada, New Zealand, Europe and the USA as well as RSA(70), RSW(11), GI(122), AAS, RI(3) & L(16). Represented in Glasgow AG(9), Greenock AG, Lillie AG(Milngavie), Perth AG.
**Bibl:** Caw 389-90; Halsby 225-6, 624; Ewan Robson, George Houston, Atelier, 1997.

**HOUSTON, John OBE RSA RSW RGI SSA** **1930-**
Born Buckhaven, Fife. Painter in oil and watercolour. Educated Buckhaven HS and Edinburgh College of Art 1948-54. Married Elizabeth Blackadder(qv). His early work was much influenced by Munch and also, to a lesser extent, by Morandi and Sironi in Italy when he travelled in that country on a travelling scholarship 1953-54. Returning to Edinburgh he joined the staff of Edinburgh College of Art becoming Deputy Head, School of Drawing & Painting 1982-89. OBE 1990. Travelled widely, in 1957 was instrumental in launching the 57 Gallery, Edinburgh and held his first one-man show there the following year. Elected ARSA 1964, RSA 1972, he won the Guthrie Award in 1964 and the Cargill prize at the GI in 1965. In 1969 visited the Museum of Fine Art and the Johnston Foundation, Racine, USA. Powerful colourist, evoking the moods of light and weather over expanses of sky and water. Lives at 57 Fountainhall Road, Edinburgh. Regular exhibitor RSA, RSW & GI(12). Represented in NGS, SNGMA, Aberdeen AG, Glasgow AG, Kirkcaldy AG, Perth AG, Lillie AG (Milngavie), Gracefield Centre, Dumfries, Liverpool AG, Abbot Hall AG (Kendal), Bradford AG, Portsmouth AG, RSA. Not to be confused with John Houston of Troon.
**Bibl:** Cardiff, Oriel 31, 'The Scottish Show', (Ex Cat 1988, Text by James Holloway & Duncan Macmillan); Gage 45, 144; Hartley 136-7; SAC, Edinburgh 'Ten 30. The work of ten Edinburgh artists 1945-75', (Ex Cat 1975); Roger Billcliffe, John Houston, Ex Cat, Oct 1996; Macmillan 2001, 105,110,112-3,115,129,133,187, illus 121,122.

**HOUSTON, John Adam Plimmer RSA RI** **1812-1884**
Born Gwydyr Castle, Wales, 25 Dec; died London, 2 Dec. Born of a Scottish family. Painter of historical scenes, narrative works and genre. Came north as a schoolboy, being educated in Dalkeith. His father was a small manufacturer in Renfrewshire, his mother distantly related to the Nasmyth family. In his third year at the RSA school won the drawing prize and in 1836 exhibited his first picture 'Don Quixote in his Study' at the British Institute. This was followed by 'French goatherds' in 1838. In 1841 moved to Edinburgh, having already travelled extensively in France, Germany and Italy. Began exhibiting RSA from 1833 and in 1841 'The watchfire: soldiers of Cromwell disputing on the Scriptures' was purchased by the Association for the Promotion of Fine Arts in Scotland. In 1844 went to Paris and in 1855 travelled, for health reasons, to Pisa, followed by visits to Florence and Sienna the next year. In 1857 he spent the summer and autumn in the Highlands before chest problems persuaded him to move to London in 1858. In the 1850s he moved towards a pre-Raphaelite style, having studied for a time with Waller Hugh Paton(qv). His watercolours, often of wild Highland landscapes, are 'well-composed, warm and luminous, and more modern in character than the rest of his work...He possesses refined and poetic feeling, his manner of painting is decisive yet delicate, and his colouring brilliant, harmonious, and quietly effective. His aim has been to do well rather than much' [James Dafforne in *AJ*]. Although his early, romantically treated historical pictures have received the most attention it is his brilliantly handled watercolours that are now best regarded. Sometimes painted single figures, often young ladies standing in mountainous landscapes. Elected ARI 1874, RI 1879, ROI 1883, ARSA 1842, RSA 1845. Exhibited RA(45) 1841-1877, RSA(221) 1833-1885, ROI(4), RI(17), GI(17), AAS & RBA(3). Lived at 10 Upper Phillimore Place, London W. Represented in NGS, Ashmolean (Oxford), Glasgow AG, Maidstone AG.
**Bibl:** AJ 1869, 69-71; Armstrong 43; Bryan; Brydall 422-3; Caw 119 et al; Halsby 102-4 et al; McKay 355; Portfolio 1887, 136; The Year's Art 1885, 229.

**HOUSTON, John Rennie McKenzie RSW** **fl 1856-1932**
Born Glasgow. Painter in oil and some watercolour of figurative subjects and interiors. Received his early art training in Glasgow, exhibiting mainly in Scotland. Worked mainly in watercolours, influenced by the Dutch school. Preferring rich colours, wet washes and subjects set in their historical context, his work was largely derivative. Lived Rutherglen before retiring to Edinburgh c1930. Elected RSW 1889. Exhibited RSA(3), RSW(36), AAS & GI(45) from 10 Rosslyn Avenue, Rutherglen.

**HOUSTON, Lilias** **c1920-1978**
Died Glasgow, Jan. Painted crowd scenes and landscapes, especially the wild fastnesses of Wester Ross and more urban continental scenes, also occasional figurative works. Had a solo exhibition at Lillie AG, Milngavie 1976. Exhibited RSA(4) & GI(7) 1970-77. Represented Lillie AG (Milngavie).

**HOUSTON, Nettie** **fl 1970-**
One time art teacher at Kircudbright Academy where she exerted a strong influence among her pupils. Participated in the exhibition 'Artists in Kirkcudbright' in Edinburgh.

**HOUSTON, Peter Denniston** **fl 1933-1936**
Painter in oil of landscapes. Exhibited a scene in Majorca and a view of Barcelona at the RSA & GI(2), from 38 Burnside Road, Rutherglen.

**HOUSTON, R Falconer** **fl 1955**
Paisley etcher. Townscapes. Exhibited GI(1), from 4 High St, Castlehead.

**HOUSTON, Robert RSW** **1891-1942**
Born Kilbirnie, Ayrshire, 5 Jne; died Glasgow. Painter in oil and watercolour of landscapes, mainly coastal scenery and lochans, and figurative subjects, also aquatintist. Studied Glasgow School of Art where he was a contemporary of Gordon Thomas(qv). Painted in a strong style, mainly landscapes of the west coast and the western isles. Also executed railway posters for which his strong sense of design and use of solid colour was ideally suited. Elected RSW 1936. Exhibited RA(6), RSA(8), RSW(11), GI(34) & L(7). Represented Glasgow AG.
**Bibl:** Halsby 227, 264.

**HOUSTON, Miss Valerie** **fl 1967-1969**
Troon watercolour landscapist. Daughter of John Houston of Troon(qv). Exhibited GI(2), latterly from 29 Scargie Rd, Caprington Estate, Kilmauns.

**HOUY, William** **fl 1878-1883**
Kelso painter in oil of landscape; exhibited a harbour scene at the RSA in 1883.

**HOW, Archibald** **?-1734**
Early painter. Son of John How of Syde. In 1704 apprenticed to Joseph Borch (or Beech) and in 1722 elected painter burgess of

Edinburgh. From 1722-33 member of the Incorporation of St Mary's. Nothing is now known of his work.

**HOW, Miss Francis Thalia** **fl 1889-1928**
Edinburgh based painter in oil; enamellist. Exhibited SWA(1) from 23 Melville Street, before moving to London. Thereafter exhibited RSA, 1912, 1915 and 1928 all from London, one a landscape and the others champlevé enamels.

**HOW, Miss Julia Beatrice** **1867-1932**
Born Bideford, N. Devon 16 Oct; died Hoddesdon, Herts 19 Aug. Figure and occasional still life painter in oil and pastel, also pencil. Member of a notable family of silversmiths, the Hows of Edinburgh. Although of Scottish descent and regarded in Scotland as a Scottish painter (her retrospective exhibition was sub-titled 'A Scottish painter in Paris'), she shared her training and residency between France and England. After her parents died she moved to Bournemouth and in about 1890 entered the Herkomer School of Art, Bushey. Moved to Paris to continue studies at the Academie Delacluse c1893. Came to know Rodin and the painters Albert Besnard and Lucien Simon. Although not formally a member of the 'Intimiste' group, alongside Bonnard and Vuillard, she was fully aware of and influenced by them and their approach. Her early work, mostly portraiture executed at her studio in Étaples, was sombre in tone. Her palette gradually brightened with a change in subject to female nudes, babies and still life. Best remembered for her sensitive portrayal of mothers and young children achieved in an intimate, unobtrusive manner. Her finest work was in pastel, using bright colours and with the broken surface adding to the feeling of lightness and vitality. "Her innate modesty and refusal to impose her own views on others stood in the way of her obtaining recognition in England, where she was convinced that her delicate, elusive work would not please. But in France she found...that discerning appreciation of her fragile transparent technique and masterly handling of luminous gradations of colour in the lowest tones that made such eminent critics as M. Arsène Alexandre say of her 'une de plus originelles artistes femmes de notre temps, et de plus penetrantes'" [The Times]. Exhibited regularly at the Paris Salon from 1902 and held several solo exhibitions in Paris, also GI & in the States. Represented in Tate, V & A, Musée du Luxembourg.
**Bibl:** Fine Art Society 'Beatrice How', (Ex Cat 1979-80); Times (obit), 22/8/1932.

**HOWARD, Henry** **fl 1854**
Exhibited a work entitled 'Willie brewed a peck o'malt' at the RSA.

**HOWARD, Ian RSA** **1952-**
Born Aberdeen. Painter in acrylic, mixed media on wood/canvas; also printmaker. Trained at Edinburgh University 1970-75 where he obtained an hons degree in Fine Art, and Edinburgh College of Art. Awarded a travelling scholarship 1976 enabling him to visit Italy. The following year appointed to the staff, Gray's School of Art, Aberdeen. In 1978 won the Guthrie Award and in 1979 a major SAC Award. In the 1985 Scottish Open Drawing Competition he won 1st Prize. Currently head of painting, Duncan of Jordanstone College of Art. Exhibits extensively at home and abroad including the RSA & AAS. Elected RSA 1998. '(His) imagery has always been abstruse, many-layered, allusive...with an obsessive interest in the archetypal and historic which has now expanded to include a kind of heraldic grandeur' [Beaumont]. Represented in Dundee AG, Aberdeen AG, Paisley AG, Clare College, Cambridge, Hunterian Museum (Glasgow). Lives at 66 Camphill Road, Broughty Ferry.
**Bibl:** Ex Cat, Fine Art Society, Sept 1991 (text by Mary Rose Beaumont).

**HOWARD, William C** **fl 1891-1909**
Wardie oil painter of portraits, figurative subjects and landscape. Exhibited RSA(13). Represented in Kirkcaldy AG.

**HOWDEN, Marion (May Aitken)** **fl 1902-1928**
Edinburgh based painter and sculptress of portraits and still life. Exhibited RSA(5), RI(1) & GI(1) from 10 Ettrick Road and latterly 10 Moray Place.

**HOWE, James** **1780-1836**
Born Skirling, Peebles-shire 31 Aug; died Newhaven, 11 Jly. Painter in oil and pencil; animals especially horses, also portraits. Second of four sons of the minister of Skirling. Excited by horses at a very early age, stimulated by the four fairs held in his own village every year. The local schoolmaster, Robert Davidson, was known in the district for his hand-writing and for the vignettes of flowers and animals that he used to illustrate his letters. Probably copying these, the young man illustrated his father's sermons. His first known work is of a boy on a pony, now in Biggar Museum. Went to Edinburgh in April 1795 to join his elder brother and became apprenticed to the Nories(qv). After painting a panorama for a Mr Marshall, he set up on his own as a portrait painter. In 1806 he was commissioned by the Earl of Buchan(qv) to paint portraits of centenarians in the belief that these were worth recording for socio-medical reasons. The Earl, who had been trained at the Foulis Academy in Glasgow, advised the young artist to travel to London. This he did in 1806 but he returned somewhat disillusioned the following year. Nevertheless he became interested in the Society of Artists founded in 1808 and their first exhibition included two of his works. In 1811 he showed 5 pictures, one a portrait of different breeds of cattle commissioned by Sir John Sinclair, another work 'Interior of a Stable', was purchased by the Earl of Buchan, having been likened by a contemporary critic to the work of George Morland. In 1812 he exhibited 2 works, 'The Colonel on the Spanish Horse' and 'Portrait of a Gamekeeper, Peter Anderson'. In 1815 he visited the battlefield of Waterloo, possibly with his pupil William Kidd(qv) and Alexander Carse(qv). This resulted in his first major achievement, a panoramic outline of the battle, described as 'this grand panoramic painting...it fixed on the moment in the battle when Napoleon was throwing the remnants of his forces against Wellington's infantry, with the Prussians in the distance advancing to help'. Two other related works were exhibited, 'The Battle of Waterloo' was shown in the British Institution in London 1816 and 'The Scots Greys in bivouac before the Battle of Waterloo' is now in the Scots Greys room of the United Services Museum, Edinburgh. There followed a series of important illustrations for various books. In 1824 14 of his drawings were published as engravings with the title *The Life of the Horse.* In 1829, collaborating with the engraver W H Lizars, Howe produced *Breeds of Domestic Animals,* which remains a classic. In 1834 Charles Turner mezzotinted 'Hawking', an outstanding work showing Mr Flemming of Barochan Castle, with John Anderson, one of the last of the old Scottish falconers and William Harvie the artist and falconer. In 1832 he published *Portraits of horses and prize cattle.* As a man he was improvident, irresolute and unstable, saved by his friends and patrons. His biographer suggests that he had two styles. 'The earlier, and the one clients expected in a portrait painter, was careful and professionally competent bringing out the character and distinguishing features of the people and the animals he painted. His second style which could be seen in the lively way he painted the country fairs, and in the *Drawings for Fun,* made marked return to his natural way of drawing and painting done with great economy of line and capacity to occupy the available space' [Cameron]. He was a lively illustrator, good at crowds and handling crowd scenes as the 'Fair at Skirving' - his most celebrated work - indicates, although the draughtsmanship is sometimes weak. Generally a much underrated artist with an innocent vitality often missing in more acclaimed work. Represented in SNPG, NGS(18), Aberdeen AG, Perth AG, Dundee AG, Glasgow AG.
**Bibl:** J R Brotchie 'James Howe' Scot Art Rev, vol 4, no 1, 1952; Brydall 424-6; A D Cameron, James Howe 1780-1836 The Man who Loved to Draw Horses, 1986; Caw 196-7; D Cleghorn-Thomson, 'A Neglected Animal Painter' The Scotsman 27.10.1956; Halsby 264; Irwin 192-3 (illus).

**HOWE, Robert** **fl 1910-1929**
Edinburgh painter; exhibited AAS during the above years.

**HOWIE, Mrs Euphan** **fl 1929-1933**
Aberdeenshire watercolour painter of landscape. Fond of evening scenes in the Highlands. Exhibited AAS(5), latterly from The Shieling, Bieldside.

**HOWIE, Ian** **fl 1919-1931**
Aberdeenshire landscape painter. Often exhibited at the AAS from Tor-na-Dee, Murtle.

**HOWIE, Mrs J Edith** **fl 1902-1935**
Aberdeenshire painter in oil and watercolour of local landscape,

harvest scenes and rural genre. Self-taught. Wife of a general practitioner in Strathdon. Exhibited RSA(1) 1925 & AAS(6) from Craig-na-Ulaidh, Strathdon.

**HOWIE, James Jnr** **fl 1845-1847**
Edinburgh portrait painter of minor consequence. Exhibited RSA(4), mostly characters of the Theatre Royal.

**HOWIE, James** **1931-**
Born Dundee. Abstract painter in oil. Studied at Dundee College of Art 1949-1954 then undertook further studies in Paris 1955. Between 1960 and 1962 was in Spain and Jamaica. Visiting lecturer at Dundee College of Art 1962-8. Exhibited RSA(11) 1953-58, 1964 & again in 1980. Represented in Dundee AG.

**HOWIE, John** **fl 1846-1852**
Sculptor. Lived at Ceres, by Cupar, Fife. Exhibited 6 portraits at the RSA including a marble bust of Major Playfair, Provost of St Andrews and in 1852 a marble statue of the Prince of Wales. Other works included portrait busts of Sir David Brewster (1848) and Major Barclay (1850).

**HOWIE, John** **fl 1951-1953**
Ayrshire portrait and genre painter; exhibited GI(2), from Gorliach, James St, Dalry.

**HOWIE, Lilias Ann** **fl 1975-1978**
Aberdeenshire artist; exhibited AAS(3), latterly from 15 Taylor Court, Aberlour.

**HOWIE, W H** **fl 1888-1906**
Glasgow painter. Exhibited GI(4) from 131 West Regent Street.

**HOWIE, William** **fl 1853-1854**
Born Kilmarnock. Painter of portraits and still life. Studied at the Trustees Academy. Exhibited RSA(3).

**HOWIESON, Charles T** **fl 1940-1942**
Edinburgh painter. Exhibited 2 landscapes at the RSA from 10 Pentland Crescent.

**HOWIESON, Lyndsay M** **1961-**
Born Edinburgh, 19 Nov. Sculptress. Trained Edinburgh College of Art 1979-84 and Edinburgh University, obtaining an hons degree. Graduated with distinction and 1984-85 was part-time teacher in the sculpture department, Edinburgh College of Art. In 1985 she set up a group to develop new landmark sculpture for Musselburgh at the Unemployed Worker's Centre. In July 1986 was the Scottish sculptress at the first International Scottish Sculpture Symposium. Member of Scottish Sculpture Workshop, Lumsden. Began exhibiting RSA 1984 from 4/5 Inchgarvie Court, Ferry Road Drive.

**HOWIESON, Miss Mary** **fl 1958-1959**
Dumbarton figure and portrait painter; exhibited GI(3) from Tilgellyn, Colgrain, Helensburgh.

**HOWISON, John** **fl 1861-1871**
Duddingston landscape painter in oil; exhibited RSA(2) including 'Portobello Manse' in 1871.

**HOWISON, Thomas** **fl 1838-1840**
Edinburgh painter of landscape and topography, especially castles. Exhibited RSA(5) during the above years.

**HOWISON, William ARSA** **1798-1851**
Born Edinburgh. Engraver. Educated at Heriot's Hospital. After training as an engraver with Wilson he was employed by D O Hill(qv) to engrave several of his works. Resided at 8 Frederick Street. Never exhibited RSA although elected Associate 1838. Contributed to the volumes published by the Association for the Promotion of the Fine Arts in Scotland favouring the works of William Allan(qv) and Thomas Faed(qv). Among his best works are 'The Curlers', after Sir George Harvey, the same artist's 'The Covenanters' Communion, The Polish Exiles', after Sir W. Allan, and 'The First Letter from the Emigrants', after Thomas Faed. An anonymous obituary referred to him as 'a man of strong native sense, integrity, honour, and insight into many things besides engraving. We never met with a finer embodiment of the sturdy, the hearty, and the tender virtues of a Scottish craftsman'.
**Bibl:** Bryan; Brydall 214; Bushnell and J C Guy, 'Edinburgh Engravers' in the book of the Old Edinburgh Club, vol 9, Edinburgh 1916; Scotsman, 1851 (obit).

**HOWSE, Mrs Henrietta Rose Chiheliana Thornton ARMS** **1892-?**
Born Waterford, Ireland 20 Jan. Watercolour artist, mainly of miniatures but also some landscapes especially Alpine views and scenery on Arran and Skye. Educated Brighton and Brussels, studied art in Brussels and London with Arthur Lindsey. Married into a naval family. Lived for many years at Ellersleigh, Kilmacolm, Renfrewshire, moved to London 1948. Elected ARMS 1938. Exhibited RMS & GI(32).

**HOWSON, Peter** **1958-**
Born Isleworth, London, moved to Scotland at the age of four. Painter of figure subjects, portraits in oil, and stage scenery. Attended Glasgow School of Art 1975-77. Joined the Royal Highland Fusiliers, an unhappy but formative period which lasted only nine months. Resumed art studies 1979-1981 when Sandy Moffat became a strong influence. Executed a series of murals at Feltham Community Association 1982-83, portraying aspects of contemporary life. Uses bold, black contours, bright colouring and socially relevant subject matter. Artist-in-residence, University of St Andrews 1985. Awards include Hospitalfield scholarship 1979, Henry Moore Foundation Prize 1988, Eastwood Publication Prize (RGI) 1992, European Young Artists Prize (Belgrade) 1992, Lord Provost's Prize (Glasgow Gallery of Modern Art) 1995 & 1998. 'The world that he depicts is a decidedly masculine one: soldiers, boxers, body-builders, sportsmen. But his attitude towards it is not celebratory or triumphant, although it might seem so at first sight. On the contrary he sees this overweening masculinity as flawed. Bulging muscles, posturing and aggression are seen as futile and destructive, if they lack the right environment and the right channels or a push too far...there is a baroque exuberance in Howson's work, a robustness of form, that comes close to caricature at times...the effect is to produce a kind of popular imagery, a folk history of Glasgow working class life' [Hartley]. In the coarse modern idiom, his work has been well received by the contemporary academic establishment, and by patronage from pop stars. Appointed war artist for Bosnia 1993. In 1995 he returned to London and since 1997 recognition and popularity have risen sharply. A sensitive man, he has overcome severe emotional problems and is a generous benefactor to many charities. A retrospective exhibition was held at the McLellan Galleries, New York 1993. Exhibited RA, RSA & RGI(6), from 37 Hillhead St, Glasgow. Represented in Aberdeen AG, British Museum, City Art Centre (Edinburgh), SNGMA, V & A, Tate AG, Paisley AG, Dundee AG, Perth AG, Walker AG, Lillie AG (Milngavie), Liverpool AG, People's Palace (Glasgow), Metropolitan Museum (New York), Museum of Modern Art (New York), Southampton AG, Fitzwilliam (Cambridge), Gulbenkian (Lisbon), Kilmarnock Museum, Ayr AG, Nat Gall of Norway, Nottingham AG, Paul Mellon Centre (Yale Univ).
**Bibl:** Hartley 136-7; Alan Jackson The Times, 'The Human Face of War', May 1, 1993; Jly 10, 1993, 24-9; T Jackson, 'Peter Howson', The Green Book Vol 12, No 6 1986; Waldemar Januszczak, 'Peter Howson' (Ex Cat, Sep 1987); Robert Heller, 'Peter Howson, Flowers East', London, ex cat 1998; Laura Campbell, *'Peter Howson, Painting the Masses'*, website biography; Macmillan 2001, 117,129, 145,148,149,151, illus 162.

**HOWY, William** **1798-c1853**
Edinburgh painter in oil of landscape and coastal scenes. Particularly fond of castles and harbours. Exhibited RSA(18) including views on Arran, Fife and the Lothians, also 'Tantallon Castle' 1847, 'Kilchurn Castle' 1849 & 'Ruins of Fast Castle' 1853.

**HUCK, James** **1875-1940**
Born Penicuik, Midlothian 8 May; died Glasgow, 23 Feb. Painter of portraits and landscapes in oil, pastel and watercolour. Early days were spent in Galashiels. In 1900 went to Glasgow, studied at Glasgow School of Art winning a Haldane scholarship and a travelling bursary which enabled him to visit France and Italy. Shortly after returning appointed to the staff of Glasgow School of Art, becoming Assistant Director 1926, retired 1938. Member, Glasgow Art Club. His

landscapes were mainly of the Western Isles, Iona and the Scottish borders around his home. Painted heads with great sensitivity but weaker with hands and costume. Exhibited RSA(7), AAS 1912-35 & GI(12), from 3 Marchmont Terrace, Glasgow.
**Bibl:** Halsby 264.

**HUDSON, F H** **fl 1842-1846**
Edinburgh portrait painter; lived at Roslin Castle, Midlothian. Exhibited RSA(5).

**HUDSON, Margaret M A** **fl 1948-1970**
Sculptress. Worked mostly in bronze and plaster, especially female sitters and figures. Lived at Drumrossie House, Insch, Aberdeenshire and exhibited 2 portrait busts at the RSA, 1948 and 1961, & AAS(3) 1964, one of an African girl; also GI(3), all from Findrassie House, Elgin.

**HUGHES, Caroline Sarah** **fl 1977-1980**
Aberdeenshire jewellery designer. Exhibited AAS from 9 Hillhead Terrace.

**HUGHES, Edith (née Burnet)** **fl 1920-1929**
Glasgow based painter and engraver. Exhibited a view of the West Church, Aberdeen RSA 1921, AAS(1) & GI(6). Possibly the **Edith M B HUGHES** (1888-1971) responsible for the Font in St Mary's Cathedral, Edinburgh (1959), the design therein of the Screen in the Chapel of St Margaret (1959) and roof details at West Colinton Cottage (c1935).

**HUGHES, Ian** **1958-**
Born Glasgow. Studied at Duncan of Jordanstone College of Art 1976-1980. From 1981-87 worked in Glasgow and Edinburgh with mental patients, an experience which powerfully affected his work. First one-man exhibition in Edinburgh 1985. This included 'The Anatomy Lesson' which with its installation of paintings on a mock operating table gained considerable critical acclaim. In 1987 his work was included in SNGMA's exhibition 'The Vigorous Imagination'. The following year was artist-in-residence, SNGMA. 'In these paintings he painstakingly reproduced elements from Old Master pictures which were then half-obliterated with gushing blood-like paint. Additionally, he produced a series of boxes containing photographs culled from medical text-books combined with religious imagery and glutinous paint. While being deeply distressing and shocking, Hughes' work has, nonetheless, a profoundly human resonance' [Hartley]. During 1989 exhibited in France, Germany and Poland. Represented in SNGMA.
**Bibl:** Hartley 137; SNGMA (Ex Cat 1988).

**HUGHES, Marianne** **fl 1983**
Painter. Exhibited three works at the AAS from 286 Hardgate, Aberdeen.

**HUGHES, Miss Rose E** **fl 1910-1914**
Dunbartonshire portrait miniaturist; painted on ivory. Exhibited RSA(2), RI(9), AAS, L(4), a portrait of the 'Bishop of Glasgow & Galloway' 1912 GI & London Salon(4), from Inchneuk, Rhu.

**HUGHES, Miss Ruth** **fl 1955-1956**
Dumbartonshire painter of figure studies and still life; exhibited GI(2), from 16 Boyle St, Whitecrook, Clydebank.

**HUGHES, T Harold** **fl 1912-1938**
Aberdeen artist, architect and topographical etcher. Exhibited RSA (2), GI(9) & AAS(4) from 8 Fonthill Rd and latterly from Glasgow.

**HUGHES, William** **1842-1901**
Born Lanarkshire; died Brighton, Dec 18. Father of Sir Herbert Hughes-Stanton(qv). Painter of still life, fruit but most often flowers. Pupil of George Lance and William Hunt. Perhaps the finest flower painter Scotland has produced. His work was always finely drawn, sensitively coloured and designed, handled in a most decorative, unassuming manner. According to Bryan he was a shy, retiring man having few friends. Little is known of his life. Commissioned by Lord Calthorpe to paint five large decorative bird paintings to adorn the staircase of his house in Grosvenor Square. Moved to Brighton in 1895/6, ending his days at 11 Belgrave Place. His first exhibited work was at the British Institution in 1862 followed by the first of 35 exhibits at the RA 1866. Represented in Hull Museum, Cape Town AG.
**Bibl:** Bryan.

**HUGHES-STANTON, Sir Herbert Edwin Pelham RA PRWS** **1870-1937**
Born Chelsea. Son of the Lanarkshire-born flower and still life painter William Hughes(qv). Landscape painter. Largely self-taught, having received elementary early lessons from his father. As a young man he was a keen copyist of the old masters but gradually developed a romantic style of landscape painting, similar to that of his contemporary Alfred East. His work is now rather out of favour. Elected RA 1920, PRWS 1915, RWS 1921, knighted 1923. Represented in Bradford AG, Liverpool AG, Australia, Barcelona, Buenos Aires, Florence, Tokyo.
**Bibl:** AJ 1910, 77-82; 1904, 271; 1906, 180; 1907, 373; 1908, 171, 1909, 285; Internat. Studio 1908, 33, 269ff; RA Pictures 1907-8, 1910-15; Studio 1908,42,269ff; Who's Who 1924; Wood 241.

**HUIE, Helen Pillans** **fl 1886**
Edinburgh landscape and topographical painter in oil. Exhibited RSA(3).

**HULTON, Phillip B** **fl 1972**
Exhibited once at the AAS from 35A Union St, Aberdeen.

**HUMBLE, J R** **fl 1833-1837**
Edinburgh based painter of landscape, still life and flowers. Probably brother of Stephen H(qv). Exhibited RSA(4).

**HUMBLE, Stephen** **fl 1828-1838**
Edinburgh painter of flowers, fruit and occasional miniature portraits and topographical sketches. Probably brother of J R H(qv), and similarly fascinated by the colour and texture of shells. Exhibited RSA(22).

**HUME, Kenneth** **fl 1953**
Glasgow landscape painter; exhibited GI(1), from 24 Balgonie Rd, Mosspark.

**HUME, Robert RBA** **1861-1937**
Edinburgh based painter in oil and watercolour of landscape and rustic genre. Lived for many years in Edinburgh until settling in London 1894, returning to Edinburgh 1913. Elected RBA 1896. Exhibited RA(10) 1891-1903, mostly landscapes, also RSA(45), RSW(5), RBA(51), GI(9) & AAS 1887, from 16 N. St Andrews St.

**HUME, Robin RGI** **1943-**
Born May 28, Bridge of Allan. Painter and sculptor. Trained Glasgow School of Art, subsequently becoming member of staff before taking early retirement in order to work full-time, concentrating particularly on finely chiselled bronze porrtraits. Elected RGI 1997. Exhibits RSA and, more regularly, at RGI.

**HUMPHRIES, Mrs Miriam** **fl 1935**
Inverness-shire painter. Exhibited RI(1) from The Grange, Fort William.

**HUMPHRIES, W H** **fl 1953-1987**
Aberdeenshire artist of local landscape subjects. Exhibited AAS(4) during the above years from Beach Brae, Milltimber.

**HUNT, Adelin** **fl 1905**
Lanark-based miniature painter. Exhibited three miniatures at the GI from Whitehall, Bothwell.

**HUNT, Cecil Arthur VPRWS RBA** **1873-1965**
Born Torquay, 8 Mar; died London. Landscape painter in oil, watercolour and tempera, mostly watercolour. Educated Winchester and Trinity College, Cambridge. A qualified barrister, he only began painting full-time in 1919, the same year that he was elected RWS. VPRWS 1930-33, RBA 1914. Deeply affected by mountain grandeur, he became profoundly attached to the Highlands and Islands, painting in these regions throughout his long working life. Exhibited GI(116), all from Mallord House, Church St, London SW3. Particularly fond of Skye to which he returned repeatedly and

faithfully recorded in all its moods. Represented in BM, V & A, Glasgow AG, Blackburn AG, Cartwright Hall(Bradford), Exeter Museum, Fitzwilliam(Cambridge), India Office Library, Leeds AG, Manchester AG, Newport AG, Portsmouth City AG.
**Bibl:** OWS Club, xxxviii, 1963.

**HUNT, Clyde du Vernet** **1861-**
Born Glasgow. Sculptor and painter of figurative subjects. Lived most of his life in London but also spent some years in Paris. Exhibited RA(2) & L(1).

**HUNT, Mrs Naomi** **fl 1971-1976**
Renfrewshire sculptress. Worked mainly in clay and plaster. Exhibited GI(3), from 12 McPherson Drive, Gourock.

**HUNT, Thomas ARSA VPRSW** **1854-1929**
Born Skipton, 24 Dec; died Glasgow, 13 Mar. Painter in oil and watercolour of landscapes and genre. Studied at Leeds and Glasgow Schools of Art also in Paris under Raphael Collin. Married Helen Salmon(qv) 1887. Fond of depicting local characters using a vigorous and unsophisticated style. Exhibited mainly in London from 1881 also occasionally in Scotland. Received an honourable mention at the Paris Salon 1895. President, Glasgow Art Club 1905-1906. Vice-president, Royal Scottish Society of Painters in Watercolour. Writing in the *AJ*, a critic found 'his personality so strong, that it is little wonder he is becoming a power for good in his adopted city'. A large work entitled 'A Royal Caledonian Hunt, Cadzow Forest' in the Old Town exhibited at the GI in 1898 attracted considerable attention as did a stirring rendering of the 'Atholl Highlanders, Glen Tilt' shown at the RSA the same year. Elected RSW 1885, ARSA 1929. Exhibited RA(22) from 1881, also RSA(64), RSW(129), GI(138), AAS 1894-1926 & L(20). Represented in Glasgow AG, Greenock AG, Leeds City AG, Wakefield AG.
**Bibl:** AJ 1898, 158; Halsby 264.

**HUNTER, A A** **fl 1940**
Amateur painter of Newport-on-Tay, Fife; exhibited a watercolour at the RSW.

**HUNTER, Agnes S** **fl 1876-1907**
Painter in oil and watercolour of figurative subjects and portrait miniatures. Exhibited RSA(3) & GI(7) formerly from Coldstream, then Dalry, Ayrshire before moving to Rothesay and finally Hunting Tower, Cathcart in 1905.

**HUNTER, Alexander** **fl 1840-1841**
Edinburgh based painter. Exhibited rural scenes and topographical subjects often in the Edinburgh area, sometimes portraying cattle and children. Exhibited RSA(6) from Doune Terrace.

**HUNTER, Andrew** **1964-**
Portrait and figure painter. Trained Edinburgh College of Art and Edinburgh University. Son of Ann Patrick(qv) and Richard Hunter(qv); brother of Julian H and Susannah H(qv). Married to the artist **Caroline WENDLING** (b1961). Assistant Curator, Gainsborough Museum, Suffolk.

**HUNTER, Miss Anne Douglas** **fl 1959**
Glasgow watercolourist of figure compositions; exhibited GI(2), from 118 Cathcart Rd.

**HUNTER, Archibald** **fl 1948-1953**
Renfrewshire landscape painter in oil and watercolour; exhibited GI(8), from 13 Whitehaugh Drive.

**HUNTER, Bella J** **fl 1893**
Edinburgh watercolour painter; exhibited RSA(1) & AAS in the same year from 9 Hope Street.

**HUNTER, Mrs Beth** **fl 1979**
Glasgow-based artist. Exhibited 'Prophecy of Spring' at the GI, from 43 Limetree Walk, Milton of Campsie.

**HUNTER, Colin ARA RI RSW RE** **1841-1904**
Born Glasgow; died Kensington. Painter and etcher of seascapes and coastal scenes. Son of a Helensburgh postmaster. Father of John Young H(qv). Began life as a clerk but was encouraged by Milne Donald(qv) to become a landscape painter. In the 1860s he turned to seascape painting on which his reputation is founded. In 1872 moved to London and the following year 'Trawler's waiting for darkness', subsequently etched by Chauvel, was his first major success. In 1879 'Their only harvest' was bought by the Chantrey Bequest. His pictures capture the mood of the sea rather than its purely visual effects. Although technically as good a painter as many other marine artists of his time, his strong greeny-black colours and thickening skies can be remarkably effective although the overall effect is often coarse. Most of his pictures were painted on the west coast or among the Hebrides. Visited Paris in about 1866 and studied briefly in the studio of Bonnet. 'He does not attempt to transfer the waves to his canvas; he understands that paint can grapple with the sea as colour and as colour he is content to take it' [Armstrong]. 'The Mussel Gatherers' of 1880 is now in Hamburg AG, 'Waiting for the Homeward Bound' is in Adelaide AG, the 'Herring Fleet at Sea' in Manchester, as is 'The Upper Rapids of Niagara', painted during a visit to the US in 1884 and exhibited at the RSA the following year. In 1898 his 'Changing Pasture', exhibited at the RA, was illustrated that year in the *AJ* (p170), described as 'a wonderfully redolent work of a summer scene on Loch Duich; the luminous atmospheric effect, the majestic loneliness of the setting enhanced by the touch of life'. Friend of McTaggart(qv), sketched with him at Tarbet over a number of years in the late 1860s. Elected ARA 1884, RSW 1879, ROI 1883, RE 1881, RI 1882. Exhibited RA, including 'Salmon Fishing on the Dee' (1895), RSA(68), GI(94), AAS 1885-1898 & L(15), after 1877 from 14 Melbury Rd, London. Represented in Glasgow AG(8), Kirkcaldy AG, Nat Gall of South Africa (Cape Town).
**Bibl:** Caw 324-6; Halsby 118, 123-4, 244, 264.

**HUNTER, David** **fl 1851-1872**
Edinburgh oil painter of portraits, figurative subjects and landscape. Related to William H(qv). Exhibited RSA(15) & GI(1), from 6 Lothian Square.

**HUNTER, Duncan** **fl 1836**
Portobello painter. Exhibited 'Moonlight' at the RSA.

**HUNTER, Ed** **1942-**
Born Glasgow. Painter of representational landscapes. Trained part-time at Glasgow School of Art and Strathclyde Univ. Member of Committee, Paisley Art Institute. Exhibits RSA, RGI, Paisley Art Institute from 35 Kilpatrick Gdns, Glasgow.

**HUNTER, Gavin** **fl 1957**
Ayr landscape painter; exhibited a Cornish scene at the GI from 33 Chalmers Rd.

**HUNTER, George Leslie** **1877-1931**
Born Rothesay, Bute, 7 Aug; died Glasgow, 6 Dec. Painter in oil of genre, landscapes, portraits and still life. Largely self-taught. Son of a Bute pharmacist. Two of his elder brothers having died of tuberculosis, in 1890 the family emigrated to California. When his father returned to Scotland in 1897, Hunter elected to remain behind, moving to San Francisco where he quickly established himself as an illustrator. Among his earliest successes were the illustrations for Bret Harte stories in *Overland Monthly*. He began to work with paint, an activity stimulated by a visit to Paris, and possibly Scotland, 1904/5. This was at the time the post-Impressionists were holding their famous exhibitions. Back in California, Hunter's first one-man exhibition was planned for 1906 but the day before it was due to open an earthquake destroyed his possessions including all his paintings. Later that year he travelled to see his mother in Glasgow, but finding no demand for his illustrations in Scotland he proceeded to London with frequent excursions to Paris, often with E A Taylor(qv) whom he had met in the metropolis. During WWI he continued to paint while working on his uncle's farm at Millburn, Lanarkshire. The dark palette of his early still lifes was replaced by more luminous colour. Some of his works were purchased by the Glasgow dealer Alex Reid. In 1916 his first solo exhibition took place at Reid's Gallery, La Société des Beaux-Arts. During this period he spent much time reading about the artists who most inspired him, especially Van Gogh and Gauguin but also William McTaggart and Whistler. He wrote 'everyone must use his own way, and mine will be the way of colour'. In 1919 he began to visit Fife, his palette becoming at this time still brighter, his handling

of paint more relaxed although executed with ever-increasing energy. By now he was being supported by collectors as well as galleries, especially in Glasgow and Dundee and his financial problems were over. In spite of this Hunter remained unable to manage his own affairs and life was a continuous struggle not only with his art but also with a mental condition which bordered on the paranoid. In 1922 and again the following year he visited Italy, calling in at Paris en route, returning for a short visit to California in 1924. Thereafter he divided his time between Fife and, increasingly, Loch Lomond where he began to undertake his largest landscapes. After an exhibition in London 1924, Cadell, Fergusson and Peploe joined Hunter for an exhibition in Paris 'Les Peintres de l'Écosse Moderne'. Shortly afterwards, however, his mental condition seriously deteriorated and at the end of 1926 he returned to France, this time to the Mediterranean. Back once more in London he was commissioned to paint C B Cochran and to produce sketches of the show *Evergreen.* In 1931 he produced a superb set of watercolours of Hyde Park. Settling in Glasgow, his physical health so deteriorated that painting became no longer possible. A most distinctive craftsman and in many ways the most exciting of the colourists, although the least predictable; an extremely important figure in the development of 20th century Scottish art. Exhibited RSA(13), GI(95) & L(8). Represented in NGS(2), SNPG(1), Dundee AG, Glasgow AG, Kirkcaldy AG, Manchester AG, a number of French museums, Sydney AG(Australia), Victoria AG(Australia).
**Bibl:** R Billcliffe, The Scottish Colourists, 26-28,45-50,62; Halsby 159, 206; W Hardie, Scottish Painting, 127-137; Hartley 137-8; T J Honeyman, Introducing Leslie Hunter, 1937; Irwin 394; RGI Glasgow, (Ex Cat 1977).

**HUNTER, George Sherwood RBA** **1846-1919**
Born Aberdeen; died Aberdeen, 18 Jne. Painter in oil & watercolour of landscape, seascape, genre, occasional flowers and sporting scenes. Studied Edinburgh College of Art, also in Paris and Rome. Painted extensively on the continent especially in France, Holland, Italy and Spain as well as in Egypt and the Middle East. Enjoyed painting scenes with fisherfolk in a strong heavy manner, although he also portrayed other subjects, such as an evocative study of 'A deerstalker in Mar Forest' exhibited RSA 1883. Won medals at Crystal Palace 1896 and 1898 and an honourable mention at the Paris Exhibition of 1900. Founder member, Aberdeen Artists' Society 1885 and a member of its Executive Committee but in 1886 moved to London, remaining there until 1898 when he moved to Newlyn. There he became friendly with Elizabeth and Stanhope Forbes at whose art school he was persuaded to teach. Stanhope Forbes' biographer refers to Hunter as 'an artist of sincere and thoughtful individuality who is always ready to supplement the teacher's efforts'. Elected RBA 1889. In addition to his work in France exhibited in Rome and Chicago 1882-1911. Elected RBA 1889. A retrospective exhibition was held at the Rendezvous Gallery, Aberdeen 1990. Exhibited RSA(48), RA(16), AAS 1887-1912, RBA(77), ROI(12), GI(24) & L(17), also many times at the AAS including a number of views of Upper Deeside.
**Bibl:** Wingfield.

**HUNTER, Harriet B** **fl 1905-1906**
Edinburgh painter; exhibited a view of Ettrick Bay, Bute at the RSA from 12 Randolph Crescent.

**HUNTER, Harry Johnson** **fl 1866-1870**
Glasgow landscape painter in oil and watercolour; exhibited a view of Cathcart Church RSA & GI(1), from 109 Dale St.

**HUNTER, Isobel** **fl 1881**
Amateur painter. Exhibited SWA(1) from Anton's Hill, Coldstream.

**HUNTER, Dr J Ewing** **fl 1893-1897**
Amateur Dunbartonshire flower painter; exhibited GI(4) from Duncairn, Helensburgh.

**HUNTER, James Brownlie** **1855-c1919**
Edinburgh artist and engraver; coastal scenes, landscapes and portraits. Exhibited RA(3) & RSA(18), latterly from Duddingston, Midlothian.
**Bibl:** Halsby 264.

**HUNTER, Jennifer** **1968-**
Born Mar 27. Painter in oil and watercolour, printmaker & teacher. Trained Glasgow School of Art 1986-1990. Jointly runs *Chrome Yellow*, an arts organisation working with children. First solo exhibition in Glasgow 1992. In 1997 she received a tavel grant from Glagow City enabling her to visit Vietnam. Exhibits RSA & RGI since 1992 & RSW from 1995.

**HUNTER, John** **1960-**
Born Perth, 18 Jne. Sculptor. Studied Edinburgh College of Art obtaining 1st class honours 1982-1986 and a postgraduate diploma in 1987. In 1986 received the Andrew Grant major travelling scholarship and the following year the John Kinross scholarship which enabled him to visit Florence. Artist-in-residence at the Glasgow Garden Festival 1988. In 1990 he won the Benno Schotz prize for the most promising work by a young sculptor domiciled in Scotland. Lecturer, Edinburgh College of Art. Exhibited SSA since 1984, RSA & AAS in 1990.

**HUNTER, John Kelso** **1802-1873**
Born Dankeith, Ayrshire, the seat of Col William Kelso, 15 Dec; died Pollockshields, nr Glasgow, 3 Feb. Artist, author and cobbler. His father had come to Ayrshire in 1799 as a gardener. In his early days Hunter was employed as a herd boy on the estate and then was apprenticed to a shoemaker. Settled in Kilmarnock where he taught himself portrait painting. Then went to Glasgow where he was employed alternately as artist and shoemaker. In 1847 his self-portrait as a shoemaker was accepted at the RA. In 1868 published his first book *The Retrospect of an Artist's Life* and in 1870 *Life Studies of Character - Recollections of Burns and other Scottish Literary Heroes,* a work which faithfully describes the society surrounding Burns including information about the song-writer Tannahill. Contributed 'Head' to the RSA 1849 and thereafter 4 further works in 1858, 1868 and twice in 1872; also GI(7) including 'An Artistic Cobbler' (1873), from Kempock Place, Gourock.

**HUNTER, John T** **fl 1940-1948**
Edinburgh based painter mainly in tempera of portraits and rural topography. Exhibited RSA(9) & GI(1), first from 47 George Square and latterly from 4 Wardie Avenue.

**HUNTER, John Young RBA** **1874-1955**
Born Glasgow, 29 Oct; died Taos, New Mexico, 9 Sep. Painter of portrait, genre, historical and landscapes in oil. Son of Colin H(qv). Studied RA Schools, gaining 2 silver medals. Visited Italy, Germany and Belgium but lived in Suffolk until settling in USA 1913. Had a liking for romantic scenes with figures in gardens and interiors in both oil and watercolour. Married to the English artist Mary Young Hunter. 'My Lady's Garden' was purchased by the Chantrey Bequest 1899. Illustrated *The Clyde* (1908). Elected RBA 1914. Exhibited RA(42), ROI(2), RI(1), RBA(3), GI(15), including 'The Duke of Argyll' (1910). Represented in Liverpool AG.
**Bibl:** Caw 452; Halsby 264.

**HUNTER, Mrs John Young (Mary)** **fl 1910**
Portrait painter. Wife of John Young H(qv), together illustrated *The Clyde,* 1908. Exhibited GI(1), from 9 Launceston Place, London.
**Bibl:** Halsby 264.

**HUNTER, K R** **fl 1966**
Glasgow genre painter; exhibited GI(1), from 21 Walton St.

**HUNTER, Miss Kate** **fl 1872-1874**
Edinburgh flower painter in oil and watercolour, occasional still life. Exhibited RSA(4) & GI(1), from Tantallon Terrace, North Berwick.

**HUNTER, Kenneth** **1962-**
Born Edinburgh. Sculptor. Trained Glasgow School of Art 1983-87. Works in the classical tradition in multi-media, plywood, bronze, stone, jesmonite & glass reinforced plastic. Held exhibitions at the SNPG and in Glasgow. Public commissions have included a garlanded sacrificial animal for Graham Square, praised by Duncan Macmillan, and other sculptures for public places in southern Scotland. Exhibits RSA. Represented in SNPG, Glasgow AG.
**Bibl:** Macmillan 2001, 141,171,181-3, illus 202.

**HUNTER, Miss Lucy** **fl 1883-1888**
Painter of figures, seascapes, flowers and animal studies in oil. Possibly related to Isobel H(qv). Exhibited RSA(5) & SWA(2) from Belchester, Coldstream & GI(2), from 56 Alexander Ave, Eaglesham.

**HUNTER, Margaret** **1948-**
Born Irvine, Ayrshire. Painter of symbolic figure subjects and semi-abstract work; sculptress. Studied at Glasgow School of Art 1981-85 and on the strength of various awards continued her studies at the Hochschule der Kunste in Berlin under George Baselitz. Thereafter divides her time between Berlin and Fairlie in West Scotland. From her earliest days as an artist the main theme has been the female form 'defined in terms of an expressive gestural brushwork.' The lifestyles in Berlin and the influence of Baselitz had a liberating effect on her work. 'Her early interest in mother/child symbolism has extended to other more complex human relationships expressed by means of a vigorous, stabbing application of paint' [Hartley]. Large corpus of work produced after stay in Majorca, inspired by colours and light but also by the socio-political complexities confronting the local population. Her sculptures, in their standing carved wooden figures, show an affinity with African forms, reminding one critic of Brancusi and Giacometti. There is a strong graphic element in her work with emotive use of strong colour. Solo exhibition Edinburgh City Art Gallery 1990. Represented in SNGMA.
**Bibl:** Bill Hare, Contemporary Painting in Scotland, Edinburgh 1993;Hartley 138; The Edinburgh 369 Gallery, 'Ideas and Images' (Ex Cat 1988).

**HUNTER, Marshall** **1905-?**
Born Glasgow. Portrait painter and teacher. Studied Edinburgh College of Art and Moray House Training College. Exhibited RSA 1931-1949 from North Lodge, Inveresk and latterly from Levenhall, Musselburgh.

**HUNTER, Miss Mary Sutherland** **1899-?**
Born Holytown, Lanarkshire. Painter in oil and watercolour of portraits, still life, landscapes, interiors, also sculptress. Studied Edinburgh College of Art and RSA School where she gained the Chalmers Jervise Award 1922. Painted extensively in Scotland, Cornwall and the South of France. Exhibited RSA(10), RSW(1), GI(3) & L(1), from 26 Hermitage Drive, Edinburgh.

**HUNTER, Mason ARSA RSW** **1854-1921**
Born Broxburn, Linlithgow; died Edinburgh, 31 Jan. Landscape and coastal painter in oil and watercolour. Early education at Dr Begg's School, Newington before studying Edinburgh School of Design and at both the Academie Colarossi in Paris and the Barbizon. Exhibited at the leading London galleries, also internationally in Berlin, Munich, Rome and Venice. Elected Chairman, SSA 1907, RSW 1929, ARSA 1913. His coastal scenes are particularly attractive, portraying evocatively the wide expanse of sea and the colourful sails. Exhibited RSA(145), RSW(86), AAS(1921-23), RI(1), RHA(3), GI(57) & L(5), after 1906 from 54 Queen St, Edinburgh.
**Bibl:** Caw 333; Halsby 264.

**HUNTER, Norman M** **fl 1878-1922**
Edinburgh watercolour painter of buildings, especially castles. Exhibited RSA(4) from 1 Bedford Place.

**HUNTER, Miss Patty** **fl 1938-1940**
Engraver; landscapes and town views. Exhibited GI(4) from Auchendrane, Alexandria, Dunbartonshire.

**HUNTER, Richard Druiett RSW** **fl 1954-**
Arbroath based painter in oil and watercolour, mainly the latter, of local coastal scenes, figure subjects, still life; often incorporated harbours and boats into his pictures. Married Ann Patrick(qv). Children also artists. Exhibited RSA(45) 1954-89, AAS 1969-85 & GI(7), from Cairniehill Lodge. Represented in Glasgow AG.

**HUNTER, Robert** **fl 1886-1889**
Edinburgh watercolour painter of landscapes and figurative subjects. Exhibited RSA(9) from 28 Queen Street.

**HUNTER, Robert A** **fl 1970-1983**
Edinburgh based painter of interiors and still life, especially plants. Exhibited RSA(3).

**HUNTER, Stephen** **fl 1942-1954**
Ayrshire engraver and watercolourist. Landsscape and harbour scenes. Exhibited 2 wood engravings and a coloured woodcut at the RSA in the above year from Hawthorn Villa, Darvel & GI(8).

**HUNTER, Susannah** **1971-**
Designer and figurative painter, generally large-scale watercolours. Trained in Fashion, Central St, London. Youngest child of Ann Patrick(qv) and Richard H(qv), sister of Andrew H(qv) and Julian H. Represented in Aberdeen AG.

**HUNTER, W** **fl 1802-1829**
Minor Edinburgh portrait painter of St Patrick's Square. Said to have been trained under John More, was made a Burgess of Edinburgh in 1802. Exhibited an unknown sitter at the RSA in 1829.

**HUNTER, William ROI** **c1890-1967**
Born Glasgow; died 29 Mar. Painter in oil of figures, conversation pieces, flowers and still life; also engraver. Studied Glasgow School of Art under Fra Newbery(qv) where he received a travelling scholarship. Visited many European cities and studied for a time under Artot in Brussels. At one time he worked with Greiffenhagen(qv) and Anning Bell(qv) in the execution of murals. Sometimes worked on Skye. Elected ROI 1928. Governor, Glasgow School of Art; President, Scottish Artists Benevolent Association. Former secretary of the RGI and President, Glasgow Art Club 1938-40. Exhibited widely not only in the UK but also at the Paris Salon and in North America; RA(1), ROI(28), RSA(20) 1915-1959, AAS 1912, GI(122) & L(4), from his home Rigside, Iain Rd, Bearsden. Represented in Glasgow AG.
**Bibl:** Glasgow Herald, 1 Apr 1967(obit).

**HUNTER, William B** **fl 1858-1868**
Edinburgh painter in oil and watercolour; landscape and wildlife. Related to David Hunter. Exhibited RSA(15), often Highland scenes, & GI(3), from 6 Lothian St.

**HUNTER, William R** **fl 1950-1964**
Renfrewshire watercolour landscape painter. Exhibited GI(9), mostly of Kircudbright and Culross, from Croftbank, Mearns Rd, Newton Mearns.

**HUNTINGDON, Beatrice M L** **1889-1988**
Born St Andrews. Painter in oil of portraits and figure subjects. All her early life was spent in St Andrews. Studied painting in Munich and Paris (1905), exhibiting at the Paris International. Married William MacDonald 1928 after which time she travelled with her husband extensively in Western Europe and in Canada. In the 1930s they moved to Edinburgh although they did not finally settle there until the early 1960s. Exhibited RSA(16) including a portrait of 'Hector Chalmers' (1938), and 'Head of a Dutchman' at the AAS in 1923 from 43, South St, St Andrews, & GI(3), from 1938 until 1946 at 116 Hanover St.

**HUNTLEY, Eric** **fl 1957-1982**
Painter of landscapes. Lived in Paxton, Berwickshire. Painted in a bold almost semi-abstract style with strong use of colour and minor attention to line. Exhibited RSA(3) between the above years.

**HUNTLY, Marchioness of** **fl 1887-1893**
Talented amateur painter in oil & watercolour. Painted mainly on her extensive travels abroad. Exhibited AAS(6) including 'The Golden Gate, Istanbul', and scenes in Japan, New Zealand, Australia, & Canada.

**HURD, Miss Margaret McFarlane** **1902-?**
Born Bothwell, Lanark. Painter, etcher, leather and craftworker. Landscape, interiors, buildings. Went to England at an early age, studied at Harrow School of Art and then moved to Grindleford, Debyshire, c1932. Exhibited between 1926 and 1940 at the RSA(15), RA(3), RCA(5), GI(18), AAS & L(1), after 1933 from Newstead, Grindleford, Derbyshire.

**HURD, Robert Andrew** **1905-1963**
Architect. Trained Edinburgh College of Art. Became assistant to Sir Frank Mears working on central Edinburgh planning 1931-1932,

especially in the Canongate area including the Tolbooth Area Redevelopment (1954-8). The leading exponent of his time of characteristic Scottish architecture, he was responsible for much restoration work in old Edinburgh and old Aberdeen and also, in 1956, at Culross Abbey House, Fife. Secretary and later President of the Saltire Society. Author of several textbooks including *Scotland under Trust* ( 1938) and (with Alan Reiach) *Building Scotland* (1941 & 44).
**Bibl:** Gifford 198,211-2; Glasgow Herald, 18 Sep 1963(obit); Scotsman, 18 Sep 1963(obit).

**HURREL, Steven** **fl 1988-**
Glasgow sculptor. Works in wood and stone. Exhibited GI(1), from 2 Bellhaven Terrace, Hillhead.

**HURT, Louis Bosworth** **1856-1929**
Born Ashbourne, Derbyshire; died Matlock, Derbyshire. Painter in oil of Highland landscape and cattle. Descended from an interesting English family, with Sitwell connections, having a long association with Derbyshire (what is now Green Hall, Ashbourne appears on a 1547 map as 'Hurt's House'). His son Colin played cricket for Derbyshire. His first training was with George Turner and his son at Barrow-on-Trent. An early example of Hurt's work shows Okeover Hall across the meadows in the sunshine. As he developed, almost all his work portrayed Highland cattle in their indigenous surroundings, often with swelling mists behind, or beside tumbling burns or mirror-still waters of some Highland loch. Also occasionally painted deer, and small landscapes done when at his holiday cottage in Snowdonia. Only one winter scene is recorded, a work commissioned by an expatriate Scot living in Pittsburgh. Kept his own Highland cattle to use as models and usually included at least one black cow in his composition. His work, always popular, has become increasingly so. Some mystery attaches to an artist who signed his work '**A. Millward**' and who exhibited twice at the GI in 1897 from Ashbourne in Derbyshire. His compositions and works seem identical to those of Louis Hurt's. To compound the mystery, Hurt's wife also exhibited 1886-1888 at the GI. It is unlikely that three artists living in the same town could have painted so similarly, especially as one became so famous but it remains unclear whether Millward was a pseudonym or a follower. Exhibited RA(19) 1891-1902, all of them Scottish scenes, also RSA(4), ROI(4), RBA(24), GI(22) & L(9), after 1887 from Ivonbrook, Darley Dale. Represented in Greenock AG, Manchester AG, Russell-Cotes AG (Bournemouth), Reading AG.

**HUSBAND, Eliza Stewart** **fl 1899-1913**
Edinburgh oil painter of portraits, especially children, still life, landscapes. Exhibited RSA(25), RSW(1), AAS & GI(11).

**HUTCHEON, Cynthia J S (née Watson)** **1946-**
Born Ponteland, Northumberland. Graphic & textile designer. School in Aberdeen followed by Gray's School of Art 1964-68. Runner-up, Cinzano Fabric into Fashion Award 1967. After a spell art teaching in Aberdeen moved to a staff appointment at Queen Margaret's College, Edinburgh 1971. First solo exhibition Aberdeen 1986. Occasional exhibitor AAS from Tigh-na-Dee, Crathes.

**HUTCHESON, James A** **fl 1831**
Edinburgh based painter of portraits, historical and literary subjects. Exhibited 3 works at the RSA in the above year, including a scene from *The Gentle Shepherd.*

**HUTCHESON, Jessie** **fl 1888-1893**
Glasgow flower painter. Exhibited GI(3) after 1889 from 6 Parkgrove.

**HUTCHESON, Miss Mary** **fl 1894-1896**
Glasgow landscape and farmyard painter. Exhibited GI(2) from 54 Albert Road, Crosshill.

**HUTCHESON, Thomas** **1922-**
Born Uddingston, Lanarkshire, 13 Nov. Landscape and figurative painter in oil and watercolour, sometimes semi-abstract. Studied Glasgow School of Art 1941-2 and 1946-9. Lived at Cumnock, Ayrshire. Member of the Glasgow Group. Preoccupied with colour used mainly as a vehicle for the expression of emotion and feeling. Exhibited RSA(39) 1950-1983, moving to Glasgow in 1953, also GI(89) & SSA, since 1966 from 73 Woodend Drive. Represented in Glasgow AG(3), Paisley AG, Bradford AG, Leeds AG, Manchester AG, Detroit AG, San Juan AG(Puerto Rico).

**HUTCHESON, Walter** **fl 1869-d1910**
Glasgow based painter in oil and watercolour of landscapes, especially scenes of Arran and the west coast, rustic scenes, genre and figurative subjects. Probably father of Miss Mary H(qv). Lived at 6 Douglas Place, Crosshill. Exhibited RSA(22) 1869-1905, RHA(2) & GI(73), after 1886 from 54 Albert Rd.

**HUTCHINSON, Miss Frances E** **fl 1849**
Portrait painter in oil; exhibited RSA(3).

**HUTCHISON, Alexander Campbell** **fl 1878**
Edinburgh landscape painter of local scenes in oil; exhibited RSA(1).

**HUTCHISON, Arthur G** **fl 1921**
Amateur Aberdeen artist. Exhibited AAS from 10 Albert St.

**HUTCHISON, Doris F (Mrs N Katz)** **fl 1939-1945**
Painter of flower pieces and still life in oil and watercolour. Exhibited RSA(6) & GI(2) from 7 Bellshaugh Road and later 15 Woodside Terrace, Glasgow.

**HUTCHISON, Emily** **fl 1895-1902**
Pollockshields designer. Exhibited GI(9) from 195 Nithsdale Road.

**HUTCHISON, George Jackson** **1896-1918**
Painter of pastoral scenes and animal subjects in oil and watercolour. Son of Robert Gemmell H(qv). Lived at 8 St Bernard's Crescent, Edinburgh and during the early years of WWI, before he was killed at Merville, France, just six months before the war ended. His favourite subjects were his pet donkey 'Neddy' and his dog 'Prince'. Exhibited RA(6), RSA(4), RSW(1), GI(4) & L(5). Represented by a single work 'Getting Ready' in Glasgow AG.

**HUTCHISON, Ian** **fl 1917**
Glasgow based painter. Exhibited GI(1) from 114 Berkeley Street.

**HUTCHISON, Ian** **fl 1956-1957**
Edinburgh based painter of landscape. Exhibited views of Perth and Edinburgh RSA from Comiston Road.

**HUTCHISON, Isabel Wylie (Mrs H Morley)** **fl 1896-1939**
Landscape painter. Often painted the rugged mountains of Greenland in a broad style making apt use of the whiteness of the paper. Also painted the lochs of Scotland and American views. Lived in Berkill, Stirling in the 1890s before moving to Glasgow 1895. Exhibited GI(6), latterly from Carlowrie, Kirliston, West Lothian.
**Bibl:** Halsby 264.

**HUTCHISON, James A** **fl 1832-1881**
Painter in oil of portraits, rustic scenes, subject paintings and occasional still life. Some confusion has been caused by the various spellings of his name, he himself used both Hutchison and Hutcheson and by the fact that he lived in a variety of addresses in Edinburgh, Glasgow and latterly at Woodlands, Lochgoil. Member of the West of Scotland Academy. Exhibited 26 works at the RSA between the above years, including 'Fugitives from the massacre of Glencoe' (1834), 'Elijah in the cave' (1840) and the portrait of the 'Rev Dr Thomas Chalmers' (1838). Also exhibited occasionally at the GI(13), latterly from Lochgoilhead.

**HUTCHISON, James Hay** **fl 1881**
Edinburgh painter. Exhibited RSA(1) a rustic scene in watercolour from 10 Breadalbane Terrace.

**HUTCHISON, John A RSA** **1833-1910**
Born Laurieston, Edinburgh; died Edinburgh, 23 May. Sculptor. Specialised in portrait and figure sculpture in bronze, marble and wood. Studied at Trustees' Academy 1848 and in Rome c1849. Studied under Robert Scott Lauder(qv) in Edinburgh and Alfred Gatley in Rome. After an apprenticeship with a wood carver in Edinburgh he clearly greatly benefited from his training. He was the only sculptor working in Edinburgh around 1900 trained by Lauder.

'He blended a national vigour and realistic propriety with a feeling for the chaste purity of the classic ideal'. Among his work was a colossal bronze statue of John Knox for the quadrangle of New College, Edinburgh. His bust of his teacher R S Lauder, illustrated in the *AJ* 1898, was said to be a good likeness. Elected ARSA 1862, RSA 1867. Librarian of the Academy 1877-1886, Treasurer 1886-1907. In 1909 he was made an 'Honorary Retired Academician'. Exhibited in London from 1861 but mainly at the RSA(179) & GI(9) marble busts, latterly from 3 Thomas St, Edinburgh. Represented in NGS, SNPG(6), Canongate Church, Greyfriars Church, New College, the gilded figure carrying the torch of learning over the dome of the Old Quad (1879), the Adam Black monument in Princes St Gdns (1876-7), the Dean Cemetery and Fitzwilliam Museum, Cambridge. His marble bust of Queen Victoria (1880) exhibited RSA 1889 was presented to the Victoria AG, Dundee.
**Bibl:** Gifford 149,155,160,185,189,284,314,316,389-90,435,438, 577.

**HUTCHISON, Maud Gemmell** **fl 1908-1925**
Painter in oil and watercolour; mainly still life and coastal scenes. Sister of Robert(qv) and George Jackson H(qv). Exhibited RSA(11), RSW(4), GI(8) & L(2), latterly from 8 St. Bernard's Crescent, Edinburgh.

**HUTCHISON, Robert Gemmell RSA RBA ROI RSW 1855-1936**
Born Edinburgh; died St Abbs, Berwickshire. Landscape figure and portrait painter. Husband of Janet Boe (of Biggar) and father of George Jackson H(qv) and Maud H(qv). After his school days he began work as a seal engraver but this was soon abandoned in favour of painting. Studied at the Board of Manufacturers School of Art, Edinburgh. Painter in oil and watercolour, concentrating on children in interiors and paddling on sun-filled beaches, illustrating the strong influence of MacTaggart. He was extremely sympathetic in his treatment of childhood which 'if somewhat literal, is fresh and individual'. His treatment of children by the sea shows the strong influence of MacTaggart. Awarded a gold medal at the Paris Salon for his 'Bairnies, cuddle doon'. Both in technique and in the way in which his composition was treated his work followed closely that of the Hague School while in his later work the influence of Joseph Israels(qv) is very apparent. He was prolific and has remained extremely popular enjoying a market reputation that currently surpasses almost all his contemporaries. During many summers he painted at Carnoustie and latterly at Coldingham. His only grandchild, **Jean Isabel MONTGOMERY** (1913-1990), nicknamed 'Snooky' completed some oil paintings and studies. Lived latterly at 8 St Bernard's Crescent, Edinburgh. Elected RSW 1895, ARSA 1901, RSA 1911. Exhibited RA(55), RSA(184), RSW(118), GI(113) & AAS, after 1912 from 8 St. Bernard's Crescent. Represented in Kelvingrove AG, Glasgow(4), Greenock AG, Walker AG, Liverpool, Paisley Art Institute, RSA, Toronto AG(Canada).
**Bibl:** AJ 1900, 321-6; Caw 427-8; Halsby 71, 166, 167, 241, 264; Hardie III 193; Studio 1913, 134, 136; 1915, 103.

**HUTCHISON, Shand Campbell** **1920-?**
Born Dalkeith. Painter in oil, watercolour and pastel of landscape and figurative subjects. Trained Edinburgh College of Art 1939-40 and again after WW2 1946-49. Thereafter travelled and studied in France and Spain. Taught part-time at Edinburgh College of Art also at Heriot Watt and Edinburgh University. President, Scottish Arts Club 1968-70. Exhibited RSA(20) 1923-64, also RSW & SSA.

**HUTCHISON, Walter** **fl 1885**
Amateur Glasgow artist; exhibited AAS from 6 Douglas Pl, Crosshill.

**HUTCHISON, Sir William Oliphant PRSA RP** **1889-1970**
Born Kirkcaldy, 2 Jly; died 5 Feb. Portrait and landscape painter. Studied Edinburgh College of Art 1909-1912 under Edward A Walton(qv), whose daughter Margery he married, and in Paris. In 1912 in association with Eric Robertson(qv), D M Sutherland(qv), Spence Smith(qv) and A R Sturrock(qv) he formed the Edinburgh Group. Became Director, Glasgow School of Art 1933-43. Lived in Kirkcaldy and Edinburgh before moving to London 1922 and to near Woodbridge, Suffolk 1936. His principal works include 'Kitchen bathroom', 'Margery in my Overall', 'A family group', and 'Black Water', also 'Derby Day', (exhibited RA 1933). Elected ARSA 1937, RSA 1943, RP 1948, PRSA 1950, VPRP 1960, knighted 1953. Exhibited RSA(63), RA(25), GI(100), L(13), RBA(2) & Paris Salon. Represented in SNPG(2), including Queen Elizabeth II, Glasgow AG(4) and Kirkcaldy AG.
**Bibl:** Halsby 220.

**HUTH, Frederick, Jnr** **fl 1881-d1906**
Edinburgh engraver and watercolour painter of landscapes, buildings, interiors and portraits. Exhibited RA(8) & RSA(24) from 43 Albany Street. One of his etchings after Rembrandt was exhibited at the RSA in 1887 and an engraving of Gainsborough's portrait of 'Mrs Graham' attracted considerable attention when first shown at the RA in 1898.

**HUTTON, Charles** **1905-1995**
Born Annan, Dumfriesshire, Jly 28; died Sep 11. Architect. Educated Bellahouston Academy, Sheffield and Bolton. A scholarship enabled him to attend Liverpool School of Architecture. Worked in Paris and London 1929-36, being involved in the building and design of Osterley Underground Station, for which he was largely responsible, and London University Senate House. One of the last surviviors of the Arts and Crafts Movement. Member various committees of the British Standards Institution and was a governor of two colleges. Finally settled in Somerset.
**Bibl:** The Times, Obituary, Sep 23 1995.

**HUTTON, D Inglis** **fl 1948-1950**
Glasgow painter in oil and watercolour of landscape and portraiture. Exhibited GI(3), from 12 Borland Rd, Bearsden.

**HUTTON, James** **1894-1957**
Born Broughty Ferry. Little known minor marine watercolourist. Exhibited GI(1).
**Bibl:** Halsby 264.

**HUTTON, John P** **fl 1913**
Edinburgh based painter. Exhibited at the Walker Gallery, Liverpool (1) from 71 Clerk Street.

**HUTTON, Katharina** **fl 1898**
Coatbridge artist. Exhibited 'Butterflies' at the GI from Briarfield.

**HUTTON, Robert** **fl 1681-d1696**
Son of Robert Hutton, Baillie of Queensferry. Apprenticed to John Munro, painter, in 1691 and made a Burgess of City of Edinburgh in 1692. Also a member of the Incorporation of St Mary's.
**Bibl:** Apted 48.

**HUTTON, Thomas Swift** **fl 1887-1906**
Landscape painter in both mediums, moved from Glasgow to England in the turn of the century, but returned to Glasgow c1906. In 1898 he exhibited a 'View of St Abb's Head' at the RA and the following year a 'View of the Needle's Eye - the glories of departing day', from 21 Charing Cross, Glasgow. Exhibited RSA(4), RA(2), GI(1) & L(5).

**HUTTON, William** **c1780-?**
Edinburgh engraver. Resided in the High Street. In 1810-11 was in partnership with George Walker(qv). By 1819 he had taken another partner, the firm being then known as Hutton and Balmain. In 1820 he engraved Gow's *Fourth Collection of Strathspeys*. Two pen sketches of the interior of Blackness Castle, both signed and dated July 22 1782, are in the NGS.
**Bibl:** Bushnell, Scottish Notes and Queries, Nov 1928.

**HUXLEY-JONES, Thomas Bayliss FRBS ARCA** **1908-1969**
Born Aberdeen. Sculptor. Lived in Aberdeen where he was head of the sculpture department, Gray's School of Art 1937-47, before moving to work in London. Retired to Essex. Specialised in portrait figures, exhibiting 27 at the RSA between 1935 and 1957 including a fine portrait bust of 'Fiddes Watt' (1942) and 'Sir William Hamilton-Fyfe, Principal of Aberdeen University' (1944); and frequently at the AAS from 1935.

**HYMANS, Henry S** **fl 1858**
Edinburgh oil painter of narrative subjects; exhibited RSA(2).

**HYNDMAN, Mrs Gwendoline** **fl 1970**
Dunbartonshire sculptress. Exhibited a portrait bust in plaster at the GI from 46 Dumbuck Crescent, Dumbarton.

**HYSLOP, Jane** **1967-**
Born Edinburgh. Painter & printmaker. Trained Edinburgh College of Art 1985-1990. Winner of several awards including the Creighton Print award (RSA) 1988, Mary Armour student prize 1989, John Kinross travelling scholarship 1989, Andrew Grant Bequest (ECA) 1989, Elizabeth Greenshields Foundation grant (Canada) 1990 & the Latimer Prize (RSA) 1997. Recipient of many commissions by Scottish local authorities. Exhibited RSA 1997-. Represented in Edinburgh City AG, NLS, RSA Archive.

# I

**IBBOTSON, Marjorie** **fl 1937-1939**
Silversmith. Although of English origin, moved to Edinburgh c1939 remaining there during the war, thereafter moving to Decor Studio, Sheffield. Exhibited RSA a silver cross set with turquoise and lapis-lazuli in 1939; also SWA(1).

**IMHOF-CARDINAL, Catherine** **c1955-**
French semi-abstract figurative painter. Trained in sculpture and drawing at the Ecole des Beaux Arts. Settled in Scotland in the early 1980s. Her work is informed by a strong sense of generally soft colours accompanied by an unusual method of composition whereby a painting gradually emerges from a series of lines thrown onto a sheet, the subject suggesting itself through the creative work process. First solo exhibition Aberdeen 1985 followed by others in England, Singapore, Switzerland, France, Canada and Scotland at annual intervals. Exhibits RSA, Australia & France from Blairs, Aberdeenshire.

**IMLACH, Miss Agnes Campbell** **fl 1867-1901**
Edinburgh painter in oil and watercolour of portraits and interiors. Sister of Archibald F I(qv). Exhibited RSA(14), including a fine portrait of her father 1875 and an historically interesting sketch of 'Sir Walter Scott's study at Astieshiel' 1887. Also exhibited a portrait at the AAS in 1894, from 48 Queen's Street.

**IMLACH, Archibald F** **fl 1879-1892**
Edinburgh painter in oil; portraits, landscape and literary subjects. Brother of Agnes I(qv). Exhibited RSA(36), GI(12), AAS(2) & L(3), after 1886 from 13 Ravelston Park.

**IMLACH, William** **fl 1966**
Aberdeenshire painter of figure studies and local scenes. Exhibited AAS(2) from 6 Foreman Drive, Peterhead.

**IMPETT, Miss Agnes L** **fl 1954**
Edinburgh-based sculptress. Exhibited a statuette in lime wood at the GI from 31 Primrose Terrace.

**IMRIE, Archibald Brown** **1900-c1968**
Born Edinburgh, 23 Dec. Painter in watercolour and oil, etcher and lithographer. Figurative works, landscape and buildings. Also commercial artist. Studied Edinburgh College of Art, RSA Life School, Paris and Florence. Travelled to the latter on a Carnegie travelling scholarship. Lived for many years in Edinburgh, exhibiting quite regularly in London & USA. Exhibited RSA(17), RSW(1) & GI(7), from 1951 at 7 Merchiston Gdns. Represented in Kirkcaldy AG.

**IMRIE, Donald S** **fl 1981**
Aberdeen printmaker; exhibited AAS(1) from 19D Ferrier Crescent.

**INCORPORATION OF ST MARY'S** **c1635-?**
Painters were first specified by name in a craft guild in a charter confirmed by Charles I 1635. Before the Reformation this was known as the **Incorporation of St. John's Chapel** but when the crafts moved to St. Mary's chapel in Niddrie's Close, it assumed the above name. At the conclusion of their apprenticeship painters were required to complete 'essays', examples recorded in Apted and Colston. Other activities included the settlement of disputes between master and apprentice, between members, and the furtherance of the interests of members (including protection against other guilds and non-members). Once qualified, a painter had to pay the equivalent of an entrance fee to become a burgess before being allowed to practice his trade. In 1709 two members (Roderick Chalmers and James Norie) suggested that painters might qualify for membership by decorating the guild's property rather than by paying a fee. In 1720 the herald painter, Chalmers(qv), executed a chimney-piece portraying the ten trades at work outside Holyrood, including a probable self-portrait as the painter sitting before an easel. This work, 'The Edinburgh Trades', can be seen in the Joint Incorporation of Wrights and Masons in Edinburgh.
**Bibl:** Apted 3-5; J Colston, The Incorporated Trades of Edinburgh, Edinburgh 1891, 65-75; George Hay, 'A Scottish Altarpiece', Innes Rev. VII,5; Macmillan [SA] 84-5; Ranald Nicholson, Scotland, The Later Middle Ages, Edinburgh 1989, 591.

**INGLEBY, Joseph** **1962-**
Sculptor. Trained Slade School & West Surrey College of Art & Design 1983-1988. Joined Glasgow Sculpture Studios 1989. Awarded RSA bursary 1988; major Artists' Award Pollock-Krasner Foundation (NY). Exhibits RSA, SSA. His work is publicly sited in several places including the William Morris Museum (Kelmscott Manor) & the University of Stirling. Lives at 4 Woodlands Drive, Glasgow.

**INGLEFIELD, Mrs Charlotte** **fl 1866-1867**
Edinburgh based landscape painter in oil. Exhibited landscapes of the Lake District and Perthshire and two paintings of Carthage at the RSA during the above years, moving later to Bedale.

**INGLES, David N ARHA** **?-d1933**
Scottish portrait painter who moved to Dublin c1917 and finally to London c1930. Elected ARHA 1919. Exhibited RSA(4), RHA(25), a portrait of 'Tom Scott RSA' at the GI(1912) & L(1), from Forest View, Selkirk.

**INGLES, George Scott ARCA (Lond)** **1874-?**
Born Hawick, 5 Mar. Painter, lithographer and wood block printer; landscape, figure studies and country buildings. Studied Royal College of Art, obtaining a travelling scholarship. Vice-principal of Leicester College of Arts and Crafts. Lived in Leicester after moving from Galashiels. Exhibited RSA(19), RA(19), GI(5) & L(3).

**INGLES, William Scott Anderson** **fl 1910-1940**
Hawick painter and engraver; genre and local landscapes. Exhibited RSA(18) & L(1).

**INGLIS, Alexander ('Rufus') MBE RSW** **1911-1992**
Born Elgin; died Kendal. Painter in oil and collage, landscapes and topographical subjects in Britain and abroad, also plaster figures and potter. Married the English artist Alice Lake. Trained Edinburgh and Munich, held an Andrew Grant fellowship in mural painting 1936-1938. Served in the Merchant Navy 1940-1945. After the war became Art Master at Sedburgh. Exhibited RSA(45) since 1932 and once - 'Canisp, Suilven and Cul Mhor' - at the GI, from 12 Westwood Ave, Kendal, Cumbria.

**INGLIS, Bessie D** **fl 1927-39**
Edinburgh based painter in watercolour; garden scenes, especially trees and rustic buildings. Exhibited RSA(13) including 'The Old Rectory, Dunkeld' and 'The Cowshed'.

**INGLIS, David M M** **fl 1948**
Edinburgh based artist; exhibited a flower study at the RSA.

**INGLIS, Mrs Deborah Margery** **fl 1951-1960**
Argyll painter; Spanish rural landscape and figurative works. Exhibited GI(3) from Rarera, Kilniver, by Oban.

**INGLIS, Esther (Mrs Bartholomew Kello)** **1571-1624**
Believed to have been born in Dieppe; died England, 30 Aug. Calligrapher and miniaturist. Daughter of Nicholas Langlois who fled to England following the St Bartholomew massacre 1572. Settled in Edinburgh as a school teacher 1578. Instructed in calligraphy by her mother, Marie Prisott. In about 1596 married Bartholomew Kello. Lived Edinburgh from 1599 until moving to England 1607. Shortly before leaving Scotland she prepared an illuminated manuscript "Cinquante Octonaires sur la Vanitex et Inconstance du Monde", containing a Self-portrait. In 1609 her manuscript *A Book of the Armes doone by me Esther Inglis, Januar the first 1609* was a gift to Henry, Prince of Wales. This contained "the skilfully limned portraiture of Esther Inglis dressed in black, with the wide-spreading ruff of the time round her neck, and a jaunty little high-peaked hat overtopping her yellow hair". The British Museum contains MSS by Inglis; two of them (ROY MS 17 D xvi and ADD MS 27, 927) contain self-portraits, also 'Self-portrait' dated 1595 is in SNPG; and the Royal Library.
**Bibl:** Apted, 48-9; Archaeol J XIX, 1862, 188; Bradley; Bryan;

Brydall 70-1; DNB (see Kello); Foskett, British Miniature Portraits, i 349; D Laing, 'Notes Relating to Mrs Esther Inglis' Proc Soc Antiqs of Scotland, vi 284-289; Long 235-6; Macmillan [SA], 65.

**INGLIS, Evelyn S** **fl 1967**
Aberdeen painter; exhibited 'A Mythological landscape' at the AAS from 188 Midstocket Road.

**INGLIS, Frank Caird** **fl 1900-1904**
Edinburgh landscape painter in oil. Exhibited RSA(5) & 'A Dutch canal' AAS in 1902 from Rock House, Calton Hill.

**INGLIS, Hazel** **fl 1978**
Aberdeen painter. Trained at Gray's School of Art, Aberdeen. Exhibited AAS(2) from 18 Holburn Rd.

**INGLIS, J A Russel** **fl 1891-1901**
Edinburgh based painter of topographical scenes, generally in Scotland and occasionally Italy. Exhibited RSA(7) between the above years.

**INGLIS, James** **fl 1866-1891**
North-east painter who lived for a time in Aberdeen & Dundee; painted figurative subjects and portraits in oil. Exhibited RSA(8) & AAS(2), latterly from 6 Comely Green Pl, Edinburgh.

**INGLIS, Jean** **fl 1918-1933**
London-based flower and figure painter; exhibited once at the AAS from 70 High St, Hampstead (1933) and once at the GI from 1 Holly Place, NW.

**INGLIS, Jessie S** **fl 1868**
Edinburgh watercolour painter; exhibited a topographical sketch at the RSA.

**INGLIS, John RSW** **1953-**
Born Glasgow. Son of a policeman. Educated Hillhead High School, Glasgow 1965-1970 and Gray's School of Art, Aberdeen 1970-1974; post-diploma 1975. Spent a year at Hospitalfield 1973. In 1975 awarded the Keith prize and in 1976 another travelling scholarship enabled him to visit Italy. In 1980 received an SAC award and in 1982 the RSA Meyer Oppenheim Award. In 1987 he won the Educational Institute of Scotland Award and 1994 the May Marshall Brown Award (RSW). Member of the Dundee Group 1979-1984. During his years as a student became friendly with Ian Mackenzie Smith(qv), then Curator of Aberdeen AG, whom he helped in the hanging of exhibitions. Subsequently worked for a year in a commercial gallery before teaching art at Clackmannan College. Works primarily in watercolour and has become increasingly abstract, although finely delineated and colourful. Pays little regard to market interests, remaining true to his own personal vision in the contemporary academic tradition. First solo exhibition overseas, Illinois, 1997. Elected RSW 1984. Exhibits regularly RSA, RSW, GI(5) & AAS 1974-86. Represented in Aberdeen AG.

**INGLIS, Johnston J** **fl 1887-1888**
Dunfermline painter in oil of landscapes, often in Argyllshire. Exhibited RSA(4) between the above years and at the GI in 1900 when living at Montrose, Donnybrook, Dublin.

**INGLIS, Miss M Haddon** **fl 1927**
Nairn painter; exhibited one painting at the Walker Gallery, Liverpool from The Little House.

**INGLIS, Matthew** **1958-**
Born Stirling. Designer and sculptor. Trained Edinburgh College of Art 1976-81, specialising in tapestry. SAC award 1984. Artist-in-residence, Univ. of St Andrews 1988. Three principal elements in his work are free standing sculpture, miniature tableaux and wall panels.
**Bibl:** Bill Hare, Contemporary Painting in Scotland, Edinburgh 1993.

**INGLIS, Sister Meeda** **1913-?**
Born Arbroath. Painter in oil and watercolour of portraits and commonplace objects and scenes; teacher and member of the International Society of the Sacred Heart. Trained Gray's School of Art and Hospitalfield School of Painting where she was the first woman in their graduate programme. Taught Dublin and Aberdeen before becoming Head of Art, Craiglockhart College of Education. Exhibited AAS from her home in Queen's Cross, Aberdeen.

**INGLIS, Michael A** **fl 1971**
Aberdeen painter; exhibited AAS(2).

**INGLIS, Robert** **fl 1899**
Painter. Exhibited a landscape at the GI from 19 North Coburg Street, Glasgow.

**INGRAM, Alexander** **fl 1884**
Glasgow-based figure painter; exhibited GI(2) from 32 Bank Street, Hillhead.

**INGRAM, Jane S** **fl 1928**
Amateur painter. Exhibited RSA(1) from 22 Great King Street, Edinburgh.

**INGRAM, Margaret K** **fl 1883-1886**
Aberdeen-based landscape painter, sometimes of Venetian scenes. Moved to Aberdeen c1885. Exhibited RBA(2) & AAS from 28 Ashley Rd.

**INGRAM, R S** **fl 1877**
Born Glasgow. Watercolour painter. Son of the Rev G S Ingram and brother of William Ayerst I(qv). Exhibited once at the RSW in the above year.

**INGRAM, William Ayerst RBA RI ROI** **1855-1913**
Born Glasgow; died Falmouth. Painter in oil and watercolour of landscapes and seascapes. Son of Rev G S Ingram, brother of R S I(qv). Pupil of J Steeple and A W Weedon. An immoderate traveller, enjoyed most painting coastal and river scenes. Hardie writes 'much of his work was in oil, but his watercolour drawings of subjects found on the coast and the open sea have a quiet, though not impressive accomplishment, lacking in bite or personality.' In 1894 he opened a gallery in Falmouth with the English artist, H S Chook. Elected RI 1907, ROI 1906. President of the Royal British Colonial Society of Artists 1888. Exhibited RA(44) from 1880 and at the RBA from 1883, also RSW(1), ROI(27), RI(53) & GI(4), from Albion House, Falmouth, but never at the RSA. Represented in V & A, National Maritime Museum, Greenwich, Sydney AG.
**Bibl:** Martin Hardie III, 82 (pl 105); RA Cats 1905, 1907, 1912; Who's Who 1913, 1914.

**INNES, Mrs Alexander** **fl 1885-87**
Amateur Kincardineshire artist. Exhibited 'Unsettled weather' and two other works at the AAS from Raemoir, Mill of Forest, Stonehaven.

**INNES, Callum** **1962-**
Born Edinburgh. Painter in oil of portraits, landscape and abstracts. Trained Gray's School of Art, Aberdeen 198-84 followed by a year at Edinburgh College of Art. In 1987 spent a further year studying in Amsterdam. First one-man exhibition in Aberdeen 1986. 'My earlier work was involved with figuration and self-expression. The new work is still an expression of self but I want the paintings to live and breathe beyond my intentions...I am trying to combine that sense of independence with the visibility of process'. Exhibits AAS. Lives in Edinburgh.
**Bibl:** Bill Hare, Contemporary Painting in Scotland, Edinburgh 1993; Third Eye Centre, Glasgow 'Scatter', (Ex Cat 1989).

**INNES, George B** **1913-1970**
Born Glasgow. Carver in stone. Spent four years at the Glasgow School of Art and in 1936 exhibited with the painter James Law Forsyth(qv) in Glasgow. In 1938 he showed four stone carvings at the Glasgow Empire Exhibition. In 1939 he volunteered for the army. During war service his hands were badly burned. Thereafter, work became difficult and his subsequent output was greatly reduced. After 1945 he became strongly influenced by the work of Henry Moore, composing heavy, simplified masses reminiscent of pre-Columbian sculpture. After 1947 he pursued a literal Cubist style, reducing figures to rigid geometrical arrangements with carved facets. Although he continued working until the end of his life, he had

become a sad almost forgotten figure. Exhibited RSA(4) 1939, 1947 and 1956, & GI(4) from 996 Pollokshaws Rd. Represented in Kirkcaldy AG.
**Bibl:** T.S. Halliday and George Bruce, Scottish Sculpture : A Record of Twenty Years, 1946; Hartley 139.

**INNES, John** **fl 1939**
Edinburgh artist; exhibited 'Timber houses at Nurnberg' at the RSA from 11 Eltringham Gardens.

**INNES, Moira** **1957-**
Born Edinburgh. Sculptress. Works are mostly in wood, plaster and ceramic constructions based on old chairs and other domestic objects to which she enjoys giving a new meaning. Trained Edinburgh College of Art 1975-1980, employed by Scottish Sculpture Trust to supervise open-air sculpture exhibitions. Since 1980 part-time lecturer at the Duncan of Jordanstone College of Art and visiting lecturer at Gray's School of Art. From 1984-1986 she was on the Board of Directors, Scottish Sculpture Workshops. In 1985 received an SAC award to represent the Scottish Sculpture Trust and the Federation of Scottish Sculptures at the International Congress in Chicago. Exhibited RSA(1) 1984.

**INNES, Robert** **fl 1827-1876**
Edinburgh portrait painter in oil, also figurative subjects. By 1837 he had an established practise at 5 Lothian Road, but after some years moved to larger studios in Frederick Street. Toured the country regularly and for a number of years visited Inverness annually. In 1843 he completed a fine portrait 'Provost Alexander Cumming' who had resigned the provostship prematurely in 1840. Another portrait was 'Dr Alexander Rose', commissioned by the Kirk Session and for many years in the vestry of the High Church; engraved 1844. Other sitters included 'Captain Fraser of Knockie', 'Dr Nicol, Provost of Inverness' (1840-1843), 'James Grant, 12th Laird of Glenmoriston'; 'Lady Saltoun of Ness Castle' (1846) and 'Bishop Eden'. In 1851 he painted the well-known Elgin personality 'Isaac Forsyth'. This large painting hung in the Assembly Rooms of the Trinity Lodge of Freemasons in that town for many years. Exhibited 67 works at the RSA, including 'Sheriff Gordon as Captain in the Highland Volunteers' (1861) and 'James Eckford Lauder RSA' (1867), the latter now in the SNPG.
**Bibl:** W Simpson, Inverness Artists, 1925, 26-28.

**INSH, K Margaret** **fl 1945-**
Dundee artist, trained at Dundee College of Art 1941-1946 where she was awarded a post-diploma scholarship. After marrying 1949 abandoned painting for about 12 years. Then resumed her artistic career, guided by a deep interest in conservation, concentrating on bird and flower studies. Her husband and three children are all amateur artists. Her bird studies are accurate, characterised by delicacy, tender colour and detail. They tend to be small with unambitious composition. Lives in Auchterarder, Perthshire.

**INSH, Richard John** **fl 1975-1988**
Aberdeen artist; exhibited mainly local landscapes at the AAS during the above period from 24 Rosebank Pl.

**INSH, Rodger** **1950-**
Born Jan 22. Abstract & landscape painter. Trained Duncan of Jordanstone College of Art 1967-71. Won first prize, Pernod Scottish Painting Show 1974. Solo exhibitions Kirkcaldy AG & elsewhere. Exhibits RSA, RSW, AAS.

**INSTITUTE FOR THE ENCOURAGEMENT OF THE FINE ARTS IN SCOTLAND** **1819-1830**
Founded on the 1st Feb, 1819 under the auspices of twenty-four directors headed by the Duke of Argyll and including the Marquis of Queensberry and the Earls of Fife, Haddington, Hopetoun, Elgin, and Wemyss and March. An inaugural exhibition was held in Raeburn's private gallery, attached to his studio in York Place. This included 92 loaned works, most of them owned by the directors. Life membership was fixed at £50 and, remarkably, no artist sat on any committee. After a second exhibition in 1820 it was agreed that contemporary artists might contribute and in 1821 there appeared works by Raeburn himself, Geddes, George Simson, Wright, Geikie, Andrew Wilson, Patrick Nasmyth, Patrick Gibson, John Wilson and Clarkson Stanfield together with sculptures by Chantrey, Josephs and Scoular. The exhibition of 1826 was held in Playfair's new Royal Institution. The building was to accommodate the Board of Trustees, the Royal Society of Edinburgh, the Society of Antiquaries of Scotland and the above Institute, the last three as tenants of the first. Exhibitions continued there for three more years but increasing hostility from the artists eventually led to the establishment of an independent Scottish Academy. For a short time rivalry between the two bodies persisted and at first the Institute had the better of it, helped by commissions given by the directors to artists who remained loyal. In 1830 their exhibition included works by living artists but it was not successful and later that year the Institute disappeared.
**Bibl:** Brydall 329-337; Irwin 187-8, 206, 236.

**INVERNESS GOVERNMENT SCHOOL OF SCIENCE AND ART** **1865-?**
Artistic endeavour and interest around Inverness wilted in the mid-nineteenth century leading to the foundation of the above School under the initial direction of Robert L Bain, a certificated teacher. In Sep 1867 an exhibition was held, the main attractions being a number of Old Master paintings including works by or after Carrachi, Claude, Cuyp, Dolci, Titian and Zucharelli. The only exhibiting local artist of note was Alexander F Sutherland(qv). A further exhibition followed in 1881 under the patronage of Queen Victoria. No fewer than ten lady artists were represented - a high proportion for those days, as well as works by Reynolds, Millais, John Phillip(qv), and the Nasmyths(qv).
**Bibl:** William Simpson, 'Inverness Artists' in Inverness Courier, 30 Dec 1924-20 Jan 1925.

**INVERNESS ROYAL ACADEMY** **1792-?**
Founded in 1792 and governed by a board of directors, a drawing master was included on the staff of the school almost from the beginning and, according to Simpson, this continued throughout the nineteenth century. A teacher called **MOODIE** taught drawing as well as arithmetic and geography. In 1805 the directors were so pleased with his work that in addition to his official duties he was permitted to offer private tuition, but in 1807 a complaint was received and the privilege was rescinded, leading to his resignation the following year. Other distinguished art teachers included John Guy Hamilton(qv), James Glen(qv), M Jastresbski(qv) and P Delavault(qv).
**Bibl:** William Simpson, 'Inverness Artists', Inverness Courier, 30 Dec 1924-20 Jan 1925.

**IRONS, Miss Agnes R** **fl 1898-1924**
Edinburgh painter in oil and watercolour, portraits, genre and landscape. Particularly fond of introducing domestic fowl into her genre paintings. Exhibited RSA(15), RSW(1) & GI(1), from 13 Glenorchy Terrace.

**IRONSIDE, Christine** **1953-**
Born Aberdeenshire, 7 Oct. Studied Edinburgh College of Art 1971-1976 and Moray House 1977. Obtained a Hospitalfield scholarship in 1974, and a travelling award enabling her to visit Greece in 1976. In 1984 she won first prize in a photographic competition and in 1986 was awarded an SAC grant. Her work is mostly still-life and figure compositions although from 1986-1988 she concentrated on flower and still-life watercolours done on fine paper. Fascinated by primitive birds and animals alongside celtic symbols, characterised by the use of rich and vibrant colour, often with black and in a stylised manner showing the influence of Egyptian art. Recently returned to working on figures in oil. Her portraits have been shown at the SNPG.

**IRONSIDE, W Dalton** **fl 1923-1926**
Amateur Aberdeen painter. Exhibited landscapes AAS(2) from 29 Rubislaw Den South.

**IRVINE, Mrs Anna M Forbes** **fl 1851-1886**
Aberdeenshire painter in watercolour who early in life moved to Edinburgh but continued painting landscapes mostly of Aberdeenshire as well as Egyptian scenes. One of the Irvines of Drum. Exhibited RSA(25) & AAS. Early works were from Edinburgh but after 1872 lived mostly at Drum Castle.

**IRVINE, Miss E** **fl 1865**
Landscape painter; exhibited at the RSA(2) from London.

**IRVINE, George G ARIBA** **fl 1906-1908**
Aberdeen architect and draughtsman. Exhibited architectural and ecclesiastical designs and drawings AAS(3) from 231A Union St.

**IRVINE, Georgina** **fl 1893**
Edinburgh artist. Exhibited 'An Aberdeenshire landscape' at the AAS from 12 Queen St.

**IRVINE, Mrs Helen** **fl 1942**
Lanark painter. Exhibited 'November' at the GI from 55 Carlisle Rd, Lesmahagaow.

**IRVINE, Hugh** **fl 1808-1829**
Landscape painter, probably itinerant. In 1811 he exhibited three works, 'An Aberdeenshire view', 'A view from Castle Street, Aberdeen', and 'A study from nature, Aberdeenshire', these were followed in 1812 by 'On the Banks of Loch Muick, Aberdeenshire', and in 1813 there was 'A View on the River Feugh, Kincardineshire'. Also many works in the area of Rome and Egypt. In 1824 he was back painting a landscape at Altyre, Morayshire, the seat of Sir William Gordon Cumming, and of Dunkeld, the seat of the Duke of Atholl. Never exhibited in Scotland. Exhibited RA(27) 1808-1829. Represented in Drum Castle (NTS).

**IRVINE, James,of Rome** **1757-1832**
Born Scotland, Mar 18. History painter and art dealer. Studied at the RA Schools in 1777. Began as a history painter but became more active as a dealer in Rome where he remained until at least 1828. In 1787 he exhibited 'Ganymede' at the Royal Academy (now in Marischal College, Aberdeen) followed by another work 1794. Visited and painted in the United States c 1818. Exhibited twice at the Institution for the Encouragement of the Fine Arts in Scotland (predecessor of the RSA), 1826 and 1828; elected an honorary member 1830. In 1828 contributed to the RSA from Italy 'Satan Rising from Chaos'. On 30 May, 1830 his membership, together with his appointment as 'Corresponding Member' was proposed by Thomas Hamilton(qv), seconded by Watson Gordon(qv). Delighted with the compliment, Irvine replied on 11 Sep that he was forwarding as a gift to the Academy the first cast from the first mould made of the Venus de Medici which he had purchased 25 years earlier from the caster himself.
**Bibl:** Esmé Gordon, The Royal Scottish Academy, Edinburgh 1976, 33-4; Waterhouse.

**IRVINE, James** **1833-1899**
Born Menmuir, Forfarshire; died Hillside, Montrose. Portrait painter in oil. Pupil of Colvin Smith(qv) at Brechin; subsequently studied Edinburgh Academy, becoming employed by Mr Carnegy-Arbuthnott of Balnamoon to paint portraits of retainers on the estate. Practised as a portrait painter for some years at Arbroath before moving to Montrose. After a period of considerable struggle, eventually became recognised as one of the leading portrait painters in Scotland of his time, receiving numerous commissions. Close friend of George Paul Chalmers(qv). Painted the occasional landscape and in his later years came to Edinburgh, where the influence of Chalmers increased. His earlier work had shown the influence of Watson Gordon(qv), his later work gained in picturesqueness but lost in individuality. 'His work was distinguished by powerful light and shade, by low-toned but rich colour, and by expressive, if somewhat ragged brush work. In characterisation, also, they were often very good. He was almost equally happy in dealing with men and women' [McKay]. One of his best male portraits was the powerful study 'Quartermaster Coull - one of the boarders of the Chesapeake and the man who steered the Shannon into action in the duel fought off Boston on 1 June, 1813' (RSA 1874). Exhibited RA(2) 1882 and 1884 but mainly RSA(47) from 1849 to 1885, also GI(5) & AAS, latterly from 52 York Place. Represented in SNPG.
**Bibl:** Caw 289; DNB; McKay 322-3; SNPG Cat 1889.

**IRVINE, James** **fl 1881**
Edinburgh painter of figurative subjects in oil; exhibited 'The Stagecoach' at the RSA.

**IRVINE, Miss Jennifer** **fl 1987-**
Glasgow painter of still life and semi-abstracts. Exhibited GI(8) from 45 Clouston St.

**IRVINE, John** **fl 1784**
Edinburgh engraver. Married in Old Greyfriars parish church, 1784.

**IRVINE, John ARSA** **1805-1888**
Born Lerwick, 5 Jne; died Dunedin, Otago, 22 Jne. Painter of portraits, marines and still-life. Primarily a portrait painter but also produced a number of figure and marine subjects as well as some delicate compositions of fruit and flowers. His father died when he was 10 and in order to earn a living and study art he went to Edinburgh 1826. Shortly afterwards proceeded to London where he studied alongside Etty and Maclise(qv). In 1828 won a medal at the RA Schools for studies from the antique. Exhibited a portrait in the first exhibition of the RSA 1827, beginning a long series which continued without a break until 1862. By 1888 he had become the Academy's oldest Associate. Returned to Edinburgh 1832-1838 with a break in London 1840-1843. In 1858, for health reasons, he went to Melbourne and then Otago. Ceased to exhibit at the RSA 1862. President, Art Society of Dunedin. Halsby incorrectly described him as an amateur. Elected ARSA 1834. Represented in NGS(3), SNPG(2), Dunedin AG.
**Bibl:** Halsby 265.

**IRVINE, Miss Lucy Douglas** **fl 1929**
Amateur Fife painter. Exhibited 'Study of a farm building' at the AAS, from Pittenweem.

**IRVINE, Mabel V** **fl 1936-1937**
Painter. Exhibited still lifes and flower pieces RSA(3) from University House, St Andrews.

**IRVINE, Margaret S** **fl 1930**
Edinburgh based portrait painter. Exhibited RSA(2) from 86 Findhorn Place.

**IRVINE, Miss Mary H** **fl 1867-1869**
Edinburgh flower painter in oil; exhibited RSA(7).

**IRVINE, Robert Scott ('Otto') RSW** **1906-1988**
Born Edinburgh, 16 Mar; died Edinburgh, 3 Sep. Landscape, topographical and occasional flower painter in watercolour; also teacher. Educated at Heriot's and Edinburgh College of Art 1922-1927 under Alison(qv), John Duncan(qv), Lintott(qv) and D M Sutherland(qv). Lived in Edinburgh for many years appointed principal art master at George Watson's School, Edinburgh 1936, returning there after the war (during which he served as liaison officer with the 8th Army), until his retirement in 1971. Visited Tetuan with John Gray(qv) and A G Munro(qv), painting a number of scenes whilst there which came to be well-regarded although his style was closer to English contemporary watercolourists than to his Scottish contemporaries. Elected RSW 1934. President, Scottish Arts Club 1952-4. Exhibited RSA(7), RSW(18), AAS(2) & GI(12), from 5 Spence St, Newington.
**Bibl:** Halsby 222,265.

**IRVING, Alan B** **fl 1945**
Ayrshire landscape painter; exhibited GI(1) from 7 Highfield Ave, Prestwick.

**IRVING, E O Bell** **fl 1885**
Edinburgh painter in oil of portraits and figurative subjects; exhibited RSA(3).

**IRVING, James** **fl 1877-1891**
Edinburgh painter in oil and watercolour of townscapes, cattle, rustic scenes and portraits. Not to be confused with James Irvine of Montrose(qv). Exhibited RA(1), RSA(35) & GI(4) from 17 Sutton Place.

**IRVING, Jean Bell** **fl 1884**
Edinburgh painter of 22 India Street; exhibited a continental landscape at the RSA.

**IRWIN, Jean** **fl 1970-1974**
Dunbartonshire painter. Exhibited 2 figure studies at the RSA between the above years, including a nude, from 13 Strathblane Rd, Milngavie.

**IRWIN, Miss Jean H** **1905-1983**
Glasgow based painter. Most early work was in watercolour but after 1970 turned increasingly to oils, with occasional pencil studies. Landscape, still life, flowers and rocks. Exhibited 'Bourg St Maurice, Savoie' at the RSA (1905), but mainly GI(58), since 1961 from 13 Strathblane Rd, Milngavie. Represented in Glasgow AG, Lillie AG (Milngavie).

**ISAAC(S), Miss Gertrude E** **fl 1889-1894**
Glasgow sculptress; mostly female figures, portrait busts and medallions. Exhibited RSA(1), GI(6) & a bas relief of 'Mrs Pirie' at the AAS(1893).

**ISHERWOOD, Miss Jessie** **fl 1887-1889**
Edinburgh watercolour painter of English townscape and buildings. Sister of Ruth Margaret I(qv). Exhibited RSA(4) from 13 Howe Street.

**ISHERWOOD, Miss Ruth Margaret** **fl 1886-1887**
Painter in watercolour of buildings. Sister of Jessie I(qv). Exhibited 'Argyle House from Castle Hill' and a 'Peep through a Doorway in the Gordon House' at the RSA in 1887.

**ISRAELS, Josef HRSA** **1824-1911**
Dutch painter who greatly influenced the development of Scottish art, especially watercolour painting. Among leading Scottish artists most influenced by him in both technique and composition were Robert Weir Allan(qv), Robert Gemmell Hutchison(qv), George Paul Chalmers(qv), Watterston Herald(qv), Henry Wright Kerr(qv), Arthur Melville(qv), Tom McEwan(qv) and James Paterson(qv). His broad wet watercolour style with an emphasis on the poetic representation of everyday life were the most significant features. Close friend of Sir George Reid(qv) and of G P Chalmers(qv). Hugh Cameron(qv) also worked with him when visiting Holland. In 1870 Israels visited Aberdeen where, in addition to the artist community, Daniel Cottar the leading art dealer in Scotland, based in Aberdeen, patronised his work. Cottar's agent in Glasgow, Craibe Angus (1830-1899) opened a gallery in Glasgow 1874 introducing the work of Israels to the general public. The other leading Glasgow dealer, John Reid, had eleven works by Israels in his gallery. Once, walking across a Highland moorland under a brilliant sunset sky, Israels explained to a friend that now he understood where Scottish painters got their love of colour. 'Their colour combines softness with intensity, and is rich, varied, beautiful.' During his lifetime his works were owned by J Dick Peddie RSA(qv), the notable Aberdeen collector John Forbes White, the Corporation of Glasgow, Kelvin AG, Glasgow and D Croal Thomson. Elected Honorary Member, RSA 1887. Exhibited RSA(25) 1870-1912, RSW(2), regularly AAS 1885-1926 & GI(33).
**Bibl:** Caw 99, 244, 249; Halsby 70, 130, 169, 243; Irwin 346, 348, 349, 351, 377-8; Macmillan [SA], 243-5, 247, 255, 258, 263.

**IVERSON, Nora A (Mrs Sloan)** **fl 1943**
Glasgow figurative painter; exhibited GI(1) from 5 Doune Terrace.

**IVEY, Sidney J** **fl 1946**
Glasgow watercolour painter; exhibited two Ceylon landscapes at the GI from 8 Nimmo Drive.

# J

**JACK, Andrew M** **fl 1907**
Stirling engraver. Exhibited 'The Curler' and another figurative work at the GI from Craigmill House.

**JACK, Charles D** **fl 1951**
Glasgow amateur watercolour painter; exhibited two landscape scenes of Treboul at the GI, from 1 Burnbank Terrace, St George's Cross.

**JACK, John** **fl 1872-1891**
Edinburgh painter in oil of landscape, local and coastal scenes. Exhibited RSA(27) & GI(1) from 1 Hermitage Place.

**JACK, Maureen E** **fl 1972-1973**
Angus potter. Married Michael J(qv). Exhibited AAS(4) from 29 Waterside, Monifieth.

**JACK, Michael B** **fl 1969-1974**
Dundee potter. Married Maureen J(qv). Exhibited AAS during the above period.

**JACK, Miss Patti** **fl 1881-1897**
Dunblane painter in oil and watercolour of landscape, interiors and flowers. Moved to St Andrews in 1884. Exhibited 'On the Moors, Galloway' at the RA (1884), also RSA(33), GI(3), latterly from Viewburn Place.

**JACKSON, A Logan** **fl 1912-1929**
Glasgow painter. Moved to Milngavie in the 1920s. Exhibited a Spanish landscape and a genre painting at the GI(2), latterly from Whinhurst.

**JACKSON, Charles d'Orville Pilkington ARSA FRBS 1887-1973**
Born Garlennick, Cornwall 11 Oct; died Edinburgh, 20 Sep. Sculptor, mainly large works and portrait busts. Educated Loretto School, Musselburgh. Studied Edinburgh College of Art gaining a travelling scholarship 1910. Served during WWI being mentioned in despatches, and in WW2 with the Royal Artillery. President, SSA 1942-5 and 1946-8 member of the Royal Fine Art Commission to Scotland. His largest work was an equestrian statue 'Robert the Bruce', unveiled 1964 by the Queen at the site of the Battle of Bannockburn to mark its 650th anniversary. In the 1930s executed 83 statuettes for the United Services Museum, Edinburgh Castle; other works in the capital include the carved Scottish regimental and corps badges and the Mercantile Marine Memorial in the National War Memorial, sculptures in the S aisle and S choir aisle of St Mary's Cathedral, panelling and plasterwork design in Acheson House on the Royal Mile, the Royal Scots Memorial in West Princes St Gdns, carvings of pelicans and angels in the Sacrament House of St Mary's Cathedral and the Font in St James' Church, Inverleith Row. Also designed the choir screen in St Serf, Ferry Rd, Granton. Elected ARBA 1922. Exhibited RSA(81), RA(10), RBA(2), AAS 1961, L(6) & GI(15), latterly from 4 Polwarth Terrace. Represented in SNPG(5), City of Edinburgh collection, Scottish National War Memorial, Paisley Abbey, Imperial War Museum, Calgary (Alberta).
**Bibl:** Gifford 100-1,115-6,215,317,366,391,572,602.

**JACKSON, Charles Ernest** **fl 1912**
Painter of topographical scenes. Exhibited 3 works at the RSA in the above year whilst living in York.

**JACKSON, David** **fl 1974**
Glasgow painter of figurative works; exhibited GI(2), from 8 Highburgh Rd.

**JACKSON, Jessie A** **fl 1887**
Edinburgh watercolour painter of local landscapes; exhibited RSA(2).

**JACKSON, John** **fl 1801-1848**
Scottish house and ornamental painter and engraver. In 1815 made a Burgess of Edinburgh and 1818 was in partnership with David Roberts, the stage painter. Together they were responsible for the oak-grained walls in the tower study of Craigcrook Castle, Craigleith; these provided the background to the 16th century Stirling heads now returned there but the walls have consequently disappeared. Excelled in his imitations of woods and marbles and was spoken of by a critic as a 'distinguished decorative painter and a sincere lover and patron of art'. Taught at Trustees Academy. Exhibited 2 studies of cattle at the RSA in 1838.
**Bibl:** Gifford 533; C Hill, Reminiscences of Stockbridge.

**JACKSON, John Baptist** **fl 1760s**
Printmaker of chiaroscuro woodcuts and textile designer. From 1765 he received an annual grant for drawing patterns and training apprentices as designers at the Trustees' Academy. In 1762 applied to succeed Charles Pavillon(qv) as Master but Alexander Runciman(qv) was preferred.
**Bibl:** Irwin 91.

**JACKSON, Matthew** **fl 1900-1909**
Glasgow sculptor. Exhibited two portrait busts and a portrait medallion at the GI, from 61 Jane St.

**JACKSON, Miss Noreen** **fl 1967-1981**
Painter and linocut artist of figurative studies, sometimes in pencil. Exhibited GI(3) in 1967 from 13 Queen's Crescent, Glasgow, in 1969 from Tigh Na Creag, Morar, and in 1971 from Diss, Norfolk.

**JACKSON, Sylvia** **fl 1980-1983**
Aberdeen painter. Exhibited AAS from 1 South Ave, Cults.

**JACKSON, William** **fl 1948**
Amateur Glasgow watercolourist, also worked sometimes in oils; landscape and figurative works. Exhibited GI(4), from 575 Scotland St.

**JACKSON, William A** **fl 1919-1921**
Aberdeen jewellery designer. Exhibited AAS from 191 Union St.

**JACOB, Violet A M F (née Kennedy-Erskine) LLD 1863-1946**
Born House of Dun, nr Montrose; died Kirriemuir, Sept. Author, poetess & occasional painter in watercolours. One of the most interesting literary and artistic personalities of her time. Among her antecedents was Sir John Erskine, Moderator of the General Assembly 1565 and King William IV (through the actress Mrs Jordan). Married an Irishman, Major Arthur Jacob, 1894. Completed many drawings of Indian flowers & plants 1897-99. In 1899, when her husband was posted to South Africa, she returned to Britain and in 1902 published her first book *The Sheep-Stealers*. The following year she published twenty-four comic poems, written in collaboration with Lady Helen Carnegie, and illustrated by herself. Several more books appeared, notably *Flemington* which John Buchan thought was the finest example of Scottish historical writing since R L Stevenson(qv). Then, in 1916, the death of her only son in battle halted her literary work. After the death of her husband in 1936, she moved to Kirriemuir where she spent the remainder of her life. Her history of the House of Dun was published in 1931 and her collected poems in 1944. Awarded LLD (Edin) 1936. Exhibited AAS 1929.
**Bibl:** Ronald Gordon, Introduction, *The Lum Hat & Other Stories*, Aberdeen UP, 1982.

**JACOBSEN, Pauline** **fl 1959-**
Aberdeen painter mainly in watercolour, landscape and figurative works; also sculptress and engraver. Trained Ealing School of Art and the Slade. Lived at 'Thornhill', Cults. Exhibits RSA and AAS including views of Aberdeen and Poolewe, Ross-shire. Elected member, Society of Wood Engravers 1954. Represented in Aberdeen AG, Utah State University and many international collections.

**JAFFRAY, Esther H P** **fl 1961**
Aberdeen artist. Exhibited AAS(2) from 71 Gairn Terrace.

**JAFFRAY, George** **fl 1709**
According to Bushnell he engraved the coat of arms on the title-page of Alexander Garden's *Theatre of the Scottish Kings,* published in Edinburgh 1709.
**Bibl:** Bushnell.

**JAFFRAY, George** **fl 1788**
Scottish architect whose main claim to fame was a design for the Town House in Old Aberdeen and part of the High Street.

**JAFFREY, Lady Helen** **fl 1935-1964**
Aberdeenshire artist, mainly painted flowers. Exhibited AAS(5) from Ladyhill, Bieldside.

**JAFRAY, James** **fl 1738**
Obscure painter. Son of an Edinburgh tailor and on 3 Feb, 1738 apprenticed to James Norie, the painter burgess in Edinburgh.

**JAMES, Miss Emily** **fl 1813**
Amateur Edinburgh artist; exhibited one figurative study at the British Institute.

**JAMES, H** **fl 1878**
Glasgow amateur painter; exhibited a west coast landscape at the GI, from 4 Doune Terrace.

**JAMES, Henry** **fl 1861**
Amateur oil painter of Highland landscapes; exhibited RSA(1) from an address in Glenshee.

**JAMES, Marion B P Mitchell** **fl 1950-1965**
Helensburgh based portrait, landscape and figurative painter in oils and watercolour. Exhibited RSA(2), GI(11) & at the AAS, from Ardblair, E King St, Helensburgh, moving to Inverlorne, Perth Rd, Dunblane, Perthshire c1964.

**JAMES, W G** **fl 1837**
Exhibited a view of the Lake of Monteith at the RSA from Glasgow.

**JAMESON, Alexander** **fl 1728**
Obscure Edinburgh engraver. In 1728 engraved the family group of 'George Jamesone, with his Wife and Son'.
**Bibl:** Bryan.

**JAMESON, Andrew** **fl 1839-1871**
Edinburgh painter in oil of local landscape and coastal scenes. Exhibited RSA(9), at first from Alloa and later from Edinburgh.

**JAMESON, Cecil RP** **fl 1910-1937**
Portrait and landscape painter. Began exhibiting when still a student at Hospitalfield, Arbroath. Subsequently joined the staff there and exhibited RA(6), RSA(1), ROI(3), RHA(1), GI(2) & L(3).

**JAMESON, George** **fl 1765-1773**
Scottish carver and author. Best known for his books *Thirty-Three Designs with the Orders of Architecture according to Palladio* (1765) and *Rudiments of Architecture: or The Young Workman's Instructor* (1773).

**JAMESONE, Mary (Mrs George Aedie)** **?-1684**
Daughter of George J(qv). Embroiderer. Believed to have worked the four large needlework panels in St Nicholas Kirk, Aberdeen: *Finding of Moses*; *Esther before Ahasuerus*; *Susanna and the Elders*; *Jephthah's Daughter*. Married George Aedie 1677.
**Bibl:** W Kelly, *Four needlework panels attributed to Mary Jamesone*, Miscellany of the Third Spalding Club, vol II, Aberdeen 1941; Margaret Swain 64-7.

**JAMESON, Middleton** **c1860-1919**
Landscape figure and flower painter. Brother of Dr Jameson of the Jameson Raid. Lived in Paris in the 1880s where he worked alongside Arthur Melville(qv), moving to London and, after a further spell at Calais, settled in Glasgow c1895. Exhibited RSA(4), ROI(4), RI(5), RA(18), L(8), GI(5, including an unusual subject 'Assegai-making, Mashonaland' 1896 & LS(4).

**JAMESON, Robert** **fl 1858**
Edinburgh oil painter of local landscapes; exhibited RSA(1).

**JAMESON, William** **fl 1638**
Sir Thomas Hope recorded in his diary that on 20 July 1638, 'at the ernest desyr of my sone Mr Alexander, William Jamesoun, painter was sufferit to draw my pictur'. It is possible this entry may refer to George Jamesone's portrait.
**Bibl:** Apted 49; 'Sir Thomas Hope's Diary', Bannatyne Club, 1843, 75-76.

**JAMESON, William** **fl c 1790**
Glasgow engraver. Studied Glasgow Academy. Published engravings of (a) a head out of Jacomo Frey's print of the 'Holy Family' by Carlo Maratta; (b) a head of 'St John'; (c) a head of 'Socrates'; (d) 'Alexander the Great'; and (e) a head of 'Virgil'. A list of twenty-three engraved plates by Jameson is given in Duncan's *Notices and Documents illustrative of the literary history of Glasgow,* 1831.
**Bibl:** Bushnell.

**JAMESONE, George** **1589/90-1644**
Born Aberdeen, probably 8 Feb; died Aberdeen, Oct/Nov, 1644. Third son and fourth child of a master mason and city architect to Aberdeen, Andrew Jameson, and his wife Marjorie. His uncle, David Anders of Finzeauch was described as 'the most skillful mechanic that ever lived in Scotland'. Educated Aberdeen University. Quickly devoted himself to art. In Edinburgh he was apprenticed for seven years to John Anderson(qv). May have visited the continent between 1615 and 1621. Married in Aberdeen 1624. His earliest patrons were from the trade and academic circles of Aberdeen but within a short time he was painting the aristocracy of the north-east and eventually of all Scotland. Until 1628 was probably in competition with Adam de Colone(qv) but although the latter had at first attracted a more aristocratic clientèle, competition ended with de Colone's departure from Scotland, leaving Jamesone with a monopoly that he was to enjoy for the rest of his life. In 1633 he painted the portrait of Charles I on the occasion of the monarch's visit to Scotland and later that year went abroad with Sir Colin Campbell of Glenorchy, reaching Rome. The first commissions from Campbell were for 'fancy portraits of his female ancestors and portraits of Scottish Kings and Queens. These were followed by the 'Glenorchy Family-tree' (1635) and a series of portraits of members of the extended Campbell family including 'The young Covenanter, the Earl Marischal'. During this time that Jamesone took his only known apprentice, Michael Wright(qv). His best portraits are those of 'James Graham, 1st Marquess of Montrose' (1629), 'The 1st Earl of Southesk' (1637), his brother 'Sir Alexander Carnegie' (1637), and 'Sir William Nisbet of Dean' (1637). Also the portrait of 'Mary Erskine, Countess Marischal' (1626), described as one of the most beautiful and satisfying of Jameson's paintings. In 1633 and 1643 he acquired rights in two estates outside Aberdeen, at Fechil, near Ellon, and at Esslemont. In 1635 he created an ornamental garden beside the Denburn in Aberdeen which the poet, Arthur Johnston, described as one of the notable features of the town. Took part on Aberdeen's behalf in a mission for the forces of the Covenant in 1639, an incident which led to his confinement in Edinburgh towards the end of that year and the inclusion of his name in a Privy Council roll of 'delinquents'. In the period of social upheaval which followed, Jameson's work deteriorated with only a few more portraits being added to the large number already completed. In 1797, Alexander Carnegie listed 89 pictures by Jameson while Brockwell lists 107. He left no successor nor any student of comparable quality other than Michael Wright(qv). Undoubtedly Scotland's first major portraitist. His characteristic style has the paint put on thinly 'with the greatest solicitude for the ground...the fruit of his stay at Antwerp. It is the first sign of what has ever since been a main feature of Scottish painting'. In those portraits which show clear signs of authenticity 'the handling is fused, the impasto thin and transparent, the features well drawn, the colour warm but wanting in variety, and the composition stiff and ingenuous'. His merit is based more on historical than on aesthetic considerations but, in addition to his prolificacy, coming at a time when Scotland was enjoying a period of peace and comparative prosperity enabling paintings to be purchased and commissioned, he was working in an age when easel paintings were still unusual but which, largely through his efforts, became far more widespread. His work brings to life some of the pages of history. Represented in NGS, SNPG(22, including the 'Glenorchy family tree'), The Binns (NTS), Craigievar Castle (NTS), Crathes Castle (NTS), Fyvie Castle (NTS), Nat Gall of Ireland (Dublin).
**Bibl:** Armstrong, 4-6; Brockwell; Bulloch, George Jamesone 1885; Caw 9-12 et al; Macmillan [SA] 9,50,58,60-67 et passim in early chs (up to 93); McKay, 7-8, 10-13; Thomson, George Jamesone, 1974.

**JAMIESON, Alexander ROI** **1873-1937**
Born Glasgow, 23 Sep; died London, 2 May. Landscape and portrait painter, mainly in oil. Studied Haldane Academy School of Art, Glasgow winning a scholarship that enabled him to spend a further year in Paris 1898. Visited Spain 1911 and served in France during WW1. First one-man show in London 1912. Married Biddy MacDonald(qv). Lived for many years at Burnside, Weston Turville, nr Aylesbury, Bucks. Elected ROI 1927. His early work showed a close affinity with the Glasgow School but, as Lavery pointed out, his later work was in the English tradition of landscape painting. Exhibited RA(14), RSA(15), ROI(2), LS(13), GI(15), AAS 1906-35 & L(12). Represented Lillie AG (Milngavie).
**Bibl:** Caw 392; Macmillan [SA] 309-10; J B Manson 'Alexander Jamieson' The Studio Vol 51, 1911.

**JAMIESON, Biddy (née MacDonald)** **fl 1895-1950**
Scottish portrait painter in oil of landscape, genre and coastal scenes. Married Alexander J(qv). Moved to London after her marriage. Exhibited RSA(2), ROI(1), SWA(4), GI(1) & LS(8).

**JAMIESON, Calder** **fl 1981**
Dundee painter; exhibited 'The Edwardian Chair' at the GI, from Ferncroft, 6 Panmure Terrace, Barnhill.

**JAMIESON, Cecil ARP** **fl 1908-1935**
Arbroath-based painter. Probably a member of the teaching staff at Hospitalfield from where he intermittently exhibited 5 works at the AAS, all local landscapes.

**JAMIESON, David A** **fl 1978**
Aberdeen printmaker. Trained at Gray's School of Art, Aberdeen. Exhibited AAS from 2c Donald's Place.

**JAMIESON, Elizabeth** **fl 1946-1951**
Glasgow based painter in gouache and watercolour of literary subjects and occasionally in oil; also wood engraver and bookplate designer. Exhibited illustrations to Spencer's *Faerie Queene* at the RSA, also GI(8), from 13 Southpark Avenue.

**JAMIESON, Ernest Arthur Oliphant Auldjo** **c1880-1937**
Architect. Became partner of J A Arnott(qv). No major legacy, their most important work being a share in the design of the Church of Scotland office, George St including its 1932-3 eastern extension, an extended hall for Davidson's Mains Parish Church, and the lodges for Astley Ainslie Hospital in Grange Loan.
**Bibl:** Gifford 305,515,548.

**JAMIESON, F E** **fl 1920-1950**
Painter, possibly Scottish, in oil of Highland lochs, often in the vicinity of Loch Katrine. Sometimes inscribed the title on the verso; often coarse canvases. Bright, rather garish colours, a weak and florid imitator of the Breanskis.

**JAMIESON, Florence** **1925-1971**
Born Glasgow. Painter in oil, watercolour, gouache & pastel of figurative subjects, still life, flowers and domestic genre. Studied Glasgow School of Art. Had her first one-man show in Glasgow 1954. Regular exhibitor at RSA(26) 1948-1962, also GI(31), SSA & SSWA, after 1961 from Coach House, Palace Estate, Callander, Perthshire. Represented in Glasgow AG.

**JAMIESON, Hazel D** **fl 1908**
Exhibited RSA(1) from The Dean, Bo'ness.

**JAMIESON, Miss Jean** **fl 1871-1872**
Edinburgh landscape painter in oil; exhibited RSA(5).

**JAMIESON, Miss Mary** **fl 1885-1886**
Aberdeen painter. Studied in Paris 1885. Exhibited flower studies and local scenes AAS & GI(2), from the Manse, Old Aberdeen.

**JAMIESON, Peter Tod** **fl 1906**
Exhibited a version of 'The Judgment of Paris' at the GI when living at Glencloy House, Brodick, Arran.

**JAMIESON, Robert** **fl 1847-1870**
Edinburgh landscape and topographical painter in oil, mainly local scenes. Exhibited RSA(18) between the above years.

**JAMIESON, Robert Kirkland RBA** **1881-1950**
Born Lanark, 19 Jan; died 3 Sep. Landscape and still life painter in oil, watercolour and occasionally ink and wash. Educated at Lanark GS, Glasgow Training College for Teachers, and Paris. In 1920 married the flower painter Dorothea Selous. Head, Westminster School of Art 1933-1939. Lived in London for many years and exhibited mainly in England at the RA(11), RSA(2), ROI(13), RI(6), RBA(101), GI(10) & L(2), after 1942 from 50 Courtfield Gdns, London SW5.

**JANSON, Mark** **1968-**
Figurative painter, portraitist & draughtsman. Trained Gray's School of Art 1988-92. First solo exhibition Glasgow 2001. Recent works in pencil and acrylic on paper. Macmillan enjoys his "beautifully drawn portraits and scenes of nostalgia like faded photographs". Exhibits RSA 1994- from Dovehill Strudios, Glasgow.
**Bibl:** Macmillan 2001, 179, illus 197.

**JAPP, Miss** **fl 1890**
Amateur painter, mainly of flowers but also landscape. Pupil of Alexander Brownlie Docharty(qv); exhibited two floral works at the GI.

**JARDINE, Miss Aeta J** **fl 1917-1943**
Painter in oil and watercolour of landscape and figure studies. Lived in Glasgow with a brief spell at Hunters Quay, Argyllshire before settling in 17 Colville Terrace, London W11 c1929. Exhibited RA(1), RSA(3), RSW(1), RBA(1), ROI(1) & GI(6).

**JARDINE, Miss Jet S** **fl 1914-1940**
Watercolour painter of Helensburgh. Influenced by the works of James Paterson(qv). Moved to 1 Porchester Sq, London c1928. Related to, possibly the sister, of Aeta J(qv). Exhibited RA(4), RSA(5), SWA(2), GI(3) & RI(5).
**Bibl:** Halsby 265.

**JARDINE, Thomas** **fl 1884**
Edinburgh landscape painter in oil; exhibited RSA(1) from 29 Brougham Street.

**JARDINE, Sir William HRSA FRSE** **1800-1874**
Born Edinburgh, 23 Feb; died Sandown, IOW 21 Nov. Naturalist, artist and illustrator, son of Sir Alexander Jardine of Applegarth, Dumfries whom he succeeded 1820. Married William Lizars'(qv) sister. Published a number of important natural history works including *Illustrations of Ornithology* (1830) and *The Naturalist Library* (1833-45) of which he was the editor. Founded (with Selby) *Magazine of Zoology & Botany* 1837 which became *Annals of Natural History* 1838. Elected HRSA 1827. Exhibited four works at the RSA 1829-1833, three of them still-lifes.
**Bibl:** DNB.

**JASINSKI, Alfons B** **1945-**
Born Falkirk, 14 Sep. Painter in oil of landscapes and domestic subjects. Educated St Medan's High School, Stirling and Edinburgh College of Art 1964-1968. Received a travelling scholarship in 1969. Encouraged by James Mowat, he held his first one-man show in Lower Largo in 1971. Particularly fascinated by symbolism in landscape. Exhibited over 20 works at the RSA since 1972, GI(5) & AAS(3), latterly from 15 Normand Rd, Dysart.

**JASTREBSKI, P A** **fl 1840-1852**
Aberdeen-based Polish painter and draughtsman. Appointed drawing master at the newly established Inverness Royal Academy(qv) on the departure of James Glen(qv) in 1851. Before that time he had been commissioned by the Spalding Club to undertake detailed drawings of the sculptured stones of northern Scotland, work which subsequently appeared in *The Sculptured Stones of Scotland.* Whilst in Inverness he opened private classes for the teaching of drawing and painting, specialising in heads and landscapes and pencil and crayon.

He also undertook portraits. In November 1852 resigned his appointment and went to Australia.

**JASTRZEMBSKI, Oktawian** **fl 1941**
Edinburgh flower painter. Exhibited once at the GI, from 12 Bruntsfield Gdns.

**JEANS, William (of Edinburgh)** **fl 1769-1771**
Sculptor. There are two statues of "Dacian Captives" signed by him in the portico of Penicuik House, Midlothian. Jeans was in Rome in 1767. According to Gunnis, Jeans was also a painter as a signed drawing of John Brown is in the SNPG. This is incorrect. The drawing is a portrait of Jeans himself by John Brown. Alexander Runciman(qv), also a friend, painted a portrait of Jeans. Exhibited at the Free Society, 1769-1771, showing models in terracotta and clay.
**Bibl:** Macmillan [GA], 43.

**JEFFERSON, Charles George** **1831-1902**
Glasgow painter in oil and watercolour of coastal scenes, still life and landscape, most often in Arran, Argyll and Perthshire. Formerly from Glasgow, after 1894 from Winchester St, South Shields. Exhibited RSA(26) & GI(32).

**JEFFREY, Edward** **fl 1953-**
Sculptor. Works in bronze, plaster, stone, terracotta & wood; mostly figurative. Trained Glasgow School of Art under Benno Schotz 1941-48. Awarded London scholarship and in 1965 appointed lecturer in Art, Dundee Coll. of Education, becoming a close friend of Neil Catchpole(qv). Subsequently head of Aesthetic Education, Northern College of Education. Fine pianist. Exhibits RSA & RGI(12) since 1974 from 20 Duntrune Terrace, Broughty Ferry.

**JEFFREY, Miss Joan** **fl 1974**
Glasgow embroiderer. Exhibited GI(1), from 101 Milngavie Rd, Bearsden.

**JEFFREY, Rachel** **fl 1901**
Edinburgh based painter. Exhibited RSA(2) from 14 Randolph Crescent.

**JEFFREY-WADDELL, John** **1876-1941**
Born, 4 May; died, 4 Dec. Architect, etcher, author and watercolourist. Studied Glasgow School of Art and Glasgow Technical College. Worked mainly in Scotland and lived at Hallside in Lanarkshire. In addition to his professional and artistic works he published a number of books including *The Architecture of Glasgow* and *Rambles Through Lanarkshire.* In 1928 his firm exhibited two designs for parish churches at the GI.

**JEFFS, James G ('Tim')** **1904-1975**
Born Dumfries; died Dumfriesshire, Oct 1. Sculptor, portraits and figures, often in wood or plaster. Originally trained as a motor engineer, he worked with Arrol Johnson in Dumfries before becoming a test driver. After the firm closed down Jeffs moved to Brooklands. Earned a national reputation as a craftsman and his services were constantly in demand by various local authorities and other public bodies for the design and execution of presentation wooden caskets and parchment scrolls. Shortly before WW2 he was assistant curator, Dumfries Observatory Museum. He completely modernised the museum and in 1939 was appointed curator. In 1941 devoted himself to teaching and was appointed arts and craft teacher to the local council; in 1945 he took up a similar post at Kirkcudbright Academy. Thereafter he became a freelance sculptor, remaining in Kirkcudbright and teaching art during the summer. Among recipients of his memorial work were Sir Winston Churchill and General Eisenhower. Drowned in a boating accident on Loch Ken. Exhibited GI(4) from the Yellow Door Studio, 41 English Street, Dumfries. Represented in the Paul Jones Crypt at the Naval College, Annapolis (USA), presented on the occasion of the sailors' bicentenary.

**JEFREE, Christopher E** **fl 1972**
Aberdeenshire silversmith and jewellery designer. Exhibited AAS(1) from Inverbervie Mains, nr Drumwhindle, Ellon.

**JELFE, Andrews** **?-1759**
Died 26 Apr. English master mason, deserves mention on account of his work 1715-1718 when he was sent by the Board of Ordnance to repair and make some forts in Scotland. Involved in the building of Inversnaid, Stirlingshire, and Kiliwhimen, Ruthven and Bernera in Inverness-shire, in collaboration with J L Romer. While in Scotland 1719, Jelfe made measured drawings of the Roman monument known as 'Arthur's O'on' which Stukeley later had engraved and which is mentioned in Stukeley's *Account of the Roman Temple and other Antiquities near Grahams-Dike in Scotland,* 1720.

**JEMELY, James** **[see GEMMELL, James]**

**JENKIN, Valentine** **fl 1617-1634**
English painter in oil who conducted some important work in Scotland. His work at Stirling, carried out 1627-1629, is still visible. This includes armorials over the inner yett, internal painting on the second floor of the palace above the royal apartments and in the hall. He was working in Glasgow 1623 and again in 1627. Although English by birth, he was made a painter burgess of Glasgow 1623 'for service done by him to the burgh, and to be done, which will extend to the sum of 100 merks'. In 1617 he may have come north to prepare for the visit of James VI along with Matthew Goodrick. In 1627 he was also working at Hamilton Palace, being paid £266 13s by the Marchioness of Hamilton, including work on the room later known as the 'Duchesses painted chamber'. Also undertook work at Falkland Palace and, in 1634, at Kinneil House for the Marchioness of Hamilton.
**Bibl:** Apted 52-3; M R Apted, Painted Ceilings of Scotland, Edinburgh 1966, 89,92; Macmillan [SA], 53; Maitland Miscellany, iii, 369n; Rosalind Marshall, The Days of Duchess Anne, London 1973, 39,58; Works Accounts, ii, 24n,77, 233, 236-7, 255-6, 314, 443.

**JENKINS, Miss A L** **fl 1904**
Amateur painter. Exhibited once at the Walker Gallery, Liverpool from The Rectory, Galashiels.

**JENKINS, A Margaret** **fl 1898-1910**
Aberdeen landscape painter. Exhibited scenery of the north-east regularly at the AAS during the above years from 46 Bon-Accord St.

**JENKINS, Arthur Henry** **1871-?**
Born Galashiels, 15 Aug. Painter in oil and watercolour of landscapes and figures subjects, sometimes of scenes in North Africa which he visited in 1901. Studied at Edinburgh College of Art and Colarossi's, Paris. Art master at King's School, Bruton, Somerset, then Trinity College, Glenalmond and finally Edinburgh Academy. Exhibited RA(16), RSA(26) 1900-1935, RSW(3), AAS(2), RCA(5), GI(9) & L(16). Represented in City of Edinburgh collection.

**JENKINS, Elizabeth Edgecombe (née Shepherd)** **fl 1900-1921**
Painter and illustrator of children's books. Lived 1907-c1920 in Edinburgh where she was an active member of the artistic community, associated with Edinburgh College of Art. Exhibited RSA(5), RSW(2), RA(1), GI(4) & L(12).

**JENKINS, Mary J** **fl 1898-1902**
Aberdeen painter of landscape and rustic scenes. Possibly related to A Margaret J(qv). Exhibited AAS(3) from 49 Bon-Accord St.

**JENKINS, Mrs Violet E** **fl 1907-1912**
Edinburgh painter in oil and watercolour; pastoral scenes and genre. Exhibited GI(4), from 20 Roseburn Cliff.

**JENNINGS-BROWN, H W** **fl 1880-1887**
Painter in oil of landscape. Her work included views of Brittany and Normandy. Exhibited RSA(18) between the above years, originally from an address in Sussex but from 1885 living in Edinburgh.

**JERDAN, James** **c1841-1913**
Minor Edinburgh architect. Father and later partner of John J(qv). Designed Gogarburn House (1893) and the 'picturesque polychrome sheds and associated housing' of the Water Depot in Drumpark Yard, Duddingston (1893-5).
**Bibl:** Gifford 216-7,503,528,557,589,623.

**JERDAN, John** **fl 1892-d1947**
Edinburgh-based architect and draughtsman. Son and erstwhile

partner of James J(qv). Designed Napier House, Colinton Rd (1934). Exhibited RSA(6) including a number of French topographical scenes.
**Bibl:** Gifford 277,349,501,595.

**JEVONS, Arthur** **fl 1889**
Exhibited a study of 'New Forest beeches' at the GI from Ben Venue, Lochgilphead, Glasgow.

**JOASS, John James ARIBA** **1868-1952**
Born Dingwall. Architect. Trained with his father before entering the offices of J J Burnet(qv). Studied Glasgow School of Art as an evening student. Moved to Edinburgh c1890, won the Pugin Prize 1893 followed by the Owen Jones Prize two years later. Elected ARIBA 1895. Interested in the formal gardens of Scotland. Worked as a draughtsman for Robert Lorimer(qv) and in 1897 entered into partnership with John Belcher in London. Exhibited the drawing of a gatehouse for Earlshall at the RSA 1893.
**Bibl:** Peter Savage, Lorimer and the Edinburgh Craft Designers, Edinburgh 1980, 26,40,156,165; Studio, vol. XI, 165.

**JOHN of Linlithgow** **fl 1329**
Early heraldic painter. Mentioned by Apted and Brydall on account of his work relating to the funeral of Robert I. On 5 Aug 1329 he received 65s 10d for 'two books of gold leaf and fine linen...and for various expenses incurred over the painting of the chapel erected over the king's body' and a further reference to '5 pieces of fine linen and 5 books of gold leaf, for the illumination and furnishing of the king's tomb'. Later presented with a further 66s 7d from the King.
**Bibl:** Apted 53-4; Brydall 23; Exchequer Rolls of Scotland, i,150, 185,193,210.

**JOHNS, Miss Lesley** **fl 1965**
Angus landscape painter in oils and watercolour. Exhibited 'Early morning - Concarneau' and another at the GI, from 6 Melville Gdns, Montrose.

**JOHNSON, A E Dorothy** **fl 1931**
Lerwick artist; exhibited a monochrome AAS from 3 Prince Alfred St.

**JOHNSON, Charles Edward RI ROI** **1832-1913**
Born Stockport, Cheshire. Painter in oil of landscapes, angling, stalking and figurative subjects. Studied at RA Schools. After working for some years in Edinburgh 1863-1896, moved to 34 Gloucester Rd, London where he ran a school of landscape painting. Painted in a direct, strong manner with a mastery of composition and sensitivity to atmosphere. Most of his exhibited work was of Highland subjects. Elected ROI 1883, RI 1882. Exhibited RA, RSA(41) 1858-1878 & GI(42), after 1895 from Carrington Lodge, 33 Sheen Rd, Richmond, Surrey.
**Bibl:** Wingfield.

**JOHNSON, Harry** **fl 1865-1870**
Scottish painter of classical scenery and landscape in oils. Exhibited GI(17), mostly Perthshire scenery, latterly from Melvin Cottage, Maryhill Rd, Glasgow. Not to be confused with an English painter of the same name working at the same time.

**JOHNSON, Helen Stirling** **1888-1931**
Born Troon, Ayrshire. Painter in oil and watercolour. Studied Glasgow School of Art 1907-1915 winning a Haldane Travelling Scholarship enabling her to visit Paris. Won Lauder prize 1922. In later life moved to Kirkcudbright where she became a close friend of A E Taylor(qv). Continued to travel on the continent visiting and painting in Brittany and Corsica. For many years an active member of the Glasgow Society of Lady Artists. Exhibited RA(5), RSA(23), GI(28) & L(5), from Glasgow and Kirkcudbright.

**JOHNSON, James** **?-1811**
Edinburgh engraver and music-seller. Published *The Scots Musical Museum* in 6 volumes, 1787-1803, with engraved title-pages, for which he engraved the plates of music. In the collection of Scots songs he was helped by Robert Burns who spoke of him as 'an honest Scotch enthusiast, a friend of mine'. According to Bushnell he was the first person to strike music upon pewter plates. Not to be confused with a London engraver of the same name.
**Bibl:** Bushnell; DNB.

**JOHNSON, Nigel I** **fl 1978**
Aberdeenshire potter. Trained Gray's School of Art, Aberdeen. Exhibited AAS(1) from Monymusk.

**JOHNSON, Robert** **1770-1796**
Born Shotley, nr Ovingham, Northumberland; died Kenmore, Oct 26. Watercolour painter and engraver. In 1788, through the efforts of his mother, he became acquainted with Thomas Bewick, being subsequently apprenticed to Beilby and Bewick in Newcastle to learn copper-plate engraving. Undertook watercolour sketches from nature, often taken from Bewick's books. His drawings for Bulmar's edition of Goldsmith's and Parnell's *Poems* were cut by the Bewicks in 1795. In later life he forsook engraving in favour of painting, taking a job with a Perth publisher called Morison. His most important work was copying Jamesone's portraits in Taymouth Castle for reproducing in Pinkerton's *Iconographia Scotica.* Whilst engaged on this commission he caught a chill from which he died. Buried in Ovingham, Northumberland where a monument was erected to his memory.
**Bibl:** DNB; Thieme Becker.

**JOHNSON, Stewart B** **fl 1966**
Glasgow painter; exhibited GI(1), from 481 Dumbarton Rd.

**JOHNSON, W H** **fl 1921-1923**
Edinburgh engraver of figurative subjects; exhibited AAS during the above years & GI(1), from 29 York Place.

**JOHNSTON, A D** **fl 1832**
Landscape painter. Exhibited two Argyllshire scenes at the RSA from an Edinburgh address.

**JOHNSTON, Alan** **fl 1939-1946**
Glasgow draughtsman in pencil; exhibited a portrait and a figure composition at the GI, from 101 Croftside Ave.

**JOHNSTON, Alan** **1945-**
Born Scotland. Painter in oil of figurative and abstract works, sculptor. Studied Edinburgh College of Art 1967-1970 and Royal College of Art, London 1970-1972, specialising in life drawing. 'He spent a period in Germany; there he began a series of Minimalist drawings done with a hard graphite pencil, many done on hand-made Japanese paper. Returned to Scotland in 1973, settling in Edinburgh. There he worked on a series of drawings based on the length of the megalithic yard. These were hieratic, vertical forms of varying width, in which tone was carefully built up and modulated through fine hatchwork pencil marks. The series was shown at the Von der Heydt Museum, Wuppertal 1974. His interest in Zen Buddhism and the relation between man and nature has informed his entire oeuvre which tends towards the quiet and discreet. More recently he has worked on large canvasses and produced several sculptures. In the 1980s his work was widely exhibited in Britain, Iceland, Japan and New York' [Hartley]. Represented in SNGMA.
**Bibl:** Bill Hare, Contemporary Painting in Scotland, Edinburgh 1993; Hartley 139; Museum of Modern Art, Oxford, 'Alan Johnston', (Ex Cat 1978); Pier Arts Centre, Stromness, Orkney, 'Alan Johnston', (Ex Cat 1978-88); Von der Heydt Museum, Wuppertal, 'Alan Johnston; Grey Marks in the Village,', (Ex Cat 1974).

**JOHNSTON(E), Alexander** **1815-1891**
Born Edinburgh; died Hampstead, London, 2 Feb. Historical, genre and portrait painter; also illustrator. Son of an Edinburgh architect. At the age of 15 he was apprenticed to a seal engraver in Edinburgh and 1831-1834 studied at the Trustees Academy. With a recommendation from Sir David Wilkie he went to London 1836, studying at the RA Schools under W Hilton. Before going south he painted a number of portraits including several of the family of a Dr Morrison. Two of these were his first exhibits at the RA (1836 and 1837). Remained in London for the rest of his life and 'dropped from the roll of Scottish painters'. In 1841 exhibited his first historical painting 'The Interview of the Regent Murray with Mary, Queen of Scots', bought by the Edinburgh Art Union. From this time on he turned increasingly to austere, sombre, historical scenes and in 1845 his 'Archbishop Tilitson administering the Sacrament to William Lord Russell at the Tower' (1845) was bought by Mr Vernon and is now in the Tate. Contributed illustrations for Charles Mackay's *The Home Affections,* 1858. His exhibit of 1846 'The Introduction of

Flora McDonald to Prince Charles Edward Stuart after his retreat from the Battle of Culloden' was awarded a premium by Glasgow Art Union although subsequently declined by the artist. Caw considered his works 'marked by sound drawing and expressive composition, which, in combination with reticent colour, give (them) a certain severe stateliness'. Altogether exhibited RA(77) 1836-1886 & RSA(8) 1833-1837; also Paris Salon 1878 (where his work was much admired), RHA(2), ROI(4), GI(36) & L(1), after 1879 from 36 King Henry's Rd, London NW. Represented in Tate AG, Sheffield AG, Sunderland AG.
**Bibl:** AJ 1857, 57; 1862, 108; 1863, 236; 1865, 336; Caw 120-121; DNB; Irwin 215.

**JOHNSTON, Mrs Alice A P** **fl 1925**
Sculptress, especially of children. Exhibited a child's head at the RSA from 7 Wester Coates Road, Edinburgh.

**JOHNSTON, Andrew** **c1700-1750**
Scottish engraver, probably resident in Edinburgh. Engraved maps of Scotland for the 1722 edition of Camden's *Britannia.* Engraved bookplates for Colonel Charles Cathcart 1720, Hon George Baillie 1724, Lord Kinsale 1730, The Earl of Wigtoune 1730, and His Excellency Robert Hunter 1740. Four mezzotint portraits are recorded by Chaloner Smith, three of them from London.
**Bibl:** Bryan; Bushnell; Butchart 7; J Chaloner Smith, British Mezzotint Portraits, 4 pts, 1878-83.

**JOHNSTON, Angus** **fl 1948-1950**
Glasgow painter of Scottish hills. Exhibited GI(2), from 126 Burghead Drive.

**JOHNSTON, Cecile E M** **fl 1951-1964**
Edinburgh painter of portraits and domestic scenes. Exhibited RSA(7) between the above years.

**JOHNSTON(E), Charles Edward** **fl 1858-1878**
Bonnington painter in oil of landscape principally of the Scottish Highlands but also of continental & Welsh subjects. Best known work probably 'The Horse Dealer' (1877). Exhibited RSA(41).

**JOHNSTON, Charles Stewart Still** **1850-c1924**
Edinburgh architect. Designed Guthrie Memorial Church (1881). His most notable private house is 28 Inverleith Place built for the shipowner Duncan McIntyre (1898). Exhibited two designs at the RSA including additions to Pollock Castle (Renfrew) for Mr and Mrs Fergusson Pollock (1890); also GI(1), from 10A North Street.
**Bibl:** Gifford 229,374,419,472,555,580.

**JOHNSTON, David E** **fl 1971-1989**
Born Laurencekirk. Part-time landscape painter in oil and watercolour, mainly around his home. Meticulous technician. Teaches English at Arbroath HS. Exhibits AAS from Woodville, Laurencekirk.

**JOHNSTON, D M** **fl 1951-1962**
Glasgow watercolour artist of country buildings and flowers. Exhibited GI(2), from 112 Keppochhill Rd.

**JOHNSTON, Ebenezer Y** **fl 1946-1949**
Galashiels painter in oil; still life and local topography. Exhibited RSA(3) during the above period.

**JOHNSTON, Mrs Elise** **fl 1961**
Edinburgh amateur painter. Exhibited 'Houses at Blackford' at the GI, from 43 W. Savile Terrace.

**JOHNSTON, Miss Elizabeth** **fl 1944-1947**
Portrait and landscape painter in oils and occasionally pencil; based in Edinburgh. Exhibited RSA(2) & GI(1), from 42 Primrosebank Rd.

**JOHNSTON, Frank** **fl 1968-1974**
Glasgow landscape artist in oils and watercolour. Exhibited GI(2), from 29 Fulbar Rd.

**JOHNSTON, George Bonar RSW** **1933-**
Painter originally from Leith, spending the war years in Caithness. Landscapes, mostly fishing and harbour scenes and interiors. Trained Edinburgh College of Art 1951-56 where he came under the influence of Gillies(qv), McTaggart(qv) and Philipson(qv). Elected RSW 1977. Moved to Dundee 1966 as Schools adviser in art and design. Exhibited RSA(20) 1961-1986, and regularly RSW.

**JOHNSTON, G** **fl 1868**
Stirling watercolourist. Exhibited 'The Landing Place' at the GI, from 20 Murray Place.

**JOHNSTON, George B** **fl 1965-1985**
West Lothian-based painter in oil and occasional watercolour. Landscape and old country buildings. Exhibited GI(15), after 1966 from 10 Collingwood Crescent, Barnhill, Dundee.

**JOHNSTON, Graham** **fl 1917**
Heraldic painter to the Lyon Court. Employee of HM Register House, Edinburgh; exhibited RSA(1).

**JOHNSTON, Helen S** **1888-1931**
Born Troon. Painter of flowers, genre and Scottish landscape. Trained Glasgow School of Art 1907-15. Won a Haldane Travelling Scholarship which took her to Paris. Returned to Glasgow before moving to Kircudbright. Visits to Corsica and Brittany produced some interesting, strong portrayals of local peasantry, especially the lacemakers of Brittany. A large mural is in Possilpark Library (Lanark). Exhibited RGI(28) and AAS.

**JOHNSTON, J A** **fl 1983**
Aberdeenshire artist; exhibited AAS(1) from 28 Forsyth Dr, Balmedie.

**JOHNSTON, J H** **fl 1828-1835**
Dumfries-based painter in oil of local scenes and teacher. Held classes in the High Street.

**JOHNSTON, James** **fl 1975**
Renfrewshire painter; exhibited GI(1), from 2 Gateside Ave, Greenock.

**JOHNSTON, Miss Janet** **fl 1863-1897**
Edinburgh painter in oil but mainly watercolour of domestic scenes, wild flowers, fruit and landscape. Exhibited RSA(32) between the above years, also GI(4), from 1 Great Stuart St.

**JOHNSTON, John** **fl 1880-1893**
Glasgow landscape painter; exhibited RSA(1) & GI(2), from 52 Portugal Street.

**JOHNSTON, Joseph Marr** **1871-1934**
Edinburgh architect. Influenced by Art Nouveau. Designed Leith Poorhouse (later Eastern General Hospital) (1903-7); Clydesdale Bank, Bernard St (1923), St Mary's Primary School, Leith (1926).
**Bibl:** Gifford 463,466,471,479.

**JOHNSTON, Margaret M** **fl 1887**
Amateur Fife painter. Exhibited RSA(1) from Balgowrie, Culross.

**JOHNSTON, N** **fl 1907-1908**
Painter. Exhibited RSA(3) from Wellwood, Ayr.

**JOHNSTON, P (E)** **fl 1842-1862**
Edinburgh painter in oil of landscapes and marines. Exhibited RSA(11).

**JOHNSTON, Robert Brown** **fl 1880-1903**
Edinburgh painter in oil and watercolour of Scottish and continental landscape, flowers, portraits and narrative subjects. Exhibited RSA(25 - four of these scenes at Carradale), GI(8), AAS(2), & L(4), after 1885 from Jane Lodge, Newbattle Terrace.

**JOHNSTON, Miss Ruth J** **fl 1919-1921**
Portrait miniaturist. Living at Ardoch House, Bearsden 1918 but moved to Mumbles, Glamorgan and thence to Swansea the following year. Exhibited RA(1), RSA(1) & GI(3).

**JOHNSTON, Sheila** **fl 1978**
Aberdeenshire amateur artist of local landscapes. Exhibited AAS(2) from Tree Cottage, 2 Colesea Rd, Cove Bay.

**JOHNSTON, Stuart** **1891-c1939**
Born Cupar, Fife. Draughtsman (usually in charcoal) and etcher, landscape and old country edifices. Studied at Glasgow School of Art. Exhibited GI(30) & L(4) from a Glasgow address between 1923 and 1938.

**JOHNSTON, Stuart** **fl 1967-1986**
Aberdeenshire painter; exhibited two works at the AAS from 1 Burnside Way, Balmedie.

**JOHNSTON, Sybil** **fl 1973**
Aberdeenshire painter. Exhibited AAS(1) from Elmbank, 4 Cairn Rd, Peterculter.

**JOHNSTON, T** **fl 1794**
Scottish engraver. Engraved a map of Tweeddale 1794.

**JOHNSTON, Thomas** **fl 1871**
Edinburgh painter in oil of figurative subjects. Apparently different to the Thomas C Johnston who was exhibiting at the RSA at the same time. Exhibited RSA(1) from 37 Thistle Street.

**JOHNSTON, Thomas C** **fl 1871-1886**
Edinburgh painter in oil of landscape and coastal scenes; exhibited RSA(11).

**JOHNSTON, Thomas Vincent** **fl 1951**
Glasgow sculptor. Exhibited two pieces in terracotta at the GI.

**JOHNSTON, Tracey** **c1970-**
Scottish painter of semi-abstract imaginative work in a variety of medium. Trained Gray's School of Art 1988-95. Winning a John Kinross scholarship in 1992 enabled her to spend a year in Florence. The use of symbolic imagery and a fascination with architecture and religious themes pervade much of her work. Exhibits AAS.

**JOHNSTON, William** **fl 1921-1967**
Landscape, flower and figure painter in both oil and watercolour. Lived for a time in Edinburgh, moved to Glasgow c1928 then to Dundee c1936. Exhibited RSA(7 - local topographical scenes) 1944-1960 from Dundee; also RSW(3) & GI(28), mostly from 10 Kinghorne Terrace, Dundee but in 1967 from 2 Striven Gdns, Glasgow.

**JOHNSTON, William Boswell** **fl 1878**
Edinburgh landscape painter in oil; exhibited RSA(1).

**JOHNSTON, William Myles** **1893-1974**
Born Edinburgh. Animal, landscape and bird painter, also ceramic designer. Studied Edinburgh College of Art under William Walls(qv), subsequently spent five years in America painting pastels, mainly of poultry. Returned to Edinburgh where he married Dorothy J(qv). Taught at John Watson's College. Specialised in decorating pottery with animal designs. Moved to Kirkcudbright 1940 where Jessie King(qv) and E A Taylor(qv) were among his friends. Worked with Sir Robert Lorimer(qv) on the Scottish National War Memorial in Edinburgh Castle, executing the heraldic blazoning. Died in a fishing accident. Exhibited RSA(8).
**Bibl:** Halsby 265.

**JOHNSTON, William P M** **fl 1914-1922**
Edinburgh-based animal painter. Exhibited RSA(3) & L(2) from 37 Fountainhall Road.

**JOHNSTONE, Dorothy ARSA (Mrs D M Sutherland)** **1892-1980**
Born Edinburgh, Dec 25. Painter in oil, watercolour and chalk of figure subjects, especially children, flowers and landscapes; also teacher. Daughter of George Whitton J(qv) and niece of James Heron(qv). Studied art in Paris and Florence and at the Edinburgh College of Art 1908. Taught Edinburgh College of Art 1914-1924. Through her friend Cecile Walton(qv) she met E A Walton(qv) and other members of the Glasgow school. In 1919, the Edinburgh Group (W O Hutchison, Eric Robertson, A R Sturrock and D M Sutherland) was reconstituted and joined by Dorothy Johnstone, Mary Newbery and Cecile Walton. During and after the war years she spent the summer at Kircudbright, staying at the Greengate Close cottage studios adjacent to the home of E A Taylor(qv) and Jessie M King(qv). Their 1920 exhibition was particularly successful; it was said that 'people look to the Edinburgh group to something unique rather than universal; for something of pagan brazeness rather than parlour propriety'. In 1924, as well as holding a joint exhibition with Cecile Walton, she married D M Sutherland(qv) who, in 1933, became Director of Gray's School of Art in Aberdeen. As a result of her marriage was forced to give up her teaching position and for the rest of her life lived at Cults, Aberdeen becoming increasingly interested in child portraiture. A delightful, friendly lady who always kept in close touch with the community of Scottish artists, first in Edinburgh and later in Aberdeen. Elected ARSA 1962. Exhibited RSA(160+), RA(3), RSW(1), GI(41), AAS, & L(9). Represented in Glasgow AG.

**JOHNSTONE, George Whitton RSA RSW** **1849-1901**
Born Glamis, Forfarshire, May 3; died Edinburgh, 22 Feb. Painter in oil and watercolour of landscapes, especially of the north-east and Scottish Highlands. Father of Dorothy J(qv). Painted in Fontainebleau forest. Arrived in Edinburgh as a cabinet maker and in 1877 enrolled at the RSA Life School during which time he painted genre and portraits. In his later years his paintings became more generalised, the foliage and composition becoming more reminiscent of Corot. In 1896 was a student of the Board of Manufacturers School of Design where he won a bronze medal for drawing from the antique. Caw found his work 'pleasant and sincere, if unemotional... (containing) a certain mannerism of touch, which results in a rough hewn and unpleasantly marked surface'. Elected ARSA 1883, RSW 1885, RSA 1895. First exhibited RSA in 1872 & RA in 1859. Exhibited RA(13), RSA(153), RSW(28), AAS 1885-1898, GI(44) & L(2), after 1890 from 4 Napier Rd. Represented in NGS, V & A ('St. Monance'), City of Edinburgh collection, Munich AG.
**Bibl:** AJ 1899, 146-9; Bryan; Caw 302.

**JOHNSTONE, Graham** **fl 1984**
Glasgow printmaker; exhibited GI(1), from 169 Queen's Drive.

**JOHNSTONE, Miss Helen** **fl 1853-1859**
Edinburgh based portrait miniaturist. Exhibited RSA(8) portrait miniatures during the above years.

**JOHNSTONE, Hugh** **fl 1949-1954**
Glasgow sculptor, usually in wood; animals and mythological subjects. Exhibited GI(4), from 63 Great George St.

**JOHNSTONE, J** **fl 1790-1840**
Edinburgh engraver. Engraved many bookplates including for the Duke of Hamilton (1830), James Boyd (1820) and James Gillespie Davidson (1840).
**Bibl:** Bushnell.

**JOHNSTONE, James** **fl 1980**
Kincardineshire artist. Exhibited AAS(1) from Mount Pleasant, Banchory.

**JOHNSTONE, Rev James Barbour** **1815-1885**
Born near Annan; died Dumfries. Part-time painter in watercolour of local scenes. Educated Dumfries Academy; foundation Minister of Wolflee 1849-1862, later moved to Warrington. Exhibited RSA(2) & at the RGI(1) from 2 Glebe Terrace, Dumfries.

**JOHNSTONE, John jnr** **fl 1926**
Aberdeenshire amateur landscape painter. Exhibited AAS(1) from 28 North St, Peterhead.

**JOHNSTONE, John ARSA** **1937-**
Born Falkirk, Stirlingshire. Painter in oil of landscape and semi-abstracts. Studied art at Edinburgh College of Art 1959-1961 obtaining a travelling scholarship enabling him to visit the West Indies and South America 1961-1962. First one-man exhibition in Bogota 1961. Won Latimer Award, RSA 1968. Has taught since 1963 at Edinburgh College of Art. Described as a soft surrealist, though with

violent contrasts of colour. Lives in Lauder, Berwickshire. Elected ARSA 1972. Regular exhibitor at the RSA. Retrospective exhibion at the Scottish Gallery, Edinburgh 1970. Represented in Aberdeen AG, City of Edinburgh collection, Hamilton AG (Canada), Museum Olinda (Brazil), SAC.
**Bibl:** Gage 62-3, 145.

**JOHNSTONE, John** **1941-**
Born Forfar. Painter in oil, watercolour and pencil; also etcher. His preferred medium is oil on hardboard and since 1977 has become increasingly interested in printmaking. Studied at Duncan of Jordanstone College of Art 1959-1964 and then travelled to Europe on a scholarship visiting Belgium, France, Germany, Holland & Spain. In 1967 he spent the year painting in Jamaica. From 1968 joined the staff of Dundee College of Art and in 1988 was elected professional member, SSA. Held many one man shows. Influenced by 15th and 16th century Flemish paintings, Expressionism, Victorian book illustrators and some caricatures. Increasingly fascinated by allegorical and narrative works, often with biblical themes. Both his exhibits at the RSA in 1989 were allegorical representations of Jonah and the whale. Lives at 22 Yeoman St, Forfar, Angus. Inspired by a visit to Jamaica in 1998. Exhibits regularly at the RSA since 1979 & GI(1), concentrating latterly on large-scale works depicting aspects of modern life. In 1992 Dundee AG purchased *Lord Mustard* (a busker). Represented in Dundee AG, collection of the Duke of Edinburgh.

**JOHNSTONE, Louise** **c1952-**
Born in Edinburgh. Graduated in English and psychology, University of Edinburgh. In 1983 enrolled at Duncan of Jordanstone College of Art concentrating on painting in oil, since when has held a number of successful exhibitions. Influenced by the art of classical Greek and renaissance Florence, also the work of the French sculptress Camille Claudel. Best known for her portrayal of the female form 'trapped on a threshold of time occupying an isolated and uncertain space' sometimes nude, sometimes draped in ethereal robes generally recumbent, seen from above. 'The hold of the past is apparent in the classical design of the poses and in the drapery which serves to reveal the form while at the same time surrounding it in mystery. The potential for movement and transformation which exists within the figures creates a tension between the figure and the careful geometry of the background. Contradictory feelings of strength and vulnerability are conveyed through the tension between the image and the surface of the board or paper on which it exists'. Her work is executed on a specially prepared board using a ground of gesso and polyfilla creating a wall-like surface. The limited palette of light-flooded colour used in the paintings echoes those found in frescoe or grisaille painting. Also executes bas-relief sculptures echoing the same concerns as her painting with their worn, broken surfaces, their bleached, stainlike colouring and the architectural unity of the image, the ground and the frame. One of the more interesting contemporary artists. Lives in Auchterarder, Perthshire. Exhibits RSA.

**JOHNSTONE, P** **fl 1842-1862**
Edinburgh painter in oil of landscapes, marine, river and pastoral scenes. Exhibited RSA(11) between the above years.

**JOHNSTONE, Robert B** **fl 1886**
Edinburgh landscape and figure painter. Exhibited AAS(2) from Newbattle Terr.

**JOHNSTONE, Valerie Ross** **fl 1964-1973**
Aberdeen jewellery designer. Exhibited a number of designs at the AAS from 162 Bon-Accord St.

**JOHNSTONE, William** **fl 1885-1913**
Edinburgh engraver; exhibited three works at the RA, 1894-5, two of them after paintings by Charles Martin Hardie(qv) and one 'In time of peace' after Robert Gemmell Hutchison(qv). Exhibited RSA(7). Represented in Glasgow AG.

**JOHNSTONE, William OBE** **1897-1981**
Born Denholm, Roxburghshire, 8 Jne. Landscape, portrait and abstract painter in oil and watercolour, ink and plaster. Studied Edinburgh College of Art 1919-1923, RSA Schools 1923-1925, Paris at the L'Hôte Academie and at Colarossi's 1925-27. As a student won a number of major awards including the Maclaine Watters prize 1924, Stuart and Keith Prizes 1925. Until his retirement in 1961 all his professional life was spent in London. Thereafter he returned to Lilliesleaf, Roxburghshire where he became a sheep farmer. During WW2 he divorced his wife, later marrying Mary Bonning. Principal, Camberwell School of Art 1938-1945 and Central School of Art, London 1946-1961. Had a profound effect on art education in Britain. Author of *Child Art to Man Art* (1960), *Creative Art in Britain* (a re-issue of *Creative Art in England* 1936) and *Points in Time : An Autobiography* (1980). Awarded OBE 1961. Prepared a report on art education in Israel for UNESCO 1962. Described as having 'a powerful, if wayward, talent'. Henry Lintott(qv) was the only teacher he confessed to admire. In 1924 awarded three RSA prizes and in 1925 the Carnegie travelling scholarship enabling him to visit France, Italy, Spain and North Africa 1925-1927, marrying an American girl in Paris who rejoiced in the name of Flora McDonald. After an unsuccessful trip to California in 1928 they returned to Scotland in 1929, moving to London 1930. 'William Johnstone is not an artist who has ever wanted to rationalise or systematise his work. He has painted in bursts, and done little work for long periods, repainted old pictures. He has not been above facing his tracks in one way or another. His character as a painter remains elusive, and his final status may well be a matter for controversy in the future' [Douglas Hall]. Exhibited at the RSA only at the beginning of his career, becoming increasingly an anti-establishment figure. Continued to paint throughout his life with exhibitions of oils, watercolours, drawings and plaster until the year of his death. Generally (but not universally) regarded as one of the most original and influential painters of his time. A friend and ally of Hugh MacDiarmid, he influenced many artists including Eduardo Paolozzi(qv) and Alan Davie(qv). After he thought he had finished painting he embarked on what was to become his last period 1971-81, a style described by Hall as 'biomorphic surrealism' culminating in 'A Point of Time', now in the SNGMA. This period was characterised by large canvases of great energy, which can either be disregarded as undirected posturing or hailed, a view to which his biographer subscribes, as 'one of the most amazing achievements of old age in the history of art'. There was a studio sale in Glasgow 12 April 1990. Represented in SNPG(1), SNGMA, Glasgow AG, Abbot Hall AG(Kendal).
**Bibl:** A T Cunningham, 'William Johnstone', Studio CXXV, Jan 1943; Gage 29 et al; Douglas Hall, William Johnstone, 1980; Hardie 151-4; Hartley 139-140; Hayward Gall, London & Edinburgh, 'William Johnstone', (Ex Cat 1980); William Johnstone, Child Art to Man Art, London 1941; William Johnstone, Creative Art in Britain, 2nd Edition London 1950 (first pub Creative Art in England, 1936); William Johnstone, Points in Time: An Autobiography, London 1980; William Johnstone, 'The Education of the Artist', Studio CXXV, Jan 1943; Duncan Macmillan, 'William Johnstone, an appreciation', Art Monthly, July 1981.

**JOHNSTONE, William Borthwick RSA** **1804-1868**
Born Edinburgh, Jly 21; died Edinburgh, Jne 5. Painter in oil of landscape, figures and historical subjects. Began life as a solicitor, but abandoned law for art at an early age. Married a daughter of J C Brown(qv). Equally interested in the history of art, qualities which led to his appointment as the first curator of the NGS 1858. His own portrait by John Philip is in the NGS. In his style he was at first a follower of Wilkie(qv), but this changed after visiting Rome in 1843. Toward the end of his life was influenced by John Philip(qv). Besides art he was fond of literature, being a friend of David Laing. He was the anonymous contributor to the *North British Review* of two interesting articles on Scottish and English art. Compiled a biographical catalogue of the NGS. Treasurer, and for many years, Trustee of the RSA. In spite of a painful illness, he remained an active member of the Academy until the end of his life. Also painted some miniatures and was a sensitive watercolourist, somewhat reminiscent in style to Turner. Received lessons in miniature painting from Robert Thorburn(qv) in London. 'Landscape with Peasant Girl carrying Pitcher', in the V & A, is a fine example of his oeuvre set in an Italianate landscape. Elected ARSA 1840, RSA 1848. Exhibited RSA(101) & GI(2) from Winsidney Lodge, Whitehouse and latterly 3 Gloucester Place, Edinburgh. Represented in NGS(3), V & A, City of Edinburgh collection.
**Bibl:** Armstrong 63; Bryan; Brydall 426-8; Halsby 265; Irwin 287; McKay 259.

**JOLLY, Miss Eveline (Eva) Isabella** **fl 1924-1946**
Watercolour painter and illuminator. Specialised in landscape, topographical compositions and still life. Exhibited RSA(2), RSW(2), AAS, & GI(6) after 1940 from Burnside Cottage, Ceres, Fife.

**JOLLY, Miss Fanny C** **fl 1863-1878**
Probably English. Exhibited widely in Scotland; regularly RSA(47), invariably pastoral scenes and flower pieces, usually in watercolour, also GI(10) & RA(6), from Oldfield, Bath.

**JONAS, Henry E** **fl 1881-1884**
Edinburgh landscape painter in oil. Several of his exhibits were moonlight scenes. Exhibited RSA(7) from 31 Wright's Houses.

**JONES, A C** **fl 1974**
Glasgow painter; exhibited GI(1), from 21 Kensington Gate.

**JONES, Anthony** **fl 1972**
Sculptor. Exhibited AAS(1) in Killearn stone from 41 Rose St, Glasgow.

**JONES, Charles Digby** **fl 1836-1892**
West Tarbert painter in oil of domestic genre and seascape. Exhibited RSA(8), latterly from 12 Chester Street, Edinburgh.

**JONES, Gillian** **1966-**
Ross-shire painter, engraver and silkscreen printmaker; oil, gouache, pastel and ink. Trained Gray's School of Art, Aberdeen 1984-8, winner of Elizabeth Greenshields Award for the most promising young artist in 1988. Inspired by colour, pattern, light and line in landscape, still life and interiors. Exhibited two still-lifes RSA in 1989 from 10 Church Street, Cromarty.

**JONES, Henry E** **fl 1892**
Exhibited 'Moonlight on the Fyfe coast' at the RSA from 17 Gillespie Crescent, Edinburgh.

**JONES, J C** **fl 1836**
Minor Edinburgh landscape painter; exhibited RSA(2) in the above year.

**JONES, Rosamund** **1944-**
Scottish printmaker. Wildlife subjects, especially game birds, and landscape. Studied Leeds College of Art, and on the proceeds of a David Murray scholarship visited Barra. Produces her work in limited editions on a Spider Wheel press. Exhibits RSA, from New Bridge, Birstwith, nr Harrogate.

**JONES, Thomas Bayliss Huxley** **fl 1937-1965**
English sculptor in terracotta, bronze, ivory and plaster. Head of sculpture dept, Gray's School of Art, Aberdeen in the 1930s. Exhibited GI(10), after 1950 from High House, Broomfield, Chelmsford, Essex.

**JONES, Vivian D** **fl 1938**
Ayrshire animal engraver, usually drypoint. Specialised in dogs. Exhibited GI(2).

**JOSEPH, Samuel RSA** **1791-1850**
Born Cambridge; died London, 1 Jly. Sculptor. Studied at the RA Schools in 1811 under Peter Rouw, awarded a silver medal in the same year and another in 1812. Came to Edinburgh 1823 where he executed many admirable portrait busts and several statues. Important figure and foundation member of the RSA. Graham, in British Literature and Art, described his busts as 'superior to any examples of sculptural art that had been produced in Scotland previous to his practice'. In 1828 he returned to London but never received the credit that is his due. The statue of 'William Wilberforce' (1838), now in Westminster Abbey, is his masterpiece. According to the RSA report of 1850 his style is more suited to bronze than marble 'having a look of decision reclaimed from hardness by the freedom of its handling'. Exhibited RA 1811-46 & RSA(54) 1827-1835. Among his major works, in addition to Wilberforce, are the statue of 'Sir David Wilkie' (1843) now in the Tate, and busts of 'Sir Walter Scott' (1825), 'George IV' (1831) and 'Voltaire'. Represented also in NGS(11) and City of Edinburgh collection (marble of 'Lord Provost William Trotter of Ballandean').
**Bibl:** Brydall 185,331; Gunnis 222-3; Scott, English Schools of Sculpture, 1871.

**JOSS, Miss Eleanor M (Mrs R Scott Irvine)** **fl 1940-1944**
Edinburgh landscape painter in oil but mainly watercolour. Married the Edinburgh watercolourist R Scott Irvine(qv) c1942. Exhibited RSA(4), RSW(1) & GI(2) from 1 Succoth Place.

**JUDGE, Michael** **fl 1985**
Glasgow painter; exhibited GI(1), from 32 Falkland St.

**JUDGE, William E** **fl 1941-1943**
Ayrshire landscape painter in oil; exhibited five west coast landscapes at the RSA during the above years.

**JUNOR, David** **1773-1835**
Probably born Edinburgh; died Perth, 14 Oct. Painter of portraits and landscape. Appointed drawing and writing master, Perth Academy 1798 and senior drawing master 1807-c1818. From 1814 until 1830 he was listed as a teacher of velvet painting. Among his pupils were Thomas Duncan(qv), D O Hill(qv) and perhaps J McLaren Barclay(qv). In 1830 he retired from teaching but continued to paint. Represented by a portrait in Perth AG.

**KAMIENSKA-PALUCH, Mrs Irma** **fl 1945**
Edinburgh-based painter; exhibited GI(1) from 5 Greenbank Row.

**KANE, John** **1860-1934**
Born West Calder. Naïve painter, the first to achieve recognition in the United States whence he emigrated 1879. First employed as a steelworker in Pittsburgh and from 1884 to 1890 as a coal miner in Alabama. After losing a leg in 1891 he worked as a night watchman on the railways, tinting and painting photographs in his spare time. His first essay into oil painting was c1910 by which time he was working as a carpenter and house painter in Ohio. Began painting portraits as well as landscapes, interiors and townscapes, combining careful detail with naïve stylization and imaginative reconstruction. First came to general attention in 1927 when some of his paintings were accepted for the Carnegie International Institute Museum of Art in Pittsburgh. Awarded the Carnegie Prize. Represented in the 'Masters of Popular Painting' exhibition at the Museum of Modern Art in New York, 1938.
**Bibl:** Harold Osborne(ed), Twentieth Century Art, 1988, 285.

**KANT, Miss Janet C** **fl 1914-1917**
Glasgow based painter and engraver. Topographical and townscapes. Exhibited RSA(4), GI(6) from 546 Argyll Street. Represented in Glasgow AG.

**KARR, Mrs W** **fl 1855**
St Andrews painter in oil of town scenes; exhibited RSA(1) from 67 North St.

**KAY, Alexander** **fl 1813-1863**
Edinburgh topographical and landscape artist. Prolific watercolour painter of Scottish landscape, shipping and coastal scenes. His style was influenced by 'Grecian' Williams, but his drawing is generally weaker. Aquatints of Edinburgh were made from his drawings, the most famous being 'View of the old Town, taken from Clarke's Circulating Library, South St. Andrew St', 1812/14 and 'View of the old Town taken from Princes Street', 1814. Both were copied in aquatint by J Clark(qv). Probably responsible for the drawings of a set of 12 hand-coloured aquatints, engraved by James Mitchell(qv), which are among the earliest Scottish aquatints depicting the Common Man. Exhibited Society of Dilettantes & RSA. Represented in V & A.
**Bibl:** Butchart 41; Halsby 265; Hugh Cheape, 'Portraiture in Piping', *Scottish Pipe Band Monthly*, 5/6,1988.

**KAY, Archibald RSA RSW** **1860-1935**
Born Glasgow; died Glasgow, 6 Sep. Landscape painter in oil and watercolour. Educated McLaren's School, Glasgow. His second wife was Mary Margaret K(qv). From a Caithness family, initially pursued a commercial career but after some years abandoned this in favour of studying at Glasgow School of Art under Robert Greenlees(qv). Then went to Paris and studied at the Academie Julian under Boulanger, Lefevre and Constant. Returning from France he taught for 18 years in Glasgow schools. After retiring lived for a number of years at Callander, Perthshire. Also worked on Iona. Vice-president, RSW. Regularly exhibited at the Society's annual show. Elected RSW 1892, ARSA 1916, RSA 1930. Exhibited RA(28), RSA(102), RSW(82), GI(141), L(25), RI(3) & AAS (during virtually all his working life 1885-1933), after 1930 from 14 Woodlands Terrace, Glasgow. Represented in Glasgow AG(3), Greenock AG, City of Edinburgh collection.
**Bibl:** Caw 392; Halsby 265.

**KAY, Arthur HRSA FSA** **fl 1881-d1939**
Glasgow painter. Married Kate Cameron(qv). A significant figure in Edinburgh artistic circles prior to WW2. A discerning and enthusiastic collector encompassing the Dutch School, Old Masters and a number of important Impressionists including Degas' 'The Absinthe Drinkers'. Chairman, Scottish Modern Arts Association. Exhibited 'Study of a Rose' at the GI in 1881 from 27 Belhaven Terrace.

**KAY, Christina McS** **fl 1889-1893**
Glasgow based flower and landscape painter in oils and watercolour. Exhibited GI(6) from 120 Mains Street.

**KAY, Miss Harriet M** **fl 1884-1902**
Edinburgh miniature painter in oil. Exhibited RA (portrait of her mother, 'Mrs A C Kay') 1902 & RSA(4) 1884-1900.

**KAY, James RSA RSW** **1858-1942**
Born Lamlash, Arran, 22 Oct; died Whistlefield, Dunbartonshire, 26 Sep. Painter in oil and watercolour, pastel, mixed media and gouache; marines, landscape, street and continental scenes. Loved dramatic contrasts of light and shade sometimes using paper of differing colours. Father of Violet K(qv). Started life in insurance but soon moved to art. Studied Glasgow School of Art. Travelled widely on the continent, especially in France and Holland. First exhibited Paris Salon 1894 and in Holland where he achieved some renown with his townscapes and coastal subjects. Maintained a studio in Glasgow and for many years lived at Whistlefield. His special love was painting the Clyde and the west coast of Scotland. Later work was distinguished by great vitality and freshness of colour. Shared a studio for a time with David Gauld(qv) and Stuart Park(qv). As well as being an active member of the Glasgow Art Club was close to the Glasgow Boys though never one of them. Enjoyed busy river scenes on the Clyde and Thames, also beach scenes and market places in Brittany and Normandy. His style underwent several changes; his later paintings had strong tones with encrusted coloured backgrounds and more attention to technique than to the subject-matter. It has been suggested that Kay may have been influenced by Adolphe Monticelli who had many works exhibited in Glasgow from the mid-1880s. Elected RSW 1896, ARSA 1893, RSA 1938. Honoured by French organisations including the gold medal of Société des Artistes Françaises 1903 and the same year won a gold medal at the 37th Exposition Municipale des Beaux-Arts de Rouen. Exhibited RA(3) from 1889, RSA, RSW, regularly at the Paris Salon from 1894, AAS 1896-1937 & GI(144), after 1916 from Crimea, Whistlefield, Dunbartonshire. Represented in Aberdeen AG, Glasgow AG(3), Greenock AG, Paisley AG, Stirling AG, Lillie AG (Milngavie), Brodie Castle (NTS), Bradford AG.
**Bibl:** Caw 333; Halsby 160, 244, 265; Glasgow Herald, 4 Jan 1942 (obit); Hardie 143; Macmillan [SA], 285, 309-10; 'James Kay', Ex Cat, Perth Festival of the Arts 1987.

**KAY, John** **1742-1826**
Born nr Dalkeith, Apr; died Edinburgh. Painter of portrait miniatures and caricatures while remaining a professional barber. Son of a stone mason who died when his son was eight years old, Kay was taken care of for five years by his mother's relations in Leith. Being unhappy, he apprenticed himself to a Dalkeith barber, after which time he set up on his own account in Edinburgh painting miniatures in his spare time as well as sketching horses, dogs and shipping. Patronised by a number of influential citizens including William Nisbet. In 1782 received an annuity of £20 and devoted his time to painting miniatures and etching portraits and caricatures, some of which landed him into trouble. In the window of his barber's shop sketches replaced wigs. He went from success to success until his premises in Parliament Street were destroyed in the Great Fire of 1824. After his death *A Descriptive Catalogue of Original Portraits* was published in 1836, with details of 356 etchings. A further Series of *Original Portraits by John Kay, Edinburgh* followed in 1877. Is said to have etched almost 900 plates. A sketch of Adam Smith is the only authentic portrait of the great man. Devoted himself full-time to art 1785. Twice married, having ten children by his first wife. Best remembered for his Edinburgh portraits, depicting local characters in a watercolour style much influenced by David Allan(qv). Later in life he was financially embarrassed, requiring the assistance of Mr Nisbet. His three brothers, of whom William(qv) is the best known, were all etchers. The usual signature on his etchings is 'I Kay' or 'IK'. Exhibited at the Edinburgh Association of Artists 1811-1816 and Institute for the Encouragement of the Fine Arts 1822. A miniature of William Low, an Edinburgh portrait painter, catalogued as by Kay, was loaned to the exhibition at the South Kensington Museum, 1865. Represented in NGS, SNPG(3, including an oil 'Self-portrait' and a watercolour portrait of 'Archibald Campbell'), Glasgow AG, City of Edinburgh collection.
**Bibl:** Brydall 205-6; Bryan; Butchart 8,16-17,21,24,91-4; Caw 52; DNB; Foskett 361; Halsby 265; McKay 326; Hilary & Mary Evans, *John Kay of Edinburgh*, 1977.

**KAY, Mary Margaret (née Thomson)** **fl 1904-1912**
Glasgow landscape painter in oils. Lived in Glasgow before moving to Callander, c1908; wife of Archibald K(qv). Exhibited GI(7), latterly from Woodend, Callander.

**KAY, Robert** **1740-1818**
Edinburgh architect. Designed the South Bridge, Edinburgh (1785-8).
**Bibl:** Gifford 188,234,293,562.

**KAY, Robertson** **fl 1892-1899**
Edinburgh minor portrait painter; moved to London in the 1890s.

**KAY, Thomas** **fl 1887**
Edinburgh painter of landscape in watercolour; exhibited RSA(1).

**KAY, Miss Violet MacNeish RSW** **1914-1971**
Born Glasgow, 18 Jne. Landscape and occasional painter in oil and watercolour. Daughter of James K(qv). Studied Glasgow School of Art under Hutchison(qv) and Shanks(qv) 1936. Painted west coast scenery in a fresh strong manner. Elected RSW 1948. Exhibited RSW(10), GI(60) & a Spanish street scene at the AAS in 1935 from 12 Ruskin Terrace.
**Bibl:** Halsby 265.

**KAY, William** **fl 1795-1830**
Painter in oil and watercolour, etcher and engraver; portrait miniatures and caricature portraits. Son of John K(qv). Best remembered for his original drawings and four prints in the Edinburgh Room of Edinburgh Central Library. These show some typical city characters, very like his brother's, including a member of the City guard, the street porter and town crier. A miniature portrait of 'Lord Byron, aged seven', signed and dated '1795', drawn in watercolour on paper, was sold at Sotheby's 1920. Represented in City of Edinburgh Collection.
**Bibl:** Butchart 94.

**KAYE, Mrs Betty** **fl 1955**
Edinburgh amateur watercolourist. Exhibited 'Edinburgh townscape' at the GI from 38 Warrender Pk Terrace.

**KEANY, Brian** **1939-**
Painter in oil of interiors and still life. Married Christina K(qv). Exhibited RSA 1977-1979 & GI(1), from 27 Solway Place, Glenrothes, Fife.

**KEANY, Mrs Christina Nicol** **fl 1979**
Painter of interiors and still life in oil. Married Brian K(qv). Exhibited once at the RSA.

**KEARNEY, Joseph** **fl 1965-1988**
Glasgow painter and etcher of informal portraits and figurative compositions. Member Glasgow Art Club. Exhibited GI(19) including a portrait of the 'Most Rev J D Scanlan, former Archbishop of Glasgow', 1975.

**KEAY, Harry** **1914-?**
Born 9 May. Painter in oil, figure studies, still life and farm scenes. Trained Dundee College of Art and Hospitalfield, Arbroath 1930-38. Lived in Dundee. In addition to exhibiting at the Dundee Art Society in the 1940s and 50s exhibited RA, RSA(17), GI(6) & SSA, from 1942 from 132a Nethergate, Dundee.

**KEDDIE, Gordon** **fl 1978**
Aberdeen artist; exhibited AAS(1) from 11a Gerrard Street.

**KEDDIE, Jessie** **fl 1861-1862**
Edinburgh landscape painter in oil; exhibited RSA(1) & GI(1), from 23 Hanover St.

**KEDDIE, Norelle C** **fl 1948-1956**
Edinburgh based sculptress of figurative works. Exhibited maquettes and figure subjects RSA(9) between the above years.

**KEDSLIE, Andrew F** **fl 1885-1894**
Landscape painter in watercolour, most often views in Fife. Lived at Ryton-on-Tyne in 1885, moving to Edinburgh c1887. Exhibited RSA(9) & RSW(1).

**KEENAN, Miss Irene** **fl 1970-1971**
Glasgow flower and semi-abstract painter; associated with Glasgow School of Art. Exhibited GI(2).

**KEENAN, John S** **fl 1902-1911**
Aberdeen painter of landscape, usually in oil. Exhibited AAS from 195 Union St.

**KEER, Peter** **fl 1599-1620**
Scottish cartographic engraver. Engraved maps of Scotland and Scottish counties, some of them with Speed.
**Bibl:** Bushnell.

**KEILLER, Mrs Dolly Phil-Morris** **fl 1914-1915**
Painter of figurative subjects. Daughter of the English caricaturist and illustrator, Philip Morris, and first wife of the son of the founder of the Keiller marmalade firm. Her husband built a studio near the top of Craigendarroch Hill, Ballater, now privately owned and known as Darroch Shiel. Exhibited RSA 'Au delas des bars' 1914 from a London address and, after her marriage, 'La fin du carnival', from Morven, Ballater.

**KEILLER, Gabrielle Muriel (née Ritchie)** **1908-1995**
Born North Berwick, Aug; died Bath, Dec 23. Art benefactor and collector; champion golfer. Ladies Open golf champion of Luxembourg, Switzerland & Monaco 1948, finalist English Open championship 1951. After two failed marriages she married the archaeologist Alexander Keiller 1951. After his death in 1955, she abandoned golf, became a Roman Catholic, and learned photography. Her interest in modern art, especially surrealism, was inspired by a visit to Peggy Guggenheim's collection in Venice and the work at the Venice Biennale of Eduardo Paolozzi(qv), whose main patron she became. Built up an outstanding collection, featured at the Edinburgh Festival of 1986, as well as donating works to the SNGMA, the Tate Gallery and the Hunterian Art Gallery, Glasgow. She bequeathed a substantial portion of her collection to the SNGMA.
**Bibl:** The Times, Obituary, Jan 1996.

**KEIR, Miss Bridget** **fl 1929-1951**
Edinburgh watercolour artist and engraver. Landscapes and townscapes including the northern Highlands, Italy and the Middle East. Exhibited a Venetian scene at the AAS (1929) & GI(18), latterly from 122 Cheyne Walk, Chelsea whence she moved c1920.

**KEIR (KIER), David** **1802-1864**
Cowen records a Glasgow glazier David Kier (sic) associate (founder ?) of the stained glass window firm J & W Keir some of whose work is in the church of the Holy Rood, Stirling.
**Bibl:** Painton Cowen, Stained Glass in Britain, 1985, 230.

**KEIR, Elizabeth E** **fl 1929-1964**
Cambuslang draughtswoman, mainly in pen. Wife of James Carnegie K(qv). Exhibited landscapes and townscapes RSA(1) & GI(10) from 16 Milton Avenue.

**KEIR, Harry/Henry** **1902-1977**
Glasgow artist. Painter mainly in wash drawings but also occasional oils; figure subjects and genre. Left school at 14 to become a house painter and sign writer. Attended Glasgow School of Art evening classes. Painted the working class areas of Glasgow in a sombre style, also sketched gypsies and travellers and prepared illustrations for Edward Gaitens' *Gorbal Novels.* Exhibited RSA(10) & GI(23) after 1946 from 68 Baldwin Avenue. Represented in Glasgow AG.
**Bibl:** Halsby 265.

**KEIR, James Carnegie** **fl 1919-1936**
Glasgow watercolourist and engraver of landscapes, townscapes and occasional figure studies. Married to Elizabeth E K(qv). Exhibited RSA(2) & GI(8) from 16 Milton Avenue, Cambuslang.

**KEIR, Miss Lindsay J** **fl 1984-1986**
Renfrewshire painter of flowers and still life. Exhibited GI(4), from 37 Low Barholm, Kilbarchan.

**KEIR, Robert** **fl 1814**
Painter. According to Graves, he painted landscapes; exhibited RA(2), GI(2) & elsewhere in the Provinces.

**KEITH, Alexander** **fl 1836-1874**
Edinburgh painter in oil of portraits, figures and animals. Brother of Haydon K(qv). Lived for many years at Brighton Crescent, Portobello. Exhibited RSA(9) & GI(4). Represented Edinburgh City collection.

**KEITH, Miss Alison** **fl 1976**
Ayrshire flower painter; exhibited GI(2), from 11 Cessnock Rd, Galston.

**KEITH, David Barrogill MC** **1891-1979**
Born Thurso, 1 Mar; died Thurso, 30 Dec. Painter in oil and watercolour; lawyer. Most of his works are landscape and topographical. Served in the army in WWI, awarded Military Cross for heroism in France. Practised as a solicitor in Thurso between the wars and then returned to active service in 1939 serving as a Staff Captain in the legal affairs department Orkney and Shetland Defence HQ 1940-44. In 1945 returned to Thurso resuming his legal practice. Appointed Sheriff 1946. Remained unmarried, living with his sister. Member, Caithness Artists Society. Exhibited RSA(23) 1937-1966 & RSW. Represented in the collection of HM the Queen Mother. Some Spanish scenes are in Thurso Museum though not normally on show.

**KEITH, Haydon** **fl 1867**
Portobello painter of figurative subjects in oil. Brother of Alexander K(qv). Exhibited RSA(1).

**KEITH, J B** **fl 1893-1896**
Aberdeen artist in oil, watercolour, pen and ink, and pencil; mainly landscapes. Often painted on Upper Deeside. Among four exhibits at the AAS during the above years was 'Lochnagar from Prony'. Lived at Bank House, Spring Garden.

**KEITH, J Stuart** **fl 1951-1953**
Glasgow sculptor in wood. Attracted to the depiction of movement, especially ballet. Exhibited GI(4), from 45 Viewmount Drive.

**KEITH, Margaret I** **fl 1979**
Amateur painter. Exhibited AAS 1979.

**KEITH, Mrs T W** **fl 1886-1890**
Aberdeen flower painter. Exhibited AAS from 301 and later 373 Union St.

**KELLAND, James** **fl 1873**
Edinburgh landscape painter in oil; exhibited RSA(2).

**KELLAR, Kenneth W** **fl 1938**
Glasgow based draughtsman in ink. Exhibited two landscape sketches at the GI from 6 West End Park St.

**KELLER, Johan** **1863-c1915**
Born The Hague, Nov 13. Sculptor, specialised in portrait busts; bronze, plaster, terracotta, ceramics. Staff member, Glasgow School of Art 1895, then Helensburgh from the turn of the century until the early part of WWI. Exhibited RA(7), RSA(5), GI(40) & L(4). Represented in Le Musée Boymans (Rotterdam).

**KELLMAN, Leonard** **fl 1952-1955**
Dundee based sculptor. Exhibited figurative works RSA.

**KELLOCK, David Taylor** **1913-**
Stained glass window designer. Studied Edinburgh College of Art 1932-1936. Began exhibiting in 1937 showing RSA(3) from Woodlea, Carnock Road, Dunfermline.

**KELLY, George** **1920-1965**
Born Aberdeen, Jly 10; died Aberdeen. Landscape and topographical painter in oils, teacher. Began working life as an apprentice house painter during which time exhibited first work at RGI 1936. Served during WW2 in RAF. Trained Gray's School of Art 1945-50. Gold medal for painting 1949. Married 1950. Father of Paul K(qv). Combined painting with teaching art from 1950 until his death. First one-man show in Aberdeen 1955, last one-man show also in Aberdeen 1965. Exhibited RSA(2), RGI(4) & AAS from Prospect Cottage, Skene.

**KELLY, Mrs Gladys May** **fl 1973**
Amateur Glasgow painter; exhibited 'Study of a Girl' at the GI, from 37 Edgemont St.

**KELLY, James** **fl 1886**
Glasgow based landscape painter. Exhibited GI(2) from 58 Great Hamilton St.

**KELLY, John Turner** **fl 1890-1907**
Edinburgh landscape painter in oil, often of views in the Lothians. Exhibited RSA(27), all scenes in East Lothian, also AAS & GI(5).

**KELLY, Joseph** **fl 1931**
Dunfermline based artist. Exhibited RSA(1) from Buchanan Street.

**KELLY, Margaret H** **fl 1861**
Glasgow painter of natural history subjects in watercolour; exhibited GI(3), from 110 N. Frederick St.

**KELLY, Nicholas** **fl 1810-1831**
Flower painter; exhibited RA in 1810 from an Edinburgh address and again in 1815 and 1831 from York.

**KELLY, Paul** **1958-**
Born Aberdeenshire, Jly 19. Painter, sculptor and photographer. Son of George K(qv). Trained Edinburgh College of Art 1977-81. First solo exhibition in Aberdeen 1984. Exhibits AAS from the family home in Skene, Aberdeenshire.

**KELLY, Robert George** **1822-1910**
Born Dublin Jan 22; died Chester, May 9. Portrait and landscape painter. Father of Robert George Talbot K and grandfather of Richard Barrett Talbot. Exhibited 6 portraits at the RSA, all in 1850, from Queen Street. It appears that he moved south shortly thereafter, at first to 36 Howland Street, London from where he exhibited a Kirkcudbright landscape at the RA before settling c1860 in Birkenhead from where he showed 4 more works at the RA; also RHA(17) & L(52).

**KELLY, Thomas Meikle** **1866-c1945**
Dunbartonshire painter and etcher. Worked in oil and watercolour mainly landscapes, topographical and figure subjects. Studied Glasgow School of Art. Founder member Milngavie Art Club 1915-1916, exhibiting there until the early 1940s. Hon President of the Club at the time of its 25th Anniversary Exhibition in Glasgow 1940. Toward the end of his life lived at Dunrowan, Milngavie, Dunbartonshire. Exhibited 1893-1940 RSA(10), RSW(14), AAS, GI(15) & L(3). Represented in Lillie AG, (Milngavie) by 3 oils, one pen and wash drawing and an etching.

**KELLY, William ARSA** **1861-1944**
Born Aberdeen; died Aberdeen. Architect & architectural draughtsman. Trained with William Smith(qv), designer of the present Balmoral Castle. Went to London for a number of years returning c1890 to work for his former employer (latterly known as Messrs Kelly & Nicol) remaining with them for 40 years. Among his most important commissions were the Aberdeen Savings Bank, St Ninian's Church, Aberdeen, new wings at Montrose Mental Hospital, and a reconstruction of the Old Infirmary, Aberdeen. Interested mainly in ecclesiastical architecture. Founder member, Aberdeen Ecclesiastical Society, becoming President. Associated with the University Senatus, restored King's College Chapel as well as designing the War Memorial. Author of *St. Machar's Cathedral* 1910, *Midmar Castle* (in *Scottish Notes & Queries*, vol 1), *S. Pittick's Belfry* (in *Scottish Notes & Queries*, vol 1), *Some Ancient Churches nr Aberdeen* (In Trans. of Aberdeen Ecclesiological Society, vol 1, part 1). For several years lecturer at Aberdeen University. Elected ARSA 1911, Honorary Retired Associate 1933. Frequent exhibitor RSA & AAS(3).
**Bibl:** Dunbar 152; RSA (obit) 1944.

**KELMAN, Donald Stewart** **1937-**
Born 10 April. Studied Grays School of Art, Aberdeen. Paints in watercolour and acrylics. Exhibited RSA, AAS, SSA. Represented in Aberdeen AG. Exhibited RSA(8) & AAS from Cove Schoolhouse, Cove, Aberdeen.

**KELMAN, Janet Harvie** **fl 1898-1900**
Edinburgh based painter of landscape and the occasional portrait. Apparently unrelated to Donald Stewart K in spite of the coincidence of having the same address separated by six decades. Exhibited RSA(2) & AAS(2), formerly from the Schoolhouse, Cove, Aberdeen and latterly from 4 Claremont Pk, Leith.

**KELSEY, Robert** **1949-**
Born Glasgow. Painter of landscape and still life. Trained Glasgow School of Art. Head, Art & Design, Renfrew HS 1971-95. Visited Tuscany and Portugal. Prefers bold contrasting colours. Regular exhibitor RGI.

**KELSO, Roberta (Bet)** **fl 1940-1953**
Paisley painter usually watercolour or charcoal; figure subjects (often children) and farm animals. In 1946 moved to Kilquharity House, Castle Douglas before returning to Paisley c1949. Exhibited GI(11) & Paisley Art Institute 1952-53.

**KEMP, Agnes** **fl 1892-1910**
Landscape, fruit, flower and figure painter who moved from Edinburgh to London c1899. Exhibited RSA(1), GI(4), RBA(2), RI(1) & SWA(2).

**KEMP, Alan** **fl 1963-1988**
Edinburgh landscape and figurative painter. Exhibited RSA(13).

**KEMP, Mrs Catriona** **fl 1966-1974**
East Glasgow flower and still life painter; exhibited GI(3), from 141 Monreith Rd.

**KEMP, Mrs Eleanor Maria Hilda** **1910-?**
Born Elie, Fifeshire. Painter of landscape and stylised figure subjects in oil. Studied Regent Street Polytechnic School and at the Slade. Painted in Canada, Italy, Yugoslavia and the USA as well as occasionally around the Inner Hebrides but mostly in Essex and her native Fife. Lived in East Anglia since 1960. Exhibited RI & SWA.

**KEMP, George Meikle** **1794-1844**
Born Moorfoot, Peeblesshire. Architect and watercolour artist. Self-taught son of a shepherd, first apprenticed to a joiner but a knowledge of building construction and a love of Gothic architecture caused him to visit the cathedral cities of Scotland and England, working in Glasgow and London - at the latter in the office of William Burn. From 1824-1826 travelled in France and Belgium sketching and measuring the ecclesiastical edifices and antiquities. Settled in Edinburgh where he was employed as an architectural draughtsman. His best known work was for the Edinburgh Scott Memorial; originally placed third of 55 entrants (using the pseudonym John Morvo) the committee were undecided and requested further drawings, eventually making Kemp the winner. 'The complex rather shaggy spire above, supported by flying buttresses, is a synthesis from continental sources adapted from the cathedral spire at Antwerp. Kemp's practical experience and consummate draughtsmanship were the link between his excited experience of the 'gorgeous decorations' of continental Gothic and their execution' [Gifford]. In 1843, Kemp drew three sketches of the Calton Hill, of interest because they all dealt with proposals for completing the National Monument. These were engraved by Nichol(qv), J West and T Dick. Died from drowning in the canal basin before the Scott Monument was completed. A number of his sketches are in the Edinburgh Room of the Central PL. Two works, one a pencil and wash study of 'Melrose Abbey' and the other a pencil study of the 'National Monument of Calton Hill' are in the NGS while a portrait of 'James Moir', attributed to Kemp, is in the SNPG. Also 4 works in Edinburgh City collection.
**Bibl:** Butchart 64-6; Colvin; Dunbar 149; Gifford 48,314-6; Halsby 265-6.

**KEMP, J** **fl 1911**
Dundee painter; exhibited 'Marche aux pommes' at the GI from Redcroft, Blackness Rd.

**KEMP, Miss Jeka (Jacobina)** **1876-1966**
Born Bellahouston, Glasgow. Landscape painter in oil and water-colour, with a penchant for colourful and bustling scenes, especially continental. Studied art in London and Paris before travelling to Italy, Holland and North Africa. Exhibited French landscapes at the Glasgow Society of Lady Artists, at the GI and in 1912 held her first one-man exhibition in Glasgow. In 1914 a critic described her as a 'distinguished disciple of Melville'; her colour and technique are derived from that artist although her style is rather cruder. Abandoned painting 1927 but remained in France until 1939 before returning to Dorset. Halsby regards her most successful watercolours as figures on beaches or in interiors, flooded with the light of southern France. Exhibited RSA(2), RA(1), GI(9) & L(16).
**Bibl:** Halsby 266.

**KEMP, John** **fl 1907-1911**
Glasgow based painter. Exhibited a Spanish watercolour GI from 20 Lansdowne Crescent.

**KEMP, John H** **fl 1973**
Aberdeen painter in pastel. Exhibited a landscape at the AAS in the above year from 60 Watson St.

**KEMP, Marjorie** **fl 1921-1955**
Born Blairgowrie, Perthshire. Stained glass artist, studied at Glasgow School of Art and lived in Edinburgh. Entered into partnership with Margaret Chilton(qv). Designed Gardiner Memorial window in Greyfriars (c1938), St Columba (1930) in the hall of Salisbury Church but most of her best known work was in collaboration with Chilton. Exhibited RSA(13), RA(6) & GI(7), latterly from 8 Fettes Row.
**Bibl:** Gifford 44-5,155,178,284,388,452,572,598,618,634.

**KEMP, Violet I** **fl 1940-1955**
Dalkeith based painter of portraits, flowers and Midlothian scenery; exhibited RSA(8) from Elm Lodge.

**KEMP, W S** **fl 1882**
Glasgow watercolour painter; exhibited a figure study at the GI, from 7 Gladstone Terrace.

**KEMP, William G** **fl 1872-1887**
Edinburgh architect and painter in oil and watercolour of buildings, interiors and landscape. Exhib RSA(7) & GI(1), from 3 Alfred Place.

**KEMPE, Charles Eamer** **1834-1907**
Stained glass window designer and decorator. Designed a window depicting saints and Old Testament heroes in the outer S nave aisle of St Giles (c1898), the Reredos (c 1900) and two other lights in St Michael and All Saints, and two lights and a vesica in St Oswald, now Boroughmuir School annexe.
**Bibl:** Gifford 44,117,257-8,366,494.

**KEMPLAY, Ms Suzanne** **fl 1988-**
Edinburgh oil painter; exhibited GI(1), from 2nd flr R, 60 Haymarket Terrace.

**KEMPSELL, Jake** **1940-**
Born Dumfries. Sculptor, semi-abstract, sometimes figurative. Studied at Edinburgh College of Art 1959-65. Lecturer in sculpture at Edinburgh College of Art 1965-75. Head of sculpture at Duncan of Jordanstone School of Art, Dundee since 1975. First one-man show in Edinburgh 1970. Elected member SSA 1967 and received SAC awards in 1968 and 1969. Involved in open air exhibitions in Scotland, England and Wales. His work is featured in D Petherbridge's *Art in Architecture,* 1987 and G Murray, *Art in the Garden,* 1988.

**KENDALL, Miss Alice R** **1896-1955**
Edinburgh painter of figurative studies, mainly illustrating scenes of childhood. After the war moved to 19a Edith Grove, London. Exhibited RSA in 1944 and 1946 & GI(3), from 14 Mayfield Gdns.

**KENDRICK, Emma Eleanora** **1788-1871**
Watercolour painter of flowers and figurative work, often with subjects taken from literature. Exhibited RSA(7) from 4 Duchess St, Portland Place, London.

**KENMORE, Mary** **fl 1861**
Renfrewshire painter; exhibited 'Moonlight' at the GI, from Greenock.

**KENNARD, Edward** **fl 1883-1888**
Little known illustrator. Specialised in scenes of Highland Games for the *Illustrated London News* 1883-86 and in *The Graphic* 1888. Wrote and illustrated *Fishing in Strange Waters* (1885). His wife was the first authoress on golf.

**KENNAWAY, Charles Gray** **1860-1925**
Born and died Perth. Landscape, portrait and figure painter in oil and watercolour; also etcher. Educated Sharp's Institution, Perth and under the Perth artist William Proudfoot(qv). Entered Royal College of Art in London where, after seven years, gained his Art Master's certificate. A travelling scholarship took him to Paris where he continued his studies at the L'Atelier Julian. Principal, **ATHANEUM SCHOOL OF ART**, Glasgow 1892-1900. Shortly before his death he installed murals depicting heroines from the Waverley novels in the family restaurant. In later life lived in Torquay. Exhibited RA(3), RSW(2), AAS(5), RI(1), L(3), GI(11) & Perth Fine Art Exhibition (from an Aberdeen address) 1911/12; posthumously at Perth AG 1937/8. Represented in Perth AG (portrait of his son and 2 self-portraits).

**KENNEDY, Alexander** **fl 1958-1967**
Glasgow painter of townscapes. Exhibited GI(2), from 11 Whittingehame Dr.

**KENNEDY, Cecil** **1905-1997**
Born England, 4 Feb; died Dec 12. Painter in oil of flowers. The most popular British flower painter of his time. Came from a Scottish family who at the instigation of Thomas Faed(qv) moved to London. After training at art school he studied under a number of artists the most influential being Nieco Jungmann. Also studied in Antwerp when serving there with 21st Army Group 1944, and Paris. Awarded silver medal at the Paris Salon 1956 and gold medal 1970. His carefully delineated flower paintings have been likened to those of the Dutch 17th Century Masters in approach and devotion to detail. Held exhibitions in London, Paris, New York and Johannesberg. Exhibited regularly RA, RSA & RHA.
**Bibl:** The Times, Obituary, Dec 1997.

**KENNEDY, Duncan** **fl 1886**
Glasgow based painter and sculptor, usually in wood. Exhibited GI(3) from 30 Steven Street.

**KENNEDY, Edward W** **fl 1892-1919**
Edinburgh sculptor and designer. His work was widely varied from religious themes, portraits and ambitious figure studies to a design for a bronze door knocker. Exhibited RSA(10), GI(6) & L(1).

**KENNEDY, James C** **fl 1870-1871**
Elgin painter in oil of buildings and landscape; exhibited RSA(2), including an illustration for a Robert Burns poem, & 'Spynie Palace by moonlight' at the GI.

**KENNEDY, John** **fl 1850**
Landscape painter. Master of the School of Art at Dundee. His watercolours are delicately drawn with clear colour. A series of five watercolours painted in 1855 relating to Burns' life are in NGS.
**Bibl:** Halsby 266.

**KENNEDY, John Davies** **fl 1920-1955**
Painter in oil and watercolour, also etcher. Portraits, still life and figure studies, also landscape especially in Flanders, France and Wales. Living in Selkirk 1920, Edinburgh 1921 and Cramond Bridge 1931. Exhibited RSA(22), RSW(10), L(3) & GI(3).

**KENNEDY, Joseph** **fl 1873**
Aberdeen based painter. Painted domestic scenes; associated with the School of Art in Aberdeen. Exhibited RSA(3).

**KENNEDY, Mrs L F (Mrs C N Kennedy)** **fl 1885-1895**
Stirling based painter in oils and watercolour. Topographical and figurative compositions. Exhibited GI(3) after 1886 from 38 Abbey Road, London.

**KENNEDY, Magnus A** **fl 1909-1916**
Dumfries sculptor of portraits and portrait busts. Moved to Liverpool c1914. Exhibited GI(3) & L(3).

**KENNEDY, Robert A** **fl 1892-1950**
Scottish painter of landscape and topographical subjects, often in Fife. Lived at various times in Glasgow, Dundee and Liberton moved to the latter shortly before WW2. Exhibited RSA(21), GI(16) & L(1), after 1947 from 61 Howden Hall Rd, Liberton.

**KENNEDY, Thomas** **fl 1830-1855**
Edinburgh landscape and subject painter in oil; exhibited RSA(8) including 'Elfin - favourite spaniel' which received critical acclaim 1852.

**KENNEDY, Tom** **fl 1974**
Banff sculptor, generally in bronze. Trained Gray's School of Art, Aberdeen. Exhbited AAS from 53, High St, Buckie.

**KENNEDY, W J** **fl 1887-1914**
Painter. Exhibited RSA(1) & GI(1).

**KENNEDY, William** **1859-1918**
Born Hutchesontown, Glasgow, 17 Jly, died Tangiers, 11 Dec. Painter of landscape and genre in oil, watercolour & latterly pastel. Orphaned at an early age and went to live with his brother in Paisley. In 1875 he won a prize at Paisley School of Art and probably attended the Glasgow School of Art as well. Studied in Paris 1880-1885 under Bouguereau, Fleury and Bastien-Lepage & at Grez-sur-Loing. Worked in Stirling 1885-1898. First exhibition in London 1886. In 1883 his painting of Millet's home in Barbizon was exhibited at the RSA. Enjoyed painting military subjects and was closely associated with the Glasgow School. In 1912 he settled in Tangiers for health reasons, painting Arab scenes and lively Arab horses. His early work was full of promise and very varied, showing the influence of Corot although the subject matter was often unusual. Friendships with Henry(qv) and Crawhall(qv), and especially Lavery(qv), contributed to his development. In 1887, when the Glasgow Boys formed themselves into a society, Kennedy was elected President. It was at Craigmill, working with Denovan Adam(qv), that Kennedy loved to paint horses, and it was there he met his wife, Lena Scott. Probably brought Joseph Crawhall and John Lavery with him to Cambuskenneth. Lived for several years in Abbey Road and painted many local scenes including the 3rd Battalion of the Argyll and Sutherland Highlanders who trained each summer in the King's Park. From about 1900 he and his wife paid extensive visits to Berkshire where he enjoyed sketching the rural scenery of southern England. 'His style developed from a meticulous attention to detail to a much greater breadth of treatment and the use of thickly applied paint, later to be dragged across the surface of the canvas in a somewhat turgid manner. He was an uneven painter and signed his name to many mediocre and some downright bad paintings, but his best work is good by any standards and is distinguished by a richness of tone and freshness and vivacity in the handling of the paint, and the presence of that vital element which makes it live for us still' [Ailsa Tanner]. Exhibited RA(1), RSA(18), RSW(2), GI(74), AAS(2) & L(11). Represented in Glasgow AG(4), Kirkcaldy AG, Paisley AG, Perth AG, Karlsruhe AG.
**Bibl:** AJ 1894, 79; The Baillie Feb 8, 1893; Billcliffe, The Glasgow Boys, 1985; Caw 445-6; Eyre-Todd, Who's Who in Glasgow 1909, 107; Halsby 150, 266; Hardie 92-3; Irwin 373-6; Macmillan [SA] 255, 259.

**KENNEDY, Mrs William (née Lena Scott)** **fl 1900-1916**
Glasgow-based artist. Painted landscapes in oil. Fond of late evening scenes and sunsets. Wife of William K(qv). Exhibited RSA(1), GI(29), AAS(3) & L(7).

**KENNEDY, William Denholm** **1813-1865**
Born Dumfries; died London. Painter in oil and watercolour of historical subjects, genre and landscape; also a discerning critic of engravings and etchings and a great music lover. As a young man he went to London where he became a friend and pupil of William Etty. Entered the RA Schools in 1833 winning the Gold Medal for historical painting 1835. A scholarship enabled him to visit Italy 1840-1842. Although at first a painter of historical scenes, Kennedy changed after his Italian journey to Italian genre and literary subjects including scenes from Byron, Spenser and Tasso. Occasionally made designs with stained glass for Thomas Willemont. Died from dropsy. Exhibited RA(52) 1833-1865 & RSA(12) 1834-1845. Represented

in National Gallery of Ireland, BM.
**Bibl:** AJ 1865, 235 (obit); Bryan; Cat of National Gallery of Ireland 1920, 64; DNB XX 1892, 437; Halsby 266; Redgrave.

**KENNEP, Andrew** **fl 1885**
Edinburgh painter in oil; exhibited 'Rustic gossip' at the RSA from 4 Montgomery Street.

**KENT, James S** **fl 1900**
Glasgow-based artist. Exhibited GI(2) from 212 St Vincent Street.

**KEPPIE, Miss Jessie RSW** **1868-1951**
Born Glasgow. Watercolour painter of flowers, architectural and topographical subjects, also designer. Studied Glasgow School of Art under Fra Newbury(qv) and James Dunlop(qv). Member of 'The Roaring Camp' at Dunure where her brother John Keppie's usual lady guests included Frances and Margaret Macdonald(qv), Agnes Raeburn(qv), Kate Cameron(qv) and Janet Aitken(qv). Originally engaged to Charles Rennie Mackintosh(qv), she never married. Awarded silver medal in the National Competition of 1889 for her design of a Persian carpet. Illustrated many flower drawings. Author of a fairy tale for *The Magazine* (1893). Lifelong member of the Glasgow Lady Artists' Club. Awarded the Lauder Prize. Latterly lived at Haddington Park, Prestwick. Exhibited extensively 1892-1940, RSA(13), RSW(36), GI(100) & L(5).
**Bibl:** Burkhauser 50,60-1,76-7,79, 117; Halsby 185, 266.

**KEPPIE, John RSA FRIBA JP** **1862-1945**
Born Glasgow; died Haddington Park, Prestwick, 25 Apr. Painter, architect and architectural draughtsman, also etcher. Brother of Jessie K(qv). Educated Ayr Academy, Glasgow University and Atelier Pascal in Paris 1883. Pupil of Campbell Douglas & Sellars(qv). After the latter's death he left to join Honeyman(qv). His first designs derived from Sellars and the Beaux Arts, but he soon collaborated with CR Mackintosh(qv). Principal partner in the firm of Keppie & Honeyman. Associated with John Honeyman in the restoration of several churches including Linlithgow church and Brechin cathedral, and the construction of many important buildings in Glasgow including the School of Art. Fellow, Institute of British Architects, President, Royal Incorporation of Architects in Scotland, Glasgow Institute of Architects, Glasgow Architectural Association and Glasgow Art Club. In 1930 Chairman of Glasgow School of Art, founded the John Keppie Scholarship in Architecture and Sculpture. Elected ARSA 1920, RSA 1931. Exhibited RSA, GI(67), RSW(6) & L(1). Represented in Glasgow AG, Edinburgh City collection.
**Bibl:** A Gomme & D Walker, Architecture of Glasgow, London 1987(rev), 293 et al.

**KER, Miss Angela** **fl 1955-1965**
Glasgow painter in oils and occasional watercolour; portraits, flowers and still life. Exhibited GI(13), latterly from Tulloch Cottage, Blanefield, Stirlingshire.

**KER, Donald** **fl 1969-1970**
Aberdeen-based potter. Exhibited AAS(5) from Gray's School of Art.

**KER, Miss Joan** **fl 1961-1973**
Painter of Norrieston, Thornhill, by Stirling. Exhibited continental and Scottish, topographical and coastal scenes RSA(9), GI(4) & AAS(1965-71).

**KER, Joanna R** **fl 1931-1973**
Painter in oil of landscape and topographical scenes. Originally working from Delmaine, Ledaig, Argyll, later moved to Strathblane 1930-1934 and finally to Rye, Sussex c1937. Exhibited RA, RSA, SWA & RBA although because of confusion with her contemporary Joan Ker(qv) it is unclear how many exhibits were shown in each.

**KER, Thomas** **fl 1656-d1686**
Son of the Aberdeen painter William K(qv). Apprenticed in 1656 to Joseph Stacie becoming a painter burgess of the Cannongate in 1667, a member of the Incorporation of St Mary's 1679-1685 and burgess of Edinburgh in 1680. Employed at Holyrood House from 30 June to 15 November, 1673 at 18 shillings per day.
**Bibl:** Apted 54-5.

**KER, William** **fl 1652-1668**
Aberdeen painter. Father of Thomas(qv). Between October 1652 and April 1657 he received £4 4s 'for guilding the phan of the pricket' at King's College, Aberdeen. Commissioned by the Earl Marischal to guild the arms at the Kirk of Rathen (1666). Received a further £6 for painting the King's arms in Aberdeen.
**Bibl:** Apted 55; GRO Aberdeen Reg. of Deaths, OPR, 168A/18; Old Aberdeen Records, i, 216.

**KERMACK, Agnes M** **fl 1891-1897**
Edinburgh flower and figurative painter in oil and watercolour. Exhibited RSA(2), GI(5) & AAS(1), latterly from 7 Lansdowne Crescent.

**KERR, Miss Caroline** **fl 1978**
Glasgow figure painter; exhibited 'Study of a Nude' at the GI, from 79 Clouston St.

**KERR, Miss Edith Miles** **fl 1925-d1930**
Died Hawick, 14 Feb. Painter of portraits in oil and watercolour. Exhibited two local landscapes at the GI from The Anchorage, Lochranza, Arran in 1930, & a portrait at the RSA five years earlier, from her home at 14 Duke Street, Hawick.

**KERR, Grace M** **fl 1890**
Glasgow-based artist; exhibited a continental townscape at the GI from 194 Bath Street.

**KERR, Lady (Harriet) Louisa** **c1815-1884**
Scottish miniaturist, died 24 Apr. Almost certainly the daughter of the 6th Marquis of Lothian. Married Sir John Stuart Forbes, Bt in 1834. Little is known about her work and she appears not to have been very prolific. The South Kensington Museum had on loan in 1865 'Portrait of a Lady in the Character of the Muse, Polyhymnia', painted on ivory 1830. Two silhouette portraits by Lady Louisa Ker (sic) are recorded on page 11 of the 1905 catalogue of portraits belonging to the 4th Earl of Lothian.
**Bibl:** Long 250.

**KERR, Henry Francis** **1855-1946**
Edinburgh architect and draughtsman of interiors. Responsible for remodelling Greyfriars (1931-8), designing New College Mission in the Pleasance (1891-3) and two interesting homes in Wester Coates, 'Redmount' in the Road and No.2 in the Avenue. Exhibited RSA(18) & GI(3), from 16 Duke St.
**Bibl:** Gifford 154,241,243,342,382,528.

**KERR, Henry Wright RSA RSW** **1857-1936**
Born Edinburgh; died Edinburgh, 18 Feb. Painter in oil and watercolour of portraits and figurative subjects. One of the most prolific Scottish artists, a fine recorder of Scottish character and the Scottish scene and a painter of considerable imagination and sympathy. Best known for his portraits of elderly, characterful gentlemen and for his book illustrations. Many of the books he illustrated remain popular today. Early education was in Dundee where he was apprenticed to a manufacturer. Then took up an appointment in Leith so that he could attend art classes at the Board of Manufacturers and Life School of the RSA. In 1882 his first watercolour landscape was exhibited at the RSA. In addition to working in Scotland he embarked on a sketching trip to Holland where he came under the influence of the Hague School. Also visited Ireland where, by his portrayal of local character, he was regarded as the natural successor to Erskine Nicol(qv). Visited Connemara 1888. Illustrated some of Galt's novels but his best known illustrations were for Dean Ramsay's *Scottish Life and Character* (1909); Mitford's *Annals of the Parish* (1911); G.A.Birmingham's *The Lighter Side of Irish Life* (1911) and Galt's *The Last of the Lairds* (1926). In 1923-24 he acted as Deputy President of the RSA. Earned a reputation as a portrait painter, two of his most important works being 'Principal Martin' (RSA 1930/1), and 'Dr Darling, Master of the Merchant Company' (now in the Merchants' Hall). Elected RSW 1891, ARSA 1893, RSA 1909. Exhibited RA(8), RSA(159), RSW(70), GI(26), AAS, RI(1) & L(12), latterly from 18 York Place. Represented in NGS, SNPG(60) including 'Robert Gemmell Hutchison' & 'Sir James Lawton Wingate', Dundee AG, Glasgow AG, Kirkcaldy AG, City of Edinburgh collection.
**Bibl:** Caw 426-7; Halsby 169, 266; RSA (obit) 1936; Scotsman (obit) 18.2.1936; Houfe 196.

**KERR, J** **fl 1800**
Scottish engraver, probably of Glasgow. Engraved a bookplate for the Rev. Robert Clarke 1800.
**Bibl:** Bushnell.

**KERR, James** **fl 1879-1883**
Glasgow landscape painter. Exhibited GI(4), latterly from 154 W. George St.

**KERR, James H** **fl 1880-1898**
Edinburgh sculptor in marble and plaster. Often depicted sports and sportsmen, especially curling and golf, also celebrities such as 'Burns' (1884) and 'Margaret Wilson, the Solway Martyr' (1884). Exhibited RSA(5) & GI(11) from Dalry Road, Edinburgh.
**Bibl:** Gifford 278.

**KERR, Miss Maree** **fl 1937-1938**
Hamilton lithographer; exhibited GI(3) from The Priory, Carlisle Road.

**KERR, Margaret** **fl 1870-1885**
Edinburgh painter of figurative and literary subjects in oil who moved to London c1880. Exhibited RSA(7) & SWA(5).

**KERR, Nesta** **fl 1886-1894**
Glasgow flower painter; exhibited GI(5), latterly from 17 Kersland Terrace.

**KERR, Miss Nora Jean** **fl 1953**
Renfrewshire watercolour painter and linocut artist. Exhibited a landscape and 'Wild Horses' at the GI, from Orcadia, Kilmacolm.

**KERR, Peter** **1857-1940**
Born Greenock, died Greenock. Painter in oil and watercolour of still-life, portrait and landscape. Trained Edinburgh College of Art winning the principal awards for three successive years. Exhibited regularly in Glasgow and Edinburgh, also a selection of British pictures exhibited in Paris. Honorary President, Greenock Art Club where he was a well-known and respected figure for many years. Exhibited RSA(4), RHA(7) & GI(18), latterly from 121 Forsyth St, Greenock.
**Bibl:** Glasgow Herald 3.1.40 (obit).

**KERR, Miss Pheona** **fl 1988**
Glasgow sculptress. Exhibited 'Autumn Prayer' in mixed media at the GI, from 26 Craigie St, Govanhill.

**KERR, R W Graham** **fl 1931-1945**
Painter and draughtsman in watercolour and ink; also miniaturist. Exhibited GI(4) since 1945 from 22 Christchurch St, London SW.

**KERR, Robert** **fl 1870**
Glasgow watercolour painter. Exhibited a military subject at the GI from 79, North St.

**KERR, Robert** **1823-1904**
Born Aberdeen. Architect. Went to London at an early age becoming a founder member and first President of the Architectural Association. From 1847-8 Professor of the Arts of Construction at King's College, London. District Surveyor, St. James, Westminster 1862-1902. Author of *The English Gentleman's House* 1864.
**Bibl:** Peter Savage, Lorimer and the Edinburgh Craft Designers, Edinburgh 1980, 165.

**KERR, William** **fl 1716**
Little is known of this painter beyond the fact that in 1716 he is recorded as painting funeral escutcheons from Forres. Possibly related to the Aberdeen painter William Ker(r).

**KERR-LAWSON, James** **1864-1939**
Born Anstruther, Fife, 28 Oct; died London, 1 May. Moved to Canada the year after he was born. Painter in oil and watercolour of landscape and portraits; also mural decorator, etcher and lithographer. Studied at the School run by the Ontario Society of Artists together with George Reid both of whom were awarded silver medals. Also studied in Rome and Paris under Lefevre and Boulanger. Then lived in Florence and London. Hartrick records that he was one of the early experimenters in the revival of lithography around the turn of the century. In 1909 he was a founder member of the Senefelder Club(qv). Later executed some fine decorations in the Senate House, Ottawa, becoming a close friend of Homer Watson. His oil paintings show the influence of the New England Art Club painters and the quieter tones of the Camden Town school. But his watercolours of Spanish and Italian towns and market scenes often sparkle. Contributed to F E Jackson's *The Neo-Lith,* 1907-8. Exhibited GI(10), ROI(1), RBA(1) & L(8). Represented SNPG by portraits of 'John Logie Baird' and 'Sir John Lavery', also in Glasgow AG.
**Bibl:** Halsby 231, 266.

**KERSHAW, Mrs** **fl 1875-1877**
Glasgow flower and natural history painter; exhibited GI(5), latterly from 40 Jane St, Helensburgh.

**KICKIUS, Apollonia** **1669-1695**
A shadowy English figure, lived and worked most of her life in Scotland. At the time of her demise she was probably working at Castle Huntly for the 1st Earl of Strathmore. Buried in Longforgan church where her monument bears the following inscription:
Interred lyes under this stone
The comely virtuous Apollone
Kickieus, a rare yea matchless one.
Exemplar for a godly life,
A constant modest loving wife.
In paintrie strange who shew more skill
Than ere Apelles could, yet still,
Tho fam'd and prais'd much, most humble.
The heavens bereav'd us of this bliss,
Now great's her gain, ah sad's our loss.
**Bibl:** Apted 55-6; J G Dunbar,'Lowlanders in the Highlands', Country Life, 8 Aug 1974.

**KIDD, Alistair D** **fl 1953**
Angus painter; exhibited GI(1), from 60 Jeanfield Rd, Forfar.

**KIDD, J (or T)** **fl 1868**
Perth oil painter of figurative subjects; exhibited RSA(1).

**KIDD, Joseph Bartholomew RSA** **1808-1889**
Born Edinburgh; died Greenwich, May. Landscape, genre and marine painter in oil; also occasional illustrator. Little is known of his early life. Exhibited Carlisle Academy 1826-28 having been a Foundation Associate of the RSA 1826. Received Hope and Cockburn Award 1829. At about this time he studied with John Thomson of Duddingston(qv). After 1836 he ceased to exhibit at the RSA and on moving to London severed all connection with Scottish art. Illustrated Sir Thomas Dick Lauder's *The Miscellany of Natural History,* 1833; also *West Indian Scenery,* 1838-40. Exhibited two works in 1826 at the Institution for the Encouragement of Fine Arts in Scotland and the following year began to show annually at the RSA (1827-1836) a total of 75 works. Sometimes confused with his near contemporary, William K(qv).

**KIDD, Scott** **fl 1960-1962**
Bute painter of still life and figure subjects. Exhibited GI(4) since 1961 from 90 High St, Rothesay.

**KIDD, Thomas H** **fl 1858-1871**
Painter in oil of Edinburgh and later Perthshire of landscape and still-life; exhibited RSA(8).

**KIDD, W Graham** **fl 1894**
Amateur Aberdeenshire painter; exhibited a landscape at AAS from 6 James Pl, Keith.

**KIDD, William HRSA** **1796-1863**
Born Scotland; died London, 25 Dec. Painter of genre, often with animals, also portraits and still-life. Studied under James Howe(qv), the animal painter, but most influenced by the work of Wilkie(qv) and Alexander Carse(qv). Went to London 1817 and between that time and 1853 exhibited regularly at the RA a total of 33 works. His scenes of Scottish life, pathetic or humorous, are in the Wilkie tradition. Although a talented and prolific artist, was unable to manage his

worldly affairs and lived in continual poverty. In London he worked for a time as a teacher at Greenwich, and towards the end of his life was supported by an Academy pension and the charity of some friends. Precocious as well as prolific, having exhibited his first painting at the age of only 13 (1809). 'His drawing was vivacious and expressive; his handling, fluent and easy, had animation and sparkle; his colour variety and some charm; and his sense of design, if lacking distinction, was apposite to what he had to say. He was not a great or even a fine artist, but his pictures possessed such definite, if modest, merit, that one wonders why they have attracted so little notice' [Caw]. McKay considered that he had a talent which should have given him a high rank among painters but for some reason this never seems to have occurred. Elected Honorary Member of the RSA 1829 he thereafter began to exhibit most of his works in Edinburgh. Exhibited three works at the Associated Society of Artists (1809-11), two at the Edinburgh Exhibition Society (1815) and then regularly at the RSA (1829-1853), a total of 38 works. Represented in NGS(1), Glasgow AG.
**Bibl:** Armstrong 48; Brydall 270-1; Caw 106-7; Butchart 24; DNB XXI 1892, 95; Macmillan [SA] 183-4; McKay 159-160; Portfolio 1878, 151 ff; Redgrave.

**KIDDS, D Gordon** **fl 1939**
Exhibited RSA(1) from 23 Charlotte Square, Edinburgh.

**KIDSTON, Miss Annabel** **1896-1981**
Born Hillend, Glasgow. Painter in oil and watercolour, wood engraver, etcher & illustrator. Studied at Glasgow School of Art 1918-21 under Greiffenhagen(qv) & Forester Wilson(qv). In 1922 embarked on further studies in L'Hôte's studio at La Grande Chaumière before spending three years as head of the art department at Laurel Bank school in Glasgow. Returned to full-time studies 1926, this time at the Slade learning the art and craft of engraving under Thomas Smith and painting under Henry Tonks and Wilson Steer. From 1941 until 1946 worked for the Committee for Education for the Forces and 1946 was elected the first chairman Art Committee of St Andrews which she formed with two other engravers working in the north-east of Scotland, the sisters Alison & Winifred MacKenzie(qv), becoming their first President 1972. Between 1947 and 1950 a part-time member of staff at Dundee College of Art. Elected President of the Art Committee of St Andrews 1972. Illustrated Mathew Arnold's *The Forsaken Merman & The Scholar Gipsy* (1927). Exhibited RA(1), RSA(16) & RGI(34), since 1959 from Kinneddar, Helensburgh. Represented in Glasgow AG.
**Bibl:** Garrett 1 & 2; Horne 277; Jaffé.

**KIDSTON, Miss Penelope** **fl 1961-1974**
Dunbartonshire painter in oils of landscape, still life and townscapes. Related to Annabel K(qv). Exhibited RSA & GI(5) during the above years.

**KILGOUR, A Wilkie** **1868-1930**
Born Kirkcaldy; died Montreal, Canada. After his migration to Canada, nothing further seems to have been recorded. Exhib 5 works at the London Salon from 8 Fitzroy Street, London, 1808-1809.

**KILGOUR, Miss Belle M** **fl 1925-44**
Edinburgh painter & sculptor of figurative compositions and portraits eg 'Pharaoh's daughter' (ex RSA 1943) - a direct carving in alder wood. Exhibited RSA(6) & GI(11), from The Blue Gate, 5 Corstorphine Hill Ave.

**KILGOUR, Sir John** **fl 1527-1541**
Chaplain and heraldic painter. Only fragments of his life are now known. In 1527 was painting the Royal Arms for which he received £3, in 1532 he was working with Alexander Chalmer 'for the laying with gold in paynting culloring and for stuff to the tua lyonis and torris upon the heid of the tua west roundis' at Holyrood'. At Holyrood again in 1535 and 1538 received 2000 francs in payment for work on the King's ships. The following year he received clothing from the King in return for his further work on the ships, again in 1540 and in 1541, according to the accounts of the Lord High Treasurer, he was paid £40 'for the making of four banneris to the trumpettis'.
**Bibl:** Apted 57.

**KILGOUR, Robert W** **fl 1831-1873**
Edinburgh landscape and occasional portrait painter in oil; most of his work was of the area around Edinburgh. Exhibited RSA(60).

**KILLAH, Jean P** **fl 1935-1937**
Aberdeen landscape painter. Exhibited AAS(2) from 46, Clifton Rd.

**KILLAH, Margaret** **fl 1935-1937**
Aberdeen painter of still life and coastal views. Possibly related to Jean K(qv). Exhibited AAS(2) from 23, Watson St.

**KILLIN, G Goldie** **fl 1920**
Amateur Lanarkshire painter who exhibited one work at the Walker Gallery, Liverpool from 7 Stewarton Drive, Cambuslang.

**KILOH, J** **fl 1830-1840**
Aberdeen engraver. Known to have undertaken work for the Skene Library in 1830 and for J W Mackenzie in 1840, probably book-plates. Also worked for David Robert Morice 1830.

**KILPATRICK, George** **fl 1947**
Ayr draughtsman. Exhibited a figure study at the GI, from 8 Fotheringham Rd.

**KILPATRICK, J Alexander** **fl 1888**
Painter of 28 Arlington Street, Glasgow; exhibited a Glasgow townscape at the GI(1). Possibly the same as represented in Glasgow AG.

**KILPATRICK, Miss Renie** **fl 1927**
Glasgow sculptress. Exhibited GI(1) from 3 Eildon Villas, Mount Florida.

**KILPATRICK, Robert** **fl 1935-1950**
Watercolour landscape painter of 153 Garthland Drive, Glasgow; moved to Perth c1938 and then to 53 Viewforth Place, Pittenweem in 1942. Exhibited RSW(4) & GI(9).

**KIMM, Alexander K** **fl 1916-1923**
Landscape painter. Exhibited RSA(2) & GI(8) from Kirkcudbright (1916), Mount Florida, Glasgow (1917) and Brampton, Carlisle (1919).

**KINCAIRD-PITCAIRN, Mary Mabel (née Thorne)** **1875-c1940**
Painter of flower studies in miniature. Studied at Colarossi's, Paris. Lived in Greenock at 80 Finnart Street from whence exhibited RSA(5), RI(23) & L(4).

**KING, Alan** **1946-**
Born Glasgow. Painter of colourful figurative subjects, often including brightly coloured musicians and other theatrical scenes with a strong Italianate flavour; art teacher. Trained Glasgow School of Art 1963-68. Exhibits RGI, Paisley Art Institute.
**Bibl:** Albemarle Gallery, London, Ex Cat 1998.

**KING, Alison** **c1948-**
Embroiderer; teacher. Trained Edinburgh University 1965-69. Member, '62 Group of the Embroiderers' Guild; founder-chairman New Scottish Embroidery Group. Her work, mostly on commission, has a painterly quality.
**Bibl:** Margaret Swain 177-8.

**KING, Andrew** **fl 1876-1877**
Paisley oil painter of local landscapes; exhibited RSA(1) & GI(1) from 3 Underwood Rd.

**KING, Benjamin B** **fl 1875-1904**
Glasgow oil and watercolour landscape painter; exhibited RSA(1) & GI(21).

**KING, Charles** **fl 1707**
Little is known about this artist. Son of Patrick Kyle, Snowdoun Herald, in 1707 was apprenticed to Henry Fraser. Thereafter worked in Kirkcaldy.

**KING, James J** **fl 1885**
Exhibited two landscapes at the GI from Glasgow.

**KING, Jessie Marion (Mrs E A Taylor)** **1875-1949**
Born New Kilpatrick, Bearsden, Glasgow; died Kirkcudbright, 3 Aug. Painter, etcher, designer and illustrator; landscape, figurative and fantasies; also jewellery designer and muralist. Daughter of the minister of New Kilpatrick. Her father was reluctant to allow her to embark upon an artistic career but eventually she won him over and enrolled at the Glasgow School of Art. There Francis Newbery(qv) excused her from the full rigours of the academic curriculum, allowing her to devote more time developing her talent for sensitive and decorative linear expression, using as her models the natural world, especially plants. After gaining a travelling scholarship which took her to Germany and Italy, where the paintings of Botticelli made a strong impression, she returned to Scotland becoming part of the Mackintosh coterie. *The Studio* was warmly enthusiastic about her work and in 1902 published a long, well-illustrated article about her. The same year she exhibited in Turin beside other Glasgow artists. Taught book and ceramic illustration at Glasgow School of Art until 1908. Among the many books she illustrated were *The Jungle Book* (1897); Arnold's *The Light of Asia,* 1898; G Buchanan's *Jeptha,* 1902; *The High History of The Holy Grail* (transl. by S Evans), 1903; 95 illustrations for William Morris' *The Defence of Guinevere* (1904); Milton's *Comus,* 1906; *Poems of Spenser,* nd; a book of plant drawings *Budding Life,*1906; P. Mantegazza's *The Legend of Flowers,* 1908; *Dwellings of an Old World Town,* 1909; *The Grey City of the North,* 1910; E Ancambeau's *The Book of Bridges,* 1911 and the same author's *Ponts de Paris,* 1912; James Hogg's *Songs of the Ettrick Shepherd,* 1912; John Keats' *Isabella and the Pot of Basil,* 1914; Oscar Wilde's *A House of Pomegranates,* 1915; *The Little White Town of Never-Weary,* 1917; *Good King Wenceslas,* 1919; Kipling's *L'Habitation Forcée,* 1921; *How Cinderella Was Able To Go To The Ball,* 1924; *Mummy's Bedtime Story Book,* 1929; *Whose London,* 1930; Arthur Corder's *Our Lady's Garland,* 1934; *Kirkcudbright,* 1934; Florence Drummond's *The Fringes of Paradise,* 1935; I Steele's *The Enchanted Capital of Scotland,* 1945; and J McCardel's *The Parish of New Kilpatrick,* 1949. Also contributed covers for International Library Editions of *The Marriage Ring* by Jeremy Taylor 1906, and for *Everyman* 1906. Her cover design for *L'Evangile de l'Enfance* c1900 won the Gold Medal at the International Exhibition of Decorative Arts, Turin 1902. Between 1905 and 1911 she painted landscapes in which accurate observation was combined with a characteristically decorative handling of vegetation. Much of her work was done on parchment, built up with carefully drawn thin pen lines, delicately coloured or tinted. Altogether she illustrated over 700 books and covers between 1899 and 1949. Also designed wallpapers, fabrics, posters, bookplates, ceramics and costumes, having been inspired by Leon Bakst's costumes for the Ballet Russes. Influences in her work can be detected from Whistler, Rosetti, Botticelli and, most of all, the Glasgow Group especially George Rennie Mackintosh(qv). In 1908 married E A Taylor(qv). Three years later they opened the 'Sheiling Atelier of Painting, Design and the Applied Arts' in Paris. At the outbreak of WW1 she returned to Kirkcudbright and each September went back to Arran where she helped organise a summer sketching class. In her delicate traceries and finely delineated gossamer-like drawings, using dots and lines somewhat reminiscent of Beardsley, she occupies a unique place in Scottish art, shared only by her friend Annie French(qv). Her reputation was consolidated by an SAC travelling exhibition 1970. Exhibited regularly RSA(48), RSW(4), GI(105), AAS (1906-23), RHA(1), SWA(4), L(22) & LS(3). Represented in NGS, SNGMA, Glasgow AG, Edinburgh City collection ('The Enchanted Capital of Scotland').
**Bibl:** Burkhauser 19,48,50,73,105,133-199,173-4,186,238; Caw 179-181 et al; Hardie passim ch vii; Hartley 140; Houfe; Irwin 401-2,403(illus); Macmillan [SA], 294,296,318,337; SAC, 'Jessie M. King' (Ex Cat 1974, Text by Cordelia Oliver); Studio Vol 25, 1902, 176-188; vol 26, 1901-2,177, illus; vol 36,1906,241-246, illus; vol 46,1909,148-150, illus; Studio Yearbook 1909,1911,1912,1913, 1919; Watson, Miss Jessie M King and her Work; Colin White, The Enchanted World of JMK.

**KING, Mrs Maitland** **fl 1893**
Aberdeenshire portrait painter; exhibited AAS(1) from Dyce.

**KING, Colonel Ross** **late 19th Cent**
Amateur painter of Tertowie, Aberdeenshire. Exhibited 2 French alpine scenes at the AAS.

**KING, William** **fl 1886**
Amateur Aberdeen painter; exhibited a local view at the AAS from 70, Rose St.

**KINGSLEY, John Everard** **1956-**
Painter in oil and acrylic; portraits, townscapes and semi-abstracts. Studied Glasgow School of Art 1973-1977. Member of the group '81 and a council member of Paisley Art Institute. Commissioned to provide the Presidential portrait for the Royal College of Physicians and Surgeons, Glasgow (1986), and a finalist in the Hunting Group art competition (London) 1988. His work shows the influence of the Camden Town school whilst more recently shades of Matisse and Hitchins can be discerned. Exhibited RSA since 1983, GI(45) since 1976, & Paisley Art Institute, since 1984 from 10 Doune Gdns, Glasgow.

**KININMONTH, Mrs Caroline** **fl 1940-1975**
Edinburgh painter of still life subjects, flowers and rural scenes; exhibited RSA(25) & GI(3) from 46A Dick Place.

**KININMONTH, Sir William Hardie PRSA FRIBA FRIAS HRA HRSW** **1904-1988**
Born Forfar, 8 Nov. Architect and draughtsman. Educated Dunfermline High School and George Watson's, Edinburgh. Studied Edinburgh College of Art 1924-9 under John Begg, and at the Slade under Albert Richardson. Began in partnership in Edinburgh 1933. Undertaken many important commissions in Scotland including the air terminal building at Renfrew, RNAS Lossiemouth, Pollock Halls of Residence (Edinburgh University), extensions to Fettes College, James Gillespie HS (1964), Adam House in Chambers St (1954-5), Mary Erskine School (1964-7) and Brunton Town Hall, Musselburgh. Elected PRSA 1969-73, knighted 1972.
**Bibl:** Gifford 75,90,223,264n,487,496,530,565,574,624.

**KINLOCH, Miss** **fl 1868-1871**
Edinburgh landscape painter in oil, particularly fond of Deeside. Exhibited RSA(2).

**KINLOCH, H C B** **fl 1892**
Scottish landscape painter of no known address. Exhibited a view of the river Spean at the GI.

**KINLOCH, M W** **fl 1890-1894**
Painter of landscape, flowers and interiors. Exhibited GI(4) from Glasgow.

**KINLOCH, Miss Shona** **1962-**
Glasgow-based sculptor; trained Glasgow School of Art. Exhibited GI(2), latterly from 59 Melbourne Ave, East Kilbride. A cement sculpture 'Pecking Hen' is in the Lillie AG, Milngavie.

**KINLOCH-SMYTH, George Washington Andrew** **1835-1896**
Born Meigle, Perthshire. Painter in oil of local landscapes, portraits and figure subjects; also sculptor. Studied in Paris under Rodin. Exhibited two works at the Perth Fine Art exhibition 1883. Exhibited RA(3) 1884, all of them bronze busts, and RSA(9) 1879-87; also represented in Perth AG (an oil portrait and 2 bronze busts).

**KINNEAR, Mrs Anthaila** **fl 1925**
Exhibited RSA(1) from Edinburgh College of Art.

**KINNEAR, Charles George Hood ARSA** **1830-1894**
Born Kinloch, Fife; died Edinburgh, 5 Dec. Architect. Showed an early taste for architecture and after two years study in Italy settled in Edinburgh where he worked under David Bryce(qv). In about 1858 he entered into partnership with Dick Peddie(qv). Associated with numerous buildings erected in Edinburgh and elsewhere, after designs by the firm of which he became senior partner in 1891. These include Threave House (1872), Dunblane Hydropathic Institution and Wauchope House, Roxburghshire (both 1877), and Princes Street

Station. Elected ARSA 1893. Exhibited altogether nine designs at the RSA.
**Bibl:** Dunbar 162; Gifford 269,373.

**KINNEAR, Harry** **fl 1882**
Glasgow painter of landscape and townscape; exhibited GI(2), from 4 Sydney St.

**KINNEAR, James Scott** **fl 1870-1917**
Edinburgh landscape painter in oil and watercolour; occasional equine portraits. A reproduction of his drawing Arthur's Seat and Salisbury Crags from the Braid Hill appeared in the *AJ* in 1894 together with six other Edinburgh drawings. An historically interesting view of St Andrews Old Course fetched over £13,000 in 2003. Exhibited fine, accurately detailed and representational landscapes at the RA 1880-92, mostly winter scenes & RSA 1871-91. Exhibited RSA(80), RSW(7), GI(19), AAS(1885-1898) & RI(1). Represented in Edinburgh City collection(3).
**Bibl:** Halsby 266; Wingfield.

**KINNEAR, Leslie Gordon** **1901-1976**
Dundee-based landscape painter usually in watercolour, etcher. Studied École d'Industrie, Bordeaux. Landscape, portrait and figure painter, mainly in watercolour. Earlier work mostly portraiture and figurative, turning increasingly to landscape, including a number of finely executed French views. Exhibited RSA(23), RSW(4) & GI(4) from Tighbeg, Invergowrie.
**Bibl:** Caw 303; Halsby 266.

**KINNELL, Fiona Thomson** **fl 1981**
Aberdeen printmaker; exhibited AAS from 32, Bedford Rd.

**KINNISON, James** **fl 1898-1900**
Associate member of Dundee Graphic Arts Association. In 1900 he exhibited a watercolour landscape at the RSA from 1 Westfield Avenue, Dundee.

**KINNOULL, Countess of** **fl c1880-1910**
Perth potter and ceramic designer. Used local red clay decoration in the production of plaques, vases, flower pots and sconces made from moulds and painted with naturalistic decoration of leaves and flowers. Exhibited Perth Arts & Crafts Exhibition 1904.

**KINROSS, John M RSA** **1855-1931**
Born Stirling, died Edinburgh, 7 Jan. Architect. Trained in Glasgow with John Hutchinson(qv) and worked with Wardrop(qv) and Reid(qv) before studying in Italy 1880 and 1881. After publishing *Details from Italian Buildings, chiefly Renaissance* he set himself up in practice 1882, based in Edinburgh. A stylist in all he did, his main influence was not on major design but on the general charm, elegance and practicality of modest buildings which helped to set the tone of Scottish architecture during his lifetime. Designed Carlskempe, North Berwick (described by Lorimer as 'infinitely finer' than anything Mitchell or Wilson ever did). His obituary spoke of his work as lying chiefly 'in domestic scenes, ranging from the the palatial stateliness of Manderstone to the charm of the gardener's cottage or the practical requirements of the stable'. Occasionally he made excursions into the realm of pure Renaissance architecture. Elected ARSA 1893, RSA 1905, Treasurer 1924-31. Exhibited RSA(37).
**Bibl:** Colvin; Gifford 65,302,349,580,599,623; Peter Savage, Lorimer and the Edinburgh Craft Designers, Edinburgh 1980, 25,83,91,98,165.

**KIPPEN, Andrew M** **fl 1848-1863**
Edinburgh painter in oil of portraits, figures and landscapes. His wife was also an artist(qv). Exhibited RSA(15) including his most ambitious project 'Embarkation of Her Majesty on Loch Tay, 10 Sept 1842', 1858.

**KIPPEN, Mrs A M** **fl 1848-1857**
Edinburgh and Perthshire artist. Landscapes, generally in the Perthshire Highlands. Married to Andrew K(qv). Exhibited RSA(2) in 1848 and 1857, both of the region around Loch Tay.

**KIRK, A Andrew** **?-1805**
Medallionist. Undertook portrait heads, often with his brother, John K(qv). Two joint works, both of the Duke of Cumberland, are in the SNPG.

**KIRK, David** **fl 1884-1900**
Glasgow landscape, townscape and rural painter in oil and occasional watercolour; exhibited RSA(5) & GI(12).

**KIRK, James** **1817-1879**
Born Tweedshaws. Portrait painter in oil. Trained Trustees Academy. For a time between 1851 & 1860 he was living in Moffat but was back in Edinburgh by 1861. Received several commissions from the Hope Johnstone family in 1848; other sitters included 'Sir G Graham-Montgomery Bt', & 'J B Hamilton Montgomery Esq of Newton'. Exhibited RSA(24) & GI(2), from 155 Gairbraid St. Sometimes confused with John Kirk(qv).

**KIRK, John** **fl 1832-1854**
Dumfries sculptor. Generally worked in marble, mainly portrait busts and figures. Joined the RA Schools in 1847 and two years later won a silver medal for the 'best model from the antique'. In 1850 was working at Birmingham School of Design. 'Feeding-time', shown in 1853, is probably his best known work. Exhibited RA(5) 1847-54; also British Institute 1849-54.

**KIRK, John** **fl 1740-1778**
Edinburgh sculptor; specialised in portrait medallions, sometimes in plaster. Often worked with his brother Andrew K(qv). Two medallions of the 3rd Duke of Athol, two of the Duke of Cumberland, and one of the 1st Earl of Mansfield are in the SNPG.

**KIRK, Thomas** **early 18th century**
Decorative landscape painter. Unusual in his time, he occasionally signed his work, the best surviving example being murals at Inveresk.

**KIRKCALDY, William** **fl 1861**
Glasgow watercolourist. Exhibited the portrait of a steamship at the GI from 4 Corunna St.

**KIRKHAM, Mrs Evelyn Buchanan** **fl 1983-1988**
Glasgow still life painter. Married Norman K(qv). Exhibited GI(10) from 6 Hampden Terrace.

**KIRKHAM, Norman** **fl 1976-1988**
Glasgow painter of portraits, genre and still life. Married Evelyn Buchanan K(qv). Exhibited RSA(15) & GI(51) from 6 Hampden Terrace.

**KIRKLAND, Alexander** **1824-1892**
Born Scotland; died Portland, Oregon. Architect and engineer. 'Stylistically his work encompassed neo-Greek, austere classical and Venetian, the two last the result of collaboration with John Bryce(qv) and the assistance of James Hamilton(qv) respectively' [Gomme & Walker]. Responsible for much work in Boswell St, including 2-26 Bothwell St (with John Bryce) and much of St Vincent Crescent, Finnieston. He moved to London c1860 but, failing to establish a successful engineering practice, emigrated to Jefferson, Wisconsin 1868 as a liquor merchant. Moved to Chicago 1871 and was appointed Commissioner for Public Buildings 1879, having designed County Building, Chicago (1882) with Egan, demolished 1909.
**Bibl:** A Gomme & D Walker, Architecture of Glasgow, London 1987(rev) 293-4.

**KIRKPATRICK, Mrs** **fl 1873**
Edinburgh landscape painter in oil; exhibited 'Marling church, near Meran, Tyrol' at the RSA.

**KIRKPATRICK, Edward** **fl 1867-1878**
Edinburgh painter in oil of interiors, portraits and figurative subjects. Among his sitters was 'James Lorimer, Professor of Public Law at Edinburgh' (1870) and, in 1874, a sketch for a larger picture of Joan of Arc in prison. Exhibited 15 works at the RSA during the above years.

**KIRKPATRICK, J** fl 1881
Glasgow-based watercolour painter; exhibited GI(1) from 148 Bellfield Street.

**KIRKPATRICK, James** fl 1948-1953
Paisley watercolourist of landscape and townscape. Exhibited GI(9), from Allanton Ave.

**KIRKPATRICK, Miss Susan Louise** fl 1940-1949
Painter in watercolour and chalk and charcoal; figurative works. Exhibited 'Ballerina' at the RSA in 1941, also GI(3), latterly from 10 Kirksyde Ave, Kirkintilloch.

**KIRKWOOD, Alexander** fl 1853-1903
Edinburgh sculptor of medals and small portrait busts. A design for the Queen's Medal was shown in 1887. Probably the same Alexander Kirkwood who was awarded a prize for sculpture from the antique at the Trustees Academy 1853. Among the collection of portrait medallions at the RSA in 1885 was one of his father and another of "an eminent golfer". Exhibited RSA(5) & AAS(1) from St James's Square.

**KIRKWOOD, Constance R B** fl 1916-1919
Edinburgh-based painter, etcher, engraver and potter. Studied Edinburgh College of Art, Dublin and Camden, London. Lived in Edinburgh from where she exhibited portraits, landscape etchings and lithographs at the RSA(6).

**KIRKWOOD, David McMillan** fl 1971-1974
Landscape painter; exhibited GI(3), from 22 Stiven Crescent, Wishaw.

**KIRKWOOD, Miss Dorothea M** fl 1914-1929
Glasgow sculptress. Exhibited RSA(1), GI(8) & L(3), first from Glasgow and then from Edinburgh.

**KIRKWOOD, Elizabeth H** fl 1909-1923
Enameller & silversmith. Worked with Alex Kirkwood & Son on the later stall-plates for Edinburgh's Thistle Chapel. Exhibited RA(3), RSA(9), RMS(1), GI(3) & L(11) from 68 Thistle St, Edinburgh.
**Bibl:** Peter Savage, Lorimer and the Edinburgh Craft Designers, Edinburgh 1980, 72, 165.

**KIRKWOOD, Fiona** fl 1971
Glasgow trained textile designer; exhibited GI(2).

**KIRKWOOD, James** fl 1792-1804
Edinburgh engraver. Entered into partnership with his son Robert, trading as James Kirkwood & Son of Parliament Square, later moving to 11, South St. Andrew Street. Engraved maps and plans 1792-1804. Possibly the same J Kirkwood who in 1774 engraved a plan of Perth from an address in Perth.
**Bibl:** Bushnell; J C Guy 'Edinburgh Engravers' in The Book of the Old Edinburgh Club, vol 9, 1916;

**KIRKWOOD, John** 1947-
Born Edinburgh. Semi-abstract painter; teacher. Works mainly in mixed media, collages and found objects. Trained Dundee College of Art 1965-70. Influenced by the Dadaists and Futurists, his interests are based firmly on the northern traditions of painting eg Breughel. Professional member, SSA 1972. Prefers to be known as a 'multi-medium practitioner', producing large sculptural relief panels, sometimes abstract, sometimes with pictorial images expressing socio-political concerns. Also produces photomontage and hand-coloured etchings. Has had a variety of jobs outside painting, including teaching children with special needs. Represented in SNGMA, Hunterian Museum(Glasgow), SAC.
**Bibl:** Bill Hare, Contemporary Painting in Scotland, Edinburgh 1993.

**KIRKWOOD, Mrs Joyce** fl 1965
Ayrshire artist; exhibited GI(1), from 8 Ellisland Drive, Kilmarnock.

**KIRKWOOD, Miss Mary H** fl 1897-1900
Flower painter in oil; exhibited RSA(6) from 18 Melville Street, Portobello.

**KIRKWOOD, Robert** fl 1790-1825
Engraver, one of the finest to have worked in the capital. Son of James K(qv). Best known for his map of 1817. In 1819 he produced an unusual combination of plan and view, the whole of the New Town, the elevations of the streets and buildings being depicted pictorially. All the buildings are numbered and in many cases the owners of the properties are also shown. A smaller scale 'Specimen of a Proposed Plan and Elevation of the Old Town of Edinburgh' subsequently appeared in reduced size but it was never produced to the scale originally intended. In 1817 Kirkwood re-engraved Gordon of Rothiemay's 'Birds-eye View' of 1647. Also engraved a number of bookplates including those for Carse 1820, J B Clarkson 1820, Henry Wilson Cleland 1810. Married 1796. Obtained a patent for improvements in the copperplate printing press, 28 February 1803. Represented in City of Edinburgh collection (2 engravings).
**Bibl:** Bushnell; Butchart 5,7,43-44; H C Timperley, Encyclopedia of Literary and Typographical Anecdote, 1842.

**KIRKWOOD, Robert** fl 1876-1883
Edinburgh painter in oil and watercolour of landscape and coastal scenes; exhibited RSA(7) & GI(1) from 37 Loudoun Street.

**KIRKWOOD, Mrs Terry F Barron** fl 1976
Renfrewshire amateur painter; exhibited GI(2), from Muskoka, Woodside Rd, Brookfield.

**KIRKWOOD, Thomas** fl 1964-1965
Ayrshire watercolour painter of townscapes. Exhibited GI(2), from 8 Ellisland Drive, Kilmarnock.

**KIRKWOOD, Thomson** fl 1861-1889
Glasgow landscape painter in oil; exhibited RSA(5) & GI(20) with some intervals in between, since 1889 from 9 Hampden Terrace, Mt Florida, Glasgow.

**KIRKWOOD, William** fl 1878
Glasgow painter of rustic scenes; exhibited GI(1), from 137 N. Dundas St.

**KITCHEN, James** fl 1855-1885
Painter in watercolour of portraits & figurative subjects; exhibited RSA(3) first from Leith and latterly from Dumbarton.

**KITFIELD, Candace Carman (Mrs Lucas)** 1948-
Born USA, 23 Feb. Painter in gouache, watercolour and oil of landscapes and figures. Trained at Rhode Island School of Design, Providence, USA, University of New Hampshire and at the Ruskin School of Drawing, Oxford University. Mainly influenced by the Scottish colourists, German expressionism and the Fauves. Most recently her style has evolved away from factual representation toward an attempted reconciliation between formal and abstract painting. Lives in Scotland, exhibiting RSA & SSWA.

**KITSON, Miss Jean** fl 1919-1921
Aberdeen landscape painter, often continental scenes. Exhibited AAS from 36, Richmondhill Pl.

**KLEBOE, Peter** fl 1969
Ayrshire painter who enjoyed painting trees; exhibited GI(2), from 56 Shawlands St, Catrine, Mauchline.

**KNIGHT, Miss Annie** fl 1889-1898
Painter in oil and mezzotint engraver of figure subjects. Exhibited RSA(3) from Eskgreen, Musselburgh.

**KNIGHT, Donald** fl 1957-1958
Edinburgh painter, draughtsman and engraver. Exhibited RSA(3).

**KNIGHT, Frederick** fl 1858
Portobello watercolour painter of local landscape scenes; exhibited 'Duddingston Loch' at the RSA.

**KNIGHT, George H** fl 1871
Dollar landscape painter in oil; exhibited 'Castle Stalker, Loch Linnhe - moonlight' at the RSA.

**KNIGHT, Miss M** **fl 1902**
Edinburgh amateur painter in pastel. Exhibited a sketch at the RSA from Queen St.

**KNIGHTON, William** **fl 1844**
Edinburgh painter in oils. Exhibited 'Newhaven fishwives selling fish' at RSA from 27, Drummond St.

**KNOPP, Gertrude M (née Curtis)** **1875-?**
Born Kilninver, Argyll. Painter in oil and watercolour. Studied art at the Slade School under Brown, Steer, Tonks and Russell 1899-1904. Married the Hungarian artist, Imre Knopp. Awarded the Esterhazy Prize in Budapest 1921. Later lived in London. Secretary of the WIAC 1910-1913. Exhibited RA, ROI & NEAC. Represented in Budapest Museum of Fine Arts.

**KNOTT, Miss Emmeline M** **fl 1876**
Edinburgh sculptress. Daughter of Tavernor K(qv). Exhibited a portrait bust of John Knox at the RSA.

**KNOTT, Tavernor M** **fl 1846-1889**
Edinburgh painter in oil of portraits, landscape and historical scenes. Father of Emmeline K(qv). Among his best known portraits was one of 'HRH Datu Tumongong Abubakar Sri, Maharajha of Jahore', now in the Public Hall, Singapore (1867), while his best-known historical pictures are 'Flora Macdonald lamenting the departure of Prince Charles Edward' (1853) and 'Knox and the Queen's Advocate' (1877). Exhibited RSA(125) & GI(39), latterly from York Place, Edinburgh. A portrait of 'Rev Norman MacLeod' (1848) is in the SNPG; also represented in Paisley AG, Edinburgh City collection.

**KNOWLES, Alexander** **fl 1887**
Edinburgh watercolour painter of coastal scenes; exhibited RSA(1).

**KNOWLES, Farquhar McGillivray** **1859-1932**
Born USA; died Toronto, Canada. Landscape painter. Although living in London 1892-1893, and in spite of his international career and the fact that his exhibits were in England - ROI(1) & RBA(1) - he was of Scottish extraction.

**KNOX, Miss Barbara G** **fl 1966**
Kirkintilloch flower painter; exhibited GI(1), from Hillcroft, Bellfield Rd.

**KNOX, Miss E A** **fl 1893-1901**
Landscape painter in oil and watercolour. Exhibited GI(2) from Bridge of Allan (1893) and from Woodend, by Callander, Perthshire (1901).

**KNOX, John** **1778-1845**
Born Paisley, died Keswick. Painter of landscape in oil. An important and influential figure in the history of Scottish landscape art. Considering the quality of his work and the dramatic intensity of his landscapes, it is remarkable how little is known of his career. Son of a yarn manufacturer, he came from the south-west of Scotland, his family moving to Glasgow in 1799. In 1809 he is mentioned as a portrait painter, although today he is known exclusively for his landscapes. It is probable that he was a pupil of Alexander Nasmyth(qv) and he would certainly have known Nasmyth's sets for the Glasgow Theatre and his many views in the west. Regular contributor to the exhibitions of the Glasgow Dilettanti Society(qv), exhibiting 'Panoramic View from the Top of Ben Lomond' 1829. Best known for his broad sweeping landscapes seen from the height of a mountainside looking down on valleys and lochs with goats feeding precipitously and travellers often beside boats admiring the scene. His compositions of the Clyde valley demonstrate a magnificent grasp of technique with remarkably fresh use of paint and the general effect, although heavy, is wonderfully dramatic. Believed to have held drawing classes in Glasgow attended by Horatio McCulloch(qv) and W L Leitch(qv) as well as by the portrait painter Daniel Macnee(qv). In 1823 a collection of lithographs were published as 'Scottish Scenery drawn upon stone by John Knox'. Exhibited RA(5), 'View in the Trossachs' and a 'View of the Town Castle of Inveraray', from 130 Jermyn Street, London in 1829; a 'View of Derwent Water, Cumberland', and 'View of Glen Coe', both in 1832 and a' View of Brougham Hall', the seat of the Lord Chancellor in 1835, these three from 1 Upper Gloucester Place, London; also exhibited British Institution(6). An exhibition of his paintings was held Glasgow AG 1974. Represented in Perth AG, Glasgow AG by eight paintings but surprisingly nothing in the NGS.
**Bibl:** Caw 143; Halsby 54,111; Irwin 243 et al; Macmillan [SA] 145,164,226-7; McClure, 'John Knox Landscape Painter', (Ex Cat Glasgow 1974); McKay 267.

**KNOX, John** **fl 1930-1932**
Kirkintilloch sculptor; exhibited RSA(2) & GI(1).

**KNOX, John (Jack) RSA RSW RGI** **1936-**
Born Kirkintilloch. Artist in oil, watercolour, charcoal and pva; also teacher. Educated Lenzie Academy and Glasgow School of Art 1951-1955 under William Armour(qv) and David Donaldson(qv), also in Paris with the painter André Lhôte. In 1959 he visited a major exhibition of American abstract expressionism in Brussels which deeply affected him. By 1965 he had adopted a style 'using bright colours in witty, obsessively detailed depictions of banal objects'. In 1971 an exhibition of his work was held in London. During the 1970s he worked on a series of table-top still-lifes of great simplicity with clear reference to 17th century Dutch painting. Taught at Duncan of Jordanstone College of Art, Dundee and since 1981 head of painting, Glasgow School of Art. Won Stuart Prize 1957; Latimer Award 1965, Guthrie Award 1968, Maude Gemmell Hutchison Prize (RSA) 1998. Member, Scottish Arts Council 1974-79, SNGMA Trustees Committee 1975-82. Secretary, RSA 1990-91. In the early 60s he lived on Bute where he painted large abstracts of landscape and sea. Participated in exhibition 'Seven Dundee Painters' 1970. Illustrated *The Scottish Bestiary* 1986, *La Potiniere* (nd). Lived in Carnoustie, Angus, now at Bearsden, Glasgow. Succeeded Robert Steedman as Secretary of the RSA 1990. Exhibits regularly at the RSA, AAS(1), GI(21), since 1980 from 31 North Erskine Pk, Bearsden. Represented in SNPG, SNGMA, Aberdeen AG, Dundee AG, Lillie AG (Milngavie), Edinburgh City collection, Hunterian Museum (Glasgow), Glasgow AG, Kirkcaldy AG, Kirkintilloch Museum, Perth AG, Manchester AG, Otis Art Institute (Los Angeles), Olinda Museum (Sao Paulo).
**Bibl:** Judith Bumpus, 'A most Vigorous Force', The Collector, Aug 1990; Gage 56-7; Hardie 198; Hartley 141; Cordelia Oliver, Jack Knox: Paintings and Drawings 1960-83, 1983; SAC, 'Scottish Art Now', (Ex Cat 1982); Macmillan [SA]; Bill Hare, *Contemporary Painting in Scotland*, 1993.

**KNOX, Robert** **?-1848**
Born Paisley. Younger brother of John K(qv). Became a shawl and dress manufacturer and a competent amateur painter. From 1842 until his death he was the tenant of Kelvingrove House, subsequently acquired by the Corporation to become the original Kelvingrove Museum. The only recorded work appears to be 'The Royal Squadron Passing Gourock, August 1847', now owned by the Corporation of Gourock.

**KNOX, Miss Rosemary E** **fl 1956**
Dunbartonshire figurative painter; exhibited GI(1), from 24 Colquhoun Square, Helensburgh.

**KOLDEWEY, B J** **fl 1936**
Possibly related to the B H Koldewey who exhibited at the ROI from Dordrecht, Holland. Exhibited RSA(1).

**KOLLACK, Albert J D** **fl 1990-**
Perthshire painter. Exhibited RSA(1).

**KONDRACKI, Henry** **1953-**
Born Edinburgh. Trained Byam Shaw School of Art 1981-2, Slade 1982-6. Expressive narrative painter, generally on a large scale, complex and somewhat raw in tone. Exhibitions in Edinburgh, London and Melbourne.
**Bibl:** Bill Hare, Contemporary Paintings in Scotland, Edinburgh 1993.

**KOSTER, Elisabeth (Betty) ARCA ARBS** **1926-**
Born in England. Lives in Scotland. Sculptress and teacher. Trained Kingston School of Art and Royal College of Art, 1945-1947. After

graduating and until 1951 was assistant to Barney Seale, working for the Festival of Britain. Thereafter became principal teacher of art in various places in Aberdeenshire and Edinburgh 1953-1975. From 1973-1980 part-time lecturer in wood carving at Edinburgh College of Art and from 1979-1983 lecturer in ceramic sculpture, Lothian District. Elected ARBS 1979, receiving the Cameron Millar Award of the SSWA. In 1982 elected Vice-president, SSWA. Exhibits RSA. Represented in Ellon Academy, Aberdeenshire, St Kentigern's church (Edinburgh), The Vatican.

**KRALE, M** **fl 1967-1989**
Edinburgh-based landscape painter. Exhibited RSA(3) from 103 Princes St.

**KROUPA, B** **fl 1880**
Exhibited RSA(1) from Fettes College, Edinburgh where he was a teacher.

**KRUSZELNICKA, Mrs Zofia** **fl 1953**
Edinburgh-based sculptress; exhibited GI(2), from 4 Chalmers Crescent.

**KRYZANOWSKI, Wladyslaw** **?-1973**
Born Poland; died Edinburgh. Trained Cracow and Paris before the war; settled in Edinburgh in the 1940s, remaining there until his death. Although his pre-war works still appear in Warsaw auctions, the absence of them in Scotland suggests that his output diminished after leaving his homeland.

**KU, Christopher** **fl 1987-1988**
Aberdeen abstract painter; exhibited GI(2) from 234 Springhill Rd.

**KUMMER, Elisabeth A von** **fl 1876**
Lived in Glasgow and painted natural life studies in oil; exhibited RSA(1).

**KUMPEL, William** **fl 1853-1879**
Painter of portraits, figurative subjects and occasional landscape; oil and watercolour. Probably of German extraction. Lived a short time in Edinburgh. Exhibited RSA(1), an unidentified sitter; RA(7) 1857-1879 & GI(1), latterly from 51 Mortimer St, London.

**KYD, Hannah** **fl 1900**
Aberdeen amateur painter of coastal scenes; exhibited AAS(1) from 74, Queens Rd.

**KYD, James** **fl 1860-1871**
Painter in oil of domestic and highland scenes. Living at Burfanside Terrace, Worcester when he exhibited 'China painters' (1860) and 'Porridge Making in a Highland Cottage' (1868) at the RA. Was back in Edinburgh by the time he exhibited his two works at the RSA (1870 and 1871): 'Home life in the Highlands' and 'The auld drover by his ain ingleside'.

**KYLE, T** **fl 1885**
Painter. Exhibited RSA(1) from 10 Derby Place, Broughty Ferry, Angus.

**KYNOCH, Miss Kathryn** **1942-**
Born Portobello. Painter of portraits, figure and animal compositions. Lived most of her life in Glasgow. Trained Glasgow School of Art 1959-64 and then for a spell in Madrid. Exhibited RSA (19) & GI(47) latterly from 425 Dumbarton Rd. Represented in Glasgow AG, Hunterian AG, Univ. of Glasgow.

**KYNOCH, Miss Minnie** **fl 1896-1912**
Dundee painter of landscapes, flowers and portraits. Associate member, Dundee Arts Association 1893-1895 and a full member 1896-1900. Exhibited RSA(2, 'An old canal' (1905) and 'Rue de l'Arche, Falaise' (1912)), AAS & GI(3), from 8 Airlie Place.

**KYRLE SOCIETY** **1878-**
English society named after the social reformer John Kyrle, with a Glasgow branch, similar in purpose to the Social Union formed in Edinburgh by Andrew Geddes. It aimed at social improvement through the arts rather than being involved in the practice of art. Especially concerned with art in hospitals and the adornment of public parks. Commissioned mural paintings by the Glasgow Boys(qv).

# L

**LACOME, Myer** **fl 1965-**
Designer and collage decorator. Member of staff, Dundee College of Art. Lives in Edinburgh. Exhibits RSA irregularly since 1965.

**'LADY'** **fl 1828-1854**
Anonymous painter of flower pieces, literary subjects, landscapes and a single portrait 1848. Exhibited 15 works at the RSA between the above years revealing neither an address nor an identity.

**'LADY'** **fl 1848-1857**
Anonymous sculptress and portrait miniaturist. Exhibited 6 works at the RSA between the above years without address or identity. Appears to have been well-connected and possibly associated with the Drummond family since among her exhibited portrait medallions are 'Mrs Drummond of Megginch' 1852, 'Gen Sir Gordon Drummond' 1852 and 'Miss Stirling Graham of Duntrune'. Possibly same as previous entry although both appear to have exhibited RSA 1848.

**LAFFERTY, Ray** **c1972-**
Landscape and figurative painter in various mediums. Trained Duncan of Jordanstone College of Art 1989-94 and at Gray's School of Art 1987-2002. Works in the classical mould. Winner of Greenshields Scholarship 1995, Macfarlane Trust Drawing Award (RGI) 1998, Hospitalfield Award (RSA) 2003.

**LAIDLAW, Jessie** **fl 1888-1896**
Glasgow painter of figurative works, mainly portraits. Exhibited GI(5) during the above years, from Linda Villa, Govan.

**LAIDLAW, Nicol** **1886-?**
Born Edinburgh, 4 Feb. Portrait and landscape painter, etcher and illustrator. Painted watercolour landscapes of the Lothians, most of his portraits are in oil; also painted conversational pieces. Studied at Edinburgh College of Art winning a medal in the life class 1909; also studied in Paris and Spain. Exhibited RA(4), RSA(24), RSW(5), GI(8) & L(5) & AAS from an Edinburgh address.
**Bibl:** Halsby 266.

**LAIDLAW, Thomas H** **1846-1915**
Born Annan, Dumfriesshire; died North Scituate, Rhode Island, USA. Painter in oil, watercolour, pencil and mixed media; also etcher and illustrator. Related to Robert Thorburn(qv) and a lifelong friend of W E Lockhart(qv). In 1860 he was apprenticed to John Cleminson, painter, of Annan. Specialised in landscapes, mostly of the Borders. Came to Hawick 1870. Illustrated Oliver's *Upper Teviotdale;* contributed to *Manchester Guardian* and *Journal of Decorative Art.* Designed Christmas cards for Raphael Tuck. Played an active role in local life being a JP, town councillor (from 1883), cricketer, bowler and curler. President of the Buccleuch Club and Border Bowling Association. An intense lover of the Border countryside, he used to say that one could spend a lifetime painting Teviotdale alone. Exhibited RSA(3). Represented in Government House, Ottawa (taken there by the Earl of Minto), and in Hawick Museum.
**Bibl:** Border Mag vol vi,65,Jne 1901,101-4.

**LAIDLAY, William James** **1846-1912**
Born London; died London, 25 October. Painter in oil; landscapes. Of Scottish extraction though lived most of his life in London. Studied in Paris 1879-1885 under Carolus Duran and Bouguereau. A founder of the New England Art Club, about which he wrote a book *The Origin and First Two Years of the NEAC* (1907). Strong opponent of the RA. His pictures showed French Impressionist influence. Exhibited at the Société des Artists Français in Paris 1880-1912 and RA(17) 1882-1896 and twice at the RSA: 'Tantallon by Moonlight' 1877 and 'Evening at Scoulton Mere' 1911; also AAS 1886 & GI(12) 1882-1912, mostly coastal scenes and all from London addresses.
**Bibl:** AJ 1890, 156; 1907, 154; Caw 308; Maas 248.

**LAING, A** **fl 1886**
Renfrewshire landscape painter. Exhibited a landscape at the RSA from Castlehead, Paisley.

**LAING, A M** **fl 1887**
Amateur painter. Exhibited 'The village smithy' at the GI.

**LAING, Alexander** **?-1724**
Early Edinburgh painter. Burgess of Edinburgh. Apprenticed to Alexander Wilson 1716. In 1713 was a member of the Incorporation of St Mary's, remaining until 1723.

**LAING, Alexander** **c1750-1823**
Architect. Designed Old HS, High School Yards, Edinburgh (1777), the Inverness Town Steeple (1789-92), and the right half of Archers' Hall, Buccleuch St (1776-7). Influenced by James Gibb(qv).
**Bibl:** Gifford 186,188,242,330,332-3,427,605.

**LAING, Andrew** **fl 1512**
Early palace painter and decorator. Undertook decorations of a now indeterminate character at the royal palaces of Stirling and Falkland for King James IV. On 13 September, 1512 he was paid £4.6s.8d for work done at Falkland.
**Bibl:** Armstrong 3; Apted 58.

**LAING, Annie Rose (née Low)** **1869-1946**
Born Glasgow, Jan 20. Figure and landscape painter, mostly of continental landscapes and interiors, also children, generally in oil but also some watercolours. Wife of James Garden L(qv). Exhibited mainly in Scotland, but after a spell in Italy settled in London. All her academy works in Scotland were conversational pieces and continental subjects including 'In a Dutch church' 1905, 'Bruges lace makers' l915 and 'In villa Torlonia, Frascati, Italy' 1925. 'A feminine and rather charming sentiment as regards children...united to considerable beauty of colour, lighting, and handling' [Caw]. Exhibited RSA(10), RA(3), GI(63), AAS(2) and L(8). Represented in Glasgow AG(2).
**Bibl:** Caw 428; Halsby 266.

**LAING, E** **fl 1888**
Amateur Glasgow Painter. Exhibited GI(2) from 24 Napiershall Street.

**LAING, Esther Martin** **fl 1954-1967**
Edinburgh sculptress. Mainly figure subjects and sometimes open air sculpture. Exhibited RSA intermittently during the above period including a portrait bust of O Wissing Esq, & GI(1) from 2 Douglas Crescent.

**LAING, Frank ARE** **1852-1907**
Born Dundee. Painter and etcher of landscapes and architectural subjects. Influential member of the artistic circle when John Duncan(qv), George Dutch Davidson(qv) and David Foggie(qv) were all working in Dundee. With Alex Grieve(qv), founded the Tayport Art Circle. His etchings show great confidence and skill and were warmly commended by Whistler. Used the method invented by Seymour Haden in which the graving is done while the plate is immersed in acid so that the drawing and bighting are simultaneous. Abandoned business for art in his 30s and after two years studying in Edinburgh, went to Paris to work under JP Laurens often returning thereafter. Eighty etchings shown in France 1898 attracted so much praise they were published in the Bibliotheque Nationale. 'Neither distinguished nor romantic, as Cameron's and Bone's city views are, his - especially perhaps the Edinburgh series - are noticeable for the admirable way in which the ready made picturesque is used' [Caw]. Towards the end of his life lived in Kirkcaldy, paying several visits to Spain. Elected ARE 1892. Exhibited Paris Salon (awarded an hon. mention 1900), RA(3), RSA(6), RSW(1), RE(33), GI(6) & AAS (1894-1906). Represented in Dundee AG, Victoria AG (Australia).
**Bibl:** Caw 462-3; Halsby 197-8,200,267.

**LAING, Gerald** **1936-**
Born Newcastle-upon Tyne. Sculptor, draughtsman, print-maker and textile designer. Trained at St Martin's School of Art, London. Spent his early professional life in the USA, mainly in New York. Since 1979 has lived and worked in Kinkell castle, Ross-shire which he restored himself. Numerous solo exhibitions, the first at the Laing AG (Newcastle) 1963. Executed statue of Sherlock Holmes at the top of Leith Walk, Edinburgh and 'The Wise and Foolish Virgins' in George St. Exhibited AAS(1). Represented in V & A, SNGMA, Nagasaka

Museum (Japan), Metropolitan Museum of Modern Art (New York), Minnesota Institute of the Arts; Aldrich Museum (Connecticut), Indianapolis Museum; Gelsenkirchen Museum (Germany).
**Bibl:** Gifford 299; SNGMA 'Gerald Laing', (Ex Cat 1971).

**LAING, J C** **fl 1879**
Glasgow watercolourist; exhibited 'St Andrews' at the RSA.

**LAING, James** **fl 1984**
Amateur Hebridean artist. Exhibited GI(1) from 25 Melbost, Stornoway.

**LAING, James Garden RSW** **1852-1915**
Born Aberdeen Oct 15; died Aug. Aberdeen painter of landscape, architectural subjects and church interiors in watercolour. Trained and worked as an architect in Aberdeen. After practising for a time he began painting in watercolour. Although he produced landscapes and coastal scenes, is now best known for his church interiors in which the influence of Bosboom and other Dutch contemporaries whom he met on sketching holidays in Holland is clearly visible. Had an architect's feeling for stonework and interiors. Husband of Annie Rose L(qv). Elected RSW 1885. Began exhibiting GI 1878, thereafter RSW(114), RSA(55), RI(6), RA(21), RBA(1), L(13), GI(80) & AAS 1895-1912, latterly from Albany Mansions, Charing Cross, Glasgow. Represented in Glasgow AG, Paisley AG, Leeds AG, Minneapolis AG (USA).
**Bibl:** Caw 392; Halsby 164,267.

**LAING, Jean** **fl 1978**
Aberdeen jewellery designer. Exhibited AAS from 80 Union Grove.

**LAING, John Joseph** **1830-1862**
Born Glasgow; died Glasgow. Wood engraver. After practising for a time in Glasgow went to London where he was mainly employed on architectural subjects for *The Builder*.
**Bibl:** Bryan.

**LAING, Joyce H** **fl 1959-1970**
Aberdeen painter of country scenes and rustic genre. Exhibited AAS (2), including 'On the Fungle, Aboyne', from 7 Royfold Crescent.

**LAING, Miss M J** **fl 1925**
Edinburgh based artist. Exhibited 'The Ferry' at the RSA from Murrayfield.

**LAING, Margaret** **fl 1940-1965**
Edinburgh painter and engraver. Mainly flower studies, topographical works of Edinburgh and its environs and conversation pieces, also coloured lithographs. Exhibited RSA(29) GI(4), latterly from 12 Ethel Terrace.

**LAING, Samuel** **1780-1868**
Born Kirkwall, Orkney; died Edinburgh. Author, soldier, traveller and amateur artist. Younger brother of Malcolm Laing (1762-1818) the historian. Studied Edinburgh University and Kiel. Joined the army 1805, fought in the Peninsular War. Returned to civilian life 1889 becoming Provost of Kirkwall. In 1834, after the failure of the kelp industry, he toured Scandinavia to study economic conditions. Important publications followed including a translation of the Icelandic Chronicle, *The Heimskringla* in 3 volumes. Spent the latter part of his life in Edinburgh and is buried in the Dean's Cemetery. Little is known of his artistic work although he is represented in the SNPG by a wash drawing of Kirkwall, 1804.
**Bibl:** DNB.

**LAING, Tomson** **fl 1890-1904**
Glasgow painter in oil and watercolour, mainly coastal and beach scenes often with horses gathering wrack, painted in a rather laboured style. Exhibited RSA(2), GI(4) and L(4) from Partick.

**LAING, William D** **fl 1879-1885**
Edinburgh oil painter of Edinburgh town scenes and more general landscapes. Exhibited RSA(14).

**LAIRD, Miss Alicia H** **fl 1835-1870**
Painter in oil; landscape, interiors, miniature portraits. Although nothing is definitely known of her nationality there is reason to believe she was Scottish. This is based partly on the fact that most of her exhibits were from various Edinburgh addresses but also because of the number of sitters who were themselves Scottish and resident in Scotland. Member of the Society of Lady Artists. Exhibited regularly RA(27) 1846-1865 including portraits of 'General Sir Hector Maclean', 'Col Juan Yturregui Persian Minister to Her Majesty's Court in London', 'General Arista' (former President of Mexico), and 'Miss Cumming', daughter of Sir Alex Gordon Cumming of Altyre. Also exhibited RSA(48) 1835-1870, including an interior of a croft in Braemar, Aberdeenshire & GI(10).
**Bibl:** Dictionary of Artists; A Graves, RA Exhibitors; Long 257.

**LAIRD, James** **fl 1971**
Amateur Glasgow sculptor. Exhibited GI(1) from 9 Firth Ave.

**LAIRD, Michael Donald** **1928-**
Edinburgh architect. Designed the police station in Gayfield Sq (1961) and the Refectory in King's Buildings (1971). Exhibited RSA(19) including designs for Astley Ainsley Hospital (1964), Standard Life Assurance building (1970) and the Garry bridge, Killiecrankie (1971), from 22 Moray Place.
**Bibl:** Gifford 69,74,229,426,488,496,506,513,pl.110.

**LAIRD, Miss Minele** **fl 1952**
Amateur Glasgow watercolourist. Exhibited GI(2).

**LAMB, Miss Elspeth** **fl 1977-**
Painter. Exhibited GI(2).

**LAMB, Helen Adelaide** **fl 1913-d1981**
Born Prestwick. Painter in watercolour and monochrome; also illustrator and illuminator of manuscripts. Trained Glasgow School of Art from which she won a travelling bursary. Taught art at St. Columba's, Kilmacolm. For many years shared a studio with her sister Mildred(qv) at Bryanston, Dunblane. Exhibited RSA(4) & GI(12) 1919-1963.
**Bibl:** Halsby 267.

**LAMB, Mildred R (Mrs Walter Connor)** **1900-1947**
Perthshire-based watercolourist and illustrator; also chalk and pen and ink. Sister of Helen Adelaide(qv) with whom she lived for many years at Dunblane. Trained Glasgow School of Art. Illustrated many books. Exhibited RSA(2) & GI(6).
**Bibl:** Halsby 267.

**LAMB, William** **fl 1861**
Amateur Edinburgh painter. Exhibited two local views at the GI from 116 Rose St.

**LAMB, William A ARSA** **1893-1951**
Born Montrose. Sculptor of figure subjects. Studied at the North Links School before serving his apprenticeship as a monumental sculptor to his brother James, c1906-12. Attended evening classes in art at Montrose Academy and 1912 worked with an Aberdeen granite merchants, simultaneously studying at Gray's School of Art. During WWI served as an infantryman and lost the use of his right hand. During convalescence in Aberdeen, he began using his left hand and from 1918-21 attended the art classes of John Myles(qv) and Lena Gaudie(qv) at Montrose Academy, moving to full-time study at the Edinburgh College of Art with Percy Portsmouth(qv) and David Foggie(qv) 1921-22. Proceeded to further studies in Paris at the École des Beaux-Arts under Boucher and embarked upon an extensive cycle tour of France and Italy. Returned to Montrose 1924. Exhibited "The Cynic' (1925) at the Paris Salon and began exhibiting RA & RSA. In 1929 won the Guthrie Award for 'Ferryden Fishwife'. In 1932 he modelled heads of the Royal family, also Hugh Macdiarmid and Pittendreigh MacGillivray, and in 1945 began a stone carving business. Modelled strong expressionistic sculptures of fisherfolk showing the influence of Meunier and Barlach. Elected ARSA 1931. Exhibited RSA(100+), RSW(3), RA(2), GI(18), AAS & L(1). His entire output of drawings, watercolours, etchings, bronzes, stone and wood carvings and plasters are housed in the William Lamb Memorial Studio, Montrose. Represented in SNGMA.
**Bibl:** Norman K Atkinson, 'William Lamb 1893-1951, Cat of the William Lamb Studio, 1979; T S Halliday and George Bruce, Scottish Sculpture. A record of twenty years, 1946; Hartley 141; Montrose Festival and SAC, Baird, Lamb, (Ex Cat 1968, text by James Morrison).

**LAMBART, Alfred** **1902-?**
Born Darlington. Portrait painter, poster artist and illustrator. Studied at Allan-Fraser College, Arbroath. Exhibited RA 1927-32.

**LAMOND, Henry** **fl 1889-1915**
Glasgow painter of landscape and conversation pieces. Exhibited GI(5).

**LAMOND, W G** **fl c1900-1915**
Architect and draughtsman. Launched his own practice in Friockheim, Angus before moving to Dundee, joining J H Langlands(qv) as chief draughtsman 1904. Alone the firm carried on the art nouveau movement in Dundee that had been led by John Duncan(qv) and George Dutch Davidson(qv). Largely responsible for the six schools designed for the Dundee School Board 1905-1913, also the Baroque façade of the Technical College, Bell St, Dundee (1907).
**Bibl:** Bruce Walker & W S Gauldie, Architects and Architecture on Tayside, Dundee 1984, 163; David Walker, 'Architects and Architecture in Dundee 1770-1914', Abertay Hist Soc publ no 3 (The design for the Eastern Schools is illus as pl X).

**LAMOND, William Bradley RBA** **1857-1924**
Born Newtyle, near Dundee. Worked for many years on the Caledonian Railway. Developed a talent for portrait painting at which he made an early reputation though later turned to landscape enjoying particularly working horses in woodland with effective portrayal of dappled sunshine through trees, also coastal scenes, often with children fishing off the rocks. Largely self-taught, this led to a direct, personal style with fine sense of colour and composition. Lived most of his life in Tayport, Fife and 27 Bank Street, Dundee. Elected RBA 1904. Exhibited RA(1), RSA(16), GI(25), AAS(1) and RBA(8). Represented in Victoria AG (Australia).
**Bibl:** Halsby 267.

**LAMONT, Mrs A F C** **fl 1940**
Amateur Glasgow painter of figurative studies. Exhibited GI(2) from Oakfield Ave.

**LAMONT, Donald** **fl 1977-1984**
Alloa painter. Exhibited RSA & GI(5) from 50 Broomknowe Drive, Kincardine-on-Forth, Fife.

**LAMONT, Elsie** **fl 1926-1940**
Landscape painter in watercolour. Often painted Italian scenes. Lived at Seaport, Elie, Fife but travelled widely. Exhibited RSA(1), RSW(5), SWA(1), RI(1) & GI(2).

**LAMONT, John Charles ARSA** **1894-1948**
Born Chryston, Lanarkshire, 2 Sep; died Kirkcudbright. Painter in oil; figurative subjects and landscapes. Only son of a doctor. Studied Glasgow School of Art under Greiffenhagen and Newbery, winning a travelling scholarship. Suffered serious war wounds while serving in WWI with the Royal Tank Corps, leaving him with ill-health for the rest of his life. He had a rare insight 'with delicious and sometimes unusual colour'. Built himself a house near that of Robert Sivell(qv) and his wife, Lamont's sister-in-law. Friend of Archibald McGlashan(qv) and James Cowie(qv). After the war worked in Ireland where he won the Torrance Award. 'His work never associates itself with the heroic or the fanciful; rather it is concerned with the complete recognition of the constant truths with which he lived in a circumscribed part of the world. His approach was completely objective, his subject the tender moods of the human, intimate, individual scenes. He painted in a low tone, yet succeeded in securing colour that was clear and vibrant, imparting to the whole effect a solemnity and quietness very impressive' [RSA obit]. His work showed the influence of Augustus John, especially in its markedly human characteristics. Lived most of his life in Kirkcudbright. Elected ARSA 1941. Exhibited regularly RSA & GI(10).
**Bibl:** RSA Obituary 1948.

**LAMONT, Lella Ramsay** **fl 1880-1889**
Painter of interiors, portraits and still life. Exhibited RSA(4) & GI(7) at first from 53 Rue Renneguin, Paris and later from Glasgow.

**LAMONT, Ramsay** **fl 1891-1899**
Painter. Lived at 9 Marine Parade, North Berwick before settling in France. Possibly related to Lella Ramsay L(qv). Exhibited GI(8).

**LAMONT, Thomas Reynolds** **1826-1898**
Born Greenock. Painter in oil and watercolour; topographical, figurative subjects and stained glass window designer. Educated in Greenock and St John's Wood, London. Studied in Paris with Du Maurier and Poynter at the Atelier Gleyre, also in Spain. His student days have been recalled by Du Maurier in his book *Trilby* in which Lamont appears as B T Laird. Painted several period pieces in watercolour, with figures dressed in elegant 18th century costume, often posed in beautiful gardens. His technique was good although he was sometimes obsessed with detail, nevertheless managing to create luminous colours, indicating a pre-Raphaelite influence. His subject matter does not always do justice to his technique. There is an interesting two-light window designed by Lamont in the south chancel of the Church of St Nicholas in North Bradley, Wiltshire, depicting portraits of his two wives, Mary and Bessie. These are more like fashion plates than religious effigies. The church historian, John Craig, refers to their 'beautiful design and finely executed work by an academic artist'. No other examples of stained glass by Lamont are recorded. Contributed to *London Society* 1865 and to *The Sheiling Magazine* 1865-6. Elected ARWS 1866. Exhibited RA(4) 1861-1880, RSA(7), RWS(18), GI(8) & L(7). Represented in V & A, Glasgow AG, Greenock AG.
**Bibl:** Halsby 108,267.

**LANDLES, William** **fl 1949-**
Sculptor. Studied under Eric Schilsky(qv) of the Edinburgh College of Art 1951-56, having gained a grant awarded from the Andrew Grant Bequest (on the basis of early work). His work developed in an abstract vein, constructing and carving in marble, slate, glass and terracotta. Represented in the 15 British Sculptors Festival Exhibition in Edinburgh 1967. In 1977 his work changed in nature returning to the production of figurative bronzes. Has undertaken a number of commissions including the Scottish Junior Rugby Trophy for the Royal Bank of Scotland, memorial to the poet Will Ogilvie nr Ashkirk, Roxburghshire 1993 and another of the same for Bourke, Western Australia. Elected SSA 1986. Exhibits regularly at the RSA, GI, AAS & SSA, latterly from 16 Longhope Dr, Hawick.

**LANDLESS, John** **fl 1876-1893**
Glasgow amateur landscape artist; mostly local scenes. Exhibited GI(2) from 2 Elliott Street, Hillhead.

**LANDSEER, Sir Edwin Henry RA** **1802-1873**
Born London, 7 Mar; died London, 1 Oct. Painter in oil of animals, portraits, landscape and narrative subjects. Although not Scottish, this great Victorian animal painter influenced the appreciation and development of Scottish art in two ways. First, his association with many of the leading figures in British life, from Queen Victoria downwards, a large number of whom were Scottish, and second, the paintings and drawings themselves which were a major factor in placing Scotland on the artistic and social map of the western world. Visited Scotland for the first time 1824 meeting Sir Walter Scott and and as a guest of the Duke of Atholl at Blair Atholl, falling in love with the Highlands. Made studies of the Duke's keepers and of red deer which eventually became part of 'Death of the Stag in Glen Tilt'. His visit to Scott was momentous for the influence of the writer was profound and long lasting. Together, with Mendelssohn in the realm of music and Horatio McCulloch(qv) in the realm of art, they gave Victorian Scotland its unique, rather sentimentalised image which survives to this day. Spent ten days at Abbotsford and in 1826 Scott described Landseer's dogs as 'the most magnificent things I ever saw - leaping, and bounding, and grinning on the canvas'. The artist was chosen to be an illustrator for the Waverley edition of his novels. Landseer visited Scotland almost every year of his life thereafter. His closest friends and patrons were in Scotland, Queen Victoria appointed him Animal Painter to Her Majesty for Scotland. His whole career was inextricably intertwined with the Scottish scene. Among his closest friends were the Duke and Duchess of Abercorn who had a lodge at Ardverikie on Loch Laggan; the 4th Earl of Aberdeen whose Scottish home was Haddo House, Aberdeenshire, where Landseer painted 'The Otter Hunt'; the 4th Duke of Atholl, at whose home Landseer was a frequent guest; the 2nd Marquess of Breadalbane, Lord Chamberlain of the Queen's household and who frequently stayed and hunted on his Perthshire estate; the politician and sportsman the 10th Earl of Wemyss; Edward Ellice, of Glen Quoich,

Secretary of War 1833-34 and deputy governor of the Hudson Bay Company. Landseer paid brief visits to Balmoral during three consecutive autumns and in 1854 Queen Victoria sat for him for the last time. His last important Royal commission was a pair of contrasting subjects 'Sunshine', a recollection of Prince Albert in the Highlands, and 'Sorrow', depicting Queen Victoria as a widow at Osborne. With advancing age his identification with the spirit of the Highlands became more pronounced. 'His was not the idealised, romanticism of the outsider, but one founded on knowledge and close association'. "There is a stern sincerity about Highland rocks" he wrote to an old friend in 1859, 'a sort of unadorned truth which you don't find in the rich combinations of the Banks of Conan - where everything is suggestive of comfort and tenderness". He might have said the same of the strong, stubborn character of the Highlanders, and he is still remembered with respect in the glens' [Ormond]. His influence on Scottish animal painting remains strong, comparable to his influence not only on the British School but throughout Europe. He was made an honorary Scottish Academician 1866, exhibiting 19 works there 1827-1872. In the RSA's official report of 1873, a point was made that is still sometimes overlooked 'no-one understood as well as he did, the working of that mysterious faculty which we call instinct, but which approaches much nearer to the human intellect than many of us are ready to allow'. Represented in NGS, SNPG(4), NG, NPG, BM, Tate AG, V & A, Aberdeen AG, Perth AG, Brodie Castle (NTS), Haddo House (NTS), Birmingham AG, Bury AG, Cambridge AG, Liverpool AG, Manchester AG, Sheffield AG, Wallace Coll (London), Preston AG, Sunderland AG, Dublin AG, Hamburg AG, Minneapolis AG (USA), Milwaukee AG (USA), Melbourne AG, Sydney AG (Australia), Yale Center for British Art (New Haven, Conn).
**Bibl:** AJ 1873, 326f (obit); 1874, 55f; 1875-77, see index; 1879, 178, 201, 245; 1905, 59; 1908, 248; A Chester, The Art of EL, 1920; Cundall; A Graves, Cat of the Works of the late Sir EL; I B Hill, Landseer, An Illustrated Life of Sir EL, 1973; Irwin, 206, 222, 313, 321-3, 328, 353, 355; C Lennie, Landseer the Victorian Paragon, 1976; C S Mann, The Works of EL, 1843; J Manson, Sir EL, 1902; D Millar, Queen Victoria's Life in the Scottish Highlands, 1985, 10, 11, 14, 16, 26-8, 32-3, 37, 39, 40, 47-52, 60, 79, 91, 97, 110, 122, 126-30, 146, 148; C Monkhouse, EL Works ill by Sketches from the Collection of Her Majesty, 1888; R Ormond, Sir Edwin Landseer, 1981; Portfolio 1871, 165f; 1872, 127; 1873, 144; 1876, 18f; 1885, 32; J Ruskin, Academy Notes, 1856-1858; J Ruskin, Modern Painters; L Scott, Sir EL, 1904; F G Stephens, Sir EL, 1880; F G Stephens, Life and Works of Sir EL, 1881; Sarah Tytler, Landseer's Dogs and Their Stories, 1877.

**LANE, Margaret R** **fl 1909-1938**
Edinburgh painter of portraits and portrait miniatures. Painted friends and acquaintances rather than high society. Exhibited RSA(19).

**LANG, Miss Amelia** **fl 1865**
Flower painter of Scottish extraction. Lived in Sunderland; exhibited RSA(1).

**LANG, A M** **fl 1885**
Paisley based landscape painter. Exhibited 'Arrochar' at the RSA, also GI(1) & L(2) from the High Church Manse, Castlehead.

**LANG, J Ramsay** **fl 1897-1917**
Rutherglen painter in watercolour of east coast scenes and genre. Exhibited RSA(1), RSW(2), GI(4) and AAS(1) from Churchill.

**LANG, Jessie M** **fl 1979-1983**
Amateur Glasgow painter. Exhibited GI(2) from Royal Bank House, Port Glasgow and Glenbuckley cottage 1979.

**LANG, Laurina** **fl 1971**
Edinburgh painter. Member SWA. Exhibited a tree study at the AAS from 2 Blackford Glen Road.

**LANG, Lila** **fl 1907**
Amateur Ayr artist. Exhibited GI(1) from Langwell.

**LANG, Marion C** **fl 1897-1913**
Renfrewshire painter; exhibited GI(3) & L(1) from Milnbank House, Milnbank, Dennistoun.

**LANG, Robert H** **fl 1981-1984**
Lothian sculptor, mainly in bronze. Exhibited RSA(4) formerly from Pathhead, Midlothian and latterly from Aberlady, East Lothian.

**LANGLADE, Pierre (Peter)** **1812-1909**
Born France; died Bonnyrigg. Painter in oil of subject studies, still-life, landscape and wild flowers. Spent most of his life in Bonnyrigg and Lasswade. Exhibited at the RSA(20), GI & AAS.

**LANGLANDS, Alexander** **fl 1922-1946**
Painter of landscape and topographical studies, mostly in water-colour. Exhibited RSA(1) & GI(5) from a Glasgow address.

**LANGLANDS, George Andrew Nasmyth RSW** **c1865-1940**
Native of the Stow district of Midlothian. Painter in oil and water-colour, landscape and portraits. Studied Edinburgh College of Art and Antwerp. Particularly fond of painting the banks of rivers and small villages. Prolific artist, spent much time sketching on the east coast of Scotland and in the Highlands as well as occasionally in Belgium and Holland. Spent most of his life in Edinburgh. Elected RSW 1896. Exhibited RA(6),RSA(88), RSW(113), GI(35), L(4) & AAS.
**Bibl:** Halsby 267.

**LANGLANDS, J H** **fl 1890-1910**
Dundee architect. With W G Lamond(qv) associated with the art nouveau movement in Dundee. Active in school design including Hawkhill School (now Blackness Primary) (1892).
**Bibl:** Bruce Walker & W S Gauldie, Architects and Architecture on Tayside, Dundee 1984, 141.

**LASKIE, Margaret G** **fl 1966-1972**
Aberdeenshire amateur flower painter. Exhibited AAS(2) from 4 Abbotshall Gardens, Cults.

**LATIMER, Elizabeth Osborne** **fl 1899-1940**
Edinburgh watercolour landscape and topographical painter of quality. Exhibited RSA(18), RSW(1), GI(8) & AAS(1) from Morningside Place.

**LAUDER, Miss Agnes (Nancy)** **1880-c1936**
Born Kilmarnock, 27 Jan. Painter in oil and watercolour of landscapes and flowers. Lived in Kilmarnock. Signed her work 'Nancy Lauder'. Exhibited RSA(5) 1907-1936, RA(1), RSW(4) & GI(28).

**LAUDER, Alexander** **fl 1857-1860**
Edinburgh based painter of religious and subject paintings. Moved to Devonshire c1860. Exhibited RSA(3).

**LAUDER, Charles James RSW** **1840-1920**
Born Glasgow; died Glasgow, Apr 27. Painter of watercolours; figurative subjects, wild flowers and architectural views. Son of James Thompson L(qv). Studied art at Glasgow School of Design under Heath Wilson(qv). Exhibited at the main London galleries from 1890, after settling in Richmond-on-Thames where he lived for 15 years. Painted often in Italy, especially Venice, and along the Thames. Late in life he returned to Scotland, living in Thorntonhill, Lanarkshire. Fine draughtsman, sensitive to the moods and fabrics of townscapes. His second wife, Gertrude(qv), was a member of the Glasgow Society of Lady Artists, best known for establishing the Lauder Prize for the finest work in their annual exhibition. Exhibited RSA(32), RSW(85), GI(86), RBA(6), GI(4) & AAS. Represented in Dundee AG, Glasgow AG, Greenock AG, Paisley AG.
**Bibl:** Caw 334; Halsby 160,267.

**LAUDER, George Dick** **fl 1843-1849**
Painter of landscapes and seascapes in oil; exhibited RSA(8), mostly Highland scenes but also 'Scene after a wreck - twilight after a storm', 1844.

**LAUDER, Gertrude Annie** **?-1918**
Glasgow painter of topographical subjects and miniatures. Wife of C J Lauder(qv). Exhibited RSA 1902-1910 including a case of miniatures, several Venetian scenes and a study of King William's state bedroom at Hampton Court 1910.
**Bibl:** Halsby 267.

**LAUDER, Miss Isabella Scott** **1839-1918**
Edinburgh painter in oil and watercolour of portraits, interiors, figure studies and landscape. Daughter of Robert Scott L(qv). Some of her work, including a portrait of her step-brother Edward Thomson, remains in the family. Exhibited RSA(44), GI & AAS 1885, from 25 Merchiston Avenue.

**LAUDER, J Scott** **fl 1865**
Edinburgh painter. Exhibited a watercolour 'The old stable, Arran' at the GI from 11 Duncan St.

**LAUDER, James Eckford RSA** **1811-1869**
Born Silvermills, nr Edinburgh Aug 15; died Edinburgh, 29 Mar. Painter in oil; genre, landscape and historical subjects. Younger brother of Robert Scott(qv), uncle of Isabella(qv). Studied Trustees Academy under Sir William Allan(qv) and Thomas Duncan(qv) 1830-33 and in Rome 1834-38 with his brother with whom he may have shared a studio. On his return settled in Edinburgh. Worked in a similar manner to his brother, though with a strong individuality of his own. McKay regarded his 'Bailie Duncan McWheeble at breakfast' in the NGS as 'one of the happiest translations ever made from the literary to the painter's art'. Besides Scottish scenes he drew heavily upon his sketches made when in Italy and these constituted a large number of his exhibits at the RSA during the few years prior to his death. Perhaps his most important and finest figure picture was 'Michael Angelo nursing his old and faithful servant Urbino' 1860. Other important works include 'The Parable of the Ten Virgins' 1855 and 'Hagar' 1857 which according to Caw has all the faults and good qualities of his average performance. After about 1857 he turned increasingly to landscape. The fact that these did not produce any stronger popular acclaim than his earlier historical work led to a certain indifference and carelessness in his work which may have contributed to his premature death. In 1847 he won a premium in the Westminster Hall competition for 'Parable of Forgiveness', now in the Walker AG, Liverpool. 'The Wise and Foolish Virgins' was engraved by Lumb Stocks for the Association for the Promotion of Fine Arts in Scotland. Elected ARSA 1839, RSA 1846. Exhibited RA(6) 1841-1846, mostly from 24 Fettes Row, Edinburgh, RSA (113) 1833-1869 & GI(1). Represented in NGS, SNPG(2), Walker Gallery, Liverpool.
**Bibl:** AJ 1869, 157 (obit); Armstrong 50; Bryan; Brydall 428-9; Caw 117-8; DNB; Hardie 31-2; Irwin 298; Portfolio 1887, 153; Redgrave.

**LAUDER, James Thompson** **fl 1830-1850**
Portrait painter in oils. Father of Charles James L(qv).

**LAUDER, Kenneth Scott ARCA** **1918-?**
Born Edinburgh, 4 Mar. Painter in oil and watercolour, mainly the latter, also teacher; coastal and hill scenes, semi-abstracts. Educated King Alfred's School, Wantage, studied art at Chelsea School of Art 1934 under Robert Medley and Royal College of Art 1936-39 under Gilbert Spencer. Influenced by Turner's later work, by Braque, Olitski and Julius Bissier. His main interest has been in coastal and hill areas giving expression to landscape without reference to man, places 'that have a remoteness that emphasises our temporal nature'. Seeks to establish a subtlety of colour and tonal change uniting with the surface to express the horizontal qualities and vitality of movement in the sky. Held many one man exhibitions. During WW2 served in the RAF as a pilot. Exhibited at the Schloss Leopoldskron, Salzburg, also Walker AG, Liverpool & Laing AG (Newcastle). Lived in Liverpool.

**LAUDER, Miss Nancy** **fl 1907-1942**
Kilmarnock flower and landscape painter, mainly in watercolour. Exhibited AAS(2) & GI(30) from 97 Dundonald Road.
**Bibl:** Halsby 267.

**LAUDER, Robert Scott RSA** **1803-1869**
Born Silvermills, nr Edinburgh Jne 25; died Edinburgh, 22 Apr. Painter in oil of historical and biblical genre. Brother of James Eckford L(qv). Studied at Trustees Academy under Andrew Wilson(qv) and under Sir William Allan(qv). When very young he made some designs for the *Arabian Nights' Entertainments* and having made the acquaintance of David Roberts, seven years his senior, found the latter's enthusiasm for the young man's abilities a source of great encouragement. Worked for three years in London, returning to Edinburgh 1826, and then from 1833 to 1838 studied in Bologne, Florence, Rome and Venice. Existed by painting portraits and some teaching at the Trustees Academy. Shortly before going to Rome he married one of John Thomson's daughters and from 1833 until 1838 Rome became their home. The 'Trial of Effie Deans', begun before he left Scotland, was taken to Rome and brought home again to be finished thanks to Gibson's encouragement. This highly original composition attracted acclaim when exhibited 1842. In 1843 scriptural subjects were 'Heralded by Ruth', followed by 'Christ Walking on the Sea' 1847, submitted for the Westminster Hall competition and subsequently purchased by Lady Burdett Coutts, and 'The Crucifixion'. From 1838-52 was in London. Then appointed Master of the Trustees Academy, Edinburgh. A most popular and successful teacher under whose leadership the Academy produced many of its best pupils including Chalmers, Peter and Thomas Graham, McTaggart, Orchardson and Pettie. After 1857, landscape and slighter figure subjects, themes of poetry and legend, became more prominent. He used colour in a manner reminiscent of Delacroix. Having had little training in the knowledge of form, this was difficult for an experienced hand to rectify especially one interested in colour. 'The nobler and graver sense of design added to his work thereby, often seems only to accent the looseness of the drawing and certain stiffness and rigidity, which mar his compositions' [McKay]. But in dignified design, and in the use of those sombre and harmonious colour arrangements which best suit the expression of graver subjects, Lauder did a great service to Scottish art. After his appointment as Director in the Antique, Life and Colour department of the Trustees Academy on 16 February 1852, he left the Ornament and Architecture classes to Christian Dallas(qv), and appointed John Ballantyne(qv) as his assistant in the Antique and Life classes. 'Taking Lauder's pupils as a whole...they set up individuality and a sincerity of self-expression in their places. They first made beautiful colour a distinct motif in Scottish art. They first substituted subjectivity and creation for realism and reflections of the actual. They pointed the way to combining imagination with polished mechanique. They first disclosed the enchantment of pure art' [Caw]. In 1861 Lauder suffered a stroke preventing him from ever painting again. Exhibited RA(25) 1827-1848 and RSA(154) 1826-1870. Foundation member, RSA when only 26. Represented in NGS, SNPG(8), Glasgow AG, Victoria AG (Australia).
**Bibl:** AJ 1850, 12ff; 1869, 176 (obit); 1898, 339-343, 367-371; Armstrong 49-50; Bryan; Brydall 429-431; Caw 115-117 et passim; Lindsay Errington, Master Class: Robert Scott Lauder and his pupils'; Halsby 109,118,220,225 et al; Hardie 54, passim ch iv; Irwin 295-9 et passim; McKay 220-232; Macmillan[SA] 201-4,208,212-3, et passim in chs xi-xiv; NGS 1983; Redgrave.

**LAUDER, T J** **fl 1862**
Painter. Exhibited 'Old Stable at Arrochar' at the RSA from an Edinburgh address.

**LAUDER, Thomas** **fl 1570-1574**
Peebles master mason. Largely responsible for one of the few partially surviving town walls in Scotland. Between the above years he directed the building of Peebles town wall. The contract specified that this had to be 'four elnis half ground and all, thre futtis half ane fut of brief' and the surviving portions indicate that these dimensions were followed closely. There were also to be blockhouses stationed at intervals, one of which is still well preserved; it is circular and its two wide-mouthed gun-ports are so placed to provide covering fire along both adjacent sections of the wall.
**Bibl:** Gunnis.

**LAUDER, Sir Thomas Dick Bt** **1784-1848**
Died East Lothian, 29 May. Author, historian, amateur landscape and portrait painter. Succeeded his father becoming 7th Baronet of Fountainhall, Haddingtonshire 1820. Married Charlotte Cumin, only child and heiress of Grange Cumin, Relugas, Moray and there he made his home. Contributed scientific papers to the *Annals of Philosophy* from 1815. In 1839 became Secretary to the Board of Scottish Manufacturers whose policy was to encourage the foundation of art and technical schools. Then became secretary to the Royal Institution for the Encouragement of the Fine Arts. Illustrated *A Voyage Round the Coasts of Scotland and the Isles* 1842, the illustrations being subsequently engraved by Charles Wilson, and *An Account of the Great Floods of August, 1829* (1830), engraved by WH Lizars(qv). Other works which he helped illustrate include *Rivers of Scotland* (1847-9), *Essays on the Picturesque* (1842), which he also edited and prefaced with an essay on 'The Origin of Taste', and *The Miscellany of Natural History* (1833-4). A pencil drawing of the

'Rev John Thomson of Duddingston' (1831) is in SNPG.
**Bibl:** DNB; Irwin 193.

**LAUDER, William** **fl 1698**
Born Haddington. Painter in oil. Son of a provost of the town. Apprenticed to the painter Thomas Warrender 1698. None of his work is now recorded.
**Bibl:** Apted 58; 'Edinburgh Apprentices 1666-1700', ed by F.J.Grant & C.B.B. Watson, Scot. Rec. Soc. 1906, 1929, p54.

**LAURENSON, Pat** **fl 1975-**
Aberdeenshire-based potter. Exhibited AAS(6) from the short-lived Glen Tanar Pottery, Dinnet.

**LAURIE, J C** **fl 1871**
Amateur Glasgow landscape painter. Exhibited GI(2) from 27 Hope St.

**LAURIE, Jessie S** **fl 1881**
Amateur Glasgow painter. Exhibited GI(2) from 11 Percy Terrace.

**LAURIE, John** **1916-1972**
Born Shrewsbury. Portrait painter; occasional landscapes and figurative studies. Studied Glasgow School of Art 1933-36 and Hospitalfield, Arbroath, 1938-1940, winning a Carnegie Travelling scholarship 1939. Taught drawing at Glasgow School of Art 1946-72. Almost all his RSA exhibits were portraits including 'Sir Daniel Stevenson, Principal of Glasgow University', 1943 and 'James Cowie RSA', 1947; also GI(44). Represented in SNPG ('James Cowie RSA').
**Bibl:** Mungo Campbell, 'The Line of Tradition', Nat Galls of Scotland, Ex cat, Edinburgh 1993; Hardie 158(illus).

**LAURIE, Katherine Ann** **fl 1887-1888**
Edinburgh painter of genre and portraits. Exhibited RSA(4) from Nairne Lodge, Duddingston.

**LAURIE, M W** **fl 1862**
Amateur Edinburgh artist. Exhibited 'Apple blossom' at the GI.

**LAURIE (LOWRY), Robert** **c1755-1836**
Born London. Engraver and mezzotinter. Of Scottish extraction, awarded premiums from the Society of Arts 1771 and 1776, the latter for an invention that aided the printing of colours in mezzotints. In addition to the plates listed by Bryan he executed a portrait of 'Elizabeth, Duchess of Argyle' after Catherine Read in 1771 and a portrait of 'John Jervis, Earl St Vincent', after T Stuart, 1794. In the catalogue of the Loan Exhibition of British Engraving and Etching, (V&A 1903), his dates are given as c1740-c1804.
**Bibl:** Bryan; Bushnell; 'Cat of the Loan Exhibition' V&A 1903; DNB.

**LAURIE, Simon RSW RGI** **fl 1989-**
Glasgow sculptor. Elected RGI 2000. Exhibits GI from 152 Craigpark, Dennistoun.

**LAURIE, Walter** **fl 1798**
Edinburgh engraver. All that is now known of his life is his appearance on the list of subscribers to David Crawford's *Poems chiefly in the Scottish Dialect,* 1798.

**LAVERY, Sir John RA RSA RHA PRP HROI LLB** **1856-1941**
Born Belfast, Mar; died Kilmagenny, Co Kilkenny, 11 Jan. Painter in oil; portraits, genre and landscape. An orphan, reared on a farm in Ulster, he had a deprived childhood. In 1874 went to Glasgow to work as a photographer's assistant and attended evening classes at the Haldane Academy of Art. Then also spent some time in London studying at Heatherley's; returning to Glasgow, he rented a studio next door to Alex Roche(qv). After the studio had been destroyed by fire the two artists travelled to Paris together for further studies, Lavery working under Bouguereau. 'The artistic events then in Paris can be fixed exactly for Lavery had a small student work, 'Les Deux Pecheurs', hung at the Salon next to 'The Bar at the Folies Bergeres' by Manet. He spent a very happy time at the village of Grez, where there was a notable Bohemian colony, before returning with Roche to his friends in Glasgow. He came back having been profoundly influenced by Bastien-Lepage and the kind of decorative treatment derived from Frank O'Meara. In 1884/5 he spent a productive period at Grez-sur-Loing in the company of Millie Dow(qv), William Kennedy(qv) and Alex Roche(qv). In 1885 he saw Guthrie's painting 'To Pastures New' which he thought better than anything he had seen in Paris. As a result the two artists were to remain firm friends becoming equally successful, Guthrie in Scotland, Lavery internationally. 1885 found him back in Glasgow and working on 'The Tennis Party', one of the most bold and innovative works to emerge from the Glasgow School. At about this time the influence of Whistler became apparent, especially in his portraits. In 1888 he painted the official picture of the Queen's state visit to Glasgow. This led to more commissions. At the end of 1890 he made the first of many visits to Morocco where in 1903 he acquired a winter home. In 1896, attracted to high society and elegant ladies, he moved to London establishing himself as a highly fashionable portrait painter, setting up a studio in Cromwell Road. Among the many important commissions to follow were several official narratives including 'The Arrival of the German Delegates on HMS Queen Elizabeth', 1918 and 'Viscount Morley moving the Address on the Irish Treaty in the House of Lords', 1922. One of his most famous portraits, and of an altogether more unassuming nature than many of the formal works he had hitherto completed, was 'The Prime Minister at Lossiemouth', 1933. This showed the plus-foured Prime Minister about to lay down a book before enjoying cherry cake and jam set out in front of a black-leaded grate. Played an important role in the formation of the International Society of Sculptors, Painters and Engravers 1898. Whistler became president and Lavery vice-president. Having acquired international recognition, Lavery spent the latter part of his life painting Hollywood stars and spending winters in his luxurious Tangier studio. As well as 'The Tennis Party' (RSA 1889), his most famous works included 'The Night After the Battle of Langside, May 13, 1568' (RSA 1893) and 'The Morning After the Battle of Langside'. These two paintings were among the very few historical pictures Lavery ever painted. Although neither received good notices in Scotland they were appreciated on the continent, one being purchased by the Royal Museum of Brussels in 1895. They demonstrated the essential difference between the academic approach and that of the young Glasgow Boys. Buchanan thought that Lavery was never to achieve such depth and understanding as depicted in these pictures of human feeling again. Caw, in the *AJ* (1898) wrote 'his sense of design, fine eye for subtle colour schemes of grey and black or white, able handling, and ideal of picture-making, are of a high order, but his interest in life seems superficial, and he paints a pretty woman not so much as she is but as a conventionalised type.' About 'The Tennis Party' it has been said that 'In it he seems to put into practise the advice received from Bastien-Lepage on capturing the human figure in action. He remembered this as 'always carry a sketch-book, select a person, watch him, then put down as much as you remember. Never look twice.' His comment was that from that day on he became 'obsessed by figures in movement'. This picture immediately stamps Lavery as having greater natural dexterity than any of the other Glasgow painters. And it is not spoiled by the over-facile virtuosity which creeps into his later work' [Hardie]. One other painting which must be mentioned is 'The Hammock - Twilight' (1884). 'At the end of a pleasantly indolent day, a young woman turns in her hammock to pick up a cup of tea beside her on a stool...but there is no indication that she has been engaged in any activity. Her face is in shadow and half-hidden from the spectator by the black rug on which she is lying. Human expression is therefore subordinated, as in most early Glasgow group works, to an interest in form and colour...the placing of objects is as refined as the restricted palette in which they have been painted...the hammock contains all the characteristics of the early Glasgow School style, and is one of the finest paintings of that School' [Irwin]. In the course of his busy and successful career Lavery received many honours including ARSA 1892, RSA 1896, RP 1893, PRP 1898, ARHA 1906, RHA 1906, ARA 1911, RA 1921, Knighthood 1918. Member of the Academies of Antwerp, Brussels, Milan, Rome and Stockholm and of the Secessions of Berlin, Munich and Vienna. Awarded the Cavalière of the Crown of Italy in 1901 and made a Chevalier of the Order of Leopold (Belgium) 1907. Won a Gold Medal at the Barcelona International Exhibition. Exhibited extensively at the RSA, RA and in all the other major places including the Paris Salon & AAS 1910-1937. His works may be seen in the NPG, SNPG(2), Tate AG, V & A, Aberdeen AG, Adelaide AG, Belfast AG, Berlin AG, Birmingham AG, Bradford AG, Brussels AG, Buenos Aires AG, Cambridge AG, Chicago AG, Cork AG, Dublin AG, Dundee AG, Edinburgh City Collection, Glasgow

AG, Greenock AG, Johannesburg AG, Leipzig AG, Limerick AG, Liverpool AG, Manchester AG, Mannheim AG, Munich AG, Ottawa AG, Louvre (Paris), Perth AG, Philadelphia AG, Pittsburgh AG, Rochdale AG, Rome AG, San Diego AG, Sydney AG, Toronto AG, Venice AG, permanent collections of RA and RSA.
**Bibl:** AJ 1904, 6-11; 1908, 3-6; Apollo, vol 2, 1925; Halsby 143,145,147 et al; Hardie passim in chvi,122,139; Irwin passim; John Lavery, The Life of a Painter, London 1940; Kenneth McConkey,'Sir John Lavery', Fine Art Society & Ulster Museum (Ex Cat 1984); Macmillan[SA] 259-60,273-4,280-2,285-310; David Scruton, 'John Lavery the early career', Crawford Centre for the Arts, St Andrews, (Ex Cat 1983); Lady Ann Semphill (Intro) 'Sir John Lavery RA', Spink & Son, London (Ex Cat 1971); Walter Shaw Sparrow, John Lavery and His Work, London 1911; Studio vol 27, 1903; vol 45, 1909.

**LAW, Alexander McCallum** **fl 1922**
Glasgow amateur painter. Exhibited GI(1) from 21 Ravenswood Drive, Shawlands.

**LAW, Andrew** **fl 1870-1873**
Glasgow painter of poetic landscapes. Exhibited GI(5) including 'Morag's Fairy Glen', 'Dunoon' and 'Baggy Burn Glen, Dunoon', from 127 Paisley Rd.

**LAW, Andrew** **1873-1967**
Born Crosshouse, Kilmarnock. Painter in oil; portraits, still lifes, animals and urban landscapes. Educated Kilmarnock and Glasgow School of Art under Fra Newbery(qv). Haldane travelling scholarship took him to the Academie Delacluse, Paris 1896-7. Active member of the Glasgow Art Club and staff member, Glasgow School of Art until his retirement in 1938. Exhibited RSA(40), GI(93), L(9) & AAS. Represented in Glasgow AG(3).
**Bibl:** Halsby 159.

**LAW, Arthur E** **fl 1926-1952**
Stonehaven painter of landscape, genre, local scenery and still lifes, often with porcelain figures. Best known for his coastal and harbour scenes. Married Jean L(qv). Art teacher at Mackie Academy in the 1930s before moving to Harris Academy, Dundee. Retired to Edinburgh where he died. Exhibited RA(8), RSA(14), AAS (1926-1935) & L(3), mostly from 14 Fetteresso Terrace, Stonehaven until c1936.

**LAW, D McKay** **fl 1933-1940**
Painter of portraits and genre. Exhibited RSA(3), first from Edinburgh and then from Leith.

**LAW, David RSW RBA RE** **1831-1901**
Born Edinburgh, 25 Apr; died Worthing, Sussex, 29 Dec. Landscape painter in oil and watercolour, and etcher. Apprenticed early to George Aikman(qv), the seal engraver. Admitted to Trustees Academy 1845 studying under Alexander Christie(qv) and Elmslie Dallas(qv) until 1850. Then became a map-engraver in the Ordnance Survey office, Southampton. It was not until 1870 that he resigned in order to pursue a full-time career as an artist. A founder member, Royal Society of Painter Etchers 1881. Among his best known etchings are two series of Thames subjects, and a 'Trossachs' series. Exhibited RA(52) 1873-1899 as well as many exhibits at the RSA and elsewhere. His plates after Turner and Corot and some modern landscape painters had many admirers and when reproductive etching was in high fashion, they were in great demand. His best and most vital etchings were of his own paintings. Elected RE 1881, RSW 1882, RBA 1884, HRBA 1893. Exhibited RE(42), RSW(9), RBA(28), GI(9) & RHA(10). Represented in Dundee AG, Sydney AG.
**Bibl:** AJ 1902, 85 (obit); Bryan; Caw 454; DNB 2nd supp; Halsby 267; Portfolio 1879, 193ff; 1880, 93; 1883, 1884; 1902.

**LAW, Miss Frances** **fl 1988-**
Angus painter. Exhibited GI(1) 1988, from Barberswells, Craigton by Kirriemuir.

**LAW, Freda Graves** **fl 1903**
Edinburgh painter. Exhibited RSA(1) from 10 Salisbury Road.

**LAW, Graham Couper RSA RIBA FRIAS** **1923-1996**
Born Scotland, 28 Sep. Architect. Educated at Merchiston Castle School, King's College Cambridge and Cambridge University School of Architecture. His design experience was largely gained working for Robert Matthew and with Richard Buckle. Interested in the theory and practice of design, his thesis on 'Greek' Thomson(qv) appeared in the *Architectural Review* (1954, no.5). Frequent exhibitor RSA, including designs for St Columbus Church, Livingstone and the Ardrossan Ferry terminal. The design for Eden Court Theatre, Inverness was exhibited at the RA 1973 and for the Pitlochry Festival Theatre in 1975, both of which received RIBA awards. Involved in the design of several major art exhibitions including the Epstein Commemorative Exhibition of 1961, 'Music and Dance in Indian Art' at the Royal Scottish Museum 1963, 'Treasures from Scottish Houses' at the RSM 1967 and 'Canada 101' at the ECA 1968. Elected ARSA 1980, RSA 1995. James Morris(qv) wrote "In many ways Graham Law belonged to an older and more sincere generation. His courteous manner, his care and interest in other people (especially those in the field of architecture and the arts) will ensure that they will remember his tall, somewhat gangly figure as one of the most distinguished gentlemen in his profession." Exhibited drawings and watercolours at the RSA.
**Bibl:** James S Morris, Obituary, RSA Annual Report, 1996.

**LAW, Helen** **fl c1880-c1890**
Glasgow amateur painter in pastel and watercolour of domestic genre and interiors. Exhibited once at the New England Art Club from Glenval, Pollokshields.

**LAW, Mrs Jean (Jane) A** **fl 1926-1929**
Painter of landscape and interiors. Wife of Arthur E L(qv). Exhibits include works in Dordrecht and Concarneau. Exhibited RSA(2) & AAS(2) from 14 Fetteresso Terrace, Stonehaven.

**LAW, John** **fl 1882-1884**
Edinburgh painter in oil; landscape and rustic scenes. Exhibited RSA(4).

**LAW, Mrs Margaret C** **fl 1986-**
Ayr painter of west coast landscapes. Exhibited GI(3) 1986-7. from 12 Abbots Way, Doonfoot.

**LAW, W B** **fl 1908**
An artist of this name presented two watercolours to the City of Edinburgh collection, 'Echo Bank village' and 'Broughton Burn', both dated 1908.

**LAWRENCE, Anne E** **fl 1887**
Aberdeen painter in oil and charcoal of coastal scenes, landscape and portraits. Exhibited AAS(8) from 2 Bon-Accord Street.

**LAWRENCE, Eileen E M (Mrs Onwin) ARSA** **1946-**
Born Leith. Studied at Edinburgh College of Art 1963-8, after which she lived and worked in London 1969-72. Then lived in Wuppertal, Germany for a year before visiting America where she became particularly interested in Indian ceremonial fetishes. Returning to UK, she held her first solo show in Edinburgh 1969, another in 1974 and in Stirling the following year. Married to Glen Onwin(qv). Specialises in the delicate portrayal of feathers and similar totemic objects, generally in watercolour and ink. 'An austere limited repertoire of...natural forms...until quite recently in monochrome, and often on scrolls of handmade paper as if in allusion to a fetishistic primitive religion...suggesting that these simple natural forms possess a power or significance of importance to man, as well as depicting them in and for themselves'[Hardie]. The content is finely drawn with immense care and feeling for detail. Elected ARSA 1997, member SSA, exhibits RSA & SSA. Represented in European Parliament; Gulbenkian Foundation, Glasgow AG, Nat. Gall of Modern Art, Canberra, SNGMA, Tate AG.
**Bibl:** Bath Festival,'Eileen Lawrence', (Ex Cat 1986); Hardie 196; Hartley 141-2; Fischer Fine Art, London, 'Eileen Lawrence: Recent Work', (Ex Cat 1980 & 1985); Macmillan[SA] 395,398.

**LAWRENCE, G W** **fl 1929-1937**
Aberdeenshire landscape painter. Exhibited AAS(2) from Hillhead, Lonmay.

**LAWRENCE, George H** **fl 1951-1955**
Edinburgh based landscape painter, often of English and French

views. Exhibited RSA(3) from 11 Warriston Crescent.

**LAWRENCE, Gordon R** **fl 1952-1986**
Glasgow based landscape and portrait painter who later moved to Merseyside. Painted a number of Cypriot landscapes when visiting the island in the 1950s. Exhibited RSA 1952, 1955, and 1986.

**LAWRENSON, Thomas** **fl 1941-1951**
Dundee painter of portraits and interiors. Exhibited GI(4) from 26 Noran Ave, Craigiebank.

**LAWRIE, Charles** **fl 1879**
Edinburgh painter of coastal scenes in watercolour; exhibited RSA(2). Represented in Greenock AG.

**LAWRIE, Hamish B** **1919-1987**
Born Dunfermline. Painter in oil and watercolour; landscape, mostly Irish and Scottish, also scene painter. Educated St John's School winning gold medal for art. Trained Gray's School of Art, Aberdeen after which he found employment as a camera man on a film set. Said to have sold his first work to Dylan Thomas. After a spell in southern Africa, on the advice of his friend J B Fergusson(qv) eventually settled in France 1951-60. Used vigorous brushwork demonstrating his unbridled enthusiasm for paint producing work that was always colourful, sometimes crude but never dull. Did not exhibit at any of the major academies although a well-known and much loved member of the Scottish Arts Club. Exhibited GI(1) 1941. Represented by an oil in Edinburgh City collection.

**LAWRIE, J C** **fl 1869-1870**
Amateur Glasgow landscape painter. Exhibited GI(2).

**LAWRIE, James** **fl 1850**
Edinburgh based topographical painter. Exhibited 'View of Stirling' at the RSA from Leith Walk.

**LAWRIE, Madelaine** **fl 1850**
Leith based painter. Possibly related to James L(qv). Exhibited 'Hullah in the Desert' at the RSA from a Leith address.

**LAWRIE, Mary H S** **fl 1887**
Edinburgh based artist. Exhibited RSA(1) from 23 Saxe Coburg Place.

**LAWRIE, Norman A** **fl 1929**
Amateur Aberdeen artist. Exhibited a study of a ship at the AAS from 14 Esslemont Avenue.

**LAWRIE, William** **fl 1898-1912**
Aberdeen painter and etcher. Exhibited AAS(6) from 37 Spa Street and later 312 Holburn Street.

**LAWRIE, William** **c1825-c1890**
Architect, specialising in public buildings. Responsible for the Primary School, Kingussie (1874-6), the Manse at Croy (1855), alterations to Ness Castle (1855), Ness House, Fortrose (1859). In mid-career entered into a successful partnership with James Matthews(qv).
**Bibl:** Gifford, H & I, 91,159,165,194,201,204,214,419 et passim

**LAWSON, Bernard** **fl 1897**
Amateur Edinburgh portrait painter in oil; exhibited RSA(1) from 4 Starbank Place, Trinity.

**LAWSON, Cecil Gordon** **1851-1882**
Born Wellington, Shropshire, Dec 3; died London, Jne 10. Painter in oil and watercolour of genre and landscape. Both his Scottish parents were artists. Went to London 1861 with his father, William L(qv) the portrait painter. Began by painting small, detailed rather laboured studies of fruit and flowers in the manner of William Hunt. After visiting the Low Countries and France in 1874 scored his first success with 'The Minister's Garden' 1878 at the opening of the Grosvenor Gallery. His death, at the age of 31, cut short a most promising career. The few pictures he completed reveal an artist 'singularly sensitive to the grandeur and bold rhythm of nature'. It was Lawson's laudable ambition to make landscape express emotion without the introduction of incident or other explanatory accessory, and in many cases he succeeded to admiration. Close in touch with Nature herself rather than with a particular mood or phase as some great landscape artists have been, he loved high summer with its thick-leaved greenery and somnalent blue skies as well as the gaiety and glad freshness of spring or the mellow austere passing of autumn, was as fond of moorland and marsh as of woodland and meadow, and was as much at home in the stone-strewn valley of desolation as in the luxuriant hot gardens of England...His pictures are pregnant with the life and change of Nature, with its growth and lusty life, its decay and its perennially renewed youth, and with those emotional symphonies which the ever-changing sky plays upon the enduring features of the earth. These he painted with an impetuous and broad and yet assured masterful touch, which, if sometimes coarse, was ever expressive and significant and in a style usually distinguished and always pictorial. His sense of colour, although somewhat lacking in delicacy, as his tone was rather wanting in fineness of modulation, was at once effective and beautiful, especially in those rich deep harmonies of blue and brown or of lush greens, blues and whites, which were the most characteristic expression of this side of his gift. An artist who had learned much from the past and yet was in touch with the best elements of his own time, a realist who had yet a passionate and original perception of the beauty and poetry of the world and a distinguished sense of style' [Caw]. Exhibited RA(18) 1870-1882 & GI(12). Represented in Tate AG, V & A, Glasgow AG, Birmingham AG, Manchester AG(5).
**Bibl:** AJ 1882, 232f (obit); 1895, 282; 1908, 122; 1909, 102; Binyon; Caw 313-6; Gosse, Lawson, a Memoir, 1883; Halsby 267; Hardie III 188-9, (pl 221); Irwin 359; Maas 228; Mag of Art 158, Dec 1893; Redgrave; D P Reynolds 155 (pl 110); Studio 66 (1916), 240; 1923, 261.

**LAWSON, Colin** **1959-**
Born Dunfermline. Abstract painter & teacher. Trained Edinburgh College of Art 1977-1982. Awarded Elizabeth Greenshields scholarship 1983 & 1985. Elected SSA 1982 but resigned 1987. Part-time lecturer at Edinburgh College of Art since 1991. Exhibits RSA 1984 onwards, from 37 Inverleith Place, Edinburgh.

**LAWSON, E** **fl 1888**
Amateur artist; exhibited at the Walker Gallery, Liverpool (1) from 13 Elm Row, Edinburgh.

**LAWSON, Elizabeth R (née Stone)** **fl 1844-1894**
Figure and flower painter in oil and watercolour. Mother of Francis Wilfred L(qv) and Cecil Gordon L(qv). Although Scottish, lived and worked most of her life in England, first of all in London and later in Bedford. Exhibited RSA(1), RHA(2), GI(2), RBA(1) & L(1).

**LAWSON, Florence** **fl 1922**
Edinburgh based painter. Exhibited St John's Close, Canongate, Edinburgh at the RSA from 30 Alva Street.

**LAWSON, Florence Graham** **fl 1897-1902**
Edinburgh painter who moved to Carlisle c1900; exhibited mainly landscapes but also flower studies and a portrait miniature in oil at the RSA(5) & GI(1).

**LAWSON, Francis Wilfred** **1842-1935**
Born Wellington, Shropshire. Painter of genre and landscape and illustrator. Son of Scottish parents, brother of Cecil Gordon L(qv). For many years worked as a designer for *The Graphic.* Lived much of his life in London, but moved to Crowhurst, near Buxton 1913. Illustrated *Poetical Works of Henry W Longfellow* (c1870); Collins: *The Law and the Lady* (1876, with Fildes & Hall). Exhibited 1867-1913 including 14 works at the RA 1867-84, and four at the RSA 1878-83 including a sketch for 'A Merry Christmas' owned by Charles Lees (1879) & GI(6).
**Bibl:** Houfe 203.

**LAWSON, George Anderson HRSA** **1832-1904**
Born Edinburgh; died Richmond, Surrey, 23 Sep. Sculptor. Studied Trustees Academy, became a pupil of Alexander Handyside Ritchie(qv). At the same time also a student at the Trustees School under R S Lauder(qv). Specialised in portrait busts usually in bronze, sometimes in terracotta or marble, also portrait medallions. Exhibited first at the RSA in 1860 and a few years later he went to London

before undertaking further studies in Rome. Designed the frieze above Glasgow City Chambers depicting Queen Victoria and the countries of Great Britain receiving homage from the Countries of the World c1888. A bronze figure of a sleeping boy depicting 'Summer' is in George Watson's College, Colinton Rd, Edinburgh. Continued to exhibit at the RSA until 1892, making three of the statues for the Scott Monument Edinburgh (Robert Bruce, Diana Vernon and Bailie Nicol Jarvie), and the Wellington Monument, Liverpool, as well as many statuettes and busts. Elected HRSA 1884. Exhibited RA(48) 1862-1893 & RSA(32) 1860-1905; also RBA(1), RI(2) & GI(15). In 1874 executed a bronze statue for the late Lord Cochrane for the Chilean government, now in Valparaiso. Represented in NGS, SNPG(2, including 'John Pettie'), Glasgow AG.
**Bibl:** Gifford 316,496; RSA Obituary.

**LAWSON, George Stodart** **fl 1881-1897**
Edinburgh watercolour painter of figurative subjects and flower studies. Lived for some years at Henfield, Sussex, before returning to Edinburgh in 1886. Exhibited RSA(1) & GI(2).

**LAWSON, Helen E** **19th century**
Scottish engraver. Daughter of Alexander L(qv).

**LAWSON, Henry R** **fl 1880-1882**
Painter in oil of genre; exhibited RSA(5) & GI(2) from 4 Coates Place, Edinburgh.

**LAWSON, Ian** **fl 1953-1987**
Painter of flowers, landscape and figurative subjects. Lived in Kirkcaldy, Dunfermline and Glasgow from 1965. Exhibited RSA(21) & GI(12). Represented in Kirkcaldy AG.

**LAWSON, Miss Isabel** **fl 1894-1898**
Edinburgh oil painter of domestic genre and interiors; exhibited RSA(2) & GI(1). Sometimes catalogued with the initial J or T.

**LAWSON, J** **fl 1898-1902**
Edinburgh painter of figurative works. Exhibited GI(4) from 7 Atholl Crescent.

**LAWSON, Miss J B** **fl 1888**
Amateur Glasgow painter. Exhibited GI(1) from 241 West George Street.

**LAWSON, James Kerr** **1865-1939**
Born Anstruther. Painter of mainly topographical works, also portraits and figurative studies. Trained Paris and Rome. Visited Morocco with his friend James McBey(qv) 1912. Exhibited GI(11) at first from Pittenweem, Fife, then Dunbartonshire, moving to London c1939 before finally settling in Canada.

**LAWSON, Jean** **fl 1942**
St Andrews landscape painter. Exhibited RSA(2).

**LAWSON, Jessie L** **fl 1920-1921**
Lanarkshire portrait painter. Exhibited RSA(1) & GI(1) from Dornoch, Cambuslang.

**LAWSON, John** **fl c1770**
Scottish engraver. Studied at Glasgow Academy. Specialised in portrait heads. Among his best known plates are: 'A head of the Virgin', after Raphael; 'A head of Horace', from Pine; 'A head of Fenelon'; 'A head of Germanicus'; 'Virgo Victrix'; 'The Amazon Penthesiela slain by Achilles'; 'Diomedes and Gleucus exchanging shields'; and a statue of Diana.
**Bibl:** Bushnell; Duncan, Notices and Documents illustrative of the Literary History of Glasgow, 1831.

**LAWSON, John** **fl 1857-1863**
Dunfermline painter in oil of portraits and domestic animals; exhibited RSA(6).

**LAWSON, John** **1869-1909**
Died Carmunnock, 9 Sep. Landscape painter and illustrator. Living at Strathbungo 1882, Sheffield 1892-1893, returning to live in Girvan, Ayrshire. Reid regards him as a very competent draughtsman of the second rank, producing excellent figure studies for popular magazines in the 1860s. Contributed illustrations to *Once a Week* (1865-67); *The Sunday Magazine; Cassell's Magazine; The Quiver* 1865; *The Children's Hour* 1865; *The Shilling Magazine* 1866; *The Argosy* 1866; *British Workman* 1866; *Pen and Pencil Pictures from the Poets* 1866; *Ballad Stories* 1866; *Golden Thoughts from Golden Fountains* 1867; *Roses and Holly* 1867; *Ballads, Scottish and English* 1867; *Nursery Time* 1867; *Early Start in Life* 1867; *The Children of Blessing* 1867; *The Golden Gift* 1868; *Original Poems* 1868; *Tales of the White Cockade* 1870; *The Runaway* 1872; *The Childrens' Garland* 1873; *The Fiery Cross* 1875; *The World Well Lost* 1877; *Clever Hans* 1883; *There Was Once* 1888 and *Childhood Valley* 1889. After 1902 most of his works were of Welsh scenes. Exhibited RSA(16), RI(1), GI(55) & L(4). Represented in Glasgow AG(5), Culzean Castle (NTS).
**Bibl:** F Reid, Illustrators of the Sixties 1928, 228-9, illus.

**LAWSON, Margaret E** **fl 1935**
Glasgow based artist; exhibited 'Self-portrait' at the RSA from 160 Onslow Drive.

**LAWSON, Oscar A** **19th century**
Scottish engraver. Son of Alexander L(qv). Spent most of his life in the US where he was chart engraver to the US Coast Survey.

**LAWSON, Ray** **fl 1972-1973**
Inverness-shire landscape painter. Exhibited AAS(3) from Errogie.

**LAWSON, Stephen** **fl 1866**
Musselburgh landscape painter in oil; exhibited RSA(1).

**LAWSON, Stephen** **1942-**
Born Glasgow. Sculptor and photographer. Studied Edinburgh College of Art 1961-7 and, having won the Latimer Award, in Boulder, Colorado 1968-70. Spent the next thirteen years teaching in the U.S. First British solo exhibition 1989. Represented Glasgow AG, SAC.

**LAWSON, T** **fl 1894**
Edinburgh flower painter. Exhibited GI(1) from 13 Moray Place.

**LAWSON, Thomas** **1951-**
Born Glasgow. Stylised painter. Studied University of St Andrews 1969-73 with a postgraduate year at Edinburgh. Migrated to New York 1975, subsequently settled in Los Angeles. Often bases his compositions on childrens' literature and newspaper cuttings; influenced by Pop art. Exhibition Edinburgh 1990. Also writes on art and is involved in mounting exhibitions of modern art.
**Bibl:** Bill Hare, Contemporary Painting in Scotland, Edinburgh 1993.

**LAWSON, William** **fl 1814-1874**
Edinburgh-based painter in oil of landscape, subject paintings, portraits and genre. Married to a painter. Father of Cecil Gordon L(qv) and Francis Wilfred L(qv). Exhibited RA(6) 1819-1863, RSA(41) 1829-1860 & GI(2).
**Bibl:** Caw 313.

**LAWSON, William Rawson** **1900-?**
Edinburgh painter in oil and watercolour, also illustrator. Studied at Edinburgh College of Art and privately under Robert Burns. Painted the reredos in Reid Memorial Church, W Savile Terrace, Edinburgh with 'The Last Supper'. Among his illustrations were those for an edition of *The Ancient Mariner* 1920. Exhibited widely 1920-1935 including RSA(13), RSW(2), GI(1), AAS & L(1).
**Bibl:** Gifford 485.

**LEA, Miss Augusta** **fl 1898**
Amateur Edinburgh topographical artist. Exhibited two Venetian scenes at the GI, from 64 Northumberland St.

**LEADBETTER, Charles** **fl c1854-c1874**
Architect. Probably related to Thomas L(qv). Designed the Curvilinear Gothic Elim Pentecostal Church, George IV Bridge (1859) and Edinburgh Blind Asylum (1874).
**Bibl:** The Building News, Dec, 1874; Gifford 162,598,636.

**LEADBETTER, Miss Kate** **fl 1873-1876**
Edinburgh flower painter in oil; exhibited RSA(7).

**LEADBETTER, Margaret M** **fl 1885-1891**
Edinburgh watercolourist of domestic and figurate subjects. Possibly related to Kate L(qv). Exhibited RSA(8) & GI(2) from 'Waterhouse', Gillsland Road.

**LEADBETTER, Thomas Greenshields** **fl 1885-d1931**
Edinburgh architect and draughtsman. Probably related to Charles L(qv). Partner in the firm of Leadbetter & Fairley later becoming Leadbetter, Fairley and Reid. Exhibited two designs at the RA - Dundhu, Aberfoyle (1890) and Grantully Castle, Perthshire (1892), also at the RSA(18) & GI(18) including Wells, Roxburghshire, 1910 for Sir Robert Usher Bt.
**Bibl:** Gifford 292,533,600.

**LEADBITTER, Margaret Fletcher (née Fletcher)** **fl 1908-1950**
Born Dunans, Argyll. Painter in oil and watercolour of landscapes and figure subjects. Studied London, Paris and Italy. Worked extensively in the Scottish Highlands concentrating on the effects of sunlight and moonlight. Lived in Lancashire, Yorkshire and London, but based mainly at Harrogate. Exhibited RSA(9), RA(1), RCA(2), RHA(1), L(5), GI(1) & London Salon.

**LEADER, Captain** **fl 1876**
Amateur Edinburgh painter. Exhibited a watercolour at the GI from 8 Lennox St.

**LEADER, Violet Eustace V (Mrs Delmege)** **1903-?**
Miniature and landscape painter, born in County Cork, Ireland but lived and worked at Barr's Lodge, Loch Etive, Taynuilt, Argyll. Exhibited RA(1).

**LEASK, Henry** **fl 1883**
Edinburgh painter in oil of rustic scenes; exhibited the study of a byre at the RSA(1) from 6 Summerhall Square.

**LEAT, James H** **fl 1910-1911**
Painter. Exhibited Walker Gallery, Liverpool (4) from a Glasgow address.

**LECKIE, John** **fl 1956-1977**
Lanarkshire painter of portraits, still life, birds and flowers. Lived in Airdrie, before moving to Tarbert, Argyll. Exhibited GI(5).

**LECKIE, John B** **fl 1861-1862**
Amateur Dunbartonshire landscape painter. Exhibited GI(2) from Bonhill.

**LECKIE, Miss Katherine J** **fl 1967**
Amateur St Andrews sculptor. Exhibited GI(1).

**LECKIE, Ronnie** **Cont**
Born Lanarkshire. Studied fine art at Nottingham Univ. Trained in both painting and digital design. Lives and paints on Mull where he also runs his own gallery.

**LECKIE-EWING, J G** **fl 1910-1928**
Watercolour painter. Landscapes including views of St Andrews area, many of the golf course, slightly dull but atmospheric. Exhibited GI(1) from Maxwell Bank, St Andrews.

**LECLAIR, Anne** **fl 1974**
Aberdeen portrait painter. Studied at Gray's School of Art, Aberdeen. Exhibited AAS(1) from 16 Westray Crescent.

**LE CONTE, John** **1816-1877**
Painter and engraver. Watercolour; landscapes, townscapes, especially Edinburgh. Lived and worked in Stockbridge, Edinburgh for most of his life. Pupil and assistant of the engraver, Robert Scott(qv). Thirty watercolours are in the Edinburgh Room or hung in Huntly House, Edinburgh. His engraving of 'Wilkie's Parliament Close' is well known. A prolific worker though many of his sketches were quite minor and not intended for exhibition. Lived at 5 Granville Place, Edinburgh. His work was accurate, colourful and seen together forms an historically important account of how Edinburgh looked in the middle of the last century. He exhibited at the RSA(24). Three of his works are in the NGS, a watercolour of 'The Old Scottish Mint, Cowgate' (1873), 'Edinburgh Castle from the Grassmarket' and 'Greyfriars Churchyard' (1884), also 26 original drawings and a considerable number of engravings are in the City of Edinburgh collection. Represented also in Glasgow AG.
**Bibl:** Brydall 214; Butchart 24,74-5; Halsby 90.

**LEDINGHAM, Miss Margaret** **fl 1902-1910**
Painter in oil of local landscape, miniatures, portraits and east coast harbour scenes. Moved around a good deal, during the nine years she was exhibiting her addresses include Aberdeen, Kincardine O'Neil, Dingwall, and Glasgow. Possibly an art teacher as in 1910 she was at Dingwall Academy. Exhibited AAS(3) & a portrait miniature at the GI.

**LEE, Mrs A H** **fl 1874-1885**
Edinburgh painter in oil of landscape and dead game; exhibited from Blairhall, Fife at the RSA in 1885 and from an Edinburgh address, two works at the RSA in 1874. Other works were exhibited at the RSA from a **Mrs E S Lee** in 1875-78. Whether there were two artists or only one is unclear.

**LEE, Bremner P** **fl 1884**
Landscape painter of local scenery. Exhibited GI(1) from 8 The College, Glasgow.

**LEE, Helen Cecilia** **1951-**
Born Southport, Lancs, 15 Jly. Painter in oil and especially watercolour, charcoal and pastel; illustrator and print maker; figures and semi-abstracts. Educated Morrison's Academy, Crieff 1966-70 and Edinburgh College of Art 1970-75 where she obtained an Andrew Grant scholarship, travelled to Switzerland, Italy and Turkey. RSA student finalist 1975. Settled in Edinburgh exhibiting regularly at the RA, RSA & RSW. 'Lee's free use of realism is heightened with poetry and impelled by a splendid certainty of action'. Held her first one-man show in Crieff 1972.

**LEE, Janet Augusta** **fl 1886-1902**
Edinburgh painter of flowers, figure subjects and portraits. Probably wife of Robert Alleyne L(qv). Exhibited RSA(4), RSW(1), GI(1) & AAS(2), formerly from Duddingston House and later from 54 Northumberland Street.

**LEE, John William** **fl 1883-1887**
Aberdeen painter of portraits, figure studies, genre and landscape in oil. Exhibited RSA(5) & AAS(4) from 2 Hill Street.

**LEE, Joseph Johnson** **1876-1949**
Born Dundee. Artist and author. Studied Slade School and Heatherley's. During WWI he served in the Black Watch before returning to work with the Thomson Publishing Company, Dundee. Published *Tales of Our Town* 1910, *Fra Lippo Lippi* 1914, *Ballads of Battle* 1916, *Work-a-day Warriers* 1917, and *A Captive at Karlsruhe* 1920. Also contributed to *Punch.*
**Bibl:** Houfe.

**LEE, Norman S** **fl 1984**
Amateur painter. Exhibited GI(1) from Latchet, Auchterhouse, by Dundee.

**LEE, Oswin Addison John** **fl 1897-1898**
Edinburgh watercolour painter of sea birds; exhibited RSA(2).

**LEE, Robert Alleyne** **fl 1901-1904**
Edinburgh portrait painter. Probably husband of Janet Augusta L(qv). Exhibited RSA(2) including 'Lord Kinnear' 1904, from 54 Northumberland Street, Edinburgh.

**LEECH, Miss Gwynneth M** **fl 1987-**
Glasgow painter of portraits and conversation pieces. Exhibited GI(5) from 70 Barrington Drive.

**LEECHMAN, James Jr** **fl 1888-1890**
Watercolour painter. Exhibited GI(3) from a Glasgow address.

**LEES, Charles RSA** **1800-1880**
Born Cupar; died Edinburgh, 27 Feb. Painter in oil of portraits, genre

and landscapes. Studied art in Edinburgh where he began his career by teaching drawing, afterwards taking to portraiture in which he had some instruction from Raeburn. Following a six month visit to Rome he returned to Edinburgh where he remained for the rest of his career. After some years of practising, during which he married, he resumed portrait painting and joined the Scottish Academy in 1830 along with the succeeders from the Royal Institution. Fond of open-air sports. In later years he devoted himself more to landscape, chiefly views on the east coast with an occasional portrait and domestic scene. Humour was often apparent in his work and a certain compositional lightness in marked contrast to some of the heavier work of the historical painters working at the same time. 'Skaters at Duddingston Loch' (1854) formed his reputation. Became best known for his skating scenes. Elected RSA 1830, treasurer 1868 until his death. Other famous works are the iconic 'A Grand Match Played over St Andrews Links', with numerous portraits (1865), purchased by the SNPG in 2002 for £2.3M, engraved by Charles Wagstaffe 1850, oil sketches for which hang in the the R &A, St Andrews; and 'Curlers' (1867). Exhibited RA(6) 1841-57 including portraits of 'The Earl of Buchan' and 'The Earl of Leven and Melville' (both 1841) and of 'Cardinal Beato(u)n', 'Archbishop Hamilton of Glasgow and Bishop Gavin Dunbar of Dunblane, with their friends, looking from the battlements of the Castle of St Andrews at the martyrdom of George Wishart' (1857). Exhibited RSA(213), 1822-80 & GI(12). One of his most famous paintings, 'The Grand Match of the Royal Caledonian Curling Club at Linlithgow' (1853) was exhibited posthumously at the RSA in 1880. Represented in NGS, SNPG(4).
**Bibl:** AJ 1880, 172; Robert Browning, History of Golf, London 1955, 55-8; Bryan; Brydall 431-2; Caw 120; DNB XXXII; McKay 223; RSA (Obit).

**LEES, Mrs Helen** **fl 1972**
Ayr landscape painter. Exhibited two Hebridean scenes at the GI from 39 Dalmilling Rd.

**LEES, Mrs Madge M G** **fl 1889**
Painter. Exhibited 'The mid-day meal' at the GI(1) from 113 St George's Road, Glasgow.

**LEGAT, Francis** **1761-1809**
Born Scotland, 8 Mar; died London, 4(or 7) Apr. Painter of figure studies and engraver. Pupil of Andrew Bell(qv) and in 1783 entered the RA Schools after earlier studies in Edinburgh. In 1793 he engraved booklets to the designs of Agnes Berry for Anna Seymour Damer, illustrated in Fincham. After studying in Edinburgh under Alexander Runciman(qv) he went to London 1780 gaining employment with Boydell and other publishers. In recognition of his engraving 'Ophelia before the King and Queen', he was, towards the end of the century, appointed Engraver to the Prince of Wales. Engraved several plates in a very finished style, appearing to have imitated the fine style of Sir Robert Strange(qv). Among his other well-known plates after Boydell, Gavin Hamilton's portrait of 'Mary Queen of Scots', Poussin's 'The Continence of Scipio', Northcote's 'The Children in the Tower' and 'Scene from King Lear' after Barry. In 1796 he exhibited 'A Girl and Pigeons' at the RA and 'Maternal Solitude' in 1800 from 3 Charles Street, by Middlesex Hospital.
**Bibl:** Bryan; Brydall 203; Bushnell; DNB; Waterhouse.

**LEGGAT, James** **fl 1909**
Amateur sculptor of portrait medallions. Exhibited GI(1) from 52 Haughhill Avenue, Ayr.

**LEGGAT, Jeannie** **fl 1902**
Aberdeenshire amateur artist. Exhibited an Aberdeen townscape at the AAS from 259 Union Grove.

**LEGGE, Arthur** **fl 1883**
Amateur Glasgow topographical painter. Exhibited GI(1) from 17 Windsor Circus.

**LEGGETT, Alexander** **c1828-1884**
Painter in oil of genre, often painted fisherfolk with a coarse, rough understanding which reached the human aspect of the work while leaving something to be desired in the scenery. He had a versatile talent; exhibited regularly at the RSA 1848-1876. In 1860 he showed 'Study of a Fishergirl on the East Coast of Scotland' at the RA from 6 Lothian Street, Edinburgh. Exhibited RSA(71) & GI(25).
**Bibl:** AJ 1869, 105.

**LEGGETT, Dora** **fl 1884**
Landscape painter in oil. Probably wife of Alexander L(qv). Exhibited two Perthshire landscapes at the RSA in the above year from 3 King's Place, Leith Walk, Edinburgh.

**LEIPER, William RSA** **1839-1916**
Born Glasgow, 21 May; died Helensburgh, 27 May. Architect and watercolourist. Studied painting in Paris. Apprenticed in Glasgow to Boucher and Cousland(qv) and afterwards studied in London under William White and J L Pearson. Began practising in Glasgow c1865. Success in a competition for the design of Dowanhill Church of Scotland(1865) made him a challenger to Honeyman(qv) as the city's leading Gothic architect. For twenty years 'he was in the vanguard of the Anglo-Japanese manner, working closely in conjunction with the decorative artist Daniel Cottier(qv)' [Gomme & Walker]. Designed many churches but his special strength lay in domestic architecture. His interiors were stamped with such a distinctive personal impress that they were referred to as 'Leiperian'. Won silver medal, Paris Exhibition 1900 for the Sun Insurance office, 147-151 W. George St, Glasgow. Designed what Dunbar describes as one of Glasgow's most extraordinary Victorian buildings, the Italian Gothic extravaganza incorporating polychromatic brickwork, that was a carpet factory built at 62 Templeton St, Glasgow Green, for the Templeton family, Kinlochmoidart House 1885. Moved from a Gothic style toward the Free School approach of Norman Shaw, designing many houses in the Helensburgh area. His watercolours were most often of the West Coast. Exhibited at the RA three designs, one for a house at Killin, Perthshire (1874), an alteration to Earnock, Lanarkshire (1876) and a new staircase for Kelly House (1899). Elected ARSA 1892, RSA 1896. Exhibited 48 designs and drawings 1870-1912 including one or two stained glass designs for the Park Church, Glasgow (1897); also RSW(3), GI(37) & AAS.
**Bibl:** Dunbar 143,154; A Gomme & D Walker, Architecture of Glasgow, London 1987(rev) 294 et passim; Halsby 268; Peter Savage, Lorimer and the Edinburgh Craft Designers, Edinburgh 1980, 79, 166.

**LEISHMAN, Robert RSW** **1916-1989**
Born Inverkeithing, Fife, 30 Oct. Painter in oil, watercolour and gouache; abstract and fantasies. Studied Edinburgh College of Art, 1934-8. Served overseas during WW2 and in 1947 abandoned abstract painting in favour of romantic work, developing a richness in the surface of oil paint to create 'fantasies lit by a source within the canvas itself'. In 1965 he turned increasingly to watercolours, showing the influence of Chagall and Maxwell, and by 1974 was working extensively in both media. "It is the pervasive moods and auras he creates that make Leishman's fantasies palatable; and it is by them that his imagery has become mature in texture and quality; for its actual contents have changed only little over the years...in subtle matters of the presentation and technique he is often entirely convincing and entirely captivating' [Gage]. Elected SSA 1950, resigned 1974, RSW 1970. Held many one-man exhibitions. Represented in Dundee AG, SAC.

**LEITCH, Miss Annie Mary** **fl 1901-1918**
Born Greenock. Landscape painter and teacher. Studied Glasgow School of Art. Lived and worked most of her life in Greenock. Daughter of Daniel Leitch of the local firm J Leitch & Son. Exhibited RSA(1), GI(10) & L(1) from the family home at 1 Finnart Terrace.

**LEITCH, D** **fl 1952-1958**
Glasgow painter in watercolour and pen and wash. Mainly topographical subjects. Exhibited GI(3) from 111 Tantallon Rd.

**LEITCH, Kitty Macdonald** **fl 1916-1921**
Glasgow sculptor, mostly in bronze. Figure studies. Moved to London in the 1920s; exhibited GI(6) from a London address.

**LEITCH, Lilian O** **fl 1938-1939**
Edinburgh painter mainly in watercolour and pencil of flowers and domestic animals. Exhibited RSA(4) from 1 Gordon Terrace.

**LEITCH, Richard Principal** **fl 1840-d1882**
Born Glasgow. Watercolourist. Brother of William Leighton L(qv),

he settled in London where he was a successful drawing master and author of several instructional books. Travelled extensively in Italy and Switzerland, visited Egypt. His watercolour style has been described as heavy, although his best work can be effective. Painted landscapes in a rather formalised manner, using a characteristic grey for all shadows. Sent by *The Illustrated London News* to Italy in 1859 to cover the Franco-Italian War. Published, with J Callow, *Easy Studies in Water-colour Painting* (1881), and contributed to the *ILN* 1847-1861; *Poets of the Nineteenth Century* 1857, *Good Words* 1864, *The Sunday Magazine* 1865, *Idyllic Pictures* 1867 and *The Quiver*. Exhibited RSA(12) 1845-1855. Represented in BM, V & A, Maidstone AG, Newport AG.
**Bibl:** Halsby 268; Houfe, 137 (illus).

**LEITCH, William Leighton RI** **1804-1883**
Born Glasgow, 22 Nov; died St John's Wood, London, 25 Apr. Painter in oil and watercolour; landscapes and figurative subjects. Son of a manufacturer who sent him first to a private school, then to the school of the Highland Society and from there to a lawyer's office. But an early love of art had been fostered by early meetings with Horatio McCulloch and Sir Daniel MacNee. He abandoned the lawyer's office and an attempt at weaving and became a house painter. Married when he was 19, was then employed at the Theatre Royal as a scene painter. In less than a year he went to Cumnock, Ayrshire. In the company of McNee, McCulloch and John Anderson, he was employed decorating snuff boxes. His work attracted the notice of the Marquis of Hastings and Dr Young of Irvine and, armed with a letter from David Roberts, went to London where he was employed at the Queen's Theatre. There he met Clarkson Stanfield, moved to the Pavilion Theatre and was patronised by a wealthy stockbroker, Mr Anderson. Began exhibiting RA 1841 and in 1854, because of ill health, visited Italy for four months with one of his pupils, Sir Coutts Lindsay. Lady Canning, a Lady-in-Waiting to Queen Victoria, asked for instruction from him. The Duchess of Sutherland had acquired a portfolio of his Italian sketches and these were well-received by the Queen. Leitch was at Blair with the Royal party in 1844 although the first session between the Queen and the artist was on 30th September, 1846 when the Queen reported finding him 'a very good simple man'. She told Lady Canning that Leitch was an excellent master whom she recommended whenever she could. Lessons with him continued for almost 20 years. In 1864, after many visits to Balmoral, Osborne and Windsor, he received a Royal annuity and at the studio sale after his death the Queen acquired many more works by her 'kind old drawing master'. His work has been variously received. Brydall considered it characterised by 'a great deal of sweetness and beauty, both in regard to form, colour and sentiment; and while sometimes suggestive of the works of Turner, Robertson, Stanfield, especially the last, have always an individuality of their own'. Armstrong thought him 'seldom brilliant as a colourist, he had a sense of harmony, and few of his drawings lacked the repose it gives'. Martin Hardie found much of Leitch's work superficial and cluttered, 'characterised by thorough observation, nicety of touch, and supreme competence'. Caw concluded that his work, especially its colour, 'is much more varied than that of Thomson, Williams or McCulloch, but at the same time it inclines to be garish and spotty and is not fused and graded in atmosphere'. More recently, Halsby described the work as having 'considerable charm and poetry which, although not totally original, is certainly very individual. His watercolours of the Italian lakes, painted in fresh blues, purples and greens, with sensitively drawn figures and buildings in ochres and reds in the foreground, can be exquisite...he was not insensitive to atmosphere...he captures the damp mists and subtle colours of the Highlands in a watercolour technique which is less incisive and precise than used for the Italian views'. Twelve fine atmospheric sketches of Edinburgh are in the City Public Library, eight of them engraved by J D Harding. Represented in BM, NGS, V & A, Williamson AG (Birkenhead), Cartwright Hall (Bradford), Dundee City AG; Glasgow AG, City of Edinburgh collection.
**Bibl:** Brydall 432-8; Butchart 63,69-71; Caw 155-6; Halsby 75-8 et al; Hardie[SP] 23-4; Irwin 314-316 et al; Andrew MacGregor, Memoir of W L, 1884; Macmillan[SA] 202,226,229; Millar, Queen Victoria's Life in the Scottish Highlands, 1985, passim.

**LEITH, A L** **fl 1882**
Comrie landscape painter; exhibited RSA(1).

**LEITH, Eliza** **fl 1861-1862**
Edinburgh portrait painter in oil; exhibited RSA(2).

**LEITH, James** **fl 1886-1901**
Glasgow-based landscape painter. Exhibited GI(2).

**LEITH SCHOOL OF ART** **1988-**
Founded by Mark(qv) and Lottie Cheverton(qv). An innovative art school housed in the Old Norwegian church, Leith, run by the founders without any additional staff. Students are selected without any formal requirements but on the basis of a portfolio of work and a 'commitment to intensive creative study'. From the beginning classes have been over-subscribed. Two weekly classes and five-day courses, held during the Festival, are open to all. In 1990 about 150 attended. 'The hallmark of the School (is) its concern for people as individuals as well as artists' [*The Times.*]
**Bibl:** The Times, 24 Oct 1991(obit).

**LEITH-HAY, Sir Andrew** **19th Cent**
Amateur Aberdeenshire painter. Author of *Castellated Architecture of Aberdeenshire,* 1849. Represented in the old family home, Leith Hall (NTS).

**LEITH-HAY, Hon Mrs Henrietta (née O'Neill)** **fl 1921-d1965**
Aberdeenshire painter of domestic genre, country scenes and portraits. Exhibited GI(4) & AAS(5) from the family home Leith Hall, Kennethmont. Represented in Leith Hall (NTS).

**LENAGHAN, Brenda RSW** **1941-**
Born Galashiels, 10 May. Attended Glasgow School of Art 1963 gaining diploma in commercial and graphic design. Worked for Bernat Klein as fabric designer in Galashiels 1963-1978. During this time she taught in Glasgow and worked freelance as an illustrator. Won Maud Gemmell Hutchison Award (RSA) 1999, Anne Redpath Award twice, SSWA Award once. Greatly enjoys travel, having visited France, Greece, India, Italy, Nepal, Russia, Scandinavia, Tibet and China. Gains inspiration from the people, colours and mythology of the places she visits. Elected SSWA 1973 serving as a member of council for three years, RSW 1985. Began exhibiting 1974 and has continued to do so at the RA, RSA, RSW, SSWA and GI, lately from 'Clouds', The Green, Tyningham, East Lothian.

**LENNIE, John** **fl 1879-1902**
Edinburgh painter in oil and watercolour; interiors, buildings and castles. Particularly interested in Rosslyn Chapel, parts of which form the subject of many of his exhibits. Exhibited RSA(14), GI(2) & L(1), from 2 Napier Road, Edinburgh.

**LENNOX, Miss Barbara** **fl 1943**
Glasgow weaver. Exhibited GI(1).

**LENNOX, Douglas** **fl 1971-1980**
Ayrshire landscape painter. Exhibited RSA(2) & GI(21) from Kilmarnock.

**LESLIE, Francis** **1833-1894**
Born Glasgow; died Edinburgh. Sculptor. Studied Glasgow School of Art and then in England Street (later to become Haldane Academy). One of her colleagues there was William Simpson(qv). Went to London where she joined John Henry Foley and associated with the sculptor, George Lawson(qv). Invited by George Ewing to return to Glasgow where she completed the statue of Robert Burns now in George Square. Joined the studio of John Mossman(qv) and remained in his employ until the latter's death in 1890. Responsible for many of the statues that came from this studio including those of David Livingstone and Sir John Moore as well as a large number of busts among them Bishop Murdoch in the Pro-Cathedral House, Glasgow. Taught Glasgow School of Art and was an active member of the Glasgow Art Club. Regular exhibitor RSW & GI. Her last exhibit was at the International Exhibition in Glasgow in 1889.

**LESLIE, Frank** **fl 1880-1892**
Painter. Exhibited GI(3) from 180 West Regent Street, Glasgow.

**LESLIE, James** **1801-1889**
Designer and engineer. Trained under William Henry Playfair(qv).

Employed by the Dundee Harbour Board. Engineer-in-charge of Castlehill Reservoir, Edinburgh (1849-50), designed the still surviving lock gates of the Old East Dock, Leith Harbour (1842-4). With John Taylor of London designed the Customs House, Dundee (1842-3), 'the last great neo-Classical building in Dundee, its Palladian composition and Greek detailing hint at the coming of Victorian eclecticism' [Walker & Gauldie].
**Bibl:** Gifford 176n,460; Bruce Walker & W S Gauldie, Architects and Architecture on Tayside, Dundee 1984, 83.

**LESLIE, Jean F D** **fl 1954-1978**
Born Edinburgh. Painter of still life, coastal and continental scenes. Studied at the Grande Chaumière in Paris and Edinburgh School of Art. Married a lawyer. Professional member SSA and SSWA. Exhibited RSA(20) & GI(2).

**LESSELS, James** **fl 1881-1904**
Kirkcudbright painter in oil of rustic scenes and landscapes. Moved to Montrose c1890 and then to Leith in 1903. Exhibited RSA(16). Not to be confused with the minor Edinburgh architect **James LESSELS** fl 1880s (son of John L(qv)).

**LESSELS, John Archibald** **1808-1883**
Edinburgh architect and painter in oil and watercolour; topographic, landscapes, interiors, churches and designer. Partner in the firm of Cousin and Lessels. Architect to the City Improvement Trust in which capacity was involved in the completion of Royal Crescent. Designed Chester St 'a highly successful Victorian-Georgian compromise' [Gifford], the E side (3-21) of Palmerston Place and St Leonard's Hall of Residence (1869-70). Exhibited RSA(40) during the above years, perhaps his best known being a 'View of the Acropolis'/painted from an original sketch - made on the spot by Lt Col Ogilvy McNiven 1861.
**Bibl:** Gifford see index.

**LESSELS, Jay** **fl 1927**
Watercolourist. Exhibited GI(1) from West Kilbride.

**LETHABY, William Richard** **1857-1931**
Architect. Most memorable work was on the island of Hoy. There he was responsible for the substantial enlargement of Melsetter House (1898), the design for Rysa Lodge (and the extension to Hoy Lodge c1900), giving the island what Gifford described as 'three of the best Arts and Crafts houses in Britain'.
**Bibl:** Gifford, H & I, 53,299,309,341-3,pl.94.

**LETHAM, Jane C** **fl 1889**
Amateur Glasgow painter of flowers, fruit and still life. Exhibited GI(2) from Tennant St.

**LETHAM, John B** **fl 1873-1876**
Edinburgh oil painter of landscapes, figurative and literary subjects, interiors. Won Stuart Prize, RSA 1874. Exhibited RSA(7).

**LETHAM, Lady** **fl 1940**
Amateur Edinburgh artist. Exhibited GI from 1a Ramsey Gardens.

**LEVACK, John** **fl 1850-1875**
Portrait painter. His origins are unrecorded and of the various places suggested, Flanders, France and the north of Scotland, the last is probably the most likely. Specialised in individual and group portraits. Three of his works are in Airdrie PL. One portrays a curling scene on Rawyards Loch with many local dignitaries, signed and dated 1857. The second is a large painting of the Rankin Family and, although undated, is probably an earlier work since some of the same figures appear as in the curling picture, but are younger. The third work was painted from a photograph and depicts the two donors of two public fountains in Airdrie, one of them the Lord Provost. A fourth work was described in John McArthur's *New Monkland Parish* 1890. This is the portrait of a local schoolmaster and churchman, 'Rev Hugh Watt', commissioned by his friends and pupils and referred to by a contemporary as 'Mr Levack's chef d'oeuvre'. Levack was active in the public life of Airdrie 1864-1870/1. Governor of Airdrie Poor House and between 1866 and 1879 listed as a shareholder for the building of Airdrie's Public Hall [after John Fox]. Although he does not appear to have exhibited in any of the Academies, he did exhibit works at Suffolk Street, London 1856-7.

**LEVEN, Miss C C** **fl 1854-1882**
Painter in oil of portraits, seascapes, still-life and flowers. Exhibited RSA(8) from Bellevue Crescent and 26 Saxe Coburg Place, Edinburgh.

**LEVEN, Marian RSW** **1944-**
Born Edinburgh. Landscape & portrait painter, mainly in watercolours. Educated Auchtermuchty & Bell-Baxter, Cupar, Fife. Trained at Gray's School of Art 1962-66 after which she taught for several years in Fife schools. Married to Will McLean(qv). Recipient of many awards including Laing landscape prizes 1991 & 1993, May Marshall Brown prize (RSW) 1995, Dundee Open prize 1996, the Mabel Mackinlay award (RGI) 1996 and Noble Grossart Painting prize 1997. Elected RSW 1993, exhibits regularly at RSA, RGI & RSW from 18 Dougall St, Tayport, Fife.

**LEWES, Miss Jane L** **fl 1849**
Edinburgh painter in watercolour of still life; exhibited RSA(2).

**LEWES, Henry (Harry)** **1819-1904**
Edinburgh painter in oil; landscape, many of the Rhine and the fishing coast of the north east, also Fife, Strathspey and Argyll. Exhibited RSA(58).

**LEWES, John** **1830-1838**
Edinburgh landscape painter, most of his subjects being in Perthshire. Exhibited RSA(14).

**LEWIS, Anthea RSW** **1948-**
Painter, mainly in watercolour. Trained Edinburgh School of Art 1966-70. Specialises in delicate paintings of animals, often in a jungle environment, intricately detailed, generally in vivid colour. Lived in Australia for four years. Develops her compositions from photographs, illustrations and visits to zoos. Possesses a firm commitment to conservation. First solo exhibition 1971. Elected RSW 1977. Frequent exhibitor at RSW & GI(2).

**LEWIS, Esther** **fl 1900s**
Marine painter and decorator. Two paintings on tiles depicting shipping on the Clyde and Mersey are in the Café Royal, Edinburgh.

**LEWIS, Henry** **fl 1866-1870**
Edinburgh landscape and topographical painter. Exhibited GI(5), mainly west coast scenes, from Clerk St.

**LEWIS, Norma** **fl 1963**
Glasgow sculptress. Exhibited two figurative studies in terracotta and plaster from 160 Fergus Drive.

**LEWIS, Whyn (Miss)** **1973-**
Born Edinburgh, April 26. Painter. Trained Glasgow School of Art 1991-95. Her first exhibit was accepted at the RSA while still a student. Awards include the Maude Gemmell Hutcheson Prize (RSA) 1994 and again in 1997, John Kinross scholarship (RSA) 1995, Meyer Oppenheim Prize (RSA) 1998.

**LEYDE, Marion E** **fl 1893-1902**
Edinburgh painter in watercolour of landscapes and coastal scenes especially in Banffshire and Fife. Daughter of Otto Theodore L(qv). Exhibited RSA(15) & RSW(3) from 17 St Bernard's Crescent.

**LEYDE, Otto Theodore RSA RSW** **1835-1897**
Born Wehlau, East Prussia; died Edinburgh, 11 Jan. Painter in oil, watercolour and pastel; also engraver, portraits and landscape. Educated in Prussia and at the Royal Academy of Fine Arts, Koenigsberg under Prof Rossenfelder. At the age of 19 he came to Edinburgh where he was employed as a lithographic artist, becoming a naturalised subject. In 1862 he had a studio in Picardy Place in a house which was also the atelier of Hugh Cameron(qv), Keeley Halswelle(qv) and George Hay(qv). Member of a sketching club which, as well as the above three artists, included W F Vallance(qv), Waller Hugh Paton(qv) and Paul Chalmers(qv). He was well favoured with influential sitters including Lady Mackenzie of Coull, Sir James and Lady Matheson of the Lews, two daughters of the Duke of Atholl. A portrait of the 'Master of the Merchant Company, Sir Thomas Boyd', now hangs in the Merchant Hall. He painted children with great sympathy and charm, and older ladies in a gentle way. A man of

quiet good humour and genial disposition and much loved. Began exhibiting RSA 1858 and in London exhibited RA(3) 1877-1888, from 3 Douglas Crescent, Edinburgh. Elected ARSA 1870, RSW 1879, RSA and librarian 1886-96. Exhibited RSA(119), RSW(45), RE(9) & GI(43). Represented in NGS by three works including a scrapbook, also City of Edinburgh collection.
**Bibl:** AJ 1897, iv (obit); Caw 274; Halsby 268; V&A Cat of Engr Brit Port, 1908-25, VI, 515, 645.

**LEYDEN, John Michael** **1908-?**
Born Grangemouth, Stirlingshire, 21 Nov. Draughtsman and cartoonist; watercolour, and monochrome. Educated at Grangemouth High School and St Aloysius College, Glasgow under William Hunter. Also studied art in Durban, at Heatherley's and Central Schools of Arts and Crafts. Held one-man shows in Durban AG and the Natal Society of Artists. The family emigrated to South Africa in 1926; Leyden became apprenticed as a lithographic artist and began drawing for the *Durban Advertiser* 1927 becoming a free lance commercial artist in 1929. His first cartoons appeared in the *Motor Cycle,* London 1930. Visited England in 1933, taking the opportunity to study under Frederick Whiting and Bernard Adams, and etching at the Central London School of Art under W Robins. Returned to South Africa 1937 and a year later joined the *Sunday Tribune* as a cartoonist. In 1939 moved to the *Daily News.* Council Member, South African Society of Artists. Exhibited watercolours, cartoons in the World Cartoon Festival, in Montreal and Johannesburg AG. Acknowledged a profound influential debt to his art master at Grangemouth, James Davie(qv), father of Alan Davie(qv). Regarded as South Africa's leading cartoonist and one of its leading watercolourists. Published 10 books of cartoons, lived in Durban. Represented in Africana Museum, Johannesburg.

**LEYS, Baron Henri** **fl 1866-1872**
Portrait and landscape painter. Lived for some years in Glasgow. Exhibited RSA. In 1866 he exhibited 'Christmas Day at Antwerp during the Spanish Occupation', purchased by John Graham of Skelmorlie Castle, and in 1872 a portrait of 'The Duchess of Parma'.

**LIBERKOWSKA, Miss C A** **fl 1975-1978**
Lanarkshire-based painter. Exhibited GI(3) from East Kilbride.

**LICHTENSTEIN, Georgette** **fl 1889**
Edinburgh based painter of figurative subjects and portraits. Exhibited RSA(2) from 22 India Street.

**LIDDELL, Charles** **fl 1862**
Amateur Glasgow watercolourist. Exhibited a local landscape at the GI from 32 Granville St.

**LIDDELL, Mary Francis** **fl 1892**
Amateur painter. Exhibited GI(1) from Apsley Place, Glasgow.

**LIDDELL, Thomas Hodgson RBA** **1860-1925**
Born Edinburgh. Painter in oil and watercolour of landscapes, continental and Scottish, and figure subjects. Educated Royal High School, Edinburgh and London. Travelled widely, especially in China, bringing back many watercolours sketched there which were displayed in London 1909. Author of *China, its Marvel and Mystery.* He moved around Britain, being resident at various times in Edinburgh, London, St Ives, Pershore and Chepstow. Exhibited RA(24), RSA(17), RBA(46), RI(1), ROI(3), GI(1), L(3) & London Salon(2).

**LIGAT, J** **fl 1888**
Amateur painter. Exhibited GI once from Myrtle Bank, Rutherglen.

**LIGHTBODY, Alex** **fl 1891**
Painter. Exhibited Walker Gallery, Liverpool (1) from Braidwood, Carluke.

**LIGHTBODY, Francis** **fl 1847**
Edinburgh based topographical painter. Exhibited 'Bothwell Castle' at the RSA from Danube Street.

**LIGHTBODY, James A** **fl 1952-1955**
Glasgow based sculptor, often of equestrian subjects. Exhibited RSA(3) GI(4).

**LILLIE ART GALLERY** **1962-**
Founded at Milngavie, Dunbartonshire with a bequest of $23,000 and a collection of paintings from Robert Lillie(qv). The emphasis is strongly on Scottish art of the twentieth century. In addition to over 300 paintings there is a small selection of glass, ceramics and sculpture as well as a growing number of prints and etchings. Three important benefactors have been Professor A L Macfie and his brother Maj-Gen J M Macfie(qv), and Mrs P M Black (who donated 59 working drawings by Joan Eardley).

**LILLIE, Robert** **1867-1949**
Born Edinburgh. Painter of still life and landscapes in watercolour, occasionally in oil; also an etcher. The eldest in a family of nine, he moved to Glasgow when he was five and eventually embarked on a career in banking remaining with the British Linen Bank for 43 years. Attended evening classes at Glasgow School of Art under Fra Newberry and later, until demands at the bank became too severe, he taught at the same evening classes. After retirement in 1925, devoted himself to painting full-time. Founder member of Milngavie Art Club (alongside Mary(qv) and William Armour(qv) inter alia). Bequeathed the bulk of his estate and collection of paintings to found the Lillie AG. Lived at 'Sprouston', Tannock Drive, Milngavie from where he exhibited RA(2), RSA(5), ROI(4), RI(5), GI(21) & L(8). Represented in Lillie AG(Milngavie).

**LINDAL, Miss Ann** **fl 1863**
Greenock painter of flowers; exhibited RSA(1).

**LINDO, Francis (Joseph Beschey)** **1714-fl c1767**
Portrait painter. Although born in Antwerp, he undertook a number of important commissions in Scotland and in spite of so little being known about his life and work, his entry seems justified. A letter of administration granted to his widow on 23 March 1767 describes him as 'Joseph Beschey, otherwise Francis Lindo of Isleworth'. There is a small portrait at Syon and there is also one done by a Beschey who apparently was a younger brother. Two pictures by him are at Pinkie House, Musselburgh, a portrait of 'Lady Hope and her husband' and one of 'Elizabeth Hope'. Several other Scottish portraits of the 1760s are known. These include 'Alexander Gordon, eighth son of the 2nd Earl of Aberdeen' and 'Colonel Cosmo Gordon' (1735-1783), seventh son of the 2nd Earl of Aberdeen.

**LINDSAY, Alister** **1962-**
Born Dundee, Jan 6. Painter, chiefly of landscape often local and Highland scenery although the latter seldom depict specific places. Also paints contemporary Dundee. Trained Duncan of Jordanstone College of Art 1979-83. Since 1992 he has drawn increasing inspiration from the surrealist school. Awards include the Iain Eaddie prize for landscape painting 1983, Elizabeth Greenshields Foundation Scholarship 1990. Began exhibiting SSA 1988 and RSA 1990. Represented in Dundee AG.

**LINDSAY, Lady Blanche (of Balcarres) (née Fitzroy) c1844-1912**
Watercolour painter. Probably her most important contribution to the arts was the establishment, with her husband, Sir Coutts Lindsay, of the Grosvenor Gallery in 1878. A watercolour entitled 'A Poet's Dream', depicting a squirrel eating a nut with flowers in a vase and an apple beside him was illustrated in R Henry's book *A Century Between,* 1937. Exhibited widely, including works at the RSA(2), RI(37), ROI(1), SWA(1), GI(2), L(4) & RHA(1).

**LINDSAY, Sir Coutts Bt RI** **1824-1913**
Painter and watercolourist; portraits, figure studies and landscape. Had a few lessons from Mulready. Friend and pupil of William Leighton Leitch(qv) with whom he visited Rome 1854. Possibly his most important work was the ceiling of a room in Halford House. With his wife, Lady Blanche(qv), he founded the Grosvenor Gallery in 1878. This was the focus of the aesthetic movement, patronised by Burne-Jones and many avant-garde artists, as well as satirised by du Maurier and Gilbert and Sullivan. Their separation in 1890 led to its closure. Lindsay then founded a new gallery. Elected RI 1879. Exhibited RA(9), including his mother, sister, wife and brother, GI(2), ROI(2), RI(5) & L(2).
**Bibl:** Champlin-Perkins, Encyclopedia of Painters 1880 iii; Halle, Notes from a Painter's Life (1909); Halsby 76; Who's Who 1912-14; Virginia Surtees, 'Coutts Lindsay 1824-1913', Michael Russell Publishing 1993.

**LINDSAY, David** **fl 1857**
Edinburgh painter of figurative subjects; exhibited Old Commodore and his pupil at the RSA from South Bridge.

**LINDSAY, Mrs Elsie M** **fl 1947**
Edinburgh painter. Exhibited a watercolour at the GI.

**LINDSAY, G S** **fl 1957-1964**
Glasgow sculptor. Figurative works in plaster and terracotta. Exhibited GI(10) from Lister Rd.

**LINDSAY, George** **fl 1827-1848**
Edinburgh portrait painter, sometimes included animals alongside his sitters; also painted genre and conversation pieces. Seems to have moved around the city a good deal. Among his exhibited works were 'Mrs Nicol of the Theatre Royal, Edinburgh in the character of Tibbie Howison', 1828, and 'Lady Jane Somerset, in the garden of Windsor Castle', 1831.

**LINDSAY, George** **fl 1886**
Dundee watercolour painter of flowers; exhibited RSA(1) from 5 Airlie Terrace.

**LINDSAY, Helen** **fl 1931-1933**
Amateur Glasgow painter; exhibited GI(3).

**LINDSAY, Ian Gordon OBE RSA FRIBA FRIAS FSA(Scot)** **1906-1966**
Born Edinburgh, 29 Jly; died Uphall, West Lothian, 28 Aug. Architect and author. Educated Marlborough and Trinity College, Cambridge. Studied at Cambridge Architectural School and was apprenticed to Reginald Fairlie. He began practising in Edinburgh 1931. Became senior partner in the firm of Ian Lindsay and Partners of Edinburgh. An authority on Georgian architecture, he did much work on old Scottish buildings including Inveraray Castle, Mertoun, Aldie Castle, Pluscarden Priory and the Canongate Church. Perhaps his most famous and important work was on Iona. Designed the plain Georgian Colinton Mains Church (1947), restored part of Canongate Church (1946-54) and Stenhouse mansion, Stenhouser Mill Crescent (1937-9 and 1962-5) - now the Stenhouse Conservation Centre. Member, Historic Buildings Council of Scotland, on the Council of the National Trust for Scotland and the Royal Fine Art Commission for Scotland. His reputation was widespread, he was greatly esteemed in Australia and throughout Scandinavia where he was a recognised authority on traditional north European architecture. Published *Old Edinburgh* (1939), *Georgian Edinburgh* (1948) and *Cathedrals of Scotland.* Lived in West Lothian. Elected ARSA 1947, RSA 1960. Exhibited regularly RSA.
**Bibl:** Colvin; Dunbar 115; Gifford 43,149,276,278,306,509,634.

**LINDSAY, James** **fl 1906**
Glasgow painter, lived latterly at Largs. Exhibited GI(1).

**LINDSAY, Robert** **?-1727**
Scottish portrait painter about whom little is known. Described in contemporary records as a 'painter in Edinburgh'. Painted the portrait of the Edinburgh surgeon, 'Alexander Birnie' (1708-32), and also another Birnie, an Edinburgh advocate, suggesting that he was highly regarded by at least the Birnie family.

**LINDSAY, Steven** **fl 1687-1704**
Painter. Son of John Lindsay, a goldsmith, he was apprenticed to George Porteous the Elder, Herald Painter Burgess of Edinburgh. It is recorded that Lord Kinnaird 'in full satisfaction of all accompts due by the said Noble Lord or his Lady portraits or others' paid £15 to Lindsay on 15 May, 1704.
**Bibl:** Apted 58; SRO Rossie Priory Muniments, GD.48/1069.

**LINDSAY, Thomas** **1882-?**
Animal and life painter, mainly in watercolour; also etcher and photographer. Studied Glasgow School of Art. Exhibited between 1908 and 1948 at the RSA & GI, latterly from Clarkston, near Glasgow.

**LINDSAY, W Caird** **fl 1893-1898**
Painter. Exhibited GI(3) from 5 Glenavon Terrace, Partick.

**LINDSAY, William K** **fl 1936-1939**
Edinburgh landscape painter; exhibited RSA(3) from 17 & 2 Boswell Terrace.

**LINDSAY-WATSON, Mrs Anna Eliza** **1848-1938**
Born Newcastle. Little is known beyond her birthplace and the fact that she was the daughter of Mr J Hedley, a Lord Mayor of that city, and that after a period during which she lived in Leadburn, she eventually settled overseas where she died at an advanced age. Exhibited at the RSA once in 1886 when living at Hawick.

**LINDSLEY, Kathleen** **fl 1985-**
Scottish wood engraver of landscapes in the style of Grinling Gibbings. Member of the Society of Wood Engravers with whom she exhibits annually.

**LINKLATER, Joyce** **fl 1978**
Aberdeen painter of figurative studies. Exhibited AAS(1) from 16 Summerfield Terrace.

**LINLEY, Joseph** **fl 1978-1979**
Glasgow painter. Exhibited GI.

**LINLITHGOW, Doreen Maude, 2nd Marchioness of HRSW (née Milner)** **c1890-1965**
Amateur watercolour painter. Daughter of Sir Frederick Milner, 7th Bt. Married the 2nd Marquis 1911. Accompanied her husband as Vicereine during his Viceroyalty of India 1936-43 and was awarded the Kaisar-i-Hind gold medal. After her husband's death in 1952 she moved to Ham Common, Richmond, Surrey. A drawing entitled 'Morning glory', presented by the artist to the SMAA(qv) in 1964 is now in the collection of the City of Edinburgh.

**LINN, M** **fl 1880**
Amateur flower painter of Pollockshields, Glasgow; exhibited GI(2).

**LINNEN, John** **1802-1888**
Born Greenlaw, Berwickshire; died New York. Portrait painter in oil. Studied RSA School. Emigrated to Toronto 1834. Eighteen of his portraits were included in the exhibition held in Parliament Buildings, Toronto by the Society of Artists. Exhibited again at the Toronto Society of Arts in 1847. Between 1847 and 1860 worked as a successful portrait painter in New York. Exhibited two portraits at the RSA 1830. Represented in Metropolitan Museum, New York.

**LINTON, John** **fl 1941-1953**
Dundee watercolour painter of topographical works. Exhibited GI from Dundee and Carnoustie.

**LINTON, Thomas** **fl 1911-1912**
Painter. Exhibited RSA(2) from 8 Albyn Place, Edinburgh.

**LINTON, Miss Violet** **fl 1931**
Amateur painter. Exhibited AAS.

**LINTOTT, Mrs Audrey** **fl 1933-1940**
Flower painter in watercolours. Wife of Henry Lintott(qv). Exhibited RSA(10) & GI(2).

**LINTOTT, Mrs Edith** **fl 1908-1919**
Painter. Member of the Lintott family of artists. Exhibited RSA(11) & GI(11), from Edinburgh.

**LINTOTT, Henry John RSA** **1878-1965**
Born Brighton. Painter in oil of portraits, figure subjects and landscape, also teacher. After studying in Brighton, London, Paris and Italy, he was appointed to the staff of the Edinburgh College of Art 1902 and remained in that city for the rest of his life. Already well known and respected as a painter, his 'Haymaking in Sussex', shown at the RSA in 1911, achieved ready approval. Became equally known as an inspirational administrator and teacher in the artistic life of Scotland. With David Foggie, Ian Sutherland, Sir William Gillies, Sir William McTaggart, John Maxwell and Ann Redpath, he founded the Edinburgh School. Painted the ceiling of the telling room in the Commercial Bank 1940, altered 1981. Showed regularly RSA(87) from 1905, also RA(13), RSW(3), RI(1), L(25), GI(56) & AAS.

Among his principal works were portraits of 'Lord Constable' (1865-1928) and 'Lord Sands' (1857-1934), both now in Parliament Hall. Represented in City of Edinburgh collection(4).
**Bibl:** Gifford 380n; Halsby 221; Hardie[SP] 37,142; Macmillan[SA] 337,366; RSA Obituary.

**LIPSCOMB, Anna** **fl 1870**
Glasgow painter of rural scenes and conversational pieces. Exhibited GI(3) from 8 Bothwell Place, Hillhead.

**LISTER, William** **fl 1878**
Glasgow painter in watercolour of landscape, especially English rivers. Exhibited RSA(3).

**LITTLE, Edith J** **fl 1881-1888**
Edinburgh watercolour painter of flowers and interiors; exhibited RSA(5) & GI(7) from 34 Palmerston Place.

**LITTLE, Helen** **fl 1905-1910**
Amateur Edinburgh artist. Exhibited RSA(3) from 17 Keir Street.

**LITTLE, Mrs Irene** **fl 1966**
Glasgow painter. Exhibited a watercolour still life at the GI from 35 Buchanan Drive.

**LITTLE, James** **fl 1875-1910**
Edinburgh painter in oil and watercolour of landscapes, townscapes and interiors. Painted in a proficient style, his colours tending towards restrained grey-green tonality. Enjoyed the texture of buildings and the contrasting lines and angles they produced. Exhibited regularly at the RSA(58) & GI(4). Represented in City of Edinburgh collection(4), Brodie Castle (NTS).
**Bibl:** Halsby 268.

**LITTLE, Lawrence S** **fl 1881**
Kirkcaldy landscape painter in oil; exhibited RSA(1).

**LITTLE, R** **fl 1877-1888**
Dunbartonshire painter of genre. Exhibited GI from Delmore, Helensburgh.

**LITTLE, Robert W RWS RSW** **1854-1944**
Born Greenock, 8 Apr; died 18 Oct. Painter in oil and watercolour of landscape, genre, interiors and flowers. Also lithographer. Son of a wealthy shipowner, he was educated at Glasgow University and studied at the RSA Schools 1876-81 before travelling overseas where he worked at the British Academy in Rome in 1882 and under Dagnan-Bouveret and Courtois in Paris (1886). He had travelled with the family as a child and developed a taste for the Mediterranean coastline. His work presents considerable variety, at first studies of interiors and groups of flowers, then Italian subjects - hill towns in Italy - and latterly landscape, all influenced by the pre-Raphaelites. Later he developed a broader, wetter style, with lively rhythms in the clouds and foliage. Caw remarked that his work 'had a certain romanticism of sentiment and a pleasing mingling of decorative quality and of classical balance and restraint in design'. Recently his work has passed into comparative disfavour. Elected RSW 1886 (resigned 1904, re-elected 1910), ARWS 1892, RWS 1899, VPRWS 1913-16 and HRWS 1933. Exhibited regularly at the RSA, RSW, RSW, GI(72) & AAS. Represented in Brodie Castle (NTS).
**Bibl:** Caw 387-8; Halsby 161-2,268; Hardie III 194; Huish 1904; Studio 23 (1901) 48; 41 (1907) 172-180; 55 (1912) 189, 190 (plts); Summer No 1900; Winter No 1917-18, pl x 28.

**LITTLEJOHN, Miss Barbara M** **fl 1964-1965**
Aberdeen enamellist and metalware designer. Exhibited AAS(3) from 9 Hilton Avenue.

**LITTLEJOHN, Henry E** **fl 1901**
Edinburgh painter. Exhibited RSA(1) from 3 Warrander Park Terrace.

**LITTLEJOHN, Robert** **fl 1861**
Glasgow oil painter of literary and figurative subjects. Exhibited RSA(2).

**LITTLEJOHN, Robert** **fl 1921**
Aberdeen painter; exhibited AAS from 19 Westburn Drive.

**LITTLEJOHN, William Hunter RSA RSW RGI** **1929-**
Born Arbroath, 16 Apr. Painter in oil; fantasies and abstract work. Educated Arbroath High School and Dundee College of Art. Won Guthrie Award 1962, David Cargill Award GI 1968. Became Head of Drawing and Painting, Grays School of Art, Aberdeen 1970. Strongly influenced by James Cowie(qv), Ben Nicholson(qv) and Braque. Until 1965, his work was a sensitive, delicate, motionless world of fantasy; thereafter movement and agitation took over 'intuitively dioramic, containing creative ambiguities of location or time, permitting seagulls in the kitchen or crockery on the harbour wall...A hint of expressionist violence allied to a vision which, under highly professional control, comprehends formal and graphic verities in objects ranging from ewers to pelicans' [Felix McCullough]. Lives in Arbroath. Has exhibited regularly RSA & AAS 1959-81. Represented in SNGMA, Aberdeen AG, Arbroath AG, Paisley AG, Abbot Hall AG (Kendal), Towner AG (Eastbourne).

**LITTLETON, Miss Lucy Ann** **fl 1863-1883**
Painter in oil and watercolour of fruit, flowers and still-life. Moved from Greenlaw to Glasgow in 1864, subsequently settled at Chideock, Dorset. Exhibited RSA from 1863, & GI(19).

**LIVESAY, F** **fl 1868-1885**
English landscape painter. Although based in Portsmouth and then the Isle of Wight he was fond of mountain scenery and a frequent visitor to both Scotland and Switzerland. Also painted country scenes and cottage interiors. Exhibited RSA(22).

**LIVESAY, William** **fl 1871-1884**
Painter in oil of landscapes. Living in Edinburgh 1871 at which time he exhibited at the RSA and subsequently moved to Sudbury, Derby from where he exhibited at the London Salon(2) & RE(2).

**LIVINGSTONE, Isobel T** **fl 1905-1907**
Glasgow based amateur painter. Exhibited GI(3) from Westfield, Shawlands.

**LIVINGSTONE, James Robert** **fl 1975-1984**
Aberdeen artist; exhibited mostly landscapes of the north-east at the AAS from 293 Balmoral Gdns.

**LIVINGSTONE, Jessie W S** **fl 1888-1913**
Lanarkshire painter of landscapes and figurative subjects. Exhibited RSA(5) & GI(4) from 17 Hill Street, Wishaw.

**LIVINGSTONE, Jim** **1953-**
Born Busby, Glasgow. Painter in watercolour and large chalk drawings with vivid, confrontational and often disturbing imagery. Trained Gray's School of Art 1972-77. Scottish Young Contemporaries Prize 1982. Clare Henry wrote that he "walks a tightrope between Dali-like Surrealism, religious iconography, and kitch" (Glasgow Herald). Represented in Glasgow AG, Aberdeen AG.

**LIVINGSTONE, John** **fl 1847-c1860**
Clydeside painter of shipping. His oil painting of the iron paddle steamer *'Loch Lomond'*, built for the Dumbarton Steam Ship Company in 1845 by William Denny & Brothers, the first ship they built, signed and dated 1847 was included in the exhibition of the 'Artists on the River Clyde', Helensburgh 1958. This was the first vessel to use a form of mechanical signalling between the bridge and the engine-room, the captain conveying his orders by a knocker which struck the engine-room hatch. An interesting oil by him of the '*Europa*' (built 1848) is in Merseyside Maritime Museum.

**LIVINGSTON(E), Nan C (née Briggs)** **c1876-1952**
Born East Lothian. Painter of landscapes and floral studies in oil and watercolour. Educated privately, studied art in Paris in the 1890s. Although her early work included studies of the Latin Quarter, painted in oil using the palette knife but with a very delicate style, sometimes mistaken for watercolour, all her exhibits were Scottish scenes in and around Edinburgh, also Fife, Dumfries-shire and Perthshire. Member, SSWA. Exhibited RSA(17), RSW(3), L(5), GI(10) & AAS 1929-37 from 3 St Bernard's Crescent, Edinburgh.
**Bibl:** Scotsman (obit 8.8.52).

**LIZARS, Daniel** **1760-1812**
Edinburgh engraver. Father of William Home L(qv) and student of Andrew Bell(qv). Executed a line engraving of Lord Braxfield (the prototype of Weir of Hermiston) after Raeburn. Six of his works are mentioned in the *Edinburgh Scene,* the most important of which is the 'View of the New Bridge of Edinburgh'. Another interesting work is the 'Perspective View of South Bridge Street' and the adjacent buildings according to the intended plan which appeared in the 1786 edition of the *Edinburgh Magazine.* Represented in the City of Edinburgh collection(3), Glasgow AG.
**Bibl:** Bushnell; Butchart 16,18,37; J C Guy, 'Edinburgh Engravers' in the Book of the Old Edinburgh Club, vol 9, 1816.

**LIZARS, William Home ASA** **1788-1859**
Born Edinburgh; died Jedburgh, 30 March. Engraver, painter of portraits and subject pictures. Educated Royal High School and apprenticed to his father, Daniel L(qv) and to John Graham(qv), Master of the Trustees Academy, where for a time he was a fellow pupil with David Wilkie. When his father died, he had to abandon painting to support his mother and her large family, so concentrated on engraving. He constantly experimented with new methods and is said to have perfected an etching process which performed all the functions of wood engraving for book illustrations. A series of 26 plates of natural history, beautifully engraved in colour, is a fine example of this development. The family business, known variously as W & D or W H & D was responsible for many important projects, one of which was a magnificent Design for the National Monument of Scotland according to the plan first conceived by the architect, Andrew Elliot. Lizars was a man of great energy and character and his assistance was sought at the foundation of the Scottish Academy in 1826. From that date until 1830 he was an engraver Associate. McKay wrote of his 'considerable dramatic ability and a keen observation of character, rendered with a touch which, in spite of a thin and precise application of the pigment, admirably suits the purpose. Somewhat wanting in taste, a forcing of the note'. Exhibited two works at the RA in 1812, both of which became well known, 'Reading the Will' and 'Scotch wedding', both now in the NGS. It is interesting to note that these paintings were painted several years before Wilkie repeated them. Together with Andrew Geddes(qv) and John Thompson(qv), he was employed to make pictorial records of the regalia of Scotland, following their discovery in 1818. He acted as host to J J Audubon(qv) during the latter's visit to Edinburgh in 1826 and undertook the engravings of the plates of his *Birds of America.* Represented in NGS(2), SNPG(4), Glasgow AG, City of Edinburgh collection(many).
**Bibl:** Armstrong 20; Brydall 209-211; Butchart 87-8 et al; Halsby 88,111; Irwin 191-2; McKay 157-8; Macmillan[SA] 147-149 et passim; Elizabeth Strong,'W H Lizars, engraver', Scottish Antiquarian Booksellers, Edinburgh, Mar 1989.

**LOCHHEAD, Edwin H** **fl 1931-1935**
Painter. Exhibited GI(2) from 29 Havelock Street, Glasgow.

**LOCHHEAD, Gordon** **1950-**
Born Keith, Banffshire. Education Gordonstoun School, 1963-7 and Essex University where he graduated in physics 1970. Then enrolled as a part-time student at Bath Academy of Arts 1972-5 having various occupations including teaching until 1986. Since then has been a full-time artist-craftsman, combining sculpture with jewellery and foundry work. He recognises many influences, including those of Cellini, Mailot, Huggins, Hepworth and Ayrton. His commissions include work for various Scottish regimental museums, including the Museum of the Royal Scots in Edinburgh Castle. Also for a number of churches, among them St Boswell's Parish Church in the Borders. Exhibited regularly at the RSA since 1987, also GI & SSA.

**LOCHHEAD, James** **fl 1891**
Amateur Glasgow painter. Exhibited a Highland landscape in watercolour at the RGI from St. Vincent Crescent.

**LOCHHEAD, John RBA** **1866-1921**
Born Glasgow; died Glasgow. Painter of landscapes, portraits and still-life. Studied art at the Life School in Edinburgh. Was for a time connected with the Craigmills School, near Stirling. Travelled extensively abroad, especially Belgium, France, Holland and Switzerland. Lived at Kilbride, Ayrshire before moving to Glasgow. His best known works include 'Summertime in the Fenn Country', 'The Evening Hour', 'Country Contempt' and 'Decking the May Queen'. Elected RBA 1911. Exhibited RA(3) 1895 and 1902, also RSA(77), RSW(5), ROI(1), RBA(56), GI(75) & AAS (1906-12). Represented in Glasgow AG.
**Bibl:** Caw 389; Halsby 268.

**LOCHHEAD, Malcolm** **fl 1974**
Glasgow embroiderer. Exhibited GI(1) from 17 Dowanside Rd.

**LOCHHEAD, Mary (née MacNee)** **fl 1894-1901**
Edinburgh-based painter in oil of English rustic scenes. Daughter of Sir Daniel M(qv). Associated with Craigmill, Stirling(qv). Moved c1900 to West Kilbride. Wife of John L(qv). Exhibited RSA(3) & GI(2).

**LOCK (or LOCH), James** **1774-1828**
Scottish portrait painter. Little is known of his work. In 1812 he sailed to India with permission to set up in Calcutta as a portrait painter, but he landed in Madras. For the next four years he was working in that city before moving to Calcutta where he remained until 1823. He then moved to Murshidabad and finally to Lucknow in 1825 where he entered the employment of the King of Oudh. Died Lucknow after a painful illness on March 12.
**Bibl:** Walpole Soc xix, 57-58.

**LOCKE, Miss Mabel Renée** **1882-1959**
Born Selkirk. Sculptress, painter and pencil artist; portraiture and figurative studies. Began to learn sculpture at the age of 9 under Frank Wood at the Buccleuch Memorial school, Hawick and later studied at Heatherley's, London, and St John's Wood Art College. Worked with a stone mason before joining Rowand Anderson as an assistant on bronze and silver work. Also worked with Robert Lorimer(qv). Founder member, SSWA. Responsible for font in Colinton church. Some models were reproduced by the Royal Crown Derby porcelain factory. Most of her exhibits were portrait busts in bronze including Sir James Caird Bt, 1924 (the model for the bronze now in the Caird Hall), and in 1936 a bust of The Rt Hon the Earl of Home. Lived latterly in Hawick. Exhibited RSA(16), RSW(1), GI(20), AAS & L(3).

**LOCKERBIE, Ethel** **fl 1913-1914**
Glasgow portrait miniaturist. Exhibited GI(2) from 13 Windsor Terrace.

**LOCKHART, A M** **fl 1891**
Edinburgh flower painter. Exhibited RSA(2) from 9 Chamberlain Road.

**LOCKHART, David RSW** **1922-**
Born Leven, Fife, 4 Nov. Worked in watercolour, oil, acrylic and ink. Son of an unemployed miner, educated at Beith High School and Edinburgh College of Art. Lockhart always remained very close to West Fife and the area around Cowdenbeath. Began as an illustrator, but with the help of Robert Leishman, turned his attention increasingly to oils. Influenced by John Maxwell(qv), James Cowie(qv) and James Cumming(qv). Particularly concerned with the need for a good volume of output for which he used screens, templates, rags, rollers and nozzles screwed to paint tubes. Most of his work centred upon literary or narrative sources with a ground swell of nostalgia. The colours are subdued. He disavowed the use of the term style, preferring to use idiom which changed according to the discovery of new media to work with, eg waterproof ink. Exhibited RSW, winning an award there in 1984, also GI 1975.

**LOCKHART, John** **fl 1881-1884**
Glasgow watercolour painter of portraits; exhibited RSA(3) & GI(1).

**LOCKHART, John Harold Bruce** **1889-1956**
Born Beith, Ayrshire. Watercolour landscape painter, schoolmaster and sportsman who became Headmaster of Sedbergh after a spell at Rugby School. Proficient watercolourist, his subjects often relate to the many visits he made overseas. Exhibited RA(1), RSA(3), RSW(7), RI(2) & GI(2).
**Bibl:** Halsby 268.

**LOCKHART, W M** **fl c1870-1912**
Glasgow ecclesiastical and topographical artist. Student of Thomas Fairburn(qv). Exhibited GI(7) from 151 Sword Street.

**LOCKHART, William Ewart RSA ARWS RSW RE** **1846-1900**
Born Eaglesfield, nr Annan, Dumfries-shire; died London, 9 Feb. Painter in oil and watercolour of genre, landscape, Spanish subjects, Scottish historical scenes and portraits. Son of a smallholder who sent his son, at the age of 15, to study art in Edinburgh under John Blake McDonald(qv). In 1863 Lockhart went to Australia for his health and on his return in 1867 settled in Edinburgh. Greatly affected by John Phillip's later pictures resulting in the first of a number of journeys to Spain. There he found material for some of his finest works marked by the strength of their execution and the brilliance of their colour. Also found subjects in the literature and romantic history of Spain, illustrating several incidents in *Don Quixote* and *Gil Blas* and the story of the Cid. He also enjoyed east coast fishing villages in which he was influenced by Sam Bough. In 1887 Queen Victoria selected Lockhart to paint 'The Jubilee Celebrations in Westminster Abbey'. Generally, it may be said that his watercolours were more effective than his oils. 'In oil he was apt to forget that there is a strength of delicacy as well as of power and erred in over-emphasis both of handling and of colour, which he employed too often in separate masses unrelated by a sense of decorative design'. Elected ARSA 1871, RSA 1878, RSW 1878, ARWS, 1878, RE 1881, RP 1897. Exhibited AAS 1890-96, also GI(32). Represented in NGS by 'Gil Blas' and the 'Archbishop of Granada' (1878), also Aberdeen AG, Broughty Ferry AG, Glasgow AG, Kirkcaldy, Paisley AG, Perth AG (El Cid), Windsor AG, Victoria AG (Australia).
**Bibl:** Armstrong 83; Bryan; Caw 264-6; Cundall; Halsby 65-6 et al; Hardie iii 174, 190; Irwin 323; McKay 359; Portfolio 1878, 84, 132, 148, 164, 193; 1883, 226; 1887, 228; RA Pictures 1891-6; Peter Savage, Lorimer and the Edinburgh Craft Designers, Edinburgh 1980, 61,166.

**LOCKWOOD, Lucy** **fl 1927**
Melrose painter. Exhibited a view of her garden at the RSA from The Priory.

**LOCKWOOD, Maurice A** **fl 1948-1959**
Glasgow sculptor. Exhibited figurative works, mostly in wood and occasionally in Portland stone. Exhibited GI(9) from Burnside, Rutherglen.

**LOCKWOOD, Percy F** **fl 1946-1959**
Glasgow topographical and flower painter. Exhibited GI(7) from 71 Croftside Ave.

**LODDER, Charles, Jnr** **fl 1876-1902**
Edinburgh painter in watercolour of seascapes, coastal scenes and landscapes, especially of the north east. Son of Capt Charles L(qv). Painted in a similar rather dour style to his father. Exhibited RSA(24) including several scenes of Arran, also RSW(1), GI(21), AAS(10), & RHA(2).

**LODDER, Captain Charles Arthur RN** **fl 1860-1885**
Painter in oil and watercolour of sea pieces, coastal scenes and landscape. Father of Charles L(qv). He painted marine subjects with all the knowledge of his professional career as a sailor. Favoured a subdued palette, sometimes very dark. Lived for a time in Edinburgh where he became friendly with Sam Bough(qv), and in 1863 was living at Borrowstone House, Kincardine O'Neil, before moving to Largs. Exhibited RSA(78), also RHA(9), RBA(2), GI(14) & L(2).

**LODGE, Joan O** **fl 1930**
Sculptress. Exhibited a portrait bust at the GI from Glasgow School of Art.

**LOGAN, David** **fl 1790-1815**
Architect of Montrose in the neo-Classical tradition. Best known for his design for Montrose Academy, Angus, completed in 1815, pre-dating Playfair's Academy and Angus's Dundee HS. Also designed the Auld Kirk, Montrose (1791), the original tower replaced 1834, Forfar Academy (1815) and the Town House, Arbroath (1803).
**Bibl:** Bruce Walker & W S Gauldie, Architects and Architecture on Tayside, Dundee 1984, 80,85.

**LOGAN, Mrs Ethel** **fl 1929-1932**
Scottish printmaker. Exhibited GI(2) from 65 Castle Street, Edinburgh.

**LOGAN, Miss E A** **fl 1866-1868**
Duddingston painter in oil of figures, landscapes and children. Daughter of R F Logan(qv). Exhibited RSA(4).

**LOGAN, George B** **fl 1898-1904**
Lived in Greenock. Well known designer of furniture and interiors for Wylie and Lochhead, also a competent watercolour painter of interiors. A number of his decorative schemes were reproduced in magazines including *The Studio*. Exhibited several times at the GI.
**Bibl:** Halsby 188,268.

**LOGAN, Miss Isa E** **fl 1939**
Amateur Glasgow watercolourist. Exhibited 'Gairloch' at the GI from Giffnock.

**LOGAN, J** **fl 1821**
Sculptor. Exhibited at the RA 'A Sculptured Stone in Aberdeenshire' from 62 Union Street, Aberdeen.

**LOGAN, James G** **fl 1968-1971**
Ayrshire sculptor. Religious groups, birds; usually worked with driftwood. Exhibited GI(4) from Tullochgorm, Caldwell Rd, West Kilbride.

**LOGAN, John Garth** **1877-?**
Aberdeen landscape painter, sculptor and commercial artist. Studied Gray's School of Art, Aberdeen. Exhibited RSA 1922 & AAS - mostly farming scenes - 1912-26, latterly from 52 King's Gate.

**LOGAN, Robert Francis** **fl 1864-1885**
Duddingston painter in oil and watercolour of marines, wildlife, fish and landscape. Father of Miss E A Logan(qv). One of several painters who had a studio at 4 Picardy Place, Edinburgh. Exhibited regularly RSA(41), GI(2) & RI.

**LOGAN, Thomas** **fl 1893-1906**
Painter. Exhibited two sttudies of heads at the GI from Glasgow.

**LOGAN, Thomas T** **fl 1843**
Glasgow painter of local landscapes and topographical subjects. Often painted old mills. Exhibited RSA(3).

**LOGAN, William** **fl 1894-1896**
Watercolour painter; exhibited RSW(1) & GI(1) from 327 St Vincent Street, Glasgow.

**LOGAN, William P** **fl 1922**
Edinburgh painter. Exhibited 'Zoo sketches' at the RSA from 4 Canaan Lane.

**LOGGAN, David** **1635-1692**
Born Danzig; died London. Miniature painter and engraver. Of direct Scottish descent. This spelling is an old form of Logan the main branch of the family coming from Ayrshire. One of the finest miniature painters working in plumbago. Studied under the engraver W Hondius and later with Crispin van der Pass in Amsterdam, where he lived for seven years before moving to London, becoming much influenced by Hollar. In 1662 Loggan was employed by the King's Printers to engrave the title page for the *Book of Common Prayer.* Apart from a short visit to Paris with his pupil Edward Le Davis, where he may have met the French plumbago painter Nanteuil, Loggan remained working in London. Because of the plague he moved to Nuffield, near Oxford, in 1665. The wisdom of the change was confirmed when in 1669 he was appointed Public Sculptor to the university. Not to be outdone, Cambridge University appointed Loggan its engraver in 1690. During this period Loggan completed the two works for which he has become best known, *Oxonia Illustrata* in 1675 and *Cantabrigia Illustrata* c1676-1690. The former incorporated a set of eleven plates entitled 'Habitus Academicorum Oxoniae a Doctore usque ad Servientem' which form a distinct set of costume plates. Also a teacher, among his pupils being Robert Shepherd, Michael Bandergucht and Robert White, the last becoming

at least the equal of his master. Naturalised 1775. His portraits are magnificently drawn and beautifully expressive, often with a buff or yellowish tinge, of which the principal are 'Charles I on horseback', 'Queen Henrietta Maria', 'Charles II' (4 plates), 'Queen Catharine of Braganza', 'James, Duke of York', 'George Monck', 'Lord Justice Coke', 'The Earl of Clarendon', 'The Earl of Derby', 'James Duke of Monmouth', 'Archbishop Sancroft', 'Pope Innocent XI', 'Archbishop Laud' and 'Archibald, Earl of Argyll'. His work is signed sometimes 'DL', or sometimes 'DL del' and occasionally 'D Loggan'. Represented in the V & A(5, including 'Cardinal Mazarin'), BM(8), including a portrait of 'Charles II', NPG, SNPG, Ashmolean (Oxford); Huntingdon Library, California (including a wonderfully detailed drawing of an unknown lady, illustrated Foskett, 29A, p134).
**Bibl:** Bryan; Conn XXXIV, 1912, 3; DNB; Foskett 134-6; Irwin 211; Long 277-8; Walpole Society Annual XIV, 55-64.

**LOGIE, Donald R** **fl 1967**
Designer of stoneware and pottery. Exhibited AAS(2) from Wellbrae, Errol.

**LOGIE, Harrison** **fl 1919-1923**
Amateur Glasgow painter; exhibited GI(2) from 100 St John Street, Craighall Rd.

**LOGIN, Helen M** **fl 1891-1905**
Edinburgh painter of flowers, buildings and portraits; exhibited RSA(7).

**LOND, William Turner de** **fl c1822-1830**
The identity of this artist remained long unclear until a letter published in *The Connoisseur* (1906) from a Douglas A Seton Stewart reported that 'William Turner 'de Lond' was employed by Sir Henry Stewart of Allanton to illustrate a book which he published in 1827, and while at Allanton he gave drawing lessons to Sir Henry's daughter. He was probably a drawing master who came to settle in Edinburgh or at any rate in Scotland not later than 1822'. Turner de Lond's best known watercolours of the Great Fire of 1824 were lithographed by Robertson and Ballantine. Six noteworthy drawings were 'Part of the Ruins of the Great Fire, Edinburgh, as seen from the Door of the Police Office'; 'A View of the Great Fire at Edinburgh 1824'; the 'Great Conflagration - Edinburgh as seen from Calton Hill'; 'Conflagration of Tron Church, Edinburgh, 16th November, 1824'; 'A View of the Great Fire and Parliament Square, Edinburgh'; 'Part of the ruins of the Great Fire from the High Street'. He did a further set of published drawings entitled *Scotia Delineata.* Another famous aquatint, engraved by Lizars, illustrated 'The Arrival of George IV at the Palace of Holyrood, 1822'. This work, dedicated to the Lord Provost, includes elegantly and colourfully dressed ladies, bringing a colour and warmth to the scene that is unusual in topographical works of this period.
**Bibl:** Butchart 60-2,88.

**LONG, Jessie M** **fl 1883**
Amateur Renfrewshire painter of still life and flowers. Exhibited GI from Royal Bank House, Port Glasgow.

**LONG, John O RSW** **?-1882**
Edinburgh painter in oil and watercolour of landscape. Moved to London c1860, continuing to paint Highland landscapes including popular views of Arran and Skye. Elected RSW 1878. Exhibited RSA(9), GI(2) & more regularly RSW.
**Bibl:** Halsby 268.

**LONG, Rosemary Ann** **fl 1976-1988**
Kincardineshire animal painter, especially of cats. Trained Gray's School of Art, Aberdeen. Exhibited AAS between the above years from 21 Marine Terrace, Muchalls.

**LONGDEN, Alfred A** **fl 1901-1908**
Landscape painter & etcher; exhibition organiser and lecturer. Specialised in atmospheric effects, painted some New Zealand scenes. Studied Royal College of Art and moved north to Aberdeen c1908. First exhibited work at the RA was 'A Steep Side of Ben Lomond' (1901). Exhibited RA(2), AAS(5) & RI(2), latterly from 16 Albyn Place.

**LONGDEN, John** **fl 1926-1929**
Glasgow sculptor. Exhibited RA(2), RI(2) & GI(2) from Drumry Road, Clydebank.

**LONGFIELD, T** **fl 1902**
Amateur Ayrshire landscape watercolourist. Exhibited GI(1) from Mauchline.

**LONGLAND, Mrs Helen** **fl 1974-1981**
Glasgow painter of flowers and woodland scenes. Exhibited GI(8) from 11 Campbell Drive, Bearsden.

**LONGMUIR, A D** **l 1864-1886**
Edinburgh painter and etcher in oil and watercolour, also teacher; landscapes and figurative subjects. Art master at King's School, Sherborne, Dorset 1872. Exhibited RSA(17), RE(2), GI(2) & AAS.

**LONIE, Alexander S** **fl 1906-1910**
Aberdeen sculptor; exhibited RSA(1) & AAS(3) from 21 Adelphi & latterly 25 Union Terrace.

**LORIMER, Ann D** **fl 1901-1907**
Edinburgh portrait painter. Exhibited RSA(3).

**LORIMER, Freida** **fl 1929-1930**
Amateur Edinburgh painter. Exhib GI(2) from 22 Great King Street.

**LORIMER, Miss Hannah Cassels** **1854-1876**
Edinburgh painter in watercolour of still-life and wild flowers; modeller and wood carver. Daughter of James L(qv), sister of Janet Alice L(qv) and John Henry L(qv). Married the Governor-General of Fiji, Sir E. im Thurm. Exhibited RSA(4) & GI(5).

**LORIMER, Henry** **fl 1890**
Amateur Glasgow landscape painter. Exhibited GI(1) from Lariotlea, Cathcart.

**LORIMER, Hew Martin CBE RSA FRBS** **1907-1993**
Born Edinburgh, 22 May; died St Andrews, 1 Sep. Architectural sculptor in stone. Second son of the architect Sir Robert Lorimer(qv). Educated Loretto School, Magdalene College, Oxford. Initially went on to study architecture but changed to sculpture at Edinburgh College of Art under Carrick. Awarded Andrew Grant Scholarship 1933 and a travelling scholarship 1934-5 enabling him to visit France, Italy and Sicily. Returned to Edinburgh following a spell with Eric Gill at Piggotts. Gill introduced him to the writings of Ananda Coomeraswami. From this association sprang the belief that artistic endeavour is part of God's continuing act of creation, a notion which remained with Lorimer in all his work. A tour of Romanesque French churches and the purchase by the NGS of Bourdelle's 'Vierge d'Alsace' inspired him to produce the columnar 'Mother and Child' 1931-46, a concept from which grew the impressive granite statue of Our Lady of the Isles on the island of South Uist which stands 27' high in which he was assisted by Maxwell Allan. Appointed sculptor in charge of carvings on the National Library of Scotland, he himself designing and sculpting the seven allegorical figures. Always worked from his own designs and always carved direct without using scale models in clay nor ever using a painting machine to make enlargements. Among a number of religious works completed during the 1930s are 'The Crucifixion' for the Dawson Burial Chapel, Fochabers, 'Our Lady Star of the Sea' for Tayport and four saints for the Reredos in St Margaret's Church, Dunfermline. An intensely serious artist of graciousness and warmth. Elected ARSA 1946, RSA 1957, Knight of the Order of St. Gregory. His work is usually unsigned. Lived at Kellie Castle, Pittenweem, Fife for many years. Exhibited regularly RSA & GI.
**Bibl:** Crawford Art Centre, St. Andrews, 'The Lorimers', (Ex Cat 1983, Text by Hew Lorimer); Hartley 142; Macmillan[SA] 331; Talbot Rice Art Centre, Edinburgh, 'Hew Lorimer Sculptor', (Ex Cat 1988, text by Duncan Macmillan); The Scotsman, 'Joy of Expression in Stone', D. Macmillan (obit), 4 Sep 1993.

**LORIMER, Janet Alice** **1857-?**
Embroiderer. Daughter of James L(qv), sister of Hannah, John and Robert. Married Sir David Chalmers.
**Bibl:** Peter Savage, Lorimer and the Edinburgh Craft Designers, Edinburgh 1980, 166.

**LORIMER, John Henry RSA RSW RWS RP** **1856-1936**
Born Edinburgh, 12 Aug; died Pittenweem, 4 Nov. Painter of portraits and contemporary genre in oil and watercolour. Son of Prof James Lorimer and brother of the architect, Sir Robert Lorimer(qv). Studied at Edinburgh University, RSA under McTaggart(qv) and Chalmers(qv), and in Paris under Carolus Duran 1884. Travelled in Spain 1877, Italy 1882 and Algiers 1891, also in the low countries. In early career he concentrated on portraiture and flower painting and was especially concerned with the study of tone. His first exhibit 'Wintry Gloamin' was at the RSA 1873; two years later a portrait of his mother at the RSA was highly praised. In 1879 a portrait of his father was hung on the line at the RA and received the praise of J E Millais and Sir Frederick Leighton. Finding himself suddenly famous he quickly became a member of the London artistic élite and by 1880 commissions began to pour in. Ninety portraits have been identified most of them having disappeared into private collections. Commissions were received from the Duke of Montrose, the 13th Duke of Hamilton, Sir David Chalmers, Lord Fraser and Lord Playfair. Later he was to win distinction as a painter of contemporary genre - mainly scenes of Scottish middle-class home life, for example, 'Winding Wool' 1890, 'Grandmother's Birthday - Saying Grace' 1893 and 'The Flight of the Swallows' 1907. 'The Ordination of the Elders in a Scottish Kirk' 1891, called by Caw 'one of the most national pictures ever painted'. Was much concerned with the effect of light and his interiors especially are luminous and transparent. Many of his garden scenes and interiors were modelled on views around his home, Kellie Castle. Liked to imagine scenes where he could place several figures involved in some action with an audacious mingling of light from different sources. This daring treatment is shown particularly in 'The White Lady', 'Our Lady Star of the Sea' and 'Summer Twilight' (Kirkcaldy AG). His 'The Eleventh Hour' hung on the line at the RA 1894 and taken to Windsor to be inspected by Queen Victoria; re-titled, 'Marriage de Convenance', the picture won the gold medal in Paris 1900 and was subsequently purchased by Philadelphia AG and is now in the Kende Gallery, New York. His 'Lullabye' also won a gold medal in Paris, this time the purchaser being the Australian Government buying for the Victoria National Gallery, Melbourne. 'Twilight', re-christened 'Le Benedicte', has been on loan to the Louvre. In addition to his other honours was corresponding member to the Institut de France but refused the Legion d'Honneur under foreign office rules forbidding acceptance of foreign decoration for services in the domain of art. His work was popular in France and in exhibitions abroad he came to be associated with the Glasgow School though he in fact was not a full member. Writing in the *AJ,* Caw observed 'while in his subject pictures, usually charming interiors with figures, he is perhaps too closely bound by what is before him, and never lets himself go, and in portraiture he retains that primary interest in character, which was the chief concern of the older school, his technical equipment is, of its kind, remarkably complete, his observation is acute, colour often delicately harmonious, his sentiment always refined'. Painted over 70 portraits and lived at Kellie Castle for 60 years. Regular exhibitor at the Paris Salon between 1880 and 1914. French critics were particularly appreciative of his paintings of landscapes and of his daring use of light from different sources. Awarded several gold medals and elected to the French Institute. In his watercolours we see much use of grey, white and cream with occasional touches of stronger colour to set off the composition. His portrait of 'Sir Robert Lorimer ARA, as a boy' 1875, was purchased by the Chantrey Bequest in 1930. Elected ARSA 1882, RSW 1885, ROI 1890, RP 1892, RSA 1900, ARWS 1908, RWS 1934. Resigned from the Academy 1921. Exhibited RA (43), RSA(123), RWS(88), RSW(33), RHA(2), RI(2), ROI(8), GI(59), AAS (1894-1929) & L(32). Seven of his portraits are in the SNPG, including one of James Lorimer and another of Sir William Quiller Orchardson; a series of studies for 'The Ordination of the Elders' is in NGS, also in Dundee AG, Glasgow AG, Kirkcaldy AG, City of Edinburgh collection.
**Bibl:** AJ 1893, 308; 1895, 321-4; 1908, 93,127; Caw 420-3; Dayot, Le Peinture Anglaise 1908, 275, 281 ff; Halsby 268; Macmillan[SA] 258; Portfolio, 1893, 104, 118, 153; Peter Savage, Lorimer and the Edinburgh Craft Designers, Edinburgh 1980; Studio: 34, 270; 45, 1909; 68,125.

**LORIMER, Miss Mary McLeod** **fl 1945-1953**
Fife painter of portraits and coastal scenes. Daughter of Hew Martin L(qv). Exhibited RSA from Kellie Castle, Pittenweem.

**LORIMER, Sir Robert Stodart ARA RSA** **1864-1929**
Born Edinburgh, 4 Nov; died Edinburgh, 13 Sep. Architect and occasional painter in oil and watercolour, pencil. Educated Edinburgh Academy and University. Articled to the Edinburgh architect Sir R R Anderson(qv) 1885-9. Came to London 1890. Worked in the office of G F Bodley for 18 months and then returned to Scotland to undertake the restoration of Earlshall, Leuchars, Fife (1892). Settled in Edinburgh and Kilconquhar, Fife. The principal source of inspiration was Scottish domestic architecture of the 16th and 17th centuries. First came to public notice with the building of the Thistle Chapel, an addition to St Giles Cathedral. Connected with work on cemeteries in Italy, Egypt and Macedonia as well as in Great Britain. Between 1903 and 1928 did a considerable amount of work in Tayside. Walker & Gauldie list the main examples as: Hallyburton, Perthshire (1903-6); Barguillean, Taynuilt, Perthshire (1906-8); Hill of Tarvit, Cupar, Fife (1907-8); St Andrews University Library (1907-9); Woodhill, Barry, Angus (1908-9); reconstruction at Monzie Castle, Perthshire (1908-12); Balmanno Castle, Perthshire (1916-21); alterations to Blair Castle, Perthshire (1920-1); Kinloch House, Collessie, Fife (1921-3); Drumkilbo, Meigle, Perthshire (1920-2); St Andrews War Memorial (1922); restoration of St. John's church, Perth (1923-8) and the interesting Kinfauns Castle Dairy, Perthshire (1928). President, Royal Scottish Incorporation of Architects. Elected ARSA 1903, knighted 1911, ARA 1920, RSA 1921. Exhibited frequently RA & RSA, also RWS(1), GI(16) & L(4). Represented by a small oil painting and many sketches at Kellie Castle (NTS).
**Bibl:** Frank Deas, 'Review of Lorimer's work', RIBA Journal 21.2.31 & 7.3.31; Ian Gow,'The Scottish National War Memorial', in 'Virtue and Vision', NGS (Ex Cat 1991); Gifford see index; Christopher Hussey, The work of Sir Robert Lorimer, 1931; Peter Savage, Lorimer and the Edinburgh Craft Designers, Edinburgh 1980 (contains list of works revised post Hussey); L.G. Thomson,'Review of Lorimer's work', RIAS Quarterly, Autumn 1929; Bruce Walker & W W Gauldie, Architects and Architecture on Tayside, Dundee 1984, 157-161.

**LORNE, Marchioness of** **[see Louise, HRH Princess]**

**LORNE, The Marquess of (later 9th Duke of Argyll)** **1845-1914**
Born 6 Aug; died 2 May. Amateur artist and illustrator. Eldest son of George, 8th Duke of Argyll. Educated Eton and Trinity College, Cambridge. In 1868 elected MP for Argyllshire and in 1871 married HRH Princess Louise(qv), fourth daughter of Queen Victoria. From 1878-83 Governor-General of Canada and MP for South Manchester 1895. Published a number of books including *Canadian Pictures* 1885, and contributed illustrations for *The Graphic* in 1883. Also illustrated *Guido & Lita, A Tale of the Riviera* (1873).
**Bibl:** Houfe 213.

**LOTHIAN, George** **fl 1840-1842**
Edinburgh landscape painter. Exhibited mainly scenes in the Falkirk/ Linlithgow/Stirling area at the RSA(8).

**LOTHIAN, Maurice** **fl 1793**
Edinburgh seal engraver. Married in 1793 and the same year was known to be working in Lady Yester's Parish.

**LOUDAN, William Mouat** **1868-1925**
Born London. Painter of genre and portraits, illustrator. His parents were both Scottish. Educated Dulwich College before attending the RA Schools for four years, winning a travelling scholarship. In Paris he undertook further studies under Bouguereau. Elected NEA 1886, RP 1891. Although in later life he devoted himself entirely to portraiture he contributed regularly to the *ILN* 1889-1894. Exhibited GI(22). Represented in V & A, Leeds AG and Walker Gallery, Liverpool.
**Bibl:** The Artist, 1899, 57-63, illus; Houfe.

**LOUDEN, Robert** **fl 1980-1983**
Midlothian landscape painter. Exhibited five seasonal scenes at the GI from 97 Forthview Crescent, Currie.

**LOUDON, John** **fl 1893-1900**
Amateur watercolour painter of Blantyre and later of Hamilton; also teacher. Trained Glasgow School of Art. Married Laura L(qv). Head

teacher, Hamilton Academy before becoming Chief Inspector in Art for Scotland. Exhibited RSA(1), RSW(1), GI(5) & Hamilton AC 1903.

**LOUDON, Laura J (née Bennie)** **1871-1945**
Ayr painter of flowers, still life and portraits. Wife of John L(qv). Studied part-time Glasgow School of Art 1887-97. Exhibited RSA(8) 1918-1938 & GI.

**LOUDON, Margery A** **fl 1980-1982**
Edinburgh painter. Exhibited 'Autumn greenhouse' and 'Night window' at the RSA.

**LOUDON, Miss Noni** **fl 1925-1928**
Ayr painter of country scenes. Daughter of Laura(qv) and John L(qv). Exhibited RSA(2).

**LOUGH, Ruth** **fl 1967-1972**
Aberdeen painter in oil of figure studies. Trained Gray's School of Art, Aberdeen. Exhibited AAS from 12 Ellerslie Rd, Bankhead, Bucksburn.

**LOUISE, HRH The Princess** **1848-1939**
**The Princess Louise Caroline Alberta, Marchioness of Lorne, later Duchess of Argyll.**
Born Windsor Castle 8 Mar; died Kensington Palace. Artist, sculptress and writer. Sixth child and fourth daughter of Queen Victoria. Studied under Edgar Boehm, designed the statue of Queen Victoria in Kensington Gardens. In 1871 she married the Marquess of Lorne, later 9th Duke of Argyll. Artistically the most talented member of the Victorian royal family, several others of whom had artistic talent. Illustrated Campbell: *Auld Robin and The Farmer* (1894). Elected HRE 1897, RMS 1897, RSW 1884. Exhibited RSA (a bronze statuette of Edward the Black Prince, now at Inverary Castle), RSW(16), RWS(14) & GI(2). Represented in St. Paul's Cathedral by 'The Angel of Salvation behind Christ on the Cross', a bronze statue commemorating Dominion soldiers who had died in the Boer War.
**Bibl:** Houfe 213; Hilary Hunt-Lewis, Appendix II in David Duff, The Life Story of HRH Princess Louise, London, 1940, 337-344; Jane Roberts, Royal Artists, London 1987, passim; Lady Elizabeth Longford, Darling Loosy; Letters to Princess Louise, 1856-1939, Weidenfeld & Nicholson, 1991.

**LOVE, Andrew** **fl 1896-1919**
Amateur watercolour painter from Newmills, Midlothian. Exhibited RSA(2), RSW(3) & GI(4).

**LOVE, Janet M** **fl 1901-1902**
Landscape painter. Exhibited GI(2) & L(1) from 21 St James Street, Paisley.

**LOVE, Lillian** **fl 1888**
Amateur flower painter of Geilsland, Leith; exhibited GI(1).

**LOVE, Mrs Margaret Joyce** **fl 1940-1965**
Painter of natural history subjects, especially trees and flower studies; exhibited GI(9) from 122 Queens Drive, Glasgow. Moved to Aberdeen some time before 1959 from where she exhibited AAS(3) from Greenacres, Milltimber.

**LOVE, Robert** **fl 1861-1867**
Glasgow oil painter of landscapes; exhibited RSA(5) & GI(5).

**LOVELL, Richard** **fl 1950-1958**
Edinburgh topographical painter. Exhibited RSA(7).

**LOW, Miss Annie Rose** **fl 1894-1900**
Glasgow painter in oil and watercolour of figurative subjects; exhibited RA(3), including 'An Arab Boy, Algiers' 1896, also RSA(3), GI(72) & AAS.

**LOW, Bet ARSA RSW RGI** **1924-**
Born Gourock, Renfrewshire, 27 Dec. Painter in oil and watercolour. Educated Greenock Academy. Studied Glasgow School of Art under James Cowie(qv) and at Hospitalfield, Arbroath 1942-46. Began as a free-lance artist, holding her first one-man exhibition in Glasgow 1946, and as a set designer at the Unity Theatre; also portrait painter and art therapist. Co-founder and co-director with John Taylor of the New Charing Cross Gallery, Glasgow 1963-68. Influenced by the German Expressionists and by social realism, but even more by the regions in which she has worked, most especially Orkney but also Arisaig and Donside. Gradually moved to organic abstract art from 1960 and since 1967 has attempted to make an amalgamation between the abstract and a more objective view of nature. Fascinated by mist and haze which she portrays with great tenderness and sensitivity. She never paints on the spot, more interested in elements than in specific places although she has for many years been in love with the Orkneys. Married Tom Macdonald L(qv). Exhibited with the Society of Scottish Independent Artists in 1947. Member of the **Clyde Group** formed before 1946. Elected RSW 1974, ARSA 1988. Exhibits regularly RSA, RSW, AAS, GI & SSA. Represented in Aberdeen AG, Glasgow AG, Abbot Hall AG (Kendal), Lillie AG (Milngavie), Waterford AG, Royal College of Physicians and Surgeons, Glasgow, Perth AG.
**Bibl:** Macmillan[SA] 371,373; Cordelia Oliver,'Bet Low', Third Eye Centre, Glasgow (Ex Cat 1955).

**LOW, Constance** **fl 1896-1898**
Aberdeen painter, mainly local scenery. Exhibited AAS(3) from The Kyles, Longside.

**LOW, D Paton** **fl 1880-1883**
Architect and watercolourist. Exhibited GI(5) from 209 Hope Street, Glasgow.

**LOW, Miss Mabel Bruce RBA** **1883-1972**
Born Edinburgh; died 3 Jne. Painter in watercolour and woodcut artist. Pupil of Walter Sickert at Westminster Art School, Robert Burns(qv) at Edinburgh College of Art and Richard Jack at the RA Schools. Principal works include 'Summer Flowers' and 'A Country Bouquet'. Married to Alexander Chisholm and lived for many years in Bournemouth. Exhibited RA(18), RSA(6), SWA(17), RBA(133), RI(3) & L(4).

**LOWE, Isabella Wylie** **1855-1925**
Born and died Perth. Painter in oil and watercolour of interiors, portraits, landscapes and miniatures. Primarily a miniature painter who painted landscapes in watercolour in a professional style. Between 1895 and 1896 she shared a studio with W M Frazer(qv) at 58 Tay Street. Exhibited RSA(5), AAS(3) & GI(12), also at Perth and Dundee Art Societies 1883-1925. Represented in Perth AG.
**Bibl:** Halsby 269.

**LOWE, J Wylie** **fl 1909**
Perth portrait miniaturist. Exhibited GI(1) from Tay St.

**LOWE, Robert** **fl 1875**
Edinburgh landscape painter in oil; exhibited 'Old Mill nr Edinburgh' at the RSA.

**LOWERY, James** **fl 1975-**
Dundee painter of country scenes in oil, acrylic and watercolour. Also potter. Exhibited AAS(1) & GI(3), from 3 Davidson St, Broughty Ferry.

**LOWES, Henry** **fl 1952-1956**
Edinburgh topographical watercolourist. Exhibited GI(4) from Lasswade Rd.

**LUBBOCK, Miss Helen A B** **fl 1959-1980**
Angus sculptor of portrait busts. Exhibited RSA(5) including busts of The Hon Jane Howard, Lord Lyell, Professor Sir John Boyd, and Col Guthrie of Guthrie, GI(7) 1962-68, including a plaster head of Rt Hon Lord Boyd Orr of Brechin, & at AAS, from Farnell Mains, Brechin.

**LUCA, Miss Isa** **fl 1952-1955**
Musselburgh sculptress. Exhibited two figurative groups and a relief at the GI in wood, from 32 Hope St.

**LUCANI, Hope** **fl 1961-1965**
Aberdeenshire-based amateur painter; painted mainly continental landscapes. Married to Mary L(qv). Exhibited AAS(3) from Wellwood, Birse, Aboyne.

**LUCANI, Mary O H** **fl 1966**
Aberdeenshire-based artist; married to Hope L(qv). Exhibited 'Summer' at AAS from Wellwood, Birse, Aboyne.

**LUCAS, Candace Karman (Mrs Kitfield)** **1948-**
Born America, 23 Feb. Painter in oil, watercolour and gouache, mainly landscapes and figurative subjects. Trained Rhode Island School of Design, Providence RI and University of New Hampshire, before coming to Britain where she continued her studies at the Ruskin School of Drawing in Oxford. Influenced by the Scottish Colourists, German Expressionists and the Fauves. She has evolved away from factual representation of the real world into one which attempts a reconciliation between formal and abstract painting. In order to avoid the purely subjective response that abstraction alone provokes, she retains a core of structural reality with abstraction achieved through manipulation of bright colour, texture and tone, along lines suggested by the Fauves. Exhibits regularly at the RSA, SSWA from Edinburgh.

**LUCAS, Marjorie A (Mrs Murray Tod) ARCA (Lond)** **1911-?**
Painter in watercolour; also embroiderer, illustrator and wood and line engraver. Studied Royal College of Art under Osborne and Robert Austin and received a Diploma in 1933. Married Murray Middleton Tod(qv) 1938. Lived in Kirkcudbright 1938-42 before moving back to Edinburgh in the 60s. Member, Society of Artist Printmakers 1935, SSA 1946. Exhibited regularly RA(2), RSA(24) 1935-63 & GI(19)

**LUCY, E Falkland** **fl 1893-1904**
Glasgow landscape artist. Exhibited GI 1903-4 and a rural scene at the AAS.

**LUDWIG, Francis Conroy (Theodore)** **1869-?**
Born Aberdeen. Painter of local townscapes and landscapes. Son of a shipbroker from Swinemunde and German Consul in Aberdeen. Worked in the family business for some time before devoting himself to painting, mainly in watercolours. Possibly a student of John Mitchell(qv). Signed his paintings 'F C Ludwig'. Exhibited AAS(9) 1906-1926, latterly from 78 Beaconsfield Place.

**LUGAR, Robert** **c1773-1855**
Born England; died London, 23 Jne. Celebrated designer of picturesque castles and lodges with an important influence on contemporary architecture in Scotland as well as being responsible for some of the visual splendours of the country. In 1811 published *Plans and Views of Buildings executed in England and Scotland* followed by *Villa Architecture, a Collection of Views with Plans of Buildings executed in England, Scotland* 1828. Responsible for the first asymmetrical Gothic house in Scotland, Tullichewan, Dumbartonshire (1792). Although now demolished, a comparable work was Balloch, its most remarkable feature being the concave ground plan of the entrance façade (1809). Lugar played an important part in the popularisation of the Picturesque movement and had among his principal students, the Aberdeen architect Archibald Simpson(qv). Also responsible for the 'spirited' Hensol, Kirkcudbright (pre-1828), with its sparkling granite masonry, ogee-roofed turrets, and specially vistaed interiors, an Italianate house, Glenlee, Kirkcudbright (1822) and Tullichewan, nr Dumbarton (c1808, now demolished). The plates for Glenlee appeared in Villa Architecture, pls 30-31 and for Hensol in the same publication, pls 26-29.
**Bibl:** Colvin, 369-371; Dunbar 122,124.

**LUKE, Mrs Nellie** **fl 1892**
Amateur Broughty Ferry painter; exhibited 'Heather and sea' at the RSA from Netherby.

**LUMSDEN, Miss Alice** **fl 1893-1906**
Aberdeenshire painter of miniatures. Probably sister of Ethel L(qv). Exhibited AAS(3) from Pitcaple Castle, Pitcaple.

**LUMSDEN, Allan** **fl 1970**
Aberdeen painter. Exhibited AAS(1) from 76, Menzies Rd.

**LUMSDEN, Ernest Stephen RSA RE** **1883-1948**
Born Edmonton, London, 22 Dec, died Edinburgh, 29 Sep. Painter of portraits and genre, also etcher and aquatintist. As a young man he entered the Navy but was forced to leave through ill-health after serving for a short time on HMS Worcester. Studied art at Reading under Morley Fletcher 1898 and in Paris 1903 at the Academie Julien as well as studying the work of Velasquez on a trip to Madrid in 1904. Velasquez and Rembrandt remained his heroes. Like McBey(qv), Lumsden, in 1905, taught himself to etch from Lalanne's *Treatise on Etching* and in 1906 eight of his etchings were shown at the International Society of Painters and Gravers, and the following year two were hung in the Paris Salon. His first solo exhibition of topographical etchings of Reading, Ludlow and France was held in Reading 1908. The same year, Morley Fletcher, who had become Principal of the Edinburgh College of Art, invited him north to a teaching post which Lumsden accepted. He exhibited in Stockholm 1909 and travelled to Berlin and Amsterdam. In 1910 held an exhibition at Dowdeswell's in London and visited Canada, China, Japan and Korea. In 1912 he abandoned teaching and travelled with his wife and former colleague, Mabel Royds(qv), to India. In order to undertake war service, he remained in India 1917-1919. During this time he prepared the three sets of Indian prints (etching and aquatint) which have come to be regarded as his highest achievement. His sympathetic rendering of townscapes, monasteries and villages celebrated the traditional way of life. Upon returning to Edinburgh he continued mainly his etching work, published *Art of Etching* in 1925 and illustrated James Bone's *The Perambulator in Edinburgh* in 1926. In 1929 became President of the Society of Artist Printmakers and in 1933 was elected RSA, consolation for having been rejected as official artist to the Everest Expedition owing to a weak heart. By now he was working in Raeburn's old studio in Queen Street painting portraits, writing and teaching until his death. His work is distinguished by traditional elegance while the influence of Whistler and Meryon are never far away. He was undoubtedly one of the finest etchers Scotland has enjoyed. Exhibited AAS 1927-19137. Represented in SNPG(1), SNGMA, Tate AG, V & A, Belfast AG, Birkenhead AG; Bogota AG, Indonesia; Cork AG; Dunedin AG, New Zealand; Fitzwilliam Museum, Cambridge; collection of the City of Edinburgh; Glasgow AG; Johannesburgh AG, South Africa; Reykjavik (Iceland); National Gallery of Canada; Toronto AG, Canada; National Gallery of Finland, Helsinki; San Francisco; Library of Congress, Washington.
**Bibl:** J Copley, 'The Later Etchings of E S Lumsden', Print Collector's Quarterly XXIII, 211; Halsby 220,269; Hartley 142; E S Lumsden, The Art of Etching, London 1925; Macmillan[SA] 308,361; M C Salaman,'The Etchings of E S Lumsden RE', Print Collector's Quarterly VII 1921, 91; The Times 2 Oct 48 (obit).

**LUMSDEN, Ethel F** **fl 1919-1933**
Aberdeenshire landscape painter. Possibly sister of Alice L(qv). Exhibited town and rural scenes at the AAS(4) from Pitcaple Castle, Pitcaple.

**LUMSDEN, Henry William** **fl 1885**
Mataeur painter. Exhibited AAS(4) all in the same year.

**LUMSDEN, W A** **fl 1868-1869**
Edinburgh landscape painter in oil; exhibited RSA(3).

**LUNAN, Alice M M** **fl 1933-1965**
Glasgow painter and erngraver; mainly flowers. Her paintings appear to have spanned two separate times, 1933-5 and 1960-5. Exhibited RSA(1), GI(4) after 1960 from Kew Terrace.

**LUNN, Miss Avril** **fl 1951-1952**
Scottish artist. Trained Glasgow School of Art. Exhibited two scenes in the Bahamas at the RGI, from Gt Western Rd.

**LUSCOMBE, Miss Gloria C** **fl 1984-1988**
East Kilbride painter of nudes and still life. Exhibited GI(2).

**LUSK, J Neilson** **fl 1950-1982**
Glasgow painter of portraits and woodland scnes, mostly in watercolour. Exhibited GI(14) from Pollokshaws Rd.

**LUTENOR, G A** **fl 1827-1829**
Edinburgh portrait painter and enamellist. Exhibited RSA(6) including 'Mr Pritchard of the Theatre Royal' 1828 from 33 Dundas Street.

**LUTENOR, J W** **fl 1838**
Glasgow animal painter. Brother of John L(qv). Exhibited a study of a cat and a sketch of an otter hound at the RSA from St Enoch's Square.

**LUTENOR, John G** **fl 1835-1838**
Glasgow painter of portraits and figure studies. Brother of J W L(qv). Exhibited RSA(2) from St Enoch's Square.

**LUXTON, Alice E** **fl 1897**
Amateur flower painter; exhibited GI(1) from 14 Ardgowan Square, Greenock.

**LYELL, Miss Isabella C** **fl 1876-1879**
Edinburgh watercolour painter of fruit, still-life and landscape; exhibited RSA(5).

**LYLE, George A** **fl 1890-1910**
Edinburgh architect. Assistant and successor to Robert Raeburn(qv). Designed most of Eyre Crescent, Edinburgh, also the Barnton Hotel (1895). Partner of **William CONSTABLE** (1863-?).
**Bibl:** Gifford 267,421,551,599.

**LYLE, Thomas Byron** **fl 1875-1891**
Glasgow figure and domestic painter in oil. Fond of country scenes, especially harvesting; was known to have painted an occasional golfing scene. Exhibited RA(1), RSA(18), GI(23), AAS(3), GI(23) & L(4), latterly from 101 Charlotte St, Fitzroy Sq, London.

**LYNCH, John Goudie** **1946-**
Born Glasgow, 9 Jly. Portrait painter in oil on wood panel and canvas. Educated Hutchison's Boys GS 1958-64 and Glasgow School of Art 1964-68. Spent a year at Jordanhill College of Education 1969 before taking up an appointment as art teacher at the International School of Amsterdam in 1970 where he remained until 1974. Major influences have been the modern Dutch realists, especially Westerik and Koch. Commissions include the 'President of the European Parliament' 1983, 'President Dankert at the European Parliament' 1989. Currently lives in France where he works as a full-time portrait painter.Exhibited in many galleries in France, Holland and Switzerland as well as at the European Parliament. Represented in the Rigaud Museum (Perpignan), European Parliament (Brussels) and Palais de l'Europe (Strasbourg).

**LYNCH, Ms Kaye** **fl 1984-1985**
Lanarkshire painter. Exhibited GI(4) from 1 Bankhouse Rd, Lesmahagow.

**LYNCH, Thomas** **fl 1948**
Amateur Glasgow landscape painter. Exhibited GI(1) from Glencairn Drive.

**LYON, Miss Alice M** **fl 1882-1891**
One of two animal painting sisters of Scottish ancestry who lived in London. Exhibited RSA(12).

**LYON, Andrew** **fl 1868-1869**
Glasgow oil painter of landscape and marine subjects often featuring fishing fleets of the Clyde. Exhibited RSA(3) & GI(4).

**LYON, Miss Edith F** **fl 1885-1887**
One of two animal painting sisters of Scottish ancestry living in London in the 1880s. Exhibited portraits of domestic animals at the RSA between the above years.

**LYON, Miss Elizabeth** **fl 1965**
Amateur Lanarkshire painter; often worked in crayons. Exhibited a study of horses at the GI, from Broomhouse, Uddingston.

**LYON, Elsie Inglis** **fl 1902**
Aberdeen illustrator and black & white artist. Exhibited AAS(1) from 52 Carden Place.

**LYON, George P** **fl 1881-1890**
Glasgow landscape painter; exhibited 'Loch Lomond' at the RA (1885), AAS & GI(20) latterly from Thornhill, by Stirling.

**LYON, John Howard** **c1870-1921**
Landscape and sporting painter who lived in Edinburgh and Strathyre, Perthshire. Worked in oil and watercolour. His work is boldly constructed with bright colours and a good feel for the landscape, especially the southern uplands of Perthshire. Exhibited RSA(18), RSW(2) & GI(6).

**LYON, Muriel** **fl 1973**
Aberdeen painter of semi-abstrracts and abstracts. Exhibited AAS from 4, Marine Terrace.

**LYON, Peter** **c1930-**
Sculptor, writer and jeweller. Son of Robert L(qv). Trained under Willi Soukop at Bryanston and under Eric Schilsky at Edinburgh College of Art. Began free-lance work 1953. Senior Lecturer, Central School of Art (London) 1969-85. Responsible for the sculptures at the Diaghilev exhibition in London 1954. Solo exhibitions London, Oxford & Cambridge. Among places where his work can be seen are Balliol College, Oxford, the Kingsway Hall, London, the Gertrude Jekyll water garden, Surrey. Designed crozier for the Bishop of Winchester. Author of *Design in Jewellery*.
**Bibl:** Martin Forrest, Robert Lyon, Ex Cat, Nov 1996.

**LYON, Robert RP RBA ARCA(Lond)** **1894-1978**
Born Liverpool, 18 Aug. Painter of portraits, still life and landscape in oil and tempera; occasional linocuts and portrait busts in plaster. His father came from Lossiemouth and his mother from Edinburgh. Father of Peter L(qv). Studied Liverpool School of Art, Royal College of Art and British School in Rome, 1924. Appointed Master of Fine Art, King's College, Newcastle 1932. While there organised a class for members of the mining industry, the Ashington Group. Head of the art department, Dumfries Academy 1938-42 before becoming Principal, Edinburgh College of Art, a position he retained until his retirement in 1960 when he went to live in Eastbourne, Sussex. Exhibited RSA(48) & GI(4).
**Bibl:** Martin Forrest, Robert Lyon, Ex Cat, Nov 1996.

**LYON, Thomas Bonar** **1873-1955**
Born Glasgow, 24 Jan; died Ayr, Jan. Painter and etcher of landscapes and figure subjects. Studied Glasgow School of Art and Royal College of Art, also in France, Belgium and Holland. Art Master at Irvine Academy and Oban HS, subsequently supervisor of art in schools with Ayrshire Education Authority, retiring at the end of 1937. Influenced by Glasgow marine artists including MacMaster(qv) and Black(qv). Popular member of the Glasgow Art Club and one of the oldest members of Ayr Sketch Club, he always gave great encouragement to the amateur members. Also a fine musician, playing the cello in his local orchestra. Among his major works are 'A Summer Idyll', 'The Blue Boat' and 'Bruges Place du Bourg'. Lived at Mosside, Ayr. Exhibited RSA(22), GI(80), RSW(2) & AAS.
**Bibl:** Halsby 269.

**LYONS, Andrew Wesley** **fl 1902-1925**
Edinburgh painter and designer of 22 Lady Lawson Street and later 12 Melville Place; exhibited RSA(6) including an unfinished oil sketch for a ceiling decoration at Falkland Palace, Fife.

# Mac/Mc

**McADAM, Walter RSW** **1866-1935**
Born Glasgow, 26 May; died Peebles. Painter in oil and watercolour; landscapes and coastal scenes. Trained Glasgow. Lived most of his life in Glasgow spending summers at his studio in Lochwinnoch, Renfrewshire, eventually retiring to Edinburgh. Vice-president RGI, regular contributor to the RSW. Closely associated with the world of music. Painted Highland and west coast scenes in a style which was competent but dull, often with subdued muddy colours. After 1918 he executed a number of sketches on Majorca. Elected RSW 1894. Exhibited RSA(3), RSW(48), RWS(2), GI(115) as well as in the English provinces and overseas. Represented in Glasgow AG.
**Bibl:** Caw 392; Halsby 269; Scotsman, Nov 16, 1935 (obit).

**McALDOWIE, James** **fl 1885-1913**
Edinburgh landscape painter in oil and watercolour. As well as Scottish scenes he exhibited several Dutch views including 'Groote Kirk, Dordrecht' and 'Dordrecht canal'. Exhibited RSA(16), RSW (2), AAS(2) & GI(4).

**MacALISTER, Archie** **1935-**
Born Glasgow. Painter in ink, pencil, & watercolour; illustrator and architect. Trained in architecture Glasgow School of Art 1953-6 followed by a spell at the Edinburgh College of Art 1956-9. A postgraduate award enabled him to study in Europe. On his return 1964, he set up practice in Edinburgh as an architect. From 1971-7 tutor at Heriot Watt University. Held his first one-man exhibition 1985. Commissioned by the Scottish Postal Board 1986 to prepare images printed in commemoration of the centenary of the Crofters Commission. Particularly interested in illustrating the work of 20th century poets. In 1988 he designed, illustrated and published *Seeker, Reaper,* a nautical poem by George Campbell Hay. The same year compiled *Edinburgh,* formed a new company 'As Albain' for the promotion of collaborative art. Commissioned 1989 to provide the watercolour illustrations for Kenneth White's *The Bird Path* and *Travels in the Drifting Dawn.*

**McALISTER, Hugh** **fl 1965**
Aberdeen painter; exhibited two figurative works at the AAS from 31 Beechgrove Terrace.

**MacALLAN, Thomas** **fl 1929-1933**
Glasgow painter of still life subjects and country scenes. Exhibited AAS(2).

**MacALLISTER, A D** **fl 1848-1853**
Edinburgh painter of subject paintings; exhibited RSA & GI(4) from Castle St and later from Glasgow.

**MacALLISTER, A S** **fl 1864**
Glasgow oil painter of figurative subjects; exhibited RSA(2).

**MacALLISTER, Miss Mary** **fl 1939 -1943**
Glasgow-based painter; exhibited a still-life at the RSA & GI.

**MacALLISTER, Stewart** **fl 1935-1937**
Wishaw artist. Exhibited 'Self-portrait' and 'Leaves from my sketch-book' at the RSA, and once at the GI, between the above years, from 'Glenholm'.

**MacALLISTER-YOUNG, Miss Elizabeth** **fl 1973**
Glasgow painter. Exhibited 'Pied Piper' at GI from Hillview Street.

**MACALLUM, Andrew** **fl 1850-1886**
Prolific landscape painter, mainly in oil. Possibly Scottish. Lived latterly at 47 Bedford Gdns, London. Exhibited RA(53) including 'The Black Wood of Rannoch, Perthshire' 1869 and 'Glassalt Shiel, Glen Muick' 1877; also GI(3). Represented by two paintings in Manchester AG.

**MacALLUM, George** **1840-1868**
Born and died Edinburgh. Sculptor. Educated Edinburgh. Trained for a time under William Brodie(qv). Modelled figures and ornamental work inside the Physicians Hall, Edinburgh and executed a number of busts full of expression and character. A marble bust of David Bryce is in the Call-Over Hall, Fettes. Supplemented the original rounded portraits originally modelled by Lazzaroni in 1845. Not as well known as his work deserves although acquired some professional recognition during his lifetime. Died before he had had time to reach the full expression of his powers. Worked mostly in miniature, also executed a number of miniature portraits. Exhibited RSA(47), a marble bust of the architect David Bryce being included posthumously in the 1880 exhibition & GI(11). This is now in the SNPG whilst an attributed version is in Edinburgh City collection.
**Bibl:** Gifford 288,573; 'Virtue & Vision, Sculpture and Scotland', NGS (Ex Cat 1991).

**MacALLUM, Hamilton** **1841-1896**
Born Kames, Argyll; died Beer, South Devon. Painter in oil of marine and coastal subjects. His parents intended him for a mercantile career but in 1864 he went to study art at the Academy Schools in London. Began to exhibit in 1866 and from then until 1896 he was a constant exhibitor at the main London exhibitions. In common with Colin Hunter(qv), he found most of his subjects on the west coast of Scotland, although a visit to Italy helped to make his pictures more sun-filled and cheerful. But his figures remained slightly sentimental. Particularly effective in depicting atmosphere but less sure in his handling of colour. 'As studies of light and air, the best works of Macallum deserve a very high place. In some of his pictures the sun palpitates through the vaporous air with a truth not surpassed by Cuyp' [Armstrong]. 'As a painter of the sea [he] just missed the first rank, for, real as his love of it was and wonderfully as he painted certain of its phases, especially its 'multitudinous laughter', his pictures lack a sense of that seeming inward life and power and of that unbroken continuance of elemental existence which are perhaps its strongest appeal to the imagination' [Caw]. In 1887 visited Capri and Salerno where he painted a number of sensitive works. Enjoyed working in full daylight, often from a glass house built especially for the purpose on Hampstead Heath. For some years he was based at Tarbert, Loch Fyne with Colin Hunter(qv) and McTaggart(qv). A competent yachtsman, he cruised on his own yacht. His last exhibited work 'The Crofter's Team' is now in the Tate. Founder member RSW and of both the RI 1882 and ROI 1883. Exhibited RA(21), ROI(25) & GI(11). Represented in Tate AG, V & A, Glasgow AG.
**Bibl:** Armstrong 77-8; Bryan; Caw 327-9; Halsby 124, 269; McKay 359; Portfolio 1870, 150; 1887, 211; 1890, 184; James Dafforne, in Studio 1900, 149-151.

**McALPINE, Helen Emmeline (Mrs Bacon)** **fl 1903-1932**
Born London. Landscape painter in watercolour. Studied at Lambeth and then in Glasgow and Edinburgh before settling in Corpach, Inverness. Exhibited RSW(7), GI(3), L(1) & London Salon(7).

**McANALLY, John J** **fl 1951-1961**
Argyll artist. Specialised in still life and local landscape. Exhibited RSA in 1951, 1958 & 1961 from Campbeltown.

**McANALLY, William** **fl 1942-1971**
Painter of landscape and subject works. Exhibited intermittently RSA from Glasgow, Uddingston and latterly from Stirling; also GI(2) 1941.

**McANDREW, Donald C** **fl 1950-1953**
Edinburgh painter. Exhibited still lifes and interiors RSA(5), from 32 Midmar Gdns. Represented in City of Edinburgh collection.

**MacANDREW, E** **fl 1959**
Inverness-shire watercolourist. Fond of depicting icy scenes, also flowers. Exhibited AAS(3) from Spean Bridge.

**MacANESPIE, Mrs A L** **fl 1984**
Amateur Milngavie landscape painter. Exhibited GI(1).

**McARA, Miss J M** **fl 1913**
Amateur Glasgow painter. Often painted harbour scenes and shipping, both Scottish and continental. Exhibited AAS & GI(2) from 19 Dundonald Rd.

**McARDLE, Miss Elizabeth** **fl 1973**
Amateur Caithness painter. Exhibited GI(2) from Wick.

**McARTHUR, Miss** **fl c1851**
Painter. All that is known about her is an association with Bell's school, Inverness in the early 1850s and that, according to Simpson, she painted miniatures on ivory and larger portraits in crayon and oil. Possibly related to Agnes(qv) and Jane M(qv) both of whom exhibited RSA in the 1870s and 1880s.
**Bibl:** W Simpson, Inverness Artists, Inverness 1925,41.

**MacARTHUR, Miss Agnes M** **fl 1873-1903**
Edinburgh painter in oil and watercolour of landscapes and figures. Sister of Jane M(qv). Exhibited RSA(43). Until 1885 most of her exhibits were of Arran and Kinross-shire, thereafter of Edinburgh and the Lothians.

**MacARTHUR, Miss Blanche F** **fl 1877-1903**
Painter in oil and watercolour of flowers, landscape, figurative subjects and genre. Spent most of her life in London at 30 John Street, Bedford Row although exhibited extensively in Scotland. At the RSA she showed 29 works, also RA(18), GI(15), L(15), RBA (14), RHA(4) & SWA(20).

**McARTHUR, Miss Christine L RSW RGI** **c1953-**
Possibly born Kirkintilloch. Painter in oils, pastel and watercolour. Trained Glasgow School of Art 1971-76. She first became known for large scale still lifes but in the late 1980s she began working in pastel before reverting again to oils as well as occasional acrylic and collage. Elected RGI 1990, RSW 1995. Won Lauder award, Macfarlane award. Become increasingly abstract. Exhibits RSW, RGI.
**Bibl:** Clare Henry, Christine L McArthur, Ex Cat, Roger Billcliffe, Glasgow, May 1998.

**MacARTHUR, Miss Jane S** **fl c1870-1885**
Edinburgh painter in oil and watercolour of flowers, portraits and figures. Sister of Agnes M(qv). Exhibited RSA(36) & SWA(1).

**McARTHUR, Lindsay Grandison** **fl 1886-1946**
Painter in oil and watercolour, also pen & ink; landscapes and rural scenes. Lived at Oban before moving in the 1890's, first to Willersey, Gloucestershire and then, in 1899, to Broadway, Worcestershire, finally settling in Winchcombe, Gloucestershire 1911. Painted pleasing rural scenes in a decorative manner with a light touch. Exhibited RA(34), RSA(4), ROI(3), AAS & L(17). 'A country pond with trees and waterfowl', shown at the RA, sold for £16,000 in 1990 - the first of his works to have reached the London auction rooms. Represented in NGS (2 pen studies of grasses and 2 designs for bookplates, one for Lady Maud Bowes-Lyon, all dating from 1946), Glasgow AG, Kirkcaldy AG(24), Edinburgh City collection(2), Perth AG.

**MacARTHUR, Miss Mary** **fl 1880-1901**
Painter in oil of portraits and figurative subjects. Sister of Blanche M(qv). Shared a studio with her sister at 30 John Street, Bedford Row from where she exhibited RA(2), RSA(5), RBA(1), RHA(18), ROI(1), GI(14) & SWA(5). Represented in Glasgow AG.

**MacARTHUR, Miss Morag D** **fl 1943**
Lanarkshire weaver. Exhibited GI(1) from Airdrie.

**MacARTHUR, Ronald M** **fl 1940**
Edinburgh painter of country scenes and buildings. Exhibited RSA(2) from 18 Wellington Street.

**MacARTHUR, Sheila** **1915-**
Glasgow painter. Studied at Glasgow School of Art and Jordanhill. Associated with R Annand(qv) and Noel Slaney(qv). Founder member of the New Scottish Group based in Glasgow.

**McARTHUR, William R S** **1946-**
Born Aberdeen. Portrait painter and printmaker. Trained Lowestoft School of Art 1961-3 and Gray's School of Art, Aberdeen 1963-7. His first job was as a visualiser at the Contemporary Theatre Company, London where he became increasingly interested in films. Painted and travelled in North Africa on a photographic project on Islamic art and architecture 1978-84 before returning to Gray's School of Art 1985-7 to undertake further studies and then to Duncan of Jordanstone College of Art 1987-8 before taking up a post as assistant workshop manager, Aberdeen Print Studio 1989. Began exhibiting at the RSA 1990. Won the award of the Highland Society of London; also exhibits at the Aberdeen Artist's Society. Lives in Inverurie.

**McARTHY, David** **c1854-1926**
Edinburgh architect. Probably related to the architect **Charles McARTHY**. Responsible for the rather drab Royal Dick Vet College ((1909-16) and many lesser Edinburgh buildings.
**Bibl:** Gifford 243,270,421,500,622.

**McARTNEY, Sylvia** **fl 1976**
Painter in oils. Solo exhibition at the Carlton Hotel, Edinburgh 1976. Represented in Edinburgh City collection.

**McARTNEY, William** **fl 1827-1831**
Edinburgh painter of genre and character studies; exhibited RSA(4).

**MacAULAY, Miss Kate** **fl 1872-1900**
Painter of coastal scenes, usually with shipping. Moved from Scotland to Capel Curig, North Wales. Her watercolours are competently composed and an obvious enjoyment of coastal scenes shines through her work. Among her main works are 'Scotch Herring Trawlers', 'Sea Cliff', 'A Corner of the Quay'. Elected ASWA 1880, SWA 1890, RSW 1879, resigning 1898. Exhibited most frequently at the SWA(72) and RSW(43), also RA(5), RSA(12), RBA(6), RI(1) & GI(19), latterly from Capel Curig, N. Wales.
**Bibl:** Halsby 269.

**MacAULAY, M M** **19th Cent**
Obscure painter of sporting still lifes.
**Bibl:** Wingfield.

**MacAULAY, William John** **1912-**
Edinburgh painter, mosaic and stained glass designer. Studied at Edinburgh College of Art 1930-35 and the British School of Archaeology 1935-36. Exhibited 'The excavation, Istanbul' at the RSA in 1937 from 80 Pilrig Street.

**McAVOY, Gladys** **fl 1969-**
Inverness painter and engraver of local views and topographical subjects. Specialises in coloured linocuts and prints. Exhibited RSA(5) 1976-1979, & AAS from 65 Old Edinburgh Road. Represented in Lillie AG (Milngavie).

**MacBEATH, Brian F** **fl 1980-1988**
Aberdeen artist trained Gray's School of Art, Aberdeen. Exhibited RSA(5), including 'Self-portrait', & AAS, latterly from Inverbervie.

**McBEE, James Grove** **fl 1908**
Painter. Exhibited 'Old Torry, Aberdeen' at the RSA from an Aberdeen address but appears never to have exhibited in Aberdeen, nor elsewhere.

**MacBETH, Ann** **1870-1948**
Born Bolton, Lancs. Painter in watercolour and pen & ink; textile designer and educationalist. Eldest of nine children, daughter of a Scottish engineer and grand-daughter of the academician R W MacBeth(qv). Trained, Glasgow School of Art 1897-1901. In 1899 won a prize for needlework. Appointed assistant to Jessie Newbery(qv) 1901. Described as a direct, slightly forbidding character but very kind and generous. Most of her early work was embroidery; designed and worked Glasgow's coat of arms for a banner presented to Professor Rucker at a British Association meeting which was later shown at an international exhibition. Won silver medal, Turin 1902. In 1906 began to teach metalwork design followed the next year by book binding. Also designed jewellery, ceramics and textiles. In collaboration with Margaret Swanson(qv) she developed a new method of teaching needlecraft to children. The method received international recognition and was enshrined in a jointly prepared book *Educational Needlecraft* 1911. Her embroidery was characterised by distinctive metal clasps and rose and heart motifs. Her style of drawing in ink, heightened with

bodycolour, was akin to that of her Glasgow contemporaries Jessie M King(qv) and Annie French(qv). Fra Newbery, quoted by Arthur, wrote 'Miss Macbeth kept her design aspirations in the background until she made herself a competent draughtswoman, and had mastered the art of drawing, without which design is as lifeless as a body without a soul'. Through her teaching and enthusiastic talent she was a central figure in the internationally renowned Glasgow School of Art during its apotheosis. In 1913 became Lady Warden at the School of Art. Her design of a carpet for Alexander Morton & Co in 1914 was illustrated in *The Studio.* Continued to write, *The Playwork Book* appeared in 1918, *Schools and Fireside Crafts* (with Mary Spence) 1920, *Embroidered Lace and Leatherwork* 1924, *Needleweaving* 1926 and *The Countrywoman's Rug Book* 1929. Retired to Patterdale in the lake district from where she continued to teach embroidery and handicrafts, especially rugmaking. Owned a kiln in which she designed a christening mug or plate for every child christened in the parish. Exhibited GI(7), L(6) & Glasgow Society of Lady Artists. Won Lauder prize twice, 1930 and 1938. Represented in Glasgow AG.
**Bibl:** Liz Arthur in Burkhauser, 153-7; Halsby 181,183; Fra Newbery 'An Appreciation of the work of Ann Macbeth', Studio, vol XXVII, 1902, 40.

**MacBETH, James** **1847-1891**
Edinburgh painter in oil and watercolour of portraits and landscapes. Son of Norman M(qv) and brother of Robert Walker M(qv). Exhibited RA(15) 1872-1884, mostly from London although he was back at 2 Polworth Terrace, Edinburgh in 1880; also RSA (21) including a portrait of 'Joseph Pease, MP' (1876) presented to the Corporation of Darlington, and an interesting picture of 'The Boat Race' (1881). Also exhibited ROI(6), RI(9), L(2) & G(11). Represented in Norwich AG.
**Bibl:** Wingfield; Houfe 217.

**MacBETH, Norman RSA** **fl 1857-1902**
Born Port Glasgow; died Edinburgh. Portrait and landscape painter in oil. Studied seal-engraving in Glasgow before proceeding to the RA Schools in London and in Paris at the Louvre. Worked in Greenock 1841 before moving to Glasgow c1848 and after 1861 moved to Edinburgh. In 1886 he went to London where he was appointed by the RA as their trustee for the British Institution Scholarship Fund. Although exhibiting regularly at the RA 1857-86 his Scottish practice was more lucrative. Caw was rather dismissive 'Few (of his portraits) possess distinctive character or merit; his handling, though careful and in a way competent, was hard and unsympathetic; his drawing had no style, his colour no charm. Yet his conventional and completely undistinguished portraiture has certain solid qualities, likeness and simplicity and the unconscious impress of a healthy tradition, which are not without value'. Father of Robert Walker M(qv) and Henry Macbeth-Raeburn(qv). Elected ARSA 1870, RSA 1880. Exhibited RA(25), RSA(196), GI(17) & RI(2). Represented NGS, SNPG(1), Glasgow AG(6), City of Edinburgh collection(2).
**Bibl:** Caw 178; Clement & Hutton; DNB; McKay 355; Portfolio 1886, 25; 1887, 233.

**MACBETH, Robert Walker RA RI RPE RWS** **1848-1910**
Bron Glasgow, Sept 30; died London. Painter of pastoral landscapes and rustic genre, also etcher & illustrator. He was the son and pupil of Norman MacBeth(qv). Studied in London and worked for *The Graphic.* He was influenced by G H Mason and Frederick Walker. His realistic scenes of rural life mostly in the fens and in Somerset, of countryfolk going about their labours and the contrasting life of gipsies and travelling showmen are his hallmark but he also loved to portray fisherfolk and attractive country girls. His colour became richer as he developed, revelling in the sparkle of sunshine. He was a highly accomplished artist technically, sure in brushwork and direct in handling. As an etcher he was influenced by Velasquez and Titian. He illustrated F G Jackson's *A Thousand Days in the Arctic* 1899 and contributed to *Once a Week,* 1870, *The Sunday Magazine* (1871) and *The English Illustrated Magazine* (1883-5). He was elected ARA 1883, RA 1903, RE 1880, HRE 1909, RI 1882, ROI 1883, ARWS 1871, RWS 1901. Altogether he exhibited 115 works at the RA between 1873 and 1904, also several times at the RSA, RWS(16), RE(49), GI(10) & at the AAS 1893-1910. 'The Cast Shoe'was purchased by the Chantrey Bequest in 1890. Represented in V & A, Aberdeen AG, Manchester AG.
**Bibl:** AJ 1883, 296; 1893, 28; 1897, 324; 1900, 289-92; 1908, 12; Caw 277-9; Graphic Arts,123,132; Hardie III, 190; Portfolio 1881, 21; 1883, 64; 1884, 224; 1887, 233; Studio, special no. 1917; Wedmore, Etching in England 1895, 152ff.

**MacBETH-RAEBURN, Henry Raeburn RA RE** **1860-1947**
Born Helensburgh, 24 Sep; died Dedham, Essex, Dec. Portrait painter and engraver. Son of Norman M(qv), brother of R W(qv), Marjorie May(qv) and J Macbeth(qv). Educated Edinburgh Academy and University, he studied art at the RSA and in Paris at Julien's. Began as a portrait painter in London but from about 1890 became increasingly interested in engraving, moving to Newbury, Berkshire. The previous year he had visited Spain and in 1896-7 etched a series of frontispieces for Osgood & Co's edition of Hardy's *Wessex Tales.* His best known works are engravings of the portraits of Sir Henry Raeburn. The popularity of his engravings increased the value of the originals and in some cases his use of colour was considered to be an improvement on the originals. In 1936 completed a portrait of 'King George V in Highland dress', later engraved with a mezzotint plate taken from it. Elected RE 1899, ARA 1921, RA 1933. Awarded a Civil List pension 1941. Frequent contributor to *ILN* 1894-1896. Exhibited RA(32) 1881-1904, also RSA & GI(2). Represented in V & A.
**Bibl:** Halsby 269; Houfe; Wingfield.

**MacBETH-RAEBURN, Marjorie May** **1902-1988**
Painter of equestrian subjects. Daughter of Henry Macbeth-Raeburn(qv) and distantly related to Sir Henry Raeburn(qv). Often copied works by other artists but also executed studies of her own. Signed using her maiden name.
**Bibl:** Wingfield.

**McBEY, James LLD** **1883-1959**
Born Newburgh, Aberdeenshire, 23 Dec; died Tangiers 1 Dec. Etcher, watercolourist and occasional painter in oils. An elegant, refined and often under-rated artist. Whilst his watercolours present an idiosyncratic vision of the world, especially the parched lands of North Africa and the coastlines of Holland, East Anglia and north-east Scotland, it is for his etchings that he is best remembered. Had an abiding love for his native corner of Scotland but sadly this was so long frustrated he once referred to the area as 'a fair but stern land that held for me sad associations and in whose rigid economy I, as an artist, had no place'. Apart from a brief period of study at Gray's School of Art, Aberdeen and some desultory lessons with John Hay(qv), both in 1901, he was self-taught, even to the extent of making a printing press out of an old mangle. It is said that he read every one of the 700 volumes then in the fine art section of Aberdeen's Public Library. The book that most captured his imagination was Whistler's *The Gentle Art of Making Enemies;* in order to frequent the exhibition in Edinburgh 1903 McBey took a job with the Kirkcaldy branch of the North of Scotland Bank. The thin application of paint and economy of line, whether in oil or watercolour, were learned from Whistler and remained a lasting characteristic of his work. In his etchings he was influenced by Rembrandt, especially in the treatment of chiaroscuro, creation of atmosphere and delicacy of characterisation, as well as by Whistler's balance and rhythm stemming in turn from the Japanese prints of Hiroshige and Hokusai. McBey produced his first known etching, a view of Aberdeen harbour, in 1902 and three years later one was accepted by the RSA and two by the RGI. The following year he established a studio at 220 Union St, Aberdeen. In 1910 he left the bank to work as an artist full-time. His first one-man exhibition was held at the John Kesson Gallery, Diamond Street, Aberdeen when five of the twenty exhibits were sold. The same year he visited Spain with his artist friend D I Smart and had a show in London with 77 prints sold. In 1912 he appointed Colnaghi as his agent and with James Kerr Lawson(qv) set forth to visit Morocco, thus beginning a long association with North Africa that continued during WW1 with the Australian Camel Patrol in Egypt and Palestine. Also worked as an official war artist in France. In 1916 he was commissioned and posted to the Army Printing and Stationery Services in Boulogne from where he was rescued by Campbell Dodgson and sent to join Allenby. At this time he began experimenting with pen washes over drawings and with watercolour. Between 1919 & 1921 three sets of etchings based on his war drawings were published and a series of illustrated letters to William Hutcheon appeared in *The Graphic.* Over the next two years he visited France, Holland and Spain and in 1923 designed the

famous label for 'Cutty Sark' whisky. There followed several visits to Venice culminating in the publication of his 'Venice Set' in 1926. He next undertook two trips to the States, incorporating an unsuccessful exhibition in Chicago and in 1931 married Marguerite Loeb of Philadelphia in New York. Together they visited Spain (1932) and Morocco (1932), buying a house in Tangiers. Returning to Aberdeen he was awarded an honorary doctorate and began concentrating more on portraiture. Among his sitters were T E Lawrence, King Feisal and General Allenby. In 1939 he was again in the States and having had his offer to resume work as a war artist rejected on grounds of age he became an American citizen. This distressed some quarters in Scotland who never quite forgave him. There is a McBey Memorial print room within Aberdeen AG given to the display of some of his finest works. McBey completed no work after 1911 owing to the discouragement of his Philadelphian patron and friend, H H Kynett. He was probably the finest and most distinctive Scottish artist never to have been honoured by his country's academy. Exhibited RA(15), RSA(12), GI(45), AAS 1906-1937 & L(74), but mostly with the Fine Art Society and Colnaghi in London. Represented in BM, Imperial War Museum, Aberdeen AG, Dundee AG, Perth AG, City of Edinburgh collection, Hunterian AG, Glasgow, Brodie Castle (NTS), Nat Gall of New Zealand(Wellington).
**Bibl:** Aberdeen AG,'James McBey Centenary' (Ex Cat 1984); Halsby 231-3; Martin Hardie, James McBey: Catalogue Raisonne 1902-24, London 1925; Martin Hardie & Charles Carter, James McBey: Etchings and Drypoints from 1924, Aberdeen 1924; Macmillan [SA] 308; Nicholas Parker (ed), The Early Years of James McBey: An Autobiography 1883-1911 (1977); Perth AG (ex cat 1988, by Tarn Brown); Malcolm Salaman, The etchings of James McBey, London 1929; Studio Vol 61,1914,97-107; Jennifer Melville, James McBey's Morocco (HarperCollins, Glasgow 1991); 'McBey and the Sea', Ex Cat, Aberdeen Art Gallery 1991; J Melville, "Manhattan to Marrakesh - the art and lives of James and Marguerite McBey", Aberdeen AG 2001.

**MacBRAYNE, A Madge** **1883-1949**
Born Glasgow. Studied at Glasgow School of Art. Painted in oil and watercolour; landscapes, also sculptures. Received the Lauder Award 1931. Lived for some years in Helensburgh. Exhibited RSA(18), RSW(2), RA(1) & GI(29).
**Bibl:** Halsby 269.

**MacBRAYNE, M** **fl 1887**
Glasgow landscape painter. Exhibited an Ayrshire coastal scene at the GI, from 4 Lilybank Terrace.

**MacBRAYNE, R D** **fl 1887**
Glasgow artist; exhibited AAS(1).

**McBRIDE, Aggie** **fl 1888-1890**
Amateur Glasgow flower painter. Exhibited GI(4) from Tollcross.

**MacBRIDE, Alexander RSW RI** **1859-1955**
Born Cathcart, nr Glasgow, 8 Mar; died Cathcart, Lanarkshire. Landscape painter in watercolour, especially river and watersides. Studied Glasgow School of Art and Academie Julien in Paris. Painted in England & Italy. Elected RSW 1887, RI 1899. Exhibited RSA(10) 1885-1916, AAS 1896-1912 & annually GI 1885-1956.
**Bibl:** Caw 392; Halsby 269.

**MacBRIDE, Alice** **fl 1914**
Glasgow artist; exhibited RI(1) from Sunnyside House, Cathcart.

**McBRIDE, Charles** **1853-1903**
Edinburgh sculptor. Portrait busts, often in marble. Lived at 7 Hope Street Lane. A bust of Andrew Carnegie (1891) is in Edinburgh Central PL. Exhibited RA(2) 1890 including a portrait bust of Archibald Campbell, 3rd Marquis of Argyll (1897) for St Giles Cathedral, Edinburgh. Exhibited RSA(4) including fine portrait busts of Thomas Carlyle 1885, Sir Alex Grant, late Principal of the University 1887 and the Principal in 1900 Sir William Muir. Also exhibited GI(5) & AAS(2), including a bust of Gladstone. Represented in SNPG, Edinburgh City collection (2, including a marble bust of Lord Provost Sir George Harrison).
**Bibl:** Gifford 115,178,284,316.

**MacBRIDE, Mrs John** **fl 1891-1893**
Glasgow amateur painter. Wife of the sculptor John M(qv) and mother of M Lawson M(qv). Exhibited GI(2) from 1 Colebrooke Place.

**MacBRIDE, John Alexander Patterson** **1819-1890**
Born 1819, died 10 Apr. Sculptor. Son of Archibald MacBride of Campbeltown, Argyll, he trained under the Chester sculptor William Spence and went to London in about 1841. In 1844 exhibited a group Margaret of Anjou and her Son at Westminister Hall. The *Literary Gazette* considered Margaret 'virago' and her son 'a poor attenuated, impudent lad,' but Samuel Joseph was so impressed by the work that he took the sculptor into his studio as a pupil without charging his usual fee of 500 guineas. MacBride later became Joseph's chief assistant, but returned to Liverpool about 1852, where he became an enthusiastic supporter of the pre-Raphaelites. As Secretary of the Liverpool Academy, he was instrumental in awarding the annual prize of 50 guineas on two occasions to Holman Hunt and Millais. His works include a statue of Dr Adam Clarke for Portrush; statues of the four seasons for Sir John Gerrard, and busts of Philip Bailey (now in the SNPG), Sir William Brown, Michael Whitby, Field Marshal Lord Combermere, Dr Raffles, Col Peter Thomson and John Millar. Also carved a tablet in memory of Dr Stevenson, 1854, for St Mary's Church, Birkenhead. His last work was a statuette of H M Stanley, replicas of which were made by Minton of Stoke-on-Trent. His wife was an amateur artist(qv), and his son also painted(qv). Exhibited RA(3) in 1848 and 1853, the latter a marble bust of General Lord Combermere, when Constable of the Tower and Provincial Grand Master of Cheshire which was presented to the Freemasons of Cheshire; also at the Liverpool Academy and elsewhere. Models of Lady Godiva were awarded by the Liverpool Art Union as one of their prizes in 1850. [After Gunnis.]
**Bibl:** Gunnis.

**McBRIDE, M Hunter** **fl 1890-1892**
Glasgow artist. Exhibited GI(4).

**McBRIDE, M Lawson** **fl 1900**
Glasgow artist. Son of John M(qv). Exhibited GI(1) from 1 Colebrooke Place.

**MacBRIDE, William** **?-1915**
Glasgow landscape painter in oil. Landscape and country activities such as sheep shearing and wood cutting. Exhibited RA(3) from 1890-1894 from Glasgow addresses, RSA(25) 1883-1913, also RSW(3), GI(79), AAS & L(12). Represented in Glasgow AG, City of Edinburgh collection. Not to be confused with the Irish artist William MacBride who painted in the 1920s.
**Bibl:** Caw 392; Halsby 269.

**MacBRYDE, Robert** **1913-1966**
Born Maybole, Ayrshire, 5 Dec; died Dublin. Painter in oil of still life and figure subjects. Left school when he was 14; after five years working in a local shoe factory, studied at Glasgow School of Art 1932-1937 under Hugh Adam Crawford(qv) and Ian Fleming(qv); also at Hospitalfield when James Cowie(qv) was teaching there. In Glasgow he met Robert Colquhoun(qv) who became a great friend. The two became so inseparable that when one was awarded a travelling scholarship, the School also awarded one to MacBryde so that they could remain together. As a result, he studied in France and Italy 1937-9 holding his first one-man show London 1943. Having moved to London in 1941, where he shared a house with John Minton and (from 1943) Jankel Adler(qv), MacBryde came under the influence of Wyndham Lewis and Adler. During this time his work became more decorative, the forms flattened and his palette lighter. From 1947-48 he collaborated with Colquhoun on Massine's ballet, 'Donald of the Burthens', which appeared at Covent Garden in 1951. That year he was commissioned to design murals for the *SS Oronsay* and also by the Arts Council to paint a large canvas for the Festival of Britain exhibition, 'Sixty Paintings for '51'. 'I set out to make clear the order which exists between objects which sometimes seem opposed...this leads me beneath the surface of things, so that I paint the permanent reality behind the passing incident'. Died as the result of being run over by a bus in Dublin. Represented in SNGMA, by a portrait of 'Robert Colquhoun' in SNPG, also Glasgow AG, Manchester AG.

**Bibl:** CAC, Edinburgh, Robert Colquhoun (Ex Cat 1981); Gage 31,32,59,147; Halsby 231; Hardie 172-3; Hartley 143-4; Mayor Gallery, London, Robert Colquhoun and Robert MacBryde (Ex Cat 1977); Rothenstein 175-6 (pl 149); Malcolm York, The Spirit of the Place; Nine Neo-Romantic Artists in Their Times, London 1988.

**McCAIG, Isobel** **fl 1938**
Helensburgh amateur portrait painter; exhibited 'Maria Antonelli' at the GI(1) from Winaisia, Abercromby Street.

**McCAIL, William** **1902-1974**
Animal painter, principally of working horses but also racing and circus scenes, farming subjects and domestic animals. His preferred media were charcoal, pastel and black litho-chalk. Mainly self-taught, began his working life as a deckhand in West Hartlepool docks at the age of 14. Shortly after apprenticing himself to a joiner he suffered a serious accident and while convalescing was given drawing lessons by his elder brother who had attended art school. In 1926 he joined the art department of D.C.Thomson the Dundee publishers and from 1940-c1948 worked as an illustrator. After the war he established an artists' agency (Strathmore Studios) in Dundee which had many well-known names among its clients and which continued until his retirement in 1963. Influenced by an early study of Lt-Col Luard's book *Horses & Movement* which led to many hours spent sketching in the stables of the old LMS railway company. His convincing and spontaneous depiction of moving horses has been likened to the work of his near-contemporary English painter, Skeaping. In later life he gave advice and encouragement to many young artists including Neil Dallas Brown(qv) whose portrait of McCail 1961 remains in the family. Held one-man exhibitions in Liverpool, Edinburgh, Pitlochry and Braemar. Exhibited a pastel of a crowded gymkhana scene at the RSA 1949. [From notes provided by his son, Ronald McCail.]

**McCALL, Charles James ROI** **1907-1989**
Born Edinburgh, 24 Feb; died London. Painter in oil and pastel; portraits, interiors, figurative subjects and landscapes. Began as a clerk to a firm of Edinburgh lawyers, but in 1933 won a scholarship to Edinburgh College of Art studying under D M Sutherland(qv) and S J Peploe(qv). In 1938 had the unusual distinction of being made a Fellow of the Edinburgh College of Art at the age of 31. Continued studies in Paris at the Academie Colarossi under Friesz and elsewhere on the Continent, 1937-8. On his return, he began almost immediately to exhibit work it the RA and with the London Group. Also held one-man shows in Manchester, Dublin 1951, New York 1955, Montreal and Winnipeg. His painting was in the tradition of Vuillard and Sickert - coming between poetic neo-romanticism of the war years and the potentially overwhelming influence of American abstraction. This is a quiet but genuinely felt and observed art, continuing to flourish in an unsensational way. At his happiest working on a small intimate scale - domestic interiors and urban scenes, using a rich solid surface of paint, simplified shapes produced by artificial lighting. In 1940 commissioned to undertake a painting for the Royal Engineers. Posthumous studio sale held by John Nicholson (Fernhurst, Surrey), Feb 4, 2004. Elected ROI 1950, NEAC 1957. Exhibited RA(1), RSA(93) & AAS. Represented in Paisley AG, City of Edinburgh collection(2), Perth AG.
**Bibl:** Mitzi McCall: *Interior with Figure; the life and painting of Charles McCall*, 1987.

**McCALL, Lizzie C** **fl 1900**
Amateur flower painter. Exhibited GI(1) from The Manse, Ardrossan.

**McCALL, Miss M** **fl 1886**
Amateur flower painter, almost certainly sister of Lizzie C M(qv). Exhibited 'Basket of flowers' at the GI(1) from The Manse, Ardrossan.

**McCALL, William** **fl 1949**
Dundee painter. Exhibited 'Camperdown - before the show' at the RSA from 18 Woodside Terrace.

**McCALLIEN, William J** **fl 1899-1913**
Argyll painter of coastal and placid fishing scenes. Exhibited RSA(2) & GI(8) from Tarbert, Loch Fyne.

*[NB In some cases the names McAllum and McCallum appear interchangeable].*

**McCALLUM, James** **c1967-**
West Highland painter, etcher and printmaker. Trained Grays School of Art. Mostly figurative work, interested in the technical side of paintings, use of different materials and techniques. Stimulated by classical mythology and mystical imagery. Awarded the John Kinross scholarship (RSA) 1990. First solo exhibition Aberdeen 1992, also Glasgow. Began exhibiting RSA 1989, also AAS.

**McCALLUM, John Gavin** **fl 1982-1984**
Sculptor. One of two brothers who exhibited RSA(2) in the 1980s, first from East Kilbride and latterly from Holm, Orkney.

**McCALLUM, Kerry J** **fl 1984**
Sculptor. Brother of John Gavin M(qv). Exhibited RSA.

**McCALLUM, Miller** **fl 1861**
Amateur Glasgow landscape painter. Exhibited GI(1) from 247 Sauchiehall St.

**McCAMMOND, David** **fl 1891-1895**
Greenock artist in oil and watercolour; pastoral scenes. Exhibited GI(6) & L(1) from 8 Margaret Street.

**McCANCE, William ('Mack')** **1894-1970**
Born Cambuslang, 6 Aug; died Girvan. Painter in oil and also sculptor. Youngest and seventh son in a family of eight. Educated Hamilton Academy, and Glasgow School of Art when Fra Newbury was Principal. Awarded a travelling bursary. Studied also under Greiffenhagen(qv) and Anning Bell(qv). Worked in London from 1919 where he was a member of the Vorticist group, producing abstract drawings in oil. Also art critic for the *Spectator* 1923-26. Illustrated under the pseudonym Mack for *Lloyds Magazine.* An ardent nationalist and friend of Hugh Macdiarmid. Exhibitions of sculpture, oil paintings and drawings were held at several London galleries and in St Andrews. From 1930-33 he controlled the Gregynog private printing press in Montgomeryshire. Published a number of books including *The Fables of Aesop* with wood engravings illustrated by his first wife, Agnes Parker. In 1933 he left Gregynog and moved first to Albrighton in the English Midlands and later to Hambledon, Berkshire. After separating from his wife 1955 moved to Girvan. Contributed a series of articles to the *New Chronicle, Reynolds News* and *Picture Post.* His articles on Epstein were subsequently reprinted in the artist's autobiography. Taught typography and book production at Reading University 1944-1959, a post in which he succeeded Robert Gibbins. Returned to Scotland and painted landscapes, especially the country near Barr. In 1963 he married Dr Margaret Chislett and from that time until his death in 1970 worked in Girvan. Hardie regards McCance as one of the most forward looking of Scottish artists during the period 1918-39 but his works remain rather obscure largely because he rarely exhibited in public and an unusually large proportion of his work was experimental. A travelling exhibition visited Dundee, Glasgow and Edinburgh in 1975. Represented in SNGMA, Dundee AG, Glasgow AG.
**Bibl:** Contemporary Scottish Studies, Edinburgh 1976; Dundee City AG, 'William McCance (1894-1970)', (Ex Cat 1975); Patrick Elliott, Scottish Masters series no. 14, Edinburgh 1990; Cyril Gerber FA, Glasgow 'William McCance', (Ex Cat 1989); Hardie 148-151 (illus); Hartley 144-5; William McCance, 'The Idea in Art', The Modern Scot, No 2, 1930; Hugh MacDiarmid,'The Art of William McCance', Saltire Review vi, no 22, 1960; 'William and Agnes McCance', Scott. Educ. J, 20 Nov 1925 reprinted; Macmillan [SA] 348-351,353, 358, 383; Reading AG,'Work by William McCance' (Ex Cat 1960).

**McCANN, Austin** **fl 1961**
Amateur Glasgow landscape painter. Exhibited GI(1).

**McCANN, Charles** **fl 1862-1875**
Glasgow painter in watercolour and occasional oil; landscapes, seascapes and coastal scenes. Exhibited GI(3).

**McCANN, Ellen Jean Wallace** **1954-**
Angus sculptress and ceramic designer and potter. Trained at Art School. Exhibited RSA since 1978, also AAS, from Kirkden Schoolhouse, Guthrie, by Forfar.

**McCANN, John P** **fl 1890-1894**
Aberdeen painter of local landscape, especially the Cairngorm mountains and the coastline around Aberdeen. Exhibited AAS(3) from Desswood Place.

**McCANN, L E** **fl 1894**
Amateur artist; exhibited GI(1).

**McCARTHY, Hamilton W** **1809-?**
Sculptor. A marble bust of Edward Irving, founder of the Catholic Apostolic Church, dated 1867, is in SNPG.

**McCARTNEY, Crear** **1931-**
Born Symington, Lanarkshire 4 Feb. Stained glass window designer and teacher. Studied Glasgow School of Art 1950-55 under Walter Pritchard(qv). After graduating worked for five years in the stained glass studio at Pluscarden Abbey, Moray. Principal art teacher, Lesmahagow 1964-1988. Since 1988 has devoted himself full-time to his own creative work. One of Scotland's leading designers. Represented by windows in St. Anthony's chapel, Fishlake, Indiana, USA 1958, Birnie kirk, Moray 1961-75, Paterson Memorial Kirk (5 windows 1976-1981), Ayr Auld Kirk 1986-90, the west window in St Magnus cathedral (to mark the 850th anniversary in 1987), St Margaret's, Banchory, Kincardineshire 1988, St Mary's, Nairn 1989, 4 windows in Dornoch cathedral 1988-91, Feteresso 1990, Biggar kirk, Lanarkshire 1991, and Fala kirk, Midlothian 1991. Currently working on a window for St Michael's, Linlithgow to celebrate the church's 750th anniversary. Exhibited GI(3) 1955.

**McCARTNEY, William** **fl 1953**
Amateur Argyll painter. Exhibited a still life at the GI from Dunoon.

**McCAY, Pat** **fl 1973-1979**
Dunbartonshire landscape artist. Exhibited GI(7) from 13 South View, Dalmuir before moving to London c1979.

**MACCHESNEY, Miss Jan** **fl 1974**
Glasgow embroiderer. Exhibited GI(1).

**McCHEYNE, Alistair Walker** **1918-1981**
Born Perth, 27 May. Painter in oil; genre and figurative subjects. Educated Perth Academy, studied art Edinburgh College of Art under David Alison(qv) 1935-40, London 1938-9 and Paris at the Academie Grande Chaumière in 1947. Awarded a scholarship in drawing and painting in Edinburgh 1939 and a travelling scholarship 1940. From 1950-56 he was BBC art critic and since 1955 principal art teacher, George Heriot School, Edinburgh and teacher of life drawing and painting in the Lauder Technical School, Dunfermline. Elected SSA 1945. Exhibited RSA(7).

**McCHEYNE, John Robert Murray FRBS** **1911-1982**
Born Edinburgh, 2 Jne. Sculptor in wood, stone, bronze and terracotta. Studied Edinburgh College of Art 1930-35, Copenhagen 1936-37, Athens and Florence 1937-38. Returning to Britain, exhibited regularly 1935-40, living latterly at Gosforth, Northumberland being attached to Kings College, Newcastle-on-Tyne as Master of Sculpture in 1939. Served in WW2 with Royal Engineers. First sculptor to carve Portsoy marble. His main sources of inspiration were Greece and Scotland. Writing in 1962 he identified two fundamental points of reference for understanding sculpture; "1) Sculpture is the occupation of space in such a way that mass and void together create an equilibrium; and 2) a sculpture is a work constructed out of material by a techique". Elected ARBS 1945. Exhibited RSA(9) & GI 1938-53. Represented in several churches and schools in the north-east of England, and in New Zealand.

**McCHLEARY, David** **fl 1924-1930**
Glasgow engraver of topographical subjects. Exhibited GI(8) & AAS from 5 Danes Drive, Scotstoun.

**McCLINTOCK, Mary (Maidhi) Howard (née Elphinstone)1888-?**
Born Bagshot, Surrey. Painter, modeller and woodcut artist. Fond of painting flowers. Studied at the Slade School, London, moving to Edinburgh 1925 where she remained for a number of years, latterly at 3 Arboretum Road. Exhibited RA(2), RSA(10), RSW(6), AAS(1), RBA(4), RI(3), SWA(2) & L(1).

**McCLORY, John** **fl 1944-1956**
Borders painter of still life, farmyard scenes and figurative works. Exhibited RSA between the above years, at first from Selkirk, after 1955 from Kelso.

**McCLURE, David RSA RSW RGI** **1926-1998**
Born Lochwinnoch, 20 Feb; died Dundee, Feb 20. Painter in oil and watercolour. Figurative subjects, still lifes and murals, often brightly coloured and with a symbolic element using flat colours and tones unaffected by light and shadow. Educated Queenspark School, Glasgow, Edinburgh University and Edinburgh College of Art 1947-52; received a travelling scholarship 1952-53 enabling him to visit Spain and Italy followed by further trips to Italy and Sicily in 1956-57. In 1955 an Andrew Grant fellowship saw him painting ceiling decorations and murals for the reconstructed King's Room at Falkland Palace. After further visits to Italy and Sicily in 1963 he spent three months in Oslo. Subsequently embarked on several sketching trips with Anne Redpath around the kingdom of Fife. Lived in Dundee and lectured at Dundee College of Art from 1957, becoming head of the painting school 1983-85. Although his health deteriorated, following his second marriage in 1988 he began to produce fine flower paintings and Scottish coastal scenes, rich in expression and colour. Published *John Maxwell*(qv) 1975, a monograph on his life and work. 'Timor Mortis', exhibited at the RSA 1989, was particularly well received. A sure draughtsman, he enjoyed bright colour and faithful attention to form. Elected ARSA 1963, RSW 1965, RSA 1971. Exhibited regularly at RSA, RSW, GI & AAS. Represented in SNGMA, Aberdeen AG, Dundee AG, Glasgow AG, Kirkcaldy AG, Lillie AG(Milngavie), Edinburgh City collection(3), Perth AG, Towner AG (Eastbourne).
**Bibl:** Gage 43,44,46,147; Anon, Obituary, RSA Annual Report 1998.

**McCLURE, Lady E T** **19th Cent**
Obscure landscape artist, probably an amateur. Represented in Edinburgh City collection by a sepia drawing on tinted paper of Dreghorn Castle.

**McCLURE, J** **fl 1820**
Engraver, probably of Edinburgh. Engraved a bookplate for John Davidson, 1820. Recorded in neither Bryan nor DNB.
**Bibl:** Bushnell

**McCLUSKEY, Miss Agnes** **fl 1865-1866**
Rothesay oil painter of flowers, fruit and still-life; exhibited RSA(2) & GI(1).

**McCLUSKEY, J M** **fl 1964**
Glasgow painter of still life and fruit. Exhibited GI(2) from Grosvenor Terrace.

**McCLYMONT, John Inglis** **fl 1880-1900**
Figure painter in oil and watercolour of domestic subjects and landscape. Lived in Edinburgh. His evocative portrait of 'Old Tom Morris' 1900 showing the by then elderly golfer standing quizzically on the green of a coastal links, putter under his arm, fetched £15,000 at auction in 1989. Lived for a time at 11a Shandwick Street, Edinburgh. Exhibited twice at the RA, 1893 and 1895, also RSA(36), GI(16) & AAS 1890-94. Represented in City of Edinburgh collection.

**McCOIG, Isobel** **fl 1970**
Kincardineshire painter of figurative subjects. Married Malcolm M(qv). Exhibited AAS.

**McCOIG, Malcolm** **1941-**
Born Greenock. Painter in oil and watercolour, printmaker. Studied Glasgow School of Art completing a postgraduate course. In 1964 he was appointed head of textile dept at Gray's School of Art, Aberdeen. Won Scot Riddley prize at the Bradford Biennale 1970 and spent most 1975 studying in Madison, Wisconsin, followed by a spell as artist in residence at Soulesquoi Printmakers, Orkney. Visiting lecturer in Nigeria 1988. Married Isobel M(qv). Exhibits RSA, AAS & overseas. Represented in SNGMA, Aberdeen AG, Hunterian AG (Glasgow University), Lillie AG(5,Milngavie), City of Edinburgh collection.
**Bibl:** Gage 68.

**MACCOLL, Dugald Sutherland** **1859-1948**
Born Glasgow, 10 Mar; died London, 2 Dec. Painter, mainly in watercolour; landscape and architectural subjects; art critic and teacher. Educated Westminster School, Glasgow, University College London and Lincoln College, Cambridge 1876-84. After studying at Westminster School of Art, went to the Slade, working under Legros 1884-92, followed by a visit to Italy and Greece. In 1890 art critic for the *Spectator* and later of the *Saturday Review*. Appointed lecturer in the history of art at University College, London and Keeper of the Tate Gallery 1906-11 and of the Wallace Collection 1911-24. Author of several art books including *Nineteenth Century Art* 1902, *Confessions of a Keeper* and *Philip Wilson Steer* 1945. His 'Crock and Cottage Loaf No 2' (1931) was purchased by the Chantrey Bequest in 1940. Elected NEA 1896, RSW 1938. Exhibited at the RA(2), RSA(10), RSW(3), AAS, L(3), & GI(10). Represented in SNPG, Glasgow AG, Kirkcaldy AG, collection of City of Edinburgh(3), Brodie Castle (NTS), Manchester AG.
**Bibl:** Caw 325,361; Halsby 240,269; Irwin 370; Harold Osborne(ed), Twentieth Century Art, 1988, 340.

**McCOLL, Mrs Kathleen** **fl 1940**
Amateur Helensburgh portrait painter; exhibited GI(2) including 'Self-portrait'.

**McCOLL, Lachlan** **fl 1973**
Amateur Edinburgh painter. Exhibited AAS(1) from 59 Ratcliffe Terrace.

**McCOMB, Leonard ARA** **1930-**
Born Springburn, Glasgow, 3 Aug. Painter in oil, watercolour, pastel, pencil and conte; portraits, interiors and flowers. Attended Junior Art School, Manchester 1945-1947, Regional College of Art, Manchester 1954-1956 and Slade 1959-1960. Immediately after graduating took up a teaching post at the West of England College of Art, Bristol remaining there until 1964 when he became head of Foundation Studies at Oxford Polytechnic 1964-1977. Held a number of one-man shows in various parts of the world including Germany, Venice, China and the USA. Received RA Award 1988 for the most distinguished work in any media. Represented in the V & A, Tate AG, Birmingham AG, Manchester AG, Swindon AG, Worcester AG.
**Bibl:** David Brown, 'The Watercolours of Leonard McComb', Arts Review, September 1979; Timothy Hyman: 'Leonard McComb Body and Spirit', London Mag, 1982; Ian Jeffrey 'Leonard McComb' Burlington Mag, 1984; John McEwen 'Stephen Buckley and Leonard McComb' Art in America, 1983.

**McCOMB, Mary** **fl 1895**
Glasgow landscape artist; exhibited GI(1) from 7 India Street.

**McCOMBIE, James** **fl 1945**
Amateur Glasgow figurative painter. Exhibited GI(1).

**McCOMBIE, Miss R** **fl 1887**
Aberdeen-based painter; exhibited RSA(1).

**McCOMISH, Roy** **fl 1950**
Exhibited a pen and wash sketch at GI from Gordonstoun School.

**McCONCHIE, John** **fl 1892-1894**
Landscape painter in watercolour. Living in Paris 1883. Exhibited GI(4) from West Kilbride.

**McCONNELL, Leslie C** **fl 1978-1979**
Fife painter of figurative and narrative subjects. Exhibited RSA(2) from Kinghorn.

**McCONNOCHIE, Mrs Alex Inkson (née Thom)** **1846-c1910**
Born Peterhead, Aug 12. Amateur Aberdeen-based portrait painter; often in pastel. Married the well known author at St Nicholas church, Aberdeen 1873. Exhibited a pastel portrait of her husband at the AAS in 1898, 'Self-portrait' 1902 and a study of 'Gerald Lawrence' 1908, when living at 88 Devonshire Rd.

**MacCONVILLE, Charles** **fl 1938-1940**
Landscape watercolour painter, especially of the Clyde. Exhibited GI(5) from Rankin Drive, Largs.

**MacCONVILLE, Gordon** **fl 1946**
Amateur Paisley landscape painter in watercolour. Exhibited 'The Old Tolbooth', Stonehaven at the GI.

**McCORKINDALE, Flora** **fl 1908-1937**
Miniature painter. Exhibited RSA(1) & GI(3) from Craiginan Lodge, Dollar, and in 1937 from Birnam, Perthshire.

**McCORMACK, John** **fl 1947-1952**
Angus topographical watercolour painter. Exhibited GI(2) from Brechin.

**McCORMACK, William W** **fl 1911-1918**
Painter. Exhibited RSA(5) & GI(2) from The Anchorage, Helensburgh and latterly from Lurgan.

**MacCORMI(A?)CK** **19th century**
Miniaturist, probably Scottish. Long records a miniature portrait of a Naval Officer signed 'McC', painted in the manner of Andrew Robertson, and catalogued as by 'McCormick'. This appeared in the salerooms 1921. Schedlof records a miniature painter of this name working in London 1860.

**McCORMICK, Fiona** **fl 1956-1964**
Edinburgh painter of Lothian and continental landscape, also flowers. Exhibited RSA(13).

**McCRACKEN, Cynthia G S** **fl 1918-1963**
Fife oil and watercolour painter of portraits, snow scenes and topographical sketches. Daughter of Lieut-General Sir F M(qv) & Lady McCracken whose portrait she painted, and was shown at the RSA 1918. An artist listed only as McCracken exhibited 'Winter' at the RSA in 1944 from the Marine Hotel, Elie. Exhibited RSA(11), RSW(1) & GI(6) from Ochter House, Elie; by 1945 she had moved to Croydon.

**McCRACKEN, David MRCVS** **1925-**
Born Glasgow, 30 Apr. Landscape painter in watercolour and pen and ink; also veterinary surgeon. Educated Queenspark, Glasgow, Marr College, Troon and Glasgow Vet College 1948. Self-taught artist, influenced by the work of Cotman, Callow, Bonnington, Crawhall(qv) and Wyeth. Since about 1970 has worked mainly in pen and ink, being particularly attracted to rustic buildings in Massachusetts and around Perth, where he lives. His portrayals of the Old Grist Mill in Sudbury, Mass, exemplified an exquisite attention to detail, the sensitive handling of line producing a quite idiosyncratic and entirely refreshing result.

**McCRACKEN, Lieut-General Sir F** **fl 1944**
Amateur artist. Took up painting after retiring from the army. Father of Cynthia M(qv). Exhibited GI(2) from the Marine hotel, Elie, Fife.

**McCRACKEN, Francis** **1879-1959**
Born Northern Ireland; died Edinburgh. Painter in oil and water-colour; mostly flower pieces, portraits, genre, interiors and still life but also occasional Scottish and continental landscapes. Emigrated to Australia with his family as a young child, thence to New Zealand. Early training Auckland School of Art before coming to Edinburgh after the war in 1921 studying at the RSA School. After winning a Carnegie travelling bursary he went to Paris studying under L'Hôte. Influenced by Cubism, exhibited at the Paris Salon. Always a rebel, he resigned from SSA shortly after joining. Member of the Scottish avant-garde, frequently visited the Middle East. A memorial exhibition was held at the RSA, Edinburgh 1960. Exhibited RSA(45), RSW(5), GI(4), AAS(3) & L(3) from 10 Forth Street. [From notes by J Chisholm.]

**MacCRAE, George** **fl 1783-1802**
Born Edinburgh. Travelled to Canada 1783 where he established himself as a successful portrait painter in Halifax remaining there until 1802. Returned to Scotland, after which nothing further is known of his work. One of the first portrait painters in Canada and a member of the first Canadian art organisation, the 'Amateur Chess, Pencil and Brush' (of Halifax) 1787-1817. Shortly after his arrival in Canada was appointed Secretary of the North British Society, Halifax.

**McCRIE, John** **fl 1870-1873**
Glasgow landscape painter. Exhibited GI(2) from Thistle St.

**McCRINDLE, Alfred D A** **fl 1928-1933**
Ayrshire watercolour artist & engraver; exhibited RSA(2), RSW(1), GI(9) & L(2) from Gowanbrae, Girvan and latterly Kilmarnock.

**McCRINK, John Henry** **fl 1973**
Amateur Aberdeen painter; exhibited AAS(1).

**McCRONE, Noni** **fl 1961-1981**
Perthshire artist in oil of landscapes, especially flora and also occasional coloured woodcuts. Exhibited RSA(30) from Crieff.

**McCROSSAN, Miss Mary** **fl 1897-1927**
Glasgow painter of harbour and fishing scenes. Exhibited RA(3) & GI(9) at first from Ann St, then Liverpool and later from Cheyne Walk, London.

**McCULLOCH, A** **fl 1878-1890**
Dundee architect. Responsible with his erstwhile partner **J C FAIRLEY** of Edinburgh for the early Renaissance style Girls HS, Euclid Crescent, Dundee (1889) and for the Public Gymnasium, Ward Rd, Dundee (since remodelled).
**Bibl:** Bruce Walker & W S Gauldie, Architects and Architecture on Tayside, Dundee 1984, 138.

**McCULLOCH, D R** **fl 1888**
Amateur painter; exhibited GI(1) from 50 West Clyde Street, Helensburgh.

**McCULLOCH, Daniel Whyte** **fl 1842**
Edinburgh portrait painter. Exhibited 'Sir John Graham Dalyell, Bt' at the RSA in 1842 from 16 Charlotte St.

**McCULLOCH, David** **fl 1871**
Amateur painter. Exhibited a still life of fruit in watercolour at the GI. No address listed.

**McCULLOCH, Elizabeth M C** **fl 1886**
Edinburgh watercolourist of landscapes; exhibited RSA(2) from 2 Alfred Place, Newington, including Turnberry Lighthouse.

**McCULLOCH, George** **fl 1852-1901**
Sculptor and painter in oil of literary subjects, landscapes and figure paintings. This versatile artist exhibited 30 works at the RA (1859-1901) latterly from St Agnes's Vicarage, Logan, Stranraer. Resident in London most of his working life. Member of the Hogarth Club. Exhibited regularly RSA(24) 1852-78, ROI(1), RBA(1) & GI(14).

**MacCULLOCH, Horatio RSA** **1805-1867**
Born Glasgow; died Trinity, nr Edinburgh, 26 Jne. Landscape painter in oil. Son of a weaver, he was born on the night Glasgow was celebrating Trafalgar Day, hence his Christian name. Employed by Lizars to colour Selby's *Ornithology* c1825 as well as a work on anatomy by Dr Lizars. After a spell in Cumnock with W L Leitch(qv) and Macnee(qv) painting snuffboxes he returned to Glasgow exhibiting with the Glasgow Dilettanti Society(qv). Began to exhibit RSA 1829. Moved to Edinburgh 1838 settling in the New Town. Studied under the landscape artist John Knox(qv), alongside Macnee and W L Leitch. Exhibited mostly at the RSA, showing only two pictures at the RA in 1843. Together with Landseer, whom he often met while painting in Argyll, he contributed more than any other painter to the popular Victorian image of the Highlands which to a large extent continues to this day. Especially attracted to the Forest of Cadzow and the lower valleys of the Clyde and Avon causing him to live in Hamilton, only moving to Edinburgh after election to the RSA. His works have a certain national character influencing the Scottish school of landscape painting to a greater extent than any other artist of his time. His early paintings were largely derivative from John Thomson(qv) but became more individual as he returned increasingly to Highland subjects. Nevertheless, he found it difficult to assimilate the finer qualities of his predecessors and exaggerated his own idiosyncrasies. 'His main failing is to overcrowd features and to force the contrasts'. He never rid himself of the conventional treatment of foliage as practised by Nasmyth and others and he had problems with water. Redgrave said of his 'Loch Achray', shown at Manchester 1857 'it is reflection without surface'. He was a man of simple habits, extensive reading, varied information and great amiability deserving the respect which he enjoyed on all sides. The generation of painters he influenced included John Fleming, Arthur Perigal, J Milne Donald, Edmond Hargitt & Alexander Fraser who wrote his biography. 'His style was vigorous, robust and refined, conveying to a spectator a grand impression of nature in all its phases. His moonlights, especially of the deer forest, are full of fine poetic feeling, and probably no artist has so truly rendered the character of Scottish scenery as exhibited in the broad expanse of lake and on loch and crag, of mountains swathed in mist, rising beyond remains of old Highland fortresses' [Brydall]. Elected ARSA 1834, RSW 1838. A major exhibition was held at Glasgow AG 1988. Exhibited 200 works at the RSA 1829-1868 & GI 1861-7. Represented in Glasgow AG, NGS, Aberdeen AG, Broughty Ferry AG, Dundee AG, Paisley AG, Perth AG, City of Edinburgh collection, Brodie Castle (NTS), Culzean Castle (NTS).
**Bibl:** AJ 1864, 187f (obit); 1867, 187-8; Armstrong 42-3; Art Union 1847, 380; Brydall 438-41; Butchart 69,77; Caw 143-5 et passim; Cundall; DNB; Alexander Fraser, Scottish Landscape. The Works of Horatio MacCulloch, Edinburgh 1872; Gott 229, pl 124; Halsby 110-112 et al; Hardie III 187-8; Irwin 353-7; McKay 266-71; Macmillan [SA] 164,210,225-9; Portfolio 1887, 135f, 207; Sheena Smith,'Horatio McCulloch', Glasgow AG (Ex Cat 1988).

**McCULLOCH, Ian ARSA** **1935-**
Born Glasgow, Mar 4. Painter in oil and acrylic. Studied Glasgow School of Art 1953-57 and Hospitalfield, Arbroath. Awarded travelling scholarship 1957. Lived in Cumbernauld, taught University of Strathclyde. Founder member, Glasgow Group. Retired to Lenzie. Included in the exhibition 'Three Centuries of Scottish Painting' at National Gallery of Canada 1968-69. Held his first one-man show in Edinburgh 1960. 1976 Artist-in-residence, Univ. of Sussex. Elected ARSA 1989. Won 1st prize, Stirling Smith Biennial 1985; winner of Glasgow International Concert Hall Mural Competition 1989-90. Many solo exhibitions in Canada, Germany, Holland, UK and USA. Exhibited RSA(33) 1959-1984, GI(3) & AAS(1) 1973, from 12 Meadow View, Cumbernauld. Represented in the City of Edinburgh collection, Glasgow AG, Univs of Glasgow & Liverpool, SAC, Smith AG (Stirling), Kelvingrove AG, Dundee AG, Perth AG. Lives at 51 Victoria Rd, Lewnzie, Glasgow G6 5AP.
**Bibl:** Gage 55,57,147.

**MacCULLOCH, James RBA RSW** **fl 1863-d1915**
Landscape painter in watercolour and oil. Lived for many years in London. Painted mostly Highland subjects, especially on the west coast in Ross-shire and on Skye. His style was tight and his colours tended to be overly sweet with purple mountains and very bright skies. Elected RBA 1884, RSW 1885. Exhibited four works at the RA 1874-1883, all of them Highland scenes, and several at the RSA, but mainly at the RBA(120) & RSW(68); also GI(34), RI(24), ROI(1) & L(4). Represented in Glasgow AG, Manchester AG.
**Bibl:** Halsby 270.

**McCULLOCH, John** **fl 1862-1872**
Glasgow oil painter of figurative subjects and pastoral scenes; exhibited RSA(1) & GI(13).

**McCULLOCH, Miss Martha** **fl 1984**
Amateur Lanarkshire painter. Exhibited GI(1) from Coatbridge.

**McCULLOCH, Mary Miller** **fl 1900-1910**
Kilmarnock flower painter. Exhibited RA(1), RSA(1), GI(8), L(6).

**MacCULLOCH, Thomas** **fl 1846-66**
Edinburgh painter in oil of genre, country interiors and still-life; exhibited RSA(11) & GI. Titles included 'Hogmanay' (1848), 'The braw pennyworth' (1854) & 'Returned from the fair' (1857).

**McCULLOUGH, Felix** **fl 1964**
Edinburgh stained glass window designer and art critic. Exhibited laminated glass panels illustrating details from the Passion of Christ for St Francis Xavier church, Falkirk exhibited RSA 1964. Worked from Outlook Tower, Castle Hill.

**McCULL(E)Y, W T** **fl 1894-1896**
Morayshire painter. Particularly attached to upper Deeside. Three of his four exhibits at the AAS were 'Shepherd's Brig over the Cluny, Braemar', 'Old Castle of Braemar', & 'On the Glenshee Rd, Braemar', all entered from Young Street, Nairn.

**McCURRACH, Margaret T** **fl 1956-1968**
Fife artist who painted flower studies, local and fishing scenes from St Andrews and later Cupar. Exhibited RSA(13).

**McCUTCHEON, John ROI** **1910-**
Born Dalmellington, Ayrshire, Jne 1. Painter in oil, watercolour, pen and ink also occasional portraits in pastel. Studied at Glasgow School of Art 1929-33. Won the McCowan prize 1929. Influenced by the French Impressionists, especially Pisarro, Sisley, Monet, Cézanne and Van Gogh. His gay, scintillating harbour scenes were inspired by Honfleur and Bruges. Until about 1960 his work was decidedly representational, thereafter a stronger sense of colour and pictorial design became apparent and the subject matter narrowed to coastal scenes, street markets and flower pieces. Visited France on a number of occasions. Elected Associate, Society of French Artists 1969, ROI 1970. Exhibited RSA(12), RSW(2), GI(40) & Paris Salon from 3 Lothian Gardens, Glasgow.

**MACCUTCHEON, Miss Mary Welsh** **fl 1946-1948**
Glasgow painter of genre. Watercolour, pen and wash. Exhibited GI(5) from Onslow Drive.

**McCUTCHION, John** **fl 1937-1954**
Glasgow landscape painter, often of the western Highlands, principally in watercolour. Exhibited GI(15) from Paisley West Rd then Forfar Ave.

**MacDONALD, A M** **fl 1875-1889**
Edinburgh painter of rural and domestic scenes and interiors, also occasional portraits. From 1887 lived at 8 York Buildings, Queen St. Exhibited RSA(52) including a portrait of the artist J C Wintour 1883, also GI(3).

**MacDONALD, Alastair James Henderson RMS FRSA** **1934-**
Born Tigh-na-bruaich, Argyll, Jly 5. Painter of landscape miniatures in watercolour and gouache. Educated at Pope Street School, New Eltham, studied art at Woolwich Polytechnic under Heber Matthews and Joan Dawson. His work, usually on card, is principally watercolour and tends to have an Oriental appearance, due to his treatment of the basic structure of plants and the constant search for simplicity. Council member, RMS 1973-4. Exhibited RMS & RI.

**McDONALD, Alexander** **1839-1921**
Aberdeen portrait painter, also occasional landscapes. Went to England at an early age. Began exhibiting RA from Bushey, Herts 1893, showing 11 works there including 'The Earl of Lichfield' 1904 and 'Frederick Morris Fry, Master of the Merchant Taylor's Company' 1896. Also exhibited RSA(1), AAS(18), & L(2) and lived latterly in Winchester, Hants.

**MacDONALD, Alice** **fl 1893-1929**
Aberdeen versatile painter of local landscape, portraits, figurative works and domestic animals, especially dogs. Moved in the 1920s to The Grange, Inverness. Exhibited regularly AAS and occasionally at the GI.

**MacDONALD, Angus William** **fl 1983-1988**
Aberdeen painter, trained Gray's School of Art, Aberdeen. Exhibited AAS(2) from 195 King St.

**MacDONALD, Archibald W** **fl 1930-1933**
Exhibited 'The entry - Crinan canal' at the RSA from a Glasgow address. Moved later to Coventry.

**MacDONALD, Arthur** **fl 1906-1943**
Edinburgh painter in oil and watercolour of interiors, coastal scenes, portraits and genre. Formerly from Glasgow but after 1902 from Sunnyside, Pittenweem, Fife. Exhibited RSA(31), RSW(3), GI(95), AAS 1910-1937 & L(3)

**MacDONALD, Miss Catriona** **fl 1984**
Amateur Glasgow portrait painter. Exhibited GI(4) from Cambuslang.

**MacDONALD, Miss Christina** **fl 1877-1878**
Dornoch watercolour painter of wild flowers; exhibited RSA(3).

**McDONALD, D** **fl 1867-1877**
Port Glasgow oil painter of landscapes, especially the West Highlands; exhibited RSA(11) & GI(6).

**McDONALD E M** **fl 1876-1888**
Edinburgh painter. Exhibited RSA(1) & GI(1) from 3 Great King Street.

**MacDONALD, Elizabeth R** **fl 1908**
Aberdeen amateur flower painter. Exhibited AAS(1) from 293 Gt Western Rd.

**MACDONALD, Flora (Mrs William Johnstone)** **20th Cent**
American sculptress. Married William Johnstone(qv) in 1927, having met her husband in Paris when working in the studio of Antoine Bourdelle. Had studied stone carving in Edinburgh with Alexander Carrick(qv).

**MacDONALD, Frances E (Mrs MacNair)** **1874-1921**
Watercolour painter of portraits and figure subjects; embroiderer and metalwork designer. One of the most important artistic figures of her generation. Sister of Margaret M(qv)(Mrs Rennie Mackintosh). Studied Glasgow School of Art 1890-c1894. Won bronze medal in a national competition for a tapestry while still a student. Collaborated closely with her sister Margaret, especially at the beginning of their careers and, with their respective husbands, they constituted the 'Group of Four'(qv). Early watercolours had a strong symbolic element. 'The Macdonalds poster work challenged the existing visual iconography of its day by providing a radical new representation of the 'feminine persona'. Their images provided an alternative reading of 'femininity' to that of the dominant discourse and created a female who was visually self-defined" [Burkhauser]. After their marriages the sisters developed in increasingly distinctive ways although the Four continued to exhibit as a group until the Turin exhibition of 1902. Between 1909 and 1915 her work shows the effects of the personal marital problems she was suffering as well as the influence of the changing social mores relating to the role of women. Whilst in Liverpool 1899-1908 she taught at University College before returning with the family to Glasgow. For the next three years taught design at Glasgow School of Art. Two of her more controversial works, 'Girl in the East Wind with Ravens Passing the Moon or (Ill Omen)', completed in 1893, and 'The Sleeping Princess' of 1895/6 were reproduced in *The Yellow Book,* July 1896. That year her work was featured in *The Studio.* Her exhibits with the Sandon Society of Artists in 1908 and subsequently at the London Salon received critical attention, but this was more for their rhythmic inventiveness and symbolism than for their relationship to feminist theory which became the main source of current interest. It is unclear whether she committed suicide or died of a cerebral haemorrhage. After her death MacNair destroyed most of what remained of his wife's work (as well as his own). In addition to the international exhibitions and later at the Salons, she exhibited at the RSW(1), GI(2) & L(3) from 9 Windsor Terrace, Glasgow. Represented in Glasgow AG, Hunterian Museum (Glasgow Univ).
**Bibl:** Burkhauser 90-95,123-132 et passim; Halsby 175-9; Hardie passim ch vii; Irwin 396,400-1(illus); Liverpool Courier 10 April 1912; London Salon Cat 1908; Macmillan [SA] 293-4,296-305; Scottish Art Review,19, no 4, 1975, 13-16, 28; Studio XI, 1897, 86-100.

**MacDONALD, Miss Frances J** **fl 1983-1985**
Argyll amateur painter. Exhibited GI(4) from Crinan Cottage, Crinan.

**MacDONALD, Fred R** **fl 1964-1965**
Edinburgh painter & designer. Taught at Edinburgh College of Art. Exhibited RSA(4) from Sciennes Rd.

**MacDONALD, Hamish** **1935-**
Born 29 Jan. Painter and teacher; landscapes and seascapes in oil,

gouache and watercolour. Trained Glasgow School of Art 1963-7 becoming Principal Art Teacher at St Patrick's High School, Coatbridge. National winner of the Laing painting competition 1989. Held several one-man shows since 1963. Commissioned by the Bell Coll. of Technology to paint the portrait of William Bell. Contributor to Arts Review broadcasts and publications. Won RGI award 1993; co-winner, Laing Art competition 1997. Exhibits at the RSA, GI, SSA and RSW annually from his home in Uddingston. Represented in Glasgow AG, Paisley AG.

**MacDONALD, Hugh** **fl 1796**
Edinburgh engraver. Married in Lady Yester's parish 18 Dec 1796.

**MacDONALD, Hugh** **fl 1906-1920**
Glasgow landscape painter; exhibited RA(1) & GI(15).

**MacDONALD, Ian** **fl 1966-1968**
Glasgow painter in oils; preoccupied with the effects of light upon colour. Exhibited RSA(2) & GI(3).

**MacDONALD, J H** **19th Cent**
Edinburgh painter in oil of rustic interiors; exhibited 'The Old Smiddy' at the RSA from 4 St Peter's Place, Edinburgh.

**MacDONALD, James** **fl 1831-1833**
Edinburgh sculptor. Portrait busts and narrative works, usually with a religious connotation. Exhibited RSA from Cumberland St.

**MacDONALD, James** **fl 1974-1975**
Haddington landscape painter. Exhibited RSA(3) & GI(8).

**MacDONALD, James** **fl 1984**
Cumbernauld painter and engraver. Exhibited RSA(1) & GI(6).

**MacDONALD, James Wilson Galloway ('Jock')** **1897-1960**
Born Thurso, Caithness; died Toronto, Canada. Son of an architect. Studied Edinburgh College of Art 1918-22. Fabric designer 1922-25 with Charles Paine; taught at Lincoln School of Art as Head of Design 1925. Migrated to Vancouver 1926 to become Head of Design at the Vancouver Art School. Sketched with Varley 1927-34 and after 1933 became interested in 20th century art, especially the work of Kandinsky, Klee and Miro. Together with Varley he founded the British Columbia College of Arts 1933-5. Lived in Nootka, British Columbia 1935-6. One of the five founding fathers of abstract art in Canada (with Brooker, FitzGerald, Brandtner and Lawren Harris). In his early days in the colony he was fascinated by the mountains and Indian life of the west coast. His first exhibited work 'Lytton church, British Columbia' 1930 is now in the Nat. Gallery of Art, Ottawa. He had painted 'Automatics' by 1934 but moved to abstract works from 1935. Lived in the local lighthouse but during the depression life was so difficult that he virtually stopped eating and was eventually removed to hospital suffering from malnutrition. In 1937 he travelled to California to visit correspondents to whom he had described his experiments. Viewing an exhibition there which he especially admired inspired him to develop what he called his 'Modalities' - an expression borrowed from Kant to connote 'expression of thought in relation to nature'. During the early years of WW2 these Modalities were sufficiently popular to allow him to live. He moved first to Calgary and then c1947 to Toronto where students at the College of Art there profited from his lucid teaching. At this time he was painting not only experimental abstracts but conventional canvases from his earlier period. Finally in 1954 his experimentation brought him to a new school of modernism and he joined the Painter's Eleven, committed to abstraction and modernism. His best known student was William Ronald. Returned to Vancouver and taught at the Canadian Institute of Associated Arts and Templeton Junior High School. Appointed Director, art department of the Institute of Technology and Art, Calgary 1942 and at Banff School of Fine Arts 1945-46. Then moved east to Toronto, teaching at the Ontario College of Art 1947-60. In 1954 he travelled to Europe on a Canadian government fellowship visiting Scotland, France and Venice. Represented in Nat. Gall. of Canada (Ottawa), Art Gall of Greater Victoria (B.C.), Ontario AG, Toronto AG.
**Bibl:** Terry Fenton & Karen Wilkin, Modern Painting in Canada, Canada 1978, 111 et passim; Harold Osborne(ed), Twentieth Century Art, 1988,340-1.

**MacDONALD, James Lock** **fl 1878-1882**
Edinburgh landscape painter in oil, also military subjects; exhibited RSA(2) from 16 Greenside Street.

**McDONALD, Jeff** **fl 1988-**
East Kilbride painter. Exhibited GI(3) 1988.

**McDONALD, Jessie M** **fl 1880-1889**
Painter in oil of landscape and topographical subjects. Lived and worked in Edinburgh, Stonehaven and Pollockshields. Exhibited RSA(6) & GI(6).

**McDONALD, John** **fl 1843-1858**
Edinburgh painter in oil of figurative subjects and genre; exhibited RSA(51).

**McDONALD, John** **fl 1885-1888**
Edinburgh painter in watercolour; possibly the son of John M. Exhibited three scenes of old Edinburgh at the RSA from 8 Leslie Place.

**MacDONALD, John** **fl c1840-c1860**
Born Edinburgh where he had a small business in the High Street as framer and vendor of artists' materials. As a young man he was reputed to have shared a studio with Wilkie. Painted in sombre colours but became more colourful. Many of his portraits were burned in an Edinburgh fire but a self-portrait is known to remain, also the study of a blind fiddler with a dwarf child and a dog 'Cleopatra'. A son, **John MacDonald Jnr**, was a landscape painter who exhibited GI(1) 1861.

**MacDONALD, John** **1967-**
Born Sep 3. Printmaker. Studied Glasgow School of Art 1986-90. His main interest is in printmaking, etching, lithography, screen prints and charcoal drawings. Worked for a time on the theme of Scottish gold mining based on his own experience around Tyndrum. Exhibited RSA 1989-90 from 68 Thornbridge Road, Garrowhill, Glasgow.

**MacDONALD, John Blake RSA** **1829-1901**
Born Boharm, Morayshire, May 24; died Edinburgh, Dec 21. Painter of historical subjects, especially Jacobite, also figurative works, domestic genre and latterly landscape. Worked in both oil and watercolour. Educated in his northern village before going to Edinburgh where in 1857 he entered the RSA Life School and in 1862 carried off first prize for painting from life. Studied under Scott Lauder(qv) with Chalmers(qv) and MacTaggart(qv). Made Edinburgh his home, paying frequent visits to France, Belgium and in 1874 Venice. Painted in a strong, bold manner using dark colours and the chiaroscuro effects encouraged by R S Lauder. His best work was effective and very 'Scottish' in feel but always rather lacking in draughtsmanship. In later life he gave up figure painting in favour of landscape. Elected ARSA 1862, RSA 1877. Started exhibiting 1846, the first being portraits of Hugh Millar and a lady. For the next twenty years he painted portraits and figure subjects, usually Highland or Jacobite, with such titles as 'Dugald Dalgety's interview with Montrose' 1862, 'Prince Charles leaving Scotland' 1863 and 'Arrest of a rebel at Culloden' 1864. Showed AAS 1887. His most famous painting was probably 'Lochaber No More; Prince Charlie leaving Scotland' 1863, now in Dundee AG, also represented in Crathes Castle (NTS).
**Bibl:** Bryan; Caw 262, 264; Halsby 270; McKay 359.

**MacDONALD, J P** **fl 1871**
Amateur Glasgow painter. Exhibited 'Old Bridge of Dee, nr Braemar' at the GI, from 13 Elm Grove.

**MacDONALD, Miss Katherine Bethune** **fl 1959**
Amateur Inverness painter in watercolour. Exhibited two continental scenes at the GI.

**MacDONALD, L A** **fl 1874-1875**
Skye painter of local landscapes in oil. Husband of Maria M(qv). Exhibited RSA(3) and later at the GI, from Fairlie, nr Largs.

**MacDONALD, Lawrence RSA HRSA** **1799-1878**
Born Gask, Perthshire, Feb 15; died Rome, Mar 12. Sculptor. Began

to carve in stone at an early age when apprenticed to a local mason, Thomas Gibson. His first recorded work is of a statue of a boy supporting a vase on his head which can be seen in the garden at Moncreiffe, Perthshire. In 1822 he went to Edinburgh, entering the Trustees Academy, and the same year proceeded to study in Rome, becoming one of the founders of the British Academy of Arts in that city. Four years later he returned to Edinburgh where he showed classical groups, a figure of the Youthful Slinger, and a number of busts including Charles Kemble, described in the *Literary Gazette* (1831) as 'fine and energetic a head as ever was modelled...considering that MacDonald is one of the most distinguished ornaments of the British School of Sculpture'. While in Edinburgh he was admitted to the Edinburgh Phrenological Society, whose founder (George Combe) he had initiated into the philosophy of art 'exercising a formative influence on Combie's exposition of phrenology in relation to the fine arts' [Smailes]. In 1832 he went back to Rome and remained there until his death 46 years later. One of the most popular portrait sculptors of his time. Writing in the *AJ* from Rome in 1851, a correspondent described his studio as 'the peerage done into marble, a plaster galaxy of rank and fashion, row after row and room after room of noble and illustrious persons of peer. All who ever figured in the *Court Journal* are here, looking as classical as drapery and hair-dressing can make them yet a patent family likeness pervades them all, a universal type reminding me of a bad dinner tasting as if every dish had been cooked in the same pot, insipid and unappetising, very'. Although unfair, this criticism contains more than a grain of truth. Elected RSA 1829, HRSA 1858. He is buried near the Porta San Paolo. Exhibited 25 works at the Institute for the Encouragement of Fine Arts in Scotland 1827-29 from 12 Pitt Street, Edinburgh and at the Scottish Academy, seven works in 1832, one (from Rome) in 1837 and at the RSA three marble busts between 1841 and 1865. His major statues are 'Girl with a Carrier Pigeon' of 1830 (Russell-Cotes Museum, Bournemouth), 'Ajax', 1831, (Powerscourt, Ireland), 'Andromeda Chained' 1848 (Haddo House) and 'Hyacinthus', 1852 (Windsor Castle). Among his most impressive busts are the Duke of Atholl 1827 (Blair Atholl), Viscountess Canning and The Marchioness of Waterford, 1838 (both at Highcliffe Castle), Lord Alexander Russell 1839 (Woburn Abbey), Lady Ebury 1839 (Apsley House), Sir Henry Taylor 1843 (NPG), Duke of Cambridge 1846 (Windsor Castle) and George Combe (SNPG). Also represented in Perth AG.
**Bibl:** AJ,1851,351; Brydall 190; George Combe, 'Notice of Laurence MacDonald', Phrenological J, Edinburgh 1832, 154-162; P H Drummond, Perthshire in Bygone days, London 1879, ch xviii 109-126; DNB; Gunnis 248-9; Frederick Moncreiffe, The Moncreiffes Vol 2,494; Helen Smailes,'Thomas Campbell and Laurence MacDonald: the Roman Solution to the Scottish Sculptor's dilemma', in 'Virtue and Vision, Sculpture in Scotland 1540-1990', NGS (Ex Cat 1991).

**MacDONALD, Margaret**
**[see MACKINTOSH, Margaret Macdonald]**

**MacDONALD, Maria C** **fl 1874-1877**
Skye painter of landscape and rustic scenes. Wife of L A M(qv). Exhibited RSA(3) & GI(2).

**MacDONALD, Martha** **fl 1985**
Dundee painter. Exhibited 'Pineapple pieces' at the RSA.

**MacDONALD, Murray J** **fl 1887-1914**
Edinburgh oil and watercolour painter of landscapes and figurative subjects. His work was generally on a small scale, finely portrayed with good colour and accurate detail. His watercolours were particularly sensitively executed. An artist whose reputation has grown with the passage of time although the small scale on which he preferred to work remains an obstacle to general recognition of his due. Painted often on Deeside and in the Angus glens. Exhibited RSA(9). Represented in Paisley AG, Royal collection ('Balmoral Castle').

**MacDONALD, Neil** **fl 1985-1987**
Glasgow portrait painter. Exhibited GI(2), from Caird Drive.

**MacDONALD, R A** **fl 1879**
Edinburgh watercolour painter of rustic scenes; exhibited RSA(1).

**McDONALD, Robert Neville** **fl 1887-1888**
Ayrshire painter. Exhibited GI(3) from Galston, nr Kilmarnock.

**MacDONALD, Dr Ronald Annandale** **1899-?**
Edinburgh etcher. Studied at Edinburgh College of Art; exhibited RSA 1928-31 from 69 Merchiston Crescent.

**MacDONALD, Samuel** **fl 1865-1891**
Edinburgh landscape painter in oil; exhibited two Highland scenes at the RSA, one of them of Skye where he was then living; also GI(1).

**MacDONALD, Somerled** **1869-1948**
Born Skye; died Inverness. Landscape and portrait painter who lived most of his life in Armadale in Skye although latterly moved for a time to Inverness where he died. Painted portraits of many Highlanders including Lord Lovat and the late Lord Lovat, both exhibited at the RA. A champion piper, winning the Scottish Piping Society's Championship several times. Exhibited RA(2), RSA(16), AAS ('Gordon piper practising', 1902), GI(3) & London Salon(3).
**Bibl:** Scotsman March 29,1948 (obit).

**MacDONALD, Stuart Wyllie** **1948-**
Born Dundee, Sep 8. Painter, mainly in oil. Educated Gray's School of Art and Hospitalfield, Arbroath 1966-71. Awarded an Italian scholarship enabling him to visit Florence 1971 and first prize at Arbroath 1973. Greatly influenced by the Tuscany landscape and by the Italian masters, particularly Mantegna, Uccello and Piero della Francesca. At home he came under the contrasting influences of William Johnstone(qv), James Cowie(qv) and Edward Baird(qv). Lived and worked at Forres, Moray during the 1980s and since 1990 from Glasgow. Regular exhibitor RSA, AAS, GI & SSA.

**MacDONALD, Thomas** **fl 1867**
Edinburgh landscape painter in oil; exhibited RSA(1).

**MacDONALD, Tom** **1914-1985**
Born & died Glasgow. Painter in oil, watercolour & gouache; semi-abstracts and figurative subjects. Trained as a marine engineer but left sea to work as a theatre designer. Proceeded to spend a year studying painting with Joseph Herman(qv) when resident in Glasgow 1937-8. In 1947 he married Bet Low(qv), with whom he had been a member of the New Art Club(qv). Between 1965 and 1975 worked intermittently with the Scottish Opera Company and from 1950 devoted himself to full-time painting. Extra-mural teacher of art in Glasgow, held his first one-man show in Edinburgh in 1961. Elected member of the SSA, founder member of the Clyde Group(qv). Exhibited RSA(10) 1965-1981, GI & AAS(2). Represented in SNGMA.
**Bibl:** Hardie 167; Wingfield.

**MacDONALD, Virginia** **fl 1964-1975**
Aberdeen painter of country scenes; exhibited AAS from 34 Victoria St and latterly from Waulkmill Cottage, Peterculter.

**MacDONALD, W** **fl 1978**
Argyll landscape painter. Exhibited two mountain scenes at the GI, from Rockvale, Shore Rd, Innellan.

**MacDONALD, William** **fl 1911-1913**
Edinburgh painter of portraits and still life. Exhibited RSA(4) from North St Andrew Street.

**MacDONALD, William** **fl 1913**
Edinburgh painter who exhibited 'Mother & child' at the RSA from 20 Harrison Rd.

**MacDONALD, William** **1883-1960**
Born Scotland; died Edinburgh. Landscape painter in oil; portraits, still life, Scottish & continental landscape; occasional etcher. Studied painting and etching in Paris & Madrid. His abiding fascination with the Spanish landscape led to the soubriquet 'Spanish' MacDonald. After several sojourns in Spain he returned to Dundee c1912 where his future wife, the artist Beatrice Huntington, was one of his students. After WW1 he moved to Edinburgh where he met Cadell and Peploe and became an active and popular member of the Scottish Arts Club. An authority on etching, partly responsible for persuading the NGS to acquire E S Lumsden's collection of etchings. Exhibited RA(4),

RSA(29), ROI(3), RBA(3), LS(2) & GI(13), latterly from 116 Hanover St, Edinburgh.
**Bibl:** Scotsman, 4 Feb 1960(obit).

**MacDONALD, William** **fl 1955**
Amateur Dunbartonshire landscape painter in watercolour. Exhibited GI(1) from Lenzie.

**MacDONALD, William Alexander** **fl 1965**
Glasgow sculptor. Worked in ciment fondu and welded metal. Exhibited a welded bronze figure of a warrior at the RSA & GI(8).

**MacDONALD, William Alister** **fl 1884-1893**
Painter in oil and watercolour; landscapes. Very little is now known about him. Exhibited 'Doubtful Weather, Loch Hourn' at the RA (1892) and another work in 1893; also in Suffolk Street, from 21 Camden Rd, London.

**MacDONALD-BUCHANAN, Elizabeth** **1939-**
Born London. Trained Ruskin School of Art, Oxford, 1957-59. After an early marriage forsook painting until 1984 when she collaborated with Anne and Graham Arnold, members of the Ruralist Group. Studied sculpture under Allan Sly. Lives at Poolewe, Wester Ross. Her work is much inspired by highland life and by the farming and wild life around her, sculpted in a strong, chunky style. Exhibited RA(4) and two works at the RSA, 'Highland Garron' 1985 and 'Blackface Ram' 1990.

**MacDONNELL, Peter** **fl 1944-1947**
Edinburgh painter of street scenes and townscapes, often either Edinburgh or Perth. Exhibited RSA(4) from 16 Danube St.

**McDOUGAL, John** **fl 1877-1903**
Landscape painter. Probably Scottish but based in Liverpool. Moved to Min-y-don Cemaes, nr Amlwch, Anglesea 1898. Exhibited RA(26) & GI(7).

**MacDOUGALL, Agnes** **fl 1894**
Amateur Dunoon painter; exhibited at the GI(1) from Sghor Bheann, Bullwood.

**MacDOUGALL, Allan** **fl 1872-1889**
Scottish landscape painter of poetic woodland scenes and flowers. Exhibited RSA(1) & GI( and RSA(1) from Hillside House, Partickhill Road.

**MacDOUGALL, Allan A** **fl 1861**
Amateur Edinburgh topographical painter. Exhibited GI(1) from 51 N. Hanover St.

**MacDOUGALL, Allan C** **c1826-1862**
Landscape painter. Related to Allan MacDougall(qv). On 9 June 1856 he entered the Trustees Academy having been recommended by Horatio McCulloch(qv). He left very shortly afterwards and nothing further is known of his career. His exhibits were all prior to that date, at the RSA(29) and in London 1851-3. A landscape, dating from 1850, is in a private collection in Glasgow.

**MacDOUGALL, Allan G** **fl 1879**
Glasgow landscape painter. Exhibited a watercolour at GI, from Kenmure St.

**McDOUGALL, Archibald** **fl 1900**
Glasgow landscape artist; exhibited GI(1) from 18 Randolf Gardens, Partick.

**MacDOUGALL, Colquhoun** **fl 1938**
Flower and landscape painter; appears to have exhibited exclusively at the Brook Street Gallery where he showed at least 29 works before WW2.

**MacDOUGALL, Jillian** **fl 1963-**
Flower painter in watercolour. Trained Canterbury College of Art 1955-60, awarded the National Diploma of Design in hand-printed textiles and machine embroidery. In recent years she has concentrated on watercolour drawings of botanical subjects deriving most of her subjects from plants in the Royal Botanic Gardens, Edinburgh. In 1978/9 the SAC used her painting of an endangered Hawaiian plant, the silver sword, for the cover of their exhibition 'The Plant'. Awarded gold medal of the RHS for watercolours of orchids 1986. Commissioned to paint the rose, 'Elizabeth of Glamis' commemorating the Queen Mother's visit to Aberdeen. Regularly exhibits in London and also in Tennessee, USA. Exhibited RSA(8). Represented in the V&A, the Royal Botanic Garden, Edinburgh, the Woodland Centre, near Jedburgh (by a commissioned watercolour of trees in the Pinery at Monteviot, commissioned by the Marquis of Lothian).
**Bibl:** R Brinsley Burbridge, A Dictionary of British Flower, Fruit and Still Life Painters.

**MacDOUGALL, Leslie Grahame RSA PPRIS FSA(Scot) FRIBA** **1896-1974**
Born Edinburgh, 14 Aug. Architect. Educated at Merchiston Castle School, Edinburgh, Edinburgh University and Edinburgh School of Architecture under Sir George Washington Browne(qv), John Begg(qv) and Carus-Wilson. Also a pupil of Sir Robert Lorimer's in 1921. Commenced private practice 1926. He assumed the surname of MacDougall in place of Grahame-Thomson on the succession of his wife to the Chieftainship of Clan MacDougall 1953. Shared the distinction with one other of being the first student to complete a full diploma course in the newly established School of Architecture. First important commission was the Reid Memorial Church, Edinburgh (1929-33), followed by a 'civilised Mediterranean inspiration' [Gifford] 6, Easter Belmont Rd (1932); also responsible (with Frank Connell(qv)) for the Guardian Royal Exchange Insurance building, George St (1938-40) and for Fairmilehead (1937) and Longstone Parish Churches (1954). After the War he found it difficult to accept the changes in architecture from traditional values of scholarship and beauty to the new idols of pragmatic functionalism. His practice continued but he did not flourish in the same way as he had done before 1939. Lived at Oban. Elected FSA(Scot) 1924, FRIBA 1936, PPRIS 1954, ARSA 1937, RSA 1946. Exhibited regularly at RSA.
**Bibl:** Gifford 43,300,307,327,421,484,504,534,566,617,632.

**MacDOUGALL, Miss Lily Martha Maud** **1875-1958**
Born Glasgow. Watercolour painter and occasionally oil; mainly portraits and floral studies. Studied in Edinburgh Royal Institution, the Hague School of Art in Antwerp, the Carrière Academie in Paris and at the studio of Jacques Emile Blanche. Daughter of the founder and first President of the SSWA of which she was herself a founder member. In 1941 elected SSA, honoured in America, being an honorary member of the Schroeder Foundation. Began exhibiting RSA (16) 1900, also RSW(7), GI(10) & AAS. Represented in Glasgow AG, City of Edinburgh collection, SAC, St Louis(USA) AG.
**Bibl:** Halsby 270; Scotsman 23 Dec 1958 (obit).

**MacDOUGALL, M O** **fl 1931-1932**
Amateur Glasgow sculptor. Worked mainly in bronze and plaster. Figurative classical studies. Exhibited GI(6) from 6 Barington Drive.

**MacDOUGALL, Miss Marion G M** **fl 1947**
Amateur Glasgow sculptress. Exhibited a plaster head at the GI from 17 Eastcote Ave.

**MacDOUGALL, Neil** **1816-1843**
Trained West of Scotland Academy. Landscape painter. Deserves greater recognition.

**MacDOUGALL, Norman M** **1852-1939**
Began his artistic career in London as a figure painter to Daniel Cottier(qv), the stained glass designer. Returned to Scotland and settled at Carmunnock with a studio in Glasgow. Known mostly for his landscapes, especially the village of Carmunnock and its surrounds. Lived at 211 West Campbell Street. Frequent exhibitor RSA & GI, also RA, RBA, AAS 1902-1910 & RI(8) 1874-1902. Represented in Lillie AG (Milngavie).
**Bibl:** Glasgow Herald, Dec 1, 1939 (obit).

**McDOUGALL, Peter G** **fl 1956-1958**
Argyll painter of Scottish and continental landscape and genre. Exhibited GI(4) from Hunter's Quay, Dunoon.

**MacDOUGALL, William Brown** **1869-1936**
Born Glasgow; died Laughton, Essex, Apr 20. Painter of landscapes and figures in oil and pastel; illustrator, etcher and wood engraver. Educated Glasgow Academy. Studied in Paris at the Academie Julien under Bouguereau, J M Laurens and R Fleury. Returned to the UK settling at Laughton, Essex. Married the poet and novelist Margaret Armour. His principal works include 'Yachts Racing at Horning', 'Bank Holiday Regatta' and 'Springtime in Epping Forest'. Illustrated a number of books including *Chronicles of Streatham* (1896), *The Book of Ruth* (1896), *The Fall of the Nibelungs* (Margt Armour, 1898), *Thames Sonnets and Semblances* (1897), *Isabella*...(1898), *The Shadow of Love and other Poems* (Margt Armour, 1898), *The Eerie Book* (Margt Armour, 1898), *The Blessed Demozel* (D G Rossetti, 1898), *Omar Khayyam* (1898), *Fields of France & St Paul* (F W Myers). Also contributed to *The Yellow Book* (1894), *The Evergreen* (1894) and *The Savoy*. Exhibited RA(2), RSA(6), GI(9), & at the Paris Salon. Represented in Glasgow AG, Manchester AG.
**Bibl:** Caw 418; Houfe; R E D Sketchley, English Book Illustrators,1902, 26, 128; Studio vol 10, 1898, 210.

**MacDOWALL, Catharine** **fl 1950-1951**
East Lothian artist. Exhibited at the RSA 'The black kitchen, St Mungo's Well', 1950 and 'The Orchard, Mungo's Well', 1951, from Drem, N Berwick.

**MacDOWALL, Mrs Flora** **fl 1915-1917**
Larbert painter of townscapes and genre. Exhibited RSA(2) & GI(2) from Carrondale.

**MacDOWALL, Miss Helen W** **fl 1866**
Edinburgh oil painter of wild life, especially wild flowers; exhibited RSA(3).

**MacDOWALL, J Stuart** **fl 1915**
Amateur sculptor; exhibited a portrait bust 'Jean' at the GI from 27 Main Street, Kilbirnie.

**MacDOWALL, James D** **fl 1973**
Glasgow sculptor. Exhibited 'African head' in walnut at the GI from Kelvindale Rd.

**MacDOWALL, John S** **fl 1941-1956**
Renfrew painter in watercolour and oil, mainly the former. Landscape and genre. Exhibited GI(11).

**McDOWALL, Stella** **fl 1977**
Aberdeen sculptress. Exhibited a standing figure at the RSA from Hazelhead.

**McDOWALL, William** **1905-1988**
Born Girvan, Ayrshire. Painter in oil of still life, flowers, fruit, topographical studies and occasional landscape. After early study in engineering and a brief spell working in the theatre he turned to art, studying at Edinburgh College of Art under S J Peploe(qv). In 1932 he went to London where he worked as a commercial artist with Thompson newspapers. Retired to East Anglia 1969. Exhibited RSA (28) 1931-1940, always from London; also RBA & RI from 1922.
**Bibl:** Wingfield.

**McDOWELL, Gordon Grant** **fl 1975-1982**
Aberdeen painter of interiors and semi-abstracts. Exhibited AAS & GI(6) from 36 Ashvale Place.

**McDOWELL, William** **fl 1577**
Master of Work. Responsible for the lowest stage of the Portcullis Gate of Edinburgh Castle, illustrated in Gifford (pl.58), replacing the Constable's Tower destroyed 1573.

**MACDUFF, Archibald** **c1850-?**
Etcher and sketcher, possibly an amateur. Plates listed by Bryan include 'The Temptation of Adam', 'Job and his Friends', 'The Birth of Venus', 'King Lear' (all after Barry), 'Holy Family' (after Raphael).
**Bibl:** Bryan.

**MacDUFF, William** **fl 1846-1879**
Believed to have been born in Perthshire, but Edinburgh-based painter in oil. Landscapes, figure subjects and genre. Exhibited RSA(68) & GI(14) 1861-1873, at one time from Falkland, Fife, latterly from Cramond before finally settling in Surrey.

**McELHINNEY, Douglas Thomas** **fl 1975-1988**
Painter of semi-abstracts, often with botanical allusion. Lived in Dundee then Leicester and most recently c/o Old Schoolhouse, Elphinstone, E Lothian. Exhibited RSA(9) & GI(2).

**McELROY, James** **fl 1973-1988**
Painter. Exhibited intermittently at the AAS.

**McELWEE, Bessie S** **fl 1910-1922**
Glasgow painter; exhibited 53 works at the Walker Gallery, Liverpool from 93 Hope Street.

**McERLEAN, John F** **fl 1930**
Amateur Glasgow painter. Exhibited an interior in watercolour at the GI(1) from 126 Castle Street.

**McEWAN, A D** **fl 1896-1905**
Painter. Exhibited GI(3) from the Glasgow area.

**McEWAN, Agnes** **fl 1899-1906**
Stirlingshire flower painter; exhibited RSA(3) & GI(4) from Alva.

**McEWAN, Angus Maywood RSW** **1963-**
Born 19 Jly. Trained Duncan of Jordanstone School of Art, Dundee 1987. Gained Elizabeth Greenshields Foundation award 1987 and postgraduate diploma in 1988 before setting up partnership with Ian Ritchie doing trompe l'oeil and mural work, leading to the opening of a gallery in Dundee 1989. Influenced by the High Renaissance as well as by Rodin, de Chirico and Burne Jones. Usually works in acrylic, pastel, charcoal and/or oil (mixed media). Realistic in manner but with strong awareness of basic abstract compositional design, often of a surrealist nature. Joined teaching staff, Dundee Further Education College 1997. Won Latimer Award (RSA) 1995, a Salvesen scholarship enabled him to visit China 1996 resulting in 50 compositions exhibited RSA, and the Alexander Graham Munro Award (RSW) 1999. Elected RSW 1995. Represented in Dundee AG. Exhibited RSA since 1987 & RGI 1988, from 7 Glenleven Drive, Wormit, Newport-on-Tay.

**McEWAN, D** **fl 1906-1907**
Glasgow draughtsman. Exhibited two black and white drawings at the GI from 1 Gray St.

**McEWAN, Daniel** **fl 1885-1888**
Glasgow landscape painter, mostly of the Clyde and west coast. Exhibited GI(3), from Mt. Florida and latterly Albert Drive.

**McEWAN, Donald** **fl c1750-1770**
Perthshire mason, based at Dunkeld. Built the four-arched bridge across the river Tummel at Kinloch Rannoch 1764, extensively repaired 1946 and again in 1976.
**Bibl:** Annette M Smith, *Jacobite Estates of the Forty-Five*, 1982, pp187-8.

**McEWAN, Dorothy Anne Wilson (née Turnbull)** **fl 1954-1963**
Born Peebles, Jan 15. Amateur painter in oil of figurative works, especially African portraits, also occasional Scottish landscape. Educated Edinburgh University. Studied painting under James Cumming(qv) and Peter White(qv). Exhibited Nat Gall of Zimbabwe 1961.

**McEWAN, John** **fl 1891**
Dundee artist; exhibited 'Through the wood' at the RSA, from 79 High St, Lochee.

**McEWAN, M** **fl 1890-1891**
Landscape painter, usually west coast scenery, also flowers. Exhibited GI(3) from Glasgow.

**MacEWAN, Mary Dempster** **fl 1896-1929**
Inverness-based artist. Possibly related to Miss M Poyntz M(qv) who was working contemporaneously from Inverness-shire, though from a different address. Exhibited country subjects and figurative works at the AAS.

**McEWAN, Miss M Poyntz** **fl 1898-1929**
Portrait and figurative painter. May have been related to Mary Dempster M(qv) and have trained at the School of Art in Bushey. Exhibited a watercolour at the RSA in 1898 from an address in Bushey, Herts and at the RA in 1902, 'Hush-a-bye Baby', from Evelix, Inverness; also RI, AAS(2) & SWA(2), in 1929 from St Michaels, Carrbridge.

**McEWAN, Mrs Patty Hunter** **fl 1959-1976**
Aberdeen artist. Landscape, local topography and tree studies. Exhibited frequently at the AAS, of which she was for many years a council member. Lived in Westfield Terrace.

**McEWAN, Peter** **fl 1888-1889**
Painter of fruit and flowers. Exhibited GI(2) from 3 Albert Drive, Crosshill, Glasgow.

**McEWAN, Thomas** **fl 1847-1848**
Edinburgh sculptor. Exhibited RSA(3) including a statuette of Dr Chalmers. Lived in Newington.

**McEWAN, Thomas (Tom) RSW** **1846-1914**
Glasgow painter in oil, but mainly watercolour; domestic scenes and genre. Born near Glasgow into a poor family with artistic inclinations, his father being an amateur artist and a friend of James Docharty(qv). Apprenticed to a pattern designer in Glasgow, in 1863 attended evening classes at the Glasgow School of Art under Robert Greenlees(qv). During the 1860s he exhibited at the GI and in 1872 embarked on a sketching holiday with James Docharty, working on Islay and Jura. Dutch influence can be seen in his work, especially that of Joseph Israels(qv). He used members of his family as models and was particularly fond of portraying grandparents and their children sewing and engaged in similar activities in the home and in open farmsteads, often with poultry in the foreground. The influence of Wilkie can occasionally be seen. At his best he was a very good artist, and was for several years President of the Glasgow Art Club. Lived for many years at Rosevale, Helensburgh. Elected RSW 1883. Exhibited RA(1) 1887, RSA(11), RSW(49), GI(97) & AAS 1898-1902. Represented in Glasgow AG, Paisley AG.
**Bibl:** Caw 273-4; Halsby 70,270.

**McEWAN, Walter** **fl 1902**
Obscure painter of uncertain origin. Exhibited at the Walker Gallery, Liverpool(1) from 11 Plas Pigalle, Paris.

**McEWAN, William** **fl 1827-1849**
Prolific Edinburgh landscape artist; he enjoyed painting old castles and coastal scenes often with figures and sometimes wrecks. Taught drawing in Edinburgh. Illustrated *Old and New Edinburgh.* Exhibited RSA (25) including 'Castle Campbell' & 'Ravensheugh Castle', both in 1827, 'Dirleton Castle' 1845 and 'Ravenscraig Castle' 1849. Represented in National Museum of Scotland.

**MacEWAN, Winnie** **fl 1906-1934**
Painter. Exhibited RA(3), SWA(1) & London Salon(5).

**McEWEN, Charles** **c1843-1892**
Born Glasgow. Painter in oil and watercolour of landscapes and figure subjects. Studied in Italy. Brother of Robert McEwen, great uncle of Professor James McEwen. Like his brother Robert, he died in tragic circumstances, disappearing over a cliff while painting in Shetland; it seems that, engrossed in his work, he took a fatal step backwards. Exhibited two works at the RA in 1890 from 79 West Regent Street, but more frequently at the RSA(9), often coastal scenes including a New Zealand landscape 1876 and 'Lee Shore, off Stornoway' 1885, also GI annually 1874-1892.

**McEWEN, D H** **fl 1861**
Little known illustrator. Contributed to Hall: *The Book of South Wales* (1861).

**MacEWEN, Helen B** **fl 1889**
Glasgow topographical painter; exhibited GI(2) from 8 Rosslyn Terrace, Kelvinside.

**McEWEN, Miss Kate** **fl 1881**
Landscape painter. Exhibited an oil RSA and 'Interior of a Highland cottage' at the GI from The Hill of Drip, nr Stirling.

**MacEWEN, Molly** **fl 1935**
Watercolourist; exhibited RSA(1) from Inverness.

**McEWEN, Robert** **c1845-1882**
Glasgow painter in oil and watercolour of landscape and rustic scenes, brother of Charles with whom he studied in Italy. Published three books of pen and ink sketches in the 1870s: *Bohemia, Extravagances* and *Among the Sassenachs. Bohemia* is particularly interesting as it contains light-hearted sketches of Glasgow artists of the time including, for example, an incident when Colin Hunter(qv), while sitting drawing in a boat at the mouth of Tarbert Harbour, was run down by the 'Mary Jane'. Other fellow artists including William McBride(qv) and Wellwood Rattray(qv) are to be found in all three volumes. Died in tragic circumstances, breaking his neck when attempting to carry his easel down steep studio stairs. Exhibited RSA(8) & GI(13). Wingfield mentions a picture 'Salmon Fishing' by an **R McEWEN** in the Hutchinson collection with the date 1822.

**McEWEN, Rory** **1932-1982**
Born Marchmont, Berwickshire. Painter, especially of flora/fauna, illustrator, folk singer, poet. Son of Sir John McEwen, diplomat, politician, poet and putative clan chief. Educated Eton and Cambridge, he received no formal art training, although at Eton he was inspired by Wilfrid Blunt, author of *The Art of Botanical Illustration.* He never described himself specifically as a 'botanical illustrator' but his paintings of flowers, leaves, fruit and vegetation are botanically accurate as well as artistically superb. In this medium, he worked in the tradition of Ehret, Ligozzi and Redouté. His favourite medium was watercolour painted on Italian calfskin vellum with images built up with minute strokes of very dry colour. The feeling of texture was obtained by modelling and over-emphasising the highlights or shadows cast by veins or other uneven structures on the surface of the leaf or petal. He was never too formal nor stylised nor 'unnaturally perfect'. His publications concentrated on the intricacies of old flowers, such as carnations, pinks, old English tulips - and the traditional flowers portrayed in 17th century still-life paintings. His paintings of onions, fallen leaves and such like are pure observations from nature. His first major exhibition was in New York in 1962, followed by a show at the Assembly Rooms, Edinburgh 1964 as part of the International Botanical Congress. Two years later a further one-man show was held in Edinburgh. A major posthumous exhibition was held at the Royal Botanic Gardens, Edinburgh 1988. Publications include *Old Carnations and Pinks* (1955), *The Auricula* (1962), *Tulips and Tulipomania* (1977). Also made table sculptures in refractive glass and executed a number of abstract paintings. Illustrated the end papers for Gavin Maxwell's *Ring of Bright Water.* Represented in V & A, SNGMA, Glasgow AG, Fitzwilliam Museum (Cambridge), Hunt Botanical Library (Pittsburgh), The White House (Washington DC).
**Bibl:** Hartley 145; Nihonbashi Gall, Tokyo, 'Rory McEwen', (Ex Cat 1980); Rich. Demarco Gall, Edinburgh 'Rory McEwen', (Ex Cat 1969); Royal Botanical Gardens, 'Rory McEwen 1932-82 - The Botanical Paintings', (Ex Cat 1988).

**McEWEN, Robin** **fl 1961**
Born Marchmont, Berwickshire. Watercolourist and illustrator. Brother of Rory McE(qv). Two illustrations in Gavin Maxwell's *Ring of Bright Water.* Exhibited RSA(2).

**McFADYEN, Jock** **1950-**
Born Paisley. Figurative painter. Studied at Chelsea School of Art 1973-7, becoming a part-time lecturer at the Slade. Interested in street scenes, his work is 'probing, edgy and humorous, as he focuses sharply on the desperate, the destitute and the dispossessed of London's east end'. His luminous paintings appear as if lit by a single light and there are no tricks concealing the harsh realities to which his work bears witness. In this he is very much a social commentator. Represented in the NG, V & A, Birmingham City AG, Manchester

City AG, Imperial War Museum (London), Hunterian Museum (Glasgow), SAC.

**McFADZEAN, Stuart** **fl 1983-**
Ayrshire painter. Exhibited RSA(9) from Dalchomie Farm, Maybole.

**MacFALL, (Major) Crawford Haldane** **1860-1928**
Born Jly 24; died London, Jly 25. Artist, author and professional soldier. Educated RMA, Sandhurst. Author of 8 volume *History of Art* (1910), wrote and illustrated *With the Zhob Field Force* 1890 (pub 1895), and *The Splendid Wayfaring* (1913). Exhibited two works at the RA - 'A Marriage in High Life, Sierra Leone' 1891 and 'British Zouaves Checking French Attack at Dawn, Warina, Dec 1893' 1894; also elsewhere in London, from 60 Wynnstay Gdns, Kensington.

**McFALL, David Bernard RA** **1919-**
Born Cathcart, Glasgow, 21 Dec. Sculptor in bronze and stone of portraits, figure subjects and animals. Educated English Martyrs, Sparkhill and in Birmingham at the Junior School of Arts and Crafts 1931-34, then at the College of Arts 1934-39 under Charles Thomas. Travelled to Athens, Paris, Rome and China. Settled in London, becoming a technical assistant in the studio of Jacob Epstein. Member of the teaching staff at Kennington from 1956. Married to the actress Alexandra Dane. In 1972 awarded the medal for the best sculpture of the Society of British Painters. His statue of Sir Winston Churchill at Woodford was unveiled by Lord Montgomery and was the last sculpture of the great man to be taken from life. Lived and worked in London. Elected ARA 1955, RA 1963. Exhibited RA from 1943 & GI 1945-79. Represented in Tate AG, Glasgow AG, NPG, Imperial War Museum, RA.

**McFARLAND, Gillian (Mrs Martin Rayner)** **1963-**
Born Fife. Painter in oil also wood carver and teacher. Trained at St Martin's School of Art, London 1982-5 graduating with BA Hons. Fascinated by working with paper. Attended Parry's Paper Workshop in Glasgow in 1989 and opened a Papier Mâché Workshop with her husband Martin Rayner in Inverness 1990. Portrays images drawn from her own experience usually a single image within a decorative frame that is carved and painted on. Lives at 32 Queen's Street, Newport-on-Tay, Fife. Her first exhibit at the RSA was in 1987, winning an award; she exhibited again 1990.

**McFARLANE, A** **fl 1897**
Glasgow painter. Exhibited RSA(1) from 7 Scott Street, Garnethill.

**MacFARLANE, Alasdair** **fl 1932-1937**
Glasgow artist; exhibited 'A misty morning 'at the RSA & GI(6) from 26 Ibrox Street, latterly from Mosspark.

**MACFARLANE, Alexander Archibald** **fl 1944-1956**
Glasgow topographical painter, mostly harbours, docks and boats. Exhibited GI(25) from 1157 Gt. Western Rd and later Wykeham Rd.

**MacFARLANE, Miss Anne** **fl 1932-1938**
Greenock painter; exhibited 'A stormy night' and 'The gypsy' at the RSA from Woodlea, 5 Fox Street.

**MacFARLANE, Mrs Anne** **fl 1909-1913**
Watercolour painter of coastal scenes and landscape; exhibited RSA(1), RSW(2) & AAS(3) from 68 Lauriston Place, Edinburgh.

**McFARLANE, Erskine** **fl c1885**
A coloured lithograph of 'The Royal Review of Scottish Volunteers, Queens Park, Edinburgh, 1881' is in the collection of the City of Edinburgh.

**MacFARLANE, Miss Florence M** **fl 1943-1945**
Argyll painter; exhibited rural genre at the RSA(4) & GI(4) from Tarbert.

**MacFARLANE, Frances** **fl 1920-1922**
Studied at Edinburgh College of Art, moved to St Andrews c1922 from where she exhibited a self-portrait at the RSA & GI(2).

**McFARLANE, Hilda J** **fl 1909-1910**
Glasgow amateur portrait painter. Exhibited GI(2) from 3 Princes Terrace, Dowanhill.

**MacFARLANE, John R** **fl 1865-1883**
Glasgow painter of portraits and genre. Exhibited GI(8) from Willowbank Crescent.

**MacFARLANE, John R** **fl 1904-1905**
Glasgow portait miniaturist. Exhibited miniatures on ivory at the GI from 39 Hamilton Terrace, Peel St. Sometimes confused with the previous entry.

**MacFARLANE, James L** **fl 1865-1869**
Still-life painter of flowers and fruit. Lived for many years in London. Exhibited RSA(9) & GI(2).

**McFARLANE, John** **fl 1858**
Inverness portrait painter; exhibited RSA(1).

**McFARLANE, John** **fl 1910-1911**
Ayr sculptor; portrait busts. Exhibited GI(2) from Thistlebank, Ashgrove Street.

**McFARLANE, John F** **fl 1968**
Glasgow watercolourist. Possibly brother or son of Alexander M(qv). Exhibited GI(1) from Wykeham Rd.

**McFARLANE, Margaret** **fl 1968**
Glasgow painter; exhibited 'Winter night' at the RSA, from Barrhead.

**McFARLANE, Miss Mary F** **fl 1919**
Glasgow watercolour painter of interiors and still life. Exhibited GI(2) from Montgomerie Crescent.

**MacFARLANE, Sheila Margaret** **1943-**
Angus painter and engraver. Exhibited RSA(4) between 1965 & 1978 including illustrations to the *Apocalypse.*

**MacFARLANE, T D** **fl 1894-1908**
Glasgow-based artist and illustrator. Specialised in illustrating children's books including Noyes: *Minstrelsy of the Scottish Borders* (1908) and *Days That Speak* (1908). Exhibited RGI(2) from 12 Dalhousie Street.

**McFARLANE, W H** **fl 1850-1865**
Engraver. Four lithographs, including a fine print of the 'Ceremony of Laying the Foundation Stone of the GPO, Edinburgh 1861', are in the City of Edinburgh collection.

**MacFARLANE, William Welsh** **fl 1867-1887**
Edinburgh painter in oil and watercolour of landscapes and domestic genre. Exhibited RSA(7).

**MacFARQUHAR, George** **?-c1799**
Coach painter in Edinburgh. In 1745 he was apprenticed to David Clelland and in 1763 became a Burgess of Edinburgh. Also a member of the Incorporation of St Mary's. In 1767 he took as an apprentice, Charles Maud and in 1777, Alexander Christie.

**MacFIE, Barbara E** **fl 1939**
Edinburgh amateur painter. Exhibited RSA(1) from 17 Westercoates Terrace.

**MACFIE, Major General J M CB CBE MC** **1891-1985**
Physician, professional soldier and amateur watercolour painter of landscape, often of the western Highlands. Graduated Glasgow Univ. 1915, the most distinguished medical graduate of his year. Joined the RAMC and served extensively overseas. Like his brother, Professor A L Macfie, he was a noted art collector and benefactor to the Lillie AG (Milngavie) who own four of his works.
**Bibl:** Lillie AG Ex Cat, 1980 (text by Elizabeth M Dent).

**McGAVIGAN, Anna** **fl 1901**
Amateur artist. Exhibited GI(1) from Jessieville, Lenzie, nr Glasgow.

**McGAVIN, Miss Ann** **fl 1948**
Amateur Glasgow artist. Exhibited a scraperboard study 'Les Vagabonds' at the GI from Harriet St. Possibly the same **Ann**

**McGAVIN** who exhibited two sculptures at the GI 1958 from Hillhead.

**McGAVIN, George MacDougall** **fl 1966-1983**
Edinburgh painter in watercolour of landscape and narrative works. married to Margaret M(qv). Exhibited RSA(8) & GI annually 1965-1988. Represented in Lillie AG (Milngavie) by 4 works.

**McGAVIN, Margaret** **1924-**
Edinburgh-based painter. Works mainly in watercolour and gouache; flowers and still life. Wife of George MacDougall M(qv). Exhibited RSA(10) & GI(14). Represented in Lillie AG(Milngavie).

**McGECHAN, David** **fl 1885**
Exhibited a rustic scene in oil at the RSA from 7 Clunebraefoot, Port Glasgow.

**McGECHAN, Margaret M** **fl 1893-1903**
Renfrewshire flower painter. Exhibited RSA(1) & GI(12) from Paisley.

**McGEEHAN, Aniza (Mrs V Murphy)** **1874-?**
Sculptress; generally portrait busts in bronze. Studied at Glasgow School of Art and at Colarossi's, Paris. Lived in Airdrie 1894, before moving to Liverpool, London and back to Liverpool. Shortly after the turn of the century she was living at 24 Platts Lane, Hampstead, London. Sister of Jessie M McGeehan(qv). Exhibited from 1894-1931 at the RA(8), RSA(3), L(11) & GI(17).

**McGEEHAN, Jessie M Miss** **1872-1961**
Born Airdrie. Painter in oil and watercolour of landscape and figurative studies. Fond of river and harbour scenes, generally with fisherfolk and brightly colour shipping; also designed glass mosaics. Sister of Aniza McGeehan(qv). After an early life in Airdrie in c1897 she moved to Glasgow. Considering her great talent and the affinities in her work with the Hague School and with McGown Coventry she is remarkably little recorded. Highly competent in handling both watercolour and oil, although sometimes with excessive strength. Exhibited RA(1) 1901, by which time she was living in Glasgow; also RSA(11), GI(34) & L(29).
**Bibl:** Caw 428.

**McGEEHAN, Margaret M** **fl 1898**
Paisley watercolour painter of flowers; exhibited RSA(1).

**McGEEHAN, Patrick** **1842-1924**
Airdrie landscape painter in oil; exhibited RSA(1). Father of Aniza M(qv) and Jessie M(qv).

**McGEOCH, George** **fl 1948-1956**
Paisley sculptor. Related to James Anderson M(qv). Portraits, fish and animals. Exhibited GI(7) in marble, plaster and wood.

**McGEOCH, James Anderson** **1913-**
Born Paisley, Dec 1. Painter in oil and pastel; sculptor in clay, wood and stone. Studied at Glasgow School of Art under W O Hutchison(qv) 1932-37 and in Paris 1938. Lived and worked in Paisley for most of his life. Exhibited at the RSA, GI, SSA and at the Paris Salon from 53 Underwood Road, Paisley.

**McGEORGE, Andrew** **1810-1891**
Glasgow lawyer, local historian and amateur painter. Occasional cartoonist of local characters. Painted meticulous views of Glasgow in watercolour and pencil.
**Bibl:** Halsby 270.

**McGEORGE, Mabel Victoria RSW (formerly Mrs Munro)** **1885-1960**
Watercolour painter; mainly landscapes, particularly the western Highlands, the Lothians and in Perthshire, often on a large scale. Niece of the Earl of Minto, her maiden name was Elliot. The centre of a minor social scandal when marrying the impecunious artist, Hugh Munro(qv), who at the time was employed cutting wood blocks for Charles Mackie(qv). A year after Munro's death in 1928, she married W S McGeorge(qv) and it was at this time that she began to paint watercolours professionally. Trained by J Campbell Noble(qv). Lived for many years in Haddington. Elected RSW 1930. Exhibited RSA(41), RSW(44) & GI(4). Represented in Glasgow AG.
**Bibl:** Halsby 270.

**McGEORGE, William Stewart RSA** **1861-1931**
Born Castle Douglas; died Gifford, 9 Nov. Painter of landscapes, portraits and figure subjects in oil. Member of the Kirkcudbright school. In 1880 entered the Royal Institution, Edinburgh as a student, studied thereafter at Antwerp Academy under Verlat, spending three years there in the company of Hornel(qv) and Wishart(qv). Hornel encouraged him to lighten the tone of his work. A small, dapper gentleman, MacGeorge fell out with Hornel after abjuring the latter on his excessive drinking. Awarded Keith prize 1888. Spent the winters in Edinburgh and the summers painting in Kirkcudbright, once with a productive summer break in Venice. His favourite subjects were brightly painted, light woodland scenes often with children picnicking or cavorting among flowers. His principal works included 'Kirkcudbright', 'Border Ballads' and 'Halloween'. Exhibited RA(3) 'In the Valley of the Dee, Kirkcudbright' 1894, 'Among the wild hyacinths, Galloway' 1900 and 'The water-sprite' 1901. Married Hugh Munro's widow, Mabel Victoria(qv) 1929. The character 'Terry McWhirter' in S R Crockett's *The Raiders* was modelled on MacGeorge. Elected ARSA 1898, RSA 1910. Exhibited RSA(148), GI(56), AAS, L(8) & RHA(3). Represented in the SNPG (a portrait of 'William Mouncey'), Aberdeen, Dundee, Glasgow and Perth AGs, City of Edinburgh collection, MacKelvie AG,(Auckland, New Zealand).
**Bibl:** AJ, 1911, 127; Caw 405-6; Hardie 77,101; Macmillan [SA] 253-5; RSA Obituary 1931; Studio vol 49, 1910, 229-230.

**McGHIE, John N** **1867-1952**
Born and died Glasgow. Painter and etcher of coastal scenes, figures and portraits also occasional watercolours. Studied Glasgow School of Art, RA Schools and in Paris at the Academie Julien. Enjoyed seascapes, coastal and harbour scenes, especially those on the east coast of Scotland near Pittenweem where, in later years, he had a studio and spent most summers. Often used coarse canvases. Particularly fascinated by the local fisher-folk as they waited by the shore for their men-folk to return, often with fish baskets on their shoulders or arms, wearing the characteristic blue and white striped dresses. A painting 'The Follow Through' is reputedly the portrait of the golfer David Rintoul. President, Glasgow Society of Etchers. Exhibited RA(8) 1891-93 whilst living in Hamilton, but mainly RSA(19), RSW(2), GI(114), L(5) & Hamilton AC 1924. Represented in Glasgow AG, Paisley AG.
**Bibl:** Wingfield.

**McGHIE, Kirsty** **1959-**
Born Edinburgh. Sculptress and occasional stained glass window designer. Studied Glasgow School of Art 1980-5. A travelling scholarship enabled her to visit Japan 1983, a first solo exhibition following in 1985. Works in a variety of materials including plastics, wire netting, resin and wax. Visiting lecturer Edinburgh College of Art.
**Bibl:** Collins Gall, Glasgow, 'Shape+Form. Six Sculptors from Scotland', (Ex Cat 1988-9); Hartley 146; .

**McGIBBON, Alexander** **fl 1886-1891**
Glasgow architect and topographical watercolour painter. Exhibited a sketch of the Palais de Justice, Rouen in 1891 at the RA & GI(3).

**McGIBBON, Andrew** **fl 1861-1938**
Glasgow watercolour landscape and subject painter; exhibited 'A Devonshire Moor' at the RSA, also GI(4). In later life moved to Southwold, Suffolk.

**McGIBBON, Bell C** **fl 1901-1912**
Edinburgh painter of landscape and figure subjects also enamellist. Husband of Jessie R M(qv). Exhibited RSA(3) & AAS(2) from 23 Learmonth Terrace.

**MacGIBBON, David** **1830-1902**
Architect, architectural historian and draughtsman. Father and latterly partner of **Alfred Lightly MacGIBBON** (1874-1915). Worked for William Burn(qv) contemporaneously with Richard Shaw(qv) and William Nesfield(qv). Started in practice in Edinburgh c1855.

Succeeded Thomas Hamilton(qv) as architectural adviser to the Merchant Company on the Grindlay Estate 1864 when he also followed David Rhind(qv) as supervisor of development on the lands of Merchiston Castle. Best known for his co-authorship of the *Ecclesiastical Buildings of Scotland* and the *Castellated and Domestic Architecture of Scotland* (5 vols) (1887-1892) and the *Ecclesiastical Architecture of Scotland* (1896-97). Designed the house at the end of Bruntsfield Crescent, Edinburgh into which Robert Lorimer's family moved 1873. Responsible for several interesting works of his own and the reconstruction of Buccleuch Parish Church (1866). His design for the Crimean Monument, Sheffield was exhibited RSA 1858. Altogether exhibited RSA(20).
**Bibl:** Gifford 240,267-9,493,499,501,503,578,621 et passim; Peter Savage, Lorimer and the Edinburgh Craft Designers, Edinburgh 1980, 1,66,142,157,167.

**McGIBBON, Jessie R** **fl 1896-1910**
Edinburgh watercolour painter of buildings and topographical scenes. Wife of Bell C M(qv). Exhibited RSA(3) & GI(2).

**McGIBBON, William Forsyth** **1856-1923**
Glasgow architect. Apprenticed to the Barclays(qv). Specialised in ecclesiastical work although Glasgow Corn Exchange indicated awareness of English fashion. 'The effectively profiled brick Italian castellated of his industrial buildings showed how resourceful he could be on a limited budget' [Gomme & Walker]. Exhibited GI(13) from 221 West George Street.
**Bibl:** A Gomme & D Walker, Architecture of Glasgow, London 1987(rev) 294 et passim.

**MacGILL, Alexander** **fl 1697-d1734**
Architect. Son of the minister of Arbilot, Angus. Apprenticed to an Edinburgh mason, Alexander Nisbett (or Nesbet) 1697. His name appears in *Vitruvius Scoticus* as joint architect of Yester House, East Lothian. Involved with Alexander Edward(qv) in alterations to Kellie Castle, Angus (1699-1705), assistance in the design of House of Nairne, Perthshire after Bruce(qv) had died (1710) and Blair Drummond, Perthshire (1715-7; dem 1870) which incorporated six separate courtyards. An association with James Smith(qv) began in 1709 when the two co-operated in drawing up a scheme for the enlargement of Cullen House, Banffshire and continued until the latter's death 1731. Some years later his name appears as one of the witnesses of an agreement concerning a pumping engine which Smith had developed. In 1710 he had been admitted to the Edinburgh masons' lodge as an 'architector', and in 1720 was appointed City Architect of Edinburgh, a position he retained until 1734. In November 1718 he had prepared plans for a new Greyfriars Church for the City Council, opened three years later, and in 1722 he added a two-storey pedimented Palladian porch covering the N doors. Seems to have been "content to work in the idiom already established by Bruce and Smith...he had a strong feeling for mass, as well as a fascination for grandiose courtyard layouts of (great) complexity" [Dunbar]. Commissioned by the 2nd Earl of Bute to design a large mansion at Mountstuart (1716-22). Another interesting work was Donibristle (1719-23, main block destroyed 1859) undertaken for the 6th Earl of Moray, built on an H-plan, and the churches of Mountstuart (Bute) 1722, Donibristle (Fife) 1729-32 and Newbattle (Midlothian) 1727. "Mountstuart is a T-plan building with a swept hipped roof which gives way at each end of the main block to a pedimented gable surmounted by an ogee-roofed bellcot. The ridges of the roof are decorated with scalloped leadwork of the kind familiar from both Smith's and McGill's drawings, while the double lancet windows are set somewhat uncomfortably restricted within rusticated surrounds. At the small private chapel of Donibristle, however, all such awkwardenesses are overcome and the result is a harmonious Gibbsian composition in miniature, complete with pedimented roof and elegant octagonal belfry" [Dunbar].
**Bibl:** Dunbar 84,87-8,93; Gifford 38,151,154,592,pl.24; Bruce Walker & W S Gauldie, Architects and Architecture on Tayside, Dundee 1984, 50.

**McGILL, David** **fl 1889-d1947**
Sculptor, probably English but with Scottish connections. Worked mainly in bronze, portrait busts, figure studies and natural history subjects. Highly competent, representational. Executed the gilded bronze profile portrait decorating the Font in St Cuthbert's Parish Church, Edinburgh. Exhibited RA(23+), often at the GI & St Sebastien at the RSA, latterly from 1 Scarsdale Villas, London but in 1927 c/o Hugh McGill (whose bust he had exhibited RA 1898) at 68 London Rd, Kilmarnock.
**Bibl:** Gifford 275.

**McGILL, Duncan T G** **1896-?**
Born 9 Jan. Edinburgh based painter of landscapes in oil and watercolour. Studied at Edinburgh College of Art. Fond of the coastlines of Cumbria and Galloway. Exhibited RSW, GI & SSA.

**McGILL, James** **fl 1924-1945**
Glasgow artist; exhibited continental and rural scenes at the RSA(6), GI(12) & L(1).

**McGILL, James** **fl 1980-1987**
Perthshire landscape painter of local and continental topography. Exhibited GI(5) from Thornhill.

**MacGILLIVRAY, Allister M** **fl 1954-1960**
Dundee painter of flowers and genre. Exhibited GI(4).

**McGILLIVRAY, F** **fl 1887-1888**
Painter of flowers and genre. Exhibited GI(6) from a Glasgow address.

**MacGILLIVRAY, George** **fl 1838-1847**
Dundee painter in oil, crayon, pen, ink and pencil; local and continental landscapes and coastal scenes. Worked in a naive but appealing manner. Exhibited 'Dutch craft at Dort' at the RSA. Represented in Dundee AG by 'The Opening of the Dundee-Arbroath Railway' (1838) and 'The Union Hall, Dundee' (1847).
**Bibl:** Hardie 26.

**MacGILLIVRAY, Ian** **c1965-**
Inverness-based painter of wildlife, especially red deer, generally in oils. Managed by his father, he has established a growing reputation, popular with naturalists and sportsmen alike.

**MacGILLIVRAY, James Pittendrigh RSA LLD** **1856-1938**
Born Inverurie; died Edinburgh, 29 Apr. Sculptor, poet and photographer. Aged 13 he entered the studio of William Brodie(qv), remaining there for six years before going to Glasgow. In 1875 he began work with John Mossman(qv) whom he helped in executing a number of Glasgow buildings including the statue of Livingstone and the new Metropole Theatre. The only sculptor associated with the Glasgow School. Enjoyed fierce argument and entered the artistic furore of the time with relish, contributing articles for the *Scottish Art Review*, of which he was a founder and editor. Directed a strong diatribe against the RSA, giving rise to the soubriquet 'Macdevilry'. 'While he carried out many portrait commissions - we must thank him for the likenesses of many of the Glasgow Boys in their hey-day - he was to receive, following his statue of Burns, a number of large public commissions culminating in the grandiose Gladstone Memorial in Edinburgh...His own attitude to public sculptor is found in a paper which he read to the Edinburgh Architectural Association (1917): 'Architecture is the necessary setting or background of sculpture. Sculpture inhabits architectural places; it is for the jewelling of cities' [Buchanan]. Writing in the *AJ* (1898), Caw found that 'he brings a wider outlook, a more cultured intelligence, and a more forceful individuality to his task than any of his fellow sculptors...fire and energy of conception, and he expresses his ideas with a vigour of style and an appreciation of decorative effect which are almost new. His range of subjects is wide, his treatment reveals a true understanding of the nature of the materials he works in, and his conception of sculpturesque motive is almost invariably appropriate.' In the mid 1890s returned to Edinburgh where he designed his own house, Ravelston Elms, Murrayfield, later the home of another sculptor, Pilkington Jackson. In Edinburgh, he prepared the report the outcome of which was the new building for the Edinburgh College of Art. He photographed his own works and had prints made to his special instructions. Published two volumes of poetry *Pro Patria* 1915 and *Bog Myrtle and Peet Reek* 1922. His figure of W E Gladstone (1916) decorates the centre of Coates Crescent, John Knox (1904-5) and Robert Fergusson are in St Giles and Dean Montgomery is in St Mary's Cathedral. A striking memorial statue in

red granite to Dr Thomas Guthrie (1908) is in Grange Cemetery. In later life was active in the affairs of the RSA, coming to recognise the value of such organisations 'for maintaining and safeguarding...the normal trend of development in Art as against what I conclude are but side issues, and vagaries, such as cubism in Painting and the weird efforts of Archipenko in Sculpture'. Exhibited three portrait busts at the RA 1891-92, RSA (137), GI (56) & AAS 1888-1929. Some of his principal sculptures are Byron (Aberdeen), The Marquis of Bute (Cardiff), Gladstone (SNPG) and Burns (Irvine). Elected ARSA 1892, SSA 1900, RSA 1901 and granted an LLD Aberdeen 1909; appointed King's Sculptor-in-Ordinary for Scotland 1921 (an office revived specially in his honour). Represented in NGS, RSA, Aberdeen AG, Glasgow AG, Kirkcaldy AG, Paisley AG, collection of Edinburgh City(10).
**Bibl:** AJ 1898, 72; Caw 224,361; Gifford 46, 48,114, 116, 284, 366, 371, 588, 596; MacGillivray, 'Sculpture in Scotland', Trans of the Edinburgh Architectural Association, vol 9, 1928; NLS (47 vols and boxes of written and photographic material); SAC,'The Glasgow Boys', (Ex cat 1968); Scots Magazine, 5,1924; Studio, vol 45, 1909, 116; Robin Lee Woodward, 'Pittendrigh MacGillivray', in 'Virtue and Vision', NGS (Ex Cat 1991).

**McGILLIVRAY, T P** **fl 1872**
Edinburgh sculptor of portrait medallions. Brother of William M(qv). Exhibited RSA(1).

**McGILLIVRAY, William E** **fl 1867-1875**
Edinburgh sculptor of portrait medallions and busts. Brother of T P M(qv). Exhibited RSA(9) & GI(6).

**McGILVRAY, Robert** **1952-**
Dundee painter of interiors, portraits and semi-abstract landscape; oil, watercolour and pastel. Trained Duncan of Jordanstone College of Art. Exhibited GI(2). Represented in Kirkcaldy AG, City of Edinburgh collection.

**McGLASHAN, Alexander** **fl 1871-1885**
Glasgow landscape painter in oil, often scenes in Arran and Perthshire. Exhibited RSA(16) & GI(29).

**McGLASHAN, Archibald A RSA** **1888-1980**
Born Paisley, 16 Mar; died 3 Jan. Painter of portraits, figure subjects and landscapes in oil. Father of John Glashan(qv). Educated Glasgow and Paisley, studied at Glasgow School of Art under Newbery(qv) and Greiffenhagen(qv) where he met three kindred spirits, all of whom had a stimulating effect on the development of Scottish art: Robert Sivell, James Cowie and Jack Lamond. This was when the Glasgow School was considered to have passed its zenith. These four students were given every encouragement to analyse and examine some of the best paintings of the Italian renaissance. McGlashan was awarded a Haldane travelling scholarship enabling him to visit Europe. He was deeply impressed by Rembrandt and Franz Hals but most of all by the Italian masters, especially Tintoretto. He was never in harmony with modern American or British art, nor with Impressionism. He preferred to paint his own immediate environment, his wife, children, still-life, flowers and fruit. Good examples are his 'Woman and Child' and 'Wife and Child' now at Glasgow AG. Member of the Society of Eight(qv). Travelled widely on the Continent, settled in Glasgow and later retired to Rothesay, Bute. Founder member, Glasgow Society of Painters and Sculptors, President, Glasgow Art Club. 'His affectionate brush seems at a touch to bring life to a face, to a hovering butterfly, or to a shaft of light, while his sense of colour and design are a constant delight, both by their originality and their brightness' [Hutchison]. He was one of the best painters of children of his time. His colour is bold and sometimes hectic but he makes flesh seem real and is especially good at conveying the 'isolated composure of sleeping babies'. He lived latterly with his daughter although he was frequently visited by his talented draughtsman son, John(qv). Elected ARSA 1935, RSA 1938. Exhibited RSA and GI(50+). Represented in SNPG, Aberdeen AG, Dundee AG, Glasgow AG, Laing AG (Newcastle-on-Tyne), Paisley AG, Edinburgh City collection(2).
**Bibl:** Hardie 148; Macmillan [SA] 332,338,348,360; RSA Obituary;

**McGLASHAN, Barry** **c1970-**
Painter of landscape often with strong figurative component, often in evocative fantasy compositions. Trained Gray's School of Art. Winner of several student awards and, more recently, the John Kinross Scholarship (RSA) 1996, the Macallan Award (RSA) 1996, Guthrie Award (RSA) 1998, and Salvesen Travelling Scholarship (RSA) 2001. Studied in Florence and USA. Invited to the Florence Biennial 2003. Exhibits RSA. Represented in Aberdeen AG, Fuller Museum (Boston, USA), El Museo de la Cuidad (Mexico).

**McGLASHAN, Miss D** **fl 1956-1961**
Ayrshire painter of pastoral scenes, flowers. Exhibited GI(8) from Pinwherry.

**McGLASHAN, Daisy A (Mrs W S Anderson)** **1879-1968**
Glasgow painter. Studied Glasgow School of Art 1903-4. After an early marriage in 1904 she was persuaded to resume painting by her friend Henry Alison(qv). Her first exhibit was at the GI in 1904 while still a student.

**McGLASHAN, Stewart** **?-1904**
Sculptor. A memorial to Robert MacLean (d1871) is in Warriston Cemetery, Edinburgh. Entered into practice with his son with whom he designed a Celtic cross memorial to the Scottish Horse (1905) adorning Edinburgh Castle Esplanade.
**Bibl:** Gifford 90.

**McGLASHAN, Violet** **fl 1894-1896**
Watercolour painter of flowers and landscape. Exhibited GI(4), first from Glasgow and after 1895 from Kirkintilloch.

**McGLONE, Arthur** **fl 1943-1944**
Amateur Glasgow flower painter. Exhibited GI(2) from Knightswood.

**McGOLDRICK, John** **fl 1985**
Glasgow painter. Exhibited GI(1) from 63 Jordanhill Drive.

**MacGOUN, Miss Hannah Clarke Preston RSW** **1867-1913**
Edinburgh painter in watercolour of portraits, especially children, figure subjects, narrative and landscapes. Also painted interiors and genre in watercolour. Studied at Edinburgh School of Art and RSA Life School. Unusually proficient at painting children in a style influenced by the Dutch School. 'Her drawings are marked by a pleasing union of breadth and delicacy of tone and local colour, her draughtsmanship, if not very constructive, is gracious and expressive' [Caw]. Illustrated *Memories* by William MacGillivray (1912), Katherine Burrill's *The Little Foxes,* Dr John Brown's children's books *Pet Marjorie, Rab and his Friends, The Little Book of Children,* also *The Five Little Miss Deacons* by Lady Kemp, Norman MacLeod's *The Gold Thread,* and an anthology *The Gift of Friendship.* Elected RSW 1903. Exhibited RA 1893 and 1895, also RSA(68), RSW(37), GI(28), AAS(11), RHA(2) & L(13). Represented in NGS, SNPG ('Self-portrait'), Paisley AG, City of Edinburgh collection(3).
**Bibl:** Caw 428; Halsby 270.

**McGOWAN, Eleanor** **1943-**
Born Glasgow. Painter in oils, acrylic and mixed media of joyous highly charged landscapes, inspired especially by the north-west coast of Scotland. Influenced by James Fullarton(qv) and the Scottish Colourists. Prizewinner, North Ayrshire Open Art Comp. 2000. Member Glasgow Society of Women Artists and RGI, where she regularly exhibits.

**McGOWAN, Raymond** **1947-**
Born 8 Mar. As a printmaker enjoys etching, viscosity printing, copper and wood engraving as well as lino and woodcuts. Educated Dundee College of Art 1964-68 and Hospitalfield, Arbroath for one year in 1967. Completed postgraduate course in Dundee College of Education 1968-69 and a further course in printmaking with S W Hayter at Atelier 17, Paris in 1973. In 1974 went to USA and set up a printmaking studio 'Kala Institute' in San Francisco. For the next two years he moved between Paris and Canada as a freelance artist, occasionally teaching in his old Atelier in Paris. Since 1988 he has been a full-time lecturer in printmaking at the Duncan of Jordanstone College of Art, Dundee, having been elected a member of the Printmakers' Council of Great Britain in 1979 and Chairman and

founder member of the Dundee Printmakers' Workshop. Influenced by Josef Sekalski(qv) and S W Hayter in Paris. He has undergone several changes in style related to movements in his environment, most recently has adopted a free abstract approach. Began exhibiting at the RSA in 1989. Represented in Dundee AG, Perth AG.

**MacGOWAN, Robert** **fl 1952-1957**
Glasgow painter of landscape and flowers. Exhibited 'Head with mask' and 'House on the island' at the RSA & GI(1) from Belhaven Terrace.

**McGOWN, Miss Christina** **fl 1982-1986**
Painter from East Kilbride and later Aberdeen. Exhibited GI(4).

**McGRATH, Joseph** **fl 1954**
Amateur Glasgow printmaker. Exhibited a linocut at the GI, from Nimmo Drive.

**McGREGOR, A Ronald** **fl 1882-1883**
Glasgow amateur painter of flowers and landscape. Exhibited GI(3) from 113 Breadalbane Terrace.

**McGREGOR, Miss Christine** **fl 1921-1925**
Glasgow painter of figure studies, portrait heads and studies of snall domestic animals, often in pastel; also etcher. Exhibited RSA(1), GI(7), AAS 1919-26 & L(1).

**MacGREGOR, George S** **fl 1887-1891**
Glasgow book illustrator and watercolour painter. Contributed to *ILN* 1887. Exhibited RSA(3) & GI(1) from 5 Huntly Gardens, Kelvinside.

**MacGREGOR, Harry** **fl 1894-1934**
Edinburgh painter in oil and watercolour of landscape and pastoral scenes, especially pools and streams in the sunrise and sunset. Moved to Glasgow for a short time in 1900, then to Peebles c1909 and Loanhead 1929, before retiring to Edinburgh. Sometimes painted in Kircudbright where he became friendly with W S MacGeorge.(qv). Exhibited RSA(83), GI(22) & RSW(5).

**McGREGOR, Miss Jenny** **fl 1875**
Pollockshields oil painter of landscapes and country buildings. Exhibited RSA(2) & GI(1).

**MacGREGOR, Miss Jessie M** **fl 1875-d1919**
Painter of flowers, genre, portraits & historical subjects, also illustrator. Working in Liverpool from 1872 before moving to London c1886. Elected ASWA 1886, SWA 1887. Exhibited RSA(2) & RGI 1875-1904, from Glengyle Lodge, Bruntsfield Place.

**MacGREGOR, John** **fl 1855-d1872**
Born probably Edinburgh; died St Petersburg. Photographer. Joined William Carrick(qv) in establishing one of the first photographic studios in Russia. According to Carrick's mother "I do not believe there were ever two souls born to live in such unity and concord together". MacGregor provided the energy, Carrick the artistry and contacts.
**Bibl:** Felicity Ashbee & Julie Lawson, William Carrick, Scottish Masters series, no. 3, Edinburgh 1987.

**McGREGOR, John** **fl 1873-1900**
Edinburgh oil painter of landscapes and sea pieces; exhibited RSA(4), latterly from 7 New Broughton Street.

**MacGREGOR, John Douglas RSW** **1891-1951**
Born St Andrews, Oct 13; died Glasgow, Sep 10. Painter in watercolour of coastal, harbour and fishing scenes; also designer of metalwork, woodwork, silk painting, china painting and embroidery including amusing, beautifully crafted puppets. Educated Madras College; apprenticed to a firm of house painters c1906. Worked with Wylie & Lochhead, Glasgow 1909-12, attending classes at Glasgow School of Art before proceeding to London, employed by Waring & Gillow as painter, gilder and furniture designer. Attended evening school at Central School of Art. Served with the Highland Light Infantry in WWI being severely wounded at Loos, right shoulder paralysed and one leg amputated. Trained Dundee School of Art 1917-21. Visited America 1921, returning to teach art, Stirling HS 1922-9. HM Inspector of Schools 1930-50. Came under the strong influence of Surrealism and neo-Romanticism. His expressive watercolours are delicate, sensitive and full of unforced symbolism. Founded Glasgow Puppet Guild 1942. Elected RSW 1950. Posthumous exhibition of watercolours, Glasgow 1952; retrospective exhibition St Andrews & Dundee 1992. Exhibited RSA(14), RSW & GI(15). Represented in Glasgow AG, RSA, SAC.
**Bibl:** Halsby 270; Dundee AG Ex cat (text by Morna MacCusbie), 1992.

**McGREGOR, John E** **fl 1953-1954**
Edinburgh portrait painter. Exhibited GI(3) from Hope St.

**McGREGOR, Lynn B RSW** **1959-**
Born Pittenweem, Fife. Portrait painter. Studied Edinburgh College of Art 1985-88, awarded a Hospitalfield scholarship 1987. Teaching part-time in the Life Classes at the ECA in 1989. Works in Scotland and Ireland, painting landscapes and seascapes in a semi-abstract manner. Awards include SAC Award 1991, SSWA Special Award 1991, Eli Lilly Purchase Prize 1996, Mabel McKinley Prize (RGI) 1999. First solo exhibition Edinburgh 1993. Elected RSW 2000. Exhibited RSA, RSW, RGI from an isolated island off the Northern Irish coast.

**MacGREGOR, Marie S** **fl 1886-1901**
Glasgow oil painter of fruit and still-life; exhibited RSA(2) & GI(3) from Garnethill and Hill St.

**MacGREGOR, Miss Marilyn** **fl 1974**
Renfrewshire embroiderer. Exhibited GI(1) from Brookfield.

**McGREGOR, Mhairi P RSW** **1971-**
Painter, mainly in oils. Trained Glasgow School of Art 1989-93 where she was awarded a Christie Bursary, a landscape drawing prize and John Kinross scholarship, this enabling her to spend three working months in Florence. Spent most of 1997 in Australia. Further travel took her to Arizona and New Mexico. Elected RSW 1999.

**MacGREGOR, P** **fl 1886**
Edinburgh painter in oil of figurative subjects; exhibited RSA(1), from 2 Danube Street.

**MacGREGOR, Miss Polly** **fl 1885-1889**
Glasgow painter of rural scenes and wild flowers. Possibly sister of Mary M(qv). Exhibited GI(5) from 113 Breadalbane Terrace.

**MacGREGOR, Patrick** **fl 1897-1898**
Glasgow painter. Exhibited GI(1) & L(1) from 3 Carfin Street.

**McGREGOR, Robert RSA** **1847-1922**
Born Bradford; died Portobello. Painter in oil and watercolour; figurative subjects. Son of a Dunfermline businessman who settled for a time in Yorkshire. At an early age he returned with his father to Dunfermline. Settling in Edinburgh, he spent a short time working for the publishers, Nelson. Although at this time he had had no regular training, he had received some tuition from a French artist. Subsequently attended the RSA Life Schools where he must have made rapid progress for his first exhibit at the RSA was in 1873, when he was still only 26. There followed an annual show of his work until 1916, a total of 203 paintings. Although he never embarked on any formal studies in France or Holland, his work more closely resembles a number of his French and Dutch contemporaries than it does any contemporary Scottish work. The effects of his almost annual visits to the picturesque districts of Normandy and Holland are clearly reflected, especially in his later works. More than any artist before James Guthrie(qv) or the Newlyn School, he seems to have absorbed the teachings of Bastien-Lepage and Millet. 'Perhaps the first Scottish genre painter to apply rigorous study of tone to his work; a capable draughtsman and pleasant, if restricted, colourist, and, although he has learned much from some of his modern Dutchmen, his pictures have an individuality and sentiment of their own' [Caw]. At the beginning he was most interested in tone but instead of combining it with full local colour, he preferred quiet values and the gentler, more subtle light of the Dutch coast. 'His colour is, of course, conditioned by his feeling for light, and if its appeal is limited, and it can scarcely be described as highly emotional, it is usually pleasant enough to

escape the reproach of being nearly negative, while at times its subdued harmonies result in quiet yet positive charm. Further, neither his handling nor his drawing is marked by emphasis. Content to render effect and incident simply and directly, he paints with an equal and fairly smooth impasto and draws without fuss or flourish'. In his earlier years he found his subjects mostly in Scotland but as he became older his subjects became more frequently Continental and the size of his paintings larger. Painted workers in the field and at the fringes of the sea going about their labours rather than the depiction of any great drama, and portrayed the innocent joys of childhood, the affinity between the very old and the very young, especially when working in the open air together on a common task. The quality of painting in his major work, such as 'The Knife Grinder' 1878, now in Dundee AG or 'Shrimping on the Seine' 1895, now in a private collection, are among the most impressive works of his time. Also painted occasionally in watercolour and often comparatively minor sketches of less interest and quality. Used the same family as models for many of his paintings. Elected ARSA 1882, RSA 1889. Exhibited RA(15), RSA & GI(100). Represented in NGS, Broughty Ferry AG, Dundee AG, Glasgow AG, Paisley AG, Edinburgh City collection, Perth AG, Preston AG, Mackelvie AG (Auckland).
**Bibl:** AJ 1903, 124; Caw 283-4; Conn 65, 108; Halsby 270; Hardie 66,78,79,85; Macmillan [SA] 254-5; Studio 68, 123; 85, 106 ff.

**McGREGOR, Sara (Mrs Charles W Holroyd)** **fl 1898-1918**
Edinburgh painter of portraits, genre and conversation pieces. Daughter of Robert McGregor(qv). Considered by some contemporaries to be at least as talented as her father, but died tragically young in childbirth. Her portrait of Ebenezer Roxburgh(qv) remains in the family. Lived in Portobello. Not to be confused with Sarah McGregor, the English flower painter working at about the same time. Exhibited RA(2), RSA(30), GI(13) & L(1), latterly from a studio in Queen St.

**McGREGOR, Miss Sheena** **fl 1973-1974**
Glasgow amateur painter. Exhibited GI(2).

**MacGREGOR, Stuart** **fl 1866-1867**
Edinburgh oil painter of landscapes and figure subjects; exhibited RSA(4).

**MacGREGOR, W T** **fl 1896**
Stirlingshire oil painter of topographical works and street scenes; exhibited RSA(1) from Bridge of Allan.

**MacGREGOR, Walker** **fl 1937**
Glasgow painter. Exhibited GI(2) from 13 Durcombe Street.

**MacGREGOR, William Firth** **fl 1921-1924**
Edinburgh painter of portraits and topographical subjects. Exhibited RSA(4) & GI(1) from 51 Albany Street.

**MacGREGOR, William York RSA RSW** **1855-1923**
Born Finnart, Dunbartonshire, 14 Oct; died Oban, 28 Sep. Painter in oil and watercolour; landscapes. Son of a well-known Glasgow ship builder. Generally regarded as the father of the Glasgow School of painters. Nine years older than Hornel(qv), he was between four and six years older than most other members of the School, while Melville(qv) and Grosvenor Thomas(qv) were the same age and Paterson(qv) and Macaulay Stevenson(qv) were a year older and Dow(qv) and Christie(qv), seven and eight years older respectively. He studied at the RSA Schools under James Docharty(qv), and later at the Slade School under Legros. At first his landscapes were conventional but under the influence of his friend James Paterson(qv), who had studied in Paris, began to develop a more robust style. 'In his pictures justness of tone, delicacy and breadth of handling, and a charming quality of pensive colour are conspicuous. The rhythm of line and mass is distinguished, the colour reticent and grave, yet resonant and finely balanced in design, the handling instinctive with strength and style, the sentiment splendidly solemn. He is not a realist in the ordinary sense, his landscape is essentially abstract, but at the same time, it is full of reality and often noble in spirit' [Martin]. From 1888-90 he went to South Africa because of asthma, thereafter his style changed, the colours became more gloomy and the forms more abstract. His pictures were never popular, although he did sell two very well in Munich in 1890. Eventually asthma led him to live at Albyn Lodge, Bridge of Allan, during which time he became actively involved in the flourishing community of Cambuskenneth. His work was not a great influence upon the Glasgow School, rather was he the father figure in more general 'common sense' matters. Thus, an often quoted sample of advice he gave to some of his younger colleagues was 'hack the subject out as you would were you using an axe, and try to realise it; get its bigness. Don't follow any school, there are no schools in Art'. Possibly his most important work was the 'Vegetable Stall' (1884), now in the NGS. 'So naturally are the vegetables placed, one feels that the knife has just been laid down and that its owner will return in a moment or two'. It is an important example of the Glasgow School, especially in the handling of paint and the keen visual enjoyment of the subjects. Elected ARSA 1898, RSA 1921, RSW 1885. Exhibited RA (2), RSA(73), RSW(19), GI(45) & AAS. Represented in Tate AG, NGS, Aberdeen AG, Glasgow AG, Greenock AG, Kirkcaldy AG, Newcastle AG, Paisley AG, Lillie AG (Milngavie), City of Edinburgh collection, Hunterian Museum (Glasgow), Perth AG, Munich AG, Buffalo AG (NY).
**Bibl:** AJ 1894, 179; 1898, 47; 1904, 172; Caw 380-2; Conn 68 (1924) 55; Halsby 150-1 et al; Hardie passim ch vi; Irwin 373-4(illus); Macmillan [SA] 255-6,267-8,313; Martin 42-4; SAC (Ex Cat 1968); Studio, 89 (1925); 92 (1926), 53, 55.

**MacGRORY, Donal** **fl 1974-**
Scottish parentage. Physician and part-time artist. Mainly watercolours with a strong interest in the sea and landscape. Studied at Ruskin School of Drawing, Oxford. First solo exhibition in Kent, 1974 followed by others in London, Edinburgh and Moscow.

**McGRUER, Stephen** **fl 1970-1972**
Aberdeenshire sculptor. Trained Gray's School of Art, Aberdeen. Exhibited AAS(3) from 5 Granton Place and latterly Artrochie Fm, Ellon.

**McGUFFIE, Miss Constance** **fl 1943**
Renfrewshire amateur artist. Exhibited a pencil and wash study 'The orange skirt' at the GI, from Newton Mearns.

**McGUFFIE, Thomas** **fl 1863-1865**
Glasgow architect and topographical watercolourist. Worked occasionally in England and Italy. In Edinburgh designed a large villa, Clerwood, Clermiston Rd (c1860) with large gables and Gothic detail. Exhibited RSA(1) & GI(6).

**McGUINNESS, Johnny** **1955-**
Painter and sculptor. Studied Dundee College of Art. In addition to painting semi-abstract works he creates three-dimensional figures from hundreds of random fragments of contemporary plastic toys. These are painted in unrelieved black presenting a detached, sinister image. His first solo exhibition was in Edinburgh 1986. Exhibits RSA & SSA.

**McHARDY, Edith** **fl 1911**
Ayr sculptress. Related to M A McHardy(qv). Exhibited a girls's head at the GI from Sunnyside.

**McHARDY, Miss Elizabeth A** **fl 1877-1889**
Edinburgh painter of domestic interiors, flowers, still life and topographical works. Exhibited at the RSA(7) and GI(1) from various addresses.

**McHARDY, James ('Calamo Currente')** **fl 1895**
Author and illustrator, probably Scottish. Illustrated and wrote *Half Hours with an Old Golfer* under the pseudonymn 'Calamo Currente'.

**McHARDY, M A** **fl 1910**
Ayr sculptor. Related to Edith M(qv). Exhibited a portrait in bronze bas-relief from Sunnyside.

**McHARG, James** **fl 1955-1968**
Glasgow painter of portraits, genre and topographical subjects. Exhibited GI(18), from Batson St.

**McHARG, Nicola ('Nicki')** **1956-**
Born, Calcutta, India, 24 Sep. Printmaker, framer and illustrator. Studied Gray's School of Art, Aberdeen 1974-78 and a post diploma

course 1978-79. Her particular interest is in mezzotints and the subjects are generally townscapes. Lives at 2 Cottage Brae, Aberdeen. Has had one-woman shows at Peacock Studio, Aberdeen and Glasgow Print Studio, also overseas. Exhibited RA, RSA & GI(1). Represented in Glasgow AG, Edinburgh City collection, SAC.

**MACHIN, John** **fl 1935-1953**
Glasgow topographical painter, mostly west coast and Glasgow scenes. Exhibited GI(14), from St. Andrews St.

**MacHUTCHEON, John C** **fl 1907**
Glasgow engraver. Exhibited GI(2).

**McIA(I)N, Mrs Fanny HRSA** **1814-1897**
Painter of figurative and historical subjects. Wife of R R MacIain(qv). Taught at Government School of Design. For a long time head of the Female School of Design in London. Now best remembered as an artist for her picture 'A Highlander defending his family at the massacre of Glencoe' which was later engraved. The first woman artist in Scotland honoured by the RSA, becoming an Honorary RSA in 1854. Exhibited five works at the RSA, 1840-1853, along similar lines to her husband. Also ten works at the RA, 1836-1847, all of them from various London addresses. A number of these were figurative studies, mostly of children. A portrait of her husband 'Robert Ronald McIain' is in SNPG.
**Bibl:** Brydall 443; Caw 120; Halsby 271.

**McIA(I)N, Robert Ronald ARSA** **1803-1856**
Born Scotland; died Hampstead, London 13 Dec 1856 or 1 Dec 1857. Painter in oil of historical genre and battle scenes; illustrator. A true Highlander, descended from the MacDonalds of Glencoe, throughout his life he retained a great energy, enthusiastic temperament and a passionate love and admiration for everything Highland. Although he began life on the stage and was quite successful, he gave this up c1840 in order to devote himself full-time to painting. Indeed, his first exhibits at the RA 1836-39 gave as his address Theatre Royal, Drury Lane. Painted episodes from Scottish history and incidents depicting Highland courage and character. During the last 17 years of his life he devoted himself to painting with great energy. In addition to his studio in London, he kept a studio for many years in Fort William. Married to the artist, Fanny MacIain(qv). A fine raconteur and singer. At an Eglinton tournament he once took the part of a medieval jester. His best known works were 'An Incident in the Revolutionary War of America' 1854 and 'A Highland Whisky Still' 1849. Elected ARSA 1852. Exhibited RA(13) 1836-1847, the first three of which were landscapes, the remainder historical scenes; also RSA(24) 1840-1855. Perhaps best remembered as the illustrator of the first major work on the Scottish clans, *Clans of the Scottish Highlands,* 2 vols (1845-47) and *Gaelic Gatherings* (1848), also *The London Art Union Prize Annual* (1845).
**Bibl:** AJ 1857, 62f (obit); Brydall 442-3; Caw 120; Halsby 271; Redgrave.

**McILHENNY, Ian** **fl 1973-1986**
Renfrewshire landscape painter, often continental subjects. Exhibited GI(7) from Eaglesham and later Glasgow.

**MacILROY, Maude G** **fl 1915-1923**
Painter and sculptress; subject paintings, often with animals especially horses. Moved from Glasgow to Turnberry c1920; exhibited RSA(12), GI(14) & L(3).

**McILWRAITH, Agnes (Mrs C F Fyfe)** **fl 1919-1920**
Glasgow portrait painter. Exhibited GI(4) from 21 Bruce Road, Pollockshields, latterly from Lily Bank, Port Glasgow.

**McILWRAITH, Andrew (or McLauraith)** **fl 1715-1753**
Edinburgh portrait painter. Married Anne, daughter of William Mossman of Kirkurd on 13 July, 1715. Elected member of the Guild of St Luke 1729 and a Burgess of the city of Edinburgh in 1735. Signed his work 'M'Lauraith Pinxit'. In 1725 he executed a portrait of 'Sir Lawrence Mercer of Meginch', 1725, also 'John, 11th Lord Gray' (1716-1782) and 'Bishop Burnet', painted for Marischal College, Aberdeen 1723. Also a number of unknown sitters, most of which are in the collection of the Earl of Stair.

**MacINNES, Alexander** **fl 1830-1853**
Inverness portrait and landscape painter in oil, also printmaker. First emerges on the scene about the year 1830 when he produced a series of views of Inverness, the artistic value of which was slight although the prints that were made are now very rare and have great value. In the summer of 1836 he returned from a sketching tour overseas and set up as a portrait painter at 23 Chapel Street. The *Inverness Courier* referred to 'a large painting of Queen Esther before King Ahasuerus'. In 1836 he produced an historically important townscape of Inverness showing Church Street as it would appear when St John's Espiscopal Church was completed. In 1837 he moved to 41 Church Street, there setting up as a teacher and restorer as well as painter. Among his earlier works of which details remain known are a view of Loch Duich, much applauded by a contemporary art critic, and a portrait of an old Highland woman, 'Isobel Mhor', a well known Inverness character 'whose face had all the deformity and deep furrowed lines of age'. In 1842, his 'Young Highland Wife' was purchased by the Art Union of Edinburgh. At about this time he also painted the portraits of 'Alexander Cumming, Provost of Inverness' (retired 1840), the well known Highland author, 'Captain Fraser of Knockie', and a portrait of one of Lord Lovat's retrievers commissioned by Sir George Gore. In 1843 he had five works at the RSA, one a portrait of 'Eddie Ochiltrie' was described 'as of great character and merit'. The only example of his art publicly exhibited in Inverness is his copy of the portrait of 'Duncan Forbes', first laird of Culloden and great-grandfather of Lord President Forbes. The copy, made from the original in Culloden House, was presented to the Town Council of Inverness in 1843 in recognition of which the Council proposed conferring the freedom of the Burgh on the artist, but this was never consummated. In April, 1845 he sold all his studio items and moved to London. Living at 4 Allason Terrace, Kensington, he exhibited three works at the RA, one a study of the lodging house where JMW Turner had died the previous year (1851) and one a landscape of Ben Alder, Inverness-shire.
**Bibl:** W Simpson: Inverness Artists, Inverness 1925, 18-25.

**McINNES, Miss Ellen** **fl 1860-1863**
Painter of portraits and figure studies and later of flowers. Worked first from Edinburgh and later from London. Exhibited RSA(6) including a portrait 'The Very Rev Dean Ramsay' 1860.

**McINNES, Mrs Elspeth** **fl 1983**
Amateur Ayrshire painter. Married John M(qv). Exhibited GI(1) from Tawthorn Smiddy, by Kilmarnock.

**MacINNES(S), Ian** **fl 1959-1967**
Orkney painter of land and seascapes. Exhibited AAS from Thistlebank, Stromness.

**McINNES, James** **fl 1881-1882**
Edinburgh landscape painter in watercolours. Exhibited RSA(2) from 22 Home Street.

**McINNES, Jock** **1943-**
Scottish painter and teacher. Trained Glasgow School of Art 1962-66. After winning a travelling scholarship enabling him to visit Europe, he joined the staff before painting full-time. Awarded Colquhoun Memorial first prize 1978, Cargill award (RGI) 1991.

**McINNES, Robert** **1801-1886**
Died Stirling. Scottish painter of genre, rural life and portraits. Spent many years in Italy, returning in about 1848. Began exhibiting at the RA in 1841 with a portrait of the 'Rt Hon Sir James Kemp' but a more important painting was 'Italian Bowlers - Seen in the Courtyard of an Osteria' (1843). Five years later he exhibited a great advance on his previous work, 'Summer's Afternoon on the Lido near Venice' 1848. This depicts the celebration of a fiesta by a party of Italian peasants assembled under a tree, and contains many effective groups of figures painted in a clear and finished manner. The same year he showed a landscape painted in the Carrara Mountains with bullocks drawing blocks of marble down a mountainside. His later work was richer in colour and well finished, unlike the freer, sometimes meaningless shadows that detracted from earlier work. His watercolour style was influenced by Wilkie(qv) and John Philip(qv) but lacked their refined draughtsmanship. Friend of W B Scott(qv). Brydall concluded that 'his pictures were more characterised by a high degree of finish and

good careful drawing and colour, than by the loftier qualities of art, such as imagination or subtlety of expression and treatment'. Produced very few finished works during latter years. Exhibited RA(27), RSA(5) & GI(1), latterly from Lago House, Tunbridge Wells. Represented in NGS ('Self-portrait'), Glasgow Corporation Collection, Paisley AG.
**Bibl:** AJ 1859, 170; Brydall 443-4; Caw 120; Halsby 271; McKay 259.

**McINNES, Roy** **fl 1984**
Glasgow painter. Exhibited 'Still life' at the GI from 9 Cedar Court.

**McINROY, Patricia** **fl 1886-1896**
Ayrshire landscape painter, also interiors and genre. Exhibited RSA(2) & GI(3) from The Birkenward, Skelmorlie. Her interior exhibits of 1886 are in the Bute collection, Glasgow AG.

**McINTOSH, A** **fl 1861**
Glasgow landscape painter. Exhibited GI(3) from Binnie Place.

**McINTOSH, A** **fl 1961**
Dunbartonshire painter. Exhibited 'Glen Falloch' at the GI, from Arrochar.

**McINTOSH, Archibald Dunbar RSW** **1935-**
Born Glasgow. Painter in oil and watercolour. Trained Glasgow School of Art 1953-57. Recipient of Torrance Award (RSA) 1964 and Guthrie Award (RSA) 1967. Elected Vice-President RSW 1995. Exhibited RSA since 1965 (78), RSW & annually GI since 1956, latterly from 10 Park Place, Dunfermline. Two watercolours of Edinburgh scenes in the Edinburgh City collection.

**MacINTOSH, Daniel** **fl 1800-1825**
Edinburgh print-seller, carver, gilder, stationer, engraver and teacher of drawing. Carried on business first in St. Andrews St and later at 49 Princes Street. Best known as the publisher of William Paterson's *Twelve Etchings of Views in Edinburgh.* With varied business interests, his well-designed business cards and property (the shop frontage is seen clearly in Joseph Ebsworth's 'Northern View from The Scott Monument'), his influence as a teacher on the artistic life of the city is likely to have been considerable, even though no original work of his is now known.
**Bibl:** Butchart 44,46.

**MacINTOSH, Frieda (? Freida)** **fl 1973**
Angus designer; exhibited AAS(1) from 17 Traill Terrace, Montrose.

**McINTOSH, Iain Redford ARSA** **1945-**
Born Peterhead, Aberdeenshire. Sculptor. Works in wood, stone, marble and clay. Studied at Gray's School of Art, Aberdeen 1962-67. Awarded Governor's prize and Founder's prize 1964. In 1965 he was granted the Queen's Award for Art and Design travelling scholarship and in 1970 won Benno Schotz prize for sculpture at the RSA, followed by the Latimer award 1971. Among his commissions is the bronze 'Girl at the Pool' at Cherrybank, Perth. Elected ARBS 1976, ARSA 1981. Exhibits regularly RSA & GI 1969-1980 from Powmouth, nr Montrose.

**McINTOSH, Irvine** **fl 1935**
Angus topographical painter. Exhibited AAS from 51 West High St, Forfar.

**McINTOSH, J** **fl 1779**
Scottish engraver. His only known work is a portrait 'William, 17th Earl of Sutherland', after Allan Ramsay 1779.
**Bibl:** Bushnell; J Chaloner Smith, British Mezzotint Portraits, 4 pts, 1878-83.

**MacINTOSH, John** **fl 1888-1914**
Landscape painter. Exhibited GI(1) & LS(8) from Strath Cottage, Galston.

**MacINTOSH, John Macintosh RBA** **1847-1913**
Born Inverness; died England, 5 Mar. Painter of landscapes, often in watercolour. Studied Heatherley's, later in Paris. Painted widely in Berkshire and was for many years Secretary of the Newbury Art Society. Member of the RBA in 1889 until his resignation 1904. Council member, Ridley Art Club. Illustrated Hayden: *Islands of the Vale* (1908). Exhibited RA(28) 1880-1901, all English landscapes, also RI(25), ROI(6), RBA(116) & GI(3), after 1895 from Woolhampton, nr Reading. Represented in the V & A.

**McINTOSH, Marion** **fl 1982-1988**
Edinburgh painter who later moved to Glasgow. Exhibited a portrait and a study of silver birches at the RSA, also GI(1).

**McINTOSH, Miss Myra** **fl 1974**
Embroiderer. Exhibited GI(1) from Uddingston.

**McINTOSH, Robert** **fl 1827**
Edinburgh painter of figurative subjects. Exhibited RSA(1) from East Richmond Street.

**McINTOSH, T H** **fl 1869**
Edinburgh painter of local landscape and coastal scenes. Exhibited RSA(1) from 75 Princes Street.

**McINTYRE, Alexander** **fl 1965**
East Kilbride painter. Exhibited GI(1).

**MacINTYRE, Archibald** **fl 1793**
Edinburgh engraver. Engraved ten views of the principal public buildings in Edinburgh, and nine in a set of thirteen similar smaller views. Also engraved a plan of Edinburgh city and its environs for Aitchison's *Edinburgh Directory,* 1793.
**Bibl:** Bushnell.

**McINTYRE, Mrs Dolina** **fl 1969-1986**
Cumbrae painter. Exhibited west coast landscapes from Glasgow and later Millport at the GI(16).

**MacINTYRE, Donald** **1923-**
Glasgow landscape painter. Moved to North Wales 1960. Exhibited spasmodically at the RSA(7) 1946-7 and again 1960-2, also GI(17) 1944-60.

**MacINTYRE, Donald Edward** **1900-?**
Born Edinburgh, 27 Aug. Painter, etcher and jeweller. Landscapes, figurative and architectural subjects. Assistant art master, George Watson's Boys College, Edinburgh and part-time member of staff at the Edinburgh College of Art. Lived in Edinburgh. Exhibited RSA(7) 1923-28 & GI(1).

**McINTYRE, Miss Doris Barton** **fl 1960-1964**
Glasgow painter of landscapes and portraits. Exhibited 'Self-portrait' and two watercolour landscapes at the GI, from Kew Terrace.

**MacINTYRE, Edith A** **fl 1923-1939**
Flower & landscape painter in watercolour and pastel. Exhibited RSA(4), AAS(2), & L(1) from Vinebank, Broughty Ferry.
**Bibl:** Halsby 271.

**McINTYRE, Hugh** **fl 1979-1983**
Dumfries painter and engraver. Exhibited RSA(4) & GI(2).

**McINTYRE, Iain** **1959-**
Born Aberfeldy. Printmaker, based in Fife. Represented Perth AG.

**MacINTYRE, James** **1880-c1950**
Born Thornliebank, 11 Dec. Painter of domestic and figurative subjects and etcher. Brother of Joseph Wrightson M(qv). Educated first at the local school in his village then at Allan Glen's School, Glasgow and later at the Glasgow and West of Scotland Technical College. Originally intending to be an architect he served an apprenticeship under James Miller(qv). His duties there included the execution of a number of drawings in pen and ink. Also attended Edinburgh School of Art as a part-time student. Finding that his love for original black and white work developed he progressed so quickly as to win the bronze medal for architectural design at the National Competition in London 1899. At Edinburgh School of Art he met Susan Crawford(qv) who, together with William Strang(qv), D Y Cameron(qv) and Muirhead Bone(qv), were pioneers of

modern etching. Under Crawford's guidance Macintyre studied the art of etching. His first plate 'The Glasgow and South-Western Railway Bridge' earned immediate success. Many of his etchings, principally of Edinburgh and Glasgow, were published by Stoddart and Malcolm. His work was distinguished by delicate draughtsmanship, poetic feeling, and technical excellence. It is remarkable how his stature has been allowed to fade over the years for at his best he was the equal of D Y Cameron(qv). Travelled a great deal of the continent and also in the United States but his best work was his Scottish subjects where his love for the countryside coupled with his profound knowledge of architecture made him particularly at home in rendering the stately aspects of the buildings drawn in the cities and towns of Scotland. During WW2 he and his brother lived on Isle of Ornsay, Skye, from where he exhibited a number of works as well as being an active member of the Observer Corps. Exhibited RA(6), RHA(8), RBA(1), GI(1) & L(1). Represented in City of Edinburgh Collection (2).
**Bibl:** F Rutter, 'James Macintyre', The Man and His Work, Edinburgh.

**MacINTYRE, James C** **fl c1880-c1911**
Amateur Perthshire landscape painter and copyist. Exhibited Perth exhibitions in 1883, 1903, 1904 and 1911-12. Represented in Perth AG(8), including copies after Sir J E Millais and W E Lockhart.

**McINTYRE, John** **fl 1908-1911**
Edinburgh painter. Exhibited RSA(4) from 28 North Bridge St.

**McINTYRE, John** **fl 1980-1985**
Paisley painter of flowers and landscape. Exhibited GI(13).

**McINTYRE, Joseph** **1940-**
Dundee figurative painter in pastel and oils. Trained Dundee Coll. of Art 1961-65 under Alberto Morrocco(qv) and James McIntosh Patrick(qv). Curator, Orchar Collection (Dundee) 1968-1988 and in 1972 joined Duncan Jordanstone College of Art as a part-time lecturer. Draws inspiration from the play of light and shadow in the city, especially at night. Won Pernod prize 1973, principal prize-winner, Robert Colquhoun competition 1975. Regular solo exhibitions in USA, Scotland & elsewhere since 1966. Represented in the Royal Collection; Dundee AG.

**McINTYRE, Joseph, Wrightson** **fl 1870-1888**
Scottish painter. Brother of James M(qv). After living most of his life in Kentish Town, London, he moved to 2 Market Place, Sheffield c1885. Exhibited RA(5), 'Stranded on Goodwin Sands' at the RSA 1870 & GI 1870-1873.

**McINTYRE, Keith** **1959-**
Born Edinburgh. Studied Duncan of Jordanstone College of Art, Dundee 1978-1982 followed by a postgraduate year. After winning the Carnegie Award 1982 spent most of 1983 studying papermaking in Barcelona Paper Workshop. Returning to Scotland he settled in Moffat, Dumfries-shire. This had a profound effect on his work as he became increasingly fascinated by the customs of rural southern Scotland. Preoccupied with the sexual stereotyping of male dominance as well as the more general theme of fertility. Received the Gillies Award 1983 and since 1984 has been a part-time lecturer at Glasgow School of Art. Represented in SNGMA, Aberdeen AG, Dundee AG, Cleveland AG(Middlesborough).
**Bibl:** SNGMA, The Vigorous Imagination, (Ex Cat 1987).

**MacINTYRE, Maggie** **fl 1889-1890**
Glasgow artist. Exhibited two scenes on the Clyde at the GI, from 139 Greenhead Street.

**McINTYRE, Michael S** **fl 1973**
Aberdeen painter of birds and local landscape. Exhibited AAS(2) from 23 Marywell St.

**McINTYRE, Patricia Elizabeth** **fl 1975-1981**
Aberdeen engraver. Trained Gray's School of Art. Exhibited RSA(4) & AAS, from 49 Regent Quay.

**McINTYRE, Paul A** **fl 1971-1981**
East Kilbride Painter. Exhibited GI.

**McINTYRE, Peter** **20th Cent**
New Zealand artist of Scottish descent. A large oil painting of Dunedin was presented to Edinburgh City by the citizens of Dunedin in 1947.

**McINTYRE, Robert** **fl 1971**
Amateur Lanarkshire sculptor. Exhibited a wooden abstract GI.

**McISAAC, James Nigel** **1911-**
Born Edinburgh. Son of a stained glass artist with Cunningham, Dickson and Walker, and a piano teacher. Educated Portobello and Edinburgh College of Art 1933-1934 under S J Peploe(qv) and Herbert Read. Completed a teacher training course at Moray House 1935, became art teacher at the Royal High, then Assistant Rector 1972-1976. Exhibited regularly at the RSA, SSA and GI. Represented in SNPG and Edinburgh City collection.

**MACK, Alastair** **fl 1987**
Edinburgh painter. Exhibited GI(1) from Orchard Brae.

**MACKAY, Alasdair Gordon Douglas** **fl 1913-1937**
Glasgow painter of portraits, character studies and coastal and topographical scenes; exhibited RSA(18), AAS(2) & GI(11) from both Edinburgh & Glasgow.

**McKAY, Alex C** **fl 1962-1970**
Dumfries landscape painter; exhibited RSA(13) from Maxwelltown.

**MACKAY, Alexander S** **fl 1868-1889**
Born Kilmarnock. Painter in oil of portraits and figure subjects, he worked from Kilmarnock before moving to 13 Cornwall Street, Edinburgh. Exhibited RSA(50) including a portrait of 'Major General Furlong of the Indian Staff Corps' 1878 and the vocalist, 'John Templeton of Drury Lane and Covent Garden' 1884, as well as a number of prominent ecclesiastics.

**MACKAY, Charles** **1868-?**
Born Glasgow, 25 Oct. Painter of landscape in watercolour, furniture designer. Studied at Glasgow School of Art and Paris at the Academie Delacluse. Lived in Glasgow before moving to Finnart, Cambuslang. Exhibited RSA(2), RSW(13), GI(12) & L(5).
**Bibl:** Halsby 271.

**MACKAY, Miss Christina (Mrs Alexander M Young)** **fl 1943-1948**
Glasgow portrait and flower painter, also occasional sculptures. Exhibited RSA & GI(4).

**MACKAY, Colin A** **fl 1988**
Glasgow amateur painter. Exhibited GI(1) from Springhill Gdns.

**MACKAY, David B** **fl 1883-1899**
Painter in oil and watercolour; landscapes, townscapes & harbour scenes. Exhibited RSA(13), RSW(2), AAS(2) GI(8) & L(1) from High Street, Crail, Fifeshire until 1883 and thereafter from Kilmarnock although he did occasionally return to Crail where he retained a studio. There may have been another **David MACKAY** who exhibited landscapes at the RSA 1884-1895 from a Kilmarnock address. Either or both David MacKays may have been related to Alexander M(qv).

**MACKAY, Dorothy M** **fl 1935**
Sculptress. Designed a statue of St Peter (1935) in St Peter (Episcopal) Church, Lutton Pl, Edinburgh.

**MACKAY, Florence Agnes** **fl 1893-1936**
Aberdeen flower and landscape painter; oil and pastel. Studied Gray's School of Art, Aberdeen, also in France and Belgium. On her return to Scotland appointed art mistress at Peterhead Academy and Aberdeen HS. Exhibited 'Roses' at the RSA in 1896 and several works at the AAS 1893-1936 from 256 Great Western Road.

**MACKAY, G D** **fl 1925**
Landscape and animal painter. Exhibited RSA(2) from 11 Boswell Quadrant, Wardie.

**MACKAY, Gordon** **fl 1884**
Lochcarron landscape painter in oil. Exhibited RSA(1).

**MACKAY, Hugh** **fl 1902-1906**
Glasgow painter. Fruit and flower studies, also Clyde scenes. Exhibited GI(5).

**MACKAY, Ian** **fl 1970**
Amateur painter. Exhibited RSA(1) from Kirkintilloch.

**McKAY, Miss Isa** **fl 1941**
Clackmannanshire sculptress. Exhibited 'Song of the Sea' at the RSA from Menstrie.

**MACKAY, Isobel M** **fl 1966**
Aberdeen sculptress. Exhibited a portrait bust at AAS from 298 Gt Western Rd.

**MACKAY, J R** **fl 1946-1949**
Glasgow engraver. Exhibited two etchings, one of 'Herring fishers at Stonehaven', at the GI, from Dryburgh Gdns.

**McKAY, John Ross RSA FRIBA FRIAS** **1884-1961**
Edinburgh architect. Responsible for many buildings in and around Edinburgh including Binns (1935) and (with James Smith Richardson(qv)) the entrance to the original Caley Picture House (1922-3). Designed hospitals and restored churches including those in Nicholson St and at Inverleith. Former President RIAS and Edin Archit. Assoc. Vice-chairman, Board of Management, Edinburgh College of Art, consultant to the Church of Scotland. Trained at Edinburgh School of Applied Art before WW1 and worked in the office of Sir Robert Lorimer(qv). Opened his own practice after the war, becoming senior partner in Dick Peddie, McKay & Jameson. Elected ARSA 1945, RSA 1954. Exhibited at RSA(19) & GI(6).
**Bibl:** Gifford 241,308,313,323,381,492,564,571,576,622.

**MACKAY, James Millar** **fl 1858-1904**
Edinburgh and Kilmarnock painter in oil of landscapes and old castles. Exhibited RSA(46) including 'Busby Castle, Ayrshire' (1866), 'Dean Castle, Ayrshire' (1868), many views around Edinburgh, 'Golfers on the Links, Troon' (1889) and 'Ellangowan Castle (vide Guy Mannering)' (1902); also 'Dunure Castle' at the AAS 1893; also GI(2).

**MACKAY, John** **fl 1841-1860**
Edinburgh oil painter; landscapes often incorporating curling scenes. Responsible for a finely executed depiction on a gold snuff box (1841) of curling on Duddingston Loch with its octagonal pavilion designed by William Playfair(qv) 1824. Exhibited 'Okehampton Castle' and 'View near Slateford' at the RSA. Represented in Dick Institute, Kilmarnock by 'Curling at New Farm Loch, Kilmarnock' (c1860).
**Bibl:** Wingfield.

**MACKAY, John** **1910-**
Born Edinburgh. Painter of landscape, portraits and subject paintings. Worked as a photographer and studied at the Edinburgh College of Art in the evenings. Freelance illustrator for Scottish publications. Exhibited RSA(24) 1930-1945 including a study of a pianoforte recital and Reid orchestral concert 1939. Represented in Edinburgh City collection by 10 watercolours and monochromes, and one oil of Sir Donald Tovey at the Usher Hall, Edinburgh 1940.

**MACKAY, Leslie** **fl 1978-1983**
Dundee painter. Married Shona M(qv). Trained at art school. Exhibited AAS from 6 Hepburn St.

**MACKAY, Lady Lucinda** **1941-**
Born Berkshire. Painter of portraits, landscape and still-life; also potter. Has developed a distinctive style and, to quote herself, 'is happiest with the sensuous versatility of oil paint'. Daughter of the Earl of Inchcape. Early childhood was spent partly in Ayrshire and partly in Vaud, Switzerland. When only 11 she won a public prize for portraiture. Studied Edinburgh University and College of Art under David Talbot Rice and Sir William Gillies(qv). Spent ten years teaching art and pottery in London. First solo exhibition in London 1974. Living in Scotland since 1977. Exhibited RSA(2) 1986.

**MACKAY, Norah** **fl 1937**
Aberdeen amateur artist. Exhibited a view in the Seychelles at AAS from The Close, Don St, Old Aberdeen.

**MACKAY, Robert** **fl 1830-1874**
Prolific Edinburgh landscape painter in oil with a marked penchant for castles; exhibited RSA(154) between the above years including 'Borthwick Castle, evening' (1839), 'Doune Castle', 'Niddry Castle' & 'Roslin Castle' (all 1842), 'Garvald Tower - moon rising' (1846), 'Ravenswood Castle' & 'Hume Castle, evening' (1848), & 'Thirlestane Castle' (1868); also GI(19) 1861-1874.

**MACKAY, Robin** **fl 1976**
Aberdeenshire artist. Exhibited 'View from an aeroplane' at the AAS from Wairds Farm, Durris.

**MACKAY, Shona** **fl 1983**
Dundee artist. Wife of Leslie M(qv). Exhibited AAS(1) from 6 Hepburn Street.

**MACKAY, T** **fl 1870**
Edinburgh landscape painter in oil; exhibited 'At Rosyth' at the RSA.

**MACKAY, Thomas** **fl 1940-1948**
Edinburgh landscape artist. Exhibited a study of Dalmeny church at the RSA from Mossmorran, Belmont Road, Juniper Green and another (watercolour) in 1948 from Rutherglen.

**McKAY, Thomas Hope** **fl 1870-1930**
Glasgow painter of fishing boats, harbours and coastal scenes in oil and watercolour. Influenced by the 'wet' Glasgow technique derived from the Hague school. Exhibited RSA(1), RSW(3), RA(2) & GI(22).
**Bibl:** Halsby 271.

**MACKAY, William** **fl 1890-1921**
Aberdeen painter of local landscapes and figurative subjects. Among his exhibits at the AAS(10) was 'On the Muick, nr Ballater', and several scenes in Easter Ross from 96 Park Street and later 38 Broomhall Rd.

**McKAY, William Darling RSA LLD** **1844-1924**
Born Gifford, Haddington; died Edinburgh, 10 Dec. Came to Edinburgh at the age of 16 and was first noticed ten years later for a series of pastorals, in which figures played an important part. 'He had a genuine, naive joy in natural beauty in rural life, which tranfuses his work and infects the spectator with something of the same feeling...but with all its truth one misses in his art that spirit of personal and emotional interest in the workers and in the deeper relationship between man and the soil which kindles one before the pictures of men whose greater insight and profounder thought confer not only greater significance but more distinguished pictorial aspect on their work. Yet, at its best, his technique, if undistinguished and lacking in brilliance and power, has spirit and precision, and with it his drawing, more deft than learned or elegant, is in close sympathy. As a colourist, he is frank and representative, rather than forceable and emotional' [Caw]. Awarded an honorary LLD by the University of Edinburgh in 1919 and thereafter known as Dr McKay. Friend of Lawton Wingate(qv). In 1872, when on a painting excursion to Cadzow Forest, became increasingly interested in watercolour painting. Best remembered as the author of *The Scottish School of Painting* (1906) which, although a pioneer work, encompassed the 18th century in a mere eight pages; also (with Frank Rinder) edited *The Royal Scottish Academy* 1826-1916 (1917). Librarian of the RSA 1896-1907, Secretary 1907-1924. Elected ARSA 1877, RSA 1883. Exhibited at the RSA(over 200), GI(46) & AAS. Represented in NGS(3), SNPG ('Self-portrait'), Glasgow AG, Kirkcaldy AG, City of Edinburgh collection, Brodie Castle (NTS).
**Bibl:** Caw 299-300; Halsby 137; Irwin 37; Macmillan [SA] 253-4,266,271; Studio, vol 59,1913,137.

**MacKEACHAN, D** **fl 1895**
Renfrewshire painter. Exhibited GI(2) from Garmoyle, Langbank.

**McKEAN, Graham** **1962-**
Scottish figurative and surrealist painter in oils. His work shows the influence of Matisse, Stanley Spencer and Beryl Cook. His compositions have an invasive humorous quality with the figures

generally bathed in sunshine. Has held exhibitions in Belgium, New York, London and Glasgow. Began exhibiting RGI 1994. Represented in British Consulate, New York.
**Bibl:** Albemarle Gallery catalogue, 1998.

**McKEAN, Hugh R MM** **1946-**
Born Broughty Ferry. Landscape painter & teacher; works in oil and acrylic. Educated George Heriots School & Edinburgh College of Art from where he was awarded a postgraduate scholarship. Won Military Medal for gallantry at Anzio Beachhead. Taught in several Edinburgh schools before becoming lecturer, Dundee College of Education. Travels in France & Holland. Exhibited RSA(3).

**McKEAN, L** **fl 1879**
Glasgow watercolour painter of wildlife; exhibited RSA(1).

**MacKEAN, Mrs Muir** **fl 1889-1893**
Paisley flower painter. Exhibited GI(9) from Oakshaw, then Milton House.

**MacKEAN, R McGillivray** **fl 1910**
Glasgow sculptor. Exhibited a relief portrait at the GI from 6 Calder St.

**MacKEAN, Robert** **fl 1925-1926**
Sculptor, mainly portrait busts. Exhibited GI(3) from Boydston, Barfillan Drive, Cardonald.

**McKEAND, Clara** **fl 1885-1888**
Glasgow painter. Sister of Lucy M(qv). Exhibited 'A quiet afternoon' at the RSA 1886 & GI(5), from 24 Royal Crescent.

**McKEAND, Lucy** **fl 1885-1896**
Watercolour painter of flowers and domestic genre. Sister of Clara M(qv). Exhibited RSA(4) & GI(4), from 24 Royal Crescent, Glasgow, after 1895 from Kelvinside.

**McKECHNIE, -** **fl 1849**
Portrait painter of unrecorded initials; exhibited RSA(2).

**McKECHNIE, Alexander Balfour RSW** **1860-1930**
Born Paisley, 18 Oct; died Milliken Park, Renfrewshire, 28 Jan. Painter in oil and watercolour of landscapes and eastern subjects. Spent three years in business and then studied at Glasgow School of Art, taking up painting full-time 1887. Travelled extensively in North Africa, Egypt and Europe. Principal works include the 'Hall of Pillars, Karmak' and the 'Second Pylon, Temple of Luxor'. Elected RSW 1900. Exhibited RA(1) 1904, RSA(13), RSW(84), RI(9), GI(87), & L(4) from Red House, Milliken Park. Represented in Glasgow AG, Paisley AG.
**Bibl:** Halsby 271.

**MACKECHNIE, C T** **fl 1831-1832**
Scottish miniaturist. Exhibited two portrait miniatures at the RSA, one of a nephew of the Earl of Fife.

**McKECHNIE, John A ARSA** **fl 1981-**
Aberdeen printmaker. Exhibits regularly RSA, RGI & AAS from 175 West Princes St, Woodside, and later from Glasgow. Elected ARSA 2003.

**McKECHNIE, Mrs Mary** **fl 1988-**
Fife painter. Exhibited GI(1), from Gateside.

**MacKECHNIE, Robert G S RBA** **1894-c1976**
Born Glasgow, 6 Jly. Educated at Glasgow Academy and Fettes, then Oxford University, returning to Scotland where he studied at Glasgow School of Art, remaining there in the 20s as a member of staff. After taking his diploma, he attempted to combine farming and painting in Stirlingshire. His first one-man show in Florence 1924. After returning from a year in Italy he joined the Seven and Five Society along with Barbara Hepworth, Ivan Hichens, Ben Nicholson and others. In 1934, suffering from ill health, he went to live in Rye. After working as a munitions worker during the War he took up weaving. Continued to visit Italy and Scotland regularly, especially Barra and Iona. His working life was interrupted by a weak constitution, although in 1975 he was still painting and had another one-man show in Rye. His wife was also an artist. Exhibited RSA(2), RBA(55) & GI(2).

**McKEE, George H** **fl 1932-1935**
Glasgow engraver. Exhibited three etchings at the GI from 99 Claythorn St.

**McKELL, Mrs Josephine** **fl 1958-1962**
Glasgow landscape painter. Exhibited GI(3) from Bearsden.

**MacKELLAR, Agnes C** **fl 1909**
Glasgow painter. Exhibited GI(1).

**McKELLAR, Archibald** **fl 1871-1888**
Glasgow painter in oil of landscape and figurative subjects. Later moved to Kenmore Street, Aberfeldy. Exhibited RSA(3) & GI(5).

**MacKELLAR, Duncan RSW** **1849-1908**
Born Inveraray, Argyll; died Glasgow, 13 Aug. Painter of genre in oil and watercolour. Studied art in Glasgow and London. Worked in a photographic studio tinting prints before becoming a full-time painter in 1875. His speciality was figure and interiors, in quaint country cottages and stately baronial halls. His technique was sensitive and delicate. Elected RSW 1885. Exhibited RA(2), RSA(49), RSW(75), GI(76) & AAS. Represented in Glasgow AG, Paisley AG.
**Bibl:** Caw 272; Halsby 271.

**McKELLAR, J E** **fl 1890**
Glasgow painter. Exhibited GI(2) from 112 Bath Street.

**MacKELVIE, Mary Baillie** **fl 1933-1938**
Edinburgh watercolour flower painter; exhibited RSA(2), RSW(1) & GI(2).

**McKENDRICK, Andrew** **fl 1936-1947**
Glasgow painter. Exhibited two rustic scenes at the RSA 1944 and 1947, also GI(16) from 150 Morningside Street.

**McKENDRICK, George Bain** **fl 1949**
Ardrossan amateur painter. Exhibited GI(1).

**McKENDRICK, J MacLellan** **fl 1945**
Ayrshire still life painter. Exhibited GI(1) from Old Cumnock. Probably the **J M McKendrick** who exhibited GI(2) 1954.

**McKENDRICK, Tom RSW RGI** **1948-**
Born Clydebank. Watercolour painter of strongly coloured abstract compositions. Influenced by a continuing fascination with the steel, rust, rivets and fire of shipyards in some of which he worked 1963-9. Trained Glasgow School of Art 1971-5 followed by a year at Jordanhill College of Education. Winner of a number of awards including the David Cargill(GI) 1977, Torrance Memorial 1979, Moray McKissok prize 1981 and Inverclyde Biennial Prize 1986. Member of the Glasgow Group 1986. Elected RSW 1985. Exhibits regularly RSA, RSW & GI. Represented Glasgow AG, Lillie AG(Milngavie), SAC.

**McKENNA, Conrad Terence** **fl 1956-1983**
Glasgow painter and engraver. Mainly Italian scenery in oil and watercolour; also wood engravings. Exhibited RSA(6) & GI(24).

**McKENNA, Hugh** **fl 1936-1984**
Glasgow painter of flowers and Scottish topography. Exhibited RSA(3) & GI(31) from 40 Midcroft Avenue until 1951, then from 49 Kingspark Ave.

**McKENNA, James** **fl 1958**
Glasgow watercolour painter. Exhibited GI(1) from Leyden Gdns.

**MacKENNA, Tracy** **1963-**
Abstract sculptress. Trained at Glasgow School of Art 1981-86, obtaining an hons degree in fine art. Postgraduate year spent at the Hungarian Academy of Fine Art, Budapest 1986-87. Invited artist at the Artists' Collective Studio, Budapest 1987. Returning to Scotland 1988 received a commission from the Forestry Commission and a

residency at Glasgow Garden Festival. Co-founder and director of Glasgow Sculpture Studios and part-time lecturer at Grays School of Art, Aberdeen. Awarded Benno Schotz prize 1985, James Torrance Memorial Award for Young Artists, GI 1986, Meyer Oppenheim Award RSA, 1987. Visited Romania 1988. Exhibits widely at the RSA, GI and SSA. Has taught in Scotland and Hungary. Represented in Limerick City AG, (Ireland), Danube Sculpture Park (Hungary), Szatmar Museum, Mateszalka (Hungary).

**MACKENNAL, Sir Bertram KCVO RA HRSA** **1863-1931**
Born Melbourne, Australia. Sculptor. Both parents were born in Ayrshire of long-descended Scottish stock. His father **John Simpson MacKENNAL** was also a sculptor. Studied in Paris and then at Birnie Rhind's(qv) studio in Edinburgh before settling in London. His first major success was in 1893 when his statue of Circe was 'mentioned' at the Paris Salon and exhibited later in London. Among his major works are three statues of Queen Victoria for, respectively, India, Australia and Blackburn, three memorials to Edward VII for Calcutta, Melbourne and Adelaide, a national memorial to Gainsborough and group 'Phoebus with the horses of the sun' for Australia House, London. 'Diana Wounded', exhibited at the RSA (1913), was purchased by the Chantrey Bequest. "One may say of his style that it is graceful and fluent, with a certain sobriety and strength of character which we shall claim as the native contribution to his achievements' [Pittendrigh MacGillivray]. Elected ARA 1909, HRSA 1920, RA 1922. Regular exhibitor RA, RSA & GI(13) 1902-1932. Represented in Edinburgh City collection(2 bronzes).

**MACKENZIE, Miss** **fl 1837-1838**
Edinburgh painter of Highland landscapes. Exhibited RSA(3) from 61 Queen St.

**MACKENZIE, Mrs** **fl 1867**
Edinburgh amateur portrait painter; exhibited two sketches at the RSA from 29, Nortumberland St one of which had the quaint title 'A surviving contemporary of Robert III of Scotland - sketched on the spot'.

**MacKENZIE, Miss A F** **fl 1939**
Edinburgh artist. Exhibited 'Horse studies' at the RSA from 37 Buckston Terrace.

**MacKENZIE, Adam** **fl 1861-1863**
Edinburgh oil painter of local scenes; exhibited RSA(11).

**MacKENZIE, Alexander** **1850-1890**
Born Aberdeen; died Aberdeen, 8 Feb. Painter in oil and watercolour of landscape and genre, also woodcarver. Son of an upholsterer. After spending his teenage period wandering around Spain, he was apprenticed to James Allan and Sons, cabinet makers and upholsterers, as a carver, studying art in the evening. Won the Queen's Prize at the Aberdeen School of Art for drawing from the cast. Left Allan's 1875, moving to Edinburgh in about 1880, visited Paris 1888, at the same time as George Sim(qv). Painted 'A Frugal Meal in Brittany', now one of three works of his in Aberdeen AG, which was exhibited at the Paris Salon. A modest, unassuming man, he was an original member of the Aberdeen Artists Society. His landscapes and figures, including character sketches and some portraits, were well received. Sometimes confused with A M MacKenzie(qv). Exhibited RSA(13) 1877-1886, GI 1883-86 & AAS 1885-1889, from 15 Adelphi. Represented in Aberdeen AG, Sydney AG (Australia).

**MacKENZIE, Alexander** **fl 1887**
Aberdeen painter of landscape, domestic genre and figure subjects. Exhibited AAS(7) from 10 Ann Place, and posthumously in 1890 & 1896.

**MacKENZIE, Alexander George Robertson ARSA FRIBA** **1879-1963**
Born Aberdeen; died Inverurie, 20 Mar. Architect & landscape painter. Son of Alexander Marshall MacKenzie. Studied architecture in London and Paris. Received a number of important commissions; elected President of the Architectural Association 1917. Articled to his father, subsequently worked with Sir Robert Edis in London and with René Sargent in Paris before joining his father as a partner. Practised in London. His principal works (with his father) included the Waldorf Hotel, Australia House, Hursley Park, Hants, as well as several ecclesiastical buildings and a number of sports pavilions at English schools. After his father died in 1933 he returned to Aberdeen and was there commissioned to design King's College Pavilion, Pittodrie Church, the Capitol Cinema, and Coull House, Aboyne. Keenly interested in preservation in both town and country. Elected PRIA 1947. He lost a leg in WWI. Exhibited RA(4), RSA, AAS(4) & L(1).

**MacKENZIE, Alexander Marshall RSA LLD** **1848-1933**
Born Elgin; died Culter House, 4 May. Architect and draughtsman in pen and ink. Son of Thomas Mackenzie of Elgin(qv) and nephew of William(qv). Educated at Elgin Academy, Aberdeen and Edinburgh. Received his professional training in the office of his father's partner James Matthews(qv) and with David Bryce(qv). Moved to Aberdeen from Elgin in 1877, becoming a partner with Matthews. Specialised in ecclesiastical works in the Gothic idiom including Craigiebuckler church (1883), the new Crathie Church, Aberdeenshire and Mar Lodge. Other buildings include the vigorous Renaissance Northern Assurance building in Union Street, Aberdeen (1885) made from Kemnay granite, a new tower fronting Broad Street for Marischal College, Aberdeen (1903-6) described as 'a surprisingly successful English Perpendicular composition which also constitutes a high watermark in granite craftsmanship', the sculpture court for Aberdeen Art Gallery, and Aberdeen's principal war memorial. In collaboration with his son, he built Australia House in the Strand, the Waldorf Hotel, London and a new clock tower at Fyvie Castle (RA 1899). Latterly lived in Aboyne, Aberdeenshire. Father of Alexander George Robertson M(qv). Elected ARSA 1893, RSA 1918. Exhibited RA(4), RSA(23) & GI(12).
**Bibl:** Colvin; Dunbar 152-3.

**McKENZIE, Miss Alison RSW** **1907-1982**
Born Bombay, 30 Aug. Painter in oil, watercolour and gouache; also wood engraver, poster designer and pen draughtswoman. Sister of Winifred M(qv) with whom she shared two shows, in London and Glasgow. Educated Piers Field School 1921-25; studied at Glasgow School of Art 1925-29 and at the Grosvenor School of Modern Art under Iain MacNab(qv) 1932-3. Awarded the Fra Newbery medal; taught for 12 years at Dundee College of Art, 1946-1958, specialising in life drawing and painting. Settled in St Andrews in Fife. A very fine wood engraver. With her sister Winifred(qv) and Annabel Kidston(qv) formed the St Andrews group of wood engravers. Commissioned by the London North Eastern Railway Company to design posters which were subsequently shown in London at an exhibition of poster art. Her work, although similar, is more clearcut than her sister's. Illustrated Milton's *On the morning of Christ's Nativity* for the Gregynog Press (1937). Elected RSW 1952. Exhibited GI(9) 1952-56. Represented in Dundee AG, Ottawa AG (Canada).
**Bibl:** Garrett 1 & 2; Horne 305; Jaffé; Linda Saunders: "Two Women Wood Engravers in Fife", *Green Book* 2, no.4 (1986); Waters.

**McKENZIE, Andrew** **1886-?**
Glasgow architect and watercolourist. Studied Glasgow's Schools of Art and Architecture. Exhibited RSA(1), RSW(8), GI(5) & L(3) 1920-1932 .
**Bibl:** Halsby 271.

**MacKENZIE, Andrew** **c1970-**
Abstract painter, basing his work on landscapes. Trained Edinburgh College of Art 1987-93. Several solo exhibitions in Scotland. Received Aeneas Award (RA) enabling him to visit Florence, also an award from the SAC 1999. Represented in Edinburgh City AG, RA and in several Scottish hospitals.
**Bibl:** Moira Jeffrey, 'Out Here: Selected paintings & drawings 1998-2001', ex cat.

**MacKENZIE, Mrs C W** **fl 1867-1873**
Edinburgh painter in oil and watercolour; landscapes and figure subjects. Exhibited RSA(4).

**MacKENZIE, Calum** **fl 1972-1974**
Glasgow painter in the modern idiom. Exhibited RSA(5) from Cambuslang.

**MACKENZIE, Miss Christine** **fl 1974**
Renfrewshire painter. Exhibited 'Waterfall' at the GI from Eaglesham.

**MACKENZIE, Colin** **fl 1879**
Glasgow amateur painter. Exhibited an interior at the GI.

**MacKENZIE, David Maitland RSA** **c1800-1880**
Painter in oil of landscapes. Some mystery surrounds this artist. He was a foundation Associate of the Institution for the Encouragement of the Fine Arts in 1826 where he exhibited some well executed landscapes in 1826 and 1830, and again during the first four years of the Scottish Academy 1827-1830. He was elected RSA in 1829 but in 1832 he forfeited his membership, apparently due to unseemly behaviour, being one of two Academicians to be deprived of their membership by disciplinary action. Six years later the same happened to John W Ewbank(qv). The ostensible reason was failing to satisfy the Council with their diploma submissions but it is probable that behaviour had more to do with it since many other artists who had never submitted works retained their membership. There then follows a series of entries from 1835 to 1874, variously catalogued as by 'D M, D W, Daniel and Donald MacKenzie', all of similar compositions although it is unclear how many of these were the work of David Maitland MacKenzie. He worked rather heavily but sometimes effectively in the manner of Horatio MacCulloch(qv).

**MacKENZIE, Donald** **1846-1874**
Edinburgh landscape painter in oil; exhibited RSA(7).

**MacKENZIE, Donald** **1944-**
Born Glasgow. Figurative and landscape painter; illustrator. Trained Duncan of Jordanstone College of Art 1963-68. Worked in London 1969-75, interrupted by a year at Atelier 17 in Paris. Visiting lecturer, Duncan of Jordanstone College of Art 1979-87. First solo exhibition in London 1972, followed by many others in Scotland and England. A visit to Morocco resulted in a series of evocative local landscapes 1989. Settled in Dundee. As his career has developed, landscapes have increasingly overtaken figurative work. Illustrated *The Shell Book of Festivals and Events*, *The Rhythm of the Glass*, *Brennan's Book*, *Glasgow since 1900*. Exhibits RSA. Represented in V & A, NLS, Glasgow AG, Edinburgh City Art Centre.

**MacKENZIE, Dorothy** **fl 1917-1924**
Portrait painter; exhibited RSA(2) & SWA(3), first from New Park, St Andrews and after 1920 from London.

**MacKENZIE, Miss Eliza J M** **fl 1866-1871**
Edinburgh landscape painter, also painted trees. Exhibited RSA(3). In 1857 a **Miss E Mackenzie** exhibited at the RA.

**McKENZIE, Elizabeth H** **fl 1954-1960**
Glasgow painter of figurative subjects and fishing scenes. Exhibited RSA(9) & GI(12).

**MACKENZIE, Frederick OWS** **1787-1854**
Born Scotland; died London, 25 Apr. Watercolour painter, architectural draughtsman and illustrator. Son of a linen draper, he studied under John Adey Repton the architect. His first employment was making architectural and topographical drawings for John Britton. Noted for his conscientious drawings of buildings, mostly ecclesiastical. Published several books including *Architectural Antiquities of St Stephen's church, Westminster* and illustrated Britton's *Salisbury Cathedral*. Illustrated *Etchings of Landscapes for the use of Students* (1812), *History of the Abbey Church of St Peter, Westminster* (1812), Britton: *Salisbury Cathedral* (1813), *History of the University of Oxford* (1814), *History of the University of Cambridge* (1815), *Illustrations of the Principal Antiquities of Oxfordshire* (1823), *Graphic Illustrations of Warwickshire* (1829), *Memorials of Architectural Antiquities of St Stephen's Chapel, Westminster* (nd). A sketch of the porch of Aylesham church, Norfolk, erected in 1488 was shown at the RA 1804. Associate OWS 1822, Member 1823, Treasurer OWS 1831-54. Represented in the NGS (pencil drawing of a monument to Joshua Reynolds), V & A, Dublin Museum, Manchester AG, Nottingham AG.
**Bibl:** Benezit; Bryan; Hardie: *Watercolour Painters in Britain*, 3, 1968, pp17-18 illlus; Houfe 219; Petter: *Oxford Almanacks*, 1974.

**MacKENZIE, George Jnr** **fl 1879**
Edinburgh oil painter of fantasy studies; exhibited a painting of fairies at the RSA.

**McKENZIE, George Findlay** **fl 1921-1940**
Edinburgh portrait watercolourist; exhibited RSA(47), RSW(1) & GI(8).

**MacKENZIE, Helen Margaret (Mrs Budd) ROI ARCA(Lond)** **c1885-1966**
Born Elgin; died London, 4 May. Painter of portraits, figure subjects, animals and interiors in oil; also etcher. Trained Royal College of Art under Moira, diploma 1906. Married the artist H A Budd 1915. principal works include 'A Country Boy', 'Farmyard Peace', 'Cat and Fruit', 'Sleeping Shepherd', 'Victorian Family' and 'Hyde Park in Summer'. Lived in London for many years. Elected ROI 1923, ASWA 1918, RSW 1923. Exhibited RA(22), ROI(46), SWA(38), GI(15), AAS(3) & L(1), latterly from Ladyhill, Elgin.

**MacKENZIE, Hugh Grant** **fl 1967**
Aberdeen sculptor. Exhibited 'Zulu bride' at the AAS from 1 Magdala Place.

**MACKENZIE, Iain** **fl 1958-1959**
Glasgow portrait painter. Exhibited GI(3) from 8 Park Terrace.

**MacKENZIE, James Charles** **fl 1881-1898**
Edinburgh painter of country subjects and landscape. Exhibited RSA(11), including 'Evening at the Red Well Links, Banff', 1890, AAS(1) & GI(2), from Greenside Place.

**MacKENZIE, James S** **fl 1878-1884**
Glasgow painter of portraits and continental landscapes. Exhibited GI(4).

**McKENZIE, James (Scarth)** **fl 1929-1937**
Edinburgh sculptor. Worked mostly in wood. Exhibited RSA 1929, 1934 & 1937; & GI 1937-8.

**MacKENZIE, James Hamilton ARSA RSW ARE** **1875-1926**
Born Glasgow; died Glasgow, 29 Mar. Painter in oil, watercolour and pastel, etcher; landscapes and architectural subjects. Trained Glasgow School of Art, Paris and, having received a Haldane travelling scholarship, in Florence. He sketched in East Africa during WWI and painted landscapes whenever possible on all his trips abroad as well as many scenes in the Western Isles when in Scotland. His works are characterised by bold black outlines, especially when depicting topographical contours. Principal works include 'Cathedral Tower, Bruges', 'Cathedral of St Francis of Assisi'. President, Glasgow Art Club 1923-1924. Killed in a railway accident. Elected RSW 1910, ARSA 1923. Exhibited RSA(49), RSW(57), AAS, RE(26), GI(75) & L(17). Represented in Glasgow AG, Paisley AG, Lillie AG(Milngavie), Edinburgh City collection.
**Bibl:** Halsby 225-6,271; Wingfield.

**McKENZIE, John** **fl 1879**
Edinburgh landscape painter in oil; exhibited RSA(1).

**McKENZIE, John** **fl 1924-1971**
Sculptor. Figure studies, still life and designs. Executed carvings in slate, wood reliefs and occasional concrete. Exhibited RSA(55) & GI(29) first from Glasgow and then, in 1940, from Arbroath.

**McKENZIE, John L** **fl 1982**
Paisley amateur painter. Exhibited GI(1).

**McKENZIE, Kenneth** **1862-1899**
Born Burgie. nr Forres. Painter in oil of landscapes, figurative and sporting subjects. He was a competent painter, able to catch the mood of grouse drives and the windswept hills of Kintyre. He moved his address a number of times, exhibiting at the RA(14) 1885-1891 from Holyhead, Wales, in 1892 (the year of his marriage) from London, four works 1893-1895 from Torrisdale Castle, Carradale, Argyll, two sporting subjects in 1896 from Drissaig, Kilchrenan and two works 1897 and 1899 from his birthplace. Also exhibited ROI(14), RHA(13), RBA(1), GI(4) & L(14) though apparently never at the RSA. Represented in Glasgow AG.

**McKENZIE, Kenneth** **fl 1968-1984**
Glasgow painter in oil of figure studies, nudes and occasional landscapes. Exhibited RSA(4) & GI(21).

**MACKENZIE, Miss L J** **fl 1894**
Aberdeenshire amateur painter. Exhibited 'A peep of the Dee' at AAS from The Manse, Aboyne.

**MacKENZIE, Miss M** **fl 1933-1945**
Glasgow watercolourist; also worked in pencil. Fairy subjects, designs. Exhibited GI(3) from Deanston Dr.

**MACKENZIE, Margaret Isobel** **fl 1952-1959**
Aberdeen painter of portraits, flower and conversation pieces. Exhibited RSA(5), AAS(2) latterly from 44 Grosvenor Place.

**MACKENZIE, Miss Margaret K** **fl 1944-1946**
Renfrewshire sculptress. Worked mainly in stone and wood. Exhibited figurative works at the RSA & GI(6) from Barrhead.

**MacKENZIE, Mary** **fl 1880**
Dundee painter. Exhibited RSA(1) from Magdalen Yard Road.

**MacKENZIE, Mary** **1888-c1957**
Aberdeen painter of landscape, portraits and figures, especially children. Trained Gray's School of Art 1909-1913. Taught Gray's School of Art until 1948. In 1986 Aberdeen Art Gallery chose her study of a young girl, 'The Little Bridal Attendant' as their picture of the month to celebrate the wedding of Prince Andrew and Sarah Fergusson. Her work is not generally known which is unfortunate because those works which have come to light show great sensitivity and a fine feel for character and colour. Bequeathed a substantial legacy to Gray's School of Art. Exhibited RSA(12) from 88 Bedford Place and later from Bieldside, also regularly at the AAS, including a tender rendering of 'Abergeldie Castle'.

**MacKENZIE, Molly** **fl 1935**
Amateur Glasgow painter. Exhibited 'Darkie jazz' at the RSA from 74 Deanston Drive.

**MacKENZIE, Muriel Alison** **fl 1884-1938**
Edinburgh landscape painter in oil, sculptor and engraver; exhibited RA(3), RSA(2), SWA(4), GI(5), ROI(2) & LS(3) from 44 Warrender Park Road and later London.

**McKENZIE, Nancy** **1965-**
Born Edinburgh. Painter. Trained Edinburgh College of Art 1983-87. Occasional exhibitor RSA, from 27 Hillside Crescent, Edinburgh.

**McKENZIE, Raymond** **fl 1973**
Glasgow painter. Exhibited a landscape at the GI from Byres Rd.

**MACKENZIE, Robert Tait** **1867-1938**
Born Almonte, Ontario; died Philadelphia, Sep. Sculptor. Scottish parentage. Originally pursued a medical career in Montreal, serving as a ship's surgeon before becoming House Physician to the Governor General of Canada 1897. In 1903 and 1904 contributed two works at the RA, also Paris Salon, chiefly of an athletic character. In 1904 he was appointed to a chair of Physical Education and in 1931 was made Research Professor. Awarded the King of Sweden's medal for sculpture at the Stockholm Olympic Games 1912. Responsible for a number of important Edinburgh statues including the Scottish American War Memorial in West Princes St Gdns, The Call (1924-7) - a bronze kilted soldier - and work at Balmoral, Oxford, Cambridge and the Metropolitan Museum in New York. A bronze plaque of John Campbell Gordon, 7th Earl & 1st Marquess of Aberdeen is in the SNPG; also represented in NGS(3).
**Bibl:** Scotsman, 8 Sep 1938(obit).

**MacKENZIE, Roderick** **fl 1850-1867**
Edinburgh oil painter of naval subjects; exhibited RSA(4).

**MacKENZIE, Roderick D** **fl 1908**
Scottish painter. Exhibited four works at the London Salon from 31 Boulevard de Port Royal, Paris.

**MacKENZIE, Samuel RSA** **1785-1847**
Born Cromarty. Originally a stone carver, but visiting Edinburgh as a young man he was introduced to Raeburn for whom he developed an intense admiration, and whose advice and assistance induced him to become a painter, greatly influencing his development. Besides portraits, he painted fancy heads, some of which were engraved. On one occasion he made such a good copy of a Raeburn portrait that the master said to him 'Well, MacKenzie, you can take your's aside now - I don't know which is mine and which is the other'. Caw found his 'handling deficient in certainty and spontaneity, the designs lacking in real significance, and the expression of character usually superficial and without force'. Patronised by the Dukes of Gordon and Roxburgh, he exhibited a portrait of the latter 1832. Elected RSA 1829. Exhibited 101 works at the RSA, including two of the Duke of Roxburgh, one of the Duchess of Roxburgh and the Marquis of Bowmont.
**Bibl:** Bryan; Caw 88-9.

**MACKENZIE, Stuart T** **1959-**
Born Feb 5. Painter and teacher. Trained Edinburgh College of Art 1979-1983. Lecturer, Gray's School of Art 1987-88, Glasgow School of Art 1988- . Solo exhibitions in USA (1984), Aberdeen, Edinburgh & Glasgow. Winner of several awards, his work is represented in Aberdeen AG, Mellon Foundation.

**MACKENZIE, Thomas** **1814-1854**
Architect. Based in Elgin although worked extensively in the Aberdeen area. Father of A. Marshall Mackenzie(qv), brother of William M(qv). Trained under Archibald Simpson(qv). Partner of James Matthews(qv).
**Bibl:** Dunbar 152.

**MACKENZIE, Thomas** **fl 1843**
Edinburgh landscape painter. Exhibited RSA(3).

**MacKENZIE, Tom** **1947-**
Born Lerwick. Etcher and engraver. Studied at Hornsey College of Art 1974 and Wimbledon College of Art 1974-75. Currently works from a Glasgow print studio and a studio in Portree, Isle of Skye. Primarily a print maker, he has held a number of one-man shows in Glasgow. Since 1970 has concentrated on the landscape of Skye and Wester Ross. Uses a three plate colour etching technique. Exhibited RSA since 1978 & AAS in the 1980s. Represented in SNGMA, Dundee AG, Glasgow AG, Inverness AG, SAC.
**Bibl:** John Taylor, Tom Mackenzie - Etchings - 1973-1993, Skye & Lochalsh Enterprise, 1993.

**MacKENZIE, Violet L** **fl 1927-1947**
Edinburgh sculptress. Exhibited figures and portrait busts at the RSA (7) & GI(2) from 42 Craighouse Avenue and later Greenbank Loan.

**MacKENZIE, Miss W J M** **fl 1886-1917**
Edinburgh landscape painter in watercolour; exhibited 'Largo from the beach' at the RSA; also ROI(1), RI(2), RBA(8), L(1) & SWA(7), formerly from Edinburgh, after 1896 from London.

**MacKENZIE, William** **1765-c1837**
Miniature painter. Possibly the William Mackenzie who went to the RA Schools in 1781. Known to have been working at 3 Castle Street, Edinburgh in 1820. A miniature portrait of 'Lord Seaforth', signed and dated 1828, was in the SNPG although, as Foskett points out, the Earldom became extinct in 1815 so this must have been copied from an earlier portrait. Probably the same 'Captain William Mackenzie' who had 20 works shown at the RSA 1832-37 including several portraits of members of the Campbell family including 'Rear-Admiral Patrick Campbell' 1833.
**Bibl:** Foskett, ii, 394.

**MACKENZIE, William M** **?-1856**
Architect. Brother of Thomas Mackenzie of Elgin(qv) and uncle of Alexander(qv). City architect of Perth. Best known for his design of an asymmetrical farmhouse at Elcho, Rhynd, Perthshire (c1830), illustrated in Loudon's *Encyclopaedia* thus influencing a whole generation of British farmhouses.
**Bibl:** Dunbar 152; J C Loudon, Encyclopaedia of Cottage, Farm and Villa Architecture, London 1833; Bruce Walker & W S Gauldie, Architects and Architecture on Tayside, Dundee 1984, 109-110.

**MacKENZIE, William Murray** **fl 1873-1908**
Edinburgh painter in oil and watercolour of landscapes, including

Continental scenes, rustic and figurative subjects, also portraits. In the early 1880s he visited southern Italy exhibiting five Italian scenes in 1883. Exhibited RSA(54), RSW(2), GI(20) & L(5). Represented in City of Edinburgh collection.

**McKENZIE, Miss Winifred** **1905-?**
Born Bombay, 23 Aug. Painter in oil and watercolour and wood engraver. Landscapes, still life and flowers. Daughter of an architect and sister of Alison M(qv). Educated at Priors Field 1921-23, trained Glasgow School of Art 1923-27 and Grosvenor School of Modern Art under Iain MacNab(qv) 1932-3. Lived first in Kilmacolm and later in London until settling in St Andrews in 1940. Received the Newbery Medal 1929. During WW2 held wood engraving classes for the services. Fascinated by the play of light on water and the reflections made by trees and buildings. Together with her sister Alison(qv) and Annabel Kidston(qv) she formed the St Andrews group of wood engravers. Taught life drawing and engraving at Dundee College of Art from 1944 until retiring in 1958. Exhibited RSA, RSW & GI. Represented in Perth AG, Liverpool AG, Belfast AG, Cork AG.

**McKENZIE SMITH, Ian OBE PRSA PPRSW RGI FRSA FSA (Scot) LLD** **1935-**
Born Montrose, 3 Aug. Painter in oil and gouache also artistic administrator. Father of Sarah M S(qv). Educated Robert Gordon's College, Aberdeen, trained Gray's School of Art 1953-9 under Henderson Blyth(qv) and Hospitalfield, Arbroath 1958-9. After leaving art school was an Education Officer with the Scottish Design Centre in Glasgow. A travelling scholarship 1958-9 enabled him to visit France, Italy, Holland, Belgium, Germany and Spain. Early influence was exerted by the American Colorfield group, notably Barnett Newman. A travelling scholarship in the 1980s to Paris introduced him to the Japanese artist Kanzo Okado who encouraged an interest in Zen philosophy and its associated art. One critic has referred to 'the combination of lyrical minimalism and an Oriental sense of balance and calligraphic finesse [that] has characterised his work ever since'. Has been in the mainstream of the abstract modern Scottish art movement both as painter and administrator. This led to works of an academic nature receiving considerable attention whereas other styles have been neglected. Appointed Director of Aberdeen AG 1968. Member of numerous Boards and Committees. Regular exhibitor RSA, RSW, AAS; also GI(4). Elected ARSA 1973, RSA 1987, RGI 1999, Treasurer RSA 1990, President RSW 1988. President, RSA 1998- .Represented in SNGMA, Abbothall Gallery, (Kendal), Aberdeen AG, Glasgow AG, Arts Council of Northern Ireland, Perth AG, Edinburgh City Arts Centre, Hunterian Museums, Glasgow.
**Bibl:** Gage 51-2; Hartley 164; Macmillan [SA] 400; SAC 'Scottish Art Now', (Ex Cat 1982).

**McKENZIE SMITH, Sarah** **1965-**
Born Glasgow, Jan 5. Painter and sculptress. Daughter of Ian M S(qv). Trained Edinburgh College of Art 1985-91. After a year as Artist-in-Residence, Repton School 1991, teaches Gray's School of Art 1992- . Has exhibited site-specific mixed media installations and related works throughout the UK and in Finland, France and North America from her home in Aberdeen.

**MacKEOWN, M G C** **fl 1955-**
Edinburgh amateur portrait painter. Exhibited RSA(3) from Brandon St.

**McKERRACKER, Robert** **fl 1923**
Topographical painter; exhibited RSA(2) from 2 Heriot Gardens, Burntisland.

**McKERRELL, Duncan** **fl 1931-1935**
Engraver. Exhibited RSA(3) & GI(5) from 3 Pine Street, Greenock.

**McKERRELL, John** **1947-**
Born Falkirk, Jan 12. Painter, mainly in watercolour, also egg tempera and oils. After a long spell of teaching at Prestwick Academy 1972-97 he began painting full-time. Since the age of 3 has lived in Troon. Educated Marr College, Troon, trained Edinburgh College of Art 1965-70. Won scholarship and the RGI's Alexander Stone award 1970 and again in 1988. He paints Scottish landscapes and seascapes in an intensely realistic style. Exhibits RSA, RSW, GI & RI from Troon.

**McKERRON, Mrs Agnes M** **fl 1908-1937**
Aberdeen landscape painter, mainly of the Aberdeenshire mountains and Perthshire. Exhibited AAS from 1 Albyn Place.

**McKERROW, J Dickson** **fl 1901-1902**
Perthshire painter. Exhibited RSA(1) & GI(1) from Craigandoran, Crieff.

**MACKERS, Miss J Stuart** **19th Cent**
Edinburgh landscape painter; exhibited AAS(2) from 2 Dillbank Terrace.

**MACKIE, A B** **fl 1859-1872**
Edinburgh painter in watercolour of local landscape and coastal scenery; exhibited at the RSA(6).

**MACKIE, Miss Annie** **fl 1887-1934**
Flower painter in oil and watercolour; also occasional sculptor in bronze. Sister of Charles Hodge M(qv). Lived in Portobello before moving to 7 Goldhurst Terrace, London NW. Exhibited RA(5), RSA(22), RSW(9), RI(1), L(1) & RBA(1).
**Bibl:** Halsby 271.

**MACKIE, Campbell** **1886-1952**
Landscape painter. Represented by a view of Loch Awe in the Lillie AG (Milngavie).

**MACKIE, Charles Hodge RSA RSW PSSA** **1862-1920**
Born Aldershot; died Edinburgh, 12 July. Painter in oil and watercolour and print maker; landscapes, portraits; also mural decorator. Brother of Annie(qv) and father of Donald(qv). Descended from two lines of potters and with a touch of gypsy blood, he was the son of an army officer. Left school at 16 in order to attend art classes at Edinburgh University but played constant truant, except from the anatomy classes which he loved. Received painting lessons from Robert Frier(qv) who persuaded his father to allow the young Mackie to study art more intensively. Went to the RSA Schools alongside his friends Garden Smith(qv), R B Nisbet(qv) and P W Nicholson(qv), concentrating on applied art and mural decoration, being especially influenced by Professor Geddes. A devout Christian, during visits to London he worked among the poor and destitute until an attack of pneumonia forced him to abandon the work. Visited Pont-Aven in northern France where he met Gauguin and his disciples, Le Sidaner and Paul Serusier. In 1903/4 he went to Spain, painting watercolours in Toledo and Madrid which were later purchased in Edinburgh by a visiting San Francisco dealer (Mr Torrey), but all were subsequently lost in the great San Francisco earthquake. At about this time he befriended Maurice Denis, and his work showed a vivid sense of colour and design. Although these remained with him, his Symbolist period ended in about 1905. In 1908 he and Adam Bruce Thomson(qv) went to Venice and a work painted at the time, 'St Mark's, Venice', is now in Perth AG. He was captivated and worked through the searing Venetian heat that entire summer. His early reputation was based on two important exhibitions in 1883, followed by a transitional period when colour interested him more than the pictorial and his work became much criticised. His reputation began to revive in 1907, when 'The Return of the Flock to the Fold' was hailed as the picture of the year. Towards the end of the century he paid short visits to Normandy and Britanny, establishing a studio near Étaples 1904-1909. In 1900 he co-founded and was President of the SSA(qv). In 1912 won a gold medal in Amsterdam. He undertook important work for the publication *Evergreen,* his design for the cover becoming the trademark of the Symbolist movement. Designed a mural for Patrick Geddes in Edinburgh. In later life he became a close and influential friend of Harold & Laura Knight. Illness prevented any more important work after 1917. Elected RSW 1901, ARSA 1902, RSA 1917. Exhibited RA(6), RSA(126), RSW(52), RHA(16), RI(35) & GI(1). Represented in NGS(3), Perth AG, City of Edinburgh collection(7), Sydney AG (Australia), Victoria AG (Australia).
**Bibl:** AJ 1911, 127; Bourne FA, Edinburgh 'Charles Hodge Mackie', (Ex Cat); Caw 423-4; Halsby 188,191-2,193,228,271; Hardie 121-4; Anne Mackie's Diary, unpublished MS in NLS; Irwin 405; Macmillan

[SA] 273,279,296,298,309,310; Studio vol 49, 1910, 229; vol 56, 1912, 150(illus).

**MACKIE, Claire Julia** **fl 1984-1985**
Aberdeenshire artist. Exhibited AAS(2), including 'Silver, silk and sycamore', from Dunnydeer Farm, Insch.

**MACKIE, Donald M** **fl 1932-1933**
Edinburgh architect. Son of Charles Hodge M(qv). Had a studio near Murrayfield; exhibited RSA(3).

**MACKIE, Miss E D** **fl 1932**
Montrose artist. Exhibited RSA(2) from 11 High Street.

**MACKIE, George RSW DFC** **1920-**
Born Cupar, Fife, 17 Jly. Painter in watercolour; designer and illustrator. Specialised in shipping and coastal scenes, especially around Aberdeen. Studied at Dundee College of Art 1937-40 and Edinburgh College of Art 1946-48. Married Barbara Balmer(qv). Head of Design at Gray's School of Art 1956-80; maintains a studio in Edinburgh. In addition to contributing drawings to the *Radio Times* also illustrated Gray: *Historical Ballads of Denmark* (with Edward Bawden, 1958) and Keith: *Aberdeen University Press* (1963). Also wrote an important monograph *Lynton Lamb, Illustrator* (Scolar Press, 1978). Design consultant to Edinburgh Univ Press 1953-82. A retrospective exhibition of his work for the EUP at the NLS 1991. Elected RSW 1965. Appointed a Royal Designer for Industry 1973. Exhibits RSA, RSW, GI(2) & SSA.
**Bibl:** Horne 306; Jacques.

**MACKIE, Gordon** **fl 1975-1979**
Glasgow painter of coastal scenes. Exhibited GI(7), from 77 Knowetop St.

**MACKIE, Isobel** **fl 1939**
Amateur Banffshire painter. Exhibited a portrait of her grandmother at the RSA from Woodside, Rothiemay.

**McKIE, Mrs J H** **fl 1906-1921**
Painter of landscape, and townscapes, especially churches. Lived variously at Stonehaven & Aberdeen. Exhibited AAS(9) latterly from 17 Golden Square, Aberdeen.

**McKIE, J M F** **fl 1961-1966**
Aberdeen sculptor and designer. Exhibited AAS(6) from 16 Belvidere St.

**MACKIE, John** **fl 1975-1976**
Glasgow landscape and portrait painter. Exhibited GI(3) from 13 Gibson St.

**MACKIE, Mary** **fl 1940-1947**
Figurative painter and waver. Worked in watercolours, pencil and did ermbroideries and wall hangings. Exhibited RSA(1) & GI(26) from Moor Croft, Milngavie.

**MACKIE, Muriel** **fl 1932-1940**
Portrait miniaturist. Exhibited RSA(12) from Edinburgh.

**MACKIE, Peter Robert Macleod ARSA** **1867-1959**
Born Edinburgh. Painter in oil, watercolour and pastel of landscapes; also stained glass window designer. Studied Edinburgh College of Art and in Paris, after which he continued to work in Dieppe and Paris. Strongly influenced by Whistler. During WW2 he served with the Red Cross, after which he spent two years in Egypt. Curator of Kirkcaldy AG 1929-1948. Most of his work was in oil although his watercolours were always delicately painted with strong atmospheric effect. Elected ARSA 1933. Exhibited RSA(96), GI(16) & L(1), latterly from an address in Culross, Fife. Represented in Kirkcaldy AG, City of Edinburgh collection.
**Bibl:** Caw 425; Halsby 271.

**MACKIE, Rachel** **fl 1979-1980**
Edinburgh-based metalwork and jewellery designer. Exhibited AAS(6) from 164 Canongate.

**MACKIE, Thomas Callender Campbell MBE ARIBA ARIAS** **1886-1952**
Born Helensburgh, Jne 17; died Milngavie, Aug 17. Painter in oil and pastel; landscapes and flowers, also lithographer, designer and etcher. Educated Larchfield School, Helensburgh and Glasgow School of Architecture. Head of design, Glasgow School of Art. Author of *Pattern*, Longmans 1935. Member, Glasgow Art Club. Exhibited regularly RSA(48) & GI(77), also once at the RA. Represented in Glasgow AG, Paisley AG, Lillie AG (Milngavie).

**MacKILL, Isa** **fl 1896-1900**
Flower painter. Exhibited GI(6) & RHA(1), first of all from Dunoon and in 1897 from Glasgow.

**McKILLOP, John** **1888-c1968**
Watercolour landscape and seascape painter, also occasional flower studies. Trained Glasgow School of Art. Was still working in 1955 when he exhibited 'Irises' at the RSA, having exhibited at the GI(35) from 6 Regent Moray Street, Glasgow and latterly Flat 10, Wyndford Rd.

**McKINLAY, Mrs A Mabel M** **fl 1956-1967**
Glasgow flower painter. Probably wife of Alister M(qv). Exhibited GI(12) from 1 Victoria Circus.

**McKINLAY, Agnes** **fl 1897-1901**
Glasgow painter of genre. Exhibited GI(2) from Woodside Crescent.

**McKINLAY, Alister** **fl 1966**
Glasgow painter. Probably husband of Mabel M(qv). Exhibited GI(1) from 1 Victoria Circus.

**McKINLAY, David** **fl 1888-1901**
Glasgow painter of landscape and portraits. Exhibited GI(3) from N. Portland St.

**McKINLAY, Duncan** **fl 1874-1901**
Landscape painter; exhibited RSA(2) & GI(20) from Glasgow and briefly from Great Malvern, Worcestershire.

**McKINLAY, D McKenzie** **fl 1882-1912**
Stirlingshire painter in oil of landscape, domestic genre & figurative subjects. Exhibited RSA(10), GI(5), AAS(2) & L(1) from Polmont and Gorebridge, Midlothian.

**McKINLAY, Kate** **fl 1887-1893**
Painter of flowers and west coast scenery including the Clyde. Exhibited GI(4) from Glasgow.

**McKINLAY, Mary C S** **fl 1937**
Amateur Glasgow watercolour artist; exhibited at the GI(1) from Alexandra House, Carmyle.

**MacKINLAY, Miguel** **1895-?**
Born Guadalajara, Spain. Painter in oil of landscapes, portraits and figurative subjects. Son of a Scottish father and Spanish mother, he spent his early life in Spain and Australia, settling in England 1921. Entirely self-taught; exhibited 1921-39 RA(10), GI(1) & L(2).

**MacKINLAY, Thomas** **fl 1853-1870**
Painter in oil of portraits, landscape and figurative subjects. Worked in London and Greenock and after 1961 in Edinburgh. Exhibited RSA(23) & GI(1).

**McKINLEY, Agnes** **fl 1897-1901**
Amateur Glasgow painter. Exhibited GI(2) from 2 Woodside Crescent.

**McKINNA, Edward Burns** **fl 1927-1935**
Landscape painter and etcher; frequently painted views on the Clyde. Exhibited RA(1), RSA(6) & GI(8) from Glasgow.

**McKINNA, Mary E Tait** **fl 1930-1952**
Painter of still-life and flowers, also occasional portraits. Prolific artist of competence and grace. Exhibited RSA(19) & GI(41) from 150 Locksley Avenue, Glasgow. Represented Glasgow AG.

**McKINNELL, J Wilson** **fl 1941-1953**
Glasgow landscape painter in oil and watercolour, chiefly the latter. Worked a lot on Arran. Exhibited GI(10) from Victoria Rd.

**MacKINNON, Aileen Robertson** **1901-?**
Born Perth. Painter in oil of country scenes including studies of farm animals; also musician. Trained Regent Street Polytechnic, London. Exhibited 1926-1930 at the RA(1), GI(1), L(1) & Perth Art Association, from 63 Shrewsbury Road, Birkenhead.

**MacKINNON, Archibald** **fl 1879**
Glasgow watercolour painter; mainly interiors. Exhibited RSA(1).

**MacKINNON, Charles** **fl 1935-1937**
Aberdeen painter of coastal scenes and landscape. Exhibited AAS(3) from 177 Queens Rd.

**MacKINNON, Miss Esther Blaikie** **1885-1934**
Born Aberdeen; died Banchory 16 Jly. Painter, etcher, lithographer and illustrator; landscape and occasional portraits. After WW1 moved to Bath in 1921 and then to Hampstead 1923-1935 where she maintained a studio before returning to Aberdeen in 1935. In spite of severe physical disability exhibited widely at home and abroad including the Paris Salon. Illustrated Cecil Sharp's *Book of Folk Songs* in silhouette. Exhibited RA(1), RSA(10), SWA(4), GI(4), L(4), London Salon(18) & AAS regularly 1900-1921, latterly from Kimberley, Banchory.

**MacKINNON, Finlay** **1865-1935**
Born Poolewe, Wester Ross. Landscape painter, mainly in watercolour. Trained South Kensington and Paris, returned to live in Poolewe with regular excursions to London. Specialised in the landscape of Wester Ross, painted with muted colours, pedestrian composition and a generally sweet palette. Illustrated a number of books the best known of which are Hugh Fraser's *Amid the High Hills,* 1923 and Seton Gordon, *The Charm of Skye*, 1929. Served as Capt in 4th Seaforth Highlanders in WW1. Always wore the kilt which, allied to a broad west coast accent, led to him being regarded in the London art world as the archetypal Scotsman. Exhibited RA(19) including a landscape of 'Gairloch' 1902, RSA(1), AAS(4) & L(16).
**Bibl:** Halsby 271.

**MacKINNON, Miss Fiona** **fl 1935-1937**
Aberdeen painter of coastal scenes and landscape, sometimes around Lake Geneva. Sister of Charles M(qv). Exhibited AAS(2) from 177 Queens Rd.

**MacKINNON, Iain** **fl 1971**
Hebridean sculptor; exhibited 'Wild geese' at the RSA from his studio on the Isle of Tiree.

**McKINNON, James H** **fl 1885-1890**
Glasgow sculptor. Worked mainly in plaster. Exhibited RSA(3) & GI(1) latterly from 324 Scotland Street.

**McKINNON, John** **fl 1874-1876**
Glasgow landscape watercolourist. Exhibited GI(6) from various addresses.

**MacKINNON, Mrs Lachlan** **fl 1900**
Aberdeen stained glass window designer. Exhibited AAS(1) from 8 Queens Rd.

**MacKINNON, M Allan** **fl 1900-1901**
Glasgow amateur flower painter. Exhibited GI(2) from 139 Greenhead Street.

**MacKINNON, Margaret Cameron** **fl 1897-1903**
Greenock flower painter in oil; exhibited RSA(2), RHA(2) & GI(3).

**MacKINNON, Robert** **fl 1896-1907**
Watercolour painter; exhibited RSW(1) & GI(11) from Govan and Wilkie Park Rd, Glasgow.

**MacKINNON, Miss Susan R M** **fl 1876**
Edinburgh painter in oil; exhibited a study of trees at the RSA.

**MacKINNON, Mrs W P** **fl 1926**
Amateur Aberdeen painter. Exhibited 'Castle Rd, Accra' at AAS from 50 St Swithin Street.

**McKINNON, William** **fl 1869**
Edinburgh oil painter of figurative studies; exhibited RSA(1).

**MACKINTOSH, Alexander** **fl 1918**
Settled in New York at an early age. Exhibited once at the RSA from 55 Bible House, Astor Place, New York.

**MACKINTOSH, Anna F** **fl 1932**
Amateur Glasgow painter of figure studies; exhibited RSA(1) from Western House, 108A University Avenue.

**MACKINTOSH, Anne H** **Contemporary**
Born Motherwell. Painter and plant physiologist. Trained Glasgow School of Art. Paints mainly in oil; portraits, still life and landscape. Commissioned by Margaret Thatcher 1990. Influenced by James Robertson(qv) and David Donaldson(qv). Exhibits RSA & GI.

**MACKINTOSH, Charles Rennie** **1868-1928**
Born Glasgow, 7 June; died London, 10 Dec. Architect, designer, watercolourist and theorist. Attended evening classes at Glasgow School of Art whilst apprenticed to the Glasgow architect John Hutchison(qv) 1884. In 1889 joined the firm of Honeyman and Keppie as a qualified draughtsman. In 1891, on the proceeds of being awarded the Alexander Thomson travelling scholarship, made visits to Italy, France and Belgium. At the School he came to the attention of the Principal, Fra Newbury who, with his wife, remained friends for the rest of his life. While studying, Mackintosh and his fellow student and later best friend, Herbert MacNair(qv), met their future wives, the artist sisters, Margaret and Frances Macdonald(qv). They became known as 'The Four'(qv) and proceeded to collaborate on designs for furniture, metal work and illustration. After their marriage in 1900 the Mackintoshes often worked closely together on commissions for interior decorations. In 1896 the Four held their first joint exhibition at the London Arts and Crafts Society. This was badly received and in England Mackintosh never overcame the mistrust created by his early work. The achievements of his mature architectural and furniture design which left such a rich heritage to his native country remained unappreciated there during his lifetime. They were, however, acknowledged on the Continent. The Four were invited to participate in the eighth exhibition of the Vienna Secession in 1900 and two years later an International Exhibition of the Modern Decorative Art brought European designers together in Turin. Among the extravagant excesses of Continental Art Nouveau, 'the restraint and clean-lined elegance of the Mackintosh/MacNair room caused a sensation'. He is alone among Scottish architects and artists in being so highly regarded in Europe but so neglected at home. The magazines *Dekorative Kunst* and *Deutsche Kunst und Dekoration* illustrated and described their work more frequently than any British publication. They were feted in Vienna and treated as geniuses in Austria and Italy. Virtually all his architectural work was executed between 1896 and 1909. Newbury arranged for him to be commissioned to design the new Glasgow School Art, a revolutionary building described as 'a major landmark in the history of modern architecture' which is probably his best and most loved work. For Kate Cranston he designed a succession of famous tea room interiors, highly original, but again making little impact at the time. He also designed a number of private homes, among them 'Windyhill' for the Glasgow businessman William Davidson, and 'Hill House' for Walter Blackie. Not only was he responsible for the architecture but also for every detail of furniture and decoration. By 1913 he had given up hope of a viable practice in Glasgow and terminated his partnership with John Keppie. With his wife he left to join the Newburys at their holiday home in Suffolk. At this time he absorbed himself in painting delicate watercolour flower studies which, while retaining a hint of an art nouveau style, even in the foliage, revealed his acute powers of observation. Plans to publish a botanical text book were abandoned owing to the War. In 1915 he and Margaret settled in Chelsea where they hoped to resume their architectural practice. Although deeply depressed, his creativity did not diminish. The textile designs produced at this time as well as interior schemes for the tea room in Glasgow and 78 Derngate, Northampton were remarkably

innovative. By 1923 they were on the move again, this time to Southern France where they settled first in Collioure and later in Port Vendres. It was here that all hope of a further architectural career was abandoned and he concentrated entirely on watercolour painting. In 1927 his wife had to spent two months in London for medical treatment and by the end of the year he himself was so ill suffering from cancer that he had to return to London. When he died, the entire contents of their home and studio, including several of his chairs and the French paintings that he had been preparing for an exhibition, were valued at £88. 6s 2d. In architecture his finest and most characteristic works were the Glasgow School of Art; the house at 78 Derngate, Northampton;Windyhill, Kilmacolm (the house was sold in 1918 but most of the furniture is now housed in the Glasgow School of Art); Queens Cross Church, Glasgow; Hill House, Helensburgh; the Willow Tea Rooms, 271 Sauchiehall Street; Scotland Street school, Glasgow; the Glasgow style gallery in the Glasgow Museum and Art Gallery, Kelvingrove; and Ruchill Church Hall, Glasgow. Among his watercolours, his drawings for the Glasgow School of Art magazine deserve mention. As he was developing his own symbolic language, we find the 'Descent of Light' painted for the 1894 magazine, the 'Tree of Personal Effort' and the 'Tree of Influence' 'both based upon natural forms combined with a geometrical construction', at the Glasgow School of Art. An exhibition of his flower drawings was held in Glasgow 1977. Other exhibitions included a memorial exhibition at the McLellan Gallery 1933, a Saltire Society and Arts Council exhibition in Edinburgh 1953, exhibition of his architecture, design and painting at the Edinburgh Festival 1968, 'Le Sedie di Charles Rennie Mackintosh': Triennale di Milano, Milan 1973; exhibition in Toronto AG 1978, exhibition of his watercolours at the Fine Arts Society, Glasgow 1978, exhibition of his Chelsea Years 1915-23 at the Hunterian AG, Glasgow 1978, his designs 1868-1928 at the Seibu Museum of Art, Tokyo 1979, 'Lost Furniture Found' at the Glasgow School of Art 1982, general exhibitions of his work in Copenhagen in 1982 and Helsinki in 1983, 'Charles Rennie Mackintosh, architect and designer' (Thomas Howarth Collection) at the Federal Reserve Board Building, Washington DC 1985, and an exhibition in Tokyo 1985-6. During his lifetime he was not particularly interested in exhibiting his watercolours and did so only on a few occasions at the RSW & GI. In the history of Scottish art, he retains a special place as the most neglected and yet one of the most remarkably influential geniuses of his time. (See also Margaret MacDonald Mackintosh and 'The Four').

**Bibl:** Alison, Charles Rennie Mackintosh as a Designer of Chairs, London 1974; Jefferson Barnes, Some Examples of Furniture by Charles Rennie Mackintosh in the Glasgow School of Art Collection, Glasgow 1968, and Some Examples of Metalwork at the Glasgow School of Art, Glasgow 1968; Billcliffe, Architectural Sketches and Flower Drawings by Charles Rennie Mackintosh, New York 1977; Billcliffe Mackintosh Watercolours, London 1978; Billcliffe Charles Rennie Mackintosh: The Complete Furniture, Furniture Drawings and Interior Designs, London 1979, 3rd edtn 1988; Billcliffe Mackintosh Textile Designs, London 1982; Billcliffe Mackintosh Furniture, London 1984; Billcliffe and Vergo, Charles Rennie Mackintosh and the 'Austrian art Revival'; Bliss, Charles Rennie Mackintosh and the Glasgow School of Art, Glasgow 1961; Buchanan, Mackintosh's Masterwork : The Glasgow School of Art, Glasgow 1989; Burlington Magazine CXIX, 1977, 739-46; Cooper, Mackintosh Architecture, the Complete Buildings and Selected Projects, London 1978; A Gomme & D Walker, Architecture of Glasgow, London 1987(rev), 294-5 et al; Halsby 172-5, 176-9, 185, 203-5, 246; Hardie ch vii; Hartley 146; Howarth, Charles Rennie Mackintosh and the Modern Movement, 2nd edtn, London 1971; Irwin 395-403; Larner, The Glasgow Style, Edinburgh 1979; McLaren Young, Architectural Jottings by Charles Rennie Mackintosh, Glasgow Institute of Architects, Glasgow 1978; MacLeod, Charles Rennie Mackintosh, Architect and Artist, 2nd edtn, London 1983; Macmillan and Futagawa, Charles Rennie Mackintosh, the Glasgow School of Art, Glasgow, Scotland, Great Britain 1887-99, 1907-09, Tokyo 1979; Pevsner, 'Charles Rennie Mackintosh' Studies in Art, Architecture and Design II, London 1968; Pamela Reekie,'The Mackintosh House', Hunterian AG, Glasgow (Ex Cat nd); Scottish Arts Review XI, No 4, 1968 (special number devoted to Mackintosh); Studio IX 1897, 203-05; XI 1897, 86f, 226f; XIX 1900, 48f; XXIII 1901, 237ff; XXVI 1902, 91f; XXVIII 1903, 283ff; XXXIX 1906; 31f; special no 1901; Studio Year Book of Decorative Art 1907.

**MACKINTOSH, Colin John** **1866-1910**

Born Nairn, Sept; died Aviemore, Sept 1. Painter in oil and watercolour of Highland landscapes and portraits; also illustrator. Son of a landscape gardener who came to Inverness in 1871. Began life as a draper with Gunn & Grant of Castle St, but on the instigation of his employer, Mackintosh was introduced to the Dingwall artist Angus Sutherland(qv). Sutherland became his teacher and remained his friend and inspiration. Entered RSA-School 1888, winning the Chalmers bursary. Soon after his marriage in 1902 he moved to Glasgow but returned to Inverness three years later, finally settling at Lynwilg, Alvey where his wife had been appointed teacher. His work was characterised by harmony of colour and a true feel for the characteristic light of the NW-Highlands. Illustrated William Mackay's *Urquhart & Glenmoriston.* Exhibited RSA(3) including 'The Findhorn, Kyllachy, Inverness-shire' in 1896, a painting subsequently purchased by Lord Kyllachy. His portrait of the Gaelic scholar 'Alexander Macbain' is in Inverness Royal Academy.

**Bibl:** 'H.P.S.' Colin John Mackintosh, privately printed, Inverness 1911.

**MACKINTOSH, Finlay** **fl 1987-**

Glasgow painter of flowers and interiors in the modern colourful, abstract manner. Exhibited GI(5) from 29 Broomfield Rd.

**MACKINTOSH, James** **fl 1882-1884**

Edinburgh painter in oil and watercolour; exhibited three still-lifes at the RSA from 42 Queen Street.

**MACKINTOSH, James S** **fl 1924-1949**

Painter of genre and pastoral scenes. Exhibited RSA(7) & GI(3) from Edinburgh.

**MACKINTOSH, Jane H** **fl 1894**

Aberdeen amateur painter of local scenery. Wife or daughter of Thomas Alexander Mackintosh(qv). Exhibited AAS(1) from 17 Golden Square.

**MACKINTOSH, John** **1931-1966**

Glasgow painter of conversation pieces, portraits and flowers. Exhibited RSA(5) 1954-8 & GI(17). 'Sunday Afternoon' is in Glasgow AG.

**MACKINTOSH, John M** **1847-1913**

Born Inverness. Landscape painter.

**MACKINTOSH, Lillian H** **fl 1908-1923**

Aberdeen painter in watercolour and jewellery designer. Probably the daughter of Thomas M(qv). Believed to have been trained at Gray's School of Art. In addition to finely detailed sensitive small-scale watercolours of landscape and occasional figurative subjects, and a few oil sketches, she designed jewellery and textiles. Exhibited during the above years AAS(9) from 58 Forest Rd.

**MACKINTOSH, Margaret MacDonald RSW (née MacDonald)** **1863-1933**

Born Staffordshire. Painter in watercolour and stained glass artist. Trained Glasgow School of Art. Married Charles Rennie Mackintosh(qv). One of The Four(qv) (with her husband, sister Frances and brother-in-law Herbert MacNair) who worked closely on commissions for interior decorations. She gave her volatile husband lifelong support and inspiration through all the vicissitudes of public disregard, economic impoverishment and severe illness. She and her sister, while studying under Fra Newbury(qv) at the Glasgow School of Art, developed an enigmatic imagery of weird skeletal female figures and metamorphic lines owing something to Aubrey Beardsley, to the symbolism of Jan Toorop, and to the 'obscurer shadows of the Celtic Twilight'. Their work earned the group the nickname 'Spook School' and in Scotland attracted much suspicion for being tainted with the 'decadence' of art nouveau. One of the first Symbolist watercolours produced by The Four was Margaret Macdonald's 'Summer'. She combined with her sister in producing an important series of four watercolours 1897-98 depicting the seasons; these were framed in elaborate beaten lead surrounds which they also designed and made. All of these are on vellum and can be seen in Glasgow AG. Between 1900 and 1910 her work was related to the commissions in which her husband was then involved.

'Mysterious Garden' 1905 is related to a series of panels executed for the Warndorfer Villa in Vienna. At this time her work was elegant, decorative, a little excessive in its symbolic component, but nevertheless meticulously prepared. From 1910 onwards she concentrated on larger works but after leaving for France in 1923 she produced no further work. Elected RSW 1900, resigned in 1923. Received Diploma of Honour, Turin International Exhibition, 1902. Exhibited RSA(1), RSW(21), GI(14) & L(4). Represented in Glasgow AG. (See also Charles Rennie Mackintosh).
**Bibl:** Burkhauser 109-122 et passim; Halsby 175-9,185,270; Hardie passim ch vii; Macmillan [SA] 293,294,324; Pamela Reekie, 'Margaret Macdonald Mackintosh', Hunterian AG, Glasgow (Ex Cat 1983).

**MACKINTOSH, Margaret** **fl 1946-1948**
Stirling landscape painter; exhibited RSA(2).

**MACKINTOSH, Thomas Alexander** **1866-1925**
Born Edinburgh. Painter in oil and watercolour of landscapes. Grandson of the Aberdeen artist James Gordon(qv). Graduated in dentistry at Edinburgh University before joining his brother's practice in Aberdeen. There he took up art when in his thirties, demonstrating unusual skill. Lived at 17 Golden Square, Aberdeen & later 58 Forest Rd. Painted in a style reminiscent of J C Mitchell(qv) and W M Fraser(qv). Began exhibiting at the Aberdeen Artists' Society in 1902, continuing to show there until 1923; also GI(1) 1906.

**MACKINTOSH, T H** **fl 1869**
Edinburgh landscape painter in oil; exhibited RSA(1).

**McKISSOCK, John F** **fl 1952**
Ayrshire portrait painter; exhibited 'Portrait of Catherine' at the RSA from Troon.

**McKNIGHT, David Moran** **fl 1946-1947**
Glasgow engraver and draughtsman. Exhibited a charcoal drawing and a lithograph at the GI, from 11 Queen's Crescent.

**MACKY, Gordon** **fl 1884**
Landscape painter. Exhibited RSA(1) from Loch Carron, Wester Ross.

**McLACHLAN, Cecile** **c1935-**
Painter, potter and teacher. Daughter of W Miles Johnston(qv) and Dorothy Nesbitt(qv). Brought up in Kircudbright whence her school had been evacuated during the war. Lecturer in art at Moray House College of Education 1955-90. Former President SSWA.

**McLACHLAN, James** **fl 1922-1938**
Architect. Designed the elaborate revivalist Morningside United Church, Edinburgh (originally Congregational) (1927-9), also St Christopher's, Craigentinny Rd (1934-8). Commissioned by Crawfords to build their premises at 15-19 Hanover St (1930).
**Bibl:** Gifford 43,307,397,618,661.

**MacLACHLAN, James M** **fl 1938-1939**
A minor watercolour painter; exhibited RSA(1) & RSW(1), from 36 Plewlands Gardens, Edinburgh.

**McLACHLAN, John** **1843-1893**
Edinburgh architect. Pupil of David Cousin. In 1868 began his own business which was quickly successful. Executed many offices of the National Bank in Scotland including the baronial branch at 179 High St, Royal Mile (1892-3)- also the old Stock Exchange, Thistle St (1890) and other public offices in St. Andrews Square, Edinburgh. His best ecclesiastical work was Wardie Parish Church (1892) 'a jolly Gothic church with Francophile detail'. Exhibited RSA(11) including a design for the new Cottage Hospital, Hawick and the new Stock Exchange in Edinburgh (1890), from 29 York Buildings, York Place.
**Bibl:** Gifford 203,263,313,323,328,380,502,563,602,644.

**McLACHLAN, Kate** **fl 1887**
Amateur painter. Exhibited GI(1) from Helensburgh.

**McLACHLAN, Rita M C** **[see SANDYS-BROWN, Mrs R M C]**

**McLACHLAN, Miss Sue** **fl 1966**
Amateur Glasgow-based watercolour painter. Exhibited 'Storm' at the GI, from Lambert Drive, Clarkston.

**McLACHLAN, Thomas Hope** **1845-1897**
Born Darlington. Painter in oil of landscapes, also etcher and drypoint engraver. Son of a Scottish banker and his wife who had settled in England. Educated at Merchiston Castle School, Edinburgh and Trinity College, Cambridge where he excelled. Then studied law at Lincoln's Inn, practising for some years in the Court of Chancery. An interest in art steadily grew and, encouraged by John Pettie(qv) and others, in 1878 he decided to abandon law in favour of painting. Without any previous academic training, he studied with Carolus Duran in Paris. Influenced by the romantic works of George Manson(qv) and Cecil Lawson(qv). Caw thought 'he painted in a manner that expressed his feelings wonderfully well, and they were such that one would readily overlook the far graver defects of methods than can be laid to his charge. Moreover, he was a refined colourist of wide range and great expressive power and possessed a sense of design which never failed in dignity and sobriety, so that the ensemble of his pictures is ever distinguished and complete and never commonplace'. Occasionally worked in oil and also executed a number of impressive etchings, some of which were reproduced in the *Magazine of Art.* Sometimes he incorporated into his solemn and often bleak landscapes a storm-buffeted peasant in a manner reminiscent of Millet. Lived in London from 1883, after 1894 at 2 Spencer St, Victoria St. Exhibited 42 works at the RA, most of them Scottish scenes but also some continental and several seascapes; also ROI(29), RE(7), RI(7),GI(1) & L(13). Represented in the Tate AG ('Evening Quiet'), NGS ('Christobel under the oak'), Kirkcaldy AG, Guildhall Museum,(London), City of Edinburgh collection.
**Bibl:** AJ 1897, 191; Bryan; Caw 316-318; DNB; Mag of Art 1903, 117ff; Studio 1907, 134ff.

**McLACHLAN, Mrs Valerie** **fl 1974-1977**
Glasgow painter of figurative works, flowers and landscape. Exhibited GI(5) from Stamperland Ave, Clarkston.

**MacLAGAN, Alexander** **fl 1873-1874**
Portobello oil painter of coastal scenes and landscapes; exhibited RSA(4).

**MacLAGAN, Mrs Dorothea Frances ('Bay')** **1895-?**
Born Greenock. Painter in oil and watercolour of portraits, figure compositions and genre until 1940, plant and botanical work after that time. Studied Byam Shaw School of Art 1914-1917 and RA Schools 1917-1922. Married Philip Douglas M(qv). Lived at Bridgetown, Devon. Held frequent solo shows after the first in Cambridge in 1947. Her work was included in the exhibition 'Flower Paintings 1652-1952', Victoria Gallery, Bath. In 1958 she began work for *Preview* in the design of a new botany gallery at the Natural History Museum, South Kensington. Also in 1958 she contributed a page for the *Book of Golden Roses* presented to Sir Winston and Lady Churchill on their golden wedding anniversary. An important retrospective exhibition was held in Dartington Hall 1975. Exhibited RA(5) & GI(2).

**McLAGAN, Miss Mary L** **fl 1881-1901**
Edinburgh flower painter; exhibited RSA(3) from 5 Eton Terrace.

**MacLAGAN, Philip Douglas** **1901-1972**
Born Swatow, China, Sep 26; died Totnes, Devon. Painter in oil and watercolour; portraits, figures and landscapes. Son of a Scottish missionary family who returned to Berwick-on-Tweed in 1905. Studied in London at St John Wood's Art School and the RA Schools. Began exhibiting 1922 including regular works at the Venice biennial until 1940. After the War he rarely showed his work publicly. He was a part-time teacher at the City of London School for 35 years. His paintings, especially of landscape, are delicate in brushwork, colour and design, and often of wistful beauty. The simple unnoticed corners of nature are affectionately and sensitively portrayed, a rocky pool and a meandering burn, a tree-stump, a momentary vista in a woodland. The palette is controlled with full tonal harmony. In 1937 he moved to the vale of Aylesbury and settled there as primarily a landscape painter. Married Dorothea M(qv). Served in WW2 in North Africa and Italy in photographic intelligence. Rarely painted thereafter. Exhibited RA(14), ROI(10), RBA(6) & L(2).

**MacLAGAN, T** **fl 1856**
Edinburgh landscape painter; exhibited once at the RSA from St Leonard's St.

**McLAGHLAN, M W** **fl 1897**
Edinburgh artist; exhibited RSA(3) from 11 Saxe Coburg Place.

**McLAREN, Charlotte Gordon (Mrs O'Flaherty)** **1869-1940**
Born Glasgow. Miniature and portrait painter in oil and chalk. Studied Glasgow School of Art 1894-1899, also at the Slade and in Paris. Lived in Millport with her husband, the cathedral Provost. Exhibited RA(11), including a fine portrait of 'Kate Cameron' 1900; also RSA(23), RSW(2), RMS(1), RHA(2), GI(18) & L(15), latterly from 121 Bath St.

**McLAREN, Dougald** **fl 1759-c1786**
Portrait painter. Son of a surgeon, he married on 25 May, 1766, Agnes, daughter of the minister of Inveresk. Apprenticed in 1759 to James Allan, painter, staying eight years before joining the Nories(qv), then moved to Runciman(qv), the Hope family paying for his indentures and maintenance. In 1766 he worked with Runciman at the Hope's Moffat House. In 1768 he took over Runciman's entire business. Was a member of the Incorporation of St Mary's and in 1786 took on a George MacKenzie as apprentice. No recorded works of his remain.

**MacLAREN, Donald Graeme** **1886-1917**
Landscape and portrait painter of Scottish parentage. Lived in London and exhibited in various London galleries. His portrait of the poet 'Dugald Sutherland MacColl (1886-1948)' is in the SNPG.

**MacLAREN, Duncan** **1884-1963**
Born Glen Etive, Argyllshire. Part-time landscape painter in oil, watercolour and pastel. Spent all his life as a gamekeeper and deer stalker in Argyll and Perthshire - mainly on the Wills family estate of Meggernie, apart from two years in the Argyllshire police and four years as a piper in the Black Watch and Lovat Scots during WWI. Wounded in France, whilst in hospital met an officer who in civilian life was an art teacher. This encouraged him to paint and after marriage (to Euphemia McEwan) 1928 he held his first one-man show. In 1959 he began to lose his sight and had to cease painting. Exhibited in Glasgow, Dundee, Inverness and Perth. Although not represented in any public gallery his work remains in many private collections throughout the Scottish Highlands.

**McLAREN, Duncan Gillies** **fl 1969-1970**
Glasgow sculptor. Worked in alabaster and plaster. Exhibited GI(3).

**McLAREN, Miss Elspeth** **fl 1961-1963**
Ayrshire painter and engraver. Worked in watercolours, pen and ink; also lithographer and etcher. Mainly topographical subjects. Exhibited GI(4) from Crosshouse, by Kilmarnock.

**McLAREN, George Miller** **fl 1944-1953**
Glasgow landscape painter. Exhibited GI(17) from Bearsden.

**McLAREN, Gilbert** **fl 1866-1868**
Perthshire painter in oil of local landscapes, especially in the region of Blair Atholl where he lived. Exhibited at the RSA(6).

**MacLAREN, Helen ROI (Mrs Flint)** **1897-?**
Born Lovat Arms hotel, Fort Augustus, Inverness-shire, April 15. Painter of landscapes and figure subjects in oil. Studied art under Bernard Adams and at the London School of Art. Married the English artist E H Flint. Lived in London and Bishops Stortford, Herts. Her principal works include 'July Evening', 'The Edge of the Wood' and 'Montreuil-sur-Mer'. Exhibited RA(1), ROI(31) & SWA(23).

**MacLAREN, James** **1829-1893**
Dundee architect. Trained under David Bryce(qv). Soane medallist. Among his more notable buildings are Erskine church, Arbroath (c1851): Congregational church, Broughty Ferry (1865); Balthayock House, Perthshire (1870) and the 282 ft high decorative brick stack at Camperdown Works, Dundee (1865-6) - sometimes incorrectly ascribed to J H Maclaren(qv). Also designed intermediate stations on the Dundee-Arbroath joint railway line and many farm buildings, especially on the Panmure estate, Angus.
**Bibl:** Bruce Walker & W S Gauldie, Architects and Architecture on Tayside, Dundee 1984, 135-6,149.

**McLAREN, James** **fl 1881-1917**
Painter. Exhibited RSA(17) & GI(5) from Edinburgh and later Garthland Ave, Glasgow.

**MacLAREN, James Marjoribanks RIBA** **1843-1890**
Born Stirling. Architect, one of the most lively exponents of the 'free style' in British architecture. Pioneer of the Arts and Crafts style. Trained at L'École des Beaux Arts, Paris. Articled to James Salmon snr(qv) of Glasgow. Worked for Campbell Douglas(qv) and Stevenson(qv) before moving to Godwin and Coad's offices in London. Disciple of Edward Godwin. The fact that farm buildings and the Fortingall cottages on the Glenlyon estate (1889-90) anticipated several features of Charles Rennie Mackintosh's houses has led Dunbar and others to conclude that the latter had been influenced by MacLaren. Another pupil was Robert Lorimer(qv) who left only when invited to work on Earlshall. Several Perthshire commissions uncompleted at his death were finished by William Dunn(qv) and Robert Watson(qv). In addition to joint exhibits at the RA when a partner with Coad he exhibited 4 designs under his own name 1887-1890 including one for the Hotel Sta Catalina, Las Palmas, from 21 King William St, Strand. Should not be confused with James Maclaren(qv).
**Bibl:** Dunbar 153,165; James M MacLaren, Architectural Association Notes, Vol 4,56; Peter Savage, Lorimer and the Edinburgh Craft Designers, Edinburgh 1980, 7,8,32,154-6,167; Bruce Walker & W S Gauldie, Architects asnd Architecture on Tayside, Dundee 1984, 155.

**McLAREN, John** **1923-1996**
Painter and design engineer, his family coming from Glen Affric. After training at Willesden, Northampton and Harrow Art Schools followed by a brief spell in commercial art, he turned to engineering. Married to **Judith M**, a painter of woodland scenes. After retirement he returned to Scotland and to painting in oils, watercolours and pastel. His compositions were landscape, especially Deeside and the Inverness-shire glens, also oil related machinery. Exhibited RSA & AAS.

**McLAREN, John Jnr** **fl 1882-1889**
Edinburgh painter in oil; interiors, landscape and figurative subjects. Son of John Stewart M(qv). Exhibited RSA(5) including an interior of the SNG (1886), also GI(10) & L(1).

**MacLAREN, John Stewart** **1860-1930**
Born Edinburgh, Sep 11. Painter in oil and watercolour; landscapes, figurative and architectural interiors. Studied at the RSA Schools and in Paris. Active member of the Scottish Arts Club. Travelled widely in France and Spain. Lived for a time in Harthill House, Moffat, Dumfries-shire. Principal works include 'Fruit Market, Seville', 'Spanish Gypsies', 'Near Concarneau', 'Cathedral Tarragona' & 'Interior of the National Gallery, Edinburgh' (1886). Lived at 53 Broadhurst Gdns, S. Hampstead. Exhibited RA(6), RSA(26), RSW(1), RBA(2), AAS & GI(25). Represented in Lillie AG (Milngavie), Edinburgh City collection.

**MacLAREN, M A** **fl 1880-1881**
Glasgow landscape painter, mainly around Loch Lomond. Exhibited GI(4) from 15 Elgin Grove Place.

**MacLAREN, Ottilie H (Mrs O Wallace)** **1875-?**
Scottish sculptress. Portrait busts and portrait medallions. Exhibited RSA 1900-04 & GI(2) from Paris, Edinburgh and London.

**McLAREN, Peter** **fl 1932-1936**
Painter. Exhibited RSA(4) from 48 Leys Park Road, Dunfermline.

**McLAREN, Peter** **1964-**
Born Edinburgh, Mar 14. Works in oil on board or marine ply; also in watercolour, collage, and is a screen printer and etcher. Trained Edinburgh College of Art 1982-1986 with a postgraduate year 1986-1987. Received a number of awards including the John Kinross Scholarship enabling him to visit Italy 1986. The Richard Ford award of the RA took him to Madrid; also won the Adam Bruce Thomson

award of the RSA and the David Cargill Trust award of the RGI. In 1987 winning the Andrew Grant Major Award enabled him to visit USA and in 1989 was the British Airways 'most promising artist' resulting in a travelling scholarship worth £10,000. The same year he was granted the John Murray Thompson Award at the RSA. Early influences were John Houston(qv) and members of his own family, especially his mother Irene Thomson and uncle James Thomson(qv). Impressed by the American abstract expressionists studied during his visit to the USA in 1990. Uses a variety of techniques in placing the paint on the canvas including pouring it, splashing it and scraping it. Many solo exhibitions in continental Europe and variously in Scotland. Exhibits RGI since 1986. Lives at Dounby on Orkney. Represented in RA, RSA, Edinburgh City Arts Centre, Perth AG, Bochum Museum (Germany), Belgium, and Oslo; also in the collection of HRH Duke and Duchess of York.
**Bibl:** "Peter McLaren" Exhibition cat., Sophie van Moerkerke Gallery, Belgium 1989; "Young Artists as Loss Leaders", Charles Hill, *Art Review* 1990.

**McLAREN, Walter** **fl 1861-1909**
Glasgow landscape and figure painter in oil. Painted young ladies and sunlit Mediterranean scenes. Spent several years on Capri and eventually settled at Sandhurst Lodge, Church Walk, Worthing. Exhibited RA(12), RSA(3) & GI(18).

**McLAREN, William H M** **1923-c1987**
Portrait and landscape painter, also murals and book engravings. Studied Edinburgh College of Art under Joan Hassall(qv). Worked independently after graduating earning considerable success with his detailed, decorative black and white engravings in the manner of Rex Whistler, and in their detailed simplicity reminiscent of a bygone era. Illustrated Wankowicz: *Sunshine and Storm* (1948), Beverley Nichols: *Merry Hall* (1953), *Laughter on the Stairs* (1953), Parker: *Surrey Gardens* (1954), Nichols: *Sunlight on the Lawn* (1956), the tenderly evocative Macleod: *Oasis of the North* (1958), Fletcher: *The Rose Anthology* (1963), Nichol: *Garden Open Today* (1963), *The Art of Flower Arrangement* (1967), *Garden Open Tomorrow* (1968), *The Gift of a Home* (1972), Sansom: *Aurora's Glade* (1973). Exhibited RSA(1).
**Bibl:** Horne (illus) 307; Brian North Lee: *British Bookplates: A Pictorial History* (David & Charles, 1979).

**McLAUCHLAN, Alexander** **c1800-c1890**
Perth house painter, decorator and minor artist. Appears in local directories 1837-1889/90. Three local views are known, the earliest dated 1822, competent and rather naive, all now in Perth AG.

**McLAUCHLAN, Archibald** **fl 1752-c1770**
Portrait painter in the style of Mosman(qv). Originally from Argyll but settled in Glasgow. Student of the Foulis Academy(qv), he matriculated from Glasgow University 1762. Married the daughter of Robert Foulis(qv). In c1770 went to Rome, partly in order to make a large copy of Raphael's 'School of Athens'. About the same time he painted what Irwin describes as 'a rather contrived, almost naïve, group of the Glasgow merchant 'William Glassford and his family' now in the Glasgow AG'.
**Bibl:** Irwin 88; W J Macaulay, Scott Art Rev, III, 1951, 14ff; Waterhouse.

**MacLAUCHLAN, D** **fl 1888**
Glasgow landscape painter. Exhibited GI(1) from 30 Carnarvon Street.

**McLAUCHLAN, William** **fl 1896-1899**
Watercolour artist of Paisley who exhibited two landscapes at the GI.
**Bibl:** Halsby 271.

**McLAUCHLAN, William** **fl 1946-1947**
Dundee subject painter. Exhibited RSA(2) from Invergowrie.

**McLAURIN, Miss Ailie R** **fl 1944**
Renfrewshire amateur landscape painter. Exhibited 'Ben Ledi after rain' at the GI, from Bridge of Weir.

**McLAURIN, Alan M** **fl 1944**
Kilmacolm painter. Exhibited a portrait 'The late Sam Fulton' at the GI.

**McLAURIN, Duncan RSW** **1849-1921**
Born Glasgow; died Helensburgh, Jan 25. Painter in oil but mainly watercolour of landscapes and cattle. Trained Glasgow School of Design and at Heatherley's. Exhibited chiefly in Scotland living in Bloomfield, Lomond Street, Helensburgh. Much of his earlier work is to be preferred to his later, somewhat limited output. His watercolours have strong romantic appeal but as he grew older the strong, glowing colours were replaced with duller dark greens and browns. Elected RSW 1878. His principal works include 'Home from the Plough' and 'Cattle by a Stream'. Exhibited RSA(11), RSW, GI(55) & L(1). Represented in City of Edinburgh collection(2).
**Bibl:** Halsby 271-2.

**McLAURIN, Isabella** **fl 1879**
Amateur Helensburgh watercolour painter of flowers and still life. Sister of Janet M(qv). Exhibited GI, from Glenan Gdns.

**McLAURIN, James N** **fl 1890-1906**
Watercolour painter of landscape and topographical subjects. Exhibited RSW(4) & GI(12) from Kelvin Cottage, Bothwell in 1890 and from Leith at the beginning of the century.

**McLAURIN, Janet** **fl 1876-1879**
Amateur Helensburgh watercolour painter of flowers. Sister of Isabella M(qv). Exhibited GI(3) from Glenan Gdns.

**MacLAURIN, Robert** **fl 1900-1904**
Amateur painter of landscapes in watercolour. Exhibited GI(3) from 39 Caldercult Road, Maryhill.

**MacLAURIN, Robert** **fl 1940-d1947**
Painter of watercolour landscapes. Exhibited GI(10) from Homesteads, Stirling.

**MacLAURIN, Robert** **1961-**
Born Yorkshire, where he spent his childhood. Painter of landscape and topographical subjects. Studied Edinburgh College of Art 1979-83. An Andrew Grant scholarship took him to Turkey, returning to Istanbul the following year on a Turkish Government scholarship. A frequent motif in his work is the essential loneliness of the individual, characterised by a large human figure set against dramatic landscape and dwarfed by it. First solo exhibition in Edinburgh 1984. Exhibited 'A Storm, Istanbul' at the RSA(1986) from Leven Terrace. Represented in SNGMA.
**Bibl:** Hartley 147; 369 Gall, Edinburgh & Art in General, New York, 'An Exchange', (Ex Cat 1987-88).

**McLAY, Colin S** **fl 1946**
Amateur Aberdeen-based painter. Exhibited a shipyard scene at the GI from 58 Queens Rd.

**McLEA, Duncan Fraser** **1841-1916**
Painter of marines and local coastal scenery. Scottish parentage. Probably brother of J W McLea(qv). Lived in Newcastle-uon-Tyne from where he exhibited RSA(8) 1870-1886.

**McLEA, John Watson** **fl 1832-1861**
Leith painter of marines, portraits and landscapes. Highly competent and pleasing artist in the traditional mould; his coastal scenes are invariably interesting and well executed, often with figures and generally on a small scale. Due recognition has never been given, evidence of the comparative neglect of native marine painting in Scotland. Exhibited RSA(44) including an unusual picture of two amateur jockeys 1858. His *Granton Harbour during the Regatta* (1859) is in the Royal Forth Yacht Club.

**McLEAN, A** **fl 1878-1880**
Glasgow watercolour painter of landscape. Exhibited GI(4) from Markland Terrace.

**MacLEAN, Alastair F** **fl 1952**
Amateur Renfrewshire watercolololourist. Exhibited an Arran land-scape at the GI from Bridge of Weir.

**MACLEAN, Alexander** **1840-1904**
Painter of genre and gentle townscape. Scottish parentage but lived

and worked solely in England. Exhibited RA(10) & GI(3) 1872-1904, latterly from 5 Holland Park Stdios, London. Died St. Leonards, Sussex.

**McLEAN, Allan** **fl 1872-1880**
Glasgow painter in oil and watercolour of landscapes and coastal scenes; exhibited RSA(11) & GI(2) from 18 Markland Terrace, Hillhead.

**McLEAN, Bruce** **1944-**
Born Glasgow. Sculptor, painter and designer. Studied Glasgow School of Art 1961-3 and St Martin's School of Art, London 1963-6 under Antony Caro and William Tucker. Quickly disillusioned by what he regarded as the pomposity of so much contemporary sculpture he embarked on his own form of performance art. In 1966 he joined the staff of Croydon School of Art and shortly after transferred to Maidstone College of Art. First solo exhibition in Dusseldorf 1969. In 1972 he held a one-day show at the Tate 'King for a Day' in which he exhibited 1000 booklets containing proposals for new sculptures. In the late 1970s he returned to more traditional idioms producing paintings and drawings somewhat reminiscent of Matisse. Continues to deride contemporary sculpture including sometimes himself, from a London base. Represented SNGMA, Tate, Lillie AG (Milngavie), Southampton City Museum, Arts Council.
**Bibl:** Hartley 147; Musee d'Art et d'Industrie, Saint-Etienne, 'Bruce McLean' (Ex Cat 1981); Scot. Gall, Edinburgh, 'Bruce Mclean', (Ex Cat 1986); Third Eye Centre, Glasgow, (Ex Cat 1980, texts by David Brown and Sarah Kent); Whitechapel Gall, London, 'Bruce McLean', (Ex Cat 1982, text by Nena Dimitrijevic).

**MACLEAN, Carnegie** **fl 1764**
Edinburgh engraver. Maried Isobell, daughter of a Stirling mariner 1764.
**Bibl:** Bushnell.

**MacLEAN, G D** **fl 1900**
Landscape painter; exhibited RSA(2) from Langsdale, Gourock.

**McLEAN, Hamish** **fl 1989-**
Dundee painter. Exhibited RSA from 1989 from 42 Sherbrook Crescent.

**MacLEAN, Hector** **fl 1982-1985**
Glasgow painter. Landscapes and genre. Exhibited GI(5) from 17 Beech Ave.

**McLEAN, Miss Isobel** **fl 1910-1923**
Aberdeenshire landscape painter, mainly in pastel. Exhibited AAS(3) from Breda House, Alford.

**McLEAN, J M M** **fl 1887**
Edinburgh watercolour painter of pastoral scenes; exhibited RSA(1).

**McLEAN, James** **fl 1871-1910**
Glasgow oil painter of landscapes, especially in the Highlands. Exhibited RSA(16) & GI(13).

**McLEAN, James C** **fl 1931**
Linlithgow-based painter; exhibited 'The Shrine' at the RSA from 295 High Street.

**McLEAN, James W L** **1878-c1930**
Born Stranraer, Feb 5. Portrait and landscape painter. Trained Glasgow School of Art. Member, Liverpool Sketching Club. Exhibited GI(1), L(10) & RCA(1).

**McLEAN, John** **fl 1933-1960**
Glasgow figure painter and sculptor. Prolific and versatile. Painted mainly in watercolour: landsacape, fishing boats and flowers; carved statuettes, often in mahogany. Exhibited RSA(5) & GI often between 1942 & 1960, from Mearns Rd, Clarkston.

**McLEAN, John Talbert** **1939-**
Born Liverpool. Abstract painter. Son of Talbert M(qv). Studied St Andrews University 1957-62 and Courtauld Institute 1963-6. From 1966 taught at a number of London colleges including Chelsea School of Art and the Slade. Lived in New York 1987-9. Currently based in London. Exhibits RSA & RSW. First solo exhibition Edinburgh 1975. Artist-in-Residence, Edinburgh University 1984-5. Commented that as a painter his greatest concern is colour. Represented in Tate AG, SNGMA, Southampton AG, Swindon AG.
**Bibl:** Hartley 148.

**MacLEAN, R** **fl c1817-1824**
Portrait and figure painter in oil. One of several enigmatic figures whose departure from the artistic scene was as sudden and unannounced as their arrival. In 1817 he was working in Scotland having studied art in Italy. He specialised in copying the old masters and in 1819 exhibited a copy of Sassoferrato's 'Holy Family' at Nairn, Forres, Elgin and Fort George. This was admired by Prince Leopold of Saxe-Coburg and the King of the Belgians when visiting the Highlands. He disposed of other copies by lottery and was successful enough to return to Italy. In 1824 he was again in Inverness where he set up practice as a portrait painter, opening a small gallery containing 'a few original paintings by Titian, Poussin, Salvator Rosa, etc', also scarce and valuable prints. At the same time he established an art class in the town, and gave anatomy lessons to medical students. Thereafter he disappeared from public notice without trace.
**Bibl:** 'Old Inverness Artists', Inverness Scientific Society, 1919.

**McLEAN, Talbert** **1906-1992**
Born Oct 15; died May 29. Abstract painter; lived and worked in Arbroath. Father of John M(qv). Studied at Dundee College of Art 1923-1927, joining the staff in 1928-1932. For the next seven years he became a free-lance artist in London and Liverpool, serving in the forces during WW 2. After the war, until 1972, taught at Arbroath High School, becoming professional member, SSA, and regular exhibitor RSA & GI. His style gradually changed from watercolour landscapes in the 1930s and 1940s to watercolour abstractions in the 1950s and 1960s, and to abstract formal shapes in the 1970s and 1980s in which he was much influenced by American expressionism. Exhibited RSA(2) & GI(2). Represented in SNGMA, Glasgow AG, Dundee AG, Arbroath AG, SAC.

**McLEAN, Tom W** **fl 1933**
Amateur watercolourist; exhibited RSA(1).

**MacLEAN, William RSA RSW RGI** **1941-**
Born Inverness. Sculptor and painter. Descended from generations of Skye fisherfolk. Associations of sea and seafaring show in his work. Trained Gray's School of Art, Aberdeen and Hospitalfield School of Art, Arbroath 1961-67, then at the British School in Rome. Received a number of awards including the Benno Schotz prize for sculpture and the RSA Gillies Award. Appointed senior lecturer, Duncan of Jordanstone College of Art 1994 becoming Professor shortly afterwards. Has held numerous one-man exhibitions in Scotland, also in Rome and in 1987 in London and at North Dakota Museum of Art 1998. His technique illustrates craft skill, this having developed from early semi-abstract paintings which already conveyed environmental emotions. Although he had been making box constructions before, after coming in contact with the box constructions of Joseph Cornell he worked on an unusual series of sculptures and constructions composed of driftwood, found objects and sculptured elements. These are fitted into box-like frames and painted. Their inspiration frequently comes from Scotland's seafaring culture as fish bones, hooks and miscellaneous objects and are arranged in bizarre tableaux evoking Scotland's pre-industrial fishing traditions. In 1973 he was commissioned by the Scottish International Education Trust to undertake a visual study of Scottish ring-net fishing for which he produced 400 drawings and diagrams. Elected SSA 1969, ARSA 1973, RSA 1991, RGI 1996, RSW 1997. Received Civic Trust award 1997 & Scottish National Heritage Supreme Award for three memorial cairns for Cuimhneachain nan Gaisgeach, Isle of Lewis. Represented in Edinburgh City AG, Forens AG (Hull), Fitzwilliam Museum, Lillie AG (Milngavie), McLaurin AG (Ayr), McManus AG (Dundee), NLS, Peterhead AG, Smith AG (Stirling), Stoke-on-Trent AG, Yale Centre for British Art (New Haven, USA), SNGMA, BM, Aberdeen AG, Glasgow AG, Hull AG, Inverness AG, Kirkcaldy AG, Perth AG, Scunthorpe AG, NTS, SAC.
**Bibl:** Mungo Campbell, 'The Line of Tradition', Nat Galls of Scotland, Ex cat, Edinburgh 1993; Gage 74-5,148; Hartley 148-9; Angus Martin with illustrations by Will Maclean, The Ring-Net

Fishermen, Edinburgh 1981; Claus Runkel Fine Art, Will Maclean: Sculptures and Box Constructions 1974-1987: A Catalogue Raisonne, London 1987; Duncan Macmillan, Symbols of Survival: the Art of Will Maclean, Edinburgh 1992.

**McLEAN, William J** **fl 1929**
Amateur Glasgow painter. Exhibited an interior at the GI, from Kirkwood St.

**MacLEAY, Kenneth RSA** **1802-1878**
Born Oban, Jly 4; died Edinburgh, 11 Nov. Painter in oil and watercolour of portraits and landscape, also portrait miniaturist. Son of Kenneth MacLeay of Glasgow and Oban(qv) and a man of considerable literary note; brother of McNeil M(qv). His mother was a Macdonald of Keppoch. Early years were spent in Crieff, entering the Trustees Academy, Edinburgh in 1822. There he obtained recognition as a miniaturist and was a founder member of the RSA in 1826, subsequently resigning but re-elected Academician 1829. Exhibited at the Institute for the Encouragement of Fine Arts in Scotland from 1822-1829 and RSA 1828-1879. In 1865 he exhibited at the RA miniature portraits of 'Prince Alfred', 'Lord George Campbell', 'Princess Arthur and Leopold', the latter being commissioned by Queen Victoria. He alone continued the tradition of William Nicholson - the small watercolour portraits of which 'Miss Helen Faucit' (RSA 1844) is a good example. His watercolour landscapes are of generally poorer quality. Queen Victoria commissioned a collection of watercolour drawings illustrative of the physiognomy, attire and ancient arms of the Highlanders. Thirty-four drawings were exhibited at 33 Old Bond St in 1869. They comprise the Royal Stuarts, Argyle men, Athole men, Breadalbane men, Camerons, Chisholms, Colquhons, Drummonds, Duff men, Farquharsons, Forbeses, Frazers, Gordons, Grahams, Grants, Harris men, Keppoch men, McDonalds, MacDougals, MacGregors, McIntoshes, McKays, McKenzies, McLeans, McLeods, MacNeills, MacNaughtens, MacNabs, McPhersons, Menzieses, Munros, Murrays, Robertson, Stewarts and Sutherland men. All were lithographed. The commission included splendid portraits of the Prince Consort and the Duke of Edinburgh as well as of some Balmoral retainers. The series was subsequently published as *Highlanders of Scotland* (1870), with hand-coloured lithographs both in book form and as frequently produced prints. Married Louise, daughter of Sir Archibald Campbell of Ardkinglas. Painted many miniatures on ivory and paper with a "soft touch rather in the manner of Thorburn(qv)...he used a sepia shading on the face and often delineated the features with a reddish colour. Frequently signed in full on the reverse 'Painted by - Kenneth MacLeay - Edinburgh', followed by a date". Said to be a fine looking man with the grand air of a Highland chieftain. 'A good draughtsman and an excellent colourist, and, handling his medium with delicate certainty, his work possesses that subtle bloom and play of tint which belonged to watercolour only, and only to watercolour when used with understanding of its limitations and possibilities. Moreover, his sense of construction was real, and gave distinction and clarity to the abstract convention which most of his portraiture is wrought...in its own way nothing could well be more delightful than the best of his work, and that portraiture of this type has not remained fashionable, or has not be revived, is a distinct loss to those who cannot afford to employ the best artists' [Brydall]. During his lifetime was known as the Raeburn of miniature painters. Represented in SNPG(5), NPG, NGS, Edinburgh City collection, Culzean Castle (NTS).
**Bibl:** AJ 1869, 97-8; Brydall 444-5; Caw 92; Foskett 394; Halsby 92,169,272; McKay 324-6; Scottish Masters series, Edinburgh 1988.

**MacLEAY, McNeil ARSA (Resigned)** **fl 1829-d1848**
Born Argyll, Dec 20; died Stirling, Jan 18. Painter in oil, watercolour and gouache. Brother of Kenneth M(qv). Prolific painter of landscapes, mostly in oil and almost exclusively Highland landscapes (though some golfing scenes), especially in Perthshire; occasional Continental scenes, particularly on the Rhine following a visit there in 1840. Elected ARSA 1836 but resigned 1848. Although a competent, colourful landscape painter, he had nothing of the facility and artistic quality of his brother, but as romanticised views of picturesque parts of the Highlands his work had a gentle charm, occasionally over-finished. In 1848 he moved from Edinburgh to Stirling, living in Lower Bridge Street, remaining there for the rest of his life. In 1992 a view of Stirling Castle in oils was sold for £30,000. Exhibited only once at the RA, 'View at the head of Loch Eil, Inverness-shire' 1839, & RSA(219). Represented in The Binns (NTS), Perth AG.
**Bibl:** Caw 92; Halsby 272.

**MacLEAY, Millicent F L** **fl 1877**
Edinburgh landscape painter in oil; exhibited RSA(1).

**MacLEAY, Miss** **fl 1824**
Little known painter, possibly sister of Kenneth(qv) and McNeil M(qv), she exhibited a flower painting at the RA in 1824.

**McLEHOSE, Mrs Agnes (Clarinda)** **1759-1841**
Born Glasgow. Moved to Edinburgh. Married James M(qv) 1776. Met and corresponded with Robert Burns. Represented in City of Edinburgh collection by two small wash drawings 'Prison Scene' and 'Family Scene'.

**McLEISH, John** **fl 1879-1904**
Edinburgh oil painter of still life, landscapes and castles. Exhibited RSA(2).

**McLELLAN, Alexander Matheson RSW RBA** **1872-1957**
Born Greenock, Jan 23; died Mar 12. Painter in oil and watercolour of portraits and figure subjects; also mural decorator and stained glass designer. Studied at the RA Schools and in Paris at the École des Beaux Arts. Worked in London, Paris, Manchester, New York, and for many years in Glasgow. His style was careful and deliberate, sometimes lacking a little in sparkle. Principal works include 'Burghers of Bruges', 'Heretics' and 'The Ancient Mariner'. Elected RBA 1910, RSW 1910. Exhibited RA(2), RSA(9), RSW(66), RBA(12), ROI(1), GI(18) & at the London Salon(5). Represented in Glasgow AG.
**Bibl:** Halsby 272.

**McLELLAN, Alexander N** **fl 1921-1934**
Glasgow watercolour painter of topographical subjects and genre. Exhibited GI(7) from 66 Norham St.

**MacLELLAN, Annie S** **fl 1887-1894**
Glasgow portrait and figure painter. Exhibited RSA(2) & GI(6) from Haghill House, Dennistoun.

**MacLELLAN, Gilleasbeag** **fl 1956-1967**
North Uist sculptor. Plaster statuettes. Moved to East Kilbride. Exhibited GI(3).

**McLELLAN, Graham L** **fl 1962**
Amateur Glasgow sculptor. Exhibited a terracotta portrait bust and a figurative group in reinforced concrete at the GI, from Hillpark.

**MacLELLAN, Janet** **fl 1936-1940**
Arbroath watercolour painter of flowers; exhibited RSA(2) & RSW(3) from Middleton, Friockheim.

**MacLELLAN, John Barland** **fl 1938-1939**
Ayrshire painter of figure studies; exhibited RSA(1) & GI(1) from 15 Parkend Cottages, Saltcoats.

**MacLELLAN, Malcolm** **1908-c1940**
Born Dunfermline, Apr 6. Landscape, flower and still life painter. Spent part of his youth in Canada before settling in Glasgow 1927. Trained Glasgow School of Art, mainly part-time. Exhibited RSA(1) & GI(25). Represented in Glasgow AG.

**McLELLAN, Miss Maureen** **fl 1945-1979**
Renfrewshire sculptress. Mainly portraits worked in plaster, terracotta and ciment fondu. Exhibited GI(20) from Whitecraigs.

**McLELLAN, Sadie (Mrs Walter Pritchard)** **1912-?**
Portrait painter and stained glass window designer. Trained Glasgow School of Art 1931-6 under Charles Baillie and at the Danish Royal Academy of Art under Prof Utzon Frank. Married Walter Pritchard(qv). Pioneered a technique using concrete and glass, a fine example of which is 'Stations of the Cross' in the church of the Sacred Heart, Cumbernauld. Lived in Canada. Exhibited RSA(2) & GI(9) from 14 Ferguson Avenue, Milngavie. Represented by a porch window in Culross Abbey, by a window 'Woman Clothed with the

Sun' in Pluscarden Abbey, Grampian and by ten windows, nine of them depicting the 'Pilgrim's Progress' in the Robin Chapel, Niddrie Mains Rd,. Edinburgh.
**Bibl:** W. Buchanan, 'The Terrible Crystal', Scott. Arts Rev, 14, 2, 1973, 22-29; Painton Cowen, Stained Glass in Britain, 1985; Gifford 538.

**McLENNAN, -** **fl c1833**
Obscure painter in oils. The Royal Caledonian Curling Club, Edinburgh has 'Curling at Curling Hall, Largs' (c1833) by an otherwise unrecorded artist.

**McLENNAN, J Forbes** **fl 1902-1905**
Painter. Exhibited RSA(2) from Edinburgh.

**MacLENNAN, Miss K C** **fl 1912**
Painter. Exhibited at the Walker Gallery, Liverpool(1) from Archnacloich, Amulree, Perthshire.

**McLENNAN, Kate** **fl 1903**
Edinburgh based marine painter; exhibited 'Sea sketch - a September squall' at the RSA from 20 Heriot Row.

**McLEOD, D** **fl 1793-1802**
Obscure miniature painter. Almost certainly Scottish. Exhibited 'A Highlander' at the RA 1793 from the Strand, London. By 1802 he was working in Edinburgh. 'Miniatures by him which I have seen were coarse, and weak in drawing' [Long].
**Bibl:** Long.

**MacLEOD, Daniel** **fl 1931**
Aberdeenshire landscape painter in watercolour. Exhibited AAS(1) from The Square, Ellon.

**MacLEOD, Duncan** **fl 1974-**
Dumbarton painter; exhibited 'A raging calm' at the RSA & GI(25) since 1974.

**MacLEOD, Miss Flora** **1907-**
Born Dalvey, Forres, Mar 24. Painter in watercolour. Educated privately and studied art under Wycliffe Eggington 1949 and Jack Merriott 1951-2. Developed from very detailed representation of flowers and landscape to a broader, simpler style, mostly landscape - the north west of Scotland, India and Cornwall. Elected BWS 1951, SSWA 1955, SWA 1960. Exhibited RSW, RI, AAS, RBA, & GI. Represented in Reading AG.

**McLEOD, Ian RSW** **1939-**
Born Port Glasgow. Painter in oil, watercolour, acrylic, pencil on canvas, panel and paper. Landscape and figurative works, generally nudes, the principal ingredient being the quality of draughtsmanship. Worked for seven years in the Burntisland Ship Building Company 1954-61 before training at Edinburgh College of Art 1961-1965 and Regent Road Institute of Further Education in Edinburgh 1965-1966, then teacher training at Moray House 1966-67. Elected RSW 1996, elected SSA 1968. Held his first one-man show in Edinburgh 1970.
**Bibl:** SAC Edinburgh 'Scatter', (Ex Cat 1971).

**McLEOD, Janette** **Cont**
Represented by a collage 'Carina' in the Lillie AG (Milngavie).

**McLEOD, John** **fl 1846-1872**
Edinburgh painter in oil; animals, especially cattle, horses and dogs, figurative subjects and landscapes, often woodland scenes. Brother of Robert M(qv). Received commissions from William Stirling, MP for Keir, also from Lord Abercrombie and the Duke of Buccleuch. He often not only signed and dated his work but even added the day and month. Exhibited RSA(150+) & GI(1).
**Bibl:** Bryan; Wingfield; Bowmill Catalogue

**McLEOD, John** **fl 1949**
Amateur Glasgow painter. Exhibited a still life at the GI from Renfrew St. Possibly the **John McLEOD** who exhibited 'The cage' at the GI in 1956 from Lanarkshire.

**MacLEOD, K H** **fl 1871**
Amateur Edinburgh sculptor; exhibited a portrait bust at the RSA.

**MacLEOD, Margaret Henderson (née Doig)** **1922-**
Born Barnet, Herts 26 Sept. Painter in oils, watercolours & gouache; also etcher & printmaker. Mainly coastal and landscape, often with buildings. Educated Elgin Academy & Edinburgh College of Art. After many years teaching in Argyll, in 1984 moved to St Andrews. Exhibited RSA, RSW, AAS.

**MacLEOD, Miss Mary W** **fl 1931-1935**
Aberdeenshire-based painter of landscape, sometimes of the US. Exhibited scenery from California & Ohio at AAS(6) from 'Craigievar', Bieldside.

**McLEOD, Robert H** **fl 1863-1871**
Edinburgh sculptor of portrait busts, medallions; also engraver. Brother of John M(qv). Exhibited RSA(5) including a study of a piper which received favourable contemporary attention 1865.

**MacLEOD, Roderick A** **fl 1961-1975**
Fife painter of topographical landscape and coastal scenes. Exhibited RSA scenes of Iona and North Queensferry, in 1961, 1973 and 1975, & GI(5) from Tayport.

**MacLEOD, Torquil James** **fl 1959-1965**
Born Inverness. Trained Grays School of Art, Aberdeen. Art master at Strathallan school. Painted mainly east coast views, especially harbour and river scenery. Moved from Inverness to Fife via Aberdeenshire and Kincardineshire. Exhibited RSA(4) & AAS from 4 Portlethen and later from Tayport.

**MacLEOD, William Douglas** **1892-1963**
Born Clarkston, Renfrewshire, Jan 1. Painter in oil and pastel of landscapes, also cartoonist and etcher. Worked in a bank 1906-1915 before serving with the Royal Artillery in WWI . After the war he turned to art, studying at Glasgow School of Art 1919-1923. Cartoonist with *Glasgow Evening News* 1920-1930. He etched views in Algeria, Spain, Italy, Belgium and elsewhere abroad, from his home at Lenzie, Dunbartonshire. Married an artist. Exhibited RSA(5), GI(60+) & L(2). Among his principal works are 'Carting Sand, Machrihanish', 'Valencia Bridge' and 'John Knox's House, Edinburgh'. Represented in Glasgow AG.

**MacLEOD, Mrs William Douglas** **fl 1930**
Amateur sculptress. Exhibited three versions of a portrait at the GI, in plaster, bronze and marble, from Kilmichael, Milngavie.

**McLERAN, James** **18th Cent**
Architect. Principal buildings are the austere Tarbat House (Ross & Cromarty) 1787, and an additional range at Dunrobin 1785, the latter commissioned by the Countess of Sutherland after her marriage to Lord Trentham, making it, as General Grant of Ballindalloch said "a convenient Lodging for all the Company you are likely to have there without any Pomposity about an antiquated Castle." (Much altered in the 1840s).
**Bibl:** Gifford, H & I, 51,462-3,572.

**McLINTOCK, John** **fl 1888**
Amateur Glasgow landscape painter of mainly local scenes. Exhibited GI(1) from 81 Eglinton Street.

**MACLISE, Daniel RA** **1806-1870**
Born Cork; died at 4 Cheyne Walk, Chelsea, Apr 25. Painter of portraits and historical scenes; illustrator. Son of a Scottish soldier and Irish mother. After a brief spell as an apprentice banker, he turned to art, training at Cork Art School during which time his study of Sir Walter Scott created a sensation. Tutorship by Dr Woodroffe in anatomy stood him in good stead for future figure drawing. Visited London in 1827, attended the RA Schools, winning gold and silver medals 1828. The former entitled him to a travelling scholarship which he declined to pursue. Returned briefly to Ireland before settling in London as a portraitist and book illustrator. Contributed eighty caricatures to *Fraser's Magazine*, each one accompanied by the humorous text of Dr Maginn. The originals, now in the British Museum, established his reputation. Began a lifetime of exhibiting at the RA in 1829. Elected ARA 1835, RA 1840. In 1840 he made a second visit to Paris. Shortly after his return he became involved in the decoration of the new Houses of Parliament. He was first assigned *The Spirit of Chivalry* and a short while later *The Spirit of Justice*. There

followed *The Meeting of Wellington and Blucher after Waterloo* and *The Death of Nelson*, the latter completed in 1864. Following the death of Sir Charles Eastlake and the refusal of Sir Edwin Landseer, Maclise was offered the RA Presidency but he too declined. He also declined a knighthood. After the death in 1865 of his sister Isabella, with whom he lived, his health steadily deteriorated. He illustrated Croker: *Fairy Legends* (1826), Barrow: *Tour Round Ireland* (1826), *Ireland its Scenery and Character* (1841), Dickens: *The Chimes: A Goblin Story* (1844), Dickens: *The Cricket on the Hearth; A Fairy Tale* (1845), Moore: *Irish Melodies* (1845), Burger: *Leonora* (1847), Moxon: *Tennyson* (1860), Tennyson: *The Princess* (1860), Tennyson: *Idylls of the King* (nd), *Story of the Norman Conquest* (1841 - forty-two drawings). Exhibited RA, RBA, BI. Represented in British Museum, National Gallery of Ireland, V & A, NPG, Ashmolean.
**Bibl:** Bryan 253-4; Chatto & Jackson, *Treatise on Wood Engraving*, 1861, p569; Houfe 219-220; Ormond: *Daniel MacLise 1806-1870*, NPG, 1972.

**MacLUCKIE, Ella R** **fl 1912-1913**
Falkirk painter of miniatures, often in pencil; exhibited RSA(1), GI(1) & L(2) from Braeside.

**McLUNDIE, R Douglas** **fl 1947-1948**
Edinburgh stained glass window designer. Associated with the Abbey Studio of glass stainers. Three windows in the Dean Parish Church, two as a war memorial and three in St Stephen's, Comely Bank. Exhibited design for a memorial window for Gillespie church, Dunfermline at RSA.
**Bibl:** Gifford 387,572.

**MacLURE, Andrew** **fl 1857-1882**
Scottish landscape painter and lithographer. At an early age went to London where he remained for the rest of his artistic career. Exhibited six works at the RA 1857-1881, all of them coastal scenes and figurative subjects. lived at 14 Ladbroke Square, from where he also exhibited at the GI. Illustrated Bushman: *Flowers and Their Poetry* (1845); *Queen Victoria in Scotland* (1842), *Highlands and Islands of the Adriatic* (1849). One of his RSA works was purchased by Sir Daniel MacNee.
**Bibl:** McKay 333; Houfe 220.

**MacLURE, D G L** **fl 1888**
Glasgow amateur landscape painter. Exhibited GI(1) from 32 Granville Street.

**McLUSKIE, Frank** **1951-**
Born Leith, Aug 23. Painter in oil, watercolour & tempera; professional restorer. Trained as a restorer, self-taught as an artist. Influenced by Annigoni. Occasional landscape but mainly tortuous figures expressing anguish, distress and mysterious foreboding. A twentieth century echo of Breughel. Since the mid-1980s, having established himself as one of Scotland's leading restorers, he has almost abandoned painting. Occasionally uses a pseudonym. Several solo exhibitions in Edinburgh. Exhibited RSA(1) 1975.

**MacLUSKY, Hector John** **1923-**
Born Glasgow, Jan 20. Painter in oil and watercolour, also illustrator. Educated Roundhay and Warwick Schools, trained Leeds College of Art 1939-40 and Slade School 1945-48. Worked for a time for television. Exhibits RA & RBA from Holly-bush House, Baines Lane, Datchworth, Herts.

**McMANUS, Harry** **1810-1878**
Edinburgh portrait painter; exhibited RSA(3).

**McMANUS, John** **fl 1973-**
Painter. An oil painting 'Old Campaigner' is in City of Edinburgh collection.

**MacMARTIN, John Rayment FRSA** **1925-**
Born Glasgow, Oct 3. Artist in oil, wood carver, sculptor in metal, model maker and product designer. Studied at Allan Glen's School, also architecture at Glasgow School of Art. Concentrates on industrial design, lecturing in the subject with Lanarkshire Education Authority. Lives in East Kilbride.

**McMASTER, Miss Elizabeth** **fl 1954-1955**
Glasgow painter of portraits and still life. Exhibited GI(2).

**MacMASTER, James RSW RBA** **1856-1913**
Glasgow painter in oil and watercolour, principally the latter; landscapes, coastal scenes and seascapes. Living at St Monance, Fife in 1890, moved to Ayr c1895. Painted mostly Highland views and coastal scenes using the 'wet' technique in watercolour in a manner reminiscent of Clouston Young(qv). Influenced by the Hague School, employed a subdued palette. Competent draughtsman but lacked inspiration. Elected RSW 1885, RBA 1890. Exhibited RA(8) 1885-1897 including 'High Tide, St Monance, Fife' 1887, 'On the Maas, Dordrecht' 1888 and 'Off to the fishing ground' 1896; also RSA(14), RSW(39), AAS, L(2), RI(3) & GI(75). Represented in Glasgow AG, Paisley AG.
**Bibl:** Halsby 161,272.

**McMEEKAN, John** **fl 1876-1897**
Glasgow landscape painter in oil; exhibited RSA(12) & GI(11).

**McMILLAN, David** **fl 1988-**
Gourock-based sculptor. Exhibited a wood carving at the GI.

**McMILLAN, Hamilton J** **fl 1875-1908**
Helensburgh landscape painter. Often woodland scenes, occasional domestic genre. Prolific, exhibited RSA(31), RHA(26), GI(31) and 'Study of a tinkers' camp' at the RA 1896. Another artist exhibited at the RSA 1886-88 and regularly at the GI throughout the 1880s from the same address in Helensburgh and listed sometimes as **Hamilton MACMILLAN Jnr** and sometimes as **Hamilton John MACMILLAN** (recorded as exhibiting GI 1887-1906). It is unclear whether the **Hamilton MACMILLAN** who exhibited at the RSA and GI from an Edinburgh address was Hamilton M junior or a third artist.

**McMILLAN, J Ross** **fl 1943-1949**
Aberdeen watercolourist. Often painted Deeside. Exhibited GI(6) from Crown St.

**MacMILLAN, John** **fl 1906-1926**
Aberdeen painter of portraits, figure studies and landscape; also some sculptures. Exhibited AAS(10) from 239 Rosemount Place.

**McMILLAN, Margaret** **fl 1956-1986**
Greenock painter of pastoral scenes, genre and still life. Moved to Gourock in later life. Exhibited RSA(9) & GI(24).

**MacMILLAN, Mary E** **fl 1901-1932**
Born South Africa. Painter and etcher; mostly portrait miniatures but also some topographical scenes. Came to Edinburgh to study under Robert McGregor(qv), also at the RSA Schools and in Paris. Remaining in the city, she exhibited at the RSA(7), AAS, L(5) & GI(6).

**MacMILLAN, Mary G** **fl 1902**
Edinburgh watercolour artist, often painted studies of children. Exhibited AAS(1) from 12 Chalmers Crescent.

**MacMILLAN, Sheila Macnab** **1928-**
Born Glasgow. Landscape painter in oils, gouache and acrylic. Geography graduate of Glasgow, studied painting under her uncle Iain Macnab(qv). Member of the Glasgow Society of Women Artists and on the council of the SSWA. Among her awards are the Lily McDougall prize (SSWA) 1984, Anne Redpath Award (SSWA) 1985, the Lauder Award of the GSWA in 1984, the Eastwood Publications award (RGI) 1993, the William Bowie award (Paisley Art Institute) 1993 and Scottish Provident Award (SAAC) 1996. Often works in Argyll, on the Moray Firth, also in Fife and France. Influenced by Joan Eardley(qv), Anne Redpath(qv), Duncan Shanks(qv) and James Robertson(qv) as shown in her flambuoyant use of colour and the quality of paint. Exhibited a lively study of *'Glasgow Docks'* at the RSA in 1989 and two further works in 1990, from 469 Kilmarnock Rd, Newlands. Has exhibited regularly at the RSA & RGI since 1976.

**McMILLAN, William CVO RA FRBS LLD** **1887-c1942**
Born Aberdeen, Aug 31. Sculptor of figure subjects and statues. Studied at Grays School of Art, Aberdeen and Royal College of Art

1908-12. Member, RA Sculpture School 1929-40. 'The Birth of Venus' was purchased by the Chantrey Bequest in 1931. Elected ARA 1925, RA 1933. Awarded the CVO. Exhibited 1917-1940 at the RA(61), RSA(15), GI(14), L(7) & ROI(2). Lived latterly at 65 Glebe Place, London SW3. Principal works include portrait statues of 'George V' (Calcutta), 'Earl Haig' (Clifton College, Bristol), 'George VI' (Carlton Gardens, London). Represented in Tate AG.

**MacMILLAN, Winifred** **fl 1880-1885**
An amateur flower painter in watercolours; exhibited RSA(3) & GI(7) from Greenock.

**McMONNIES, Frederick William** **1863-c1936**
Born Brooklyn, New York 28 Sep. Family emigrated from Galloway. Painter of mainly military subjects, also occasional portraits; sculptor. Studied at Art Students' League of New York, at the École des Beaux-Arts, Paris and in Munich under Augustus Saint-Gaudens. Received an honourable mention at the Paris Salon 1889, 1900 and 1901, and the grand prix d'honneur at the Paris Exhibition of 1900. Made a Companion of the Legion of Honour 1933. Exhibited RA(1) 1902 from Giverny, Eure, France. Distantly related to Richard Goble(qv) and possibly to **Mary Louise McMONNIES** (b. New Haven, Conn.) who studied under Bouguereau and Carolus Duran, was awarded a bronze medal at the Paris Exhibition of 1900 and who is represented in Rouen Museum.

**MacMORLAND, Arthur** **1888/9-1952**
Watercolour painter; mainly continental scenery but also the west coast especially Arran. Exhibited RA(10), RSA(20) & GI(28), first from Dunfermline, after 1935 from Troon and latterly from Fairlie, Ayrshire.

**McMORELAND, Mrs G A** **fl 1968**
Amateur Ayrshire landscape painter. Exhibited GI(2) from Ballantrae.

**MacMOR(E)LAND, Patrick John** **1741-c1810**
Born in Scotland. Miniature portrait painter on ivory and enamel. Worked in Scotland, Manchester 1774-77, London 1777, Liverpool c1781 returning to Manchester 1793. Lectured on art and taught at Manchester 1809. Painted miniatures on ivory and enamel miniatures for rings, 'stained' portrait sketches, tinted drawings of landscapes, Italian views and seascapes. Although his work varied, at its best it was of a high quality. Exhibited RA(9) 1776-1782, Society of Artists 1774-75 & Liverpool 1784-1787. Represented in V & A while the British Museum has an engraved portrait of 'Elizabeth Raffald'; a miniature of an unknown man signed 'P Mc 1803' is in SNPG.

**McMORRINE, H** **fl 1893-1897**
Painter. Exhibited GI(3) from a Glasgow address.

**McMORRING, Andrew** **fl 1969**
Glasgow painter. Exhibited RSA(2).

**McMURDO, Wendy** **1962-**
Born Edinburgh. Painter. Trained Edinburgh College of Art 1980-7 and Pratt Institute, New York 1986-7. First solo exhibition in Edinburgh 1986. Uses images taken from photography, generally of parts of the human body, reassembling and redefining them in ways which stimulate a fresh look at what appears to be natural. Deep red is a favourite colour. Part-time lecturer at the Edinburgh College of Art since 1988.
**Bibl:** Third Eye Centre, Glasgow 'Scatter', (Ex Cat 1989).

**MacMURRAY, Mrs Elizabeth Hyde** **1891-1982**
Born Banchory, Kincardineshire, Mar 2. Painted in oil, educated at the University of Aberdeen and studied art privately in London with Roy de Maistre and Martin Bloch. Wife of the philosopher Professor John Macmurray. Exhibited RSA, SSA and SSWA, from 8 Mansionhouse Rd, Edinburgh.

**McMURTRIE, Mary** **1902-2003**
Born Skene, Aberdeenshire; died Aberdeen, 1 Nov. Flower painter, illustrator, botanical author and gardener. Mother of Elspeth Haston(qv). Trained Gray's School of Art. One of the most remarkable, modest and highly regarded botanical artists Scotland has produced, she continued to paint into her 101st year when she was Britain's oldest working artist, with an emphasis on accurate physical attractiveness rather than botanical analysis. For over 40 years she ran a nursery of alpines and garden flowers at the Manse of Skene until the death of her husband in 1949, then at Springbank Lodge, Aberdeen, and finally at Balbithan House, Kintore, purchased in 1959. Collected and painted wild flowers in Kenya, Scotland and the Algarve. Member, Society of Botanical Artists. Publications include *Wild Flowers of Scotland, Plantas do Algarve* (commissioned & published by Lisbon Univ, 1991), *Wild Flowers of the Algarve* (4 vols 1981-94), *Shrubs of the Algarve* 1997, *Trees of Portugal* 1999, *Scots Roses* 1998 & *Scottish Wild Flowers* 2001. Also illustrated Roy Genders' *Growing Old Fashioned Flowers* 1975. *Old Pinks* was published posthumously in 2004. Exhibitions of her work have been held in France, at the RHS London, Portugal, Scotland & Kenya.

**McNAB, Chica (Mrs James Munro)** **1889-1960**
Born Philippines; died Glasgow. Wood engraver, painter in oil and watercolour; teacher. Sister of Iain Macnab(qv). Taught wood engraving at Glasgow School of Art 1926-7.

**McNAB, Eilidh** **fl 1946**
Fife painter; exhibited a view of 'The Marchmont bridge, Berwickshire' at the RSA, from Kirkcaldy.

**MacNAB, Mrs Fiona** **fl 1930-1940**
Glasgow sculptress. Worked in bronze, wood, lead and plaster. Mainly statuettes in wood. Exhibited GI(7) latterly from 10 Hamilton Drive.

**MacNAB, Iain PROI RE** **1890-1967**
Born Iloilo, Philippines, Oct 21; died London, Dec 24. Painter, etcher and woodcut artist of landscape and figure subjects. Son of an official of the Hong Kong & Shanghai Bank. Brother of Chica M(qv). Arrived in Scotland and resided in Kilmacolm 1894. Educated at Merchiston Castle School, Edinburgh. Trained Glasgow School of Art 1917 and Heatherley's School of Fine Art 1918. Served in France during WWI with the Argyll & Sutherland Highlanders. After being wounded was subsequently invalided out in 1916. After the war became joint Principal at Heatherley's School of Art 1919-25, then founder and first Principal of Grosvenor School of Art 1925-40, spending a year in Paris studying at the Academie Julien 1928. Elected associate of the Royal Society of Painter-Etchers & Engravers 1923, fellow 1935. Joined the RAF 1941 and invalided out 1945. He then regained possession of the premises formerly used by the Grosvenor School and in 1946 leased them to Heatherley's, becoming its Director of Studies 1946-63. In 1959 elected President of the ROI and governor of the Federation of British Artists. Chairman of the Imperial Arts League 1962. MacNab wrote & illustrated *Figure Drawing* (Studio, 1936) and *The Students' Book of Wood Engraving* (Samson Press, 1951). He also illustrated *Nicht at Eenie: The Bairn's Parnassus* (1932), Burns: *Tam O'Shanter* (1934), Whyte: *Towards a New Scotland* (1935), Browning: *Selected Poems* (1938) and Landor: *The Sculptured Garland* (1948). "The fundamental disciplines of Paleolithic art and engraving engaged his lifelong interest...the designing of books (he) dealt with as an applied art" [Garrett]. A master of bold shading and perspective and an influential teacher. Elected ARE 1923, RE 1934, ROI 1932. Exhibited RA(12), RSA(24), ROI(27), RE(40), RCA(2), GI(28) & L(11). Represented in SNGMA, Glasgow AG, V & A, Ashmolean Museum, Porsmouth AG, Manchester AG, Perth AG, Nat Gall of New Zealand (Wellington).
**Bibl:** Blond Fine Art, London, 'Iain Macnab and his circle', (Ex Cat 1979); Albert Garrett, Wood Engravings and Drawings of Iain Macnab of Barachastlain, Tunbridge Wells 1973; Herbert Grimsditch,'Iain MacNab',The Artist, April 1937; Hartley 149; Deane; Garrett 1 & 2; Horne 307-8; Peppin; Waters.

**MacNAB, Ian** **1944-**
Born Dundee, Jne. Painter in oil, with generous use of the palette knife. Landscape, especially of the Highlands often incorporating water, and townscapes, usually Glasgow where he settled in 1959. Largely self-taught, he attributes the greatest influence to Maurice Utrillo, Paul Cézanne and, in the treatment of his beloved Highlands, to Horatio McCulloch(qv). Won 2nd prize in a public painting

competition when he was fifteen. Held his first one-man show 1977 and won the Latimer Award 1980. Practises xylography (a form of woodburning or engraving). Exhibits RSA regularly since 1977, and GI, from 16 Sherwood Drive, Orchard Park, Glasgow.

**MacNAB, J** **fl 1854**
Edinburgh painter. Exhibited two river scenes, one of the Clyde and one of the Tweed, at the RSA.

**McNAB, Janice** **1964-**
Born Aberfeldy. Painter in oils. Educated Breadalbane Academy, trained Edinburgh College of Art 1982-86. Divides her time between Edinburgh and Amsterdam. Represented Perth AG.

**McNAB, John S** **fl 1876-1891**
Glasgow painter in oil and watercolour of figurative subjects and landscapes. Moved to 9 Harrington Gardens, South Kensington c1889. Exhibited RSA(3), ROI(2), L(3) & GI(4).

**MacNAB, Peter RBA** **fl 1861-d1909**
Landscape and rustic genre painter, illustrator.Started life in Glasgow before moving to London c1868. Visited Brittany and Spain. Elected RBA 1879. Contributed to *Illustrated London News* (1882-83), *Cornhill Magazine* (1884) and *The English Illustrated Magazine* (1885). Exhibited RA(17), RSA(13), RI(37), RBA(9), L(7) & GI(37), after 1881 from 219 Maida Vale.

**McNAB, William Hunter** **fl 1902-1929**
Architect and draughtsman in pen and ink as well as watercolour. Related to Mrs Fiona M(qv). Exhibited GI frequently from 121 West George St, Glasgow.

**McNAE, James** **fl 1956-1959**
Glasgow painter in watercolours. Exhibited GI(3) from Giffnock.

**MacNAIR, Charles J** **fl 1932**
Amateur painter who exhibited at the GI(1) from 112 Bath Street, Glasgow.

**McNAIR, James Herbert** **1868-1955**
Painter of portraits and figures in oil but mainly watercolour. Trained at Glasgow School of Art. Came from a Skelmorlie military family. His artistic fame is indelibly related to his association with Charles Rennie Mackintosh(qv), his wife Frances Macdonald(qv), and her sister Margaret(qv). His first training was in Rouen where he spent a year studying watercolour. On returning to Glasgow he was apprenticed to the architect, John Honeyman, but found architecture uncongenial and entered evening classes at the Glasgow School of Art. There he came under the influence of the charismatic headmaster Fra Newbery(qv) who introduced him to to the Macdonald sisters(qv). Together they developed a distinctive watercolour style (see 'The Four' and the 'Spook School', both of which McNair was a member; also cf Charles Rennie Mackintosh). It is interesting to note that in 1891 he purchased Hornel's painting 'The Brook' as a result of winning a lottery; as Billcliffe comments, one can only speculate on the effect this picture and others by Hornel and Henry had on the Spook School. In 1894 he set up as a designer and decorator but he never achieved recognition as an artist and his work was always strongly derivative from the other three members of The Four. 'He seems to have accepted wholeheartedly the mysticism and feminine naïveté of the Macdonalds' work. As Mackintosh grew away from the Four, McNair became more and more obsessed with its Celtic and medieval imagery, melancholic and sinister images gradually pervading his later work' [Billcliffe]. His Glasgow office was destroyed by fire (1897) and with it disappeared many of his drawings. Executed a number of illustrations, mainly for legends and poems including the *Legend of the Birds* and *Border Ballads.* Later in 1897 he was offered a position at Liverpool University in the School of Art and Applied Art but this ended when the School closed in 1905. After a short period teaching in that city he returned impecuniously to Glasgow. One last exhibition was held with his wife in London 1911 but its failure, together with the death of his wife in 1921, finally disillusioned him. Although he lived for another 34 years, he was a broken man and undertook no further work. Exhibited RSA(2), GI(4), L(3) & London Salon(5).
**Bibl:** Billcliffe; Burkhauser 90-2,124-4 et passim; 'J H McNair in Glasgow and Liverpool' Walker AG Annual Report 1970-1, 48-74; Halsby 173, 175-7, 179.

**MacNAIR, Mrs Mareka** **fl 1944**
Edinburgh painter; exhibited 'Study of a nude' at the RSA.

**MacNAIR, Robert** **fl 1851**
Paisley landscape artist, usually country scenes; exhibited RSA(1).

**MacNAIR, Tom M** **fl 1949-1951**
Kilmarnock sculptor of portrait busts and figures; exhibited RSA(5) & GI(5).

**McNAIRN, Arthur Stuart** **fl 1900-1902**
Edinburgh stained glass decorator; exhibited RA(1) & RSA(3) from 12 Hart Street.

**McNAIRN, Caroline** **1955-**
Born Selkirk. Painter in oil, watercolour and pastel. Daughter of John M(qv). Studied Edinburgh College of Art 1972-8. Seeks to present a complex of opposing images in a hard style intended to depict the life of a city-dweller. First solo exhibition 1980 in Edinburgh. Best work generally regarded as being in pastel. Her paintings have a strong Parisian flavour, becoming bolder in design and colour, larger in scope and size and her images more expressive.
**Bibl:** Hardie 214(illus); Hartley; 369 Gallery, Edinburgh 'Caroline McNairn' (Ex Cat 1987).

**McNAIRN, John** **1881-1946**
Edinburgh landscape painter in oil and watercolour with a bold technique. Publisher of the *Hawick News*. Exhibited RSA(4) from East Arthur Place.

**McNAIRN, John** **1910-**
Glasgow painter of landscape in oil and watercolour using bold strong colours. Father of Caroline(qv). Studied Edinburgh College of Art under DM Sutherland(qv) and William Gillies(qv); also in France at the Academie Scadinare under Othon Friesz, and in Spain 1933. After WW2 he eventually settled in Hawick. Influenced by the colourists and by contemporary French painting. Exhibited RSA(15) 1933-69 & GI(2). Represented in Glasgow AG.
**Bibl:** Halsby 272; Hardie 145,214.

**McNAMARA, James McNeil** **fl 1955-1980**
Leith painter and sculptor. Specialised in sculpture using welded brass and steel, also copper; painted topographical scenes. Exhibited RSA(8) & GI(2).

**McNAMEE, Jacqueline Karen** **1959-**
Born Belfast, June 1. Sculptor. Trained Edinburgh College of Art 1988-1992 where she won a travel award (1989), the Helen A Rose Bequest for Drawing (1992) and subsequently the Myer Oppenheim award (RSA 1994). Works mainly in stone and wood. Exhibits Royal Ulster Academy, SSA, RSA and with the Edinburgh Sculpture Workshop. Lives in Buccleugh Terrace, Edinburgh.

**McNAUGHT, James** **1914-**
Born Glasgow, Dec 28. Painter of landscape in oil and watercolour. Began as textile designer, taking evening classes at Glasgow School of Art. Father of James M(qv). Exhibited RSW & GI from 20 Ruel St.

**McNAUGHT, James Jnr** **1948-**
Glasgow painter of figure studies in oil. Studied Glasgow School of Art. Son of James M(qv). Warden of Glasgow School of Art hostel at Culzean Castle 1972-3 and resident tutor and warden in Glasgow 1973-4. Since 1976 has been assistant principal teacher at St Mungo's Academy. Although his style has changed since 1974 his work is highly characteristic. Fat ladies are portrayed in various guises often with erotic undertones and considerable humour. Influences of Picasso, Paul Klee, Lucien Freud, Juan Gris and John Byrne are apparent. In addition to his popularity in Scotland he has become widely known in Germany where his first one-man show was held in 1983, four years after his first solo exhibition in Amsterdam. Began exhibiting at the GI in 1964 when only 16 years old, also at the RSA. Many of his paintings have been chosen to illustrate books and reproduced as posters. Lives in Darvel, Ayrshire. Exhibits RSA.

**McNAUGHT, James** **1960-**
Born Glasgow 31 Jly. Painter in oil and mainly watercolour, occasional pastel, townscapes and topographical views, also teacher. Trained Glasgow School of Art 1979-1983. Although exhibited at the RSA while still at art school, after joining the staff of Glasgow Academy became so preoccupied with teaching duties that his own artistic work has taken second place.

**McNAUGHT, John** **1966-**
Born Glasgow, Dec 21. Studied at Gray's School of Art, Aberdeen 1988, graduating with an honours degree in fine art. Since then has worked as a self-employed printmaker and artist working mainly in lithography with silk screen and relief painting. His preferred subjects are narrative accounts of Scottish happenings, both historical and contemporary. Influenced by European medieval painting and by Daumier. Represented in Paisley AG, Greenock AG.

**McNAUGHT, R** **fl 1882**
Amateur Glasgow landscape painter. Exhibited GI(1) from Bath Crescent.

**MacNAUGHTAN, Alan G** **fl 1935-1940**
Glasgow watercolour painter, generally of West Highland views, also topographical works. Exhibited RSA(5), RSW(2), AAS, & GI(24).

**MacNAUGHTON, Colin** **fl 1928-1933**
Edinburgh figurative abstract painter. Studied at Edinburgh College of Art. Exhibited RSA(3) from 39 Braid Road.

**MacNAUGHTON, Iris Carruthers** **fl 1955-1966**
Edinburgh painter of flowers, still life, landscape and continental scenes. Exhibited RSA(15) & GI(3).

**MacNAUGHTON, Jessie** **fl 1900-1902**
Edinburgh painter. Exhibited RSA(2) from 3 Hope Terrace.

**MacNEE, Sir Daniel PRSA** **1806-1882**
Born Fintry, Stirlingshire; died Edinburgh, Jan 17. Portrait painter in oil and chalk. Father of Mary Lochhead(qv). Moved to Glasgow on the death of his father when he was six months old. Studied under John Knox(qv), together with Horatio MacCulloch(qv) and William Leighton Leitch(qv). Worked for Lizars, the Edinburgh engraver, while still training at Trustees Academy. In 1832 returned to Glasgow where he soon established himself as a portrait painter, becoming the leading Scottish portraitist of his day. His best work was done between 1845 and 1860. A great conversationalist, most of his life was spent among the merchants of Glasgow but on the death of Sir George Harvey in 1876 he was unanimously elected President of the RSA and moved back to Edinburgh where his success increased further. Knighted the following year. It is said that when he died 'all Edinburgh followed him to the grave'. 'While his portraits showed the true artistic taste in the arrangement and composition of colour, he never attained the highest quality of warmth or luminosity and, especially in the painting of flesh, was apt to fall into a coldish, chalkiness...No-one suffered from constraint or tedium in sitting for his portrait to MacNee'. Brydall believed that he used too much of 'fugitive kind of Naples yellow' in his lighter flesh tints. In 1855 he received a gold medal at the Paris International Exhibition for his portrait of the 'Rev Dr Ralph Wardlaw', now in Glasgow AG. Member of the Dilettante Society(qv) and of the West of Scotland Academy, of which he became President 1866. Awarded an honorary doctorate by the Universities of Glasgow and Edinburgh; appointed a Deputy Lieutenant of the County of the City of Edinburgh. Raeburn and Andrew Geddes were significant influences. At his most appealing when painting the portrait of an artist friend, such as 'Horatio MacCulloch'. He and MacCulloch spent some time together in Ayrshire where as young men they had painted the lids of snuff boxes and drawn coloured plates for W H Lizars. Exhibited RA(100) 1832-1881, including many famous contemporary figures, 15 works at the Institute for the Encouragement of the Fine Arts in Scotland 1827-29; also RSA(313) - almost more than any other artist - as well as occasionally at the GI & AAS. Represented in NGS, SNPG(14), Glasgow AG, Paisley AG, Edinburgh City collection.
**Bibl:** Armstrong 46-7, 177-8, 203, 474, 487; Bryan; Brydall 445-448; Irwin 222, 243, 308, 310-11, 315, 354, 418n; McKay 129, 134-8; Macmillan [SA] 164,226,229; Portfolio 1887, 139.

**McNEE, John** **fl 1902**
Exhibited 'Holyrood Abbey - west front' at the RSA from 33 Montpelier Park, Edinburgh.

**MacNEE, Margaret B** **fl 1901**
Paisley flower painter. Exhibited GI(1) from 20 Caledonia Street.

**MacNEE, Maxwell** **fl 1861-1871**
Edinburgh landscape painter in oil; frequently exhibited RSA (27) including a view of 'Deeside, near Ballater' 1868.

**MacNEE, Patricia** **fl 1886**
Edinburgh portrait painter in oil. Wife of Thomas Wiseman M(qv). Exhibited RSA(1).

**MacNEE, Robert Russell GI** **1880-1952**
Born Milngavie, Dumbartonshire. Painter in oil and watercolour of landscapes and figures. Enjoyed particularly the rural farm scenes of Perthshire and the east coast. Trained at Glasgow School of Art, moving to Edinburgh, Dundee then c1923 to Dunkeld, settling finally in Barnhill, Angus. He enjoyed bright, sunlit scenes, often in dappled sunlight coming through trees falling on farm buildings with usually a working horse and foraging poultry. The bright, pastoral pleasures of the scene made his work more popular among the public than among critics. Signed his work 'R Russell MacNee'. Exhibited RA(3), RSA(35), RSW(3), AAS, GI(115) & Paris Salon. Represented in Kirkcaldy AG, Culzean Castle (NTS).
**Bibl:** Caw 392; Halsby 272.

**MacNEE, Thomas Wiseman** **fl 1886-1894**
Edinburgh sculptor and portrait medallionist. Married to Patricia M(qv). Exhibited RSA(3), including a portrait of 'Clark Stanton', RSA & GI(2).

**McNEE, William Cairns** **fl 1953**
Dundee painter of local landscapes. Exhibited RSA(1).

**MacNEIL, Alexander** **fl 1913-d1950**
Glasgow engraver & drypoint etcher. Exhib RSA(14), RSW(2), L(1) & GI(50). There are in Glasgow AG no fewer than 57 works by him.

**McNEIL, Andrew** **fl c1920-c1930**
Glasgow artist. Painted views of Glasgow, Edinburgh and other towns in oil, watercolour and pen and ink.
**Bibl:** Halsby 272.

**McNEIL, D** **fl 1967**
Edinburgh sculptor; exhibited a portrait head at the RSA.

**McNEIL, George** **fl 1928**
Paisley-based amateur painter; exhibited GI(1) from 5 Arthur Street.

**McNEIL, Norman S** **fl 1934-d.c1970**
Army officer and amateur painter. Portraits, flowers, genre and landscape. Trained Glasgow School of Art. Exhibited RSA(12) and GI(10) from 56 Newark Drive, Pollockshields, Glasgow, then from 2nd Batt Highland Regt 1942, then back to Newark Drive; died Tighnabruach.

**McNEILL, Mrs A** **fl 1867**
Amateur Oban landscape painter in oil; exhibited RSA(2).

**MacNEILL, Alyson** **1961-**
Versatile artist: works in watercolour, gouache; also wood engraver, linocuts & book illustrator. Trained Duncan of Jordanstone College of Art. Won Josef Sekalski prize for printmaking. Post-graduate year at Glasgow School of Art studying design. Provided illustrations for Eliot: *The Mill on the Floss* (1986), Mackay: *The Song of the Forest* (1986), *Twenty-Three Wood Engravings from Colin Mackay's "The Song of the Forest"* (1987), *Benedicite Omnia Opera* (1987), *A Second Book of Scottish Poetry*.
**Bibl:** Folio 40; Horne 309; Linda Saunders: "Two Women Wood Engravers in Fife", *The Green Book*,2, no.4 (1986),pp37-43.

**McNEILL, Miss Catriona** **fl 1950**
Amateur Glasgow sculptress. Exhibited a negro head in plaster at the GI, from Randolph Rd.

**McNEILL, Duncan** **fl 1963-1969**
Dollar sculptor. Moved to Edinburgh. Exhibited portrait heads RSA & GI(8), including a posthumous portrait of 'Dr Rudolph Steiner'.

**McNEILL, Mrs Jean Ross** **fl 1950**
Amateur Glasgow painter. Exhibited 'The shore road' at the GI from Fifth Ave.

**McNEILL, Robert C** **fl 1939-1948**
Glasgow sculptor usually portrait studies, often of Maya people. Exhibited RSA(11) & GI(17), from 875 Mosspark Drive, Cardonald.

**McNEISH, Alexander** **1932-**
Born Bo'ness. Apprenticed in coachpainting and lettering. Trained Edinburgh College of Art 1953-57, participating in group exhibitions in Edinburgh 1958 and 1960, also in Newcastle in 1959, York in 1959, Salzburg in 1960 and Vienna in 1960. Principal lecturer in Painting, Exeter College of Art. Included in Four Young Scottish Painters' Exhibition, SAC 1960-61. Represented in Edinburgh City collection(2).
**Bibl:** SAC, 'Painters in Parallel', (Ex Cat 1978).

**McNICOL, Bessie (Mrs Alexander Frew)** **1869-1904**
Born Glasgow, Jly 15; died Glasgow, Jne 4. Painter of portraits, genre and landscape in oil and watercolour. Elder of twin daughters of a schoolmaster. One of the most important Glasgow painters of her time, perhaps the foremost lady painter Scotland has produced. Trained Glasgow School of Art 1887-92 and in Paris at the Academie Colarossi. In 1896 opened her first studio at 175 St. Vincent St. The same year visited Kircudbright where she met Hornel(qv), William McGeorge(qv) and William Mouncey(qv). Among other Scottish artists of the period with whom she was friendly were David Gauld(qv), John Keppie(qv) and George Henry(qv). An early portrait of Hornel, exhibited at the GI in 1897, now adorns the Hornel museum in Kircudbright. An early 'Self-portrait' c 1894, now in Glasgow AG, suggests the stuffed heaviness of the hay fever sufferer which in summer she was. Although primarily an oil painter of sensitive portraits, she also executed a number of delicate maternal scenes in watercolour. Her only solo exhibition was held at Stephen Gooden's Art Rooms 1899 - the year she married Alexander Frew(qv). Together they acquired D.Y.Cameron's former home, encompassing a large studio, in Hillhead. The influence of Hornel remained with her and can be seen in many of her works as, less frequently, is the style of Bastien-Lepage. With William Arthur Gibson(qv) and her husband, she was the principal exhibitor at the first show of the Glasgow Society of Artists 1902. Their fourth exhibition was held at the Dore gallery in London when her work was shown posthumously. Died tragically in childbirth at the end of the previous year. Exhibited 'A Fifeshire interior' at the RA (1893) from 175 St Vincent St, Glasgow; at the Women's International Exhibition, London in 1900 (illus in *The Studio,* Vol XX), and RSA(5), RSW(1), GI(22) & L(4). Represented in Aberdeen AG, Glasgow AG, City of Edinburgh collection, Hornel Museum (Kircudbright).
**Bibl:** Caw 436-7; Halsby 272; Scottish Art & Letters 1904, vol III, no 3, 198; Ailsa Tanner in Burkhauser, 193-199, 227-232 et passim.

**NcNICOL, Ian** **fl 1928-1938**
Best known as the owner of the leading Scottish gallery of his time with an unerring eye for quality and rising talent. Also an accomplished watercolourist using light colours and touch principally in landscapes. Son of John McNicol(qv). Exhibited RSA(1) 1935; also RSW(2) & GI(16) from his home in Kilmarnock, Ayrshire.
**Bibl:** Halsby 272.

**McNICOL, Ian Cameron** **1965-**
Born Paisley. Architect, artist and printmaker. Trained Glasgow College of Building 1987-90, Mackintosh School of Architecture 1983-86. Buildings and urban topography are depicted in a variety of mediums & techniques. Exhibited Portland, Oregon (winning the Purchase Prize 1997), Finland, RSA, RGI.

**McNICOL, John** **1862-c1940**
Born Partick, Glasgow. Landscape painter in oil and watercolour; also master-gilder. Father of Ian McNicol(qv). Lived and worked in Ayrshire. Exhibited watercolours GI(34) & L(3).
**Bibl:** Halsby 272.

**McNICOL, Robert A** **fl 1930**
Kilmarnock amateur landscape painter; often painted on Arran. Exhibited GI(8) from 8 Dunure Drive, then Walker Ave.

**McNICOL, Rona Munro** **fl 1986**
Sculptor. Exhibited 'Flight of imagination' at the RSA when a member of the Scottish Sculpture workshop in Lumsden, Aberdeenshire.

**McNIE, Jean Cooper Dods** **fl 1965**
Edinburgh sculptress. Exhibited 'Teenagers singing' at the RSA; also GI(1).

**MacNIVEN, John RSW** **fl 1886-d1895**
Born Glasgow. Painter and sculptor. Coastal and fishing scenes in the manner of Clouston Young(qv) and James McMaster(qv). Worked with Glasgow Corporation's Water Department before turning to full-time art in oil and watercolour; also portrait sculptures. Self-taught. One of many artists who, in the latter part of the 19th century, was working on Arran. His first exhibit at the RSA was an Arran landscape. Elected RSW 1891. An oil painting 'Clutha at Whiteinch', 1887 was included in 'The Artist & the Clyde' exhibition, Helensburgh 1958. (A clutha being a river bus within Glasgow harbour). Exhibited RA(4), RSA(5), RSW(4) & GI(35).
**Bibl:** Halsby 272.

**McNIVEN, Colonel Thomas William Ogilvie** **fl 1846-1855**
Serving officer and painter of military and historical subjects. Exhibited RSA(11) including 'The Attack of the light French Cavalry at the Battle of Orthez' (1850) from a Musselburgh address.

**McNULTY, James** **fl 1981-1984**
Kinross painter of rustic scenes. Exhibited RSA(5).

**MacPHAIL, Alex** **fl 1896**
Amateur watercolourist; exhibited RSW(1) from 13 Ann Street, Hillhead, Glasgow.

**McPHAIL, John** **fl 1881**
Amateur painter; exhibited GI(1) from 9 West Princes St, Glasgow.

**McPHAIL, N** **fl 1873-1878**
Glasgow sculptor. Mainly medallion portraits. Exhibited GI(5) from Buchanan St.

**McPHAIL, Rodger** **c1955-**
English wildlife and sporting artist and illustrator; occasional cartoons. Established as one of Europe's leading painters of country pursuits. A keen angler, shot, stalker, and naturalist, with a lovely strain of droll humour. A remarkable facility for capturing a country scene accurately, with unusual speed, and with a sensitive eye for colour and composition. Much of his work is centred upon the hills and glens of Scotland. Holds highly successful solo exhibitions in London. Travels widely in Europe, Africa and North America. Illustrated Willock: *The ABC of Shooting* 1978; Lord Home: *Border Reflections* 1979; Mursell: *Come Dawn, Come Dusk* 1982; Wodehouse: *Sir Agrivane* 1984; Brian Martin: *Sporting Birds of the British Isles* 1984; *Open Season: An Artist's Sporting Year* 1986; Bold et al: *Scottish Poetry Book* 1987; *Jagd rund um's Jahr* 1987; Tryon: *The Quiet Waters By* 1988; Dennis: *How to Cook Pheasant* 1988; Hayes: *How to Cook Trout* 1989; *Fishing Season* 1990; Curtis et al: *The* Best *of My Fun* 1991; McKelvie: *A Country Naturalist's Year* 1993; Willock: *The New ABCs of Shooting* 1994; *A Hill Farmer's Year* 1995; Rodger McPhail: *Rodger McPhail; Artist, Naturalist, Sportsman* 2002. Undertakes commissions from collectors and organisations worldwide including Kenya, Spain, Norway, Britain, and the United States. Fine examples may be seen in the House of Bruar, Perthshire.

**MacPHAIL, Tom A** **fl 1964**
Aberdeenshire textile designer of 16 Gladstone Terrace, Turriff; exhibited AAS.

**McPHEE, John** **fl 1976-1986**
Aberdeen painter of subject paintings. In 1979 he moved to Oban. Exhibited RSA(7).

**MACPHERSON, A J** **fl c1860**
Printmaker. A coloured lithograph after J W McLea(qv) is in the collection of the City of Edinburgh.

**MacPHERSON, Aeneas** **fl c1785-1790**
Little is known of this portraitist and engraver beyond the fact that in 1789 he published a collection of engravings entitled *Edina Delineata;* or 'picturesque perspective views of the public and remarkable buildings, etc. in the City of Edinburgh and its environs. With an account, descriptive and historic, accompanying each view. Designed, drawn, engraved and written by Aeneas MacPherson'. These engravings, competent but unexciting, appeared in four parts, each with four views. They are: 'Holyrood Palace - St Anthony's Chapel - The North Bridge' (Part 1); 'St Roque's Chapel - Hume's Tomb Chapel - The Castle - St Cuthbert's Church' (Part 2); 'Ruins of Holyrood Chapel - The New Bridewell - North-west View of Heriot's Hospital - High Street from the Tron Church' (Part 3); 'St George's Chapel - Episcopal Chapel, Cowgate - St Andrew's Church - Trinity College Church - Royal Infirmary and Royal Exchange - Parliament House' (Part 4). In 1799 he was a candidate for membership of the Trustees Academy when living at 7 South Richmond St.
**Bibl:** Bushnell.

**MacPHERSON, Alexander VPRSW** **1904-1970**
Painter, mainly in watercolour of landscapes. Studied Glasgow School of Art. Lived in Paisley for many years before spending a short spell, c1934, in Wembley and then returning to Glasgow in 1935. Worked mainly on the west coast, often on Arran & Mull, also frequently in France. His watercolours are solidly composed with strong outlines in charcoal and sometimes pencil. Elected RSW in 1932, becoming vice-president. Exhibited RSA(89), RSW(37), RA(1), GI annually 1926-1970, AAS & L(1). Represented in Glasgow AG, Paisley AG, City of Edinburgh collection.
**Bibl:** Halsby 229,272.

**MacPHERSON, Annie W** **fl 1894**
Fife amateur painter of Towershiel, Lenzie. Exhibited GI(1).

**MacPHERSON, Archibald** **fl 1876-1906**
Edinburgh architect of mainly R.C. church interiors and private houses. Exhibited at the RSA(13) including marble and bronze decoration in the Church of the Sacred Heart, Edinburgh & GI(6).
**Bibl:** Gifford 220,256,382,426,504,594,644.

**MacPHERSON, Miss Barbara H** **fl 1900s**
Watercolour painter of landscapes. Lived in London for many years before returning north to Glasgow in c1906. Exhibited RSA(3), RBA(2), RI(5), L(2) & GI(2).

**MacPHERSON, Betty F** **fl 1906**
Amateur Glasgow draughtswoman of religious works. Exhibited GI(2) from Gt. Western Rd.

**MacPHERSON, Constance M** **fl 1898**
Inverness-shire flower painter of Invergoyle. Lived and worked at Streatham in London.

**McPHERSON, D Reid** **fl 1895**
Glasgow landscape painter. Exhibited GI(1) from 57 Dalhousie St.

**MacPHERSON, Douglas** **1871-?**
Born Aberidge, Essex. Son of John M(qv) and, like his father, an illustrator. Trained Westminster School of Art. On the staff of the *Daily Graphic* and *The Graphic* 1890-1913 and *The Sphere* from 1913, in which capacity he covered the Spanish-American War of 1898, the St Petersburg Revolt of 1905 and the Assassination of Don Carlos in 1908. He served with the RNVR during WW1 and represented *The Sphere* at the opening and investigation of Tutankhamun's Tomb 1923-24. Illustrated King George V's Coronation for the *Daily Mail* and during WW2 acted as a war artist for *The Sphere*, *Daily Telegraph* and *Daily Mail*. Exhibited RA 1907.
**Bibl:** Halsby 272; Houfe 220.

**MacPHERSON, Miss E** **fl 1911-1913**
Elgin portrait miniaturist. Exhibited L(5) & GI(2) from 23 High St.

**MacPHERSON, George Alexander ARSA** **1935-**
Born Invershin, Sutherland. Abstract and landscape painter; oil and pastel. Studied Edinburgh College of Art 1954-8 followed by a postgraduate year. In 1958 won the Stuart Prize (RSA) and in 1966 the Latimer & Guthrie Awards of the RSA. First one-man exhibition in Edinburgh 1957. Taught Edinburgh College of Art. In 1989 won the Borders' Biennial Art competition with 'Reivers' Song and *Eildon Drum*. Won Highland Society of London prize 1995 and the Guthrie Award 1990. Elected ARSA 1987. Regular exhibitor RSA since 1961 from 21 West Maitland St, Edinburgh; also GI(2). Represented in City of Edinburgh collection.

**MacPHERSON, Guiseppe (or James or Joseph)** **1726-c1779**
Born Florence, Mar 19. Son of Donald Macpherson, running footman to the Duke of Gordon. One of the great Scottish miniaturists who unfortunately never worked in Scotland. Unravelling all available information it is almost certain that this artist, known variously as Guiseppe, James or Joseph Macpherson, was one and the same. In Rome he studied under Pompeo Batoni and by the 1750s was working in London, Milan and Paris, although by the early 1760s he had returned to Florence. He executed many life-size portrait groups in oil, generally commissioned by English visiting aristocrats. His best miniatures were painted in an oval; a writer observed in 1776 that Macpherson was "almost the only painter in Europe who possesses this art to perfection, as may be seen in the many works in this medium produced by his hand". One patron was the 3rd Earl of Cowper, a connoisseur who had settled in Florence in the 1760s. In 1767 the Earl loaned 60 miniature copies by the artist of the Uffizi self-portraits to the Florentine Academy. These were subsequently presented to George III and now form part of the Royal Collection. Foskett records that in 1778 Macpherson was persuaded to present his own self-portrait, painted in miniature on goatskin, to the Grand Duke of Tuscany for inclusion among those by famous painters in the collection. The Director of the Grand Ducal gallery recommended its acceptance as "it would do honour to Florence to enrich the collection with a work which shows that we still have some men of true merit". For this Macpherson was awarded a gold medal. The work may still be seen in the Uffizi Gallery and a canvas replica, by the artist, hangs in Apsley House, London, having been exhibited at the RA in 1960. Copies after Uffizi artists are now in Windsor. An enamel miniature of an unknown lady signed 'Macpherson 1741', formerly in the Nachemsohn Collection, is now in Dublin AG. Long found it reminiscent of the manner of Allan Ramsay. According to Clouzot the artist sometimes signed his work 'Macson'. A fine enamel portrait of an unknown lady, c1740, in the V & A is signed 'Macpherson Pinx'. Schidlof quotes Zania that Macpherson's christian name was Joseph, hence part of the confusion.
**Bibl:** Clouzot; J Fleming, Conn, Nov 1959, 166-7; Irwin 108; Long 285; M Webster 'A Scottish Miniaturist in Florence', Country Life Jne 8, 1972, 1445-6.

**McPHERSON, Henry** **fl 1913-1923**
Glasgow amateur painter of narrative subjects; exhibited GI(3) from 57 Rolland Street, Maryhill.

**MacPHERSON, Mrs J L** **fl 1917**
Amateur watercolourist; exhibited RSW(1) from Barrogill, Bothwell, Lanarks.

**MacPHERSON, James** **fl 1881**
St. Andrews painter in oil of landscapes, especially castles; exhibited RSA(1).

**MacPHERSON, John** **fl 1858-1884**
Watercolour landscape painter, also commercial artist and illustrator. Father of Douglas M(qv). Lived in St Andrews and Edinburgh before settling in London 1882. He worked in a dense manner but with contrasting freedom in his skies. His son was also a press illustrator. Collaborated with Otto Leyde(qv) with whom he shared a studio. Exhibited landscapes and coastal scenes at the RSA(34), RBA(1), RHA(1), GI(6) & RI(1).
**Bibl:** Halsby 272.

**MacPHERSON, Margaret Campbell** **fl 1885-1904**
Edinburgh painter in oils and pastels of portraits, figures, landscapes and coastal scenes and still-life. Lived for some years in St John's,

Newfoundland from where she first exhibited, before moving to Edinburgh in 1886 and to Paris at the turn of the century. Exhibited 'Daydreams' at the RA, RSA(33), AAS(2), GI(17) & L(5), latterly from 6 Shandwick Place.

**MacPHERSON, Neil** **fl 1983-**
Caithness painter; moved c1986 to Ayrshire. An award winner at the Young Artists '86 exhibition organised by the RSA. Exhibited local scenes at the RSA. Developed an interest in depicting people in their encompassing physical environment, including some of the animals that surround them. Exhibited RSA & AAS from Dalehornie Farm, Maybole. Represented in Glasgow AG, SAC.

**MacPHERSON, Nora G** **fl 1883**
Edinburgh flower painter; exhibited RSA(1) from 31 Melville Street.

**MacPHERSON, Robert** **fl 1863-d 1873**
Edinburgh portrait painter in oil; exhibited RSA(2). A work after this artist is in SNPG.

**McPHERSON, Robert Turnbull** **fl 1835-1839**
Edinburgh portrait painter, often in crayons and generally with sitters accompanied by their pets. In 1837, for example, exhibited 'William Stewart of Glenmoriston with favourite dogs' at the RSA. Exhibited RSA(15).

**McPHERSON, William** **1905-?**
Born Glasgow, 7 May. Landscape and portrait painter, shipping scenes - some continental - also decorative figure compositions. Trained Glasgow School of Art winning a prize for landscape. Exhibited RA(3) 1925-1951, RSA(16), RSW(3) & GI annually 1927-1954.

**MacQUARRIE, Donald** **fl 1896-1932**
Greenock landscape painter in oil and watercolour who moved to Maybole in 1903 and then to Gladsmuir, Kilmacolm c1920. Exhibited RSA(2), GI(8), RSW(1), AAS & L(2).

**MacQUEEN, Alison** **fl 1917-1919**
Amateur watercolourist; exhibited RSW(2) from 2 Danube Street, Edinburgh.

**MacQUEEN, Charles T K RSW** **fl 1967-**
Glasgow painter in oil and watercolour. Moved to Falkirk and Dunfermline. Exhibits RSA regularly since 1970, & GI since 1967, latterly from 3 Park Place, Dunfermline.

**McQUEEN, Isabella** **fl 1953-1954**
Edinburgh designer of cheerful stained glass windows. Exhibited RSA(2).

**MacQUEEN, Miss Jane Una** **fl 1905-1938**
Born Aberdeen. Prolific painter of local landscapes, flowers and still life. Landscape painter who lived for many years at West Cults and then at Fae-me-Well, Cothal, Aberdeenshire. Exhibited 'Early spring on the Don' at the RSA & regularly at the AAS.

**MacQUEEN, Jessie Kennedy** **fl 1921**
Amateur Banff animal painter. Exhibited AAS(1) from Fife Cottage, Macduff.

**MacRAE, Ebeneezer James** **1881-1951**
Edinburgh architect and occasional painter of topographical subjects on the continent, around London and Edinburgh. City Architect for many years. Primarily responsible for the vestibule and stair-hall of the City Chambers (1936-8); also Greyfriars Hotel (1930) and the Curator's House, Lauriston Castle (1927). Exhibited RSA(12).
**Bibl:** Gifford, see index.

**MacRAE, Mrs Eleanor M** **fl 1943**
Aberdeen painter, probably an amateur. Exhibited a farmyard scene at the RSA.

**MacRAE, Eliza** **fl 1879**
Glasgow amateur flower painter. Exhibited GI, from Wilson St.

**MacRAE, Grace H** **fl 1891-1898**
Amateur Edinburgh painter in watercolours of portrait medallion, land and seascapes. Probably the wife of John M(qv) since in 1891 her RSA exhibit was a medallion of 'John Macrae Esq'. Exhibited RSA(2), RI(1), GI(1) & AAS(1).

**MacRAE, Iain** **fl 1956**
Glasgow amateur portrait painter. Exhibited GI(1) from 11 Ashcroft Drive.

**MacRAE, John** **fl 1873-1883**
Edinburgh painter in oil and watercolour of landscapes and coastal scenes. Possibly related to Grace M(qv). Exhibited RSA(8).

**MacRAE, L C** **fl 1894-1899**
Edinburgh landscape and figure painter, also domestic animals, flowers and still-life. worked mainly in oil. Exhibited RA(2), RSA(9), AAS(8), ROI(4), RI(1) & GI(10) from 6, Chalmers Crescent.

**MacRAE, Mary** **fl 1900**
Amateur Dundee watercolourist. Exhibited 'Temple grounds, Kyoto' at the GI, from Balruddery.

**McRAEBURN, Agnes** **fl 1901**
Amateur Glasgow painter; exhibited RSA(1) from 1 Hillhead Street.

**MacREDIE, Mrs G Cunningham** **fl 1873**
Edinburgh landscape painter in oil; exhibited 'Winter' at the RSA.

**MacRITCHIE, Alexina** **fl 1885-1932**
Painter in oil of portraits and domestic genre. Studied at the Slade and Juliens in Paris. Moved to Edinburgh in the 1880's and 1890's after interludes in Paris and London where she finally settled. Exhibited RA(3), RSA(12), GI(5) & L(4).

**MacROBBIE, Ella Macfarlane** **fl 1900-1935**
Aberdeenshire watercolour painter of country and woodland scenes, local landscape. After a spell at the Free Church Manse, Premnay moved to Heathville, Culter. Regular exhibitor at the AAS during the above years.

**McROBBIE, Ian** **fl 1948**
Edinburgh watercolourist. Exhibited GI(1) from Belford Ave.

**McROBERTS, Edward C** **fl 1899-1953**
Glasgow sculptor of portrait busts and heads, usually in plaster. Exhibited GI(11) formerly from Pollockshields, and latterly from Dumbreck.

**McSHANNON, Miss A** **fl 1894**
Amateur painter; exhibited once at the Walker Gallery, Liverpool from 7 Scot Street, off Sauchiehall Street, Glasgow.

**McSKIMMING, Elizabeth E** **fl 1915**
Amateur Glasgow painter; exhibited GI(1) from 12 Campden Drive, Bearsden.

**MacSYMON, John** **1876-?**
Born Greenock. Painter and black and white artist and critic. Exhibited RSA 1911-1929, RCA(2) & L(14), latterly from Birkenhead.

**McTAGGART, Betty** **1895-1986**
Painter in oils and watercolour; mainly still life. Daughter of William McTaggart(qv) by his second wife Marjory, and aunt of Joseph McTaggart(qv). Exhibited RSW(2) & GI(1) from Dean Park, Bonnyrigg.
**Bibl:** Fine Art Society,'The McTaggarts', Edinburgh Ex cat,1974.

**McTAGGART, Joseph** **1947-**
Born near Carrbridge, Inverness-shire. Sculptor. Grandson of William M(qv), he was educated at Grantown GS and Banff Academy before attending Edinburgh College of Art 1966-72 where he specialised in sculpture. Concentrates on three-dimensional carvings and sculptures of birds and animals with foliage characteristic of their native woods. Has held a number of solo exhibitions in Scotland and also in continental Europe. In 1990 he became interested in carved furniture, larger wooden sculptures and other architectural works

developing a style which incorporates delicate carving into strong massive basic forms. Lives near Aberfeldy.

**McTAGGART, William RSA RSW** **1835-1910**
Born Aros, nr Campbeltown, Argyll; died Dean Park, Broomieknowe, Midlothian, Apr 2. Son of a crofting family. As a boy was first apprenticed to a chemist in Campbeltown but left home at 16 and went to Edinburgh. His childhood days on the Mull of Kintyre induced a love of the sea that stayed with him for the rest of his life. In Edinburgh he trained at the Trustees Academy under Scott Lauder(qv) 1852-1859. Among his contemporaries were Hugh Cameron(qv), George Chalmers(qv), Tom Graham(qv) and John Pettie(qv). Began exhibiting at the age of 18 and won several prizes as a student, obtaining portrait commissions in his early days. His first exhibits were all portraits. By 1857 he decided to concentrate entirely on landscapes and figure subjects limiting himself to portraits, mainly of children, only when he badly needed money. A pre-Raphaelite approach was evident in his early landscapes, it is said he spent three months painting one particular view on Kintyre. These early works were predominantly anecdotal, a feature that gradually disappeared as he developed. After his marriage in 1863 he settled in Fairlie, near Largs. During the winter he worked on large oils, spending the summer sketching on the coast. His 'Grandmother Knitting' 1864, now in Glasgow AG, and 'Spring' (1864, NGS) are perhaps his most important works from this period. By 1860 his interest in impression and mood was overtaking his interest in detail, and his lack of 'finish' was beginning to find criticism. His diploma work illustrating a scene from Tennyson's *Dora* 1868/9 illustrates this transition while further development can be seen in 'On the White Sands' painted two years later, now in Broughty Ferry AG. In 1868 he painted on Loch Fyne with Colin Hunter(qv). Irwin has commented that the fluency of his swiftly executed watercolours influenced the loosening of his handling of oil paint, a new found freedom which burst into a more turbulent, aggressive view of nature in the 1880s. About this time he began to use rougher canvasses with more dramatic compositions. In 1883 he introduced the idea of completing a work in only one session, thus his 'Carradale' 1883, now in Kirkcaldy AG. On this was based a larger stormy canvas (1890) purchased by Andrew Carnegie. From 1876 he painted 'On the Atlantic Shore' at Machrihanish and after 1889 moved from Edinburgh to Broomieknowe, Midlothian where he spent the rest of his life, although continuing to regularly visit the coast. In later work there is a weakness in his handling of form, especially human figures. The broken colour surfaces of the children dissolve into their surroundings and whilst this is all part of portraying the unity of man with nature, it is never entirely successful and the great praise lavished upon his work during his lifetime seems now perhaps a little exaggerated. Nevertheless his voyage into impressionism certainly hastened the development of Scottish art in this direction and helped delineate the battle lines for the surging Glasgow School. Hardie believes that even Turner did not excel McTaggart in the latter's knowledge of swift movement, 'the scudding foam and spray, the changing light and colour of the sea'. For his main biographer and protagonist Caw, he painted the sea 'with a passion and insight, a profound knowledge of Nature and an assured mastery of expression, which makes him incomparable. Other men paint the form and colour of the sea; he expresses its apparent life', and, in the *Art Journal,* 'a picture such as 'Storm', surely one of the most wonderful renderings of the tumultuous agitation of a great elemental disturbance ever painted...in variety, power, and originality he is the most imposing figure in Scottish art today, and one of the few great artists of our time'. McTaggart's work remains of seminal importance, not only because of its influence upon succeeding generations of Scottish artists, but also because of its unique qualities. Elected ARSA 1859, RSA 1870. 'Harvest Moon' (1899) was purchased by the Chantrey Bequest. Friendship with Sam Bough was instrumental in arousing an interest in watercolours and in 1878 he was elected President of the newly formed Society of Scottish Watercolour Painters. Grandfather of William MacTaggart(qv). Exhibited 107 works at the RSA between 1855 and 1911, eight works at the RA 1866-1875, and RHA, RSW, GI(100+), AAS(1), & L(10). Represented in the Tate AG, NGS, SNPG ('Self-portrait'), Aberdeen AG, Broughty Ferry AG, Glasgow AG, Kirkcaldy AG, Paisley AG, Perth AG, RSA, Edinburgh City collection(6), Brodie Castle (NTS), Sydney AG (Australia), Nat Gall of Canada (Ottawa).
**Bibl:** AJ 1894, 243-6; Burlington Magazine 32 (1918) 227ff; Caw, William McTaggart.A Biography and an Appreciation, Glasgow 1917; Caw 248-254 et al; Conn 50 (1918), 1060ff; P M Dott, Notes technical and explanatory on the Art of William McTaggart', Edinburgh 1901; Lindsay Errington, 'William McTaggart', NGS 1989; Fincham, William McTaggart,1935; Halsby 117-120; Hardie ch v; Hardie III 195-8 (pl 230); Irwin 365-371; Macmillan [SA] 231-3,240-253 et passim; National Gallery of NGS and Tate Galleries, 'Centenary Exhibition of Paintings by William McTaggart', (Ex Cat 1935; Studio XLVII, 1909, 83-93.

**MacTAGGART, Sir William PPRSA RA FRSE HonRSW LLD** **1903-1981**
Born Loanhead, Midlothian, May 15. Painter in oil and occasional watercolour of landscape and still-life. Son of Hugh Holmes M, marine engineer and Roberta Little; grandson of William M(qv). Educated privately, trained Edinburgh College of Art, later in France and Italy. Taught and influenced by D M Sutherland(qv), Henry Lintott(qv) and Adam Bruce Thomson(qv). Although he did not attend Lhôte's Academy, he learned of its teaching from William Crozier. His first exhibit at the RSA was in 1921 and in 1922 he was elected SSA and became a founder member of the 1922 Group. The following year he paid the first of many annual visits to France and in 1924 held his first one-man show at Cannes. Elected member of the Society of Eight (1927) and two years later held his first one-man show, in Edinburgh. Elected President, SSA 1933. Became a part-time member of staff, Edinburgh College of Art. In 1937 married Fanny Aavatsmark, the daughter of a Norwegian General awarded the St Olaf medal for war service in 1947. That year he was elected ARSA. In 1938 he moved to 4 Drummond Place, Edinburgh where he remained for the rest of his life. Although he enjoyed longevity, he had had more than his share of illness, which in early years had been one of the formative influences on his art. During WW2, his paint became thicker and the composition more fluid. Influenced by the 1952 exhibition of Roualt. Shortly afterwards he abandoned symbolism and freely interpreted the forces of nature with a strong emphasis on colour. 'MacTaggart has kept a wary eye on the passing show of artistic fashions, and has rejected all the models recently exhibited. He should be considered with his French, German and Russian masters, with whom he has so much in common; and in that company he can appear with confidence' [Harvey Wood]. Elected RSA 1948 and Secretary of the RSA in 1955, President in 1959, the same year that he was made an Honorary Royal Academician, Honorary Royal Hibernian Academician, Honorary member of the RSW. Awarded an LLD from Edinburgh 1961; knighted 1962. Elected a Fellow of the Royal Society of Edinburgh 1967, RA 1973. Represented in the Tate AG, SNGMA, Aberdeen AG, Dumfries AG, Dundee AG, Kirkcaldy AG, Paisley AG, Lillie AG (Milngavie), City of Edinburgh collection(4), RSA, Sydney AG (Australia).
**Bibl:** Halsby 217-8; Hardie 158 et passim ch x; Hartley 150; Macmillan [SA] 351-2,358,365-9; SAC, 'Retrospective', (Ex Cat 1968); Scottish Field, Sept 1960, 22-24; SNGMA 'Sir William MacTaggart', (Ex Cat 1968); Studio Oct, 1959, 70-74; Who's Who; H Harvey Wood, William MacTaggart, Edinburgh 1974.

**McTAGUE, George** **fl 1940**
Amateur painter of 7 Chancelot Terrace, Edinburgh. Exhibited RSA(1).

**MacTAVISH, Grant Robert** **fl 1987-**
Renfrewshire painter. Often used mixed media. Exhibited GI(6) from Newton Mearns.

**McVARISH, Fergus Thomas** **fl 1973-1976**
Glasgow painter. Exhibited GI(3) from Clarkston.

**MacVEAN, Mrs H E** **fl 1934**
Argyllshire amateur watercolourist. Exhibited RSW(1) from Kilchrenan, by Taynuilt.

**McVITIE, D J Graham** **fl 1964**
Dundee sculptor. Exhibited 'Paddy' at the RSA.

**McWHINNIE, Ian** **fl 1982**
Amateur Glasgow painter. Exhibited GI(1) from Allison St.

**MacWHIRTER, Miss Agnes Eliza** **1837-1878**
Edinburgh painter in oil occasionally but mainly watercolour of still-

life, landscape and flowers. Sister of John M(qv). 'A Panegyric upon Folly', exhibited at the RSA in 1871, was described by an anonymous contemporary critic as 'wonderful'. Painted on Arran where she was a leading member of the artistic community in the 1860s. Her work was highly detailed in its execution and naturalistic in its conception. Exhibited RA(3) and regularly at the RSA(43); also GI(14).
**Bibl:** Halsby 109.

**MacWHIRTER, John RA HRSA RI RE** **1839-1911**
Born Slateford, nr Edinburgh, Mar 27; died London, Jan 28. Son of an Edinburgh paper manufacturer who was also an amateur draughtsman, botanist and geologist. Father of Agnes Eliza M(qv). At the age of 15 he absconded from his job in a book shop in order to study art entering the Trustees Academy, going later with Chalmers(qv), Pettie(qv) and others to London. In 1855 undertook the first of many visits to Austria, Germany, Italy and the Alps. Spent two summers in Norway making detailed sketches of wild flowers which came to the attention of Ruskin who wrote 'I have never seen anything like it'. Some of these were subsequently purchased by Ruskin and bequeathed to the Ashmolean Museum while an album (1861) is in the NGS and a further study in Glasgow AG. After studying at the Trustees Academy under Robert Scott Lauder(qv), he became more interested in broader atmospheric studies than in finely detailed work. Increasingly attracted to Scottish landscapes using strong colours and subordinating detail to the general effect but in due course he developed a preoccupation with trees, especially silver birch, for which following his painting 'The Three Graces', he became best known. Elected ARSA 1867, HRSA 1882, ARA 1879, RA 1893. Friend of William McTaggart(qv) and some of his freedom of technique shows the influence of this relationship. 'Illustrations of the Yarrow' were reproduced in the *Art Journal* in 1893. Published several books including *The MacWhirter Sketch Book* (1906), *Landscape Painting in Watercolour* (1907) and *Sketches from Nature* (1913). In addition to 'The Three Graces', his other most famous work was 'The Lady of The Woods'. 'The Three Graces' stood close to the head of Loch Katrine. 'June in the Austrian Tyrol' was purchased by the Chantrey Bequest 1892. Armstrong considered that he was 'often weak in design, never robust in constitution, his pictures breathe a sympathy with the subtlest forms and tenderest tints of nature which are scarcely to be seen elsewhere'. Exhibited RA(126), RSA(118) 1854-1911, also RSW, RHA, AAS 1893-1910, ROI(9) & GI(50+). Represented in SNG, Broughty Ferry AG, Glasgow AG, Paisley AG, Edinburgh City collection, permanent Collection of the Royal Academy of Arts, Brodie Castle (NTS), Sydney AG (Australia).
**Bibl:** AJ 1879, 1911 et passim, 1898, 86-7,369-370; Christmas Annual 1903; Armstrong 74-5; Caw 256-8 et passim; Halsby 108-9,120-3,131; Hardie 62-4; Irwin 359-60,364-5,et al,pl 186; Macmillan [SA] 229,231,242; Spielman, The Art of J MacWhirter, 1904; John MacWhirter, Sketches from Nature, London 1913; The MacWhirter Sketchbook, London 1906; Hints to Students on Landscape Painting in Watercolour, London 1900; Landscape Painting in Watercolour, London 1906; Wingfield.

**McWHIRTER, William Ewing ARIBA ARIAS** **1934-1996**
Born Ross-shire. Architect and landscape artist; lecturer. From Aberdeen GS 1946-51 he trained in architecture at the Scott Sutherland School of Architecture, Aberdeen 1952-58. His first post was in the housing division of the London Architect Dept 1958-9 before doing national service with RAF; in 1961 returned to Aberdeen as Lecturer in Design, Gray's School of Art, until 1967. Involved in design of Edinburgh Royal Infirmary whilst with Robert Matthew, Johnson Marshall & Partners (1963-67), in 1967 appointed Chief Architect, Ross & Cromarty CC 1967-75. His final position was Depute Director of Architectural Services, Highland Regional Council 1975-96. Designed Alness Academy in the mid-1970s. Throughout his life he painted Highland landscapes with a sensitivity and understanding of the unique colours, textures and atmosphere of the region. Held regular exhibitions at Eden Court, Inverness, with a retrospective 1997. Exhibited RSA(4).

**McWHOR, Alice Fergusson** **fl 1925-1928**
Amateur painter. Exhibited at the Walker Gallery, Liverpool(8) from 4 Frankby Road, Great Meols, Cheshire.

**McWILLIAM, John** **fl 1970**
Edinburgh painter of coastal scenes. Exhibited Pittenweem harbour at the RSA, from Dalhousie Terrace.

**MAAN, Alex** **fl 1887-1888**
Glasgow painter; exhibited RSA(2) from 136 Wellington Street.

**MABON, Tom** **fl 1978-1982**
Aberdeen painter who in 1981 moved to Inverness. Exhibited AAS (4), latterly from 32 Culcabock Ave.

**MACH, David** **1956-**
Born Methil, Fife. Sculptor. Studied Duncan of Jordanstone College of Art, Dundee 1974-79. For the next three years pursued post-graduate work at the Royal College of Art, London winning the RSA drawing prize in his final year. Attracted to the waste products of the consumer society he constructed his first work, a Rolls Royce car built from thousands of old books. Later work has included old car tyres, furniture, magazines, bottles and toys. Hartley argues that his work, while being 'figurative' in the sense that recognisable objects are depicted, belongs also to the realm of performance art in that the audience is able to observe its construction. He works quickly enabling him to get closer to the energy inside the materials so that "it is impossible for me to have total control". An enormous confidence trick on a gullible public or a fresh approach to sculpture as an art form? Since 1982 he has been a part-time lecturer at the Kingston Polytechnic in the Sculpture department. Interested in 'on site' constructions made with found objects as exhibited at the SNGMA in 1987, eg an avalanche of magazines, with some cascading down through the windows of the gallery. His hallmark is the sculpting of known physical objects in unexpected material. The artistic and/or spiritual content of the work is questionable. He has exhibited and had exhibitions in Barcelona, Brussels, New York and Toronto. Represented in SNGMA.
**Bibl:** Galerie t'Venster, Rotterdam, 'David Mach, Master Builder', (Ex Cat 1983, Text by Tom Bendham); Hartley 150-1; Riverside Studios, London, 'David Mach, Fuel for the Fire', (Ex Cat 1986, Text by Mel Gooding); SNGMA 'The Vigorous Imagination', (Ex Cat 1987); Tate Gall, London, 'David Mach, 101 Dalmatians', (Ex Cat 1988).

**MACHELL, Iain H** **fl 1978**
Aberdeen artist; studied Gray's School of Art, Aberdeen. Exhibited AAS(1) from Craigentath, Blairs.

**MACHIN, John** **fl 1935-1938**
Elected SSA 1989. Exhibited RSA, RSW & GI(7) since 1987 and at the SSA since 1988, latterly from 42 Orchard Brae Ave, Edinburgh. Represented in the City of Edinburgh Art collection, Heriot Watt University.

**MACK, Alastair** **1955-**
Born Edinburgh 4 May. Painter and printmaker. Works with acrylic on paper and, for larger works, on canvas; also collage. Employed as a laboratory technician 1971-1983 before enrolling at the Edinburgh College of Art where he graduated in 1987, spending a postgraduate year 1987-8. Won the Keith Prize 1987 and the RSA major print-making award 1967; the following year received first prize for printmaking at the Edinburgh College of Art. Influenced by Robert Callender(qv), Alan Davie, Matisse, and Paul Klee, the major source of his work is science and nature. He is 'concerned with exploring the form, colour and pattern found in science and nature from one end of the scale of life to the other, by identifying the interplay between the properties of simple shapes and the complex organisation according to which they are arranged and the consideration of the individual unit by placing each in its own space within the larger group. The abstract images emphasise these views by placing simple signs and symbols on blocks of strong colour which occasionally touch, interfere and overlap'. First solo exhibition in Edinburgh 1989. Elected SSA 1989. Exhibited RSA, RSW, & GI since 1987 and at the SSA since 1988, latterly from 42 Orchard Brae Ave, Edinburgh. Represented in City of Edinburgh collection, Heriot Watt University.

**MACK, Hilda Muriel (née Watkinson)** **1895-?**
Born Glasgow, 17 May. Painter and etcher. Studied at Slade School and Academie Colarossi in Paris. Lived at Aigburth, Liverpool. Exhibited RA & Walker Gallery, Liverpool(13).

**MACK, J C** **fl 1857-1871**
Perthshire landscape painter; exhibited RSA(2) from Bridge of Earn.

**MAGAZINE, THE** **1893-1896**
Edited from Glasgow School of Art and handwritten by Lucy Raeburn(qv), it was an important if limited outlet for the early vision of the Spook School(qv). Four volumes only appeared, between November 1893 and the Spring of 1896. Original illustrations were included - in addition to rare, early watercolours and designs by Charles Rennie Mackintosh, there were designs by the Macdonald sisters as well as photographs by James Annan(qv). Other contributors included Janet Macdonald Aitken(qv), Kate Cameron(qv), Jessie and John Keppie(qv), and Agnes Raeburn(qv).
**Bibl:** Ian Monie, 'The Magazine', in Burkhauser 76-79.

**MAGEE, Frank FSA(Scot)** **fl 1971-d.c1980**
Aberdeen amateur artist. Painted watercolours of architectural and topographical subjects in a meticulous, architectural manner with considerable skill and fidelity. Active member of the city council and Art Gallery committee. Exhibited AAS(5) from 2 Woodburn Gdns.

**MAGEE, Gregg** **1966-**
Born Johnstone. Painter, mixed media. Trained Edinburgh College of Art where he won the Helen Rose bequest. Mainly still life in a melancholic ambience. Participated in Borders Biennial and Perth AG exhibition.

**MAGUIRE, J E** **fl 1914**
Renfrewshire amateur landscape painter. Exhibited GI(1) from Eaglesham.

**MAGUIRE, J T** **fl 1934-1936**
Amateur etcher and batik designer. Exhibited RSA(1) & GI(4) from 8 Wilton Street, Glasgow.

**MAGUIRE, John T** **fl 1950-1955**
Glasgow painter of figurative and landscape studies, some harbour scenes. Exhibited mainly watercolours at the GI(4) from Ballieston.

**MAIDMAN, Edward Charles Henry** **fl 1897-1909**
Edinburgh architect. Gifford gives only a single mention: 434 (1902) and 442 Lanark Rd (1904), the latter known as 'The Gair'. Exhibited RSA(16) between above years.
**Bibl:** Gifford 512.

**MAIN, -** **fl 1830**
Leith engraver. Engraved a bookplate for Stodart of Kailzie and Ormiston, 1830.
**Bibl:** Bushnell.

**MAIN, Edith A** **fl 1912**
Aberdeen amateur artist; painted topographical subjects. Exhibited AAS(2) from 38 Loanhead Terrace.

**MAIN, George** **fl 1700-1742**
Edinburgh engraver. Engraved bookplates for Campbell of Monzie (2 varieties); Royal College of Physicians, Edinburgh, 1700. Engraved the plates for Nisbet's *System of Heraldry,* 1742.
**Bibl:** Bushnell; Ex Libris Journal, 5,75.

**MAIN, Miss Helen Barbara** **fl 1939**
Amateur Renfrewshire watercolourist. Exhibited GI(1) from Kilmacolm.

**MAIN, Miss Irene Lesley** **1959-**
Born Glasgow. Educated at Park School, Glasgow. Trained Glasgow School of Art 1976-80 under Donaldson(qv), Shanks(qv) and Rae(qv); Hospitalfield and in Italy. Won Lauder award. Flower and still life painter, also figuratives and landscape. Influenced by Colourists, especially J D Fergusson(qv). Solo exhibitions Edinburgh. Associated with the Main Gallery, Glasgow. Exhibits GI(12). Represented in SAC.

**MAIN, John P RBA** **fl 1893-1928**
Glasgow watercolour and oil painter of landscapes; sculptor. Sculptures include decorative panels, statuettes and in 1909 a memorial bust to Dr Wilson (erected at Govan). Exhibited RSA(9), RSW(4), GI(24), AAS, L(1) & London Salon(1), latterly from Clarkston, Busby. Represented by a silkscreen print in City of Edinburgh collection.

**MAIN, Kirkland ARSA RSW** **1942-**
Edinburgh-based painter in oil and watercolour. Teaches at Edinburgh College of Art. Elected ARSA 1989, RSW 1990. Exhibited RSA(26) since 1976, from 15 Cramond Village.

**MAINDS, Allan Douglas(s) ARSA** **1881-1945**
Born Helensburgh, 23 Jan; died Gosforth, 4 Jly. Painter of portraits and figure subjects; watercolours were mainly landscape and still-life; also designed costumes and posters. Son of William Reid M(qv). Trained Glasgow School of Art where he won the Haldane Travelling Scholarship enabling him to study in Holland and Brussels under Jean Delville(qv) before proceeding to Rome. Staff member, Glasgow School of Art 1909-1931 and Professor of Fine Art, Kings College, Durham from 1931. Elected ARSA 1929. Member of Glasgow Art Club when living at Hillhead, before moving to Gosforth. His style was strong bearing the marked influence of French artists stemming from his time in that country. Exhibited RA(1), RSA(38), RSW(1), GI(58) & L(2).
**Bibl:** Halsby 273.

**MAINDS, William Reid** **fl 1885**
Dunbartonshire landscape painter in oil. Lived at 2 Iona Terrace, Helensburgh. Father of Allan Douglas M(qv). Exhibited RSA(1) & GI(1).

**MAIR, James H** **fl 1958**
Renfrewshire artist. Exhibited 'Nightfall' at the GI from Johnstone.

**MAITLAND, Alister** **fl 1930-1936**
Glasgow landscape and topographical painter, also shipping scenes. Worked in oil, watercolour and pencil. Exhibited RSA(3) & GI(15) from 13 Stephen Drive, Linthouse.

**MAITLAND, Andrew** **1802-1894**
Architect. Formed partnership with his sons **James MAITLAND** (1845-1929), **Andrew MAITLAND Jnr** (1847-1889) and his grandson **Andrew Gordon MAITLAND** (1880-1983). Undertook first design for Gairloch Hotel (1872), enlarged by the partnership (1880). Responsible for baronial additions to Kincraig House (1872), also the Old Schoolhouse, Ardgay (1852), Migdale Hospital, Bonar Bridge (1863). The partnership designed the Tain Parish Church (1891-92), Tain Town Hall (1874-76), the Free Church School Nairn (1847-48), the Dalmore Distillery (1893-96) and Averon Youth Centre (1898), both at Alness, the Free Church, Aultbea (1872-73), Victoria Hall (1887) & Primary School (1875-76), both at Cromarty, Edderton School (1876), Kiltearn Parish Church (1893), extensions to Flowerdale House (1904), Free Church, Poolewe (1889), Glenmorangie Distillery (1888-89), Free Church, Ullapool (1908-09), Gair Memorial Hall, Bonar Bridge (1879), Clydesdale Bank, Dornoch (1893) and many other public buildings in the north.
**Bibl:** Gifford, H & I, 392,406,421,432,447,555-6,558,630 et passim.

**MAITLAND, Ann Emma** **fl 1890-1940**
Painter of flowers and landscape in oil and watercolour. Lived in Glasgow c1893 before moving to Bexley 1896 and finally to London c1902. Exhibited widely including RA(9), RI(8), ROI(1), RBA(3), GI(12), SWA(20) & L(11). Probably the same as **Annie R MAITLAND** of West Cults House, Cults, Aberdeenshire who exhibited flowers and local landscapes at the AAS 1894-1908, including 'Lochnagar', 1898.

**MAITLAND, C J** **fl 1869**
Painter. Exhibited two works at the RSA including 'Boy and rabbits'.

**MAITLAND, Mrs F J** **fl 1897**
Edinburgh based painter. Exhibited 'At the hills, Shanghai' at the GI, from Craighead.

**MAITLAND, Moira RSW** **1936-**
Born Aberdeen. Painter of still life and landscape including views in Ibiza. Trained Gray's School of Art 1951-55 obtaining a post diploma in 1955-56; also at Hospitalfield, Arbroath. Travelled in France, Italy and Spain. First solo exhibition was in Edinburgh 1958. Lives at Newton Rd, Newtonhill, Kincardineshire. Awarded the Keith Prize, RSA 1959; elected RSW 1998, SSA 1960. Exhibits RSA, AAS(8) 1959-64 & SSA.

**MAKINSON, Trevor Owen** **1926-?**
Born Southport, 8 Jne. Painter of portraits and landscapes. Educated privately, studied at Hereford Art School and Slade School. Came to Scotland to take up an appointment at Glasgow School of Art and a Chair at Glasgow University, remained in Glasgow ever since. His first one-man show was in 1944. In his early days he was especially encouraged by Laura Knight and was once described as 'an unrepentant adherent of the traditional representational school of British painters'. His 'Susan Ritchie' is a modern masterpiece. After retiring from Glasgow School of Art, he directed a gallery in Glasgow. Exhibited RBA from 1942, RA from 1943, also RSA, GI & SSA. Represented in Hereford AG, Salford AG, Stoke-on-Trent AG, Stockholm AG, National Museum of Wales, Newport AG, Glasgow AG, Buxton AG.

**MALCOLM, Alister James** **c1950-**
Born Glasgow but lives and works in Aberdeen. Works mainly in acrylic. Painter of two sharply contrasting styles: surrealist subjects and naturalistic, highly finished still lifes, box contructions and meticulous studies of insects, especially butterflies, bees and wasps. Father and brother also paint. Trained Gray's School of Art, Aberdeen from where a travelling scholarship enabled him to visit the continent. Awarded SAC Bursary 1982. Lived for a time in France. Exhibits RSA, RGI & AAS from 22 Bright St. Represented in the collections of HRH The Duke of Edinburgh and Prince Edward.

**MALCOLM, Anne** **fl 1969-1970**
Dundee sculptress; mainly portrait busts. Exhibited RSA(2).

**MALCOLM, Edward** **c1916-?**
Born Peterhead, Aberdeenshire. Trained Grays School of Art, Aberdeen and Eastbourne College of Art. Father of Alister M(qv). Paints mainly watercolour landscapes. War service 1941-6. Exhibited AAS(4) from 22 Bright St.

**MALCOLM, Ellen RSA (Mrs Gordon S Cameron)** **1923-?**
Born Grangemouth, 28 Sep. Painter in oil; flowers, still life and landscape. Educated Aberdeen Academy and Gray's School of Art 1940-1944, under Robert Sivell(qv) and Ian Sutherland(qv). Awarded Chalmers-Jervise Prize 1946 and Guthrie Award 1952. Married Gordon Cameron(qv). Lived at 7 Auburn Terrace, Invergowrie, Perthshire. Elected ARSA 1968, RSA 1976. Exhibited RSA regularly from 1945, GI(26) 1944-83 & AAS 1959-66. Represented in Lillie AG (Milngavie), Perth AG, Edinburgh City collection, Southend AG.

**MALCOLM, George A** **fl 1951**
Motherwell painter; exhibited 'Dee estuary, Kircudbright' at the RSA; also GI(1).

**MALCOLM, Isobel** **fl 1969**
Aberdeen amateur artist. Exhibited a painting of fishing boats at the AAS from 16 Wallfield Crescent.

**MALCOLM, Margaret I** **fl 1983-1988**
Aberdeen painter of interiors and still life. Exhibited RSA in 1983, 1984 & 1988.

**MALCOLM, Thomas** **fl 1888**
Amateur painter; exhibited GI(1) from 1 Salmond Place, Edinburgh.

**MALCOLMSON, James C** **fl 1932**
Minor Paisley engraver; exhibited a drypoint etching at the GI from 3 Lonsdale Drive.

**MALIPHANT, George** **fl 1806-1829**
Architect and painter of architectural and topographical subjects in oil

and watercolour. Exhibited RA(11) including a design for a villa in the Highlands for R. Douglas 1815, and a cenotaph to the memory of Princess Charlotte 1818, latterly from 20 Blenheim St, London. (Halsby gives his initial as H).
**Bibl:** Halsby 273.

**MALKOWSKA, Janina E (Janka)** **1912-?**
Born Poland. Printmaker and free-lance illustrator. Studied at Warsaw Academy and Vienna Kunstgewerbe Schule. Settled in Edinburgh 1947, then in Perthshire. During 1934-39 she illustrated the first edition of a book of poems by Julian Turwin. After WW2 settled in Krakow then moved to the British Zone 1946-47 exhibiting with Polish displaced artists. In 1947 she arrived in Edinburgh and joined the Edinburgh College of Art. In 1985 she joined the Glasgow Print Studio. Best known for her woodcuts. First exhibited three prints at the RSA in 1948 and continued to exhibit regularly there, also at the RA & AAS(3), from 8 Grinnan Rd, Braco, Perthshire.

**MALLINSON, Ethel M** **fl 1917-1940**
Landscape painter. Although she lived most of her life at Fairleigh, Ilkley, Yorkshire, almost all her exhibited works were executed in Scotland: at the RSA(6), GI(27) & RSW(2), also at the Walker Gallery, Liverpool(4).

**MALLOCH, George Stirling** **1865-1901**
Born Perth, Feb 3; died Patterson, NJ, USA. Painter in oil and watercolour; figure subjects, landscapes and portraits. Trained Edinburgh College of Art, Paris and Italy. Due to ill health he travelled in the Baltic during the 1880s undertaking watercolour sketches. Later executed views in Perthshire in a style somewhat reminiscent of the Hague School, often in an engagingly fresh manner. Drowned while bathing off the New Jersey coast. Exhibited RSA(11), RSW(1), GI(1), AAS(5) & L(3). Represented in Perth AG, including his last picture, 'Maple Leaves'.
**Bibl:** Halsby 273.

**MANDS, Irene S** **fl 1984**
Aberdeen amateur artist; exhibited once at the AAS from 7 Walker Rd.

**MANGAN, Stephen** **1964-**
Born Edinburgh. Painter of stong figurative compositions. Trained Duncan of Jordanstone College of Art 1984-1989, winning the Dalgetty Prize (1988). Exhibits RA, RSA, winning the Saltire Prize (1995), John Murray Thomson award (1996) and Guthrie award (1997); also AAS.

**MANGIN, Mrs Constance W** **fl 1884-1886**
Amateur painter of figure subjects and animals from Catstackburn, Selkirk. Exhibited RSA(2).

**MANIS, John P** **fl 1897**
Amateur Glasgow artist; exhibited once at the Walker Gallery, Liverpool from Cardowan Road, Stepps.

**MANN, Alex** **1923-2004**
Born Ayr, 23 Feb. Painter in acrylic. Former gallery director, educated at Pollockshields Academy and Sidcup School of Art. Intrigued by the combination of colour and sound. Lived for many years in Mosely, Warwickshire before moving to Aberdeenshire, first to Braemar, then to Aboyne then back to Braemar. Represented in Leamington AG.

**MANN, Alexander ROI** **1853-1908**
Born Glasgow; died Glasgow, 26 Jan. Painter in oil of landscape and genre, also photographer. Son of a prosperous business man. Father of Mary Gow M(qv) and Sir James Mann (sometime Director of the Wallace Collection and Suveyor of the Royal Works of Art). Received art lessons from Robert Greenlees when he was barely ten years old. After joining his father's firm, Mann Byers, he left in 1877 to go to Paris where he studied first at Julian's before, in 1881, moving to the studio of Duran, where he remained until 1885. By 1877 he was established as a painter, living at 45 Rue Vivienne near to the atelier of Carolus-Duran whose daughter married the playwright George Feydeau. Mann's sketchbooks from this time show a number of Feydeauesque scenes. His first exhibit at the GI was in 1879 and at the Salon 1882. Influences can be seen of Millet and the Barbizon painters, also Bastien-Lepage. Spent some time in Aberdeenshire, at Stonehaven 1881 and Collieston 1882, with Millie Dow(qv). In 1884 his 'A Bead Stringer, Venice' received an honourable mention, the first Glasgow picture to receive such an award. The draughtsmanship was excellent, the colour clear and bright. By 1886 he had returned to landscape and in a number of pictures painted during the next few years - 'By the Findhorn' 1887 and 'Nearing the Sea: Findhorn' 1888 were the most important - he showed a fine feeling for light and mood, subdued by harmonious colour, competent brush work and draughtsmanship. Travelled extensively and frequently in Italy, France and Morocco painting a number of fine Tangier scenes as well as a portrait of 'Kaid Maclean', 1894. A posthumous exhibition was held in Edinburgh and Glasgow in 1988. Elected ROI 1893. In 1896 he settled in London and continued to show at the RA(21) 1884-1904. Exhibited also RSA(11), RBA(18), GI(69), ROI(48), RBA(18) & AAS 1885-1908. Represented in Glasgow AG, Kirkcaldy AG, Liverpool AG, Nottingham AG.
**Bibl:** Caw 384-5; Fine Art Society, London & Glasgow 'Alexander Mann', (Ex Cat 1983, Text Christopher Newall); Macmillan [SA] 268; Studio 426 (1909), 300-305; Who's Who 1908.

**MANN, Allan R** **fl 1975-1984**
Dundee painter, later moved to Ayr. Exhibited RSA(2).

**MANN, Cathleen S (Marchioness of Queensberry) RP ROI** **1896-1959**
Born Scotland; died London, 9 Sep. Daughter of Harrington(qv) and Florence Sabine M(qv). Painter of portraits, still-life and flowers. Trained Slade School and in Paris. Married the Marquis of Queensberry 1926 and, following a divorce, J R Follett 1946. Spent most of her life in London. Elected ROI 1935, RP 1931, SWA 1932. Exhibited regularly RA(23), RSA(2), GI(16), ROI(4), SWA(8) & L(1). A portrait of the actuary 'Ludovic MacLellan Mann' (1869-1955), is in SNPG; also represented in Glasgow AG.

**MANN, Catriona** **1955-**
Born London. Painter in oil & watercolour. Educated Aberdeen, trained Edinburgh College of Art 1975-1979. Further studies Edinburgh Univ., graduating LLB 1983. Elected SSWA 1986, founder member of Trustees, Paintings in Hospitals 1991. Particularly interested in landscape & buildings. Venice a constant inspiration. Exhibits RSA, RSW.

**MANN, Florence Sabine (née Pasley)** **fl 1895-1923**
Painter in oils of portraits and portrait miniatures. First wife of Harrington(qv) and mother of Cathleen M(qv). Lived at Duncryne, Alexandria, Dunbartonshire before moving to London at the turn of the century. Exhibited three portraits at the RA in 1885 and 1886 from 51 Hamilton Terrace, Edinburgh, also GI(2).

**MANN, G Harrington RP RE** **1864-1937**
Born Glasgow, 7 Oct; died New York, 28 Feb. Painter of portraits in oil, also landscapes and subject paintings; illustrator and stained glass window designer. Father of Cathleen M(qv) and son of John M(qv). Trained Glasgow School of Art and Slade School under Legros before going to Paris for further studies under Boulanger and Lefevre. Also worked in Italy before returning to live in Glasgow from 1890 to 1900, finally settling in London. Attained a wide reputation and spent several seasons in the USA painting portraits, maintaining a home in New York. He wrote an autobiography but it was never published. When returning to Glasgow in 1888, became associated with, though arguably not a full member of, the Glasgow School. Member of the Society of Eight(qv). Selected compositions which lent themselves to decorative treatment, specialising in portraiture after 1892. He records that 'the greatest compliment of his life' was the fact that Sargent, two weeks before his death, expressed an intention to vote him into the RA. 'With a broad, competent brushwork, Mann combines something of the deeper characterisation of Guthrie. He shows great skill and interest in organising compositional detail decoratively and in arranging groups, particularly of children' [Sara Henderson]. First came to attention by his acutely observed rendering of scenes in Yorkshire fishing villages, and subjects from the Waverley Novels, a series that culminated in the 'Attack of the MacDonalds at Killiecrankie' 1891. A portrait of his wife 1891 was a fine example of the animated, broad style of his

portraiture combined with a refinement that is somewhat redolent of Sargent at his best. Worked as an illustrator for both *The Daily Graphic* and *The Scottish Art Review.* Author of *The Technique of Portrait Painting,* 1933. Died while visiting New York. Member of the New English Art Club and International Society, being elected to both. Elected RE 1885 (resigned 1891), RP 1900, NPS 1911, NEAC 1891. Exhibited RA(46), RSA(27), RBA(1), RE(1), RI(1), GI(60), AAS & NEA(8). A 'Self-portrait' is in the SNPG. His portrait 'Sir John Lavery' is in Glasgow AG; represented also in Belfast AG, Glasgow AG, City of Edinburgh collection, House of Dun (NTS), Melbourne AG, Sydney AG, Victoria AG (Australia), and by stained glass windows in St. Andrew's church, Ardrossan.
**Bibl:** The Artist,Aug 1897,363-9; Caw 431; Painton Cowen, Stained Glass in Britain, 1985, 230, 235; Hardie 142; Houfe; Macmillan [SA] 283; SAC 'Glasgow Boys', (Ex Cat 1968); Studio 1903, Vol XXIX; Wingfield.

**MANN, James** **fl 1936-1948**
Glasgow flower and genre painter; also engraver. Exhibited RSA(1) & GI(10) from 67 Croftfoot Rd and after 1942 from Carluke, Lanarkshire.

**MANN, James Scrimgeour RI** **1883-1946**
Born Dundee, 30 Aug; died England, 1 Jne. Painter in oil of marine subjects, also poster artist. Trained Liverpool School of Art. Member of the Liverpool Academy of Art. Principal works include 'The Pilot Jack', 'The Great Days' and 'The Coming of the Westerlies'. Settled in Liverpool and later at Caldy, Cheshire. One of many artists who, although Scottish, worked most of his life in England and was more a part of the English artistic scene than the Scottish. Elected RI 1932. Exhibited RA(2), RI(55), RCA(27), L(49), RBA(4) & GI(1).

**MANN, John** **1796-1827**
Scottish portrait painter. Married Catherine McLellan (1795-1887). Now best known as the father of John (1827-1910), and Harrington M(qv). Did not live long enough to establish a reputation.

**MANN, Julia A (Mrs Doak)** **fl 1891-1903**
Painter of flowers, topographical subjects and landscape. Lived in Glasgow, moved to 15 Queen's Rd, Aberdeen c1896. From there she exhibited GI(8) & AAS(3).

**MANN, Kathleen (Mrs Hugh Crawford)** **c1905-?**
Born Kent. Painter also embroiderer and illustrator. Trained Croydon School of Art 1924-28 under Rebecca Crompton. Gained a scholarship to the Royal College of Art where she developed an interest in peasant dress. Published her first book *Peasant Costume in Europe* 1931. After a year on the staff of Cheltenham College of Art became head of the embroidery department, Glasgow School of Art, succeeding Anne Knox Arthur(qv). There she introduced machine embroidery. In 1934 she married a colleague Hugh Crawford(qv) as a result of which she was required to resign, forcing her to hold private classes in her home. Exhibited widely and her work featured in a special volume of *The Studio* 'Modern Embroidery' (1933). Some years later she published *Appliqué Design and Method* (1937), *Embroidery Design and Stitches* (1937) and in 1939 *Designs from Peasant Art.* Moved to Aberdeen 1939 where she continued to teach. By 1955 she had abandoned embroidery to concentrate on painting and illustration. Member, SSA. Exhibited GI(2) in 1935 from 3 Park Terrace, Glasgow.
**Bibl:** Liz Arthur in Burkhauser, 183.

**MANN, Mary Gow** **1888-?**
Painter in watercolour. Daughter of Alexander M(qv). Studied at Goldsmith College and under Norman Garstin 1923. Showed RA(1) 1927 from Ledard, Henley-on Thames, Oxfordshire.

**MANN, Nathaniel** **fl 1965**
Dunbartonshire amateur landscape painter in watercolour. Exhibited GI(1) from Old Kilpatrick.

**MANNIX, Robert** **fl 1880-1898**
A quite prolific artist of considerable competence in the traditional manner. Exhibited RSA(34) & GI(3) from Glasgow 1898 having earlier lived in Dublin.

**MANSEL, Miss Henrietta Cecilia** **fl 1883**
Painter in oil and pastel of portraits; exhibited RSA(2) from Flakedale, Hamilton, Lanarks.

**MANSON, Donald** **1948-**
Born Ayr, Apr 25. Painter in oil,watercolour & pastel of still life, landscape and semi-abstracts. Studied Glasgow School of Art 1966-71 & Hospitalfield, Arbroath under John Knox(qv) 1969. First one-man exhibition in Edinburgh 1988. Attracted to Cornwall and the NW Highlands. Exhibits GI since 1987, RSA(2) 1990, from 25 Ranfurly Rd, Bridge of Weir, Renfrewshire.

**MANSON, George** **1850-1876**
Born Edinburgh, 3 Dec; died Lympston, Devonshire, 27 Feb. Wood engraver and painter in oil and watercolour. One of the tragic figures of Scottish art. Although he died of consumption when only 26 years old, he established himself as one of the most sensitive and artistic painters that Scotland has produced. After leaving school he began as a punch cutter, making dyes for type with Messrs W & R Chambers. His style of engraving was direct and artistic, using Bewick as his model. Some of the woodcuts that he executed when he was 16 years old still remain. In 1870 he competed for a prize offered by the Edinburgh Society of Engravers on Wood to apprentices. 'The competitors all engraved the same landscape, the drawings on block, which were provided for them, and finished with the pencil point in the usual way to indicate texture and foliage. Manson, unlike the others, entirely ignored these stencillings; and, following his own ideas, produced the effect of the drawing by the means of simple lines, all running in one direction across the block, the light and shade being preserved by the varying breadth of the lines. The engraving was executed with such originality and fine sense of atmosphere, that the judge, while unable to award the first prize for anything so unlike the conventional method of engraving, sent the young man a special prize from himself to mark his "admiration of the engraver's artistic feeling in landscape"'. A gentle, diffident young man but said to be full of inflexible determination and self-reliance, with a singular care for justice in both word and deed. In 1869, for example, on the anniversary of Wordsworth's death, he went out to paint the lesser celandine, the poet's favourite flower. 'Quiet and undemonstrative as he was, there was something singularly fascinating about him, an undefinable power of attracting to himself those with whom he came into contact, of making himself "a beautiful acquisition to their existence"'. He joined a local art club, the Craigmillar Sketching Association. His first exhibit at the RSA was 'The Study of a Doorway at Craigmillar Castle' 1869, followed the next year by 'Milking Time'. In 1871 he began practising as a professional painter, mainly in watercolour. Visited London and in 1873 continental Europe with the artist W D McKay(qv). In Paris he spent several days studying at the Louvre being especially attracted to the works of Giorgone. In 1874 ill-health forced him to visit Sark and the following year went to Paris where he began to etch. Among his works at this time are 'The Fisherboy', 'The Smuggler' and his own portrait, almost all dealing with the sea. Returning from Sark he undertook a Highland tour, then divided his time between Edinburgh and Galashiels. In January 1875 he visited Paris with P W Adam(qv) and there began to etch, receiving instruction from M Cadart. While at St Lo he painted a distant view of the city but this was never finished for while working in the snow he contracted pneumonia. On his return he settled near Shirley, near Croydon, there producing 'Girl with a Donkey'. Shortly before his death in 1874 he expressed his intention of executing a Scottish subject but there only remained time for a small study of a scene from Ramsay's *Gentle Shepherd.* 'He was above all things a colourist, colour being quite the sweetest and tenderest quality of natural objects. And the human face being of all coloured things the subtlest and most lovely, he painted this oftenest, in all its aspects of pink rounded babyhood, rose flushed girlhood, bronzed prime, and wrinkled age. By the beauty of his flesh painting, by the importance which he gives to the human countenance in all his pictures, his work is separated from most of the rustic subjects of younger Scottish painters...the characteristic notes of the art of George Manson are its perception of natural beauty, and its perception of the mingled pathos and loveliness of human life. He was a true artist, learning from all around him, but shaping all that he learned into his own forms of beauty, and stamping it with the impress of his own clearcut personality' [J M Gray]. After his death, an exhibition of watercolours was held in London 1881, exciting great interest. Armstrong

compared him to Frederick Walker while Bryan refers to delicacy and tenderness 'scarcely surpassed by any other painter of his school'. Among contemporary collectors of his paintings were several artists including James Cassie, James Orchar and, later, Partick Adam, W D McKay and J Kent Richardson. Exhibited once at the RA, a portrait of 'Bertha, a young child' 1873, RSA(12) & ROI(7). Represented in V & A, NGS, SNPG (2 'Self-portraits'), Broughty Ferry AG, City of Edinburgh collection.
**Bibl:** Bryan, Vol 3, 276; Caw 279-280; Gray, George Manson and His works, 1879; Halsby 70,126,241; Hardie 66,78,79.

**MANSON, J Wellwood** **fl 1930-1952**
Glasgow painter of landscapes, especially the Western Highlands. Exhibited RSA(3) & GI(12) from Bearsden and latterly Albert Drive.

**MANSON, Robert Kirk** **fl 1954**
Glasgow amateur painter. Exhibited 'Calm morning' at the GI.

**MANUEL, John** **fl 1900-1904**
Edinburgh painter of topographical subjects and ecclesiastical sketches. Moved for a time to Hawick before returning to Edinburgh. Exhibited RSA(5).

**MANWELL, James Barr** **fl 1937**
Paisley amateur engraver; exhibited an etching 'Paisley Town Hall' at the GI, from 5 Gray's Crescent.

**MARCELLINO, Paola** **c1965-**
Born in Italy. Tapestry weaver and fashion designer. Studied Edinburgh College of Art 1984-5 and Heriot Watt University followed by two years in London before settling in Edinburgh 1987. Prepared a tapestry after a painting by William Baillie(qv). Seeks to incorporate tapestries into fashion design. Influenced by early mosaics. Exhibited in Australia and Sardinia.

**MARECHALL, J** **fl 1882**
Edinburgh amateur portrait miniaturist. Exhibited RSA(1) from 57 Frederick St.

**MARIE, -** **fl 1861-1863**
Edinburgh-based painter in oil of fruit and still life. Exhibited RSA(4).

**MARK, Brenda RSW** **1922-1960**
Born Hull. Painter in oil and watercolour, principally the former. Moved to Edinburgh as a young girl. Trained Edinburgh College of Art before travelling in France, Germany and Italy. Married Robin Philipson(qv) 1949. Her work is characterised by a very marked decorative sense, cool colour and strenuous lyricism. Won the Guthrie Award. Close friend and sketching companion of Anne Redpath(qv). Lecturer at Moray House. Exhibited RSA, RSW, GI(3) & SSA.
**Bibl:** Scotsman, 21 Sep 1960(obit).

**MARLE, Edward** **fl 1971-1976**
East Kilbride painter. Exhibited GI(7).

**MARQUIS, Alexander** **fl 1839-1841**
Edinburgh painter of domestic genre, portraits and rustic scenes. Exhibited RSA(4) from George St.

**MARQUIS, James Richard RHA** **fl 1858-d1885/7**
Although not Scottish, he lived for some years in Edinburgh painting seascapes and landscapes, especially of Skye. Elected ARHA 1861 and RHA later the same year. Exhibited RSA(20) in 1871 from Callander, RHA(25), GI(20), ROI(1) & L(3).

**MARR, Miss Edith** **fl 1874-1876**
Edinburgh watercolour painter, specialising in wild birds and domestic animals. Spent a year at St Helier in Jersey, where she undertook many sketches. Exhibited RSA(3).

**MARR, G Dixon** **fl 1890**
Aberdeen artist; exhibited a sailing picture at the AAS from 121 West Montrose Street.

**MARR, Jessie** **fl 1881-1883**
Amateur landscape painter of Oxhill Village, Dumbarton; mainly poetic scenes on Arran and the east coast. Exhibited GI(6).

**MARR, William ('Bill')** **fl 1972-**
Aberdeen-based painter of landscape and still life. Exhibits AAS, latterly from 57 School Crescent, Newburgh.

**MARRIOTT, Helen** **c1957-**
Silversmith. Trained Glasgow School of Art 1975-79 followed by three years at the Royal College of Art 1980-83. Works mainly on commission including presentation pieces for the City of Glasgow. Exhibits London, Milan and in Scotland. Represented in the collection of the Worshipful Company of Goldsmiths (London).

**MARSHALL, Annie** **fl 1880-1903**
Edinburgh amateur miniature painter of portraits; exhibited RMS(1) & GI(2) from 1 Park Grove Terrace.

**MARSHALL, Annie E** **fl 1879-1894**
Glasgow painter of flowers, fruit and birds. Moved to Redpool, Auchmill, Aberdeenshire c1894. Exhibited GI(3) & AAS.

**MARSHALL, Miss Clemency Christian Sinclair RMS** **1900-?**
Born St Andrews, Fife, 22 Nov. Painter in oil and watercolour of portraits and portrait miniatures. Sister of William M(qv). Lived in London. Elected ARMS 1926, RMS 1930. Exhibited RA(3), Paris Salon & RMS(42).

**MARSHALL, David** **fl 1808**
Obscure portrait and landscape painter who arrived in Inverness in March 1808 taking up residence in East Street where he advertised himself as a portrait painter. Notices stated that 'he draws most striking likenesses by means of an improved pentograph which is constructed on a principal which cannot fail to secure the desired effect'.

**MARSHALL, David** **fl 1842-1843**
East Kilbride landscape painter; exhibited two local scenes at the RSA.

**MARSHALL, David George** **fl 1986**
Glasgow painter. Exhibited 'The Cock of the North' and 'The gilded cage' at the RSA from Clarkston.

**MARSHALL, George** **?-1732**
Edinburgh painter of portraits and still-life. Said to have studied under the younger Scougal(qv) and under Kneller in London; also in Rome. His best known work is a portrait of the non-juring 'Bishop of Dunblane'. Elected President of the then newly established Edinburgh Academy of St Luke.
**Bibl:** Brockwell 6; Bryan; Brydall 112; Caw 26; Macmillan [SA] 104.

**MARSHALL, George D** **fl 1881-1889**
Amateur Glasgow painter of genre and topographical subjects. Exhibited GI(3) from 73 Elderslee Street.

**MARSHALL, J W** **fl 1831-1832**
Scottish sculptor of portrait busts. Exhibited RSA(5) including 'Mr John Langford Pritchard of the Theatre Royal in the character of Mark Antony'.

**MARSHALL, James** **fl 1831-1851**
Edinburgh landscape painter, especially of Highland scenery. Exhibited RSA(6) from Broughton St.

**MARSHALL, John** **fl 1883**
Edinburgh landscape painter. Taught art at Edinburgh High School; exhibited RSA(1).

**MARSHALL, John** **fl 1905-1946**
Landscape painter, especially west Highland scenes; oil and watercolours. Exhibited RSA(4), RSW(3), AAS(2) & GI(23) from 123 Kingsheath Avenue, Rutherglen.

**MARSHALL, John** **fl 1929-1948**
Edinburgh sculptor. Mainly figurative subjects, often in Portland or Caen stone. Exhibited RSA(17).

**MARSHALL, John Blyth** **fl 1898-1946**
Prolific artist who painted mainly landscapes in watercolour; lived at 3 Rosefield Place, Portobello; exhibited RSA(38), RSW(6), AAS(2) & GI(3).

**MARSHALL, John Dalrymple** **fl 1846-1889**
Edinburgh painter of portraits and figure subjects including many biblical and literary studies. Moved from Edinburgh to Glasgow in the late 1880s; exhibited RA(5), RSA(47) & GI(2).

**MARSHALL, Maud E G (Mrs R J Wilson)** **1878-1967**
Born Co. Antrim. Painter and sculptress. Domesticated animals and farming scenes. Came to Ayrshire as a child. Trained Glasgow School of Art and Frank Calderon School of Animal Painting. During WWI painted horses for the Imperial War Museum and after the war embarked on much charitable work for retired and ill working horses.. Exhibited RSA(2) & GI(54) from Little Turnberry.

**MARSHALL, Peter** **1762-1826**
Although he worked as a painter he is best remembered for his invention of a mechanical contrivance known as a peristrophic panorama.
**Bibl:** Bryan.

**MARSHALL, Peter Paul** **1830-1900**
Born Edinburgh; died Teignmouth, Devon. Surveyor and engineer, grandson of Peter M(qv). Painter of subject paintings, landscape and occasional portraits. Educated Edinburgh HS and attended life classes at the Academy. His engineering work took him to London where he met Madox Brown, through whom he became associated with the Morris group. Painted many views of Arran and in East Anglia, especially around Gorleston nr Yarmouth where he had a studio. Poor health caused his retirement to Devon. His son became vice-president of the Norwich Art Circle. Exhibited a portrait at the RA(1877) & RSA(4) including "Stevenson modelling engines in clay by the light of the boiler fire - his wife and favourite rabbits', from Rose St.
**Bibl:** Bryan.

**MARSHALL, Mrs R J Wilson** **fl 1926**
Ayrshire portraitist in pencil and monochrome. Exhibited GI(1) from Maidens.

**MARSHALL, Richard Y** **fl 1953-1968**
Motherwell sculptor. Mostly figurative subjects in plaster, terracotta, ciment fondu and wood. Exhibited GI(7).

**MARSHALL, Robert C** **fl 1867**
Aberdeen landscape painter in oil; exhibited two works at the RSA including 'Mill at Braemar' 1867.

**MARSHALL, Rosamund C** **fl 1907**
Amateur painter of Priorsgate, St Andrews; exhibited RSA(1).

**MARSHALL, Mrs Rose** **fl 1880-1910**
Edinburgh-based painter of flowers, fruit, figures and landscapes, mostly in oil. After a spell in Leeds moved to Edinburgh 1882 living latterly at St Bernard's Crescent. Exhibited RA(22), RSA(19), ROI(6), RBA(14), AAS(3) & GI(2).

**MARSHALL, W J** **fl 1830**
Edinburgh painter of still life; exhibited 'Dead game' at the RSA from Rose St.

**MARSHALL, William Calder RA HRSA** **1813-1894**
Born Edinburgh, Mar 18; died London, 16 Jne. Sculptor and draughtsman in pencil. Son of a goldsmith. Educated at Edinburgh HS and University but decided to adopt sculpture as his profession. Studied under Chantrey and Baily and in Rome. Also joined the RA School, winning a silver medal 1835. In 1841 he gained a gold medal from Manchester for his 'Bacchus and Ino' and in 1844 sent statues of Chaucer and Eve to Westminister Hall. In 1857 won first prize for his design for a national monument to the Duke of Wellington; but the memorial was eventually entrusted to Alfred Stevens, leaving Marshall to carve only a series of bas-reliefs in the Chapel of St Paul's. Worked in Edinburgh but removed to London in 1839. Elected ARSA 1840 but resigned, becoming ARA 1844, RA 1852. Subsequently reinstated at the Scottish Academy, being elected HRSA 1861. Honoured by the French government for services rendered in connection with the Paris International Exhibition of 1878. Another example of a Scotsman who developed his career in England where he became very much better known and more influential than ever he was in his own land. Exhibited no fewer than 141 works at the RA 1835-1891. These included a bronze statue 'Sir Robert Peel' commissioned for Manchester 1853, a marble statue of Sir George Grey erected in Capetown 1862, a statue of James, 7th Earl of Derby, beheaded in 1651, for the town of Bolton in memory of his execution, 1865. 'The Prodigal Son' 1881 was purchased by the Chantrey Bequest. Executed idealised and classical subjects as well as memorial statues, including the group depicting 'Agriculture' on the Albert Memorial. Memorial statues for Lord Clarendon and Lord Somers are in the Houses of Parliament, Sir Robert Peel in Manchester, and Jenner is in Kensington Gardens. C B Scott, quoted by Gunnis, said he was 'a man with some resources of the tangible Philistine sort, but no more poetry, fancy or classic perceptions than a cow. One wonders how this sensible, commonplace person has ever attempted to realise any ideals or to touch a modelling-tool; or how, when he did attempt it, he had ever succeeded so far as he had'. Represented in NGS, SNPG ('Self-portrait'), Palace of Westminster, Westminster Abbey, Kensington Gardens, Arbroath, Bolton, Capetown, Coventry, Glasgow AG, Leicester Square ('Sir Isaac Newton', 1874), Walker AG (Liverpool), Montrose AG, Salford AG.
**Bibl:** AJ 1894, 286; Bryan; Gunnis 256-7.

**MARSKELL, Miss Muriel** **fl 1964-1978**
Renfrewshire-based painter of landscape and flowers. Exhibited GI(5) from Bearsden, then Kilmacolm.

**MARTEN, Elliot H** **fl 1886-1910**
Landscape painter in watercolours. Lived in Hawick, painted generally in the Borders and North of England. Exhibited 'Autumn Leaves' at the RA 1886.
**Bibl:** Halsby 273.

**MARTHY, David** **fl 1916**
Edinburgh-based amateur painter; exhibited RSA(2) from 25 Frederick Street.

**MARTIN A D** **fl 1835-1843**
Leith landscape and topographical painter; exhibited RSA(5).

**MARTIN, Adam M** **fl 1954**
Fife landscape painter; exhibited RSA from Kelty.

**MARTIN, Agnes** **fl 1877**
Dundee flower painter in watercolours; exhibited RSA(1).

**MARTIN, Mrs Agnes Fulton** **1904-?**
Born Glasgow, 11 Sep. Painter in oil of street scenes and figure subjects. Trained Glasgow School of Art. Lived some years at Cove, Dunbartonshire before settling at South Godstone, Surrey. Exhibited RSA(4), RBA(2), SWA(3), ROI(2), RCA(1), GI(4), AAS ('Tomintoul') & Paris Salon.

**MARTIN, Alex** **fl 1893-1917**
Amateur Glasgow watercolour painter; flowers and Clyde landscapes. Exhibited RSW(1) & GI(14).

**MARTIN, Allan D** **fl 1977-1979**
Renfrewshire painter. Exhibited GI(5) from Eaglesham.

**MARTIN, Charles C** **1832-?**
Penicuik artist. Son of John M(qv). Entered Trustees Academy April 2 1851 and left on May 5th the following year after which he disappears without trace. A **Charles Martin** exhibited three watercolours at the GI in 1861 but he is more likely to have been the English portrait painter of that name.

**MARTIN, D D** **fl 1883**
Amateur Glasgow painter; exhibited GI(1) from 26 Carrington Street.

**MARTIN, D Kay** **fl 1907-1908**
Amateur painter. Living in Crieff 1907, moved to Cardwell Bay, Gourock 1908. Exhibited GI(2).

**MARTIN, David** **1737-1797**
Born Anstruther, Fife, Apr 1; died Edinburgh, Dec 30. Portrait painter in oil and chalk, mezzotint and line engraver. Son of the village schoolmaster at Anstruther. Pupil of Allan Ramsay(qv) in London from c1752, he continued to work in the studio as well as studying at St. Martin's Lane Academy until the 1760s, accompanying the great man to Rome 1755-7. After Ramsay had secured Royal commissions, Martin, his chief assistant and copiest, produced many of the state portraits which now appear under his name. Married a woman of property and remained in London 1779-1782. Returning to Edinburgh 1785 after the death of his wife, he became associated with Raeburn, whose first instructor he had been, continued to practise as a portrait painter in London and was appointed Limner to the Prince of Wales. Much influenced by Reynolds although maintaining a more circumspect approach. Among his sitters was 'Benjamin Franklin', commissioned when the sitter was in London 1767, now in the White House, Washington. Other prominent sitters included the philosopher, 'Lord Kames' 1794 (SNPG), 'General Watson of Muirhouse', the brilliant advocate 'Andrew Crosbie' (now in the Faculty of Advocates, Parliament Hall), 'James Brodie of Brodie' 1785, the innovative chemist 'Joseph Black' 1787, (now in the Royal Medical Society, Edinburgh), Glasgow's Lord Provost, 'George Murdoch' 1793, (now in Glasgow AG) and the politician 'Robert Cunninghame-Graham' c1794-7 (SNPG). In 1791 the Royal Company of Archers commissioned him to paint their President, 'Sir James Pringle of Stitchell', and the portrait still hangs in their premises, the sitter having had to choose between Martin and Raeburn. Was most successful with his feminine portraits, though without the tonal subtleties of Ramsay, and at his best with three-quarter lengths. Although his work was uneven and never attained the level of vigour and elegance of Ramsay or Reynolds, often experiencing particular difficulty over hands, he was an important bridge between Raeburn and Ramsay and ranks among the top second line Scottish portrait painters. Among his best known engravings are 'L.F. Roubiliac', the sculptor, after A. Carpentiers,1765; 'Lady F. Manners', daughter of the Marquis of Granby, 1772; 'Jean-Jacques Rousseau', after Ramsay; and 'David Hume', after Ramsay. In 1780 he engraved a bookplate for Jno. Huddlestone. Two works of his were in the RA in 1779 (when he was described as 'principal painter to HRH the Prince of Wales for Scotland) and again in 1790. His own portrait, painted by Robert Adam, is in NPG. Represented in NGS(12), SNPG(16), Glasgow AG, The Binns (NTS), Brodie Castle (NTS).
**Bibl:** Armstrong 10; Bryan; Brydall 167-8; Bushnell; Caw 46-7; DNB; Halsby 141,150; Irwin 65-8 (pls 23,26,59); McKay 29; Macmillan [SA] 109-110,138,150-1; Wingfield.

**MARTIN, David McLeod RSW RGI SSA** **1922-**
Born Glasgow, 30 Dec. Painter in oil and watercolour, also gouache; teacher. Trained Glasgow School of Art 1940-1942. Served in the RAF in WW2 until 1946 when he returned for two further years' study in Glasgow, studying under Hugh Crawford(qv) and David Donaldson(qv), and at Jordanhill Training College 1948-49. Taught in various Glasgow schools until 1972 when he became Principal teacher at Hamilton Grammar School 1973-1983. Awarded May Marshall Brown Award (RSW) 1984. Retired early in order to devote himself full-time to painting. Early influences include the work of Cézanne because of its strong structural content and Bonnard because of his visual poetry, seductive colour and handling of pigment. His work is mainly derived from landscape from which he extracted rhythmic lines and related shapes sometimes echoed in other areas of the painting. Also painted still-life. Commissioned by Lord Bute to paint the island of Bute to decorate new premises in Rothesay. Elected SSA 1949, RSW 1961, RGI 1981, member of the Paisley Art Institute 1984, invited Artist at Perth Art Society, Art Gallery & Museum 1987. Exhibited at the RA, RSA, GI from 1949 & AAS 1981 and 1985. Represented in City of Edinburgh collection, Dick Institute (Kilmarnock).

**MARTIN, David Owen** **fl 1884-1935**
Glasgow painter of landscapes and coastal views, especially in the Kingdom of Fife; oil and watercolour. Author of *The Glasgow School of Painting,* 1897. Exhibited RSA(6), RSW(4), RI(1) & GI(3).

**MARTIN, Edwin** **fl 1913-1938**
Born Forfar, Angus. Portrait and landscape painter in oil; also portraits and occasional still lifes. Trained Glasgow School of Art. Moved to London shortly after graduating. Exhibited RA(10), RSA(7), GI(6), RI(1) & L(5).

**MARTIN, Elizabeth M** **fl 1850-1853**
Glasgow landscape painter; exhibited local scenes RSA in 1850 & 1853 from Union St.

**MARTIN, Miss Ella Maria** **fl 1855**
Edinburgh landscape painter; exhibited RSA(1).

**MARTIN, Emily J** **fl 1894-1898**
Edinburgh landscape painter; exhibited AAS(3) from 12 Glencairn Crescent.

**MARTIN, Francis Patrick** **1883-1966**
Born Anstruther, 18 Dec. Painter of genre and landscape in oil and watercolour; poster designer. Trained Glasgow School of Art. Principal works include 'Making Hay', 'The Garland' and 'March'. Prepared poster designs for the GPO. President, Glasgow Arts Club, Secretary, RGI. Exhibited RSA(52), GI(50+), AAS ('The Awakening of Spring' 1926) & L(3) from 3 Caird Drive, Glasgow. Represented in Glasgow AG.

**MARTIN, H Fulton** **fl 1884-1889**
Glasgow amateur landscape painter of 19 Broompark Drive, Dennistoun; exhibited GI(7), all scens at Cove.

**MARTIN, Henry Harrison** **fl 1853-1879**
Glasgow-based figurative and topographical painter. Often painted Spanish subjects, including 'At the bull fight' RA 1858. Moved to London c 1854. Exhibited RA(10) & GI(4), latterly from 132 Ebury St.

**MARTIN, Mrs Isobel** **fl 1976-1987**
Renfrewshire landscape painter. Exhibited GI(9) from Gilmour St, Eaglesham.

**MARTIN, Ivan** **1947-**
Born Glasgow. Primarily a watercolour painter; teacher. Trained Glasgow School of Art 1964-68, followed by a year at Aberdeen College of Education 1969. Won Hospitalfield scholarship, John & Mable Craig Bequest, Hutcheson Drawing prize. First solo exhibition in St Andrews 1986. Taught part-time Forgan Art Centre 1975-93 and Dundee College 1993-98. His work displays a sensitive treatment of light and colour.

**MARTIN, J Bruce** **fl 1879-1905**
Edinburgh painter who spent some time in Glasgow. Painter in oils; flowers and church interiors. Exhibited RSA(4) & GI(6).

**MARTIN, James** **fl 1853-1856**
Glasgow painter of landscapes, topographical works and nature studies. Son of an Edinburgh carver. Entered Trustees Academy 9 Nov 1853 having been recommended by Horatio McCulloch(qv). In 1854 moved to Claremont Place, Edinburgh. Exhibited RA(1) as an hon. exhibitor & RSA(17).

**MARTIN, James** **fl 1982-**
Banff amateur painter; exhibited RSA(13) 1982-88 and a figure subject at the AAS from Mill of Eden House, King Edward.

**MARTIN, James** **fl 1951**
Edinburgh sculptor; mainly wood carvings. Exhibited RSA(3) & GI(2) from Orchard Drive.

**MARTIN, James B** **fl 1902-1910**
Edinburgh landscape painter; also decorative book illustrations. Moved to London c1910. Exhibited RSA(2) from Shandwick Place & AAS(3).

**MARTIN, Jean B RSW** **c1946-**
Born Glasgow. Painter in watercolours. Trained Glasgow School of Art 1964-68. Awarded a Hospitalfield scholarship and the Hutcheson Drawing prize. "If there is a unifying theme running through my paintings", she says, "it is light...different seasons, times of day, and different locations present me with endless inspiration from the subtle

distinctions of light". Fond of bright colours quietly arranged in semi-abstract form. Elected RSW 2003.

**MARTIN, John** **fl 1846**
Edinburgh landscape painter; exhibited RSA(1).

**MARTIN, Lawrence** **fl 1860**
Perthshire painter; exhibited two local scenes at the RSA from Dunkeld.

**MARTIN, Matthew** **fl 1798**
Edinburgh engraver. Named as a subscriber to David Crawford's *Poems chiefly in the Scottish Dialect...1798*.

**MARTIN, Norman** **fl 1961-1968**
Lanarkshire sculptor of figures and animals. Exhibited RSA(10) & GI(10) from Carmunnock.

**MARTIN, Ronald** **1948-**
Born Glasgow. Sculptor. Trained Duncan of Jordanstone College of Art, 1975-80; after undertaking a postgraduate year, appointed part-time lecturer in the sculpture department 1982 and visiting lecturer 1983-84. Travelling scholarships enabled him to visit Germany and New York. The Blackness Project in Dundee commissioned a public sculpture 1984. Has held one-man exhibitions in Dundee and New Zealand.

**MARTIN, Samuel** **fl 1866-1877**
Paisley painter in oil and watercolour of coastal scenes and landscapes; exhibited RSA(8) & GI(8).

**MARTIN, William** **fl 1888-1889**
Amateur painter of Edinburgh who latterly moved to Walton, Surrey. Exhibited 'A country cobbler' at the RSA(1) & L(1).

**MARWICK, Thomas Purves** **1854-1927**
Edinburgh architect. Joined in partnership by his son Thomas Craigie M. A minor figure, best remembered for The Royal Bank of Scotland building, Palmerston Pl (1894).
**Bibl:** Gifford, see index.

**MARWICK, Thomas Waller** **c1901-1971**
Edinburgh architect. Son of Thomas Craigie M, grandson and later partner of Thomas Purves M(qv). Designed the Sun Alliance Assurance offices, 68 George St 'two fashionably framed-up elevations meeting perfunctorily at the corner of Frederick St with an ugly splay' [Gifford].
**Bibl:** Gifford 237,263,303,313.

**MARX, Enid** **1902-?**
Born London. Painter, designer and engraver. Trained Royal College of Art. Worked in St Andrews 1956-1959, returned south to join the staff of Croydon College of Art. First one-man exhibition at the Danish Institute, Edinburgh. Included in the annual Exhibition of Lady Artists in Glasgow. Represented in the V & A, USA and Sweden.

**MARY, Queen of Scots** **1542-1587**
Distinguished embroiderer. During her spell at the French court during her betrothal to the Dauphin 1548-58 instruction in needle-work was given by the Dauphin's mother, Catherine de' Medici herself a distinguished embroiderer. When Mary returned to Scotland 1561 she had with her two French embroiderers Pierre Oudry and Servais de Conde who for a time were her closest companions. According to the contemporary Nicholas White (an envoy of Queen Elizabeth) she also carved and painted. Surviving examples of her work are the Oxburgh hangings, now broken up; segments are in the V & A, Hardwick Hall (Derbyshire) and at Holyrood.
**Bibl:** Jane Roberts, Royal Artists, London 1987, 38-41, 39(illus), 41(illus); Margaret Swain, The Needlework of Mary Queen of Scots, Van Nostrand Reinhold 1973; Wardle: *The Embroideries of Mary Queen of Scots: Notes on the French Background*, Bulletin of the Needle and Bobbin Club, NY, vol 64, nos 1 & 2, 1981, pp3-14; Margaret Swain 32-40 (incl illus).

**MASON, Agnes Mabel Murray** **fl 1899-1903**
Little known Glasgow flower painter. Exhibited RSA(3) & GI(2) from Fern Tower, Kelvinside.

**MASON, David** **fl 1862-1869**
Leith painter of coastal and harbour scenes, mainly around the Firth of Forth. In 1863 moved to London, continuing to exhibit at the RSA where he showed six works.

**MASON, G R** **fl 1873-1877**
Edinburgh oil painter of landscapes; exhibited RSA(2).

**MASON, George** **fl 1844**
Edinburgh painter of naval subjects and marines. Exhibited 'The close naval engagement - boarding the prize' at the RSA, from Leith Walk.

**MASON, John jnr** **fl 1829-1831**
Architect and architectural draughtsman. Exhibited a number of topographical studies in watercolour at the RSA.

**MASON, Marion** **fl 1908**
Aberdeen amateur sculptor; exhibited AAS(1) from 24 Dee Place.

**MASON, William** **fl 1835-1855**
Edinburgh topographical artist. Often painted castles. Exhibited RSA (21) including 'Scene on the Marquis of Lothian's Grounds, Newbattle' 1846. His 'St. John's Chapel, Princes St, from Castle Terrace' was engraved as a coloured lithograph by Nichol c1845 as was 'Canongate Tolbooth' c1840.
**Bibl:** Butchart 66.

**MASSARD, F Victor** **fl 1905-1935**
Watercolour painter and teacher. Maintained a studio in Quarry Hall Terrace, Hamilton. Taught French at Hamilton Academy 1907-35. Founder member of Hamilton Art Club 1907. Exhibited RSW(1), RI(1) & GI(1).

**MASSIE, Ian J** **1937-**
Born Aberdeen. Works in watercolour, pen and ink, also sepia. Trained Gray's School of Art 1955-59 with a post-diploma year 1959-60. Visited Austria, France, Italy and Switzerland. First one-man show in Edinburgh 1962. Lives in Dunfermline. Exhibited RSA, AAS since 1959 & GI(5) latterly from 8 Alexandra St.

**MASSON, A S** **1806-1834/5**
Painter in oil and watercolour; landscapes; also teacher. A little known artist and Edinburgh drawing master. His superbly mature work depicting the first George Watson's Hospital was published when he was only 13 years old. The drawing was engraved by Robert Scott and issued in 1819. Butchart described it as 'undoubtedly one of the engraver's best efforts'. The sketch is full of movement with pupils practising archery, parents strolling among them, and kites flying overhead. (The Royal Infirmary took over the school in 1879). Another Edinburgh scene done much later, 'Leith from the Pier', was engraved by J Gellatly. Little more is known about the artist which given the quality of the known drawings, is as disappointing as it is remarkable. Between 1829 and 1835 he exhibited 40 works at RSA.
**Bibl:** Butchart 47; Halsby 273.

**MASSON, Andrew** **1750-1825**
Born nr Edinburgh. Landscape painter and drawing master. In 1824 he assisted Turner by making wave studies from the Bell Rock Lighthouse.
**Bibl:** Bryan.

**MASSON, Cecilia** **fl 1888-1896**
Amateur painter of game; exhibited GI(4), from Oakshaw Side, Paisley.

**MASSON, Gordon C** **fl 1964-1974**
Glasgow painter of coastal subjects. Exhibited GI(5).

**MASSON, Kenneth F** **fl 1951-1966**
Giffnock painter and sculptor. Topographical works. Moved to Thornliebank, Renfrewshire. Exhibited GI(6).

**MASSON, Linda** **fl 1970-**
Aberdeenshire sculptress. Trained Gray's School of Art, Aberdeen.

Favours figurative subjects in a quasi-abstract manner. Exhibited RSA(6) 1978-1983 & AAS since 1970, latterly from The Old Schoolhouse, Insch.

**MASTERTON, Eric Ritchie** **fl 1968-1969**
Glasgow artist; exhibited 'Black landscape' at the RSA; also GI(3).

**MATHER, George Marshall** **fl 1827-1857**
Edinburgh portrait painter in oil; also miniaturist and figurative painter. Trained Trustees Academy 1847-9. Exhibited RSA(41).

**MATHER, John** **1848-1916**
Hamilton painter in oil and watercolour of landscape. Trained Glasgow School of Art, subsequently painted in England, Scotland and France, exhibiting mostly in Glasgow. In 1878 visited Melbourne and went on to New Zealand. Founder member, Australian Art Association; President, Victorian Artists' Society; Trustee, Nat. Gall, Victoria (Australia). Exhibited RSA(2) & GI(2).

**MATHERS, Beatrice** **fl 1972**
Amateur Aberdeen landscape painter; exhibited AAS(1) from 41 Burnieboozle Crescent.

**MATHERS, David S** **fl 1938-1948**
Edinburgh painter, most probably a serving officer. Portraits and landscapes. Exhibited RSA(9) & GI(2) from a variety of addresses in Scotland and England including the Black Watch (Royal Highland Regiment), Edinburgh and finally Suffolk.

**MATHERS, Helen Mann** **fl 1906-1910**
Minor Stirling flower painter; exhibited AAS(1) & GI(1) from 31 Snowden Place.

**MATHESON, Andrew K M** **fl 1978-1979**
Aberdeen artist; exhibited AAS(3) from 2 Polmuir Rd.

**MATHESON, Miss Gertrude A** **fl 1935-1953**
Edinburgh animal, landscape, flower and figure painter in oil and watercolour. Exhibited RSA(18), RSW(1), GI(5) & AAS (Oban, 1935), latterly from Eglington Crescent.

**MATHESON, K Munro** **fl 1885**
Edinburgh artist. Exhibited a study of the old fortified church at Royat in the Auvergne at the RSA(1) from 19 Northumberland Street.

**MATHESON, Norman A** **fl 1959**
Aberdeen watercolour painter of landscape. Exhibited AAS(2) from 54 Richmondhill Place.

**MATHESON, Miss Pat** **fl 1974**
Stirlingshire painter. Exhibited 'Spring Carnival' at the GI from Killearn.

**MATHESON, Robert** **1807-1877**
Edinburgh architect. Attached for many years to the Office of Works, he worked in a restrained Italianate manner, elegantly displayed in the New Register House (1856-62) and General Post Office (1861-5). Also erected the monumental Royal Scottish Museum (1861-74), the chief architect of which was Francis Fowke; the Fountain in the forecourt of Holyrood (1858-9) and the Stables and Guardroom (1860-2); designer of both Lansdowne Crescent (1865) and Grosvenor Gdns as well as the New Palm House at the Royal Botanic Gdns (1856-8).
**Bibl:** Dunbar 149; Gifford, see index.

**MATHESON, Teresa A** **fl 1984**
Aberdeen jewellery designer. Exhibited AAS(1) from 8 Kingsland Place.

**MATHIE, D W** **fl 1847-1861**
Painter of portraits, genre and animal studies. Exhibited RSA(4) & GI(1) latterly from Rothesay, Bute.

**MATHIE, Emily** **fl 1890**
Minor Glasgow flower painter. Exhibited GI(1) from 15 South Park Terrace, Hillhead.

**MATHIE, James** **fl 1897-1938**
Ayrshire landscape painter. Possibly husband of Emily M(qv). Exhibited RSA(3), AAS(2), GI(25), & L(1) from Newmills 1897 and Kilmarnock 1906.

**MATHIESON, Charles** **fl 1974-1977**
Glasgow painter. Exhibited 'The Quarry' and 'Autumn leaves' at the GI, from Bearsden.

**MATHIESON, James Muir** **fl 1892-1922**
Musician from Bridge of Allan who painted watercolours of marine and coastal scenes. Moved to Glasgow c1905. Exhibited RA(3), RSA(4), GI(10) & L(9).
**Bibl:** Halsby 273.

**MATHIESON, John George** **fl 1918-1940**
Painter and etcher. Lived at 16 Allan Park, Stirling. His work shows the influence of D Y Cameron(qv). Painted and etched landscapes and views of towns in a highly constructed style. Although not a member of the Craigmill Group he was active in the neighbourhood and must have benefited from the presence of such neighbouring artists as Denovan Adam(qv), Jessie Algie(qv) and Nelly Harvey(qv) all of whom were living and working around Cambuskenneth at the same time. Exhibited RA(1), RSA(21), RSW(1), AAS)4), GI(32) & L(3).
**Bibl:** Halsby 273.

**MATHIESON, William** **fl 1878**
Edinburgh oil painter of landscape; exhibited RSA(1).

**MATHISON, John RGI** **fl 1956-**
Prolific Glasgow landscape painter. Generally painted the north-west coastline, especially Skye, in both oils and watercolour, mainly the former. Elected member RGI. Exhibits annually GI since 1956, latterly from Albert Dr.

**MATTHEW** **fl 1434**
King's painter. Payment of £37 16s recorded at Linlithgow palace for 'various materials of colours' delivered.
**Bibl:** Apted 61; J Stuart et al(eds), The Exchequer Rolls of Scotland, Edinburgh 1878-1908.

**MATTHEW, Charles** **fl 1886-1890**
Scottish portraitist in pencil and designer of bronze portrait medallions. SNPG holds thirteen examples including the portraits of several artists.

**MATTHEW, Miss Jessie** **fl 1901-1904**
Amateur Edinburgh painter of portraits and figure subjects. Exhibited RSA(2) & AAS(2), from 15 Ainslie Place.

**MATTHEW, John Fraser FRIBA FRIAS FSA(Scot)** **1875-1955**
Architect and draughtsman. Son of an Edinburgh military tailor whose interest in pageantry was shared by his son. Became known as 'the military man'. His first job was as a page in the retinue of the Lord High Commissioner at Holyrood. Lorimer's sister Louise was so impressed by a model of the building made by Matthew (for which he had won a prize at James Gillespie's school) that she took it home to show her brother. He was sufficiently enthusiastic to take on the young man as his first articled pupil, 1893. Trained also at Edinburgh School of Applied Art and Heriot Watt College. Served in the Boer War with the Edinburgh Volunteers and in WW1 as a Major in the Signals. Became a partner of Lorimer's 1927 after running the office for twenty-five years. Savage wrote that he was such a good office administrator (and Lorimer sometimes so temperamental) that 'they complemented each other's failings and the excellence of Lorimer's later work in the Gothic as well as in country houses rests almost as much on the support provided by Matthew as in Lorimer's vision' (p.27). Harry Hubbard recalls that he was 'an inveterate humourist with a keen awareness of the ridiculous and seemed never too busy to enjoy a joke' [Savage]. Primarily responsible for the Zoology building at Edinburgh University (1927) and, in spite of severe migraines, deeply involved with Lorimer in the design and planning of Edinburgh's War Memorial. After Lorimer's death Matthew took over the practice but in the slump that followed no further important work came their way, the only memorable building being the interdenominational Robin Chapel, Niddrie Mains Rd (1950-3).

**Bibl:** Gifford 118,487,538,601; Peter Savage, Lorimer and the Edinburgh Craft Designers, Edinburgh 1980, 13-14,26,27,35,40,53-4,66,87,126,142-5,151,153,167.

**MATTHEW, Margaret** **fl 1969**
Aberdeen-based potter. Exhibited AAS(2) whilst at Gray's School of Art, Aberdeen.

**MATTHEW, Sir Robert Hogg ARSA PRIBA** **1906-1975**
Born 12 Dec; died 21 Jne. Architect. Received many public and private commissions. Elected President, Royal Institute of British Architects 1962 and knighted the same year; relinquished the Presidency in 1964. Prolific exhibitor at RSA & GI.
**Bibl:** Gifford 323.

**MATTHEWS, Douglas** **fl 1974**
Glasgow painter. Exhibited GI(1) from Barmulloch.

**MATTHEWS, James** **1820-1898**
Architect. Had one of the largest practices in Scotland, based on Aberdeen and partnered by Thomas Mackenzie of Elgin and later by William Lawrie(qv). With Thomas Mackenzie(qv) designed St Columba High Church, Inverness (1851), the Free Church school, Nairn (1847-8), Craig Dunain Hospital, Inverness (1860-4), the Bank of Scotland, High St, Inverness (1847), the baronial Aldourie Castle, Inverness (1853-61), the 'baronialisation' of Cawdor Castle for the 1st Earl (1854-5). Later, with William Lawrie, he designed the excessively baronial Aigas House, Beauly (1877), the courthouses of Kingussie, Grantown-on-Spey (1867), Portree (1865), and Lochmaddy (1875), the Town House, Inverness (1876), the beginning of the Market Arcade in Inverness (1869), the Bank of Scotland, Kincraig (1865-7) & Kingussie (1875-6), the austere Free Church, Kingussie (1877-9), Beauly parish church (1877-9), the U-plan Drumnadrochit Hotel (1881-2), Drumnadrochit School (1876-7), the Free Church, Fasnakyle (1868), Invermoriston School (1876), the old head office of the Highland Railway Co, 28-34 Academy St, Inverness (1873-5), the Tomnacross primary school, Kiltarlity (1867), the Sheriff Court, Fort William (1876), the Free Church, Gairloch (1878), the nearby shooting lodge at Tournaig (1878), the Free Church, Arnisdale (1888), the tall twin-gabled house at Duisdale, Skye (1867), and the old Caledonian Bank, Lochmaddy, N Uist (1877). Best known for his ecclesiastical work.
**Bibl:** Dunbar 152; Gifford, H & I, 68,126,167,191,193-2,278,283, 385 et passim, plts 93,105.

**MATTHEWS, Jenny** **fl 1987-1988**
Edinburgh flower painter. Exhibited RSA in both above years.

**MATTHEWS, Robert Wilson** **1895-**
Landscape painter, illustrator and commercial designer. Trained Edinburgh College of Art and the RSA Schools. Awarded a Carnegie travelling scholarship 1922 and a Chalmers Bursary the same year. Exhibited RSA(3) 1920-1922 GI(1).

**MATTHIE, David** **fl 1873**
Edinburgh figure painter in oil; exhibited RSA(1).

**MAUGHAN, Miss Eliza** **fl 1863-1875**
Edinburgh painter in oil of landscapes, buildings and wild flowers. Moved to Melrose 1872-4 before returning to Edinburgh. Exhibited RSA(11), latterly from Mollendo Terrace.

**MAUGHAN, Paula A** **fl 1981**
Aberdeen-based jewellery designer. Trained at Gray's School of Art, Aberdeen. Exhibited AAS(2) from 19 King's Crescent.

**MAULE, John** **fl 1838**
Edinburgh sculptor. Exhibited a design for a Gothic monument to the memory of Sir Walter Scott at the RSA, 1838 from Broughton St.

**MAUNSELL, Geraldine (née Mockler)** **1896-?**
Born Bahmo, Burma. Coloured woodcut engraver; mainly landscapes. Studied at Glasgow and Edinburgh Schools of Art. Exhibited RSA(1), GI(4), AAS(2) & L(4) from Clyde Cottage, Lanark.

**MAVOR, Osborne Henry (James Bridie)** **1888-1951**
Born Glasgow. Physician, playwright and occasional painter. Studied medicine at Glasgow University; served with the RAMC in both wars. Better known as James Bridie, Mavor painted caricatures and illustrations to plays in a lively, colourful, idiosyncratic style signing his work 'OHM'. It is unclear whether or not he endeavoured to exhibit any of his watercolours, two of which - 'Gallstone Leaving the Common Duct' and 'The Train' - are in SNGMA.
**Bibl:** Mungo Campbell, 'The Line of Tradition', Nat Galls of Scotland, Ex Cat, Edinburgh 1993; Halsby 273.

**MAXTON, John Kidd** **1878-1942**
Born Perth. Studied interior design and stained glass design at Glasgow School of Art. Also painted landscape in watercolour in a basic style that sometimes totally failed. Moved to Edinburgh as a young man. Exhibited 'Springtime by the Old Cramond Bridge' at the RSA from 39 Marchmont Road.
**Bibl:** Halsby 273.

**MAXWELL, Alexander** **fl 1901**
Amateur Glasgow painter. Exhibited GI(1) from Douglas Gardens, Bearsden.

**MAXWELL, Miss Constance** **fl 1942**
Edinburgh amateur flower painter. Exhibited RSA(2) from Atholl Crescent.

**MAXWELL, George** **fl 1973**
East Kilbride abstract painter. Exhibited GI(2).

**MAXWELL, Hamilton RSW** **1830-1923**
Born Glasgow, 27 Dec; died Glasgow, 5 Feb. Painter of landscapes and architectural subjects, principally in watercolour. Educated Glasgow HS. Originally trained for a business career and lived in Australia 1852-56 where he dug for gold. Returned to England and worked in Derbyshire for two years before going to Bombay in 1859 where he became Sheriff and Chairman of the Bank of Bombay, 1878. In 1881 he returned to Scotland and took up full-time painting. President of Glasgow Art Club 1909. As well as working in Scotland, he painted widely in France, Italy and Germany and kept a studio in Paris 1893-98. Occasionally worked in North Africa using a style which, if sometimes clumsy and insensitive was, as Halsby points out, possibly the result of attempting large scale works without having sufficient draughtsmanship. Elected RSW 1885. Exhibited RSA(6), RSW(113), RIA(1), RI(2), GI(100), AAS(1890-1910) & L(6).
**Bibl:** Halsby 273.

**MAXWELL, Herbert** **fl 1875-1878**
Fort William painter of landscapes in watercolour; exhibited RSA(2).

**MAXWELL, James** **fl c1770**
Engraver who worked in Scotland and was probably Scottish. Studied Foulis Academy(qv) which supported a visit Italy to pursue his studies. Engraved 'Ovidius Naso', after Bellori; 'Hippocrates', after Sandrart; 'Sophocles', after Sandrart; a head of 'Joseph', after Jacomo Frey's print of Joseph and 'Potiphar's Wife', by Carlo Maratta; 'The lame man's head' (an etching), after Raphael; 'A muse', from the Museum Florentinum; 'Apollo', a statue, from the same museum.
**Bibl:** Bushnell; Duncan, Notices and Documents illustrative of the Literary History of Glasgow, 1831; Murray, Robert & Andrew Foulis, Glasgow 1913.

**MAXWELL, John RSA** **1905-1962**
Born Dalbeattie, 12 Jly; died Dalbeattie, 3 Jne. Painter in oil and watercolour, also occasional gouache, chalk and pen & ink; figurative subjects, landscapes and portraits. Educated Dalbeattie HS and Dumfries Academy; trained Edinburgh College of Art 1921-1926. Awarded a post-diploma scholarship and a travelling scholarship travelled to Paris 1927, working at the Academie Moderne under Leger and Ozenfant. Visited Italy and Spain, a trip during which he became acquainted with the Primitives. Returning to Scotland he embarked on a teacher training course at Moray House 1928 being appointed to the staff of Edinburgh College of Art 1929. Awarded the first Andrew Grant Fellowship of the ECA 1933 during which time he painted an important mural at Craigmillar School. The same year he was elected SSA. In 1935 returned to the ECA, remaining there until his retirement to paint full-time 1946. His first major exhibition was

held in London jointly with William Gillies(qv) 1954. Exhibited with 'Six Scottish Artists' at Nottingham and 'Contemporary Scottish Artists' in Stirling 1959. Retired from all teaching owing to ill health 1961, returning to Millbrooke nr Dalbeattie, returning for a brief spell to teach in Edinburgh 1955. Although much influenced by Braque, Chagall and Soutine when in France, and by the work of the symbolist Odilon Redon, he returned from the Continent somewhat unsettled. This mood was changed by Gerald Moira. At the time that Maxwell was at the ECA in 1929, Moira was the Principal and was also engaged on a large scale mural for St Cuthbert's Church, Niddrie, Edinburgh. An assistant being required Maxwell was appointed. He and Gillies, encouraged by a happy and productive working visit to Kircudbright together subsequently went to the Ardnamurchan peninsular. He retired from the Glasgow School of Art for health reasons in 1943 and went to live in Dalbeattie, returning for a brief spell to teach in Edinburgh 1955. As his work developed, 'we find a completely personal vision, blossoming into a number of fine, original paintings which have their basis in flowers and figure and birds...Large bouquets of flowers intermingled with female shapes, with birdlike and butterfly forms, the moon and stars above village houses and churches with wrought-iron gates and balconies. Work of this period also shows something more deeply characteristic of the atmosphere and quiet colour of his native Galloway - an area to which he frequently returned - and also connects with the impression received from the early mural at Niddrie. His colour scheme, built on a basis of rich grey, was composed mainly of golden yellows, russets, umbers and greens, contrasted with violet and blue-grey. When the theme demanded, he could play a sparkling tune with the gayest colour notes. Yellows, both in oil and watercolour, he managed with great skill and subtlety, ranging from the palest citron to the deepest orange. In green, also a difficult colour, as in the plumage of some exotic bird's wing or in a bower of spring foliage framing a sheltering figure, he could judge quality to perfection....His palette was in keeping with his method of painting. Its wooden surface, thickly encrusted with layers of hard paint, had several craters of varying depth form and rounded.....Into these cavities were squeezed fresh paint which took on a mysterious quality and become part of an exquisite harmony. In striking contrast was his method of painting watercolours, the most personal of all his work. They vary from gouache, to a mixture of gouache and watercolour. Some were reinforced by the addition of pen and ink. Their effect was usually got by flooding the paper with a basic colour, and on the moist surface skilfully suggesting forms, be they cliffs or trees or birds or figures, and guiding the spreading colour into a suggested pattern as it soaked into the paper...Among the finest and most satisfying of his watercolours are his later examples in which female nudes, flowers and bird forms are the chief motives. Maxwell was a complex character, generally quiet and thoughtful and given to contemplation...but he was a clubbable person and on occasion he could take part in a convivial evening with real enjoyment' [D M Sutherland]. Maxwell was unique in that 'alone among his group, he sought to extend the range of his art beyond the confines of both hedonism and expressionism. He did so by exploring the invisible spirit that is imminent in nature.'[McClure]. Elected ARSA 1945, RSA 1949. Exhibited regularly RSA & AAS(9). Represented in Tate AG, SNGMA, RSA, Aberdeen AG, City of Edinburgh collection, SAC, Gracefield Art Centre (Dumfries), Glasgow AG, Kirkcaldy AG, Manchester, Paisley AG, Perth AG, Sydney AG (Australia).
**Bibl:** Gage 28-30 et al; Hardie 162-4; Halsby 213-215 et passim; Hartley 151; David McClure, John Maxwell, Edinburgh 1976; Rothenstein 176 (plts 106, 107); SAC, Three Scottish Painters (Maxwell, Eardley, Philipson) 1963; Scot Art Rev v, 4, 1956; Studio 118, July 1939; 126, Sept 1943; June 1945; 146, Sept 1953; 152, Aug 1956; 154, Aug 1957; Aug 1960; D M Sutherland, 'John Maxwell 1905-1962' (Ex Cat 1963); R H Westwater,'John Maxwell', Scottish Arts Rev, v, 4, 1956.

**MAXWELL, Sir John Stirling RSW** **1866-1956**
Born Jne 6; died May 30. Amateur watercolourist who lived in Pollokshaws, Glasgow. Expert on rhododendrons. 'His watercolours have an unusual frozen style which can be charming at times, especially when he is concerned over detail' [Halsby]. Painted views in Scotland and on the Continent and was a Trustee of the Wallace Collection and the National Galleries of Scotland. Elected RSW 1936, HRSW 1938. In addition to many exhibits at the RSW also showed GI(4) & RWS(1). Represented in Paisley AG.
**Bibl:** Caw 215; Halsby 273.

**MAXWELL, Joseph RSW** **1925-?**
Born Kilmarnock, 25 Nov. Painter in oil, but mainly watercolour. Portraits, landscapes, seascapes and interiors. Trained Edinburgh College of Art, also trained as a cartographer/draughtsman. Interested in line, rhythm and shape. Influenced by the work of Paul Nash, Ravilious, Gillies(qv) and John Maxwell(qv). Elected RSW 1960. Lived in Tayport, Fife. Staff member, Dundee College of Education. Exhibited RSA(31) & GI(23). Represented in Dundee AG, Glasgow AG, Paisley AG, Khan AG (New York).

**MAXWELL, Marion M** **fl 1900**
Minor flower painter of 10 Northpark Street, Glasgow. Exhibited GI(1).

**MAXWELL, Robert** **fl 1835-1839**
Glasgow painter of still life and dead game; exhibited RSA(4) from Maxwelton Place.

**MAXWELL, Tom** **?-1937**
Born Glasgow. Self-taught etcher; mainly landscape, topographical and harbour scenes. On the staff of the *Evening Times.* Lived in Glasgow and Kilbridge, Ayrshire. Exhibited GI(36) & L(13). Represented in City of Edinburgh collection.

**MAXWELL, Miss Ursula C** **fl 1942**
Edinburgh amateur sculptress. Exhibited two portrait busts at RSA.

**MAXWELL, William Hall** **fl 1877-1886**
Edinburgh painter in oil of landscapes and still-life. Spent some time studying and living in Barbizon, France c1884. Exhibited Paris Salon & RSA(12) including two Barbizon subjects in 1883 and other French scenes in 1882 and 1884; also GI(16) 1877-1886.

**MAY, Elizabeth L ('Elsie')** **fl 1959-1964**
Aberdeen painter and printmaker; still life and genre. Exhibited AAS(6) latterly from 14 The Chanonry, Old Aberdeen.

**MAY, Frederick F** **fl 1896**
Amateur Aberdeen landscape painter; exhibited 'On the Don' at the AAS, from 334 King St.

**MAY, J C** **fl 1906**
Minor Glasgow painter of Woodbourne, Partickhill; exhibited GI(1).

**MAY, James** **fl 1855-1879**
Edinburgh painter in oil and watercolour of landscapes, figure subjects and portraits. Lived in many different places within the city. A competent painter although sometimes his work lacked finish. Prolific in his lifetime, but surprising how seldom his paintings are now seen. Proficient at painting children, generally in interiors. Exhibited RA 1866 & GI(9), but mainly RSA(72).

**MAY, Mrs Philip** **fl 1875**
Edinburgh portrait painter. Wife of Phil May. Exhibited a landscape at the RSA in 1875.

**MAYNE, Arthur** **fl 1892**
Minor Edinburgh painter; exhibited 'Cramond ferry' at the RSA from 56 Bruntsfield Place.

**MAYO, Drummond** **fl 1980-**
Stirling painter of flowers and semi-abstract subjects. Exhibited RSA & GI(1) since 1980 from Rait, Perthshire.

**MAZZINI, Torquato** **fl 1875**
Portrait painter. Although presumably of Italian origin, lived in Edinburgh and exhibited RSA(1).

**MEAD, Thomas** **fl 1858**
Edinburgh oil painter of landscape, also theatre scene painter. Exhibited RSA(1) when working at the Queen's Theatre.

**MEADOWS, Christopher** **1863-c1914**
Born Hungarford, Leics, May. Brother of Robert M(qv). Glasgow-based painter. Moved to Renfrewshire 1890 then to Saltcoats, Ayr at the turn of the century. Member of the Society of Six (the others being

George C Guthrie, Albert Beard, Tom Gilfillan, C H Lilley and R Clouston Young). Painted a view of Routenburn golf course. Exhibited GI(15). Represented in Paisley AG.

**MEADOWS, Kenny** **fl 1863-1870**
Edinburgh oil painter of literary subjects; exhibited RSA(3) & GI(2).

**MEADOWS, Robert** **1846-fl 1896**
Born Hungarford, Leics, April. Brother of Chris M(qv). Painter in watercolour, mostly landscapes. Married into an Aberdeen family 1870 and settled in Scotland. Lived at various times in Campsie, Leicester, Glasgow and eventually Houston, Renfrewshire. Exhibited RSA(1) & 'Old Aberdeen' at RGI 1874 and eight more works thereafter.

**MEARS, Sir Frank Charles PRSA** **1880-1953**
Born Tynemouth, 11 Jly; died New Zealand, 25 Jan. Architect. Studied at Edinburgh School of Applied Art. Practised for some years in Scotland. Apprenticed to Lorimer(qv) after schooling at George Watson's. Prior to 1914 he worked with Ramsay Traquair, also with Sir Patrick Geddes on the studies of Edinburgh and Dublin. For a short time he was with Sir Edwin Lutyens with whom he went to Jerusalem, working there also with Geddes on the new Hebrew University on Mt Scopus. Contributed an interesting article 'Primitive Edinburgh' to *The Early Views and Maps of Edinburgh,* 1544-1852, RGS 1919. Returned to Edinburgh in the 1920s. Responsible for the George V Bridge in Aberdeen, Livingstone Memorial at Blantyre, Royal Scots Monument in Princes Street Gardens, Edinburgh, and, with Geddes, the layout of the Zoological Gardens, Edinburgh. His principal contributions were in the footsteps of Geddes, developing in a practical way the latter's theoretical teaching. Elected ARSA 1936, RSA 1943 and President, RSA 1944, the year he was knighted. Exhibited many designs at the RSA & GI.
**Bibl:** Gifford 116,195,214,527,571,pl.2.

**MEDINA, Sir John (Juan) Baptiste de** **1659-1710**
Born Brussels; died Edinburgh. Painter of portraits, occasional history subjects; illustrator. Son of Medina de l'Asturias described as a Spanish Captain of Brussels. Worked in oils and sometimes chalk. Trained under François Duchatel before moving to London 1686, quickly establishing a successful practice as a portrait painter, becoming the leading portraitist in Scotland between 1689 and 1710. Illustrated Ovid's *Metamorphoses* and Milton's *Paradise Lost,* the latter published by Jacob Ponson, 1688. In 1691 he met the Earl of Leven in London, painted his portrait and that of his parents, the Earl and Countess of Melville. They were so impressed by his work that they persuaded the young artist to visit Scotland, aided by Lord Leven's wife Anna, his mother, the Countess of Melville and his second cousin, Margaret, Countess of Rothes.There it is said he subsequently painted half the nobility. Walpole observed that he took with him to Scotland a number of bodies, to which the heads of commissioned sitters were then added. 'His work, at its best far from robust, often descends to a feeble and vapid imitation of Lely' [McKay]. In Edinburgh 1693-4, he set up a new studio and as well as portraits, painted figure subjects, several of which are at Penicuik House. Knighted 1707. Remained in Scotland almost entirely until his death. Buried in Greyfriars Churchyard. His practice was not confined to portrait painting, several of his figure subjects being in the collection of the Earl of Wemyss and Sir David Forbes (brother to Duncan Forbes of Culloden). Stirling, in his *Annals of the Artists of Spain* (quoted by Brydall) said of the Medina portraits in the possession of the Earl of Leven 'of the beauties of the family, for whose fair heads Medina had the honour of finding bodies, the most pleasing are a pretty 'Lady Balgonie of Northesk' and the lovely 'Margaret Nairne', wife of Lord Strathallan, slain at Culloden, and herself imprisoned in Edinburgh Castle. The first Duke of Argyll was also one of his patrons. He painted a large and excellent picture of a nobleman and his two sons who were both Dukes in their turn - John, who claimed the victory at Sheriffmuir, and Archibald, better known as Lord Islay, Walpole's viceroy beyond the Tweed. The Highland heads of these chieftains Medina fitted upon Roman bodies; and he represented the sire in boots of lustrous brass, giving a laurel wreath to his eldest boy, thus vindicating his claims to the national faculty of second-sight, as he stands pictured among his ancestors at Inveraray. Also painted a large family group for the Gay Gordon, who held out Edinburgh for James II. His best figure painting is regarded as 'Apelles and Campaspe'. During his time in Scotland his style changed from the 'full, sonorous Baroque portraits of the 1690's to the lighter, freer, less formal portraits of the following decade'. Some of his best work, likened not unfavourably to Hogarth, were his informal portraits of his own children. Represented in NGS, SNPG(14), NGS, Inveraray Castle, Blair Castle, Royal College of Surgeons (Edinburgh), Brodie Castle (NTS), Drum Castle (NTS; portrait of 'Lord Forbes'). Apted lists all known portraits.
**Bibl:** Apted 61-64; Brydall 94-96; Caw 20-21; Holloway 33-42 et passim; Irwin 39-41,47,65,98-9; Macmillan [SA] 82-4,92,95-6; Rosalind K Marshall,'John de Medina', NGS 1988; R K Marshall, 'Childhood in XVIIth Century Scotland', SNPG Cat, Edinburgh 1976,66-7; McKay 8; Scottish Records Office, registers of testaments, 8/8/85, dated 16 March 1711.

**MEDINA, John** **1721-1796**
Born and died Edinburgh. Grandson of Sir John M(qv). His son (also **John Medina**) was an artist whose portrait John Medina painted and which is now in the NGS. A portrait painter though of quite minor consequence. In early life he worked as a copiest and repaired some paintings at Holyrood. His main claim to attention is his portrait of 'Andrew Gairdner', founder of the Orphan Hospital. It is supposed that this work, probably painted shortly before the sitter's death 1739 was presented to the hospital 36 years later. One interesting feature, noted by Irwin, is that a building related to the sitter's interests is shown through an open window, behind the seated figure. Exhibited six works in London, 1772-74, but none in the Academy. From 1782 to 1792 living in Hyndford's Close, Edinburgh. In the *European Magazine,* Oct 1776, it was written 'his peculiar talent was the rescuing from decay and ruin of some of the best collections of pictures in Scotland; a recent instance of which was afforded in the Collection of Kings in the Palace of Holyroodhouse, the rescue of which will long appear a monument to his merit'. Represented in SNPG(copies).
**Bibl:** Brydall 96-7; Caw 21.

**MEEK, Miss Doris** **fl 1943**
Lanarkshire weaver. Exhibited GI(7), mostly homespun designs using native dyes, from Airdrie.

**MEGGET, John** **fl 1831-1832**
Edinburgh portrait painter and associate of the Norie family. Exhibited RSA(3), latterly from 5 Calton St.

**MEIKLE, Henry** **fl 1874-1875**
Glasgow oil painter of landscape and figure subjects; exhibited RSA(2) & GI(1).

**MEIKLE, William** **fl 1894-1910**
Glasgow stained glass window designer. Founder and senior partner of old Glasgow stained glass design business, Wm Meikle & Sons. Their work can be seen in St Michael's, Linlithgow, 'The Boy Samuel'; the east window of the Clark Memorial church, Largs; and four lancet lights depicting the Evangelists (1900) in Mayfield Church. The firm exhibited corporately at the GI(21) 1895-1928.
**Bibl:** Gifford 45,635; Painton Cowen, Stained Glass in Britain, 1985, 234, 238.

**MEIKLEJOHN, Mrs Dudley** **fl 1882-1883**
Lasswade watercolour painter of animals and landscapes. Lived latterly at Mount Lothian, Dalkeith. Exhibited twice at the RSA, on the second occasion a landscape in Iceland bore the signature 'Dudley Meiklejohn'.

**MEIN, Miss Margaret J** **?-1896**
Edinburgh painter in oil and watercolour of flower studies, figure studies and country scenes. Probably related to Thomas M(qv) and William G M(qv). Exhibited RA(1), RSA(10), RSW(2), RI(1), RBA(1), GI(13), AAS & L(4) from 12 Glencairn Crescent.

**MEIN, Thomas** **fl 1873-1887**
Edinburgh painter in oil and watercolour of landscapes, especially loch and river scenery. Probably related to Margaret M(qv) and William G M(qv). Exhibited RSA(9) including several of the Clyde, Loch Awe and Loch Earn; also GI(1).

**MEIN, William Gordon** **fl 1866-1925**
Figure and landscape painter in oil, watercolour and pen & ink; also illustrator. Moved from Kelso to Edinburgh in 1894 and to London in the early 1900s. Specialised in illustrating boys' stories including Nigel Tourneur's *Hidden Witchery* 1898 and S R Crockett's *My Two Edinburghs* 1913. Also worked for *The Dome* (1899-1900). Probably related to Margaret M(qv) and Thomas M(qv). Exhibited RA(1), RSA(3), RI(2) & GI(2).
**Bibl:** Caw 418; Houfe.

**MELDRUM, David G (or S)** **fl 1884-1885**
Minor Kirkcaldy painter; exhibited 'The duckpond 'at the RSA from Kirkcaldy and a picture entitled 'September' at the AAS in 1885.

**MELDRUM, George Hamilton** **fl 1941-1946**
Glasgow painter in pastel and watercolours. Exhibited GI(3) from St. Vincent St.

**MELDRUM, George William** **fl 1917-1920**
Sculptor. Mainly portrait busts. Exhibited RA(1) & RSA(1).

**MELDRUM, Max** **1875-c1950**
Born Edinburgh. Painter in oil, teacher and theorist. Migrated to Melbourne 1889 and enrolled at the National Art Gallery School of Victoria under Bernard Hall. Here he acquired a life-long concern with tonal values, a predeliction for the artfully designed lights of studio interiors as well as developing an interest in the rational theory of painting. In 1893 he joined the Prehistoric Order of Cannibals, a club of young artists founded in Melbourne 1893. In 1899, having won a travelling scholarship, went to Paris but disliked the 'ineptitude and academic conventions of the schools which persuaded him to study instead in the school of nature which he found in Brittany'. In spite of this he frequently exhibited at the Paris Salon and in 1908 became an Associate of the Société Nationale des Beaux Arts. Remained in France for thirteen years during all of which time his dislike of modern art increased. Lengthy studies at the Louvre persuaded him that all great art had been impersonal and was primarily concerned with the objective depiction of appearance. In 1913 he returned to Melbourne and four years later established a school in which he developed, practised and taught his theory. This had a great effect on the development not only of Australian art but extended as far as the United States. He believed that the artist's aim was to transfer an exact illusion within the limitations of painting of the objects present in the act of perception. He linked this theory with criticism of society, becoming an ardent pacifist. 'For many his single-mindedness and resistance to personal corruption by social and financial success made him a symbol of artistic integrity in a philistine community where the idea of art as a way of life was a poor joke. In his own art he was a capable and honest but not an inspired craftsman. Much of it has the air of pedantry one finds in his writings. But an early portrait of his mother reveals a precocious mastery of his craft and a truly superb impersonalisation of sympathy reminiscent of the young Rembrandt. The latent humanism of such early works, however, did not survive the intellectual rigour which his arid theory imposed upon his own painting....His theory..is probably the last of those attempts..to deduce a naturalistic theory of painting from scientific or pseudo-scientific presuppositions. Yet, oddly enough, in his later work the very breadth with which Meldrum painted his planes of tones, and his refusal to add detail and polish, had the effect of introducing into his art a kind of tonal, cubic reduction akin in many ways to the modified, post-impressionist methods adopted by many painters during the 1920s' [Smith]. He exerted great influence not only with his teaching but also among a wide range of pupils including Archibald Colquhoun, who was to establish a school in Melbourne 1927, Hayward Veal and Percy Leason, who transferred the theory to America and taught a modified version at Statton Island and at his own summer school on the shores of Lake Champlain. Meldrum himself embarked on a lecture tour in the United States 1931. Close friend of his fellow Scot George Frater(qv). Has been described as 'the greatest figure in Australian art in the period between the wars', but was unpopular among many sections of society, especially during 1937-45 when a trustee of the National Gallery of Victoria. Represented in Sydney AG(Australia), Melbourne AG (Australia).
**Bibl:** C Colahan (ed) Max Meldrum: His Art and Views, Melbourne 1917; R R Foreman (ed) The Science of Appearance as formulated and taught by M Meldrum, Sydney, 1950; Harold Osborne(ed) Twentieth Century Art, 1988, 365; B Smith, Australian Painting 106,110,128,130,161,177-9,181,189,191-3,195-6,199-201,215, 217,271,308.

**MELDRUM, William** **1865-1942**
Glasgow watercolour landscape painter. Highland views usually in sombre tones heightened with bodycolour. Friend of several of the Glasgow Boys and J Q Pringle(qv). Exhibited RSA(1) 'The Knoydart hills from Skye'; irregularly RSW & GI(11). Represented in Glasgow AG.
**Bibl:** Halsby 273.

**MELLIN (MELVILLE), Andrew** **fl 1611-1634**
Aberdeen painter. Married Isobel Jamesone, possibly a relative of George Jamesone(qv) 1613. An indication that there was a relationship between the two artists is strengthened by the fact that in 1634 both Mellin and Jamesone were godfathers to the same child. In 1611 he painted 'the new beir' in St Nicholas Kirk, Aberdeen.
**Bibl:** Aberdeen City Archives, Kirk and Bridge Works Accounts 1571-1670; Apted 64; Apted 64; Thomson 39.

**MELLIN (MELVILLE), John** **fl 1587-1605**
Early Aberdeenshire painter. In 1587 he painted an imitation tapestry at the rear of the rood loft at St Nicholas Kirk, Aberdeen as well as the east clock. Probably responsible for decorated ceilings at Delgatie Castle, Aberdeenshire, signed 'J M' and dated 1592/3 and 1597. In 1604 was accused by the Church of painting a crucifix for the burial of Isobel Auchterlony, wife of William Gordon of Gight. Mellin admitted that he had done this but that it was at the Laird's request for which he produced the necessary proof. In 1604/5 he painted the arms on the 'Tolbuithe dur' in Aberdeen.
**Bibl:** Apted 64; SRO, Aberdeen Kirk-Session Records, CH 2/448/2, 13 May 1604; Thomson 38-9.

**MELLIS, Margaret Nairne** **1914-**
Born Wu-kung-fu, China, 22 Jan. Landscape and figurative painter. Of Scottish descent, she came to Britain when only a year old. Trained Edinburgh College of Art 1929-33 under S J Peploe(qv). An Andrew Grant postgraduate award enabled her to visit Paris, where she studied under André Lhôte, also Cornwall and the South of France. Began as a figurative painter but soon turned to constructivism, using paper, cardboard, wood, slate, stone and eventually, marble, to make collages and reliefs. After a difficult divorce from the artist Adrian Stokes, whom she had married in 1938 and with him becoming a seminal figure in the St Ives group, she remarried and from 1948 until 1950 lived in France. Returned to figure painting in oil, gradually moved towards simplification and pure colour abstraction. Her work has been dominated by colour, using unbleached and unprepared linen canvasses. Exhibition in Edinburgh 2004. Lives and works in Suffolk. Represented in Tate AG, V & A, SNGMA, Sheffield AG, SAC, Ferens Gallery (Hull).
**Bibl:** Hartley 152; Pier Art Centre, Stromness, Orkney, 'Margaret Mellis 1940-1980', (Ex Cat 1982); Redfern Gall, London, 'Margaret Mellis 1940-1987', (Ex Cat 1987).

**MELLISH, Mrs Joyce Carol** **fl 1973-1987**
Glasgow painter of nudes and portraits. Exhibited GI(18) from Gardner St.

**MELROSE, Walter B** **fl 1887-1910**
Edinburgh landscape painter of mainly rustic scenes in oil. Lived for a time in Musselburgh before moving back to Edinburgh. Exhibited RSA(22), GI(12) & L(1).

**MELROSE, William** **fl 1988-**
Edinburgh painter of marine pictures in a semi-abstract style. Exhibits RSA from Silverknowes Drive.

**MELVILLE, Alexander** **fl 1846-1878**
Painter in oil; portraits, miniatures, allegorical subjects. Worked for most of his life in London. His wife Eliza Smallbone was also an artist. Exhibited regularly Royal Academy 1846-1868, GI(1), BI & SBA. The Melville A Jamieson collection included a miniature on ivory of a man, 2" x 1 5/8", signed on the reverse 'Painted by Alex: Melville, 1858'.

**MELVILLE, Arthur ARSA RSW ARS** **1855-1904**
Born Loanhead-of-Guthrie, Forfar, 10 Apr; died Witley, Surrey, 28 Aug. Painter of landscape and figure subjects in watercolour; also occasional illustrator. Son of a large family, as a child he moved to East Lothian where he worked in a shop, studying art in Edinburgh in the evening. Eventually enrolled as a full-time student at the Edinburgh College of Art studying under John Campbell Noble(qv). After three years in Edinburgh, in 1878 he embarked on his first trip overseas, going to Paris where he met Robert Weir Allan(qv), studying for a time at the Ateliers. He preferred studying contemporary French work and stayed for a while at Grez-sur-Loing where a number of artists from various countries were working. Became particularly friendly with a young Scottish painter called Middleton Jameson(qv), brother of the famous Dr Jameson. Here he became increasingly concerned with the translucent qualities of his chosen medium. In 1880 travelled to the Middle East visiting Baghdad, Cairo, Istanbul and Karachi. In Baghdad he narrowly escaped death after being assaulted by bandits, remaining there until August 1882. During this time we find a heightened colour, a suggestion of romanticism and a gradual trend towards a greater discrimination in what he sought to record although his 'looseness of touch and firmness of intention' was retained. His preoccupation with Eastern subjects remained throughout the 1880s and although by this time he was already associated with the Glasgow group and visited France with them in 1886 and 1889, he did not return to Algiers and Spain until 1890. Indeed in 1885 he visited Orkney. Returned to Algiers 1891 and 1892 with Frank Brangwyn and in 1894 he visited Venice for the first time. Married and settled in Witley, Surrey 1899. Here he began experimenting in oils but the enthusiasm for travel remained and that year he was back in Spain, in 1902 in Italy, and in 1904 embarked upon what was to be his final trip to Spain where he and his wife both contracted typhoid from which he died at the tragically early age of 49. Although his general style and technique never changed, his output may be divided into four periods. The first tentative time of development during his early visit in France of which 'Kincup Meadow' 1879 is regarded as the best example, with its hints of Corot; the second phase was during his first Eastern expedition where his own distinctive type of impressionism came to the fore. A mastery of controlled wetness was not yet apparent. His chief motif is light, his interest in the romantic impressions and the mood of mystery and poetry with little concern for specifics; in the third phase called by his biographers his 'Spanish period' there is 'an extremely personal synthesis of form expressed with force and dexterity. In bullfights, Spanish markets and landscapes, immediate beauty and truth are revealed in the glory of colour...His colour has became more transparent, his tone more dazzlingly clear, his whites more resonant'. The last phase was best captured in Venetian Nocturnes where the full development of his genius finds its expression. 'He could lay on colour with the freshness of a shower of rain. His control of touch was masterly. Moreover, he drew by mass. It was always wrong to call his work watercolour "drawings" for they are watercolour paintings from first to last. His second great quality was his power of controlling and combining strong colours to produce harmonious effects.. He was able to compose a picture to grasp the pictorial aspects of a scene, where others saw only confused movement and formalist glitter, Melville imposed rhythm and shape' [McKay]. He was one of the great artistic innovators of his time and perhaps, with his contemporary, Crawhall(qv), the most masterful and innovative watercolourist of his age. His position with the Glasgow Boys was ambiguous. He had already developed his highly individual art before meeting them but, having become their friend, he spent a great deal of time in their company until he abandoned Edinburgh 1889. Contributed occasionally to *The Graphic* (1882). Elected RSW 1885, ARSA 1886, ARWS 1880, RWS 1900, RP 1891. Exhibited RSA(82) 1875-1905, also RA(15), RI(8), GI(35), RWS (24), AAS & L(29). Represented in the BM, Tate AG, V & A, Metropolitan Museum (New York), Musée de L'Art Moderne (Paris), NGS, Aberdeen AG, Glasgow AG, Liverpool AG, Dundee AG, Kirkcaldy AG, Leith City AG, Edinburgh City collection, Paisley AG, Brodie Castle (NTS), Walker AG (Liverpool), Preston AG.
**Bibl:** AJ 1904, 336, 381 (obit); Caw 394-8 et al; Dundee AG 'Arthur Melville' (Ex Cat 1977); Halsby 131-4 et passim; Hardie 94-6 & passim ch vi; Houfe; Irwin 380-392; Edward McCurdy, 'A.M.' Scottish Art & Letters, Glasgow 1950; Agnes Ethel McKay, Arthur Melville, Scottish Impressionist, 1855-1904, Leigh-on-Sea, 1951; Macmillan [SA] 254-5,261-4,276-7,268-8; OWS Club ,1,1923; W Graham Robertson, Time Was, London 1931; Studio 37 (1906), 284-293; 42 (1908), 143-5; 82 (1921), 227, 251, 257; 83 (1922), 132-5; Iain Gale, Arthur Melville, Atelier, 1996.

**MELVILLE, Miss Frances Annie** **fl 1886**
Amateur painter in oil of local landscapes; exhibited RSA from 41 Townsend Place, Kirkcaldy.

**MELVILLE, Mary** **fl 1883-1886**
Amateur flower painter of Glasgow; exhibited GI(5).

**MELVILLE, Walter** **fl 1681-1729**
Early Edinburgh painter. Son of William Melville, painter. Apprenticed 1681 to the herald painter George Porteous(qv). In 1687 he was made a Burgess of the City of Edinburgh and in 1691 Burgess of the Canongate. Named as the Rothesay Herald in July, 1697 and again as a herald painter in 1700. In 1690-1697 he was working at Holyrood House, in 1690 'whitening and painting severall places in the King's apairtment', also worked for Lord Forfar in the Castle and in 1693 was painting the Commissioner's bedchamber, the Secretary's apartment and other rooms. From 12 October 1697 he was working on ceilings in the Earl of Annandale's lodgings. During the same period also employed at Edinburgh Castle. Gifford suggests that a panel on the W wall of Magdalen Chapel in the Cowgate depicvting the City arms may have been his. He had as apprentices John Waitts 1696 and John Cochrane 1699.
**Bibl:** Apted 65-6; Gifford 164; Scottish Record Office E.28/ 579/ 14/ 1-2;E; E. 25/580/2/7; E. 28/581/17.

**MELVIN, Mrs Gladys Georgie S** **fl 1919-1921**
Glasgow miniaturist. Exhibited three miniature portraits at the GI.

**MELVIN, Grace** **1892-1977**
Born Glasgow; died Vancouver. Glasgow-based designer, embroiderer and illustrator; taught illumination at the Glasgow School of Art 1920-27 before moving to Vancouver. Appointed head of the design department at that city's School of Art, remaining there until 1952. Retrospective exhibition, Vancouver 1980. Represented in permanent collection of Glasgow School of Art.
**Bibl:** Burkhauser 75, 154, 186.

**MELVIN, James William** **1860-1934**
Born Fife; died Wallasey, Apr. Part-time painter, mostly landscape in oils; also portraits but less successfully. Most of his work was in and around Angus where he worked in the hotel business, latterly owning the Kinloch Arms, Carnoustie 1908-28, before retiring to Wallasey. Exhibited GI(1) 1892 from 43 Peddie Street, Dundee.

**MELVIN, R G** **fl 1867**
Glasgow painter of watercolour topography. Exhibited GI(1) from 124 St. Vincent St.

**MENDELOW, Anne** **fl 1985-**
Born in South Africa, moved to Scotland in the late 70s. Self-taught painter of interiors, landscape and figurative work in a variety of mediums. Owns her own Gallery in Glasgow. Exhibits RSA & RGI.

**MENELAWS, Adam** **c1775-1835**
Scottish architect, originally from Edinburgh. He reached Russia c1787, possibly as the result of a note in the *Edinburgh Evening Courant* 1784. There he met Charles Cameron(qv) and worked as his assistant, mainly at Tsarskoe Selo, building the ruined chapel with an Egyptian sarcophagus from Alexandria (1827), an elephant house in the Turkish style, a 'Tour des Heritiers', and at the Peterhof he added a 'Kottedzh', built for the Tsarina Alexandra Feodorova. Also built the Egyptian Gate, between the villages of Kousmina and Tsarskoe Selo, at the entrance to the Imperial park.
**Bibl:** Tait, AA, British Architects in the Service of Catherine II.

**MENELAWS, William Brown** **fl 1901-1942**
Amateur Edinburgh watercolour painter, quite prolific shortly before WW2. Working from Monkwood, Colinton. Exhibited 16 portraits, still lifes and flower pieces at the RSA, also RSA(10), GI(1) & RSW(23).

**MENINSKY, Philip** **1922-?**
Educated Herts. Painter of figure studies, still life, trees and vegetation. Younger son of the painter Bernard M. Prisoner-of-war Singapore and on the Burma Railway sketched with Ronald Searle, thirty of the drawings now in the Imperial War Museum. After the war moved to Glasgow and became associated with the Glasgow School of Art receiving encouragement from Mary and William Armour(qv). First one-man exhibition Glasgow 1961. Became especially interested in the world of dance, painting members of the London Ballet Festival. Exhibited RSA(3) & GI(15). Represented in Lillie AG (Milngavie), Imperial War Museum, HRH Duke of Edinburgh.

**MENZIES, Alexander F** **fl 1981-1984**
Aberdeen jewellery designer; exhibited AAS from 95 Union Grove.

**MENZIES, Donald P** **fl 1891**
Minor watercolour landscape painter. Exhibited 'Vera Cruz on the Gulf of Mexico' at the GI from 53 Bentinck Street, Glasgow. Possibly the **Donald MENZIES** who was at the Trustees Academy 1882-4.

**MENZIES, Gordon** **fl 1975**
Edinburgh engraver. Exhibited a lithograph at the RSA from Atholl Place.

**MENZIES, Isobel (Mrs Irvine)** **fl 1958-1973**
Ayrshire painter. Landscapes in watercolour including 'Iona' and continental scenes. Exhibited GI(3) from Brandon House, Troon.

**MENZIES, James** **fl 1958**
Topographical painter. Husband or brother of Isobel M(qv). Exhibited views of York Minster and Ripon cathedral at the GI from Brandon House, Troon.

**MENZIES, J** **fl 1809-1831**
Scottish engraver. Engraved a plan of Perth, 1809. With a **G Menzies** (possibly his brother), he engraved several maps of Scottish counties, railways and towns 1816-1831.
**Bibl:** Bushnell.

**MENZIES, John** **fl 1871-d.1939**
Born Scotland; died Edinburgh. Landscape and decorative painter in oil and watercolour; also illustrator. After a spell in Hull he returned to Edinburgh where he became quite prolific. Married Maria M(qv). Taught drawing and composition at the Edinburgh College of Art. Spent some time painting in Cockburnspath and at East Linton. Exhibited RA(4), RSA(46), GI(10), RI(1), AAS (1898-1923) & L(1), latterly from 1 Beaufort Rd. His last two works at the RA in 1885 and 1892 were both Highland scenes.

**MENZIES, Mrs John (Maria)** **fl 1880-1900**
Landscape and figure painter, mostly of the Highlands and north-east. Her three works at the RA were all of Scottish subjects, even though she was living at Hull at the time: 'On the Coast near Aberdeen' (1880); 'A Shieling; top of Loch Vennachar' (1884); 'On the moor -the Trossachs' (1885). Wife of John M(qv). Exhibited RA(3), RSA(3), RI(3), GI(1) & AAS(5) from Hull and latterly Edinburgh.

**MENZIES, Robert** **fl 1948**
Dunbartonshire amateur painter. Exhibited GI(1) from Hardgate.

**MENZIES, W C** **fl 1929**
Amateur painter of 22 Braeside Avenue, Rutherglen; exhibited GI(1).

**MENZIES, William** **fl 1955**
Grangemouth engraver. Exhibited lithograph portraits of workmen at RSA, also pen and ink sketches.

**MERCER, Andrew** **1775-1842**
Born Selkirk; died Dunfermline, 11 Jne. Miniature painter and poet. After early intentions to enter the Church with a year spent studying theology at Edinburgh University 1790, he abandoned the idea, concentrating instead on writing poetry, painting miniatures and teaching drawing. Settled in Dunfermline, drawing patterns for damask manufacturers, writing a *History of Dunfermline,* and a few poems published in 1828. Seems to have been unable to cope with the financial burdens of life and died in extreme poverty.
**Bibl:** Bryan; DNB; Long 293; Foskett 403-4.

**MERCER, Vera Cockburn** **1921-**
Born Galashiels. Painter in oil, watercolour and pastel of landscapes, portraits, flower studies and still-life. Trained Gray's School of Art, Aberdeen under Robert Sivell(qv) 1937-40. Married Alberto Morrocco(qv) 1941. That year she undertook further studies at Edinburgh College of Art, especially drawing under John Maxwell(qv). Travelled extensively, painting on the way, in France, Italy, Sicily, Spain, also in China and Tunisia. Solo exhibition London 1999. Exhibiting RSA & GI.

**MERCER, William** **fl 1954**
East Lothian painter; exhibited a 'Stewartry Farm' at the RSA from Tranent.

**MERCIER, Philip** **fl c1780**
Engraver. Possibly resident in Edinburgh in some teaching capacity, but apart from seven very formal aquatints of city subjects, little is known of his life or work. These aquatints, executed 1780-1781, were of the Castle, Heriot's Hospital, Holyrood House and general views from the four quarters of the compass. The set is to be found in monochrome and hand tinted; the drawing is crude but there is an attractive naivete about them. Two other views may have been the work of Mercier, 'View of Part of old Stokebridge (looking West)' and 'Bridge at Water of Leith, about 1750 (looking West)'. These were reproduced in Cumberland Hill: *Historic Memorials and Reminiscents of Stockbridge.* Represented in Edinburgh City collection(4 watercolour drawings of Old Edinburgh). Not to be confused with the Frenchman Philippe Mercier who died c1760.
**Bibl:** Butchart 18.

**MERRILEES, Margaret** **fl 1894-1896**
Aberdeen painter of landscape, especially small rivers and burns. Exhibited AAS(3) from 14 Schoolhill.

**MERRY, Mabel** **fl 1896**
Minor Glasgow painter; exhibited GI(1) when living at 6 Rosebery Terrace, Kelvinbridge.

**MERRYLEES, A Russell** **fl 1893**
Amateur portrait painter who had a studio in Albert Hall, Edinburgh; exhibited 'Dorothy' at the RSA.

**MERRYLEES, Miss Annie R (Mrs A M Arnold)** **fl 1893-1900**
Miniature painter of quality. Wife of Reginald E Arnold. Although of Scottish parentage and well-connected north of the Border, she married an Englishman and lived and worked most of her life in England. Her sitters included 'Mrs Cameron Corbett', 'Hon Thomas Erskine', younger son of the Earl of Mar and Kellie, 'The Countess of Mar & Kellie', and 'Hon Francis Erskine'. Exhibited RA(46), RSA(1), RMS(21), RI(21), GI(6) & L(3) from 1 Lennox St, Edinburgh and latterly 26 Bassett Road, Ladbroke Grove, London.

**MERY, Eugenie** **fl 1869-1889**
Glasgow-based landscape artist, born Paris. Worked in oils and watercolour. Studied under Mme Cave and de Pommayrac. Painted mainly portrait studies including domestic animals; also flowers and still life. Exhibited Paris Salon from 1869 & GI(1) from 136 Wellington Street.

**MESNARD, William** **fl 1862**
Glasgow-based portrait painter. Exhibited GI(1) from 77 W. Nile St.

**MESTON, A C** **fl 1900**
Amateur Aberdeen painter in watercolours; exhibited two topographical works at the AAS.

**MESTON, Meta** **fl 1943-1959**
Kincardineshire painter of landscape, domestic genre and portraits; exhibited RSA(16), GI(4) & AAS from 44 Arduthie Road, Stonehaven.

**METHVEN, C W** **fl 1883**
Renfrewshire painter of harbour scenes and coastal views. Exhibited GI(2) from Greenock.

**METHVEN, Robert** **1937-**
Born Glasgow. Painter in oil and gouache of abstracts and semi-abstracts. Trained Glasgow School of Art 1955-58, winning a travelling scholarship 1959 enabling him to travel across Europe. Settled in Glasgow.

**MICHAEL, Peter** **1964-**
Born Singapore. Architect and watercolour painter of architectural subjects. Lived for some years in Ireland where he attended St Columba's College, Dublin 1975-1983. Trained as an architect at Thames Polytechnic 1983-1986 followed by three years at the Scott Sutherland School of Architecture. Since 1987 has lived in Edinburgh. Awarded the Sir Robert Lorimer prize in 1989 and again in 1990 and the Sir John Kinross award 1989. His main interest as a painter is in composition, depicting interesting buildings using unusual combinations of colour and with particular attention to texture. Exhibited RSA 1990 & SSA.

**MICHIE, Alastair ARBS RWA** **1921-?**
Born France. Dorset-based painter in oil, gouache and acrylic; also sculptor. Often landscape, figurative works and conversation pieces. Elder son of Anne Redpath(qv) and James Michie(qv), brother of David(qv). Exhibited 'Gold Relief 21' at the RSA. Represented in Edinburgh City collection.

**MICHIE, David Alan Redpath RSA RGI FRSA(Scot)** **1928-?**
Born St Raphael, Var, France, 30 Nov. Painter in oil and watercolour of figurative subjects and semi-abstracts. Younger son of James Michie the architect(qv) and Anne Redpath(qv). Trained Edinburgh College of Art 1947-53 and, as a result of winning a travelling scholarship, in Italy 1953-54. Joined Gray's School of Art as a lecturer in painting in 1958, remaining there until 1962, in 1969 moved to the staff of Edinburgh College of Art. Vice-Principal, Edinburgh College of Art 1974-1977 and visiting professor of painting, Belgrade Academy of Arts 1979. In the course of his career he rather abandoned the rich textures inherited from his mother's work, and developed a more flat and straightforward style in which although colour remains a vital ingredient, it is more thinly applied and decorative elements of line and pattern are accentuated. One detects an affinity with Matisse. His work sometime appears contrived, seldom beautiful. Elected PSSA 1961-3, ARSA 1964, RSA 1972. His first one-man show was in London in 1967, repeated several times thereafter. Exhibited RSA regularly, GI(19) & AAS 1959 and 1981, from 55 Osborne Place, Aberdeen. Represented in SNGMA, Aberdeen AG, Glasgow AG, Edinburgh City collection, RSA, Royal Collection, Gracefield Art Centre (Dumfries), Kirkcaldy AG, Perth AG.
**Bibl:** Gage 44-5; Hardie 164; Macmillan [SA] 369,392,394.

**MICHIE, James Beattie** **1891-1960**
Born Inverness; died Bristol. Architect & landscape painter in oil and tempera. Married Anne Redpath(qv). Designed war graves and memorials for the War Graves Commission in N.France. Worked on murals at Chapelle St.Rosline in the Alps Maritime. Lecturer in architecture at RWA.

**MICHIE, James Coutts ARSA** **1861-1919**
Born Aboyne, Aberdeenshire, 29 Jly; died Haslemere, Surrey, 18 Dec. Painter in oil of landscape and portraits. Brother of Mary Coutts M(qv). Studied under Joseph Farquharson(qv) and in Edinburgh, at the Trustees School 1877-78 and RSA life class, also Rome and Paris, under Carolus Duran. In 1893 settled in London, leaving Aberdeen where he had been an active member of the Aberdeen Artists' Society and the second President of the Society of Scottish Artists. Subjects were peaceful rural scenes, sometimes with figures. His technique was occasionally deficient in draughtsmanship. Close friend of the collector George McCulloch. After the latter's death in 1909, he married Mrs McCulloch. In 1898 he was awarded a medal (3rd class) and an honorable mention in 1900 at the Universelle Exhibition in Paris. Finally settled in Haslemere, Surrey. Elected ARSA 1893. Exhibited RA(45), RSA(99), ROI(18), RBA(2), GI(27), AAS (1885-1919) & L(27). Represented in Aberdeen AG, Walker AG (Liverpool), Sydney AG (Australia), Montreal AG.
**Bibl:** AJ 1902, 290-3; 1905, 122; 1907, 164; Arts in 1898, Special No; Caw 311; Conn 56 (1920) 126; Studio 38 (1906) 15, 16,21.

**MICHIE, John** **fl 1858**
Kelso painter; exhibited an angling scene at the RSA.

**MICHIE, John D** **fl 1858-1892**
Edinburgh painter in oil of figure subjects, historical scenes, landscapes, especially in Brittany and Sussex. His wife was also an artist living at 8 St Peters Place, Viewforth and in London 1872-77 before returning to Edinburgh. Two works which attracted favourable attention were 'Jedburgh Abbey' 1887 and 'A Wounded Seagull' 1884. Exhibited RSA(74) & GI(8).

**MICHIE, Mrs John D** **fl 1878-1880**
Painter of flowers in watercolour. Married John D M(qv). Exhibited RSA(1) & SWA(1).

**MICHIE, John M** **fl 1844-1873**
Edinburgh painter in oil of figures and landscape subjects, often continental especially Brittany. Exhibited 'Kilmeny in the Fairy Glen' RA 1864; also RSA(81), from 31 North Bridge.

**MICHIE, Miss Mary Coutts** **fl 1885-1919**
Aberdeen flower painter in watercolour. Sister of James Coutts M(qv). Moved to London 1897, the date of her last known work. Exhibited 'Autumn flowers' RA 1892 from 1 Crown Place, also RSA(2), GI(1), AAS (1885-1919, mostly from Marywell, Aboyne) & L(1).

**MICHIE, T C** **fl 1881**
Edinburgh-based painter of genre. Exhibited GI(2) from Picardy Place.

**MICHIE, T S** **fl 1880-1881**
Glasgow amateur landscape painter. Local scenes. Exhibited GI(5), latterly from Cadzow Street, Hamilton.

**MIDDLEMAS, A** **fl 1895-1902**
Edinburgh painter. Exhibited RSA(3) from 2 St Peter's Place, Viewforth.

**MIDDLETON, Alexander Bell** **1830-1880**
Born Edinburgh. Painter in oil of portraits, genre and figure subjects. Trained Trustees Academy 1850-56. Moved to Arbroath when young. Actively involved in the development of Hospitalfield through his friend Patrick Allan-Fraser(qv). Exhibited RSA(24) and in 1880 posthumously 'A Newspaper Boy'.

**MIDDLETON, J R** **fl 1846**
Edinburgh landscape painter; exhibited RSA(1).

**MIDDLETON, James** **fl 1893**
Edinburgh painter of figure subjects. Exhibited 'A Moorish type' at the RSA, from Grosvenor Crescent.

**MIDDLETON, James Godsell** **fl 1827-1872**
English painter of genre, portraits and literary subjects, especially Scott. Probably his best known work is his portrait of 'Prince Albert' RA 1862, painted for the Hon. Artillery Company. In addition to exhibiting RA(78) 1827-1872, exhibited a scene from the *Heart of Midlothian* at the RSA 1846 and from *Woodstock* 1850; also from *Bride of Lammermoor* GI 1870.

**MIDDLETON, James Raeburn** **1855-c1910**
Born Glasgow, 11 Nov. Painter in oil and watercolour of genre and portraits. Worked extensively in Burma and Morocco, although lived most of his life in Glasgow. Exhibited RA(4), RSA(5), RSW(2), RBA(1), GI(57), L(5) & Paris Salon after the early 1890s from 132 West Regent St. Represented by three works in Glasgow AG.

**MIDDLETON, Janet** **fl 1906**
Amateur portrait miniaturist. Exhibited GI(1) from Manorhead, Stow, Midlothian.

**MIDDLETON, John** **fl 1855-1871**
Edinburgh painter in oil of rural scenes and landscapes. One of the band of artists who enjoyed sketching on Arran, two of his oil paintings executed on the island being among his exhibits at the RA in 1854. Exhibited RA(14), 1847-1855, latterly from Surrey Street, Norwich; also RSA(4). Represented in Paisley AG.

**MIDDLETON, Rowan** **fl 1926-1929**
Aberdeen painter of mountain landscapes. Exhibited AAS(3) from 94 Queen's Rd.

**MIDDLETON, Mrs Sandra H** **fl 1981**
Glasgow amateur painter. Exhibited GI(2) from Bearsden.

**MIDDLETON, W Diack** **fl 1964**
Aberdeen printmaker. Exhibited AAS from 109 Gairn Terrace.

**MIDGLEY, James Herbert** **fl 1882-1883**
Edinburgh oil painter of landscapes. Exhibited RSA(2) from 18 Hope Terrace.

**MIERS, John** **1757-1821**
Born Quarry Hill, Leeds; died Jne. Renowned profile miniaturist. Son of a coach painter, believed to have been descended from the Dutch artist Frans van Mieris. The first painter to develop a method for introducing shades on a composition of plaster of Paris. In 1786 visited Edinburgh, completing 18 portraits of the family of Sir John Steuart, 4th baronet of Allanbank. These included the '14th Earl of Erro', two of his sisters, and 'Robert Dundas' (later Lord Armiston), President of the Court of Session. This visit influenced a number of Scottish miniaturists, notably J. Smith of Edinburgh(qv), who was probably a pupil before becoming his assistant in 1785. Represented in City of Edinburgh collection by two of the silhouettes originally executed for the Steuarts.
**Bibl:** Arthur Mayne, British Profile Miniaturists, London 1970, 48-60.

**MIKULA, Stanislaw** **fl 1941-1942**
Edinburgh-based painter of landscape and still life. Exhibited RSA(4) from Bruntsfield Place.

**MILL, Alex George** **fl 1904**
Minor painter of 121 St Vincent Street, Glasgow; exhibited GI(1).

**MILL, J W** **fl 1943**
North Queensferry painter; exhibited GI(1).

**MILLAR, Alexander** **fl 1711-1742**
Early painter. Son of a Dalkeith weaver. Apprenticed to James Norie in 1711. Became a burgess of Edinburgh in 1720, and 1722-42 member of the Incorporation of St Mary's.

**MILLAR, Alexander** **fl 1774-1779**
Portrait painter who lived in Writer's Close, Edinburgh and advertised as such 1776-1790.

**MILLAR, Bruce David** **fl 1967-1980**
Fife sculptor. Exhibited four figure subjects at the RSA from Newport-on-Tay. also two works in steel at the AAS when living in Dunfermline 1967

**MILLAR, C R Leslie** **fl 1919-1931**
Aberdeen landscape painter. Related to Roderick M(qv) who worked from the same address. Exhibited AAS from 103 Osborne Place including a striking picture of Loch Fyne.

**MILLAR, E C Frenes** **fl 1938**
Minor Glasgow engraver; exhibited an etching of a chinchilla at the GI.

**MILLAR, Effie** **fl 1981**
Paisley artist. Exhibited 'The miner' at the RSA.

**MILLAR, Miss Elizabeth L** **fl 1959-1971**
Glasgow landscape painter and sculptress. Statuettes and Highland scenery, especially around Carradale. Exhibited GI(6) from Ashcroft Drive.

**MILLAR, Elizabeth ('Lizzie') Rodger** **fl 1891-1896**
Glasgow painter of genre and flowers. Exhibited GI(4) from Albert Drive.

**MILLAR, Elsie M** **fl 1965**
Aberdeenshire painter of local landscape and flowers. Married John A Garland M(qv). Exhibited AAS from Smith Cottage, Fawells, Keith Hall, Inverurie.

**MILLAR, G** **fl 1830**
Edinburgh engraver. Engraved a bookplate for Thomas W E Robson, 1830.
**Bibl:** Bushnell.

**MILLAR, James** **fl 1954-1972**
Glasgow watercolour painter, occasionally also in oils. Genre and topographical works. Exhibited GI(16), many of scenes in the vicinity of Ostend, from Invergyle Drive.

**MILLAR, John A Garland** **fl 1967-1970**
Aberdeenshire watercolourist. Married Elsie M(qv). Exhibited AAS(4).

**MILLAR, Harold R** **fl 1891-d1935**
Born Dumfries. Painter and illustrator. Intended to study engineering but studied art instead, enrolling in Birmingham. First known works were for Birmingham magazines such as *Scraps* and *Comus.* Derived a very strong style in pen and ink based on the work of Vierge and Gigoux. Illustrations for a series of eastern stories were greatly in demand on account of their authenticity. Illustrated George Sand's *The Golden Fairy Book* (1894); *The Humour of Spain* (1894); *Fairy Tales from Far and Near* (1895); Morier's *The Adventures of Haji Baba* (1895); Bernhardt's *The Silver Fairy Book* (1895); Peacock's *Headlong Hall, Nightmare Abbey* (1896); Marryat's *The Phantom Ship* (1896); Bellerby's *The Diamond Fairy Book* (1897); Harraden's *Untold Tales of the Past* (1897); Marryat's *Frank Mildmay* (1897); *Snarleyow* (1897); Anthony Hope's *Phroso* (1897); Kinglake's *Eothen (1898);* Nesbitt's *The Book of Dragons* (1900); Nesbitt's *Nine Unlikely Tales for Children* (1901); Hugo's *The Story of the Bold Pecopin* (1902); *Queen Mab's Realm* (1902); Nesbitt's *The Phoenix and the Carpet* (1904); *The New World Fairy Book* (1904); Nesbitt's *Oswald Bastable and Others* (1905); Myra Hamilton's *Kingdom Curious* (1905); Kipling's *Puck of Pook's Hill* (1906); Nesbitt's *The Enchanted Castle* (1917); *The Magic City* (1910); Nesbitt's *The Wonderful Garden* (1911); Nesbitt's *Wet Magic* (1913); *The Dreamland Express* (1927) & Hakluyt's *Voyages* (1929). Contributed to many publications including *Judy* (1890), *The Girl's Own Paper* (1890-1900), *Fun* (1891-2), *The Strand Magazine* (1891, 1905), *The English Illustrated Magazine* (1891-2), *Chums* (1892), *Good Words* (1893), *Good Cheer* (1894), *The Sketch* (1898), *Black & White* (1899), *The Quiver* (1900), *Punch* (1906-9), *The Ludgate Monthly, Pick-Me-Up,* Cassell's *Family Magazine, The Idler, The Minister & Eureka.* Exhibited RA(3) 1892-1903, after 1900 from 7 Tunley Rd, Upper Tooting, London. Represented in V & A.
**Bibl:** Houfe; The Idler, vol 8, 228-236; Brigid Peppin, Fantasy Book Illustrators, 1975, 188-189, illus; R E D Sketchley Eng Bk Illustrators, 1903, 109, 112, 167.

**MILLAR, John Hutcheson** **fl 1876-1885**
Glasgow painter in oil of landscapes and flowers who, in 1885 moved to Hamilton. Exhibited RSA(3).

**MILLAR, L Roger** **fl 1893-1896**
Glasgow artist; exhibited GI(3) from 7 Albert Drive, Queen's Park.

**MILLAR, Robins** **fl 1918-1964**
Glasgow watercolour painter of genre. Exhibited GI(5) from 67 Hope Street, after 1953 from Quadrant St.

**MILLAR, Roderick** **fl 1967**
Aberdeen sculptor. Related to C R Leslie Millar(qv). Exhibited AAS(1).

**MILLAR, Thomas** **fl 1864**
Edinburgh medallion portraitist; exhibited once RSA.

**MILLAR, Thomas W** **fl 1877**
Landscape painter in oil from Paisley; exhibited RSA(1).

**MILLAR (or MILLER), William** **fl 1751-1784**
Scottish portrait painter about whom little is known. Son of Alexander M(qv), painter burgess of Edinburgh. Burgess of Edinburgh 1768 and a member of the Incorporation of St Mary's the same year. His portrait of 'Thomas Trotter' (b1682) is in the NGS. The earliest known work is a copy of a Ramsay portrait of the 3rd Duke of Argyll 1751. Also copied portraits by Gavin Hamilton in the 1760s. His 'John Home' 1762 is in SNPG. His work was developed from the style of Denune, later showing the influence of David Martin(qv), his principal rival as a portraitist in Edinburgh from 1767, and of Ramsay's earlier work. From 1773 to 1776 he was living in Writer's Court, Edinburgh, was advertising as a limner at the same address 1773-4 and as a portrait painter 1775-6. Between 1780-1784 described himself as a painter, living in Blackfriars Wynd. Completed a number of portraits at Oxenfoord Castle including 'Professor Fergusson', 'Thomas and Elizabeth Hamilton of Fala' and 'Baron C Montesquie'. Represented in NGS.
**Bibl:** Holloway 144; Macmillan [SA] 109.

**MILLAR, W J** **fl 1870**
Glasgow landscape painter in watercolours. Exhibited 'View on the Clyde' at the GI from 16 Arlington St.

**MILLER Miss** **fl 1871**
Dunbar landscape painter in oil; exhibited once at the RSA.

**MILLER, Alec** **1879-?**
Born Glasgow, 12 Feb. Sculptor and teacher; stone, marble and wood. Trained Glasgow School of Art 1900-1902 and Florence 1908. Taught at Campden School of Arts and Crafts 1902-1914 and Oxford City School of Art 1919-1923. Lived in Campden, Gloucestershire and Monterey, California. Elected ARMS 1921. Exhibited RA(12), RSA(2), RMS(3), GI(4) & L(5).

**MILLER, Alexander** **fl 1867**
Landscape painter. Exhibited GI(1) from Glasgow.

**MILLER, Andrew** **c1700-1763**
Engraver. Probably of Scottish descent although born in London. Father of William M(qv). Lived in Dublin from c1740 until his death. Studied under Faber. Engraved the designs of Frank Hayman with whom he shared a drink problem. Best known works are mezzotint portraits, among them 'Dean Swift', after F. Bindon, 1743; 'Robert Boyle', the philosopher; 'Charles Lucas MD of Dublin'; 'Robert Jocelyn', 'Lord Newport, Chancellor of Ireland', 1747; 'Josiah Hort, Archbishop of Tuam'; 'Eaton Stannard, Recorder of Dublin'; and 'Joseph Baudin', the painter.
**Bibl:** Bryan; Bushnell; DNB; Chaloner Smith; C.E. Russell, English Mezzotint Portraits and their States, 2 vols,1926.

**MILLER, Andrew** **fl 1967-**
Sculptor mostly in stone. Exhibited RSA(1) when attached to the Scottish Sculpture Workshop, Lumsden, Aberdeenshire; also GI91) 1967.

**MILLER, Andrew Stephen** **fl 1861**
Musselburgh painter in oil of still-life; exhibited RSA(1).

**MILLER, Aphra M (Mrs Bremner)** **fl 1944-**
Scottish portrait painter and photographer. Trained Gray's School of Art. Moved to London before settling in Poole. Married **Taylor BREMNER** 1949 and in 1980 turned to photography. Gained a Fellowship, Royal Photographic Society 1987 and an AFIAP (Artist in Federation Internationale de l'Art Photographique) 1989. Exhibited RSA(3).

**MILLER, Archibald Elliot Haswell RSW** **1887-?**
Born Glasgow, 10 Jne. Painter in tempera, oil and watercolour; landscapes, architectural subjects and portraits, also book illustrator. Trained Glasgow School of Art 1906-1909 and in Munich 1909-10, Berlin, Vienna and Paris. Taught Glasgow School of Art 1910-14 and again after the War until 1930 when he was appointed Keeper and Deputy Director of the National Galleries of Scotland, a position he held until his retirement in 1952. Made a special study of military uniforms and Highland dress. Married Josephine Cameron and lived for some years at Gillingham, Dorset. Elected RSW 1924. One of the principal figures in Glasgow art circles between the wars. A retrospective exhibition of his drawings of military apparel was held at the Imperial War Museum, London 1971. Exhibited RA(5), RSA(23), RSW(26), GI(34), RSW(26), GI(18), AAS(3) & L(6). A good example of his 'constructive use of line on flat areas of colour' is 'Rocher St Michel Le Puy' in Glasgow AG.
**Bibl:** Halsby 224-5,273.

**MILLER, C R Leslie** **fl 1907-1908**
Kilmarnock-based painter and sculptor. Watercolours and portrait busts. Exhibited GI(3)

**MILLER, Captain Charles Keith** **fl 1874-1880**
Glasgow-based ship painter. *'Braemar Castle* in a Storm', now owned by John Brown & Co, sgd 'CKM', was included in the exhibition 'The Artist and the Clyde', Helensburgh 1958. The *Braemar Castle,* built in 1872, was the first ship to be launched from Clydebank shipyard. Exhibited 'After the squall' at the RSA.

**MILLER, David T FRBS** **1931-**
Born Banffshire. Sculptor; wood, stone, bronze, steel and fibreglass-resin. Educated Mortlach School, Dufftown. Trained Gray's School of Art 1948-50, Edinburgh College of Art 1950-53 under Eric Schilsky(qv) and, when awarded a travelling scholarship, went to Paris and Vallauris. Served in the Queen's Own Cameron Highlanders 1954-6. Returned to Scotland to teach. His later work has been mainly in stone and wood, but sometimes in welded steel, clay and bronze. Elected SSA 1959, received Latimer Award, RSA 1961. Fellow, RBS 1970. Exhibited RSA 1958-72 & SSA. Represented in SAC.

**MILLER, George** **fl 1889-1898**
Glasgow painter, mainly in watercolour, of landscapes and seascapes. Exhibited RSA(5) & GI(9) from Hillhead from Observatory Rd and Ailsa Terrace.

**MILLER, George L** **fl 1962-1977**
Greenock figurative painter, also landscape, genre & still life. Exhibited 'Girl with a guitar' at the RSA & GI(8).

**MILLER, George M** **fl 1880-1882**
Minor landscape painter; exhibited GI(4) from 3 Osborne Terrace, Govan.

**MILLER, Graham M** **fl 1950**
Dundee painter; exhibited a continental scene at the RSA.

**MILLER, Ian George** **fl 1962-1965**
Dundee painter of landscapes and still life; exhibited RSA(2).

**MILLER, J** **fl 1887**
Edinburgh painter of landscape; exhibited 'On Braid burn' at the RSA, from Clerk St.

**MILLER, Miss J** **fl 1883**
Dundee painter. Exhibited RSA(2) from 23 South Tay Street.

**MILLER, J Hutcheson** **fl 1880-1893**
Lanarkshire painter of genre and topographical subjects; professional photographer who took over Annand's business after the latter's death. Exhibited RSA(1) & GI(12) from Hamilton and later Glasgow.

**MILLER, J McKenzie** **fl 1950-1955**
Caithness sculptor. Exhibited four portrait busts of local notables at the RSA from his studio in Wick.

**MILLER, J Nina (Mrs Charles L Davidson)** **1895-?**
Born Hamilton, Lanarks. Painter and black and white artist and teacher. Studied mural painting at Glasgow School of Art 1920-2, subsequently in France and Italy. Married Charles Lamb Davidson(qv). Exhibited RSA(6) 1922-1935, RSW(1) & GI(10). A cartoon for a window in St. Margaret's church, Duns, Berwickshire, was shown at the RSA 1951.

**MILLER, J Robertson** **fl 1880-1912**
Watercolourist who painted coastal scenes and harbours in Scotland and Holland using broad washes. Exhibited GI(19).
**Bibl:** Halsby 274.

**MILLER, James** **fl 1853**
Portrait painter. SNPG has 'The Duke of Wellington' on panel, signed and dated 1853.

**MILLER, James** **fl 1865-1888**
Leith oil painter who later moved to Edinburgh; landscape, buildings and flowers; exhibited at the RSA(9).

**MILLER, James RSA RSW** **1893-1987**
Born Dennistoun, Glasgow, 25 Oct. Painter of portraits, still-life and animals sometimes in oil but mainly watercolour. Trained Glasgow School of Art under Greiffenhagen(qv) and Anning Bell(qv), subsequently in Paris. His watercolours are strongly composed with sharp outlines and subdued washes. In the 1920s and 30s he travelled extensively abroad, working in the Mediterranean area and also on the west coast of Scotland, especially on Skye where he had a home. In Paris he made studies of the street scenes of the period and continued to make the architecture of the major cities of Europe his principal subject matter, with special affection for the architectural heritage of Spain. During WWI he executed a number of sketches of war damage and of Glasgow, subjects well-suited to his rather heavy treatment. Elected RSW 1934. Exhibited 1921-87 more than 100 works at the RSA, also RSW(32), GI(85) & AAS(1), latterly from 114 W Campbell St. Represented in Aberdeen AG, Bradford AG, Dundee AG, Edinburgh City Collection, Glasgow AG, Millburn AG, Newport AG, Paisley AG, Perth AG.
**Bibl:** Halsby 274; Scot Arts Rev, VII, 2; Francis Walker, RSW Obituary, 1987.

**MILLER, James RSA FRIBA FRSE** **1860-1947**
Born Auchtergavin, Perthshire; died Stirling, 28 Nov. Architect. Studied under Andrew Heiton(qv). In 1888 he entered the service of Caledonian Railway Company before starting on his own account 1893. Designs for the Glasgow International Exhibition of 1901 brought him to public attention. Designs for Bombay Museum were accepted in 1908, two years after his election as ARSA. Member, Royal Fine Art Commission for Scotland and Architectural Advisory Committee. From 1903 'became the most persistent creator of massive mercantile monuments in Glasgow, at first neo-baroque but from 1920 onwards American classic.' [Gomme & Walker]. In this he was assisted by **Richard GUNN**. Main works include the reconstruction of the Royal Infirmary, the Infirmaries of Perth and Stirling, Broadcasting House, Belfast, the Royal Scottish Automobile Club, Glasgow and the Medical and Natural Philosophy Schools of Glasgow University. Other designs included work at Turnberry Hotel, Ayrshire, the *SS Lusitania* (1910), Newington Synagogue (1929-32) and Kildonan Mansion, Barrhill (1915). Elected RSA 1930. Exhibited RA(3), RSA(50) & GI(25).
**Bibl:** Gifford 260,552,636; A Gomme & D Walker, Architecture of Glasgow, London 1987(rev), 295-6; Halsby 274.

**MILLER, James** **fl 1912**
Glasgow-based amateur watercolourist. Exhibited 'Campsie Fells' at the GI from Wilton Drive.

**MILLER, James Brash** **fl 1863-1878**
Edinburgh painter in oil and watercolour; landscapes and portraits. Married an artist. Exhibited RSA(32) & GI(12).

**MILLER, Mrs James Brash** **fl 1862-1863**
Edinburgh painter of landscape and nature studies. Married James Brash M(qv). Exhibited RSA(3) including a view on Arran, from Duncan St.

**MILLER, Miss Jane** **fl 1883**
Edinburgh watercolour painter of still-life and flora; exhibited RSA(2).

**MILLER, Jean** **fl 1970-1972**
Edinburgh painter of topographical subjects; exhibited RSA(4) from Craiglea Drive.

**MILLER, John** **fl 1873-1909**
Glasgow landscape painter in oil and watercolour. Generally English scenes and figure subjects. Almost all his exhibits were at the GI(64), also RA(3), RSA(7) & L(1), firstly from 70 Robertson St then 40 W. Nile St.

**MILLER, John RSA PRSW** **1893-1975**
Born Glasgow, 21 Mar; died Glasgow, 17 Jan. Painter in oil and watercolour of still-life, landscapes, especially the Clyde. Educated Queens Park Secondary School, then went into a bank but whilst ill in hospital his enthusiasm was fired by Charles Davidson(qv). Decided to change course and enrolled at Glasgow School of Art under W O Hutchison(qv) 1936-41, with a spell at Hospitalfield, Arbroath under James Cowie(qv) 1938. Postgraduate diploma 1941. Senior Lecturer in Drawing and Painting at Glasgow School of Art 1944. The greatest influence on his work was Impressionism. France was an early mecca of his travelling but in later life he turned to Iona and his home ground of Rhu. Water and boats often figured in his landscapes, in later life he turned increasingly to flowers. His composition became richer in colour with the years. An anonymous critic wrote 'occasionally a canvas that is disturbingly woolly and perhaps ill-resolved, but most of his still-lifes and the landscapes in oils are imbued with a golden classic quality that warms the eye and spirit. His style and quietude invest his work - his pictures whisper, they never exclaim'. Elected President, RSW 1970-1972 having been elected RSW 1952, ARSA 1957, RSA 1966. Exhibited often at the RA, RSA, RSW, GI, AAS(4) & SSA. Represented in Dundee AG, Glasgow AG, Lillie AG (Milngavie), Paisley AG, Edinburgh City collection, SAC, Newport AG.
**Bibl:** Edward Gage, RSW Obituary, 1976; Halsby 274.

**MILLER, John William** **fl 1936-1940**
Edinburgh watercolourist; exhibited RSA(2) & RSW.

**MILLER, Josephine Haswell (née Cameron) ARSA** **1890-1975**
Born Glasgow, 1 Oct; died Dorset. Painter in oil, watercolour and tempera, also etcher; portraits and landscapes. Educated Woodside School. Trained Glasgow School of Art 1909-1914 under Greiffenhagen(qv) and Anning Bell(qv), in Paris (through winning a Haldane travelling scholarship), and in London under Sickert. As a student she completed a mural Science (c 1913) which remains in Possilpark Library, Glasgow. Married Arthur H M(qv) 1916. Member of the Board of Management, Edinburgh College of Art 1941-1945. The first woman to be elected a member of the RSA. From 1924 until 1932 taught etching and printmaking at Glasgow School of Art. Much of her work was the result of visits to Austria, Belgium, France, Germany, Italy and Spain. Moved from Glasgow to Edinburgh 1932. Elected ARSA 1938. In 1941 she joined Mary Armour and Anne Redpath in the execution of a series of brightly coloured, broadly painted murals for the Rosyth naval base. On her husband's retirement in 1952 as Keeper of the SNPG, they moved to Dorset, thereby debarring her from RSA rank, although she continued to exhibit there. Her career was interrupted by WW1 and WW2, but she continued working, combining great sensitivity and charm with outstanding artistic gifts and exceptional achievements. A perfectionist, she often destroyed her own work. Won the Lauder Award 1922. Exhibited RA(3), RSA(26), RSW(3), GI(48) & L(3). Represented in Glasgow AG, City of Edinburgh collection.
**Bibl:** Burkhauser 237; Halsby 225,274.

**MILLER, Miss Lila Webster** **fl 1915-1960**
Amateur Edinburgh watercolourist; portraits, townscapes, still lifes and topographical subjects. Exhibited RSA(10), RSW(1), GI(7), AAS (2) & L(1), from 34 St Andrews Square and 6 Cobden Rd, Edinburgh.

**MILLER, Miss Lydia H** **fl 1917**
Dunbartonshire artist; exhibited a monochrome figure study at the GI from Lenzie.

**MILLER, Miss M G** **fl 1894**
Aberdeen painter of flowers, fruit and still life; exhibited AAS(2) from Rubislaw Den N.

**MILLER, Maggie** **fl 1884**
Minor Glasgow flower painter; exhibited GI(1) from 2 Ettrick Terrace, Kelvinside.

**MILLER, Mary M** **fl 1941**
Flower painter; exhibited a study of chrysanthemums at the RSA from Dunedin, Stow, Berwickshire.

**MILLER, May** **fl 1973**
Aberdeen metalwork designer; exhibited AAS(1) from 18 Hilton Place.

**MILLER, Mrs Molly** **fl 1947-1949**
Portrait painter. Exhibited two pencil portraits at the GI from 256 Tantallon Rd, Glasgow.

**MILLER, Molly** **fl 1970-1971**
Edinburgh painter in oil of topographical subjects; exhibited RSA(3).

**MILLER, Ninian** **16th Cent**
Scottish professional embroiderer. Attached to the Court of Mary Queen of Scots(qv). Unfortunately it is impossible to attribute the making of the surviving embroideries, known to have been designed and made by the several Court embroiderers, to any one person. When Mary fled to England in 1568, Miller remained behind, establishing his own workshop in Edinburgh.

**MILLER, P Fraser** **fl 1863**
Dunbartonshire landscape painter in oil; exhibited RSA(1).

**MILLER, Miss P Graham** **fl 1932**
Edinburgh artist. Exhibited RSA(1) from 21 Lennox Street.

**MILLER, Peter** **fl 1941-1943**
Edinburgh painter of biblical scenes and landscape; exhibited RSA(3) from Balcarres St.

**MILLER, Peter Weir** **fl 1965-1966**
Glasgow watercolourist. Topographical works. Exhibited GI(3) from Bishopbriggs.

**MILLER, Miss R Binnie** **fl 1937**
Minor sculptor of Crossford, Dunfermline. Exhibited a plaster Madonna at the GI(1).

**MILLER, Robert** **fl 1897**
Edinburgh painter. Exhibited GI(1) from 24 Broughton Place.

**MILLER, Robert A** **fl 1950**
Lanarkshire sculptor; mainly figurative works in coloured plaster. Exhibited RSA(2) from Bellshill.

**MILLER, Robert R** **fl 1934-1980**
Part-time artist, teacher and journalist. Rural scenes and still life, often with flowers. Art Editor, *Homes & Gardens.* Retired to Eastbourne where he had taught for many years. Exhibited RSA(6) when living at 3 Beaconsfield Terrace, Hawick.

**MILLER, Ronald Timothy** **fl 1983**
Aberdeen sculptor; exhibited AAS(1) from Viewfield Rd.

**MILLER, Miss Ruby** **fl 1943-1947**
Dunfermline sculptress of portrait heads. Exhibited GI from Crossford.

**MILLER, Stanley** **fl 1940**
Ayrshire engraver. Exhibited an etching at the GI from 11 Kellie Place, Alloa.

**MILLER, Sydney Houghton** **c1884-1938**
Edinburgh architect and architectural draughtsman, mainly ecclesiastical subjects. Responsible for the large Bank of Scotland building, 3 Hope St (1930). Exhibited RSA(10) including sketches of Ely and Lincoln cathedrals.
**Bibl:** Gifford 308.

**MILLER, Major W** **fl 1882**
Edinburgh painter of 67 George Street, who was in the Madras Army. Exhibited 'Indian landscape' at the RSA.

**MILLER, Walter** **fl 1894-1949**
Painter in oil and watercolour. Exhibited RSA(1), RSW(3) & GI(80), from Kilmarnock and later Glasgow.

**MILLER, Watt Muir** **fl 1892-1893**
Uddingston painter of landscapes and townscapes. Moved to Glasgow in mid-career. Exhibited GI(3). Represented in Glasgow AG.

**MILLER, Walter** **fl 1965-1984**
Glasgow artist; exhibited RSA(7).

**MILLER, William** **[see MILLAR, William]**

**MILLER, William HRSA** **1796-1882**
Born Edinburgh, May 28; died Sheffield, Jan 20. Engraver and watercolourist, lived most of his life in Edinburgh. A Quaker, and twice married. Apprenticed to William Archibald, but in 1819 went to London where he studied under George Cooke. Returned home to Millerfield, nr Edinburgh 1821. In the estimation of Ruskin, Miller was the best engraver of Turner's work. 'The work of William Miller interpreted quite peculiar exquisiteness those refinements of light which in Turner's middle and later time so much engaged his effort' [Wedmore]. In addition to engraving drawings of Edinburgh by James Skene, Clarkson Stanfield, David Octavius Hill, Edward Leighton Leitch and Turner, he engraved H W Williams' fine watercolour of 'Edinburgh from Arthur's Seat' (1845). Four years after his death a privately printed catalogue of Miller's works was published, together with a memoir. Foundation Associate Engraver of the RSA in 1826, but was one of the nine artists who withdrew after the first meeting, being reinstated in 1862 and elected HRSA. Engraved for Turner's *England and Wales* series, Rogers' *Poems,* Scott's *Waverley* novels and poetical works, and Campbell's *Poems.* Exhibited RSA(40) 1827-1882, including a study of the 'Summit of Lochnagar' 1858. Represented in SNPG, Glasgow AG, City of Edinburgh collection(27). (According to Butchart he was born in 1801).
**Bibl:** Bryan; Brydall 214; Bushnell; Butchart 59,62-3,68,70; DNB; J C Guy,'Edinburgh Engravers',in The Book of the Old Edinburgh Club, vol 9, 1916; Halsby 274.

**MILLER, William** **fl 1879-1933**
Painter of landscape and domestic genre in oil and watercolour. A prolific artist, he moved between Glasgow, Bridge of Allan (1907), Edinburgh (1924) and Prestwick (1929). Exhibited RA(1), RSA(11), RSW(8), GI(62) & L(3).

**MILLER, William G** **fl 1891-1908**
Glasgow painter who moved to London for a short time in 1901 after some success at the RA where he exhibited six works, also domestic scenes at the GI(29), RI(7) & L(1).

**MILLIGAN, Robert F** **fl 1910-1917**
Minor stained glass designer. Exhibited GI(5) from 58 Bain Street East, Glasgow.

**MILLIGAN, Thomas R** **fl 1871-1902**
Glasgow landscape painter in oil and watercolour. Moved to Greenock c1902. Exhibited RSA(2), RSW(1) & GI(9).

**MILLMAKER, John T** **fl 1862-1885**
Obscure Glasgow landscape painter also some still lifes and Mediterranean coastal scenes. Exhibited RSA(2) & GI(5) and once at Manchester City AG, from McAslin St.

**MILLONS, Captain Thomas** **1859-?**
Born Edinburgh. Painter and sailor; marine and architectural subjects in oil and watercolour. Went to sea and took the opportunity to study the formation of waves and sea effects, which greatly helped in the development of his artistic skills. Particularly fond of the coastline around Dunbar. Finally settled in Lasswade, Midlothian. Exhibited 1885-1927 at the RA(1), RSA(2), RSW(1), GI(1), RCA(6) & L(1).

**MILLOR, Lizzie R** **fl 1891**
Amateur painter of 7 Albert Drive, Crosshill, Glasgow. Exhibited GI(1).

**MILLS, Beryl** **fl 1959-1965**
Aberdeenshire landscape and still life painter. Exhibited AAS(6) latterly from Kintra, Beaconhill Rd, Milltimber.

**MILLS, Charles S** **1859-1901**
Dundee painter and poet. Painted landscapes and coastal scenes in oil but mainly watercolour, generally around Dundee and Tayport; also photographer. Educated West End Academy, Dundee. Worked for most of his life at Dundee in a shipping company. Founder member of the Tayport Art Circle. Painted landscapes with sensitive attention to light and mood although appears never to have exhibited beyond his immediate environment. Friend of George Dutch Davidson(qv) and closely associated with the Dundee Graphic Arts Association in the 1890s. Exhibited AAS(1) in 1893.
**Bibl:** Halsby 274.

**MILLS, Edward** **fl 1871-1918**
Painter of landscapes, seascapes and coastal scenes. Visited Rome 1882, returning to Edinburgh 1883 before settling in London 1890. Exhibited RA(13), RSA(10), RI(2), ROI(1) & L(3).

**MILLS, Georgina** **fl 1965-1967**
Edinburgh painter of still life and coastal scenes, especially the harbours of the Firth of Forth; exhibited RSA(4) from India St.

**MILLS, Humphrey** **?-1692**
Edinburgh-based clockmaker. Introduced new style of clockmaking to Scotland c1655. Admitted a freeman of the Edinburgh Hammermen c1660, becoming Deacon of the Incorporation. His work is distinguished from English clocks of the period by his name appearing at the base of the ornamental front brass fret. Other characteristics are the use of two separate weights for the chiming mechanism and the narrow chapter ring with squat figures. Represented in National Museum of Scotland, Glasgow Museum.

**MILLS, J Donald** **1872-1958**
Dundee architect. Educated Morgan Academy and Dundee HS. Studied architecture in Dundee and the Midlands. Among his best known buildings are those for Dundee and St Andrews Universities. Restored many Scottish castles including Fingask, and was invited by Queen Mary to help in the re-design of Balmoral Castle Gardens. Exhibited a memorial in Portland stone at the RSA in 1919.

**MILLS, John** **fl 1907**
Minor Glasgow engraver of topography. Exhibited GI(2) from 50 Kent Rd.

**MILLWARD, James** **fl 1862-1866**
Edinburgh landscape painter in oil; exhibited RSA(4) & GI(2). Probably the same as **John MILLWARD** listed as exhibiting GI(2) 1865.

**MILN, Robert** **fl c1710**
Scottish engraver. Responsible for several engraved plates in *Miscellanea quaedam Eruditae Antiquitatis,* Edinburgh, 1710.
**Bibl:** Bryan.

**MILNE, Arthur E** **fl 1914-1919**
Edinburgh painter. Exhibited only during WWI, RSA(3), including 'Dawn on the ridge, Passchendaele' 1919.

**MILNE, Arthur P** **fl 1896**
Amateur Aberdeen painter of local scenes; exhibited AAS(1) from 10 Queen's Rd.

**MILNE, Miss C M** **fl 1919**
Aberdeen amateur figure painter;exhibited once at the AAS from 26 Rubislaw Terrace.

**MILNE, Catherine W** **1908-1950**
Painter in oil and watercolour also etcher and draughtswoman. Daughter of J M M(qv). Educated Morgan Academy, Dundee, studied etching at evening classes at Dundee College of Art under James Macintosh Patrick 1930-39. First exhibit at the RSA was 'Careworn' 1937 while working for James Keiller and Sons, Dundee. Member, Dundee Art Society with whom she exhibited mainly landscapes.

**MILNE, David M** **fl 1974-1989**
Aberdeenshire sculptor. Exhibited AAS(6) from Collonach, Drumoak.

**MILNE, Ellis R** **fl 1926-1976**
North-east wood engraver and etcher of landscapes; exhibited RSA(9) and frequently at the AAS over a span of fifty years, latterly from Mill O'Campfield, Glassel.

**MILNE, George** **fl 1900-1933**
Aberdeen painter of local coastal scenes and landscape; especially fond of the Findhorn. From a variety of addresses exhibited often at the AAS between the above years. Possibly the **George MILNE** who exhibited a still life at the RSA in 1943 from Murrayfield, Edinburgh.

**MILNE, H Clifton** **fl 1908**
Aberdeen amateur painter; exhibited 'A snowy day in March' at the AAS from 108 Clifton Rd.

**MILNE, J T** **fl 1920-1921**
Edinburgh painter; specialised in oriental scenes. Exhibited RSA(2) and the following year at the AAS, from 21 Nelson St.

**MILNE, James** **fl 1811-1834**
Architect. Designed St Bernard's Parish Church, Saxe-Coburg St, Edinburgh (1823), St Bernard's Bridge (1824), the lay-out of Ann St and St. Bernard's Crescent (1824) and the unfinished Saxe-Coburg Place (1821).
**Bibl:** Gifford 188n,340,361,374,402,404-7,409,413-4,pl.123.

**MILNE, James** **1860-1918**
Aberdeen landscape and portrait painter in oil and watercolour, also etcher and teacher. Trained Gray's School of Art becoming Art Master at Peterhead and later joined the staff of Gray's School of Art. Spent several summers working with George Davidson(qv) in Skye and Wester Ross. Lived at 17 Beechgrove Terrace, Aberdeen. Exhibited 'Hillside, Cromarty' at the RSA in 1913 and AAS(45), including several portraits, 1881-1917.
**Bibl:** Halsby 274.

**MILNE, Jean** **fl 1904-1917**
London based sculptor of Scottish extraction; exhibited RA(5), RSA(6), GI(3) & L(9).

**MILNE, John** **1823-1904**
St Andrews architect and draughtsman of architectural subjects. Trained under David Bryce(qv). In Edinburgh he designed the now disused St Bernard's Free Church, Henderson Row (1854-6). Exhibited RSA(8) including a design for the memorial arch in Fettercairn to commemorate the visit of Victoria & Albert in September 1861 (1866).
**Bibl:** Gifford 415,417.

**MILNE, John Maclauchlan RSA** **1886-1957**
Born Edinburgh; died Isle of Arran, 28 Oct. Son of Joseph M(qv). Painter in oil and watercolour of landscapes. Educated George Watson's, Edinburgh. After a spell at Kingoodie, nr Dundee, spent some years in Canada working as a cowboy. On his return visited Paris and, like Peploe, 'saw Cézanne and was immediately conquered' [Gaudie]. His wife was French and the patronage of Alex Keiller, head of the Dundee marmalade firm, enabled him to absorb the French atmosphere free of financial worry. Between 1919 and 1932 he spent part of every year in France, first in the rue des Quatres-Vents in Paris but then in the Mediterranean, at Cassis and St Tropez, often with Peploe(qv), Duncan Grant(qv) and Cadell(qv). Strongly influenced by the Impressionists and post-Impressionists, the impact of his French experience remained in all his subsequent work. Shortly before WW2 he settled in Corrie on Arran when his palette became more direct. A year before he died became Warden of Hospitalfield at Arbroath. His personality was 'attractive, ebullient and urbane' [Hardie]. Painted numerous works under the generic title of 'Paysage de Provence'. Elected ARSA 1934, RSA 1938. Exhibited RSA(47), GI(50+), AAS(1) & L(1). Represented in Glasgow AG(2), City of Edinburgh collection.
**Bibl:** Dundee AG 'A Centenary Exhibition', (Ex Cat 1985); Sinclair Gauldie, John Maclauchlan Milne, 1885-1957; Halsby 274; Hardie 143-4; RSA Obituary 1957.

**MILNE, John R H** **fl 1957-1958**
Lanarkshire sculptor. Exhibited RSA(2) from Hamilton.

**MILNE, John Stephen** **fl 1959-1965**
Aberdeenshire portrait and landscape painter. Exhibited AAS(5) from Windsmuir, The Craigs, Ellon.

**MILNE, Joseph** **1857-1911**
Born and died Edinburgh. Painted landscapes and seascapes in oil and occasionally watercolour. Father of John Maclauchlan M(qv), brother of William Watt M(qv). Lived in Edinburgh but also worked in Ayrshire and the Tay valley. Developed a personal style of painting using strong, bright tones with free use of bodycolour. Exhibited RA(6), latterly from 13 Granville Terrace, but mainly RSA(81), GI(45), AAS(1886-1893) & L(5).
**Bibl:** Halsby 274.

**MILNE, Margaret** **fl 1984**
St Andrews amateur portrait painter; exhibited AAS(1) from 48 Albany Park.

**MILNE, Mary** **fl 1908**
Amateur Aberdeen painter of local landscapes; exhibited AAS(1) from 45 Argyll Place.

**MILNE, Oswald Partridge** **fl 1918-1943**
Scottish portrait painter and etcher of topographical subjects. Lived at Leith Fort, near Edinburgh before moving to London 1933. Exhibited spasmodically at the RSA, in 1918(3) and then again in 1933 and 1943(3). Possibly the same as the architect **Oswald P MILNE** who exhibited RA 1903.

**MILNE, Robert** **fl 1950**
Lanarkshire watercolour landscape painter and stained glass window designer also teacher. Taught Hamilton Academy. Designed war memorial window in Cadzow parish church. Exhibited GI(1) from Hamilton. Represented in Hamilton Museum.

**MILNE, Samuel F** **fl 1938**
Amateur Glasgow watercolourist. Exhibited GI(1) from 437 Duke St.

**MILNE, William** **fl 1839-1843**
Edinburgh landscape painter, often worked on Arran. Exhibited RSA(6) from George St.

**MILNE, William Watt** **1869-1949**
Born Edinburgh, died St Ives, Hunts., Mar 10. Painter in oils of landscape, coastal scenes and interiors. Brother of Joseph M(qv). Attended Edinburgh College of Art, also RSA Life School 1885-1889. Won Maclaine Watters prize 1887 and a Chalmers bursary 1889. Visited Normandy. As a young man, his work was exhibited in Barcelona, Budapest, Munich, Venice and Vienna. Spent early life at St Monance, Fife, 1899 moving to Cambuskenneth, Stirling 1908-1913. Although not directly associated with Craigmill, he was active in the village at the time of great artistic endeavour, benefiting from the association of A K Brown(qv), Archibald Kay(qv), Henry Morley(qv) and William Wells(qv). During this time he visited France, painting in the village of Berneval, nr Dieppe. Married with three daughters, in 1916 the family moved to St Ives, Huntingdonshire after which time, although establishing a studio there, he found life increasingly hard. At some time, for a reason never discovered, William added Watt as a second christian name, creating a source of confusion ever since. Exhibited RSA(29), RGI(32), & between 1885 & 1912 at the AAS & L(1). Represented in Kirkcaldy AG, Smith AG (Stirling), Norris Museum (St Ives).

**MINTO, James** **fl 1884-1887**
Edinburgh painter in oil and watercolour of landscapes and flowers; exhibited RSA(5) from Ivy Cottage, Ivy Terrace.

**MINTY, Joan** **fl 1937**
Aberdeen amateur painter; exhibited a shore scene at the AAS from 18 Ashley Park S.

**MIRYLEES, M W** **fl 1879**
Edinburgh watercolour landscape painter; exhibited RSA(1). Possibly father of the London artist, Rita M.

**MIRYS, Silvestre de** **c1700-1788/93**
Born probably in France, Jan 8; died Bialystok, Poland. Painter in oil of portraits, historical and religious subjects, also murals. Son of a Scottish Jacobite who escaped with James to France. Father of Silvestre David de M(qv). Pupil at the Academie de Paris where he was awarded a gold medal. In 1729 was in Rome painting for the French Duc de St-Aignan while continuing his studies, before leaving was decorated by the Pope with the Order of the Golden Spur. Invited to Poland by Prince Jablonovski to undertake commissions in Warsaw but after various adventures including imprisonment and fighting a duel, left there and settled in Danzig. Some time later worked for Count Branicski in Bialystok where he was an offical at the Hetman's court 1788-1793, where he died. Made a baron 1788. A true eccentric, abjuring meat and all warm food. Painted on dish cloths which he maintained were the best 'canvases' of all. Although preferring a cold palette his compositions were skilfully composed, the drawing accurate and imaginative. Represented in collection of King Stanislaus Augustus Poniatowski, Bialystok palace, Wieliczka palace, Mielynski Museum ('Self-portrait'), National Museum (Warsaw), (portrait of 'Susanne Poltz', wife of the chief court painter), National Museum (Krakow), (portrait of 'K. Wegierski' 1772), Lubomirski Museum (Lvov), Posen Museum ('Self-portrait'), Lemberg, Univ Library (Warsaw).
**Bibl:** Thieme-Becker.

**MIRYS, Silvestre David de** **1742-1810**
Born Poland; died France, 23 Nov. Painter in oil and gouache; illustrator and miniaturist engraver. Son of Silvestre de M(qv). In 1769 went to Paris and between 1771 and 1775 worked under Vien. Painted biblical stories and Roman, Chinese and Japanese history stories for the children of the Duc d'Orleans. Painted a portrait of 'Mme de Genlis' 1781. Drew designs and preliminary sketches for the works of Delilles 1806-08.

**MITCHELL, Miss -** **fl 1898**
Aberdeen amateur painter; exhibited a study of King's College at the AAS from 72 Ashley Rd.

**MITCHELL, Agnes** **fl 1833-1837**
Edinburgh painter of flowers, fruit and still life. Exhibited RSA(4), latterly from Glamis Castle, Angus where she may have been employed as an art teacher to the family.

**MITCHELL, Alexander** **fl 1858-1871**
Edinburgh oil painter of landscapes and fruit; exhibited at the RSA(5).

**MITCHELL, Alex F** **fl 1959**
Fife landscape and portrait painter. Lived at various times in Aberdeen, Tayport and Edinburgh. Exhibited RSA(4), GI(4) & AAS(1).

**MITCHELL, Ann** **fl 1921**
Amateur Aberdeen portrait painter; exhibited 'Self-portrait' at the AAS from 45 Elmfield Avenue.

**MITCHELL Anne M** **fl 1986**
Stirling painter; exhibited two works at the RSA: 'Afternoon light' and 'On reflection'.

**MITCHELL, Archibald** **fl 1935-1941**
Landscape and figurative painter. Exhibited 'The pink cart' 1941 at the RSA and an Italian landscape at the AAS from Glenfoot, Newmilns.

**MITCHELL, Arthur George Sydney** **1856-1930**
Architect. Pupil of Rowand Anderson(qv). After serving his apprenticeship with Anderson & Browne entered into partnership with J. Wilson(qv) and later E A O Auldjo Jamieson(qv). Extensively remodelled Lennoxlove, nr Haddington. Exhibited RSA(10) 1883-1888 including the United Presbyterian church, Oakfield, Glasgow (1883), Montrose Asylum (1887) and additions to the Commercial Bank of Scotland's head office in Glasgow and a library for Bonaly Tower (1888). Designed his own home, 'The Pleasance', nr Gullane (referred to by Herman Multhesius in *Das Englische Haus* 1904-5). Among his better known erections in Edinburgh are the remodelled

Mercat Cross in the High St (1885); Well Court, the 'picturesque fantasy' in the Dean Village (1883-6); the Archway at the foot of Observatory Rd (1887); the remodelled St Cuthbert's Parish Church, Dell Rd (1907-8); Craighouse, Craighouse Rd (1889-94); and his last work, the Church of Scotland offices, George St (1909-11).
**Bibl:** Gifford, see index; Peter Savage, Lorimer and the Edinburgh Craft Designers, Edinburgh 1980, 91,110,167.

**MITCHELL, B** **fl 1902**
Aberdeen amateur landscape painter; exhibited two continental scenes at the AAS from 8 Queen's Terrace.

**MITCHELL, C K** **fl c1890-1900**
Little known marine painter. Lived and worked in Dundee during the last decade of the nineteenth century. His '*SS Perth* leaving Dundee' is in Perth AG.

**MITCHELL, Charles** **fl 1968-1972**
Glasgow watercolour painter of topographical subjects; exhibited AAS(1) from 73 Clouston St.

**MITCHELL, Charles L** **1860-1918**
Born Laurencekirk; died Pittsburgh, 30 May. Painter in oil and watercolour of landscapes and portraits, also restorer. Son of a farmer. Educated in Montrose and Aberdeen before travelling to Germany where he briefly studied art. Began his career as a bank clerk and joined the Dundee Graphic Arts Association 1891 exhibiting with them until 1900 from a studio in Ward Road, Dundee. Gained a local reputation as a landscapist and painter of Highland interiors and later of portraits. Commissioned to restore a collection of 18th century portraits belonging to Lord Gardenstone. Paid frequent visits to America eventually settling in Pittsburgh. Exhibited RSA(3) including a portrait of the Sheriff substitute of Forfarshire 1900, GI(16) & AAS including several Deeside scenes.

**MITCHELL, Colin C** **fl 1933-1940**
Edinburgh watercolourist. Exhibited RSW(12), RSA(2) & GI(1) from Clermiston Rd. Represented in Glasgow AG.

**MITCHELL, Colin Gillespie** **c1870-c1938**
Glasgow landscape painter in oil and watercolour. Fond of portraying scenes on the Clyde and Tweed. Trained Glasgow School of Art. Spent some time in Tunbridge Wells, Kent c1934. Secretary, Glasgow Art Club. Exhibited RA(3), RSA(6), RSW(3), GI(60+) & L(3).

**MITCHELL, David** **1946-**
Born Glasgow, Aug 8. Trained Glasgow School of Art 1964-8 under William Armour(qv) and David Donaldson(qv). Represented in Lillie AG (Milgavie) by a pen and ink drawing 'Wild Garden'.

**MITCHELL, David H** **fl 1938**
Minor painter of 3 Saffron Hall Crescent, Hamilton; exhibited RSA(1).

**MITCHELL, David L** **fl 1870**
Edinburgh landscape painter in oil; exhibited RSA(1).

**MITCHELL, Donald** **fl 1950-1953**
Paisley painter of coastal scenes and shipping in watercolour. Exhibited GI(5).

**MITCHELL, Edward** **fl c 1780**
Edinburgh engraver. Engraved Northcote's 'Death of Sir Ralph Abercromby'. Known chiefly for his portraits of 'Rev J Grey', after Douglas, and 'Rev Andrew Thomson', after Raeburn. The stipple engraver George Walker was a pupil.
**Bibl:** Brydall 205; Bushnell.

**MITCHELL, Edward D** **fl 1896-1910**
Aberdeen painter of Scottish and Dutch landscape; exhibited AAS from 33 King's Crescent.

**MITCHELL, Elspeth (Mrs Alan Cuthbert)** **fl 1940**
Glasgow watercolour painter and engraver. Exhibited GI(2) from 7 Grosvenor Crescent.

**MITCHELL, Emily Grace (Mrs Paul Henry) HRHA** **1868-1953**
Born Peterhead, Aug 11; died Ireland. Landscape, flower and portrait painter. One of ten children of Rev. John M whose grandmother was Lord Byron's cousin. Studied in Brussels, worked at Blanc Gavrin's Academy before studying under Francois Quelie and Andre Lhôte. Met the Irish painter, Paul Henry, in Paris, married him in London 1903. Began exhibiting at the RA 1904 and RHA 1910, from a London address. Moved to Achill Islands 1912. Separated from Henry 1934 but never divorced. Exhibited AAS(7), Dublin, Belfast & London until 1946. A rather neglected artist due partly to having a well-known, forceful husband and partly because since her death consent has been withheld for the publication of reproductions. A retrospective exhibition of her and her husband's work was held at the Hugh Lane Municipal Gallery of Modern Art, Dublin 1991.
**Bibl:** Snoody.

**MITCHELL, Enid M** **fl 1959-1965**
Painter of still life, portraits and landscape. Exhibited AAS(7) latterly from 8 Laverock Park, Glenrothes.

**MITCHELL, Francis** **fl 1835-1837**
Edinburgh painter of portrait miniatures. Exhibited RSA(2) from Buccleuch St.

**MITCHELL, Francis N** **fl 1862**
Edinburgh landscape painter. Exhibited 'Lettermay, Lochgoil' at the RSA from Dublin St.

**MITCHELL, George** **fl 1943-1951**
Glasgow painter of landscapes. Exhibited RSA(5).

**MITCHELL, George J** **fl 1921**
Dundee portrait painter and watercolourist. Exhibited a portrait of 'Lieut Horsefall VC' (killed in action) at the RSA from Braeside, Lawside Road. Represented in Kirkcaldy AG.

**MITCHELL, Gordon K ARSA RSW RGI** **1952-**
Born Edinburgh, 16 Feb. Painter in oil, watercolour and acrylic of portraits, still life and murals. Trained Edinburgh College of Art 1970-75. Commissioned by the Royal Navy, Commonwealth Institute and University of Edinburgh. One of the finest contemporary Scottish draughtsman and imaginative painters. 'His perspectives can dare to the point of recklessness, yet need no safety net. Whatever the subject, he summons it with hair breadth precision' [Gordon Smith]. Solo exhibitions Glasgow 1990, 1993. Major awards include a First Prize (RSA), William Gillies award (RSA), J Murray Thomson Award (RSA). Elected President, SAAC 1993; RGI 1998, ARSA 1999. Represented in Paisley Art Institute, Kansas City Art Institute, Old City AG (Jerusalem). Lives at 10 Argyll Terrace, Edinburgh. Member of the SSA. Exhibits RSA 1977,1984,1990 & GI.
**Bibl:** Billcliffe Gall. Ex Cat (text by W Gordon Smith), May, 1993.

**MITCHELL, Grierson Gordon** **fl 1863-1873**
Edinburgh oil painter of figures and townscapes; exhibited RSA(4).

**MITCHELL, Helen H** **fl 1899-1904**
Edinburgh landscape painter of local scenery. Exhibited RSA(8) & GI(4).

**MITCHELL, Henry** **fl 1882-1902**
Architect and watercolour draughtsman. Possibly English. Moved from Rock Ferry, Cheshire in the early 1890s to the Glasgow area from where he exhibited GI(10) & L(9).

**MITCHELL, Ian** **20th Cent**
Amateur Aberdeenshire artist; exhibited AAS from 8 Alexandra Terrace, Fraserburgh.

**MITCHELL, J Edgar** **1871-1922**
Dundee watercolour painter of landscapes and rural genre. Moved to Edinburgh 1895 and in 1915 to Newcastle. Exhibited RSA(4) & RSW(1).

**MITCHELL, James (or John)** **1791-1852**
Edinburgh-based line engraver. His best known plates are after

Wilkie, especially *'Alfred in the Meatherd's Cottage'* and *'The Rat-Catchers'*. Engraved several plates for the Raphael Bible as well as Rubens' picture *'Daniel in the Den of Lions'*. But perhaps historically his most important engravings were the set of 12 hand-coloured aquatints depicting the Common Man, drawn by 'A Kay', which can be seen in the NLS and in the Highland Folk Museum, Kingussie.
**Bibl:** Bryan; Brydall 129; Bushnell; DNB.

**MITCHELL, James** **fl 1875-1902**
Edinburgh painter in oil and watercolour of landscapes, mainly pastoral scenes and latterly some topographical works. Moved to Prestonpans c1900. Exhibited RSA(17) & AAS(1).

**MITCHELL, Jeannie** **fl 1891**
Minor painter of Haslewood, Langside, Glasgow; exhibited GI(1).

**MITCHELL, Jemima W** **fl 1899-1900**
Amateur Edinburgh miniature painter of 31 Alva Street, exhibited at the RSA(2).

**MITCHELL, John** **Early 19th Century**
Peterhead artist. Uncle of the Aberdeen John M(qv). Studied under John Phillip(qv) at the Trustees Academy and under James Forbes(qv). Friend of P C Auld(qv).

**MITCHELL, John** **1837-1926**
Born Woodside, Donside; died 14 Jly. Attended evening classes under James Giles(qv) in Aberdeen, also taught by his uncle the Peterhead artist John Mitchell(qv). After an apprenticeship at a local lithographic company (Keith and Gibb) where George Reid(qv) also worked, went to London to study at the Slade under Legros. Returning to Aberdeen he painted many scenes around the city including Balmoral, under the patronage of Queen Victoria. Gave lessons in painting to the Royal Family. His landscapes are highly coloured with dominant blues and purples in the hills and with vivid greens and yellows in the foreground, subtly fused and never garish. His talent as a colourist overcomes weak draughtsmanship. Also lithographed sketches for John Stewart's *The Sculptured Stones of Scotland,* 2 Vols, 1856-57, illustrated *Under Lochnagar* 1894, edited by the Balmoral factor of the time, Dr R A Profeit. His landscapes of Aberdeenshire are highly prized especially in the area in which he lived. Also painted in the Mearns which some regard as his best work. Most of his exhibits were of local scenes. In 1875 he painted an interior of Culter Castle and its Chapel which was subsequently purchased by the owner and in 1883 showed a portrait of his mother. Lived latterly at 10 Gladstone Place, Queen's Cross, Aberdeen. Exhibited RA(5), GI(2) and very frequently at both the RSA(34) 1865-1900, also AAS 1885-1926. Represented in Aberdeen AG.
**Bibl:** Halsby 274.

**MITCHELL, John** **fl 1867-1890**
Edinburgh landscape painter in oil; exhibited RSA(3) & GI(4).

**MITCHELL, John RSW** **1937-**
Born Glasgow, 21 Dec. Painter in watercolour, silkscreen engraver, also teacher. Educated Glasgow Academy and Edinburgh RHS. Trained Edinburgh College of Art 1956-61. Paints fine watercolours from his home in Fife. Elected RSW 1967.

**MITCHELL, John** **fl 1944**
Midlothian still life painter; exhibited RSA(1) from Dalkeith.

**MITCHELL, John** **fl 1984-1985**
Fife painter. Exhibited GI(4) from Glenrothes.

**MITCHELL, John Campbell RSA** **1862-1922**
Born Campbeltown, Argyll; died Edinburgh, 15 Feb. Painter in oil and occasionally watercolour; landscapes and marine scenes. Started life in a lawyer's office but at the age of 22 abandoned his legal ambition and entered Edinburgh College of Art where he worked in the RSA life class and later in Paris under Benjamin Constant. Two very early works, both scenes from the hunting field, dated 1879 appeared on the market in the 1990s. On his return to Scotland 1890 settled in Edinburgh where he remained for the rest of his life. In 1891 shared the Keith Prize. First exhibited at the RSA 1886 and in 1901 spent some time in Galloway developing a great attraction for and technique in portraying changeable skies. Painted large expanses of moorland and rolling countryside as well as wide expanses of beach and ocean. Had a strong feeling for sunlight and fluctuating shadow. In about 1904 moved to Corstorphine when there was a change reflecting his new environment, from the breezy to a more pensive sentiment. Elected ARSA 1904, RSA 1918. Exhibited RA(8), RSA(99), RSW(2), GI(67), AAS & L(3). Represented in Aberdeen AG, Glasgow AG, City of Edinburgh collection, Walker AG (Liverpool), Manchester AG.
**Bibl:** Caw 390-1; Halsby 165-274; Wingfield.

**MITCHELL, Miss L C** **fl 1899-1908**
Stirling painter of genre. exhibited GI(7) & RHA(1).

**MITCHELL, Laurence** **fl 1796**
Dumbarton engraver. None of his work is recorded. In 1796 married in Edinburgh.
**Bibl:** Bushnell.

**MITCHELL, M** **fl 1887**
Amateur landscape painter in watercolour; exhibited RSA(1) from Kinghorn.

**MITCHELL, Madge Young** **1892-1974**
Born Uddingston, Glasgow. Watercolourist; portraits, figure studies, landscapes, seascapes and coastal scenes. Trained Gray's School of Art, Aberdeen, becoming a member of staff 1907. Painted many portraits in both mediums, also produced sensitively portrayed effulgent landscapes of the north-east. Exhibited RSA(27), RSW(1), GI(13) & AAS 1919-1973, latterly from Flat 33, Salisbury Court, Salisbury Terrace, Aberdeen.
**Bibl:** Halsby 274.

**MITCHELL, Margaret** **c1940-**
Born Edinburgh. Evacuated to Bermuda 1947. Returning to the UK after the war studied art first at Dartington Hall Art Centre, Devon followed by three years at Edinburgh College of Art. After her marriage, completed her diploma at Dundee College of Art. Settled in Angus and later in Perthshire. Her delicately worked and colourful landscapes are recognised more by the general public than by the academic establishment and most of her exhibitions have been in Edinburgh and Perthshire, with successful shows at the Pitlochry Festival.

**MITCHELL, Miss Marion B P ('Mysie')** **fl 1919-1921**
Painter of landscapes. Exhibited AAS(5), all of the Beauly area, from a Sefton address.

**MITCHELL, Miss Mary M** **fl 1921-1923**
Aberdeenshire etcher of considerable talent. Exhibited drypoints of local landscape and figurative works at the AAS(4) from Central Schoolhouse, Skene.

**MITCHELL, Mary W** **1902-?**
Aberdeen painter in oil of landscapes and teacher. Trained Gray's School of Art, Aberdeen 1920-1923 before joining Albyn School for Girls as art teacher; there she wrote 'Art Notes' for the magazine and began exhibiting at the AAS in 1923 and again in 1926 from Mount Cottage, Mount St. Probably the **Molly Were Mitchell** who exhibited in London 1927-1929.

**MITCHELL, Miss Meg** **fl 1984**
Glasgow artist. Exhibited GI(1) from Kenmuir Ave.

**MITCHELL, Peter McDowall** **1879-c1940**
Born Galashiels, 30 Jly. Painter in oil and watercolour, also etcher. Trained Glasgow School of Art from which he received a travelling scholarship. From his studio in Glasgow he painted landscapes, mostly of the west Highlands. Exhibited RSA(6), RSW(16), GI(5) & L(8), latterly from 84 Mossgiel Road, Yewlands, Glasgow.
**Bibl:** Halsby 274.

**MITCHELL, Robert** **fl 1775-1801**
Aberdeen architect. Established himself in practice in London c1775.

Designed Preston Hall, Midlothian for Alexander Callendar 1791-1800, described by Dunbar as a'singularly accomplished example of the fully developed neo-Palladian country house, complete with matching retinue of estate buildings". Subsequently obtained commissions for a number of English country houses including Moore Place, Much Hadham, Herts for James Gordon 1777-1779, Silwood Park, Berks for Sir James Sibbald 1796, Heath Lane Lodge, Twickenham for Isaac Swanson and extensive alterations to Cottesbrooke Hall, Northants for Sir W Langham c1770, including the bridge and lodges in the Park. At Preston Hall, as in some of his other houses, while the main lines of the composition are conventional, there is an important refinement of detail particularly regarding the interior decoration. 'The plan of the main block revolves about a top-lit staircase, whose first-floor gallery, with its elegant iron balustrade, Corinthian screens and enriched ceiling, provides a focal centre of quite unexpected grandeur' [Dunbar]. Published an important work *Plans, etc of buildings erected in England and Scotland; with An Essay to elucidate the Grecian, Roman and Gothic Architecture* 1801. Exhibited six designs at the RA 1782-1798, latterly from 42 Newman St.
**Bibl:** Colvin 392; Country Life, Feb 15/22, 1936; Dunbar 120, 123; Robert Mitchell, Plans of Buildings Erected in England and Scotland, 1801.

**MITCHELL, Sheila** **fl 1976-1979**
Aberdeenshire painter of figure studies. Trained Gray's School of Art, Aberdeen. Exhibited AAS(6) from Balfour Cottage, Durris.

**MITCHELL, Sydney** **fl 1950-1965**
Glasgow portrait painter. Exhibited RSA(24) between the above years.

**MITCHELL, Thomas** **fl 1881-1885**
Glasgow landscape painter in oil; exhibited RSA(2) & GI(1), from 21 Drury Street.

**MITCHELL, William** **fl 1820**
Edinburgh engraver. Engraved a bookplate for Charles Lawson, 1820.
**Bibl:** Bushnell.

**MITCHELL, William** **fl 1880-1903**
Glasgow landscape and genre painter. Exhibited GI(11) from 18 Kew Terrace.

**MITCHELL, William B** **fl 1884-1902**
Edinburgh painter in oil of figure subjects and landscape. Caretaker at St George's Free Church, Stafford Street, Edinburgh. Exhibited RSA(5), GI(1) and 'Newark Castle', Fife at the AAS in 1900.

**MITCHELL, William Sydney** **fl 1949-1960**
Glasgow painter of portraits, genre and topographical works. Mostly drawn in pencil, pen and wash, chalk. Exhibited GI(9) latterly from Dinmont Rd.

**MITCHELL, Miss Wilma M** **fl 1962**
Fife watercolourist. Landscapes, sometimes continental; townscapes. Exhibited GI(2) from Dunfermline.

**MITCHELSON, David** **fl 1758**
Edinburgh seal cutter. Married in Edinburgh 1758. No recorded work remains.
**Bibl:** Bushnell.

**MODEEN, Mary** **1953-**
Born Madison, Wisconsin. Printmaker, author, teacher and sculptress. Settled in Scotland 1989. Senior lecturer, Duncan Jordanstone College of Art. First solo exhibition 1976, followed by many others in Australia, USA & Scotland. Exhibits RSA, SSA & AAS. Represented in Hungarian Nat. Museum of Art, Hood Museum (Dartmouth, NH), Dundee AG. Lives in Blairgowrie, Perthshire.

**MOFFAT, Alexander** **1943-**
Born Dunfermline. Painter in oil, pencil; also etcher, writer and teacher. Portraits and figurative works. Studied at Edinburgh College of Art 1960-64 and thereafter worked in an Edinburgh engineering factory until 1966 when for the next eight years he worked as a photographer although at the same time practised painting, sometimes in association with his friend, John Bellamy(qv), with whom he may be said to have initiated a fresh approach to realism in Scottish painting. Chairman, '57 Gallery' in Edinburgh 1968-78. Primarily a portraitist, before 1967 he employed earth colours, but later adopted a brighter palette. Influenced by Max Beckmann's figure paintings, using sharp black contour lines and high key colour. Also influenced by R B Kitag. First solo exhibition at SNPG 1973. Since 1979 has taught at Gray's School of Art. His writings on art have appeared in many art reviews, also involved in the selection of several exhibitions of contemporary work. Represented in SNPG, SNGMA.
**Bibl:** Gage 66-69; Hardie 198; Hartley 152; Macmillan [SA] 369,401,404,406; SNPG, 'A view of the Portraits by Alexander Moffat (Ex Cat 1973); SAC Edinburgh 'Scatter', (Ex Cat 1971); Third Eye Centre, Glasgow 'Seven poets: an exhibition of paintings and drawings by Alexander Moffat', (Ex Cat 1981).

**MOFFAT, Alison G** **fl 1958-1963**
Glasgow painter of informal portraits. Moved to Edinburgh. Exhibited GI(3).

**MOFFAT, Anne** **fl 1978**
Aberdeenshire painter. Wife of Cecil M(qv). Exhibited a landscape at the AAS from Firdael, Drumlithie.

**MOFFAT, Arthur Elwell** **fl 1880-1902**
Edinburgh painter in oil and watercolour; landscapes, often wooded, and townscapes. An interesting, competent painter adept at conveying atmosphere as well as natural contour. Spent a short time in London in the late 1880s but returned to Edinburgh 1889. Exhibited three works at the RA in 1886 and 1887 including 'The Dee at Banchory' (1886); but mainly at the RSA(24), RSW(1), GI(5), RHA(2), RI(3) & AAS 1885-1902.

**MOFFAT, Betsy Burns** **fl 1930-1938**
Painter of flowers, interiors and informal portraits; also woodcuts. Possibly sister of Isobel M(qv). Exhibited oils and watercolours RSA (12), RSW(3) & GI(3) from Clairinch, Milngavie and latterly Glasgow.

**MOFFAT, Cecil H** **fl 1976-1978**
Aberdeen artist; trained at Gray's School of Art, Aberdeen. Married Anne M(qv). Exhibited AAS(2).

**MOFFAT, David G** **fl 1986-1988**
Glasgow sculptor and painter. Exhibited figurative works at the GI in plaster and terracotta, from Clarence Drive.

**MOFFAT, George** **fl 1953**
Perthshire painter of genre; exhibited RSA from Dunblane.

**MOFFAT, Gordon T** **fl 1961-1980**
Aberdeen landscape and portrait painter, sometimes continental scenes. Exhibited AAS often from 6 Osborne Place, and GI(1) 1948.

**MOFFAT, Hugh** **fl 1965**
Aberdeen amateur painter. Exhibited GI(2) from Hartington Rd.

**MOFFAT, Isobel** **1906-1961**
Milngavie painter. Sister of Betsy Burns M(qv). Exhibited RSA(1) from Clairinch.

**MOFFAT, J** **fl 1800-1827**
Edinburgh-based engraver. Specialised in Scottish maps which he is known to have been working on 1821-1827. Also engraved book-plates including one for Hay of Linplum, 1800 and one for C.R. Hay,1800. An engraved portrait of 'George Heriot' after Scougal and a mezzotint of the same sitter are in the collection of the City of Edinburgh.
**Bibl:** Bushnell.

**MOFFAT, J Frederick** **fl 1879-1888**
Edinburgh oil painter of landscapes and figure studies. Some Continental landscapes were included in his work, particularly sketches of Normandy in the early 1880s. Exhibited RSA(34), GI(6) & AAS from The Avenue, Greenhill Gdns, Edinburgh.

**MOFFAT, Mrs Jane L** **fl 1855**
Edinburgh flower painter; exhibited RSA(2) from Danube St. Possibly the same **Mrs W W MOFFAT** who exhibited fruit and flower studies at the RSA 1857-1860, also from Danube St.

**MOFFAT, Miss Janet S** **fl 1846-1858**
Midlothian based painter of portraits and portrait miniatures, especially children. Lived for a time in Leith. Exhibited RSA(27).

**MOFFAT, John S** **fl 1900-1906**
Stirlingshire sculptor. Exhibited a portrait bust at the RSA from Larbert & GI(2).

**MOFFAT, Menzies** **1829-1907**
Lanarkshire-based embroiderer, photographer and tailor. An eccentric recluse, he never married. Two panels hang in the Town House, Biggar. *The Royal Crimean Hero Tablecloth* has a centrepiece of Queen Victoria surrounded by ladies of the Court and no fewer than 81 pictorial scenes as well as the portrait of a local doctor, Dr Pairman, whose life story Moffat incorporated into a wallpaper pattern book, now destroyed.
**Bibl:** Margaret Swain, pp130-2.

**MOFFAT, Muirhead** **fl 1916-1932**
Amateur Glasgow draughtsman. Exhibited GI(2) from 134 Douglas St.

**MOFFAT, Miss Nan Muirhead** **fl 1930-1931**
Glasgow amateur artist, mostly in pen and ink. Probably daughter of Muirhead M(qv). Exhibited GI(6) from 11 Dungoyne Gardens.

**MOFFAT, Thomas Gordon** **fl 1939-1970**
Helensburgh-based painter of landscape, portraits and genre. Exhibited RSA(5) & GI(9) from Balmaha and latterly Aberdeen.

**MOFFAT, William Lambie** **1808-1882**
London land surveyor who undertook historically important work in Edinburgh. His *Geometrical and Geological Landscape,* published Edinburgh c1837 contained tables of the relative altitudes of the 'principal public and other edifices, squares and hills situate in the City of Edinburgh and the Environs'. The engravings were done by W H Lizars(qv) and include 300 small pictures. A steel engraving of 'Edinburgh and Environs' 1837 is in the City of Edinburgh collection.
**Bibl:** Butchart 64; Gifford 74,319,620.

**MOHR, Mrs** **fl 1899**
Aberdeen landscape painter; exhibited a Highland loch scene at the AAS from 61 Argyll Place.

**MOIR, Mrs Ellen** **fl 1867-1874**
Edinburgh painter in oil and sculptor of animals and figure subjects. Exhibited RSA(17) and in provincial galleries including in England.

**MOIR, George** **fl 1834**
Edinburgh figurative painter; exhibited 'Portrait of a young guitarist' at the RSA from George St.

**MOIR, Mrs James** **fl 1902**
Minor Glasgow painter; exhibited GI(3) from 16 Hamilton Drive, Pollockshields.

**MOIR, John** **1775-1857**
Died Peterhead, 28 Feb. Scottish portrait and occasional landscape painter. Son of the Rev Dr George Moir of Peterhead. Educated in Aberdeen, he learned the rudiments of drawing in Edinburgh 1803 where he was described as a landscape painter. Went to Italy, studying antiquities in Rome. On his return initially painted mainly landscapes but also portraits. Portraits of 'Captain Barclay', 'Mr Niven Lumsden' and 'Captain Adam Cumine' were all exhibited in Edinburgh, also 'William Livingstone MD' (1760-1840). Other sitters included the violinist composer of strathspey and reels, 'William Marshall' (1748-1833), and the advocates 'William Carnegie' (1772-1840) and 'Henry Lumsden' (1784-1856). In 1843 exhibited 'View on the River Don, nr Aberdeen' at the RSA. His portrait '4th Duke of Gordon, Keeper of the Great Seal of Scotland' (1743-1827), signed and dated 1817, is in SNPG. Represented also in Drum Castle (NTS), Leith Hall (NTS).
**Bibl:** Aberdeen Journal, 8 Jan 1927; Caw 90.

**MOIR, John** **fl 1884-1887**
Glasgow landscape and portrait painter; exhibited GI(3) from 4 Selbourne Terrace, Woodlands Road. Represented in Glasgow AG(2).

**MOIR, John H M** **fl 1942**
Midlothian landscape painter; exhibited RSA(2) from Currie.

**MOIR, Miss Margaret** **fl 1875**
Edinburgh oil portrait painter; exhibited RSA(1). A portrait of 'Margaret, Lady Burnett, wife of the 7th Baronet of Leys', is in Crathes Castle (NTS).

**MOIR, William** **fl 1878**
Edinburgh watercolourist; exhibited a French landscape at the RSA.

**MOIRA, Gerald Edward ARA PROI VPRWS RWA** **1867-1959**
Born London, 26 Jan; died Northwood, Middlesex, 2 Aug. Painter in oil and watercolour of landscapes and figure subjects, also mural decorator and teacher. Although English by birth, both parents were Portuguese, his influence on the development of Scottish art in the 1930s was considerable largely on account of being Principal of the Edinburgh College of Art 1924-1932. Studied at RA Schools 1887-89 and in Paris. Exhibited RA from 1891. 'Washing Day' was purchased by the Chantrey Bequest 1938. Whilst in Edinburgh worked on murals in the chancel vault depicting the four evangelists for St Cuthbert's Church in collaboration with John Maxwell(qv). Illustrated Walter's *Shakespear's True Life* 1890. Elected ARA 1904, ARWS 1917, RWA 1919, RWS 1932, PROI 1945, VPRWS 1953. Exhibited RA(47), RSA(11), RWS(102), RSW(2), ROI(36), GI(38), L(28) and London Salon (5). Represented in V & A, Glasgow AG.
**Bibl:** Gifford 275; Halsby 213,245; Watkins, J H, The Art of Gerald Edward Moira, 1922.

**MOLLISON, M T** **fl 1887**
Minor Glasgow figure; exhibited GI(1) from 4 Windsor Terrace.

**MOLYNEAUX, Elizabeth Gowanlock RSW** **1887-1969**
Painter in watercolour of landscapes. Painted in Scotland, often on Arran, also in France and Italy. Lived in Edinburgh and painted in a fluent style using washes. Her treatment of watercolour has been likened to that of Emily Paterson(qv) and Anna Dickson(qv). Received Lauder Award 1924. Elected RSW 1923. Exhibited RSA(6), RSW(76), GI(34), SWA(2) & Paris Salon.
**Bibl:** Halsby 274.

**MONAGHAN, George C** **fl 1912-1913**
Glasgow watercolour painter and engraver; principally figure studies. Probably father of Robert J M(qv). Exhibited RSW(1), GI(1) & AAS(1) from Darnley, Barrhead.

**MONAGHAN, John** **fl 1987-**
Glasgow painter. Exhibited 'Unloading at the Granary' at the GI, from Dorchester Ave.

**MONAGHAN, Robert J** **fl 1935-1939**
Glasgow painter of still life, portraits and pastoral scenes. Possibly son of George C M(qv). Exhibited RSA(7) & GI(1) from 34 Brighton Street, Glasgow.

**MONAGHAN, Samuel R** **fl 1958-1983**
Linlithgow landscape artist. Moved to Edinburgh c1975. Exhibited RSA(4).

**MONCRIEFF, Colonel Sir Alexander FRS KCB** **1829-1906**
Born Edinburgh. Educated Edinburgh University and Aberdeen. Served in the artillery during the Crimea and was present at the Siege of Sevastapol. Notable innovator in artillery and munitions. Married Harriet Rimington 1875; elected FRS 1871, knighted 1890. In later life travelled extensively in Canada, the Middle East and South Africa. Highly competent amateur watercolourist of military subjects and landscape. Exhibited RSA(5) including 'Camp of the 2nd English Division before Sebastopol and Balaclava' from the United Services Club, Edinburgh. Lived at Barnhill, nr Perth and latterly Bandillon.

**MONCRIEFF, David Scott** **fl 1853-1874**
Edinburgh watercolour painter of landscape; exhibited 'A view of Niagara' and two local Edinburgh scenes at the RSA.

**MONCRIEFF, Jean** **fl 1972-1984**
Kincardineshire painter and printmaker; works mainly in watercolour depicting still life and interiors. Trained Gray's School of Art, Aberdeen. Exhibited AAS(2) from 10 Christie Crescent, Stonehaven.

**MONCRIEFF, Mary M** **fl 1911**
Minor painter; exhibited RA(1) from 13 Dean Park Crescent, Edinburgh.

**MONCRIEFF, Robert Scott** **fl 1871**
Amateur caricaturist. Possibly brother of David Scott M(qv). His drawings of Scottish lawyers 1816-1820 were published as *Scottish Bar* 1871.
**Bibl**: Houfe.

**MONCRIEFF, W Dundas Scott** **fl 1878**
Glasgow-based painter of interiors. Exhibited GI(1) from 27 Buchanan St.

**MONCRIEFF, W W Scott** **fl 1852**
Painter. Probably related to David(qv) & Robert Scott M(qv). Lived at Dalkeith Park; exhibited 'A view of the Park' at the RSA.

**MONRO, Alexander Binning HRSA (resigned 1847)** **1805-1891**
Edinburgh-based painter in oil of landscapes; also sculptor. After first studying for law changed to art, painting in Italy before returning to Edinburgh. Father of Charles C Binning M(qv). Favoured dramatic landscapes, generally in the Highlands, stormy scenes across rivers and near the coasts. His main home was in Auchinbowie House, Stirling but also had a studio at 28 Rutland Square, Edinburgh and from 1884-1886 lived on Rothesay. Exhibited RA(2), 'A stormy coast scene' 1842 and 'Lochranza Castle, Arran - Evening' 1847. Elected HRSA 1835 but resigned in 1847. Exhibited RSA(86) 1832-1867; also GI(8).

**MONRO, Charles Carmichael Binning** **1851-c1910**
Painter in oil and watercolour of landscape, coastal and shipping scenes. Fourth son of Alexander Binning M(qv). Moved to the south of England in 1870, returning to Scotland 1891. Queen Victoria purchased at least one of his watercolours, 'View across Gairloch toward Eilean Horisdale'. Exhibited RA(10) 1874-1890, also RSA(31), often in the Highlands, including a 'View below the Linn of Dee' (1878), & AAS(5) in 1885 from Auchinbowie, Stirling.

**MONRO, David T/F** **fl 1834-1837**
Edinburgh topographical painter, fond of depicting castles. Exhibited RSA(2).

**MONRO, Miss Helen (Mrs Turner)** **fl 1934-1957**
Edinburgh engraver, mainly wood engravings, also illustrator and occasional watercolourist. Exhibited RSA(5), mostly flowers and fruit, from Queen St. Represented by a watercolour and pencil drawing of the 'Keys of the City of Edinburgh' (1934) in the Edinburgh City collection.

**MONRO, Hugh** **1861-1931**
Landscape painter in oil and watercolour of 16 Picardy Place, Edinburgh. A portrait of 'Mary of Guise' (1515-1560), after the Hardwick portrait, was purchased in 1924 by the SNPG as was his portrait of the 'Regent Moray' (c1531-1570) copied after an unknown artist 1925. Exhibited RSA(20) & RSW(2).

**MONRO, James N** **fl 1893**
Minor painter of 28 Bath Street, Glasgow; exhibited GI(1).

**MONRO, Mrs M V** **fl 1929**
Edinburgh watercolourist. Exhibited a landscape at the GI from Queen St.

**MONRO, Dr Thomas** **1759-1833**
Born London; died Bushey. Physician, collector, patron and watercolourist. Worked in watercolour, Indian ink, charcoal and chalk, mainly landscape details especially trees and rocks. Third in a line of Scottish doctors who specialised in mental health each being at Bethlem Hospital. Educated Harrow and Oriel College, Oxford. Occupied a position of outstanding importance in the history of British watercolour painting, mainly on account of the positive encouragement he gave to young watercolourists and above all to Thomas Girtin and J M W Turner. In 1794 he moved from Bedford Square to Adelphi Terrace and there established an academy 'where, during the winters, Girtin, Turner, John Varley and others copied and composed variations upon Gainsborough, Hearne and most especially J R Cozens'. In addition the young men had full and free access to Monro's fine collection of watercolour drawings and books. He was a student of John Laporte but followed Gainsborough most whom as a young man he had known. Dr Foxley Norris wrote of Monro's sketches that they 'were made out of doors on the pad in Payne's grey or Indian ink wash, sometimes on grey, sometimes on blue, sometimes on white paper; then they were taken home to be worked over with charcoal, crayon or Indian ink. In some of the sketches the figures - single or in groups - and animals were cut out in white paper, stuck on to the sketch in the appropriate place with gum, and then treated with brush or crayon to bring them into tone with the rest'. In 1811 and 1812 was consulted by George III at Windsor. All his children also drew to some extent, most particularly **Henry** (1791-1814), **John** (1801-1880) and **Alexander** (1802-1844). Examples of Henry's works are in the Ashmolean and the Fitzwilliam. Represented in BM, V & A, Aberdeen AG, Ashmolean, Exeter Museum, Fitzwilliam AG, Abbot Hall AG (Kendal), Leeds City AG, Newport AG, Ulster Museum.
**Bibl:** AJ 1901; Conn XLIX, 1917; Hardie III, 177-280; OWS Club, II, 1924; VAM (Ex Cats 1917, 1976); Walpole Soc, V, XXIII, XXVII; Williams 247-248.

**MONTEATH, Miss Catherine** **fl 1868-1898**
Perthshire painter. Turned increasingly to painting wild flower pieces as her career advanced, at which she was extremely competent. Lived at Glenhead Cottage, Dunblane. Exhibited landscapes and flower paintings in oil and watercolour RSA(25) & GI(4).

**MONTEITH, Harold E** **fl 1947-1951**
Amateur Stirling watercolourist. Exhibited GI(2) from Cambusbarron.

**MONTEITH, John A** **fl 1885-1903**
Glasgow painter in oil of local and rural scenes; exhibited RSA(6), GI(34), AAS(2) & L(1) from 79 W Regent St.

**MONTEITH (or Montieth), Kathryn** **fl 1978**
Kincardineshire painter of figurative subjects; exhibited AAS(2) from 89 Barclay St, Stonehaven.

**MONTEITH, William** **fl 1893**
Minor painter of Springdale, Langside; exhibited GI(1).

**MONTGOMERY, Lady Alice A Graham** **1822-1890**
Died Stobo, Peebleshire, 16 Dec. Amateur painter in oil of portraits and figure subjects. Third daughter of John Hope-Johnstone of Annandale and the wife of Sir Graham Montgomery whom she married 1845. Lived at Stobo Castle, Peebleshire. Exhibited RSA(8).

**MONTGOMERY(IE), Miss Snookie** **fl 1932**
Edinburgh painter. Exhibited RSA(1) from 8 St Bernards Crescent.

**MONTGOMERY, Miss Iona A E** **fl 1989-**
Bearsden narrative painter. Daughter of James A M(qv). Exhibited GI(1) from Iona Ave.

**MONTGOMERY, James A** **fl 1975-1979**
Glasgow landscape painter. Father of Iona M(qv). Exhibited GI(4) from Iona Ave.

**MONTLAKE, Eli** **fl 1943**
Renfrewshire sculptor; exhibited 'Man' at the RSA, from Giffnock.

**MOOD, John** **fl 1863-1867**
Edinburgh landscape painter in oil; exhibited RSA(8) from Rosehall House.

**MOODIE, Donald RSA PSSA** **1892-1963**
Born Edinburgh, 24 Mar; died 19 Jne. Painter in oil and watercolour; landscapes, still-life, portraiture and murals. Educated George Heriot's and Edinburgh College of Art. Awarded postgraduate scholarship 1914. In 1919 appointed to the staff of ECA, shortly afterwards painted a large mural for their dining hall. Sketched extensively in Brittany, later in the borders and the west Highlands. A skilled watercolourist, sympathetic to the ideas of the progressive students under his care who included Gillies(qv), Maxwell(qv) and MacTaggart(qv). His murals are notable for their fine conception, design and beauty of line. Elected ARSA 1943, RSA 1952, President, SSA 1937-1942. In 1959 became Secretary, RSA remaining in office until shortly before his death in 1963. Exhibited extensively RSA(100+), GI(34), AAS & L(2) from Beechbank, Ratho Station, Midlothian. Represented in Aberdeen AG, Glasgow AG, Kirkcaldy AG, Edinburgh City collection.
**Bibl:** Halsby 211,219,220,275.

**MOODIE, Helen C** **fl 1894**
Glasgow artist. Exhibited once at the GI from 256 Great Western Rd.

**MOODIE, Margaret** **fl 1959-1967**
Edinburgh landscape and portrait painter. Fond of Iona. Exhibited RSA(7) from Drumsheugh Place.

**MOODY, Rona** **20th Cent**
Dalmellington stained glass window designer. Represented by the David Muir memorial window in Gladsmuir church, Midlothian.

**MOONEY, John Francis ARSA RSW** **1948-**
Born Edinburgh. Painter of still life, botanical works, metaphorical and abstract compositions, often seeking to introduce wit into his work. Trained Edinburgh College of Art 1966-70. Travelling scholarship enabled him to visit Greece, Turkey and Spain and from 1972-1990 held a teaching post at Edinburgh College of Art. Elected RSW 1983, ARSA 1984. Won Guthrie Award, RSA 1982. First one-man exhibition in Edinburgh 1973. 'He develops the idea of a theme and variations to create a subtle and often ironic series of metamorphoses on a set of given images, an irony that is enhanced by the way in which he contrasts high finish with an expressly artificial mode of composition' [Macmillan]. Regularly exhibits RSA, RSW & GI(1) from 14 Stanley St, Edinburgh. Represented in SNGMA, Dundee AG, Perth AG, Hunterian AG (Glasgow).
**Bibl:** Macmillan [SA] 395.

**MOONIE, Mrs Janet** **fl 1940**
Edinburgh amateur painter of domestic genre. Exhibited RSA(13) & GI(2) from 78 Newbattle Terrace.

**MOORE, Miss Dorothy Winifred** **1897-?**
Born Cork. Painter in oil and watercolour of portraits and landscapes, also teacher. Trained Edinburgh College of Art 1915-20. Appointed to a teaching post in Shrewsbury 1920. Daughter was also an artist, Miss M M(qv). Exhibited from 1919-1931 at the RA(1), RSA(4), RSW(3), RHA(11), AAS(4) & L(9), from 24 Buccleuch Place, Edinburgh.

**MOORE, Eleanor Allen (Mrs R C Robertson)** **1885-1955**
Born Glenwhirry, Co Antrim, Jly 26; died Edinburgh, Sep 17. Painter of portraits, landscape and genre, often in China. A daughter of the manse, her mother came from St Cyrus, Angus. Moved with her family to Scotland 1888, first to Edinburgh and then to Newmilns, Ayrshire. Began training at Glasgow School of Art 1902, working under Delville(qv) and Artot. Her first exhibit was at the GI 1909. During the war served as a nurse at Craigleith Hospital, Edinburgh. Being unable to afford models many of her early works were self-portraits; her first real success was 'The silk dress', shown at the GI in 1919 and illustrated in the catalogue (reproduced in colour in Burkhauser). This is a painting of outstanding character and charm, a self-effacing self-portrait. In 1922 married Dr Robert Cecil Robertson. On his appointment to a public health position with the Shanghai Municipal Council, she moved to China 1925. Fascinated by the people and towns of the Yangtse Delta, she painted many sketches, some of which were exhibited by the Glasgow dealer Ian McNicol in Kilmarnock 1934. Not influenced by oriental art, capturing the strange scenes around her with fidelity but through western eyes. Evacuated with her husband from Shanghai to Hong Kong during the Sino-Japanese War in 1937. Following the death of her husband in 1942 she returned to Scotland but painted very little more. Exhibited RSA(7), GI(14) & L(1).
**Bibl:** Halsby 275; Ailsa Tanner in Burkhauser 210-213, 229, 233.

**MOORE, Mrs Hilary** **20th Cent**
Glasgow painter. Exhibited GI(2) from Eastwood Ave.

**MOORE, Letitia A** **fl 1890-1893**
Minor flower painter of Uladh Tower, Dalmuir, Dunbartonshire; exhibited GI(3).

**MOORE, Miss M** **fl 1927**
Minor Edinburgh painter. Daughter of Dorothy Winifred M(qv). Exhibited RHA(1) from 24 Buccleuch Place.

**MOORE, Sarah** **fl 1980-1981**
Aberdeen portrait and figure painter; exhibited AAS(2) from 12 Springbank Terr.

**MOORE, Temple L** **fl 1872**
Glasgow amateur watercolourist of shipping. Exhibited GI(1) from Parkhead.

**MOORE, Thomas F** **fl 1937-1938**
Dundee painter. Exhibited RSA(2) from 40 Rankin Street.

**MOORES, Alfred N** **fl 1942**
Helensburgh painter. Exhibited 'Candlemas moon' at the RSA.

**MOORHEAD, Ethel** **fl 1901-1920**
Dundee painter of portraits and figurative studies; moved to London c1916, to Dublin c1918 and Arbroath 1920. Exhibited RSA(8), GI(4), AAS(3) & L(1) from Pitalpin House, Lochee.

**MOORWOOD, Ruth F (Mrs Graham Munro)** **fl 1922-1937**
Edinburgh painter of informal portraits, continental scenes, flower pieces and oriental subjects. Faithful and much travelled observer. Exhibited RSA(5) & GI(2), latterly from 6 Church Lane Sq.

**MORA-SZORC, Maria (Mrs David Donaldson)** **fl 1959-1972**
Painter and sculptress. Moved from Glasgow to Drymen c 1962. Exhibited GI(5).

**MORAN, Frank W** **fl 1984**
Perthshire landscape artist. Exhibited a Welsh scene at the RSA 1984, from Dunkeld.

**MORDAUNT, Miss Elsie E** **fl 1919-1926**
Aberdeen painter and etcher; landscape, topographical, figurative. Exhibited AAS(8) from 39 Albert St.

**MORE, David** **1954-**
Born Dingwall, Sep 16. Illustrator, especially of trees. Schooled in England but without any formal training in art. In addition to producing a poster for the Countryside Commission and several book covers, he illustrated Rushforth: *Trees* (1979), Fitter: *Gem Guide to Trees* (1980), Jennings: *Trees* (1981), *The Country Life Pocket Guide to Trees* (1985), Mitchell: *The Complete Guide to Trees of Britain and Northern Europe* (1985), *The Guide to Trees of Canada and North America* (1987), *Tree* (1988).
**Bibl:** Horne 324; IFA.

**MORE, Jacob FSA** **1740-1793**
Born Edinburgh; died Rome, 1 Oct. Painter in oil, pencil and wash, gouache and watercolour; landscapes. Began his working life as an apprentice goldsmith but very soon turned to art, apprenticing himself with James Norie's firm in 1764. He must have been already accepted by Alexander Runciman(qv) as he became a member of the latter's club and was involved in painting scenery for an Edinburgh theatre production 1769. In 1771 he had begun to exhibit paintings of the Falls of Clyde at the Society of Artists in London, one of which came to the attention of Sir Joshua Reynolds. These early works were among the most innovative and skilful executed in his lifetime. One of the 'Falls of Clyde' is now in the NGS, 'Cora Linn' (1771) is also in

the NGS while 'Stonebyres Linn' (1771-3) is in the Tate. Another painting of note from this period is 'Bonnington Linn' (1771-3), now in the Fitzwilliam Museum, Cambridge. In 1773 he went to Italy, remaining there until his death in 1793. Whilst there he assisted in the decorations and laid-out gardens of the Villa Borghese. In 1787 Goetat was taken by Angelica Kauffmann to More's studio and was greatly impressed. One of a very small number of British artists in the 18th century to achieve a reputation abroad in their lifetime. His 'Self-portrait' 1783 is in the Uffizi. Almost all his Italian output was landscape including many of the famous Roman and Neopolitan sites, especially the Tivoli. He had a strong sense of place, being more interested in this than the historical or purely aesthetic nature of the composition. Loved the open air and nature and when drama could be introduced as from moonlight or erupting volcanoes, these became an intrinsic part of his oeuvre. Two large paintings from his Italian sojourn are among his best works: 'Mount Vesuvius in Eruption : The Last Days of Pompeii' 1780 (now in the NGS) and 'An eruption of Mount Etna' RA 1788. A leading member of the Scots community in Rome, accompanied Ramsay in the latter's search for Horace's Villa 1775. Laid out an English garden for the Villa Borghese which, although extensively altered, can still be seen. Exhibited 11 works at the RA between 1783 and 1789 by which time he was called in London 'More of Rome'. He was paid more for his pictures than Claude and generally thought of as one of the finest landscape painters of his time. Joshua Reynolds thought him 'the best painter of Air since Claude'. Represented by a 'Self-portrait' in Uffizi (Florence); also in Villa Borghese (Rome), NGS, Glasgow AG and Perth AG.
**Bibl:** Bryan; Brydall 158-161; Caw 38-9; Halsby 20-22 et al; Irwin, "Jacob More, Neoclassical Landscape painter", Burlington Mag, CXIV, 1972, 774-9; Irwin 133-138; James Holloway, "Jacob More", NGS (Ex Cat, 1987); Macmillan [GA] 137-140, 142-3.

**MORE-GORDON, Harry** **1928-**
Born England. Painter in oil and watercolour of portraits, also textile designer, teacher and illustrator. Came north to study at Edinburgh College of Art 1949-1953, remaining to become a lecturer in the design department, a position he retained until his retirement in 1988. Has been magazine editor, freelance artist, illustrator and textile designer including fabrics for Liberty's. Married Marianne M-G(qv). His interiors are closely detailed and naturalistic with a strong sense of design, in later career he specialised in portraits and watercolours. Represented in permanent collection of the SAC.

**MORE-GORDON, Mrs Marianne** **fl 1975-**
Born London. Studied in St Albans and Central School of Art. Obtained a diploma in sculpture and ceramics. Until 1976 worked with handicapped children, thereafter turning to full-time designing, producing fabrics and sewn works. Has a strong sense of colour and creates delicately detailed design. Married to Harry M-G(qv). A talented artist, exhibits RSA & SSA.

**MORGAN, -** **Early 19th Cent**
There is a watercolour in the NGS of the 'Tower and Pier of Leith' catalogued as by 'Morgan'.

**MORGAN, Miss Annie W** **fl 1900-1951**
Prolific oil and watercolour painter from Edinburgh; gardens, rustic genre and landscape, especially Iona. Exhibited at the RSA(60), RSW(1), GI(49) & AAS(4), from Woodville, Laverockbank, Trinity, then Drummond Place.

**MORGAN, Birgitte Livingston** **fl 1970**
Edinburgh painter; exhibited at the RSA 'Marie Lloyd revisited' and 'Wherever the book opens'.

**MORGAN, Hugh** **fl 1923-1931**
Aberdeen painter of country scenes and landscape. Married Kathleen M(qv). Exhibited AAS from 58 Midstocket Rd.

**MORGAN, John C B** **fl 1906**
Amateur Glasgow sculptor; exhibited GI(1) from 20 Minerva Street.

**MORGAN, Kathleen I** **fl 1926-1929**
Aberdeen-based painter of figurative works and landscape. Married Hugh M(qv). Exhibited AAS(3).

**MORGAN, Miss Ruby J** **fl 1919-1926**
Aberdeenshire landscape artist, including Grampian scenery. Moved to Buckfastleigh, Devon 1923. Exhibited AAS from Newton, Methlick.

**MORGAN, William** **fl 1898-1900**
Amateur Glasgow sculptor, specialising in portraiture. Exhibited GI(3) from 61 Jane Street.

**MORGAN, William Evan Charles** **1903-c1970**
Painter in watercolour, line engraver and etcher. Trained at the Slade School, obtained Prix de Rome Scholarship 1924 enabling him to undertake further studies in Italy. Came to the Ardtornish Estate in Argyll through the patronage of Mr Owen Hugh Smith who had purchased it in 1929. Several watercolours of local scenes as well as a number of etchings remain in private hands locally. During WW2 he worked for the War Office designing camouflage. From 1928-1936 exhibited RA(11) & L(7), latterly from Craigbhea, Ardtornish, Morvern, Argyll.

**MORHAM, Robert H Jnr** **1839-1912**
Edinburgh architect and occasional painter in watercolour of landscapes and architectural drawings. Sometime Edinburgh City Superintendent of Works; President, Institute of Scottish Architects 1870-1. Designed City Hospital (1896-1903) and the elegant fire station in Lauriston Place (1897-1901) as well as many minor buildings in the city. Represented in City of Edinburgh collection by a watercolour and sepia drawing. Exhibited at the RSA(7) including a wayside sketch in 1869, from 11 Royal Exchange.
**Bibl:** Gifford, see index.

**M0RIES, Fred G** **fl 1905-1954**
Painter in watercolour and charcoal of portraits and figure studies. Lived in Greenock before settling in London c1937. Exhibited RA (2), RSA(5), RBA(1) & GI(26). Represented in Glasgow AG.

**MORISON, Bessie** **fl 1890**
Edinburgh amateur flower painter. Sister of Rosie J(qv). Exhibited a study of wild flowers at the AAS from 108 George St.

**MOR(R)ISON, Miss Christian Graham** **fl 1867-1880**
Stirling painter in oil and watercolour; pastoral scenes, domestic animals, flowers and conversation pieces. Exhibited RSA(16) & GI, latterly from Drummond Place.

**MORISON, Colin** **1732-1810**
Born Deskford, Banffshire; died Rome. Painter in oil of portraits, also sculptor. Studied King's College, Aberdeen from 1748 to 1752 under Thomas Blackwell. A son of the manse, he went to Rome in 1754 helped by his local patron, Lord Findlater. His intention had been to study painting, with this in mind, and with the help of Lumsden, he established himself with Mengs. Unfortunately a gun shot wound damaged his eyesight so that he was forced to turn instead to sculpture. In 1763, finding this insufficiently profitable, he became a dealer in antiquities and paintings. He bequeathed a collection of 300 paintings, mostly by Italian painters, to King's College, Aberdeen, but owing to the French occupation of Italy the paintings were removed from Rome to Paris and never seen again. In 1755 he toured Naples in the company of Robert Adam(qv) and Charles Hope and ten years later accompanied Boswell on his tour of the Roman sites. Boswell said that he had 'such a prodigious quantity of body that it would require at least two souls to animate it'. His only known painting, formerly at Castle Grant, is 'Andromache offering sacrifice to Hector's shade'. Irwin comments that 'the style shows a moderately successful attempt to master early neo-classicism as evolved by Gavin Hamilton(qv), Meng and Vien, with geometrically arranged architecture in the background, reminiscent of Poussin. But the quality of his painting hardly suggests a promising future'. Another recorded work mentioned by Irwin, although now lost, was a copy of a miniature of 'Sir James Grant', based on the Gavin Hamilton portrait in the Seafield collection. No examples of his sculpture have appeared although several pieces were mentioned in a letter addressed by Morison to Sir James Grant in Rome in 1778 (mss Register House, Edinburgh GD 248-227-2). Exhibited a sculpture at the RA 1778.
**Bibl:** J Fleming, Robert Adam and his Circle, 1962, 153-4; Irwin 64,104-52; Basil Skinner, Burlington Mag, XCIX, Jly 1957, 238.

**MORISON, David** **1792-1855**
Perth engraver and lithographer. Member of a well-known local family of printers. A man of great energy and versatility. Although self-taught, his lithographic work was highly regarded. Illustrated many works published by the family business; of one of these, *The Catalogue of the Kinfauns Library,* Sir Walter Scott referred to the great honour done to himself by "the scholarlike and artistic manner in which he has accomplished the interesting task...the execution of the tasteful illuminations are in the first character of ancient art, and remind us of the work of Holbein chastened by a more elegant and refined period of the arts...I have seen no work of the kind more beautifully or more classically designed and executed". Morison designed and master-minded the erection of the building for the Literary and Antiquarian Society of Perth,1824.
**Bibl:** Bushnell; J. Minto 'The Morisons of Perth' in The Library, vol 1, 1900, 254-263.

**MORISON, Duncan M** **fl 1948-1966**
Edinburgh landscape painter, mostly scenes in Sutherland. Exhibited RSA(20) & GI(13).

**MORISON, George** **fl 1843-1848**
Edinburgh portrait painter. Exhibited RSA including several portraits of military men, from Little King St.

**MORISON, J R M** **fl 1905**
Exhibited two architectural studies of buildings at the RSA from 33 Craiglea Drive, Morningside, Edinburgh.

**MORISON, John M** **fl 1877-1912**
Glasgow painter in oil of landscapes, rustic scenes and figure subjects. Moved to Kilmacolm 1882. Exhibited RSA(6) & GI(14) from Copswood, Kilmalcolm.

**MORISON, Margaret Heron** **fl 1936-1939**
Perth painter of pastoral scenes; exhibited RSA(3) & RCA(3) from Newmiln.

**MORISON, Rosie J** **fl 1889-1903**
Edinburgh painter in oil of landscape, domestic genre & flowers. Sister of Bessie M(qv). Exhibited RSA(38), GI(13) & AAS(6) from 108 George St.

**MORISON, William Leslie** **fl 1878**
Dundee watercolourist; exhibited 'The Cricketer' at the RSA.

**MORLEY, Henry** **1868-1937**
Born Nottingham, 29 Dec; died Stirling, 19 Jly. Painter in oil and watercolour of landscapes, figures, animals, also an etcher and pastelier. Trained Nottingham School of Art and Academie Julien in Paris. Married Isabel M(qv). Moved from Nottingham to Stirling 1895, spending the summers in Cambuskenneth at the time of great artistic activity, attending the active animal painting school of Craigmill. Principal works included 'Ploughing in Spring', 'March Morning' and 'Hauling Timber'. A very competent artist who painted confident, strong works, particularly good at cattle and dogs. Member, Glasgow Arts Club. Exhibited at leading British galleries and on the Continent including RSA(48), RSW(4), GI(77), AAS, L(12) & Paris Salon.
**Bibl:** Caw 392; Halsby 275.

**MORLEY, Mrs Isabel** **fl 1902-1916**
Painter in oil and watercolour. Wife of Henry M(qv). Exhibited GI(17), AAS(2) & L(1) from St Ninian's, Stirling.
**Bibl:** Halsby 275.

**MORNAY, Charles de** **1902-1969**
Ayr landscape painter in oils. Exhibited Ayr Art Society over many years but never sought to show elsewhere.

**MORRICE, Alan Fergusson** **fl 1966-1973**
Aberdeen landscape and figurative painter, mostly local views. Exhibited AAS from 19 Mayfield Gdns.

**MORRIS, Andrew** **fl 1834-1838**
Edinburgh painter of informal portraits and genre. Lived in Hanover St and India St. Exhibited RSA(12) such subjects as 'An orphan girl' 1834, 'A peasant girl leaving home to go to service' 1836 and 'Oyster woman' 1837.

**MORRIS, Mrs Annie** **fl 1918**
Edinburgh sculptor. Exhibited a bronze altar cross at the GI from Morningside Rd.

**MORRIS, Gerard A** **fl 1976**
Glasgow part-time painter. Exhibited GI(1).

**MORRIS, James Archibald RSA FRIBA FRSA** **1857-1942**
Born Ayr, 14 Jan; died Ayr, 28 May. Architect and draughtsman. Educated Ayr Academy, he was apprenticed early to L Miller of Glasgow. Went on to train at Glasgow School of Art, Slade School and RA Schools. Travelled widely in Italy, France and Germany but practised in England and Scotland. Member, Art Workers' Guild 1892. Elected ARSA 1916, RSA 1931. Among the churches he designed was St Ninians, Troon. Probably best known for his efforts to save and restore the 'Auld Brig' of Ayr. In 1896 he collaborated with C A Chastel de Boinville in the design for the proposed new Battersea Polytechnic, also submitted a design the same year for St Andrews Church, Ayr, in collaboration with Hunter(qv). Exhibited RA(1), RSA(42) & GI(18).
**Bibl:** Gifford 512.

**MORRIS, James Shepherd RSA FRIAS RIBA** **1931-**
Born St Andrews, Aug 22. Architect and watercolour artist. Hon. Treasurer, RSA 1992-. Studied under Charles Pulsford(qv), Sir William Gillies(qv) & Sax Shaw(qv) at Edinburgh College of Art and at the Univ. of Pennsylvania. Member of many committees, winner RIBA Heritage Year Award 1974. Involved in the design of Strathclyde University, several large hospitals and the Institute of Terrestrial Ecology, Penicuik. Keen sportsman. Exhibits RSA from Edinburgh.

**MORRIS, Margaret (Mrs J D Fergusson)** **1891-1980**
Born London; died Glasgow. Professional dancer and artist. Wife of J D Fergusson(qv). Met her future husband in Paris 1913. Together they built a little house and studio before returning to Britain at the outbreak of war. In London she had a small theatre club which she ran whilst living with her mother and aunt. At weekly concerts Margaret was patronised by Bernard Shaw, the Sitwells, Ezra Pound, Gordon Craig and Wyndham Lewis among others. Soon Charles Rennie Mackintosh and his wife joined the group and Margaret began taking a serious interest in painting herself under the tutelage of Fergusson. Throughout the 1920s Margaret & Fergusson took their pupils and followers to France. Moved from France to live in Glasgow shortly before WW2 1939. In 1940 she established the Celtic Ballet in Glasgow and in 1963 established the J D Fergusson Art Foundation. Published *The Art of J D Fergusson; A Biased Biography* 1974. Not to be confused with Margaret Morris (1891-1980), the English portrait miniaturist.
**Bibl:** R Billcliffe: The Scottish Colourists, 37,41,58; Hardie 167-169; Macmillan [SA] 316,322-5,347,369,373.

**MORRIS, Miss Mary** **fl 1893-1950**
Glasgow landscape painter, often Iona, Mull and elsewhere in the western Highlands. Lived at Pollockshields, exhibiting GI(50), AAS (1) & L(1) from 53 Glencairn Drive. Represented in Glasgow AG.

**MORRIS, Oliver** **fl 1895**
Obscure portrait painter, possibly Scottish. A portrait of 'John Traill, master of "Greyfriars Bobby'' is in the Edinburgh City collection.

**MORRIS, Roger** **1695-1749**
Architect. Although English some of his most important and influential work was done in Scotland. Responsible for introducing the neo-Gothic style to Scotland. His designs for the 3rd Duke of Argyll's new home at Inveraray were prepared in 1745-6. 'A great square block with circular-angle towers and the clear-storeyed central hall which rises above the main roof-line as a battlemented keep. Apart from the crenelated parapets, the only external Gothic features are the pointed windows and hood-moulds' [Dunbar]. Also prepared designs 1744 for remodelling and Gothicising the Duke of Argyll's house at Roseneath, Dunbartonshire, a building subsequently des-

troyed by fire 1802. An interesting structure for which he was responsible is the celebrated Carolinian dovecote at Inveraray 1747-8.
**Bibl:** Colvin 90,92,115,125,129; Dunbar 120; Bruce Walker & W S Gauldie, Architects and Architecture on Tayside, Dundee 1984, 69.

**MORRIS, W V** **fl 1907**
Amateur Edinburgh painter of portrait miniatures; exhibited RSA(1) from 13 George St.

**MORRIS, William** **fl 1875-1876**
Glasgow amateur landscape painter, especially of view on Arran. Exhibited GI(2) from 4 Keir Terrrace.

**MORRISON, A Neil** **fl 1970-1972**
Glasgow painter & sculptor. Exhibited RSA(2) & GI(2), latterly from Helensburgh. An acrylic 'Apple' is in the Edinburgh City collection.

**MORRISON, A W** **fl 1969**
Edinburgh painter; exhibited 'Storm brewing' at the RSA.

**MORRISON, Albert** **1872-?**
Glasgow etcher and University administrator. Trained Glasgow School of Art. In 1904 appointed assistant to the Clerk of Senate at Glasgow University, becoming Registrar 1913-1921, being forced to retire due to ill-health. Between 1929 and 1931 exhibited four works at the GI from 12 Austen Road, Jordanhill.

**MORRISON, Alexander** **fl 1864-1894**
Elgin painter in oil of portraits and figure subjects. Moved to Glasgow c1888. Exhibited RSA(33) including an imposing portrait of 'Alex Cameron of Mainhouse, Lord Provost of Elgin' (1873), also GI(2) & AAS(3) from 147 High St.

**MORRISON, Miss C Graham** **fl 1872-1876**
Stirling painter of genre and flowers. Exhibited GI(4).

**MORRISON, C W M J** **fl 1839-1840**
Dalkeith landscape painter; exhibited RSA(2).

**MORRISON, Charles L** **fl 1921-1923**
Aberdeen painter of landscape, often continental. Exhibited AAS(3) from 78 Fountainhall Rd.

**MORRISON, David** **fl 1820-c1830**
Building designer. Not a trained architect but as Secretary, Perth Literary and Antiquarian Society designed The Monument, Perth (1822; remodelled 1854) as accommodation for the Society and Perth Public Library.
**Bibl:** Bruce Walker & W S Gauldie, Architects and Architecture on Tayside, Dundee 1984, 81(illus),82-3.

**MORRISON, David** **1958-**
Born 5 Oct. Trained Duncan of Jordanstone College of Art, Dundee 1985-1989. Painter in oil, pastel, collage and mixed media, also printer and lithographer. Most influenced by the environmental and political issues of Scotland and of the landscape of the west coast. In 1989 awarded the second Macallan Scottish Art Prize. Exhibits RSA, AAS(2) & Dundee Arts Society from 3 Polmuir Rd, Aberdeen.

**MORRISON, George** **fl 1912-1931**
Aberdeen painter of landscape and topographical works; exhibited AAS from 58 Hardgate.

**MORRISON, Iain Alexander** **fl 1983**
Aberdeen painter; exhibited AAS(3) from 13 Roslin St.

**MORRISON, J C** **fl 1873-1887**
Banff landscape painter in oil, also executed figure studies; exhibited RSA(4) & AAS(4).

**MORRISON, John Lowrie (Jolomo)** **1948-**
Born Maryhill, Glasgow. Painter in watercolours and oils, landscape and religious themes. Studied Glasgow School of Art 1967-1971. Awarded the WO Hutchison prize for outstanding achievement in drawing and in 1973 won a scholarship from the RA Schools. Taught art at Lochgilphead HS 1973-97. Visited France, Holland and Italy but is most attracted to the scenery of Argyll, the latter being the primary source of his localised fame. Very prolific, since 1985 has used the abbreviation 'Jolomo'. Extremely popular, with a family business 'Jolomo Ltd'. Uses strong, vibrant colours without too much attention to detail. Some religious works have been commissioned by the Church of Scotland. Exhibits RGI.
**Bibl:** Rosalind Jones, *John Lowrie Morrison: The Colour of Life* (Scottish Christian Press 2003); Sunday Times, Sept 28, 2003, 1-2.

**MORRISON, J T McD** **fl 1830**
Edinburgh sculptor; exhibited two male portrait busts at the RSA from Pitt St.

**MORRISON, James (or John)** **1778-1853**
Born Dumfriesshire; died 8 Jne. Painter and poet. Portraits and landscape. Educated Dumfries school, went to Edinburgh to study engineering and art under Alexander Nasmyth(qv). Returned to Dumfries to paint portraits and became assistant engineer to Telford; later joining Rennie(qv) and then Lismore. In 1821 he executed a plan for Abbotsford and in 1832 published a volume of poems. Exhibited 'Balloch, the pass from Ayrshire into Galloway' RSA 1832.

**MORRISON, James** **fl 1870**
Edinburgh still life painter; exhibited RSA(1) from Haddington Place.

**MORRISON, James F T RSA RSW LLD** **1932-**
Born Glasgow, 11 Apr. Painter in oil and watercolour of landscapes. Educated Hillhead High School, trained Glasgow School of Art 1950-54. In 1965 lecturer at Dundee College of Art. Won the Torrance Memorial Prize 1958. Founder member of the Glasgow Group. Moved to Catterline, Kincardineshire (Joan Eardley's village) 1959. Artist-in-residence at Hospitalfield, Arbroath 1962-3; member, SSA Council 1964-1967. Settled in Montrose 1965, obtaining a travelling scholarship to visit Greece 1968. Especially fond of the valleys of the South and North Esk, his paintings have moved between realism and abstraction. In his early days he was one of the "Dundee Seven'(qv). 'Morrison's sense of composition is classical...but his inspiration and his sense of atmosphere are local, his method, his low horizon and large sky, his concern for detail and precise naturalisation, is northern' [Neat]. Recently has concentrated on large, usually rectangular, oil paintings, often with wide expanse of sea and sand. Has also painted overseas, visiting Iceland in 1990 & Greenland 1991. Became disenchanted with the artistic establishment and at the same time increasingly individualistic in his artistic development. Elected RSW 1970, ARSA shortly afterwards, RSA c1989. His first exhibition was in Glasgow 1956. This brought immediate recognition for his portrayal of run-down tenement Glasgow. Held regular shows in Britain, Florence and West Germany. Exhibits regularly RSA, GI & AAS 1959-1965, latterly from Craigview House, Usan, Montrose, Angus. Represented in Aberdeen AG, Dundee AG, Glasgow AG, Perth AG, SAC, Ridderkerk (Holland).
**Bibl:** Hardie 198-200; H McLean,'James Morrison', Scottish Art Review, 1, 1959; Macmillan [SA] 392,400; James Morrison & David Walker, 'James Morrison: The Glasgow Paintings', William Hardie Gallery, Glasgow (Ex Cat 1990).

**MORRISON, James Prentice** **fl 1959**
Amateur Glasgow landscape painter. Exhibited a continental scene at the GI from Cowan St.

**MORRISON, John, Snr** **fl 1871**
Glasgow landscape painter in oil. Father of John M(qv). Both father and son rather confusingly exhibited at the RSA for the first time in the same year and both exhibited a painting of Loch Long.

**MORRISON, John, Jnr** **fl 1871-1875**
Glasgow landscape painter in oil. Son of John M(qv). Exhibited RSA(5).

**MORRISON, John A** **fl 1943**
Glasgow painter of figure subjects and informal portraits; exhibited RSA(1) from Ardgowan St.

**MORRISON, Miss K F** **fl 1943**
Aberdeen painter; exhibited 'Autumn gold' at the RSA.

**MORRISON, Kay** **fl 1959**
Aberdeen amateur watercolourist; exhibited a landscape at the AAS from 72 Beaconsfield Place.

**MORRISON, Laura May** **fl 1987**
Edinburgh painter; exhibited a work entitled 'And the pursuit of happiness' at the RSA.

**MORRISON, Marjorie** **fl 1927-1933**
Minor Edinburgh painter of flowers and still life; exhibited RSA(3) from 4 Belford Rd.

**MORRISON, Mary H** **fl 1896**
Aberdeen amateur flower painter; exhibited AAS(1) from 48 Queen's Rd.

**MORRISON, Michael** **fl 1827-1837**
Edinburgh sculptor; mostly executed miniature portrait busts. Exhibited RSA(6).

**MORRISON, W McIvor** **fl 1880-1893**
Possibly of Irish origin. He was living on Rothesay, on the Isle of Bute, 1884 from where he exhibited GI(3).

**MORROCCO, Alberto OBE RSA RSW RP RGI LLD D Univ** **1917-1998**
Born Aberdeen, 14 Dec, died 10 March. Painter in oil, watercolour, gouache and tempera. Brother of Valentino M(qv). Trained Gray's School of Art 1932-1938 under Robert Sivell(qv), James Cowie(qv) and D M Sutherland(qv); also in France, Italy and Switzerland 1939. Won Guthrie Award 1943. Head of the school of painting, Dundee College of Art 1950-83. Travelled extensively in Italy, France and Switzerland. During the war he fell victim to Churchill's insistence that suspected aliens should be rounded up, and since he held dual nationality, Morrocco was confined for 8 months in Edinburgh Castle. During this time he drew realistic pictures of wounds to allow medical orderlies to use them on manouevres. His observations of the human body (studied in the morgue) and anatomy were always significant. Later, when teaching part-time in Aberdeen he was commissioned to provide drawings to illustrate *Anatomy of the Human Body* by Robert Lockhart. Awarded San Vito Prize (Rome) 1959, Hon. LLD (Aberdeen) 1980, appointed OBE 1993. Founder member of the 47 Group of Artists who exhibited annually in the Aberdeen AG 1947-1950. A successful portrait painter as well as landscapes, still-lifes and genre. His work is strong, without recourse to overmuch subtlety. Elected ARSA 1951, RSA 1963. Among his more important commissions are portraits of 'The Queen Mother', 'President of Iceland', 'Lord Cameron' and 'The Earl of Mar & Kellie'. Exhibited regularly RSA & AAS 1959 and 1961, from 28 Springfield, Dundee. Represented in SNGMA, Aberdeen AG, Dundee AG, Glasgow AG, Gracefield Art Centre (Dumfries), Kirkcaldy AG, Paisley AG, Perth AG, Lillie AG (Milngavie), City of Edinburgh collection, Bristol AG, SAC.
**Bibl:** Gage 37; Hardie 183-4; Macmillan [SA] 360,392; Sir Anthony Wheeler, Obituary, RSA Annual Review 1998

**MORROCCO, Elizabeth A G** **fl 1973-**
Jewellery and metalwork designer; watercolour painter of landscape and decorative still life. Trained Duncan of Jordanstone College of Art 1969-1974, specialising in jewellery and silversmithing. Married Nicholas M(qv) 1973. Teaches in Dundee. Exhibits RSA, AAS.

**MORROCCO, Jack B** **1953-**
Painter of portraits, genre, still life and figurative works, mainly in oils but occasionally in acrylics. Younger son of Valentino M(qv) & Rozelle M(qv), brother of Nicholas M(qv). Educated Madras College, St Andrews, trained Duncan of Jordanstone College of Art 1970-5. Worked for five years as a free-lance illustrator when the demand grew so great that he established a marketing and design consultancy in Dundee 1980, which he continued to run with a staff of fifteen until 1996 at which time he began painting full-time. His compositions and associated styles vary to an unusual degree. His still life studies and studio designs are bathed in colour with a slightly angular quality while his figurative work while warm and sensual portray the images more pictorially, more faithfully. Founder member, Dundee Group of Artists. Exhibits RSA(6) 1977-1984, GI(6) & AAS(1) from 275 Hawkhill, Dundee.

**MORROCCO, Leon Francesco ARSA** **1942-**
Born Edinburgh. Painter in oils and other mediums, also muralist. Son of Alberto M(qv), brother of Valentino(qv), father of Leon(qv), Laurie(qv) & **ANNA-LISA**, an illustrator resident in Paris. Educated Harris Academy, Dundee and Dundee College of Art 1958-9 under his father, at the Slade under Sir William Coldstream(qv) 1959-1960 and Edinburgh College of Art 1960-63 under Robert Philipson(qv). Frequent one-man shows. Lecturer in painting, Glasgow School of Art 1965-68 and again 1969-79. Spent year at the Academia di Brera, Milan on an Italian scholarship. Went to Australia 1979 as Head of Fine Art Dept at the Chisholm Institute, Melbourne, moving 1991 to Ballarat Univ. College before returning to London 1992. Awards include Andrew Grant Travelling scholarship 1965, Latimer prize (RSA) 1970. Lives in London. Elected ARSA 1971, RGI 1996. Regular exhibitor RSA & RGI. Represented in SNGMA, Lillie AG (Milngavie), Leeds AG, Australian Govt collection, Queensland Govt collection, City of Edinburgh collection.

**MORROCCO, Nicholas E** **fl 1971-**
Perthshire sculptor, specialises in figurative works, often in cold-cast bronze. Eldest son of Valentino M(qv). Trained Duncan of Jordanstone College of Art 1968-75. Teaches art. Exhibits RSA(7) & GI(1) from Coupar Angus.

**MORROCCO, Mrs Rozelle** **fl 1966-**
Aberdeen portrait painter, also figure and flower studies in oils,. Daughter of Margaret Auld(qv), sister of Eric A(qv). Married Valentino M(qv). Exhibits RSA(10), GI(11) & AAS from 12 Norwood, Newport-on-Tay.

**MORROCCO, Valentino** **fl 1966-**
Fife-based portraitist and landscape painter, usually in watercolours. Trained in architecture, Aberdeen. Brother of Alberto M(qv). Married Rozelle M(qv) whose portrait he exhibited AAS 1966. Father of Jack B(qv) and Nicholas(qv). Lecturer, Duncan of Jordanstone College of Art for many years until retiring 1990.

**MORTIMER, Miss Eleanor M** **fl 1876-1878**
Amateur Edinburgh watercolour painter of flowers; exhibited RSA(2).

**MORTIMER, John (?Jack)** **fl 1933-1952**
Glasgow sculptor. A bronze relief memorial portrait of Very Rev. John White (1952) is in South Leith Parish Church. Exhibited a bronze statuette at the RSA from 56 Croftburn Drive, Kings Park.

**MORTON, Alastair** **1910-1963**
Born Carlisle where his father owned a textile manufacturing firm. In 1926 the family moved to Edinburgh and after a year reading mathematics at Edinburgh University and a shorter spell at Oxford, joined the family business in 1931. Became artistic director to a new textile design company 1932 and from about 1935 began his association with leading British artists, including Ben Nicholson and Barbara Hepworth, involving them in contemporary textile design. During the late 1930s he commissioned them and other Constructivist artists to design fabrics. From 1936 produced his own paintings exhibiting them at group shows from 1937. Represented in SNGMA.
**Bibl:** Hartley 152-3; Jocelyn Morton, Three Generations of a Family Textile Firm, London 1971.

**MORTON, Miss Annie Wilhelmina** **1878-c1940**
Born Edinburgh, 20 Apr. Painter in oil and watercolour of birds, genre and landscape. Trained Edinburgh College of Art and Academie Julien in Paris. Assistant teacher of design at the Edinburgh College of Art. Exhibited regularly RSA(26), RSW(9), GI(6) & L(2).
**Bibl:** Halsby 275.

**MORTON, Cavendish RI ROI** **1911-**
Born Edinburgh, 7 Feb. Painter in oil and watercolour of landscapes, marines, industrial subjects including motor cars, and country houses; also woodcut artist and theatre designer. Lived in Eye, Suffolk for many years. Illustrated Dorothy Hammond Innes' *Occasions* (1972). Vice-President, Norfolk Contemporary Arts Society. Lives on the Isle of Wight. Exhibited RA(4), RSA, RSW, RI, ROI, RBA. Represented in BM, Glasgow AG, Kilmarnock AG, Kirkcaldy AG, Norwich Castle Museum, Wolverhampton AG.

**MORTON, Denness** **fl 1964**
Edinburgh painter; exhibited RSA(2).

**MORTON, J** **fl 1829**
Mysterious artist; exhibited 'View of Mar Lodge & Braemar' at the RSA from an unrecorded address.

**MORTON, John Shirlaw** **fl 1914**
Edinburgh artist; exhibited a gothic interior at the RSA.

**MORTON, James B** **fl 1904**
Minor Edinburgh painter; exhibited RSA(1) from 15 Pitt Street.

**MORTON, K** **fl 1984**
Kirkcaldy painter; exhibited 'Electric tree' at the RSA.

**MORTON, Robert Harold** **fl 1924-1955**
Edinburgh landscape painter in oil; also engraver. Lived in Glasgow, later Stirling. Painted a wide variety of scenery including France, Italy, Spain and the Highlands. Exhibited RSA(40), GI(24) & AAS(2) from 44 Clermiston Rd. Represented in Glasgow AG, Paisley AG.

**MORTON, Robert Scott** **fl 1932-1936**
Minor Edinburgh painter of architectural subjects; exhibited RSA(5).

**MORTON, S C** **fl 1892-1904**
Little known painter from Glasgow; exhibited at the Walker Gallery, Liverpool (3).

**MORTON, Thomas** **fl 1878-1911**
Glasgow landscape painter, usually in watercolours. Exhibited GI (17), latterly from Partick.

**MORTON, Thomas Corsan** **1859-1928**
Born Glasgow; died Kirkcaldy, 24 Dec. Painter in oil, occasionally watercolour and pastel; landscapes. Trained Glasgow School of Art and Slade, also in London under Legros and later in Paris under Boulanger and Lefevre. He and Whitelaw Hamilton where the last two Glasgow Boys to settle in Cockburnspath for the annual painting seasons en plein air. Only two works survive from this period which give any indication of the direction his work was going, 'An Autumn Day, Berwickshire Coast' painted with a downward eye showing sheep in a deciduous woodland with very little skyline and the trees cut off one-third of their height, the ewes fuzzy and the light artificial. 'The Duck Pond' is an altogether more interesting work, recalling David Gauld's Normandy oeuvre in its dappled sunlight on the bark of the trees and the sides of the buildings. Worked with Paterson(qv), Henry(qv) and Walton(qv) studying at W Y McGregor's(qv) Bath Street studio in the early 1880s. 'Scots Artist' was shown at the Grosvenor Gallery Exhibition 1890. In Glasgow University there is a painting dedicated to Morton by Newbery. Conservative by nature, he once wrote to Hornel 'my own heart is with the old 'uns, and modern manifestations don't appeal to me much unless based on the great ones of old'. When not suffering from inferior draughtsmanship, his work is surprising in the revelations of design and handling. Appointed Keeper of the Scottish National Galleries 1908. For the last few years of his life was the first Keeper of Kirkcaldy AG. Exhibited RSA(47), GI(102), RSW(2), RBA(1), AAS (1906-1921) & L(4). Represented in Glasgow AG, Kirkcaldy AG.
**Bibl:** Billcliffe, The Glasgow Boys 107,157,160,197; Caw 386; Halsby 139,151,275; Irwin 374-5; SAC 'The Glasgow Boys' (Ex Cat 1968, 63, W R Hardie).

**MORTON, W G** **fl 1896-1940**
Prolific Glasgow oil painter and watercolourist; informal portraits, pastoral, genre and figurative studies. Exhibited RSA(2), RSW(3), GI(40) & AAS (1921-1933) from Lymnerscroft, Hillpark.

**MORTON, William Scott** **fl 1874-1902**
Edinburgh architect and painter in watercolour of contemporary landscapes, also furniture designer. Lived in Edinburgh until moving to London c1894. Exhibited RA(2) & RSA(9) from Dalry House.

**MOSMAN, James** **?-1573**
Celebrated Edinburgh goldsmith and deacon. The stone front of John Knox House, Edinburgh was built for him. He was executed for supporting Mary, Queen of Scots.

**MOSMAN, William** **c1700-1771**
Born Aberdeen; died Middlefield, nr Aberdeen, Nov. Painter in oil of portraits and occasional landscapes. Active from about 1730, mainly in Aberdeen where he taught drawing at King's and Marischal Colleges under the patronage of Lord Deskford. Spent a short time with Aikman(qv) in London. Painted mainly portraits, only one landscape is known. In 1731 he was working for Patrick Duff of Premnay as his interior decorator, painting history pictures for the staircase and created a map room with maps pasted on the walls for decorative effect. Continued working for Duff when in Rome, producing large works for Culter. In 1732 returned to Rome as an agent with John Urquhart. During the visit the latter became probably the first Scotsman to commission Batoni. During this last part of his stay in Rome 1737/8 he was working under Imperiali beside the young Allan Ramsay(qv), copying Jacobite portraits and painting further studies for Culter House as well as acting as agent for the son of Sir John Clark of Penicuik, also for Patrick Duff himself and for his cousin John Urquhart. His landscape view 'Aberdeen from the south' 1756 is in Aberdeen AG. In 1759 he was known to have been working for the library at Monymusk and teaching drawing again in Aberdeen in the early 1760s having been provided with models of foliage by Delacour. Apart from a fine red chalk copy of Kneller's portrait of Bishop Burnet, now in a private collection in New Zealand, nothing further is known of his work of the 1760s. One of the most competent portrait painters of his time working in Scotland but his style not being in accord with the then fashionable London manner he returned home to Scotland. In 1741 painted a portrait, now in Kinnaird Castle, 'which shows a successful manipulation of a rococco palette of pinks, light blues and cinnamon, but in which the poses are strained and unconvincing, a characteristic of many of his portraits' [Irwin]. The full-length portrait 'Sir Thomas Kennedy of Culzean' (Culzean Castle) is perhaps his finest work, somewhat in the manner of Ramsay and Batoni in its casual elegance. Represented in NGS ('Elizabeth Drummond'), SNPG, Aberdeen AG, City of Edinburgh collection ('Lord Provost James Stuart'), Culzean Castle (NTS), Haddo House (NTS), House of Dun (NTS).
**Bibl:** Holloway 92-9, 110-13, 144-5 et passim; Irwin 44-5(illus).

**MOSS, Mrs Elizabeth Campbell** **fl 1935-1938**
Painter in watercolour of flowers. Trained Glasgow School of Art. Limited her extensive number of exhibited works to Walker's Gallery, Liverpool(79).

**MOSS, Janet Boyd** **fl 1959-1971**
Glasgow sculptress. Exhibited mainly portrait busts at the RSA(3) including one of the neurosurgeon 'Sloan Robertson' 1971, now in Glasgow's Institute of Neurological Sciences; also GI(2).

**MOSS, Thomas** **fl 1913**
Art master. Taught at The School House, Scorton, near Garstang and exhibited Walker Gallery, Liverpool(1).

**MOSSES, W Innes** **fl 1866-1868**
Burntisland landscape painter in oil; exhibited RSA(4).

**MOSSMAN, David** **1825-1901**
Edinburgh painter of landscape and figure subjects, also distinguished miniaturist. This prolific and versatile artist moved first to Newcastle and then c1860 to London where he built up an aristocratic clientele. Exhibited RA(10) 1853-1888 including portraits of HRH the Prince and Princess of Hesse 1868; also RSA (18) 1853-1870 & GI(5), latterly from 4 Brook St, Hanover Square, London.

**MOSSMAN, George** **1823-1863**
Born Edinburgh. Sculptor. Son of William M(qv), younger brother of John M(qv). Went to Glasgow as a child and later studied there under his father. When 21 went to London and joined the RA Schools, having been recommended by the English sculptor William Behnes, whose studio he worked in. J. Foely, in whose studio he also worked, thought highly of the young Mossman, although writing in the *AJ* after the sculptor's death he suggested that Mossman's constitution was insufficiently robust to deal with the 'day and night application'. Returned for a time to Glasgow where he shared a studio with his brother, but died when only 40. Left an unfinished life-size figure of Hope referred to in the *AJ* as 'a noble statue, giving evidence of true genius'. His statue of Alexander Wilson had been executed for Paisley the previous year while shortly before his death he had been

commissioned to execute a monument to John Galt for Greenock Cemetery. Exhibited RA(2) including 'Prince Charles Edward Stuart after Culloden' 1846, RSA(4) & GI(5), from 5 Greenland Place, Brunswick Sq, London.
**Bibl:** AJ, 1864, 12; Gunnis 266; Robin Lee Woodward,'Nineteenth Century Sculpture in Glasgow' in 'Virtue and Vision' NGS (Ex Cat 1991).

**MOSSMAN, Isabella** **fl 1854-1858**
Edinburgh (Corstorphine) painter in oil of portrait miniatures; exhibited RSA(6) including a miniature portrait of 'Capt Thomas Thomson RN' 1854.

**MOSSMAN, John G HRSA** **1817-1890**
Sculptor. Brother of George M(qv), eldest son of William M(qv). Studied under his father in Glasgow where he spent almost all his life. Most of his work was done in Scotland, a large proportion of which remains in Glasgow. After further studies in Edinburgh, went to London working under Baron Marochetti before returning to Glasgow. Elected Hon. RSA 1885. In Glasgow AG can be seen the statues of Peel (1853), Livingstone (1876), Thomas Campbell (1877), Provost Lumsden and Norman Macleod (1881), the bust of William Connal (1856), Alexander Thomson (1877) and 'Rosalind' (1879). In 1854 he completed a monument to Henry Monteith in Glasgow Necropolis and in 1872 cast the bronze figure of the Lady of the Lake for the Loch Katrine fountain in West End Park. Exhibited RA(6) 1868-1879, RSA(17) 1840-1886 & GI(55) from 21 Elmbank Crescent, Glasgow. A statue of Rev Patrick Brewster 1863 is in Paisley Cemetery and the bust of the Duke of Hamilton for the Hamilton Monument is at Cadzow. A bust of Sheriff Henry Bell 1874 and a cameo of Sam Bough are in SNPG.
**Bibl:** Gunnis 266; Robin Lee Woodward,'Nineteenth Century Sculpture in Glasgow, 'Virtue and Vision', NGS (Ex Cat 1991).

**MOSSMAN, Mary S** **fl 1880**
Amateur Glasgow painter. Exhibited GI(1) from 2 Chatham Place.

**MOSSMAN, William** **1793-1851**
Born Glasgow. Sculptor of portrait busts and medallions. Son of the parish schoolmaster of West Linton; father of John M(qv). Trained Trustees Academy and was a pupil of Sir Francis Chantrey. Practised for a time in London but in 1831 returned to his native Glasgow where he remained for the rest of his life. In 1842 he was employed by Blore, the architect, on 'sculpture' for Glasgow Cathedral and in 1848 he made a gothic monument to Lord Cathcart for Paisley Abbey [after Gunnis]. It is said that his bust of Dr Clelland was the first bust done in Glasgow. Exhibited RSA(4) & GI(6). Represented in Paisley AG.
**Bibl:** Brydall 185; Gunnis 266; Roger: The Monuments of Scotland; Robin Lee Woodward,'Nineteenth Century Sculpture in Glasgow', in 'Virtue and Vision', NGS (Ex Cat 1991).

**MOSSMAN, William** **?-1884**
Scottish sculptor. Probably related to the Mossman family of sculptors although this is unclear. Specialised in figurative works and portrait busts. Among his 25 exhibits at the RSA were a bust of Shakespeare(1868), a bust of the metaphysician Professor Alexander Campbell Fraser, Flora Macdonald and, shown posthumously in 1916, a plaster statuette of Robert Burns.

**MOTLEY, David** **fl 1898**
Minor landscape painter; exhibited GI(1) from a Glasgow address.

**MOUAT, Fiona Mary** **fl 1955**
Edinburgh painter of still life; exhibited RSA(1).

**MOULDER, Michael** **fl 1979-1980**
Stirlingshire engraver of topographical works. Exhibited a study of 'Kilmorlich church, Cairndow, Argyllshire' from Killearn; also GI(2).

**MOULDS, Thomas** **fl 1963-1967**
Lanarkshire painter and etcher. Exhibited GI(3) from Hamilton.

**MOULES, George Frederick RSW** **1918-1990**
Born Manchester, 18 Feb. Painter in watercolour, wood engraver and designer. Trained Glasgow School of Art. Married Noel Slaney(qv) whom he met at art school. An early interest in etching and wood engraving, inspired by Lennox Paterson(qv), developed into a love of watercolour painting in which he was influenced by the early English masters especially Cotman and Girtin. Lived in Glasgow where for a time he taught at the art school in the department of interior design. During the war served in North Africa and the Mediterranean. Elected RSW 1949. Exhibited 1936-40 RA(1), RSA(13), GI(50+), also RSW & Walker Gallery, Liverpool. Represented in Glasgow AG.
**Bibl:** Bill Baillie, RSW Obituary, 1991.

**MOULES, Miss Odette** **fl 1968-1970**
Glasgow painter of abstract works. Related to (?daughter of) George M(qv). Exhibited GI(6) from Southpark Terrace.

**MOULTRAY, James Douglas** **fl 1855-1883**
Edinburgh oil painter of landscapes, often in the Highlands, and genre; exhibited RA(2) 1870 and 1872; also RSA(50) & GI11), latterly from 130 George St.

**MOUNCEY, William** **1852-1901**
Born and died Kirkcudbright. Painter in oil and watercolour of landscapes. Largely self-taught. Married E O Hornel's(qv) sister. Initially a tradesman but in 1886 abandoned his work as a house decorator in favour of full-time art, becoming a member of the Town Council. Visited Bedfordshire on a sketching holiday in 1896, was enamoured with the picturesque countryside of the south-east of England and came back resolved to work even harder which he did until his death. From about 1888 his artistic powers as a sympathetic interpreter of nature developed gradually. Used paint thickly and with restrained but telling use of colour, helped initially by Hornel from whom he later becamed estranged. 'His best efforts were clear and luminous in colour, and the sentiment in many of his pictures had much in common with Monticelli, Corot, Hobbema, Linnell, Constable and Maris, whose works he greatly admired...With longer life and health to prosecute his art...he might have produced greater works...He was happy and contented, he quietly worked in his studio, honoured and respected by all his artistic friends' [Harper]. Influential member of the Kircudbright School. Exhibited RSA(37), GI(26), AAS & L(3). Represented in Glasgow AG, Kirkcaldy AG, Paisley AG.
**Bibl:** Caw 405; M M Harper, The Gallovidian Vol 1, 1904.

**MOWAT, Isobel** **fl 1966**
Kincardineshire painter; exhibited a wintry country scene at the AAS from 66 Portlethen.

**MOXON, John** **fl 1854-1880**
Edinburgh painter; figure subjects, rustic scenes and landscapes. Exhibited RSA(10) & RBA(2), after 1870 from 3 Kilgraston Rd.

**MUEGO, Douglas** **fl 1974-1986**
Painter. Exhibited GI(4) from Glasgow and Annan.

**MUILL, Miss Christian** **fl 1887-1900**
Aberdeen painter of flowers and portrait medallions. One of two artistic sisters. Exhibited a medallion 'Miss Lumsden of Midmar' at the AAS.

**MUILL, Miss Lottie** **fl 1896-1900**
One of two Aberdeen sister painters. Exhibited two flower studies at the AAS from the family home 28 Fountainhall Rd.

**MUIR, Miss Anne Davidson RSW** **1875-1951**
Born Hawick. Watercolour painter of flower and head studies. Trained Edinburgh College of Art and Heriot Watt. Settled in Glasgow 1905 becoming recognised for her delicate flower studies, exhibiting with Jessie King(qv), Jessie Algie(qv) and Louise Perman(qv) in London at the Baillie Gallery as well as in Glasgow. Her style was fluent, with the use of broad transparent washes. Also painted heads of old people, similar to those of Henry Wright Kerr(qv). Elected RSW 1915. Exhibited RA(2), RSA(30), RSW(72), GI(79), AAS & L(7). Represented in Glasgow AG, Brodie Castle (NTS), Hill of Tarvit (NTS).
**Bibl:** Halsby 275.

**MUIR, Catherine C** **fl 1973**
Glasgow painter; exhibited a view of the lily pond in Culzean Park at the RSA.

**MUIR, David** **fl 1879-1888**
Watercolour painter of buildings and landscape. In the early 1880s he moved from Edinburgh to 7 New Court, Lincoln's Inn, London. Exhibited RA(1), RSA(5), RSW(4) & RBA(1).

**MUIR, Gavin R** **fl 1881-1883**
Leith painter in watercolour of buildings and rustic scenes including cattle. Exhibited RSA(5) from 49 Cowper Street.

**MUIR, Gordon** **1962-**
Born Glasgow. Painter in oils of abstract works with a strong figurative and rhythmic component. Trained Glasgow School of Art, with a year's student exchange spent in Baltimore, Maryland. His work has developed from a strong interest in modern pop music and painting to a more international awareness, especially the ethnic visual arts of South America and Islam and the Celtic tradition. Associate Member of the Glasgow Group. Exhibited in Germany, USA and Britain. Lives at 23 Carnavon St, Glasgow.

**MUIR, J Stewart** **fl 1904**
Edinburgh painter; exhibited 'After death - transition' at the RSA, from 22 Caledonian Rd.

**MUIR, James** **fl 1876**
Amateur oil painter from Paisley of still-life and flowers; exhibited RSA(2).

**MUIR, James** **fl 1863-1876**
Glasgow painter of rustic scenes; exhibited RSA(1) & GI(3).

**MUIR, Jean Seaton (née Chapman)** **fl 1904-1929**
Painter of flowers and landscapes. Although born in London, trained in Paris and Scotland, eventually settling in Ayrshire from where she exhibited RSA(2). In 1929 exhibited a rustic scene and a flower painting at the AAS when living at 'St Monenna', Troon.

**MUIR, John H** **fl 1942-1954**
Glasgow painter of watercolour landscapes. Exhibited GI(7) from Bernard St.

**MUIR, Mrs John** **fl 1935-1939**
Amateur watercolourist; exhibited RSW(5) from 27 Merchiston Crescent, Edinburgh.

**MUIR, Lilian B** **fl 1948-1950**
Glasgow portrait painter; exhibited RSA(3) & GI(3).

**MUIR, Miss Lily** **fl 1974**
Minor Glasgow flower painter. Exhibited GI(1), from Ormiston Ave.

**MUIR, Maria** **fl 1889**
Glasgow amateur flower painter. Exhibited GI(1) from 18 Monteith Row.

**MUIR, William Temple** **fl 1871-1907**
Ayrshire painter of landscape. Moved to London c1884. Exhibited RA(5), RSA(3), RI(2), ROI(1), RHA(2), GI(2) & L(1), after 1898 from 162 Merton Rd, Wimbledon.

**MUIRHEAD, Andrew** **fl 1855-1871**
Edinburgh landscape painter in oil; exhibited RSA(14).

**MUIRHEAD, Daniel** **fl 1895-1896**
Edinburgh portrait painter. Moved to London 1896. Exhibited a portrait of 'Miss Gordon Mackenzie RA' 1895, from 60 Castle Street, Edinburgh and the following year 'Miss Charlotte', from Blantyre Lodge, Blackheath. Appears not to have exhibited in Scotland.

**MUIRHEAD, David Thomson ARA ARWS** **1867-1930**
Born Edinburgh. Painter in oil, pencil and watercolour of landscapes and portraits. Brother of John M(qv). Trained as an architect before studying at the RSA Schools and Westminster School of Art under Fred Brown. Moved to London 1894, becoming associated with the NEAC. Painted estuaries and landscapes with broad vistas, often in East Anglia, in a competent but pedestrian manner, using quiet colours and subtle harmonies. Belonged essentially to the English School in spirit and style. Member, Society of 25 Artists and New English Art Club. Elected ARWS 1924, ARA 1928. Exhibited RA(10), RSA(37), RSW(1), RWS(47), RHA(39), GI(22), AAS, NEA(274) & L(14). Represented in Glasgow AG, Kirkcaldy AG, Paisley AG, City of Edinburgh collection(2), Brodie Castle (NTS), Manchester AG, Nat Gall of Canada (Ottawa).
**Bibl:** Caw 425; Halsby 275.

**MUIRHEAD, George Jnr** **1861-1938**
Born Perth, 8 May; died Essex (?). Taught by William Proudfoot(qv). Specialised in landscape views around Perth, usually in watercolour; also portraits. Employed as a cast-painter by Malloch's of Perth. By 1937 he had moved to Essex. Father of Katie Campbell M(qv). Exhibited in Perth with the city's Art Association c1883-1937. Represented in Perth AG.

**MUIRHEAD, Mrs Jane Burns** **1850-1920**
Flower painter. Exhibited 'Christmas Roses' with the RSA 1888.

**MUIRHEAD, John Jnr RSW** **1863-1927**
Born Edinburgh; died Houghton, Huntingdonshire, 21 Nov. Painter in oil and watercolour of landscape; also etcher. Studied at the Border Manufacturers' School in Edinburgh 1880. Worked in Belgium, France and Holland painting in a similar, if slightly looser manner to his brother David M(qv). Illustrated Belloc's *River of London.* Principal works include 'Declining Day and Ebbing Tide', 'Houghton Mill', 'Towing Path Bridge' and 'Huntingdon Landscape'. Elected RSW 1893, RBA 1902. Exhibited extensively on the Continent, RA(10), RSA(85), RSW(112), ROI(13), GI(76), AAS & L(11).

**MUIRHEAD, John B** **fl 1880-1895**
Glasgow watercolour painter of landscapes; exhibited RSA(5) & GI(7).

**MUIRHEAD, John R** **fl 1884-1888**
Edinburgh watercolour painter of landscape; exhibited RSA(3).

**MUIRHEAD, Katie Campbell** **fl 1910-1924**
Edinburgh based sculptress. Specialised in portrait busts and portrait medallions. Daughter of George Muirhead Jnr(qv). Shared the Guthrie Award with D M Sutherland(qv). Exhibited RSA(12) including 'Pittendrigh MacGillivray' 1919, and 'Principal Sir Alfred Ewing of Edinburgh University' 1924; also GI(5).

**MUIRHEAD, Ronald A** **fl 1960-1961**
Edinburgh sculptor. Exhibited two works at the RSA including a bust of Moultrie R Kelsall 1961, & GI(2).

**MUIRWOOD, Helen** **fl 1882-1892**
Minor Glasgow flower painter in watercolour. Exhibited GI(3) from Rosslyn Terrace, Kelvinside.

**MULHERN, Robert** **fl 1959-1970**
Glasgow painter and teacher. Figurative works, usually in watercolour, pastel or ink. Shared an exhibition with Rosaleen Orr(qv) in Glasgow 1960. Exhibited RSA(6) & GI(15).

**MULHERN, Mrs Rosaleen (née Orr)** **fl 1956-1970**
Painter of portraits and genre. Married Robert M(qv). Exhibited GI(7).

**MULDER, Nancy** **fl 1981**
Edinburgh printmaker; exhibited AAS(2) from 8 Buccleuch Place.

**MULHOLLAND, Craig** **1969-**
Born Glasgow. Painter in oils. Trained Glasgow School of Art 1987-91. First solo exhibition 1992 in Glasgow. Armour prize for still life (RSA) 1992. Seeks to have his paintings mediate between thoughts and things. "Remarkable technical facility...producing complex images containing many ideas and references always carefully composed and elegantly painted" (Andrew Patrizio).
**Bibl:** "Craig Mulholland. New Paintings and Drawings", ex cat, Duncan Miller Fine Arts 1996.

**MULLAN, Nigel** **1955-**
Edinburgh-based sculptor. Studied sculpture and fine art at Norrie's School of Art, 1979-1982 and Newcastle University 1982-1984. In

1984-1988 was a Fellow-in-sculpture with the Didgewell Art Trust, Welwyn Garden City. Works mainly in stone, sometimes in collaboration with the Edinburgh Sculpture Workshop. Exhibits RSA from 77 Bellevue Road.

**MULLEN, David** **fl 1983-1986**
Falkirk artist. Exhibited GI(3).

**MULLEN, Sam** **fl 1977-1979**
Lockerbie landscape painter; exhibited RSA(1) & GI(2), latterly from Dunoon.

**MUMFORD, Andrew Angus** **fl 1952-1965**
Greenock watercolour painter of landscapes, especially Arran. Exhibited GI(4).

**MUNGALL, Frances** **fl 1948-1951**
Edinburgh painter and sculptor. Landscapes and figurative works. Exhibited RSA(4) from India St.

**MUNGALL, John B** **fl 1936**
Amateur Glasgow painter. Exhibited RSA(2) from 31 Garnethill Street.

**MUNNOCH, John** **c1895-1915**
Edinburgh painter of landscape, portraits and genre. Before the war he was considered a most promising young artist. Served as a private in the 5th Btn., Royal Scots in WWI. Killed in action June 1915. Exhibited RSA(8) & GI(1).

**MUNRO, Alexander** **1825-1871**
Born Inverness, 26 Oct; died Cannes, France, 1 Jan. Sculptor. Probably the most distinguished artist or sculptor to have come from Inverness. Oldest son of an Inverness dyer. While a boy at Inverness Academy he showed a remarkable aptitude for carving. At that time a kind of thick square-headed slate pencil was used with a soft, smooth grain. Munro carved fancy figures such as 'Minerva' and 'Napoleon' on these pencils which were discovered by the headmaster of the Academy. Recognising the boy's ability, the head introduced him to several people of artistic awareness in the area including Sheriff Fraser-Tytler of Aldourie, chairman of the Academy directors. Fraser-Tytler placed his considerable library at the disposal of the boy and together they spent Saturday afternoons walking through the oak woods of Aldourie discussing some of the rare treasures on the book shelves. Another early patron was Hugh Cameron, County Clerk of Ross-shire, who provided a special clay which Munro was able to use for more refined modelling. In 1845 examples were submitted to the RSA and with the help of Harriet, Duchess of Sutherland (wife of the 2nd Duke), he proceeded to London in 1848 to study under Sir Thomas Barry who employed the young man on the sculptured works then being built for the Houses of Parliament . Near his lodgings in Westminster he rented a coach-house, converting it into a studio where he worked on portrait sculpture. In 1849 he exhibited a work of high originality at the Academy which attracted the plaudits of the press. His first important group Paulo and Francesca, cast from the clay, was submitted to the RA in 1851. The group attracted the attention of Gladstone who enquired if the work could be put into marble. This was agreed and the work found a home in the Prime Minister's gallery at Hawarden. In 1853 he was commissioned by the town of Oldham to execute a large bust of Sir Robert Peel who had died three years earlier. Redgrave said that his works were 'of true genius and feeling and graceful and spirited, but sketchy in their execution'. But it was as a sculptor of children that he most excelled. Among the most noteworthy of his 97 exhibits at the RA were 'The Ingram Children' 1853, 'The Gathorne Hardy Children' 1859, 'The Matheson Children' 1861, and 'The Crompton Roberts Children' 1865. 'The Gladstone Children' 1856 was shown at Hawarden and 'The Hardy Children' in Chilham Church, Kent. In 1856 the *ILN* published an engraving of Gladstone and his children remarking that the sculptor drew his inspiration from classic sources, 'embuing his conceptions with a poetry and domestic beauty of his own'. In 1856 he secured the patronage of the Prince Consort who visited the sculptor's studio. At the Academy that year one of his works was a fine bust of Dante. Although the general exhibition of sculpture was described as 'abominable as ever,'...'the sole exception (was) Munro's excellent productions'. At the request of the Prince Consort, Munro was commissioned to make three statues erected in Oxford Museum 'Praxitiles', 'Sir Isaac Newton', and 'James Watt', while busts of 'Hippocrates', 'Galileo' and 'Sir Humphrey Davy' were later added. The full-length statue of 'Mary, Queen of William III', which stands in the entrance hall of the House of Commons is by Munro. Toward the end of his life he developed tuberculosis requiring him to live in Cannes where he died on New Year's day, 1871. The *AJ* wrote 'few artists ever numbered a larger, more various or more deeply attached circle of friends, by whom his memory will always be cherished as among the purest, sweetest and most loveable of men'. His original plaster model of 'The Sweeping Child' is in Birmingham AG. Among his miscellaneous works mention should be made of the well-known fountain in Berkeley Square 1865, and the boy and dolphin fountain by Grosvenor Gate, Hyde Park, of about the same date. Also carved a number of chimney pieces for the Duke of Sutherland at Dunrobin Castle 1849. Napoleon III commissioned him. Exhibited 97 works at the RA between 1849 and 1870. Among these were bronzes of 'J E Millais' 1854, 'Gladstone' 1855, and the marble group of 'Gladstone's children, Agnes and Herbert' 1856. His last two exhibits from the Villa de la Tourelle, Cannes, France were portrait busts of the 'Earl of Dalhousie' and 'W Cosmo Gordon of Fyvie, Aberdeenshire' 1870. In addition to his artistic work he was distinguished for his literary ability as well as his remarkable conversational powers, the latter being appreciated by Thomas Carlyle who wrote in 1869 'I know no more amiable, clear, and gentle-hearted fellow man'. He was a close friend of Ruskin, who was godfather to one of his sons, as well as of Thackeray, Trollope and Joseph Mazzini. Represented in SNPG, Central Criminal Court, Houses of Parliament, Inverness Town Hall, Oxford Museum, Birmingham AG, Bodleian Library (Oxford), Newcastle Literary and Philosophical Society, Gravesend Town Hall, University Museum (Oxford).
**Bibl:** AJ 1871, 79; Brydall 191; Gunnis 267-8; ILN, Jan 28, 1871(obit); Feona Pearson,'Sir John Steell and the idea of a Native School of Sculpture', in 'Virtue and Vision', NGS (Ex Cat 1991); W Simpson, Inverness Artists, Inverness 1925, 4-16.

**MUNRO, Alexander Graham RSW** **1903-1985**
Born Mid Calder, Midlothian. Painter in oil, pastel and watercolour; also teacher. Educated George Heriot school and Edinburgh College of Art, winning a drawing prize and a travelling scholarship. In 1925 won Chalmers-Jarvis bursary and Keith prize, RSA. Studied in Paris under André Lhôte. In early years was an associate of a famous group of etchers including McBey(qv) and Muirhead Bone(qv). Turned to book illustration with Nelson's under the direction of Walter Grieve(qv). After further travels in western Europe he and John Weeks(qv) visited Algiers, Morocco and Tunis, remaining in north Africa for three years. Returned to Edinburgh 1929 and married Ruth Morwood 1932 with whom he later made a home in North Africa above Tetuan. Art master at Loretto and Glenalmond schools. His only one-man exhibition was in Edinburgh 1984. A studio sale took place in Glasgow, 2 Jly 1987. Apart from one or two scenes in Finland and the Highlands, almost all his 49 exhibits at the RSA were of North African and Spanish people and scenery. He did not show at the RSA after 1952, restricting his work to the RSW of which he was elected a member 1956, & GI, first from Corstorphine and after 1960 37 Heriot Row.
**Bibl:** R Scott Irvine, RSW Obituary 1986.

**MUNRO, Alexander R** **fl 1937-1940**
Minor Musselburgh sculptor. Exhibited works in alabaster and plaster at the RSA(4) from 2 Harbour Rd.

**MUNRO, Andrew Oswald** **fl 1904**
Glasgow painter; exhibited GI(1) from 3 Victoria Terrace, Mt Florida.

**MUNRO, Annie W** **fl 1894**
Arbroath artist; exhibited the study of a building in Tenerife at the AAS from Abbey House.

**MUNRO, Arlette** **c1950-**
Born Belgium. Textile designer & screen orintmaker. Attended school in Belgium, trained at Winchester School of Art and Gray's School of Art. Married Ian M(qv). Exhibits AAS from Dingwall.

**MUNRO, Campbell Mrs Henrietta Maria** **fl 1876-1888**
Scottish portrait painter. Lived most of her life at 27 Eaton Place, London. Exhibited RSA(3) and elsewhere in the English provinces.

**MUNRO, D F** **fl 1828-1830**
Landscape painter; exhibited Edinburgh and Perthshire views at the RSA(5).

**MUNRO, D R** **fl 1888**
Minor Glasgow painter who once exhibited at the GI from 5 Westbank Quadrant, Hillhead.

**MUNRO, Daniel** **fl 1846-1873**
Glasgow painter in oil of portraits, landscape and figure subjects; exhibited often at the RSA, a total of 45 works between the above years & GI(50+). Represented in Glasgow AG, Paisley AG.

**MUNRO, David** **fl 1839**
Edinburgh painter of landscape and coastal scenes. Exhibited RSA (1) from Leith Walk.

**MUNRO, David** **fl 1846-1872**
Painter of genre and portraits, probably from Edinburgh. His portrait of 'John Macfie (1783-1852), Provost of Leith during the visit of George IV' in 1822, is in the Edinburgh City collection.

**MUNRO, Donald of Tain** **fl 1841-1865**
Architect & builder. Best remembered for his design of Edderton Parish Church (1841-42), described, a trifle unkindly, by Gifford as 'ambitious but earthbound'. In association with Andrew Maitland(qv) designed the free Church at Resolis (1865).
**Bibl:** Gifford, H & I, 38,410,425, pl.34.

**MUNRO, Duncan** **fl 1984**
Marine artist. Exhibited '*HMS Glasgow*' 1984 and one other at the GI.

**MUNRO, Gordon** **fl 1988-**
Midlothian-based sculptor. Began exhibiting RSA 1988 from 45J Promenade, Musselburgh.

**MUNRO, Hugh RGI** **1873-1928**
Born Glasgow, 23 Dec. Painter in oil and watercolour of landscape, genre and flowers, also sunlit, evocative beach scenes; illustrator. Worked for Charles Mackie preparing woodblocks. First husband of Mabel Victoria MacGeorge(qv). His flower pieces are often effective with vibrant colours and good draughtsmanship without being excessively showy. Augmented his income by working as an art critic for the *Glasgow Herald.* Principal works include 'A Scottish Herd Girl', 'The Renfrewshire Road' and 'Children of the Storm'. Exhibited RSA(5) & GI(60). Represented Glasgow AG, Paisley AG.
**Bibl:** Halsby 275.

**MUNRO, Ian** **1935-**
Born Aberdeen. Painter in oil, watercolour and pastel of landscape, plant life and general illustration. Trained Gray's School of Art, Aberdeen. Joined Aberdeen University Press as a graphic designer. In Newcastle became head of graphics in the University's audio-visual centre. Past President, AAS. After retiring from teaching settled in Dingwall where he works as a full-time artist. Exhibits regularly at RSA, RWS, ROI, RGI & AAS.

**MUNRO, James Burnet** **1925-**
Born Musselburgh. Sculptor. From 1944-1947 he served in the army as a Lieutenant with the 2nd Btn., Royal Scots. Enrolled at Edinburgh College of Art studying sculpture 1947-52. In 1980 he received Associateship of the RSBS and in 1981 elected Council Member, SSA. Participated in the Scottish Sculpture Open in 1981 at Kildrummy Castle, Aberdeenshire and in 1978 shared the RSA Ireland Alloys Award, winning it outright in 1979 and gaining the Benno Schotz Award in 1979, the Ireland Alloys Award again in 1980. Finalist in the Scottish Sculpture Open 1981. Exhibits regularly RSA, GI & SSA.

**MUNRO, Miss Janet** **fl 1872-1873**
Amateur watercolourist from Glasgow of flowers and fruit; exhibited RSA (2) & GI(5).

**MUNRO, John** **fl 1671-d1694**
Painter. Son of an Edinburgh tailor. Apprenticed to Charles Wilson, painter 19 April, 1671. Made Burgess of Edinburgh 13 July, 1681. In 1679 painted a 'peice of landskip' for Mary's Chapel, the same year he was elected a member of the Incorporation of St Mary's. In 1681 he took as an apprentice Robert Hutton and in 1694, John Clerk.
**Bibl:** Apted 67-8.

**MUNRO, John** **fl 1865-1866**
Stirlingshire painter of pastoral scenes in watercolour. Exhibited GI(3) from Lennoxtown.

**MUNRO, Kenny** **1954-**
Born 24 May. Sculptor. Works in bronze, wax, concrete and plaster cast. Trained at Edinburgh College of Art 1972-1976. Helped by a post-graduate scholarship, travelled to Norway, returning to complete his studies in Edinburgh 1966-7. From 1977-9 was an environmental artist with Livingstone Development Corporation, then spent a year of further studies at the Royal College of Art, London. After completing the course, he formed a partnership to establish the 'M & M Fine Art Bronze Foundry', leaving in 1982 in order to undertake solo commissions. Held his first one-man show 1988. Seeks to 'cross the traditional barriers between community education, gallery art, the mysterious role of the artist in society'. Lives at Cross Roads, Ormiston, East Lothian. Exhibited RSA(2) 1989.

**MUNRO, Miss Margaret (Minnie)** **fl 1885-1894**
Glasgow oil painter of landscapes and flowers; exhibited RSA(4), GI(11), AAS(1) & L(3) from 241 W George St.

**MUNRO, Mary** **fl 1970**
Inverness landscape painter; specialised in local scenes. Exhibited AAS(1) from 2 Hill St.

**MUNRO, Peter** **1954-**
Born Easter Ross. Painter in acrylic and oil of wildlife and country scenes and objects. Trained Burslem School of Art 1972-73 and Chelsea School of Art 1973-76. Returned to northern Scotland to work in the family business but visiting Canada in 1982 he discovered the work of Robert Bateman. Inspired by the discovery, he became a full-time artist 1987. His work to date has been exclusively directed to wild life, especially the birds, flowers and mammals of north Britain, often embellished with rustic objects. His favourite medium is acrylic, worked in a naturalistic style with a smooth, rather flat finish. A great love of nature is accurately and sensitively evinced with a delicate use of colour.

**MUNRO, Robert** **1784-c1855**
Born Ferintosh, by Nairn. Painter in oil and watercolour. Copyist and restorer. Had a varied career and although adept with the pencil it was comparatively late in life before he took up painting. As a young man he served in the army, joining the 26th Cameronians 1803 and in 1805-6 took part in the Battle of Corunna. Later served in the Walcheren Expedition and was present at the siege of Flushing. Military service affected his health although he served again in Portugal 1811-12 and was at the Battle of Waterloo. Settled in Aberdeen where he applied himself to painting. By October 1822 he had gathered together a large collection of pictures but his efforts as a dealer met with little success. Befriended by John Phillip(qv), when the latter left Aberdeen for London he presented Munro with his easel and many paints. In May 1850 Munro visited Inverness where among his commissions was a full-length portrait of and for the 'Duke of Gordon', in General's uniform after Sir Thomas Lawrence's portrait. This subsequently hung for many years in northern meeting rooms. Another of his successful copies was Winterhalter's portrait of 'Queen Victoria, Prince Albert and the Royal family'. 'The Prince Consort in Highland Costume' was purchased by Inverness Town Council for the Council Chambers.
**Bibl:** W Simpson, Inverness Artists 1925, 28-31.

**MUNRO, Robert** **fl 1876-1907**
Glasgow painter in oil of landscape, especially Highland river scenes, sometimes with Highland cattle. Possibly brother of Thomas M(qv). Exhibited RSA(18), GI(35), AAS(1) & L(2) from 74 Elvan Terrace, Ibrox.
**Bibl:** Caw 341 (spells his name Monro).

**MUNRO, Robert Henry** **1886-?**
Born Belfast, 27 Nov. Painter in oil and watercolour of figures and architectural subjects. Trained Edinburgh College of Art and RSA

School of Painting. After graduating remained in Edinburgh. Exhibited regularly RSA(5), RSW(3) & GI(2) 1914-1925.

**MUNRO, Thomas** **fl 1879-1904**
Glasgow painter in oil and watercolour of landscape. Probably brother of Robert M(qv). Exhibited RSA(8), including an Arran landscape 1886; also GI(41), AAS(4) & RSW(5) from 1 Bright Place, Paisley Rd, then Elvan Terrace.

**MUNRO, William** **1895-1927**
Died Fraserburgh, Jan 1. Fraserburgh-based painter and art teacher. A fine study of Fraserburgh harbour is in Fraserburgh Academy. Member of the 1922 group who exhibited in Edinburgh where his landscapes of the western Highlands received critical acclaim, one of them 'South Morar' being singled out by the *Scots Observer* as the best on show, preferred to McTaggart et al. His tragically premature death denied him the reputation that his talents would assuredly have earned. Held several solo exhibitions in Fraserburgh.

**MUNRO, William D** **fl 1919-1920**
Edinburgh painter and engraver; landscapes, architectural subjects, also etchings and lithographs. Prolific over a short span, exhibited RSA(12) & GI(2) from 21 Macdonald Road.

**MURDOCH, Ada M** **fl 1904**
Edinburgh miniaturist. Exhibited GI(1).

**MURDOCH, Agnes A** **fl 1887-1889**
Minor Glasgow flower, fruit and still life painter. Exhibited GI(3) from 9 Newton Place.

**MURDOCH, Miss Dorothea Burn** **[see BURN-MURDOCH]**

**MURDOCH, J A** **fl 1881-1885**
Oil painter of landscape of Antigua Villa, Cambuslang. Exhibited RSA(1) & GI(1).

**MURDOCH, John** **fl 1844-1865**
Edinburgh landscape painter in oil; exhibited RSA(8) including a view 'Rannoch Moor' (1865).

**MURDOCH, John S** **fl 1850**
Whilst at the Government school of design, Glasgow exhibited a painting 'The soldier's visit to the tomb of his ancestors' at the RSA.

**MURDOCH, Morag** **fl 1896-1908**
Edinburgh sculptress. Portrait busts, bas relief and narrative works. Exhibited GI(6) latterly from Shandwick Place.

**MURDOCH, Tom C** **fl 1971-1986**
Glasgow-based painter who later moved to Elderslie. Exhibited RSA(3) & GI(7).

**MURDOCH, William Duff** **fl 1899-1923**
Born Dumfries-shire. Painter in oil, occasional pen and ink, also pencil; portraits, figures and landscape. Trained Regent Street Polytechnic School of Art and Slade. From his home in Sanquhar, Dumfriesshire he exhibited a rather gruesome genre painting, 'Sin and Death' (1899) at the RA, and having moved to London in 1900, exhibited two further works, 'War' (1901) and 'Putney Bridge' (1902) from 16 Rigault Road, Fulham. Exhibited also RSA(1) & L(3).

**MURDOCH, W G Burn** **[see BURN-MURDOCH]**

**MURE, James** **fl 1868-1877**
Paisley oil painter of fruit and flowers; exhibited RSA(1) & GI(4).

**MURGATROYD, E Winnifred (Mrs Tom Gentleman)** **fl 1926-1929**
Glasgow born painter. Moved to London shortly after her marriage 1927. Exhibited RSA(1) & GI(3).

**MURISON, Mrs** **fl 1902**
Aberdeen painter of estuarial views; exhibited AAS(1) from 140 Hamilton Place.

**MURPHY, Alexander (Sandy) RSW RGI** **fl 1981-**
Ayrshire painter of landscape, still life and flowers. Elected RSW 2000, RGI 2000. Exhibited GI(9) from Stevenson.

**MURPHY, Miss Annie** **fl 1890**
Painter. Exhibited a Dutch church interior at the GI giving the Royal Botanic Gardens, Edinburgh as her address.

**MURPHY, D F** **fl 1864**
Edinburgh oil painter of genre; exhibited 'The first lesson' at the RSA.

**MURPHY, E Benley (or Bailey)** **fl 1905-1908**
Edinburgh painter. Exhibited RSA(2), latterly from 28 North Bridge.

**MURRAY, A McE** **fl 1923-1926**
Painter of minor consequence. Exhibited GI(2) from 74 Cairns Road, Cumbuslang.

**MURRAY, Mrs Alastair** **fl 1898-1901**
Edinburgh watercolour painter; exhibited RSA(1) & RSW(1) from 21 Grosvenor Street.

**MURRAY, Alexander J** **fl 1893-1910**
Aberdeen landscape watercolourist. Painted mainly local views. Active member, Society of Aberdeen Artists with whom he exhibited regularly between the above years. Two watercolours, 'The Well House, Aberdeen' 1893 and 'The Wallace Tower, Aberdeen' 1893/5, are in Leith Hall (NTS).
**Bibl:** Halsby 275.

**MURRAY, Andrew** **1865-c1932**
Etcher and engraver. Trained Glasgow School of Art and British Museum. Between 1831 and 1832 living at Rumbling Bridge, Kinross from where he exhibited RSA(2) & GI(2).

**MURRAY, Anne M** **fl 1971**
Amateur painter. Exhibited AAS(1) while still a student at Gray's School of Art, Aberdeen.

**MURRAY, Miss Annie B** **fl 1884-1904**
Edinburgh landscape painter; exhibited RSA(5), including a view on Arran (1886), from 17 Cumin Place.

**MURRAY, Archibald** **fl 1912-1956**
Painter of portraits, figure studies and landscape; lived in Glasgow, Dundrennan, Kircudbright and Inveresk. During WW1 served with the 1st Brigade, RFC. Exhibited RSA(2), GI(30) & AAS(4).

**MURRAY, Charles** **1894-1954**
Born Aberdeen, Apr 21; died London, Mar 17. Painter in oil, watercolour and gouache; also etcher and wood engraver; figure subjects, landscapes and still-life. Son of a journeyman woodcarver. Studied 1908-1911 and later taught etching, line and wood engraving Glasgow School of Art 1919-1923. Studied British School, Rome 1923-1925, distinguishing himself by winning the Prix de Rome in engraving, the only Scot, trained outwith the London Schools, to have achieved this honour. An excellent teacher numbering among his pupils Ian Fleming(qv) and Merlyn Evans. In 1922 he left Glasgow in peculiar circumstances settling in the Leeds area. Little of his work from the 30s, when he was living in a caravan with fellow artist Jacob Kramer, is known although some were purchased in the Leeds area of Yorkshire. A painter of uneven quality whose best work was his early etchings and wood engravings. His watercolours, influenced by contemporary stage design and illustration, were not always successful. Many of his figure subjects were of theatrical personalities. His use of extenuated, mannerist form, curved lines and dynamic positions give his prints of the late 1920's great vitality. Travelled widely in Europe, including visits to Russia and Iceland. In 1935 he married and moved to Middlesex where he began to paint landscapes in oil and gouache, also religious subjects. His first solo exhibition was in London 1946. A memorial exhibition was held in Leeds 1955 and a posthumous exhibition in Aberdeen AG 1978. Exhibited RA, RSA(6), GI(7), AAS (2) & L(1). Represented in the SNGMA, Aberdeen AG, Glasgow AG.
**Bibl:** Halsby 275-6; Hartley 153; Macmillan [SA] 359,361; E I

Musgrave, Charles Murray 1894-1954; Studio, Vol CXLIX 747, June 1955, 180-183; Temple Newsam House, Leeds 'Charles Murray Memorial Exhibition', (Ex Cat 1955).

**MURRAY, Charles Oliver RE** **1842-1923**
Born Denholm, Roxburghshire; died Dec 11. Painter and etcher of landscapes, architectural and figure subjects; also illustrator. Educated Minto School, Edinburgh School of Design and RSA Schools winning the Keith Prize. Exhibited in the main London galleries from 1872. Elected RE 1881. Received international awards including a gold medal in 1884, silver medal in Munich 1893, gold medal in Paris 1900. Worked as an engraver and illustrator for English magazines but later devoted himself entirely to etching, working mainly on pictures after famous artists. Elected RPE on its foundation 1881; member of the Art Workers Guild. His etching 'Golf at St Andrews' after W G Stevenson(qv) was published by the Fine Art Society 1892. Illustrated *Spindle Stories* by Ascot Hope 1880; contributed to *Golden Hours* (1869), *Good Words* (1880), & *The English Illustrated Magazine* (1891-2). Exhibited RA(47) 1880-1904 including an etching of 'Mrs Scott Moncrieff' after Sir Henry Raeburn 1880; also RE(153), RSA(7) & L(13). Lived most of his life in South Croydon. Represented in British Museum.
**Bibl:** Houfe.

**MURRAY, Mrs C Croll** **fl 1902**
Edinburgh landscape painter; exhibited two views of St. Andrews at the RSA, from Gayfield House.

**MURRAY, D Gustavus R** **fl 1885-1886**
Edinburgh oil painter of figurative subjects; exhibited RSA(1) & AAS(2) from 12 Woodburn Terrace.

**MURRAY, David** **fl 1733**
Obscure Scottish painter. Described by Waterhouse as 'a sort of Scottish Wootton'. A picture of 'The Caledonian Hunt', signed and dated 1733, is in The Binns, Linlithgow (NTS).

**MURRAY, Sir David RA HRSA PRI RSW** **1849-1933**
Born Glasgow, 29 Jan; died London. Painter in watercolour and oil of landscapes and seascapes; also occasional illustrator. From an Appin family. Trained Glasgow School of Art under Robert Greenlees(qv) and spent 11 years in a mercantile firm before taking up painting. At first he worked in Scotland, but a visit to London 1883 broadened his horizons; then travelled on the Continent, spending time in Italy and in 1886 working in Picardy. Influenced by Greenlees' style, his early work was preoccupied with detail and his watercolours were freshly and delicately drawn with bright colour. As his career developed he increasingly abandoned watercolours for oils and became recognised in England whence he moved in 1886. 'In the Country of Constable', shown at the RA in 1903, was bought by the Chantrey Bequest. 'It was with the hues of things that his heart was engaged' [Armstrong]. He had great skill in the use of blue and depicted the onset of spring wonderfully well. Elected ARSA 1881, HRSA 1919, ARWS 1886, PRI 1917, ARA 1891, RA 1905; knighted 1918. In later years his watercolours suffered from an excessive use of bodycolour and metallic tints. Contributed illustrations to *The English Illustrated Magazine,* 1887. His photo by James Cox is in the SNPG. Exhibited RA(248), RSA(83), RSW(60), RWS(45), RI(68), ROI(39), GI(100+) over a span of 63 years, AAS 1885-1894 & L(77). Represented in Aberdeen AG, Glasgow AG, Paisley AG, Edinburgh City collection, Manchester AG, Williamson AG (Birkenhead), Sydney AG (Australia).
**Bibl:** AJ 1892, 144-148; 1895, 98; Armstrong 75-6; Caw 304-6 et al; Halsby 165-7; Houfe; Macmillan [SA] 253,254-5.

**MURRAY, David Scott** **1866-1935**
Born Dundee; died Scone, 15 Nov. Painter in oil and watercolour. Educated Dundee High School, studied art at South Kensington winning an award. Appointed assistant art master, Dundee HS c1889, art master, Morgan Academy, Dundee and in 1899 art master at Perth Academy. Founder member, East of Scotland Art Teachers' Association. In 1920 published a set of lithographs. He was President of the Perth Art Association and painted many attractive landscapes of the area in watercolour in a 'wet' style with a subtle sense of colour. When at Morgan Academy exhibited RSA (1892) and also quite regularly at Dundee, AAS and Perth. Represented in Paisley AG, Perth AG.
**Bibl:** Halsby 276.

**MURRAY, Dawson RSW** **1944-**
Born Glasgow. Trained Glasgow School of Art and Academy of Fine Arts, Venice. Works mainly in acrylic, watercolour; also etcher. Abstract visions exploring space and the images that surround his studio and garden. Member of the Glasgow Group. Lives and works at 7 Glencart Grove, Kilbarchan, Renfrewshire. Regular exhibitor RSW & RGI(5).

**MURRAY, Diona Vere Magdala** **1909-1975**
Edinburgh sculptress, mainly in bronze. A bronze memorial bust of Rev Dr Charles Warr (1969) is in ther W aisle of the Canongate Church. Exhibited portraits busts at the RSA(5) & GI(2). Represented in SNPG.
**Bibl:** Gifford 150.

**MURRAY, Donald** **1940-**
Born Edinburgh. Watercolourist, calligrapher & teacher. Educated George Heriot's School, trained Edinburgh College of Art 1958-63, winning an Andrew Grant post-graduate travelling scholarship. Illustrations of his work appeared in *Christian Symbols Ancient and Modern, Calligraphic Styles*, and *An Leabhar Mor (The Great Book of Gaelic)*. Elected professional member SSA 1963. Retired as Head of Art, Robert Gordon's College, Aberdeen 2000, to paint full-time. Exhibits RSW, SSA, AAS & Pitlochry Festival Theatre. Represented in collections of Aberdeen Council, Edinburgh City Council and HRH The Princess Royal.

**MURRAY, Ebenezer H** **fl 1863-1886**
A competent and prolific Edinburgh painter in oil of landscape, genre and literary subjects. Spent some time in Musselburgh c1883, before returning to central Edinburgh 1885. Exhibited RSA(43), GI(11) & L(2). Represented in Paisley AG.

**MURRAY, Edward** **fl 1945-1946**
Glasgow engraver. Exhibited three topographical etchings at the GI.

**MURRAY, Lady Evelyn Stuart** **1868-1940**
Embroiderer. Daughter of the 7th Duke of Atholl. Excessively shy, embroidery was her means of escape. After training from a private tutor, she spent several years in Belgium, specialising in the exacting technique of Brussels *point de gaze*. Her whitework panel of the British Royal Arms, remaining at Blair Castle, has been described as one of the finest pieces of Scottish embroidery of the twentieth century. Toward the end of her life she became blind.
**Bibl:** Margaret Swain156-8.

**MURRAY, Frank** **fl 1908-1935**
Edinburgh-based painter of Highland scenery. Exhibited RSA(2), including 'The Ghillie's house' and 'On the moor', & AAS(3) from 16 Hillside Crescent.

**MURRAY, Gail** **fl 1975-1987**
Renfrewshire painter of flowers and still life; exhibited RSA(10) & GI(19) from Bridge of Weir.

**MURRAY, George** **?-1822**
Born Scotland; died Philadelphia, 2 Jly. Engraver. Organised the banknote and engraving firm of Murray, Draper, Fairman & Co, 1810-11; they became the best of the banknote engravers in America of their time. An engraving of Robert Burns is in City of Edinburgh collection.
**Bibl:** Bushnell; Stauffer, American Engravers, vol 1, 186; vol 2, 375.

**MURRAY, George S** **fl 1850-d1899**
Scottish oil painter of figure subjects, portraits and landscape. Moved around a great deal between Edinburgh, Hamilton and Glasgow before settling on Arran 1871. Exhibited RSA(10) & GI(4) including several views on Arran.

**MURRAY, George ARCA** **1875-1933**
Born Blairgowrie. Painter and decorative designer. Specialised in decorative painting and mosaics, also landscapes in Italy and Spain as well as Scotland, and portraits in watercolour and oil. Trained

Edinburgh College of Art and Royal College of Art. Used a vigorous style with many crossing brush strokes to create a pattern of colour which, combined with strong tints, introduced a sense of movement in his landscapes. A title page design was reproduced in *The Studio,* vol 14, 1898, p71. In the 1920s lived at 11 Margaret St, Aberdeen. Exhibited RA(25), always from London, and subsequently, after his return to Scotland, at the RSA(4), GI(3), RI(3), AAS(1) & L(4). Represented in Glasgow AG, Perth AG.
**Bibl:** Halsby 276.

**MURRAY, George** **fl 1941-1954**
Glasgow painter of portraits, still life and flowers. Exhibited RSA & GI(22), from Austen Rd.

**MURRAY, George** **fl 1961-1967**
Aberdeen painter of landscape and fruit. Trained Gray's School of Art, Aberdeen; exhibited AAS(6, including 'Aberarder, Deeside'), from 45 Salisbury Terrace.

**MURRAY, Gordon Cameron RIAS RIBA** **1952-**
Born Airdrie, 26 Jly. Architect. Graduated with first-class hons Strathclyde University 1974; awarded Rowand Anderson medal of the ARIAS 1976 and Dundas and Wilson Award, RSA 1989/1990. After three years working as a part-time architectural assistant in Airdrie his first full-time professional appointment was with Richard Moira and Partners in Edinburgh. In 1977 joined the Cunningham Glass Partnership of Glasgow. In addition to his designs, exhibited at the RSA, was primarily responsible for Grampian House, Aberdeen (1983), Highlander House, Glasgow (1989) and Wellington House, Glasgow (1989); also an interesting private house at Madderty, Crieff (1989).

**MURRAY, Graham** **fl 1929-1983**
Prolific Glasgow painter of landscape, townscapes, still life and flowers. A French influence became steadily more pronounced in his work. Exhibited RSA(28), & GI throughout the above period, from Cambuslang.

**MURRAY, Greta Fraser** **fl 1961-1966**
Aberdeenshire painter. Specialised in local landscape. Exhibited AAS(4) latterly from 3 Rathburn St, Buckie.

**MURRAY, J** **fl 1860**
Edinburgh landscape painter; exhibited RSA(2), from Princes St.

**MURRAY, J Oswald** **fl 1849**
Edinburgh portrait painter in oil; exhibited RSA(6).

**MURRAY, Sir James** **?-1634**
Clerk of Works to King James VI. Designed Parliament House in Edinburgh (1632-40). Probably responsible with **Sir Anthony ALEXANDER** (d 1637, joint Master) for the major overhaul of Holyrood Abbey Church. Probably also involved in remodelling parts of Magdalen Chapel in the Cowgate.
**Bibl:** Gifford 93,119,121,133,163.

**MURRAY, James** **fl 1871-1876**
Oil painter of Philipshaugh, Selkirk; hunting scenes, landscapes, portraits and figure subjects. Member of the Reform Club, London. Exhibited RSA(8).

**MURRAY, Mrs James** **fl 1894-1906**
Aberdeen painter of flowers, especially roses, and townscapes. Exhibited AAS(6) from Glenburnie Park, Rubislaw Den N.

**MURRAY, James G ARE** **fl 1886-d1906**
Aberdeen painter in oil and watercolour of portraits, landscape and interiors; also etcher. Illustrated several of Alex McConnochie's books about the north-east of Scotland. Elected ARE 1895. Exhibited two portraits at the RA (1904) from 5 West Regent Street, Glasgow, and RSA(11) including an interior of the old School of Art, Aberdeen 1886, RSW(1), RE(25), GI(15), AAS & L(3).

**MURRAY, James J/M** **fl 1835-1838**
Edinburgh painter and draughtsman; oil, watercolour, pen & ink, and pencil; landscape & topographical. Exhibited RSA(7) from Union Pl.

**MURRAY, James T RSW** **fl 1892-d1931**
Aberdeen painter in oil and watercolour of landscapes and coastal scenes; generally on the east coast; also occasional narrative subjects. Elected RSW 1927. Exhibited from 1888 RSA(52), RSW(9) & GI(16).
**Bibl:** Caw 463; Halsby 276.

**MURRAY, Joan Gail** **1947-**
Born Scotland, 15 May. Trained Glasgow School of Art, earning her diploma in printed textile. Specialises in coloured drawings of flowers, influenced by the drawings of Alice Coats and the Spanish artist, Joan Porc. Lives in Paisley. 'A geometric delicacy outside the mainstream of contemporary artistic endeavour - and suffering not at all for that'.

**MURRAY, John George** **19th Century**
Scottish engraver. The City of Edinburgh has 3 engravings, one of 'Queen Mary landing at the Port of Leith, 1561' after Allan, and 2 after Alexander Johnston: 'The Introduction of Flora MacDonald to Prince Charles after the Battle of Culloden, 1746' and 'The Meeting of Bonnie Prince Charlie and Flora MacDonald'.

**MURRAY, John Reid** **1886-1906**
Born Helensburgh; died Prestwick. Studied in Glasgow before going to Antwerp Academy with E A Hornel(qv). Exhibited with the Glasgow Boys in Europe. A landscape painter, his work is distinguished by the frequent use of heavy impasto with a fine feel for seasonal colouring, often with extensive foreground and a low horizon. Sadly, although gaining a gold medal in Munich 1897, he died before his full potential was realised. Exhibited RSA(45), RA(1), GI(50), RHA(7) & L(2). At the time of his RA exhibit 1892 was living at 136 Wellington Street, Glasgow. Represented in Glasgow AG(3).
**Bibl:** Caw 407.

**MURRAY, Liz** **fl 1979**
Renfrewshire painter; exhibited RSA(3) from Kilbarchan.

**MURRAY, Lizzie** **fl 1900-1906**
Paisley painter of portraits and figurative subjects of Primrose Bank, High Carriage Hill. Exhibited GI(3).

**MURRAY, Loveday (Mrs J M McPherson)** **fl 1891-1902**
Aberdeen painter in oil and pastel of portraits, occasional flower pieces and landscape. Shared a studio in Aberdeen with her architect brother Alex J Murray(qv). May have been trained in Edinburgh; after her marriage 1900 went to live at the Manse, Birsay, Orkney and ceased to work professionally. Exhibited AAS(12) 1893-1902, mostly portraits, from 3 Huntly St.

**MURRAY, M** **fl 1880**
Amateur Stirling landscape painter. Exhibited GI(1) from 27 Victoria Place.

**MURRAY, M A** **fl 1885**
Perthshire-based landscape painter; exhibited RSA(1) from Dollerie, Crieff.

**MURRAY, Mrs Mary M RWS** **fl c1920-1955**
Painter in watercolour of landscapes. Studied briefly under Walter Severn, otherwise self-taught. Lived at Polmaise Castle, Stirling before moving in the 1930s to 5 Pembroke Street, Glasgow. Elected RWS 1920, SSWA 1938. Exhibited RSA, RSW & GI.

**MURRAY, Patrick** **fl 1862**
Bute topographical and landscape painter. Exhibited GI(1) from Rothesay.

**MURRAY, Peter** **fl 1933-1937**
Aberdeen painter of architectural subjects, especially around Aberdeen. Exhibited AAS(3) from 141 & 146 Blenheim Place.

**MURRAY, Robert** **1888-1967**
Born Edinburgh; died Aberdeen. Painter in oil of landscapes, often in the Highlands, and portraits, also teacher. Principal art master, Robert Gordon's College, Aberdeen for 25 years. Held several one-man

shows in Aberdeen. Exhibited RSA 1942-3 & more frequently at the AAS & SSA; also GI(1).
**Bibl:** Glasgow Herald, 7 Dec, 1967 (obit).

**MURRAY, Paul** **fl 1984-1987**
Greenock painter of still life. Exhibited GI(4).

**MURRAY, Robert D** **fl 1975-1988**
Paisley artist. Liked painting scenes from the lives of fisherfolk; moved to Bridge of Weir, Renfrewshire. Exhibited RSA(11) & GI(29).

**MURRAY, Sarah** **fl 1886-1894**
Aberdeenshire painter of landscapes and portraits. Exhibited AAS(5), latterly from 20 Kintore Place.

**MURRAY, T G B** **fl 1886**
Minor figure; exhibited RSA(1) from 12 Woodburn Terrace, Edinburgh.

**MURRAY, Thomas** **1663-1735**
Born Scotland; died London Jne 1. Portrait painter. Went to London at an early age, studied under John Riley. Had great success as a portraitist; likened by Waterhouse to Closterman. It is said that he was remarkable for his personal beauty and elegance of manner. Owing to his association with John Riley, the painter of William and Mary, he had access to the aristocracy and royalty. His method of painting faces and leaving the accessories to others, detracted from the worth of his work. 'While those painted by himself were frequently delicate and expressive, the others are too often heavy in handling and inferior in style. There is little variation even in his impasto, however, his drawing is careful rather than delicate or expressive; and if his colour is refined in tone, it is negative and monotonous and lacking in modulation. But, although his handling of oil paint is rather dry and sapless, it is simple and refined, and he had a considerable sense of character, which redeems his portraiture from the taint of manufacture, which might otherwise have asserted itself' [Caw]. 'Queen Anne' 1703 and 'William III' 1725 are in the Middle Temple, London, while a life-size portrait of 'John Murray, 1st Duke of Atholl' 1705 is in Blair Castle showing the Duke in a relaxed pose, standing before an archway through which the old Dunkeld House is visible. A 'Self-portrait' is in the Uffizi (1708) in Florence and an engraving in the Museo Florentino, also represented in NPG, Fishmonger's Hall, Royal Society, Royal College of Physicians, Blair Castle, Middle Temple.
**Bibl:** Apted 68; Brockwell 6; Bryan; Brydall 97-8; Caw 15; Anna Maria Crino,'Thomas Murray', in Rivista d'Arte, xi, 1963; Irwin 45; McKay 10; Macmillan [SA] 81; Waterhouse 106; Wingfield.

**MURRAY, Thomas** **fl 1799**
Edinburgh glass engraver. Married in Edinburgh 1799.
**Bibl:** Bushnell.

**MURRAY, Thomas P F** **fl 1968**
Glasgow painter of portraits and genre. Exhibited RSA(3) including 'Self-portrait'.

**MURRAY, William** **fl 1800-1807**
Little known Scottish artist who painted small pictures of dogs, especially hounds. 'A Foxhound Outside a Kennel', inscribed 'W Murray Pinxt 1803' is in the Paul Mellon collection, Upperville, VA, USA.
**Bibl:** Wingfield.

**MURRAY, William** **fl 1830**
Glasgow sculptor; exhibited a male bust at the RSA, from Queen St.

**MURRAY, William** **fl 1884**
Edinburgh watercolour painter; exhibited a study of buildings at the RSA from 1 Rosslyn Crescent.

**MURRAY, William Grant ARCA(Lond)** **1877-1950**
Born Portsoy, Banffshire, Aug 11; died Swansea, Nov 17. Painter in oil of landscape and figure subjects, also coastal scenery off the Aberdeenshire and Moray shores. Trained Edinburgh College of Art and Royal College of Art where he received a diploma 1904. Then went to Paris for further studies at the Academie Julien. Lived in Swansea for many years where he was Principal, School of Arts and Crafts, also Curator of Swansea AG. Exhibited RA(4), RCA(2) & RI(1), though never in Scotland. Represented in Aberdeen AG.
**Bibl:** Halsby 233-4.

**MURRAY, William J B** **fl 1868**
Edinburgh painter of coastal and harbour scenes. Exhibited 'Newhaven from the east' at the RSA, from Trinity.

**MURRAY, William Miller Graham** **1907-?**
Born Langside. Painter in oil and watercolour of landscape, also etcher and wood engraver. Trained Glasgow School of Art, Paris and Istanbul. Exhibited 1928-1940 at the RA(2), RSA(9), RSW(2), GI(14) & L(2) from 5 Stewarton Drive, Cambuslang, Glasgow.

**MURRAY-JARDINE, Katherine** **fl 1911-1927**
Sculptress. Exhibited RA(6), GI(1) & L(3) from London and Moffat, Dumfriesshire.

**MUSGRAVE, Lewis Russell** **c1835-fl 1856**
Edinburgh portrait and topographical painter. Probably son of William Thomas M(qv) and Mary Ann Heaphy(qv). Entered Trustees Academy 1853, having been recommended by Horatio McCulloch(qv), but left after only a year. Between 1851 and 1856, encouraged by the Young family from whom he received a number of commissions, he exhibited 18 works at the RSA, mostly portraits but also 'View of an iron suspension bridge across the Thames' 1856, from 32 Royal Circus.

**MUSGRAVE, Mrs William (née Mary Ann Heaphy)** **fl 1821-1858**
Miniaturist. Wife of the portrait painter, William M(qv); probably mother of Lewis Russell M(qv). Worked in London until c1837, but moved to Edinburgh 1841. Thereafter exhibited in her maiden name. A fine miniaturist who worked in the manner of Sir W J Newton. Enjoyed a brief working visit to the US 1850. Lived at 32 Royal Circus, Edinburgh. Exhibited RA(36) & RSA(104), mostly portrait miniatures of children but also, in 1858, 'The Crimean legacy - a Highland soldier bringing to the widow of his officer the favourites of her slain husband'.

**MUSGRAVE, William Thomas** **fl 1841-1849**
Edinburgh portrait painter, husband of the miniaturist Mrs W M(qv), probably father of Lewis Russell M(qv), whose portrait he exhibited at the RSA in 1846. Exhibited the portrait of a young lady at the RA 1841 and a study of children 1847, also RSA(18).

**MUSGROVE, A J** **fl 1913-1933**
Minor Glasgow painter in watercolours; exhibited RSA(1) & RSW(1).

**MUSGROVE, Alexander Johnston** **1890-1952**
Born Edinburgh. Painter in oil and watercolour. Son of an artist, his father died before he was born. Trained Glasgow School of Art and later under Maurice Greiffenhagen(qv), also under M Artot and Professor E Baltus in Brussels. In Glasgow he had been attracted to etching, working under S F Crawford(qv) and Sir D Y Cameron(qv). After graduating, joined the staff of the Glasgow School of Art exhibiting his first works at the GI, the Walker Gallery in Liverpool and RSA. In 1923 went to Winnipeg where he established the Winnipeg School of Art and the city's first public gallery. The following year he founded the Winnipeg Sketch Club and two years later co-founded, with W J Phillips, the Manitoba Society of Artists. In 1925 opened his own studio teaching as well as painting landscapes. Among his students were Charles Comford, Eric Bergman and Clarence Tillanius. Writing in 1941 Valerie Condé said 'oils are Musgrove's favourite medium, though he also works in watercolour and does occasional etchings and woodcuts. His coloured woodcuts have been exhibited with the printmakers of California. Contemporary life and living are his favourite subjects, though he does considerable landscapes too. His method is to ponder and visualise a subject, until he has a clear mental picture of what he wants to do, as regards colour, drawing, arrangement and major details. He then quickly paints the picture, using large brushes on the canvas, without any preliminary drawing'. 'Manitoba Fishing Post' won first prize at the Canadian National Exhibition 1940 and was later included

in a London exhibition. A greater number of his works were watercolours to which only a few relate to the known oils painted several years later. A retrospective exhibition entitled 'The Forgotten Innovator' took place at Winnipeg AG 1986. Represented in Royal Canadian Academy, Winnipeg AG, Glen Bow Museum (Canada).
**Bibl:** Dictionary of Canadian Artists Vol 4 1974, 1344-46; Nancy E Dillow (Ex Cat) 1986; J Russell Harper, Painting in Canada, 1966, 343-344; W F Perry & L Hobbs, A Brief History of the Winnipeg Sketch Club, 1970; A H Robson, Canadian Landscape Painters, 1932, 186.

**MUSGROVE, William** **fl 1881-1883**
Edinburgh oil painter of landscape; exhibited RSA(2).

**MUSZYNSKI, Leszek** **1923-?**
Born Poland. Settled Aberdeen where he joined the staff of Gray's School of Art c1950. Exhibited Institut Français d'Ecosse, Edinburgh. Represented in SNPG by portrait of Anne Redpath(qv).

**MUTCH, George Kirkton** **1877-?**
Born Strichen, Aberdeenshire, Nov 11. Painter in oil and watercolour, also etcher and teacher. His main compositions were of mountainous landscapes in north Scotland. Trained Gray's School of Art, Aberdeen winning a life painting prize and gold medal for modelling. Taught Hamilton Academy 1907-1919. Exhibited 1906-1932 RSA(8), RSW(1), GI(4), AAS 1902-1921 & L(1), settling eventually in Edinburgh.

**MUTTER, John** **fl 1829**
Lanarkshire landscape painter; exhibited RSA(2) - 'Craigmillar Castle' and 'Fall of Stonebyres, Lanarkshire', from Lanark.

**MUZNI, Paul** **c1975-**
Painter in oil of semi-abstract colourful figurative paintings. Trained Gray's School of Art 1990-95 and at the Slade, under Euan Uglow(qv) until 1998. Following a year teaching life studies at the Slade and then at Gray's, he settled in Edinburgh. Awarded Keith Prize (RSA) 1998. First Prize student award, Paisley 1997. Solo exhibitions at the Rendezvous Gallery (Aberdeen).

**MYDDLETON, James M** **fl 1872**
Painter in watercolour of landscapes. Worked in London. Exhibited RSA(1).

**MYERS, (or MYRES) Miss Jane** **fl 1881-1907**
Kincardine painter in watercolour of landscapes and flowers. Lived at Bervie 1881, moving to Montrose c1885, then to Edinburgh c1898. Exhibited RSA(9), GI(1) & AAS(2).

**MYHILL, Liz** **c1980-**
Scottish landscape painter in oil and watercolour; printmaker. Trained Duncan of Jordanstone College of Art 1998-2002, graduating with 1st class hons in illustrating and printmaking. Devoted to the landscape of the West Highlands and Hebrides. Exhibits AAS.

**MYLES, John** **fl 1858-1873**
Edinburgh painter in oil of landscapes, portraits, figure subjects and domestic animals. Exhibited RSA(15). A portrait of the Albany Herald is in the Lord Lyon's offices, Edinburgh.

**MYLES, Kenneth** **fl 1951-1963**
Sculptor. Portrait busts and figure compositions. Exhibited 9 works at the RSA whilst at Dundee Art College; later moved to Stirling.

**MYLES, Miss Margaret** **fl 1874**
Painter of still life in watercolours and occasional oils. Came from a Forfar family but lived and worked most of her life in Birkenhead. Possibly the daughter of William M(qv).Exhibited RSA(1).

**MYLES, William Scott** **fl 1850-1911**
Forfar painter of landscape, still life usually of freshwater fish, in oil and watercolour.. Worked in Broughty Ferry before moving to Arbroath 1895. Painted scenes around the east coast and Perthshire. Friend of John Waterston Herald(qv). Exhibited RSA(2).
**Bibl:** Halsby 276; Wingfield.

**MYLIUS, Andrew** **1935-**
Born London. Sculptor. Studied agriculture at Edinburgh but transferred to art studies 1959-62, enrolling at Camberwell and the Slade. Spent 1968 in the USA. Designed and collaborated in the manufacture of Gropa racing cars 1968-72. Competent painter before turning to sculpture, then became increasingly involved as a designer, business executive and racing driver. Executed a 35-foot long work by the shore of a man-made loch in Fife. Based at Newport-on-Tay, Fife.

**MYLNE, Alexander** **1613-1643**
Sculptor. Second son of John M(qv), died tragically young, probably of the plague then sweeping through Edinburgh, fourteen years before his father. Married Anna Vegilman 1632. Father of Robert Mylne(qv). Assisted his father in the erection of a sun-dial standing to the north of Queen Mary's Tower at Holyrood for Charles I. Admitted into the Edinburgh Lodge and made a Fellow of his craft in 1635, the same year that he executed a sculpture of the King's Arms for the entrance of Parliament House, Edinburgh (now over the S door). Carved the tympanum with the City arms in the Tron Church. Elected burgess of Edinburgh, 1643. Buried in the Abbey of Holyrood.
**Bibl:** Gifford 121,123,174; David Howarth,'Sculpture in Scotland 1540-1700' in 'Virtue and Vision', NGS (Ex Cat 1991); R S Mylne: The master-masons to the Crown of Scotland, 115, 130-132.

**MYLNE, John of Perth** **c1585-1657**
Master mason. Son of John M(qv), renowned for his work in the erection of the bridge over the Tay at Perth. In 1610 he married, in 1616 departed from Perth in favour of Edinburgh, and in 1621, following the death of his father, assumed an important place in Edinburgh's masonic circles. Became involved in the making of a statue of King James VI for the Netherbow Port for Charles I who had expected to visit the city the following year. Left Edinburgh 1618 and returned to either Perth or Dundee and the next year was involved in building a church at Falkland in association with his elderly father. In 1622 he was advising Aberdeen over the building of a new steeple for their Tolbooth and in 1629-30 he executed alterations and additions to Drummond Castle for the Earl of Perth including most of the gateway. Subsequently returned again to Edinburgh, this time to work for the king. His first task was the building of a large pond beside Holyrood. After the death of William Wallace(qv) he succeeded as Principal Master Mason to the Crown. But held this position for only five years before resigning in favour of his eldest son. In 1633, in collaboration with his sons Alexander and John, he completed the famous sundial in Holyrood with its varied emblems of the House of Stuart. Made a Burgess of Kirkcaldy 1643 and between 1644 and 1651 was actively involved on buildings in Dundee including the church steeple, the Tolbooth and various fortifications.
**Bibl:** Gifford 147,183; David Howarth,'Sculpture and Scotland 1540-1700' in 'Virtue and Vision', NGS (Ex Cat 1991); Robert S. Mylne, The Master Masons to the Crown of Scotland, 1893, 104-130; Bruce Walker & W S Gauldie, Architects and Architecture on Tayside, Dundee 1984, 33-5.

**MYLNE, John, the younger** **1611-1667**
Born Perth. One of the most distinguished members of the notable family of Scottish master-masons and architects. Father of Alexander Mylne(qv). In 1633 was assisting his father in the execution of the sundial at Holyrood. Appointed master-mason for the Crown in 1636 and for the Burgh of Edinburgh c1640. In the latter capacity he designed the Tron Kirk, Edinburgh (begun 1637, the building was altered and truncated in the late 18th century with the original south aisle entirely removed). During the Dutch War of 1665-7 he was responsible for designing a small fortification at Lerwick to guard the Sound of Bressay (largely reconstructed & renamed Fort Charlotte). His work at Leslie House, with William Bruce, constituted a turning point in the history of Scottish architecture. Shortly before his death he provided a number of alternative schemes for the building of the Linlithgow Tolbooth. Unfortunately, the restoration of 1848 makes it impossible to determine the precise nature of Mylne's original building. A fine example of a municipal hospital, intended primarily for the elderly and poor, is Cowane's Hospital, Stirling (1637-49), built to a charming courtyard plan with a prominent lead-roofed steeple. The architect himself carved the portrait statue of the founder.

**Bibl:** Dunbar 54,163,201,205; Gifford 37,84,108n,109,126,172, 180, pls 16,23; David Howarth,'Sculpture and Scotland 1540-1700' in 'Virtue and Vision', NGS (Ex Cat 1991); Mylne, The Master-masons to the Crown of Scotland 1893; Bruce Walker & W S Gauldie, Architects and Architecture on Tayside, Dundee 1984, 33-5.

**MYLNE, John M** **fl 1886-1919**
Glasgow landscape painter; exhibited RSA(3) & GI(30).

**MYLNE, Robert (of Balfarge)** **1633-1710**
Born Edinburgh; died Inveresk, Dec 10. Edinburgh architect and builder. Member of the long line of Scottish master masons, son of John M(qv). First important work was a new Cross of Perth 1668. Worked with Sir William Bruce(qv) in the restructuring of Holyrood House and Thirlestane. Mylne succeeded his uncle as Master-Mason to the Crown 1668. His drawings for the site-plan, first floor plan and elevation of the east range of Holyrood House are now in the British Museum. Largely responsible for remodelling Leslie Castle following the death of his uncle in 1666, work which continued until its completion in 1672. A photograph of an engraving of the remodelled west elevation is in William Adam, *Vitruvius Scoticus* (1810). A statue to Heriot is in George Heriot's School. Other Edinburgh buildings, some now demolished, are listed in Gifford. Further details are among the Rothes papers at Kirkcaldy AG. In about 1670 Mylne was employed by the Duke of Lauderdale to remodel his principal Scottish home, Felstone Castle, under the general direction of William Bruce. His daughter married the architect, James Smith(qv).
**Bibl:** Dunbar 77-8,84,89; Gifford 126,140,142,144,157-8,160,162, 180-1,191,194,203,214,449,472,548,590,604n,pl 48; Robert S. Mylne, The Master-Masons to the Crown of Scotland, 1893, 213-248.

**MYLNE, Robert FRS** **1734-1811**
Born near Edinburgh, Jan 4; died Amwell, Herts, May 5. Architect, draughtsman and master-mason. Son of the Master-mason for the Crown and Surveyor to the City of Edinburgh, he was one of a remarkable line of Scottish master-masons employed by the kings of Scotland since the end of the 15th century. In 1747 was apprenticed for six years to Daniel Wright(qv). Then joined his father as an assistant and worked for a spell as carver at Blair Castle, remodelled for the Duke of Atholl. In 1754 went to Paris where his brother William(qv) was already studying architecture. In 1755 they proceeded to Italy where Robert remained for four years, mainly in Rome. In 1757 executed drawings of Greek temples intending to publish *Antiquities of Sicily.* This, however, was never completed, and he returned to London in July, 1759. In 1758 he was awarded a silver medal for architecture at the Concorso Clementino, St Luke's Academy, the first Briton to receive the honour. The medal is now in the Guildhall Museum. Elected a member of the Academy 1759, also member, Academies of Bologne and Florence. His return to London coincided with a competition to build a bridge at Blackfriars in which he was successful over 70 rivals. This success was not altogether popular in London, where there was hostility against the award going to an unknown Scot, inspiring a poem by Charles Churchill 'The Ghost' (1763). The new bridge was opened in November, 1767 (dem 1868). Throughout his life he combined being an engineer with being an architect. His most important engineering works were connected with the Gloucester and Berkeley Ship Canal and Fen drainage above King's Lynn. In 1767 he was made joint engineer to the New River Company with Henry Milne and the same year was appointed surveyor to St Paul's Cathedral, carrying out extensive structural repairs to the south transepts 1781-1782. Designed a new pulpit, carved by Edward Wyatt and a Frenchman called Mouette. Later the same year he became surveyor to Canterbury Cathedral and in 1775 succeeded William Robinson as clerk of works of Greenwich Hospital, being eventually dismissed 1782 after a disagreement with the surveyor over the rebuilding of the Chapel. Surveyor to the Thames Commissioners from c1788, undertaking many improvements to navigation on the river. Elected a Fellow of the Royal Society in 1767 and was an original member of the Architects' Club 1791. Described by a contemporary as 'a man of austere manners, (and) of violent temper (who) appeared to have a contempt for every art but his own, and for every person but himself'. One of his own workmen said that 'Mr Mylne was a rare jintleman, but as hot as pepper and as proud as Lucifer'.Very sociable, much disposed to conversation. As an architect Calvin ranks him alongside Dance, Wyatt and Holland 'as one of the leading members of the profession at the end of the 18th century, and his work has all the refinement and elegance of the period at its best'. T Cooley, R W Dowthwaite, J Matthews and A Tod were pupils and his son, W C Mylne(qv), succeeded to his practice. Buried in the crypt of St Paul's Cathedral near the remains of Sir Christopher Wren. The rest of his family are buried at Amwell in Herts where he had built a mausoleum in the churchyard. His portrait, drawn by Brompton in Rome in 1757, was engraved in Paris by Vangeliste 1783. A pencil portrait by George Dance (now in the NPG) was published in Daniell's *Collection of Portraits* (1808-1814). Among his bridge works were widening the Old Bridge in Glasgow (1774), building the bridge over the Medway at Tunbridge, Kent (1775, dem 1808), and the bridge over the Test on Salisbury Road at Broadlands, Hants. In general architecture, responsible for many domestic alterations, including refitting the salon, drawing room, dining room and hall at Inverary Castle, Argyllshire (1772-1782) for the Duke of Argyll, building a house for Lord Garlies (Galloway House, Wigtownshire (1763), alterations and additions to Roseneath Castle, Dumbartonshire (1783-1784), the east front of Stationers Hall, Ludgate Hill, London (1800), the splendid Maam steading at Inverary (1790), and Callay House, Kirkcudbrightshire for James Murray of Broughton (1763-5).
**Bibl:** Colvin 399-403; Dunbar 118,166,177,197,218,226,242,246; S Esdaile 'A Forgotten Episode in the History of Robert Mylne', RIBA Jnl, Feb 1944; Gents Mag, lxxxi (i), 1811, 499-500; Gifford 67,140, 163,187,216; Gotch, 'The Missing Years of Robert Mylne' Arch Rev Sept 1951; R S Mylne, The Master-masons to the Crown of Scotland 1893, Chap xiii; J Nichols, Literary Anecdotes, ix 1815, 231-3.

**MYLNE, Robert** **fl 1700-1720**
Edinburgh engraver. Son of a well-known antiquary. Engraved some of the plates for Nisbet's *Heraldry,* also some Scottish antiquities for *Miscellanea quaedam Eruditae Antiquitatis,* Edinburgh 1710. Engraved bookplates for Charles Batchelor, 1710; Rev John Gould; the Rev John Govean, 1700; Meldrum of Halton, 1710; Oliphant of Kinnedder, 1700; John Pollock, 1720; James Udny, 1710; Rev David Walker, 1700.
**Bibl:** Bushnell.

**MYLNE, Robert William FRIBA** **1817-1890**
Born Jne 14; died Great Amwell, Herts, Jly 2. Architect and engineer. Son of William Chadwell M(qv). In 1836 settled in Sunderland. Helped Sir Richard Gibney in the construction of a new pier on the northern side of the mouth of the river Wear. Visited Paris with James Watt 1839. Returned from a European tour with many architectural sketches and spent 1843-53 working with his father in London, mainly in matters related to the river and the city's water supplies. Elected ARIBA 1839, FRIBA 1849, Fellow of the Geological Society 1848, and Geological Society of France in recognition of his advice overt the construction of the Canal du Midi; also Fellow, Edinburgh Society of Antiquaries 1863. Published *Geological Map of London.* Surveyor to the Stationers' Company 1863, designed and rebuilt houses in Ave Maria Lane and Amen Corner (1887). Responsible for drawing attention to the fact that one of the powder stores in Edinburgh Castle had been the chapel of Queen Margaret, the redesigning of which was subsequently entrusted to Hippolyte Blanc(qv).
**Bibl:** Robert S. Mylne, The Master-Masons to the Crown of Scotland, 1893, 290-298.

**MYLNE, Thomas** **?-1763**
Died March 5. Member of the celebrated family of master masons, the eldest grandson of Robert(qv). Active in Edinburgh during the whole of the reign of George II, being for many years Surveyor to the City as well as a Burgess and magistrate. Involved in freemasonry, he was a Grand Treasurer of Scotland 1737-1755. Designed Edinburgh Infirmary (1743-5, now demolished), Inveresk Manor House (1745) and many other houses in and around Edinburgh. 'He was genial and popular amongst his companions, and was highly respected in his day..he was considerate and careful in regard to the proper education of his sons, but did not himself rise to the first rank of the architectural profession' [Mylne].
**Bibl:** Dunbar 111; Robert S. Mylne, The Master-Masons of the Crown of Scotland, 1893, 249-252.

**MYLNE, William** **1662-1728**
Mason. Member of the famous family of masons. In 1710 completed a Mausoleum of the Trotters of Mortonhall in Greyfriars churchyard, begun by Robert M(qv).
**Bibl:** Gifford 158.

**MYLNE, William** **1734-1790**
Born Edinburgh; died Dublin Mar 6. Architect and engineer. Younger son of Thomas(qv) and brother of the more famous Robert(qv). Remained in Edinburgh with his father, becoming a member of the Town Council. Primarily responsible for what became known as the North bridge, the foundation stone of which was laid Oct 21, 1763. Also worked in Glasgow, being involved with his brother Robert(qv) in designing and building the Jamaica Street bridge over the Clyde (1767-72), the work being superintended by John Adam(qv). In 1769 made a burgess of Dumbarton. In later life settled in Dublin becoming Engineer to the Waterworks. His departure from Edinburgh marked the end of several centuries of architectural services to Scotland by one of the country's most celebrated families.
**Bibl:** Gifford 66,285; Robert S. Mylne, The Master-Masons to the Crown of Scotland, 1893, 253-260.

**MYLNE, William Chadwell FRS** **1781-1863**
Born London, April 5/6; died Amwell, Herts, Dec 25. Engineer, surveyor and probably topographical draughtsman. Second son of Robert M(qv). By the time he was sixteen was already helping his father to stake out the lands purchased for the Eau Brink Cut and was soon employed in helping to build the Gloucester and Berkeley ship canal. Appointed assistant engineer to the New River Company 1804. When his father died in 1811, he succeeded to the control of the works, retaining his appointment for 50 years. Also followed his father as Surveyor to Stationers Company in 1811, retaining the position until 1861. Although mainly engaged in the engineering works connected with water-supply and draining, he also practised as an architect and designed several country houses and was in demand as a surveyor and valuer. In 1815 he supervised the repair of Caversham Bridge, nr Reading, for Lord Cadogan, and Garret Hostel Bridge over the River Cam at Cambridge (illustrated in Hann & Hosking, *Bridges* (1843)). Elected FRS 1826, member, Institute of British Architects at its foundation 1834. Treasurer of the Smithonian Society of Civil Engineers for over 50 years and in 1842 became a member of the Institute of Civil Engineers. His son, R W M(qv), was the last of the 12 generations of the family to practise architecture, a quite remarkable tradition. Probably exhibited two works at the RA, 'A Temple at Tivoli' 1797, "made out and restored from actual measurements" and 'A View in Hertfordshire' 1802.
**Bibl:** Builder xii, 1864, 7; Calvin 403; Country Life, Jan 28, 1939; Mylne: The Master-masons to the Crown of Scotland, 1893, chap xiv; Bruce Walker & W S Gauldie, Architects and Architecture on Tayside, Dundee 1984, 33-5

# N

**NAGAHIRO, Keijo** **fl 1976-1989**
Painter who settled in Aberdeenshire. Exhibited stylised nature subjects, especially trees, at the AAS(5) from the Old Manse of Bourtrie, Oldmeldrum.

**NAGL, Hazel Anna RSW RGI** **1953-**
Born Glasgow. Painter in watercolour and mixed media. Landscapes, garden scenes and seascapes. Won the RGI's Alexander Stone prize 1987 and 1990. Member of Glasgow Group and Glasgow Art Club. Elected RSW 1988, RGI 2000. Has exhibited at the RSA since 1985 and regularly at the RSW & RGI. Lives at 4 Lawnmarnoch House, Troon Dr, Bridge of Weir, Renfrewshire.

**NAIRN, Andrew** **fl 1924-1940**
Glasgow based artist of landscape, topography and flower studies. Exhibited RSA(4) & GI(10).

**NAIRN, Frederick C** **fl 1884-1905**
Glasgow based artist of landscape, especially Deeside. Exhibited GI(7) including 'The Dee nr Ballater' 1903.

**NAIRN, James McLachlan** **1859-1904**
Born Lenzie, nr Glasgow; died Wellington, NZ, 22 Feb. Landscape, figurative and portrait painter in oils, watercolours and pastel. Had Nairn remained in Europe he would have had an international rather than a national reputation. Worked for five years in a Glasgow architect's office before deciding to pursue art as a full-time career. Trained Glasgow School of Art and Academie Julien in Paris. Follower of the Glasgow school, influenced by W Y McGregor(qv), James Paterson(qv), George Henry(qv) and Edward Walton(qv). Arrived in New Zealand on the *Forfarshire,* landing at Dunedin on 2nd January 1890, having migrated for health reasons. Moved to Mataura, then back to Dunedin, finally settled in Wellington 1891. Vice-President, Council of New Zealand Academy of Fine Arts. Appointed instructor of a new Life Class at Wellington Technical School 1891 where he was described as "helpful, even-tempered and popular". Earned reputation as an excellent teacher. Organised the first annual exhibition of the Wellington Art Club 1893, a newspaper critic accusing Nairn and his followers of "chromatic lunacy". His 'Tess' (1893), now in the National Art Gallery, Wellington, shows the marked influence of the Glasgow boys. A believer in *plein air.* At the time of his death was regarded as "pre-eminently the foremost artist in New Zealand". In association with a group of artists including Nugent, Welch, Fred Sedgwick and Mabel Hill, he established the first Wellington Art Club in protest of the fact that the New Zealand Academy of Fine Arts had no artists on its committee. As well as landscapes and seascapes Nairn painted occasional portraits, three of which hang in the Supreme Court of Wellington. He was happy, carefree and generous, living life to the full, unconventional, quite without pretence and commercially disinterested. He once said "always spend your last shilling as though you had 50 more behind it". Exhibited RSA (5) 1879-1885, also GI. Represented by 28 works in National AG of New Zealand, also Auckland AG, 'Kildonan' 1866 is in Glasgow AG.
**Bibl:** Brown and Keith, 10,13,49,52,56-58,60,68,74-76,77,79-86, 104,119; Caw 384; N Harrison, 'The School that Reilly built' , Wellington Technical College, New Zealand 1961; J Magurk, 'James Nairn and his Pumpkin Cottage', The Evening Post, Wellington, New Zealand 8th October 1946; C McCahon, James Nairn and Edward Firstrom, Auckland City Art Gallery 1954; A H O'Keeffe, 'Art in Retrospect - Earlier Dunedin Days - Paint and Personality', Art in New Zealand, 47, March 1940; M E R Tripe, James McLachlan Nairn, Some postal reminiscences in Art in New Zealand, 2nd December 1928; C Wilson, 'James McLachlan Nairn in Art in Australia', The Freelance in the NCE, Wellington, New Zealand, 27.2.1904.

**NAIRN, James T** **fl 1812-?**
Portrait painter. Associated with the Scottish Academy at its birth, exhibited a portrait of 'Dr Adam Ferguson' 1812. A large oil portrait of the agriculturalist 'George Dempster of Dunniston' (1732-1818) is in the SNPG. Possibly the **J T NAIRNE** who exhibited A group of fruit and 'Pomona's offering' at the RSA 1853-4 from Kirkcaldy.
**Bibl:** Brydall 243.

**NAIRN, Margaret (née White)** **1903-1990**
Died May 18. Painter in oils and watercolour. Landscapes and figurative works. Trained Glasgow School of Art where she first met her lifelong friend and fellow student Mary Armour(qv). Married Bryce Nairn, a Glasgow vet who later joined the Foreign Service. Painted a great deal in Morocco, often with Winston Churchill, also in France, Spain and Madeira. Studied for a time in the States with Oscar Kokoschka.
**Bibl:** Burkhauser 15,233.

**NAISMITH, Eileen** **fl 1980-**
Milngavie-based painter of still life, pastoral and topographical works. Exhibited RSA(2) & GI(21).

**NAISMITH, Margery H** **fl 1933-1939**
Glasgow amateur watercolour painter; exhibited RSW(2), RSA(1) & GI(4) from 12 Albert Gate.

**NAKESKA, Eleanora** **fl 1900-1902**
Edinburgh landscape painter. Exhibited scenery in northern France and Scotland at the RSA(5) from 11 Dundas Street.

**NAPIER, Caroline Margaret** **fl 1899**
Edinburgh painter. Exhibited 'Old snuff mill, Juniper Green' at the RSA(1) from 5 Morningside Drive.

**NAPIER, Charles Goddard RSW** **1899-1978**
Born Edinburgh, 1 Aug. Painter of landscape and architectural studies mostly in watercolour, also pottery painter. Educated George Watson's School and Edinburgh College of Art. First one man show at Brook Street AG 1934. Lived for some years in Oxford before returning to Edinburgh. Had a clear almost primitive style with close attention to detail. Elected RSW 1914. Exhibited regularly RSA(62), RSW(59), GI(100+), AAS(2), RBA(4) & L(11), from 35 Mardale Crescent. Represented in City of Edinburgh collection.
**Bibl:** Halsby 222,276.

**NAPIER, E G** **fl 1792**
Engraver, thought to be Scottish. Engraved a bookplate for the Rev Edward Napier 1792.
**Bibl:** Bushnell.

**NAPIER, George Alexander** **1823-1869**
Born Montrose, 26 May; died Tradeston, Glasgow 30 Apr. Marine painter in oil; also worked for a time as a railway superintendent. Married Margaret Fotheringham at Fettercairn, 1853. His painting of the *'Shenandoah'* was included in the Helensburgh exhibition 'Painters of the Clyde'. A number of his works appeared on the market 1972-88 mostly barques, clippers, sailing ships and whalers. Exhibited RSA(2) & GI(9).

**NAPIER, Gertrude Primrose** **fl 1900-1902**
Cathcart landscape painter; exhibited AAS(3) from 37 Queens Crescent, Cathcart.

**NAPIER, James** **fl 1872**
Edinburgh painter of still life. Exhibited GI(1) from Sylvan Place.

**NAPIER, James** **1859-1905**
Painter. Nephew of John James N(qv). Exhibited GI(7) from Carment Drive, Strathbungo, then Glasgow.

**NAPIER, James Brand** **fl 1861-1885**
Painter in oil, watercolour of landscapes, still life, flowers and portraits; also teacher. Father of James Harold N(qv). Exhibited RSA(30).

**NAPIER, James Harold** **fl 1912-1926**
Born Edinburgh. Painter in oil and watercolour, writer and art critic. Son of James Brand N. Studied Edinburgh University. Settled in London c1912. Exhibited RI(6) & London Salon(3).

**NAPIER, James MacVicar** **1839-1904**
Landscape painter in oil who in 1885 was living at Dungarvan, Gourock and in 1890 at Birdston, Kirkintilloch. Exhibited 2 works at the RA in 1889 and 1890 including a fine study of Machrihanish Bay; also RSA(4), GI(14) & L(2).

**NAPIER, John** **fl 1885-1898**
Painter of Edinburgh and Greenock mostly watercolours of landscapes and interiors. Exhibited RSA(6) & RSW(1).

**NAPIER, John James** **1831-1877**
Born Glasgow, 29 Jly; died London, 20 Mar. Painter in oil of portraits and figure studies. Educated Glasgow HS and Andersonian University. Member of the Greenock shipbuilding family (co-founders of the Cunard line). Uncle of James N(qv). Showed an early ability in art and regarded at University as excelling his teachers. In 1847, when only 16, exhibited landscapes and portraits in both Glasgow and Edinburgh. In 1852 moved to London and exhibited his first portrait, 'The Principal of Haileybury College' 1856, from 8 Park Terrace, Westbourne Street. Continued to exhibit at the RA until 1876, a total of 32 works, also RSA(51) & GI(36). Better known portraits include 'Sir Samuel Cunard' 1859, 'Admiral Sir Charles Napier', the African missionary 'The Rev Dr Robert Moffat' 1873, 'J C Schetky' 1874 - when marine painter to the Queen - and 'David Roberts RA' 1861. 'George Duncan MP' is in Dundee AG.

**NAPIER, of Magdala, Lady Mary Cecilia** **fl 1889-1906**
Landscape painter. Daughter of Maj-Gen Edward Scott and 2nd wife of General Lord Napier whom she married 1861. (Lord Napier was unrelated to the famous family of that name having been a Fletcher and changing his name to Napier by deed poll). Exhibited RA(3) - 'The Falls of the Luing, Ross-shire' 1889, 'Our last hole' 1896 and 'Summer on Loch Linnhe' 1898; also ROI(4), from 9 Lowndes Sq, London.

**NAPIER, N S** **fl 1892**
Dumbarton flower painter. Exhibited GI(1) from Omaha, Helensburgh.

**NAPIER, Robert Twentyman** **1850-1921**
Glasgow landscape painter in oil. Elder brother of John McVicar N(qv). Exhibited RSA(2), GI(10) & L(1).

**NAPIER, Robert West FRSA FSA(Scot)** **1871-1939**
Born Edinburgh, Nov; died Edinburgh, 13 Mar. Artist, restorer and author. Painted in oil and watercolour, landscape and figures. An exhibition of his work in the 1930s in Edinburgh illustrated an idiosyncratic style with studies of nature and cartoons with a socio-political flavour. Secretary, Fine Art Guild (Scotland). Published *Essays on Art* and *John Thomson of Duddingston, Landscape painter.* Killed by falling out of a window.

**NAPIER, Gen Sir William** **1785-1860**
Skilled amateur painter and sculptor. Brother of Sir Charles N and grandson of the 6th Lord Napier, historian of the Peninsular War. Honorary exhibitor at the RA. In 1821 exhibited a sculpture 'Juan and Haidee' (from a Byron quotation) and in 1858 a bronze statuette: 'The Death of Alcibiades'.

**NARDINI, Peter Anthony** **1947-**
Born Glasgow, 16 Aug. Painter, musician, playwright and poet. Educated Glasgow School of Art where he won the Cargill Award. Inspired by literature, his work is invested with a dream-like quality, partly due to the subjects he selects and partly to his controlled and subtle use of design and colour. Nardini lives in the land of make-believe and symbolic imagery, enhanced by a remarkable feel for texture and the place of the human figure in the grand design. Lives in Hamilton, exhibits RSA & GI.

**NASMYTH, Alexander** **1758-1840**
Born Edinburgh, 9 Sep; died Edinburgh, 10 Apr. Painter in oil of portraits and landscapes. Son of a master builder involved in the building of George Square in Edinburgh. After attending Royal High School apprenticed to a Mr Crichton, coach painter. Then entered the Trustees Academy studying under Alexander Runciman(qv). In 1774, when he was still only sixteen, his work came to the attention of Allan Ramsay(qv) who took the young Nasmyth to London as his assistant. Ramsay was a great collector of Old Masters and it was here that the young Nasmyth became acquainted with the landscapes of Claude, Cuyp and Ruisdael. In 1778 he returned to Edinburgh where he began to paint full-length portraits and family groups. One of his patrons was Patrick Miller of Dalswinton who financed a visit to Italy 1782. In 1783 James Byres reported that Nasmyth had decided to take up landscape painting and was already involved in copying Claude Lorrain. In 1785 returned to Edinburgh and resumed portrait painting. About this time he became friendly with Robert Burns whose portrait he painted in 1787. There is no doubt that the poet and the artist each influenced the other in their interpretation and love of nature and general attitude to life. In the early 1790s he established a drawing school. Among his early pupils was Andrew Robertson of Aberdeen(qv) who referred to Nasmyth as 'the first landscape painter in Edinburgh or even in Britain'. He was now painting Scottish landscapes, especially in the Clyde area and Perthshire, somewhat in the classical manner of Claude. Historically, his work is a bridgehead between the classicism of Claude and the early stirrings of 19th century romanticism. In addition to his work as an artist he was a man of many other accomplishments: a mechanical genius, who in 1806 designed a bridge for Lord Breadalbane for the grounds of Taymouth; bridges and a castellated lighthouse with Gothic windows for the Duke of Argyll; an architect who designed St Bernard's Well (1788), a classical temple based on Tivoli, erected for Law Lord Gardenstone on the Water of Leith; also his own house in Edinburgh; designed the earlier version of the Dean Bridge; invented the bow and string bridge and was involved with Miller and Symington in the development of steam navigation. From about 1810 'the open vista gives way to more enclosed scenes, often with rocks flanking a river which flows smoothly or cascades in shallow falls in the manner of von Ruisdael'. For the Earl of Cassilis he executed two views of Culzean Castle, both exhibited at the RA in 1816. His paintings of Edinburgh are of two types, the panoramic view made popular by various engravers, especially Robert Barker(qv), and more circumscribed views of the city's architecture. In 1821 sixteen engravings of vignettes of Scottish landscapes, each associated with a Waverley novel were engraved by W H Lizars(qv) and published by Constable. In the 1820s exhibited a number of continental views in Edinburgh although there is no reason to suppose that he revisited mainland Europe. As he grew older he fell into a more automatic mode of painting; when, for example, commissioned to paint Castle Grant, instead of visiting himself he sent his son James to make a sketch from which he then completed the finished work. Opinion has always been sharply divided as to the artistic merit of his art. Undoubtedly his middle period (1800-1820) saw the apotheosis of his genius. According to Armstrong, the weakness of his landscapes 'lies in the want of sympathy with colour and an almost total absence of the faculty for composition', whilst McKay thought that 'at no time had Nasmyth much of the painter's delight in, or mastery over, his material; in this respect his pictures remain cold and timid to the end'. 'His composition was frequently well ordered on classic lines, his tone was harmonious and pleasant though mannered and his drawing was careful, precise, and not wanting in character, but in detail his touch was apt to be formal, and in foliage and such like even tea-trayey; and while his colour possesses considerable refinement and unity it has, possibly from his practise of underpainting with burnt sienna, little variety, and is, whether the motif be Spring or Autumn, low, brown and monotonous in tint' [Caw]. His portrait painting, although wanting in both power and grace, was of considerable accomplishment, had it not been for the fact that his outspokenness combined with the fact that his politics varied from that of most of his clients, he might have gone on to achieve equal stature to that of his teacher Ramsay. Five daughters were artists as were his eldest and youngest sons. Elected hon. RSA 1832. Illustrated Scott's *The Border Antiquities of England and Scotland* (1917). Exhibited RA(9) 1813-1826 & RSA & its predecessors(122). Represented in NG, NGS, SNPG (including his 4 portraits of Robert Burns), Aberdeen AG, Glasgow AG, Edinburgh City collection, Brodick Castle (NTS), Culzean Castle (NTS), Drum Castle (NTS), Fyvie Castle (NTS), House of Dun (NTS), Bristol AG, Nottingham AG, Mellon Coll (Connecticut).
**Bibl:** Armstrong 16-17; Caw 47-8, 139-40; Janet Cooksey, Alexander Nasmyth, London 1991; Crawford Art Centre, St Andrews, 'Alexander Nasmyth', (Ex Cat 1979); Houfe; Irwin 72-3, 138-145 et passim; P Johnson & E.Money, The Nasmyth Family of

Painters, 1977; McKay 175-7; Macmillan [GA] 140-151, 159-60 et passim; [SA] 136-145; Alexander Nasmyth, Sixteen Engravings from Real Scenes, supposed to be described in the Novels and Tales of the 'Author of Waverley' Engr by W H Lizars, Edinburgh, 1821; James Nasmyth, An Autobiography, 1883; Basil Skinner, 'Nasmyth Revalued', Scottish Art Review, new series, X, 3, 1966, pp 10-13, 28.

**NASMYTH, Anne Gibson (Mrs Bennett) 1798-1874**
Painter in oil and watercolour of landscapes. Daughter of Alexander Nasmyth(qv). Married the Manchester engineer William Bennett. Painted mainly Scottish and especially Highland landscapes often with storm effect in the manner of her father, generally with great competence but little originality. Exhibited RA 1830, RSA(7) 1834-44, & Paris Salon 1829-1837.
**Bibl:** see Nasmyth, Alexander.

**NASMYTH, Miss Barbara 1790-1870**
Painter in oil and watercolour of landscapes. Daughter of Alexander N(qv). Taught at York Place School moving with her brother James(qv) to Patricoft, nr Manchester after her father died in 1840. In about 1850 returned to London. Painted in the manner of her father, often in the Lake District and around Edinburgh. Particularly skilled in the handling of woodland scenery. Exhibited RSA(34) & GI(2).

**NASMYTH, Charlotte 1804-1884**
Born Edinburgh. Painter of landscapes in oil and watercolour. Youngest daughter of Alexander N(qv). Painted in the style of her father and arguably the most talented of the sisters. Exhibited RA(6) 1840-1862, five of the works being Essex landscapes. Reserved her Scottish landscapes for the RSA, exhibiting (63) there; also GI(1) & Paris Salon 1840-1862. Her portrait, by William Nicholson, is in the SNPG.
**Bibl:** see Nasmyth, Alexander.

**NASMYTH, Elizabeth (Mrs E Terry) 1793-?**
Landscape painter. Daughter of Alexander N(qv). Represented by 'The Falls of Clyde' in the NGS. Exhibited Paris Salon 1816-1829.

**NASMYTH, James 1808-1890**
Born Edinburgh, Aug 19; died London, May 7. Youngest son of Alexander N(qv). Successful engineer, having been inspired by James Watt whom he visited in 1817. His autobiography remains the main source of information about the family. After a spell in London moved to Lancashire. Married 1840. Played a significant part in the development of the steam engine and related machinery, opening his own factory at Paticroft, nr Manchester 1836. Invented the steam hammer as well as machine tools of various kinds. Also a noted astronomer. Retired to Penshurst, Kent 1856 devoting himself to painting landscapes, fantasies and foreign views in watercolour and pastel. Exhibited RSA in 1834. Represented in NGS by a pastel 'Self-portrait'; Aberdeen AG.
**Bibl:** Halsby 34-9; Irwin 140-145,226,229,234,239-40.

**NASMYTH, Miss Jane 1788-1867**
Landscape painter in oil and watercolour. Eldest daughter and pupil of Alexander N(qv) and organiser of the York Place School. Affectionately known as 'Old Solid'. Painted landscapes mainly in Scotland and the English Lakes in the manner of her father and teacher, whose work her's more closely resembles than do any other member of the family. Exhibited RSA(66), GI(8) & BI 1826-1866. Represented in V & A, Montreal AG.

**NASMYTH, Jean Burns (Mrs McKirdy) fl 1912-1953**
Edinburgh landscape and flower painter. There was a remarkable span of 41 years between her isolated exhibits at the RSA one of which was 'In Glen Gairn, near Ballater'; also GI(1), from 18 Mayfield Gardens.

**NASMYTH, Miss Margaret 1791-1869**
Edinburgh landscapist. Daughter and pupil of Alexander N(qv). She painted more Highland subjects than her sisters and was more interested in introducing figures into her compositions. Painted in the manner of her father. Went to Lancashire 1836 in order to keep house for brother James(qv). Her work was firmer than that of her sisters, but she was renowned for her free handling of paint. Exhibited RSA(40) & GI(2).

**NASMYTH, Patrick 1787-1831**
Born Edinburgh, 7 Jan; died Lambeth, London, 17 Aug. Landscape painter. Eldest son and pupil of Alexander N(qv). In his young days often toured the surrounding countryside of Edinburgh sketching with his father and in 1807 travelled with the family to London. Particularly attracted to 17th century Dutch landscapes and these influenced him for the rest of his comparatively short life. He sketched in London and quite soon showed a greater interest in foliage than his father's more stylized versions. Because of an injury to his right-hand he painted with his left, an additional handicap being deafness. It is said that, unlike his father, he was fond of low company and drink. 'The skies in his pictures have been praised for their truth and beauty, and in contrast with the dark landscapes over which they float they seem clear and bright, but they are monotonous in colour and wanting in sense of motion'. Armstrong wrote that 'his work is never empty, it is full of thought, and care, even love; but of fancy, of power to invent, it is almost destitute, and for a defect of that sort the only cure is to see and learn as much as possible'. Another author wrote somewhat mischievously 'the technique of his pictures is of the dexterous mechanical sort which takes no account of the mysterious or the infinites, but which, for that very reason, commended itself to the dilettanti'. He rarely dated his earlier paintings although after c1820 dating became more common. During his stay in London he absorbed the work of Hobbema. The influence of van Ruisdael becomes increasingly apparent, both in his more 'open landscapes with the light and shade organised into horizontal bands under high arching luminous skies, and also in his enclosed forest scenes'. One of the best examples of this period is 'View of Leigh Woods' 1830 now in the Fitzwilliam Museum, Cambridge. He was only forty-four when he died whilst watching a thunderstorm. His work was often forged during his life-time so great care is needed to determine what is genuine. Exhibited RA(20) 1811-1830; also RSA, most posthumously. Represented in NG, Tate AG, V & A, Glasgow AG, City of Edinburgh collection, Fitzwilliam Museum (Cambridge), Sheffield AG, Cape Town AG (SA), Montreal AG (Laermont coll.), Hamburg AG.
**Bibl:** AJ 1908, p36; Armstrong 41-2; Caw 157-9; Conn 35 (1913), 75ff; 53 (1919), 40; 73 (1925), 30, 51; Irwin 238-240; McKay 177-9; Macmillan [SA] 143-4,227,229; Portfolio 1887, 143; Whitehall Review Apr 1910, 22ff.

**NASMYTH-LANGLANDS, George A ?-1940**
Edinburgh painter best known for his Border landscapes; exhibited RSA(95) between 1884 & 1917.

**NATIONAL GALLERY OF SCOTLAND 1850-**
Its origins can be traced back to the Treaty of Union (1707) when a Board of Manufacturers was established to relieve poverty with Treasury funds to encourage manufacturing. To this end a Drawing Academy(qv) had been set up in 1760 and in 1822 Playfair was commissioned to design a building on the Mound which would house the Academy as well as other institutions (see Trustees Academy). When these premises proved inadequate Playfair designed another immediately to the south (on the site of Wombwell's menagerie), with an interior designed by D R Hay(qv). The first of a distinguished line of Keepers to be appointed was the academician William Johnstone(qv). After Playfair's death in 1757 plans were completed by his assistant James Hamilton and the foundation stone was laid by Prince Albert on March 22, 1859. The basis of the collection, initially comprising 150 works, was provided by some important continental paintings including 26 purchased in Genoa and Florence in 1830-1 for the Institution for Encouragement of Fine Arts(qv) by the painter Andrew Wilson (with some advice from David Wilkie). These were augmented by pictures, sculptures, vases and bronzes from the Torrie Bequest, provided on permanent loan by the University, and by works from the Board of Manufacturers and the Royal Association(qv). In 1861 Lady Murray of Henderland presented a significant collection that incorporated the Allan Ramsay collection with its Ramsays, a Watteau, Lancret, Pater, Boucher and Greuze. Among further additions were Rembrandt's 'Woman in Bed' and a pair of Frans Hals portraits from William McEwan MP (1827-1913), and Vermeer's 'Christ in the House of Martha and Mary' from the Coats family. In 1903/4 the Treasury initiated an annual purchasing budget. Many other important gifts followed, among them the Marquis of Lothian's collection that included Cranach's 'Venus and Cupid' (given in 1941), and 22 Impressionists from Sir Alexander

Maitland QC (1877-1965); also several permanent loans of which the finest came from the Duke of Sutherland in 1946. Considered with others of comparable size it is among the finest, if not the finest, national gallery in Europe.
**Bibl:** Brydall 350-353; Caw 66,213-217,228; Esmé Gordon, The Royal Scottish Academy, Edinburgh 1976 passim; Irwin 242,286,289,305,338,345.

**NATTES, John Claude** **c1765-1822**
English artist. Landscape and topographical painter in oil and watercolour. Trained under Hugh Deane. Foundation member, Old Watercolour Society. His primary influence in Scotland resulted from drawings and etchings of Edinburgh commissioned for *Scotia Depicta* 1799-1804. All were engraved by J Fittler. In 1801 he completed two interesting sketches of Edinburgh castle subsequently reproduced as aquatints by J Merigot. Exhibited RA(50) including Edinburgh views 1801 and 1802 and 'Fingal's Cave' 1803. Represented in BM, V & A.
**Bibl:** Butchart 39-40.

**NAUGHTON, Miss Elizabeth** **fl 1867-1885**
Inverness painter in oil and watercolour of Highland landscapes, portraits, still life, interiors and coastal scenes. Exhibited RSA over a long period a total of 24 works, sometimes from a London address and occasionally from Edinburgh but most years from Inverness.

**NAVELLIER, Edouard Felicien Eugene** **1865-1945**
Amateur Parisian painter and sculptor who had strong affinities with Scotland. Exhibited RSA(4 bronze animal figures) & GI(5), from 4 Rue Royer Collard, Paris. Represented in Paris (Luxembourg), Paris (Museum of Modern Art).

**NEALON, Lynne S** **fl 1976-1978**
Dundee painter of interiors and still life. Trained Dundee School of Art. Possibly related to David N(qv). Exhibited a continental interior at the AAS; also GI(2), from 2 Wilkie's Lane.

**NEALON, David** **fl 1989-**
Edinburgh painter; probably related to Lynne S Nealon(qv). Exhibited 'Hollow tree' at the RSA; also GI(1) from 28 Balmoral Pl.

**NEAVE, David** **1773-1841**
Architect. Practice in Dundee. Believed to have designed the Episcopal chapel, Castle St, Dundee (1810-2). Best remembered for the neo-classical street architecture of Dundee's Union Street, especially Thistle Hall (1833). Also the terrace houses in S. Tay St, Dundee (1817-29) and the former Queen's College Library.
**Bibl:** Bruce Walker & W S Gauldie, Architects and Architecture on Tayside, Dundee 1984, 81-2.

**NEEDLE, Kym A** **1946-**
Born Gawler, Australia, Nov 26. Painter in mixed media & collage, also ceramicist; teacher at South Australia School of Art. Settled in Scotland 1972. Exhibited RSA from 1995, from 2 Brown's Place, Edinburgh.

**NEELE, Samuel John** **1758-1824**
Engraver. Worked on Scottish maps and views, 1799-1824. By 1823 he had taken a son into partnership.
**Bibl:** Bryan; Bushnell.

**NEIL, Andrew** **fl 1976-1987**
Edinburgh painter of semi-abstracts and still life; exhibited RSA(13) & AAS(2), latterly from Cupar, Fife.

**NEIL, Angus** **1924-**
Born Kilbarchan, Renfrewshire. Painter of portraits, flowers and still life. Studied Glasgow School of Art 1950-53, awarded the Chalmers Jervise Prize and an RSA Award. Included in the SAC exhibition 'Painters in parallel' (1978), also in an exhibition of flower paintings, RSA(12) & two works - a portrait and a flower piece - at the AAS 1969-61 & GI(13) from The Old Post Office, Catterline. Represented in Aberdeen AG, Glasgow AG, SAC.

**NEIL, George** **fl 1888-1930**
Glasgow watercolour painter of genre and pastoral scenes. Worked in the conventional 'wet' style of the time. Exhibited GI(8).
**Bibl:** Halsby 276.

**NEIL, John** **fl 1865-1872**
Glasgow landscape painter, mostly in watercolour. Spent some time in Birmingham during the early 1870s before returning to Glasgow 1872. Painted mainly in Aberdeenshire and Ayrshire. Exhibited GI(12).

**NEIL, Miss Marilyn R** **fl 1970-1972**
Ayr painter of flowers and topographical subjects. Exhibited GI(3).

**NEIL, Miss Mary E** **fl 1906**
Aberdeenshire amateur landscape painter. Encouraged by her neighbour Rudolphe Christen(qv). Lived at Fasnadarach, nr Ballater. Exhibited Normandy landscapes made on sketching holidays, at the AAS(2).

**NEIL, Thomas** **fl 1881-1882**
Glasgow based artist. Exhibited GI(2).

**NEILL, David** **fl 1916-1917**
Greenock portrait painter. Exhibited RSA(3) from 5 Caddlehill Terrace.

**NEILSON, Miss Agnes** **fl 1881**
Glasgow amateur flower painter in oil. Exhibited RSA(2) from 10 Somerville Place, Glasgow.

**NEILSON, Andrew P** **fl 1951**
Born Dundee. Painter in oils and watercolour of portraits and landscape. Trained Dundee College of Art. Lives and works in Dundee. Exhibited RSA(2) from a Glasgow address. A watercolour view of 'The Overgate', Dundee is in Dundee AG.

**NEILSON, Duncan H** **fl 1907**
Paisley portrait painter in pen and ink, pencil. Exhibited at the GI(3) from Roselea, Renfrew Road.

**NEILSON, Edward Little** **c1837-fl 1865**
Edinburgh watercolour painter of landscapes often of the Highlands, especially Argyllshire. Trained Trustees Academy 1856. Exhibited RSA(17) &GI(1).

**NEILSON, Elmer M** **fl 1897**
Amateur landscape painter of Scottish extraction; exhibited a Sussex view at the RSA(1) from The Studio, Berpham, near Arundel, Sussex.

**NEILSON, Gail** **fl 1973**
Renfrewshire painter of flowers, still life and semi-abstract works. Exhibited RSA(3) & GI(4) from Kilbarchan.

**NEILSON, Henry Ivan** **fl 1900-1909**
Kirkcudbright figurative and landscape painter who moved to Edinburgh c1908. Most of his landscapes were scenes in Kircudbright. Exhibited RSA(17), GI(9), AAS(2) & L(5).
**Bibl:** Caw 407.

**NEILSON, James** **fl 1917**
Glasgow artist; exhibited GI(1) from Eastwood, Mount Vernon.

**NEILSON, Jennie L** **fl 1908-1912**
Amateur Glasgow portrait miniaturist. Exhibited GI(5) & L(2) from Springburn and later Glasgow.

**NEILSON, Lilian** **1938-1998**
Born Kirkcaldy, Fife; died Jan 6. Studied Dundee College of Art 1955-60 obtaining post-diploma award 1961. In 1960, whilst attending a summer school at Hospitalfield, Arbroath, she met Joan Eardley, beginning an important pupil/teacher relationship which developed until in 1963, shortly before Eadley's death, Neilson bought No.3 Catterline. Visited Greece 1973, India 1982 & 1991, and several central Asian republics 1985. A major retrospective exhibition was held at Aberdeen AG and Stirling Univ. 1999. After visiting France and Italy settled at Catterline, Kincardineshire from where she exhibited landscape and scenes depicting the life of the fisherfolk of the north-east at the AAS 1966-1973; GI(6) & SSA.

**NEILSON, Miss Marian** **fl 1873**
Edinburgh landscape painter in oil; exhibited 'Loch Lisken' at the RSA.

**NEILSON-GRAY, Miss Norah RSW** **1882-1931**
Born Helensburgh; died Glasgow, 27 May. Painter in oil and watercolour of portraits. Trained Glasgow School of Art. Based in Glasgow, her principal works include 'The Refugee', 'Little Brother' and 'The Missing Trawler'. A highly competent and sensitive painter. Elected RSW 1914. Exhibited Paris Salon where she received a bronze medal 1921 and a silver medal in 1923, also at the RA. Represented in Glasgow AG(2).

**NEISH, Mrs Violet** **fl 1947-1966**
Glasgow painter of flowers, still life and occasional topography; mainly watercolours. Exhibited GI(24) from 32 Minerva St, later Royal Terrace.

**NELLIS, Miss Margaret** **fl 1934**
Edinburgh painter of genre and figurative studies. Exhibited RSA(1).

**NELSON, James** **fl 1843-1847**
Edinburgh portrait painter; exhibited RSA(6).

**NELSON, John** **fl 1973-**
Born Edinburgh. Painter and printmaker. Trained Edinburgh College of Art from which he obtained a postgraduate scholarship. Exhibitions organiser of the Glasgow League of Artists. Exhibits GI(3). Represented in Kirkcaldy AG.

**NELSON, Meta** **fl 1878**
Amateur flower painter in oil; exhibited RSA(1) from an Edinburgh address.

**NESBITT, Dorothy (Mrs William Myles Johnston)** **1893-1974**
Born Musselburgh. Landscape painter. Trained Edinburgh School of Art. Worked as a studio assistant to Burns. Founder member, Kircudbright school. Served as a town councillor, only the second woman to have done so. Close friend of Lena Alexander(qv). Her paintings presented a straightforward and strong sense of atmosphere.

**NESBITT, John** **1831-1904**
Painter of landscape, interiors and marines. Enjoyed painting river mouths and shore lines using a quiet palette, achieving his effects with skilful use of chiaroscuro. Exhibited 'A Spate on the Feugh, Banchory' at the RSA (1886) and 16 works at the RA (1870-88), most of them from 24 George Street. Titles include 'After a Gale' (1870); 'Rhu Mhor, Loch Alsh, Ross-shire' (1880) and 'Looking East from the Roundell, Gullane' (1888). Also exhibited 128 works at the RSA, RSW(1), RHA(1), GI(32) & AAS(1885-1893). Represented in Glasgow AG.
**Bibl:** Caw 331; Halsby 276.

**NESBITT, John Robinson** **fl 1885**
Edinburgh landscape painter. Exhibited 'A November afternoon - near Edinburgh' at the RSA from 6 Howe St.

**NESS, Anne W K** **fl 1933**
Edinburgh portrait painter. Exhibited RSA(1) from 7 South Gray Street.

**NESS, James** **1870-1946**
Painter, sculptor and engraver; landscape and genre. Exhibited RSA(4), including a bronzed plaster portrait bust of 'The late Rev Robert Milne DD, of Perth', GI(8) & L(1) first from Paisley and then from Perth, finally in 1910 from London.

**NESS, John Alexander ARE** **?-1931**
Born Edinburgh. Painter of landscape and marines in oil and watercolour. Elected VPNSA in 1920, ARE 1903. Exhibited from 1903 mainly at the RE(30) but also GI(3), most often at the Nottingham Gallery, latterly from 18 Bridgford Rd.

**NEUFELD, Ingeborg(Mrs Winter)** **fl 1941-1946**
Glasgow sculptress. Portraits and figures in various kinds of wood. Exhibited RSA between the above years.

**NEVAY, Heather** **1965-**
Glasgow-based painter of landscape, figurative subjects and portraits. Trained Glasgow School of Art 1983-88. First solo exhibition Glasgow 1995. Regular exhibitor RSA since 1992.

**NEVAY, James** **fl 1755-1796**
Scottish history painter, engraver and antiquary. Pupil of Gavin Hamilton(qv). Lived and worked in Rome 1760-1784, armed with an introduction to Andrew Lumsden and studying under Mengs. Paintings recorded by him include two done on commission for James Grant of Grant (Lord Strathmore): 'Agripina with the ashes of Germanicus' and 'Saving of young Cyrus by the Shepherd'. According to a letter from the Abbé Grant to Sir James, the commission included payment of $100 a year until the works were completed - and not unnaturally Nevay took ten years. Taught Anne Forbes(qv) and was involved in a feud with the Runciman brothers(qv) in Rome 1768. Alexander Runciman seems to have held Nevay in some way responsible for the death of John R 1769.
**Bibl:** Irwin 421,n.38; Macmillan [GA] 42-4; Seafield Papers, GRO 248/609; Basil Skinner, Scots in Italy, 1966, 25, 29, 33.

**NEVILL, Miss Sarah** **fl 1989-**
Renfrewshire sculptress in the modern abstract manner. Exhibited a work in steel at the GI, from Barrhead.

**NEVILLE, A Munro** **fl 1923-1968**
Glasgow watercolour painter. Exhibited RSA(1), RSW(3) & GI(46), formerly from Dumbreck, Glasgow and latterly from Barassie, Troon.

**NEVILLE, Louis** **fl 1887-1914**
Watercolour landscape painter. Employed for some years on the Forth Bridge works and from South Queensferry began exhibiting ships and seascapes. Eventually moved to the Infantry Barracks, Ballinrobe, Co. Mayo where he continued exhibiting until the outbreak of WWI. Exhibited RSA(7) 1887 including *'HMS Britannia,* Dartmouth' and 'A Brigantine Ashore on Forty-Mile Beach, NW'; also RHA(4) & L(10) and over 70 works at Walker's Gallery in London.

**NEVILLE, Winifred** **fl 1932**
Glasgow draughtsman. Exhibited a pencil sketch of Amsterdam at the GI from 41 Mosspark Drive.

**NEW ART CLUB** **1940-1942**
Formed in December 1940 by J D Fergusson(qv). He wished to join the Glasgow Art Club(qv) but he considered it inappropriate for an artist to have to pay an entrance fee and so constituted his own club, using as his premises Margaret Morris's dancing academy for which he paid no rent. Subscription was £1 'which may be paid in quarterly instalments' and exhibits were not subjected to any jury (a practice Fergusson had met at the Salon des Independants). But, according to Schotz, there were hardly any members of real talent or even with an art school training. After desultory bi-weekly meetings and monthly exhibitions the Club folded up, replaced by the New Scottish Group(qv).
**Bibl:** Hardie 168; Harris & Halsby; Benno Schotz, Bronze in my Blood - Memoirs of Benno Schotz, Edinburgh 1981.

**NEW SCHOOL OF APPLIED ART** **1892-1906**
Formed in Edinburgh by subscription from mainly the architectural profession, under the jusidiction of a committee of the Board of Manufacturers organised by the architect Sir Rowand Anderson(qv). 'Intended to teach not drawing, but art used in industry - eg decorative painting, furniture, sculpture, wood, metal and plaster work - also typography, silver and goldsmiths work, bookbinding and lithography' [Rowand Anderson]. Combined with the rump of the Trustees Academy until 1902 when a Departmental committee made a number of recommendations which resulted in the formation of the Edinburgh School of Art(qv) four years later.
**Bibl:** Caw 223-224.

**NEW SCOTTISH GROUP** **1942-c1951**
Founded in November 1942 in Glasgow by J D Fergusson following the demise of the New Art Club(qv) and The Centre(qv). In addition to Fergusson himself, members included the painters Jankel Adler (who left Glasgow a year later), Louise Annand, Isabel Babianska,

Donald Bain, Marie de Banzie, Anne Cornock-Taylor, William Crosbie, Taylor Elder, Robert Frame, Millie Frood, George Hannah, Josef Herman, Sheila MacArthur and Tony St Clair; and the sculptors T S Halliday and George Innes. As with the New Art Club, no jury was employed but there seem to have been only three exhibitions following the first one in April, 1943, the last one being held in 1946. In 1947 several members provided works for an exhibition of modern Scottish painting at the first Edinburgh Festival and in 1951 there was a retrospective exhibition in Glasgow. 'The informal, at times anarchic nature of the NSG, and the greatly varying aspirations, styles and talents of its members, would not lead us to expect much stylistic common ground among them. Individualism was greatly prized and encouraged, particularly by Fergusson. But three main strands of influence, running from Fergusson, Herman and Adler are clearly visible' [Hardie]. Its main achievement was to broaden the horizons of art in Scotland beyond the limitations of local establishment and contemporary national fashion.
**Bibl:** Hardie 169-172.

**NEWBERY, Fra(ncis) Henry RWA ARCA (Lond) 1855-1946**
Born Membury, Devon; died Corfe, Dorset, 18 Dec. Painter in oil and watercolour of genre and landscape, art teacher and administrator, possessing great flair for encouraging and recognising talent. Educated at Bridport and at the Royal College of Art. Became a member of the teaching staff at the RCA before transferring to Glasgow School of Art 1885 as Director, a post he retained with outstanding distinction until ill-health forced his retirement in 1918. During his period in office the School developed rapidly from providing mostly part-time evening classes into an important centre of art training with a reputation that extended far beyond the boundaries of Scotland. Married Jessie Rowat(qv) 1918. Although Newberry was not a great artist, he was a fine administrator and stimulator. He spent several holidays with Mackintosh at Walberswick, Suffolk. His 'Summer's Day (Looking across the Estuary from Walberswick to Southwold)' fetched £62,000 at auction in the 1990s. In 1902 he organised the Scottish section of the International Exhibition in Turin, possibly the single most important showpiece for the Glasgow style. Played a critical and influential role in the artistic life of Scotland for almost half a century. His directorship of the GSA corresponded with the flowering of the artistic genius of Charles Rennie Mackintosh(qv) and the early days of the Glasgow school. Retired to Castle Corfe, Dorset. Whilst in Glasgow he exhibited 4 works at the RA 1890-1900, RSA(46), RSW(4), GI(68), AAS(3) & L(21). Represented in SNPG (by a portrait of 'Charles Rennie Mackintosh'), Glasgow AG, Edinburgh City collection (illus in Margaret Swain, *Costume,* no.12,1978,70), Perth AG.
**Bibl:** Burkhauser 58-9,64-9,160-1 et passim; Caw 225; Halsby 40,159,175-6; Irwin 372,399-403; Macmillan [SA] 256,273,291-4 et passim in chs xiv-xviii; Scotsman 20.12.46 (obit).

**NEWBERY, Mrs Jessie Rowat 1864-1948**
Born Paisley; died Corfe Castle, Dorset. Embroiderer and teacher. Mother of Mary Newbery(qv). Childhood was spent in Paisley where her family were engaged in the shawl business. Educated in Edinburgh before studying textile design and stained glass at Glasgow School of Art. Taught embroidery, enamel work and mosaics at Glasgow School of Art 1886. Married Principal Fra Newbery(qv) 1889. Her 'great achievement was that she established a Department of Embroidery at the GSA in which the teaching took a revolutionary new form, with embroidery seen as a specialist subject linked to the other arts. Her main aim, to encourage and develop the individual skills of each student, was a complete break with the prevalent belief that laborious execution was more important than originality which had resulted in stereotyped work of little artistic merit' [Arthur]. In 1890 she won a bronze medal at South Kensington for a stained glass design 'Tempestas'. Also designed textiles, book covers and costumes. Her designs influenced the development of many celebrated students among them Ann Macbeth(qv) and the 'Four'(qv) (the two Macdonald sisters who were to form such an artistically potent quartet with Charles Rennie Mackintosh and Herbert MacNair). She once avowed 'nothing is common or unclean: the design of a pepper pot is as important, in its degree, as the conception of a cathedral'. Exhibited RSA(1), RSW(3) & GI(8). A design for the cover of Matthew Blair's *The Paisley Thread And the Men Who Made It* is in Paisley AG and illustrated in Burkhauser (fig 35); also represented in V&A, Glasgow AG, Paisley AG. and by a chalice and paten, executed to her design, in St Bride's Scottish Episcopal church, Glasgow.
**Bibl:** Liz Arthur in Burkhauser, 147-151; Halsby 175-6,179,181, 183; Irwin 404; Studio, vol XII,1897,48; vol 26,99,103.

**NEWBERY, Mary (Mrs A R Sturrock) 1892-?**
Born Glasgow. Watercolour painter and embroiderer. Daughter of Fra(qv) and Jessie Newbery(qv). Trained Glasgow School of Art. Influenced by Charles Rennie Macintosh(qv), using brilliant bright wools in bold colours. In her flower drawings was much affected by the work of Aubrey Beardsley. Close friend and associate of Cecile Walton(qv), spent the summers in Walberswick, Suffolk together with her and their two neighbours Eric Robertson(qv) and W O Hutchison(qv). In 1919 joined the Edinburgh Group(qv) together with Cecile Walton(qv) and Dorothy Johnstone(qv). During WW1 worked in the De Havilland Aircraft Co as a tracer in their drawing office. In Norwich she met Alick Sturrock(qv) whom she subsequently married. Exhibited RSA(21), RSW(6), GI(40) & L(12).
**Bibl:** Halsby 220,285; Macmillan [SA] 294,331-2.

**NEWLANDS, Anne fl 1913**
Edinburgh painter of still life, portraits, genre and interiors. Exhibited RSA(18) from Lauriston Pl.

**NEWLANDS, Hunter fl 1934-1935**
Amateur watercolourist; exhibited RSW(2) from 7 Carlyle Gardens, Haddington.

**NEWLANDS, James fl 1840-1876**
Edinburgh landscape and historical narrative painter in oil. Fond of sunset scenes. Exhibited RSA(20).

**NEWLANDS, Roderick Kenneth fl 1972-1975**
Aberdeen painter; exhibited RSA(3) & AAS(7), latterly from 22 Tanfield Walk, Woodside.

**NEWMAM, Ethel fl 1937-1938**
Dunbartonshire painter. Exhibited at the RSA(1) & GI(1) from 6 The Avenue, Craigendoran.

**NEWMARCH, C Strafford fl 1858-1866**
Glasgow landscape painter in oil of modest ability; mostly Argyllshire scenery. Exhibited RSA(10) & GI(28).

**NEWTON, Alfred Pizzey RWS 1830-1883**
Born Rayleigh, Essex; died Rock Ferry, Cheshire. Landscape painter in watercolour. Italian ancestry. Most of his early and better known work was done in and of the Scottish Highlands. When working in the vicinity of Inverlochy, Inverness-shire his work came to the attention of Queen Victoria who subsequently patronised him. Visited Italy 1861, Greece 1882. Elected AOWS 1858, OWS 1879. Studio sale, London 29 Apr, 1884. Exhibited RA(5) 1855-1881, latterly from 44 Maddox St - all except one, scenes in the central Highlands. Represented in V & A, Stalybridge AG.
**Bibl:** Mallalieu; Wingfield.

**NEWTON, H 1840-1843**
Edinburgh-based painter of portraits and topographical subjects. Moved for a spell to London before settling in Edinburgh 1842. Between the above years exhibited 21 works at the RSA including two Swiss views and a portrait of 'The Hon Martha Rollo'. Possibly the **H J NEWTON** who exhibited the portrait of an artist at the RA 1833.

**NEWTON, John Harry fl 1983-1988**
Aberdeen painter. Trained at Gray's School of Art, Aberdeen. Exhibited AAS from 53a Nelson St.

**NIBLETT, Frederick Drummond fl 1882-1913**
Edinburgh watercolour painter of churches; also illustrator. Illustrated *Dulcima's Doom and Other Tales* by Willis, c1880. Enjoyed large-scale coloured caricatures, exemplified by his parodies on the mottoes of peers produced for the short-lived periodical *Crown* 1906-07. Moved from Edinburgh to London. Exhibited RSA(2).

**NIBLOCK, Steven J** **fl 1977-1988**
Edinburgh sculptor. Moved to Helensburgh in the 1980s. Exhibited nudes and portrait busts, most in terracotta, at the GI(6).

**NICHOL, -** **fl c1840-1850**
Obscure Edinburgh engraver of ability. Appears to have specialised in old buildings, including 'St John's Chapel in Princes Street', after W Mason c1845 and the same artist's 'Canongate Tolbooth', done a few years earlier. Also produced some notable coloured lithographs of old Edinburgh including 'Edinburgh from the North c1840', 'Princes St, looking West; with proposed Scott Monument c1840' (both after J. Gordon jnr) and 'Head of the West Bow', also c1840. Represented in the Edinburgh Room of Edinburgh PL.
**Bibl:** Butchart 65-6.

**NICHOL, George Smith** **fl 1870-1880**
Edinburgh painter in oil, watercolour and sepia of landscapes often in the Edinburgh and Musselburgh localities, also portrait miniatures. His topographical watercolours were carefully drawn and finely detailed, generally views of Edinburgh. Exhibited RSA(14) mostly portrait miniatures. Represented in the NGS by 15 works, being small studies of Edinburgh views including four Holyrood interiors.

**NICHOL, Regi** **fl 1933**
Amateur watercolour painter; exhibited RSW(2).

**NICHOLAS, Kathleen L** **fl 1922**
Amateur artist. Exhibited GI(1).

**NICHOLL, J L** **fl 1904**
Edinburgh painter. Exhibited RSA(1) from 98 Marchmont Crescent.

**NICHOLSON, Ben** **1894-1982**
Born Denham, Bucks 10 Apr; died London Feb 6. Abstract painter in oil and relief. Eldest son of Sir William Nicholson and the Scottish painter Mabel Pryde(qv), maternal nephew of James Pryde(qv). Trained for one term at the Slade 1910-11 before proceeding to study languages in France, Spain and Italy. Lived briefly in Pasadena 1917-18. Began by painting landscape and still life but later developed into pure abstract works influenced by Synthetic Cubism and by 1927 developed a primitive style after Henri Rousseau. First one-man show in London 1922. Moved to London 1931, beginning his association with Barbara Hepworth and Henry Moore. Visited Picasso, Arp, Braque and Brancusi in France 1932. After joining Abstraction-Creation 1933 made his first wood relief and in 1945-6 changed to linear, abstract paintings for which he is now best remembered. Edited *Circle: International Survey of Constructivist Art* 1937. Resumed landscape compositions and introduced colour to his abstract reliefs after settling in Cornwall 1939. Retrospective exhibitions in Venice 1954, Tate AG and Amsterdam 1955, Buffalo (USA) 1978. Migrated to Switzerland 1955 and reverted to painted reliefs. Awarded Order of Merit 1968. Married first the artist Winifred Nicholson 1920, then Barbara Hepworth. 'Le Quotidien' was purchased by the Chantrey Bequest 1965. Exhibited internationally & London Salon, GI and various provincial galleries. Represented in Tate AG, V & A, Guggenheim Museum, San Francisco Museum of Modern Art, Abbot Hall AG (Kendal), Cleveland AG, Hyde Art Museum (New York), Manchester City AG, Museo Nacional de Bellas Artes (Argentina), London Museum, Nat Gall of Wales, Norton Simon Museum (Pasadena), Yale Center for British Art.
**Bibl:** York City AG,' The Nicholsons', (Ex Cat 1988).

**NICHOLSON, Ian G B** **fl 1975-1987**
Aberdeen portrait and figurative painter. Trained Gray's School of Art, Aberdeen. Exhibited AAS(2), latterly from 14B Ferryhill Place.

**NICHOLSON, J B R** **fl c1815**
Illustrator, possibly Scottish. A set of watercolour drawings of soldiers and bandsmen, having a Scottish flavour including a sketch of Edinburgh Castle, appeared in the London auction rooms Nov, 1976.
**Bibl:** Houfe.

**NICHOLSON, Jim** **1924-1994**
Born Yorkshire. Studied Leeds College of Art, in 1955 moved to Edinburgh. After serving with the RAF during the closing years of the war, he became Art Director of the National Trust for Scotland 1964. Specialised in landscape watercolours in the colourist tradition with strong use of washes. In the 1950s he formed his own Scottish Dance Band, 'The Jim Nick Band'. Represented in Tate AG, SNGMA ('Homage to Modern Art' in partnership with Ian Hamilton Finlay(qv)), City of Edinburgh collection.

**NICHOLSON, Mrs Mabel (née Pryde)** **1871-1918**
Born Edinburgh. Figure and portrait painter. Sister of James Pryde(qv), first wife of Sir William Nicholson, mother of Ben N(qv), sister of James Ferrier Pryde(qv). Trained in art at Bushey, Herts. Married William Nicholson 1893. During a short life she exhibited only between 1910-1920, at the GI(3) & L(4). A memorial exhibition was held at Goupil Gallery 1920.
**Bibl:** Derek Hudson, James Pryde, London 1949.

**NICHOLSON, Michael Angelo** **c1796-1842**
Architect. Son of Peter N(qv) by his first wife. Studied architectural drawing at the school of P Brown in Wells Street and became a pupil of John Fulston. Admitted RA Schools 1814. Engraved plates for his father's works and collaborated with him in the publication of *The Practical Cabinetmaker* 1826. Also lithographed the plates for *Erectheion* (1826), published his own *The Carpenter's and Joiner's Companion* (1826), *The Five Orders, Geometrical and in Perspective* (1834); and *The Carpenter's and Joiner's New Practical Work on Handrailing* (1836). Ran a school for architectural drawing in Euston Square. Although principally an architectural draughtsman, designed a house at Carstairs, Lanarkshire, the plan and elevation of which are illustrated in his father's *The New Practical Builder* (1823) p566. Exhibited RA 1812-1828, latterly from 1 Euston Crescent.
**Bibl:** Colvin.

**NICHOLSON, Peter** **1765-1844**
Born Prestonkirk, East Lothian, 20 Jly; died Carlisle, 18 Jne. Architect. Son of a stonemason, he was apprenticed to a cabinet maker at Linton in what was then Haddingtonshire. On the conclusion of his apprenticeship, he worked as a journeyman in Edinburgh, and at the age of 23 moved to London where he taught evening classes for mechanics at the same time pursuing his own craft. This enabled him to finance his first publication, *The Carpenter's New Guide* (1792), for which he also engraved the plates. This described an original method of constructing groins and niches of complex forms. There followed soon afterwards *The Carpenter's and Joiner's Assistant* (1792) and *Principles of Architecture* (1795-8). In 1800 returned to Scotland setting up practice in Glasgow and remaining there until 1808. Among his designs were two pavilioned terraces on the slopes of Blythswood Hill, Glasgow (1802). In 1806 he was patronised by the 12th Earl of Eglinton for whom he laid out the coastal burgh of Ardrossan. "Built on a regular plan, the streets are wide, straight, and cross at right-angles. The houses are all of two storeys, well finished, neat and comfortable" [New Statistical Account]. Also at this time he erected a timber bridge over the Clyde, Carlton Place, Partick for Fulton Alexander as well as making additions to a number of college buildings. Designed a coffee room at Paisley. The harbour at Ardrossan was built under the direction of Thomas Telford, on whose recommendation Nicholson was appointed Surveyor to the county of Cumberland 1808. There he surveyed the buildings with new Courts of Justice at Carlisle to Telford's designs until 1810, when he returned to London, leaving the Courts to be completed by Sir Robert Smirke. Between 1812 and 1819 he produced *The Architectural Dictionary,* 2 vols, containing plates of many of his own works (re-edited and re-written by Lomax and Gunyon 1855-62). In 1827 he began publication of *The School of Architecture and Engineering,* planned for completion in 12 volumes, but after the fifth volume this was abandoned owing to the publisher's insolvency. Nicholson lost heavily, and as a result went in 1829 to Morpeth where a small property there had been left him by a relative. In 1832 he moved on to Newcastle-on-Tyne, where he opened a school but two years later had to obtain public assistance and in 1835 he was elected President of the Newcastle Society for the Promotion of the Fine Arts. During his last years he was helped by the generosity of Thomas Jamieson of Newton. A monument to his memory, designed by R W Billings(qv), was erected in Carlisle Cemetery 1856. Twice married, he had two sons and a daughter. His eldest son Michael Angelo(qv) was also an architect. Devoted his life to the application of scientific methods in building, using his great ability as a mathematician to simplify old methods as well as to invent new ones. His improvements in the construction of handrailing was rewarded with a gold medal by the

Society of Arts 1814. The first author to write on the construction of hinges and the hanging of doors and the first to notice that Grecian mouldings were conic sections. His invention of the centro linead, an instrument for drawing lines which are required to converge towards an inaccessible point, resulted in a gift of £20 from the Society of Arts in 1840 as well as a silver medal. Other publications of this remarkable architect were *The Student's Instructor* (1804); *Mechanical Exercises* (1811); *A Treatise of Practical Perspective* (1815); *An Introduction to the Methods of Increments* (1817); *Essays on the Combinatorial Analysis* (1818); *The Rudiments of Algebra* (1819); *Essay on Inverlution and Evolution* (1820); *Treatise on the Construction of Staircases and Handrails* (1820); *Analytical and Arithmetical Essays* (1820); *Popular Course of Pure and Mixed Mathematics* (1822); *Rudiments of Practical Perspective* (1822); *The New and Improved Practical Builder and Workman's Companion* (1823); *The Builder and Workman's New Director* (1824); *The Carpenter and Builder's Complete Measurer* (1827); *Popular and Practical Treatise on Masonry and Stonecutting* (1827); *Practical Masonry, Bricklaying, and Plastering* (1830); *Treatise on Dialling* (1833); *Treatise on Projection with a Complete System of Isometrical Drawing* (1837); *Guide to Railway Masonry* (1839); *The Carpenter, Joiner and Builder's Companion* (1846); *Carpentery* (ed Ashpitel), (1849); *Carpentery, Joining and Building* (1851); with John Rowbotham Nicholson, *A Practical System of Algebra* (1824); and with his son Michael Angelo N *The Practical Cabinetmaker, Upholsterer, and Complete Decorator* (1826).
**Bibl:** Brydall 181; Colvin; Dunbar 117-8; A Gomme & D Walker, Architecture of Glasgow, London 1987(rev), 296.

**NICHOLSON, Peter Walker** **1856-1886**
Born Cupar, Fife; died Nigg, Cromarty. Edinburgh-based lawyer and watercolour painter mainly of landscape, buildings and rustic genre. Educated Universities of Edinburgh and St. Andrews. Trained RSA Schools, Ruskin School Oxford, at the Slade, and Bonnat's studio, Paris 1881. Friend of Charles Hodge Mackie(qv), Garden Smith(qv) and R B Nisbet(qv). Published an essay in the Round Table series on D.G. Rossetti, and in 1835 began to exhibit at the RSA. An illustrated memorial volume by H.B. Baildon and J.M. Gray was published privately in Edinburgh 1886. Drowned in a boating accident in the Cromarty Firth when only 30 years old. Exhibited RSA(15) & GI(3).
**Bibl:** Bryan; Caw 280; Halsby 126,276.

**NICHOLSON, William RSA** **1781-1844**
Born Ovingham-on-Tyne, Northumberland, 25 Dec; died Edinburgh, 16 Aug. Portrait painter, miniaturist & etcher. Second son of a schoolmaster who became master of the grammar school at Newcastle-on-Tyne, and his Scottish wife. Self-taught in art. Early in life he moved to Hull where he painted miniatures of serving officers. In 1814 settled in Edinburgh remaining there for the rest of his life. Founder member of the RSA 1817, foundation academician 1826 and first Secretary of the RSA 1826 a post he held until 1830. After resigning but withdrawing his resignation two years previously in April 1830 he wrote to the Academy, 'although I never for a moment despaired of ultimate success, yet I soon found that it could only be attained by the greatest activity and attention. Accordingly, I found it necessary to make my own affairs give way to those of the Academy, resulting in a very serious sacrifice on my part and I may mention in confidence that I cannot estimate my loss at less than £200 a year. Under the circumstances the Council will not impute it to any indifference that this has to be my last General Meeting. I have now laboured upwards of four years, and never shunned any duty, however disagreeable. I therefore think it only fair and reasonable that another member should take the labouring over'. The Academy accepted this request and elected David Octavius Hill(qv). Nicholson exhibited RSA annually between 1827 and 1844. Among his most famous works were a portrait of 'Sir Adam Ferguson' 1817, the poet 'James Hogg' 1827, 'William Etty RA' 1850 and 'Sir Walter Scott with his dog Maida' 1815, exhibited RSA 1834. Also painted landscapes and a few etchings, some of which were published including portraits of notables such as 'Robert Burns' and the architect 'Playfair'. Brydall found his miniatures 'delicate and refined' but McKay thought 'his average work has a lack of grit in the treatment of the flesh, which gives something of effeminacy to the male portraits, and of oversoftness to the female'. His later portraits show the influence of Raeburn. Exhibited RA(7) 1808-1822 including a portrait of 'Thomas Bewick' 1816, also OWCS, Edinburgh Exhibition Society 1814-16 & Institute for the Encouragement of the Fine Arts in Scotland 1821-25. Represented SNPG by a large 'Self-portrait' in oil, together with 17 other works; also in NGS ('Charlotte Nasmyth'), Kirkcaldy AG.
**Bibl:** Armstrong 34; Bryan; Brydall; Bushnell; Caw 89-90; Foskett 422; Esmé Gordon, 4,14-18,21-22,25,27,32,39-41,47,49-50,53-54, 57,90,127; Halsby 51; McKay 127, 320-22; Macmillan [SA] 162-3.

**NICHOLSON, William** **fl 1870-1872**
Edinburgh architect whose main claim to attention was his design of the Presbyterian church on Capital Hill, Washington. Exhibited RSA 1870-2.

**NICOL, Miss** **20th Century**
Aberdeenshire painter; exhibited AAS on an unrecorded date from High St, Inverurie.

**NICOL, Miss Beatrice** **fl 1972-1973**
Glasgow painter of still life. Exhibited GI(3), from Kinghurst Ave.

**NICOL, Erskine RSA ARA** **1825-1904**
Born Lochend Road, Leith; died Feltham, Middlesex, 8 Mar. Painter in oil and watercolour; genre, often of a humorous character, figurative subjects. After a spell as a house-painter's apprentice he entered the Trustee's Academy 1838 studying under William Allan(qv) from whom he inherited a strong tradition of expression based upon the work of Wilkie. In 1846, after a brief spell as drawing master at Leith High School, went to Ireland obtaining by chance an appointment as an art master in Dublin. Whilst there he developed the humorous side of his work, later becoming the most humorous painter Scotland has produced. It was in the cabins and potato patches of Ireland that he first found material for his lively sketches. 'You turn to a picture by Nicol, as you go to see a favourite comedian, expecting to laugh heartily, and you are seldom disappointed'. He saw the comic in every situation and, although overfond of the Irish man of farce, his insight into certain types of character was great. A prolific painter, so that the quality work varied. But the influence of his Irish visit lasted with him throughout his career. His paintings are less fine than Thomas Faed's but the expressions he gave to his characters are more distinctive. 'His brush seldom portrayed beauty...but his adroit touch is singularly happy in its application to the suntanned faces of pronounced physiognomy and dilapidated costume' [McKay]. Towards the 1860s the subject of his paintings became more Scottish, with thinner shadows and more umber and a well conceived light and shade veil. All this was exemplified in his diploma picture 'The Day after the Fair'. Settled in London 1862 but continued to make an annual visit to Ireland to study his subjects at first hand. Later, when he travelled less, he turned more to Scottish genre, working for a time in Pitlochry. In 1885 he retired finally to Feltham, Middlesex where he died. In his early career he had been attacked for the strong element of caricature in his work but this was replaced as his similarity to Wilkie became more apparent. A good example of this is 'The Rent Day, Signing the New Lease' 1868, now in Leicester AG, redolent of Wilkie's 'Letter of Introduction', in the setting of the figures and the treatment of still life objects. Occasionally he turned to subjects in which more profound levels of human emotion were involved such as immigration, emigration and shipwreck, exemplified by 'The Missing Boat' 1876 now at the Royal Holloway College. Illustrated A M Hall's *Tales of Irish Life and Character,* 1909, and W Harvey's *Irish Life and Humour,* 1909. Contributed occasional illustrations to *Good Words* (1860). Elected ARSA 1855, RSA 1859, ARA 1868. Exhibited RA(53), RSA(172) 1841-1905; also AAS 1896 & GI 1862-1911. Both his sons Erskine E N(qv) and John Watson N(qv) were painters. In addition to places already mentioned, he is represented in the BM, Tate AG, V & A, NGS, SNPG (two 'Self-portraits'), Aberdeen AG, Dundee AG, Glasgow AG, Harrogate AG, Sheffield AG, Ulster Museum.
**Bibl:** Armstrong 81; AJ 1870, 65-7; 1893, 301; 1904, 170; Caw 163-4; Gaunt 232 plate 127; Halsby 69-70; Irwin 304-5; Maas 116-7; McKay 347-51; Macmillan [SA] 186,213,215,216,218,231; Portfolio 1879, 61ff; 1887, 227; Ruskin, Acad Notes 1875; Joyce M Wallace, Further Traditions of Trinity and Leith, Edinburgh 1988.

**NICOL, Erskine E Jnr** **?-1926**
Died at Cabanets, Log, France 13 May. Painter in oil and watercolour of landscapes. Son of Erskine N(qv), brother of John Watson N(qv).

Travelled widely, painting sometimes in watercolour, with quiet colours and broad washes; influenced by the Dutch school. Exhibited RA(7), RSA(6), RSW(1), ROI(1) & GI(4).
**Bibl:** Halsby 69,148,276.

**NICOL, Gavin** **1927-**
Born Scotland, 22 May. He works in all media: oil, tempera, acrylic and watercolour. Trained Glasgow School of Art 1949-53 and Hospitalfield Summer School 1953. Held several one man shows 1971-73 and 1989. After graduating in 1953 part of every summer was spent around the Mediterranean. Influenced by the light there, by his reading in philosophy, by the New Testament, the pyschology of Jung, by Cézanne's later work and the cubism of Braque. Attempts to integrate figurative compositions which reflect his own experiences and in which it is possible to see the surreal in the real and the real in the surreal. Exhibits RSA & GI(3). Represented in Lillie AG (Milngavie), Greenock AG, Hunterian Museum (Glasgow Univ).

**NICOL, G Gordon** **fl 1959-1964**
Aberdeen artist. Portraits and figurative works; exhibited AAS(2) from 88 Desswood Place.

**NICOL, George S** **fl 1876**
Edinburgh amateur watercolour landscape painter. Exhibited 'On the Esk, nr Musselburgh' at the GI, from Cumberland St.

**NICOL, Miss Iris E D** **fl 1939-1942**
Renfrewshire watercolourist. Trees, flowers and garden scenes. Exhibited GI(2) from Kilmacolm.

**NICOL, John Watson ROI** **1856-1926**
Painter in oil of genre, portraits and historical subjects; also illustrator. Son of Erskine(qv), brother of Erskine E N(qv). Exhibited 32 works at the RA between 1876 and 1903 including a portrait of the German Emperor, commissioned by the United Services Club 1903, some prominence was given to his 'Lochaber No More', the tragedy of a Highlander who has to leave his shepherd's life, illustrated in the *AJ* (1884) and exhibited RA 1883. A brushwork drawing of a tulip for a bookcover was illustrated in the *Art Journal* 1906. Elected ROI 1888. Contributed to *Good Words* (1860) and *Black and White* (1896). Sheffield AG has 'For better, for worse (Rob Roy and the Bailie)', exhibited RA 1886. Other works include 'A young cavalier', (1877), 'Before Culloden' (1882), and 'Westward Ho!' (1901). He illustrated *Good Words,* six of the illustrations being shown at the RSA 1887. Also exhibited RSA(19), ROI(19), GI(4) & L(7).
**Bibl:** AJ 1884, 348; 1906, pl 150; Gazette des Beaux Artes 1879, II 371; Caw 272; Houfe.

**NICOL, William W** **fl 1840-1873**
Edinburgh painter in oil of landscapes, portraits and figure subjects. Lived briefly in Edinburgh, Innerleithen, Southampton, Worcester, Cheltenham, London and Somerset before settling in Edinburgh 1865. Some of his works were painted on a grand scale, eg 'Charles I surrendering himself to General Leslie' 1841, 'Sir Walter Raleigh writing the History of the World while a prisoner in the Tower' 1842 and 'Sir Walter Scott collecting the Border Minstrelsy, accompanied by Hogg and Laidlaw' 1843. One work at the RSA was described by a contemporary critic as 'more like a rice paper drawing than a painting, hard and poor and vulgar'. Exhibited RA(9), RSA (39) & GI(10).

**NICOLE(L), Andrew Keith** **fl 1983**
Dundee painter; exhibited a figurative work at the AAS from 138 Hilltown.

**NICOLL, Archibald Frank/Frederick** **1886-c1935**
Born Christchurch, New Zealand. Painter in oil and watercolour of portraits and landscape. Settled in Glasgow 1912 and after a short interlude in Kew, Surrey returned to Edinburgh 1917, remaining in Scotland until going south again to London 1930. Exhibited RSA(3), RA(2), RSW(1), GI(2) & L(1).

**NICOLL, Ian Scott** **fl 1964**
Aberdeen-based painter; exhibited RSA(2) - 'Sea wall' and 'First snow'.

**NICOLL, John M** **fl 1952-1955**
St Andrews landscape painter, mainly local scenes, also pen and ink sketches of Rome and Sicily. Exhibited RSA(10) & GI(3).

**NICOLL, Miss Maggie** **fl 1897-1937**
Greenock flower painter. Studied at Glasgow School of Art. Exhibited RSA(1), GI(9) & AAS(2) from 52 Union St.

**NICOLL, Mrs Mary** **fl 1980-**
Glasgow painter. Exhibited GI(2) from Bishopbriggs.

**NICOLL, Lady Catherine Robertson** **fl 1910-1937**
Competent amateur landscape and interior painter. Divided her time between London and Aberdeenshire. Author of two interesting books of family reminiscences. Exhibited AAS(8), mainly Strathdon scenes including 'Auchindoir churchyard'; 'Craig Castle'; 'The Old Manse garden, Lumsden'; and 'Library at the Old Manse, Lumsden'. Lived at Bay Tree Lodge, Frognal, Hampstead, London and during the summer at The Old Manse, Lumsden.

**NICOLSON, John A** **fl 1948-1950**
Edinburgh painter of informal portraits and figure subjects. Exhibited 'Indian woman' and 'Art class' at RSA.

**NICOLSON, John** **1843-1934**
Born John O'Groats; died Caithness. Little known self-taught painter in oils; also sculptor & farmer.

**NICOLSON, John P** **fl 1891-1921**
Leith painter in oil and watercolour of still life, landscape and buildings. Exhibited 7 works at the RA 1891-4 including a lively portrayal of the 'River Deveron in spate' (1893), RSA(41), RSW(1), AAS 1890-1921, RBA(2), RHA(3), GI(9) & L(2).

**NICOLSON, William Campbell** **1880-1965**
Scottish watercolour painter of genre and figure studies; also poster artist and illustrator. Most of his professional life was spent as a commercial artist. After an apprenticeship in Leith and Edinburgh, where he worked alongside Russell Flint(qv), moved to Mosspark, Glasgow as chief artist with McCorquodale & Co. Among works for this firm was a limited edition centenary calendar of Mary, Queen of Scots (1946). Contributed many covers for the *Wide World Magazine* and posters for British Rail. His last major commercial work was a vast map of the Clyde produced in sections which was displayed for many years at Glasgow Central station. Exhibited RSA(2) - 'Idle moments' and 'A street in Algiers', RSW(2), AAS(3) & GI(9) from 18 Mosspark Drive, Glasgow.

**NICOLSON, Winifred Ursula (Mrs Wightman) RMS** **1881-?**
Born St Petersburg, Russia. Miniature painter. Trained Edinburgh. Painted miniatures at the Russian Court 1901-1908. Elected ARMS 1907, RMS 1909. Lived for a time in Scotland, settling in Cheshire. Continued to exhibit RA(5), RSA(3), RSW(1), GI(1), RMS(19) & L(1).

**NIGHTINGALE, Charles Edward** **fl 1874**
Edinburgh still life painter in watercolour; exhibited RSA(1).

**NIMMO, Harry** **fl 1939-1940**
Edinburgh watercolour painter of English and Scottish landscapes; exhibited at the RSW(5), GI(1) & RSA(3) from 16 Craig's Avenue, Corstorphine.

**NIMMO, James** **fl 1881-1898**
Edinburgh painter in oil and watercolour of landscapes and buildings, especially the castles and buildings of old Edinburgh. Possibly related to Harry(qv) and John Jules N(qv). Exhibited RSA(9) & GI(5).

**NIMMO, Robert H** **fl 1827-1829**
Edinburgh engraver and lithographer; portraits, birds, animals and topographical works. Exhibited RSA(6), including a portrait of 'Robert Pollock', author of *The Course of Time,* from St David St. Represented in Glasgow AG.

**NIMMO, John Jules** **fl 1856-1877**
Edinburgh-based painter in oil and watercolour of portrait minia-

tures, usually on ivory, and townscapes. Lived for some years in Paris. Exhibited RSA(44).

**NINETEEN TWENTY-TWO GROUP** **1922-1932**
A group of Edinburgh College of Art students who graduated in 1922. Founded by William Gillies(qv) and William MacTaggart(qv), it included A V Couling(qv), William Crozier(qv), William Geissler(qv), David Gunn(qv), George Wright Hall(qv), Alexander Graham Munro(qv) and George C Watson(qv). Characterised as being 'Francophile, colourful, serious and civilised' [Hardie]. Annual exhibitions were held in Edinburgh. The Group was the closest approximation to an Edinburgh School, a label they have in places attracted. (See also under individual artists.)
**Bibl:** Hardie 158,160.

**NISBET, Miss A Holmes** **fl 1890-1891**
Glasgow painter. Exhibited GI(2) from Mavisbank, Partick Hill.

**NISBET, Alexander** **1682-?**
Leith painter who frequently gave Vertue information and was responsible for repainting the landscape background of Van Somer's painting of Lord Bacon. Brydall records him as Alexander NESBITT.
**Bibl:** Brydall 108.

**NISBET, Dr Alexander F R** **?-1975**
Born New Abbey, Kirkcudbrightshire; died Dumfries, 24 Jly. Painter in oil of landscapes, flowers and portraits. Nisbet came from a farming family, studied agriculture at Glasgow University from where he received a doctorate. Lecturer, West of Scotland College of Agriculture. Upon his retirement 1964 he took up art full-time, achieving success commercially as well as in national exhibitions. Best known for his landscapes of his beloved Stewartry, also painted in Spain, in the Hebrides and Northern Ireland; occasionally turned to flower pieces and portraits. Exhibited GI(3). His painting of 'Paul Jones' birthplace' hangs in Kirkcudbright Museum.

**NISBET, E** **fl 1889**
Painter, possibly Scottish. Exhibited GI(1) from Park Road, Havistock Hill, London.

**NISBET, H Crockett** **fl 1898**
Edinburgh landscape painter in oil. Exhibited RSA(1) from 2 Western Terrace, Murrayfield.

**NISBET, H Hume** **1849-1923**
Born Stirling, Aug 8; died Eastbourne. Painter and author; illustrator. Travelled widely. Father of Noel Laura N(qv). Trained under Sam Bough(qv). When sixteen he began to travel and spent years exploring Australia. On his return became art master at Watt College and Old Schools of Art, Edinburgh. Resigned 1885 and was sent by the publishers Cassell & Co to Australia and New Guinea 1886. Visited China and Japan 1905-6. In later years spent increasing time writing. Illustrated *Her Loving Slave* (1894), *A Sappho of Green Springs* (Bret Harte, 1897) and *The Fossicker* (Ernest Glanville, 1897). Contributed to *The English Illustrated Magazine* (1890-1). Seems to have ceased exhibiting 1885 possibly on account of extensive travelling. Exhibited RSA(5) from Edinburgh, usually town views; also GI(2) & RHA(4).
**Bibl:** Houfe.

**NISBET, James** **fl c1770-1785**
Architect and plasterer. Best known for his classical treatment of the galleried hall church at Kelso (1773). Also responsible for an intricate ceiling (1782) in the High Dining Room on the 1st floor of Tweeddale Court on Edinburgh's Royal Mile and detailed plaster work at Leuchie House, E. Lothian. In 1792 he designed the long-fronted Tontine Building (120-124 George St), although never completed, it became a cavalry barracks during the Napoleonic War and afterwards a government office, the front now restored retaining the interesting staircase in no. 118.
**Bibl:** Dunbar 124; Gifford 210,293,305n,306.

**NISBET, James D** **fl 1932-1961**
Glasgow-based watercolour painter of country genre. Moved later to Aberdeen. Exhibited 'Barbara' and 'Winter feeding' at the RSA, also RSW(3), RGI(1) and AAS(3), latterly from 52 Ashgrove Rd W.

**NISBET, Miss Jane** **fl 1875-1906**
Glasgow painter in oil and watercolour of landscapes, still life, flowers and fruit. Exhibited RSA(21), GI(30), AAS(3) & L(3) from 11 Westminster Gdns, Hillhead.

**NISBET, John** **fl 1903-1940**
Architect and painter in oil and watercolour; also etcher. Topographical subjects. Lived in Glasgow and later Edinburgh. Exhibited RSA(6), RSW(4), GI(9), AAS(2) & L(4).

**NISBET, Mrs Margaret Dempster (née Dempster)** **fl 1886-1932**
Edinburgh painter in oil of portrait miniatures, portraits and figurative subjects. Wife of Robert Buchan N(qv). Trained at Royal Institution in Edinburgh and in Paris. After a spell in Edinburgh moved to Comrie, Perthshire, finally settling in Crieff. One of her best known works was 'Stonehaven Harbour from Bervie Braes' RSA 1897. Exhibited RSA(37), RA(1), RI(7), RBA(1), GI(16), AAS(1896-1931), L(5) & London Salon(4).

**NISBET, Noel Laura (Mrs Harry Bush)** **1887-?**
Painter and black and white artist. Daughter of H Hume H(qv). Trained South Kensington 1910. Married the English artist Harry Bush. Exhibited RA 1914-1940, RI(62), ROI(13), L(10) & GI(2).

**NISBET, Pollok Sinclair ARSA RSW** **1848-1922**
Born Edinburgh, 18 Oct; died Edinburgh, 28 Dec. Painter in oil and watercolour of townscapes and coastal scenes, landscape and architectural subjects. Elder brother of Robert Buchan N(qv). Educated Edinburgh Institution, having started in a lawyer's office. Pupil of Horatio McCulloch(qv). Travelled extensively in Italy, Morocco, Algeria, Tunis and Spain; also Holland and Belgium. His Scottish landscapes are rather formally handled and conventionally composed, his best and most characteristic works are his paintings of market places and the characteristic buildings of Morocco and Spain. Elected RSW 1881, ARSA 1892. Exhibited RSA(165), RSW(119), GI(89), AAS(1897), RHA(3) & RI(2). Represented in Glasgow AG, City of Edinburgh collection.
**Bibl:** Caw 298; Halsby 276-7; Studio, special RSA issue, 1907.

**NISBET, Robert Buchan RSA HRSW RBA RSW RI** **1857-1942**
Born Edinburgh, 1 Jly; died Crieff, 15 Aug. Prolific painter in watercolour of landscapes (some golfing), occasionally in oil. Son of a house-painter. First apprenticed in a shipping office before committing himself to art 1880. Joined his brother Pollok(qv) in Venice. Then entered the Board of Manufacturer's School, Edinburgh and the RSA Life Classes 1882-85, before proceeding to Paris for further studies under Bouguereau. Whilst at the RSA Schools influenced by Sam Bough(qv) and the mainstream English watercolour tradition of Cox, Girtin and de Wint. Returning from France he settled in Crieff. Married Margaret Dempster(qv). Sometimes his more important drawings were rubbed until little of the original surface remains giving a certain gritty appearance to his colour. 'Although his apprehension of Nature is neither very personal nor very profound, and has been chastened unduly by respect for certain traditions and restricted by exercise on too limited a range of effects, his work is refined in tone, broad and harmonious in effect, and marked by considerable dignity of style. His favourite colour schemes are subdued brown and blue, dull saffron and grey green, while his compositions are generally built upon simple albeit distinguished lines' [Caw]. Won many awards including medals overseas. Founder member and chairman, Society of Scottish Artists 1892. Honorary member of the Royal Belgium Watercolour Society, HRSW 1934, having been elected RSW 1887, RBA 1890, RI 1892, RAS 1907, ARSA 1893, RSA 1902. Exhibited RA(21) 1888-1901, 'Evening stillness' 1890 being purchased for the Chantrey bequest; also RSA(214), RSW(185), RI(100), RHA(10), RBA(25), GI(125), AAS(1890-1933) & L(39). Represented in the V & A, Dundee AG, Glasgow AG, Paisley AG, Kirkcaldy AG, City of Edinburgh collection, Derby AG, Leeds City AG.
**Bibl:** AJ 1898, 71; Caw 303,312-313,362,388,483; Halsby 165,241, 277.

**NISSEN, Mary Still** **fl 1982**
Aberdeen painter; exhibited a country scene at the AAS from 66 Sluie Dr.

**NIVEN, Forrest** **fl 1888-1911**
Painter. Exhibited GI(6) from Pollockshields, nr Glasgow.

**NIVEN, Jean** **fl 1933-1936**
Greenock portrait and figurative engraver. Wife of William N(qv). Exhibited 'Segovia' at the RSA, & GI(2) from 4 Fox Street.

**NIVEN, Katherine** **fl 1893**
Glasgow painter. Exhibited GI(1) from 75 Hill Street.

**NIVEN, William** **fl 1941**
Renfrewshire engraver. Husband of Jean N(qv). Exhibited a portrait etching at the GI from Greenock.

**NIXON, Alfred J** **fl 1876-1887**
Edinburgh watercolour painter of portraits and townscapes. Best known for his recording of Edinburgh Old Town eg 'Bull's Close, Cowgate - taken down 1873' (1876) and 'Cowan's Close, Cowgate' (1887, now demolished). Exhibited RSA(3) from 501 Lawnmarket. Represented in City of Edinburgh collection (2 watercolours of old Edinburgh).

**NIXON, Jacqui** **1964-**
Kincardineshire-based figurative artist in a semi-abstract manner. Honours graduate. Exhibits RSA since 1989, latterly from 17 Strathmore Rd, Glamis.

**NIXON, James ARA** **c1741-1812**
Miniaturist. Little is known of his early life. Trained RA Schools 1769. Member, Society of Artists and exhibiting with them 1765-1771. Painted portraits in oil and watercolour, also historical subjects and book illustrations. Influenced by Sir Joshua Reynolds. Numbered many actresses among his sitters. One pupil was Augustus Toussant. Appointed Limner to the Prince Regent 1790 and Miniature Painter to the Duchess of York two years later. Living in Edinburgh 1796-8 but later moved to Devonshire where he ended his days. His work is of very high quality, deserving more recognition than has yet been given. 'He painted with strong bright colours, and used a lot of gum with his paints. Many of his portraits have a dark background or thick foliage. His miniatures of ladies often depict them holding a bird; the faces of his sitters are usually shaded with irregular soft cross-strokes, the hair being painted in broad sweeping strokes without much detail' [Foskett]. Sometimes signed with a hidden small 'N'. Elected ARA 1778. Exhibited RA 1772-1807 a total of 100 works, including a portrait of 'Lady Belhaven' (or Lady Balcarres) executed in Edinburgh 1796 and a portrait of 'Major-General Sir Eccles Nixon' (1800), presumably a relative. Represented in V & A, BM, Liverpool AG.
**Bibl:** Foskett.

**NIXON, Ronnie** **fl 1977-1981**
Glasgow amateur painter. Exhibited GI(2).

**NIXON, William** **c1810-1848**
Edinburgh architect. After the Lords Ordinary abandoned their sittings in Parliament House 1844, Nixon was commissioned to design four new courtrooms, the W pair (VII & VIII) still intact. Also responsible for the classical Police Chambers, Parliament Square (1845-9).
**Bibl:** Gifford 120,124,129,186.

**NOBBS, Percy Erskine** **1885-1964**
Architect. Trained Edinburgh University and then under Sir Robert Lorimer(qv). Won Tite Prize 1900, Owen Jones Prize 1903. Said to have been an irascible man but wrote a moving tribute to Lorimer when hearing of his death. Went to London before being appointed to the chair of Architecture at McGill Univ, Canada c1903. Elected FRIBA 1930, RCA 1919. Photographs of some of his baronial designs in Canada were included at the Empire Exhibition, Wembley, 1926.
**Bibl:** Peter Savage, Lorimer and the Edinburgh Craft Designers, Edinburgh 1980, 26,51,131,152,167.

**NOBLE, David** **fl 1882-1890**
Edinburgh oil painter of landscapes, particularly local scenes and farm animals. Younger brother of Robert N(qv) who died tragically young, student of his cousin J Campbell Noble(qv); related also to G Inglis N(qv). Exhibited RSA(21) & AAS(8) from 6 Comeley Green Place & London Rd.

**NOBLE, Donald John Robert FSA(Scot)** **1950-**
Born St Andrews, 24 Jly. Painter in watercolour and oil, and sculptor; landscapes and portrait busts generally in bronze. Educated Glenalmond, under the art teacher Ronald Craig(qv). Self-taught thereafter except for some tuition from Birgitte Nielson(qv). Devoted to the north-west coast of Scotland where he lives and works. Since graduating at Cambridge in 1972 his Impressionistic style has given way to comparative simplification. Scenes of the mountainous north-west are painted with a brooding richness of colour and an unsentimental but accurate sense of atmosphere.

**NOBLE, Dougal** **1945-**
Edinburgh-based painter; exhibited 'Northern dreamtime' at the RSA 1990, from 20/13 Caledonian Crescent.

**NOBLE, G Inglis** **fl 1884-1906**
Edinburgh landscape painter in oil, mostly scenes of rural life. Related to David(qv) and Robert N(qv). Exhibited RSA(11) & AAS(11) from 6 Comeley Green Place.

**NOBLE, James Campbell RSA** **1846-1913**
Born Edinburgh, 22 Jly; died Ledaig, Argyll 25 Sep. Painter in oil of landscape, portraits and rustic genre, also lithographer and occasional watercolourist & etcher. Cousin of Robert N(qv). Trained RSA Schools under Chalmers(qv) and McTaggart(qv) and, being favoured by the former, was considerably influenced by him. His early work made figures the central features of his rural scenes. Worked closely with two companions John R Reid(qv) and John White(qv). Gradually, however, he became more of a quintessential landscapist, favouring scenes of shipping, rivers, ports and pictures on the Medway, Tyne, Seine and Clyde. In the early 1880s lived at Coldingham, painting the rocky coast of Berwickshire. Taught for a time at Edinburgh School of Art having Arthur Melville(qv) among his pupils. Revisited Holland 1900 and thereafter his most characteristic works were of Dutch waterways. Won the Keith prize 1873. President, Scottish Arts Club. Elected ARSA 1879, RSA 1892. Exhibited RA(10) 1880-1896, latterly from Gogar Mains, Corstorphine, Edinburgh; also RSA(160), RSW(1), GI(20), AAS 1885-1912 & L(19). Represented in NGS, City of Edinburgh collection (etching), Glasgow AG, Kirkcaldy AG.
**Bibl:** Caw 309-10; Halsby 132,277; RSA, ed Charles Holme 1907; Studio 44 (1908) 232; 58 (1913) 66; The Year's Art, 1914, 445.

**NOBLE, Robert RSA PSSA** **1857-1917**
Born Edinburgh; died East Linton, 12 May. Painter of landscape and genre in oil and occasional watercolour. Studied under his cousin J C Noble(qv) at Trustees School and RSA Life Class 1879-84. Shared Keith prize 1892. First came to notice with a number of large cottage interiors with figures, deep-toned in their contrasting effects of light and shade, in about 1880. After studying in Paris under Carolus Duran, he turned to landscape, a development confirmed when he moved to East Linton. Foundation member and first President, Society of Scottish Artists 1892. In 1886, after viewing a number of paintings by Monticelli, he produced a series of pictures with brilliantly costumed figures among the blaze of the Tynninghame rhododendrons in full bloom. Always conscious of the design element in his work he employed a subdued palette liking warm and luminous colour 'a very distinct leaning to warm colour forced to an unnatural intensity, qualities which impressed themselves upon the spontaneous outgoings of his sympathies when face to face with nature, but giving his pictures a certain artificial and made look. On the other hand their refined handling, rich low tone and varnish quality, added to the respect for and skilful use of traditional design fit them admirably alongside pictures of the older schools' [Halsby]. Elected ROI 1897, ARSA 1892, RSA 1903. Exhibited RSA(134), RA(20), RSW(1), ROI(18), GI(37), AAS 1890-1912 & L(7). Represented in Tate AG, NGS, City of Edinburgh collection(2).
**Bibl:** AJ 1890, 159; Conn 1919, 99; Halsby 132,277; Macmillan [SA] 254,262,266; Studio 58 (1913) 66; 64 (1915) 60; 65 (1915) 100ff; 68 (1916) 125; 70 (1917) 44; 73 (1918) 73; 92 (1926) 53.

**NOGUES, J** **fl 1842**
Edinburgh painter of portraits and genre. Exhibited RSA(4) from 93 Princes St.

**NOLAN, Geoffrey** **fl 1982-1984**
Aberdeen painter of semi-abstract works. Exhibited AAS(2) from 168 Crown St.

**NOLAN, John** **fl 1938-1939**
Dundee painter. Exhibited RA(1) & RSA(1) from 22 Urquhart St.

**NOON, Martin** **fl 1981-1983**
Glasgow painter. Exhibited GI(6) from Bearsden.

**NORIE, Miss Christina** **fl 1870**
Perth animal painter; exhibited 'The rival pets' at the RSA.

**THE NORIE FAMILY**
Members of the the family were the leading decorative and landscape painters in Scotland during the first half of the 18th century. Their business was founded by James Norie and continued for four generations until eventually sold 1850. However, only members of the first two generations were artists of note in their own right and of these only two, James 'Old Norie' (1684-1757), the founder of the firm, and his younger son Robert (after 1711-1766) can be said to have an identifiable style of their own.
**Bibl:** Caw 23,40,159,196; Gifford 211,626,639; James Holloway, The Norie Family, Scottish Masters no. 20, 1994; Irwin 126-8,129, 134,192,233,242.

James Norie (Old Norie)
1684-1757

George N
fl 1740-1760

Robert Norie II
1766-1821

Robert Norie III

James N yngr
1711-1736

Robert Norie I m Jean Yetts
1711-1766

John Norie
fl 1774

**NORIE, George** **d pre-1763**
Painter and decorator. Son of James Norie the 1st. In 1742 was made a Burgess of Edinburgh and five years later a member of the Incorporation of St Mary's. He died some time before 1763.

**NORIE, James** **1684-1757**
Born Knockando, Morayshire; died Edinburgh. Father of James Norie Jnr(qv). Founder member with his son, Academy of St Luke(qv), established in Edinburgh 1729. Admitted a Freeman of St Mary's Chapel, Incorporated Trades of Edinburgh 1708 and two years later had taken on his first apprentice, Alexander Miller(qv). Largely responsible for establishing the prosperous family firm of interior decorators who collaborated with architects in the design and execution of decoration including landscape canvases, murals and panels. Best known for mountains and waterfalls, often with classical ruins. The firm employed and trained assistants among whom were James Howe(qv), Alexander Runciman(qv) and John Wilson(qv). In 1718 he painted the chimney-piece in the convening house of St Mary's Chapel and during the next two years was working for the Earl of Hopetoun. Friend of the poet Allan Ramsay and in 1721 subscribed to the first edition of Ramsay's poems. In the 20s he continued working at Hopetoun and at Marchmont. In 1729 signed the Charter establishing the Academy of St Luke. His earliest known canvas is 1756 but its whereabouts is no longer known. Often difficult to know whether canvases signed James Norie are by the father or one or both sons. In 1743 became Deacon of the Wrights. In the late 40s his firm was working for the government at Fort William and in 1750 at Fort Augustus and Edinburgh Castle. In 1753 he received 5 gns for painting the organ at St Cecilia's Hall and the following year sketched a coat of arms for Robert Adam. A view of Melrose is inscribed on the back 'James Norie 1757'. An interesting classical landscape with trees and lake 1736 is in the NGS and a similar classical landscape with women bathing is in Aberdeen AG. An interesting view of 'Biel House near Dunbar', painted probably in the 1740s for the 4th Lord Belhaven in a private collection, was executed in grisaille, although again there is some doubt as to which member of the family was actually responsible. Another interesting decorative landscape in a beautifully ornate frame is in Caroline Park, Edinburgh. Represented in NGS, SNPG ('Self-portrait' and 'Panorama of Taymouth Castle').
**Bibl:** Brydall 108,111,159,162; Gifford 558; Daniel A Werschmidt, James Norie, privately printed Edinburgh 1890; Holloway 145; Irwin; Macmillan [SA] 73-4,84-7.

**NORIE, George W** **fl 1833**
Watercolourist. Possibly a member of the celebrated family of painters and decorators. Represented in the NGS by two works, the study of a bootblack and an old man with a stick, both signed and dated 1833.

**NORIE, James, Jnr** **1711-1736**
Born Knockando, Morayshire; died Edinburgh. Decorative and landscape painter in Edinburgh. Eldest son of James Norie, he signed the Charter of the Academy of St Luke in 1729 the year of its establishment. Travelled to London with his brother Robert(qv) to study under George Lambert. No work can now be identified for certain although a number of canvases attributed to his father might be his.
**Bibl:** J Holloway, 'Robert Norie in London and Perthshire', Conn, Jan 1978; Macmillan [SA] 86-7,119.

**NORIE, John** **1766-1821**
Recorded as born and died Edinburgh. Son of Robert Norie I. Elected Burgess of Edinburgh 1825 and a Guild Brother 1841. No work of his is now known.
**Bibl:** McKay, 187.

**NORIE, John** **fl 1774**
Aberdeen painter whose advertisement appeared in the *Aberdeen Journal* 7.iii.1774 saying that he was in partnership with James Wales of Banff and that 'they undertook house, landskip, ornament, coach and sign-painting and guilding'.

**NORIE, Marie L J RSW** **fl 1880-1889**
Edinburgh watercolour painter of landscapes, portraits and rustic scenes. Particularly fond of Arran. Elected RSW 1887. Exhibited frequently RSA(12) & RSW from Coltbridge Hall, Murrayfield, Edinburgh.
**Bibl:** Halsby 277.

**NORIE, Orlando** **1832-1901**
Military artist and illustrator. Descendant of the celebrated Edinburgh family of artist-designers. Spent his entire working life in England, retaining a studio in Aldershot. Best known for his accurate and finely detailed portrayal of British regimental costume, custom and history. Illustrated *The Memoirs of the 10th Royal Hussars* (R S Liddell, 1891). Exhibited two works at the RA in 1882 & 1884 - 'The Battle of Ulundi'; 'Charge of the 17th Lancers and Tel-el-Kebeer, 13th September 1882'. Represented in V & A, Royal collection, Nat Army Museum, India Office library and many regimental museums.
**Bibl:** Houfe.

**NORIE, Robert I** **1711-1766**
Landscape painter. He trained in London under George Lambert to whom he was sent with his brother James(qv). After the dissolution of the Academy of St Luke(qv) they were forced to seek work outside Scotland but by the early 1740s they were back in Edinburgh. In 1747 he was a Guild Member of the Incorporation of St Mary's taking on as apprentices Cumming in 1747 and Alexander Runciman(qv) 1750. Signed and dated two of four decorative landscapes now in the Duke of Hamilton's apartments at Holyrood. One is Ben Lawers as seen from the east end of Loch Tay and the other a waterfall and castellated ruins. Painted identifiable Scottish views of the sort George Lambeth had been painting in the 1730s. Alexander Runciman(qv) and Jacob More(qv) were among his pupils.
**Bibl:** J Holloway, 'Robert Norie in London and Perthshire', Conn Jan, 1978; Irwin 106,126,131,134; Macmillan [SA] 86,110,133-4; [GA] 137-8.

**NORIE, Robert II** **fl 1742-1747**
Son of Robert Norie I. Elected a Burgess of Edinburgh in 1742, member, Incorporation of St Mary's 1747. No work attributed to him with certainty remains.

**NORIE, Robert III** **fl 1840-1850**
Landscape painter. The last member of the family to be associated with the decorative business, it was he who sold it. Exhibited 25 landscapes at the RSA and one at the RA in 1846 - 'Dort on the Meuse', from 30 St James's Square, Edinburgh.

**NORMAN, Brian** **fl 1979**
Edinburgh painter; exhibited 'Thaumaturgus' at the RSA.

**NORMAN, George Mathieson** **1919-?**
Landscape painter. Exhibited RSA in 1968 & 9 from Fraserburgh; also GI(20) some of the time from Glasgow.

**NORMAN, Richard** **fl 1977-**
Painter of topographical subjects and genre. Son of George N(qv). Exhibits GI(5) since 1977.

**NORQUAY, Brenda** **fl 1980**
Orcadian painter of local landscapes. Trained Gray's School of Art, Aberdeen. Exhibited AAS from Holland, S. Ronaldsay.

**NORRIE, Miss Daisy M** **1899-?**
Born Fraserburgh, 10 Jne. Etcher, aquatinter and dry point artist. Studied Aberdeen Art School gaining a travelling scholarship enabling her to visit Italy. Between 1919 and 1923 living at 77 Bon-Accord St, Aberdeen from where she exhibited eleven local scenes and etchings at the AAS. Settled in London and exhibited 1924-25 RSA(3) & GI(1) from 28 Cross Street, Fraserburgh. In the mid-1970s she moved to Buckley, Cheshire.

**NORST, Miss Ellen** **fl 1932**
Glasgow amateur watercolour painter; exhibited RSW(1) from 2 Kensington Gate.

**NORTHEY, Mrs Elma (née Thomson)** **1876-**
Born Glasgow, 4 Nov. Watercolour painter of landscape, flowers and still life. Lived for a time in Callander, Perthshire before settling in Ayr. Exhibited 1900-1940 at the RSA(4), RI(5), GI(3), RSW(1), L(2) & London Salon(3).

**NORTON, C** **fl 1718-1722**
Edinburgh engraver. Possibly father of the engraver **Christopher NORTON** who studied in Rome 1769. Subscribed to Nisbet's *Essay on...Armories,* 1718. Engraved plates for *Nisbet's System of Heraldry,* 1722.
**Bibl:** Bushnell.

**NORTON, Marjorie** **fl 1928**
Exhibited 'Mademoiselle' at the RSA from 20 Dalkeith Street, Joppa.

**NOTMAN, Marion** **1952-**
Born Portobello. Painter of interiors, still life and landscape. Trained Edinburgh College of Art 1970-75, winning a travelling scholarship 1975. Since 1991 paints full-time from Tain. First solo exhibition 1992 followed a year later by her first exhibit RSA. Represented in Robert Gordon Institute, Aberdeen.

**NOVICE, George William** **fl 1849-1871**
Edinburgh-based painter in oil of landscape, still life, dead game, fruit and birds. Brother of Percival N(qv). Moved from London to settle in Edinburgh c1834. Exhibited RA(3) from various London addresses 1828-33, & RSA (31) thereafter.

**NOVICE, Percival** **fl 1858-1868**
Edinburgh-based oil painter of landscape and interiors. Brother of George William N(qv). Exhibited RSA(4). Represented in SNPG.

**NUGENT, Mrs Jane (née MacTaggart)** **1947-**
Landscape painter. Niece of Sir William MacTaggart(qv).

**NUTTER, William Henry** **1821-1872**
Edinburgh painter in oil of landscapes, generally in the Carlisle & Dumfries areas, on the continent, and elsewhere in Scotland. Exhibited RSA(17) & GI(9). Represented in Glasgow AG.

**OAKE, Herbert Walter** **fl 1922-1931**
Painter and teacher. Trained Edinburgh College of Art, RSA Schools and Royal College of Art. Painted mainly in watercolour and for many years lived in Kings Lynn, Norfolk. Exhibited RA(1), RSA(5) & RSW(2).

**OAKES, John Wright ARA HRSA** **1820-1887**
Born Sproston House, Middlewich, Cheshire, Jly 9; died Leam House, Addison Rd, London, Jly 9. Landscape painter, mainly in North Wales although also undertaking a tour in Switzerland and occasionally in Scotland. Moved early in life to Liverpool where he was educated and apprenticed to a house painter. First exhibit was a picture of fruit at the Liverpool Academy 1839. Four years later began landscape painting, an occupation he was able to pursue full-time from c1846. Elected a full member of Liverpool Academy 1850 and in 1853 became Secretary. His landscapes are naturalistic, in the tradition of Leader and Vicat Cole. Visited Deeside 1864 and again in 1870, painting 'The falls of the Garrawalt, Balmoral' during the first visit RA 1865 and the 'Linn of Muick' RA 1871 during the second. After being elected ARA 1876 he was one of the few painters who used photography to develop the precision and freshness of feeling in landscape painting. This was recognised by the Scottish artistic establishment who in 1883 elected him HRSA. Remained a considerable influence on succeeding generations of Scottish landscape painters. A contemporary described him as a 'man of sturdy appearance, more like a sea-captain than a painter, much marked by small-pox, and addicted to wearing black satin waistcoats'. Habitually carried his left hand in his pocket and, unlike most artists, never allowed anyone watch him paint. Exhibited RA(90), RSA(59) from 1849, including 'On the Sannox Water' 1856, 'A Creek on the Leven' 1863, 'The foot of Goatfell, Arran' 1864; also GI(30). Represented in Glasgow AG.
**Bibl:** AJ 1879, 193-6; 1887, 287 (obit); Bryan; Caw 233; Marillier 182-8 (pl p186); Portfolio 1887, 186 (obit).

**OAKESHOTT, Sheila (Mrs Kelly)** **fl 1959-1970**
Aberdeenshire designer; favoured floral motifs. Exhibited designs at the AAS(12) from Prospect Cottage, Westhills, Skene.

**OATES, Ian Richard** **1950-**
Born Perthshire. Painter of wildlife and sporting scenes, especially deer-stalking, primarily in watercolours. Trained Gray's School of Art 1968-72. Awarded Hospitalfield scholarship. First solo exhibition London 1981, with others following regularly in England and Scotland. Spends time each year as a professional stalker, giving him an intimate understanding of the sport in its varied and changing scenery. Illustrated two stalking classics, 'Lays of the Forest' (1985) and 'The High Tops of Black Mount' (1987). His studies of dogs, although fewer than his stalking subjects, are finely executed and popular. Recently commissioned to paint two ceilings in a Robert Adam mansion. Keen curler and former captain, Comrie Cricket Club.

**O'BRIEN, L R PRCA** **fl 1890**
Edinburgh landscape painter; exhibited AAS(2) from 108 George St.

**O'BRIEN, Nora (Mrs Charles Chadwick)** **fl 1944-**
Painter of portraits, flowers and topographical scenes, especially in France, latterly structured semi-abstracts. Trained Edinburgh College of Art. After two years in Paris, where she was awarded a *mention honorable* at the Salon des Artistes Français, joined the staff of Edinburgh College of Art. Following marriage and a period in Liverpool from 1954, moved to Aberdeen 1968. Exhibited RSA(27) & GI(2).

**OCHTERLONY, Miss** **fl 1812**
Landscape painter. Exhibited 'A View on the North Esk and Grampian Hills' at the RA in 1812 from an address in London. Possibly the same **Henrietta OCHTERLONY**, an engraver working in Scotland during the early nineteenth century.

**OCHTERLONY, Miss C A** **fl 1894**
Edinburgh amateur portraitist. Exhibited AAS(1) from 2 Eildon St.

**OCHTERLONY, Sir Matthew Montgomerie Bt ARSA FRIAS FRIBA** **1880-1946**
Born Juniper Green, Edinburgh, 28 Feb; died Edinburgh, 4 Oct. Architect. Also a skilled craftsman in metal, wood, and stained glass. Educated in Edinburgh and privately, he was apprenticed to John Kinross and thereafter assisted Lorne Campbell until 1916. After the war was assistant to F E B Blanc(qv) and Dick Peddie(qv). Commenced practice on his own account c1927, subsequently becoming a partner with H O Tarbolton(qv). Succeeded to the title 1931. Among his works are the Warrior's Chapel in Old St Paul, Jeffrey St (1924-6); additions to St Cuthbert's (1934); Commercial Bank of Scotland and St Ninian's Cathedral, Perth. Lived all his life in Edinburgh. In 1939 elected ARSA , also member, Institute of British Engineers. Exhibited RSA(9) & GI(2).
**Bibl:** Gifford 166-7,514,521-2,580.

**O'CULAIN, Calum Edmund** **fl 1984**
Aberdeenshire-based sculptor. Exhibited once at the AAS while resident in Lumsden at the Scottish Sculpture Workshop.

**ODLING, Elizabeth** **fl 1955**
Stirlingshire painter; exhibited 'The pinetum 'at the RSA; also GI(2), from Fintry.

**ODLING, Henry Edward ARCA** **1921-?**
Born Sheffield. Painter of still life and landscapes. Trained Sheffield and Glasgow School of Art. Executed murals at Chatelherault Visitor Centre, Hamilton, Lanarks. Lived Isle of Lismore, Argyll. Exhibited RSA(5), at first whilst at Glasgow School of Art, after 1949 from 13 Huntly Gdns, Glasgow; also GI(17) 1949-80.

**O'DONNELL, Roanne** **1965-**
Born St Andrews. Painter in various media. Trained Edinburgh College of Art 1983-88 and in Barcelona. Recipient of various international commissions including from Italy, Spain, USA & Scotland. Commissioned by the Scottish Office for commemorative work at St Andrew's House, Edinburgh.

**O'DONNELL, Ron** **1952-**
Born Stirling. Innovative photographer. Trained University of Stirling 1970-76 since when he has worked as a technical photographer in the Civil Engineering Department of Edinburgh University. During the 1970s and early 80s he photographed the decaying interiors of old-fashioned shops and slum dwellings. In about 1984 he began making alterations to the interiors of disused buildings, adding Surrealist-inspired motifs - Egyptian frescoes were painted over the peeling wallpaper of a tenement interior; a cardboard nuclear mushroom cloud appears in the middle of the sitting room. Adapts existing interiors rather than creating entirely new settings. Shown at many exhibitions in Britain and held a solo exhibition in Edinburgh 1985. In 1987 he created the tableau for 'The Great Divide' at the SNGMA. Represented at the SNGMA.
**Bibl:** Hartley 153; SAC, 'The Vigorous Imagination', (Ex Cat 1987); The Photographers' Gallery, London, 'Constructed Narratives: Photographs by Calum Colvin and Ron O'Donnell', (Ex Cat 1986).

**O'FLAHERTY, Mrs Charlotte G** **fl 1933**
Portrait miniaturist, probably an amateur. Exhibited GI(3) from Millport, Isle of Cumbrae, Bute.

**OGG, A C A** **fl 1957-1961**
Glasgow watercolourist; mostly foreign topographical subjects. Exhibited GI(6).

**OGG, Bessie F A** **fl 1923**
Aberdeen painter of local landscape. Wife of Robert O(qv). Exhibited AAS from 6 Hammerfield Ave.

**OGG, James** **fl 1935-1941**
Aberdeen landscape artist. Exhibited RSA(2) & AAS(2) from 11 Springbank Terrace.

**OGG, Robert A** **fl 1888-1929**
Aberdeen landscape & still life painter. Husband of Bessie O(qv). Exhibited a still life of vegetables at the RSA(1) & local landscapes at the AAS, from 26 Stanley Street.

**OGILVIE, Charles H E** **fl 1903-1928**
Portrait painter. Lived in Glasgow and Ayrshire. Exhibited RSA(2), L(1) & GI(11) mainly from Saltcoats.

**OGILVIE, Mrs Clare Mary** **fl 1930-1938**
Portrait miniature painter; exhibited RMS(7).

**OGILVIE, Elizabeth** **1946-**
Born Aberdeen. Sculptor and draughtsman. Trained Edinburgh College of Art 1964-69 specialising in sculpture under Eric Schilsky(qv). Completed a postgraduate course 1969-70, received a postgraduate award in 1974 and the SAC major award 1977. Turned increasingly from low relief to pure monochrome drawings on paper. First solo exhibition was in Edinburgh 1974. President, SSA 1981-3. Visiting lecturer, Hull and Glasgow School of Art; currently lecturer at Edinburgh College of Art, living in Leith. Essentially an artist of the sea, its associations having been for many years an intrinsic part of her art. Progressed through figurative sculpture to pure landscape in white plaster relief, an austerity translated directly into two dimensions. Her first essays in this form of landscape were in the medium she still employs: monochromatic drawing, creating images with only shallow space on large sheets of paper. Together with others of her generation in Edinburgh, (Michael Docherty(qv), Eileen Lawrence(qv) and especially Will McLean(qv)), she reacted against the loose painterliness of the previous generation. The colour in her work when it appears is very slight, the merest fleck. Her main source of inspiration is from the wild seascapes around the lighthouse at Point of Stoer, Sutherland which she and Bob Callender(qv) own. Since 1984 has been using a wash and collage plus the use of acetate cheesecloth. This was used, for example, in her first book of Haiku poems. Some of her latest work has been on a very large scale with St Kilda (the home of her maternal grandfather) used as a new source of imagery. Represented in SNGMA, Glasgow AG.
**Bibl:** Hartley 153-4; Macmillan [SA] 396,398; SAC, 'Watermarks', (Ex Cat 1980, Text by Robert Callender & Elizabeth Ogilvie); Talbot Rice Centre, Edinburgh, 'Sea Papers', (Ex Cat 1984); Talbot Rice Centre, Edinburgh 'Sea Sanctuary', (Ex Cat 1988).

**OGILVIE, Frederick Dove** **fl 1875-1917**
Edinburgh painter in watercolour of landscapes and coastal scenes. Moved to England at the turn of the century settling first in Harrogate 1901 and subsequently at Dunster, Somerset c1914. Exhibited RA(1), RSA(11), RSW(7), RI(4), RHA(1), GI(12) & L(4).

**OGILVIE, Frederick F** **fl 1907-1920**
Watercolour landscape painter; travelled extensively in the Middle East based in London. Exhibited RA(1) & RSA(2) but mainly at Walker's Gallery, London (100+).

**OGILVIE, George** **?-1723**
Scottish painter. Born deaf and dumb. Remarkably little seems to be known of this artist who in 1703 was appointed His Majesty's Limner in Scotland. In 1715 he took part in the Jacobite Rising and in 1719 a petition to restore to him his salary as His Majesty's Limner appears to have succeeded because on his death in 1723 there was a rivalry between Jervas(qv) and Aikman(qv) for the succession.

**OGILVIE, J C** **fl 1835-1858**
Aberdeen painter in oil of marines and landscapes; exhibited RSA (6), including 'Battle of St Vincent from the description of Capt Maryatt in his work, *Peter Simple'* 1858.

**OGILVIE, J D** **fl 1885**
Edinburgh watercolour landscape painter; exhibited 'In the Hermitage glen' at the RA in 1885 from 1 Bellhaven Terrace, Edinburgh.

**OGILVIE, Miss J M** **fl 1907-1941**
Edinburgh topographical, flower and portrait painter in oil and watercolour. Sister of Lilian(qv) and R Ogilvie(qv). Exhibited RSA (7), RSW(4) & GI(10) & a miniature portrait of the 'Hon Mrs Dalrymple' at the AAS in 1910, latterly from 14 Campbell Ave.

**OGILVIE, Miss Lily (Lilian) L APRMS** **fl 1924-1945**
Edinburgh painter of portrait miniatures, landscape & birds. Lived with her sister J M Ogilvie(qv). A finely executed portrait of 'Lady Mary Baillie', daughter of the Earl of Haddington, painted in the 1940s, is illustrated in Foskett: *Collecting Miniatures,* p457. Exhibited RSA(12), mostly harbour and street scenes in France & Cornwall, and animals and flowers, also GI(17) & AAS(8), latterly from 14 Campbell Ave.

**OGILVIE, R** **fl 1933**
Edinburgh miniaturist. Exhibited RSA(1) from 16 Coatbridge Terrace, Edinburgh. Probably brother of the Misses J M(qv) and Lilian L(qv).

**OGILVIE, Sara** **1971-**
Born Edinburgh, Feb 24. Printmaker & illustrator. Trained Edinburgh College of Art 1989-94, where she later taught part-time. Awards include Heriot Watt prize for 1991-92, Watt Club Medal 1993, Edinburgh Printmaker's Workshop 'Homage to Senefelder' 1996. First solo exhibition 1994. Exhibited Belgrade, Germany, Int. Centre for Graphic Arts, Ljubljana & London. Member of Printmaker's Workshop since 1994.

**OGILVIE, Miss V** **fl 1894-1921**
Perthshire painter of figurative compositions. Exhibited AAS(4) from Inchture and later Ballyoukan Lodge, Pitlochry.

**OGILVIE, William FRIAS** **c1895-1939**
Edinburgh architect, draughtsman and humorous poet. Trained Edinburgh College of Art. Member Scottish Arts Club. Published a volume of poems (Porpoise Press). Exhibited RSA(3) from 10 Cameron Park, including a book plate for the 9th Batt, Royal Scots.
**Bibl:** Scotsman, 31 Jan 1939(obit).

**OGILVIE, W A** **fl 1933**
Amateur watercolourist; exhibited RSW(4).

**OGILVY, James** **fl 1846-1871**
Edinburgh painter in oil of landscapes and figurative subjects, among his paintings were several studies of Rabiis, one exhibit being described by an anonymous contemporary critic as 'awful', 1867. Exhibited RSA(14).

**OGILVY Miss N (or Violet)** **fl 1888-1904**
Dundee painter in oil and watercolour of figurative subjects. Exhibited RSA(4) & RSW(1), latterly from Baldovan, Strathmartine.

**OGSTON, Miss Elliot M** **20th Cent**
Aberdeenshire painter of flowers, figurative works and landscape; exhibited AAS(5) from Ardoe House, Aberdeen.

**OGSTON, Thomas** **fl 1846-1847**
Edinburgh figurative painter; exhibited RSA(3).

**OLDRIEVE, William Thomas HRSA** **1853-1922**
Architect. Employed for many years at HM Office of Works, Edinburgh. Partner in Oldrieve, Bell & Paterson. His Majesty's Principal Architect for Scotland 1904-14. Elected HRSA 1914. Among his most important work were a new roof and oak carvings for Glasgow Cathedral (1913) and an extension to Edinburgh's General Post Office (1908-9).
**Bibl:** Gifford 70,121,124,144,147,187,258,283,288-9,301,437, 511, 576.

**OLIPHANT, Alexander G** **fl 1934-1936**
Grangemouth portrait painter. Exhibited RSA(2) from 25 Marshall St.

**OLIPHANT, Miss Janet Mary** **fl 1895-1900**
Forfarshire painter of narrative subjects and portraits; exhibited AAS (2) from Elmwood, Lochee. A pencil and chalk drawing of the novelist 'Margaret Oliphant (1828-1897)', signed & dated 1895, is in SNPG.

**OLIPHANT, John** **fl 1732**
Scottish portraitist about whom very little is now known. The portrait

of an unknown gentleman appeared in an Edinburgh saleroom 1956 signed & dated 'Johannes Oliphant, 1732', the negative of which is in SNPG.

**OLIPHANT, John** **fl 1832-1843**
Edinburgh painter of landscape and portraits; worked in both oils and watercolour. Painted many Highland scenes, often with cattle, especially on Arran. Exhibited RSA between the above years, latterly from Shakespeare Sq.
**Bibl:** Halsby 277.

**OLIVER, Catherine** **fl 1927**
Painter. Exhibited once at Manchester City AG from an address in Argyll.

**OLIVER, Miss Dora M** **fl 1885-1890**
Edinburgh painter in oil and watercolour, mostly flowers; exhibited RSA(4) & AAS(1) from Moston Terrace, Mayfield.

**OLIVER, Dorothy** **fl 1905-1914**
Painter of interiors and portrait medallions. Exhibited RSA(3) - including 'Interior of St Mary's Cathedral, Edinburgh' and two portrait medallions; also GI(1) & L(4), from Liberton House, and latterly Greenend, Glasgow.

**OLIVER, Miss E A (Lizzie)** **fl 1896-1902**
Glasgow-based painter of topographical and pastoral subjects. Exhibited GI(5).

**OLIVER, Miss L Campbell** **fl 1900-1901**
Edinburgh landscape artist. Exhibited two views in the Cramond area of Edinburgh at the RSA from Olive Lodge, Polwarth Terrace.

**OLIVER, George A** **fl 1947**
Glasgow amateur watercolourist. Exhibited 'Faiz Bazar, Delhi' at GI.

**OLIVER, Thomas** **1791-1857**
Born Crailing Hall, nr Jedburgh, 14 Jan; died Newcastle, Dec. Architect and cartographic draughtsman. Son of a weaver. Educated Jedburgh School before moving as a young man to Newcastle-upon-Tyne where he was assistant to John Dobson and where he remained for the rest of his life. Thus all his work was undertaken in England. In 1814 married Margaret Lorimer, the daughter of a Kelso mason. In 1821 set himself up in independent practice. Although best known for his maps of Newcastle, he shares with Dobson the credit for much of the early 19th century development of the city. In 1824 he designed two houses for John Baird at the entrance to Elswick Court from Northumberland Street, which he claimed to be the first stone-fronted dwelling-houses built in Newcastle for more than a century. He was consulted by the Common Council in connection with the laying out of the new streets between Newgate and the Fickett Tower and the new houses in Blackett Street were built in accordance with his plans. Designed Leazes Crescent and the adjoining houses, and the large block known as Leazes Terrace, begun 1829. Designed the Londonderry Institute at Seaham Harbour, Durham, executed in the Greek Doric style. Four sons, **Adam** (b1815), **James** (b1820), **Thomas** (b1824) and **John** (b1826). Thomas practised as an architect in Sunderland until 1857 when he returned to Newcastle, later becoming the founder of the firm of Oliver Leeson and Wood. Adam and James both became civil engineers. In addition to the plans of Newcastle issued in 1830, 1844, 1849, 1851, and (posthumously) in 1858, Oliver was the author of *The Geographical Synopsis of the World*, also *A Topographical View of Great Britain and Ireland,* both pre-1831, and *A New Picture of Newcastle upon Tyne* (1831). Also published a *Reference* to accompany his maps of 1830 and 1844, and in 1851 *The Topographical Conductor, or Descriptive Guide to Newcastle and Gateshead.*
**Bibl:** Colvin; Jones and Honeyman, 'Thomas Oliver and his Plans for Central Newcastle', Archaeologia Aeliana, xxix, 4th ser., 1951.

**OLIVER, Mrs Torfrida** **fl 1942-1953**
Selkirkshire watercolour painter. Generally worked in England and Malta. Exhibited GI(5) from Kelso.

**OLIVIA, Miss Pauline** **fl 1966-1969**
Edinburgh sculptress. Exhibited in bronze and fibreglass at the GI (3), from Merchiston Crescent.

**O'NEIL, Bernard** **fl 1951-1955**
Edinburgh sculptor. Exhibited RSA(8) during the above period such titles as 'Bull moose', 'Siesta' - lignum vitae, 'Bronco buster' and 'Ballerina', from 14 Warrender Park Cr.

**O'NEIL, Francis** **fl 1844**
Edinburgh landscape painter; exhibited RSA(1), from 16 Queen St.

**ONWIN, Glen ARSA** **1947-**
Born Edinburgh. Studied painting at Edinburgh College of Art 1966-71. Near the end of his studies began experimenting with natural chemical substances applying, for example, salt on to papier mâché. In March 1973 he discovered a salt marsh near Dunbar and was immediately struck by the constantly changing nature of the marsh as the tide altered the shape and size of the pools and the plant life gradually died. He photographed the site at different times and from different angles, evoking a sense of natural decay in drawings and constructions on to which he applied wood, glass, wax and salt itself. In this way he created salt as a symbol, a life-giving force and a destroying substance. Works based on this idiosyncratic discovery formed the basis of a 1975 SAC touring exhibition and led to the introduction of a further variety of natural substances in the 1980s. Recently elected ARSA. Exhibited RSA & widely in group and one man shows; also AAS(2). Represented in SNGMA, SAC.
**Bibl:** FMG, Edinburgh, 'Revenges of Nature:Glen Onwin' (Ex Cat 1988); Gage 76-8; Hartley 154; Inst. of Cont. Arts, London, 'Essentials for Life...The Recovery of Dissolved Substances' (Ex Cat 1978, Essay by David Brown); Macmillan [SA] 396,399; Glen Onwin, Saltmarsh, Edinburgh 1974; Glen Onwin, The Recovery of Dissolved Substances, Bristol, 1978; SAC, 'Glen Onwin Saltmarsh', (Ex Cat 1975, Text by David Brown).

**OPPENHEIMER, Charles RSA RSW** **1876-1961**
Born Manchester; died Kirkcudbright 16 Apr. Painter of landscapes in oil and watercolour, especially Ayrshire and Kircudbright, also Florence & Venice. Son of Ludwig O (who had been engaged in mosaic decoration of cathedral interiors). Trained under R H A Willis and Walter Crane at the Manchester School of Art, subsequently in Italy. Served with the Royal Artillery during WW1 and after the war returned to live in Kirkcudbright, next door to his friend EA Hornel(qv). There he remained for the rest of his life. His work depicted the changing seasons. An enthusiastic angler, he established himself as a sensitive painter of nature, quiet pastoral views and running water, preferring the gentler moorlands and fields of the south-west of Scotland to the more rugged Highlands. Designed a number of posters for British Rail, using local beauty spots as his subjects, and the badge and motto of the Scottish Police Force 'Semper Vigilo'. Was himself a member of the Special Constabulary. A well-known figure in the artistic community. Elected ARSA in 1927, RSA 1934, RSW 1912. Exhibited RA(46), RSA(83), RSW(98), GI(74), AAS 1929-1937 & L(17), latterly from 14 High St, Kircudbright. Represented in SNPG (portrait of 'W S McGeorge'), Glasgow AG, City of Edinburgh collection, Castle Douglas AG, Manchester AG(5).
**Bibl:** Halsby 229,277; RSA Obituary, 1961.

**ORAM, Ann RSW** **1956-**
Born London. Painter in watercolour, occasionally gouache, mixed media and sometimes oil. Trained Edinburgh College of Art 1976-82 obtaining an honours degree and a postgraduate diploma with distinction. In 1983 joined the staff of the College as a part-time lecturer remaining there for two years until 1985 began increasingly to teach privately. Elected RSW 1986. From 1987 settled in Spain for two years, painting assiduously. Her main influences have been the Scottish watercolour school of the mid-20th century: Redpath(qv), Gillies(qv), Maxwell(qv) and Blackadder(qv). Favoured subjects are interiors, architectural subjects and sketches done whilst travelling although more recently turned increasingly to flowers and portraiture. Exhibited often RSA since 1983; also GI(4) since 1986, from 39 Barony St, Edinburgh.

**ORCHAR, James Guthrie** **fl 1872-1885**
Broughty Ferry collector and painter in oil and watercolour of landscapes and seascapes, often in the Highlands and sometimes on the European continent. A great collector and benefactor of the arts, it is to him that Dundee Art Gallery owes its fine McTaggarts, Orchardsons,

Petties, Boughs and other Scottish painters of the time. In his Will he provided for the building and maintenance of Broughty Ferry AG. Lived at Angus Lodge, Broughty Ferry. Exhibited RSA(14).
**Bibl:** Caw 222; Irwin 337,344.

**ORCHARDSON, Charles** **fl 1854-d1917**
Edinburgh painter in oil of figure subjects; exhibited RSA(2).

**ORCHARDSON, Charles M Quiller ROI** **1873-1917**
Died London, 26 Apr. Painter in oil of portraits and landscapes. Son of Sir William Quiller O(qv). Painted several portraits of huntsmen in the saddle. Died of war wounds inflicted in the Middle East. Elected RBA 1902, ROI 1907. Exhibited RA(30), also ROI(15), RBA(6), GI(4), AAS(1896-1931) & L(13), after 1902 from 3 Wychcombe Studios, England's Lane, NW.
**Bibl:** Wingfield.

**ORCHARDSON, Sir William Quiller RA HRSA** **1832-1910**
Born Edinburgh, Mar 27; died London, Apr 13. Painter in oil of genre and portraits. Father of Charles M Q(qv). Of Highland descent, began studying at the Trustees Academy when only thirteen, staying to work under R Scott Lauder(qv) alongside his contemporary Thomas Faed(qv), a student until 1855. His early work is in the mainstream of Scottish genre, pictures such as 'The Flowers of the Forest' 1864, now in Southampton AG, and 'The Broken Tryst' in Aberdeen AG. Moved to London 1862, sharing a house with Tom Graham(qv) and John Pettie(qv), and began exhibiting at the RA the following year. At first he painted historical genre taken mainly from Shakespeare and Scott but later he turned to psychological dramas of upperclass life, such as 'Le Marriage de Convenance' and 'The First Cloud', for which he is now best remembered. There is a theatrical quality in the way he groups his figures and the feeling he has for the value of empty spaces and the elegant postures of so many of the subjects. His technique was equally refined and distinctive, using subdued colours - mostly yellow and brown 'as harmonious as the wrong side of an old tapestry' [Chesneau]. First came to prominence in 1877 with 'The Queen of the Swords' (a version of which is in the NGS), the title taken from the description of a character in Sir Walter Scott's *The Pirate.* His varied output included social scenes in 18th century costume, episodes of the revolutionary and Napoleonic periods - he was a great admirer of Napoleon, his 'Napoleon On board the *Bellerophon'* (now in the Tate Gallery) was a Chantrey Bequest in 1880. Painted many pictures illustrative of contemporary manners as well as a number of portraits. A Chevalier de Legion d'Honneur 1895. Knighted 1907, Hon RSA 1871. Among his best portraits are 'Mrs Ralli' RA 1885 and 'Mrs Joseph' 1887, both illustrating subtle individuality and a rich technique. 'Orchardson does not cover so much ground as Hogarth, he does not hit so hard a blow as Rembrandt, but the mantles of both touched him as they fell' [Armstrong]. Writing in the *AJ* Stevenson said his 'convention, though clever and original, stands in overwhelming proportion to his sentiment for nature. He is connected with truth by drawing chiefly; his colour, tone, air and light are many degrees removed from an interest in reality. He arranges all his pictorial elements, however, with unquestionable taste, and he always stamps his work with an unmistakeable individuality'. While Pinnington, also writing in the *AJ,* remarked that Orchardson 'paints action and expression, throws a volume into a gesture, a biography into a figure and face...he neither preaches in colour nor makes it the vehicle of homiletic prosing. He is essentially a well-bred man of the world, who leaves the curtain hanging over the dark places of life, and sees in passion chiefly a disagreeable disturbance of the tranquillity of culture'. Collected French furniture which he used as props in his paintings. He himself regarded 'Master Baby' (NGS) as his best work. Sickert had expressed admiration for this 'marvellous' picture and was puzzled that Degas whilst agreeing in principle, said that he had liked other things better. An occasional illustrator, he contributed to *Good Words* 1860-1 and again in 1878, and to *Touches of Nature* 1866. Elected ARA 1868, RA 1877, HRMS 1900, RP 1897, HRSA 1871. Exhibited AAS 1890-1931. Represented in NG, NGS, SNPG, Tate AG, Arbroath AG, Southampton AG, Broughty Ferry AG, Aberdeen AG, Forbes Magazine Collection, New York; Glasgow AG(7), Kirkcaldy AG, City of Edinburgh collection, Manchester AG(3), Florence (Offices); National Gallery of Victoria, Melbourne, Nat Gall of South Africa(Cape Town).
**Bibl:** AJ 1867, 212; 1870, 233 ff; 1894, 33 ff; Armstrong: The Art of W Q O (Portfolio mono) 1895, reprint 1904; Caw 236-240; Hilda Orchardson Grey, The Life of Sir W Q O (1830); Halsby 243; Hardie 58-62 et passim ch iv; Houfe; Irwin 339-342; Little, 'Life and Works of W Q O' Art Annual, 1897; J Maas passim; Macmillan [SA] 231-240 et passim.

**O'REGAN, H B** **fl 1873**
Sculptor. Exhibited 'Bust of Tenfeldsrock' at the GI.

**ORMAN, Alexander** **fl 1869-1870**
Edinburgh landscape painter in oil; exhibited RSA(4).

**ORMISTON, Eileen (Mrs Murray)** **1949-**
Born Glasgow, Nov 16. Printmaker, teacher, embroiderer. Trained Glasgow School of Art 1968-72. Founder member, Glasgow Print Studio. Retired from teaching 1989 in order to concentrate on drawing. Glasgow AG purchased 4 etchings 1972. First exhibited RSA 1973 and at RGI from 1989, from Napier Ave, Cardross.

**ORMOND, Mrs Kate** **fl 1900-1901**
Landscape painter; exhibited RSA(3) & GI(1) from Overton, Kilmacolm.

**ORMONDE, Kenneth D** **fl 1959**
Painter. Exhibited two works at the AAS whilst at Gray's School of Art, Aberdeen.

**ORPHOOT, Burnett Napier Henderson RSA** **1880-1964**
Born Peebles 13 Apr; died Murrayfield, Edinburgh, 8 Apr. Architect and etcher. Educated Rugby School and Edinburgh University. Proceeded to train at Edinburgh School of Applied Art and in Paris under Gustave Umbdenstack. His early work in London and Edinburgh brought him into contact with Sir Rowand Anderson(qv) and George Washington Browne(qv). Concentrated on domestic architecture, although responsible for Peebles War Memorial and the restoration of Haddington Episcopal Church. Partner in Orphoot, Whiting and Bryce who designed a select series of villas on the S side of Easter Belmont Rd. Elected ARSA 1936, RSA 1943. Exhibited RSA(10), GI(6), AAS(3), L(8) and regularly at the Paris Salon, latterly from 25 Queensferry St. Represented Glasgow AG.
**Bibl:** Gifford 632.

**ORPHOOT, Miss M J C** **fl 1907-1909**
Painter. Possibly related to Burnett O(qv). Exhibited RSA(2) & L(1) from Greenhithe, North Berwick.

**ORR, Agnes M** **fl 1887**
Edinburgh amateur still life painter; exhibited a work at the AAS from 3 Fingal Pl.

**ORR, Alex** **fl 1940s**
Glasgow painter of flowers and quiet pastoral scenes. Exhibited GI(5) from 15 Blythswood Square, then from Bellevue Rd, Ayr.

**ORR, Donald Macrae** **fl 1973**
Paisley amateur artist. Exhibited GI(2).

**ORR, Ina R** **fl 1883-1887**
Glasgow painter. Exhibited RHA(2) & GI(6) from 136 Wellington St.

**ORR, Miss J F** **fl 1888-1890**
Glasgow amateur painter; exhibited GI(3) from Langside.

**ORR, Jack** **1888-1961**
Painter in oil and watercolour of portraits, landscapes and animals, especially birds. Brother of Monro(qv) and Stewart Orr(qv). Trained Collegiate School, Glasgow and Hospitalfield, Arbroath. Illustrated a number of children's books including *Periwinkle* and *The Farmer's Boy.* Became Head of the College of Commercial Art in London, resigning at the outbreak of WW2 1939. His watercolours of parrots and exotic birds are often large and painted in a dashing style on silk or linen in the manner of Joseph Crawhall but without the latter's distinction. Completed a number of sporting subjects including lawn bowls ('A Good Delivery', 1919) and a coaching scene 'Happy Reunions at the Inn'. His figures were generally depicted in costume of an earlier period. Exhibited RA(1), RSA(7), RSW(11), GI(20) & L(1). Represented in Edinburgh City collection.
**Bibl:** Halsby 277; Wingfield.

**ORR, Miss Jackie** **fl 1978-1985**
Ayrshire painter, usually of still life. Probably daughter of James O(qv). Exhibited GI(10), from Prestwick.

**ORR, James R Wallace** **1907-?**
Painter and engraver of landscape, genre and topographical studies. Probably father of Jackie O(qv). Trained Glasgow School of Art 1929-33. Member SSA and Council member, Society of Artist Printmakers. Served in the Auxiliary Fire Service and RAF during WW2. Awarded Royal College of Physicians & Surgeons Prize (RGI) 1997. Exhibited RA(1), RSA(23) & GI(28), at first from Glasgow then in 1933 from Kircudbright, Helensburgh 1936 and finally Prestwick 1984-8. Represented in SNGMA.
**Bibl:** Mungo Campbell, 'The Line of Tradition', Nat Galls of Scotland, Ex cat, Edinburgh 1993.

**ORR, Jessie F** **fl 1888-1890**
Glasgow flower painter. Exhibited GI(3), from Langside.

**ORR, Monro Scott** **1874-1955**
Born Irvine, 7 Oct. Painter and etcher of figurative subjects, also illustrator. Brother of Jack and Stewart Orr(qv). Educated Bellahouston Academy and Glasgow School of Art. Painted mainly in watercolours using clear bold outlines and a simplified style. His illustrations appeared in several books including *The Arabian Nights* (1913), *Grimm's Fairy Tales, Mother Goose, Jane Eyre* (1921) and *Two Years Before the Mast.* Painted an alphabet, the original pictures being purchased by Queen Mary and hung in Queen Mary's Hospital for Sick Children. His work is characterised by care, clarity and precision. Exhibited RSA(2), RSW(3) & L(9) but mainly GI(28).
**Bibl:** Caw 468; Bertha E. Mahony et al, Illustrators of Children's Books 1744-1945, Boston(USA), 1948, 343.

**ORR, Patrick William** **fl 1889-1932**
Glasgow painter in watercolour of landscape and figurative subjects. Exhibited RA(2), RSA(4), RSW(1), AAS(2), GI(58) & L(5).

**ORR, Rosaleen (Mrs Mulhearn)** **fl 1956-1970**
Glasgow painter of portraits and genre. Exhibited GI(7).

**ORR, Stephen(s)** **fl 1980-1986**
Bute painter of flowers and topography. Exhibited GI(4), from Millport.

**ORR, William E A** **1907-?**
Glasgow amateur watercolourist of minor consequence; exhibited RSW(1) & GI(3) from Old Auchendrane, Bearsden.

**ORR, William Stewart RSW** **1872-1944**
Born Glasgow, Jan 21. Painter of landscape in watercolour and oil, book illustrator. Educated Bellahouston Academy, read architecture at Glasgow University before completing formal art studies at Glasgow School of Art. Lived for a time with his brother Monro Scott O(qv) at Corrie, on Arran. Having worked earlier in an Essex architect's office, later moved to the west and in addition to his love of Arran also painted Iona. Illustrated a number of children's books including *Two Merry Mariners* and *Gammon and Spinach.* Employed a bright palette lightly applied in fluid washes; especially good at portraying light on moving water. Elected RSW 1925. Exhibited RA(2), RSA(36), RSW(44), RI(6), GI(68), AAS & L(20), latterly from Corrie House, Corrie, Arran. Represented Glasgow AG, Manchester AG.
**Bibl:** Halsby 277; Houfe; Studio 'Modern Book Illustrators and Their Work', 1914.

**ORROCK, James RI** **1829-1913**
Born Edinburgh; died Shepperton, Middlesex, May 10. Painter in oil and watercolour of landscapes; collector, lecturer and writer. Educated at Irvine Academy, where he copied engravings and was taught by a drawing master called White. At Edinburgh University he studied medicine and dentistry. After qualifying as a dentist he studied art in Leicester under James Fergusson and John Burgess, and with Stewart Smith at the Nottingham School of Design until 1866, when he moved to London. Illustrated a number of works including Crockett's *In the Border Country* (1906) W Wood's *Mary Queen of Scots* (1906) and W Shaw Sparrow's *Old England* (1908). Went to London 1866, undertaking further studies with William Leighton Leitch(qv). Became a great admirer of David Cox whose style and subject matter were both reflected in his work. He himself thought that 'Bradgate Park near Leicester' was his best and most important watercolour drawing, (now, together with other works, in the V & A). Ardent collector of Chippendale furniture and Nankin porcelain, and was a patron of Thomas Collier. Elected ARI 1871, RI 1875, ROI 1883. Exhibited RA(3), RSW(1), RI(123), ROI(57), GI(1) and many works at the Fine Art Society. Represented in V & A, Cardiff AG, Cartwright Hall (Bradford), Leicester AG, Maidstone Museum, Newport AG, Castle Museum (Nottingham), Portsmouth City AG, Ulster Museum.
**Bibl:** Caw 156; Halsby 277; Hardie III 159-160; Houfe; Mag of Art 1904, 161-7; Studio 30 (1904) 360ff; Who's Who 1913-14.

**OSBORN, Miss Emily Mary** **1834-c1885**
Glasgow painter in oil and watercolour of portraits and genre. Prolific artist of considerable quality. Moved to London at an early age. Trained Dickinson's Academy, Maddox Street. Lived in Munich 1870-4 but continued to exhibit at the RA. Her work bordered on the tendentious but was typically Victorian in its fine attention to detail, slightly sullied by sentimentality. Exhibited RA(43) 1851-1884 including a rather romanticised version of 'The Escape of Lord Nithsdale from the Tower' 1716 1861; also RSA(3), SWA(58), GI(50+) & L(3).

**OSBORNE, Mrs Cherrie** **fl 1936**
Painter of flower studies and informal portraits. Exhibited 'Self-portrait' at the RSA & GI(1), from the Manse, Cockenzie and latterly Learmonth Terr, Edinburgh.

**O'SULLIVAN, Michael John** **fl 1982**
Aberdeen-based painter. Shared studio with Robert Ogg(qv). Exhibited AAS(3) from 13 Northfield Pl.

**OSWALD, John Harvey** **fl 1851-1899**
Edinburgh painter in oil of landscapes, coastal scenes. Father of Mary O(qv). Enjoyed the wilder aspects of nature. Occasionally included Highland cattle in his scenes but in these he was less successful. Worked occasionally in northern France. 'Banff Harbour in a Gale', exhibited RSA 1882, received favourable mention at the time. Exhibited RA(7) 1874-1890 including 'Highland Burn in Spate' 1884 and the dramatic 'Fast Castle' 1874, but mostly at the RSA(150+); also at the RSW(1), RHA(6), AAS, ROI(1), GI(50+) & L(5), latterly from 28 London St.

**OSWALD, Miss Mary** **fl 1888-1905**
Edinburgh painter in oil and watercolour, still life and brightly coloured rural scenery principally around Edinburgh and the Lothians. Daughter of John O(qv). Lived for a time at 28 London Street, Edinburgh. Exhibited RSA(41), GI(9) & AAS(5).

**OTTEWELL, Benjamin John HRI OWS** **1847-1937**
Born Streatham, Sep 11; died Bath, Mar 21. Watercolour painter of landscape. Trained South Kensington. For many years he spent a large part of every summer in Braemar, Aberdeenshire, painting scenes of the valley of the upper Dee being often guided to the most picturesque places by the head keeper of Mar Estate whom he befriended. These works, whilst occasionally woolly, capture the changing colours and moods of this part of the Highlands in watercolour more accurately than any other artist. Remembered as an irascible but dedicated bachelor artist. Queen Victoria thought highly of him, while taking tea at Danzig Shiel in June 1895 she 'saw some beautiful sketches by an artist by the name of Ottewell, who had spent several months in Braemar painting, having been snowed up for some weeks, in the winter, at the Linn of Dee'. Subsequently painted a number of watercolours for the Queen, and for the Prince of Wales and the Duke and Duchess of York. Like Everett Green before him, he taught Princess Beatrice. Elected Hon. RI 1895; founder member, Old English Watercolour Society. Committee member, Braemar Golf Club 1911-12. Exhibited RA(4), RI(21), RBA(1), RHA (1) & GI(1), from 11 Mansell Rd, Wimbledon. His watercolour of 'Danzig Shiel' 1896, a cottage on Balmoral estate, is in the Royal collection.

**OUDNEY, David** **fl 1987-1988**
Dundee painter of figurative subjects worked in a semi-abstract

manner with strong use of colour and with musical allusions in the titles eg 'Tennessee waltz' and 'Accordion girl'. Exhibited RSA(3).

**OVENS, James** **fl 1674**
Early painter. Son of a Tranent indweller. Apprenticed to Joseph Stane (or Stacie), painter. Possibly the **James HOVENS** who married a Janet Bruce 4 Jly 1679.
**Bibl:** Apted 48,69; Edinburgh Marriages 1595-1700, 339.

**OVENS, W Roberts jnr** **fl 1927**
Amateur watercolour painter; exhibited 'Ruins of St Mary's chapel', (Wales) at the RSA; also RSW(3) from an Edinburgh address.

**OVENSTONE, Margaret** **fl 1959-1961**
Aberdeen painter of still life and portraits. Exhibited AAS(2) from 212 Rosemount Pl.

**OVERWEG, Lily** **fl 1887**
Aberdeenshire-based painter; exhibited three portraits at the AAS from an address in Kincardine O'Neil.

**OWEN, G Elmslie** **fl 1929-1931**
Stirling painter of still life and topographical works. Exhibited AAS(3) from The Studio, Lovilands Gate.

**OWEN, G J** **fl 1887**
Glasgow amateur painter; exhibited GI(1) from 107 Buchanan St.

**OWEN, John J** **fl 1883-1887**
Minor Glasgow painter of still life and topographical studies. Exhibited GI(3) from 10 Corunna Street.

**OWER, Charles** **fl 1876-1939**
Dundee architect and topographical watercolourist. In popular partnership with his brother **Leslie OWER**(qv). Responsible for the florid Pearl Insurance Building, Meadowside, Dundee (1898). Exhibited RSA(7), including a design for the North of Scotland Bank, Lochee.
**Bibl:** Bruce Walker & W S Gauldie, Architects and Architecture on Tayside, Dundee 1984, 144.

**OZANNE, Mrs Pearl** **fl 1967-1970**
Aberdeen painter. Trained Gray's School of Art, Aberdeen. Exhibited highly coloured flower pieces and still lifes at the AAS(5) from Hillcrest, Shielhill.

# P

**PADDOCK, William** **fl 1892-1920**
Glasgow painter in oil and watercolour; flowers and portraits. Exhibited RSA(2), RA(3), RSW(3) & GI(14).

**PAGAN, Jack** **fl 1969-1970**
Dundee painter of still life. Exhibited RSA(3).

**PAGE, James** **fl 1887**
Portobello watercolour flower painter; exhibited 'Strawberry blossoms' at the RSA.

**PAGE, Jane L** **fl 1889**
Portobello amateur painter. Probably wife of James P(qv). Exhibited 'A corner of Park Neuk' at the RSA, from 2 Royal Terr.

**PAILLOU, Peter Jnr** **c1757-c1832**
Born Dec 1. Miniature portrait painter, sometimes larger portraits. Son of the bird painter Peter Paillou. Entered RA Schools 1784; exhibited RA(24) 1786-1800. Working in Glasgow 1820. Sitters were often painted against a sunset background; they are generally well executed with flesh colours smoothly painted, not stippled. Sometimes employed a foliage background. Foskett records the latest known work as dated 1831. Represented in NGS(3).
**Bibl:** Foskett; Waterhouse.

**PAIRMAN, George** **c1828**
Edinburgh landscape painter. In 4 April 1849 entered the Trustees Academy in Edinburgh having been recommended by William Alexander of Leith, but in 1850 he left. Exhibited from Edinburgh a view of the 'Mouse River, nr Lanark' at RSA 1850 and the following year, this time from Glasgow, a view in the west Highlands.

**PAIRMAN, John** **fl 1827-1880**
Born Biggar, Lanark. Edinburgh painter in oil and watercolour of landscapes, genre, rustic scenes and figures. Probably related to George P(qv). His name appears in the first Scottish Academy Catalogue, 1827. Preferred simple titles such as 'A woman resting'. Exhibited regularly at the RSA during the above years from various Edinburgh addresses. Three of his pencil drawings are in the NGS, all dating from 1835-6, all heightened with white. The SNPG has three portraits including 'Lord Jeffrey' (1773-1850) and 'Self-portrait'.

**PAIRMAN, John R** **fl 1868-1884**
Portobello landscape painter, particularly fond of sunsets often around Edinburgh. Exhibited RSA, latterly from Samiston Lodge, Portobello.

**PAISLEY ART INSTITUTE** **1876-**
Formed primarily for the purpose of holding exhibitions with occasional lectures and discussion groups arranged in association with the local public art gallery. Exhibitions held annually; local artists showing alongside others from Glasgow and Edinburgh, as well as from further afield by invitation. Three classes of membership: artists, honorary, and lay, the former two being elected. Since 1911 their collection has been on permanent loan to the Paisley Museum and Art Gallery. Many well-known artists began their exhibiting career in Paisley.
**Bibl:** Caw 212.

**PALMER, David** **fl 1989**
Exhibited 'Portrait of a megalith' at the RSA, from 103 Ralston Path, Glasgow.

**PALMER, Joan** **1941-1984**
Glasgow painter in watercolour and engraver. Generally wild life subjects, especially flowers and trees. Exhibited paintings and etchings at the RSA(11) & GI(37) from 34 Hillhead St and latterly from Lenzie. Represented in Lillie AG (Milngavie).

**PALMER, Ken** **1944-**
Born Glasgow. Abstract painter pre-occupied with light and ideas derived from science and technology. Trained Glasgow School of Art 1962-6. Exhibits in USA, Germany, Holland and the UK. Member of the Glasgow Group. Lives and works at 23 Oakfield Avenue, Glasgow.

**PALMER, Robin** **fl 1982**
Kincardineshire painter; exhibited two abstract works at the AAS from The Whins, Auchattie, Banchory.

**PALMER, Mrs Rosemary** **fl 1964-1974**
Aberdeenshire landscape and topographical artist. Exhibited AAS(4) from Old Aberdeen, latterly from 7 Park Rd, Cults.

**PAOLOZZI, Sir Eduardo RA FRIAS DLitt(hon)** **1924-**
Born Leith, 7 Mar. Sculptor. Lithographer and designer. Of Italian parentage, studied at Edinburgh College of Art 1942 and Slade School 1943-7. Worked in Paris 1947-50 being influenced by Giacometti and Paul Klee. Upon outbreak of WW2 was interned at Saughton Jail, Edinburgh, but after three months was released, returning to the parental shop to sell ice-cream. After a short spell with a firm of tea importers, enrolled at Edinburgh College of Art 1943 but after six months was called up and served in the Pioneer Corps. Whilst with them in Buxton, Derbyshire he alighted on Ozefont's *The Foundations of Modern Art,* a book which changed his life. Transferred to Oxford where at the time the Ruskin School of Art was sharing quarters with the Slade; after showing them some of his drawings he was accepted without paying fees on condition that he worked as a fire watcher, sleeping in the Ashmolean Museum and earning 4/6d a night, which remained his only income for a year. In the mid 1940s became interested in the works of Chirico, Dada and Surrealism, with a particular disposition toward the sort of collage defined by Max Ernst as 'the systematic exploitation of the chance or artificially provoked encounter of two or more substantially alien realities on a seemingly unsuitable level'. First one man exhibition in London 1947. In the early 1950s became a central figure in the Independent Group, a proto-Pop gathering of artists and critics centred around London's ICA. In 1953 commissioned by Hamburg City Council to design a large fountain for a new park. His work was included in the British Pavilion at the Venice Biennale 1952. Taught textile design at the Central School of Art and Design London 1949-55 and sculpture at St Martin's School of Art 1955-58. Awarded the David E Bright prize for a sculpture shown at the British Pavilion in Venice 1960. Has made collages, lithographs, and designed wallpapers. Often executed portrait and figure subjects in bronze and concrete as well as painting in watercolour and gouache. Since 1986 has been Her Majesty's Sculptor-in-Ordinary for Scotland and is currently working on sculptures for the New British Library and a Design Museum. In the 1980s received several major public commissions including the large entrance doors of Glasgow University's Hunterian Museum (1976) and the mosaics for Tottenham Court Tube Station in London (1980). Professor of Sculpture at the Akademie der Bildenden Kunste in Munich and tutor in ceramics, Royal College of Art. Knighted in 1989. In 1988 the NPG held an exhibition of his portraits and in 1991 his large bronze *Manuscript of Monte Cassino* was placed at Picardy Place, Edinburgh. Elected FRIAS 1991. Gifted the Paolozzi collection to the NGS 1994. Commissioned by Nat. Museum of Scotland for twelve bronze figures and the following year worked on the doors of the west front of St Giles. Exhibited AAS(1) 1966. The Tate Gallery held a major retrospective exhibition 1971. Represented in SNGMA, Dundee AG, Glasgow AG, City of Edinburgh coll, Manchester AG(5).
**Bibl:** Connolly,'A Childhood: Sir Edouardo Paolozzi', The Times, 8 Sept 1990; Hardie 192-3; Hartley 154-5; Diane Kirkpatrick, Eduardo Paolozzi, London 1970; Winfred Konnertz, Eduardo Paolozzi, Cologne 1984; Macmillan [SA]; Rosemary Miles, 'The Complete Prints of Eduardo Paolozzi', V & A 1977; Harold Osborne(ed), Twentieth Century Art, 1988, 425; Rothenstein 178; Schneede, Eduardo Paolozzi, London 1971; Tate Gallery, 'Eduardo Paolozzi' (Ex Cat 1971).

**PARIS, Alexander** **fl 1932**
Amateur artist; exhibited RSA(2) from 10 Provost Road, Linlithgow.

**PARK, Alistair** **1930-1984**
Born Edinburgh, 22 Apr. Painter in oil; teacher. Educated at Kirkcaldy High School and trained Edinburgh College of Art 1947-52. Taught for many years at Newcastle-upon-Tyne Polytechnic. Based in Edinburgh. After National Service in 1953-55 he taught

part-time at the Edinburgh College of Art and at an Edinburgh Secondary School 1957-63. Lecturer, Bradford College of Art 1963, moving to Newcastle-upon-Tyne's College of Art 1967 where he remained until his death. During the 1960s exhibited extensively throughout Britain. 'From the figurative work of the late 1950s to the abstract paintings of the 1960s, his work has showed a very natural evolution'. In 1963 he wrote 'I was interested in elementary images which have usually resolved into forms with human connections. In late paintings, these human images have been appearing in the forms of squares and circles and ovoids, it was an obvious step to move into the non-figurative world'. His first one-man show was in Edinburgh 1957, the last 1983. Regular exhibitor RSA & SSA. Represented in SNGMA, Abbot Hall AG (Kendal), Perth AG, SAC.
**Bibl:** Edinburgh City Art Centre, 'Alistair Park', (Ex Cat 1983); Hartley 155.

**PARK, Andrew** **fl 1909-1918**
Minor painter; exhibited GI(2) & Walker Gallery, Liverpool(2) from 152 George Street, Paisley.

**PARK, Carton Moore RBA** **1876-1956**
Born Scotland; died New York, Jan 23. Portrait, decorative and animal painter, also illustrator. Trained Glasgow School of Art under Fra Newbery(qv). First success was the publication of some of his illustrations in *The Glasgow Weekly Citizen* and *St Mungo.* A talented caricaturist, illustrated animals in a strong manner redolent of Japanese prints. Elected RBA 1899 but resigned 1905. Moved from Glasgow to Chelsea at the turn of the century and emigrated to America c1910. Editor and illustrator for George Allen's *Child's Library.* Illustrated *An Alphabet for Animals* (1899), *A Book of Birds* (1900), *A Book of Dogs, A Child's London* (1900), *The Child's Pictorial Natural History* (1901), La Fontaine's *Fables for Children, The King of the Beasts,* S.L. Bensusan's *A Countryside Chronicle, The Bee, Biffel,* and *The Story of a Trek-ox.* Also executed mural panels for *The Zoo* and *The Farmyard,* and lithographs for *Uncle Remus, Tales of the Old Plantation* and *Breer Rabbit.* Contributed illustrations to *The Butterfly* (1899) and *The Idler.* Exhibited RA(1), RBA(15), GI(4) & L(2) but mainly at the Baillie Gallery(91) 1897-1910.
**Bibl:** Houfe (illus 408); R.E.D. Sketchley, Eng. Bk. Illus., 1903, 118, 168; Studio, Winter no.,1900-01,16-17 & Modern Book Illustrators and Their Work, 1914.

**PARK, D S** **fl 1886**
Glasgow minor painter; exhibited GI(1) from 101 St Vincent Street.

**PARK, Francis E C** **fl 1937**
Fife minor painter, exhibited RSA(1) from Loseberry, Elie.

**PARK, George Harrison** **fl 1875-1887**
Inverness painter in oil of portraits, landscapes, churches and still life. Possibly related to the sculptor Patric Park(qv). Moved to Edinburgh 1878 living at 6 Shandwick Place. Exhibited RSA(24) including a commissioned portrait of the 'Children of John Noble of Inverness' 1885; also GI(8) & RHA(1).

**PARK, J Eddington** **fl 1894**
Aberdeenshire painter of coastal scenes; exhibited AAS(1) from Ardaros, Fraserburgh.

**PARK, (James) Stuart** **1862-1933**
Born Kidderminster, 29 Apr; died Kilmarnock, 3 Sep. Painter in oil of flowers, portraits and figure subjects. Occasionally painted in watercolour. Born of Ayrshire parents, his father being a carpet designer. His mother's name was Stewart which was incorporated in his own name J Stuart Park until 1890. Thereafter he preferred Stuart Park and this is how he is generally known and invariably catalogued. His early life and education are uncharted although he may have been apprenticed to an engineer. Painted in his spare time, taking up painting professionally in 1888. Trained Glasgow School of Art and in Paris under Lefevre and Boulanger. At this time he also painted portraits, mainly of young girls framed by flowers, and developed an association with the Glasgow Boys with whom he is now identified. Moved from Glasgow to Kilmarnock 1896. Developed a very individual technique using thick and rapid strokes against a dark background, suggesting rather than defining the texture and colour of flowers. Produced work of markedly varying quality, his better delicate paintings, often rectangular, are markedly superior to his run-of-the-mill still lifes, often of roses, which during his lifetime he sold for £5. These stereotyped paintings diminished his reputation although his finest work ranks among the best flower paintings Scotland has produced. 'With almost oriental skill he used the fully loaded brush to describe in single strokes the twist of a petal or the shape of a leaf. In such painting there is no room for fumbling or the tentative approach. After a day's work he would ride home on a bicycle with two canvases strapped to his back and contemplate them through the evening, either to let well alone, or scrape the paint off to start afresh' [Tanner]. A conservatory was attached to his studio and probably a greenhouse as well providing a great variety of subjects. Held a successful exhibition every year in Glasgow. Caw said of his art 'if exceedingly limited, (it) has a note and distinction of its own. Although somewhat lacking in form, his pictures show real passion for the beauties of texture and colour in flowers, and his technique...with its exquisite impasto is admirably suited for their expression'. As a person he was given to intemperance, sometimes arrogant, never suffering fools gladly. On the other hand he was more open-minded and better informed about developments in art than any other members of the Glasgow School. He once wrote 'in the first place there should be beauty of colour, also decorative effect, then adequate carrying power. A distinguished painter recently said - in relation to carrying power - that a picture was not fulfilling its proper function, unless it could convey across a Gallery, and he was right. There should also be, of course, the natural and realistic effect of the flowers themselves'. The best work was done 1889-92, mainly pink, yellow and red roses. An early watercolour of strawberries 1886 was shown at the RSW that year. This is an interesting example of earlier work and of the lightness of touch at the outset of his career in spite of uncertainty of design. Member, International Society of Sculptors, Painters and Engravers. Exhibited RA(1), RSA(29), RSW(2), GI(116), AAS(1) & L(27). Represented in Dundee AG, Kilmarnock AG, Kirkcaldy AG, Glasgow AG(8, including one of his best portraits 'A Gipsy Maid'), Perth AG, Lillie AG (Milngavie).
**Bibl:** AJ 1898, 70; Billcliffe 172 (pl 168) 172 268-9; Caw 449-450; Conn 37 (1913) 121; Halsby 150,160,277; Irwin 373,375,383; Macmillan [SA] 268; Studio 29 (1903) 296; 31 (1904) 67, 163; 37 (1906) 200; SAC Cat 'The Glasgow Boys' 64-66.

**PARK, M Alexander** **fl 1896-1904**
Helensburgh amateur painter; exhibited GI(2) from Greenburn.

**PARK, Matthew James** **1878-1963**
Born and died Glasgow. Painter in oil, watercolour and pencil; mainly landscapes but also architectural drawings, portraits and textile designs. Attended evening classes at Glasgow School of Art 1904-5. Began working life as a house decorator and painter. Little known due to his extreme reclusiveness and limited output, most of his known works remaining with his descendants.

**PARK, Patric RSA** **1811-1855**
Born Glasgow; died Warrington, Lancs 18 Aug. Sculptor. Both his father Matthew and his grandfather were statuaries and masons in Glasgow. Aged 14 apprenticed to Mr Connell, mason, who was at the time building Hamilton Palace. It was here that Park, after working for two years as a stonecutter, was entrusted with carving the coat-of-arms above the main entrance. In 1828, when still only 17, he was employed by the architect Gillespie to carve decorative details at Murthly Castle. In 1831 went to Rome and after studying for two years under Thorwaldsen returned home. In 1839 he submitted a fearsome design for the Nelson Memorial, which unfortunately showed Nelson grasping his sword by the blade. Two years later he moved from Glasgow to Edinburgh and in 1845 sent a figure of a Greek huntsman to an exhibition held to select suitable works of art for the new Houses of Parliament. In 1846 his statue 'Modesty Unveiled', entered for the Art Union competition, was censored, causing him great anger. In 1850 he decided to erect a gigantic figure of Wallace on the hills near Edinburgh and prepared a model which stood 15 feet high and required 10 tons of clay. Lack of encouragement led him to abandon the project, according to *The Builder* he 'destroyed with his own mallet the model he had so laboriously made'. In 1855 he died at Warrington Railway Station bursting a blood vessel when helping a porter lift a hamper of ice. His portrait busts are remarkable for expressing great energy and in many instances embodying a feeling of much tenderness. He was in

particular demand as a sculptor. *British Literature and Art* opined that 'Park's appreciation of beauty and subjects of a more ideal kind was not equal to his appreciation of character in portrait busts' while *The Building Chronicle* considered that 'all his works are marked by a vigorous originality, a grace of style and a delicate beauty of finish which few equalled'. Close family ties with Inverness. Married the second daughter of Dr Carruthers of the *Courier.* Among his many commissions was one from Napoleon III to execute the portrait bust of Sir Charles Napier. An excellent example is the bust of 'Sheriff Fraser Tytler of Balnain and Aldourie', which stood for many years in a niche on the wall facing the entrance staircase to Inverness Castle. Before the battleground of Culloden was clearly marked he completed 'Statue of a Highlander' to be placed on the moor for the guidance of visitors. Before this could be erected a monument on the battlefield had been planned, although Park's sculpture received a prominent place at the Inverness exhibition of September 1867 and its present whereabouts is unknown. Elected ARSA 1849, RSA 1851. Exhibited 54 works at the RA 1836-1855 including busts of several famous artists of the day, 87 works at the RSA 1839-1856 and 10 exhibited posthumously. Busts of 'Sir Archibald Alison', 'Lord Jeffrey', 'David Octavius Hill', 'James Jardine' and 'Professor Simpson' are in the SNPG, those of 'James Oswald' and 'Adam Smith' in Glasgow AG, busts of 'James Hutton' and 'Sir James Hall' are in the Geological Museum, London. Also represented in NGS, V & A, ('Napoleon III' 1855), NGS, Huggins College (Gravesend), New College (Edinburgh), Manchester Free Library, Royal Society, RSA ('Horatio McCulloch' 1849 and 'Sir John Watson-Gordon' 1851). A bust of 'David Hamilton' is in Glasgow Museum.
**Bibl:** Brydall 191; Colvin 290-291; Scottish Family History, vol II, 276; Gifford 316,438; Simpson, 'Inverness Artists', Inverness Courier, 1925 16-18; Robin Lee Woodward, 'Nineteenth Century in Glasgow', in Virtue & Vision, SNPG, (Ex Cat 1991).

**PARK, William** **fl 1868-1870**
Edinburgh sculptor of portrait busts and medallions; exhibited RSA(17).

**PARK, W Mason** **fl 1905**
Minor Glasgow portrait miniaturist. Exhibited GI(1) from 65 Kelvindale St.

**PARKER, Miss Agnes Miller (Mrs McCance) RE** **1895-1980**
Born Irvine, Ayrshire, 25 Mar; died Ravenscraig Hospital, Greenock. Painter in oil and tempera, wood engraver and book illustrator. Educated Whitehill Higher Grade School, trained Glasgow School of Art 1911-17 under Greiffenhagen(qv), Forrester Wilson(qv), James Dunlop(qv) and Professor Baltus. Awarded Haldane travelling scholarship. Also studied wood engraving under Gertrude Hermes and Blair Hughes-Stanton 1926. Worked as an instructress in Glasgow 1918-20 but after a while went to England, returning to Scotland 1955. In 1918 married William McCance(qv) and went to live on Arran. From 1920-1928 taught art at Maltman's Green School, Gerrard's Cross, then at Clapham HS. Visited Paris 1926 and 1927 St. Tropez. At this time she shared her husband's Vorticist approach. Between 1930 and 1933 taught and engraved at the Gregynog Press, Newton, Montgomeryshire, illustrating *The Fables of Aesop* (1931). Elected ARE 1939. Her work is marked by a strong sense of design and a sturdy realism sometimes seasoned with allegory and by abundant vitality and clarity, her work is "quite distinctive, being filled with fine cross-hatching and stippled dots"[Horne]. Hodnett considered that, when at her best, few engravers were her equal. Illustrated *The Fables of Aesop* (1931), H E Bates' *Through the Woods* (1936), *Down the River* (1937). Later worked extensively for the Limited Editions Club of New York c1938 during which time she illustrated Thomas Gray's 'Elegy written in a Country Churchyard', the works of Shakespeare (1959), *How It Happened* (1930), Davies: *Daisy Matthews and Three Other Tales* (1932), Sampson: *XXI Welsh Gypsy Tales* (1933), Bates: *The House with the Apricot* (1933), Le Corbeau: *The Forest Giant* (1935), Hardy: *The Return of the Native* (1942), Furst: *Essays in Russet* (1944), Jefferies: *Spring of the Year* (1946), *Life of the Fields* (1947), *The Old House at Coats* (1948), *Field and Hedgerow* (1948), *The Open Air* (1948), McCormick: *The Gold Torque* (1951), Roche: *Animals under the Rainbow* (1952), Lewis *Honey Pots and Brandy Bottles* (1954), Powys: *Lucifer* (1956), Hardy: *Far from the Madding Crowd* (1958), *The Mayor of Casterbridge* (1964), *Jude the Obscure* (1969); *A Shropshire Lad* (1942), *The Faerie Queen* (1953), and *Tess of the D'Urbevilles* (1956). Separated from her husband 1955, the marriage was dissolved 1963 when she reverted to her maiden name. Lived in Glasgow, later moved to Lamlash, Arran. Exhibited RSA(5), RE(4), GI 1956-62 and overseas. Represented in SNGMA (transferred from NGS), V&A, and by photographs of her work at the NLS.
**Bibl:** Burkhauser 235-6; Hartley 156; Albert Garrett, A History of British Wood Engraving, 1978; SAC, 'Graven Images', (Ex Cat 1979); Hugh MacDiarmaid, 'William and Agnes McCance' in Scott. Educ. J.,20 Nov 1925; Macmillan [SA] 348-350; Society of Wood Engravers, London, 'Engraving Then and Now' (Ex Cat 1987); Horne 343; Dorothy A Harrop: *A History of the Greynog Press* 1980; Jaffé; Deane; Hodnett; Waters; Rogerson & Dreyfus: *Agnes Miller Parker: Wood-Engraver and Book Illustrator*, Fleece Press 1990.

**PARKER, Cushla** **fl 1921**
Painter. Exhibited RSA(2) from 9 Ann Street, Edinburgh.

**PARKER, Miss Elizabeth Rose ARMS SSWA** **1868-1953**
Born Renfrewshire. Landscape and miniature portrait painter and teacher. Trained Glasgow School of Art 1895-1901, Paris, London and Edinburgh. Lived in Partick and Glasgow. Exhibited mainly in Scotland at the RSA(12) & GI(48); also the RA(3), RMS(34) & L(1).

**PARKER, Janetta** **fl 1965-1970**
Perthshire sculptress. Specialised in portrait heads and figure studies. Exhibited RSA(5) from Coupar Angus.

**PARKER, Miss Joan M** **fl 1967-1968**
Glasgow-based painter of landscape and still life in watercolour. Exhibited GI(2).

**PARKER, Miss Kate Callow** **fl 1870-1878**
Edinburgh painter in watercolour of flowers, figurative subjects and still life. Exhibited RSA(5).

**PARKER, Phyllis M** **fl 1906**
Edinburgh portrait miniaturist. Exhibited RSA(4) from 15 George St.

**PARKES, Jane** **fl 1937**
Glasgow ceramic designer and sculptor. Exhibited GI(3) from 7 Westwood Avenue, Giffnock.

**PARKS, Lilias Ann** **fl 1892-1894**
Aberdeen painter; exhibited AAS(3) from 49 Powis Pl.

**PARKINSON, Sydney** **c1745-1771**
Born in Scotland. Painter of botanical, topographical and zoological works. Went to London 1767 where he was introduced to Joseph Banks by the horticulturalist James Lees. This led to his being appointed official artist with Captain Cook's first expedition to Australia and New Zealand 1768-1771. During this time he produced an illustrated journal which formed the official account of the expedition and included many hundred works in watercolour and gouache. During the return journey he died and was buried at sea. His work showed accuracy and great sensitivy with a feel for colour and design that would have assured attention and fame had he lived.

**PARKYN, John Herbert RWA ARCA (Lond)** **1864-?**
Born Cumberland, 16 Oct. Painter in oil, pastel and watercolour; genre. Trained Clifton School of Art, Royal College of Art and Academie Julien, Paris. Awarded Prix de Rome 1891 and again in 1893. Headmaster of Kingston-upon-Hull School of Art for eleven years and subsequently Headmaster of Ayr Academy. Highly competent artist who painted a variety of subjects from cats to elegant ladies in elegant landscapes, always with competent handling and a fine sense of design, often with idiosyncratic canvas sizes. Retired to Dalry, Galloway where he painted his last exhibits. Exhibited RA(7) 1884-1903, mainly still lifes; also RI & L(2).

**PARKYNS, L B** **fl 1808-1817**
Landscape painter in oil; hon. exhibitor RA(4) 1808-1817 where he showed a number of Scottish castles including 'Creighton Castle' 1808, 'Doune Castle' 1809, also 'Bamburgh Castle' 1810.

**PARRY, Jacki/y** **1941-**
Born Wonthaggi, Victoria, Australia. Printmaker and engraver. Early studies and initial teaching experience in Australia before enrolling in

Glasgow School of Art 1970-1974, specialising in printmaking. Founder member, Glasgow Print Studio 1972. Awarded Cargill scholarship 1975 enabling her to visit Poland and in 1988 visited Japan. Honoured the same year by an award from the Glasgow Society of Lady Artists. Lecturer Glasgow School of Art 1981-5. Studied with Laurence Barker at Barcelona Paper Workshop and in 1984 had her first solo exhibition in Compass Gallery. Exhibited widely overseas including Int. Print Biennale in Poland 1985 and in Germany 1986. Worked also in Orkney. An intensely energetic artist. Exhibited GI(3) & AAS(4) from 23 Kelvinside Gdns. Represented in SNGMA, Hunterian Museum (Glasgow Univ), Lillie AG (Milngavie).

**PARSONAGE, George G** **fl 1966-1977**
Glasgow sculptor. Worked in wood and metal, mostly figurative subjects. Exhibited GI(9) from Humane Society House, Glasgow Green.

**PARSONS, John Whitehill RBA RMS** **1859-1937**
Born Greenock 10 Jly; died England, 7 Jan. Painter in oil and watercolour; marines, landscapes, portraits and miniatures. Educated Edinburgh, studied art at the RSA Schools and in Paris under Paul Delance. A fine athlete, held records for both high and long jumps. Lived for a time at Pulborough, Sussex from 1904. Exhibited RA(3) including a portrait of his wife, RSA(33), RSW(3), RMS(18) & GI(31).

**PARTRIDGE, John** **1790-1872**
Born Glasgow, 28 Feb; died London, 25 Nov. Painter of portraits and genre. In 1843 he was appointed Portrait Painter Extraordinary to Her Majesty and to Prince Albert. This followed a commissioned portrait of 'The Queen' painted by command of Her Majesty for the King of the French and a portrait of 'Prince Albert' painted for the Duchess of Kent, both exhibited RA 1842. Other portraits included 'Leopold Prince of Belgium' 1837 and 'John, 4th son of Sir Robert Peel' 1834. Few biographical details of him are known. Also painted a number of Scottish sitters among them 'George Granville, 2nd Duke of Sutherland' (1786-1861) 1850, 'John Campbell, son of Colin Campbell', 'Sir Islay Campbell', 'Lord Succoth, Lord President of the Council' and the '10th Earl of Haddington'. Exhibited RA(72) 1815-1846, and 'Portrait of a gentleman' RSA 1849. Curiously for so distinguished an artist, he is not represented in any public Scottish collection although examples are in NPG, BM, Dublin AG, Liverpool AG, Nottingham AG, Salford AG, Oxford Univ; also in private collections of the Duke of Sutherland, Earl of Haddington, Sir Islay Campbell of Crarae, and at Mellerstain.

**PASQUOLL, Robert D** **1881-1927**
Painter in oil who lived and worked in Glasgow. Painted dockland scenes on the Clyde in a competent, realistic manner. Exhibited RSA (2), L(3) & GI(9). Represented in Glasgow AG.

**PATALONO, Enrico** **fl 1869-1890**
Glasgow-based painter in oil of portraits and figurative subjects. Although nothing is known of his background he was living in Glasgow 1869-1886 but had moved to 1 Langham Place, London by 1890. Exhibited once at the RA 1890; also RSA(2) & GI(32).

**PATERSON, A A** **fl 1915**
Amateur landscape painter; exhibited 'Loch-na-Cuilc - Loch of the rushes' at the RSA from the United Free church manse, Dervaig, by Tobermory, Argyll.

**PATERSON, Miss Ada Elma** **fl 1894-1906**
Kincardineshire portrait and landscape painter; exhibited AAS(7) from Birkwood, Banchory.

**PATERSON, Agnes** **fl 1897**
Amateur Edinburgh painter in oil of portraits and figurative subjects living at 5 Leamington Terrace. Exhibited RSA(1).

**PATERSON, Alexander** **fl 1846**
Glasgow landscape painter; exhibited RSA(1).

**PATERSON, Alexander** **fl 1883-1902**
Aberdeen oil painter of local and continental landscape including coastal scenes of the north-east and shipping; exhibited RSA(2) & AAS(7), latterly from 18 Links St.

**PATERSON, Alexander Nisbet ARSA RSW FRIBA** **1862-1947**
Born Glasgow; died Helensburgh, 10 Jly. Architect and painter in watercolour. Husband of Maggie P(qv), father of Mary Viola P(qv) and younger brother of James P(qv). Educated Glasgow Academy, studied at the École des Beaux Artes in Paris. 'A fastidious, comfortably off and retiring architect, whose best work is too little known' [Gomme & Walker]. Attended Atelier Pasal, Paris 1883-1886. Friend and partner of Campbell Douglas(qv) 1903-1910. Visited Holland, Italy and America on a bursary awarded by the RIBA. Worked in the offices of Sir John Burnet(qv) and Sir Aston Webb, set up in practice Glasgow 1891-1892. Painted many works in France as well as in Scotland. Designed a number of buildings in Glasgow including the Club House for the Liberal Club, National Bank of Scotland and in Edinburgh, and Carnegie Aquarium in the Zoological Park (1924-7); also a memorial tablet in the Preston Aisle, St Giles to R S Lorimer (1932). Elected ARSA 1912, RSW 1916. Exhibited 'Interior of the Baptistry, Florence' RA 1890 from 13 Portland Terrace, London; also RSA(105), RSW(108), RI(1) & GI(101). Represented in Glasgow AG.
**Bibl:** Gifford 115,527n,580; Halsby 154,277; A Gomme & D Walker, Architecture of Glasgow, London 1987(rev), 296.

**PATERSON, Anda Carolyn (Mrs James Spence) RSW RGI** **1935-**
Born Glasgow. Painter in oil, gouache, chalk and polyvinyl; figures and portrait studies; also etcher. Trained Glasgow School of Art 1952-58 with a year at Hospitalfield 1957-58. Received a highly commended postgraduate diploma and in 1966 won RSW Latimer Award. First one man show in Glasgow 1963 and the following year won a Glasgow Civic Prize. Co-founder, with her husband James Spence(qv), of the Glasgow Group. Principal teacher of art, Jordanhill and evening lecturer at Glasgow School of Art. Her work shows the influence of Goya, Daumier, Millet and the German expressionists. Portrays the disadvantaged and confused eg washer-women and beggars. Believes herself to be 'developing a strong resemblance to my own paintings'. To this extent she is a social painter with a strong sympathy for her subjects glowing through the vigorous composition and colours, depicting in her own words 'the messy untidyness of human life, on one hand ridiculous and comic, on the other struggling, anxious and tragic". Lives and works at 55 Bainfield Rd, Cardross, Dunbartonshire. Elected SSA 1967, SSW 1968, winning Anne Redpath prize at the RGI 1978. Exhibits regularly RSA & RSW, and once at the AAS in 1973 from 223 Nithsdale Rd. Represented in Inverness AG, Dundee AG, Hunterian Museum (Glasgow Univ), Glasgow AG, Lillie AG (Milngavie).

**PATERSON, Andrew** **fl 1864-1874**
Edinburgh sculptor of portrait busts. Exhibited RSA(18), from Greenside Pl.

**PATERSON, Andrew** **fl 1869-1873**
Midlothian landscape artist, mostly of local scenery. Exhibited RSA in 1869 from Roslin and in 1871 from Lasswade.

**PATERSON, Anne** **fl 1969**
Aberdeenshire amateur figurative painter. Married Bruce P(qv). Exhibited AAS(1) from the Post Office, Pitcaple.

**PATERSON, Miss Annie M** **fl 1887-1923**
Glasgow painter of flowers and rural genre. Exhibited quite frequently at the AAS from 231 W Regent St. Possibly the **A M PATERSON** who exhibited three works at the AAS from Cranfurd, Lasswade, Midlothian in the 1920s.

**PATERSON, Bruce** **fl 1974-1984**
Aberdeenshire painter of figurative subjects and semi-abstracts. Trained Gray's School of Art, Aberdeen. Married Anne P(qv). Exhibited three works at the AAS from the Post Office, Pitcaple.

**PATERSON, C M** **fl 1885**
Edinburgh amateur painter; exhibited 'Treasure trove' at the RSA from 6 Merchiston Crescent.

**PATERSON, Catherine W** **fl 1920-1930**
Amateur painter of informal portraits and figure studies. Exhibited RSA(1), SWA(1) & L(1), latterly from a Glasgow address.

**PATERSON, Charles** **fl 1894-1896**
Aberdeen landscape painter; exhibited AAS(2) from 63 Jasmine Terr.

**PATERSON, David** **fl 1937-1940**
Falkirk amateur watercolour painter exhibited 'The Pool of London' at the RSA, also RSW(2) from 36 Napier Place.

**PATERSON, Derek G** **fl 1972-1988**
Aberdeen painter; exhibited AAS(3), latterly from 263 Gt Western Rd.

**PATERSON, Donald M RSW** **1950-**
Born Kyleakin, Isle of Skye. Painter in oil and watercolour mainly the latter; also sculptor. Trained Glasgow School of Art 1968-72. First one man show 1974 and in 1986 obtained the RSA Highland Society of London Award. Retains a strong sense of belonging to North-west Scotland. Said that 'although it is the product of a combination of direct experiences, observations, and memories centred upon the north-west, each drawing, painting, print or construction becomes concerned with achieving a personally coherent and meaningful balance and the result can sometimes be oblique, departing by varying degrees from the original source'. Lives at Blaven, Tor Rd, Bridge of Weir. Elected RSW 1983. A regular exhibitor RSA, RSW & GI.

**PATERSON, Miss Emily Murray RSW** **1855-1934**
Born Edinburgh; died London. Painter in oil and watercolour of landscape and flowers. Trained Edinburgh College of Art, London and Paris. Worked in Austria, Holland, Belgium, Norway, Switzerland and Venice, in later life living in London. Used broad, translucent washes producing luminosity, especially in her treatment of cascading water, snow-capped mountains and the dappled shifting sunlight of Venice. Influenced by, though not a member of, the Glasgow School and seems to have had no personal contact with any of the Glasgow Boys. Strong extrovert and keen Alpinist. Walks in the Austrian Tyrol resulted in a London exhibition. In 1918 her watercolours of the Ypres battlefield were exhibited in London. Elected RSW 1904, ASWA 1910. Exhibited widely including RA(17), RSA(91), RSW(108), RI(24), RMS(12), RHA(2), GI(57), AAS 1900-1933, RBA(4), L(8) & SWA(68). Represented in V & A, Glasgow AG, Dundee AG, Imperial War Museum, Brodie Castle (NTS), Manchester AG, Musee Royal de l'Armee (Brussels).
**Bibl:** Caw 393; Halsby 167,277.

**PATERSON, George M** **fl 1866-1904**
Painter in oil and watercolour of landscape, still life, figures and portraits. Shared a studio at 5 Picardy Place but later moved to Liberton. Exhibited twice at the RA, in 1881 and in 1886 'Marshall Keith's last battle, Hochkirch, 1758'; also RSA(24), including the prophetically titled 'Road versus Rail' 1881, GI(12), AAS(3) & L(6).

**PATERSON, George William Lennox ARE** **1915-1986**
Born Glasgow, 7 Jan. Painter of portraits, battle scenes, landscape and still life; engraver, woodcut artist and teacher. Son of well-known Glasgow architect, George Andrew P. Trained Glasgow School of Art winning Guthrie Award 1946. Elected ARE 1947. Lecturer in wood engraving and book illustration, Glasgow School of Art, becoming Deputy Director. Lived in Helensburgh. His development and output suffered from the administrative burdens of his academic post, his conscientiousness as a teacher allied to an unambitious temperament. Designed a banknote for Clydesdale Bank. Keen sailor and member, Royal Marines Reserve. Spent most summers on Eilean Horisdale, Wester Ross. A warm hearted, friendly man always actively occupied whether painting or sailing or latterly building his own sailing dinghies at which he was highly skilled. Illustrated Moray McLaren & Major-Gen Stewart's *Fishing as We Find It*, 1960. Regular exhibitor RSA 1938-78, RE, GI & AAS(3). Elected ARE 1947. Published two manuals: *Scraperboard* (1960) and *Making a Colour Linocut* (1963). Illustrated Fairless: *The Roadmender* (1950), Dunnett: *Land of Scotch* (1953), Burns: *Poetical Works* (1958), Mitchison: *A Fishing Village on the Clyde* (1960). Represented in SNGMA, Glasgow AG.
**Bibl:** Horne 344; Peppin; Waters.

**PATERSON, Hamish Constable** **1890-1955**
Born Moniaive; died Moniaive. Architect and painter of portraits and landscape. Third son of James P(qv). Trained Edinburgh College of Art. Seriously wounded in WWI. Turned increasingly to watercolour painting producing many fine landscapes of the south of France during the 1920s and 1930s. The quality of his work varied and in later life the psychological scars of war caused a marked deterioration. A celebrated work, portrait of 'The Duchess of Atholl', was drawn at Blair Castle during her parliamentary election campaign 1938-9. Solo exhibition London 1922 and on a canoe on the river Ouse 1927. Returned to Moniaive 1953. Exhibited RA(3), RSA(56), RSW(10), RHA(1), L(4) & GI(19). Represented in City of Edinburgh collection (watercolour portrait of 'Sir William Oliphant Hutchison' 1926).
**Bibl:** Halsby 277; Lillie AG 'James Paterson, Moniaive and following Family Traditions', (Ex Cat 1983, text by Anne Paterson Wallace).

**PATERSON, Hannah Frew** **fl 1967-**
Embroiderer; teacher. Trained under Kathleen Whyte at Glasgow School of Art 1963-67, winning the Newbery Medal 1967. Completed an important triptych for Cardross Church 1981-84. Teaches part-time, Glasgow School of Art.
**Bibl:** Margaret Swain 175-7; H Frew, *Three Dimensional Embroidery*, Van Nostrand, 1975.

**PATERSON, Hugh Scott** **fl 1860-1877**
Inveresk landscape painter in oil. Exhibited RSA(8) including several works in the Inveresk and Kircudbright areas, also on Arran 1877.

**PATERSON, Ian Watson** **1917-1996**
Born Nairn, June 17; died Aberdeen, Sept 15. Architect, painter & teacher. Educated Nairn Academy, graduated Aberdeen School of Architecture 1947 having been interrupted by war service in the Middle East 1940-46. Awarded travelling scholarship. Joined German firm of Ernest May, working in East Africa, before returning to Aberdeen to teach at the School of Architecture 1950-82. During his earlier years he continued to paint, mostly landscape and boating scenes, and in 1982 worked almost full-time as a painter, regularly visiting Italy. Exhibited RSA(3) & AAS in the 1960s and again in the 1980s, from his home which he designed himself, 141 Garthdee Rd. (From notes provided by his niece, Jean Heddle)

**PATERSON, J C** **fl 1917-1918**
Edinburgh amateur painter in oil and watercolour, mostly portraits. Exhibited RSA(2), RWS(3) & RSW(1) from 17 India Street.

**PATERSON, J F** **fl 1882**
Watercolour painter. Exhibited 'On the Tweed, Norham' at the GI, from The Professional Hall, George St.

**PATERSON, J S** **fl 1896**
Amateur painter of Whitehill, New Deer, Aberdeenshire; exhibited GI(1).

**PATERSON, James** **fl 1846-1875**
Dundee painter in oil and watercolour of landscapes and topography, sometimes with figures; exhibited RSA(11).

**PATERSON, James PRSW RSA RWS** **1854-1932**
Born Hillhead, Glasgow, 21 Aug; died Edinburgh. Landscape painter, mainly in watercolour. After a short spell at the Western Academy, where he first met W Y MacGregor(qv) starting a life-long friendship, later attended Glasgow Academy. An intention toward painting showed itself early but his father insisted on his son first going to University. After a year at University Paterson entered the business, also attending the local art school with landscape lessons from A D Robertson(qv). Exhibited RSA(2) 1874, a year later exhibited for the first time GI. Reassured by these signs of talent, his father eventually agreed to the young man abandoning business so, in 1877, at the age of 23, Paterson went to Paris to continue art studies under Jacquesson de la Chevreuse. Subsequently joined the atelier of Jean Paul Laurens. Whilst in Paris Paterson paid short visits to Switzerland, Italy and Egypt, but long summer vacations were spent in Scotland and in the summer of 1878 he and M Y MacGregor(qv) painted at St Andrews. Returning to Glasgow in the spring of 1882 he became associated with the group of slightly younger men then gathering under a banner of artistic revolt. "Most of them - Guthrie, Crawhall and Henry at least - had been self-taught, and painting the country together they had been cultivating a broad and powerful manner of painting, which would represent the weight and mass of

things and secure the unity and fullness of tone which had been neglected by most Scottish artists in favour of the more elaborate and less closely related rendering of nature. Paterson joined this coterie and, with his more informed command of values acquired in Paris, did finished studies while the others were still struggling over technical difficulties...After marriage in 1884 to Eliza Ferguson, the couple settled in Moniaive in Dumfries-shire...perhaps of all the French romanticists, Corot was the painter whose work he appreciated most...These things, however, were contributory to the expression of Paterson's personal sentiment for nature. Informed by true if not special feeling, good and occasionally quite beautiful in colour and taste, and designed on lines in which decoration and realism were happily blended, the pastorals he painted there possess an idyllic quality of their own...His affection for the district of Moniaive and the spirit in which he painted it appear in the letterpress as well as in the illustrations of his monogram title *Nithsdale,* 1893' [Caw]. Paterson loved the harmonies of blues and browns and although sometimes a little vague was generally a fine watercolourist. Founder member, Edinburgh Society of Eight 1912, having moved to the capital seven years previously. Appointed Librarian and then Secretary of the RSA. After losing his wife 1910 spent increasing time on the continent, especially Tenerife. The Mediterranean sun was echoed in a brighter palette. After 1898, although continuing to return to Moniaive, Edinburgh became the immediate source of his inspiration. The late development of his art was now taking place, with a stronger preference for picturesqueness of subject and a more decorative ensemble and a wider range of colour. Also painted portraits especially after 1900. Co-founded the *Scottish Art Revue,* and received a gold medal at the Munich International 1885. In 1890 he had been among those chosen to hang at the GI exhibition and was responsible for what became known in the City as the Impressionist room. This attracted exhibits from Steer, Clausen and others and although arousing bitter controversy at the time it can now be seen an achievement of distinction and quality. Elected ARSA 1896, RSA 1910, RSW 1885, President, RSW 1916, RWS 1898. Exhibited RA(29), RSA(177), RWS(193), RSW(152), RHA(2), GI(130), AAS(1885-1931) & L(57). Represented in NGS, SNPG(9), Glasgow AG, Lillie AG (Milngavie), City of Edinburgh collection, Manchesterc AG, Abbot Hall AG (Kendal), Nat Gall of New Zealand (Wellington).
**Bibl:** AJ 1894, 77, 79; 1905, 184, 352f; 1906, 186; 1907, 187,282; 1908, 28; Art News 30 (1932),20,12; Roger Billcliffe, The Glasgow Boys, London 1985; Caw OWCS, 1933; Caw 382-3; Halsby 137-9, 145,154,202,277; Irwin 373-4,393; Lillie AG, Milngavie 'James Paterson, Moniaive and following family traditions', (Ex Cat 1983); Macmillan [SA] 255-6,270,278-9,282,285,310; Martin, cont 1968; Studio 45, 1909, 116,119(illus); 63 (1915) 112f also indexed 1903-1918.

**PATERSON, James C** **fl 1885-1904**
Amateur painter; exhibited GI(2) from a Glasgow address.

**PATERSON, James Phillips** **fl 1902-1905**
Dunfermline portrait painter; exhibited RSA(3) from 31 High St.

**PATERSON, Miss Janet** **fl 1898**
Inverness amateur painter; exhibited once at the AAS from Larkfield, Southside Rd.

**PATERSON, Jeannie Sinclair** **fl 1890-1896**
Versatile Aberdeenshire painter of portraits, landscape and coastal scenes of the north-east. Exhibited AAS(6), latterly from the Manse, Whitehill, New Deer.

**PATERSON, Jentie** **fl 1904**
Glasgow amateur painter; exhibited GI(1) from 2 Windsor Quadrant, Kelvinside.

**PATERSON, John** **fl c1795-d1832**
Architect. Little known of his early life. Carried on a successful career running the Adams' office in Edinburgh after both brothers had died, with important commissions on both sides of the border. His most celebrated work was the great Sham Castle built at Eglinton, Ayrshire for the 12th Earl of Eglinton 1798 (now gutted). His most important classical house, Montgomerie, Ayrshire was built for the same patron 1804. This is a long low building in the Adam Wyatt manner with an imposing colonnaded bow-front. In c1806 commissioned by the 4th Earl of Breadalbane to remodel and enlarge Taymouth Castle, Perthshire, already altered by William Adam, but Lord Breadalbane changed his mind and decided to have a new building and dismissed Paterson. Another successful building was the castellated house of Monzie, Perthshire for Colonel Campbell (c1795; reconstructed by Lorimer following a fire 1905-12). Probably responsible for Leith Bank (1804-6), a two-storey Ionic columned villa. Also designed the Georgian Gothic revival church of St. Paul's, Perth (1807).
**Bibl:** Colvin; Dunbar 121,125; Gifford 188n,442,470n,475,516; Bruce Walker & W G Gauldie, Architects and Architecture on Tayside, Dundee 1984, 69,90(illus),93.

**PATERSON, John** **fl 1884**
Amateur landscape painter; exhibited GI(1) from Newlands, Ayr.

**PATERSON, John** **1832-1877**
Edinburgh architect. Partner with R Thornton Shiells(qv). Designed the Georgian Beehive Inn (1867-8) in Edinburgh's Grassmarket.
**Bibl:** Gifford 223,228,425,471.

**PATERSON, John** **fl 1895**
Aberdeenshire painter of local coastal and harbour scenes; exhibited AAS(1) from 5 Queen St, Peterhead.

**PATERSON, John Ford** **fl 1869-1883**
Edinburgh oil painter of landscape and rustic scenes. Frequently painted views of the Tweed, especially around Norham. Exhibited RSA(16) & GI(1).

**PATERSON, John Wilson** **1887-1970**
Edinburgh architect. H M Officer of Works 1922-1943. Remodelled the interior of what became the Scottish United Services Museum (1928-30). Designed the pannelling in the King's Dressing Room and Wardrobe at Holyrood (c1930) and was responsible, with A J Pitcher(qv), for the Sheriff Courthouse in the Lawnmarket. Designed the Children's Farm along the lines of small Cape Dutch ranges at Edinburgh Zoo (1956-8) and the 'pompous' telephone building in Newington (1923).
**Bibl:** Gifford 91,98,144-5,188,200,407,527,570,628,642.

**PATERSON, Joseph Henry** **fl 1976**
Aberdeenshire painter. Trained Gray's School of Art, Aberdeen. Exhibited a portrait and a figurative work at the AAS from 31 Bryson Cr, Buckie.

**PATERSON, Kate W** **fl 1898-1911**
Amateur Glasgow sculptress. Exhibited RSA(1) & GI(4) from 25 University Gardens and latterly London.

**PATERSON, Miss L** **fl 1887-1888**
Glasgow amateur flower painter; exhibited GI(3) from 1 Athole Gdns Pl, Hillhead.

**PATERSON, Mrs** **fl 1879**
Biggar watercolourist; exhibited a study of game birds at the RSA.

**PATERSON, Maggie** **[see HAMILTON, M]**

**PATERSON, Maggie C** **fl 1890**
Amateur painter. Exhibited GI(1) from Cordoba, Bothwell.

**PATERSON, Margaret S** **fl 1951-1965**
Dumfriesshire painter of landscapes including scenery in Spain, Ibiza and Cumberland. Exhibited RSA(4) & GI(4), from Langholm.

**PATERSON, Mary** **fl 1887-1890**
Glasgow flower painter; exhibited GI(4) from 193 Renfrew St.

**PATERSON, Mary Stewart** **fl 1892**
Amateur painter; exhibited RSA(1).

**PATERSON, Miss Mary Viola** **1899-1981**
Born Helensburgh, 19 Feb; died Helensburgh. Painter in oil; also lithographer and colour printer. Daughter of Alexander Nesbit P(qv), niece of James Paterson(qv), founder member of the Glasgow School.

Trained at the Slade School under Greiffenhagen 1918-1921. Her portrait was painted by Russell Flint under the title 'The Fawn Habit'. Went to Paris, studied at the Academie de la Grande Chaumière under Lucien Simon Besnard and at the Academie L'Hôte under André L'Hôte. France became her base. Painted classical studies of French subjects. Travelled with her mother Maggie Hamilton to St Tropez, Venice and Malta. Although not herself a landscape painter these surroundings inspired her. As well as painting in oil and watercolour she designed three stained-glass windows for St Bride's Church, Helensburgh completed by Guthrie & Wells of Glasgow 1924-31. Involved in printmaking, etching, lithography, wood engraving and a unique form of colour printing which she called 'Wood Types'. This involved engraving a line drawing on a wood block which separated the different areas of colour brushed in before printing - a method which permitted a greater realisation of form. At the outbreak of WW2 was in France but managed to leave on the last sailing through the Mediterranean. During the war worked with the Admiralty at Oxford. Lived in Helensburgh for many years. Toward the end of her life illness prevented her painting. Exhibited regularly RA, RSA, SSA & GI. Represented in V & A, NGS, BM ('Highland Games' - a coloured woodcut, c1935).
**Bibl:** Belgrave Gall, London 'The Paterson family', (Ex Cat 1977); Halsby 278; Lillie AG 'James Paterson, Moniaive and following Family Traditions, (Ex Cat 1983, text by Anne Paterson Wallace).

**PATERSON, Matt Hope** **fl 1889-1892**
Glasgow painter of west coast scenery. Exhibited GI(4) from Dennistoun.

**PATERSON, O M** **fl 1887**
Glasgow amateur painter; exhibited GI(1) from Laurieville, Crosshill.

**PATERSON, Oscar** **fl c1890-c1920**
Glasgow stained glass window and jewellery designer. Executed many windows in Scottish churches of which perhaps the best known is the Argyll window in the SE corner of St. Giles cathedral, Edinburgh; also designed windows depicting the 'Crucifixion' in the Church of the Good Shepherd, Murrayfield and 'Nativity' (1912) in Mayfield Church. Exhibited GI(3).
**Bibl:** Gifford 45,117,628,635.

**PATERSON, Robert** **1712-1801**
Sculptor. Based in Galloway. Carved hundreds of headstones for churchyards in that county and in Wigtownshire. Many years after his death, in 1855, Sir Walter Scott's publishers, Messrs Black, erected a tombstone to his memory in Caerlaverock churchyard. He had a son **Walter (1749-1812)** who was also a stone-engraver. His history and 'wayward mode of life' suggested to Walter Scott the novel *Old Mortality.*
**Bibl:** Colvin 293; Ramage, Drumlanrig and the Douglases.

**PATERSON, Robert** **1825-1889**
Edinburgh architect. Trained under William Beattie(qv) but quickly forsook the neo-classical and Italianate traditions. Latterly entered into partnership with his son **Robert PATERSON Jnr**. Remembered for his Café Royal (1861) in West Register St, Edinburgh the quadrant corners of which 'have many precedents in Edinburgh's Georgian housing, but are an innovation in the architecture of commerce' [Gifford]. Also did some church work including Salisbury Church, Causewayside (1862). The Town Council Office, Portobello (1877), now the police station.
**Bibl:** Gifford 205,250,312-3,330,380,595,618,620,652.

**PATERSON, Robert** **fl 1863-1889**
Edinburgh engraver. Exhibited RA(6), mostly landscapes with dramatic settings such as 'Farmyard - moonlight' 1870 and 'Heath - evening effect' 1871. Engraved the 'Burial of Wilkie' after J M W Turner 1888. Moved to London in the mid-1870s, latterly at White-friars St, E.C. Exhibited RSA(1) 1878 & 4 wood engravings at the GI.

**PATERSON, Robert Edward Stirling** **fl 1889-1940**
Edinburgh painter in oil and watercolour of shipping, harbour and coastal scenes. Employed a rather sombre style and is now an almost forgotten artist. The 'Corner of Peterhead Harbour' 1897 received favourable attention at the time. Lived at Northwood House, Russell Place, Trinity, Edinburgh. Exhibited RA(2), RSA(33), RSW(11), GI(9), 'The Deer Sanctuary, Cluanie' at the AAS 1931 & L(1).
**Bibl:** Halsby 278.

**PATERSON, Robert Tod Gow** **1866-c1934**
Edinburgh painter and pencil portrait artist. Trained Edinburgh School of Art. Travelled extensively. Exhibited RSA 1927-1931 & GI(2) from 6 Morningside Park. Represented City of Edinburgh collection by a watercolour portrait of the artist's mother.

**PATERSON, Susie** **c1955-**
Printmaker. Trained Duncan of Jordanstone College of Art 1975-79. Appointed printmaking technician, Glasgow School of Art 1998. Involved in all aspects of photography. Exhibits RSA, AAS & SSA. Represented in Edinburgh City AG, Alvar Alto Museum (Finland), and the Royal Collection.

**PATERSON, T Graham** **fl 1987-**
Glasgow abstract painter. Exhibited GI(1) from 65 Gardner St.

**PATERSON, Thomas** **fl 1919-1925**
Glasgow amateur painter of coastal scenes in watercolour, often with children. Exhibited RSA(2), GI(2) & AAS(2) all in the same year, from 196 St Vincent Street.

**PATERSON, Thomas Tolmie** **?-1933**
Edinburgh architect. Designed the Celtic cross memorial to General Wauchope now in Niddrie Mains Primary school.
**Bibl:** Gifford 382,543,579-81,599.

**PATERSON, William** **fl c1810-1820**
Edinburgh etcher. In 1816 there appeared in Edinburgh *Twelve Etchings of Views in Edinburgh;* the work was dedicated to Sir Walter Scott and the anonymous etcher was William Paterson. These were so well received that a further selection of 12 more was published in the same year, this time by Archibald Constable. In 1819 there appeared a companion work *Scenery and Antiquities of Midlothian* included in which are 'Edinburgh and its Environs - from the Fife Coast', the 'View from Corstorphine Hill', and the 'View from Stockbridge (incorporating buildings being erected in the grounds of Sir Henry Raeburn RA)', 'St Anthony's Chapel', 'Merchiston Tower', and 'Craigmillar Castle'.
**Bibl:** Butchart 44-6.

**PATERSON, William** **?-c1955**
Edinburgh architect. Partner in Oldrieve, Bell & Paterson. Designed the Trustee Savings Bank in Hanover St 'monumental American Neo-Classical in the McKim tradition' [Gifford] with charming Italian Renaissance detail; also Bristo Baptist Church (1932-5).
**Bibl:** Gifford 69,308,385.

**PATERSON, William** **fl 1879-1939**
Glasgow landscape painter in oil and watercolour; often river scenes. Latterly appears to have returned to Glasgow following a period in York Place, Edinburgh. Exhibited 'Moorland at Poolewe, Wester Ross' RA 1900. More frequently exhibited RSA(12), GI(9), AAS(1) & L(1).

**PATERSONE, George** **fl 1718**
Edinburgh engraver. Subscribed to Nisbet's *Essay on...Armories,* 1718.
**Bibl:** Bushnell.

**PATON, Agatha Waller** **fl 1895**
Edinburgh landscape painter. Exhibited 'In the Dalmeny woods' and 'A calm day at sea' at the RSA from 4 George Square.

**PATON, Amelia Robertson** **[see HILL, Mrs D O]**

**PATON, Archibald G** **c1880-1963**
Glasgow etcher of architectural and topographical subjects. An artist of considerable ability and interest; exhibited RA(2), RSA(8), GI(36) 1916-1963 & L(1), including 'Interior, British Museum' 1927 and 'Interior, St Stephen's, Walbrook'.

**PATON, David** **fl 1660-1698**
Miniature portrait painter; mostly in plumbago, pencil and sepia. One of the few Scottish miniature painters of the 17th century. As far as is known he worked only in Scotland. Long records that he drew highly finished miniatures in plumbago, some copied from pictures. Some were engraved eg 'Sir James Dalrymple', engraved by R White. Accompanied the Hon William Tollemache, youngest son of the Duchess of Lauderdale, on the Grand Tour. In Turin 1671. Manuscripts relating to the tour are at Ham House. A fine example of his work is 'Viscount Dundee', in the SNPG, and a rectangular miniature of 'Charles II' also in plumbago and inscribed 'D Paton fecit 1669-/s Couper invenit 1665'. The receipt is at Oxenfoord Castle, Midlothian in which David Paton, Limner of Edinburgh acknowledges 'having received from David McGill, Professor of Philosophy, in the name of Robert, Viscount Oxford, £186.8s. as interest on £780 Scots money from 20 May, 1690 to 20 May, 1695 as payment for a miniature portrait of The Prince of Wales set in silver and for two silver frames for other pictures' (5 June 1695). Settled in London c1700. A drawing of one of the Dukes of Argyll was shown at Inverary Castle 1974. A plumbago on vellum portrait of two gentlemen, 'The Yester Lords' and a pen portrait of 'John Graham of Claverhouse, Viscount Dundee' are in the NGS, and of 'Thomas Dalyell' (1599-1685) is in The Binns (NTS).
**Bibl:** Brydall 94; Caw 19; Conn LII, 1918, 73; Foskett 438-9; Long 330; Macmillan [SA] 77.

**PATON, David** **1801-1881**
Architect. Son of an Edinburgh builder. Emigrated to practise in S Carolina. Designed Nos 1-3 York Place and 15-19 North St Andrew St; also 59-73 Cumberland St, 25-29 Dundas St as well as several other properties built by his father.
**Bibl:** Gifford 332,342,344-5,349,411.

**PATON, David** **fl 1883-1892**
Glasgow artist; later moved to Pittenweem c1892. Exhibited RSA (1), GI(2) & an Arran view AAS 1885 from Eastbank, Johnstone.

**PATON, David William** **fl 1891-1925**
Sculptor in bronze of domestic genre and figurate subjects. Exhibited RSA(10), all from Edinburgh.

**PATON, Donald** **1866-1949**
Landscape painter in watercolour. Lived and worked on Arran, also in Edinburgh. Possibly related to Waller Hugh P(qv) & Noel P(qv). Sometimes used the pseudonym 'E H Thompson'. Exhibited 'Moor and mountain - Arran' at the RSA; also GI(4).
**Bibl:** Halsby 278.

**PATON, Eliza L M** **fl 1940**
Midlothian amateur painter; exhibited GI(1) from Midfield, Lasswade.

**PATON, Frederick Noel** **1861-1914**
Edinburgh watercolour painter of landscapes. Younger son of Sir Joseph Noel P(qv), brother of Ranald Noel Paton(qv). Exhibited RSA (5) including an imposing study of 'Dunluce Castle' 1887; also GI(1).
**Bibl:** Halsby 278.

**PATON, H** **fl 1879-1880**
Amateur Glasgow landscape painter. Exhibited GI(2) from St. Vincent St.

**PATON, Herbert** **fl 1984**
Aberdeen printmaker; probably brother of James P(qv). Exhibited AAS(1).

**PATON, Hubert** **fl 1886-1888**
Edinburgh painter of fairy subjects and west coast mountain landscape. Exhibited GI(3), from George Sq.

**PATON, Hugh ARE** **1853-1927**
Born Glasgow, 5 Feb; died England, 24 Oct. Painter, etcher, pastellier and author. Educated at Glasgow Academy, he was self-taught in art. Began etching c1880. Met with almost immediate success. In 1896 published *Etching, Drypoint, Mezzotint,* and this was followed in 1909 by *Colour Etching.* In later years he lived at Arden Adam, Marple, Cheshire. Elected ARE 1887. Exhibited Paris Salon, also RA(1), RE(112), GI(1), L(26) & RCA(1).

**PATON, J** **fl 1820**
Aberdeen engraver. Engraved a bookplate for Marischal College, Aberdeen, 1820.
**Bibl:** Bushnell.

**PATON, James** **fl 1778-1802**
Edinburgh miniature painter about whom little is known. Advertised as limner opposite the foot of Niddry's Wynd, Edinburgh, 1778-1781, then set up as miniature painter there 1783-84, re-introduced the term limner 1784-86. Shortly thereafter moved to the Cowgate, opposite Niddry Street, setting up again as a miniature painter, moving 1793 to a position opposite the Concert Hall where he remained until 1802.

**PATON, James** **fl 1984**
Edinburgh artist. Same address as Herbert P(qv). Exhibited AAS(1).

**PATON, James Fraser** **fl 1903-1912**
Greenock amateur scenery artist. Exhibited 'In Tangiers' and 'In Duddington Manse garden' at the RSA & GI(1) and at the London Salon (11) from 52 Eldon Street.

**PATON, Jessie G (Mrs D N Rolls)** **fl 1905**
Glasgow amateur artist; exhibited GI(1) from 3 Yarrow Gdns, Kelvinside.

**PATON, John M** **fl 1900-1902**
Edinburgh landscape artist. Exhibited AAS(2) from 5 Windsor St.

**PATON, Sir Joseph Noel RSA FSSA** **1821-1901**
Born Dunfermline, 13 Dec; died Edinburgh, 26 Dec. Painter in oil and watercolour of religious, historical, mythical and allegorical scenes; genre and landscape. Also sculptor, illustrator and occasional wood engraver. Son of a keen collector of Scottish antiquities (an interest he was later to share), and Fellow, Scottish Society of Antiquaries. His mother was related to the Earls of Atholl, his father was a pattern-designer in Dunfermline. Brother of Waller Hugh P(qv). Had 11 children several of whom became artists. First employed 1839-42 in Paisley as a designer of muslins but in 1843 went to London, enrolling at the RA Schools where he met John Everett Millais who was to become a life-long friend. In 1845 won prizes in the Westminster Hall Competition for his Spirit of Religion and 1847 won the premium of £300 for two oils, 'Christ Bearing His Cross' and the 'Reconciliation of Oberon and Titania'. Two years later 'Quarrel of Oberon and Titania' was bought for the NGS. In 1854-5 painted with his brother at the family holiday home on Arran. In 1855 received an honourable mention in Paris and exhibited a major work 'Pursuit of Pleasure at Home'. Although he greatly sympathised with the aims of the pre-Raphaelite brotherhood, he never became a member because of his return to Scotland where in 1876 he was given a doctorate from the University of Edinburgh. Elected ARSA 1847, RSA 1850, appointed Her Majesty's Limner for Scotland in 1865, a position he held until his death 1901. Knighted 1866. Published two works, *Poems of a Painter* (1861) and *Spindrift* (1867), and helped to illustrate S.C. Hall's *Book of British Ballads.* A man of wide learning and culture, the subjects of his pictures being drawn from a broad range of sources. Attracted to Swedenborgian mysticism and the work of William Blake, after 1870 devoted himself increasingly to religious works. Nevertheless, probably his most original works were his paintings of fairies, such as 'Oberon and Titania' and 'The Fairy Raid'. 'His technique was laborious and pre-Raphaelite in detail, but he was primarily a painter of the intellect, and cared more for ideas than technique. moving towards a cold and academic style, often compared to the Nazarenes. The sketches for these late works - usually in brown monochrone - are often livelier and more interesting than the finished picture'. Like David Scott(qv), he owes little to the traditions of Scottish art. McKay speaks of his 'lightsome and exuberant fancy and flowing line...His strength lies in his faculty of composition...That mastery of the brush so conspicuous in many Scottish painters was not among his gifts, though many of his earlier work show a delicate and tender craft'. In his early days had been greatly affected by the novels of Sir Walter Scott for many of which he had provided illustrations. But after visiting London 1843

he became more interested in the English poets, especially Shelley, Tennyson and Milton. Contributed outline engravings for Shelley's *Prometheus Unbound* (1844) and *The Tempest* (1845), also for Milton's *Comus*. Other illustrations include those for James Wilson's *Silent Love* (1845), Coleridge's *Life of the Ancient Mariner* (1863), W E Aytoun's *Lays of the Scottish Cavaliers* (1863), Charles Kingsley's *The Water Babies, Gems of Literature* (1866), *The Story of Wandering Willie* (1870), E Strivelyne's T*he Princess of Silverland and other Tales,* and John Brown's *Rab and his Friends* (1878); also illustrations for *A Book of British Ballads* (1842), Pennell's *Puck on Pegasus* (1861) and *The Cornhill Magazine* (1864). Irwin comments that he was the only Scottish painter of his generation to make extensive use of the nude in his paintings. Ruskin's assessment referred to him as 'the genius of Edinburgh, more of a thinking and feeling man than a painter, but not a bad painter'. His work is becoming more favourably reassessed, his occasional watercolours, especially from the early years, are wonderfully detailed and with a great feeling for nature, prepared in a detailed manner that for most artists would be described as too laborious but with his technique were unsurpassed of their kind. Sometimes he succeeded in rendering the inner spirit of the subject. This is especially the case in 'Luther at Erfurt' 1861 'one of its author's most perfect things, in which the moment chosen is that in which the monk who shook the world after a night of mental anguish, finds with the coming of dawn the light of a sure belief which was to revolutionise medieval Europe'. Exhibited RA(14) 1856-1869, including a portrait of 'Princess Helena' 1864 and the 'Fairy Raid' 1867, now in Glasgow AG. Did designs for a statue of 'Bruce and Psyche Watching the Sleep of Eros'; 'Spindrift' (sea-sprites poised on a wave), a portrait head of 'Professor Wilson' and several heads of Christ. Also designed a stained-glass window of Robert the Bruce for Dunfermline Abbey 1882. Refused nominations for the Presidency of the RSA 1876, again in 1891. In 1882 he was granted the Freedom of the Royal Burgh of Dunfermline. Exhibited RSA(132), GI & AAS(3) in 1885 and 1893. Represented in NGS, SNPG, Glasgow AG, Royal Shakespeare Company (Stratford), Kirkcaldy AG, City of Edinburgh collection (oil and woodcut), Royal collection, Montreal Museum, Melbourne AG (Australia), Dunfermline City Chambers, Perth AG.
**Bibl:** AJ 1861, 119; 1863, 64; 1866, 140; 1869, 1-31; 1881, 78-80; 1895, 97-128; 1902, 70-72; Alastair Auld, 'Fact and Fancy: Sir JN Paton', SAC 1967; Bate 71ff; Caw 167-70; Grant 233, pl81; Halsby 278; Hardie 32-5; Houfe; Irwin 265-6, 285-295, 357-8, pls 138-141; Maas 152-3; Mag of Art III (1880) 1-6; 'L'Art' 59 (1894) 386ff; 61 (1902) 30; Macmillan [SA] 212-13,230-2; Noel-Paton, Tales of a Grand-daughter, 1970; Ruskin, Academy Notes 1856.

**PATON, Mrs Margaret** **fl 1866-1892**
Edinburgh landscape painter in oil and watercolour. Wife of Waller Hugh P(qv). Lived for many years at 14 George Sq. Exhibited RSA(6) including 'The church at Fetteresso' 1867 and 'Trout Pool on the Dochart' 1890; also AAS.

**PATON, Mary Irene** **fl 1966**
Glasgow painter. Exhibited 'Nocturne' at the GI, from Crown Rd South.

**PATON, Mary Richmond** **fl 1959-**
Aberdeenshire painter, especially of garden scenes and local landscape. Trained Gray's School of Art, Aberdeen. Exhibited RSA (6) 1956-84, GI(3) & AAS(16), from Lonmay manse and latterly Rathen Lodge, Fraserburgh.

**PATON, Peter** **fl c1830-1850**
Born Galashiels. Painter in watercolour, pen and pencil; also woodcutter. Few details of his life are known. There is a group of sepia drawings in the NGS originally executed for the Abbotsford edition of Sir Walter Scott's novels (1842-1847) where they appear as woodcuts. The drawings are clearly done by a highly competent hand. Also sketched Edinburgh and Italian scenes.

**PATON, Ranald Alexander Noel** **1864-1943**
Portrait painter. Oldest son of Sir Joseph Noel P(qv). Lived at 33 George Square. Exhibited a portrait of his father at the RA 1895 and the portrait of an artist, perhaps also his father, at the RSA 1890. Represented in SNPG by a pencil portrait of his father 1890.

**PATON, Miss Sophia M** **fl 1865-1868**
Selkirk painter in oil of landscapes, especially castles, flowers and fruit. Moved to Edinburgh in 1866. Exhibited RSA(14) & GI(2).

**PATON, Victor Albert Noel** **fl 1902**
Sculptor. Son of Joseph Noel P(qv). Exhibited a portrait bust of his father at the RSA 1902.

**PATON, Waller Hubert** **fl 1881-1932**
Sculptor and watercolour painter of portraits, figure subjects and wildlife. Not to be confused with his father Waller Hugh P(qv). A very competent modeller gaining several public commissions in the 1890s and early 20th century. In 1902 established a studio at 39 Bruntsfield Gardens, Edinburgh. Specialised in decorative work, for example statues of 'Cardinal David Beaton' and 'Sir James Douglas' now in the SNPG, a statue of 'Robert the Bruce' in marble, freestone and wood, a recumbent figure for St Conan's Church, Lochawe, a Boer War Memorial to the Argyll and Sutherland Highlanders 1907 at Stirling Castle and a statuette of 'Victory' in bronze for the NGS 1881. Also exhibited several paintings at the RSA among them several scenes in Colorado 1897. In 1887 went on a sketching trip to Wester Ross, one result of which was 'At Garve Inn' RSA 1887.
**Bibl:** Gifford 262; M.H.Noel Paton, Tales of a Grand-Daughter, Edinburgh 1970; Wingfield.

**PATON, Waller Hugh RSA RSW** **1828-1895**
Born Wooers-Alley, Dunfermline Jly 27; died Edinburgh, Mar 8. Painter in oil but principally watercolour of landscapes; illustrator. Son of a Dunfermline damask designer, antiquarian and religious mystic. Brother of Joseph Noel Pqv). Father of Waller Hubert P(qv). Began by assisting his father. In 1848 he became increasingly interested in landscape painting and took lessons in watercolour from John Adam Houston(qv). Joined his brother on sketching holidays at the family's summer home on Arran. In 1858, with his brother, illustrated Ayton's *Lays of the Scottish Cavaliers* (1863); also *Poems and Songs* by Robert Burns (1875). His wife was also an artist. From 1859 he lived in Edinburgh although spending long spells in London 1860. In 1861 and again 1868 toured the continent. Queen Victoria commissioned him to undertake a drawing of Holyrood Palace 1862. The first Scottish painter to work entirely in the open air, most of his compositions being of the hill and river scenery of Perthshire, Aberdeenshire and especially Arran, often at sunset. A most prolific artist, all his major works and many of the smaller studies were reproduced in postcard size in 4 volumes, all of which remained in the family until sold at auction and subsequently dispersed. His portrayal of the Scottish Highlands in pre-Raphaelite detail and with a predeliction for sunset is unsurpassed. Unfortunately his habit of using strong bodycolour for highlights and depth has led to fading, especially in the sky. The sheer number of his watercolours which appear on the market and his brother's greater fame as an oil painter, have resulted in insufficient attention being given to the many fine large oils that he produced. His prevailing colour was the purple of the northern sunset for which in his lifetime he was criticised by Caw and others, although on occasion was defended by Ruskin. Those who loved the dramatic qualities of the Highlands without the intrusion of Highland cattle or deer and very often of people, find in Paton's work peaceful charm that is seldom found elsewhere. Went to great lengths to locate places of historical and local interest as well as views having special aesthetic appeal. Elected FSA (Scot) 1869, RSW 1878, ARSA 1857, RSA 1865. Exhibited RA(15) 1860-1880, RSA(345); also GI & AAS 1885-1900, latterly from 14 George Square. Represented in NGS, Aberdeen AG, Dundee AG, Greenock AG, Glasgow AG, Cardiff AG, Victoria AG (Australia).
**Bibl:** AJ 1895, 169 (obit); Bryan; DNB; Caw 172,194-5; Halsby 100-102; Houfe; Irwin 357-8; McKay 317-8; Macmillan [SA] 230,253.

**PATON, William** **fl 1869**
Glasgow animal painter. Exhibited 'English terrier dog' at the GI, from St. George's Rd.

**PATRICK, Ann** **1937-**
Born Dundee. Concentrates on landscapes and still life in Angus, north-west Sutherland, France, Spain and Italy; also flowers. Daughter of James McIntosh P(qv). Trained Dundee College of Art and Hospitalfield, Arbroath 1954-58. In 1960 married the painter Richard Hunter(qv); children also artists. Motivated by a great love of

the sun, music and colour and influenced by clarity of colour wherever it is found, especially in early Italian and Persian painting but also in the more modern works of Monet, Bonnard and Balthus. Has held several solo shows throughout Scotland. Exhibits regularly RSA(70+), occasionally RA & GI(25) 1870-1988; also AAS(2). Represented in Aberdeen AG, Dundee AG.

**PATRICK, Mrs Cordelia McIntyre** **fl 1945-1968**
Glasgow painter of portraits, flower studies and topographical works. Exhibited RSA(6) & GI(5).

**PATRICK, Elizabeth** **fl 1861-1892**
Glasgow landscape painter in oil. Studied Glasgow School of Art 1875-80, later joined the staff. Founder member, with Georgina(qv) & Robert Greenlees(qv), Glasgow Society of Artists(qv). Exhibited RSA(3) but mainly GI(30).

**PATRICK, James** **fl 1880-1905**
Edinburgh painter in oil and watercolour of rustic interiors, churches and landscape; also a number of golfing subjects including a watercolour portrait of 'Tom Morris' c1890 and 'The Links Fair, Kirkcaldy' 1894. Related to John(qv) and John Rutherford P(qv). Exhibited RSA(25) & GI(2), initially from Wemyssfield, Kirkcaldy, later from Edinburgh.
**Bibl:** Wingfield.

**PATRICK, James** **fl 1926**
Fife landscape painter. Exhibited AAS(1) from Lu-Mara, Pittenweem.

**PATRICK, James** **fl 1947**
Glasgow watercolour painter; topographical works. Exhibited GI(1), from Sandyford Place.

**PATRICK, James Baxter** **fl 1884**
Edinburgh painter in oil. Exhibited RSA(2) from 17 Barony Street.

**PATRICK, James McIntosh RSA ROI ARE LLD** **1907-1998**
Born Dundee, 4 Feb, died Dundee, 7 April. Painter in oil and watercolour of landscapes and portraits; also etcher. Son of an architect, father of Ann P(qv). Educated Morgan Academy, Dundee and trained Glasgow School of Art 1924-8 under Maurice Greiffenhagen(qv), and then in Paris. Studied etching under Charles Murray(qv). Worked in a clear detailed manner in the pre-Raphaelite tradition but with greater attention to light. As an etcher is regarded as one of the first in a new generation of etchers producing highly finished images in the early 1930s inspired by 16th and 17th century artists, especially Breughel. Based in Dundee for many years, 'Winter in Angus' was purchased by the Chantrey Bequest 1935. Received many awards including the Guthrie prize, RSA 1935. Taught at the Duncan of Jordanstone College of Art. First became known for his finely executed etchings and in 1928 negotiated a substantial contract with a London dealer for prints. When the market for prints collapsed he diversified, accepted a part-time post at Dundee College of Art 1930 and began painting seriously in oils, exhibiting his first work RA 1928. The Tate purchased their first Patrick in 1935. His paintings are generally of cultivated landscapes presented panoramically around Dundee and the Carse of Gowrie executed in minute, delicately captured detail which has been likened to Breughel. Exfoliated trees are precisely delineated like the skeleton of a carefully dissected fish. A one-man exhibition was held at Dundee AG 1967 and a travelling exhibition 1987. Elected ROI 1949, ARSA 1949, RSA 1957. Exhibited regularly RA, RSA, RE, RBA & GI(25). Represented in SNGMA, Aberdeen AG, Dundee AG, Glasgow AG, City of Edinburgh collection, Brodie Castle (NTS), Manchester AG, Perth AG, National Gallery of South Africa, NG of South Australia, Sydney AG (Australia), Carnegie Institute (Pittsburg).
**Bibl:** Roger Billcliffe, 'James McIntosh Patrick', FAS London (Ex Cat 1987); Dundee AG, 'McIntosh Patrick', (Ex Cat 1967); Halsby 234,235,243,278; Hardie 146-7; Hartley 156; Macmillan [SA] 359-360,361-2.

**PATRICK, Jessie G** **fl 1902-1905**
Glasgow sculptor. Exhibited GI(2) & L(2) from 59 Bath Street.

**PATRICK, John** **fl 1871-1886**
Kirkcaldy painter in oil and watercolour; mainly landscapes especially of the east coast, also wild plants and figure subjects. Related to John Rutherford(qv) and James P(qv). Exhibited RSA(32) & GI(7), formerly from Wemyssfield, Kirkcaldy and latterly from Edinburgh.

**PATRICK, John Rutherford** **fl 1882-1904**
Painter in oil of landscape and genre. Probably brother of James(qv) and John P(qv). Lived in Edinburgh. Exhibited 'Through wind and rain' at the RA (1891) from East Linton, Preston Kirk; also RSA(23), GI(6) & AAS(1).

**PATRICKSON, Miss** **fl 1817-1829**
Edinburgh painter in pastel, crayon and watercolour. Mostly portraits, occasional figure subjects. In August, 1817 was living in Dumfries. Exhibited at Carlisle Academy 1824 from Great King St, Edinburgh. Thereafter exhibited 12 works at the RSA, latterly from South Castle St. In 1827 one of her exhibits was 'Mr Mackay of the Theatre Royal...in the character of Caleb Balderston'.

**PATTERSON, Gregory J** **fl 1988-**
Glasgow painter. Began exhibiting GI 1988 from Gibson St.

**PATTERSON, Iain** **1946-**
Born Ayr. Abstract painter, a minimalist. Lives in Edinburgh, teaches Edinburgh College of Art where he studied 1964-9. In 1969 awarded an Andrew Grant Travelling Scholarship enabling him to visit Albania, Czechoslovakia and Yugoslavia. Won SAC Award 1972. Has held several one man exhibitions including in Venice 1975 and another in Poland 1977. Represented in SAC.

**PATTERSON, J Ford** **fl 1885**
Dundee painter of coastal scenery. Exhib AAS(2) from 19 Albert Sq.

**PATTERSON, James** **fl 1885-1904**
Amateur flower painter, generally in oils. Exhibited RSA(1) & L(1) from Ancrum Manse, Ancrum.

**PATTERSON, Janet** **1941-**
Born Edinburgh. In 1949 moved to Liverpool and in 1960 went to London to study for four years at the Slade School under Patrick George. Won several drawing prizes and after graduating was awarded a French Government Scholarship enabling her to visit Aix-en-Provence. On her return took up a position as lecturer at Liverpool and Wallasey College of Art 1966-68, in 1969 returned to Edinburgh. Received an SAC Bursary 1981. Elected member of the London Group and professional member SSA 1983. Compositions, often in watercolour, depict the isolated human figure contained in an environment. Often a geometric element - austere grids of patterns representing walls and windows - pinioning and supporting more voluptuous forms within the image. Photographs are used as an aid towards accuracy. 'For her the starting-point of a picture lies not so much in the physical appearance of a figure - or of any other object - as in that figure's quality of mysterious particularity in relation to its surroundings. The resulting images haunt and disconcert in the manner of powerful narrative, deriving their strength from her capability as both visionary and draughtswoman, and from her capacity to summarise and condense and, in the context of a single gesture, simultaneously to record and invent' [Mary Taubman]. In 1987 her work was selected for inclusion in the British-Australian bicentennial exhibition. For five months was artist-in- residence at various Australian institutions. Represented in Sheffield AG, SAC, Chatsworth.

**PATTERSON, John/James** **fl 1829-1830**
Edinburgh landscape and genre painter, also cabinet portraits. Animals occasionally appear in his work. Exhibited RSA(8).

**PATTERSON, Miss M S** **fl 1881**
Edinburgh amateur painter; exhibited RSA(1) from 28 Rutland St.

**PATTERSON, (George) Malcolm** **fl 1921-1938**
St Andrews-based printmaker and versatile painter of portraits, genre and townscapes. Worked in France, Italy and Spain. Exhibited RSA(28) & AAS(1), from Dauphin Hill.

**PATTERSON, Matthew** **fl 1889-1890**
Glasgow amateur painter; exhibited GI(2) from Rockhill, Dennistoun.

**PATTISON, George** **fl 1884**
Amateur painter; exhibited GI(2).

**PATTISON, James** **1955-**
Born Dundee, 2 Nov. Painter in acrylic on canvas; also etcher and printmaker. Trained Duncan of Jordanstone School of Art 1973-79 where he studied architecture. Influenced by a year spent in Amsterdam and three months in Vienna. The influences of Rothko, Matisse, and the Cubists can be seen in his abstract compositions. Solo exhibition Glasgow 1990. Exhibits RSA since 1980 & regularly AAS since 1982 from 33 Commercial St. Represented in Dundee AG, Elvar Aalto Museum (Finland), SAC.
**Bibl:** Bill Hare, Contemporary Painting in Scotland, Edinburgh 1993.

**PATTISON, Robert T** **fl 1876-1877**
Edinburgh flower and fruit painter; exhibited RSA(5).

**PATTULLO, Lin** **1949-**
Born Glasgow. Landscape painter. Self-taught. First solo exhibition in Glasgow 1993. Winner Lauder Award (GSWA) 1994, Neville Award (Paisley Art Institute) 1997, Trevor & Webster Award (RGI) 1997. Exhibits RSA 1993- and RGI since 1991. Represented in collection of HRH Prince Charles.

**PAUL, Andrew** **fl 1870s**
Scottish engraver and landscape painter. In their catalogue the Foulis refer to Paul's 'essays in landscape that were done before his death (and) have that simplicity which promises superior excellence'. His view of the West Street, called the Trongate, is the last and most capital of his works, and was finished after his death by William Buchanan(qv).
**Bibl:** Brydall 129; Foulis Academy catalogues (see Foulis Academy bibl).

**PAUL, Arthur Forman Balfour** **1875-1938**
Edinburgh architect. Designed many minor buildings in the city including St George's School, Upper Coltbridge Terrace (1911-14).
**Bibl:** Gifford 242,244,276,295,348,368,391,418,521,531,574,580, 628,635.

**PAUL, D** **fl 1846**
Greenock landscape painter; exhibited RSA(4).

**PAUL, David Scott** **fl 1869-1870**
Glasgow landscape painter in oil; exhibited RSA(2) & GI(2).

**PAUL, Elizabeth (Mrs J A D Paton)** **fl 1940**
Amateur Bothwell portrait painter and portrait miniaturist. Exhibited GI(7) from 13 Dunlop Crescent, and after her marriage from Gowanlea, Largs, Ayrshire.

**PAUL, Miss Florens A J** **fl 1900-1931**
Aberdeenshire landscape and flower painter in watercolours and occasionally oils. Descended from a French Huguenot family, one of whom fled to Aberdeen 1696. Sister of the poetess Ella Mary Gordon (Seton Gordon's mother) whose books Miss Paul illustrated. Her family acquired the small estate of Newseat, near Peterhead. Studied in London at the Queen Square School of Art and in Paris at the Atelier Ludovici. Exhibited ROI and RBA. Held a solo exhibition in London 1922 and again in 1931, the latter devoted to the scenery of upper Deeside, especially in the vicinity of Balmoral and Crathie where she lived. Included in Sir Joseph Duveen's Hull exhibitions. A contemporary critic wrote that 'the next best thing to visiting Deeside itself is to spend an hour studying Miss Paul's subjects'. Published *Sketches of Deeside* (c1931) which include 20 sepia illustrations.
**Bibl:** F A J Paul, Sketches of Deeside (privately printed, nd c1931); Walker's Monthly, April-May, 1931.

**PAUL, Mrs G M** **fl 1873**
Edinburgh landscape painter; exhibited 'On the Cowie, Stonehaven' at the RSA.

**PAUL, H S** **fl 1887-1888**
Dumbarton amateur painter; exhibited GI(2) from Kirkton.

**PAUL, J G** **fl 1880-1884**
Amateur landscape and marine painter. Lived in Glasgow before moving to Kensington, London. Exhibited GI(1) & RBA(3).

**PAUL, James B** **fl 1873-1891**
Glasgow oil painter of landscapes; exhibited RSA(2).

**PAUL, John M** **fl 1947**
Glasgow watercolour painter. Exhibited GI(1).

**PAUL, Robert** **1739-1770**
Glasgow-based engraver, probably Scottish. Trained at the Foulis Academy, Glasgow and engraved several views of the city one of which, of the cathedral, is dated 1762.
**Bibl:** Bryan; Bushnell; D Murray, R and A Foulis, Glasgow 1913.

**PAUL, Robert** **fl 1840-1845**
Scottish portrait painter about whom very little is known. Commissioned to undertake several works by Lord Cochrane of Cults. In the collection is a posthumous portrait 'George Boyle, 4th Earl of Glasgow (1765-1843)', signed 'R Paul, Edin 1843'. In 1844 a portrait of the 'Revd Edward B Ramsay (1793-1872), Dean of Edinburgh' signed again 'R Paul, fl Edin 1844'. Exhibited RSA(7), mostly portraits but also 'Bothwell Castle' 1841.

**PAUL, Robert** **fl 1865**
Stirlingshire amateur watercolourist. Exhibited a pastoral scene at the GI from Lennoxtown.

**PAUL, Robert Duncan** **fl 1971-1983**
Glasgow printmaker. Exhibited GI(4) & AAS(1), from 12 Cresswell St.

**PAULIN, George Henry ARSA FRBS** **1888-1962**
Born Muckart, Perthshire, 14 Aug; died Swindon, Wiltshire, 10 Jly. Portrait and figure sculptor. Brother of Jeanie Wright Ellis(qv). Educated Dollar Academy and Edinburgh before embarking on a six year course at Edinburgh Institution and College of Art under Percy Portsmouth(qv), then in Rome and for four years in Florence, and Paris 1911-14. Returning to this country he settled in Glasgow becoming an active member of the Glasgow Art Club(qv). Principal works are the War Memorials in several Scottish towns including Denny, Dollar, Kirkcudbright and Milngavie. Also memorials of Sir William Ramsay at Glasgow University and of Dr MacEwen in Claremont Church, Glasgow. Elected ARSA 1920. Exhibited RA (27), RSA(61), RI(16), GI (50+), AAS 1929-33 & L(7). Represented in SNPG ('Sir William MacEwen, Glasgow surgeon, 1848-1924').

**PAULIN, J W (Mrs Dewi Ellis)** **fl 1917**
Milngavie amateur painter. Exhibited GI(1).

**PAULL, Myra C** **fl 1902-1908**
Aberdeen painter of figurative subjects and landscape. Exhibited AAS(7) from 13 Albyn Terrace.

**PAVILLON, Charles** **1726-1772**
Born Aix-en-Provence, France, 26 Mar; died Edinburgh, 14 Jne. Painter of mythological subjects and administrator. May have been in Edinburgh 1766, in 1767 succeeded another Frenchman William Delacour(qv) as Master of the Trustees Academy, a post he retained until c1771. John Brown(qv) and Alexander Nasmyth(qv) were among his pupils. Exhibited 2 works in London 1768-70, also at the Scottish Academy in 1768 & 1770.
**Bibl:** Brydall 145; Esmé Gordon, The Royal Scottish Academy 66; Irwin 91; Scots Mag, vol 34,333.

**PAXTON, John** **1725-1780**
Born Scotland; died Bombay, Feb 19. Portrait and history painter. Of Scottish parentage. Brother of Sir William Paxton of the Bengal Civil Service. Trained Foulis Academy and in Italy. In 1776 went to India where he died. Painted a portrait of 'Signorina Zamperini as 'Cechina'', and 'James Tassie', a fellow student at the Foulis Academy. A contemporary writer (Catherine Read) clearly did not think much of the artist, writing in Calcutta 'we have now another named Paxton but he is a very indifferent hand, and yet he gets employment'. Exhibited regularly at the Society of Artists of which he was elected a member 1765; also RA(6) 1769 and 1770. All unknown sitters except for a 'Mr Estwick' 1770. (In the RA exhibitors

list a further 8 works are mentioned 1802-1807 under John Paxton but unless the date has been incorrectly recorded this must be a different artist since John Paxton died in 1780). Represented in SNPG by 'James Tassie'.
**Bibl:** Brydall 129; Bryan; Forster; Scot. Hist. Rev. Vol 2, 46; Irwin 90; David Murray, Robert and Andrew Foulis and the Glasgow Press, Glasgow 1913.

**PAYNE, Arthur E** **fl 1906-1912**
Aberdeen landscape and figurative painter in oil and tempera. Exhibited RA(1) & AAS(5) from 44 Hammerfield Avenue.

**PAYNE, G T W** **fl 1965-1977**
Glasgow painter in oil and watercolour of figurative and topographical subjects. Exhibited GI(7), from Bishopbriggs.

**PAYNTER, Hilary RE FRSA** **1943-**
Born Dunfermline. Wood engraver and art therapist. Lived in China as a child 1949-51 and then Malta 1956-8. Trained Portsmouth College of Art under Gerry Tucker 1959-64. Taught in Putney 1965-7 and for two years in USA. Teacher in charge at Hammersmith Remand Home 1967-72. Elected member, Society of Wood Engravers 1972, becoming Secretary 1983; elected RE 1984, FRSA 1984. Illustrated Weatherhead: *The Imprisoned Heart* (1979), *Astrologer's Pocket Almanac* (1980), *Alternative Holidays* (1981), *Hilary Paynter's Picture Book* (1984), Jones: *Bwyta'n Te* (1989), Shakespeare: *King Lear* (1989), *Richard II* (1989). Exhibits RA, RE.
**Bibl:** *Hilary Paynter: Wood Engravings* (1991); Brett; Garrett 1 & 2; Horne 346; Jaffé; Mahoney.

**PAYTEN, Miss Peggy** **fl 1934-1939**
Ayrshire landscape and bird painter. Exhibited 'Fog on the Clyde' and 'A morning ride at the RSA'; also GI(2) & AAS from Shirley, 26 Fullarton Drive, Troon, latterly Glasgow.

**PAYTON, Mrs Emily (née Smith)** **fl 1916-1936**
Painter. Wife of Robert Payton R(qv). Exhibited RSA(3) at first from Huntingdonshire and Sussex, latterly from Edinburgh.

**PEACEY, Jessie M Lawson ARBS** **1885-?**
Born Edinburgh. Sculptress and painter. She lived for a time in New York as well as in London from where, at 4 Pembroke Studios, London W8, she worked mainly on portraits and figures. Known as Jess Peacey.

**PEACH, Dorothy** **fl 1945-1955**
Edinburgh-based painter of landscape, genre, still life and flowers. Exhibited RSA(20), latterly from 5 Alva St.

**PEACH, Margaret** **fl 1976**
Roxburghshire painter of local street scenes, portraits and landscape. Exhibited RSA(3) from Kelso.

**PEACOCK, Alex** **fl 1880**
Glasgow amateur watercolour painter; exhibited 'Charge of the 17th Lancers at Ulundi' at the GI from 48 Overnewton Square.

**PEACOCK, Alexander W** **fl 1885-1887**
Edinburgh landscape painter in watercolour. Local scenery. Exhibited RSA(2) from 9 McLaren Road.

**PEACOCK, Miss Catherine C** **fl 1865-1876**
Glasgow oil painter of landscape, flowers and figure studies; exhibited RSA(4) & GI(12).

**PEACOCK, J Neil** **fl 1935-1937**
Glasgow amateur watercolourist; exhibited GI(4) from 279 Mosspark Drive.

**PEACOCK PRINTMAKERS** **1974-**
Aberdeen non-profit making distributing company providing facilities for artists in north-east Scotland to make and market original prints. Membership is open to all, and the workshop is controlled by a 5-person management committee. Work is conducted at four levels: classes of instruction - members working - custom printing by staff - publication and distribution of artists' work. Located in Castle St (tel 01224 51539).

**PEARSE, Mrs Annette** **fl 1932-1940**
Prolific amateur Dunbartonshire artist. Delicate portrayals of lace, velvet and crinoline gowns, mostly in pen and ink. Exhibited GI(16) from Woodend, Dullatur.

**PEARSON, Dorothy** **fl 1938-1940**
Amateur watercolourist who lived at 16 Learmonth Terrace, Edinburgh. Exhibited RSW(3).

**PEARSON, Iain** **fl 1971-1975**
Greenock sculptor; figurative works mostly in wood. Exhibited GI(5).

**PEARSON, Miss Katherine** **fl 1987**
Glasgow sculptress. Exhibited a work in metal at the GI.

**PEASTON Nancy G** **fl 1928-1940**
Greenock painter in watercolour and stained glass designer. Conducted a business with her husband/brother/father as 'designers, arts and crafts' at 21 Brougham St, Greenock 1938-40. Exhibited two stained glass designs and a mural panel at the RSA; also GI(7), from 79 South St.

**PEDDIE, Archibald** **1917-?**
Born Helensburgh, 15 Aug. Painter in oil, watercolour and tempera. Local views and still life. Trained Glasgow School of Art 1935-39. Exhibited regularly RSA, GI & SSA from Perthshire.

**PEDDIE, Barbara S** **fl 1878-1908**
Edinburgh painter in oil, watercolour and pastel of flowers, portraits, townscapes and landscapes including continental studies. Exhibited RSA(40) including a portrait of her father 'Dr Peddie' 1896, GI(11), AAS 1885-1902, RI(1) & SWA(2).

**PEDDIE, Christina (Mrs J A Henderson Tarbet)** **fl 1892-1937**
Edinburgh painter in oil and watercolour of buildings, still life, miniature portraits on ivory, and landscapes. Married to Henderson Tarbet(qv). Exhibited RSA(35), RSW(13), AAS(1) & GI(4).
**Bibl:** Halsby 278.

**PEDDIE, George S** **1883-1911**
Dundee watercolour painter and illustrator. His life was cut short before he had had an opportunity of establishing a reputation.
**Bibl:** Halsby 278.

**PEDDIE, James Dick** **1885-1918**
Edinburgh painter in oil and watercolour of landscapes and portraits. Moved to London c1906. Exhibited RA(5) including an imposing painting of 'Ben Cruachan' 1895, RSA(37), RSW(2), GI(4), AAS(1) & L(2).
**Bibl:** Halsby 278.

**PEDDIE, John Dick MP RSA** **1824-1891**
Edinburgh architect. Partner in the firm of Peddie and Kinnear, Peddie concentrating on the Italian style leaving Kinnear to the baronial. Among his many designs were Dryburgh House (1877), Dunblane Hydropathic Institution (1877), Craiglockart Hydropathic Institution (1878) and branches of the Royal Bank of Scotland and the National Bank in Paisley (1879); also the XVth century French Gothic Morgan Hospital, Dundee (1863-6), Kinnettles Castle, Angus (1867) and the University Club in Princes St, Edinburgh (1866). Designed monuments to Rev James Peddie and Thomas Scott in Warriston Cemetery. A good example of his domestic work is his own home, now North Trinity House, 114-6 Trinity Rd (1858). Elected ARSA 1868, RSA 1891, Secretary, RSA 1870-76. Exhibited RSA(29) 1854-1890 & GI(2). Represented in City of Edinburgh collection.
**Bibl:** Dunbar 162; Gifford 68,318,323,325,336,376,576,614; A Gomme & D Walker, Architecture of Glasgow, London 1987(rev), 296 et passim; Bruce Walker & W S Gauldie, Architects and Architecture on Tayside, Dundee 1984, 131.

**PEDDIE, John More Dick** **1853-1921**
Edinburgh architect. Erudite son of John Dick Peddie(qv). Specialised in restorations. Partner of Sir George Washington

Browne(qv). Responsible in Glasgow for the National Bank, 47 St. Vincent St and the Scottish Provident Building, 17-29 St Vincent Place whilst in Edinburgh he designed the College of Art (1906-10); Commercial Union Insurance offices, George St (1908-9); Bank of Scotland, George St (1883-5); Longmore Hospital, Salisbury Place (1879) and the churches of St Kentigern, St Peter's Place (1897) and Holy Cross, Cramond (1912). Exhibited RSA 1879-1921.
**Bibl:** Gifford 43,185,234,258,301,304,494,548,636,pl.109; A Gomme & D Walker, Architecture of Glasgow, London 1987(rev), 296 et passim.

**PEDDIE, Tom Hutchinson** **1871-1954**
Born Musselburgh, Oct 4; died Jne 18. Painter in oils, watercolour, pen & ink. Portraits, genre, murals, landscape. Studied under Sir Alma Tadema. Worked for *Illustrated London News.* Executed murals for several hotels in England and Scotland, including Douglas hotel, Aberdeen. A retrospective posthumous exhibition was held at the Rendezvous Gallery, Aberdeen.

**PEEBLES, Mrs Eleanor** **fl 1923**
Amateur painter, wife of the minister at Uddingston, Lanarkshire. Exhibited a miniature portrait, 'The Rt Rev John Smith DD, Moderator of the General Assembly' at the RSA.

**PEEBLES, Mrs G S** **fl 1910**
Aberdeen portrait miniaturist. Exhibited AAS(1) from 65 Osborne Pl.

**PEFFERS, Barbara Douglas** **1943-**
Born in Edinburgh of Scottish parents. Sculptress in ceramics. Trained in ceramics in Denmark with Gutte Eriksen and Helle Allpass 1962-63 before returning to this country for further studies at Duncan of Jordanstone College of Art 1965-70. Qualified as a teacher 1973 and taught in Caithness 1975-80 and Wester Ross 1984-1988. Awarded travelling scholarship and the Helen Ottilie Wallace prize, also an Andrew Carnegie travelling scholarship enabling her to visit Turkey 1968-9. Travelled in France 1979 from whence she returned in 1987 and 88. Initially her work was based on the human figure, later developing through landscape to constructions based on aspects of the sea. Currently uses a wide variety of materials and techniques and is also returning to ceramic work. Lives and works at Millhouse, Isle Martin, near Ullapool, Wester Ross, with her sister Evelyn P(qv). Exhibits RSA 1971, 1980 & 1981; also AAS(1) 1969.

**PEFFERS, Evelyn** **1939-**
Born Hawick. Sculptress. Painter in oil mostly landscapes and seascapes also draws in pencil and works in terracotta, bronze and bronze resin specialising in figurative work, also works in glass and natural forms for making abstract sculpture as well as sculptures of portrait heads and equestrian sculpture including polo. Trained Edinburgh and Dundee. Private pupil of the late Scott Sutherland(qv). Her aim in abstract work is to portray "beautiful or arresting objects with menace". Exhibits RSA 1986 & 1989, also SSA & SSWA. Lives and works at Millhouse, Isle Martin, near Ullapool, Wester Ross, with her sister Barbara Douglas P(qv).

**PELLY, Frances RSA ARBS** **1947-**
Born Edinburgh. Sculptor with a preference for natural media - clay, stone and wood. Studied Duncan of Jordanstone College of Art, Dundee 1965-71. Lecturer Gray's School of Art, Aberdeen 1978-83. Received many awards including the Carnegie (1969), Guthrie (1970) and Gillies (1982) prizes. In 1986 was one of four artists in residence Edinburgh. A retrospective exhibition was held at St. Andrews University 1987. Her work is sensitively carved; she has a preference for displaying on the floor or wall rather than on a plinth. Often uses 'found' objects, re-arranged to create inherent friction and tension. Fascinated by graveyards. Elected ARSA 1976, RSA 1990. Exhibits regularly RSA, GI & SSA; also AAS(4) 1980-3, latterly from Windbreck, Burry, Orkney.

**PENDER, William** **fl 1885**
Edinburgh painter of minor consequence; exhibited 'The head of a cavalier' at the RSA, from 6A Salisbury Street.

**PENDER, Walter L** **fl 1904**
Glasgow minor painter of 10 Grantly Street, Shawlands; exhibited GI(3).

**PENDER-CRICHTON, A** **fl 1934**
Glasgow amateur topographical painter; exhibited RSA(3) from 24 Gibson Street.

**PENNEY, Andrew Matthew** **fl 1865-1907**
Edinburgh painter in oil and watercolour of landscapes, narrative paintings and an occasional portrait. In 1880 exhibited a miniature portrait on ivory at the RSA and in 1905 'A bit of Old Edinburgh'. Exhibited RSA(18), RSW(1) & GI(1).

**PENNY, William** **fl 1800-1838**
Painter in watercolour, pen and ink; also engraver. Working in the early part of the century. Painted views of Edinburgh in pen and ink and engraved other artists' work. Engraved a miniature portrait of 'Robert Fergusion of Raith, Fife' (from a bronze medal). Also engraved, for the *Bannatyne Club Miscellany,* vol 2, Gordon of Rothiemay's 'Views of Edinburgh Castle' and 'Parliament House'. Responsible for the frontispiece to Bishop Lesley's *History of Scotland,* also engraved the plates for Cosmo Innes's *Chronicle of Melrose,* and a plate showing a sugar bowl belonging to John Trotter Brockett Esq of Newcastle. Lived in Midcalder, nr Edinburgh. Represented in Glasgow AG.
**Bibl:** Bushnell; Halsby 278.

**PEPLOE, Denis Frederic Neal RSA** **1914-1993**
Born Edinburgh, 25 Mar; died Edinburgh, 21 May. Painter in oil of still life, landscape and figurative subjects; also sculptor. Son of Samuel John P(qv). Educated Edinburgh Academy and Edinburgh College of Art 1931-6, followed by a period in Paris at the Academie André L'Hôte 1937. Lived in Edinburgh; taught Fettes College for two years followed by war service in the Intelligence Corps and Special Operations Executive. Taught at Edinburgh College of Art 1954-79. Travelled on a scholarship to Yugoslavia, Greece and Italy. Enjoyed depicting the form and texture of natural objects although latterly became more interested in pattern and tone. Elected ARSA 1956, RSA 1966. Librarian, RSA 1966-1973. 'An air of shyness and reserve concealed a fine, lively intellect and a wide appreciation of all things aesthetic' [Gage]. Exhibited regularly RSA & GI(5). Represented in Glasgow AG, Kirkcaldy AG, Perth AG, Edinburgh City collection, SAC.
**Bibl:** Edward Gage, The Scotsman, 22 May 1993(obit).

**PEPLOE, Mrs Margaret (née Mackay)** **fl 1935**
Edinburgh painter. Wife of Samuel John P(qv). Exhibited RSA(1) from 13 India Street.

**PEPLOE, Samuel John RSA** **1871-1935**
Born Edinburgh, 27 Jan; died Edinburgh, 11 Oct. Painter in oil of still life, landscapes and figure subjects. Son of Robert Peploe, Assistant Secretary, Commercial Bank of Scotland, and Anne Watson. Educated Edinburgh Collegiate School, trained under Charles Hodder at Trustees Academy and at RSA Life Classes 1892-96 and 1902. His father having died when he was 13 the young man entered the legal offices of Scott and Glover, but in 1893 he persuaded the Trustees to allow him to enter Edinburgh School of Art where his best friend was Robert Brough(qv). Another friend was R C Robertson(qv) with whom he sailed among the Western Isles, discovering Barra. Up to 1910 his work was painted within a small tonal range in a fluid medium with sure, incisive brushwork. The portraits, many of them models of Orkney girls, were assured, lyrical and tender. In 1910 he went to Paris for three years attending classes at the Academie Julien and the Academie Colarossi 1894, winning a silver medal at the latter. During this time he shared a studio with Brough. He had many friends including J D Fergusson(qv), Anne Estelle Rice(qv), Joseph Davidson(qv) the sculptor, and his wife Yvonne. During three years there working under Bouguereau (who Peploe later described as a 'damned old fool') he visited the south of France with his artist friends and became pre-occupied with the use of colour, struggling with simple masses of pure colour. This new enthusiasm for colour produced a series of still lifes, studio interiors and small landscapes which was to remain his métier for the rest of his life. His son has written 'his painting was unusually free of the psychological overtones common to much romantic art. The fact is that his response to the visual world was profound but lyrical; it was quite simply one of love. The emotions of fear, hate and impending doom which give impetus to much great romantic painting are almost

entirely absent...he achieved romantic ends by classical means in that he arrived at the particular through a stern preoccupation with the generalities of pure form. The subject of his paintings are never symbolic but realistic; yet they are quintessential, as an apple may be seen as containing within it the elements of life, fruitfulness and death'. After 1920, following Cézanne's theory, he became interested in the predominance of the arrangement of the picture space. In later years he was happiest painting landscapes. During most of his later summers he left Edinburgh to paint with his friend Cadell on Iona 1920-34. During these visits he produced a series of views of Ben More as seen from Iona, 'his quintessential statement about landscape painting' [Billcliffe]. In 1924 took his family to spend the summer in Cassis with Cadell and the following year was painting Sweetheart Abbey nr Dumfries with renewed excitement in portraying the landscape, especially the trees, in the warmer colours he was now developing. The only one of the four Colourists to become a teacher, for the last 18 months of his life he taught part-time at Edinburgh College of Art. In about 1934 he became increasingly depressed, a condition which moving to a new studio did little to alleviate. A full catalogue raisonné can be found in the SNGMA exhibition cat 1985. Elected ARSA 1918, RSA 1927. Exhibited RSA(82), GI(43) & AAS 1921-61. Represented in NGS, SNPG ('Self-portrait'), Aberdeen AG, Glasgow AG(18), Kirkcaldy AG, Lillie AG(Milngavie), City of Edinburgh collection(4), Brodie Castle (NTS)(Douglas Hall), Manchester AG, Perth AG, Nat Gall of New Zealand (Wellington), Sydney AG Australia)(4), Victoria AG (Australia).
**Bibl:** AJ, 1907, 282; Roger Billcliffe The Scottish Colourists, 1989, 15, 17, 20, 22, 23, 24, 25, 60; Stanley Cursiter, Peploe: An intimate memoir of an artist and his work, 1947; J D Fergusson, 'Memoir of S J Peploe' - written in 1945, republ. in Scott. Arts Rev.,Jan 1962; Halsby 159,208,278; Hardie 127 et passim ch viii; Hartley 157-8; SNGMA Exhibition: 'S J Peploe 1871-1935' (Ex Cat 1985, with introduction by Guy Peploe); Studio 45, 1909, 116.

**PEPLOE, William Watson** **1869-1933**
Born Edinburgh. Painter in oil, watercolour and pen and ink. Brother of Samuel John P(qv). Bank manager with the Commercial Bank of Scotland in Stockbridge. His artistic career has been overshadowed by other members of his family, especially his younger brother. In the early 1890s he and his brother and R C Robertson(qv) painted together on Barra where Robertson had built himself a studio. When his brother married and moved to Paris in 1910, he published a volume of poetry, *The Heart of a Dancer.* His black and white drawings prior to 1918, when he came under the influence of the Vorticists, were influenced by Aubrey Beardsley. In 1918 produced two tiny abstract colour sketches but his family believe that these were merely 'another manifestation of his playfulness'. Exhibited RSA(14) from his home in Edinburgh. Represented in SNGMA, Kirkcaldy AG.
**Bibl:** Halsby 278; Hartley 158; Stanley Cursiter, Peploe, 1947.

**PERCIVAL, A F** **fl 1894-1897**
Glasgow amateur sculptor. Exhibited three informal portraits at the GI from Alma Place, Shawlands.

**PERIGAL, Arthur Snr** **1784-1847**
Born in England; died Edinburgh. Portrait and landscape painter, also historical narrative works. Father of Arthur P(qv). Trained at the RA School under Fuseli. Settled with his family in Edinburgh c1830. Awarded RA gold medal 1811 for 'Themistocles taking refuge with Admetus'. Abandoned an early career in the Admiralty in favour of art. Exhibited RA(9), latterly from Ship St, Northampton & RSA(16) 1839-1846.
**Bibl:** Bryan.

**PERIGAL, Arthur RSA RSW** **1816-1884**
Born London; died Edinburgh, 5 Jne. Painter in oil and watercolour of landscapes. Son of Arthur P(qv). Came with his father to Edinburgh c1830. Studying under his father, otherwise self-taught but soon established a reputation in both oil and watercolour. Influenced by Horatio McCulloch(qv) and to a lesser degree by the pre-Raphaelites. With the exception of some views in Switzerland and Italy, his landscapes were entirely of Scottish scenery, treated in a crisp, breezy manner often verging on hardness but always bold and firm in handling. His diploma picture was of a moorland, near Kinlochewe. Some of his watercolours painted in Italy in the early 1840s show a lightness of touch missing in his later work. His views of the fishing villages of the east coast have historical interest not always appreciated. Elected ARSA 1841 when he was only 25; RSA 1868. Treasurer, RSA 1880 until his death in 1884. Prolific worker, exhibiting RA(11) 1861-84, RSA(355); also RSW, GI & Carlisle Academy 1846-50. Represented in NGS, Dundee AG, Glasgow AG(3), Paisley AG, City of Edinburgh collection, Brodie Castle (NTS) ('Beach scene at Nairn' 1878).
**Bibl:** AJ 1884, 224; Bryan; Brydall 448; Caw 146; Halsby 86-7,278; Irwin 356; McKay 318; Macmillan [SA] 229; Redgrave.

**PERMAN, Louise Ellen (Mrs James Torrance)** **1854-1921**
Born Eastwood, nr Glasgow; died Helensburgh. Trained Glasgow School of Art, married James Torrance 1912. Painted flowers in watercolour and oil; often exhibited with Jessie Algie(qv), Jessie King(qv) and Anne Muir(qv). Her oils were nicely composed with an excellent sense of form and colour. An underestimated painter whose true qualities are only beginning to be realised. Exhibited RA(6) 1899-1904 from 131 West Regent Street, Glasgow; also RSA (28), AAS 1900-19, ROI(1), GI(79), L(24) & SWA(8). Represented in Glasgow AG(2).
**Bibl:** Caw 456; Halsby 278.

**PERROTT, Sylvia** **fl 1964-1971**
Edinburgh engraver. Exhibited RSA(5), from Dalhousie Terr.

**PERRY, Alice Bertram** **fl 1916**
Amateur Glasgow sculptress. Exhibited 'Abandoned' at the GI, from Woodlands Tce.

**PETER, Rev James** **fl 1874**
Aberdeen watercolour painter of landscapes; exhibited RSA(1).

**PETERKIN, Katherine D** **fl 1908-1910**
Aberdeen landscape painter, primarily of local views. Exhibited AAS from 45 Queen's Rd.

**PETERS, Miss Helen** **fl 1974-1975**
Glasgow nature painter. Exhibited GI(3), from Gt Western Rd.

**PETERS, Miss Joyce** **fl 1941**
Landscape painter. Exhibited a local scene at the GI from St. Fillans.

**PETERS, William** **fl 1897**
Glasgow amateur sculptor. Exhibited 'Triptych inspiration' at the GI.

**PETERSON, Christine** **fl 1969-1976**
Aberdeen painter of portraits and still life. Exhibited AAS from 91 Beaconsfield Pl.

**PETRIE, George** **c1789-c1840**
Aberdeen engraver. Engraved bookplates for Thomas McCombie, 1820 and Alex Brebner, 1830. Bryan mentions an engraver **George PETRIE PRHA**, the son of James Petrie of Aberdeen, who was born in Dublin 1789, dying there in 1866, and who visited Scotland in 1845. It is unclear whether the two G Petries were related or a confusion concerning the same man.
**Bibl:** Bryan; Bushnell.

**PETRIE, James** **c1760-1819**
Born and died Dublin. Painter of landscapes and miniatures in oil; engraver. Although born in Dublin where he lived most of his life, both of his parents were Scottish, his father coming from Aberdeen and his mother from Edinburgh. Studied at Dublin Society's schools, he practised as a miniaturist at 82 Dame Street where he also conducted an antique and coin business as well as drawing illustrations for various magazines. Exhibited in Dublin 1801-1815. At the time of the Rebellion he was arrested on suspicion of having connections with the United Irishmen. After a spell in the Provost Prison he was released on the intervention of a Major Sandys, whose portrait he painted. By his first wife, Elizabeth, who came from Edinburgh, they had a son George Petrie PRHA. Represented in National Gallery, Dublin, including a watercolour portrait of 'Edward Fitzgerald' inscribed on the reverse 'Painted from life'; also a miniature of his son 'George Petrie', and 'Self-portrait'.
**Bibl:** Bryan; G W Stokes, Life of G Petrie 1868; Strickland; Wilson's Dublin Directory 1816, 115.

**PETRIE, James B** **fl 1965**
Dundee topographical painter. Exhibited GI(1), from Logie St.

**PETRIE, John** **fl 1796-1825**
Edinburgh engraver. Possibly father of John Petrie Jnr(qv). Contributed to the *New Picture of Edinburgh,* 1816; engraved six views and two plans for *The Original Description of the Monastery and Chapel Royal of Holyrood House,* published in 1819. The name 'John Petrie, Engraver' appears on the upper storey of a building behind St Giles in a south view of the church illustrated on page 54 of *New Picture of Edinburgh.*
**Bibl:** Bushnell; Butchart 57.

**PETRIE, John jnr** **fl 1878-1880**
Edinburgh painter in oil and sometimes chalk of portraits and figure studies. Related (?son) to John P snr(qv). Exhibited RSA(4) including 'The late John Petrie, student', RSA 1880 and 'The late John Petrie, Deputy Keeper of Sasines, Aberdeen' 1880.

**PETRIE, William McWhannel** **1870-1937**
Glasgow painter in oil, watercolour, pastel and tempera of domestic genre, topographical and figure studies, also etcher and sculptor. Studied at Paris and Italy. Versatile artist who taught for several years at Glasgow School of Art. Made a particular study of furniture and interior decorating. At Glasgow School of Art taught modern poster work and design. Active member, Glasgow Art School and frequent exhibitor in Glasgow, principally of tempera painting. Exhibited RSA(8), RSW(5), AAS(2) & GI(44) from 248 West George Street, Glasgow.
**Bibl:** Glasgow Herald, Jan 11 1937 (obit).

**PETRIE, William P** **fl 1914**
Edinburgh amateur portrait painter of 54 Shandwick Place; exhibited GI(1).

**PETTIE, John RA HRSA** **1839-1893**
Born Edinburgh, 17 Mar; died Hastings, 20 Nov. Painter of historical and literary subjects in oil, also illustrator. His parents hoped that he would go in for business but, supported by his uncle Robert Frier(qv), a well-known teacher of drawing, he chose art. When sixteen began studying Trustees Academy under Scott Lauder(qv) alongside Orchardson(qv), Hugh Cameron(qv) and others. There he met McTaggart(qv) who was to become a life-long friend, also Tom Graham(qv) and Orchardson with whom he later shared a studio in London. James Drummond(qv) was impressed by Pettie's earlier sketches. His first picture 'The Prison Pet', exhibited at the RSA in 1859 was purchased for £35 by the Society for the Promotion of Fine Arts in Scotland. His diploma picture was 'Jacobites, 1745'. Worked as an illustrator for *Good Words* (1861-3), *The Sunday Magazine* (1868-69), Wordsworth's *Poetry for the Young* (1863), *Pen and Pencil Sketches from the Poets* (1866), *Good Words for the Young* (1869) and *Touches of Nature by Eminent Artists* (1866). Provided all the illustrations for J de Lefde's *The Postman's Bag* (1865), L G Seguin's *The Boys of Axelford* (1869) and *Rural England* (1881). Leading member of the Sketching Club formed at the Waverley Temperance Hotel which continued until 1861. In 1862 he moved to London with Orchardson with whom he shared a studio. His earlier work, in which he often placed his friends, was marked by a well-developed sense of humour. Particularly attracted to illustrating themes from Shakespeare and Sir Walter Scott. His interpretations of historical scenes and literary events were always dramatic and imaginative, sometimes even theatrical. Excelled in costume pieces, producing figures of striking force even when using only grey washes. Caw compared his work to the novels of Dumas. Particularly attracted to military episodes, the best known being 'The Drumhead Court Martial'. His style was vigorous and in its richness of texture shows the influence of Van Dyck and Rubens. He was extremely generous, giving many of his paintings to friends, refusing any remuneration. He had a simple, straightforward nature and was very hospitable. 'Pettie is all decision and strength, he is sensuous where Orchardson is intellectual. He seizes an incident and paints a paean, a ballad, a joke; but whatever it may be, he sets out with a clearly defined purpose, and never wanders from the strict line leading to its attainment' [Hardie]. Although his work may now seem a little mannered, in his portrayal of incidents from Highland life he has never been bettered. The *AJ,* writing of 'The Chieftain's Candlesticks', noted, 'there is not another artist who could have painted with such trenchant force and truthfulness of effect those two stalwart Highlanders with flambeau in one hand and claymore in the other standing in their native dignity by the side of their Chieftain's chair in this bare and rugged hall'. After 1870 he experimented with chiaroscuro effects and turned more to portrait painting, often depicting his sitters in historical costume. 'The Vigil' was purchased for the nation by the Chantrey Bequest in 1884. Elected ARA 1866, RA 1873. Exhibited RA(119) 1860- 1893, RSA(71) 1858-1894; also ROI, RHA, GI(45), AAS & L(20). Represented in NG, V & A, NGS, SNPG(7), Aberdeen AG, City of Edinburgh collection, Broughty Ferry AG, Dundee AG, Glasgow AG, Ashmolean (Oxford), Bristol AG, Manchester AG, Sheffield AG, National Gallery, Perth AG, Victoria (Melbourne), Montreal AG.
**Bibl:** AJ 1869, 265-7; 1893, 206-10; 1907, 97-116; Armstrong 84-5; Bryan; Caw 240-243 et passim; Hardie 46,54 et passim ch iv; M.Hardie John Pettie 1908; Irwin 342-4 et passim; McKay 358-9; Macmillan [SA] 231,233-5,254,256,258; Reynolds 36,95.

**PETTIGREW, David** **1948-**
Born Meikle Wartle, Aberdeenshire, 1 Dec. Painter in oil of landscapes. Studied at Gray's School of Art 1967-71 and Hospitalfield 1971. Gained 2nd prize at Arbroath Exhibition 1971, won the Keith Award 1972 and was awarded a Travelling Scholarship 1973 and the Latimer Award the following year. Teaches art in Aberdeenshire where he lives. Most influenced by the north-east environment, by his visits to Italy and by the music of Poulenc and Debussy. Exhibited RSA 1972-6 & AAS(2) from 24b Kirk St, Oldmeldrum.

**PETTITT, George** **fl 1857-1863**
Probably English but painted and exhibited many works in Scotland. Landscapes, generally mountainous, often with lakes/lochs. Exhibited RA(2) and RSA (37) during the above years, including 'Kilchurn Castle, Loch Awe' 1862 and 'Loch Achray and the Trossachs' 1863. Lived at Rose Cottage, Grasmere, Westmoreland.
**Bibl:** AJ 1858, 78; 1859, 81; 1861, 71.

**PEVIE, George** **fl 1893-1906**
Aberdeen landscape and portrait painter. Exhibited AAS(3) including 'Culblean and Dinnet Moor', latterly from 2 Westburn Rd.

**PHEMISTER, Thomas C** **fl 1941-1973**
Aberdeen painter of local topography, especially buildings in Old Aberdeen and local villages. Exhibited RSA(11) & AAS 1959-73, from 5 The Chanonry, Old Aberdeen and latterly 6 Maryville Park, Aberdeen.

**PHILIP, Jackie** **1961-**
Born Edinburgh. Painter in oil of interiors, still life and landscape. Trained London. Depicts vibrant, colourful studio interiors and a lyrical interpretation of the Tuscany landscape which she came to admire when teaching in Florence. Awarded Andre de Segonzac scholarship at the RA Schools 1983-6. Exhibits RA from her London studio.

**PHILIP, M** **fl 1892-1896**
Amateur Glasgow painter of flowers and interiors; exhibited GI(3).

**PHILIPSON, Sir Robin J RA PRSA FRSA RSW RGI DLitt LLD** **1916-1992**
Born Broughton-in-Furness, Lancs, 17 Dec; died Edinburgh 26 May. Attended school at Whitehaven, Cumberland but when he was fourteen his family moved to Gretna. Attended Dumfries Academy before enrolling Edinburgh College of Art 1936-1940. Then joined King's Own Scottish Borderers, serving in India during WW2. After the War he joined the staff of the College of Art in Edinburgh where his work quickly showed the influence of Gillies(qv) and Maxwell(qv). Enjoyed the sensuous handling of strong colour, sometimes harsh composition and often satirical in mood. In the early 1950s began a series of paintings depicting cockfights, a theme which remained with him for some years. During the 1960s became interested in church interiors, crucifixions and more general figurative subjects. Compositions became increasingly abstract although the subjects generally remained identifiable. In the 1970s he searched for greater clarity of design, more frequently using animals, especially zebras with a pervasive menace and strong hint of

sexuality. Retired as Head of the School of Drawing and Painting at ECA 1982. Used heavy impasto and developed his own highly distinctive oeuvre. Member, Royal Fine Arts Commission for Scotland and of the Council of the Edinburgh Festival Society. Elected SSA 1948, ARSA 1952, RSW 1954, RSA 1962, FRSA 1965, PRSA 1973 remaining in office for 10 years; knighted 1976. Regular exhibitor RSA, RSW & GI. Made a belated appearance RA as an honorary associate Academician 1973, and as a full Academician 1980. Married Brenda Mark 1949, the artist Thora Clyne(qv) 1962 and Diana Mary Pollack 1976. Represented in SNGMA, Aberdeen AG, Glasgow AG, Kirkcaldy AG, City of Edinburgh collection, Paisley AG, Perth AG, Lillie AG (Milngavie), Leeds AG, Laing AG (Newcastle), Manchester, Middlesburgh, Southport AG, Sunderland AG,s, Walker Gallery (Liverpool), North Carolina AG (USA).
**Bibl:** Roger Billcliffe, 'Robin Philipson', ECA (Ex Cat 1989); Elder Dickson, 'Robin Philipson', Scott Gall (Ex Cat 1961 and 1983); Hardie 184-5; Hartley 158-9; M Lindsay, Robin Phillipson Edinburgh 1976; Macmillan [SA] 367,375 et passim; Scotsman, 29 May 1992(obit); Scott Art Rev VIII, 2, 1961, 20-23, 32; Studio, Oct 1962, 142-5; W Gordon Smith, Philipson, Atelier, 1995.

**PHILLIP, Colin Bent RWS RSW** **1855-1932**
Born Kensington, 20 Dec; died Devon, 8 Jly. Landscape painter, principally in watercolour. Son of John Phillip(qv). Studied drawing for a short period at Lambeth School of Art and Edinburgh, St Andrews University and privately under David Farquharson(qv). His watercolours are almost entirely of Highland scenery although most of his life was spent in Devon and London, returning to Scotland regularly to paint. His large depictions of Highland scenes can be extremely effective although occasionally unduly large and repetitious. Caw remarked that 'he is perhaps more draughtsman than painter, and his landscapes often large in size are marked by careful and learned drawing of mountain form and structure, rather than by justness of tone, fullness of colour, or fineness of atmospheric relationship and effect'. Elected RSW 1890 (resigning in 1907), ARWS 1886, RWS 1898. Exhibited RA(15), RSW(20), RWS (114), RI(9), GI(2), AAS 1888-1933 & L(11). Represented in Aberdeen AG, Glasgow AG, Exeter Museum.
**Bibl:** Caw 308; Halsby 278; Paviere; Who was Who 1929-40.

**PHILLIP, John RA HRSA** **1817-1867**
Born Oldmeldrum, Aberdeenshire, 19 Apr; died Kensington, London, 27 Feb. Painter in oil of portraits and Scottish domestic life and genre. Son of a shoemaker. Sometimes known as Spanish Phillip on account of his success in painting Spanish subjects. Father of Colin Bent P(qv). After an unhappy early apprenticeship with a local house-painter in one of the poorest parts of Aberdeen (Wallace Nook), Philip went to a Major Bryce Gordon to repair a broken window but became absorbed in a painting; the Major, coming down to breakfast, found the window untouched but admired the painting and offered Philip his first encouragement. When 17 he ran away to London as a stowaway on a boat. There he spent an absorbing day at the Royal Academy, firing an enthusiasm to become a painter. When he returned to Aberdeen Major Gordon introduced him to Lord Panmure. Two years later a gift from Lord Panmure, who had seen a painting done by the young artist in the manner of Wilkie, enabled him to return to London, there to study first under T M Joy 1836 (pupil of Samuel Drummond), and then enrolling at the RA Schools 1837. From this time he became a member of the Clique(qv), a coterie which included Augustus Egg, W P Frith, Richard Dowd (who married Phillip's sister) and H N O'Neil. At this time his intentions were directed towards history painting. 'Bruce about to receive the Sacrament on the morning previous to the Battle of Bannockburn' (now in Brechin Town Hall) illustrates this interest. In 1839 returned to Aberdeen although continuing to exhibit at the RA as well as the RSA and British Institution. In 1846 returned to London and undertook a series of Scottish subjects, all exhibited at the RA. His work showed the strong influence of Wilkie not only in its composition but in the manner of preparation. 'His finished pencil drawings and oil studies of single figures or small groups, show fine perception of character and a sensitivity to his subjects'. 'Scotch Washing', RA 1851, was subsequently engraved for the Glasgow Art Union using the more evocative title 'Heather Belles'. This consisted of 'groups of bare-footed Scots maidens performing ablutions to themselves in their garments in the shallow waters of a most picturesque burn' *[AJ]*. In 1851 ill-health caused him to undertake what was to be the first of several visits to Spain, journeys which were to change his art. Receiving the approval of Landseer, who brought the young artist to the attention of Queen Victoria, Phillip became the Queen's favourite Scottish painter. Returning from Spain the Queen bought 'Spanish Gypsy Mother' as a Christmas present for Prince Albert. In 1856 he returned to Spain, this time with Richard Ansdell. There they produced several joint works, Ansdell painting the animals while Phillip executed the figures. From this second visit there enters in his work a slight vulgarity, partially offset by a greater feeling for light and colour, matters which were noted by Ruskin who described 'The Huff', RA 1859 as being 'full of powerful and dexterous painting but ungraceful and slightly vulgar'. At this time he began experimenting in the use of chalk and watercolour. In 1860 returned once more to Spain and proceeded to undertake what many regarded as his finest works, including 'La Gloria: A Spanish wake' and 'Spanish Boys Playing at Bullfighting' (both in the NGS), and in 1865 'Early Career of Murillo' for which the Keillers of Dundee paid 3,800 gns. Phillip himself regarded 'La Gloria' as his finest work - the Spanish equivalent of Wilkie's 'Penny Wedding'. In 1866 he embarked on journeys to Florence and Rome. Recognised by his contemporaries to have been delightfully warm-hearted, 'simple and single-minded, he could not make an enemy, while on his intellectual side he had a large share of that quiet humour which his countrymen do not lack but for which they seldom get the credit'. Of his earlier portraits one of the finest examples, a full-length study of 'Prince Albert' in Highland dress is now in the Town House Aberdeen and his commission work for the Queen 'The marriage of the Princess Royal' (1858) the oil sketch for which is now in Aberdeen AG. After his death the Queen requested Landseer to find out whether she could purchase a picture and some sketches from the contents of Phillip's studio. In 1873 there was a comprehensive exhibition of 220 of his paintings at the V&A. At his death there were 56 half-finished works in his studio, according to McKay 'enough of the higher quality to place him in the front rank of British painters'. Brydall said that 'he has given to his Spanish works a nationality and peculiar animation, which even the great native artists have not surpassed: from Velasquez and Murillo down to the latest painter of the Peninsula, none has more faithfully and forceably registered the genuine nationality'. Exhibited 55 works at the RA 1838 to 1867 including 'Prince Albert' painted for the City of Aberdeen 1858, a portrait of the 'Earl of Dalhousie' 1864 and a portrait of the 'Rt Hon Duncan McNeill of Colonsay, Lord Justice General of Scotland and Lord President of the Court of Session' 1866; also AAS posthumously. Represented in NGS, SNPG(7) including the artist 'Samuel Bough', 'William Borthwick Johnstone' and 'Self-portrait'.
**Bibl:** Aberdeen AG, 'John Phillip' (Ex Cat by Carter, 1967); AJ XXIX, 1867, 127, 153-7; 1859, 132; 1894, 58; Bryan; Brydall 448-454; Caw 179-184; Conn 38 (1914) 123; Gaunt 233 (172-73); Halsby 63-5,278; Irwin 322-3,326-31; Hardie 50-3,54,56; Maas 95-6 et passim; McKay 278-293; Macmillan [SA] 146,186,192,214,217; Port 1887, 157ff, 175ff; Reynolds 10, 11, 56, 62, 322-3, 326-31 et passim.

**PHILLIPS, Miss Ann** **fl 1972**
Stirling painter of still life. Exhibited GI(2), from Blairlogie.

**PHILLIPS, Charles Gustav Louis** **1863-1944**
Born Montevideo. Painter and etcher. Came from an Aberdeenshire family and spent his early years in Aberdeen. Fond of depicting Highland river scenery. Moving to Dundee received his art training at the local art school under W M Grubb(qv). In 1881 won a national bronze medal but abandoned teaching in order to devote himself to painting full-time. Helped to found the Dundee Graphic Arts Association. His success was largely the painting of open air studies; essentially a colourist painter. Described as 'bold and daring, possessing considerable character and distinction but...the colour hard in parts and lacking something in finish'. Exhibited RSA(22), AAS(3) & GI(9). His 'Gypsy Cook' is in Dundee AG.
**Bibl:** Halsby 279.

**PHILLIPS, Miss Deborah** **fl 1979-1980**
Dundee amateur painter. Exhibited GI(2) from Strathmore Ave.

**PHILLIPS, Douglas** **1926-**
Born Dundee. Painter, mainly in watercolour; landscape and sea-scapes, also illustrator. Studied Dundee Art College before serving in WW2 in India and Ceylon with the RASC. After the war became an

illustrator, working for eighteen years with D C Thomson of Dundee contributing to *Great Moments in Boxing* 1974, *My Favourite Mountaineering Stories* 1978. His work has featured in *The Artist Magazine* on several occasions and in the *International Artist Magazine*, Oct 1998 'Atmosphere versus Accuracy'. Books illustrated include Ottley: *Brumbie Dust* (1969), William: *Gallipoli* (1969), Catherall: *Big Tusker* (1970), Borer: *The Boer War* (1971), Patchet: *Roar of the Lion* (1973), Tate: *The Runners* (1974), Cook: *Sea Adventures* (1974), Hynds: *Dolphin Boy* (1975), Sibley: *Adam and the FA Cup* (1975), Sibley: *Adam and the Football Mystery* (1979), Furminger: *Bobbie Takes the Reins* (1981), *Bobbie's Sponsored Ride* (1982), Stranger: *The Honeywell Badger* (1986). Most enjoys action subjects, often with horses. Taught illustration and watercolour painting, his work has appeared in the British and French *Reader's Digest.* Several paintings published as limited edition prints. Exhibits regularly RSA, RSW, RGI & SW.
**Bibl:** Wingfield; Horne 350; Peppin.

**PHILLIPS, F D** **fl 1951-1952**
Amateur Dundee painter. Exhibitred two watercolours of Cannes at the GI, from North Court St.

**PHILLIPS, Ian** **fl 1961-1964**
Greenock painter of still life and topography. Exhibited GI.

**PHILLIPS, J** **fl 1779-1790**
Edinburgh engraver. Engraved a view of North Bridge and Register House for Arnot's *History of Edinburgh,* 1779.
**Bibl:** Bushnell.

**PHILLIPS, James** **fl 1870**
Dumbartonshire landscape painter. Exhibited GI(2) from Helensburgh.

**PHILLIPS, James Edward** **fl 1952-1972**
Painter of topographical subjects and nature studies. Exhibited RSA(5) & GI(3) first from Edinburgh and latterly from Blairlogie, Stirlingshire.

**PHILLIPS, Mrs May** **fl 1951**
Amateur Greenock flower painter. Exhibited GI(1).

**PHILLIPS, Roderick** **fl 1976**
Aberdeen-based metalwork designer. Exhibited AAS(3) from 13 Larch Rd.

**PHILP, William** **fl 1984**
Angus amateur painter. Exhibited GI(1) from Forfar.

**PHIN, J** **fl 1766**
Scottish engraver. Guy distinguishes him from Thomas Phin but doubt remains over their respective identities. A J Phin engraved a portrait of Charles I in 1766.
**Bibl:** J C Guy, 'Edinburgh Engravers', in The Book of the Old Edinburgh Club, vol 9, 1916.

**PHIN, Thomas** **fl 1746-1759**
Edinburgh engraver. Probably related to J Phin(qv). Working in the NW parish in 1752. Engraved various maps of Scotland 1746-1759.
**Bibl:** Bushnell.

**PICKERING, Beryl** **fl 1957-1961**
Stirlingshire landscape painter, mostly local scenes. Exhibited RSA in 1957 and 1961.

**PICKERING, Ruby** **1873-fl c1893**
Glasgow amateur flower painter of 20 Montgomerie Quadrant; exhibited GI(3) while still a student at Glasgow School of Art 1889-1893.

**PICKFORD, James Gillanders** **fl 1902**
Aberdeen amateur painter in pen and ink; exhibited a sketch of a cavalier at the AAS from Seaview Cottage, Links.

**PICKUP, M Holmes** **fl 1970-1974**
Painter of estuarial scenes and fishing boats. Lived for a time in Edinburgh and often painted scenes on the Forth. Exhibited GI(3), latterly from Tighnabruich, Argyll.

**PIERCE, Charles E RI** **1908-?**
Born Edinburgh. Painter, etcher and wood engraver, in oil, watercolour and pastel. Educated George Heriot School, Edinburgh College of Art and RA Schools. Moved to London. Exhibited RA, RSA(4) and GI.

**PILKINGTON, Frederick Thomas** **1832-1898**
Edinburgh architect. Designed the unusual house Inchglas, Brioch Terrace, Crieff (1859), a number of churches and the Eastern Club, Albert Square, Dundee (1868, dem 1966) a 'rich Venetian Romanesque palace with touches of Renaissance detail (showing) Pilkington at his best and, although flambuoyant in execution, the building had a dignity entirely lacking in the bland Bank which replaces it' [Gomme & Gauldie]. Dunbar regards his 'Ruskinian Gothic' Barclay-Bruntsfield Church (1862-4) as one of the outstanding monuments of the Scottish Gothic Revival. Designed Dean Park House (now Daniel Stewart's Boarding House) in his later (Second Empire) style (1874); built for the geologist S L Jolly. Gifford regards this as his best work in this manner; also designed Viewforth St David Church (1871). Exhibited RSA(30) & GI(6).
**Bibl:** Dunbar 149; Gifford 40,58,64-5,255,265,388-9,408,494-5, 502,598-9,631, pls 40,73; Bruce Walker & W S Gauldie, Architects and Architecture on Tayside, Dundee 1984, 133-5.

**PILLANS, William S** **fl 1862**
Edinburgh painter of North American scenes. Exhibited 'The prairie on fire' and 'Wild horses of the prairie' at the RSA.

**PINKERTON, Mary H** **fl 1892-1893**
Edinburgh landscape painter. Exhibited 'On the Fife coast' at the RSA, AAS(1) & GI(1), from 14 East Claremont Street.

**PINTNER, D** **fl 1918**
Glasgow stained glass designer. Exhibited GI(2) from 20 Ruthven Street, Hillhead.

**PIRIE, Miss Annie A** **fl 1889-1893**
Aberdeen flower and portrait painter in oils and pastel; exhibited a portrait at the RSA, also GI(2) & AAS(7), latterly from The Chanonry.

**PIRIE, Sir George PRSA HRSW LLD** **1864-1946**
Born Campbeltown, Argyll, 5 Dec; died Torrance, Stirlingshire, 17 Feb. Painter in oil, watercolour and pencil; animals, landscape and birds. Son of a Glasgow doctor. Attended Glasgow University and studied art at the Slade School, London and in Paris under Boulanger, Fremlet and Lefevre at the Academie Julien. After a visit to Texas spent some years at the village of Midhurst in Surrey before returning to Glasgow, finally settling in Stirlingshire. Never much in sympathy with the theories held by most of the Glasgow Boys so is now regarded as a member of the Glasgow School rather than a Glasgow Boy. His art was intimate, undecorative, sensitive and elusive, his draughtsmanship and technique sound but not brilliant. The subdued tones and bold brushwork that he used at the beginning of his career gradually gave way to higher tones, more fluid brushwork and more sophisticated design. Latterly this liquidity is at the expense of the penetrating characteristics of his earlier work. In his pencil drawings he often added watercolour in a free manner with extensive use of bodycolour and occasionally pastel. Elected ARSA 1913, RSA 1923, HRA 1933 and PRSA 1933-44; knighted 1937. Exhibited in Buffalo, St Louis, Stuttgart and Ghent as well as at the RA(21), RSA(86), GI(120), AAS(1) & L(18). Represented in Glasgow AG, Paisley AG, City of Edinburgh collection, Gracefield AG (Dumfries), RSA.
**Bibl:** Caw 442-3; Halsby 150,279.

**PIRIE, Ian McDonald** **fl 1976-1985**
Aberdeen potter and ceramic designer. Trained Gray's School of Art, Aberdeen. Exhibited AAS during the above years from 305 Union Grove.

**PIRNIE, Jackson G** **fl 1899**
Edinburgh amateur painter; exhibited 'Mandolin player' at the RSA from 10 North Street, David Street.

**PIRRETT, John** **fl 1933-1940**
Kirkintilloch engraver & etcher. Exhibited RSA(10) & GI(4) from 37 Eastside and latterly the Schoolhouse, Craigton, Milngavie.

**PIRRETT, Miss Vivien Louise** **fl 1965**
Amateur painter. Probably daughter of John P(qv). Exhibited GI(2), from Milngavie.

**PITCAIRN, Mrs M M K** **fl 1937-1939**
Greenock still life and flower painter; exhibited RSA(3).

**PLATT, John Edgar** **1886-1967**
Born Leek, Staffs. Colour woodcut artist. Trained at Royal College of Art eventually becoming Principal, Leicester College of Arts and Crafts and Blackheath School of Art. Taught for some years at Edinburgh College of Art during which time he exhibited RA, RSA & GI 1924-1934.

**PLAYFAIR, James** **1755-1794**
Architect. Father of William Henry P(qv). Third son of the minister of Liff & Benvie, Angus. Between 1788 and 1794 was living in Fitzroy Square, London and appears to have built numbers 21 and 23 whilst retaining his professional activities in Scotland where in fact most of his main works were executed. The most important of these was the neo-classical mansion built 1791-7 for Charles Gordon of Buthlaw, Cairness, in the remote north-east corner of Aberdeenshire. This house was remarkable for its bold stylistic eclecticism, Greek, Roman and Egyptian elements being grouped in striking, if not always harmonious, apposition. 'The house comprises a tall, severe looking main block of H-plan half encircled at the rear by a low flat-roofed court of offices. The terminal pavilions of the office range are rusticated all over and incorporate the resting Egyptian tomb-portico motifs, while the arched entry to the courtyard is of correspondingly primitive form. Most of the interiors are Greek but there is one notable Egyptian room decorated with stucco panels containing hieroglyphs' [Colvin & Dunbar]. In Edinburgh there is a modest example of his work, nos 3-5 Roxburgh Place (1791-2). Exhibited RA 1783-1793 and published *A Method of Constructing Vapour Baths* (1783), other works include the entrance to Hawkshead Park for the Countess of Glasgow (1785), Farnell church, nr Brechin (c1789) and Kinnaird Castle, Forfarshire remodelled for Sir David Carnegie (1785-93). In the Sir John Soane Museum there is a portfolio of drawings by him which includes designs for Anniston House, Forfarshire for John Rait (1786; dem), Cullen House, Banffshire for the Earl of Findlater and Seafield (1787), an entrance Lodge and other works at Keith Palace, Midlothian for the Duke of Buccleuch (1786), Dunninald House and Village, Forfarshire, for David Scott (1787) as well as additions to Dupplin Castle, Perthshire, for the Earl of Kinnoull (1789), Kippinross, Perthshire for John Stirling (1789), additions to Langham Lodge, Dumfries-shire for the Duke of Buccleuch (1786) and a church at Kirriemuir, Angus (1786-90). Designed the neo-classical Town Hall, Forfar (1786-8) and a remarkable mausoleum in the churchyard of Methven, Perthshire (1793).
**Bibl:** Colvin; T A Cherry & I G Brown, 'Scottish Architects at Home and Abroad', NLS, Ex Cat 1978,71; Dunbar 115,117; Gifford 247; Bruce Walker & W S Gauldie, Architects and Architecture on Tayside, Dundee 1984, 66(illus),67.

**PLAYFAIR, William Henry RSA** **1789-1857**
Architect & architectural watercolourist. Younger son of James P(qv). Studied Edinburgh and under William Stark(qv) in Glasgow. Worked in London for Robert Smirke and James Wyatt 1813-5. After a brief visit to France, launched an Edinburgh practice and in 1815 won a competition for the completion of Robert Adam's scheme for Edinburgh University. The townscape of Edinburgh owes more to him than to any other single architect. Responsible for designing New College (1845-50); the vast octagonal St Stephen's Church (1828); the National Gallery (1848); the interior of the Old Quad (1819-27); the Royal Scottish Academy (1822-6 & 1831-6); Surgeons' Hall (1829-32); Donaldson's School (1841-51) - described by Gifford as his 'great Jacobean palace'; the National Monument (1824-9); the Dugald Stewart Monument (1831) and Observatory (1818) on Calton Hill; Bonaly Tower for Lord Cockburn (1836); Duddingston Manse (1823) for Rev John Thomson(qv), and for Lord Mackenzie the only thoroughgoing Italianate villa in Edinburgh, Belmont (1828). He was concerned for the quality of townscape, for the relation of a building to its neighbours and to the surroundings in which it is placed. This is well illustrated in his plan for the Calton Hill Terraces and the London Road area of Edinburgh (detailed in Gifford pp 444-8). In 1819 he was commissioned by the Heriot Trust to design what became known as Royal Circus and NW Circus Place. Patronised by Lord Lynedoch on Tayside, designing an Italianate farmhouse at Dalcrue, Perthshire (1832), and a bridge in the same village (1832-6). Also responsible for the design of Dollar Academy (1818), one of the most imposing of the Burgh Schools erected in the opening quarter of the 19th century in Scotland. He was a man of warmth and tenderness long beset by ill-health and a sense of deep loneliness. Represented in NGS by three sketches including a water colour of Edinburgh Castle and the proposed National Gallery.
**Bibl:** Dunbar 112,117,158,161; Gifford see index; Irwin 187,229, 289; Peter Savage, Lorimer and the Edinburgh Craft Designers, Edinburgh 1980, 126,133,168; Bruce Walker & W S Gauldie, Architects and Architecture on Tayside, Dundee 1984, 67.

**PLAZALSKI, Raymond** **fl 1985-1986**
Glasgow sculptor. Exhibited two 'Seascapes' in terracotta at the GI.

**PLENDERLEITH, Mungo** **fl 1881-1918**
Glasgow landscape painter in oil and watercolour. Lived for a time in Edinburgh c1901. 'Dunluce Castle' RSA, 1896 received favourable attention. Exhibited RSA(6), RSW(1), RI(2) & GI(37).

**PLENDERLEITH, Thomas Donald RE** **1921-?**
Born Peebles. Wood engraver, etcher and painter; also teacher. Educated at St Clement Danes GS. Trained Ealing College of Art under James Bostock, and at Hornsey Art College 1945-6, studying etching under Norman Jones. Between 1947 and 1954 he taught art at Pinner GS. From 1954 until 1974 head of the art department at St Nicholas GS. Elected RE 1962.

**PLOWRIGHT, Rosamund ARCA** **fl 1964-1966**
Inverness-shire landscape artist; mainly depicted scenes close to her home. Exhibited AAS(4) from Balchraggan, Drumnadrochit.

**POETT, Lucy M ARBS** **fl 1975-**
Born Edinburgh. Sculptress and painter. Schooled in both England and Scotland, studied at Heatherly's but following the death of her grandfather and the need to help on the family farm near Dundee returned to Scotland for further studies at Dundee College of Art under Scott Sutherland(qv). Returned to her studio in Chelsea doing portrait commissions and animal drawings. In 1986 a portrait head of Sir Alec Guinness was purchased by the Duke of Atholl for permanent display at Blair Castle. In 1989 her 'Old Bilt', a bronze head was bought by Aberdeen AG. Regularly exhibits portraits at the Royal Society of Portrait Painters in London. While her paintings are generally of people, being especially fascinated by faces, her sculpture is more varied and includes bird and animal studies. Elected ARBS 1983, also member SSA and SSWA. Exhibits sculptures, drawings and watercolours at the RSA and in 1981 was awarded RSA prize for the best sculpture by a woman artist. Lives at Aberdona House, by Alloa.

**POGGI, Pat** **c1936-**
Born USA. Scientist, mathematician, philosopher and textile designer. Originally trained in chemistry and philosophy, teaching the latter for a time at Michigan State University. In 1962 married and moved to Florence, before settling in Edinburgh 1964. After a short spell teaching maths at Edinburgh University and the birth of her first child she began working professionally in textiles, especially tapestry, designing and teaching in her own studio. Exhibited SSWA 1976-83, at the 'Gli Arazzi nell' Arte Contemporanea, Bologna 1980 and in Scotland and USA. Elected SSWA 1979, member of Council 1982. Won Peter Rae Weaving Award 1983.

**POLLEY, Ivan** **fl 1981**
Born Colchester, Essex. Printmaker. Originally trained as an engraver. Studied graphics at Colchester and NE Essex School of Art before moving to Edinburgh. Particularly fond of the old sailing craft found in the Essex marshes and dykes. Exhibited AAS(1).

**POLLITT, Mrs Mary E** **fl 1927-1955**
Edinburgh-based painter of landscape, still life, interiors, genre and topographical works; in oil and watercolour. Studied in London and

Paris and travelled extensively in Europe especially in Spain and Morocco. Exhibited RSA(21), RSW(17), AAS(5), GI(20) & SWA(2), latterly from 50 Queen St.

**POLLOCK, Andrew D** **fl 1930-1933**
Edinburgh engraver of topographical works. Exhibited at the RSA (8 including 'The harbour, St Monance' 1933), from 5 West Montgomery Place.

**POLLOCK, Fred** **1937-**
Born Glasgow. Abstract painter, preoccupied with colour and colour relationships. Studied Glasgow School of Art 1955-9. Guest artist at Triangle Workshop, New York 1984. First solo exhibition Glasgow 1963.

**POLLOCK, George A** **fl 1929**
Kilmarnock painter of rustic scenes; exhibited AAS(1) from 2 Loanhead St.

**POLLOCK, Jackson N** **1912-1956**
Edinburgh professional painter although he only exhibited once at the RSA - 'York cathedral' - from Medway Bank, Gylemuir Road.

**POLLOK, Netta** **fl 1929-1931**
Amateur painter and draughtswoman. Exhibited three romantic illustrations in monochrome at the GI 1929 from Langside, Glasgow and 1931 from an address in Rutherglen.

**POMEROY, Frederick William** **1857-1924**
Sculptor. Designed the Dr Thomas Guthrie memorial statue in West Princes St Gdns (1910).

**POMEROY, Timothy Allen** **1957-**
Lanarkshire painter of landscape and figurative compositions; also sculptor in wood and sandstone. Trained Gray's School of Art, Aberdeen. Exhibited GI(10) & AAS(5), from 16 Barriedale Ave, Hamilton, latterly from Carnwarth.

**POMPHREY, Helen Frances** **fl 1980**
Aberdeen-based painter of still life; exhibited AAS(1) from 159 Hardgate.

**POOLE, Dunbar** **fl 1894-1896**
Glasgow amateur watercolour painter. Exhibited RSW(1) & GI(3) from 59 Bank Street, Hillhead.

**POPE, James H** **fl 1871**
Edinburgh painter in oil of equestrian subjects; exhibited RSA(3).

**POPE, Perpetua MacNaughton** **1916-**
Born Solihull, Warwicks, 29 May. Painter in oil. Born of an Aberdonian family. Educated at Albyn School, Aberdeen and trained Moray House College of Education and Edinburgh College of Art where she was influenced by the work and teaching of Gillies(qv), Maxwell(qv) and Leonard Rosoman. Remained in Scotland where she spent virtually the whole of her working life. Concentrated on Scottish landscapes and views in Cyprus and Greece. Her colour tends towards the cool and much of her best work depicts the cold sea and the dull rich ochres of autumn. Worked in heavy impasto in a semi-impressionistic style. Resigned from a lectureship at Moray House in order to paint full-time. Lived and worked in Carlops. Regular exhibitor RA, RSA, AAS 1959-78, GI(5), SSA & SSWA. Represented in City of Edinburgh collection, Royal collection, Nuffield Foundation, SAC.

**POPE, Ronald Ernest** **fl 1961-1981**
Kinross-shire landscape painter of mainly local scenery. Exhibited RSA(7) & GI(2) from Milnathort.

**POPE, Samuel Jnr** **fl 1896-1940**
Aberdeen landscape painter. Painted mainly the scenery of upper Deeside and although achieving neither the fame nor quality of John Mitchell(qv), Melvin Rennie(qv) or Benjamin Ottewell(qv), his best work reflects his love of the region and his skill in capturing its essential charms and subtle colours. Exhibited 'October - Loch of Park' at the RSA in 1900 and AAS(35) 1896-1937 & GI 1940, at first from 28 Victoria St and later from 8 Albert St.

**PORDON, William** **fl 1861**
Edinburgh painter in oil and watercolour of coastal scenes also scene painter. Working at the Queen's Theatre in 1861, the year he exhibited twice at the RSA.

**PORTEOUS, George Jnr** **1663-1713**
Born Edinburgh; died 19 Nov. Painter. Son of George P(qv). Apprenticed to his father in 1687 and made a burgess and guild brother of Edinburgh 1696. Unusually, it is recorded that in 1711 he acquired Craighouse to which he added a new wing and then let it for £100 Scots per annum.
**Bibl:** Apted 75; Laing MSS,IV,26, Edinburgh Univ. Lib.

**PORTEOUS, George The elder** **fl 1660-d1698**
Heraldic painter. Son of John Porteous, a Leith tailor. Apprenticed to John Telfer, herald painter, 1663. Burgess of Edinburgh 1669. He was undertaking heraldic work for Edinburgh Town Council 1678-9, painting the arms for the funeral of Lady Ann, daughter of the Earl of Morton 1683 and for the funeral of the Earl of Lauderdale 1691. Drew the arms for the Duke of Hamilton's monument 1698. In 1686 he was involved in a scandal when his apprentice James Bontine accused him of robbery, imprisonment and violence. Defended himself on the grounds that Bontine had been stealing his pencils and colours and entering into a combination to raise his wages with his fellow journeymen. Porteous won the case on the grounds that his apprentice was bound to him and therefore the materials belonged to Porteous. In 1660 he painted the Mercat Cross of Edinburgh after it had been repaired for Charles II's Restoration. Involved in work for the funeral of Lady Margaret Leslie, Dowager Countess of Wemyss, 1688 and employed with Henry Fraser the elder, for painting Coats of Arms of Viscount Dundee and the Earl of Dunfermline and 'other persons forfeited for High Treason'.
**Bibl:** Apted 72-75; Fountainhall 'The Historical Notices' 749 and 772.

**PORTEOUS, Jessie G** **fl 1898**
Edinburgh watercolour painter of landscapes; exhibited 'Largo bay' at the RSA, from 6 Mansfield Place.

**PORTEOUS, Mrs Lee** **fl 1972**
Berwickshire painter of pastoral subjects. Exhibited GI(1) from Lauder.

**PORTEOUS, William** **fl 1861-1882**
Prolific Edinburgh painter of Highland scenes especially in Argyll. Exhibited RSA(73), latterly from 5 Kerr Street, Stockbridge. Represented by a watercolour of the Cowgate in Edinburgh City collection.

**PORTEOUS WOOD, James RSW** **1919-**
Born Edinburgh, Sep 12. Painter of portraits, murals and landscapes in oil, watercolour and black and white; also designer. Educated at George Heriot's School, studied art at Edinburgh College of Art 1936-40 obtaining a travelling scholarship; also worked under R H Westwater and W F Rainer and with Sir D Y Cameron(qv). Held several one man shows. Commissioned to undertake work at the Royal Palace, Kathmandu. Lived for a time in Ripon, Yorkshire, before becoming chief designer to Asprey's. Abandoned commercial art to resume full-time painting independently in Scotland 1976. Illustrated Hancock: *East and West of Severn: Midland Riches* 1956 and Harrison (Ed): *Yorkshire Dales*. Youngest person ever elected RSW 1945. Lives on the north-west coast of Scotland. Exhibits regularly RSW and spasmodically at the RA & RSA.

**PORTER, Frederick J** **fl 1901-1937**
Amateur watercolour painter of still life, flowers and local scenery, he lived for a time at Earnhope, Comrie, Perthshire before moving c1937 to Morningside Road, Edinburgh. Exhibited RSA(7), RSW (1), GI(1) & London Salon(14). Probably the same as **Dr Frederick Porter**, oil and watercolour painter and S J Peploe's brother-in-law, who was influenced by Peploe and for whom a memorial exhibition was held at the Scottish Gallery, Edinburgh 1949.

**PORTER, Hilda** **fl 1894-1925**
Figure painter originally from Ireland. Moved to London 1899 before settling first in Falkirk and then c1920 at Kippen, Stirlingshire,

where she worked for a time beside Sir D Y Cameron(qv). Exhibited RA(2), GI(1) ROI(2), SWA(4), RHA(22), RCA(1) & L(7).

**PORTER, Miss Margery** **fl 1940**
Minor Edinburgh landscape painter of 65 Morningside Road. Daughter of Frederick J P(qv). Exhibited RSA(1).

**PORTER, Sir Robert Ker** **1777-1842**
Born Durham; died St Petersburg, May 2. Painter of battles, portraits and figure studies; also author. Following the death of his father, a serving army officer, his mother moved to Edinburgh where the young man was brought up. Whilst there he met the celebrated Flora Macdonald. His admiration was fired by a battle-piece in that lady's possession. From this moment his imagination took off and his determination was born to become a battle painter. In 1790 his mother introduced her precocious son to West, President of the RA, who immediately admitted him as a student to the RA Schools. His subsequent career encompassed visits to Russia 1804, where he was appointed historical painter to the Emperor, to Finland and Sweden, and in 1808 he accompanied Sir John Moore to the Peninsula and was present at the battle of Corunna. On a second visit to Russia he married Princess Mary, daughter of Prince Theodore de Schertkoff. Returning to England 1813 he was knighted and published *Travelling Sketches in Russia and Sweden.* He next visited the East and many of the sketches made there are now in the British Museum. A further historically important travel book followed which incorporated many engravings of costumes, portraits and antiquities relating to Georgia, Persia, Ancient Babylon and North America. In 1826 he became British consul in Venezuela, remaining there until 1821 during which time he painted a portrait of Bolivar. A last visit to St Petersburg in 1841 proved fatal; he died there while preparing to return home. A deeply religious man, he often referred to his formative young years in Edinburgh and the chance influence of Flora Macdonald. Exhibited RA(38), latterly from 6 Gerrard St, Soho.
**Bibl:** Bryan; Irwin 207.

**PORTSMOUTH, Percy Herbert RSA** **1874-1953**
Born Reading, 2 Feb; died Hitchin, Herts, 29 Oct. Sculptor of portrait and figure subjects. Spent five years as an engineer before studying at Royal College of Art under Walter Crane and Morley Fletcher. Then went to Paris and Brussels before returning to London for further studies at the Royal College of Art under Lanteri. After successful exhibitions he moved to Edinburgh to become head of the sculpture department at Edinburgh College of Art. Executed 'Phoenix rising from the ashes' in the deep cusped recess over the entrance to the Scottish National War Memorial in Edinburgh; a bronze statue of 'Prudence' in the Commercial Union Insurance building and a memorial head of 'George Rowe' in John Watson's School. Retired 1929, his later years being spent at Rushton, Herts. Elected ARSA 1906, RSA 1923. His diploma work was 'The Captive', exhibited at the RSA 1906. Exhibited RSA(101), RA(35), GI(49), RMS(1), AAS 1921-35 & L(6). Represented in City of Edinburgh collection(2), including a bronze bust of Sir D Y Cameron.
**Bibl:** Gifford 100,301,392; Macmillan [SA] 331; Peter Savage, Lorimer and the Edinburgh Craft Designers, Edinburgh 1980, 150,168.

**POTTER, Beatrix (Mrs William Heelis)** **1866-1943**
Born 28 Jly, Kensington; died Sawrey, Cumbria 22 Dec. Celebrated English author and illustrator of childrens' books, also painted occasional landscapes. Worked exclusively in watercolour, pencil and crayon. Entirely self-taught, she led a very sheltered life living with her parents until she was almost 40. Her first book, T*he Tale of Peter Rabbit* appeared in 1902 and in 1905 she acquired a farm near Windermere where she remained for the rest of her life. Married a local solicitor 1913. Her home was bequeathed to the National Trust. An association with Scotland was central to her fame and literary work. Her family owned Dalguise House in Perthshire and there, around Birnam and Dunkeld, she spent twelve successive summers 1874-1886. Her first book evolved from a letter she wrote from Scotland to a sick friend. 'Jeremy Fisher' was based on an angling friend of her father's, 'Mr Tod' on a tame fox kept by a local gamekeeper while 'Mrs Tiggy-winkle' the hedgehog was inspired by the family home-help Kitty MacDonald. A sculpted garden dedicated to her memory is at Birnam, Perthshire.

**POTTIE, Evelyn Scott** **20th Cent**
Inverness painter; trained Gray's School of Art, Aberdeen. Exhibited AAS(8) from Broombank, Loch Flemington, Gollanfield.

**POTTINGER, Frank RSA** **1932-**
Born Edinburgh. Sculptor and painter, mainly in wood, clay and fibreglass. Studied Edinburgh College of Art 1958-63 and with the proceeds of a post-diploma scholarship travelled to Greece and Turkey. In 1973 became lecturer in art at Aberdeen College of Education a post he retained until 1985 before resigning in order to pursue a career as a full-time artist based in Leith. A broad vernacular theme has been dominant in his work with music and dialect speech the starting points in many of his sculptures. Occasionally a coarseness appears, as often in modern painting and sculpture. An edition of small bronzes for the Scottish Sculpture Workshop helped revive an interest activity in lithographic printmaking. Elected SSA 1972, ARSA 1979 - the same year as he won the William Macaulay prize and other awards, RSA 1991. Exhibits RSA & AAS 1974-87. Represented in Hunterian Museum (Glasgow), Paisley AG.

**POTTINGER, John I D** **fl 1943-1951**
Edinburgh portrait painter. Exhibited RSA(4). In 1943 he was with the 74th Medium Regt of the RA; in 1951 was living at 11 Darnaway St.

**POULEVOIR (or POLNOIR), Hames (or Hannes or Heuves)** **fl 1420-1431**
A mysterious figure whose Scottish connection has yet to be positively confirmed. Brydall recounts that in the French royal accounts of 1420 there appears an artist of this name then probably at Poitiers and 'with more certainty' at Tours between 1428 and 1436. He goes on "It was this Poulevoir who painted the white banner of Jeanne d'Arc...His daughter was a friend of La Pucelle, and she was married at the cost of the bourgeois of Tours. When it is considered that the name Polwarth is a well-known Scotch one; that the name Poulevoir is not native French, and not unlike Polwarth; and also that Hames is the ancient Scoto-French form of James,- we may believe that a Scottish artist was the author of the portrait described by Joan in her examination (she said she had seen in the hands of a Scotchman a picture resembling her in armour, kneeling on a cushion in the act of presenting a letter to the king)- a not unreasonable supposition to anyone familiar with the transformation of Scottish surnames in old French history. Another of these strangers, if not the same, followed La Pucelle in all her campaigns, and did not quit her till he had witnessed the barbarous tragedy at Rouen, and afterwards ended his life as a monk at Dunfermline...it is supposed that the monk, the painter of the white banner and the portrait, was the same". An additional point, referred to by Hill Burton, is that Polwarth was an old patronymic of the house of Home or Hume. Brydall concludes 'that Sir Alexander, the head of the house, was one of Douglas's companions slain at the battle of Verneuil, and left three sons, thus suggesting the idea that one of these remained in France and was the painter of the portrait'.
**Bibl:** Annals of Dunfermline; Brydall; Hill Burton, Scot Abroad.

**POULTER, Miss Annie** **fl 1884**
Amateur Greenock watercolourist; exhibited 'Girl's head' at the GI from 18 Ardgowan Square.

**POULTON, James** **fl 1853-1856**
Edinburgh painter of fruit, flowers and still life. Exhibited RSA(3) from Rose St.

**POULTON, Richard** **fl 1927**
Rutherglen figurative painter; exhibited 'The Cowpuncher' at the GI from 80 High Street.

**POUNCY, Benjamin Thomas** **?-1799**
Draughtsman and engraver, probably Scottish. Engraved several views of St. Andrews, after drawings by J Oliphant, and plates after Clevely and Kitchingman.
**Bibl:** Bushnell.

**POW, Patrick** **fl 1537**
Heraldic painter working at Falkland Palace in November, 1537.
**Bibl:** Accounts of the Master of Works, vol i, ed. H M Paton, Edinburgh 1957; Apted 75; Macmillan [SA] 35.

**POW, Thomas** **fl 1929**
Minor landscape painter; exhibited 'A mountain road, Killin' at the RSA from 62 South Street, Armadale, W Linlithgow.

**POWELL, Edward George** **fl 1939-1969**
Glasgow painter of figures, portraits, rural scenery and farm life. Exhibited RSA(14) & GI(3) from 34 Falkland Mansions, Hyndland & later Partickhill Rd.

**POWELL, Sir Francis RWS PRSW** **1833-1914**
Born Pendleton, Manchester; died Dunoon. Watercolour painter of landscape and coastal scenes. Son of a merchant. Trained for three years at Manchester School of Art winning a medal for figure drawing. In 1878 when living in Glasgow, was one of the founders of the Royal Scottish Society of Watercolour Painters becoming its first President. Knighted 1893. Most of his watercolours were marine and lake views. 'His own enthusiasm as an admirable painter of sea subjects, coupled with his enthusiasm, tact and personal charm, did much to advance the personal advancement of watercolour in Scotland' [Hardie]. He went to live in Dunoon in 1857 and in 1877 won the Haywood prize for the best watercolour exhibited in Manchester. Main works include 'Ben Nevis from Locheil', 'The Channel Tug', 'Loch Corruisk', 'The Sea Belle', 'The Isles of the Sea' and 'A Summer Breeze'. A contemporary critic of the Seventh Winter Exhibition of the Society of Painters in Watercolour wrote of Powell's 'The North of Arran', 'he is as yet unmarred by mannerism or unspoilt by frequent reiteration. From Mr Powell...we may expect much; his style is healthy and manly, his treatment shows an eye watchful of nature in moods of majesty and mystery'. Although English by birth his influence on the development of Scottish art, especially watercolour painting, is as great as almost any Scotsman and this fact together with the many years he spent in Glasgow and Dunoon confirms a respected place in the development of Scottish art. Elected ARWS 1867, RWS 1876. Exhibited RSA(2), RSW(51), RWS(62), GI(9), AAS(4) & L(6). Represented in V & A, Dundee AG, Glasgow AG, Manchester City AG, Portsmouth City Museum.
**Bibl:** AJ 1869, 11, 1893, 272; Caw 211,334; Halsby 141,279; Hardie III, 82, 174-5; Studio 63 (1915) 220; 67, 256; Who was Who 1897-1915.

**POWELL, Kate** **fl 1885-1888**
Edinburgh oil painter of animals, landscape and interiors. Exhibited RSA(4) including a view of 'The interior of Edinburgh National Gallery' and 'The Braids from Powburn' 1888, from 3 Bright's Crescent.

**POWER, Ronald J** **fl 1933**
Glasgow topographical painter. Exhibited GI(1), from Dunearn St.

**POWER, William A** **fl 1865**
Painter in oil of landscapes, often of the Hebrides. Exhibited RSA(3).

**POWLEY, Elizabeth** **fl 1969-1971**
Dundee painter of local scenery and gardens; exhibited RSA(5).

**PRAGNALL, Valerie** **1942-**
Born Worthing. Sculptress. Worked in several different jobs in London and Paris before coming to Glasgow 1972. Studied stained glass design at Glasgow School of Art 1981-5. Uses natural materials such as twigs and moss, many being site-specific. There is repeated allusion to fertility, growth and survival. Artist-in-residence Glasgow Garden Festival 1988. Lives and works in Glasgow.
**Bibl:** Collins Gall, Glasgow, 'Shape and Form: Six Sculptors from Scotland', (Ex Cat 1988); Hartley, 159.

**PRASAD, V N** **fl 1934**
Amateur artist; exhibited a continental landscape at the RSA from 19 Esplanade Terrace, Joppa.

**PRATT, Anna (Mrs John Burnett)** **fl 1843-1868**
Aberdeenshire landscape painter of local scenes in oil and watercolour. Specialised in painting castles. Lived at Cruden Bay. Exhibited RSA(13) including 'Maiden Castle' 1843, 'Doune Castle' and 'The Castle of Pitfichie, Monymusk', both 1854, 'Dunottar Castle' and 'The Ruins of Old Slains Castle', both 1864. Also exhibited in the English provinces 1843-1848.

**PRAT(T), David** **fl 1496-d1503**
Figure painter. Worked for James IV of Scotland at Cambuskenneth and Stirling. According to an inventory taken in 1505 paintings at Stirling included one in three compartments bearing the figure of Our Lady with her Son in her arms, and two angels bearing musical instruments. In 1497 he undertook altar paintings for the king and between 1501 and July 1508 received several payments for work in connection with the burial place of James III at the Abbey of Cambuskenneth. After his death the king granted 'the rents of money and grain to the said David's relict for the marriage of her daughter' [Apted].
**Bibl:** Accounts of the Lord High Treasurer of Scotland (ed T Dickson et al, 1877-1916); Apted 75-7; Brydall 46; Exchequer Rolls of Scotland (ed J Stuart et al, 1878-1908)xii, 8, 13, 135,140,190; 'History of Chapel Royal', Grampian Club, 1882, xlix; Macmillan [SA] 30.

**PRATT, David Camden** **fl 1878-1940**
Glasgow watercolour landscape painter. Possibly son of David P(qv). Exhibited RSW(1), GI(5) and two views of Skye at the AAS in 1926, latterly from 14 Shaftesbury Terrace.

**PRATT, David** **fl 1873-1874**
Glasgow landscape painter in oil; exhibited RSA(3) GI(6).

**PRATT, Edward** **fl 1880-1881**
Edinburgh painter in oil of domestic scenes. Exhibited 'Premeditating' at the RA 1880, also RSA from 74 Princes Street.

**PRATT, James** **fl 1880**
Minor Glasgow painter. Exhibited GI(1) from 103 Renfrew Street.

**PRATT, John** **fl 1496**
Decorator of the Royal Palaces at Stirling and Falkland for King James IV. On the 12 July 1496 he was paid the sum of £5 19s by the King and on the 14 September a further £3 'for paynting of the pailzoune thanis and the Kingis Cotearmour'.
**Bibl:** Apted 77; Armstrong 3.

**PRATT, John** **fl 1892**
Amateur Fife painter of High Street, Crail; exhibited GI(1).

**PRATT, Thomas M** **fl 1883-1898**
Glasgow painter of nature subjects and genre in oil; exhibited 'The haunt of the entomologist' at the RSA; also GI(9).

**PRATT, William Henry** **fl 1923-1932**
Edinburgh engraver. Lived for a time in Edinburgh but mainly in London from where he exhibited English and continental views at the RSA(3).

**PRATT, William M** **1854-1936**
Born Glasgow, 17 Apr; died Lenzie. Painter in oil and watercolour of landscapes, marines and figure subjects. Trained Glasgow School of Art and Academie Julien, Paris. Lived at Kirkintilloch, moving to Lenzie c1910. Exhibited RA(6) 1880-1936, RSA(64), RSW(7), GI(161), AAS(3) & L(23). Represented in Glasgow AG, City of Edinburgh collection.
**Bibl:** Halsby 279.

**PREHN, Eric Thornton** **1894-1985**
Born Moscow; died Edinburgh. Landscape painter in oils. Left Russia with his parents 1922. Studied in Florence under Nicola Lochoff. Settled in Scotland 1941, living in Oban before moving to Edinburgh 1945. Frequent visitor to Italy. Memorial exhibition at Fine Art Society 1986. Exhibited RSA (7) & RGI.

**PRENTICE, D R** **fl 1868-1898**
Little known watercolourist of landscapes and coastal scenes; worked in the Highlands and on the east coast.
**Bibl:** Halsby 278.

**PRENTICE, John B** **fl 1956-1958**
Lanarkshire painter in watercolour and pen and ink. Landscapes, especially Clydeside. Exhibited GI(3), from Kirkmuirhill.

**PRENTICE, John R** **fl 1849-1875**
Edinburgh painter in oil of landscapes, especially local scenes. Exhibited RSA(45) including several views on Arran, & GI(11)

**PRENTICE, Miss Marie Y** **fl 1905-1913**
Glasgow miniature painter of Albany Chambers, Charing Cross and Airdrie. Exhibited RA and Society of Miniature Painters 1908-1910; also 13 miniatures at the GI.

**PRESTON, George** **fl 1947-1948**
Cambuslang landscape and topographical painter. Exhibited GI(3).

**PRESTON, Laurence ARCA** **fl 1912**
Aberdeen-based painter of rural genre and country scenes; exhibited AAS(4) from 77 Stanley St.

**PRICE, Miss Marion** **fl 1960**
Glasgow amateur still life and flower painter. Exhibited GI from Elm St.

**PRICKETT, M** **fl 1923**
Exhibited 'The blue coat' at the RSA from 9 Greenhill Pl, Edinburgh.

**PRIEST, Mrs Margaret** **fl 1947**
Amateur Renfrewshire sculptress. Exhibited 'Head of a young girl', carved in rosewood, at the GI, from Barrhead.

**PRIMROSE, Jean Logan** **1910-?**
Born Glasgow, Jne 16. Painter in oil and watercolour of portraits and figurative studies, also illustrator of the books of Rumer Godden. Trained Hammersmith School of Art and at the City and Guilds. Sister of William Primrose, the viola player. Illustrated Godden: *Miss Happiness and Miss Flower* - runner-up for the Greenaway Award - (1961), *St Jerome and the Lion* (1961), *Little Plum* (1963), *Home is the Sailor* (1964), de Gasztold: *Prayers Told from the Ark* (1963), *The Beasts' Choice* (1967). Exhibited RA, RBA and Paris Salon.
**Bibl:** Horne 357; Mahoney; Peppin; Waters.

**PRINGLE, Alexander** **fl 1880-1882**
Edinburgh landscape painter in oil; exhibited RSA(2) from 32 Fountainbridge.

**PRINGLE, David Wauchope** **fl 1876**
Edinburgh watercolour landscape painter; exhibited RSA(1).

**PRINGLE, Elizabeth S (Mrs W R Rutherford)** **fl 1935-1938**
Edinburgh landscape watercolourist; also painted figure studies including nudes. Exhibited RSA(5), RSW(1) & AAS from 31 Craiglockart Crescent.

**PRINGLE, Miss Helen** **fl 1881-1888**
Edinburgh watercolour painter of figurative subjects. Exhibited RSA(2) from an Edinburgh address.

**PRINGLE, J Connell** **fl 1930**
Edinburgh amateur watercolour painter; exhibited RSW(1) from 120 Polwarth Tce.

**PRINGLE, John J** **fl 1896-1898**
Glasgow amateur painter. Exhibited GI(5) from 788 London Road.

**PRINGLE, John Quinton** **1864-1925**
Born and died Glasgow. Painter of portraits, still life and landscapes mostly in watercolour although increasingly in oil following a visit to Shetland 1931. Son of the station master of Langbank, nr Glasgow. One of those unusual but, to admirers and friends, intensely irritating people who steadfastly refused throughout his life to dedicate himself to his finest talents. In his case this was painting and an unwillingness to abandon his optical and general repair shop at 90 Saltmarket. Fra Newbery(qv) said 'my one regret, and it is a deep and lasting one, is that (Pringle) absolutely refused to abandon his daily tradework'. Nevertheless his shop was always a focal point for artists much to the detriment of the business itself. He attended evening classes 1883-5 and, with the aid of a bursary, continued evening classes at Glasgow School of Art until 1895. In 1910 he visited Normandy. Among many prizes, he won a gold medal for life drawing at a national competition in South Kensington 1891. From 1911-1920 he worked only in watercolour although returning to oil during his last years. Because of his life-style his output was small and he held only a single solo exhibition 1922. In 1919 he became acquainted with Hunter(qv) and Peploe(qv) both of whom were impressed with his talents, an important encouragement which helped launch his one exhibition. In 1923 ill-health together with the persuasion of his friends led to the sale of his business and a move to Ardersier, Inverness-shire. He visited the Shetlands 1921 and again in 1924 shortly before his death. His work was intensely personal although influenced by Bastien-Lepage, Guthrie(qv) and Hornel(qv) as well as by other Glasgow artists of the period. Remained as idiosyncratic in his art as in his life. Although his earliest works now seem rather laboured, from 1894 they became increasingly colourful, delicate and imbued with the artist's own personal style. Two of his best known works are 'Muslin Street, Bridgeton', subsequently acquired by the Scottish Modern Arts Association, a work showing remarkable topographical detail which took a year to complete, and 'The Loom', described as 'a direct and convincing transcript of the weaver's life'. In 1923 James Simpson wrote of 'the obscure optician; the self-effacing worker; the artist with imperishable fragments of beauty in his soul, which he sustained, nurtured, and exemplified in odd moments of release from his consecrated toil. He did not wake one morning to find himself famous - the vulgar concept did not occur to him; but he awoke late in life to realise the permanent character of the kingdom of dreams, and to receive with muted feelings the astonishing assurance that he, the least among men, should have been the creator of masterpieces. Not for the first time has the workman's jacket been drawn tightly across the bosom of genius'. Since his death critics have acclaimed his work and this, together with its comparative rarity, makes it extremely desirable. 'In many ways [he was] the most gifted of all his contemporaries in Scotland. Never tempted to overproduce for exhibitions, he created works of consistent quality that can be astonishingly original in technique and both dreamily poetic and painstakingly observant. His colour is jewel-like and his paintings show the most fastidious execution, and a personal form of the pointillisme of the neo-Impressionists, whose work Pringle almost certainly never saw' [Hardie]. Represented in Glasgow AG, Dundee AG, City of Edinburgh collection, Hunterian Museum (Glasgow).
**Bibl:** Halsby 158-60,172; Hardie 107-8; Hartley 159-160; SAC,'John Quinton Pringle' (Ex cat 1981); Scott Art Rev, new series, IX, 2, 1963, 1-4, 28; new series, IX, 3, 1964; new series, XV, 2, 1979; Glasgow AG, 'John Q Pringle 1864-1925: A Centenary Exhibition' (Cat by J Meldrum and A Auld, 1964); Irwin 394; Macmillan [SA] 295-6; J S Simpson, Scott Country Life, Dec 1923, 464-466.

**PRINGLE, Kate** **fl 1897-1901**
Edinburgh oil painter of still life, interiors, landscapes and portraits. Exhibited RSA(9) & GI(4) from 7 Fettes Row & latterly from Russell Place, Trinity.

**PRINGLE, Thomas** **fl 1863-1875**
Edinburgh oil painter of landscapes, especially the Highlands and local Edinburgh scenes. Exhibited RSA(13).

**PRIOLO, Paolo** **fl 1857-1890**
Painted costumes, interiors and historical narratives. Probably a Sicilian he lived for a time at various Edinburgh addresses 1857-60 and subsequently in London at 64 Stockwell Park Road. Exhibited RA(7), RSA(6) & GI(3).

**PRIOR, Mark Anthony Morpheus** **fl 1980-1981**
Aberdeen printmaker. Trained at Gray's School of Art, Aberdeen. Exhibited AAS(3) from 39 Desswood Pl.

**PRITCHARD, Walter** **1905-?**
Born Dundee. Painter and stained glass artist; teacher. Studied at Dundee School of Art where he obtained both an ordinary and a travelling scholarship. Husband of Sadie McLellan(qv). After visiting Europe he became stained glass instructor at Edinburgh College of Art where he encouraged and taught many important pupils including Crear McLellan(qv). Exhibited RA(2), RSA & GI(2).

**PROCTER, Robert Field** **1879-1931**
Born in Scotland; ded Melbourne. Arrived in Christchurch, New Zealand with his family at the age of 7. Trained Canterbury School of

Art and privately with van ver Velden. Pursued further studies in Antwerp, Italy and Paris before returning to Christchurch 1898. Member, Council of the Christchurch Art Society 1899-1902 and Christchurch School of Art 1910-15. By 1916 was in Auckland, teaching at the Elam School of Art until 1920. Migrated to Melbourne 1928 where he joined the staff of the Business & Technical College. Represented by 'In the Campo Del Fioro, Rome' in Nat Gall of New Zealand (Wellington); also Canterbury AG, Christchurch AG, Auckland AG, Hocken Library (Univ of Otago).
**Bibl:** Una Platt, Nineteenth Century New Zealand Artists, Avon Fine Prints, 1980.

**PROCTOR, - fl c1740**
Edinburgh-based seal engraver. Taught William Berry(qv).
**Bibl:** Bushnell.

**PROSSER, Douglas fl 1966**
Aberdeenshire sculptor. Exhibited AAS(1) from 57 Kellands Rd, Inverurie.

**PROUDFOOT, Alexander RSA 1878-1957**
Born Liverpool, 7 Nov; died Perth 10 Jly. Sculptor of figurative works, mainly portrait busts. Trained Glasgow School of Art and in 1908 gained a Haldane travelling scholarship. After the war many commissions awaited him mainly for of war memorials. Head of the sculpture department of Glasgow School of Art 1912-1928. Twice President, Glasgow Art Club 1924-6 and 1939-41. Married the sculptress Ivy Gardiner(qv) 1955. Elected ARSA 1920, RSA 1933. Exhibited RA(6), RSA(62), RSW(2), GI(54) & L(4). Represented in SNPG.

**PROUDFOOT, James RP ROI 1908-1971**
Born Perth, 3 Mar; died London, 15 Jly. Landscape and portrait painter and black and white artist. Educated Perth Academy and St Andrews University. Worked in his father's carpet business before studying art at Heatherly's, Goldsmiths College and in Paris. Received an honourable mention at the Paris Salon for a portrait of 'Peter Ustinov', now in Perth AG. Elected ROI in 1934, and RP 1947. Exhibited from 1933 RA(5), RSA(3) & ROI(11). Represented in Perth AG (including an early 'Self-portrait').

**PROUDFOOT, Mrs Jane (Ivy) Hunter Ferguson 1894-1975**
Born Greenock. Sculptress of mainly figurative works. Trained Glasgow School of Art becoming assistant to Benno Shotz(qv) and Alexander Proudfoot(qv) whom she married. Best known for her fine sculptural portraits of children. Hon. member, Soroptomists International. Exhibited under the name of Ivy Gardiner at the RA, RSA, Walker Gallery (Liverpool) & GI(34).
**Bibl:** Glasgow Herald, March 27 1975 (obit).

**PROUDFOOT, John fl 1836-1862**
Perth painter in oils of flowers, landscapes, portraits and figure studies from literature. Brother of William P(qv). Exhibited RSA(30).

**PROUDFOOT, William 1822-1902**
Born Perth, Oct 27; died Perth Jan 7. Brother of John P(qv). Worked in oil and watercolour; landscapes, dead game, portraits and interiors. Educated Perth Academy. Studied art in Italy c1844 before settling in Perth. Friend of John Gibson(qv), Lawrence MacDonald(qv) and Thomas Smith(qv). It was not until he was about 70 that he began painting in watercolour, which he called 'diluted art'. His landscape watercolours are fresh and effective but his still lifes are more highly finished and sometimes overlaboured. A good teacher, running a life class in Perth in the 1880s attended by George Muirhead(qv). Prolific painter who during his life-time exhibited RSA(124) & GI(10), most from Edinburgh. Represented in Perth AG.
**Bibl:** Halsby 279.

**PROVAN, Mrs Elizabeth G fl 1879-1912**
Glasgow painter in oil of flowers and portraits. Her work is colourful and the quality of her drawing stands the test of time. Exhibited RA (4), RSA(14), RSW(1), GI(62) & L(1), from 189 Hill St.

**PROVAN, George W fl 1911-1912**
Glasgow amateur topographical painter. Exhibited GI(2) from 6 Westercraigs, Dennistoun.

**PROWETT, James Christie fl 1892-d1946**
Born Bannockburn. Of French extraction. Painter in oil and watercolour. Educated Stirling HS, later going to Paris where he was a prize winner at the Paris School of Art. On his return he became a member of both the Glasgow Art Club and Stirling Fine Art Association, contributing to the triennial exhibitions in the Smith Institute. A very good colourist and craftsman. Exhibited RSA(10), GI(55), RSW(2), AAS(1900-26), RHA(1) & L(3).

**PRYDE, James Beugo fl 1888**
Edinburgh portrait painter. Member of the Nicholson/Pryde(qv) families of painters, directly descended from John Beugo(qv). Exhibited 'David Pryde Esq MA, LLD' at the RSA, from Fettes Row.

**PRYDE, James Ferrier 1866-1941**
Born Edinburgh 30 Mar; died London, 24 Feb. Painter in oil, watercolour, gouache and pastel; architectural and figure subjects; also lithographer and postal designer. Only son of the headmaster of Queen Street Ladies' College, his mother was a niece of R S Lauder(qv) and J E Lauder(qv). Educated George Watson's, trained RSA Schools 1866-7 and at Academie Julien, Paris under Bouguereau. This was followed by a short spell at Herkomer's School, Bushey where he met William Nicholson(qv) 1893. This led to the latter's marriage to Pryde's sister and to collaboration between the two men. Together they began to produce posters using the pseudonym 'J & W Beggarstaff'. These had a profound effect upon poster design in the 1890s. They also experimented with woodcuts and together produced *The Page* (1898) based on archaic chap-book printing. Pryde worked for a time as an actor, touring Scotland in 1895 with Gordon Craig. His best paintings were completed during the years 1900-1925, mostly portraits in grisaille, gouache and oil; also architectural subjects. More of a designer than an illustrator he nevertheless provided the illustrations for Wilhelm Hauff's *The Little Glass Man* (1893), and contributed to *Tony Drum* (1898). Around 1909 began a sequence of paintings inspired by Mary Queen of Scots' bed at Holyrood Palace. Altogether he painted 12 of this subject with a 13th only interrupted by his death. His first one-man show was 1911. Lady Cowdray was among many who saw and admired his work, buying several of the more important examples and commissioning more. Altogether 18 works were hung along the side walls of the library at Dunecht, Aberdeenshire. His last important picture, 'The Grave', was acquired by the Tate in 1929. In 1930 he designed sets for Paul Robeson's 'Othello'. Bedridden for two years before his death. Regarded by some as one of the greatest imaginative painters since Turner. 'He is commonly appreciated by those who have an understanding for music. By the subtlety of his low tones, and by his deliberate and legitimate exaggerations of emphasis, he works on the emotions with some of the magic of his sister art...as in all great art the spectator comes away from his pictures not depressed but uplifted' [Hudson]. 'The Doctor' was purchased by the Chantrey Bequest in 1940. Friend of Guthrie and Walton, often meeting with them and William Nicholson in the 1890s at Joseph Crawhall's house in Yorkshire. His health was damaged by alcohol and he produced little work after 1925. A retrospective exhibition was held in Edinburgh 1992 as part of the International Festival. Exhibited widely including RSA(8), RHA(1), GI(8), AAS 1919-37 & London Salon(4). Represented in Tate AG, V & A, SNGMA, City of Edinburgh Collection, Nat Gall of Canada (Ottawa).
**Bibl:** Caw 448-9; Halsby 146,155,240; Hartley 160; Hardie 103-4; Houfe; Derek Hudson, James Pryde 1866-1941, London 1949; Leics Gall, 'The art of James Pryde', (Ex cat 1933); Redfern Gall, 'James Pryde', (Ex Cat 1988 - Text by John Synge); Harold Osborne(ed), Twentieth Century Art, 1988, 449; Wingfield.

**PRYOR, Sybil fl 1962**
Edinburgh landscape painter; exhibited RSA(1).

**PRYSE, Tessa Spencer fl 1968-1982**
Ross-shire painter of portraits and flowers. Exhibited RSA, from Fortrose.

**PULSFORD, Charles Denis ARSA 1912-1989**
Born Leek, Staffordshire, 8 Jne. Painter and worker in three dimensions. Brought up in Fife, educated at Aberdour and Dunfermline HS. Trained Edinburgh College of Art 1933-7, being awarded a fellowship in 1939; also studied in France and Italy. His first one-man

show at the French Institute, Edinburgh 1951 followed by another in London two years later. In the 1940s was influenced by the Surrealists and in the 1960s by the development of the Apollo/Demeter - Hephaes 2/Demeter themes. Also by the work of Duchamp and subsequently by the advent of the Creative Cell. This resulted in his becoming involved in experimental vision and sound, culminating in Tuscany with the composer Robert Majek. Supported by the British Council and the Fondazione Romacs. The Creative Cell formed by Pulsford Sculpture/Theatre Group called GASP occupied much of his time. Staff member, Edinburgh College of Art 1948-1960, subsequently Head of Fine Art, Wolverhampton College of Art and part-time lecturer, Edinburgh Department of Architecture. A contemporary critic wrote 'a rugged and aesthetic intellectual, odd-man-out who has, with admirable tenacity, followed an independent and highly original path that owes little or nothing to outside influences. He is intent on making abstract symbols of great, classic dignity, that will reflect the more durable kind of philosophical or mystical concepts of Man and the Universe which found expression in Ancient Greece...his qualities of unconformity, aloofness and mysticism have combined with his expatriate position to deprive us of the opportunity of honouring his gifts' [Gage]. Hardie likens his work to Jackson Pollock ' the same transatlantic painterly abstract style' and to 'the flickering, flame-like colour field painting of Clyfford Stills'. Published *The Creative Cell* (1973). Lived in Staffordshire. Elected ARSA 1958, SSA 1950. Exhibited regularly RSA, RSW, GI & SSA. Represented in SAC.
**Bibl:** Gage 34-5; Hardie 185.

**PURDIE, Ian C** **fl 1954-1960**
Glasgow painter and etcher. Exhibited ships and views in Amsterdam at the GI.

**PURDIE, James** **fl 1881**
Amateur Fife watercolour painter of landscape. Exhibited RSA(1) from Aberdour.

**PURDOM, Dorothy** **fl 1918-1919**
Roxburghshire painter from Langheugh, Hawick. Daughter of a well known solicitor, Sir John Purdom. Painted animals, especially dogs and horses. Exhibited RSA(2).

**PURDOM, Patricia** **fl 1987-**
Hawick artist. Daughter of Dorothy P(qv). exhibits colourful semi-abstracts at the RSA, beginning in 1987; currently lives at 41 Hepburn Gdns, St Andrews.

**PURVES, James E** **fl 1863-1869**
Edinburgh painter in oils, genre and landscapes. Exhibited RSA(19). Probably the same Purves who drew 'Smolett's House, High Street', now in the Edinburgh City collection.

**PURVES, James M** **fl 1932**
Glasgow topographical painter; exhibited GI(2) from 22 Wilton Dr.

**PURVES, Robert** **fl 1934**
Amateur Glasgow painter; exhibited 'At the pool' at the RSA(1), from 9 Walmer Terrace, Ibrox.

**PURVIS, John Milne** **1885-1961**
Born Perth, Aug 31; died Dundee, Oct 30. Painter of figurative subjects. Educated Perth Academy, trained Glasgow School of Art 1905-08 where he was a Haldane scholar. Travelled in Europe and North Africa. Assistant master of drawing & painting, Dundee Technical College 1910, becoming Head of department until his retirement in 1950. Exhibited oil and watercolours, based on his many trips abroad, particularly to Spain, North Africa and Turkey. Designed sets for the Dundee Dramatic Society and was a member of the Perth Art Association and President of the Dundee Art Society 1936. Exhibited RSA(9), RSW(5), RA(1), GI(3) & L(5). Represented in Perth AG.
**Bibl:** Halsby 279; R H Rodger, John Milne Purvis (1885-1961), Perth AG 1994.

**PYPER, William** **fl 1900-1906**
Aberdeenshire landscape and topographical painter. Exhibited AAS(4) including 'Muchalls Castle', from Hillhead of Pitfodels.

**PYRSE, G Spencer** **fl 1930-1938**
Painter, possibly Scottish. Exhibited GI(7) through his agents: Twenty-One Gallery, Glasgow.

# Q

**QUAIL, Gerald** **fl 1963**
Glasgow ceramicist; exhibited a pottery statuette of a lady at the GI.

**QUAST, Henry** **fl 1869-1873**
Glasgow landscape painter in watercolour; exhibited RSA(2) GI(6) all of Arran.

**QUEENSBERRY, The Marchioness of** **[see MANN, Cathleen]**

**QUESNEL, Augustin the First** **1595-1661**
Born Paris, 18 Dec. Painter and print-seller. Member of a celebrated Franco-Scots family of artists; son of Francois(qv), grandson of Pierre Q(qv). De Marolles records that he painted portraits, but the only known work is 'A Flute-player', engraved by Ganieres. Represented in Budapest AG.
**Bibl:** Benezit; Bryan.

**QUESNEL, Francois** **1543-1619**
Born Holyrood, Edinburgh; died Paris. Member of the celebrated Franco-Scottish family of artists. Eldest son of Pierre Q(qv). Painter of portraits and tapestry designer, worked in oil, pastel, black chalk. Most distinguished as a portraitist. The ablest member of the family and a great favourite with Henry III and his court, especially Chancellor Chiverny. De Marolles records that his portraits were often confused with those by Janet. Compiled 'Le Premier Plan de Paris, en douze feuilles'. A modest, retiring disposition prevented wider fame and greater honours. Many of his tapestry designs were used for the entries of Marie de Medici and the consecration of Louis XIII, some being engraved by Thomas de Leu. Represented in the Louvre (bust portrait of a woman in black chalk), French National Library (two pastels 'Portrait of a Man' and 'Gabrielle d'Estrees'), Florence (Palais Pitti), Le Mans AG, Versailles Palace.
**Bibl:** Benezit; Bryan.

**QUESNEL, Jacques** **?-1624**
Born Paris; died Paris, May 11. Third son of Pierre Q(qv). Painted churches and according to de Marolles decorated the Zamet hotel. Bryan records a quatrain of de Marolles:

> Jacques peignit des Saints, des voutes, des chapelles.
> Il peignit des tableaux pour l'hotel de Zamet,
> Il en fit pour le prince a qui tout se soumet,
> Et l'on connut de lui mille beautes nouvelles.

**Bibl:** Benezit; Bryan.

**QUESNEL, Nicolas** **?-1632**
Born Paris; died Paris Aug 7. Second son of Pierre Q(qv). Portrait painter. Dean of the Society of Painters and Sculptors. A pastel portrait of his father is in the National Library, Paris.
**Bibl:** Benezit; Bryan.

**QUESNEL, Pierre** **fl 1538-1580**
Stained glass window designer. Scion of a celebrated family of Franco-Scottish artists, descended from an ancient Scottish house. Protected by Mary of Guise (Lorraine), who presented him to her husband, James V. Married Madeleine Digby in Scotland where their eldest son François(qv) was born in 1543. Shortly afterwards the family settled in Paris where he was known to have been living 1580. His only recorded work is a design, executed in 1557, for the east windows in the church of the Grand Augustins, Paris, the subject of which is the ascension, with Henry II and Catherine de Medici as spectators. Apted suggests that he may have been the anonymous painter who in 1542 received payment from the Queen for work done at Falkland and as general wages.
**Bibl:** Apted 77; Benezit; Bryan; R.K. Marshall, Mary of Guise, 1977, 203; Sheila M. Percival, French Artists, unpub. thesis, Edin Univ, 1962, 5-10, 156.

**QUESNEL, Toussaint** **1594-1651**
Born Paris, Dec 15; died Paris. History painter. Son of Nicolas Q(qv). In 1651 he painted history subjects in collaboration with Freminet and Dubreuil. The same year he was a signatory to the act of union between the master painters and the academicians.
**Bibl:** Benezit; Bryan; Marolles.

**QUICK, G Graham** **fl 1954**
Ayrshire amateur watercolour painter. Exhibited GI(1).

**QUIGLEY, Jim** **fl 1985-1987**
Glasgow painter. Exhibited GI(2).

# R

**RAE, Barbara RA RSA RSW** **1943-**
Born Crieff. Painter in oil, watercolour and pastel. Uses acrylic paint and collage to build up a rich decorative surface. Studied Edinburgh College of Art 1961-5, awarded travelling scholarship 1966 before proceeding to Moray House 1966-7. Received a number of prestigious awards including the Guthrie Medal 1977, May Marshall Brown award, RSW 1979, Sir William Gillies award, RSA 1983 and the Alexander Graham Munro award, RSW 1989. Has held numerous one-man shows and taught in various Edinburgh schools. A painter of large semi-abstract enigmatic landscapes with the merest hints of specific places and the marks left by man on the landscape. Her works are not conventionally picturesque and on occasion are positively ugly. In 1983 she began experimenting with printmaking, her first monotypes being made in New Mexico 1986. Her work, which is sometimes repetitive and even clichéd, has been likened to Hitchens and Piper. Elected RA 1997, RSW 1975, ARSA 1980, RSA 1992, President, SSA 1983. In 1990 exhibited at the Madrid International Art Fair. Regular exhibitor at RSA, RSW, GI & AAS 1974-5 and 1985 when living at 65 Dunbar St, latterly from her studio at 30 Elbe St, Leith. Represented in Aberdeen AG, SAC, Dundee AG, British Museum, McLaurin AG (Ayr), Kelvingrove AG (Glasgow), SGMA, Lillie AG (Milngavie), Hunterian Museum (Glasgow), Edinburgh City collection, Perth AG.

**RAE, Edna M W** **fl 1931-1933**
Glasgow landscape painter & wood engraver. Exhibited a harbour scene at the RSA, another at the GI; also AAS(1), from 93 St Andrews Dr.

**RAE, Miss Elsie** **fl 1982-1983**
Glasgow still life painter. Exhibited GI(2), from Bearsden.

**RAE, Henrietta (Mrs Normand)** **fl 1896-1906**
Painter of figure subjects. Exhibited AAS(3) from London.

**RAE, Iain Logie** **fl 1972-1976**
Aberdeenshire painter of marine subjects and topography. Exhibited AAS(3) including a study of a schooner and another of a trawler, from 124 Kirkhill Rd, Tullos.

**RAE, James B** **fl 1962**
Clackmannanshire amateur artist. Exhibited GI(1), from Dollar.

**RAE, Jennifer** **fl 1973-1974**
Kincardineshire jewellery designer. Exhibited AAS(3) from South Barns, Laurencekirk.

**RAE, John Taylor ARBS** **fl 1971-1987**
Aberdeenshire sculptor. Trained Glasgow School of Art. Exhibited RSA(2) & AAS(2) from 9 Glen Rd, Dyce and Blairgowrie.

**RAE, Lizzie C** **fl 1896**
Aberdeenshire amateur painter of genre and still life. Exhibited AAS(2) while employed at the Town & County Bank, Aberdeen.

**RAE, Mary** **fl 1883-1887**
Watercolour portrait painter, also garden scenes and figurative subjects. Of Scottish parents lived most of her life in London, latterly at 23 Phillimore Gardens, Kensington. Exhibited a portrait RA 1886, also RSA(5) & RI(1).

**RAE, Muriel** **fl 1970**
Aberdeenshire artist; exhibited AAS(1) from 3 Hillview Terrace, Cults.

**RAE, Peter Eric** **fl 1979-1980**
Aberdeen painter. Trained Gray's School of Art, Aberdeen. Exhibited AAS(3) from 6 South Mount St.

**RAE, Robin** **fl 1961-1962**
Edinburgh landscape and portrait painter; exhibited RSA(3) including 'Self-portrait'.

**RAE, Ronald** **1946-**
Born Ayr. Sculptor, works in granite, bronze (hand carved), and wood. Also graphic artist. Prefers to work in Kemnay stone. Part-time student, Glasgow School of Art 1966-7, becoming a technical assistant 1967-8 and a full-time student Edinburgh College of Art 1968-70. For the next seven years was a self-employed artist and sculptor. Then sponsored by an American art collector to work in the United States for one year. Returning to Ayr in 1978 he was commissioned to carve five granite sculptures for Rozelle Park, Ayr and was involved in the restoration of the sculptures in Dunfermline City Hall 1980-81. The next year was working at Royal Edinburgh and General hospitals, also at the world headquarters of the General Accident Company in Perth for which he executed the 'Return of the Prodigal'. A sculpture was recently commissioned by Glenrothes to mark their 40th Anniversary.

**RAE, Wendy H** **fl 1979-1980**
Aberdeen artist. Trained Gray's School of Art, Aberdeen. Exhibited AAS(4) from 177A Crown St.

**RAEBURN, Miss Agnes Middleton RSW** **1872-1955**
Born Glasgow; died Glasgow, 3 Aug. Painter in oil and watercolour of landscapes and flowers. Sister of Lucy Raeburn(qv). Trained Glasgow School of Art under Fra Newbery 1887-1901. Member of Charles Rennie Mackintosh's circle, contributing to *The Magazine* 1893-96 for which publication she was primarily responsible; her frontispiece 'Winged Woman' for the April 1894 issue is illustrated in Burkhauser (fig 47, p49). One of the 'Immortals' who contributed watercolours, drawings, prose and poetry to the development of Glasgow as a European cultural centre. Her early work was influenced by Glasgow Symbolism but her later landscape, continental watercolours as well as the flower studies are freely painted, being characteristically 'wet' in style. Art mistress, Laurelbank School and President, Glasgow Society of Lady Artists(qv) 1940-1943. Although her output was large it was consistent. Her coloured lithograph poster for the Glasgow Lecture Association, illustrated by Burkhauser in colour (p98), is now in the Hunterian Museum, Glasgow University. Elected RSW 1901, won Lauder Award 1927. Exhibited RSA(35), RSW(144), GI(98), AAS 1906 & 1931 & L(13). Represented in Dundee AG.
**Bibl:** Burkhauser 48-9,59-60,76,79,96 illus; Halsby 279; Irwin 400.

**RAEBURN, Elizabeth A** **fl 1937**
Edinburgh artist. Exhibited 'Solitude' at the RSA from 33 Heriot Row.

**RAEBURN, Ethel Maud** **1867-1953**
Edinburgh artist painted landscapes in watercolour often of Venetian scenes; also flower pieces and occasional portraits. Exhibited regularly RSA(40), RSW(27), also GI(22), RI(2), L(5) & London Salon(10). Represented Edinburgh City collection(2).
**Bibl:** Halsby 279.

**RAEBURN, Sir Henry RA** **1756-1823**
Born Stockbridge, Edinburgh, 4 Mar; died Edinburgh, 8 Jly. Painter in oil of portraits and portrait miniatures. Son of a weaver and mill owner, by the time he was nine both his parents had died. Attended George Heriot's Hospital School but left when he was 15 to become an apprentice with the Edinburgh goldsmith James Gilliland (27.6.1772). His first recorded work, executed c1773, was a portrait miniature of the etcher and steel engraver 'David Deuchar' (now in the SNPG) inscribed 'the second portrait done by him during the time he was apprentice with Mr Gilliland, Jeweller, Parliament Square, Edinburgh'. A later miniature portrait was the '2nd Earl Spencer', painted in Rome after a study by the Irish painter Hugh Douglas Hamilton 1785. The first known full-length portrait is 'George Chalmers of Pittencrieff' 1776, now in the City Chambers, Dunfermline. In 1775, David Deuchar introduced Raeburn to David Martin(qv) who allowed the young man to copy examples of his (Martin's) work. Two further momentous events followed. In 1780 he married Anne Edgar, a wealthy widow, enabling him to acquire property and land in Stockbridge, subsequently extended from 1813 onward in the style of the New Town to become one of Edinburgh's first suburbs. The second event was visiting London and meeting Reynolds in 1783/4 (according to Redgrave he spent two months in Reynolds' studio). In July 1784 he went to Rome, studying at the

Vatican and cultivating the friendship of James Byres(qv). After returning to Scotland 1786 the extension of his powers was continuous and remarkable. 'Seldom has an artist's technique shown a growth so gradual and uninterrupted' (McKay). He moved steadily to what has been described as enlarged portrait miniatures, eg 'Sir William Forbes of Craigievar' 1788 to full-length figures in landscape settings, eg 'Sir John and Lady Clark of Penicuik' 1791, finally reaching an apotheosis in grand portraits of Highland chieftains and other notables, eg 'The MacNab', 'Alastair Macdonell of Glengarry' 1812 and 'John, 2nd Marquess of Bute' 1821. His shadows became less black, his backcloths more ambitious, his use of colour more assured. In 1798 he moved to a new studio built in York Place but in 1810, shortly after Hoppner's death and following the failure of a business enterprise, he sought richer rewards in London though soon returned to Edinburgh. His style was better suited to painting older rather than younger women. 'He succeeded best where features were pronounced and modelling could be deep and sculptured' [Irwin]. 'Mrs Scott Moncrieff' c1814 NGS, and 'Mrs William Urquhart' c1814 Glasgow AG are among his most successful female portraits. But it is by his paintings of Highland chieftains that he is popularly remembered. Majestic, dignified and colourful but without pomposity or unnatural drama, and with character predominating over effect. Other famous portraits are 'Dr Nathaniel Spens' 1791, 'Dr Alexander Adam', 'Major William Clunes', his diploma picture 'The Boy and Rabbit' 1821, and his own 'Self-portrait' in the SNPG. 'His best portraits show a unity and coherence of conception, combined with a free certainty of handling, that is only to be excelled in the work of two or three very famous men. His colour is of the negative kind. It gives neither pain nor much active pleasure. Now and then it shows a tendency to heat, but as a rule, it is simply quiescent...His pictures seldom give an opening for positive criticism. So far as they go they come near perfection, but the range of his chiaroscuro is too short; his shadows and his highlights are too near each other, which leads to a want of depth and roundness in his modelling, and generally to a want of force. This comes partly, no doubt, from his habit of painting without a rest for his hand...It is undoubtedly to the strong and original personality of Henry Raeburn that we owe the existence of a Scottish School of Painting' [McKay]. 701 portraits have been recorded. Elected ARA 1812, President, Society of Artists 1812, RA 1815, knighted shortly after being appointed His Majesty's Limner and Painter for Scotland 1823. Exhibited RA(53) 1792-1823. Represented in SNPG(24), NGS, Aberdeen AG, Glasgow AG, Kirkcaldy AG, City of Edinburgh collection, Fyvie Castle (NTS)(an important group of 13 portraits), The Baird Flat (NTS), Hill of Tarvit (NTS), Craigievar Castle (NTS), Drum Castle (NTS), Hill of Tarvit (NTS).
**Bibl:** Armstrong 10-16; Sir Walter Armstrong, Sir Henry Raeburn (1901); Arts Council of GB, Raeburn Bicentenary Exhibition, Edinburgh 1956; Brydall 219-228; Caw 69-78 et passim; E R Dibdin, Raeburn, London 1925; A.Duncan, A Tribute of Regard to the Memory of Sir Henry Raeburn, 1824; Greig, Sir Henry Raeburn, (1911); Irwin 146-164, 219-221 et passim; McKay 32-68; Macmillan [GA] 74-80, 129-137 et passim; Macmillan [SA] 150-54, 158-163 et passim; John Morrison 'Reminiscences of Sir Walter Scott, the ettrick shepherd, Sir Henry Raeburn etc', Taits Edin Mag X, 1843 & XI, 1844; RSA 1886 (Ex Cat); Sir Robert Louis Stevenson 'Some Portraits by Raeburn' in Virginibus Puerisque, London 1881.

**RAEBURN, Lucy (Mrs Alfred Spottiswoode Ritchie) 1869-1952**
Born Glasgow(qv). Writer and occasional metal designer. Sister of Agnes Middleton R(qv). Trained Glasgow School of Art 1894-1895 but left prematurely on account of her success in editing the first numbers of *The Magazine.* As a result of this literary work became a close friend of Charles Rennie Mackintosh(qv) and his wife(qv) and an influential member of the circle. Her only recorded work is a hammered brass panel exhibited at the Arts and Crafts Exhibition Society, 1896. In 1898 she married and moved to Edinburgh. Ian Monie records that the hammerwork she exhibited at the GSA Exhibition was good enough to be commended in a local press notice.
**Bibl:** Ian Monie in Burkhauser, 76,78,109,119.

**RAEBURN, Robert 1819-1888**
Edinburgh architect. Designed mostly ecclesiastical works including the Livingstone Memorial Medical Mission in the Cowgate (1877-8); Roseburn Free Church, West Coates (1867) later to become the parish church; and St Colm, Dalry Rd (1881). His assistant and successor was George Lyle(qv).
**Bibl:** Gifford 164,255,311,318,502,504,547,580,593,598-9,611, 622.

**RAIMBACH, Miss Emma Harriet 1810-c1882**
Born London, Jly 6; died Caen, France. English miniature portrait painter; also painted occasional landscapes and portraits in water-colour and pencil. Eldest surviving daughter of the miniaturist engraver and friend of Wilkie, Abraham R (Swiss father and English mother). Awarded silver medal by the Society of Arts in 1826. Entered the Convent of the Good Shepherd, Hammersmith c1847 where she was known as 'Sister Mary of St. Arsène'. Her close connections with Scotland are evidenced by the fact that of her 55 exhibits at the RA 1835-1855 at least 15 were of Scottish sitters including 'Maj-Gen Sir Patrick Ross' 1836, 'Viscount Drumlanrig' and 'Viscountess Drumlanrig' both 1842, the 'Lovat children of Beaufort Castle' 1844, and the 'Family of James Campbell of Loch Awe' 1846. Furthermore, in 1845 and 1846 she exhibited 15 works at the RSA, mostly portraits of children of the Scottish nobility. Represented in V & A.
**Bibl:** Foskett; Long.

**RAIMES, Miss Bessie fl 1873-1887**
Edinburgh watercolour painter of landscape; exhibited RSA(4).

**RAINE, Paul c1945-**
Painter in oil of landscape, flowers and domestic genre. During his studies as a mature student at Gray's School of Art, Aberdeen he completed a dissertation on Tibetan Thangka painting, an art form which continues to influence him. Paints in a rather heavy style often in sombre hues lightened by compositional devices such as copper and pewter pans, and flower heads. Lectured for two years at Aberdeen College of Commerce. Paints full-time in Aberdeenshire.

**RAINY, Anne fl 1925**
Amateur sculptress, working mainly bronze figures. Exhibited GI(2) from Rose Valley, Croy, Inverness-shire.

**RALPH, George Keith fl 1752-c1798**
Portrait and history painter of Scottish extraction. Lived and worked all his life in London. Born in September, entered the RA Schools 1775. His most ambitious work is a competent full-length 'Alderman John Spink' 1791, now in the Guildhall, Bury St Edmunds. Three of his portraits were engraved at Bury 1788. In 1794 appointed Portrait Painter to the Duke of Clarence. Exhibited regularly RA(35) 1778-1811.

**RALSTON, J McL fl 1868-1889**
Glasgow oil and watercolour painter of genre; also illustrator. Left Scotland to work in England c1873. Illustrated Dickens' *A Child's History of England,* 1873 and *The Pilgrim's Progress,* 1880 edition. Contributed to *ILN* 1872-3 and again 1880-1. Exhibited RSA(1) and occasionally at the Dowdeswell Galleries.
**Bibl:** The Brothers Dalziel, A Record of Work, 1840-1890, 1901; Houfe.

**RALSTON, Mrs Margaret fl 1954-1987**
Lanarkshire painter of still life, genre and informal portraits. Exhibited GI(10) from Bothwell and subseqently from Edinburgh.

**RALSTON, William 1848-1911**
Born Dumbarton; died Glasgow, Oct. Black and white artist and illustrator, especially of humorous studies. After abandoning an early career as a photographer believed to have studied under a younger brother. Contributed many drawings to *Punch* 1870-1886, especially genre and military subjects. Later became expert at episodic illustration and strip cartoons. Living in Glasgow at the turn of the century but spent his last years in London. Illustrated Thackeray's *Barry Lyndon* (1894) and contributed to *The Graphic* 1870-1911, *Sporting & Dramatic News* 1895, *Cornhill Magazine* 1883-4, and *Daily Graphic.* Exhibited GI 1902 and 1910.
**Bibl:** Caw 295-6; Houfe; M.H. Spielmann, The History of Punch, 1895, 543; Wingfield.

**RAMAGE, James c1825-1887**
Died 21 Nov. Painter of landscapes, draughtsman and pioneer of photo-lithography which he studied with W H Lizars(qv). Probably brother of Jessie Ramage(qv). For some years head of the artistic

department, T Nelson & Son of Edinburgh. Exhibited RSA(5), from 17 Torphichen Street, Portobello.

**RAMAGE, Miss Jessie** **fl 1869-1877**
Portobello painter in oil and watercolour of figures, literary subjects and landscape. Probably sister of James Ramage(qv). Exhibited RSA(14) & GI(2).

**RAMAGE, Peter** **fl 1915**
Glasgow amateur sculptor of 181 Shamrock Street; exhibited GI(1).

**RAMAGE, William** **?-1828**
Born Leith. Naval artist. Began as a sailor and in 1793 was serving on the frigate *Iris.* In 1798-99 he obtained his Commission and was the Signal and Flag Lieutenant to Admiral Earl St Vincent. In 1807 promoted to the rank of Commander and in 1817 was commanding the brig *Cherokee.* Several pictures of naval scenes were exhibited at the Royal Naval Exhibition, Chelsea, in 1891 including a series of watercolours of the Battle of St Vincent (1797). Of Scottish interest was 'His Majesty George IV proceeding to the Port of Leith in the land of his Ancestors' which was subsequently published as a coloured lithograph (1822).

**RAMSAY, -** **c1831-?**
Son of the Rev William Ramsay of Crieff. Entered Trustees Academy, Edinburgh 16 November 1849 on the recommendation of Thomas Brown Jnr but left on 24 April the following year. No record remains of his work.

**RAMSAY, Miss Alice** **fl 1926-1928**
Renfrewshire painter of landscape and genre. Daughter of James R(qv). Attended Glasgow Art School as a contemporary of Mary Armour(qv) but was unable to complete the course owing to the ill-health of her mother and brother. Nevertheless she resumed painting in later years both in Ayrshire and also in America. There is a painting in the Weaver's Cottage originally executed for Glasgow AG. Exhibited 'The MacDougal tartan' at the RSA and also once at the GI, from the Old Manse, Kilbarchan.

**RAMSAY, Allan** **1713-1784**
Born Edinburgh, 13 Oct; died Dover, 10 Aug. Portrait painter in oil; thinker and writer. Eldest son of Allan Ramsay, poet and author of *The Gentle Shepherd.* James Norie(qv) was a family friend and neighbour although whether he ever taught the young artist is unclear. His first known work, a chalk drawing of his father made in 1729, coincided with the founding of the Academy of St Luke of which young Ramsay became a founder member (the only one to decorate the pages of history). In 1732 he went to London to study under Hans Hysing and may have attended the Academy in St Martin's Lane which at that time was directed by Hogarth. Returned to Edinburgh 1733, setting himself up as a portrait painter. Only a few works can be safely attributed to this early period, among them 'Margaret Calderwood' and 'Kathleen Hall of Dunglass'. There is a trend away from Hysing's stylization back towards the mould of Aikman (another family friend). In 1736, with Dr (later Sir) Alexander Cunynghame, he went to Rome to study under Imperiali, then at the French Academy under Vleughels. In 1737 he moved to Naples for further studies under the ageing Francesca Solimena. The summer of 1738 found him back in London, a profound interest in French art and an enhanced understanding of draughtsmanship both established. Rapidly gained a reputation that rivalled Hogarth's - he had become the first Scottish painter to invade England successfully. The next year he married Anne Bayne, great grand-daughter of Sir William Bruce of Kinross(qv) and daughter of the 1st Professor of Municipal Law at Edinburgh (of which subject, according to Boswell, 'he was very ignorant'). The two portraits of Anne and himself are elegant, finely delineated and very personal in their intimate appeal. 'The treatment of reflected light on the shadow of her cheek and on the dark edges of her sleeve reveals a fidelity to the phenomena of nature of a kind not seen before in British painting' [McMillan]. Throughout the 1740s he completed a succession of important works, from the full-length child portrait of the 'Hamilton children' 1740, the gentle, refined 'Janet Dick' 1748 to the severely imposing '3rd Duke of Argyll' 1749. Hereafter, technique and intention changed. The use of red underpaint was abandoned, the paint became thinner, the colours more delicately matched. In 1752, his first wife having died after only six years of married life, Ramsay married Margaret Lindsay, niece of Lord Chancellor Mansfield. His first royal portrait was 'George III' 1757. There followed a succession of royal commissions for the execution of which he employed several assistants including Philip Reinagle(qv) (1749-1812), David Martin(qv) - who had been with Ramsay on his first visit to Italy), and Alexander Nasmyth(qv). Appointed Painter-in-Ordinary to the King 1760, subsequently declined a knighthood. One of his last great portraits was 'Mrs Bruce of Arnot' 1765. In 1775 he again visited Italy and shortly after his return suffered an accident to his right arm. This and general weakening health persuaded him to retire to Italy there to attempt to identify the site of Horace's Sabine villa, but the outcome was never published. Overcome with homesickness, in 1784 he came back to Britain only to die in Dover. In addition to being a painter, Ramsay was a rational, empiricist thinker. Friend of Rousseau and Hume (whose portrait he painted 1766), he was the author of three works: *A Letter to the Earl of - concerning the Affair of Elizabeth Canning* (1753), *On Ridicule* (1753) and *Dialogue on Taste* (1755). He was also a linguist, his fluency in German enhancing his popularity at Court. His Edinburgh home, once known as the House of the Muses, remains on Castlehill. The beauty, charm, elegance, poetic sensitivity to character and his refined use of colour place Ramsay in the forefront of British art. His work wielded an indelible influence on the future of Scottish painting. In the words of his biographer 'few portrait-painters have shown a more fastidious taste than Ramsay. As a man he impressed his friends by his correctness of judgement and by his profound scholarship. Superficially excitable, but fundamentally calm and thoroughly balanced, Ramsay was in nothing more typical of his age than in his power to be considered a man of reason who knew how to exercise a rigid control over his emotions. His temperament is mirrored in his portraiture, which is serene, urbane, altogether charming, but lacking in much passion...His work as a whole shows little experimentation or adventure; and the tender theme which is so often repeated might become monotonous were it not for the subtlety of its variation. His vision is serene, contemplative and delicate almost of fragility. The portraits which we best remember have the allure of a sweet but faint perfume. They reveal a refined sensibility and an impeccable taste, and these are his special virtues. If they reveal less passion or enthusiasm the reason is not hard to find. He possessed genius, but was not possessed by it' [Smart]. Represented in Tate AG, NPG, NGS, SNPG(18), Glasgow AG, City of Edinburgh collection, The Binns (NTS), Brodie Castle (NTS), Crathes Castle (NTS), Hill of Tarvit (4-NTS), Craigievar Castle (NTS), Manchester City AG; Ashmolean Museum, Oxford; St John's College, Oxford; Trinity College, Cambridge; Jesus College, Cambridge; Emmanuel College, Cambridge; Hunterian Museum (University of Glasgow), Copenhagen AG, Nat Gall of Canada (Ottawa), Nat Gall of Ireland (Dublin), Dulwich AG, Minneapolis AG (USA), The Louvre (Paris).
**Bibl:** Ian G Brown 'Allan Ramsay's Rise & Reputation', Walpole Society, 104-110, 1984; Ian G Brown 'Poet and Painter, Allan Ramsay, Father and Son', NLS, 1984; Caw 28-33 et al; Caw 'Allan Ramsay, Portrait-Painter' Walpole Society, XXV 1936-7, 33ff; James Holloway, 'Portrait of an Artist', Antique Collector, July 1992, 38-43; Irwin 51-64 et passim; Macmillan [GA] 17-36 et passim; Macmillan [SA] 91-92,94,97-98 et passim; Allan Ramsay, The Investigator: I On Ridicule, II On Elizabeth Canning, III On Naturalisation, IV On Taste, London 1762 (1st edition 1755); Alastair Smart, The Life and Art of Allan Ramsay, 1953.

**RAMSAY, Allan** **1852-1912**
Born Forfarshire; died Edzell, Angus. Painter in oil and watercolour of genre, still life and portraits but principally landscape. Until at least 1886 he lived at various addresses in Dundee and by 1889 had moved to Edzell. After leaving school he was apprenticed to a chemist but, in his own words, "could never keep his hands frae the brushes". Abandoning pharmaceuticals, he became associated with a designer-painter and some designs made at this time are in an RC church in Dundee. Subsequently became friendly with George Whitton Johnstone RSA(qv) with whom he often worked and who struggled to command Ramsay's skill at depicting running water. Married early and a study of his young daughter was the first picture accepted by the RSA. Best known for his tender evocations of the woods and streams of the Angus glens. Generally painted on a small scale 'with the low, red dying rays of sunset flaming duskily through the sombre branches and lying blood-red among the reeds; silvery evening effects, with

fading sunshine outlining shadowy birch, and deepening the congregated shades in the warm, rich depth of autumnal foliage, whose soft, unchequered reflections lie on untroubled depths, the loneliness unrelieved, or only accentuated, by a low-toned solitary figure stealing silently through the gathering dusk' [Obituary]. Also a skilled portraitist, commended by Agnew the London connoisseur and dealer. A commissioned work for the brother of a young man drowned in Lochlee was described as 'not a portrait but a resurrection'. A modest, softly-spoken retiring man and a genial companion. An accomplished violinist. Exhibited RSA(19), GI(4) and regularly Dundee Art Society. Represented in Dundee AG by 'The Old Bridge at Inverlochy, Glenorchy' 1885 and 'William H Phin, Esq.' 1884-5.
**Bibl:** Arbroath Guide, 19 Oct 1912 (obit).

**RAMSAY, Miss Catriona S** **fl 1975-**
Glasgow painter. Flowers, fruit and the landscape of the west coast of Scotland. Exhibits GI(13) since 1975, from Bearsden.

**RAMSAY, Colin Cameron** **fl 1918-1928**
Amateur Glasgow painter; exhibited RSA(2), L(2) & GI(1).

**RAMSAY, Coin S** **fl 1918-1928**
Dundee potter. Exhibited AAS(3) whilst at Duncan of Jordanstone School of Art.

**RAMSAY, David** **1869-?**
Born Ayr, Nov 14. Painter of landscape, principally in watercolour. Trained Glasgow School of Art. Art Master, Greenock Academy for many years. Exhibited chiefly in Scotland, at the RSA(6), RSW(13), GI(10) & L(1).

**RAMSAY, David A** **fl 1947**
Glasgow painter of informal portraits. Exhibited 'Girl in a white blouse' at the RSA.

**RAMSAY, David M** **fl 1942-1951**
Glasgow landscape painter, principally in watercolour. Worked mainly along the north-west coast and on Tiree. Exhibited GI(11), from Kelvinside.

**RAMSAY, David Prophet** **1888-1944**
Born Perth, Jly 6; died Trochrie, nr Dunkeld, Jan 11. Portrait, figure & landscape painter. Studied textile design with Coates Bros of Perth 1904-9 before proceeding to Glasgow School of Art 1909-12. On the proceeds of a Haldane scholarship visited Paris, Italy & Spain. In WW1, as an officer in the Black Watch he was seriously wounded at Pilken Ridge and was invalided out in 1917. Produced a series of caricatures under the pseudonym 'Sam Ray'. Elected President, Dundee Art Society 1930. Moved to Dunkeld 1933. Commissioned to paint 'Princess Margaret' 1934. Exhibited RA(3), RSA(16), GI (13), AAS(1929 & '33) & L(5) from various addresses in Perthshire. Represented in Dundee AG, Paisley AG, Perth AG, Oldham AG.
**Bibl:** R H Rodger, D P Ramsay, Centenary Ex Cat, Perth AG 1988.

**RAMSAY, Eilbert** **fl 1904**
Amateur artist of Ellenlee, Kilmacolm; exhibited a monochrome drawing of 'The Aisle of Caterque, Glasgow cathedral' at the GI.

**RAMSAY, G B** **fl 1848**
Edinburgh landscape painter; exhibited 'On the Blackwater' at the RSA.

**RAMSAY, Gilbert** **c1880-1915**
Glasgow-based painter. Killed in WWI. Exhibited GI(1) 1902, a similar composition to that shown 1904 by Eilbert R(qv).

**RAMSAY, Gladys C** **fl 1937-1939**
Amateur Edinburgh watercolour painter of landscape, still life and rustic scenes, mostly in the vicinity of Edinburgh. Exhibited RSA(6), RSW(1) & GI(1) from 18 West Castle Rd.

**RAMSAY, Hugh** **1877-1906**
Portrait painter of Scottish descent. Born and died in Melbourne, Australia after a tragically short life. Represented by 'Self-portrait' in Melbourne AG.

**RAMSAY, Hugh McD** **fl 1938-1946**
Glasgow amateur painter of figure studies; exhibited 'Portrait of a boy' at the RSA and once at the GI from 101 Clarence Drive.

**RAMSAY, J M** **fl 1966-1968**
Ayrshire watercolour painter. Exhibited GI(2), from Irvine.

**RAMSAY, Jack** **fl 195-1951**
Glasgow artist. Exhibited chalk drawings, also pen and ink studies, at the GI.

**RAMSAY, James** **fl 1846-1871**
Edinburgh landscape and still life painter; exhibited RSA(2).

**RAMSAY, James** **fl 1911-1912**
Amateur painter. Father of Alice R(qv). Exhibited GI(2) & L(1) from the Old Manse, Kilbarchan, Renfrewshire.

**RAMSAY, James A** **fl 1919-1940**
Amateur Edinburgh watercolourist; mostly continental scenes but also views in the south of England. Most of his Scottish subjects were of fishing scenes and fisherfolk. Exhibited RSA(11) & RSW (11).

**RAMSAY, Nancy H (Mrs W S Hewison)** **fl 1951-1969**
Orkney landscape painter; exhibited mostly local topography at the RSA 1951-3 & AAS(1), from Newark, Weyland Bay, Kirkwall.

**RAMSAY, Lady Victoria Patricia Helena Elizabeth RWS** **1886-1974**
Born Mar 17. Painter in oil and watercolour of flowers and landscapes. Grand-daughter of Queen Victoria, daughter of the Duke & Duchess of Connaught and Strathearn. Married Admiral The Hon. Sir Alexander Ramsay 1919, and by royal permission renounced the style and titles of "H.R.H.' and 'Princess'. Worked for a time in Ceylon and the Bermudas. A skilful painter who worked in a bold style, benefitting from a wide contact with many leading contemporary artists. Present when Queen Victoria laid the foundation stone for the new church at Crathie on Sept 11, 1893, a watercolour of which by John Mitchell is illustrated in *Under Lochnagar* (1894). Elected NEAC 1931, HRI, RSW 1932, ARWS 1940. Exhibited widely including RA(3), GI(2), RHA(2), RWS(4) & SWA(3) but mainly at the Goupil Gallery, London(113), mostly from her home at Windlesham, Surrey. 'Tiger Lilies' is in Manchester City AG.

**RAMSAY, Susan E** **fl 1914-d1931**
Watercolour painter. Topographical subjects, sometimes in black and white. Daughter of Professor G.G. Ramsay. Lived at Drumore, Blairgowrie, Perthshire and later at 16 Queens Gdns, St Andrews. Exhibited GI(1) & L(3).

**RAMSAY, William** **fl 1600-1620**
Edinburgh painter. Son of a plasterer who in 1600 was apprenticed to James Workman(qv). Elected burgess of Edinburgh 1605. His success was marked by taking three apprentices, John Ryllye 1608, John Milles 1613 and George Brown 1620. There are no records of his work. He was paid £8 for executing ensigns for a weapon showing on 29 July 1607 and his name was among those painters working at Edinburgh Castle 1617.
**Bibl:** Apted 77; Edinburgh Burgh Records 1604-26, 30.

**RAND, Keith John** **fl 1984-**
Born Rinteln, Germany. Artist/craftsman/sculptor specialising in metal and wood sculpture and furniture. Works are abstract and constructed rather than carved. Trained Winchester School of Art 1979-82. Then established a studio in Winchester where he designed and made sculptural furniture for general exhibition. In 1984 he moved to Scotland to work at the Scottish Sculpture Workshop making large-scale sawdust drawings of landscape and public places in Aberdeenshire, Dunbartonshire and Yorkshire. In 1985 commissioned by Gordon District Council to design and make furniture in bent steel for the sculpture walk at Lumsden. In 1987 appointed part-time lecturer at Gray's School of Art and the following year became artist-in-residence at Duthie Park, Aberdeen where he executed a large sculpture for the Japanese garden. In 1989 joined the Board of Directors of Scottish Sculpture Workshop and was commissioned to undertake work for Shell. Received the Benno Schotz Award 1987

and the Latimer Award 1989. Presently working mostly in wood, some figurative but mostly abstract work. Exhibits regularly at the RSA & AAS; also GI(1), from Quarry Hill cottage, Craig, Rhynie, Aberdeenshire. Permanently sited sculpture can be seen in many places including the Lumsden Sculpture walk, Braemore, Duthie Park (Aberdeen).

**RANKEN, William Bruce Ellis ROI RI RP VPROI 1881-1941**
Born Edinburgh, Apr 11; died London, Mar 31. Painter in oil and watercolour of portraits, interiors, flowers and landscapes; also decorator. Educated Eton, trained Slade School. Lived mostly in England and France. Prolific worker, at his best the watercolours are freshly handled although some are too large and laboured. His sketches of gardens are generally attractive. Silver medal, Salon des Artistes Françaises 1928. A good example of his work 'A View of Hampton Court' is in Dundee AG. Commissions include portraits of the Royal family and interiors of Buckingham Palace and Windsor; also painted 'The Coronation of King George VI'. Lived in Edinburgh, London, Dumfries and eventually Eversley, Hampshire. First exhibited at the New English Art Club. For many years was President of the Royal Institute of Painters in Watercolour, also of the Pastel Society, Royal Society of Portrait Painters and the National Society of Portrait Painters. Elected RI 1915, ROI 1910, RP 1916, VPROI 1920. Exhibited RA(22), RSA(22), ROI(60), RI(99), L(28) & GI(4). Represented in Dundee AG, Glasgow AG, Hamilton Museum, City of Edinburgh collection(3).
**Bibl:** Halsby 279.

**RANKIN, Alexander (or Andrew) Scott 1862-1942**
Born Aberfeldy, Perthshire; died Pitlochry, Perthshire. Painter of domestic genre, animals and rustic buildings mostly in oil but occasionally in watercolour, also illustrator and caricaturist. Studied at the Manufacturers' School, Royal Institute and Life School, Edinburgh. Staff member of *Today* and caricaturist of *The Idler* c1893. Lived and worked at Strathtay from 1902 until 1914. Painted in a sickly if competent manner. Illustrations for the *AJ* included 'Aberfeldy and its Neighbourhood', and an article on the Glasgow Exhibition. Towards the end of his life settled in Pitlochry. Exhibited RA(3), RSA(27), RSW(2), RCA(1), AAS(3), GI(5) & L(7).
**Bibl:** Halsby 279; Houfe; Wingfield.

**RANKIN, Miss Arabella Louisa 1871-c1935**
Born Muthill, Perthshire. Painter and colour woodcut artist, also engraver. She lived for a time in London before returning to Abbotsbrae, Crieff c1913 going back once more to Kensington, London 1922-35. Exhibited RSA(24), RSW(3), SWA(6), RI(1), GI (18) & L(8).
**Bibl:** Halsby 279; Houfe; Studio, 8, 1896, 252(illus).

**RANKIN, Jim fl 1976**
Painter. Exhibited AAS from 105 Hayton Rd, Aberdeen. Subsequently moved to Edinburgh.

**RANKINE, John P fl 1922-1928**
Amateur artist from Hamilton; exhibited two pencil drawings at the GI.

**RANKINE, Walter D fl 1883-1895**
Amateur Glasgow and Hamilton painter. Possibly father of John P R(qv). Exhibited GI(3).

**RANNIE, Henry A fl 1888-1910**
Glasgow landscape painter, mainly in watercolour. Painted Highland and moorland scenes generally on a small scale and in a delicate hand. Exhibited GI(4) from 11 Nelson Terrace, Hillhead.

**RATHBONE, Edward fl 1891**
Edinburgh painter; exhibited 'Whins in bloom' at the RSA, from Queens Place.

**RATTRAY, Alexander William Wellwood ARSA RSW 1849-1902**
Born St Andrews, 21 Jly; died 17 Apr. Painter in oil and watercolour of landscapes, flowers, shore and coastal scenes; almost always of the Highlands, east coast or Mull of Kintyre. Son of a Glasgow minister. Educated Glasgow University, trained Glasgow School of Art under Robert Greenlees(qv). Travelled to Paris where he studied under the landscape artists Damoye and Daubigny. Received honourable mentions at the Paris Salon and Paris International 1889 where his 'Salmon stream' and 'Ferry, Loch Ranza' received acclaim. On his return he settled in Glasgow. If at times a little clumsy his work nevertheless captures the feel of the Highlands very well and the restrained colours of the east coast fishing villages. Widely known as 'Wellwood Rattray'. Lived in Glasgow and at Fellowhills, Berwickshire. Elected RSW 1885, ARSA 1896. Exhibited RA(23) 1883-1898, RSA(71) 1876-1902; also RSW(37), RI (2), RHA(2), AAS 1885-1906 & GI(69). Represented in Glasgow AG.
**Bibl:** Bryan; Caw 303; Halsby 280.

**RATTRAY, David fl 1875-1878**
Glasgow landscape painter. Worked on Arran and Clydeside. Exhibited GI(5) from Buccleuch St and then Mains St.

**RATTRAY, John William fl 1842-1887**
Edinburgh portrait painter in oil and crayon. Most sitters are now unknown but those that can be identified are of the gentry or professional classes in Edinburgh. His work is rarely seen, probably because it remains in the families for whom it was painted. Exhibited RSA(42), latterly from 45 Cumberland Street.

**RAWLE, John S fl 1868-1887**
Glasgow painter of portraits, figurative works and landscape; teacher. Moved to Government School of Design, Nottingham. Exhibited RA(14) & GI(9), after 1883 from 35 St. Augustin Rd, London NW.

**RAWLIN, Mrs Alexander fl 1904-1912**
Amateur Dumfries painter of architectural subjects and local scenes; exhibited RA(1), AAS(1), L(8) & SWA(1), from Mairsgrove.

**RAWLING, Brian c1930-**
English painter of mainly Scottish subjects. Began life as a commercial artist before joining the staff of the Milk Marketing Board. After thirty years of part-time painting in oils, acrylic and watercolour, he left the Board to become a full-time artist 1972. Specialises in stalking scenes, sporting dogs, farming subjects and heavy working horses, in watercolours. First solo exhibition 1974 followed by many, almost annually, in Scotland, where he lived 1978-2001, and England. Commissions by many sporting estate owners.

**RAWLINSON, Ralph fl 1629-1648**
Carver. All that is known, and this from the Hamilton Archives, Lennoxlove, is that in 1629 he carved heraldic beasts for Ballachastell and in 1649 executed a sundial for Hamilton Palace.

**RAYER, William fl 1944-1945**
Glasgow painter of portraits and still life. Exhibited GI(3) including a portrait of 'Chief Constable M.M.McCulloch, Glasgow City Police.'

**RAYNER, Louise J 1832-1924**
Born Derby; died St. Leonards on Sea, Sussex. One of the finest topographical watercolourists of the 19th century. She was English and lived all her life south of the border. The reason for her inclusion is that she is best known for her evocative portrayal of the old streets and wynds of Edinburgh, London, Chester and other old British and French towns. Unfortunately, although her refined and sensitive watercolour depictions of Old Edinburgh are not to be found in any of the major Scottish public collections, they remain a touchstone for work of this nature; in the general artistic life of Scotland they are well known if sometimes neglected on account of her English origins. In 1872 she settled in Chester. Exhibited 30 works at the Society of Women Artists as well as at the RA, RBA, RHA and RI. Represented in the V & A, Coventry AG, Derby AG, NG of Ireland (Dublin), Newport AG, Reading AG.

**RAYNER, Martin 1946-**
Born Nov. Sculptor. Childhood spent in the south-east Scottish fishing towns of North Berwick and Dunbar. After working as a newspaper journalist for 12 years, a businessman in New Zealand and for a short time as a greaser on an Israeli cargo ship, he enrolled at Duncan of Jordanstone College of Art, Dundee 1975, gaining a highly commended postgraduate diploma. Married to Gillian MacFarland(qv). In 1984-6 he was based at the Scottish Sculpture

Workshop in Aberdeenshire and throughout 1987 was SAC's Artist-in-Industry at Blair Atholl, Perthshire. Commissioned 1990 to carve two wooden coats-of-arms for Dundee's twin town of Wurzburg, Bavaria. In addition to his sculpture, mainly in wood generally having association with ships and the sea, he also occasionally paints. Exhibits RSA from 32 Queen St, Newport-on-Tay. Represented in Aberdeen AG, Blair Castle (Perthshire).

**RAYNER, William F** **fl 1932-1955**
Edinburgh artist of landscape and portraits; exhibited RSA(4) first from Maitlandfield, Haddington and just before WW2 from Edinburgh.

**READ, Catherine** **1723-1778**
Born Forfarshire, Feb 3; died on voyage from India, 15 Dec. Daughter of Forfarshire family of Jacobite leanings (her father was Laird of Torbeg). After early education in Edinburgh, in about 1750 she travelled to continue her art studies first in Paris where she studied under the French pastellists Blanchet and La Tour and then in Italy where she gained most from the Venetian pastellist Rosalba Carriera. Painting notabilities in oil and crayon, she received the patronage of the connoisseur Cardinal Albani, whose portrait she drew, and who recommended her to Lord Bolingbroke. 'An outstanding British pastellist of the 18th century' [Irwin]. At the time of the rebellion she was painting portraits of Isabella Lumsden and her brother Andrew, afterwards Secretary to the exiled Prince. Smollett, Hayley, and Fanny Burney all spoke of her crayon portraits with enthusiasm. In 1754 she was in London, painting portraits of many of the celebrated ladies of the age, at first from St. James's Place, then from Jermyn St. In Italy she had been friendly with Anne Forbes(qv) and fell under the protection and the guidance of Peter Grant (1708-1784). Unfortunately, in Italy young Scottish students found it very difficult to earn enough to live. She wrote 'I painted two princesses for which they gave me by way of a present two medals...I expect in a few days to begin a picture of the brother of Princess Cheresina from whom I shall have perhaps some such useless trinket. For you must know that the Italians despise people so much that are obliged to do anything for money that Mr Grant thought it proper to name no price when the question was asked'. 'Working in a graceful and refined manner she was specially successful in pictures of women and children, and in 1763 painted 'Queen Charlotte with the Prince of Wales', and two years later the Prince and his brother, while engravings by Finlayson of her portraits of the beautiful Gunnings, 'The Duchess of Hamilton' and 'The Duchess of Argyll' and 'The Countess of Coventry', have remained popular. Such pictures as 'Miss Harriott Powell' show the influence of Allan Ramsay, and pictures like 'Miss Jones' that of Reynolds. Perhaps the most charming and personal of her portraits is 'Lady Georgiana Spencer as a child', in Lord Spencer's collection. In 1775 she went with her niece, later to become Lady Oakeley, to India and died in tragic circumstances on the voyage home. Fanny Burney said of her work 'nothing can be so soft, so delicate, so blooming'. Exhibited RA(4) from 27 Wellbeck Street, 1773, 1774 and 1776. Represented at Lennoxlove, East Lothian.
**Bibl:** Bryan; Caw 49; LXXXIX (Jan 1932) 35-40; (Mar 1932) 171-178; Irwin 70, 74, 76; McKay 27-8; Scottish Antiquary 1904; Macmillan [SA] 110-111; Victoria Manners, 'Catherine Read' Conn, LXXXVIII (Dec 31), 376-386; A.F. Steuart, Asiatic Quarterly Rev, Jan 1902; Scottish Hist. Rev.,2, 1904.

**READ, James** **fl 1759**
Edinburgh engraver. His name occurs in Bremner's *Curious Collection of Scots Tunes,* 1759; also in Stewart's *Collection of the Best and Newest Reels,* 1761.
**Bibl:** Bushnell; Davidson Cook in Scottish N & Q, Nov 1928.

**READ, W** **fl 1825**
Engraver. He engraved the maps and plates in Shaw's *History of the Province of Moray,* 1827, the plates being after drawings by John Grant and C.S. Allan Hay. Bushnell believes he probably resided in Elgin.
**Bibl:** Bushnell.

**READMAN, William R** **fl 1920**
Amateur Bishopbriggs painter of little consequence; exhibited two black and white landscapes at the GI, from Freeland.

**READY, Andrew** **fl 1775-1793**
Glasgow engraver. Engraved a map of Glasgow 1775. His daughter Agnes married an Edinburgh bookseller 1793.
**Bibl:** Bushnell.

**RECOMIO, Michael C** **fl 1978**
Aberdeenshire-based amateur artist; exhibited AAS(2) from 6 Mortlach Gdns, Aboyne.

**REDDICK, Peter** **fl 1966**
Dunbartonshire watercolourist and wood engraver. Exhibited GI(4).

**REDDOCK, A** **?-1843**
Portrait painter; lived in Falkirk. All that is now known of his work is a portrait of 'Sir James Dalyell 5th Baronet (1774-1841)' inscribed on the reverse 'A Reddock, Falkirk', now at The Binns, and a portrait of 'Lady Janet Dundas (1720-1805)'.

**REDFEARN, W D (Also catalogued as W B REDFARN)** **fl 1862-1871**
Glasgow painter in oil, landscape, wild life, animals (especially terriers) and dead game; also occasional watercolour. Exhibited RSA (15) & GI(20), latterly from St Vincent St.

**REDFERN, June** **1951-**
Born in Fife. Painter in oil and watercolour, also collage. Trained Edinburgh College of Art 1968-72. Awards include Andrew Grant scholarship 1972, SAC Award 1982. After graduating she taught at a comprehensive school in Leith, an experience which influenced her so that from using images found in various publications she began recording her immediate surroundings in a broadly realistic way. Works from this period were included in her first exhibition 'Real Lives' held in 1981. Subsequently became disillusioned with her previous development and began making collages from fragments of paintings, sticking them on to silver backgrounds. After a brief spell teaching at Preston Polytechnic 1982-3 joined the staff of Cardiff College of Art having in the meantime returned to oil painting although now using a bold expressionist use of the brush and colour to produce strong, highly dramatic compositions redolent of contemporary German and Italian painting. In 1985 she left Cardiff to become Artist-in-residence at the NGS. Over the next six months her work was the basis of an exhibition at the NG in 1986. Guest artist, University of Minnesota 1986. First solo exhibition 1996. Participates in various BBC art programmes. Exhibits regularly in Edinburgh and London. Represented in Aberdeen AG, Bradford AG, Dundee AG, Glasgow AG, Kirkcaldy AG, Laing AG (Newcastle), Lillie AG (Milngavie), National Gallery (London), SNGMA.
**Bibl:** Hartley 161; Hartley, 'June Redfern to the River', (Ex Cat 1985); NG, London, 'June Redfern; Artist-in-Residence', (Ex Cat 1986); Marina Vaizey 'Drawing out the Feminine' *Sunday Times* 1990; Duncan Macmillan, review *The Scotsman* 1996.

**REDMOND, Eric** **1932-**
Born Edinburgh; trained Edinburgh College of Art 1951-55. Held group exhibitions in Edinburgh, Newcastle and York 1959. Included in 'Four Young Scottish Painters' exhibition, 1960 and '61. Exhibited RGI(1) 1959. Sometime teacher to adult mentally handicapped in West Lothian, Supervisor, West Lothian Senior Occupation Centre.

**REDPATH, Anne OBE RSA ARA LLD ARWS ROI RBA** **1895-1965**
Born Galashiels, 29 Mar; died Edinburgh, 7 Jan. Painter in oil and watercolour of landscapes, figure subjects, interiors and still life. Daughter of a tweed designer. Educated Hawick HS where she was strongly encouraged by her art teacher John Gray. Overcame parental objection to entering art school by obtaining a teacher's certificate at Moray House. Then enrolled Edinburgh College of Art 1913-1917 studying under Robert Burns(qv), Henry Lintott(qv) and D M Sutherland(qv). In 1917, having qualified as an art teacher and obtaining a travelling scholarship in 1919, visited Brussels, Bruges, Paris, Florence and Sienna. She said that it was only after her visit to Sienna, when she became familiar with the Primitives, that she knew that they were much greater than most artists who have painted since 'and I have never changed my mind'. Married James Beattie Michie(qv), then an architect with the Imperial War Graves Com-

mission 1920. Lived in France until 1934, the last four years at Cap Ferrat, before returning to Hawick, and in 1934 resumed her work as a painter. At the time of her first solo exhibition in Edinburgh 1947 she was painting landscapes and still life interiors in white and grey although gradually moving towards a brighter palette inspired by Gauguin and Matisse and by oriental manuscripts and Far Eastern textiles. Visited Paris again in 1948 and moved to Edinburgh 1949. A visit to Spain that year inspired her to adopt a new expressive handling of paint and to incorporate a sense of drama into otherwise rather dull compositions of peasants, hill towns and church interiors. A visit to Corsica in 1954 stimulated a still more brilliant use of colour and a fascination with the organic nature of rocks, buildings, plants and jewel-encrusted altar pieces. In 1955 she became seriously ill and although recovering in 1959 suffered a second serious illness which left her unable to use her right-hand. With her output now seriously limited she went to the Canary Islands 1959, Portugal 1961 and Holland 1962. During these trips her works incorporated red, brown, blue and purple paint scumbled, scraped and piled upon the canvas until buildings, rocks and water, flowers and cloth or holy relic and screen became a unified, vibrant whole. She was always looking at the world afresh and capturing unsuspected beauty. In her oils, paint is almost alive, handled with a tortuous yet controlled vision. She was most noted for her still lifes and for her east coast, French and Spanish subjects. Her visit to Paris, Brussels and Italy influenced her firstly towards the style of Botticelli, although she describes herself as a contemporary rather than a modern painter. Elected ARBA 1946, ARSA 1947, President of the Scottish Society of Women Artists 1944-7, ROI 1948, RSA 1951, OBE 1955, ARA 1960. Frequent exhibitor RSA, RA & GI. Represented in SNGMA, Glasgow AG, City of Edinburgh collection(3), Kirkcaldy AG, Lillie AG(Milngavie), Brodie Castle (NTS), Manchester AG, Abbot Hall AG (Kendal), Nat Gall of New Zealand (Wellington), Sydney AG (Australia).
**Bibl:** Patrick Bourne, Anne Redpath, 1989; George Bruce, Anne Redpath 1974; Gage 29; Halsby 215-6,280; Hardie 164-6; Hartley, 161; Macmillan [SA] 366-7 et passim; Scott Arts Rev, V, 3, 1955, 11-14; Studio, CLIX, 803, March 1960, 86-89.

**REDPATH, Babs (Barbara Mary) (née Lawford)** **1924-?**
Born London, 31 January. Painter in oil, landscapes and still life. Trained Edinburgh College of Art; awarded Andrew Grant travelling scholarship enabling her to visit Florence. Influenced in Edinburgh by Gillies(qv) and in Italy by the works of Tintoretto. Arrived back in Glasgow 1956. Became inspired by the pigeon lofts on the Maryhill section of the canal, also Govan Ferry and the general desolation of the City of Glasgow. Married Anne Redpath's nephew. Member, Glasgow Society of Women Artists(qv). Exhibited AAS(1) 1973 from 32 Glasgow St; also GI(34), SSA & SSWA.

**REDPATH, Caroline (née Tennant)** **1895-1939**
Figurative and portrait artist; often worked in stencil and on a small scale. Married Anne Redpath's older brother William; mother of Kim Redpath(qv).

**REDPATH, Kim** **1925-?**
Portrait and figurative painter; teacher. Daughter of Caroline Tennant(qv) and niece of Anne R(qv). In mid-career taught for a time at Earnock HS, Hamilton. Exhibited RSA 1944,'52 & '55, at first from Hawick, later from St Boswell's.

**REED, John** **fl 1863-1868**
Dalkeith painter in oil, portraits and figures. Exhibited RSA(7) & GI(1) from Harford House, Eskbank.

**REES, C B** **fl 1955**
Edinburgh painter. Exhibited 'Converted boathouse, Port Ballintrae' at the RSA.

**REES, Sir Richard Lodowick Edward Montagu Bt** **1900-1970**
Born Oxford, 4 Apr; died London, 24 Jly. Painter in oil and watercolour. Son of Sir J D Rees MP. Educated Eton and Trinity College, Cambridge. Studied watercolour painting in Yorkshire under Fred Lawson 1936 and at St John's Wood Art School 1937 also at Camberwell under Coldstream, Rogers, Passmore and Gowing 1945-6. Then came north, lived in Edinburgh for many years, finally returning to London shortly before his death. Exhibited RA, RSA, RBA & SSA.

**REEVE, Burgess** **fl 1857**
Edinburgh sculptor. Exhibited a medallion portrait of a child at the RSA, from Alva St.

**REEVES, Philip Thomas Langford RSA RSW ARCA RE RGI** **1931-**
Born Cheltenham, 7 Jly. Etcher, also painter in oil and watercolour and teacher. Trained Cheltenham School of Art 1945-9 under Seaton White, R S G Dent and Gerald Gardiner, also RCA 1951-4 under Robert Austin and Edwin Ladell. Appointed lecturer in printmaking, Glasgow School of Art from 1954, subsequently becoming Head of Department. His influence in the development of Scottish printmaking since 1960s was considerable, being responsible for having printmaking upgraded into a separate department at GSA and a founder member of the Printmakers Workshop, Edinburgh 1967, also the Glasgow Print Studio. In 1970 won the May Marshall Brown watercolour Award and Cargill Award 1976. Member, Glasgow Group. Elected ARSPE 1954, FRSPE 1965, RSW 1959, ARSA 1971, RSA 1976. Frequent exhibitor RSA, AAS 1972-81, RSW & GI throughout 1955-1988. Represented in SNGMA, V & A, Aberdeen AG, Glasgow AG, Inverness AG, Lillie AG (Milngavie), Paisley AG, City of Edinburgh collection, Manchester AG, SAC.
**Bibl:** Mungo Campbell, 'The Line of Tradition', Nat Galls of Scotland, Ex cat, Edinburgh 1993; Gage 49-50.

**REEVES, Thomas** **fl 1884**
Glasgow amateur sculptor. Exhibited a portrait medallion of 'Rev Dr Norman Macleod' at GI, from 145 Finlay Drive, Dennistoun.

**REGENT, Peter** **1929-**
Edinburgh sculptor. Works in granite bronze and stone. Moved to Newport-on-Tay, Fife. Exhibited RSA(15) including a resin bronze head of Alberto Morrocco 1983; also GI(13) since 1981. Represented in Lillie AG (Milngavie).

**REGNORDSON, W Birch** **fl 1880-1900**
Painter of landscape in oils and watercolours, most often of the Perthshire highlands, mainly in watercolour. Pleasant, faithful representations. Represented in Perth AG.
**Bibl:** Halsby 288.

**REIACH, Alan OBE RSA RSW RBI** **1910-1992**
Born London, 2 Mar; died Edinburgh 23 Jly. Educated Edinburgh Academy. Son of Bertie Reiach, Scottish naval architect and founding editor of *Yachting Monthly,* and a Polish mother. Came to Edinburgh 1922 and after studying at Edinburgh Academy and Edinburgh College of Art was apprenticed to the architect Robert Lorimer(qv) 1928-32. From 1928-35 he studied architecture at the Edinburgh College of Art, winning many prizes including the Andrew Grant Scholarship, enabling him to travel widely in the USA (where he stayed for a time at Frank Lloyd White's school at Taliesin), Europe and the USSR. These experiences, together with a research fellowship to study vernacular buildings in Scotland formed the basis of his first book *Building Scotland,* published in 1940, with Robert Hurd. From 1944-47 he was on the Clyde Valley regional planning committee and from 1947-54 taught architecture at ECA. Member, Fine Arts Commission for Scotland 1966-80. Senior partner in the firm of Reiach and Hall. Influenced by Asplund and Alto, also Frank Lloyd Wright and Le Corbusier. Principal buildings include the Appleton Tower in Edinburgh, the New Club in Edinburgh(1966), the church of St John, Oxgangs (notable for its long clerestoried nave facing a hall across a paved square) and two churches at Cumbernauld. 'The abiding character of his buildings [is] serious cultural intent; their particular Scottish features being an insistent plainness, heavy modelling, geometric massing and a clever use of northern light' [Obituary]. Exhibited regularly RSA and occasionally RA. Retired 1975 although remained a consultant until 1980. His plans for a Gallery of Modern Art to be built in Edinburgh, a model of which was made by Stanley Cursiter, remains in the SNGMA archives. Awarded OBE 1964, ARSA 1969, RSA 1986.
**Bibl:** Gifford 43,74,312,418,487,502,567,570,659; Hartley 162; McKean, The Scottish Thirties an Architectural Introduction (1987); A Reiach and R Hurd, Building Scotland - A Cautionary Guide (1940), 2nd rev ed 1944; The Times Aug 13, 1992(obit).

**REID, Miss** **fl 1864-1870**
Portobello portrait painter in oil; exhibited RSA(5).

**REID, Miss Agnes L (Mrs James Jardine) 1902-?**
Born Musselburgh, 22 Dec. Portrait and figure painter in oil also watercolour, landscapes and etcher. Studied at Edinburgh College of Art under David Alison(qv), Percy Portsmouth(qv), Henry Lintott(qv) and D M Sutherland(qv). Exhibited RSA(6) and in provincial galleries from her home at Slateford, Midlothian, latterly from Greenhill Pl, Edinburgh.

**REID, Alex fl 1974**
Aberdeenshire painter; exhibited AAS(1) from 12 Manse St, New Aberdour'

**REID, Alexander 1747-1823**
Born Kirkcudbrightshire. Painted oil portraits, landscapes and portrait miniatures. Was in Paris before the Revolution, subsequently worked in Dumfries. Burns sat for him in January 1796. Reid succeeded to a family estate in Kirkeenan near Dalbeattie, in 1804, where he settled and remained unmarried. Exhibited Society of Artists 1770. The SNPG has a miniature on ivory of Burns believed to be the portrait for which the poet stated in a letter (Jan 29 1796) he was sitting.
**Bibl:** Bryan; Caw 50.

**REID, Alexander fl 1874-1881**
Glasgow watercolour painter of landscape. Became Scotland's leading art dealer of his time having trained at Gimpel Fils with Theo Van Gogh, the latter having once painted his portrait. Exhibited RSA(1) & GI(3) from 37 & 103 St Vincent Street.

**REID, Alexander 1930-**
Born Perth. Designer of costumes and decorative figures. Educated Perth Academy and Dundee School of Art. After a time spent working for the theatre in London he returned to Perth where he taught art. Member of the Scottish Craft Centre. An exhibition 'Figures in Costume' was presented under the auspices of the SAC at the Edinburgh Festival, 1961. His work demonstrates great flair and attention to detail with a satisfying marriage between historical accuracy and artistic merit. Exhibited AAS(1) 1974 from 12 Manse St, New Aberdour, Aberdeenshire.

**REID, Alexander fl 1977-1985**
Renfrewshire-based painter of landscape and still life. Exhibited GI(6), latterly from Newton Mearns.

**REID, Andrew fl 1881-1932**
Edinburgh oil painter of rustic scenes, landscapes and figure subjects. Most of the time lived in Edinburgh but was in Paisley 1908. Exhibited RSA(26), GI(24), AAS(5) & L(23).

**REID, Annie fl 1925-1938**
Minor portrait painter of Heathfield, Campbeltown; exhibited 'Mrs Milne Rae' at the RSA, also RSW(5).

**REID, Miss Annie Wallace fl 1900-1908**
Aberdeen painter of landscape and flowers. Exhibited AAS(3) from Abergeldie Cottage, Balmoral Place.

**REID, Archibald David ARSA RSW ROI 1844-1908**
Born Aberdeen; died Wareham, Dorset, 30 Aug. Painter in oil and watercolour of landscapes. Brother of Sir George(qv) and Samuel(qv). His early education was in Aberdeen. Spent several years in mercantile offices before entering the RSA Schools 1867 and studying painting in Paris at the Academie Julien 1878. Although his figures are often modern the influence of the Dutch School, especially in his watercolours, is strongly visible with their careful composition and restrained colour. Most of his subjects were Scottish coastal scenes although he also travelled and painted in France, Holland and Spain. Elected RSW 1883, ARSA 1892, ROI 1898. Exhibited at the RA(18) from 1872 and extensively RSA(100), RSW, GI(35) 1872-1906 & AAS 1885-1910. Represented in Kirkcaldy AG, Edinburgh City collection.
**Bibl:** Caw 301-2; Halsby 280.

**REID, Arthur fl 1976-1978**
Aberdeenshire painter. Trained Gray's School of Art, Aberdeen. Exhibited AAS(3) from Orchard Cottage, Pitmedden Gdns.

**REID, Mrs Beryl fl 1916-1930**
Edinburgh-based painter in oil and watercolour. Wife of William Bernard R(qv). Exhibited RSA(11), RSW(2), GI(1) & L(2). Represented in City of Edinburgh collection(2).

**REID, David fl 1887-1910**
Aberdeen painter; exhibited AAS during the above years.

**REID, Miss E fl 1867-1880**
Edinburgh portrait painter, also painted domestic genre and figurative subjects, some with literary associations. Illustrated RL Stevenson's *Child's Garden of Verses* (1922). Exhibited RSA(3), from Portobello.

**REID, Florence A fl 1917**
Minor Lanarkshire miniaturist of Craigpark House, Thorntonhall; exhibited GI(1).

**REID, Miss Flora Macdonald M fl 1879-d1938**
Born Scotland. Painter in oil and watercolour of genre and figurative subjects. Sister and pupil of John Robertson R(qv). Although she received some training at the Edinburgh College of Art her main teacher was her brother. Lived for many years at Looe, Cornwall and later in London but painted widely on the continent, visiting Belgium, France and Norway. In Europe she particularly enjoyed the bustling market scenes painted with great colour, feeling and strength, also landscapes. Her style remains similar to her brother's although the brush work was sometimes stronger, the figures more colourfully portrayed and the scenes more lively. Fascinated by the colour contrasts between 'the sunlit houses and the shadow-chequered pavements, the green trees and the canvas boothes' [Caw]. Won a medal at the Paris International Exhibition 1900. Exhibited RA(8); from 1881 elsewhere in England, also RSA(14), GI(88) 1880-1938 & AAS 1898-1931. Represented in Leeds AG, Walker Gallery Liverpool, Manchester AG, Rochdale AG.
**Bibl:** Caw 283; Halsby 280.

**REID, Sir George PRSA HRSW LLD 1841-1913**
Born Aberdeen, 31 Oct; died Oakhill, Somerset, 9 Feb. Painter in oil and watercolour, also illustrator; portraits and landscapes. Educated Aberdeen GS. At the age of 13 apprenticed to a lithographer but in 1862 moved to Edinburgh to study at the Trustees Academy before proceeding to further studies in Paris and Utrecht in the studio of Alexander Mollinger. This visit to Holland in 1866, supported by his patron the Aberdeen collector John Forbes White, heralded a change in his career. He became a close friend of Josef Israels, whose portrait he painted when visiting The Hague. In 1870 Israels visited Aberdeen and the effects of his association with Reid became increasingly apparent. In 1872 Reid professed to preferring landscape painting to portraiture although he continued the latter throughout his life. His assured and vivid style quickly attracted notice and he soon established himself as Scotland's leading portrait painter. Moved from Aberdeen to Edinburgh 1884. One of his best known paintings 'The Passage of the Army of Montrose during Winter, through the Pass of Strathfillan' 1877, now in the Aberdeen AG, was an austere work subsequently used to illustrate *The Legend of Montrose.* Encouraged by White who was particularly fond of a flower painting by Diaz, Reid painted a number of flower pieces during the late 1870s and early 1880s, of which one example is in Aberdeen AG. His diploma picture 'Dornoch' shows a strong Dutch influence 'grey in colour, elaborate in gradation, solemn in sentiment'. Armstrong said that 'of all living Scotsmen, Reid perhaps most completely deserves to be called a master in the Continental sense'. He had more in common with the older French painters, notably J P Laurens, than with any of his own colleagues. Writing in the *AJ* in 1898 Caw observed 'we have become so accustomed to Sir George Reid's great power of rendering likeness and character, that we are too apt to forget its value and rarity, and to ask for a more truly artistic expression is perhaps compatible with the qualities his work possesses in so uncommon degree...the more obvious defects of style, the excess of small and over-incisive drawing in his heads, and the detachment of head from background, are of the kind that time deals kindly with'. His watercolours were most often executed in pen and monochrome washes of which 'Traquair House' (NGS) is a good example. Elected ARSA 1870, RSA 1877, President, RSA 1891-1902, knighted 1891. Illustrated *The Selected Writings of John Ramsay* (1871), Smiles' *Life of a Scotch*

*Naturalist* (1876), *George Paul Chalmers* (1879), W. Alexander's *Johnny Gibb* (1880), *Twelve Sketches of Scenery* (1882), *Natural History and Sport in Norway* (1882), *The River Tweed* (1884), *The River Clyde* (1886), *Salmon Fishing on the Ristigouche* (1888), *Lacunar Basilicae* (1888), *St. Giles' Edinburgh* (1889), Mrs Oliphant's *Royal Edinburgh* (1890) and *Familiar Letters of Sir Walter Scott* (1894). Also contributed illustrations for *The English Illustrated Magazine* (1890-1). Exhibited RA(21) 1877-1903 & RSA (197); also GI 1862-1913 & AAS 1885-1919, some from his home at St Luke's, Kepplestone, Aberdeen and latterly from his home in Edinburgh at 22 Royal Terrace. Represented in NGS, SNPG(21), Aberdeen AG, Glasgow AG(7), Edinburgh City collection, Brodie Castle (NTS), Haddo House (NTS), Manchester AG.
**Bibl:** AJ 1882, 361-5, 1893, 3; Armstrong 82-3; Caw 286-9 et passim; Halsby 127-9,280; Houfe; Irwin 350-352; Mag of Art 1892, 196-203; Macmillan [SA] 242-4; J. Pennell, Pen Drawing and Pen Draughtsmen, 1904, 277-279 (illus); R.E.D. Sketchley, Eng. Bk. Illus., 1903, 31 141; Studio 55 (1912) 167-178; 1907 Special Number.

**REID, George Ogilvy RSA** **1851-1928**
Born Leith; died Edinburgh, 11 Apr. Painter in oil and watercolour, historical genre, especially the Jacobite and earlier periods, also landscapes and occasional portraits. Worked as an engraver for ten years before taking up painting. Had exhibited at the RSA, at which he was later a student in 1872, but it was not until 1884 that he showed the promise which was to eventually sustain his art. His early pictures were small costume-pieces painted with great technical dexterity and clear delineation of character. Although his 'sparkle and vivacity' were generally approved and his renderings of 18th century life accurate and interesting Caw found that 'a finer and more delicate sense of colour and tone, and more finesse in the style of touch and drawing' would have given them more artistic distinction. In 1891 Queen Victoria commissioned him to paint the christening at Balmoral of the infant son of the Prince and Princess of Battenberg. The finished work included a portrait of Queen Victoria and about 30 other royal and distinguished people. This attracted great attention at the time and, together with his 'Cromwell's Reflections on seeing the Portrait of Charles I', was illustrated in the *AJ*. His paintings of Scottish life are in the Wilkie tradition as modified by the Orchardson/ Petty coterie. Often painted in and around Killin in Perthshire. Among his better known historical works especially the powerful, dramatic, later compositions were 'After Killicrankie' 1897, 'The Prince's Flight' 1899, 'Kidnapped' 1902, and 'The Smugglers' 1903. In the last three the settings are interiors rather than the open air and the ceaseless sea. Among his cosier items may be numbered 'The New Laird' 1891, 'A Literary Clique, The Catechising' 1889 and 'Oor Laird's Coort Day' 1888. Elected ARSA 1888, RSA 1898. Exhibited RA(12), RSA(182) almost annually 1872-1928; also AAS 1893-1902 & GI 1882-1928. Represented in SNPG, Glasgow AG, Kirkcaldy AG, Edinburgh City collection.
**Bibl:** AJ 1893, 152; 1903, 123; Caw 271-272; Hardie 62,64 et passim ch v; Studio 43 (1908) 134, 137.

**REID, Hamish** **1929-**
Born Dalkeith. Painter in oil; landscape, buildings, figures and still life. Trained Edinburgh College of Art, travelled in France, Spain and Italy. Taught Edinburgh College of Art until 1990. Exhibited RSA(24) 1954-1979 & SSA.

**REID, Henry J Macphail** **fl 1931**
Glasgow amateur painter of 4 Finnieston Quay; exhibited 'The Quarry bridge, Arran' at the GI.

**REID, Miss Isabella E** **fl 1878-1936**
Aberdeen painter in oil of still life and also miniature portrait painter. Among her sitters was her relative Professor Reid FRCS. Exhibited RA(7), RSA(6), GI(1), AAS(7) & RI(6) in the 1880s from Hawthorn Lodge, Aberdeen and in the early part of the 1890s from London before returning to 37 Albyn Place, Aberdeen.

**REID, Miss Isobel H** **fl 1941**
Edinburgh landscape painter. Exhibited RSA(2), from Murrayfield.

**REID, J** **fl 1901**
Glasgow amateur painter; exhibited 'Cottage nr Kilkerran' at the GI, from 49 Queen Mary Ave, Crosshill.

**REID, J T Rennie** **fl 1880-1896**
Edinburgh painter in oil and watercolour of landscape, often fishing and coastal scenes, also genre and interiors. Especially fond of coastal scenery around Banff and Stonehaven. Exhibited RSA(55) including several views of Stonehaven, and at the AAS(6) when living at West Lauriston Place and 34 St Andrews Square. Often confused with John Thomas Reid qv).

**REID, J Watson** **fl 1897-1901**
Amateur Glasgow painter; exhibited GI(3).

**REID, James** **fl 1902**
Kincardineshire amateur painter; exhibited a local scene at the AAS from Moray Bank, Stonehaven.

**REID, James** **fl 1968**
Lanarkshire sculptor; exhibited 'Composition 3' in black at the RSA, from Carluke.

**REID, James Brown** **fl 1861-1863**
Edinburgh oil painter of genre, topographical and figurative subjects. Exhibited RSA(10) & GI(2).

**REID, James Campbell** **fl 1906-1911**
Glasgow topographical painter. Exhibited three monochromes at the GI.

**REID, James Eadie** **fl 1885-1906**
Painter of figurative works and landscape; oil and watercolours. Exhibited RSA(6) from 19 Picardy Place, Edinburgh & GI(1) before moving to Paris c1908, then to near Kew Gardens, London from where he exhibited London Salon(7).

**REID, Miss Jane C** **fl 1887-1896**
Kincardineshire amateur painter; probably a daughter of the manse. Exhibited at the AAS(6), mainly interiors especially of churches, at first from the Free Church Manse, Banchory, later from 13 Beaconsfield Place, Aberdeen.

**REID, Janet** **fl 1912-1927**
Edinburgh artist mainly of watercolours; exhibited RSA(2) & RSW(8).

**REID, John** **fl 1718**
Edinburgh engraver. Subscribed to Nisbet's *Essay on...Armories,* 1718.
**Bibl:** Bushnell.

**REID, John** **fl 1879-1882**
Edinburgh painter in oil and watercolour of landscapes and topographical subjects. Exhibited RSA(6), from 10 Nicholson Street.

**REID, John** **fl 1959-1960**
Kincardineshire painter of local scenery; exhibited RSA(4), from Stonehaven.

**REID, John G** **fl 1903**
Glasgow painter; exhibited 'At the Botanic Gardens, Glasgow' at the RSA.

**REID, John Robertson RI RBA ROI** **1851-1926**
Born Edinburgh, 6 Aug; died Hampstead, London 10 Feb. Painter of genre, landscape and coastal scenes in oil and watercolour. Brother and teacher of Flora Macdonald R(qv) and pupil of George Paul Chalmers(qv) and William MacTaggart(qv). Also trained RSA Schools. Went to Cornwall 1881 where he remained for twenty years. His watercolour style was as dramatic and vigorous as his oil paintings, with deep blues and greens predominant. Although fond of depicting all aspects of rural life, for example 'Toil and Pleasure', (purchased by the Chantrey Bequest 1879) and 'Country Cricket Match', he was mainly drawn to scenes of fisherfolk and the fishing life. Thus such titles as the 'Waterman's Wife', 'The Boatman's Lass', 'Pilchard Fishers, Cornwall'. The content of these pictures is sometimes a little sentimental but his style is strong and vigorous, influenced by Bastien-Lepage and the social realists. In the mid 1880s his style began to change, the handling becoming coarser and more mannered and the subjects more dramatic although he remained able

to produce fine work of an earlier quality. Most of his life was spent in England but he knew many of the Glasgow Boys and himself made a considerable contribution to the development of the Glasgow School. An exhibition of his work was held at the Fine Art Society in London in 1899, although by this time - apart from a fine group of Venetian watercolours - his work had deteriorated with repetitious content and indelicate control. Many of his fishing paintings were done in and around Polperro. Contributed illustrations to *The Graphic* (1892) and *The Sketch* (1894). Elected RBA 1880, ROI 1883, RI 1891. Exhibited RA(29) from 1877, RSA(37) from 1875, GI 1873-1924 throughout & AAS 1906-21. Represented in V & A, Glasgow AG, Leicester AG, Liverpool AG, Manchester AG.
**Bibl:** AJ 1884, 265-8; Armstrong 89; Caw 281-3; Conn 74 (1926) 250; Halsby 280; Hardie III 192; Houfe; Macmillan [GA] 254; R. Mutner, Gesch b Malerei im 19 Jahr, 1893; Wingfield.

**REID, John Thomas** **1843-1917**
Scottish landscape painter, illustrator and writer. Attended Logie school, Causewayhead 1855-6 and after some tuition from a drawing master exhibited his paintings at the RSA for the first time in 1865 when living at 2 George's Place, Leith Walk. In 1866 went by steamship to London, painting en route on the Isle of Wight, and the following year travelled, again by sea, to Shetland. He appears to have remained there until returning to Georges Place in 1869. That year he published the first of three books *Art Rambles in Shetland.* In 1870 he was living at 10 North St Andrews St, Edinburgh before moving c1873 to 8 London St and in 1875 to 18 Picardy Place followed two years later with a move to 21 Broughton Place. Throughout these years he continued to exhibit at the RSA, showing 48 works between 1865 and 1884, including views of Fair Isle, Shetland and the Niagara Falls. In 1876, basing himself at Gaul House, Murthly, Perthshire, he undertook an extensive tour of the Highlands leading to his second book *Art Rambles in the Highlands and Islands* (1878), the engravings of which were done by the Dalziel brothers(qv). *Pictures from the Orkney Islands* appeared in 1881. In 1884, having left Perthshire, he was living in London at 62 Park Rd, Haverstock Hill. Three years later he answered a call from the CIM (now called the Overseas Missionary Fellowship) for missionaries to go to China. He and his wife reached there in January, 1888. This seems to have marked the end of his painting and writing. He died intestate at Iyang, Kiangsai Province, China on May 6. Exhibited GI(1). [From notes kindly provided by Margaret Campbell.]
**Bibl:** Mairi Hedderwick, Highland Journey, A Sketching Tour of Scotland, Edinburgh 1992; John T Reid, Art Rambles in the Highlands and Islands 1878.

**REID, Katherine M** **fl 1887-1891**
Glasgow flower painter. Exhibited GI(5).

**REID, Miss Lizzie** **fl 1880-1918**
Painter of domestic genre. Sister of Flora McDonald(qv) and John Robertson R(qv). Spent most of her life in England, partly in Sussex and partly in Hampstead, London. Exhibited RA(5) including 'Over the Sea' 1884 and 'The Music Lesson' 1886; also RSA(6), ROI(4), RBA(16), GI(2) & L(4).

**REID, Mrs Marell** **fl 1935**
Minor Glasgow flower painter of Uplands, Bearsden; exhibited GI(1).

**REID, Mrs Mary** **fl 1935**
Ross-shire amateur painter; exhibited 'Shadows' at the AAS from Arabella House, Nigg.

**REID, May** **1891-1987**
Glasgow painter of figurative subjects and informal portraits. Trained Glasgow School of Art under Greiffenhagen(qv) 1915-1921. Her impressive graduation work 'Night and Day', redolent of the pre-Raphaelites, is illustrated in colour, Burkhauser (p216). Lived and worked for a spell in Monte Carlo before marrying and settling in London after which no further work has been recorded.
**Bibl:** Burkhauser 214,216.

**REID, Miss Mary Peach** **1854-1921**
Landscape painter in watercolours. Brought up in Powburn and painted country and rustic scenes. Emigrated to Toronto 1913. Exhibited RSA(1) 1875, and 6 works at the London Salon 1912-1913.

**REID, Sir Norman** **c1915-?**
Born London, 27 Dec. Scottish extraction. Educated Wilson's GS London, winning a scholarship to study at Edinburgh College of Art 1933-7. Elected SSA 1935. Awarded a major travelling scholarship 1938-9. Art administrator and painter, mainly of still life in oil. Served during WW2 with the Argyll and Sutherland Highlanders. Joined the staff of the Tate Gallery 1946, becoming Keeper and deputy Director 1959, Director 1964-79. Knighted 1970. Member, first as Secretary-General and later as Vice-Chairman, of the Int. Inst. for Conservation 1963-79; chairman British Council fine art committee 1968-75, President of the Rome Centre 1969-77, member of the council of the Mellon Centre 1971-8, Council of the Royal College of Art 1974-7, President, Penrith Society of Artists, member Arts Council 1964-74. 'Without straining after originality, Norman Reid succeeds in expressing through familiar forms an individual, private vision of the world. He paints for himself. not for the public, and it is this sense of being allowed to look into a secret garden that gives his work its quality' [Bullock]. Exhibited RSA but only resumed full-time painting after retirement from the Tate, holding his first one-man exhibition in London 1991. Represented Tate AG, Nat. Art Collection.
**Bibl:** Lord Bullock, 'Norman Reid Paintings', in Montpelier Studio (Ex Cat London, 1991).

**REID, Miss P Rox** **fl 1850-1868**
Edinburgh painter of portraits and literary subjects; fond of illustrating Tennyson. Exhibited RSA(22) from Cumberland St, later Gt King St and after 1857 from Portobello.

**REID, Miss Pattie** **fl 1893-1917**
Portobello and Paisley flower and landscape painter. Exhibited RSA(3) & GI(1) from 3 Cart Street, Paisley and after 1915 from Glasgow; also Paisley Art Institute 1893-1917.

**REID, Paul** **1975-**
Born Scone, Perthshire. Painter inspired by the classical tradition, with a strong fascination with mythology. Trained Duncan of Jordanstone College of Art 1994-98, winning a Carnegie scholarship and a John Kinross travelling scholarship in his final year, enabling him to visit Madrid & Florence. First solo exhibition Aberdeen 1999. Represented in Perth AG.

**REID, Robert** **1776-1856**
Edinburgh architect. Chief government architect for Scotland 1803-1838. Played a leading role in the development of Georgian Edinburgh, responsible with William Sibbald(qv) for the layout of much of the Northern New Town (1801-2). His principal buildings are St George's Church, Charlotte Square, Edinburgh (1811-1814), the Old Academy, the centrepiece of Rose Street in Edinburgh, and the rather gloomy Custom House, Leith (1811-12). 'Contemporary critics who compared his work unfavourably with that of Robert Adam may seem in retrospect to have missed the point, for while Reid's Adamesque designs, such as the Parliament Square complex, were no doubt undistinguished, some at least of his buildings should be judged rather as early if tentative essays in pursuit of the Greek ideal. This is particularly the case with St George's Charlotte Square and the Leith Custom House, where simple geometric massing is in each case the dominating feature of the composition, while in the picture-gallery at Paxton House (Berwickshire) Reid created an elegant neo-classical interior incorporating arched exedrae and a central oculus' [Dunbar, 116]. Crown Architect for Scotland 1806-1836. Submitted unsuccessful competitive design for the National Monument and completed the building of Edinburgh University. Responsible for the County buildings in Perth and the war prisons of Perth and Greenlaw.
**Bibl:** The Builder, 10 Jne 1882; Dunbar 112,115-6; Gifford, see index.

**REID, Robert Dow** **fl 1956**
Glasgow sculptor. Exhibited two statuettes made from whale ivory at the GI.

**REID, Robert Payton ARSA** **1859-1945**
Born Edinburgh, 22 Oct; died 17 Jan. Painter and book illustrator. Educated George Watson's College, Edinburgh (where he was a founder pupil) and RSA Schools, winning the Stuart prize and the

Maclaine-Watters medal. In 1887 he went to study at the Munich Academy under Johann Herterick, remaining there four years. This led to further trips abroad, to Holland where he enjoyed painting in the manner of the Hague School, to Venice where he became familiar with the Macchiaioli group which profoundly influenced his further development, and to Paris where he enrolled at Academie Julien under Bouguereau, Robert Fleurie and Fernand Cormon. His next journey was to Italy and in Palermo he shared a villa with Richard Levick. Returning to Britain he rented a studio in London, became friendly with J W Waterhouse but soon returned home to Edinburgh. There he became a founder member of the SSA and was elected ARSA 1886. Interested in classical history, displayed his knowledge in treating classical and mythological themes, varied by cavalier subjects. A quiet, sensitive shy man, friend of William Miller Frazer(qv) and Robert Noble(qv). Returned regularly to the continent, wintering in Monte Carlo or Tangiers. Married Emily Smith, a fellow artist, 1916 and moved back to England until he returned finally to Edinburgh 1933. First exhibited RSA in 1880 and continued to do so with few interruptions for the rest of his life showing 181 works there; also RA(2), GI(30), ROI(2), AAS 1906-33 & L(3). Two of his works are in the Mackelvie AG, Auckland, New Zealand.
**Bibl:** Caw 272; M.A. Forrest, 'Robert Payton Reid' (Ex Cat, Forrest McKay, 1990).

**REID, Robert S** **fl 1880-1881**
Leith painter in oil and watercolour of landscapes; exhibited RSA(2).

**REID, Samuel RSW** **1854-1919**
Born Aberdeen, 4 Jly; died April. Watercolour painter of landscapes and illustrator. Younger brother of Archibald David(qv) and Sir George(qv). Educated Aberdeen Grammar School, went to London 1896. Won a gold medal at the Crystal Palace Exhibition 1899. Also an author and poet; his collected poems *Pansies and Folly-bells* were published in 1892. Contributed illustrations to several magazines. Lived in Glasgow in the early 1880s before moving to Alloa and then to England eventually settling in Chorley Wood. His watercolours, often depicting architecture, cathedrals and landscape, are carefully drawn in a manner similar to an oil. Competent rather than exciting. Illustrated John Kerr's *History of Curling* (1890). Elected RSW 1884. Exhibited RA(16), RSA(48), RSW(22), GI(69), AAS (1887-1912) & L(6).
**Bibl:** Halsby 280.

**REID, Stephen RBA** **1873-1948**
Born Aberdeen, 30 May; died London, 7 Dec. Painter of portraits, rural scenes, still life, historical and classical subjects; illustrator. After leaving school entered his father's office but left after four years and remained at home for a year while commencing studies at Gray's School of Art. Went to Edinburgh in 1893 where he spent three years at the RSA Schools before proceeding to London with £1 in his pocket. There he began illustrating various magazines with monochrome drawings and colour illustrations for children's books. During WW1 started painting large canvases, historical and decorative. Married Kate Cato 1902. As a young man he was greatly influenced by the work of Edwin Abbey, favouring Georgian costumes and settings. His principal works include 'Ophelia', 'Macbeth', 'Thomas a'Becket' and 'Choosing a Mare'. Elected RBA 1906. Illustrated *Rime of the Ancient Mariner*(1906), Alfred Noyes' *The Magic Casement*(1908), *Seven Champions of Christendom* (1907), *Boys' Book of Cuchulain*(1910), *Boys' Book of Pirates* (1916), Masefield's *Jim Davis*(1924), *Cruise of the Cachalot*(1926), Frank Brown, *Sea Apprentice*(1926). Provided illustrations to *The Windsor Magazine, The Temple Magazine* (1896-7), *The Idler, The Strand Magazine* (1906), and *The Connoisseur* (1910). Exhibited RA(24), RSA(2), RBA(19), RI(2), AAS(8) & L(10).
**Bibl:** Bertha E. Mahony et al, Illustrators of Children's Books 1744-1945, Boston(USA), 1948, 351.

**REID, Stuart** **fl 1914**
Glasgow watercolour painter. Exhibited RSW(3) & GI(1) from 79 West Regent Street.

**REID, Tammy Y** **fl 1976**
Aberdeenshire artist; exhibited AAS(1) from Easter Cultercullen, Udny.

**REID, William** **fl 1891-1906**
Glasgow watercolour painter; exhibited 'Amongst the trees' at the RSA & GI(4).

**REID, William Bernard** **fl 1916-1938**
Edinburgh flowers, domestic genre, landscape and portrait painter. Moved to London in the late 1930s. Married Beryl R(qv). Exhibited RA(3), RSA(12), RSW(1), GI(3) & L(2).

**REID, William E** **fl 1940**
Amateur Edinburgh portrait watercolourist of 13 Duke Street; exhibited RSA(5) & RSW(2).

**REID, William Robert** **1854-1919**
Architect. Best remembered for his late Georgian Edinburgh villa Easter Park (1905-6) 'faultlessly executed and quite devoid of feeling' [Gifford].
**Bibl:** Gifford 58,550-2.

**REID, William S** **fl 1943**
Glasgow amateur watercolour painter. Exhibited GI(1) from Bearsden.

**REID-MURRAY, J** **fl 1906**
Glasgow landscape painter; exhibited RSA(1).

**REINAGLE, Miss Charlotte** **fl 1798-1808**
Painter of landscape and animals. Daughter of Philip R(qv). Lived in London. Exhibited RA(6), latterly from 5 Gloucester St, New Rd.

**REINAGLE, Miss Fanny** **fl 1799-1820**
Painter of portrait miniatures and occasional landscape. Daughter of Philip R(qv). Lived with her sister until 1810 when she was at 47 Warren St. Exhibited RA(12).

**REINAGLE, George Philip** **1802-1835**
Born London; died London, Dec 6. Marine painter, mostly of battle scenes. Youngest son of Ramsay Richard R(qv). Studied under his father and began copying Dutch masters. At the Battle of Navarino 1827 and with Lord Napier's fleet off Portugal in 1833, producing a number of lithographs of the engagement. Published *Illustrations of the Battle of Navarin, and illustrations of the occurrences at the entrance of the Bay of Patras...*1828. A pen and wash drawing 'The Landing of George IV at Leith' c1825 is an interesting historical record of the occasion. Exhibited RA(37) 1822-1835, latterly from 11 Great Randolph St, Camden Town. Represented in BM, Victoria AG (Australia).
**Bibl:** Bryan; Butchart 89.

**REINAGLE, Miss O G** **fl 1831-1832**
Member of the celebrated family of artists, daughter of Philip R(qv). Landscape painter, mainly of the Cotswolds. Her exhibits at the RA were limited to two consecutive years only, during which 11 works were accepted, from 5 Park Place, Chelsea.

**REINAGLE, Philip RA** **1749-1833**
Born Scotland, probably Edinburgh; died Chelsea, London, 27 Nov. Portrait painter who later took up animal painting and sporting pictures, also botanical subjects and landscape. Son of a Hungarian musician. Entered the RA Schools in 1769 and in the early 1770s worked under Allan Ramsay; it is said that Ramsay embarking on a foreign visit instructed Reinagle to paint fifty pairs of 'Kings and Queens' at ten guineas each. This so angered Reinagle that thereafter he abandoned portraiture in favour of sporting subjects, especially gun dogs and landscapes. From 1780 he spent some time in Norwich working on conversation pieces in the manner of Walton. He painted a miniature in c1800. Helped Barker(qv) in the execution of the latter's panoramic views of Rome, Florence, Gibraltar and the Bay of Naples. Produced an important series of falconry blackline etchings illustrating various modes of hawking. Sometimes collaborated with others including John Russell RA and George Morland. A famous pugilistic contest is depicted in a work now in Broderick Castle. Made a number of book illustrations including botanical drawings used in Thornton's *Sexual Systems of Linnaeus,* 1799-1807, *Philosophy of Botany,* 1809-1810, Taplin's *Sportsman's Cabinet* 1803 containing

many kinds of sporting dogs, engraved by John Scott, and *The Sportsman's Repository* (1820). Elected ARA 1787, RA 1812. Exhibited RA(114) 1773-1827. Represented in BM, V & A.
**Bibl:** AJ 1898; Bryan; Foskett; Houfe; Macmillan [SA] 109,138; Paviere; Waterhouse; Wingfield.

**REINAGLE, Ramsay Richard POWS** **1775-1862**
Born England; died Chelsea, London. Painter of portraits, landscape and figurative subjects in both oil and watercolour. Son and pupil of Philip R(qv). Helped in the preparation of some of Barker's Panoramas. Visited Italy and Holland and the Lake District. Assistant to Hoppner c1810 and painted most of the versions of Hoppner's portrait of Pitt. His best portraits are very competent but lack sparkle. One of the first associates of the OWS in 1805 becoming President 1812. Thereafter he concentrated on oil painting. In 1848 he was forced to resign after exhibiting another artist's work as his own. In his last years he was mainly employed in copying and restoring Old Masters. Less highly regarded than his father. Elected ARA 1814, RA 1823. Exhibited RA(112), latterly from 8 Robert St, King's Rd, Chelsea. Represented in BM, V & A, Williamson AG (Birkenhead), Maidstone Museum, Castle Museum (Nottingham), Wakefield AG.
**Bibl:** Bryan.

**RENCOULE, Marcel Armand** **fl 1923-1926**
Born Paris. Amateur painter of fruit, still life and topographical subjects. Became a naturalised British subject 1919 having acquired the Regent Gallery in Glasgow. Exhibited RSA(1), GI(5) & L(2).

**REILLY, Miss Freda Ellen** **1894-?**
Born Paris, 6 Sep. Painter in pastel. Educated at Woodridings School, Pinner, and Chateau d'Ai, Geneva. Taught by her parents and influenced by Fred and Mary Yates. Lived and worked at South Ledaig, Argyll. Elected PS 1931. Exhibited all over Britain in the main provincial galleries.

**RENISON, William jnr** **fl 1893-1938**
Born Glasgow. Painter, engraver and etcher. Frequently moved, living in Glasgow, Dublin, Manchester and London before settling in Auchterarder, Perthshire. Sensitive etcher whose best work was his landscapes and buildings. Also undertook figure subjects executed with great sympathy. His principal works include 'The Great Clock at Rouen', 'The Cobbler', and 'Ben Lomond'. Exhibited RA(2), RSA(4), RHA(9), GI(39) & L(2); also Paris Salon.

**RENNET, Miss G F** **fl 1965**
Aberdeen amateur artist; exhibited AAS(1).

**RENNIE, Alex** **1977-**
Born England, Scottish parentage. Painter. Trained Wimbledon School of Art and Cheltenham & Gloucester College of Art. Lives and works in England where his first solo exhibition was in 2003; exhibits also in Scotland and Nothern Ireland. A self-portrait exhibited NPG.

**RENNIE, George** **1802-1860**
Born Haddingtonshire; died London, 22 Mar. Sculptor. Son of George Rennie the agriculturist (1749-1828), nephew of John Rennie the architect(qv). In 1834 he carved a series of bas-reliefs for the Dividend Office of the Bank of England including 'Mercury', 'Britannia', 'Ceres', 'The Thames', 'Industry', and 'Calculation'. In 1836 his suggestion to Sir William Ewart that a parliamentary committee should be formed led to the establishment of the School of Design at Somerset House. Helped Joseph Hume to obtain freedom of access to all monuments and works of art in public buildings and museums. In 1841 he decided to enter Parliament and was returned as the Liberal member for Ipswich. Six years later became Governor of the Falkland Islands where it is said he was 'an unqualified success'. His best known sculpture, 'The Archer', 1828, was exhibited at the RA 1833 and is now at the Athenaeum Club. A contemporary critic thought it showed 'an admirable knowledge of anatomy though (it was surprising) in contemplating the excellencies to find that the very inferior statue of 'The Gleaner' (RA 1828) is from the chisel of the same artist'. But the writer omitted to mention that the latter was the sculptor's very first exhibit. The bust of his uncle 'John Rennie' 1831, a figure of 'Mars' and a bust of 'Alexander' can be seen at Chatsworth. One of the first artists to suggest bringing Cleopatra's Needle to London. According to the design and plan he submitted for the 1839 competition it was to be erected in Trafalgar Square as the main feature of the National Monument to Nelson. As a young man he went to Rome to study sculpture and shortly after his return when still only 26 he had his first two exhibits at the RA from 6 George Street, Portland Square. Continued to exhibit at the RA(14) for the next 7 years.
**Bibl:** Athenaeum, 31.3.1860 (obit); Gunnis.

**RENNIE, George Melvin** **1874-1953**
Born Macduff, 9 Sep; died Edinburgh, 26 Jne. Painter in oil, watercolour, pastel, charcoal and pencil and pen and ink; landscape, especially Upper Deeside. Son of an interior decorator and amateur artist, he served his apprenticeship in the family business which was involved in extensive work at Duff House, then owned by the Duke and Duchess of Fife. After the death of his father, he and his brother John Irvine R(qv), sold the business and moved to Aberdeen. During this time he attended Gray's School of Art as a part-time student under James Hector(qv), and at the Aberdeen School of Design. He was already combining business with painting seascapes of the north-east. In 1916 he suffered an accident which badly damaged his right shoulder and changed the direction of his life. As a result he sold his share of the business to his brother and concentrated almost exclusively on landscape painting, with an occasional portrait and still life. In 1924 he opened a studio in Braemar, Aberdeenshire where he spent most of every year 1926-46. An enthusiastic explorer of the hills and glens, he had a Clyno motor car for reaching the more remote areas. Among his commissioned work was a view of Birkhall House, Ballater for Queen Mary, some large murals for a restaurant in Aberdeen, Jewish religious scenes for a synagogue, and landscapes for Lazenby Hall, Cumbria. His love and knowledge of Upper Deeside and the Grampian mountains enabled him to paint this part of Scotland in all seasons, especially autumn. His work, if sometimes a little static, captures the contours and light to a remarkable degree. He also painted extensively in the West Highlands when on holiday, and in the Lothians and Borders. In 1946 he left Braemar, finally retiring to Edinburgh in 1948 where he died. He was survived by his second wife and eight children. Apart from exhibiting at Paisley Art Institute he sold direct to the public rather than through the academies although he did exhibit with the AAS(8) between 1900 and 1929. A posthumous exhibition of his work was held at the McEwan Gallery in 1990.

**RENNIE, H A** **fl 1888-1897**
Glasgow amateur painter of 11 Nelson Terrace, Hillhead; exhibited GI(4).

**RENNIE, Henry J** **fl 1910**
Aberdeen minor artist; exhibited an illuminated poem at the AAS from 78 Hardgate.

**RENNIE, James G** **fl 1929**
Edinburgh painter who exhibited A Normandy inn at the RSA, from 3 Warriston Place.

**RENNIE, John** **1761-1821**
Born Phantassie, East Lothian, 7 Jne; died London, 4 Oct. Architect, millwright and general engineer. The younger son of a Scottish farmer, he exemplified a young man from a modest background successful through his own exertions. As a result of working for three years as a millwright he was able to finance himself to study at Edinburgh University for three years. At the age of 23 he went to Birmingham to help Boulton and Watt in designing and executing machinery for flour mills in London. These were destroyed by fire but not before the mechanism had aroused great interest launching Rennie's growing reputation as a mechanical engineer. His main claim for entry is as a designer of bridges, docks and harbours. His first bridge was built over the Water of Leith 1783. At the beginning of his career he was invited to design a number of other bridges, mainly in Scotland, though some remained uncompleted. His first major work was the bridge at Kelso which, with its semi-elliptical arches separated by pairs of Doric pilasters, its well-defined masonry and its level roadway, anticipated the chief characteristics of his later bridges over the Thames. In June 1810, having criticised earlier plans, he supervised the construction of a new bridge over the Thames at Somerset House, one of the principal features of which was laying the foundations in coffer dams instead of in the caissons that had been

recommended by others. This method secured a firm base for the bridge which was called the Strand Bridge (opened by Prince Regent 1817). Declined a knighthood. His last great work was to design a new bridge to replace the old London Bridge but he died before this could be completed. After his death the practice was taken over by his younger son John(qv). Among his principal works in addition to those mentioned above were the Musselburgh Bridge (over the River Esk), the bridge over the Great West Road at Virginia Water (1805), Wolseley Bridge, Staffs (1798-1800), New Galloway Bridge, Kirkcudbrightshire (1811), Newton Stewart Bridge (over the River Cree, 1812), bridge at Bridge of Earn, Perthshire (1819), Cramond Bridge (1819), the Ken Bridge, New Galloway, Kirkcudbrightshire (1820) Kelso Bridge over the Tweed - one of the first bridges in Britain to have a level roadway - and the Lune Aquaduct near Lancaster. Involved in the development of Leith harbour 1799. Primarily responsible for the design of the Bell Rock Lighthouse, off Arbroath (1817).
**Bibl:** Colvin 486-8; Dunbar 216, 218, 226; Gifford 460.

**RENNIE, Sir John** **1794-1874**
Died Bengeo, nr Hertford, 3 Aug. Son of John Rennie(qv). Engineer and architect. Having acquired his father's practice he received a knighthood in 1831 for his work in designing and completing new London Bridge. He was also an engineer to the Admiralty in which capacity he completed various works in the Royal Dockyards including the Great Breakwater across Plymouth Sound, begun by his father in 1811 and completed thirty years later. Responsible for designing the Royal Victualling Yard at Stonehouse, near Plymouth (1830) described as 'amongst the finest works of the engineer-architect in England'. This was his only important architectural work. Retired c1862.
**Bibl:** Rennie, The Autobiography of Sir John Rennie (1875); Smiles, Lives of the Engineers, ii, 1861, 11.

**RENNIE, John Irvine** **fl 1900-1919**
Aberdeen landscape artist and domestic decorator. Brother of George Melvin R(qv). Painted atmospheric local landscapes but did not have the talent of his brother. His daughter was an art teacher who married the artist R.H. Condie(qv). Exhibited AAS(6) including 'The Colonel's Bed on the River Ey' 1919.

**RENNIE, Mike** **fl 1972-1976**
Aberdeen painter; exhibited AAS from 23 Cameron Way, Bridge of Don.

**RENNIE, Miss Moira** **fl 1932**
Helensburgh artist; exhibited Fisherman's houses at the RSA.

**RENNIE, Stephen James** **fl 1984-1986**
Aberdeen printmaker. Exhibited AAS(7), latterly from 8 Walker Rd, Torry.

**RENNIE, William** **fl 1945-1946**
Glasgow painter. Exhibited GI(3), from Dunchattan St.

**RENNIE, William** **fl 1954-1963**
Glasgow painter and sculptor. Worked in chalk and in wood. Exhibited GI(6), from Woodside Rd.

**RENNIE (RENNAY), William** **fl 1684-1688**
Dundee painter. In 1684 he was paid £40 and 'a boll of meal' by Patrick, 1st Earl of Strathmore for painting the 'roofs of the quir' (chancel ceiling) of Longforgan Church. Later employed on a course of decorative painting at Castle Lyon and Glamis. One of the Earl of Strathmore's grievances against Jacob de Witt was that he had allowed Rennie to execute parts of his artistic work.
**Bibl:** Apted 79; Glamis Book, ppxlii, 68.

**RENNIE, William John** **fl 1885-1886**
Angus watercolour painter; exhibited RSA(4) & GI(1), from 8 Douglas Terrace, Broughty Ferry.

**RENNY, James** **1946-**
Born Sri Lanka, 11 Oct. Wildlife artist in oil, acrylic, watercolour and gouache. Moved with his family to Zimbabwe 1951. Educated in South Africa where he obtained a diploma in art and a degree in Fine Art studies at the University of Witswatersrand 1964-8. Returned to Zimbabwe to teach for two years; lived rough in the bush studying wildlife under the guidance of an elderly native. Then travelled to Greece and Switzerland before reaching Scotland 1974, becoming a full-time painter the following year. His first one-man exhibition 1980 was opened by HRH Prince Philip and was a sell-out; his second exhibition in London 1986 was sold out on the opening day. Commissions worldwide including the birds of New South Wales and the birds of Canada. Displays of his early work may be seen at the National Trust properties at Killiecrankie and St Abb's Head. As well as a fine painter he is a keen observer and naturalist with an almost pre-Raphaelite attention to detail and devotion to accuracy. His colours tend to be strong and his compositions sometimes suffer from a preoccupation with the wildlife which dominate to the detriment of pure aesthetic considerations. In strength and accuracy he is one of the finest wildlife painters of his time. Lives in Perthshire.

**RENTON, D S Stewart** **fl 1933**
Amateur Edinburgh watercolour painter; exhibited RSW(1) from 106 Thirlstone Road.

**RENTON, Joan RSW (née Biggins)** **1935-**
Born Sunderland, 11 Aug. Painter in oil and watercolour and occasional drawing; sometimes uses acrylic, also etches. Landscapes, seascapes, still life, flowers and simplified abstracts. Educated Hawick HS, trained Edinburgh College of Art 1953-7 plus a diploma year 1958. A travelling scholarship in 1979 enabled her to visit parts of Europe. Influenced by Gillies, Redpath, Joan Eardley and the MacTaggarts. Member, RWS & SWA and President for several years of the SSWA which in 1985 she led to its becoming the Society of Scottish Artists and Artist Craftsmen(qv). Exhibits regularly RSA, RSW, SSA & GI, from 9 Lennox Row, Edinburgh. Represented in Royal Collection.

**RENWICK, Mrs Emily** **fl 1887**
Glasgow amateur painter of The Terrace, Gartcosh; exhibited GI(1).

**REOCH (Beech), John** **fl 1700-1742**
Painter. Son of a perfumer and Deacon of Wrights. Apprenticed to Joseph Beech, painter, in May 1700. In 1741 made burgess of the City of Edinburgh and the following year a member of the Incorporation of St Mary's, he married the daughter of a merchant in 1744 and in 1747 took on as an apprentice James Watson, indicating some success in his professional life.
**Bibl:** Apted 79.

**RESTALL, Andrew** **1931-**
Born Headington, Oxon, Jan 12. Landscape painter, designer (especially of postage stamps), teacher. Moved with his family to Edinburgh 1934 when his father was appointed Head of Printing Dept at Heriot Watt College. Trained Edinburgh College of Art 1948-54, winning an Andrew Grant scholarship in his final year. Undertook various designer jobs before taking a part-time teaching position at Edinburgh College of Art 1962. Moved to assume senior teaching appointments in Coventry & Brighton 1964-1990, before returning to Edinburgh as Head, Dept of Visual Communications at Edinburgh College of Art. Retired from teaching 1996. Received many commissions for postage stamps including the commemoration of the opening of the Forth road bridge 1964, IXth Commonwealth Games 1970. Exhibited RSA 1991 and 1997.

**RESTALL, Miss Barbara** **fl 1945-1956**
Edinburgh painter of interiors, domestic genre and landscape. Exhibited RSA(4).

**REVEL, John Daniel RP ROI IS ARCA (Lond)** **1884-1967**
Born Dundee, 2 Feb; died nr Reading, 25 Nov. Painter in oil and watercolour of portrait and figurative subjects. His father, of French extraction, came from Holland. Trained Royal College of Art, London. Received diplomas for architecture 1908 and for painting 1911. Exhibited RA and other leading galleries elsewhere. Head-master of Chelsea School of Art 1912-1924 being the youngest ever director at the time. Then moved to Glasgow on his appointment as Director of the Glasgow School of Art 1925-32. His time at Glasgow was not happy; Revel felt his hands were tied by uninformed businessmen directors at a time when the Glasgow School of Art, after

the wonderful reign of Fra Newbery, was beginning to grow inward-looking. In 1901 awarded a National Medal from the Board of Education at South Kensington. He and his wife, the artist Lucy Revel(qv), retired first to Cornwall and finally in 1937 to Blewbury, nr Didcot. In WW1 served in the artillery in India where he executed many fine watercolours. Appointed war artist there and later in Mesopotamia and in Russia. After his wife's death in 1961 became a recluse. Exhibited RA(6), RSA(11), ROI(6), GI(22) & L(1). Represented in Dundee AG, Glasgow AG, Reading AG.
**Bibl:** G M Ellwood, Drawing and Design April 1924, new series XLVIII vol 3.

**REVEL, Lucy Elizabeth Babington (née Mackenzie) 1887-1961**
Born Elgin. Painter of portraits & flowers. Her uncle was the renowned architect Alexander Marshall Mackenzie(qv). Wife of John R(qv) whom she met at the Royal College of Art when they were students together. Lived in London, then Glasgow and Blewbury, Berkshire. Taught illustration and lettering at Chelsea Art School. Had a good sense of colour and a fine feel for sitters but her output was always limited by her teaching. Lucy Revel and her husband are remembered as a warm, charming, hospitable and delightfully unassuming couple whose original talents never fully flowered. Elected member, Society of Women Artists. Exhibited RA(4), RSA(5) and SWA(40), GI(1) & L(1). Represented in Glasgow AG.

**REVILLE, James RSW 1904-2000**
Born Sheffield, died Dundee. Painter in watercolours and oils, mainly the former; also occasional etcher. Painted mainly flowers, still life, portraits & landscape, often in vibrant tones. Trained Sheffield Technical School of Art. Went to London 1923-25, working as a freelance illustrator. In 1925 he moved to Dundee, joining John Leng & Co (later D C Thomson & Co) as an illustrator. He remained in Dundee for the rest of his life, where he was a friend and contemporary of James McIntosh Patrick(qv) and Neil Catchpole(qv). Served with the RAF during WW2. Joined Dundee Art Society 1928 becoming President 1948-50. Greatly admired & respected as a fine gentleman and highly accomplished artist. Elected RSW 1960. Exhibited RA(3), RGI(19), RSA (48) & RSW. A retrospective exhibition of his work was held at the Eduardo Alessandro Studios, Broughty Ferry, 2002. Represented in Dundee AG.
**Bibl:** Halsby 280; "The Art Master", *Dundee Courier* May 4, 2002

**REY, Loris fl 1934-1939**
Sculptor. Mainly portrait busts. Of French descent. Took to art because he was unable to afford to be a scientist. Lived in Bridge of Weir 1934 and was at one time head of the Sculpture department at Leeds University before moving to London shortly before the outbreak of WW2, where he held a major exhibition. Exhibited RA(2), RSA(3) & GI(6).
**Bibl:** Observer, 8 Jan 1939.

**REYNOLDS, Lyn fl 1926-1932**
Painter and sculptor.nd wood engraver. Trained Glasgow School of Art. Exhibited for the first time while still a student. Moved to Hyde, Cheshire in c1930. Exhibited RSA(1) & L(1).

**REYNOLDS, Margaret K fl 1920-1950**
Glasgow painter and wood engraver of landscape and flowers. Lecturer, Glasgow School of Art 1929. Elected ASWA 1940; won the Lauder Award 1948. Exhibited before and during the first year of WW2 at the RSA(3), GI(3) & L(1).

**REYNOLDS, Warwick RSW 1880-1926**
Born Islington; died Glasgow, 15 Dec. Illustrator, watercolourist and engraver. Son of the artist Warwick Reynolds Snr. Studied life drawing at the Grosvenor Studio in Vauxhall Bridge Road, and then at St John's Wood Art School, and later at the Academie Julien in Paris 1908. His watercolours have a strong sense of graphic design often with clearly drawn animals against flat coloured backgrounds. Spent a large amount of time at London Zoo observing animals 1895-1901. Illustrated for several magazines from 1895. Elected RSW 1924. Exhibited RA(8), RSA(18), RSW(8), GI(36) & L(15). Represented in Aberdeen AG.
**Bibl:** Halsby 223,225,280.

**RHIND, Alexander fl 1861-1887**
Edinburgh sculptor and oil painter of portrait busts, figures and landscape subjects. Related to J S Rhind(qv). Exhibited RSA(45) almost annually between the above years, including a rather poor portrait of 'John Phillip' 1868 and a rather more refined and delicate statuette of 'Highland Mary' 1884; also GI(9). Represented in SNPG.

**RHIND, Alexander fl 1919-1935**
Minor Edinburgh sculptor. Member of the well-known family of sculptors. Probably son of Douglas R(qv). Exhibited RSA(3) from Belford Rd.

**RHIND, Alexander fl 1929-1955**
Dunfermline portrait and still life painter who spent some time also in Falkirk and Edinburgh; often worked in Berwickshire and Fife. Exhibited RSA(23) & GI(3).

**RHIND, David 1801-1883**
Edinburgh architect and draughtsman. Served apprenticeship in London. Designed the Commercial Bank, Gordon St, Glasgow (1857), based on the Renaissance palazzo, also the Scott Monument, George Sq, Glasgow(1838), Life Association building, Princes St, Edinburgh (1855-8, now demolished), the Graeco-Roman Commercial Bank in George St, Edinburgh (1846-7) and the multi-turreted Daniel Stewart's College (1848). Represented in Edinburgh City collection by a pen and watercolour drawing of 'Capriccio: The Monuments of Edinburgh' c1862.
**Bibl:** Dunbar 141,147; Gifford see index; A Gomme & D Walker, Architecture of Glasgow, London 1987(rev), 296.

**RHIND, Douglas H fl 1902-1904**
Minor Edinburgh portrait sculptor. Member of the distinguished family of sculptors. Probably father of Alexander R(qv). Exhibited RSA(3) from Belford Rd, including a relief portrait of the artist 'Tom Marjoribanks Hay RSW'.

**RHIND, Jessie A (Mrs Bonnar) fl 1894-1896**
Minor Edinburgh painter and illustrator; exhibited RSA(2) from 9 Mardale Crescent.

**RHIND, John c1836-1889**
Architect. Responsible for the excessively baronial Ardverikie (1874-78), recently featured in the BBC's *Monarch of the Glen* dramas, the simple Free Church, Laggan (1867, partly dem.), Invermoriston manse (1880), Clydesdale Bank, Academy St, Inverness, originally the Royal Hotel (1864, refronted by **William MACKINTOSH**, 1872-73), Invergarry Hotel (1885), the Free Church Dingwall (1867-70), Knockbain Parish Church, Munlochy (1884-86).
**Bibl:** Gifford, H&I, 39, 53, 70, 77-8, 93, 181, 439-40 et passim, pl.40.

**RHIND, John ARSA 1828-1892**
Born Banff. Sculptor. Son of a master mason descended from a family of masons established in Banff since the early eighteenth century; father of John Massie R(qv) and William Birnie R(qv). Studied sculpture in the studio of Alexander Handyside Ritchie(qv). Sitters included the 'Earl of Mar and Kellie' 1886 and 'William Gladstone' 1886, executed for the Scottish Liberal Club. Elected ARSA 1892 but sadly died a few days after the election before signing the membership roll. A number of portrait busts including 'Victoria and Albert', 'Darwin', 'Michaelangelo' and 'Newton' (1859) are in the Royal Scottish Museum; a statue of William Chambers (1888-1891) is in Chambers St and of Dick (1883) at the Royal (Dick) Vet College.Exhibited 50 portrait busts and designs at the RSA 1857-1892, also RA & GI(6). Represented in NGS, SNPG(2), St Giles Cathedral, Edinburgh (statue to Dr Chambers).
**Bibl:** Gifford see index.

**RHIND, John Jnr fl 1887**
Edinburgh sculptor of portrait busts. Son of John R(qv). Exhibited a bust of his mother at the RSA 1887.

**RHIND, John Massey RSA 1858-1936**
Born Edinburgh; died 21 Oct. Sculptor. Son of John R(qv), brother of William Birnie R(qv). Trained in his father's studio and then for six years at the RA Schools in London where he was awarded the silver

medal for sculpture. Then spent two years working with Sir Albert Gilbert and Sir Thomas Brock. In 1896 went to USA and was a successful candidate in an open competition for a large bronze door for Old Trinity Church, New York. This was followed by a series of more public commissions including a bronze equestrian memorial to George Washington for Newark, New Jersey and four heroic statues of modern presidents. Other portraits included 'Andrew Carnegie', 'General Grant', 'General Sherman'. In Pittsburg he decorated the Carnegie Institute with symbolic figures and a statue of 'Robert Burns'. In Canada where he also worked he is represented by four war memorials and a large bronze of Cornwallis. His diploma work was a bronze of a Red Indian 'The Scout'. Awarded gold medals for sculpture at the Buffalo, St Louis and New York exhibitions. In 1929 he returned to Scotland having his last exhibit at the RSA in 1931. A memorial portrait of 'David Rhind' in low relief is in Warriston Cemetery. President of the Salmagundi Club, New York and President of the Scottish Arts Club in Edinburgh. Elected ARSA 1931, RSA 1934. Exhibited RA(3), RSA(20) & GI(5). Represented in Edinburgh City collection (where he is incorrectly catalogued).
**Bibl:** Gifford 577.

**RHIND, John Stevenson** **1859-1937**
Edinburgh sculptor. Related to Alexander R(qv). Won third prize for a statue of Robert Burns RSA 1890. An obelisk in memory of Sir James Steel (1906) is in the Dean Cemetery, a bronze statue of 'Queen Victoria' (1907) with added panels six years later adorns central Leith; 'Edward VII' is in Victoria Park, Newhaven Rd and a memorial obelisk and bronze relief portrait of 'Dr Balfour' (1907) is in Portobello Cemetery. Exhibited RSA(53) including a bas-relief of 'Christ before Pilate', awarded the Stuart prize 1883, a composition repeated in another exhibit four years later; also exhibited GI(12) & AAS(2) from 59 Torpichen St in 1893. Represented in SNPG(2).
**Bibl:** Gifford 248,390,467,603,652.

**RHIND, Margaret Scott (née Taylor)** **1935-**
Born north-east Aberdeenshire, 23 Feb. Painter, mainly in watercolours. Prefers this medium on account of their translucent qualities. Specialises in landscape and still life, focusing on the changing seasons, growth and decay. Studied at Gray's School of Art, Aberdeen 1952-6 concentrating on drawing and sculpture. Taught in Glasgow and Aberdeen 1957-65 and in 1971 at Breadalbane Academy. Influenced by William Gillies(qv) and Paul Nash. There is a tendency toward increasing abstraction. Exhibits regularly RSA, RSW, AAS & GI, from Rannoch Lea, Taybridge Rd, Aberfeldy. Represented in Perth AG.

**RHIND, Sir Thomas Duncan ARIBA** **1871-1927**
Edinburgh architect and occasional etcher, mainly architectural and topographical subjects. Third son of John(qv), brother of John Massey R(qv) and William Birnie R(qv). Began his artistic career by studying sculpture but quickly turned to architecture. Trained Edinburgh School of Art. Served in WW1 as a major in the 5th Batt. Royal Scots. Exhibited RSA(23), often in collaboration with his brothers, also GI(1) & L(4).

**RHIND, William Birnie RSA** **1853-1933**
Born Edinburgh; died Edinburgh Jly 9. Sculptor. Son of John R(qv). Educated Edinburgh, studied under his father before enrolling at the Edinburgh School of Design under Hodder and five years at the RSA Life School. He carved portraits, decorative works and memorial groups as well as busts and figures. His first exhibit was in 1878. Outside Scotland was responsible for public monuments in Winnipeg, Canada, India and Australia. At home he executed the memorial to the 42nd Regiment at Aberfeldy (1888), a statue of Queen Margaret for the entrance to the SNPG (1891), Burns statue for Montrose (1891), an alto-relievo panel 'The Ruder Arts' for the porch of the SNPG (1893), a monument to Thomas Coates for Paisley Corporation Museum (1894), statues of 'King Robert the Bruce' and 'Wallace' for the SNPG (1895) a group sculpture for the Kelvingrove Gallery, Glasgow (1899), design for Hawick Patriotic Memorial (1903), two allegorical groups 'The Sciences' and 'The Fine Arts' (for Shipley AG, Gateshead 1915) and allegorical groups for the New Parliament Buildings in Winnipeg (1916), his last exhibit. Also undertook work at Fettes College and in Buckie. Elected ARSA 1893, RSA 1905. Exhibited RA(10), RSA(133), GI (41), RHA(3), AAS(2) & L(8), latterly from St Helens, Cambridge St. Represented Edinburgh City collection.

**RHIND, William James** **fl 1883-1884**
Edinburgh watercolour painter of landscapes and rustic scenes; exhibited RSA(3) from 30 Kemp Place.

**RIACH, May Johnstone** **fl 1929**
Painter. Exhibited 'The Corner House, Glamis' at the AAS from 74 Beaufort Mansions, London.

**RICHARD, Dorothy** **fl 1926**
Lanarkshire subject painter. Exhibited GI(1), from Kirkton, Carmyle.

**RICHARDS, Robert Steel** **fl 1966**
Glasgow watercolour painter. Exhibited GI(1).

**RICHARDSON, A M S** **fl 1910**
Aberdeenshire painter of landscapes. Exhibited 'Murcar Links' and a Dutch canal scene at the AAS, from Ladysmith, Bieldside.

**RICHARDSON, Alexander** **fl 1843-1850**
Edinburgh painter of landscape, domestic genre & informal portraits; exhibited RSA(15).

**RICHARDSON, Andrew** **fl 1828-1830**
Edinburgh artist; exhibited RSA(9) including 'The grave of the murdered traveller' and several landscapes.

**RICHARDSON, Andrew** **fl 1841-1852**
Edinburgh painter of landscapes and portraits. Exhibited RSA(66), three of them landscapes of Glen Nevis and one of the Catskill Mountains in the USA.

**RICHARDSON, Mrs Frances** **fl 1947-1961**
Edinburgh painter of flowers, still life and topographical subjects. Exhibited GI(13) from Edinburgh, latterly Rothesay Terrace.

**RICHARDSON, James Smith FSA(Scot) FRIAS Hon RSA** **1883-1970**
Born North Berwick. Architect and monumental carver. Cousin of the colourist F.C.B. Cadell(qv) and second cousin to Phyllis Bone(qv). Trained with McIntyre Henry. Worked for Robert Lorimer(qv) c1903-6. Elected FGSA(Scot) 1912, appointed HM Inspector of Ancient Monuments for Scotland 1913 a position he held until 1946 except for war service with the Royal Scots. In this capacity he had occasion to differ with Robert Lorimer, especially over the latter's plans for a national war memorial. Appointed to the RSA Chair of Antiquities 1953. Member, Société Prehistoric Française. British representative, League of Nations International Institute 1922. Curator, National Museum of Antiquities of Scotland 1925. His work led to the discovery of Skara Brae and the recovery of the Traprain Silver in East Lothian. Delivered the Rhind Lectures 1948. Designed the formal gardens at Edzell and Pitmedden and was the inventor of a gramophone driven by weights. Works include Church of St. Baldred, North Berwick - memorial oak panelling at back of pulpit and memorial chancel gates (1910). Exhibited RSA(11) & L(5).
**Bibl:** Colvin; Peter Savage, Lorimer and the Edinburgh Craft Designers, Edinburgh 1980, xx,26,78,86-7,120,126,147,151,168.

**RICHARDSON, Jenny** **1944-**
Born Edinburgh. Painter. Trained Edinburgh College of Art 1962-66. Exhibits at RSA & in Ireland from West Cork.

**RICHARDSON, Joseph Kent RSW** **1877-1972**
Edinburgh artist and dealer, also connoisseur collector, sportsman and watercolourist. He was a fine pencil draughtsman, rather in the manner and style of D Y Cameron(qv). His watercolours of country landscapes are colourful and tranquil. Elected RSW 1917. Exhibited RA(1), RSA(37), RSW(94) & GI(17). Represented in Edinburgh City collection.
**Bibl:** Halsby 280.

**RICHARDSON, Rosemary Rowan** **fl 1967**
Aberdeen watercolour landscape artist; exhibited AAS(2).

**RICHARDSON, Miss Sybil** **fl 1944**
Glasgow illuminator. Exhibited GI(1).

**RICHARDSON, William** **19th Cent**
Scottish engraver. Three works are in the collection of the city of Edinburgh: 'Old and New Edinburgh' and 'Barskimming on the Ayr', after D.O. Hill and a scene from 'The Cottar's Night' after John Faed.

**RICHEY, Mary E** **fl 1927-1938**
Edinburgh painter who moved to Polperro, Cornwall in about 1932 and thence to Bridport, Dorset 1935. Worked mainly in watercolour. Exhibited RA(1), RSW(1) & SWA(10).

**RICHMOND, Andrew** **fl 1868-1899**
Glasgow painter of landscapes, seascapes and figure subjects. Painted mainly scenery around the Clyde, Loch Fyne and on Arran. Exhibited RSA(18) & GI(60), from St Vincent Street.

**RICHMOND, Cathy G** **1949-**
Born Liverpool. Painter in oils and watercolours. Launched herself into art training as a mature student, Glasgow School of Art 1992-96, winning the Kelly Prize for first year students and the Emmy Sachs award for final year students; also the Keith Prize (RSA). Exhibits RGI since 1994, RSA from 1995 and RSW 1995, from 1 Caird Drive, Kyndland.

**RICHTER, John** **fl 1907**
Glasgow-based painter. Lived at 288 New City Road and exhibited RSA. Represented in Birmingham AG, Manchester AG.

**RICHTER, Otto** **fl 1885**
Minor Glasgow landscape painter of 2 Ailsa Terrace, Hillhead. Possibly father of John R(qv). Exhibited 'The Reed pool, Braes o' Balquhidder' at the RSA(1).

**RICKEY, Jane** **fl 1933**
Minor Dunbartonshire sculptor of Clarendon, Helensburgh; exhibited a portrait bust at the GI.

**RIDDEL(L), Daisy** **fl 1901-1902**
Minor Berwickshire painter of still life and dead game; exhibited RSA(2), from Cocklaw, Cockburnspath.

**RIDDEL, James ARSA RSW** **1857-1928**
Born Glasgow, 27 Mar; died Balerno, nr Edinburgh, 14 Mar. Painter in oil and watercolour; landscape, portraits and genre, also an illustrator. Influenced by his close friend J L Wingate(qv). Trained Glasgow School of Art and later in Edinburgh, living in Forfar, Colinton and from 1922 in Ayrshire. Active member of the Glasgow Art Club. Undertook extensive journeys to Belgium and Canada where he completed a number of paintings. Head of the Art Department of Heriot Watt College for 20 years. Favoured large watercolours 'using rubbed paper to achieve a hazy, indecisive effect'. His seascapes and coastal scenes are his most highly regarded works. Elected RSW 1905, ARSA 1919, Treasurer of the RSW for many years. Provided the coloured illustrations for the 1949 edition of R. Chalmers' *Traditions of Edinburgh* described as 'the standard and classic work on the traditions and antiquities of the Scottish capital'. Exhibited RA(7), RSA(128), RSW(51), GI(100), RHA(2), AAS(2) & L(11). Represented in Glasgow AG.
**Bibl:** Caw 391; Halsby 280.

**RIDDELL, James** **fl 1886**
Forfar painter of topography and figure studies. Exhibited RSA(2).

**RIDDELL, R A** **fl 1793-1795**
Remarkably little is known of this landscape painter who was an honorary exhibitor at the RA. In 1793 he exhibited a view of Dumfries from the south-east. In 1795 a fine view of Edinburgh from the north west, the castle silhouetted against Arthur's Seat, was published as an aquatint by Archibald Robertson(qv).
**Bibl:** Butchart 18.

**RIDGWAY, Richard** **fl 1944**
Painter of North Berwick. Exhibited RSA(1).

**RIEGLER, Maggie** **fl 1969-1975**
Aberdeen textile designer; exhibited AAS from 35 Louisville Ave.

**RIFAT, David** **fl 1961**
An Edinburgh painter who exhibited a study of a church at the RSA.

**RIGG, J E** **fl 1882-1884**
Edinburgh painter in oil and watercolour of still life; exhibited RSA(2), from 39 Inverleith Row.

**RIGG, William** **fl 1907**
Minor Glasgow painter. Exhibited GI(1), from 79 West Regent St.

**RILEY, Miss Jessie** **fl 1888**
Minor Glasgow painter; exhibited GI(1), from 6 Royal Terrace, Crosshill.

**RILLIE, A** **fl 1900-1901**
Ayrshire watercolourist. Exhib GI(2) from Fenwickland, nr Ayr.

**RINTOUL, Alexander** **fl 1884**
Minor Edinburgh landscape painter in oil. Exhibited RSA(1), from 27 Elder St.

**RINTOUL, David** **fl 1892-1919**
Glasgow painter. Flowers, landscape (especially on Arran) and figures. Moved to Renfrew c1904; exhibited GI(9).

**RIPPIN, Miss Dorothy C** **fl 1931**
Dunbartonshire portrait painter. Sister of Everilde R(qv). Exhibited RSA(1), from Hughenden, Lenzie.

**RIPPIN, Miss Everilde** **fl 1934**
Painter. Sister of Dorothy C R(qv). Exhibited 'The raising of Lazarus' at the RSA, from Hughenden, Lenzie, Dunbartonshire.

**RISK, Kathleen** **fl 1929**
Minor Edinburgh portrait painter of Gogarbank House, Corstorphine. Exhibited RSA(1).

**RITCHIE, Miss -** **fl 1900**
Aberdeen flower painter; exhibited 'Christmas roses' at the AAS, from 90 Irvine Pl.

**RITCHIE, Alexander A** **fl 1833-1880**
Edinburgh painter in oil and watercolour of figurative, historical, topographical scenes and portraits; also an engraver. Many of his works carried strong literary allusions often from Scott or Shakespeare. Exhibited RSA(24). Represented in Edinburgh city collection by an oil and a watercolour view of old Edinburgh.
**Bibl:** Halsby 280.

**RITCHIE, Alexander Handyside ARSA** **1804-1870**
Born Musselburgh; died Edinburgh. Sculptor. Son of a brickmaker who after studying architecture turned to sculpture. Then went to Rome 1829 where he studied under Thorwaldsen and in 1844 exhibited 'Sophronia and Olinda at the Stake' in Westminster Hall. Brother of John Ritchie(qv). His principal practice lay in ornamental sculpture but also executed many busts, statues and groups. Responsible in Edinburgh for the ornamental figures on the Commercial and British Linen Banks, for a group of children for the Western Bank (1848), and for decorative details on the office of the Life Association of Scotland (1859). In London he was employed under John Thomas on decorative sculpture for the Houses of Parliament. Among his busts were the 'Countess of Lincoln' (1837), 'Marquis of Huntly' (1838), and 'Sir Charles Eastlake' (1866). He also carved the busts of the 'Rev Charles Findlater' (1836) for Newlands Church, 'Dr Andrew Thomson' (1837) for the Presbyterian Hall, Edinburgh, the 'Rev George Leigh' (1838) for the Mechanics Institute, Hull while those of 'George Kemp' (1845) and 'David Stowe' (1852) are in the SNPG and the Kelvin AG respectively. Executed a number of statues including those of 'Sir Walter Scott' (1839), at Selkirk, 'Mr Ferguson of Raith' (1843) at Dirleton, Haddington; 'Prince Charles Edward Stuart' (1844) for the Scott Memorial in Edinburgh, 'Eustace de Vesci and William de Mowbray' (1848) for the House of Lords; 'Queen Victoria' (1851) now at Holyrood Palace; 'Peel' (1852) at Montrose; 'Dr Moir' (1853), at Musselburgh; 'Hugh Miller' (1858) at Cromarty; and

'Wallace' (1858) at Stirling. He undertook a series of statues in 1845 for the New Physicians Hall in Edinburgh and also for Stirling Cemetery. His group 'The Rev David Dickson blessing children' (1844) stands outside St Cuthbert's Church, Edinburgh, while his monument to 'Charles Marjoribanks' (1836) is at Coldstream and his tablet to the Rev John Patterson (1848) is in Falkirk Church. He executed a pair of lions (1852) for Hamilton Palace Mausoleum. Exhibited RA(11) 1830-1868, RSA(127) 1825-1869. Represented in NGS by his sketch for the Selkirk monument to Sir Walter Scott, in the SNPG by a plaster bust of the designer of the Scott memorial, 'George Meikle Kemp (1795-1844)', Edinburgh City collection by a plaster cast of George Meikle Kemp, and Glasgow AG (bust of D. Stow Esq).
**Bibl:** Brydall 192; Gifford 207,226,277,288,300,316,326,458; Gunnis 322-3.

**RITCHIE, Alexander Hay** **1822-1895**
Born Glasgow; died New York. Painter of portraits, genre and historical works. Trained under Sir William Allan. Emigrated to New York 1841.

**RITCHIE, Alick P F** **?-1938**
Born Dundee; died 25 May. Dundee draughtsman and illustrator. Began his drawing career in the shipyard of Brown & Simpson, the latter being his uncle. After a short time proceeded to London, specialising in theatrical posters, and then to Antwerp for further training. Executed many street scenes, mostly in monochrome.
**Bibl:** Celtic Annual, 'Dundee Artists', 393, 16; Dundee Advertiser, 26 May, 1938 (obit).

**RITCHIE, Miss Annie W** **fl 1876**
Minor amateur Edinburgh oil painter of local scenes; exhibited RSA(1).

**RITCHIE, Charles E ROI** **fl 1894-d1940**
Portrait and landscape painter. Began working life as a barrister but changed to art and studied in Paris. Lived in London but moved to Dunottar House, Stonehaven (1894-1900), then to Redcraig, Muchalls and finally to St Andrews. Whilst in Aberdeen was a member of the then flourishing Aberdeen Artists' Society. Exhibited RA(23), RSA(3), RBA(1), ROI(27), RI(2), GI(4), AAS(33) & L(12).

**RITCHIE, David** **19th Cent**
Obscure artist, probably Scottish. A watercolour of 'The Old Mint, South Gray's Close' is in the Edinburgh City collecton.
**Bibl:** Halsby 281.

**RITCHIE, David J** **fl 1937-1957**
Aberdeen sculptor of portrait busts and figurative works; often used ivory. Exhibited 'Salome' (1948), 'Persephone' (1955) and 'Exodus II, v 5' (1957) at the RSA, two wood carvings at the GI & an ivory carving at the AAS, from 33 Chestnut Row.

**RITCHIE, Duncan S** **fl 1888**
Glasgow painter. Exhibited GI(1) from 13 Rosslyn Terrace, Kelvinside.

**RITCHIE, 'of Dundee'** **fl 1929**
Shadowy figure who painted landscapes and coastal paintings from 18 Collingham Gardens, London. Described himself as Ritchie 'of Dundee'. Exhibited mainly at the Ridley Art Club.

**RITCHIE, Miss E C** **fl 1927-1930**
Painter. Probably English, she settled in Montrose c1928 from where she exhibited Ludlow at the RSA, also L(2).

**RITCHIE, Eric** **1934-**
Born Aberdeen. Painter in oil and watercolour of landscapes, abstracts, theatre designs and panels. Trained Edinburgh College of Art becoming a part-time member of staff. Travelled in France and Italy. On his return designed and painted murals in London and Cheshire. Awarded the Keith prize 1955. Held the first of several one-man shows in Edinburgh 1960. Became increasingly concerned with the landscape of East Lothian and Berwickshire. Enjoys strong fresh colours. Lives at Anwoth Cottage, Cockenzie. Exhibited GI(1) & AAS(3) 1976, from 29 Jeffrey St, Edinburgh. Represented in London, Edinburgh, Glasgow, New Orleans and Rome.

**RITCHIE, Fullarton** **fl 1873-1880**
Edinburgh watercolour painter of landscape. Exhibited RSA(3).

**RITCHIE, George** **fl 1948-1952**
West Lothian painter of topographical watercolours. Exhibited GI(4) from Linlithgow.

**RITCHIE, Henry** **fl 1858-1880**
Edinburgh painter in oil and watercolour principally landscapes. Two favourite subjects were Highgate pond and the Water of Leith. Exhibited regularly RSA(64), mainly from 9 Gardiner's Crescent, also GI 1869-1876.

**RITCHIE, Miss Hope K** **fl 1920-1939**
Little known Edinburgh painter of figurative subjects, genre, flowers and still life. Exhibited RSA(5), RSW(4), AAS(1) & GI(5) from 2 Armidale Terrace.

**RITCHIE, Ian Cameron** **fl 1987-**
Dundee-based painter fond of using enigmatic titles such as 'Acid rain', 'Tide of change'. Exhibits RSA & GI, from 248 Blackness Rd.

**RITCHIE, Professor James** **fl 1938-1955**
Amateur watercolourist of buildings, landscape and topographical subjects. Professor at the University of Aberdeen (living at Castleton Hse, Old Aberdeen) & from 1937 in Edinburgh (living at 31 Mortonhall Road). Exhibited RSA(7), GI(8) & AAS(6) including 'Building of the New Infirmary', Oct 1932 1937.

**RITCHIE, Janet A K** **fl 1962**
West Lothian painter of still life; exhibited RSA(1), from Kirkliston.

**RITCHIE, John** **1809-1850**
Died Rome, 30 Nov. Sculptor; visionary. Younger brother of Alexander Handyside(qv). Largely self-taught although he became his brother's assistant when the latter returned from Rome. His one exhibit at the RA was 'The Flood' in 1840 which he had modelled in clay eight years previously. Some years later this came to the attention of a Mr Davidson who was so impressed that he commissioned a group in marble, enabling the sculptor to visit Rome. He left Scotland in September 1850 but on a visit to Ostia contracted malaria from which he died after only a few days illness. His principal works in Scotland are the statue of 'Sir Walter Scott' in Glasgow and the figure of 'The Last Minstrel' (1844) for the Scott Memorial in Edinburgh. Owing to his being left-handed, the statue of Scott has the plaid thrown over the wrong shoulder, a mistake noticed too late. Exhibited the statue of Scott, together with one of 'Lord Byron', in Bond Street, London (1833) and his marble statue of 'A Poetess' was exhibited posthumously at the Great Exhibition of 1851. Exhibited RSA(13) including a cabinet statue of 'The Duke of Wellington' (1840) in 1849. Represented in MCC, Lords (London) by 'Village Cricket' 1855.
**Bibl:** AJ, 1851, 44; Brydall 192; Gunnis 323; Scotsman, 3 Sep 1938; Wingfield.

**RITCHIE, John** **fl 1849-1865**
Edinburgh painter in oil of figurative subjects and rural genre, often with a strong humorous element. Exhibited RSA(42) from London 1860-1 & GI(6), mostly from Edinburgh.

**RITCHIE, Mary E** **fl 1923-1926**
Aberdeen painter and etcher of landscape, portraits and figurative compositions. Exhibited AAS(4) including 'Self-portrait', from 5 Devanha Terrace.

**RITCHIE, Paul Stephen** **fl 1976-1979**
Aberdeenshire painter of genre; exhibited AAS from Seaview, Collieston.

**RITCHIE, Thomas L** **fl 1861-1875**
Glasgow painter in oil of portraits, especially women. In 1863 was commissioned to paint the portrait of the 'Master of Trinity House, Leith'. Other exhibited works include the 'Provost of Cupar, Fife' 1854 and 'James Syme, Surgeon and Licentiate of the Royal College of Physicians, Edinburgh'. Exhibited GI(2) 1861.

**RITSON, Mrs Claire (née Stuart-Brown)** **1907-?**
Born Maryhill, Glasgow, 23 Nov. Painter in oil, watercolour and gouache. Educated St Leonard's School, St Andrews, trained Edinburgh College of Art and Arthur Segal and Frobisher Schools of Art. Often signed her work simply 'Claire'. Exhibited GI(1) 1954, RBA, ROI, SWA and in Paris. Represented in Bendigo AG (Victoria, Australia).

**ROBARTS, Miss H G** **fl 1877**
Selkirk painter of landscape; exhibited 'On the Inver, Sutherland' at the RSA.

**ROBB, Alan** **1946-**
Born Glasgow. Painter, teacher and administrator. Portraits, landscapes and shipping scenes. Educated Robert Gordon's College, Aberdeen and from 1964-9 at Gray's School of Art including a year at Hospitalfield, Arbroath 1968. Art master, Oundle School 1969-72, then lecturer in painting, Crawford School of Art, Cork 1975-8, becoming head of painting 1978-80. Further promoted to Head of Fine Art Studies 1980-82 during which time he was also chief examiner in fine art to the Republic of Ireland. Since 1983 has been Head of Fine Art at the Duncan of Jordanstone School of Art. Director of WASPS, director of Art in Partnership. External assessor in painting and printmaking, Sheffield Polytechnic. Published *Irish Contemporary Art* (1982). Exhibits RSA and AAS(5), latterly from 59 Cupar Rd, Newport-on-Tay. Represented in SAC, Crawford AG (Cork), Arts Council of Northern Ireland, Arts Council of Ireland.

**ROBB, Alexander H** **fl 1893**
Aberdeen amateur painter. Exhibited 'Old and New Bridges of Don' at the AAS from 6 Schoolhill.

**ROBB, Alexander R** **1950-**
Born Kirkwall. Painter of still life, landscape & portraits in oil, gouache and pastel. Trained Glasgow School of Art 1968-72. His work is characterised by strong drawing and rich use of colour. Exhibits RSA & RGI, from Dumfriesshire.

**ROBB, Bill** **fl 1974-1976**
Aberdeen painter. Trained Gray's School of Art, Aberdeen. Exhibited AAS(4), from 4 Polmuir Rd.

**ROBB, Carole** **1943-**
Born Renfrewshire. Painter. Studied Glasgow School of Art and Reading University. First one-man exhibition London 1966, followed by others in Glasgow and New York.

**ROBB, Emma M** **fl 1886-1896**
Glasgow watercolour painter of landscapes, portraits, flowers and animals. Lived at Busby House, Busby, Renfrewshire. Exhibited RSA(3) & GI(10).

**ROBB, George** **fl 1858**
Ayrshire painter of landscapes in oil; exhibited RSA(3).

**ROBB, Grace Elspeth** **fl 1900-1935**
Aberdeen watercolour painter of flowers and local landscape. Exhibited AAS from 19 Kings Gate and latterly Holmsdale, Cults.

**ROBB, J R Beith** **fl 1932**
Lanarkshire sculptor. Exhibited a plaster figure at the GI from Gartcosh.

**ROBB, John S** **fl 1901-1902**
Glasgow landscape painter; exhibited GI(1) & AAS(1) from Ferryhill.

**ROBB, Mrs Lena** **fl 1947-1969**
Edinburgh painter of portraits and flower studies. Exhibited GI(37) from Trinity Rd.

**ROBB, Thomas** **fl 1853**
Edinburgh sculptor. Exhibited portrait bronze medallions at the RSA, from 25 Thistle St.

**ROBB, William George** **1872-1940**
Born Ilfracombe, Devon. Landscape and figure painter. Trained Aberdeen School of Art and under Bouguereau and Aman Jean in Paris. Returned to England, where he mainly exhibited, including RA(10) though most of his work was shown in provincial galleries including AAS 1890-1937.

**ROBBIE, Alexander** **fl 1948-1986**
Glasgow landscape and topographical painter; exhibited RSA(6) & GI(1) , mainly east coast scenery especially Arbroath and the Firth of Forth, latterly from Bearsden.

**ROBBIE, Frank** **fl 1963-1987**
Edinburgh painter of landscape and still life. Exhibited RSA(4).

**ROBBIE, Karen** **1965-**
Born Dundee, 19 Dec. Works in mixed media, mostly acrylic, oil, pastel and pencil on canvas and paper. Trained Duncan of Jordanstone College of Art, Dundee, obtaining a scholarship at Hospitalfield 1989, enabling her to visit Paris, Turkey, India, Nepal and Pakistan. Her work is mainly abstract with 'gestural forms depicting space and atmosphere, creating a tension, depth and lyrical flow'. Lives at 11 Rosefield Street, Dundee. Exhibits regularly RSA.

**ROBBINSON, Mrs Margaret** **fl 1854-1870**
Edinburgh painter of figurative studies; also painted historical and literary subjects. Moved to London where she soon established a reputation, showing 13 works at the RA between 1854 and 1870, latterly from 12 Lincoln's St, Chelsea. Her portrayal of 'Straw-rope twisting in the Highlands' 1858 is an interesting record of a now vanished rural skill. Also exhibited RSA(3).

**ROBERT, Charles** **1806-1872**
Born Edinburgh; died Edinburgh. Engraver. Trained Trustees Academy. His earliest works were vignette portraits. Employed by the London Art Union from its inception, producing several excellent plates for subscribers. Among the best known are 'The Expected Penny', 'The Rush-plaiters' and 'The Widow'.
**Bibl:** Bryan.

**ROBERTON, Mrs Henrietta Jane** **c 1850-1935**
Born Glasgow. Painter of still life, interiors, landscape and flowers in oil. Founder member of the Glasgow Society of Lady Artists. Married 1871. Exhibited RSA(22), GI(24) & L(13), mostly from Markland Terrace, Hillhead.

**ROBERTON, Thomas** **fl 1876-1877**
Edinburgh oil painter of local scenes; exhibited RSA(3).

**ROBERTS, Arthur Spencer** **1920-?**
Painter in oil and watercolour, animals and fish. Son of a musician, he moved from Scotland to the south of England in 1927 being educated at Hastings GS and trained Brassey School of Fine Art. Joined the RAF, serving in Burma and India during WW2. After returning to England he studied art for five years before becoming a wildlife artist and a teacher of art, specialising in big game but later turning his attention to all branches of animal art, including birds, sporting dogs, and fish. Prints of his work have been published. One of his major works is a giant mural, depicting 200 species of Asian jungle animals commissioned by the Aspinall Zoo at Port Lympne.

**ROBERTS, C** **fl 1871**
Amateur Glasgow painter. Exhibited a still life of fruit at the GI.

**ROBERTS, Claire** **1971-**
Born Aberdeen, March 20. Painter & printmaker. Trained Gray's School of Art 1989-93 and at the Slade School of Art 1995-97. Occasional lecturer, Gray's School of Art 1998-. Winner of various awards including RSA printmaking award 1993. Uses the print medium in an imaginative sometimes rather stark way to express the complexities of the human condition. Exhibits AAS & SSA since 1993, RSA 1995. Represented in Aberdeen AG, Kinross Archive (RSA).

**ROBERTS, David RA HRSA** **1796-1864**
Born Stockbridge, Edinburgh, 24 Oct; died London, 25 Nov. Painter in oil and watercolour of architectural subjects, also illustrator. Son of a shoemaker. Apprenticed to Gavin Beugo(qv), a former heraldic painter, but by then a house painter. Whilst working there he came

into contact with William Kidd(qv) and the two young men, together with a man named Mitchell, started a small life class. Being unable to pay for a model they took it in turn themselves, sometimes interspersed by using a donkey, and mounted an exhibition of their work, Robert's contribution being a large picture of the 'Battle of Trafalgar'. After seven years as an apprentice he went to Perth where he was employed by a London decorator called Conway who was undertaking work at Scone Palace. The next year he went to Edinburgh where he joined a circus as a scene painter. Visited Carlisle, Newcastle and York, but there the company failed. Returned to Edinburgh working as a foreman-decorator at a mansion being built at Abercairney. After further adventures in Edinburgh he joined the Glasgow Theatre Royal as a scene painter. By 1820 he changed to the Theatre Royal in Edinburgh, marrying later the same year. In 1822 he exhibited 3 pictures at the RI in Edinburgh; 'The Foot of the Cowgate', 'The Interior of Newby Abbey', and a view of the 'Nether Bow'. The same year he went to London becoming a scene painter at Drury Lane. There he renewed his acquaintance with Clarkston Stanfield who became a life-long friend and associate. Their joint work earned a reputation for both. When the Society of British Artists was formed in 1823, Roberts became its Vice President and in 1830 President. He was by now gradually abandoning scene painting in favour of architectural subjects. In 1827 he alone was responsible for designing the sets for the first London production of Mozart's 'Il Seraglio'. In 1832 he embarked on his first extensive continental expedition visiting Spain where he painted a number of pictures including the interior of a cathedral during Corpus Christi Day and the 'Tower of the Giralda'. Returning to England the following year he continued to paint Spanish subjects, exhibiting at the RA 1826 until 1864. In 1838-9 visited Egypt and the Holy Land, making sketches sufficient to keep him working for ten years, and in 1851 and '53 he twice toured Italy. 'He became one of the best known of the later topographers, and the results of his many journeys exist not only in oil paintings and watercolours but in the form of coloured reproductions which were highly popular and brought him a considerable fortune' [Hardie]. Some of his most pleasing and lively works were done before 1840; his drawings done in the east are monotonous in their uniform scheme of grey, red, brown and yellow although Ruskin praised his endurance, his exquisite drawings and his statements of facts but said that among his sketches he saw 'no single instance of a downright study in which the real hues and shades of sky and earth had been honestly realised or attempted nor were there, on the other hand, any of these invaluable blotted five minute works which record the unity of some simple and magnificent impression'. Among his publications are *Picturesque Sketches in Spain During the Years* 1832 and 1833, and *Views in the Holy Land, Syria, Idumea, Arabia, Egypt and Nubia* (6 vols 1842-9). Also contributed to Jennings' *Landscape Annual* (1835-8), *The Chaplet* (c 1840), Lawson's *Scotland Delineated* (c 1845), and Lockhart's *Spanish Ballads.* In 1849 he visited Belgium with Louis and Charles Haag, the latter also accompanying him on a tour to Scotland, and for a second time to Rome. In 1851 his artistic reputatation was recognised by his being made a Commissioner for the Great Exhibition. When in Edinburgh 1858 he was granted the Freedom of the City. His diploma picture at the RA was 'Baalbec'. Opinion of his work varies, Brydall considers that 'few artists have ever approached Roberts in his delineation of architectural subjects, more especially Gothic. In his very noble interiors of medieval cathedrals, invariably animated by well disposed groups of figures, the quality of height and space is most successfully managed by the gradual losing of detail in line, form, and colour...In his wealth of resource, beauty of colour and finish, and breadth of effect he is unequalled.' Armstrong considered that 'as an artist, Roberts shone rather by the quality than by the extent of his powers. His range was narrow. He had scarcely a trace of invention. His colour, as a rule, was very poor in quality, reminding us rather of the scene painters pot than of the oil painter's palette; while as for atmosphere the best equivalent he could devise for it was a mechanical degradation of tint, and yet, as far as it goes, his work is always artistic. He composed well, his sense of architectural effect was fine, and his drawing of detail suggestive. His colour was for the most part harmonious, and sometimes, in his best work - in his Spanish pictures for example - not deficient in warmth'. In his artistic development three phases can be distinguished: Spanish 1838-48, Italian 1851-60 and London 1860-64. McKay considered that 'within his limits he shows great talent, and few painters have brought more pleasure to their countrymen'. As an artist, especially a watercolourist, he was unusually dispassionate, a quality which together with his finely balanced composition sometimes led to a mistaken criticism of dullness. The architectural balance which he sought and so often obtained revealed an inner freshness beyond apparent repetition. Lived at 7 Fitzroy St, Fitzroy Square, London. Elected Hon. RSA 1829, ARA 1838, RA 1841. Exhibited RA(101) 1826-1864, RSA(31) 1822-1865 & GI 1861-2. Represented in BM, V & A, NGS, Aberdeen AG, Glasgow AG, Edinburgh City collection, Brodick Castle (NTS), Brodie Castle (NTS), Blackburn AG, Bury AG, Doncaster AG, Dudley AG, Leeds City AG, Leicester AG, Manchester AG, Newport AG, Williamson AG (Birkenhead), Fitzwilliam (Cambridge), Portsmouth City Museum, Ulster Museum, Nat Gall of Canada (Ottawa), Nat Gall of South Africa (Cape Town), Victoria AG (Australia), Sydney AG (Australia).

**Bibl:** AJ 1858, 201; 1865, 43; 1867, 21; Armstrong 43-45; J. Ballantine, The Life of David Roberts RA, 1866; Barbican AG, London 'David Roberts', (Ex Cat 1986); Kenneth Bendiner, 'David Roberts in the Middle East: social and religious themes', Art History 6, Mar 1983; Bryan; Brydall 313-323; Caw 153-5; Conn 51 (1918) 51, 59; 68 (1924) 48; 69 (1924) 195; 86 (1930) 402, 406; Helen Guiterman, David Roberts RA, London 1878; Halsby 78-82; M. Hardie, Vol III, 1968, 179-183 illus; Houfe; Irwin 331-4; Maas 95; McKay 260-266; Macmillan [SA] 142,145-7 et passim; Old English Watercolour Society 1947, III 179-183 et passim; Portfolio 1887, 45, 136-7; Reynolds 'British Artists Abroad, Roberts in Spain' etc, Geog. Mag XXI 1949; J. Ruskin, 'Modern Painters II', Acad Notes chap vii, 1855-9.

**ROBERTS, Derek** **1947-**
Born Berwick-upon-Tweed. Painter of abstracts in watercolour, oil, ink and pastel. Trained Edinburgh College of Art 1966-71. Composes 'complex configurations of form and colour, transforming them into harmonious abstract paintings which are an analogue of nature'. Held his first one man show in 1977. His work was included in the exhibition 'Scottish Art Since 1900' at the SNGMA,1989. Lives and works in a farmhouse on the northern edge of the Pentland Hills. Represented in SNGMA.

**Bibl:** Hartley 162; Laing AG, Newcastle-upon-Tyne, 'Four Seasons,: paintings by Derek Roberts' (Ex Cat 1988); Macmillan [SA] 400; SAC Edinburgh, 'Derek Roberts: Summer Shadows, Winter Footpaths' (Ex Cat 1985).

**ROBERTS, Elspeth** **fl 1984-**
Aberdeen and Glasgow-based painter mainly of still life and semi-abstracts. Exhibits RSA(11), GI & AAS, latterly from 81 Blairbeth Rd, Burnside.

**ROBERTS, Miss H G** **1851-1947**
Amateur watercolourist from Selkirk. Exhibited a landscape at the RSA in 1877.

**ROBERTS, John** **1768-1803**
Born Scotland; died New York. Miniature painter; also portraits in crayons, mezzotints and stipple engraving. Went to New York 1793 but soon afterwards abandoned art in favour of experimentations in steam navigation. Keen amateur musician, and an alcoholic. In 1799 he engraved a portrait of Washington.

**Bibl:** Bolton; Bushnell; Fielding; Long, 365; Stauffer vol 1,223; vol 2,446.

**ROBERTS, John** **fl 1882-1930**
Edinburgh painter in oil and watercolour of flowers, animals, cattle and landscape. Married Janet, oldest daughter of Joseph Denovan Adam(qv), settling in Drummond Lodge, Callander. Travelled the country extensively, living in Liverpool 1882, Edinburgh 1889, Stirling 1891, Glasgow 1896 and Dunblane 1897 where for a brief time he taught at the Craigmill school(qv), and Callander (1906). Although a cattle painter his work was inferior to that of David Gauld(qv) whose compositions he sometimes sought to emulate. Exhibited RSA(17), RSW(4), GI(38) & L(3).

**ROBERTS, Kenneth** **1932-1995**
Born Arbroath, Mar 26; died Fowlis Easter, Feb 15. Painter of landscape, rural scenery and still life; also lithographer. Studied Duncan of Jordanstone College 1950-55 under Alberto Morrocco(qv). The influence of McIntosh Patrick(qv) was apparent

in most of his work. Specialised in local landscape in all its changing moods and seasons. Produced some memorable lithographic images of Dundee in the 1950s. After teaching in Aberdeen and Brechin, became principal art teacher, Harris Academy (Dundee) 1956-93. Trustee of the Orchar Gallery (Broughty Ferry). Important retrospective exhibition 1996. In 1984 he moved to Balloch, Foulis Easter, by Dundee. Exhibited 18 works at the RSA from 1954, occasionally at the AAS. In 1953 and again in 1987 exhibited a coloured lithograph at the GI.
**Bibl:** David M Walker, 'Kenneth Roberts: the Angus Year' ex cat 1996.

**ROBERTS, Miss Laura** **fl 1954**
Glasgow portrait miniaturist. Exhibited GI(2) from Woodlands Terrace.

**ROBERTS, M L W** **fl 1887**
Edinburgh watercolour painter of flowers and figure subjects; exhibited RSA(2).

**ROBERTS, Mrs Margaret A** **fl 1949**
Edinburgh watercolourist. Exhibited GI(1) from Ravelston Dykes.

**ROBERTS, Richard James** **fl 1898-1907**
Painter of dead game, landscape and flowers. Exhibited RSA(5), GI(4) & L(2) from addresses in Stirling and later Dollar.

**ROBERTSON, Miss A K** **fl 1908-1914**
Painter. Exhibited RA(2), RSA(1) and GI(1), formerly from London and then at the outbreak of WWI from Edinburgh.

**ROBERTSON, A Struan** **fl 1897-1918**
Painter in oil and watercolour of landscapes and country scenes. Probably father of Miss Struan Robertson(qv), with whom he is often confused. His work was powerful, clear-cut and attractive although sometimes suffering from overly broad handling of paint accentuated by the use of coarse-grained canvases. Exhibited GI(14) from 79 West Regent Street, Glasgow, latterly from Eaglesham, nr Glasgow.

**ROBERTSON, Adam** **fl 1799-1827**
Edinburgh artist. All that is known of his life is that in 1799 he was apprenticed to John Donaldson and William Neilson and in 1831 he was elected a Burgess of Edinburgh. That year he took on as apprentices Benjamin Findlay and David Aitken Ogilvy.

**ROBERTSON, Agnes Muir** **fl 1898**
Painter in watercolour of buildings. Exhibited a view of the 'Old Leper Hospital, near Durham' at the RSA from the UP Manse, North Berwick.

**ROBERTSON, Ailsa** **fl 1943-1954**
Edinburgh painter of continental scenes and Scottish landscapes. Exhibited RSA & GI from Ainslie Place.

**ROBERTSON, Aitken** **fl 1963-1970**
Edinburgh landscape and topographical artist; exhibited RSA(4) & GI(1).

**ROBERTSON, Alan Keith** **fl 1910-1927**
Architect. Responsible for Moray House College of Education (1910-13); Moredun Research Institute (1924-7) and began the East Suffolk Rd hostels for lady students (1917).
**Bibl:** Gifford 184,582,638.

**ROBERTSON, Alec R** **fl 1896-1906**
Aberdeen painter of landscape and coastal scenes. Exhibited AAS(3) including a view of the Muchalls coastline, from 59 Duthie Terrace.

**ROBERTSON, Alexander** **1772-1841**
Born Aberdeen 13 May; died New York. Portrait miniaturist also landscape painter and etcher. 4th son of William R. of Drumnahoy, Cluny parish, Monymusk, Aberdeenshire. Brother of Andrew(qv) and Archibald R(qv). Apprenticed to Andrew Bell. In London he studied under Samuel Shelley before going to New York 1791 where together with his brothers he started the Columbian Drawing Academy at 79 Liberty St. In 1799 went to the Lakes and to Canada, painting many pictures. After 1802 his reputation and demand as a teacher prevented much further painting. Married 1800. In his early days he etched a number of illustrations for early issues of the *Scots Magazine* from drawings by Clerk of Eldin. Among his pupils was the engraver Robert Scott(qv). Because all three brothers often signed themselves only 'A Robertson' it is sometimes difficult to identify which of the trio did the work. Named as a subscriber to David Crawford's *Poems chiefly in the Scottish Dialect,* 1799. Elected Secretary of the American Academy 1817-25 and Keeper 1820-1835; he was intensely interested in public education and was an original incorporator of what later became the huge public school system of New York. Contemporaries spoke of his hard-working, studious and gentle nature. Exhibited American Academy from 1817.
**Bibl:** Bryan; Brydall 203; ; Bushnell; Foskett 471.

**ROBERTSON, Alex** **fl 1957**
Glasgow landscape painter in watercolours. Exhibited 'Lister Burn, Lamlash' at the GI, from Loanfoot Ave.

**ROBERTSON, Alexander** **1927-1978**
Born Scotland. Painter and sculptor. Studied forestry at Edinburgh University and attended evening classes at the Edinburgh College of Art. Forestry officer in Malaya and Hong Kong 1946-59. Returning to Europe he enrolled at the Accademie de Belle Arte, Florence. Settled in the Trossachs 1960 and began painting full-time. First one-man exhibition in Glasgow 1964. The following year he moved to Norfolk where he established a community of artists. In 1968 began creating environmental installations and in the 1970s moved into sculpture and painted wooden constructions. Exhibited GI(1).

**ROBERTSON, Alexander Duff** **1807-1886**
Glasgow painter in oil, watercolour and charcoal of landscapes and portraits. Taught drawing in Glasgow and painted a number of very good views of the city in pencil and watercolour. Exhibited RSA(3) from 48 Dundas Street. A fine sensitively rendered charcoal portrait of the artist 'John Milne Donald' is in SNPG; represented also in Glasgow AG.
**Bibl:** Halsby 281.

**ROBERTSON, Canon Alfred J** **fl 1934-1938**
Obscure watercolour painter. Exhibited mainly at the Walker Gallery, London. A work of his was sold at Sotheby's Feb 25, 1975.

**ROBERTSON, Miss Alison** **fl 1943**
Glasgow designer. Exhibited a block and screen printed fabric design GI.

**ROBERTSON, Alison M** **fl 1943-1946**
Aberdeen portrait and landscape artist; exhibited RSA(6).

**ROBERTSON, Anderson Bain** **fl 1957-1988**
Glasgow-based painter of figurative works and architectural subjects. Moved in 1961 to Saltcoats and then, in 1981, to Troon, Ayrshire. Exhibited RSA(14) & GI(25) 1957-1988.

**ROBERTSON, Andrew ARHA** **1777-1845**
Born Aberdeen, 14 Oct; died Hampstead, London, 6 Dec. As a boy he studied as a scene painter, also as a portraitist and miniaturist. Before leaving Scotland he studied under Nasmyth and Raeburn, but still found time for more general academic studies enabling him to graduate MA in 1794. In 1797 he entered the RA Schools and after some hesitation settled in London, establishing a practice as a miniature painter. In this he was extremely successful, painting a number of distinguished sitters including members of the Royal family over a career spanning forty years. Both his brothers, Alexander(qv) and Archibald(qv), were also miniaturists. Always fond of music - at the age of 16 he was Director of Concerts in Aberdeen and his weekly private concerts were known to a wide range of people in London. His work was noticed by Benjamin West whose miniature portrait he painted. In 1803 was among those responsible for establishing the Artists' Volunteer Corps. Appointed miniature painter to the Duke of Sussex 1805. Visited Paris 1804 and 1808, and in 1809 was a member of the Associated Artists in Watercolours with whom, in 1808, he exhibited portraits of five princesses. Among his pupils were Francis Cruickshank(qv) and Sir William Charles Ross(qv) who for a time was his assistant. He used watercolour in a meticulous but delicate manner. Foskett records that his best miniatures were reminiscent of Raeburn and that 'he sketched

in the features in brown monochrome, and when painting, placed his table so that the light slanted over his left shoulder, his sitter being in front of him, rather to the right'. Personally very popular, on his retirement 1841 was presented with a testimonial inscribed 'To the Father of Miniature Painting'. Generally considered to be one of the finest miniaturists of the 19th century. He married twice, one son (Edward) becoming a miniaturist and a daughter Emily (of his second wife), who edited *Letters and Papers of Andrew Robertson.* Exhibited RA(292) and elsewhere, after 1830 from his studio at 19 Berners St. Represented in V & A, NPG, NGS, Ashmolean Museum, Royal collection.
**Bibl:** Bryan (long entry); Butchart 18-19,35,40; Caw 90; Foskett; Halsby 281; Irwin 217-9 et passim; Long; Macmillan [SA] 151,161-2,166; Emily Robertson(ed), Letters and Papers of Andrew Robertson AM, London 1895, 4.

**ROBERTSON, Archibald Lt-Gen** **1745-1813**
Died Lawers, Perthshire Feb 13. Amateur landscape painter. First cousin of Robert Adam(qv). Professional soldier and trained engineer who attained the rank of Lt-Gen. Served in America and his book, *Diaries and Sketches in America* (1762-1780) was published in 1930. While involved in the War of Independence he sketched landscapes in monochrome watercolour showing firm drawing and sensitive composition. In 1916 a sketchbook, previously in the possession of Baroness Semphill and Mary Grey of Northants, was presented to Rev. CDR Williamson of Lawers. The sketches then found their way to New York PL 1919 who published them as being an important reference for life in the USA at that time. Other drawings appeared in vol 5 of *The Iconography of Manhattan Island.* After peace was declared in 1783 he married and settled down on the family estate in Lawers. Most of his work is in New York but there are examples in NGS and the National Gallery of Wales.
**Bibl:** Arch. Robertson, his diaries and sketches in America 1762-1780, New York 1930.

**ROBERTSON, Archibald** **1765-1835**
Born Monymusk, Aberdeenshire, 8 May; died New York, 6 Dec. Painter of miniatures in oil and watercolour and of landscapes, often in crayon; also designer, aquatintist and etcher. Elder brother of Andrew(qv) and Alexander Robertson(qv). Became friendly with Raeburn in Edinburgh where he first studied. Went to London 1786 where he studied under Shirreff(qv) and an artist called Peacock. He also seems to have been a pupil of Reynolds. In 1791 he was sent to New York. The Earl of Buchan had asked him to deliver a box made from part of an oak tree that had sheltered William Wallace so the young man took the opportunity of also visiting Philadelphia where he painted a miniature of Washington on a slab of marble now in the New York Historical Society. Settled in New York establishing the Columbian Academy with his brother Alexander, who joined him in 1792. In 1795 he executed a fine aquatint of 'Edinburgh from the north-west' after Riddell and in 1802 published his *Elements of the Graphic Arts.* Co-founder and director of the American Academy of Art. His paintbox is now in the Rossenbach Museum, Philadelphia. Foskitt records an oil portrait of 'George Washington (1732-1799)' at Sulgrave Manor, Northampton, commissioned by David Stewart, 11th Earl of Buchan and presented to Sulgrave Manor by the 15th Earl of Buchan 1951. Represented in Edinburgh City collection, Smithsonian Institute (Washington), Metropolitan Museum of Art (New York), Philadelphia Museum of Art.
**Bibl:** Bryan; Bushnell; Fielding's American Engravers, Supplement to Stauffer, 1927,36-7; Foskett 472; Irwin 150,217; Macmillan [SA] 151.

**ROBERTSON, Barbara** **1945-**
Born Broughty Ferry. Printmaker and illustrator. Trained Gray's School of Art, Aberdeen. Fond of strong colours and absract design. First solo exhibition in Dunblane 1980 followed by Glasgow 1981. Exhibits RSA & AAS(1) from 10 The Row, Dougalstown. Represented Aberdeen AG, Glasgow AG, Lillie AG(Milngavie).

**ROBERTSON, Bella T** **fl 1896**
Aberdeen flower painter; exhibited AAS(1) from 82 Blenheim Place.

**ROBERTSON, Bessie M** **fl 1897-1922**
Edinburgh painter in oil of portraits and domestic genre; exhibited RSA(27) & AAS(1), from 37 Drummond Place.

**ROBERTSON, Bruce** **fl 1910**
Fife landscape painter and etcher; exhibited AAS(2) from The Studio, Pittenweem.

**ROBERTSON, C H** **fl 1824-1840**
Painter in oil of figurative studies and sporting subjects. Possibly related to J Robertson(qv). Best known for his painting of 'Caddie Willie' c 1839 (alias William Gunn) which he may have painted twice. The Royal Burgess Golf Club of Blackheath owns one of the originals, the second went missing after its inclusion on loan in the Glasgow Exhibition 1911. A lithograph by Ballantine of Edinburgh was dedicated to the 'Clubs of Edinburgh and Leith'. Painted the portrait of 'Kittie Fell winning a horse race at Tinwald Downs, Dumfries' 1833.
**Bibl:** Wingfield.

**ROBERTSON, Caroline** **fl 1981**
Dundee painter. Trained at one of the Scottish Schols of Art. Exhibited AAS(1) from 45 Lyon St.

**ROBERTSON, Charles** **fl 1790-d1799**
Died before May 1799. Son of James Robertson, minister at Loch Broom. In 1790 he was apprenticed to Alexander Weir remaining with him for seven years. The same year he was elected a Burgess of Edinburgh and had among his apprentices David Martin, John Michie, Andrew Mitchell and John Ronald. At about this time there was in Edinburgh an auctioneer and seller of artists' material called **Charles ROBERTSON**, reported by Thomson to have also had a decorative painting business. It is possible that this was the same person.

**ROBERTSON, Charles** **fl 1860-1869**
Edinburgh-based painter in oil of landscapes and local scenes. Moved to Glasgow 1867. Not to be confused with the English painter Charles Robertson RE RWS (1844-1891). Exhibited RSA(5) & GI(1).

**ROBERTSON, Charles Kay** **fl 1877-1931**
Edinburgh painter in oil and watercolour of mainly portraits but also landscape, game, interiors, buildings and flowers. Married to Jane R(qv). Exhibited RSA(57), including a portrait of 'Mrs David Octavius Hill' 1883, also RA(14), GI(11) & L(1).

**ROBERTSON, Mrs Charles Kay (Jane)** **fl 1885-1923**
Dundee miniature portrait painter; also occasionally painted domestic genre. Settled at first in Edinburgh but shortly after her marriage to Charles Kay R(qv) 1897, she moved to London. In 1899 her portrait of the 'Earl of Hopetoun, Lord Chamberlain' was shown at the RA. Exhibited RA(10), RSA(1), AAS(2) & SWA(1), latterly from 28 Tite St, Chelsea.

**ROBERTSON, Charlotte Bryce** **c1948-**
Born England but has lived and worked for most of her life in Scotland. Painter of landsdcape and seascape; teacher. Trained Carlisle College of Art 1969-70 and Edinburgh College of Art 1970-74 followed by a year at Hospitalfield. Awarded Andrew Grant Travelling scholarship 1975, Governor's Prize (Hospitalfield) 1974. Especially fascinated and impressed by the importance of the sky to light and texture. First solo exhibition Symington, 1974. Combines painting with teaching from her home in Fochabers, Moray. Exhibits Lillie AG (Milngavie), Dick Institute (Kilmarnock).

**ROBERTSON, David** **fl 1897-1901**
Kilmarnock painter in oil of landscapes; exhibited 'Afterglow' at the RSA & GI(2).

**ROBERTSON, David ARSA** **1834-1925**
Born Strathblane, Perthshire; died Edinburgh, 20 Feb. Architect and etcher. Trained Glasgow School of Art. Served an apprenticeship in the office of the Edinburgh City Architect, his early career was as a consulting architect for the United Presbyterian Church of Scotland, a position which brought him into contact with current ecclesiastical affairs. Became President, Edinburgh Architectural Association 1865, re-elected 1887. Co-founder of the Scottish Arts Club. Elected ARSA 1893. Responsible for the North Morningside United Free Church (1879-81), designed in the Norman style; Gorgie Memorial Hall (1887) and the John Ker Memorial Church, Polwarth Gardens,

Edinburgh. Served during WW1 with the Artists Rifles. Not to be confused with the painter David M Robertson(qv) who was working about the same time and who was incorrectly assignated ARSA in the RA list, nor with the minor Kilmarnock painter of the same name. Exhibited RSA(19) between 1878 and 1902. His first exhibit was a design for additions to David Bryce Mansion at Caerlee, Innerleithen. **Bibl:** Gifford 433,507,519,618.

**ROBERTSON, David** **fl 1942-1943**
Edinburgh portrait and figurative painter; exhibited RSA(3), from Alderbank Terrace.

**ROBERTSON, David** **fl 1953**
Glasgow painter of rural topography. Exhibited GI(2) from Battlefield Rd.

**ROBERTSON, David M** **fl 1883-d1909**
Born Edinburgh; died Douglas, IOM, Mar 7. Painter in oil and watercolour of landscapes and buildings. Principal, School of Art, Douglas, Isle of Man 1884-1909, having previously taught at Douglas Secondary School. Exhibited 'Irish landscape' at the RA 1892. Not to be confused with David Robertson the architect and etcher nor with the minor Kilmarnock painter of the same name. Exhibited RA(1), RSA(9), GI(2) & L(1). Represented in Manx Museum.

**ROBERTSON, Derek** **1967-**
Born St Andrews, 13 Jly. Trained at Duncan of Jordanstone School of Art 1985-9 graduating with an honours degree in Fine Art. In 1986 and 1987 runner-up for the Richardson Award and in 1987 obtained the Pat Holmes Memorial Prize. Won the James Guthrie Orchard Prize 1989. His works include an extensive range of material making three-dimensional constructions, installations and two-dimensional drawings, paintings and prints. Gains inspiration from the natural environment and man's relationship with it, extracting imagery from wildlife, landscape and agriculture. His first one man show was held in 1987. His work has been published by the Scottish Ornithologist Club, Nature Conservancy, The British Trust for Ornithology, Angus Bird Report and the Perthshire Bird Report. Illustrated a book on Scottish vernacular architecture.

**ROBERTSON, Duncan** **1966-**
Born Perth, Jan 18. Sculptor and printmaker. Educated Perth Academy, trained Edinburgh College of Art 1984-90 and Academie Bildenden Kunste (Munich) 1992-94. Gained Andrew Grant scholarship enabling him to visit New York and John Kinross scholarship which took him to Florence, both in 1990. Represented in Perth AG.

**ROBERTSON, Eleanor Moore** **1885-1955**
Born Glenwherry, Co Antrim, 26 Jly. Trained Glasgow School of Art 1905-8 under Fra Newbery(qv) and Jean Delville(qv). Father of the art critic Ailsa Tanner. Painter of figurative subjects and occasional landscapes. After marrying Dr RC Robertson(qv) went to Shanghai 1925-37 during which time was a member, Shanghai Art Club. Evacuated during the Sino-Japanese War 1937, returned to Scotland. First one-man exhibition with Ian MacNicol, Kilmarnock 1934. Represented in Lillie AG (Milngavie), Dick Institute, Kilmarnock (2).

**ROBERTSON, Edward** **1809-**
Scottish portrait miniaturist. Son of Andrew Robertson(qv) from his first marriage. Studied under his father before going to the RA Schools 1827. A miniature by him of his brother 'Captain Charles Robertson' was included in the Edinburgh Exhibition of 1965 (Captain Robertson was present at the signing of the Maori Treaty 1840 and Cape Robertson, New Zealand is named after him). It is believed that he died in Dublin but the exact date is unclear. His work closely resembles that of his father. Exhibited RA(11) 1830-1837 and visiting Dublin in the early 1830s (staying at 27 Dame Street) he exhibited a number of portrait miniatures at the RHA. A 'Self-portrait', painted in Dublin 1831, was sold at Sothebys on Jne 24, 1974. Exhibited RSA(6) 1833-1857. Represented in SNPG.
**Bibl:** Foskett 473.

**ROBERTSON, Edward Walton** **1919-**
Painter of landscape, portraits and domestic genre. Son of Eric and Cecile W(qv). Exhibited RSA(21) and two watercolours at the GI 1947.

**ROBERTSON, Ellen McT** **fl 1901-1919**
Edinburgh watercolourist; landscapes and rural genre. Exhibited RSA(7) & RSW(1) & GI(1).

**ROBERTSON, Elsa D** **fl 1902**
Edinburgh flower painter; exhibited RSA(1), from 205 Newhaven Rd.

**ROBERTSON, Emily C** **fl 1896**
Minor watercolour artist. Exhibited RSW(2) from Naparina, Cambuslang.

**ROBERTSON, Eric Harald Macbeth** **1887-1941**
Born Dumfries, 13 Feb; died Cheshire. Painter of portraits, landscapes and figure subjects in oil, occasional watercolour, chalk, pencil and pastel. Came to Edinburgh around the turn of the century, studied architecture at the Royal Institution School and Edinburgh College of Art. Influenced by the work of Burne-Jones and Rossetti. In Edinburgh he became friendly with John Duncan(qv) who introduced him to the world of Celtic myth and the Symbolist painters. In Duncan's studio he met Cecile Walton(qv), daughter of E A Walton(qv), who became his wife. In 1912 he showed in Edinburgh with J R Barclay, W O Hutchison, J G Spence Smith, A R Storrock and D M Sutherland; after more exhibitions in 1913 and 1914 the Edinburgh Group was formed 1919. Robertson's unconventional morality together with the nudity found in many of his works at the time scandalised Edinburgh. In 1917-18, while working with the French Ambulance Unit in France, he turned to landscapes in oil and pastel. In 1923, having been ostracised in Edinburgh, he parted from his wife and moved to Liverpool, sharing a studio with Sydney Merrills and joining the Merseyside Art Circle. His murals for a local public house, 'The Grapes', are still intact. He re-married but continued to drink heavily and after 1930 became increasingly depressed and his work declined. During his lifetime his pre-Raphaelite and Vorticist predelictions were out of fashion. A contemporary wrote that 'he had genius no one who ever came into contact with him could possibly doubt.' His son-in-law became his biographer. Principal works include 'The Picnic', 'Summer Clad', 'Dance Rhythm', and 'The Satin Stole'. Exhibited RA(2), RSA(47), RSW(3), GI(12) and in France. Represented in Glasgow AG(2), City of Edinburgh collection.
**Bibl:** 'Eric Robertson' (Edin. Ex Cat, 1974; intro by John Kemplay); Halsby 192-5,220; Hardie 142-3; John Kemplay, The Two Companions, Edinburgh 1991; Macmillan [SA] 335-7,339-340.

**ROBERTSON, Eva H** **fl 1931-1945**
Edinburgh painter of genre, usually in watercolours. Exhibited RSA (5) & GI(3).

**ROBERTSON, Ewan B** **fl 1911-1913**
Minor Edinburgh landscape painter and engraver. Mostly Northumbrian and Lothian views; also exhibited a drypoint etching 'On the Seine'. Exhibited RSA(5), AAS(2) & L(4) from 8 Murrayfield Drive.

**ROBERTSON, Fiona GRANT[see GRANT ROBERTSON, Fiona]**

**ROBERTSON, G** **fl 1866**
Edinburgh painter in oil, mostly domestic pets; exhibited RSA(1).

**ROBERTSON, Helen H** **fl 1890-1892**
Glasgow painter; exhibited 'Her best and only Bonnet' at the GI(1) from Dowanhill Gdns.

**ROBERTSON, I Murray** **1961-**
Glasgow graphic artist and printmaker. Trained Glasgow School of Art 1979-83 obtaining a post-graduate diploma 1984. From 1986 worked as a lithographer technician at the Glasgow Print Studio helping to further enhance the high degree of technical ability. This resulted in finely detailed line engraving technique of etching and dramatic effects achieved in the handling of coarse-grained wood blocks. Most scenes are typical industrial tableaux with figures and lowering skies. Participated in 1986 Bradford Print Bienniale. Exhibited extensively since 1983 at the RA, RSA in 1986 and 1989. Represented in SAC.

**ROBERTSON, Iain** **1949-**
Born Glasgow. Studied University of Reading 1968-72, trained

Chelsea School of Art 1972-3. Maker of painted constructions. Exhibits RSA since 1983 and at the AAS, from 8 Marine Terrace; also GI, latterly from Edinburgh.

**ROBERTSON, Iain** **c1960-**
Born Nicosia, Cyprus of Scottish parents. Abstract painter. Trained Cumbria College of Art 1978-9, Exeter College of Art 1979-82. Remained in Exeter to work at Spacex Studios. Won Pollock-Krasner Foundation award 1988, SAC award 1990. Returned to Edinburgh 1988. Takes 'visual delight that colour and texture can express in themselves' [Hare]. Early work was tentatively wrought in muted colours, with clear negative and positive areas. Prefers canvases in vertical or square form.
**Bibl:** W. Hare, Contemporary Painting in Scotland, 1993.

**ROBERTSON, Iain Murray** **1941-**
Glasgow lithographer. Trained Glasgow School of Art. Lithographic technician with Glasgow Print Studio. Exhibited GI 1984 from Bolton Drive.

**ROBERTSON, J B** **fl 1920-1944**
Glasgow painter of portraits, flowers and townscapes. Exhibited RSA(4) & GI(17), from Kelvinside Terrace and later Lubnaig Rd.

**ROBERTSON, James** **fl 1758-1770**
Minor early architect. His lasting memorial is the mansion Redhall House (1758) in Craiglockhart Drive, Edinburgh built for George Inglis of Auchendinny. Responsible for designing the parkland around Duddingston House (c1768) now largely incorporated into a golf course.
**Bibl:** Gifford 56,536,561.

**ROBERTSON, James** **fl 1821**
Scottish engraver and lithographer. Engraved maps of Scottish counties, 1821-2, working sometimes with Ballantyne(qv).
**Bibl:** Bushnell.

**ROBERTSON, James** **fl 1855-1856**
Amateur artist, illustrator and photographer. Married Christina Sanders(qv). Contributed an illustration of the Crimea to *ILN* 1855 and made daguerrotype pictures of the War after the photographer Roger Fenton had left the front. Later worked with Felice Beato and became an offical British photographer. Drawings based on his photographs appeared in *ILN* 1856.
**Bibl:** Houfe; 'The Camera goes to War', SAC, 1974-5, 58.

**ROBERTSON, Dr James** **fl 1937**
Amateur Aberdeenshire artist; exhibited a local landscape at the AAS, from Clifton House, Peterhead.

**ROBERTSON, Mrs James (née Christina Sanders) HRSA** **1775-1856**
Born Edinburgh. Portrait painter in miniature and full size portraits in both oil and watercolour; also painted occasional subject pieces and copied works of Correggio, Velasquez and Le Brun. Niece (or daughter) of the Fifeshire coach painter George Sanders. Married the artist James R(qv) 1823. Elected Hon. RSA 1829. In 1843 went to St Petersburg and painted the portraits of the Czar and Czarina, and was promptly made a member of the Imperial Academy in St Petersburg. In Paris 1836/7. By 1841 she was back in London. In 1844 her work was accompanied with an announcement that she had been elected to the Imperial Academy of Arts, St. Petersburg. Her work was widely known and respected for its excellent draughtsmanship and her particular skill at drawing hands. Many of her miniatures are large. In the Musée des Arts Decoratifs in Paris there is a large oval miniature by her dated 1848. According to Foster's catalogue of the Duke of Northumberland's miniatures, the collection contains a miniature of the '3rd Duke of Northumberland' and two of the '3rd Duchess of Northumberland", both large and both signed CR 1825. She exhibited 129 works at the RA including portraits of the 'Lord Chief Commissioner of the Jury Court of Scotland' 1827, 'The Duchess of Buccleuch' 1831, 'The Duke of Buccleuch' and 'The Marchioness of Lothian', both 1832, 'Baroness de Rothschild' 1837 and the 'Grand Duchesses Olga and Alexandrina, daughters of the Emperor of Russia' 1841. In 1843 her portrait of 'Czar Nicholas I and Czarina Alexandra Feodoravna' was exhibited at the RA. In 1860 her paintings of the Russian royal family were auctioned in London. Lived for many years at 36 Harley St before moving to 6 Bentinck St 1844. Exhibited RSA(11) 1829-1839. At the end of the 1980s the first British exhibition of her work was held at Edinburgh City Art Centre. She is represented by several royal portraits in the Winter Palace, St Petersburg.
**Bibl:** Long 369-70; Foskett 473-4; McKay.

**ROBERTSON James D** **fl 1863-1879**
Glasgow-based painter in gouache & watercolour. Worked in Scotland, Norfolk and Spain. Exhibited RSW, GI(1) from Ure Place.

**ROBERTSON, James Downie RSA RSW RGI** **1931-**
Born Cowdenbeath, Fife. Paints in oil and gouache, mainly landscapes and seascapes many of them based on local Renfrewshire scenes. Trained Glasgow School of Art 1950-1956, spending a post-diploma year in France, Holland, Italy, North Africa and Spain. Joined the staff at Glasgow School of Art in 1959. In 1967 became a full-time lecturer at the GSA, and between 1962 and 1972 ran a summer school in Kircudbright. Visiting lecturer Rhodes, Capetown 1970. Senior lecturer, Glasgow School of Art 1975-96. Joined Gray's School of Art in Aberdeen 1986 and the same year Dundee College of Art. In 1987 spent a year at Millersville University, Pennsylvania. Received several awards including the Cargill Award of the RGI 1971, May Marshall Brown Award of the RSW 1976, Gillies Award RSW 1981, Cargill Award RGI 1982, and the Graham Munro Award 1987. Regards himself less a landscape painter than one who uses the landscape as a starting point for works aimed at observation, memory and mood. Exhibits regularly RA, RSA, RGI, RSW. Lives in Kilbarchan, Ayrshire. Elected RSW 1962, ARSA 1974, RSA 1989. Represented in Glasgow AG, Edinburgh City collection, Lillie AG (Milngavie), Hunterian Museum (Glasgow University), RSA, SAC, Royal collection.

**ROBERTSON, James G** **fl 1880-1886**
Edinburgh painter in oil of landscapes and figures; exhibited RSA (8).

**ROBERTSON, James H** **fl 1868-1870**
Glasgow landscape painter in oil; scenery in Berwickshire and the Lothians. Exhibited RSA(3).

**ROBERTSON, Mrs J H** **fl 1900**
Glasgow flower and landscape painter; exhibited AAS(2) from 18 Markland Terrace, Hillhead.

**ROBERTSON, John** **fl 1875-1900**
Inverness architect. Worked in Edinburgh where he designed a number of dwellings in the West Port (18-26) and the lanceted Gothic St Andrew Church, Craigmillar (1900).
**Bibl:** Gifford 505,538.

**ROBERTSON, John** **fl 1880-1900**
Dunfermline painter in watercolour of landscapes, especially in Fife. A competent watercolourist who often signed with a monogram. Moved to Edinburgh c1891. Exhibited RSA(6).

**ROBERTSON, John Ewart** **1820-1879**
Born Edinburgh. Animal and portrait painter of Kelso who later moved to Liverpool; specialised in equestrian portraits. Between 1838 & 1863 exhibited 22 works at the RSA including a portrait of the 'Duke of Roxburgh' 1844. Represented by a portrait of 'Robert Andrew Macfie' in the Edinburgh City collection, also Manchester AG.

**ROBERTSON, John Morton** **fl 1868-1885**
Perth and Edinburgh painter in oil of landscapes and figurative works. Married to an artist. In 1869 was living in Methven, near Perth. Exhibited RSA(3) & 'Leith pier' at the AAS, latterly from Regent Terrace, Edinburgh.

**ROBERTSON, Mrs John Morton** **fl 1871**
Perth figurative painter in oil. Wife of John Morton R(qv). Exhibited 'An unexpected visitor' at the RSA.

**ROBERTSON, John Murray** **1844-1901**
Architect. Trained under Andrew Heiton(qv). 'By far the most progressive and able of the late Victorian architects in this area...he seemed unable to accept commissions as offered...had he taken a

partner or restricted his output he might have become one of the greatest architects of his age' [Walker & Gauldie]. Narrow religious beliefs prevented him taking a partner while overwork led to stress and an early death. In the Egypto-Greek style favoured by Alexander Thomson(qv) he designed India Buildings, 86 Bell St, Dundee (1874). Turning to a half-timbered manner designed The Bughties, 76 Camphill Rd, Broughty Ferry, Angus (1822-95). Regularly visited the Low Countries. His last favoured style was akin to the Jacobean exemplified in Seathwood, Perth Rd, Dundee (1883) and the Caledonian Insurance Co. office, Meadowside, Dundee (1886). Pioneered the design of mass-concrete mansion houses in Scotland: Beachtower, Ralston Rd, Dundee (1875) and Moyness, 76 Grove Rd, West Ferry (1876).
**Bibl:** Bruce Walker & W S Gauldie, Architects and Architecture on Tayside, Dundee 1984, 136-8,139(illus).

**ROBERTSON, Jonathan** **fl 1968-1986**
Glasgow painter and printmaker. Trained Gray's School of Art, Aberdeen. Exhibited GI(13) 1968-1986 & AAS 1983-6, from 13 Spence St and latterly Kingsborough Gdns.

**ROBERTSON, Kay** **fl 1892-1899**
Portrait painter. Married Christina Saunders(qv) and moved to London. According to a correspondent in the *Scots Magazine* (Jan 1977) he exhibited at the RA and in 1892 was living at 146 Princes St. But there is no record of an exhibit at the RA, the confusion being caused by separate entries in the RA lists, although all exhibits were by his wife. It was also said that in 1895 he painted the portrait of a beautiful young woman, possibly Lily Langtry, Edward VII's mistress. After his marriage lived at 28 Tite St, Chelsea.

**ROBERTSON, M Hope** **fl 1950**
Moffat portrait and landscape painter; exhibited RSA(2) & GI(1) from The Lodge.

**ROBERTSON, McCulloch** **fl 1905-1916**
Painter of landscapes in watercolour, especially river scenes. Lived for a time at Nethermoss, Muckart, by Dollar, then Dunkeld 1912 and London 1913. Exhibited RI(12), GI(1), AAS(1), L(6) & London Salon(2).
**Bibl:** Halsby 231.

**ROBERTSON, Margaret (Mrs M McGeetyan)** **1919-?**
Born 16 Jan. Painter in oil most often of landscapes. Trained privately by Bernard Adams. The major influence on her work was Cézanne. Showed at Pitlochry Theatre Festival 1975. As the years passed her colourful landscapes became more abstract with a fuller interpretation of colour and less attention to detail. Exhibited RSA, GI and Paisley Institute.

**ROBERTSON, Miss Mary** **fl 1920-1927**
Minor Glasgow landscape painter. Exhibited at GI(2) & L(2) from 10 Grafton Sq.

**ROBERTSON, Mary I** **fl 1966-1974**
Aberdeen painter of townscapes and fishing scenes. Exhibited AAS (8), from 20 Mosman Place.

**ROBERTSON, Minnie B** **fl 1909**
Little known Ayr sculptor; exhibited a bas relief of a boy's head at the GI from Bellarina.

**ROBERTSON, Murray** **fl 1989-**
Scottish engraver. Exhibited 'Inheritance' at the RSA in 1989.

**ROBERTSON, Richard Ross RSA FRBS** **1914-**
Born Aberdeen, 10 Sep. Sculptor; clay, wood, bronze, stone and ivory, with a preference for carving in stone or wood. Trained Glasgow School of Art 1933-34 and Aberdeen 1934-39 under T B Huxley-Jones(qv). Lectured at Gray's School of Art, Aberdeen from 1946 until retiring 1979. Also executed portraits including 'The late Lord Boothby'. His work aims at a synthesis of the figurative in the abstract, influenced by natural objects after Greek sculpture and the sculptures of Chartres, Egypt and India. Lived in Blairgowrie. Elected SSA 1947, ARBS 1951, FRBS 1963, ARSA 1969, RSA 1977. Exhibited regularly RA, RSA, GI, AAS & SSA, latterly from 7 Polmuir Rd, Aberdeen. Represented in Aberdeen AG, Metropolitan Museum (New York), Princeton University (USA), Boston University (USA).

**ROBERTSON, Robert** **fl 1957-1958**
Angus painter of genre and interiors; exhibited RSA(2), from Arbroath.

**ROBERTSON, Robert** **fl 1957-1965**
Glasgow painter of topographical landscapes. Exhibited GI(5) from Ormonde Ave.

**ROBERTSON, Robert Cantley** **fl 1927-1940**
Edinburgh painter, stained glass designer and engraver. Portraits and landscapes. Not to be confused with three other artists with the same initials all working at the same time from Edinburgh and Kilmarnock. Exhibited RSA(16) & GI(2).

**ROBERTSON, Dr Robert Cecil** **fl 1932-1940**
Painter of landscapes in oil, specialising in oriental subjects; also engraver. Public health specialist. Skilled technician. Married the artist Eleanor Moore R(qv). Employed the Glasgow dealer Ian McNicol(qv) as his agent. Exhibited RSA(5), RA(1) & GI(9) from Kilmarnock and Edinburgh.

**ROBERTSON, Robert Cowan** **1863-1910**
Born Glasgow, 25 Dec; died London. Painter mainly in oil of marines and landscapes. His main claim to attention is probably his close friendship with and informal influence upon Samuel John Peploe(qv). Together they visited the Outer Hebrides 1897 on a small sailing yacht owned by Robertson who had private means. Robertson built a studio at Borve on Barra and with Peploe paid several visits to the island, painting furiously. When only 25 he had already come to the attention of Caw who thought the artist 'shows promise and good qualities'. In 1896 he exhibited 'A Mountain Torrent' at the RSA and in 1898 'Lobster Fishers'. Enjoyed working on a large scale, Cursiter records how he had no hesitation about taking a six foot canvas into the open. He had a fine feeling for open air and the rushing movement of the sea. Cursiter says that 'his pale, sparkling sea-pieces with dancing waves, missed excellence by the narrowest margin'. A lovely Orkney girl called Maggie Leask was a favourite model of Alexander Roche's whom Robertson introduced to Peploe, also her younger sister Nell. Retained a studio at 15 Shandwick Place, Edinburgh. Not to be confused with either of his contemporaries, Robert Cantley Robertson(qv) or Dr Robert Cecil Robertson(qv) nor with Robert Currie Robertson(qv). Exhibited RSA(16), also AAS(1), GI(4), L(5) & RHA(2).
**Bibl:** Caw 333.

**ROBERTSON, Robert Currie** **fl 1911-c1973**
Painter and etcher of architectural subjects and landscapes. Lived at 59 Dean Street, Kilmarnock and later at Juniper Green. Exhibited RSA 1973, RSW & GI(5).

**ROBERTSON, Ruth S** **fl 1970**
Aberdeen painter. Trained Gray's School of Art, Aberdeen. Exhibited once at AAS, from 4 Oakdale Terrace.

**ROBERTSON, Miss S Isabella** **fl 1864-1874**
Edinburgh painter in oil of portraits, often women, and occasional landscapes. Her first non-portrait was in 1872 when she showed a study sketched on board a Rhine steamer, and the following year exhibited 'Bridge on the Moselle'. Exhibited RSA(32).

**ROBERTSON, Seonaid Mairi** **1912-?**
Born Perth, 27 Jan. Potter, psychologist and teacher. Educated Perth Academy, Edinburgh University and Edinburgh College of Art, also on the continent. Fellow of Edinburgh College of Art 1945-48 and lecturer, Goldsmith's College 1945-6, Assistant Art Adviser, WRCC and Senior Lecturer in Art at Bretton Hall 1949-56. Research Fellow 1953-4 and Senior Research Fellow in Education at Leeds University 1957-9. Lived in England. Signed her work 'SMR' and exhibited widely at the SSA and in the provinces.

**ROBERTSON, Sheila Macleod RSMA SWA** **c1940-**
Scottish painter in oils of marines, seascapes and coastal scenes. Trained at Watford and the Central School, London. She quickly

developed a particular interest in the light and mood of sea, coast and landscape. Held many successful solo shows in London and in Scotland. Elected member, Royal Society of Marine Artists 1969, also professional member, St Ives Society of Artists. To increase her knowledge of the weather and sea conditions of the western seaboard she cruises as a crew member on an ocean yacht. Her work, produced mainly with the palette knife, is regularly exhibited at the RI, ROI & RSMA. When not sailing she lives in Edinburgh.

**ROBERTSON, Miss Struan** **fl 1935-1948**
Painter in oil, watercolour, pastel and gouache. Probably the daughter of A. Struan Robertson(qv), with whom she is often confused, although his work was handled more broadly and is on a larger scale and generally harder in its presentation. One of the most neglected and underrated Scottish painters. Her work showed a strong affinity with the Dutch School and in its strong harmonious balance of colour with the finer examples of Robert McGown Coventry(qv). Fond of portraying Dutch canal scenes and fisherfolk by the shore often with colourful sails reflected in sparkling water. Most of her work is small-scale, fine and softly coloured, conveying a sense of tranquillity mirrored in the peaceful nature of her compositions. At the time of her only exhibit at the RSA in 1938 she was living at 149 Warrender Park Road, Edinburgh.

**ROBERTSON, Thomas** **fl 1846-1880**
Leith painter in oil of landscapes and marines. Moved to Edinburgh c1847. Not to be confused with Thomas Robertson(qv) who was painting at the same time in Glasgow. Exhibited RSA(21) among them 'The SS *Mercator* running up the Forth' (1849)), latterly from 15 Haymarket Terrace.

**ROBERTSON, Thomas** **fl 1856-1896**
Glasgow oil painter of flowers and landscape. Not to be confused with Thomas Robertson of Edinburgh(qv) nor with the Glasgow animal and flower painter Thomas R(qv). Exhibited RSA(14) & GI(4).

**ROBERTSON, Thomas** **fl 1861-d1866**
Glasgow painter of portraits, mostly military, and domestic animals. *The Glasgow Herald* referred to a print of a posthumous exhibit 1867 'The Volunteers of Glasgow' as 'the masterpiece of a clever artist, who had already brought himself into notice by studies of a similar character'.

**ROBERTSON, Thomas Saunders** **1835-1923**
Born Blairgowrie, Perthshire; died Broughty Ferry, 2 Mar. Architect, occasional watercolour draughtsman; also writer. Educated Perth Academy. Trained under Edward(qv), joined Andrew Hamilton of Edinburgh as a draughtsman before becoming partner in the firm of Edward & Robertson, responsible for the final version of Carbet Castle, Camphill Rd, Broughty Ferry. Designed a number of churches including St Stephen's, Broughty Ferry, St Enoch's parish church, Rosebank parish church and the Catholic church, Constitution Rd, Dundee. Executed interesting if rather coarse landscapes. Wrote and illustrated *The Progress of Art in English Church Architecture*. Member and Vice-president, Dundee Art Committee. Associated with his friend J G Orchar(qv) in the collection which led to the Orchar Gallery. Keern angler, curler and golfer. Exhibited 'At Carnoustie' at the RSA & GI(4), all architectural drawings.
**Bibl:** Dundee Courier, 5 Mar 1923(obit); Proceedings, Antiquaries of Scotland, 3rd ser, vol 8, 1897-8; Transactions of the Scottish Ecclesiological Soc.,vol 6,pt 3, no.18,1920-21; Bruce Walker & W S Gauldie, Architects and Architecture on Tayside, Dundee 1984, 142(illus),144; David M Walker, 'Architects & Architecture in Dundee 1770-1914', Abertay Hist. Soc., No 18; 1977.

**ROBERTSON, Thomas W** **fl 1906-1912**
Minor painter of 74 Norse Road, Scotstoun; exhibited GI(2).

**ROBERTSON, Tom ROI RBA RI** **1850-1947**
Born Glasgow, 25 Jne; died Eastbourne, 3 Feb. Painter in oil, pastel and watercolour; landscapes and marines. Trained Glasgow School of Art and in Paris under Benjamin Constant. In 1898 visited Morocco where he painted in the south of the country and in the Atlas Mountains. Worked for a time in Venice frequently returning to Paris where he received an honourable mention at the Paris Salon 1904, and a gold medal at Nantes 1910. Painted in an impressionist style with gentle tones; when using watercolours he employed bright colours and was particularly good at depicting dappled sunlit, often reflected on water. His work is idiosyncratic, sometimes reminiscent of the pointillistes. His principal works include 'En Ecosse', 'The Haven under the Hill', 'Silvery Sea' and 'Nocturne, Venice'. Elected RBA 1896, ROI 1912, RI 1912, Hon retd ROI 1937. Lived in London before retiring to Eastbourne. Exhibited RSA(7), RSW(4), ROI(51), RI(2), RHA(1), RBA(52), RA(15), AAS(2), GI(92) & L(11).
**Bibl:** Caw 392; Halsby 281; Wingfield.

**ROBERTSON, Walter Wood** **1845-1907**
Architect. Succeeded Robert Matheson(qv) at H M Office of Works. 'A good caretaker and adapter but less distinguished in new buildings' [Gifford]. Designed the 'purple-faced authoritarian' Royal Observatory (1892) and the more unassuming attractive neo-Jacobean Post Office (1904) in Portobello.
**Bibl:** Gifford 70,125,186,286,437,443,486,575,653.

**ROBERTSON, Warde** **fl 1874-1877**
Glasgow portrait painter in oil; exhibited RSA(3) & GI(1).

**ROBERTSON, William** **fl 1752-1766**
Leven architect. Practice in Dundee. Mainly industrial designs, all now demolished although some photographs remain including one of the 'Packhouses', Dundee.
**Bibl:** Bruce Walker & W S Gauldie, Architects and Architecture on Tayside, Dundee 1984, 116(illus),117.

**ROBERTSON, William** **fl c1735-c1753**
Very little known of this artist beyond the fact of his marriage on 1 June 1735 in Edinburgh, then on 24 April 1753 we find him seeking refuge as a debtor in Holyrood Abbey Sanctuary, at which time he is described as a 'limner'. Possibly the same **W ROBERTSON** who signed a small whole-length portrait of 'Prince Charles Edward Stuart' which appeared on the market in 1948, and by the same hand another work of 'Flora MacDonald', now in Glasgow AG, in a style similar to that of Charles Phillips.

**ROBERTSON, William** **fl 1775-1784**
Edinburgh 'painter' who was working at the Old Playhouse Theatre 1775-1779, probably as a scene painter and was then listed in the *Edinburgh Directories* for the period as a painter living at Meal-Market Stairs 1780-1784. May have been brother of Andrew(qv) and Archibald R(qv) who worked alongside Raeburn under Alexander Runciman(qv).
**Bibl:** Macmillan [SA] 151.

**ROBERTSON, William** **1786-1841**
Northern architect. Designed the RC churches of Wick (1836) and Inverness (1836), 'a joyous display for carpenter's Gothic' [Gifford], Reelig House (1837-38), the houses of Dochfour and Dochgarroch (1839), Lochluichart Lodge (1840), transforming it into a *cottage orné*, with an Italianate tower at one corner and a rear extension, Inverness Public Library, originally Dr Bell's school, (1839-41), and the Union Hotel, Inverness (1838).
**Bibl:** Gifford, H & I, 37-8,52,67,69 et passim, pls.32,107,112.

**ROBERTSON, William Aitken** **fl 1856-1861**
Leith painter of landscape, still life and shipping and river scenes. Exhibited RSA(3) & GI(3).

**ROBERTSON, Wilma I** **fl 1966-1972**
Aberdeenshire landscape painter; exhibited AAS during the above years, RSA(5) 1968-1970 & GI(4) from addresses in Cults and at Tigh-na-Mara, Beaconhill Rd, Milltimber.

**ROBERTSON-BROWN, J S** **fl 1941-1946**
Edinburgh painter, sculptor, singer and teacher. Trained Edinburgh College of Art. and Royal School of Music. Director of Art, Merchiston Castle School 1943-1960 before moving to Sherborne. Changed his name to I S Robertson. Exhibited RSA (5).

**ROBERTSON-FIDDES, K Beth** **1972-**
Born Edinburgh. Sculptress of portraits and figurative work. Trained Edinburgh College of Art 1990-95. Won Benno Schotz Award (RSA) 1997 for a portrait bust. Has her own foundry. Works from Greenhead Farm, West Saltoun, Pencaitland.

**ROBERTSON-ROSS, Miss** **fl 1885**
Edinburgh-based amateur portrait painter. In 1885 exhibited a portrait of her father 'Maj-Gen Robertson-Ross of Glenmoidart, Inverness-shire' at the RSA.

**ROBINSON, Basil** **fl 1965**
Morayshire-based wood carver of religious subjects. Moved to Wales. Exhibited two works at the AAS, from Pluscarden Priory, Elgin.

**ROBINSON, Carol Anne** **fl 1954**
Fife painter; exhibited AAS(1), from 37 High St, Kingham.

**ROBINSON, Douglas** **fl 1900-1903**
Glasgow-based portrait painter. Moved to London c 1902. Exhibited GI.

**ROBINSON, Eleanor** **fl 1895**
Glasgow flower and still life painter; exhibited GI(1) from La Mancha, Langside.

**ROBINSON, Frederick Cayley** **1862-1927**
London painter in oil also decorator, illustrator, poster artist and theatrical designer. Trained St John's Wood School of Art, RA Schools and Julien's, Paris 1890-92. Influenced by Puvis de Chavannes. The early part of his working life was led in London but he spent the last period of his life in Scotland. Appointed Professor of Figure Composition and Decoration at Glasgow School of Art 1914 remaining there for 10 years until his retirement 1924. His influence as a teacher was considerable, partly because it occurred at a time when the School was being transformed after the war following the departure of Fra Newbury(qv). A gentle theatricality permeates his work. Reference has been made to the reliance he placed 'on the compositional value of the horizontal and the sudden assymetrical vertical - frequently taking the form of cypress trees - making him an intriguing psychological study'. Exhibited RA(14), RWS(30), RSW(1), RSA(4), ROI(7), RBA(37), GI(16), L(21) & London Salon(7). Represented in Tate AG.
**Bibl:** Fine Art Society, London 'Frederick Cayley Robinson', (Ex Cat 1977); Macmillan [SA] 338,361;

**ROBINSON, H L** **fl 1905-1930**
Berwickshire painter of rural scenes and Lowland landscape. Exhibited 'Feeding the sheep - evening' at the RSA & L(1) from The Cottage, Hutton.

**ROBINSON, Harry Watt** **fl 1897-1934**
Glasgow artist of coastal and harbour scenes. At the turn of the century moved to Bridge of Weir. Worked in oil and watercolour, exhibiting RSA(5), RSW(3), GI(50) & London Salon (12). Represented in Glasgow AG.

**ROBINSON, Iain** **fl 1986-**
Glasgow-based painter. Exhibited GI 1986, from Huntly Gdns.

**ROBINSON, Joan (Mrs Dow)** **fl 1943-1966**
Glasgow painter of flower, still life and occasional portraits. Exhibited RSA(3), including 'Self-portrait'; also GI(25), latterly from Cleveden Drive.

**ROBINSON, John H** **19th Cent**
Engraver. Six important engravings are in the collection of the City of Edinburgh: 'Regent Murray', 'The Marquis of Argyll', 'Sir Walter Scott', 'Viscount Dundee', 'Robert Burns' (after Alexander Nasmyth) and 'Charles I' (after van Dyck).

**ROBINSON, M Y** **fl 1847**
Edinburgh flower and still life painter. Exhibited RSA(1), from Beaumont Place.

**ROBINSON, Malcolm J** **1948-**
Born Jarrow-on-Tyne. Commercial artist, illustrator, specialising in wildlife, craftsman. Trained Edinburgh College of Art 1967-71. Spent a year sign-writing in Turkey and stewarding on a Greek ship before settling with his wife near Galashiels. Illustrated *Alternative Scotland* and *A Scottish Bestiary* 1978.

**ROBINSON, Miss Margaret H** **fl 1885-1886**
Minor Edinburgh oil painter of flowers, figures and country scenes; exhibited RSA(2) & AAS(2), from 16 Greenslade Place.

**ROBINSON, William** **fl c1714**
Obscure portrait painter. His portrait of 'Andrew Allen'(qv) was engraved by Richard Cooper. Other sitters included 'William Forbes', Professor of Law at Glasgow(1714) and 'Dr John Arbuthnot' in the SNPG.
**Bibl:** Brydall 171.

**ROBINSON, William** **fl 1955**
Glasgow painter; exhibited 'The Headland' at the RSA & GI.

**ROBINSON, William Howard** **fl 1902-1932**
Born Inverness-shire. Portrait and figure painter; also occasional sporting subjects. Trained Slade School and under S J Solomon. Lived in London. Painted many fencing scenes and portraits of fencers, also boxing and greyhound racing. Exhibited RA 1902 and at the Walker Gallery, Liverpool(2); also other provincial galleries including NEAC.
**Bibl:** Wingfield.

**ROBSON, A H** **fl 1933**
Minor Scottish watercolour painter; exhibited RSW(1).

**ROBSON, Adam** **1928-**
Born Hawick, 16 Aug. Painter in oil dedicated to ships and the sea, also landscape especially around Dollar where he lived from 1956. Trained Edinburgh College of Art. Confesses to having been influenced by Cézanne over structure, Paul Nash over imaginative content, Joan Eardley(qv), Turner and McTaggart(qv) over atmosphere, Peploe(qv) and Gillies(qv) with regard to colour and Anne Redpath(qv) concerning texture. Regularly visits the Shetlands which remain a constant inspiration. Designed 21 stall cushions and 42 kneelers for the Abbey Church, Iona. Exhibited regularly RSA 1951- 1974; also RGI(25) 1958-1978. Represented in Glasgow AG.

**ROBSON, Albert Lockie** **fl 1963-1985**
Edinburgh painter of still life and landscapes, usually in the Borders. Exhibited RSA(6) & GI(1), latterly from Newport-on-Tay.

**ROBSON, Allan Watt** **fl 1949-1966**
Edinburgh landscape painter; exhibited RSA(5), mostly local scenery, from Edinburgh, later from Dunning, Perthshire.

**ROBSON, Gavin** **1950-**
Born Edinburgh. Painter in oil. Trained Edinburgh 1968-74, travelled to France on a scholarship. Fellow in Fine Art, Nottingham Univ 1975. First solo exhibition in Nottingham the same year.

**ROBSON, James W** **fl 1948-1957**
Glasgow painter of west coast and Arran landscape. Exhibited RSA(7) & GI(4), from Bearsden.

**ROBSON, Lorraine** **1962-**
Born 18 Mar. Employed 1980-84 as a cartographic assistant in the Scottish Office before enrolling at Edinburgh College of Art 1984-8, graduating with a BA Hons degree in Fine Art. Won the Scotland Today Fashion Designer Award 1984, having won the Selina Good memorial prize 1988. Though starting as an abstract sculptor she has begun recently to use glass fibre and is fascinated by the fetishes worn and used by primitive cultures to depict fertility ritual magic. Her later work has become more figurative. Exhibited RSA 1989 from 7, West Preston St.

**ROBSON, Maggie** **fl 1880-1881**
Glasgow amateur painter of flowers and genre. Exhibited GI(4), from 14 Royal Crescent.

**ROBSON, T** **fl c 1820-1830**
Engraver, probably Scottish. Possibly related to to the copperplate engraver turned actor **Thomas Frederick ROBSON (?1822-1864)** whose original name was Thomas Robson Brownhill. Engraved bookplates for, inter alia, Brown 1820; W.B. Clarke 1830; Hon.

Archdeacon Cochrane; Croudace 1830; Havelock; William Hutton; Lambton; Henry Stapylton 1830; & Thomas Wood 1830.
**Bibl:** Bushnell.

**ROBSON, William** **1868-1952**
Born Edinburgh. Painter in oils and pastel of landscape, rustic scenes and animals. Youngest son of Lord Sinclair. Trained Edinburgh College of Art and in Paris at Julien's, also in Florence where he met and married the daughter of a Neopolitan fisherman. Returned to Edinburgh 1900 before moving to Kirkcudbright 1904, sharing a studio with the English etcher William P Robins and other lesser known artists. Prolific, exhibiting RSA(64), RA(5), GI(18), AAS(2) & L(7), latterly from The Studio, Kircudbright.

**ROCHE, Alexander Ignatius RSA** **1861-1921**
Born Gallowgate, Glasgow, 17 Aug; died Slateford, Midlothian, 10 Mar. Painter of landscapes, portraits, murals and figure subjects. Son of a milliner. After leaving St Mungo's Academy began to train as an architect but quickly turned to painting, enrolling at the Glasgow School of Art. In the early 1880s went to Paris for further training under Lefebre, Boulanger and Jerome. Among his fellow students were Willliam Kennedy and John Lavery(qv). With the latter he found the current enthusiasm for Bastien-Lepage much to his liking, forming an influence that was to last for the rest of his life. In France the Scots painted together at Grez-sur-Loing. Returned to Glasgow 1885 settling in an unpretentious home in rural Dumbartonshire. First exhibited at the Glasgow Institute in 1881 and had his first big success there four years later with 'The Dominie's Favourites'. In 1889 exhibited 3 works at the GI which received great acclaim establishing him as one of the acknowledged leaders of the new movement which became known as the Glasgow School. In 1887 his 'Good King Wenceslas' showed the influence of Bastien-Lepage. Most of 1888 was spent in Capri where he became known to a cosmopolitan group of artists including Fabbi and Harold Speed. Spells in Florence and Venice followed and it was in Florence that he met his Italian wife. Also influenced by Whistler, especially in his feminine portraits, as in 'Miss Lou' 1889. 'His style is characterised by a fluid technique, subtle colour schemes and an elusive charm that stemmed from his avowed concern with beauty in nature'. In the 1890s, invigorated by further visits to Italy, he was rewarded with a number of honours and distinctions, not least a commission to paint a large mural for the banqueting hall of Glasgow's new municipal buildings. This depicted the legend of St Mungo and is his most ambitious figure composition. During this time he visited America. Settled in Edinburgh 1896 becoming increasingly interested in portraiture, the success of which resulted in a trip to N. America. In Edinburgh, 1906 he married a daughter of Robert Alexander(qv). Sadly a few years later a cerebral haemorrhage paralysed his right-hand. He taught himself to paint with his left hand and was later to produce some of his best landscapes. 'The most striking qualities in Roche's pictures are a quaint and decidedly romantic element in the informing sentiment, an exceptional grasp of the material aspects of nature, and technically an exquisiteness of handling and of surface that are very delightful...a genuinely poetic strain, a combination of the sensuous beauty and colour that pervade the verse of Keats, and the fervid earth-worship that inspires Meredith's nature poetry, joined in his best work to a quaintness that is quite medieval in flavour' [Caw]. In another place the same author affirmed 'Roche was more in love with beauty than his fellow artists and all his work is coloured by a delicate fantasy'. Awarded the gold medal in Munich 1891, an honourable mention, Paris Salon 1892 and a gold medal at Dresden 1897. One of the leaders of the Glasgow Group(qv), being highly respected both as a person and as a painter. Elected NEA 1891, RP 1898, ARSA 1893, RSA 1900. Exhibited RA(10), RSA(82), RSW(1), RHA(2), ROI(1), L(15), GI(72) & AAS 1894-1921. Represented in NGS, SNPG ('Self-portrait' + 2), Glasgow AG, Kirkcaldy AG, Edinburgh City collection (6, including a 'self-portrait' and one of 'Lord Provost Sir Robert Cranston'), Adelaide AG, Berlin AG, Kunsthaus, Zurich.
**Bibl:** AJ 1894, 79; 1898, 48-9; Caw 373-6 et al; Anne Donald, SAC Ex Cat 1968, 72-3; Haldane Macfall,'Alexander Roche' The Artist, 1906; Halsby 149,150; Irwin 389-390 et al (illus); Macmillan [SA] 259,273-4,280-2.

**ROCHE, Hugh** **fl 1984**
Aberdeenshire painter. Married Kate R(qv). Exhibited AAS(1) from 8 Marine Terrace, Muchalls.

**ROCHE, Kate** **fl 1982-**
North-east artist of local landscapes and genre. Married Hugh R(qv). Exhibited AAS from 8 Marine Terrace, Muchalls.

**ROCHEAD, John Thomas** **1814-1878**
Born Edinburgh. Glasgow architect and monochromatic artist. Pupil of David Bryce(qv). Spent two years as draughtsman with Hurst & Moffatt of Doncaster. Returned to Scotland settling in Glasgow as chief draughtsman with the Hamiltons(qv). Launched his own practice 1841. In 1844 designed the Royal Arch, Dundee commemmorating the visit of Queen Victoria (dem to make way for the Tay road bridge). Retired to Edinburgh 1870 when he completed a number of villas in Morningside Place (Nos 13-15 & 17-19). Exhibited a number of pen and ink drawings as well as architectural designs at the RSA where altogether he exhibited 15 works including a design for the War Office (1858), for Speirs College (1866) and the first premium design for the Wallace Monument (1860). Contributed to the development of Glasgow in the mid-Victorian era by the boldly Italianate Grosvenor Square (1855) and other buildings.
**Bibl:** Colvin; Dunbar 138; Gifford 622; A Gomme & D Walker, Architecture of Glasgow, London 1987(rev), 296-7; Bruce Walker & W S Gauldie, Architects and Architecture on Tayside, Dundee 1984, 131(illus),132.

**ROCHESTER, Ralph** **fl 1949**
Renfrewshire painter of genre and local landscape. Exhibited GI(2) from Paisley.

**RODGER, George** **fl 1890-1893**
Minor painter of Braiffauld, Tollcross; exhibited GI(2).

**RODGER, Gwen** **fl 1990-**
Painter. Exhibited 'Dusk' at the RSA, from The Luggie, Lauder.

**RODGER, Tom** **fl 1893**
Glasgow painter of rural scenes. Exhibited GI(1) from Hillside St.

**RODGER, Willie ARSA** **1930-**
Born Kirkintilloch. Best known as a relief process printmaker of linocut and woodcut prints, printed without use of press. Also worked in etching and drypoint, lithography, oil, gouache, acrylic and stained glass design. Trained Glasgow School of Art 1948-52, specialising in graphic design and continuing for a post diploma year 1952-3. Well known also for his pen and ink drawings, many deploying a semi-autographical persona 'Gilmour Whitecross' and bold black drawings in conte crayon of urban topography. Influenced by the work of the German Expressionists and fascinated by the inherent qualities of printing surface. Favourite compositions are figurative and architectural subjects. First one man-show was in Glasgow 1964. In 1970 elected a member of the Glasgow Group and in 1971 Artist-in-Residence, Sussex University. The following year he received first Prize, Kirkintilloch Art Exhibition and in 1975 1st Prize for the Scottish Design Council's annual award (given for a set of Scottish historical playing cards). More recent designs include over 70 linocut illustrations for *The Field of the Thistles* by Monica Clough 1984, two stained glass windows for St. Mary's Parish church, Kirkintilloch 1991-2, linocut designs for 40 banners to commemorate the bicentenary of Union St, Aberdeen. Elected RGI 1994. Elected Council Member, SSA 1979-81, won Benno Schotz Award 1985. Elected ARSA 1989. Exhibits regularly at the RSA, AAS(6) & GI from Stenton, Bellevue Rd, Kirkintilloch. Represented in V & A, Aberdeen AG, Dundee AG, Glasgow AG, Perth AG, Edinburgh City collection, Lillie AG(Milngavie).
**Bibl:** 'In Between the Lines, Willie Rodger - a Retrospective', Foreword by Wm Buchanan & Cordelia Oliver: U. of Strathclyde Touring Exhibition 1986-7.

**ROE, Andrea** **1968-**
Born Beverley, Yorkshire, April 18. Sculptress. Trained at Humberside College of Further Education and Edinburgh College of Art 1987-90. Won several awards including Edinburgh District AC award 1995, Hope Scott Trust Award 1996. First solo exhibition in Edinburgh 1995. Exhibited Mauritius, Lithuania & Sweden. Sometimes uses unconventional materials like sponges, PVC and feathers in order to portray more vividly human reaction to physical confrontations. Artist-in-residence at the Royal Crichton Hospital

(Dumfries) 1998, she rather quaintly describes an interest "in the physical reactions of the body, its systems and its invountary release of liquids". Lives and works in Edinburgh.

**ROE, Clarence H** **fl c1870-d1909**
Painter in oil of Highland landscapes, often with red deer. Athough his work is quite often seen little is known about him. Son of Robert Henry Roe(qv). Lived for a time at 9 South Crescent, Tottenham Court Road, London. His dark brooding landscapes and clumsy brushwork are not greatly appealing although they portray mountain mood quite well. Exhibited RHA(2) & GI(1).

**ROE, Robert Henry** **1793-1880**
Painter in oil of Highland sporting scenes, including animals and birds. Considering the frequency with which his Highland landscapes are to be seen very little is known about his life. Father of Fred and Clarence Roe(qv) and of Colin Graeme(qv). Among his best known works are 'A Highland Shooting Party - Loch Kinnard, Perthshire' 1852, 'Highland Keeper waiting for a shot at an eagle', and 'Highland poachers' 1857. A study of 'Highland Poachers' at the RSA had been commissioned but whether by the poachers or the landlords is not recorded. Sometimes spoken of as the poor man's Landseer but this is unfair as it is only his compositions that are similar, his style and treatment are quite different, generally not bearing comparison, although they are evocative of the Highland stalking season. Exhibited RA(10) 1852-1868, all of them Highland scenes. Living at Sandbank, Argyll and later Glasgow 1854-57. Exhibited extensively in the English provinces.
**Bibl:** Conn: 63 (1922) 232; Smith: Recollections of the BI (1860), 125ff.

**ROEMELLE Mrs** **fl 1906**
Glasgow artist; exhibited 'A quiet evening' at the GI from 34 Kelvinside Gdns.

**ROGER, Anne** **fl 1953-1961**
Glasgow painter; portraits and Clydeside scenes. Exhibited 'Elliot station' at the RSA; also GI(6), from Jordanhill.

**ROGER, George A** **fl 1955**
Lanarkshire-based painter; exhibited 'Woman reading' at the RSA, from Biggar.

**ROGER, William** **fl 1830-1831**
Aberdeen painter of portrait miniatures. Exhibited RSA in both the above years, from Bon Accord St.

**ROGERS, Neil** **fl 1953**
Glasgow painter of still life. Exhibited GI(1), from Morningside St.

**ROGERS, R** **fl 1791-1792**
Painter in watercolour, aquatintist. Drew and engraved several scenes at Leith races, forming a commentary on Robert Fergusson the Edinburgh poet.
**Bibl:** Caw 52.

**ROGERS, William** **fl 1849-1857**
Edinburgh portrait painter in oil; exhibited RSA(35) including 'Argyle Robertson Esq MD, President of Royal College of Surgeons'.

**ROGERSON, John** **fl 1920-1921**
A little known Glasgow painter of landscape, mainly continental. Exhibited GI(2) from 202 Hope Street.

**RÖHL, Frieda (Mrs James Pittendrigh Macgillivray)** **c1877-fl 1886**
Glasgow painter in oil of landscapes, still life, figure subjects. Competent artist fond of depicting trees. Married 1886, moved to Edinburgh 1894. Co-founder and Treasurer of the Glasgow Society of Lady Artists. Exhibited RSA(12), AAS(1), RHA(8) & GI(18), from 130 Wellington St.

**ROLAND, Miss** **fl 1850**
Edinburgh landscape artist; exhibited a Yorkshire view at the RSA, from Dublin St.

**ROLLAND, Helen M** **fl 1923-1935**
Watercolour painter of landscapes who lived in Peebles before moving c1930 to Edinburgh. Exhibited RSA(5), RSW(12), SWA(4) & GI(3).

**ROLLAND, Mrs Martha Suhr** **fl 1970**
Edinburgh-based painter. Exhibited 'Littoral' and 'Poppies of the field' at the GI.

**ROLLINSON, Sunderland** **1872-?**
Edinburgh portrait painter of character studies, also engraver. Exhibited RSA(3) & GI(1).

**ROLLO, Alex** **fl 1914**
Glasgow landscape artist; mainly continental scenes. Exhibited GI(2) from 9 Carlton Gardens.

**ROLLO, Alison Dorothy (née Brown)** **1950-**
Born Dundee, Sept 15. Sculptress. Spent most of her childhood in Malaysia before returning to Scotland in 1964. Trained Duncan of Jordanstone College of Art 1968-72. After a short spell teaching at Inverurie, took up a lecturing post in Auckland (NZ) 1976-93. Returned again to Scotland 1993. A permanent exhibition of her sculpture is in Pitlochry. Undertook a study tour of the Pacific Islands 1995-96. Exhibited a large stoneware sculpture at RSA 1997 from her home in Pitlochry.

**ROLLO, J B** **fl 1840-1844**
Edinburgh painter of town and country buildings; exhibited RSA(6), from Nicholson St.

**ROMANES, Margaret C** **fl 1935-1945**
Edinburgh engraver of rural scenes, still life and flowers; mainly wood engravings. Exhibited regularly RSA(11) during the above years from 3 Whitehouse Terrace.

**RONALD, Alan Ian RSW** **1899-1967**
Born Edinburgh, 6 Jne; died Dunfermline. Painter in oil and watercolour; harbours, quaysides and country scenes. Trained Edinburgh College of Art. Worked on the east coast of Scotland and in Germany in a powerful, effective style. Lived for a time in Edinburgh before settling in Charlestown, Fife. Elected RSW 1935. Exhibited RSA(49), RSW(37), GI(12), AAS(2) & L(7), latterly from 34 Nile Grove.
**Bibl:** Halsby 281.

**RONALD, Margaret E** **fl 1954-1961**
Edinburgh landscape and still life painter. Exhibited RSA(4).

**RONALDSON, Mrs Elsie** **fl 1942**
Edinburgh painter of figurative works. Exhibited a study of a Malay boy at the RSA.

**RONALDSON, Thomas Martine** **1881-1942**
Born Edinburgh, 13 Dec; died London, 12 Mar. Painter in oil and watercolour of portraits. Educated Merchiston Castle School, Edinburgh and Trinity College, Oxford. Returned to Scotland to train at Edinburgh College of Art, then in London at the Cope and Nicoll School and Paris at the Academie Julien under J P Laurens. Exhibited Paris Salon, winning a silver medal 1926; also RA(26), RSA(42), ROI(1), GI(2), L(13), & London Salon(5).

**RONEY, John J** **fl 1943-1945**
Painter of genre portraits. Exhibited RSA through an agent in Paisley.

**ROONEY, Pat** **fl 1931-1932**
Landscape painter. Exhibited two Yorkshire views RSA.

**ROQUES, Casimir** **fl 1877-1886**
Painter in oil; flowers, fruit, still life, portraits, figure subjects and landscape. Lived for many years in Edinburgh. Exhibited RSA(14) from 16 George Street.

**ROSA, Frederick A** **fl 1884-1888**
Edinburgh painter in oil and watercolour of figure subjects,

landscapes and coastal/fishing subjects. Exhibited RSA(7) from 40 Frederick Street.

**ROSCHLAU, Michael** **fl 1971-1986**
Glasgow-based engraver. Exhibited GI(14), several from Glasgow School of Art.

**ROSE, Miss Alison Helen** **1900-?**
Born Edinburgh, 3 Feb. Painter in oil of landscapes. Trained Heatherley's. Lived at Newlyn, Cornwall and exhibited RA(6) 1924-39; also RSA(1) & SWA(3).

**ROSE, Caroline A** **fl 1923**
Morayshire portrait miniaturist. Exhibited two works - one a portrait of her mother - at the AAS, from the United Free Church manse, Cawdor, by Nairn.

**ROSE, David Thomas** **1871-1964**
Born Glenluce, Wigtownshire, 9 May; died Brighton. Painter in oils and watercolour, mainly the latter, occasional etcher; professional civil engineer. After an unhappy early spell in the family butchery was apprenticed to an Inverness engineering firm. This took him to Glasgow 1896 where he discovered the Glasgow Boys(qv), becoming most influenced by Arthur Melville(qv). Studied at night classes, Glasgow School of Art under Fra Newbery(qv). Involved in the extension of the Highland line from Connel Bridge to Ballachulish. In Malta 1904-7, working on the breakwater, Valetta harbour. Returning to UK via Italy and France he completed many sketchbooks of drawings, mostly street scenes and local characters. Published cartoons in *Punch* and c1926 began etching but the loss of an eye led to abandonment of this art 1934. Lived in Yorkshire 1920-35. Painted almost full-time after retirement to Brighton, becoming an active member of the Brighton & Hove Art Club 1935-64. Sensitive to atmosphere and character, many busy scenes with extensive use of quiet blues, greys and browns. Retrospective exhibition at the Calton Gallery, Edinburgh 1993. Exhibited RA, RSA, GI. Represented in Imperial War Museum, Science Museum, Edinburgh PL, Hove AG, Southwark AG, Bradford Industrial Museum, Harrogate AG, Portsmouth Museum, Malta Museum.
**Bibl:** Ex Cat, Calton Gall, Edinburgh 1993 (text by Fiona Sturrock).

**ROSE, Marion** **fl 1891-1900**
Edinburgh painter of portraits and flowers. Exhibited RSA 1891, 1892 & 1900.

**ROSE, Robert C** **fl 1943-1950**
Kirkcaldy sculptor, mainly portrait busts. Exhibited 5 works at the RSA including a bust of 'Mary, Queen of Scots' 1944.

**ROSE, Robert Traill** **1863-1942**
Born Newcastle, 12 Mar; died Edinburgh, 3 Dec. Painter of landscape and figures in oils and watercolour and book illustrator. The Rev. Robert Traill of Greyfriars, famous in covenanting times, was a distant forbear while Rose's paternal grandfather was founder of the Edinburgh Geological Society 1834. Apart from a short time at the old Edinburgh School of Art he was self-taught, though influenced at one remove by the work of Walter Crane and William Morris. An increasing deafness from the age of nine led Rose to an inward approach to life and to a deep love of art and books. He once said "I do know that it has thrown me very much in on myself...but I don't like it". Within his art there was a spiritual conception of the mystery yet fundamental simplicity of life. A strong sombre element affected much of his work, a preoccupation with the thought of birth and death, of sacrifice and suffering. This was clearly seen in the illustrations Rose prepared for the deluxe edition of the *Book of Job,* (Abbey Press 1902). An article on the Society of Artists Exhibition of 1911 referred to "the profundity of thought and grandeur of conception which marked many of the designs characteristic of most of Mr Rose's work". Illustrated *The Dream of Gerontius, Edinburgh Vignettes* and *Pilgrim's Progress.* Rose abandoned his art at the onset of WWI when the strain of long hours working in a munitions factory led to a severe breakdown. After a gradual but complete recovery spent in the borders, in 1925 his sight began to fail and for the last 15 years he endured the tragedy of blindness. For much of his life he lived at Tweedsmuir, Peebles-shire. Illustrated 25 books and covers including Buchan and Paton's *History of Peebles-shire* (1927). In the words of his wife, Mary Tweedie-Stodart, "few artists have known greater adversity, yet to the end, despite the sombre strain in his character, he had an extraordinary quick and witty humour and, at times, the almost impish fun of a small boy". 'Treated in simple masses of black and white, rich and full in tone and balanced with fine decorative effect, his drawings are frequently so arresting that whether one comprehends their actual meaning or not, one receives from them an impression of seriousness and sincerity' [Caw]. Other works include a large bronze for Partick Church, Glasgow, another for St Mary's Kirk in Biggar and a Border cairn at Swinton, Berwickshire. Exhibited RSA, RSW, GI(2), Paris, Munich, Liepzig, Prague and the United States. Represented in NGS(6), Edinburgh City collection.
**Bibl:** Caw 418; Glasgow Herald 5.12.42 (obit); Halsby 96-7; Houfe; Scotsman 5.12.42 (obit); Studio, 55,1912,312 illus; 'Modern Bk Illustrators & Their Work', 1914.

**ROSEBURG H William** **fl 1907**
Midlothian landscape artist. Exhibited 'A Border stream' at the RSA from Loanhead.

**ROSS, -** **fl 1810**
Glasgow engraver. Engraved a bookplate for William Steele 1810.
**Bibl:** Bushnell.

**ROSS, Aitken M** **fl 1890-1893**
Glasgow painter of modest consequence; exhibited GI(2) from 114 West Campbell St.

**ROSS, Alastair Robertson ARSA FRBS FSA(Scot) FRSA Hon FRIAS** **1941-**
Born Perth, 8 Aug. Sculptor in clay, bronze, stone, metal and perspex. Specialises in female torsos and half length nudes, metal abstract figures. Educated St Mary's Episcopal School, Dunblane and McLaren High School, Callender. Studied art at Edinburgh College of Art under Alex Schilsky(qv) and Norman Forrest(qv) 1960 and Dundee College of Art 1960-66 under Hugh Crawford(qv) and Scott Sutherland(qv); also in Amsterdam, Athens, Florence, Rome and Vienna. Awarded the Dickson Prize for sculpture 1962, travelling scholarship 1963, RSA Chalmers Bursary 1964, RSA Carnegie travelling scholarship 1965, Duncan of Drumfork scholarship 1965, and a postgraduate scholarship 1965-6. Also award winner in sculpture at the Paris Salon 1966-7, Société des Artistes Français bronze medal 1968, silver medal 1970. Member, Scottish Arts Club 1971; Council of the SSA 1972; Council, RBS 1972. Lecturer in sculpture at Dundee College of Art. Lived in Dunblane before moving to 28 Albany Terrace, Dundee. A strong sensual element runs through all his figure work. Elected FRSA 1966, ARBS 1968, SSA 1969, FSA (Scot) 1971, ARSA 1980, vice-President of the Royal Society of British Sculptors 1988. Awarded the Sir Otto Beit medal of the RBS 1989, made a Freeman of the City of London 1989. Most recent work includes a life size bronze of the Albany Herald, Sir Iain Moncreiffe of that Ilk, in the New Register House, Edinburgh. Exhibits regularly RSA, Paris Salon, Holland and elsewhere overseas as well as in the UK. Represented in Perth AG.

**ROSS, Alexander** **1834-1925**
Inverness architect who practised at 42 Union Street. His design for St Mary's Cathedral, Edinburgh (1872) was well received but not finally chosen.Exhibited a design for the modified interior of Inverness Cathedral at the RA 1870 and further designs for Inverness Cathedral and Rosehaugh House, Inverness-shire at the RSA 1872.
**Bibl:** Gifford 363.

**ROSS, Miss Alice E** **fl 1886-1937**
Painter in watercolours. Rural scenes, domestic genre, still life, animals, flowers and occasional portraits. Lived Edinburgh before moving for a short time to Alloa. Exhibited RSA(55), RSW(6), RA(2), GI(29), AAS(2 - 'A cockatoo' and 'A quiet corner') & L(13), latterly from 18 Glenorchy Terrace.

**ROSS, Ann(e) RSW** **1945-**
Born Edinburgh. Painter in oil, watercolour and gouache, fantasies, plant forms, figurative studies and abstracts. Studied Edinburgh College of Art 1962-67 and travelled to France and Italy on an Andrew Grant Travelling Scholarship 1967 and in 1971 received an

SAC Award. First solo exhibition was Edinburgh 1970. Designer/illustrator with the Royal Scottish Museums, Edinburgh 1971-72, then Art Editor/Designer with Chambers of Edinburgh 1972-81. Thereafter has worked as a freelance with first solo exhibition Edinburgh 1997. Favours interiors and still life scenes depicting well-loved objects. Elected RSW 1999. Regular exhibitor RSA, RSW from 22 India St, Edinburgh. Exhibited AAS(3) between 1959 & 1961, latterly from 29 South Constitution St, Aberdeen. Represented in SAC, Glasgow University (Hunterian Museum).

**ROSS, Arran Campbell** **1965-**
Born Perth, Feb 11. Sculptor. Trained Edinburgh College of Art 1983-87 and Duncan of Jordanstone College of Art 1987-88. Inaugural winner of JD Fergusson award 1997. Lecturer Edinburgh College of Art. Represented in Perth AG.

**ROSS, Cameron** **1963-**
Born Inverness. Etcher and lithographer. Trained Glasgow School of Art 1981-85. Much of his work depicts social issues. Works as a printmaking technician at Gray's School of Art, Aberdeen. Part-time tutor with Peacock Press, the Aberdeen printmakers. Founder member, Highland Printmaking Workshop. First solo exhibition in Inverness 1988. Exhibits RSA and AAS, from 20 Richmond Terrace.

**ROSS, Carol H** **fl 1912**
Inverness painter of figurative subjects. Exhibited 'The jeweller' at the AAS, from Riverfield.

**ROSS, Miss Catherine Henderson** **fl 1878-1913**
Edinburgh painter in watercolour of domestic scenes. Moved to Riverfield, Inverness c1910. Sister of Miss Ellie R(qv). Exhibited RSA(3).

**ROSS, Christina Paterson RSW** **1843-1906**
Born Edinburgh. Watercolour painter of landscapes and figure subjects. Daughter of Robert Thorburn R(qv) and sister of Joseph Thorburn R(qv). Keen observer of village life, she lived mostly in Edinburgh and painted in a broad light wash often on quite a large scale with figures in interiors; also fishing scenes and romantic landscapes. Her colours are sober but often produce a fine harmony. Visited the continent on several occasions, some of the sketches made there being exhibited RSA 1878 and again in 1886. One of her best works is 'Crail Harbour' RSA 1897. Elected RSW 1880. Exhibited RA(2), RSA(77), RSW(66), RI(7), RHA(1), RBA(2), GI(31), AAS (1887-1902) & L(32). Represented Edinburgh City collection by two watercolour drawings 'Sailmaking' and 'The Salmon Fishers' Leisure Hour'.
**Bibl:** Caw 428; Halsby 281.

**ROSS, Christine** **fl 1978**
Glasgow painter; exhibited RSA(2), from Hamilton Drive.

**ROSS, Donald Sinclair** **fl 1973**
Aberdeen landscape painter. Exhibited AAS(1) from 7 Hopetoun Grange, Bucksburn.

**ROSS Mrs E C (née E C Thomson)** **fl 1858-1891**
An Edinburgh painter in oil and watercolour on ivory of portraits and portrait miniatures. Pupil of Signor Casella and mother of Eleanor Madge R(qv). Exhibited RSA(17) & GI(3).

**ROSS, Miss Eleanor Madge** **fl 1880-1925**
Edinburgh miniature painter in oil and watercolour also figurative subjects, flowers and landscapes. Daughter of Mrs E C Ross(qv). Lived in North Berwick before moving to Edinburgh and finally London. Exhibited 6 portrait miniatures in ivory at the RSA 1890-1902, including several members of the aristocracy, and 20 other works between 1882-1919; also RA(4), GI(9), AAS(2 - 'Lady Henry Gordon Lennox' and 'Emeritus Professor Blackie') & L(3).

**ROSS, Miss Ellie** **fl 1902**
Inverness painter of portrait miniatures. Sister of Catherine Henderson R(qv). Exhibited a case of miniatures at the RSA, from Riverfield.

**ROSS, Miss Elizabeth T** **fl 1878**
Edinburgh watercolour painter of flowers; exhibited RSA(1).

**ROSS, Mrs Frances (née Trufitt)** **fl 1892**
Edinburgh portrait painter. Exhibited 'The Hon Leonore Hamilton', daughter of Lord Belhaven at the RSA, from 6 Salisbury Place, Newington Road.

**ROSS, George** **fl c1710**
Scottish portrait painter. Waterhouse records 'a quite professional portrait' of 'Col John Somerville' c1710 at Hopetoun.

**ROSS, Helen** **fl 1937**
Aberdeen painter of interiors; exhibited AAS(2), from 133 S. Anderson Drive.

**ROSS, Hugh** **1800-1873**
Portrait miniaturist in watercolour, sometimes in pencil. Came from an artistic Ross-shire family (his father was gardener to the Duke of Marlborough) although he himself worked all his life in England. Brother of Sir William Charles(qv) and Magdalena R(qv). Awarded prizes by the Society of Arts in 1815, 1816 and 1820. A portrait of him by E W Hatton was exhibited at the RA in 1845. First exhibit at the RA 1815 when aged 15; subsequently exhibited 34 more portraits there 1815-1845, latterly from 24 Russell Place. A miniature of his brother 'Sir William Ross' is in NPG.

**ROSS, Hugh** **fl 1950**
Glasgow amateur landscape watercolourist. Exhibited GI(1) from Dumby Gdns.

**ROSS, Isabella S** **fl 1868-1873**
Perthshire painter of landscape and flowers; exhibited RSA(3) & GI(2) from Alyth.

**ROSS, James** **fl 1849**
Edinburgh landscape painter in oil; exhibited RSA(2).

**ROSS, James M** **fl 1887**
Angus painter of landscape; exhibited AAS(1), from Hillside, Montrose.

**ROSS, Jane W** **fl 1883-1897**
Glasgow painter in oil of still life and flowers. Exhibited RSA(3) & GI(11), from 26 Huntly Gdns.

**ROSS, Miss Jean M** **fl 1944**
Edinburgh painter; exhibited once at the RSA, from Manor Place.

**ROSS, Jenepher Wendy** **fl 1966-**
Glaswegian sculptress. Won 2nd prize at sculpture exhibition at miniature town Madurodan in The Hague. Work influenced by stalactite and stalagmitic forms helping in the combination of an abstract with a naturalistic approach. First solo exhibition in Glasgow 1966. Exhibits RSA intermittently, latterly from 103A Gower St.

**ROSS Miss Jessie S** **fl 1866-1896**
Edinburgh painter of topographical and flower studies. Eventually settled at Ballagan, Strathblane, Perthshire. Exhibited a sketch of the Dean cemetery and two other works at the RSA, also RSW(2), GI(1) & L(1).

**ROSS, John** **fl 1535-1536**
Linlithgow painter. Known to have been painting in Linlithgow Palace during the above years. It is recorded that he painted 'ane lyon thua unicornis that suld stand upone the forentres and the salutatiun of our lade with the wle pege and pape the knyght and laborius man...with all the new irne wyndoys that is put wp, in the first with red led and syne with wermione with all the prekkettis that the thanis standis on and sall gylt the crossis and ballis so mony as wantis'. He received further sums for painting the lining of the Chapel and decorations in the Chapel loft.
**Bibl:** Apted 80.

**ROSS, John** **fl c1776-c1833**
Edinburgh painter. Apprenticed to James Cumming, painter 1776-1782. In 1786 elected Burgess of Edinburgh. Took as apprentices Archibald Cameron 1793, James Hutchison 1795, John Austin 1798, Alexander Robertson 1801 and George Kinnear 1803. In 1833 he was still painting in Edinburgh. None of his work is now known.

**ROSS, Sir John** **1777-1856**
Born Inch, Wigtonshire, Jne 24; died London, Aug 30. Celebrated Arctic explorer, amateur artist and illustrator. Joined the East India Company 1794 and the Royal Navy in 1805. Commander in the Baltic and North Sea 1812-1817 and undertook his famous expeditions in search of the North-West Passage in 1818 and 1829-33. Consul in Stockholm 1839-46, promoted to Rear-Admiral in 1834, receiving a knighthood the same year. Author and illustrator of *A Voyage of Discovery* (1819) and *Narrative of a Second Voyage in Search of a North-West Passage* (1835). His portraits are in SNPG, NPG and Royal Geographical Society. Represented in BM, National Maritime Museum (Greenwich).
**Bibl:** DNB; Houfe; J. Roy Geog Soc, vol xxviii,130.

**ROSS, John** **1956-**
Born Cullen. Painter in oil, watercolour and pastel of wildlife also figurative subjects and landscapes. Trained Gray's School of Art 1973-78 obtaining the Governor's Award 1976, George Davidson Scholarship 1977, the first award of the Contemporary Art Society 1977, the MacLaine Watters medal 1978 and was the first winner of the Colquhon Memorial Prize 1981. After leaving Art School he painted Highland cattle and red deer in brooding, misty landscapes, somewhat in the style of Louis B Hurt(qv) although the cattle are more diminutive. In the early 1980s he turned increasingly to bright pastel colours with children playing on sunlit beaches after the manner of Gemmell Hutchison(qv); later we find a more impressionistic style in a semi-pointillist manner. In the 1990s his attention turned increasingly to portraying red deer and other wildlife subjects in their Highland habitat and sunlit beach and country scenes reminiscent of pointillism. Seeks to develop beyond the popular to what he describes as 'conceptual art'. Exhibited AAS in 1976 & 1987, latterly from Inverness-shire.

**ROSS, John E** **fl 1886-1930**
Glasgow painter. Moved to Birkenhead c1910; exhibited GI(10) & L(8).

**ROSS, John Ferguson** **fl 1928-1937**
Glasgow painter of shipping scenes, figurative works and landscape. Exhibited RSA(9) & AAS(2), from Rossbank, Carmyle.

**ROSS, John Halford** **1866-**
Born Rossshire. Painter and teacher, studied at Wolverhampton, Leicester, Nottingham and London. Settled in Nottinghamshire and exhibited 1892-1909, mainly in the Midlands.

**ROSS, Joseph Thorburn ARSA** **1849-1903**
Born Berwick-on-Tweed; died Edinburgh, 28 Sep. Painter of landscapes and figurative subjects, coastal scenes and seascapes, often with figures and birds. Son of Robert Thorburn R(qv) and brother of Christina R(qv). Educated Scottish Institute and in Dr Graham's private classes. His father put him into a merchant's office in Leith where he spent some years but after a short spell in Gloucester returned to Edinburgh 1876. Enrolled Trustees School winning several prizes including a gold medal for drawing. Admitted to RSA Life School 1877 and in 1879 awarded the Stuart Prize for composition and design. First exhibited RSA 1872. In 1880 went to the continent which he frequently visited thereafter. His watercolours have a spontaneity missing in his larger oils. Elected ARSA 1896. Genial and generous, he died in an accident. Exhibited RA(5), RSA(93), RSW(5), RI(1), RHA(3), GI(36), AAS (1885-1898) & L(23) from 78 Queen St. Represented in NGS(2).
**Bibl:** Bryan; Caw 331-2; Halsby 281.

**ROSS, June** **fl 1966**
Aberdeenshire amateur portrait painter. Exhibited AAS(1), from Moss-side House, Dunecht.

**ROSS, Launcelot Hugh** **1885-?**
Born Aberdeen. Architect. Studied Gray's School of Art, Aberdeen and London University. Assistant to Sir John James Burnet. Exhibited designs and drawings RSA(2) & GI(17) 1914-40.

**ROSS, Lesley Ann** **fl 1977-1978**
Aberdeen painter of figurative works, genre and topographical subjects. Trained Gray's School of Art, Aberdeen. Exhibited 'Doris' at the RSA (1978) & AAS(2), from 47 Justice St.

**ROSS, Lucy** **fl 1990-**
Edinburgh-based painter; exhibited RSA(2) from 13 Park Rd, Newington.

**ROSS, Miss M** **fl 1887**
Aberdeen painter of flowers and interiors; exhibited AAS(2), from 134 King St.

**ROSS, Madge** **fl 1890-1923**
Portrait and figure painter, mainly of girls and women. She had a varied life, living first in Paris where she studied under Bouguereau and Fleury, then London (21 Arkwright Rd, Hampstead) and went to Helensburgh c1895 where until 1910 she ran a studio at Craigendoran. with Miss Park. Norah Neilson Gray(qv) was one of their pupils. Exhibited Paris Salon, RA(2), AAS(2) & GI(9), mostly from Greenburn, Helensburgh and latterly from Crow Rd, Glasgow.

**ROSS, Magdalene/a (Mrs Edwin Dalton)** **1801-1874**
Miniaturist and portrait painter. Daughter of William Ross(qv) and his wife Maria, sister of Sir W C Ross(qv) and Hugh Ross(qv). Probably the Miss M Ross who won awards from the Society of Arts in 1823 and 26. Married 1841. Exhibited under her married name from 1842. In 1850 appointed Miniature Painter to the Queen. Many portraits were of children. Exhibited a miniature of her mother Mrs Maria Ross(qv) 1835. Said to have been a favourite of Delacroix, with whom she painted. Exhibited Paris Salon, RA(49) 1820-1856, latterly from 52 Upper Charlotte St, London where she lived with her sister and brothers. A miniature portrait of her by her brother is in the V & A. Miniatures of 'King Leopold I of the Belgians' and 'Louise, Queen of the Belgians' (this after Sir W C Ross), both executed 1840, are in the collection of HM the Queen.
**Bibl:** Foskett.

**ROSS, Margaret** **fl 1911-1923**
Montrose land and seascape painter who moved to Glasgow in the early 20s. Exhibited 'Waves' at the RSA; also GI(2) & L(2).

**ROSS, Margaret** **fl 1975-1978**
Midlothian landscape and figure painter; exhibited RSA(2), from Balerno.

**ROSS, Mrs Maria** **fl 1833**
Portrait painer. Wife of Hugh Ross(qv), mother of Sir W.C. Ross(qv). Exhibited 'Portrait of a Gentleman' at the RA 1833, from the family home at 52 Upper Charlotte St, London.

**ROSS, Miss R** **fl 1885**
Minor Edinburgh painter of 28 Walker Street. Exhibited RSA(1).

**ROSS, R McAllister** **fl 1927-1937**
Glasgow landscape painter; exhibited AAS(2) & GI(5), from 50 Nithsdale Road.

**ROSS, Robert, Jnr** **fl 1868-1890**
Edinburgh painter in oil and watercolour of genre, portraits, landscapes. Son of Robert Thorburn R(qv), brother of Christina R(qv). His work was similar in style and subject to his father under whom he studied as a young man. Exhibited RSA(62), GI(11) & L(2).

**ROSS, Robert Henry Alison** **fl 1898-1940**
Edinburgh oil painter of buildings, landscapes, portraits, figure subjects and topography. Among his sitters were 'Sir Andrew H.L.Foster, former Lt-Governor of Bengal' 1915, 'Rt Hon Charles Scott Dickson, Lord Justice-Clerk' 1920 and 'Rt Rev Dr Norman MacLean, Chaplain to the King' 1920. Exhibited RA(1), RSA(36), AAS(3), GI(12) & L(2).

**ROSS, Robert Thorburn RSA** **1816-1876**
Born Edinburgh; died Edinburgh, 13 Jly. Painter in oil and watercolour of genre, portraits and country scenes; also mezzotintist. Father of Joseph Thorburn R(qv) and Christina Paterson R(qv). At the age of 15 he began studying art under George Simson(qv), then the leading art teacher in Edinburgh, followed by three years at the Trustees Academy under Sir William Allan(qv). Settled in Glasgow as a portrait painter and in 1842 visited Berwick-on-Tweed where his father was a master gunner. He remained there for ten years increasing his output although his portraits, mostly in crayon, were painted in

Glasgow. Whilst in Berwick he sent his first contribution to the RSA, 'The Spinning Wheel' (1845). In mid-career he turned increasingly to homely scenes of Scottish life in the manner of the Faeds and Erskine Nicol, although lacking their humour or technical accomplishment. Illustrated *The History of a Pin* (1861). Caw praised his fresh watercolour sketches, one of the finest being 'Study of ferns, grasses and stones' 1865, now in the NGS. Particularly skilled at the characterisation of children and their childish sports and amusements. He lived for many years at 6 Atholl Crescent, Edinburgh. Elected ARSA 1896. Exhibited RA(6), RSA(125) 1872-1904 & GI(9). Represented in NGS(7), City of Edinburgh collection.
**Bibl:** AJ Dec 1871 281-3; 1876, 295 (obit); 1900, 287; Bryan; Brydall 454-6; Caw 166; Cundall; Halsby 129, 281; McKay 355; Studio 39,(1907),258.

**ROSS, Miss Sally** **fl 1983**
Glasgow painter. Exhibited 'Pattern of Vines' at the GI, from Clarence Dr.

**ROSS, Thomas FSA(Scot) Hon RSA** **1839-1930**
Architect and writer. Apprenticed to Kirkland and Charles Wilson in Glasgow. Appointed assistant to David MacGibbon 1862, later to become a partner. Awarded LLD from Edinburgh University 1910 and appointed Professor of Antiquities, RSA 1918. Associated with Lorimer as Editor of the *National Art Survey for Scotland,* for vol 2, 1923 and vol 3, 1925. Co-author with David MacGibbon, of the *Castellated and Domestic Architecture of Scotland* and other works. Combined artistic and architectural skills. His work as an architectural draughtsman is of the highest order, ranking him beside R W Billings(qv). He was the original architect chosen to design a side chapel for St Giles in Edinburgh. Restored the W side of Abbey Strand (Edinburgh, 1916) and designed Prestonfield Church (1900, dem 1975). Fifty-three drawings, executed between 1890 and 1920, are in the Edinburgh Room, Edinburgh City Library.
**Bibl:** Butchart 78; Gifford 218,636n,660; Peter Savage, Lorimer and the Edinburgh Craft Designers, Edinburgh 1980, 1,84,168.

**ROSS, Tom** **1876-1961**
Dundee artist of Birkhill, Lochee best known for his lithographs of the city. Also worked in oil and watercolour, the latter in strong colour and wet washes. Remarkably, as the result of a street accident most of his work was painted with his toes. Exhibited RSA(4), GI(8) & L(4).
**Bibl:** Halsby 281.

**ROSS, William, Snr** **fl 1809-dc1843**
Miniature landscape and portrait painter and teacher of drawing. His family came from Ross-shire. Married Maria Ross(qv); father of Sir William Charles R(qv), Hugh(qv) and Magdalene(qv) - all of them miniaturists. Exhibited RA(5) 1809-25 including portraits of his children 1809 and also two landscape studies of the village of Pitchford, Shropshire 1825. A chalk portrait of the artist by his son William dated 1842 is in the V & A, while another fine miniature of him was exhibited at the Edinburgh Festival Exhibition of 1965.

**ROSS, William** **fl 1753**
Portrait painter. Nothing is known of this artist beyond one recorded work. This is a slightly coarse but well observed portrait of 'Lewis Rose of Culmoney', signed and dated 'Wm Ross pinxit 1753' and measuring 30 x 24 inches, in the Kilravock private family collection, by Nairn.

**ROSS, William** **fl 1908-1935**
Aberdeen painter of local landscape and still life. Exhibited AAS(2), from 10 Thomson Street.

**ROSS, Sir Willliam Charles RA** **1794-1860**
Born London, 3 Jne; died 20 Jan. Portrait painter and portrait miniaturist also historical, classical and biblical subjects painted in oil. Son and pupil of William(qv) and Maria Ross(qv). In 1808 entered the RA Schools winning numerous prizes; also received seven premiums at the Society of Arts 1807-21. In 1814 became for a time an assistant to Andrew Robertson(qv) to whom he was related on his mother's side. Gradually abandoned historical painting in favour of portrait miniatures. He built up a large practice in the highest circles, including Queen Victoria and the Prince Consort. In 1837 The Queen and Duchess of Kent sat to him, and later Queen Adelaide, Prince Albert, the Royal children and various other members of the Royal families of France, Belgium, Portugal and Saxe-Coburg. The following year he won £100 premium at the Westminster Hall competition for the cartoon 'The Angel Raphael discussing with Adam'. He remained pre-eminent among portrait miniaturists until 1857 when he was struck down with paralysis. Said to have been extremely amiable and benevolent as well as a fine draughtsman having great skill in the use of colour and the arrangement of his sitters. Reynolds notes that 'it was his special gift to catch his sitters at their most genial and agreeable, and his miniatures of Prince Albert, Melbourne and Louis Philippe rank among the most attractive and effective portraits of the epoch'. 'An exquisite draughtsman and colourist; he designed skilfully, arranged gracefully and used elaborate finish or bold treatment as required' [Long]. 'He used a pale flesh tint and shaded the features with soft grey-blue strokes; the hair is drawn in loose masses rather than in detail and the costume often picked out with opaque white' [Foskett]. An exhibition of 220 of his works was held in London the year he died, the complete list being published in J J Foster: *Miniature Painters, British and Foreign,* vol 1. He is said to have painted over 2,200 miniatures. From 1845 he lived at 38 Fitzroy Square, remaining unmarried. Elected ARA 1838, RA 1843 and knighted in 1842. Exhibited RA(298) 1819-1859, the first three when he was aged only 15. Represented in the V & A, NPG, BM, SNPG, Wallace Collection, Nottingham AG, Royal Collection.
**Bibl:** AJ 1849, 76; 1860, 72; AU 1839, 35; Bryan; Caw 90-1; Clement & Hutton; Conn 31 (1911) 210, 261; 55 (1919) 93-4; 61 (1921) 314; 40 (1922) 154; 41 (1922) 99; 46 (1925) 33; DNB; Foskett 480-481; Gents Mag 1860 I, 513; Irwin 219,323; Long 375-6; Redgrave; Reynolds 174, 177 (pl); Sandby, History of the Royal Academy,1862,II,121-4.

**ROSS, William H A** **fl 1883-1891**
Edinburgh architect and part-time painter of architectural subjects in oil, watercolour, pen and pencil. Exhibited RSA between the above years including sketches of old Edinburgh.

**ROSS, William Leighton** **fl 1907-1908**
Minor Edinburgh painter of rural genre; exhibited RSA(3) & GI(2), from 18 Glenorchy Terrace.

**ROSSI, Eugenio Federico Carlo RSW** **1921-**
Born Johnstone, Renfrewshire, 13 Feb. Painter in oil and watercolour, also printmaker. Both parents Italian. Trained Glasgow School of Art. Influenced by Cézanne, Picasso, Braque, Matisse and Rembrandt. A brief encounter with Fauvism produced 'Portrait of a Girl' 1941. In his youth Rossi concentrated on still life becoming interested in figures in the late 1950s. The landscape which most excited him is in Tuscany. From the early 1960s there was a development away from oils to mixed media, including the use of collage. We find a preoccupation with shapes interfused with angular perspective. 'By creating a whole succession of horizontals and verticals that both overlay and underly the architecturally positioned shapes...he achieves a dignity of design and subtle rhythmic flow that have something of the quality, and sophistication, of pieces of music listened to in private. His compositions are beautifully ordered and ascetic in feeling; figurative in spite of vague hints towards abstraction than one need not take seriously...lacking the fire and depth and sense of exploration that one would hope to experience in paintings that seem content to perpetuate a theme' [Coia]. Worked consistently alone, away from any group influence, spending most of his life in Glasgow where his first one-man show was held in 1968. Combined painting with being principal teacher of art in a Glasgow school. Exhibited regularly RSA, RSW & GI. Represented in Glasgow AG.

**ROSSI, Mario** **1958-**
Born Glasgow. Painter and sculptor. Studied sculpture at Glasgow School of Art 1975-9 and Royal College of Art, London 1979-81. Gulbenkian scholar at the British School in Rome 1982-3. Although most of this early training led to the production of bronze sculptures he has moved increasingly to painting. Using classical forms such as urns and Ionic capitals he has tended toward surrealism. This led to an exhibition 'The Archaeologist' at Edinburgh City art centre (1984), a theme developed in charcoal drawings employing motifs taken from contemporary industrial landscape. 'Rossi's art is concerned with evanescence, with the fact that nothing lasts intact, everything is subject to the same laws of change and decay' [Hartley]. Represented

in SNGMA.
**Bibl:** Hartley 162; 'The Vigorous Imagination', Ex cat, Edinburgh, SNGMA 1987, 102-3 et passim; TEC, Glasgow, "New Image Glasgow', (Ex Cat 1985).

**ROSSI, Silvio Anthony** **fl 1936-1940**
Airdrie-based painter of still life, figures and flowers; exhibited RSA(11).

**ROSSVOL, Christine** **fl 1969**
Aberdeen-based designer. Married Ronning R(qv). Exhibited AAS, from 17 Rubislaw Den N.

**ROSSVOL, Ronning R** **fl 1969-1984**
Aberdeen-based watercolour artist. Trained Gray's School of Art, Aberdeen. Married the designer Christine R(qv). Exhibited regularly at the AAS between the above years, moving from Aberdeen to Dyce and then to 22 Cuninghill Avenue, Inverurie.

**ROUGH, Charles** **fl 1877**
Aberdeen topographical painter in oil; exhibited RSA(1).

**ROUGH, Helen M** **fl 1888**
Minor Glasgow figure of 35 Kersland Terrace, Hillhead; exhibited GI(1).

**ROUGH, James Johnston** **fl 1920-1972**
Edinburgh painter in oil and watercolour; local scenery, continental landscape and figure compositions. In later life he moved to the Isle of Man and finally to Lancashire. Exhibited RSA(19), RSW(3) & GI(17).

**ROUGH, William Ednie** **1892-1935**
Born Kirkcaldy. Painter in oil and watercolour of landscapes; teacher. Trained Edinburgh College of Art where his studies were interrupted by the outbreak of WW1. During the war served in the 5th Royal Scots and Northumberland Fusiliers. Awarded a diploma at the ECA 1920. Art teacher, George Heriot School and subsequently principal art teacher at Dumfries Academy. In 1932 he returned to Edinburgh to become art master at Daniel Stewart's College. Fond of Highland scenery and continental scenes especially around Honfleur and Concarneau. Exhibited RSA(7), RSW(10) & GI(3).

**ROUGVIE, Walter** **fl 1930-1936**
Fife watercolour painter of local scenery. Exhibited RSA(9) & RSW(4), from 136 High St, Leslie.

**ROUNTREE, David** **fl 1957-1958**
Glasgow topographical watercolourist. Exhibited GI(3) from Dunearn St.

**ROWAN, William Gardner** **1845-1924**
Glasgow architect and oil painter; architectural subjects, usually ecclesiastical. Pupil of **George KENNEDY**, former assistant to Barry. Specialised in church work, often beautifully detailed though he seldom designed on a large scale. Later work became increasingly Gothic. Exhibited RSA & GI(19).
**Bibl:** A Gomme & D Walker, Architecture of Glasgow, London 1997(rev), 297.

**ROWAND, M** **fl 1893**
Minor Glasgow figure; exhibited GI(1) from 227 West George St.

**ROWAND, (or ROWLAND), William** **fl 1777**
Born Glasgow(?). Miniature painter and portraitist, also teacher. All that is known of him is that by 1777 he was in New York where he became established as a painter and teacher of drawing. Grose, Long and Wallace refer to the name as Rowand but Fielding, Foskett and Schidlof prefer Rowland.
**Bibl:** Bolton; Fielding; Foskett; W Kelby: Notes on American Artists (1922) 14; Long; Schidlof.

**ROWANTREE, Frederick** **fl 1898-1903**
Glasgow painter who moved to London in the early 1900s; exhibited GI(3).

**ROWAT, James** **fl 1889-1925**
Glasgow painter in watercolour of landscapes, architectural subjects, interiors and flowers. Brother of Jessie Rowat(qv) (Mrs Fra Newbery). Exhibited 'View of Glasgow Cathedral' at the RA in 1892, also RSA(3), RSW(1), GI(31) & L(2), from 234 West George St and after 1897, West Regent St.
**Bibl:** Halsby 281.

**ROWAT, Mary** **fl 1887-1893**
Little known Paisley painter of Warriston. Exhibited GI(1) & Paisley Art Institute annually 1887-1893.

**ROWE, Irene** **fl 1970**
Edinburgh painter; exhibited 'Drying nets' at the RSA, from Barnton.

**ROWE, J Lincoln** **fl 1988**
Edinburgh artist; exhibited 'Moonlight in the Indian Ocean' at the RSA, from Sandport St.

**ROWE, Lorna** **fl 1991-**
Painter in oils of figurative subjects and genre. Enjoys contrasting patterns of colour and human movement. Exhibition 'Images of Turkey' Aberdeen 1993.

**ROWLAND, Mrs Evelyn Graham** **fl 1930-1931**
Glasgow engraver of flowers and narrative subjects. Exhibited RSA(2), AAS(2), GI(2) & L(1), latterly from 4 Camphill Avenue, Langside.

**ROWLE (or Roule) Archibald** **fl 1539-1546**
Early Edinburgh painter. In 1539 he was painting the King's Ship and in 1540 was painting artillery at Edinburgh Castle. In 1542 he was working in Register House and was painting rooms in the Governor's lodging at Edinburgh Castle in 1546.
**Bibl:** Apted 80.

**ROWSON, Hugh T** **fl 1967-1988**
Aberdeen painter and engraver of still life, domestic genre. Exhibited RSA(4) & AAS from 10 Pentland Rd and latterly from flat H, Dunecht House, Skene.

**ROXBURGH, Ebenezer B** **fl 1862-1897**
Dunfermline painter in oil and watercolour of religious subjects, portraits, landscapes, figurative subjects and interiors. Father-in-law of Robert McGregor(qv). Prolific painter although his work is now seldom seen. Among his better known works are 'Doune Castle' 1884 and 'Lochleven Castle' 1897. Exhibited RSA(49) between the above years and AAS(1) 1885, from 6 Elm Row, Edinburgh.

**ROXBURGH, Miss Josephine Maud** **fl 1881-1882**
Edinburgh painter in oil of domestic genre. Possibly sister of Ebenezer R(qv). Exhibited RSA(1) & GI(2) from Newington Lodge.

**ROXBURGH, William** **fl 1906**
Midlothian amateur landscape painter in watercolours. Exhibited GI(1) from Lasswade.

**ROYAL ASSOCIATION FOR THE PROMOTION OF THE FINE ARTS IN SCOTLAND**
**[see Association for the Promotion of the Fine Arts in Scotland]**

**ROY, J** **fl 1946-1947**
Glasgow painter. Mostly Indian subjects in watercolour. Exhibited GI(4), from Byres Rd.

**ROYAL GLASGOW INSTITUTE OF THE FINE ARTS** **1861-**
Its immediate antecedent was a public meeting convened in Glasgow on the initiative of Lord Provost Sir James Campbell for the purpose of organising annual art exhibitions in view of the West of Scotland Academy's weakening position (30 Sept 1851). Four years later an exhibition was organised by twelve local architects and held in Bath St where among the works on show were 60 drawings by David Roberts(qv) and others by Grecian Williams(qv) and Andrew Wilson(qv). In 1861 the RGI opened its first exhibition in the Corporation Galleries. When the town council refused further use of

the rooms the Institute was forced to raise the money for a building of its own and this was opened in Sauchiehall St in 1880. Although mounting debts forced it to sell a portion of its permanent collection, the crisis was overcome and in 1896 a royal charter was granted. Then in 1904, the new rooms proving too small, and the whole of the Corporation galleries becoming available again through the transfer of the city collections to Kelvingrove, exhibitions returned to their previous quarters. Managed by a council of twelve, seven laymen and five artists chosen by its members, the object of the Institute has been defined as 'to diffuse among all classes a taste for Art generally, and more especially for contemporary Art'. A successful Art Union was organised along the English model. It is interesting to note that whereas the RSA has been criticised for its insularity, at the turn of the century the Institute was criticised for being 'disdainful of native talent'. This might partially account for the fact that although there has been an internationally recognised Glasgow School there has been no Edinburgh equivalent.
**Bibl:** Brydall 365; Caw 210-211.

**ROYAL SCOTTISH ACADEMY 1826-**
Founded 27th May, 1826 when a group of artists, frustrated by the élitist policies of the Institute for the Encouragement of the Fine Arts in Scotland(qv), met to draw up plans for a rival organisation. This was first propounded in a document written and circulated by William Nicholson(qv). With Patrick Syme(qv) in the chair, an Academy was proposed having twenty-four artist members (thirteen academicians, nine associates and two associate engravers). Nine of these resigned almost at once, having subsequently appreciated the responsibilities they had been asked to incur, and at a second meeting (on Boxing Day, 1826), the remaining fifteen resolved to proceed toward a first public exhibition the following February. A Council of four was elected: Patrick Syme (chairman), James Stevenson, William Nicholson (secretary) and Thomas Hamilton (treasurer). The first exhibition, held concurrently with the Institution's (to whom a majority had remained loyal), produced 282 works from 67 artists. Duly encouraged and supported by the large number of artists who had now deserted The Royal Institution, amalgamation was achieved, largely through the good services of Lord Cockburn and Lord Justice Hope. The first general meeting took place on 11 November 1829. Exhibitions continued in Waterloo Place until the expiry of the lease in 1834. George Wilson(qv) was the first President until his death in 1837 when he was succeeded by William Allan (soon to be knighted). An application for a charter of incorporation was refused but a second was successful. On 13 August 1838 the academy became the Royal Scottish Academy of Painting, Sculpture and Architecture. Hostility with the Royal Institution continued so that in 1846 the RSA was informed that only two of the four exhibition rooms would remain available. This they refused to accept and Playfair(qv) was commissioned to design a new building the foundation stone of which was laid by Prince Albert on 30th August 1850. Work was completed in 1855 with general custody and maintenance vested in the Board of Manufacturers, the RSA having exclusive charge of the public galleries, council room and library. The first exhibition in the new building, the 29th, assembled probably the best ever seen at one time in Scotland. Donations began to arrive, establishing funds to support needy artists and to provide awards for the young. Among the first bequests were £10,000 in 1826 from Peter Spalding of Heriot Row (a former superintendent of the Calcutta Mint), £1,000 from Alex Keith of Dunottar in 1852 and a similar amount from the recently bereaved mother of George Paul Chalmers. There has accrued a substantial number of bursaries, prizes and scholarships primarily for the benefit of younger exhibitors. The most important are the **W & J Burness Award** (for an outstanding work in any medium by a young Scottish artist), **Chalmers Bursary** (bequeathed by Mrs Collie, mother of G P Chalmers, for distinguished work in the Life School, the first winner of which in 1882 was T Austen Brown(qv)), **Chalmers-Jervise Prize** (donated by Andrew Jervise of Brechin for the most deserving students in painting, sculpture, architecture, wood engraving or etching, first won in 1890 by Allan Stewart), **City of Edinburgh Award** (to encourage young Edinburgh artists of particular merit), **McGrigor Donald Sculpture Award** (for the most outstanding sculpture in the annual exhibition), **Guthrie Award** (instituted by the 17th Earl of Moray to commemorate the presidency of Sir James Guthrie, given to the most outstanding work in the exhibition by a Scottish artist under 33 years old), **Highland Society of London Award** (for the best work in any discipline by a Highland artist), **Maude Gemmell Hutchison Prize** (2, for the best paintings or drawings of an animal or animals), **Ireland Alloys Award** (for an outstanding work in any medium by an artist under the age of 35), **Keith Prize** (donated in 1851, originally for the best student in the Life School, and first won in 1854 by Robert Herdman(qv), now given for the best work shown by a student), **Latimer Awards**(2, for meritorious works by Scottish artists below the age of 33), **Maclaine-Watters Medal** (donated by a friend of G P Chalmers, and designed by Sir Noel Paton in 1877 for the best student in the Life Class - first awarded in 1878 to Patrick W Adam(qv)), **Meyer Oppenheim Prize** (for a painter or sculptor under 35 years old), **RSA Medal for Architecture** (for outstanding work, preferably a drawing), **Saltire Society Purchase** (for a purchase of a drawing, painting or sculpture by a Scot under the age of 30 living and working in Scotland, as a gift for the RSA permanent collection), **Benno Schotz Prize** (for the most promising work by a sculptor under the age of 33 living in Scotland), **Scottish Arts Club Prize** (for a painting, drawing or print), **Scottish Post Office Board Award** (for a painting in any medium or a drawing by an artist living and working in Scotland), **Stuart Prize** (donated in 1864 by Lady Stuart of Allanbank for a student sculpture), **John Murray Thomson Award** (for a young artist of promise) and the **Ottilie Wallace Scholarship Fund Prize** (for the best work by a sculptress). In spite of the conflicting enticements of London and the continent, and the emergence of the Glasgow Institute(qv) in 1861, the RSA has retained its position as the dominant force in Scottish contemporary art, with a large majority of Scotland's leading artists among its members and associates. If at times it has succumbed to a conservatism endemic to establishment institutions, and more recently, to a numbing Edinburgh parochialism, these are characteristics other academies in larger places have experienced and ones which will assuredly again be overcome.
**Bibl:** Brydall 334-349; Caw 62-7,209-210,223; Esmé Gordon, The Royal Scottish Academy 1826-1976, Edinburgh 1976; Sir George Harvey, Notes on the Early History of the Royal Scottish Academy, Edinburgh 1873; Irwin 187-8,283-288 et passim; James Paterson, The Royal Scottish Academy, A Retrospect, Edinburgh 1911; 'Royal Scottish Academy', (ed Chas Holme), Studio, special issue, 1907.

**ROYAL SCOTTISH WATER-COLOUR SOCIETY 1878-**
Founded in Glasgow in 1878 by a number of artists, Sir Francis Powell and Austen K Brown (secretary of the RSA in 1906) in the vanguard, who felt that the art of water-colour painting was neglected in existing exhibitions. Founder members numbered 25 and then, as now, they were drawn impartially from across the nation, and beyond, making the RSW in Caw's words 'of all the art societies in Scotland perhaps the most representative'. Exhibitions are generally held in Glasgow - the Society has always been based in the west - but they have also taken place in Edinburgh, Dundee and even London. A royal charter was granted in 1888. During the first hundred years there were only ten Presidents of whom the first was Sir Francis Powell(qv). Sam Bough(qv) was the first Vice-President but his death within a year of the Society's foundation led to the election of William McTaggart(qv) 1879. The first Treasurer was Charles Blatherwick(qv).
**Bibl:** Caw 211; Halsby (with Appendices listing original and more recent members).

**ROYDS, Mabel Alington (Mrs E S Lumsden) 1874-1941**
Born Bedfordshire. Painter in oil and watercolour, also woodcuts. In addition to teaching and producing prints and woodcuts also executed book illustrations. Her woodcuts were prepared in an unique manner in which the colour was applied by brush giving each cut individuality. Sometimes plans were laid down in collage, some of which still survive. Studied under Tonks at the Slade, later visiting Paris where she met Sickert. Then went to Canada, returning to Britain 1911 to join the staff of the ECA where she became friendly with Fergusson(qv) and Peploe(qv). Married the etcher Ernest Lumsden(qv) 1914. Sketched extensively during a honeymoon in India and Tibet, 1916. Returned to Edinburgh 1917. Favourite subjects were children, animals and landscape, all treated with a delicate sensitivity and charm and a vibrant yet quiet use of colour that deserve greater recognition. Exhibited RSA(45), RHA(1), L(6), GI(3) & SWA(1). Represented in BM, V&A, Ulster Museum of Art, Iowa AG (USA).
**Bibl:** Herbert Furst (ed), The Modern Woodcut, London, 1924; Hartley 163; 'Modern British Woodcuts and Lithographs by British

and French Artists' Studio, special number, 1919; Malcolm C. Salaman (ed), Fine Prints of the Year, 1923, London, 1924.

**RUDD, David Heylin** **1894-c1960**
Glasgow painter, wood engraver, etcher and engraver. Studied Glasgow, London, Basle, Paris and Zurich. Became Curator, Glasgow Corporation AG before retiring for medical reasons 1951. Served with distinction in the RFC during WWI and again in WW2. Exhibited RSA(2), GI(4) & L(4) between 1928-1931, from 48 Clifford St.

**RUFFINI, Luigi** **fl 1782-1801**
Italian born professional embroiderer who settled in Scotland 1782. Introduced a form of white embroidery - Dresden work and tambouring - no longer made commercially in Scotland. Established a workroom in Edinburgh employing twenty apprentices, and in 1783 the Board of Trustees gave him a grant. A further application in 1784 drew no response and having no fewer than seventy apprentices in March 1785, a further application enabled him to move to larger premises. By this time knowledge of his work had extended to western Scotland. A modification using water-soluble dye led to the western trade establishing their own tambour workshops which in turn led to the development of Ayrshire embroidery. A further appeal to the Board in 1801 was turned down.
**Bibl:** Margaret Swain 93-8; M Swain, *Tamboured muslin in Scotland*, Embroidery, vol XIV, no 1, Spring 1963, p20.

**RULE, Robert** **fl 1890**
Glasgow landscape painter; exhibited 'Montrose harbour' at the AAS, from Kelvinside.

**RULLAN, Ayrton** **fl 1883**
Midlothian watercolour painter of landscape; exhibited RSA(1) from St Ann's Mount, Polton.

**RUNCI(E)MAN, Belle** **fl 1902**
Aberdeenshire amateur artist. Exhibited a coastal and a river scene at the AAS, from Castletown, King Edward.

**RUNCIMAN, Alexander** **1736-1785**
Born Edinburgh, 15 Aug; died Edinburgh, 21 Oct. Son of an architect and builder and the elder brother of John R(qv). Apprenticed to John Norrie(qv), the decorator, before continuing his studies at Foulis' Academy in Glasgow and in Rome where he went with his brother in 1766, returning to London in 1774 whereupon he resided in Leicester Square with Hogarth's widow. First came to notice with 'Nausicaa and Ulysses', painted in Italy. A contemporary critic spoke of 'the fine drawing of Julio Romano' and 'the deep juicy lustre of Tintoret'. His style at this time was an exaggeration of his friend Fuseli's but 'sometimes he dropped into simplicity and pleasantness'. In one of his paintings Allan Cunningham had inscribed on the back of a stretcher 'other men talked meat and drink, but Runciman talked landscape.' Appointed Master of the Trustees Academy 1772-1786, succeeding Charles Pavillon(qv). Although at the time of his appointment the Trustees were pleased to appoint someone 'whose genius had been well known to the people of taste in this country', his disinterest in the Academy's industrial aims and the licence he gave students to attend who wished to make drawings merely for amusement attracted their displeasure, so that in 1774 they asked him to amend his policy. However, his services were neither thanked nor praised and it seems that perhaps he was less diligent than he might have been and certainly less than his successor David Allan(qv). In 1766 he painted 'A Pagan Sacrifice' in grisaille on the ceiling of the portico of Sir James Clark's house in Penicuik but after his return from Italy, where he concentrated on large scale figure compositions, he began to paint a vast Homeric work 'Ulysses surprising Nausicaa' shown at the Academy in 1772. Other classical scenes were the 'Judgement of Hercules' (the drawing for which is in the NGS), 'Orpheus and Eurydice', 'The Birth of Venus' and 'Orestes pursued by the Furies' (now in the NGS). He was also inspired by the works of Milton and Shakespeare but his work at Penicuik, 'the most ambitious series of murals commissioned in Scotland in the 18th century' [Irwin] were destroyed by fire in 1899. Other wall panels include 'The Ascension', 'Prodigal Son', 'Christ and the Samaritan Woman' and 'Moses & Elijah' for the Church of St Patrick in the Cowgate, Edinburgh. Lockhart, quoted by Irwin, commented that 'there is about his often miserably drawn figures, and as often miserably arranged groups, a certain rudeness of character and grandeur, a certain indescribable majesty and originality of conception, which shows at once, that had he been better educated, he might have been a princely painter' (Peter's letters, II, 277-8). His interest in landscape painting, although secondary to his classical subjects, remained with him throughout his life. 'An Italian Landscape' (NGS) shows his skill in achieving atmosphere and handling paint. It also shows that, contrary to what some critics argue, he was a fine colourist although much of his work suffers from its present poor condition. In his drawings of the classical ruins 'he is particularly skilful in capturing their romantic quality which rise dramatically from his foregrounds with an almost exaggerated scale reminiscent of Piranesi...he is interested in these drawings in the crumpled remains of the Roman past, including the partially buried or the overgrown...Drawings such as 'The Tomb of the Horatii' are among the finest re-interpretations of ruins by an 18th century British artist, and are amongst the best demonstrations of the romantic fascination in ruins and desolation' [Irwin]. As a man he was Falstaffian and flambuoyant, earning the soubriquet 'Sir Brimstone'. Topham referred to him as 'the Sir Joshua Reynolds of this country, whose invention is perhaps equal to that of any painter in Europe'. There is a portrait group in the SNPG of Alex Runciman and John Brown by themselves. His drawing, 'East View of the Porch of Holyrood House' c1779 was engraved by A Cameron and used in Arnot's *History of Edinburgh.* Represented in Tate AG, NGS, SNPG (3) including Self-portrait.
**Bibl:** Armstrong 8; Susan E. Booth, 'Alexander Runciman in Italy and his work for Sir James Clark, of Penicuik, 1766-1773', MA Thesis Univ of London 1967, partially published in Journal of Warburg and Courtauld Inst, XXXII, 1969, 332-343; John Brown, Obit of Alexander Runciman 'Caledonian Mercury' 26.10.1785; Bryan; Brydall 162-4; Burlington Mag, CXII, Jan 1970, 29-31; Bushnell; Butchart 17; Caw 40-43; DNB; Gifford 169; Halsby 22-4 et al; Irwin 78, 91-2, 105-111, 130-3 et passim; Mcmillan[GA] 41-65 et passim; 'Alexander Runciman and the influences that shaped his style', unpub PhD thesis, Edin Univ 1974; 'Alexander Runciman in Rome', Burlington Mag. cxii, 1970; Scots Mag, August 1802, 'Biographical Sketch of Alexander Runciman'; Topham, Letters from Edinburgh, London 1776 passim.

**RUNCIMAN, John** **1744-1768**
Born Edinburgh; died Naples. Painter of portraits and classical and historical scenes in oil and chalk; also an etcher. Younger brother of Alexander R(qv). Although his life was short the works that remain show the highest promise. His paintings were generally small with an unusual quality of colour. Visited Rome with his brother 1767. Although he died so young he absorbed strong influences from the work of Teniers, Rembrandt and Dürer. Fuseli thought that he 'excited much livelier expectations of his abilities as an artist' than his brother Alexander. 'His chalk drawings have a vitality of line that his brother hardly ever equals' [Irwin]. His earliest known work is an etching 'The Taking down of the Nether Bow Port' 1764, the earliest known Scottish etching of importance; the last known work to survive is his 'Self-Portrait' 1767-8. This shows him reflecting on Michelangelo with the classical figure from one of the Medici tombs visible behind him. He was an exceptionally accomplished draughtsman, exemplified in 'Bacchus reclining against a wine sack' (NGS), a work which shows the influence of Rubens. His 'Salome receiving John the Baptist's head' (NGS) is based on a Dürer woodcut, while perhaps his best known painting 'King Lear in the Storm' (1767, NGS) again shows the influence of Rubens. *In The Art of Etching,* Lumsden speaks of John Runciman as 'the first Scottish etcher of importance'. Shortly before his death he is said to have destroyed all his studio work. It was a tragic loss to Scotland's artistic heritage when he died of tuberculosis aged only 24. There is a monument to him in the Canongate Church, Edinburgh. Represented in SNPG ('Self-portrait').
**Bibl:** Armstrong 8; Bryan; Brydall 164-5; Bushnell; Butchart 17-18,54,78; Caw 43; DNB; Halsby 282; Irwin 111-112 et passim; E.S. Lumsden, The Art of Etching, 1925, 192-6; McKay 21-2; Macmillan [GA] 43-50; Macmillan [SA] 118-9 et passim; W.M. Merchant, 'John Runciman's Lear in the Storm', J of Warburg & Courtauld Inst, XVII, 1954, 385-6.

**RUNCIMAN, Miss Mary E** **fl 1913-1945**
Glasgow painter of informal portraits and genre; exhibited 'Portrait and Reflections' at the RSA 1913, and, many years later, GI(1) 1945.

**RUSHTON, William C** **c1875-1921**
Painter originally from Cambuslang who went to Edinburgh and then to Yorkshire. Exhibited GI(5) & L(9).

**RUSKIN, John** **1819-1900**
Born London, Feb 8; died Coniston, Jan 20. Art critic and historian, author and watercolourist, especially of buildings and topographical subjects. Only son of **John James RUSKIN**, a Scottish wine importer with artistic interests who had studied under Nasmyth. Trained at King's College, London and studied drawing under Copley Fielding and J.D. Harding. Enrolled at Christ Church, Oxford 1836 and in 1839 won the Newdigate Prize. Travelled around Europe 1840-1. Met Turner in 1840 and visited Venice for the first time in 1841. *Modern Painters* was published in 1843; begun as a defence of Turner it developed into an examination of the general principles of art criticism. Thus, by 1860 when the series ended, he had become Britain's leading art critic and an ardent advocate of the pre-Raphaelites. In 1869 became Slade Professor of Art at Oxford. Elected HRWS, 1873. Illustrated *The Seven Lamps of Architecture* with 14 etched plates (1849), *The Stones of Venice* (1853), *The Poems of John Ruskin* (1891) and *Poetry of Architecture* (1893). Retired to Coniston 1871 and became increasingly a recluse, dying there from pneumonia. His personality has been well summarised by Martin Hardie 'Typical of the age in his compound of wild prejudice and generous enthusiasm and in the firm belief, which he shared with Gladstone, in his own straightforwardness and honesty of opinion. Like Gladstone, he showed 'equal readiness to fight for the shadow or the substance, a comma or a creed'. He was censorious and fastidious like Matthew Arnold. In all the great Victorians, Carlyle and Tennyson among the writers, Landseer and Leighton among the painters, there was the same mixture of high intellect, religious faith, self-assurance, intractability, partisanship, dignified presence, sometimes a suspicion of hypocrisy. And yet they had character and a common heroic quality'. One of the towering figures of British art criticism, influential even when out of fashion. Represented in BM, V & A, Glasgow AG, Ashmolean (Oxford), Birkenhead AG, Birmingham AG, Brantwood AG, Fitzwilliam Museum (Cambridge), Sheffield AG, Nat Gall of Canada(Ottawa).
**Bibl:** Caw 132,139,154,169,180,182,195; W.G. Collingwood, The Art Teaching of JR, 1891; J. Evans, JR, 1954; Halsby 93-4,108-9 et al; Martin Hardie, II,43-5; Houfe; Irwin 244-5 et al; M. Lutyens, Millais and the Ruskins, 1967; P. Quennell, JR, 1949; P.H. Walton, The Drawings of JR, 1972; T.J. Wise & J.P. Smart, Bibliography, 1893.

**RUSS, Annie L R** **fl 1896-1904**
Amateur watercolourist and flower painter. Exhibited RSA(1), RSW(1) & GI(3) from Pollockshields.

**RUSSEL, George** **1810-1898**
Aberdeen sculptor. The bachelor son of a leading confectioner in the city he first came to attention for his execution of elaborate figureheads for ship's prows. Later specialised in portrait busts, sometimes with a narrative component. It is recorded that on one of his Aberdeen properties there was a basement containing a bakery and because of poor sanitation and the proximity of a sewer the Town Council resolved to close the building. Russel deemed an adjacent ironmonger, Alexander Stephen, responsible for the complaint and proceeded to execute a grotesque gargoyle of poor Stephen which he placed on the nearest street corner so that the shopkeeper suffered a contemptuous daily reminder. The gargoyle now decorates the south-east corner of Provost Skene's House, Aberdeen. Exhibited RSA(2).
**Bibl:** John A Soutar, The Deeside Field, 18,1984,107.

**RUSSELL, Miss -** **fl 1887**
Aberdeen still-life painter; exhibited AAS(2), from Rosemount Terrace.

**RUSSELL, A W** **fl 1919**
Amateur Edinburgh painter of 81 Balgreen Road, Murrayfield; exhibited RSA(1).

**RUSSELL, Alastair B** **fl 1950**
Renfrew painter; exhibited 'Killin church' at the RSA.

**RUSSELL, Alexander L** **fl 1929-1956**
Dundee stained glass designer. Exhibited RSA, including a design for a stained glass window in St. Mary's Episcopal church, Newport, Fife depicting the Nativity (1951); also GI(5), latterly from Perth Rd.

**RUSSELL, Charles** **fl 1866-1873**
Painter in oil of topographical and natural history subjects. Although he worked in Glasgow he also lived for a time in Edinburgh. Exhibited RSA(5).

**RUSSELL, Charles RHA** **1852-1910**
Born Dumbarton 4 Feb; died Blackrock, Ireland 12 Dec. Painter in oils of portrait and genre. Son of John Bucknell R(qv). Those who remember him as a young lad at Fochabers speak of him as a 'gey wild boy'. Moved to Dublin as a young man in 1874. Elected ARHA 1891, RHA 1893. Exhibited Royal Hibernian Academy from 1878. Exhibited 'A Rival in the Studio' at the RA 1889, also RHA(86) & L(2), latterly from 6 St Stephen's Green.

**RUSSELL, Daisy** **fl 1928**
Amateur Greenock painter of 11 Ardgowan Square; exhibited GI(1).

**RUSSELL, David** **fl 1945**
Glasgow amateur landscape painter in watercolours. Exhibited a view on Iona at GI, from Hector Rd.

**RUSSELL, Miss Dhuie (Mrs Tully)** **fl 1875-1921**
Painter in oil and watercolour of landscapes, flower paintings and angling scenes. Daughter of John Bucknell R(qv), became locally well known for her pictures of the Spey. Working from her home at Spey Cottage, Fochabers, in her early career specialised mainly in flower paintings, later becoming a competent painter of Speyside landscapes. Her happy disposition was reflected in her paintings - sometimes a fisherman is shown on the point of landing a good fish. Her views of Old Fochabers and her landscapes of the Upper Spey are delicately executed. Also modelled fish caught on the river with her brother John(qv), at first with her father and later with her husband John Tully who became a leading expert in modelling salmon in wood with Dhuie executing the painting in which she captured precisely the natural colour of the fish. Examples of their work can still be seen in local houses and even some fishing huts on Speyside. Later they moved to their own home on West Street. Exhibited RSA(2) 1894 and 1897; also 'Grilse Pool, Fochabers' AAS 1921.

**RUSSELL, George Horne PRCanA** **1861-1933**
Born Banff. Painter in oil of portraits and marines. Trained Aberdeen School of Art and South Kensington. Moved to Montreal 1890 becoming the fashionable painter of Montreal society and 'even followed it during the summer months to St Stephens in the Bay of Fundy, where he painted seascapes of the holiday resorts'. Like other academic artists his canvases were pleasing and gave the subjects a dignified and stately air beyond the capabilities of the camera...their paintings had a taste that seldom allowed for harsh colour...they were interested to please or charm and made no immediate demand on the minds and emotions. They gave satisfaction by following convention' [Harper]. Elected Associate of the Canadian Academy 1909, full member 1918; President 1922-6. Exhibited Canadian Academy. Represented in Nat Gall of Canada.
**Bibl:** J. Harper, Painting in Canada, 1977.

**RUSSELL, Captain Harald Alain** **1893-?**
Born Belle-Ile-en-Mer, France, Sep 24. Painter in oil and watercolour of landscapes, seascapes, fish and insect life. Son of John Peter R(qv). After a spell in Berkshire settled at Killinver, Oban, c1924 and from there exhibited RSA(1), RSW(2) & GI(2).

**RUSSELL, J Galloway** **?-1917**
Dunfermline artist in oil of considerable promise whose career was tragically cut short when he was killed in action on May 3 1917.

**RUSSELL, James** **1754-1786**
Professor of Surgery at Edinburgh University and amateur draughtsman. Also collector of Old Master drawings. A pen, pencil and sepia wash drawing 'View in Ayrshire' is in NGS. A portrait of Russell and his father, Professor of Natural Philosophy at Edinburgh, by David Martin, painted when the young man was fifteen, is in the SNPG.

**RUSSELL, James A** **1865-fl 1886**
Painter in oils. Third son of John Bucknell R(qv) by his second

marriage and brother of Dhuie R(qv). He specialised in angling scenes and fish, especially salmon and trout, very much in the manner of his father. Often signed his work 'John B Russell' in distinction to his father who signed 'John Russell'. Exhibited RHA 1886 from the family home Spey Cottage, Fochabers.

**RUSSELL, James** **fl 1952**
Amateur Glasgow landscape painter. Exhibited GI(1), from Keir St.

**RUSSELL, John Bucknell** **1819/20-1893**
Born Edinburgh; died Fochabers, 4 May. Painter in oil of fishing scenes and landscape, also murals. Brought up in Aberdeen where he began life as a house painter. Soon turned to art and one of his first assignments was the painting of an altar piece for St Mary's Chapel, Huntly Street, Aberdeen. Later he returned to Edinburgh for a number of years exhibiting at the RSA. Settled in Fochabers c1868, probably being attracted there by the possibility of work with the Duke of Richmond and Gordon and his friends who came to Gordon Castle for the sporting season. Also a fine woodcarver, his models of Spey salmon made to the exact measurements of the originals added to his reputation. The modelling was done in the old laundry workshop at Gordon Castle and later painted in his studio, with his daughter Dhuie(qv) as his assistant. Executed 11 very large panel paintings with scenes taken from Aesop's fables in Haddo House for the 7th Earl of Aberdeen and did fresco work at Kelly Castle, Fife. Other work completed in the neighbourhood was at the Chapel in Buckie. Enjoyed the patronage of Lord Lovat for whom he worked in Inverness. An active member of the local community in both church and politics, founder of the Fochabers Conservative Association and a Knight of the Primrose. An extremely generous, hospitable and popular figure, interested in all the arts. Conductor of the choir of St Mary's, Aberdeen and later at St Mary's Chapel, Fochabers. Married twice. Held his first one man show in Fochabers on 26 Sept 1885. One of the finest Scottish painters of fish against a background of appropriate landscape. In 1989 one of his paintings realised £26,000. A portrait of a lady by 'John Russell' is in Castle Fraser (NTS). [From notes provided by Gordon Baxter, personal communication.]

**RUSSELL, Kathleen Barbara** **1940-**
Born Edinburgh. Painter in watercolour of flowers, plants, landscapes & seascapes. Trained Edinburgh College of Art under Philipson(qv) and Gillies(qv). In 1970 married the head gardener of King's College University, London, before coming north to join the staff at the Edinburgh College of Art. In 1975 returned south to combine teaching in London while continuing her own artistic career. Exhibited RSA(14) 1963-72. Represented in City of Edinburgh collection by a large oil 'St. Abbs, Storm' (1965).

**RUSSELL, Marie** **fl 1910**
Glasgow painter of minor consequence; exhibited GI(1) from Cleveden, Kelvinside.

**RUSSELL, Neil** **fl 1938-1948**
Fife landscape painter; exhibited 'Spring landscape' and 'Garden in winter' at the RSA, from Blairburn, Culross.

**RUSSELL, Nicola** **1962-**
Scottish painter & textile designer. Trained Duncan of Jordanstone School of Art 1987-91 coming under the influence of Will McLean(qv) and Peter Collins(qv). After graduating became primarily a designer while still continuing to paint. Won Incorporation of Weavers of Glasgow Award (best final year student) 1997. Her designs have been shown in London & Paris. Exhibits RSA since 1992 from Dunesk Lodge, Green Lane, Lasswade.

**RUSSELL, Peter J** **1948-**
Born Portsmouth. Stirling-based painter and former teacher. Studied mathematics and the history of art, Edinburgh University 1966-69 before proceeding to art training at Duncan of Jordanstone College of Art 1969-73. Retired from teaching 1991 in order to devote himself to full-time painting and the development of art appreciation and creation in Scotland's central region. The same year elected to the Council of the Society of Scottish Artists. First solo exhibition in the Collective Gallery, Edinburgh 1985, followed annually by others. Excited by industrial activity, stimulated by visits to Germany, and by notions of conflict and reconstruction. Continues to enjoy an involvement with education, especially with those who have experienced mental illness. Member, Hanging Together group(qv). Occasionally collaborates with Karen Strang(qv). Major exhibition *Building 2000* at the Smith AG, Stirling, 1995. Exhibits RSA, RGI, RSW, AAS 1980-94.
**Bibl:** Andrew Guest, Building 2000, Ex Cat, Smith Art Gallery, Stirling 1995.

**RUSSELL, Rhona I C** **fl c1920**
Aberdeen flower painter; exhibited AAS(1), from 47 Nelson St.

**RUSSELL, Robert Ramsay** **fl 1876-1912**
Edinburgh miniature painter usually on ivory, also watercolourist. Exhibited RSA(10) & GI(1) at first from 7 Panmure Place, Edinburgh, after 1911 from Glasgow.

**RUSSELL, Wallace** **fl 1887-1897**
Glasgow painter of domestic, topographical and figure subjects. Exhibited RA 1889, giving his address as the 'Palette Club, Glasgow'; also RSA(2), GI(4) & L(1).

**RUSSELL, William H** **fl 1926-1934**
Lanarkshire engraver, mostly woodcuts. Exhibited RSA & GI(2) from Carstairs.

**RUSSELL, William** **fl 1937-1951**
Glasgow landscape and figure painter. Exhibited 'Tomato pickers, Antibes' at the RSA 1951, GI(1) 1949 & a view on Arran at the AAS, from 33 Whitehall Avenue. Possibly the same as previous entry.

**RUSSELL-HALL ROI** **1905-?**
Born 28 Feb. Painter in oil of figurative subjects and landscape. Trained Dundee School of Art and in Paris. Elected ROI 1959. Exhibited RA, ROI, RP and in the provinces, from a London base.

**RUTHERFORD, Alexandra Victoria ('Alexa')** **1952-**
Born Dunfermline, 24 May. Sculptress and printmaker. Educated at Bell-Baxter High School, Cupar and Duncan of Jordanstone College of Art, Dundee. Specialised in printmaking, mostly of landscapes, has worked increasingly in linocuts. Lives in Edinburgh. Exhibited RSA 1971 and 1975.

**RUTHERFORD, Miss Ann C** **fl 1877-1881**
Painter of The Scuars, Jedburgh, who exhibited 2 studies of wild-flowers in oil at the RSA.

**RUTHERFORD, Archibald** **1743-1779**
Born Jedburgh. Painter in oil and watercolour of landscapes. Became drawing master at Perth Academy. In 1776 he intended to settle in Edinburgh but the Board of Manufacturers encouraged him to live in Glasgow and to teach there. In 1779 there was a sale of his drawings in Edinburgh shortly after his premature death. Represented in NGS(4).

**RUTHERFORD, Christine** **fl 1969**
Aberdeen sculptress and silver designer. Exhibited AAS(1), from 37 Woodend Place.

**RUTHERFORD, George Jnr** **fl 1932-1933**
Little known engraver of 12 Watt Street, Greenock, exhibited two linocuts at the GI.

**RUTHERFORD, George** **fl 1953**
Edinburgh artist. Exhibited a study in pen at the GI, from Buckingham Terrace.

**RUTHERFORD, Helen Copeland** **fl 1910-1929**
Portrait painter including portrait miniatures, from Ardnadam, Argyllshire. She moved to London before finally settling in Edinburgh from where she exhibited at the RA(1), RSA(6), RI(7) & L(2).

**RUTHERFORD, Mrs James** **fl 1894**
Amateur Glasgow painter; exhibited 'A street in Constantinople' at the GI, from 2 Ailsa Terrace, Hillhead'.

**RUTHERFORD, Mrs Joyce Watson (née Watson)** **fl 1920-1942**
Landscape painter in watercolour; mostly Scottish scenes. Lived at

Rhu, Dunbartonshire, before settling in Huelva, Spain c1935, returning to Scotland before the outbreak of war. Exhibited RSW(6), RSA(2) & GI(5).

**RUTHERFORD, Louisa Marion** **fl 1977**
Aberdeenshire printmaker; trained Gray's School of Art, Aberdeen. Exhibited AAS, from the Schoolhouse, Newtonhill.

**RUTHERFORD, Maggie A** **fl 1908-1929**
Glasgow watercolourist and etcher who painted landscapes and flowers from Govanhill. Exhibited 'A close, Stonehaven' at the RSA, also AAS(2) & GI(4), latterly from 28 High St, Jedburgh.
**Bibl:** Halsby 282.

**RUTHERFORD, Mary W** **fl 1895-1920**
Edinburgh watercolour painter of landscape, still life, domestic animals and portrait heads. Exhibited regularly RSA(21), also GI(8), AAS(4) & L(4), from 12 Shandwick Place.

**RUTHERFORD, Patrick J** **fl 1889-1891**
Minor Edinburgh painter; exhibited GI(1) & L(1).

**RUTHERFORD, Stewart** **fl 1927-1947**
Glasgow painter of Scottish topography; exhibited GI(9) & NEA(2), latterly from, Bearsden.

**RUTHVEN, Lady Mary (née Campbell)** **1789-1885**
Amateur painter in oil and watercolours of still life and classical landscape. Daughter of Walter Campbell of Shawfield. Married James, Lord Ruthven 1813, living at Winton House, East Lothian where her friend and mentor Sam Bough(qv) was a frequent guest. Her watercolours of Greek temples, vases and sculpture after Lusieri are skilfully executed. Exhibited RSA(2) 1880. Represented in NGS(4).
**Bibl:** Halsby 114,282; Irwin 361.

**RUXTON, Charles C** **fl 1933**
Arbroath painter; exhibited 'A friend' at the RSA, from 18 Glover St.

**RYAN, John Gerald Christopher** **1921-?**
Born Edinburgh, Mar 4. Book illustrator and cartoonist. Educated Ampleforth College 1930-43. After war service in Burma 1943-46 undertook art training Regent Street Polytechnic 1946-48. Assistant Art Master, Harrow School 1948-54 before becoming a full-time freelance artist. Influenced by Ardizzone, HM Bateman and Ronald Searle, his most popular work was Captain Pugwash, first created 1950 with many subsequent appearances in book form, on the radio and on television. Most of his originals are with the centre for the Study of Cartoons, University of Kent. Ryan wrote and illustrated *Captain Pugwash* (1956), *Pugwash Aloft* (1958), *Pugwash and the Ghost Ship* (1962), eleven additional Pugwash titles, *The Story of Tiger-Pig* (1977), *Dodo's Delight* (1977), *Doodle's Homework* (1978), *Tiger-Pig at the Circus* (1978), *Crockle Saves the Ark* (1979), *Crockle Takes a Swim* (1980), *All Aboard* (12 stories, 1980-83), *Crockle Adrift* (1981), *Crockle and the Kite* (1981), *The Floating Jungle* (1981), *Frisco and Fred* (1985), *Frisco and Fred and the Space Monster* (1986). Cartoonist for the *Catholic Herald* from 1963 until shortly before his death. Commissioned by *Radio Times, Eagle, Girl.* He also illustrated, with Sylvia Stokeld, Wilson: *The Second Young Eve* (1962). Exhibited RA. Represented in the collection of the Univ. of Kent.
**Bibl:** Driver, Horne 380; Mahoney; Peppin.

**RYMER, James** **fl c1775-1795**
Edinburgh engraver. Bushnell gives two entries but probably the same. No known work remains.
**Bibl:** Bushnell.

**RYMER, William C** **fl 1868**
Edinburgh landscape painter in oil; exhibited RSA(4).

# S

**SADLER, Patricia** **1946-**
Born Selkirk. Landscape and flower painter in watercolours and acrylic. Especially inspired by the challenging patterns of light and colour of Provence and the Scottish Borders. Her work is a personal response to the scenes she remembers so that representation of their natural source is not always apparent.

**ST GEORGE, Joseph** **fl 1815-1847**
Sculptor and painter. At the exhibition of works by Scottish artists held in Edinburgh in 1815 he showed a portrait bust of the Duke of Wellington. This was reported in the *Scots Mag* as being 'freely modelled and the drapery very well cast...this young artist seems to be making rapid advancement and to feel his art'. Later moved to London exhibiting two works at the RA 'A Scene in Kensington Gardens' 1843 and 'A view in Saxony, the fortress of Koenigstein in the distance' 1847, from 50 Jermyn Street.
**Bibl:** Gunnis; Scots Mag, Aug 1815, 100.

**ST GEORGE, Sylvia** **fl 1905-1940**
Painter in oil of landscapes. Trained Edinburgh. Moved to Colchester, Essex c1915. Exhibited RA(6) 1905-1940, RSA(5) & NEA(6); also a number of provincial galleries.

**ST LUKE'S ACADEMY** **1729-1731**
The first but short-lived Edinburgh public academy modelled on the Roman academy of the same name(qv), formed 'for the encouragement of these excellent arts of Painting, Sculpture, Architecture, etc and Improvement of the Students'. Sometimes called the 'Missing Academy'. The twenty-nine original signatories included James McEuen, William Adam, the young Allan Ramsay, two members of the Norie family of decorators, John Alexander and Allan Ramsay snr. George Marshall was elected President, the engraver Richard Cooper Treasurer and Roderick Chalmers Secretary. Altogether there were 18 artist members and 11 honorary members. Meetings were held November-February and June-July with facilities available for a total of eight hours weekly.
**Bibl:** Brydall 110-113; Irwin 83-5.

**SALMON, Miss Helen Russell (Mrs Thomas Hunt)** **1855-1891**
Born Glasgow. Glasgow-based painter in oil of flowers, figure subjects and portraits. Daughter of an architect. Trained Glasgow School of Art. Married the artist Thomas Hunt 1887. Lived latterly at Woodlands, Gairlochhead, Dunbartonshire. Exhibited RA(6) 1884-1890; also RSA(6), GI(23), AAS(2) & L(4). Represented in Glasgow AG.

**SALMON, James Snr** **1805-1888**
Glasgow architect. Father of WF Salmon; grandfather of James S, jnr(qv). Apprenticed under John Brash(qv). By 1830 he was in practice on his own but 1843-1854 joined with **Robert BLACK** (1800-1869), architect of the Exchange courts and Adelaide Place. In 1868 joined forces with **James RITCHIE**. Member, Glasgow Town Council 1860 and Convenor of Parks & Galleries, he promoted the first extension of Kelvingrove. A man of wide interests and narrow beliefs. Author of *Gowandean.* Designed the Mechanics Institute (1861), Langside College(1866) and several Glasgow churches. Described by a contemporary as "a moral man, a grave man...aware of the uprightness and integrity of his motives, he would, if he were a commissioner or member of a prison board, employ himself as architect without any of the hesitation which less eminently respectable persons might feel out of deference to the proprietors' *[The Baillie].*
**Bibl:** A Gomme & D Walker, Architecture of Glasgow, London 1987(rev), 297.

**SALMON, James Jnr** **1873-1924**
Glasgow architect and designer; also occasional watercolourist. Son of the architect **W Forrest SALMON**(1843-1911); grandson of James S sen(qv). Apprenticed to his father and to William Leiper(qv). Partner in the firm of Salmon, Son & Gillespie, it is difficult to apportion design responsibility as between Salmon and Gillespie, WFS being the business head. Designed 142-144 St. Vincent St, Glasgow (1899) - known as the 'Hatrack' on account of its ten storeys on a frontage of less than 30 feet - and Lion Chambers, Hope St (1906) with its advanced kind of reinforced concrete construction (devised by L.G. Mouchel) which, according to Dunbar, made possible the introduction of membrane walls and floors only four inches thick. Held strong and unpopular views about art. According to a writer in *The Baillie* (quoted in Gomme & Walker), 'he might be ready to call himself a social and municipal Bolshevik and smile all the more if some chuckle-headed people were shocked at the announcement...he thinks Glasgow so ugly that the more there is the more's the pity and declares himself annoyed that nobody else is proud enough of it to be ashamed of it'.
**Bibl:** Dunbar 145; A Gomme & D Walker, Architecture of Glasgow, London 1987(rev), 297-8; Halsby 188.

**SALMON, James Marchbank** **1916-**
Painter in oil and watercolour also pen and ink, potter and lithographer. Educated George Watson's School and studied at Edinburgh College of Art and Berlin Academy. Lecturer, St Paul's Training College, Cheltenham 1938-47, Principal of Lincoln School of Art 1947-60 and Croydon College of Art 1960-1973. Then migrated to Canada to become Dean at the University of Calgary, Alberta. President of the National Society for Art Education 1968-9 and Chairman, Association of Art Institutions 1972-3. As a young man he lived at Murrayfield. Exhibited RSA(2) & RSW(2).

**SALMOND, Mary A** **fl 1927-1955**
Amateur Edinburgh flower painter in watercolour; exhibited RSA 1943 & 1945 from Ravelston Dykes, GI(4) & RSW(6) from 7 St Margaret's Road.

**SALTER, P** **fl 1849**
Edinburgh sculptor. Exhibited a portrait bust of a lady at the RA 1849.

**SALVESEN, George William** **fl 1921-1926**
Edinburgh sculptor and carver of figurative works mostly in bronze and plaster. Surprisingly little known of his life. 'Peace and Mercy' is in Scottish National War Memorial; also his carving of 'The Planets' designed by Douglas Strachan(qv). Exhibited RSA(5) & GI(1).
**Bibl:** Gifford 100-1; Peter Savage, Lorimer and the Edinburgh Craft Designers, Edinburgh 1980, 148,151,illus(pl 309).

**SAMPSON, J E** **fl 1933**
Minor watercolourist; exhibited RSW(1).

**SAMSON, Alfred George Law** **1889-1943**
Edinburgh artist. His Majesty's Herald Painter and Writer to the Court of the Lord Lyon. Began his artistic career with the publisher Thomas Nelson and in 1906 became assistant to Graham Johnston, former H M Herald Painter, whom he succeeded 1927. Exhibited RSA(1) from The Lyon Court.
**Bibl:** Scotsman, 24 Mar 1943(obit).

**SAMUEL, Andrew** **fl 1893-1898**
Aberdeen painter of country scenes, coastal saubjects and flowers. Related to James P S(qv). Exhibited AAS(5), latterly from 103 Bon Accord St.

**SAMUEL, James P** **fl 1894-1896**
Aberdeen painter of local landscape and rustic scenery. Related to Andrew S(qv). Exhibited AAS(3). latterly from 103 Bon Accord St.

**SANANIKONE, Kanita** **fl 1965**
Aberdeen-based painter of still life and figure subjects. Exhibited AAS(2) from 60 Brighton Place.

**SANDEMAN, Archibald** **fl 1930-1940**
Glasgow watercolourist of Lochend Farm, Bearsden. Father of Margot Sandeman(qv). Painted west coast scenery, especially around Mull, Skye and Arran. Exhibited RSW(16), GI(14) & L(1).

**SANDEMAN, Miss Margot** **1922-?**
Born Glasgow. Painter in oil and sculptress; also occasional ceramic designer. Daughter of Archibald S(qv) and friend of Joan

Eardley(qv). Trained Glasgow School of Art 1939-43. Received Guthrie Award 1957. Exhibited RSA(22) 1942-72, GI(7) & SSA, from Lochend Farm, Bearsden, latterly from Rubislaw Drive, Bearsden.

**SANDERS, George** **1774-1846**
Born Kinghorn, Fife; died London, 26 Mar. Educated in Edinburgh. Uncle of Christina Sanders (Mrs James Robertson)(qv). Served his apprenticeship alongside Sir William Allan(qv) with a coach painter called Smeaton. During this time he was working as a portrait miniaturist, then as drawing master and book illustrator. Experimented with marine subjects having a panoramic view of Edinburgh taken from the guard ship in Leith Roads publicly displayed, but thereafter restricted himself to painting portrait miniatures. Settled in London in about 1805, the same time as Wilkie. In about 1812 seems to have turned his attention almost entirely to painting life-size portraits in oil which were in great demand. His forte, however, was miniature painting; and the opinions of his brethren in art being more in favour of his miniatures than his other works, piqued him, causing him to become estranged from the main body of the profession, and declining academic honours. In London he was well patronised; from his studio at 15 Edward St, Portman Square, he painted a miniature of 'Byron' 1807 and an oil portrait of the poet two years later. Another sitter was Princess Charlotte and in 1811 Farington records that Sanders had abandoned miniature painting for large size portraits for each of which he received 250 gns. A number of miniatures are in the collection of the Duke of Marlborough including 'The Marquess of Blandford' 1818, 'The Marchioness of Blandford' 1819 and 'Lady Caroline Susan Pennant' 1823, all of which were lent to an exhibition at the V&A in 1865. A miniature of 'Lady Shelley' was reproduced in *The Diary of Frances, Lady Shelley* (1912). His work was attractive, his copies of Old Masters being executed in a crisp and dainty wash. Some of his work was engraved. Although he suffered in later life from ophthalmia he exhibited RA(7) from 1844. Three portrait miniatures were exhibited posthumously at the RSA in 1887. His portrait by Andrew Geddes is in the SNPG. Twenty-six watercolours after Dutch and Flemish paintings are in the NGS. There is a suggestion of the influence of Raeburn, particularly apparent in two of his miniatures in the SNPG; also represented in NGS by two portraits and 26 watercolours. Not to be confused with George Lethbridge Sanders.
**Bibl:** Brydall 243-5; Caw 91; Conn XXX, 1911, 157; Foskett 489-490; Halsby 282; Irwin 80-1,143,188,198(pl 22); Long 384-5; McKay 323-4.

**SANDERS, Gertrude E** **fl 1881-1922**
Edinburgh based watercolour and pastel painter of rural scenes, flowers and occasional portraits; also miniaturist. Exhibited RSA(16) & RGI(4), from 3 Eildon St.

**SANDERSON, Miss** **fl 1838**
Glasgow portrait miniaturist; exhibited a 'Head of Christ' at the RSA from Renfield St.

**SANDERSON, Ivan Terence** **1911-?**
Born Edinburgh, Jan 30. Traveller, zoologist and illustrator. Left Scotland at the age of five to live in London. Educated Eton and Cambridge University. As a schoolboy he sailed in the Mediterranean and the North Sea visiting Scandinavia and the north Atlantic islands. Visited the Orient to collect animals. In 1932, after graduating, led a small zoological expedition on behalf of the Linnean Society, the Royal Society and the British Museum, to the British Cameroons. Married 1934. In 1936 he was in West Indies and spent several months on Mt. Aripo studying the vampire bat and the famous Diablotin birds that live only in the cave. Later travelled in the Caribbean and British Honduras studying and illustrating animal distribution. Served in Naval Intelligence during WW2 and transferred to the Ministry of Information in New York 1947. Settled in the USA, opening a private zoo in New Jersey. Wrote and illustrated *Animal Treasure* (1937), *Animals Nobody Knows* (1940), *Living Treasure* (1941), *Caribbean Treasure* (1942), *Inside Living Animals* (1947), *How to Know the American Mammals* (1951), *Silver Mink* (1952), *Living Mammals of the World* (1955). Also illustrated Waldeck's *Treks across the Veldt* (1944).
**Bibl:** Bertha E. Mahony et al, Illustrators of Children's Books 1744-1945, Boston(USA), 1948, 355; Horne 381.

**SANDERSON, Miss Joan** **fl 1880-1882**
Edinburgh oil painter of figure subjects. Daughter of Robert S(qv). Exhibited RSA(2) from Forest Road.

**SANDERSON, Mary** **fl 1894-1896**
Edinburgh painter of country subjects and portraits; exhibited AAS(3), from Talbot House, Ferry Rd.

**SANDERSON, Nicola Elspeth** **fl 1978-1979**
Fife printmaker and designer; exhibited AAS(4), from East Pitscaff, Newburgh.

**SANDERSON, Robert** **fl 1865-1905**
Edinburgh painter in oil and watercolour of townscapes, figure subjects, genre, coastal and angling scenes. Father of Joan S(qv). Prolific and skilful painter whose work has never attracted quite the attention it deserved. Exhibited RSA(106), including an interesting view of Milne's Court, Lawnmarket (demolished 1883-1884), RSW (1), GI(17), AAS (1885-7) & L(1). Represented in Glasgow AG, Edinburgh City collection.
**Bibl:** Halsby 282.

**SANDILANDS, The Hon Alison M** **fl 1909**
Painter. Exhibited at the Walker Gallery, Liverpool (1) from Calderhouse, Mid Calder.

**SANDILANDS, Miss Euphemia D** **fl 1943**
Falkirk weaver. Exhibited 'Homespun' in native dyes at the GI.

**SANDILANDS, George Somerville** **1889-1961**
Born Glasgow, 6 Apr. Painter and etcher, also art critic. Studied art in Paris, Berlin, Dresden, Munich, Rome and Athens. Art critic of the *Daily Herald* 1928-39; published several books including *The Watercolours of Frank Brangwyn, The Watercolours of R P Bonnington* and *In Praise of Lakes.* Registrar, Royal College of Art 1939. Exhibited RA(2); also RBA, RI, NEAC & ROI. Lived most of his life in the south of England, settling finally at Kingswood Way, Sanderstead, Surrey.

**SANDS, J** **fl 1862-1888**
Scottish amateur draughtsman, illustrator and minor poet. Trained as a solicitor, became a close friend of the writer Charles Keene whom he first met in 1862. There followed several expeditions made together through Scotland, in 1869, 1871 and 1874, Sands acting as guide. After contributing to a newspaper in Buenos Aires in the early 1860s, he began an association with *Punch* in 1870, as well as helping Keene with material for his humorous writing. In later life he became increasingly difficult, falling out with *Punch* on the grounds that Keene's nephew (Aster Corbould(qv)) was receiving preferential treatment. Retired to Shetland ending his days as a recluse. Signed his work with an hour-glass symbol. Illustrated and wrote *Out of this World or Life in St. Kilda* (1876). Represented in V & A (by an album).
**Bibl:** Houfe; G.S. Layard, The Life and Letters of Charles Samuel Keene, 1892, 123-128.

**SANDY-BROWN, Mrs J A (Rita M C MacLachlan)** **fl 1913-1940**
Argyll painter of landscape, mainly the west coast of Scotland especially Iona & Mull; also etcher. An exhibition of her work was held at the Modern Gallery, New Bond St, London 1913. Exhibited RSA(1), from Stronsaule, by Connel.

**SANDYS-LUMSDAINE, Leesa** **1936-1985**
Born Malvern, Worcestershire; died Edinburgh. Painter in oil of equestrian subjects and landscape. Early life was spent in India where her father was a tea merchant. Educated in England and Switzerland she spent one 'slightly disillusioning year' at Cheltenham Art College before settling in an isolated old school house 12 miles from Hawick 1974. There she remained, surrounded by up to 14 dogs and a variety of other animals, until dying tragically young after a long illness. Her paintings often showed a great sense of humour, some being reproduced as prints. Painted many of the most famous race-horses of her time in Ireland, Jamaica, France, Belgium, Hong Kong and the US as well as in Britain. Also executed portraits of Masters of Fox Hounds and their families, dogs and stalking scenes. Completed occasional sculptures, including a tombstone for a former race handicapper.
**Bibl:** Wingfield.

**SANDYS-LUMSDALE, Amy** **fl 1891-1902**
Minor painter. Lived at Blanerne, Edrom. Exhibited Royal Society of Artists in Birmingham(2).

**SANG, Rev A M** **fl 1885**
Paisley landscape painter in oil. Exhibited a scene at Arrochar at the RSA from the High Church Manse, Castlehead.

**SANG, Geraldine** **fl 1926-1931**
Midlothian watercolour painter and wood engraver. Exhibited RSA(1) & RSW(2) from Westbrook, Balerno.

**SARGENT, GT** **fl 1833**
Edinburgh painter of interiors; exhibited 'Interior of the Abbey of Holyrood' at the RSA, from Newington.

**SASSOON, David** **1888-1978**
Born Walton-on-Thames. Landscape painter. Moved to 45 Castle St, Kirkcudbright in the early 1920s where he painted mainly local scenery. Exhibited 1912-1934 RSA(2), AAS(1), L(1) & London Salon(21).
**Bibl:** Halsby 282.

**SAUNDERS, David** **fl 1952-1959**
West Lothian oil painter of continental and lowland landscape, trees and boating subjects. Exhibited RSA(14) from Bo'ness.

**SAUNDERS, E S** **20th Cent**
Edinburgh landscape painter. Exhibited two Devon views at the AAS from 34 Fountainhall Rd.

**SAUNDERS, Miss Edith** **fl 1931**
Scottish amateur painter, domiciled in England. Exhibited a study of a farmstead at the AAS in 1931 from Clova, Mayfield Rd, Sutton, Surrey.

**SAUNDERS, Mrs Eleanor Nora** **fl 1918-1922**
Glasgow portrait miniaturist; exhibited RSA(3), RA(1), GI(4) & L(2).

**SAUNDERS, Miss Margaret** **fl 1831-1836**
Edinburgh painter of portrait miniatures; exhibited RSA(14) at first from Queen St and latterly York Place.

**SAUNDERS, Robert A** **fl 1982**
Paisley artist; exhibited RSA(2) & GI(1).

**SAVIDGE, Henry T** **fl 1942-1943**
Edinburgh painter of genre and figure subjects; exhibited 'War effort' 1912 and 'Village politics' at the RSA, from Redford Rd, Colinton.

**SAVILLE, Major John** **fl 1961-1962**
Perthshire watercolour painter of local topography; exhibited 'Street scene' at the RSA, from Strathyre.

**SAWERS, J L** **fl 1882**
Edinburgh watercolour landscape painter. Exhibited GI(2) from Picardy Place.

**SAWERS, John the elder** **fl 1591-d1628**
Heraldic painter of Edinburgh. Made a painter Burgess of the City on 16 November 1591 and the following day was paid for services to the town. Recorded as a herald painter to the Lyon Court 1599. His wife and son were also artists. He received 10s and a pint of wine for 'drawing ye stane to be set above the foir yet heid' at Magdalen Chapel, Edinburgh 1614. Working at Edinburgh Castle and Linlithgow 1617 and was painting for the King in June of that year. Between March and April 1618 he was among those working at Edinburgh Castle, again for the King. Also working at Linlithgow 1628, the year of his death. Had as apprentices John Stewart 1595, Gilbert Henryson 1603, John Scott 1607, and John Binninge 1610.
**Bibl:** Apted 81-2; Gifford 164.

**SAWERS, John the younger** **fl 1617-d1651**
Only son of John Sawers the elder(qv) painter Burgess of Edinburgh and Guild Brother of Glasgow. Recorded as a herald painter in 1628 and Burgess of Edinburgh and was working for the Carrick Pursuivant 1637 and the Snowdoun Herald 1643. His eldest son was appointed the Carrick Pursuivant 5 June 1650. His younger son was also a painter. Working at Edinburgh Castle 1617 and again 1633. In 1637-9 he was working on the New Parliament House, Edinburgh and in 1637 working on the exterior, colouring the King's arms and pictures. He also painted the High Gallery of the Tolbooth. In 1647 painted the arms for the funeral of Lady Anna Cunningham, 2nd Marchioness of Hamilton. Had as apprentices Andrew Gibson 1629, James Stalker 1632, Charles Wilson 1639 and Andrew Henryson 1649.
**Bibl:** Apted 82-3.

**SAWERS, Thomas Lauder** **fl 1881-1894**
Edinburgh painter in oil and watercolour of townscapes, figure and literary subjects, buildings, and lithographer. Exhibited RSA(50), including 'The Unveiling of the Mercat Cross by Gladstone, November 1855' (ex 1886), of which a large watercolour illustrating the presentation was presented to the Magistrates in Council by Mr Gladstone measuring almost 4 ft x 3 ft. This records an important event in the history of Edinburgh and is now in Huntly House. Represented in the collection of the City of Edinburgh.
**Bibl:** Butchart 77.

**SAWYER, Mrs Elaine** **fl 1981**
Largs amateur painter. Exhibited still life at GI.

**SAXON, Miss Ruth B** **fl 1987-**
Dundee painter. Exhibited GI(1).

**SAXTON, Miss Anna M** **fl 1943-1978**
Glasgow painter and sculptress. Related to Donald S(qv). Flowers, portraits and genre. Exhibited RSA(11) & GI(18) from Kilmarnock Rd.

**SAXON, Donald D** **fl 1936-1951**
Glasgow painter of figure studies, portraits, still life and genre; exhibited RSA(8), AAS(1) & GI(16) from 903 Sauchiehall St.

**SAXTON, James** **?-1817**
Born Manchester. Brydall mentions this artist as having settled in Edinburgh for several years from where, in 1805, he painted a portrait of Sir Walter Scott. Also 'Crihee the taylor, dealer in old shoes, broker, and picture pimp, the son of an Aberdeen appleman, ironically represented in the character of a connoiseeur criticising a picture' together with 'the honest old Edinburgh eggman, companion to ditto' [*Gentle Shepherd,* 1808].
**Bibl:** Brydall 242.

**SAYER, Miss Alice** **fl 1982-**
Renfrewshire painter of still life, genre and topographical works. Began exhibiting GI 1982.

**SCADDING, Mark** **c1974-**
Painter of landscape and figurative subjects, mostly in watercolours. Won Mary Armour Award, 1990; John Kinross scholarship RSA 1992. Trained Gray's School of Art, Aberdeen 1989-93. Received Elizabeth Greenshields scholarship enabling him to visit North America and Russia 1993. Solo exhibitions in Rendezvous Gallery, Aberdeen. Exhibits AAS. Represented in RSA permanent collection.

**SCARBOROUGH, F W** **fl 1896-1898**
Ayr painter of landscapes, fishing scenes; oils and watercolours. Exhibited GI(4) from St. John's studio, Cromwell place.

**SCHAW, William** **1550-1602**
Born Scotland; died Apr 18. Architect and landscape draughtsman. Master of Works to James VI. There are drawings in Holyrood amongst Crown property which are attributed to him. In 1590 employed at both Holyrood and Dunfermline and accompanied James to Denmark. Sketches made on this visit are in Fredensborg Palace. His main claim to fame was the restoration of Dunfermline abbey; according to Brydall he built the steeple, the north porch, some of the buttresses, the roofs of the north and south aisles, and the portion of the gable above the great western door; also possibly designed the queen's house, and houses for the bailie and constabulary. He attracted the attention of Queen Anne of Denmark

becoming President of Sacred Ceremonies and her chamberlain in Scotland. There is a memorial tomb at Dunfermline Abbey. It seems he was held in high esteem by all who knew him, especially in the royal households. Not recorded by Apted.
**Bibl:** Bryan; Brydall 87; Gifford 91,pl 58; Henderson, Annals of Dunfermline.

**SCHENK, Frederick E E** **fl 1877-1907**
Edinburgh sculptor of portrait busts, figure and allegorical subjects'. Possibly son of Joseph S(qv). Carved a figure of 'Peace' for the *Scotsman* Buildings. Left Edinburgh for Stoke-on-Trent c1886. Exhibited RSA(2), RA(21), GI(8) & L(4). Represented in Oxford Town Hall, Council Hall Stafford, Municipal Council Chamber, Bath.
**Bibl:** Gifford 232.

**SCHENK, Joseph Jnr** **fl 1876**
Edinburgh sculptor, portrait busts, related to Frederick. Exhibited RSA(1).

**SCHETKY, Miss Caroline (Mrs Richardson)** **1790-1852**
Born Edinburgh, 3 Mar; died 14 Mar. Painter in oil of landscape, still life, portraits and portrait miniatures. Daughter of Maria Reinagle(qv), younger sister of John Christian(qv) and John Alexander S(qv). Travelled to Philadelphia 1818 to live with one of her brothers and while there exhibited at the Pennsylvania Academy 1818-1826 and later at the Athenaeum, Boston. Also a church organist. An example of her work was shown at the Metropolitan Museum, New York 1927. Fielding records that she married T M Richardson but this is doubtful; Groce and Wallace record that she married a Samuel Richardson of Boston in 1825.
**Bibl:** Fielding; Foskett; Groce; Long; Wallace.

**SCHETKY, John Alexander** **1785-1824**
Born Edinburgh; died Cape Coast Castle, Sierra Leone, 5 Sep. Painter in oil and watercolour of marine subjects. Descended from an old Transylvanian family, the son of a German musician who played the cello in the Edinburgh Musical Society; brother of John Christian S(qv). Studied simultaneously medicine at Edinburgh University and art at the Trustees Academy under John Graham(qv). After graduating, joined the army as a surgeon in the Peninsular War and served with distinction under Lord Beresford. In 1808 he exhibited his first work at the RA and in 1814 returned to Edinburgh and began drawing again but in 1819 was recalled to active service, first in Ceylon and then in Sierra Leone where he had hoped to illustrate the land made famous by the explorations of Mungo Park. Deputy-Inspector of Hospitals for Service on the coast of Africa. Illustrated Scott's *Provincial Antiquities* together with Turner, Thomson and Calcott. In 1821 exhibited 'Recollection of the Serra da Estrella, Portugal' at the RA and in 1825 two posthumous collaborative works, both with his brother, *'The Brune* taking the French Frigate *Oiseau,* 1768' 1825 and 'HM frigate *Brune,* running from the French ship *Constant,* 1762'. His work was much admired by John Thomson(qv), quoted in a biographical sketch by Schetky's friend Dr Maclagan, 'inventive, romantic and (with) poetical imagination'. Executed several Portuguese scenes in watercolour at the RWS. Between 1811 and 1821 showed at both the Associated Artists and RWS.
**Bibl:** Armstrong 40; Brydall 307-8; Caw 160,322; Halsby 282.

**SCHETKY, John Christian** **1778-1874**
Born Edinburgh 11 Aug; died, Scarborough, York, 29 Jan. Painter in oil and watercolour of marines, also illustrator and teacher. Painted ships, naval incidents from history and contemporary life. Descended from a Transylvanian family, son of a Hungarian cellist who settled in Edinburgh and Maria Reinagle(qv); brother of John Alexander S(qv). Educated Edinburgh High School, subsequently studied under Alexander Nasmyth(qv) although Schetky claimed he learned more from Van der Velde. In his early life he helped his mother run drawing classes for young ladies in Edinburgh which he continued to do after she died until 1795. After a short spell as a scene painter in 1801 he visited Paris and Rome on foot. On his return journey he narrowly escaped arrest as a spy when in Toulon while sketching two captured men-of-war in the dockyard. Settled in Oxford where he practised as a teacher. In 1808 he was made Professor of Drawing at the Royal Military College, Marlow (later to become the Royal Naval College, Portsmouth) remaining there until 1836; he next joined the East India College at Addiscombe, retiring 1855. In 1815 appointed Painter in Watercolours to the Duke of Clarence and in 1844 Marine Painter-in-Ordinary to Queen Victoria. Between 1840 and 1845 produced his best known works including 'The Sinking of the Royal George'. 'Simplicity in conception, good drawing, and colour which, without being in any sense good, is at least clear and not unharmonious' [Armstrong]. He helped Turner by making sketches of the picture in the Neptune for the great man's painting of the Battle off Cape Trafalgar, commissioned by George IV. Subsequently Schetky painted the same subject. Twice received commissions to paint the Royal Yachts and in 1860 Prince Albert bought his drawing of the Departure of the Prince of Wales from America, sketched in Plymouth Sound. A contemporary writer said that he distanced all other Professors by his great height as well as by his marked individuality; 'a fine breezy old fellow with gaunt spare frame, stray white hairs and clothes thrown on him from at least a mile'. Illustrated the Duke of Rutland's *Sketches and Notes of a Cruise in South Waters* (1850) and H S Rous' *Court Martial*; also published *Reminiscences of the Veterans of the Sea* (1867). Exhibited RA(71) 1805-72, including an unusual and historically interesting landscape 'Fort Augustus, Loch Ness' 1870, painted from aboard a yacht; also RSA, after 1859 from 11 Kent Terrace, Regent's Park, London. Represented in BM, NGS, National Maritime Museum (Greenwich), Manx Museum.
**Bibl:** AJ, 1874, 1877,160; Armstrong 40-41; Brydall 306-7; Caw 160, 322; Halsby 282; Houfe; Irwin 223,316-7(pl 114); McKay 167; S.F.L. Schetky, Ninety Years of Work and Play, A Life of JCS, 1877.

**SCHETKY, Mrs John George Christoff (née Maria Anna Theresa Reinagle)** **?-1795**
Born Edinburgh. Painter of portrait miniatures, singer. Member of the distinguished artistic family who settled in Edinburgh. Her father was the Hungarian composer Reinagle, her brother was R R Reinagle RA(qv), J C(qv) and J A Schetky(qv) were two of her sons and Caroline S(qv) one of her daughters. In 1774 she married in Edinburgh an Hungarian musician by whom she had 11 children.

**SCHLAPP, Otto** **fl 1904-1932**
Musselburgh-based sculptor of Swiss origin. Exhibited RSA(5) including 'Walter Scott as a student' 1932, latterly from Edinburgh.

**SCHILSKY, Eric C T RA RSA** **1898-1974**
Born Southampton, Oct 22; died Edinburgh, Apr 29. Sculptor of portraits in stone and bronze. Born of an ardent musical family (his father was leader of the Queen's Hall Orchestra), music was as important to him as painting and sculpture. Educated at Haberdashers School in London and at the College de Genève. Spent holidays in Paris, Florence, Venice and Rome. Studied art at the Slade under Harvard Thomas and drawing and anatomy sculpture at the École des Beaux Artes. Married the artist Victoria Foot(qv). During his time at Westminster School of Art he executed many well-known portraits including 'Ernest Thesiger', 'Nijinsky', 'Earl Beatty' and Modigliani's model 'Gabrielle'. He defined sculpture as 'basically the expression of man's emotions and spiritual aspirations conveyed by and externalised into the language of form, in a concrete medium'. He never moved away from figurative sculpture believing that the most direct method of expressing the essence of man came through the use of the image of man as a vehicle. His work was never concerned with violence of movement but rather the subtle juxtaposition of refined form, arrangements of planes and masses within a unified basic mass. Assessor of sculpture, Royal College of Art. Appointed Head of the School of Sculpture, Edinburgh College of Art 1946-69. Elected ARSA 1952, RSA 1956, ARA 1957. Exhibited frequently RSA, RA, GI, AAS 1964 & L. Represented in SNPG ('Sir William Gillies'), Aberdeen AG, Paisley AG, City of Edinburgh collection, Stoke-on-Trent AG.

**SCHILSKY, Mrs Eric** **[see FOOT, Victorine]**

**SCHOFIELD, David** **c1970-**
Painter in oils, specialising in works of fantasy and imagination; printmaker. Trained Duncan of Jordanstone College of Art, winning the Sekalski Award for printmaking 1993. After one year lecturing in the Dundee Design School he turned to painting full-time. Won Latimer Prize (RSA) 2000, Macfarlane Trust Award (RGI) 2002.

Exhibitions in London, Scotland, New York & the Channel Islands. Regular exhibitor RSA, RGI.

**SCHOFIELD, K R** **fl 1963-1967**
Edinburgh painter of still life, flowers and buildings; married to Rosemary S(qv). Exhibited RSA(7), from Park Rd.

**SCHOFIELD, Rosemary** **fl 1971**
Edinburgh-based artist. Married K R Schofield(qv). Exhibited 'Reflections' at the RSA.

**SCHOTZ, Benno RSA LLD Hon FRIAS** **1891-1984**
Born Arensburg, Estonia, 28 Aug. Portrait sculptor. Son of a watchmaker. In 1911 he travelled to Darmstadt, Germany to study engineering, transferring to Glasgow Royal Technical College. Then began work as a draughtsman with the Clyde shipping firm John Brown & Co and enrolled for evening classes at Glasgow School of Art. A visit to the Ivan Mestrovic exhibition in London 1915 decided him to become a sculptor. First exhibit was at the GI 1917. In 1920 elected President of the Society of Painters and Sculptors, Glasgow, and three years later became a sculptor full-time. First one man show 1926 at Reid & Lefevre's in Glasgow followed by a London show 1930. Head of Sculpture and Ceramics Departments, Glasgow School of Art 1938. Appointed Her Majesty's Sculptor-in-Ordinary for Scotland 1938. His earlier work, especially his portrait busts, had been inspired by Rodin whereas his later work owed more to Epstein. His wood carvings of the 1940s demonstrate a close affinity with modernism. Retired from teaching 1961. Lived in Glasgow for most of his life playing an active role in the Jewish life of the city; buried in Jerusalem. Author of *Bronze in my Blood,* 1981. Elected ARSA 1934, RSA 1938. Major exhibitions of his work were mounted by the SAC 1962, the RSA 1971 and at Kelvingrove AG (Glasgow) 1978. Exhibited RSA(56), RA(13), GI(100+), AAS & L(9). Represented in SNPG, RSA, Aberdeen AG, Dundee AG, Glasgow AG, Paisley AG, Perth AG, Edinburgh City collection, Stoke-on-Trent AG, Jerusalem AG, Tel Aviv AG, House of Commons.
**Bibl:** Hartley 163; Glasgow, Alex Reid & Lefevre, 'New Sculpture by Benno Schotz' (Ex Cat 1929); Glasgow, 'Benno Schotz. Portrait Sculpture' (Ex Cat 1978); SAC, 'Benno Schotz Retrospective Exhibition' (Ex Cat 1971).

**SCHUELER, John (Jan)** **c1930-**
Born Milwaukee, Wisconsin. Landscape painter. Studied at University of Wisconsin, Los Angeles and California School of Fine Art, San Francisco. After a period in New York 1951-70 with spells abroad, including a prolonged visit to Mallaig, settled there 1970. Since that time has concentrated on capturing the atmosphere and light of the Scottish western seaboard in a style which retains a semblance of abstraction. First solo exhibition in New York, latterly at Pitlochry Festival theatre and galleries throughout Scotland.

**SCHULTZ, Robert Weir** **1860-1951**
Born Scotland. Architect. Changed his name to Weir at the outbreak of war (1914). Studied under Sir Robert Rowand Anderson(qv); worked for both Norman Shaw and Sir Ernest George before travelling widely in Greece and establishing himself as an authority on Byzantine architecture. Opened a London practice 1891. 'Schultz's architecture is conspicuous for the imaginative quality of its workmanship in the variety of different styles, often chosen to be subtly subservient to existing buildings. Some of his most important work was undertaken for the 3rd and 4th Marquesses of Bute, two remarkable patrons of architecture. The 3rd Marquess, who had employed Burgeo to create medieval fantasies at Cardiff Castle, was Schultz's first client and he commissioned Byzantine chapels, characteristically dominated by recondite symbolism, at St John's Lodge in London and at Dumfries House in Scotland. He also worked at the House of Falkland in Fife and began the restoration of several Scottish castles. For the 4th Marquess he designed a chapel in Edinburgh, furniture for the old Place of Mochrum and St Andrew's Chapel in Westminster Cathedral, this last a remarkable Arts and Crafts interpretation of Byzantine styles' [Stamp]. Close friend of the English architect Francis Troup, he was associated with Robert Lorimer(qv) for a time, touring France together with Jack Lorimer and Louis Davis(qv) until temperamental differences intervened. Designed the Scots Renaissance villa Lowood (1910-12) behind Craigiehall. Member and subsequently Master of the Art Workers Guild and Council member of the Design and Industries Association (DIA) established 1915. Employed up to five assistants but never delegated design.
**Bibl:** David Ottewill in Architectural History, vol 20, 1979; Gifford 593,615; Peter Savage, Lorimer and the Edinburgh Craft Designers, Edinburgh 1980, 25,67,127,168; Gavin Stamp, R W Schultz, Architect and his work for the Marquess of Bute, Mountstuart 1981.

**SCHUNEMANN, L** **fl 1666-1674**
German painter working in Scotland during the above years. Sometime after 1660 he painted 'Anne, Countess of Balcarres', and made a drawing of 'William, 3rd Earl of Lothian'. In 1666 he painted 'Lady Margaret Hamilton' and the following year 'John Leslie, 7th Earl of Rothes'. Represented in SNPG by 5 works, 3 of which are attributed.
**Bibl:** Apted 83; SNPG Artists' files.

**SCHWABEN, Hans W** **fl 1894-1914**
German painter living in Edinburgh 1894, moved to London c1910. Exhibited GI(1), L(1) & LS(11).

**SCLATER, Miss Annie** **fl 1875**
Edinburgh painter in watercolour of natural history subjects; exhibited RSA(1).

**SCOBIE, Andrew** **fl 1877**
Dunfermline amateur painter in watercolour of topographical subjects; exhibited RSA(1).

**SCOBIE, Gavin** **1940-**
Born Edinburgh. Sculptor. Studied painting Edinburgh College of Art 1958-1962 and shortly after graduating became art teacher in Edinburgh until 1974. His first sculptures were executed in 1966 developing from the formal minimalist tradition of Judd, Turnbull and King. In 1976 won the Invergordon Sculpture prize but in 1974 abandoned teaching in order to sculpt full-time, moving to Ross-shire. After 1972 began producing works using long pieces of aluminium balanced in precarious harmony. In 1976 commissioned to execute a large steel sculpture for Eden Court Theatre, Inverness. Its unveiling in 1977 coincided with a solo exhibition at Inverness AG. The same year he began a series of bronze 'books', comprising hinged single 'pages' which opened to reveal sculptural elements. Since 1983 has also worked in terracotta. Now lives in London and teaches at the Byam Shaw School of Art. A major retrospective exhibition was held in 1984. Represented in SNGMA, Edinburgh City collection, Eden Court Theatre (Inverness).
**Bibl:** Hartley 163-4; Duncan Macmillan, Gavin Scobie, John Donald, Edinburgh 1984; SAC, 'Gavin Scobie - Sculpture' (Ex Cat 1974).

**SCOBIE, George** **fl 1957**
Dundee sculptor. Exhibited 'Penguin' at the RSA.

**SCOT, Patrick** **fl 1718-1722**
Edinburgh engraver. Subscribed to Nisbet's *Essay on...Armories,* 1718. Engraved plates for Nisbet's *System of Heraldry,* 1722.
**Bibl:** Bushnell.

**SCOTLAND, Isabel G** **fl 1930-1936**
Painter of landscape, still life and flowers; exhibited RSA(6) & GI (4), from Biggarton, Airdrie.

**SCOTLAND, John Thomas** **fl 1878-1884**
Painter who lived in Banff 1880, moving to Edinburgh c1884 worked in oils. Interiors, flowers, coastal scenes and landscape. Exhibited RSA(7).

**SCOTLAND, T M** **fl 1910**
Minor Glasgow painter; exhibited GI(1) from Tolcross.

**SCOTLAND, Miss W Winifred** **fl 1943**
Glasgow weaver. Exhibited GI(1).

**SCOTT, A** **fl 1826**
Engraver, probably Scottish. Engraved a bookplate with the armorial insignia of Thomas J Scotland, 1826.
**Bibl:** Bushnell.

**SCOTT, Miss -** **fl 1875-1878**
Glasgow sculptress. Exhibited portrait busts in plaster at the GI(7), from Elmbank Crescent and after 1876 Albert Rd.

**SCOTT, A Hamilton** **fl 1900-1926**
Paisley landscape painter. Later moved to Shawlands, Glasgow. Exhibited 'The salmon cobble' at the RSA, also GI(7), AAS(1) & L(5).

**SCOTT, Andrew Robb** **fl 1885-1905**
Minor Edinburgh architect. Partner of W Hamilton Beattie(qv). Exhibited a study of the Queen's chair in St Giles cathedral at the RSA from 10 Primrose Terrace, Slateford Road.
**Bibl:** Gifford 231n,311.

**SCOTT, Ada** **fl 1900-1907**
Landscape and genre painter. Lived on the Isle of Wight 1900 and settled in Edinburgh c1907. Exhibited RA(1) & GI(1), from 4 High St, Ventnor.

**SCOTT, Alexander** **fl 1865-1870**
Edinburgh landscape painter in oil; exhibited RSA(7).

**SCOTT, Alexander** **fl 1923**
Aberdeen amateur flower painter; exhibited AAS(1), from 561 Gt. Western Rd.

**SCOTT, Anne McGregor** **fl 1948**
Selkirk painter of informal portraits; exhibited RSA(1).

**SCOTT, Archibald** **c1798-1871**
Architect. Designed the old Portsburgh Church (1828) in Edinburgh's Grassmarket, now demolished; also the disused Lauriston Place United Presbyterian Church (1859); Stockbridge Market (1824-5) for David Carnegie (only the entrance now surviving).
**Bibl:** Gifford 227,255,404,413,454n.

**SCOTT, Arthur** **fl 1880-1884**
Edinburgh painter in oil and watercolour of ships, coastal scenes, landscapes and flowers. Moved to Islay 1884. Exhibited RSA(10), including a view of 'The Atlantic', & L(2).

**SCOTT, Miss Bessie Dundas** **fl 1874-1904**
Edinburgh painter in oil and watercolour of landscapes. Exhibited RSA(2) from 25 Inverleith Row.

**SCOTT, Cameron R** **fl 1969**
Aberdeen designer; exhibited AAS(1), from 75 Dee St.

**SCOTT, Charles** **1886-1964**
Born Newmilns, Ayrshire; died Vancouver. Painted primarily landscapes in oil. Trained Glasgow School of Art, also in Belgium, Holland and Germany. Moved to Canada 1912, going first to Calgary and then to Vancouver where he became Director of the Vancouver School of Art 1925-1952.

**SCOTT, Charles Hepburn** **fl 1907-1912**
Landscape and topographical painter often with figures in oil and watercolours. Exhibited RSA(3) & GI(3) from Edinburgh and latterly from Glasgow.

**SCOTT, Charles Marriott Oldrid** **1880-1952**
Architect. Son of Sir George S(qv); brother of John O S(qv). Executed the W spires of St Mary's Cathedral, Edinburgh (1913-7).
**Bibl:** Gifford 363.

**SCOTT, David RSA** **1806-1849**
Born Edinburgh, 10 Oct; died Edinburgh, 5 Mar. Painter in oil of historical subjects; etcher and illustrator. Son of Robert S(qv) and younger brother of William Bell S(qv). Apprenticed to his father as a line engraver but being ambitious to excel left his father's workshop and enrolled at the Trustees Academy 1827, becoming one of the founder members of the Edinburgh Life Academy Association. Visited Italy 1832-4, making anatomical studies in the Hospital for Incurables. Settled in Edinburgh. Tried to revive the tradition of grand historical painting using biblical or mythological subjects. His first major canvas was 'The Hopes of Early Genius dispelled by Death' 1828. In 1830 he undertook an enormous canvas 'Discord', intended to convey the revolt of a new order against the old. This was exhibited at the RSA in 1840. In 1831 he published *The Monograms of Man* incorporating a set of engravings recording the life of man in a brooding, pessimistic manner. The same year he etched a series of illustrations for the *Ancient Mariner* (1837) but this had little success. Exhibited only twice at the RA; after one had been 'skied' and another rejected he declined to submit again. His largest picture 'The Discovery of the Passage to India, rounding the Cape of Good Hope' (Vasco de Gama), having a length of 18', was exhibited at his own expense but failed to gain appreciation and is now in Trinity House, Leith. He also failed in the 1842 competition for paintings to the new Houses of Parliament. In 1848 he met Emerson, having read his essays, and that year painted his portrait (now in Concord, Massachusetts); also painted his friend 'Dr Samuel Brown' 1844, (NGS). For most of his life interested in mysticism and the supernatural, and chronically frustrated at being unable to transcend the life of the senses. He had 'an inextinguishable longing for paradise regained'. His last years were marked by increasing gloom intensified by unrequited love and accentuated by illness. His works are romantic and mystical, 'they breathe a particular intellectual and spiritual atmosphere, and hence whatever their defects, they possess a life and...interest of their own' [Caw]. But, as McKay said, 'he is uneasy when he departs from the colossal and the abstract...his designs and illustrative work in black and white furnish a more suitable vehicle for forms of art addressed to the intellect, and get rid of the sensuous element inseparable from colour'. Although influenced by Etty and pre-occupied in much of his work with death he never deviated from the ideal which he set out. His technique was inadequate for a comprehensive expression of his thought. 'He remains a warning to his successors that not even genius can afford to despise the means through which it has to be expressed' [McKay]. He wrote verse and some stories including 'A Dream in my Studio', published in the *Edinburgh University Souvenir* of 1835. Illustrated Coleridge's *The Ancient Mariner* (1837), Nichol's *Architecture of the Heavens* (1851) and *Pilgrim's Progress* (1860). His RSA obituary noted that he was unfortunate to 'exhibit works which nobody pretended to admire...yet...his art, like all art came of intense egotism, had a character and occasionally impressiveness difficult to describe'. Armstrong likened him to B R Haydon 'though endowed with active minds and feelings sensitive to imagination, they were without that reciprocity between brain and sense in which artistic judgement consists. Aspiration they mistook for power, and impossibilities for feats within their reach'. His works are now seen as too heavy to command much attention. Elected ARSA 1829, RSA 1834. Exhibited 89 works at the RSA, 1828-1880 (the last 7 posthumously), & AAS(1) 1896. One of his most famous paintings 'The Traitor's Gate' (1842) is now in the NGS while his portraits of 'William Dyce' and 'William Bell Scott' are in the SNPG. Many of his works in pencil, crayon and oil are in the NGS, also BM, Glasgow AG, Kirkcaldy AG, Edinburgh City collection.
**Bibl:** AJ 1849, 144; Armstrong 50-53; Brydall 456-465; Butchart 37; Mungo Campbell,'David Scott', NGS 1990; Caw 122-8; Gaunt, 236, pl 44; John M Gray, David Scott RSA and his Works, Edinburgh 1884; Halsby 99-100,282; Hardie 35-7; Houfe; Irwin 263-277 et passim; McKay 234-244, 253-5; Macmillan [SA] 202, 205-7,212-3; Portfolio 1887, 153ff; W.B.Scott, Memoir of DS, 1850; W.B. Scott, Autobiographical Notes of the Life of, vol 2, 1892, 216-219, 259-268.

**SCOTT, David** **fl 1956-1962**
Glasgow painter of west coast topography. Exhibited GI(3) from Newhaven Rd.

**SCOTT, David Henry George** **1945-**
Born Edinburgh, Jan 29. Book illustrator and landscape painter. Educated Eton, trained at the Byam Shaw School of Art 1963-66 followed by two years at RA Schools 1966-67. Illustrates children's books for Methuen and Walker. Exhibits RA, RBA.
**Bibl:** Horne 384; Who.

**SCOTT, Mrs Dorothy** **fl 1965-1970**
Aberdeen amateur draughtswoman; exhibited AAS(2), from 81 Osborne Pl.

**SCOTT, Miss Elizabeth Y** **fl 1960**
Amateur Coatbridge sculptress. Exhibited a figure in terracotta at the GI.

**SCOTT, Frieda Ewart** **fl 1964-1979**
Ayrshire painter of landscape and rustic genre; sometimes continental and once a New Zealand subject. Exhibited GI & AAS, from Hayhill, Woodside Gdns, Carmunnock.

**SCOTT, Gavin** **fl 1889-1909**
Glasgow oil painter of landscape and coastal scenes. Moved to Uddingston 1898 and then to Edinburgh c1903. Exhibited RSA(12), GI(16) & L(3).

**SCOTT, George** **fl 1851-1863**
Edinburgh oil painter of still life, flowers and fruit; exhibited RSA(4).

**SCOTT, George** **fl 1862**
Aberdeen portrait painter; exhibited RSA(2).

**SCOTT, Sir George Gilbert** **1810-1878**
London-based architect. Father of Charles(qv) and John(qv). Although English he designed some important Scottish landmarks including Glasgow University(1870), St Mary's Episcopal cathedral, Edinburgh(1874), St. James's Episcopal church, Leith (completed by R.W. Billings under Scott's direction, 1862), St. Paul's Episcopal church, now the cathedral, Dundee (1853-5), and the Albert Institute, Dundee (1867) including the flambuoyant elliptical staircase at the west end. His younger son John(qv) completed his Glasgow buildings and did other work in the city, sometimes in collaboration with J J Burnet(qv).
**Bibl:** Dunbar 145,147,149-51; Gifford 40,277-8,363-5,375,454, 476,pl 45; A Gomme & D Walker, Architecture of Glasgow, London 1987(rev), 298; Bruce Walker & W S Gauldie, Architects and Architecture on Tayside, Dundee 1984, 132-3.

**SCOTT, George T** **fl 1896**
Forfar landscape painter. Exhibited 'On the Gairn' and another work at the AAS, from 11 St. James's Terrace.

**SCOTT, Gordon M** **1965-**
Born Glasgow. Painter of portraits. Graduated from Glasgow School of Art in 1986, his first exhibit at the RSA, 'Into the Labyrinth', was in 1989, the year he held his first solo exhibition in Inverness. Most enjoys realistic narrative works with unusual slants. An admirer of the work of Breughel, Rembrandt and Caravaggio. Fascinated by mythology and symbols. Undertakes portrait commissions and has painted many historical sites in the Inverness area. Lives at Gorthleck, Inverness. Exhibits GI since 1989. Represented in Inverness AG ('Self-Portrait').

**SCOTT, Harold** **fl 1893**
Glasgow painter of seascapes. Exhibited GI(2).

**SCOTT, Hugh** **fl 1959-1968**
Greenock landscape and topographical painter; exhibited RSA(1) & GI(7).

**SCOTT, Ian McLachlan** **fl 1966-1970**
Glasgow amateur landscape painter. Moved to Dunoon, then Rothesay. Exhibited GI(4).

**SCOTT, Ian Charles** **1957-**
Born Nov 29. Figurative painter in the modern idiom. School at Wick, from where he commutes to New York. Trained Duncan of Jordanstone College of Art 1981-86. Alistair Salveson Award (RSA) 1992, Elizabeth Greenshields Scholarship. Appeared on several television programmes and his work has featured in *Modern Painters* and *Arts Review*. Exhibits RSA since 1997.

**SCOTT, Ian William Ligertwood FRBS** **1940-**
Born North Ronaldsay, Orkney, 23 Apr. Painter and sculptor. Figurative studies, local landscape. Trained Gray's School of Art, Aberdeen 1958-61. Worked for some years as a lobster fisherman, generally combining farm assistance and road repairing with work as a painter and sculptor. Gained two RSA prizes for sculpture including the Latimer Award 1965. Concentrates on sea and rockscapes, usually natural formations of lava and rock. Elected Fellow, RSBS 1972. Exhibited AAS(4) 1965-6. Represented in SAC, Faroese Art Society, while a portrait of 'Professor Evans-Pritchard' adorns the Institute of Social Anthropology in Oxford and a fine portrait of 'Stanley Cursiter' is in Orkney County Library.

**SCOTT, Irene Mary** **1942-**
Born Penicuick, Midlothian, 31 Dec. Painter in watercolour and collage, also printmaker and etcher. Graduated from Edinburgh College of Art 1965 and visited the continent on a postgraduate scholarship. Attended the Open University 1988. Elected to the Council, Society of Scottish Artists 1986-8. In 1989 became a member of the Scottish Sculpture Workshop committee. Her main professional interest is the cultural landscape of Scotland. Her work reflects the influence of Paul Nash, Ben Nicholson and Lionel Feininger. Exhibits in Scotland with the RSA, RSW & SSA.

**SCOTT, Isobel Maclagan (Mrs Chalmers)** **1900-?**
Glasgow etcher and designer. Trained Glasgow School of Art. Exhibited RSA & GI in 1925 from 25 Hamilton Drive .

**SCOTT, J** **fl c1820-1830**
Glasgow-based engraver. Engraved bookplates for John Vincent Leach, 1830; Dr Macfadyen, 1820; William Ramsay, 1820; Edward Thompson, 1830; Ligonier Treadway, 1820. Not to be confused with the English engraver of the same name.
**Bibl:** Bushnell.

**SCOTT, John Beattie** **fl 1886-1919**
Aberdeen painter in oil of landscape, fishing and coastal scenes. Had a studio at 58 Tay St, Perth 1893-94. Exhibited RA(2), RSA(2), RHA(12), AAS 1886-1919 & L(13), latterly from Thornton, Fyvie. Represented in Perth AG.

**SCOTT, James** **fl 1564-1592**
Early Glasgow heraldic painter. Burgess and Freeman of Glasgow 1574. In 1577 was granted 'fynes' for his 'bountetht and labouris done be him in culloring of the knok, moyne and orlage, and wther commowne work of the towne'. Worked also for the burgh of Ayr, including adding the crown to the Queen's arms. His son, **George SCOTT**, also became a burgess painter.
**Bibl:** Apted 83-4; Ayr Burgh Accounts 42,142,146,173.

**SCOTT, James** **fl 1828-1856**
Born Jedburgh. Painter of genre and portraits; exhibited RSA(36) from various Edinburgh addresses.

**SCOTT, James Maxwell** **fl 1929-1956**
Draughtsman and engraver, principally of architectural subjects, especially Old Edinburgh. Exhibited regularly at the RSA(15), at first from Middlesex and after 1952 from Barnton, Edinburgh.

**SCOTT, James V** **fl 1866-1892**
Edinburgh painter in oil and watercolour of landscape. Brother of John Russell S(qv). Lived for a time in Surrey. Exhibited RA(3) 1877-1888, two of them views on Arran, but mainly RSA(30) 1866-1887 including more views of Arran; also RI(10) & GI(8), latterly from 13 Duke St.

**SCOTT, John** **?-1666**
Important wright. Master Wright to Edinburgh in which capacity he built the great hammerbeam roof of Parliament House (1637-9) and collaborated with John Mylne jnr(qv) in building the Tron Church (1636-47) planned to house the congregation after St Giles became a cathedral.
**Bibl:** Gifford 84,121,174-5,180,pl 75.

**SCOTT, John** **fl 1832-1865**
Edinburgh oil painter of still life and landscape; exhibited RSA(7).

**SCOTT, John** **fl 1908**
Amateur Edinburgh painter; exhibited 'Westminster' at the RSA from 52 Dalry Rd.

**SCOTT, John Douglas** **fl 1863-1885**
Scottish landscape painter, usually the scenery of Perthshire and the western Highlands. Lived and worked at Roslyne Cottage, Bridge of Allan, before moving to 24 George Street, Edinburgh. Exhibited 3 landscapes at the RA 1872 and 1880-81, AAS(1) & GI(14), but mainly confined his exhibits to the RSA where between 1866 and 1882 he exhibited 45 works.

**SCOTT, John Halliday** **fl 1876-1889**
Architect and landscape painter. Living at 39 Brunswick Rd, Brighton in the late 1870s and early 1880s from where he exhibited 3 landscapes at the RA. Moved to Edinburgh c1889 exhibiting two New Zealand coastal scenes at the RSA; also RI.

**SCOTT, John Oldrid** **1841-1913**
Architect. Son of Sir George(qv); brother of Charles(qv). Involved in work at St Mary's Cathedral (Edinburgh) mostly after his father's designs.
**Bibl:** Gifford 363,365-6.

**SCOTT, John Russell** **fl 1836-1876**
Edinburgh oil painter of landscapes, especially Perthshire views. Brother of James V S(qv). Exhibited 85 works at the RSA and occasionally at the GI, including a number of scenes on Arran.

**SCOTT, Kathleen (Lady Scott, later Lady Kennet)** **1878-1947**
Born Mar 27, Carlton-in-Lindrick, nr Worksop; died 24 July, London. Sculptress. Related on her mother's side to James Skene(qv) and more distantly to Lord Pitsligo. Privately trained in Paris under Rodin. Sitters included Asquith, Neville Chamberlain, Florence Nightingale, George V, George VI, members of the Norwegian Royal Family, Lloyd George, Queen Mary, Marquess of Reading, Lord Reith, J M Barrie, Bernard Shaw. Also designed several war memorials and undertook many sculptures of mothers and children subjects of special appeal to her. Bronzes of her first husband, Captain Scott, are in Waterloo Place, London and in Auckland (NZ). Regular exhibitor at RA, Paris Salon, Royal Society of Portrait Painters. Represented in Westminster Abbey and in the Tate AG (a bust of Asquith, presented by Lord Duveen).
**Bibl:** Louisa Young: *A Great Task of Happines: The Life of Kathleen Scott* (Macmillan 1995).

**SCOTT, Keith** **1939-**
Born London. Painter, printmaker and teacher. Trained Hornsey College of Art 1958-63. Taught at Luton School of Art, Hornsey College of Art and the Byam Shaw School of Drawing and Painting before moving to Scotland 1964 to teach at Edinburgh College of Art. First one-man exhibition in Edinburgh 1964. Exhibited RSA(6). Represented by a pastel in the City of Edinburgh collection.

**SCOTT, Laura** **fl 1887-1888**
Minor Edinburgh still life painter; exhibited RSA(1) & GI(1).

**SCOTT, Mary** **fl 1940**
Perthshire artist. Exhibited RSA(1) from Ardchoile, Aberfoyle.

**SCOTT, Mary J** **fl 1898**
Amateur Glasgow watercolourist; exhibited RSW(1) from 2 Teviot Terrace.

**SCOTT, Mary J F M** **fl 1935-1989**
Aberdeen-based artist, moved to Brechin c 1937. Painted rustic scenery and landscape, sometimes around Concarneau, France. Exhibited AAS(4), latterly from Annfield, Brechin and after an interval of almost forty years exhibited two works at the RSA, from 44 Merchiston Ave, Edinburgh.

**SCOTT, Maureen** **fl 1984**
Edinburgh-based printmaker. Exhibited AAS(1), from 32 Lady Menzies Pl.

**SCOTT, Menzies** **20th Cent**
Amateur Hamilton painter and librarian. Deaf and dumb. Painted mostly landscapes in watercolour. Represented in Hamilton Museum ('Birthplace of David Livingstone from the R. Clyde' & other works).

**SCOTT, Michael** **1946-**
Born Peterhead. Painter. Studied political science at Liverpool before becoming a self-taught artist though attended life classes at the Glasgow School of Art for a short time. His paintings are figurative, often of literary themes in a manner that varies from neo-cubist to grotesque realism. Principally influenced by Dutch and Flemish 'primitives', new Rennaisance painters and the Cubists. Since 1978 has exhibited RA, RSA & GI, winning the David Cargill senior award 1989, latterly from 1 Wilmot Rd, Glasgow.

**SCOTT, Michael Muir** **fl 1882-1934**
Edinburgh painter of genre and portrait miniatures; sometimes in watercolour. Exhibited RSA & GI(1).

**SCOTT, Capt R** **fl 1851**
Edinburgh amateur marine painter; exhibited 'Hove to for a pilot' at the RSA, from Register St.

**SCOTT, R McDonald** **fl 1953-1970**
Melrose landscape watercolour painter & tapestry designer. Trained Edinburgh College of Art in textile design and with a travelling scholarship visited western Europe, Russia and the United States. Designed and wove the carpet for the chancel of Glasgow cathedral in Coronation year. Won design competition for a second carpet in the same building. Other examples are in St Giles cathedral, Vaughan College (Leicester) and many churches. Exhibited a number of sketches done whilst on war service in the Middle East. Exhibited RSA(9), RSW, GI(12) & AAS(8), from The Pendstead.
**Bibl:** Carnegie Festival of Music and the Arts (Ex Cat 1970).

**SCOTT, R Menzies** **fl 1946-1960**
Lanarkshire watercolour painter of flowers, still life and genre. Exhibited GI(5) from Hamilton.

**SCOTT, Robert** **1771-1841**
Born Lanark, 13 Nov; died Jan. Engraver. Father of David(qv) and William Bell S(qv). Apprenticed to A Robertson 1787. Studied under David Allan(qv) at the Academy 1788. Taught John Burnett(qv) and also his sons David(qv) and William Bell S(qv). 'The best Scottish engraver of his time' [Bryan]. He and his sons occupied a leading place in the artistic life of Edinburgh. His business was on Parliament Stairs where he employed several assistants. In 1795-6 engraved 'The Views of Seats and Scenery chiefly in the environs of Edinburgh', from drawings by Alexander Carse(qv) and Alexander Wilson(qv). Head of the best Atelier in Edinburgh 1800. Among his many works was a series of engravings for the 1808 edition of the *Gentle Shepherd* after Carse and John Stevenson. Also worked for the *Scots Magazine,* executing prints of country seats for twenty years. In 1800 he married Miss Ross, daughter of a Musselburgh mason. Engraved bookplate for Cupar library. Brydall reports that his workshop, in the uppermost flat opposite the west side of Parliament House, had only two windows - a work-table ran mid-way along these supported by brackets, enabling each window to accommodate two tenants, the uppermost of whom were perched on chairs nearly six feet high. Kept printing presses, his principal customer being a Gainsborough publisher called Mosely. Among his apprentices was the celebrated engraver Samuel Allardyce whose reputation was made in the United States. A watercolour 'Lord Milton, Lord Justice-Clerk' (1692-1766), after Allan Ramsay, is in the SNPG. A pen and wash drawing 'Cotton mills of Lanark' and an album containing drawings and related engravings are in the NGS, also represented in City of Edinburgh collection (26).
**Bibl:** Armstrong 30; Bryan; Brydall 203-4; Bushnell; Butchart 35-6; Halsby 61,90; Irwin 92-3, 195, 272-3 and 277.

**SCOTT, Robert** **fl 1864**
St Andrew painter in oil of marines, exhibited RSA(2).

**SCOTT, Robert Hepburne** **fl 1893-1919**
Painter in watercolour of landscapes. Lived for a time in Cambridge before coming north to Merton House, St Boswells c1898 and thence to Edinburgh. Exhibited RSA(2) & RSW(2), but mainly at the Baillie Gallery(48).

**SCOTT, Thomas (Tom) RSA** **1854-1927**
Born Selkirk, 12 Oct; died Selkirk, 31 Jne. Scottish watercolour

painter of figures and landscapes. Son of a local builder. Trained Edinburgh School of Art and RSA Life Class 1877. During the first year that he devoted himself full-time to art he exhibited at the RSA and continued to do so until almost the end of his life, being one of only a few Scottish artists and academicians to have worked solely in watercolour. Eldest of a family of five. After leaving Selkirk Grammar School became an assistant to his father in the tailoring trade. Moving to Edinburgh 1877, ostensibly to learn the trade as a tailor's cutter, he attended evening classes at the Royal Institution. His paintings soon attracted the attention of Sam Bough(qv), whose own paintings show a close affinity with the English watercolour school, particularly David Cox. Bough exerted a strong influence on the young painter and, much against his father's wishes, Scott soon turned to painting full-time. After training in Edinburgh, and with the assistance of a generous patron, Scott went on a foreign tour. Visited Switzerland, Italy and Tunis, but it was the art of Holland, and in particular of France that had the greatest affect on his painting. Like other Scottish painters of the time, including members of the Glasgow School, Scott was drawn to the world of French realist painters such as Bastien-Lepage and J F Millet. But his work lacks the 'social realism' of Lepage; what he learned from the French painters was the means of imparting a sensitivity to nature and a way of recording everyday life in the Borders. On his return to Edinburgh, Scott interspersed his landscape paintings with historical painting of Border incidents and landscapes painted further afield in northern Scotland, also in North Africa, Holland and Italy. Remained in Edinburgh until 1889 when he moved to Earlston. Here, he was able to indulge his life-long interest in archaeology, amassing a large collection of antiquities. After living for a few years at Bowden, he settled at Leslie Cottage, Selkirk 1901. From Selkirk he made excursions up the Ettrick and the Yarrow valleys searching for subjects to paint. His work is always highly competent reflecting visual intimacy and feel for the changing moods of local scenery. Thinly painted in transparent colour and, at times, with loose touches of broken colour, his paintings display a sureness of touch. There is always a grasp of detail without losing the broad sweep of design. Disliked insincerity and the 'Kailyard' School, an attitude reflected in his art. Never, whatever the subject, is there a forceful or robust quality about his paintings, rather a simple and sincere feeling for nature. The young William Johnstone(qv) was befriended by Tom Scott and accompanied him on many painting excursions. 'It is his quiet and unobtrusive mastery which makes his best work so vital' [MAF]. A distinguished antiquarian, possessing a valuable collection of Border relics and stone implements. Elected ARSA 1888, RSA 1902. Exhibited frequently at RSA, RSW, GI 1882-1912 & AAS 1893-1919, latterly from Leslie Cottage, Selkirk. Represented in NGS.
**Bibl:** Edward Pinnington,'Tom Scott RSA', AJ 1907, 17-21; Caw 302-3; Halsby 162-5,241,282; Hardie 152; RSA Obituary 1927.

**SCOTT, Thomas R** **fl 1831-1832**
Painter. Exhibited two Border landscapes at the RSA (no address).

**SCOTT, W A** **fl 1887**
Edinburgh landscape painter; exhibited a scene in Kirkudbright, from Hope St.

**SCOTT, W B** **fl 1899**
Minor figure of 13 Dalrymple Crescent, Edinburgh; exhibited GI(1).

**SCOTT, W Guild** **fl 1896-1909**
Gourock figurative painter; exhibited 'A Russian nobleman' at the GI 1909 and An old salt at the AAS, from Hillside House.

**SCOTT, W W** **fl 1852-1854**
Edinburgh painter of dead game and angling sketches; exhibited RSA(2), latterly from St Bernard's Court.

**SCOTT, Walter (A)** **fl 1899-1938**
Painter in watercolour of landscapes, also etcher. Studied and lived in Edinburgh. Exhibited RSA(9), RSW(7), AAS 1896-1926, GI(4), RCA(2) & L(2), latterly from 13, Queen's Park Ave.
**Bibl:** Halsby 282.

**SCOTT, Walter Schomberg ARIBA** **1910-?**
Born Sep 14. Architect, specialising in the restoration of old historic buildings. Trained Edinburgh School of Architecture 1929-36 and in the office of Sir Reginald Fairlie. Subsequently worked in London with Sir Edward Maufe and in Edinburgh with Ian Lindsay, joining the latter as a partner after WW2. Designed Dupplin Castle, nr Perth and Gannochy Lodge, Edzell; also House of Crathes and extensions to Crathes Castle. Enthusiastic devotee of Scottish traditional architecture. Lived at Northfield House, Prestonpans, E Lothian. Exhibited RSA(1) 1934.

**SCOTT, William** **fl 1798**
Edinburgh engraver. His name appears among the subscribers to David Crawford's *Poems chiefly in the Scottish Dialect.*
**Bibl:** Bushnell.

**SCOTT, William ('Bill') RSA FRBS** **1935-**
Born Moniaive, Dumfries-shire. Sculptor. Trained Edinburgh College of Art 1953-8 obtaining a postgraduate scholarship 1958-9 enabling him to travel to study at the École des Beaux Arts in Paris. Some time after his return became senior lecturer at the College. Has held numerous one-man exhibitions including 'Built in Scotland', in Edinburgh (1983). Often works on a small scale making use of the visual impact of the plinth, which while raising small works also isolates them. 'Scott selects out different parts of the stand as plinths and sculpture. The interaction between the two echoes Barancusi's concern for the pedestal of the traditionally presented sculpture becoming part of the whole work' [Michael Tooby]. There is a speculative element in his work which stems from the exploration of devices which refer to the outside world - of fusion of images of human forms and of landscape which was seen in his earlier, cast works. His later works are larger, often wooden and 'totemic'. He marks and paints the surface of his works. Elected ARSA in 1973, RSA 1984, Secretary RSA 1998- Exhibits regularly RSA, SSA, AAS and with the Glasgow Group.
**Bibl:** Michael Tooby, text in 'Built in Scotland", Ex Cat, Campden Art Centre, 1983.

**SCOTT, William B** **fl 1899**
Edinburgh amateur figurative painter. Exhibited GI(1), from S. Gray St.

**SCOTT, William Bell HRSA LLD** **1811-1890**
Born Edinburgh, Sep 12; died Penkill Castle, 14 Jly. Pre-Raphaelite painter and muralist in oil and watercolour, also illustrator and poet. Son of Robert Scott the engraver(qv), brother of David S(qv). Studied under his father and Trustees Academy 1831 under Sir William Allan(qv). Fearful of being forced to remain with the family business he escaped to London 1837. Having arrived there he found that landscape was out of fashion so took up illustrative work in the manner of Maclise(qv), becoming friendly with Augustus Egg and W.P. Frith. His first London painting 'The Old English Ballad Singer', was exhibited at the BI. Like his brother he entered the Westminster Hall competition 1842 but was unsuccessful; this encouraged him to accept the offer of appointment as master of the Government School of Design at Newcastle-upon-Tyne 1843. For the next 20 years he remained there, travelling to London every summer largely on account of his friendship with Rossetti and Holman Hunt. Also a poet, contributed poems to *The Germ.* Met Millais and Ruskin in 1853 but did not altogether approve of the latter. In 1854 commissioned to paint a series of works depicting the history of Northumberland for Wallington Hall, Morpeth, shown in London 1861. The eight scenes were 'St Cuthbert on Farne Island', 'The Building of the Roman Wall', 'The Death of Bede', 'The Danes descending on the Coast of Tynemouth', 'The Spur in the Dish', 'Bernard Gilpin taking down the Gage of Battle at Rothbury Church', 'Grace Darling', and 'Iron and Coal', the last being one of the few British 19th century pictures to show men working under contemporary factory conditions. His most successful work was done comparatively late in life. Was already 46 when he began to paint the Wallington series. Eleven years later he completed both wall paintings on the staircase at Penkill Castle, Ayrshire, based on *The Kingis Quair.* The pre-Raphaelite style did not come readily and his oil paintings are often laboured in detail and harsh in colour, the drawing indecisive and uneven. His subjects, 'although well chosen and historically accurate are often sentimentally superficial'. Said to have been inspired in his compositions but clumsy in their execution. His watercolours were usually more effective. His work at Penkill Castle, the home of the Boyd family, led to a life-long friendship with Alice Boyd who was

the model for his picture 'Grace Darling', and also for 'Una and the Lion' 1860. Fortunately the many watercolour drawings of the Penkill staircase frescoes remain in place. During his lifetime he was better known for his poetry and his writings on art than for his large historical pictures. Among other works he published *The Life of Albert Dürer* (he was a great admirer of Dürer and a collector of his prints); *Antiquarian Gleanings in the North of England* (1851); *Half-hour Lectures...of the Fine and Ornamental Arts* (1861); *On British Landscape Painters* (1872); and *William Blake* (1878). Elected HRSA 1887. During his lifetime he had the capacity of forging many friendships with interesting figures of his time yet curiously his written accounts were remarkably acerbic without charity or grace. Exhibited RA(7) 1842-1869, RSA(45) 1833-1870, also AAS(1). Represented in Tate AG, NG, V & A, NGS, SNPG ('Self-portrait'), Aberdeen AG, Manchester AG, Laing AG (Newcastle), Abbot Hall AG (Kendal), Nat Gall of Canada (Ottawa).
**Bibl:** Apollo, May 1969, 386-390; Sept 1977; Bryan (long entry); Butchart 36-7; Caw 171-2; Halsby 97-9,282; Hardie 35,78,87(illus); Houfe; Irwin 277-282 et passim; Macmillan [SA] 207-8; W. Minto, Autobiographical Notes of the Life of William Bell Scott, 2 vols (1892); William Bell Scott, Illustrations to the Kingis Quair of King James I of Scotland painted on the Staircase of Penkill Castle, Edinburgh 1887.

**SCOTT, William George CBE RA** **1913-1989**
Born Greenock 15 Feb; died of Alzheimer's disease nr Bath, Dec 28. Painter in oil, landscapes, still life and figure subjects; latterly abstracts. Brought up in Northern Ireland, studied Belfast College of Art 1928-31 and RA Schools 1831-5, greatly influenced by the writings of Clive Bell and Roger Fry. His early works were mainly figurative showing the influence of Cézanne and Bonnard. In 1936 spent some time in Cornwall with Dylan Thomas and two years in Pont-Aven, Brittany. In the later 1940s he concentrated on still life, especially kitchen objects. By 1950 he was turning to pure abstract art and his contact with American artists in 1953 was an important factor in gaining American acceptance of contemporary British art. His later work was largely abstract. First one-man exhibition was in the Leger Gallery, London 1942. Elected member of the London Group in 1949. Became senior painting master at Bath Academy of Art and was represented in the British Pavilion at the Venice Biennial in 1958 and at the Sao Paulo Biennial in 1961 where he won the International Critics' Purchase Prize. Between 1963 and 1965 was the Ford Foundation's resident artist in Berlin. Awarded CBE 1966. Elected RA 1977. Major prize winner at the RA 1985. Illustrated Dickinson: *Soldiers' Verse* (1945). Exhibited RA. Retrospective exhibitions Zurich 1959, Hanover 1960, 1961, 1962, Berne 1963, Belfast 1963, Tate AG 1972. Represented in Tate AG, V & A, SNGMA, Dundee AG.
**Bibl:** Harold Osborne(ed), Twentieth Century Art, 488; Rothenstein 179 (plts 137,138); Atley: William Scott: Art in Progress (Methuen 1963); St Ives 1939-1964: Twenty Five Years of Painting and Pottery (Tate AG 1975), William Scott: Paintings, Drawings and Gouaches (1972); Horne 385; Waters; Who.

**SCOTT, Winifred Kennedy** **c1899-c1940**
Perthshire potter and embroiderer. Studied Glasgow School of Art 1920-24 where she was a partial contemporary of two other Perthshire potters and designers of distinction **Mary RAMSAY** (1896-c1963) and **Jessie WILSON**(1888-1966). Having failed to obtain a teaching post worked from her home Birchwood, Burnam. Her pottery often had Egyptian or oriental motifs executed in cool colours. Died of tuberculosis. Exhibited Glasgow Society of Women Artists 1925.

**SCOTT-ELLIOT, Marjorie A** **fl 1923-1933**
Aberdeenshire painter of genre, portraits and landscape; exhibited AAS(5), from Belhelvie Lodge, Whitecairns.

**SCOTT-MARTIN, David** **fl 1985**
Ayr painter. Exhibited 'Distant surf' at the GI.

**SCOTTISH ART REVIEW (Old Series)** **1888-1892**
Short-lived influential journal, first appeared June, largely initiated by E A Walton(qv) and James Paterson(qv). The idea was to educate the public to enjoy and understand the kind of art favoured by its founders - a number of the Glasgow Boys(qv) principally Henry, Lavery, McGillivray, Paterson and Roche. The editor was R Macaulay Stevenson(qv). They gained the support of George Clausen, Walter Crane and Frank Short, with contributions from J M Barrie, Prince Kropotkin et al. After only eighteen months the effort of production proved too great. The new owners, Messrs Walter Scott, re-christened it *The Art Review* but after only two more years it ceased publication.
**Bibl:** Caw 349-50,357; Irwin 371,374,376,378,382.

**SCOTTISH ARTIST AND ARTIST CRAFTSMEN** **1990-**
Founded from the former Society of Scottish Women Artists(qv). Although particular emphasis is given to 'artist craftsmen', in the words of Joan Renton, the first President, 'we plan to identify with the decorative arts, although the new organisation will continue to embrace all the visual arts'. The inaugural Council consists of the President, Marj Bond RSW, Jane Butler, June Carey, Jean Donaldson, Marie Goodenough, Jenepher Wendy Ross, Sheena Stephen, Christine Tainsh and Christine Woodside. A new prize is the Nancy Massey Travel award, worth £4,000 open to under 25 year-olds.

**SCOTTISH ARTISTS' BENEVOLENT ASSOCIATION** **1889-**
Formed in the above year to provide assistance to distressed deserving artists, their widows and dependents.

**SCOTTISH ARTS CLUB** **1873-**
Edinburgh-based. Formed in 1873 when a group of nine practising artists met in the Prince of Wales hotel, Edinburgh. The inaugural committee comprised Robert Herdman RSA (elected first President), William Brodie RSA, Hugh Cameron RSA, James Cassie ARSA, George Paul Chalmers RSA, George Hay ARSA, Clark Stanton ARSA, J. Oswald Stewart and W.F. Vallance (later RSA). In 1892 it broadened to include all the arts, and lawyers. Meetings were held at the Architectural Association, 37 George St until in June 1874 moving to 24 Castle St, above Aitken Dott. Between 1882 and 1894 the Club met at 28 Queen St moving to its own premises at 24 Rutland Square. In the same year its present title was agreed. 'I drop into the SAC with the feeling that I am coming into my own home...with the certainty of finding a group of individuals with whom I can agree or disagree as I please but who never alter their opinions for anything I may say...I know I shall find comment sometimes shrewd, sometimes absurd, sometimes ultra conservative, sometimes near revolutionary, but always lively on contemporary Scottish and artistic matters' [Moray McLaren]. A cultural haven whose influence has been no less potent for being almost entirely intangible. A studio was added to their premises 1997.
**Bibl:** Caw 211; The Scottish Arts Club 1874-1974, SAC, Edinburgh 1974.

**SCOTTISH COLOURISTS**
The group name given to four Scottish painters of approximately similar age, sharing middle-class backgrounds and, although seldom if ever all working together, having a similar approach to painting, most especially a preoccupation with colour and light. They were Samuel John Peploe (1871-1935), John Duncan Fergusson (1874-1961), George Leslie Hunter (1877-1931) and Francis Campbell Boileau Cadell (1883-1937). Peploe and Fergusson talked and worked together 1900-1914, Cadell and Peploe from 1918 to 1930. Hunter kept in touch with the others but was a more private figure, preferring to work alone. Less ambitious than the Glasgow Boys(qv) but sharing a determination to eschew current fashion, they left behind no school, only one of the four (Peploe) involved himself in any teaching. Recognition came belatedly. 'There seems to be in the Scottish character a sense of responsibility, caution and respect for convention that is balanced in almost equal amount by an element of irresponsibility, rebelliousness, even aggression. The latter qualities are all too often suppressed until they erupt, perhaps with uncontrolled vigour, this lack of control sometimes ensuring that little is achieved by the outburst. The Colourists were capable of harnessing this underlying aspect of their nature. Their achievements came from the expression of emotions which - if the Kirk and the Estalishment were to be believed - were uncontrollable once unleashed...[apart from Hunter] the other three [maintained] the balance between order and disorder, aggression and convention, passion and Calvinist retraint sufficiently to allow them to achieve much that fellow Scots aspired to and often failed to achieve and which many English painters, working on a less emotional plane, perhaps never experienced at all' (Billcliffe). In the 1980s the Colourists received sensational acclaim in the market place, not only in Scotland but also

in Europe and Japan; however, by 1990 this had abated to a more sustainable level. (See also individual entries.)

**Bibl:** Roger Billcliffe, The Scottish Colourists, London 1989; Guildford House Gall, 'Three Scottish Colourists' (Ex Cat 1980, Text by Richard Calvocoressi); William Hardie, Scottish Painting 1837-1939, London 1976; T J Honeyman, Three Scottish Colourists, London 1950.

**SCOTTISH MODERN ARTS ASSOCIATION 1907-1964**

Founded in Edinburgh by a group of subscribers to the Royal Association for the Promotion of Fine Arts(qv) 'to ensure the preservation of representative examples of Scottish art, more particularly by acquiring works of contemporary Scottish artists and also to assist in the enriching of Scottish public art collections'. In 1932 the chairman, Arthur Kay, pressed for 'a modern place of art in Edinburgh - a Tate Gallery', a concept that, based more on the Luxembourg in Paris than the Tate, came to pass 28 years later in the form of the SNGMA(qv). In 1964 the majority of works owned by the Association were donated to the City of Edinburgh who acquired the old Royal High School building for the purpose.

**Bibl:** Caw 228n; A Eddington,'The Scottish Modern Arts Association', Studio, vol 45,1909,114-119.

**SCOTTISH NATIONAL GALLERY OF MODERN ART 1960-**

Opened by Sir Kenneth Clark at Inverleith House 10 August 1960. The gallery exhibits the continuation of the NGS collection and is currently in a building designed by William Burn(qv). Dedicated to twentieth century art, it is supported by private gifts and public grant, the most important of the former having come from the Maitland and Richmond-Traill collections, and gifts from Sir DY Cameron in 1945, R R Scott Hay 1967 and Dr R A Lillie 1977. In 1987 Mrs Black presented 250 sketches by her sister, Joan Eardley(qv), while in 1995 a significant bequest was received from Muriel Keiller(qv).

**SCOTTISH NATIONAL PORTRAIT GALLERY 1882-**

The concept of a national portrait gallery had its origins among a community of antiquarians and literati against a background of late 18th century fashion for compiling inventories of portraits in royal and aristocratic possession. In 1780 there was formed **THE SOCIETY OF ANTIQUITIES OF SCOTLAND,** convened by David Erskine, 11th Earl of Buchan(qv). Buchan recommended 'biographical gleanings of illustrious persons, with drawings of their unengraved portraits and proofs of their authenticity'. But the idea foundered causing him to collaborate with the historian John Pinkerton to produce *Iconographica Scotica* (1797) and its sequel *The Scottish Gallery of Portraits of Eminent Persons of Scotland* (1799). In the statutes of the Society of Antiquities (1783) Buchan requested 'A room or gallery shall be appropriated for the collection of the best Portraits...denominated the Temple of Caledonian Fame'. This led to portrait drawings of the first members of the Society executed by John Brown(qv). At the suggestion of David Laing, an influential member of the Society of Antiquities, they approached the Trustees of the Board of Manufacturers proposing an exhibition of Scottish portraiture, an idea simultaneously under consideration by the RSA so that, with strong public support, a series of exhibitions was held between 1859 and 1876. In 1882 the SNPG was founded as the result of an offer of £10,000 from John Ritchie Findlay of Aberdour, proprietor of *The Scotsman,* on condition that a matching grant would be forthcoming from the Government. The President of the RSA relayed the offer to the Board of Manufacturers on 7th December 1882. In May 1884 the same donor provided a further sum of £20,000 for a building combining the new Gallery with the National Museum of Antiquities, conditional on a site being provided. The building, designed by Rowand Anderson(qv), was opened by the Marquis of Lothian on 15th July, 1889, its great central hall decorated with murals depicting scenes from Scottish history, by William Hole(qv). At the beginning the Gallery owned 324 portraits with a further 71 on loan. The collection of paintings, drawings, sculpture, prints and stained glass - by English and foreign as well as Scottish hands - has steadily increased by private benefaction and public funding in addition to which there is a fine library including a photographic archive of all important known portraits in private Scottish hands.

**Bibl:** Brydall 353-4; W G Burn-Murdoch, Description of a Procession of Scottish History, Edinburgh 1902; Caw 217; J M Gray, The Scottish National Portrait Gallery. The Building and its Contents. Also a Report of the Opening Ceremony, Edinburgh 1891; Irwin 410; Helen Smailes, A Portrait Gallery for Scotland, Edinburgh 1985; Colin Thomson, Pictures for Scotland, Edinburgh 1972.

**SCOUGAL(L), David fl 1654-1677**

Portrait painter. There is a recorded account to the Earl of Panmure in respect of four small pictures. Also he sold paintings to the Earl of Mar, Sir John Foulis 1672, Viscount and Viscountess Oxenfoord 1666 and 1669 respectively; and Lord Murray 1681. His portrait of 'Lady Jean Campbell' 1654 is the only signed painting extant. Also painted the 'Marquess of Argyll (1598-1661)' now in the SNPG, and two finely delineated late works of Sir John and Lady Clerk of Penicuik. Other portraits believed to have been by this artist are 'David, 2nd Earl of Wemyss' 1656; 'Countess Margaret Leslie' 1657 and 'James Grant of Freuchie and his wife' 1658. Holloway notes that 'a characteristic of the male portraits of the 1650s is the way the artist modelled his heads out of angled planes, accentuating the cheek-bone, his women have softer features'. Modelled his work upon Van Dyck and Michael Wright(qv) although whether he ever studied under the latter is unclear. Represented in SNPG(2), City of Edinburgh collection (portrait of 'Sir James Stewart of Coltness, Lord Provost of Edinburgh 1648-50 & 1658-60', the first known portrait of a Lord Provost), The Binns (NTS), Brodick Castle (NTS), House of Dun (NTS - though these may be by John Scougal).

**Bibl:** Apted 84-5; Caw 217; Holloway 14-17,33-4; Macmillan [SA] 75-7.

**SCOUGAL(L), George fl 1694-1737**

Portrait painter. Son of John Scougal Jnr(qv). Until c1900 his identity was in doubt but from records in Merchant House, Glasgow, we know that in 1715 he was commissioned to paint James Govane. In 1718 he painted the portraits of George and Thomas Hutcheson and in 1723 'Robert Saunders of Auldhouse'. In 1724 he received £3.10s for painting the Dean of Guild Thomson. Most of his surviving pictures are of ladies but his work was of poor quality. Writing in 1772 Sir George Chalmers said that the artist's 'great run of business brought him into an incorrect stiff manner void of expression. His carelessness occasioned many complaints'. The National Library of Scotland have the translation by Sir William Hope of Jacques de Solleysell's *Manual of Equitation and Farriery,* the title page of which was engraved by John Sturt after an original design by George Scougal. Waterhouse considered his work 'almost beneath consideration'.

**Bibl:** Apted 85-6; Bryan; Caw 17-19; Records of Trades House of Glasgow 1713-77, ed Lumsden, Glasgow 1834; View of the Merchant's House of Glasgow, Glasgow 1866, 152; Waterhouse.

**SCOUGAL(L), John c1645-1737**

Born Leith; died Prestonpans. Portrait painter. According to Brydall was cousin to Patrick Scougal, consecrated Bishop of Aberdeen 1664. Father of George(qv) and the son or nephew of David S(qv). Married a Margaret Gordon in St Machar's Cathedral, Aberdeen April 28th 1680. He was known to have lived in Edinburgh in 1694 and to have painted portraits for Lady Ravelston the same year in which he apparently purchased the fishing rights above and below Balgownie Bridge. One of his earliest portraits is of the '4th Earl of Panmure' c1689 (now at Glamis), while the portraits of Sir Francis and Lady Grant can be dated 1700. Working as a portrait painter in 1690 with a house and studio in Advocate's Close. Between 1693 and 1702 was copying portraits for the University at Glasgow. Commissioned to paint full-length portraits of 'King William' and 'Queen Mary' for Glasgow Council and also of Queen Anne 1708. In 1682 the Earl of Panmure paid £9 4s sterling for his own framed portrait and two frames. The 4 works attributed to Scougal are in the SNPG, including his portrait of 'Lord Harcarse' of which McKay wrote 'a careful modelling, with no attempt at an artistic treatment of light and shade, and all want that lightness of touch which can give charm and esprit to the most conventional arrangements'. According to Holloway 'his style became increasingly perfunctory and some of his last portraits...seem almost to have been assembled from kits, with almond-shaped eyes a speciality'. Appears to have given up painting more than 20 years before his death in 1737. Represented in NGS (attributed 'self-portrait'), SNPG (attributions), Glasgow AG, City of Edinburgh collection(3), The Binns (NTS), Fyvie Castle (NTS).

**Bibl:** Apted 86-8; Armstrong 6; Bryan; Brydall 92-3; Caw 17-19; Extracts from the Records of the Burgh of Glasgow, 422; Holloway 45-9, 147-8 et passim; Foulis Account Book, 198 et seq; McKay 13; Records of Old Aberdeen (New Spalding Club); Wilson, Memorials of Old Edinburgh.

**SCOULAR, W G** **fl 1925**
Minor Edinburgh painter; exhibited RSA(1) from 40 West Preston St.

**SCOULAR, William** **1796-1864**
Born Scotland; died Soho, London, 23 Jly. Sculptor. Studied at the Trustees School of Design under John Graham and in 1814 went to London becoming a pupil of Sir Richard Westmacott at the RA Schools. In 1816 he received a silver medal from the Society of Arts for a statue of 'Faunus' and in 1820 the Isis gold medal for a group 'Brutus and his Son'. Received RA gold medal for sculpture 1817 and the silver medal for modelling at the Life Academy. Travelled periodically between London and Edinburgh maintaining a studio in Mound Place, partly in order to receive patrons and to exhibit his work, where he was described as the 'Edinburgh sculptor'. In 1825 won an RA travelling scholarship and went to study in Rome, remaining there for several years though it was reported at the time that his 'modest and retired habits estranged him from his countrymen visiting Rome'. In 1823 appointed Sculptor to the Duke and Duchess of Clarence, having executed a small figure of their child the infant Princess Elizabeth, (now in Windsor Castle) 1821. In 1825 the *Literary Gazette* referred to his figure of 'Narcissus' by saying 'we have scarcely ever seen a more beautiful model, chaste in design, just in its proportions and graceful in action'. But some years later (1844) the *Art Union* referred to a bust of the Prince Consort as 'among the worst of the portraits we have seen'. In 1840 his 'Italian Peasant Boy' was awarded a prize by the Scottish Art Union and in 1843 he designed a medallion of John Hampton for the memorial erected on the site of the Battle of Chalgrove Field. A bust of 'Sir John Dashwood King' is at West Wycombe Park. Exhibited RA(59) 1815-1846 including a bust of 'Prince Albert' 1844, and many at the BI 1816-1843. His statue of 'James Watt', shown in Birmingham, which fetched £136 at Christie's in 1889, is probably the one now in Glasgow AG, Represented also in SNPG.
**Bibl:** Gents Mag, 1854, pt II, 316; Gunnis 345-6; Redgrave; Scots Mag, 1816, 207.

**SCOULE/AR, James** **1740-1812**
Born Edinburgh, 13 Jan; died London, 22 Feb. Miniaturist and crayon portraitist. Youngest of four children but his elder brother predeceased his father making James the family heir. It seems probable that there was a younger brother Robert. Uncle of the miniaturist John Brown(qv), whose mother Agnes Scouler was James's sister. Evidence of this is a miniature in the collection of Lord Thomson exhibited in Edinburgh 1965, signed and dated 'J Scouler/ 1768', and inscribed on the reverse 'Robert Scouler/Ensign in India/ Brother to James Scouler/Portrait Painter/1768'. James Scouler studied at the Duke of Richmond's Gallery in London and at St Martin's Lane Academy. Awarded a premium for drawing in 1755 by the Society for Arts. According to Foskett 'he used a lot of gum with his paints, giving the impression of oil paintings. His later works are often signed parallel to the edge of the miniature, and sometimes scratched in the paint'. Exhibited Society of Artists 1761-8, Free Society 1767 & RA(33) 1780-1787. Represented in V & A, ('David Garrick and his wife'), NGS(2), Glasgow AG.
**Bibl:** Foskett, 497-8.

**SCOULE/AR, Robert** **fl 1768**
Portrait miniaturist. Probably younger brother of James S(qv). That so little is known of this artist can be attributed to his prolonged stay in India.

**SCOULLER, Glen RSW** **1950-**
Born Glasgow. Painter in watercolour and oil, of landscape and still life. Studied Glasgow School of Art 1968-73 followed by a scholarship year spent in Greece. Received the Lauder Award, Glasgow Art Club 1987. Since then has painted mainly landscapes of Provence though is also interested in still life. Influenced mainly by his teachers at Glasgow, Donaldson, Shanks and Robertson, and inspired by Paul Klee's watercolours of Tunisia 1914. Taught for 15 years at the Glasgow School of Art before becoming a full-time artist 1989. Regular solo exhibitions in England, Scotland and South Africa since 1977. Employs a wet style with concentrations of high colour and disregard of either detail or form. Elected RSW 1997. Exhibits regularly RSA; also GI(1). Represented in Lillie AG (Milngavie), SAC.

**SCRAGG, Michelle** **1963-**
Born Glasgow. Painter in oils and watercolours, also textile designer. Trained Glasgow School of Art 1982-86 and at Winchester School of Art. Benno Schotz Prize 1986. A visit to Malaysia inspired a series of watercolours 1993-94. Selected by the Design Council to exhibit in the 'Young Creators' exhibition in London & Glasgow. First solo exhibition London 1995. Exhibits RGI.

**SCROPE, William** **1772-1852**
Author, sportsman and artist. Painted landscape and literary subjects in oil. Son of Richard Scrope DD and direct descendant of Richard, 1st Baron Scrope of Bolton, Lord Treasurer to Edward III. An excellent classical scholar, he lived most of his life at 13, Belgrave Square, London with frequent sortis to northern Scotland. He rented Lord Somerville's fishing lodge nr Melrose where he became a close friend of Sir Walter Scott and the artist William Simson(qv). Best known for his classic sporting books *The Art of Deer-Stalking* (1838) and *Days and Nights of Salmon Fishing on the Tweed* (1843), illustrated by the Landseer brothers and Simson. Member, Academy of St Luke in Rome and Fellow of the Linnean Society. Accomplished artist, he exhibited RA(6) 1801-1832 where he was an 'honorary exhibitor', and was a founder member of the BI. All the pictures were of Scottish landscapes except the first (a scene from Schiller).
**Bibl:** Athenaeum 1852, 800; DNB; Gent. Mag. 1852, ii, 201; Graves; G.P. Scrope, History of Castle Combe, 1852; Wingfield.

**SCRYMGEOUR, James M** **fl 1828-1836**
Edinburgh portrait and religious painter; exhibited RA(3), including 'The Earl of Airlie', 1832 and 'Christ crowned with thorns', 1836 & RSA(1), from St James Sq, Edinburgh and later 63 Frith St, London.

**SCULLIN, Miss Mary S** **fl 1957**
Glasgow watercolour painter. Shipping subjects. Exhibited GI.

**SCULLION, Claire** **1962-**
Born Helensburgh. Landscape painter. Exhibits GI(3) including several seascapes and coastal scenes.

**SCULLION, George** **fl 1954**
Dumbarton painter of rustic scenes. Exhibited GI(1).

**SCULLION, Louise** **1966-**
Born Helensburgh. Sculptress. Trained Glasgow School of Art 1984-88. Interested in the interplay between the natural world and man-made urban environment, a fascination stimulated by a visit to Dallas. First one person exhibition in Glasgow 1988. One of seven contemporary artists presented under the rubric 'Scatter' at the Third Eye Centre, Glasgow 1989.

**SEARS, Heather Clella** **fl 1979-1982**
Aberdeen artist. Trained Gray's School of Art, Aberdeen. Exhibited AAS(3), from 39 Holburn Rd.

**SEATON, R** **Early 19th Century**
Aberdeen artist. Painted watercolour views in and around the city of Aberdeen in a highly competent style. His figures are well drawn, the topography detailed and of considerable historical interest delineated in a manner reminiscent of Paul Sandby. Alexander Nasmyth used Seaton's work when preparing his own views of Aberdeen. Two works included in the 1991 exhibition of watercolours at Aberdeen AG. Represented in Aberdeen AG.

**SEATON, Rosemary** **fl 1970**
Edinburgh artist; exhibited 'Spanish carnival' at the RSA from Chessels Court.

**SEATON, William** **19th Cent**
A small oil painting 'Man Playing a Penny Whistle' is in Edinburgh City collection.

**SEGGIE, Miss Elizabeth A** **fl 1871-1875**
Edinburgh painter in watercolour of birds and flowers also landscape. Exhibited RSA(4).

**SEHACHER, C** **fl 1860**
Edinburgh-based artist; exhibited 'Dalgetty church, on the Fife coast' at the RSA, from Castle St.

**SEIVWRIGHT, Miss Georgie** **fl 1900**
Aberdeenshire flower painter, probably amateur. Exhibited AAS(1), from The Elms, Bieldside.

**SEKALSKI, Jozef ARE** **1904-1972**
Born Turek, Poland, 25 Sep. Printmaker, designer, mural painter, wood engraver, etcher and illustrator; also designed book plates. After schooling at Turek Boys' GS, studied medicine for three years 1925-8 before enrolling at the Faculty of Fine Arts, Wilno University, trained in painting by Ludomir Slendzinski, lettering with Bonawentura Lenart and engraving under Jerzy Hoppen, (whose assistant he became during his last year), 1929-34. Then spent three years painting church murals in Turek, Doleszczyn, and Poreba and in 1937 became head of an artist's and designer's studio in Lodz. During this time he visited Vienna and Italy. In 1940 he escaped to Hungary and in Budapest held a solo exhibition of prints. He then travelled through Zagreb to Italy and France, there enlisting in the Polish army under French command. Captured in the Ardennes and marched to Saxony whence he escaped, finally reaching Britain 1942. Joined the Polish forces in Scotland and during the latter days of the war settled in St Andrews where he became one of an important group of wood engravers, including the sisters Alison(qv) and Winifred McKenzie(qv) and Annabel Kidston(qv). Married Roberta Hodges(qv), art teacher at St. Leonard's School, St Andrews. A leading figure in the establishment and development of what became known as the St. Andrews school of wood carving. At the end of the war he was involved in illustrating and designing for the Polish Library and Publishing House in Glasgow and in 1945 produced illustrations for Anstruther's *Old Polish Legends* and for Rostorowski's poems, *The Fourteen Hours of the Night* (1946). In 1949 he illustrated Alastair Reid's *Poems.* From 1957 was lecturer in printmaking at Dundee AG. Elected ARE 1949, SSA 1950. Exhibited paintings and wood engravings RA & RSA. Represented in SNGMA, Perth AG.
**Bibl:** Dundee AG, 'Jozef Sikalski ARE SSA 1904-1972' (Ex Cat 1978); Albert Garrett, A History of British Wood Engraving, 1978; Gill & Fraser, Jozef Sikalski, Dundee 1976; Hartley 164.

**SELBIE, James** **fl 1959-1961**
Fife painter of portraits, local harbour scenes; exhibited AAS(2), from 148 Grange Cottages, West Wynd, Pittenweem.

**SELCRAIG, J K** **fl 1895**
Minor Glasgow painter of 10 Montgomerie Terrace; exhibited RSA(1).

**SELKIRK, Mrs Isabel** **fl 1935**
Glasgow amateur painter of flowers; exhibited AAS(1), from 42 Millbrae Rd.

**SELLAR, Charles A RSW** **1856-1926**
Born Edinburgh; died Perth, Apr. Painter in oil and watercolour; portraits, especially ladies, and landscape. Graduated in law at Edinburgh University before turning to art. Had a studio in Perth establishing a local reputation, painting east coast fishing villages and Perthshire views. His style is rather sweet, with good colours and a nice sense of light although the draughtsmanship can be imprecise. Moved to take up a commission with the Dewar whisky family. Committee member, Perthshire Artists' Association 1921-5. Elected RSW 1893. Exhibited RA(2), RSA(73), RSW(63), RHA(2), RI(1), AAS (1886-1923), RBA(1), GI(20) & L(7), mostly from 11 Charlotte St, Perth.
**Bibl:** Halsby 282.

**SELLAR, Jennie D** **20th Cent**
Aberdeenshire textile designer; exhibited AAS(3), from Clinterty House, Bucksburn.

**SELLARS, David Ramsay** **1854-1922**
Edinburgh painter in watercolour of coastal and farmyard scenes, and landscape especially on Tayside and the Fife shore-line. Exhibited RSA(18), AAS(4) & GI(2) having moved from 23 Union Place to Dundee c1889.
**Bibl:** Halsby 282.

**SELLARS, James** **1843-1888**
Glasgow architect. Apprenticed 1857-64 to Hugh Barclay(qv). Joined Campbell Douglas(qv) c1870. Won the first and second Stewart Fountain competitions 1870-1. The following year went to France and from 1874 developed a style influenced by late 16th century French architecture. Won 1888 Exhibition competition. Designed Kelvinside Academy(1877) in the neo-classical mould with added severity, Wylie & Lochhead's (now Fraser's), 45 Buchanan St (1883), New Club 144-146 West George St(1879) and several churches.
**Bibl:** Dunbar 141; A Gomme & D Walker, Architecture of Glasgow, London 1987(rev), 298-9.

**SELLARS, Jeannie A** **fl 1907**
Glasgow silversmith; exhibited GI(2) from 13 Loudon Terrace, Kelvinside.

**SELLARS, William** **fl 1870**
Glasgow amateur topographical watercolourist. Exhibited GI(2).

**SELLARS, William W** **fl 1885-1889**
Dundee landscape painter in oil; exhibited RSA(3) from 28 Longwynd.

**SEM, Agnes** **fl 1929**
Montrose amateur portrait painter; exhibited AAS(1), from Lochside.

**SEMMENCE, John O** **fl 1953-1984**
Aberdeenshire painter of portraits and landscape. Exhibited RSA frequently during the above years having moved from the Schoolhouse, Cults to Kent 1979. Represented in Edinburgh City collection.

**SEMPHILL, Lady** **fl 1935**
Amateur landscape painter. Member of well-known Aberdeenshire family, associated with Craigievar Castle. Exhibited a view of Craigievar at the AAS from Fintray House, Fintray, Aberdeenshire.

**SEMPLE, Carol** **1974-**
Semi-abstract sculptress. Exhibits RSA & GI (of which she is a member), from 27 Elmwood Terrace, Edinburgh.

**SEMPLE, Pat RSW** **1940-**
Brought up in Kintyre, Argyll. Landscape painter in watercolour, also occasionally oil. Trained Edinburgh College of Art 1958-63 with a postgraduate year 1963-4. In the late 1980s moved from Strathdon, Aberdeenshire to Inverness-shire and in 1991 back to the north-east. Her lines are convulsive, tormented and twisted with great movement and a sense of semi-explored mystery. Finds inspiration in the wilderness, dramatic skies and sunsets. Paintings have 'bold, brave curves and sweeps with clouds billowing overhead in multi-clouded splendour charged with hot, thundery hue' [Henry]. Endeavours to convey her feelings for 'timelessness, strength, melancholy, history'. Had her first solo exhibition in Stirling 1980. Elected SSA 1980, RSW 1987. Exhibits regularly RSW & AAS since 1977. Represented Aberdeen AG, SAC.

**SEMPLE, R S** **fl 1876**
Edinburgh painter; exhibited 'A quiet corner' at the RSA, from St Andrews Sq.

**SEMPLE, Dr Robert** **fl 1959-1961**
Aberdeenshire amateur painter of country scenes and topography; fond of the Plockton area of Wester Ross. Exhibited AAS(5), from Greenbank, Milltimber.

**SEMPLE, William** **fl 1927-1953**
Little known Glasgow painter; worked in both oil and watercolours. Continental landscapes, some on Clydeside and Arran. Exhibited GI(20).

**SENIOR, Susan K** **fl 1963**
Edinburgh painter of landscapes, especially Norwegian; exhibited RSA(3), from Nether Lennie.

**SENIOR, William** **fl 1940s-1960s**
Glasgow painter. Flowers, still life and semi-abstracts. Member of the Clyde group(qv) with Bet Low(qv) and Tom MacDonald(qv). Exhibited GI(2).

**SEN(N)EFELDER CLUB** **1913-**
Formed 1913. An association of etchers and lithographers named after the Prague playwright and founder of colour lithography in 1798, Alois Sen(n)efelder (1771-1834). Although not based in Scotland, where there is no equivalent, engravers, etchers and lithographers from north of the border have been members and exhibit with the Club at its annual shows in London.

**SERVANT, John** **fl 1768**
Scottish portrait painter who worked for Lord Linton of Traquair House. In 1768 he painted the portrait of 'Charles, 7th Earl of Traquair (1766-1827)' signed 'John Servant, pinxit 1768'. No other works of his are known.

**SETON, Isabel Margaret** **fl 1898-1915**
Edinburgh painter of portrait miniatures, still life and conversation pieces. Exhibited RSA(6), GI(5) & L(2).

**SETON, John Thomas (sometimes appears as 'SEATON')** **c1758-1806**
Portrait miniaturist. Son of Christopher Seton, a gem engraver. Studied under Francis Hayman at St Martin's Lane Academy. In Rome 1758-9. In 1766 he settled in Bath and had been elected a member of the Incorporated Society of Artists. Went to Calcutta 1776 remaining nine years apart from a brief interlude in Edinburgh 1780. Given leave to proceed to Bengal to practise portrait painting. Portraits painted during these years included 'Col Allan MacPherson', his wife, and brother (Col John MacPherson). These were all published in W C MacPherson's *Soldiering in India 1764-1787,* (1928). Returned to Scotland 1785 and known to be living in Edinburgh 1806. Dated works include 'Lord Adam Gordon (1726-1801)' painted in 1768, 'John 5th Lord Carmichael' and '4th Earl of Hyndford (1710-1787)' both painted in 1773, and a British officer signed and inscribed 'Calcutta 1779'. Exhibited SA 1761-9 and three half-length portraits of ladies at the RA in 1774 from St Andrew's St, New Town, Edinburgh. Represented in NGS(3), SNPG (4) including a portrait of 'Katherine Walkinshaw 1776'.
**Bibl:** Archer, 99-107; Bryan; Forster; Walpole Soc, xix (1930-1), xxi (1933), xxxvi, 74.

**SETON, Mary E** **fl 1923-1940**
East Lothian landscape watercolourist she moved from Dirleton to Gullane in the late 1920s. Exhibited RSA(1), RSW(8) & RI(1).
**Bibl:** Halsby 282.

**SEYMOUR, Edward** **fl 1851-1854**
Edinburgh painter of local scenery. Married an artist(qv). Exhibited RSA(4).

**SEYMOUR, Mrs Edward** **fl 1872-1873**
Edinburgh landscape painter in oil especially of the north west and around Inverness. Married Edward S(qv). Exhibited RSA(4).

**SHALDERS, George** **fl 1885**
Edinburgh painter of interiors; exhibited AAS(1), from 6 Kilgraston Rd.

**SHAND, Barbara Sinclair** **fl 1890-1896**
Aberdeen artist. Over a comparatively brief period exhibited 14 portraits, flower paintings and landscape at the AAS, from 41 Osborne Pl.

**SHAND, Brian Cook** **fl 1970-**
Aberdeen potter; moved to Banff to set up the Portsoy Pottery. Exhibits regularly AAS since 1970.

**SHAND, Edward Arthur** **fl 1884-1885**
Edinburgh painter of pastoral scenes; exhibited RSA(2).

**SHAND, George** **fl 1890**
Edinburgh designer; exhibited AAS(1), from 12 Atholl Place.

**SHAND, Lizzie** **fl 1902**
Aberdeenshire amateur landscape artist; exhibited 'On the Dee' at the AAS, from Huntly.

**SHANKLAND, Miss Jennie C** **fl 1895**
Greenock flower painter; exhibited RSA(2).

**SHANKS, Alastair** **fl 1950**
Aberdeenshire amateur watercolourist. Exhibited a view on Islay at the GI from Strichen.

**SHANKS, Alexander** **fl 1940-1950**
Landscape painter; often scenes on Islay. Possibly brother of Alastair S(qv). Exhibited GI(4) from 7 Kirkwood Street, Glasgow.

**SHANKS, Duncan Faichney RSA RSW** **1937-**
Born Airdrie 30 Aug. Landscape painter, potter and ceramic designer. Trained Glasgow School of Art. Part-time lecturer in Glasgow School of Art for many years until retiring 1979 in order to become a full-time painter. Held many one man shows including Toulouse and Edinburgh, and participated in a group show, Rio de Janeiro 1985. Married Una S(qv). Won a number of awards including the Latimer and Macaulay Prizes of the RSA and the Cargill and Torrance Awards of the RGI. Lives in the Clyde Valley, drawing inspiration from its landscape. His work, which has become increasingly abstract, reflects an emotional reaction to landscape rather than literal recording of it. Increasingly kaleidoscopic in his use if colour, much influenced by music. Elected RSW 1990, RSA 1990. Regular exhibitor RSA, RSW, GI & AAS(2) 1972, from Davingall House, by Carluke, Lanarkshire. Represented in Glasgow AG, Lillie (Milngavie), Hunterian AG (Glasgow), SAC.
**Bibl:** Duncan Macmillan, 'Duncan Shanks, Falling Water', Talbot Rice Gallery, Edinburgh, (Ex Cat 1988); Macmillan [SA] 400-1; Roger Billcliffe, Duncan Shanks,Capriccios, Ex Cat, Oct-Nov 1998.

**SHANKS, George F** **fl 1943-1955**
Glasgow-based architect and engraver. Exhibited an etching of Pontevecchio, Florence at the GI 1943 and architectural drawings subsequently.

**SHANKS, George F** **fl 1967-1969**
Potter and ceramic designer. When at Duncan of Jordanstone College of Art, Dundee exhibited 4 works at the AAS during the above years.

**SHANKS, Lewis** **fl 1871**
Glasgow memorial sculptor. Exhibited a design for a memorial fountain at the RSA.

**SHANKS, Mrs T** **fl 1959**
Watercolour painter. Wife of Thomas S(qv). Exhibited GI(1) from Kilbarchan.

**SHANKS, Thomas (Tom) Hovell RSW RGI** **1921-**
Born Glasgow. Watercolourist; landscapes, mostly west Highland. Stemming from childhood visits to Skye he was most fascinated by the dramatic effects of light and shade on landscape. Member of the Glasgow Group. Regular exhibitor RSW, RSA(15), GI(100+) & AAS(2). Represented in Glasgow AG, Paisley AG, and by two pen washes - 'Loch Ewe' and 'Carn a'Ghobhair, Sleat' - in Lillie AG (Milngavie), SAC. Lived at Rosehill Well Rd, Kilbarchan, Renfrewshire.

**SHANKS, Mrs Una B** **fl 1982-1983**
Lanarkshire-based flower painter. Married Duncan S(qv). Exhibited RSA & GI(1) from Carluke.

**SHANKS, William Somerville RSA RSW** **1864-1951**
Born Gourock, 28 Sep; died Glasgow, 30 Jly. Painter in oil and watercolours of portraits, interiors and still life in a style better suited to oils. Developed a dashing style with freedom allied to good draughtsmanship. Began as a pattern designer with a curtain manufacturer, studying drawings in the evening at Glasgow School of Art under Fra Newbery. Determined to take up painting full-time went to Paris 1889 working under J P Laurens and Benjamin Constant for three years. In 1922 received a silver medal at the Société des Artistes Français, his work bearing the influence of Manet, also Sir John Lavery(qv). Teacher of drawing and painting, Glasgow School of Art 1910-39 before moving to Stirling. Frequent exhibitor at the Paris Salon. Returned to Gourock 1949, but following his wife's death a

year later settled in Glasgow. 'His work was characterised by an amazingly skilful technique which distinguished all his subjects - still lifes, landscapes, interiors and portraits - by a fine sense of colour and by its tonal qualities'. His diploma work was 'The Visitor' and his best known portraits were the artists 'Archibald Kay' and 'Tom Hunt'. Elected ARSA 1923, RSW 1925, RSA 1933. Exhibited RSA(74), RSW(36), RA(6), GI(122), AAS (1926-31) & L(9). Represented in Glasgow AG(3) including a portrait of 'John Q. Pringle', Edinburgh City collection.
**Bibl:** Halsby 159,283; RSA Obituary 1951.

**SHANNAN, Archibald McFarlane ARSA FRBS** **1850-1915**
Born Glasgow, 28 May; died Glasgow, 28 Sep. Sculptor. Executed busts in marble and bronze. Educated Glasgow University and trained Royal College of Art, he worked in Paris after serving as an apprentice in stonecutting and building. Caw spoke of his 'admirable character and expressive, sound modelling, united to a certain feeling for style, which suggest possibilities of power'. Married Louise G S(qv). Elected ARSA 1902. Exhibited at the RA(5), RSA(33), GI(40) & AAS(2) in 1906 latterly from his studio, 36 Buccleuch St, Glasgow.
**Bibl:** Robin Lee Woodward, 'Nineteenth Century Sculpture in Glasgow', Virtue & Vision, NGS, Edinburgh (Ex Cat, 1991).

**SHANNAN, Mrs Louise G(?E)** **fl 1895-1910**
Painter of figurative subjects. Wife of the sculptor Archibald McFarlane S(qv). Exhibited GI(15).

**SHANNON, Donald** **fl 1952-1964**
Perth painter of portraits and figurative subjects. Exhibited RSA(5), including a self-portrait.

**SHARP, Alistair** **1926-**
Born Cowdenbeath. Sculptor. Studied Edinburgh College of Art. Visited Paris. Taught in Fife and Edinburgh until 1975. Lives and works in Edinburgh. Represented by a bas-relief on paper in the Edinburgh City collection.

**SHARP, Christopher** **fl 1978**
Aberdeen artist; exhibited AAS(1) from 30 Hill St.

**SHARP, Daphne Dyce** **fl 1954-1983**
Edinburgh sculptress. Migrated to Canada. Exhibited RSA(7).

**SHARP, Mrs Doreen K** **fl 1977**
Perthshire painter of figurative works. Exhibited GI(1) from Braco.

**SHARP, Mrs Elizabeth H** **fl 1980**
Glasgow-based amateur painter. Exhibited GI(1).

**SHARP, J H** **fl 1880**
Glasgow painter of landscape and figurative subjects. Exhibited GI(2) from Doune Terrace.

**SHARP, James** **fl 1894-1911**
Aberdeen landscape painter; exhibited AAS, from 8 Albury Rd.

**SHARP, John** **fl 1916-1926**
Sculptor. Mostly figurative works, informal busts including a portrait bust of Alexander Findlay Esq, MP for Motherwell, 1921. Lived in Duns, Berwickshire in 1916 before moving to Glasgow. Exhibited GI(14).

**SHARP, Joseph** **fl 1876-1910**
Glasgow landscape painter in oil and watercolours. Often painted rural and harbour scenes. Exhibited RSA(3) & GI(42).

**SHARP, Lois** **fl 1976**
Dundee painter of flowers and still life; exhibited RSA(1).

**SHARP, Mrs Louie E** **fl 1906-1912**
Kincardineshire painter of portraits and figurative works; exhibited AAS(6) & GI(1), from Union Bank House, Banchory.

**SHARP, Nellie H** **fl 1887**
Amateur Glasgow painter of 4 Doune Terrace, Hillhead; exhibited GI(1).

**SHARP Robert S W** **fl 1927-1951**
Amateur Glasgow flower and genre painter of 585 Argyle Street; exhibited GI(2).

**SHARPE, Charles (of Hollam)** **late 18th Cent**
Scottish figurative painter. Father of Charles Kirkpatrick S(qv). Died in Edinburgh. A miniature study of a man and a little girl, reproduced in *Charles Kirkpatrick's Letters* (ed by A Allardyce, 1868) is in NGS.

**SHARPE, Charles Kirkpatrick** **1781-1851**
Born Hoddam Castle, Dumfries-shire, 15 May; died Mar. Scottish artist of caricature portraits and etchings; also illustrator, antiquarian, musician and poet. Member of the old Scottish family of Mar, related to the royal house of Stuart. Studied Edinburgh University and in 1798 entered Christ Church, Oxford to read classics but quickly established a reputation as an artist with watercolour portraits of the Dean and some fellow students. Settled in Edinburgh where his interest in Scottish antiquities deflected him from entering the church. Close friend of Sir Walter Scott and David Scott(qv), he was essentially an amateur artist involved in literature and the theatre. One of his first etchings was a striking caricature of Mme. de Stael on the occasion of her visit to Edinburgh, 1813. Mainly executed pen and wash drawings illustrating literary subjects and watercolours of theatrical scenes. His caricatures are quite successful, showing the influence of Rowlandson but his watercolour portraits are amateurish. A volume of ballads, etchings and prose was published in Edinburgh 1869. Contributed illustrations for Hogg's *Witch of Fife* (1820), *Fugitive Scottish Poetry* (1823), *The Romances of Ottuel, Roland and Vernagu* (1836) and *Flora's Fete.* A volume of ballads, prose fragments and etchings was published by Blackwoods 1869. Represented in NGS(17), SNPG(copies), BM, NLS (2 vols of watercolour portraits dated 1813), Edinburgh City collection.
**Bibl:** A. Allardyce, CKS's Letters, 1868; A. Allardyce, The Etchings of CKS, 1869; Bryan; Bushnell; Halsby 283; Houfe; Charles Kirkpatrick Sharpe, Etchings with a Memoir, Edinburgh 1869.

**SHARPE, Gregory** **fl 1732**
A large pen drawing 'The East Prospect of Aberdeen', signed and dated 1732, appeared as a reduced etching in *Description of Aberdeen,* 1661 published by the Spalding Club in 1842. The drawing is in NGS.

**SHATWELL, Val** **Contemporary**
Dunblane-based jeweller and silversmith. Trained Glasgow School of Art. Professional member SSA. Member, Hanging Together group(qv). Solo exhibition, Univ of Strathclyde 1997. Seeks to evoke contrasting emotions from single images and experiences as, for example, change which may be regretted or welcomed.

**SHAW, A Wilson** **fl 1911-1915**
Amateur Glasgow painter of Dennistoun; exhibited GI(1) & L(8).

**SHAW, Cameron** **fl 1973**
Mintlaw painter; exhibited two portraits at the AAS, from Kirnknockie Croft.

**SHAW, Charles B** **fl 1850**
Glasgow painter. Exhibited a still life of fruit at the RSA.

**SHAW, Isabel** **fl 1964**
Aberdeenshire watercolourist; exhibited a landscape at the AAS, from The Stables, Davah, Inverurie.

**SHAW, J Crawford** **fl 1887-1899**
Glasgow painter in oil of figures and landscape; exhibited RSA(4), GI(26) & L(4), from Dowanhall Gdns and later W. George St.

**SHAW, James** **fl 1883-1902**
Edinburgh landscape painter in oil; also illustrator. Worked for *Punch.* Exhibited RSA(24), GI(7) & L(1). Represented in V & A.
**Bibl:** Houfe.

**SHAW, James Howie** **fl 1960-1962**
Glasgow painter of country subjects, often with angling themes; exhibited RSA(5).

**SHAW, Miss Jean L Crawford** **fl 1971-1972**
Lanarkshire artist. Possibly daughter of J Crawford S(qv). Exhibited GI(2) from Lesmahagow.

**SHAW, John, Jnr** **fl 1862-1863**
Amateur Edinburgh landscape painter in oil; exhibited RSA(4).

**SHAW, Michael** **fl 1885**
Painter of 7 Campbell Street, Riccarton, Kilmarnock. Exhibited two rustic scenes at the RSA.

**SHAW, Richard Norman RA HRSA** **1831-1912**
Born Edinburgh, 7 May; died London, 17 Nov. Architect. The leading British domestic architect of the late Victorian age. Educated in Edinburgh, his working life was spent almost entirely south of the border. As a young man was apprenticed to William Burn(qv), working alongside David McGibbon(qv) and others. Won the RA Schools Medal. Following a European tour published *Architectural Sketches* 1858. After a spell working for A. Salvin and then as a draughtsman with G.E. Street, he opened his own practice 1862, sharing offices with William Nesfield(qv). Member, RIBA but resigned over a policy disagreement. Elected Hon. RSA 1911. One of his most interesting designs, Tudor on the outside and Renaissance within, was featured in the exhibition 'Scottish Architects at Home and Abroad' at the NLS 1978. This was Dawpool, built in Cheshire 1882-6 (since demolished) for the shipping magnate Thomas Ismay. The total affect of the ornate interiors was described as 'overwhelming'. His best known building was (the old) New Scotland Yard (1890). Elected ARA 1871, RA 1877, HRSA 1911. Exhibited 38 designs at the RA 1870-1900, RSA(10) 1907-1912, all of them of London buildings, apart from one house in Sussex (Whispers) and one in Surrey (Pierrepont).
**Bibl:** Colvin; Peter Savage, Lorimer and the Edinburgh Craft Designers, Edin. 1980, 7,8,29,31,38,39,42,51,71,104,152,168.

**SHAW, Rita** **fl 1932-1934**
Amateur Glasgow painter of flowers and still life. Exhibited RSA(1) & GI(2), from 17 Balmeg Avenue, Giffnock.

**SHAW, Robert (Bob)** **Contemporary**
Lawyer and part-time etcher. No formal training but developed through his membership of the Edinburgh Printmakers Workshop. In the German Expressionist tradition, following Bellany(qv) and Stephen Campbell(qv). People in humorous and bizarre settings. Settled in Orkney where he established the Soulisquay Printmakers at Hatston, Kirkwall. First solo exhibition in Edinburgh 1976.

**SHAW, Sax Ro(w)land** **1916-2000**
Born Berrbrow, Huddersfield, Dec 5; died Edinburgh, Sept. Painter in watercolours of continental scenes, topography & still life; also tapestry and stained glass window designer. Grandfather's second name Rowland, father used the 'w' arbitrarily, Sax dropped it altogether. Educated Almondbury GS, trained Edinburgh College of Art 1936-38, Huddersfield College of Art 1938-40 and post-graduate scholar at Edinburgh 1946-47 before embarking on a travel scholarship to France during which he studied tapestry at the Gobelin, Paris. Lectured in architecture and interior design, Edinburgh College of Art 1948; director of weaving, Dovecote studios, Edinburgh 1955-60. Also lectured Glasgow School of Art. Best known for his stained glass and tapestries. Helped in later years by his son, **Christian Gerard S**, whose main work is restoration although also a stained glass window designer (largely responsible, for example, for the window in Ballater parish church). Fellow, Master Glass Painters 1979. Exhibited RSA, RGI & in France, Finland and the USA. Represented by stained glass windows also in Glasgow Cathedral, and the churches of St Andrews (Bute); Iona, St Andrews Parish; St Ninian's, Kilmarnock; Church of Scotland,Accra; St Kentigern's, Edinburgh (with tapestries); Netherlea (Glasgow); Hyndhead (Glasgow); Dunfermline Parish; St Mary's (Haddington); West Mayfield Parish; Lochgilphead Parish; Loch Fyneside & Ballater (opened by the Queen Mother 1986). Other windows at Bell's Whisky Reception Centre (Perth); Warriston Crematorium (Edinburgh); Scottish Development Agency (Edinburgh). Tapestries can be seen in Coventry Cathedral and elsewhere in England and Scotland.
**Bibl:** Gifford 45,524,660.

**SHEARER, Charles Manon** **fl 1978-1980**
Aberdeen printmaker and engraver; moved to Kirkwall c 1980. Trained Gray's School of Art, Aberdeen. Exhibited AAS(4), latterly from Edgecot, Scapa Flow.

**SHEARER, Donald M** **1925-**
Born Kyle of Lochalsh, Wester Ross. Popular but under-rated painter of landscape, somewhat in the manner of Mackintosh Patrick(qv). His subjects are most often the north-west Highlands and the Moray Firth, especially around its northern shores near his home. Trained Gray's School of Art, Aberdeen 1949-53, winning an Academy award 1954. Became interested in golf courses and designed a series of links views published as prints. Received many commissions to paint golfing scenes at St Andrews and Carnoustie, later produced as prints. Since 1990 his style has changed from detailed representational to a broader brush, using sharp contrasts to intensify dramatic appeal. Lives at Rossal, Seabank Rd, Invergordon. Exhibited regularly RSA, GI & AAS 1959-1964 from his home at Invergordon.

**SHEARER, Helen** **fl 1971**
Kincardineshire landscape painter; exhibited 'The auld kirkyard, Kirkwall' at the AAS, from Drumnalan, Laurencekirk.

**SHEARER, James** **1853-1931**
Born Dunfermline, May. Damask designer and painter in oil and watercolour; landscapes, townscapes, rustic scenes, coastal scenes and figure subjects; also etcher. Father of James S(qv), grandfather of Moira Shearer (Mrs Ludovic Kennedy) the ballerina. Founder and President of the Dunfermline Art Society and the Dunfermline Orchestra. Fond of Crail and Anstruther which he often painted. Exhibited RSA(15) from Morton Lodge, Dunfermline (which he built); also GI & AAS(6), sometimes from 24 Shandwick Place, Edinburgh. Represented in Dunfermline AG(12).

**SHEARER, James OBE RSA FRIBA FRIAS** **1880-1962**
Born Dunfermline. Architect. Son of James S(qv). Partner in firm James Shearer and Annand. Consulting architect to the Carnegie UK Trust for almost 37 years. Designed the Andrew Carnegie memorial in Dunfermline, also the new Scottish Central Library, Fishers Close, Edinburgh. Elected ARSA 1943, RSA 1948. Representative of the RSA with the National Trust for Scotland. Exhibited RSA 1940-57 & GI 1940-61.

**SHEARER, James Elliot** **1858-c1940**
Born Stirling, 23 Sep. Painter in oil and watercolour of landscapes, mainly in watercolour, also flowers. Lived at Benview, Stirling 1880s before moving to Manchester and returning to Edinburgh c1895. Exhibited RSA(76), RSW(22), RA(1), GI(16) & L(1).
**Bibl:** Halsby 283.

**SHEARER, John W** **fl 1965**
Fife painter of local scenery; exhibited RSA(1) from Pittenweem.

**SHEARER, Robert** **fl 1884**
Watercolour painter of uncertain origin. Represented in Edinburgh City collection with a drawing of Saughton Bridge(1884).

**SHEARER, Mrs Rosa L** **fl 1899-1912**
Watercolour painter; mainly flowers and still life. Wife of James Elliot S(qv). Exhibited RSA(1), GI(10) & L(1).

**SHEMILT, Elaine** **1954-**
Born Edinburgh. Sculptress & printmaker. Trained Winchester School of Art (sculpture) and Royal College of Art (printmaking). Since 1989 senior lecturer, Duncan of Jordanstone College of Art. In 1997 her exhibition "Behind Appearance" toured the American midwest. Her work has been exhibited in Holland, Switzerland and USA. Represented in Dundee AG.

**SHEPHERD, Anna** **fl 1985**
Aberdeen jewellery designer. Trained Gray's School of Art, Aberdeen. Exhibited AAS from the Jewellery Gallery, 2 Station Rd, Cults.

**SHEPHERD, Annie M** **fl 1894-1902**
Aberdeen painter and metalwork designer; exhibited landscape,

figure studies and metalwork designs at the AAS(7), from 15 Fonthill Terrace.

**SHEPHERD, John** **fl 1853-1855**
Edinburgh painter of landscape and dead game; exhibited RSA(4), from George St.

**SHEPHERD, Margaret Isabel** **fl 1973-1977**
North-east silversmith. Trained Gray's School of Art, Aberdeen. Exhibited AAS(6), from Woodend Cottage, Barras, nr Stonehaven.

**SHEPHERD, Sydney Horne** **1909-?**
Born Dundee, 30 Dec. Painter in oil, watercolour and pastel, also lithographer. Trained Glasgow School of Art under Greiffenhagen(qv) 1927-30. Lived in Chelsea for many years before moving to Glasgow to teach at the Glasgow School of Art 1929-31. Exhibited RSA, GI & in the USA.

**SHEPHERD, Thomas Hosmer** **1792-1864**
Watercolour painter and engraver of buildings and townscapes. Son of an Edinburgh merchant. Spent most of his life in England and is best known for 38 important drawings of Edinburgh made for *Modern Athens Displayed, or Edinburgh in the 19th Century,* 1829. Executed a series of over 100 small sketches which were engraved by 19 different engravers. Burgess of Edinburgh 1821. Had as apprentices James Shepherd 1822, David Hill 1825 and Charles Robertson 1828. Another important engraving is the large 'View of Edinburgh showing the communication between the Old and the New Town as proposed by Alexander Trotter Esq, of Dreghorn' 1834. Other historically interesting works include four fine watercolours of the contemporary Edinburgh scene 'Charlotte Square', 'Regent Murray's House in the Canongate', the 'Levee Room in Regent Murray's House' and the 'West Bow from the Lawnmarket'.
**Bibl:** Butchart 55-6.

**SHEPLEY, Clifford** **1908-?**
Born Bonnyrigg, Midlothian, 5 Aug. Medical illustrator in pencil, pen and ink, watercolour and pastel. Educated in Edinburgh, trained Edinburgh College of Art 1928-32 followed by a year at Moray House Teacher Training College 1932-3. Founder member, Medical Artist's Association 1949. Elected AMI 1951, AIMBI 1969. Author of *Preparation of Drawings and Diagrams for Scientific Publications* and *Development of Medical Illustrations.* Exhibited a chalk drawing at the RSA 1932, from 11 Restalrig Avenue, Edinburgh.

**SHEPPARD, Elizabeth A C** **fl 1983**
Aberdeen painter; exhibited AAS(2), from 8 West Mount St.

**SHEPPHERD, Mrs Nancy (née Huntly)** **1890-?**
Born Nasirabad, India. Painter in oil, watercolour, black and white; landscape, portraits and figurative subjects. Worked in a strong realistic style devoid of frills and mannerism. Trained Edinburgh College of Art, Kunstgewerbe Schule, Dusseldorf and RA Schools, London. Regular summer visitor to her native Scotland. Painted one of the few known pre-war pictures of a Highland Games 1939. Exhibited RA(7) 1913-1937 & L(1), latterly from Welwyn Garden City, Herts.

**SHERAR, Robert F** **fl 1885-1903**
Edinburgh landscape and topographical painter in watercolour and oil; exhibited RSA(5).

**SHERIDAN, Christina D** **fl 1933**
Painter of interiors and still life; exhibited RSA(2) from Glasgow School of Art.

**SHERIFF, Charles** [see SHIRREFF]

**SHERIFF, Flora (Mrs McDowall)** **1887-1965**
Born Larbert, Stirlingshire. Painter, mainly in watercolour. Taken by father to Egypt and Germany where she received instruction in drawing. Studied etching under D Y Cameron(qv) and at Glasgow School of Art. Fra Newbery(qv) admired her equestrian sketches saying 'very few could draw horses as she did'. Married and settled in Galloway 1914. Although comparatively unrecognised as an artist, an exhibition of her work took place at the Hornel AG 1982. Three exhibits at the RSA all predated her marriage.

**SHERIFF, G Vincent** **fl 1877-1890**
Born Scotland. Landscape painter in oil. Lived and worked most of his life in Liverpool where he exhibited 22 works at the Walker Gallery. Also exhibited 'A view in Glenfalloch' RA 1877, from 21 Leigh St, Liverpool.

**SHERIFF, John ('Dr Syntax') ARSA** **1816-1844**
Born Glasgow; died Edinburgh, 9 Dec. Painter in oil of animals, particularly dogs and horses; caricaturist. Worked as a clerk for some years in Glasgow before taking up painting and in spite of his short life - he died when he was only 28 - achieved some fame. His portrait of a famous greyhound 'Mountain Dew with the gamekeeper George Parker', exhibited RSA 1840, attracted considerable attention. His patrons included Sir William Maxwell Calderwood, Archibald Brodie of Arran, Sir David Dundas and Lord Rossmore. 'He painted animals with such elaboration and taste, as to give promise of attaining a high position' (RSA cat 1863). Elected ARSA 1839 when he was only 23. Exhibited RSA(33) 1830-1844, including 2 posthumous exhibits, 1863 and 1880. A large selection of his pen and ink drawings is in City of Edinburgh collection.
**Bibl:** Caw 198; Halsby 283; McKay 355; Wingfield.

**SHERIFF, William** **fl 1861-1900**
Glasgow painter in oil and watercolour of seascapes and views around Glasgow. Exhibited RSA(3) & GI(11) latterly from 5 Minard Terrace, Partickhill.
**Bibl:** Halsby 283.

**SHERIFF (or SHIRREFF), William Craig** **1786-1805**
Born Camptoun, nr Haddington, 26 Oct; died Edinburgh (in John Graham's house) 17 Mar. Painter of historical subjects and genre. Son of a farmer. Together with Wilkie(qv) was a pupil of John Graham's(qv) at Trustees Academy 1802-1805. When he died, only six months after his 18th birthday, he had almost finished 'a very clever' 'Escape of Queen Mary from Loch Leven'. This was engraved by William Lizars and gained the highest prize for the best historical picture done by a student at the Trustees Academy, an award introduced by the Master, John Graham. His talent was recognised by Wilkie who spoke of his 'great promise'. 'Queen Mary's escape' was exhibited RSA 1863. Represented in NGS.
**Bibl:** Armstrong 34; Bryan.

**SHE/IRRIFFS, A J** **fl 1890-1894**
Aberdeen landscape painter of local scenery; exhibited AAS(3), from 10 Crimon Place.

**SHERRIFFS, John** **fl 1888-1937**
Aberdeen painter in oil and watercolour. Painted Highland landscape with figures and crofting interiors, also occasional portraits. Moved to England shortly after the turn of the century. Elected RSW 1895 but removed from the list 1909. Exhibited RSA(3) & AAS(16) when still at 14 Union Row, Aberdeen.

**SHERRIFFS, Robert Stewart** **1906-1960**
Born Edinburgh. Heraldic artist, illustrator, cartoonist, author, cricketer. Educated Arbroath HS, trained Edinburgh College of Art, with particular interest in heraldry. Provided weekly illustrations for the *Radio Times.* Following service with the Tank Regiment in WW2 appointed film caricaturist to *Punch,* a position retained until his death. Illustrated Marlowe: *Tamberlaine the Great* (1930); Arkell: *Playing the Game* (1935); *The Rubaiyat of Omar Khayyam* (1947); Dickens: *Captain Boldheart* (1948); *Mrs Orange* (1948). Wrote and illustrated *Salute If You Must* (Jenkins 1945). Retrospective exhibitions at the National Film Theatre 1975, National Theatre 1982.
**Bibl:** Driver; Feaver; Horne 390; Peppin; Price.

**SHEWAN, Jennifer A** **fl 1969-1984**
St Andrews painter of continental and Scottish landscape, especially Sutherland. Exhibited RSA(5).

**SHIACH, James Alex** **fl 1898**
Minor Edinburgh watercolourist of 7 Duddingston Crescent, Portobello; exhibited RSW(1).

**SHIACH, John S** **fl 1935-1963**
Aberdeen landscape painter; also occasional informal portraits, genre and flower studies. Moved to Edinburgh and later to Roxburghshire.

Exhibited RSA(30), GI(16) 1944-1960 & AAS(6) including 'On the Gairn' and 'Dee at Invercauld', after 1952 from 6 Crofts Rd, Kelso.

**SHIELD, Miss Jane Hunter RSW(res)** **fl 1870-1895**
Edinburgh watercolour painter and pen and ink artist of portraits, flowers and birds. Established a reputation for her studies of birds and flowers but ceased to work after 1895. Elected RSW 1885 but resigned 1903. Exhibited RSA(9) & RSW(4).
**Bibl:** Halsby 283.

**SHIELDS, D Gordon** **1888-1943**
Edinburgh painter of portraits, flowers, landscape and interiors; also etcher. Moved to Perth during WWI before returning to Edinburgh immediately after the war. Son of Harry S(qv). Exhibited RA(1), RSA(50), GI(23), AAS(2) & L(1), from 72 Polwarth Terrace. Represented in SNPG, Glasgow AG, Edinburgh City collection, Brodie Castle (NTS), Hill of Tarvit (NTS).

**SHIELDS, Henry (Harry) Gordon RBA** **1859-1935**
Born Cromwell Park, Nr Perth, 18 May; died St Andrews 23 Dec. Amateur painter in oil and watercolour of landscapes, yachting scenes and flower pieces. Educated Dollar and St Andrews. Father of Gordon S(qv). Went to London 1879 studying for a time at the Slade although he retained business interests in Perth as chairman of John Shields & Co, manufacturers of table linen, also of Shields Motor Company. A series of *Famous Clyde Yachts* were published as thirty-one lithographs by J Meikle 1888. Returned to Scotland 1894 finally settling in St Andrews. Regarded painting as only a hobby but achieved widespread recognition. Exhibited RA(8), RSA(13), RBA(62), ROI(10) & GI(25).
**Bibl:** Wingfield.

**SHIELDS, Thomas W** **1850-1920**
Born St. Johns, New Brunswick; died USA. Scottish parentage. Painter of figurative subjects. Lived at 45 Avenue Villiers, Paris 1880 while training under Carolus Duran and Gerome. Eventually migrated to USA, studying in New York under Wilmarth. Exhibited 'Portrait of a cavalier' at the RA 1880. Represented in Brooklyn Museum (USA).

**SHIELS, Peter** **fl 1878-1883**
Minor Edinburgh painter in oil of rustic scenes, townscapes and figure subjects. Exhibited RSA(5) from 20 Tobago Street.

**SHIELLS, Robert Thornton** **1833-1902**
Edinburgh architect and painter in watercolour, especially churches. Probably brother of William Thornton S(qv). Close friend of the young Russell Flint(qv) who encouraged him to move to London. Designed Tron Free Church (1876-7) in Chambers St. Partnered with James M Thomson(qv) until moving to England from 1898, working as an illustrator and watercolourist. Exhibited RSA(13).
**Bibl:** Gifford 223,226,267,504,598,733; Halsby 235,283.

**SHIELLS, William Thornton** **fl 1898-1910**
Landscape painter in watercolour. Probably brother of Robert Thornton S(qv). Exhibited RA(8), RSA(1), RSW(4), RI(3), L(18) & GI(1).

**SHIELS, Nicholas** **fl 1884-1889**
Edinburgh watercolour painter of landscapes and figure subjects. Exhibited 'An Oak Tree on the Banks of the Tummel' at the RSA 1884 and two in 1887 including a study of Buffalo Bill, followed by 3 further works 1889, from Rye, Sussex.

**SHIELS, William RSA** **1785-1857**
Born Berwickshire; died Edinburgh, 27 Aug. Painter in oil of rural genre, animals and mythological subjects; occasional watercolours. Also teacher, William Yellowlees(qv) being his best-known pupil. Divided his interests between painting domestic animals and genre after Wilkie. Very little known of his life. Best remembered for his series of pictures of different breeds of horses for the Agricultural Museum, University of Edinburgh, later used to illustrate Lowe's *The Breeds of the Domestic Animals of the British Islands.* In 1808 and 1830 was in London, exhibiting RA(8), the first, 'Ulysses and Laertes' 1808, being one of the few examples of his mythological work. 'Interior of a Scottish Fisherman's Cottage' (1851) is a fine example of Scottish domestic genre showing what a greatly underestimated artist he remains. His animals are especially well painted, often in Highland surroundings. Founder academician, RSA 1826. Exhibited RSA(113) 1808-1856.
**Bibl:** Bryan; Brydall 243; Caw 198; McKay 355; Macmillan [SA] 181; Redgrave; Cat of Engraved British Art, BM 3 (1912) 105.

**SHILLABEER, Miss Mary** **fl 1915-1961**
Edinburgh painter of flowers and domestic genre. Exhibited RSA 1915-16 and again 1959-61, at first from Queen St and latterly Windmill St.

**SHILLINGHAM, J E** **fl 1830**
Edinburgh bird painter; exhibited 'Specimens of birds in Poonah' at the RSA, from Nicholson St.

**SHIRLAW, Walter** **1838-1910**
Born Paisley, Aug 6; died Malta, 26 Dec. (According to Benezit he died in Madrid). Genre and landscape painter, also illustrator. Designed letters for books. Widely travelled, studied at Munich Academy and with Raab, Wagner, Ramberg and Lindenschmidt. Awarded medals in Munich and in Philadelphia 1876; received hon. mention at Paris Exposition Universelle, gold medal in Buffalo (USA) 1901 and St. Louis (USA) 1904. First President of the Society of American Artists. Exhibited RA(3) between 1881 and 1891, latterly from 3 New Burlington St and after settling in USA showed regularly in Chicago and New York.
**Bibl:** Benezit; Houfe.

**SHIRRAS, Miss Margaret G** **19th Cent**
Aberdeen flower painter; exhibited AAS(2), from 19 Beaconsfield Place.

**SHIRREFF (or SHERIFF), Charles** **c1750-c1830**
Born Edinburgh; died Bath. Painter in oils and crayon; portraits, portrait miniatures and historical subjects. Deaf and dumb from the age of four. First practised in Edinburgh but was in London in 1768 and entered the RA Schools the following year. Won a silver medal 1772. Worked in Bath 1791-6 before proceeding to India, staying first in Madras and then Calcutta c1799-1809. Returning to England he retired to Bath, occasionally working in Brighton, Cambridge and Deptford, sometimes in collaboration with the English miniaturist E Miles. Many sitters were from the stage, including Mrs Siddons. According to Foskett 'characteristics of his work are the use of a criss-cross hatching to model the face and shape the background. His portraits were precise but not flattering, with the eyebrows often thickly delineated and the contours of the face clearly defined'. Sometimes likened to Cosway, occasionally signed his work 'C Sherriff pinxt' with date. Exhibited RA(77) 1771-1831 & Free Society of Artists 1770-73. Represented in V & A, BM has several engravings after his portraits, Brodie Castle (NTS).
**Bibl:** Bryan; Caw 45; Foskett; Long; Waterhouse.

**SHIR(R)EFF(S), John** **1853-d1933**
Born Aberdeen, painter in oil and watercolour of portraits and domestic genre, also interiors. Painted Highland cottages and landscapes, generally with figures; also portrait oils. Related to Charles S(qv), both lived for a spell at 7 South St, Greenwich. Elected RSW 1895 and although written off in 1909 continued to occasionally exhibit there into the early 1930s. Exhibited RA(4), RSA(18), RSW(5), RI(5), RHA(1), RBA(11) & L(2).
**Bibl:** Halsby 283.

**SHIRREFFS, Grace** **fl 1964-1965**
Aberdeen painter of portraits, figure studies (especially fishwives) and local landscape. Married William S(qv). Exhibited AAS(4), from 487 Great Western Rd.

**SHIRREFFS, William** **fl 1883-1900**
Glasgow sculptor of portrait busts and figurative studies. Worked mostly in bronze and marble. Exhibited RSA(2), GI(21) & AAS(10) including a bust of the artist 'David Gauld' (RSA, 1896), from 207 West Campbell St.

**SHIRREFFS, William** **fl 1964-1967**
Aberdeen ceramic designer. Married Grace S(qv). Exhibited AAS (2), from 487 Gt Western Rd.

**SHIVAS, Edwin** **fl 1896-1900**
Aberdeenshire landscape painter; exhibited local scenery AAS(4), from 46 Queen St, Peterhead.

**SHIVAS, James** **fl 1874-1886**
Peterhead painter in oil of coastal scenes and interiors; exhibited RSA(3) from 46 Queen Street.

**SHORE, Bertha Emma Louisa** **fl 1891-1914**
Painter in oil of landscape. Exhibited GI(3), L(4), LS(20) & RBA(1) from Cambuskenneth, Stirling.

**SHORE, Captain the Hon Frederick William John** **fl 1880-1888**
Edinburgh painter in oil and watercolour of landscape and wild-flowers. Brother of Henry Noel S(qv). Lived in Gibraltar 1882 and then Clonmell, Ireland. Many of his subjects were scenes in Morocco and Gibraltar. Exhibited RA(2) 1883 and 1888, RSA(9), GI(1), RBA(1) & ROI(4).

**SHORE, Hon Henry Noel (later Lord Teignmouth)** **1847-1925**
Painter in watercolour of shipping, often oriental. Brother of F W J S(qv). Lived in Edinburgh before moving to London, then north to Greenock before settling in Thomastown, Co Kilkenny, c1921. Worked for some years as a coastguard. Exhibited RSA(5), RHA(6), RI(2) & GI(4).

**SHORT, Ian James Bruce RSW** **1926-1996**
Born Watford, 6 Feb. Painter in gouache and watercolour; landscape, still life and semi-abstracts. Trained Edinburgh College of Art 1949-53. Awarded an Andrew Grant post diploma scholarship 1953-4 enabling him to study in France and Spain. Then spent a year at Moray House College of Education and after a spell of teaching became Principal Lecturer in Art, Aberdeen College of Education. Mainly influenced by William Gillies(qv), Leonard Rosoman and Robin Philipson(qv). Worked exclusively in gouache from 1967, specialising in north-east coast fishing villages. His paintings showed a tendency towards greater abstraction over the years. Lived in Edinburgh. Elected RSW 1972. Exhibited regularly RSA (from 1961), RSW, GI & AAS 1969-82.

**SHORTREED, Anne** **fl 1969-1970**
Livingston painter of portraits and landscape; exhibited RSA(3).

**SHULVER, William F** **fl 1921**
Aberdeen amateur landscape painter; exhibited 'On the Dee' at the AAS, from 11 Mid Stocket Rd.

**SHUTER, Edmund F** **fl 1934-1967**
Edinburgh pastellist and engraver of flowers, topographical subjects; specialises in woodcuts. Exhibited RSA(4). Represented City of Edinburgh collection by a pastel 'Calton Jail by night' 1934.

**SIBBALD, William** **?-1809**
Architect. With Robert Reid(qv) was responsible, in his capacity as Superintendent of Works, for designing Edinburgh's northern New Town (1801-2). Other work in Edinburgh included the Gothic Lady Yester's Church (1803-5) and Portobello Old and Windsor Place Parish Church (1809). Won competition to design St Andrew and St George Church, George St (1785) but the contract was awarded Andrew Frazer(qv). Lived at 13 Charlotte Sq.
**Bibl:** Gifford 163,229,296,335,339-40,343-5,352-3,460,629, 650.

**SIBLEY, David C G** **fl 1938-1942**
Amateur landscape artist in sepia, line and wash. Perhaps an art teacher as when living at Wilton Place, Sheffield he was attached to King Edward VIII School. Exhibited RSA(6), GI(2) & RBA(2), until 1942 from Ballater, Aberdeenshire.

**SIDAWAY, David** **fl 1944-1954**
Glasgow painter of figure subjects and landscape, sometimes in watercolour. Exhibited GI(6).

**SIDEBOTTOM, N** **fl 1914**
Minor Edinburgh painter. Exhibited RA(1) & RSA(1) from 143 Warrender Park Road.

**SIDEY, David H** **fl 1956-1957**
Edinburgh painter of flowers and still life. Exhibited 'Autumn still life' at the RSA; also GI(2), from Forth St.

**SILCOCK, William** **fl 1932-1934**
Little known painter of 41 Carron Road, Falkirk; exhibited RSA(2).

**SILK, C** **fl 1872**
Glasgow-based painter. Probably brother of Thomas S(qv). Exhibited 'Campsie Hills, with cattle' at the GI.

**SILK, Thomas** **fl 1863-1869**
Glasgow-based landscape and cattle painter. Related to C Silk(qv). Exhibited GI(5).

**SILLARS, Caroline** **fl 1955-**
Painter in oil and watercolour; portraits, still life, interiors, flowers and landscape, sometimes with a musical theme. Paints in a pleasing traditional style with heavy use of ochre. Trained in Paris and later at Byam Shaw School of Art, London. Since 1955 has lived in the West of Scotland exhibiting regularly RA & RSA.

**SILLARS, D** **fl 1886-1900**
Glasgow landscape and figure painter. Exhibited GI(6), some in watercolour, latterly from Wellington St.

**SILLARS, William** **fl 1871-1875**
Glasgow oil painter of shore scenes; exhibited RSA(2) & GI(1).

**SILLARS, William Kennedy** **fl 1929-1935**
Little known Kilmarnock painter of country scenes and flowers; exhibited GI(4) & AAS(2), from 63 Picken St. Moved c1934 to Lytham St Annes, Lancs.

**SILLERS, David** **fl 1886-1900**
Minor Glasgow painter of figurative subjects and flowers. Exhibited RSA(2) & GI(6) including 'Returning to his regiment' RSA 1887.

**SILVER, Margaret E** **fl 1975**
Aberdeenshire painter of country subjects; exhibited AAS(1), from 8 Arnhall Crescent, Westhill, Skene.

**SILVESTRE, Gilles** **1590-c1631**
Born and died Nancy, France. Descended from a Scottish family called originally Sylvester who settled in Lorraine at the beginning of the 16th century, he was the first of a long line of distinguished artists whose last artistic representative was Baron Augustin de Silvestre (1762-1851). After his marriage to the daughter of Claude Henriet, painter to the Duke of Lorraine, devoted himself to painting. Descendants, well recorded in the literature, were all born and active in France.
**Bibl:** Benezit.

**SIM, Miss Agnes Mary RSW (Mrs Smythe)** **1887-1978**
Painter in watercolour. Specialised in portraits, figure subjects and landscape. After a short spell in Paris lived at Lochside, Montrose. Sister of Nan S(qv). Elected RSW 1927. Exhibited RSA(26), RSW (46), AAS (1931-7) & GI(5). Represented in City of Edinburgh collection.
**Bibl:** Halsby 283.

**SIM, George** **fl 1886-1893**
Aberdeen painter of topography, continental landscape & local scenery. Exhibited AAS(5), from 16 Constitution St.

**SIM, James** **fl 1870-1895**
Painter of genre and landscape in oil, subjects often continental, especially France & Italy. Lived for a time in Chelsea before settling in Edinburgh c1895. Exhibited RA(12) 1870-1893; also RSA(1) & RI(2).

**SIM, Mary E** **fl 1906-1910**
Glasgow topographical painter; usually worked in monochrome. Exhibited GI(2).

**SIM, Nan** **fl 1926**
Amateur Montrose watercolourist. Sister of Agnes S S(qv). Exhibited RSW(1) from Lochside.

**SIM, Miss Sheila** **fl 1975**
Glasgow engraver. Exhibited GI(2).

**SIM, Stewart** **fl 1929**
Amateur landscape painter of 16 Melville Terrace, Edinburgh; exhibited RSA(3).

**SIME, David** **fl 1846**
Amateur Edinburgh artist; exhibited a figurative subject RSA.

**SIMMERS, Miss Connie** **fl 1982-**
Stirlingshire painter of flowers, still life, topography and figure studies. Began exhibiting GI 1982 from Killearn.

**SIMON, Edith (Mrs E C R Reeve)** **c1912-2002**
Painter and sculptor; writer and historian. Trained Slade, enrolling when she was 15, and Central School of Arts & Crafts, but abandoned her studies in order to write and become a founder member of the AIA. Published 17 fiction and non-fiction works, the first when she was 23. In 1972 she returned to full-time painting and sculpting. One innovative technique she employs ('scalpel painting') is to make paper cutouts as bas reliefs; shapes are cut out of layers of variously coloured paper with a scalpel producing delicate designs reminiscent of painting. Specialised latterly in portraits, often delineated in appropriate settings. Held regular one-man exhibitions. A major figure in the cultural life of Edinburgh, as much by precept as by social contact. Exhibited RSA from Edinburgh.

**SIMON, Frank W** **1862-1933**
Architect and landscape painter in oil. Trained with J. Cotton in Birmingham, and at Atelier Pascale, École des Beaux Arts, Paris 1883-1886. Professor of Applied Arts, 1892. Entered into practice 1894 entering into partnership with C.E. Tweedie 1899 and in 1899 with Rowand Anderson(qv) and Hunter Crawford(qv). For his father Professor Simon he designed Outwood (no. 8) Blackford Ave (1889) 'beautifully detailed in pale orange sandstone with spreading piend roofs'. Emigrated to Canada 1902. His firm Simon and Tweedie exhibited RA(1). Exhibited a landscape RSA 1886 and 16 other works; also GI(3), 2 in collaboration with W Allan Carter.
**Bibl:** Gifford 264,380,502,599; Peter Savage, Lorimer and the Edinburgh Craft Designers, Edinburgh 1980, 6,163,168.

**SIMONS, Gertrude C** **fl 1919-1968**
Painter of interiors, still life and flower studies; mostly in watercolours. Exhibited RSW(3), RSA(1), GI(9), AAS(4) & L(2), from 13 South Exchange Place, Glasgow, then Biggar and finally Bathgate, Midlothian.

**SIMPSON, Miss Alice M** **fl 1887**
Aberdeen amateur flower painter; exhibited AAS(2), from 1 Albyn Terrace.

**SIMPSON, Archibald** **fl c1820-1835**
Minor Aberdeen artist who painted local scenes in oil. His principal claim to attention was that in 1827, with his friend James Giles(qv), founded the first Aberdeen Art Society.

**SIMPSON, Archibald** **1790-1847**
Born at 15 Guestrow, Aberdeen, May 4. Aberdeen architect. Suffered all his life with a handicapped left arm. Pupil of Robert Lugar in London 1810-1812. Then visited Italy before returning to Aberdeen 1813. By now his lifelong rival John Smith(qv) had already been working in Aberdeen for eight years. Most of his buildings were of a classical style. Particularly good in adapting the Grecian vocabulary to the requirements of Aberdeen granite, hitherto regarded as an inferior building material. His first commissions, in 1813, were both for the Forbes family of Donside: Castle Forbes near Keig, and a modern neo-classical wing Druminnor (later demolished). His first public commission in Aberdeen was for St Andrew's Chapel, now St Andrew's Episcopal Cathedral in King St. The best of his work is at Park House, Aberdeenshire(1822), Boath House, Nairn(c1830) and Stracathro, Angus (1827-30) 'whose external grandeur (was) complemented by sumptuous interior decoration in paint, scagliola and marble' [Dunbar]. Another interesting building is the broad-eved Italianate house at Thainston, Aberdeenshire (c1820-30). Responsible for the original Letham Grange, Angus (c1825-30) and Inverbrothock church, Arbroath (1828). Involved in ecclesiastical architecture, the best example being St Giles's, Elgin (1828) while in his native city was largely responsible for the design of Bon Accord Crescent, Marine Terrace, the Old Infirmary (1833-40), the New Market (1840-2, now demolished) and the Music Hall (1820). An able violinist, with his flautist brother Alexander, refounded Aberdeen Musical Society and later, with his friend James Giles(qv) was a founder member of the AAS. Simpson's portrait, by James Giles, hangs in Marischal College, Aberdeen. The local historian G M Fraser considered that Simpson, 'in the course of his 35 years professional life did much - more we might say than any other single person - to give character and beauty to the City of Aberdeen'.
**Bibl:** Dunbar 118-9,124,152; Irwin 410; Bruce Walker & W S Gauldie, Architects and Architecture on Tayside, Dundee 1984, 77(illus),75-8,89. Archibald Simpson, Architect of Aberdeen, Aberdeen Civic Society, 1978.

**SIMPSON, Betty** **1903-1960**
Glasgow dancer, artist and teacher. Founder member of the New Art Club in Glasgow and of the Margaret Morris Movement School. Associated with J.D. Ferguson(qv) and his wife Margaret Morris(qv).

**SIMPSON, Miss Christine** **fl 1974**
Falkirk weaver. Exhibited GI(1).

**SIMPSON, Mrs Edith** **fl 1935-1938**
Edinburgh flower painter; exhibited RSA(3), from 22 Strathearn Rd.

**SIMPSON, Miss Elizabeth** **fl 1969**
Renfrewshire still life painter. Exhibited GI(1) from Barrhead.

**SIMPSON, Ethel H** **fl 1862-1890**
Amateur Edinburgh painter; exhibited landscapes and figure subjects RSA(10), latterly from Eastwood, Ferry Rd.

**SIMPSON, Eva G** **fl 1900**
Aberdeenshire landscape painter. Lived with her sister Gerby(qv) at Whinhurst, Fordoun from where she exhibited 'Summer' at the AAS.

**SIMPSON, George** **fl 1825**
Obscure painter and teacher. Master at Edinburgh Drawing School(qv) established in Hill St 1825.

**SIMPSON, George** **c1861-1944**
Architect. Son of James S(qv). Designed Leith Victoria Baths (1896-9); finished his father's Northern General Hospital (1893).
**Bibl:** Gifford 464-5,602-3,610.

**SIMPSON, George** **fl 1878**
Edinburgh watercolourist; exhibited a study of buildings at the RSA.

**SIMPSON, Miss Gerby B** **fl 1900-1902**
Aberdeenshire landscape and figure painter. Lived with her sister Eva(qv) at Whinhurst, Fordoun. Exhibited AAS(2).

**SIMPSON, H D** **fl 1909**
Minor watercolourist; exhibited RSW(1) from 9 Kemp Street, Hamilton.

**SIMPSON, Miss Helen F** **fl 1957**
Renfrewshire amateur watercolourist. Exhibited GI(2) from Newton Mearns.

**SIMPSON, Henry** **fl 1870-1876**
Edinburgh landscape painter in oil; exhibited RSA(5).

**SIMPSON, Henry Jackson MC** **1893-1963**
Born Aberdeen, 12 March. Painter, engraver, teacher, printseller, restorer, framer. Nephew of Alec Fraser(qv). Served in Tyneside Scottish Regiment during WW1; awarded the MC for bravery. After the war, studied at Gray's School of Art. His delicate brushwork first

found employment at Foresterhill, painting studies of diseased eyes, some of which were published in medical journals. Especially fond of outdoor pursuits, in 1949 published 13 plates for *The Young Angler* (John Steele Allan). Painted seascapes, still-life, animal studies, topographical views and miniatures. His delicately painted watercolours of local scenes and his sensitive etchings have always been popular. Member of the Northern Arts Club. Studio for many years at 4 Diamond St, Aberdeen. Represented the main London auction houses in the north-east of Scotland. Exhibited RSA(3), RGI(1) and irregularly at AAS 1908-37. A centenary exhibition at Aberdeen AG 1993. Lived at Laurelwood Ave during his first marriage and Craigton Rd during his second marriage.

**SIMPSON, Hugh D** **fl 1898**
Kilmarnock painter. Exhibited 'Interior, King's Coll. chapel, Cambridge' at the GI.

**SIMPSON, James** **1831-1934**
Architect. Father of George S(qv). Architect to Leith School Board. Designed the grandiose No 25 Learmonth Terrace (1891-3) for Arthur Sanderson with an interior 'the most sumptuous in the city'. Responsible for the Scandinavian Lutheran Church (1868-9) and many other buildings in Leith.
**Bibl:** Gifford 75,399,457,463-71,473-4,476,478,481,602,645, 655.

**SIMPSON, James B** **fl 1950-1963**
Caithness painter of local scenery, also topographical subjects and Spanish views. Related to John W S(qv); exhibited RSA(14) & AAS from Olrick, Kenneth St, Wick.

**SIMPSON, James C M** **fl 1953**
Dumbartonshire amateur artist. Exhibited a chalk drawing at the GI from Dalmuir.

**SIMPSON, Jessie M** **fl 1946-1969**
Edinburgh sculptress, narrative subjects. Mainly in wood especially lime, cherry and chestnut. Exhib RSA(34) & GI(48) from Nelson St.

**SIMPSON, John Hutchison** **fl 1887-1890**
Edinburgh portrait painter in oil and watercolour. Exhibited RSA 1887, also GI(3). Possibly the J H Simpson who exhibited RA 1877 & GI 1890.

**SIMPSON, John W** **fl 1970**
Caithness painter of local views. Related to J R Simpson(qv). Exhibited AAS(1), from Olrick, Kenneth Rd, Wick.

**SIMPSON, Joseph W RBA** **1879-1939**
Born Carlisle; died 30 Jan. Painter and etcher of portraits and landscapes also caricaturist and illustrator. Received encouragement as a young man from J G Hodgson so that after schooling in Carlisle trained at Glasgow School of Art. Worked as a designer for a Carlisle printer before becoming a full-time artist, settling in Edinburgh where he had a studio in Castle St which became a meeting place for many artists. Peploe(qv), J D Fergusson(qv) and Robert Hope(qv) joined him in forming a sketching club - the **SPO** - named after their favourite food: sausages, potatoes and onions. Went to London where he had a studio next to his friend Frank Brangwyn. Also close friend of Sir D.Y. Cameron(qv). Elected RBA 1909. In 1918 official war artist to the RAF in France. Designed bookplates and covers for several Edinburgh publishers, many of which were exhibited overseas. Published *Twelve Masters of Prose and Verse* (1912), *God Save the King in La Grande Guerre* (1915) and *War Poems From The Times* (1915). Illustrated *Simpson, His Book* (1903), *The Book of Book Plates* (1903), *Ibsen* (1907), *Lions* (1908), *Literary Lions* (1910) and *Edinburgh* (1911). Exhibited in London from 1897, also at the RSA(8), RSW(1), RBA(20), GI(4), L(4), LS(8) & overseas. Principal works include portrait of 'Frank Brangwyn', 'The Bombed House' and 'The Priest'. In later life maintained a studio in Kirkcudbright. A memorial exhibition was held in Carlisle AG 1939. Represented in SNPG (Edward VII).
**Bibl:** Houfe; Scotsman,'Edinburgh Memories', 1 Feb 1939; Studio, 1905-6, 21-25.

**SIMPSON, Lizzie Jane** **fl 1883**
Edinburgh landscape painter of 22 London Street. Exhibited RSA(1).

**SIMPSON, Mary** **fl 1887-1888**
Minor Edinburgh watercolour painter of landscape. Exhibited RSA(2) from 2 Moredun Crescent.

**SIMPSON, Reginald A** **fl 1978-1979**
Aberdeen printmaker; trained Gray's School of Art, Aberdeen. Depicts interiors with parties and active night life. Exhibited AAS (3), from 49 Regent Quay.

**SIMPSON, Robert** **fl 1872-1879**
Dundee oil painter of seascapes; exhibited RSA(2).

**SIMPSON, Thomas** **fl 1768-1787**
Edinburgh engraver. Engraver to the Edinburgh Mint before 1787. Engraved 18 plates, after S. Wale, for W. Wilkie's *Fables,* 1768.
**Bibl:** Bushnell.

**SIMPSON, T** **fl 1963**
Edinburgh sculptor. Exhibited 'Dancing girl in wood' at the GI, from Barnton.

**SIMPSON, W** **fl 1881**
Perthshire artist; exhibited a scene in Normandy at the RSA, from Aberfeldy.

**SIMPSON, W H** **fl 1837**
Edinburgh landscape painter; exhibited 'Road scene on the Water of Leith' at the RSA, from Tobago St.

**SIMPSON, Miss Wilhelmina Euphemia** **fl 1851-1859**
Portrait painter; in 1851 she was living in Edinburgh and in 1859 was in Perth; exhibited RSA(2).

**SIMPSON, William RI FRGS** **1823-1899**
Born Carrick St, Glasgow, 28 Oct; died Willesden, London, 17 Apr. Painter in oil but chiefly watercolour of topographical and architectural subjects, also war artist, illustrator and engraver of current events. Educated Perth and Glasgow. Intended to become an engineer but in 1839 was apprenticed to Macfarlane, a lithographic printer, then to Messrs Allan and Ferguson, a Glasgow firm of lithographers. Enjoyed going into the countryside with Robert Carrick(qv) to paint landscapes in watercolour. One of the first students at the Glasgow School of Design 1845. In 1851 he went to London where he became a close friend of Louis Haghe and was employed by Messrs Day and Sons, the foremost lithographers of their time. On the outbreak of the Crimean war, the London dealer Colnaghi commissioned Simpson to go to the Crimea to make sketches for publication so that he became the first official war artist (Agnew despatched a mobile photographic van under Roger Fenton at about the same time). The result of his expedition was two folios of lithographs containing 81 plates, dedicated to Queen Victoria and published as *The Seat of War in the East* (1855-6). After the war was attached to the Duke of Newcastle's party which explored Circassia 1875-6. Wanted to accompany the Italian Campaign but was discouraged by the Queen and instead travelled 1859-62 in India, Kashmir and Tibet making architectural and archaeological sketches. After problems of publication due to the publisher's financial difficulties, his work finally appeared in a series of 50 plates, with a text by Sir John Kaye, *India Ancient and Modern* (1867). In 1871 he witnessed the Paris Commune. Travelled to India again in 1875 after which he held an exhibition of his watercolours in London, four of them being purchased for the Royal Collection. In 1866 joined the *ILN* on whose behalf he attended the marriage of the Czarevitch Alexander III to Princess Dagmar at St Petersburg. Thereafter followed Lord Napier's Magdala expedition and the Franco-German War of 1870. Attended the opening of the Suez Canal 1869. Visited China for the Emperor's marriage and recorded the Prince of Wales's Indian tour 1875-6. Illustrated Dr Schliemann's excavations of 1877. In 1881 he went north to paint a series of watercolours of Balmoral and the surrounding countryside, staying with the Prince of Wales at Abergeldie. The finished works are dated 1882; these include the interior and exterior of the old Crathie Church, a cricket match between Abergeldie and Balmoral, and a garden cottage at Balmoral. His final overseas journey was with the Afghan Boundary Commission 1884. The last years of his life were spent completing a series of watercolour drawings Glasgow in the Forties, acquired by

Glasgow AG in 1898. Published Brackenbury's *Campaign in the Crimea* (1855). His life was recorded in *Meeting the Sun* (1874). Illustrated *War in the East* (1855-6), *Meeting the Sun, a Journey Round the World* (1873), *Picturesque People and Groups from all Quarters of the Globe* (1876), *Shikar and Tamasha* (1876), *The Buddhist Praying Wheel* (1896), *The Jonah Legend* (1899) and *Glasgow in the Forties* (1899). Contributed to *The Quiver* (1890), *The Picturesque Mediterranean* (1891) and *The English Illustrated Magazine* (1893-6). Hardie notes that Simpson's work, 'like that of Roberts, was spirited and dexterous. Much of what he produced in colour (his output in pencil and wash was prodigious) was in the nature of a tinted sketch, but his more thoughtful work, as in some of the watercolours made in India and Egypt, has considerable merit'. At his best he was imaginative and romantic but inevitably, given the nature of his travelling life, much of his work was commonplace and rather uninspired. Elected ANWS 1874, NWS 1879, helping to gain the Society's Royal Charter 1884. Exhibited RI(36), RSA(6), GI(4), ROI(5) & L(5). Represented in BM, V & A, NGS, Glasgow AG, Kirkcaldy AG, Paisley AG, Greenwich AG, Royal Collection.
**Bibl:** AJ 1866, 258; Bryan; Brydall 465-6; Caw 291-2; Halsby 82-3; Hardie III 96, 186-7; Houfe; Irwin 334-6; Maas 97; W Simpson, Autobiography, 1903.

**SIMPSON, William** **fl 1862-1865**
Glasgow sculptor. Exhibited a medallion of a young lady and an 'Alto-Relievo' at the GI.

**SIMPSON, William** **fl 1866-1887**
Edinburgh painter of landscapes in oil. Lived for a time at Aberlady. Exhibited RSA(12) & GI(1)

**SIMPSON, Will(iam)** **fl 1893-1939**
Aberdeen landscape painter; exhibited AAS from 187 King St.

**SIMSON, Miss** **fl 1855-1857**
Edinburgh portrait painter, generally in chalk. Probably sister of George(qv) and George W Simson(qv). Exhibited RSA from 54 North Frederick St.

**SIMSON, David** **1803-1874**
Born Dundee. Painter painter and sculptor. Brother of William(qv) and George S(qv). Co-founder with his brother of the New Drawing Academy in Edinburgh 1831; also taught at Heriot's Hospital and the Scottish Institution. Lover of rural scenes and pursuits, especially fishing. A much loved man of gentle demeanour and great sensitivity. Possibly the **David SIMSON** who painted coastal scenes and landscape and who Brydall mentions as 'having a good position as a Scottish landscape painter', and who may have exhibited at the RSA during the first half of the 19th century. Exhibited RSA(c43). Represented in SNPG ('William Simson').
**Bibl:** Scotsman, 30 Mar 1874(obit).

**SIMSON, E R** **fl 1886**
Amateur Jedburgh landscape painter in oil; exhibited RSA(1) from Bedrule.

**SIMSON, Miss F K** **fl 1886-1888**
Edinburgh painter of landscapes and architectural subjects in oil; exhibited RSA(3) from 25 Nile Grove, Morningside.

**SIMSON, George RSA** **1791-1862**
Born Dundee; died Edinburgh 11 Mar. Painter in oil, also chalk, of portraits and landscapes. Brother of William(qv) and David S(qv). His work echoes the style and subjects of his more able brother William. Started life as a printer and did not direct his attention to art until he was 29. His first works contributed to the modern exhibition held at the Royal Institution, Edinburgh and these attracted considerable notice. Continued to be a regular contributor to all the exhibitions of modern art works until he died. Foundation associate of the RSA although was one of nine artists who withdrew after the first meeting. Fancy figures and portraits first engaged his attention but he later practised chiefly landscape painting. Taught drawing and painting and was held in high regard as a teacher. His diploma work, 'Peasant Girl', shown in 1831 was renamed 'Girl at a Well'. Enjoyed recording the dramatic effects of water, painting several scenes on Arran, stormy sunsets, dramatic moonlight effects and river scenes. Elected RSA 1829. Exhibited RSA(91), latterly from 54 North Frederick St.
**Bibl:** Bryan; Caw 120; McKay 259.

**SIMSON, George W** **fl 1851-1868**
Edinburgh painter in oil of buildings and landscape; exhibited RSA (23) from Broomieknowe, Lasswade. Possibly the same **George SIMSON** as in addition to having the same first name they overlapped in time and had the same address; on the other hand the titles of their respective exhibits seem quite distinctive.

**SIMSON, John Aberdein** **fl 1905**
Amateur Edinburgh painter of 9 Eton Terrace, exhibited RSA(1).

**SIMSON, R** **fl 1848**
Exhibited once - 'Dr Chalmers preaching in the West Port' - at the RSA (no address).

**SIMSON, William RSA** **1800-1847**
Born Dundee; died Chelsea, 29 Aug. Painter in oil of landscapes, portraits, sporting subjects and historical genre. Son of a Dundee merchant, his brothers and one sister were also artists(qv). Trained Trustees Academy under Andrew Wilson(qv). Began by painting coastal scenes and landscapes near Edinburgh but in 1827 visited the Low Countries. On his return his work gained the admiration of Sir William Allan(qv), R S Lauder(qv) and Sir Frances Grant(qv), all of whom purchased landscapes. There followed a trip to Italy 1834-35. Returned to the continent 1838 before settling in London at the end of the year. After this time his attention was directed mainly to historical genre from English and Italian history, interspersed with the occasional portrait and sporting subject. The RSA catalogue of 1863 recorded 'it is much to be regretted that he abandoned landscape painting, as he possessed so true a feeling for nature, and such admirable execution, that had he devoted himself to it exclusively, he would have attained still higher eminence'. Among his principal historical works are 'The Murder of the Princes in the Tower' and 'Cimabue and Giotto', both 1838, 'Salvator Rosa's first Cartoon on the Wall of Certosa' and 'The Temptation of St Anthony' 1844. An atmospheric depiction of 'The Twelfth of August at Badenoch' 1829 is in NGS. Shortly after his death a series of lithographs from his landscape drawings was made and published by his brothers. Caw refers to 'two lovely sketches of children and two clever drawings of dogs'; the same author considered 'Solway Moss' (NGS) 'by far his finest work...the quiet beauty rather than the lustiness or power of nature...for him the desolation and vastness made little appeal...but Solway Moss is pregnant with meaning and beauty. The benediction it breathes is as significant as the turmoil of winds and passing seas'. This work was regarded by Armstrong as 'possibly the best example of the old school of Scottish landscape in the entire gallery'. As his work developed it became richer in tone and colour and more detailed in composition. Rather an isolated figure among his contemporaries although sometimes compared to Thomson of Duddingston. A wash drawing of Sir Walter Scott is in the SNPG. Exhibited 25 works at the RA between 1830 and 1847 only two of them straight portraits, 'John Burnet FRS' 1841 and the 'Nieces of the late Sir David Wilkie' 1846. Perhaps his best known exhibit is 'Prince Charles Edward Stewart at the Battle of Preston' (1745) 1834. Illustrated *Sinbad the Sailor.* Exhibited RSA(139) 1821-1887 including 19 exhibited posthumously. 'The Arrest of William Tell in Altdorf' 1846 is now in the V & A as part of the John Sheepshanks Gift of 1857, as is his sketch of 'Gil Blas' 1847. Represented in NGS(6+), V & A, Birkenhead AG.
**Bibl:** Armstrong 62; Art Union, 1847, 353 (obit); Bryan; Brydall 465-6; Caw 156-7; DNB; Halsby 46,63,88,283; Irwin 227; Macmillan [SA] 183-4,202,229; Robin Nicholson, 'William Simson RSA 1800-1847', Fine Art Society, London (Ex Cat 1989); Studio Special Number: RSA, 1907, vii, xiv; Wingfield.

**SINCLAIR, Alexander Garden ARSA** **1859-1930**
Edinburgh painter in oil and watercolour of landscape, genre and portraits. Primarily an oil painter. Member, Society of Eight(qv). His wife was also an artist(qv). Produced some good watercolours in the Dutch manner, including landscapes in Northern France and Scotland especially Iona. His loose handling of paint and expansive skies gave vitality to his work. Helped to illustrate *Evergreen* in his earlier years. Elected ARSA 1918. Exhibited RSA(74), RSW(2), GI(5), AAS (1887-1923) & L(2). Represented in NGS, Kirkcaldy AG.
**Bibl:** Caw 389; Halsby 283.

**SINCLAIR, Alastair Brown** fl 1966
Kircudbright sculptor. Exhibited 'Adam and Eve' in wood at the GI, from Gatehouse of Fleet.

**SINCLAIR, Mrs Alexander Gordon** **fl 1919-1920**
Edinburgh landscape painter. Married Alexander Gordon S(qv). Exhibited RSA(3).

**SINCLAIR, Andrew** **fl 1937**
Painter. Exhibited RSA(1).

**SINCLAIR, Archibald** **fl 1830**
Painter. Exhibited RSA(1) - 'Sketch in the pleasure grounds of the Rt. Hon. the Earl of Wemyss - Gosford'. No address shown.

**SINCLAIR, Callum** **fl 1989-**
Glasgow-based sculptor; exhibited RSA(1) & GI in wood and sand.

**SINCLAIR, David RSW** **1937-**
Painter & engraver. Studied Glasgow School of Art under William(qv) & Mary Armour(qv) and David Donaldson(qv). Exhibits delicately delineated small etchings, printed on his own press. Won Murray Thomson Award (RSA) 1995, Morrison Portrait Award (RSA) 1997. Elected RSW 2001. Exhibits RSA, RSW, RGI, SSA, from Rosebank, Berwick-on-Tweed.

**SINCLAIR, David M** **fl 1886**
Castle Douglas painter of landscape and trees; exhibited RSA(2).

**SINCLAIR, Miss F E** **fl 1940**
Amateur Midlothian watercolourist. Exhibited RSW(1) & GI(1) from Lasswade.

**SINCLAIR, George** **fl 1899-1925**
Glasgow architect and watercolourist. Moved to Edinburgh. Exhibited GI(1). Represented by a watercolour of George Square in the City of Edinburgh collection.

**SINCLAIR, James** **fl 1830-1831**
Berwick-on-Tweed portrait and genre painter; exhibited RSA(2). Represented in SNPG.

**SINCLAIR, James R** **fl 1896**
Amateur Edinburgh landscape painter in oil; exhibited RSA(1) from 29 Queen Street.

**SINCLAIR, Miss Jean** **fl 1944**
Aberdeen painter; exhibited 'Bombed church' RSA & 'Nannie' at the GI.

**SINCLAIR, Mrs L H** **fl 1920**
Edinburgh painter. Exhibited RSA(1) from 18 Ann Street.

**SINCLAIR, Mary** **fl 1886-1890**
Edinburgh painter of landscape and figure subjects in oil and watercolour; her landscapes were directly in the Nasmyth tradition. Exhibited RSA(1) from 3 Gloucester Place.

**SINCLAIR, R W** **fl 1867**
Edinburgh oil painter. Exhibited RSA(2).

**SINCLAIR, Mrs Sophia M** **fl 1869-1889**
Edinburgh painter in oil and watercolour of rustic buildings, wild birds, landscape, portraits and still life. Wife of William Sinclair(qv). Exhibited RSA(31) from 16 Hart Street.

**SINCLAIR, William** **fl 1861-1878**
Edinburgh painter in oil and watercolour also black and white, of townscapes, interiors and still life. Married Sophia S(qv). Exhibited RSA(50) & GI(1).

**SINCLAIR, William** **fl 1875-1878**
Glasgow landscape and figure painter in oil and watercolour. Not to be confused with William Sinclair of Edinburgh who was painting at the same time. Exhibited 'On the east coast, nr Dunbar' at the RSA (1); also GI(2).

**SINCLAIR, William** **fl 1961-1967**
Glasgow painter of landscape, genre and portraits. Most of his views are local scenes. Exhibited RSA(8) & GI(15), latterly from Port Glasgow.

**SIVELL, Robert RSA** **1888-1958**
Born Paisley 16 Oct; died Kircudbright, 17 Apr. Painter in oil of portraits, figure subjects and occasional large murals; also teacher. Trained Glasgow School of Art 1908-10 where he gained the Guthrie and Torrance Awards, also Paris and Florence. He had trained for a time as an engineer and spent two years in North America but returned to Glasgow in 1916 after serving in the Merchant Navy on the South American route during WW1. Close friend of Archibald McGlashan(qv) and James Cowie(qv). President of the short-lived Society of Painters and Sculptors. Married and settled in Kirkcudbright 1923. There is a flavour of Boticelli about his paintings. His love of the Renaissance grew into a passion and stayed with him undimmed all his days. In 1921, after a visit to Italy, 'he returned refreshed, invigorated and convinced that his own painting was in the true spirit of this great tradition'. Executed murals in the student's Union, Aberdeen, but now probably best known as a teacher who, while inspiring some by his example inhibited others by his inflexibility. Numbered many famous names among his pupils. Distinguished by keen draughtsmanship and solidity of form, a deep and mellow colour used with careful discrimination. During WW2 worked for the Imperial War Museum. Principal of Drawing and Painting at Gray's School of Art, Aberdeen 1936-54. Elected ARSA 1936, RSA 1943. Exhibited RA(1), RSA(91), GI(50+), AAS(1931-1937) & L(7). Represented Glasgow AG(2), Edinburgh City collection.
**Bibl:** Arts Council, 'Robert Sivell', (Ex Cat 1960); Hardie 142,147; Macmillan [SA] 338-9,348,360.

**SKEA, Ralph** **fl 1976-1982**
Broughty Ferry painter; exhibited RSA(4).

**SKELTON, Miss E M** **fl 1907**
Painter. Exhibited RSA(1) from The Hermitage of Braid, Edinburgh.

**SKENE, James of Rubislaw** **1775-1864**
Born Aberdeen, 7 Mar; died Oxford, 27 Nov. Amateur artist and etcher. Youngest child and second son of the laird of Rubislaw. His father died when he was only a year old and in 1783 the family moved to Edinburgh. There Skene made his first sketches with whiting on a cellar door, followed by drawings of nearby houses on the West Bow. This might have been the beginning of a successful career as a professional artist, but in 1791, while still a pupil at the High School, his elder brother died and James succeeded to the family estate in Aberdeen. Proceeded to Edinburgh University to read law, which he rarely practised although called to the Scottish Bar on his return from an educational trip to Germany in 1796. His first journey abroad whetted his appetite for travel and stimulated an interest in the language and literature of Germany, a fact which greatly endeared him to Sir Walter Scott who held a commission in the Edinburgh Light Horse when Skene was appointed cornet in 1797. During military camps at Musselburgh they used to ride and talk together thus beginning a life-long friendship. In a letter to Lady Dalkeith in 1806 Scott described the artist as "an amiable and accomplished young man, and for a gentleman the best draughtsman I ever saw". In 1802 Skene set out on an extended tour of the continent, exploring France, Belgium, Germany, Switzerland and Italy, making sketches and writing in script diaries wherever he went. After his marriage to Jane Forbes in 1806, he and his wife settled at Invery nr Banchory for the next ten years, except for brief visits to Edinburgh and Ashesteil. In 1816 they returned with their young family to live in the New Town in Edinburgh and became quickly involved in the activities of many literary, scientific and artistic societies. He was made Secretary of the Royal Society, and member of the Society of Antiquaries to whose publication he contributed. At about this time Scott conceived the idea of a descriptive volume on Edinburgh with illustrations by Skene. Many of the drawings made after 1816 were intended for the work but 'Reekieana' (as it was to be called) never materialised as a book, although the sketches have survived. Shortly after returning to Edinburgh 1821, following a prolonged stay in the South of France, Skene toured the Borders with Scott and Hogg, collecting material for etchings to illustrate the Waverley Novels. The layout of Princes Street

Gardens was entrusted to him and he wrote a paper for the Society of Antiquaries on the discoveries made during the excavations around the Castle. A journey along the Rhine in 1824 produced more sketch books, and in September 1830 Skene was appointed Secretary of the Board of Trustees for Manufacturers in Scotland, a position which enabled him to promote finances for the fine arts in Scotland. To him fell the sad task of organising the fund launched in October 1832 for the Memorial to his beloved friend. Visiting his son who had settled in Greece, Skene was so charmed with the country that he bought a villa near Athens. His family remained there for the next seven years during which time the artist travelled round the Greek islands making hundreds of sketches, keeping diaries and being a frequent and welcome guest at the Royal Palace. Returned to Britain 1845 and after a short stay at Leamington spent his remaining years at Frewin Hall, Oxford. The academic atmosphere of Oxford was eminently suited to his literary, scientific and artistic taste. "His sense of colour, his appreciation of the architectural refinement of the subjects he chose for his pen and brush, and above all his technique give him a high place among artists who specialised in this kind of work. Unfortunately he was not equally skilled in the art of engraving and his attempts to master lithographic methods of reproduction did not lead him very far" [Butchart]. Published *A Series of Sketches of Existing Localities alluded to in the Waverley Novels,* illustrated with his own etchings and commended by Scott. In 1943 Edinburgh City library purchased at auction three volumes of Skene's watercolours totalling 222 works, most of them between 1817 and 1819, though one dates from 1804 and some are as late as 1837. These can be seen in the Edinburgh room of the Public Library. Other works are in the NGS (including two large folios of continental watercolours 1820-1 and 1824-8).
**Bibl:** Bushnell; Butchart 4,5,39,63,73,88-9,96-108; DNB; Halsby 50; Meta Viles, personal communication.

**SKENE, Robert** **fl 1615**
Aberdeen painter and glasswright. Made a burgess of Aberdeen on account of his work for Sir James Skene (Skeyne) of Curriehill, a Lord of Session.
**Bibl:** Aberdeen Burgesses 1399-1630, 114; Apted 88; Thomson, George Jamesone, 27,133-5.

**SKETCHING CLUB** **c1875-c1884**
The immediate successor in London of the Auld Lang Syne club(qv) comprising mainly Scottish artists of note resident in London. The same traditions were followed and it is not clear why the name was changed nor when the Sketching Club precisely came into being nor last met. Members included John Burr, Thomas Graham, Frank Holl (who was secretary for many years and whose death precipitated the group's dissolution), Colin Hunter, C.E.Johnson, George Paul Chalmers, George A Lawson, John MacWhirter, W.Q.Orchardson, John Pettie and FR Stock. Later members were Edwin Abbey, A.Parsons, David Murray and EJ Gregory. Meetings were held weekly at members' homes in rotation and the member chosing the subject was allowed to retain the consequent sketches, many of which were later worked into full-scale works (eg Pettie's 'Challenge', Holl's 'Child's Funeral'). Unlike the Auld Lang Syne group, unfortunately no Minutes were kept.
**Bibl:** Martin Hardie, John Pettie, London 1908, 44-48; Martin Hardie, The Artist, Jan 1902, with illus; Martin Hardie, Chamber's Journal, Jan 1906.

**SKINNER, Anne** **fl 1977-1978**
Dundee painter; exhibited RSA(2).

**SKINNER, William** **fl 1892-1903**
Edinburgh landscape painter in oil and watercolour, also occasional figurative works and decorative illustrator. Exhibited Scottish and Spanish scenes at the RSA(23), RSW(1), AAS(5) & GI(5), from 24 Shandwick Place.

**SKINNER, Lieut-General William** **1700-1780**
Military architect. Designed Fort George 1747-67. This was intended to house almost 2,000 troops and was equipped with the fullest possible complement of defence. "The buildings are just as expressive of military might, the pedimented gatehouse flaunting the royal coat of arms, the barrack blocks symmetrically disposed round a large central square, the occasional use of a Doric order reinforcing rather than lightening the purposeful severity" (Gifford). Skinner repaired Fort Augustus, adding a dry moat and glacis 1747-48.
**Bibl:** Gifford, H & I, 57,168-9,174,177,plts 28, 76-78.

**SKIRVING, Archibald** **1749-1819**
Born Athelstaneford, Nr Haddington; died Inveresk. Son of an East Lothian farmer said to have been the author of 'Hey Johnnie Cope', and who certainly wrote the ballad 'Tranent Muir'. Began work as a painter of miniatures but after returning from Italy devoted himself almost entirely to pastel. Remembered as much for his eccentric habits as for his art. Went to Rome c1786 remaining there for eight years, being captured by the French on his homeward journey and imprisoned for a year. One result of this experience was an eye disease (unocular elipopia) which led to him having to abandon miniature painting. Some of his pastel portraits are masterpieces of technical ability. 'His miniatures are excellent for their drawing, colour and admirable expression. He possesses great taste, was ingenious, eccentric and aspired to wit' [Redgrave]. He was lazy and examples of his work are comparatively rare. During his lifetime he demanded a fee considerably more than that received by Raeburn. His contemporary Patrick Gibson(qv) wrote 'his enthusiasm and genius were equally divided between painting, darning stockings, turning egg-cups, mending his old clothes, and other useful offices'. The lovely chalk drawing 'Robert Burns' is his most famous work although it is doubtful if it was painted from life. Buried in Athelstaneford churchyard. His own portrait was painted several times including examples by Raeburn, Geddes, and George Watson. Represented by an oil portrait of his father and of 'Dr Alexander Carlyle of Inveresk' (nicknamed Jupiter) and 6 other works in the SNPG; also in NGS.
**Bibl:** Brydall 169; Caw 45-6; McKay 26-7; Irwin 80; Edward Lloyd, Archibald Skirving, Scottish Masters series, Edinburgh 1994; Macmillan [SA] 151-2; Basil Skinner, 'Archibald Skirving', Trans. of the East Lothian Antiquarian Soc.,xii 1970; Tanja Sundström, 'Archibald Skirving', MA thesis, St Andrews University, 1994.

**SKIRVING, Christina A** **fl 1896-1903**
Watercolour painter of flowers, country buildings and rustic scenes; exhibited RSA(2), RSW(2) & AAS(3), from Croys, Nr Dalbeattie

**SKIRVING, J** **19th Cent**
Portrait painter. A portrait of 'Lord Woodhouselee' appeared in the RSA 1880, lent by G.M. Tytler Esq of Edinburgh.

**SLACK, Iain Ross** **fl 1989-**
Glasgow painter and sculptor; exhibited 'The James Watt Dock, Greenock' at the RSA; also GI(3).

**SLANEY, Miss Noel (Mrs G F Moules) RSW** **1915-**
Born Glasgow, 26 Dec. Painter in oil and watercolour of still life. Trained Glasgow School of Art. Married George Moules(qv). Lived in Glasgow for many years. Elected RSW 1946. Exhibited RA(1), RSA(39), RSW & GI(88). Represented Glasgow AG, Lillie AG (Milngavie).

**SLATER, Francis** **fl 1839-1841**
Glasgow landscape painter; exhibited RSA(2).

**SLATER, John** **fl 1920**
Amateur Edinburgh painter of 12 Craigmillar Park. Exhibited 'Poultry' at the RSA.

**SLATER, Peter** **1809-1860**
Born Edinburgh; died London. Sculptor. Son of a marble cutter, he entered the studio of Samuel Joseph as a carver and assistant. Went with Joseph to London and studied there for some years at the RA Schools having been recommended by Wilkie Collins. In 1844 exhibited 'Canute Reproving his Flatterers', a work which the *Literary Gazette* said 'we must decline being one'. In 1853 executed the statue of James Watt for Adam Square, Edinburgh, being a copy of one made by Chantrey. His statue of George Heriot (1854) was placed on the south-west niche of the Scott Monument on Princes Street, while a monument of Dr Carson (1855) in St Giles is another example of his work. Exhibited RA(30) 1846-1870, the first being a marble bust of John Gladstone of Fasque (1846 ) & RSA(57), latterly from 37 Great Russell St having returned to London shortly before his death. Represented in SNPG.
**Bibl:** Gifford 115,182,316.

**SLAVEN, Miss Kate** **fl 1987-**
Aberdeen painter. Began exhibiting figurative works at the GI 1987.

**SLEZER, Capt John** **c1645-1717**
Died Scotland 24 Jne 1714 (or 1717). Dutch draughtsman and engraver. Worked and died in Scotland, arriving from Holland 1669. Patronised by Charles II and the Duke of York. Made captain of an artillery company 1690. Best known for his great work *Theatrum Scotiae* (1693). The identity of the artist of these drawings is generally regarded as Slezer although a doubt over this attribution remains. 'From the accounts connected with the publication of the book and the abortive history of Present State of Scotland it appears that the engravings from the drawings were done by Robert White, but the drawings passed through the hands of John Wyck (a Flemish painter who had settled in London), who introduced the figures to render the views more attractive, and that an artist (whose name is nowhere mentioned) was brought over from Holland to draw the views. This mysterious and persistent anonymity may point to the fact that the artist from Holland was Slezer who wanted to secure for himself the requisite fees due to the artist' [RSA catalogue]. The only known drawing by Slezer definitely used in the publication was 'Dumbarton' (plate 5), now in the SNG. Butchart argues that 'it is well-nigh impossible to over-estimate the value of these early topographical delineations of Scottish townships, and the two Edinburgh plates which occupy the place of honour at the beginning of the volume are excellent examples of early engraving'. At some time he was a superintendent of ordnance and sent to Holland for guns and gunners in 1680. Although awarded with a grant to be shared with one other to enable him to continue work on a sequel to be called *Scotia Illustrata,* Slezer became more and more in financial toil, until eventually he was forced to take refuge in Holyrood sanctuary where he spent the last years of his life. He did produce work after *Theatrum Scotiae,* a number of pencil and wash drawings having been acquired by Edinburgh library in 1939. Devised a scheme for additional fortification for Edinburgh Castle (1675), partly completed 1677-80 when the area within the west wall was levelled and the eastern defences recast. Represented in NGS(6 attributed), City of Edinburgh collection.
**Bibl:** Bushnell; Butchart 11-13; DNB; Gifford 86.

**SLIGHT, Daisy** **fl 1906**
Minor flower painter of North Mains, Ormiston, East Lothian; exhibited GI(1).

**SLIMMON, Thomas M** **fl 1947**
Ayrshire painter of coastal scenes; exhibited AAS(1), from 43 High St, Newmilns.

**SLOAN, Christine Scott P** **1887-1975**
Born Glasgow. Watercolourist; informal portraits and topography. Trained Glasgow School of Art 1907-15. After war service she taught for a time at Laurel Bank School. Lived at 2 Crown Circus, Dowanhill, Ayrshire. Exhibited RSA(1), RSW(5) & GI(8).
**Bibl:** Halsby 283.

**SLOAN, Jack Faulds** **fl 1980-1987**
Lanarkshire painter; trained at art school. Exhibited GI(11) 1980-1987 & AAS(4) from 12 Berriedale Ave, Hamilton.

**SLOAN, Mrs Jean** **fl 1960**
Glasgow painter of still life. Exhibited GI(2) from Kelvin Court.

**SLOANE, James Fullarton** **1866-1947**
Born Ibrox, Glasgow, 13 May; died Glasgow Jan. Painter of landscapes, figure subjects and still life in oil and watercolour, also poster artist. His favourite haunts were Scottish country towns and fishing harbours, places such as Peebles, Kelso and Callander. The 7th son of an accountant and his amateur artist wife; his paternal grandfather had been rector of Peebles GS and has a section devoted to his memory in Peebles museum. His brother **Robert H SLOANE** was also a part-time artist, having studied at the Glasgow School of Art where in 1887 he was awarded the Haldane medal. Educated Glasgow HS. Studied art, probably as an evening student, at the Glasgow School of Art under Fra Newbery(qv) and possibly also at the Atheneum under James Campbell. His first job was as a clerk in a shipping office, from there he became a draughtsman before becoming a full-time artist c1900. Married 1895. His only attempt at exhibiting at the Royal Academy was successful but he was so disillusioned by the expense involved that he neither visited the exhibition nor ever sought to exhibit in London again. Several of his exhibits at the RSA were the subject of favourable notices in the Parisian as well as the Scottish press. From his Glasgow studio exhibited RA(1), RSA(7), RSW(9), GI(49) & L(3).
**Bibl:** Revue du Vrai et du Beau, Paris, 25 June 1924; Robert W Sloane (son), personal communication.

**SLOANE, Ninian** **fl 1965**
Morayshire-based landscape painter and stained glass window designer. Output affected by drink. Exhibited AAS(2), from Pluscarden Priory, Elgin.

**SMAIL, A D** **fl 1866**
Edinburgh topographical painter in oil. Probably father or possibly brother of Miss A Y L S(qv). Exhibited 'Moreau's monument, nr Dresden' at the RSA 1866.

**SMAIL, Miss A Y L** **fl 1868-1869**
Edinburgh landscape painter in oil. Related to A D S(qv). Exhibited RSA(3).

**SMAIL, Bettie C** **fl 1936**
Amateur Edinburgh flower painter; exhibited RSA(2) from 1 Grange Terrace.

**SMAIL(L), Elizabeth M A(?H)** **fl 1879-1886**
Edinburgh painter in oil and watercolour of contemporary townscapes and flower studies. Exhibited RSA & GI(1).

**SMAIL, G F** **fl 1878**
Edinburgh watercolour painter of landscapes. Exhibited 'A View at Aboyne, Aberdeenshire' at the RSA.

**SMALL, Catherine E (Kate)** **fl 1914-1940**
Prolific and competent Edinburgh painter; flowers and fruit. Exhibited RSA(33), RSW(21), GI(20) & L(1), latterly from 32 Braid Crescent.

**SMALL, David** **1846-1927**
Glasgow watercolour painter of landscapes and coastal scenes; also stained glass window designer. Painter of Old Glasgow, he produced topographical sketches for *By'gone Glasgow;* also views of Edinburgh, Stirling and Dundee. Worked in a tight style but had great sensitivity for old buildings and their environs. Illustrated *Sketches of Quaint Bits in Glasgow* (1887). Responsible for a window in St Giles' Cathedral (1879). Moved to 4 Airlie Terrace, Dundee c1890. Exhibited RSA(3), RSW(1), AAS(3) but mainly GI(16). Represented in Edinburgh City collection.
**Bibl:** Gifford 116; Halsby 283.

**SMALL, James E** **fl 1880**
Edinburgh painter; exhibited RSA(1) from 6 Washington Place.

**SMALL, John** **1862-1938**
Aberdeen painter of marines, shipping and coastal scenery; also topographical subjects. Related to Leo James S(qv). Exhibited a study of rocks at the RSA in 1894 and at the AAS regularly 1893-1935, latterly from 38 S. Constitution St.

**SMALL, John William** **fl 1875-1883**
Edinburgh-based architect and watercolourist, also furniture designer. Lived for a time in Stirling before moving to Edinburgh. Painted topographical views of Stirling and adjacent towns and in his later years Edinburgh townscapes. Exhibited RSA(11), latterly from 56 George Street.
**Bibl:** Halsby 283.

**SMALL, Leo James** **fl 1923-1935**
Aberdeen topographical painter. Related to John S(qv). Exhibited AAS(5) from 38 S. Constitution St.

**SMALL, McKenzie** **fl 1894**
Minor painter of Rose Villa, Ibrox, Glasgow; exhibited GI(1).

**SMALL, William RI HRSA** **1843-1929**
Born Edinburgh, 27 May; died Worcester 23 Dec. Painter, watercolourist and illustrator, also lithographer. Studied at the RSA Schools, winning a bronze medal in the Life Class, and after a spell in Edinburgh working in the art department of the publisher Messrs Nelson, moved to London 1865. Remained there until c1915 when he finally settled in Worcester. A very prolific and quick worker, his illustrations appeared in many magazines and his watercolours were romantic and superbly executed, reminiscent of the work of Fred Walker. Among his exhibited works were a water polo scene and one of the Prince of Wales driving a sleigh along London embankment 1881. Illustrated *Words for the Wise* (1864), *Miracles of Heavenly Love* (1864), *Marion's Sundays* (1864), *Washerwoman's Foundling* (1867) and Bret Harte's *A Protégée of Jack Hamilton's* (1894). Contributed to many periodicals including *Shilling Magazine* (1865-66), *Once a Week* (1866), *Good Words* (1866-68), *The Sunday Magazine* (1866-8, 1871), Cassell's *Family Paper* (1866,1870), *Sunday at Home* (1866), *Pen and Pencil Pictures From the Poets* (1866), *Touches of Nature by Eminent Artists* (1866), *Ballad Stories of the Affections* (1866), *London Society* (1867-69), *The Argosy* (1867), *The Quiver* (1867), *Poems* by Jean Ingelow (1867), *Idyllic Pictures* (1867), *Two Centuries of Song* (1867), Foxe's *Book of Martyrs* (1867), Heber's *Hymns* (1867), *The Spirit of Praise* (1867). Illustrated *Book of Sacred Poems* (1867), *Golden Thoughts from Golden Fountains* (1867), *Ode on the Morning of Christ's Nativity* (1867), *North Coast and Other Poems* (1868), *The Graphic (*1869-1900), *Pictures from English Literature* (1870), *Good Words for the Young* (1871), Novello's *National Nursery Rhymes* (1871), *Judy's Almanac* (1872), Thornbury's *Legendary Ballads* (1876), Dalziel's *Bible Gallery* (1880), *Chums* (1892), *Fun,* and *The Gypsy* (1915). His work 'The Last Match' was purchased by the Chantrey Bequest in 1887. Elected ARI 1870, RI 1883, HRSA 1917. Exhibited RA(32) 1869-1900, including original drawings for Fielding's *Tom Jones* and the same author's *Joseph Andrews* (1882) and for *Prince Fortunatus* (1893); also RSA(30), GI(6), RHA(3), RI(10), ROI(9) & L(7), latterly from 294 Camden Rd, London. Represented in NGS(2), SNPG (2 of Ramsay Macdonald), Edinburgh City collection, Leicester AG, Liverpool AG, Manchester AG, Birmingham (St George's Soc).
**Bibl:** Caw 292-4; Clement and Hutton; Halsby 283-4; Hardie III, 96; Hayden, Chats on Old Prints 1909; Houfe; Pennell, Modern Illustrators, 1895; Forrest Reid, Illustrators of the Sixties, 1928, 216-227 illus; Wingfield.

**SMALL, William Farquharson** **fl 1941**
Stirlingshire watercolourist. Exhibited GI(1) from Lennoxtown.

**SMART, -** **fl 1810**
Edinburgh engraver; possibly the father of the engraver **John SMART** (b Leith 1838). Engraved a bookplate for WGC Kent, 1810.
**Bibl:** Bushnell.

**SMART, Alastair RSA ARBS** **1937-**
Born Aberdeen. Sculptor. Specialises in figure subjects. Trained Gray's School of Art 1955-60 with a postgraduate year 60-61. In 1960 won the Keith Prize, the Benno Schotz Award and the Latimer Award; was also granted the Brough Memorial Travelling Scholarship and the Elizabeth Greenshields Award, enabling him to visit Toronto. Married the artist Elizabeth S(qv). Since 1965 lecturer at the Duncan of Jordanstone School of Art, Dundee; lives Muirhead, by Dundee. Elected ARSA 1976, RSA 1992. Exhibited regularly RSA & AAS 1961-1981. Represented in Kelvingrove AG, Glasgow AG, Carnoustie Library (coat-of-arms), Adelaide AG (South Australia).

**SMART, Bessie** **fl 1889**
Hamilton artist. Exhibited once at the GI from Balgreen.

**SMART, Betty Hunter** **fl 1950-1951**
Edinburgh painter; exhibited 'Autumn view' and 'December afternoon' at RSA.

**SMART, David** **fl 1866-1867**
Perth architect. His design for Perth Station Hotel was exhibited RSA; also exhibited plans for the restored and enlarged Balhousie Castle, Perth for the Earl of Kinmont.

**SMART, Mrs Elizabeth** **fl 1965**
Dundee-based painter of still life and flowers. Married to Alastair S(qv). Exhibited AAS(1) from 242 Coupar Angus Rd, by Dundee.

**SMART, Ian Douglas** **fl 1975-1983**
Aberdeenshire artist. Trained Gray's School of Art, Aberdeen. Exhibited AAS during the above years, from 22 Loirston Ave, Cove.

**SMART, J Gordon** **fl 1897-1898**
Edinburgh watercolour painter of building, topographical subjects. Son of John S(qv). Exhibited RSA(5) from 13 Brunswick Street, Hillside.

**SMART, John RSA RSW RBA** **1838-1899**
Born Leith; died Edinburgh, 1 Jne. Landscape painter in oil and watercolour; often with a sporting involvement. Studied privately with Horatio McCulloch(qv) whose influence remained throughout his working life. Earlier landscapes were often painted in England and Wales but as time went by he turned exclusively to Highland scenery. They were 'drowned in a deeper dose of brown than his master ever used, and in it one notes that love of Highland scenery that was to be his most outstanding quality. Painting much out of doors, however, the brown gradually lessened on his palette, and, though he never attained real success as a painter of light or as a colourist, a dark substratum vitiating his tones and hues, his pitch became truer and his colour fresher and more naturalistic. His handling also gained in boldness and breadth, and towards 1880 when at the height of his powers, if rather heavy-handed, it was marked by verve and incisiveness, quite in harmony with the rugged scenery and striking effects of which he was so fond...If coarse in handling and wanting in subtlety of feeling, they are simple and effective in design, vivid in effect, and powerful in execution, and breathe an ardent passion for the landscape of his native land...Later, as his technique and sentiment weakened, conventionality reasserted itself, and after 1890 he appeared to be working less from fresh impressions than past experience...A fervid enthusiast for everything Scottish, he wrote and sang Scots songs, played the pipes, and wore the kilt' [Caw]. Writing of his 'Pass of Leny' (Dundee AG), David Webster considered it 'a delightful piece of colouring, poetically rendered, and suggestive of the wilder grandeur of our northern passes when robbed of their burden of summer beauty. He excelled in personal pictorial renderings of autumnal charm and in each his colouring was always exceedingly true, natural, and appropriate'. As well as a number of golfing scenes, one reproduced in Kerr's *History of Curling* (1896), he completed many angling and shooting pictures. Published *A Round of the Links: Views of the Golf Greens of Scotland,* engraved by George Aikman(qv) (1893) - a scarce and greatly valued book, and illustrated Crucelli, *Mistura Curiosa* (1869) and Sidey, *Reminiscences of a Medical Student* (1886). Founder member of the Scottish Watercolour Society. Elected ARSA 1871, RSA 1877, RSW 1878. Exhibited RA(28) 1870-1899, RSA(268) 1860-1900; also RSW(61), RBA(6), RHA(3), ROI(2), AAS 1885-1891 & GI(104), after 1884 from 13 Brunswick St, Edinburgh. Represented in Glasgow AG, Brodie Castle (NTS).
**Bibl:** Bryan; Caw 297-8; Clement and Hutton; Who was Who 1897-1915; Halsby 125,284; Wingfield.

**SMART, John McF** **fl 1873**
Glasgow still life painter. Exhibited GI(1) from Dumbarton Rd.

**SMART, Miss Lenore** **fl 1919-1929**
Kincardineshire landscape painter; exhibited AAS, from Hillhead, Cockney, Stonehaven.

**SMART, Miss Maude N** **fl 1919**
Aberdeenshire sculptor of portrait heads; exhibited AAS(3), from 37 Salisbury Terrace.

**SMART, Robert jnr** **fl 1853**
Edinburgh painter; exhibited 'Sketch at Liberton' at RSA, from Shakespeare Sq.

**SMASHERS' CLUB** **1848-1863**
Edinburgh sketching club composed entirely of practising artists. Original members were James Archer, John Ballantyne, William Crawford, John Faed, Thomas Faed and William Fettes Douglas.

The Minutes were kept in doggerel, with each member adopting a persona for the meeting (eg John Ballantyne(qv) was 'Butterworth'). Each member drank from his own rummer, the side of which he had autographed with a diamond. At meetings a theme would be introduced (eg 'death', 'conspiracy', 'boyhood'), sketches made accordingly and the topic discussed. Some of the originals are in the Print Room of Glasgow AG. When most of the members had become established and moved to London the migrants reconstituted themselves there as the Auld Lang Syne Club(qv) and later 'The Sketching Club'(qv).
**Bibl:** Martin Hardie, John Pettie, London 1908, 42-3; Mary McKerrow, The Faeds, Edinburgh 1982, 15.

**SMEAL, R W** **fl 1924**
Amateur watercolour painter, probably Scottish. Lived in Kent. Exhibited RSW(1).

**SMEALL, Miss E M** **fl 1932**
Edinburgh painter. Exhibited at the RSA once from 5 Nile Grove.

**SMEALL, James E** **fl 1880-1882**
Edinburgh artist; topographical and marines; exhibited RSA(3) from 5 Newton Terrace, East Tynecastle.

**SMEALL, Tom** **fl 1869**
Minor landscape painter; exhibited a scene near Monzie, Perthshire at the RSA.

**SMEALL, William** **1790-1883**
Edinburgh painter in oil and watercolours. Shoemaker by trade but preferred sketching and painting although continued to do both throughout his working life. Said to have visited America c1835. Published two volumes of pencil drawings of Old Edinburgh covering the period 1815-1870, important in the history of the city because of the number of buildings no longer in existence. Exhibited RSA(72) 1832-1873; also GI(2). Represented in Edinburgh City collection(5).
**Bibl:** Butchart 57.

**SMEATON (SMITON), Walter** **fl 1782-1799**
Painter. Son of a bookbinder, now best known for his apprentices than for his own work. It seems that he and a man called Chancellor were coach painters in the Canongate. He was a bailie of the Canongate. This must have been quite a large firm since it compared favourably in the number of apprentices with only two taken by the Nories over a comparable period. Probably died 1799 since the year before there had been a sale of his books, pictures and prints and in 1797 only Mrs Smeaton's name is recorded at their home at the head of New Street, Canongate; also Chancellor appears to have died about the same time. By far the best known apprentice was James Howe(qv), taken on in 1795, the others were **Thomas Boston** 1782, **Alexander Cumin** 1784, **Robert Aitken** 1785, **Alexander Graham** 1785, **James Paterson** 1786, **Alexander Wright** 1789 and **John Houston** 1796.
**Bibl:** Book of the Old Edinburgh Club (1935), xx, 21.

**SMELLIE, G R** **fl 1877**
Edinburgh painter of landscape; exhibited 'On Gala Water' at the RSA, from Hope Pk Sq.

**SMELLIE, John** **fl 1909-d1925**
Glasgow artist in oil and watercolour; fond of depicting beach scenes. Exhibited from 1909 RSA(9), RSW(5) & GI(22).

**SMELLIE, Robert D** **fl 1858-1908**
Edinburgh painter in oil and watercolour of landscapes, figure subjects, animals. In 1898 was working from London where he appears to have settled. Regular exhibitor RSA(56) 1858-1908 including 'The Otter Hunt' and 'Spaniel with Wild Duck', both 1884, 'The Dog Show' 1885 and 'Going to Oban Market' 1896; also GI(9) & AAS(1) when living at 2 Watt Terrace.
**Bibl:** Wingfield.

**SMELLIE, Mrs S M** **fl 1895**
Edinburgh painter. Possibly wife of Robert S(qv). Exhibited RSA(1) from 13 Union St.

**SMELLIE, Thomas** **fl 1932-1934**
Minor engraver of 46 Portland Road, Kilmarnock; exhibited topographical drawings in pencil, also etchings at the GI(3).

**SMIBERT, John** **1688-1751**
Born Grassmarket, Edinburgh 24 Mar; died Boston, USA, 2 May. Painter of portraits, occasional portrait miniatures, landscapes and architect. Son of a dyer. An outstanding example of a Scotsman whose success was achieved beyond his own shores. Studied under an Edinburgh house painter Walter Marshall, after serving his apprenticeship in 1709 went to London studying at the same academy that Aikman(qv) had attended. Then took a job as a coach painter and in 1716 returned to Edinburgh. There he became patronised by Sir Frances Grant(qv) who in 1709 became Lord Cullen. In 1713 Cullen purchased the House of Monymusk; there Smibert painted his most famous Scottish portrait, a family group (measuring 83 x 129 ins) of 'Lord Cullen and his family'. The exact date of this work is unknown but it was probably completed some time before 1722. A medallo of the painting (17 x 27‹÷¢ ins) was executed 1718-19. Both works remain in the possession of the family. During this time he became friendly with Allan Ramsay(qv) whose portrait Smibert painted on two occasions. In August, 1719 he visited Italy and during his first year in Florence purchased paintings by a number of Italian masters. Holloway suggests that in view of Smibert's friendship with the dealer Andrew Hay these paintings may have been purchased for re-sale in London. Whilst in Florence he painted a picture of 'Siberian Tartars' for the Grand Duke of Tuscany which was subsequently presented to the Czar. On returning he went for a short time to Edinburgh but by 1722 was established as one of the leading painters in London and in 1727 Lord Cullen's successor and his wife sat for him in London. This elegant painting also remains in the family. It is recorded in the George Vertue *Notebooks* that because 'he could not well relish the false, selfish griping, overreaching ways, too commonly practiz'd', the artist resolved to leave London which he did in the company of his friend Bishop Berkeley who was leaving to found a college in Bermuda with the aim of converting the American Indians. Landing in Virginia, they sailed north to Rhode Island and after six months Smibert went to Boston where he finally settled, marrying Mary Williams, daughter of Dr Nathaniel W, a rich American 20 years his junior. Proceeded to execute probably his best work. His large group Bishop Berkeley and family is at Yale University, the portrait of an aged clergyman, Dr Robinson of Salem, is in the Essex Institute. He was also the architect of Faneuil Hall, Boston. It is unclear whether he painted any miniatures. The first exhibition of his work since 1730 was held at Yale University 1949. Represented in NPG, NGS, SNPG, Boston AG (Mass), Brooklyn AG, Buffalo (USA), Dublin AG, New Haven AG (Conn), Metropolitan Museum (New York), Worcester AG (USA).
**Bibl:** Bryan; Brydall 106-8; Caw 26; Miles Chapell, 'A note on Smibert's Italian Sojourn', Art Bulletin, cxiv, Mar 1982; H.W. Foote, John Smibert, Painter, Cambridge (Mass) 1950; Holloway 48, 74-81, 123, 148; Irwin 47,100; Macmillan [SA] 91-2,94-5 et passim ch v; Mass.Hist.Soc. 'The Notebook of John Smibert', Boston, Mass, 1967; S.T. Riley, 'John Smibert and the business of portrait painting' in American Painting to 1766: A Reappraisal, Charlottesville (Virginia) 1971; R.H. Saunders, 'John Smibert (1688-1751), Anglo-American Portrait Painter' (PhD Yale, 1979); R.H. Saunders & E.G. Miles, American Colonial Portraits 1700-1776 (Ex cat 1987); Yale University AG, 'The Smibert Tradition: The first selected showing of John Smibert's Paintings since 1730' (Ex cat 1949).

**SMIBERT, Nathaniel** **1734-1756**
Born Boston, Mass Jan 20; died Boston, Mass 3 Nov. Portrait painter. Son and pupil of John S(qv). A tragically premature death prevented any lasting memorial.

**SMIETON, Mrs J P** **fl 1872-1883**
Broughty Ferry painter in oil and watercolour of landscape, often with buildings. Wife of Thomas S(qv). Exhibited RSA(17).

**SMIETON, James** **1869-1935**
Born Carnoustie; died Edinburgh. Mostly painted views of Perth in watercolour with a restricted, almost subdued palette. Left Elgin for Perth 1894 becoming art master at Sharp's Institution until its amalgamation in 1915 with Perth Academy. Then, until 1925, assistant to D S Murray(qv). Possibly related to Thomas S(qv).

Committee member, Perth Artists Association 1911 and 1923-29. Exhibited 1904-29 in Dundee & Perth. Represented in Aberdeen AG. **Bibl:** Halsby 284.

**SMIETON, Thomas A** **fl 1883**
Broughty Ferry painter. Married an artist(qv). Exhibited RSA(1) from Panmure Villa.

**SMIRKE, Sir Robert** **1781-1867**
Architect. Although an Englishman - perhaps the most successful British architect of the 19th century - his influence in Scotland was twofold. As one of the most prolific exponents of the Greek Revival style a number of important houses designed in Scotland had a considerable influence on the development of Scottish architecture in the early 19th century. Among them were Whittinghame, East Lothian (1817) for James Balfour, Kinmount, Dumfries-shire (pre 1819), for the Marquis of Queensberry, and the 'uncompromisingly austere' Cultoquhey, Perthshire (1819). Designed picture galleries for Erskine House, Renfrewshire, Kinfauns Castle, Perthshire (1820-22) for Lord Gray, and Strathallan Castle, Perthshire, while in more sombre mood is the Doric style Perth County Buildings (1815-9). The second field of great influence was his teaching, William Burn(qv) being his most famous Scottish pupil.
**Bibl:** Colvin 545-548; Dunbar 123,127,129; Bruce Walker & W S Gauldie, Architects and Architecture on Tayside, Dundee 1984, 75,78(illus),125.

**SMITH, Mrs** **fl 1890**
Glasgow painter; exhibited an interior at the GI.

**SMITH, A F** **fl 1862**
Glasgow sculptor; exhibited a portrait medallion of a gentleman at the RSA.

**SMITH, A Harold** **fl 1900-1920**
Painter of landscapes and topographical subjects, also engraver. Came from London to Stirling c1910 before moving to Glasgow in 1920. Exhibited RA(4), RSA(11), GI(19) & L(2).

**SMITH, Agnes Harrison** **fl 1896-1900**
Aberdeen painter of figurative works and informal portraits. Exhibited AAS(5), latterly from Craigielea, Mannofield.

**SMITH, Alan** **1941-**
Sculptor. Describes himself as a 'conceptual artist'. Trained Edinburgh College of Art 1960-64. Co-founder and chairman, Ceramic Workshop in Edinburgh 1969. Then spent two years working in Italy before returning in 1977. Exhibited 1974 VII Biennale d'Arte della Ceramica at Gubbio, Italy. Work was shown at Aberdeen AG and permanently represented in SNGMA, SAC.

**SMITH, Alex J** **fl 1940**
Minor Falkirk painter of 6 Wall Street, Camelon. Local topography, especially around Stirling. Exhibited RSA(1) & GI(2).

**SMITH, Alexander** **fl 1874-1885**
Edinburgh watercolour painter of buildings and topographical scenes. Exhibited RSA(6) from 11 Albany Street.

**SMITH, Alexander Cormack** **1875-1922**
Amateur painter and naturalist. Lived in Perth and painted mainly birds in oil and watercolour. Cousin of Spence-Smith(qv). Exhibited Dundee and Perth 1911-1921. Represented in Perth AG.
**Bibl:** Halsby 284.

**SMITH, Alexander Monro** **1860-1933**
Born Falkirk. Painter in oil and watercolour of portraits, figure subjects, also illustrator. Educated Falkirk GS, trained Glasgow School of Art. Worked in London 1884-1915 before returning north of the border to live in Edinburgh and Glasgow. President, Scottish Arts Club. Principal works include 'The Pedlar' and 'Francesca da Rimini'. Exhibited RSA(7), RSW(2) & L(3).
**Bibl:** Halsby 284.

**SMITH, Alexander Ritchie** **fl 1878**
Amateur Edinburgh watercolourist; exhibited 'On old High School Wynd' at the RSA. Represented by a watercolour 'Mealmarket Stairs, Cowgate' in Edinburgh City collection.

**SMITH, Alfred** **fl 1926**
Aberdeen amateur painter; exhibited 'Gulls' at AAS, from 130 Hamilton Place.

**SMITH, Alison Margaret** **fl 1965-1969**
Aberdeen painter of local landscapes; exhibited AAS(3), from 167 Craigievar Crescent.

**SMITH, Miss Amelia** **fl 1851**
Perth painter of figurative subjects; exhibited RSA(3).

**SMITH, Andrew** **c1934-**
Born Cockpen, Midlothian. Painter of Edinburgh life and allegory. Trained Edinburgh College of Art in the 1950s. Visited Italy on a travelling scholarship, became a teacher in Midlothian. Encouraged by bursaries and commissions took early retirement to concentrate on painting. Held two one-man exhibitions in Edinburgh 1990: 'The Desperate Elements' and 'Paintings of Edinburgh Life'. Executed several large panels and also smaller works for the new Standard Life Assurance building at Canonmills. Exhibited 'Autumn nights' and 'Three figures' at the RSA.
**Bibl:** Observer Scotland, 1 Jly 1990.

**SMITH, Andrew Lawrenson (Anders Lauritzen)** **c1630-c1694**
Born Orkney/Shetland; died Sola, nr Stavanger, Norway. Painter and sculptor. Father of Knud S(qv). Travelled to Norway as a young man; although his life is clouded in mystery, on the basis of stylistic similarities with Peter Nagelsen of Bergen it is supposed that Smith had been his pupil in Bergen. Summoned to Stavanger 1658 to design a new pulpit for the Cathedral. This survives as the finest example of baroque wood carving in Norway and among the finest anywhere. Responsible for many meticulously sculpted figures in the churches of Bergen and Stavanger. Represented in Bergen Museum, Stavanger Museum.
**Bibl:** Sigrid Christie, 'Den lutherske ikonografi i Norge inntil 1800', Oslo 1973; Henrik Grevenor: Norsk malerkunst under renessanse og barokk, Oslo 1927; Dorotha Platou, Andrew L. Smith, Stavanger 1928.

**SMITH, Andrew MacDonald** **fl 1984**
Dundee amateur artist; exhibited AAS(1) from 58 Provost Rd.

**SMITH, Arthur** **fl 1857-1867**
Aberdeen oil painter of marines, continental and local scenes; exhibited RSA(6) & GI(6), latterly from Lichfield, Staffs. Represented in Leith Hall (NTS).

**SMITH, Arthur** **fl 1879**
Edinburgh oil painter of flower studies; exhibited RSA(1).

**SMITH, Mrs Barbara** **fl 1879-1885**
Glasgow amateur sculptress. Exhibited a portrait bust at the RSA, also GI(6) & L(1) from 12 Sandyford Street.

**SMITH, Berta** **fl 1899-1908**
Dunblane painter of genre, interiors and domestic animals. Moved to Jedburgh c1906. Exhibited RSA(18) & GI(5).

**SMITH, Miss Bradshaw** **fl 1865**
Dumfries-shire amateur painter in oils of landscapes mostly of southern Scotland; exhibited RSA(2).

**SMITH, Bryan** **fl 1986-**
Dollar painter; began exhibiting GI 1986 and RSA 1987.

**SMITH, C B** **fl 1878**
Edinburgh oil painter of wildlife; exhibited RSA(1).

**SMITH, C B J** **fl 1960**
Glasgow painter of still life. Exhibited GI(2).

**SMITH, C F O** **fl 1912-1933**
Amateur painter of Eskbank who moved to Edinburgh in 1918. Exhibited RSA(5), RA(1), GI(1) & ROI(1).

**SMITH, C Snodgrass** **fl 1875-1898**
Amateur Glasgow landscape painter in oil. Exhibited RSA(2) & GI (4), from Meadow Row, Lenzie.

**SMITH, Campbell** **fl 1968-1973**
East Kilbride painter of landscapes, portraits and still life. Moved to Glasgow. Exhibited GI(3).

**SMITH, Campbell Lindsay** **1879-1926**
Born Forfarshire. Painter of portraits, figure studies, wildlife and landscape. More influenced by pre-Raphaelitism than by the contemporary art scene as exemplified by either the Glasgow School or the Colourists, a backwater shared with J Young Hunter(qv) and Andrew Turnbull(qv). His figure studies especially are embued with elaborate detail likened to the work of Holman Hunt and Millais. In 1903 he was living at 113 High Street, Old Aberdeen, from where he exhibited a portrait at the RA of 'Crawford Noble'. The following year was at 58 Beaconsfield Place, Aberdeen, from where he exhibited a study of a farm girl, also at the RA. Exhibited RA(6), RSA(6), AAS 1902-26, GI(5) & L(1).
**Bibl:** Caw 453.

**SMITH, Charles** **1750-1824**
Born Orkney, Sept; died Leith, 19 Dec. Painter in oil and watercolour of portraits and historical scenes; occasional etcher. Studied in RA Schools 1771 under Mortimer. Intended to go to India in 1777 but delayed until 1783. Travelled extensively whilst there and was patronised by several Princes. Later had his portrait engraved with the title 'Painter to the Grand Mogul'. Among his other talents was writing musical entertainments of which the best known was 'A Trip to Bengal' in two acts. In 1796 returned to London exhibiting mythological subjects such as 'Cymon and Iphigenia' and a portrait of an unidentified nobleman 1797. Also painted a 'Self-portrait' in watercolour. Exhibited RA(15) 1789-1797 & at the Scottish Academy 1776. Represented by a sketchbook in the SNPG.
**Bibl:** Archer; Bryan; Bushnell; DNB; Sir William Foster, 'British Artists in India 1760-1820', Walpole Soc, xix (1931) & xxi (1933).

**SMITH, Charles** **fl 1815-1829**
Possibly English portrait painter who came to live in Edinburgh at 22 York Place in 1829. Whilst still in London he had exhibited a portrait of 'Lord Erskine' 1821 and in 1823 a famous painting of the Culloden veteran 'Patrick Grant' then aged 109, also the same year a portrait of 'Sir James Macintosh', Lord Rector of the University of Glasgow. In 1829 exhibited two works both painted in Rome, one of them a portrait of 'David Wilkie'. At this time he was residing at 32 York Place, Edinburgh. Sometimes confused with the Orcadian painter of the same name (previous entry).

**SMITH, Charles** **fl 1971-1978**
Aberdeen-based silversmith. Exhibited AAS from 231 Queens Rd.

**SMITH, Charles Frederick Ortmann** **fl 1912-1933**
Edinburgh painter; exhibited pastoral scenes occasionally at the RSA (in 1912, 1927 & 1933).

**SMITH, Miss Charlotte Elizabeth** **1871-1951**
Aberdeenshire painter in oil and watercolour of flowers and landscapes; also etcher and teacher. Although mainly self-taught trained for a short time Royal College of Art, also Glasgow, France and Holland. On her return became art teacher at Peterhead Academy. From there she exhibited RA(1), RSA(1) & AAS (1908-1937), residing at 51 St. Peter St. Died Peterhead.

**SMITH, Miss Christian Aikman** **fl 1929-1937**
Minor Edinburgh painter of of flowers and still life; exhibited RSA(3) from 40 Blacket Place.

**SMITH, Clare (née Fullerton)** **1938-**
Born Newport-on-Tay, Nov 9. Potter. Daughter of Leonard Fullerton(qv). Trained Edinburgh College of Art 1956-60. Works with oxidised stoneware thrown on the wheel, also Raku vases. Strongly influenced by plants and wildlife including fish. Her husband is also an artist. Exhibits Scottish Potters' Association and throughout Scotland, from Urquhart, Moray.

**SMITH, Colvin RSA** **1795-1875**
Born Brechin; died Edinburgh 21 Jly. Portrait painter, especially of men. Coming from a well-connected family, he studied at the RA Schools in London and thereafter worked in Italy studying the Old Masters. On his return journey he visited Antwerp where he undertook some work after Rubens. In 1827 set up as a portrait painter in Raeburn's old studio in Edinburgh. Caw was rather harsh, commenting that his talent was 'neither original nor assimilative' and that his portraiture seldom rose above the 'competent commonplace'. On the other hand the same writer recognised that 'he drew correctly, had a certain appreciation of character, and arranged his pictures simply...at times he did admirable work in the Raeburn manner, not infrequently designed a full-length with considerable dignity and excellent feeling for the relationship, in character and scale, of figure and background'. Armstrong found his portraits 'well drawn and modelled and in spite of great simplicity, full of truth and vitality'. Seceded from Royal Institution 1830 and remained an ardent supporter of the Academy throughout his long career. His main deficiency was perhaps the difficulty he had in portraying flesh which alternated between a ruddy low tone and a rather earthy impasto as exemplified in 'Lord Jeffrey'. 'Lord Provost Sir James Spittal' is in the Council Chambers, Edinburgh, where it can be compared in the same room to portraits by Watson Gordon and Graham Gilbert. His best known work is a portrait of 'Sir Walter Scott', painted in 1827; of this the writer noted 'whether he had genius or no I am no judge. My own portrait is like, but I think too broad about the jowls, a fault they fall into I suppose, by placing their subject on a high stage and looking up to them, which foreshortens the face'. Elected RSA 1829. Probably related to Charles Smith(qv) with whom he shared an Edinburgh address (32 York Place). Exhibited RA(13) 1843-1871 including a commissioned portrait of 'George Anderson, Provost of Kirkcaldy' 1848, the 'Lord Justice General of Scotland' 1850, the 'Solicitor General of Scotland' 1853 and 'Alexander Guthrie of Brechin' 1864. Exhibited RSA(219) 1826-1871, including 5 posthumously 1880, & GI(3). Represented in SNPG(10), Ashmolean Museum (Oxford), NPG, University of Edinburgh (Senate Hall), Edinburgh City collection, Glasgow AG (4), County Hall, Grantown-on-Spey AG, Nairn AG, Manchester AG, Montreal (Learmonth AG).
**Bibl:** AJ 1875, 304 (obit); Armstrong 46; Bryan; Brydall 240-1; Caw 88; Irwin 219-221; RCM Colvin Smith, Life and Works of Colvin Smith, 1939; McKay 124-5; Poole, Cat of Brit Paint BM 6 (1925) 550.

**SMITH, Miss Constance T** **fl 1898**
Minor watercolour painter of 13 Royal Crescent, Crosshill, Glasgow; exhibited RSW(1) & GI(1).

**SMITH, D J** **fl 1932**
Minor painter; exhibited GI(1) from 26 Dunbar Avenue, Rutherglen, Nr Glasgow.

**SMITH, D Caldwell** **fl 1893**
Motherwell amateur painter. Exhibited 'An Ingle Neuk' at the GI.

**SMITH, David** **fl 1769**
Edinburgh engraver. Lived in Lady Yester's parish and married the daughter of an Edinburgh merchant, 17 Dec 1769.
**Bibl:** Bushnell.

**SMITH, David** **1861-1926**
Minor Fife painter; exhibited RSA(3), from Mossgiel, Wormit.

**SMITH, David** **fl 1938-1939**
Amateur Edinburgh painter of 53 Frederick Street; exhibited RSA(2).

**SMITH, David H** **fl 1871-1878**
Edinburgh amateur painter in oil of landscapes and figure subjects. Exhibited RSA(5), including one of Arran.

**SMITH, David Murray RWS RBA** **1865-1952**
Born Edinburgh, Jly 4; died Dorking, Surrey, 29 May. Landscape painter in oil and watercolour but mainly the latter; also etcher. Educated George Watson's College in Edinburgh, trained Edinburgh College of Art and RSA Schools. In 1893 went to London and exhibited at the principal galleries from that time. Elected RBA 1905,

ARWS 1916, RWS 1933. Moved from London to Long Crendon (Bucks) 1924, then to Gomshall (Surrey) and on to Abinger Hammer. He continued to paint until the day he died. His landscapes were rather austere with broad skies, and with only occasional figures. Worked in Venice and Wales. His paintings show a strong Dutch and Barbizon influence, and, in his watercolours, the English landscape tradition of Cox and de Wint. The subject of several positive articles in *The Studio.* A memorial exhibition was held at Walker's Galleries, London 1954 and another at the Calton Gallery, Edinburgh 1991. During his working career he was successful but since his death, the memorial exhibitions apart, his work has been neglected. Exhibited RA(19), RSA(18), RSW(16), RWS(199), ROI(6), RBA(118), GI(27) & L(28). Represented in Nat Gall of Wales, Nat Gall of NSW (Sydney), Auckland AG (New Zealand), Boston Museum of Fine Arts (USA), Harvard Univ, Toronto AG, Manchester AG, Bury AG, Harrogate AG, Newcastle AG, Plymouth AG, Preston AG, Southport AG, Wednesbury AG, Worthing AG.
**Bibl:** Caw 464; Halsby 284; Studio 1914-1916.

**SMITH, Donald** **fl 1959-1971**
Aberdeenshire artist; exhibited ten works, mostly fishing subjects, at the RSA (1961-71) and four figure studies and genre paintings at the AAS, from Orrock House, Balmedie.

**SMITH, Dorothea Nimmo** **fl 1932-1943**
Edinburgh painter and engraver. Informal portraits and genre. Exhibited RSA(8) & GI(9) from 35 Heriot Row.

**SMITH, Miss E R** **fl 1871-1872**
Edinburgh watercolourist of interiors and bird nests. Sister of Jessie Smith(qv). Exhibited RSA(3).

**SMITH, E W** **fl 1926**
Edinburgh amateur hand; exhibited a pastel study at the AAS from 18 Church Lane.

**SMITH, Edward H** **fl 1966-1984**
Banffshire painter of topographical views. Exhibited RSA(3), GI(1) & AAS between the above years from 5 Commerce St, Findochty.

**SMITH, Edwin Dalton** **1800-?**
Painter in oil and watercolour, mainly the latter. Portraits, portrait miniatures and flowers.
**Bibl:** Halsby 284.

**SMITH, Edwin J** **fl 1934-1935**
Amateur Angus painter of landscape and flower studies. Exhibited GI(2) from 7 Guthrie Terrace, Broughty Ferry.

**SMITH, Elizabeth Pentland** **fl 1906**
Minor Renfrewshire sculptor; exhibited GI(1) from The Knowe, Kilbarchan.

**SMITH, Miss Emma** **fl 1870**
One of four Edinburgh sisters all of whom first exhibited at the RSA in the same year. Painted river scenes in oil of which she exhibited 2 at the RSA.

**SMITH, Eric** **fl 1971**
Glasgow silversmith. Exhibited two silver gilt goblets at the GI.

**SMITH, Mrs G B Elliot** **fl 1890-1897**
Edinburgh painter in oil and watercolour of animals, landscape and interiors. Exhibited RSA(22) including a study of a 'Wee Highlander' 1890 and 'Foxhounds' 1896, also GI(9) & AAS (2) where described as 'Miss' Elliot Smith, from 47 Inverleith Row and latterly 24 York Place.

**SMITH, G Comrie** **fl 1900-1912**
Glasgow portrait miniaturist, mostly on ivory. Exhibited RSA(4), GI(15), & L(2) from the Studio, Giffnock, Nr Glasgow.

**SMITH, G Mackenzie** **fl 1881**
Minor Edinburgh watercolour landscape painter; exhibited RSA(2) from 27 Lauder Rd.

**SMITH, Garden Grant RSW** **1860-1913**
Born Banchory, Kincardineshire; died Hammersmith 25 Aug. Watercolour painter of landscapes and topographical scenes, especially golfing scenes; illustrator, author and editor. Son of Aberdeen's second city architect William Smith(qv) who lived in Banchory; brother of Charles (author of *The Aberdeen Golfers)* with whom he founded Aberdeen Univ. Golf Club 1877 and designed a small course (now abandoned) at Kirkton of Fetteresso. Educated Chanonry School, Old Aberdeen and Aberdeen University; trained Aberdeen School of Art and in Paris under Carolus Duran. Best known as a painter of golfing subjects. Illustrated a number of golfing books including *Golf* (1897), *The World of Golf* (1898), *Sidelights on Golf* (c1907) and his monumental work, a classic of golf literature, *The Royal and Ancient Game of Golf* (1912), produced jointly with Hilton. An inveterate traveller, he sketched in North Africa, Spain and Southern France, but loved especially Seville. Influenced by Arthur Melville(qv) although without the latter's vitality. Enjoyed a working association with Charles Hodge Mackie(qv), Peter Nicholson(qv), RB Nisbet(qv) and AG Sinclair(qv). Elected RSW 1890. Toward the end of his life abandoned painting in favour of playing golf and editing *Golf Illustrated* 1895-1913. One obituary, by Ernest Lehmann, described Smith as 'a true Scot, tenacious of his point of view, dour and able in argument, but always with a saving sense of pawky and delightful humour which enabled him to laugh at his own foibles while meeting and parrying the attack of his adversary'. Elected RSW 1890. Exhibited RSA(41) including some Spanish scenes 1897; also RA(3) 1894-96 including a watercolour 'Autumn' described in the *Whitehall Review* (May 19, 1894) as of 'superlative beauty', RSW(12), RI(5), AAS 1888-98 & GI(11).
**Bibl:** Country Life, Obit, 6 Sep 1895; Glasgow Herald, 22 April, 1895; Halsby 154-5,284; The Times, Obit, 26 Aug 1913; Whitehall Gazette, 26 May 1894; Wingfield.

**SMITH, Gary** **fl 1984**
Stirlingshire painter. Exhibited GI(1) from Killearn.

**SMITH, George** **1793-1877**
Born Aberdeen. Architect. Apprenticed to David Hamilton(qv). Faced with the rivalry of Alexander Simpson(qv) and John Smith(qv) found difficulty in earning a living in Aberdeen, so opened a drawing academy but in 1823 moved to Edinburgh becoming principal clerk to William Burn(qv). Launched his own architectural practice in Edinburgh 1827, later taking on **Henry HARDY** (1831-1908) as a partner. 'His Exchange Coffee House (now David Winter, printers), Dundee (1828) is the most subtle and finely detailed of the neo-Classical buildings on Tayside' [Walker & Gauldie]. Responsible for enlarging and remodelling Tayfield House, Fife (1829) in a Jacobean style. The first to establish a distinctive Glasgow style for the terraces in the West End. In Edinburgh designs included the unusual St John Church, Victoria ST (1838-40) 'less like a church than three bays of a Jacobean country house' [Gifford]; an interesting link between styles of domestic architecture at 87 West Bow (1850); the Tudor-style Buccleuch Parish School (1839) and a number of lesser buildings showing Jacobean characteristics.
**Bibl:** Gifford 168,203,230,235-6,250,319,357,412,417; A Gomme & D Walker, Architecture of Glasgow, London 1987(rev), 299; Bruce Walker & W S Gauldie, Architects and Architecture on Tayside, Dundee 1984, 74(illus),78-80.

**SMITH, George RSA** **1870-1934**
Born Mid Calder, Midlothian 2 Feb; died Edinburgh 26 Nov. Painter in oil of landscapes and animal subjects, especially scenes involving working horses. Educated George Watson's College, studied art at Board of Manufacturers School, Edinburgh and Antwerp under Verlat. On his return worked in the RSA Life School. Painted many works in Stirling, also in the Hebrides, Holland, Belgium and North Africa. Won gold medal at the Antwerp International Exhibition and was a member of the International Société des Beaux-Arts, Paris 1924. Large works were commissioned by both the King of Italy and the Prince of Bavaria. His paintings had charm, capturing the spirit of the heavy horses as they worked on farms and under dappled sunlight in woodlands. Caw found his work 'effective in design, good in colour and very powerfully painted'. Elected ARSA 1908, RSA 1921. Exhibited RA(5), RSA(128), RHA(3), GI(87), AAS 1896-1931 & L(9). Represented in Aberdeen AG, Glasgow AG(3), Kirkcaldy AG,

Edinburgh City collection, International Gallery of Modern Art, Venice; Chadwick Museum, Bolton; Nuneaton AG, New Zealand.
**Bibl:** Caw 442; RSA Obituary 1934.

**SMITH, George A** **fl 1953-1959**
Aberdeenshire-based amateur landscape painter; exhibited RSA(1) 1953 & AAS(2) including 'Dee above Braemar - winter', from 55 Beach Hill Gdns.

**SMITH, George L** **fl 1890-1906**
Aberdeen painter of landscape and shipping compositions. Exhibited AAS(4) from 151 King St.

**SMITH, Gerald Johnston** **fl 1916-1929**
Edinburgh landscape painter in oil and watercolour; exhibited RSA(8), RSW(1) & GI(2).

**SMITH, Gilbert** **?-1726**
Master Mason at a time when master masons performed also as architects. Son of the master mason James Smith(qv). Appointed King's Master-Mason in Scotland 1715.
**Bibl:** Dunbar 84.

**SMITH, Gregor Ian** **1907-c1985**
Born Helensburgh. Trained Glasgow School of Art, winning a travelling scholarship and the Newbery Medal. Influenced by the Scottish Colourists. His work is characterised by sure but crude, broad brushwork and the chunkiness that is more at home with buildings than living creatures. Has worked as a caricaturist and teacher. Illustrated over a score of children's books. Exhibited RSA(5) 1952-1975 & GI(56) 1952-1984. Lived nr Helensburgh.

**SMITH, Gregor McFarlane RSW** **1944-**
Painter. Trained Edinburgh College of Art 1962-7. Founder member and former chairman, Glasgow League of Artists. Held his first one-man show in Edinburgh 1976. Paints landscape in a semi-abstract manner, generally in watercolour, with an emphasis on colour rather than form. Elected RSW 1983, the same year that he began exhibiting at the RSA, from 14 Muirside Ave, Mount Vernon, Glasgow. Represented in Pecs Cathedral (Hungary), Royal collection.

**SMITH, Miss Helen** **fl 1870**
Landscape painter. One of four Smith sisters who exhibited RSA 1870. A landscape was her only exhibit.

**SMITH, Henry** **fl 1741-1769**
Portrait painter. Active in the 1740s at Wemyss Castle. Painted 'Lady Margaret Wemyss' and 'Elizabeth Clephane, Lady Geddes', both 1740, and 'Lord Murray' 1741. Portraits by him are in the collection of the Duke of Sutherland at Dunrobin. Signed his work in a monogram 'HS' and painted in a style somewhat reminiscent of Highmore. Working in Devonshire 1742. Possibly the same as the 'obscure Norwich portraitist Henry Smith' who died in January 1769 mentioned by Fawcett in '18th Century Art in Norwich' published by the Walpole Society, XLVI (1978), 71-90.
**Bibl:** Wemyss Castle Muniments at SNPG; Farrington Oct 13, 1809.

**SMITH INSTITUTE** **1874-**
Stirling public art gallery. The city gave the site and a local amateur artist/collector, Thomas Stewart Smith(qv), gave the building, his collection of paintings including works by Sam Bough(qv), David Cox, J D Harding, William Hunt and John Phillip(qv), and £22,000 bequeathed under trustees. The building, designed by Lessels, was opened 11th August 1874. Annual exhibitions were held from c1880 but later discontinued.
**Bibl:** Brydall 368; Caw 222.

**SMITH, Miss Isobel** **fl 1950**
Kilmarnock figurative painter. Exhibited GI(1). An **Isobel SMITH** exhibited GI 1975 from Eaglesham, Renfrewshire.

**SMITH, Isobelle Margaret Campbell** **1937-**
Born 25 Feb. Trained Glasgow School of Art. Works in watercolour and mixed medium, developing increasingly towards abstraction. Influenced by Philip Reeves and John Piper. Lives at Balvicar House, by Oban. Exhibits RSA 1960, 1988-9, RSW & GI.

**SMITH, J** **fl c1787-1820**
Edinburgh painter of silhouettes, an art in which he was one of only few Scots to excel (the others being S Houghton(qv) and George Bruce(qv)). Described himself as a 'Hair and Pearl Worker', working in North Bridge St. Member of the Miers(qv) school. In his profiles he aimed at resembling the sitter rather than following the precepts of Miers. probably succeeded Houghton and Mrs Lightfoot as an assistant to Miers 1785, remaining until his departure for London 1788. Returned to Edinburgh a short while later, advertising his services in the *Caledonian Mercury*.
**Bibl:** Arthur Mayne, British Profile Miniaturists, London 1970 62-3 (illus).

**SMITH, J Morrison** **fl 1937-1940**
Glasgow painter of flowers and still life. Exhibited GI(10) from 146 Park Rd.

**SMITH, J Moyr** **fl 1888-1923**
Watercolour painter who came to live at Kilcreggan on the Firth of Clyde in 1911. Exhibited RA(3), RSA(1), RSW(2), GI(3), RBA(3) & L(9).

**SMITH, J Myrtle** **fl 1891-1899**
Montrose painter. Moved to Edinburgh c1899. Exhibited RSA(1).

**SMITH, J R Hunter** **fl 1934**
Glasgow landscape painter. Exhibited RSA(2) & GI(1) from 14 Stirling Ave, Westerton.

**SMITH, J Stewart** **fl 1865-1892**
Edinburgh topographical painter in oil and watercolours. Exhibited RSA(1), GI(5) & L(1) from 2 Hill Street.

**SMITH, J W** **fl 1847-1850**
Edinburgh painter, later moved to Darlington c1850. Produced landscapes and topographical works, including several views on Arran. Exhibited RSA(3).

**SMITH, James** **c1646/7-1731**
Mason and architect. Began working life as a mason, soon becoming a master mason, and eventually one of the most influential Scottish architects of his time, recognised as the 17th century pioneer of 18th century Palladianism. Father of James and Gilbert(qv). Studied originally for the priesthood but left 1675. In 1677 Sir William Bruce singled him out for a special assignment when Smith was master-mason at the remodelling of Holyrood House. In 1698 he, together with his son, was superintending buildings at Hamilton Palace. Between 1679 and 1700 the remodelling of Drumlanrig Castle, Dumfries-shire for the 1st Earl of Queensberry was carried on and it seems that what has been described as the 'exuberant Caroline show-front, enriched with a lavish display of carved ornamental detail', was executed by Smith. After becoming an Edinburgh Burgess 1679 he married the daughter of the King's master mason Robert Mylne(qv). In 1683 appointed overseer of the Royal Works in Scotland, a position held previously by Bruce. He remained in this office for 35 years. Involved in the construction and repair of various Highland garrisons and forts in the years immediately following the Union. Acquired the estate of Whitehill nr Musselburgh for himself and although dismissed from his official position 1719 continued a busy professional life to the end, pursuing a law suit against the Earl of Leven for work done at Melville House when aged 80. Other designs for which he was responsible were the remodelling of Dalkeith House for the Duchess of Buccleuch (1701) and his only major building on Tayside, Melville House, Fife (1697-1701), Ruthven Barracks (in 1718 Smith was Surveyor and Chief Director for carrying on the Barracks in North Britain in which capacity he inspected the site and almost certainly prepared designs for this and probably the forts of Bernera, Fort Augustus and Inversnaid before being dismissed in 1719). The small country mansion built for his own use on his estate, later re-christened New Hailes, has since been greatly extended. His last major building project was the design of Yester House, East Lothian, although the final building was not completed until much later by William and Robert Adam. In this he was joined by a former colleague Alexander Macgill(qv), with whom he had co-operated some time previously over the enlargement of Cullen House, Banffshire. Also responsible for the only Edinburgh church to be

built in the late 17th century, Canongate Church, (1688-91). The fact that its basilican plan is more reminiscent of continental catholicism than of presbyterianism is hardly surprising since Smith was an ardent catholic (credited with having sired 32 children). There is a similarity with the later parish church of Durisdeer, Dumfries-shire, also said to have an association with Smith although to what extent is unclear. Also responsible for the first Mausoleum in the city (c1685-91) built in Greyfriars for Sir George Mackenzie of Rosehaugh, 'the most advanced architectural work of its period in Scotland' [Gifford]; Old Surgeons' Hall (1697); supervised the fitting out of the Thistle Chapel (1687) for James VII.
**Bibl:** Colvin, Howard, 'A Scottish Origina for English Palladianism', Archit. History, xvii, 1974; Dunbar 17,55,61,101-4,125,159, 164; Gifford 38,47,55,66, 128n,149,162,180,186,203, 217, pls 26-7,50; Mylne et passim; Bruce Walker & W S Gauldie, Architects and Architecture on Tayside, Dundee 1984, 50-1; Marcus Binney, 'Don't let the preservation become an excuse for neglect', The Times, 13 Oct 03.

**SMITH, James** **1808-1863**
Born Alloa; died Polmont. Father was a builder, responsible for Alloa parish church (designed by Gillespie Graham(qv)). Moved to Glasgow 1826. In 1837 he took over from his father and entered into partnership with his brother-in-law James Hamilton 1843. The practice failed but after further difficulties became again successful, though overshadowed by the trial for murder of his daughter Madeleine. This forced him to move to Helensburgh; finally retired to Polmont. Responsible for Royal Exchange Square (1850) (with David Hamilton(qv) and A. Elliot) and for the front of McLellan Galleries(1855); also Bellahouston parish church(1863).
**Bibl:** Gifford 154,208; A Gomme & D Walker, Architecture of Glasgow, London 1987(rev), 299-300.

**SMITH, James** **fl 1952-1959**
Glasgow-based painter of informal portraits, still life and flower studies. Exhibited GI(3) from Weir St and latterly Kersland St.

**SMITH, James Mackie** **fl 1885-1901**
Montrose oil painter of rustic scenes. Moved to Glasgow at the turn of the century. Exhibited RSA(5), AAS(2) & GI(1), latterly from 13 Castle Place.

**SMITH, Jamus J K** **20th Cent**
Aberdeen painter of local landscape in watercolour; exhibited AAS (7) from 11 Murray Terrace.

**SMITH, Miss Jane H** **fl 1881-1890**
Edinburgh artist; probably sister of Mary H Smith(qv). Exhibited RSA(2), latterly from 10 Learmonth Terrace.

**SMITH, Mrs Jane Stewart** **1839-1925**
Edinburgh topographical artist and occasional painter of flowers and portraits in oil and watercolour. Worked sometimes on the continent. Author of *The Grange of St Giles* (1898) and *Historic Stones and Stories of Bygone Edinburgh* (1924). Took great care over the accuracy of her compositions, often working between 4 and 8 on summer mornings 'to catch the reverberating echoes of the past as they linger round the old historic buildings'. Exhibited RSA(48) 1866-1876. Some of her original work can be seen in Huntly House where a recently acquired drawing of Holyrood Chapel is among her finest work. Represented also in City of Edinburgh collection which has 60 watercolours of old Edinburgh.
**Bibl:** Butchart 78-9; Halsby 284.

**SMITH, Jervel (?) Barrack** **fl 1959**
Aberdeenshire figure painter; exhibited AAS(1) from the same address as Donald S(qv).

**SMITH, Miss Jessie E B** **fl 1871**
Landscape painter. Sister of E R S(qv). Exhibited a watercolour RSA 1871.

**SMITH, Jim** **fl 1921**
Ayrshire painter of local scenes; exhibited AAS(1), from Kylerigg, Mauchline.

**SMITH, John** **fl 1800-1837**
Edinburgh stipple engraver. Engraved Reynolds' portrait of 'William Hunter, MD'. Not to be confused with English painters and engravers of the same name.
**Bibl:** Bushnell.

**SMITH, John (of Darnoch)** **fl 1817**
Sculptor. According to the *Gentleman's Magazine* (1817, pt I, p621) he was commissioned by Lord Buchan to carve a very large statue of Wallace at Dryburgh 1817.

**SMITH, John ('Tudor Johnny')** **1781-1852**
Aberdeen architect. Son of an Aberdeen builder and father of the architect William S(qv). Spent some time learning his profession in London, developing a penchant for the Tudor style. City architect of Aberdeen for many years, responsible for the 'very pretty little' Town's Schools (1841) and for the graceful North church (1830). Best known for Banchory House, Banchory-Devenick and alterations to old Balmoral Castle for Sir Robert Gordon.
**Bibl:** Dunbar 118-9,152; Fenton Wyness, Royal Valley, 1968, 236, 277-8.

**SMITH, John** **fl 1880-1886**
Aberdeenshire painter in oil and watercolour of landscapes and figure subjects, also coastal and river scenes. Exhibited RSA(6) & AAS(26), latterly from Hunterhill, Old Meldrum & 56 Marischal St.

**SMITH, Mrs John** **fl 1865-1885**
Minor Glasgow sculptor; portrait busts; exhibited AAS(3) & GI(5), from 12 Sandyford Place.

**SMITH, John D** **fl 1979**
Painter. Exhibited AAS(1). (No address).

**SMITH, John Guthrie Spence RSA** **1880-1951**
Born Perth, 14 Feb; died Edinburgh, 22 Oct. Landscape painter in oil and illustrator. Educated at Dundee School for the Deaf and Dumb, and College of Art in Dundee where he gained prizes 1906. Trained Edinburgh School of Art 1908-1910 under Robert Burns(qv) and RSA Schools where he won several prizes. When between two and three years old years old he suffered a severe attack of scarlet fever which rendered him deaf and dumb for the rest of his life. Having a highly developed sense of humour he began to produce caricatures though in adult life these became fewer. Went to France 1911 and 1912 with his mother and made a considerable number of pictures in watercolour many depicting donkeys pulling carts. Participated in the Edinburgh Group exhibitions of 1912 & 1913 and again with the resuscitated group 1919-21. After the outbreak of war 1914 painted at Haddington and Perth, chiefly landscapes notable for their strong sense of colour and their decorative quality. Remained unmarried, spending his last years with William Mervyn Glass(qv). Elected ARSA 1930, RSA 1939. Exhibited RA(1), RSA(83), RSW(3), GI (81), AAS 1912-37 & L(11), latterly from 6 St. Vincent St. Represented City of Edinburgh collection, Brodie Castle (NTS), Perth AG.
**Bibl:** Halsby 193,220,222,284; R H Rodger, J G Spence Smith RSA, Perth AG 1986.

**SMITH, John Maxwell Dalrymple** **1841-1913**
Fraserburgh painter in oil of landscapes and seascapes especially along the Scottish north-east coast. Exhibited RSA(8) & AAS(4) 1893 and again in 1910.

**SMITH, Joseph Calder** **1876-1953**
Born Arbroath. Worked in his home town and Dundee. A competent if rather uninspired artist; exhibited RSA(1) & GI(1), latterly from Motherwell.
**Bibl:** Halsby 284.

**SMITH, Joseph Linden** **1862-fl 1897**
Galashiels watercolour painter; exhibited a moorland landscape at the RSA.

**SMITH, Julia** **fl 1897**
Little known Glasgow flower painter. Exhibited GI(1) from 5 Blythswood Square.

**SMITH, Karen Ann** **fl 1987-1988**
Edinburgh sculptress; exhibits bronzes RSA.

**SMITH, Kenneth** **fl 1700-1707**
Portrait painter. Although English he came to Scotland in 1700 as painter and servant of the Duke of Queensberry (Lord High Commissioner). Petitioned Edinburgh Town Council where it was written he 'brought to Scotland for various noblemen some pictures and frames for staircases and lobbies' and sought permission to auction off the remainder. Stayed in Scotland and in 1707, after being made a Burgess of Edinburgh, was one of several 'distinguished aliens', including Medina(qv), to be naturalised. That year he was lining pictures and copying portraits of Queen Mary for the Duchess of Buccleuch.
**Bibl:** Apted, 89; Edinburgh Burgh Records 1689-1701, 272; Acts Parl. Scot., xi, 485; Macmillan [SA] 81.

**SMITH, Knud** **c1670-?**
Painter. Little is known of this obscure artist, son of Andrew Lawrenson S(qv). According to Benezit he was born in Stavanger, where his father lived and worked, and died in Scotland. A portrait of his brother Lauritz S is in Oslo Museum of Industrial Art.
**Bibl:** Benezit.

**SMITH, Leonard Findlay** **fl 1978-1984**
Aberdeen jewellery and metalwork designer. Trained Gray's School of Art, Aberdeen. Exhibited AAS during the above period.

**SMITH, Leonard John** **1885-1958**
Born Newport-on-Tay, Tayside; died Sussex. Painter and etcher; figure studies, often of sporting activities such as boxing, skating, athletics; also nudes. Grandson of Sir John Leng, Lib MP for Dundee. Studied in Toronto, Canada and New York. His work is delicately delineated with minimal line, in the mould of James McBey(qv), though less subtle. Illustrated for magazines including *Punch, Pall Mall, Gaiety.* Built Windyshields Links, nr Seafield, East Sussex. Exhibited RSA(2) 1928-39 & L(3) from London and latterly from Windyshields.

**SMITH, Leonora B** **fl 1888-d1921**
Glasgow oil painter of figures and flowers; also portrait miniatures on ivory. Lived for a time in Argyll, then Glasgow. Exhibited RSA (7) & GI(10).

**SMITH, Lesley N** **fl 1912-1930**
Stirlingshire artist of Allanbank, Bridge of Allan; linocut miniatures. Exhibited GI(1) and elsewhere in the provinces.

**SMITH, Lizzie Elmslie** **fl 1887**
Aberdeen amateur flower painter; exhibited AAS(1) from Summerhill.

**SMITH, Miss M Campbell** **fl 1885-1887**
Edinburgh painter of country subjects; exhibited AAS(6), from 27 Lauder Rd.

**SMITH, Miss Madeline** **fl 1870**
Painter. One of four sisters who exhibited at the RSA the same year; showed two river scenes.

**SMITH, M M** **fl 1897**
Edinburgh amateur painter; exhibited a townscape at the AAS from 21 Napier Rd.

**SMITH, Marian** **1951-**
Born Kelso. Painter, mainly in oil, of still life. Trained Edinburgh College of Art. Lives and works in Edinburgh. Represented in Edinburgh City collection.

**SMITH, Marjorie R** **fl 1931-1945**
Edinburgh painter of figure studies, genre and domestic animals; ; exhibited RSA(9) from 22 Inverleith Gardens.

**SMITH, Miss Mary** **fl 1870-1884**
Edinburgh flower and landscape painter; one of four sisters working from the Canongate. Exhibited RSA in the 1870s and 1880s.

**SMITH, Mrs Mary H** **fl 1879-1900**
Edinburgh painter in oil and watercolour, landscape, figure subjects and flower pieces. Related to Jane S(qv). Exhibited RSA(8) from Raeburn Place.

**SMITH, Matthew** **fl 1886-1888**
Glasgow painter of 131 Anfield Street, Denistoun; moved to Edinburgh 1888. Exhibited flowers, landscapes and town scenes at the RSA(4).

**SMITH, Nathaniel L** **fl 1946-1965**
Glasgow painter, principally in watercolour. Flowers, still life and topography. Exhibited GI(7).

**SMITH, Miss Nellie Gordon** **fl 1893-1896**
Aberdeen painter of still life and portraits; exhibited AAS(6) from 32 St. Swithin's St.

**SMITH O Ramage** **fl 1905**
Amateur Glasgow portrait miniaturist. Exhibited GI(1) from Cambuslang.

**SMITH, O S** **fl 1891**
Minor painter of Meadow View, Lenzie, Nr Glasgow; exhibited at the GI(1).

**SMITH, Olive** **fl 1966**
Edinburgh-based painter; exhibited a still life at the RSA from Cammo Hill.

**SMITH, Paul** **fl 1859**
Edinburgh painter of figurative studies; exhibited RSA(2) from St. David St.

**SMITH, Paul L** **fl 1972**
Edinburgh sculptor; exhibited 4-piece group at the RSA from East Hermitage Pl.

**SMITH, Peggy L** **fl 1938**
Amateur painter of View Park, East Newport, Fife; exhibited RSA(1).

**SMITH, Peter** **fl 1888**
Obscure Edinburgh painter; exhibited RSA(1) from 2 Queen's Stt.

**SMITH, Peter** **fl 1908-1912**
Aberdeen painter of local landscape; exhibited AAS(5) from 56 Holburn St.

**SMITH, Phyllis** **fl 1927**
Amateur Edinburgh sculptress of 30 Alva Street; exhibited a bronze bust at the RSA.

**SMITH, Mrs R A** **fl 1873-1885**
Edinburgh painter in oil and watercolour of portraits, figure subjects and flower pieces. Exhibited RSA(9) from 27 Raeburn Place.

**SMITH, R C** **fl 1847-1865**
Edinburgh painter of landscape and church interiors. Moved to Durham and thence to Surrey. Exhibited RSA(7) including views of Arran and the borders and the interior of Durham cathedral.

**SMITH, R G Edington** **fl 1893-1937**
Glasgow landscape and country genre painter who spent a short time in the 1900s at 75 Buccleuch St, Dumfries before returning to Glasgow. Exhibited RSA(3), AAS 1900-1906, GI(5) & L(1).

**SMITH, Miss Rachel M** **fl 1965**
Edinburgh watercolourist. Exhibited 'Bowl of Roses' at the GI.

**SMITH, Raymond Maynard** **fl 1893**
Amateur painter of 7 Ashton Place, Dowanhill, Glasgow; exhibited 'Head of a donkey' at the GI.

**SMITH, Richard A** **fl 195-1957**
Glasgow painter in watercolour and gouache. Continental and British topography. Exhibited GI(6), from Walnut Crescent.

**SMITH, Robert Turnbull Haig** **1938-**
Born Dunfermline. Edinburgh-based abstract painter principally in oil and educational administrator. Trained Edinburgh College of Art. Exhibited RSA(6) 1963-1965 from Nether Lennie Farmhouse. Represented in SAC.

**SMITH, Ronald F RGI** **fl 1969-**
Glasgow painter of marine and harbour scenes, often in the Mediterranean. Elected RGI 1999. Exhibits GI(29) since 1969, latterly from 60 Abbey Drive.

**SMITH, S B Elliot** **fl 1889-1893**
Edinburgh painter of landscape and country subjects; exhibited RSA(2) & AAS(2) from 47 Inverleith Row.

**SMITH, S Catterson** **fl 1872-1882**
Glasgow painter of pastoral scenes. Moved to Dublin 1880. Exhibited GI(6).

**SMITH, Sally** **fl 1970-1983**
Edinburgh sculptress; exhibited RSA 1970 and 1983.

**SMITH, Samuel** **1888-c1940**
Born Glasgow, 5 May. Painter in oil and watercolour and etcher; mainly landscape and topography. Trained Glasgow School of Art. Lived in Glasgow. Exhibited 1927-32 RA(1), RSA(8), GI(7) & L(2). Represented in Brodie Castle (NTS), Leith Hall (NTS).

**SMITH, Miss Sarah Adams** **fl 1881**
Minor Edinburgh flower painter of 10 Duncan Street, Drummond Place. Exhibited RSA(1).

**SMITH, Sidney** **fl 1885**
Amateur Glasgow painter of 10 Smith Street, Hillhead; exhibited a watercolour of a local scene at the RSA.

**SMITH, Mrs Stewart** **fl 1869-1882**
Edinburgh painter of landscape and topographical scenes. Exhibited GI(3).

**SMITH, Sydney Goodsir** **fl 1947-1958**
Edinburgh landscape painter; exhibited 9 works at the RSA, most of Wester Ross.

**SMITH, Thomas** **fl 1744**
Edinburgh engraver. Engraved a map of the Lothians 1744.
**Bibl:** Bushnell.

**SMITH, Thomas** **fl 1912-1919**
Minor Glasgow painter of 152 St Vincent Lane; exhibited GI(3) & L(5).

**SMITH, Thomas B** **fl 1918-1945**
Paisley painter of the sea and coastline. Moved to Cardonald, Glasgow c1935. Exhibited RSA(4), GI(6) & L(4), latterly from Oldhall, Paisley.

**SMITH, Thomas Stuart** **1815-1869**
Born Stirling; died Avignon, Dec 31. Studied in Italy. Of uncertain parentage, his early working life was spent in Nottingham where he built up a successful practice as a portrait painter. According to a local report his first exhibit at the Royal Academy was entitled 'The Monk's Welcome' shown in 1850 and subsequently purchased by the artist's benefactor Professor Owen, but the RA catalogue contains no reference such a work; however, the artist executed a replica now in Stirling AG. Of the original, Sir William Stirling Maxwell wrote that the work "was so great a favourite of the late Sir Edwin Landseer that he never visited him (Owen) without taking it down from the wall and examining it with new expressions of admiration for the masterly qualities of the work". In 1856 the Crown granted Smith the estates of Glassingall and Canglour as his rightful inheritance. These he sold shortly afterwards to enjoy again a career as an artist, untrammelled by the cares of running a country estate. Returned to England taking up residence at 35 Fitzroy Square, painting, collecting and becoming friendly with many English artists of the time such as John Orrock who said "Mr Smith was the best and clearest demonstrator...of interpreting nature by the art of oil painting I have ever known; and his method was perhaps as perfect as it could be, for it was founded upon the best methods of the greatest painters, ancient and modern". In addition to Landseer(qv), other contemporary artists to applaud the work of this almost forgotten artist included Ruskin(qv), George Cole and John Phillip(qv). Died suddenly whilst on holiday in France. Unmarried and without heirs, he bequeathed his considerable collection, as well as c140 of his own works, to found what became the Smith AG & Museum, Stirling(qv). In addition to at least one exhibit at the RA, 'A Fellah of Kinneh' 1869, now in the Smith AG, he exhibited two interiors at the RSA from Dunblane.
**Bibl:** Smith Institute, Anon., Cat, 'Memoir of Thomas Stuart Smith', Stirling, 1934.

**SMITH, Tom** **fl 1914-1943**
Edinburgh watercolourist. Painted buildings in Scotland, England and Holland. Exhibited RSA(7) & RSW(7). Represented in City of Edinburgh collection by a watercolour of 'Bakehouse Close, Edinburgh'.
**Bibl:** Halsby 284.

**SMITH, Tom** **fl 1975**
Aberdeen painter; exhibited 'Jaguar' at the AAS, from 26 Bank St.

**SMITH, Walter B** **fl 1856-1878**
Edinburgh oil painter of portraits and landscapes including continental scenes; exhibited RSA(12).

**SMITH, William** **fl 1818-1829**
Montrose architect. St John's Free Church, Montrose (1829) is attributed to him, also an upper storey to Hutcheson's Palladian Town House, Montrose (1763-4).
**Bibl:** Bruce Walker & W S Gauldie, Architects and Architecture on Tayside, Dundee 1984, 80.

**SMITH, William** **fl 1850**
Ayrshire painter; exhibited 'The birth of Burns' at the RSA from Mauchline.

**SMITH, William (A)** **1754-c1795**
Miniaturist and portrait painter. Entered the RA Schools 1772 and exhibited RA 1774. Exhibited the half-length miniature portrait of a lady and two other miniatures at the RA in 1774 and a miniature of 'Major Drummond' in 1802. Occasional larger works exemplified by 'Sportsman with Dog and Game' 1791 which measured 49 in x 39ins. Painted portraits of 'Alexander, 4th Duke of Gordon' and three of the 'Countess of Westmoreland', one on ivory. Foskett refers to three examples all signed differently: 'WS /1780'; 'W A Smith 1791'; 'W/ A Smith 1791' and another of the same Duke signed 'W Smith delint, 1782'. The NGS has three watercolours, two signed 'W A Smith' and dated 1790. Represented in Brodie Castle (NTS), Leith Hall (NTS).
**Bibl:** Foskett 523; Long 413.

**SMITH, William** **1817-1891**
Aberdeenshire architect and designer. Son of 'Tudor Johnny' Smith(qv), architect of Sir Robert Gordon's additions to old Balmoral. Father of Garden Smith(qv) and the author Charles Smith. Aberdeen city architect. Now best known for Balmoral Castle (1853) and the spire of Aberdeen's Mither Kirk. Produced a number of Gothic buildings including a replacement spire for St. Nicholas's church (1878-80) and a block in Union St (1846). It was the latter's impression on Prince Albert that supposedly led to Smith being commissioned to design the new Balmoral. William Kelly(qv) was his best known pupil. Lived for many years in Banchory, Kincardineshire.
**Bibl:** Dunbar 152; Fenton Wyness, Royal Valley, 1968, 236, 279.

**SMITH, William snr** **fl 1891-1901**
Edinburgh painter of animals, genre and landscape. Father of William S(qv). Exhibited RSA(7) & GI(3).

**SMITH, William jnr** **1865-1941**
Painter in oil and watercolour of figure subjects, country scenes, landscape and genre; also engraver and illustrator. Son of William S(qv); had his portrait painted by John Phillip(qv) of which he himself executed a mezzotint which was exhibited at the RSA.

Illustrated *Deeside* (1911) and S R Crockett's *Abbotsford.* Lived at 1 Ramsay Gdns, Edinburgh in 1889 and Aberdeen 1896; exhibited RA(1), RSA (8), AAS(10) & GI(3), latterly from 46 Holburn Rd. There may have been a third **William SMITH** painting in Aberdeen at the same time.
**Bibl:** Caw 469.

**SMITH, William James** **fl 1920-1937**
Glasgow architect and watercolour painter. Exhibited GI(6) including a design for Canadian national war memorial 1926.

**SMITH, William Ryle** **1862-1945**
Broughty Ferry art teacher and watercolourist. Uncle of Sir William Gillies(qv). Exhibited locally.
**Bibl:** Halsby 211,284.

**SMYLIE, Ernest K** **fl 1912-1913**
Amateur Glasgow sculptor. Figurative works, often in plaster. Exhibited GI(3), from 591 Alexandra Parade, Dennistoun.

**SMYTH, Miss Dorothy Carleton** **1880-1933**
Born Glasgow. Irish/French parentage with family connections in Fife. Painter in oil, watercolour and pastel of figures and portraits, also costume designer, illustrated several books. Lifelong attraction to exotic clothes led her naturally to an interest in the theatre and dramatic costume. Sister of Olive Carleton S(qv). Began her art training in Manchester but transferred to Glasgow School of Art under Fra Newbery(qv) 1898-1905. During her student days became interested in stage design, spending some time as designer and producer in Stockholm and Paris. Her stained glass window 'Tristan and Iseult' was exhibited at the Glasgow 1901 Exhibition. The following year a Glaswegian doctor commissioned two portraits and an anonymous well-wisher sponsored an overseas study tour resulting in an extended stay in Florence. Then spent several years in Paris and Stockholm designing and producing for the stage. In 1910 she designed the costumes for several London productions and in 1914 worked with Granville Barker on his production of 'A Midsummer Night's Dream', her costumes (influenced by Leon Bakst) receiving more attention than the performance. Commissioned to design and superintend the making of costumes for the world tour of the Quinlan Opera Company, the Frank Benson Shakespearean Company and Glasgow Rep Theatre. Contributed illustrations for de luxe editions of Kipling, Shakespeare and Stevenson. Also designed carvings in stone for Greenock War Memorial. Taught GSA 1914-33 and selected as successor to John Revel(qv) as Director of the School but died before she could take up the appointment. Broadcast talks to children on BBC under the name 'Paint Box Pixie'. Exhibited RA(1), RSA(1), GI(10), L(3) and regularly from 1902 with the Glasgow Society of Lady Artists. Represented in V & A, Glasgow AG.
**Bibl:** Bulletin, 16 Feb 1933 (obit); Burkhauser 167-9, 171-2; Glasgow Herald, 16 Feb 1933 (obit); Halsby 284; Houfe; Studio, winter no, 1900-01, 55; vol 25, 1901-2, 281-286.

**SMYTH, James** **fl 1920-1944**
Edinburgh painter in watercolour and oil of landscape and flower studies, also teacher. Assistant design master, Edinburgh College of Art. Exhibited RSW(10), RSA(13) & L(5).
**Bibl:** Halsby 284.

**SMYTH, John** **c1968-**
Figurative painter, mainly in oils. Trained Gray's School of Art 1995-2000. Influenced by Joyce Cairns(qv). Enjoys depicting the human figure, both male and female, in unusual semi-nude poses. One man exhibitions in Aberdeen & Edinburgh. Winner of David Gordon Memorial Trust Award 2002. Exhibits RSA.

**SMYTH, John Talfourd** **1819-1851**
Born and died Edinburgh. Engraver. Trained Trustees Academy and under Sir William Allan(qv), although mainly self-taught. Went to Glasgow 1838 but returned to Edinburgh shortly before his death. Among his best engravings are 'Knox distributing the Lord's Supper' (after Wilkie), 'Tartars dividing their Booty' (after Allan) and 'The Last in' (after Mulready).
**Bibl:** Bryan.

**SMYTH, Margaret Learmond** **1961-**
Born 30 Apr. Painter in gouache, acrylic, oil, charcoal and pastel. Trained Edinburgh College of Art 1979-84. Elected SSA 1987. Held solo exhibition in Edinburgh 1985 followed by another in Greenock 1986 and Pittenweem 1988-9. Since 1985 has been art teacher, St Leonard's School, St Andrews. Exhibits regularly RSA, RSW & SSA from her home in Pittenweem.

**SMYTH, Miss Olive Carleton** **1882-1949**
Born Glasgow, 11 Dec; died Cambuslang. Painter in oil, watercolour and gouache of portraits and figure subjects; also illuminator, decorator, designer, gesso and fresco artist. Sister of Dorothy Carleton S(qv), with whom she remained close throughout their days; friend and associate of De Courcy Dewar(qv). Like her sister, she developed an early interest for the theatre and in 1906 assisted the American actress Mrs Ross Whytell in organising shows in Glasgow for the benefit of the survivors of the San Francisco earthquake. Trained Glasgow School of Art 1900-1909, joining the staff there 1902-14 and, following the death of her sister, becoming head of design 1933. Exhibited Turin 1902. Joined Glasgow Society of Lady Artists 1905. Her early work 'shares an affinity with that of the Viennese Secessionist Gustav Klimt in the employment of jewel-like highlights, and in shared design motifs particularly the Japanese inspired use of patterned clothing as a design element' [Burkhauser]. Early watercolours were in a visionary style that have been compared to Nora Nielson Gray(qv). Subsequently influenced by Chinese brush drawing in a naive, rather stylised manner. In 1917 her exhibit at the exhibition of the 'Foire de Lyon' in France of a Celtic subject, 'The Two Hunters of Terg Thoun', was the only British work shown. Exhibited RA(9), RSA(9), RSW(3), RHA(3), GI(19), AAS, L(11) & Paris Salon. Represented in Nat. Gall of Canada (Ottawa), Glasgow AG, Paisley AG.
**Bibl:** Burkhauser 73,75,170-2 (illus).

**SNEDDON, Andrew** **fl 1988-**
Glasgow abstract painter. Exhibited GI(1) from Crathie Drive.

**SNEDDON, Carol Anne** **fl 1983-**
Aberdeenshire jewellery designer; trained Gray's School of Art, Aberdeen. Exhibits AAS since 1983 from Milton of Crathes Studios, Crathes.

**SNEDDON, John Douglas** **fl 1980-**
Bo'ness painter and engraver. Exhibits RSA, from 5 Hope Cottages, Muirhouses.

**SNELL, Robert** **fl 1923**
Lived at Stell, Kirkcudbright; exhibited Walker Gallery, Liverpool (1).

**SNELLING, Julian** **fl 1966-1967**
Midlothian painter of figurative works; exhibited RSA(3) from Stow.

**SNODGRASS, J B** **fl 1940**
Minor Glasgow watercolourist; exhibited GI(2) from 148 Saracen St.

**SNODGRASS, Jane (or Jame)** **fl 1841**
Stranraer artist; exhibited 'The vacant chair' at the RSA.

**SNODGRASS, Robert Nisbet** **fl 1927-1953**
Glasgow painter and etcher of buildings and interiors; exhibited RSA(11), AAS(2) & GI(13) from 983 Sauchiehall St, latterly Glasgow School of Art.

**SNOWDEN, Michael Alan RSA** **1930-**
Born Lincolnshire. Sculptor, figurative subjects. After his national service he attended Teacher Training College at York and then studied at Camberwell School of Art specialising in sculpture under Karel Vogel. Until 1962 member of staff at Camberwell and in 1964 joined Edinburgh College of Art. In 1965-72 was a member of the SAC lecture panel. Best known for his sensuous interpretation of the human figure. Most works have a monumental quality, even the smallest pieces. The first solo exhibition was at Leicester Galleries 1971. Commissions include work at Southwark Cathedral, Livingstone New Town, and an 8 ft bronze group 'Mother and child' for Cumbernauld New Town. In Edinburgh he sculpted 'Baptized Christ' (1968) for Craiglockhart Coll. of Education. Elected ARSA 1974, RSA 1985. Exhibits regularly RSA & RA.

**SOCIETY OF EIGHT** **1912-19**
Edinburgh group of like-minded established artists tending to the use of bright colour. Held an opening exhibition at the New Gallery, 12 Shandwick Place. Foundation members were P W Adam, David Alison (the only one originally associated with the Edinburgh Group), F C B Cadell, James Cadenhead, John Lavery, Harrington Mann, James Paterson and A G Sinclair. By 1919 - the year the parallel Edinburgh Group(qv) was reconstituted - W Y MacGregor had replaced Harrington Mann who was in turn replaced about six years later by Peploe. Subsequent members included John Duncan, W G Gillies, Lintott, Archibald McGlashan and William MacTaggart. Members were allowed to show 20 works each at the annual exhibition while sculptors such as Percy Portsmouth were invited as guest exhibitors.
**Bibl:** Hardie 142.

**SOCIETY OF INCORPORATED ARTISTS** **1808-1813**
Sometimes referred to as the Society of Associated Artists. A group of artists trained Trustees Academy and under Alexander Nasmyth(qv). The Society was founded for the purpose of mounting exhibitions of their work. Apart from the Foulis Academy(qv), this was the first organisation of its kind in Scotland, attempts to form an academy having been made by Nasmyth in 1791, 1794 and 1797. The inaugural exhibition of 178 works was highly successful and included miniatures by William Douglas, chalk and medallion heads by John Henning and work by Alexander Carse, Alexander and Patrick Nasmyth, John Thomson, Patrick Syme, James Foulis, J. Woolford, William Findlater, James Stevenson, J. Brooks, John Beugo, J Morrison, Alexander Galloway, James Howe, Walter Weir, Peter Gibson, John Moir, Nathaniel Plimer, W H Lizars, Michael Morrison and R Morrison. George Watson was elected first President. A second exhibition opened 20 May, 1809 with 48 artists including Raeburn represented and almost 500 guineas taken at the door. This, and the two exhibitions that followed, were held in Raeburn's studio, 32 York Place. Success stimulated the establishment of a life class and in 1812, with Raeburn having been elected the year before, the fifth and final exhibition was held. 209 works were presented by 68 artists. The Society had accumulated over £1600 and a shopkeeper called Core had presented the artists with a building of their own, later known as the Lyceum. But in 1813, under the presidency of Raeburn, a majority of members, wishing to divide the funds among themselves, called for dissolution. In spite of an attempt by Raeburn, Beugo, Foulis, Galloway, Henning, Alexander Nasmyth and Watson to annul the resolution, the Society was duly dissolved. 'Had their efforts been successful, the Society might now have been one of the richest and most influential public bodies in Scotland, and the later contentions between the Royal Institution and the Scottish Academy would never have occurred' [Brydall].
**Bibl:** Brydall 324-7; Alexander Campbell, A Journey from Edinburgh through Parts of North Britain etc, London 1810, 276; Irwin 186,189,190-1,215; Esme Gordon, The Royal Scottish Academy, Edinburgh 1976, 4-12; Macmillan [SA] 161-2.

**SOCIETY OF SCOTTISH ARTISTS** **1891-**
Founded 16th February, 1891 at a meeting in the Albert Hotel, Edinburgh with Robert Noble in the chair. Its declared aims were 'to induce younger artists to produce more important and original works by providing opportunities to display them and to procure educative examples of modern and past art on loan for purposes of exhibition'. Open to both professional and 'ordinary' members who compete on equal terms for places in the annual exhibition and in the election of office-bearers 'to represent the more adventurous spirits in Scottish Art'. Sections are divided into painting, sculpture, architecture and applied art. Originally women were only eligible for membership as 'honorary lay members' but this was later changed to allow full professional status. Based in Edinburgh but with wide geographical representation across the country, until WW2 the Society included in its annual exhibition distinguished foreign artists such as Munch, Paul Klee, Paul Nash and Rodin. Craft work is incorporated in its exhibitions and in 1984 photography was included in the annual exhibition for the first time. Although a progressive outlook has subsequently been retained, the Society has become increasingly an exhibiting vehicle for young Scottish painters.
**Bibl:** Caw 211; Hardie 142; Cordelia Oliver, *The First 100 Years*, SSA 1988.

**SOCIETY OF SCOTTISH WOMEN ARTISTS** **1924-1990**
Founded by Lily McDougall's(qv) father William, 'to give encouragement and opportunity to women artists'. The first President was W H McDougall. Originally there were professional and lay members, the former limited to women only, the latter being open to both sexes. A third category, that of associate members, was later added. Professional members were divided into three sections: painting, sculpture and crafts with associates being limited to women under 25. The major awards were Anne Redpath prize for Painting and the Lily McDougall Open award. In the 1940s standards fell until Anne Redpath assumed the Presidency in 1944. From 1983 candidates for professional membership had to be nominated by two professional members. Thereafter submitted work was voted upon before the opening of the annual exhibition. From 1946 the annual exhibition was always held at the RSA with one other held annually outside Edinburgh; in 1985 this was taken outside Scotland, to Bristol. In 1990 the Society was replaced by the Scottish Artists and Artist Craftsmen(qv).
**Bibl:** Patrick Bourne, Anne Redpath, Edinburgh 1989 passim.

**SOEBORG, Knud Christian** **1861-1906**
Born Viborg, May 31; died Copenhagen, 4 Sep. Norwegian painter of portraits and interiors; also illustrator and writer. Trained Copenhagen Academy. Brother of the artist Axel S. Lived for a short time in Glasgow before moving to London c1897. Exhibited RA(1) & GI(2).

**SOHNS, Frederick** **fl 1878-1901**
Edinburgh-based painter of Nahant Villa, Juniper Green. Worked in oil and watercolour, landscapes, topographical subjects. Exhibited RSA(34) including 'The Old Bridge at Cramond' 1887 and 'The Ancient Church of St Jacob, Thom, Poland' 1898, also GI(1).

**SOMERVILLE, Alec P** **fl 1932-d1948**
Glasgow amateur watercolourist of 40 Langside Drive; mainly west coast topographical. Exhibited RSW(1) & GI(21).

**SOMERVILLE, Alexander** **fl 1898**
Edinburgh landscape painter in oil; exhibited 'The Maas from Dordrecht' at the RSA from 32 Hillside Street.

**SOMERVILLE, Andrew RSA** **1808-1834**
Born Edinburgh; died Edinburgh, Jan. Painter in oil, landscapes and figure subjects. Son of a wire-worker. Educated Royal HS, studied art under William Simson(qv) until Simson went to London 1825. Fascinated by the border ballads. First exhibited at the Institution for the Encouragement of Fine Arts in 1826, a chalk portrait of a young gentleman. Continued to exhibit at the Institute and its successors a total of 27 works before his premature death at the age of 26, long before his talent could be fully expressed. His best known works are 'Bride of Yarrow' 1833, 'Cottage Children' in the NGS, and a humorous 'Donnybrook Fair' 1834. Elected ARSA 1831, RSA 1832. Represented in NGS.
**Bibl:** Bryan; Brydall 466; Caw 120.

**SOMERVILLE, Charles** **1870-1939**
Born Falkirk 29 Jly; died, Fox House, Wigginton, Herts, May 9. Painter of landscape, figure and portraits in oil and watercolour, also teacher. Father of Stuart Scott S(qv) and Margaret Scott(qv). Educated Falkirk Academy but completely self-taught in art except for short periods with the landscape painter William Tindall. Left Scotland as a young man, married Ann Otley 1894 but, after having three children, his wife died tragically young and in 1905 he married Rose Ann Chantrey by whom he had six children. Founder of Doncaster Art Club, and friend of Joseph Crawhall(qv) with whom he worked. Patronised by the Garter King of Arms, Sir Alfred Scott-Gattie. Exhibited RSA, RHA(2) 1908-29, in London and the provinces.

**SOMERVILLE, Daniel** **c1780-1834**
Born Dalkeith. Engraver, etcher and watercolour artist, also worked in pencil and was a teacher. Specialised in views of Edinburgh. Started as a line engraver and pencil artist, living 1825-32 at 7 St James's Square. Concentrated on fine book illustrations and topographical plates, all executed with a wonderful eye for detail. In 1817 published 'Sixteen Original Sketches of Edinburgh', followed in 1826 by '30 Drawings', drawn meticulously and attractively. Sir Daniel Wilson

used them when preparing his *Memorials of Edinburgh.* Somerville was also an experimenter and several of his copper plates can be seen in Lady Stair's House, Lawnmarket, Edinburgh. *The Print Collector's Quarterly* (1934) referred to 'a Sketch from a Mutilated Bass Relief drawn and executed on marble by corroding away the lights surrounding the lines, and printed on the surface in the manner of the letterpress prints of the early engravers,' by Daniel Somerville, Edinburgh 1818. That Somerville's exhibits were considered important can be gleaned from the fact that whereas descriptions of the works of the great majority of exhibitors are accorded a single line his entry occupied a full page, yet his name and the inventions to which he laid claim seem to have been omitted from the records of the art of lithography. By 1833 he had moved to 5 St James's Square and the same year was elected an Associate of the Royal Institution. Two of his works were exhibited posthumously at the RSA 1887, 'The Weigh-House Edinburgh', the property of the Lord Justice General and - also his property - 'Bakehouse Close, Edinburgh'. Represented in NGS (2 pencil sketches); City of Edinburgh collection.
**Bibl:** Brydall 213; Bushnell; Butchart 47-8; J.C. Guy, 'Edinburgh Engravers' in The Book of the Old Edin Club, vol 9, 1916; Halsby 284.

**SOMERVILLE, Howard** **1873-1952**
Born Dundee; died Bristol 2 Jly. Painter of portraits, interiors, still life and figure subjects in oil and sketches of women in ink; also etcher. After a private education studied science and engineering at Dundee Technical College. Became an engineer but gave this up in favour of art. Settled in London 1899 and began to contribute to *Punch* and other magazines. Then moved to Glasgow and on to New York before returning in 1899 to London. Elected RPE 1917. Exhibited principal London Galleries, in the provinces and Paris Salon where he won a silver medal 1928. Contributed to *Moonshine* (1900), *Punch* (1903-6) & *ILN* (1911). Exhibited RA(14), RSA(8), GI(28), L(17) & LS(14). Represented in SNPG, Walker Gallery (Liverpool).
**Bibl:** Houfe.

**SOMERVILLE, James** **fl 1962-1969**
Fife painter who moved from Glenrothes to Edentown by Ladybank in the mid-1960s. Exhibited RSA(2).

**SOMERVILLE, John Whyte** **fl 1902-d1916**
Painter in oils and watercolour of animals, informal portraits and figure studies, also the occasional landscape. Lived in Glasgow until moving to Dalkeith c1911, to Edinburgh 1912 and finally to Heriot 1915. Founder member of the Edinburgh Group. Killed in action Jne 22, 1916. Exhibited RA(2), RSA(13), RSW(2) & GI(1).

**SOMERVILLE, Miss Margaret (Peggy) Scott** **1918-1975**
Born Old Ford Farm, Ashford, Middlesex, Jne 2. Painter in oil and watercolour of landscapes, flower pieces and figure subjects. Youngest daughter of Charles(qv), sister of Stuart S(qv). Trained under her father and RA Schools. Lived in East Anglia for many years. Exhibited Royal Drawing Society at the age of three, and Royal Hibernian Academy when she was only seven. Held her first solo exhibition in the Claridge Gallery when she was nine (1928), repeated the following year. When she was twelve, Sickert noticed her and encouraged her to attend the RSA Schools. Basically a naturalistic artist equally at home in all mediums painting genre, landscapes, still life and seascapes. The strongest influence on her work was nature itself. Moved to East Anglia in the early 1930s and apart from a short period in Hertfordshire just before and after WW2 remained in Suffolk until her death. Eric Sandon wrote of her 'we know at once that we are in the presence of a mystic for whom reality does not cease at the outward appearance of things but must be sought in the essence that hides beneath the shape...for her there is no need to invent a new language of forms that are outside those of nature, because nature is filled with magical depths unplumbed except by the poet and the painter...it is this insight into the heart of things that gives especial tension to her vibrant forms and luminous colours. Above all, it is this which gives her work the objective timelessness of true art, isolating it from all that is transitory, facile or merely cerebral'. Several posthumous exhibitions including at the Aldeburgh Festival 1977, Ipswich AG 1997 and at the David Messum gallery (London). Exhibited ROI(2). Represented in Norwich Castle Museum, Norfolk AG (Virginia).
**Bibl:** John Somerville (personal communication); Stephen Reisas, 'The Child Art of Peggy Somerville', Herbert Press 1990; Stephen Reisas, 'Peggy Somerville: an English Impressionist', Antique Collectors' Club 1996.

**SOMERVILLE, Nicol** **fl 1735-d1770**
Edinburgh painter. Elected Burgess of Edinburgh 1739 and from 1740-42 a member of the Incorporation of St Mary's. Had as apprentices D Lindsay 1745, John Cochrane 1762, James Boyd 1766 and William Simpson 1770.

**SOMERVILLE, Mrs Robert** **fl 1882**
Dalkeith oil painter of flower pieces; exhibited RSA(1).

**SOMERVILLE, Stuart Scott** **1908-1983**
Born Arksey, nr Doncaster, Feb 6; died Suffolk. Painter in oil of portraits, flowers, still life, interiors, figures and landscape. Third son of Charles S(qv), brother of Margaret S(qv). Studied art under his father. Became known for his flower pieces. 1934/5 was spent in East Africa where he was the official artist with the Oxford and Cambridge University expedition, sponsored also by the British Museum and Royal Geographical Society, to the Ruwenzori mountains. Upon returning spent some time in Paris where he exhibited. Married 1942 and three years later moved from Cornwall to Suffolk. It is not widely known that he worked quite extensively in watercolour, pastel and chalk painting landscape, abstract works and nudes but these he never sought to sell. Exhibited 1925-26 RA(10), RSA(1), ROI(12), RHA(4) & L(2).
**Bibl:** John Somerville (personal communication); Rosamund Somerville, Mountains of the Moon; Stuart Scott Somerville, Ex Cat, Bernheimer Fine Arts, London, May 1990; Patrick Synge, Mountains of the Moon, Drummond, London 1937.

**SOMERVILLE, Ward O** **fl 1964-1968**
Glasgow painter of still life, dead game and pastoral scenes. Exhibited GI(5).

**SOMERVILLE, William** **fl 1940-1958**
Minor Glasgow topographical watercolourist; exhibited GI(5) from 29 Lawnmoor St. and latterly Castlemilk Drive.

**SOMMERVILLE, Isabella** **fl 1901**
Glasgow artist. Landscape and flower studies. Exhibited GI(2) from Mossfield, Maxwell Park.

**SOMMERVILLE, John** **fl 1840**
Edinburgh artist; exhibited 'George IV's first approach to Holyrood' in 1822 at the RSA, from Brunswick St.

**SOMMERVILLE, Tom** **fl 1829**
Edinburgh amateur landscape painter; exhibited a view of the Firth of Forth at the RSA, from Rose St.

**SOUDEN, Miss E B** **fl 1929**
Minor watercolour painter of Mount Rideau, North Berwick; exhibited RSW(1).

**SOUTAR, Charles G** **fl 1940**
Dundee architect and painter. Exhibited GI(2).

**SOUTAR, Hamish Ferguson** **fl 1960-1973**
Dundee artist; exhibited RSA(2)) & GI(15), mostly watercolour landscapes.

**SOUTAR, Hilda M** **fl 1940**
Little known Dundee painter of flowers and topographical studies; possibly related to Hamish S(qv). Exhibited RSA(3) from 85 Magdalen Yard Road.

**SOUTER, George** **fl 1885-1908**
Elgin watercolour painter of landscape; exhibited RSA(6), AAS(5) & L(2), from Rose Cottage.

**SOUTER, John Bulloch** **1890-1972**
Born Aberdeen; died Aberdeen, 10 May. Painter in oil and watercolour, etcher. Trained Gray's School of Art and Allan Fraser School, Arbroath. A travelling scholarship took him to Belgium, France, Italy,

Germany, Spain, and Switzerland. Copied Old Masters on the way, especially Velasquez, Chardin and Vermeer. Served in the RAMC during WWI. Enjoyed early success at portraiture including Ivor Novello and Gladys Cooper among his sitters; also painted street scenes and by 1922 was established in London. In 1927 his portrait 'Fay Compton' was exhibited at the RA. The year before he had completed 'The Breakdown', a painting showing a white nude girl dancing beside a black musician. The work, destroyed and repainted in 1962, was withdrawn from the RA at the request of the Colonial Secretary who thought it might 'increase our difficulties in ruling coloured people'. Held his first one-man exhibitions in London in the 1930s. In 1952 moved to Aberdeen remaining there for the rest of his life painting landscapes, still life, flower studies; also executing wood engravings and linocuts. Exhibited GI(47) & AAS 1910-1937 from 1 Springbank Terrace. Represented in Edinburgh City collection, Manchester AG.
**Bibl:** Bourne Fine Art, (Ex Cat, Edinburgh 1986); Macmillan [SA] 334-5; Rendezvous Gallery, Aberdeen (Ex Cat).

**SOUTHBY, Lucy** **fl 1873**
Glasgow watercolourist. Exhib a still life of fruit and flowers at the GI.

**SOUTTAR, Miss Anna** **Early 20th Cent**
Watercolour painter of informal portraits, landscape and figurative works; exhibited AAS from Edenville, Aberdeen and subsequently East Grinstead.

**SOUTTER, Florence Margaret** **fl 1902**
Aberdeenshire amateur painter of country scenes; exhibited AAS(1) from The Manse, Echt.

**SOUTTER, Rose Stanley** **fl 1892-1893**
Minor figure of Church Lane, Kirkcaldy; exhibited GI(4), all narrative works.

**SPARK, Samuel Robin Halévy** **1938-**
Born Bulawayo, Zimbabwe. Portrait painter in the modern idiom; oil and watercolour. Arrived in Scotland at the age of 7 when awarded Andrew Grant Scholarship. After working in the Civil Service 1966-82 enrolled Edinburgh College of Art 1983-7. Exhibits RA, RSA & RSW. Represented in SNPG.

**SPARKE, Frank S** **fl 1928-1934**
Amateur Edinburgh watercolour painter of topography, especially around Edinburgh, Dalmeny and Stirling. Exhibited RSA(7), RSW(1) & GI(1).

**SPARROW, -** **fl 1788-1789**
Obscure engraver. Engraved 9 plates for Francis Grose's *The Antiquities of Scotland* 1797, including a fine view of 'Edinburgh castle', 'Holyrood', 'Holyrood chapel', 'St Roque's chapel', 'the Wryte's houses', 'St Anthony's chapel' and two of Craigmillar castle. Further plates were produced in collaboration with James Newton. A **Thomas SPARROW** was working as a wood engraver in Philadelphia 1765-1780.
**Bibl:** Butchart 28.

**SPECK, E Blanche** **fl 1911-1912**
Minor Airdrie watercolour painter. Exhibited GI(2) from Wesley Manse.

**SPEDDING, Sidney** **1916-**
Born Ashington, Northumberland. Sculptor. Studied Armstrong College, Durham University 1832-36 and then at Edinburgh College of Art 1936-9. Exhibited RSA 1939.

**SPEEDWELL, Jane Hunter** **fl 1883-1885**
Edinburgh amateur watercolour painter of flowers. Exhibited RSA(1), GI(2) & L(1).

**SPEIR, Guy** **fl 1925-1928**
Painter who lived at the Abbey, North Berwick; exhibited RSA(2) but mainly Walker's Gallery, London(86).

**SPEIRS, Catharine S** **fl 1951-1962**
Glasgow sculptress; mainly in bronze and plaster. Exhibited a portrait bust at the RSA; also GI(3).

**SPEIRS, Daniel** **fl 1870**
Glasgow figure painter. Exhibited 'The young artist' at the GI, from William St.

**SPEIRS, John** **fl 1885-1897**
Minor Glasgow oil painter of portraits, flower and figure studies; exhibited RSA(4), GI(4), AAS(3) & L(1) from Langside.

**SPEIRS, John A** **fl 1877-1883**
Glasgow topographical watercolourist. Exhibited GI(7).

**SPEIRS, Robert** **fl 1909**
Amateur Paisley artist; exhibited GI(2) & L(1) from 34 High Street.

**SPEIRS, William** **fl 1906-1912**
Glasgow artist; exhibited GI(2).

**SPENCE -** **19th Cent**
Obscure artist. A watercolour of Bakehouse Close, Canongate, Edinburgh is in the Edinburgh City collection.

**SPENCE, Barbara** **fl 1973**
Morayshire painter; exhibited AAS(1) from Glencairn, Reidhaven St, Elgin.

**SPENCE, Sir Basil Urwin OM OBE RA ROI PPRIBA ARSA** **1907-1976**
Born Bombay 13 Aug. Architect. Educated at George Watson's College, Edinburgh and the Schools of Architecture in Edinburgh and London. In 1931 began a flexible partnership with William Kinninmonth although remaining largely independent. In 1934 a flat-roofed house for Dr John King and a garage at Causewayside were among the first examples of modernist architecture built in Britain. A year later he collaborated with Tommy Tait for the two Scottish Pavilions and the Empire Exhibition in Glasgow 1936. In his later work he reverted to more traditional steep-pitched roofs and incorporated details from Scottish vernacular architecture. Designed two exhibitions at the Royal Scottish Museum 'Scottish Every Day Art' (1936) and 'Enterprise Scotland' (1947). In 1951 won a competition for a new cathedral at Coventry, finally consecrated in 1962. From the early 1950s he and his firm designed numerous airports, schools, housing estates, churches throughout Britain including the University of Sussex and the headquarters of the Scottish Widows Fund and Life Assurance Society, Edinburgh. Also involved in the British Embassy (Rome), Southampton University, buildings at Edinburgh and Glasgow Universities, Broughton Place, Quathquhan Lodge, St Andrew Church, Clermiston (1957), and Gribloch Keppen. Designed the War Memorial in St Giles to the 94th (City of Edinburgh) Regiment. RA Professor of Architecture 1961-1968. Received OBE 1948, elected ARSA 1952, RA 1960, PPRIBA 1960, knighted 1960, awarded Order of Merit 1962. President, Royal Institute of British Architects 1958-60. A Basil Spence Collection is with the Royal Commission on the Ancient and Historical Monuments of Scotland.
**Bibl:** Gifford 43,46,115,244,305,388,395,612,633,640; Hartley 165; C. McKean, The Scottish Thirties: an Architectural Introduction, 1987.

**SPENCE, Harry RBA** **1860-1928**
Born London. Painter of portraits and landscapes in oil and water-colour. Both parents were Scottish. Trained Glasgow, London and Paris. Settled in Glasgow 1885. Particularly fascinated by the landscape of Galloway. Elected NEAC 1887, RBA 1909. Exhibited in many places including RA (where the 'Valley of the Dee' was shown 1899), RSA(21), RSW(3), RBA(38), ROI(3), RCA(1), GI (63) & L(16). Represented in Glasgow AG.
**Bibl:** Caw 407; Halsby 145,285.

**SPENCE, James Allan Stewart RSW RGI** **fl 1959-**
Glasgow landscape painter, primarily in watercolour. Since retiring from teaching has become increasingly interested in the printing methods of lithography, etching and woodcuts. Related to Judith(qv) and Paul S(qv). Married Anda Paterson(qv) with whom he founded the Glasgow Group(qv) 1958, being president/chairman until 1990. Has said that his dominant theme is always 'the human drama of athletes under stress, and the changing elemental drama of sky and sea'. Elected RSW 1989, RGI 1996. Exhibited RSA(18), GI

throughout 1955-1989 and two landscapes at the AAS, one of Ballater, latterly from 55 Bainfield Rd, Cardross, Dumbartonshire. Represented in Glasgow AG(2), Dundee AG, Royal collection, SAC.

**SPENCE, John** **fl 1768-1789**
Early painter. Son of William S, painter Burgess of Edinburgh. Elected Burgess 1768 and a member of the Incorporation of St Mary's. Took as apprentices Robert Kerr 1781 and Robert Waterstone 1789.

**SPENCE, John Simpson** **fl 1919-1936**
Edinburgh amateur painter; exhibited RSA(6).

**SPENCE, Judith Anna** **fl 1981-**
Cardross sculptress and engraver of figurative works. Related to James Allan(qv) and Paul S(qv). Exhibits RSA & GI(10) since 1981.

**SPENCE, Paul** **fl 1987**
Cardross painter; related to James Allan and Judith S(qv). Exhibited a nude at the RSA.

**SPENCE, William** **c1806-1883**
Born Glasgow; died Helensburgh. Architect. Assistant to John Bryce(qv). Working on his own 1837. Designed several theatres and other buildings 'all showing an adventurous and resourceful mind' [Gomme & Walker]. His best known existing design is 21-31 Buchanan St (c1879); on Tayside was responsible for the Rennaissance Clydesdale Bank, High St, Dundee (1876). Hugh Barclay(qv) was a pupil. Retired to Helensburgh.
**Bibl:** A Gomme & D Walker, Architecture of Glasgow, London 1987(rev), 300; Bruce Walker & W S Gauldie, Architects and Architecture on Tayside, Dundee 1984, 135.

**SPENCER, Leonard** **fl 1908**
Galashiels painter of Waitknowe Terrace; exhibited 'The lake' at the RSA.

**SPENDLER, J E** **fl 1890**
Minor Edinburgh painter; exhibited GI(1) from 15 Leopold Place.

**SPENLOVE, Francis Raymond** **1897-?**
Born London 11 Nov. Son of Frank S(qv). Painter of portraits and figure subjects. Lived in Cornwall with a studio at St Ives. Exhibited ROI, RP & Paris Salon.

**SPENLOVE-SPENLOVE, Frank RI ROI RBA** **1868-1933**
Born Bridge of Allan, Stirlingshire, 24 Feb; died London, 30 Apr. Painter of landscape and genre in oil and watercolour. Father of Francis Raymond S(qv). Studied London, Paris and Antwerp. Founder and principal, Spenlove School of Painting (The Yellow Door Studio) from 1896. His first exhibit RA 1887; won a gold medal Paris Salon 1901. Painted genre for a number of years before turning to landscape. Worked in Holland, Belgium and widely in England. Exhibited RA(79), RBA(144), RHA(5), RCA(42), RI (106), ROI(91), GI(23) & L(38). Represented in Glasgow AG.

**SPIERS, Daniel** **fl 1875**
Amateur Glasgow wildlife painter. Exhibited 'Nest Harriers' at the GI, from Thistle St.

**SPIERS, Diane** **fl 1985**
Glasgow minor sculptress; exhibited an untitled work at the RSA.

**SPIERS, John A** **fl 1880-1897**
Glasgow portrait painter and teacher; exhibited GI(10) & L(2).

**SPILLER, Eric** **fl 1977-1981**
Aberdeen jewellery designer; exhibited AAS from 9 Hillhead Terrace.

**SPINDLER, James Gustavus H** **1862-1916**
Dundee painter in oil and watercolour of landscape, especially in the Dundee vicinity but also in Italy, Germany and Switzerland. Father of Jane S(qv). Arrived in Britain c1880, settling in Dundee. His work is of modest quality and traditional in its rendering of landscape although often with excessive use of browns and blues. Exhibited RSA(41), RA 1895, GI(11) & L(1), from 7 Ward Rd. Represented in Dundee AG (a golfing scene entitled 'St. Andrews').
**Bibl:** Wingfield.

**SPINDLER, Miss Jane Elizabeth** **fl 1870-1903**
Dundee painter in oil and watercolour of landscapes, rustic scenes and interiors. Daughter of James Gustavus S(qv). Studied under her father whose work her own closely resembles. After a spell in Edinburgh settled in Blairgowrie during the late 1880s. Exhibited RSA(29) from 1870, AAS (2 in 1885) & GI(8). Her painting 'Spring' is in Dundee AG.

**SPITTAL, Jean** **fl 1931**
Aberdeenshire amateur artist; exhibited 'Loch Davan' at the AAS, from 128 Mid Stocket Rd.

**SPOOK SCHOOL** **[see GLASGOW FOUR]**

**SPRAGUE, Hilda G Vaughan** **fl 1895-1897**
Minor Edinburgh portrait painter of 29 Buckingham Terrace. Possibly related to the miniature painter Edith Sprague. Exhibited RSA(2).

**SPRENGER, Charles** **fl 1888-1906**
Glasgow painter of flowers, local topography and interiors. Moved to 3 Glenbank Terrace, Lenzie c1906. Exhibited GI(7).

**SPRING, A** **fl 1883**
Unknown artist; exhibited GI(1) from Glasgow.

**SPRY, Graham G J** **fl 1971-1987**
Kincardineshire-based artist; trained Gray's School of Art, Aberdeen. Exhibited AAS from 74 High St, Banchory.

**SQUIRE, Geoffrey ARSA RSW PRSW RGI** **1923-**
Portrait painter, also landscapes. Elected ARSA 1978, RSW 1983. Regular exhibitor RSA, GI & RSW. Exhibited a portrait of the 'Lord Lyon King of Arms' RSA 1990 from his studio at Elie, Fife. Represented Glasgow AG(2), Lillie AG (Milngavie).

**SQUIRE, Maud H** **fl 1909**
Fife landscape painter in watercolours. Exhibited a Spanish scene at the GI, from Kirkcaldy.

**STACIE, Isaac** **fl 1681-d1692**
Edinburgh painter. Son of Joseph S(qv). Painter burgess by right of his father 13 Sep 1682. Apart from his marriages and the date of his burial - 22 Oct - nothing is known of his life and work.
**Bibl:** Apted 89; Edin. Marriages 1595-1700, 650; Greyfriarts Interments, 612.

**STACIE, Joseph** **1625-1686**
Born Notts, Mar. Heraldic painter. In May, 1643 he came to Scotland. Married a daughter of the Sawers family of painters, 2 Jne 1650, and ten days later became a painter burgess. Appointed Herald painter (conjoint) 1663-86, Ross Herald 30 Sep 1663. Records exist of work done at Trinity House, Leith, for the town of Edinburgh, and at Edinburgh castle; painted arms for the funerals of George, 2nd Earl of Panmure 1675 and Mary, Marchioness of Douglas 1676, also Sir Archibald of Stewart of Castlemilk. Apprentices included Thomas Ker 1656, James Ovens 1674 & Andrew Ker 1677.
**Bibl:** Apted 89-90; Edin. Marr. 1595-1700, 650; Lyon Court, 29; Registrum de Panmure, ed J. Stuart, Edinburgh 1874, xlv.

**STAFFORD, Mrs Sarah** **fl 1873-1875**
South Queensferry painter in watercolours of castles and local landscapes. Exhibited RSA(5).

**STALKER, Colin J** **fl 1885-1925**
Edinburgh painter in oil and watercolour of landscapes and church interiors; also interior designer. Exhibited RSA(6) including 'A Choir Screen at Ludlow' 1885 & RSW(2).

**STALKER, James** **fl 1632-1638**
Early Scottish painter. Son of David S(qv). Apprenticed to John Sawers the younger(qv) 1632. There is a painted ceiling of his in the Skelmorlie Aisle, Largs, dated 1638 bearing the signature 'J Stalker'.
**Bibl:** M R Apted, Painted Ceilings of Scotland, Edinburgh 1966,

89,91(illus); Apted 144; Dobie W: 'The Skelmorlie Aisle and Monument at Largs', Arch and Hist Coll relating to Ayrshire and Galloway, vi, 1889, 58-76.

**STALKER, Mary A** **fl 1908**
Aberdeen flower painter; exhibited AAS(1) from 534 King St.

**STANDEN, Peter** **1936-**
Born Surrey, 3 Apr. Printmaker and painter. Trained Nottingham College of Arts and Crafts, 1954-6 attaining an Andrew Grant Junior Open Bequest enabling him to continue his studies at the Edinburgh College of Art 1956-9. After doing National Service in Germany settled in Edinburgh 1962 becoming a member of the council of the Printmakers Workshop 1974-87 and chairman 1979-82. In addition to teaching in schools 1969-86 he worked on his own account most assiduously whilst enjoying a sabbatical leave in 1979 and 1980. Enjoys depicting people at work. Has held a number of exhibitions, also shown at the Ljubiana Biennale 1987. His work is representational, often allegorical. It includes a number of recurring images such as broken statues, vegetation, ruins, children playing and rusting machinery. More recently scenes of an imaginery and ironic future have predominated. Lives in Edinburgh. Exhibits regularly RSA & AAS 1981, from 5 Lee Crescent, Edinburgh. Represented in Edinburgh City collection, SAC, Hamilton AG (Canada).

**STANLEY, Montague ARSA** **1809-1844**
Born Dundee, Jan; died Ascog, Bute, 5 May. Father was in the navy, crossing to New York when young Stanley was only 14 months old. When he was three his father died. 'Natural affection formed one of the most prominent features in his character, and his mind was imbued with the most fervent aspirations and indomitable activity'. It was said that he was a saintly person. His mother married again and moved to Nova Scotia 1815. There he became associated with native Indians, becoming proficient with bow and arrow. When his step-father died of yellow fever in Jamaica the young man took to the stage and in 1819 came to England. He went to Suffolk but in 1824 engaged as an actor in York, coming to the Edinburgh theatre in 1828 and remaining for the next ten years. His first drawing from nature was 'Roslin Castle'. In Edinburgh he had lessons from Ewbank(qv) and in 1833 married an Edinburgh girl. Five years later he left the stage for religious reasons and in 1843 in failing health he settled in Bute. It was said rather unmercifully that he had 'all the weaker elements and few of the redeeming qualities of Fenwick and Ewbank' but he enjoyed a good reputation in his lifetime though the lack of great talent led to his subsequent neglect. He contributed verse to a book published by Oliphant in Edinburgh, also to the *Christian Treasury.* After his death the contents of his studio were completely destroyed by fire on their way to auction. Elected ARSA 1838 having been an honorary member for the preceeding three years. Exhibited RSA(83) 1828-1845, almost all of them landscapes, some Welsh, some of the Lake District but mostly Scottish.
**Bibl:** Bryan; Brydall 467-9; Caw 145; Rev D T K Drummond, The Life of Montague Stanley, 1848; McKay 199.

**STANMORE, H** **fl 1865-1868**
Amateur Edinburgh oil painter; exhibited continental landscapes at the RSA including views in France, Switzerland and the Roman Campagna.

**STANTON, George Clark RSA** **1832-1894**
Born Birmingham; died Edinburgh, 8 Jan. He was both a painter of portraits, rustic scenes and portrait miniatures, and a sculptor. Educated King Edward's Grammar School and Birmingham School of Art, where he studied silversmithing. Subsequently worked for the firm of Elkington and Mason who sent him to Florence to study Italian renaissance sculpture and metalwork. In Italy became associated with Garibaldi. Several drawings of Garibaldi dating from the late 1840s and early 50s are recorded. In 1855 he settled in Edinburgh where his fiancée Clara Gamgee had returned from Italy. There he remained for the rest of his life. He executed several statues for the niches of the Scott Monument, mostly busts and portrait medallions; also bronze panels illustrating the history of the Scott family in the Royal Mile; statues to the Army and Navy in Charlotte Square. In later life he turned his attention increasingly to painting and book illustrating, including interesting work in watercolour. His subjects include romance, history and often literary themes sometimes from Shakespeare. 'His heroines wore richly coloured dresses and his backgrounds are finely detailed, yet his pictures carry great conviction and never appear like theatrical charades'. Close friend of Sam Bough(qv) and much influenced by the pre-Raphaelites. Among works he illustrated was his father-in-law (John Gamgee's) books on horses. Taught for a time at the Life Schools and was curator of the Life School of the Academy 1881-1893/4. Sold few works during his lifetime and was continuously in debt. He lived at 1 Ramsay Lane. Elected ARSA 1862, RSA 1885. In 1857 and annually until 1894 exhibited RSA(210); also RSW(2), GI(55) & L(4). "La Fruttajuola', exhibited at the RSA (1862), was purchased by Kelvin AG, Glasgow while his busts of 'Sam Bough' (1859) and 'Erskine Nicol' (1860) are in SNPG, also in Dundee AG, Glasgow AG.
**Bibl:** Bryan 115; Gifford 203,294,316; Halsby 108,285.

**STANTON, John G** **fl 1883-1886**
Edinburgh flower painter. Son of George Clark S(qv). Exhibited RSA(3).

**STAPLES, Sir Robert Ponsonby** **1853-1943**
Born Dundee. 12th Bt. Painter in oils, watercolour and pastels; also illustrator. Portraits, figurative and sporting subjects. Trained Louvain Academy of Fine Arts 1865-70, Dresden 1867 and in Brussels under Portaels 1872-4. Taught art at the People's Palace, Mile End Rd, London 1897. Contributed cartoons and more serious illustrations for *The Sketch, ILN* and *The Graphic.* Lived for some years in Ireland. Exhibited RA(12) 1875-1901, latterly from 3 Comeragh Rd, West Kensington; also RHA & SS. Represented in Worthing AG ('The Last Shot for the Queen's Prize at Bisley' 1887); MCC collection, Lords, London ('England v Australia at Lords', in collaboration with G H Barrable, 1886).
**Bibl:** Wingfield.

**STARFORTH, John** **1823-1898**
Architect. Specialised in Gothic church design. In Edinburgh responsible for Davidson Church, Eyre Place (1879-81, now a warehouse), London Road Church (1874) and the demolished United Presbyterian Church, Granton (1878).
**Bibl:** Gifford 415,435,447,611.

**STARK, James** **fl 1933-1937**
Minor painter of Burngreen, Kilsyth; exhibited 'John Knox House' RSA, also L(1).

**STARK, James D** **fl 1915**
Minor figure of 6 East Savile Road, Edinburgh; exhibited 'A city corner' at the RSA.

**STARK, Miss M B** **fl 1919-1921**
Edinburgh artist. Exhibited RSA(2) from 6 Warrender Park Cres.

**STARK, Malcolm** **fl 1861-1892**
Glasgow architect and watercolourist of town views. Partner in Malcolm Stark & Rowntree who designed several churches and municipal buildings in and around Scarborough; also Gilfillan church, Whitehall Crescent, Dundee (1888) although the fine wooden cupola which enriched the design has been vandalised. Exhibited RSA(1) & GI(11).
**Bibl:** Bruce Walker & W S Gauldie, Architects and Architecture on Tayside, Dundee 1984, 135.

**STARK, Marjorie** **fl 1955-1980**
Edinburgh painter of landscape (mainly continental Italian), still life and fruit; exhibited RSA(39), and a Venetian scene at the AAS, from 31 Midmar Gardens and subsequently, after 1975, from Kelso.

**STARK, W S** **fl 1933-1937**
Minor Glasgow painter of townscapes; exhibited 'A bit of old Edinburgh' at the RSA; also GI(2), AAS(1) & L(1), from Woodstock Drive, Newlands.

**STARK, William** **1770-1813**
Born Dunfermline; died Glasgow, Oct 13. Architect. Teacher of James Playfair(qv). Regarded by many of his contemporaries as Scotland's most promising architect. Visited St Petersburg 1798. Few of his buildings survive; the asylum at Bell's Park(1809) was believed to be the first in Britain to employ a radiating plan while the equally advanced Court House, Edinburgh (1809) has been compared to

Smirke's Covent Garden. Designed Dundee hospital(1812) and Gloucester hospital(1822-3). As Playfair's master, has a claim to be regarded as the originator of the neo-Gothic in Scotland. In 1811 health problems led to his moving to Edinburgh where he designed the interior of the library of the Writers to the Signet (1812), and the Advocates' Library (1812) 'Stark's mastery is shown in his transformation of an oppressive tunnel into a marvellously light space' [Gifford]. Reviewed entries for the Calton scheme 'condemning the imposition of formal plans on uneven ground, stressing the beauty of the site and the importance of following natural contours, and of combining architecture with trees' [Gifford]. The month he died Sir Walter Scott wrote in a letter to a friend [quoted by Brydall] 'This brings me to the death of poor Stark, with whom more genius has died than is left among the collected universality of Scottish architects'.
**Bibl:** Brydall 180-1; Dunbar 117-8; Gifford 120,123-4,435n,444, pl 84; A Gomme & D Walker, Architecture of Glasgow, London, 1987(rev), 300.

**STARK, William S** **fl 1936-1944**
Glasgow landscape painter, mostly west coast of Scotland, but also in the Baltic. Exhibited GI(6) from Langside Drive.

**STAUNTON, W L** **fl 1841**
Edinburgh amateur painter; exhibitied 'A blink of rest' at the RSA, from 26 George St.

**STAVELEY, William** **fl 1785-1805**
Painter of portraits and portrait miniatures. Descended from an old Yorkshire family with Scottish connections through his mother's side. Lived all his working life in London although undertaking a number of important commissions in Scotland. His father was a York framemaker. Portraits of 'John Balfour of Pilrig' and 'Captain John MacIntosh RN' were in Mount Melville while the Countess of Seafield has 'Sir James Grant of Grant', signed 'W Staveley 1796' and 'Dr Gregory Grant' (c1720-1803). Commissioned by the Rose family of Kilravock to paint the portrait of the 20th laird 'Col Hugh Rose' (1780-1827) which according to a signed inscription on the reverse was painted in 1798. His son became a Lt-Gen and inherited a talent for drawing, as well as undertaking much of Wellington's reconnaissance work in the Peninsular War. Exhibited RA(51) 1785-1805. Represented by two portraits in SNPG.

**STAYERS, J** **fl 1851-1853**
Glasgow painter of land and townscapes; exhibited RSA(6) from Portland St.

**STEAD, Tim** **c1950-**
Carver. Trained at art school. Devoted to wood carving of all kinds. Designed furniture for Cafe Gadalfi, Glasgow and recently a lectern and rood screen in St Nicholas Church, Aberdeen. Inspired by the Austrian artist and environmental activist Hundertwasser. First solo exhibition, Edinburgh 1993. Lives and works at The Steading, Blainslie, Galashiels.
**Bibl:** Cathy Coll, Sunday Times, 15 Aug 1993; Giles Sutherland, Explorations in Wood, Edinburgh 1993.

**STECHAN, Louis** **fl 1885-1886**
Amateur Edinburgh painter in oil and watercolour of landscapes and trees. Exhibited RSA(7) from 13 Elm Row.

**STEDMAN, Ralph E** **fl 1942-1945**
Dundee painter of landscapes, often in Cornwall and the Highlands. Exhibited RSA(9).

**STEEDMAN, A** **fl 1900**
Amateur Edinburgh watercolour artist; exhibited two Venetian scenes at the GI from 11 Greenhill Gardens.

**STEEDMAN, Miss C L** **fl 1903**
Selkirk painter. Exhibited SWA(2) from Ravenhough.

**STEEDMAN, Miss E M** **fl 1921-1939**
Edinburgh painter in oil and watercolour. Continental scenes including topographical views in Venice and southern England. Exhibited RSA(19), RSW(27), GI(9) & L(2) from 2 Heriot Row & later Strathearn Rd.

**STEEDMAN, Mary** **fl 1898**
Edinburgh painter. Wife of A Steedman(qv). Exhibited once at the Royal Society of Artists in Birmingham from 11 Greenhill Gardens.

**STEEL, Miss Dorothy** **fl 1950-1980**
Born on the Clyde coast. Landscape painter, based in Gourock. Trained Glasgow School of Art in the 1940s where she became a friend of Joan Eardley(qv) with whom she travelled to France and whom she introduced to the Clydeside shipyards. At that time their styles were similar but in later years Steel's work became simplified and dominated by landscapes of the Clyde coastline. An exhibition of her work was held in Glasgow 1990. Exhibited RSA(2) with a gap of twenty-four years between; also GI(3).

**STEEL, Grace** **fl 1892-1893**
Ayrshire flower painter. Exhibited GI(3) from Cumnock.

**STEEL, Mrs H Eadie** **fl 1910-1911**
Minor Glasgow portrait miniaturist. Exhibited GI(2) from 142 Cambridge Drive, Kelvinside.

**STEEL, Helen** **fl 1888**
Glasgow flower painter. Exhibited GI(1) from 66 South Portland St.

**STEEL, James Jnr** **fl 1865**
Glasgow sculptor. Exhibited a portrait bust at GI from Holmhead St.

**STEEL, James Dawson** **fl 1935-1937**
Aberdeen landscape and topographical painter; exhibited AAS(2) from 28 Erskine St.

**STEEL, John Sydney** **1863-1932**
Born Perth; died Balquhidder. Painter of animals and stalking scenes. Educated Perth Academy and Madras College, St Andrews. Father was a close friend of Sir John Millais, who recommended that he should be sent to London for art training at the Slade School. Steel maintained a lifelong friendship with J G Millais, son of the President, with whom he collaborated on several of the latter's published works notably *British Deer and Their Horns.* He also numbered Archibald Thorburn(qv), Lionel Edwards and Ernest Briggs(qv) among his friends, sharing a studio in London with the latter. Unfortunately he suffered much from long periods of ill-health which necessitated sojourns in North Africa. His best work was done in oils but also painted watercolours and produced some admirable etchings. His pictures of deer are best known but he also painted some fine pictures of African and Arab life studies. Steel's work was not in the clearcut style usually beloved by sportsmen but was as a rule low in tone, with mist, snow or rain as the prevailing motif. Cherished a wintry day on a steep hillside with deer grazing their way through mist or snow; few painters could capture the gleam of wintry sunlight on the high hills as he did. 'In a somewhat enfeebled body he combined a complex personality for he was an accomplished artist as well as a keen student of natural science and a sportsman who dearly loved the Scottish highlands, its rivers, moors and mountains, its deer and wild game. It was because he knew so much about stags and hinds, highland ponies and grouse that he pictured them all so well on canvas' [Flatt]. Works of his were a regular feature at local art exhibitions. Towards the end of his life, urged by friends and admirers, held his first highly successful one man show in London. Dearly loved by many friends who knew him as 'Stag' or, on account of his accustomed heavy brogues, 'Tackets'. Exhibited RA(6), RSA(15), RBA(9), RE(2), ROI(7), AAS(2), GI(1) & L(2) from 1 Rosemount Pl. Represented in Perth AG, Nat Gall of South Africa (Cape Town).
**Bibl:** R J Flatt, Scottish Field, 15 Jan 1930; Wingfield.

**STEEL, Miss Mary L** **fl 1943**
Perthshire flower painter; exhibited 'Poppies' at the RSA, from Rumbling Bridge.

**STEEL(E), Margaret R** **fl 1901**
Amateur Glasgow figure of 3 Dowanhill Terrace, Partick. Exhibited GI(1).

**STEELE, A** **fl 1870**
Glasgow watercolour painter. Exhibited West Highland landscapes at the GI(4), from Monteith Row.

**STEELE, Miss Alice A** **fl 1883**
Amateur Edinburgh portrait painter. Exhibited RSA(1) from 55 Albany Street.

**STEEL(E), Grace** **fl 1892-1893**
Minor Ayrshire figure of Polquhirter, New Cumnock; exhib GI(2).

**STEELE, Mrs Katherine** **fl 1963-1965**
East Lothian landscape painter, mostly local scenery. Exhibited RSA (3) & GI(2), from Longniddry.

**STEEL(E), Robert** **fl 1863-1867**
Glasgow amateur landscape painter in oil; exhibited RSA(2) & AAS(2).

**STEELL, David George ARSA** **1856-1930**
Born Edinburgh; died Edinburgh, 7 Mar. Painter in oil and watercolour of animals and birds. Son of Gourlay S(qv); nephew of the sculptor Sir John Steell(qv). Studied at the Mound School of Art. Began exhibiting RSA 1873 and continued annually until shortly before his death. His 'Laird of Cockpen', RSA 1866, was poorly received, an anonymous critic writing that it was 'crude and raw in colour, much overdone otherwise'. Throughout his career he showed an interest in animals, painting mainly creatures of the field, forest and mountains, especially birds, and deer depicted in their natural surroundings. Enjoyed country sports until failing eyesight intervened. Worked very much in the manner and style of his father under whom he had studied. Elected ARSA 1885. Exhibited RSA(202); also RA(1), GI(15), AAS(2) & L(4).
**Bibl:** Caw 340; Wingfield.

**STEELL, Gourlay RSA** **1819-1894**
Born Edinburgh; died Edinburgh, 31 Jan. Painter in oil and watercolour and tempera of animals, still life and character studies. Son of **John STEELL**, a well-known Edinburgh woodcarver, and younger brother of Sir John S(qv). In his early life he taught modelling at the Watt Institute in Edinburgh and modelled animal groups for silversmiths. Preferred painting and enrolled at Trustees Academy where he studied under Sir William Allan(qv) and for a time R S Lauder(qv). When only 27 he was elected ARSA 1846, RSA 1859 - the same year that he was appointed painter to the Highland Agricultural Society. Selected to succeed Sir Edwin Landseer(qv) as Animal Painter to Her Majesty for Scotland, a position retained until his death in 1894. Enjoyed an almost monopoly of animal paintings in Scotland and executed many commissions for the aristocracy somewhat in the style of Landseer although, in the opinion of Caw, 'his handling had not Howe's gusto, nor his colour Forbes's quality, and it is questionable if he had a truer sense of pictorial fitness as either of them. It was a narrow and conventional view of picture making into which ensemble and decorative effect did not enter...but he drew horses, dogs and cattle with considerable skill and distinct sense of character and form, painted with neatness and finish, and conceived his subjects in the manner that proved attractive to many people'. Among his best known works were 'Lord President Inglis' and a 'Shooting-party at Glencorse' 1868, 'The Earl of Wemyss with his huntsman and pack' 1863 and 'Col Carrick Buchanan'. 'The Pass of Leny' is in the Royal Collection but perhaps his best known work of all is 'A Cottage Bedside at Osborne' - showing the Queen reading the Bible to an aged fisherman. It was engraved and became extremely popular. Also exhibited sketches of Queen Victoria's three dogs, 'Noble, Corran and Waldmann' at the RA 1874 'painted by command'. Among other patrons were the Duke of Buccleuch, the Earl of Rosebery, the Duke of Atholl, and the Earl of Haddington. From c1870 he lived in Randolph Place until moving c1876 to 4 Palmerston Place. Kept a studio at 123 George Street. Contributed illustrations to *Poems and Songs* by Robert Burns (1875). Curator of the NGS 1882-1894. Exhibited RA(1) 1865-1880, GI(5) & no fewer than 277 works at the RSA between 1835 and 1894; also once at the AAS 1887. Represented in Glasgow AG(3), Edinburgh City collection, Haddo House (NTS).
**Bibl:** AJ 1893, 125; 1894, 125 (obit); Bryan; Caw 198-9; DNB; Halsby 285; Houfe; Irwin 323 (pl 177); McKay 355-6; Wingfield.

**STEELL, Gourlay Jnr** **fl 1862-1874**
Animal and subject painter, often of a literary character, in the style of his father Gourlay S(qv). Exhibited RSA(7), GI(1) & AAS(2) from 8 Mary Place.

**STEELL, James H** **fl 1845**
Dundee portrait painter; exhibited the portrait of a local mother and her children at the RSA from the High St.

**STEELL, Sir John RSA** **1804-1891**
Born Aberdeen, 18 Aug; died Edinburgh, 15 Nov. Sculptor of figures in monumental groups; also draughtsman. Son of John S(qv), carver and gilder, and brother of Gourlay S(qv). His family moved to Edinburgh in 1805 and in 1818 he was apprenticed to a woodcarver at the same time as he began studies at the Trustees Academy under Graham(qv). At the end of his apprenticeship he decided to become a sculptor and went to Rome remaining there for several years. In 1827 he executed a large statue in wood for the North British Fire and Insurance Corporation and in 1833 modelled the group 'Alexander taming Bucephalus' which attracted great attention. Urged to go to London by Sir Francis Chantrey but declined in order to devote all his energies to the improvement of art in Scotland. His seated figure of Sir Walter Scott in Princes Street, Edinburgh is thought to be the first marble statue ever commissioned in Scotland by a Scottish artist. He was the first sculptor to introduce artistic bronze casting into the country and at his own expense he built a foundry so that not only his own works but those of others could be reproduced in metal. In 1868 he carved a group for the tympanum of the Bank of Montreal in Canada, and the parable of 'The Ten Virgins' for the Standard Assurance Office, Dublin. Principal works are the statues of 'Lord de Saumarez' (1840) at the National Maritime Museum, Greenwich; 'Professor Blaikie' (1844), the West Church, Aberdeen; 'Queen Victoria' (1844), The Royal Institution Edinburgh; 'Sir Walter Scott' (1846), Princes Street, Edinburgh; 'The Countess of Elgin' (1849), in Jamaica; 'Allan Ramsay' (1850), in Edinburgh; 'Wellington' (1852), in Edinburgh; 'Lord Jeffrey' (1855), Parliament House, Edinburgh; 'Professor Wilson' (1856), Princes Street, Edinburgh; 'Lord President Boyle' (1856), Parliament House, Edinburgh; 'Sir David Baxter' (1863), Dundee; 'Lord Dalhousie' (1864), Calcutta; 'Sir Walter Scott' (1870), New York; 'Dr Chalmers' (1871), for the Free Church College, Edinburgh; 'Burns' (1874) New York; 'The Prince Consort' (1876) in Edinburgh and 'Burns' (1884) on The Embankment, London. Busts include his diploma work at the RSA, 'David Scott' (1831), 'Lady Stuart of Allanbank' (1838) in the SNPG, 'Earl Grey' (1839) The Council Hall, Edinburgh; 'Lord Campbell' (1843), SNPG; 'The Duke of Wellington' (1845) The Upper School, Eton and another in 1846 for Apsley House, London; 'The Duchess of Buccleuch' (1846) for Dalkeith Palace; 'Lord Cockburn' (1857) for Parliament House, Edinburgh; 'Florence Nightingale' (1859) for the Royal United Service Institution; 'Florence Nightingale' (1862) for Derby AG with a replica in the NPG; 'Thomas de Quincey' (1876) for the SNPG; 'Dr Walburton Begbie' (1879) for the Royal College of Physicians, Edinburgh; and 'Robert Burns' (1885) for Westminster Abbey. His main monuments included those for the Countess of Elgin in Jamaica Cathedral (1843), Dr Alison in St Paul's, Edinburgh (1845), and for the 78th Highland Regiment in St Giles Cathedral, Edinburgh (1845), the Duke of Atholl for Blair Atholl Castle, Perth (1864); the Revd Dr Gordon for the Free High Church, Edinburgh (1866); Officers and Men of the 93rd Highlanders for Glasgow Cathedral (1869); Officers and Men of the Black Watch for Dunkeld Cathedral (1872) and Dean Ramsay for St John's Church, Edinburgh (1875). In 1887 he was one of the subscribers setting up the Edinburgh Life Academy which preceded the Royal Institution. In 1829 he was elected RSA and in 1838 was appointed Her Majesty's Sculptor for Scotland. In 1876 he was knighted on the occasion of the inauguration of his statue of the Prince Consort. Exhibited RSA(66) 1827-1880, RA(9) 1837-1876, all from his studio at 9 Randolph Place, Edinburgh. Represented in NGS(4), SNPG(24), Edinburgh City collection(3).
**Bibl:** Caw 199; Gifford 48,90,116,123,151,178,281,287,289,293, 298,305,314, 316,376,390,pl 55; Gunnis 370-1; Irwin 65,319,418n,; Fiona Pearson,'Sir John Steell and the Idea of a Native School of Sculpture', in Virtue & Vision, Edinburgh (Ex Cat NGS 1991); Steell, Scrapbooks, vols 1-4, NLS Edinburgh; Robin Lee Woodward, 'Nineteenth Century Scottish Sculpture', unpub PhD thesis, Univ. of Edinburgh 1977.

**STEEN, Ben** **fl 1961-1983**
Renfrewshire painter of landscapes, figure studies and still life; exhibited RSA(7) & GI(14) from Whitecraigs, latterly Glasgow.

**STEIL, Aitken** **fl 1841-1849**
Perth flower and topographical painter; partial to painting castles, local landmarks and groups of flowers in vases. Exhibited RSA(4).

**STEIN, James** **fl 1836-1864**
Coldstream-based painter in oil and occasional watercolour, landscapes especially Scottish romantic buildings such as castles and old cottages. Moved to Edinburgh and then (c1847) to Haddington. Kinsman of Robert Stein(qv). Exhibited RSA(112).
**Bibl:** Halsby 285.

**STEIN, Nettie H** **fl 1936-1940**
Minor Edinburgh watercolour painter of figure studies and genre; exhibited 'Breton peasant' at the RSA; also RSW(2).

**STEIN, Robert** **fl 1813-1844**
Edinburgh landscape painter; exhibited 'Cumberland landscape', 'A scene on the Firth of Forth, nr Aberdour' and 'A View of Edinburgh from the west' at the RA from St John's Street 1813-14, also RSA(31) 1832-1844, mainly the Scottish Highlands and Arran but also such subjects as 'Chepstow Castle' and 'Windsor Castle', both 1839, and 'Eton, from Windsor' 1844. In 1863 a painting was lent for exhibition at the RSA by Sir G.S. Montgomery. Kinsman of James Stein(qv).

**STENBERG, Ron** **fl 1980**
Fife painter of informal portraits and heads. Exhibited GI(3) from Wormit.

**STENHOUSE, Andrew J ARSA** **1954-**
Born Renfrew, 30th May. Sculptor and draughtsman. Began as an architectural technician. Trained Duncan of Jordanstone College of Art, Dundee, with a year at Hospitalfield 1977. Member of Dundee group 1979-81. Worked at the Scottish Sculpture Workshop in Lumsden before establishing his own studio in Fife. Benno Schotz award (RSA) 1983. Elected ARSA 1987. Spent a year in New York City 1987-8 during which time he fell under the influence of 'primitive' art and the architecture of site. Attracted toward the work of Cézanne and Joseph Beuys. Between 1984 and late 1985 was involved with the 'Neoists'. In 1988 helped to establish the Edinburgh Sculpture workshop. Exhibits RSA & AAS from 13 Kirk St, Markinch, Fife. Represented in SAC.

**STENHOUSE, Charles** **1878-c1946**
Born Dundee, 15 Oct. Painter of landscape in oil and occasionally watercolours. Trained Glasgow School of Art. Father of Kathleen S(qv). Lived in Glasgow before moving to Crail. Exhibited RSA(9) 1906-1937, RSA(9), GI(60) & L(3).

**STENHOUSE, James** **fl 1942-1948**
Ayrshire landscape painter; exhibited RSA in 1942 and 1948 from Troon.

**STENHOUSE, Kathleen R** **fl 1937**
Amateur Glasgow painter. Daughter and pupil of Charles S(qv). Exhibited GI(2) from 653 Shields Road.

**STENHOUSE, May** **fl 1900-1901**
Minor Edinburgh painter; exhibited at the RSA(3) from Lothian Vale, Holyrood.

**STEPHEN, Agnes M** **fl 1932-1970**
Dunbartonshire engraver. Mainly landscapes in woodcut and linocut. Trained Glasgow School of Art c 1917. Treasurer, Glasgow Society of Lady Artists 1962-1970, Vice-President 1964-5. Exhibited RSA(1) & GI(7) from Invergare, Rhu.

**STEPHEN, Annette J** **1910-1990**
Born Stonehaven, Kincardineshire. Painter in oils of turbulent seas, fishing subjects and the landscape around her home. Studied in Edinburgh and France. In 1950 settled in Watch House, Catterline. Responsible for introducing Joan Eardley(qv) to Catterline. Exhibited AAS regularly.

**STEPHEN, Daniel** **1921-?**
Born Aberdeen. Painter of portraits, landscape, still life and large-scale murals, also sculptor. Trained Gray's School of Art, Aberdeen 1940-5. An important RSA travelling scholarship enabled him to visit France & Italy. Worked in London 1949-52 before returning to Aberdeen. Began exhibiting RGI, RSA 1946 and RA 1957. In 1974 developed 'Optiken', a new form of kinetic painting. Moved to Perth 1981. A large 2m high wooden sculpture 'Helios - a tower project' appeared at the RSA 1986.

**STEPHEN, Frank** **fl 1983**
Aberdeenshire painter; exhibited AAS(2) from 16 Beechwood Ave, Ellon.

**STEPHEN, George** **fl 1972**
Aberdeenshire amateur artist; exhibited AAS(1) from 1 West Rd.

**STEPHEN, George B** **fl 1926**
Aberdeen topographical painter; exhibited AAS(4) from 9 Smith St.

**STEPHEN, James** **fl 1912-1923**
Aberdeen landscape painter, especially of local scenes including the Dee valley; exhibited AAS(9) from 31 Holburn St.

**STEPHEN, Ralph A** **1922-fl 1979**
Born Edzell, Angus. Educated Montrose Academy. Trained by his father as a blacksmith but began painting seriously after meeting James Morrison 1964. Most interested in local scenery, particularly the coast around St Cyrus. Held a one-man exhibition in Florence and others subsequently. Lives at 28A S. Esk St, Montrose; exhibited RSA, AAS & SSA until 1979.

**STEPHEN, T** **fl 1920-1922**
Amateur Glasgow engraver. Exhibited RSA(1) & GI(4) from 6 Hillside Place, Springburn, latterly St. Vincent St.

**STEPHEN, William Gow** **fl 1921**
Aberdeen painter; exhibited a townscape at the AAS from 26 Esslemont Ave.

**STEPHENSON, Dorothy** **fl 1910**
Little known painter; exhibited L(3) from Newburgh.

**STEPHENSON, Miss Elizabeth H** **fl 1886-1887**
Aberdeen painter of flowers, still life and interiors. Married R Tydd S(qv). Exhibited AAS(3) from 297 Union St.

**STEPHENSON, George** **fl 1882-1885**
Minor Glasgow etcher exhibited RE(6) & L(1) from 12 Waterloo St.

**STEPHENSON, James** **1828-1886**
Born Manchester, Nov 26; died May 30. Engraver in line and mezzotint, also draughtsman in crayon. Trained under Finden. Settled in London 1847. Although an Englishman he was particularly attracted to the Scottish artistic tradition and most of his best known works are of Scottish subjects. In 1856 his first exhibit at the RA was a series of drawings illustrating 'Tam O'Shanter', after John Faed, followed two years later by a further set of engravings after the same artist illustrative of the soldier's return. There followed 'My ain fireside', after Thomas Faed, 1861, a portrait of 'HRH Prince of Wales', after Sir John Watson Gordon 1864, and 'The Wayfarers', after Tom Graham 1873. One of his most celebrated engravings is 'The Highland Whisky-Still' after Landseer; also several works after David Roberts. Represented in City of Edinburgh collection by 8 engravings, including one after Gourlay Steell.
**Bibl:** Bryan 125 (by Martin Hardie).

**STEPHENSON, R B Tydd** **fl 1887-1891**
Perthshire topographical artist. Husband of Elizabeth H S(qv). Exhibited AAS(4) latterly from Perth District Asylum, Murthly.

**STERLING, Mrs John L** **fl 1893**
Glasgow landscape and flower painter. Exhibited GI(2) from 26 Albion Crescent, Dowanhill.

**STERLING, Muriel (Mrs Antony Caton-Woodville)** **1898-1940**
Designer, scene painter and teacher. Trained Glasgow School of Art 1919-22 and at the Academie de la Grande Chaumière. Worked as a scene painter in Bath and Birmingham and later at the Malvern

festival. Associated with Sir Barry Jackson. Taught at Laurel Bank. Killed in an air raid during WW2 in London.

**STEUART, (or STEWART) Miss Catherine** **fl 1862-1875**
Landscape painter, occasional buildings but mainly scenery in Argyll and on Arran. Varied the spelling of her name, preferring Stewart in later years. Exhibited RSA(12) between 1862-9 from Rothesay and subsequently from Edinburgh.

**STEUART, Charles** **fl 1762-1790**
Landscape painter, probably born Perthshire. Nothing known of his early life, the first recorded landscape being exhibited at the Free Society in London 1762, although circumstantial evidence persuades Macmillan that he had probably been a pupil of Robert Norie, coeval with Runciman and James Cumming. Selected by the 3rd Duke of Atholl to decorate the dining room at Blair Castle. This had been completed c1751 and the large wall panels were executed by Steuart 1766-1778. Three of the five large canvases depict waterfalls, one the ruin of Dunkeld Cathedral 1767 and the other the Perthshire peaks of 'Craig-y-Barns and Craigvinian from Torvald' 1768. Also worked for the Earl of Bute at his various homes and for the Earl of Breadalbane at Taymouth. For the former he painted a variety of English-type landscapes, more varied than at Blair, including a pastoral haymaking scene, and one of Lord Bute's other home Highcliffe. Described by Irwin as a 'mysterious, isolated figure who made an interesting contribution to landscape painting in the second half of the century'. Represented in Glasgow Univ ('Rumbling Brig over the Bran') 1765. The paintings done for the Duke of Atholl and the Earl of Bute remain in situ.
**Bibl:** Apollo, xcix 1975 (Irwin); cvi, Oct 1977, 300ff; Irwin 128-130, notes on 426; Macmillan [SA] 133-4,135(illus).

**STEUART, George** **?-1806**
Born Atholl, Perthshire; died Douglas, Isle of Man, Dec. Architect. Thought to have begun as a housepainter. In 1770 he planned and built a house in Grosvenor Place, London for the 3rd Duke of Atholl and was subsequently practising as an architect, first in Berners St and afterwards in Harley Street. Designed several country homes, and the remarkable Church of St Chad, Shrewsbury, which, with its circular nave and free-standing tower, has been described as 'one of the most boldly conceived buildings of the whole Georgian epoch' [Whiffen-Stuart]. Other buildings for which he was responsible include Attingham Hall, Salop for Lord Berwick (1783-5), Lythwood Hall, Salop (1785, dem 1950); Baron's Court, co Tyrone, Ireland for the Marquis of Abercorn; and Wellington church, Salop (1788-90). He was almost certainly undertaking commissions, among them the two rectangular courtyard-plan farms of Rotmell and Blairuachdar, for the 4th Duke of Atholl who owned estates on the Isle of Man and who was Governor of the island at the time of Steuart's death.
**Bibl:** Colvin 571; Dunbar 181; Whiffen-Stuart, Georgian Churches, 1948, 53.

**STEUART, James** **fl 1877-1900**
Glasgow painter in oil and watercolour of landscapes, generally Highland scenes. Author of *Sketching in Watercolours,* and *Sketching Ways and Sketching Days.* Over 50 topographical watercolours of Edinburgh by him are in the Edinburgh City Library. Exhibited at the RSA(4) & RSW. Probably the same **James STEUART** who is separately listed in RSA records as exhibiting 1897-1900, mainly Cheshire subjects from Northumberland St, Edinburgh.
**Bibl:** Butchart 79.

**STEUART (OR STEWART), Sir John James** **1779-1849**
Born Rome. Watercolour painter of battle scenes, historical subjects, landscape and equestrian studies, also etcher. Inherited the baronetcy of Allanbank, Berwickshire, becoming the 5th Baronet 1817. Published the first of several sets of etchings including titles from Scott and Byron, *The Visions of an Amateur,* published by Carpenter of London and *Gleanings from the Portfolio of an Amateur (*1821). Painted in England and Scotland, often on Rothesay and the islands of the Clyde. These are more colourful than his figure drawings which are usually in monochrome washes heightened with white. His main works were large battle scenes executed in the manner of Borgnone. There are in the NGS two scrapbooks and two albums together containing more than 60 drawings, pencil studies and etchings; also represented in BM, Glasgow AG, Ulster Museum.
**Bibl:** PCQ, April 1942.

**STEUART, T** **19th Cent**
Engraver. Executed an interesting early print 'The North British Railway from the North Bridge', 1846. Four engravings by him after Sir Daniel Wilson(qv) are in City of Edinburgh collection.
**Bibl:** Butchart 77.

**STEVEN, A** **fl 1947-1957**
Glasgow painter of landscapes and informal portraits. Moved to Callander, Perthshire c 1952. Exhibited GI(4).

**STEVEN, Helen M** **fl 1888-1891**
Glasgow painter of flowers and domestic genre. Exhibited RSA(1) & GI(4) from 34 Berkeley Terrace.

**STEVEN, George** **fl 1859-1860**
Leith landscape painter; exhibited 'A mountain gorge' and 'A Highland lake' at the RSA.

**STEVEN, Jane** **fl 1893**
Glasgow flower painter. Exhibited GI(1) from 44 Grandby Terrace, Hillhead.

**STEVEN, Maria J (G)** **fl 1886-1891**
Edinburgh watercolour painter of landscapes; exhibited RSA(2).

**STEVENS, Alexander** **c1730-1796**
Died 20 Jan. Architect. His obituary in the *Gents Mag* records that 'in the course of the last 40 years, he erected more stone bridges, and other buildings in water, than any other man in these kingdoms'. Designed the Sarah Bridge over the River Liffey (1783-91) and many works in the north of England and Scotland, including the aquaduct over the River Lune near Lancaster co-designed by John Rennie(qv). Responsible for the small castellated house of Raehills, Dumfries-shire, built for the 3rd Earl of Hopetoun (1786). 'This building, altered and enlarged by William Burn in 1834 had in its original design an L-shaped block with a conventional entrance front to the north but an imposing east facade overlooking landscaped gardens, and a curiously double-bowed re-entrant angle...The only castellated features are the battlemented upperworks' [Dunbar]. Built and probably designed the spire for St Cuthbert's Parish Church (1789-90); involved in the north side of Charlotte Square including the design of nos. 1 & 2 (among the finest interiors in the city). May have designed Hyndford Bridge, Lanarkshire (1773), 'with its corbelled parapet and rounded, turreted cutwaters, it exemplifies the more sophisticated approach of the bridge builders of the turnpike era' [Dunlop].
**Bibl:** Colvin 571; Dunbar 126, 218; Gifford 273-4,294; Gents Mag lxvi (i) 1796, 169.

**STEVENS, Gordon W** **fl 1955**
West Lothian stained glass designer. Exhibited a glass panel at GI, from Grangemouth.

**STEVENS, John RSA** **1793-1868**
Born Ayr; died Edinburgh. Painter of genre and portraits. Practised painting in Ayr before going to London but once there distinguished himself by obtaining two silver medals at the RA Schools in 1818. His exhibit RA 'Portrait of a lady" 1815 was the first of 14 works exhibited there between 1815 and 1857. Cultivated a close study of the Old Masters during several years spent in Rome where he painted one of his most important works 'Pilgrims at their devotions', exhibited in 1831. In 1826 painted 'Queen Mary', a work described at the time as 'excellent, finished in a style breathing the spirit and the power of the Old Master. The figure of the Queen is graceful, the drapery beautiful, and the accessory parts of the picture chaste and finished'. Elected ARSA 1826, RSA 1829. In 1868 he suffered a railway accident in France which eventually led to his death shortly after his return home. 'The Standard-Bearer' is in NGS.
**Bibl:** AJ 1859, 141; Bryan; Brydall (where he is incorrectly referred to as Steven) 278-9; Cat of Eng Brit Port BM 2 (1910) 409, 658; Wingfield.

**STEVENS, Robert H** **fl 1970**
Angus designer; trained Gray's School of Art, Aberdeen. Exhibited two works at the AAS in the above year from the Manse of Glenesk, Brechin.

**STEVENS, William** **fl 1866**
Glasgow minor figure; exhibited 'Still life with fruit' RSA.

**STEVENSON, -** **fl 1830**
Aberdeen engraver. Engraved a bookplate for Aberdeen Mechanics' Institution, 1830.
**Bibl:** Bushnell.

**STEVENSON, A Ross** **fl 1856-1860**
Edinburgh painter; exhibited illustrations of Roslin Chapel at the RSA in 1856(2) & 1860.

**STEVENSON, Ada P** **fl 1893-1900**
Anateur painter of flowers and west Highland landscape. Wife of the minister of Rutherglen; exhibited GI(4).

**STEVENSON, Alan FRSE LLB** **1807-1865**
Born Edinburgh; died Portobello, Dec 23. Civil engineer, member of the Stevenson family, specialising in the building of lighthouses. Eldest son of Robert Stevenson(qv), succeeding his father as engineer to the Northern Lighthouses Board 1843. Educated High School & Edinburgh University, winning the Fellowes prize in nat. phil. Designed ten lighthouses including the keepers' houses of Cromarty (1846), Fortrose (1846) and Noss Head (1849), Skerryvore (1838-43) & North Ronaldsay Lighthouse (1851-54), with David S(qv). Author of *A Rudimentary Treatise on the History, Construction, and Illumination of Lighthouses* (1850). Recipient of medals from the Emperor of Russia and the Kings of Holland & Prussia.
**Bibl:** DNB; Gifford, H & I, 62,124,347,399,418,626,629,pl.122; Bella Bathurst, The Lighthouse Stevensons, HarperCollins, 1999.

**STEVENSON, Anthony W** **fl 1889-1907**
Obscure animal painter, mainly dogs. Wingfield records a pair of black and tan and white greyhounds dated 1889.
**Bibl:** Wingfield.

**STEVENSON, Bessie** **fl 1879**
Minor Edinburgh watercolour painter; exhibited a study of continental buildings at the RSA.

**STEVENSON, Christina Russell** **fl 1887-1888**
Obscure Glasgow flower painter. Exhibited GI(2) from Wardend, Milliken Park.

**STEVENSON, David FRSE FRSSA** **1815-1888**
Born Edinburgh, Jan 11; died North Berwick, July 17. Designer & civil engineer. Third son of Robert S(qv). Educated Edinburgh High School and University. Author of *The Application of Marine Surveying and Hydrometry to the Practice of Civil Engineering* 1842, the first work of its kind. Toured North America 1837 resulting in *Sketch of the Civil Engineering of North America* republished with additions 1859. Other books followed. Joined his father and brother Alan(qv) as partner 1838 in which capacity he assumed responsibility for the entire business management. Succeeded brother Alan as engineer to the Northern Lighthouses Board 1853 and, with his brother Thomas(qv), designed and built no fewer than 28 beacons and 30 lighthouses, the optical machinery of the latter being in almost every case novel. Stemmming from his report of 1870 lighthouses worldwide began using paraffin for lighting rather than colza oil. Also involved in lighthouse design and construction in India, Newfoundland, New Zealand and Japan. Because of earthquake dangers in Japan, Stevenson devised the 'aseismic' arrangement to protect delicate optical equipment. Elected FRSE 1844, President, Royal Scottish Society of Arts 1869.
**Bibl:** DNB; Gifford, H & I, 123n, 347 et passim.

**STEVENSON, David Watson RSA** **1842-1904**
Born Ratho, Midlothian, 25 Mar; died Edinburgh, 18 Mar. Brother of William Grant S(qv). Sculptor of portrait busts and idealised subjects. Trained Trustees School and Life School at the same time, and studied for eight years under William Brodie(qv). Also studied in Rome. Whilst at the Trustee School won the South Kensington national prize for a statuette reproduction of the Venus of Milo. In Rome 1876 and frequent visitor to Paris. When an assistant to Sir John Steell(qv) he was involved in Steell's commission for the Scottish National Memorial to the Prince Consort and for the Wallace memorial outside Stirling. Statues to 'Science,' 'Learning' and 'Labour 'adorn Charlotte Square while 'Robert Burns' (1898) is in Leith. His terracotta bust of 'James Drummond'(qv), now in the RSA collection, was exhibited in 1876, other exhibits included a portrait bust of 'Kenneth MacLeay' 1877, the model for a bronze statue to 'Robert Tannahill', now in Paisley AG, 1884, 'Sir John Steel when sculptor to Her Majesty for Scotland' 1887 and 'Napier of Merchiston' 1898, now in SNPG. Writing in the *AJ* Caw commented that he 'suffers from a conscientious desire for a finish and completeness beyond that which his artistic impulse demands; but it is always sincere, and marked by sterling qualities of its own. His portraiture is admirable in its simple veracity, and if his more imaginative figures are lacking in high poetry and style, they are always refined, and in their own way completely realised'. Elected ARSA 1877, RSA 1886. Exhibited RA(15) 1868-1898 including portrait busts of 'George McDonald' (1871), 'the Earl of Hopetoun, Governor of Victoria' (1891), a bronze statuette of 'Robert Louis Stevenson'(1895) and a marble bust of RLS (1898). At the RSA he exhibited almost annually a total of 172 works from 1859 until his death in 1904; also GI(40), L(6) & RHA(2). Represented in SNPG (7), Paisley AG, Edinburgh City collection(6) including four studies of R L Stevenson.
**Bibl:** AJ 1898, 72; Gifford 147,203,275,281,284,294,304,316,404, 470, pl 8; Fiona Pearson,'Sir John Steell and the Idea of a Native School of Sculpture', in Virtue and Vision, (Ex Cat NGS 1991); RSA (obit).

**STEVENSON, E L** **fl 1914-1921**
Minor Glasgow figure; exhibited Walker Gallery, Liverpool(5).

**STEVENSON, F** **fl 1885**
Amateur Glasgow artist; exhibited RSA(1) from Rosewood Villa, Crosshill.

**STEVENSON, Mrs Frances** **fl 1953**
Renfrewshire topographical painter. Exhibited GI(1) from Whitecraigs.

**STEVENSON, George Cunningham** **fl 1919-1957**
Edinburgh watercolour landscape painter. Trained Hospitalfield and served in WW2. Moved to Hamilton 1932, Airdrie 1934 where he was head of art at the Academy, and Pittenweem 1954. Exhibited RSA(12), RSW & GI(6).
**Bibl:** Edinburgh Evening News, 1 Aug 1957.

**STEVENSON, George V** **fl 1940-1953**
Glasgow painter of genre, military portraits and local scenery; many in watercolour, chalk and/or pencil. Exhibited RSA(4) & GI(2) from 36 Woodlands Drive.

**STEVENSON, Hamilton** **?-1788**
Scottish portrait and landscape painter. Pupil, with his brother John, at the Foulis Academy but shortly afterwards emigrated to Charlestown, South Carolina, then to Jamaica where he and his brother set up in partnership. On September 21 1773 an advertisement appeared in the *Carolina Gazette and Country Journal* 'Stevenson, limner - history, portrait, landscape and miniature, family and conversation pieces, size of nature or small whole length style of Zoffani: perspective views from nature'. Sometime after 1775 they established an Academy for Drawing and Painting at Charlestown where they professed to teach after the manner taught in the Roman schools.

**STEVENSON, Miss Helen G** **fl 1923-1935**
Edinburgh colour woodcut artist, fond of Highland subjects including boats. Trained Edinburgh College of Art 1923. Exhibited RSA(14), AAS(7), GI(15) & L(10), from 87 Comiston Drive, latterly Pentland Crescent.

**STEVENSON, James RSA** **c1785-1844**
Edinburgh painter in oil and watercolour; landscapes and seascapes. Painted landscape in the Lothians, Dumfries-shire and occasionally in Wales but most especially in Perthshire; also seascapes of the south east coast of Scotland. Foundation academician 1826, and one of the most neglected. His diploma work was 'Edinburgh, from the Old Pier, Kinghorn' 1831. Landscapes around Newhall House were engraved for Robert Burns' *The Gentle Shepherd with illustrations of the Scenery* (1808). Moved from 68 to 74 George Street 1842. Exhibited

RSA(111) 1808-1844 yet is not mentioned in any of the early histories.
**Bibl:** Butchart 36; Halsby 51.

**STEVENSON, Mrs Jean(n)ie Grant** **fl 1886-1937**
Edinburgh painter in watercolour and pastel of rustic scenes, portraits and atmospheric landscape, sometimes with fishing boats. Married William Grant S(qv). Exhibited frequently RSA(47); also RSW(1), AAS 1906-1912 & GI(31), latterly from the Dean Studio.

**STEVENSON, Jean Macaulay** **fl 1931-1966**
Painter of figure studies in oils. Trained Glasgow School of Art 1926-31. Daughter of John Macaulay S(qv). Visited France 1910. Won Lauder award 1933. Secretary, Glasgow Society of Lady Artists 1955-9. Exhibited GI(5).

**STEVENSON, John** **fl 1851-1871**
Portrait painter. Worked many years in Ardrossan. Specialised in portraits of children, also figure subjects. Exhibited RSA(5) & GI(3).

**STEVENSON, John** **fl 1856**
Edinburgh painter of figure studies; exhibited 'Contemplation' at the RSA from Hanover St.

**STEVENSON, John Jnr** **fl 1940**
Glasgow stained glass designer. Possibly son of John S of Ardrossan(qv). Exhibited GI(1), from 4 Gray Street.

**STEVENSON, John James** **1831-1908**
Architect with strong Perthshire connections. Related to Robert Louis S(qv) and to the engineer Stevensons. Began adult life as a theology student but following a visit to Italy decided to take up architecture, becoming articled to David Bryce(qv) in Edinburgh 1856-8. Moved to the offices of Gilbert Scott in London and in 1860 became a partner in Glasgow with Campbell Douglas(qv) but returned to London 1869, entering into partnership with **E.R. ROBSON**, architect to the School Board. Continued to build churches. houses and University buildings in England. Pioneered the Queen Anne revival in his own home. His office was known as the Scotsman's stepping-stone to London. Stevenson proposed Robert Lorimer for associateship of the RIBA 1891. Practised only from London 1874-1890 from Red House, Bayswater and subsequently 4 Porchester Gardens. Among his best known designs in Scotland were those for the Free Church, Crieff (ex RA 1882), the tower for St Leonard's Church at Perth (1884), Westerlea, Murrayfield (remodelled by Lorimer), Kelvin Stevenson Church, Glasgow (1898), the Peter Memorial Church, Stirling (1899) and another church in Stirling (1901). Author of *House Architecture* (1880). Exhibited RA(25), RSA(1) & GI(7).
**Bibl:** Gifford 633; A Gomme & D Walker, Architecture of Glasgow, London 1987(rev), 300; Peter Savage, Lorimer and the Edinburgh Craft Designers, Edinburgh 1980, 4,7,30,39,97,111,142,156,169.

**STEVENSON, Joseph** **fl 1876**
Amateur Edinburgh sculptor; exhibited RSA(1).

**STEVENSON, Miss M** **fl 1871**
Amateur watercolour painter of wildlife subjects; exhibited RSA(1).

**STEVENSON, Martin William** **1954-**
Born Peebles, Jan 31. Portrait and figure painter in oils and acrylic; trained Duncan of Jordanstone College of Art, Dundee 1974-9. Influenced by Lucien Freud, Frampton and Andrew Wyeth. Won BP Portrait Award, NPG 1990. Exhibits RSA since 1983; also AAS, from 400 King St. Represented in Aberdeen AG.

**STEVENSON, Pasley** **fl 1887**
Amateur watercolour painter who lived at Crossgates, Fife; exhibited a rural scene at the RSA in the above year.

**STEVENSON, Robert FRSE FSA (Scot)** **1772-1850**
Born Glasgow, June 8; died Edinburgh July 12. Civil engineer. Trained Andersonian Institute, Glasgow & Edinburgh University. Taken into partnership by Thomas Smith, the first engineer to the Northern Lighthouses Board, 1796. Superintended the design and construction of no fewer than 20 lighthouses around Scotland. Undertook voyage round Scotland with Sir Walter Scott 1814. An originator of Edinburgh's Royal Observatory, while his experiments on the destruction of timber by *Limnoria terebrans* led to the universal use of greenheart oak for structures in the sea.
**Bibl:** DNB, Gifford, H & I, 62, 117, 350, 510, 625-6.

**STEVENSON, Robert** **fl 1876-1879**
Glasgow landscape painter; fond of Arran and the west Highlands. Exhibited RSA(4).

**STEVENSON, Robert** **fl 1960s**
Four studies by an artist of this name are in the City of Edinburgh collection, all purchased from the artist 1961 and all studies of R L Stevenson's house at Swanston (one oil, three watercolours).

**STEVENSON, Robert Alan Mowbray** **1847-1900**
Born Edinburgh, Mar 28; died Chiswick, London, 18 Apr. Painter in oil of landscape; also critic. Studied in Edinburgh, Cambridge, Antwerp and Paris under Carolus Duran. Professor of Fine Art, Liverpool University College 1880-1893; influential art critic of *Pall Mall Gazette* 1893-1900. Exponent of impressionist theory. Pioneered the trend toward an appreciation of the pictorial rather than the literary or sentimental. Published a book on Velasquez 1896. Lived in London. Exhibited RA(5) 1879-1885; also RSA(9), ROI(3) & RBA(1) from 16 St. Leonard's Terrace, Chelsea.
**Bibl:** Benezit; Caw 142,307,349,360-1,374; Irwin 345,370,375,376, 394.

**STEVENSON, Robert Louis** **1850-1894**
Born Edinburgh, 13 Nov; died Samoa, 4 Dec. Celebrated author and amateur woodcut artist. Studied engineering at Edinburgh University and admitted as an advocate in the city 1875. In the 1870s publication began of his series of best-selling classics including *An Inland Voyage* (1878), *Travels with a Donkey in the Cevennes* (1879), *Treasure Island* (1882, partly written in Braemar), *Kidnapped* and *Dr Jekyll and Mr Hyde* (both 1886). Ill-health forced him to travel abroad, first to North America (1887) then, via Australia, to Samoa. None of his very competent woodcut illustrations were published before his death. Pennell records a whole series of little books, virtually unknown, which he illustrated including *Moral Emblems* (c1881), with its third edition retitled *The Graver and the Pen, or scenes from Nature with appropriate verses, The Black Scalper, The Black Canyon, The Pirate* and *The Apothecary*. Most of his landscapes were executed in pencil. Met many of the most distinguished continental artists of his time during sojourns at Barbizon and in Paris. In 1879 met an American, Mrs Osbourne(qv), an habitué of the art coteries of Paris and Fontainebleau, whom he followed to California, marrying her 1880. His own style is best seen from the sketch book he carried to the Cevennes although in landscape he adopted a more sophisticated, naturalistic style.
**Bibl:** Caw passim; DNB; Houfe; J. Pennell, 'RLS, Illustrator', Studio, vol 9, 1897, 17-24 illus.

**STEVENSON, Mrs Robert Louis (Fanny van de Grift Osbourne)** **1840-1914**
Born Indianapolis. Moved and painted among the art circles of Fontainebleau and Paris. Married R L Stevenson(qv) 1880. Settled in Samoa 1890. Returned to California after her husband's death. Represented in Edinburgh City collection by an oil 'The Bridge at Grez, Forest of Fontainbleau'.

**STEVENSON, Robert Macaulay RSW** **1854-1952**
Born Glasgow, 4 Jne; died Bardowie, Milngavie 20 Sep. Painter in oil and watercolour, landscape and figure scenes. Married Stansmore Dean(qv). Father of Jean Macaulay S(qv). Member of the Glasgow School. Trained Glasgow School of Art and although not one of the most original members of the group he became its principal spokesman after about 1888. Deeply involved in the artistic life in Glasgow, as much in its administrative complexities as in the substance of its art. Contributor to *Quiz*. Largely responsible for ensuring that the Glasgow Art Club was won over to the new movement. Best known for his paintings of river scenes, often in moonlight with a dependence on a rich impasto giving a rather gloomy but romantic aspect to the scene. Elected RSW 1906, largely on account of his small-scale landscapes, but struck off 1913. Profoundly influenced by Corot; he himself called his work 'constructive idealism' which he described thus 'the colours fade, the aspect changes, the leaves die, the picture as it was in Nature ceases to be: the recollection remains, and that memory I transcribe on to canvas. And since the remembrance stays

with us, while the actuality fades and perishes, is not the memory that does not perish the essential human fact, the really living part?' His studio, called the Macaulaypol, was open to all and sundry. Lived in France 1910, remaining there until after WW1 and then from 1932-51 lived in Kirkcudbright before retiring to his former home at Robinsfield, Milngavie. Member Glasgow Art Club 1886 until shortly before his death. Of all the Glasgow Boys it is said he was closest to Hornel and Henry in style although popular with all of them; Melville would never stay anywhere else when visiting Glasgow. For a short time edited *Scottish Art Review*(qv). Lavery(qv) called him the prophet of the School, having survived all the other Glasgow Boys he became a symbol of what they stood for. The *Art Journal* of 1938 recorded that 'he is so in love with twilight over woodland and lake, with dim shadowy colour betwixt green and gray, that he will not or cannot see nature otherwise; and, if his pictorial ideas seem to be derived in this respect, his pictures have qualities which are personal to himself'. His brother, Sir Daniel S, became Lord Provost of Glasgow. Exhibited RA(2), in 1884 and 1892, but mainly RSA(17), RSW, AAS 1894-8 & GI(75). Represented in Glasgow AG(10), Greenock AG, Paisley AG, City of Edinburgh collection, Barcelona AG, Berlin AG, Brussels AG, Munich AG, Prague AG, St Louis AG, Weimar AG (Germany), Zurich AG (Switzerland).
**Bibl:** AJ 1898, 70; Billcliffe 41, 173; Caw 385-6,485; Halsby 126,150,285; Irwin 373-4,378,381; Studio, (1901) vol 22.

**STEVENSON, Stansmore Richmond Leslie Dean** **[see DEAN]**

**STEVENSON, Thomas FRSE FRSSA** **1818-1887**
Born Edinburgh, July 22; died Edinburgh (in his home, 17 Heriot Row), May 8. Designer, engineer, meteorologist. Youngest son of Robert S(qv); father of Robert Louis S(qv). Apprenticed in his father's office, published the first of many learned papers the same year as qualifying 1842, and by 1883 this total had reached 44. Entered family partnership 1846 becoming, with his brother David(qv), engineer to the board of northern lighthouses 1853-85, with whom he designed several lighthouses and harbours including Holbornhead lighthouse and keepers' houses at Scrabster (1860-2), the outer harbour at Wick (1862-67) and the attractive small lighthouse and adjacent keepers' houses at Corran, Loch Linnhe (1860). Main contribution was his development of lighthouse illumination. Elected FRSE 1848, becoming President 1885; President, Royal Scottish Society of Arts 1859-60. Originator and one-time secretary, Scottish Meteorological Society 1871. Invented the Stevenson screen for barometers (still in use) 1864.
**Bibl:** DNB.

**STEVENSON, Thomas** **fl 1885**
Glasgow oil painter of figure subjects; exhibited RSA(1).

**STEVENSON, William** **fl 1882-1900**
Edinburgh still life and figure painter in oils. Exhibited RSA(18) & GI(4).

**STEVENSON, William Grant RSA** **1849-1919**
Born Ratho, Midlothian, 7 Mar; died Edinburgh, 6 May. Sculptor and painter of animal subjects. Younger brother of David Watson S(qv). Educated at the parish school, trained Edinburgh College of Art and RSA Life Class where he gained one gold and two silver national medals. His most important works in sculpture are statues of Robert Burns at Kilmarnock, Denver and Chicago and Sir William Wallace in Duthie Park, Aberdeen (1883). Some of his best work is modelled in silver and on a much smaller scale than his statues, for example, 'The Return of the Spies with the Grapes of Esheol' executed for the Marquess of Bute, and a bronze statuette of Harry Vardon. The humour with which he depicted some of his paintings, particularly of domestic animals, was in contrast to the hardness of his style and the coldness of his colour. Probably less serious in purpose than his brother although occasionally more lively in manner. Contributed to Kerr's *History of Curling* (1890). C O Murray(qv) etched an original work 'Golf at St Andrews' 1892. Elected ARSA 1885, RSA 1886. Exhibited RA(9) 1874-1895; also RSA(190), GI throughout 1872-1919 & AAS 1885-1912. Represented in SNPG (Sam Bough), Edinburgh City collection.
**Bibl:** AJ 1885,335; 1898,72,128; Caw 340; Gifford 203,284,316, 390,426,443; Who was Who 1916-1928; Wingfield.

**STEWART, Mrs A** **fl 1887**
Renfrewshire landscape painter. Exhibited GI(1) from 6 Percy Street, Paisley.

**STEWART, Alan** **fl 1890-1894**
Edinburgh artist, (sometimes spelled Stuart). Landscape and figure studies. Exhibited AAS(8) from 108 George St.

**STEWART, Alan D** **fl 1959**
Aberdeen landscape painter; exhibited 'Winter landscape, Strathdon' and 'Mellon Udrigle' at the AAS from 17 Belvidere St.

**STEWART, Alexander** **fl 1864-1876**
Edinburgh-based oil painter of landscapes and figure subjects. Moved to Aberfeldy, Perthshire. Exhibited RSA(17).

**STEWART, Alexander** **fl 1897-1902**
Glasgow painter, mostly Surrey landscapes in watercolour. Exhibited GI(5).

**STEWART, Alexander** **fl 1917-1967**
Painter in watercolour, etcher and draughtsman. Scottish landscapes. Exhibited GI(5) from a variety of addresses, latterly from Paisley.

**STEWART, Alexander B** **fl 1950**
Alloa portrait painter; exhibited RSA(1).

**STEWART, Alexander C** **fl 1847-1848**
Landscape painter. Lived Dundee then Edinburgh 1848. Exhibited mainly west Highland and Arran scenery at the RSA(6).

**STEWART, Allan** **1865-1951**
Born Edinburgh, 11 Feb; died Dalry, 29 Jan. Painter in oil and watercolour; portraits, landscapes, military and historical subjects, also illustrator. Trained RSA Schools and Edinburgh Institution. At the former he gained the Maclaine-Watters award and the Stuart and Chalmers prizes. Further studies in Paris and Spain. Staff of *ILN* from c1895 and accompanied Edward VII on an Mediterranean cruise. Was their special artist in South Africa. Worked at Kenley, Surrey until c1925, moved to Castle Douglas, Kircudbright. 'His pictures are somewhat cold in tone and too heavy and black in colour...but capably and effectively drawn and designed...his illustrative drawing is more capable and effective than distinguished and searching [Caw]. Illustrated Grierson's *Children's Book of Edinburgh* and *Children's Tales from Scottish Ballads* (both 1906), the same author's *Book of Celtic Stories* (1908), S.R. Crockett's *Red-Cap Adventures* (1908), Grierson's *Tales of Scottish Keeps and Castles* (1928) and Scott's *Tales of a Grandfather* (1934). In the spring of 1946 his painting 'King Edward VII inspecting the Royal Company of Archers, the King's Bodyguard for Scotland' was purchased for Holyrood Palace. Among other principal works were 'The Charge of the Scots Gray's at St Quentin', 'Queen Mary Going to Her Execution' and 'Prince Charlie's Last Look at Scotland', RA 1894, is now in a New Zealand private collection. Another effective work that received much publicity at the time, partly through a popular engraving, was 'To the Honour of Brave Men', a moving rendering of Major Wilson's last stand at the Shangani river, while another of the same ilk was 'The Gordons at Dargai'. Exhibited RA(9), RSA(27), RSW(1), GI(8) & L(6), latterly from 3 Randolph Gdns, Maida Vale. Represented in United States Golf Association Museum ('The First International Foursome', painted in Carolean costume).
**Bibl:** Caw 466; Bertha E. Mahony et al, Illustrators of Children's Books 1744-1944, Boston(USA), 1948, 362-3; Wingfield.

**STEWART, Miss Amy** **fl 1889-1901**
Edinburgh painter in oil and watercolour of portraits and figure subjects. Exhibited RA(3), RSA(9), RSW(1), GI(2) & L(1).

**STEWART, Anthony** **1774-1846**
Born Crieff; died Stockwell, London. Painter of portrait miniatures and occasional portraits. Both his daughters Grace Campbell(qv) and Margaret(qv) were his pupils and became skilled miniaturists. Studied landscape under Alexander Nasmyth(qv) but preferred miniature painting which he practised in Scotland and later in London. Married the daughter of Alexander Weir. Had a fashionable clientele including members of the Royal family. Painted the first miniature ever done of

'Princess Victoria'. Exhibited RA(12) 1807-1820. Specialised in children, commissioned to paint the portraits of 'Princess Charlotte' and 'Princess Victoria'. Most of his sitters were painted full-face. When portraying adults the result was less effective than when working with children. Often used light, clear colours with much stippling in the background. He was supposedly patronised by the daughters of Campbell of Monzie and Inverawe and to have painted allegorical panels for a summer-house at Monzie Castle, Gilmerton, Perthshire but no records of either now exist. Illustrated Hume: *Douglas, a tragedy* 1797. Represented in NGS(5), V & A, Royal collection.
**Bibl:** Bryan 128; Brydall 247; Caw 91.

**STEWART, B** **fl 1897**
Minor landscape painter of Balshagray House, Partick, Glasgow, exhibited GI(1).

**STEWART, Col B H Shaw** **fl 1928-1938**
Amateur watercolourist. Living at Spean Bridge, Inverness-shire 1918 and in 1938 was in Glasgow. Exhibited RSA(1), RSW(1) & GI(6).

**STEWART, Betty** **fl 1955-1957**
Aberdeen sculptress; exhibited religious works in wood at the RSA(2).

**STEWART, Catherine M** **fl 1862-1870**
Bute painter of still life, west Highland landscape and portraits. Exhibited GI(8) from Rothesay.

**STEWART, Charles Edward** **fl 1887-1938**
Born Glasgow. Painter in oil of genre, historical subjects and country sports especially hunting. Trained RA Schools and Academie Julien in Paris. Lived for a time in Glasgow and London, and Dunning in Perthshire, moved to Little Kimble, Bucks c1920. Exhibited RA(37) including his best known work 'Every Dog Has His Day', RSA(3), ROI(3), RHA(2), GI(19) & L(2). Represented in Glasgow AG.
**Bibl:** Wingfield.

**STEWART, Charles E** **fl 1931-1949**
Glasgow stained glass window designer. Exhibited GI(10).

**STEWART, Colin H** **fl 1986**
East Lothian landscape painter of local views. Exhibited RSA from Haddington.

**STEWART, Douglas Gordon** **fl 1936-1947**
Dundee subject painter; exhibited RSA(6) including 'Bull ring' (1947).

**STEWART, Douglas** **fl 1965**
Aberdeen painter; exhibited AAS(1) from 6 Sunnybank Rd.

**STEWART, Edward** **fl 1982-**
Glasgow painter. Began exhibiting GI(3) 1982.

**STEWART, Elizabeth D** **fl 1907**
Edinburgh painter; exhibited two Venetian scenes RSA from 10 Salisbury Rd.

**STEWART, Miss Elizabeth E** **fl 1974**
Ayrshire amateur painter. Exhibited GI(1), from Troon.

**STEWART, Frederick Craik** **fl 1923-1931**
Etcher. Portraits and topographical subjects. Exhibited RSA(3), GI(17) & L(1). Living at Blackhall, Midlothian after 1926.

**STEWART, Miss Frances E** **fl 1939-1948**
Glasgow painter of portraits, genre & still life; exhibited at the RSA(12) & GI(7), latterly from Beaconsfield Pl, Aberdeen.

**STEWART, George** **fl 1896**
Aberdeen amateur painter of country scenes; exhibited AAS(1) from Cuparstown Row.

**STEWART, Miss Grace Campbell** **fl 1843-d1863**
Portrait miniaturist. Daughter and pupil of Anthony S(qv), sister of Margaret(qv). Worked in London and built up a reputation as a fine miniaturist. Among 14 exhibits at the RA (1843-56) was 'Lady Rachel Scott, daughter of the Earl of Eldon' 1843, 'Lady Selina Scott, daughter of the Earl and Countess of Eldon' 1846 and 'Helen Mary, daughter of Sir William Heathcote' 1856. Lived latterly at 10 Union Rd, Clapham.

**STEWART, Graham** **c1956-**
Goldsmith, silversmith and jeweller. Trained Gray's School of Art 1973-78. Recognised as one of Britain's leading silversmiths. Employs smithing techniques including forging, raising, carving and engraving. His work echoes the curves and rhythms of nature while latterly he has become more interested in creating what he calls 'table sculpture'. Solo exhibitions in England & Scotland since 1992. Made a Freeman of The Worshipful Company of Goldsmiths 1996. Represented in Birmingham AG, Aberdeen AG, Goldsmiths Company (London), City of Edinburgh collection, collections of Queen Elizabeth and the Princess Royal. Lives and works from his studios in the High St, Dunblane.

**STEWART, Henry** **1897-?**
Born Glasgow, Jan 20. Painter in watercolour and etcher. Exhibited 1923-37, RSA(2), RSW(3), GI(2) & L(2), from Bridge of Weir, Renfrewshire.
**Bibl:** Halsby 285.

**STEWART, Hope James** **fl 1839-d1883**
Prolific painter in oil, watercolour and pencil; portraits, subjects and landscapes. In Rome 1842. Various Edinburgh addresses, latterly Prestonfield. Exhibited RSA(100+) including 'HM The Queen and HRH Prince Albert meeting a Highland Funeral in the Pass of Killiecrankie' 1869. Represented in SNPG(15).

**STEWART, Ian** **fl 1923-1935**
Glasgow portrait, flower, interior and still life painter; mostly in pencil. Moved to England c1931 exhibited 'Sacristy door, Iona cathedral' at the RSA (1929); also RA(3), GI(4) & L(1).

**STEWART, Isabel** **fl 1917-1918**
Glasgow sculptress. Exhibited RSA(1) & GI(1) from 49 Polwarth Gardens, Hyndland.

**STEWART, J Smith** **fl 1938**
Kilmarnock watercolour painter; exhibited GI(1) from 53 Holehouse Rd.

**STEWART, J Tytler** **fl 1905**
Minor painter of pastoral scenes. Exhibited GI(1) from Craigend, Cardross.

**STEWART, James** **fl 1856-1861**
Edinburgh painter of nature subjects; exhibited RSA(3) from Broughton St.

**STEWART, James** **fl 1858-1859**
Edinburgh painter of conversation pieces and informal portraits; exhibited RSA from Hanover St. Possibly the same **James Stewart** employed as a 'Master' at the Edinburgh Drawing Institution in Hill St 1825.
**Bibl:** Prospectus of a Drawing Academy in Edinburgh, (1825), MS in Edinburgh PL.

**STEWART, James** **fl 1878**
Perthshire landscape painter in oil; exhibited 'Scene in Strathardle' RSA.

**STEWART, James** **fl 1944**
Fife watercolour painter; exhibited 'Mending the nets at Pittenweem' RSA 1944, from Cardenden; 'The Fishing Fleet, Pittenweem' at the GI 1944.

**STEWART, James Jnr** **fl 1870-1876**
Glasgow painter in oil of trees and figures in landscape, exhibited 3 scenes on Arran at the RSA, and 13 Arran landscapes at the GI.

**STEWART, James (John) Oswald** **fl 1864-1894**
Painter in oil and watercolour of figure subjects and literary interiors.

Much influenced by Mollinger. May have visited Arran 1872. Apart from a spell at Fordyce Castle, Portsoy 1880-5, lived in Edinburgh and Seafield St, Cullen, Banff. Exhibited RSA(43), AAS(2) & GI(5).

**STEWART, James Lawson** **fl 1829-1905**
Edinburgh painter in oil of landscapes occasionally north west Highlands but more often on the continent, also topographical subjects. Divided his time between Edinburgh and London. Exhibited RA(3), RSA(79), RBA(2) & L(1). Among his better known exhibits was 'The Cirque of Garnarvie, Pyrenees' 1864, the highest waterfall in Europe, and 'Slioch, Loch Maree', the same year.

**STEWART, James Malcolm** **1829-1916**
Glasgow painter in oil of figure subjects, portraits and landscapes, coastal scenes. Exhibited RA(1), RSA(47), GI(59) 1861-1897 & RBA(1). Represented in Glasgow AG.

**STEWART, James Scott** **fl 1854-1919**
Painter originally from Falkirk of figure subjects and portraits in oils. Moved to Glasgow from where most of his exhibits were entered. Exhibited RSA(32), RSW(1), GI(68) 1863-1919 & L(1).

**STEWART, James (?Struthers) HRSA** **1791-1863**
Born Edinburgh; died Cape Colony. Engraver and painter of portraits, landscape and genre. Articled to Robert Scott the engraver(qv); studied drawing at the Trustees Academy under Graham(qv). Became a competent line-engraver, engraving many of Sir William Allan's paintings including 'Circassian Captives' 1820 and the 'Murder of Archibishop Sharpe' 1824. Engraved Wilkie's 'The Penny Wedding'. Foundation member, RSA 1826 but moved to London 1830, exhibiting there until 1861. Owing to lack of money in 1833 he emigrated to Algoa Bay, Cape Colony settling there as a farmer; but within a year lost everything due to the Kaffir War. Then went to live in Somerset, Cape Colony, where he taught and painted portraits. Many of his works were destroyed when the family fled from marauding tribesmen. Resigned his academic membership 1858 but was granted honorary membership the following year. Among his plates were: 'Tartar Brigands dividing their Spoil' after Allan; 'The Murder of Archbishop Sharp', after Allan; 'The Abdication of Mary Stuart', after Allan; 'The Gentle Shepherd', after Wilkie; 'The Pedlar', after Wilkie; and 'The Penny Wedding', after Wilkie. Exhibited 21 works at the Institution for the Encouragement for the Fine Arts in Scotland and 5 works at the Scottish Academy 1830-34 including a diploma landscape 1831; also RA(21) 1825-59. Represented in SNPG, Glasgow AG, City of Edinburgh collection.
**Bibl:** AJ 1863, 165; Bryan; Brydall 204-5; Bushnell; DNB; Fine Arts Quart Rev, 2, 1864, 209; Print Coll Quart, 16, 1929, 273; Redgrave.

**STEWART, Jamie B** **fl 1870-1871**
Amateur Greenock portrait and landscape painter. Moved from Craigard, Pollockshields to Greenock c1871. Exhibited an oil RSA; a crayon portrait GI.

**STEWART, Jane Gertrude (Mrs John)** **fl 1891-1908**
Edinburgh miniature painter. Lived at Twynham, Kirkcudbright, before moving to Garscube Terrace, Edinburgh 1896. Exhibited RSA(9), GI(1) & L(1).

**STEWART, Janet Elizabeth H** **fl 1977-1978**
East Lothian sculptress; exhibited RSA(3) in rosewood, alabaster and lignum vitae, from Humbie.

**STEWART, Jess K** **fl 1926**
Aberdeen-based painter; exhibited a view of Banff at the AAS from 51 Elmbank Terrace.

**STEWART, John** **fl 1595-1617**
Early Edinburgh painter. Apprenticed to John Sawers snr(qv) 25 Mar 1595. Associated with John Workman(qv) who described Stewart as 'my man'. Received payment for work done at Edinburgh Castle, 9 and 16 Jne, 1617. Brother **William STEWART** (fl 1617-1632) also a painter burgess.
**Bibl:** Apted 91; Accounts of the Masters of Works, ii, 78,80.

**STEWART, John** **fl 1839-1841**
Edinburgh portrait and genre painter; exhibited RSA(5) from Buccleuch St.

**STEWART, John** **fl 1841-1863**
Edinburgh landscape painter; exhibited RSA(11).

**STEWART, John** **1860-1928**
Amateur Ross-shire artist, draughtsman, poet and designer. Lived for many years in Maryburgh before becoming sub-master at Ullapool. Sketched and painted Highland landscapes in pencil and watercolour. Illustrated work for Lady Aberdeen c1900, also for the *Ross-shire Journal*. Designed Ullapool War Memorial.

**STEWART, John** **fl 1865-1901**
Born Greenock. Painter and ship's chandler. Father of Col. Arthur Stewart, who purchased Glengarden from Rodolphe Christen(qv) and distant cousin of Hugh Clapperton(qv). Friend of John Pettie(qv). Commissioned by the sugar magnate, Lord Lyle. Lived for a time in Kilmacolm & Gourock. Exhibited RSA(6) & RGI(9).

**STEWART, John Anderson** **1800-1866**
Dundee oil painter of landscape, genre and rustic portrait figures, often illustrative of the work of Robbie Burns. Father of John Anderson S(qv). Exhibited RSA(10). Represented by 'Rev. G Gilfillan' in Victoria AG (Australia).

**STEWART, John Anderson Jnr** **fl 1883-1893**
Dundee painter of landscape and topographical works, sometimes in pen & ink, also pencil. Son of John Anderson S(qv). Exhibited RSA(10) & GI(1).

**STEWART, Ken** **fl 1977-1979**
Aberdeen painter. Trained Gray's School of Art, Aberdeen. Exhibited AAS(6) from 48 Stanley St.

**STEWART, Kenneth** **fl 1978**
Aberdeen printmaker. Exhibited AAS(1) from 1 Abbotswell Drive.

**STEWART, Kenneth Gunn** **fl 1971**
Aberdeenshire artist; exhibited AAS(2) from 1 Golf Rd, Bieldside.

**STEWART, M** **fl 1897**
Amateur watercolour painter. Exhibited GI(1) from The Schoolhouse, Roseneath.

**STEWART, Miss M C** **fl 1867**
Bute landscape painter. Probably sister of Catherine S(qv). Exhibited a view on Arran at the GI, from 20 Argyle Pl, Rothesay.

**STEWART, Maggie P** **fl 1893-1898**
Amateur watercolourist of Kelvindale, Maryhill, Glasgow; exhibited RSW(1) & GI(4).

**STEWART, Malcolm** **1829-1916**
Painter of portraits and genre. Represented by 'Roundell Palmer' in NPG, Glasgow AG(3) including a portrait of 'Dr Livingstone'.

**STEWART, Miss Margaret (Mrs John Seguier)** **19th Century**
Portrait miniaturist. Elder daughter and pupil of Anthony S(qv), sister of Grace Campbell S(qv). Said to have been a competent portrait miniaturist but no recorded works remain. Married the English artist John Seguier (1785-1856), who succeeded his brother as superintendent of the BI. Her son wrote *A Dictionary of Painters* (1870).

**STEWART, Mary (Lady Elton)** **1773-1849**
Born Castle Stewart, Kirkcudbright; died Clevedon, Somerset, 6 Dec. Married Sir Abraham Elton 1823. In 1820 she produced a set of 'Four Panoramic Views of Edinburgh and the Surrounding Country from the Top of Blackford Hill'. These were engraved by Hullmandel. Not entirely satisfied with this work, in 1823 she produced four further views, this time from the Calton Hill, which were engraved by J Westall. All these works have a rural quality, as well as a geographic range that at the time made them unique. After marrying moved to England and nothing more of importance seems to have been produced.
**Bibl:** Butchart 82-4.

**STEWART, Minnie R** **fl 1888-1918**
Minor Glasgow painter of flowers, especially roses; also occasional topographical works. Exhibited GI(9).

**STEWART, Neil C** **fl 1985**
Edinburgh landscape painter; exhibited once at the RSA, from Mentone Terrace.

**STEWART, Miss Nellie** **fl 1900-1935**
Painter in oil and watercolour of landscapes and garden scenes. In 1900 she was living in Kirkcaldy but by 1920 had moved to Edinburgh. Exhibited RSW(10), RSA(2), GI(2) & L(1).
**Bibl:** Halsby 285.

**STEWART, Peter** **fl 1870-1874**
Kirkcaldy oil painter of buildings and landscape; exhibited RSA(7).

**STEWART, R Lees** **fl 1906-1916**
Amateur Glasgow painter; exhibited GI(5).

**STEWART, Robert** **1924-**
Born Glasgow. Textile and ceramic designer, printmaker and poster artist. Studied Glasgow School of Art, later joining the staff to become head of printed textiles. Commissioned by Liberty's. Exhibited AAS.

**STEWART, Robert J** **fl 1937-1948**
Renfrewshire watercolour painter. Exhibited GI(4), from Newton Mearns.

**STEWART, Robert Wright ARE ARCA (Lond)** **1878-1953**
Born Dysart, Fife. Painter in watercolour, etcher and mezzotinter of landscapes, portraits, figures, and architectural subjects. After gaining experience in the art department of the Allen Lithographic Company of Kirkcaldy, enrolled Edinburgh College of Art where he gained a scholarship which took him to the RCA, Kensington. Studied etching under Sir Frank Short, then travelled to France and Germany. Prominent member of the Chelsea Arts Club, chairman of its house committee prior to WW2. Lectured Chelsea School of Art. Elected ARE 1911. Exhibited RA(21), RSA(5), RE(31), ROI(3), GI(11) & L(12). Represented in Kirkcaldy AG.

**STEWART, Mrs S A** **fl 1917**
Edinburgh amateur enamellist; exhibited a study of Huntly Castle at the RSA.

**STEWART, Sara (Zara)** **fl 1884**
Minor Glasgow landscape artist; exhibited 'A Showery Day' at Kinnaird, Perthshire at the RSA; also GI(2), from 7 Loudoun Terrace, Kelvinside.

**STEWART, Miss Scott F** **fl 1970**
Renfrewshire sculkptress. Exhibited a woodcarving at the GI, from Whitecraigs.

**STEWART, Susan C** **fl 1886-1901**
Greenock painter in oil of domestic animals and occasional topographical works. Later lived at Skelmorlie c1894. Exhibited RSA(7) & a view near Rio de Janeiro at the GI 1901.

**STEWART, Sydney Birnie ARSA FRBSA RCA** **1914-1976**
Born Stirling Village, nr Peterhead. Sculptor and painter in oil and watercolour. Trained Gray's College of Art, Aberdeen gaining a gold medal and a travelling scholarship, and RCA, London. Best known for his stone sculptures of figures. Regular exhibitor RSA, occasionally GI. 'The Tilted Chair' was included in a touring exhibition of Scottish sculpture 1965. Lived latterly in Duddingstone, Midlothian. Represented in Edinburgh City collection.

**STEWART, Sylvia** **1968-**
Born Dunfermline, Jan 17. Sculptress. Trained Gray's School of Art 1986-90, followed by studies at Cyprus College of Art 1991-92. Works in natural organic materials. Uses discarded materials to create sculptures which evocatively relate to the material itself. Runs workshops for the handicapped. Won Chalmers Fervise Award (RSA) 1991, David Gordon Memorial Award (RSA) 1993, Helen Ottile Wallace scholarship (RSA) 1994 & Benno Schotz Award (RSA) 1996. Exhibited at Nat. Museum of Scotland 1996 and at exhibitions Aberdeen AG 1997 and Cardiff 1998. Exhibits RSA since 1993, from Montgomery St, Edinburgh.

**STEWART, Thomas** **fl 1890**
Minor Greenock still life painter. Exhibited GI(1) from 45 Brougham Street.

**STEWART, William** **1823-1906**
Painter in oil and watercolour of rustic interiors, still life and landscape. Trained Paisley School of Design. Originally from Edinburgh, moved to Paisley. Frequent exhibitor RSA(72), GI(33), AAS(2) & L(1). Lived latterly in Greenock. Represented City of Edinburgh collection.

**STEWART, William** **1886-fl 1922**
Paisley engraver; interiors and topography including French churches and buildings. Exhibited studies of local buildings RSA 1914 & 1921; GI(8) 1912-1922.

**STEWART, William B** **fl 1974**
Ayrshire painter. Exhibited GI(2) from Troon.

**STIGAND, Miss Helen M** **fl 1868-1884**
Edinburgh landscape painter in oil who moved to London early in her career. Most of her works were either continental landscapes, for example 'Lucerne Cathedral and the Rhigi' (ex RA 1868) and 'St Peter's, Rome' (1872) or views in the south of England (eg 'Beeches in Knowle Park, Kent' ex RA 1870). Exhibited RA(5), RSA(23), GI(14) & SWA(3), latterly from 31 Conduit St.

**STILL, Kenneth M** **fl 1926-1935**
Aberdeenshire painter of local views, buildings and army life. Attached to the 30th battalion, Gordon Highlanders. Exhibited RSA 1912-15 & AAS(3) from 139 Glenbervie Rd.

**STILL, William** **fl 1887**
Aberdeen painter of townscapes and local landscape; exhibited AAS (4), latterly from 18 View Terrace.

**STIRLING, A P** **fl 1878**
Musselburgh amateur landscape painter of local views; exhibited RSA(1).

**STIRLING, Miss Alison** **fl 1984**
Glasgow engraver. Exhibited GI(1)

**STIRLING, Mrs Betty M** **fl 1965**
Glasgow amateur painter. Exhibited GI(2).

**STIRLING, Dorothy** **1939-**
Born Glasgow. Sculptress. Trained Glasgow School of Art 1983-7. First solo exhibition in Edinburgh 1989. Her work is governed by casual objects found from the lonely beaches of Wester Ross and the busy banks of rivers in the Forth Clyde basin. Interested in the texture and colour of weatherbeaten, rusty or sea-bleached objects. Uses a box form of construction often to protect the image but the work is painted to become part of the whole assemblage. Larger finds become supports for painted panels or for a collage of findings to form relief icons celebrating the image and moods of the Scottish landscape. Lives in Stirling. Exhibits RSA, GI(1) & SSA.

**STIRLING, Edwin** **1819-1867**
Born Dryburgh, Jly 27; died Liverpool Jan 6. Sculptor. Clay figures which he had modelled as a child were shown to his neighbour Sir David Erskine. Erskine was so impressed that he arranged for the young man to be apprenticed to a stone-carver at Darnick, possibly John Smith(qv), after which time he enrolled at Edinburgh School of Art. Later settled in Liverpool, working for an architectural carver called Canavan whose partner he later became. In 1857 executed most of the decorative carving for the offices of the Liverpool and London Insurance Company, also responsible for the statues on the south front of Horton Hall, Cheshire and for the memorial to the Prince Consort at Hastings (1863). A monument in his memory and to the memory of his infant son stands in the Liverpool Necropolis where he is buried.
**Bibl:** AJ 1867, 84; Builder, 1857, 40; Gunnis 374.

**STIRLING, Florence Hutchison** **fl 1882-1895**
Minor Edinburgh oil painter of figures, flowers and portraits; exhibited RSA(5) & GI(5).

**STIRLING, John** **1820-1871**
Born Aberdeen; died overseas. Painter of portraits, rustic genre, dogs, literary subjects and fairy tales; also subjects in Morocco. After 1855 his addresses vary between London and Aberdeen. In 1868-9 visited Morocco. Began exhibiting London 1852 and continued to do so until 1871. Ruskin noted his 'Scottish Presbyterians in a Country Parish Church - The Sermon' (ex RA 1855) regarding it as 'a very noticeable picture, showing careful study and good discrimination of expression. But the painter cannot do all he wants to do; and he should try to work more delicately, and not attempt so much at once'. Exhibited RA(24) & RSA(17), until 1858 from Broadford Bank, Kingsland Place, Aberdeen and after 1860 from his London home at 5 Langham Chambers.
**Bibl:** AJ, July 7, 1934; G.M. Fraser in Aberdeen Journal, Jly 7, 1934; J. Ruskin, Academy Notes, 1855; Christopher Wood, Dict. of Victorian Painters.

**STIRLING-BROWN, A E D G** **fl 1900-1913**
Obscure but highly talented equestrian artist. Usually worked in oils; also engraver. Probably Scottish. Possibly related to **Thomas STIRLING-BROWN** (fl 1902-1915). Wingfield records several portraits of hunters, polo ponies and a racehorse, jockey up, dated 1911.
**Bibl:** Wingfield.

**STIRLING-MAXWELL, Sir John** **fl 1914-1938**
Glasgow author and occasional watercolour artist. Exhibited 'Church interiors' at the GI from Pollok House.

**STIRRAT, Eliza B** **fl 1887-1898**
Painter of flowers and landscape. Exhibited GI(5) from 11 Derby Crescent, Kelvinside, Glasgow.

**STITT, Fanny H** **fl 1886**
Painter of Woodburn, Dalkeith; exhibited RSA(1).

**STIVEN, Charles** **1960-**
Born Aberdeen. Painter in the modern idiom. Son of Fred S(qv). Trained Edinburgh College of Art 1981-5; travelled to Amsterdam on a postgraduate scholarship. First one-man exhibition 1985. Awarded Greenshields prize 1986 and again in 1988, and the RSA City of Edinburgh award 1989. In 1990, having won the Alastair Salvesen scholarship, visited USA. Began exhibiting RSA 1988. Represented in Edinburgh City collection.

**STIVEN, Fred ARSA** **1929-1997**
Born Fife. Sculptor in mixed media (boxed constructions), designer, teacher, typologist. Trained Edinburgh College of Art 1947-51 gaining a postgraduate scholarship in 1952. Appointed to the Arts staff of Fife Education Authority 1954. In 1958 joined the staff of Gray's School of Art, Aberdeen becoming head of design 1987. Elected SSA. First one man exhibition in Edinburgh 1969, repeated in 1974. Creates 'enlarged and highly evocative responses to the marine mystery and the ambience of the seashore. Originally these assemblages were mostly of driftwood and other flotsam. Though since Stiven is both a consummate craftsman and designer even these were never used unaltered, partly because of their intrinsic qualities, but mainly because such objects carry intimations of human involvement, and a link with some tradition' [Cordelia Oliver]. His work has been likened to that of Ben Nicholson(qv) and Will McLean(qv). Lived in Echt and subsequently at Sheallagan, Golf Course Rd, Blairgowrie. Regular exhibitor RSA, AAS 1967-1986 & SSA. Represented in Aberdeen AG, SAC.
**Bibl:** Gage 50-1; Hardie 196; Anon, Obituary, RSA Annual Report 1996.

**STIVEN, Mrs Ruth** **fl 1974-1986**
Textile designer and painter of semi-abstracts and still life. Exhibited AAS during above period, latterly from Castlefield, Cupar, Fife.

**STOBIE, Alex** **fl 1987**
Perth painter; exhibited 'Still-life with turnip' at the RSA.

**STOCKAN, Brenda M N** **fl 1964-1965**
Aberdeen enamellist; exhibited AAS(3) from 38 Gilcomston Pk.

**STOCKS Eben** **fl 1896-1897**
Amateur artist of 136 Wellington Street, Glasgow, exhibited GI(2).

**STOCKS, Miss J Christian** **fl 1934**
Minor watercolour painter of Osborn House, Kirkcaldy, exhibited RSW(1).

**STOD(D)ARD, Mary Tweedie Oliver** **fl 1897-1901**
Portrait and landscape painter. Lived in Tweedsmuir, Peebleshire 1897 moving to Edinburgh c1900. Exhibited RSA(2) & GI(1).

**STODDART, Alexander** **1959-**
Born Edinburgh. Sculptor; mainly mythological subjects in the modern idiom, derived from French and Scottish styles of the 19th century. Trained Glasgow School of Art under Cliff Bowen. Awarded Emmy Sachs prize.

**STODDART, Christina Mary** **fl 1893-1914**
Edinburgh-based painter in oil and watercolour of figure subjects. Exhibited 'The Noon-Day Rest - India' RA 1904; also RSA(14) including a vivacious rendering of 'Whitebait Fishing in Normandy' 1898, GI(3), L(4), AAS(1) & London Salon (3), latterly from 26 Castle St.

**STODDART, D McKay** **fl 1899**
Glasgow topographical painter; mostly continental. Exhibited GI(2).

**STODDART, Miss Frances** **fl 1837-1867**
Landscape painter in oil; Scottish, Welsh and continental subjects with particular attention to Highland rivers. Unlike most Scottish artists resident in Scotland, exhibited RA before RSA. Exhibited RA(3) including 'Dunkeld Abbey' 1837, and in 1840 'Highland Landscape' and 'A View Over the Vale of Comrie with Sir David Baird's Monument', but at the RSA no less than 110 including 5 Deeside scenes 1840 among them 'Balmoral' and 'Cottages on the Gairden Water'. Another exhibit to attract favourable attention was an evocative, powerful 'Loch Maree' 1864; also GI(4). Lived at 10 Belle Vue Crescent, and later Heriot Row, Edinburgh.

**STOD(D)ART, Miss Grace H** **fl 1889-1922**
Born Chesterhall, Lanarkshire; painter of landscapes, genre and figure subjects in oil and pastel. Studied with Christina Ross(qv) at Edinburgh and Paris at Colarossi's. Used a bright fresh palette with great effect. Exhibited such paintings as 'Spring in East Lothian' and 'Primrose Day' at the RSA(38), RSW(1), AAS(5), GI(4) & L(8), latterly from Wintonhill, Pencaitland.

**STODDART, Sarah C** **fl 1893**
Painter. Exhibited GI(1) from 16 Lansdowne Crescent, Glasgow.

**STONE, Nicholas** **fl 1617**
English sculptor. Member of a group sent north by James VI in preparation for his visit to Scotland in 1617. Although nothing of his work survives in Scotland, work in his style can be seen in Dunbar church and Culross Abbey.
**Bibl:** Macmillan [SA] 49,53,61.

**STONES, Robert C** **fl 1951**
East Kilbride painter; exhibited 'Birnie Hill Farm' at the RSA.

**STONOR, Winifred M** **fl 1918-1929**
Probably an English artist. Came to live in Glasgow c1929. Exhibited GI(1) & SWA(3).

**STORER, Henry Sargant** **fl 1814-d1837**
Born Cambridge(?); died London, Jan 8. Engraver, probably English but with strong Scottish connections, of whom little is known beyond the fact that, with his father **James STORER**, he produced in 1820 an important collection of engraved *Views in Edinburgh and its Vicinity*, published by Constable. Most of the principal buildings in the city were included among the 100 engravings. Butchart considers them of 'considerable importance from a topographical viewpoint, (but) in themselves a trifle formal and rather lacking in human interest'. For most of his working life lived in Chapel Street, Pentonville, where work was more readily available with English publishers rather than in Scotland. Exhibited RA(2) between the above years including

'Panoramic View of the City of Edinburgh' 1819 and 'The Tron church, Edinburgh' 1821, latterly from 146 Whitechapel. Represented in City of Edinburgh collection.
**Bibl:** Butchart 48-9,99,106; Bryan 132-3.

**STOREY, Harold** **1888-1965**
Landscape painter in oil and watercolour; also etcher and draughtsman in pencil. Lived for many years at Newton Mearns, Renfrewshire. Exhibited RA(7), RSW(1), RSA(21), AAS(1929-35), GI(43) & L(9). Represented in Glasgow AG.

**STORIE, Andrew** **fl 1911-1919**
Edinburgh painter; mainly continental landscapes but also illustrations for *Hans Anderson* (1911). Exhibited RSA(5).

**STORIE, Jan** **fl 1984-1985**
Aberdeenshire painter; exhibited AAS(2) from Old Bourtreebush Farm, Newtonhill.

**STORK, Philip** **fl 1871**
Glasgow amateur painter. Exhibited 'Study of a head' at the GI, from Hope St.

**STORRAR, David** **fl 1875-1886**
Kirkcaldy landscape painter in oil and watercolour; exhibited RSA(11), AAS(3) & GI(1).

**STORTZ, Philip C (G)** **fl 1871-1882**
Portrait painter living in Glasgow in the early 1870s; exhibited RSA(2) in 1871 & at the Walker Gallery, Liverpool 1882 from 19 King's Road, Brighton.

**STORY, Miss Elma** **1886-1941**
Born Edinburgh. Painter in watercolour of landscapes and interiors, especially churches. Trained Glasgow School of Art, Edinburgh and Paris. Often painted views of Iona. A memorial exhibition of her work, together with Janet Aitken(qv) and Kate Wylie(qv), was held at the Glasgow Society of Lady Artists 1942. Exhibited RSA(5), RSW(1), AAS(1), GI(30) & L(1), latterly from 21 Ashton Rd, Glasgow.
**Bibl:** Halsby 285.

**STORY, Gordon** **fl 1902-1922**
Edinburgh painter; unusually combined topographical compositions with miniature portrait painting. Exhibited RSA(4), GI(1) & L(1).

**STOTT, Andrew Thomson** **fl 1959**
Aberdeen flower painter and sculptor. Exhibited AAS(3) from 685 Gt Northern Rd.

**STOTT, Susan** **fl 1982-1984**
Aberdeen textile designer; trained Gray's School of Art, Aberdeen. Exhibited AAS(2) from 33 Wallfield Place.

**STOTT, William R S** **fl 1897-1930**
Aberdeen painter of portraits, figure studies and genre; exhibited AAS(7) from 33 St. Swithin St; also GI(4) including a portrait of 'Sir A Lyon, Lord Provost of Aberdeen' 1909, latterly from Cheyne Row, London.

**STRACHAN, Alexander** **fl 1929-1946**
Stained glass artist of 5a Balcarres Street, Edinburgh. Brother of Douglas S(qv). Exhibited RSA(3) & L(3). Represented by the clerestory windows in the church of Holy Trinity, St. Andrews, and by 'Christ in the Temple' and a Livingstone window in Dunfermline Abbey (1932) whilst in Edinburgh there is the 'convincing' pair of narrative windows depicting 'Pilgrim's Progress' (1934) and five lights 'Revelation' (1928) in Greenbank Church, Morningside; 'Peace' (1939) in Cramond Parish Church; and three examples in Priestfield Church, Newington.
**Bibl:** Gifford 45,547,617,636.

**STRACHAN, Alice** **fl 1887**
Aberdeen amateur flower painter, especially roses; exhibited AAS (2) from 14 Irvine Place.

**STRACHAN, Andrew** **fl 1616-d1673**
Born Aberdeen; died Aberdeen, 14 Feb. Painter of armorials. In 1630 George Jamesone made him godfather to his son, and in 1633 was a witness to an instrument of sasine in favour of Jamesone. In 1614 he was painting and illuminating Sir Alexander Hay's name and arms on the Brig of Don. The same artist varnished three pulpits and a loft in Greyfriar's Kirk, Aberdeen. Also painted sundials and the Town's arms on the New Kirk 1643. Buried in Aberdeen.
**Bibl:** Apted 92; Duncan Thomson, George Jamesone, 20; Thomson 39.

**STRACHAN, Arthur Claude** **1865-?**
Born Edinburgh 15 Mar. Painter in watercolour of landscape especially English cottages. Studied art in Liverpool. In the early 1920s returned to Scotland from Somerset where he had been living. Exhibited RA(4), L(64) & RI(4) 1885-1932.

**STRACHAN, Arthur W** **fl 1920**
Miniature portrait painter of Netherley, Dollar; exhibited RA(1).

**STRACHAN, Dorothy W** **fl 1965**
Dundee amateur landscape painter; exhibited AAS(1) from Clepington Rd.

**STRACHAN, Eddie** **1940-**
Born Forfar, Angus. Painter and teacher. Trained Duncan of Jordanstone College of Art 1957-62. Principal art teacher, Harris Academy, Dundee 1964. Exhibits RSA.

**STRACHAN, Eric** **fl 1961-1970**
Glenrothes sculptor; moved to Connel, Argyll in the late 1960s. Exhibited torsos RSA 1961 and 1970.

**STRACHAN, George** **1939-**
Born Peterhead. Landscape & marine painter in oil and watercolour; local historian. Mainly self-taught. Worked in the fishing industry before retiring 1997, now a full-time artist. His work is in collections in Brazil, Canada, Australia, Holland & Norway. Exhibits AAS from Station House, Inverugie, Peterhead.

**STRACHAN, Ian** **fl 1959-d c1999**
Aberdeenshire landscape and wildlife painter, wood carver, art teacher and photographer. Unassuming dedicated art master at Aboyne Academy for many years. Author and illustrator of *Upper Deeside and the Grampians.* Exhibited AAS(4) from Birse, Aboyne.

**STRACHAN, Lizzie S** **fl 1896**
Aberdeen amateur flower painter; exhibited AAS(1) from King's College.

**STRACHAN, Olive** **19th Cent**
Painter. Exhibited AAS from The Tower, Fort George. No date.

**STRACHAN P R Douglas** **20th Cent**
Aberdeen portrait painter; exhibited AAS(2) from 480 Union St.

**STRACHAN, Robert Douglas HRSA LLD** **1875-1950**
Born Aberdeen; died Lasswade, Midlothian, Nov 20. Painter in oil and watercolour of portraits, topographical and figure subjects; also stained glass window designer and mural decorator. Educated Robert Gordon's College, Aberdeen and RSA Life School 1894-95. Left to become political cartoonist on the *Manchester Chronicle.* Much of his early work was devoted to mural painting and portraiture including a mural in the Music Hall, Aberdeen in 1898 depicting 'Ancient and Modern Labour'. In 1899 studied in France and Italy, visiting Morocco 1902 and Holland 1904. Commissioned to make stained glass windows for the Palace of Peace in the Hague. Elected HRSA 1920. Returned to Italy in 1906 and again in 1908 and in 1914 visited Egypt, Palestine, Greece, Turkey and Vienna before going to London. His reputation is based on his stained glass work which he continued to do in Aberdeen until shortly before his death when he moved once again to Midlothian. His reputation is world-wide. In addition to his work at the Hague he undertook important work for the Scottish National War Memorial, Edinburgh Castle and the Goldsmith's Window at St Paul's Cathedral (destroyed during the

war). Other important work includes windows for King's College chapel (Aberdeen), a window evoking 'Womanhood' (1944) in All Saints, Cambridge, a memorial to Thomas Hardy in Stinsford church (Dorset), Hotham church (Humberside), the west window in the north aisle of St Mary, Kemsing (Kent), windows in St Andrew's Presbyterian church, Frognal, Hampstead (London), 'Childhood' in Shellingford (Oxfordshire), Woldingham (Surrey), a window depicting the 'Empty Tomb and Supper at Emmaus' (reputed to be his last work) in the east window of the south aisle of St. Mary, Eastbourne (1949), the east window in Eryholme church (N. Yorks), Dunblane cathedral, Dunfermline Abbey (1916), eleven windows in Holy Trinity, St Andrews, the library of New College Hall, Edinburgh (1911-34), many churches in Aberdeen including St. Machar's cathedral and King's College chapel, Castle chapel (Edinburgh), St Giles cathedral (Edinburgh), St Cuthbert's, Lothian Rd (Edinburgh), Iona abbey, the north aisle of Glasgow cathedral, Glasgow University chapel, St John, Perth, Paisley abbey, and the war memorial window in Brechin cathedral. Recipient of an honorary LLD from Aberdeen Univ. In 1921 exhibited a portrait of 'Mrs John Harrower' at the AAS. Frequent exhibitor RSA, AAS 1902-1929 & occasionally GI, latterly from 4 Douglas Crescent, Edinburgh, which he had remodelled by Robert Lorimer(qv).
**Bibl:** Caw 413-5; Painton Cowen, Stained Glass in Britain, 1985, 230-5, 237-9 et passim; Gifford 44,92,100-1,114,116-8,145,185, 274,276,454,506,555,572,595,629; Irwin 410; Peter Savage, Lorimer and the Edinburgh Craft Designers, Edinburgh 1980, 87-8, 108,141-2,150,169; Douglas Strachan, Stained Glass Windows of Douglas Strachan, privately printed 1972.

**STRACHAN, Sydney M** **fl 1945-1947**
Ayr engraver; woodcuts, linocuts and drypoint. Exhibited GI(3).

**STRAIN, Euphans Hilary (Mrs Harold Wylie)** **1884-1960**
Born Alloway, Ayrshire; died Jne 2. Painter of portraits and marines. Educated Germany and trained Glasgow School of Art winning the Director's prize 1922 followed by diploma 1923. Married Harold Wyllie(qv). Lived for many years in Glasgow and Dunkeld before finally returning to Ayrshire. Exhibited RA(1), RSA(9), Paris Salon, GI(24), L(3) & RCA(1).

**STRANG, David Rogerson** **1887-1967**
Born Dumbarton Jly 14. Portrait painter and etcher. Printed many of his father's etchings. Son of William(qv), brother of Ian S(qv). Studied at Glasgow University. Exhibited RA(1) from a London address.

**STRANG, Ian RE** **1886-1952**
Born London Apr 11; died Wavendon, Bletchley, Bucks Mar 23. Etcher and draughtsman of architectural and figure subjects. Eldest son of William(qv), brother of David S(qv). Educated Merchant Taylors' School; studied art at the Slade 1902-1906 and Academie Julien, Paris under J P Laurens 1906-8. Worked in Belgium, France, Italy, Sicily and Spain. When in Italy became a member of the Faculty of the British School in Rome. Author of *The Student's Book of Etching* (1938); illustrated Frances Strang's *Town and Country in Southern France* (1937). Elected ARE 1926, RE 1930. Exhibited RA (36), RSA(8), RE(47), RHA(1), GI(3) & L(5). Represented in V & A, Manchester AG(7).
**Bibl:** Houfe.

**STRANG, James** **fl 1897-1902**
Amateur painter; exhibited RSA(1) & GI(3) from Westwood, Busby, Lanarkshire.

**STRANG, Karen** **1963-**
Born Falkirk. Painter and performance artist. Trained Glasgow School of Art 1981-85, graduating with First class Hons, followed by a year at the Academy of Fine Arts, Warsaw. First solo exhibition Warsaw 1986. Particularly concerned with the history of women, Polish affairs and politics generally. Professional member SSA, member of the Hanging Together group(qv). Sometimes works in collaboration with Peter Russell(qv). Held an interesting exhibition 'Insanadiorama' at the Stirling AG 1995. Represented in SNGMA.
**Bibl:** Elspeth King, 'Stirling Girls; Towards a Women's History of Stirling', Smith AG (Stirling) 2003.

**STRANG, Margaret Kippen** **fl 1888-1905**
Lanarkshire artist; exhibited GI(3), latterly from Bosfield, East Kilbride.

**STRANG, Maggie** **fl 1882**
Glasgow amateur watercolour painter. Exhibited GI(1).

**STRANG, William RA RPE** **1859-1921**
Born Dumbarton Feb 13; died Bournemouth Apr 12. Painter, etcher and engraver. Worked in oils, silverpoint, charcoal and chalk. Father of David(qv) and Ian S(qv). Educated Dumbarton Academy, went to London when he was 16 to study at the Slade under Legros. Began by painting allegorical subjects and portraits in oil but very quickly turned increasingly to etchings, drypoints, line engravings, mezzotints, aquatints, and woodcuts. In 1889 awarded the silver medal for etching at the Paris International Exhibition. In later life he turned again to painting chiefly in oil but also a few watercolours and in 1897 received first-class gold medal for painting at the Dresden International Exhibition. Made a particular study of Rembrandt, Holbein and Millet. Essentially a Scottish artist, in the vanguard of those who advanced the quality and use of etching as a mode of artistic expression. 'As with most Scots, a persistent racial flavour tinges all Strang's work'. He was conscious of the unseen, the spiritual and the drama of life as man pits himself against the fortunes of nature, destiny and death. 'With him life is not complex and refined but passionate and elemental. And in his grim, rugged and tragic yet romantic interpretations, one comes into close touch with elemental passion, primal superstition or unswerving faith. Questions of dogma and creed apart, he is of the breed of Calvinistic Scots' [Caw]. In his watercolours as in his sketches his working folk are 'strong and rude in build and angular in form and action' more at home in shadow and storm than in sunshine. In 1905 the class of Associate-Engraver was revived by the RA, Strang being one of only two elected in 1906. He had a dignified, potent and severe sense of style. Binyon records that he produced over 750 etchings and prints. Elected RE 1881, RP 1904, RA 1921. President, International Society of Sculptors, Painters and Gravers 1918-1921. Medallist at Paris Exhibition of 1897. Among the works he illustrated were *The Earth Friend* (1892), *Death and the Ploughman's Wife* (1894), *Nathan the Wise* (1894), Ian Hamilton's *The Ballad of Hadji* (1894), *Baron Munchausen* (1895), *Pilgrim's Progress* (1895 edition), *Christ Upon the Hill* (1895), *Sinbad the Sailor and Ali Baba* (1896, with J.B. Clark), *Paradise Lost* (1896 edtn), Alice Sargant's *A Book of Ballads* (1898), *A Book of Giants* (1898), Laurence Binyon's *Western Flanders* (1899), *Etchings from Rudyard Kipling* (1901), *The Praise of Folie* (1901), Walton's *The Compleat Angler* (1902 edtn), *Tam O'Shanter* (1902 edtn), Coleridge's *The Rhyme of the Ancient Mariner* (1902) and *Thirty Etchings of Don Quixote* (1903). Contributed to *The English Illustrated Magazine* (1890-1), *The Yellow Book* (1895) and *The Dome* (1898-1900). A 'Self-portrait' 1919 was purchased by the Chantrey Bequest. Exhibited RSA(18), RA(69), GI(18), L(32), RHA(3) & posthumously AAS(2). Seven works including 2 self-portraits are in SNPG, also represented in NGS, V & A, Glasgow AG(8), Kirkcaldy AG, Lillie AG (Milngavie), City of Edinburgh collection, Manchester AG(20), Leeds AG, Ashmolean (Oxford), Nat Gall of Canada (Ottawa) (11).
**Bibl:** Laurence Binyon, 'The Etchings of William Strang', Print Collectors' Quarterly, viii, 1921; Caw 454-7; Houfe; Maas 250; Macmillan [SA] 300-304,310,334; Sir Frank Newbolt, The Etchings of William Strang, London (nd); Catalogue Raisonné of the Print Work of W S, London 1962; F. Sedmore, 'Frank Short and WS' in Eng.Illus.Mag., vol 8, 1890-1, 457-466; Sheffield City AG, 'William Strang' (Ex Cat, 1981); RED Sketchley, Eng Bk Illus, 1903, 58, 154.

**STRANGE, Sir Robert FSA** **1721-1792**
Born Pomona, Orkney Jly 14; died London, Jly 5. Miniature painter and engraver. Had one of the most romantic and adventurous biographies of any Scottish artist. His family traced back to John Strange of Balcaskie, Fife in the 14th century, who had settled in Orkney at the time of the Reformation. Until 14 was educated in Kirkwall and then, following the death of his father, went to sea but was shortly afterwards persuaded to join a law firm in Kirkwall, later joining his brother, an Edinburgh lawyer. There he became apprenticed to Richard Cowper(qv) in whose house he lived. Shortly afterwards he fell in love with a Miss Lumsden, sister of the secretary

to Bonnie Prince Charles. She required him to enrol for the Prince if they were to marry and this he did, fighting at the battle of Culloden - having been named engraver to the Prince whose portrait, together with those of several of the officers, he drew and engraved. This was inscribed probably later (when re-issued in France) 'À Paris, chez Chevreau, Rue St Jacques'. The next recorded work was a design for a bank note when the army was billeted in Inverness prior to Culloden. He married Miss Lumisden 1747 and in 1748 accompanied the Prince to Rouen. They remained there for about a year during which time Strange studied under Descamps. Temporarily abandoned the idea of becoming a miniaturist and went to Paris to study under Le Bas 1749. Returned to London in October 1750 and took up engraving. Visited Paris several times, spent four years in Italy copying the work of Old Masters in chalk and watercolours. Elected member Academy of St Luke in Rome 1763. A highly skilled engraver and painted a number of miniatures. Among the bookplates he designed were those for Dr Thomas Drummond [see Hardy's Book Plates, 64] and Andrew Lumisden [see Eng. Bk. Plts, 2nd ed, 135]. His own portrait was painted by several distinguished artists including Greuze, Raeburn and Romney. During one of his spells in London he engraved Benjamin West's picture 'The Apotheosis of the Children of George III' 1787 which so pleased the King that the same year he was granted a knighthood. Painted several portraits of Prince Charles Edward Stuart and members of his family several of which were included in the South Kensington Exhibition of 1865. 'He worked in pure line, and his plates are remarkable for delicate clearness and precision, united to admirable feeling for the structure and the relationship of the component parts in the pictures he interpreted. They gave him the foremost place amongst British line engravers, and the honours showered upon him show the high esteem in which his work was held abroad' [Caw]. 'His style shows a combination of purity, breadth and vigour which has scarcely been equalled' [Bryan]. Published *A Descriptive Catalogue of a Collection of Pictures, and of thirty-two Drawings,* collected by him in Italy; also *An Inquiry into the Rise and Establishment of the Royal Academy of Arts; to which is prefixed a letter to the Earl of Bute.* Exhibited Society of Artists 1760-1775; elected FSA 1772. Three works are in SNPG including 'Self-portrait'; also represented in City of Edinburgh collection, National Library of Scotland (many).
**Bibl:** Bryan 135 (includes a list of his best works); Brydall 113,194-202; Bushnell; Caw 33; James Dennistoun, The Memoirs of Sir Robert Strange and of Andrew Lumisden, 2 vols, 1855 (Lumisden was Strange's brother-in-law); DNB; Foskett 534; Irwin 84-5,88; Long 422-423; McKay 323.

**STRATH, Miss Elizabeth (Lizzie)** **fl 1896-1919**
Aberdeenshire painter of portrait heads, flowers and interiors; exhibited AAS(6) from 39 Forest Rd.

**STRATH, Nan** **20th Cent**
Banff amateur painter; exhibited 'Orkney harbour' at the AAS, from 12 Campbell St, Banff.

**STRATHEARN, A S** **fl 1907-1911**
Amateur Glasgow painter; exhibited GI(2) latterly from Giffnock, Renfrewshire.

**STRATHERN, Edward Matheson** **fl 1965**
Perth painter; exhibited 'Cane chair' RSA.

**STRATHIE, Thomas J** **fl 1897**
Glasgow painter. Exhib GI(2) from 2 Lansdowne Place, Shawlands.

**STRATHMORE & KINGHORNE, Cecilia, Countess of** **?-1938**
Amatuer embroiderer. Mother of the late Queen Elizabeth, the Queen Mother. A pelmet and bedhead, still at Glamis, of thistle design and with the inner pelmet richly embroidered bearing the Strathmore arms, with the initials of the Countess's ten children, is a fine example of what can be accomplished using silks on cream satin. A superb embroidered set of bedroom furnishings was designed for her daughter, Lady Elphinstone, in whose family it remains.
**Bibl:** Margaret Swain 153-5.

**STREET, F** **fl 1810**
Edinburgh engraver. Engraved a bookplate for Alexander Maxwell Adams, 1810.
**Bibl:** Bushnell.

**STRONACH, Alexander** **17th/18th Cents**
Master mason. Built, and probably designed, the massive Tolbooth & Sheriff Court at Tain (1706-08), the elegant storehouse at Portmahomack (1699), and restored Dornoch Castle (1720).
**Bibl:** Gifford, H & I, 65,74,445,460,569,plts.99,121.

**STRONACH, Ancell ARSA** (withdrawn) **1901-1981**
Born Dundee, Dec 6. Painter of portraits and figure subjects, also mural and church decorator and stained glass designer. Trained Glasgow School of Art. Won Guthrie Award, a travelling scholarship and the Torrance Memorial Prize. Modelled his work on the Early Renaissance combined with developments in ecclesiastical stained glass. Lived in Glasgow where for many years he was Professor of Mural Painting, Glasgow School of Art until resigning 1939. An eccentric, he was attracted to the circus and, abandoning Glasgow, he trained and managed a troupe of acrobatic birds known as 'Ancell's Painted Pigeons' which toured the provinces with his wife, a professional acrobat. Among his principal works are 'The Pilgrims', 'Where Sinks the Voice of Music into a Silence' and 'And Thou Art Wrapped and Swayed in Dreams'. Awarded ARSA 1935 but withdrawn forty years later. Exhibited RA(2), RSA 1925, RSW(3), GI(20) & L(5). Represented in Edinburgh City collection.

**STRONG, Albert** **fl 1947-1949**
Ayr still life painter. Exhibited GI(2).

**STRONG, C Gordon** **fl 1905**
Painter. Exhibited RSA(1) from 69 Montpelier Park, Edinburgh.

**STRONG, Edgar** **fl 1945**
Glasgow painter. Exhibited 'Winter afternoon' at the GI.

**STRONGMAN, B** **fl 1883-1884**
Glasgow landscape painter in oil and watercolour. Exhibited RSA(1) & GI(2) from 56 Hill Street, Garnethill.

**STRONGMAN, William** **fl 1891**
Painter. Exhibited GI(1) from School of Art, Dumbarton.

**STRUTHERS, Andrew** **fl 1891**
Amateur Glasgow watercolourist. Exhibited GI(2) from 287 Duke St.

**STRUTHER(S), Agnes J** **fl 1901**
Glasgow amateur flower painter. Exhibited GI(1) from 2 Kelvingrove Terrace.

**STRUTHERS, Anna S** **fl 1881**
Glasgow painter. Sister of Margaret S(qv). Exhibited GI(1) from 5 Oakfield Terrace.

**STRUTHERS, M Fleming** **fl 1895-1910**
Stirling painter; birds and landscapes mainly in watercolour. Involved with the Craigmill Group. Exhibited RSA(1), RHA(1), GI(2) & L(1).
**Bibl:** Halsby 285.

**STRUTHERS, T R Margaret** **fl 1881**
Painter. Exhibited 'Oyster shells' at the GI, the same year as her sister Anna(qv) showed, from 5 Oakfied Terrace, Glasgow.

**STUART, A** **fl 1893**
Glasgow amateur painter. Exhibited GI(2) from 11 Kersland Terrace, Hillhead.

**STUART, Miss Agnes Easton** **fl 1876-1877**
Edinburgh minor oil painter of local landscapes; exhibited RSA(4).

**STUART (also STEWART), Alan** **fl 1893-1894**
Edinburgh figurative painter; exhibited AAS(4) from 35 Dick Place.

**STUART, Alexander** **fl 1835**
Aberdeen artist; exhibited 'An evening tropical scene in the autumn of 1826' RSA.

**STUART, Alexander Y** **fl 1864**
Minor Dundee painter in oil of local scenes; exhibited RSA(1).

**STUART, Mrs Burnett** **fl 1912**
Amateur Aberdeenshire landscape painter. Exhibited AAS(1) from Crichie, Stuartfield.

**STUART, Charles FSA** **fl 1861-1904**
London-based painter about whom surprisingly little is known. Painted in oils, often on a large-scale, specialising in red deer in the Highlands depicted dramatically, sometimes amidst bright purple heather, less often against storm-ridden skies and brooding mountains; his early work was also of flora and fauna. Exhibited RA (36) 1880-1904 - the last 17 works all Highland scenes; also RSA 1863-1883, GI(31) & AAS(2), from The Hermitage, Cleve Rd, West Hampstead. Not to be confused with the nineteenth century still life and landscape painter Charles Stuart who also exhibited RA.

**STUART, F D** **fl 1868-1871**
Amateur Edinburgh painter of interiors and portraits in oil; exhibited RSA(9).

**STUART, Gilbert Charles ('American Stuart')** **1755-1828**
Born Narragansett, Rhode Island, USA Dec 3; died Boston, Oct 9. Miniature painter and portraitist. Son of a Scottish snuff-grinder from Perth and an American mother. Studied under Cosmo Alexander(qv), working as his assistant during the latter's tour of the Southern States of the USA 1771 and returning with Alexander to Scotland the following year. After a brief spell at Glasgow University returned to America 1755. Four years later was in Dublin where he established himself as a portrait miniaturist. Unfortunately he seemed unable to organise his financial affairs so that within a year of being in Ireland he was imprisoned for debt. In 1793 returned once more to America. Better known for his larger portraits than for his miniatures, and best known for his oil portraits of George Washington. Exhibited RA(13) 1777-1785. Two miniatures were in the Guelph Exhibition 1891. Survived by his wife and 14 children, of whom **Jane** was also an artist who sometimes worked with her father. One of the most gifted painters of his time in North America and one of the best exponents of the Reynolds tradition. Moved to Boston c1805 where he remained until his death. Represented in National Museum, Washington, Metropolitan Museum, New York.
**Bibl:** Bryan; Lawrence Clark, Gilbert Stuart; Foskett, 1, 535; Strickland.

**STUART, Henry** **fl 1959-1964**
Lanarkshire painter of figurative studies and still life, sometimes in watercolour. Exhibited GI(5) from East Kilbride.

**STUART, I** **fl 1897**
Glasgow landscape painter. Exhibited 'Arran from the Ayrshire coast' at the GI, from 1 Doune Quadrant.

**STUART, Ian M** **fl 1964**
Aberdeen amateur painter of buildings and topographical subjects; exhibited AAS(1) from 13 Fonthill Rd.

**STUART, Isa** **fl 1885-1897**
Painter in oil of flowers and still life studies. Moved to Glasgow c1897. Exhibited RSA(1) & GI(1).

**STUART, James 'Athenian' FRS FSA** **1713-1788**
Born Ludgate Hill, London; died London, Feb 2. Architect and watercolourist. Son of a Scottish mariner, spent all his working life in London and Rome and is little recognised in Scotland. As a young man he displayed a considerable talent for drawing. When his father died he obtained employment with Lewis Goupy, a well-known London fan painter. Became interested in classical antiquity and studied mathematics and anatomy, developing skills at drawing as well as working in gouache and watercolour and teaching himself Latin and Greek. After his mother's death in 1742 visited Rome travelling most of the way on foot. In 1748 he accompanied Gavin Hamilton(qv), Matthew Brettingham and Nicholas Revett to Naples and in 1750 published *De Obelisco Caesaris Augusti.* In 1748 he and Revett began plans to produce *Antiquities of Athens* and in 1751 was elected to the Society of Dilettanti. After a spell with Revett in Greece he returned to England 1755 and began the first drawing for *Antiquities* which appeared in 1762. Stuart's contribution to the book was mainly in the general topographical views based on his original gouache sketches, many of which are now in the RIBA. Elected FRS and FSA in the early 1760s and in 1763 appointed Painter to the Royal Society being succeeded by Reynolds 1769. In 1758 became Surveyor of Greenwich Hospital and in 1764 succeeded Hogarth as Serjeant-Painter, an appointment finally abolished in 1782. Exhibited with the Free Society of Artists, mainly Athenian watercolours. Also executed some decorative painting for the houses of his patrons, among them Mrs Montagu of Sandleford Priory. Undertook monuments and medallions and was frequently consulted by Josiah Wedgwood. It was 26 years before the second volume of *Antiquities* appeared, it having been delayed by the author's sudden death. It was finally published by his widow with the help of William Newton in 1787. The third volume, for which he left the completed drawings, appeared in 1795 with Willey Reveley as editor, and in 1816 a further volume of papers and drawings by Stuart and Revett was published with a supplementary volume appearing in 1830. Exhibited FS 1765-1783. Miniature portraits of Stuart and his second wife are in the NPG, a 'Self-portrait' is in the RIBA. A volume of his gouache drawings are in the RBA as well as a notebook containing his observations on Italian painters. Among his architectural works were a Doric temple at Hagley Park for Lord Lyttelton (1758); the interior of the first floor of Spencer House, Green Park; the interior decorations of Londonderry House for Lord Holdernesse (c1750-5); Portman House, Portman Square (c1775-82), and the Chapel at Greenwich Hospital (1779-88). Among his monuments, the only Scottish one is the elegant 'Lady Catherine Paulet' (1775-6) in Greyfriars Churchyard, Edinburgh and two in Westminster Abbey: 'Admiral Watson' and 'Viscount Howe'. Among the medals he designed were one to celebrate the birth of the Prince of Wales (1762), one for the Society for the Formation of Arts, Manufacturers and Commerce (1757, used until 1805), and those to commemorate Clive's victory at Plassey, the capture of Guadaloupe (1759) and the Battle of Minden.
**Bibl:** R. Blunt, Mrs Montagu, Her Letters and Friendships, 1923, Vol 1, 164, Vol 2, 82-3; Bryan; Colvin 581-5; Journal of the Warburg Inst, ii, 1938-9; Gifford 157; Macmillan [SA] 32, 50; Stuart & Revett, Antiquities of Athens 1762; Waterhouse.

**STUART, Sir James** **1779-1849**
Born Rome; died Edinburgh. Amateur painter and etcher. The 5th Baronet of Allanbank, Berwickshire. Friend and neighbour of Sir Walter Scott. In 1821 Colnaghi published two sets of 6 etchings by Stuart illustrating Scott and Byron. Seven years later, a further set of etchings 'Gleanings from the Portfolio of an Amateur' appeared. Prolific watercolourist painting landscapes and battle scenes in a fluent pen and wash style; also painted subjects inspired by literature and occasional sporting subjects. His best works are probably his landscape sketches of Scotland, most especially his vibrant views of Arran. Represented in NGS (2 albums and 2 scrapbooks), Culzean Castle(NTS, many).
**Bibl:** B.M. Cat. of Drawings by British Artists, vol 4,167; Bushnell; Halsby 285; Wingfield.

**STUART, John** **fl 1880-1886**
Amateur landscape painter of 91 North Hanover Street, Glasgow. Exhibited GI(2), latterly from Douglas Terrace, Largs.

**STUART, John Sobieski Stolberg** **c1795-1874**
Part-time painter, linguist, author, poet and sportsman. Collaborated with his brother **Charles Edward**. Claimed to be grandsons of the Young Pretender. Born Hay-Allen but changed their name when moving to Eilean Aegas, nr Beauly, Inverness-shire. Author of *Vestiarum Scoticum* (1842), *The Tales of the Century* (1847) and *Lays of the Deer Forest* (1848) which he also illustrated. Died Feb; buried Eskadale, nr Beauly, Inverness-shire. SNPG has two ink copies by him of the 3rd Duke of Perth and Lord Seaforth.
**Bibl:** 'The Sobieski Stuarts, a romantic claim to Royal descent' [by A.C.], reprinted from The Southern Echo & Reporter, Sept, 1921.

**STUART, K G** **fl 1929**
Dalkeith-based amateur painter. Possibly husband of Katharine(qv). Exhibited RSW(1) from the Old Parsonage.

**STUART, Mrs Katherine Sheila** **1905-1949**
Born Edinburgh; died Dalkeith, Midlothian, Dec 10. Painter in oil and watercolour. Trained Edinburgh College of Art and in Paris. Related to K G Stuart(qv). Married 1926. A memorial exhibition was held at the Scottish Gallery 1950. Signed her work 'S.Stuart' and sometimes

'KS Stuart'. Lived at the Old Parsonage, Dalkeith from where she exhibited RSA(13), RSW(12) & SSA, of which she was elected a member.

**STUART, Leslie P** **fl 1946-1967**
Dundee landscape and still life painter, also flower studies. Exhibited RSA(5).

**STUART, Morton G** **fl 1899-1900**
Edinburgh painter. Exhibited RSA(2) from 2 Bedford Park.

**STUART, Robert Easton** **fl 1887-1940**
Edinburgh watercolour painter of landscapes, portraits and still life; often painted farm scenes with figures working. Trained RSA Schools. Exhibited RSA(51), AAS 1893-1926, GI(14) & L(6). Represented Edinburgh City collection.

**STUART, Sheila** **1905-1949**
Dalkeith-based painter of local landscapes. Trained Edinburgh College of Art 1922-28 and then in Paris.

**STUART-BROWN, H G** **fl 1924-1931**
Painter of figures and topographical studies; exhibited RSA(6), latterly from Cathlaw, Torpichen.

**STUBBS, Samuel** **fl 1870-1875**
Minor Edinburgh-based marine painter in oil; exhibited RSA(1) & GI(1).

**STURGIS, Mrs H** **fl 1913**
Edinburgh painter. Exhibited in the provinces from 47 York Place.

**STURROCK, Alick Riddell RSA** **1885-1953**
Born Edinburgh Jne 10; died St Abbs whilst on holiday, May 16. Landscape painter in oil and watercolour, especially farming subjects in SW England, and occasional still life. Painted in a broad, flat style with a subtle often hard palette. Started his working life as an apprentice to a lithographic artist. Educated George Watson's College. Trained Edinburgh College of Art and RSA Life School. Member of the Edinburgh Group 1912. With Eric Robertson(qv) and Spence Smith(qv) developed a mild form of vorticism. A travelling scholarship enabled him to visit Paris, Italy, Munich and Holland. President, SAC. Married Mary Newbery(qv) 1918, daughter of Fra Newbery(qv). Elected ARSA 1929, RSA 1938; Treasurer RSA 1938-47, Secretary 1953. During WW2 served as a captain in the Royal Scots. Exhibited RA(4), RSA(78), RSW(3), AAS (1910-12), GI(87) & L(8). Represented in Dundee AG, Glasgow AG, Paisley AG, City of Edinburgh collection.
**Bibl:** Halsby 220,222,285.

**STURROCK, Angus P** **fl 1935**
Dundee painter. Exhibited RSA(1) from 14 Marshall Street, Lochee.

**STURROCK, David Woodburn** **fl 1887-1909**
Glasgow architect and painter. Exhibited GI(11), mostly topographical works.

**STURROCK, Mrs Mary Arbuckle Newbery (née Newbery)** **1890-1955**
Painter of flowers in watercolour, also ceramic designer and embroiderer. Daughter of Fra and Jessie Newbery(qv). Trained Glasgow School of Art, where she met her lifelong friend Cecile Walton(qv). Married Alick Riddell S(qv) 1918. Member of the reconstituted Edinburgh Group 1919. Earlier work was influenced by another of her friends Charles Rennie Mackintosh(qv), but her later work became more naturalistic. Exhibited RSA(51), RSW(6), GI(18) & L(2).
**Bibl:** Halsby 220,285.

**SUMMERS, Douglas W** **fl 1943-1946**
Banffshire portrait painter; exhibited RSA(2), from Cullen.

**SUMMERS, Miss G M** **fl 1952**
Amateur Glasgow landscape painter. Exhibited GI(1).

**SUMNER, Alice** **fl 1897-1900**
Aberdeen flower painter; exhibited AAS(2) from 7 Devanha Terrace.

**SUMSION, Peter** **fl 1980-1987**
Glasgow painter of topography and coastal scenery, sometimes in Sutherland. Exhibited GI(8) from Clarence Drive, latterly Dudley Drive.

**SUNTER, Miss Jessie C** **fl 1877-1889**
Edinburgh oil painter of flowers, portrait and figure studies. Exhibited RSA(3).

**SURENNE, D T** **fl 1830-1831**
Edinburgh portrait and figure painter, also teacher of drawing in Edinburgh. Father of Mary(qv) and the Trustees Acaddemy pupil **James G SURENNE**. Exhibited RSA, from George St.

**SURENNE, Miss Mary H** **fl 1880-1884**
Watercolour and oil painter of portraits and figure studies; probably daughter of the Edinburgh drawing master D T Surenne(qv) and sister of **John** who was also an artist. Taught drawing in Edinburgh. Exhibited RSA(8) from 6 Warriston Crescent, Edinburgh.

**SUTCLIFFE, John** **fl 1845-1853**
Edinburgh painter of animal and figure studies sometimes with literary allusions. Exhibited RA(2) from 22 Grafton St, Fitzroy Square in 1853 & RSA(8) 1845-1848.

**SUTHERLAND, Miss A** **fl 1869-1876**
Stirlingshire painter of flowers and landscape. Moved to Edinburgh c1974. Exhibited GI(4).

**SUTHERLAND, Alexander Nicolson** **fl 1949-1961**
Orkney painter; local topography, scenery and buildings. Moved to Wick, Caithness in the 1950s. Exhibited RSA(17), and a study of old buildings at the AAS, from Ash Villa, Wick.

**SUTHERLAND, Alan G D HRSA LLD** **c1931-**
Edinburgh portrait painter. Educated Loretto School, trained Edinburgh College of Art under P H Westwater. Painted 'Lord Provost John G Banks'. Exhibited RSA(20) including 'Sir William MacTaggart PRSA' 1969 and 'The Duke of Hamilton' 1970; also GI(7). Represented in Edinburgh City collection by 'Lord Provost Sir Duncan Weatherstone' (1898-1972).
**Bibl:** Edinburgh Evening News, 15 Nov 1954.

**SUTHERLAND, Alexander F** **c1846-1884**
Edinburgh painter in oil and watercolour of landscape, interior portraits, figure subjects. Often painted smugglers. Exhibited RSA (25). Seems to have had an association with Dingwall, being there 1872 and again 1875.

**SUTHERLAND, Mrs Alice** **fl 1929**
St Andrews amateur painter; exhibited RSA(1).

**SUTHERLAND, Allan Newton** **fl 1908-1919**
Aberdeen painter, mainly portraits. Moved to Glasgow c1913 before returning to Glasgow the following year and then to Aberdeen. Exhibited RSA(2), RSW(2), AAS(15) & GI, including 'Lord Provost Taggart of Aberdeen', latterly from 259 Union St, Aberdeen.

**SUTHERLAND, Angus F** **fl 1880s**
Born Dingwall; died Inverness. Painter of portraits and occasional landscapes. Began life as a house painter but was soon encouraged by local patrons to study in Edinburgh. Teacher and friend of Colin Mackenzie(qv) in whose arms he died. His best known work is the portrait of 'Dr Kennedy', Free Church minister of Dingwall. His early death prevented the fulfilment of his remarkable talent or the establishment of a national reputation.

**SUTHERLAND, Miss C** **fl 1934**
Minor Edinburgh painter. Exhibited a nursery decoration for the Princess Margaret Rose hospital for children, Edinburgh, in collaboration with **Miss C FORSYTH,** at the RSA, from 27 Grange Loan.

**SUTHERLAND, Carol Ann** **fl 1980-**
Originally from Fortrose. Painter of fishing scenes and fishing boats. Began regularly exhibiting RSA 1980.

**SUTHERLAND, David Macbeth RSA LLD** **1883-1974**
Born Wick, Caithness; died Plockton Sep 20. Painter in oil of portraits, figure subjects but especially landscape. Educated at Wick. After two years in a law office moved to Edinburgh with the intention of pursuing legal studies but instead began to work with a lithographic firm. Attended evening classes at Heriot Watt College before becoming a full-time student at the RSA under Charles Mackie(qv). A Carnegie travelling scholarship enabled him to visit France, Belgium, Holland and Spain 1911 & 1913. Studied in Paris and Madrid. In about 1913 appointed to teach painting and drawing from life, a position he resumed after WW1. In 1919 involved in resuscitating the Edinburgh Group and a camping holiday spent with Gillies(qv) and Maxwell(qv) in the north-east led to a series of landscapes of the region in which the influence of Gillies is clearly visible. Married the artist Dorothy Johnstone(qv) 1924. Received Guthrie Award and appointed Head of Gray's School of Art, Aberdeen 1933, persuading James Cowie(qv) and Robert Sivel(qv) to join him. Retired in 1948 having established himself as one of the most influential and popular art teachers and administrators in Scotland. Became a Governor of Gray's and was a trustee of Aberdeen Art Gallery for many years, receiving an hon LLD from Aberdeen Univ. Maintained that drawing was the foundation for an artist's work. An early association with the sea and fishing harbours found an echo in his paintings of Brittany and his drawings and subsequent landscapes of Scottish harbours. His diploma work 'The Breton Fisherwoman' was noteworthy in its portrayal of an archetypal fisherwoman of the north sea. The north-west coast of Scotland always had a special appeal inspiring much of his best work. The last years of his life were lived at Cults, Aberdeen. Elected ARSA 1922, RSA 1937. Exhibited RA(1), RSA(110), RSW(1), AAS 1908-1973, GI(19) & L(8). Represented in Aberdeen AG, City of Edinburgh collection(3).
**Bibl:** Aberdeen AG, 'D M Sutherland 1883-1973', (Ex Cat 1974); Halsby 193,211,219-220,285; Hardie 142.

**SUTHERLAND, Donald** **fl 1948**
Glasgow painter of local scenery; exhibited RSA(1).

**SUTHERLAND, Elizabeth, Duchess of** **1765-1839**
Landscape painter and etcher. Daughter of William, 17th Earl of Sutherland. Married Earl Gower, later Marquis of Stafford and 1st Duke of Sutherland. Studied drawing under Girtin. Painted and sketched on the continent and in the north of Scotland, many of the former being engraved. In 1807 she published *Views on the Northern and Western Coasts of Sutherland,* and in 1809 *Views in Orkney* containing 43 etchings after her own drawings. Her work is delicate and precise.
**Bibl:** Bushnell; Houfe; The Scots Peerage, 1911, viii, 359-362,

**SUTHERLAND, Miss Elspeth B** **fl 1944-1945**
Dumbarton flower painter, generally in pencil. Exhibited RSA(4) & GI(2).

**SUTHERLAND, Miss F E Sinclair** **fl 1939-1946**
Edinburgh watercolour painter of continental scenery. Exhibited GI(6) from Colinton Rd.

**SUTHERLAND, George** **fl 1884**
Obscure artist, commissioned by the Marquis of Lothian to illustrate the 1st International Forestry Exhibition held in Edinburgh 1884. A large oil painting of the event, measuring 53" x 95", is in Edinburgh City collection.

**SUTHERLAND, Helen** **fl 1984**
Sutherland engraver. Exhibited 'Dornoch landscape' at the GI, from Dornoch.

**SUTHERLAND, J** **fl 1800-1820**
Aberdeen engraver. Designed bookplates for Aberdeen Mechanics' Institution, 1810, John Forbes, 1820, Archibald N. Macleod, 1810, and Gordon Cuming Skene, 1800.
**Bibl:** Bushnell.

**SUTHERLAND, James** **fl 1920-1936**
Die cutter. Studied under Alexander Kirkwood of Edinburgh at Edinburgh College of Art for eight years. Also an instructor in heraldic die casting at the ECA. Exhibited RSA(14), from 23 Belle Vue Road, Edinburgh.

**SUTHERLAND, John** **fl 1853-1865**
Edinburgh oil painter of buildings and figure subjects including children, their pets, and fruit; exhibited RSA(10).

**SUTHERLAND, J Ralston** **fl 1963**
North Berwick painter; exhibited 'Night bird awakened' at the RSA.

**SUTHERLAND, John Robert** **1871-1933**
Born Lerwick. Edinburgh painter in oil and watercolour of landscapes and heraldic subjects, also designer. Studied Heriot Watt College and Edinburgh College of Art. Heraldic artist to the Court of the Lord Lyon, Edinburgh. Exhibited RSA(23), RSW(3), & L(3).

**SUTHERLAND, Mrs M Alice** **fl 1929-1935**
Painter in watercolours. Exhibited RSA(1) & RSW(3) from Carron Lodge, St Andrews.

**SUTHERLAND, R** **fl 1851-1853**
Midlothian painter of local views; exhibited RSA including 'The ruins of Roslin castle after sunset' (1851), from Roslin.

**SUTHERLAND, Robert Lewis** **fl 1890-d1932**
Born Glasgow; died Glasgow Jly 4. Painter in oil and watercolour of landscapes. Began his working life in the employment of Messrs John McCallum & Company, booksellers. His love of literature remained an abiding interest. Left to enrol Glasgow School of Art, gaining a Haldane Scholarship; thereafter went to Paris continuing his studies at the Academie Delacluse with further studies at South Kensington, London. Returned to Glasgow teaching art in various schools. Distinguished himself in the painting of landscapes and marine subjects. Regular exhibitor GI. President, Glasgow Art Club 1922-3. Member of Council, Royal Glasgow Institute of Fine Arts where his ability as an administrator was appreciated. Exhibited RSA(13), RSW(6), GI(90) & L(6).
**Bibl:** Glasgow Herald, 5 Jly 1932(obit).

**SUTHERLAND, Scott RSA FRBS** **1910-1984**
Born Wick, Caithness May 15. Sculptor in bronze and stone. Educated Wick HS. Trained Gray's School of Art 1928-9 and Edinburgh College of Art under Alexander Carrick(qv) 1929-33, then at the École des Beaux Arts, Paris 1934 and more briefly in Egypt, Germany, Greece and Italy 1934-5. Won Guthrie award 1940. Executed several sculptures of famous Scotsmen for the Empire Exhibition in Glasgow 1936. Taught at Dundee College of Art from 1947, where he became instructor in sculpture. Elected ARSA 1950, RSA 1970, ARBS 1954, FRBS 1961. Executed the Royal Arms above the door of the National Library. Exhibited regularly RSA from Tayport, Fife.
**Bibl:** Gifford 184.

**SUTHERLAND, Stewart** **fl 1861-1865**
Minor Edinburgh painter in oil of landscapes and castles; his favourite sketching grounds were Ireland, Northumberland and Argyll. Exhibited RSA(4).

**SUTHERLAND, Susan** **fl 1979**
Amateur painter. Exhibited AAS(1); no address given.

**SUTHERLAND, William** **fl 1868-1870**
Minor Edinburgh landscape painter in oil; exhibited RSA(4).

**SUTTER, Katherine Eugenie** **fl 1887**
Painter of minor consequence; exhibited 'Queen Mary's Audience Room, Holyrood' at the RSA from 6 Belle Vue Terrace, Edinburgh.

**SUTTON, J** **fl 1876-1891**
Edinburgh watercolour landscape painter, painted mainly English and Welsh scenes. Exhibited RA(8) 1876-1890, also RSA(3), latterly from 77 George St.

**SVEINEJORNSSON, Miss H MacLeod** **fl 1916**
Painter of Icelandic extraction. Lived at 94 Thirlestane Road, Edinburgh, from where exhibited 'Larch and beetles' at the RSA.

**SWAN, Miss Alice Macallan ARWS** **c1860-1939**
Painter in oil but mostly watercolour of flower pieces and landscape.

Related to, probably sister of, John Macallan S(qv). Lived at Sun Mount, Cork, until moving to Glasgow in 1887 and then London 1890. Elected ARWS 1903. Exhibited RA(12) 1882-1898; also RSA(4), RWS(88), SWA(2), RI(2), GI(4) & L(14).

**SWAN, Donald Sinclair** **fl 1944-1981**
Glasgow painter of portraits and still life. Exhibited RSA(4) & GI(10), since 1974 from Millport, Isle of Cumbrae.

**SWAN, Douglas** **1930-**
Born Connecticut. Semi-abstract painter in oils. Trained Dundee College of Art 1948-53 and Hospitalfield. Awarded RSA scholarship 1954 and Italian Government scholarship 1958. Lived in Carnoustie c1932-59 then moved to Milan. When in Scotland painted mostly north-east coastal scenes. Exhibited RSA(3).

**SWAN, John Macallan RA RWS** **1847-1910**
Born Brentford, Middlesex, 9 Dec; died Isle of Wight, 14 Feb. Painter and sculptor of animal subjects. Born of Scottish parents, studied at Worcester and Lambeth before proceeding to the RA Schools and subsequently in Paris under Jerome and the sculptor Fremière, and was much influenced by Barye. Returning to London he spent much time studying and drawing animals in the Zoological Gardens and became a distinguished draughtsman and colourist. Exhibited the first of his 52 works at the RA in 1878. Early studies were all of animals especially the large cats. Later produced idyllic compositions with human figures, often in the nude. In 1889 the Chantrey Bequest purchased 'The Prodigal Son'. Elected ARA 1892, ARWS 1896, RWS 1899, RA 1905. Turned increasingly to modelling until he was devoting as much time to sculpture as to painting. A fastidious and careful worker whose output was never great. 'Walking Leopard' is at Manchester. Commissioned to produce eight large lions for the Rhodes monument at Capetown. Gained early recognition on the continent receiving many awards but a small output prevented him from achieving greater popularity at home. On his death a fund was raised to purchase his many unfinished paintings. The *AJ* recorded 'he delights in the sharp realistic contrasts of fresh greens, rude rosy flesh, blue skies and water'. In his early days studied anatomy at St. Bartholomew's and St Thomas's hospitals in London. Fremière reminded him that art is not science and Swan was inspired to immediately complete a splendid painting of a jaguar in 24 hours. One of his finest works 'The American Puma' 1897 was sold to the United States before the exhibition opened. Related to Alice M S(qv). For a short spell in 1880 he lived in Cork before returning c1884 to London. In addition to his works at the RA, he exhibited RWS(10), RSA(17), RHA(10), AAS (1894-1906), GI(19) & L(16), but mostly at the Fine Art Society (217+), usually from 3 Acacia Rd, St. John's Wood. Represented in NGS(4), SNPG, Tate AG, V & A, Aberdeen AG, Kirkcaldy AG, Brodie Castle (NTS), Manchester AG, Nottingham AG, Amsterdam (Musée National), Bath AG, Bradford AG, Preston AG, Dublin Nat Gall, Groningen AG, Melbourne AG, Philadelphia AG, Rotterdam (Musee Boymans), Stuttgart AG, Sydney AG.
**Bibl:** AJ 1894, 17-22, 1896, 68, pl pp78; DNB; Maas 82; M.H. Spielman, British Sculptures and Sculptor and Sculptures of Today, 1901; Studio II (1897), 236-242; 32 (1901) 75-86, 151-161;

**SWAN, Joseph (or Joshua)** **fl 1820-1840**
Glasgow engraver. Engraved many book illustrations and portraits of the period. According to Fincham he engraved over 30 bookplates.
**Bibl:** Bushnell; H.W. Fincham, Artists and Engravers of British and American Bookplates, 1897.

**SWAN, Mrs Mary Rankin** **fl 1906**
Portrait painter, especially children. Married John McAllan S(qv). Exhibited AAS(2).

**SWAN, R H** **fl 1860**
Edinburgh painter of rustic scenes and old buildings; exhibited RSA (2), from Ann St.

**SWANN, John** **fl 1981**
Cumbernauld sculptor. Exhibited a wood carving 'Still life with Plant' at the GI.

**SWANSON, Margaret** **fl 1899-1903**
Glasgow designer and teacher. Trained Glasgow School of Art where she subsequently became associated with Helen Paxton Brown(qv), Ann Macbeth(qv) and Anne Arthur(qv) in teaching embroidery and needlework. Probably the **Margaret Swanson** who exhibited watercolour landscapes at the RSA(1) & GI(3) 1899-1903, from 23 Bellevue Crescent, Ayr.
**Bibl:** Burkhauser 73, 154.

**SWANSON, Graeme G** **fl 1980-1985**
Aberdeen artist; trained Gray's School of Art, Aberdeen. Exhibited RSA(3) & AAS(5) from 4 Braemar Place.

**SWANSON, Miss Violet E** **fl 1943-1945**
Glasgow landscape painter; exhibited RSA(2) & GI(1).

**SWANSTON, J D** **1869-1956**
Kirkcaldy architect. Designed the King's Theatre, Edinburgh (1905-6) in collaboration with **James DAVIDSON** of Coatbridge. Exhibited GI(2) from 196 High Street, Kirkcaldy.
**Bibl:** Gifford 72,259.

**SWARBRECK, Samuel Dunkinfield** **fl 1830-1865**
Painter of land and townscape and lithographer. Although a London artist, the works for which he is probably best known and which helped mould the Victorian perception of Scotland were those depicting Scottish scenes. His major RA work 'The bedroom of Mary, Queen of Scots, Holyrood Palace: showing the anteroom where Rizzio was dragged and murdered, and the secret staircase by which the conspirators entered' was exhibited 1856. Earlier, in 1839, he had issued a folio set of 26 tinted lithographs under the title *Sketches in Scotland, drawn on stone from nature.* These well known prints incorporated stereotyped Scots including Highlanders in kilts, Newhaven fishwives in voluminous skirts, and portly gentlemen in top hats and chequered trousers. Exhibited RA(8) latterly from 31 Oakley Square. Represented in City of Edinburgh collection, Culzean Castle (NTS), Manchester AG.
**Bibl:** Bryan; Butchart 14.

**SWEET, George** **fl 1876-d1923**
Minor Glasgow landscape painter. Member, Hamilton Art Club. Exhibited RSA(1) & GI(11) from Pollockshields and latterly from Hamilton.

**SWINBURN, Miss V** **fl 1927**
Painter. Exhibited Walker Gallery, Liverpool(1), from 104 West George Street, Glasgow.

**SWINBURNE, Thordur J W** **fl 1918**
Edinburgh amateur portrait painter. Exhibited RSA(1) from 94 Thirlestane Rd.

**SWINNERTON, Joseph William** **fl 1869**
Amateur Edinburgh sculptor; exhibited a portrait bust at the RSA.

**SWINTON, Emily** **fl 1907**
Topographical artist. Exhibited sketches of Dunfermline Abbey RSA from Albany Street, Dunfermline.

**SWINTON, James Rannie** **1816-1888**
Born nr Duns, Berwickshire, Apr 11; died Dec 18. Portrait painter. His sisters **Catherine** and **Elizabeth** were also artists though neither exhibited nationally. After pursuing various studies finally persuaded his parents to allow him to train as an artist and in 1838 studied at the Trustees Academy in Edinburgh. Encouraged by Sir William Allan(qv) and Sir John Watson Gordon(qv), in whose studio he worked. In April 1839 travelled to London and the following year enrolled at the RA Schools. After that he went to Italy where he remained for three years, incorporating a visit to Spain. In Rome he found many sitters and laid the foundation of his subsequent popularity as a painter of the fashionable beauties of the day. In London established himself in Berners Street, building up a thriving practice. His works are chiefly life-sized, boldly executed, often in crayon, many of them subsequently completed in oils. One of the paintings which led to his popularity was the large portrait group of the three beautiful Sheridan sisters, 'Lady Dufferin, The Hon Mrs Norton and Lady Seymour (Duchess of Somerset)' exhibited at the RA in 1852. Also drew and painted the portraits of eminent men including 'Napoleon III', 'the Duke of Argyll' and 'the Grand-Duke

of Mecklenburg-Strelitz' 1865. His portrait of 'John Steel, Her Majesty's Sculptor for Scotland' was exhibited at the Academy in 1873. His health began to fail 1869 causing a suspension of painting with a brief resumption 1874. Exhibited RA(85) 1844-1874, RSA (41) 1843-1875, latterly from 33 Warwick place, Pimlico. Represented in NGS, SNPG (the physician 'Dr John Brown'), Dublin AG.
**Bibl:** Bryan; Cat of Engr Brit Portr BM 6 (1925) 554 692; DNB.

**SYKES, Henry** **1855-1921**
Glasgow painter in oil of landscapes, townscapes and genre. Moved to Derby 1887 before going to London two years later, finally settling in Dublin 1901. Exhibited RSA(2), RHA(2), RA(8), RBA (16), GI(1), & L(6).

**SYKES, Steven** **fl 1938**
Edinburgh amateur painter; exhibited RSA(1) from 22 Great King St.

**SYM, E B** **fl 1910**
Edinburgh portrait miniaturist; exhibited RSA(1) from 60 Murrayfield Gdns.

**SYM, Mary G** **fl 1927-1937**
Watercolour landscape painter, fond especially of the mountainous north-west of Scotland. Probably related to E B Sym(qv). Exhibited RSA(2), RSW(10) & AAS(1) from various Edinburgh addresses.

**SYME, James P W** **fl 1961-1988**
Edinburgh painter; exhibited RSA(47).

**SYME, John S (C) RSA** **1795-1861**
Born Edinburgh; died Edinburgh. Portrait painter in oil. Attended the Trustees Academy and began his career as a flower painter working with his uncle Patrick S(qv). By the age of 20 he had become increasingly interested in portrait painting which became his exclusive domain for most of his working life. A contemporary of Colvin Smith(qv), it was his association with Raeburn(qv) for which he is now best known. To some extent he was a pupil of Raeburn and later became his assistant (although probably only on replicas and studio pieces). After Raeburn's death, completed all the unfinished works remaining in the studio. 'The observation, if deficient in subtlety is sincere, and drawing and modelling, while lacking grace and fullness, express the salient characteristics of the sitter with commendable simplicity and directness' [Caw]. Two of his best portraits, 'Alexander Henderson' and 'Archibald Mackinley' are now with the Merchant Company of Edinburgh, showing how close he could become to Raeburn. In 1827 completed the portrait of 'J J Audubon'(qv), an uncharacteristically romantic portrayal which the sitter did not particularly like, regarding it as 'a strange looking figure, with gun, strap and buckles, and eyes that to me are more those of an enraged eagle than mine'. Other important works were a commissioned portrait of 'Sir James Baird' for the County Hall of Haddingtonshire 1828, 'the Solicitor General' (his diploma work, exhibited 1831, subsequently in Parliament House), 'Robert Stevenson' 1833, now in the SNPG, an equestrian portrait of 'Raeburn', the horse being painted by Sir Henry 1834. Towards the end of his life turned increasingly to landscapes, especially the Perthshire Highlands. Thus both his RSA exhibits in 1851 were scenes in the Trossachs, whilst in 1852 they were two Italian figures and the following year there was another Perthshire scene. Worked from the same address as his uncle Patrick S(qv), but by 1825 he was established at 32 Abercrombie Place and in 1839 set up home at 14 Brighton Crescent, Portobello. A bust portrait of himself, probably c1840, is at the RSA. Founder member, RSA and claimed to have been the originator. Exhibited RSA(141) & RA(2), latterly from 4 Queen St. Represented in NGS(3), SNPG (including 2 'Self-portraits'), Glasgow AG.
**Bibl:** Armstrong 17; Bryan; Brydall 241; Caw 89; Esme Gordon, 18, 25, 31, 42, 47, 57, 60, 91; Irwin 219-20; McKay 126-7;

**SYME, Patrick RSA** **1774-1845**
Born Edinburgh, 17 Sep; died Dollar, Jly. Painter in oil of flowers and portraits. Uncle of John S(qv). Best known for his work as a flower painter, his productions received high praise in the early exhibitions of the Society of Artists from 1808 onwards. Also teacher of art in Edinburgh and published *Practical Directions for learning Flower-drawing* 1810. In 1814 published a translation of Werner's *Nomenclature of Colours,* accompanied by a diagram. Married the daughter of Lord Balmuto. Their son was the eminent botanist Dr John Boswell, editor of Sowerby's *Botany.* Syme was a foundation member of the RSA at which he exhibited 54 works 1808-1845. Also taught for several years at Dollar Academy from where he exhibited his diploma work 'Flowers' 1831. Exhibited RA (3), all in 1817, from 47 North Frederick St, Edinburgh. In addition to finely detailed paintings of flowers, he produced meticulous watercolours of plants, mosses, birds and insects. Represented in NGS (an album containing 67 sketches).
**Bibl:** Bryan; Brydall 241-2; Conn, Dec 1974; Halsby 51; Irwin; McKay 126.

**SYME, W H** **fl 1876**
Edinburgh painter of topographical subjects; exhibited 'Melrose Abbey' RSA.

**SYMINGTON, J Ayton** **fl 1890-1908**
Illustrator. Probably Scottish. Specialised in illustrations for adventurer stores; also sporting subjects including curling. Contributed to Michael Scott's *Tom Cringle's Log* (1895), Captain Marryat's *Peter Simple* (1895), J.S. Fletcher's *The Wonderful Wapentake* (1896) and the same author's *The Enchanting North* (1908). Also worked for *The Sporting and Dramatic News* (1890), *Good Words* (1893), *Chums* and *The Windsor Magazine.*
**Bibl:** Houfe; Wingfield.

**SYMINGTON, Robert S** **fl 1885-1889**
Glasgow artist, topography some in watercolour. Moved to Paisley c1888. Exhibited GI(4).

**SYMON, Miss Elizabeth** **fl 1865-1866**
Wild life painter. Exhibited studies of wild birds at the RSA.

**SYMON, James** **fl 1978-1980**
Glasgow landscape painter. Exhibited GI(4), from Southbrae Drive.

**SYMONDS, Eliza G** **fl 1840-1844**
Edinburgh portrait painter and miniaturist; exhibited RSA(16).

**SYMONS, David** **fl 1910-1931**
Aberdeen landscape painter, mainly of local scenes including Glen Gairn and Dinnet moor. Exhibited AAS regularly between above years, latterly from 33 Abergeldie Terrace.

# T

**TAGGART, Eleanor** **fl 1890**
Glasgow amateur painter of wild flowers. Exhibited GI(1), from Sutherland Dr.

**TAIT, Anne Fraser** **fl 1892-1900**
Minor flower painter; exhibited GI(7), first from Busby, latterly from Glasgow.

**TAIT, Gillian** **fl 1969**
Aberdeen jewellery designer; exhibited AAS(2), from 117 Spittal.

**TAIT, George Hope JP FSA(Scot)** **1861-1943**
Born Innerleithen; died Quair House, Galashiels, Jan 24. Painter of decorative items and designer. Trained Edinburgh School of Art and lived at Galashiels. In 1903 won first prize in a competition open to all 'master painters of Great Britain'. Exhibited 'Young Starlings' at the RSA 1886 from 318 Gala Park Road, Galashiels.

**TAIT, J A** **fl 1894-1899**
Partick amateur landscape painter; exhibited GI(5), latterly from Dowanhill.

**TAIT, James** **c1762-1834**
Architect. His best work has now disappeared but at the beginning of the last century he designed the north side of the original Shandwick Place in Edinburgh's western new town.
**Bibl:** Gifford 321,377,380,454n.

**TAIT, James** **fl 1877**
Leith watercolour painter of townscapes; exhibited RSA(1).

**TAIT, James** **1868-1938**
Hawick artist. Studied Hawick Art School after working as a house painter. After obtaining a certificate with distinction he was appointed assistant art master at the School, a position he held for eleven years. Known for his landscapes and illuminated lettering, also portraits. 'Provost Fisher' is in Hawick Municipal Buildings where other work may also be seen. Exhib regularly in Hawick, Selkirk and Newcastle.
**Bibl:** Scotsman, 22 Dec 1938(obit).

**TAIT, Janet** **fl 1966**
Aberdeen painter of flowers, still life and figure studies; exhibited AAS(3), from 51 Whitehall Rd.

**TAIT, John** **fl 1656-d1692**
Early Scottish painter. Son of Thomas T of Bo'ness, apprenticed to John Telfer senior in 1656 and painter burgess of Edinburgh 1667, guild brother 1677. Had as apprentices James Anderson 1667, Thomas Warrander 1673 and Thomas Tock 1678. Member, Incorporation of St Mary's 1670-1691.
**Bibl:** Apted 94; Edin. Marr. 1595-1700, 675; Greyfriars Interments, 635.

**TAIT, John** **1787-1856**
Architect. Worked in Edinburgh for John Learmonth in the latter's development of Rutland Square (1830) and the Heriot Trust Development north-east of Queensferry Rd.
**Bibl:** Gifford 361,379,398,454n,578-9.

**TAIT, Margaret E F** **fl 1932-1934**
Minor sculptress of 6 Park Terrace, Ayr; figure subjects. Worked in plaster, lead, bronze and cement. Exhibited 'Turkey boy' RSA; also GI(1).

**TAIT, Margaret Fraser** **fl 1982-1984**
Aberdeen textile designer; trained at Gray's School of Art, Aberdeen. Shared a studio with Brenda Haldane Temple(qv). Exhibited AAS(3), latterly from Lismore Cottage, Candlehill Rd, Kilbarchan.

**TAIT, Miss Margaret T** **fl 1855-1879**
Crieff painter in oils of buildings and local landscapes; exhibited at the RSA (18).

**TAIT, Mary** **fl 1874-1882**
Edinburgh painter in oil and watercolour, landscapes and local buildings. Exhibited RSA(12) & GI(5), latterly from Somerset Cottage, Raeburn Place.

**TAIT, Robert S** **fl 1836-1875**
Edinburgh portrait painter, also painted occasional domestic interiors. In 1849 moved to London where he built up a substantial practice first from a studio at 12 Harley St and from 1853-1869 at 12 Queen Anne St. Exhibited RA(24) 1845-1875 including a portrait of 'Captain Sir Baldwin Wake Walker, Suveyor of the Navy, late Admiral of the Turkish Fleet' 1851, RSA(11) including 'A Chelsea interior in 1858' 1866, lent by the Dowager Lady Ashburton who had purchased it at the Royal Academy; also GI(1).

**TAIT, Stephen** **fl 1861-1871**
Amateur Edinburgh landscape painter in oil; exhibited RSA(6).

**TAIT, Thomas Smith** **1882-c1952**
Born Paisley. Architect. Studied at Paisley, Glasgow and the RA Schools winning the King's Prize for architecture and decorative art. Among his works are Adelaide House and Selfridges, whilst in Edinburgh he designed St Andrew's House (1936-9) 'the most impressive work of architecture in Scotland between the wars' [Gifford]. Senior partner in the firm of Sir John Burnet, Tait and Lorne of London and Edinburgh. Director of Standardisation, department of the Controller of Building Materials. Exhibited RA(7) 1928-1940, RSA(13) & GI(11) from 1 Montague Place, London.
**Bibl:** Gifford 40,441,pl 100.

**TAIT, William** **fl 1943-1945**
Glasgow watercolour painter of portraits and landscape. Exhibited GI(4), from *The Evening Citizen,* Albion St.

**TALBOT, Miss R** **fl 1865-1876**
Edinburgh painter of street scenes and buildings in oil; exhibited RSA(3) before moving to Bath from where she exhibited twice more, in 1874 and 1876 including The Sacristy, Lacock Abbey, Wiltshire 1876.

**TALBOT RICE, Alexander** **c1980-**
Portrait painter. Scottish father and half-Greek mother, great nephew of Professor Talbot-Rice. Educated Stowe School, winning top art scholarship enabling him to train Florence Academy of Art 1999-2001 and Repin Academy of Fine Art, St Petersburg. Influenced by Van Dyke, Velazquez and Sargent, he belongs to the traditional school of portraiture, seeking to depict character, mood and soul from the form while remaining true to the original. His rise to fame has been meteoric, working exclusively on commissions which have already included a memorable portrait of The Duke of Edinburgh (2003) - likely to hang in the NPG before going to St George's House, Windsor Castle; Signora Vivia Farragamo; Altynia Assylimoratovna (Prima Ballerina of the Kirov); The Bishop of London; Mrs Winston Guest; and the Lord Mayor of London presenting the Queen with the Pearl Sword on the occasion of the Jubilee.

**TALLACH, David A** **1951-**
Born Glasgow, 24 Feb. Sculptor, also painter and draughtsman. Trained Glasgow School of Art 1974-8 and awarded Haldane travelling scholarship. Works mainly in wood and pigments in three-dimensional pieces; draws in charcoal, pastel and watercolour. Mostly abstract but lately has indulged in animalistic forms. Exhibited 'Night creatures' at the RSA; also GI(1) 1983.

**TANNER, Miss Ailsa** **fl 1964-**
Helensburgh painter of Galloway and local landscape. Exhibited GI(15).

**TANNOCK, James** **1784-1863**
Born Kilmarnock; died London. Portrait painter. Known as 'Tannock of Kilmarnock'. Brother of William T(qv). Remarkably, he continued practising as a shoemaker in Kilmarnock during most of his artistically active life in spite of exhibiting 44 portraits at the RA 1813-1841. Received remarkably little recognition in his own country, either during his lifetime or since. In 1803 he went to Edinburgh becoming a student under Alexander Nasmyth(qv). Then practised

for two years in Paisley as well as working in Irvine, Greenock and Stirling, where he was patronised by Mrs Grant of Laggan, author of *Letters from the Mountains.* Moved to London 1810 becoming a student at the RA School, then presided over by Benjamin West and attended anatomical lectures by Sir Charles Bell. Painted a portrait of 'George Chalmers FRS', author of *Caledonia* (1824), also 'Sir James Shaw, Lord Mayor of London' 1817, now in Kilmarnock Town Hall. In 1826 his portrait of Irvine's 'Dean of Guild, Robert Fullarton', commissioned by the town for their Town House, was shown at the RA. His works are characterised by a pure execution and truthful delineation. Painted a number of portraits of Burns including one from Nasmyth's portrait, the only one the poet ever sat for. Among other exhibited portraits was 'Walter Denoon, a native of Inverness', aged 102, 1817. Four portraits of his are in the SNPG including one of 'George Chalmers'.
**Bibl:** Bryan; Brydall 238; Caw 90; McKay 319; Mackay, History of Kilmarnock.

**TANNOCK, William** **fl 1818-1831**
Portrait painter. Even less is known of him than his brother, James T(qv). They appear to have been living at the same address, 16 Newman Street, Kilmarnock, in the 1820s. Painted portraits of 'Sir William John Shaw' and of 'Sheriff Substitute Benjamin Bell', both now in Kilmarnock Town Hall. In later life he was an enthusiastic photographer. Exhibited 14 portraits at the RA 1818-1831 including one of 'James Thom', the sculptor 1830.
**Bibl:** Brydall 238; Kilmarnock Standard, Aug 25, 1877.

**TARBET, J A Henderson** **c1865-1937**
Prolific Edinburgh painter of coastal scenes, mountain and moorland. Commonly known as 'Henderson Tarbet'. A painter in oil and watercolour of landscapes. Married Christian Peddie(qv). His colours are invariably strong perhaps influenced by Cadell(qv). His paintings have an impressive realism conveyed in nicely harmonised colour, in the MacWhirter tradition. Active member of the Scottish Arts Club(qv). Exhibited RA(4) 1883-1912, RSA(108), RSW(25), RHA(1), GI(31), AAS 1902 & 1935 & L(4).
**Bibl:** Halsby 285; Scotsman, 21.12.37 (obit).

**TARBOLTON, Harold Ogle RSA FRIBA** **1869-1947**
Born Nottingham; died Edinburgh Jne 31. Architect. Educated at Chigwell, Essex. Studied at RA School of Architecture 1892-95. Articled to George Hine. After travelling abroad settled in Edinburgh and in 1900 was working with Ian Kinross. President, Edinburgh Architectural Association 1904-06. Worked in Bermuda where he was responsible for the completion of Bermuda Cathedral. In 1907 joined the firm of Hay and Henderson and in 1933 entered into partnership with M M Ochterlony(qv). Work in Edinburgh included the Elsie Inglis Memorial Hospital (1923); Bank of Scotland, Princes St (1926); and St David (Episcopal) Church, Newhaven (1939). Member of the Royal Fine Art Commission for Scotland for ten years. Elected ARSA 1931, RSA 1934. Exhibited regularly RA, GI & RSA.
**Bibl:** Gifford 280,313,556,580,601; Scotsman, 2 Aug 1947 (obit).

**TARENGHI, Enrico** **1848-fl 1875**
Born Rome, 14 Apr. Painter of landscape, topography and genre. Lived for a spell in Edinburgh during the 1870s. Highly competent, his best work combined strong colour, sensitivity and bravura. Exhibited RSA(1); also in Livourne, Milan, Rome & Turin. Represented in Brussels AG, Rome (Galerie d'Art Moderne).

**TARLTON, Valerie A** **fl 1976-1980**
Aberdeen printmaker, mainly figurative designs and flowers. Trained Gray's School of Art, Aberdeen. Exhibited AAS(4) latterly from 7 Mearns Walk, Stonehaven.

**TASSIE, James** **1735-1799**
Born Pollokshaws, Glasgow, Jly 15; died London, Jne 1. Eldest son of a family who probably arrived in Glasgow from Italy about a hundred years earlier. Trained as a stonemason although the only known completed work was a monument to his father (1759). Trained Foulis Academy, possibly under the Italian Torri brothers who taught modelling, moulding and casting in plaster-of-Paris. In 1763 went to Dublin as an assistant to Henry Quinn, Professor of Physics, and there learned to imitate antique cameos and intaglios. Together they invented a formula for vitreous paste which Tassie was to use in all his subsequent work, making gems and portrait medallions. In 1766 he moved to London, remaining there for the rest of his life. Exhibited for the first time at the Society of Artists (two wax models) 1767 and continued to show there annually until 1791. His earliest portraits were half-lengths, mounted on oval glass, with a coloured paper backing. Subsequently learned to cast portrait and background in the same material. By 1780 he had become the leading portrait modeller in the country with sitters including the Lord Chief Justice, his friend the art dealer James Byres, the Earl of Mansfield and the contemporary hero Admiral Keppel; also leading commercial and intellectual figures in Scotland. Although in his lifetime it was the reproduction of antique gems for which he was internationally renowned, having been greatly helped by James Byres, it is his portrait medallions which seal his place in the hall of artistic acclaim. In 1782 commissioned by Catherine the Great to produce 12,000 'pastes' for which he was paid £2,310 plus £294 for the 200-drawer cabinet, itself adorned with almost 100 heads and figures. In this he collaborated with his friend and rival, Josiah Wedgwood. These cabinets were described rapturously by Raspe for 'the elegance and simplicity of their forms, the propriety of their external ornaments which were basso relievos in white enamel, with gilt mouldings, set on a ground of green satinwood and the high finishing of the whole, (which) qualified them, at any rate for ornaments in the noble apartments of Her Imperial Majesty's superb Palace at Czarsko Zelo'. In 1791, encouraged by his collaborator Raspe, Tassie produced the most lavish of three catalogues of his work. This was illustrated by Sir William Allan (then Master of the Trustees Academy) with a frontispiece and 57 plates. After his death, the business continued in the hands of his assistant and nephew, William Tassie(qv). Exhibited RA(35) 1769-1791, after 1777 from 4 Leicester Fields. Over 150 of his medallions are now in SNPG; also in Edinburgh City collection.
**Bibl:** Bryan; Brydall 135-138; Caw 34; Country Life, cxxix, 8.6.1961, 1351-2; M M Delholm, James Tassie and Josiah Wedgwood: A Study in Parallels, Chicago, 1962; J M Gray, James and William Tassie, 1894; J Holloway, James Tassie 1735-1799 NGS 1986; Irwin 86,90,116,151,153; Y O Kagan, The Cabinet of Gem stone reproduction by James Tassie in The Hermitage. Trans State Hermitage XIV, Leningrad 1973, 82 ff; NGS,1986; Duncan Thomson, 'Two Medallionists in Georgian London, the letters of James and William Tassie', Country Life, 27.1.1972, 214-219.

**TASSIE, William** **1777-1860**
Born London; died South Kensington, London, 26 Oct. Nephew of James T(qv). Carried on the family business of reproducing ancient gems and modelling portraits. A medallion of William Pitt proved so popular that it facilitated his early retirement. Exhibited RA(5) 1798-1804, including the 'Six Kings of Scotland' 1799. Twenty-two bequeathed portrait medallions are in SNPG including two of his uncle, as well as the original casts of his and his uncle's collections of gems.
**Bibl:** AJ 1894, 96; Bryan; Brydall 138-9; John M Gray, James and William Tassie, 1894.

**TATHAM, Edmund** **fl 1846-1848**
Amateur Edinburgh landscape watercolourist; exhibited RSA(6).

**TATTON, Alistair** **fl 1977**
Aberdeen amateur painter; exhibited AAS(1), from 36 Ashvale Pl.

**TAYLER, Miss Constance J D** **fl 1885-1886**
Obscure Aberdeenshire painter of still life and figure studies; exhibited AAS(2), from Rothiemey House, Huntly.

**TAYLER, George** **fl 1864**
Little known amateur painter; exhibited RSA(1).

**TAYLOR, Agnes E** **fl 1891-1910**
Minor flower painter and sculptress. Exhibited 'A study of chrysanthemums' at the RSA & 'Boy's head' at the GI from Dalkeith and latterly Fernbank, Ayr.

**TAYLOR, Alasdair Grant** **1936-**
Born Edderton (Ross-shire). Portrait, genre and semi-abstract painter in a variety of media. Trained Glasgow School of Art 1955-59, winning Governor's Prize 1958. For many years caretaker of Glasgow Chaplaincy Centre and part-time lecturer. Fond of collage and poster paints. Exhibits RSA & RGI.

**TAYLOR, Alexander** **fl 1774-d1804**
Died Calcutta 4 Apr. Painter of portraits and portrait miniatures in oil. Probably the Alexander Taylor who entered RA Schools 4 Dec 1775 and mentioned in Walpole Society. In 1797 he went to India and remained in Calcutta by permission of the Governor-General in Council. Advertised from 69 Cossitollah Street, announcing his painting of portraits in oil and miniatures. Possibly the artist mentioned by Farington as being in Rome 1790. Exhibited regularly at the Society of Arts 1774-1778 & RA(17) 1776-1796. Foskett records that a miniature of 'Don Manuel de Goday', favourite of Queen Marie Louise of Spain, by Taylor c1796, was mounted in the name-board of a piano, according to W Dale's *Tschudi the Harpsichord Maker,* 1913.
**Bibl:** Foskett; Walpole Society, vol xix, 74.

**TAYLOR, Alexander** **fl 1867-1875**
Amateur oil painter of Highland landscape; exhibited RSA(3) & GI(3).

**TAYLOR, Sir Andrew Thomas RCanA** **1850-1937**
Born Edinburgh, 13 Oct; died 5 Dec. Architect and watercolour painter. Trained RA Schools. Emigrated to Canada 1883 and established a practise in Montreal, returning to London 1904. Chairman, Bartlett School of Architecture, London University. Exhibited RA(5) from 1875, the last work being a design for Roslin Chapel; also RSA(11).

**TAYLOR, Andrew** **fl 1885-1914**
Glasgow and London painter of pastoral scenes. Exhibited RSA(1) & GI(11).

**TAYLOR, Miss Anne** **fl 1844-1847**
Edinburgh oil painter of portraits and landscape, also sketches from nature; exhibited RSA(11) including a portrait of a gentleman in Highland dress 1844. Lived for a time in Bellevue Crescent.

**TAYLOR, Annie Anderson** **fl 1906-1913**
Minor Edinburgh watercolourist; exhibited a study of the interior of Corstorphine church at the RSA, also RA(1), from 7 Royal Crescent.

**TAYLOR, Arthur John** **fl 1920-1940**
Glasgow painter in oil and watercolour; also engraver. Mainly local Clydeside landmarks and fishing scenes, also landscape. Exhibited RA(1), RSA(16), RSW(3), GI(39) & L(6).

**TAYLOR, Benson** **fl 1917-1918**
Little known Glasgow sculptor; mainly portrait busts. Exhibited GI(3) from 18 Beechwood Drive, Jordanhill.

**TAYLOR, Charles** **fl 1929**
Milngavie painter; exhibited AAS(1), from Drummond Place.

**TAYLOR, David R** **fl 1974**
Painter. Exhibited 'Figure on the beach' at the RSA from Bo'ness.

**TAYLOR, Elizabeth** **fl 1968-1971**
Painter. Exhibited several works at the RSA from St Andrews.

**TAYLOR, Elizabeth R** **fl 1906**
Painter. Exhibited RSA(3) from Edinburgh.

**TAYLOR, Ernest Archibald** **1874-1951**
Born Greenock. Painter in oil and watercolour of landscape. Married Jessie M King(qv). His artistic talents ran in several directions; as well as painting in oil and watercolour he etched, designed interiors, stained glass windows and furniture. Joined Wylie & Lochhead as a trainee designer 1893. This led to a lecturing post in furniture design at the Glasgow School of Art. Designed the drawing room for the firm's Pavilion at the Glasgow Industrial Exhibition which in turn led to major commissions. His early watercolours 1900-1910, often painted on Arran, show much of the sensitivity to design typical of the period. After marriage to Jessie King 1908, moved to Manchester as a designer with George Wragge Ltd. Between 1911 and 1914 lived in Paris and whilst there exhibited regularly at the Paris Salon as well as running a small school of painting known as the Shieling atelier. Returning to Scotland 1914, they settled in Kircudbright and established a summer school on Arran. Received Diploma of Honour and medal at the Turin International Exhibition and in Budapest. Toward the end of his life his work became stronger and less delicate, with black charcoal outlines and forceful colour, closer to the colourists than the symbolists. Finally settled in Kirkcudbright 1916. Exhibited RSA(48), RSW(6), GI(71), AAS(3) & L(2). Represented in Glasgow AG, Castle Douglas AG.
**Bibl:** Halsby 181,185,188,191,208,220; Irwin 403; Scotsman, 22 Nov 1951(obit); Studio, 33, 1905, 217-226.

**TAYLOR, Ernest E** **fl 1891-1902**
Belfast artist of conversational pieces. Was in Bushey, Herts (at Herkomer's ?) 1895 and Belfast 1898. Exhibited RSA(6) & GI(3).

**TAYLOR, George** **fl 1864**
Liberton landscape painter in oils; exhibited RSA(2).

**TAYLOR, George** **fl 1895-1927**
Edinburgh painter of genre and nature studies. Exhibited RSA(11) & GI(5), latterly from Picardy Place.

**TAYLOR, Harry Ramsay** **c1864-1922**
Edinburgh architect. Partner of David Cousin(qv) and **William ORMISTON** (d c1919) and later John Lessels(qv). Designed the 'gingerbread Renaissance' St Andrew Hotel (1900), the single storey Stockbridge Library (1898-1900) and the Edinburgh Geographical Institute, Newington (1909), now commercial offices.
**Bibl:** Gifford 327,370,404,426,642.

**TAYLOR, Isobel** **fl 1961**
Edinburgh landscape painter; exhibited RSA(2).

**TAYLOR, James Fraser** **fl 1877-1913**
Edinburgh painter in oil and watercolour of landscape, portrait, figure scenes and literary subjects. Among his portraits was 'Professor Copland, Astronomer Royal for Scotland' RSA 1890. Exhibited RSA(64), AAS 1885-1912 & GI(6), latterly from 27 Nile Grove.

**TAYLOR, Miss Jean C** **fl 1960-1966**
Edinburgh painter and engraver. Exhibited landscape and topographical subjects at the GI(4).

**TAYLOR, John** **fl 1862-1883**
Painter based for most of his working life in Glasgow but sometimes Edinburgh. Specialised in watercolours and pen and pencil studies of literary subjects and genre; exhibited RSA(16), including illustrations for Longfellow's *Excelsior* (1881) & GI(15), mostly from Gt Hamilton St, Glasgow. Not to be confused with other painters of the same name.

**TAYLOR, John** **1936-**
Born Ayrshire. Trained Glasgow School of Art and Birmingham Polytechnic. Painter and printmaker. Style changed from early cool abstracts to more figurative works. Lives and works in Glasgow. Exhibited RSA(5) & AAS(1), from 23 Kelvinside Gdns E. Represented in SNGMA, Aberdeen AG, Lillie AG (Milngavie), Birmingham AG, SAC.

**TAYLOR, John** **fl 1875-1885**
Kirkcaldy sculptor. Executed portrait busts and biblical scenes. Established a thriving practice in Chelsea before returning to Kirkcaldy 1881. Exhibited RA(6), RSA(8) & GI(1). Among his RA exhibits were marble busts of 'Commander Lord Charles William Beresford, MP' 1879, 'Lady Monteagle' 1880, and 'Basil Bradley' 1880, latterly from Tolbooth St.

**TAYLOR, John D** **fl 1876-1890**
Prolific painter in oil of figure subjects, marines, rustic scenes and landscape. President, Glasgow Art Club 1884-5. Exhibited RA(4) 1884-88 & RSA (16) 1876-1890; also GI(54) & L(1) from 65 West Regent Street, Glasgow.

**TAYLOR, John Stavers** **fl 1888-1945**
Greenock-based etcher and watercolourist. Exhibited RSA(7), RSW(2) & GI(5) from 19 Roxburgh St, Greenock.

**TAYLOR, Linda** **1959-**
Born Stranraer, Galloway. Painter of abstract form based on conceptualised reality. Trained Edinburgh College of Art 1976-80. Won Andrew Grant travelling scholarship 1980 and in 1983 awarded a Young Artist's Bursary by the SAC. First solo exhibition Edinburgh 1985. Exhibited at the Trigon Biennale, Graz 1987, and in New York. Her work is experimental, idiosyncratic and intellectually provocative. To 'reveal' a whole tree, for example, she composed a screen consisting of 64 sheets of paper, each sheet containing a unique watermark drawing of a fragment of a tree of the same species (Scots Pine); the screen being illuminated by a vertical lightbox. Lives in Glasgow. Represented in SNGMA.
**Bibl:** Mungo Campbell, 'The Line of Tradition', Nat Galls of Scotland, Ex cat, Edinburgh 1993; Third Eye Centre, Glasgow 'Scatter', (Ex Cat 1989).

**TAYLOR, Lydia M** **fl 1921**
Aberdeenshire portrait painter and etcher; exhibited AAS(2) from the Schoolhouse, Kintore.

**TAYLOR, M Arrol** **20th Cent**
Aberdeenshire flower painter; exhibited AAS(4), from Gowanlea, Ruthrieston.

**TAYLOR, Miss Medland P** **fl 1865-1893**
Edinburgh painter in oil and watercolour of landscapes, interiors, literary subjects and flower studies; also stained glass window designer. Widely travelled. Among 63 exhibits at the RSA 1865-1893 were several Canadian scenes, an American subject 1882 and two Dutch landscapes 1885, as well as subjects such as 'Ben Wyviss from Loch Luichart' 1886; also exhibited a stained glass window design RA 1893, GI(2) & AAS(5), latterly from 9 Viewforth Terrace. Represented in Edinburgh City collection by a watercolour of Allan Ramsay's house and shop in the High St.

**TAYLOR, Peter (Patrick)** **1756-1788**
Born Edinburgh; died Marseilles, 20 Dec. Portrait painter. In 1787 made a burgess of Edinburgh. *The Burlington Magazine* illustrated an oval portrait of the artist with hat and palette. There is also recorded a still-life with his wife and child, the artist sitting on a log while his wife stands holding the child on the back of a horse and with a view of Edinburgh behind. In 1788 he struggled to establish the manufacture of floor cloth and linoleum but although extremely successful after his death, during his lifetime there was little reward and the hard work was instrumental in causing his early death. Represented in SNPG by two portraits of 'Robert Burns', one painted in 1786, the other undated (and attributed only), City of Edinburgh collection.
**Bibl:** Bryan; Burlington Mag, vol 74, 1939, 74.

**TAYLOR, R Sutherland** **fl 1858-1861**
Glasgow amateur landscape painter in oil; exhibited RSA(7).

**TAYLOR, Simon** **c1730-c1798**
Eminent painter of botanical subjects. Patronised by Lord Bute c1760 and later by Dr Fothergill whose collection of plants which he painted was sold to the Empress of Russia for £2,000. Also engraved portraits, among them 'General Joshua Guest, the defender of Edinburgh Castle against Prince Charles Edward', and 'John Ure, alias Campbell'. Authorities differ as to his date of death.
**Bibl:** Benezit; Bryan; Bushnell; DNB.

**TAYLOR, T L** **fl 1919**
Engraver. Exhibited GI(1) from Glasgow.

**TAYLOR, Thomas G** **fl 1861-1868**
Edinburgh landscape painter in oil; exhibited RSA(10).

**TAYLOR, William** **fl 1836-1877**
A Campsie painter in oil and watercolour of figures and local landscapes, particularly views in the Trossachs and Arran, mostly in watercolour. Illustrated Sir Andrew Leith-Hay's *Castellated Architecture of Aberdeenshire,* 1849. Exhibited RSA(64) & GI(29).
**Bibl:** Halsby 285.

**TAYLOR, William** **fl 1885-1886**
Aberdeen watercolour painter of local landscape; exhibited AAS(5), from 17 Adelphi.

**TAYLOR, William G** **fl 1866-1880**
Amateur painter in oil, painted landscape, especially around Dollar, and flower pieces. Exhibited RSA(8).

**TAYLOR, William W** **fl 1880-1896**
Sculptor. Lived in Kirkcaldy, Fife and in 1880 exhibited a bust of Caius Cassius at the RA. Living in Cardiff 1896 from where he exhibited a marble bust at the Walker Gallery, Liverpool.

**TAYLOR, Willison FRSA** **1918-?**
Born Lennoxtown, Feb 16. Painter in oil of portraits, landscapes, figures and abstracts. Trained Glasgow School of Art and Melbourne University. Influenced by J D Fergusson(qv) and Picasso. His output was limited by preoccupation with the mental techniques of his art. Exhibited GI from Whitfield Lodge, Lennoxtown.

**TEBBUTT, Miss J R** **fl 1964**
Glasgow landscape painter in watercolour. Exhibited GI(1).

**TEH, Hock-Aun** **fl 1973-**
Painter. Trained Glasgow School of Art. Exhibits AAS & GI(5) from 3 Morven Ave, Bishopbriggs, Lanarks.

**TELFER, Henry Monteith** **fl 1878-1886**
Edinburgh painter in oil and watercolour; local landscapes and figure subjects. Exhibited RSA(28) & GI(4).

**TELFER (TAILEFER or TAILYFIER or TOLPHUR), John** **fl 1646-d1670**
Herald painter. Only son of Robert T(qv). Worked 1661-70 with Marchmont Herald 1 February, 1661. On 8 October, 1663 arraigned before the Lyon Court and told not to molest or strike another herald painter, Joseph Stacie(qv) 'but to live Christianly and worthily hereafter'. Had as apprentices, S James Torrie 1647, John Tait 1656, James Alexander 1660, George Porteous 1663 and George Wallace 1667. In 1659 paid £30 for painting Mr Heriot and in 1664 received £216/12s/4d for work in connection with Lady Oxfuird's funeral. In August, 1666 employed by the Earl of Linlithgow for gilding and painting the colours of his regiment and in 1668 he was involved in work for the funeral of the Earl of Cassillis at which time he was described as 'His Majesty's Painter at Holyrood'. There were two John Telfers working in Edinburgh at the same time, making it difficult to distinguish them. (The other **John Telfer** is thought to have flourished from 1653 until his death in 1676).
**Bibl:** Ailsa Mss GD 25.9.18; Apted 94-5; Greyfriars Interments, 638-9; Lyon Court, 4.9.30-1; Mylne, Master Masons, 140; Roll of Edinburgh Burgesses 483.

**TELFER, Mrs Meg** **fl 1985**
Ayrshire landscape painter. Exhibited GI(3), from Largs.

**TELFER (TAILEFER or TAILYFIER or TOLPHUR), Robert** **fl 1617-1639**
Early painter. Only son of mastermason Henry T of Edinburgh. Working at Edinburgh Castle from 16 March, 1618 for which he received £4 per week. In 1633 working at Holyrood and in 1639 again working at Holyrood 'painting and dressing...the King's galry'. In 1636 employed painting the Royal Arms over the great doorway of Parliament House.
**Bibl:** Apted 96; Book of Old Edinburgh Club xiii, 50; Hollyrood Works Accounts ii, 94-5, 318, 325; Lyon Court, 4.9.30; Roll of Edinburgh Burgesses 483.

**TELFER, William Walker** **1907-?**
Born Falkirk, Oct 3. Painter in oil and watercolour of portraits, still life, flowers and landscape; etcher. Immediately after service in WW2 enrolled at Falkirk Art School under James Davie(qv). Director of Thomas Paul Limited, colour printers of Falkirk. Trained first in music and was a graduate of the College of Violinists, then became a banker, member of the Institute of Bankers in Scotland. Began painting in 1925 and, moving to Edinburgh, met Harold Morton(qv), Robbie Robertson(qv) and Willie Wilson(qv), all of whom had a considerable influence, as did Peploe(qv). Conductor of the Falkirk orchestra 1960-69. President, Falkirk Art Club 1933-48. Sponsored by Adam Bruce Thomson, elected member SSA. Held several one-man shows in Edinburgh and elsewhere. An authority on the painter

John Thomson(qv). Exhibited RSA(7), RSW(1), GI(4) & AAS(1), latterly from Nelson St, Falkirk.

**TELFORD, Jessie R** **fl 1885**
Amateur flower painter. Exhibited GI(1).

**TELFORD, Thomas** **1757-1834**
Born Glendinning, Westerkirk, Dumfries-shire. Architect and engineer. Son of a shepherd. he was apprenticed to a country mason and worked for a time in Edinburgh on the building of the New Town before travelling to London 1782. There he found work as a mason at Somerset House and, having acquired a working knowledge of architecture, was subsequently employed by William Pultney to make plans for the alteration of the latter's father's house at Wester Hall, Eskdale, and at the vicarage at Sudborough, Northants where Pultney was the patron. Next employed in supervising the building of the Commissioner's house at Portsmouth dockyard to the design of Samuel Wyatt (1784-6). Then moved to Shrewsbury to work on the castle. In due course, probably through Pultney's influence, was appointed Surveyor to the County. In 1788, having warned those responsible that a church (St Chad) was about to crumble, the accident indeed occurred bringing him considerable acclaim. As a builder of bridges he was one of the first to appreciate the possibilities of iron and his bridge at Buildwas was a pioneer structure. In 1793 he was appointed Architect, Engineer and Surveyor to the Ellesmere Canal and in 1820 became the first president of the Institution of Civil Engineers. With the death of John Rennie(qv) in 1820, became head of a new profession. In Scotland he is remembered for a variety of reasons. About 40 of his 'parliamentary manses' were built in the Highlands during the second quarter of the 19th century. There were two standard plans for these buildings, one for a two-storeyed T-plan building and the other for a more modest, single-storeyed H-plan building. Among those still extant are manses in Duror, Iona, Kilmeny, Kinlochspelvie, Lochgilphead, Portnahaven, Salen, Tobermory and Ulva. He was partly responsible for designing the model fishing town at Pultneytown, nr Wick, in 1808 and, more importantly, he was largely responsible for the construction of the Caledonian Canal (1814-1822). At the southern end of the Canal the ascent to Loch Lochy required eight large locks, christened 'Neptune's Staircase', and at the northern end the entrance to Clachnaharry Basin was founded upon piles more than 60ft deep. His greatest individual contribution was probably his bridge building, especially in the Highlands, two of his most notable being the fine seven-arch bridge across the Tay at Dunkeld and the splendid cast-iron bridge over the Spey at Craigellachie, Banffshire. In the south of the country, mention should be made of his bridge at Tongland, Kirkcudbrightshire (1805) and the Dean Bridge, Edinburgh (1831), the latter coming 'almost at the end of what was certainly one of the most productive and diversified careers ever achieved in the field of civil engineering'. Other works for which he was responsible were alterations at Shrewsbury Castle (1787), the Courts of Justice at Carlisle (begun by Telford), Broomielaw Bridge over the Clyde (1833-5; dem 1899) and Cartlandcrags Bridge over the Mouse Water, Lanarkshire (1821-2).
**Bibl:** Colvin 606-7; D and B; Dunbar 88, 198, 215, 218-9, 221; A. Gibb, The Story of Telford, 1935; Gifford 68,385,387; J Rickman,(Ed), The Life of Thomas Telford, 1839; L T C Rolt, Thomas Telford, 1958; Atlas to the Life of Thomas Telford, 1838.

**TEMPLE, Miss Brenda Haldane** **fl 1982**
Kilbarchan-based designer; trained Glasgow School of Art. Lived for a time with the designer Margaret Fraser Tait(qv). Exhibited AAS(2), from Lismore Cottage, Candlehill Rd.

**TEMPLE, John S** **fl 1860-1861**
Edinburgh amateur painter of figure studies in oil; exhibited RSA(3).

**TEMPLE, Robert Scott** **fl 1874-1905**
Edinburgh landscape painter. Lived in London and Lammas, Norfolk. Painted in oil and watercolour. Retired to The Lodge, Lammas, Norfolk c1900. Exhibited RA(13) 1874-1900 including 'Among the Pentland Hills' 1879 and several Perthshire landscapes 1884-86; also RSA(30), AAS(1) & L(3).

**TEMPLETON, Ellis** **fl 1860**
Edinburgh painter; exhibited 'Vesper Thale' at the RSA.

**TEMPLETON, J M** **fl 1888-1889**
Minor Glasgow topographical painter; exhibited GI(3).

**TEMPLETON, Rosa Isobel (Mary)** **c1868-1936**
Born British Guiana. Painter in watercolours. Settled in Helensburgh c1898 where she died. Exhibited GI(2).
**Bibl:** Halsby 285.

**TENNANT, Barbara S** **fl 1898-1937**
Aberdeen minor painter of local landscape and buildings. Married James T(qv). Exhibited AAS from 6a St Swithin St including a view of Glen Ey.

**TENNANT, Charles H J** **fl 1912**
Minor landscape artist of 2 West Coates, Edinburgh; exhibited 'The Jungfrau' at the RSA.

**TENNANT, James L** **fl 1885-1902**
Painter of local landscape and figurative compositions. Married Barbara T(qv). Exhibited AAS including 'On the Gairn' 1902. This was the year Rodolphe Christen(qv) was building his home on Gairnside so it is likely they would have been friends.

**TENNANT, Hon. Stephen James Napier** **1906-1987**
Born Apr 21; died Feb 28. Painter, poet, illustrator, aesthete. Son of Lord Glenconner. Father died 1960 leaving his son a large fortune and two properties including Dryburgh Abbey, Berwickshire. Suffered from tuberculosis in early life. First exhibited 1921 but his early promise was never quite fulfilled. Lived and worked in London, friend of Cecil Beaton, Rex Whistler, the Sitwells and Siegfried Sassoon with whom he partnered for several years. Wrote and illustrated *The Vein in the Marble* (Allen 1925), *Leaves from a Missionary's Notebook* (Secker 1929), *My Brother Aquarius* (Nash Publications 1961). Illustrated Olivier: *The Mildred Book* (1926), *The Treasure Ship* (with others 1926), Grey: *The White Wallet* (1928), Sassoon: *To My Mother* (1928), *In Sicily* (1930), *To the Red Rose* (1931). Exhibited in various London galleries 1921-87.
**Bibl:** Horne 411; Hoare: *Serious Pleasures: The Life of Stephen Tennant* (Hamilton 1990).

**TENNANT, Virginia S** **fl 1888-1898**
Ayr painter of portraits, domestic genre and figure subjects. Moved to Glasgow c1895. Exhibited RSA(1) & GI(6).

**TENNENT, R** **fl 1877-1891**
Glasgow painter, mostly of watercolours; flowers and garden scenes. Exhibited GI(4) from Clydeview Terrace.

**TERGIMAN, Marie Dominique** **fl 1975**
Aberdeen-based ceramic designer; exhibited AAS(2) from 13 Royal Court.

**TERNENT, George** **fl 1915**
Obscure Glasgow engraver. Exhibited 'The visitor' RSA & GI(1) from 34 Wilton St.

**TERRAS, Ainslie** **fl 1896**
Minor Banff landscape painter of local views; exhibited AAS(2) from 24 Fife St.

**TERRIS, John RI RSW** **1865-1914**
Born Glasgow; died Glasgow, 16 Mar. Probably related to Tom T(qv). His family moved to Birmingham in the early 1880s. As a young man studied Birmingham School of Landscape Art. In 1891, when only 26, elected RSW, and RI 1912. Travelled extensively in France and the Low Countries as well as working in England and Scotland. Much of his work is large with a bold, confident, but pleasing effect. Some of his work was sombre, the result of his fascination with contrasting colours of buildings and boats in shadow against a sunset sky. Married an artist(qv). His early death prevented adequate recognition of his art. At the turn of the century was living in Rustic Bank House, Bridge of Allan, Stirlingshire. Exhibited RA(4), RSA(36), RSW(68), GI(61), RI(13) & L(46). Represented in Brunswick AG, Venice, Galerie d'Art, Vienna (Galeri Liechenstein).
**Bibl:** Benezit; Halsby 153-4,285.

**TERRIS, John (Mrs)** **fl 1894-1897**
Painter. Wife of John T(qv). Exhibited GI(5) when living at 4 Ailsa Terrace, Hillhead, Glasgow. After moving to Stirling and Bridge of Allan she ceased exhibiting.

**TERRIS, Tom** **fl 1897-1940**
Glasgow landscape artist, mainly in watercolour. Probably related to John T(qv). Painted extensively in Holland, especially around Dort. Exhibited RSA(5), GI(45), AAS(2) & L(3), from 62 Fergus Drive.

**TERRY, Miss Pauline M** **fl 1952-1980**
Edinburgh painter in oils, watercolour and pastel. Moved to Auchtermuchty, Fife c1980. Flowers, topography and landscape, sometimes in the Highlands, sometimes local scenery. Exhibited GI(21).

**TEUNON, Clara M (Mrs Shiach)** **fl 1953-1966**
Galashiels painter of landscape, still life and country genre. Sister-in-law of John Shiach(qv). Exhibited RSA(6) & AAS(3) including 'Late summer on the Gairn' 1966, from St Peter's Schoolhouse, Little Outlands.

**THAIN, Phillip Thomas** **fl 1974-1985**
Aberdeen artist; exhibited AAS from 83 Laws Rd.

**THEW, Mary Russell (Mrs)** **1876-1953**
Painter and jewellery designer from Arisaig, Craigendoran, Helensburgh. Trained Glasgow School of Art 1894-96. Temporarily abandoned work as a professional artist until her family had grown up. Then turned to jewellery design. Believed to have had lessons from Rhoda Wager(qv) before launching her own studio in Glasgow. Subsequently moved to Green Gate Close, Kirkcudbright becoming a working member of an active local group of women artists. Belonged to the Glasgow Society of Lady Artists(qv), employing motifs derived from Celtic art. Won Lauder award 1925 for what was described as 'a particularly fine case of jewellery - brooches in metal and precious stones, rings, necklaces and other articles' [after Burkhauser]. Exhibited Walker Gallery, Liverpool(13). Represented in Glasgow AG.
**Bibl:** Burkhauser 177,181,185-6; Glasgow AG, 'The Glasgow Style', 1984, 198.

**THIELKE, Henry D** **fl 1832**
Portobello-based painter of biblical scenes. Exhibited 'Christ and the adulterous woman (St John VIII,7)' at the RSA.

**THIRD, William Chalmers** **fl 1908**
Elgin amateur painter; exhibited a work of genre at the AAS, from Glenview.

**THOM, James** **c1785-?**
Born Edinburgh. Painter of figurative works. After studying in Edinburgh moved to London. Although Bryan mentions an exhibit at the RA 1815 this is not confirmed in the RA catalogues. Exhibited British Institution(2). His 'Young Recruit' was engraved by Duncan 1825. Redgrave gives John as his christian name.
**Bibl:** Benezit; Bryan; Redgrave.

**THOM, James** **1802-1850**
Born Lochlee, April 17; died nr Ramapo, USA, April 17. Sculptor. Brother of Robert T(qv). Apprenticed as a boy to a builder at Kilmarnock employed on ornamental carving. This apart he was largely self-taught, executing a bust of Burns in 1827 and, as a result of the favourable impression this made, decided on sculpting as a career. Without a preliminary sketch, he carved life size figures of Tam O' Shanter and Souter Johnnie. These were purchased for the Burns Monument at Alloa; when shown in London in 1829 they were hailed as 'inaugurating a new era in sculpture'. Thus encouraged, he showed two further works in London 1834 but these were not well received and in 1836 he went to America in search of his agent who had absconded with earlier proceeds. The offender was eventually found in Newark, New Jersey and there Thom decided to stay. He discovered the quarries at Little Falls which provided the stone for a number of important buildings including Trinity Church, New York, for which he did most of the Gothic carving. As a result of his considerable income he purchased a farm at Ramapo, Rockland County. His portrait by William Tannock(qv) was exhibited at the RA 1830. The replicas of the two statues referred to above can be seen at Beaufort Park, Sussex. Work in Scotland includes 'Old Mortality' at Maxwelltown in Dumfries, and a statue of 'Wallace' at Ayr for which there is a replica at Kinfauns Castle, Perth. In Alloway are the figures of the 'Landlord' and the 'Landlady'. Other American work includes another replica of his 'Old Mortality' group for Laurel Hill Cemetery, Philadelphia.
**Bibl:** Brydall 186-7; Builder, 1851, 48; Building Chronicle, Vol II, 66; Gentleman's Magazine, 1850, Part II, 98; Gunnis 387-8; Swan, Views of the River Clyde, 158.

**THOM, James Crawford** **1838-1898**
Born Newark, NJ; died Atlantic Highlands, USA, 16 Feb. Painter of genre, animals and landscape. Son of James T(qv). Trained in Paris under Edward Frere. Worked in England and the USA, exhibiting RA(7) and Suffolk St; also at National Academy, New York and the Boston Exhibition of 1878. In Rheims Museum there is a painting 'Children in a Wood', signed J C Thom, although unclear whether this was the work of father or son, we believe it probably the painting exhibited RA 1864 as 'Returning from the wood'.
**Bibl:** Benezit; Catalogue of Musée de Reims (text by Sartor).

**THOM, R Riach** **fl 1876**
Glasgow landscape painter. Exhibited 'A Quiet spot - Inchbuie, Killin' GI.

**THOM, Robert** **1805-1895**
Sculptor. Younger brother of James T(qv). Apprenticed to a firm of Kilmarnock builders, Howie & Brown. Encouraged by his older brother, he worked as a carver. Little of his career is known but in 1839 he sculpted the monument at Drumclog commemorating the victory of the Scottish Covenanters over Grahame of Claverhouse. The monument was in the Gothic style and stood over 23 ft high.
**Bibl:** Art Union, 1839, 153.

**THOMAS, Albert Gordon RSW** **1893-1970**
Born Glasgow, Nov 17. Painter in oil, watercolour and tempera; figure subjects, topography and landscapes generally of the western seaboard; also teacher. Studied at Glasgow School of Art where he received a Haldane travelling bursary. Lived in Glasgow before settling in Milngavie. Elected RSW 1936. Exhibited RSA(13), RSW(24), GI(96), AAS(1) & L(1). Represented by two works in Lillie AG (Milngavie).
**Bibl:** Halsby 226-7,286.

**THOMAS, Miss Anne** **fl 1849-1878**
Lasswade portrait miniaturist and painter in oil of fruit, figure subjects and landscapes. Often included grapes in her still-lifes. Exhibited regularly RSA(44); also GI(4).

**THOMAS, Barry W G** **fl 1973-1974**
Glasgow painter. Exhibited GI(2) from Giffnock.

**THOMAS, Edward** **fl 1855**
Edinburgh artist; exhibited a sketch of the temple of Mars Utor, Rome at the RSA.

**THOMAS, Frederick** **fl 1940**
Portobello landscape painter. Exhibited 'Bleak morning' at the RSA from 32 Park Ave.

**THOMAS, George Grosvenor RSW** **1856-1923**
Born Sydney, New South Wales; died London, Feb 5. Self-taught painter in oil and watercolour of landscape and flower pieces, also collector and dealer. Came to England as a young man. Educated at Warminster GS. Began painting when he came to Glasgow 1885/6, probably as a result of meeting members of the Glasgow Boys. Influenced by Corot, Daubigny and the Barbizon School. Exhibited 'Evening' RA 1892, from 50 Gordon Street, Glasgow. Extending his interest to the Continent, won gold medals at both Munich and Dresden 1901. Occasionally worked in watercolour, portraying river views with an abundant use of colour. Regarded as one of the Glasgow Boys although on account of his London residence and his frequent visits overseas, only a peripheral member. Elected RSW in 1892 but resigned in 1908, SSA 1893. Dealt in Japanese curios and

other art objects and acquired an important collection of stained glass which he subsequently sold to Sir William Burrell, now in the Burrell Collection. In 1898 Caw expressed the view that Thomas's later landscapes were beginning to show a closer study of nature without losing their artistic grace. Member, Society of 25 Artists. Exhibited RA(1) 1892, RSA(9), RSW(16), GI(26) & L(6) as well as overseas. Represented in Glasgow AG, Budapest AG & Weimar AG.
**Bibl:** AJ 1898, 70; 1904, Nov; Glasgow AG: Calendar of Events, May/June 1965; Halsby 150,286; Studio, 1907, Vol 41.

**THOMAS, John** **1813-1862**
Glasgow sculptor & oil painter of landscapes and still-lifes. Carved the small statues of historical figures designed by Charles Doyle(qv) for the grounds of Holyrood 'confused and miserable, ugly in outline and puerile in detail' *[The Builder]*. Exhibited RSA(4) including 'Tam O'Shanter' and a marble bust of Daniel Maclise both in 1859.
**Bibl:** Gifford 141.

**THOMAS, Margaret** **1916-?**
Born London. Painter of flowers and still life. Based in England, trained Slade and RA Schools under Thomas Monnington and Ernest Jackson. A one-man exhibition in Edinburgh brought her to the city in 1954 and two years later she acquired a base there where she remained. Winner of the 1981 Hunting Group 'Oil Painting of the year' award. 'The delicacy and strength of her flower paintings, in which the design springs from the growth of the flowers and the colour from a luminosity almost abstract in its freedom, is never the same, but is, in every new study, a response to some moment and some mood which poses a problem happily confronted, radiantly solved' [Greenham]. Exhibited regularly RA & RSA from1951, usually from London but after 1985 from Ellingham Mill, nr Bungay, Suffolk. Represented in Paisley AG, Lillie AG (Milngavie), Carlisle AG, Hull AG, Edinburgh City collection; Royal West of England Academy (perm coll.), Wakefield AG, Arts Council, Royal collection.
**Bibl:** Sally Hunter FA, (Ex Cat, notes by Peter Greenham RA, London 1988).

**THOMPSON, Alfred James** **1853-1924**
Born Perth; died Hamilton. Painter in watercolours of buildings and landscapes; art teacher & photographer. Father of Evelyn T(qv). Began his teaching career at Fechney Industrial School, Perth 1876 before moving to Ayr Academy in 1877. Added 'Alfred' when in Ayr to avoid confusion with another teacher. Founder member, Ayr Sketch Club 1901. Exhibited RSA(2) 1887.

**THOMPSON, Bonnie** **c1975-**
Painter of still life. Trained Edinburgh College of Art 1992-97 followed by a year at Norwich School of Art. Won several awards while still a student. Enjoys finely observed, delicately painted "magically austere" still life. Exhibits RSA, Norwich AG.
**Bibl:** Macmillan 2001, 179-80.

**THOMPSON, David** **fl 1889-1893**
Minor Glasgow figure; exhibited GI(4).

**THOMPSON, E H** **[see PATON, Donald]**

**THOMPSON, Elise** **c1870-1933**
Animal painter of Irish extraction. Trained Paris, with Denovan Adam(qv) at Craigmill, Stirling, and in Dresden. Elected ASWA 1904. Settled in Greystones, County Wicklow c1903. Exhibited RA (4), RSA(2), RHA(15), ROI(6), SWA(40), GI(2) & L(5).

**THOMPSON, Evelyn** **1884-1973**
Born Ayr, the eldest daughter of A J Thompson(qv), art master at Ayr Academy. Painter in watercolour & teacher. Studied art at South Kensington School of Art, winning a silver medal for a bas relief of a male head 1910. Continued studies at Glasgow School of Art under Fra Newberry. Appointed art teacher, Ayr Academy 1910. Married R W Brown(qv) 1918. After the war returned to her position in Ayr, where she died 1973. Exhibited flowers, landscapes & portraits at GI(19) 1909-1951, Ayrshire Artists 1954-9, Ayr Sketch Club 1908 and Hamilton Art Club, where she was secretary, c1926. Her sister **Alexandrina Guthrie Murdoch THOMPSON** (1888-1978) was also an artist, gaining a First Class Cert. for Drawing from the Antique, RCA 1911.

**THOMPSON, Fred** **fl 1906**
Aberdeen painter; exhibited AAS(1) from 72 Union Grove.

**THOMPSON, J Johnston** **fl 1891**
Amateur Pollockshields watercolour painter; exhibited GI(1) from Doon Terrrace.

**THOMPSON, M D'Arcy** **fl 1930**
Minor St Andrews painter. Exhibited at the New England Art Club from 44 South St.

**THOMPSON, N** **fl 1809-1813**
Miniature painter, mainly young women and children. Although the first record of Thompson is that she was living at 33, Newman St, London 1809, the year of her exhibit at the RA, she was working in Edinburgh 1813. A portrait executed at this time was 'Miss Thompson of Duddingston'.

**THOMPSON, Sydney L** **fl 1904-1923**
Edinburgh painter of figure subjects. Spent several summers at Concarneau, Finisterre, France. Eventually settled in his native city c1920 from where he exhibited RA(2) and a north African street scene at the RSA.

**THOMS, Colin** **1912-1997**
Aberdeen landscape and abstract painter. Brother of Kenneth T(qv) and Patrick T(qv). Studied Edinburgh College of Art, then with the aid of a scholarship travelled extensively in Europe and the Middle East. Lecturer, Aberdeen School of Art 1951-1977. President, SSA 1949-51. Moved back to Edinburgh 1990, taking up active membership of Edinburgh Printmakers Workshop. Frequent exhibitor RSA(91) 1928-1990, RSW, GI(6) & AAS from 101 Hamilton Place, Aberdeen and 14 Coates Gdns, Edinburgh. Latterly concentrated on more abstract work with a vaguely figurative connotation. Represented SNGMA, Aberdeen AG, City of Edinburgh collection, SAC.

**THOMS, D J** **fl 1868-1871**
Edinburgh landscape painter in oil; exhibited RSA(8), latterly from Dundee.

**THOMS, Kenneth O** **fl 1932-1934**
Amateur Edinburgh painter, brother of Colin(qv) and Patrick T(qv). Exhibited RSA(3) from 14 Coates Gardens.

**THOMS, Patrick** **fl 1940**
Edinburgh artist, mainly in oils. Brother of Colin(qv) and Kenneth T(qv). Exhibited RSA(1) from the family home, 14 Coates Gardens.

**THOMS, Patrick** **1872-1946**
Dundee architect. Trained under the Owers(qv) and Thomas Cappon 1894. Established his own practice c1898 being joined as a partner by **William WILKIE**. Together they designed many unusual houses in the Perth Rd area of Dundee including The Hirsel (now Ardsheil, 389 Perth Rd)(1904) and, for himself, Greywalls, 452 Perth Rd (1929). The latter incorporates personal variations on the Arts and Crafts and Scots Baronial styles as well as showing the influence of WG Lamond(qv) and Harry East.
**Bibl:** Bruce Walker & W S Gauldie, Architects and Architecture on Tayside, Dundee 1984, 160(illus),161.

**THOMS, Vanessa** **fl 1976**
Edinburgh painter; exhibited AAS(1) from 18 Dundonald St.

**THOMSON, Miss A K** **fl 1844**
Edinburgh landscape painter; exhibited RSA(2).

**THOMSON, Adam Bruce OBE RSA PPRSW HRSW** **1885-1976**
Born Edinburgh, Feb 22; died Edinburgh. Painter in oil and watercolour, also pen and wash. Trained Royal Institution and Edinburgh College of Art, also in Paris and Madrid. Member, teaching staff of Edinburgh College of Art. Influenced by Gillies(qv) in the 1930's. Particularly attached to Edinburgh, the West Highlands, Berwickshire and Tweedside. His best work showed a great sensitivity for nature and accuracy in the colours depicting the varying moods of Scottish landscape. President, RSW 1956-63, treasurer RSA 1949-56. Elected

PSSA 1937, ARSA 1937, RSA 1946, RSW 1947, PRSW 1956-63, OBE 1963. Exhibited RSA(200+), RSW, GI(100), AAS (1926 & 1937) & L(9). Represented in Aberdeen AG, Dundee AG, Glasgow AG, City of Edinburgh collection(5), RSA.
**Bibl:** Halsby 192,211,215,220-1,286; Macmillan [SA] 332,358,361; RSA Obituary 1976;

**THOMSON, Alan Robert** **fl 1976**
Aberdeen painter; exhibited AAS(1) from 30 Louisville Avenue.

**THOMSON, Alastair W** **fl 1952-**
Glasgow painter in oils and watercolour; landscapes, mainly of the west coast and western isles. Exhibited GI(31) 1952-1989, since 1960 from Giffnock.

**THOMSON, Alexander** **fl 1775-1776**
All that is known of this artist is that he was described as a 'limner' living at the head of Niddry Wynd, Edinburgh during the above years.
**Bibl:** Edin. Directory 1775-6.

**THOMSON, Alexander "Greek"** **1817-1875**
Born Balfour, Stirlingshire. Architect. Seventeenth son of twenty children of a piously strict covenanting family. Worked for Robert Foote, Glasgow and John Baird the elder c1844. Entered partnership with John Baird the younger 1847 and later with his own brother **George THOMSON**. Married the granddaughter of Peter Nicholson(qv). Known particularly for his neo-Greek houses and churches, the best of which are the Glasgow churches in Caledonia Road(1856) and St. Vincent Street(1858) - 'monumental compositions of great power and originality' - and the Great Western Terrace house remodelled by Robert Lorimer for Burrell. A church of advanced design, Queen's Park(1867), was destroyed during WW2. Worked mainly in the south of the city, succeeding Charles Wilson(qv) as President of the Glasgow Institute of Architects 1871. Strongly condemned Gilbert Scott's design for the University; otherwise his writings were rare, the most notable being his Haldane Lectures 1874. His mid-century terraced houses are 'meticulously composed and exquisitely detailed, now recognised as among the most advanced of their kind' [Dunbar]. Clunas, one of his assistants, said that his master was 'unassuming...considerate and even affectionate, alternating in mood between dreamy unrest and bursts of productivity'. Never travelled outside Britain.
**Bibl:** Dunbar 138-141; A Gomme & D Walker, Architecture of Glasgow, London 1987(rev) 300-302; Peter Savage, Lorimer and the Edinburgh Craft Designers, Edinburgh 1980,49,169; Graham Law, "Greek Thomson", Architectural Review CXI, May 1954; Graham Law "Colonades and Temples. Greek Thomson's Style", Glasgow Herald, 8 June 1954.

**THOMSON, Alexander H** **fl 1938**
Minor figure of 7 Victoria Place, Airdrie; exhibited GI(1).

**THOMSON, Alexander P RSW** **fl 1909-d1962**
Glasgow watercolourist. Specialised in Highland views depicted in a conventional style, being little affected by contemporary artistic movements. Worked on rough paper and in a competent manner, often on a large scale. Although pleasing his work is not of major consequence. Elected RSW 1922. Exhibited RA(12) from 1906; also RSA (63) 1909-1943, RSW(76), GI(100+), RI(6), AAS(1926-1935) & L(60).
**Bibl:** Halsby 286.

**THOMSON, Alfred Stanley** **fl 1881-1882**
Amateur Edinburgh painter of 2 West Tollcross; exhibited RSA(2).

**THOMSON, Alison H** **fl 1931**
Minor figure of 20 Lochend Road, Bearsden; exhibited GI(1).

**THOMPSON, Ally** **c1960-**
Figurative painter. Trained Glasgow School of Art in the early 1980s. A friendly critic [Peter Howson] considers his work 'masterfully executed, uncompromising and stark in its beauty and he can be regarded as a visionary, in the mould of William Blake'. First solo exhibition in Glasgow 1989. Usually works on a large scale.
**Bibl:** Observer Scotland, May 1990.

**THOMSON, Andrew Ronaldson** **fl 1880-1892**
Edinburgh landscape painter in oil, mainly Border views eg 'Smailholme Tower, Roxburghshire' 1887. Moved to Glasgow 1882. Exhibited RSA(9) & GI(19).

**THOMSON, Miss Annie Bruce** **fl 1878-1889**
Edinburgh painter of flower studies and interiors. Exhibited RSA(4) including a study of 'Queen Mary's Chamber, Holyrood' 1879. Latterly lived at Cloverfords, nr Galashiels.

**THOMSON, Professor Arthur** **fl 1858-1935**
Amateur watercolour painter of landscape. Professor of Anatomy, RA from 1900. Before then lived in Edinburgh and Oxford. Exhibited RA(4) & RSA(5).

**THOMSON, Bessie** **fl 1883-1891**
Glasgow watercolour painter of flower pieces; exhibited GI(10), RBA(3), RHA(3) & SWA(1). Later moved to London.

**THOMSON, Bethia C** **fl 1880-1908**
Glasgow oil painter of fruit and flowers; probably mother of Bethia J T(qv). Exhibited RSA(2) & GI(6).

**THOMSON, Bethia J** **fl 1932-1937**
Painter. Probably the daughter of Bethia C T(qv). Lived at Springfield, Clarkston, Airdrie; exhibited GI(4).

**THOMSON, Cameron** **late 19th Cent**
Perthshire painter; exhibited AAS from the Toll House, Aberfeldy.

**THOMSON, Cecilia Gibson** **fl 1867-1885**
Edinburgh oil painter of portrait studies from life (especially young children) and still-life. Exhibited RSA(6) from 14 York Place.

**THOMSON, Charles** **fl c1800-1830**
Edinburgh engraver. Engraved plans of Scottish towns 1823-7 and many bookplates. An engraving 'View of Leith from the Marbello Tower', 1819 after David Roberts, is in Edinburgh PL.
**Bibl:** Bushnell; Butchart 59; Fincham.

**THOMSON, D C** **fl 1879-1881**
Edinburgh landscape painter in oil. Moved to London c1881. Exhibited RSA(3).

**THOMSON, David** **fl 1807-1813**
Edinburgh painter in oil of landscape and rustic interiors. Moved to London in mid-career. Exhibited the inside of a stable at the RA 1807 from 212 Piccadilly, also in the provinces.

**THOMSON, David** **fl 1853**
Edinburgh amateur landscapist. Exhibited a view of Ravenscraig Castle, Fife at the RSA, from Arthur St.

**THOMSON, David F** **fl 1932**
Minor painter of 7 Infirmary Street, Edinburgh; exhibited RSA(1).

**THOMSON, David N** **fl 1977-1980**
Edinburgh painter; exhibited RSA & GI(2), from Ferry Rd.

**THOMSON, Douglas** **1955-**
Born Greenock, Renfrewshire. Landscape and figurative painter & engraver. Trained Glasgow School of Art 1974-8 and Hospitalfield, Arbroath 1977. First solo exhibition in Glasgow 1982, followed by others in Germany and Scotland. Member of the Glasgow Group(qv). Exhibited RSA, GI(8) & AAS(2) latterly from Otago St.

**THOMSON, Miss E C** **fl 1846-1849**
Edinburgh portrait miniaturist in oil; exhibited RSA(26).

**THOMSON, Mrs E M Murray** **fl 1955-1971**
Edinburgh painter of portraits and flowers. Exhibited RSA(13) including a portrait of the artist's relative 'John Murray Thomson'(qv) 1970; also GI(12).

**THOMSON, Edward W** **fl 1869-1884**
Edinburgh sculptor and painter in oil of portrait medallions, portrait

busts and landscapes. Lived at 36 George Street. Exhibited RSA(9). Not to be confused with the English miniaturist of the same name (fl 1832-1849).

**THOMSON, Elma** **fl 1900**
Ayr amateur landscape painter. Exhibited 'A woodland path' at the GI.

**THOMSON, Elsie/Elizabeth** **fl 1946-1947**
Paisley painter of figurative works; exhibited RSA(2).

**THOMSON, Miss Elizabeth C** **fl 1967**
Glasgow sculptress. Exhibited two works in terracotta at the GI.

**THOMSON, Miss Emily Gertrude RMS** **?-1932**
Born Glasgow. Portrait painter, miniaturist, illustrator and stained glass artist. Trained Manchester School of Art. Elected ARMS 1911, RMS 1912. In 1908 was living at 11 Queens Mansions, Brook Green, London. Illustrated *A Soldier's Children* 1897 (with E Stuart Hardy), and *Three Sunsets and Other Poems with Twelve Fairy Tale Fancies* by EGT (1898). Exhibited RMS(51), L(20) & GI(1); also overseas.

**THOMSON, Emmeline W** **fl 1949-1950**
Edinburgh landscape painter; exhibited RSA(2).

**THOMSON, Ernest** **?-1925**
Glasgow oil and watercolour painter of landscape. Brother of Horatio T(qv). Married an artist. Exhibited from 1883 RSA(1), GI (49), RSW(5), AAS(1) & L(3).

**THOMSON, Mrs Ernest** **fl 1897-1898**
Amateur painter of Hillhead, Glasgow; married Ernest T(qv). Exhibited GI(3).

**THOMSON, Dr Francis Hay** **fl 1861-1870**
Glasgow amateur painter in oils, also sculptor; portrait busts and landscapes. Exhibited RSA(8) GI(14).

**THOMSON, G G** **fl 1893**
Amateur watercolour painter of 28 Napier Road, Edinburgh; exhibited RSW(1).

**THOMSON, George** **1860-1939**
Born Towie, Aberdeenshire, Apr 2; died Boulogne, Mar 22. Painter of town scenes, also portraits, landscapes and flower pieces; illustrator. Trained as an architect but took up painting instead. Studied RA Schools from 1882. Lecturer, Slade 1895-1914 before going to live in France at Chateau Letoquoi, Samer, Pas de Calais, where he died. Elected to the New England Art Club 1891. Contributed to *The Pall Mall Budget* (1891-2). Exhibited RA(14), RSA(2) ROI(1), RI(1), RHA(2), RBA(2), NEA(88), GI(8) & L(5).
**Bibl:** Houfe.

**THOMSON, George L** **fl 1946**
Edinburgh landscape artist; painted in France as well as in Scotland. Exhibited RSA(2), from Salisbury Rd.

**THOMSON, George McKelvie** **fl 1948-1964**
Paisley landscape artist; Cornish and continental subjects. Exhibited RSA(2) & GI(8).

**THOMSON, Graham** **fl 1902**
Lanarkshire amateur painter of country subjects; exhibited AAS(2) from 2 Braehead Ave, Larkhall.

**THOMSON, Helen P** **fl 1928**
Figure painter. Exhibited 'Gentleman reading' RSA from 45 Pentland Terrace, Edinburgh.

**THOMSON, Hetty D** **1904-c1976**
Glasgow painter of flora/fauna and landscapes. Exhibited RSA(8) & GI(9). Represented in Lillie AG (Milngavie).

**THOMSON, Horatio** **fl 1884-1906**
Glasgow watercolour painter; specialised in street scenes in London and Glasgow, also country studies. Brother of Ernest T(qv). Lived at 14 Great George Street, Hillhead. Exhibited AAS(4) & GI(10).
**Bibl:** Halsby 286.

**THOMSON, Miss Isabella Lauder** **fl 1878-1896**
Edinburgh watercolour and oil painter of still-life and landscape. Exhibited RSA(3).

**THOMSON, J B** **fl 1885**
Minor figure of 9 Newhall Terrace, Glasgow; exhibited GI(1).

**THOMSON, J Bell** **fl 1934**
Painter of flowers and pastoral scenes. Exhibited GI(2) from 6 Stair Park Terrace, Girvan.

**THOMSON, James** **1835-1905**
Glasgow architect. Trained under James Brown. Joined John Baird(qv) as a draughtsman, becoming a partner shortly before the latter's death. Early work was Italianate but became freer in mid-career. Undertook considerable work for the ironmasters. Designed Glasgow HS(1878). With his sons **James Baird THOMSON**(d 1917) and **William Aitken THOMSON**(d 1947), developed a style after the early German Renaissance. Unrelated to Alexander T(qv).
**Bibl:** A Gomme & D Walker, Architecture of Glasgow, London, 1987(rev), 302.

**THOMSON, James** **fl 1855-1858**
Edinburgh landscape and figure painter; exhibited RSA(5).

**THOMSON, James** **fl 1902-1919**
Airdrie painter; landscape and topography. Sometimes in monochrome. Exhibited RSA(3), GI(11) & L(2).

**THOMSON, James H F** **1951-**
Born Edinburgh, 26 Feb. Painter in oils, generally on gesso board; also scene painter & landscape gardener. Trained Duncan of Jordanstone College of Art 1973-77. Prefers working on small scale figurative and landscape compositions. Combines teaching with painting. Exhibits RSA. Lives and works in South Queensferry.

**THOMSON, James L** **fl 1832-1891**
Edinburgh sculptor of portrait busts; exhibited RSA(6) & GI(1).

**THOMSON, Rev John (of Duddingston) HRS** **1778-1840**
Born Dailly, Ayrshire, Sep 1; died Duddingston, Oct 20. Landscape painter in oil and occasional wash drawings. Known as 'Thomson of Duddingston'. Fourth son of the Minister of Dailly. Began studying theology at the University of Glasgow 1791-92, transferring to Edinburgh 1798-99. There he studied for about a month under Alexander Nasmyth. Returned to Ayrshire 1799, the year his father died, and in 1800 succeeded his father as Minister of Dailly. During his life was regarded most highly both by critics and by his fellow artists. Raeburn, for example, thought of asking him to paint in a sea but decided that if he did "it might put my part of the picture to the blush". Writing a little later, McKay said 'he is a personality and this is what lifts him above the Nasmyths, and makes share with John Wilson the honour of having given the first impulse to the Scottish school of landscape. He was a born painter...but lacked thoroughness of technique...a want of knowledge of the underlying structure of things gives an air of unreality to his compositions...but for vigour of conception and imaginative power none of his Scottish followers have excelled him'. The few wash drawings that remain show a firm outline with free use of wash in an almost modern way. His 'Edinburgh from Corstorphine Hill', engraved by W Wolnoth (1819), is a masterly interpretation of the scene between the hill and the dominant rock. Appears in *Provincial Antiquities of Scotland* by his friend, Sir Walter Scott. His friendship with Scott began in the early 1790's when his brother and the writer were both qualifying as lawyers. It was largely through Sir Walter's persuasion that Thomson became Minister at Duddingston 1805. Because of his parallel profession, Thomson preferred not to join any body of artists nor did he seek to exhibit beyond Edinburgh although as an Honorary Exhibitor he did show one landscape at the RA 1813. During the 1830's he painted a number of scenes for the 5th Duke of Buccleuch and during this time embarked on a trip of the north-east which resulted in the 'Glen of Altnarie', exhibited 1832. There was a close relationship between Thomson, Turner (who visited him in 1822) and

H W Williams(qv). Irwin points out that Thomson's most famous painting, 'Fast Castle', is remarkably similar in composition to Williams's 'Temple of Poseidon, Cape Sunion' 1822. 'The parallel between Scottish and Greek scenery so often remarked on by Williams, would make the adaptation seem rightly appropriate. Thomson would accord to Williams the deference due to a professional as opposed to himself as an amateur painter, whilst Williams' dedication of the first volume of his *Travels* to Thomson is ample evidence of a mutual esteem' [Irwin]. Unfortunately, his lack of early training limited his powers as a draughtsman and must account for the unsound technical methods, especially the excessive use of bitumen which flawed much of his best work. To the modern eye his paintings appear heavy and even dull but, placed in their historical context, they represent an important development in the history of Scottish landscape. His followers exceeded his skills but were influenced by his designs and subjects, most notably Horatio McCulloch(qv) and John Knox(qv). Exhibited 102 works at the RSA and its predecessor 1808-1841. Elected HRSA 1830. Represented in NGS, SNPG (Scott), Glasgow AG(5), Kirkcaldy AG, Edinburgh City collection(4), Brodie Castle (NTS), Haddo House (NTS), Manchester AG, Walker AG (Liverpool).
**Bibl:** Armstrong 17-18; W. Baird, John Thomson of Duddingston, 1885; Bryan; Brydall 294-8; Butchart 46-7; Caw 140-44 et passim; Halsby 34,37,111,286; Irwin 231-7 et passim; McKay 179, 180-187; Macmillan [SA] 222-5 et passim; R W Napier, John Thomson of Duddingston, 1919; William W. Telfer, 'John Thomson of Duddingston', (Ex Cat, Falkirk 1950).

**THOMSON, John** **1859-1933**
Glasgow architect. Elder son of Alexander T(qv). Went to London and trained RA schools under R P Spiers 1881-4. After working for a time with **William FLOCKHART**, in 1886 entered partnership with Sandilands(qv).
**Bibl:** A Gomme & D Walker, Architecture of Glasgow, London 1987(rev), 302-3.

**THOMSON, John Leslie RSW RBA RI** **1851-1929**
Born Aberdeen; died London, Feb 23. As a young man he moved to London and began exhibiting at the RA 1873. His landscapes showed a mixture of French, Dutch, English and an occasional Scottish subject, but mainly the scenery of the southern counties of England and the wide open spaces of Normandy and the Dutch coast. In 1906 the *AJ* described his reproduced 'Washing Place: Normandy' saying that its atmosphere, colour-correspondences, were admirably exemplified. Awarded a medal at the Chicago Institute and an honourable mention in Paris. Elected RBA 1883, NEAC 1887, ROI 1892, ARWS 1910, RWS 1912, HROI 1921. Influenced considerably by David Muirhead(qv). 'Informed by sincere love for Nature and a personal note, his pictures occupy a distinct, if modest, place in contemporary landscape [Caw]. R.A.M. Stevenson regarded him as essentially an English landscape painter. Exhibited RA(56), RBA(40), RI(13), ROI(55), RSW(38), GI(13) & L(27), latterly from 98 James St, Buckingham Gate. Represented in Kirkcaldy AG, Perth AG ('Washing Place, Normandy').
**Bibl:** AJ 1898, 53-75; 1904, 195; 1906, 87; 1907, 162; Cat de l'Exp de Cenn d b Artes 1889-1900, Paris, 1900, 302; Caw 307-8; Connoisseur 84 (1929) 60; Halsby 286; Studio, Summer No 1900; Who's Who 1929-1930 (obit).

**THOMSON, John Murray RSA RSW PSSA** **1885-1974**
Born Crieff, Dec 17; died Edinburgh, Oct 16. Painter of animals and birds in oil and watercolour. Educated Morrison's Academy, Crieff and Edinburgh School of Art, where he received a Carnegie Travelling Scholarship in the RSA Life Classes, enabling him to journey to Paris where he undertook further studies at the Academie Julian. Returned to Edinburgh and to his favourite subjects, animals and birds in their natural settings. Whilst abroad he worked in zoos and on his return was appointed a member of staff, Edinburgh College of Art, where he taught animal drawing and painting for eleven years. Serious eye trouble prevented him doing any painting for five years but partial recovery then enabled him to resume his work at a reduced level. Author and illustrator of *Animals We Know*. Had many interests outside art and natural history, including rugby football, alpine gardening, collecting and identifying Scottish provincial silver. Exhibited RSA(100+), RSW(73), RA(5), GI(50+) & L(13). Represented in Aberdeen AG, Paisley AG, Perth AG, Edinburgh City collection.
**Bibl:** Halsby 223,286; RSA Obituary.

**THOMSON, Kate W** **fl 1907**
Glasgow silversmith. Frequently collaborated with W Armstrong Davidson(qv). Exhibited GI(1) & L(3) from 137 West Regent Street.

**THOMSON, Mrs Lauder** **fl 1895-1896**
Amateur artist of 25 Merchiston Avenue, Edinburgh; exhibited RSA(2).

**THOMSON, Miss Lesley** **fl 1986**
Angus painter of rural scenes. Exhibited GI(1) from Arbroath.

**THOMSON, Leslie** **fl 1959**
Edinburgh landscape painter and printmaker. Exhibited RSA(2), from Saughton Crescent.

**THOMSON, Miss Margaret** **fl 1872-1897**
Edinburgh painter in watercolour of flowers and churches. Later moved to Birkenhead. Exhibited RSA(4) & L(2).

**THOMSON, Miss Margaret** **fl 1942**
Glasgow artist in pastels. Exhibited GI(2).

**THOMSON, Mary** **fl 1982**
Edinburgh painter; exhibited a work entitled 'January' at the RSA, from Leamington Terrace.

**THOMSON, Paton** **c1750-1821**
Engraver working in London, said to have been of Scottish extraction. Specialised in portraits including plates of 'E. Jerningham' 1794, 'John Anderson', after Allan 1799, 'Charles Kemble as Romeo' 1819 and the same actor as 'Vincentio' 1821 and 'Edmund Kean as Coriolanus' 1820.
**Bibl:** Bryan; Bushnell.

**THOMSON, Peter** **1962-**
Born Glasgow. Lives and works in Glasgow. Compositions reflect alienation, despair and social malaise. Exhibition Glasgow 1990. Represented in SAC.
**Bibl:** Bill Hare, Contemporary Painting in Scotland, Edinburgh 1993.

**THOMSON, R Millar** **fl 1883-1884**
Amateur landscape Airdrie painter in oils. Exhibited 'Birches in Arran' at the RSA & GI(2) from Park Villa, Rochsalloch.

**THOMSON, Robert** **fl 1867-1885**
Lasswade painter of interiors and country scenes; exhibited RSA(4), latterly from 2 Orwell Terrace, Dalry Road, Edinburgh.

**THOMSON, Robert** **fl 1959-1963**
Glasgow painter of Scottish and continental topography. Exhibited GI(3) from Bishopbriggs.

**THOMSON, Robert Sinclair ARSA RSW** **1915-1983**
Born Glasgow of a Caithness family; died Ballantrae. Landscape and flower painter in oil, watercolour and pastel, also murals; potter. Most of his pottery was finished in strongly coloured glazes reflecting the robust character of the potter himself. Educated Allan Glen's where an injury sustained playing rugby led to a leg amputation which caused pain for the rest of his life. Trained Glasgow School of Art under Hugh Adam Crawford(qv). During WW2 served as dispatch rider. Lecturer, drawing and painting at Glasgow School of Art 1960-65. Resigned in order to launch a pottery business with his wife **Florence JAMIESON**, producing both decorative and functional slipware. Commissioned to undertake large murals made of pottery tiles for schools in Lanarkshire. A popular teacher, Joan Eardley(qv) was among his pupils. Elected ARSA 1952, RSW. Exhibited regularly RSA 1948-1984 & at RSW & SSA. Represented Edinburgh City collection.

**THOMSON, Robert Stewart** **fl 1958-1967**
Glasgow portrait and landscape painter. Exhibited GI(7), latterly from Woodside Rd.

**THOMSON, Stuart Brodie** **fl 1977**
Amateur Edinburgh-based painter. Exhibited RSA(1).

**THOMSON, Thomas** **fl 1838-1839**
Painter of no known address; exhibited RSA(3), a local view, a study of a falcon, and a still life of fruit.

**THOMSON, Thomas** **fl 1861-1873**
Paisley landscape painter in oil and watercolour, often on Arran. Exhibited RSA(7) & GI(8).

**THOMSON, W G** **fl 1887-1908**
Aberdeen landscape painter, often painted in the Moray Firth and Fochabers areas. Moved to London at the turn of the century. Exhibited AAS(3), from 22 Belmont St.

**THOMSON, William Hill RMS** **1882-1956**
Born Edinburgh, Mar 13. Portrait painter and miniaturist in both oil and watercolour. Elected ARMS 1916, RMS 1924. Sole Scottish member of the Royal Society of Miniature Painters of his time. Exhibited in Australia during WW2; thereafter principally RA(1), RSA(47), RMS (47), GI(19) & L(21).
**Bibl:** Scotsman, 16 April 1956(obit).

**THOMSON, William John RSA** **1771-1845**
Born Savannah, Georgia; died Edinburgh, Mar 24. Painter of portraits and portrait miniatures. One of the most important figures in the history of Scottish miniature painting. Both parents were Scottish and he was brought to Britain by his father when the latter lost his job as a result of the rebellion. His father retired and settled in Edinburgh. Thomson went to London where he began exhibiting at the RA 1796 showing there a total of 45 works until 1843. Towards the end of 1812 returned to Edinburgh and remained a prolific worker until his death. Painted mostly in watercolour. Foskett likens his work to that of Samuel Stump. Often employed a greenish paint to his shading of the sitter's clothes and background. 'To accuracy of execution he added great richness of effect, preciousness of finish, and depth of tone' [Brydall]. Among his Scottish patrons were the Hunter-Blairs of Ayrshire, who still own several examples, as does the V & A. H W Williams, writing of Italian artists in his *Travels in Italy, Greece and the Ionian Islands,* said 'in portrait painting, which of them can compare with a Lawrence, a Raeburn, or a Geddes? Or in miniature with a Sanders or a Thomson?'. Elected RSA 1829. His last exhibit at the RA 1843, was a portrait of 'Tom Yarker, "the King of deerstalkers", with favourite animals'. Exhibited RSA and its predecessors a total of 190 works. Represented in NGS.
**Bibl:** Bryan; Brydall 245-6; Caw 91.

**THORBURN, Archibald** **1860-1935**
Born Dumfries, May 31; died Godalming, Surrey, Oct 9. Some authorities give his birth place as Lasswade, Midlothian. Britain's foremost wildlife artist. Although occasionally painted in oil, it is for his watercolours that he is now most highly regarded; also an occasional sculpture. Son of the miniaturist, Robert T(qv). Educated at Dalkeith and Edinburgh before studying at the newly founded St Johns Wood School of Art in London whose principal at the time was the animal painter Calderon. Remained in London for some years becoming an extremely popular illustrator and painter of birds. Married the daughter of C.E. Mudie, the proprietor of Mudie's Libraries. Friendly with other naturalist artists with whom he went on extended sketching trips, among them George Lodge(qv) and Joseph Wolf, whose influence on Thorburn's development was strong. His first important illustrations were for Swaysland's *Familiar Wild Birds,* 4 vols, 1883-1888. Then commissioned by Lord Lilford to complete the illustrations for his major work *Coloured Figures of the Birds of the British Islands.* This had been begun by Keulemans but that artist had become ill. This resulted in over 250 plates in the seven volumes. Other important works which he illustrated were Yerby's *The Ornithology of the Straits of Gibraltar* (1895), the supplement to Dresser's *Birds of Europe* (1895-6), Hudson's *British Birds,* and Thorburn's own major works, the four volume *British Birds* (1915), the two volume *British Mammals* (1900), *The Naturalist's Sketchbook* (1900) and *Game Birds and Wildfowl.* Contributed to *The Sporting and Dramatic News* (1896), *The Pall Mall Magazine, ILN* (1896-98), *The English Illustrated Magazine* (1897) and *British Diving Ducks* (1913). The first of the great wildlife painters whose works were reproduced photographically, marking an important change from the tradition of Audubon and Gould. More prints have been produced of his work than of any other wildlife artist. His compositions are minutely detailed, remarkably accurate although sometimes lacking in artistic fluency. Keen sportsman and Fellow of the Zoological Society. With Gibson(qv) and McBey(qv), both representing quite different branches of art, he was arguably one of the three greatest Scottish artists since the foundation of the RSA never to have been honoured by the academic establishment. There is now an art gallery dedicated to his memory and work. Exhibited RA(21) 1880-1900. Represented in NGS(7), BM, V & A, Woburn, Thorburn AG (Devon).
**Bibl:** Halsby 169-171; Houfe; John Southern, Archibald Thorburn Landscapes; The Major Natural History Paintings, London 1981; Studio, vol 91, 1926; Simon Taylor, Archibald Thorburn ex cat. Sotheby's, 1993.

**THORBURN, Miss Dorothy** **fl 1919-1920**
Edinburgh still life and portrait painter. Exhibited RSA(5).

**THORBURN, J Pasley Hay** **fl 1876**
Scottish sculptor of portrait busts; exhibited RSA(1).

**THORBURN, Robert ARA HRSA** **1818-1885**
Born Dumfries, Mar 10; died Tunbridge Wells, Nov 2. Portrait and miniature painter in oil and occasionally watercolour. His father was engaged in trade, his brother was a successful woodcarver. Educated Dumfries Academy where he received encouragement from a Dumfries lady with whose help he went to Edinburgh 1833 to learn drawing at the RSA Schools under Sir William Allan(qv). There he won two first prizes before proceeding to London 1836 for further studies at the RA Schools. There he took up miniature painting, and helped by the patronage of the Duke of Buccleuch and members of the Royal family, attained pre-eminence in his chosen field. His first commission from the Queen was in 1846. Exhibited RA(258) 1837-1884, RSA(17) 1835-1856 including 'Prince Alfred and Princess Helena', commissioned by Prince Albert 1851, 'The Duchess of Buccleuch and her children' 1847, 'Prince Albert' 1852. Elected ARA 1848, HRSA 1857. In 1855 won a gold medal in Paris. The advent of photography persuaded him to undertake an increasing amount of work in oil and to do portraits in chalk. Examples can be seen in Windsor Castle. One characteristic of his work is that the pupil of the eye is often enlargened to an almost perfect round. Although resident in London he kept a home in Lasswade and the last years of his life were spent at Kelso. His miniatures are often large in size and subject to cracking owing to the use of large pieces of ivory. A list of his miniatures was published by Foster in the *MPVF,* Vol I, pp 96-7. A most attractive group portrait 'Sir Robert Dalyell, 8th Baronet and his family with the family pet', 1835, is in The Binns, Linlithgow (NTS).
**Bibl:** AJ, Dec 1896, 368; Bryan; Brydall 470-1; Foskett 548-9; Long 437; McKay 326.

**THORNBURN, Walter** **fl 1896**
Elgin landscape painter of 7 Culbraid Street; exhibited RSA(1).

**THORNLEY, Mrs Betty E** **fl 1963**
Castle Douglas painter. Exhibited 'Harbour Cottage - Kircudbright' at the GI.

**THORNTON, Miss Annie** **fl 1882-1883**
A Lochearnhead painter who moved to Edinburgh. Executed flower pieces in oil and watercolour. Exhibited RSA(4).

**THORNTON, George** **fl 1973-1976**
Aberdeenshire printmaker; trained Gray's School of Art, Aberdeen. Exhibited AAS(4), from Dyce and latterly Fridayhill, by Inverurie.

**THORNTON, George Boyd** **fl 1879-1889**
Edinburgh landscape painter in oil; often painted in the Trossachs and on Arran. Exhibited RSA(24) & GI(6).

**THORNTON, Rev R H** **fl 1940**
Minor Glasgow-based watercolourist; exhibited GI(2) from 61 Hamilton Drive.

**THORNTON-KEMSLEY, Sir Colin** **1903-1977**
Born 2 Sep; died 17 Jly. Amateur landscape painter, professional politician. Exhibited a border landscape at the AAS shortly before his death.

**THOULOW, Fritz** **fl 1885**
Amateur Edinburgh-based painter of landscapes in oil; exhibited two views of Buckhaven at the RSA.

**THULBOURNE, Cynthia** **fl 1983-1984**
Dundee artist; landscape, wild flowers and garden scenes. Exhibited RSA(2) & GI(4), from Auchterhouse.

**THWAITES, Frances** **1908-1987**
Sculptress and abstract painter of landscapes. Lived in India until the age of 12 and attended school in the Himalayas. A deep interest in Chinese calligraphy remained with her and influenced her work. Subsequently lived in Scotland with prolonged intervals spent in London and Paris. Studied stained glass design at Edinburgh College of Art and won several prizes and travelling scholarships. From 1946-48 studied sculpture before turning to landscape painting. Held several solo exhibitions and exhibited frequently at the RA & RSA(9).

**TIMMINS, William** **fl 1906-1956**
Glasgow painter of landscape, buildings and general topography; exhibited RSA(1), GI(16), AAS(5) & L(1), latterly from Glenfarg St.

**TINDAL, Miss Annie** **fl 1861-1873**
Flower painter. Lived London, Greenock and latterly Bothwell. Exhibited RSA(1) & GI(8).

**TINDAL, Elfrida** **fl 1959-1962**
Edinburgh painter of landscape and rustic scenes. Exhibited RSA(2), from Lauder Rd.

**TINDAL, Susan A C** **fl 1887-1894**
Kincardineshire painter of local landscape and harbours; exhibited RSA(1) & AAS(7) from Stonehaven.

**TIPPING, Gladys** **fl 1959-1962**
Midlothian painter of genre; exhibited RSA(3), from Barnton.

**TITTLE, Robina** **fl 1916**
Painter. Exhibited RSA(1) whilst a student at Edinburgh College of Art.

**TOD, David Alexander** **fl 1882-1919**
Edinburgh sculptor of animals and portrait medallions, also figure subjects. Living in Glasgow during the early 1880's before settling in Edinburgh 1886. Executed a portrait bust of the 'Very Rev Principal Caird' RSA 1887 and a bronze of 'A Golfer' 1899. Exhibited RA(1), RSA(25) & GI (16).

**TOD, James** **fl 1869**
Edinburgh landscape painter in oil; exhibited at the RSA(1).

**TOD, Murray Macpherson RSW RE RGI SSA ARCA FRSA** **1909-1974**
Born Glasgow. Painter in oil and watercolour, also etcher. Educated at Kelvinside Academy, Glasgow. Trained Glasgow School of Art 1927-31 and Royal College of Art under Malcolm Osborne and Robert Austin. Awarded RAC diploma in 1935 before proceeding to the British School in Rome 1935-37. Became part-time teacher of etching, Edinburgh College of Art 1949-59 having been art master at Dalbeattie High School 1941-46. Elected ARE 1947, RE 1953, RSW 1953, ARCA 1955, FRSA 1949. Etched landscapes and townscapes in Italy and Spain as well as Scotland, often with a slight hint of caricature and always with an assured lightness of touch. From the late 1940s suffered from muscular dystrophy. Exhibited RA(5), RSA (93) & GI(54).
**Bibl:** Aberdeen AG, Great Scottish Etchers (Ex Cat 1981); K M Guichard, British Etchers 1850-1940, London 1977; Hartley 166; Scotsman, 15.8.1974 (obit).

**TOD, Richard** **fl 1901-1917**
Scottish painter of portrait miniatures. Lived in Edinburgh 1901 before moving to Inverkeithing 1913. Exhibited a miniature portrait RA 1910 & RSA(8), from 26 Frederick Street.

**TOD, Thomas** **fl 1873**
Leith landscape painter; exhibited 'View on the Avon' at the RSA in the above year.

**TODD, C Stanley** **1923-2004**
Born Northumberland Aug 10; died Monzie Mar 17. Self-taught watercolourist of wildlife. As a teenager he was inspired by Archibald Thorburn, encouraged by a grandfather who shared his enthusiasm. Entering the family insurance business 1940, declared unfit for war service due to a severe leg injury, he subsequently joined the Territorials reaching the rank of Major. Abandoned business life in favour of painting 1956, moving first to Crieff 1968 and then, with his sister, to Monzie 1970. First solo exhibition Perth c1972. Became one of Britain's leading wildlife artists and Thorburn expert. Specialised in the birds and mammals of northern Scotland, depicted in their natural habitats with delicate precision, often from models donated by friendly keepers. Commissioned by Grouse whisky to illustrate their brand label. Prints of his work initially in great demand but unfortunately subject to premature fading. A modest, friendly man, a perfectionist in all things, he ceased to paint when he could no longer retain the accuracy and quality he demanded, owing to the onset of arthritis c1989.

**TODD, Graeme** **1962-**
Born Glasgow. Painter of semi-abstract works. Trained Duncan of Jordanestone College of Art, Dundee 1980-5. First one-man exhibition Stirling 1986. A highly skilled doodler, generally working on a large scale, often with tracery rather than broad line and with a bright but sensitive palette. Recurring themes that serve as inspiration include 'ecology and references to time, science and matter'. Exhibits RSA & GI(1) from Dundee, with an interlude in Edinburgh.
**Bibl:** Third Eye Centre, Glasgow 'Scatter' (Ex cat, 1989).

**TODD, James Henry** **fl 1898-1913**
Glasgow painter in oil and watercolour of riverside landscapes and flowers. Exhibited RSA(2), RSW(1) & GI(6).

**TODD, Robert** **fl 1893-1905**
Minor Glasgow landscape and topographical painter; exhibited RSA (2) & GI(10).

**TODD, W G** **fl 1841**
Edinburgh landscape painter; exhibited 'View near Currie' at the RSA.

**TODD, William** **fl 1845-1847**
Edinburgh painter; exhibited 'A water mill' and 'Evening' at the RSA.

**TODD, William James Walker ARSA FRIBA** **1884-1944**
Born Glasgow, Feb 6; died Edinburgh, Apr 29. Architect. Studied Edinburgh College of Art 1902-1907; awarded a travelling scholarship 1906. In 1909 began private practice in partnership with Dick Peddie(qv). Designed many important buildings for local authorities and large firms, usually in the Scottish classical tradition. Among those for which he was mainly responsible are the Bank of Scotland at the corner of High St and Hunter Square (1923); and the wings and some outbuildings (including the Sanitorium) of Merchiston Castle School. Elected ARSA 1931. Lived at 8 Albyn Place, Edinburgh. Exhibited regularly RSA.
**Bibl:** Gifford 234,277-8,496,504,516-7.

**TODD-BROWN, William ROI** **1875-1952**
Born Glasgow; died Carbis Bay, Cornwall, Mar 25. Trained Glasgow School of Art and the Slade under Brown, Tonks and Steer. Principal, Redhill School of Art 1922-1940. Elected ROI 1935. Lived most of life in England. Exhibited RA(3), RSA(4), ROI(23), GI(2), RI(5), RE(7), RCA(2) & at the London Salon(5).

**TOGNERI, Veronica** **fl 1962-**
Freelance embroiderer. Member, Glasgow Schoolof Art Embroidery and Tapestry Society. Started a weaving workshop on Colonsay 1962. Moved to Tomintoul 1983. Artist-in-Residence, Univ of

Sussex 1978. Awarded Scottish Development Craft Fellowship 1983, enabling her to develop a very personal style of colourful, rich patchwork. Swain describes her embroidery as 'strongly disciplined'. Exhibited regularly.
**Bibl:** Margaret Swain 176-7.

**TOLAND, Peter P** **fl 1861-1871**
Minor Glasgow painter in oil of landscapes and figure subjects; exhibited RSA(3) & GI(10.

**TOLLEMACHE, Hon Duff** **1859-1936**
Edinburgh-based portrait and genre painter. Moved to London c1898. Exhibited two portraits at the RSA 1892 (from 32 York Place), and again 1902. Represented in Bristol AG.

**TOMBLESON, Christopher** **fl 1936-1940**
Painter of genre, old buildings and still life; also art teacher. Taught at John Watson's, Edinburgh from 1936 before moving via Greenlaw, Berwickshire to Russell Hill School, Surrey 1940. Exhibited RSA(10), RBA(2) & NEA(2).

**TOMKINS, William ARA** **c1730-1792**
Born London; died London, 1 Jan. Topographical and landscape painter. Both his sons were also artists. Commissioned by the Duke of Fife to paint large-scale views of his properties in London and at Elsick. Irwin refers to him 'offering his services' to Sir James Grant of Grant. Elected ARA. Exhibited RA(79) including 'The Earl of Fife's property Belvena, Banffshire' 1769, the 'Earl of Findlater's seat at Cullen, Banffshire' 1770 and 'Mar Lodge, Aberdeenshire' 1787.
**Bibl:** Irwin 130.

**TOMLIN, Anne D (Mrs Lewis T)** **fl 1930-1958**
Amateur watercolour painter of flowers and still life; lived in Edinburgh. Exhibited RSA(1), RSW(7) & GI(14), latterly from Abbotsford Crescent.

**TOMLINS, James** **fl 1886-1887**
Amateur watercolourist of 5 Gauze Street, Paisley; exhibited a study of dead birds at the RSA; also GI(1) & L(1).

**TONER, David** **fl 1976-**
Glasgow painter of topographical subjects. Made some notable paintings of Glasgow tenements, one exhibited at the RSA 1976 and another 1988; also three other exhibits & GI(37) most recently from Holyrood Crescent.

**TONER, William D** **fl 1932-1935**
Minor Cambuslang flower painter. Exhibited RSA(1) & GI(1) from 17 Prospect Ave.

**TONGE, Kenneth Hodgson** **fl 1976-1989**
Aberdeenshire textile and ceramic designer; exhibited AAS(2) from 19 Nethermains Rd, Muchalls.

**TONNER, William J** **fl 1893-1912**
Glasgow sculptor. Portrait busts, memorials and figure groups. Exhibited RSA(4) & GI(29).

**TORRANCE, A H** **fl 1937**
Amateur Dunfermline landscape painter; exhibited RSA(1) from 29 Halbeath Road.

**TORRANCE, James A S** **1859-1916**
Born Glasgow; died Helensburgh. Worked in London as a book illustrator and portrait painter; pen, wash, gouache and watercolour. Joined the Glasgow **BLACK & WHITE CLUB** 1876 when only 17. Specialised in fairy books for children. Settled in Glasgow. Married the flower painter Louise Perman(qv). Illustrated Sir George Douglas' *Scottish Fairy Tales and Folk Tales* (1893), some of the originals being in both the V & A and Glasgow AG; also *The Works of Nathaniel Hawthorne* (1894). Exhibited 'The pigfeeder's daughter' at the RSA (1926) where it was purchased by George Pirie RSA(qv); also at the GI(14). Represented in V & A, NGS(8), Glasgow AG(2), Kirkcaldy AG, Edinburgh City collection(3).
**Bibl:** Caw 430; Halsby 188; Houfe.

**TORRANCE, J B** **fl 1947-1949**
Kilmarnock portrait painter. Exhibited GI(3).

**TORRIE, Alexander** **fl 1906-1912**
Little known artist of 8 Walmar Crescent, Ibrox. Exhibited GI(5) & L(2).

**TORRIE, John J F** **fl 1934**
Minor Edinburgh watercolourist; mainly west coast landscapes. Exhibited RSW.

**TOUGH, Alexander Paul** **fl 1966-1967**
Edinburgh sculptor. Exhibited abstract wood-carvings at the RSA 1966 and 1967.

**TOUGH, D J** **fl 1889**
Minor figure of 13 North St., Andrew St., Edinburgh; exhibited RSA(1).

**TOUGH, Margaret** **fl 1969**
Aberdeen amateur flower painter; exhibited AAS(1) from 14 Whitehall Rd.

**TOUNER, William J** **fl 1898-1900**
Glasgow sculptor. Exhibited RSA(1) & GI(1) from 114 West Campbell St.

**TOWERS, Walter** **fl 1924**
Minor figure of Ardmore, Grangemouth; exhibited L(2).

**TOWNSEND, Miss Annie** **fl 1887-1896**
Amateur painter of flowers and informal portraits. Moved around the Glasgow area. Exhibited GI(10).

**TOWNSEND, J P H** **fl 1838**
Edinburgh painter; exhibited a beach scene at the RSA, from Greenside Place.

**TOWNSEND, W H** **1803-1849**
Edinburgh landscape watercolour painter; also portraitist and miniaturist, and teacher of drawing. In 1841 produced his 'Panorama from the Calton Hill', described as one of 'most interesting of all the panoramic views by reason of the extraordinary scope of the print, with its wonderful variety of figures worked into the foreground, and the great detail in which the outstanding buildings and features of the landscape are given' [Butchart]. It was a considerable achievement to have introduced such animation. Exhibited RSA(30) 1830-1849. Probably the W J Townsend who exhibited a landscape at Carlisle Academy 1830. Represented in NGS(7), collection of the City of Edinburgh (coloured lithograph in 6 sections of Edinburgh as seen from the Calton hill, 1841).
**Bibl:** Butchart 83-4.

**TRAILL, Miss Alice Margaret** **fl 1882-1907**
Kirkwall watercolour painter of still-life, landscape and dead game. Moved to Edinburgh c1889, then to Gullane c1907. Exhibited RSA(9), RSW(1), AAS(1) & GI(1), from The Ayre.

**TRAILL, Mrs Isabel** **fl 1982**
Edinburgh painter. Exhibited a still life at the GI, from Colinton Rd.

**TRAIN, Thomas** **1890-c1977**
Born Carluke, Dec 20; died Aberdeen. Portrait and landscape painter. Trained Glasgow School of Art. Exhibited chiefly in Scotland from his home near Aberdeen. Delightful person with a great love for the wild places, especially the north-west coast and the Grampian mountains. His work was rather coarsely done with a curious perspective and weak draughtsmanship but with a quaint almost primitive charm, a sort of twentieth century naïve painter. Exhibited RSA(3) 1945-1948 and regularly at the AAS 1921-1976, latterly from Church cottage, Skene.

**TRAQUAIR, Phoebe Anna (née Moss) HRSA** **1852-1936**
Born Dublin, May 24; died Edinburgh, Aug 4. Painter in oil of murals and figurative works including informal portraits, also enamellist & textile designer. Only recently has begun to receive due recognition as one of Scotland's foremost lady artists and illustrators. Daughter of a

Dublin physician; mother of Ramsay T(qv). Trained Dublin School of Art c1869-72; gained Queen's prize for a fan and a medal for studies from the Greek. At the age of 20 married Ramsay H. Traquair, an authority on fish fossils. When her husband was appointed Keeper of Natural History at the Royal Scottish Museum, Edinburgh, she settled in the capital at 8 Dean Park Crescent 1784, remaining there for the rest of her life. The emergence of her creativity came through embroidery used in large pictorial panels influenced by Burne-Jones. Also worked in illumination and enamel. Designed several bookplates and began her first illuminated MS 'The Psalms of David' c1884. Her first large figural embroidery 'The Angel of Death and Purification' 1886-7 formed the central panel for 'The Salvation of Mankind' completed 1893. Remembered for her mural paintings executed in the mid 1880's and for the part she played with John Duncan(qv) in promoting the Celtic revival. She undertook some murals for the mortuary at the Sick Children's Hospital later transferred to the chapel 1885-6. Frequently employed by Lorimer(qv) who wrote of her (quoted in Savage) "I don't think I know anyone who is as sympathetically to me artistically. She's so sane, such a lover of simplicity, and the things that give real lasting pleasure are the simplest things of nature. The singing of birds, the bleating of sheep in the distance, morning and evening, everything and everyone she finds interesting and all this without a trace of self-consciousness". Helped establish the Scottish Society of Arts and Crafts 1898. At the rear of every stall in the Thistle Chapel are enamelled armorial plates. There followed a series of panels for St Mary's Cathedral, Edinburgh on the theme of 'Benedicite'. Between 1893 and 1900 she was painting at the Catholic Apostolic Church in East London Street a large oil on plaster, using a watercolour technique depicting the 'Worship of Heaven' from the *Book of Revelation.* Examples may also be seen in St Cuthbert's Church (1939) and at the Royal Hospital for Sick Children (1885, reinstated 1895). In 1900 the RSA declined to admit her as an hon. member but relented 1920 when she became the first woman so honoured. Her painted grand piano for Lympne Castle 1909-10 is illustrated in Savage (pl 169). 'The Progress of a Soul' was exhibited at the World Fair, St Louis 1904, the year that she decorated the chancel of St Peter, Clayworth, Notts, finished in 1905. In 1912 was commissioned to execute a triptych altarpiece for the Chapel of St. Andrew, Cathedral of St James, Chicago. Painted altarpieces for three Glasgow churches including All Saints Church in St Mary's Cathedral, Glasgow 1920. Illustrated several books edited by Grace Warrack (1901 onwards). An exhibition of her work was held at the SNPG 1993. Exhibited RSA(19) & AAS(5). Represented in NGS(5, including a portrait bust of 'Pittendrigh MacGillivray'), SNPG ('Self-portrait').
**Bibl:** Elizabeth Skeoch Cumming, 'Phoebe Traquair', unpub PhD thesis, Edinburgh Univ 1987; Elizabeth Skeoch Cumming, 'Phoebe Anna Traquair', Ex cat, SNPG, Edinburgh 1993; Gifford 118,366,424-5,514,597; Peter Savage, Lorimer and the Edinburgh Craft Designers, Edinburgh 1980, 20,74,77,82-3,88,169.

**TRAQUAIR, Ramsay R** **c1874-1952**
Architect. Son of Phoebe T(qv). Trained under Lorimer(qv). Designed First Church of Christ Scientist, Inverleith Terrace (1910-11) based on Elgin's St Giles; also Mackenzie House (1910), Inverleith Place.
**Bibl:** Gifford 43,570,580.

**TRAUTSCHOLD, Wilhelm** **1815-1877**
Edinburgh portrait painter in oil; exhibited RSA(5).

**TREVELYAN, Lady Pauline Jermyn** **fl 1850-1851**
Painter of nature studies. Lived at Wallington Hall, Cambo, Northumberland but exhibited at the RSA from Melville St and latterly from Shandwick Place.

**TREVENA, William G** **fl 1951-1952**
Glasgow landscape painter in watercolours. Mainly Scottish and Dutch scenery. Exhibited GI(3), from Randolph Drive.

**TREVORROW, Mrs Doris E** **fl 1932**
Minor Glasgow painter of genre and informal portraits. Married James S T(qv). Exhibited GI(3) from 30 Claremont St.

**TREVORROW, James S** **fl 1953**
Portrait painter. Married Doris T(qv). Exhibited GI(1) from Eaglesham.

**TRITSCHLER, F D** **fl 1945-1946**
Glasgow-based sculptor; figurative works. Exhib RSA(4) & GI(8).

**TROTTER, Alexander** **1755-1842**
Ayrshire architect and draughtsman of Dreghorn. His plan for having Edinburgh Old Town enter the High St at St Giles, submitted 1829 in collaboration with Archibald Elliot II(qv), was rejected.
**Bibl:** Gifford 283,309,515.

**TROTTER, Alexander Mason ARSA RSW** **1891-1946**
Died, Ravenshall, Gatehouse of Fleet, Dec 16. Painter in oil and watercolour of interiors and architectural subjects. A spinal accident in childhood led to an interest in drawing and a wish to devote himself to art. Trained Edinburgh College of Art. For several years on the staff of Thomas Nelson and Sons, working under the direction of Walter Grieve(qv). Painted very detailed 'frozen' interiors and still-life. Used watercolour as a deliberate and highly worked style, his large still-lifes can be striking in effect. Painted decorations in *HMS Renown* and other ships of the Navy. During WW2 he executed several humorous wall drawings for the naval canteen at Rosyth. Elected RSW 1930, ARSA 1942. Exhibited RA(2), RSA(14), RSW(24) & GI(12). Represented City of Edinburgh collection, Sydney AG (Australia)(2).
**Bibl:** Halsby 286.

**TROTTER, Mrs Barbara** **fl 1937**
Minor watercolour painter; exhibited RSW(2) from 16 West Castle Rd, Edinburgh.

**TROTTER, James** **fl 1885-1907**
Edinburgh painter in oil and watercolour; contemporary buildings and townscapes; exhibited RSA(3).

**TROTTER, William** **1772-1833**
Distinguished furniture designer and cabinet maker. In Edinburgh he was responsible for designing the furniture (now replaced) for Register House; his bookcases for the Library and President's Room in the Royal College of Physicians may still be seen.

**TROUP, Francis William** **1859-c1933**
Born Huntly, Aberdeenshire. Architect. Trained RA Schools and RIBA. Consulting architect to the Home Office and supervising architect for the rebuilding of the Bank of England. Other work included designs for St John's College, Oxford and a new university settlement in Canningtown, London; also Spalding Hall, Hendon. Exhibited RA(18) & RSA(5) 1889-1933.

**TROUP, James** **fl 1833-1835**
Obscure Aberdeen landscape painter. Exhibited 'Highland views' at the RSA(5) and in London.

**TROUP, Mary Winifred** **fl 1923**
Aberdeen figurative painter; exhibited AAS(2) from 273 Rosemount Place.

**TRUEFITT, Miss Frances** **fl 1849-1877**
Edinburgh painter in oil and crayon of portraits, still-life and landscape. Related to William T(qv). Exhibited a portrait at the RA in 1873 from 65 Princes St & RSA(43) including 'The Archbishop of Canterbury' 1872. Probably responsible for the pastel study of a young boy in Edinburgh City collection (catalogued as by 'Truefill').

**TRUEFITT, Miss Jane** **fl 1847-1854**
Edinburgh painter of fruit, still life and landscape. Sister of Frances(qv) and William T(qv). Exhibited RSA(7).

**TRUEFITT, William P** **fl 1851-1870**
Edinburgh oil painter of castles, landscapes and figure subjects. Brother of Frances(qv) and Jane T(qv). Exhibited RSA(13).

**TRUNINGER, Mrs A C** **fl 1925-1935**
Minor watercolour painter of The Roundel, Gullane; exhibited RSA(2) & RSW(2).

**TRUSTEES ACADEMY** **1760-c1906**
With its origin in the Act of Union, on the initiative of Lord Kames a fund was established in 1760, administered by 21 trustees, for the purpose of starting an academy of design to promote "a taste among

workmen and youth of both sexes in Scotland", primarily in the linen industry. Classes opened in Edinburgh College. The first Master was a Frenchman, William Delacour(qv) who was succeeded by another Frenchman, Charles Pavillon(qv), before Alexander Runciman(qv) took charge c1771. He was followed by David Allan 1785-1796. The only eminent product was Alexander Nasmyth. The next Master was John Wood but he held the post for only a year before the trustees discovered that his application had been fraudulent. Between 1798 and 1817 John Graham(qv) was the Master during which time art education prospered, among the students being William Allan(qv), David Wilkie(qv) and John Watson Gordon(qv). The first painting competition was won by David Thomson(qv), brother of the secretary. In 1803 Wilkie won with 'Calisto in the Bath of Diana'. In 1821 the Academy moved to larger premises in Picardy Place, Edinburgh. When Andrew Wilson succeeded Graham the students included D O Hill(qv), R S Lauder(qv) and William Simson(qv). A complication arose in 1819 with the emergence of the Institution for the Encouragement of the Fine Arts(qv). Funds had become available to build an academy on the Mound with exhibition rooms for the Institution and teaching accommodation for the Trustees Academy. In 1826 William Allan replaced Wilson and immediately set about inculcating a sense of history among staff and students who by this time included Thomas Duncan(qv), George Harvey(qv) and J A Houston(qv). In 1827-8 David Scott(qv), who had started giving informal life classes together with Daniel Macnee(qv) and eight others, pleaded to have morning tuition. Two more Masters were appointed to add to the Director's scope: Duncan (colour and later drawing) and Charles Heath Wilson (ornament and design). From 1837-8, following Allan's accession to the Presidency of the RSA, William Dyce(qv) was appointed Headmaster. In 1844 Duncan became Director, assisted by W Crawford(qv) and J Ballantyne(qv). In 1845 he was succeeded by George Christie(qv) whose pupils included Thomas Faed(qv) and John Macdonald(qv). The work of the Academy was then described as 'one class for the study of drawing from the ancient statues, under one master; a class for the study of pictorial colouring under another master; a life academy under the especial care of the head-master; a school for instructing pupils in all the various departments of ornamental design, both in form and colour, including architecture, geometry, perspective, modelling, fresco and encaustic painting, etc, divided into classes and under the superintendence of one master and an assistant; to all of which is added a course of lectures on pictorial anatomy. The number of pupils is about 150, all of whom receive instruction gratis' [Statistical Account]. The summit of instructional achievement arrived in 1850 with the appointment of Robert Scott Lauder(qv) as Master. Among students were the Burrs(qv), Hugh Cameron(qv), George Paul Chalmers(qv), Peter Graham(qv), Robert Herdman(qv), William McTaggart(qv), John MacWhirter(qv) and W Q Orchardson(qv). The art of wood carving was later introduced and in 1858 the Academy was affiliated to the Art Department of South Kensington as one of many Goverment Schools of Design. Thereafter the life class was handed over to the Scottish Academy, an Edinburgh School of Art(qv) eventually emerged and the Trustees Academy disappeared.
**Bibl:** Brydall 142-153; Caw 67-8,217,223-224,230-235; Irwin 90-97 et passim; J. Mason, 'The Edinburgh School of Design', Book of the Old Edinburgh Club,XXVII,1949,67-96; Statistical Account of Scotland, 1845.

**TUCKER, Carlyle** **fl 1908**
Minor Glasgow sculptor of portrait busts. Exhibited GI(1) from 22 Charing Cross Mansions.

**TUCKER, Alice Evelyn** **fl 1937**
Amateur painter of 79 Glencairn Drive, Glasgow; exhibited GI(1).

**TUCKER, Violet H** **fl 1934-1940**
Amateur watercolour painter of 14 Northumberland St. Edinburgh; exhibited RSW(4).

**TUDHOPE, Alice** **fl 1902**
Edinburgh portrait miniaturist. Exhibited RSA(1) from 28 Lauriston Gdns.

**TUDHOPE, Andrew H** **fl 1885-1886**
Glasgow painter in oil of still-life; exhibited RSA(2) & GI(2) from 3 Victoria Place, Mount Florida.

**TUKE, Charles W** **fl 1870-1871**
Edinburgh oil painter of landscapes; exhibited RSA(4) & GI(1).

**TULLOCH, Miss M** **fl 1806**
Obscure flower painter. Probably Scottish. As an Hon. Exhibitor showed 'Auricula' RA 1806.

**TULLOCH, Violet M** **fl 1953**
Edinburgh sculptress; exhibited 'Giraffe' at the RSA.

**TUNNY -** **fl 1902**
Edinburgh flower painter; exhibited 'Chrysanthemums' at the RSA from 11, Castle St.

**TURBITT, Ian** **fl 1979**
Glasgow sculptor. Exhibited portraits in terracotta and ciment fondu at the GI.

**TURLEY, Miss Lorraine R** **fl 1986-**
Glasgow painter. Exhibited GI(5).

**TURNBULL, Adam Ogilvie** **?-c1834**
Architect and builder. In Edinburgh designed the north-east side of Saxe-Coburg St.
**Bibl:** Gifford 413-4.

**TURNBULL, Mrs Ancrum** **fl 1899**
Landscape oil painter. Lived in Edinburgh. Exhibited RSA(1).

**TURNBULL, Andrew Watson** **1874-?**
Painter and etcher of landscape, figurative works and architectural subjects; also stained glass window designer. Trained Royal College of Art 1895-1896 and RA Schools 1897-1902. Lived at Ingleside, Argyle Crescent, Joppa until moving south to England c1910, remaining there for the rest of his life. Principal works, close to the pre-Raphaelite tradition in which his name has been coupled with Campbell Lindsay Smith(qv), include 'The Glorious St Paul's', 'Lady Godiva', RA 1899, 'Loch Lomond, the dreaming beauty of an autumn day' and 'Summer Afternoon'. Exhibited RA(9), RSA(8), GI(7), L(5) & Paris Salon.
**Bibl:** Caw 443.

**TURNBULL, David Lynn** **fl 1885**
Topographical painter of minor consequence; exhibited 'Edinburgh from Craigmillar' at the RSA from 35 South Bridge, Edinburgh.

**TURNBULL, Frederick J** **fl 1940-1941**
Edinburgh-based landscape painter; exhibited RSA(2) from 18a Morningside Place.

**TURNBULL, J F** **fl 1949-1973**
Glasgow landscape and topographical painter. Moved in mid-career to Newton Mearns. Exhibited GI(12), often harbour scenes.

**TURNBULL, Miss Margaret** **fl 1965**
Aberdeenshire landscape painter; exhibited a winter scene at the AAS from 6 Abbotshill Crescent, Cults.

**TURNBULL, Mrs Marion** **fl 1908**
Edinburgh watercolourist. Exhibited 'In Harbour' at the GI, from Wardle St.

**TURNBULL, Michael** **fl 1965**
Edinburgh painter; exhibited RSA(1), from Albert Terrace.

**TURNBULL, Robert** **c1839-1905**
Glasgow architect. Partner with Alexander Thomson(qv) 1873-5. Thomson & Turnbull formed 1876 and in 1883 became Turnbull & Son when he was joined by his son **Alexander TURNBULL**. Among his principal designs were Cockburn Hotel, 135-143 Bath St, now demolished, and Salisbury Quadrant, 52-58 Nithsdale St, Strathbungo (1880).
**Bibl:** A Gomme & D Walker, Architecture of Glasgow, London 1987(rev), 303.

**TURNBULL, William** **1922-?**
Born Dundee. Sculptor and painter. Attended evening classes in art at Dundee College of Art; worked as an illustrator for the D C Thomson group, 1939-41. During WW2 served as a pilot in Canada, India and Ceylon. In 1946 enrolled at the Slade 1946-8 and from 1948 to 1950 was living in Paris where he met Giacometti and Brancusi. Painting large canvases in the 1940s he was one of the first British artists to understand the abstract painting of the New York School during the 1950s following a visit to New York in 1957. First exhibited sculpture in London 1950 with Paolozzi(qv) and in 1952 participated in 'New Aspects of British Sculpture' at the Venice Biennale. He had been sharing a studio with Paolozzi(qv) and up to that time the central theme for both sculptors was the head or mask (a term which Turnbull used to disassociate from the subject in the interest of the abstract). Visited Japan in 1962. Became increasingly fascinated with the physical presence of the surface and the substance of pigment, often painting monochromatically. By the early 1960s had moved to totem-like abstracts, becoming entrenched in the European Modernist movement, showing the influence of Rothko. Preferred to have his work displayed on the ground, dispensing with pedestals. 'Turnbull's work flatters, makes visible, brings to life, any setting in which it is placed. But its ability to so strongly act as a catalyst in the spectator's awareness of his environment, and also to reflect so wide a range of experience, functions only because the undramatic, "everyday" forms of Turnbull's work are the product of the acts of concentration, choice and affirmation of a richly human imagination' [Morphet]. Six bronzes and four drawings were included by invitation in the RSA 1990. A retrospective exhibition was held at the Tate 1973. Represented in Dundee AG.
**Bibl:** Gage 40; Hardie 189-191; SAC Edinburgh, (Ex Cat 1974, Text by Richard Morphet); Harold Osborne, Twentieth Century Art, 1988, 549.

**TURNER, Annie M** **fl 1912**
Minor painter of 24 Lynedoch Street, Glasgow; exhibited GI(1).

**TURNER, Arthur H** **fl 1934-1953**
Little known painter of landscape, boats and boatyards. Exhibited GI(3) from 33 Cranworth Street, Glasgow.

**TURNER, Barr** **fl 1919-1929**
Greenock artist; exhibited landscapes AAS(3), latterly from 21 Denholm Terrace.

**TURNER, David C** **fl 1933-1934**
Dunfermline painter; exhibited RSA(3) from Loanhead, Lambkilns.

**TURNER, Miss Helen M** **fl 1957-**
Glasgow topographical and flower painter, textile designer. Works in oils and pastels. Works in the Scottish Colourist tradition with broad brushstrokes and bold colours, reminiscent of the north-west coast. Chief designer for a leading Scottish carpet manufacturer. Began exhibiting RGI 1957 and at the Paisley Institute 1959. Member, Ayr Sketch Club. Lives in Prestwick.

**TURNER, Hugh** **fl 1884**
Edinburgh landscape painter in oil; exhibited RSA(1) from 7 Polwarth Crescent.

**TURNER, John** **fl 1873-1880**
Dumfries landscape and subject painter in watercolour. Moved to Glasgow c1880. Exhibited RSA(1) & GI(4).

**TUTTLE, Mrs J B** **fl 1889**
Glasgow landscape painter; exhibited a village scene at the RA from William Street, Greenland.

**TWEED, John** **1869-1933**
Born Glasgow, Oct 21; died London, Nov 12. Sculptor. Trained Glasgow School of Art, Lambeth School of Art and RA Schools; also École des Beaux Arts under Falguière. Entered the studio of William Hamo Thornycroft 1890. The Chantrey Bequest purchased his 'Lord Clive' (1910/12) in 1934. When in France he met and became friendly with Rodin. His sketch for a statuette of Major Allan Wilson for the Zimbabwe Memorial was shown at the RA 1897. Exhibited RA(64), RSA(12), RI(2), LS(5), L(7) & GI(49), latterly from 14a Cheyne Row, London.

**TWEEDIE, Miss Agnes** **fl 1882-1892**
Perthshire painter of local landscape, especially harvest scenes, in oil. Lived at Abernyte, Inchture from where she exhibited RSA(11) & AAS(3).

**TWEEDIE, Miss Christina F** **fl 1967-1973**
Renfrewshire landscape and topographical painter. Exhibited GI(5), from Newton Mearns.

**TWEEDIE, Jim** **1951-**
Glasgow abstract and decorative painter. Associate member of the Glasgow Group. Several solo exhibitions, mostly in and around Glasgow, also participated in group exhibitions in Belfast and Nurnberg, Germany. Exhibits GI.

**TWEEDIE, William Menzies** **1828-1878**
Born Glasgow, 28 Feb; died London, 19 Mar. Portrait painter in oil. Son of a Lieutenant in the Marines (whose portrait was shown at the RA in 1860), he entered Edinburgh Academy at the age of 16 and remained there for four years, gaining a prize for the best copy of Etty's 'The Combat'. In 1843 he exhibited a portrait at the RSA. Travelled to London 1846 entering the RA Schools, before studying for a further three years in Paris under Thomas Couture. Between 1856 and 1859 lived in Liverpool but in 1859 finally settled in London. His work declined and in later years he failed repeatedly to have work accepted by the Academy. From 1863 he lived at 44 Piccadilly. Exhibited RA(33) 1847-1874, including portraits of 'Thomas Faed' 1861, 'Samuel Wilberforce, Bishop of Oxford' 1863, 'James Dyce Nicol, MP for Kincardineshire' 1868, 'Prince Arthur' 1873 and 'The Rt Hon Gathorne Hardy, Secretary of State for War' 1874; also RSA(10) 1844-1875. His 'John McDiarmid' 1852 is in SNPG and 'The Duke of Devonshire' is in Univ. of London.
**Bibl:** Bryan; DNB; Ottley; Poole, R L, Catalogue of Portraits...Oxford 3, 1925; Cat of Engr Brit Ports BM, 6, (1925), 189; Redgrave.

**TYLER, Adam Albert** **fl 1903-1908**
Edinburgh sculptor; exhibited RSA(4), GI(1) & AAS(2) from 74 Bonaly Rd, Merchiston.

**TYRE, David Maxwell** **fl 1901**
Glasgow painter; exhibited RSA(1) from 27 Windsor Terrace.

**TYRE, John** **fl 1851-1863**
Glasgow painter in oil, figure subjects and wild flowers; exhibited RSA(5) & GI(3).

**TYRIE, Peter** **fl 1984**
Lanarkshire artist of wild birds; exhibited 'The Kestrels' RSA & 'The Barn Owl' GI, from Strathaven.

**TYTLER, Miss Eleanor Fraser** **fl 1871**
Member of the artistic Edinburgh family of painters and lithographers. Exhibited two landscapes at the RSA in 1871, 'A sunset near Forres' and 'Dorf Mutters, Tyrol'.

**TYTLER, George** **c1798-1859**
Born Edinburgh; died London, Oct 30. Portrait painter and topographical artist. Father of George Fraser T(qv). In 1822 he prepared a 'Panoramic View of Edinburgh from the Calton Hill'. These were published as three coloured lithographs. In addition to the buildings, the roads and Leith Port, the scenes are given an added appeal by the inclusion of the ladies of the Hill inspecting a washing, while small craft of all types sail in Leith Roads. In 1823, having moved to 10 Villiers St, off the Strand in London, he exhibited at the RA a view of the interior of St Peter's, Rome from a drawing on the spot. The same year was appointed Lithographic Draughtsman to the Duke of Gloucester. In 1824 exhibited a portrait of 'Sir English Dolben,' now in the BM, and the following year an Italian clergyman. Died in great poverty. Represented in City of Edinburgh collection by a lithographic View of Edinburgh from the Calton Hill; BM.
**Bibl:** Benezit; Butchart 83.

**TYTLER, George Fraser** **fl 1883-1885**
Edinburgh oil painter of landscape and portraits. Son of George T(qv) and husband of Margaret Fraser T(qv). Exhibited a portrait of his sister 'Miss Eleanor Fraser Tytler' RSA.

**TYTLER, James A** **fl 1971-1973**
Aberdeen landscape artist; exhibited AAS(3), latterly from 188 Gt Western Rd.

**TYTLER, Margaret Fraser** **fl 1871**
Member of the Edinburgh family of artists, wife of George F T(qv); painter of 1andscape and wildlife; exhibited RSA(4).

**TYTLER, R A Fraser** **fl 1887-1893**
Midlothian landscape painter and amateur sculptor; related to George(qv) and George Fraser T(qv). Exhibited AAS(3), latterly from Auchendinny House, Midlothian.

# U

**UGLOW, Geoffrey** **1978-**
Born England, Aug 7. Painter of urban townscapes in traditional style. After early education in Falmouth, he moved to Scotland, studying at Glasgow School of Art 1997-2000. Recipient of many awards including the Mary Armour Painting prize 1998, Landscape award (RSA) 2000, David Cargill award 2001, Macfarlane Trust award (RSA) 2001 and the John Murray Thomson award (RSA) 2001. His paintings often make a point of featuring the jumble of architectural styles characteristic of Edinburgh Old Town.

**UNDERHILL, Joan E** **fl 1930**
Minor Glasgow engraver, mainly woodcuts. Exhibited GI(1) from 29 Barnbank Gdns.

**UNDERWOOD, Mrs Mary** **fl 1939**
Amateur painter. Married Robert U(qv). Exhibited RSA(1), from 1 Louvain Terrace, Berwick-on-Tweed.

**UNDERWOOD, Robert** **fl 1937-1940**
Painter, mainly in watercolour. Moved c1939 to Berwick-on-Tweed. Married Mary U(qv). Exhibited RSA(4) & GI(2).

**URE, Alan McLymont** **fl 1915-1933**
Glasgow amateur sculptor; portrait busts. Exhibited GI(10).

**URE, Miss Beth** **fl 1938**
Stirlingshire amateur sculptress; exhibited a plaster head GI from Bonnybridge.

**URE, Isa R** **fl 1881-1885**
Helensburgh flower painter in oils. Exhibited RSA(2) & GI(8) from Cairndhu.

**URE, James L** **fl 1893**
Obscure Glasgow painter. Exhibited 'The Harvest Moon' at GI from 45 Queen's Sq, Strathbungo.

**URE, T H** **fl 1905**
Dunfermline painter; exhibited RSA(1) from 43 Carnegie Street.

**URIE, Daniel** **fl 1861**
Greenock landscape painter in oil and teacher; taught Greenock School of Art. Exhibited an Arran landscape at the RSA.

**URIE, Miss Jean** **fl 1961**
Ayrshire flower painter. Exhibited 'Roses' at the GI, from Turnberry.

**URIE, Joseph** **1947-**
Born Glasgow. Painter. Trained Duncan of Jordanstone College of Art, Dundee 1977-81 and RA Schools 1981-4. Won a number of important awards including the Chalmers Jervis Prize and British Institute Prize 1980, Farquhar Reid travelling scholarship 1981 and the J van Beuren Wittman prize 1984. First one-man exhibition in Cardiff 1984. Much of his work is 'obsessively and remorselessly' autobiographical accompanied with a degree of symbolism that helps to transcend the purely personal. A favourite device is the appearance of a howling dog, vulnerable but potentially dangerous. Exhibited GI(2). Represented in City of Edinburgh collection, SAC.
**Bibl:** Roger Francis Gallery, London (Ex Cat 1985); SNGMA, 'The Vigorous Imagination', (Ex Cat 1987).

**URQUHART, Miss** **fl 1868**
Minor amateur landscape painter in oil; exhibited RSA(3) from Edinburgh.

**URQUHART, Miss Annie Mackenzie** **1879-1928**
Born Glasgow. Watercolour painter and black and white artist. Trained Glasgow School of Art under Fra Newbury(qv) and under M Delville(qv) in Paris. Enjoyed painting children in country settings, sometimes executed on vegetable parchment with the colour stippled on to an outline drawing. Works include 'Spring' and 'Blossoms'. Towards the end of her life lived at Summerlea, Clarkston, nr Glasgow. From Bishopton, later Glasgow and then London 1928. Exhibited RA(1), RSA(3), GI(14), AAS(1) & L(1).
**Bibl:** Halsby 183; Houfe; Studio, 47, 1909, 60-63.

**URQUHART, Donald** **1959-**
Born Bankfoot, Perthshire. Artist in mixed media including photography. Trained Edinburgh College of Art 1978-82 followed by a period at the RA Study Course, The Prado, Madrid. Awards include Lowson Smart medal 1978, Andrew Grant travelling scholarship 1981/2, Richard Ford award (RA) 1982, Hope Scott Trust award 1994 and a further grant 1997. First solo exhibition in Glasgow 1990, followed by Slovenia, Austria, Edinburgh and Stornoway. His work, very much in the modern idiom, often based on the Scottish landscape, is austere and minimal.
**Bibl:** Macmillan 2001, 184, illus 204.

**URQUHART, Dorothy** **c1947-**
Born Kirkcaldy. Designer and weaver of tapestries. Trained Edinburgh College of Art 1965-9. A scholarship enabled her to visit Tunisia. In 1975 commissioned by the City of Edinburgh to design and weave tapestries for the City Chambers. Elected Vice-President, SSWA 1976.

**URQUHART, Miss Edith Mary** **fl 1910-1940**
Born Edinburgh. Portrait, figure and landscape painter in oil and watercolour. Trained Newlyn and Heatherley's. Elected ASWA 1930. Exhibited RBA(2) & SWA(32).

**URQUHART, Gregor** **c1799-?**
Born Green of Muirtown, Inverness. Portrait painter and copiest. Son of an Inverness church officer. Studied Inverness Academy and 1818-1825 in Rome. Working in London in the 1830's but in 1844 returned to Inverness where he had a studio at 75 Church Street. In London 1855 exhibited 'The Berkshire rose' at the RA from 41 Chepstow Place, Westbourne Grove. Represented in NGS by 'The Transfiguration' (after Raphael).

**URQUHART, H H** **fl 1884**
Minor Glasgow artist; exhibited 'Drying the Salmon Nets' at the GI from 12 Albert Drive, Crosshill.

**URQUHART, Helen** **fl 1913**
Painter of Murray House, Perth who exhibited at the Walker Gallery, Liverpool(1).

**URQUHART, Maggie** **fl 1880**
Amateur Glasgow landscape artist. 'Exhibited A wintry day at Camphill' at the GI(1) from Langside.

**URQUHART, Murray McNeel Caird RBA** **1880-c1940**
Born Kirkcudbright, April 24. Painter in oil and watercolour of figures, portraits, animals and landscape. Trained Edinburgh College of Art, Slade, Westminster School of Art under Sickert, Frank Calderon's Animal School and Academie Julien in Paris under J P Laurens. His style is direct and free demanding attention. Employed a pointilliste technique in his landscapes. His watercolour 'Fishing Boats, Concarneaux' was illustrated in 'Watercolour Painting of Today', *Studio* Special no, 1937. Elected RBA 1914. Last known to have lived in Meopham, Kent. Exhibited RA(16), RBA (152), RHA (5), GI(4) & RI(3).
**Bibl:** Benezit; Halsby 238,240,286; Wingfield.

**URQUHART, Samuel A** **fl 1949-1953**
Paisley watercolour painter of landscape and boats. Exhibited GI(5).

**URQUHART, Theresa** **fl 1984-1985**
Aberdeen painter of landscape and figure studies; exhibited AAS(2), latterly from 43 Menzies Rd, Torry.

**URQUHART, Thomas C** **fl 1940**
Minor Greenock painter; exhibited RSA(1) from 74 Forsyth Street.

# V

**VALENTINE, John** **1867-1944**
Born Aberdeen. Little known horse painter in oil and watercolour. His work in the late 1980s began to enjoy popular success. In the 1880's travelled to York, where he took an appointment in the press department of the local newspaper. In 1904 came north to Newcastle to work for the *Newcastle Chronicle* as an illustrator. There he remained until his retirement 1937 when he went to live in Norham where previously he had purchased a house. Here spent his remaining years painting rural scenes and landscapes, but mostly horses. His style was direct, with accurate draughtsmanship and a good sense of natural colour, if without great originality. Deserves greater recognition.

**VALLANCE, David James** **fl 1870-1887**
Edinburgh painter in oil of genre, portraits and landscapes, especially around Perthshire. Exhibited RSA(32) & GI(1).

**VALLANCE, Robert Bell** **fl 1885-1901**
Son of William Fleming V(qv). Painted in oil and watercolour, landscapes and portraits. Lived in Wardie, nr Edinburgh. Exhibited RSA(22) including 'Scene on the Dee, nr Aberdeen' 1897.

**VALLANCE, Tom** **fl 1897-1929**
Glasgow painter of farmyard scenes and genre; exhibited RSA(3) & GI(8).

**VALLANCE, William Fleming RSA** **1827-1904**
Born Paisley, Feb 13; died Edinburgh, Aug 30. Painter of landscape and marines, also illustrator. In early life his family moved to Leith and in 1841 was apprenticed as a carver and gilder to Messrs Aitken Dott of Edinburgh. During his apprenticeship began to paint portraits and genre but did not receive proper instruction until he was 23. Studied for a short time at the Paisley School of Design and Trustees Academy under E Dallas(qv) and from 1855 under R S Lauder(qv). At the Academy he was a contemporary of McTaggart's. Started exhibiting RSA 1848 but did not pursue art as a profession until 1857. After 1870 painted a series of pictures of Irish life and character, principally in Wicklow, Connemara and Galway. Now most remembered for his paintings of the sea and shipping and for his atmospheric watercolour sketches of sea and sky, often including children in a manner reminiscent of McTaggart(qv) and sometimes Erskine Nicol(qv). In the 1870's travelled in Southern France and Italy where he revelled in the quality of light. Founder and active member of the Scottish Arts Club(qv). Elected ARSA 1875, RSA 1881. 'Venice' 1877, now in Perth AG, is a good example of work at this time. Contributed illustrations for *Pen and Pencil Pictures From the Poets* (1866). His diploma work was 'Reading the War News' 1871. Exhibited RA(5), RSA(241), RSW(8) & GI(56). Represented in NGS(3), Dundee AG, Victoria AG (Australia).
**Bibl:** AJ 1898, 370 ff; Bryan; DNB, 2nd Supp 1912; Caw 263; Halsby 124,286; Houfe.

**VAN HAECKEN (VANHAECKEN, VANHACKEN, VAN HAEKEN, VANHEKEN, van AKEN), Josef** **c1709-1749**
Born Antwerp; died London, 4 Jly. Drapery painter of quality, he was much used by British artists working in London during the early part of the 18th century. Particularly associated with Allan Ramsay(qv), making it sometimes difficult to distinguish the art of each. His remarkable lifelong devotion to what Smart called 'the mysteries of silk and satin' earned him the soubriquet 'the tailor'. The 55 drawings now in the NGS, most in black and white chalk, illustrate the closeness of this collaboration. Smart cites as typical instances of portraits commissioned from Ramsay, in which the draperies were the work of Van Haecken, and for which studies by Van Haecken have been preserved, 'Countess of Strafford' 1743 and 'Mrs Madan' 1745. Van Haecken's own portrait was painted by Ramsay. After his death the practice was continued by his brother Alexander. The Earl of Wemyss and March has a painting 'The Game of Shuffleboard' that has been doubtfully attributed to this artist. Represented in SNPG.
**Bibl:** Smart, The Life and Art of Allan Ramsay, 1952, 40-42, 187 et passim; J Steegman: 'A Drapery Painter of the Eighteenth Century', Conn, June 1936, vol xcvii, 309ff.

**VANNET, William Peters** **1917-?**
Born Carnoustie, Angus, Feb 15. Painter in oil and watercolour, also etcher. Painted harbour and shipping scenes, sometimes in Holland, often around Arbroath. Trained Dundee College of Art 1935-40. Lived at 56 Howard Street, Arbroath until 1947, thereafter Broughty Ferry. Exhibited from 1939 RSA, RSW & GI(41).

**VANSON, (VANYONE, VAN SON) Adrian** **fl 1581-1602**
Court portrait painter in oil. Probably related to the Edinburgh goldsmith Abraham Vanson as for the baptism of one of the latter's children in 1595 Vanson was a witness. According to Thomson he had close ties with Sir Adrian van Damman who in 1584 was Ambassador from the Confederate Provinces to the Scottish court. In May 1594 they had joined in surety for three Dutch sailors in trouble. Succeeded Bronckhorst(qv) as court painter and between 1580 and 1600 was probably the only painter at court undertaking portraiture. All relatively sophisticated Royal portraits of that time are attributed to his hand. It is not known exactly when he first came to Scotland as he was employed before being granted an official office. However, in June 1581 he was paid for two pictures despatched to a client in Geneva and at the end of 1585 became a Burgess of Edinburgh for 'guid and thankfull seruice to be done to the guid towne be Adriane Danyone, Dutchemen, paynter, speciallie for the seruice quhairin he is to be imployet be the towne in his craft, and that he tak and instruct prenteissis'. Married the artist Susanna de Colone(qv). In 1587 and 1590 received payment for painting banners and for including those for the trumpeters at the Queen's Coronation. In December 1601 he received £20 for a miniature portrait of the King which was attached to a gold chain made by George Heriot for the Duke of Mecklenburg. (The chain alone cost £611.13s 4d). Portraits now attributed to Vanson include 'Patrick Lyon, Lord Glamis' 1583, 'James VI' 1586; 'Sir Thomas Kennedy of Culzean' 1592, two of 'James VI and Anne of Denmark' 1595 and 'Agnes Douglas, Duchess of Argyll' 1599. A number of engravings and coins related to his work can be seen in the SNPG and in the National Museum of Antiquities of Scotland. Attributed work is in SNPG(4).
**Bibl:** Apted 98-99; Caw 2; Thompson 25, 31.

**VARDY, John D** **fl 1926**
Aberdeen landscape and topographical painter; exhibited AAS(1) from 25 St Swithin St.

**VAST, William C** **fl 1927-1931**
Edinburgh watercolour painter and etcher; exhibited RSA(3).

**VAUGHAN, Huw** **fl 1986-**
Edinburgh painter. Exhibits GI since 1986.

**VAUGHAN, Thomas** **1776-1856**
Born Newington, Surrey; died Bethnal Green. Landscape and miniature portrait painter. Elder of two sons of the miniaturist Edward Vaughan. Entered the RA Schools in June 1800 but before that trained in Edinburgh under Alexander Nasmyth. Married 1808. For many years Assistant Secretary to the Royal Academy becoming its first full-time Clerk 1822, a position he retained until his death. There is a fine portrait of him by J.P. Knight commissioned by the RA 1852. Exhibited RA(16), including 'Highland landscape' 1812 and a portrait of 'Abraham Cooper RA' 1820, latterly from 22 Felton St, Hoxton.
**Bibl:** Farrington, Diaries, in BM, passim; Emily Robertson (Ed), Letters and Papers of Andrew Robertson, 2nd ed 1897,41; Anthony Vaughan (descendant), personal communication.

**VAUGHAN-LEE, Elizabeth** **[see CAMERON, Elizabeth]**

**VEITCH, John W** **fl 1872**
Duns artist, probably an amateur; exhibited a work entitled 'Sticks and stones' at the RSA, from Southside Villa.

**VEITCH, Kate** **fl 1897-1920**
Edinburgh oil painter of flower studies and landscape; exhibited RA(2), RSA(21), AAS(1) & GI(11), latterly from her studio at 45 Queen St.

**VEITCH, M Campbell** **fl 1887**
Edinburgh painter. Possibly husband of Kate V(qv). Exhibited RSA (1) from 18 Drummond St.

**VENABLES, S** **fl 1890-1891**
Amateur Glasgow painter who moved later to Liverpool; exhibited GI(1) & L(1).

**VERNON, S U** **fl 1980s**
Aberdeenshire costume and jewellery designer; trained Gray's School of Art, Aberdeen. Exhibited AAS(4) from Heathcot, Blairs, Aberdeen.

**VERRI, Miss Violet E** **fl 1947-1953**
Lanarkshire flower painter. Exhibited GI(3), latterly from Milngavie.

**VETTRIANO, Jack (Jack Hoggan) OBE Hon LLD** **1951-**
Born Methil, Fife. Painter in oils of figurative subjects, often evocative of Hollywood film material. No formal training. After training to be a miner, taught himself to paint, often copying from Impressionist still lifes. His first exhibits at the RSA, in 1988, were both sold, his first solo exhibition was sold out 1992 and his work has become increasingly popular ever since, with solo exhibitions in London, Kirkcaldy AG and elsewhere. Not without reason, he has been dubbed 'the people's artist'. The most controversial Scottish painter of his time, the academic establishment unable to accept the merits of his achievement, the market place elevating him to his position as the most popular and expensive Scottish artist. His work is idiosyncratic and instantly recognisable: slightly stiff figures, often in seedy or sinister settings, with implicit sexual undertones. He also portrays brighter beach and country scenes, reminiscent of the spirit of Noel Coward. Prints of his paintings are in constant public demand. In April 2004, his best known work 'The Singing Butler' sold at auction for £740,800, making it the most expensive painting by a contemporary Scottish artist to date. This phenomenon serves to highlight a significant but often overlooked or misunderstood distinction. Current financial value and artistic worth lie along a different continuum. Before the arrival of 'modern art' and the age of the celebrity, those who set financial standards were a comparatively few knowledgeable collectors. As an examination of Reitlinger illustrates, while the number of those able to afford expensive art has increased, financial standards are now set by a larger number of wealthy but - what some regard as - artistically unsophisticated buyers prepared to pay any price to purchase whatever takes their fancy. Thus, when an artist captures the *zeitgeist*, inflamed and nourished by the media, his work is liable to reach mesmeric heights of financial value. Alongside this modern affluence there is an entrenched artistic establishment, fostering the academic fashion it itself creates, praising those who follow its guidelines while dismissing or ignoring those who deviate. This accounts for deep divisions over the merits of Vettriano's oeuvre, on one hand those who rejoice in its unadorned atmosphere of casual sexual tension, its immediacy and redolence - sexual fantasy and nostalgia are for many an irresistible combination; on the other hand, those who denigrate what they see as the untutored handling of paint. The place of Vettriano in the pantheon of Scottish artists is far from being resolved - time will be the final arbiter. Granted Hon LLD (St Andrews) 2003. First solo exhibition was sold out 1992. OBE 2003. Exhibits worldwide including RSA, with a strong international following. Represented Kirkcaldy AG.
**Bibl:** Gerald Reitlinger, The Economics of Taste, vol II, The Rise and Fall of Picture Prices 1760-1960, Barrie & Jenkins, 1970.

**VIBART, M J** **fl 1869**
Edinburgh painter of landscape; exhibited mountain scenes at the RSA from Queen's Crescent.

**VICKERS, William** **fl c1890-c1910**
Glasgow sculptor. Responsible for several statues in St Margaret's Church of the Ursulines, Edinburgh.

**VINCENT, Brian** **fl 1979**
Edinburgh painter; exhibited 'An approaching storm' at the RSA.

**VISITELLA, Isaac** **fl 1649-d1658**
Died Edinburgh. Portraitist. Very little is known of this artist and none of his works can now be identified. Died in the Canongate and in his will reference is made to four portraits of the 'Earl of Caithness', two of the 'Earl of Winton' and one each of 'Lord Forrester', the 'Lord of Mey', 'Captain Douglas' and others. There is a written record of the 3rd Earl of Lothian writing to John Clerk of Penicuik in 1649 about a picture "..if it may be had for 25 or 30 shillings...I shall pay you again. I imagine it Visitella his hand. I would desire you if you be acquaint with him to tell I would have him come out to Newbattle to drawe a picture for me and it should be Margaret Fasides" [Clerk of Penicuik Muniments].
**Bibl:** Apted 99-100; SRO Clerk of Penicuik Muniments, GD. 18/ 2499.

**VOLTI, Carl** **fl 1889**
Glasgow-based watercolour painter; exhibited GI(1) from 77 South Portland St.

**VON KUMMER, Elizabeth A** **fl 1875-1887**
Painter of flower and nature studies. Exhibited GI(6), latterly from Laurel Bank.

**WADDELL, D Henderson** **fl 1881-1882**
Edinburgh painter in oil and watercolour of landscapes. Exhibited RA 1882 'Dunbar-evening' from 12 Percy Circus, King's Cross and the same year a landscape at the RSA 'On the Clyde'.

**WADDELL, Miss Sheila Buchanan** **fl 1967**
Glasgow watercolourist. Exhibited GI1).

**WADDELL, Gavin** **fl 1964-1965**
Edinburgh painter; exhibited RSA.

**WADDELL, John Holms** **fl 1877-1886**
Edinburgh painter of interiors and domestic genre; exhibited RSA 1877 & GI 1886 when living in Glasgow.

**WADDELL, William** **fl 1877-1896**
Painter in oil and watercolour of rustic scenes, coastal landscapes and interiors. Often painted scenery in the north-east of England. Exhibited RSA(27) including 'Edinburgh Castle' 1883, 'An interior of Glasgow Cathedral' 1887, the 'Rood Screen, Glasgow Cathedral' and the 'Choir at Norwich Cathedral', both 1890; also GI(2). The RSA catalogues also list a **William WADDEL** who exhibited landscapes 1877-1888 from an address in Edinburgh, probably the same artist.

**WADE, Heather Joanne** **fl 1989-**
Aberdeen artist; exhibited 'The Gamekeeper's Daughter' at the AAS, from 6c Hayton Rd.

**WAGER, Rhoda** **c1875-1953**
Jewellery and metalwork designer, associated with the Glasgow School. Trained Bristol Art School before moving to Glasgow where later she joined the staff of Kilmacolm Girls' school c1903. Combined teaching art with further studies at Glasgow School of Art. Exhibited her work at the School's art club and at an exhibition in Cork 1902. Returned to Bristol where she worked under Bernard Cuzner. Eventually emigrated to Fiji with her brother and from there finally settled in Sydney, Australia opening a production studio specialising in hand-wrought jewellery. Reported to have recorded at least 12,000 pieces in meticulous sketchbooks. "A Strong-willed, determined and a clear-headed and industrious business woman" [Burkhauser]. Exhibited Glasgow Lady Artists' Club 1919; also several works at Walker Gallery, Liverpool from 7 West Regent Street, Glasgow. Represented in Glasgow AG.
**Bibl:** Burkhauser 159, 178-181.

**WAIGHT, Michael J** **fl 1987-**
Aberdeen painter in the modern abstract idiom; exhibited AAS from 53 Raedon Court, Midstocket Rd.

**WAITE, D P** **fl 1945**
Edinburgh painter; exhibited 'Iranian coast' at the RSA.

**WAITE, Vicky** **1919-?**
Born High Wycombe, Bucks. Self-taught, sensitive, observant natural history and wildlife artist, illustrator. Worked in oil, pen and pencil. During WW2 served in the Women's Land Army and as a nurse at St. Dunstan's. Two years after her marriage to an RAF pilot he was killed. In 1975 met and eighteen months later married Garth Waite. They retired prematurely in order to live on Easdale, Argyll. Illustrated in colour their joint book *Island; Diary of a Year on Easdale* 1985. Exhibited RWS & ROI.

**WAITT, Richard** **fl 1708-d1732**
Birthplace unknown, but possibly north-east of Scotland. Painter of portraits and still-life. Although prolific during his short working life, remarkably few details are known about his career. One of the most under-estimated Scottish painters. Throughout Scottish art history in the last hundred years, critics have belittled an artist regarded as a 'savage minor painter'. His ability to paint texture and his success in capturing character and pose without stiffness was remarkable. One of the most impressive portraitists Scotland has produced. Tradition has it that he trained under John Scougal(qv) and possibly with Kneller. But the only supporting evidence is that some of his figures were similar in style to Scougal's and the sitters were members of the same families that the older artist had painted. However, allowing for the limited number of Scotsmen who, at the time, were interested in commissioning portraits, this is not strong evidence. In 1707 he married the daughter of David Freebairn who was to become Bishop and eventually Primus of the Episcopal Church in 1739. The following year painted the arms of the Earl of Hopetoun for the Church at Abercorn. Over the next few years he painted portraits of 'Mrs Boswell' 1709, 'Bethia Dundas' 1710, & 'Patrick Smythe' 1713. But his main patron was Alexander Grant, chief of the clan. His first painting of the laird was c1713 and there were companion full-length portraits showing great skill and verve, one of 'William Cummine, the laird's piper' 1714 and one of 'Alastair Grant Mor, the laird's Champion' 1714. Both of these are remarkable for their quality as well as being historically interesting in various particulars. In the portrait of the piper, he is shown dressed in livery with Castle Grant in the background, not as it was but with the right wing of the main block appearing symmetrical, a project which was never completed. His portrait of the Champion shows the sitter again wearing livery and with a tartan similar to the piper's. An appropriately fierce looking figure, with long barrelled-musket, pistol, dirk and scimitar-bladed sword. In addition to these works the laird's family were painted together, forming the beginning of a clan portrait gallery in the castle. In 1715 his commission with the family ended and apart from a mysterious painting dated 1716, nothing further is heard of the artist until 1722. The sitter of the 1716 work is thought to be Baltus Barents van Kleek, a Dutchman who settled at Poughkeepsie. Holloway suggests that if this identity is correct, then Waitt may have emigrated after the Jacobite rising. Other portraits painted during this first series of commissions, were 'Alexander Grant of Grantsfield', 'Ludovic Grant of Knockando', 'James Grant of Wester Elchies' and 'Patrick Grant of Milton, hereditary standard-bearer', and a number of other members of the family. In 1715 he painted a magnificent portrait of 'Sir Archibald Grant of Monymusk (1697-1778)' showing him in the splendid tartan uniform of the Queen's Bodyguard for Scotland, now in the possession of the Royal Company of Archers. After 1722 he began again to paint for the Grant family, now under Sir James Grant. Completed many portraits including a remarkable 'Nic Ciarain, Henwife of Castle Grant' and a rather splendid child portrait of 'General James Grant of Ballindalloch, aged 5' - 'besides its considerable charm, it shows Waitt's ability to use every square inch of his canvas, so that the spaces round the figure have a tension which gives liveliness to the whole design. This confidence to think of his pictures two-dimensionally like courtcards, is new in Waitt's work and begs the question where he was and what he was doing between 1716 and 1721' [Holloway]. In the background of this painting is placed an edge of Edinburgh Castle. Holloway points out that he was a cheap artist: whereas his most expensive double portrait was only £6, William Aikman working contemporaneously was charging 30 to 40 guineas for a single portrait. For 'The Henwife', for example, Waitt was only paid 25 shillings. Two of his most remarkable works were a still-life showing cauliflowers, poultry and a leg of mutton on a shelf 1724, now in the NGS, and a caustic 'Self-portrait' 1728 now in the SNPG. Even his critics have recognised the quality of the former, while the latter was reproduced on the back cover of *Patrons and Painters.* Until recently his last known recorded work was the arms of Great Britain, painted for Elgin courthouse in 1730, but in 2000 the SNPG acquired a fine unusual portrait of a gardener dated 1731. Represented in SNPG, Glasgow AG.
**Bibl:** Brydall 94; Cheape, DHG, 'Portraiture in Piping', Scottish Pipe Band Monthly, No6, Jan 1988; Holloway 70-74, 80-83, 148; J. Holloway, Antique Collector, July 1989.

**WALDEN, G R de** **fl 1858**
Edinburgh painter of coastal scenes in oil; exhibited RSA(1).

**WALES, James** **1747-1795**
Born Peterhead; died Thana, India, Nov 18. Painter of portraits and topographical subjects, engraver. Educated Marischal College, Aberdeen, but as an artist was virtually self-taught. An excerpt from the *Aberdeen Journals* 1774 advertises a partnership between Wales and John Norrie(qv), announcing 'they have engaged proper hands and entered into partnership. They perform house, landskip, ornament, coach and sign painting and gilding...in the newest and best

methods. Mr James Wales continues to copy pictures as usual'. By 1783 he had arrived in London exhibiting that year at the Society of Artists and, in 1788 and 1789, exhibited three portraits at the RA from addresses in Bloomsbury and Hampstead. In London he met James Forbes, the author of *Oriental Memoirs.* In 1790 he published two engravings (by James Phillips) from paintings of his own based on sketches by Forbes. Through this friendship Wales was encouraged to go to Bombay with the East India Company, travelling as a portrait and landscape painter. Once in India, his time was divided between portrait painting and architectural drawings. Among his portraits were 'Baji Rao', 'Nana Farnaris' and 'Mahdaji Sindia', many being utilised in the large painting in the possession of the Malet family, representing Sir Charles Malet (the artist's son-in-law) handing the ratified Treaty of Alliance to the Peshawar of Mahratta at a durbah held at Poonah in 1790. This picture, begun by Wales, was finished by Thomas Daniell and exhibited at the RA 1805. Wales married the daughter of William Wallace of Dundee and their eldest child, Susanna, married Sir Charles Warre Malet. In 1791 and 1792, Wales engraved a series of plates from his own sketches published in London posthumously *Twelve views of the Island of Bombay* and its vicinity. Toward the end of his life he visited the caverns which had recently been discovered near Ellore, resulting in a set of engravings issued in London 1803 'Hindoo excavations in the Mountain of Ellora from drawings by James Wales'. Other dated portraits include 'Dr Adam McDonald' (b 1703) done in watercolour and dated 26th June, 1772 (Dr McDonald was known as the Prophet of Bethelmie), and 'Keith Urquhart of Meldrum' 1778. Whilst on a sketching trip he caught a fever and died. A mural brass memorial was erected to him and his wife in St Thomas's Cathedral, Bombay. Represented in SNPG.
**Bibl:** Archer, 333-355; Bryan; Brydall 172; Caw 50; Forster; Walpole Soc, 19, 1930-31, 74; Wingfield.

**WALES, James** **fl 1971-1972**
Glasgow painter of still life. Exhibited GI(3).

**WALKDEN, John S** **fl 1944**
Edinburgh painter; exhibited 'Gullane sands' at the RSA.

**WALKER, Archibald** **fl 1888**
Amateur Glasgow landscape painter. Exhibited GI(1), from 149 Firpark Street, Dennistoun.

**WALKER, A Y L** **fl 1878**
Edinburgh painter; exhibited an oil study of a ruined mosque at the RSA.

**WALKER, A Emslie** **fl 1898-1900**
Aberdeenshire flower painter; exhibited AAS(2) from Richmond, Peterhead.

**WALKER, Miss Ada Hill** **1879-1955**
Born St Andrews, Fife. Painter in oil and watercolour of landscapes, portraits, still life and flowers. Studied under Mrs Jopling in London, also Glasgow School of Art and in Paris. In later life returned from England to live in St Andrews where she painted the local coastline and vigorous figure studies in a characteristically dashing style. In 1930 was commissioned to paint scenes of St Andrews for the local cinema where they can still be seen. Exhibited RSA(6) & RSW(8) from her home at Dauphin East, St Andrews.
**Bibl:** Halsby 286.

**WALKER, Alexander** **fl 1894-1933**
Glasgow painter in watercolour of landscape, figure studies and architectural subjects; also an etcher and stained glass window designer. Lived at Garnethill before moving to England in the early 1910's. Retired to Cockermouth. Exhibited RA(4), RSA(4), RSW (3), AAS(1) & GI(20). Represented by a Nativity window in Jedburgh church 1902 and a good Ascension window in St. James, Pollok (Glasgow) c1896. The RSA lists an **Alec WALKER** who exhibited narrative subjects from Garnethill and latterly from Orkney 1924-1927.

**WALKER, Miss Alice A S** **fl 1919-1931**
Aberdeen painter of landscape, harbour scenes and buildings; exhibited AAS(10) from 42 Hamilton Place.

**WALKER, Alison G** **1893-1981**
Painter and stained glass window designer. Trained Glasgow School of Art 1912-1913 and 1919-1923.

**WALKER, Andrew** **1959-**
Born Aberdeen. Landscape painter. Trained Edinburgh College of Art 1977-81. First solo exhibition Edinburgh 1982, followed by many others in London and around Scotland. Frequent visits to France. Published *The Book of Job* 1985. Exhibits RSA since 1994. Represented in Aberdeen AG, Edinburgh City Art Centre. Lives in Kelso.

**WALKER, Anne Robson** **fl 1873**
Amateur Edinburgh watercolourist; exhibited a bird study at the RSA in the above year.

**WALKER, Blair F** **fl 1986**
Dundee artist; trained Gray's School of Art, Aberdeen; exhibited AAS(3), from 42 Provost Rd, Dundee.

**WALKER, David Bruce** **fl 1969-1973**
Dundee architect and semi-abstract painter in watercolour; exhibited RSA 1961-1967 architectural designs and also 'Boat on beach' 1963 and 'Death of Christ'; also AAS from 49 Strathearn Road, West Ferry.

**WALKER, David Morrison** **fl 1955-1965**
Dundee painter of architectural subjects; exhibited RSA(4) including 'Spanish buildings in Gerona'.

**WALKER, Dougald** **1865-fl 1929**
Perth painter; exhibited RSA(1) from 11 Pitcullen Terrace.

**WALKER, E** **fl 1887-1891**
Glasgow painter of flowers and topography. Exhibited RI(1), GI(3) & L(1).

**WALKER, Euan L** **fl 1912-1928**
Amateur painter; schoolmaster. Educated Hamilton Academy. Taught at George Watson's, Edinburgh. Exhibited 'The Workshop' at the GI from Barncluith Rd, Hamilton.

**WALKER, Elizabeth** **1800-1876**
Born London; died London. English miniature painter and engraver. Daughter of the engraver and watercolourist Samuel William Reynolds. Married the Scottish engraver William Walker(qv). Studied engraving under T G Lupton but later took up miniature painting having received instruction from G Clint. Appointed miniature painter to William IV. Exhibited RA 1818-1850, latterly from 64 Margaret St.
**Bibl:** Bryan; Bushnell; DNB.

**WALKER, Elizabeth** **fl 1965-1967**
Angus painter of still life and nature subjects in watercolour. Married Syd W(qv). Exhibited AAS(5) from 12 India St, Montrose.

**WALKER, Mrs Ella L** **fl 1929**
Amateur watercolourist of Bramall, Bothwell; exhibited RSW(1).

**WALKER, Miss Elma R** **fl 1932**
Glasgow amateur artist; pen and ink, pastel. Exhibited RSA(1) & GI(2) from St Leonards, Bearsden.

**WALKER, Dame Ethel ARA RBA RP DBE** **1861-1951**
Born Edinburgh, Jne 9; died London, Mar 2. Painter in oil of portraits, flower studies, figures, landscape, seascapes and still-life. Began painting with very little training, only undertook formal studies in 1899 when already 38. Trained Radley School of Art, Putney School of Art and Slade under Sickert and Wyndham Lewis. Member of the London Group 1936. Her 'Miss Jean Warner Laurie' 1927-8 was purchased by the Chantrey Bequest in 1931 as was her 'Seascape: Autumn Morning' c1935 in 1939. She was best known for her flowing nudes painted in the open air, of which her watercolour 'The Judgement of Paris' was a fine example. Also for her flower studies, 'glittering showers of colour superbly modulated...and the sensitiveness of their treatment, applied to a subject as different as the

sea, makes the artist one of our best marine painters...she renders perfectly the changing moods of the expanse of waves' [Earp]. CBE 1938, DBE 1943. Elected NEA 1900, ARA 1940, ARBA 1921, RBA 1932, RP 1933. First solo exhibition in London 1936. 'She attempted, often with success, the difficult undertaking of fulfilling the claim of Camille Pisarro that impressionism was a way of seeing compatible with the free play of the imagination' [Rothenstein]. Described as 'energetic, witty and wild about small dogs'. Lived and worked at The White Gate, Robin Hood's Bay, Yorkshire and in London, where she died. Exhibited widely including RA(44), RSA(11), RI(1), RHA(1), SWA(20), RBA (59), LS(19), GI(19) and over 200 works with her London agent, Lefevre Gallery. A retrospective exhibition with Gwen John and Frances Hodgkins was held at the Tate Gallery 1952. Represented in Tate AG, Courtauld AG, Leeds AG.
**Bibl:** Harold Osborne(ed), Twentieth Century Art, 1988, 581; Rothenstein 16, 181 (pl 13); Wingfield; Yorkshire Post (obit) 3 Mar 1951.

**WALKER, Ethel** **fl 1986-1988**
Argyll painter of local landscape; exhibited RSA from Kirkmichael Glassary, Lochgilphead.

**WALKER, Ferguson** **fl 1949-1953**
Glasgow watercolour painter of mainly coastal scenes. Exhibited GI(3), from Rutherglen.

**WALKER, Miss Frances RSA RSW** **1930-**
Born Kirkcaldy, Fife. Studied at Edinburgh College of Art and Hospitalfield, Arbroath. Landscape painter in oil and watercolour. Awarded Andrew Grant travelling scholarship 1953 and an RSA travelling scholarship the same year. Worked in Europe, Iceland and Ireland. Visiting art teacher on the islands of Harris and North Uist 1956-58 before taking up a position as lecturer at Gray's School of Art. First one-man show in Edinburgh 1957. There is an emphasis on intricate line, often with flat colour, especially the intricacies of stone buildings and dykes and the misty moodiness of the north and north west. Elected ARSA 1970, RSA 1982. Regular exhibitor RSA, AAS (since 1959) & SSA. Settled at 5 Crimon Place, Aberdeen. Represented in Aberdeen AG, Hamilton AG, Canada, Royal Collection, RSA, SAC.

**WALKER, Rev G Barron** **fl 1884-1886**
Amateur watercolour painter of figures and landscapes. Minister of St. James's, Cruden, Aberdeenshire. Exhibited RSA(2) & AAS(2).

**WALKER, Gavin** **?-1980**
Hamilton-based amateur painter and administrator. First curator, Hamilton Museum.

**WALKER, George** **fl 1775-1803**
Edinburgh portrait and landscape painter in oil and watercolour; engraver. Son of an Edinburgh fruit seller. Apprenticed to George Hutchison 1775, later studied under Runciman(qv) and at the Foulis Academy in Glasgow. In 1786 was a candidate for the Mastership of the Trustees Academy. Appointed Landscape Painter to the King. Best remembered for his illustrations for Cririe's *Scottish Scenery* (1803), engraved by W.Byrne. He envisaged these illustrations becoming part of a gallery of Scottish landscapes which in 1804 he intimated to the Earl of Buchan was to be sent to London. The British Museum hold an engraving inscribed 'G W 1797 and T Foster 1689 from a pencil drawing by himself in the possession of G Walker, Esq, published by A Bengo, 22 June 1803'. In 1800 exhibited three Scottish landscapes at the RA from an Edinburgh address, two of them views of Loch Tay. Represented in Edinburgh City collection (2 views of Edinburgh, an oil and a watercolour).
**Bibl:** Brydall 160,293; Bushnell; Macmillan [GA] 145; David Murray, Robert and Andrew Foulis and the Glasgow Press, Glasgow 1913; George Walker: Letter to Earl of Buchan, 18 Dec 1804, Edinburgh PL.

**WALKER, George** **fl 1832**
Edinburgh painter; exhibited once - 'The tinkers' - at the RSA.

**WALKER, H** **fl 1935**
Amateur Glasgow painter. Exhibited GI(1) from 92 Newlands Rd.

**WALKER, H C** **fl 1881**
Painter. Exhibited GI(1) from Exchange Square, Glasgow.

**WALKER, Harry ARWA** **1923-?**
Born Pollokshaws, Glasgow, Jan 6. Painter in oil and sculptor in metal. Educated at Sir John Maxwell School and Polloc Academy; trained Bath Academy of Art, Central School of Arts and Crafts, and RCA. Lecturer, faculty of art and design, Bristol Polytechnic. Lived in Bath, Somerset. Represented in Royal West of England Academy.

**WALKER, Heather Elizabeth** **1959-**
Born Dunfermline. Sculptor. Trained Gray's School of Art, Aberdeen 1981-4 and Chelsea School of Art 1984-5. Awarded a Carnegie Commission for public sculpture in Falkirk Park 1981. First public exhibition 1982, her work was included in an exhibition of British young artists chosen to tour Australia. Exhibited AAS(2) latterly from 47 Gt. Northern Rd.

**WALKER, Hugh** **fl 1862-1868**
Glasgow painter of nature and still life. Exhibited GI(2), from Paisley Rd.

**WALKER, Hugh** **fl 1935**
Glasgow etcher. Exhibited GI.

**WALKER, Miss Jadwiga** **fl 1941-1944**
Edinburgh portrait painter; exhibited RSA(8).

**WALKER, James** **1748-c1802**
Born Edinburgh; died (?)St. Petersburg. Engraver, lived in Old Greyfriars parish; married 28 Feb, 1768. Believed to have been working as an engraver in St. Petersburg 1784-1802. Engraved view of Edinburgh after Francis Nicholson c1798.
Bibl: Bushnell; Butchart 26.

**WALKER, James** **fl 1906**
Aberdeen painter of local buildings and figure studies; exhibited AAS(2) from 75 Rosemount Place.

**WALKER, James B** **fl 1849**
Glasgow landscape painter; exhibited RSA.

**WALKER, James Forbes W** **fl 1944-1976**
Dundee watercolour painter; local scenery and portraits; exhibited RSA(12) & GI(13) 1947-1953.

**WALKER, Miss Janette Lennox** **fl 1866-1883**
Edinburgh painter in oil and watercolour of landscape and coastal scenes. In 1880 appointed painter to Her Grace the Dowager Countess of Roxburgh. Exhibited RSA(18).

**WALKER, Jean** **fl 1932**
Printmaker. Exhibited an aquatint at the RSA from Edinburgh College of Art.

**WALKER, Jeanette** **fl 1880-1883**
Edinburgh landscape painter, generally of the Highlands but also sometimes Somerset. Exhibited RSA(22).

**WALKER, Jenny Bird** **fl 1935-1938**
Glasgow watercolourist; exhibited RSW(1) & GI(5) from St Leonards, Bearsden.

**WALKER, Jim** **fl 1982-1989**
North-east printmaker; trained Gray's School of Art, Aberdeen. Exhibited AAS(5), latterly from 15 Millfield Drive, Hopeman, Moray.

**WALKER, Miss Joanna** **fl 1870**
Leith figure painter; exhibited an oil study at the RSA.

**WALKER, John** **fl 1970**
Obscure Dundee painter; exhibited 'Monkey group' at the RSA.

**WALKER, John Beresford** **1878-?**
Born Edinburgh. Gold and silversmith, teacher and examiner.

Trained Edinburgh School of Art and Sheffield School of Art. Exhibited RA(1) & RSA(3) 1915-1919.

**WALKER, John Russell** **?-1891**
Architect. Designed Brunstfield Evangelical Church (1882-3).
**Bibl:** Gifford 198,493.

**WALKER, Kirsten R** **fl 1986**
Portrait painter; exhibited 'Self-portrait' at the AAS from 12 Hudson Square, Montrose.

**WALKER, Mary D** **fl 1906-1935**
Aberdeen linocut artist, local scenes and views; exhibited AAS during the above years from 15 Dee Place.

**WALKER, May** **fl 1967**
Aberdeen semi-abstract painter; exhib AAS(1) from 30 Fonthill Rd.

**WALKER, Richard** **1955-**
Born Cumbernauld. Pollokshields painter, trained Glasgow School of Art, 1973-7. Awarded first prize at the Inverclyde Bienniale 1986. Exhibited AAS(1) from 32 Keir St.

**WALKER, Robert** **fl 1876-1886**
Edinburgh painter in oil and watercolour of townscapes, flowers, figure studies and landscapes. Exhibited RSA(13).

**WALKER, Robert** **fl 1948-1949**
Renfrewshire watercolour painter of conversation pieces. Exhibited GI(3), from Clarkston.

**WALKER, Robert J** **fl 1892-1944**
Glasgow landscape and flower painter, also occasional architectural subjects. Moved to Bath. Exhibited RSA(7) & GI(50), at one time from 37 Garnethill St, latterly from Killearn.

**WALKER, Robert McAllister** **1875-?**
Born Fleetwood, Apr 6. Painter in watercolour and oil; etcher. Headmaster, Hamilton Academy. Member, Hamilton Art Club 1905. Moved to Bothwell. Exhibited RSA(3), RSW(3), GI(2) & L(1).

**WALKER, Ronald E** **fl 1947**
Glasgow amateur landscape painter. Exhibited GI(1).

**WALKER, Ruth M L** **1942-**
Born Brechin, Angus. Works in oil and watercolour, painting out of doors. Trained Edinburgh College of Art 1959-1963 gaining her post diploma with a high commendation enabling her to travel on a scholarship to study stained glass designs with Patrick Reyntiens. In 1967 received the Worshipful Company of Glaziers Award, the same year completed a window for Kemback Church, Fife with further commissions following for churches in Staffordshire and a private house in Ireland. That year she became an Associate of the Glass Painters Society. In 1975 returned to Scotland to teach at St Leonards School, St Andrews, remaining as art mistress until 1984. In 1986 awarded the Anne Redpath Prize of the SSWA. Has a deep love of the local Fife landscape, especially around Kemback, where her father was minister (1952-69). Abiding interest is in colour and its emotional affect. The influence of the German Expressionists, of Munch and Van Gogh can be seen in her work. Regular exhibitor RSA, RSW, RGI, from 1 Woodburn Place, St Andrews.

**WALKER, Syd** **fl 1961-1983**
Angus painter of local landscapes and buildings; married to Elizabeth W(qv). Exhibited RSA(4), GI(2) & AAS from 12 India St, Montrose.

**WALKER, T Johnson** **fl 1937-1955**
Minor Edinburgh artist; exhibited RSA(2) & GI(1) from 427 Queensferry Road, Barnton and later Newton Mearns.

**WALKER, Thomas** **fl 1989-**
Exhibited 'Roses' at the RSA.

**WALKER, W** **fl 1710**
Bushnell mentions an engraver, thought to be Scottish; engraved a bookplate for John Mouat of Ballquholle 1710.
**Bibl:** Bushnell.

**WALKER, William** **1791-1867**
Born Musselburgh; died London 7 Sep. Engraver. Studied in Edinburgh under James Mitchell(qv). Went to London 1816, studying stipple engraving under T. Woolnoth(qv). Returned to Scotland 1819 engraving some fine plates in stipple after Sir Henry Raeburn. Among them were 'Sir Walter Scott' and a 'Self-portrait'. He commissioned Raeburn to paint 'Lord Brougham'. With Cousins he engraved the well-known plate of 'Robert Burns', after Nasmyth. Established a studio at 64 Margaret St, Cavendish Square, London 1832. Married Elizabeth W(qv). Published his own plates, among them 'The Passing of the Reform Bill'; 'Reformers at the Diet of Spires', after Cattermole, 1847; (3) 'Caxton and Edward IV', after Maclise; 'The Aberdeen Cabinet', 1857; and 'Distinguished Men of Science living in Great Britain' 1807.
**Bibl:** Bushnell; Bryan; DNB; Delaborde, Engraving and its Processes, with article by his son.

**WALKER, William** **fl 1847-1849**
Leith sculptor. Mainly portraits including 'Alberto Thorwaldsen' RSA 1847 and a vase modelled in the Trustees Academy, RSA 1848.

**WALKER, William ARE** **1878-1961**
Born Glasgow, Nov 19; died Edinburgh, Mar 10. Painter of architectural and topographical subjects; etcher. Studied in Glasgow, London, Paris and Rome. Lecturer in the history of art, Chelsea Polytechnic 1919-21. Elected ARE 1914. Lived in Greenock and London before returning north to live in Stirling, Edinburgh, Callander and finally, Dollar. Exhibited RA(7), RSA(22), RHA(3), AAS 1906-23, NEA(2), L(31) & GI (16). Represented in City of Edinburgh collection (9) including lithographs, stipple engravings and mezzotints.

**WALKER, William T C** **1913-**
Architect. Educated Broughton Secondary, trained Edinburgh College of Art. Winner of the Lorimer award and Keith Prize 1936. In July 1937 was the first-time winner of the Rome Prize in Architecture.

**WALL, Cynthia (Mrs William Birnie) RSW** **1927-**
Watercolour painter and art teacher. Trained Glasgow School of Art 1946-1950. Spent frequent working spells in France. Elected RSW 1971. Exhibited RSA(8), GI(51) & Paisley Institute. Represented in Paisley AG.

**WALLACE, (Mrs) A** **fl 1888**
Painter. Exhibited GI(1) from 4 Newton Place, Glasgow.

**WALLACE, Alastair** **fl 1987**
Edinburgh artist; exhibited AAS from 12 St Mary's Place, Stockbridge.

**WALLACE, Anne Paterson** **1923-**
Born Montrose. Painter in oil and watercolour of landscape. Granddaughter of James P(qv). Attended Perth Academy. After serving with the WRNS during WW2 trained at Chelsea School of Art 1947-50. First solo exhibition in Suffolk 1960. Combined painting with running her own fine art gallery 1960-69. Illustrated J&D Hay *East Anglia by the Sea* (1977). Her work combines immediacy and imaginative decorative invention. Lives in Suffolk. Fond of portraying the moist, misty atmosphere and dark masses of trees and reflected water, all painted against the light in the Constable tradition. Married 1951. Handles the darker colours with great skill and understanding. Exhibits RA.

**WALLACE, Miss Edith E** **fl 1887-1893**
Aberdeen painter of domestic and rustic scenes. Exhibited AAS(3) including 'Guinea pigs' and 'Rabbits feeding', from 47 Waverley Pl.

**WALLACE, Mrs Effie** **fl 1921-1927**
Amateur Perth watercolour painter; exhibited RSW(2) from Hamilton House.

**WALLACE, George** **fl 1667-1693**
Early painter. Son of an Edinburgh painter; apprenticed to John Telfer(qv), herald painter, 1667. Between 1672 and 1677 employed at Holyroodhouse 'grinding oyle collour and laying on the same twyce over upon the two turratts or turnpyck heads on the top of the

leads of the east quarter'. Probably the **George Wallace** employed at Hamilton Palace from 1678 painting windows, cornices, chimney pieces and coats of arms using linseed oil, white lead, lamp black, umber, 'brown red', indigo and verdigris. Also worked at Kinneil Castle. On the Edinburgh register of apprentices 1693.
**Bibl:** Apted 100-101; Hamilton Archives, Lennoxlove, 1678 account f.1/422; 1686 account f.1.548/17; 1692 account HA.479/22/ 59; Mylne, 200.

**WALLACE, Harold Frank** **1881-1962**
Born Mar 21; died Sep 16. Educated Eton and Christchurch College, Oxford. Called to the Bar 1908. Exhibited regularly in London and Scotland, specialising in red deer. In addition to his home in Pelsall, Staffordshire, maintained a home in Glenurquhart, Inverness-shire. An expert stalker, he illustrated numerous articles in black and white on his favourite subject which, set in well painted Highlands scenery, gave them great authority. During WW2 was Deer Controller for Scotland. Held annual exhibitions of stalking pictures in London and Edinburgh, often with Balfour-Browne(qv). Books include *Stalks Abroad* (1908), *The Big Game of Central and Western China* (1913), *Hunting Winds* (1949) and, with Lionel Edwards, *Hunting & Stalking the Deer* (1927). Although his work suffered by comparison to the finer quality of Balfour-Browne and Archibald Thorburn(qv), his knowledge of the Highlands and the accuracy of his animal paintings maintain his popularity, especially among sportsmen. Exhibited RSW(4) & RI(1).
**Bibl:** Wingfield.

**WALLACE, Helen P** **fl 1907**
Exhibited 'Old church, St Monans' at the RSA from 13 Mayfield Gardens, Edinburgh.

**WALLACE, Henry** **fl 1897**
Amateur landscape painter in watercolour. Exhibited a view on Arran at the GI from 257 Saracen Street, Possilpark, Glasgow.

**WALLACE, Miss Isabel H** **fl 1941-1942**
Edinburgh watercolour painter of rural scenes and flower studies. Exhibited GI(4).

**WALLACE, Isabella** **fl 1896**
Amateur flower painter of 3 Crown Circus, Glasgow. Married J Wallace(qv). Exhibited GI(1).

**WALLACE, J** **fl 1893**
Painter and husband of Isabella W(qv) who also exhibited once at the GI in the above year.

**WALLACE, James** **c1880-1937**
Landscape painter from Berwick-on-Tweed who later lived in London and Paisley. Trained Paisley School of Art. Friend of William Barr(qv). Taught clay modelling, Paisley School of Art 1889-c1910. Exhibited RA(5), RSA(5) & GI(5).

**WALLACE, James** **fl 1980**
Renfrewshire landscape artist. Exhibited 'Girvan harbour' GI from Johnstone.

**WALLACE, John** **fl 1801-1866**
Edinburgh portrait painter, also painted figure studies and some landscapes. Exhibited a portrait of the artist 'Rev John Thomson of Duddingston'(qv) 1841 RSA.

**WALLACE, John C(?) ('George Pipeshank')** **1841-1903**
Edinburgh painter in oil and watercolour of portraits, landscapes, coastal scenes, literary subjects and figurative subjects; illustrator. Trained at Trustees Academy under R S Lauder(qv) and John Ballantyne(qv) and Life School, RSA 1865-73, winning prizes for drawing. At first turned his attention to lithography. In 1870 he moved to 11 Melbourne Place where he remained for the rest of his life. Now best known for his golfing pictures. Began an association with the Liverpool tobacco firm Cope Bros 1870, illustrating the engraved title page of Cope's *Tobacco Plant,* replaced 1889 by *The Smoker's Garland* and from 1890 by *Smoke Room Booklets* for both of which Wallace prepared the illustrations. His watercolour 'Saturday Morning, Reiss Golf Club, Wick, Caithness' (1895) sold at auction for £27,000 in the 1980s. This depicts well-known golfing gentlemen of the time including the Mayor and other local dignitaries playing golf with, in the distance, Ackergill Tower, Noss Lighthouse and the ruins of Sinclair and Girnigoe Castles. A similar watercolour, also signed and dated September 1895, sold for slightly less a year previously. Of interest to golfing historians is the fact that the caddy boys are using canvas bags. At about the turn of the century four lithographs were published by Cope Brothers Limited, illustrating parliamentary figures of the time including A J Balfour and the legendary golfer, Tom Morris. The originals were all painted the same size and complements a rare set of 50 cigarette cards distributed by Cope c1900, many illustrated by Wallace. The originals were of identical size making them unique as golfing miniatures. His landscapes were often painted at sunset, sunrise or in moonlight as, for example, 'Loch Achall by moonlight'; 'Rhiddoroch deer forest, Ross-shire' RA, 1901. Used the pseudonym 'George Pipeshank' for many of his golfing items. Illustrated John Galt's *Works* (1895) and M R S Craig's *In Borderlands* (1899). Exhibited RA(3), from 1868 at the RSA(46), RSW(2), L(9) & GI(9). Represented in Liverpool Central Library, Westminster Palace (Smoke Room). (His name sometimes incorrectly appears as Wallis and may be confused with the Newcastle artist John Wallace).
**Bibl:** Bryan; Caw 263; Wingfield.

**WALLACE, Miss Mary** **fl 1970-1974**
Renfrewshire painter and embroiderer. Exhibited GI(3) from Eaglesham.

**WALLACE, Mrs Ottilie (née McLaren)** **1875-?**
Born Edinburgh. Sculptress. Studied under Rodin in Paris. Returned to live in Edinburgh 1901, moving to London 1905. Exhibited 1900-1935 RA(4), RSA(11), RMS(1), GI(2), L(3), SWA(1) & Paris Salon.

**WALLACE, Walter** **fl 1868-1878**
Edinburgh sculptor of portraits in bronze and plaster. Exhibited RA a marble bust 'Mrs Lyon of Appleton Hall' 1873 from his studio at 65 Frederick Street; also RSA(37) including marble and plaster busts of 'Rev Sir Henry Wellwood Moncrieff' 1869, 'The late Sir James Simpson MD' 1871 and 'W.E. Lockhart ARSA' 1876.

**WALLACE, William** **?-1631**
Master mason. Appointed Principal Master Mason to the Crown 1617 and as such was partially responsible for the practice of placing two sets of rooms side by side within the width of a building. This was done in his execution of the King's Lodging at Edinburgh Castle (1615-17) and again in the north quarter of Linlithgow Palace (1618-21). 'An arrangement of this kind, made for more compact plan than the traditional method of placing rooms end to end, while the dividing wall could conveniently be utilised to house the chimney flues, allowing the stacks to be grouped together for decorative effect. (It is also noteworthy) that the north range at Linlithgow is unvaulted and that the ground floor is given over to the living accommodation' [Dunbar]. The conversion into three-dimensional form of the Italianate symmetrical courtyard-plan evidenced by probably the best known building of the early 17th century in Scotland, Heriot's Hospital, was the work of three successive Mastermasons of whom Wallace was the first (his successors being William Ayton(qv) and John Mylne the Younger(qv)). It is probable that the north and west sides of Moray House in Edinburgh (called thus in 1643) were his work. Designed at least the first floor of Heriot's School (1628); the monumental aedicule to John Byres of Coates in Greyfriars churchyard.
**Bibl:** Brydall 47,91; Dunbar 74,93,97,100; Gifford 93,159,179-81,pls 76-7.

**WALLACE, William** **18th Cent**
Builder. Collaborated with his architect son **Lewis Alexander WALLACE** (1789-1861). Worked in Edinburgh New Town, especially in Drummond and Gloucester Places, Heriot Row (1817) and India St (1819).
**Bibl:** Gifford 343,348-50.

**WALLACE, William** **1801-1866**
Born Falkirk; died Glasgow, 8 Jly. Painter of portraits, genre and figurative subjects. Lived in Edinburgh until 1833 then moved to Glasgow. Exhibited RSA(1) 1858 & GI(8). Represented in SNPG(2, both of John Thomson), Glasgow AG ('Annie Laurie').
**Bibl:** Bryan.

**WALLIS, George Augustus** **1770-1847**
Born Merton, Surrey, 15 Feb; died Florence 15 Mar. Born of a Scottish family. Landscape painter much affected by contemporary German art, also dealer in Old Masters. In about 1786 he embarked on a journey through France, Switzerland and Italy with his wife, spending some time in Naples where he appears 1789. However, from 1794 to 1806 he was mostly in Rome where he acquired the pseudonym the English Poussin, in spite of associating mainly with the German painters Carstens and Koch. Painted a number of Ossianic subjects one of which was exhibited at the RA 1807. From then until 1810 was tracking down Old Master paintings in Spain moving then to Heidelberg where he painted a number of landscapes. In 1818 finally settled in Florence becoming a member of the Academy. Both his daughters married German artists. Exhibited RA (16) 1785-1836 including a number of watercolours and drawings. Bryan incorrectly refers to this artist as John William Wallis.
**Bibl:** Bryan; Thieme-Becker; Waterhouse; Whitley 1800-20, 122ff.

**WALLIS, Water Cyril** **fl 1929-1939**
Minor painter of 53 Spottiswood Street, Edinburgh; exhibited RSA(2).

**WALLS, James** **fl 1889**
Amateur painter; exhibited RSA(2) from 18 Queen Anne's Street, Dunfermline.

**WALLS, William RSA RSW** **1860-1942**
Born Dunfermline, Sep 1; died Jun 25. One of six children; son of a Dunfermline miller and Lord Provost of the town three times, and his Braemar wife. After leaving school was apprenticed to a linen draper but soon decided that he wanted to be an artist. Educated Edinburgh Academy. Trained RSA Schools under Hodder. Awarded the Keith prize. Studied two years in Antwerp under Verlat. His career developed at the time of an upsurge of interest in the artistic community for animal painting. At the outset was influenced by Joseph Crawhall(qv) and Edwin Alexander(qv), whose sister he married 1896. While in Antwerp during the early 1880's he paid frequent visits to the zoological gardens and on his return continued the same practice in London and Edinburgh. During this time he first met W.S. McGeorge(qv) who was to become a lifelong friend, and with whom, in 1892, he spent three months sketching and touring Scotland by caravan, being joined by Robert Burns(qv) and Peter Wishart(qv). During this trip he met Andrew Carnegie. The millionaire subsequently commissioned Walls to paint a number of animal portraits as the result of which the artist acquired a country studio at Spinningdale, Sutherland where he spent every summer (except for three war years) between 1905 and 1923. Visited Hamburg Zoo and, with T.H. Gillespie, was one of the founders of the Edinburgh Zoological Gardens. Painted a lot in the English fens as well as in the Scottish Highlands, often in Perthshire and around the Dornoch Firth, establishing a winter studio in Nether Liberton. In his watercolours he tended to use tinted, often rough paper creating highlights with bodycolour, but sometimes with a rich finish and close attention to detail. 'He shows sympathetic and highly skilled craftsmanship...few artists have shown greater appreciation of animal life or of its relationship with its landscape environment' [Hardie]. His earlier work showed a propensity to painting the large cats and occasional parrots, in later life he preferred more conventional domestic animals, especially dogs. In middle life was a renowned teacher at Edinburgh College of Art. Related by marriage to Charles Hodge Mackie(qv). Among his few portraits were 'Provost Walls of Dunfermline' 1897 and his mother (now in the NGS). His last works were among his best, especially 'The End of the Chase' 1905, 'A Kildalton Group' 1906 and his diploma work 'The Wounded Swan' 1908. 'If one might not go so far as to describe them as distinguished or masterly, they are at least remarkably able and accomplished. Drawn with refinement and a vital sense of form, painted with much quiet dexterity but no parade of cleverness, arranged simply and with fine feeling for the relationship between the animals and their landscape environment, and instinct with appreciation of animal life and of its pictorial possibilities, the sum of their qualities is very considerable' [Caw]. One of very few Scottish artists who thought to portray wild animals in their natural habitat. Elected ARSA 1901, RSW 1906, RSA 1914. Exhibited RA(18), RSA(204), RSW(128), RHA(5), GI(98), AAS 1885-1937 & L(27). Represented in NGS (portrait of the artist's mother), Glasgow AG, Kirkcaldy AG, City of Edinburgh collection(2), Brodie Castle (NTS).
**Bibl:** Caw 441-2;; Halsby 171,192,222,286; Hardie III 109; Macmillan [SA] 309; RA Pictures 1896; Studio 1907, 10; 22 (1901) 180; 43 (1908) 137; 68 (1916), 125, 152; 69 (1916) 96.

**WALSH, Thomas** **fl 1962-1974**
Glasgow topographical engraver. Moved c1970 to Bishopbriggs. Exhibited GI(12).

**WALTHEW, Susan Faed** **1827-1904**
Amateur painter. Exhibited RSA(1) from Ardmore, Gatehouse of Fleet. Her sister Louise W was also an artist, though lived and exhibited in England.

**WALTON, Allan** **fl 1944**
Glasgow-based painter. Exhibited GI(1).

**WALTON, Cecile (Mrs Eric Robertson)** **1891-1956**
Born Glasgow, Mar 22; died Edinburgh, Apr 26. Painter in oil and watercolour, sculptor and illustrator. Daughter of Edward Arthur W(qv). Studied in London, Edinburgh, Paris and Florence. Won the RSA Guthrie Award. After graduation became a member of the Edinburgh Group (with Barclay, Sutherland, Dorothy Johnstone and Spence Smith). Lived in Edinburgh for some years before moving to Cambridge and then back to Edinburgh. Her first exhibits at the RSW 1909 were illustrations from Hans Christian Andersen and Tannhauser's *Farewell.* John Duncan introduced her to the symbolist movement. In 1911 she illustrated *Andersen's Fairy Tales,* work showing the strong influence of Jessie King(qv). Later, after her marriage in 1914 to Eric Robertson(qv), she fell under the sway of John Duncan(qv) and Caley Robinson(qv) as shown in her illustrations for *Polish Fairy Tales* (1920), begun in France when her husband was serving in the Friends' Ambulance Unit, 21 of the originals being included in the Edinburgh Group's exhibition of 1921. This followed a successful exhibition of the reconstituted Group in 1919. After the breakdown of her marriage in 1923 she moved to Cambridge, working with Tyrone Guthrie on theatre designs and, returning to Edinburgh, worked for children's radio. In 1949 she wrote and illustrated (with E Robertson) *The Children's Theatre Book* (Black). Resumed painting in the late 1940's but without the success of her earlier years. Exhibited RA(6), RSA(46), RSW(5), RBA(1), GI(11) & L(19). Represented Edinburgh City collection, Liverpool AG, Dunedin AG (NZ).
**Bibl:** Caw 450; Hardie 142-3; Halsby 193-195,220; John Kemplay, The Two Companions, Edinburgh 1991; Macmillan [SA] 294,331 et passim in ch xix; Jessica Walker, 'Cecile Walton and Dorothy Johnstone', Studio 88, (1924) 80-87; Horne 433; Peppin; The Times *obit.* 26 Apr 1956.

**WALTON, Constance (Mrs W H Ellis) RSW** **1865-1960**
Born Glasgow. Flower painter in watercolour of flowers and occasional landscapes. Sister of Edward Arthur(qv), Helen(qv), Hannah More(qv), George(qv) and Richard W(qv). Trained in Paris but spent most of her early life in Glasgow before moving to Milngavie after marrying William Henry Ellis 1896. Whereas her work before she was married was figurative, after her marriage she became almost exclusively interested in painting flowers which she did with great decorative effect. Elected RSW 1887. Exhibited RA(2) 1886-7, RSW(93), GI(98) 1883-1947 throughout, AAS 1885-1890 & occasionally L(6), from 5 Belmont Terrace.
**Bibl:** Burkhauser 166, 224; Halsby 286.

**WALTON, Edward Arthur RSA PRSW HRWS** **1860-1922**
Born Glanderston House, Renfrew, Apr 15; died Edinburgh, Mar 18. Painter in oil and watercolour; landscape, portraits and genre. Son of an amateur painter. Father of Cecile W(qv). When 17 he had a spell at Dusseldorf Academy before enrolling at Glasgow School of Art at the time Fra Newbery(qv) was in charge. He formed a lasting friendship with Guthrie(qv) and Crawhall(qv), whose sister married Walton's brother, these together becoming the focal point, in personal terms, of the Glasgow School. The three began working at Roseneath sending many exhibits to the GI; also painted at Brig o' Turk in the Trossachs, where George Henry(qv) first joined the group. Walton's first exhibit, a landscape painted in Germany, was shown at the GI 1878. In these formative years he was painting with many friends in different parts of the country, reflecting his own congenial

temperament and personality - it was said that he was the only one of Whistler's aquaintances with whom the latter never quarrelled. He painted in Stonehaven with W I MacGregor(qv), with Guthrie in Lincolnshire, at Ballantrae with J D Taylor(qv) and in Surrey with A K Brown(qv). In 1883 he and Guthrie spent the summer at Cockburnspath where they were joined by Crawhall and Whitelaw Hamilton(qv) and the next year Henry(qv), Melville(qv) and Corsan Morton(qv) also came. At an early age his watercolours had earned the respect of the RSW who elected him a member 1885, impressed equally by his intimate English country landscapes as by the clarity and colour of his Clydeside views. In 1886 he established a studio at Cumbuskenneth and at about the same time joined the New English Art Club. Four years later, in the company of Melville and Sargent, he visited Paris. From 1894 to 1904 he was in London becoming a friend and neighbour of Whistler, while spending several holidays with the Newbery family at their home in Suffolk. Returned to Scotland 1904, elected RSA the same year and settled in Edinburgh, although continuing to travel regularly. In 1907 he and Guthrie went to Algiers and Spain and in 1913, once more with Guthrie, visited Brussels and Ghent. During WWI he was in Galloway, the countryside of which became an increasing source of inspiration. Elected President, RSW 1914, remaining in post until his death. Like others of the Glasgow School, his prime concern was decorative quality, achieved by careful design and balanced tones. Although first and foremost a landscape painter, he enjoyed a reputation as a portraitist, especially for his sympathetic portrayal of children. If at times these may have been over-sentimental, lacking the vigour of Guthrie or Lavery, their colour and tone are always superb. Noted for his skilful depiction of hands. Often his landscapes were enlivened by figures or animals. 'Bravura of any kind seems to have been anathema to Walton, who worked hard throughout his life to refine his vision and talent, rather than to expand them to the limits of his capacity or beyond. What is certain is that Walton's work, more than that of any of the other [members of the School], remained unspoiled by success and fame' [Oliver]. Elected NEA 1887, RP 1897, ARSA 1889, RSA 1905, RSW 1885. President of the RSW 1915. Contributed to *The Yellow Book* (1895-1897). Exhibited RA (12), RSA, RSW, GI 1878-1921 throughout and posthumously 1922-87, & AAS 1885-1921. Represented in NGS, SNPG(3), Aberdeen AG, Dundee AG, Glasgow AG, Kirkcaldy AG, Gracefield AG (Dumfries), Edinburgh City collection(3), Lillie AG (Milngavie), Leeds AG, Budapest AG, Ghent AG, Karlsruhe AG, Munich AG, Pittsburgh AG, Venice AG.
**Bibl:** AJ 1894, 77f; 1906, 312ff; Billcliffe 44-53, 106-8, 126-137, 202, 215-216; Bourne Fine Art,'E A Walton', (Ex Cat Edinburgh 1981, Text by Martin Forrest); Caw 370-3 et al; Halsby 138-141 et passim; Hardie 85-7 et passim ch vi; Houfe; Irwin 389-390 et al; Macmillan [SA] 255,259,264,274 et passim ch xv-xvii; Fiona MacSporran, Edward Arthur Walton, Glasgow 1987; SAC, 'Oliver', (Ex Cat 1968); Studio 25 (1902) 207ff; 26 (1902-3) 161-170; 58 (1913) 260-270; 87 (1924) 10-16; Special No 1917.

**WALTON, Ellen** **fl 1906**
Minor Edinburgh painter; exhibited RSA(1) from 7 Bedford Park.

**WALTON, George** **fl 1883-1899**
Artist and designer. Son of Edward Arthur(qv), brother of Cecile W(qv). Began life as a bank clerk. Designed the furniture and fittings for several of the progressive tea-rooms organised by Catherine Cranston. Established a reputation as an ecclesiastical and house decorator, later undertook work for a number of important business and private patrons including stained glass windows for William Burrell and a series of shop interiors for Kodak. In 1897, after various wanderings, settled in London. Exhibited RA(11) & GI(11).
**Bibl:** Irwin 402.

**WALTON, Hannah More** **1863-1940**
Born and died Glasgow. Sister of Edward Arthur W(qv). Miniature painter and painter on china and glass. Shared a craft studio in Glasgow with her sister Helen(qv). Exhibited GI(3) from 2 Bothwell Terrace, Hillhead. Represented in Glasgow AG.
**Bibl:** Burkhauser 166, 224; Halsby 286.

**WALTON, Helen** **1850-1921**
Born Cardross. Painter of genre and portraits, also ceramic designer and decorator. Member of the Walton family of artists. She and her sister, Hannah More W(qv), shared a studio in Glasgow. Taught ceramic design and decoration at Glasgow Art School 1893-1904, and worked often in collaboration with her sister in the production of finely detailed glassware with hand-painted insects, figures and flowers. Exhibited RSA(3) & GI(9) including 'Cecile Walton' and 'Jessie M King'. Represented in Glasgow AG.
**Bibl:** Burkhauser 166, 224.

**WALTON, Jackson** **1808-1873**
Landscape painter in oil. Painted on glass and board as well as on canvas. Scion of the Walton family of painters, father of Edward Arthur(qv), Constance(qv) and George(qv), grandfather of Cecile(qv) and great-grandfather of Edward W(qv). His oldest child Richard married Joseph Crawhall's sister Judith, while his two female grandchildren married respectively Eric Robertson(qv) and Sir William Oliphant Hutchison(qv).

**WALTON, Michael K** **fl 1969-1975**
Penicuik painter; exhibited RSA(5).

**WALTON, W G** **fl 1875**
Glasgow landscape painter. Exhibited 'Loch Long from Arrochar' at the GI from Hillsborough Sq.

**WANDESFORD, James Buckingham** **1817-1872**
Born Scotland; died San Francisco. Painter in oil and watercolour of portraits and portrait miniatures, occasional landscapes and flower studies; also sawmill operator. Emigrated to Ontario 1847 remaining there until the mid-1850s when he moved to New York remaining there five years before moving on to California during the gold rush. Elected first President of the San Francisco Art Association 1872 and died shortly afterwards. In the early days in Canada won many prizes with his watercolour portraits, landscapes and flower studies. Well-known locally as a painter of miniatures on ivory. When the mill failed he took to full-time painting of portraits, working them up from photographs if the subject was unavailable. An unsigned portrait, 'Col Thomas Talbot', an aristocratic Squire of Talbotville on Lake Eerie, is attributed to Wandesford. Later became an itinerant in New York State. At Eldon House, London, Ontario there is a large collection of his Victorian ladies with their hair hanging in ringlets and painted with some slight depth of character.

**WANDLESS, Andrew** **fl 1871**
Dundee painter; exhibited 'Girl vending artificial flowers' at the RSA.

**WANDS, Charles** **fl 1800-1829**
Glasgow engraver. Engraved a 'Head of St. Peter,' after Rubens, also topographical works. Exhibited RSA(4) 1828-9.
**Bibl:** Bushnell.

**WANDS, William** **fl 1833-1835**
Edinburgh painter of genre and figurative subjects; exhibited RSA(3).

**WANE, Marshall** **19th Cent**
Portrait painter and photographer who worked in Edinburgh. A portrait of 'James Watt, Provost of Leith' is in Edinburgh City collection.
**Bibl:** James Campbell Irons, Leith and its Antiquities from the Earliest Times to the Close of the Nineteenth Century, vol 2, 535(illus).

**WARBURTON, Miss Joan** **1920-**
Edinburgh painter. Studied in the studio of the Belgian artist Oswald Poreau and at the East Anglian School of Painting. Served in the WRENS and in an arms factory during WW2. First exhibited Women's International Art Club. Closely associated with Herbert Morris. Later exhibited RSA.

**WARD, Gordon** **fl 1986-**
Cheltenham-based painter. Exhibits still life and topographical works at the RSA.

**WARD, James** **fl 1963-1986**
Edinburgh artist of flowers and landscape; exhibited RSA(7).

**WARD, Miss Mary** **fl 1974**
Lanark embroiderer. Exhibited GI(1).

**WARDEN Peter Campbell** **fl 1978-1983**
Dumfriesshire painter and engraver. Mostly biblical themes. Exhibited RSA(11) & GI(4) from Moffat.

**WARDLAW, Miss Jacqueline** **fl 1973-1975**
Bearsden sculptress. Exhibited three works in ciment fondu at the GI.

**WARDROP, Hew Montgomery** **1856-1887**
Edinburgh architect. Son of James Maitland(qv), he succeeded to his father's practice in 1884, taking Rowand Anderson(qv) and G. Washington Browne(qv) as partners and Robert Lorimer(qv) as an apprentice. Lorimer often recalled a remark Wardrop once made to him 'there are three things of vital importance in architecture, the first is proportion, the second is proportion and the third is - proportion'. In spite of his early death Wardrop had a marked influence on the development of Scottish domestic architecture, especially through his pupil Lorimer who christened his second son after him. One of the few recorded works to survive is the half-timbered Place of Tilliefour (Aberdeenshire), completed by Lorimer.
**Bibl:** Gifford 579,623; Peter Savage, Lorimer and the Edinburgh Craft Designers, Edinburgh 1980, 4,5,39,169.

**WARDROP, James Maitland** **1824-1882**
Architect. Follower of David Bryce and father of Hew Montgomery W(qv). Entered into partnership first with Thomas Brown(qv) and subsequently with Charles Reid(qv). His two best known designs are the well proportioned Callendar House (Stirlingshire) 1869-77 and Beaufort Castle (Invernessshire) 1880-2. Responsible for major internal alterations to Minto House (Roxburghshire) 1859. His own home in Forbes Rd, Edinburgh is not without interest (c1865).
**Bibl:** Dunbar 162-3; Gifford 621; Peter Savage, Lorimer and the Edinburgh Craft Designers, Edinburgh 1980, 4,93,169.

**WARE, Miss Armyne** **fl 1931-1942**
Edinburgh painter and engraver. Had a versatile approach including flora and fauna, landscape, topography; also an etcher. Moved to Gloucester 1940. Exhibited RSA(19) including an etching 'Rievaulx Abbey' 1942.

**WARE, Harry Fabian** **fl 1932-1942**
Edinburgh painter and engraver. Executed similar compositions to Armyne W(qv) and worked from the same addresses. Exhibited RSA (18) including an etching of 'Stonehenge' 1942.

**WARMER, Miss A C** **fl 1872**
Edinburgh painter; exhibited 'Through the wood' at the RSA.

**WARNEUKE, Mrs Amy J** **fl 1893-1909**
Minor painter of portrait miniatures. Daughter of John Glover, Glasgow scenery painter. Exhibited GI(8), originally from Glasgow, then from Milngavie and latterly from 60 Lauderdale Gardens, Hyndland.

**WARRACK, Harriet G** **fl 1887-1892**
Painter in watercolour of landscape, interiors and flowers. Lived in Montrose in the late 1880's before moving to St Andrews. Exhibited RSA(5) & AAS(6), latterly from 113 North St, St Andrews.

**WARREN, Miss Kathleen M** **fl 1876-1884**
English painter, in oil and watercolour of portraits, landscape and game studies. Settled in Edinburgh c1886. Exhibited RSA(5) including an interesting view of the 'Broch of Borwick in course of excavation, Orkney' 1883; also in the provinces.

**WARRENDER, Thomas** **fl 1673-1713**
Born Haddington. Son of John W who was a burgess of the town. Apprenticed to John Tait, a painter whose work is now unknown. Became a burgess and guild brother of Edinburgh on 17th August, 1692. In 1696 was working at Hamilton Palace painting bedchambers with imitation marbling, garlands of fruits and flowers, etc., also Cramond Kirk where he was commissioned by Lady Margaret Hope to decorate the Hope monument 1697, and Craigie Hall, painting the Order of the Thistle on the Marquess of Annandale's coach 1698-1705. Later was at Hopetoun where he received £171 Scots for painting the panels of the Countess's bedchamber in 'fyne landscape work of walnut tree collour in oyll and the styles Japand on'. In 1704 painted an gilded 28 batons belonging to the constable of Edinburgh. After 1710 his son John maintained the family tradition. A still-life now in the NGS (purchased in 1900) is the only work known to have survived. This is an extraordinarily accomplished painting (illustrated as pl 44 in Holloway, 61) containing a coded political message. It is a trompe de l'oeil, itself unusual for the period, adding to the mystery which surrounds this interesting artist. Had as apprentices **William HOGG** 1695 and **William LAUDER**, who joined him 1698.
**Bibl:** Apted 101-2; Edinburgh Burgh Records, 1701-1718, 95; Edinburgh Register of Apprentices, 94, 47; Foulis Account Book, 210; Hamilton Archives, Lennoxlove, F1/691/21; Holloway 61-2, 148-9; Macmillan [SA] 78,85; Marshall, Days of Duchess Anne, 203, 205; Roll of Edinburgh Burgesses 512.

**WARRILOW, David Ross** **fl 1976-**
Glasgow-based painter of still life and flower pieces, colourful and semi-abtract. Exhibits RSA since 1984 & GI since 1976, from 18 Botanic Crescent, Glasgow.

**WASHINGTON, G** **fl 1873-1875**
Edinburgh artist; exhibited an oil painting 'Falconers in a landscape' at the RSA 1875 and 'Arab Horsemen crossing a Ford' at the GI 1873.

**WATANABE, Miss Musme** **fl 1923-1940**
Edinburgh-based artist and printmaker. Settled in Edinburgh exhibiting mainly watercolours and coloured woodcuts at the RSA(2), RSW(2), GI(8), AAS(2) & L(2) from 87 Shandwick Place.

**WATERLOW, Miss Hinemoa (Mrs Thomas)** **fl 1923-1934**
Painter of portrait miniatures, generally on ivory. Probably a Londoner who settled in Edinburgh in the early 1930's from where she exhibited RA(1), RSA(1), RBA(4) & SWA(1).

**WATERS, David B** **fl 1887-1910**
Edinburgh artist. Moved to London c1895. Exhibited RA(1) & RSA(2).

**WATERS, John** **fl 1866**
Glasgow amateur landscape painter. Exhibited 'A Highland loch' GI, from York St.

**WATERS, June L** **fl 1978-**
Aberdeen-based artist, exhibited at the AAS(3) but exhibits no longer. Lives at 141 N Deeside Rd, Milltimber.

**WATERSON, David RE** **1870-1954**
Born Brechin; died Brechin Apr 12. Trained Edinburgh College of Art, becoming a full-time artist 1890. After constructing his own press and teaching himself the art of etching, he sent examples to Seymour Haden, then President of the Royal Society of Painter-Etchers and Engravers. Haden responded "Here at last is genius". In 1901, at the Society's annual exhibition, Waterson's work was warmly acclaimed and, as a direct result, the British Museum requested a portfolio of 70 etchings for their own collection. Shortly afterwards there began a long association with a number of prosperous clients in Sweden, including King Gustav who became a personal friend. In addition to the use of mezzotint for original composition, Waterson executed coloured etchings, fine pastoral drawings (often when the weather was too intemperate for the use of watercolours) and delicate watercolour drawings. Also undertook commissions for portraits and in later life became increasingly interested in lettering and illumination. Among work in this metier was the Address from the people of Angus to Lady Elizabeth Bowes-Lyon, now the Queen Mother, on the occasion of her marriage. Another example was the beautiful 'Lockit Book' containing the roll of the Freemen of Brechin, an honour later accorded the artist himself. His portrait of 'Lord Dalhousie', sometime Governor General of Canada, adorns Brechin Castle with a copy by the same hand in Government House, Ottawa. A quiet, shy man he lived all his life in his beloved Brechin. Elected ARE 1901, RE 1910. Exhibited RSA (14), RE(89), AAS 1894-1910 & L(3). Represented in SNPG (the north-east composer 'James Scott Skinner').
**Bibl:** Houfe; R W Stewart, Scottish Field, November 1954; Studio, 34, 1905, 346-348 (illus).

**WATERSTON, Dorothea** **fl 1914-1935**
Edinburgh watercolour painter; exhibited RSA(3) & RSW(3).

**WATERSTON(E), John** **fl 1846-1866**
Prolific Edinburgh landscape painter in oil; often unsigned and exhibited anonymously. Most favoured subjects were in the Borders, Perthshire and around Loch Lomond. Exhibited RSA(78) & Roslin Castle at the GI 1865.

**WATERSTON, William** **fl 1885-1886**
Edinburgh watercolour painter particularly of tree studies; exhibited RSA(2).

**WATERSTONE, Josiah John** **fl 1902**
Obscure Edinburgh painter; exhibited RSA(1) from 10 Claremont St.

**WATKINS, Dudley Dexter** **1907-1969**
Born Nottingham; died Broughty Ferry, Aug 20. Illustrator and painter in oil and watercolour of landscapes; also teacher. Although English he spent most of his working in life in Scotland where he achieved the work for which he has become best known. Showed great talent at an early age being featured in the *Children's Newspaper* 1918 when only 11 years old. After training at Nottingham School of Art 1925 he moved to Dundee to join the publishing firm of Thomson-Lang (later known as D C Thomson and Co). There he combined illustrations for various publications with teaching life drawing at Dundee College of Art. Burst on the scene in 1934 with his creation of the characters 'The Broons' and 'Oor Wullie'. Acquired a large property in Broughty Ferry and from there poured out a continuous stream of brilliant, rapidly drawn comic characters including 'Desperate Dan', 'Lord Snooty', 'Wullie', 'Ginger', 'Tom Thumb', etc. Active supporter of the Church of Christ and a lay preacher given to providing children with religious chats illustrated with his own cartoons. Illustrated for the *World Evangelistic Crusade* and *The Adventures of William the Warrior.* Occasionally painted easel work, generally landscape, but the results were not good. Exhibited at Nottingham AG where he showed 25 works before travelling to Scotland 1925, after which time no more work was formally exhibited.
**Bibl:** Scotsman, 14.6.1975.

**WATKINS, Robert A** **fl 1965**
Fife painter of local scenery; exhibited RSA(1) from East Wemyss.

**WATLING, Thomas** **1762-c1810**
Painter in oil, watercolour, pen and wash. Believed to have been born in Dumfries where he was baptised on 19 Sept 1762 and where he was a coach painter. Orphaned in early childhood, brought up by an unmarried Dumfries lady (Marion or May Kirkpatrick) who in 1790 was 'nearly 50'. In 1788 he was transported to Australia for forging guinea notes of the Bank of Scotland. On the journey he played an important part in a mutiny. To judge from his work he appears to have been professionally trained and he either taught or offered to teach drawing. At his trial a document was produced reading 'Ladies and Gentlemen taught drawing at Watling's Academy. Admission per month One Guinea'. He had received a good education and from his subsequent work it is clear that he had absorbed a great deal of the romantic sentiment current at the time. Arrived Sydney in October and remained in the colony until at least 1796 at which time he received a conditional pardon. During the period of his conviction he made many drawings of birds, indigenous people and views of the settlement. These were commissioned by such local notables as John White the Surgeon-General, and David Collins, the Judge Advocate. Some of his drawings are in the BM (Natural History), while many of his letters home were published in *Letters from an Exile at Botany Bay,* to his Aunt in Dumfries (Penrith, c1794). Painted local scenes especially old and gnarled trees, winding mountain paths, peasant cottages, jagged and rocky cliffs, in the romantic mode. He wrote to his aunt 'I confess that were I to select and combine, I might avoid that sameness, and find engaging employment. Trees wreathing their old fantastic roots on high; dissimilar intent in foliage; cumbent, upright, fallen or shattered by lightning, may be found at every step; whilst sympathetic blues of twilight, glimmering groves, and wildest nature lulled in sweet soft repose, might much inspire the soul'. Some of his views and drawings of natives were illustrated and re-engraved by Edward Dayes for Collins's *Account of the English Colony in New South Wales* (1798-1802). Watling had plans to publish his own book but this came to nothing. His drawings were used to illustrate George Shaw's *Zoology of New Holland,* J.E. Smith's *Specimen of the Botany of New Holland,* John Latham's *Second Supplement to the General Synopsis of Birds* and the same author's *Index Ornithologicus* (1801). In 1796, having received his pardon, it is possible he travelled home via Calcutta where in 1801 and 1803 there is recorded a miniature painter of the same name. But by 1804 he was definitely back in Dumfries for that year he was alleged to have again forged £5 notes, a charge found 'not proven'. Nothing is known of his subsequent history. He occupies an important place as one of the first artists to record the growth of Australia and to combine topographical view with picturesque landscape. Represented by 'A Direct North General View of Sydney Cove...in 1794' now in the Dixson Galleries, Sydney, while 'Historic View of the West Side of Sydney Cove' is in BM.
**Bibl:** H S Gladstone 'Thomas Watling Limner of Dumfries', Trans of the Dumfries and Galloway Natural History and Antiquarian Society, 3rd ser xx (1935-6), 70-133, 225; B Smith, Australian Painting 1788-1970, 11-15; T Watling, Letters from an Exile at Botany Bay to his Aunt in Dumfries.

**WATSON, A** **fl 1869-1875**
Leith-based painter of local topography and figures; moved to Elder St, Edinburgh c1870. Exhibited RSA(4).

**WATSON, Mrs A E Lindsay** **fl 1899-1901**
Painter. Exhibited RSA(2) from Briary Yards, Hawick.

**WATSON, A R** **fl 1923-1939**
Topographical painter. Exhibited GI(2) from 150 Easterhill St, Tolcross, Glasgow.

**WATSON, Alan G D** **1957-**
Born St Andrews. Painter of sea birds and figure studies under the rubric of social realism. Trained Duncan of Jordanstone College of Art 1976-81. Won many awards including RSA travelling scholarship 1981, SAC Young Artist bursary and the Latimer Award 1985. First one-man exhibition in Edinburgh 1982. In the late 1980s concentrated on depicting the history of whaling in the 19th century, with particular reference to the east coast of Scotland. Exhibited RSA from Auchtermuchty. Represented in Dundee AG, Edinburgh City collection, SAC.

**WATSON, Alexander** **fl 1874**
Edinburgh landscape painter, especially local scenery; exhibited RSA(3) from Balfour St.

**WATSON, Alexander G** **fl 1942-1943**
Edinburgh painter of still life and buildings; exhibited RSA from Colinton.

**WATSON, Alison E F (Mrs Boshell)** **fl 1942-1963**
Glasgow sculptress; exhibited a 'Self-portrait' bust and one other at the RSA; also GI(7), mostly figurative works.

**WATSON, Andrew** **fl 1539-1560**
Heraldic painter. Received payment for working on various banners 1539 and 1541 and in July, 1541 was working for Queen Magdalene from whom he received £5 for 'the painting of five dusan armes'. In 1542 he undertook similar further work for the same patron and later that year was involved in preparing the gilt and coloured banner for the funeral of James V. In 1543 he painted further banners. In 1560 a painter named Andrew Watson, probably the same, was working with John Samson and John Foster for the City of Edinburgh.
**Bibl:** Apted 102; Brydall 53.

**WATSON, Andrew** **fl 1864-1876**
Edinburgh painter in oil and watercolour of figurative subjects and topographical scenes. Exhibited RSA(15).

**WATSON, Andrew** **fl 1917-1925**
Falkirk sculptor; often symbolic pieces eg 'North wind' (1920). Exhibited RSA(1), GI(1) & L(2) from Ingleside, Woodlands.

**WATSON, Annie** **fl 1884**
Minor Glasgow figure; exhibited GI(2) from 11 Belmont Crescent.

**WATSON, Arthur J ARSA** **1951-**
Born Aberdeen. Sculptor and screen printer. Trained Gray's School of Art and obtained a diploma in print making and printed textiles. Received various awards from the SAC. Director of the Peacock Printmakers, Aberdeen before moving to teach at Duncan of Jordanstone College of Art, Dundee. Enjoys the challenge and 'feel' of working with found objects. Inspired by the 'proximity of the north-east coasts and harbours which sustain a lifetime of artistic activity'. His works begin as imagined reconstructions sketched in notebook drawings of old structures observed around his home and the harbour area of Aberdeen. Often uses the same timbers which prompted the original studies. Elected ARSA 1986. Exhibits RSA & AAS. Represented Aberdeen AG, Hunterian AG (Glasgow), Inverness AG, SAC.

**WATSON, Miss B W** **fl 1894**
Morayshire painter of local country scenes; exhibited AAS(1), from 14 North St, Elgin.

**WATSON, C M West** **[see WEST-WATSON, C Maud]**

**WATSON, Cynthia** **fl 1966-1967**
Landscape and topographical painter working from same address as Emmie W(qv). Exhibited AAS(3), from 7 Greenbank, Primrosehill, Cults.

**WATSON, Rev David** **fl 1894-1899**
Amateur watercolour painter; exhibited RSW(1) & GI(2) from 40 Granby Terrace, Glasgow.

**WATSON, Donald** **fl 1944-1959**
Edinburgh-based landscape painter; moved to Castle Douglas, Kirkcudbright 1952. Exhibited landscapes, often with figures, at the RSA including several views on Arran; also GI(12) 1948-1958.

**WATSON, E Vernon** **fl 1938-1939**
Minor Edinburgh watercolourist whose career was cut short by WW2. Exhibited RSW(3) from Wardle Crescent.

**WATSON, Edward** **fl 1869**
Minor watercolourist; exhibited a landscape at the RSA.

**WATSON, Mrs Elizabeth** **fl 1942-1944**
Edinburgh painter of conversation pieces. Exhibited GI(3), from George St.

**WATSON, Miss Emma** **1842-1905**
Born Greenock. Painter in oil of domestic genre, garden scenes and landscapes. Trained Glasgow School of Art 1880-1889. Exhibited 'In a market garden' RA 1895; also RSA(14), RSW(1), GI(31) & L(6), from 183 West George St.

**WATSON, Emmie** **fl 1964**
Aberdeenshire painter, probably sister of Cynthia W(qv). Exhibited AAS(2) from Primrosehill, Cults.

**WATSON, Fred** **fl 1990**
Sculptor. Exhibited RSA(2) from the Scottish Sculpture Workshop, Lumsden, Aberdeenshire.

**WATSON, George** **c1680-1742**
Early painter. Apprenticed to George Porteous the painter 1694 when said to be 14. In 1709 he became Burgess of Edinburgh and from 1713-43 took as painter apprentices John Couper 1713, Hugh Ure 1717, Alexander Fraser 1736 and Thomas Cochrane 1743. Member of the Incorporation of St Mary's 1713-42.
**Bibl:** Apted 102; Roll of Edinburgh Burgesses 211; Register of Edinburgh Apprentices.

**WATSON, G L** **1851-1904**
Marine artist; also yacht designer and illustrator. Son of a Glasgow physician. Started life as a draughtsman with the Lancefield Shipyard on the Clyde. After an apprenticeship lasting three years he joined A & J Ingles as a yacht designer at their Point House Yard. In 1872 entered business on his own account. A superb draughtsman of racing craft.
**Bibl:** Wingfield.

**WATSON, George PSA** **1767-1837**
Born Overmains, Berwickshire; died Edinburgh, Aug 24. Portrait painter in oil. Son of John Watson of Overmains and Frances Veitch of Elliott, wealthy landowners. Father of William Smellie W(qv) and uncle of Sir John Watson-Gordon(qv). Received some instruction from Alexander Nasmyth before travelling to London when he was 18, studying for two years under Sir Joshua Reynolds. On returning to Scotland he set up as a portrait painter on his own account in Edinburgh and married Rebecca Smellie, eldest daughter of one of the founders of the Scottish Society of Antiquaries. Became the first President of the Society of Scottish Artists, remaining in office until 1812, also first President of the fifteen artists who inaugurated the Scottish Academy. Throughout most of his professional life he was virtually an understudy to Raeburn but as his careeer developed, his likeness to Reynolds and his attempted emulation of Raeburn lessened. He left many excellent portraits of leading figures of the time. The portrait of his father-in-law c1795 in the SNPG is 'a laboured attempt to copy Raeburn's broad and simple efforts' [Caw]. One of his best works is his impressive 'Self-portrait' and another his portrait of 'Benjamin West' 1821 in NGS. These obtained a degree of dignity which 'in combination with the reticence which belonged to the current convention, made his better things look distinguished and sincere' [Caw]. His handling was heavier than Raeburn's, the brush strokes less sure, the tone duller and the colour less interesting. On account of the favourable impression made at the Academy, he was invited to London c1815 where he painted portraits of the 'Dean of Canterbury', 'Lord and Lady Combermere' and a duplicate of his portrait of 'Sir Benjamin West' sent to the Academy of Art in South Carolina. Other portraits of note are 'Alexander Skirving' (NGS) and 'Dr Alexander Wood', now at the Royal College of Surgeons, Edinburgh. Elected RSA 1826, PSA 1826-1837. Exhibited RA(21) 1808-1823 including 'The Young Chevalier' 1817 and 'Sir Ewan Macgregor, Chief of the Clan' 1823; also RSA(141). Represented NGS, SNPG(8), Kirkcaldy AG, Edinburgh City collection.
**Bibl:** Armstrong 17; Brydall 228; Caw 79-80; Gaunt 239, pl 16; Irwin 215-216; McKay 105-8; Macmillan [SA] 160,162.

**WATSON, George** **fl 1873**
Edinburgh painter; exhibited RSA(1) from Hope St.

**WATSON, George Cuthbert** **fl 1921-d1965**
Landscape, portrait and still life painter in oil, gouache and watercolour. Taught Dunfermline HS and Trinity Academy, Edinburgh. Founder member of the 1922 Group(qv). Exhibited RSA(40), RSW(1), GI(8) & L(1), formerly from Dunfermline and latterly Edinburgh.

**WATSON, George Mackie** **1859-1948**
Edinburgh architect. Articled to Rowand Anderson(qv) becoming his chief assistant. Worked on McEwan Hall, Edinburgh and designed Bardrochat, Ayrshire, for the McEwan family; also Coldstream Lodge, Merchiston (1900); St Cerf, Granton (1901) and St James Church, Portobello (1910-12). Became first teacher of architecture in the School of Applied Art. Exhibited design for St James' church, Rosefield Pl, Portobello at the GI 1927.
**Bibl:** Gifford 502,602,650; Peter Savage, Lorimer and the Edinburgh Craft Designers, Edinburgh 1980, 23,169.

**WATSON, George Patrick Houston RSW** **1887-1960**
Born Edinburgh. Painter in watercolour, also architect. Trained Edinburgh College of Art. Married Elizabeth Isabelle Armour(qv). Painted delicate watercolours using pencil outlines with a light touch. Generally favoured landscapes, also figure studies. Elected RSW 1938. Exhibited RA(1), RSA(26), RSW(19), GI(49), AAS(5), L(6) & Paris Salon, latterly from 5 Morningside Pk.
**Bibl:** Halsby 287.

**WATSON, Homer Ransford RCA** **1855-1930**
Born Doon, Ontario, Canada; died Ontario, May 30. Landscape painter in oils. For the most part self-taught although when visiting Britain became associated with Sir George Clausen and E.J.Gregory. Worked in his native Doon but frequently visited Europe, the first time in 1887. Elected RCA 1882. In technique he has been likened to Daubigny and Rousseau. His development can be traced through several periods: early meticulous attention to detail, more solid naturalism and, during the last ten years of his life, a strong accent on

colour. Attracted to the fishing villages of Fife, in 1889 exhibited 'The village by the sea' at the RA 1889 when living and working from Charles St, Pittenweem; also GI(7) 1889-1903. Represented in Nat. Gall. of Canada (Ottawa), Montreal AG, a small museum dedicated to his memory in Doon, Ontario.
**Bibl:** Donald W Buchanan (ed), Canadian Painters, 1945, 6-7, plts 6,7.

**WATSON, Irene** **fl 1966-1970**
Aberdeen painter of flora, especially trees, and still life; exhibited AAS(5) from 14 Burnieboozle Place.

**WATSON, J Hannan** **fl 1892-1908**
Glasgow painter of landscape and country subjects who moved a number of times, to Houston, Renfrewshire 1899 and subsequently to Ochilnan, Gargumnock, Stirling before returning to Glasgow. Exhibited RSA(2), AAS(3), GI(28) & L(1).

**WATSON, J Hardwick** **fl 1885-1888**
Edinburgh painter; exhibited RSA(3) & GI(2).

**WATSON, James** **fl 1747-c1790**
Early painter. Son of an Edinburgh brewer. Apprenticed 1747 to John Reoch and made a Burgess of Edinburgh in 1768 and a member of the Incorporation of St Mary's. Elected Guild brother of Edinburgh 1788. During his career he took on a number of apprentices, among them Thomas Wilson 1778, David Alexander 1782, William Mellis 1782, Thomas Home 1786 and John Reid 1790. Little is known of his work although some engravings on glass at The Binns, Linlithgow (NTS) may have been by him.

**WATSON, James** **fl 1910-1932**
Landscape painter in watercolour, also teacher. Head, art department at Morgan Academy, Dundee. Painted landscapes and figure studies in France, Spain and Scotland in a manner reminiscent of Melville(qv). Exhibited RSA(11), RA(1), AAS(4), GI(8) & L(5), latterly from 28 Ward Rd, Dundee.
**Bibl:** Halsby 287.

**WATSON, James A** **fl 1883-1890**
Glasgow landscape painter in oil and watercolour. Lived for some years at 29 High Glencairne St, Kilmarnock. Exhibited RA(1), RSA(2) & GI(2).

**WATSON, Jenny J** **fl 1894**
Glasgow painter. Exhibited 'The Birch Wood' at the GI.

**WATSON, Jessie** **fl 1885-1891**
Minor painter of flowers and genre; exhibited RSA(4) from Wilton Bank, Hawick.

**WATSON, John** **1685-1768**
Born Scotland (probably Edinburgh); died USA, Aug 22. Portrait painter. Emigrated to the American Colonies c1715. Trained Trustees Academy, Edinburgh. Drew and painted members of the Scottish community and others in New Jersey. Portraits recorded by him at the Smithsonian Institute, Washington, include 'William Burnet (1688-1729)', 'James Henderson and Family (b1643)' and 'Tessie Henderson and her children', all dated c1726, and 'Mrs Schuyler (?)', 'Jacobus van Rensselaer (1713-62)' and 'Jan Baptist van Rensselaer (1717-1763)'; also in Phildaelphia AG.
**Bibl:** Benezit; Bryan.

**WATSON, John** **1863-1928**
Amateur painter in oil and watercolour of landscapes, topography, figure subjects and flowers. Watson was a decorative confectioner of national renown, gaining major awards at the London Exhibition and being a respected judge in both England and Scotland. Master baker and for a time chairman of the Ayrshire Master Bakers Association. His greatest delight was painting; it was customary for him to be in the bakehouse at three in the morning until two or three in the afternoon, and then to sketch until dusk. His favourite places were Riccarton, Symington and Kilmaurs. Watson revelled in the nearby countryside, the locals as they toiled in the fields, and the joy of children. In later life he abandoned business to devote himself full-time to painting but surprisingly, and without abandoning his art, returned to the bakehouse. Twice married. Founder member of the Kilmarnock Art Club where he lived all his life. Exhibited GI(12), Paisley & Stirling.

**WATSON, John** **fl 1900**
Aberdeen amateur landscape painter; exhibited AAS(1), from 104 Holburn St.

**WATSON, John** **fl 1940-1946**
Glasgow amateur still life painter. Exhibited GI(3) from Kennoway Drive, latterly from Crathie Drive.

**WATSON, John** **fl 1958**
Stirlingshire landscape painter in watercolour. Exhibited two views of St. Andrews at the GI, from Kilsyth.

**WATSON, John B** **fl 1887-1889**
Minor Glasgow painter. Exhibited RSA(3) & GI(2) from 102 Belgrave St.

**WATSON, Joseph** **fl 1902**
Glasgow amateur painter; exhibited GI(1) from 13 Cromwell Square, Queens Park.

**WATSON, Mrs L** **fl 1886**
Hawick amateur painter. Exhibited RSA(1) from Leaburn.

**WATSON, Mrs Lena** **fl 1978**
Paisley amateur flower painter. Exhibited 'Shirley Poppies' at the GI.

**WATSON, M** **fl 1887**
Edinburgh painter of portraits and still life; exhibited RSA(2) from Tweedie.

**WATSON, Miss M A E** **fl 1902-1935**
Aberdeen painter of interiors, genre and landscape; exhibited AAS throughout the above period from Broomlee, W. Cults.

**WATSON, Miss M W** **fl 1908-1914**
Possibly an English artist. Living and working in Glasgow during the early 1910s from where she exhibited GI(2), L(7) & SWA(1).

**WATSON, Miss Maggie Petrie** **fl 1908-1921**
Aberdeen flower painter. Exhibited AAS(6) from 543 Holburn St.

**WATSON, Malcolm** **fl 1872-1887**
Glasgow landscape painter in oil. Moved to 49 Grange Road, Edinburgh. Exhibited RSA(3).

**WATSON, Miss Mary** **fl 1869**
Edinburgh landscape and castle painter in oil; exhibited RSA(2).

**WATSON, Miss Mary C S** **fl 1955**
Glasgow watercolourist. Exhibited GI(2), from Cambuslang.

**WATSON, Mary F** **fl 1987**
Aberdeen flower painter; exhibited AAS(4), from 83 Cairnwell Dr.

**WATSON, Mary M** **fl 1932-1935**
Amateur painter of Blairgowrie House, Blairgowrie. Exhibited RSA(2) & RSW(2).

**WATSON, P G** **fl 1888**
Edinburgh amateur painter; exhibited RSA(1) from 16 Charlotte Sq.

**WATSON, Patrick** **fl 1914**
Edinburgh topographical engraver; exhibited GI(1) from 4 Morningside Park.

**WATSON, Robert** **1865-1916**
Architect. Trained in Edinburgh with Paterson and then articled to Hippolyte Blanc(qv) before becoming assistant to Wardrop, Anderson and Browne. Moved to London there embarking on an association with James Maclaren(qv). Later joined William Dunn as a partner in 1890; together they completed Fortingall Inn (1891) and Glenlyon House, Perthshire (1891) after the original architect (Maclaren) died. Robert Lorimer(qv), who became a friend, and Robin Dods(qv) were among their assistants.
**Bibl:** Dunbar 165; Peter Savage, Lorimer and the Edinburgh Craft Designers, Edinburgh 1980, 7,154,169.

**WATSON, Ronald** **fl 1959-1990**
Aberdeen-based painter of country susbjects, flowers, interiors and landscape; moved to Lanark 1977. Exhibited RSA(16), GI(4) & AAS(10) from addresses in Aberdeen, Cove Bay and latterly Hamilton.

**WATSON, Mrs S** **fl 1860**
Edinburgh landscape painter; exhibited 'Rocks on the beach, Dalmeny Pk, Cramond' at the RSA, from Howe St.

**WATSON, Stewart** **fl 1849-1864**
Edinburgh painter in oil of Continental scenes, especially Italian, historical subjects and portraits. Exhibited RSA(13) & GI(5). Represented in NGS.

**WATSON, T** **fl 1819**
Edinburgh painter of figure subjects; exhibited two landscapes at the Old Watercolour Society.

**WATSON, T R Hall** **fl 1890-1914**
Glasgow painter in oil and watercolour. Specialised in landscapes of Scottish scenes. Later lived in London. Exhibited RA(1), RSA(1 from a summer address in Gairloch, Wester Ross), GI(16), LS(11) & L(3).
**Bibl:** Halsby 287.

**WATSON, Thomas A** **fl 1888**
Forfar painter; exhibited GI(1) from St. James's Rd.

**WATSON, Thomas Lennox** **c1850-1920**
Glasgow architect. Apprenticed to James Boucher 166-1871, leaving to work in London with Waterhouse. After a short partnership with **Henry MITCHELL**, he worked mainly on his own, aided by distinguished assistants including W J Anderson(qv). President, Glasgow Institute of Architects 1895. Among his interests was designing the interiors of luxury yachts. From his offices in 108 West Regent St and, after 1895, 166 Bath St, exhibited RA(5) 1890-1900, including offices for the *Glasgow Evening Citizen,* the Church of St. Peter, Drogheda, and 59 Bath St. Also designed Monument in Glasgow Cathedral to the late James Hedderwick LLD RSA 1903 & GI(22) 1871-1918.
**Bibl:** A Gomme & D Walker, Architecture of Glasgow, London 1987(rev), 303.

**WATSON, W F** **fl 1844**
Topographical artist. There is a small red chalk and watercolour drawing of the 'Braid Farm, Edinburgh' in NGS.

**WATSON, Wilhelmina M** **fl 1878**
Edinburgh portrait painter in oil; exhib RSA(1) from Inverleith Row.

**WATSON, William jnr** **fl 1885-1886**
Leith architect and architectural watercolourist; exhibited RSA(2), from Wallis Place, Easter Rd.

**WATSON, William** **fl 1934-1937**
Edinburgh painter; exhibited bird paintings and 'The dead sheep' at the RSA(5).

**WATSON, William F** **fl 1975-**
Aberdeen painter; exhibits AAS from 42 Baxter St.

**WATSON, William Ferguson** **1895-**
Born Glasgow. Painter and journalist. Studied in Leicester and lived there most of his life. Exhibited Nottingham AG(8).

**WATSON, William Smellie RSA** **1796-1874**
Born Edinburgh; died Edinburgh, Nov 6. Portrait and occasional landscape painter. Son of George W(qv). When 19 he went to London and spent five years studying at the RA Schools and a similar period with Wilkie. Enjoyed a fine reputation in Edinburgh and was for some years assistant to Wilkie. Foundation member of the Scottish Academy together with his father. Never studied abroad. Sometimes painted fanciful subjects although these are rare. A keen ornithologist, bequeathed his collection of birds to Edinburgh University museum. His 'Self-portrait' was 'painted with considerable spirit, and in its monotonic scheme, shows more the influence of his cousins than of his father or Raeburn' [McKay]. Elected RSA 1826. Exhibited RA(5) 1816-89, latterly from 70 Charlotte St; also RSA and its predecessors no fewer than 297 works & GI(5). Represented in SNPG, Edinburgh City collection ('Bailie John Macfie - 1783-1852').
**Bibl:** Armstrong 17; Bryan; Caw 90; Irwin 219; McKay 125-6.

**WATSON, William Stewart** **1800-1870**
Place and date of birth unknown; died Nov 18. Obscure painter of portraits and genre. Worked for a time in America but settled finally in Edinburgh at 56 Queen Street. Many subjects were Italian peasants and Italian genre; also other compositions eg 'Installation of His Grace the Duke of Athole as Grand Master of Religious and Military Order of the Templars' 1850. Exhibited RSA(61) 1828-1869, most from Edinburgh but also from Rome 1840 and London 1843-7; also Carlisle Academy 1830. Represented NGS(3), SNPG (Burns).
**Bibl:** Scotsman, 19 Nov, 1870 (obit).

**WATSON, William Thomas** **fl 1883-1893**
Glasgow painter of harbour and winter landscapes. Exhibited GI(5).

**WATSON GORDON, Sir John RA PRSA** **1788-1864**
Born Edinburgh; died Edinburgh, 1 Jne. Painter in oil of historical subjects and portraits. Son of Captain James Watson RN, and nephew of George Watson(qv) first President of the RSA. Assumed the name Gordon in 1826 to distinguish himself from his well-known family. Studied at Trustees Academy under John Graham(qv); at first painted genre and historical subjects but quickly discovered that his talent lay in portrait painting. His early style was closely modelled on Raeburn, a friend as well as a teacher. During the 1820s his work sometimes came close to Raeburn exemplified by the full-length portrait 'John Taylor, Captain of the Honourable Company of Edinburgh Golfers' 1824 still in the company's possession and engraved by Will Henderson 1914 and again by W A Cox 1926. In 1822 painted "The Earl of Hopetoun as Captain General of the Royal Company of Archers', to commemorate the visit of George IV to Edinburgh. The original was later destroyed, but a smaller version is at Hopetoun. After Raeburn's death assumed the mantle of leading Scottish portrait painter. One of the most prolific Scottish artists. Late in his career he evolved a more personal style influenced by his admiration for Velasquez. 'His portraiture, whatever it lacks in brilliance, is simple, sincere, and at its best gravely beautiful' [Caw]. His first exhibit was a scene from *Lay of the Last Minstrel.* Painted men more sympathetically than women. His development was towards the simpler style, beginning in the middle period with 'Lord President Hope', now in the Signet Library (1832). 'There is neither the mosaic-like laying together of planes of Raeburn's early practise nor the rich effusion of his full development; but a method which never quite gets rid of a picturesque incompletion. This is why he succeeds best where the character of his sitter has been well accented by the wear and tear of life, and, for the same reason, he fails as an exponent of the charming grace of womanhood...the monitor and clothing of the period did not help colour; he is said to have mixed bath-brick with his colour and something of the dullness of that material cleaves to his paint. Grasp of character and a pictorial touch were his principal assets' [McKay]. Succeeded Sir William Allan as President of the RSA in 1850 and the same year was appointed Queen's Limner for Scotland, knighted and made an academician. Irwin considers that 'Roderick Gray, Provost of Peterhead', painted for the Governors of the Merchant Maiden Hospital, Edinburgh had 'all the best qualities that had come to be associated with the finest of Scottish portraiture'. This picture was shown in London 1853 and in Edinburgh the following year and received a first class medal at the Paris International Exhibition 1855. Exhibited RA(123) 1827-1864 & RSA(294). Represented by 40 portraits in SNPG, NGS(15), Glasgow AG, Edinburgh City collection, Perth AG, Brodie Castle (NTS), Craigievar Castle (NTS), Haddo House (NTS), Hill of Tarvit (NTS).
**Bibl:** AJ 1850, 373; 1864, 215; 1903, 301-4; BM Cat of Eng Brit Port VI (1925) 489; Bryan; Brydall 229-231; Caw 80-83; Irwin 308-10 et al; Macmillan [SA] 163-4,204,208; Maas; McKay 108-118; Portfolio 1887, 138; Redgrave; Reynolds; Studio, see index.

**WATT, Alastair** **fl 1953-1956**
Glasgow sculptor. Moved to Clarkston, Renfrewshire c1954. Exhibited GI(3).

**WATT, Albert George Fiddes** **1901-1986**
Painter of landscape, mainly of the north-east of Scotland; restorer. Son of George Fiddes W(qv). Lived and worked for many years in London where he combined painting with dealing in art and restoring.

**WATT, Alexander** **fl 1867-1877**
Glasgow architect and part-time painter. Exhibited landscape and flowers at the GI(8).

**WATT, Alison ARSA** **1965-**
Portrait painter. 'Realist painter with an original vision and a fascination with the self-portrait'. Trained Glasgow School of Art 1983-5. First solo exhibition in Glasgow 1986 and RA the same year. Received the first John Player portrait prize 1986 and the following year the Armour prize for still life. Elected ARSA 2003. Commissioned by the NPG to paint 'The Queen Mother' 1989. Represented in NPG.
**Bibl:** Spalding.

**WATT, Daisy** **fl 1939-1940**
Amateur watercolour painter. Sister of Katherine W(qv). Exhibited RSW(4) from Argyll Cottage, Clackmannan.

**WATT, David** **fl 1989-**
Glasgow painter; exhibited two Indian scenes in the modern idiom at the RSA.

**WATT, Elizabeth Mary** **1886-1954**
Born Dundee. Portrait painter (mainly of children), flower pieces, landscape; also potter. Trained Glasgow School of Art 1906-1917. Frequent visitor to Iona. Painted mostly watercolours in the manner of Jessie King(qv) although more coarsely and with less intricacy. Nevertheless, her work is not without interest. Also produced hand-painted wooden boxes and decorated ceramics. Never married. Exhibited RSA(2) & GI(16) from 328 Renfrew Street, Glasgow. Represented in Glasgow AG.
**Bibl:** Burkhauser 185-6 (illus).

**WATT, George Fiddes RSA RP LLD** **1873-1960**
Born Aberdeen 15 Feb; died Aberdeen 22 Nov. Portrait painter in tradition of Dyce, Raeburn and Watson-Gordon, also occasional landscapes and figures subjects. After a short spell working as an apprentice lithographer in Aberdeen he trained Gray's School of Art 1894-1897, developing a friendship with Robert Brough(qv). Proceeded to the RSA Schools in Edinburgh gaining Chalmers Bursary for painting. Became an extremely popular portrait painter, aided by the artistic influence of Sir George Reid(qv). Elected RP 1914, ARSA 1910, RSA 1924. Lived in London for some years but returned to Aberdeen. Among his most famous sitters were 'Lady Stormonth Darling' 1907 and 'Lord Balfour of Burleigh' 1916, painted for the Church of Scotland. 'The Artist's Mother' 1910 was purchased by the Chantrey Bequest 1930. Painted a number of fine landscapes of the River Dee, especially between 1895 and 1900. Exhibited RA(32), RSA(99), GI(26) & L(16). Represented SNPG (3), Glasgow AG(3, including 'Sir William Lorimer'), Aberdeen AG, City of Edinburgh collection(3), Culzean Castle (NTS).
**Bibl:** Caw 392.

**WATT, Gilbert F** **fl 1847-1889**
Aberdeen painter and sculptor. Exhibited portraits and portrait heads at the RSA(6); also a plaster group 'Adam & Eve' at the GI.

**WATT, Hugh** **fl 1851-1854**
Edinburgh sculptor. Exhibited RSA including a bust of 'David Watt', the seal engraver.

**WATT, James RSW RGI** **1931-**
Born Port Glasgow. Painter in oil; marine and coastal scenes. Trained Glasgow School of Art, travelled extensively in France, held his first one-man show in Greenock 1954. For many years he was Principal Art Teacher at St Columba's High School, Greenock. Essentially a winter painter who has been preoccupied for many years with the effects of winter light and winter skies, especially where the industrial Clyde merges with the unspoiled stretches of river. His work is characterised by the use of a very limited dark palette, with strong pattern and a preference for dramatic, apocalyptic skies. Since 1978 has spent his summers on the Faroe Islands, painting local landscapes and each year holding an exhibition in Torshavn. Occasionally painted industrial 'scapes from his studio at 95 Albert Rd, Greenock. Member of the Glasgow Group. Elected SSA 1965, RSW 2002, RGI 2002. Exhibits regularly RSA since 1959, RGI & SSA from 95 Albert Road, Gourock. Represented in Greenock AG, murals in the Town Hall, Port Glasgow, Royal collections.
**Bibl:** James Watt - The Clyde, cat, Oct 1995.

**WATT, James Cromer** **1862-1940**
Aberdeen jewellery designer and enamellist. Exhibited RSA (1902).

**WATT, James George** **1862-c1940**
Aberdeen painter in oil and watercolour of landscapes and coastal scenes; also occasional portraits. Younger son of a local advocate and brother of Mary W(qv). Specialised in local scenes particularly coastal subjects depicting the local fisherfolk and boats of the period. 'A study of a fighting cock' bearing the signature J G Watt made a public appearance at Bonham's, London 1983. Exhibited RSA(5) including 'At the Colonel's Cave, nr Braemar' 1885 and 'Summer Morning on the Dee' 1886; also GI(2) & regularly at the AAS from 1881.

**WATT, Katherine K** **fl 1940-1941**
Painter of flowers and pastoral scenes. Sister of Daisy W(qv). Exhibited RSA(3) & GI(2), from Argyll Cottage, Clackmannan.

**WATT, Malcolm B** **fl 1911**
Hamilton painter in oils. Exhibited 'Hamilton Art Club' 1911 from 7 McDonald St.

**WATT, Mary** **fl 1918-1920**
Minor Aberdeen figure; exhibited RSA(2) from 23 Horsfield Ave.

**WATT, P B** **fl 1843**
Edinburgh landscape painter. Exhibited 'Beach scene', west of Fife at the RSA, from St. James Sq.

**WATT, Stratton** **fl 1943**
Edinburgh painter of portraits and pastorals; exhibited RSA(3) from Blackhall.

**WATT, T Archie Sutter RSW** **1915-**
Born Edinburgh. Painter in oils and watercolour, mainly the latter, landscape and flowers. Trained Glasgow School of Art 1939 and Edinburgh College of Art 1946-49 under Maxwell(qv), Gillies(qv) and MacTaggart(qv). Lived in Galloway where he was deeply involved in local summer schools. Founder member, Glasgow Arts Festival. Elected RSW 1966. Exhibited RSA, GI13) & SSA.

**WATT, T Milne** **fl 1871**
Glasgow landscape painter; exhibited RSA(1).

**WATT, Thomas M B** **fl 1945-1954**
Edinburgh-based painter, moved to Perth 1954. Landscapes and coastal scenes of the east coast. Exhibited RSA(4).

**WATT, William R** **fl 1950-1952**
Lanarkshire painter of topographical watercolours. Exhibited GI(3), from Motherwell.

**WATTERS, Capt James Maclaine** **1847/8-1878**
Edinburgh painter in oil and watercolour of Continental landscapes; exhibited RSA(7). His memory is marked by his gift of the Maclaine Watters medal (see RSA).

**WATTS, C H (Mrs)** **fl 1936**
Minor Edinburgh painter; exhibited RSA(2) from 100 Netherby Rd.

**WATTS, Charles** **1953-**
Born Edinburgh. Painter. Trained Gloucester College of Art 1979-82 and the Royal College of Art 1983-6. On the proceeds of a travelling scholarship visited Berlin 1984 and Madrid 1985. Represented in Cheltenham AG.

**WATTS, Dougal (Dugard)** **fl 1901-1938**
Landscape watercolourist; painted mainly east coast views; exhibited RA 1901 from Boxted, Colchester.

**WATTS, William** **fl 1896**
Edinburgh landscape painter; exhibited a study of Lerwick pier at the AAS, from Nether Liberton.

**WEARNE, Miss Helen** **fl 1874-1885**
Edinburgh watercolour painter of portraits and figure studies; exhibited RSA(8) & AAS(1), latterly from 51 York Place.

**WEATHERHEAD, Isabel** **fl 1876**
Amateur watercolour painter of still-life; exhibited RSA(1).

**WEATHERLEY, Paul E** **fl 1967-1974**
Aberdeen landscape painter, especially of Highland scenes. Exhibited AAS(2), 'Stornoway' and 'Girnock burn', entered from 8 The Chanonry, Old Aberdeen.

**WEBB, Joseph ARE** **1908-1962**
Painter in oil of portraits, also mural decorator, engraver and etcher. Trained Hospitalfield, Arbroath, becoming etching master, Chiswick Art School and Instructor in Painting and Sculpture. His working life was spent in England. Elected ARE 1930. Exhib RA(12), RSA(2), RE(15), RHA(2) & L(1), latterly from Farnham Common, Bucks.

**WEBB, Thomas** **fl 1841-1869**
Edinburgh painter in oil and watercolour of figurative and topographical subjects. Exhibited RSA(22).

**WEBSTER, A H** **fl 1899**
Glasgow amateur landscape painter. Exhibited GI(1) from 134 St Vincent St.

**WEBSTER, Alexander** **1841-1913**
Born Fraserburgh, Dec 21. Painter in oil and watercolour of marine and coastal scenes. House painter and member of a well-known local family of artists, he had seven sons, all artists. Combined his artistic work with the family business. Received many commissions from overseas to paint local scenes. Exhibited RSA(15) & AAS(3).

**WEBSTER, Alexander Jnr** **fl 1893-1911**
Painter of coastal and marine subjects. Eldest son of Alexander W(qv). Continued the family business and painted in oil part-time, though less fluently than his father. Painted a draught screen portraying six local scenes on panel including the old Castle of Cairnbulg. Travelled to New York 1911, returning to Fraserburgh some years later but in 1922 set sail again for Boston after which no further work is recorded.

**WEBSTER, Alfred A** **fl 1906-1913**
Glasgow artist and stained glass window designer. Worked with Stephen Adam jnr(qv) before c1910. Father of Gordon W(qv). Killed on war service. Exhibited GI(3). Represented in St Michael church, Dumfries, and the rich, colourful four-light war memorial in St. Michael, Linlithgow; also three windows in St Anne, Corstorphine (1917) and one window, 'The Beautitudes' (1913), in St Andrew and St George;
**Bibl:** Gifford 45,274,525; Painton Cowen, Stained Glass in Britain, 1985, 230-1,234.

**WEBSTER, Douglas James** **fl 1982-**
Aberdeen artist; trained Gray's School of Art, Aberdeen. Exhibited AAS, latterly from 282 Hardgate.

**WEBSTER, Frederick** **fl 1895-1896**
Fraserburgh painter of marine scenes and landscape in oil and watercolour. Son of Alexander W(qv). Occasionally painted angling scenes which have been favourably compared to those by his better known contemporary John Russell(qv).

**WEBSTER, George** **fl 1864-1907**
Edinburgh painter and sculptor of busts and portrait medallions, sometimes in marble. Prolific worker, among his exhibits were 'Queen Victoria' RSA, 1903, 'Charles Dickens' RSA, 1871, 'William McTaggart RSA' RSA, 1874, 'Waller Hugh Paton RSA', RSA 1876 and 'Hector Chalmers' 1888. Represented among the statues on the Scott Memorial and a portrait medallion by the Fountain, Inverleith Park (c1900). Exhibited RSA(70) & GI(50).
**Bibl:** Gifford 316,575.

**WEBSTER, Gordon MacWhirter** **1908-1987**
Born Fairlie, Ayrshire, Jul 1; died Glasgow, Jan 24. Stained glass artist and designer. Son of Alfred W(qv). Educated Glasgow High School, trained Glasgow School of Art under Douglas Strachan(qv), and abroad. Possessed of a fine sense of colour, in his glass work he insisted on the best quality, hand-blown glass. Worked entirely from his studio in Cleveden Crescent, Glasgow, aided by his wife and two leadworkers (Hugh Ingram and latterly Neil Hutcheson). Decorated churches throughout Britain from a base in Glasgow, among his best work being in Tinwald church, Dumfriessshire (1938-55), the Bruce memorial in the north transept of Dunfermline abbey (1974), Dunblane cathedral, Dornoch cathedral, the rose window in St Columba, Inverness (1957), Glasgow cathedral, Glasgow University chapel, and windows in the choir of Paisley abbey (1951). Also 'Christ in Majesty' (1970) in Corstorphine Old Parish Church, three in St Cerf, Granton (1970) and two in St Anne's, Corstorphine (1953). Keen member of the Territorial Army, he served with the Royal Engineers during WW2 and in 1953 was made Hon. Colonel of his regiment. Exhibited in London, RSA 1957 and 1959 & GI, from 5 Newton Terrace, Glasgow.
**Bibl:** Gifford 45,524-5,602; Painton Cowen, Stained Glass in Britain, 1985, 230-2, 237-8; Scotsman 27 Jan 1987 (obit).

**WEBSTER, James** **fl 1894**
Aberdeen amateur artist; exhibited 'On the links' at the AAS from 14 Ashvale Place.

**WEBSTER, John** **fl 1892-1895**
Painter in oil and watercolour of landscapes. Son of Alexander W(qv). In addition to painting local scenes worked on lower Deeside and on the Spey. An exhibition of his work was held in Fraserburgh 1895.

**WEBSTER, Lawrence** **fl 1918-1920**
Fraserburgh landscape and coastal painter in oil and watercolour. Youngest son of Alexander W(qv). Specialised in local scenery.

**WEBSTER, Miss Lorna** **fl 1939**
Edinburgh painter in watercolour. Related to Robert Bruce W(qv). Exhibited GI(1), from Colinton Rd.

**WEBSTER, Malcolm Scott** **fl 1967**
Edinburgh architect and part-time painter. Exhibited two harbour scenes at the RSA.

**WEBSTER, Margaret** **fl 1862**
Fife painter; exhibited two landscapes of scenes near Moffat (Dumfriessshire) at the RSA, from Cupar.

**WEBSTER, Mary** **fl 1830-1840**
Amateur artist about whom little is known. Left an album of pleasant watercolour sketches of Scottish landscapes, including 20 views of Edinburgh. Exhibited RA(10) & RSA(1), latterly from 5 Belmont St, Southport, Lancs.
**Bibl:** Butchart 63.

**WEBSTER, Nellie** **fl 1893-1923**
Aberdeen painter of still life, fish and flowers. Exhibited AAS(11) from 15 Deemount Rd.

**WEBSTER, Peter** **fl 1904-1907**
Fraserburgh painter in oil and watercolour. Son of Alexander W(qv). Landscape works of mainly local scenes. Emigrated to Florida 1907.

**WEBSTER, R Wellesley** **fl 1887-1903**
Landscape and seascape painter. Lived in West Anstruther, Fife during the 1890s. Exhibited RA(10) & RSA(1), latterly from 5 Belmont St, Southport, Lancs.

**WEBSTER, Robert Bruce** **1892-1959**
Edinburgh-based painter in oil and watercolour who moved from Dollar in 1940. Painted mainly coastal scenes of the north-east littoral, also topographical subjects. Related to Lorna W(qv). Exhibited RSA(9) & RSW(8).

**WEBSTER, Robin** **fl 1959-1960**
Glasgow painter. Exhibited GI(2).

**WEBSTER, Thomas** **c1772-1844**
Born Orkney; died London, Dec 26. Architect. Entered the RA

Schools 1793 but subsequently became proficient as an artist, a geologist and natural philosopher. In 1880 helped Count Rumford design the Lecture Theatre, Library and Repository of the Royal Institution in Albemarle Street, plans subsequently revised by James Spiller. Buried in Highgate Cemetery.
**Bibl:** Colvin.

**WEBSTER, William** **fl 1886**
Painter. Member of the Fraserburgh family of artists; exhibited AAS(2).

**WEBSTER, William Scott** **1867-fl 1939**
Fraserburgh painter in oil and watercolour of landscapes and heraldic scenes. Second and perhaps most talented of Alexander Webster's sons. His first recorded work was a portrait of 'Mr Scott' the local dancing teacher, executed when the artist was only 17. Some time in the early part of the century migrated to Halifax, Nova Scotia earning a reputation as a painter of portraits, landscapes and heraldic subjects. An enthusiastic student of heraldry, painted coats-of-arms for three consecutive sovereigns: the first for Queen Victoria's Golden Jubilee celebrations, then in 1902 for the Duke of York on the occasion of his visit to Halifax. When this was illuminated the Duke was so impressed that he paid a special visit at night in order to see it again. His third coat-of-arms was for King George and Queen Elizabeth on the occasion of their visit to Nova Scotia in 1939. On a return visit to Fraserburgh he exhibited a watercolour of beech trees which a contemporary critic commended as being 'the equal of a Birket Foster'.

**WEDDERBURN, Janet Scrymgeour ARBS FRBS** **fl 1971-1985**
Fife sculptress. Specialises in portraits; her exhibited works include 'Sir Ian Moncrieff of that Ilk', RSA 1972, 'Hew Lorimer', RSA 1975 and 'Nicholas Fairbairn QC MP', RSA 1982. Exhibited RSA (17), from Cupar.

**WEDDERBURN, Jemima** **[see BLACKBURN, Jemima]**

**WEDDERSPOON, Kate** **fl 1892-1895**
Perthshire artist; country scenes and farm animals. Exhibited RSA(3), AAS(2) & GI(2) from Wallaceton, Bridge of Earn.

**WEDGWOOD, Harold Roland ARSA ARIBA** **1929-**
Born Sussex. Architect. Studied at the Polytechnic School of Architecture in London 1945-51 and worked during 1947 at the International Building Volunteer Camp at Pestalozzi, Kinderdorf, Switzerland. The following year awarded a Robert Mitchell scholarship enabling him to return for a fourth year to Switzerland. Elected ARIBA 1951. After two years of National Service, he settled in Edinburgh in 1959 as a member of the Housing Research Unit of the University and Deputy Director and Lecturer in Building Science. In 1960 seconded as Housing Advisor to the Maltese Government and in 1963 completed his PhD thesis 'The problem of motor vehicles in housing areas...' Taught part-time Heriot Watt University 1983-4, since when embarked upon private practice with over 250 commissions. Awards include 1973 RIBA Architectural Award, and the same year an RSA Gold Medal, RIBA Architectural Award for Scotland 1980 and Saltire Award for Lynedoch House sheltered housing scheme. In 1978 was an Award Assessor for the RIBA and has been a Civic Trust Assessor. Played a leading role in architectural developments in Scotland.

**WEEKES, Joseph** **fl 1933-1944**
Glasgow architect and part-time watercolour painter of topographical subjects. Exhibited GI(18), from Park Circus.

**WEEKS, John** **fl 1924-1925**
Painter. Exhibited RSA(4) from 10 Forth St.

**WEGMULLER, Ann RSW** **1941-**
Born Gourock, Renfrewshire. Painter of still life, landscape and semi-abstracts. Works mostly in oils but also occasionally in acrylic and watercolour. Attended art college as a mature student and in 1985 graduated with honours from Duncan of Jordanstone College of Art. Professional member, SSWA. Paints landscape in a colourful, semi-abstract manner. Elected RSW 2001. Has exhibited regularly RSA since 1987, GI(1) & AAS(4). Currently lives at 136 The Feus, Auchterarder, Perthshire.

**WEIR, Alexander** **fl 1757-d1797**
Painter. Son of a stabler. In 1747 apprenticed to James Miller, painter, and in 1757 became a burgess of Edinburgh and member, Incorporation of St Mary's. During the next 30 years he had as apprentices James Neilson 1768, John Arnot 1779, Thomas Young 1782, Charles Robertson 1786 and John Yellowlees 1786. In 1773-4 was living in Baillie Fyfe's Close, Edinburgh. In 1786 he sold to the University a natural history collection which he had formed and six years later opened a second public collection (called a museum) at 16 Princes Street. After his death this was offered to the City in 1800 for £1,600 but the offer was declined.

**WEIR, Mrs Emily** **fl 1921-1926**
Aberdeenshire amateur painter of rustic scenes, landscape and old buildings. Exhibited AAS(5) from Hill of Newe, Strathdon.

**WEIR, Helen** **fl 1970**
Edinburgh sculptress; exhibited 'Winged Victory' at the RSA.

**WEIR, Major James** **fl 1789-1803**
Little known Scottish landscape and marine painter, possibly from Aberdour. Amateur artist, probably self-taught, his work was stylised and sketchy in the treatment of landscape but accurate asnd carefully detailed in the depiction of shipping, especially naval craft. Served in the Royal Marines under Nelson in the Mediterranean 1795-1808. In March 1799 sent to Malta where he assisted in the siege of Valetta and raised a Company of Maltese Fencibles whose uniform he designed. Remained on Malta until 1803 when his rank was officially confirmed. On *HMS Audacious* at the Battle of the Nile and also on *HMS Northumberland.* Present at both the capture of Fort Elmo and of the French batteries at Porto Ferrago. After returning to England several of his watercolours completed whilst on service were engraved including two aquatints of 'Valetta', engraved by Francis Chesham, and 'The Battle of the Nile', engraved by Hellyer 1800 both of which can be seen in the National Maritime Museum, Greenwich.
**Bibl:** National Maritime Museum (correspondence).

**WEIR, James T** **fl 1876**
Edinburgh oil painter; exhibited a woodlands scene at the RSA.

**WEIR, Jessie** **fl 1880-1888**
Painter. Sister of Mary W(qv). Exhibited GI(8) from Paisley Road, Glasgow.

**WEIR, John** **fl 1878-1879**
Amateur Edinburgh landscape painter in oil; exhibited RSA(2).

**WEIR, Mary** **fl 1884-1896**
Watercolour painter of nature studies and flowers. Sister of Jessie W(qv). Exhibited RSW(1) & GI(4).

**WEIR, Peter Ingram** **fl 1885-1888**
Edinburgh watercolour painter of landscape; exhibited RSA(5), RI(1) & L(1).

**WEIR, R W S** **[see R W SCHULTZ]**

**WEIR, Robertson** **fl 1923**
Amateur Glasgow painter. Exhibited L(1) from 61 Roselea Drive, Dennistoun.

**WEIR, Walter** **fl c1782-d1816**
Edinburgh genre painter. Painter in oil and watercolour. Studied in Italy and worked in a style influenced by David Allan(qv). His faces are more like caricatures than Allan's, suggesting that he may have been acquainted with the work of Geikie(qv). In 1781 he presented a portrait 'Mr Harry Erskine' to the Public Dispensary of Edinburgh who subsequently loaned it for posthumous exhibition RSA 1880. In 1796 was a candidate for the mastership of the Trustees Academy but was not successful. In 1809 exhibited RA(2), 'Halloween' and 'The cottar's Saturday night'. Shortly after the miniature painter Archibald Robertson(qv) had arrived in Edinburgh from Aberdeen 1782, he and Weir joined with Raeburn and George Watson(qv) to use the Green Room at the theatre for three nights a week as a life class. Alexander Runciman(qv) was involved as an instructor. Sometimes confused with William Weir (RA 1855-1865) who had no Scottish

connection. Represented NGS(4).
**Bibl:** Brydall 271; Irwin 205; Macmillan [SA] 165,179-180.

**WEIR, William** **fl 1926-1949**
Glasgow watercolour painter of coastal scenery; exhibited GI(4) & AAS(1) from 463 Eglington St and latterly Bellwood St.

**WEIR, Mrs Wilma Law** **fl 1912-1940**
Born Glasgow. Painter in oil and watercolour of landscapes and coastal scenery, also leather worker. Trained Edinburgh College of Art. On the strength of a travelling scholarship visited Italy and Paris. Moved in the early 1920s to Glasgow. Exhibited RSA(4), RSW(1), AAS(7) & GI(6).
**Bibl:** Halsby 287.

**WEIRTER, Louis RBA** **1873-1932**
Born Edinburgh; died Hertfordshire, Jan 12. Artist, lithographer and illustrator. Son of a Professor of Music, apprenticed to a lithographer while studying at the RSA and the Board of Manufacturers Schools; continued further studies in Paris. Elected RBA 1905. Worked in London 1907 and Baldock 1914, featuring pictures of current events, the Diamond Jubilee and the War in the Air 1914-18. Principal works include 'The Battle of Courcelette', 'War in the Air', 'Albert Cathedral', 'The Taking of Peronne' and 'Queen Victoria's Diamond Jubilee'. Illustrated *The Story of Edinburgh Castle* and *Stories and Legends of the Danube.* Signed his paintings 'Louis Weirter' and his etchings 'Louis Whirter'. Exhibited RA(4), RSA(1) & RBA(53). Represented in V & A.
**Bibl:** Houfe.

**WEISSE, F H** **fl 1854-1868**
Edinburgh painter of landscapes and local scenes; exhibited RSA(21).

**WELCH, John** **fl 1837-1848**
Edinburgh portrait and miniature painter. Exhibited RSA(6) including portraits of the two sons of the Earl of Caithness.

**WELLS, Archibald** **1874-?**
Born Glasgow, 10 May. Portrait miniaturist and landscape painter in oil, watercolour and pastel. His miniatures were mostly enamel on copper. Went to Australia as a child and was educated at the Sydney Arts Society. Some years later returned to Britain and in 1909 was living in Glasgow before settling in Rye, Sussex. Exhibited RA(1), GI(10) & L(6).

**WELLS, Bella Hunter** **fl 1898**
Leith painter of local scenery; exhibited AAS(2) from 48 Dudley Gdns, Bonnington.

**WELLS, James** **fl 1896**
Portrait painter of no known address. In 1896 exhibited portraits of the Rev & Mrs Thomas Forbes at the AAS.

**WELLS, Margaret** **fl 1932-?**
Wood engraver and writer. Trained Glasgow School of Art 1928-32 and at Brook Green School, London 1932-36. Wrote and illustrated *Margaret Wells: A Selection of Her Wood Engravings* (Wakefield Fleece Press, 1985).
**Bibl:** Horne 440.

**WELLS, William Page Atkinson** **1872-1923**
Born Glasgow; died Isle of Man. Painter in oil and occasional watercolour of landscapes and figurative subjects. Lived in Glasgow until 1885 when he went to Sydney, Australia with his parents, remaining there and in Melbourne for five years. On returning to Europe, worked for a time in Paris where he became familiar with and inspired by the Barbizon School. Studied at the Slade under Legros and in Paris under Bouguereau and Ferrier. Whilst establishing a reputation he worked as a scene painter in Preston for seven years, finally setting in Appledore, North Devon where he remained until shortly before his premature death. In his oils, there is a predilection for large, open vistas with a low skyline, often a peasant girl herding geese or poultry. The watercolours have a particular quality which places him outside the mainstream of the Glasgow School. Used a rough paper with rich colours added on top of a base of charcoal and deep grey washes. The result is an overall darkness but a romantic, almost dreamlike, quality. Painted several golfing scenes including 'The Royal North Devon GC (Westward Ho!) with players'. Elected RBA 1906. Exhibited RA(3), RSA(3), RSW(1), GI(33), RBA(6), ROI (4) & L(14). Represented in Glasgow AG(2), City of Edinburgh(3).
**Bibl:** Caw 392; Halsby 162,163,287; Studio (1910) 48, 314(illus); 1910, 50, 266-275; Wingfield.

**WELLS-GRAHAM, Mrs Catherine** **fl 1904-1907**
Leith topographical painter; mainly cathedrals and churches. Exhibited RSA(2) including a study of Ely Cathedral.

**WELSH, Bessie** **fl 1896**
Kircudbright watercolourist of pastoral scenes. Probably wife or daughter of Joseph W(qv). Exhibited GI(2) from Newton Stewart.

**WELSH, Effie (Mrs James W)** **fl 1901-1931**
Amateur watercolour painter of landscape and portrait miniatures. Exhibited at the RSA(11), RSW(3), GI(1) & RMS (1) from a Liberton address.

**WELSH, John Mason** **fl 1906-1914**
Glasgow painter. Exhibited RSA(1) & GI(2) from Mount Florida.

**WELSH, James Bain** **fl 1960-1961**
Edinburgh painter; moved from Portobello to Clermiston c1960. Exhibited RSA(2).

**WELSH, Joseph** **fl 1881-1896**
Painter in watercolour of local landscapes; probably husband or father of Bessie W(qv). Exhibited RSA(2) & GI(3) from Newton Stewart.

**WELSH, Lizzie T** **fl 1893-1894**
Amateur painter. Related to Bessie(qv) and Joseph W(qv). Exhibited GI(3) from Newton Stewart.

**WELSH, Miss M B C** **fl 1936**
Edinburgh stained glass window designer. Exhibited RSA from 41 York Place.

**WEMYSS, Countess of (Grace Blackburn)** **fl 1906-1908**
Amateur painter who exhibited four works at the New Gallery from 23 St James's Place, London. Second wife of the Earl of Wemyss and step great-grandmother of the present Earl.

**WEMYSS, Earl of** **fl 1905-1907**
Amateur painter. Husband of Grace Blackburn(qv). Exhibited 'Venus at her toilet' RSA; also at the New Gallery(12).

**WEMYSS, Janet, Countess of** **?-1778**
Embroiderer. Daughter of Col. Francis Charteris, she married the 5th Earl of Wemyss 1720 from whom she separated c1731. What Swain describes as "an enchanting set of four bed curtains" with the initials of herself, her husband and children, with the dates of their birth embroidered on each curtain, remain in use today at Wemyss Castle.
**Bibl:** Margaret Swain 68-9.

**WEMYSS, Lady Victoria Alexandrina Violet** **1890-?**
Embroiderer and needlewoman. Designed and worked many carpets, bedcovers and chair covers all still at Wemyss Castle. After her marriage to Captain Wemyss 1918, she ran the Wemyss School of Needlwork. 'Her taste and expertise has had a profound influence on much of the canvas work done for the home in Scotland' [Swain].
**Bibl:** Margaret Swain 156.

**WEMYSS, Zibella** **fl 1895**
Amateur painter of informal portraits. Exhibited GI(1) from Durie House, Helensburgh.

**WERNIER, G H** **fl 1857**
Edinburgh artist; exhibited 'French quarters, Gallipoli' at the RSA, from Blenheim Place.

**WEST, David RSW** **1868-1936**
Born Lossiemouth; died Lossiemouth, Oct 8. Painter in watercolour; landscape and marines. Son of a ship's captain, in his youth he went to sea and when he was thirty-two participated in the Klondyke gold rush, but returned to Lossiemouth where he remained for the rest of

his life, apart from a short visit to South America in the 1920s. Highly regarded in his native Moray Firth area for his excellent portrayal of the characteristic light of the North Sea in that part of the world. Most of his work has a low skyline giving wide range for the depiction of the interplay of water and sky whilst the fishing towns and villages of the Firth coastline are painted accurately and without affectation. Favoured by copyists care is required over attribution. Elected RSW 1908 and later Vice-President. His work was shown on the Continent and in Buenos Aires where a one-man exhibition was held 1927. Exhibited RA(9) 1890-1902 from various addresses in Aberdeen and after 1902 from Lossiemouth; also RSA (94), RS(97), RHA(3), RI(2), AAS(1897-1935), GI(25) & L(3). Lived at Chilkoot, Lossiemouth. Represented in Aberdeen AG, Haddo House (NTS). **Bibl:** Halsby 232-4.

**WEST, James** **fl 1815-1827**
Edinburgh painter, apprenticed to Thomas Clephane. In 1815 made a burgess of Edinburgh. In 1817 took as apprentice William West and in 1827 James Scott. In 1823 painted 15 heads for the library of Traquair House. Lived at 2 Mansfield Place where in 1826 he decorated the walls of his apartment. These were restored in 1974. **Bibl:** Gifford 341.

**WEST, Richard William ('Dick')** **1887-1970**
Born Aberdeen, 22 May. Painter in oil and occasional watercolour; portraits, genre and landscape, also etcher. Trained Grays School of Art and Hospitalfield, Arbroath. As the result of a scholarship he travelled for two years in Holland and around Marseilles. In WW2 served with Allenby in Palestine. Following a spell as assistant art master at Gordon's College, Aberdeen he became principal art master at Forfar Academy and was an active member of the Aberdeen Artists Society. On retirement he spent two years in Somerset before emigrating to Wellington, New Zealand where he executed paintings and posters for the national railways. Shortly before his death returned to Somerset. A fine portrait of his wife, possibly his best work, painted in 1921, remains in the family. Guichard praised his swiftly drawn and amusing drypoints and illustrations for *The Trollus* (1921). Exhibited RSA(5) from Aberdeen & AAS 1906-1929.

**WEST, Samuel** **1810-1869**
Glasgow oil painter of portraits and figure subjects; exhibited RSA (10) & GI(16). Represented in Glasgow AG.

**WEST, William** **fl 1955**
Aberdeenshire painter; exhibited RSA(2) from Peterhead.

**WEST OF SCOTLAND ACADEMY** **1840-1886**
A resurrection of the old Glasgow Dilettanti Society(qv), formed at almost the same time as the Glasgow Art Union. The principal promoters were John Mossman the sculptor(qv) and J A Hutchison (drawing master at Glasgow HS) who was elected secretary. Membership was divided into three categories: academicians, associates and others, John Graham-Gilbert(qv) being elected President. By 1842 support had arrived in the form of the **ASSOCIATION FOR PROMOTING THE FINE ARTS IN GLASGOW & THE WEST OF SCOTLAND**. This body purchased £3,000 worth of paintings from the Academy's exhibitions of 1840 and 1842. In 1886, the success of the RGI(qv) and difficulty over accommodation proved too difficult to resolve causing the Academy to be finally wound up, its funds and library being donated to the RGI. **Bibl:** AJ 1840; Brydall 362-4; Caw 67; Irwin 222;

**WESTMACOTT, Henry HRSA** **1784-1861**
Sculptor. Although English, the thirteenth child of Richard Westmacott, he lived for a number of years in Edinburgh making a strong impression at the Academy who elected him HRSA 1830. His busts at the RSA included those of 'Paganini', 'Sir Walter Scott' and 'General Jackson, President of the US'. In 1836 he showed 'a model of a cenotaph in granite, surmounted by a bust in marble, in memory of the Bard of Abbotsford, to be erected by subscription in New York'.His bust of Scott was lot 59 in the studio sale at Christie's 1864. His first wife, Eliza, whom he married in 1810, was the daughter of the Town Clerk of Montrose; his second marriage was to Hannah Rowe, a descendent of the Poet Laureate Nicholas Rowe, 1827. He was a sculptor of competent, but not outstanding, talent. One of his best works was 'Lord William Gordon' (1824) at Whitkirk in Yorkshire, a delightful small full-length relief of 'Lord William in Highland dress'. Exhibited RA(3) 1833-1835 & Liverpool Academy 1831; at the RSA in 1832 he showed a model of 'a marble medallion erected by the inhabitants of St Elizabeth, West Indies, to Andrew Miller Esq'. Lived latterly at 5 Royal Terrace, Edinburgh. His principal works are in Scotland, although perhaps the best known is the monument to John Beresford in Westminster Abbey.
**Bibl:** Gunnis 421-2; M Whinney, Sculpture in Britain 1530-1830, London 1964, Part 7.

**WESTMACOTT, Henry Mrs (née Hannah Wilkinson Rowe)** **fl 1863**
Painter in oil of still-life. Second wife of Henry W(qv). Exhibited RSA(1).

**WESTMACOTT, James Sherwood** **1823-1900**
Born London, 22 Aug. Sculptor. Son of Henry W(qv) by his first marriage to Eliza Stewart and therefore half Scottish but spent the whole of his life in England. In 1855 "The Peri at the Gates of Paradise' was shown at the Paris Exhibition and later illustrated in the *AJ* and elsewhere. In 1863 he executed the figure of 'Alexander', now in the Mansion House. He modelled all the figures for the reredos of Newcastle Cathedral. Exhibited regularly RA 1846-1885; also British Institution 1852-1867 from 21 Wilton Place.
**Bibl:** Gunnis 422.

**WESTON, Charles Frederick** **fl 1982**
Aberdeen sculptor; exhibited AAS(1) from 32 Woodend Crescent.

**WESTWATER, Robert Heriot ARSA** **1905-1962**
Born Edinburgh; died Southfleet, Kent, Nov 16. Painter in oil of portraits and figure subjects. Educated Royal High School, trained Edinburgh College of Art and, with the aid of a travelling scholarship, undertook further studies in Europe. Returning to London, he taught for three years before joining the staff of the Edinburgh College of Art, remaining ten years. Awarded Andrew Grant Fellowship 1934. Taught for several years as Art Master at Fettes College before returning again to London where he practised as a full-time painter. Elected ARSA 1948. Sometime art critic of *The Scotsman.* His portraits included 'The Duke of Montrose', 'Sir Compton Mackenzie', 'Lord Boothby' and 'Hugh McDiarmid (Dr C N Grieve)'. He was a great admirer of Cézanne. In his obituary the RSA noted that 'an echo of the influence of Degas and the way he eschewed the conventional, inclined him to intimate and natural sittings appropriate to his sitters'. Also exhibited GI(2).

**WEST-WATSON, Miss C Maud** **fl 1886-1938**
Glasgow watercolour painter, often in pastel. Exhibited RSA(3), RSW(1), AAS(1), GI(19) & L(7) from 7, Grosvenor Crescent, latterly from Louisville Rd, London.

**WESTWOOD, Adam** **fl 1881-1901**
Dunfermline painter in oil and watercolour of landscapes and figurative subjects; exhibited RSA(9) & GI(4) from 19 Guildhall St.

**WESTWOOD, Dennis** **fl 1958-1970**
Sculptor. Moved across the border from Cumberland to settle in Dumbarton 1966. Subsequently went to Staffordshire. Exhibited RSA(28) & GI(3).

**WESTWOOD, Henry Roy** **fl 1886-1898**
Edinburgh watercolour painter of landscape and figure subjects. Exhibited RSA(11) & GI(2) from 8 West Newington Place.

**WESTWOOD, William** **1844-1924**
Dunfermline painter in oil and watercolour. Exhibited at Dunfermline Fine Art Association 1883-1902 & GI(2) from his studio at the Carnegie Library, Dunfermline which he shared for many years with his son, a professional photographer. Represented in Dunfermline District Museum.

**WHAITE, James** **fl 1874-1916**
Painter in oil and watercolour of landscapes, often in the Highlands. Spent most of his life until the mid-1880's in England, eventually settling in Portobello c1885. Married Lilias W(qv). Exhibited RA(4), RSA(13), RI(1), GI(2) but principally at the Walker Gallery, Liverpool (92).

**WHAITE, Lilias (Mrs)** **fl 1885**
Painter. Married James W(qv). Exhib 'Hanging the Mistletoe' RSA.

**WHALEN, A Carrick** **fl 1950-**
Sculptor and stained glass window designer. Designed an heraldic window in St Vincent Church Edinburgh (1975); collaborated in windows in Greenbank Church with William Wilson(qv), **BLAIR** & **D SAUNDERS**; and a carved wooden 'Tree of Life' in the Childrens' Chapel, St Philip Church, Pilrig (1950).
**Bibl:** Gifford 339,617,645.

**WHALEN, Thomas RSA** **1903-1975**
Born Oct 16; died Feb 19. Sculptor. Educated at St Thomas School, Leith 1908-1917. Inspired by John Hislop's weekly bible classes so that a lot of his works have scriptural titles. Became a shipwright 1914-1918. Quite unexpectedly his early work was recognised and he obtained a scholarship enabling him to attend Edinburgh College of Art as a full-time student. The first recipient of the Andrew Grant Fellowship and in 1932, with the help of a Carnegie travelling scholarship, he spent a year working in Europe. Later won the Guthrie Award. Throughout his professional career he disdained studio assistance. 'All he did was his' [Esmé Gordon]. Examples of stone heraldry stand in Edinburgh in the Lawnmarket, St Andrew's Square, also at the North of Scotland Hydro Electric Board projects. At Brunton Hall, Musselburgh there is a gilded decoration of the sun and on the stone gable of Dalkeith HS, a bronze ballerina. In each Church of Scotland canteen during WW2, there was a roundel of the burning bush on the communion table. A carved 'Christ's entry into Jerusalem' (1953) is in St Anne's Church, Corstorphine. Elected ARSA 1940, RSA 1954. His obituary referred to the 'masterliness in his direct stonework, he was probably happier as a carver with his chisel taking away than as a modeller, adding with his spatula. In all he did there was a very real sense of style exemplified clearly in his virile lettering and more recently his gentler works in Portsoy marble, rich in colour with the grey-green of our constant seas under cloudy skies, these may prove to be his most memorable works'. In 1951 commissioned to do a 'Mother and Child' for the Festival of Britain exhibition. Exhibited RSA(130+) in bronze, lead, cement, wood, glass and polystyrene; also GI(44).
**Bibl:** Gifford 307,311,525; T S Halliday & George Bruce, Scottish Sculpture. A Record of twenty years, Dundee 1946; Hartley 167-8; Saltire Soc. Fest., Hamilton,'Tom Whalen', (Ex Cat 1973, by Esme Gordon).

**WHARTON, Janet** **fl 1887**
Edinburgh painter in watercolour; exhibited an interior of Holyrood Palace at the RSA in the above year and 'A sketch in Advocates Close' - now demolished.

**WHEATLEY, Lawrence** **fl 1934-1936**
Painter in watercolour of landscapes. Lived at Bardowie, by Milngavie, before moving to England in the late 1930's. Exhibited RA(1) & RSA(1).

**WHEATLEY, Penny** **1939-**
Born Jun 2. Sculptress. Trained in music at Trinity College of Music, London before proceeding to study sculpture under David Wynne (who had been trained by Epstein whose influence was conveyed to his pupils). Initial work was cast in bronze including a number of portraits. A more abstract period followed when she experimented with various media including welded and stainless steel. Then moved on to naturalistic bronze animal sculpture, an example of which was her life-size bronze otter for the Maxwell Memorial (1977). Received many commissions for horse sculptures but from 1987 has become again more abstract, working in bronze and welded bronze. Her interest is in sculpture in landscape as an adjunct to architecture. Has had several solo exhibitions. Won the Ottilie Helen Wallace Award 1989. Exhibits RSA from her home in Lilliesleaf, Roxburghshire.

**WHEELER, Eleanor Teresa** **fl 1989-**
Aberdeen sculptress; exhibites AAS from 253c Holborn St.

**WHEELER, Sir Harold Anthony KBE PRSA HRA HFRBS FRIAC FRIBA** **1919-**
Born Stranraer, Nov 7. Architect, architectural draughtsman and planner. Educated Stranraer High School, studied architecture at Glasgow School of Architecture under Professor W J Smith and at Glasgow School of Art. A John Keppie scholar and a medallist; also a life drawing prizeman. Awarded the Bellahouston travelling scholarship as well as the Rowand Anderson studentship at the RIAS 1948, RIBA Grissell Gold Medal 1948 and an RIBA Neale bursary 1949. Trustee of the Scottish Civic Trust and Senior Lecturer at Dundee School of Architecture 1952-1958. Member of the Royal Fine Art Commission for Scotland since 1967. Influenced by Dudok, Jacobsen and Aalto, the domestic architecture of Charles Rennie Mackintosh(qv) and Frank Lloyd Wright, also by early Renaissance town planning in Italy and by early Scottish burgh architecture. Designed Hunter Building, Lauriston Place, Edinburgh (1972); his own home 3 Hawthornbank Lane (1974) and Old Farm Court, Colinton Rd (1976) for the Viewpoint Housing Association. Regular exhibitor RSA and responsible for housing in many new towns, including the Woodside Shopping Centre in Glen Rothes, as well as a number of churches including St. Columba's (Glenrothes); Templehall parish church; St. Peter's Episcopal church, Kirkcaldy; Boghall (Bathgate); and St. John's, Galashiels; also reconstructions, educational buildings (student residences at Heriot Watt Univ., Students' Union at St. Andrews and Heriot Watt Univs), and hospital extensions. Received five Civic Trust awards 1960-65 and 13 Saltire housing awards 1966-73. A good watercolourist, his sensitive use of the medium being apparent in delicate architectural drawings with clean lines, finely proportioned perspectives and close attention to functional interior detail. A leading influence on Scottish architecture for many years. In 1989 he exhibited a plan for the Scula di San Marco, Venice and a design for the Leonard Horner Hall at Heriot-Watt University. Awarded OBE 1973, ARSA 1963, PRIAS 1973, RSA 1970, PRSA 1983-1990. Lived at Hawthornbank House, Dean Village, Edinburgh.
**Bibl:** Gifford 259,395,519.

**WHEELER, Mary E** **fl 1885-1888**
Edinburgh watercolourist of landscapes, figure subjects and still-life; exhibited RSA (4) & GI(1) , latterly from Hillhead.

**WHIPPLE, J Lawton** **fl 1886-1893**
Edinburgh landscape painter; exhibited AAS(2) from St John's, Colinton.

**WHISTON, Peter RSA** **1912-1999**
Irish descent, spent childhood in Leith, educated Holy Cross Academy. Architect. Specialised in church work. Designs in Edinburgh include the tall St Margaret, Davidson's Mains (1950); the 'distinguished' St Mark (R C) Church, Fairmilehead (1959) and St Paul, Muirhouse (1968). Perhaps his most significant building is the Cistercian Monastery, Nunraw, East Lothian, the first new Scottish monastery since the Reformation. Elected RSA 1977.
**Bibl:** Gifford 43,548,567,624; Anon, Obituary, RSA Annual Report 2000.

**WHITACRE, Rev Aeired** **fl 1934-1937**
Amateur sculptor; exhibited RA(1) & RSA(2) from 24 George Square, Edinburgh.

**WHITCOMBE, Susie** **1957-**
Painter in watercolour and oil of horses; also sheep, champion cattle and foxhounds. Anglo-Scottish artist, daughter of a farming family. Has a natural talent exercised with little outside help, although attended Heatherley School of Art, London intermittently. A competent and competitive horsewoman, holds an amateur jockey's permit. Commissioned from many parts of the world, including Australia, New Zealand, Brazil, Kenya, the USA and Nigeria and has depicted famous racehorses as well as Olympic dressage mounts.

**WHITE, Captain RE** **fl 1873**
Amateur landscape painter in watercolour; exhibited RSA(2).

**WHITE, Alan Hamilton** **fl 1974-1978**
Aberdeenshire figurative painter; trained Gray's School of Art, Aberdeen. Exhibited AAS(6) from The Glebe, Collieston.

**WHITE, Alice** **fl 1887**
New Galloway painter in watercolour of landscape and flower pieces; exhibited RSA(1). Possibly the same **Alice White** who exhibited 1880-1889 RA(1), RBA(2), RI(1) & SWA(29) from Kensington, London.

**WHITE, Miss Blanche M L** **fl 1870**
Aberdour amateur painter in oil of flower pieces. One of a family of sisters, all of whom were artists. Exhibited RSA(1).

**WHITE, Charles** **fl 1788-1820**
Aberdeen-based heraldic painter and copyist. Guild burgess of Aberdeen 1695. Worked at Marischal College 1698-1707 including Dr Sibbald's coat of Arms for the Principal's room, a portrait of 'Robert Low' and a copy of Jamesone's portrait of 'Robert Gordon of Straloch', for which he received £10.
**Bibl:** Apted 103.

**WHITE, Miss Chrissie** **fl 1974**
Bearsden embroiderer. Senior lecturer, Glasgow School of Art. Exhibited GI(1).

**WHITE, Dennis** **1918-?**
Born Jan 27. Painter. Knew and worked with the artist, Mark Tobey 1936-7 but, being unable to afford art college and having no grant, was discouraged by his family. Eventually, in 1983, he attended Dundee Art School, obtaining an honours degree, and held his first one-man exhibition 1989. In his final year as a student sold an etching of the art historian Christopher White to the subject himself. Exhibited frequently RSA from West Hendersons Wynd, Dundee.

**WHITE, Donald** **fl 1988-**
Edinburgh artist; exhibited 'Elephant's graveyard' at the RSA, from Sciennes Rd.

**WHITE, Dyke (Charles G McClure)** **?-c1931**
Watercolour painter of portraits and cartoons. Living in Glasgow 1916 and in Lenzie, Dumbartonshire 1931. Exhibited RSA(1) & GI(7).

**WHITE, Edward** **fl 1884-1886**
Edinburgh oil painter, mainly castles; exhibited RSA(3) from St James's St.

**WHITE, Miss Elsie G** **fl 1972**
Glasgow painter. Exhibited 'Pears' at the GI.

**WHITE, F P** **fl 1869-1870**
Amateur landscape painter in oil; exhibited RSA(2).

**WHITE, Mrs Grace P (née Paterson)** **fl 1925-1928**
Ayrshire landscape and figure painter; exhibited RSA(4) & GI(3), from Galston.

**WHITE, Hannah Catherine** **1980s**
Aberdeenshire-based abstract artist; trained Gray's School of Art, Aberdeen. Exhibited AAS(3) from Cranley, Newburgh, Ellon.

**WHITE, J G** **fl 1885**
Minor Glasgow painter; exhibited GI(1) from 9 Fitzroy Place.

**WHITE, J P** **fl 1880**
Amateur Glasgow painter. Exhibited GI(1) from 79 West Regent St.

**WHITE, James M** **fl 1879-1904**
Minor Edinburgh painter in oil, landscapes and figure subjects. Lived at Whitebank. Exhibited RSA(5) & GI(1).

**WHITE, Jane G** **fl 1900**
Minor figure; exhibited a water colour at the GI from 55 Alexander St, Clydebank.

**WHITE, Miss Jessie F D** **fl 1871**
Member of the Aberdour family of amateur sister painters. Worked in watercolour; exhibited one landscape at the RSA.

**WHITE, John RI ROI** **1851-1933**
Born Edinburgh, Sep 18; died Beer, Devon, Dec 21. Painter in oil and watercolour of landscape, marines, portrait and rustic genre. His parents emigrated to Australia when he was five and he was educated at Dr Brunton's School, Melbourne. Entered the RSA Schools 1871, awarded Keith Prize for Design four years later. Moved south 1877 and continued working from London before moving to Axminster, Devon and finally Heavitree, Exeter 1901. Highly regarded for his design and the gentle subtlety of his silvery palette and sensitive atmosphere. Exhibited RA(40), RSA(37), ROI(106), RI(190), RBA(43), GI(34) & L(16). Elected RBA 1880, RI 1882, ROI 1886. 'A Village Wedding, Shere, Surrey' is in Exeter Museum.
**Bibl:** Caw 281; Halsby 287; Pavière, Landscape; Who's Who in Art 1934; Who was Who 1941-1950.

**WHITE, John Henry** **fl 1966-1972**
Largs sculptor. Exhibited works in wood and metal at the GI(11).

**WHITE, M W G** **fl 1891**
Amateur painter of Sudbrook, Pollokshields. Exhibited 'Narcissus' at the GI.

**WHITE, Mary Macrae (Mrs Martin W)** **fl 1893-1919**
Painter in oil of figure subjects and landscape. Living at Balruddery, nr Dundee in the 1900's. Exhibited RBA(2), RI(2), AAS(3), GI(1) & LS(3).

**WHITE, Miss Mary S L** **fl 1865-1877**
Sculptress and painter. The most distinguished member of the White family of sister artists. Specialised in portrait medallions, also painted flower pieces. Lived in Aberdour with her sisters; exhibited RSA(20).

**WHITE, Peter** **fl 1929**
Amateur watercolourist; exhibited RSW(1) from 9 Falcon Gardens, Edinburgh.

**WHITE, Peter A** **1959-**
Born Ayrshire. Painter of challenging equivocal figurative work. Trained Edinburgh College of Art 1981-85. Works in muted tones. Exhibits RGI & AAS.

**WHITE, Peter R** **fl 1954-1956**
English artist who, temporarily abandoning commercial art, moved to Ardachie, Fort Augustus, Inverness-shire 1954 where he spent three artistically rich years concentrating on portraiture and local landscape. Painted in a rumbustious, realistic style in strongly coloured oils. Returned to London 1956 to resume career as a commercial artist, gaining important contracts with the Ministry of Defence.

**WHITE, T A** **fl 1867**
Amateur Oban painter in oil of landscapes; exhibited RSA(2), one a view in South Africa.

**WHITE, T Brown** **fl 1896**
Amateur Aberdeen landscape painter; exhibited AAS(1) from 53 Thistle St.

**WHITE, T P** **fl 1869-1871**
Edinburgh landscape painter. Exhibited RSA(3) including 'Tantallon Castle' 1870, from Drummond Place.

**WHITE, W P** **fl 1882**
Edinburgh painter in oil and watercolour of buildings, sometimes overseas. Exhibited RSA(2), one an interior of Siena Cathedral, the other 'The Temple of Kermac, Upper Egypt', from 18 Carlton Terr.

**WHITEFORD, Kate** **1952-**
Born Glasgow. Artist working in mixed media. Studied drawing and painting Glasgow School of Art 1969-1973, from 1974-6 enrolled at Glasgow University reading history of art. A scholarship enabled her to visit Rome 1977 where the classical iconography, together with limited colour range of the frescos at Pompeii and Herculaneum, influenced her future. Her first one-man exhibition was at Stirling 1978. 'Her early work is minimal and non-figurative but, from about 1980 she began incorporating classical lettering and archaelogical imagery into her work. Roman urns and columns together with Celtic and Pictish signs were employed to create a symbolism suggestive of ancient myths and cultures' [Crawford Centre cat]. In 1978 moved to London, returning to Scotland 1982-3, becoming artist-in-residence, St Andrews University. In 1984-5 was artist-in-residence, Whitechapel AG, London. Since 1983 much of her work has been large-scale, executed in a limited but bright colour range created for

particular spaces. In 1987 she produced three large land-works for the Calton Hill, Edinburgh, reminiscent of prehistoric images such as the Ceine Abbas Giant. These were composed of white stone chippings laid in a shallow trench describing fish and spiral motifs. Represented in SNGMA.
**Bibl:** Crawford Centre for the Arts, St Andrews, (Ex Cat 1983); Hartley 168; Riverside Studios, London, 'Puja : Ritual Offerings to the Gods' (Ex Cat 1986); TEC, Glasgow, 'Kate Whiteford : Rites of Passage' (Ex Cat 1984).

**WHITEFORD, William G** **fl 1933-1939**
Ayrshire painter of flowers, portraits and landscape, mainly continental. Exhibited RSA(5) & GI(12) from Prestwick and latterly St Leonard's Rd, Ayr.

**WHITEHOUSE, Mrs Jocelyn M** **fl 1979**
Midlothian engraver; exhibited RSA(3), two of Scottish and one of New Zealand scenery, from Pathhead.

**WHITELAW, Alexander N** **fl 1923-1936**
Landscape painter in oil and watercolour, mainly the latter; also fishing boats and the occasional lino and woodcuts. Exhibited RSA (4), RSW(7), AAS(2), GI(12) & L(1) from Callander and later Giffnock.

**WHITELAW, C H/K M** **fl 1908-1911**
Edinburgh painter of figurative works. Exhibited RSA(2), AAS(2) & L(1).

**WHITELAW, George** **1887-1957**
Born Kirkintilloch, died London. Painter, illustrator, cartoonist. Educated Lenzie Academy and Glasgow HS. Trained under Maurice Greiffenhagen(qv) at Glasgow School of Art. Joined the art staff of the *Glasgow Evening News* while still a student. Served in the Tank Corps in WW1 after which he moved to London. Working as a free-lance artist, illustrating a series of cockney characters for *Punch*, and in other publications, he became cartoonist with the *Daily Herald* 1938. Exhibited RGI(6) and L(3).
**Bibl:** Bradshaw; Feaver; Horne 443.

**WHITELAW, Thomas** **fl 1929**
Amateur Leith painter; exhibited RSA(1) from 8 Craighall Crescent.

**WHITHAM, George** **fl 1928**
Minor Edinburgh figure who exhibited a fairground scene at Berwick-on-Tweed at the RSA from 60 Burnscourt Terrace.

**WHITTET, Andrew** **fl 1861-1921**
Edinburgh painter in oil and watercolour, mainly local landscape and some topographical. Prolific artist, exhibiting RSA(33), AAS 1884-1921, GI(10) & L(2).

**WHITTET, Mathew H W** **fl 1909-1912**
Coatbridge painter; exhibited GI(5).

**WHITTLE, Andrew** **fl 1863**
Edinburgh painter of country buildings; exhibited GI(1).

**WHITWORTH, Mrs** **fl 1886**
Amateur Coldstream painter; exhibited a genre painting at the RSA from Belchester.

**WHONE, Herbert** **fl 1956-1960**
Glasgow painter of portraits and figure subjects. Exhibited RSA(5) & GI(3).

**WHYT (WHITE), Charles** **fl 1688-1720**
Aberdeen heraldic and portrait painter. In 1688 made Guild Burgess of Aberdeen and on 10th October, 1695 commissioned by Lyon King of Arms, with the consent of George Porteous(qv) and Henry Fraser(qv), herald painters, to paint all funeral and other heraldic honours. Worked at Marischal College 1698-1707 and drew Dr Sibbald's coat of arms in the Principal's chamber 1698. In 1701 he drew Robert Low by order of the Principal, and the same year was commissioned to gild and paint the frame for the portrait. In 1701 he executed a copy of George Jamesone's portrait 'Robert Gordon of Straloch' for Marischal College and was also undertaking work as late as 1720. Not to be confused with several early English artists of the same name.
**Bibl:** Aberdeen Burgesses 1631-1700, 461; Apted 103; Fasti Academiae Mariscallanae Aberdonensis, i, 118ff,358; Old Aberdeen Records, i, 226; Thomson, George Jamesone, 81.

**WHYTE, A C** **fl 1890-1894**
Amateur Glasgow painter. Exhibited GI(2).

**WHYTE, Miss Catherine Spence** **fl 1921-1963**
Amateur painter of topographical subjects and still life. Exhibited RSA(5) & GI(1) from The Weisha, Dundee, subsequently Lincoln and Edinburgh.

**WHYTE, Clement** **fl 1862**
Edinburgh painter who specialised in portraying Shakespearean characters. Exhibited RSA(2).

**WHYTE, David** **?-c1830**
Angus architect. Worked in the style of Robert Lugar(qv). Best remembered for Keithick House, Perthshire, dating from 1818-23.

**WHYTE, Duncan MacGregor** **1866-1953**
Born Oban, Argyll, May; died Oban. Painter in oil and watercolour of portraits, landscapes and seascapes. Son of an Oban minister. Trained Glasgow, Antwerp and Paris. First became known for his portrait painting for which he travelled widely when undertaking commissions. During his overseas visits, often portrayed figures enjoying sunlit beaches. Although largely overlooked during his life, these warm, airy scenes have become increasingly popular since the contents of his two studios, at Oban and Tiree, appeared in the Glasgow salerooms in the 1970's. Married Mary Barnard(qv). Exhibited RSA(13), RSW(2), GI(50+) & L(4). Represented Glasgow AG.

**WHYTE, John B N** **fl 1938**
Argyll-based still life watercolour painter. Exhibited GI(1) from 2 Battery Terrace, Oban.

**WHYTE, John Gilmour RSW** **1836-1888**
Painter in oil, but mainly watercolour, of landscapes, especially woodland scenes, and occasional still life. Son of a Glasgow teacher. Trained as a dentist, as well as being an amateur artist was an art critic and founder member of the RSW. Also a keen collector of the paintings of the Glasgow Boys, whose work greatly influenced his own. Moved to Helensburgh c1870. Elected RSW 1878. Member, Glasgow Art Club(qv) and patron and friend of James Guthrie(qv). He was a friendly, likeable man, greatly missed by his many friends in Glasgow's artistic circles and beyond. Died of typhoid fever. Exhibited RA(5) RSA(7), RSW(19) & GI(28) from Eastwood, Helensburgh and latterly Fitzroy Place, Glasgow.
**Bibl:** Caw, Sir James Guthrie, 1932; Glasgow Herald, 24 April, 1888 (obit); Halsby 287; T Wemyss Reid, William Black, Novelist, 1924; Quiz, 22 April, 1888, 80.

**WHYTE, John S** **fl 1940-1953**
Painter of topographical watercolours. Exhibited RSA(7) & GI(3) from Helensfield, Clackmannanshire.

**WHYTE, Miss Kathleen** **fl 1974**
Eaglesham embroiderer. Exhibited GI(15).

**WHYTE, Margaret M** **fl 1889-1890**
Morayshire painter. Exhibited RSA(2) from North View, Elgin.

**WHYTE, Morna A** **fl 1978**
Aberdeen printmaker; exhibited AAS(2) from 8 Carnegie Crescent.

**WHYTE, Robert** **fl 1900-1921**
Scottish naval architect associated with Clyde shipbuilders. Among his RSA exhibits were the lounge smoking room for an Orient liner 1921. Exhibited RSA(3) & GI(6) from Helensburgh.

**WHYTE, William Patrick** **fl 1882-1905**
Painter in oil but mainly watercolour; also painted church interiors in a heavy, sombre manner. Lived in Edinburgh before moving for a

time to Paris and settling in London 1885; eventually retired to Kent 1895. Exhibited RA(3), RSA(4), GI(17), RI(2) & L(4) from his studio on Primrose Hill, London.

**WHYTE-SMITH, Mrs Jean W** **fl 1959-1962**
Edinburgh topographical and flower painter. Exhibited GI(2) from Gt. King St.

**WIATREK, Richard** **fl 1977-1984**
Fife-based painter; exhibited RSA(6) from Kennoway and later Auchtertool.

**WIENER, Ruth** **fl 1987**
Aberdeen designer in metalwork; exhibited AAS(1) from 11 Auchinyell Gdns.

**WIGGLESWORTH, Miss Lena** **fl c1945**
Aberdeen flower painter; exhibited AAS(1) from Gordondale House.

**WIGHT, Miss Elspeth S** **fl 1898-1905**
Edinburgh oil painter of fishing boats and figurative subjects; exhibited RSA(11) from Hawkhill Village, Lochend Road.

**WIGHT, John Rutherford** **fl 1870-1883**
Edinburgh painter in oil and watercolour of landscapes, especially in the border. Also an architectural draughtsman. Exhibited RSA(9) including a design for a memorial cross to a Wamphray notable (1872).

**WIGHTON, William** **fl 1861-1876**
Glasgow painter in oil of portraits, also occasional domestic animals and landscape; moved to Dundee 1868. Exhibited RSA(9) & GI(30). Represented Glasgow AG(2) including 'Burns'.

**WILDER, Aeneas** **1967-**
Born Mar 29. Sculptor. Trained Duncan of Jordanstone College of Art 1989-93 and Edinburgh College of Art 1993-94. Awarded John Kinross scholarship (RSA) 1993, Andrew Grant Bequest 1994. Sculpture tutor, Edinburgh Sculpture Workshop 1998. Specialises in large-scale works often most suitable for outdor sites. Exhibits Japan, Wales, Germany, Italy, England & Scotland, from 44 Montgomery St, Edinburgh.

**WILKIE, Alexander D** **fl 1939-1956**
Glasgow painter of flowers, topography and some portraits. Exhibited GI(17) from Tweedsmuir Rd.

**WILKIE, Sir David RA** **1785-1841**
Born Cults, Fife, Nov 18; died at sea Jun 1. Third son of a minister of Cults by his third wife, the daughter of the owner of Pitlessie Mill. Educated at the Parish School, and enrolled at the Trustees Academy, Edinburgh when only 14. His first success came when he was 18, winning ten guineas for a picture 'Calisto in the bath of Diana'. In 1804 he left John Graham and the Trustees Academy to return to Cults and to launch himself by painting the annual fair in the neighbouring village of Pitlessie. With its 140 figures, many taken from sketches made in his father's church, this was a quite remarkable work for a boy of 19. In 1805, from the income of 'The Fair' (£25) and some portraits, notably the wonderfully expressive 'Chalmers Bethune family' portrait 1804, he travelled to London, entering the RA Schools. The next year, 1805, 'Village Politicians' was in the RA and with it were sown the seeds of his southern fame. The simple, unaffected homeliness of the picture in such contrast to the artificial contrivances of most contemporary genre, marked a turning point in British art. In 1809, when still only 24, he was elected ARA and by 1812 had become an RA. Two visits to the Continent, the first to Paris with Benjamin Haden in 1814 and the second to the Netherlands in 1816, appeared to have little effect on his art, although during the latter trip he must have made first-hand aquaintance with the work of Teniers, Ostade, Brouwers and especially Rembrandt. All of these Dutch masters greatly influenced his subsequent work and it is probable that his first awareness of them came from engravings that he would have seen in Edinburgh. In 1817 he was back in Scotland visiting Sir Walter Scott and the Ettrick shepherd. In 1822 embarked upon the 'Entry of George IV to Holyrood' although not completed until some years later. In 1825, suffering a conflict over his artistic development, stressed by overwork and several times bereaved, he suffered a nervous collapse. Unable to paint, he embarked on a journey to Italy via Paris, taking the opportunity to study old masters in Dresden, Florence, Naples, Parma, Rome and eventually Spain. After his return he forsook rustic genre in favour of more robust, firmer and quickly constructed compositions of weightier substance. In 1823 appointed King's Limner for Scotland and in 1830 George IV made him his Principal Painter In Ordinary. In 1836 William IV bestowed a knighthood upon him. In 1834 he went back to Scotland, pausing in Edinburgh and sketching awhile in Perthshire. At Fern Tower, Lady Baird commissioned 'Sir David Baird discovering the body of Tippoo Sahib', completed in 1838. The next year he was sketching in Ireland. Just as he was the first British artist to thoroughly explore Spain, so were his many watercolours of the Middle East among the most impressive ever created in the region by a Briton. In 1840 visited the Holy Land. Returning full of ideas for scriptural subjects, he became suddenly ill and died at sea, off Gibraltar, moving Turner to paint the famous 'Peace: Burial at Sea'. Many of the sketches from this journey were published in 1843 as *Sketches in Turkey, Spain and Egypt* (1840-41). After the early success of 'Pitlessie' and 'Village Politicians', he continued to depict amusing aspects of Scottish life including 'Blind Man's Buff' 1812, now in the Royal Collection, 'The Blind Fiddler' 1806, 'Village Festival' 1809, Tate AG, 'The Penny Wedding' 1818, Royal collection, 'Reading of the Will' 1820, now at the Neue Pinakothek, Munich and 'Parish Beadle'. At the RA in 1822 his 'Chelsea Pensioners reading the Waterloo Despatch' struck such a resounding chord in the public mind that for the first time at the RA a protective rail had to be erected. After his first Spanish expedition, during which he was so affected by the works of Murillo and Velasquez, the new titles reflected the grander compositions: 'Napoleon' and the 'Pope and John Knox preaching before the Lords of the Congregated' 1832, Tate AG. Continued with his portrait painting after Lawrence's death in 1833, notably 'Augustus, Duke of Sussex' (attired in Highland dress, 1833, in Royal Collection), 'King William IV' 1832 and 'Mohamed Ali' 1841, Tate AG. Completed 14 etchings of which a variation of his own 'Reading a Will' is perhaps the finest. Together with Geddes(qv), he revived the art of etching in Scotland. His influence was immense and lasting in England as well as in his native Scotland. With Raeburn, he was a founding father of what has become known as the Scottish School. The verdict of history is unclear. Armstrong thought him 'an almost unique example of a great artist without a great individuality'. Delacroix, who had met Wilkie in 1825 and again in 1841, wrote that 'his finished pictures had always displeased me, but indeed his rough sketches and studies are beyond all praise'. Caw concluded that 'although Wilkie drew his subjects from the life of the Scotch peasantry, he only touched it at certain points. The shrewdness and greed of gain, the boisterous good humour and the pawky dry wit, the tendency to argument and the inclination to drink, these...characteristics are admirably expressed...but one looks almost in vain for that austere sense of responsiblity and duty, and for that stern and dour Covenanting spirit, which are at once the glory and the reproach of the Scottish people...nor did he touch the hard toil and struggle for existence which have made us what we are...but his work is not wanting in tenderness, and his reading of character, if not very profound, was sure and strong. He was no moralist, but he was a keen observer...and his technique was excellently well fitted to express the results of his insight and observation'. As a man he was described by one contemporary as 'a raw, tall, pale, queer Scotsman', while his lifelong friend Benjamin Haden reported that 'notwithstanding Paris was filled with all the nations of the earth, the greatest oddity in it was unquestionably David Wilkie. His horrible French, his strange, tottering, feeble carriage, his carrying about his prints to make bargains with print-sellers; his resolute determination never to leave the restaurant until he got his change right to a centime...but there is a simplicity in his manners, a soundness and originality in his thinking, which makes him a most instructive companion'. More recently McMillan has delineated the social context and contemporary creative activity into which the distinctly Scottish aspects of Wilkie's art fit: the teaching of Bell(qv), the novels of Scott, the poetry of Burns, the paintings of Raeburn and Ramsay, with the manner and meaning of Rembrandt behind it all. There remained differences of opinion regarding contrasting merits of Wilkie's differing aims and subjects. It is perhaps natural for Scottish writers to give pre-eminence to his early work, but as Irwin has written 'it is time that the balance was redressed so that Wilkie's total achievement can be appreciated within its historical context'. Sir John Millais, writing in 1885, thought that 'in the history of art there has been no superior to him for knowledge of

composition, beautiful and subtle drawing, portrayal of character and originality'. He was defeated by Martin Archer Shee for the Presidency of the Academy, only Collins and Leslie voting for him. Illustrated *Old Mortality* (1830), *Sketches in Turkey, Syria and Egypt* (1843) and *Sketches Spanish and Oriental* (1846). Also contributed to *The Keepsake* (1830) and *Heath's Gallery* (1836). Exhibited RA (100) 1806-1842; also Institute for the Encouragement of Fine Arts in Scotland(6) & the Scottish Academy during his life-time(8). Represented in NGS, SNPG(14), V & A, Aberdeen AG, Glasgow AG(4), Kirkcaldy AG, Brodie Castle (NTS), Hill of Tarvit (NTS), The Binns (NTS), Cardiff AG, Manchester AG, Fitzwilliam (Oxford), Bedford AG, Worcester AG, Berlin AG, Besancon AG, Nat Gall: Dublin, Gratz AG, Lille AG, Wallace Collection, Minneapolis AG, Montreal (Learmont), Munich AG, Toledo AG, Victoria AG (Australia).
**Bibl:** AJ 1859, 233ff; 1860, 236ff; 1896m 183-188; Armstrong 21-29; Art Union, 1840, 10ff; 1841, 115ff; W. Bayne, Sir David Wilkie, 1903; Bryan; Brydal 254-266; Bushnell; Butchart 24-31,75,89; Caw, 95-104; Cundall; A. Cunningham, The Life of Sir David Wilkie, 1843; Lindsay Errington,'Sir David Wilkie, paintings and drawings', NGS 1975; Halsby 52-59; Hardie III, 175-6; C. Heaton, The Great Works of Sir David Wilkie, 1868; Lord G. Gower, Sir David Wilkie, 1902; Houfe; Irwin, 165-185; David Laing, Etchings by Sir David Wilkie and Andrew Geddes, Edinburgh 1875; McKay 69-98; McMillan[GA] 157-185 et passim; [SA] passim chs ix & x; Maas, 93, 104-5; J.W. Mollett, Sir David Wilkie, 1881; Marcia Pointon, 'From Blind Man's Buff to Le Colin Maitland: Wilkie and his French Audience', Oxford AJ(7) 1984; Portfolio 1887, 90-97; RA (Ex Cat, 1958); A. Raimbach, Memoirs of Sir David Wilkie, 1853; Redgrave; Reynolds 7-8, 45-7 et passim; Ruskin, Modern Painters; Ruskin, Academy Notes; A.L. Simpson, The Story of Sir David Wilkie, 1879.

**WILKIE, John D** **fl 1861-1870**
Edinburgh oil painter of landscapes and figurative subjects; exhibited RSA(10).

**WILKIE, Robert** **1888-?**
Born Sinclairtown, Kirkcaldy, Jul 10. Painter of landscapes and interiors, also lithographer, photographer and teacher. Trained Edinburgh College of Art. Often painted mountain burns and cascading rivers. Married Mary Ballantine(qv). Lived in Glasgow. Exhibited RSA(4) 1924-1930, GI(4) & L(1).

**WILKIE, Robert** **fl 1953-1955**
Findhorn painter of landscapes. Exhibited GI(3).

**WILKIE, T(or J)** **fl 1858**
West Coates oil painter of genre; exhibited RSA(1).

**WILKIE, Thomas** **fl 1670-1680**
Edinburgh master-mason. Designed Gallery house (Angus), built in 1680 for John Falconer of Balmakellie. This is a most handsome tall building having a central staircase and a long gallery that comprises the whole of the first floor of the main block.
**Bibl:** Dunbar 58-9 (illus 58).

**WILKIE, W P** **fl 1859-1861**
Edinburgh oil painter; exhibited three Continental landscapes at the RSA in 1859 followed by Scottish landscapes in 1860 & 1861.

**WILKINS, William** **1778-1839**
English architect. Best remembered for his part in the English Greek Revival exemplified by Grange Park (Hampshire). Introduced the Tudor style into Scotland with his design for Dalmeny House, West Lothian (1815-19).
**Bibl:** Colvin; Dunbar 120,124.

**WILKINSON, Mrs Evelyn Harriet (née Mackenzie)** **1893-1968**
Born Wu-King-Fu, Swatow, China, Jun 7. Both parents Scottish. Trained Edinburgh School of Art. Married the English artist Norman W and from a London base exhibited RA(2), RI(1), ROI(5) & SWA(2) 1918-1938.

**WILLIAMS, Andrew** **1954-**
Born Barry, South Wales. From 1972-77 studied art and art history at Edinburgh and Edinburgh College of Art. Exhibits widely in Britain and overseas, his first one-man show in Edinburgh. From 1979-80 he worked in the south of France where he administered the Karolyi Foundation at Vence. Worked in New York 1984. 'He applies his paint with bold, thick brushstrokes in works allied to contemporary European figurative art. His preferred theme is the male figure, often athletes and body builders though recently he has turned to landscape' [Hartley].
**Bibl:** 369 Gallery, Edinburgh, 'Andrew Williams' (Ex Cat 1986); Hartley 168.

**WILLIAMS, Charles Sneed** **fl 1906-1914**
Painter of figurative subjects and portraits. His portrait of 'Earl Gardener' exhibited at the GI in 1906 aroused considerable favourable critical attention at the time but his work has since become little known. Exhibited GI(7) from Glasgow.

**WILLIAMS, David** **fl 1936-1937**
Painter. Exhibited RCA(4) from Dundee.

**WILLIAMS, Gertrude Alice (Mrs Morris Meredith W)** **1877-1934**
Born Liverpool. A versatile artist: sculptor, decorative painter, illustrator and stained glass window designer. Trained School of Architecture and Applied Art, Liverpool and in Paris. Married the painter Morris W(qv) and settled in Edinburgh 1907 remaining there twenty years before retiring to Devon. Associated with Robert Lorimer and frequent collaborator with her husband, including the stained glass windows for Lorimer's chapel at Ardkinglas, Argyll and four lights in St Peter (RC) Church, Morningside, having 'lovely colour and and very small-scale drawing' [Gifford]. The war memorial at Paisley, an equestrian statue, designed by her and Robert Lorimer, won a competition from over two hundred entrants. But her best known work is in the Scottish National War Memorial, windows depicting the angels of 'Courage', 'Fortitude', 'Faith', 'Hope' and 'Magnanimity'; and figures of 'Knowledge'. Exhibited work included pen and ink book illustrations, terracotta and bronze portrait busts, and continental landscape. During their stay in Scotland exhibited RA(7), RSA(37), RSW(3), GI(25+) & L(22).
**Bibl:** Gifford 100-1,114,619; Peter Savage, Lorimer and the Edinburgh Craft Designers, Edinburgh 1980, 100,133,142,170.

**WILLIAMS, Hugh 'Grecian' William** **1773-1829**
Born at sea; died Edinburgh, Jun 23. Son of a Welsh ship's captain, his mother was the daughter of Colonel Lewis, Deputy Governor of Gibraltar. Early orphaned, he was reared in Edinburgh by his maternal grandmother who had married, as her second husband, an Italian named Ruffini. His step-father encouraged the young man to become a painter, sending him to study with David Allan(qv), and this he did, remaining in Scotland for the rest of his life. As well as being based in Edinburgh painting the southern Highlands, he also worked in Argyllshire, on Arran and occasionally in Angus on the east coast. There is no doubt that had he been based in London, his fame and recognition as a watercolour painter would have exceeded that to which history presently accords him. Irwin and Caw suggest that the reason why from about 1810 his style began to broaden, was the result of an increasing amount of work in oil. A contemporary spoke of him as 'warm hearted, gentle and modest'. Armed with a congenial temperament and with the financial and social help of his wife, he moved in Edinburgh high society. The V and A hold a manuscript by him, 'Method of drawing in Watercolours as Practised by Mr Williams', quoted in full by Halsby (pp 42-45)). Highly regarded by Turner, a respect Williams warmly reciprocated. His early works were chiefly Scottish landscapes but he sometimes painted Welsh or north of England subjects - a view of 'Bangor Cathedral' 1806 is in V & A. In 1817-1818 he toured Italy and Greece and in 1820 published *Travels in Italy, Greece and the Ionian Islands* - an account of his travels with engravings from his own drawings. His watercolours of Greece attracted considerable attention and between 1827 and 1829 he published *Select Views in Greece,* a work which became so well known that he was afforded the nickname 'Grecian' Williams. The British Museum has a view on the Acropolis while the other watercolours by him are in the NGS although his Scottish drawings are now more familiar in England than any other of his work. His purple-browns and dark greens sometimes resemble the hues of De Wint and even J R Cozens. Often, however, he was content to depict in conventional terms Highland scenery and ruins and his colour, when it becomes expansive, tends to lapse into less pleasant blue-greens and hot passages of high light in brownish-red and yellow. His most characteristic drawings are

executed in broad transparent washes over a carefully pencilled outline. James Nasmyth mentions Williams as an artist whom his father helped so that the young man probably attended the Nasmyth School in York Place for a brief spell. Represented in NGS, V & A, Tate AG, SNPG(Burns), Glasgow AG, Dundee AG, Perth AG, Aberdeen AG, Edinburgh City collection(2), Brodie Castle (NTS).
**Bibl:** Bryan; Brydall 299-302; Bushnell; Butchart 39,60,63; Caw 150-152; Halsby 40-45; Irwin 228-231; McKay 192-6; Macmillan [SA] 144-7,222-7,300; Williams 64-6.

**WILLIAMS, Isabella S** **fl 1879-1883**
Amateur Glasgow oil painter; landscapes and river scenes. Exhibited RSA(4) & GI(1).

**WILLIAMS, J E** **fl 1848**
Edinburgh landscape painter; exhibited RSA(1) from Saxe Coburg Pl.

**WILLIAMS, J L** **fl c1930**
Aberdeenshire painter in oils of Highland landscape and topography; exhibited AAS from The Cross, Turriff.

**WILLIAMS, Mrs J S** **fl 1880-1883**
Amateur Glasgow landscape and topographical painter; exhibited RSA(3) & GI(5), latterly from Edinburgh.

**WILLIAMS, James Anderson** **1860-1935**
Edinburgh architect. Designed a number of schools include a design for Dumfries Academy (1896). Exhibited RSA(14) 1894-1917 from the City Chambers and other addresses in the city.

**WILLIAMS, John** **fl 1861-1875**
Prolific Campsie oil painter of landscapes, especially local scenes and in Argyllshire. Exhibited RSA(65) including a fine study of 'Eilean Donan Castle' 1863; also GI 1863-1875, latterly from Lennoxtown, Stirlingshire.

**WILLIAMS, John (or James) Francis RSA** **1785-1846**
Born Perthshire; died Glasgow, 31 Oct. Landscape painter in oils and watercolour. Went to England as a young man and practised for some years as a scene painter before returning to Scotland c1810 when he worked in the Edinburgh Theatre. First exhibited with the Associated Artists 1811. Subsequently abandoned the theatre to work full-time as a landscape painter and part-time teacher. A local character and a favourite with the caricaturists of the time. Foundation member Scottish Academy being elected RSA 1863, later becoming its Treasurer for seven years. One of nine artists who withdrew from the Academy after its first meeting, although continuing to be associated with it. In 1800 exhibited a view of Loch Tay at the RA and four further works followed, all from 6 George Street, Edinburgh, two in 1823 and two more Scottish landscapes 1840. His watercolours are restrained, the general tone being influenced by the early topographical artists. Exhibited RSA(197). His diploma work was a scene on the Ayrshire coast: 'Storm Passing Off' (1831) now in the RSA. Represented in NGS(7).
**Bibl:** Bryan; Brydall 302-3; Halsby 287.

**WILLIAMS, Morris Meredith** **1881-1873**
Born Cowbridge, Glamorgan; died Devon. Painter, stained glass window designer and illustrator. Trained Slade, Paris and Italy. After his marriage to Gertrude Alice W(qv) settled in Edinburgh as art master at Fettes College. During the war made many sketches while serving which were used by Alice in her work on the Scottish National War Memorial 1927. Five charcoal cartoons, made for his wife's frieze composed to illustrate every type of uniform and equipment used by Scotland's servicemen and women during WW1, are now in SNGMA. In collaboration with his wife designed the stained glass windows for Robert Lorimer's Ardkinglas House, Argyll; also four lights at St Peter (RC) Church, Morningside. Also in St Peter is a large mural 'Feeding of the Five Thousand' while the Reredos in St Giles Cathedral shows the 'Adoration of the Angels' painted in low relief in collaboration with his wife. Exhibited both oils and watercolours at the RA(13), RSA(53), RSW(2), GI(2) & L (33). Retired to Devon. Represented Edinburgh City collection(2), Walker AG (Liverpool).
**Bibl:** Gifford 100-1,114,619; Peter Savage, Lorimer and the Edinburgh Craft Designers, Edinburgh 1980, 100,142,170.

**WILLIAMS, Thomas** **fl 1851-1881**
Glasgow then East Kilbride landscape painter in oil and watercolour. Painted views of the Clyde and of the countryside around Glasgow. His watercolour, 'Govan Ferry' 1860 was exhibited in Glasgow 1901, again in 1912 and in 1958 at the Helensburgh exhibition 'The Artist and the River Clyde'. Exhibited RSA(6) & GI(25+) 1861-1867.
**Bibl:** Halsby 287.

**WILLIAMS, W** **fl 1815**
All that is known of this painter is that he exhibited a view in Glencoe at the RA in 1815 from 23 George Street, Edinburgh. Probably the artist whose watercolour 'Culzean from the Seashore' is in Culzean (NTS).

**WILLIAMSON, Andrew** **fl 1880-1884**
Edinburgh landscape painter; exhibited RSA(2) from 14 Moray Pl.

**WILLIAMSON, Charles** **fl 1989-**
Aberdeen painter; exhibits AAS(2) from 10 Wallfield Crescent.

**WILLIAMSON, David** **fl 1867**
Hamilton topographical painter; exhibited RSA(1) & GI(2).

**WILLIAMSON, David Whyte** **fl 1869-1889**
Edinburgh landscape painter in oil originally from Hamilton; exhibited RSA(11), latterly from 13 Melville Terrace.

**WILLIAMSON, J J** **fl 1973-1978**
Midlothian sculptor. Works in wood, especially elm, beech and oak. Exhibited RSA(4), from Roslin.

**WILLIAMSON, James** **fl 1886-1888**
Itinerant Edinburgh painter in watercolour of figurative subjects. Spent a year in Italy 1887. Exhibited RSA(1) & L(3).

**WILLIAMSON James Anderson** **1860-1935**
Edinburgh architect. Succeeded Robert Morham(qv) as City Architect 1910. Designed many minor buildings and alterations. Responsible for Portobello Town Hall (1909-12); Portobello Golf House (1910); and Morningside Public Library (1917).
**Bibl:** Gifford 194,231,259,507-8,526,535,557,588,620,653.

**WILLIAMSON, Janetta B** **fl 1879-1882**
Amateur Glasgow flower painter of 13 Queens Crescent; exhib GI(4).

**WILLIAMSON, John** **1826-1885**
Born Scotland; died Glenwood, USA, 28 May. Landscape painter. Emigrated to USA at an early age and settled in Boston. Known for his depiction of the scenery along the Hudson river and in the Catskill mountains.

**WILLIAMSON, John** **fl 1885-1896**
Edinburgh painter in oil of portraits and figure subjects, also illustrator. Specialised in costume subjects, working in Edinburgh 1885-1890 from 6 Shandwick Place, and in London from 1893 at 48 Flanders Rd, Bedford Pk. Illustrated Reed's *Kilgonan* (1894) and Crawford's *The Wild Flowers of Scotland* 1897; contributed to *The English Illustrated Magazine* (1895-6). Refined delineation, accurate detail and considerable sensitivity, somewhat in the manner of Kenneth Macleay(qv). Exhibited RA(4) including the portrait of 'Mariella, daughter of Professor F. York Powell' 1895; also RSA(11) & RBA(1).
**Bibl:** Houfe.

**WILLIAMSON, Katherine H** **fl 1987**
Aberdeen jewellery designer; exhibited AAS(1) from 3 Carden Pl.

**WILLIAMSON, Lawrie FRSA** **1932-**
Scottish landscape and figurative painter in oils and watercolour. Trained Nottingham College of Art and L'Ecole des Beaux Art. Winner of both 'Stanley Grimm' and 'Cornellison' prizes at ROI. Keen fisherman. Most of his colourful, highly charged work and solo exhibitions have been in England. Moved to Ireland 2002.

**WILLIAMSON, Robert Chisholm** **fl 1885-1887**
Amateur Aberdeen painter; exhibited RSA(1) and 'Feeding time' at the AAS from 6 Admiral Terrace.

**WILLIAMSON, Dr W H** **fl 1893-1900**
Aberdeen part-time painter in oils of coastal scenery and topography. Exhibited AAS(5) from 15 Union Terrace.

**WILLIAMSON, William Kilgour** **c1828-1856**
Edinburgh animal and heraldic painter. Entered Trustees Academy 1850 on the recommendation of James Drummond(qv) but left a year later. Married Barbara Newton of Biggar 1856. In 1853 exhibited 'The Dispute, or the Game Laws, natural and practical' RSA and 'Wood pigeon, squirrel and wild flowers' 1855, from Brighton St.

**WILLIS, Rosamund ARCA** **fl 1964-1967**
Aberdeen painter in watercolours, also textile designer. Elected ARCA. Exhibited AAS between the above years from 20 The Chanonry, Old Aberdeen.

**WILLISON, George** **1741-1797**
Born and died Edinburgh, April. Nephew of George Dempster of Dunnicken who sent him to study in Rome to study under Anton Mengs. As a very young man he had shown promise by winning a Premium in 1757 for the best drawing of an antique sculpture. His early taste in art was encouraged by a prize for a drawing of flowers in 1756 (awarded by the Edinburgh Society for the Encouragement of Arts and Sciences) and the following year second prize, and in 1758 a third prize for 'drawing from a busto'. On his return settled in London where he practised for ten years until, in 1777, he went to India where he painted a large number of portraits including one of the 'Nabob of Arcot', now at Hampton Court. Having been left a fortune bequeathed by a wealthy gentleman whose dangerous wound he had cured, he returned home pursuing his art in Edinburgh. There his work included a pleasing portrait of 'John Beugo'(qv), the engraver, now in the SNPG. 'Though slight and rather thin, it is the work of an expert brushman'. His work is widely regarded as average, but occasionally showing a glimpse of real ability. While Cunningham referred to the fact that he 'drew indifferently and coloured worse', Caw thought his works 'pleasant in colour, graceful in design, fair if not searching in character, and painted in an easy, though somewhat thin, manner'. 'The Duke of Queensberry', RA 1771 is in the Archers' Hall, Edinburgh and his smaller personal study of young 'James Boswell' 1765 is in the SNPG. Irwin regards as one of his 'most delightful creations' the portrait of 'Mrs Haughton', a celebrated London beauty of the time. In later life he sometimes identified sitters with classical characters, a practice more common among his English than his Scottish contemporaries. An attractive small-scale portrait 'Nancy Parsons', in BAC, Yale, was engraved 1771. Visited India 1774-1780 whence he sent portraits of his main patron, the Nawab of Arcot, to the Society of Artists 1777-1778. Exhibited RA(7) 1771 and 1772. Represented in SNPG(3), Victoria AG (Australia).
**Bibl:** Archer 99-107; Benezit; Bryan; Brydall 168-9; Caw 49; Irwin 74-5; McKay 27; Macmillan [SA] 111-2; Waterhouse.

**WILLOCK, Annie M** **fl 1893-1902**
Aberdeen painter of local harbour scenes, especially at sunrise and sunset. Exhibited AAS(8) from 4, Golden Square.

**WILLOCKS, Mrs Elizabeth M** **fl 1971-**
Pollockshields painter of flowers and still life. Exhibits GI since 1971.

**WILLOX, Miss Jeannie B** **fl 1894-1902**
Aberdeenshire painter of local harbour scenes, flowers; exhibited AAS(8) from Lonmay and subsequently 7 King St, Peterhead.

**WILLS, John Whyte** **fl 1923**
Polmuir sculptor. Exhibited AAS(1) from South Cottage.

**WILLSHIRE, William Hughes** **fl 1835-1836**
Edinburgh painter of interiors and landscape; exhibited RSA(2), from Trinity.

**WILSON, A Ure** **fl 1895-1896**
Amateur Dundee painter of figurative studies; exhibited AAS(2) & GI(4) from 13 Westfield Place.

**WILSON, A Maxwell** **fl 1965-1982**
Glasgow landscape painter. Exhibited GI(11).

**WILSON, Agnes E** **fl 1954-1965**
Edinburgh landscape and genre painter; exhibited RSA(4) from Seton Pl.

**WILSON, Aileen** **fl 1985**
Aberdeen printmaker. Exhibited AAS(2) from 61D Nelson St.

**WILSON, Alexander** **1766-1813**
Born Paisley, Jly 6; died Philadelphia, Aug 23. Bird painter. Son of a weaver. Apprenticed to that trade 1779 and although remaining for ten years, his temperament was unsuited for the work. He nurtured an ambition to be a poet and when 23 abandoned the loom and took to the life of a pedlar, trying to sell his poems. Several had been published anonymously and in 1790 he published a volume of poetry. Unfortunately this resulted in his imprisonment owing to the satire of a local mill owner. In 1794, in the company of his nephew, he migrated to the United States landing at Newcastle, Delaware and proceeding on foot to Philadelphia. En route he killed and preserved a red-headed woodpecker, arousing his interest in American ornithology. In 1802 he acquired a school on the Schuykill River, just below Philadelphia, where one of his neighbours was the naturalist, William Bartram. Bartram gave the young man free access to his library and Wilson quickly realised the deficiency in most American ornithological writing until that time. He, therefore, decided to write an American ornithology to which end he studied drawing and etching. Although failing to master these arts to his satisfaction, he subsequently enlisted the help of Alexander Lawson. From 1808 to 1813 he worked continuously to see the seven volumes of his master work *American Ornithology* in print. Although the mixtures of birds on each plate are often crowded and curiously placed, the research, the text and the conception of the work justifies his fame. The work covers the eastern part of the United States from Florida northwards and the thoroughness was such that despite the fact that there were only ten years from the conception of the work to his death, few species were omitted from the record. The scientific detailing of American birds rests firmly on Wilson's pioneering work. He was said to be relentless and unforgiving, driving others as hard as he drove himself and that it gave him pleasure to acknowledge error when the conviction resulted from his own judgement but found it hard to endure being told of his mistakes by others. Whereas Katesby was the first significant naturalist in America, Wilson was the pioneering ornithologist and ornithological artist.
**Bibl:** Halsby 287; Houfe; Skipworth: The Great Bird Illustrators, 1979, 24-29.

**WILSON, Alexander** **fl 1862-1870**
Glasgow watercolour landscape painter. Exhibited GI(8), mostly scenes on Arran.

**WILSON, Alice** **1876-1974**
Born Dalmuir, Dumbartonshire. Painter in oil, watercolour, pastel and pen and ink; landscapes, interiors and portraits. Second daughter of John W, a well known Clyde shipyard manager. Trained at the Slade. Her best work was in watercolour but she also painted small, decorative landscapes in oil. Achieved considerable distinction in portraiture in both oil and most particularly in pastel. Eventually settled in London. Exhibited at the RSA(28), RSW(3), AAS(1) & GI(1) from 17 Breadburn Terrace.
Bibl: Glasgow Herald, 8.2.74 (obit).

**WILSON, Miss Alice E J** **20th Cent**
Aberdeen painter of flowers and interiors; exhibited AAS from 43 Beaconfield Place.

**WILSON, Alison** **fl 1901-1908**
Minor Edinburgh painter; exhibited RSA(5) from 20 Anne St.

**WILSON, Andrew** **1780-1848**
Born Edinburgh; died England, 27 Nov. His family suffered from the Jacobite cause. Father of Charles Heath W(qv). After a brief spell of study under Alexander Nasmyth, in 1797 went to London and enrolled at the RA Schools, shortly afterwards proceeding to Rome. There he met a wealthy collector, Mr Champernon, and James Irving, artist and collector. At the same time he began studying ancient art and brought home many sketches of architectural monuments and similar subjects around Naples as well as Rome. On returning home he saw the opportunity for commercial gain in acquiring pictures and went

back to Italy in 1803-5. After many hazards he reached Genoa where, disguised as an American citizen, he obtained the protection of the American Consul. Spent three years there being elected a member of the Ligurian Academy of Arts. This was a profitable visit as he acquired 54 pictures including Rubens' 'Moses and the Brazen Serpent', now in the NGS, and Titian's 'Adoration of the Magi', now in the SNG. It is said that whilst in Genoa as a member of the local Academy he visited Napoleon. Buonaparte, on pausing to examine Wilson's picture, was informed by a fellow Academician that it was by an Englishman, whereupon Napoleon sternly replied 'Le talent n'a pas de pays'. Wilson travelled home through Germany, settling once again in London where he took up watercolour painting, an art for which his delicacy was more suited than oils. Following his marriage, became Professor of Drawing at Sandhurst Military College. Resigned 1811 to become Master of the Trustees Academy, Edinburgh where he did yeoman service in the early training of artists including R S Lauder(qv), D O Hill(qv) and William Simson(qv). Remained there for eight years before returning to Italy, painting in Rome, Genoa and Florence as well as collecting works of art for Sir Robert Peel, the Earls of Pembroke and Hopetoun, sometimes acting with Wilkie (who thought Wilson's work 'very fine and much in the style of Poussin'). Said to have been responsible for sending 27 Van Dycks to England and largely responsible for many of the old masters now in the SNG. Although he sometimes painted Scottish subjects, is best known for his Continental work and for his topographical watercolours and pencil drawings. One of the original members of the Associated Artists in Watercolour. At the RA (where he is incorrectly listed as Alexander Wilson) he exhibited 19 works 1803-1813, almost all of them Italian views including 'The Temple at Tivoli'. A grossly underrated and unrecognised artist, largely because of the small number of his works seen in Britain. 'The crispness and competence of line is not lost in the finished watercolours, which have remarkable freshness, achieved by clear washes over simple outline. In his handling of architecture, Wilson reveals an ability to sum up the construction and perspective of a building in clear and simple pencil lines, over which he places light washes...In addition to being a fine draughtsman, he had also a good sense of colour. He exploits watercolour by using the white paper beneath to create luminosity' [Halsby]. Sometimes his work is in the Claudian tradition as, for example, his 'View North Across the Forth, with Hopetoun Castle in the Foreground' 1820. He executed a line engraving of Allan Ramsay for the 1814 edition of *The Gentle Shepherd.* Helped to illustrate *Twelve Views in the Vicinity of the Metropolis of Scotland,* some engraved by himself and some by Alex Carse(qv) with whom he sometimes collaborated. Contributed to Britton's *Beauties of England and Wales* (1813-1815) and designed bookplates for Charles Craigie Halkett, 1820; David Kennedy, 1810; and D. Robertson, 1820. Represented in NG, Tate AG, NGS(8), V & A, BM, Whitworth AG (Manchester), Glasgow AG.

**Bibl:** Armstrong 18; Bryan; Brydal 303-5; Bushnell; Butchart 35,36, 43; Caw 152-3; DNB; Halsby 45-7; Houfe; Irwin 241-2 et passim; McKay 190-192; Macmillan [SA] 142-3,183,201,209; RSA, 1880 (post).

**WILSON, Andrew Stout** **fl 1949-1950**

Edinburgh landscape painter, fond of Lothian harbour scenes. Exhibited RSA(4).

**WILSON, Miss Anna Dove** **fl 1895-1899**

Prolific Aberdeen portrait painter; a portrait of 'Miss Forbes-Lumsden' at the AAS 1896 received favourable attention . Exhibited RSA(1), AAS(28), GI(1) & L(1) from 17 Rubislaw Terrace.

**WILSON, Annie Heath** **fl 1875-1920**

Painter in oil and watercolour of landscapes and figures subjects. Related to William Heath W(qv). Lived for a time in Florence c1884, Genoa 1888 and Tangier 1913 before finally settling in Suffolk. Exhibited extensively RA(5), RBA(20), ROI(3), GI(11), LS(2), SWA(14), L(8) & Paris Salon.

**WILSON, Miss B Y** **fl 1921**

Moray miniaturist and enamellist. Exhibited two miniature portraits at the RSA from Nairn.

**WILSON, Charles** **1810-1863**

Glasgow architect. Son of a local builder, he worked for ten years in the office of David Hamilton(qv) before launching his own practice 1837. Major figure in the development of Glasgow. A shy, retiring man, in 1841 visited Paris and thereafter a French influence was apparent in many of his designs. President, Glasgow Institute of Architects. Best remembered for his Woodlands Hill scheme (1855-7) carried on in association with Sir Joseph Paxton's development of nearby Kelvingrove Park. 'The contrast between the solid Gothic dignity of the hill-top Park Circus and the thrusting Victorian assertion of the encircling Park Terrace is singularly effective, the whole composition being crowned by the triple towers of the picturesque Free Church College (1856)' [Dunbar]. Also responsible for the Queen's Rooms (1857), now a Christian Science church, the Royal Faculty of Procurators, St George's Place (1854) and an interesting early mill, the Alexander Mill, in Duke Street (1849), now a hotel. Designed several mansion houses in Dundee of which the best was Hazel Hall (1853), since demolished.

**Bibl:** Dunbar 138,141,151,153; A Gomme & D Walker, Architecture of Glasgow, London 1987(rev), 303-4; Bruce Walker & W S Gauldie, Architects and Architecture on Tayside, Dundee 1984, 131.

**WILSON, Charles Heath ARSA (resigned)** **1809-1882**

Born London; died Florence, Jly 3. Architect, teacher and painter in oil and watercolour of landscape, also illustrator. Son of Andrew W(qv), father of William Heath W(qv). In addition to his work as an artist was a fine teacher, administrator and writer. Studied under his father with whom he travelled to Italy 1826, remaining until 1833. Thereafter he returned to Edinburgh practising as an architect and teaching at the School of Art. There followed a succession of senior administrative appointments, first as Director of the Edinburgh School of Art, then of Somerset House School (after Dyce resigned 1843) and, finally, Headmaster of the new Glasgow School of Design 1849. From this last appointment he resigned 1869 so as to live in Italy. Knowledgeable on fresco painting and stained glass design. In Italy he published a *Life of Michelangelo* (1876). Although his watercolours are somewhat trite in design and architectural in mood and composition, he was able to create the transparent effects of reflections on still water aided no doubt by his skill as a landscape gardener. Elected ARSA 1835, resigned 1858. Illustrated P. Pifferi's *Viaggio Antiquario* (1832) and *Voyage Round the Coasts of Scotland* (1842). In 1869 finally settled in Florence. Exhibited RSA(38) including a design for the competition for a new Nelson Monument in Trafalgar Square (1840). Represented in NGS.

**Bibl:** Brydall 149,305; Caw 129; Halsby 83-4,95,287; Houfe; Irwin.

**WILSON, Colin** **fl 1976-1979**

Renfrewshire painter of portraits and figurative works. Exhibited GI from Barrhead.

**WILSON, Cyril** **1911-?**

Born High Wycombe, April. Painter in oil, watercolour, gouache and ink, also lithographer. Trained Reading College of Art. Married Jane Bennie Fyfe(qv). In 1948 moved to Dumfries and after 1959 spent part of the year in Ibiza. President of the Forces Art Club in Cairo 1941-7 and from 1954-1958 President of Dumfries and Galloway Fine Arts Society. Elected SSA 1955. One-man shows in Cairo 1945, Beirut 1946, Edinburgh 1967 & 1970 and regularly at Ibiza since 1966. Professor Federici wrote 'in Wilson's personality there are two strands, at first sight contradictory, which intertwine in various ways and continuously...a vital passion which could be called romantic and a cultured tear, a discerning meditation which ensures for his idiom its own special nobility...he knows how to resolve symbols and formal themes, from which he starts a discourse which though exaggerated in tone knows how to achieve true and complete intensity'. Exhibited AAS(3) 1959. Represented in SNGMA, Dundee AG, Dick Institute (Kilmarnock), Gracefield AG (Dumfries), SAC, Egyptian Museum of Modern Art (Cairo).

**WILSON, D R** **fl 1880-1894**

Glasgow topographical painter. Moved to London in the 1880's and eventually to Bushey, Hertfordshire. Exhibited ROI(1), RBA(2), GI(4) & L(1).

**WILSON, Sir Daniel** **fl c1842-1850**

Edinburgh print-seller, artist's colour man and watercolourist. Apprenticed to William Miller. Went to London to gain experience, studying under Charles Turner. Returned to Edinburgh 1842 setting up business as a print-seller in West Register St. Became Secretary,

Society of Antiquaries of Scotland, in which capacity he was an influential figure in the artistic life of the city. His most important work, *Memorials of Edinburgh in the Olden Time,* appeared in 24 parts in 1847, then in two volumes the following year. These contained over 120 engraved illustrations and, in the artist's words, comprise 'pen-and-pencil sketches, professing in general considerable minuteness of outline, though with a rapid touch that precluded very elaborate finish. Accuracy has been aimed at through art, not without knowingly incurring the risk of occasionally being somewhat dry'. Wilson's drawings were engraved mostly by William Forrest(qv). Represented in City of Edinburgh collection.

**WILSON, David Forrester RSA** **1873-1950**
Born Glasgow, Apr 4; died Islay, Jan 8 or 9. Painter of portraits and decorative subjects, also etcher. Son of a lithographer; educated Gorbals Public School and Glasgow School of Art. Commissioned by Glasgow Corporation to paint one of a series of large decorative panels in the banqueting hall of the Glasgow municipal buildings. In 1890 abandoned a business career in order to study at the Glasgow School of Art under Professor Delville winning a Haldane Scholarship 1901. In 1905 he went to Europe and continued to study in Italy, Belgium, Paris and London. From 1931-38 was Head of Drawing and Painting, Glasgow School of Art. During the greater part of his teaching life lived at Milngavie, later moving to Glasgow and finally to Ayr. Elected ARSA 1922, RSA 1932, retired member 1942. Exhibited in Chicago, Pittsburg and Buffalo, USA. 'His painting is characterised by fine drawing and colour and a strong sense of decoration. It is poetical in feeling which he often expressed through allegory. All his work is founded in the best historical tradition' [Halsby]. Among his principal works are 'Fieldworkers', 'The Song', 'The Valley of Melting Snow', 'Time and History'. His few watercolours date from his early symbolist period. Frequent exhibitor RSA, also occasionally RSW, AAS 1931-1937 & GI(79). Represented in Glasgow AG, Lillie AG (Milngavie)(5) including 'Self-portrait'.
**Bibl:** Halsby 287.

**WILSON, David L** **fl 1897-1900**
Minor Glasgow painter and illustrator. Exhibited GI(2) from 3 Maxwell Pl.

**WILSON, Edith** **fl 1935-1944**
Flower painter in watercolour of 51 Dreghorn Loan, Edinburgh; exhibited RSA(1) & RSW(1), latterly from Craighouse Avenue.

**WILSON, Edward Arthur** **1886-?**
Born Glasgow, Mar 4. Illustrator, author, stage designer and designer of furniture, bookplates and silks. As a young child went with his family to Rotterdam and in 1893 migrated to the USA, settling in Chicago where he attended the Art Institute. Quickly established his own studio working in Brooklyn, NY and Truro, Massachusetts. Married Dorothy Roe 1913. Won many awards including the Art Director medal 1926 and again 1930, the Isidor prize 1927 and the Shaw prize 1942. One of America's finest and best known illustrators. Wrote and illustrated *Pirate's Treasure* (1926); illustrated Overton's *Long Island's Story*(1929), *Robinson Crusoe*(1930), Dana's *Two Years before the Mast*(1930), Cooper's *Last of the Mohicans*(1932), Hale's *Man without a Country*(1936), McMurtrie's *Wings for Words*(1940), *Jane Eyre*(1944), and Kingsley's *Westward Ho!*(nd). Represented in Metropolitan Museum (NY), New York PL, Library of Congress (Washington, DC).
**Bibl:** Bertha E.Mahony et al, Illustrators of Children's Books 1744-1945, Boston(USA), 1948, 373, 336.

**WILSON, Elaine** **1974-**
Born Kilmarnock. Sculptress. Trained Duncan of Jordanstone School of Art 1977-1981 and RA Schools 1981-4. Won several awards and a travelling scholarship enabling her to visit and work in Italy 1991. First solo exhibition 1987.

**WILSON, Francis** **1876-1957**
Born Glasgow, Dec 30; died Glasgow, Oct 7. Painter of portraits and landscape in oil and watercolour. Trained Glasgow School of Art where he won a travelling scholarship enabling him to study further in Florence, Paris and Rome. Exhibited RSA(14), RSW(3), AAS(2), GI(75), L(1) & Paris Salon. Represented in Glasgow AG.

**WILSON, Gavin W** **fl 1870-1875**
Amateur Glasgow landscape in oils; often west coast. Exhibited RSA(2) & GI(6).

**WILSON, George** **1848-1890**
Born Tochieneal, nr Cullen, Banffshire, Nov 18; died Huntly, Apr 1. Landscape and figure painter in oil, watercolour, and pen and ink. Son of a factor to the Earl of Seafield, the eleventh of thirteen children. Educated Aberdeen Gymnasium and Edinburgh University. In 1866 went to London, enrolling at the Heatherley School of Art. Later attended the RA Schools and the Slade studying under Sir Edward Poynter. There he became friendly with other artists, notably the portrait painter J B Yeats. With John Nettleship, Sidney Hall and Edwin Ellis, they formed 'the brotherhood'. Although each followed his own artistic path, the influence of them all on Wilson was considerable. He lived with the Yeats brothers, becoming imbued as much with their poetry as with their painting, accounting for the poetic quality that suffused his work. He suffered chronic ill health, depression and self-doubt. 'Modest and retiring of disposition, he lived in an idealistic thought-atmosphere created by his natural refinement of mind and visionary nature' *[Studio].* His landscapes were often autumnal and devoid of human figures; personal statements never intended for public scrutiny. Exhibited twice at the RA in 1877 and 1878, the latter a tender portrayal of 'Alastor', the poet-subject of Shelley's poem. Probably the same **George Wilson** who exhibited GI(2), RI(3) & L(1) 1882-1886. Although based in London, Wilson embarked on frequent sketching tours with Yeats to Scotland, Italy and in 1885 Algeria. His landscapes have a tender, sweet, if lonely quality with soft colours and sensitive draughtsmanship. The influence of the pre-Raphaelites and symbolists, working contemporaneously, can be clearly seen. His work, of great delicacy and sensitivity, is now seldom seen. Represented in NGS, Aberdeen AG where a retrospective exhibition of his paintings was held 1990.
**Bibl:** Aberdeen AG (Ex Cat, 1990); Caw 275-6; Halsby 107; Tod Hunter, Eng Illus Mag, Aug 1891, 771-778; Leonore van de Veer in Studio, vol 30, 1904.

**WILSON, George** **fl 1890-1893**
Aberdeen landscape painter; exhibited AAS(2) from 64 Esslemont Avenue, including 'On the Ey, nr Braemar'. Not to be confused with two other George Wilsons working at about the same time.

**WILSON, George** **fl 1987**
Banffshire artist; exhibited 'Zulu' at the RSA.

**WILSON, George Renfrew** **fl 1931-1940**
Glasgow landscape and portrait painter. Exhibited RSA(1) & GI(4) from 27 Stamperland Gdns, latterly from Dunfermline.

**WILSON, George Washington** **1823-1893**
Born Waulkmill of Carnoustie, Banff; died Aberdeen, 9 Mar. Landscape painter in watercolour and pencil but best known for his innovative photographic work. Son of a farmer who had enlisted in the British army during the French Revolutionary Wars having been press-ganged in Leith when on his way to court in connection with the family estate at Culvie, Banffshire. Father remarried and George was the second son of 11 children. Father served for 24 years having married in Portugal, begetting three children all of whom drowned with their mother on their way home to Scotland. Educated at the village school and apprenticed to a builder, in 1846 (having had an illegitimate child 1842 by a lady who refused to marry him) he moved to Edinburgh to study painting. After visiting London, where he attended open classes at the RA and received lessons from E H Corbould, travelled around western Europe before setting himself up in Crown St, Aberdeen as a miniature portrait painter. In 1849 he married Maria Cassie in Banff. In 1852 adapted photography as 'a suitable complement to his existing skill - taking advantage of the new wet collodian process'. Thereafter he considered himself an 'artist and photographer'. When Balmoral was being remodelled in 1854 he and his partner John Hay(qv) came under the patronage of Prince Albert and, following her bereavement, of Queen Victoria. They were commissioned to photograph Balmoral throughout its rebuilding. In 1855 the partnership was dissolved following the bankruptcy of the Hay family. His photographic interest began to encompass stereoscopic work and landscape. Much influenced by the writings of John Burnet, in the 1850s he produced a book of urban photos of

Aberdeen, and then published a series of slender volumes entitled *Photographs of English and Scottish Scenery* (1868). Queen Victoria's two volumes *Leaves from the Journal of our Life in the Highlands* used illustrations taken directly from Wilson's photographs. Aided by technical developments, especially the capability of making instant images, he became the leading figure in the establishment of commercial photography in Scotland. On his retirement in 1888 the business passed to his sons. Exhibited AAS(15) from Queen's Cross, Aberdeen. Some early watercolour sketches may be seen in Aberdeen PL.
**Bibl:** Roger Taylor, George Washington Wilson: Artist and Photographer, Aberdeen 1981.

**WILSON, Graham W** **fl 1970**
East Kilbride sculptor; worked in fibreglass and bronze. Exhibited GI(2).

**WILSON, Helen F RSW** **1954-**
Born Paisley. Primarily a watercolour painter. Trained at Glasgow School of Art and Hospitalfield, Arbroath 1974-76. Awarded the Governor's prize (GSA) 1974, a Cargill travelling scholarship enabled her to visit Colonsay and Italy 1976-7; won the Lauder Award 1979. Visited Italy and Yugoslavia 1975. First solo exhibition Glasgow 1978 and first exhibit RSA 1987. Elected RSW 1997. Exhibits RSA since 1987 & GI since 1977 from Beaver St. Represented in Glasgow AG.

**WILSON, Henry** **fl 1862-1871**
Edinburgh painter of Highland landscapes. Exhibited RSA(5) from Mr Wright's, 143 Princes St.

**WILSON, Hugh Cameron** **1885-1952**
Born Glasgow, Dec 22. Painter in oil of landscapes, figure subjects and portraits. Trained Glasgow School of Art under Fra Newbery(qv). Visited and painted Oronsay. Exhibited 1920-1952 RSA(17), AAS(1), GI(52) & L(1), latterly from Westbourne Gdns. Represented Glasgow AG.

**WILSON, Isabel** **fl 1975-1976**
Edinburgh amateur sculptress; exhibited 'Lilies' and 'Resting Pigeon' at the RSA.

**WILSON, Isobel** **fl 1965**
Aberdeenshire painter of country scenes; exhibited AAS(2) from 7 Loirston Place, Cove Bay.

**WILSON, Miss J M** **fl 1882-1883**
Little known painter of Banknock, Denny, Stirlingshire; exhibited L(2).

**WILSON, James HRSA** **1795-1856**
Edinburgh zoologist and amateur painter of portraits, figure studies and birds. Elected HRSA 1827. Exhibited RSA(9) from 26 St James' Sq.

**WILSON, James** **fl 1831-1847**
Berwick painter of figurative subjects and genre; exhibited RSA(6) from the Pier House.

**WILSON, James** **fl 1838-1888**
Glasgow painter in oil of figure subjects, portraits and landscapes. Exhibited RA(11), RSA(6) & GI(37), latterly from 11 Belgrave Terr.

**WILSON, James** **fl 1920-1937**
Obscure Glasgow figure. Moved in the early 1920's to Cheshire. Exhibited GI(3) & L(5).

**WILSON, James C L** **fl 1885-1911**
Minor Glasgow watercolour landscape and topographical painter. Exhibited GI(1) but mainly at Walker's Gallery, London (82).
**Bibl:** Halsby 288.

**WILSON, Joan** **fl 1952-**
Born Aberdeen. Trained Gray's School of Art 1948-52 under Hugh Adam Crawford(qv) and Robert Sivell(qv). Paints transparent watercolour directly from the countryside around Aberdeen. Mother of Robin William W(qv). Her work is not strictly topographical but aims to capture the mood of the landscape and the quality of light peculiar to the north-east. Also works in silk screen, being an ideal printing technique for emphasising the flat pattern and textures of the landscape. In 1985 won the Lily McDougal Award of the SSWA. Member, SSWA and AAS. Exhibits RSA, AAS & RSW, latterly from 3 Oakdale Terr.

**WILSON, John** **fl 1877**
Minor Edinburgh landscape painter in oil; exhibited RSA(1).

**WILSON, John Gillies** **fl 1885-1890**
Minor Glasgow painter; exhibited GI(3).

**WILSON, John H ('Jock') HRSA** **1774-1855**
Born Ayr, Aug 13; died Folkestone, Apr 29. Painter in oil and watercolour of marines and occasional landscape. Father of John James W(qv) with whose work his own is sometimes confused. When he was only 14 was apprenticed to John Norie(qv) and Alexander Nasmyth(qv). Went to Montrose c1796 where for nearly two years he taught drawing before proceeding to London. There was employed as a scene painter at Astley's Theatre and began to exhibit RA 1807 from his studio in Lambeth. Also exhibited British Institution of which he became a longstanding member. Painted 'Battle of Trafalgar' in unsuccessful competition for a prize offered by the BI, this being purchased by Lord Northwick. Although remaining in London exhibited regularly RSA and was elected an Hon. member 1827. Endowed with keen observation and a wonderful memory. Had great conversational powers rendering him immensely popular with other artists and with dealers. Most of his work portrays the coastlines of southern England and the neighbouring shores of France and Holland, seldom the open sea. 'At times he over-emphasises the ambers and siennas of bill and prow in his slanting luggers, but he comes a long way nearer the true conditions of colour than did Thomson' [McKay]. One of the founders, Society of Great Britain Artists in Suffolk Street. Visited Flanders 1818 and in 1824 travelled with his friend David Roberts(qv) to Dieppe, Rouen and Le Havre. The last entry, according to the RA catalogue records, is puzzling. He died in April in Folkestone and a portrait of 'Prince Albert' was quite out of character, nevertheless it is clearly listed that from Briarly House, Folkestone this was his exhibit. Otherwise all his other works were English and Scottish landscapes and coastal scenes although he did paint 'The embarkation of His Majesty from Ramsgate on 25th September, 1821' 1823. A leading marine artist of his time and one of the most impressive marine painters that Scotland has produced, depicting the sea and coastal shipping in a vibrant, realistic and pictorially pleasing manner. Exhibited RA(76) from 'Fall of the Clyde' 1807 to 'Prince Albert' (?) after a painting of Sir W C Ross in 1855; also RSA and its predecessors 81 works between 1821 and 1848. Represented in SNG, V & A; National Maritime Museum, Leeds AG, Salford AG, Sheffield AG, Budapest AG.
**Bibl:** AJ 1855, 192,204 (obit); 1875, 108(obit); Armstrong 18-19; British Marine Painters 25,38; Brydall 305-6; Caw 159-160; Halsby 49-50,79; Irwin 242; McKay 187-190; Portfolio 1888, 71; T. Smith, Recollections of the British Institution, 1860, 83; Studio Special No, 1919.

**WILSON, John James** **1818-1875**
Died Folkestone, Jan 30. Son of John H Wilson(qv) with whom he is often confused. Studied under his father and painted in a very similar style. Began as a landscape artist but became increasingly interested in marines. Generally his work is bright and attractive although lacking the finer touch of his father's work. His early pictures often painted farmyard scenes with cattle. Exhibited over 500 works in London between 1831 and 1875 including RA(55); also RSA(3) & GI(3). Represented in Sheffield AG.
**Bibl:** Brydall 306.

**WILSON, John L** **fl 1880**
Glasgow amateur painter. Exhibited GI(1) from 25 Napiershall St.

**WILSON, Miss June** **fl 1948-1952**
Glasgow painter of landscape and portraits. Exhibited GI(4), from Briar Rd.

**WILSON, Kenneth** **1946**
Painter and sculptor. Grew up in Dundee, trained Duncan of Jordanstone College of Art 1971-75. Worked as a medical illustrator

before devoting himself to painting full-time 1984. Moved to Edinburgh c1980. Recently has concentrated on semi-abstract landscapes and seascapes, murals and wood engravings. Exhibits RSA.

**WILSON, Mrs Leonora B Macgregor** **fl 1905-1922**
Glasgow miniature portrait painter of 21 Highburgh Rd, Dowanhill. Exhibited GI(17), mostly from Glasgow but also from Dunoon.

**WILSON, Mrs M** **fl 1868-1897**
Amateur Perthshire painter of fruit; exhibited RSA(1) & GI(5), from Methven.

**WILSON, Maggie T** **fl 1889-1901**
Painter from Cambuslang; moved to Springburn c1892. Exhibited RSA(3) & GI(14).

**WILSON, Mrs Malcolm** **fl 1890-1897**
Renfrewshire landscape painter in watercolour; mainly Arran. Exhibited GI(5), from Kilmacolm.

**WILSON, Margaret Elizabeth** **fl 1902-1927**
Edinburgh watercolour painter who moved to London after 1929. Mainly figurative and topographical. Exhibited RSA(40), RSW(7) & GI(6).

**WILSON, Mrs Margaret Evangeline** **fl 1938-1949**
Flower painter based, based in London but probably Scottish. Exhibited GI(5).

**WILSON, Margaret Thomson (Mrs James Hamilton Mackenzie)** **1864-1912**
Born Cambuslang. Genre painter in oil and watercolour, generally the latter; also continental landscape and flowers. Trained Glasgow School of Art. Worked for a time in Holland and, after her marriage, in Italy. Exhibited RA(1), RSA(10), RSW(1), GI(26) & L(2). Represented in Glasgow AG.
**Bibl:** Halsby 288.

**WILSON, Marion Henderson** **1869-1956**
Glasgow painter, sculptress and metalwork designer. Trained Glasgow School of Art 1884-1896 and worked very much in the Glasgow style. Lived for a time at 9 Windsor Terrace. 'Her repoussé work, like that of the Gilmour sisters, was mainly in brass, copper and tin. Her Celtic design inspiration is seen on a variety of objects, many employing the cabbage roses and hearts, so much a trademark of the Glasgow Style. (Her) flowing linear designs are distinctive and she often uses faces as a design motif' [Burkhauser]. Exhibited GI(18) & L(4). Represented in Glasgow AG by a repoussé tin triptych girl seated in a rose arbour flanked by rose trees.
**Bibl:** Burkhauser 182, 105-6.

**WILSON, Miss Mary Georgina Wade** **1856-1939**
Born Falkirk. Trained Edinburgh and Paris and worked mainly in watercolour and pastel, although also occasionally used oils; also book illustrator. Her best work was in pastel and her favoured compositions were of the north-east coast and harbours, flowers and still life. Executed a series of drawings of Highland mountain scenery and sea and shore scenes of the Western Isles. Exhibited pastel drawings at leading exhibitions and also held her own solo shows regularly in Edinburgh as well as exhibiting in London and, occasionally, on the Continent. Later in her career garden scenes became favoured, drawn at her home in South Bonteskine, nr Falkirk which had its own fine rock garden. Noted for exceptional quality of colour and harmony, rhythmic composition, realism and persuasive beauty. Exhibited RSA(73), AAS(8), GI(18), L(7), SWA(2) & Walker Gallery, London (73). Represented in NGS.
**Bibl:** Glasgow Herald, 5 Dec, 1939 (obit); Halsby 288.

**WILSON, Mary McIntyre** **fl 1899-1919**
Aberdeen watercolour painter who moved to Edinburgh c 1911. Mainly portraits and local landscape. Exhibited RSA(8), RSW(1), AAS(3) & GI(3) from 2 N. Charlotte Street and 20 Ann St.

**WILSON, Mary R L** **fl 1886-1887**
Edinburgh amateur watercolour painter of landscape and flowers; exhibited RSA(6).

**WILSON, Mary W** **fl 1917**
Minor watercolour painter; exhibited RSW(1) from 50 Melville St, Glasgow.

**WILSON, Peter Macgregor RSW (res 1926)** **c1856-1928**
Born Glasgow; died Sep 25. Painter of portraits, genre, landscape and marines, usually in watercolour. Studied Glasgow School of Art, London and Antwerp. Travelled widely visiting North America, Europe, Egypt, Arabia, India, Persia and Russia. Lived for a time in Edinburgh but moved to Glasgow in 1882 becoming President, Glasgow Art Club. His watercolours are executed with firm command using solid colours but his draughtsmanship is sometimes poor. Elected RSW 1885, resigned 1926. Exhibited RSW(60), RSA(9), AAS(2), GI(64) & L(9).
**Bibl:** Halsby 288.

**WILSON, Mrs Peter Macgregor** **fl 1898-1901**
Amateur Glasgow artist, guided by her husband whose work she copied. Exhibited GI(4).

**WILSON, Patrick** **fl 1850-1865**
Edinburgh architect. Designed what is now the Wilkie House Theatre, Cowgate (1859-60); the 'old Flemish' Protestant Institute (1860) on George IV Bridge; the disused College UP Church (1856); Fountainbridge FC (1854) and the adjacent Chalmers Buildings (1854); and St Catherine Argyle Church, Grange (1865).
**Bibl:** Gifford 192,225-6,240,255,264,430,593,647.

**WILSON, R A** **fl 1911**
Minor figure; exhibited GI(1) from Hastings House, Maxwell Road, Glasgow.

**WILSON, Rachel** **fl 1898**
Aberdeenshire illustrator and engraver, specialising in bookplate design. Exhibited AAS(4) from Castle Park, Huntly.

**WILSON, Robert** **?-1901**
Architect. Appointed architect to Edinburgh School Board c1882. "Although a good hand at Gothic (eg Marchmont Rd, 1882) and deferred to the Scots tradition in Canongate (Milton House School, 1886), he developed a school style known even then as Queen Anne - of frequently amazing invention and grandeur, but cheerful and beautifully detailed withal' [Gifford]. Responsible for a large number of school buildings listed in Gifford.
**Bibl:** Gifford, see index.

**WILSON, Robin William** **fl 1983-**
Aberdeen artist. Son of Joan W(qv). Exhibits AAS.

**WILSON, Ronald** **1948-**
Born Hull. Painter in oils & watercolours, occasional sculptures; also bookseller. With his parents (Scottish mother), moved to Edinburgh 1955. Trained Duncan of Jordanstone College of Art. After a brief spell in an advertising studio, moved to *The Scotsman* as a designer 1975. Many of his paintings feature Italian architecture, Palladio and his contemporaries providing a major source of inspiration. Exhibits RSA.

**WILSON, Samuel** **fl 1890-1930**
Architectural modeller of great skill. Together with Thomas Beattie(qv) responsible for most of Robert Lorimer's decorated hand-modelled ceilings including the vine ceilings at Kellie and Ardkinglas, the dining room at Dunrobin, the stairs and library at Hill of Tarvit(Fife) and the ceilings at Balmanno Castle, Dron.
**Bibl:** Peter Savage, Lorimer and the Edinburgh Craft Designers, Edinburgh 1980, 19,61-2,83,96,102,109,123,130,170.

**WILSON, Sarah R** **fl 1886-1893**
Aberdeen landscape and flower painter; exhibited AAS(12), from 26 Ferryhill Place.

**WILSON, Scottie (Robert) RSA RSW** **1889-1972**
Born Glasgow, Jun 6. Naive painter of imaginative subjects, also designer. Christened Robert Wilson, he left school at 9, volunteered for the army after running away from home at the age of 16, serving in India and South Africa. Buying himself out of the army, he

returned to Scotland, working his passage as a stoker, but later went to Toronto remaining there for 15 years. Began doodling with an unusually fine pen. Thus launched, he held his first exhibition in Toronto at the Picture Loan Society 1943. Two years later went to London and his first London one-man show was held in the Arcade Gallery. In 1914 rejoined the army and fought with the Scottish Rifles on the Western Front. After the War he returned to Glasgow before proceeding to London to work as a street trader. In 1947 represented in the Exposition International du Surrealisme, Paris. His work has been shown in France, Switzerland and USA. He was admired by the Surrealists and in 1952 went to Paris to meet Dubuffet. When 74 years old became professional designer to the Royal Worcester porcelain factory. Executed tapestry designs for the Aubusson centre in France and the Edinburgh Tapestry Co. Commissioned to do a mural for a Zurich bank. Usually signed his name 'Scottie'. Regular exhibitor RSA & RSW. Elected ARSA 1939, RSW 1946, RSA 1949. Represented in Tate AG, SNMGA, Glasgow AG, Museum of Modern Art (Paris), Metropolitan Museum of Art (New York), Nat Gall of Canada (Ottawa - 30 drawings).
**Bibl:** Barbican Art Gallery, London, 'Aftermath:France 1945-54' (Ex Cat 1982); Brook St Gallery, London, 'Scottie Wilson' (Ex Cat 1966, Text by Mervyn Levy); Hardie 154-5; Hartley 169; George Melly, 'It's all writ out for you'. The Life and Work of Scottie Wilson, London 1986; Harold Osborne(ed), Twentieth Century Art 1988, 588.

**WILSON, Sissie** **fl 1892-1893**
Minor Edinburgh watercolour painter; exhibited RSA(1), RSW(1) & GI(2) from 2 North Charlotte St.

**WILSON, Susan** **fl 1989-**
Fife artist; exhibits AAS(2) from 56 King St, Newport-on-Tay.

**WILSON, T Shaw** **fl 1930**
Obscure Glasgow sculptor; worked in bronze, marble and wood. Exhibited GI(2) from 3 Scott Street.

**WILSON, T** **fl c1850**
Mysterious figure. There is a portrait of the '2nd Earl of Egremont' in Dulwich (no. 561) inscribed on the back 'T. Wilson/Edinburgh'. Waterhouse believed the attribution to a 'Benjamin Wilson' incorrect.
**Bibl:** Waterhouse.

**WILSON, Thomas** **fl 1878-1879**
Glasgow sculptor. Portrait busts. Exhibited GI(3), from West End Park St.

**WILSON, Thomas** **fl 1875-1914**
Edinburgh painter in oil and watercolour of landscape, portraits, interiors, figures and still-life; occasional stained glass window designer. Uncle of the celebrated window designer Willie W(qv). Exhibited RSA(49), RSW(1), AAS(3), GI(20) & L(6) from 42 George Street. Overlooking the Oyster bar in the Cafe Royal, Edinburgh are eight splendid sportsmen and women designed by Wilson in the 1890s and executed by Ballantines.
**Bibl:** Painton Cowen, Stained Glass in Britain, 1985, 233; Halsby.

**WILSON, Thomas** **1954-**
Painter and administrator. Trained Edinburgh College of Art. Works in pencil, crayon and occasionally oil and watercolour. Combines his modern art with being managing director of The Open Eye Gallery in Edinburgh. Exhibits regularly RSA & GI. Semi-abstract and portraits. Represented in Museum of Fine Arts, Valetta (Malta).

**WILSON, Tryphena** **fl 1889**
Amateur flower painter. Exhibited GI(1) from Cairnview, Kirkintilloch.

**WILSON, Mrs V McGlashan** **fl 1897-1904**
Cathcart painter. Moved to Milngavie c1904. Exhibited GI(5).

**WILSON, W G** **fl 1882-1884**
Minor Glasgow painter; exhibited GI(2).

**WILSON, W Stuart** **fl 1953**
Edinburgh landscape painter; exhibited 'Tweed valley at Elibank' at the RSA, from Henderson Row.

**WILSON, William Jnr** **fl 1824-1852**
Painter. Son of John 'Jock' Wilson(qv) and brother John James W(qv). Lived in Lambeth, London and latterly at 2 Surrey Place, Old Kent Rd. It is unclear whether he was responsible for a number of exhibits at the RSA 1868-1878 or whether these were the work of another **William WILSON** or possibly William A W(qv). The RA records certainly confused them. In 1868 'Salisbury Crags' was shown at the RSA from Old Assembly Close, 'Time gun' 1870 from 101 West Port, 'Leith Harbour' 1873 from Greenside Row and 'Crichton Castle' 1878 from Albert Place. Exhibited RA(8) 1825-1852 and RSA, mostly landscapes, although he also did a hunting scene after Henry Alken 1825. Represented in Edinburgh City collection by a painting of 'the Douglas Cross, Braes of Yarrow', originally commissioned by Sir Walter Scott c1824.

**WILSON, William** **fl 1884-1892**
Dundee landscape and coastal painter in oil. Exhibited RA(4), RSA(17), GI(3) & L(2); mostly local scenes. Lived at 87 Commercial Street, W. Dock St 1887, after 1890 at 10 Shore Terrace.

**WILSON, William** **fl 1876-1884**
Glasgow painter of landscape and narrative works; exhibited RSA(2) & GI(4), especially Arran, from Dowanhill Gdns.

**WILSON, William** **fl 1881-1916**
Kirkcaldy watercolour painter of landscapes, rivers and shore scenes. Living in Blantyre 1914. Exhibited RSA(18), AAS(2) & GI(4).

**WILSON, William** **fl 1920**
Painter. Exhibited L(1) from Hallside House, Hallside, Lanarkshire.

**WILSON, William** **fl 1937-1940**
Minor landscape and still life painter of Kinchracknie, Milngavie; exhibited AAS(3) & GI(2).

**WILSON, William A** **fl 1846-1873**
Edinburgh oil painter of landscapes, also scene painter. Working at the Theatre Royal, Edinburgh in 1846 and later at the Theatre Royal, Adelphi, London. A number of his subjects were continental, particularly around Abbeville. Exhibited RA(12) & RSA(8) 1834-1859 including 'The Castle from the Market, Edinburgh' 1850, but exact details are uncertain owing to possible confusion between the several William Wilsons known to have been working at the same time (see previous entries).

**WILSON, William (Willie) A OBE RSA RSW** **1905-1972**
Born Edinburgh, Jul 21; died at his sister's home in Bury, Mar 16. Painter in oil and watercolour, also stained glass designer, etcher and engraver. Apprenticed 1920 in a stained glass studio before going on to study at Edinburgh College of Art and then Royal College of Art, London. Opened his own studio in Edinburgh 1937. Between 1945 and 1970 designed windows for more than 150 churches. After studying in Edinburgh a Carnegie Scholarship enabled him to visit Spain where he made a series of drawings from many of which he later made engravings and etchings. Also greatly influenced by 20th century French art, visiting Provins 1926, Chauvigny 1927. In 1947 acquired Phyllis Bone's studio. Drew extensively in England and Italy and at about this time resumed painting in watercolour. Returning to Edinburgh he began a career in his own studio as designer and maker of stained glass windows. Received many ecclesiastical commissions, also for commercial buildings in Britain and overseas, including the Warrior's Chapel at Canterbury Cathedral, the regimental window at Liverpool Cathedral and Bishop's Wynd in St Andrews Cathedral. He did 14 windows for Beacon Cathedral (1950) and the Great West Window in St Machar's Cathedral, Aberdeen. 'Wilson's monogram and lively lettering style are always attached to brilliantly coloured and rather crowded windows, of which [in Edinburgh] those at St Luke, East Fettes Ave (late 1950s), are among the last he designed himself; his later windows are by his assistants, including John Blyth' [Gifford]. His watercolours were influenced by his association with Gillies(qv) and Maxwell(qv). The large drawings of the 1930s show an affinity with the Expressionist work of the Edinburgh Group. Interest in architecture was clear in much of his work in this medium. Also painted some fine views in the Italian Dolomites and northern France in the mid '30s. Acclaimed by Ian Fleming as the master of Scottish 20th century printmaking. Pearson has recorded 138 etchings, engravings, wood engravings, lithographs and

scraperboard prints, 155 watercolours and over 300 stained glass windows. 'Wilson was the Scottish printmaker *par excellence* during the inter-war period and the leading postwar exponent of contemporary British stained glass' [Pearson]. Elected ARSA 1939, RSA 1949, RSW 1946; OBE 1961. Exhibited RA(3), RSA(150), RSW(3) & GI(12). In addition to Canterbury and St Giles Cathedrals and churches throughout Scotland he is represented in SNGMA, Lillie AG (Milngavie), City of Edinburgh collection, Perth AG, Museums in New Jersey (USA), New Zealand, Nairobi, Malawi.
**Bibl:** H.J. Barnes, Prospect 1960, 23; Mungo Campbell, 'The Line of Tradition', Nat Galls of Scotland, Ex cat, Edinburgh 1993; Painton Cowen, Stained Glass in Britain, 1985, 127, 230-5, 237-9; Gifford 44-5,117,300,387,494,504,515,525,556-7,572,617-8,629, 636,660; Halsby 216-7,288; Hartley 169; Nigel McIsaac, 'William Wilson', Scott. Art Rev., vol VII, 2, 1959, 20; Feona Pearson, William Wilson, Scottish Masters, 19, 1994; SSA, Annual Exh (Ex Cat 1959).

**WILSON, William Heath** **1849-1927**
Born Glasgow. Painter of landscape and genre, mainly in oil but occasionally in watercolour; administrator and teacher. Son and pupil of Charles Heath W(qv), grandson of Andrew W(qv). Head, Glasgow School of Art. Spent a lot of time in Italy. His first exhibit at the RA was an Italian sunset scene 1884 entered from Florence. In 1961 blindness tragically ended his career. Lived latterly at Brockham Green, Betchworth, Surrey. Exhibited RA(15), RSA(4), ROI(12), RBA(15), GI(2) & L(4). Represented in Glasgow AG(9).
**Bibl:** Halsby 288; Pavière, Landscapes.

**WINGATE, Alexander** **fl 1905-1906**
Glasgow topographical watercolour painter. Exhibited GI(2) from 4 Bowmont Terrace.

**WINGATE, Miss Anna Maria Bruce** **1873-1921**
Born Orkney, Jun 18; died Mar 28. Figure, landscape and portrait painter; author. Daughter of the Rev Thomas Wingate, noted evangelist, temperance reformer and author. Started her artistic life from The Manse, Stromness, Orkney in 1899. Author of *Wordsworth and Tolstoy* (1922) published one year after her death. In 1900 had 5 works accepted at the AAS, including a striking portrait of a negress. After 1902 was living at 9 Pentland Terrace Edinburgh from where she exhibited RA(3), RSA(6) & L(4).

**WINGATE, Helen Ainslie (Mrs Thornton)** **fl 1911-1938**
Edinburgh watercolour painter. Daughter of Sir James Lawton W(qv). Exhibited RSA(25), RSW(11), GI(10) & L(4).
**Bibl:** Halsby 288.

**WINGATE, J C Paterson (Mrs)** **fl 1896-1900**
Painter. Wife of J Crawford Paterson W(qv). Exhibited RSA(1) & GI(3).

**WINGATE, J Crawford Paterson** **fl 1880-1912**
Glasgow landscape painter in oil. Married an artist(qv). Exhibited RSA(8), AAS, GI(24) & L(10) from 180 West Regent St.

**WINGATE, Sir James Lawton RSA** **1846-1924**
Born Kelvinhaugh, nr Glasgow; died Apr 22. Painter. In 1864 he had had his first exhibit at the GI, followed a year later by one at the RA. In 1867 embarked upon a tour of Italy which lasted six months during which he began painting directly from nature. Completed over 150 watercolour drawings as well as some well executed oils. Arriving home he took up residence in Hamilton. Began to study seriously 1872, the year during which possibly the most significant event in his artistic life occurred when he met W D McKay(qv). This decided Wingate to gain further instruction so in the autumn of that year he moved to Edinburgh and enrolled at the Manufacturers School of Design. The following year Wingate met Hugh Cameron(qv) who drew attention to the lack of apparent feeling in Wingate's work; from then on, Wingate concentrated on depicting rural life. Later the same year he entered the RSA Life Class, studying under William McTaggart(qv) and George Paul Chalmers(qv). This experience led Wingate to become familiar with a number of important fellow artists working in the Lothians at the same time, all of whom had been influenced to varying degrees by the Barbizon and Hague schools. These included Robert McGregor(qv), J C Noble(qv), and J R Reid(qv). In 1874 he discovered the village of Muthill, buried in the Perthshire foothills, and then began a series of paintings depicting domestic rural life many of which were shown at the RSA and GI. Elected ARSA 1879 and in 1880 had his first exhibit accepted at the RA. In 1881 he settled in Muthill where he was to remain for six years during which time he was elected RSA 1886. Next moved to Colinton just outside Edinburgh where he developed a heightened awareness of atmosphere and starting giving less attention to detail. The apotheosis of this transition came in the early 1910s when his landscape increasingly became evocations of the countryside and less depictions of particular places and events. Like many other Scottish artists visits to Arran captivated him, especially sunsets across the empty sea. Elected President, RSA 1919 and the same year received a knighthood. Caw referred to him as "the chosen priest at the shrine of dying day". In the *AJ* 1898 Caw wrote, "as works of art, (Wingate's pictures) are faulty in design and lacking in monumental impressiveness but like snatches of the most exquisite song they are pregnant in suggestion, and thrilled with the rapture of infinite contact with nature...these little pictures of his, so simple in motive, so slight in subjective interest, are likely to retain their charm far longer than most of the ambitious art which makes a stir in the world today". Exhibited RA(11) & regularly at the RSA; also AAS 1886-1926. Represented in NGS(6), Glasgow AG(6), Kirkcaldy AG, Edinburgh City collection(3), Brodie Castle (NTS).
**Bibl:** AJ 1896, 73-76; Caw 318-321; Conn 37 (1913) 55; 69 (1924) 181; Dayot, La Peinture Anglaise 1908 262, 282 (pl); Fine Art Society,'Sir James Lawton Wingate', (Ex Cat, Edinburgh 1990); Halsby 167,288; Holme 'The "RSA"', Studio 1907; Irwin 371; Macmillan [SA] 253-4,259,270; Scots Pict V 22.3.1913, 547; Studio 68 (1916) 124ff - also indexes to 28, 34, 37, 43, 62, 65, 69, 80.

**WINKLES, Henry** **fl 1819-1832**
Topographical painter and draughtsman. Probably from Karlruhe, Germany. Living in London during the above years, exhibiting RA(8) of which 3 were of Edinburgh. A collection of 120 sepia drawings of old Edinburgh, intended for publication 1829 as *Views of Edinburgh* seems never to have been published. These were augmented by twelve pencil studies of Holyrood, four of St. Giles and several others.
**Bibl:** Butchart 53-4.

**WINKLEY, James** **fl 1850s**
Aberdeen itinerant landscape and portrait painter. An ordinary house-painter who developed the ability to paint in oils. Taught Sir George Reid(qv) and Thomas Bunting(qv), the latter regarded as his particular protégé. In 1853 visited Inverness where among his sitters was 'Dr George Mackay' of the North Church. The work hung for many years in the Session Room of the Free North Church. Exhibited AAS(7) from 80 Blenheim Place.

**WINRAM, Elspeth Christine** **fl 1984**
Aberdeen designer. Exhibited AAS(1) from 11 Salisbury Terrace.

**WINSHIP, Miss** **fl 1871**
Edinburgh painter; exhibited a watercolour drawing of 'Mitford Castle, Northumberland' at the RSA.

**WINSLOE, Miss Phil** **fl 1908-1918**
Minor Glasgow watercolour painter; conversation pieces. Exhibited RSA(3), GI(9) & L(10), from 28 Montgomerie St.

**WINTER ACADEMY** **1735**
Established mainly at the instigation of Richard Cooper(qv) the Edinburgh engraver. For a subscription of one guinea (half a guinea according to Irwin) members of St. Luke's Academy and others were offered instruction and the use of Cooper's extensive portfolios of Old Master engravings. Cooper's most famous pupil, Sir Robert Strange(qv), was probably a student.
**Bibl:** Brydall 113; Irwin 84.

**WINTER, James** **fl 1743-1758**
Architect. Son of Thomas W(qv). His background is unclear and much of his work is now unknown. Employed by the 2nd Duke of Atholl to build a new stable wing at Blair Castle, Perthshire in 1743-44 and subsequently to remodel the castle itself 1747-58. The alterations to the castle exterior were destroyed in 1869 when the building was recastellated by David Bryce(qv) for the 7th Duke. The Georgian interiors remain unaltered, but Winter was not responsible for their decoration. It is unclear how much of the remodelling of the main

castle and completion of the south wing were the work of James and how much of his father Thomas, but in the archives all references after July 1747 were only to James. In 1757 he was named as arbiter in connection with a dispute over the erection of the new Town Hall at Berwick.
**Bibl:** Colvin 687; Berwick Guild Books, Jan 14, 1756.

**WINTER, Thomas** **fl 1740-1750**
Architect. Father of James W(qv). Very little is known of his work beyond the fact that in 1743 he began working with his son James at Blair Castle and in 1747 was working for Lord Minto and for the Duke of Roxburgh at Floors.

**WINTON, Susan M** **fl 1984**
Dundee painter of still life and topographical works. Trained Dundee College of Art. Exhibited AAS(3) from 246 Perth Rd.

**WINTOUR, Alexander Mitchelson** **fl 1807-1813**
Little is known of this painter beyond the fact that from 1801 to 1807 he was apprenticed to Nicol Somerville. Father of **John Maitland WINTOUR** a minor painter. Made a Burgess of Edinburgh 1809 and in 1813 took as his apprentice John M Wintour, son of William Wintour, supervisor of excise.

**WINTOUR, John Crawford ARSA** **1825-1882**
Born Edinburgh, Oct; died Edinburgh, Jul 29. Trained Trustees Academy, Edinburgh under William Allan(qv) and, like his contemporary Alexander Fraser(qv), his first works were figurative subjects but after a visit to Perthshire 1850 became increasingly interested in landscape. His best work was achieved during the last twelve years of his life. 'It was the great defect of Wintour's talent that he was never able to engraft (his early sensitiveness to form and an apprehension of the densities and surfaces of things) on the idealistic compositions to which his maturer life was devoted...the want of the pervading influence of light is more keenly felt in the open, and this is just the quality to which the umber ground does not readily lend itself. After his earlier middle period and the passing away of the naturalistic impulse, Wintour fell back on the variation of the old method. Generally, a lack of cohesion, and of the solidity and restfulness of the earth's surface. In a word, his work is deficient in backbone' [McKay]. Nevertheless, there was generally a touch of romance in much of what he did, even although he achieved this by the use of conventional tones, 'varnishy browns', from which he never emerged. His early watercolours were influenced by the work of Leitch(qv) although his best works in this medium, achieved in the 1860's, have a strong personal flavour with broad brush strokes over tightly drawn pencil and charcoal outlines. His subjects were nearly always taken from the neighbourhood of Edinburgh, Dumfries, Berwickshire and occasionally Warwickshire which he visited in the autumn of 1861. It is interesting to note that in 1852 'The Bathing Pool' was purchased by the Farquharson family of Finzean. 'His daylight pictures were wanting in freshness and brilliance. This is especially so in the shadows, which lacked vibration and atmospheric quality. But in the time when sun sets and all the land grows dark, when after the glorious glow of the gloaming comes the mirk, and through the gathering darkness there rises in the east the silver disc of the moon to flood the world in solemn and subdued light, Wintour was at home...With him formula is less conscious than with Thompson for, if his compositions seem as considered and as balanced, they are more spontaneous. He had almost an unfailing sense of what makes for beauty of design; the simplicity and dignity of his composition, and the noble repose in which his landscape is usually steeped, are essentially classic qualities, and, at his best, he almost tempts comparison with the incomparable grace of Corot...the solemn beauty of moonrise with breathes from Blairlogie, the splendour of the 'Gloaming on the Eye' have rarely been surpassed in art'. Although never popular in his life-time, his best work shows a striking originality. Elected ARSA 1859 but never made a full Academician, due as much to his predisposition to drink as to the quality of his work. Exhibited RSA (230) 1843-1882, GI & AAS 1890-1906. Represented in NGS(8), Orchar AG (Broughty Ferry), Glasgow AG, Kirkcaldy AG, Brodie Castle (NTS).
**Bibl:** AJ 1898, 340; Brydall 471; Caw 186-188 et passim; Halsby 125-6,288; Irwin 361-362; McKay 308-313; Scot Art Rev, old series 1, 1888, 28-9.

**WINTOUR, William Jnr** **fl 1863-1884**
Edinburgh painter in oil and watercolour of landscapes and local rustic scenes. His relationship with William W Snr is not clear although they were working contemporaneously and may have been brothers. Exhibited RSA(40).

**WINTOUR, William, Snr** **fl 1883**
Landscape painter. Exhibited a Forfarshire castle at the RSA from Hawthornbank, Murrayfield, Edinburgh.

**WIRE, T Cyril** **fl 1939**
Glasgow portrait and figurative painter. Exhibited RSA(4) & GI(1) from 46 Southbrae Drive.

**WISE, Henry T** **fl 1905**
Edinburgh painter. Exhibited RSA(1) from 5 Craighouse Terrace.

**WISEMAN, Thomas Thorburn** **fl 1888-1913**
Painter of genre. Exhibited GI(2) & RHA(7), first from Hamilton, Lanarkshire and in the 1890's from Dublin.

**WISHART, Dora** **fl 1940**
Aberdeen flower painter. Exhibited RSA(1) from 458 Great Western Rd.

**WISHART, Peter ARSA** **1846-1932**
Born near Aberdour, Fife; died Edinburgh, May 31. Landscape painter in oils, pastel and watercolour. Spent several years in business in Edinburgh studying art at night school before enrolling at the Royal Institution and subsequently at the Academy in Antwerp under Verlat, alongside C H Mackie(qv), Hornel(qv), MacGeorge(qv) and Walls(qv). While in Antwerp painted a large number of landscapes inspired by the Scheldt which had a strong influence on his contemporaries. Later found inspiration in the hills and rushing streams of Scotland, sketching from nature on the Fife coast and later at Brig O'Turk alongside David Murray(qv) and E A Walton(qv). William McTaggart(qv) had been an early mentor whose influence is seen in the brush work and dynamic skies. His watercolours were idiosyncratic, veering toward the Expressionist as exemplified in 'Riders on the Beach' which appeared on the market in April, 1991. Lived in Edinburgh and worked up to his death. Elected ARSA 1925. Exhibited RSA (114), RSW(18), RHA(4), AAS 1900-1931, GI (25) & L(2). Represented in Kirkcaldy AG, Edinburgh City collection.

**WISHART, Sylvia** **1936-**
Born Stromness, Orkney. Orcadian landscape artist. Trained Gray's School of Art, Aberdeen, won postgraduate scholarship. Subsequently joined the staff as a teacher of drawing and painting. Returned to Orkney to paint 1987. Solo exhibitions in London, Edinburgh, Northumberland & Glasgow. Winner of RA Landscape prize. Exhibits RA, RSA(20) between 1963 & 1985, RGI(1) & AAS from 5 Well Park and latterly Heatherbraes. Represented Aberdeen AG.

**WISHART, Thomas** **fl 1947-1948**
Midlothian landscape painter; exhibited RSA from Gorebridge.

**WISSAERT, Paul** **1885-fl 1917**
Born Brussels, 13 May. Sculptor and medallionist. Son of the Belgian medallionist Francois W. Trained Brussels, Paris and Florence. Living in Edinburgh 1915 and shortly afterwards moved to London. Exhibited RSA(5), GI(1) & L(2), but apparently never in London. A bronze medallion of Rev Alexander Whyte (1836-1921), Principal of New College, Edinburgh, executed in 1915, is in SNPG.

**WISZNIEWSKI, Adrian** **1958-**
Born Glasgow. Painter of figurative subjects in acrylic, charcoal, oil and watercolour; also etcher. Of Polish extraction, he trained Mackintosh School of Architecture 1975-79 and Glasgow School of Art 1979-1983. Between 1982 and 1984 he won a series of scholarships including the Cargill Award 1983 and a grant from the Mark Rothko Memorial Trust Fund 1984. Achieved rapid success, his first work being bought by the Tate when he was only 27 and others going to the Museum of Modern Art in New York. In 1986 moved from Glasgow and settled in Alnmouth, Northumberland. 'Wiszniewski's

paintings depict an Arcadian world populated by awkward-looking young men, many of which are covert self-portraits'. Much of his early work was done with charcoal on paper, but latterly he has concentrated on larger oil paintings. 'Densely worked, patterned surfaces of the early work have given way to greater clarity of design while the imagery has remained obscure, suggesting an arcane symbolism of suppressed sexual desire. Melancholy young men struggle to comprehend their unfathomable environment in a reconstructed world that recalls de Chirico and the Surrealists' [Hartley]. 'A totem of Scottish cultural assertion...everything presented in an overall texture of rolling corrugations'. Represented in Lillie AG (Milngavie).
**Bibl:** Margaret Garlake,'Adrian Wiszniewski', Art Monthly, Nov 1985; Hardie 213-5; Hartley 170; Oona Strathearn,'Adrian Wiszniewski' in Arts Rev Yearbk 1987; Clive Turnbull,'Signs of Dreaming. The Work of Scottish Artist Adrian Wiszniewski', The Green Book, vol 2, no 4, 1986; 'The Vigorous Imagination' SNGMA (Ex Cat 1987); Walker AG, Liverpool, 'Adrian Wiszniewski' (Ex Cat 1987).

**WITHER, Kirsty** **1968-**
Born Tidworth, both parents Scottish. Trained Gray's School of Art 1986-90. Painter in oils of strong figurative and floral studies. Uses traditional techniques including palette knife, her work has been described as 'tense and moody'. Influenced by Sir Robin Philipson(qv), Joan Eardley(qv) and Keith Vaughn(qv). Exhibits RGI, from Brighton.

**WITHEROW, Mrs Nina** **fl 1940s**
Scottish watercolourist of landscape and flowers. Local landscapes, often in the Crieff and Bridge of Allan areas. One continental scene 'The old Gateway in Perugia' was shown at the RA; exhibited a study of tulips GI 1941.

**WITT (WET), Jacob (or James) de** **1640-1697**
Born Harlem; died Amsterdam, 11 Nov. Painter of portraits, heraldic decoration and landscape. Son of the Haarlem historical painter Jacob Willemsz de W. Came to Scotland c1673, being commissioned by Sir William Bruce to work at the Palace of Holyroodhouse, in collaboration with the sculptor Jan van Santvoort. Together they joined forces, working in other parts of Scotland, notably at Glamis where de Witt was commissioned to paint the chapel and Santvoort the royal Arms. Also worked at Balcaskie and Kinross under the patronage of Bruce. At Holyrood he worked mainly on allegorical and mythological scenes including a ceiling painting 'ane piece of history', portraying the King himself 1673, also 'The triumph of Galatea', in the King's antechamber. Seems to have commuted quite regularly between Holland and Scotland for he was elected to the Painters' Corporation of Cologne 1677 and in 1688 again embarked on a continental journey from his home in the Canongate. On 26 February, 1684 he was commissioned by the King to paint not only Charles II but all the previous 110 Scottish kings for the completion of which he was allowed two years. These were to be hung in the long gallery of Holyrood where they still remain. At Glamis he was assisted by William Rennie(qv). Also worked for the Makgills of Cousland and the Clerks of Penicuik. Among his finest works are the '1st Marquis of Atholl' and, on a smaller scale, 'Kenneth Mackenzie, 3rd Earl of Seaforth' (sister to the Countess of Mar). His son Theodore was living in Edinburgh 1686. Returned to Haarlem 1691. Signed his work 'Jacob de Wet' or 'J de Wet'. Represented in Holyrood Castle, NG, Aix-La-Chapelle AG, Amsterdam AG, Breslau AG, Brunswick AG, Budapest AG, Cassel AG, Copenhagen AG, Darmstadt AG, Gratz AG, Haarlem AG, Halle AG, Hamburg AG, Helsinki AG, Hermannstadt AG, Kiev AG, Leipzig AG, Hermitage Museum (Leningrad), Munich AG, Munster AG, Schleissheim AG, Schwerin AG, Stuttgart AG, Warsaw AG, Wurzbourg AG.
**Bibl:** Apted 105-7; M R Apted, Painted Ceilings of Scotland, Edinburgh 1966, 85(illus); Bannatyne Club, Miscellany, iii, 325-342,; Benezit; Brydall 84; J G Dunbar, 'Lowlanders in the Highlands', Country Life, 8 Aug 1974; Gifford 143-6; Irwin 40,169; Croft Murray, Decorative Painting, i, 260; Thomson, George Jamesone, 100.

**WOLFSON, Alma R** **fl 1971-1988**
Glasgow landscape and flower painter. Sister of Lyn W(qv). Exhibited RSA(1) & GI(11) up to 1988.

**WOLFSON, Lyn** **fl 1969-1987**
Glasgow sculptress. Sister of Alma W(qv). Exhibited RSA(2) & GI(7).

**WOLSTENHOLME, Pamela** **fl 1974**
Aberdeen landscape painter. Trained Gray's School of Art, Aberdeen. Exhibited AAS(1) from 138 Ashvale Place.

**WOOD, Alice M Collins** **fl 1879-1886**
Amateur watercolour painter of still-life, dead game and figurative subjects. Lived at Keithick, Coupar Angus from where she exhibited RSA(2) & GI(2).

**WOOD, Andrew** **fl c1535**
Carver. Assistant to John Drummond(qv). Involved in carving the splendid roof, now destroyed, of the Presence-chamber at Stirling Castle.

**WOOD, Christopher** **1962-**
Born Leeds. Painter in oils & watercolour. Trained Edinburgh College of Art 1980-84. First solo exhibitions, Edinburgh 1987 followed by London, Oxford, Newcastle, Glasgow & Edinburgh. Exhibits RSA since 1990, also RGI, SSA & RSW, from East Lothian.

**WOOD, David Innes Sandeman** **1933-1996**
Born Glasgow; died London. Painter of historical subjects and landscape. Trained Edinburgh College of Art and Sir John Cass College in London. Grandson of Frank Watson W(qv). Lived in Norfolk for most of his life. Exhibited RSA & RBA.

**WOOD, Flora (Mrs Kenneth Maclay)** **1910-c1980**
Born Portobello. Painter of flowers, street scenes and figurative works; also sculptress. Spalding describes her as a 'figurative artist who had a number of styles but frequently displays a bias towards the geometric rather than the organic'. Studied in Florence and for a short time in Paris under André l'Hôte. Enrolled Edinburgh College of Art 1930 and then spent two terms at Edinburgh College of Art. Moved to Glasgow 1946. First solo exhibit at the Lillie AG (Milngavie) 1979. Exhibited RSA & GI 1947-1979 throughout. Represented in Lillie AG (Milngavie)(2).
**Bibl:** DBA, vol I.

**WOOD, Frank Crichton** **1965-**
Born July 23. Architect and draughtsman. Trained Dundee University 1984-90. Particularly interested in Scottish baronial architecture, he received a travelling scholarship on graduating, visiting & recording all the castles in Scotland. 'Honorary' architect to Scottish Arts Club 1994. Part-time tutor Dundee University 1995. Involved in restoration of Castle Dhu 1996, the drawings for which in RSA 1996. Converted listed buildings into four modern housing units (drawings & model, RSA 1998).

**WOOD, Frank Watson** **1862-1953**
Born Berwick-on-Tweed, Sep 19; died Edinburgh, Mar 23. Watercolour painter of marine subjects, landscapes, including many golfing subjects in which the figures are unusually well drawn, and portraits. Trained London and Academie Julien in Paris. On his return he became assistant master, Newcastle School of Art 1883-9, leaving to become Headmaster, Hawick School of Art 1889-99. From his time in the borders, he turned increasingly to marine subjects and it is for these that he is best known. Worked mainly around Northumberland and Berwickshire but also in the vicinity of Gullane where he eventually lived. Painted sailing ships and warships in strong colour and line. Exhibited RA(1), RSA(15), RSW(8) & GI(5).
**Bibl:** Halsby 288; Wingfield.

**WOOD, George W** **fl 1898**
Edinburgh landsape painter; exhibited AAS(1) from 2 Warriston Crescent.

**WOOD, Miss Helen Muir** **1864-1930**
Glasgow painter and enamellist. Trained with the Mackintosh group 1882-c1900 and subsequently taught enamelling at Glasgow School of Art. Also designed stained glass and painted ceramics. Exhibited Glasgow Society of Lady Artists, Glasgow Exhibition 1901 and Cork 1902. Painted some church interiors and occasional genre. Exhibited

RSA(1), AAS(2) & GI(9), latterly from 17 Rosslyn Terrace, Kelvinside. Represented in Glasgow AG.
**Bibl:** Burkhauser 73, 182.

**WOOD, Henry Harvey** **fl 1923-1931**
Edinburgh painter in oil, watercolour and pencil; portraits and occasional interiors. Trained Edinburgh College of Art under John Duncan(qv). Exhibited RSA(9) & RSW(1).

**WOOD, Ian** **fl 1945-1946**
Milngavie painter of nature studies. Exhibited GI(2).

**WOOD, J Leslie** **fl 1871-1881**
Edinburgh oil painter of portraits and figure subjects; exhibited RSA(2).

**WOOD, Jacqueline H** **fl 1970-1975**
Aberdeen trained artist; trained Gray's School of Art, Aberdeen. Exhibited AAS(3) from 3 Marchbank Rd, Bieldside.

**WOOD, James** **fl 1917-1933**
Genre and landscape painter of Paisley; exhibited RSA(4), AAS(3), GI(6) & L(1), moving in the late 1920s to Englewood, Kilmacolm, then to Greenock.

**WOOD, James Porteous RSW** **1919-**
Born Edinburgh, Sep 12. Painter in oil and watercolour of portraits, landscapes and murals. Studied at Edinburgh College of Art 1936-40 from where he received a travelling scholarship. Lived for a time in Ripon, Yorks before becoming chief artist and designer to Aspreys of London. Abandoned commercial art to resume full-time painting independently in Scotland 1976. Elected RSW 1945, at the time the youngest person to have achieved the honour. Executed murals in the Royal Palace, Kathmandu, Nepal. Illustrated Hancock's *Midland Riches* and Harrison's *Yorkshire Dales.* Lives and works in Arisaig, Inverness-shire.

**WOOD, James Scott** **fl 1956**
Glasgow-based sculptor. Exhibited GI(2).

**WOOD, James T** **fl 1965-1985**
Aberdeen sculptor; exhibited RSA(3) & AAS, from 3 Marchbank Rd.

**WOOD, L** **fl 1881**
Amateur painter of 3 Chapel Street, Edinburgh; exhibited RSA(1).

**WOOD, Louise** **fl 1888-1893**
Amateur Glasgow painter of narrative works; exhibited GI(2), from 16 Queen Mary Avenue, Crosshill.

**WOOD, Marshall** **fl 1856**
Edinburgh sculptor. Exhibited two portrait busts/head studies at the RSA from S. Castle St.

**WOOD, Mary Isobel** **fl 1925-1940**
Little known Edinburgh painter, engraver and stained glass designer; also woodcuts. Collaborated with Douglas Hamilton(qv) over a series of windows depicting the trees of the Bible in Priestfield Church; also represented in Burdiehouse Church. Exhibited RSA(8), including a memorial window for the parish church on the island of Lismore 1928.
**Bibl:** Gifford 45,484,636.

**WOOD, Matthew** **fl 1864-1869**
Minor oil painter of Edinburgh who painted still-life and birds and birds' nests something in the manner of the Clares. Exhibited RSA(11) including an unusual composition of wild bees 1865.

**WOOD, Miss Muir** **fl 1901**
Glasgow sculptress. Exhibited 'Study in white metal' at the RSA.

**WOOD, Robert** **fl 1700-1722**
Edinburgh engraver. Best known work is a portrait of 'Sir George Mackenzie'. Engraved plates for Nisbet's *System of Heraldry,* 1722; bookplates for George Balderston (see Grigg's *Armorial Book Plates,* 2nd xser.,86), 1700; John Birbie of Broomhall, 1700; Plenderleith of Blyth, 1710. Subscribed to Nisbet's *Essay on...Armories,* 1718.
**Bibl:** Bushnell.

**WOOD, Roy** **fl 1967-1986**
Linlithgow etcher. Member of staff, Edinburgh College of Art. Exhibited RSA in 1967 and again 1986.

**WOOD, Shakespere** **1827-1886**
Leith sculptor. Exhibited RSA in 1847 and again 1865 including a bust of the Rev Dr Duncan, Professor of Oriental Languages, New College, Edinburgh (1847).

**WOODBURN, Miss J J** **fl 1868**
Amateur Glasgow painter. Exhibited 'Fruit' at the GI.

**WOODBURN, W S** **fl 1876**
Glasgow landscape painter in oil; exhibited RSA(1).

**WOODFORD, James** **fl 1931-1935**
Scottish sculptor, mainly in bronze; portrait busts. Worked from Greenock before moving to London. Exhibited AAS(6).

**WOODHOUSE, Andrew Lawrence** **fl 1965**
Aberdeen painter of local landscape and semi-abstracts; exhibited AAS(2), from 77 Queen St.

**WOODLARD, B G** **fl 1898**
Amateur painter of 25 Comeley Bank Ave, Edinburgh; exhibited GI(1).

**WOODMAN, Miss May** **fl 1919-1921**
Landscape painter and etcher, especially of town and street scenes. Exhibited AAS(4) at first from 93 Argyll Place and subsequently from London.

**WOODSIDE, Christine A RSW RGI** **fl 1975-1976**
Perth painter of townscapes and landscapes; trained Gray's School of Art, Aberdeen. Elected RSW 1999, RGI 1999. Exhibited RSA & AAS from 8 Woodlands, Perth, and latterly Annan.

**WOOLARD, William** **fl 1883-1908**
Edinburgh painter in oil and watercolour of landscapes, seascapes and townscapes; exhibited RSA(23), RSW(2), AAS(5) & GI(2), latterly from 16 Picardy Place. Represented in Edinburgh City collection by 13 watercolours and pencil studies of old Edinburgh.

**WOOLFORD, Charles Halkerston** **1864-1934**
Born Edinburgh. Painter in oil and watercolour of buildings, interiors, still-life and landscape, mainly the last. Father of Harry W(qv). Trained School of Board of Manufacturers. Lived for many years at Eskbank House, Musselburgh. His best known works include 'Progress of the Forth Bridge' 1885, 'A house in the Cowgate occupied by Sir Thomas Hope, King's Advocate of Charles I in 1626', 'Edinburgh from Arthur's Seat', both 1887 and 'Strathallan from near Gleneagles' 1896. Member of the naturalist school who painted nature as he saw it with a clear, warm and strong palette and a good sense of design, though occasionally his scenes are over-worked. Like many painters of his kind, his popularity has worn well. Exhibited RA(2) 1892 and 1894, but mainly RSA(104), RSW(10), AAS(1893-1912) & GI(45). Represented in City of Edinburgh collection.
**Bibl:** Caw 389.

**WOOLFORD, Harry Halkerston Russell** **1905-?**
Born Edinburgh. Landscape painter in oil and watercolour and picture restorer. Trained at Edinburgh RSA; a Carnegie Scholarship enabled him to visit France, Italy and (later) North Africa. Enjoyed a fine reputation as a picture restorer working for the national galleries as well as for a number of private and trade clients. His output after retirement became limited by alcohol. His most productive years were between 1922 and 1939. Exhibited RSA(6), RSW(5), AAS(2) & GI(4).

**WOOLFORD, John Elliott H** **fl 1815**
Scottish artist. Lived at Tichbourne Street, London; exhibited two landscapes at the RA - 'View of Edinburgh Castle from the Canon

Mills' and another landscape, both in 1815. Emigrated to North America.

**WOOLNOTH, Alfred** **fl 1872-1896**
Edinburgh painter in oil and watercolour of landscapes and figure subjects. Lived at 28 Ruthvengate, Edinburgh, before moving to 14 Well Walk, Hampstead, London in the late 1880's. In 1886 his 'View of the Old Town of Stonehaven' was well received. Exhibited 'Pass of Glencoe' 1872 and 'Falls of Unach, nr Loch Lee' 1889 at the RA; also RSA (11), GI(2) & L(3).

**WOOLNOTH, Charles Nicholls RSW** **1815-1906**
Born London; died Glasgow, 25 Mar. Painter in oil and watercolour of landscapes and coastal scenes. Moved to Scotland at an early age, living in Glasgow and studying at the RSA Schools. Founder member, RSW 1878. His work is of variable quality, sometimes depicting the grandeur of the Highlands majestically and sometimes appearing commonplace and over-worked. Among his better known works are 'Lochnagar from Invercauld' 1872, 'Loch Maree' 1873, 'A view on Arran' 1875 and 'Loch Restal, Glen Croe' 1887. Much of his good work was carefully detailed with Highland cattle and red deer sometimes appearing but always subservient to the landscape. Exhibited RSA(53), RSW(87) & GI(100+). Represented in Glasgow AG.
**Bibl:** Halsby 107,288.

**WOON, Miss Annie K** **fl 1868-1907**
Edinburgh painter in watercolour, also sculptress, etcher and teacher. She concentrated on portraits, landscapes and flower pieces. Sister of Rosa W(qv) probably related to E A W(qv). Exhibited RSA(12), including a sculptured bust of 'The Astronomer Royal for Scotland, Professor Copeland' (1901); also GI(8), L(2) & SWA(1).

**WOON, Miss E A** **fl 1890-1895**
Exhibited two shipping scenes in watercolour at the RSA from 4 Walker Street, Edinburgh, also a figure study at the AAS in 1894. Related to Annie and Rosa W(qv).

**WOON, Miss Rosa Elizabeth** **fl 1875-1914**
Edinburgh painter in oil of figure subjects, portraits and domestic interiors. Sister of Annie W(qv). Moved to London at the turn of the century. Commissioned by Lord Craighill to paint his two daughters, RSA 1876. Exhibited RSA(14), AAS(1), SWA(1), GI(1) & London Salon(15).

**WORK, George Orkney** **c1870-1921**
Painter from Bridge of Dee, Castle Douglas. Moved to Liverpool in the 1900s then to Skipton, Yorks c1913. Exhibited RSA(1), GI(2) & L(31).

**WORKMAN, Charles** **fl 1591-d1605**
Early Edinburgh painter. Son of David W(qv), painter. Died Aug 16 of the plague. Made Burgess of Edinburgh 1521. Working in the city 1591-1605 during which time he took as apprentices John Henryson 1601 and John Scott 1605. At the time of his death his debtors included the Master of Glamis.
**Bibl:** Apted 107.

**WORKMAN, David** **fl 1554-d pre1591**
Father of Charles(qv), James(qv) and John W(qv), all painters. In 1581 he was painting the ceiling of the Inner Tolbooth of Edinburgh and in 1585-6 was made a Burgess. Although known to have done other work in the city, none is now recorded. In 1554 he was involved in a quarrel with Walter Binning(qv) and a group lead by the Deacon of Wrights. In 1586 he painted the walls of the 'lords inner counsalehous'.
**Bibl:** Apted 107; Edinburgh Burgh Records 1573-1589, 194-5,226,461.

**WORKMAN, Evelyn Jane (or H?) Lochhead** **fl 1900-1907**
Minor painter of 5 Woodside Terrace, Glasgow; exhibited RSA(3) & GI(4).

**WORKMAN, James the elder** **fl 1587-1633**
Edinburgh painter, son of David W(qv). Made a Burgess of Edinburgh, 27 January, 1587. Listed as a herald painter 1592. Owned property at Burntisland. Apted considers that his residence there may be relevant to the authorship of painted ceilings discovered in Burntisland. In 1589 he and his brother John(qv) worked for the Queen including 'gilding the gret armeis at the Nether bow, and for gilding of tua armeis quhilk ar to be put up at the West port and for malloring and cullering of the Nether bow about the armeis, and for drawing of alscheller draughtis within the bow, and for cullouring of the cros'. Also known to have worked between 1616 and 1633 at Edinburgh Castle and Linlithgow Palace. On 24 March, 1629 received £240 with John Binning for work at Linlithgow Palace, including painting all the King's rooms. Possibly responsible for the Processional Roll at the funeral of Margaret Ross, Lady Keir of Holyrood. Late in life attracted the criticism of the Lord Lyon, Sir James Balfour, who thought the artist should be punished for being ignorant of the arms of England which is 'expreslie contrair the othe of al thes quho proffessis the knoledge of honor and armes within the kingdome of Scotland'. Had as apprentices William Symington 1594, William Ramsay 1600 and George Reid 1606.
**Bibl:** Accounts of the Masters of Works, vol ii, 62,78-9,81; Apted 107-110; Edinburgh Burgh Records 1589-1603, 328,330; Fraser, The Stirlings of Keir and their Family Papers, Edinburgh 1858, 51-3; Macmillan [SA] 48,52,85; J H Stevenson, Heraldry in Scotland, Glasgow 1914, 114,118.

**WORKMAN, James the younger** **fl 1617-d pre1664**
Early painter. Son of James W(qv). Painter Burgess of Edinburgh 1641. Painted the Queen's Chamber in the Abbey of Holyrood for which he was paid £3.6s 8d.
**Bibl:** Apted 110; Greyfriars Internments, 704; Master of Works Accounts, ii, 76.

**WORKMAN, John** **fl 1589-d1604**
Edinburgh painter. Son of David W(qv). On 14 November, 1592 appointed by the King 'paynter of the armes of all knichtis lordias erles and dukes at the tymes of thair belting and promotion and alsua at the tymes of thair foirfaltiers restitution and funerallis and all uther tymes and occasionis'. Died of the plague 31 October, 1604. Working in connection with the Queen's entry to Edinburgh including gilding two arms and the Nether bow and was paid 20 shillings for a painting of the 'Bachus' 1589-90. In 1592 was responsible for funereal paintings after the death of James, Earl of Moray and Patrick Dunbar, sheriff of Moray. In 1603 he painted the coach in which Queen Anne departed for England.
**Bibl:** Apted 110-111; Edinburgh Burgh Records 1589-1603, 328-332; Macmillan [SA] 47-8; Thomson, 34.

**WORKMAN, Nellie B** **fl 1900-1912**
Figure and topographical painter; sometimes in monochrome. Probably originally Irish, perhaps from Co. Down. Moved to Scotland c1910, living in Glasgow 1912 from where she exhibited a figurative work RA; also GI(2) & SWA(1).

**WORKMAN, Robert S** **fl 1886**
Amateur still-life watercolour painter; exhibited RSA(1) from Windmill St, Saltcoats.

**WOTHERSPOON, James Jnr** **fl 1889-1891**
Minor Glasgow painter; exhib RSA(1) & GI(5) from 4 Lynedoch Pl.

**WOTTON, Thomas E** **fl 1889-1890**
Glasgow painter; mainly river scenes. Moved to London 1890. Exhibited GI(4).

**WRATE, Judy** **fl 1982-**
Aberdeenshire printmaker; trained Gray's School of Arty, Aberdeen. Exhibited AAS(2) from 8 Kirkhill Drive, Old Meldrum.

**WRENCH, Arthur Edwin** **fl 1923-1924**
Amateur Glasgow engraver. Exhibited GI(2) & L(2) from 165 St Andrews Rd, Pollokshields.

**WRIGHT, Alan James** **fl 1966**
Edinburgh painter; favoured large figure groups and large, dashing landscapes. Trained Edinburgh College of Art. An exhibition of his work in Edinburgh 1966. Exhibited 'Fish vendors' at the RSA, from Lauriston Pl.

**WRIGHT, Mrs Anne** **fl 1984**
Helensburgh still life painter. Exhibited 'Blue Vase' at the GI.

**WRIGHT, Bill RSW** **1931-**
Born Sep 1, Glasgow. Painter, mainly in watercolour, gouache and acrylic, the latter on both canvas and paper and executed in a loose, 'wet' style. Trained Glasgow School of Art 1949-53. Derived his inspiration from the sea and the Atlantic coastline, especially the west coast of Kintyre. First solo exhibition in Irvine 1974. For twenty years was art adviser to Strathclyde Regional Council before becoming a full-time painter. "At my most recent one-man show, people commented on how peaceful the atmosphere was; I ask no more". Professional member, SSA and member, Glasgow Group. Elected RSW 1977. Awarded William Gillies Prize 1995 and winner UK section of the Laing Competition in the same year. Frequent exhibitor RSA & RSW; also GI(63) since 1952. Lived at Old Lagangarve Cottage, Bellochantuy, Argyll. Represented Lillie AG (Milngavie).

**WRIGHT, Catherine M** **fl 1879-1891**
Landscape and figure painter who lived in Crieff for some years before moving c1887 to London. Painted mainly still-life and figure subjects in oil, also occasional watercolours. Exhibited RA(3) 1887-1889; also RSA(5), ROI(4), RBA(1), GI(4), SWA(4) & L(3), latterly from 149 Tachbrook St, London.

**WRIGHT, Miss Cathleen Honoria Moncrieff** **fl 1913-1922**
Amateur sculptress of Kinmouth, Bridge of Earn, Perthshire. Exhibited a portrait bust RSA(1).

**WRIGHT, Charles** **fl 1979-1981**
Fife painter. Exhibited RSA(3), from Lower Largo.

**WRIGHT, David** **fl 1911**
Edinburgh painter. Exhibited RSA(1) from 15 Wilton Rd.

**WRIGHT, Mrs E** **fl 1885-1900**
Aberdeenshire landscape painter; exhibited local scenes at the AAS from Ellon.

**WRIGHT, Miss Elsie** **fl 1940-1946**
Glasgow watercolour painter. Exhibited GI(6), mainly topographical scenes in west Scotland and the English Lakes.

**WRIGHT, Elsie M** **fl 1893**
Minor Glasgow painter. Exhibited two country cottage subjects at the GI, from 14 Belhaven Terrace, Kelvinside.

**WRIGHT, Miss Eveleen** **fl 1987-**
Helensburgh engraver. Exhibited GI(1) - 'Aquarius'.

**WRIGHT, G** **fl 1866**
Obscure Edinburgh landscape painter; exhibited RSA(2), one a view on Arran, from Alva St.

**WRIGHT, G Rutherford** **fl 1920-1926**
Painter of Rowancliffe, Giffnock; exhibited GI(2).

**WRIGHT, George** **1860-1942**
Born nr Leeds; died Seaford, Sussex. Sporting painter and illustrator. Lived for several years at Ednam Street, Annan. Brother of Gilbert Scott W, with whom he often collaborated. Moved to London c1894. His subjects included coaching scenes, hunting scenes, polo and country scenes, somewhat in the manner of Heywood Hardy. Used a lively, realistic style with bright colours, often painted in pairs. Illustrated *'King', the Story of a Dog* (1936), *'Pinto' the Mustang* (1935) and *Wild Horse Silver* (1934). In later life lived at Gilshaw Lodge, Bilton Rd, Rugby. Exhibited RA(16) 1892-1904 but principally RSA (33) & GI(15) including several landscapes around Annan, Dumfriesshire.
**Bibl:** Paviere, Sporting Painters, 93.

**WRIGHT, George Gibson Neill** **fl 1956-1961**
East Lothian landscape painter. Exhibited 'Willows on the Tyne' RSA; also GI(2), from Dunbar.

**WRIGHT, George H B** **fl 1936-1940**
Angus painter of landscape and pastoral scenes. Exhibited RSA(9) from 55 Princes St, Monifieth.

**WRIGHT, H Cook** **fl 1917-1930**
Painter of historic buildings. Exhibited AAS(2) 1923 and intermittently GI(3) from Morven, Helensburgh.

**WRIGHT, H Guthrie** **fl 1866-1867**
Amateur landscape painter in oil; exhibited RSA(4).

**WRIGHT, Isabel (Mrs Thomas Calder)** **1880-1958**
Born Renfrew. Trained Glasgow School of Art 1901-1904. Exhibited exclusively at the Walker Gallery, Liverpool(49) from Glasgow.

**WRIGHT, Miss Isabella M** **fl 1864-1871**
Edinburgh painter in oil and watercolour of landscapes, churches and castles; spent 1870 in Aboyne, Aberdeenshire. Exhibited RSA(3).

**WRIGHT, James RSW** **c1885-1947**
Born Ayr. Painter in oil and watercolour, mainly the latter, and stained glass designer; landscape and figure subjects. Brother of Margaret Isabel W(qv). Educated Ayr Academy. Inspired in watercolour at an early age by instruction received from James McMaster(qv). Pursued further studies at Glasgow School of Art and after graduating took up a position as cartoonist to Stephen Adam(qv), then one of the leading stained glass artists in Glasgow. This interest in stained glass design remained with him for the rest of his life co-existing with his work as a painter in various media. His landscapes were generally breezy coastal views in bright, vibrant colours with exuberant brush work. Also worked in France. Elected RSW 1920. Some of his best glass work can be seen at Kilbarchan, Culross and Pittenweem. Subsequently elected Vice-President, RSW. Lived latterly at Garelochhead, Dumbartonshire. Exhibited RA(3), RSA(36), RSW(82), AAS(2), GI(57) & L(5), latterly from Old Mill, Kilbarchan. Represented in Glasgow AG(2), Edinburgh City collection.
**Bibl:** Halsby 288.

**WRIGHT, James Coupar** **?-1968**
Born Orkney; died California. Watercolour painter and stained glass window designer. Trained Edinburgh College of Art, obtaining a scholarship that enabled him to study stained glass design in Dusseldorf. Subsequently moved to Santa Barbara, California where he concentrated on painting in watercolour. Represented in several U.S. public collections.

**WRIGHT, Jeremiah** **fl 1671-1685**
Edinburgh painter. Brother of John Michael Wright(qv). Responsible for executing the arms inscriptions on the Guild Hall judges' pictures by his brother 1671. In 1685 was made a member of the Court of Assistance of the Painter-stainer's company.

**WRIGHT, John** **fl 1863-1865**
Minor Edinburgh painter in oil of figure subjects; exhibited RSA (5).

**WRIGHT, John Michael** **1617-1694**
Portrait painter. *(Benezit* records birthplace Scotland c1623; died London 1700). Although one of the most important and impressive European portrait painters of the 17th century, remarkably little is known about his life. It is not even known for certain where he was born and whether or not his parents were Scottish. The probability is that, although living in London, his parents were Scottish and that he was born in London. What is known for certain is that from 6 April, 1636 until about 1641, he was in Edinburgh serving an apprenticeship under George Jamesone(qv). These details, together with the fact that many of his most important works were of Scottish sitters, justifies his inclusion here. After departing for Rome in 1641, it cannot be said with certainty whether or not he was ever again in Scotland although it is possible. Little known of his life in Rome until 1647; he must have been studying not only painting but also obtaining a scholarly knowledge of classical antiquities. In 1648 he was elected to the Academy of St Luke alongside Nicolas Poussin, Claud Mellan and Velasquez. In 1647 he produced his only known etching - 'Virgin and Child, after Carracci'. By 1653/4 his reputation as an antiquarian persuaded the Archduke Leopold, Governor of the Spanish Netherlands, to appoint him his antiquary. In 1656 he had returned to London and in 1860, Charles II, having been restored to

the throne, commissioned the artist to paint the ceiling of the king's bedchamber in Whitehall Palace. After the great fire of 1670 the City Aldermen appointed a committee to commission a number of portraits. A competition was held in which Wright was successful, ahead of Huysmans, Hale and another. He executed 22 full-length portraits 1671-75 for which he received £36 each. When John Evelyn visited the Guildhall in 1673, although biased against the unfashionable painter, he wrote 'I went home, turning in, as they went through Cheapeside to see the Pictures of all the Judges and Eminent men of the Long road newly painted by Mr Write...most of them were very like the Persons they are made to represent, though I never took Write to be any considerable artist'. In addition to his contacts within the city, Wright travelled around the English countryside painting members of the aristocracy who rarely visited London. An important group of pictures was commissioned by Sir Walter Bagot in 1675 and from this contract there survives a series of letters revealing a great deal about the artist's methods and himself. His health began seriously to fail in 1694 and he was buried in St Martins in the Fields on 1 August that year. Described by a contemporary as of middle stature 'free and open, innocently merry in his conversation (especially amongst his friends), of great plainness and simplicity, and of a very easy temper'. His biographers note that this description conveys the feeling of many of his own portraits. The ceiling for the king's bedchamber (now in Nottingham AG) has been described as 'the most accomplished and thoroughgoing baroque decoration painted by a British artist' [Holloway]. For Queen Catherine's chamber he painted a chimney piece depicting St Catherine. His most impressive work of this period were two portraits of 'King Charles II' 1661. The first is in the Royal Collection and the second, until recently unrecorded, is in private hands. Throughout the 1670s he styled himself 'Pictor Regius' although, in contrast to his contemporary Lely, he never received a formal appointment. Also at this time he curiously adopted the additional christian name John. From the mid 1660s can be dated two of his most important works, a portrait of 'John Leslie, Duke of Rothes' and a portrait of one of his patrons, 'Sir William Bruce of Kinross, Surveyor of the Royal Works', now in the SNPG. He was in Ireland 1679-83 and probably dating from this period is the fine 'Lord Mungo Murray (1668-1700)', also in SNPG. Two versions of this portrait are known, one dated 1684 the other 1689 being one of the historically most interesting depictions of full Highland hunting costume of the period. Other paintings of figures in Scottish costume include the actor 'John Lacy', dressed as a Scotsman in full Highland costume, painted for the King. In 1685 King James VII appointed Lord Castlemaine as Ambassador to the Pope and Wright was made artistic director with responsibility for organising the ceremonials, important for successful political negotiation. This task took him back to Italy where he remained from 1685-87 before greatly suffering from the King's departure in 1688. Among his best domestic works is a family portrait of 'The children of the 3rd Earl of Salisbury, Lady Catherine Cecil and James Cecil, later 4th Earl of Salisbury', a remarkably fine, carefully constructed work which, in spite of complicated dresses worn by the children, retains a feeling for the simplicity of youth. A wonderful artist and still somewhat underestimated. Known during his lifetime by various pseudonyms including 'Michael Ritus' when in Rome (in which name he registered at the Rome Academy) and on the reverse of one portrait 'Jos. mick Wrilps Londonensis Pictor Caroli Regis'. Represented in SNG, SNPG(3), V & A, Culzean Castle(3) (NTS), Nottingham AG, Sudbury Hall (National Trust), Claydon House (National Trust), Manchester AG, Tower of London, Hampton Court, Royal Collection, Manchester AG, Wolverhampton AG, National Gallery of Ireland.
**Bibl:** Bryan; Burlington Mag, Vol cxxx, Oct, 1988; Brydall 98-100; D. Farr, 'A Rediscovered John Michael Wright's Signature' in Burlington Mag, Feb, 1961; J. Fenlon, 'John Michael Wright's 'Highland Laird' identified'; Holloway 18-22, 27-31,149-150; McKay 9,15-16; W.J. Smith, 'Letters from Michael Wright', Burlington Mag, xcv, 1953, 233-6; Stevenson and Thomson, John Michael Wright, the King's Painter, 1982; Thomson 71-74; H.Walpole, Anecdotes of Painting in England, 1876, ii, 123-5; Walpole Society, Vertue Notebooks, i, 22-4,31,44,50,81,83-4,91,97, 111,117,136; ii, 4,66,135,138; iii, 12; iv, 3,6,31,68,92,102-5, 122, 159,163,177,189; v, 1,9,14,50-1,68; Waterhouse, Painting in Britain 1530-1790, 1962, 66; Guy Wilson,'Greenwich Armour in the Portraits of John Michael Wright', Conn, Feb, 1975, 108-115; J.M. Wright, An Account of His Excellence Roger, Earl of Castlemaine's Embassy...to his Holiness Innocent XI, London 1688.

**WRIGHT, M I** **fl 1888**
Amateur Glasgow landscape artist. Exhibited GI(1) from 34 Burbank Gdns.

**WRIGHT, Margaret** **fl 1966-1969**
Glasgow painter, mainly of landscapes. Moved to Peterborough and then St. Albans. Exhibited RSA(7) & GI(2).

**WRIGHT, Margaret Isobel** **1884-1957**
Born Ayr; died Gourock. Sister of James W(qv). Trained Glasgow School of Art 1902-1908, continuing her studies in France. Like her brother, painted watercolours of the west coast and its harbours; also fond of painting children at play. Married 1921 and settled in Gourock. Helped to illustrate *Recording Scotland* (1952). Her work was characteristed by the use of dense watercolour showing clearly the influence of George Henry(qv) and other members of the Glasgow School. Increasingly recognised as a painter of substance and vitality. Exhibited RSA(35), GI(76) & L(3).
**Bibl:** Halsby 288.

**WRIGHT, Miss Meg** **1868-1932**
Edinburgh painter in oil and watercolour of landscape, portraits, figure subjects and interiors. Caw found her work weak in observation and careless in handling but with a real and charming feel for landscape. Exhibited RA(3), RSA(83), RSW(7), RBA(3), RHA(2), AAS 1893-1921, GI(39) & L(2), from 12 Queen Street and from 1910 12 Grange Rd.
**Bibl:** Caw 391.

**WRIGHT, Moncrieff (Mrs)** **fl 1904-1909**
Edinburgh sculptress. Probably mother of Cathleen Honoria W(qv). Moved to Milnathorpe 1906 and Bridge of Earn 1909. Exhibited RSA(3), all portrait busts.

**WRIGHT, Rosemary** **fl 1966-1968**
Aberdour painter of flora, fauna, landscape and still life. Influenced by Mary Armour(qv) and Gillies(qv), she painted in a spontaneous, dashing manner with a light palette and great freshness. First one-man exhibition in Edinburgh 1966. Exhibited RSA(3).

**WRIGHT, Professor Stanley** **fl 1970**
Architect, occasional painter and teacher. Principal of Edinburgh College of Art. Exhibited a landscape at the RSA.

**WRIGHT, Thomas** **fl 1893-1910**
Ayrshire landscape painter. Exhibited a view of St. Monans AAS 1931 from Hazlewood, Stevenston.

**WRIGHT, Tom** **fl 1888**
Minor Glasgow painter. Probably brother of W W(qv). Exhibited GI(1) from 31 Queen Mary Ave, Crosshall.

**WRIGHT, Will J E** **fl 1906-1929**
Glasgow architect and painter of townscapes and churches; exhibited intermittently at the GI, from Laurelhill, Bearsden.

**WRIGHT, William** **fl 1805-1806**
Glasgow artist. Probably brother of Tom W(qv) who was exhibiting at the same time and from the same address. Exhibited RSA(2) from 31 Queen Mary Ave.

**WRIGHT, William** **fl 1886-1896**
Falkirk painter in oil and watercolour; exhibited RSA(1) & RSW(1).

**WROUGHTON, Julia ARCA ARWA** **1934-**
Born Bridge of Allan, Stirlingshire, Oct 24. Painter in oil and watercolour. Educated at the Beacon School, Bridge of Allan; trained Colchester School of Art 1953-57 under John O'Connor and Hugh Cronyn, continuing at Royal College of Art 1957-1960 under Carel Weight and Colin Hayes. Held her first solo exhibition at the Torrance Gallery, Edinburgh 1960. Lives on Mull. Exhibits RA. Represented in Royal West of England Academy of which she was elected a member.

**WYATT, Miss A M B** **fl 1901**
Amateur Orkney artist. Exhibited RI(1) from The Manse, Stromness.

**WYLD, Eleanor** **fl 1878**
Painter from Gartcosh; exhibited local landscapes and wildlife scenes in oil at the RSA(2).

**WYLIE, Duncan P C** **fl 1981**
Edinburgh painter; exhibited AAS(1).

**WYLIE, Edward Grigg** **c1885-1954**
Glasgow architect. Apprenticed with W F McGibbon. Lecturer, Glasgow School of Architecture 1912. His design for Hillhead HS 1921 won a competition and, with **Alexander WRIGHT**, designed the award-winning Scottish Legal Life Building, Bothwell St. Consultant to the Scottish Industrial Estates 1930s, designing many factories showing the influence of the 1936 Exhibition. Responsible for the Dental Hospital, Renfrew St.
**Bibl:** Gomme & Walker, Architecture of Glasgow, L 1987(rev), 304.

**WYL(L)IE, G Kinloch** **fl 1887-1890**
Amateur Glasgow topographical painter; exhibited RSA(2) & GI(7).

**WYLIE, Georgina Mossman (Mrs Greenlees) RSW** **fl 1870-1918**
Painter in watercolour of landscapes. Lived in Glasgow for many years before moving c1896 to Prestwick. Elected RSW 1878. Exhibited RA(1), RSW(89), RSA(18) & GI(42).

**WYLIE, James** **fl 1931-1959**
Ayrsher watercolour landscape painter; often on Arran. Exhibited RSW(2), AAS(1) & GI(14) from Hazlewood, High Road, Steventon.

**WYLIE, Miss Kate** **1877-1941**
Born Skelmorlie, Ayrshire. Painter in oil and watercolour of portraits, flower studies and landscapes, now best known for her flowers. Trained Glasgow School of Art. Often painted on Arran where she had a cottage at Blackwater Foot. In 1942 a memorial exhibition of her work, and that of Janet Aitken and Elma Story, was held at Glasgow Society of Lady Artists. Exhibited RA(4), RSA(19), RSW(19), AAS(1), GI(47) & L(1). Represented in Glasgow AG(2).
**Bibl:** Halsby 288.

**WYLLIE, George ARSA** **1921-**
Born Glasgow. Sculptor. Began life as a customs officer in Northern Ireland. Returned to Gourock in the 50s and enrolled in art courses. Inspired by an exhibition of Italian metal sculpture at the Glasgow School of Art, this led to him attending welding classes. Much of his work contains a humorous element. Member of the Glasgow Group. His 'Paper Boat' was awarded the Gulbenkian prize. Lives at 9 McPherson Drive, Gourock. Elected ARSA 1989. Exhibited RSA since 1967, GI(35) & AAS(2). Represented in Glasgow AG, SAC, Worcester AG (Mass).

**WYLLIE, Miss Gladys Amy** **fl 1902-d1942**
Embroiderer and textile designer. Trained Edinburgh College of Art and later took diploma in the City of London Guilds course in church embroidery. Founder of the Modern Embroiderers' Society, with whom she exhibited from 1923. Exhibited banners, copes and altar frontals RSA(8) & SSA from her home in Edinburgh, and later Blairgowrie. Represented in V & A, Scottish church, Jerusalem, St. Mary's cathedral, Edinburgh.

**WYLLIE, Gordon H RSW** **fl 1954-**
Greenock watercolour painter of landscapes, also works in gouache and pastel. Elected RSW 1967. Exhibited RSA(24) & RGI(66). Represented in Lillie AG (Milngavie)(3).

**WYLLIE, Lt Col Harold OBE VPRSMA** **1880-1973**
Born London, Jne 20/29; died Dunkeld Dec 22/3. Painter of marines in oil, watercolour, gouache, pencil; also sculptor, etcher- drypoint, bitten etching and aquatintist. Son of W L Wyllie. Educated at Smyths Littlejohns, studied art under his father and with Sir T Graeme Jackson, Edwin Abbey and Sir Frank Short. Appointed marine painter to the Royal Victoria Yacht Club, Ryde. One of the few men to have been commissioned in all three services. Re-created with meticulous accuracy the battles and exploits of the Royal Navy, and with his encyclopaedic knowledge, was still receiving commissions at the age of 92. Member of the Committee with direct responsibility for rebuilding and rerigging Nelson's Flagship, *HMS Victory*. In 1900 commissioned in the Royal West Kent Regiment and later served with the Buffs. One of the first men to fly in action, having joined the Royal Flying Corps in 1914. Later commanded squadrons in France and England and in 1916 obtained a commission in the Wiltshire Regiment. Mentioned in despatches. Awarded OBE. From 1925-1930 served in the RAF Reserve reaching the rank of Wing Commander. During WW2 was with the RNVR as a Lieut-Commander. Settled in Dunkeld, Perthshire where he lived for many years, painting till the end of his life. Exhibited RA(11), RI(2) & GI(3). Represented in Cape Town AG, Imperial War Museum, National Maritime Museum.
**Bibl:** Scotsman, 24.12.73 (obit).

**WYLLIE, Miss Marion** **fl 1965**
Glasgow figurative painter. Exhibited GI(1) from Bearsden.

**WYLLIE, Robin H** **fl 1958-1963**
Glasgow landscape painter. Moved to Balloch. Exhibited GI(4).

**WYLLIE, William** **fl 1922**
Paisley landscape painter in oil and watercolour; rural scenes and animals. Exhibited RSW(1) & GI(4) from Johnstone, Renfrewshire. Not to be confused with William Lionel W.

**WYNESS, J Fenton FRIBA ARIAS** **1903-c1980**
Born Aberdeen, Aug 15; died Aberdeen Mar 12. Painter in monochrome and watercolour, also sculptor, writer, historian, architect and art critic. Educated at Aberdeen GS. Trained Gray's School of Art. Author of *Second Book of Legends, Donside, Kincardineshire, Let's Look Around Aberdeenshire, Mediaeval Edinburgh, Mediaeval Elgin, North-Eastern Journey, Royal Deeside* and *City by the Great North Sea* (1965). Exhibited RSA, GI(2) & AAS(10) from 25 Belmont St. Represented in Imperial War Museum, Aberdeen AG.

**WYPER, Jane Cowan RSW** **1866-1898**
Born Glasgow. Painter in oil and watercolour of coastal scenes, landscape and figure subjects. First exhibited RSA 1890 and again in 1896 (when incorrectly catalogued as 'I C') and in 1897. Elected RSW 1896. Died in tragic circumstances, falling off a cliff on the Isle of Sark. During her short life she exhibited RSA(7), GI(17), L(2) & RSW, mostly marines.
**Bibl:** Halsby 288.

**WYSE, Henry Taylor** **1870-1951**
Born Glasgow, Feb 6; died Edinburgh, Mar 24. Remarkably versatile in many artistic and literary fields. Painter in oil, watercolour and pastel of landscape and flower studies; also potter, author & teacher. Painted scenery in Scotland and the Netherlands. Trained Dundee School of Art, Glasgow School of Art and Colarossi's, Paris. Lectured in art at Coatbridge, Arbroath and then Edinburgh. Close friend and working associate of James Waterston Herald(qv). Published *Modern Methods of Art Instruction, Memory and Imaginative Drawing* and other works on art. An unpublished monograph on J W Herald(qv) was used extensively in Kenneth Roberts' biography (1988); frequent contributor to *The Studio*. Designed the interior of the Arcadian Gallery, Glasgow 1907, including a pastel drawing, and produced ten panels for D M Brown's Tearoom, Dundee; also panels for a hotel in Gravadona, Italy. Chairman, Edinburgh Repertory Theatre 1924-34. Lived in Arbroath where he taught at the High School 1893-1904 before moving to Edinburgh to teach at George Watson's Ladies College, 1904-22 (seconded for part of this time to Merchiston Castle School). After teaching at Moray House Training College 1922-35, retired, remaining in Edinburgh. Ran Holyrood Pottery during the 1920s; this was managed by his elder daughter. Used leadless glazes which Wyse pioneered; the limited output of the factory is now eagerly collected. Exhibited RSA(8), AAS(4), GI (3), L(2) & London Salon(6), latterly from 5 Craighouse Terrace, Edinburgh. Represented in Huntly House Museum, Edinburgh (pottery).
**Bibl:** Halsby 157; Ann Smith (granddaughter) in personal communication.

# Y

**YARRINGTON, Claire H** **1958-**
Born Jan 23. Works in pastel, charcoal, oil and mixed media, also lithographs and monoprint. Her main interest is in creating prints, drawings and paintings which explore the boundaries of the man-made environment, where land meets sea, the tamed gives way to the wild, light meets shadow, past meets present. Studied Edinburgh University, graduating with honours in archaeology 1980. Continued her studies in Sheffield, obtaining BA Hons in Fine Art 1986. Archaeological illustrator for Aberdeen AG. Exhibits RSA since 1987. First solo exhibition 1989. Lives in Lumphanan, Aberdeenshire.

**YARROW, Lady Annette** **fl 1974**
Renfrewshire sculptress. Exhibited 'Orion' at the GI, from Kilmacolm.

**YATES, James Bennett** **fl 1978**
Fife painter; exhibited 'The apple of my eye' at the RSA; also GI, from Culross.

**YATES, Peter** **fl 1978**
Perthshire painter; exhibited RSA(1) from Callander.

**YEATES, Nicholas** **fl 1682**
Engraver. One of the earliest depictions of Leith port is his etching 'Prospect of Leith', 1682 dedicated to the Lord Provost and Council. Probably the portrait painter who collaborated with John Collins and was responsible for a well-known work 'General Sir William Waller'. Represented in Edinburgh PL.
**Bibl:** Benezit; Butchart 10-11.

**YEATS, George** **1850-1852**
Edinburgh portrait painter, also figure compositions. Exhibited RSA (9) including a portrait 'Miss Forbes of Pitsligo' (1852) from Howe St.

**YELLAND, John** **fl 1868-1880**
Edinburgh painter in oil and watercolour, portraits and landscape. Exhibited RSA(19) & GI(2), from 24 George St.

**YELLOWLEES, John** **fl 1786-c1818**
Early painter. In 1786 was apprenticed for six years to Alexander Weir, painter, and the same year made a Burgess of Edinburgh. Subsequently took as apprentices John Rodgers 1805, Charles King 1807, James Law 1808, William Doig 1815 and Richard Clark 1818. This number of apprentices suggests a substantial business but nothing further is known.

**YELLOWLEES, William** **1796-1856**
Born Mellerstain, Berwickshire; died London. Portrait painter. Studied under William Shiels(qv). Foundation member of the Scottish Academy, practising in Edinburgh for about fifteen years before going to London c1830 where he became a protégé of Prince Albert. In London he enjoyed an aristocratic clientele, his portraits including the 'Earl of Denbigh" 1830, two of 'His Majesty's Aides-de-Camp', both 1837 and 'General Sir William Anson' 1845. Because of the similarity of his style to that of Raeburn and the small size of many of the heads, became known as 'the Little Raeburn'. Sir William Fettes Douglas(qv) was a great admirer of his work, which was often little larger than miniature although distinguished by rich impasto and a beauty of colour not often seen in oil painting on so small a scale. His work suffered from an excess of bitumen. First exhibit RA 1829, followed by 20 works between then and 1845. Represented in NGS(2) ('Mother' and 'Father'), SNPG(3) including 'Rev Dr Jamieson'.
**Bibl:** Bryan; Brydall 243; Caw 90; McKay 127-8; Port BM 6, 1925.

**YEOELL, William J** **fl 1886**
Edinburgh amateur painter in oils; exhibited a rustic interior at the RSA, from 26 Rosemount Buildings.

**YGLESIAS, Vincent P** **fl 1882-1901**
Glasgow-based landscape and topographical painter. Moved to London c1889 from Fitzroy Square. Exhibited GI(35).

**YOOLL, Miss Helen Annie Graham** **fl 1877-1898**
Obscure watercolour painter from Pittenweem, Fife. Painted flowers and local landscape. Exhibited RSA(5), latterly from Jessfield House, Newhaven Rd, Edinburgh.

**YORSTON, George** **fl c1740**
Edinburgh engraver. Married in S.W. parish 5 July 1752. No work now recorded.
**Bibl:** Bushnell.

**YOUNG, A** **fl 1885**
Minor Edinburgh painter; exhibited RSA(2) from 18 Morningside Terrace.

**YOUNG, Miss A** **fl 1920**
Amateur Glasgow artist; exhibited L(1), from 100 N Frederick St.

**YOUNG, Aggie Thoms** **fl 1898**
Amateur Glasgow painter; exhibited GI(1) from 15 Kelvingrove St.

**YOUNG, Alan** **fl 1989-**
Aberdeen portrait painter; exhibited AAS from 8 Tollohill Place.

**YOUNG, Alex** **fl 1961**
Aberdeenshire still life painter; exhibited AAS(1) from Glendee Lodge, W Cults.

**YOUNG, Alex M** **fl 1949-1988**
Glasgow landscape painter, mainly in watercolour. Exhibited 'Tree study' at the RSA, from Ashkirk Drive; also GI(11), latterly from Milngavie.

**YOUNG, Alexander** **1865-1923**
Fife-based painter of landscape, coastal scenes and figures. In the 1890s he was living at Croft Cottage, Pittenweem. In a loose, rather rough style he enjoyed the mists and moody weather as in 'Turnip gathering after heavy rain on the Braid Burn' 1885 and 'Guddlers' 1886. Exhibited RA(8), RSA(10), ROI(2), AAS(2), GI(1) & L(1). Represented in Glasgow AG.

**YOUNG, Alexander Ayton** **fl 1925**
Alloa-based artist. First exhibit at the RSA was a pastoral scene entered from the Edinburgh College of Art when still a student. Subsequently exhibited once more, in 1925, from 15 Glebe Terrace.

**YOUNG, Alexander W** **fl 1892-1933**
Glasgow sculptor; figure studies in various media. Exhibited GI(28).

**YOUNG, Andrew** **fl 1874-1919**
Painter from Burntisland in oil and watercolour; local shipping scenes, landscape and conversation pieces. Exhibited RSA(8), LS (15), GI(6) & L(8).

**YOUNG, Anna Denholm** **fl 1875**
Ayr portrait painter. Exhibited RSA(1) & RBA(1).

**YOUNG, Arthur Denoon RMS** **fl 1896-1900**
London-based portrait and portrait miniaturist. Elected RMS 1897. Sometimes confused with Anna Denholm Y(qv). Exhibited RSA(9) & RMS(17).

**YOUNG, Miss Bessie Innes** **1855-1936**
Born Glasgow. Painter of landscape, genre, flowers and still life, also garden painter and teacher. Trained Glasgow School of Art and in Paris at the Academie Delacluse. Shared a studio in Glasgow with Annie French(qv) and Jane Younger(qv) c1902-1910; their work was often exhibited together. Most of her paintings were in oil but also painted watercolour studies of landscape and flowers. Exhibited RSA(24), AAS 1900-1919, GI(25), L(3) & NEA(3). Represented Glasgow AG.
**Bibl:** Halsby 288.

**YOUNG, Buchan** **fl 1871**
Inverkeithing painter; exhibited two sketches of historical buildings RSA.

**YOUNG, Mrs Catherine (née McMillan)** **1928-**
Born Elgin, Morayshire. After raising a family embarked on a part-time course Edinburgh College of Art 1976-1983. Influenced by Nicolaes de Stael and Joan Eardley(qv). Attained considerable success showing works at the RSA, RSW, SSA & SSWA. First solo exhibition in Leith 1980.

**YOUNG, Charles** **fl 1885**
Edinburgh watercolourist; exhibited 'Athens restored' at the RSA, from St. Andrews Square.

**YOUNG, Miss Christian** **fl 1932**
Stirlingshire painter; exhibited 'Mural decoration - India' at the RSA from Bonnybridge.

**YOUNG, Mrs Christina McKay** **fl 1949-1980**
Glasgow painter and sculptress. Moved to Milngavie. Landscape and still life watercolours; plaster and terracotta portrait sculptures. Exhibited GI(9).

**YOUNG, Clement** **fl 1967-1972**
Banchory painter; exhibited several times at the RSA and at the AAS between the above years, from 13 Silverbank Crescent.

**YOUNG, Miss E J F** **fl 1869-1870**
Edinburgh oil painter of alpine landscape; exhibited RSA(2).

**YOUNG, Edmund Drummond** **1876-1946**
Born Edinburgh. Flower and still life painter, also genre, landscape, portraits and figurative studies. Worked mainly in oils but occasionally in watercolour. Son of William Drummond Y(qv). Combined work as a painter with being a professional photographer, establishing an international reputation in the latter. Author of *The Art of the Photographer* 1931. Exhibited RA(5), RSA(48), RSW(1), AAS, GI(16) & L(5). Represented Edinburgh City collection(2), The Binns (NTS).

**YOUNG, Elizabeth McAllister** **fl 1968**
Glasgow topographical painter, mostly watercolours. Exhibited 'Fetteresso church, nr Stonehaven' RSA; also GI(8).

**YOUNG, Eric H** **fl 1974-1975**
Lanarkshire painter. Exhibited GI(2) from Bothwell.

**YOUNG, Mrs Evelyn** **fl 1967**
Kincardineshire figure painter. Married Clement Y(qv). Exhibited 'Nude in Ochre' at the AAS.

**YOUNG, Miss Frances** **fl 1862-1871**
Edinburgh painter in oils of buildings, figures and fruit. Exhibited RA(2) 1862 & 1867, the second a view of 'The old Priory, Hampstead'; also RSA(5), from 12 Springfield Villas, Fulham Priory.

**YOUNG, Gabriel** **fl 1965**
Lanarkshire topographical painter. Exhibited 'Grangemouth Docks' at the GI, from Quater.

**YOUNG, George Penrose Kennedy** **fl 1887-1905**
Perth architect. Specialised in public buildings. Practised from 42 Tay St. His design for St Stephen's church, Craigie, Perth was exhibited at the RSA (1899), also four other works between the above years.

**YOUNG, Miss Gertrude E** **fl 1910-1923**
Aberdeen landscape painter. Exhibited 'The Gairn valley' and several continental townscapes at the AAS(7), from 57 Queens Rd.

**YOUNG, Harry** **fl 1965**
Aberdeen designer of jewellery and precious stones. Exhibited AAS(1) from Mendick, Bieldside.

**YOUNG, Henry** **fl 1896-1900**
Aberdeen landscape and figure painter. Exhibited AAS(4), from 23 Spa St.

**YOUNG, J Ian** **fl 1978-**
Aberdeen painter. Exhibits AAS from 63 Craigton Rd.

**YOUNG, James A** **fl 1918**
Glasgow amateur sculptor; exhibited 'Madonna and Child' at GI, from Argyle St.

**YOUNG, James B** **fl 1874**
Glasgow painter; mainly continental topography. Exhibited GI(2).

**YOUNG, Janet B B** **fl 1914-1923**
Glasgow painter of portrait miniatures and topographical works; sometimes in monochrome. Exhibited RSA(1), GI(6) & L(1).

**YOUNG, John** **fl 1893-1907**
Forfar painter. Moved to Glasgow c1907. Exhibited GI(2).

**YOUNG, John** **fl 1859-1860**
Edinburgh landscape painter; exhibited Ayrshire views at the RSA (3), from Canongate.

**YOUNG, John R P** **fl 1875-1879**
Amateur Glasgow landscape watercolourist; mostly west coast subjects, especially around Lochgilphead. Exhibited RSA(2) & GI(6).

**YOUNG, John William** **fl 1877-1884**
Edinburgh painter in oils and watercolour. Sporting subjects, harbours and country buildings. Exhibited an energetic painting 'Steeplechase' RSA 1877 and two other works; also GI(1), from 22 Royal Circus and latterly Charles St.

**YOUNG, Joyce McLellan** **fl 1884-1886**
Sutherland landscape painter; exhibited RSA(3) from Lairg.

**YOUNG, Keith O B** **fl 1887-1892**
Edinburgh watercolour painter of landscape and still life; exhibited at the RSA(5) including 'A dead blackbird', from 3 Tipperlin Rd.

**YOUNG, Margaret H K** **fl 1888**
Obscure Glasgow watercolour painter; topographical subjects. Exhibited GI(1) from 110 N. Frederick St.

**YOUNG, Mary-Rose** **fl 1889-1890**
Glasgow flower and wild-life painter. Exhibited RA(1), GI(3) & L(1).

**YOUNG, Norman** **fl 1942-1948**
Glasgow artist. Exhibited three works at the RSA: 'Air raid', 'Brewing storm' and 'Girl in mirror'; also GI(1).

**YOUNG, Miss Rachel R B** **fl 1910-1911**
Glasgow miniature painter. Exhibited a miniature portrait of a gentleman at the RA (1910) from 5 Great Western Terrace; also GI(2).

**YOUNG, Rebeka Mary** **fl 1977-1981**
Aberdeen painter. Moved to Edinburgh. Trained Gray's School of Art. Exhibited AAS(2).

**YOUNG, Robert** **fl 1878-1898**
Edinburgh painter in oil and watercolour of rustic scenes. Exhibited RSA(5) & GI(6), moving eventually to Edinburgh. Not to be confused with Robert Clouston Y(qv).

**YOUNG, Robert Clouston RSW** **1860-1929**
Painter in watercolour, enjoyed depicting children playing by the seaside and in country streams. Unpretentious but competent watercolourist who worked mainly on the Clyde and amid the surrounding villages. Elected RSW 1901. Lived in Glasgow and latterly at Ardrossan. Exhibited RSA(9), RSW(100), GI(75) & L(2). Represented in Culzean Castle (NTS).
**Bibl:** Halsby 160-1,289.

**YOUNG, Shirelle** **fl 1987**
Aberdeen amateur portrait painter. Exhibited AAS(1) from 326 Clifton Rd.

**YOUNG, Stephen** fl 1887
Glasgow minor figure; exhibited RSA(1) from 134 Bath St.

**YOUNG, Thomas Jnr** **fl 1865-1904**
Prolific Edinburgh painter in oil of landscapes, interiors and portraits. Particularly fond of depicting the rolling countryside of the Borders in a style similar to that of Tom Scott(qv). Exhibited RSA (52).

**YOUNG, Thomas P W** **fl 1919-1938**
Glasgow watercolour painter and engraver; many etchings, often of churches. Exhibited RSA(4), RSW(1) & GI(13).

**YOUNG, Miss Wilhelmina M** **fl 1943**
Edinburgh painter; exhibited 'Sunny showers' at the RSA.

**YOUNG, William** **fl 1883-1900**
Architect. Preferred lavish, Renaissance-style design. Rebuilt Gosford House, East Lothian 1883 and the Banqueting Hall, Glasgow city chambers, subsequently decorated by Alexander Roche(qv).
**Bibl:** Dunbar 112; Irwin 389.

**YOUNG, William RSW** **1845-1916**
Landscape painter, often of the Highlands, chiefly in watercolour. Together with William Dennistoun(qv) and James Cowan(qv), founded the Glasgow Art Club(qv) 1867. For many years an amateur but began painting profesionally in 1878. Enjoyed portraying the west coast and Arran in a detailed and mannered, slightly melancholic style. A local historian and authority on early art and archaeology. Elected RSW 1880. Exhibited RA(4), RSA(48), RSW(88), GI(101) & L(2). Represented in Glasgow AG.
**Bibl:** Caw 299; Halsby 289.

**YOUNG, William** **fl 1869-1890**
Edinburgh landscape painter in oil; also occasional portraits. Exhibited RSA(6) & GI(1). Represented in SNPG ('Thomas Carlyle'). Not to be confused with William Young RSW(qv).

**YOUNG, William Drummond ('C.W. Drummond Young')** **1855-1924**
Born Glasgow. Painter of informal postraits and country subjects. Father of Edward Drummond Y(qv) & William Drummond Y jnr(qv). Founder of the 'Pen and Pencil Club', Rustic Arts Club, the Trotters, and other societies. Exhibited RSA(22) & GI(10). Represented in Edinburgh City collection.

**YOUNG, William Drummond Jnr** **fl 1898-1903**
Edinburgh landscape painter in oil. Son of William Drummond Y(qv). Exhibited RSA(3).

**YOUNG, William Mclellan** **fl 1912-1926**
Glasgow painter; still l;ife, interiors and subject studies. Moved to Bridge of Allan c1921. Exhibited RSA(2), AAS(1), GI(8) & L(3).

**YOUNG, William Norman** **fl 1951-1952**
Ayrshire painter of portraits and old buildings. Exhibited RSA(3) & GI(1), from Catrine, by Mauchline.

**YOUNGE, John C** **fl 1862-1863**
Edinburgh-based landscape painter and sculptor. Living in Perth 1864. Exhibited RSA(4).

**YOUNGER, Elspeth** **fl 1964-1974**
Scottish embroiderer. Exhibited AAS & GI(1) during the above years, sometimes from 34 Strachan St, Arbroath and sometimes from Coull Schoolhouse, Tarland, Aberdeenshire.

**YOUNGER, Jane** **1863-1955**
Born Glasgow. Daughter of a prosperous family involved in the cotton trade. Educated Park school, trained Glasgow School of Art 1890-1900; also at Craigmill School of Animal Painting(qv). Painted mostly landscape in watercolour in a strong, colourful style; also bookplate designer and embroiderer. Her devotion to painting was probably accentuated by progressive deafness. Her sister married Walter Blaikie the publisher, who had commissioned designs for Hill House, Helensburgh from Charles Rennie Mackintosh(qv). Worked in Paris during the early 1890s and 1895-1910 shared a studio with Annie French(qv) and Bessie Young(qv) at 227 W. George St, Glasgow. Often visited and painted on Arran and in 1902 visited northern Italy and Switzerland with the Blaikies. Some of her textile designs are still in Hill House. Exhibited RSA(16), RSW(22), AAS 1910-1933, including several west Highland scenes, one of them a study made at Flowerdale, Gairloch, GI(23), SWA(11) & L(5).
**Bibl:** Anne Ellis (in Burkhauser) 174-5; Halsby 289.

**YOUNGSON, Mary** **fl 1896**
Aberdeen painter of still life, fruit and fish; exhibited AAS(2) from Mannofield.

**YOUNGSON, William Coutts** **fl 1933-1972**
Aberdeen landscape painter; exhibited AAS over a long period, from 'Ardmore', Inchgarth Rd, Pitfodels.

**YUILL, Helen C** **fl 1932-1934**
Minor Falkirk artist; exhibited a mural decoration and two other works at the RSA, from 34 Learmonth St.

**YULE, Ainslie** **1941-**
Born North Berwick, East Lothian. Abstract sculptor. Trained Edinburgh College of Art 1959-1964, post-graduate scholar in his final year. After graduating he worked as a free-lance graphic and interior design consultant for several large organisations including the BBC. Gregory Fellow in sculpture, Leeds University 1974-5. Lecturer in design, Gray's School of Art, Aberdeen and visiting lecturer in sculpture, Chelsea School of Art. Head of sculpture at Kingston Polytechnic. Exhibits RSA & AAS from 68 Desswood Place, Aberdeen. Represented in SNGMA, BM, Aberdeen AG, Kirkcaldy AG, Ulster AG, Perth AG.

**YULE, Forbes W** **fl 1952-1986**
Glasgow painter of portraits, flora and fauna. Exhibited RSA(3) & GI(30).

**YULE, Mary A** **fl 1923-1926**
Aberdeen landscape painter. Exhibited 'On the Gairn' and one other work at the AAS, from 25 Whitehall Rd.

**YULE, William James** **1869-1900**
Born Dundee; died Nordrach-on-Mendip. Portrait painter in oils and chalk, also figurative studies and colourful market scenes. Son of a whaling captain. Trained Westminster School of Art under Fred Brown and in Paris under J-P Laurens, also in Spain. Laurens said that Yule painted like a cello, giving happy expression to the rich full sweetness of the low-toned colour harmonies he loved. A contemporary of George Dutch Davidson(qv) and John Duncan(qv) in the Dundee Graphic Arts Association. Worked for a few years in Edinburgh and 1897-8 moved to London with his friend David Muirhead(qv), but precarious health interfered with his work. Came back to Edinburgh in 1893, sharing a studio with A E Borthwick(qv). Toured Spain 1894-5 and then went back to London. A painter of exceptional ability and character whose career was tragically cut short at the age of only 31. Caw referred to his 'technical expression of a high order, and personal vision of great charm. He possessed that simple, serious and scrupulous style which, according to Saint-Beuve, goes far. The simple and unforced beauty, the sincerity of observation, the delicacy and distinction of statement in his pictures promise great things'. By his death Scottish painting lost one of the most sensitive, unaffected talents of his time. Exhibited RSA(5) & GI(6). Represented in NGS.
**Bibl:** AJ 1898, 71; Caw 433-5; Hardie 104.

**YULE, Winifred J** **fl c1905-1915**
Edinburgh-based portrait painter. Living in Aberdeen 1910. Exhibited 'St Agnes' at the AAS that year from Roslin Villa, Bieldside; also RSA.

# Z

**ZEZZOS, Alessandro** **1848-1914**
Born Venice, Feb 12; died Vittorio Venetio. Painter of genre and figure compositions in watercolour. Trained Venice Academy. Lived for a spell in Edinburgh c1889-1906 before returning to Paris. From his studio at 11 Hanover St exhibited a study of 'A Venetian' at the RA 1889; also RBA(1), RI(3), LS(5), L(5); also in Milan, Paris, Rome & Turin. Represented in Walker AG (Liverpool), Chemnitz AG, Florence (Palais Pitti), Rome (Galerie d'Art Moderne), Venice (Galerie d'Art Moderne).

**ZICHY, Count Mihaly von** **1827-1906**
Born Zala, Hungary, Oct 15; died St. Petersburg, Feb 28. Hungarian landscape and sporting painter, and lithographer. Studied in Pest and under Waldmuller in Vienna. Painter to the Russian Court from 1847, illustrator of several Russian poems. A keen shot, invited by the Prince of Wales to visit Abergeldie (beside Balmoral) on several occasions in the 1870s to join the stalking parties there. Working mainly in ink with sepia and grey washes he produced an evocative series of seventeen drawings complementing those made by Carl Haag for Queen Victoria. As a result of one of his visits ten works commissioned by the Prince were exhibited at the RA 1873; these included 'Stormy day near Loch Muick', 'Stags shown by torchlight at Abergeldie Castle' and several stalking subjects. All were well received, providing some of the better depictions of deer stalking. Represented in Royal collection, Budapest AG, Leningrad AG, Galerie Tretiakoff (Moscow).
**Bibl:** Benezit; D. Millar, Queen Victoria's Life in the Scottish Highlands, 1985, 136-8.

**ZIMMERER, F J** **fl 1919**
Kircudbright-based landscape painter in watercolours; exhibited GI(2) from The Green Gate.

**ZIMMERMAN, Amy Mary** **fl 1885-1888**
Glasgow painter. Moved to Fallowfield, Manchester in the late 1880s. Exhibited GI(1) & L(1).

**ZIMMERMAN, Miss Emma** **fl 1886**
Glasgow painter. Exhibited 'Gorse' at the GI.

**ZINKEISEN, Anna Katrina (Mrs Guy Heseltine) RP ROI** **1901-1976**
Born Kilcreggan, Ayrshire, Aug 28; died London. Portrait and landscape painter, also flowers and murals. Sister of Doris Z(qv). Educated privately at home, trained RA Schools, London winning silver and bronze medals. First exhibited at the Royal Academy when only 18. During the war served as a medical artist as well as painting hospital subjects and air-raid victims. Married to an army colonel, a fact which increased her interest in military subjects. Among her sitters were HRH Prince Philip, Sir Alexander Fleming, Lord Beaverbrook, Lord Todd, Lord Portal and Sir Robert Mark. Commissioned by both Queen Elizabeth and Queen Mary to execute a number of murals. Undertook extensive commercial work including posters, her best remembered example being the soigné aristocrat featured in the De Reszke cigarette advertisements. Designed the dust jacket for Alan Herbert's *Plain Jane,* commissioned to paint the Queen's coronation bouquet in 1953. Illustrated Herbert: *She-Shanties* (1926); *Plain Jane* (1927); Brahms: *The Moon on My Left* (1930); Buergel: *Oola-Boola's Wonder Book* (1932); Sharp: *The Nymph and the Nobleman* (1932); Quaglino: *The Complete Hostess* (1935); Farjeon: *Nice Sharp and Earlier* (1938); Streatfield: *Party Frock* (1946); Abrahall: *Prelude* (1947); Phoenice: *A Rainbow of Paths* (1965). Exhibited RA(24), RSA(6), ROI(30), RHA(2), RBA(1), RMS(1) & L(12); also regularly at Paris Salon from 1926. Represented in National War Museum, Beaverbrook AG (Fredericton, Canada), Castle AG (Nottingham), Bradford AG, Vancouver AG.
**Bibl:** Harold Osborne(ed), Twentieth Century Art, 1988, 598-9; Horne 453; Peppin; Waters.

**ZINKEISEN, Miss Doris Clare ROI** **1898-1991**
Born, Gareloch, Dumbartonshire, 31 Jly; died 3 Jan. Portrait and landscape painter, also theatrical designer and keen horse painter. Sister of Anna Z(qv). Won a scholarship to the RA Schools in London. Deeply interested in horses, she hunted with the Pytchley. At the Paris Salon, where she exhibited regularly from 1929, won gold medal 1930 and bronze medal 1929. During WW2 joined the St. John's Ambulance Brigade and the Red Cross appointed her their official war artist to record medical work at the front. After the liberation of Europe she completed a number of paintings at Belsen now in the Imperial War Museum. Lived most of her life in London, latterly moving to Suffolk. Had a distinctive, individual, decorative style with bright, fresh but not hard colouring. Published *Designing for the Studio* (Studio, 1938). Illustrated Priestley: *The High Toby* (1945). Elected ROI 1928. Exhibited RA(19), RSA(7), GI(1), SWA(3), RHA(1) & Paris Salon. Some of her costume and theatrical designs are in the V & A. Represented also in Melbourne AG, Sydney AG, York AG.
**Bibl:** *Guardian*, obit Jan 8.91; Horne 453; Waters.

**ZUNTERSTEIN, Nama** **fl 1968-1969**
Sculptress. Wife of Paul Z(qv). Exhibited two figure works at the RSA, latterly from Kilmacolm.

**ZUNTERSTEIN, Paul ARBS** **1921-c1968**
Sculptor. His 'Eurydice' in plaster was included in the touring Exhibition of Scottish Sculpture 1965. His wife Nama(qv) was also a sculptor. Exhibited RSA(18) 1952-68 & GI(22) 1950-1968, latterly from Kilmacolm.

**ZYW, Adam Leslie** **1948-2003**
Born Edinburgh, May 26; died Edinburgh, June 18. Architect and sculptor. Son of Aleksander Z(qv). Educated Edinburgh Academy, trained Architectural Association School of Architecture. After qualifying 1974, he studied landscape architecture for two years at Edinburgh Univ. Investigator with the Fine Art Commissions of Scotland. Set up in private practice 1981 and at about this time became lecturer, Mackintosh School of Art (Glasgow), and subsequently at the Universities of Edinburgh & Aberdeen. Also worked as a draughtsman, painter, gilder and furniture maker, in most of which activities he exhibited. His brother **Michael ZYW** was also an artist. Married three times. Received public commissions from the Royal Fine Art Commission for Scotland, SNGMA, and Podere Fonte Ferrata Castagneto Carducci (Italy).

**ZYW, Aleksander** **1905-1995**
Born Lida, Poland, Aug 29. Painter of landscape and figure subjects in oil, watercolour and pen and ink. Father of Adam L Z(qv). Trained Warsaw Academy of Fine Arts 1926-32, continuing studies in Athens, Paris 1934-9 and Rome. Came to Britain 1940, settling in Edinburgh where he held his first solo exhibition 1945 having been appointed an official war artist with the British Forces. Illustrated *Edinburgh as the Artist Sees It* (1945). Second home in Tuscany. Interested in movement and energy as, for example, illustrated in the group of 95 works together entitled 'An Instant of Water' 1975, for the preparation of which he used photographs of the Water of Leith. His later work explored religious themes, including Christ and the Resurrection. An exhibition of his paintings *The Nature of Painting* was held at the SNGMA 1986. Exhibited RSA 1941-1957 & GI(2) 1959. His work quickly became known internationally and can be seen in the SNGMA, Glasgow AG, City of Edinburgh collection (Parliament Hall 1946), Brodie Castle (NTS), State Collection of Poland (Warsaw), National Gallery of Poland, Tate AG, Rhodes NG (Zimbabwe).
**Bibl:** Gage 32.

# REFERENCES

(ALBEMARLE GALLERY) *Scottish Figurative Painting - Iain Faulkner, Stuart Gatherer, Alan King, Graham McKean* (Albemarle Gallery, London c2001)
ALDERSON, Brian *Looking at Picture Books* (National Book League 1973)
APTED, Michael R & HANNABUSS, Susan *Painters in Scotland 1301-1700* (The Edina Press Ltd, Edinburgh 1978)
ARMSTRONG, Sir Walter *Scottish painters, a critical study* (Seeley & Co 1888)
BALDRY, A L *British Marine Painting* ('The Studio' 1919)
BALSTON, Thomas *English Wood Engraving 1900-1950* (Art & Technics 1981)
BATE, Percy H *Art at the Glasgow Exhibition 1901* (Virtue 1901)
---------- *Modern Scottish Portrait Painters; with an introductory essay* (Edinburgh 1910)
BATEMAN, Michael *Funny Way to Earn a Living* (Leslie Frewin 1966)
BEETLES, Chris *The Illustrators: The British Art of Illustration 1780-1993* (Chris Beetles Ltd, London 1993)
BELLAMY, B E *Private Presses and Publishing in England since 1945* (Bingley 1980)
BENEZIT, Emmanual *Dictionnaire des Peintres, Sculpteurs, Dessinateurs et Graveurs* 8 vols (2nd edtn, Librarie Grund 1960)
BILLCLIFFE, Roger *The Scottish Colourists* (John Murray 1985)
---------- *The Glasgow Boys: the Glasgow School of Painting* (John Murray 1985)
---------- (Comp) *The Royal Glasgow Institute of the Fine Arts 1861-1989* 4 vols (Glasgow, The Woodend Press 1982)
BILLINGS, Robert William *The Baronial and Ecclesiastical Antiquities of Scotland* (Edinburgh 1845-52)
BOLTON, Theodore & WEHLE, H B *American Miniatures 1730-1850* (New York 1937)
BRADLEY, J W *A Dictionary of Miniaturists, Illuminators, Calligraphers and Copyists, with reference and notices of their patrons, from the establishment of Christianity to the Eighteenth Century*. 3 vols. (Bernard Quaritch, London 1887-89)
BRADSHAW, Percy V *They Make Us Smile* (Chapman & Hall 1942)
BRETT, Simon *A Handbook for the Nineties* (Swavesey: Silent Books 1987)
BROCKWELL, Maurice Walter *George Jamesone and some primitive Scottish Painters; based on unpublished MSS.* (Privately printed 1939)
BROOK-HART, Denys *British 19th Century Marine Painting* (Antique Collectors' Club, Woodbridge 1974)
---------- *British 20th Century Marine Painting* (Antique Collectors' Club, Woodbridge 1981)
BROWN, Gordon H & KEITH, Hamish *An Introduction to New Zealand Painting 1839-1967.* (Collins 1969)
BRYAN, Michael *Bryan's Dictionary of Painters and Engravers* (G Bell & Sons, rev edtn, 1930-34)
BRYDALL, Robert *Art in Scotland, its Origins and Progress* (Edinburgh, Blackwood 1889)
BUCHANAN, William et al *The Glasgow Boys*. 2 vols (Scottish Arts Council 1968 & 1971)
---------- "Mr Henry and Mr Hornel visit Japan" (Scottish Arts Council 1978)
BULLEY, Margaret Hattersley, *Ancient and Medieval Art; a short history* (Methuen 1914)

BUMPUS, Judith *Elizabeth Blackadder* (Phaidon 1988)
BURBRIDGE, R Brindley *A Dictionary of British Flowers, Fruit and Still Life Painters* (Leigh-on-Sea, Lewis 1974)
BURKHAUSER, Jude (Ed) *Glasgow Girls: Women in Art and Design 1880-1920* (Canongate 1990)
BUSHNELL, George Herbert (comp) *Scottish Engravers: a biographical dictionary of Scottish engravers and of engravers working in Scotland to the beginning of the 19th century*, (Oxford UP 1949)
BUTCHART, R *Prints & Drawings of Edinburgh* (C J Cousland & Sons Ltd, Edinburgh 1955)
CAMPBELL, Mungo *The Line of Tradition* (National Galleries of Scotland 1993)
CARPENTER, Humphrey & PRICHARD, Mari *The Oxford Companion to Children's Literature* (OUP 1984)
CAW, James L *Scottish Painting Past and Present 1620-1908* (T C & E C Jack, Edinburgh 1908)
---------- *Scottish Portraits*. 2 vols (T C & E C Jack, Edinburgh 1902-03)
CHAMBERS, Robert *A Biographical Dictionary of Eminent Scotsmen* 9 vols, new edition (Blackie & Son 1852)
CHILVERS, Ian A Dictionary of Twentieth Century Art, (OUP 1999)
CLEMENT, Clara Erskine & HUTTON, Laurence *Artists of the Nineteenth Century and Their Works* (Boston, Jas R Osgood 1879)
CLOUZOT, Henri-Georges *Dictionnaire des Miniaturistes* (Paris 1924)
COLVIN, H M *A Biographical Dictionary of British Architects 1600-1840* (Yale Univ. Press, 3rd edtn 1995)
CORDINGLY, David *Marine Painting in England 1700-1900* (Studio Vista 1974)
COSH, Mary *"The Adam Family at Arniston"*, Arch. Hist. 27 1984, pp214ff
CUNDALL, Herbert Minton *A History of British Watercolour Painting; with a biographical list of painters* (John Murray, London 1908)
CUNNINGHAM, Allan *Lives of the Most Eminent British Painters*, 6 vols (John Murray, London 1829-1833)
CURSITER, Stanley *Scottish Art to the Close of the Nineteenth Century* -(George Harrap & Co 1949)
D'ANCONA, Paolo & AESCHLIMANN, Erhard *Dictionnaire Miniaturistes du Moyen age et de la Renaissance dans les differentes contrees de l'Europe* (Milan, Hoepli 1949, reprinted 1982)
DEANE, Yvonne & SELBORNE, Joanna *British Wood Engraving of the 20s and 30s* (Portsmouth City Museum & Art Gallery 1983)
D N B *Dictionary of National Biography* (Smith, Elder & Co 1908)
DRIVER, David *The Art of the "Radio Times": The First Sixty Years* (BBC 1981)
DUNBAR, John G *The Historic Architecture of Scotland* (Batsford 1966)
----------*The Architecture of Scotland* (Batsford, rev edtn, 1978)
EVANS, Francis M *A Rough Sketch of the British School of Painting* (Harrogate Art Galleries 1912)
FEAVER, William *Masters of Caricature* (Weidenfeld & Nicolson 1981)
FERGUSSON, John Duncan *Modern Scottish Painting* (Glasgow, Wm Maclennan 1943)
FIELDING, Mantle *Dictionary of American Painters, Sculptors and Engravers* (Paul A Struck, New York 1945)
FINLAY, Ian *Art in Scotland* (Longmans 1945, reprinted 1948)

FLEMING, John *Robert Adam and his Circle in Edinburgh and Rome* (John Murray 1962, re-printed 1978)
FOSKETT, Daphne *British Portrait Miniatures* (Spring Books 1963)
---------- *A Dictionary of British Portrait Miniatures* 2 vols (Praeger Publishers 1972)
FOSTER, Joshua James *A Dictionary of Painters of Miniatures 1525-1850* (Philip Allan & Co 1926)
----------*English Miniature Painters of the XVII Century*, 2 vols (Dickinsons, London 1914-16)
GAGE, Edward *The Eye in the Wind: Contemporary Scottish Painting since 1945* (Collins 1977)
GARRETT, Albert *A History of British Wood Engraving* (Tunbridge Wells, Midas Books 1978)
---------- *British Wood Engraving of the 20th Century: A Personal View* (Scolar Press 1980)
GAUNT, William *British Painting* (Avalon Press 1945)
GIFFORD, John *Highlands and Islands (The Buildings of Scotland)*, (Penguin Books 1992)
GIFFORD, John et al *The Buildings of Scotland* several vols by region (Penguin 1989-92)
GILBEY, Sir Walter *Animal Painters* 2 vols (Vinton & Co 1900)
GEDDES, Patrick (Ed) *Evergreen; A Northern Seasonal* 4 vols (Edinburgh 1895-96)
GOMME, Andor & WALKER, D *Architecture in Glasgow* (Lund Humphries 1968, rev 1987)
GORDON, Esmé *The Royal Scottish Academy* 1820-1976 (Skilton, Edinburgh 1976)
GRANT, Maurice Harold *A Dictionary of British Etchers* (Rockcliff 1952)
GRAVES, Algernon *A Dictionary of Artists 1760-1893* (Kingsmead Reprints 1970)
---------- *The British Institution 1806-1867* (Kingsmead Reprints 1969)
---------- *The Royal Academy of Arts 1769-1904* 4 vols (Kingsmead Reprints 1970)
GUNNIS, Rupert *Dictionary of British Sculptors 1660-1851* new rev edtn (The Abbey Library n.d.)
HALSBY, Julian *Scottish Watercolours 1740-1940* (Batsford 1986, rev 1990)
HARDIE, Martin *Watercolour Painting in Britain*, 3 vols (Batsford 1966-68)
HARDIE, William R *Scottish Painting 1837-1939* (Studio Vista 1976, rev 1990)
---------- *Three Scottish Colourists* (Edinburgh, Scottish Arts Council 1970)
HARE, Bill *Contemporary Painting in Scotland* (Sydney, Craftsman House 1992)
HARRIES, Meirion & HARRIES, Susie *The War Artists: British Official War Art of the Twentieth Century* (Michael Joseph 1983)
HARTLEY, Keith *Scottish Art since 1900* (Lund Humphries 1989)
---------- et al *"The Vigorous Imagination; New Scottish Art"* (SNGMA exhib. cat. 1987)
HIND, Arthur M *A History of Engraving & Etching from the 15th Century to the year 1914* (Dover Publications Inc 1963)
HODNETT, Edward *Five Centuries of English Book Illustration* (Aldershot, Scolar Press 1988)
HOLLOWAY, James *The Norie Family* (Scottish Masters series no.20, NGS 1994)
---------- *Patrons and Painters; Art in Scotland 1650-1760* (SNPG 1989)
HONEYMAN, T *Three Scottish Colourists* (Edinburgh, T Nelson & Sons 1950)
HOLME, Charles *The Royal Institute of Painters in Watercolours* ('The Studio' 1906)
HOOK, Philip & POLTIMORE, Mark *Popular 19th Century Painting* (Antique Collectors' Club, Woodbridge 1986)
HORNE, Alan *The Dictionary of 20th Century British Book Illustrators* (Woodbridge, Antique Collectors' Club 1995 reprint)
---------- *20th Century British Book Illustrators* (Antique Collectors' Club, Woodbridge 1994)

HOUFE, Simon *The Dictionary of 19th Century British Book Illustrators and Caricaturists 1800-1914* (Antique Collectors' Club, Woodbridge 1978, reprinted 1996)
HUTCHISON, Sidney C *The History of the Royal Academy 1768-1986* (Robert Royce Ltd 1986)
ICB. MAHONEY, Bertha et al *Illustrators of Childrens' Books 1744-1945* (Boston, Horn Books, 1947 + three supplements 1958, 1968 & 1978)
IRWIN, David & Francina *Scottish Painters at Home and Abroad 1700-1900* (Faber & Faber 1975)
JACQUES, Robin *Illustrators at Work* (Studio Books 1963)
JAFFÉ, Patricia *Women Engravers* (Virago Press 1988)
JOHNSON, Jane (comp) *The Royal Society of British Artists 1824-1893* (Antique Collectors' Club, Woodbridge 1975)
---------- & GREUTZNER, A *Dictionary of British Art 1880-1940* (Antique Collectors' Club, Woodbridge 1980)
LEES-MILNE, *The Age of Adam* (B T Batsford 1947)
LONG, Basil S *British Miniaturists* (Geoffrey Bles, London 1929)
MAAS, Jeremy *Victorian Painters* (Barrie & Rockliff 1969)
MACKAY & RINDER *The Royal Scottish Academy 1926-1916* (Glasgow, J Maclehose 1917)
MACKAY, William Darling *The Scottish School of Painting* (Duckworth & Co 1906)
McKEAN, Charles *The Scottish Thirties; an Architectural Introduction* (Scottish Academic Press 1987)
MACMILLAN, Duncan *Painting in Scotland: The Golden Age* (Phaidon 1986)
---------- *Scottish Art 1460-1990* (Edinburgh, Mainstream 1990)
---------- *Scottish Art in the 20th Century* (Edinburgh, Mainstream 2001 edtn)
McWILLIAM, Colin *The Buildings of Scotland - Lothian, except Edinburgh* (Penguin Books 1978)
MAHONY. Bertha et al *Illustrators of Children's Books 1744-1945* (Boston 1948)
MALLALIEU, Hugo L *The Dictionary of British Watercolour Artists up to 1920* 3 vols (Antique Collectors' Club, Woodbridge 1976-1979)
MARILLIER, H C *The Liverpool School of Painters* (John Murray, London 1904)
MARTIN, David *The Glasgow School of Painting* (George Bell & Sons 1897)
MAYNE, Arthur *British Profile Miniatursts* (Faber & Faber 1970)
MITCHELL, Sally *Dictionary of British Equestrian Artists* (Antique Collectors' Club, Woodbridge 1985)
MURDOCH, W G Blaikie *The Art Treasures of Edinburgh* (J & J Gray, Edinburgh 1924)
MURRAY, David *Robert and Andrew Foulis and the Glasgow Press* (Glasgow 1913)
MYLNE, Robert Scott *The Master-Masons to the Crown of Scotland* (Scott & Ferguson and Burness & Co, Glasgow 1893)
(NATIONAL GALLERIES OF SCOTLAND) *Virtue and Vision; Sculpture in Scotland 1540-1990* (1991)
NOEL-PATON, M H *Tales of a Grand-daughter* (Privately printed by author 1970)
OSBORNE, Harold (Ed) *Twentieth Century Art* (Oxford University Press 1981)
OTTLEY, William Young *An Inquiry into the Origin and Early History of Engraving upon Copper and in Wood, with an account of engravers and their works, from the invention of chalcography by Masco Finguerra, to the time of Marc Antonio Raimondi* 2 vols (Univ of Chicago Press, 2003 reprint)

PAINTON, Cowen *Stained Glass in Britain* (Michael Joseph 1985)
PAVIERE, Sydney Herbert *A Dictionary of British Sporting Painters* (Leigh-on-Sea, Lewis 1965)
---------- *A Dictionary of Flower, Fruit & Still Life Painters* (Leigh-on-Sea, Lewis 1965)
---------- *A Dictionary of Victorian Landscape Painters* (Leigh-on-Sea, Lewis 1968)
PAYNE, Christopher *Animals in Bronze* (Antique Collectors' Club, Woodbridge 1982)
PEPPIN, Brigid & MICKLETHWAIT, Lucie *Dictionary of British Book Ilustrators: The Twentieth Century* (John Murray 1983)
PRICE, R G G *A History of Punch* (Collins 1957)
REDGRAVE, Samuel *A Dictionary of Artists of the English School* (Kingsmead Reprints 1970)
REID, J M & HONEYMAN, T J *Glasgow Art Club 1867-1967* (Glasgow Art Club 1967)
ROBERTS, Jane *Royal Artists; From Mary Queen of Scots to the Present Day* (Grafton Books 1987)
ROE, F Gordon *Sea Painters of Britain* (F Lewis Publishers Ltd 1948)
ROTHENSTEIN, John *British Art Since 1900. An Anthology* (Phaidon 1962)
---------- *Modern English Painters* 3 vols (2nd edtn New York, St Martin's Press 1976)
RYDER, John *Artists of a Certain Line* (Bodley Head 1960)
RYKWER, Joseph *The Brothers Adam* (Collins, London 1985)
S A C *The Scottish Arts Club, Edinburgh 1874-1974* (The Scottish Arts Club 1974)
SALAMAN, Ferdinando *A Collector's Guide to Prints and Printmakers* (Thames & Hudson, London 1972)
SAVAGE, *Lorimer and the Edinburgh Craft Designers* (Paul Harris Publishing, Edinburgh 1980)
SCHIDLOF, Leo R *The Miniature in Europe* 4 vols (Akademische Druck-U. Verlagsanstalt, Graz 1964)
SIMPSON, W *Inverness Artists* (Inverness Courier 1925)
SKETCHLEY, R E D *English Book Illustration* (Kegan Paul, Trench, Trubner & Co, London 1903)
SKINNER, Basil *Scots in Italy in the Eighteenth Century* (Edinburgh, SNPG 1966)
SKIPWITH, Peyton *The Great Bird Illustrators* (The Hamlyn Publishing Group 1979)
SMAILES, Helen (Comp) *The Concise Catalogue of the Scottish National Portrait Gallery* (National Galleries of Scotland 1990)
SNOODY, Theo *Dictionary of Irish Artists of the 20th Century* (Merlin & Co, Dublin 1966, rev 2002)
SPALDING, Frances & COLLINS, J *Twentieth Century Painters and Sculptors (*Antique Collectors' Club, Woodbridge 1991)
SPARROW, Walter Shaw *British Sporting Artists* (John Lane 1922)
STRICKLAND, W G *Dictionary of Irish Artists* 2 vols (Maunsell & Co, Dublin 1913, revised Irish Academic Press 1969)
SWAIN, Margaret, *Scottish Embroidery; Medieval to Modern*, (Batsford, London 1986)
THOMPSON, Francis *A Scottish Bestiary* (Molendinar Press, Glasgow 1978)
THOMSON, Duncan *Painting in Scotland 1570-1650* (SNPG, Edinburgh 1975)
---------- *George Jamesone* (OUP, Oxford 1974)
THIEME, Ulrich *Allgemeines Lexikon der Bildenden Kunstler* 37 vols (W Englemann, Leipzig, 1992 reprint)
USHERWOOD, R D *Drawing for the "Radio Times"* (Bodley Head 1961)
VERTUE, George *Note Books. Walpole Society 1930-1955.* 6 vols

WALKER, Bruce & GAULDIE, W Sinclair *Architects and Architecture on Tayside* (Dundee Institute of Architects 1984)
WALKER, Stella A *Sporting Art in England 1700-1900* (Studio Vista 1972)
WALPOLE, Horace *Anecdotes of Painting in England 1762-1771* 5 vols (John Major & Robert Jennings, London 1828)
WALPOLE SOCIETY *Vols I-XLII 1911-1970*
WATERS, Grant M *Dictionary of British Artists Working 1900-1950* 2 vols (Eastbourne Fine Arts 1975)
WATERHOUSE, Ellis *Painting in Britain 1530-1970* (Antique Collectors' Club, Woodbridge 1981)
WHITLEY, William Thomas *Artists and Their Friends in England 1700-1799* 2 vols (Medici Society, London 1928)
WHO *Who's Who in Art* (Havant Art Trade Press 1986 22nd edtn)
WHO'S WHO IN ART *Who's Who in Art* 17th edition (The Art Trade Press Ltd 1974)
WILLIAMS, Iolo *Early English Watercolours* (The Connoisseur, London 1952)
WILLIAMS, Julia Lloyd *Dutch Art and Scotland: A Reflection of Taste* (NGS 1992)
WILLIAMSON, G C *Signed Enamel Miniatures of the XVIIth, XVIIIth & XIXth Centuries* (Jacob Nachemsohn 1926)
WINDSOR, Alan *Handbooks of Modern British Painting 1900-1980* (Scolar Press 1992)
WINGFIELD, Mary Ann *A Dictionary of Sporting Artists 1650-1980* (Antique Collectors' Club, Woodbridge 1992)
WISHART, Anne (Ed) *The Society of Scottish Artists: The First 100 Years* (SSA 1991)
WOOD, Christopher *A Dictionary of Victorian Painters* (Antique Collectors' Club, Woodbridge 1971)
WOOD, Lt-Col J C *British Animal Painters* (F Lewis Publishers Ltd 1973)